Abbreviations Used in This Dictionary

Abbr.	abbreviation	n.	noun
adj.	adjective	nom.	nominative
adv.	adverb	obj	object
Brit.	British	obj.	objective
cm	centimeter(s)	part.	participle
compar.	comparative	pers.	person
def.	definition	pl.	plural
defs.	definitions	poss.	possessive
E	East	pp.	past participle
Eng.	English	prep.	preposition
esp.	especially	pres.	present
ft.	foot, feet	pron.	pronoun
in.	inch(es)	pt.	past tense
interj.	interjection	S	South
km	kilometer(s)	sing.	singular
m	meter(s)	superl.	superlative
mi.	mile(s)	v.	verb
mm	millimeter(s)	W	West
N	North	yd.	yard(s)

STAFF

Project Editor: Carol G. Braham

Editors: Robert Cohen, Madeline Kripke, Georgia Maas,
   Trudy Nelson, Karen Osborne, Enid Pearsons
Copyeditors: Lisbeth Dyer, Trumbull Rogers
Managing Editor: Jan Berman
Database Manager: Constance A. Baboukis
Programming Consultant: Paul Hayslett
Director of Production: Patricia W. Ehresmann
Editorial Production Services: Jennifer Dowling, Seaside Press

Editorial Director Emeritus: Sol Steinmetz
Publisher: Charles M. Levine

Random House
Webster's
Basic Dictionary
of American
English

Random House

House Webster's Basic Dictionary of American English

.ght © 1998 by Random House, Inc.

.ights reserved under International and Pan-American Copyright Conventions. No part this book may be reproduced in any form or by any means, electronic or mechanical, .ncluding photocopying, without the written permission of the publisher. All inquiries should be addressed to Reference & Information Publishing, Random House, Inc., 201 East 50th Street, New York, NY 10022. Published in the United States by Random House, Inc., New York and simultaneously in Canada by Random House of Canada Limited.

This work is based on the *Random House Webster's Dictionary of American English* published in 1997.

The Random House Living Dictionary Database™ is a trademark of Random House, Inc.

Library of Congress Cataloging-in-Publication Data
Random House Webster's basic dictionary of American English.
   p.   cm.
   ISBN 0-679-78005-X
   1. English language—Dictionaries. 2. English language—United States—Dictionaries.
PE1628.R276   1998
423—dc21   98-2885
                                          CIP

This book is available for special purchases in bulk by organizations and institutions, not for resale, at special discounts. Please direct your inquiries to the Random House Special Sales Department, toll-free 888-591-1200 or fax 212-572-4961.

Please address inquiries about electronic licensing of this division's products, for use on a network or in software or on CD-ROM, to the Subsidiary Rights Department, Random House Reference & Information Publishing, fax 212-940-7370.

Visit the Random House Web site at: www.randomhouse.com

Typeset and printed in the United States of America.

First Edition

0 9 8 7 6 5 4 3 2 1

ISBN 0-679-78005-X

New York   Toronto   London   Sydney   Auckland

Contents

New Words in American English

The vocabulary of English, especially American English, is growing at a remarkable rate. Among all the varieties of English around the world, including British English, it is American English that changes the fastest, adding more new words each year. New words and phrases have entered the language mostly as a result of recent inventions or knowledge in the fields of science and technology. Social and cultural trends and fashions have also contributed to the great expansion of the English vocabulary. These new terms represent a variety of subject categories, both general and specialized.

Many new words and phrases are borrowed from other languages, such as *fajitas* (from Spanish) and *karaoke* (from Japanese). Others are formed by combining or blending two or more existing words, such as *camcorder* (from *camera* and *recorder*) and *alternative medicine*. The creation of abbreviations is another common method of word formation in English. The abbreviation *ATM* is certainly more convenient to use than the full phrase "automated-teller machine"; the shortened form *PIN* is easier to pronounce and remember than the full form "personal identification number." New words are also commonly formed from existing words by the addition of a prefix or suffix, such as *microbrewery* (prefix *micro-*) and *cyberspace* (prefix *cyber-*).

Not only does the language add new vocabulary, but existing words change, broaden, or narrow their meanings over time. The new sense of *rocket scientist* (highly intelligent person) extends the original meaning (specialist in rocket design).

New words and phrases become popular and are given life in our newspapers, magazines, books, and electronic documents, not to mention radio and television shows, movies, and plays. Some new expressions last only for a few months and are forgotten soon after their introduction. Others are controversial because of their slang status, or because they are thought to be offensive. It is not possible to predict the future of a particular word. As for the future of English, the language is certain to continue its expansion in the course of the 21st century.

A careful study of the following selection of words will reveal a great deal about our changing world. You will find the definitions for these and many more new words in the A–Z dictionary.

abs
aromatherapy
body piercing
chocoholic
control freak
digerati
dis
dweeb
factoid
food court
high-definition television
hot-button
in-your-face
Kwanzaa

latte
microbrewery
newbie
no-brainer
PCS
rightsize
shock jock
snail mail
snowboard
soccer mom
spam
sport-utility vehicle
V-chip
voice mail

Guide to the Dictionary

Random House Webster's Basic Dictionary of American English is intended for learners of English as a second or foreign language. This dictionary covers the most common words and phrases in the English language. Spellings, usages, and pronunciations are based on American English. Definitions have been written in a clear and simple style that is easy for a beginner to understand.

The Main Entry

The main entry (sometimes called the "headword") is printed to the left of the rest of the text in heavy black type. Main entries are listed in alphabetical order, regardless of whether they are single words, compounds of two or more words, abbreviations, prefixes, or suffixes.

Different spellings or forms of the main entry are also printed in heavy black type. They are placed to show whether they apply to all definitions or only to particular meanings. A different form that applies to only one definition is placed after the definition number. These different forms are introduced by the words "or," "also," or "Also called."

Single-word entries have centered dots to show where the word can be divided into syllables. This is a guide to where to add a hyphen (-) at the end of a line. In

es•say•ist /ˈɛseyɪst/ *n.* [*count*] a writer of essays.

ˈair ˌbag, *n.* [*count*] a bag that inflates automatically inside a motor vehicle to protect the driver and passengers in a collision.

ESL, an abbreviation of: English as a second language.

re-, a prefix meaning: back or backward (*repay*); again or once more (*recapture*).

-ness, a suffix meaning quality or state (*goodness; darkness*).

go•fer or **go-fer** /ˈgowfər/ *n.* [*count*] *Slang.* an employee whose chief duty is running errands.

ball•point /ˈbɔlˌpɔynt/ *n.* [*count*] a pen in which the point is a small ball that rolls against a supply of ink. Also called **ˈballpoint ˈpen.**

check•out /ˈtʃɛkˌawt/ *n.* **1.** [*noncount*] the time by which a guest at a hotel must leave a room. **2.** [*count*] Also called **ˈcheckout ˌcounter.** a counter where customers pay for purchases, as in a supermarket.

ea•gle /ˈiygəl/ *n.* [*count*] a large, powerful, broad-winged bird having claws to catch its prey.

main entries composed of two or more words, individual words are not usually divided into syllables if they are entered at their own alphabetical places.

Homographs are words that have the same spelling but different origins and meanings. Each homograph is given a separate main entry and is marked with a small raised number following the word.

'**flight at,tendant,** *n.* [*count*] an airline employee who attends to passengers' comfort and safety.

cape[1] /keyp/ *n.* [*count*] a piece of clothing without sleeves, fastened at the neck and falling loosely from the shoulders.

cape[2] /keyp/ *n.* [*count*] a piece of land extending out into the sea.

Pronunciation

This dictionary shows the pronunciation for any main entry that is not a combination of two or more other main entries. A pronunciation key showing the system of symbols used to represent sounds in this book appears on the inside front cover. The pronunciation system is a modified version of the International Phonetic Alphabet (IPA). This version of the IPA is commonly used in teaching American English. Many learners of English are already familiar with this system and can use knowledge of their own native languages to determine the sound that each IPA symbol represents.

The pronunciation is enclosed in slash marks after the entry. If more than one pronunciation is possible, the more common one is listed first. After the first pronunciation, only the part that is different is shown, and the part that is the same is replaced with a hyphen. In words of two or more syllables, a primary stress mark /'/ comes before the syllable having the greatest stress. A secondary stress mark /ˌ/ comes before a syllable that has secondary stress (stress that is less strong). Syllables are not separated by spaces.

can•di•date /'kændɪ,deyt, -dɪt/ *n.* [*count*] **1.** a person who seeks a political office or other job: *presidential candidates.* **2.** a student studying for a degree: *a candidate for a doctoral degree.* —**can•di•da•cy** /'kændɪdəsiy/ *n.* [*noncount*]

Parts of Speech

Part-of-speech labels refer to a word's grammatical category, or how the word functions in a sentence. The parts of speech are *adjective, adverb, conjunction, interjection, preposition, pronoun, noun,* and *verb.* The abbreviations used for these parts of speech are explained in the chart on page i.

If a main entry has more than one grammatical category, a part-of-speech label appears before each group of definitions given for that part of speech.

au•thor /'ɔθər/ *n.* [*count*] **1.** someone who creates a book, article, etc.; writer. **2.** the maker of anything: *the author of the new tax plan.* —*v.* [~ + *obj*] **3.** to be the author of: *to author a novel.*

Inflected Forms

Inflected forms are the changed forms, like plurals of nouns or past tenses of verbs, that a word may have depending on how it is used in a sentence. Inflected forms appear in heavy black type toward the beginning of the main entry. Most verbs form the past tense and past participle by adding *-ed* and the present participle by adding *-ing: They dressed, They have dressed, They are dressing.* Most nouns form their plural by adding *-s* or *-es: dogs, churches.* This dictionary shows inflected forms for all nouns and verbs that have irregular forms. Also, the dictionary shows inflected forms for regular nouns and verbs whenever there might be confusion about spelling.

For nouns, the inflected plural forms are indicated by the abbreviation *pl.* before them.

de•i•ty /'diyɪtiy/ *n., pl.* **-ties. 1.** [*count*] a god or goddess. **2. the Deity,** God.

For verbs, inflected forms are listed in the following order: the past tense, the *-ed/-en* form or past participle (if it is different from the past tense), and the *-ing* form or present participle.

for•give /fər'gɪv/ *v.,* **-gave** /-'geyv/, **-giv•en, -giv•ing. 1.** to stop blaming someone for a mistake, crime, etc.: [~ + *obj*]: *to forgive a sin.* [*no obj*]: *Forgive and go forward.* **2.** [~ + *obj*] to cancel a debt: *to forgive the interest owed on a loan.*

For adjectives and adverbs, inflected forms are shown for those that form the comparative and superlative with a change in form or by adding *-er* and *-est.*

hap•py /'hæpiy/ *adj.,* **-pi•er, -pi•est. 1.** very pleased; glad: *I'm happy to hear the good news.* **2.** satisfied with one's condition: *a happy baby.*

Grammatical Information

Grammatical information is contained within "grammar codes" that have brackets [ ] around them. In general, a swung dash or tilde (~) within a bracketed grammar code stands for the main-entry word.

If the grammar code applies to only one definition, it is placed after the definition number.

base•ball /'beys,bɔl/ n. **1.** [noncount] a game played with a bat and a ball by two teams of nine players each. **2.** [count] the ball used in baseball.

If it applies to the entire entry or part of speech, it is placed after the part-of-speech label.

el•e•ment /'ɛləmənt/ n. [count] **1.** one of the parts of a whole: Cells are the basic elements of the human body. **2.** one of a class of substances that cannot be chemically separated into simpler substances: Hydrogen and oxygen are the elements that make up water.

Noun Grammar Codes

[count] This is a count noun; it can be counted and has a plural. It can be used with the word a or an before it.

boat /bowt/ n. [count] a vessel for traveling by water: Both of those fishing boats belong to my neighbor.

[noncount] This noun does not have a plural. It can be used with the word much or the phrase a lot of, but cannot be used with the word a or an.

laugh•ter /'læftər/ n. [noncount] the action or sound of laughing: The audience roared with laughter at the comedian's jokes. There was a lot of laughter in the classroom.

[noncount][count] Some nouns are both countable and noncountable, depending on their use. If one definition covers both count and noncount meanings, both grammar codes will be shown.

en•mi•ty /'ɛnmɪtiy/ n., pl. **-ties.** a feeling of bitter hostility or hatred: [noncount]: Great enmity exists between the two countries. [count]: Enmities between the two tribes prevented cooperation.

[plural] This noun is only used in the plural with a plural verb.

pants /pænts/ n. [plural] a piece of clothing reaching from the waist to the ankles, with a separate section for each leg: His pants were too tight.

[singular] This noun is only used in the singular with a singular verb. It can be used with a or an before it.

'free 'hand, n. [singular] unrestricted freedom or authority: a free hand to cut the budget.

[the + ~] This noun is used with the word the before it.

lime•light /'laym,layt/ n. [the + ~] a position at the center of public attention: He'd always enjoyed being in the limelight.

Verb Grammar Codes

Transitive Verbs

[~ + *obj*] This is a transitive verb. It is followed by an object, usually a noun or pronoun. The example sentence or phrase will sometimes have a passive construction, in which the subject receives the action expressed by the verb.

A transitive verb may be followed by an indirect object and then a direct object.

A transitive verb may be followed by a clause beginning with the word "that" or some other word.

A transitive verb may be followed by the word "to" and then the infinitive form of another verb.

A transitive verb may be followed by another verb in the -*ing* form.

Intransitive Verbs

[*no obj*] This is an intransitive verb. It is not followed by an object.

An intransitive verb may be followed by a prepositional phrase consisting of a preposition and its object. Often, an example sentence or phrase will show the correct or appropriate preposition.

Verbs that can be either Transitive or Intransitive

[*no obj*] [~ + *obj*] Some verbs can be either transitive or intransitive.

earn /ɜrn/ *v.* [~ + *obj*] to receive in return for one's work or service: *to earn $50,000 a year.*

o•blige /ə'blaydʒ/ *v.* [~ + *obj*], **o•bliged, o•blig•ing.** to require, as by law, conscience, or force: *We were obliged to invite them to our party.*

find /faynd/ *v.*, **found** /fawnd/, **find• ing.** [~ + *obj*] to locate or get by search or effort: *I found her an apartment.*

sup•pose /sə'powz/ *v.*, **-posed, -pos• ing.** [~ + *obj*] to assume something, as for the sake of argument: *Suppose (that) you won a million dollars in the lottery.*

pre•fer /prɪ'fɜr/ *v.* [~ + *obj*], **-ferred, -fer•ring.** to like better than someone or something else: *I'd prefer to leave now.*

hate /heyt/ *v.*, **hat•ed, hat•ing.** [~ + *obj*] to dislike intensely: *They hate violence. I hate getting up early.*

e•vap•o•rate /ɪ'væpəˌreyt/ *v.*, **-rat•ed, -rat•ing.** [*no obj*] to disappear; vanish: *His hopes evaporated.*

em•bark /ɛm'bɑrk/ *v.* [*no obj*] **1.** to board a ship or aircraft. **2.** to start a difficult activity or project: *to embark on a long journey.*

fail /feyl/ *v.* **1.** [*no obj*] to be unsuccessful: *The experiment failed.* **2.** [~ + *obj*] to be of no use or help to; to disappoint: *His friends failed him.*

Adjective Grammar Codes

[*before a noun*] This adjective must come before the noun it refers to; it cannot appear after a form of the verb *be*.

im•i•ta•tion /ˌɪmɪ'teyʃən/ *adj.* [*before a noun*] not real; artificial: *imitation leather.*

[*be* + ~] This adjective must follow a form of the verb *be* and cannot appear before the noun it refers to.

li•a•ble /'layəbəl/ *adj.* [*be* + ~] **1.** legally responsible: *You are liable for the damage.* **2.** likely: *She's liable to win.*

Definitions

Within a main entry, a single series of numbered definitions includes all parts of speech, phrasal verbs, and idioms. Usually, the most common or frequently occurring meanings appear first among the definitions.

Definitions that are cross references to another part of the alphabet, where the entry with the full definition is given, are shown in small capital letters. If there is no grammar code at a cross-reference definition, it will be found at the entry with the full definition.

'**mercy ˌkilling,** *n.* EUTHANASIA.

When transitive and intransitive meanings of a verb or count and noncount meanings of a noun are similar, often one definition will cover both uses. If there are example phrases or sentences, the appropriate grammar code appears before each example. If there are no examples, both grammar codes appear before the definition.

stat•ute /'stætʃuwt/ *n.* a law passed by a legislature: [*count*]: *a statute against littering.* [*noncount*]: *Working conditions are regulated by statute.*

egg•plant /'ɛg,plænt/ *n.* [*count*] [*noncount*] a dark-purple vegetable shaped like a large pear.

Examples

Example sentences or phrases inform the reader about the meaning of the word and how the word behaves grammatically in a sentence.

Examples clarify the grammar codes and definitions. However, they are most useful in showing which kinds of words regularly combine with the word being defined.

fair /fɛər/ *adj.*, **-er, -est. 1.** honest; just: *a fair trial; a fair wage.* **2.** of a light color; not dark: *fair skin.*

Phrasal Verbs

Phrasal verbs (sometimes called "verbal phrases" or "two-word verbs") combine a verb and one or more prepositions or adverbs. Phrasal verbs are listed in heavy black type in a single alphabetical group after all other verb definitions.

For some phrasal verbs that take an object, the object can either follow the verb or follow the preposition or adverb. Example phrases or sentences show both alternatives.

break /breyk/ *v.*, **broke** /browk/, **bro•ken** /'browkən/, **break•ing. 1.** to divide into parts violently: [~ + *obj*]: *He broke the vase.* [*no obj*]: *The vase broke.* **2. break down,** to (cause to) stop working: *The car broke down; to break down her resistance* or *to break her resistance down.* **3. break in, a.** to enter by force or unlawfully: *A thief broke in last night.* **b.** to train to a new situation: *to break in a new assistant* or *to break a new assistant in.*

For other phrasal verbs, the object must follow the preposition or adverb.

look /lʊk/ *v.* **1.** [*no obj*] to use one's eyes in order to see: *I'm looking at this book. She looked out the window.* **2. look after,** to take care of: *Who will look after the children?*

Idioms

Idioms are expressions whose meanings cannot be predicted from the usual meanings of the individual words. Idioms are listed alphabetically in heavy black type as the final numbered definitions in an entry. They are preceded by the label **—Idiom.**

Some idioms are followed by an object, and other idioms do not take an object. Example phrases or sentences show how an idiom is used.

end /ɛnd/ *n.* [*count*] **1.** the last part; the point where something stops: *the two ends of a rope.* **—Idiom. 2. put an end to,** to stop; finish: *Let's put an end to this constant arguing.*

Run-on Words

Run-on words are words that are formed from the main entry without great differences in meaning or spelling. They are usually formed by adding a suffix to the main entry word, and are usually a different part of speech.

If you are not sure about the meaning of a run-on, look up the suffix in the dictionary. For example, the word *enlightenment* uses the first sense of *-ment*, and means "the act of enlightening someone" or "the state of being enlightened."

Run-on words appear in heavy black type at the end of an entry, following the last definition.

en•light•en /ɛn'laytn̩/ *v.* [~ + *obj*] to give understanding or knowledge to. —**en•light′en•ment,** *n.* [*noncount*]

-ment, a suffix meaning: an action or resulting state (*government; abridgment*); a product (*fragment*); a means (*ornament*).

Usage Notes and Labels

Usage notes are intended to help learners avoid common errors in writing and speaking. These notes appear at the end of many entries. They are preceded by the label —**Usage.**

al•right /ɔl'rayt/ *adv., adj.* ALL RIGHT. —**Usage.** The one-word spelling AL-RIGHT is used in informal writing, but the phrase ALL RIGHT is preferred in formal, edited writing.

Several usage labels are used in this dictionary, such as *Informal, Slang, Offensive.* These labels serve as a guide to the attitudes that speakers have toward a word. *Informal* language is usually used in casual conversation, for example when speaking with someone you know well. It is also used in letters to friends, short notes, etc. *Slang* is extremely informal language, such as the new words and phrases used by young people. *Offensive* language includes words and phrases that tend to upset or insult a particular person or group.

bud•dy /'bʌdiy/ *n.* [*count*], *pl.* **-dies.** *Informal.* a friend.

British and American Pronunciations and the International Phonetic Alphabet

English, like other languages, exists in a variety of forms called *dialects*. Dialects are different in vocabulary, grammar, and pronunciation. They usually show a speaker's geographic origins and—because people can, to some extent, change the way they speak—dialects can also show how much education someone has.

Despite the ocean that separates England from America, the standard British and American dialects—the two dialects shown in most dictionaries—have remained surprisingly similar since British settlers first brought their language to America nearly 400 years ago. There are differences in vocabulary (for example, the British say *lift* when Americans say *elevator*), but the major difference between British English and American English is in the way they sound.

However, the differences in pronunciation are *not* as great as British and American learning materials seem to suggest. British and American pronunciations appear to be more unlike than they actually are because some of the International Phonetic Alphabet (IPA) symbols usually used by British linguists and teachers are different from those used for the same purpose by their American counterparts. Nevertheless, many of these symbols—British and American—represent substantially the same sounds.

Below we describe some of the real differences between British and American pronunciation. We then show the traditional differences in IPA symbols between British and American dictionaries. The accompanying chart reveals that many words in the two countries are actually said in much the same way, in spite of the different symbol systems.

1. Differences in Pronunciation

There are many dialects of English in both Great Britain and the United States. In dictionaries intended for general use, dictionary makers do not try to show how words are pronounced in all these dialects. Instead, British dictionaries show the usual pronunciations of England's educated upper class (referred to as *Received Pronunciation,* or *RP*). American dictionaries reflect the pronunciations used by most national radio and television broadcasters (a dialect often referred to as *Broadcast Network Standard,* or *BNS*).

Certain categories of sounds are consistently different in these two dialects. Most noticeable is the *r*. In British RP, the *r* is silent after a vowel, except when followed immediately by another vowel in the same word or the next word. Although some dialects of American English similarly omit the sound of *r* after a vowel, in American BNS the *r* is normally pronounced in all positions. Thus *bird, star,* and *port* are shown as /bɜːd/, /stɑː/, and /pɔːt/ in British materials, but as /bɜrd/, /stɑr/, and /pɔrt/ in American materials that use IPA.

Another letter pronounced differently is *a*. British speakers tend to use a "broad a" /ɑ/ in a group of words that includes *half, dance, plant,* and *rather*. Most Americans use a "flat a" /æ/ in these words.

Yet another general difference is the tendency of Americans to pronounce the "long u" sound of such words as *tune, due,* and *new* without the initial *y* sound (represented in British IPA by /j/) usually heard in British pronunciation.

In addition to general differences like these, there are individual words that have come to be pronounced differently in Great Britain and America. For example, the initial *sch-* of *schedule* is pronounced /sk/ in America but /ʃ/ in Britain (although *school* is pronounced the same—with an initial /sk/—in both places). Some other words that sound strikingly different in Britain and America are:

ate (past tense of *eat*)	Br. /et/	Am. /eyt/
charade	Br. /ʃə'rɑːd/	Am. /ʃə'reyd/
clerk	Br. /klɑːk/	Am. /klɜrk/
leisure	Br. /'leʒə/	Am. /liyʒər/
laboratory	Br. /lə'bɒrətrɪ/	Am. /'læbrə‚tɔriy/
lieutenant	Br. /lef'tenənt/	Am. /luw'tɛnənt/
missile	Br. /'mɪsaɪl/	Am. /'mɪsəl/
privacy	Br. /'prɪvəsɪ/	Am. /'prayəvsiy/

2. Differences in Use of Symbols from the International Phonetic Alphabet

In any dialect, no two people pronounce words in exactly the same way. IPA symbols can therefore only approximate the sounds that an individual speaker might make in pronouncing a word. Linguists who study phonetics—the sounds of languages—sometimes reach different conclusions about what symbol (or combination of symbols) best represents the usual sound of a particular word in a particular dialect. Thus even among scholars in the same country, different representations are used for the same sound. This is true, in both Great Britain and the United States, especially for vowel sounds, which are difficult to describe precisely.

In the United States, more traditional sets of IPA symbols have been joined by a number of additional variations. The American scholars and teachers who prefer these symbols think that they better represent extremely subtle differences in sound. They have found them especially useful in helping students to understand how English vowels differ from those in other languages. The following chart shows some common IPA symbols used in dictionaries and other English-language learning materials.

While some of the symbol choices differ in British and American materials, they represent sounds that are the same or very similar in standard British and American dialects. The symbols in **bold print** are the ones used in this dictionary.

Initial sound in	British IPA	American IPA
*y*es	/j/	/j/ or **/y/**
*sh*eep	/ʃ/	/ʃ/ or /š/
*ch*eap	/tʃ/	**/tʃ/** or /č/
*J*eep	/dʒ/	**/dʒ/** or /dž/

Indicated vowel sound in	British IPA	American IPA
*fa*ther	/ɑ:/	**/ɑ/** or /a/
c*i*ty	/ɪ/ or /i/	/ɪ/ or /i/ or **/iy/**
s*ee*	/i:/	/i/ or **/iy/**
s*e*t	/e/ or /ɛ/	/e/ or **/ɛ/**
s*aw*	/ɔ:/	/ɔ/
t*oo*	/u:/	/u/ or **/uw/**
b*i*rd	/ɜ:/	/ɜ/
t*a*ke	/eɪ/ or /ei/	/eɪ/ or /e/ or /ei/ or **/ey/**
t*i*me	/aɪ/ or /ai/	/aɪ/ or /ai/ or **/ay/**
t*ow*n	/aʊ/ or /au/	/aʊ/ or /au/ or **/aw/**
t*oy*	/ɔɪ/ or /ɔi/	/ɔɪ/ or /ɔi/ or **/ɔy/**
t*o*p	/ɒ/	/ɑ/ or **/ɒ/**
t*oe*[1]	/ɛʊ/ or /ɛu/ or /əʊ/ or /əu/	/oʊ/ or /o/ or /ou/ or **/ow/**

[1] Unlike the other sounds in this list, the "long o" sound in words like *toe* and *boat* is noticeably different in RP from BNS, as indicated by the initial /ɛ/ or /ə/ symbol and the absence of the /o/ symbol from all of the representations for that sound in British IPA. This entry is included in the chart, however, for the convenience of the reader in comparing the British and American materials.

A

A, a /ey/ *n.* [*count*], *pl.* **A's** or **As, a's** or **as.** **1.** the first letter of the English alphabet. **2.** a grade or mark given to a student in school to indicate excellence: *She received an A in English.*

a /ə; *when stressed* ey/ *indefinite article.* [*usually before count nouns*] **1.** one: *a friend of mine; a month ago.* **2.** (used to refer to the class of things the noun belongs to): *A dog has four legs.* **3.** (used to refer to a rate or measurement with the noun) per; each: *My dentist charges $50 a filling.* **4.** (used before words like *little, lot, few*): *a little time; a few stars.* **5.** (used before a proper name) a work of art by: *The investor paid $5 million for a Van Gogh.* ——**Usage.** A is used before words beginning with a consonant sound (*a book*); AN is used before words beginning with a vowel sound (*an apple*). Words that begin with the letter *h* sometimes cause confusion. When the *h* is not pronounced, the word is preceded by AN: *an hour.* When *h* is pronounced, the word is preceded by A: *a hundred.* Adjectives such as *historian, historical, heroic,* and *habitual* are commonly preceded by A in both speech and writing (*a historian of ancient China; a habitual criminal*), but AN is also common, especially in British English (*an historian, an historic event*).

a-¹, a prefix meaning: on, in, or into (*ashore*); toward or at (*aside*).

a-², a prefix meaning: not (*atypical*); without (*amoral*).

AA, an abbreviation of: Alcoholics Anonymous (a group that helps its members with problems caused by alcohol.)

A.A., an abbreviation of: Associate of Arts (a degree from a two-year college).

AAA, an abbreviation of: American Automobile Association.

A.B., an abbreviation of: Bachelor of Arts.

ab•a•cus /ˈæbəkəs/ *n.* [*count*], *pl.* **ab•a•cus•es, ab•a•ci** /ˈæbə,say, -,kay/. a frame with rods on which balls or beads are moved, used for calculating.

a•ban•don /əˈbændən/ *v.* **1.** [~ + *obj*] to leave completely and finally; desert: *to abandon a sinking ship.* **2.** [~ + *obj*] to give up; withdraw from: *to abandon hope.* —**a'ban•don•ment,** *n.* [*noncount*]

a•bashed /əˈbæʃt/ *adj.* embarrassed or ashamed.

a•bate /əˈbeyt/ *v.,* **a•bat•ed, a•bat•ing.** [*no obj*] to become less in amount, degree, or intensity. —**a'bate•ment,** *n.* [*noncount*]

ab•bey /ˈæbiy/ *n.* [*count*], *pl.* **-beys.** a home for a group of monks or nuns connected with a particular church.

abbr. or **abbrev.,** an abbreviation of: abbreviation.

ab•bre•vi•ate /əˈbriyviy,eyt/ *v.* [~ + *obj*], **-at•ed, -at•ing.** to shorten (a word or phrase) to a form that represents the whole word or phrase.

ab•bre•vi•a•tion /ə,briyviy'eyʃən/ *n.* [*count*] a shortened form of a word or phrase used to represent the whole, as *Dr.* for *Doctor.*

ABC's or **ABCs** /ˈey,biy'siyz/ *n.* [*plural; used with a plural verb*] the English alphabet: *Children learn their ABC's in kindergarten.*

ab•di•cate /ˈæbdɪ,keyt/ *v.,* **-cat•ed, -cat•ing.** to give up (an important position, a high office, etc.): [~ + *obj*]: *He abdicated the throne of England.* [*no obj*]: *He decided to abdicate.* —**ab•di•ca•tion** /,æbdɪ'keyʃən/, *n.* [*noncount*]

ab•do•men /ˈæbdəmən/ *n.* [*count*] the part of the body between the chest and the legs; belly.

ab•dom•i•nal /æbˈdɒmənəl/ *adj.* of, relating to, or located in the abdomen: *abdominal pains.*

ab•duct /æbˈdʌkt/ *v.* [~ + *obj*] to carry off (a person) illegally and by force; kidnap. —**ab•duc•tion** /æbˈdʌkʃən/, *n.* [*count*]

ab•er•ra•tion /,æbəˈreyʃən/ *n.* [*count*] behavior or a condition that is not normal or usual.

a•bet /əˈbɛt/ *v.* [~ + *obj*], **a•bet•ted, a•bet•ting.** to help (someone) to do something wrong: *abetting the enemy.*

ab•hor /æbˈhɔr/ *v.,* **-horred, -hor•ring.** to hate very much; detest: *Gandhi abhorred violence all his life.* —**ab•hor•rence** /æbˈhɔrəns, -ˈhɒr-/, *n.* [*noncount*] —**ab'hor•rent,** *adj.*

a•bide /əˈbayd/ *v.,* **a•bode** /əˈbowd/ or **a•bid•ed, a•bid•ing.** **1.** [*no obj*] to dwell; reside; live. **2. abide by,** to agree to behave according to: *to abide by the court's decision.*

a•bil•i•ty /əˈbɪlɪtiy/ *n.,* *pl.* **-ties.** power or skill to do, make, or think; talent: [*noncount*]: *He has much ability in music.* [*count*]: *Her abilities are many.*

a•blaze /əˈbleyz/ *adj.* [*be* + ~] **1.** on fire: *The forest was ablaze.* **2.** gleaming with or as if with light: *The sky was ablaze with stars.*

a•ble /ˈeybəl/ *adj.* (for def. 2) **a•bler, a•blest. 1.** having the power, skill, or knowledge to do something: *able to read music.* **2.** having or showing unusual talent, intelligence, skill, or knowledge: *an able leader.* —**a'bly,** *adv.*

-able, a suffix meaning: able to be (*readable*); tending to (*changeable*); worthy of (*loveable*). Compare -IBLE.

ab•nor•mal /æbˈnɔrməl/ *adj.* not normal or usual: *His wild behavior is clearly abnormal.* —**ab•nor•mal•i•ty** /,æbnɔrˈmælɪtiy/, *n.* [*count*], *pl.* **-ties.** —**ab'nor•mal•ly,** *adv.*

a•board /əˈbɔrd/ *adv., prep.* on, in, or into (a ship, train, airplane, etc.): *The ship sank, drowning all who were aboard. They went aboard the ship.*

a•bode¹ /əˈbowd/ *n.* [*count*] a place in which a person lives; residence; home.

a•bode² /əˈbowd/ *v.* a pt. and pp. of ABIDE.

a•bol•ish /əˈbɒlɪʃ/ *v.* [~ + *obj*] to remove completely: *to abolish slavery.* —**ab•o•li•tion** /,æbəˈlɪʃən/, *n.* [*noncount*]

a•bom•i•na•ble /əˈbɒmənəbəl/ *adj.* **1.** very hateful: *an abominable murder.* **2.** very bad; awful: *abominable taste in clothes.*

ab•o•rig•i•ne /,æbəˈrɪdʒəniy/ *n.* [*count*] one of the original inhabitants, esp. of Australia. —**ab•o•rig•i•nal** /,æbəˈrɪdʒənl/, *adj.*

a•bort /əˈbɔrt/ *v.* **1.** [~ + *obj*] to cause to give birth to (a fetus) before it is able to live. **2.** to stop too early: [*no obj*]: *The missile flight aborted.* [~ + *obj*]: *They aborted the space flight.* —**a•bor•tion** /əˈbɔrʃən/, *n.* [*noncount*] [*count*]

a•bound /əˈbawnd/ *v.* [*no obj*] to exist in great amount or numbers; be well supplied: *The land abounds in coal.*

a·bout /ə'bawt/ prep. **1.** concerning; on the subject of: a novel about the Civil War. Compare ON. **2.** near; close to; approximately: She's about my height. **3.** here or there; in or on: The dog wandered about the neighborhood. —adv. **4.** nearly; almost: Dinner is about ready. **5.** nearby; not far away: My papers are somewhere about. **6.** here and there: to move furniture about. —Idiom. **7. be about to,** be ready to do something: We're about to eat dinner. **8. not about to,** not intending to: I'm not about to lend you money. **9. what about,** what plans do you have concerning (the person or thing mentioned)? What about the money you owe me? **10. how about,** (used to make an offer or suggestion): How about a cup of tea? **11. it's about time,** the time has arrived to do (something): It's about time to leave. —Usage. Both ON and ABOUT mean "concerning"; ABOUT is used when the information given is general and not too technical: a novel ABOUT the Civil War. ON is used when the information is particular, as by being scholarly or technical: an important article ON the Civil War.

a·bove /ə'bʌv/ adv. **1.** at or to a higher position: We saw the birds above. **2.** higher in number; over: persons age 18 and above. —prep. **3.** in or to a higher place than; over: to fly above the clouds. **4.** more in number; over: persons above 18 years of age. **5.** higher in rank or authority than: A major is above a captain. —adj. **6.** said, mentioned, or written earlier: the above remarks. —n. [noncount] **7.** [the + ~] things mentioned earlier in the same document: All the above proves that we're right. —Idiom. **8. above all,** most importantly; principally.

a·bra·sion /ə'breyʒən/ n. **1.** [noncount] wearing down or damaging by scraping or friction. **2.** [count] a scraped spot or area: There were many abrasions on his leg.

a·bra·sive /ə'breysɪv, -zɪv/ adj. **1.** rough enough to cause abrasion. **2.** annoyingly harsh: an abrasive personality. —n. [count] **3.** any material used for grinding, polishing, etc., as sandpaper.

a·breast /ə'brɛst/ adv., adj. **1.** side by side: They walked two abreast. —Idiom. **2. be** or **keep abreast of,** be informed about: He kept abreast of the news.

a·bridge /ə'brɪdʒ/ v. [~ + obj], **a·bridged, a·bridg·ing.** to make (a book, article, etc.) shorter. —a'bridg·ment, a'bridge·ment, n. [count]

a·broad /ə'brɔd/ adv. in or to a foreign country: He often travels abroad.

a·brupt /ə'brʌpt/ adj. **1.** sudden or unexpected: an abrupt departure. **2.** quick; unfriendly and impolite: an abrupt reply. —ab'rupt·ly, adv. —ab'rupt·ness, n. [noncount]

abs /æbz/ n. [plural; used with a plural verb] Informal. the muscles of the stomach; abdominal muscles.

ab·scess /'æbsɛs/ n. [count] a swelling in the body caused by pus: a painful abscess in her gums.

ab·scond /æb'skɒnd/ v. [no obj] to leave suddenly and secretly: The cashier absconded with the money.

ab·sence /'æbsəns/ n. **1.** [noncount] the condition of being away: Absence makes the heart grow fonder. **2.** [count] a period of time being away: an absence of a few days. **3.** [noncount] lack; nonexistence: the absence of proof.

ab·sent /'æbsənt/ adj. **1.** not in a certain place;

not present: absent from class again. **2.** lacking; nonexistent: Books were absent from their lives.

ab·sen·tee /ˌæbsən'tiy/ n. [count] a person who is absent.

'ab'sent-mind·ed, adj. unaware or forgetful of what is happening or what one is doing.

ab·so·lute /'æbsə,luwt/ adj. **1.** [before a noun] total and complete: That's an absolute lie! **2.** not limited: an absolute monarch.

ab·so·lute·ly /ˌæbsə'luwtliy/ adv. **1.** completely; totally: It is absolutely necessary to finish on time. **2.** (used as an interjection) certainly: Do you want the job? —Absolutely!

ab·solve /æb'zɒlv, -'sɒlv/ v. [~ + obj], **-solved, -solv·ing.** to free from guilt, blame, responsibility, or sin.

ab·sorb /æb'sɔrb, -'zɔrb/ v. [~ + obj] **1.** to suck up or drink in (a liquid); soak up: A sponge absorbs water. **2.** to get the full attention of: This book will absorb the serious reader. **3.** to take in and use: to absorb information.

ab·sorb·ent /æb'sɔrbənt, -'zɔr-/ adj. able to absorb liquid: absorbent cotton.

ab·sorp·tion /æb'sɔrpʃən, -'zɔrp-/ n. [noncount] the process of absorbing or being absorbed.

ab·stain /æb'steyn/ v. [no obj] to keep oneself from doing something immoral, unhealthy, etc.: to abstain from smoking.

ab·sten·tion /æb'stɛnʃən/ n. [noncount] the act of abstaining.

ab·sti·nence /'æbstənəns/ n. [noncount] the giving up of pleasures that are immoral, unhealthy, etc.: abstinence from alcohol.

ab·stract /æb'strækt, 'æbstrækt/ adj. **1.** existing in the mind; not being something one can touch, see, hear, taste, or smell: an abstract idea. **2.** difficult to understand: an abstract theory.

ab·surd /æb'sɜrd, -'zɜrd/ adj. without sense, good reason, or common sense: Spending more money than you earn is clearly absurd. —ab'surd·i·ty, n., pl. -ties. [noncount]: the absurdity of cleaning the house before the cleaner comes. [count]: full of jokes and other absurdities. —ab'surd·ly, adv.

a·bun·dant /ə'bʌndənt/ adj. present in an amount that is more than enough: an abundant supply of water. —a·bun·dance /ə'bʌndəns/, n. [count] [noncount] —a'bun·dant·ly, adv.

a·buse /v. ə'byuwz; n. ə'byuws/ v., **a·bused, a·bus·ing,** n. —v. [~ + obj] **1.** to use wrongly or improperly; misuse: to abuse authority. **2.** to harm; treat badly. —n. **3.** wrong or improper use; misuse: [noncount]: drug abuse. [count]: Firing her from the job was an abuse of power. **4.** [noncount] harsh treatment. —a·bu·sive /ə'byuwsɪv/, adj.

a·bys·mal /ə'bɪzməl/ adj. extremely bad or severe: abysmal weather.

a·byss /ə'bɪs/ n. [count] **1.** a deep space or hole too large to be measured. **2.** the lowest or most hopeless depths; hell.

AC, an abbreviation of: **1.** air conditioning. **2.** Also, **ac, a.c., A.C.** alternating current.

A/C or **a/c,** an abbreviation of: **1.** account. **2.** air conditioning.

ac·a·dem·ic /ˌækə'dɛmɪk/ adj. **1.** [before a noun] of or relating to a school, esp. one for higher education: academic studies. —n. [count] **2.** a student or teacher at a college or university. —ˌac·a'dem·i·cal·ly, adv.

a·cad·e·my /ə'kædəmiy/ n. [count], pl. -mies. **1.** a secondary or high school, esp. a private one.

A

2. a school or college for special training: *a military academy.*

ac•cede /æk'siyd/ *v.* [~ + *to* + *obj*], **-ced•ed, -ced•ing.** to agree: *to accede to a request.*

ac•cel•er•ate /æk'sɛlə,reyt/ *v.*, **-at•ed, -at•ing.** to (cause to) develop, progress, or advance faster: [*no obj*]: *The unemployment rate accelerated.* [~ + *obj*]: *Those policies accelerated unemployment.* —**ac•cel•er•a•tion** /æk,sɛlə'reyʃən/, *n.* [*noncount*]

ac•cel•er•a•tor /æk'sɛlə,reytər/ *n.* [*count*] a device, esp. a pedal, for controlling the speed of a motor vehicle engine.

ac•cent /'æksɛnt/ *n.* [*count*] **1.** the force of a spoken sound, shown by pronunciation, pitch, loudness, or a combination of these: *The accent in the word "absorb" is on the second syllable, "-sorb".* **2.** a mark showing relative force (as ´, ` or ', ,), vowel quality (as French grave `, acute ´, circumflex ^), pitch, etc. Also called **accent mark.** **3.** a way of speaking that is typical of a particular person, group, or place: *a Southern accent.* **4.** special emphasis: *Our boss puts an accent on getting to work on time.* —*v.* [~ + *obj*] **5.** to pronounce (a sound) with extra loudness, extra length, or higher pitch: *Accent the second syllable in the word "absorb".* **6.** to emphasize.

ac•cen•tu•ate /æk'sɛntʃuw,eyt/ *v.* [~ + *obj*], **-at•ed, -at•ing.** to give special emphasis or importance to: *Try to accentuate the student's progress.*

ac•cept /æk'sɛpt/ *v.* [~ + *obj*] **1.** to take or receive (something offered) willingly: *She accepted my apology.* **2.** to agree to: *We can't accept the terms of the contract.* —**Usage.** Because of similarity in pronunciation, ACCEPT and EXCEPT are sometimes confused in writing. ACCEPT is a verb meaning "to receive willingly": *Please accept my gift.* EXCEPT is usually a preposition meaning "other than": *Everybody came except you.* When EXCEPT is used as a verb, it means "to leave out": *Certain types of damage are excepted from coverage under this insurance policy.*

ac•cept•a•ble /æk'sɛptəbəl/ *adj.* **1.** worthy or capable of being accepted. **2.** barely adequate or satisfactory. —**ac•cept•a•bil•i•ty** /æk,sɛptə'bɪlɪtiy/ **ac'cept•a•ble•ness,** *n.* [*noncount*] —**ac'cept•a•bly,** *adv.*

ac•cept•ance /æk'sɛptəns/ *n.* [*noncount*] **1.** the act of accepting or state of being accepted or acceptable. **2.** favorable reception; approval: *She got a letter of acceptance from the college.*

ac•cess /'æksɛs/ *n.* [*noncount*] **1.** an approach or entrance: *The back door was the only access to their house.* —*v.* [~ + *obj*] **2.** to get (information) from a computer: *She accessed the files through the network.*

ac•ces•si•ble /æk'sɛsəbəl/ *adj.* easy to approach, enter, or use: *The house was easily accessible.*

ac•ces•sion /æk'sɛʃən/ *n.* [*noncount*] the act of taking on the responsibilities of a high office´ or position.

ac•ces•so•ry /æk'sɛsəriy/ *n.* [*count*], *pl.* **-ries.** **1.** an extra part that improves or completes the basic part: *The car's accessories included power windows.* **2.** *Law.* a person who, although absent, helps someone else to commit a crime.

ac•ci•dent /'æksɪdənt/ *n.* [*count*] **1.** something damaging that happens without anyone intending it to happen: *a three-car accident on the icy road.* **2.** any event that happens unexpectedly: *Meeting her again was a happy accident.* **3. by accident,**

unexpectedly: *I met her quite by accident.* —,**ac•ci'den•tal,** *adj.* —,**ac•ci'den•tal•ly,** *adv.*

ac•claim /ə'kleym/ *v.* [~ + *obj*] **1.** to praise or greet with great approval: *The critics acclaimed the book.* —*n.* [*noncount*] **2.** loud or enthusiastic approval or praise; acclamation.

ac•cla•ma•tion /,æklə'meyʃən/ *n.* [*noncount*] a strong demonstration of welcome or approval: *The speech was greeted with acclamation.*

ac•cli•mate /'æklə,meyt/ *v.* [~ + *obj*], **-mat•ed, -mat•ing.** to accustom or become accustomed to a new climate or environment: *The goldfish acclimated (themselves) to the new tank.*

ac•co•lade /'ækə,leyd, -,lɑd/ *n.* [*count*] any award, honor, or notice of praise.

ac•com•mo•date /ə'kɒmə,deyt/ *v.* [~ + *obj*], **-dat•ed, -dat•ing.** **1.** to do a favor to or for; help: *The store accommodated both new and old customers.* **2.** to provide enough room or lodging for; to make room for: *The convention center can accommodate over 400 guests.*

ac•com•mo•da•tion /ə,kɒmə'deyʃən/ *n.* [*count*] Usually, **accommodations.** [*plural*] lodging: *The accommodations at that hotel are comfortable.*

ac•com•pa•ni•ment /ə'kʌmpənimənt/ *n.* [*count*] something that accompanies, esp. music to support the featured musical performance: *a piano accompaniment to the violin.*

ac•com•pa•nist /ə'kʌmpənɪst/ *n.* [*count*] a performer of musical accompaniments.

ac•com•pa•ny /ə'kʌmpəniy/ *v.* [~ + *obj*], **-nied, -ny•ing.** **1.** to go with: *She accompanied me home.* **2.** to play or sing an accompaniment to: *I accompanied her song on guitar.*

ac•com•plice /ə'kɒmplɪs/ *n.* [*count*] a person who knowingly helps another in a crime.

ac•com•plish /ə'kɒmplɪʃ/ *v.* [~ + *obj*] to succeed in finishing; achieve: *The pilot accomplished his mission.* —**ac'com•plished,** *adj.* —**ac'com•plish•ment,** *n.* [*noncount*] [*count*]

ac•cord /ə'kɔrd/ *v.* **1.** [*no obj*] to agree: *Being rude to customers doesn't accord with the store's policy.* **2.** [~ + *obj*] to give; grant; bestow: *They accorded the president great honor.* —*n.* [*count*] **3.** an agreement, esp. an international agreement: *an accord banning nuclear weapons in space.* —**Idiom. 4. in accord with,** in agreement with: *Your promotion was in accord with my wishes.* **5. of one's own accord,** voluntarily or willingly: *She did the extra work of her own accord.*

ac•cord•ance /ə'kɔrdns/ *n.* —**Idiom. in accordance with,** in agreement with: *to act in accordance with the law.*

ac•cord•ing•ly /ə'kɔrdɪŋliy/ *adv.* **1.** therefore; so: *Dinner was at eight o'clock; accordingly we arrived at 7:45.* **2.** in a way that fits: *If you are rude to others, expect to be treated accordingly.*

ac'cord•ing ,to, *prep.* **1.** in accord with or in a way that fits: *They were paid according to how much work they did.* **2.** as stated by: *According to my dictionary, that word´ has three meanings.*

ac•cor•di•on /ə'kɔrdiyən/ *n.* [*count*] a musical instrument that can be carried, with a keyboard and a pair of bellows for forcing air through small reeds.

ac•cost /ə'kɔst, ə'kɒst/ *v.* [~ + *obj*] to approach and speak to, esp. in an unfriendly, demanding way.

ac•count /ə'kawnt/ *n.* [*count*] **1.** a description of events or situations: *a truthful account.* **2.** an amount of money deposited with a bank: *a savings account.* —*v.* **account for, 3.** to give an explanation for: *Can you account for your finger-prints on the gun?* **4.** to be the cause or source of: *The New York market accounts for a lot of our sales.* —*Idiom.* **5. on account of,** because of: *The game was postponed on account of rain.* **6. on no account,** absolutely not: *On no account should you be afraid to ask questions.* **7. take account of,** to consider; think about; allow for: *We took account of the chance of rain.* **8. take into account,** to take into consideration: *I didn't take the cost of the project into account. I took into account all the expenses of the project.*

ac•count•a•ble /ə'kawntəbəl/ *adj.* [*be* + ~] obligated to answer (to); responsible (for): *I am accountable to my supervisor. I am accountable for my own work.*

ac•count•ant /ə'kawntnt/ *n.* [*count*] a person whose profession is accounting.

ac•count•ing /ə'kawntɪŋ/ *n.* [*noncount*] the work of organizing and maintaining financial re-cords, esp. for a business.

ac•cred•it /ə'krɛdɪt/ *v.* [~ + *obj*] **1.** to recog-nize as meeting official standards. **2.** to provide with credentials: *to accredit a diplomatic envoy.* —**ac,cred•i'ta•tion,** *n.* [*noncount*]: *accreditation of the college.*

ac•crue /ə'kruw/ *v.,* -crued, -cru•ing. to grow or increase over time, esp. by adding gradually: [*no obj*] *The interest accrued at 6% a year.* [~ + *obj*]: *The account accrued interest.*

acct., an abbreviation of: **1.** account. **2.** account-ant.

ac•cu•mu•late /ə'kyuwmyə,leyt/ *v.,* -lat•ed, -lat•ing. to gather or collect, esp. a little at a time: [~ + *obj*]: *The teacher had accumulated a large collection of papers and books.* [*no obj*]: *Dust accumulated on the shelves.* —**ac•cu•mu•la-tion** /ə,kyuwmyə'leyʃən/, *n.* [*noncount*][*count*]

ac•cu•rate /'ækyərɪt/ *adj.* without any error: *ac-curate calculations.* —**ac•cu•ra•cy** /'ækyərəsiy/, *n.* [*noncount*] —'**ac•cu•rate•ly,** *adv.*

ac•cuse /ə'kyuwz/ *v.* [~ + *obj*], -cused, -cus-ing. to charge with a fault, offense, or crime: *They accused him (of murder).* —**ac•cu•sa•tion** /,ækyʊ'zeyʃən/, *n.* [*count*] [*noncount*] —**ac'cus•er,** *n.* [*count*]

ac•cus•tom /ə'kʌstəm/ *v.* [~ + *obj* + *to* + *obj*] to make (oneself) familiar with something by use or habit: *had to accustom themselves to the climate.*

ac•cus•tomed /ə'kʌstəmd/ *adj.* **1.** [*before a noun*] usual: *The student took her accustomed seat in class.* —*Idiom.* **2. accustomed to,** used to; in the habit of: *was accustomed to winning.*

ace /eys/ *n.* [*count*] **1.** a playing card with a sin-gle spot: *an ace of hearts.* **2.** (in tennis, etc.) a point made on an untouched serve. **3.** an expert: *the ace of the pitching staff.*

ache /eyk/ *v.,* ached /eykt/, ach•ing, *n.* —*v.* [*no obj*] **1.** to have a continuous dull pain: *His back ached from lifting.* **2.** to want something very much; yearn; long: *was aching for a hot shower.* —*n.* [*count*] **3.** a continuous dull pain. —'**ach•y,** *adj.,* -i•er, -i•est.

a•chieve /ə'tʃiyv/ *v.,* a•chieved, a•chiev•ing. **1.** [~ + *obj*] to get by effort: *She achieved her goal of becoming a vice-president.* **2.** [*no obj*] to perform successfully: *Some smart children do not achieve in school.* —**a'chieve•ment,** *n.* [*non-count*]: *We all had a feeling of achievement.* [*count*]: *He was proud of his daughter's achieve-ments.* —**a'chiev•er,** *n.* [*count*]

ac•id /'æsɪd/ *n.* **1.** a chemical substance that

when strong enough can burn holes in what it touches and that can turn blue litmus paper red; a substance with a sour taste, like lemon or vine-gar: [*noncount*]: *How much acid is in the soil?* [*count*]: *An acid dissolves grease.* —*adj.* **2.** be-longing or relating to acids. **3.** sharp or biting to the taste; sour. **4.** (of remarks, writing, etc.) sharp, biting, or sarcastic. —**a•cid•ic** /ə'sɪdɪk/ *adj.* —**a'cid•i•ty,** *n.* [*noncount*]

ac•knowl•edge /æk'nɒlɪdʒ/ *v.* [~ + *obj*], -edged, -edg•ing. **1.** to admit to be real or true: *The loser acknowledged defeat.* **2.** to show that one is aware of: *The teacher acknowledged me with a smile.* **3.** to thank someone for: *He wrote a note to acknowledge the gift.* —**ac'knowl•edg-ment;** (*esp. Brit.*) **ac'knowl•edge•ment,** *n.* [*noncount*] [*count*]

ac•ne /'ækniy/ *n.* [*noncount*] a disorder of the skin, marked by pimples.

a•corn /'eykɔrn/ *n.* [*count*] the nut of an oak tree.

a•cous•tic /ə'kuwstɪk/ also **a'cous•ti•cal,** *adj.* [*before a noun*] **1.** concerning hearing or sound. **2.** sounded without electric or electronic strength-ening: *an acoustic guitar.*

a•cous•tics /ə'kuwstɪks/ *n.* **1.** [*noncount; used with a singular verb*] the study of sound and sound waves. **2.** [*plural; used with a plural verb*] the qualities of an enclosed space that determine how sounds are carried to a listener: *The acous-tics of the concert hall were good.*

ac•quaint /ə'kweynt/ *v.* [~ + *obj*] to make fa-miliar with something; inform: *I acquainted them with the rules for using e-mail.*

ac•quaint•ance /ə'kweyntns/ *n.* **1.** [*count*] a person whom one knows but does not know well: *only a business acquaintance.* **2.** knowledge or information about something: [*noncount*]: *his acquaintance with African literature.* [*count*]: *I have some acquaintance with computers.*

ac•qui•esce /,ækwiy'ɛs/ *v.* [*no obj*], -esced, -esc•ing. to agree to do something: *The president acquiesced to the plan.* —,**ac•qui'es•cence,** *n.* [*noncount*]

ac•quire /ə'kwayʳr/ *v.* [~ + *obj*], -quired, -quir•ing. to get or gain through one's own ef-forts: *The child acquired new skills.*

ac•qui•si•tion /,ækwɪ'zɪʃən/ *n.* **1.** [*noncount*] the act of acquiring. **2.** [*count*] something ac-quired: *His latest acquisition is a new car.*

ac•quit /ə'kwɪt/ *v.,* -quit•ted, -quit•ting. **1.** [~ + *obj*] to declare not guilty of a crime or offense: *The jury acquitted her of all charges.* **2.** [~ + *oneself*] to behave: *acquitted himself well in his first game.* —**ac'quit•tal,** *n.* [*noncount*] [*count*]

a•cre /'eykər/ *n.* [*count*] a unit of land measure, equal to 43,560 square feet.

ac•rid /'ækrɪd/ *adj.* strong in taste or smell: *acrid fumes.*

ac•ro•bat /'ækrə,bæt/ *n.* [*count*] a person who performs gymnastic feats, esp. difficult and dar-ing tricks: *The circus hired an acrobat who could walk on a tightrope.* —,**ac•ro'bat•ic,** *adj.*

ac•ro•bat•ics /,ækrə'bætɪks/ *n.* [*plural; used with a plural verb*] feats of an acrobat; gymnas-tics: *The acrobatics were thrilling.*

ac•ro•nym /'ækrənɪm/ *n.* [*count*] a word formed from the first letters or groups of letters of the words in a name or phrase, as *AIDS* from *ac-quired immune deficiency syndrome.* Compare AB-BREVIATION.

a•cross /ə'krɔs, ə'krɒs/ *prep.* **1.** from one side to the other of: *There is no bridge across that river.*

2. on or to the other side of; beyond: *My country is across the sea.* **3.** so as to cross: *The path cut across the meadow.* —*adv.* **4.** from one side to another; wide: *The crater was a mile across.* **5.** on the other side: *If we run, we'll soon be across.*

a•cryl•ic /ə'krɪlɪk/ *n.* [*noncount*] a synthetic material used to make paint and fiber for cloth.

act /ækt/ *n.* [*count*] **1.** anything done or to be done; deed: *Giving money to the poor is an act of mercy.* **2.** [*sometimes:* Act] a formal decision, law, or the like; a decree: *An act of Congress changed welfare laws in the U.S.* **3.** one of the main divisions of a play or opera: *We saw a drama in three acts at the theater.* **4.** a short performance by one or more entertainers, usually part of a variety show, circus, etc.: *an acrobatic act.* **5.** [*usually singular*] a display of insincere behavior assumed for effect; pretense: *We could tell from her voice that her apology was all an act.* —*v.* **6.** [*no obj*] to do something: *They acted quickly to put out the fire.* **7.** [*no obj*] to conduct oneself or function in a particular way: *The assistant acted as manager.* **8.** to perform as an actor: [*no obj*]: *That television star has acted on Broadway.* [~ + *obj*]: *to act Macbeth.* **9. act out, a.** to show or express by gestures or actions: *He acted out his frustrations by throwing things.* **b.** to perform: *The students acted out the roles in the play; to act the roles out.* **10. act up, a.** to behave badly; cause mischief: *The tired, cranky child acted up during the wedding.* **b.** (of an illness) to become troublesome: *His rheumatism is acting up.*

act•ing /'æktɪŋ/ *adj.* [*before a noun*] serving temporarily, esp. as a substitute during another's absence: *an acting mayor.*

ac•tion /'ækʃən/ *n.* **1.** [*noncount*] the process or state of acting or functioning; the state of being active: *We saw the team in action.* **2.** [*count*] something done or performed; act; deed: *His heroic actions on the battlefield earned him a medal.* **3.** [*noncount*] military combat: *My uncle saw action in the war.* **4.** a lawsuit: [*count*]: *The owner of the stolen automobile brought an action against the thief.* [*noncount*]: *to bring action against the thief.*

ac•ti•vate /'æktə,veyt/ *v.* [~ + *obj*], **-vat•ed, -vat•ing.** to make active; cause to function or act: *Pushing the switch activates the car alarm.* —**ac•ti•va•tion** /,æktə'veyʃən/, *n.* [*noncount*]

ac•tive /'æktɪv/ *adj.* **1.** characterized by action or activity: *an active life.* **2.** of or relating to a voice in grammar, a verb form, or construction in which the subject is usually the person or thing that performs or causes the action of the verb. In the verb form *write* in *I write letters every day*, the verb *write* is active (opposed to *passive*). —*n.* [*count*] **3.** the active voice, or a form in this voice: *Put that verb into the active.* —'**ac•tive•ly**, *adv.*

ac•tiv•ism /'æktə,vɪzəm/ *n.* [*noncount*] the belief in or practice of direct involvement to achieve political or other goals. —'**ac•tiv•ist**, *n.* [*count*], *adj.*

ac•tiv•i•ty /æk'tɪvɪtiy/ *n.*, *pl.* **-ties.** **1.** [*noncount*] the state or quality of being active or lively. **2.** [*count*] a specific deed, action, or function: *The family's social activities included going bowling.*

ac•tor /'æktər/ *n.* [*count*] a person who acts in stage plays, motion pictures, etc.

ac•tress /'æktrɪs/ *n.* [*count*] a woman who acts in stage plays, motion pictures, etc.

ac•tu•al /'æktʃuwəl/ *adj.* [*before a noun*] existing in act, fact, or reality; real: *The actual cost of the dinner includes a 10% tax.*

ac•tu•al•ly /'æktʃuwəliy/ *adv.* as a matter of fact; really.

ac•u•punc•ture /'ækyu,pʌŋktʃər/ *n.* [*noncount*] a Chinese medical practice that treats illness or provides local pain relief by inserting needles at certain places in the body.

a•cute /ə'kyuwt/ *adj.* **1.** sharp or severe; intense: *He was in acute pain after the accident.* **2.** extremely sensitive: *Because of her acute hearing, she heard them whispering in the next room.* **3. a.** (of an angle) less than 90°. **b.** (of a triangle) containing only acute angles. —a'**cute•ly**, *adv.*

ad /æd/ *n.* [*count*] an advertisement.

A.D. or **AD,** an abbreviation of Latin *anno Domini* (in the year of the Lord); since Christ was born (used before dates): *Charlemagne was born in* A.D. *742.* Compare B.C.

ad•age /'ædɪdʒ/ *n.* [*count*] a well-known, common saying; proverb: *The old adage, "a stitch in time saves nine," means that handling problems immediately saves trouble later.*

ad•a•mant /'ædəmənt, -,mænt/ *adj.* unyielding; inflexible: *an adamant refusal.* [*be* + ~ (+ *that clause*)]: *He was adamant that he was in the right.* —'**ad•a•mant•ly**, *adv.*

'**Adam's ,apple** /'ædəmz/ *n.* [*count*] a lump of cartilage at the front of the throat that, esp. in men, sticks out.

a•dapt /ə'dæpt/ *v.* [~ + *obj*] to make suitable to new or different conditions; adjust or modify appropriately: *They adapted the movie for a TV miniseries.* —**a•dapt•a•bil•i•ty** /ə,dæptə'bɪlɪtiy/ *n.* [*noncount*] —a'**dapt•a•ble**, *adj.* —**ad•ap•ta•tion** /,ædəp'teyʃən/ *n.* [*count*]

add /æd/ *v.* **1.** [~ + *obj*] to unite or join so as to bring about an increase: *We added a few more students to the class.* **2.** [~ + *obj*] to find the sum of: *We added the four numbers together.* **3.** [*no obj*] to perform arithmetic addition: *She could add almost as fast as a calculator.* **4.** [*no obj*] to be an addition: *His illness added to the family's troubles.* **5. add up,** to amount to the correct total: *These figures don't add up right. Add up the numbers* or *Add the numbers up.*

ad•den•dum /ə'dɛndəm/ *n.* [*count*], *pl.* **-da** (-də). something added; esp., a section added to a book.

ad•dict /*n.* 'ædɪkt; *v.* ə'dɪkt/ *n.* [*count*] **1.** one who is addicted to a substance, activity, or habit: *a drug addict; a sports addict.* —*v.* [~ + *obj*; *usually:* be + *addicted* + *to* + *obj*] **2.** to cause to become dependent on an addictive substance: *was addicted to cocaine.* **3.** to devote (oneself) excessively: *was addicted to jogging.* —**addiction,** *n.* [*noncount*] [*count*] —ad'**dic•tive,** *adj.*

ad•di•tion /ə'dɪʃən/ *n.* **1.** [*noncount*] the act or process of adding or uniting. **2.** [*count*] anything added, such as a room added to a building. —*Idiom.* **3. in addition,** besides; also. **4. in addition to,** as well as; besides.

ad•di•tion•al /ə'dɪʃənəl/ *adj.* added; extra: *She wore an additional sweater for warmth.* —ad'**di•tion•al•ly,** *adv.*

ad•di•tive /'ædɪtɪv/ *n.* [*count*] a substance added to another to change or improve its quality.

ad•dress /*n.* ə'drɛs, 'ædrɛs; *v.* ə'drɛs/ *n.* [*count*] **1.** the place where a person, organization, or the like is located. **2.** a usually formal speech or written statement. —*v.* [~ + *obj*] **3.** to direct a speech or statement to: *The president addressed the nation.* **4.** [~ + *obj* + *as* + *obj*] to use a specified form or title in speaking or writing to: *Address him as "Sir."* **5.** to deal with or discuss: *to address the problem.* **6.** to put the directions for delivery on: *to address a letter.*

ad•dress•ee /ˌædrɛˈsiy, ˌədrɛˈsiy/ *n.* [*count*] one to whom a piece of mail is addressed.

a•dept /əˈdɛpt/ *adj.* very skilled; expert: *adept at juggling.*

ad•e•quate /ˈædɪkwɪt/ *adj.* **1.** fully enough for some requirement or purpose: *adequate rainfall for farming.* **2.** barely satisfactory: *His work was adequate, nothing more.* —**ad•e•qua•cy** /ˈædɪkwəsiy/, *n.* [*noncount*] —**ad•e•quate•ly,** *adv.*

ad•here /ædˈhɪər/ *v.* [*no obj*], **-hered, -her•ing. 1.** to stay attached; stick fast: *The glued areas adhered. Mud adhered to my boots.* **2.** to stay with; be faithful to: *to adhere to a plan.* —**ad•her•ence** /ædˈhɪərəns, -ˈhɛr-/, *n.* [*noncount*]

ad•her•ent /ædˈhɪərənt, -ˈhɛr-/ *n.* [*count*] one who stays faithful to a belief, party, etc.: *a strong adherent of justice.*

ad•he•sive /ædˈhiysɪv, -zɪv/ *adj.* **1.** coated with a sticky substance: *adhesive bandages.* —*n.* [*noncount*] **2.** an adhesive substance, as glue.

adj., an abbreviation of: adjective.

ad•ja•cent /əˈdʒeysənt/ *adj.* lying near or close; touching or facing: *an adjacent page; Their yards were adjacent.* [*be* + ~ + *to*]: *a field adjacent to the house.*

ad•jec•tive /ˈædʒɪktɪv/ *n.* [*count*] a word that describes nouns, as *nice* in *a nice day,* or *beautiful* in *She is very beautiful. Abbr.:* adj.

ad•join /əˈdʒɔyn/ *v.* to be close to or in contact (with): [*no obj*]: *Our rooms in the hotel adjoined.* [~ + *obj*]: *The lobby adjoined the dining room.*

ad•journ /əˈdʒɜrn/ *v.* **1.** [~ + *obj*] to suspend the meeting of (a legislature, court, etc.) to a future time, another place, or indefinitely. **2.** [*no obj*] to go to another place: *Let's adjourn to the living room.* —**ad'journ•ment,** *n.* [*count*]

ad•junct /ˈædʒʌŋkt/ *n.* [*count*] something added to another thing but that is not essential to it.

ad•just /əˈdʒʌst/ *v.* **1.** [~ + *obj*] to change (something) so that it fits, corresponds, looks, or works better: *to adjust the picture on a TV set.* **2.** to adapt oneself; become adapted: [~ + *to* + *obj*]: *to adjust to new demands.* [~ + *oneself* + *to* + *obj*]: *They adjusted themselves to life in the city.* —**ad'just•ment,** *n.* [*count*] [*noncount*] —**ad'just•a•ble,** *adj.*

ad lib /ˈæd lɪb, ˈæd/ *adv.* freely and without planning: *The speaker added a few remarks ad lib.*

ad-lib /ˈæd lɪb, ˈæd-/ *v.,* **-libbed, -lib•bing,** *adj.* —*v.* **1.** to improvise all or part of (a speech, etc.): [~ + *obj*]: *He ad-libbed his speech.* [*no obj*]: *He ad-libbed for an hour.* —*adj.* **2.** unrehearsed: *ad-lib remarks.*

ad•min•is•ter /ædˈmɪnəstər/ *v.* [~ + *obj*] **1.** to direct or manage: *He administered the department.* **2.** to give out; dispense, as justice. **3.** to apply, as medicine.

ad•min•is•tra•tion /ædˌmɪnəˈstreyʃən/ *n.* **1.** [*noncount*] management, as of a government or business. **2.** [*count*] a body of executive officials, esp. (*often cap.*) the executive branch of a government. —**ad'min•is,tra•tor,** *n.* [*count*]

ad•min•is•tra•tive /ædˈmɪnəˌstreytɪv, -strətɪv/ *adj.* of or connected with administration; executive.

ad•mi•ral /ˈædmərəl/ *n.* [*count*] the commander in chief of a naval fleet.

ad•mire /ædˈmayⁿr/ *v.* [~ + *obj*], **-mired, -mir•ing. 1.** to regard with pleasure or approval: *She admired the scenery.* **2.** to regard highly; respect: *The boy admired his father.* —**ad•mi•ra•ble** /ˈædmərəbəl/ *adj.* —**ad•mi•ra•tion** /ˌædməˈreyʃən/ *n.* [*noncount*] —**ad'mir•er,** *n.* [*count*]

ad•mis•sion /ædˈmɪʃən/ *n.* **1.** [*noncount*] [*count*] the act of allowing to enter; entrance. **2.** [*noncount*] the price paid for entrance. **3.** [*count*] acknowledgment of the truth of something: *an admission of guilt.*

ad•mit /ædˈmɪt/ *v.* [~ + *obj*], **-mit•ted, -mit•ting. 1.** to allow to enter; let in: *The theater admits adults only.* **2.** to acknowledge; confess: *He admitted his guilt. He admitted that he was guilty. He admitted robbing the bank. She admitted to the crime.* —**ad'mit•ted•ly,** *adv.*: *Admittedly, I could have tried harder.*

ad•mit•tance /ædˈmɪtns/ *n.* [*noncount*] permission to enter.

ad•mon•ish /ædˈmɒnɪʃ/ *v.* [~ + *obj*] **1.** to caution or advise about something; warn: *The judge admonished the jury to disregard the outburst.* **2.** to correct or scold gently: *She admonished the children to be home on time.*

ad•mo•ni•tion /ˌædməˈnɪʃən/ *n.* **1.** [*count*] a gentle warning. **2.** [*noncount*] mild criticism or advice.

a•do /əˈduw/ *n.* [*noncount*] **1.** delaying activity: *We left without further ado.* **2.** energetic activity: *much ado about party plans.*

ad•o•les•cence /ˌædlˈɛsəns/ *n.* [*noncount*] the period in human development between puberty and adulthood.

ad•o•les•cent /ˌædlˈɛsənt/ *adj.* **1.** relating to or being in adolescence: *an adolescent child.* **2.** immature; juvenile: *Adolescent behavior is not acceptable in an adult.* —*n.* [*count*] **3.** a teenager.

a•dopt /əˈdɒpt/ *v.* [~ + *obj*] **1.** to take up and use or practice: *to adopt a nickname; to adopt a relaxed attitude.* **2.** to take and rear (the child of others) as one's own child, esp. by a formal legal act. —**a•dop•tion** /əˈdɒpʃən/ *n.* [*noncount*] [*count*]

a•dor•a•ble /əˈdɔrəbəl/ *adj.* very attractive or charming.

a•dore /əˈdɔr/ *v.* [~ + *obj*], **a•dored, a•dor•ing. 1.** to worship as divine: *to adore God.* **2.** to like or admire very much: *I adore your new shoes. They adored shopping.* —**ad•o•ra•tion** /ˌædəˈreyʃən/, *n.* [*noncount*]

a•dorn /əˈdɔrn/ *v.* [~ + *obj*] to decorate or add beauty to, as by ornaments: *Garlands of flowers adorned their hair.*

a•drift /əˈdrɪft/ *adj.* [*be* + ~] **1.** floating without control; drifting: *The boats were adrift in the sea.* **2.** without aim or direction: *After he lost his job, he felt adrift.*

ad•u•late /ˈædʒəˌleyt/ *v.* [~ + *obj*], **-lat•ed, -lat•ing.** to admire or flatter too much: *fans adulating a rock star.* —**ad•u•la•tion** /ˌædʒəˈleyʃən/, *n.* [*noncount*]

a•dult /əˈdʌlt, ˈædʌlt/ *n.* [*count*] **1.** a person who is fully grown or of legal age: *Only adults may purchase alcohol.* —*adj.* [*usually: before a noun*] **2.** having reached full size and strength; mature: *adult plants.* **3.** of or intended for adults: *an adult film.* —**a'dult•hood,** *n.* [*noncount*]

a•dul•ter•y /ə'dʌltəriy/ *n.* [*noncount*] [*count*], *pl.* **-ies.** (an act of) voluntary sexual intercourse between a married person and someone other than his or her lawful spouse. —**a'dul•ter•er,** *n.* [*count*] —**a'dul•ter•ess,** *n.* [*count*] —**a'dul•ter•ous,** *adj.*

adv., an abbreviation of: **1.** adverb. **2.** advertisement.

ad•vance /æd'væns/ *v.,* **-vanced, -vanc•ing,** *n.,* *adj.* —*v.* **1.** to move, send, or bring forward: [~ + *obj*]: *to advance a deadline; The general advanced his armies to the border.* [*no obj*]: *The army advanced to the border. He advanced on the city.* **2.** [~ + *obj*] [*no obj*] to raise in rank; promote. —*n.* **3.** [*count*] a forward movement: *the advance of the troops.* **4.** [*count*] a development showing progress: *The prize is awarded for advances in science.* **5.** Usually, **advances.** [*plural*] attempts made to become acquainted, reach an agreement, or gain favor. —*adj.* [*before a noun*] **6.** going or placed before: *an advance guard.* **7.** made, given, or issued ahead of time: *an advance payment.* —*Idiom.* **8. in advance,** beforehand: *Get your tickets in advance.* —**ad'vance•ment,** *n.* [*count*]

ad•vanced /æd'vænst/ *adj.* **1.** far along in progress, development, or time. **2.** beyond the beginning, elementary, or intermediate: *advanced mathematics.*

ad•van•tage /æd'væntɪdʒ/ *n., v.,* **-taged, -tag•ing.** —*n.* **1.** [*count*] a circumstance favorable to success: *the advantages of a good education.* **2.** [*noncount*] benefit; gain: *It will be to your advantage to study Chinese.* **3.** [*count*] a position of superiority: *Knowledge of foreign policy gave the candidate an advantage.* —*Idiom.* **4. take advantage of, a.** to make good use of: *to take advantage of an opportunity.* **b.** to impose upon in a selfish way: *You took unfair advantage of our friendship.* —**ad•van•ta•geous** /ˌædvən'tey dʒəs/, *adj.*

ad•vent /'ædvɛnt/ *n.* **1.** [*count*] an arrival; a coming: *the advent of the holiday season.* **2.** [*usually: Advent*] the coming of Christ into the world.

ad•ven•ture /æd'vɛntʃər/ *n.* **1.** [*count*] an exciting and unusual experience. **2.** [*noncount*] a liking for danger, excitement, etc.: *a spirit of adventure.* —**ad'ven•tur•er,** *n.* [*count*] —**ad'ven•tur•ous, ad'ven•ture•some,** *adj.*

ad•verb /'ædvɜrb/ *n.* [*count*] a word that modifies or describes a verb, an adjective, or another adverb. Adverbs usually express some relation of place (*here, there*), time (*now, then*), manner (*well, quickly*), degree (*very, extremely*), etc. *Abbr.:* adv.

ad•ver•sar•y /'ædvər,sɛriy/ *n.* [*count*], *pl.* **-ies.** a person, group, etc., that opposes or attacks; opponent; enemy.

ad•verse /æd'vɜrs, 'ædvɜrs/ *adj.* [*before a noun*] **1.** unfavorable or hostile: *adverse criticism.* **2.** being in an opposite direction: *adverse winds.* —**ad'verse•ly,** *adv.*

ad•ver•si•ty /æd'vɜrsɪtiy/ *n.,* *pl.* **-ties** for 2. **1.** [*noncount*] misfortune; trouble. **2.** [*count*] an unfavorable or unfortunate event or circumstance: *to cope with life's many adversities.*

ad•ver•tise /'ædvər,tayz, ˌædvər'tayz/ *v.,* **-tised, -tis•ing.** to announce or praise (a product, service, etc.) in newspapers, radio, or television, in order to sell it: [~ + *obj*]: *to advertise a new car.* [*no obj*]: *They advertised in the paper.* —**'ad•ver,tis•er,** *n.* [*count*]

ad•ver•tise•ment /ˌædvər'tayzmənt, æd'vɜrtɪsmənt, -tɪz-/ *n.* [*count*] a paid public announcement intended to advertise something.

ad•vice /æd'vays/ *n.* [*noncount*] an opinion offered as a guide to action.

ad•vis•a•ble /æd'vayzəbəl/ *adj.* [*be* + ~] wise or sensible, as a course of action: *Preparing for an interview is advisable. It's advisable to get a second opinion.* —**ad•vis•a•bil•i•ty** /æd,vayzə'bɪlɪtiy/, *n.* [*noncount*] —**ad'vis•a•bly,** *adv.*

ad•vise /æd'vayz/ *v.,* **-vised, -vis•ing. 1.** to give advice (to), esp. to recommend as wise or sensible: [~ + *obj*]: *She advised secrecy. I advised the new student to take a music course.* [*no obj*]: *We did as she advised.* **2.** [~ + *obj*] to give (a person, group, etc.) information or notice; tell or inform: *The police advised the suspect of his rights. They advised him that he might face imprisonment.*

ad•vis•er or **ad•vis•or** /æd'vayzər/ *n.* [*count*] a person who gives advice; counselor.

ad•vi•so•ry /æd'vayzəriy/ *adj.* **1.** giving or containing advice: *an advisory letter to shareholders.* **2.** having the power or duty to advise: *an advisory council.*

ad•vo•ca•cy /'ædvəkəsiy/ *n.* [*noncount*] the act of supporting something publicly.

ad•vo•cate /*v.* 'ædvə,keyt; *n.* -kɪt, -,keyt/ *v.,* **-cat•ed, -cat•ing,** *n.* —*v.* [~ + *obj*] **1.** to support or urge by argument: *to advocate higher salaries for teachers.* —*n.* [*count*] **2.** a person who speaks or writes in support of a cause, person, etc.

aer•i•al /'ɛəriyəl/ *adj.* **1.** of, in, produced by, or done in the air: *aerial photography.* **2.** of or relating to aircraft: *aerial combat.* —*n.* [*count*] **3.** a radio or television antenna.

aer•o•bics /ɛə'rowbɪks/ *n.* exercises, as jogging or swimming, that stimulate and strengthen the heart: [*noncount; used with a singular verb*]: *Aerobics is a good way to lose weight.* [*plural; used with a plural verb*]: *The aerobics were fairly tiring.*

aer•o•dy•nam•ic /ˌɛərowday'næmɪk/ *adj.* able to flow smoothly and easily through air: *an aerodynamic design.*

aer•o•nau•tics /ˌɛərə'nɔtɪks, -'nɒtɪks/ *n.* [*noncount; used with a singular verb*] the science or art of flight.

aer•o•plane /'ɛərə,pleyn/ *n.* Brit. AIRPLANE.

aer•o•space /'ɛərow,speys/ *n.* [*noncount*] **1.** the earth's atmosphere and the space beyond. —*adj.* [*before a noun*] **2.** of or relating to aerospace, or to the industry concerned with the design and building of spacecraft.

aes•thet•ic or **es•thet•ic** /ɛs'θɛtɪk/ *adj.* of or relating to a sense of beauty or an appreciation of the arts: *a keen aesthetic sense.* —**aes'thet•i•cal•ly,** *adv.*

a•far /ə'fɑr/ *adv.* —*Idiom.* **from afar,** from a distance: *We saw him coming from afar.*

af•fa•ble /'æfəbəl/ *adj.* warm and friendly: *affable neighbors.* —**af•fa•bil•i•ty** /ˌæfə'bɪlɪtiy/, *n.* [*noncount*] —**'af•fa•bly,** *adv.*

af•fair /ə'fɛər/ *n.* [*count*] **1.** something requiring action or effort. **2. affairs,** [*plural*] matters of commercial or public interest: *affairs of state.* **3.** a private or personal concern: *That's not your affair.* **4.** an often brief sexual relationship between two people not married to each other. **5.** a social gathering.

af•fect[1] /ə'fɛkt/ *v.* [~ + *obj*] **1.** to produce an effect or change in; act on: *Cold weather affected the crops.* **2.** to impress the mind or move the feelings of: *The tragedy affected him deeply.* —**Usage.** Because of similarity in pronunciation, AFFECT and EFFECT are sometimes confused in writing. The verb AFFECT means "to act on" or "to move" (*His words affected the crowd so deeply that many wept*). The verb EFFECT means "to bring about, accomplish": *The new taxes effected many changes in people's lives.* The noun EFFECT means "result, consequence": *the tragic effects of the hurricane.*

af•fect² /ə'fɛkt/ *v.* [~ + *obj*] to pretend: *to affect concern for others.*

af•fec•ta•tion /ˌæfɛk'teyʃən/ *n.* **1.** [*noncount*] the pretense of having a knowledge, standing, etc., that is not actually possessed: *the affectation of great wealth.* **2.** [*count*] an artificial way of behaving.

af•fec•tion /ə'fɛkʃən/ *n.* [*noncount*] [*count*] fond devotion or love.

af•fec•tion•ate /ə'fɛkʃənɪt/ *adj.* showing fondness or love: *an affectionate hug.* —**af'fec•tion•ate•ly,** *adv.*

af•fil•i•ate /v. ə'fɪliy,eyt/ *n.* -ɪt, -,eyt/ *v.,* -at•ed, -at•ing, *n.* —*v.* **1.** to bring into close association or connection: [*no obj*]: *The two groups affiliated.* [~ + *obj; often:* be + affiliated + with + *obj*]: *The research center is affiliated with the university.* [~ + *oneself* + *with*]: *affiliated themselves with a political party.* —*n.* [*count*] **2.** an affiliated person or organization; a member: *a TV network's affiliates.* —**af•fil•i•a•tion** /ə,fɪliy'eyʃən/, *n.* [*count*] [*noncount*]

af•fin•i•ty /ə'fɪnɪtiy/ *n.* [~ + *for/with/to/ between*], *pl.* -ties. **1.** [*noncount*] [*count*] a natural liking for or attraction to a person, thing, idea, etc. **2.** [*count*] [*noncount*] relationship, esp. by marriage.

af•firm /ə'fɜrm/ *v.* [~ + *obj*] **1.** to assert positively; declare: *to affirm one's loyalty; He affirmed that he would not reveal my secret.* **2.** to confirm formally, as a court decision. —**af•fir•ma•tion** /ˌæfər'meyʃən/ *n.* [*count*] [*noncount*]

af•firm•a•tive /ə'fɜrmətɪv/ *adj.* **1.** expressing agreement or consent: *an affirmative reply.* —*n.* [*count*] **2.** [*in the* + ~] a manner or mode that indicates assent: *a reply in the affirmative.*

af'firmative 'action, *n.* [*noncount*] a policy to increase opportunities for women and minorities, esp. in employment and education.

af•fix /v. ə'fɪks; *n.* 'æfɪks/ *v.* [~ + *obj*] **1.** to fasten, join, or attach: *to affix stamps to a letter.* —*n.* [*count*] **2.** (in grammar) an element such as a prefix or suffix, added to a base or stem of a word to form another word. Examples are the past tense suffix *-ed* added to *want* to form *wanted,* or the negative prefix *im-* added to *possible* to form *impossible.*

af•flict /ə'flɪkt/ *v.* [~ + *obj; often:* be + afflicted + *with*] to cause distress or great trouble with mental or bodily pain: *to be afflicted with arthritis.* —**af•flic•tion** /ə'flɪkʃən/, *n.* [*count*]

af•flu•ence /'æfluwəns/ *n.* [*noncount*] the state of having an abundance of money and material goods. —**af•flu•ent,** *adj.*

af•ford /ə'fɔrd/ *v.* [~ + *obj*] **1.** to be able to undergo without serious consequence: *The country can't afford another drought. We can't afford to take the chance.* **2.** to be able to meet the expense of or pay for: *Can I afford a new car?* **3.** to supply; give: *The sale of the house afforded them a profit.* —**af'ford•a•ble,** *adj.*

af•front /ə'frʌnt/ *n.* [*count*] a deliberate act or display of disrespect; insult.

Af•ghan /'æfgæn/ *n.* [*count*] **1.** [*afghan*] a soft knitted or crocheted blanket, often in a geometric pattern. **2.** a hunting dog with long, silky hair.

a•field /ə'fiyld/ *adv.* Usually: **far afield,** away (from home): *The students came from far afield.*

a•float /ə'flowt/ *adj., adv.* **1.** floating or staying on the surface of the water: *The ship was still afloat. We kept the raft afloat.* **2.** financially solvent: *The company was barely afloat after the recession. He kept the company afloat.*

a•foul /ə'fawl/ *adj.* [*after a noun*] —**Idiom. run** or **fall afoul of, 1.** to become entangled with: *The boat ran afoul of the seaweed.* **2.** to come into conflict with: *He ran afoul of the law.*

a•fraid /ə'freyd/ *adj.* **1.** feeling fear: *He suddenly became afraid. I'm afraid of heights. She was afraid to go outside.* **2.** [~ + *(that) clause*] feeling regret or unhappiness: *I'm afraid we can't go.*

Af•ri•can /'æfrɪkən/ *adj.* **1.** of or relating to Africa. —*n.* [*count*] **2.** a person born or living in Africa.

'African-A'merican, *n.* [*count*] **1.** a black American of African descent. —*adj.* **2.** of or relating to African-Americans.

Af•ro /'æfrow/ *n.* [*count*], *pl.* **-ros.** a full, bushy hairstyle of very curly or frizzy hair.

Af•ro-A•mer•i•can /ˌæfrowə'mɛrɪkən/ *n., adj.* AFRICAN-AMERICAN.

af•ter /'æftər/ *prep.* **1.** behind in place or position: *We marched one after the other.* **2.** later in time: *Tell me after supper.* **3.** in search of: *I'm after a better job.* **4.** in agreement with: *a man after my own heart.* **5.** with the same name as: *They named her after my grandmother.* —*adv.* **6.** behind: *The marchers came first and the floats came after.* **7.** later in time; afterward: *They lived happily ever after.* —*conj.* **8.** following the time when: *After the boys left, we cleaned up the house.* —**Idiom. 9. after all,** nevertheless: *We were angry with her, but, after all, she was our child and we had to forgive her.*

af•ter•life /'æftər,layf/ *n.* [*noncount*] [*count*] life after death.

af•ter•math /'æftər,mæθ/ *n.* [*count; usually singular*] something that follows from an event: *in the aftermath of the war.*

af•ter•noon /ˌæftər'nuwn/ *n.* **1.** the time from noon until evening: [*count*]: *every afternoon.* [*noncount; by* + ~]: *I'll get it done by afternoon.* —*adj.* **2.** of, relating to, or occurring during the afternoon: *an afternoon nap.*

af•ter•taste /'æftər,teyst/ *n.* [*count; usually singular*] a taste remaining in the mouth.

af•ter•thought /'æftər,θɔt/ *n.* **1.** [*noncount*] a later thought. **2.** [*count*] something added later.

af•ter•ward /'æftərwərd/ also **'af•ter•wards,** *adv.* at a later time: *We had dinner and watched TV afterward.*

a•gain /ə'gɛn/ *adv.* **1.** once more; another time: *Try again.* **2.** back into a former state: *well again; home again.* —**Idiom. 3. again and again,** often. **4. then again,** on the other hand; however: *It might rain, but then again it might not.*

a•gainst /ə'gɛnst/ *prep.* **1.** in opposition to; contrary to: *to fight against crime.* **2.** in resistance to or defense from: *protection against mosquitoes.* **3.** in an opposite direction to: *sailing against the wind.* **4.** in or into contact with; upon: *to lean against the door.*

age /eydʒ/ *n., v.,* **aged, ag•ing** or **age•ing.** —*n.*

1. the length of time during which a being or thing has existed: [*noncount*]: *Trees of unknown age.* [*count*]: *Their ages are 10 and 13.* **2.** [*noncount*] a period of human life. **3.** [*noncount*] old age: *His eyes were dim with age.* **4.** [*count; often: Age*] a particular period of history: *the Stone Age.* **5.** [*count; often plural*] a long period of time: *I haven't seen you for ages.* —*v.* **6.** to (cause to) grow old: [*no obj*]: *She is aging gracefully.* [~ + *obj*]: *Worry aged him overnight.* **7.** [*no obj*] [~ + *obj*] to (cause to) ripen or become mature, as cheese or wine. —*Idiom.* **8. be** or **come of age,** to reach an age at which one may vote, buy alcohol, etc., legally.

-age, a suffix meaning: action or process (*coverage*); result of (*wreckage*); residence of (*parsonage*); charge (*postage*).

a•ged /'eydʒɪd *for 1;* eydʒd *for 2, 3* / *adj.* **1.** of advanced age; old. **2.** of the age of: [*after a noun*]: *a man aged 40 years.* [*be* + ~]: *My daughter is aged 13.* **3.** brought to a desired state, as wine or cheese.

a•gen•cy /'eydʒənsiy/ *n.*, *pl.* **-cies. 1.** [*count*] an organization, company, or bureau representing or doing business for another: *an insurance agency; an employment agency.* **2.** [*count*] a government bureau. **3.** [*noncount*] a means of doing something.

a•gen•da /ə'dʒɛndə/ *n.* [*count*], *pl.* **-das** or **-da.** a list of things to be done: *Make up an agenda for the meeting.*

a•gent /'eydʒənt/ *n.* [*count*] **1.** a person or thing that acts. **2.** a person or business authorized to act for another: *The pitcher's agent got him a higher salary.* **3.** a means by which something is done: *an agent of change; a chemical agent.* **4.** a person who works for or manages an agency: *a travel agent; a government agent.*

ag•gra•vate /'ægrə,veyt/ *v.* [~ + *obj*], **-vat•ed, -vat•ing. 1.** to make worse or more severe; intensify: *Arguing only aggravated our problems.* **2.** to annoy; irritate: *The constant noise aggravated us.* —**ag•gra•va•tion** /,ægrə'veyʃən/, *n.* [*noncount*] [*count*] —**Usage.** In formal speech and writing, the meaning "to annoy" (*Stop aggravating me!*) is sometimes criticized and is used less often than the meaning "to make worse" (*His angry words aggravated the tense situation*).

ag•gre•gate /'ægrɪgɪt, -,geyt/ *n.* [*count*] **1.** a sum, mass, or collection of individual items: *an aggregate of some 500 points earned over 5 years.* —*Idiom.* **2. in the aggregate,** considered as a whole.

ag•gres•sion /ə'grɛʃən/ *n.* [*noncount*] hostility toward or attack upon another, whether in words or other acts.

ag•gres•sive /ə'grɛsɪv/ *adj.* **1.** marked by or tending toward aggression; warlike; hostile. **2.** forcefully energetic: *an aggressive salesperson.* —**ag'gres•sive•ly,** *adv.* —**ag'gres•sive•ness,** *n.* [*noncount*]

a•ghast /ə'gæst/ *adj.* [*be* + ~] filled with sudden fear, horror, or amazement: *was aghast after witnessing the accident.*

ag•ile /'ædʒəl, -ayl/ *adj.* **1.** quick and skillful in movement; nimble: *agile athletes.* **2.** quick and keen: *an agile mind.* —**a•gil•i•ty** /ə'dʒɪlɪtiy/, *n.* [*noncount*]

ag•i•tate /'ædʒɪ,teyt/ *v.* [~ + *obj*], **-tat•ed, -tat•ing. 1.** to move or shake violently: *The strong winds agitated the plane.* **2.** to disturb emotionally; upset: *Please don't agitate the pa-*

tients. —**ag•i•ta•tion** /,ædʒɪ'teyʃən/, *n.* [*noncount*]

a•glow /ə'glow/ *adj.* [*be* + ~ (+ *with*)] glowing: *The room was aglow with sunlight.*

ag•nos•tic /æg'nɒstɪk/ *n.* [*count*] a person who believes that no one can know for certain about the existence of God. —**ag•nos•ti•cism** /æg'nɒstə,sɪzəm/, *n.* [*noncount*]

a•go /ə'gow/ *adj.* [*after a noun*] **1.** gone by; past: *She got here five days ago.* —*adv.* **2.** in the past: *It happened long ago.*

ag•o•nize /'ægə,nayz/ *v.* [~ + *over* + *obj*], **-nized, -niz•ing.** to suffer great mental pain or anxiety, as by thinking about something continuously: *They agonized every night over their decision.*

ag•o•ny /'ægəniy/ *n.* [*noncount*] [*count*], *pl.* **-nies.** extreme mental or physical pain or suffering.

a•gree /ə'griy/ *v.*, **a•greed, a•gree•ing. 1.** [*no obj*] to have the same opinion: *We don't agree on politics. I agree with what you say.* **2.** [*no obj*] to give consent: *Do you agree to those conditions? Do you agree to accept those conditions?* **3.** to be the same as or similar to: [*no obj*]: *His story and mine agree.* [~ + *with* + *obj*]: *Her story agrees with mine.* **4.** [~ + *with* + *obj*] to be healthful or pleasing: *Hot weather doesn't agree with me.* **5.** [~ + *that clause*] to admit as true: *We all agree that you did your best.* **6.** (of a subject and a verb in English, or of a pronoun and the word it stands for) to correspond by having the correct forms: [~ + *with* + *obj*]: *The subject agrees with the verb.* [*no obj*]: *The subject and verb agree.*

a•gree•a•ble /ə'griyəbəl/ *adj.* **1.** to one's liking; pleasing: *agreeable manners; an agreeable voice.* **2.** willing to agree: *Are you agreeable to my plans?* —**a'gree•a•bly,** *adv.*

a•gree•ment /ə'griymənt/ *n.* **1.** [*noncount*] the act of agreeing or of coming to a mutual arrangement. **2.** [*count*] an arrangement accepted by all parties: *At long last we had an agreement.* **3.** [*noncount*] the correspondence in form between the subject and verb in certain tenses, or between a noun and a possessive pronoun.

ag•ri•cul•ture /'ægrɪ,kʌltʃər/ *n.* [*noncount*] the science, art, or work concerned with cultivating land and raising crops and livestock; farming. —,**ag•ri'cul•tur•al,** *adj.*

a•ground /ə'grawnd/ *adv.* onto the ground beneath a body of water: *The ship ran aground.*

a•head /ə'hɛd/ *adv.* **1.** in, at, or to the front: *Can you see ahead in the dark?* **2.** in a forward direction; onward: *The traffic moved ahead slowly.* **3.** into or for the future: *It's wise to plan ahead.* —*adj.* [*be* + ~] **4.** winning or leading: *Our team was ahead at halftime.* —*Idiom.* **5. ahead of,** before: *I always arrived ahead of the others.* **6. get ahead,** to move onward to success.

a•hoy /ə'hɔy/ *interj.* (used at sea to call to another ship, attract attention, etc.): *Ahoy, there!*

aid /eyd/ *v.* **1.** to help: [~ + *obj*]: *to aid a needy family.* [*no obj*]: *They aided in the development of the country.* —*n.* [*noncount*] **2.** help or support; assistance: *financial aid.*

aide /eyd/ *n.* [*count*] an assistant or helper, esp. a confidential one: *an administrative aide.*

AIDS /eydz/ *n.* [*noncount*] acquired immune deficiency syndrome: a disease of the immune system that makes the person less able to resist infection, cancer, etc.

ail /eyl/ *v.* **1.** [~ + *obj*] to cause pain or trouble to: *What ails you?* **2.** [*no obj*] to be ill: *She's been ailing all day.*

ail·ment /'eylmənt/ *n.* [*count*] a physical disorder or illness, esp. a minor one.

aim /eym/ *v.* **1.** to point (a firearm, ball, etc.) so that the thing discharged or thrown will hit a target: [~ + *obj*]: *The police officer aimed the pistol and fired.* [*no obj*]: *He turned, aimed, and fired. She aimed at the target.* **2.** [~ + *obj*] to direct toward a particular goal: *The lawyer aimed his remarks at the jury.* **3.** [*no obj*] to direct one's efforts: *We aim at pleasing everyone. We aim to please.* —*n.* [*noncount*] the act of directing anything at or toward a target. **5.** [*count*] purpose; intention: *It is my aim to reform the program.*

aim·less /'eymlɪs/ *adj.* being without purpose: *aimless violence.* —**'aim·less·ly,** *adv.*

ain't /eynt/ *v.* **1.** *Nonstandard except in some dialects.* am not; are not; is not. **2.** *Nonstandard.* have not; has not.

air /ɛər/ *n.* **1.** [*noncount; often: the* + ~] the mixture of nitrogen, oxygen, and other gases that surrounds the earth and forms its atmosphere. **2.** [*noncount; often: the* + ~] the sky. **3.** [*count; singular*] general character or appearance; aura: *had an air of mystery about him.* **4. airs,** [*plural*] affected manners: *Stop putting on airs.* —*v.* **5.** to expose to the air; ventilate: [~ + *obj*]: *to air (out) a room; Let's air the room (out).* [*no obj*]: *Let the room air (out).* **6.** [~ + *obj*] to bring to public notice: *to air one's opinions.* **7.** [~ + *obj*] [*no obj*] to broadcast or televise; to be broadcast or televised. —*Idiom.* **8. clear the air,** to get rid of misunderstandings. **9. off the air,** not broadcasting: *Suddenly the station went off the air.* **10. on the air,** broadcasting: *The President is on the air tonight.* **11. up in the air,** not decided; unsettled: *Their plans are still up in the air.*

'air ,bag, *n.* [*count*] a bag that inflates automatically inside a motor vehicle to protect the driver and passengers in a collision.

air·borne /'ɛər,bɔrn/ *adj.* **1.** carried by the air: *airborne pollution.* **2.** [*be* + ~] in flight: *The plane was soon airborne.*

'air con,ditioning, *n.* [*noncount*] a system for reducing the temperature and humidity of the air in an enclosed space. —**'air-con,ditioned,** *adj.* —**'air-con,ditioner,** *n.* [*count*]

air·craft /'ɛər,kræft/ *n.* [*count*], *pl.* **-craft.** any machine that can fly, esp. airplanes, gliders, and helicopters.

'air ,force, *n.* [*count*] the military unit of any nation that carries out air operations.

air·line /'ɛər,layn/ *n.* [*count*] **1.** a company or system furnishing air transportation between specified points. —*adj.* [*before a noun*] **2.** of, for, or on an airline: *an airline pilot; airline tickets.*

air·lin·er /'ɛər,laynər/ *n.* [*count*] a passenger aircraft operated by an airline.

air·mail or **air-mail** /'ɛər,meyl/ *n.* [*noncount*] Also, **'air ,mail. 1.** a system of sending mail by airplane. —*adj.* [*before a noun*] **2.** of or relating to airmail: *airmail delivery.* —*adv.* **3.** by airmail: *to send letters airmail.* —*v.* [~ + *obj*] **4.** to send by airmail: *He airmailed the letters. He airmailed the letters to us. She airmailed us the letters.*

air·plane /'ɛər,pleyn/ *n.* [*count*] a vehicle that has wings and flies by means of propellers or jet engines. Also, *esp. Brit.*, **aeroplane.**

air·port /'ɛər,pɔrt/ *n.* [*count*] a place that has facilities for the landing, takeoff, shelter, supply, and repair of aircraft.

air·sick /'ɛər,sɪk/ *adj.* [*often: be* + ~] ill with motion sickness during air travel.

air·tight /'ɛər,tayt/ *adj.* **1.** sealed so as to prevent the entrance or escape of air or gas: *an airtight container.* **2.** having no weak points: *an airtight argument.*

air·waves /'ɛər,weyvz/ *n.* [*plural*] the radio waves used for radio and television broadcasting.

air·way /'ɛər,wey/ *n.* [*count*] the passageway from the nose or mouth to the lungs.

air·y /'ɛəriy/ *adj.*, **-i·er, -i·est. 1.** open to the air; breezy: *airy rooms.* **2.** light in manner; lively: *airy songs.*

aisle /ayl/ *n.* [*count*] a walkway between or along sections of seats or shelves, as in a theater or department store.

a·jar /ə'dʒɑr/ *adj., adv.* partly open: *The door was ajar. She had left the door ajar.*

AK, an abbreviation of: Alaska.

a.k.a. or **aka,** an abbreviation of: also known as: *Clark Kent, a.k.a. Superman.*

a·kin /ə'kɪn/ *adj.* [*be* + ~ + *to*] having similar properties, qualities, preferences, etc.: *Her thoughts on the subject were akin to mine.*

-al¹, an adjective suffix meaning: of or relating to (*tribal*); having the character of (*natural*).

-al², a noun suffix meaning act or process of (*refusal*).

AL, an abbreviation of: Alabama.

Ala., an abbreviation of: Alabama.

al·a·bas·ter /'ælə,bæstər/ *n.* [*noncount*] a kind of white, chalklike substance used for ornaments and statues.

à la carte or **a la carte** /ɑlɑ'kɑrt, ,ælə/ *adv., adj.* from or according to a menu having a separate price for each item: *We ordered à la carte. Everything is à la carte.*

a·lac·ri·ty /ə'lækrɪtiy/ *n.* [*noncount*] cheerful readiness and quickness: *She responded with alacrity when he invited her to the dance.*

a·larm /ə'lɑrm/ *n.* **1.** [*noncount*] a sudden fear caused by danger; fright. **2.** [*count*] a warning of approaching danger: *The neighbors raised the alarm.* **3.** [*count*] an automatic device that warns of danger: *The smoke alarm went off at 4 a.m.* —*v.* [~ + *obj*] **4.** to make fearful; frighten: *The news of the robbery alarmed the neighbors.* **5.** to warn of danger.

a'larm ,clock, *n.* [*count*] a clock with a bell or buzzer that can be set to sound at a particular time, as to awaken someone.

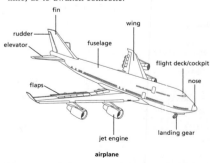

airplane

a·larm·ing /ə'lɑrmɪŋ/ *adj.* frightening; worrisome: *an alarming rise in crime.*

Alas., an abbreviation of: Alaska.

a•las /ə'læs/ *interj.* (used to express regret or concern): *We lost the money, alas.*

al•ba•tross /'ælbə,trɔs, -,trɒs/ *n.* [*count*], *pl.* **-tross•es**, (*esp. when thought of as a group*) **-tross** for 1. **1.** a large, web-footed bird of southern tropical oceanic waters. **2.** a burden: *This huge debt is the company's albatross.*

al•bi•no /æl'baynow/ *n.* [*count*], *pl.* **-nos.** a person with pale skin, white hair, pinkish eyes, and vision problems due to a genetic inability to produce a certain pigment.

al•bum /'ælbəm/ *n.* [*count*] **1.** a book made up of blank pages for collecting or displaying photographs, autographs, stamps, etc. **2.** a long-playing musical record or a set of such records: *The album sold several million copies.*

al•co•hol /'ælkə,hɔl, -,hɒl/ *n.* [*noncount*] **1.** an intoxicating colorless liquid found in wine, beer, and liquor. **2.** any drink containing this liquid.

al•co•hol•ic /,ælkə'hɔlɪk, -'hɒlɪk/ *adj.* **1.** of or relating to alcohol; containing or using alcohol: *alcoholic beverages.* —*n.* [*count*] **2.** a person suffering from alcoholism.

al•co•hol•ism /'ælkəhɔ,lɪzəm, -hɒ-/ *n.* [*noncount*] a disease marked by strong and long-term dependence on alcohol, failing physical health, and difficulty in functioning in society.

al•cove /'ælkowv/ *n.* [*count*] a recessed space in a room: *a dining alcove.*

ale /eyl/ *n.* [*noncount*] [*count*] an alcoholic beverage that is made from malt and is darker and more bitter than beer.

a•lert /ə'lɜrt/ *adj.* **1.** giving full attention; wideawake: *The children were alert, listening carefully to the teacher's instructions.* —*n.* [*count*] **2.** a warning or alarm before a military attack, a storm, etc.: *a tornado alert.* —*v.* [~ + *obj*] **3.** to make aware of; warn: *alerting the townspeople to the danger.* —a'lert•ly, *adv.* —a'lert•ness, *n.* [*noncount*]

al•fal•fa /æl'fælfə/ *n.* [*noncount*] a plant of the legume family used esp. to feed animals.

al•gae /'ældʒiy/ *n.pl.; sing.:* **-ga** (-gə). one-celled plants containing chlorophyll and usually found in water.

al•ge•bra /'ældʒəbrə/ *n.* [*noncount*] a branch of mathematics that uses letters and other symbols to represent numbers or values. —**al•ge•bra•ic** /,ældʒə'breyɪk/, *adj.* —,al•ge'bra•i•cal•ly, *adv.*

a•li•as /'eyliyəs/ *n.* [*count*], *pl.* **-as•es.** an additional or false name: *The thief used an alias instead of his real name.*

al•i•bi /'ælə,bay/ *n.* [*count*], *pl.* **-bis.** the proof of a claim by an accused person of having been elsewhere when a crime was committed: *He has a good alibi for the night of the murder.*

al•ien /'eylyən, 'eyliyən/ *n.* [*count*] **1.** a foreign-born person without legal citizenship in the country where he or she lives. **2.** a being or creature from outer space; an extraterrestrial. —*adj.* **3.** [*before a noun*] foreign; strange: *His alien style of dressing gave him an odd appearance.* **4.** unlike one's own; strange: *frightened by the alien environment; alien ideas.*

al•ien•ate /'eylyə,neyt, 'eyliyə-/ *v.* [~ + *obj*], **-at•ed, -at•ing.** to cause (someone) to stop having friendly feelings or interest: *He has alienated most of neighbors.* —al•ien•a•tion /,eylyə'neyʃən, 'eyliyə-/ *n.* [*noncount*]

a•light /ə'layt/ *v.* [~ + *obj*], **a•light•ed** or **a•lit** /ə'lɪt/, **a•light•ing. 1.** to get down from a horse or out of a vehicle: *She alighted gracefully from*

the limousine. **2.** to come down to a state or position of rest: *The bird alighted on the branch.*

a•lign /ə'layn/ *v.* [~ + *obj*] **1.** to arrange in a straight line: *He aligned the gun with the target before he started shooting.* **2.** to bring into agreement with a particular group, cause, etc.: *He aligned himself with the minority party.* [*be* + *aligned* + *with*]: *He was aligned with the minority party.* —a'lign•ment, *n.* [*noncount*] [*count*]

a•like /ə'layk/ *adv.* **1.** in the same manner; equally: *to treat all customers alike.* **2.** similar or comparable: *Not all people are alike.*

al•i•men•ta•ry /,ælə'mɛntəriy/ *adj.* [*before a noun*] of or relating to food.

al•i•mo•ny /'ælə,mowniy/ *n.* [*noncount*] a sum of money regularly paid to a spouse or former spouse for maintenance following a divorce or legal separation.

a•live /ə'layv/ *adj.* **1.** [*be* + ~] living; existing; not dead: *He was still alive after being buried in the snow for five days.* **2.** in operation; active: [*after a noun*]: *to keep hope alive.* [*be* + ~]: *Their hopes were still alive.*

al•ka•li /'ælkə,lay/ *n.*, *pl.* **-lis, -lies.** a chemical substance that neutralizes an acid to form a salt: [*noncount*]: *Alkali turns red litmus paper blue.* [*count*]: *Some alkalis are harmful to crops.*

al•ka•line /'ælkəlayn, -lɪn/ *adj.* of, containing, or like an alkali: *Use alkaline batteries in this flashlight.*

all /ɔl/ *adj.* [*usually before a noun; but see definition 1*] **1.** the whole or full amount of or number of: [~ + *the* + *noncount noun*]: *She ate all the cake.* [~ + *some nouns of time*]: *I waited for her call all afternoon.* [~ (+ *the*) + *plural noun*]: *all (the) students.* [*with the subject of a sentence*]: *The girls all enjoy camping.* [*after a pronoun object of a sentence*]: *I've seen them all.* **2.** entirely: *The coat is all wool.* —*pron.* **3.** the whole quantity, number, or amount: *Did you eat all of the peanuts?* —*n.* **4.** [*noncount*] the entire area or place: *All is calm, all is bright.* **5.** [*plural; used with a plural verb*] every one; everybody (a formal use): *All rise, the court is in session.* **6.** [*noncount*] everything: *Is that all you want?* —*adv.* **7.** wholly; completely: *all alone.* —*Idiom.* **8.** all but, almost; very nearly: *These batteries are all but dead.* **9.** all in all, in general: *All in all, we were satisfied.* **10.** all out, with one's best effort: *The team went all out to win the game.* **11.** at all (used to give emphasis to a word or phrase, esp. a word or phrase with "any" in it): **a.** in the slightest degree or amount: *Aren't there any cookies left at all?* **b.** for any reason: *Why try to please him at all?* **12.** in all, all included; all together: *There were forty in all.* **13.** of all, (used to give emphasis after a word like "first," "last," "best"): *First of all, welcome to our college.*

Al•lah /'ælə, 'ɑlə/ *n.* the Muslim name for the Supreme Being; God.

al•lege /ə'lɛdʒ/ *v.* [~ + *obj*], **-leged, -leg•ing.** to state or claim (something) without proof: [~ + *that clause*]: *You allege that he stole the car.* [*be* + *alleged* + *to* + *verb*]: *He was only alleged to have stolen the car.* —al•le•ga•tion /,ælɪ'geyʃən/ *n.* [*count*]

al•le•giance /ə'liydʒəns/ *n.* loyalty or devotion to some person, group, or cause, esp. loyalty of citizens to their government: [*count*]: *The players felt a strong allegiance to their team.* [*noncount*]: *He pledged allegiance to his new country.*

al•le•go•ry /'ælə,gɔriy/ *n.*, *pl.* **-ries.** [*count*] a story or poem conveying a moral lesson through the use of characters and events that serve as symbols: *the allegory of the Pied Piper.* —**al•le•gor•i•cal** /ˌæləˈgɔrɪkəl, -ˈgɒr-/, *adj.*

al•ler•gic /əˈlɜrdʒɪk/ *adj.* [*be* + ~ (+ *to*)] having an allergy: *She's allergic to dust.*

al•ler•gy /ˈælərdʒiy/ *n.* [*count*], *pl.* **-gies.** a strong sensitivity to a normally harmless substance, causing a physical reaction such as a skin rash, swelling in the nose or throat, sneezing, or wheezing.

al•le•vi•ate /əˈliyviy,eyt/ *v.* [~ + *obj*], **-at•ed,** **-at•ing.** to make easier to endure: *to alleviate pain.* —**al•le•vi•a•tion** /ə,liyviy'eyʃən/, *n.* [*noncount*]

al•ley /ˈæliy/ *n.* [*count*], *pl.* **-leys. 1.** a narrow passage or street, such as behind a row of houses. —*Idiom.* **2. (right) up** or **down one's alley,** highly suited to one's interests or abilities.

al•li•ance /əˈlayəns/ *n.* **1.** [*noncount*] the act of allying or the state of being allied. **2.** [*count*] a formal agreement or treaty between nations or groups to cooperate for specific purposes.

al•li•ga•tor /ˈælɪ,geytər/ *n.* [*count*] either of two crocodile-like reptiles of the southeastern U.S. and E China, having a broad snout.

al•lo•cate /ˈælə,keyt/ *v.* [~ + *obj*], **-cat•ed,** **-cat•ing.** to set apart or hold in reserve for a particular future use; assign: *to allocate space; They allocated the money for purchasing computers. They allocated him a small room.* —**al•lo•ca•tion** /ˌælə'keyʃən/, *n.* [*noncount*] [*count*]

al•lot /əˈlɒt/ *v.* [~ + *obj*], **-lot•ted, -lot•ting. 1.** to set apart for a purpose: *to allot money for a park.* **2.** to divide or give out by shares or portions: *to allot the farmland among the heirs; They allotted him a share.* —**al'lot•ment,** *n.* [*count*] [*noncount*]

al•low /əˈlaw/ *v.* [~ + *obj*] **1.** to give permission to or for; permit: *I won't allow it. How often does she allow a student to miss class? The school does not allow smoking on campus.* **2.** to let have; give as one's share: *The school allowed each person $100 for expenses.* **3.** to assign or allocate (time to do something); set apart in reserve: *Allow an hour for changing planes.*

al•low•ance /əˈlawəns/ *n.* [*count*] **1.** an amount or portion set aside for a purpose: *a dietary allowance of 900 calories a day.* **2.** a sum of money given regularly: *Each child got a weekly allowance.* —*Idiom.* **3. make allowance(s) for, a.** to overlook the existence or nature of: *We made allowances for her faults.* **b.** to allow for, as by reserving time, money, etc., for: *We made allowances for the traffic.*

al•loy /*n.* ˈælɔy, əˈlɔy; *v.* əˈlɔy/ *n.* [*count*] **1.** a substance made up of two or more metals. —*v.* [~ + *obj*] **2.** to mix (metals or metal with nonmetal) so as to form an alloy.

,**all 'right,** *adv.* **1.** yes: *All right, you can go.* **2.** (used in a question) do you agree?: *We'll meet tomorrow, all right?* **3.** satisfactorily: *Her work is coming along all right.* —*adj.* [*be* + ~] **4.** safe; healthy: *Are you sure you're all right?* **5.** acceptable: *His performance was barely all right.* —*Usage.* See ALRIGHT.

al•lude /əˈluwd/ *v.* [*no obj*], **-lud•ed, -lud•ing.** to make an allusion; refer: *He alluded to my research in his report on smoking.*

al•lure /əˈlʊr/ *v.*, **-lured, -lur•ing,** *n.* —*v.* [~ + *obj*] **1.** to attract or tempt by something flattering or desirable: *Her beauty allured him.* —*n.* [*noncount*] **2.** fascination; charm; appeal: *the allure of money.*

al•lu•sion /əˈluwʒən/ *n.* **1.** [*count*] a passing or casual reference to something: *an allusion to Shakespeare.* **2.** [*noncount*] the act of alluding: *No allusion to his criminal record was allowed in the trial.*

al•ly /*n.* ˈælay, əˈlay; *v.* əˈlay/ *n.*, *pl.* **-lies,** *v.*, **-lied, -ly•ing.** —*n.* [*count*] **1.** a nation, group, or person cooperating with another or others toward a common cause or purpose. —*v.* **2.** to unite formally, such as by treaty, league, or marriage: [~ + *oneself* + *obj*]: *Russia allied itself with France.* [*no obj*]: *They allied against the common enemy.*

-ally, a suffix used to form adverbs from certain adjectives ending in -IC: *terrifically.*

al•ma ma•ter /ˈɑlmə ˈmɑtər, ˈæl- ˈælmə ˈmeytər/ *n.* [*count*] a school, college, or university at which one has studied.

al•ma•nac /ˈɔlmə,næk/ *n.* [*count*] an annually published calendar for the coming year, containing important dates and the times of sunrises and sunsets.

al•might•y /ɔl'maytiy/ *adj.* **1.** having unlimited power; omnipotent, as God: *a concept of an almighty being.* —*adv.* **2.** *Informal.* extremely: *It's almighty hot.* —*n.* **3. the Almighty,** God.

al•mond /ˈɑmənd, ˈæmənd/ *n.* [*count*] the edible nut of a tree of the rose family.

al•most /ˈɔlmowst, ɔl'mowst/ *adv.* very nearly: *to pay almost nothing for a car.*

alms /ɑmz/ *n.* [*plural*] money, food, or other donations given to the needy.

a•loft /əˈlɔft, əˈlɒft/ *adv.* **1.** in or into the air: *were aloft seconds after takeoff.* —*prep.* **2.** on or at the top of: *flags flying aloft the castle.*

a•lone /əˈlown/ *adj.* **1.** [*be* + ~] separate; by oneself: *alone in the wilderness.* **2.** [*after a noun or pronoun*] excluding all others or all else: *You can't live by bread alone.* —*adv.* **3.** by oneself: *She lives alone.* **4.** solely; exclusively: *This jewelry is sold by us alone.* —*Idiom.* **5. leave** or **let alone,** to refrain from bothering or interfering with: *We left him alone with his thoughts.* **6. leave** or **let well enough alone,** to leave things as they are: *Let's leave well enough alone and stop tinkering.* **7. let alone,** not to mention: *too tired to walk, let alone run.*

a•long /əˈlɔŋ, əˈlɒŋ/ *prep.* **1.** over the length or direction of: *walking along the highway at night.* **2.** in conformity with: *Let's keep going along the lines we proposed earlier.* —*adv.* **3.** parallel: *He ran along beside me.* **4.** so as to go forward or onward: *Move along.* **5.** as a companion: *She took her brother along.* —*Idiom.* **6. all along,** from the start: *has been hiding something all along.* **7. along with, a.** together with: *They escaped along with a few other prisoners.* **b.** in cooperation or company with: *He planned the project along with his associates.* **8. be along,** *Informal.* to arrive at a place: *They should be along soon.*

a•long•side /əˈlɔŋ'sayd, əˈlɒŋ-/ *adv.* **1.** along or at the side of something: *We brought the boat alongside.* —*prep.* **2.** by the side of: *We brought the boat alongside the dock.*

a•loof /əˈluwf/ *adj.* **1.** reserved; not showing interest. —*adv.* **2.** distant in feeling or manner: *He remained aloof from his classmates.* —**a'loof•ness,** *n.* [*noncount*]

a•loud /əˈlawd/ *adv.* with the speaking voice: *I read the story aloud to the children.*

al•pha•bet /ˈælfə,bɛt, -bɪt/ *n.* [*count*] **1.** the letters of a language in their usual order. **2.** basic facts; ABCs: *the alphabet of biology.*

al•pha•bet•i•cal /ˌælfə'bɛtɪkəl/ *adj.* arranged according to the order of the letters in the alphabet. —,**al•pha'bet•i•cal•ly,** *adv.*

al•pha•bet•ize /'ælfəbɪˌtayz/ *v.* [~ + *obj*], **-ized, -iz•ing.** to put in alphabetical order: *The computer quickly alphabetized the list.* —**al•pha• bet•i•za•tion** /ˌælfəˌbɛtə'zeyʃən, -bɪ tə-/, *n.* [*noncount*]

al•pine /'ælpayn, -pɪn/ *adj.* of or relating to any high mountains: *alpine slopes.*

al•read•y /ɔl'rɛdiy/ *adv.* **1.** [*often with a perfect tense like present perfect or past perfect*] previously; before some specified or understood time: *I'm sorry, she has already left for the day. She had already arrived and was waiting for you.* **2.** so soon; so early; sooner than expected: *I can't believe she is already here.*

al•right /ɔl'rayt/ *adv., adj.* ALL RIGHT. ——**Usage.** The one-word spelling ALRIGHT is used in informal writing, but the phrase ALL RIGHT is preferred in formal, edited writing.

al•so /'ɔlsow/ *adv.* **1.** in addition; too; besides: *He was thin, and he was also tall.* **2.** likewise: *They have a dog and we have one also.*

al•tar /'ɔltər/ *n.* [*count*] a raised platform where religious rites are performed.

al•ter /'ɔltər/ *v.* **1.** to change; (to cause to) be different in some way, as size, style, course, or the like: [~ + *obj*]: *to alter a coat.* [*no obj*]: *Her schedule has altered drastically.* **2.** [~ + *obj*] to castrate or spay: *The cat had been altered.* —,**al• ter'a•tion,** *n.* [*count*] [*noncount*]

al•ter•nate / *v.* 'ɔltər,neyt; *adj., n.* -nɪt/ *v.,* **-nat•ed, -nat•ing,** *adj., n.* —*v.* **1.** to interchange one regularly with another in time or place: [*no obj*]: *Day alternates with night.* [~ + *obj*]: *They alternated hot and cold compresses on the injury.* **2.** to take turns: [*no obj*]: *The children alternate in doing chores.* [~ + *obj*]: *The children alternate chores.* —*adj.* [*before a noun*] **3.** interchanged repeatedly one for another: *alternate periods of clouds and sun.* **4.** every second one of a series: *Read only the alternate lines.* **5.** allowing for a choice; alternative: *Do you have an alternate plan?* —*n.* [*count*] **6.** a person authorized to take the place of another: *I sent my alternate to the meeting.* —**al•ter•na•tion** /ˌɔltər'neyʃən/, *n.* [*count*] [*noncount*]

al•ter•na•tive /ɔl'tɜrnətɪv, æl-/ *n.* [*count*] **1.** a choice limited to one option among two or more possibilities: *You have the alternative of riding, walking, or biking.* —*adj.* [*before a noun*] **2.** allowing for a choice between two or more things: *an alternative plan.* **3.** being different from the usual: *alternative lifestyles; alternative energy sources.* —**al'ter•na•tive•ly,** *adv.*

al'ternative 'medicine, *n.* [*noncount*] health care and treatments, including traditional Chinese medicine and folk medicine, that try to avoid the use of surgery and drugs.

al•though /ɔl'ðow/ *conj.* in spite of the fact that; even though: *Although we miss you, we will not ask you to return.*

al•ti•tude /'æltɪˌtuwd, -ˌtyuwd/ *n.* the height of a thing above a certain point, esp. the height above sea level on earth: [*noncount*]: *Maintain your altitude at 30,000 feet.* [*count*]: *flew down to a lower altitude.*

al•to /'æltow/ *n.* [*count*], *pl.* **-tos. 1.** the lowest female voice or voice part. **2.** a singer with this voice.

al•to•geth•er /ˌɔltə'gɛðər,' ɔltə,gɛðər/ *adv.* **1.** wholly; completely: *altogether fitting praise.* **2.** including all or everything: *The debt amounted altogether to twenty dollars.*

al•tru•ism /'æltruwˌɪzəm/ *n.* [*noncount*] concern for the welfare and well-being of others. —'**al•tru•ist,** *n.* [*count*]

a•lu•mi•num /ə'luwmənəm/ *n.* [*noncount*] a silver-white metallic element, used in alloys and for lightweight products. Also, *esp. Brit.,* **aluminium.**

a•lum•na /ə'lʌmnə/ *n.* [*count*], *pl.* **-nae** /-niy, -nay/. a woman who is a graduate or former student of a specific school, college, or university.

a•lum•nus /ə'lʌmnəs/ *n.* [*count*], *pl.* **-ni** /-nay, -niy/. a man who is a graduate or former student of a specific school, college, or university.

al•ways /'ɔlweyz, -wiyz/ *adv.* **1.** every time; on every occasion: *We always sleep late on Saturday.* **2.** all the time; without interruption: *The light is always burning.* **3.** in any event; if necessary: *If it rains I can always stay home.*

'Alzheimer's dis,ease /'ælzhaymərz, 'ɑlts-, 'ɔlz-, 'ɔlts-/ *n.* [*noncount*] a disease usually beginning in late middle age, characterized by progressive memory loss and mental deterioration.

am /æm; *unstressed* əm, m/ *v.* 1st pers. sing. pres. indic. of BE.

AM, an abbreviation of: **1.** amplitude modulation, a method of broadcasting a signal by means of a radio wave. **2.** a system of broadcasting using this method. Compare FM.

A.M., an abbreviation of Latin *Artium Magister*: Master of Arts, a title awarded to a student at a particular level of scholarship.

a.m. or **A.M.,** an abbreviation of Latin *ante meridiem*: **1.** before noon (used with hours of a day). **2.** the period from midnight to noon, esp. the period of daylight before noon. Compare P.M.

a•mal•ga•mate /ə'mælgəˌmeyt/ *v.,* **-mat•ed, -mat•ing.** to mix or merge so as to make a combination: [~ + *obj*]: *They planned to amalgamate the two companies.* [*no obj*]: *The three schools decided to amalgamate.* —**a•mal•ga•ma• tion** /əˌmælgə'meyʃən/, *n.* [*count*] [*noncount*]

a•mass /ə'mæs/ *v.* [~ + *obj*] to collect or gather together into a mass: *amassing sufficient evidence to convict the thief.*

am•a•teur /'æməˌtʃʊr, -tʃər, -tər/ *n.* [*count*] **1.** a person who engages in an activity for pleasure rather than for money. **2.** a person inexperienced in a particular activity.

a•maze /ə'meyz/ *v.* [~ + *obj*], **a•mazed, a•maz•ing.** to overwhelm with surprise: *The magician's tricks amazed the children. The children were amazed at his tricks. We were amazed to see so many people.* —**a'maze•ment,** *n.* [*noncount*] —**a'maz•ing,** *adj.*: *What an amazing view!*

am•bas•sa•dor /æm'bæsədər, -,dɔr/ *n.* [*count*] **1.** a high-ranking diplomat sent by one country to live in another. **2.** an unofficial representative.

am•ber /'æmbər/ *n.* [*noncount*] **1.** a yellow, red, or brown translucent substance used in making jewelry. **2.** the yellowish brown color of resin.

am•bi•dex•trous /ˌæmbɪ'dɛkstrəs/ *adj.* able to use both hands equally well.

am•big•u•ous /æm'bɪgyuwəs/ *adj.* **1.** having several possible meanings or interpretations: *He gave an ambiguous answer to that question.* **2.** doubtful; uncertain: *in an ambiguous position.* —**am•bi•gu•i•ty** /ˌæmbɪ'gyuwɪtiy/ *n.* [*noncount*] [*count*]

am•bi•tion /æm'bɪʃən/ *n.* **1.** [*noncount*] a strong desire for achievement. **2.** [*count*] the object or state desired: *A career on the stage is one of her ambitions.*

am•bi•tious /æmˈbɪʃəs/ *adj.* **1.** characterized by ambition: *an ambitious lawyer.* **2.** requiring a great deal of effort, cost, ability, etc.: *an ambitious program for fighting crime.*

am•biv•a•lence /æmˈbɪvələns/ *n.* [*noncount*] uncertainty, esp. the inability to make a choice between two opposite things. —**am'biv•a•lent,** *adj.*

am•ble /ˈæmbəl/ *v.,* **-bled, -bling,** *n.* —*v.* [*no obj*] **1.** to go at a slow, easy pace: *She ambled along.* —*n.* [*count*] **2.** a slow, easy walk.

am•bu•lance /ˈæmbyələns/ *n.* [*count*] a specially equipped vehicle for carrying sick or injured people to a hospital.

am•bush /ˈæmbʊʃ/ *n.* **1.** [*noncount*] an act of lying hidden to attack by surprise: *The robbers waited in ambush near the house.* **2.** [*count*] an attack from a hidden position. —*v.* [~ + *obj*] **3.** to attack from ambush.

a•mel•io•rate /əˈmiylyəˌreyt/ *v.,* **-rat•ed, -rat•ing.** to make or become better; improve: [~ + *obj*]: *Her apology ameliorated the situation.* [*no obj*]: *The situation ameliorated when both sides shook hands.* —**a•mel•io•ra•tion** /əˌmiylyəˈreyʃən/, *n.* [*noncount*]

a•men /ˈeyˈmɛn, ˈɑˈmɛn/ *interj.* (used after a prayer to express agreement) it is so; so be it.

a•me•na•ble /əˈmiynəbəl, əˈmɛnə-/ *adj.* [*usually: be + ~ + to*] ready or willing to answer, act, or agree: *The author was amenable to making a few changes.*

a•mend /əˈmɛnd/ *v.* [~ + *obj*] to modify or rephrase (a bill, constitution, etc.) formally: *Congress may amend the proposed tax bill.*

a•mend•ment /əˈmɛndmənt/ *n.* **1.** [*noncount*] the act of amending. **2.** [*count*] an alteration of or addition to a bill, constitution, etc.

a•mends /əˈmɛndz/ *n.* [*count*] —**Idiom. make amends,** to pay back, as for an injury, loss, or insult: *He promised to make amends. How can I make amends to you for my mistake?*

a•men•i•ty /əˈmɛnɪtiy/ *n.* [*count*], *pl.* **-ties. 1.** an agreeable way or manner; courtesy: *She observed the social amenities.* **2.** any feature that provides comfort, ease, or pleasure: *The hotel has a swimming pool and other amenities.*

A•mer•i•can /əˈmɛrɪkən/ *adj.* **1.** of or relating to the United States of America. **2.** of or relating to North or South America; or relating to the Western Hemisphere. —*n.* [*count*] **3.** a person born or living in the United States of America, esp. a citizen. **4.** a person born or living in the Western Hemisphere.

'American 'Indian, *n.* [*count*] a member of any of the original peoples of the Western Hemisphere, usually excluding the Eskimos.

am•e•thyst /ˈæməθɪst/ *n.* **1.** [*count*] a purple or violet quartz, used as a gem. **2.** [*noncount*] a purplish color.

a•mi•a•ble /ˈeymiyəbəl/ *adj.* **1.** having agreeable qualities; friendly: *an amiable gathering.* **2.** pleasant: *an amiable little village.*

am•i•ca•ble /ˈæmɪkəbəl/ *adj.* marked by goodwill; friendly: *The divorce was amicable.*

a•mid /əˈmɪd/ also **a•midst** /əˈmɪdst/ *prep.* in the middle of; surrounded by; among: *A few flowers grew amid the weeds.*

a•miss /əˈmɪs/ *adv.* **1.** out of the right order or condition: *Things went amiss.* —*adj.* [*be + ~*] **2.** improper; wrong: *Something is amiss.*

am•mo•nia /əˈmownyə/ *n.* [*noncount*] a colorless, strong-smelling gas or liquid, used chiefly for cleaning, refrigeration, and explosives.

am•mu•ni•tion /ˌæmyəˈnɪʃən/ *n.* [*noncount*] material fired in combat.

am•ne•sia /æmˈniyʒə/ *n.* [*noncount*] loss of memory caused by brain injury, shock, etc.

am•nes•ty /ˈæmnəstiy/ *n.,* *pl.* **-ties.** a general pardon for offenses, esp. political offenses, against a government: [*noncount*]: *The ruler promised amnesty for all prisoners.* [*count*]: *The rebel soldiers returned home under a general amnesty.*

a•mong /əˈmʌŋ/ *prep.* **1.** in, into, or through the middle of: *She was among friends.* **2.** with a share for each of: *Divide the fruit among you.* **3.** in the class or group of: *That is among the things we must do. New York is among the cities I will visit.* —**Usage.** See BETWEEN.

a•mor•al /eyˈmɔrəl, eyˈmɒr-/ *adj.* neither moral nor immoral.

am•o•rous /ˈæmərəs/ *adj.* relating to or expressing romantic love: *amorous glances.*

a•mor•phous /əˈmɔrfəs/ *adj.* lacking definite form; shapeless: *amorphous clouds.*

a•mount /əˈmawnt/ *n.* [*count*] **1.** the sum total of two or more quantities; whole: *the final amount that we actually pay for this car.* **2.** quantity; measure: [~ + *of* + *noncount noun*]: *There was a great amount of resistance to the plan.* [~ + *of* + *plural noun*]: *Huge amounts of crops lay unharvested.* —*v.* [*no obj*] **3.** to total; add up to: *The bill amounts to $300.* **4.** to be equal in value, effect, or extent; mean: *All those fine words amount to nothing.* —**Usage.** AMOUNT refers to quantity that cannot be counted (*the amount of paperwork; the amount of energy*), while NUMBER refers to things that can be counted (*a number of songs; a number of days*).

amp /æmp/ *n.* [*count*] ampere.

amp., an abbreviation of: ampere.

am•pere /ˈæmpɪər, æmˈpɪər/ *n.* [*count*] a unit of electrical current.

am•per•sand /ˈæmpərˌsænd/ *n.* [*count*] a character or symbol (&) used to mean "and," as in *Smith & Wesson, Inc.*

am•phib•i•an /æmˈfɪbiyən/ *n.* [*count*] an animal such as a frog that can live in both land and water. —**amphibious,** *adj.*

am•phi•the•a•ter /ˈæmfəˌθiyətər/ *n.* [*count*] an unroofed building or room with rows of seats rising around a central area.

am•ple /ˈæmpəl/ *adj.* **1.** fully sufficient for the purpose: *an ample reward.* **2.** large; roomy: *The apartment has ample storage space.*

am•pli•fi•er /ˈæmpləˌfayər/ *n.* [*count*] an electronic device that strengthens or intensifies sound, current, voltage.

am•pli•fy /ˈæmpləˌfay/ *v.* [~ + *obj*], **-fied, -fy•ing. 1.** to make (sound) louder by mechanical or electronic means: *The sounds are amplified and then sent through the speakers.* **2.** to add to or expand by giving further details: *They asked him to amplify (on) his reasoning.* —**am•pli•fi•ca•tion** /ˌæmpləfɪˈkeyʃən/, *n.* [*noncount*] [*count*]

am•pli•tude /ˈæmplɪˌtuwd, -ˌtyuwd/ *n.* [*noncount*] the state or quality of being ample; fullness; largeness.

am•pu•tate /ˈæmpyʊˌteyt/ *v.* [~ + *obj*], **-tat•ed, -tat•ing.** to cut off surgically (an arm, leg, finger, or other body part): *The doctor was forced to amputate her toe.* —**am•pu•ta•tion** /ˌæmpyʊˈteyʃən/, *n.* [*noncount*] [*count*]

am•pu•tee /ˌæmpyʊˈtiy/ *n.* [*count*] a person

who has lost all or part of an arm, hand, leg, etc., by amputation.

amt., an abbreviation of: amount.

a•muck or **amok** /ə'mʌk/ *adv.* **Idiom. run** or **go amuck** or **amok,** to go or rush about wildly; be out of control: *The mob had run amuck.*

a•muse /ə'myuwz/ *v.* [~ + *obj*], **a•mused, a•mus•ing. 1.** to hold the attention of (someone); entertain: *The video games amused them for hours.* **2.** to cause (someone) to laugh, smile, or the like: *His jokes amused everyone.*

a•muse•ment /ə'myuwzmənt/ *n.* **1.** [*noncount*] the state of being amused; enjoyment. **2.** [*count*] an activity to pass time enjoyably: *The city offers many amusements.*

a'musement ˌpark, *n.* [*count*] a park with games and rides such as a Ferris wheel, roller coaster, and shooting gallery.

an /ən; *when stressed* æn/ *indefinite article.* the form of A used before an initial vowel sound: *an arch, an honor, an hourly wage.* **—Usage.** See A.

-an, 1. an adjective suffix meaning of, belonging to, or resembling (*American*). **2.** It is used to form adjectives with the meaning "of or like (someone); supporter of or believer in": *Christ* + *-(i)an* → *Christian; Freud* + *-(i)an* → *Freudian.* **3.** a noun suffix meaning: a person belonging to or living in (*Hawaiian*); a person who works with or is skilled in (*comedian; electrician*); a supporter of or believer in (*Christian*).

a•nach•ro•nism /ə'nækrə,nɪzəm/ *n.* [*count*] **1.** a mistake of placing someone, something, or an event at an incorrectly early time period: *It is an anachronism to write that atomic bombs were used in the Civil War.* **2.** a thing or person that belongs to an earlier time and is out of place in the present. **—a,nach•ro'nis•tic,** *adj.*

an•a•gram /'ænə,græm/ *n.* [*count*] a word, phrase, or sentence formed from another by rearranging its letters: *"North" is an anagram of "thorn."*

a•nal /'eynl/ *adj.* [*before a noun*] of, relating to, or near the anus.

an•al•ge•sic /,ænl'dʒiyzɪk, -sɪk/ *adj.* [*before a noun*] **1.** causing a reduction or elimination of pain: *an analgesic drug.* **—n.** [*count*] **2.** a drug that reduces or eliminates pain.

an•a•log /'ænl,ɔg, -,ɒg/ *adj.* [*before a noun*] **1.** a method of audio recording in which sound waves are converted into electrical signals. **2.** a display of information by means of a pointer or hands on a dial, rather than by numerical digits (opposed to *digital*): *an analog wristwatch.*

a•nal•o•gous /ə'næləgəs/ *adj.* having similar characteristics: *The human brain is analogous to a computer.*

a•nal•o•gy /ə'nælədʒiy/ *n.* [*count*], *pl.* **-gies.** a comparison made on the basis of similar features: *an analogy between the heart and a pump.*

a•nal•y•sis /ə'næləsɪs/ *n., pl.* **-ses** /-,siyz/. **1.** the process of analyzing: [*noncount*]: *analysis of a problem.* [*count*]: *chemical analyses.* **2.** [*count*] a statement of the results of this process: *The newspaper article was a good analysis of the problem.* **—an•a•lyt•ic** /,ænl'ɪtɪk/ *adj.*

an•a•lyst /'ænlɪst/ *n.* [*count*] **1.** a person who analyzes or who is skilled in analysis. **2.** a psychoanalyst.

an•a•lyze /'ænl,ayz/ *v.* [~ + *obj*], **-lyzed, -lyz•ing.** to examine or study something by separating it into its parts and figuring out its essential

features: *to analyze the blood on the murder weapon.*

an•ar•chy /'ænərkiy/ *n.* [*noncount*] the absence of a governing body or laws with which to rule a people: *They favored anarchy over tyranny.*

a•nat•o•my /ə'nætəmiy/ *n., pl.* **-mies. 1.** [*noncount*] the science dealing with the structure of animals and plants. **2.** [*count*] the structure of an animal or plant, or of any of its parts. **—an•a•tom•i•cal** /,ænə'tɒmɪkəl/ *adj.*

-ance, a suffix used to form nouns either from adjectives ending in -ANT or from verbs, and meaning: act or example of (*appearance*); state or quality of being (*brilliance*).

an•ces•tor /'ænsɛstər/ *n.* [*count*] **1.** a person from whom one is descended: *Their ancestors were pioneers.* **2.** an earlier prototype; forerunner: *The horse and buggy was an ancestor to the automobile.*

an•ces•tral /æn'sɛstrəl/ *adj.* [*before a noun*] of or inherited from ancestors: *an ancestral home.*

an•ces•try /'ænsɛstriy/ *n., pl.* **-tries. 1.** [*count; usually singular*] the group of people from whom someone is descended: *She had an ancestry of Puritan settlers.* **2.** [*noncount*] line of descent from an ancestor: *of Chinese ancestry.*

an•chor /'æŋkər/ *n.* [*count*] **1.** a heavy device attached to a ship or boat and thrown into the water to keep the vessel from drifting away. **2.** a person or thing that can be relied on for support: *In times of distress she was our anchor.* **3.** the main broadcaster on a news or sports program. **—v. 4.** [~ + *obj*] to hold in place as if by an anchor: *to anchor the ship in the harbor.* **5.** [*no obj*] to cast anchor: *The ship anchored in the harbor.* **6.** to serve as a radio or television anchor (for): [~ + *obj*]: *She anchored the evening news.* [*no obj*]: *She anchored for seven years.* **—Idiom. 7. at anchor,** kept in place by an anchor: *The ship was at anchor while repairs were being made.*

an•chor•man or **-wom•an** or **-per•son** /'æŋkərmən/ or /-,wumən/ or /-,pɜrsən/ *n.* [*count*], *pl.* **-men** or **-wom•en** or **-per•sons.** AN-CHOR (def. 3).

an•cho•vy /'æntʃowviy, -tʃə-, æn'tʃowviy/ *n.* [*count*], *pl.* **-vies.** a small salted fish often made into a paste.

an•cient /'eynʃənt/ *adj.* **1.** of, dating from, or in a time long ago, esp. before the end of the Western Roman Empire A.D. 476: *ancient civilizations of Greece and Egypt.* **2.** very old; aged: *an ancient wise man.*

-ancy, a suffix meaning state or quality (*brilliancy*).

and (*and; unstressed* ənd, ən, *or, esp. after t, n,* or d, n), *conj.* **1.** (used to connect words, phrases, or clauses) with, as well as, or in addition to: *pens and pencils.* **2.** added to; plus: *2 and 2 are 4.* **3.** then; afterward; after that: *He finished and went to bed.* **4.** *Informal.* (used between two verbs) to: *Try and do it (= Try to do it).* **—Idiom. 5. and so forth** or **so on,** and more of the same or similar kind: *first, second, third, and so forth.*

and/or /'ænd'ɔr/ *conj.* (used to indicate that one or both of two things may be included): *You can buy accident and/or health insurance from that company.*

an•drog•y•nous /æn'drɒdʒənəs/ *adj.* having both masculine and feminine characteristics: *androgynous plants or animals.* **—an•drog•y•ny** /æn'drɒdʒəniy/ *n.* [*noncount*]

an•ec•dote /'ænɪk,dowt/ *n.* [*count*] a brief account of an interesting or amusing incident or event, often biographical.

a•ne•mi•a /ə'niymiyə/ *n.* [*noncount*] a lack of hemoglobin in the red blood cells, causing weakness and paleness. **—a'ne•mic,** *adj.*

an•es•the•sia /ˌænəs'θiyʒə/ *n.* [*noncount*] loss of sensation in the whole body or in certain areas: *drugs that bring on anesthesia in surgical patients.*

an•es•thet•ic /ˌænəs'θɛtɪk/ *n.* [*count*] **1.** a substance that produces anesthesia. **—adj. 2.** of, relating to, or causing anesthesia: *an anesthetic drug.* **—an'es•the‚tize,** *v.* [~ + *obj*], **-tized, -tiz•ing.**

a•new /ə'nuw, ə'nyuw/ *adv.* again; once more (often in a new way): *to start anew.*

an•gel /'eyndʒəl/ *n.* [*count*] **1.** a spiritual creature that serves God, often represented in the form of a human being with wings. **2.** a person resembling an angel, as in beauty or kindliness: *You're an angel to help with the children.* **3.** one who provides finances for a project, as a theatrical work. **—an•gel•ic** /æn'dʒɛlɪk/, *adj.*

an•ger /'æŋgər/ *n.* [*noncount*] **1.** a strong feeling of displeasure or rage: *His anger rose at the insult.* **—v.** [~ + *obj*] **2.** to make (someone) angry: *His selfishness angered me.*

an•gle¹ /'æŋgəl/ *n.* [*count*] **1. a.** the shape made by two lines meeting at a common point or by two surfaces meeting along an edge: *to place a chair in the angle of the wall.* **b.** the figure so formed: *a right angle.* **2.** a viewpoint: *She looked at the problem from a fresh angle.*

an•gle² /'æŋgəl/ *v.,* **-gled, -gling. 1.** [*no obj*] to fish with hook and line: *He was angling all morning.* **2.** [~ + *obj*] to use sly means to attain: *was angling for compliments.* **—'an•gler,** *n.* [*count*]

An•gli•can /'æŋglɪkən/ *adj.* **1.** of or relating to the Church of England. **—n.** [*count*] **2.** a member of the Church of England or of a church connected to it.

An•gli•cize /'æŋglə‚sayz/ *v.* [~ + *obj; sometimes: anglicize*], **-cized, -ciz•ing.** to make English in form or character.

an•gry /'æŋgriy/ *adj.,* **-gri•er, -gri•est. 1.** feeling or showing anger or strong resentment: *an angry parent; She was angry at the boss. I am angry with them today. I was angry about the insult.* **2.** [*usually: before a noun*] showing qualities related to anger: *an angry sea.* **—'an•gri•ly,** *adv.*

an•guish /'æŋgwɪʃ/ *n.* [*noncount*] great suffering or pain: *the anguish of grief.* **—'an•guished,** *adj.*

an•i•mal /'ænəməl/ *n.* [*count*] **1.** a living creature able to move on its own, to get and process its own food, and to respond to its surroundings by means of its senses and nervous system. **2.** a creature other than a human being: *We believe we are higher than the animals.*

an•i•mate /*v.* 'ænə‚meyt/ *adj.* -mɪt/ *v.,* **-mat•ed, -mat•ing,** *adj.* **—v.** [~ + *obj*] **1.** to give life to; make alive: *Her presence animated the party.* **2.** to give motion to: *The swaying leaves were animated by a cool breeze.* **—adj. 3.** alive; possessing life: *animate beings.* **—'an•i mat•ed,** *adj.* **—an•i•ma•tion** /ˌænə'meyʃən/, *n.* [*noncount*]

an•i•mos•i•ty /ˌænə'mɒsɪtiy/ *n.,* *pl.* **-ties.** strong hostility: [*noncount*]: *felt great animosity toward the tyrant.* [*count*]: *The old animosities emerged.*

an•ise /'ænɪs/ *n.* [*count*] a Mediterranean plant that produces aniseed.

an•i•seed /'ænə‚siyd, 'ænɪs‚siyd/ *n.* [*noncount*]

the seed of the anise plant, used in food and drink for its licorice flavor.

an•kle /'æŋkəl/ *n.* [*count*] the joint between the foot and leg.

an•klet /'æŋklɪt/ *n.* [*count*] a sock that extends just above the ankle.

an•nex /*v.* ə'nɛks, 'ænɛks; *n.* 'ænɛks, -ɪks/ *v.* [~ + *obj*] **1.** to attach or add, esp. to something larger: *They annexed a new lunch room to their headquarters.* **2.** to take control of (territory) from another country, often by force: *Germany annexed Czechoslovakia.* **—n.** [*count*] Also, *esp. Brit.,* **an'nexe. 3.** something annexed: *an annex to a treaty.* **4.** a building or an addition to a building. **—an•nex•a•tion** /ˌænɛk'seyʃən/, *n.* [*noncount*]

an•ni•hi•late /ə'nayə‚leyt/ *v.* [~ + *obj*], **-lat•ed, -lat•ing.** to destroy completely: *The mad scientist planned to annihilate the world.* **—an•ni•hi•la•tion** /ə‚nayə'leyʃən/, *n.* [*noncount*]

an•ni•ver•sa•ry /ˌænə'vɜrsəriy/ *n.* [*count*], *pl.* **-ries. 1.** the yearly recurring date of an important past event: *That date was the anniversary of the invasion.* **2.** the celebration of an anniversary, esp. of a wedding: *had 200 guests at their anniversary.*

an•no•tate /'ænə‚teyt/ *v.* [~ + *obj*], **-tat•ed, -tat•ing.** to supply (a text) with explanatory notes. **—annotation,** *n.* [*noncount*] [*count*]

an•nounce /ə'nawns/ *v.* [~ + *obj*], **-nounced, -nounc•ing.** to make known publicly or officially: *She announced her candidacy for the presidency. She announced that she would run for president.* **—announcer,** *n.* [*count*]

an•nounce•ment /ə'nawnsmənt/ *n.* [*noncount*] **1.** the act of making known publicly. **2.** a short advertisement in the newspaper: *announcements about apartments to share.* **3.** [*count*] something announced **4.** [*count*] a formal written or printed notice, as of a wedding.

an•noy /ə'nɔy/ *v.* to disturb or bother in a displeasing or irritating way: [~ + *obj*]: *My neighbor's loud television annoys me.* [*It* + ~ + *obj* + *that clause*]: *It annoyed me that my neighbors played their TV so late.* **—an'noy•ance,** *n.* [*noncount*] [*count*]

an•noy•ing /ə'nɔyɪŋ/ *adj.* causing annoyance; irritating: *an annoying cough.* **—an'noy•ing•ly,** *adv.*

an•nu•al /'ænyuwəl/ *adj.* [*before a noun*] **1.** of or for a year; yearly: *my annual salary.* **2.** occurring or returning once a year: *an annual celebration.* **—n.** [*count*] **3.** a plant that lives for one growing season. **—'an•nu•al•ly,** *adv.*

an•nul /ə'nʌl/ *v.* [~ + *obj*], **-nulled, -nul•ling.** to make or declare (something to be) no longer legally in force: *to annul a marriage; to annul a contract.* **—an'nul•ment,** *n.* [*noncount*] [*count*]

a•noint /ə'nɔynt/ *v.* [~ + *obj*] to rub oil or ointment on the body so as to make sacred or holy in a ceremony.

a•nom•a•ly /ə'nɒməliy/ *n.,* *pl.* **-lies. 1.** [*noncount*] a difference or change from the usual type or form; irregularity; abnormality. **2.** [*count*] someone or something that differs from the expected or usual: *A dog with two tails is an anomaly.* **—a'nom•a•lous,** *adj.*

a•non•y•mous /ə'nɒnəməs/ *adj.* having no named author, writer, etc.: *an anonymous poem.* **—a•no•nym•i•ty** /ˌænə'nɪmɪtiy/, *n.* [*noncount*]

an•oth•er /ə'nʌðər/ *adj.* [*before a noun*] **1.** being one more; being more of the same; further; additional: *Have another piece of cake.* [~ +

A

number word + plural count noun]: *Let's meet again in another three weeks.* **2.** different; of a different kind: *to visit another country and see how different life is there.* —*pron.* **3.** one more; an additional one: *I finished one book and started another.* **4.** a different one; something different: *I have one belief and she has another.*

an•swer /ˈænsər/ n. [count] **1.** a spoken or written reply to a question, request, letter, etc.: *My answer was "yes."* **2.** a solution to a problem: *never claimed to have all the answers.* **3. in answer (to),** for use as a response: *I offer these arguments in answer to your criticism.* —v. **4.** to speak or write in response (to); make answer (to); reply (to): [*no obj*]: *She answered quietly.* [~ + obj]: *The nominee answered the questions with humor.* **5. answer back,** to reply impolitely or rudely (to): *Don't answer back. Don't answer your teacher back like that.* **6. answer for, a.** to suffer as a result of one's own action: *He must answer for his criminal acts.* **b.** to be or to declare oneself responsible: *to answer for the President's safety.*

'answering ma,chine, n. [count] a device that automatically answers telephone calls and records the callers' messages.

ant /ænt/ n. [count] **1.** a small insect that lives in highly organized colonies. —*Idiom.* **2. have ants in one's pants,** *Slang.* to be impatient or eager to act.

-ant, a suffix meaning: person or thing that performs, promotes, or brings about something (*contestant; pollutant; deodorant*); performing, promoting, or being (*pleasant*).

an•tag•o•nism /ænˈtægəˌnɪzəm/ n. active hostility or opposition: [*noncount*]: *The proposal provoked antagonism among committee members.* [*count*]: *Antagonisms rose sharply among the committee members.* —**an'tag•o•nist,** n. [count]: *He considered his opponent a dangerous antagonist.* —**an,tag•o'nis•tic,** *adj.*

an•tag•o•nize /ænˈtægəˌnaɪz/ v. [~ + obj], **-nized, -niz•ing.** to cause to become hostile; make an enemy or opponent of: *His speech antagonized many voters.*

ant•arc•tic /æntˈɑrktɪk, -ˈɑrtɪk/ adj. of, at, or near the South Pole.

ante-, a prefix meaning: before, in front of (*anteroom; antedate*).

ant•eat•er /ˈæntˌiytər/ n. [count] an animal having a long snout, a sticky tongue, and strong claws, that feeds on ants and termites.

an•te•ced•ent /ˌæntəˈsiydnt/ adj. **1.** preceding; coming before: *an antecedent event.* —n. [count] **2.** something that comes or happens before another: *A few gunshots were antecedents of the war.* **3.** a word, phrase, or clause, usually a noun, that is replaced by a pronoun or other substitute: *Jane* is the antecedent (of the pronoun *she*) in the sentence: *Jane lost a glove and she is upset.*

an•te•lope /ˈæntlˌowp/ n. [count], pl. **-lopes,** (*esp. when thought of as a group*) **-lope.** a deerlike animal of Africa and Asia.

an•ten•na /ænˈtɛnə/ n. [count], pl. **-ten•nas** for 1, **-ten•nae** /-ˈtɛniy/ for 2. **1.** an aerial; a device for sending or receiving radio or television signals by means of a wire or wires connected to metal rods. **2.** one of the two long, thin, movable parts located on the heads of insects, lobsters, and some animals, having the function of feeling or sensing things in the surroundings.

an•te•ri•or /ænˈtɪəriyər/ adj. located before or

at the front of (opposed to *posterior*): *the anterior fin of a fish.*

an•them /ˈænθəm/ n. [count] **1.** a song, such as of praise or patriotism. **2.** a hymn.

an•thol•o•gy /ænˈθɒlədʒiy/ n. [count], pl. **-gies.** a collection of selected writings: *an anthology of poetry.* —**an'thol•o•gist,** n. [count]

an•thra•cite /ˈænθrəˌsayt/ n. [noncount] a hard coal that burns slowly with little smoke or flame.

an•thro•pol•o•gy /ˌænθrəˈpɒlədʒiy/ n. [noncount] the science that deals with the origins, development, physical features, and customs of humankind. —**,an•thro'pol•o•gist,** n. [count]

anti-, a prefix meaning: against or opposed to (*antislavery*); preventing or counteracting (*antifreeze*); opposite or contrary to (*anticlimax*); rivaling (*Antichrist*).

an•ti•bi•ot•ic /ˌæntɪbayˈɒtɪk, -biy-/ n. [count] a chemical substance, as penicillin, that can slow or stop the growth of bacteria.

an•ti•bod•y /ˈæntɪˌbɒdiy/ n. [count], pl. **-bod•ies.** a protein produced by the body to fight substances that cause disease.

an•tic /ˈæntɪk/ n. [count] Usually, **antics.** [*plural*] a playful or silly act or action: *Her antics in class got her into trouble.*

an•tic•i•pate /ænˈtɪsəˌpeyt/ v. [~ + obj], **-pat•ed, -pat•ing. 1.** to realize or feel beforehand: *We anticipate a large crowd tonight. We anticipate running into problems. The government hadn't anticipated that the economy would decline.* **2.** to look forward to, esp. with pleasure: *I was anticipating my promotion.* —**an•ti•ci•pa•tion** /ænˌtɪsəˈpeyʃən/, n. [noncount]

an•ti•cli•max /ˌæntiyˈklaymæks, ˌæntay-/ n. [count] something that is far less important or exciting than expected; a disappointment: *After a great series, the final, losing game was an anticlimax.*

an•ti•dote /ˈæntɪˌdowt/ n. [count] **1.** a medicine or other remedy used to fight poison, disease, etc. **2.** something that prevents or works against harmful or unwanted effects: *One antidote for crime is more police on the street.*

an•ti•freeze /ˈæntɪˌfriyz, ˈæntiy-/ n. [noncount] a substance used to keep water from freezing in the cooling system of a vehicle.

an•tip•a•thy /ænˈtɪpəθiy/ n. [noncount] a deep, habitual dislike: *antipathy toward inhuman behavior.*

an•ti•per•spi•rant /ˌæntɪˈpɜrspərənt/ n. [count] a preparation for reducing perspiration.

an•ti•quated /ˈæntɪˌkweytɪd/ adj. old-fashioned; outdated: *We replaced our antiquated computer system.*

an•tique /ænˈtiyk/ adj. [before a noun] **1.** in the style of an earlier period: *antique cabinets.* **2.** concerned with selling or buying old objects such as furniture: *an antique dealer; an antique shop.* —n. [count] **3.** an object produced in an earlier period, or, according to U.S. customs laws, 100 years old or before date of purchase: *beautiful and rare antiques.*

an•tiq•ui•ty /ænˈtɪkwɪtiy/ n. [noncount] **1.** the quality of being ancient: *a drinking glass of great antiquity.* **2.** ancient times: *in the days of antiquity.*

an•ti-Sem•ite /ˌæntiyˈsɛmayt, ˌæntay-/ n. [count] a person who discriminates against or is prejudiced or hostile toward Jews. —**an•ti-Se•mit•ic** /ˌæntiysəˈmɪtɪk, ˌæntay-/, adj. —**an-**

apartment

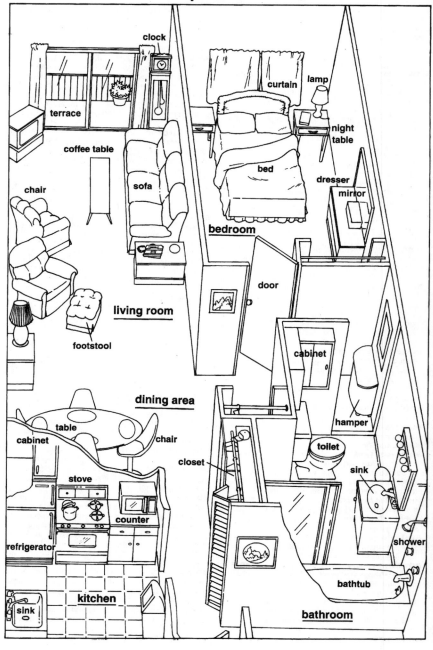

clock

curtain

lamp

terrace

night table

coffee table

dresser

mirror

chair

sofa

bed

bedroom

door

living room

cabinet

footstool

hamper

dining area

toilet

table

chair

sink

cabinet

closet

stove

counter

refrigerator

shower

sink

kitchen

bathtub

bathroom

ti•Sem•i•tism /ˌæntiy'sɛmɪˌtɪzəm, ˌæntay-/, n. [noncount]

an•ti•sep•tic /ˌæntə'sɛptɪk/ adj. **1.** [before a noun] destructive of microorganisms that cause disease: an antiseptic solution. **2.** free from microorganisms that cause disease: The surgical instruments are antiseptic. —n. **3.** a solution or substance that can destroy bacteria: [noncount]: The doctor put antiseptic on the wound. [count]: I bought an antiseptic at the drugstore.

an•ti•so•cial /ˌæntiy'sowʃəl, ˌæntay-/ adj. avoiding normal or friendly relations with other people: an antisocial recluse.

ant•ler /'æntlər/ n. [count] one of the branched horns of an animal of the deer family.

an•to•nym /'æntənɪm/ n. [count] a word opposite in meaning to another: Fast is an antonym of slow. Compare SYNONYM (def. 1).

ants•y /'æntsiy/ adj., -i•er, -i•est. Informal. nervous; impatient.

a•nus /'eynəs/ n. [count], pl. **a•nus•es.** the opening at the lower end of the digestive system through which waste passes out of the body.

anx•i•e•ty /æŋ'zayitiy/ n., pl. **-ties. 1.** [noncount] concern or fear about possible misfortune: She was full of anxiety over the delay. **2.** [count] a cause of such concern: the anxieties of modern life.

anx•ious /'æŋkʃəs, 'æŋ-/ adj. **1.** fearful of possible danger or misfortune; concerned: She felt anxious about her health. **2.** [before a noun] causing distress or fear: We had a few anxious moments when the baby fell. **3.** [be + ~] eager: She's very anxious for promotion. I was anxious to meet you. I was anxious for them to meet you. —'anx•ious•ly, adv.

an•y /'ɛniy/ adj. [before a noun] **1.** one, a, an, or some; one or more without specifying or identifying: [in questions]: Do you have any cigarettes? [with negative words or phrases]: I wasn't in any danger. [in sentences with "if"]: If you have any time, let's meet. **2.** every; all: Any child would know that. —pron. **3.** an unspecified person or persons; anyone: He did better than any before him. **4.** a single one or ones; an unspecified thing or things; a quantity or number: [with negative words]: We do not have any left. [in questions]: Don't you have any? —adv. **5.** in whatever degree; to some extent; at all: [in questions]: Do you feel any better? [with negative words]: I can't go on any longer. —**Usage.** See SOME.

an•y•bod•y /'ɛniyˌbɒdiy, -ˌbʌdiy/ pron., n., pl. **bod•ies. 1.** somebody; someone: [with negative words or phrases]: There wasn't anybody able to help. [in questions]: Isn't there anybody who can help me? **2.** [only in affirmative sentences] everyone or everybody: Anybody there will know where the train station is.

an•y•how /'ɛniyˌhaw/ adv. in any case; in spite of that: I told her not to go, but she did anyhow.

an•y•more /ˌɛniy'mɔr/ adv. any longer: [with negative words or phrases]: She said she couldn't see me anymore. [in questions]: Do you play tennis anymore?

an•y•one /'ɛniyˌwʌn, -wən/ pron. any person at all; anybody: [in questions]: Did anyone see the accident? [with negative words or phrases]: I didn't see anyone there.

an•y•place /'ɛniyˌpleys/ adv. ANYWHERE: [in questions]: Would you like to go anyplace tonight? [with negative words or phrases]: I don't want to go anyplace tonight.

an•y•thing /'ɛniyˌθɪŋ/ pron. **1.** any thing whatever; something: [in questions]: Do you have anything for a toothache? [with negative words or phrases]: I don't have anything for you today. **2.** no matter what: She'll do anything to get promoted. —adv. **3.** in any way; at all: Does it taste anything like chocolate?

an•y•time /'ɛniyˌtaym/ adv. at any time; whenever: When should I come? —Anytime is fine.

an•y•way /'ɛniyˌwey/ adv. **1.** in any case; anyhow; regardless: I don't need help, but thanks anyway. **2.** (used in continuing a story, an explanation, a conversation, etc.): Anyway, we finally solved the problem.

an•y•where /'ɛniyˌhwɛər, -ˌwɛər/ adv. **1.** in, at, or to any place: [with negative words or phrases]: She won't go anywhere without her doll. [in questions]: Is there a doctor anywhere? **2.** to any extent or degree: [with negative words or phrases]: I'm not anywhere near finished. [in questions]: Is dinner anywhere near ready? —**Idiom. 3.** get or **go anywhere,** to make progress to achieve success: You'll never get anywhere with that attitude.

a•or•ta /ey'ɔrtə/ n. [count], pl. **-tas, -tae** /-tiy/. the main artery of mammals, carrying blood from the heart to the rest of the body.

AP, Associated Press.

a•part /ə'pɑrt/ adv. **1.** into pieces or parts; to pieces: to take a watch apart. **2.** separated or away from in place, time, or point of view: cities thousands of miles apart. **3.** to or at the side, with respect to place, purpose, or function: He kept apart from the group. **4.** so as to distinguish one from another: I can't tell the sisters apart. —**Idiom. 5.** apart from, aside from; except for: had no money, apart from some loose change.

a•part•heid /ə'pɑrtheyt, -hayt/ n. [noncount] **1.** in the Republic of South Africa, a former policy of keeping people of different races apart by law. **2.** any similar system of segregation.

a•part•ment /ə'pɑrtmənt/ n. [count] **1.** a room or a group of rooms used as a residence. **2.** an apartment house.

a'partment ˌhouse or a'partment ˌbuilding, n. [count] a building containing a number of apartments.

ap•a•thy /'æpəθiy/ n. [noncount] lack of interest in or concern for things; indifference. —**ap•a•thet•ic** /ˌæpə'θɛtɪk/ adj.

ape /eyp/ n., v., **aped, ap•ing.** —n. [count] **1.** a large, humanlike monkey, with long arms, a broad chest, and no tail. —v. [~ + obj] **2.** to imitate; mimic: The boys tried to ape the teacher's mannerisms. —**Idiom. 3.** go ape over, to be wildly enthusiastic about: Our teenager goes ape over rock stars.

ap•er•ture /'æpərtʃər/ n. [count] an opening, such as a hole or slit.

a•pex /'eypɛks/ n. [count], pl. **a•pex•es, a•pi•ces** /'eypəˌsiyz, 'æpə-/. **1.** the highest point: the apex of a mountain; the apex of a career. **2.** the tip or point: the apex of the tongue.

aph•o•rism /'æfəˌrɪzəm/ n. [count] a short, clever saying that carries a general truth.

aph•ro•dis•i•ac /ˌæfrə'diyzeˌæk, -'dɪziyˌæk/ n. [count] a food, drug, or other agent that arouses or is believed to arouse sexual desire.

a•pi•ces /'eypəsiyz/ n. [plural] a pl. of APEX.

a•piece /ə'piys/ adv. [after a noun] for each one; each: The muffins cost a dollar apiece.

a•pol•o•get•ic /əˌpɒlə'dʒɛtɪk/ adj. **1.** containing an apology: an apologetic letter. **2.** presented in defense: apologetic arguments.

appliances and devices

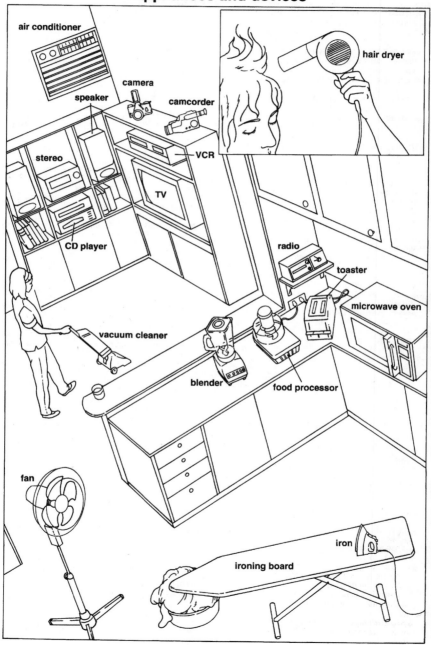

a•pol•o•gize /ə'pɒlə,dʒayz/ v., **-gized, -giz•ing.** to make an apology: [no obj]: He apologized when he spilled the coffee. [~ + obj]: I apologized to her. I apologized for my rudeness.

a•pol•o•gy /ə'pɒlədʒiy/ n., pl. **-gies.** an expression of regret for having made an error or for being rude: [count]: I sent an apology to her right away. [noncount]: a gesture of apology.

a•pos•tle /ə'pɒsəl/ n. [count; sometimes: Apostle] any of the original 12 disciples called by Jesus to preach the gospel.

a•pos•tro•phe /ə'pɒstrəfiy/ n. [count] the sign ('), used to indicate the omission of one or more letters in a word, as in we'll for we will, or gov't for government.

ap•pall /ə'pɔl/ v. [~ + obj], **-palled, -pall•ing.** to fill or overcome with horror, shock, or fear: The terrible fire appalled the neighbors.

ap•pa•rat•us /,æpə'rætəs, -'reytəs/ n., pl. **-tus, -tus•es.** **1.** [noncount] a group of instruments, tools, or materials having a particular function: firefighting apparatus. **2.** [count] the means by which a system functions: the apparatus of government.

ap•par•el /ə'pærəl/ n. [noncount] clothing, esp. outer garments: winter apparel.

ap•par•ent /ə'pærənt, ə'pɛr-/ adj. **1.** open to view: The crack in the wall was apparent. **2.** capable of being easily understood; obvious: The solution was apparent. It was apparent (to everyone) that they had cheated on the test. **3.** seeming to be real or true but not necessarily being so: He was the apparent winner of the race.

ap•par•ent•ly /ə'pærəntliy/ adv. it seems; it appears (that); seemingly: Apparently, you won the prize.

ap•pa•ri•tion /,æpə'rɪʃən/ n. [count] a ghostly appearance: The soldier's dreams were haunted by the apparition of his wounded captain.

ap•peal /ə'piyl/ n. **1.** [count] a strong plea or request: an appeal for help. **2.** [noncount] attractiveness: The game has lost its appeal. —v. **3.** [no obj] to make a strong plea: We appealed to the public for help. **4.** [~ + to] to be attractive: The red hat appeals to me.

ap•peal•ing /ə'piyliŋ/ adj. having great appeal; attractive: an appealing smile.

ap•pear /ə'pɪər/ v. **1.** [no obj] to come into sight; become visible: A man suddenly appeared in the doorway. **2.** to have the appearance of being; seem: [~ + adjective]: to appear wise. [~ + to + verb]: She appears to be sleeping. **3.** [no obj] to become available for use; come out: Your new book will appear next year.

ap•pear•ance /ə'pɪərəns/ n. **1.** [count] the act or process of appearing: He made a brief appearance at the party. **2.** [noncount] outward looks: a person of noble appearance. **3. appearances,** [plural] outward show, impressions, or indications: By all appearances, they enjoyed themselves.

ap•pease /ə'piyz/ v. [~ + obj], **-peased, -peas•ing.** **1.** to satisfy; relieve: The fruit appeased his hunger. **2.** to lessen anger or prevent fighting by agreeing to someone's demands. —**ap'pease•ment,** n. [noncount]

ap•pend /ə'pɛnd/ v. [~ + obj] to add as a piece at the end of a writing: to append a note to a letter.

ap•pend•age /ə'pɛndɪdʒ/ n. [count] a smaller or less important part attached to a central structure.

ap•pen•di•ci•tis /ə,pɛndə'saytɪs/ n. [noncount] inflammation of the human appendix.

ap•pen•dix /ə'pɛndɪks/ n. [count], pl. **-dix•es, -di•ces** /-də,siyz/. **1.** additional or extra material at the end of a text: An appendix to the travel guide lists all the nearby hotels. **2.** an outgrowth on the large intestine, shaped like a worm.

ap•pe•tite /'æpɪ,tayt/ n. **1.** [noncount] a desire for food or drink: Loss of appetite may be a sign of illness. **2.** [count] a strong desire or taste for something: an appetite for luxury.

ap•pe•tiz•er /'æpɪ,tayzər/ n. [count] a small portion of a food served before or at the start of a meal to stimulate the appetite.

ap•pe•tiz•ing /'æpɪ,tayzɪŋ/ adj. **1.** appealing to or stimulating the appetite: appetizing smells from the kitchen. **2.** appealing; tempting: Working late didn't sound appetizing to him.

ap•plaud /ə'plɔd/ v. **1.** to clap the hands in approval or appreciation (of): [no obj]: His fans applauded wildly. [~ + obj]: They applauded her performance. **2.** [~ + obj] to express approval of; praise: I applauded his decision. —**ap'plause,** n. [noncount]

ap•ple /'æpəl/ n. [count] **1.** the usually round red, green, or yellow fruit of a small tree of the rose family. **2.** the tree itself.

ap•ple•sauce /'æpəl,sɔs/ n. [noncount] a food made of apples stewed and ground to a soft mass and sometimes spiced with cinnamon.

ap•pli•ance /ə'playəns/ n. [count] a device or machine used esp. in the home to perform a specific task, as toasting bread or chilling food.

ap•pli•ca•ble /'æplɪkəbəl, ə'plɪkə-/ adj. capable of being applied; relevant: a solution applicable to the problem; a rule applicable to everyone.

ap•pli•cant /'æplɪkənt/ n. [count] a person who applies for or requests something: an applicant for a job.

ap•pli•ca•tion /,æplɪ'keyʃən/ n. **1.** [noncount] the act of applying: application of common sense. **2.** [count] the use to which something is put: new applications of the technology. **3.** [count] a form to be filled out by an applicant: Fill out and sign the application.

ap•pli•ca•tor /'æplɪ,keytər/ n. [count] a simple device for applying medication, cosmetics, or other substances.

ap•ply /ə'play/ v., **-plied, -ply•ing. 1.** [~ + obj] to make use of as relevant or suitable: The scientist applied the theory to the problem. **2.** [no obj] to be relevant; to be suitable: The theory doesn't apply in this case. **3.** [~ + obj] to put to use; put into effect: to apply the brakes. **4.** [~ + obj] to assign as appropriate: Don't apply that kind of term to me. **5.** to lay or spread on: [~ + obj]: She applied the paint to the wall. [no obj]: This paint applied easily. **6.** [no obj] to make an application or submit a request: She applied to several colleges. He applied for the job.

ap•point /ə'pɔynt/ v. [~ + obj] **1.** to name or assign officially: The committee appointed him chairman. They appointed him to the position of chairman. **2.** to fix; set: to appoint a time for the meeting. —**ap•point'ee** n. [count]: He was the youngest appointee ever to hold the office.

ap•point•ment /ə'pɔyntmənt/ n. **1.** an agreement for a meeting arranged in advance: [count]: We made an appointment to meet again. [noncount]: You can visit the museum by appointment. **2.** [noncount] the act of appointing or choosing, as to an office or position: the appointment of the chairman.

ap•por•tion /ə'pɔr-ʃən/ v. [~ + obj] to divide (parts or shares) and distribute by some rule: to apportion expenses among the three men.

ap•praise /ə'preyz/ v. [~ + obj], **-praised, -prais•ing.** to determine or estimate the worth (of something), esp. its monetary value: The art collector appraised the painting. —**ap'prais•al,** n. [noncount] [count]

ap•pre•ci•a•ble /ə'priyʃiyəbəl, -ʃəbəl/ adj. enough to be noticed; considerable: an apprecia-ble sum of money.

ap•pre•ci•ate /ə'priyʃiy,eyt/ v., **-at•ed, -at•ing. 1.** [~ + obj] to be grateful or thankful for: I appreciate your help. **2.** [~ + obj] to value or re-gard highly: They appreciate good food. **3.** to be fully aware of; understand fully: [~ + obj]: She appreciates the dangers of the situation. [~ + that clause]: I can appreciate that the situation is difficult. **4.** [no obj] to increase in value: The property appreciated rapidly. —**ap•pre•ci•a•tion** /ə,priyʃiy'eyʃən/ [noncount] [count] —**ap•pre•ci•a•tive** /ə'priyʃətɪv, -ʃiyə-/ adj.

ap•pre•hend /,æprɪ'hɛnd/ v. [~ + obj] **1.** to take into custody; arrest: The police apprehended the burglars. **2.** to grasp the meaning of; per-ceive: The student couldn't apprehend the differ-ence between the two words.

ap•pre•hen•sion /,æprɪ'hɛnʃən/ n. **1.** suspicion or fear of future trouble: [count]: had apprehen-sions about the results. [noncount]: I was filled with apprehension. **2.** [noncount] ability to un-derstand: her apprehension of the danger. **3.** [noncount] the act of arresting; seizure: prompt apprehension of criminals.

ap•pre•hen•sive /,æprɪ'hɛnsɪv/ adj. uneasy or fearful about the future: I was apprehensive as I waited for the test results.

ap•pren•tice /ə'prɛntɪs/ n., v., **-ticed, -tic•ing. —n.** [count] **1.** a person who works for another in order to learn a trade: an apprentice to a plumber. —v. [~ + obj] **2.** to send (someone) or go to work for another to learn a trade: We ap-prenticed him to a plumber. —**ap'pren•tice,ship,** n. [count]: an apprenticeship as an electrician. [noncount]: Apprenticeship lasts two years.

ap•proach /ə'prowtʃ/ v. **1.** to come nearer (to): [~ + obj]: The plane approached the runway. [no obj]: We watched as the plane approached. **2.** [~ + obj] to make contact with, usually for ne-gotiations: We approached the company with an offer. **3.** [~ + obj] to begin work on; set about: to approach the problem from a new angle. —n. [count] **4.** an act or instance of approaching: the approach of a train; the approach of winter. **5.** the method used or steps taken in setting about a task: The problem needs a different approach.

ap•proach•a•ble /ə'prowtʃəbəl/ adj. friendly and easy to talk to: His boss and his co-workers were very approachable.

ap•pro•pri•ate /adj. ə'prowpriyɪt; v. -,eyt/ adj., v., **-at•ed, -at•ing. —adj. 1.** particularly suitable; fitting: appropriate behavior; remarks appropriate to the occasion. —v. [~ + obj] **2.** to set aside for a specific purpose: The company appropriated money for travel expenses. **3.** to take for oneself; steal: They appropriated my ideas as their own. —**ap'pro•pri•ate•ly,** adv.

ap•pro•pri•a•tion /ə,prowpriy'eyʃən/ n. **1.** [noncount] the act of setting money aside for a specific purpose. **2.** [count] money that is set aside.

ap•prov•al /ə'pruwvəl/ n. **1.** [noncount] the act of approving or acceptance: Her idea was met

with approval. **2.** permission; acceptance: [non-count]: The new drug has government approval. [count]: an approval for a mortgage. **3.** [non-count] a feeling of liking, or favoring: She smiled at her son with approval.

ap•prove /ə'pruwv/ v., **-proved, -prov•ing. 1.** to have a favorable view of: [~ + obj]: I can't approve rude behavior. [no obj]: My parents didn't approve of my friends. **2.** [~ + obj] to find to be acceptable: Do you approve the plan? **3.** [~ + obj] to confirm formally; pass: The Sen-ate voted to approve the bill.

approx., an abbreviation of: **1.** approximate. **2.** approximately.

ap•prox•i•mate /adj. ə'prɒksəmɪt; v. -,meyt/ adj., v., **-mat•ed, -mat•ing. —adj. 1.** nearly ex-act; not perfectly accurate: The approximate time was 10 o'clock. —v. [~ + obj] **2.** to approach closely to; to come close (to): He approximated the ideal of a perfect leader. **3.** to estimate: She approximated the distance at a mile. —**ap'prox•i•mate•ly,** adv. —**ap•prox•i•ma•tion** /ə,prɒksə'meyʃən/ n. [count]

Apr or **Apr.,** an abbreviation of: April.

ap•ri•cot /'æprɪ,kɒt, 'eyprɪ-/ n. [count] the yel-lowish orange, peachlike fruit of a tree of the rose family.

A•pril /'eyprəl/ n. the fourth month of the year, containing 30 days.

a•pron /'eyprən/ n. [count] a garment that covers part of the front of the body and serves to protect the clothing.

ap•ro•pos /,æprə'pow/ adj. **1.** being appropriate and timely; well-suited: I found his remarks on war to be very apropos. —**Idiom. 2. apropos of,** with reference to; concerning: Apropos of his claim, can you tell us any more?

apt /æpt/ adj. **1.** [~ + to] likely; having a ten-dency: It's apt to be cold in the evenings. **2.** being quick to learn; bright: a very apt pupil. **3.** suited to the purpose or occasion; suitable: an apt re-mark.

apt., an abbreviation of: apartment.

ap•ti•tude /'æptɪ,tuwd, -,tyuwd/ n. natural ability or skill; talent: [count]: an aptitude for mathematics. [noncount]: musical aptitude.

aq•ua•ma•rine /,ækwəmə'riyn, ,ɑkwə-/ n. **1.** [noncount] [count] a transparent, light blue or greenish blue gem. **2.** [noncount] a light blue-green or greenish blue color.

a•quar•i•um /ə'kwɛəriyəm/ n. [count], pl. **-i•ums, -i•a** /-iyə/. **1.** a glass-sided, water-filled tank in which fish or other underwater animals or plants are kept. **2.** a building or institution in which fish or other underwater animals or plants are kept for exhibit and study.

a•quat•ic /ə'kwætɪk, ə'kwɒt-/ adj. **1.** living or growing in water: aquatic plant life. **2.** [before a noun] taking place or practiced on or in water: Swimming is an aquatic sport. —n. [count] **3. aquatics,** [plural] sports practiced on or in water.

aq•ue•duct /'ækwɪ,dʌkt/ n. [count] an artificial passage or canal for conducting water from a dis-tance.

-ar, 1. a suffix attached to some nouns to form adjectives: circular. **2.** a noun suffix attached to some verbs and meaning one who does or per-forms an action: beggar.

Ar•ab /'ærəb/ n. [count] **1.** a person born or liv-ing in an Arabic-speaking nation. **2.** a member of a group of people who have lived since ancient times in the Arabian Peninsula. —adj. **3.** of or re-lating to Arabs.

A·ra·bi·an /ə'reybiyən/ *adj.* of or relating to Arabia or Saudi Arabia.

Ar·a·bic /'ærəbɪk/ *n.* [*noncount*] a language spoken in countries of the Arabian Peninsula, or in other countries in the Middle East and North Africa.

¹Arabic 'numeral, *n.* [*count*] any of the number symbols 0, 1, 2, 3, 4, 5, 6, 7, 8, 9, in general European use since the 12th century.

ar·a·ble /'ærəbəl/ *adj.* capable of or suitable for producing crops: *arable land; Can the desert be made arable?*

ar·bi·ter /'ɑrbɪtər/ *n.* [*count*] a person empowered to decide matters at issue; judge.

ar·bi·trar·y /'ɑrbɪˌtrɛriy/ *adj.* **1.** decided on or done without the use of reason: *an arbitrary decision.* **2.** having unlimited power: *an arbitrary government.* —**ar·bi·trar·i·ly** /ˌɑrbɪ'trɛrəliy/, *adv.* —'**ar·bi,trar·i·ness,** *n.* [*noncount*]

ar·bi·trate /'ɑrbɪˌtreyt/ *v.,* **-trat·ed, -trat·ing.** to act or decide as arbitrator or arbiter; decide between two sides: [*no obj*]: *She has been asked to arbitrate between the two sides.* [~ + *obj*]: *She has been asked to arbitrate the issue.* —**,ar·bi'tra·tion,** *n.* [*noncount*] —'**ar·bi,tra·tor,** *n.* [*count*]

ar·bor /'ɑrbər/ *n.* [*count*] a leafy shelter formed by or covered with tree branches, shrubs, etc.

arc /ɑrk/ *n.* [*count*] **1.** any unbroken part of the curved line of a circle: *an arc of twenty degrees.* **2.** something curved or arched like a bow.

ar·cade /ɑr'keyd/ *n.* [*count*] **1.** an arched or covered passageway, usually with shops on each side. **2.** commercial space containing coin-operated games.

ar·cane /ɑr'keyn/ *adj.* known or understood only by those with special knowledge; mysterious: *arcane rituals.*

arch /ɑrtʃ/ *n.* [*count*] **1.** a curved construction over an opening. **2.** anything curved like an arch: *the arch of the foot.* —*v.* **3.** to form (into) an arch: [*no obj*]: *The elms arched over the road.* [~ + *obj*]: *The cat arched its back.*

ar·chae·ol·o·gy /ˌɑrkiy'ɒlədʒiy/ *n.* [*noncount*] the scientific study of ancient peoples and their cultures by analyzing their remaining objects, utensils, and other objects. —**ar·chae·o·log·i·cal** /ˌɑrkiyə'lɒdʒɪkəl/, *adj.* —,**ar·chae'ol·o·gist,** *n.* [*count*]

ar·cha·ic /ɑr'keyɪk/ *adj.* out-of-date; antiquated: *archaic attitudes.*

arch·bish·op /'ɑrtʃ'bɪʃəp/ *n.* [*count*] a bishop of the highest rank.

arch·en·e·my /'ɑrtʃ'ɛnəmiy/ *n.* [*count*], *pl.* **-mies.** a chief enemy.

ar·che·ol·o·gy /ˌɑrkiy'ɒlədʒiy/ *n.* ARCHAEOLOGY.

arch·er /'ɑrtʃər/ *n.* [*count*] a person who shoots with a bow and arrow.

ar·cher·y /'ɑrtʃəriy/ *n.* [*noncount*] the practice of shooting with a bow and arrow at a target.

ar·chi·tect /'ɑrkɪˌtɛkt/ *n.* [*count*] **1.** a person who designs buildings. **2.** the main person responsible for making or designing something: *the architects of the plan.*

ar·chi·tec·ture /'ɑrkɪˌtɛktʃər/ *n.* [*noncount*] **1.** the profession of designing buildings. **2.** the character or style of building: *the architecture of Paris.* —,**ar·chi'tec·tur·al,** *adj.*

ar·chive /'ɑrkayv/ *n.* [*count; usually plural*] **archives,** a place where public documents are preserved.

-archy, a combining form meaning rule or government (*monarchy*).

arc·tic /'ɑrktɪk, 'ɑrtɪk/ *adj.* **1.** [*often: Arctic*] of, relating to, or at or near the North Pole: *the arctic region.* **2.** extremely cold: *an arctic winter.* —*n.* [*the* + ~; *often: Arctic*] **3.** the region lying north of the Arctic Circle.

ar·dent /'ɑrdnt/ *adj.* intensely devoted; enthusiastic: *an ardent baseball fan.*

ar·dor /'ɑrdər/ *n.* [*noncount*] **1.** great warmth of feeling; passion: *ardor between lovers; revolutionary ardor.* **2.** zeal; enthusiasm. Also, *esp. Brit.,* ar'dour.

ar·du·ous /'ɑrdʒuwəs/ *adj.* **1.** requiring great energy or exertion: *arduous tasks.* **2.** full of hardship; severe: *an arduous winter.*

are /ɑr; *unstressed* ər/ *v.* a form of the verb BE, used in the present tense when the subject is *you* or when the subject is a plural noun or pronoun: *You are all I have. The boys are all here. Are they coming in?*

ar·e·a /'ɛəriyə/ *n.* [*count*], *pl.* **-as. 1.** a part of a space or a surface: *the dark areas in the painting.* **2.** a place or part of the world; geographical region: *the downtown area.* **3.** a particular subject of study or knowledge; field: *new areas of interest.* **4.** a measurement of a surface, equal to the length multiplied by the width.

¹area ,code, *n.* [*count*] a three-digit number used before a telephone number for dialing a long-distance call.

a·re·na /ə'riynə/ *n.* [*count*], *pl.* **-nas. 1.** a central area used for sports or other forms of entertainment and surrounded by seats. **2.** a building that contains an arena. **3.** a field of competition or activity: *the arena of politics.*

aren't /ɑrnt, 'ɑrənt/ *contraction of* **1.** are not: *You aren't really angry, are you?* **2.** (used in a question) am not: *Aren't I good enough for the job?*

Ar·gen·tine /'ɑrdʒən,tiyn, -,tayn/ *n.* **1.** [*count*] a person born or living in Argentina. —*adj.* **2.** of or relating to Argentina. Also, **Ar·gen·tin·e·an** /,ɑrdʒən'tiniyən/.

ar·gu·a·ble /'ɑrgyuwəbəl/ *adj.* **1.** open to argument; debatable. **2.** likely to be proved correct by argument: *It's arguable that Einstein was the greatest scientist of his time.*

ar·gue /'ɑrgyuw/ *v.,* **-gued, -gu·ing. 1.** to present reasons for or against a thing: [*no obj*]: *argued in favor of capital punishment.* [~ + *for/against* + *obj*]: *argued for capital punishment.* [~ + *obj*]: *to argue a case.* [~ + *that clause*]: *She argued that he was not guilty.* **2.** [*no obj*] to disagree or quarrel: *They argued all day.* —**ar·gu·ment** /'ɑrgyəmənt/ *n.* [*count*] [*noncount*] —**ar·gu·men·ta·tive** /,ɑrgyə'mɛntətɪv/ *adj.*

-arian, a suffix meaning: a person whose work is connected with (*librarian*); a person who supports or practices certain principles (*vegetarian; authoritarian*).

ar·id /'ærɪd/ *adj.* extremely dry: *the arid desert.*

a·rise /ə'rayz/ *v.* [*no obj*], **a·rose** /ə'rowz/, **a·ris·en** /ə'rɪzən/, **a·ris·ing. 1.** to get up from sitting or lying; rise: *He arose from his chair.* **2.** to awaken; wake up: *She arose at 6 a.m.* **3.** to move upward: *Smoke arose from the chimney.* **4.** to appear; spring up: *Problems arise daily. What questions will arise from this?*

ar·is·toc·ra·cy /,ærə'stɒkrəsiy/ *n.* [*noncount*] a class of persons holding high rank or special privileges, esp. nobility.

a•ris•to•crat /ə'rɪstə,kræt/ *n.* [*count*] a member of an aristocracy. —**a,ris•to'crat•ic,** *adj.*

a•rith•me•tic /*n.* ə'rɪθmətɪk; *adj.* ,ærɪθ'metɪk/ *n.* [*noncount*] **1.** the process or study of adding, subtracting, multiplying, and dividing numbers. —*adj.* **2.** Also, ,ar•ith'met•i•cal. of or relating to the rules of arithmetic: *arithmetical calculations.*

Ariz., an abbreviation of: Arizona.

ark /ɑrk/ *n.* **1.** [*sometimes: Ark*] (in the Bible) the vessel built by Noah for safety during the Flood. **2.** Also called **ark of the covenant.** a wooden chest containing two stone tablets inscribed with the Ten Commandments.

Ark., an abbreviation of: Arkansas.

arm¹ /ɑrm/ *n.* [*count*] **1.** the upper limb of the human body. **2.** any part or attachment that resembles an arm, as a support on a chair. **3.** a branch or part of an organization: *an arm of the government.* —*Idiom.* **4. an arm and a leg,** a great deal of money: *That will cost an arm and a leg.* **5. arm in arm,** with arms linked together: *walking along arm in arm.* **6. at arm's length,** at a distance that prevents familiarity: *She kept her associates at arm's length.* **7. twist some-one's arm,** to put strong pressure on someone. **8. with open arms,** cordially; hospitably: *We welcomed her with open arms.*

arm² /ɑrm/ *n.* [*count*] **1.** Usually, **arms.** [*plural*] weapons, esp. guns, rifles, or firearms. **2. arms,** [*plural*] the designs or symbols on a shield. —*v.* **3.** to (cause to) be supplied with weapons: [*no obj*]: *The country is arming for war.* [~ + one-self]: *The rebels armed themselves.* [~ + *obj*]: *They armed their troops.* **4.** [~ + *obj*] to activate, equip, or prepare (something) for a specific purpose: *to arm the security system.* —*Idiom.* **5. bear arms, a.** to carry weapons: *to claim the right to bear arms.* **b.** to serve in the armed forces: *He had to bear arms as a young man.* **6. up in arms,** angry; indignant: *is up in arms about the effort to discredit him.*

ar•ma•da /ɑr'mɑdə, -'mey-/ *n.* [*count*], *pl.* **-das.** [*Often: Armada*] a fleet of warships: *The Spanish Armada was defeated by the English navy.*

ar•ma•dil•lo /,ɑrmə'dɪlow/ *n.* [*count*], *pl.* **-los.** an animal related to the anteater and covered with jointed plates of bone and horn.

ar•ma•ment /'ɑrməmənt/ *n.* [*noncount*] the arms and equipment with which a military unit is supplied.

arm•chair /'ɑrm,tʃɛər/ *n.* [*count*] a chair with supports at the sides for a person's arms.

armed /ɑrmd/ *adj.* **1.** carrying a weapon: *an armed police officer.* **2.** [*before a noun*] involving people with weapons: *armed robbery.* **3.** [*be + ~ + with*] having in one's possession ready for use: *was armed with the facts.*

'armed 'forces, *n.* [*plural*] the military, naval, and air forces of a nation or nations.

ar•mi•stice /'ɑrməstɪs/ *n.* [*count*] an agreement to stop fighting and discuss peace; truce.

ar•mor /'ɑrmər/ *n.* [*noncount*] a metal covering that serves as a defense or protection against weapons. Also, *esp. Brit.,* '**ar•mour.**

ar•mored /'ɑrmərd/ *adj.* covered with or protected by armor: *an armored car.*

ar•mor•y /'ɑrməriy/ *n.* [*count*], *pl.* **-ies. 1.** a storage place for weapons. **2.** a factory where weapons are made.

arm•pit /'ɑrm,pɪt/ *n.* [*count*] the hollow place under the arm at the shoulder.

arms /ɑrmz/ *n.* [*plural*] See ARM².

ar•my /'ɑrmiy/ *n.* [*count*], *pl.* **-mies. 1.** the mili-tary forces of a nation, esp. those on land. **2.** any large group: *an army of cheering fans.*

a•ro•ma /ə'rowmə/ *n.* [*count*], *pl.* **-mas.** a strong pleasant odor; fragrance: *the aroma of fresh coffee.* —**ar•o•mat•ic** /,ærə'mætɪk/, *adj.*: *aromatic oils.*

a•ro•ma•ther•a•py /ə,rowmə'θerəpiy/ *n.* [*noncount*] **1.** the use of pleasant fragrances to affect or change a person's mood or behavior. **2.** treatment of the skin by the application of fragrant oils from flowers or herbs.

a•rose /ə'rowz/ *v.* pt. of ARISE.

a•round /ə'rawnd/ *adv.* **1.** in a circle or in a ring; on all sides: *The crowd gathered around and watched.* **2.** in all directions (when viewed from a central point): *could see for miles around.* **3.** in or to another, opposite direction: *She twisted her head around to see who was there.* **4.** somewhere near; somewhere about: *I'll be around for an hour.* —*prep.* **5.** about; on all sides; surrounding: *to wrap paper around the package.* **6.** on the edge or outer part of: *a skirt with fringe around the bottom.* **7.** in all or various directions from: *She looked around the room.* **8.** in the vicinity of; near to: *the countryside around Boston.*

a•rous•al /ə'rawzəl/ *n.* [*noncount*] the state or condition of being alert or stimulated.

a•rouse /ə'rawz/ *v.* [~ + *obj*], **a•roused, a•rous•ing. 1.** to stir to action or strong response; excite: *The fiery speech aroused the crowd.* **2.** to stimulate sexually. **3.** to wake (someone) up: *She aroused them at noon.*

ar•range /ə'reyndʒ/ *v.* [~ + *obj*], **-ranged, -rang•ing. 1.** to place in proper or desired order; organize: *arranged the flowers attractively.* **2.** to make plans or preparations (for): [*no obj*]: *Let's arrange for a conference.* [~ + *obj*]: *Please arrange a meeting for next week.*

ar•range•ment /ə'reyndʒmənt/ *n.* **1.** [*noncount*] the act of arranging. **2.** [*count*] something that has been arranged: *a flower arrangement.* **3.** [*count*] Often, **arrangements.** [*plural*] preparations; plans: *to make funeral arrangements.* **4.** [*count*] [*noncount*] an agreement or settlement.

ar•ray /ə'rey/ *v.* [~ + *obj*] **1.** to place, position, or set out in order: *to array troops for battle.* **2.** to dress or decorate with beautiful clothing: *arrayed in their finest clothes.* —*n.* **3.** [*noncount*] order or arrangement, as of troops assembled for battle. **4.** [*count*] an impressive grouping: *The speaker presented them with an array of facts.*

ar•rest /ə'rɛst/ *v.* [~ + *obj*] **1.** to seize (a person) by legal authority: *The police arrested the burglar.* **2.** to catch and hold: *A loud noise arrested our attention.* **3.** to stop (something) or to cause (something) to slow down: *The drug arrested the progress of the disease.* —*n.* [*count*] **4.** the act of arresting. —*Idiom.* **5. under arrest,** confined and guarded by the police.

ar•ri•val /ə'rayvəl/ *n.* **1.** [*noncount*] the act of arriving. **2.** [*count*] a person or thing that arrives.

ar•rive /ə'rayv/ *v.,* **-rived, -riv•ing. 1.** [*no obj*] to come to a place in a journey; reach one's destination: *They have just arrived in town.* **2.** [*no obj*] to come; happen: *The moment of truth has arrived.* **3. arrive at,** to reach or attain; come to: *We arrived at an agreement.*

ar•ro•gant /'ærəgənt/ *adj.* feeling or acting more important than others; rude and arro-gant officials. —'**ar•ro•gance,** *n.* [*noncount*] —'**ar•ro•gant•ly,** *adv.*

ar•row /'ærow/ *n.* [*count*] **1.** a long, slender stick, with a pointed tip and feathers, that is shot from a bow. **2.** anything resembling an arrow, as a symbol used to show direction or movement.

ar•row•head /'ærov̩,hɛd/ *n.* [*count*] a pointed tip on an arrow: *arrowheads of flint.*

ar•se•nal /'ɑrsənḷ/ *n.* [*count*] a place for producing and storing military supplies.

ar•se•nic /'ɑrsənɪk/ *n.* [*noncount*] a grayish white chemical element that can be made into a dangerous poison.

ar•son /'ɑrsən/ *n.* [*noncount*] the crime of setting fire to property. —**'ar•son•ist,** *n.* [*count*]

art /ɑrt/ *n.* **1.** [*noncount*] beautiful objects, such as paintings and sculptures: *a great collection of Japanese art.* **2.** [*noncount*] the activity, skill, or study concerned with producing such objects: *He majored in art in college.* **3.** [*count*] a category of art: *Dance is an art.* **4.** [*count; usually singular*] skill in conducting any human activity: *the art of conversation.* **5. arts,** [*plural*] languages, music, philosophy, literature, etc., as opposed to scientific subjects.

art., an abbreviation for: article.

ar•ter•y /'ɑrtəriy/ *n.* [*count*], *pl.* **-ies. 1.** a tube that carries blood from the heart to other parts of the body. **2.** a main route or highway.

art•ful /'ɑrtfəl/ *adj.* slyly crafty or cunning; tricky: *artful in twisting stories.*

ar•thri•tis /ɑr'θraytɪs/ *n.* [*noncount*] a painful inflammation and swelling of a joint.

ar•ti•choke /'ɑrtɪ,tʃowk/ *n.* [*count*] a tall plant with a head and edible leaflike scales.

ar•ti•cle /'ɑrtɪkəl/ *n.* [*count*] **1.** a piece of writing appearing in a newspaper, etc.: *She wrote a magazine article.* **2.** any individual member of a class or group of things: *an article of clothing.* **3.** one of a small class of words in English, *a, an,* and *the,* that are linked to nouns and that show whether the noun is definite or indefinite. Compare DEFINITE ARTICLE, INDEFINITE ARTICLE.

ar•tic•u•late /*adj.* ɑr'tɪkyəlɪt; *v.* -,leyt/ *adj., v.,* **-lat•ed, -lat•ing.** —*adj.* **1.** capable of or showing clarity: *an articulate campaign speech.* —*v.* **2.** to pronounce (speech sounds) clearly and distinctly: [*no obj*]: *The actor articulated so as to be understood.* [~ + *obj*]: *She articulated the vowels carefully.* **3.** [~ + *obj*] to put (an idea) clearly into speech: *He articulated his philosophy clearly.* —**ar•tic•u•la•tion** /ɑr,tɪkyə'leyʃən/ *n.* [*noncount*]

ar•ti•fact /'ɑrtə,fækt/ *n.* [*count*] any object made by human beings, esp. a tool from an earlier time found at an archaeological site.

ar•ti•fice /'ɑrtəfɪs/ *n.* **1.** [*count*] a clever trick: *Makeup is an artifice used by actors.* **2.** [*noncount*] the use of a clever trick; craftiness.

ar•ti•fi•cial /,ɑrtə'fɪʃəl/ *adj.* **1.** made by human skill; not natural: *an artificial satellite.* **2.** lacking naturalness; false: *an artificial smile.* —**,ar•ti'fi•cial•ly,** *adv.*

arti'ficial in'telligence, *n.* [*noncount*] the capability of computer programs and devices to perform functions similar to human abilities to learn and to make decisions.

ar•til•ler•y /ɑr'tɪləriy/ *n.* [*noncount*] **1.** large guns or missile launchers mounted on wheels. **2.** the branch of military forces using these weapons.

ar•ti•san /'ɑrtəzən/ *n.* [*count*] a person who practices a craft or trade requiring skilled use of the hands.

art•ist /'ɑrtɪst/ *n.* [*count*] a person who practices or is skilled in one of the arts.

ar•tis•tic /ɑr'tɪstɪk/ *adj.* **1.** beautiful; attractive:

an artistic flower arrangement. **2.** of or characteristic of art or artists: *fought for artistic freedom.*

art•ist•ry /'ɑrtɪstriy/ *n.* [*noncount*] skill, ability, or workmanship of an artist.

art•work /'ɑrt,wɜrk/ *n.* [*noncount*] an object or objects produced by artists: *the artwork on the ceiling of an old cathedral.*

-ary, a suffix meaning: relating to or connected with (*elementary*); a place or container for (*library*).

as /æz; *unstressed* əz/ *adv.* **1.** to the same degree or amount; equally: *It costs three times as much.* **2.** for example: *a number of flowers, as the tulip.* **3.** thought or considered to be: *the square as distinct from the rectangle.* —*conj.* **4.** to the same degree that: *I like to do as I please.* **5.** in the degree or manner of; in the same way that: *Do as we do.* **6.** at the same time that; while; when: *Pay as you enter.* **7.** since; because: *As you are leaving last, lock the door.* **8.** though: *Strange as it seems, it is true.* **9.** [*so + adjective + ~ + to + verb*] that the result or effect was: *His voice was so loud as to make everyone stare.* —*pron.* **10.** [*the same + ~*] that; who; which: *I have the same trouble as you had.* **11.** a fact that: *She spoke the truth, as can be proved.* —*prep.* **12.** in the role, function, or status of: *to act as leader.* —*Idiom.* **13. as ... as,** (used to express similarity or equality between two people or things): *She is as rich as Croesus* (= *She and Croesus are equally or similarly rich*). **14. as far as,** to the degree or extent that: *It is a good plan, as far as I can tell.* **15. as for,** with respect to; about; concerning: *As for the accident, I can't remember how it happened.* **16. as good as, a.** equivalent to: *After the repair, the clock was as good as new.* **b.** true to; trustworthy as: *He has always been as good as his word.* **17. as if** or **as though,** as it would be if: *It was as if the world had come to an end.* **18. as is,** in whatever condition something is in when offered, esp. if damaged: *You must buy the car as is.* **19. as of,** beginning on; on and after: *This price is effective as of next Sunday.* **20. as such,** as being what is indicated; because of what someone or something is: *An officer of the law, as such, is entitled to respect.* **21. as yet,** up to the present time: *I don't, as yet, have a good salary.*

ASAP or **A.S.A.P.** or **a.s.a.p.,** an abbreviation of: as soon as possible.

as•bes•tos /æs'bɛstəs, æz-/ *n.* [*noncount*] a fiber-like substance formerly used for making fireproof articles and in building insulation.

as•cend /ə'sɛnd/ *v.* **1.** to move, climb, or go upward (upon or along); mount: [*no obj*]: *The elevator ascended to the top floor.* [~ + *obj*]: *She ascended the stairs gracefully.* **2.** [*no obj*] to rise to a higher point, rank, degree, etc.: *The secretary ascended rapidly to the position of office manager.*

as•cend•an•cy /ə'sɛndənsiy/ also **as'cend•ance,** *n.* [*noncount*] the state of being in power, or of governing or controlling.

as•cent /ə'sɛnt/ *n.* [*count*] **1.** movement upward from a lower to a higher state, degree, grade, or status; advancement: *rapid ascent through the ranks.* **2.** the degree of tilting upward: *a steep ascent.*

as•cer•tain /,æsər'teyn/ *v.* to find out definitely; get to know: [~ + *obj*]: *We tried hard to ascertain all the facts in the case.* [~ + (*that*) *clause*]: *We ascertained that she told the truth.*

as•cribe /ə'skrayb/ *v.* [~ + *obj*], **-cribed, -crib•ing. 1.** to believe or consider (something or someone) to be the cause or source of (something): *She ascribed her failures to bad luck.* **2.** to believe that (something) was made or done by (someone): *The experts have ascribed this painting to Picasso.*

ash¹ /æʃ/ *n.* **1.** (pieces of) the gray or black powdery matter that remains after burning: [*noncount*]: *ash from a fire.* [*count*]: *cigarette ashes.* **2.** [*noncount*] fine lava thrown out by a volcano in eruption: *The city was covered with ash from the eruption.* **3.** [*noncount*] a light, silvery gray color. **4. ashes,** [*plural*] ruins, esp. the remains of something destroyed or lost forever: *left only with the ashes of former victories.*

ash² /æʃ/ *n.* [*count*] any of various trees of the olive family.

a•shamed /əˈʃeymd/ *adj.* feeling shame: [*be + ~ + of*]: *He was ashamed of himself.* [*be + ~ + verb*]: *He was ashamed to cry.* [*be + ~ + that clause*]: *She was ashamed that she had failed the test.*

ash•en /ˈæʃən/ *adj.* ash-colored; gray; extremely pale: *His face turned ashen with fear.*

a•shore /əˈʃɔr/ *adv.* to or onto the shore: *She swam ashore from the raft.*

ash•tray /ˈæʃˌtrey/ *n.* [*count*] a bowl or small dish for cigarette or cigar ashes.

A•sian /ˈeyʒən/ *adj.* **1.** of or relating to Asia. **—n.** [*count*] **2.** a person born or living in Asia.

a•side /əˈsayd/ *adv.* **1.** on or to one side: *She put her book aside and got up.* **2.** away from one's thoughts: *to put one's cares aside.* **3.** in reserve; in a separate place, as for safekeeping: *I put some money aside.* **4.** away from a group or area, esp. for privacy: *He took her aside to discuss the plan.* **—Idiom. 5. aside from, a.** in addition to; besides: *Aside from being too small, the jacket is ugly.* **b.** except for: *Aside from a few minor mistakes, this is a fine report.*

ask /æsk, ɑsk/ *v.* **1.** to put a question (to); inquire (of): [*no obj*]: *I asked but I never got an answer.* [*~ + obj*]: *I asked her but she didn't answer. I asked him if they were going home.* **2.** to request (of): [*~ + obj*]: *I asked for a little more time. I have to ask a favor of you. Could I ask you a favor? I asked her to leave with me, but she wanted to stay.* [*~ + to + verb*]: *I asked to go with her.* **3.** [*~ + obj*] to invite: *to ask guests to dinner.* **—Idiom. 4. ask for it** or **ask for trouble,** to invite problems by continuing with risky or annoying behavior: *He's really asking for it, coming in late. With an attitude like that, he's asking for trouble.*

a•skew /əˈskyuw/ *adj.* [*be + ~*] crooked; not level or straight: *Your tie is askew.*

a•sleep /əˈsliyp/ *adv.* **1.** in or into a state of sleep: *The baby was lying fast asleep in the crib.* **—adj.** [*be + ~*] **2.** sleeping: *He is asleep.* **3.** numb: *My foot is asleep.* **4.** not paying attention: *He was asleep on the job.* **—Idiom. 5. fall asleep, a.** go into a state of sleep. **b.** (of a part of the body) become numb: *My foot fell asleep after a few hours of sitting still.*

as•par•a•gus /əˈspærəgəs/ *n.* **1.** [*noncount*] an edible plant of the lily family, having green shoots, or spears. **2.** [*count*] the shoots themselves.

ASPCA, an abbreviation of: the American Society for the Prevention of Cruelty to Animals.

as•pect /ˈæspɛkt/ *n.* [*count*] **1.** a particular part or feature of something: *There are many aspects to this problem.* **2.** a look, appearance, or expres-

sion, esp. of the face: *His narrowed eyes gave him a threatening aspect.*

as•pen /ˈæspən/ *n.* [*count*] a kind of poplar tree of Europe and North America, having leaves that tremble in the slightest breeze.

as•phalt /ˈæsfɔlt/ *n.* [*noncount*] any of several kinds of dark-colored substances mixed with gravel, crushed rock, or the like used for paving: *They laid the asphalt for the driveway.*

as•pire /əˈspayᵊr/ *v.* [*no obj*], **-pired, -pir•ing.** to long for, aim for, or try to get: *He aspired to a fine career.* [*~ + to + verb*]: *She aspired to become a professor.* **—as•pi•ra•tion** /ˌæspəˈreyʃən/ *n.* [*noncount*] [*count*]

as•pi•rin /ˈæspərɪn, -prɪn/ *n., pl.* **-rin, -rins. 1.** [*noncount*] a medicinal substance used to reduce pain and fever. **2.** [*count*] a tablet of aspirin: *Take an aspirin.*

as•pir•ing /əˈspayᵊrɪŋ/ *adj.* [*before a noun*] longing or aiming to be: *an aspiring actor.* **—as'pir•ing•ly,** *adv.*

ass /æs/ *n.* [*count*] **1.** Also called **donkey.** a long-eared mammal related to the horse, and used for carrying things. **2.** a stupid, foolish, or stubborn person.

as•sail /əˈseyl/ *v.* [*~ + obj*] **1.** to attack vigorously or violently; assault: *The Marines assailed the enemy camp.* **2.** to attack verbally: *The press assailed the candidates.*

as•sail•ant /əˈseylənt/ *n.* [*count*] an attacker: *Although she was robbed, she managed to escape from her assailant.*

as•sas•sin /əˈsæsɪn/ *n.* [*count*] a murderer, esp. one who kills a politically well-known person.

as•sas•si•nate /əˈsæsəˌneyt/ *v.* [*~ + obj*], **-nat•ed, -nat•ing.** to murder (a politically well-known person). **—as•sas•si•na•tion** /əˌsæsəˈneyʃən/ *n.* [*noncount*] [*count*]

as•sault /əˈsɔlt/ *n.* **1.** [*count*] a sudden violent attack: *launched an assault on the enemy battleship.* **2.** *Law.* an unlawful physical attack upon another, esp. an attempt or threat to do bodily harm: [*count*]: *several assaults with deadly weapons.* [*noncount*]: *convicted of assault.* **—v.** [*~ + obj*] **3.** to make an assault upon: *The Marines assaulted the hilltop.*

as•sem•ble /əˈsɛmbəl/ *v.,* **-bled, -bling. 1.** to come or bring together; gather into one place; meet: [*no obj*]: *The family assembled in the waiting room.* [*~ + obj*]: *The guides assembled the tourists in the bus.* **2.** [*~ + obj*] to put together the parts of: *to assemble model airplanes.*

as•sem•bly /əˈsɛmbliy/ *n., pl.* **-blies. 1.** a gathering or coming together of a number of persons: [*noncount*]: *an assembly of children.* [*count; usually singular*]: *A great assembly of people appeared at the wedding.* **2.** [*usually: Assembly*] a legislative body, esp. a lower house: *elected to the Assembly for a term of two years.* **3.** [*noncount*] the putting together of parts, as of machinery: *assembly of the new plane.*

as'sembly ,line, *n.* [*count*] an arrangement of machines, tools, and workers in which a product is assembled part by part as it is moved along a line.

as•sem•bly•man /əˈsɛmbliymən/ *n.* [*count*], *pl.* **-men.** a member of a legislative assembly.

as•sent /əˈsɛnt/ *v.* [*no obj*] **1.** to agree; give agreement: *They assented to the new proposal.* **—n.** [*noncount*] **2.** agreement, as to a proposal: *He gave his assent to the plan.*

as•sert /əˈsɜrt/ *v.* **1.** to state strongly or positively; declare: [*~ + obj*]: *He asserted his inno-*

cence. [~ + (that) clause]: *He asserted that he was innocent of the crime.* **2.** [~ + obj] to make a claim to: *Minorities are now asserting their right to be heard.* **—Idiom. 3.** assert oneself, to claim one's rights or declare one's views firmly. **—assertion,** *n.* [count] [noncount]

as•ser•tive /ə'sɜrtɪv/ *adj.* confidently aggressive or forceful: *an assertive personality.*

as•sess /ə'sɛs/ *v.* [~ + obj] **1.** to estimate officially the value of (property) for tax purposes: *They assessed the house at one million dollars.* **2.** to evaluate the importance or character of: *They met to assess the crisis.*

as•sess•ment /ə'sɛsmənt/ *n.* [count] **1.** an act of assessing: *a quick assessment of the situation.* **2.** an amount of money something, as property, is judged to be worth.

as•set /'æsɛt/ *n.* [count] **1.** a useful and desirable thing or quality: *Math skill is an asset in business.* **2. assets,** [plural] the total resources of a person or business.

as•sign /ə'sayn/ *v.* [~ + obj] **1.** to give out as a share or task: *They assigned rooms at the hotel. They assigned us a room. They assigned a room to us.* **2.** to appoint to a post or duty: *They assigned her to the day shift.* **3.** to designate; name; specify: *Let's assign a day for a meeting.*

as•sign•ment /ə'saynmənt/ *n.* [count] **1.** something assigned, as a task: *homework assignments.* **2.** a position or post of duty to which one is assigned: *an assignment as ambassador to France.* **3.** [noncount] the act of assigning.

as•sim•i•late /ə'sɪmə,leyt/ *v.,* **-lat•ed, -lat•ing. 1.** [~ + obj] to take in and use as one's own; understand: *He tried to assimilate new ideas.* **2. a.** [no obj] (of a person from a different background) to adjust (oneself) to the dominant cultural group or national culture: *The immigrants assimilated rapidly.* **b.** [~ + obj] to bring (people from a different background) into a more dominant cultural group or national culture: *to assimilate the new immigrants.* **—as•sim•i•la•tion** /ə,sɪmə'leyʃən/, *n.* [noncount]

as•sist /ə'sɪst/ *v.* to give support or aid to; help: [~ + obj]: *She assisted me with my homework.* [no obj]: *He was asked to assist with the investigation.* **—as•sis•tance,** *n.* [noncount]: *Can I be of assistance?*

as•sis•tant /ə'sɪstənt/ *n.* [count] **1.** a person who assists; helper: *was an assistant to the manager.* **—adj.** [before a noun] **2.** serving in a subordinate position: *an assistant secretary.*

as'sisted 'suicide, *n.* [count] suicide in which a person is helped to die by a physician, friend, etc.

as•so•ci•ate /v. ə'sowʃiy,eyt, -siy-; *n.* -ɪt, -,eyt/ *v.,* **-at•ed, -at•ing,** *n.* **—v. 1.** [~ + obj] to connect or bring together in the mind: *I associate rainy days with spring.* **2.** [~ + with + obj] to keep company as a friend or companion: *Her parents wouldn't allow her to associate with anyone who smoked or drank.* **—n.** [count] **3.** a person who shares actively in an enterprise; co-worker. **—as•so•ci•a•tion** /ə,sowsiy'eyʃən, -ʃiy-/ *n.* [noncount] [count]

as•sort•ment /ə'sɔrtmənt/ *n.* [count] a collection of various kinds of things; mixed collection. **—as'sort•ed,** *adj.*

asst., an abbreviation of: assistant.

as•sume /ə'suwm/ *v.* [~ + obj], **-sumed, -sum•ing. 1.** to take for granted without proof: *to assume that everyone wants peace.* **2.** to take upon

oneself: *to assume responsibility.* **3.** to pretend to have or be: *to assume a humble manner.*

as•sump•tion /ə'sʌmpʃən/ *n.* **1.** [count] something taken for granted: *an assumption that all was well.* **2.** [noncount] the act of assuming: *Their assumption of his innocence won't change without convincing evidence.*

as•sure /ə'ʃʊr/ *v.* [~ + obj], **-sured, -sur•ing. 1.** to declare positively or confidently to: *She assured us that everything would be all right.* **2.** to make (a future event) sure; guarantee: *This contract assures the company's profit this month.* **3.** *Chiefly Brit.* to insure against loss. **—as'sur•ance,** *n.* [count] [noncount]

as•ter•isk /'æstərɪsk/ *n.* [count] a symbol (*), used as a reference mark or to indicate omission, doubtful matter, etc.

as•ter•oid /'æstə,rɔyd/ *n.* [count] any of the small bodies that orbit the sun chiefly between Mars and Jupiter.

asth•ma /'æzmə, 'æs-/ *n.* [noncount] a breathing disorder often caused by an allergic reaction and characterized by spasms in the lungs, wheezing, and difficulty in breathing out.

asth•mat•ic /æz'mætɪk, æs-/ *n.* [count] **1.** a person who suffers from asthma. **—adj. 2.** suffering from or caused by asthma.

as•ton•ish /ə'stɒnɪʃ/ *v.* [~ + obj] to fill with sudden wonder; amaze: *The victory astonished everybody.* **—as'ton•ish•ment,** *n.* [noncount]

as•tound /ə'stawnd/ *v.* [~ + obj] to overwhelm with amazement; astonish: *We were astounded by his amazing display of skill.*

a•stray /ə'strey/ *adv.* **1.** off the correct path or route; lost: *The letter must have gone astray.* **2.** away into error or confusion: *Wicked companions led her astray.*

a•stride /ə'strayd/ *prep.* with a leg on each side of; straddling: *She rode astride the horse.*

as•trin•gent /ə'strɪndʒənt/ *adj.* **1.** causing the skin to contract and the blood to stop flowing: *astringent lotion.* **—n.** [count] **2.** an astringent substance: *Apply an astringent to the cut.*

as•trol•o•gy /ə'strɒlədʒiy/ *n.* [noncount] the belief that heavenly bodies influence human affairs; the study of such influence. **—as'trol•o•ger, as'trol•o•gist,** *n.* [count]

as•tro•naut /'æstrə,nɔt, -,nɒt/ *n.* [count] a person trained for space flight.

as•tro•nom•i•cal /,æstrə'nɒmɪkəl/ also ,**as•tro'nom•ic,** *adj.* **1.** [usually: before a noun] relating to, or connected with astronomy. **2.** huge: *astronomical debts.* **—,as•tro'nom•i•cal•ly,** *adv.*

as•tron•o•my /ə'strɒnəmiy/ *n.* [noncount] the science that deals with the moon, planets, stars, and the universe beyond earth. **—as'tron•o•mer,** *n.* [count]

as•tute /ə'stuwt, ə'styuwt/ *adj.* very perceptive; wise: *an astute analysis.*

a•sy•lum /ə'sayləm/ *n.* **1.** [count] (esp. formerly) an institution for the care esp. of the mentally ill, orphans, or the poor. **2.** [noncount] protection given to political refugees.

at /æt; *unstressed* ət, ɪt/ *prep.* **1.** (used to indicate a point, place, or location, as an address): *We met at the library.* **2.** (used to indicate a point of time): *It happened at midnight.* **3.** (used to indicate amount, degree, or rate): *went at great speed.* **4.** (used to indicate a direction, goal, or an attempt to do something): *Look at that; aimed at the target.* **5.** (used to indicate occupation or involvement): *watching the children at play.* **6.**

(used to indicate a state or condition): *at peace with the world.* **7.** (used to indicate a cause or source): *amazed at her skill.*

ate /eyt/ *v.* the pt. of EAT.

-ate, a suffix meaning: of, having, or resembling: (*compassionate*); to become or cause to become (*agitate*); office, rule, or function (*consulate*).

a•the•ism /'eyθiy,ɪzəm/ *n.* [*noncount*] the belief that there is no God. —**'a•the•ist,** *n.* [*count*]

ath•lete /'æθliyt/ *n.* [*count*] a person trained or skilled in athletics. —**athletic,** *adj.*

'athlete's 'foot, *n.* [*noncount*] ringworm of the feet.

ath•let•ics /æθ'lɛtɪks/ *n.* [*plural; used with a plural verb*] athletic sports, such as running, rowing, or boxing.

-ation, a suffix meaning: act or process of (*consolation*); state or condition of (*deprivation*); result of (*combination*).

-ative, a suffix meaning: of or relating to (*qualitative*); tending or serving to (*talkative*).

at•las /'ætləs/ *n.* [*count*] a book of maps, charts, plates, or tables illustrating a subject: *a world atlas; a road atlas.*

ATM, an abbreviation of: automated-teller machine.

at•mos•phere /'ætməs,fɪər/ *n.* [*count*] **1.** the gases surrounding a planet, esp. the earth; air. **2.** a mood that seems to fill a place, event, or situation: *An atmosphere of tension filled the classroom.* —**at•mos•pher•ic** /,ætməs'fɛrɪk, -'fɪər-/, *adj.*

at•om /'ætəm/ *n.* [*count*] the smallest part of an element that still has the chemical properties of the element. —**atomic,** *adj.*

a'tomic 'bomb or **'atom 'bomb,** *n.* [*count*] a bomb whose power comes from splitting atoms of certain elements. Also called **A-bomb.**

a'tomic 'energy, *n.* NUCLEAR ENERGY.

a•tone /ə'town/ *v.* [~ + *for* + *obj*], **a•toned, a•ton•ing.** to make amends, as for an offense or sin. —**a'tone•ment,** *n.* [*noncount*]

a•top /ə'tɒp/ *prep.* on the top of: *atop a hill.*

a•tri•um /'eytriyəm/ *n.* [*count*], *pl.* **a•tri•a** /'eytriyə/ **a•tri•ums. 1.** a central courtyard open to the sky. **2.** one of the two upper chambers of the heart.

a•tro•cious /ə'trowʃəs/ *adj.* **1.** terribly wicked or cruel: *an atrocious crime.* **2.** very bad or tasteless: *atrocious table manners.* —**a•troc•i•ty** /ə'trɒsɪtiy/ *n.* [*noncount*] [*count*], *pl.* **-ties.**

at•tach /ə'tætʃ/ *v.* [~ + *obj*] **1.** to fasten or affix; join; connect: *to attach papers with a staple; She attached the check to the tax form.* **2.** to connect: *I wouldn't attach any significance to his remark.* —**at'tach•ment,** *n.* [*noncount*] [*count*]

at•tack /ə'tæk/ *v.* **1.** to attempt to harm in an aggressive way; begin fighting with: [~ + *obj*]: *The dog attacked the burglar.* [*no obj*]: *The mugger attacked and ran away.* **2.** [~ + *obj*] to blame or criticize severely: *The politician attacked his opponent's ideas.* **3.** [~ + *obj*] to set about doing or working on vigorously: *The starving man attacked the meal.* —*n.* **4.** the act of attacking; assault: [*count*]: *Several attacks took place at night.* [*noncount*]: *The village came under attack from the air.* **5.** [*count*] an episode of suffering from a disease or other condition: *a heart attack.* —**at'tack•er,** *n.* [*count*]

at•tain /ə'teyn/ *v.* [~ + *obj*] to come to or arrive at; gain; achieve: *to attain one's goals.* —**at'tain•ment,** *n.* [*noncount*] [*count*]

at•tempt /ə'tɛmpt/ *v.* [~ + *obj*] **1.** to make an effort at; try: *They attempted a long hike. He will attempt to finish the race. She attempted driving around the fallen tree.* —*n.* [*count*] **2.** an effort made to accomplish something: *The sketch was my first attempt.*

at•tend /ə'tɛnd/ *v.* **1.** [~ + *obj*] to be present at: *Children attend school each day.* **2.** to go with or happen as a result; accompany: [~ + *obj*]: *Fever may attend the flu.* [*no obj*]: *The events that attended on the assassination were mysterious.* **3.** to take care (of); look after; deal with: [~ + *obj*]: *The nurse was attending her patient.* [*no obj*]: *We were attending to the burn victims.* —**at'tend•ance,** *n.* [*noncount*] [*count; singular*]

at•tend•ant /ə'tɛndənt/ *n.* [*count*] a person who waits on, cares for, or looks after someone or something.

at•ten•tion /*n.* ə'tɛnʃən; *interj.* ə,tɛn'ʃʌn/ *n.* [*noncount*] **1.** the act of using the mind to concentrate on something: *listening with attention to the speech.* **2.** thoughtful consideration with a view to action: *I promise to give that matter my personal attention.* —**Idiom. 3. pay attention (to),** give full thought or consideration to: *Pay attention while I'm talking. Pay attention to your driving!*

at•ten•tive /ə'tɛntɪv/ *adj.* showing attention: *attentive students.* —**at'ten•tive•ly,** *adv.*

at•test /ə'tɛst/ *v.* to give proof or evidence of: [*no obj*]: *I can attest to her reliability.* [~ + *obj*]: *This essay attests your writing ability.* —**at•tes•ta•tion** /,ætɛs'teyʃən/ *n.* [*count*]

at•tic /'ætɪk/ *n.* [*count*] the part of a building, esp. of a house, directly under a roof.

at•tire /ə'tayᵊr/ *v.,* **-tired, -tir•ing.** —*v.* [*usually: be attired*] **1.** to dress or adorn, esp. for fancy occasions or ceremonies. —*n.* [*noncount*] **2.** clothes, esp. rich or fine garments.

at•ti•tude /'ætɪ,tuwd, -,tyuwd/ *n.* [*count*] **1.** manner or way one thinks about, behaves toward, or feels toward someone or something: *a cheerful attitude.* **2.** position or posture of the body: *to kneel in a prayerful attitude.*

attn., an abbreviation of: attention.

at•tor•ney /ə'tɜrniy/ *n.* [*count*], *pl.* **-neys.** a lawyer.

at'torney 'general, *n.* [*count*], *pl.* **attorneys general, attorney generals.** [*often cap.*] the chief law officer of a country or state and head of its legal department.

at•tract /ə'trækt/ *v.* [~ + *obj*] **1.** to cause to approach or come near; pull: *Magnets attract metal.* **2.** to draw by appealing to the emotions or senses: *The hearings attracted publicity.*

at•trac•tion /ə'trækʃən/ *n.* **1.** [*noncount*] the act, power, or quality of attracting. **2.** [*count*] an attractive quality or feature. **3.** [*count*] a person or thing that attracts. **4.** [*noncount*] the electric or magnetic force drawing oppositely charged bodies together.

at•trac•tive /ə'træktɪv/ *adj.* **1.** providing pleasure or delight, esp. in appearance or manner: *an attractive personality; an attractive face.* **2.** arousing interest; appealing: *an attractive idea.* —**at'trac•tive•ly,** *adv.* —**at'trac•tive•ness,** *n.* [*noncount*]

at•trib•ut•able /ə'trɪbyətəbəl/ *adj.* [*be* + ~ + *to*] believed to have been caused by: *Some mistakes were attributable to fatigue and human error.*

at•trib•ute /*v.* ə'trɪbyuwt; *n.* 'ætrə,byuwt/ *v.,* **-ut•ed, -ut•ing.** —*v.* [~ + *obj*] **1.** to designate someone or something as the cause of (something else): *She attributes his bad temper to ill health.* —*n.* [count] **2.** a quality or property believed to belong to a person or thing: *Sensitivity is one of his attributes.*

at•tuned /ə'tuwnd, ə'tyuwnd/ *adj.* [be + ~ + to] **1.** being in harmony with; adjusted to: *She was attuned to country living. My ears were not attuned to so much noise.* **2.** keenly alert to: *attuned to any criticism.*

au•burn /'ɔbərn/ *n.* [noncount] **1.** a reddish brown color. —*adj.* **2.** of this color: *auburn hair.*

auc•tion /'ɔkʃən/ *n.* **1.** a publicly held sale at which property or goods are sold to the person who offers the most money: [count]: *They held an auction to sell the equipment in the barn.* [noncount]: *They sold the house at auction.* —*v.* [~ + obj] **2.** to sell by auction: *The bank auctioned (off) the house.*

auc•tion•eer /,ɔkʃə'nɪər/ *n.* [count] a person who runs an auction.

au•da•cious /ɔ'deyʃəs/ *adj.* extremely bold or daring: *an audacious plan to row a boat across the Atlantic.* —**au•dac•i•ty** /ɔ'dæsɪtiy/ *n.* [noncount]

au•di•ble /'ɔdəbəl/ *adj.* capable of being heard: *His answer was barely audible.*

au•di•ence /'ɔdiyəns/ *n.* [count] **1.** the listeners or spectators at a public event. **2.** a formal meeting: *an audience with the Pope.*

au•di•o /'ɔdiy,ow/ *adj.* [before a noun] **1.** of, relating to, or used in the sending, receiving, or producing of sound: *audio equipment.* —*n.* [noncount] **2.** the elements of television that deal with sound: *The audio was OK but there was no picture.*

au•di•o•tape /'ɔdiyow,teyp/ *n.* [count] magnetic tape on which sound is recorded; cassette.

au•di•o•vis•u•al or **au•di•o-vis•u•al** /,ɔdiyow'vɪʒuwəl/ *adj.* [before a noun] **1.** of, relating to, or involving both hearing and sight: *Audiovisual facilities included a VCR, a tape player, and a television monitor.* —*n.* **2.** **audiovisuals,** [plural] teaching aids using audiovisual equipment.

au•dit /'ɔdɪt/ *n.* [count] **1.** an official examination of financial records: *an audit of the university's accounts.* —*v.* **2.** [~ + obj] to make an official examination of (accounts, records, etc.): *They audited our tax returns last year.* **3.** to attend (classes, lectures, etc.) without receiving credits: [~ + obj]: *She audited the class.* [no obj]: *She's not officially registered, so she's just auditing.*

au•di•tion /ɔ'dɪʃən/ *n.* [count] **1.** a trial performance by an actor, singer, musician, etc., to judge suitability for a part in a play, film, musical group, etc. —*v.* **2.** [~ + obj] to hear or view in an audition: *The director auditioned several hundred actors.* **3.** [no obj] to compete in an audition: *She auditioned for the part.*

au•di•to•ri•um /,ɔdɪ'tɔriyəm/ *n.* [count], pl. **-to•ri•ums** or, sometimes, **-to•ri•a** /-'tɔriyə/. a space in a theater, school, or other public building for seating an audience: *The school band performed in the auditorium.*

au•di•to•ry /'ɔdɪ,tɔriy/ *adj.* relating to hearing or to the ear.

Aug or **Aug.,** an abbreviation of: August.

aug•ment /ɔg'mɛnt/ *v.* [~ + obj] to make larger; increase in size, number, or strength: *He taught English after work to augment his income.* —,**aug•men'ta•tion,** *n.* [count]

Au•gust /'ɔgəst/ *n.* the eighth month of the year, containing 31 days.

aunt /ænt, ɑnt/ *n.* [count] **1.** the sister of one's father or mother. **2.** the wife of one's uncle.

au pair /'owpɛər/ *n.* [count] a person, esp. a young foreign visitor in a country, employed to take care of children, do housework, etc., in exchange for room and board.

au•ra /'ɔrə/ *n.* [count], pl. **-ras.** a quality or character surrounding something or someone: *He had an aura of respectability.*

au•ral /'ɔrəl/ *adj.* of or relating to the ear or to the sense of hearing: *aural stimulation.*

au•ro•ra /ə'rɔrə/ *n.* [count], pl. **au•ro•ras, au•ro•rae** /ə'rɔriy/. bands of colored light in the upper atmosphere, visible at night in polar areas.

aus•pic•es /'ɔspəsɪz/ *n.* [plural] Usually, **under the auspices of,** with the support and approval of: *a program under the auspices of the government.*

aus•pi•cious /ɔ'spɪʃəs/ *adj.* **1.** promising success; favorable: *auspicious signs.* **2.** favored by fortune; prosperous: *an auspicious year.*

aus•tere /ɔ'stɪər/ *adj.* **1.** severe in manner, appearance, or morals; strict; serious: *an austere man of the church.* **2.** without excess, luxury, or ease: *an austere life.* —**aus•ter•i•ty** /ɔ'stɛrətiy/ *n.* [noncount] [count]

Aus•tral•ian /ɔ'streylyən/ *n.* **1.** [count] a person born or living in Australia. **2.** [noncount] any of the languages spoken by the aboriginal peoples of Australia. —*adj.* **3.** of or relating to Australia.

Aus•tri•an /'ɔstriyən/ *n.* [count] **1.** a person born or living in Austria. —*adj.* **2.** of or relating to Austria.

au•then•tic /ɔ'θɛntɪk/ *adj.* not false; genuine; real: *an authentic dinosaur bone.* —**au•then•tic•i•ty** /,ɔθɛn'tɪsɪtiy/ *n.* [noncount]

au•thor /'ɔθər/ *n.* [count] **1.** someone who creates a book, article, etc.; writer. **2.** the maker of anything: *the author of the new tax plan.* —*v.* [~ + obj] **3.** to be the author of: *to author a novel.*

au•thor•i•tar•i•an /ə,θɔrɪ'tɛəriyən, ə,θɒr-/ *adj.* **1.** favoring or requiring obedience to authority: *an authoritarian military code.* —*n.* [count] **2.** a person who favors or acts according to authoritarian principles.

au•thor•i•ta•tive /ə'θɔrɪ,teytɪv, ə'θɒr-/ *adj.* **1.** having or showing authority; official: *authoritative orders.* **2.** supported by evidence and accepted; able to be trusted: *the authoritative account of the story.*

au•thor•i•ty /ə'θɔrɪtiy, ə'θɒr-/ *n.*, pl. **-ties. 1.** [noncount] the right, power, or ability to control, command, or decide. **2.** [noncount] power or right officially given; authorization; permission. **3.** [count] Usually, **authorities.** [plural] persons having the power to make and enforce the law; government: *He surrendered to the authorities.* **4.** [count] an accepted source of information: *That book is the authority on the subject.*

au•thor•ize /'ɔθə,rayz/ *v.* [~ + obj], **-ized, -iz•ing. 1.** to give authority to: *I am not authorized to pay you.* **2.** to give authority for: *He authorized increased spending on research.* —**au•thor•i•za•tion** /,ɔθərə'zeyʃən/ *n.* [noncount] [count]

au•tism /'ɔtɪzəm/ *n.* [noncount] a disorder characterized by reduced ability to communicate, a withdrawal into oneself, and detachment from reality. —**au•tis•tic** /ɔ'tɪstɪk/ *adj.*

au•to /'ɔtow/ *n.* [count], pl. **-tos.** an automobile; car.

auto-, a combining form meaning self or same (*autograph*).

au•to•bi•og•ra•phy /ˌɔtəbay'ɒgrəfiy/ *n.* [*count*], *pl.* **-phies.** a history of a person's life written or told by that person. —**au•to•bi•o•graph•i•cal** /ˌɔtəbayə'græfɪkəl/ *adj.*

au•to•crat /'ɔtə,kræt/ *n.* [*count*] **1.** a ruler who has unlimited power. **2.** a person who makes decisions or gives orders to others in an autocratic manner: *an office autocrat.* —**au•to'crat•ic,** *adj.*

au•to•graph /'ɔtə,græf/ *n.* [*count*] **1.** a person's signature, esp. that of a famous person for keeping as a memento. —*v.* [~ + *obj*] **2.** to write one's name on or in: *The pitcher autographed the baseball for a fan.*

au•to•mate /'ɔtə,meyt/ *v.* [~ + *obj*] [*no obj*], **-mat•ed, -mat•ing.** to use machines instead of people to perform a task. —**au•to•ma•tion** /ˌɔtə'meyʃən/, *n.* [*noncount*]

'automated-'teller ma,chine, *n.* [*count*] an electronic machine that provides banking services when it is activated by means of a special plastic card. *Abbr.:* ATM

au•to•mat•ic /ˌɔtə'mætɪk/ *adj.* **1.** having the capability of operating by itself without human aid: *an automatic sprinkler system.* **2.** occurring without conscious thought, as certain muscular actions; involuntary; reflex: *The blink of an eyelid is an automatic action.* —*n.* [*count*] **3.** a machine or device that operates automatically: *Most washing machines are automatics.* —,**au•to'mat•i•cal•ly,** *adv.*: *The car doors lock automatically.*

au•tom•a•ton /ɔ'tɒmə,tɒn, -tŋ/ *n.* [*count*], *pl.* **-tons, -ta** /-tə/. **1.** a mechanical figure built to act and move as if by its own power; robot. **2.** a person who acts mechanically.

au•to•mo•bile /ˌɔtəmə'biyl, 'ɔtəmə,biyl/ *n.* [*count*] a passenger vehicle usually having four wheels and a gasoline or diesel engine; car.

au•to•mo•tive /ˌɔtə'mowtɪv, 'ɔtə,mowtɪv/ *adj.* [*before a noun*] of or relating to automobiles or other motor vehicles: *automotive parts.*

au•ton•o•mous /ɔ'tɒnəməs/ *adj.* **1.** self-governing: *an autonomous nation.* **2.** able to act on one's own; independent: *With your own business you will be autonomous.* —**au'ton•o•my,** *n.* [*noncount*]

au•top•sy /'ɔtɒpsiy/ *n.*, *pl.* **-sies,** *v.*, **-sied, -sy•ing.** —*n.* [*count*] **1.** the examination of a dead body to determine the cause of death. —*v.* [~ + *obj*] **2.** to perform an autopsy on: *to autopsy the body.*

au•tumn /'ɔtəm/ *n.* the season between summer and winter; fall: [*noncount*]: *In autumn the leaves fall.* [*count*]: *Autumns are mild here.*

aux•il•ia•ry /ɔg'zɪlyəriy, -'zɪlə-/ *adj.*, *n.*, *pl.* **-ries.** —*adj.* **1.** additional; secondary; used as a substitute or reserve when needed: *an auxiliary power station.* —*n.* [*count*] **2.** a person or thing that gives aid; helper. **3.** an auxiliary organization: *The women's auxiliary raised money for the school.*

aux'iliary 'verb, *n.* [*count*] a verb used with a main verb to express time, aspect, mood, etc. Examples of auxiliary verbs are: *Did* in *Did you fall?*; *have* in *We have gone*; and *can* in *They can see.*

a•vail /ə'veyl/ *v.* **1.** to be of use or value to: [~ + *obj*]: *Our efforts availed us little.* [*no obj*]: *Nothing you do will avail.* —*n.* [*noncount*] **2.** use or advantage. —*Idiom.* **3.** avail oneself of, to make use or take advantage: *You should avail* yourself of every chance for help. **4. to no avail,** without success: *I tried, but to no avail.*

a•vail•a•ble /ə'veyləbəl/ *adj.* **1.** ready for use; at hand: *I used whatever tools were available.* **2.** free or ready to be seen, spoken to, etc.: *She is not available for comment.* —**a•vail•a•bil•i•ty** /ə,veylə'bɪlɪtiy/ *n.* [*noncount*]

av•a•lanche /'ævə,læntʃ/ *n.* [*count*] **1.** a large mass of snow, ice, etc., that slides down from a mountain. **2.** anything like an avalanche in suddenness and volume: *an avalanche of fan mail.*

a•vant-garde /ɑ,vɑnt'gɑrd, ,ævɑnt-/ *n.* [*plural; used with a plural verb*] **1.** the group of artists, writers, musicians, filmmakers, etc., whose work is considered modern, advanced, or experimental. —*adj.* **2.** characteristic of or belonging to the avant-garde: *The paintings were very avant-garde.*

av•a•rice /'ævərɪs/ *n.* [*noncount*] extreme greed for wealth. —**av•a•ri•cious** /,ævə'rɪʃəs/, *adj.*

ave., an abbreviation for: avenue.

a•venge /ə'vɛndʒ/ *v.* [~ + *obj*], **a•venged, a•veng•ing. 1.** to take or get revenge for (something): *He avenged the murder of his sister.* **2.** to take or get revenge for or on behalf of (someone): *Her husband avenged her by finding her murderers.*

av•e•nue /'ævə,nyuw, -,nuw/ *n.* [*count*] a wide street or main road.

av•er•age /'ævərɪdʒ, 'ævrɪdʒ/ *n.*, *adj.*, *v.*, **-aged, -ag•ing.** —*n.* **1.** [*count*] the number that results from adding several quantities together and then dividing that total by the number of quantities that were added: *Their exam averages were very high, usually 97 or above.* **2.** a typical, usual, or normal amount, rate, degree, etc.: [*count; usually singular*]: *The villagers lived for an average of seventy years.* [*noncount*]: *Her work is above average.* —*adj.* [*before a noun*] **3.** of, relating to, or forming an average: *The average rainfall is only six inches a year.* **4.** typical; common; ordinary: *the average person.* —*v.* [~ + *obj*] **5.** to find an average of: *She averaged her test scores and came up with 93.* **6.** to do, have, or get on the average: *to average seven hours of sleep a night.* —**Idiom. 7. on the** or **an average,** usually; typically: *On the average I see about two movies a month.*

a•verse /ə'vɜrs/ *adj.* [*be* + ~ + *to*] having a strong feeling of opposition to; unwilling: *averse to spending a lot of money.*

a•ver•sion /ə'vɜrʒən, -ʃən/ *n.* [*count*] a strong feeling of dislike, disgust, or hatred toward something and a desire to avoid it: *She has an aversion to snakes.*

a•vert /ə'vɜrt/ *v.* [~ + *obj*] **1.** to turn away or aside: *to avert one's eyes.* **2.** to prevent; avoid: *to avert an accident.*

avg., an abbreviation of: average.

a•vi•ar•y /'eyviy,ɛriy/ *n.* [*count*], *pl.* **-ies.** a large enclosed area in which birds are kept.

a•vi•a•tion /,eyviy'eyʃən/ *n.* [*noncount*] **1.** the design, production, or operation of aircraft. **2.** military aircraft.

a•vi•a•tor /'eyviy,eytər/ *n.* [*count*] a pilot of an airplane or other aircraft.

av•id /'ævɪd/ *adj.* **1.** [*before a noun*] enthusiastic; ardent: *an avid sports fan.* **2.** [*be* + ~ + *for*] greedy; eager: *avid of fame.*

av•o•ca•do /,ævə'kadow, ,avə-/ *n.* [*count*], *pl.* **-dos.** a pear-shaped fruit having dark green skin and a soft, buttery inside part that can be eaten.

av•o•ca•tion /,ævə'keyʃən/ *n.* [*count*] a secondary occupation: *The surgeon's avocation is teaching the handicapped.*

a•void /ə'vɔyd/ *v.* **1.** [~ + *obj*] to keep or stay away from: *to avoid taxes; to avoid danger.* **2.** to prevent from happening: *She wore boots to avoid slipping.* —**a'void•a•ble,** *adj.* —**a'void•ance,** *n.* [*noncount*]

a•vow /ə'vaw/ *v.* to declare openly; acknowledge: [~ + *obj*]: *He avowed an interest in the issue.* [~ + (*that*) *clause*]: *He avowed that he had indeed made those remarks.* —**'a'vow•al,** *n.* [*count*]

a•wait /ə'weyt/ *v.* [~ + *obj*] **1.** to wait for; expect; look for: *She was still awaiting an answer.* **2.** to be about to happen: *A pleasant surprise awaited her.*

a•wake /ə'weyk/ *v.,* **a•woke** /ə'wowk/ or **a•waked** /ə'weykt/, **a•woke** or **a•waked** or **a•wo•ken** /ə'wowkən/, **a•wak•ing,** *adj.* —*v.* **1.** to rouse from sleep: [*no obj*]: *She awoke at dawn.* [~ + *obj*]: *The noise awoke me.* **2.** to (cause to) become stirred to action: [*no obj*]: *My interest awoke when I saw the chance for profit.* [~ + *obj*]: *The project awoke his interest.* —*adj.* [*be* + ~] **3.** waking; not sleeping: *I was awake all night.*

a•wak•en /ə'weykən/ *v.* to wake up: [*no obj*]: *She awakened at dawn.* [~ + *obj*]: *She awakened the children.*

a•ward /ə'wɔrd/ *v.* [~ + *obj*] **1.** to give in recognition of merit: *The panel awards the prizes. The committee awarded him $1,000. The committee awarded the poetry prize to her.* —*n.* [*count*] **2.** something awarded, as a payment, medal, prize, or judgment.

a•ware /ə'wɛər/ *adj.* **1.** having conscious knowledge of: [~ + *of*]: *Be aware of the danger.* [~ + *that*]: *I wasn't aware that it was dangerous.* **2.** informed; knowledgeable: *politically aware.* —**a'ware•ness,** *n.* [*noncount*] *her keen awareness of others' feelings.*

a•way /ə'wey/ *adv.* **1.** from this or that place; from here or from there; off: *to go away.* **2.** out of one's possession or use: *to give money away.* **3.** in or into a place for storage or safekeeping: *to put the clothes away.* **4.** out of existence: *The memory faded away.* —*adj.* **5.** [*be* + ~] absent; gone: *is often away from home.* **6.** [*after a number or amount*] distant in place or time (from): *The town is six miles away.*

awe /ɔ/ *n., v.,* **awed, aw•ing.** —*n.* [*noncount*] **1.** an overwhelming feeling of reverence, fear, or wonder regarding someone or something. **2. in awe of,** feeling reverence, fear, or wonder: *I stood in awe of the huge mountain.* —*v.* [~ + *obj*] **3.** to cause (someone) to feel awe: *The storm awed us with its fury.*

awe•some /'ɔsəm/ *adj.* causing or showing awe: *an awesome sight.*

aw•ful /'ɔfəl/ *adj.* **1.** extremely bad; unpleasant: *the awful smell of gas.* **2.** causing shock or fear; terrible: *an awful accident.* **3.** [*before a noun*] *Informal.* very great: *knows an awful lot about art.* —*adv.* **4.** *Informal.* very; extremely: *It's awful hot in here.* —**aw•ful•ly** /'ɔfliy, 'ɔfəliy/ *adv.*

a•while /ə'hwayl, ə'wayl/ *adv.* for a short time: *Stay awhile.* —**Usage.** The adverb AWHILE is always spelled as one word: *We rested awhile.* A WHILE is a noun phrase (an article and a noun) and is used after a preposition: *We rested for a while.*

awk•ward /'ɔkwərd/ *adj.* **1.** clumsy; not having much skill: *an awkward dancer.* **2.** lacking social graces or manners: *always feels awkward at parties.* **3.** difficult to use or handle: *an awkward tool.* **4.** requiring skill or tact; difficult: *an awkward situation.* —**'awk•ward•ly,** *adv.* —**'awk•ward•ness,** *n.* [*noncount*]

awn•ing /'ɔnɪŋ/ *n.* [*count*] a piece of canvas or other material over a door, window, etc., used for protection from the weather.

a•woke /ə'wowk/ *v.* a pt. and pp. of AWAKE.

AWOL /*pronounced as initials, or as* 'eywɔl, 'eywɒl/ *adj.* **1.** absent without leave; away from military duties without permission, but without the intention of deserting. —*adv.* **2.** into AWOL status: *He's gone AWOL.*

a•wry /ə'ray/ *adj.* **1.** [*be* + ~] turned or twisted aside: *His jacket was awry.* —*adv.* **2.** away from the expected or proper direction: *Our plans went awry.*

ax or **axe** /æks/ *n.* [*count*], *pl.* **ax•es** /'æksɪz/. **1.** a tool with a blade on a handle, used for cutting, chopping, splitting, etc. —*Idiom.* **2. have an ax to grind,** to have a personal or selfish motive: *I have no ax to grind, so I'm willing to listen to all sides.*

ax•i•om /'æksiyəm/ *n.* [*count*] a statement that is regarded to be true without proof or argument; an accepted principle or rule: *It is an old axiom that the richest candidate always wins.*

ax•is /'æksɪs/ *n.* [*count*], *pl.* **ax•es** /'æksiyz/. **1.** the line around which a rotating body, as the earth, turns. **2.** a line used in a graph to figure the position of a point.

ax•le /'æksəl/ *n.* [*count*] the pin, bar, or rod on which a pair of wheels rotates.

aye or **ay** /ay/ *adv., interj.* **1.** yes: *Aye, sir.* —*n.* [*count*] **2.** an affirmative vote or voter: *"Sixteen ayes, ten no's: the ayes have it."*

AZ, an abbreviation for: Arizona.

a•zal•ea /ə'zeylyə/ *n.* [*count*], *pl.* **-eas.** a shrub of the heath family, with funnel-shaped flower clusters.

az•ure /'æʒər/ *n.* [*noncount*] the blue of a clear or unclouded sky; light, purplish blue.

B

B, b /biy/ *n.* [*count*], *pl.* **Bs** or **B's, bs** or **b's.** the second letter of the English alphabet, a consonant.

B.A., an abbreviation of: Bachelor of Arts.

bab•ble /'bæbəl/ *v.,* **-bled, -bling,** *n.* —*v.* **1.** to talk too much or foolishly: [*no obj*]: *The two friends babbled (on) for hours.* [~ + *obj*]: *The spy babbled state secrets.* **2.** [*no obj*] to make a continuous murmuring sound: *a babbling brook.* —*n.* [*noncount*] **3.** the act or sound of babbling.

ba•boon /bæ'buwn/ *n.* [*count*] a large monkey of Africa and Arabia.

ba•by /'beybiy/ *n.,* pl. **-bies,** *v.,* **-bied, -by•ing.** —*n.* [*count*] **1.** an infant or very young child. **2.** *Informal* (*sometimes offensive*). a girl or woman. —*v.* [~ + *obj*] **3.** to pamper: *to baby a sick child.* —**'ba•by•ish,** *adj.*

'baby ,boom, *n.* [*count; sometimes: Baby Boom*] a period of sharp increase in the birthrate, as that following World War II. —**'baby ,boomer,** *n.* [*count*]

'baby-,sit or **'baby,sit,** *v.,* **-sat, -sit•ting.** to take care of (a child) while the parents are away: [*no obj*]: *I baby-sat while she went shopping.* [~ + *obj*]: *She baby-sat our children.* —**'baby-,sitter, 'baby,sitter,** *n.* [*count*]

bach•e•lor /'bætʃələr/ *n.* [*count*] an unmarried man.

'bachelor's de,gree, *n.* [*count*] an undergraduate college degree.

back /bæk/ *n.* [*count*] **1.** the rear part of the human body from the neck to the end of the spine or the corresponding part of an animal's body. **2.** the part farthest from the front: *I sat at the back of the room.* —*v.* **3.** [~ + *obj*] to support, as with money: *We'll back his plan.* **4.** [~ + *obj*] [*no obj*] to (cause to) move backward. **5. back down** or **off,** to give up an argument or position: *She backed down from her refusal.* **6. back out,** to withdraw: *Don't try to back out of the deal.* **7. back up, a.** to bring or come to a complete stop: *Traffic is backed up to the bridge. Traffic backed up quickly because of the accident.* **b.** to copy (a computer file or program) in case the original is lost. —*adv.* **8.** at, to, or toward the rear: *Please step back.* **9.** in, at, or toward a starting place, time, or condition: *He went back to his home town.* —*Idiom.* **10. back and forth,** backward and forward: *pacing back and forth.* **11. behind one's back,** without one's knowledge: *They talked about me behind my back.* **12. go back on,** to fail to keep: *He went back on his word.*

back•ache /'bæk,eyk/ *n.* [*count*] a pain in the back.

back•bone /'bæk,bown/ *n.* [*count*] **1.** the spine. **2.** the main strength or support of something: *The small farmer was the backbone of the republic.*

back•break•ing /'bæk,breykɪŋ/ *adj.* requiring great effort or strength.

back•er /'bækər/ *n.* [*count*] a person who supports or aids a cause or activity.

back•fire /'bæk,fayᵊr/ *v.* [*no obj*], **-fired, -fir•ing. 1.** (of a car engine) to have a loud explosion that occurs too soon for proper combustion. **2.** to have a result opposite to the one expected; go wrong.

back•gam•mon /'bæk,gæmən/ *n.* [*noncount*] a board game for two persons.

back•ground /'bæk,grawnd/ *n.* **1.** [*count; usually singular*] the people or things at the rear, as of a picture. **2.** [*count*] a person's family, education, and experience: *He comes from a musical background.* **3.** [*count*] the things that happened before or caused an event: *The book explores the background of the war.*

back•hand /'bæk,hænd/ *n.* [*count*] a stroke, as with a tennis racket, made with the back of the hand turned forward.

back•lash /'bæk,læʃ/ *n.* [*count*] a strong negative reaction: *a backlash by voters to rising property taxes.*

back•log /'bæk,lɔg, -,lɑg/ *n.* [*count*] a group of unfinished tasks.

back•pack /'bæk,pæk/ *n.* [*count*] **1.** a pack carried on one's back. —*v.* [*no obj*] **2.** to hike using a backpack.

back•slide /'bæk,slayd/ *v.* [*no obj*], **-slid, -slid** or **-slid•den, -slid•ing.** to return to bad habits or undesirable activities.

back•stage /'bæk'steydʒ/ *adv.* behind the stage in a theater.

back•stroke /'bæk,strowk/ *n.* [*noncount*] a swimming stroke done lying on one's back.

'back ,talk, *n.* [*noncount*] a rude answer.

back•track /'bæk,træk/ *v.* [*no obj*] to return over the same path.

back•ward /'bækwərd/ *adv.* Also, **'back•wards. 1.** toward the back: *I leaned backward.* **2.** with the back end first: *The helicopter flew backward.* —*adj.* **3.** [*before a noun*] directed toward the back or past: *a backward look.* **4.** behind in progress or development: *backward countries.* —*Idiom.* **5. backward(s) and forward(s),** thoroughly. **6. bend** or **lean over backward,** to make a serious effort: *He bent over backward to be polite.*

back•yard /'bæk'yɑrd/ *n.* [*count*] the yard behind a house.

ba•con /'beykən/ *n.* [*noncount*] **1.** salted or smoked meat from the back and sides of a hog. —*Idiom.* **2. bring home the bacon,** to support oneself and one's family.

bac•te•ri•a /bæk'tɪriyə/ *n.* [*plural*], *sing.* **bac•te•ri•um** /bæk'tɪriyəm/. extremely small organisms, some of which cause infectious diseases. —**bac'te•ri•al,** *adj.*

bad /bæd/ *adj.,* **worse** /wɜrs/, **worst** /wɜrst/, *n., adv.* —*adj.* **1.** not good: *a bad movie.* **2.** wicked or evil: *the bad witch.* **3.** disobedient or naughty: *She was a bad girl today.* **4.** causing harm: *Sugar is bad for the teeth.* **5.** sick; ill: *He felt so bad yesterday that he stayed in bed.* **6.** spoiled or rotten: *The milk has gone bad.* **7.** not pleasant: *bad dreams.* **8.** severe; intense: *a bad flood.* **9.** sorry or sad: *He felt bad about leaving.* —*n.* [*noncount*] **10.** something that is bad: *to take the bad with the good.* —*adv.* **11.** *Informal.* Badly: *She wanted it bad enough to steal it.* —**Usage.** The adjective BAD, meaning "unpleasant, unattractive, unfavorable, spoiled, etc.," is the usual form after such verbs as *sound, smell, look,* and *taste: The music sounds bad. The locker room smells bad. You look pretty bad; are you sick? The water tasted bad.* After the verb *feel,* the adjective BADLY

balloon

may also be used (*She was feeling badly that day*), although BAD is more common in formal writing. BAD as an adverb appears mainly in informal situations: *He wanted to win pretty bad.*

bade /bæd/ *v.* a pt. of BID.

badge /bædʒ/ *n.* [count] an object worn as a sign of membership, rank, or achievement.

badg•er /ˈbædʒər/ *n.* [count] **1.** a small mammal that lives in holes in the ground and is active at night. —*v.* [~ + obj] **2.** to annoy continuously; pester: *Reporters seemed to enjoy badgering the president.*

bad•ly /ˈbædliy/ *adv.*, **worse** /wɜrs/, **worst** /wɜrst/, *adj.* —*adv.* **1.** in a bad way: *He speaks French badly.* **2.** very much: *She wants the job badly.* —*adj.* **3.** sick: *He felt badly and had a high fever.* **4.** sad or sorry: *I feel badly about your loss.* —*Idiom.* **5. badly off,** not having much money. —*Usage.* See BAD.

bad•min•ton /ˈbædmɪntn̩/ *n.* [noncount] a tennis-like game in which players use light rackets to hit a small plastic object over a high net.

'bad-,mouth or **'bad,mouth,** *v.* [~ + obj] to criticize, often in a disloyal way: *He badmouthed his boss.*

baf•fle /ˈbæfəl/ *v.* [~ + obj], **-fled, -fling.** to confuse; mystify: *I was baffled by her odd behavior.* —**'baf•fle•ment,** *n.* [noncount]

bag /bæg/ *n.*, *v.*, **bagged, bag•ging.** —*n.* [count] **1.** a container made of a soft material that is open at the top. **2.** a piece of luggage. **3.** a purse. **4.** something, as skin, hanging loosely: *bags under his eyes.* —*v.* [~ + obj] **5.** to pack or put in a bag. —*Idiom.* **6. in the bag,** *Informal.* almost certain to be achieved: *I thought victory was in the bag.*

ba•gel /ˈbeygəl/ *n.* [count] a chewy, doughnut-shaped roll made of dough that is simmered in water and then baked.

bag•gage /ˈbægɪdʒ/ *n.* [noncount] luggage.

bag•gy /ˈbægiy/ *adj.*, **-gi•er, -gi•est.** hanging loosely: *baggy trousers.*

'bag ,lady, *n.* [count] a homeless woman who carries her belongings in shopping bags.

bag•pipe /ˈbæg,payp/ *n.* [count] Often, **bagpipes.**[plural] a reed instrument made up of a melody pipe and other pipes sounded by air forced out of a leather bag.

bail¹ /beyl/ *n.* [noncount] **1.** money given to a court of law to guarantee that a person released from jail will return at an appointed time. —*v.* [~ + obj] **2. bail out, a.** to pay the bail for: *Her father bailed her out. We bailed out the protesters.* **b.** to help (someone) get out of a difficult situation: *I bailed her out with some money. I bailed out the child by explaining why he was late.*

bail² /beyl/ *v.* **1.** [~ + obj] to remove (water) from a boat so it won't sink: *They bailed gallons of water from the boat.* **2. bail out,** to make a parachute jump from an airplane: *The pilot told his crew to bail out. They bailed out of the fiery jet.*

bail•iff /ˈbeylɪf/ *n.* [count] an officer who keeps order in the court, makes arrests, etc.

bait /beyt/ *n.* **1.** [noncount] something, esp. food, used to attract and catch fish or animals. **2.** [noncount] [count; usually singular] something that tempts or entices. —*v.* [~ + obj] **3.** to prepare (a hook or trap) with bait. **4.** to torment, esp. with cruel remarks: *An angry man baited the speaker.*

bake /beyk/ *v.*, **baked, bak•ing. 1.** to cook in an oven: [~ + obj]: *My wife bakes delicious pies.* [no obj]: *Her husband likes to bake.* **2.** [no obj] to become baked: *It took the bread an hour to bake.* **3.** [~ + obj] to harden by heating: *We baked clay pots in a special oven.* —**'bak•er,** *n.* [count]

bak•er•y /ˈbeykəriy, ˈbeykriy/ *n.* [count], *pl.* **-er•ies.** a place where baked goods are made or sold.

'baking ,powder, *n.* [noncount] powder that causes dough to rise.

'baking ,soda, *n.* [noncount] sodium bicarbonate.

bal•ance /ˈbæləns/ *n.*, *v.*, **-anced, -anc•ing.** —*n.* **1.** a state of being steady; equilibrium: [noncount]: *Gymnasts need excellent balance.* [count; usually singular]: *a balance between work and play.* **2.** [count] an instrument for weighing objects. **3.** [count; usually singular] something that remains: *I'll do the balance of the work after vacation.* **4.** [count] the amount of money in a bank account. —*v.* [~ + obj] [no obj] **5.** to bring to or hold in a state of balance.

bal•co•ny /ˈbælkəniy/ *n.* [count], *pl.* **-nies. 1.** a platform on the outside wall of a building. **2.** an upstairs seating area in a theater.

bald /bɔld/ *adj.*, **-er, -est. 1.** having little or no hair on the head. **2.** [before a noun] blunt: *a bald lie.* —**'bald•ness,** *n.* [noncount]

'bald 'eagle, *n.* [count] a large eagle of the U.S. and Canada having a white head: the national bird of the U.S.

bald•ing /ˈbɔldɪŋ/ *adj.* becoming bald.

bale /beyl/ *n.* [count] a large, tightly tied bundle: *a bale of cotton.*

balk /bɔk/ *v.* [no obj] to stop abruptly and refuse to go on: *The horse balked at the wall. He balked at committing murder.*

ball¹ /bɔl/ *n.* [count] **1.** a round object: *a ball of yarn.* **2.** a round object used in games, as baseball. —*v.* **3.** to form into a ball: [~ + obj]: *She balled her fists and glared at him.* [no obj]: *Snow balled on the dog's paws.* **4. ball up,** to make into a mess; confuse: *I balled up the assignment. He balled it up badly.* —*Idiom.* **5. on the ball, a.** paying attention; alert: *You were really on the ball when you spotted that mistake.* **b.** intelligence and ability: *Your daughter has a lot on the ball.*

ball² /bɔl/ *n.* [count] **1.** a large, formal party for dancing. —*Idiom.* **2. have a ball,** *Informal.* to have a good time.

bal•lad /ˈbæləd/ *n.* [count] a simple poem or song that tells a story.

bal•last /ˈbæləst/ *n.* [noncount] heavy material carried on ships to make them heavier and easier to control.

'ball 'bearing, *n.* [count] a small hard ball placed in a groove between two moving parts of a machine to allow the parts to move smoothly.

bal•le•ri•na /ˌbæləˈriynə/ *n.* [count], *pl.* **-nas.** a female ballet dancer.

bal•let /bæˈley, ˈbæley/ *n.* [noncount] a form of theatrical dance that involves graceful movements.

bal'listic 'missile /bəˈlɪstɪk/ *n.* [count] a missile that is powered and guided at the beginning of its launch and then falls freely.

bal•lis•tics /bəˈlɪstɪks/ *n.* [noncount; usually used with a singular verb] the scientific study of the movement of objects shot through the air.

bal•loon /bəˈluwn/ *n.* [count] **1.** a rubber bag that floats when filled with air, used as a toy. **2.** a bag of strong, light material filled with gas to make it rise through the air. —*v.* [*no obj*] **3.** to ride in a balloon. **4.** to puff out like a balloon.

bal•lot /'bælət/ *n.* **1.** [*count*] a sheet of paper on which a vote is written. **2.** the method or act of secret voting: [*count; usually singular*]: *He was elected in a secret ballot.* [*noncount; by* + ~]: *She was chosen by ballot.*

ball•point /'bɔl,pɔynt/ *n.* [*count*] a pen in which the point is a small ball that rolls against a supply of ink. Also called **'ballpoint 'pen.**

ball•room /'bɔl,ruwm, -,rʊm/ *n.* [*count*] a large room for dancing.

balm /bɑm/ *n.* [*noncount*] a sweet-smelling oil used to lessen pain.

balm•y /'bɑmiy/ *adj.,* **-i•er, -i•est.** mild and refreshing: *balmy weather.*

bam•boo /bæm'buw/ *n.* [*noncount*] [*count*], *pl.* **-boos.** a tall tropical grass with hard, usually hollow stems.

ban /bæn/ *v.,* **banned, ban•ning,** *n.* —*v.* [~ + *obj*] **1.** to forbid. —*n.* [*count*] **2.** a legal order forbidding something: *a ban on smoking.*

ba•nal /bə'næl, -'nɑl, 'beynl/ *adj.* not interesting because commonplace. —**ba'nal•i•ty,** *n.* [*count*]

ba•nan•a /bə'nænə/ *n.* [*count*], *pl.* **-nan•as.** a curved, yellow fruit.

band¹ /bænd/ *n.* [*count*] **1.** a group acting or working together: *a band of protesters.* **2.** a group of musicians: *a school band.* —*v.* [*no obj*] **3.** to come together in a group: *The men banded together.*

band² /bænd/ *n.* [*count*] **1.** a thin, flat strip of material used to fasten things together or as decoration. **2.** a stripe, as of color: *white paper with a red band.* **3.** a plain ring: *a gold wedding band.*

band•age /'bændɪdʒ/ *n., v.,* **-aged, -ag•ing.** —*n.* [*count*] **1.** a strip of material used to cover a wound or sprain. —*v.* [~ + *obj*] **2.** to tie or cover with a bandage.

ban•dan•na /bæn'dænə/ *n.* [*count*], *pl.* **-nas.** a large, usually brightly colored handkerchief often worn around the neck or head.

B and B or **B&B,** an abbreviation of: bed-and-breakfast.

ban•dit /'bændɪt/ *n.* [*count*] a robber, esp. a member of a band of thieves.

bang¹ /bæŋ/ *n.* **1.** [*count*] a sudden loud noise. **2.** [*count*] a strong, violent blow: *a nasty bang on the head.* **3.** [*count; usually singular*] *Informal.* thrill; excitement: *gets a bang out of mud wrestling.* —*v.* **4.** to strike violently or noisily: [*no obj*]: *The police banged on the door.* [~ + *obj*]: *She banged the table with her fists.* **5.** [*no obj*] [~ + *obj*] to bump painfully.

bang² /bæŋ/ *n.* [*count*] Often, **bangs.** [*plural*] a portion of hair cut to fall over the forehead.

ban•gle /'bæŋgəl/ *n.* [*count*] a bracelet worn around the wrist or ankle.

ban•ish /'bænɪʃ/ *v.* [~ + *obj*] to send (someone) away, esp. to exile. —**'ban•ish•ment,** *n.* [*noncount*]

ban•is•ter or **ban•nis•ter** /'bænəstər/ *n.* [*count*] Sometimes, **banisters.** [*plural*] a bar or rail and its supporting posts at the side of a staircase.

ban•jo /'bændʒow/ *n.* [*count*], *pl.* **-jos, -joes.** a stringed musical instrument with a neck and a round body.

bank¹ /bæŋk/ *n.* [*count*] **1.** a long pile or heap: *a bank of clouds.* **2.** the slope of land beside a stream or river. —*v.* [*no obj*] **3.** to tip to one side: *The plane banked to the left.*

bank² /bæŋk/ *n.* [*count*] **1.** a business for lending and keeping money safe. **2.** a small container for holding money, esp. coins. **3.** a storage place: *a blood bank.* —*v.* **4.** [~ + *obj*] [*no obj*] to keep or deposit (money) in a bank. **5. bank on** or **upon,** to depend on: *You can bank on my help.* —**'bank•er,** *n.* [*count*]

bank³ /bæŋk/ *n.* [*count*] a row of objects: *a bank of phones.*

bank•rupt /'bæŋkrʌpt, -rəpt/ *adj.* **1.** not having enough money to pay debts. —*v.* [~ + *obj*] **2.** to make bankrupt. —**'bank•rupt•cy,** *n.* [*count*] [*noncount*]

ban•ner /'bænər/ *n.* [*count*] a piece of cloth with a sign on it.

ban•quet /'bæŋkwɪt/ *n.* [*count*] a large public dinner.

ban•ter /'bæntər/ *n.* [*noncount*] **1.** playful speech. —*v.* [*no obj*] **2.** to speak playfully: *The president bantered with reporters.*

bap•tism /'bæptɪzəm/ *n.* [*noncount*] a ceremony in which a person is sprinkled or covered with water as a sign of acceptance into the Christian church. —**'bap•tize,** *v.* [~ + *obj*] [*no obj*], **-tized, -tiz•ing.**

bar /bɑr/ *n., v.,* **barred, bar•ring,** *prep.* —*n.* [*count*] **1.** a long piece of solid material, used esp. to keep safe or prevent from entering or leaving: *the bars of a cage.* **2.** a piece of solid material that is longer than it is wide: *a bar of soap.* **3.** something that blocks one's path or progress: *His accent is a bar to his becoming a radio announcer.* **4.** a counter or place where drinks are served. **5.** a measure of music. —*v.* [~ + *obj*] **6.** to close with a bar: *Bar the door.* **7.** to prevent: *a religion that bars divorce.* —*prep.* **8.** except: *We were all invited bar none.*

barb /bɑrb/ *n.* [*count*] **1.** a curved point of a hook or arrowhead. **2.** an unkind remark.

bar•bar•i•an /bɑr'bɛəriyən/ *n.* [*count*] an uncivilized person.

bar•bar•ic /bɑr'bærɪk/ *adj.* **1.** not civilized. **2.** cruel.

bar•be•cue or **bar•be•que** /'bɑrbɪ,kyuw/ *n., v.,* **-cued** or **-qued, -cu•ing** or **-qu•ing.** —*n.* [*count*] **1.** a grill for cooking food over an open fire. **2.** a meal at which food is cooked over an open fire. —*v.* [*no obj*] [~ + *obj*] **3.** to cook (food) over an open fire.

'barbed 'wire /bɑrbd/ *n.* [*noncount*] wire with sharp points used esp. for fences.

bar•ber /'bɑrbər/ *n.* [*count*] a person whose job is to cut men's hair.

'bar ,code, *n.* [*count*] a series of lines printed on a consumer item for identification by a computerized scanner.

bare /bɛər/ *adj.,* **bar•er, bar•est,** *v.,* **bared, bar•ing.** —*adj.* **1.** not covered: *bare legs.* **2.** empty: *bare walls without pictures.* **3.** [*before a noun*] being just enough: *the bare necessities.* —*v.* [~ + *obj*] **4.** to uncover: *The dog bared its teeth.* **5.** to let (something) be known: *He bared damaging new facts.*

bare•back /'bɛər,bæk/ also **'bare,backed,** *adj., adv.* on a horse with no saddle.

bare•foot /'bɛər,fʊt/ also **'bare,foot•ed,** *adj., adv.* without shoes and socks: *a barefoot boy; He ran barefoot down the hill.*

bare•ly /'bɛərliy/ *adv.* no more than: *barely enough money to pay the rent.*

bar•gain /'bɑrgən/ *n.* [*count*] **1.** a purchase made at less than the usual cost. **2.** an agreement between parties: *They made a bargain to take*

B

turns driving. —*v.* **3.** to discuss the terms of an agreement: [*no obj*]: *bargained skillfully.* [~ + *obj*]: *Management bargained with labor.*

barge /bɑrdʒ/ *n.*, *v.*, **barged, barg•ing.** —*n.* [*count*] **1.** a flat-bottomed boat. —*v.* **2.** [*no obj*] to move aggressively and clumsily: *The police barged through the crowd.* **3. barge in on,** to interrupt rudely: *She barged in on our meeting.*

bar•i•tone /ˈbærɪˌtoʊn/ *n.* [*count*] a male singing voice lower than a tenor and higher than a bass.

bark[1] /bɑrk/ *n.* [*count*] **1.** the sharp cry of a dog. —*v.* **2.** [*no obj*] (of a dog) to make a bark. **3.** to speak harshly: [~ + *obj*]: *He barked orders.* [*no obj*]: *He barked at his subordinate.*

bark[2] /bɑrk/ *n.* [*noncount*] the tough outside covering of a tree.

bar•ley /ˈbɑrliy/ *n.* [*noncount*] a grain used as food and in making beer and whiskey.

barn /bɑrn/ *n.* [*count*] a building for storing hay and grain, and often for keeping animals.

bar•na•cle /ˈbɑrnəkəl/ *n.* [*count*] a shellfish that attaches itself to ship bottoms and is difficult to remove.

barn•yard /ˈbɑrnˌyɑrd/ *n.* [*count*] a yard that is next to a barn.

ba•rom•e•ter /bəˈrɑmɪtər/ *n.* [*count*] an instrument that measures atmospheric pressure.

bar•on /ˈbærən/ *n.* [*count*] **1.** a member of the lowest rank of nobility. **2.** a powerful, wealthy person: *a railroad baron.*

bar•rack /ˈbærək/ *n.* [*count*] Usually, **barracks.** [*plural*] buildings in which soldiers live.

bar•rage /bəˈrɑʒ/ *n.* [*count*] **1.** heavy continuous gunfire. **2.** a very large amount: *a barrage of questions.*

bar•rel /ˈbærəl/ *n.*, *v.*, **-reled, -rel•ing** or (*esp.* *Brit.*) **-relled, -rel•ling.** —*n.* [*count*] **1.** a round container for liquids. **2.** the tubelike part of a gun from which the bullet comes out. —*v.* [*no obj*] **3.** to drive or move at high speed: *They were barreling along at 95 miles an hour.*

bar•ren /ˈbærən/ *adj.* not able to produce children or crops.

bar•rette /bəˈrɛt/ *n.* [*count*] a clasp for holding a woman's hair in place.

bar•ri•cade /ˈbærɪˌkeyd/ *n.*, *v.*, **-cad•ed, -cad•ing.** —*n.* [*count*] **1.** a barrier of large objects, intended to stop an enemy or prevent people from entering. —*v.* [~ + *obj*] **2.** to block with a barricade.

bar•ri•er /ˈbæriyər/ *n.* [*count*] something that prevents movement, entrance, or progress.

bar•ring /ˈbɑrɪŋ/ *prep.* except for: *Barring further delays, I'll be there.*

bar•ri•o /ˈbɑriyˌoʊ, ˈbær-/ *n.* [*count*], *pl.* **-ri•os.** a section of a U.S. city inhabited chiefly by Spanish-speaking people.

bar•tend•er /ˈbɑrˌtɛndər/ *n.* [*count*] a person who serves drinks at a bar.

bar•ter /ˈbɑrtər/ *v.* [*no obj*] [~ + *obj*] to trade goods for other goods.

base[1] /beys/ *n.*, *v.*, **based, bas•ing.** —*n.* [*count*] **1.** the part on which something stands: *the base of a lamp.* **2.** a main part from which other parts develop: *a base for further research.* **3.** a place from which military operations proceed: *an army base.* **4.** any of the four corners of a baseball diamond. —*v.* [~ + *obj*] **5.** to make or form: *He based the book on his own life.* **6.** to put at a base: *an air squadron based on Guam.* —*Idiom.* **7. off base,** *Informal.* seriously

wrong. **8. touch base,** to get into contact: *Touch base with me before you leave.*

base[2] /beys/ *adj.*, **bas•er, bas•est.** **1.** not honorable; immoral. **2.** of little value.

base•ball /ˈbeysˌbɔl/ *n.* **1.** [*noncount*] a game played with a bat and a ball by two teams of nine players each. **2.** [*count*] the ball used in baseball.

base•ment /ˈbeysmənt/ *n.* [*count*] the story of a building that is underground.

ba•ses[1] /ˈbeysiyz/ *n.* pl. of BASIS.

bas•es[2] /ˈbeysɪz/ *n.* pl. of BASE[1].

bash /bæʃ/ *v.* [~ + *obj*] [*no obj*] **1.** to hit hard; smash. —*n.* [*count*] **2.** a blow: *a bash on the nose.* **3.** a lively party.

bash•ful /ˈbæʃfəl/ *adj.* shy.

ba•sic /ˈbeysɪk/ *adj.* **1.** [*before a noun*] most important; fundamental: *a basic principle.* —*n.* [*count*] **2.** Often, **basics.** [*plural*] something that is essential.

BASIC /ˈbeysɪk/ *n.* B(eginner's) A(ll-purpose) S(ymbolic) I(nstruction) C(ode): a high-level computer programming language that uses English words and punctuation marks.

ba•si•cal•ly /ˈbeysɪkliy/ *adv.* most importantly.

ba•sin /ˈbeysən/ *n.* [*count*] **1.** a round container to hold liquid. **2.** an area of land drained by a river.

ba•sis /ˈbeysɪs/ *n.* [*count*], *pl.* **-ses** /-siyz/. a base; foundation: *no basis for your opinion.*

bask /bæsk/ *v.* [*no obj*] **1.** to be exposed to pleasant warmth: *basking in the sun.* **2.** to take great pleasure: *basking in applause.*

bas•ket /ˈbæskɪt/ *n.* [*count*] **1.** a container made of flexible, woven material. **2.** an open net hanging from a metal ring in basketball.

bas•ket•ball /ˈbæskɪtˌbɔl/ *n.* **1.** [*noncount*] a game played by two teams who try to throw a ball through a basket. **2.** [*count*] the ball used in basketball.

bass[1] /beys/ *adj.* **1.** of the lowest musical pitch: *a bass clarinet.* —*n.* [*count*] **2.** a bass voice, singer, or instrument. **3.** the largest instrument of the violin family.

bass[2] /bæs/ *n.* [*count*], *pl.* (*esp. when thought of as a group*) **bass,** (*esp. for kinds or species*) **bass•es.** an edible freshwater or saltwater fish.

bas•soon /bæˈsuwn, bə-/ *n.* [*count*] a large woodwind instrument of low range.

bas•tard /ˈbæstərd/ *n.* [*count*] **1.** a child of unmarried parents. **2.** *Offensive.* a hateful person.

baste[1] /beyst/ *v.* [~ + *obj*], **bast•ed, bast•ing.** to sew with long, loose temporary stitches.

baste[2] /beyst/ *v.* [~ + *obj*], **bast•ed, bast•ing.** to moisten (meat or other food) with fat or juices while cooking.

bat[1] /bæt/ *n.*, *v.*, **bat•ted, bat•ting.** —*n.* [*count*] **1.** a stick used in certain games, as baseball, to strike the ball. —*v.* [~ + *obj*] **2.** to hit with or as if with a bat. **3.** [*no obj*] to take one's turn at hitting the ball. —**bat•ter,** *n.* [*count*]

bat[2] /bæt/ *n.* [*count*] a flying, mouselike mammal that is active at night.

bat[3] /bæt/ *v.* [~ + *obj*], **bat•ted, bat•ting.** —*Idiom.* **not bat an eye,** to show no emotion: *She didn't bat an eye when I told her the bad news.*

batch /bætʃ/ *n.* [*count*] a group taken together: *a batch of tickets.*

bath /bæθ/ *n.* [*count*] a washing of one's body in a bathtub.

bathe /beyð/ *v.*, **bathed, bath•ing,** *n.* —*v.* **1.**

[~ + *obj*] to give a bath to; wash. **2.** [*no obj*] to take a bath. **3.** [~ + *obj*] to apply water or other liquid to. **4.** [~ + *obj*] to cover or surround: *Sunlight bathed the room.* **5.** [*no obj*] to swim for pleasure: *They went bathing in the sea.* —'**bath•er,** *n.* [*count*]

'**bathing ,suit,** *n.* [*count*] a garment worn for swimming. Also called **swimsuit.**

bath•robe /'bæθ,rowb/ *n.* [*count*] a loose, coat-like garment worn after bathing or over pajamas or a nightgown.

bath•room /'bæθ,ruwm, -,rʊm/ *n.* [*count*] **1.** a room containing a bathtub and a sink and toilet. —*Idiom.* **2. go to** or **use the bathroom,** to urinate or defecate.

bath•tub /'bæθ,tʌb/ *n.* [*count*] a container to sit in while bathing.

ba•ton /bə'tɒn, bæ-/ *n.* [*count*] **1.** a light, thin stick with which a conductor directs an orchestra. **2.** a metal rod twirled by a leader of a marching band.

bat•tal•ion /bə'tælyən/ *n.* [*count*] an army unit made up of two or more companies.

bat•ter[1] /'bætər/ *v.* [~ + *obj*] to beat hard and repeatedly.

bat•ter[2] /'bætər/ *n.* [*noncount*] a mixture of flour, eggs, and milk, used in cooking.

bat•ter•y /'bætəriy/ *n.* [*count*], *pl.* -**ter•ies. 1.** a device that produces electricity: *The car battery was dead.* **2.** a group of large guns: *a battery of anti-aircraft guns.* **3.** a group of similar things: *a battery of tests.*

bat•tle /'bætl/ *n.*, *v.*, -**tled, -tling. —***n.* **1.** [*count*] [*noncount*] a fight between two military forces. **2.** [*count*] any conflict: *the battle of the sexes.* —*v.* [*no obj*] [~ + *obj*] **3.** to fight or struggle.

bat•tle•field /'bætl,fiyld/ *n.* [*count*] a place where a battle is fought.

bat•tle•ship /'bætl,ʃɪp/ *n.* [*count*] the most heavily armored kind of warship.

bawl /bɔl/ *v.* **1.** [*no obj*] to cry or shout loudly and strongly. **2. bawl out,** *Informal.* to scold vigorously: *to bawl the students out for cheating* or *to bawl out the students for cheating.*

bay[1] /bey/ *n.* [*count*] a body of water enclosed by a curve of the land around it.

bay[2] /bey/ *n.* [*count*] a part of a structure used for a particular purpose: *She backed the truck into the loading bay.*

bay[3] /bey/ *v.* [*no obj*] to howl with a deep, long sound: *A hound was baying at the moon.*

bay[4] /bey/ *n.* LAUREL (def. 1).

bay•o•net /'beyə,nɛt, ,beyə'nɛt/ *n.* [*count*] a long knife attached to the end of a rifle.

ba•zaar /bə'zɑr/ *n.* [*count*] **1.** a marketplace or shopping district, esp. one in the Middle East. **2.** a sale of various things to raise money for a charity, etc.: *a church bazaar.*

B.C. or **BC,** an abbreviation of: before Christ (used after dates): *Caesar was assassinated in 44* B.C. Compare A.D.

B.C.E., an abbreviation of: before the Christian (or Common) Era (used after dates).

be /biy; *unstressed* biy, bɪ/ *v.* and *auxiliary verb.* *Present forms: singular; 1st person form:* **am,** *2nd person form:* **are,** *3rd person form:* **is.** *Present plural form:* **are.** *Past forms: singular; 1st person form:* **was,** *2nd person form:* **were,** *3rd person form:* **was.** *Past plural form:* **were.** *Present subjunctive form:* **be.** *Past subjunctive form:* **were.** *Present participle form:* **be•ing.** *Past participle*

form: **been.** —*v.* [*usually: not: be* + ~*-ing*] **1.** to have (the quality, etc., mentioned); used to connect the subject with an adjective, or to another noun or a phrase in order to describe, identify, or say more about the subject: *Wilt is tall. I am Barbara.* **2.** to exist or live: *Shakespeare's famous line "To be or not to be" asks if life is worth living.* **3.** to occur: *The wedding was last week.* **4.** to occupy a place: *The book is on the table.* **5.** to continue as before: *Let things be.* **6.** (used as a verb to introduce a question or in a command, request, or piece of advice): *Is that right? Be quiet!* —*auxiliary verb.* **7.** (used with the *-ing* form (the present participle) of another, main verb to show continuous activity): *I am waiting.* **8.** (used with *to* plus the root form (the infinitive) of another verb to express a command or indicate future action): *He is to see me today (= He will see me today).* **9.** (used with the past participle of another verb to form the passive voice, that is, to show the action of the verb has been done to the subject of the sentence): *The policeman was shot.*

be-, a prefix meaning: to make, become (*be friend*); to treat as (*belittle*).

beach /biytʃ/ *n.* [*count*] **1.** an area of sand along a shore. —*v.* [~ + *obj*] [*no obj*] **2.** to run (a boat) onto a beach.

bea•con /'biykən/ *n.* [*count*] a light that acts as a guide, esp. for ships or aircraft.

bead /biyd/ *n.* [*count*] **1.** a small ball of glass, wood, etc., with a hole through it, often put on a string with others to make necklaces, etc. **2.** **beads,** [*plural*] a necklace of beads. **3.** a small drop of liquid: *beads of sweat.*

bea•gle /'biygəl/ *n.* [*count*] a small dog with short legs and drooping ears.

beak /biyk/ *n.* [*count*] the curved, horny part of a bird's mouth.

beak•er /'biykər/ *n.* [*count*] **1.** a large drinking cup with a wide mouth. **2.** a small glass container used in a laboratory.

beam /biym/ *n.* [*count*] **1.** a long piece of metal, wood, etc., used to support a building. **2.** a stream of light or other radiation: *a beam of light; a beam of electrons.* —*v.* [*no obj*] **3.** to send out beams, as of light or heat: *The sun beamed through the clouds.* **4.** [~ + *obj*] to send out (a signal) in a particular direction: *We beamed the signal to the satellite.* **5.** [*no obj*] to smile radiantly or happily.

bean /biyn/ *n.* [*count*] **1.** the seed of various plants, eaten as a vegetable. **2.** any of various other beanlike seeds: *coffee beans.* —*Idiom.* **3. spill the beans,** *Informal.* to tell a secret.

bear[1] /bɛər/ *v.,* bore /bɔr/, borne or born /bɔrn/, **bear•ing. 1.** [~ + *obj*] to support: *The columns can bear the weight of the roof.* **2.** [~ + *obj*] to give birth to. **3.** [~ + *obj*] to produce: *That tree bears fruit.* **4.** [~ + *oneself*] to conduct (oneself, etc.): *She bore herself bravely.* **5.** [~ + *obj*] to suffer without complaining: *I can't bear your nagging anymore.* **6.** [~ + *obj*] to carry; bring. **7.** [*no obj*] to go in a (certain) direction: *Bear left here.* **8. bear up,** to face hardship bravely: *She has been bearing up well since the tragedy.* **9. bear with,** to be patient with: *Just bear with me for a few minutes.*

bear[2] /bɛər/ *n.* [*count*], *pl.* **bears,** (*esp. when thought of as a group*) **bear.** a large mammal with thick fur.

bear•a•ble /'bɛərəbəl/ *adj.* able to be endured or tolerated: *The pain was bearable.*

beard /bɪərd/ n. [count] hair growing on the lower part of the face.

bear·ing /'bɛərɪŋ/ n. **1.** the way in which a person behaves: [noncount]: a person of dignified bearing. [count; usually singular]: a very regal bearing. **2.** [noncount; usually: ~ + on] relation or connection: That has no bearing on the problem. **3.** [count] Often, **bearings.** [plural] direction or relative position: The pilot radioed the plane's bearings.

beast /biyst/ n. [count] **1.** a large, four-footed animal. **2.** a cruel person.

beat /biyt/ v., **beat, beat·en** or **beat, beat·ing,** n., adj. **1.** [~ + obj] to hit forcefully and repeatedly. **2.** [~ + obj] to stir forcefully: Beat the eggs well. **3.** [~ + obj] to defeat in a contest: She finally beat him at the game. **4.** [~ + obj] Informal. to be better than: Making reservations on the phone beats waiting in line. **5.** [no obj] to move regularly: My heart was beating wildly every time she looked at me. **6. beat up,** to hit repeatedly: The gang beat him up. They beat up on him. —n. **7.** [count] a stroke or the sound made from such a stroke: two beats on the drum. **8.** [count; usually singular] the major rhythm of a piece of music: All her songs have a great beat. **9.** [count; usually singular] one's area of responsibility: the police officer's beat. —adj. **10.** [be + ~] Informal. tired; worn out: I was really beat after staying up all night. —**Idiom. 11. beat it,** Informal. to go away: He was bothering me, so I told him to beat it.

beat·er /'biytər/ n. [count] **1.** a person who beats: a wife-beater. **2.** a tool for beating something: an egg beater.

beau·ti·ful /'byuwtəfəl/ adj. having beauty. —'**beau·ti·ful·ly,** adv.

beau·ti·fy /'byuwtə,fay/ v. [~ + obj], **-fied, -fy·ing.** to make beautiful.

beau·ty /'byuwtiy/ n., pl. **-ties. 1.** [noncount] a quality that gives pleasure to the mind or the senses: Beauty is only skin deep. **2.** [count] a beautiful person or thing: She's a real beauty.

'**beauty ,parlor,** n. [count] a place where women get their hair cut or styled and receive other beauty treatments. Also called '**beauty ,shop.**

bea·ver /'biyvər/ n. [count], pl. **-vers,** (esp. when thought of as a group) **-ver.** a large rodent that lives in water and on land and builds dams across streams.

be·came /bɪ'keym/ v. a pt. of BECOME.

be·cause /bɪ'kɔz, -'kʌz/ conj. **1.** for the reason that: I was late because it took so long to get dressed. —prep. **2. because of,** for the reason of: I was late because of bad weather.

beck·on /'bɛkən/ v. [~ + obj] **1.** to silently call (someone) to come near, as by waving the hand: He beckoned (to) me. **2.** to call to; attract: Fame and fortune beckoned (to) him.

be·come /bɪ'kʌm/ v., **-came, -come, -com·ing. 1.** [~ + adjective] to come to be (as specified): I became tired. **2.** [~ + noun] to come into being: She became a ballerina. **3.** [~ + obj] to be attractive when worn by: That dress becomes you. See BECOMING.

be·com·ing /bɪ'kʌmɪŋ/ adj. attractive: a becoming hairdo.

bed /bɛd/ n. [count] **1.** a piece of furniture on which one sleeps. **2.** an area of ground for growing plants: a flower bed. **3.** the bottom of a body of water. —**Idiom. 4. get up on the wrong**

side of the bed, to be in a bad mood. **5. make a bed,** to fit a bed with sheets and blankets.

bed·ding /'bɛdɪŋ/ n. [noncount] the sheets and blankets on a bed.

bed·lam /'bɛdləm/ n. [noncount] a place of noise and confusion.

be·drag·gled /bɪ'drægəld/ adj. untidy, as with rain or dirt.

bed·rid·den /'bɛd,rɪdn/ adj. staying in bed because of illness, injury, etc.

bed·room /'bɛd,ruwm, -,rʊm/ n. [count] a room used for sleeping.

bed·side /'bɛd,sayd/ n. [count; usually singular] the side of a bed: He was at my bedside when I was ill.

bed·spread /'bɛd,sprɛd/ n. [count] a decorated covering for a bed.

bed·time /'bɛd,taym/ n. [noncount] [count] the time a person goes to bed.

bee /biy/ n. [count] a stinging insect that makes honey.

beech /biytʃ/ n. [count] a tree having a smooth gray bark and small, triangular nuts.

beef /biyf/ n., pl. **beefs** for 2, v. —n. **1.** [noncount] the meat of a cow or steer. **2.** [count] Slang. a complaint. —v. **3.** [no obj] Slang. to complain; grumble. **4. beef up,** to add strength or force to: Beef up that report.

bee·hive /'biy,hayv/ n. [count] a place where bees live.

been /bɪn/ v. pp. of BE.

beep /biyp/ n. [count] **1.** a short, high-pitched tone made by an electronic device: the beep of the computer. —v. **2.** to (cause to) make such a sound: [no obj]: When the timer beeps, take the cake out of the oven. [~ + obj]: The driver beeped her horn.

beep·er /'biypər/ n. [count] a pocket-size device that beeps when the person carrying it receives a telephone message.

beer /bɪər/ n. [noncount] [count] **1.** an alcoholic drink made from fermented grains. **2.** any of various drinks made from roots, etc.: root beer; ginger beer.

bees·wax /'biyz,wæks/ n. WAX¹ (def. 1).

beet /biyt/ n. [count] a plant with a large red root that is eaten as a vegetable.

bee·tle /'biytl/ n. [count] an insect with hard, horny front wings.

be·fall /bɪ'fɔl/ v. [~ + obj], **-fell, -fall·en, -fall·ing.** to happen to (someone), esp. by chance: What had befallen them?

be·fit·ting /bɪ'fɪtɪŋ/ adj. suitable for.

be·fore /bɪ'fɔr/ prep. **1.** earlier than: before noon. **2.** in front of: standing before the window. **3.** rather than: They would die before surrendering. —adv. **4.** previously: Haven't we met before? **5.** earlier: I saw her the week before. —conj. **6.** previous to the time when: before you go. **7.** rather than: I will die before I give in.

be·fore·hand /bɪ'fɔr,hænd/ adv. earlier: Anticipate the problems beforehand.

be·friend /bɪ'frɛnd/ v. [~ + obj] to act as a friend to: She befriended the new student.

beg /bɛg/ v., **begged, beg·ging. 1.** [~ + obj] to ask for something with great feeling: to beg for help; to beg forgiveness. **2.** [no obj] to ask someone for money: They begged in the streets.

be·gan /bɪ'gæn/ v. pt. of BEGIN.

beg·gar /'bɛgər/ n. [count] a person who begs.

be·gin /bɪ'gɪn/ v. [no obj] [~ + obj], **-gan** /-'gæn/, **-gun** /-'gʌn/, **-gin·ning.** to start.

be•gin•ner /bɪ'gɪnər/ n. [count] a person who has just started to learn something: *a beginner at computer programming.*

be•gin•ning /bɪ'gɪnɪŋ/ n. [count; usually singular] the starting point: *the beginning of the term.*

be•gun /bɪ'gʌn/ v. pp. of BEGIN.

be•half /bɪ'hæf/ n. [noncount] —*Idiom.* **in** or **on behalf of.** Also, **in** or **on someone's behalf.** as a representative of (someone): *on behalf of the president.*

be•have /bɪ'heyv/ v. [no obj], **-haved, -hav•ing. 1.** to act in a particular way: *The car behaves well in traffic.* **2.** to act properly.

be•hav•ior /bɪ'heyvyər/ n. [noncount] way of behaving: *bad behavior in class.*

be•head /bɪ'hɛd/ v. [~ + obj] to cut off the head of.

be•held /bɪ'hɛld/ v. pt. and pp. of BEHOLD.

be•hind /bɪ'haynd/ prep. **1.** at or toward the rear of: *behind the house.* **2.** later than: *behind schedule.* **3.** making less progress than: *We had fallen behind our opponents.* **4.** in support of: *Are you behind me in this?* —*adv.* **5.** at or toward the rear: *to lag behind.* **6.** in a place or stage already passed: *We left our bad times behind.* —*adj.* [be + ~] **7.** late: *I'm behind with the rent.* —*n.* [count] **8.** Informal. the buttocks.

be•hold /bɪ'howld/ v. [~ + obj], **-held, -hold•ing.** to see: *He beheld the splendor of the city.*

beige /beyʒ/ n. [noncount], adj. a light grayish brown.

be•ing /'biyɪŋ/ n. **1.** [noncount] existence: *They brought this council into being.* **2.** [noncount] life: *How did we come into being?* **3.** [count] a living thing: *Are there intelligent beings on other planets?*

be•lat•ed /bɪ'leytɪd/ adj. coming too late: *a belated birthday card.*

belch /bɛltʃ/ v. **1.** [no obj] to send out gas noisily from the stomach through the mouth. **2.** to come forth; send forth: [no obj]: *Smoke belched (out) from the chimney.* [~ + obj]: *The chimney belched (out) smoke.*

bel•fry /'bɛlfriy/ n. [count], pl. **-fries.** a tower for a bell.

Bel•gian /'bɛldʒən/ n. [count] **1.** a citizen of Belgium. —*adj.* **2.** of or relating to Belgium.

be•lief /bɪ'liyf/ n. **1.** [count] something believed: *a deep belief in his honesty.* **2.** [noncount] faith; trust: *children's belief in their parents.*

be•lieve /bɪ'liyv/ v. [~ + obj], **-lieved, -liev•ing. 1.** to have faith in the truth of: *I can't believe that story.* **2.** to hold as an opinion: *I believe (that) they are out of town.* **3. believe in, a.** to be sure of the truth or existence of: *to believe in God.* **b.** to accept that (something) is a good idea: *I believe in getting to work early.* —**be'liev•a•ble,** adj. —**be'liev•er,** n. [count] —**be'liev•ing•ly,** adv.

be•lit•tle /bɪ'lɪtl/ v. [~ + obj], **-tled, -tling.** to cause to seem unimportant: *Don't belittle your accomplishments.*

bell /bɛl/ n. [count] **1.** a hollow metal instrument that makes a ringing sound when struck. **2.** any device that makes a similar sound, as a doorbell.

bel•lig•er•ent /bə'lɪdʒərənt/ adj. showing readiness to fight: *a belligerent tone.* —**bel'lig•er•en•cy,** n. [noncount]

bel•low /'bɛlow/ v. to shout in a loud voice: [no obj]: *The teacher bellowed at us.* [~ + obj]: *He bellowed a warning at us.*

bel•lows /'bɛlowz/ n. [count; used with a singular or plural verb] a device for blowing air into a fire.

bel•ly /'bɛliy/ n. [count], pl. **-lies. 1.** the stomach. **2.** the rounded part of something: *the belly of the plane.*

bel•ly•but•ton or **'belly ,button** /'bɛl,iy bʌtn/ n. Informal. NAVEL.

be•long /bɪ'lɔŋ, -'lɒŋ/ v. **1.** [no obj] to be in the right place: *This book belongs on the shelf.* **2. belong to, a.** to be the property of: *The scarf belongs to me.* **b.** to be a member of: *They belong to three clubs.*

be•long•ing /bɪ'lɔŋɪŋ, -'lɒŋ-/ n. **1. belongings,** [plural] possessions: *Put your belongings away.* **2.** [noncount] a feeling of being welcome: *I had a sense of belonging.*

be•lov•ed /bɪ'lʌvɪd, -'lʌvd/ adj. **1.** greatly loved: [before a noun]: *my beloved wife.* [be + ~]: *She was beloved of everyone.* —*n.* [count; singular only] **2.** a greatly loved person: *Her beloved had died.*

be•low /bɪ'low/ adv. **1.** in or toward a lower place: *Look out below!* —*prep.* **2.** lower than; under: *below cost; below the sea.*

belt /bɛlt/ n. [count] **1.** a band of flexible material worn around the waist: *a leather belt.* **2.** a circular band used to drive machinery or carry objects: *The fan belt in the car snapped.* —*v.* [~ + obj] **3.** to fasten with a belt: *He belted (on) his raincoat.* **4.** Slang. to hit hard: *He belted his wife.* —*Idiom.* **5. below the belt,** unfair: *That nasty lie was really below the belt.* **6. under one's belt,** as part of one's background: *Get some experience under your belt.*

bench /bɛntʃ/ n. **1.** [count] a long seat for several people: *a park bench.* **2.** [noncount] a symbol for the office of a judge: *He was appointed to the bench.* **3.** [count] a long worktable: *a carpenter's bench.*

bend /bɛnd/ v., bent /bɛnt/, **bend•ing,** n. —*v.* **1.** [~ + obj] to force (something) from a straight form into a curved form: *He could bend steel with his bare hands.* **2.** [no obj] to become curved: *This wire bends easily.* **3.** to (cause to) lean away from an upright position: [~ + obj]: *She bent her head in prayer.* [no obj]: *She bent over my desk.* —*n.* [count] **4.** the act of bending: *a bend to the pressures of politics.* **5.** something that is bent: *a bend in the road.* —*Idiom.* **6. bend over backward,** to help as much as possible: *The teacher bent over backward in giving you extra time.*

be•neath /bɪ'niyθ/ adv. **1.** below: *From the mountain he looked down to the lake beneath.* —*prep.* **2.** below; under: *They lived beneath the same roof.* **3.** not worthy of: *Your remarks are beneath you.*

ben•e•fac•tor /'bɛnə,fæktər/ n. [count] a person who does a good deed.

ben•e•fi•cial /,bɛnə'fɪʃəl/ adj. doing good: *the beneficial effect of sunshine.*

ben•e•fi•ci•ar•y /,bɛnə'fɪʃiy,ɛriy, -'fɪʃəriy/ n. [count], pl. **-ar•ies.** a person who receives money or property from a will.

ben•e•fit /'bɛnəfɪt/ n. **1.** [noncount] advantage; gain: *I did this for your benefit.* **2.** [count] money paid to help someone: *The company provided many health-care benefits.* —*v.* **3.** [~ + obj] to do good to: *a health-care program that will benefit everyone.* **4.** to gain good from: [no obj]: *When the blood drive was over, the Red Cross had clearly benefited.* [~ + from + obj]: *I learned to benefit from experience.*

be•nev•o•lence /bə'nɛvələns/ n. **1.** [noncount] desire to do good: She was praised for her benevolence. **2.** [count] an act of kindness: His benevolence made it possible for me to attend college. —**be'nev•o•lent,** adj.

be•nign /bɪ'nayn/ adj. **1.** kind or gentle: a benign smile. **2.** not malignant: a benign tumor.

bent /bɛnt/ adj. **1.** curved: a bent back. **2.** [be + ~] determined: He was bent on finding the truth. —n. [singular] **3.** a special talent: She has a bent for painting.

be•queath /bɪ'kwiθ, -'kwiy θ/ v. [~ + obj (+ to) + obj] to give (property or money) by means of a will: I bequeath the house to my wife. —**be'quest,** n. [count]

be•reaved /bɪ'riyvd/ adj. greatly saddened by the death of a loved one.

be•ret /bə'rey/ n. [count] a soft cap with a flat, round top.

ber•ry /'bɛriy/ n. [count], pl. **-ries.** a small, soft fruit with seeds.

berth /bɜrθ/ n. [count] **1.** a shelflike sleeping space, as on a ship. **2.** a space in a harbor where a ship ties up.

be•seech /bɪ'siytʃ/ v. [~ + obj], **-sought** /-'sɔt/ or **-seeched, -seech•ing.** to beg or ask for strongly or urgently.

be•set /bɪ'sɛt/ v. [~ + obj], **-set, -set•ting.** **1.** to attack on all sides: He was beset by an angry crowd. **2.** to trouble very much: He was beset by problems.

be•side /bɪ'sayd/ prep. **1.** by the side of; near: Sit down beside me. **2.** compared with: Beside her, other writers are boring. —**Idiom. 3. beside oneself,** frantic; feeling strong emotion about: She was beside herself with anger.

be•sides /bɪ'saydz/ adv. **1.** in addition to; also: I'd really like to go and besides, I promised them I would come. —prep. **2.** in addition to: Besides his mother he has a sister to support.

be•siege /bɪ'siydʒ/ v. [~ + obj], **-sieged, -sieg•ing. 1.** to surround and attack: The city was besieged by the enemy. **2.** to crowd around: The president was besieged by reporters.

be•sought /bɪ'sɔt/ v. a pt. and pp. of BESEECH.

best /bɛst/ adj., superlative form of GOOD. **1.** of the highest quality; the most excellent: the best students. **2.** most suitable or appropriate: Is this the best way to handle the problem? —adv., superlative form of WELL. **3.** most excellently: That song best suits her voice. **4.** to the highest degree; most: She is the best-known actress of our time. —n. [count] **5.** [the + ~] someone or something that is best: Even the best of us makes mistakes. **6.** [one's + ~] a person's highest degree of ability or effort: We're trying to do our best. **7.** [one's + ~] good wishes: Give them my best. —**Idiom. 8. make the best of,** to do as well as one can with: to make the best of a loveless marriage; We're only going to be living here for a year; let's make the best of it. See BETTER.

be•stow /bɪ'stow/ v. [~ + obj] to give. —**be'stow•al,** n. [count; singular]

best•sell•er /'bɛst'sɛlər/ n. [count] something that sells very well. —**'best-'selling,** adj.: a best-selling novel.

bet /bɛt/ v., **bet** or **bet•ted, bet•ting,** n. —v. **1. a.** to risk money on the result of an uncertain future event: [~ + obj]: She bet $5.00 on that horse. [no obj]: Do you want to bet? **b.** [~ + obj] to make an agreement with (someone) on such a risk: She bet me $5.00. **2.** [~ + obj] to be certain of: I bet (that) you forgot it. —n. [count] **3.**

an agreement to risk money on an uncertain future event: I made a bet with my wife. **4.** something that is bet on: That looks like a good bet. —**'bet•tor** or '**bet•ter,** n. [count]

be•tray /bɪ'trey/ v. [~ + obj] **1.** to be unfaithful or disloyal to: to betray one's friends. **2.** to tell (a secret): to betray a plan. **3.** to show unintentionally: Her nervousness betrays her guilt. —**be•tray•al,** n. [count]

bet•ter /'bɛtər/ adj. comparative form of GOOD. **1.** of higher quality or excellence: We got a better view. Those politicians are no better than thieves. This is a better time for action. **2.** larger; greater: This homework assignment will take the better part of a day to finish. **3.** healthier: Are you feeling better today? —adv., comparative form of WELL. **4.** in a more appropriate way: Behave better when your grandparents are visiting. **5.** to a greater degree: She knows the way better than I do. —v. **6.** to (cause to) improve: [~ + obj]: She worked hard to better herself. [no obj]: Economic conditions have not bettered. —n. [count; usually singular] **7.** something that is preferable: the better of two choices. —**Idiom. 8. better off,** [be + ~] more fortunate; happier: You are better off without him. **9. get** or **have the better of,** to win over: Her curiosity got the better of her.

be•tween /bɪ'twiyn/ prep. **1.** in the space, time, or degree separating: between New York and Chicago; between one and two o'clock; the difference between good and evil. **2.** in equal portions for each of: The couple split the profits between them. **3.** among: a treaty between three countries. **4.** by the actions of: Between us, we can finish the job. **5.** by the combined effect of: They were both married before, so they have seven children between them. **6.** existing as a secret with: Between you and me, I think he's a fool. —adv. **7.** in the space or time that separates two points: two windows with a door between. —**Idiom. 8. few and far between,** very rare: Their visits became few and far between. **9. in between,** in a middle position: Our house is in between a school and a church. —**Usage.** Traditionally, BETWEEN is used to show relationship involving two people or things (to decide between tea and coffee), while AMONG expresses more than two (The four brothers quarreled among themselves). BETWEEN, however, is also used to express relationship of persons or things considered individually, no matter how many: Between holding public office, teaching, and raising a family, she has little free time.

bev•er•age /'bɛvərɪdʒ/ n. [count] any liquid drink except water.

be•ware /bɪ'wɛər/ v. [~ + obj; usually in a command] to be careful (about): Beware of the dog!

be•wil•der /bɪ'wɪldər/ v. [~ + obj] to confuse: The rules of baseball bewilder me. —**be'wil•der•ment,** n. [noncount]

be•witch /bɪ'wɪtʃ/ v. [~ + obj] **1.** to work magic on. **2.** to charm: She bewitched me with her smile.

be•yond /biy'ɒnd/ prep. **1.** on, at, or to the farther side of: beyond the fence. **2.** outside the limits of: pain beyond endurance. —adv. **3.** farther away: Go as far as the house and beyond.

bi-, a combining form meaning: twice (bi annual); two (bicuspid).

bi•as /'bayəs/ n., v., **-ased, -as•ing** or (esp. Brit.) **-assed, -as•sing.** —n. [count] **1.** a tendency to judge something without full knowledge of it;

prejudice: *He has a bias against anyone who is black.* **2.** a particular tendency toward something: *She has a natural bias for music.* —*v.* [~ + *obj*] **3.** to influence unfairly: *The lawyer made a tearful plea to bias the jury.*

bib /bɪb/ *n.* [*count*] a piece of cloth tied under the chin to protect the clothing while eating.

Bi•ble /'baybəl/ *n.* [*count; the* + ~] the sacred writings of the Jewish and Christian religion. —'**Bib•li•cal,** *adj.*

bib•li•og•ra•phy /ˌbɪbliy'ɒɡrəfiy/ *n.* [*count*], *pl.* **-phies.** a list of writings about one subject: *a bibliography on the topic of horses.*

bi'carbonate of 'soda, *n.* SODIUM BICARBONATE.

bi•ceps /'baysɛps/ *n.* [*count*], *pl.* **-ceps, -ceps•es** /-sɛpsɪz/. the large muscle on the front of the upper arm.

bick•er /'bɪkər/ *v.* [*no obj*] to argue about something unimportant: *bickering over TV shows.*

bi•cy•cle /'baysɪkəl/ *n., v.,* **-cled, -cling.** —*n.* [*count*] **1.** a two-wheeled vehicle driven by pushing pedals. —*v.* [*no obj*] **2.** to ride a bicycle: *They bicycled to the store.* —**bi•cy•clist** /'baysɪklɪst/, *n.* [*count*]

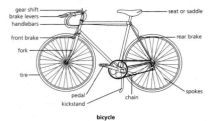

bicycle

bid /bɪd/ *v.,* **bade** /bæd/ or **bid, bid•den** or **bid, bid•ding,** *n.* —*v.* **1.** to command (someone to do something): [~ + *obj*]: *Do as I bid you.* [*no obj*]: *Do as I bid.* **2.** [~ + *obj*] to say as a greeting, etc.: *She bid him goodnight.* **3.** to offer (a certain amount of money) as the price one will charge or pay: [~ + *obj*]: *They bid $25,000 (for the job) and got the contract.* [*no obj*]: *I can't bid (for that vase); I don't have enough money.* —*n.* [*count*] **4.** an act or instance of bidding.

bide /bayd/ *v.* [*no obj*], **bid•ed** or **bode** /bowd/, **bid•ed, bid•ing.** —*Idiom.* **bide one's time,** to wait for a favorable opportunity: *He bided his time, planning revenge.*

bi•en•ni•al /bay'ɛniyəl/ *adj.* **1.** happening once every two years. **2.** lasting for two years. Also, **biyearly.**

bi•fo•cals /'bayˌfowkəlz/ *n.* [*plural*] eyeglasses or contact lenses with two portions, one for near and one for far vision.

big /bɪɡ/ *adj.,* **big•ger, big•gest. 1.** large in size, amount, etc.: *a big house.* **2.** [*before a noun*] of major importance: *a big problem.* **3.** [*be* + ~] popular: *Rock music is big today.* —*Idiom.* **4. be big on,** *Informal.* to have a special liking for: *That teacher is big on neatness.*

big•a•my /'bɪɡəmiy/ *n.* [*noncount*] marrying one person when still married to someone else. —'**big•a•mist,** *n.* [*count*] —'**big•a•mous,** *adj.*

big•ot /'bɪɡət/ *n.* [*count*] a person affected by bigotry. —'**big•ot•ed,** *adj.*

big•ot•ry /'bɪɡətriy/ *n.* [*noncount*] extreme unwillingness to accept the possibility that an idea differing from one's own may be correct.

'big ˌshot, *n.* [*count*] *Informal.* an important person: *He was a big shot in the film industry.*

bike /bayk/ *n., v.,* **biked, bik•ing.** —*n.* [*count*] **1.** a bicycle or motorcycle. —*v.* [*no obj*] **2.** to ride a bike: *We biked across Holland.* —**biker,** *n.* [*count*]

bi•ki•ni /bɪ'kiyniy/ *n.* [*count*], *pl.* **-nis.** a very small two-piece bathing suit for women or one-piece bathing suit for men.

bile /bayl/ *n.* [*noncount*] **1.** a bitter liquid produced by the liver that aids in digestion. **2.** bad temper.

bi•lin•gual /bay'lɪŋɡwəl/ *adj.* **1.** able to speak two languages equally well. **2.** using two languages: *bilingual VCR directions.*

bill¹ /bɪl/ *n.* [*count*] **1.** a statement of the money owed for goods or services: *a bill for car repairs.* **2.** a piece of paper money: *a ten-dollar bill.* **3.** a proposal for a law: *a gun-control bill.* —*v.* [~ + *obj*] **4.** to send a list of charges to: *We'll bill you later for the car repairs.*

bill² /bɪl/ *n.* [*count*] a bird's beak.

bill•board /'bɪlˌbɔrd/ *n.* [*count*] a flat surface on which large advertisements are placed.

bil•liards /'bɪlyərdz/ *n.* [*noncount; used with a singular verb*] a game played by driving balls with a long stick into holes in the corners of a table.

bil•lion /'bɪlyən/ *n.* [*count*], *pl.* **-lions,** [*or, after a number*] **-lion.** the number 1,000,000,000 in the U.S. (1,000,000,000,000 in Great Britain). —**bil•lion'aire,** *n.* [*count*]

bil•low /'bɪlow/ *n.* [*count*] **1.** very large mass like a wave: *billows of smoke.* —*v.* [*no obj*] **2.** to rise in waves; to swell out: *The sails billowed in the wind.*

'billy ˌgoat, *n.* [*count*] a male goat.

bin /bɪn/ *n.* [*count*] a large container for storing grain, coal, etc.

bi•na•ry /'baynəriy, -nɛriy/ *adj.* **1.** consisting of two parts or things. **2.** of or relating to a system of numbers that uses only 0 and 1.

bind /baynd/ *v.,* **bound** /bawnd/, **bind•ing,** *n.* —*v.* [~ + *obj*] **1.** to tie (something) with a string, rope, etc.: *She bound her hair with a ribbon.* **2.** to join by a tie: *to be bound by a contract.* **3.** to fasten or secure (sheets of paper) within a cover: *to bind a book in leather.* —*n.* [*count; usually singular*] **4.** a difficult situation: *This tight schedule has us in a bind.*

bind•er /'bayndər/ *n.* [*count*] a hard cover for holding sheets of paper together: *She keeps her class notes in a three-ring binder.*

bind•ing /'bayndɪŋ/ *n.* [*count*] the cover in which book pages are bound.

binge /bɪndʒ/ *n., v.,* **binged, bing•ing.** —*n.* [*count*] **1.** a period in which an activity is done too much: *a shopping binge before Christmas.* —*v.* [*no obj*] **2.** to go on a binge.

bin•go /'bɪŋɡow/ *n.* [*noncount; sometimes: Bingo*] a game of chance that involves matching numbers on a card with numbers called out by an announcer.

bin•oc•u•lars /bə'nɒkyələrz, bay-/ *n.* [*plural*] an instrument for looking at distant objects.

bio-, a combining form meaning life or living organisms (*biodegradable*).

bi•o•de•grad•a•ble /ˌbayowdɪ'greydəbəl/ *adj.* capable of decaying through the action of living organisms.

bi•og•ra•phy /bay'ɒɡrəfiy, biy-/ *n.,* *pl.* **-phies.** [*count*] a written account of another person's life.

The labels on the bicycle diagram:
gear shift, brake levers, handlebars, front brake, fork, tire, pedal, kickstand, chain, seat or saddle, rear brake, spokes

B

—**bi•og•ra•pher,** *n.* [*count*] —**bi•o'graph•i•cal,** *adj.*

bi•ol•o•gy /bay'ɒlədʒiy/ *n.* [*noncount*] the scientific study of living things. —**bi•o'log•i•cal,** *adj.* —**bi'ol•o•gist,** *n.* [*count*]

bi•on•ic /bay'ɒnɪk/ *adj.* having normal bodily functions strengthened or improved by electronic devices: *a bionic hand.*

birch /bɜrtʃ/ *n.* [*count*] a tree having smooth bark and thin branches.

bird /bɜrd/ *n.* [*count*] a creature with wings and feathers, usually able to fly.

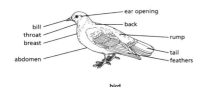

bird

'bird's-,eye, *adj.* [*before a noun*] seen from far above: *a bird's-eye view of the city.*

birth /bɜrθ/ *n.* **1.** [*noncount*] an act or instance of being born. **2.** [*count*] the act or process of bringing forth young; childbirth. **3.** [*noncount*] nationality: *Greek by birth.* **4.** [*count; usually singular*] beginning: *the birth of democracy.* —*Idiom.* **5. give birth to,** to bear (a child): *She gave birth to a boy.*

'birth con,trol, *n.* [*noncount*] methods of limiting the number of children born.

birth•day /'bɜrθ,dey/ *n.* [*count*] the anniversary of a birth.

birth•mark /'bɜrθ,mɑrk/ *n.* [*count*] an unusual spot on a person's skin at birth.

birth•place /'bɜrθ,pleys/ *n.* [*count*] place of birth.

birth•rate /'bɜrθ,reyt/ *n.* [*count*] the number of births for every 1,000 people in a given place in a given time.

bis•cuit /'bɪskɪt/ *n.* [*count*] **1.** a small, soft, raised bread. **2.** *Chiefly Brit.* **a.** a cracker. **b.** a cookie.

bi•sect /bay'sɛkt, 'baysɛkt/ *v.* [~ + *obj*] to divide into two equal parts.

bish•op /'bɪʃəp/ *n.* [*count*] **1.** a high-ranking member of the Christian clergy who supervises a diocese. **2.** a chess piece that is moved diagonally.

bi•son /'baysən, -zən/ *n.* [*count*], *pl.* -son. a North American buffalo.

bit[1] /bɪt/ *n.* [*count*] **1.** the mouthpiece of a horse's bridle. **2.** a tool part for drilling holes.

bit[2] /bɪt/ *n.* **1.** [*count*; *noncount*] a small piece or amount of something. **2.** [*a* + ~] a short time: *Wait a bit.* —*Idiom.* **3. a bit,** a little: *I'm a bit tired today.* **4. bit by bit,** a little at a time; gradually. **5. every bit,** quite; just: *The movie was every bit as good as you said it was.*

bit[3] /bɪt/ *n.* [*count*] a single unit of computer information.

bit[4] /bɪt/ *v.* pt. and a pp. of BITE.

bitch /bɪtʃ/ *n.* [*count*] **1.** a female dog. **2.** *Slang.* an unpleasant woman: *She's a real bitch today.* —*v.* **3.** *Slang.* to complain. —**bitch•y,** *adj.,* -i•er, -i•est.

bite /bayt/ *v.,* bit /bɪt/, bit•ten /'bɪtn/ or bit, bit•ing, *n.* —*v.* **1.** [~ + *obj*] to cut or tear with the teeth: *The cat bit me.* **2.** (of an insect) to sting:

[~ + *obj*]: *A mosquito bit me.* [*no obj*]: *The flies are biting today.* **3.** [*no obj*] (of fish) to take bait (and hence get caught): *Are the fish biting today?* —*n.* **4.** [*count*] an act of biting. **5.** [*count*] a wound made by biting. **6.** [*count*] a piece bitten off: *Chew each bite carefully.* **7.** [*count; usually singular*] a small meal. —*Idiom.* **8. bite someone's head off,** to respond with extreme anger: *Don't bite my head off!*

bit•ing /'baytɪŋ/ *adj.* **1.** sharp; painful: *biting cold.* **2.** cruel: *a biting remark.* —**'bit•ing•ly,** *adv.*

bit•ten /'bɪtn/ *v.* a pp. of BITE.

bit•ter /'bɪtər/ *adj.* **1.** having a harsh, unpleasant taste. **2.** [*before a noun*] causing pain or sorrow: *a bitter pill; a bitter disappointment.* **3.** characterized by hatred: *bitter enemies.* —**'bit•ter•ly,** *adv.: a bitterly cold night.* —**'bit•ter•ness,** *n.* [*noncount*]

bit•ter•sweet /'bɪtər,swiyt/ *adj.* **1.** both bitter and sweet to the taste: *bittersweet chocolate.* **2.** both pleasant and painful: *a bittersweet memory.*

bi•zarre /bɪ'zɑr/ *adj.* very strange.

blab /blæb/ also **blab•ber** /'blæbər/ *v.* [*no obj*], **blabbed** also **blab•bered, blab•bing** also **blab•ber•ing.** to tell a secret.

blab•ber•mouth /'blæbər,mawθ/ *n.* [*count*] a person who talks too much, esp. one who reveals secrets.

black /blæk/ *adj.,* -er, -est, *n.,* *v.* —*adj.* **1.** of the color black: *black ink.* **2.** characterized by absence of light: *a black night.* **3.** [*sometimes: Black*] of or relating to any of various peoples having brown to black skin, esp. those peoples whose ancestors came from Africa. **4.** very dirty. **5.** gloomy; dismal: *a black future.* **6.** (of coffee) without milk or cream. —*n.* **7.** [*noncount*] the color at one end of the gray scale, opposite to white. **8.** [*count; sometimes: Black*] a member of any of various dark-skinned peoples. —*v.* **9. black out,** to lose consciousness: *He blacked out from lack of air.* —*Idiom.* **10. in the black,** operating at a profit: *The company was operating in the black again.*

'black-and-'blue, *adj.* discolored, as by bruising: *a black-and-blue mark on my knee.*

black•ber•ry /'blæk,bɛriy, -bəriy/ *n.* [*count*], *pl.* -ries. the black or dark purple fruit of certain plants of the rose family.

black•bird /'blæk,bɜrd/ *n.* [*count*] a bird with black feathers.

black•board /'blæk,bɔrd/ *n.* [*count*] a sheet of smooth material on which one writes with chalk.

black•en /'blækən/ *v.* **1.** [~ + *obj*] [*no obj*] to (cause to) become black. **2.** [~ + *obj*] to speak evil of: *He blackened his opponent's good name.*

'black 'eye, *n.* [*count*] a blackening of the skin around the eye, resulting from a blow.

black•head /'blæk,hɛd/ *n.* [*count*] a small, black-tipped spot on the skin.

black•jack /'blæk,dʒæk/ *n.* **1.** [*count*] a short, leather-covered club used as a weapon. **2.** [*noncount*] a card game in which a player needs to get more points than the dealer to win, but not more than 21.

black•list /'blæk,lɪst/ *n.* [*count*] **1.** a list of persons who are under suspicion or not in favor. —*v.* [~ + *obj*] **2.** to put on a blacklist.

black•mail /'blæk,meyl/ *n.* [*noncount*] **1.** an act of demanding money from someone by threatening to reveal secrets. —*v.* [~ + *obj*] **2.** to obtain money by blackmail.

'black 'market, *n.* [*noncount*] the illegal buying

and selling of goods: *the black market for American blue jeans in Russia.*

black•out /'blæk,awt/ *n.* [*count*] **1.** the turning off or covering over of all visible lights, usually as a precaution against air raids. **2.** a period of failure of all electrical power. **3.** a temporary loss of consciousness.

black•smith /'blæk,smɪθ/ *n.* [*count*] one who makes objects from iron, esp. horseshoes.

blad•der /'blædər/ *n.* [*count*] a hollow organ in the body in which urine collects.

blade /bleyd/ *n.* [*count*] **1.** the flat cutting part of an implement, as a knife. **2.** the leaf of a plant, esp. of a grass. **3.** the metal part of an ice skate that touches the ice.

blame /bleym/ *v.,* **blamed, blam•ing,** *n.* —*v.* [~ + *obj*] **1.** to hold (someone) responsible for something bad: *Don't blame me for the fire.* **2.** to place responsibility for (something bad) on: *He always blames his mistakes on me.* —*n.* [*noncount*] **3.** responsibility for something bad: *She took the blame for our mistake.* —'**blame•less,** *adj.*

blanch /blæntʃ/ *v.* **1.** [~ + *obj*] to boil (food) briefly: *Blanch the vegetables in boiling water ten seconds.* **2.** to make or turn pale: [~ + *obj*]: *A long illness had blanched her cheeks.* [*no obj*]: *He blanched at the bad news.*

bland /blænd/ *adj.,* **-er, -est. 1.** gentle or agreeable: *a bland, pleasant manner.* **2.** not highly flavored or spicy: *That sauce is too bland.* —'**bland•ness,** *n.* [*noncount*]

blank /blæŋk/ *adj.,* **-er, -est,** *n.* —*adj.* **1.** having nothing on it: *blank paper; a blank videotape.* **2.** expressionless: *a blank look.* —*n.* [*count*] **3.** an empty space: *Her mind is a blank about that episode.* —*Idiom.* **4. draw a blank,** to fail to remember. —'**blank•ly,** *adv.*

'**blank 'check,** *n.* [*count*] a bank check with a signature but without the amount written in.

blan•ket /'blæŋkɪt/ *n.* [*count*] **1.** a piece of thick cloth, used as a warm covering on a bed. **2.** any covering over something: *a blanket of snow.* —*v.* [~ + *obj* (+ *with* + *obj*)] **3.** to cover: *to blanket the neighborhood with advertisements for the concert.*

blare /blɛər/ *v.,* **blared, blar•ing,** *n.* —*v.* **1.** to make a loud, unpleasant sound: [*no obj*]: *No one could sleep because his radio was blaring.* [~ + *obj*]: *Her radio was blaring rock music.* —*n.* [*count; singular*] **2.** a loud, unpleasant noise: *the blare of the television.*

bla•sé /blɑ'zey, 'blɑzey/ *adj.* indifferent to or bored with something: *You're being very blasé about winning a new car.*

blas•phe•my /'blæsfəmiy/ *n.* [*noncount*] [*count*], *pl.* **-mies.** (an act of) speaking or acting disrespectfully about God or holy things. —'**blas•phe•mous,** *adj.*

blast /blæst/ *n.* [*count*] **1.** a sudden, strong gust of wind. **2.** a loud, sudden noise: *a harsh blast from the radio.* **3.** an explosion. —*v.* **4.** [~ + *obj*] [*no obj*] to make a loud, blaring noise. **5.** [~ + *obj*] to break apart by an explosion: *They blasted the enemy communications center.* **6. blast off,** (of a rocket) to leave a launch pad. —*Idiom.* **7. (at) full blast,** at maximum capacity or ability: *The radio was on at full blast.*

blast•off /'blæst,ɔf, -,ɒf/ *n.* [*count*] the launching of a rocket or spacecraft.

bla•tant /'bleytnt/ *adj.* very obvious in a bad way: *a blatant error.*

blaze¹ /bleyz/ *n., v.,* **blazed, blaz•ing.** —*n.* **1.**

[*count*] a bright flame or fire. **2.** [*count*] a very bright glow of color or light: *a blaze of jewels.* **3.** [*count; usually singular: a* + ~] a sudden, strong outburst: *a blaze of anger.* —*v.* [*no obj*] **4.** to burn or shine brightly: *The bonfire blazed for hours.*

blaze² /bleyz/ *v.* [~ + *obj*], **blazed, blaz•ing. 1.** to make marks on a path for others to follow: *to blaze a trail.* **2.** to lead the way in forming or finding: *to blaze the way for space travel.*

blaz•er /'bleyzər/ *n.* [*count*] a sports jacket.

bleach /bliytʃ/ *v.* **1.** to make whiter or lighter in color, as by a chemical agent: [~ + *obj*]: *Don't bleach this red sweater.* [*no obj*]: *A few old bones had bleached in the sun.* —*n.* [*noncount*] **2.** a chemical that makes things whiter in color.

bleach•er /'bliytʃər/ *n.* [*count*] Usually, **bleachers.** low-priced seats at a stadium, made of boards and not covered by a roof.

bleak /bliyk/ *adj.,* **-er, -est. 1.** cold and unpleasant: *the bleak winter landscape.* **2.** without hope: *a bleak future.* —'**bleak•ly,** *adv.* —'**bleak•ness,** *n.* [*noncount*]

blear•y /'blɪəriy/ *adj.,* **-i•er, -i•est.** (of the eyes) sore and tired: *His eyes were bleary after staying up all night.*

bleat /bliyt/ *v.* **1.** to make the sound of a sheep or goat: [*no obj*]: *The sheep were bleating in the field.* [~ + *obj*]: *The goats bleated a warning.* —*n.* [*count*] **2.** the sound of a sheep or goat.

bleed /bliyd/ *v.,* **bled** (bled), **bleed•ing. 1.** [*no obj*] [~ + *obj*] to lose blood. **2.** [*no obj*] to feel pity: *My heart bleeds for you.* —*Idiom.* **3. bleed dry,** to take away all money through extreme demands.

blem•ish /'blɛmɪʃ/ *v.* [~ + *obj*] **1.** to spoil the perfection of: *His reputation was blemished by scandal.* —*n.* [*count*] **2.** a mark that spoils the appearance of something: *a blemish on her nose.* **3.** a defect or flaw: *the one blemish on his academic record.*

blend /blɛnd/ *v.* **1.** to mix together: [~ + *obj*]: *Blend the flour and eggs together.* [*no obj*]: *Oil and water do not blend.* **2.** [*no obj*] to combine in a pleasing way: *Their voices blend beautifully.* —*n.* [*count*] **3.** a mixture: *a blend of coffee.*

blend•er /'blɛndər/ *n.* [*count*] an electric machine used to liquefy foods.

bless /blɛs/ *v.* [~ + *obj*], **blessed** or **blest** /blɛst/, **bless•ing. 1.** to make (something) holy: *The priest blessed the offering.* **2.** to ask for God's favor for: *Bless this house.* **3.** to give some benefit to: *Nature blessed me with strong teeth.* **4. Bless you!** (used to express polite concern after someone has sneezed): *"Ahchoo!" she sneezed. "Bless you," he responded.*

bless•ed /'blɛsɪd; *esp. for 2* blɛst/ *adj.* **1.** holy: *the Blessed Virgin.* **2.** favored (as by God): *blessed with common sense.*

bless•ing /'blɛsɪŋ/ *n.* [*count*] **1.** the act or words of a person who makes holy: *The priest gave his blessing to the soldiers.* **2.** a gift (as bestowed by God): *the blessings of liberty.*

blew /bluw/ *v.* **1.** the pt. of BLOW². **2.** the pt. of BLOW³.

blight /blayt/ *n.* **1.** [*noncount*] a disease of plants. **2.** the state or result of ruin or damage: [*noncount*]: *Crime is one cause of urban blight.* [*count*]: *Pollution and war are blights on the planet.* —*v.* [~ + *obj*] **3.** to destroy: *Illness blighted her hopes.*

blimp /blɪmp/ *n.* [*count*] a nonrigid aircraft with a motor but no wings.

blind /blaynd/ *adj.*, **-er, -est**, *v.*, *n.* —*adj.* **1.** unable to see. **2.** [*be* + ~] unwilling or unable to notice: *They were blind to the faults of their children.* **3.** [*before a noun*] without reason: *blind obedience.* —*v.* [~ + *obj*] **4.** to make unable to see: *The bright lights blinded him.* **5.** to take away reason: *Her charm blinded me to her faults.* —*n.* [*count*] **6.** Also, **blinds.** a window covering made of cloth, wood, or metal. —'**blind•ly,** *adv.* —'**blind•ness,** *n.* [*noncount*]

'**blind 'date,** *n.* [*count*] a social meeting arranged by a third person between two people who have not met before.

blind•er /'blayndər/ *n.* [*count*] **1.** flat pieces of leather attached to a horse's bridle to prevent it from seeing sideways. **2.** Usually, **blinders.** [*plural*] something that gets in the way of seeing or understanding something: *She has blinders on where her boyfriend is concerned.*

blind•fold /'blaynd,fowld/ *v.* [~ + *obj*] **1.** to prevent (a person's) sight by covering the eyes with a cloth. —*n.* [*count*] **2.** a cloth for covering the eyes.

blink /blɪŋk/ *v.* **1.** to open and close (the eyes) quickly: [*no obj*]: *He blinked when I opened the curtains.* [~ + *obj*]: *She blinked her eyes rapidly.* **2.** to shine (something) quickly on or off: [*no obj*]: *The lights blinked in the darkness.* [~ + *obj*]: *He blinked his lights to warn other drivers.* —*n.* [*count*] **3.** an act of blinking.

bliss /blɪs/ *n.* [*noncount*] perfect happiness. —'**bliss•ful,** *adj.*

blis•ter /'blɪstər/ *n.* [*count*] **1.** a thin, watery swelling under the skin: *I have a blister on my heel.* —*v.* [~ + *obj*] [*no obj*] **2.** to (cause to) become swollen; to (cause to) get a blister on.

blitz /blɪts/ *n.* [*count*] **1.** a sudden, heavy military attack. **2.** any swift, strong burst: *an advertising blitz.*

bliz•zard /'blɪzərd/ *n.* [*count*] a severe snowstorm.

bloat•ed /'blowtɪd/ *adj.* **1.** swollen: *a bloated corpse.* **2.** too full, as from eating too much.

blob /blɒb/ *n.* [*count*] a lump of a thick, liquid substance: *a blob of glue.*

block /blɒk/ *n.* [*count*] **1.** a large, solid piece of wood, stone, etc. **2.** one of a set of cube-shaped pieces used as a child's toy. **3.** anything that stops movement: *The sink has a block in it.* **4.** a section of a town between two streets: *They live on my block.* —*v.* [~ + *obj*] **5.** to get in the way of: *Your car is blocking my driveway.* **6. block up,** to (cause to) have a block in: *The toilet blocked up all the time. Try to block up those holes* or *Try to block those holes up.* —'**block•age,** *n.* [*count*] [*noncount*]

block•ade /blɒ'keyd/ *n.*, *v.*, **-ad•ed, -ad•ing.** —*n.* [*count*] **1.** the closing off of a place to prevent goods or people from coming in or going out. —*v.* [~ + *obj*] [*no obj*, etc.)

blond /blɒnd/ *adj.*, **-er, -est**, *n.* —*adj.* **1.** (of a male) having light-colored hair. —*n.* [*count*] **2.** a blond man.

blonde /blɒnd/ *adj.* **1.** (of a female) having light-colored hair. —*n.* [*count*] **2.** a blonde woman or girl. —'**blonde•ness,** *n.* [*noncount*]

blood /blʌd/ *n.* [*noncount*] **1.** the red fluid that flows through the body. **2.** something regarded as a source of energy: *The company needs new blood.* **3.** family relationship: *He is of noble blood.* —*Idiom.* **4. bad blood,** deep, long-lasting hatred: *There has been bad blood between the two families for years.* **5. make one's blood**

boil, to cause great anger: *Such injustice makes my blood boil.* **6. make one's blood run cold,** to fill with great fear: *The dark, deserted street made her blood run cold.*

blood•bath /'blʌd,bæθ/ *n.* [*count*] the killing of many people at one time: *A bloodbath followed the overthrow of that dictator.*

blood•cur•dling /'blʌd,kərdlɪŋ, -,kərdlɪŋ/ *adj.* [*usually before a noun*] causing fear: *a blood curdling scream.*

blood•hound /'blʌd,hawnd/ *n.* [*count*] a dog used in tracking people.

'**blood ,pressure,** *n.* a measure of the force of blood in the arteries: [*noncount*]: *Eating salty foods raises one's blood pressure.* [*count; usually singular*]: *a blood pressure of 120 over 80.*

blood•shed /'blʌd,ʃɛd/ *n.* [*noncount*] killing, as in war or murder.

blood•shot /'blʌd,ʃɒt/ *adj.* (of the eyes) having the white part colored red.

blood•stream /'blʌd,striym/ *n.* [*count; singular; the* + ~] the blood flowing through the body.

blood•thirst•y /'blʌd,θərstiy/ *adj.* eager to kill: *a bloodthirsty criminal.*

'**blood ,type,** *n.* [*count*] any of the four groups into which human blood can be divided.

'**blood ,vessel,** *n.* [*count*] any tube of the body through which the blood flows.

blood•y /'blʌdiy/ *adj.*, **-i•er, -i•est. 1.** covered with blood: *a bloody shirt.* **2.** characterized by wounding and killing: *bloody battles.* **3.** *Chiefly Brit. Slang.* (used before a noun or adjective to convey strong feeling) [*before a noun*]: *That was a bloody shame* (= *a very great shame*). [*before an adjective*]: *That was bloody awful* (= *very awful*).

bloom /bluwm/ *n.* **1.** [*count*] the flower of a plant. **2.** [*noncount*] the state of flowering: *lilacs in bloom.* **3.** [*noncount*] the time of greatest beauty, strength, etc.: *the bloom of youth.* —*v.* [*no obj*] **4.** to produce flowers: *The roses bloom every year.* **5.** thrive: *His talent for languages bloomed.*

blos•som /'blɒsəm/ *n.* **1.** [*count*] the flower of a plant: *apple blossoms.* **2.** [*noncount*] the state of flowering: *The cherry trees are in blossom.* —*v.* [*no obj*] **3.** to produce blossoms: *The tree blossomed quickly.* **4.** to develop successfully: *His talent blossomed at the university.*

blot /blɒt/ *n.*, *v.*, **blot•ted, blot•ting.** —*n.* [*count*] **1.** a spot or stain: *blots of ink.* **2.** a fault: *a blot on her character.* —*v.* [~ + *obj*] **3.** to make a blot. **4. blot out,** to hide: *Clouds blotted out the sun.*

blotch /blɒtʃ/ *n.* [*count*] a large spot or mark: *blotches on her neck.* —'**blotch•y,** *adj.*, **-i•er, -i•est.**

blot•ter /'blɒtər/ *n.* [*count*] **1.** a piece of special paper that absorbs ink. **2.** a book in which events are recorded: *a police blotter.*

blouse /blaws, blawz/ *n.* [*count*] a garment for women reaching from the neck to the waist.

blow¹ /blow/ *n.* [*count*] **1.** a hard stroke with one's hand or a weapon. **2.** a sudden misfortune. —*Idiom.* **3. come to blows,** to begin to fight physically. **4. strike a blow for,** to further or advance the cause of: *to strike a blow for civil rights.*

blow² /blow/ *v.*, **blew** /bluw/, **blown, blow•ing. 1.** (of the wind or air) **a.** [*no obj*] to be moving: *The wind blew all night.* **b.** [~ + *obj*] to move something along with a current of air: *The wind*

B

blew dust in my eyes. **2.** [*no obj*] to move along, carried by the wind: *The dust blew into my eyes.* **3.** to produce a current of air, as with the mouth: [*no obj*]: *She blew into the microphone.* [~ + *obj*]: *He blew smoke into my eyes.* **4.** (of a horn, etc.) to (cause to) make a sound: [*no obj*]: *The trumpets were blowing.* [~ + *obj*]: *Drivers were blowing their horns.* **5.** [*no obj*] (of a fuse, etc.) to (cause to) stop functioning: *The fuse blew. The tire blew (out).* **6.** *Informal.* [~ + *obj*] to waste (money): *I blew $100 on dinner.* **7.** [~ + *obj*] *Informal.* to make a stupid mistake: *He blew his lines in the play.* **8. blow out,** to (cause to) stop burning: *She blew out the candles. The fire finally blew out.* **9. blow over, a.** to pass away: *The storm blew over in minutes.* **b.** to be forgotten: *The scandal will blow over soon.* **10. blow up, a.** to (cause to) explode: *The bridge blew up. They blew up the embassy* or *They blew the embassy up.* **b.** to exaggerate; enlarge: *You're blowing this whole thing up out of all proportion.* **c.** to lose one's temper: *I blew up at the kids.* **d.** to fill with air or gas: *to blow up a balloon* or *to blow a balloon up.* **—Idiom. 11. blow one's mind,** to fill (someone) with strong feelings, as with pleasure or dismay: *That movie blew my mind.* **12. blow one's stack** or **top,** to become very angry.

'blow-,dry, *v.* [~ + *obj*], **-dried, -dry•ing.** to dry or style (hair) with a small electrical appliance that blows out heated air. **—'blow-,dryer,** *n.* [*count*]

blown /blown/ *v.* pp. of BLOW[2].

blow•out /'blow,awt/ *n.* [*count*] **1.** a sudden bursting of an automobile tire. **2.** a big, expensive party: *She had a big blowout for her graduation.*

blow•torch /'blow,tɔrtʃ/ *n.* [*count*] a device that shoots out a very hot flame.

blub•ber /'blʌbər/ *n.* [*noncount*] **1.** the fat below a whale's skin. **2.** excess body fat: *With all that blubber, you should go on a diet.*

blue /bluw/ *n., adj.,* **blu•er, blu•est.** —*n.* [*noncount*] **1.** the color of a clear sky. —*adj.* **2.** of the color blue: *a beautiful blue sky.* **3.** sad or depressed: *I'm feeling a little blue today.* **4.** indecent; obscene: *a blue movie.* **—Idiom. 5. till one is blue in the face,** unsuccessfully for a long time: *to argue till one is blue in the face.* **6. out of the blue,** suddenly and unexpectedly: *Out of the blue, she inherited a fortune.* See BLUES.

blue•ber•ry /'bluw,bɛriy, -bəriy/ *n.* [*count*], *pl.* **-ries.** a bluish berry that can be eaten.

blue•bird /'bluw,bɜrd/ *n.* [*count*] a North American songbird.

'blue-'collar, *adj.* [*often: before a noun*] of or relating to manual laborers. Compare WHITE-COLLAR.

blue•grass /'bluw,græs/ *n.* [*noncount*] a kind of country music played on the banjo, fiddle, guitar, and bass.

'blue ,jay, *n.* [*count*] a bird of E North America.

'blue ,jeans, *n.* [*plural*] trousers made of blue denim.

blue•print /'bluw,prɪnt/ *n.* [*count*] a photographic print made up of white lines on a blue background, used chiefly for architectural or mechanical designs.

blues /bluwz/ *n.* **1. the blues,** [*noncount; used with a plural verb*] sadness: *I usually get the blues after the holidays.* **2.** [*noncount; used with a singular or plural verb*] a type of slow, sad, black folk music.

bluff /blʌf/ *v.* **1.** to deceive (someone) by pre-

tending to be stronger, cleverer, etc. than one is: [~ + *obj*]: *Don't try to bluff me; I know all your tricks.* [*no obj*]: *He's bluffing; I'm sure he can't overrule you.* —*n.* [*count*] [*noncount*] **2.** an act of bluffing.

blun•der /'blʌndər/ *n.* [*count*] **1.** a stupid or careless mistake: *His first blunder was to make fun of the teacher's name.* —*v.* [*no obj*] **2.** to move or act clumsily or stupidly. **3.** to make a careless or stupid mistake.

blunt /blʌnt/ *adj.,* **-er, -est,** *v.* —*adj.* **1.** having an edge or point that is not sharp: *a blunt pencil.* **2.** without politeness: *He asked blunt questions about my son.* —*v.* [*no obj*] [~ + *obj*] **3.** to (cause to) become blunt. **—'blunt•ly,** *adv.* —'blunt•ness, *n.* [*noncount*]

blur /blɜr/ *v.,* **blurred, blur•ring,** *n.* —*v.* **1.** to (cause to) become hard to see or hear: [*no obj*]: *Her eyes blurred with tears. His speech blurred the more he drank.* [~ + *obj*]: *The fog blurred the outline of the car.* —*n.* [*count; usually singular*] **2.** something that cannot be seen or remembered clearly: *The ship was a blur on the horizon. Parts of the trip were just a blur.* —'blur•ry, *adj.,* -i•er, -i•est.

blurb /blɜrb/ *n.* [*count*] a brief description of the contents of a book.

blurt /blɜrt/ *v.* [~ + *obj*] to say (something) suddenly without thinking: *He blurted (out) the secret. He blurted the secret (out).*

blush /blʌʃ/ *v.* [*no obj*] **1.** to become red in the face, as from embarrassment. —*n.* [*count; usually singular*] **2.** a reddening of the face.

blus•ter /'blʌstər/ *v.* [*no obj*] **1.** (of wind) to blow roughly. **2.** to make loud but empty threats: *He blustered about how he would beat me up.* —*n.* [*noncount*] **3.** loud noise and violence: *the bluster of a storm at sea.* **4.** noisy, empty threats: *That's just bluster; he won't fire you.* —'blus•ter•y, *adj.*

B.O., an abbreviation of: *Informal.* body odor.

bo•a /'bowə/ *n.* [*count*], *pl.* **bo•as.** a non poisonous tropical snake that kills its victims by crushing them.

boar /bɔr/ *n.* [*count*] **1.** a male pig kept for breeding. **2.** a wild pig.

board /bɔrd/ *n.* **1.** [*count*] a long, thin, flat piece of wood. **2.** [*count*] a flat piece of hard material used for a special purpose: *Write your sentence on the board* (= *a blackboard*). **3.** [*count*] a piece of wood, cardboard, etc., on which a game is played: *a chess board.* **4.** [*count*] an official group that directs an activity: *the company's board of directors.* **5.** [*noncount*] the cost of daily meals: *How much is room and board at that hotel?* —*v.* **6.** [*no obj*] [~ + *obj*] to supply or take meals and lodging at a fixed price. **7.** [*no obj*] [~ + *obj*] to go on board (of a ship, etc.). **8. board up** or **over,** to cover with boards: *to board up the old house* or *to board the old house up.* **—Idiom. 9. across the board,** applying to all equally: *to raise salaries across the board.* **10. on board,** on or in a ship, or other vehicle.

board•er /'bɔrdər/ *n.* [*count*] **1.** a person who pays to live and receive regular meals at someone's house. **2.** a pupil at a boarding school.

'boarding ,school, *n.* [*count*] a school at which pupils live as well as receive an education (distinguished from *day school*).

board•walk /'bɔrd,wɔk/ *n.* [*count*] a footpath made of boards.

boast /bowst/ *v.* **1.** [*no obj*] to speak too proudly, esp. about oneself: *He was always boast-*

ing. **2.** [~ + *obj*] to be lucky to possess: *The town boasts two new schools.* —*n.* [*count*] **3.** a cause for pride. **4.** an expression of self-praise. —'**boast•ful,** *adj.* —'**boast•ful•ly,** *adv.*

boat /bowt/ *n.* [*count*] **1.** a vessel for traveling by water. —*Idiom.* **2. in the same boat,** in the same difficult circumstances: *We're all in the same boat, so we should work together.* **3. miss the boat,** *Informal.* to fail to take advantage of an opportunity: *He missed the boat when he applied too late.*

bob[1] /bɒb/ *n., v.,* **bobbed, bob•bing.** —*n.* [*count*] **1.** a short, jerky motion: *A bob of her head told me she had noticed me.* —*v.* **2.** to move (something) quickly down and up: [~ + *obj*]: *She bobbed her head.* [*no obj*]: *The stick bobbed up and down in the water.*

bob[2] /bɒb/ *n., v.,* **bobbed, bob•bing.** —*n.* [*count*] **1.** a short, caplike haircut. —*v.* [~ + *obj*] **2.** to cut (hair) short: *to bob one's hair.*

bob•bin /'bɒbɪn/ *n.* [*count*] a round object upon which thread is wound.

bob•sled /'bɒb,slɛd/ *n.* [*count*] a long sled for two or four riders for racing down a snowy slope.

bode[1] /bowd/ *v.* [~ + *well/ill/evil* + *for*] **bod•ed, bod•ing.** to be a sign of things in the future: *The new job bodes well for his future.*

bode[2] /bowd/ *v.* a pt. of BIDE.

bod•i•ly /'bɒdliy/ *adj.* [*before a noun*] of or relating to the body: *bodily injuries.*

bod•y /'bɒdiy/ *n.* [*count*], *pl.* **bod•ies. 1. a.** the complete structure of a person or animal. **b.** a corpse: *The body was cremated.* **2.** the main part of a thing: *the body of a car.* **3.** a large amount of something: *a body of water.* **4.** a group or organization: *the student body.*

bod•y•build•ing or **bod•y-build•ing** /'bɒd,iy bɪldɪŋ/ *n.* [*noncount*] the developing of muscles through lifting weights.

bod•y•guard /'bɒdiy,gard/ *n.* [*count*] a person hired to guard another person.

'**body ,piercing,** *n.* [*count*] the piercing of a part of the body, such as the navel or the nose, in order to insert a metal ring or other ornament.

bog /bɒg, bɔg/ *n., v.,* **bogged, bog•ging.** —*n.* [*count*] **1.** an area of soft, wet ground. —*v.* **2. bog down,** to sink in or as if in a bog: *The truck bogged down in the snow. The slow computer bogged us down.* —'**bog•gy,** *adj.,* **-gi•er, -gi•est.**

bog•gle /'bɒgəl/ *v.* [~ + *obj*] [*no obj*], **-gled, -gling.** to (cause the mind to) be overwhelmed: *Vast distances boggle the mind.*

bo•gus /'bowgəs/ *adj.* false; not real: *The thief gave a bogus address.*

boil[1] /bɔyl/ *v.* **1.** to heat a liquid to the temperature at which it changes to steam: *When the water boils, turn off the heat.* [~ + *obj*]: *Boil some water for tea.* **2.** to cook (something) in boiling water: [*no obj*]: *The eggs boiled for three minutes.* [~ + *obj*]: *Boil the eggs for three minutes.* **3.** [*no obj*] to be very upset: *boiling with anger.* **4. boil down to,** to be equal to: *His statement boils down to a failure to support you.* —*n.* [*count; singular*] **5.** the act or state of boiling: *Bring the water to a boil.*

boil[2] /bɔyl/ *n.* [*count*] a painful swelling on the skin.

boil•er /'bɔylər/ *n.* [*count*] a container in which water is heated to make steam: *Call the landlord; the boiler is broken again.*

bois•ter•ous /'bɔystərəs, -strəs/ *adj.* rough and noisy: *boisterous laughter.*

bold /bowld/ *adj.,* **-er, -est. 1.** not afraid of danger. **2.** inventive or imaginative: *a bold solution to a troubling problem.* **3.** striking to the eye; very noticeable: *a shirt with a bold pattern.* —'**bold•ly,** *adv.* —'**bold•ness,** *n.* [*noncount*]

bo•lo•gna /bə'lowniy, -nə/ *n.* [*noncount*] a sausage made of beef and pork.

bol•ster /'bowlstər/ *n.* [*count*] **1.** a long, tube-shaped pillow. —*v.* [~ + *obj*] **2.** to add to; support: *They bolstered their claim with new evidence.*

bolt /bowlt/ *n.* [*count*] **1.** a strong screw used with a nut to hold things together. **2.** the part of a lock moved back by the action of the key. **3.** a sudden escape: *The thief made a quick bolt.* —*v.* **4.** [~ + *obj*] to fasten with a bolt: *He bolted the shelf to the wall.* **5.** [*no obj*] to run away quickly: *He bolted from the room.*

bomb /bɒm/ *n.* [*count*] **1.** a container filled with explosives. —*v.* **2.** [~ + *obj*] to attack with bombs. **3.** [*no obj*] *Slang.* to fail completely: *The play bombed in Boston.*

bom•bard /bɒm'bard, bəm-/ *v.* [~ + *obj*] **1.** to attack with bombs or gunfire. **2.** to attack verbally: *Reporters bombarded the candidate with questions.* —**bombardment,** *n.* [*noncount*] [*count*]

bomb•er /'bɒmər/ *n.* [*count*] **1.** an airplane that drops bombs. **2.** a person who puts bombs in buildings and other places.

bomb•shell /'bɒm,ʃɛl/ *n.* [*count*] a great surprise or shock: *His resignation came as a bombshell.*

bo•na fide or **bo•na-fide** /'bownə,fayd/ *adj.* genuine; real: *a bona fide work of art.*

bo•nan•za /bə'nænzə, bow-/ *n.* [*count*], *pl.* **-zas.** a source of great and sudden wealth or luck: *a bonanza for the gold miners.*

bond /bɒnd/ *n.* [*count*] **1.** something that holds together: *This glue creates a strong bond.* **2.** a feeling that unites one person to another: *the bond of friendship.* **3.** an agreement in which a government or business promises to pay back with interest money that has been loaned. —*v.* **4.** [*no obj*] [~ + *obj*] to join together (two materials). **5.** [*no obj*] to establish an emotional tie: *The baby and its mother bonded.*

bond•age /'bɒndɪdʒ/ *n.* [*noncount*] slavery.

bonds /bɒndz/ *n.* [*plural*] chains or ropes used to tie up a prisoner.

bone /bown/ *n., v.,* **boned, bon•ing.** —*n.* **1.** [*count*] one of the parts of the skeleton of an animal's body: *He broke a bone in his arm.* **2. bones,** [*plural*] **a.** the skeleton. **b.** a body: *to rest one's weary bones.* —*v.* [~ + *obj*] **3.** to remove the bones from: *to bone a fish.* —*Idiom.* **4. feel in one's bones,** to be sure of something without knowing why: *I'm not going to get this job; I can feel it in my bones.* **5. have a bone to pick with someone,** to have a reason for arguing with someone: *I have a bone to pick with you: Why were you late?* **6. make no bones about,** to act or speak openly: *She made no bones about her dislike for her boss.*

bon•fire /'bɒn,fayᵊr/ *n.* [*count*] a large outdoor fire: *a big bonfire to celebrate our victory.*

bon•go /'bɒŋgow, 'bɔŋ-/ *n.* [*count*], *pl.* **-gos, -goes.** one of a pair of small drums, played by beating with the fingers.

bon•net /'bɒnɪt/ *n.* [*count*] **1.** a hat tying under the chin. **2.** *Brit.* an automobile hood.

bo•nus /'bownəs/ *n.* [*count*], *pl.* **-nus•es.** pay-

B

human body

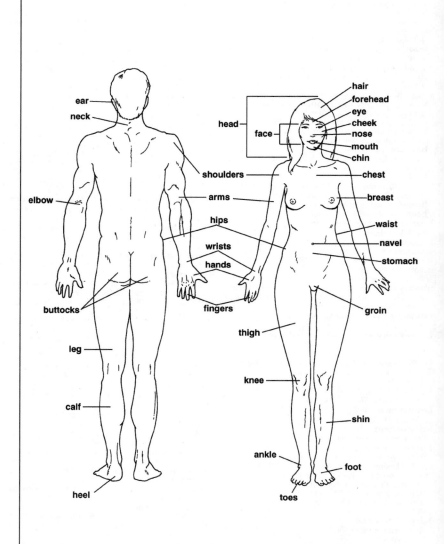

ment that is more than what is usual: *All workers received a Christmas bonus.*

bon•y /'bowniy/ *adj.*, **-i•er, -i•est. 1.** full of bones: *This fish is very bony.* **2.** very thin; having bones that can be clearly seen.

boo /buw/ *interj.* **1.** (used to express disapproval or to frighten): *"Boo! Did I scare you?" she asked.* —*v.* **2.** to cry "boo" (at someone): [*no obj*]: *The fans booed when their team lost again.* [~ + *obj*]: *The audience booed the bad singer.*

'boo•by ,prize /'buwbiy/ *n.* [*count*] a prize given as a joke to the one who comes in last in a game.

'booby ,trap, *n.* [*count*] a hidden bomb that explodes when a seemingly harmless object is touched.

book /bʊk/ *n.* [*count*] **1.** a work printed on sheets of paper bound together within covers: *a book of poems.* **2.** a set of similar things bound together like a book: *a book of stamps.* **3.** a division of a literary work: *the books of the Bible.* **4. books,** [*plural*] the financial records of a business. —*v.* [~ + *obj*] **5.** to write down the name of after being arrested: *The police booked him for murder.* **6.** to make a reservation for (a hotel room, plane trip, etc.): *We booked a flight to New York.* —**Idiom. 7. by the book,** according to the rules. **8. know** or **read like a book,** to know or understand (someone or something) completely: *He knew the city like a book.*

book•case /'bʊk,keys/ *n.* [*count*] a set of shelves for books.

book•end /'bʊk,end/ *n.* [*count*] a support placed at each end to hold up a row of books.

book•ie /'bʊkiy/ *n.* BOOKMAKER.

book•ing /'bʊkɪŋ/ *n.* RESERVATION: *Please confirm our booking for flight 270.*

book•keep•ing /'bʊk,kiypɪŋ/ *n.* [*noncount*] the system or occupation of keeping business accounts. —'**book,keep•er,** *n.* [*count*]

book•let /'bʊklɪt/ *n.* [*count*] a little book with paper covers.

book•mak•er /'bʊk,meykər/ *n.* [*count*] a person who accepts the bets of others on sports contests, esp. illegally.

book•mark /'bʊk,mɑrk/ *n.* [*count*] something put between the pages of a book to mark one's place.

book•shelf /'bʊk,ʃelf/ *n.* [*count*], *pl.* **-shelves.** a shelf for holding books.

book•store /'bʊk,stɔr/ *n.* [*count*] a store that sells books. Also called **book•shop** /'bʊk,ʃɒp/.

book•worm /'bʊk,wɜrm/ *n.* [*count*] a person who greatly enjoys reading.

boom¹ /buwm/ *v.* [*no obj*] **1.** to make a deep, hollow sound: *The cannons boomed.* **2.** to say with a booming voice: *"Back inside!" he boomed as the tornado struck.* **3.** to grow quickly and strongly: *Business is booming.* —*n.* [*count*] **4.** a deep, hollow sound: *the boom of the battleship's guns.* **5.** a rapid growth or increase: *a housing boom.*

boom² /buwm/ *n.* [*count*] a pole sticking out from a ship's mast and used to extend sails, handle cargo, etc.

boo•mer•ang /'buwmə,ræŋ/ *n.* [*count*] a curved piece of wood that will return after being thrown, used as a weapon.

boon /buwn/ *n.* [*count; usually singular*] something to be thankful for: *The lower fares are a boon to students.*

boost /buwst/ *v.* [~ + *obj*] **1.** to lift by pushing from below: *I boosted the baby into his highchair.*

2. to increase; raise: *to boost prices.* —*n.* [*count*] **3.** an upward shove or lift. **4.** an increase; rise. **5.** an act or remark that makes one feel good: *The praise from the coach gave the team a boost.*

boost•er /'buwstər/ *n.* [*count*] **1.** an enthusiastic supporter. **2.** Also called **boost′er shot′.** a dose of a medicine given to maintain the effect of a previous one.

boot /buwt/ *n.* [*count*] **1.** a strong, heavy shoe: *hiking boots.* **2.** *Brit.* the trunk of an automobile. —*v.* [~ + *obj*] **3.** to kick; move by kicking: *He booted the ball across the field.* **4.** to start (a computer) by loading the operating system.

booth /buwθ/ *n.* [*count*], *pl.* **booths** /buwðz, buwθs/. **1.** a stall or small tent for the sale or display of goods. **2.** a small compartment big enough for one person: *a telephone booth.* **3.** a partly enclosed place in a restaurant with a table between two long seats.

boo•ty /'buwtiy/ *n.* [*noncount*] valuable things taken by thieves or from an enemy in war.

bop /bɒp/ *v.*, **bopped, bop•ping,** *n. Slang.* —*v.* [~ + *obj*] **1.** to strike; hit. —*n.* [*count*] **2.** a blow: *a bop on the head.*

bor•der /'bɔrdər/ *n.* [*count*] **1.** edge: *a book with a red cover and a black border.* **2.** the line that separates one country from another. —*v.* [~ + *obj*] **3.** to form a border along: *Tall trees bordered the road.* **4.** to share a border (with): *The United States borders Canada.* **5. border on,** to be almost the same as: *This ridiculous situation borders on comedy.*

bor•der•line /'bɔrdər,layn/ *n.* [*count*] a boundary line; something marking a division.

bore¹ /bɔr/ *v.*, **bored, bor•ing,** *n.* —*v.* **1.** to pierce (a solid substance) with a drill: [~ + *obj*]: *He bored a hole into the wall.* [*no obj*]: *He bored through the walls.* —*n.* [*after a number*] **2.** the inside diameter of a hollow round object, such as a gun barrel.

bore² /bɔr/ *v.*, **bored, bor•ing,** *n.* —*v.* [~ + *obj*] **1.** to make (someone) tired and uninterested: *The long speech bored me.* —*n.* [*count*] **2.** an uninteresting person or thing: *She's such a bore. The play was a bore.* —'**bore•dom,** *n.* [*noncount*]

bore³ /bɔr/ *v.* a pt. of BEAR¹.

born /bɔrn/ *adj.* **1.** [*be* + ~] brought into existence: *She was born on October 27. That's when the idea was born.* **2.** [*before a noun*] having a natural ability: *a born musician.* **3.** a pp. of BEAR¹.

borne /bɔrn/ *v.* a pp. of BEAR¹.

bor•ough /'bɜrow, 'bʌrow/ *n.* [*count*] **1.** (in certain U.S. states) a self-governing town. **2.** one of the five counties of New York City: *the borough of Brooklyn.* **3.** (in Great Britain) a self-governing urban community.

bor•row /'bɒrow, 'bɔrow/ *v.* **1.** [~ + *obj*] [*no obj*] to take or get (something) with a promise to return it. **2.** [~ + *obj*] to adopt as one's own: *English borrowed many words from French.* —'**bor•row•er,** *n.* [*count*] —**Usage.** Do not confuse BORROW and LEND. One way to keep the meanings distinct is to think of BORROW as "take," while LEND is "give." So you can *borrow* something you don't have, and you can *lend* something you do have.

bos•om /'bʊzəm, 'buwzəm/ *n.* [*count*] the chest of a human being, esp. a woman's breasts.

boss /bɔs, bɒs/ *n.* [*count*] **1.** a person who is in charge: *I asked my boss if I could leave early. Who's the boss in this house?* —*v.* [~ + *obj*] **2.** to control; give orders.

B

boss•y /'bɔsiy, 'bɒsiy/ *adj.*, **-i•er, -i•est.** given to ordering people about.

bot•a•ny /'bɒtṇiy/ *n.* [*noncount*] the scientific study of plants. —**bo'tan•i•cal,** *adj.* —'**bot•a•nist,** *n.* [*count*]

botch /bɒtʃ/ *v.* to spoil by poor or clumsy work: [~ + *obj*]: *He botched the job interview.* [~ + *up* + *obj*]: *He botched up the job* or *He botched the job up.* [*no obj*]: *He always botches up.*

both /bowθ/ *adj.* [*before a noun*] **1.** [~ + (*the* +) *plural noun*] one and the other; two together: *I met both sisters. I met both the sisters.* —*pron.* **2.** the one as well as the other: *Both were ill.* [~ + *of*]: *Both of us were ill.* **3.** alike; equally: *I can speak both English and Russian.*

both•er /'bɒðər/ *v.* **1.** [~ + *obj*] to give trouble to; annoy or worry: *Noise bothers me.* **2.** [*no obj*] to take the trouble: *Don't bother with her. Don't bother to call. Should I bother finishing this book?* —*n.* [*noncount*] **3.** trouble or inconvenience: *Gardening takes more bother than it's worth.*

both•er•some /'bɒðərsəm/ *adj.* causing worry: *a bothersome problem.*

bot•tle /'bɒtḷ/ *n.*, *v.*, **-tled, -tling.** —*n.* [*count*] **1.** a container for holding liquids, having a narrow neck. **2.** the contents of a bottle: *He drank a whole bottle of wine.* —*v.* **3.** [~ + *obj*] to put into a bottle: *to bottle grape juice.* **4. bottle up,** to hold in; control: *to bottle up your anger* or *to bottle your anger up.* —*Idiom.* **5. hit the bottle,** *Slang.* to drink alcohol to excess.

bot•tle•neck /'bɒtḷˌnɛk/ *n.* [*count*] **1.** a narrow space in a road that slows down traffic. **2.** a stage at which progress is slowed: *They hit a bottleneck in preparing the business plan.*

bot•tom /'bɒtəm/ *n.* [*count; usually: the* + ~] **1.** the lowest or deepest part of anything: *the bottom of a page.* **2.** the under or lower side: *the bottom of a vase.* **3.** the far end: *the house at the bottom of the road.* **4.** *Informal.* the buttocks. —*adj.* [*before a noun*] **5.** of or at the bottom: *the bottom floor.* —*Idiom.* **6. bet one's bottom dollar,** to be completely certain: *You can bet your bottom dollar I'll be on time.* **7. from the bottom of one's heart,** very sincerely: *Thank you from the bottom of my heart.* **8. get to the bottom of,** to determine the cause of: *to get to the bottom of this mystery.*

bough /baw/ *n.* [*count*] a large branch of a tree.

bought /bɔt/ *v.* a pt. and pp. of BUY.

boul•der /'bowldər/ *n.* [*count*] a large rock.

boul•e•vard /'bʊləˌvard/ *n.* [*count*] a broad street, often with trees on each side.

bounce /bawns/ *v.*, **bounced, bounc•ing,** *n.* —*v.* **1.** to (cause to) strike something hard and spring back: [*no obj*]: *The box bounced down the stairs.* [~ + *off* + *obj*]: *The ball bounced off the wall.* [~ + *obj*]: *He bounced the ball.* **2.** [*no obj*] to move or walk in a lively way: *She bounced out of the room.* **3.** [*no obj*] (of a bank check) to be refused payment by a bank because there is not enough money in one's account. **4. bounce back,** to recover quickly: *She bounced back from the flu.* —*n.* **5.** [*count*] the act or action of bouncing. **6.** [*noncount*] energy; liveliness: *He had a bounce in his step after the good news.* —'**bounc•y,** *adj.*, **-i•er, -i•est.**

bound¹ /bawnd/ *v.* **1.** a pt. and pp. of BIND. —*adj.* **2.** fastened as if by a bond. **3.** fastened within a cover: *a bound book.* **4.** under an obligation: [*usually: be* + ~]: *Even the police are bound by laws.* [~ + *to* + *verb*]: *I felt bound to tell you what they say about you.* **5.** certain; sure:

[*be* + ~ + *to* + *verb*]: *He's so fast he's bound to win the race.* [*It* + *be* + ~ + *to* + *verb*]: *It is bound to happen.*

bound² /bawnd/ *v.* [*no obj*] **1.** to move by leaps; jump: *He bounded out the door.* —*n.* [*count*] **2.** a leap; jump: *With a single bound, he was over the fence.*

bound³ /bawnd/ *n.* [*count*] **1.** Usually, **bounds.** [*plural*] limit or boundary: *within the bounds of reason.* —*v.* [*usually: be* + *bounded by*] **2.** to limit by or as if by bounds: *Spain is bounded on the east by Portugal.* —*Idiom.* **3. out of bounds,** beyond or past official boundaries: *She threw the ball out of bounds.*

bound⁴ /bawnd/ *adj.* [*be* + ~ + *for*] going or intending to go: *I'm bound for Denver.*

bound•a•ry /'bawndəriy, -driy/ *n.* [*count*], *pl.* **-ries.** something that marks a limit: *The river forms a boundary between the two countries.*

boun•ti•ful /'bawntəfəl/ *adj.* abundant; plentiful: *a bountiful harvest.*

boun•ty /'bawntiy/ *n.*, *pl.* **-ties. 1.** [*count*] money given as a reward: *The bounty for a captured snake is $50.00.* **2.** [*noncount*] generosity: *She is noted for her bounty to the arts.*

bou•quet /bow'key, buw-/ *n.* [*count*] a bunch of flowers: *a bouquet of roses.*

bour•bon /'bɜrbən/ *n.* [*noncount*] Also called '**bourbon 'whiskey.** a type of whiskey.

bout /bawt/ *n.* [*count*] **1.** a contest, as of boxing; match. **2.** a short period: *a bout of illness.*

bou•tique /buw'tiyk/ *n.* [*count*] a small shop, esp. one that sells fashionable items.

bo•vine /'bowvayn, -viyn/ *adj.* [*before a noun*] of or relating to a cow or ox.

bow¹ /baw/ *v.* **1.** [*no obj*] [~ + *obj*] to bend the knee, body, or head to show respect or to greet. **2.** to bend or curve downward: [*no obj*]: *The pines bowed low in the storm.* [~ + *obj*]: *The heavy snow bowed the trees down low.* **3.** [~ + *to* + *obj*] to (cause to) give in or yield; to (cause to) submit: *You'll have to bow to your father's wishes.* **4. bow out,** to stop doing something: *He bowed out of the presidential campaign.* —*n.* [*count*] **5.** a downward movement of the head or body in respect, thanks, etc.: *She made a short bow after the play.*

bow² /bow/ *n.* [*count*] **1.** a piece of wood bent by a string stretched between its ends and used for shooting arrows: *He went hunting with a bow and arrow.* **2.** an easily loosened knot for joining the ends of a ribbon or string: *She wore a pretty bow in her hair.* **3.** a flexible rod used for playing a musical instrument like a violin.

bow³ /baw/ *n.* [*count*] the front end of a ship or airplane.

bow•el /'bawəl, bawl/ *n.* [*count*] **1.** Usually, **bowels.** [*plural*] the intestine. **2. bowels,** [*plural*] the inside parts: *The silver mine was deep in the bowels of the earth.*

'**bowel ,movement,** *n.* [*count*] the sending of waste matter out through the bowels.

bowl¹ /bowl/ *n.* [*count*] **1.** a deep, round dish for food or liquids. **2.** a rounded, hollow part: *the bowl of a pipe.*

bowl² /bowl/ *v.* **1.** [*no obj*] to play at bowling: *He likes to bowl* (or *go bowling*) *on Saturday night.* **2. bowl over, a.** to surprise greatly: *That news really bowled us over. The news really bowled over her friends.* **b.** to knock down by crashing into: *He nearly bowled us over as he rushed out.*

bow•leg•ged /'bow,lɛgɪd, -,lɛgd/ *adj.* having

the legs curved outward at the knees: *He had become bowlegged after riding horses for years.*

bowl•er /'bowlər/ *n.* [*count*] a man's hard, round hat.

bowl•ing /'bowlɪŋ/ *n.* [*noncount*] a game in which players roll balls at standing objects.

'bow 'tie /bow/ *n.* [*count*] a small necktie tied in a bow at the collar.

box[1] /bɒks/ *n.* [*count*] **1.** a container with stiff sides and often with a lid: *They put their books in boxes.* **2.** a partly enclosed area in a theater in which a few people can watch a performance. **3.** a small enclosed area: *a sentry's box.* —*v.* [~ + obj] **4.** to put into a box: *The apples were boxed and shipped.*

box[2] /bɒks/ *v.* [~ + obj] [*no obj*] to fight against (someone) in a boxing match.

box•car /'bɒks,kɑr/ *n.* [*count*] a completely enclosed railroad freight car.

box•er /'bɒksər/ *n.* [*count*] **1.** a person who fights or boxes as a sport. **2.** a German breed of medium-sized, shorthaired dogs.

box•ing /'bɒksɪŋ/ *n.* [*noncount*] the act or profession of fighting with the fists.

'box ,office, *n.* [*count*] the office of a theater, etc., at which tickets are sold.

boy /bɔy/ *n.* [*count*] **1.** a male child. **2.** *Informal.* a grown man, esp. when referred to familiarly: *I think the boys in the lab need a vacation.* —*interj.* **3.** (used to show wonder or approval or worry, displeasure, or contempt): *Boy! Just look at that!*

boy•cott /'bɔykɒt/ *v.* [~ + obj] **1.** to refuse to do business with or take part in: *The neighborhood boycotted the overpriced supermarket.* —*n.* [*count*] **2.** an instance of boycotting: *a lettuce boycott.*

boy•friend /'bɔy,frɛnd/ *n.* [*count*] **1.** a frequent or favorite male companion or lover. **2.** a male friend.

boy•ish /'bɔyɪʃ/ *adj.* of or like a boy; youthful: *a cute, boyish smile.* —**'boy•ish•ness,** *n.* [*noncount*]

'boy ,scout, *n.* [*count; sometimes: Boy Scout*] a member of an organization of boys (**'Boy ,Scouts,**) whose goal is the development of character.

bra /brɑ/ *n.* [*count*] a woman's undergarment, worn to support the breasts.

brace /breys/ *n., v.,* **braced, brac•ing.** —*n.* [*count*] **1.** something that holds parts in place or makes something stronger: *He nailed in a brace to support the wall.* **2.** Usually, **braces.** [*plural*] a set of wires used to straighten crooked teeth. **3.** a device worn to support a weak part of a person's body: *He wears a back brace.* —*v.* [~ + obj] **4.** to strengthen with a brace: *He braced the sagging wall with a piece of wood.* **5.** [~ + *oneself*] to prepare (oneself) for something unpleasant: *She braced herself for the crash.*

brace•let /'breyslɪt/ *n.* [*count*] an ornamental band for the wrist, arm, or ankle.

brack•et /'brækɪt/ *n.* [*count*] **1.** a supporting piece sticking out from a wall to support a shelf, etc. **2.** Also called **square bracket.** one of two marks, [or], used in writing to enclose information that is not essential. **3.** a group sharing a particular quality: *His raise puts him in a higher tax bracket.* —*v.* [~ + obj] **4.** to support with a bracket. **5.** to place (words, etc.) within brackets. **6.** to group in a class together.

brag /bræg/ *v.,* **bragged, brag•ging.** to boast; to say something in a proud way: [*no obj*]: *She's al-*ways bragging about her wonderful children. [~ + obj]: *He bragged that he had shot a lion.* —**'brag•gart,** *n.* [*count*]

braid /breyd/ *v.* [~ + obj] **1.** to weave together three or more strands of (hair, etc.): *She braided her hair.* —*n.* [*count*] **2.** a braided length, esp. of hair.

Braille /breyl/ *n.* [*noncount; often: braille*] a system of printing with raised dots, used by blind people.

brain /breyn/ *n.* [*count*] **1.** the nerve tissue in the head that is the center of the nervous system. **2.** Sometimes, **brains.** intelligence: *He has a good brain for math.* **3.** *Informal.* an extremely intelligent person: *She's a real brain in chemistry.* —*Idiom.* **4. pick someone's brains,** to get information by questioning another person.

brain•storm /'breyn,stɔrm/ *n.* [*count*] a sudden clever idea: *She suddenly got a brainstorm that solved the problem.*

brain•wash /'breyn,wɒʃ, -,wɔʃ/ *v.* [~ + obj] to cause (someone) to obey or change beliefs by very forceful techniques: *The enemy brainwashed all the prisoners.*

brain•y /'breyniy/ *adj.,* **-i•er, -i•est.** *Informal.* very intelligent.

braise /breyz/ *v.* [~ + obj], **braised, brais•ing.** to cook (food) by frying quickly in fat and then simmering in liquid in a covered pot.

brake /breyk/ *n., v.,* **braked, brak•ing.** —*n.* [*count*] **1.** a device for slowing or stopping movement. **2.** anything that has a slowing or stopping effect. —*v.* [~ + obj] [*no obj*] **3.** to slow or stop by or as if by a brake.

bram•ble /'bræmbəl/ *n.* [*count*] a prickly shrub.

bran /bræn/ *n.* [*noncount*] the flakes that are left when grain is ground up.

branch /bræntʃ/ *n.* [*count*] **1.** an armlike division of the stem of a tree or shrub. **2.** a division of a main system: *a branch of a bank; a branch of knowledge.* —*v.* [*no obj*] **3.** [~ + off] to divide into separate parts: *The road branches off to the left.* **4. branch out,** to expand in new directions: *The company branched out into electronics.*

brand /brænd/ *n.* [*count*] **1.** a particular kind or make of a product: *the best brand of coffee.* **2.** a mark made by burning, to show kind, ownership, etc. **3.** a particular kind: *an unfunny brand of humor.* —*v.* [~ + obj] **4.** to mark with a brand: *The cowboys branded the calf.* **5.** to label (someone) as being or having done something shameful: *He was branded as a thief.*

bran•dish /'brændɪʃ/ *v.* [~ + obj] to wave (something), esp. in a threatening way: *The robber brandished a gun.*

brand-new /'bræn'nuw, -'nyuw, 'brænd-/ *adj.* entirely new.

bran•dy /'brændiy/ *n.* [*noncount*] [*count*], *pl.* **-dies.** an alcoholic drink usually made from wine.

brash /bræʃ/ *adj.,* **-er, -est. 1.** impolite or rude: *a brash young man.* **2.** hasty or rash: *a brash decision.*

brass /bræs/ *n.* [*noncount*] **1.** a bright yellow metal, a mixture of copper and zinc. **2. the brass,** [*used with a plural verb*] musical instruments made of brass. **3. the brass,** [*used with a plural verb*] high-ranking military officers: *You'd better ask the brass about that first.*

bras•siere or **bras•sière** /brə'zɪər/ *n.* [*count*] BRA.

brat /bræt/ *n.* [*count*] a badly behaved child. —**'brat•ty,** *adj.,* **-ti•er, -ti•est.**

B

bra•va•do /brə'vɑdow/ n. [noncount] an overly showy, often false display of courage: He tried to answer his accusers with bravado.

brave /breyv/ adj., **brav•er, brav•est,** n., v., **braved, brav•ing. —adj. 1.** not afraid of danger: The brave soldier rescued his wounded friend. **—**n. [count] **2.** a warrior, esp. among North American Indians. **—**v. [~ + obj] **3.** to face with courage: She braved her father's anger. —'**brave•ly,** adv. —'**brav•er•y,** n. [noncount]

bra•vo /'brɑvow, brɑ'vow/ interj., n., pl. **-vos.** **—**interj. **1.** (used to praise a performer). **—**n. [count] **2.** a shout of "bravo!": The bravos rang out for the tenor.

brawl /brɔl/ n. [count] **1.** a noisy fight. **—**v. [no obj] **2.** to fight noisily: The demonstrators brawled in the street.

brawn /brɔn/ n. [noncount] muscular strength: It was a case of brains winning out over brawn. —'**brawn•y,** adj., **-i•er, -i•est.**

bray /brey/ n. [count] **1.** the loud cry of a donkey. **2.** any similar sound. **—**v. **3.** to utter a bray: [no obj]: The donkey brayed. [~ + obj]: He brayed a warning.

bra•zen /'breyzən/ adj. bold and shameless: brazen disrespect. —'**bra•zen•ly,** adv. —'**bra•zen• ness,** n. [noncount]

Bra•zil•ian /brə'zɪlyən/ n. [count] **1.** a person born or living in Brazil. **—**adj. **2.** of or relating to Brazil.

breach /briytʃ/ n. **1.** [count] [noncount] an act of breaking a law or promise. **2.** [count] an opening or hole made in a wall, line of soldiers, etc.: a breach in our defenses. **3.** [count] a break in friendly relations: a breach in our friendship. **—**v. [~ + obj] **4.** to make an opening or hole in (defenses, etc.).

bread /brɛd/ n. [noncount] **1.** a baked food made of flour, water or milk, and yeast. **2.** Slang. money. **—**v. [~ + obj] **3.** to coat (meat, etc.) with breadcrumbs for cooking.

bread•crumb /'brɛd,krʌm/ n. [count; usually plural] a very small piece of bread.

breadth /brɛdθ, brɛtθ/ n. [noncount] **1.** the distance from side to side; width. **2.** the extent or range of something: the breadth of her knowledge.

bread•win•ner /'brɛd,wɪnər/ n. [count] a person who earns enough money to support someone.

break /breyk/ v., **broke** /browk/, **bro•ken** /'browkən/, **break•ing,** n. **—**v. **1.** to divide into parts violently: [~ + obj]: He broke the vase. [no obj]: The vase broke. **2.** to (cause to) stop working: [~ + obj]: I broke my watch. [no obj]: My watch broke. **3.** [~ + obj] to disobey or disregard (a law, promise, etc.). **4.** to interrupt (something): [~ + obj]: A scream broke the silence. [no obj]: Let's break for lunch. **5.** [~ + obj] to make a way through: The stone broke the surface of the water. **6.** [~ + obj] to better (a record): When he jumped over eight feet he broke the old record. **7.** [~ + obj] to train away from a habit: She tried to break him of his smoking habit. **8.** [no obj] (of the day or dawn) to grow light: Day was breaking. **9.** (to cause the heart) to be overwhelmed with sorrow: [no obj]: His heart broke. [~ + obj]: He broke her heart. **10.** [no obj] (of the voice) to waver or change tone abruptly: When she started to talk about the attack, her voice broke. When he turned fourteen his voice began to break. **11. break down, a.** to (cause to) stop working: The car broke down; to break down

her resistance or to break her resistance down. **b.** to separate into component parts: These proteins will break down in your stomach. Enzymes in your stomach break down proteins. **c.** to lose control over one's emotions: She broke down and cried. **12. break in, a.** to enter by force or unlawfully: The thief broke in yesterday. **b.** to train to a new situation: to break in a new assistant or to break in a new assistant in. **c.** to wear or use (something new) and thereby ease stiffness, tightness, etc.: to break in his new shoes; to break them in. **13. break out,** to begin suddenly: A fight broke out. **14. break up, a.** to (cause to) come to an end; discontinue: The cops broke up the fight. The lovers broke up. **b.** to (cause a personal relationship to) end: They decided to break up after five years. Their children didn't break up their marriage; to break it up. **—**n. [count] **15.** a brief rest: Let's take a break from studying. **16.** a piece of good luck: What a lucky break!

break•down /'breyk,dawn/ n. [count] **1.** an instance of failure: The car had another breakdown. **2.** a division into parts, etc.; analysis: a breakdown of the sales figures.

break•er /'breykər/ n. [count] a large wave that breaks into foam.

break•fast /'brɛkfəst/ n. [noncount] [count] **1.** the first meal of the day. **—**v. [no obj; (~ + on + obj)] **2.** to eat breakfast.

'break-,in, n. [count] an illegal act of entering a building by force.

break•through /'breyk,θruw/ n. [count] an important discovery, as in science, that will lead to more discoveries: a breakthrough in the treatment of cancer.

breast /brɛst/ n. [count] **1.** either of the two parts of a woman's chest that produce milk. **2.** the front part of the body from the neck to the waist; chest.

'breast-,feed, v. [~ + obj], **-fed, -feed•ing.** to feed (a baby) with milk from the breast.

breast•stroke /'brɛst,strowk, 'brɛs-/ n. [count] a swimming stroke done face down in the water, in which the arms pull backward.

breath /brɛθ/ n. **1.** [noncount; usually: one's + ~] the air taken into and sent out of the lungs: It's cold enough to see your breath. **2.** [count] a single act of taking in air and sending it out of the lungs: Take a deep breath. **3.** [noncount; usually: one's + ~] the ability to breathe easily and normally: I stopped to catch my breath. **4.** [count] a slight hint: a breath of scandal. **—Idiom. 5. below** or **under one's breath,** in a low voice or whisper. **6. hold one's breath,** to stop breathing for a short period of time. **7. out of breath,** breathless from exertion. **8. take one's breath away,** to make one as if breathless with astonishment: The beauty of the sea took my breath away.

breathe /briyð/ v., **breathed** /briyðd/. **breath•ing. 1.** to take (air, etc.) into the lungs and send (it) out: [no obj]: The patient began to breathe normally. [~ + obj]: Just breathe that pure mountain air! **2.** [~ + obj] to put in as if by breathing: She tried to breathe life into the party.

breath•er /'briyðər/ n. [count] a pause, as for breath; a break: "I need a breather," he puffed.

breath•less /'brɛθlɪs/ adj. **1.** without breath, or breathing with difficulty: breathless after running up five flights of stairs. **2.** causing loss of breath, as from excitement, fear, etc.: a breathless ride.

breath•tak•ing /'brɛθ,teykɪŋ/ adj. amazing; astonishing: a breathtaking view.

bred /brɛd/ v. a pt. and pp. of BREED.

breech•es /'brɪtʃɪz/ n. [plural] **1.** knee-length trousers. **2.** Informal. TROUSERS.

breed /briyd/ v., **bred** /brɛd/, **breed•ing,** n. —v. **1.** [no obj] to produce young: Mosquitoes breed in still ponds. **2.** [~ + obj] to cause (plants or animals) to produce improved offspring: They breed cattle. **3.** [~ + obj] to cause: Dirt breeds disease. —n. [count] **4.** a certain type of animal: What breed is your dog?

breed•ing /'briydɪŋ/ n. [noncount] the result of one's upbringing as shown in good manners: a woman of good breeding.

breeze /briyz/ n., v., **breezed, breez•ing.** —n. **1.** [count] a light, gentle wind. **2.** [count; usually singular] an easy task: That quiz was a breeze. —v. **3.** [no obj] to move in a carefree and confident manner: He breezed into the classroom and sat down. **4. breeze through,** to complete (work, etc.) quickly and easily: We breezed through the test. —**Idiom. 5. shoot the breeze,** Slang. to talk aimlessly: The two old men were shooting the breeze.

breez•y /'briyziy/ adj., **-i•er, -i•est. 1.** having many breezes: a breezy day at the beach. **2.** light; cheerful: a breezy style of writing.

brev•i•ty /'brɛvɪtiy/ n. [noncount] shortness (of speech, etc.): the brevity of life.

brew /bruw/ v. **1.** [~ + obj] [no obj] to make (beer, etc.) by fermenting the ingredients. **2.** [~ + obj] [no obj] to prepare (tea, etc.) with boiling water. **3.** [no obj; usually: be + ~ -ing] to begin: A storm is brewing in the Atlantic. —n. [count] **4.** a brewed beverage.

brew•er•y /'bruwəriy, 'bruriy/ n. [count], pl. **-er•ies.** a place where beer is made.

bri•ar /'brayər/ n. BRIER.

bribe /brayb/ n., v., **bribed, brib•ing.** —n. [count] **1.** money given to persuade someone to do something illegal: The customs official agreed to take a bribe. **2.** something given to persuade or influence someone: The children were given cookies as a bribe to be good. —v. [~ + obj] **3.** to give or promise a bribe to. —'**brib•er•y,** n. [noncount]

bric-a-brac or **bric-à-brac** /'brɪkə,bræk/ n. [noncount; used with a singular verb] [count; used as a plural with a plural verb] small decorations of little value.

brick /brɪk/ n. **1.** (a block of) baked clay used for building: [count]: He replaced the broken bricks. [noncount]: Our house is brick on the outside. —**Idiom. 2. like a ton of bricks,** with sudden force: The news hit him like a ton of bricks.

bride /brayd/ n. [count] a newly married woman or one about to be married. —'**brid•al,** adj.

bride•groom /'brayd,gruwm, -,grum/ n. [count] a newly married man or one about to be married.

brides•maid /'braydz,meyd/ n. [count] a woman who attends the bride at a wedding.

bridge[1] /brɪdʒ/ n., v., **bridged, bridg•ing.** —n. [count] **1.** a structure that reaches across a river, road, etc., and provides a way of crossing. **2.** the upper line of the nose between the eyes. **3.** an artificial replacement of missing teeth. —v. [~ + obj] **4.** to join by or as if by a bridge: to bridge a river; to bridge a cultural gap.

bridge[2] /brɪdʒ/ n. [noncount] a card game for two teams of two players each.

bri•dle /'braydl̩/ n., v., **-dled, -dling.** —n. [count] **1.** part of the harness of a horse that goes on its head. —v. **2.** [~ + obj] to put a bridle on: They bridled the horses. **3.** [~ + obj] to control

or hold back: You've got to bridle your temper. **4.** [no obj] to show contempt or anger by raising the head: He bridled at the suggestion that he get a job.

brief /briyf/ adj., **-er, -est,** n., v. —adj. **1.** lasting a short time: He took a brief nap. **2.** using few words: Write a brief outline. **3.** very small: a brief bathing suit. —n. [count] **4.** a short statement or a written item using few words: Please prepare a brief for the president. **5. briefs,** [plural] close-fitting legless underpants with an elastic waistband: a pair of briefs. —v. [~ + obj] **6.** to instruct (someone) or give necessary information to: I briefed the new teacher on the cafeteria rules. —'**brief•ly,** adv.

brief•case /'briyf,keys/ n. [count] a flat leather case for carrying books, papers, etc.

bri•er or **bri•ar** /'brayər/ n. [count] a prickly plant or shrub with thorny stems.

bri•gade /brɪ'geyd/ n. [count] **1.** a military unit. **2.** an organization for performing certain duties: a fire brigade.

bright /brayt/ adj., **-er, -est, 1.** giving off or reflecting light: a bright, sunny room. **2.** (of colors) strong: bright red. **3.** clever or smart: a bright idea. **4.** showing hope or signs of success: a bright future. —'**bright•ly,** adv. —'**bright•ness,** n. [noncount]

bright•en /'braytn̩/ v. [no obj] [~ + obj] to become or make bright or brighter.

bril•liant /'brɪlyənt/ adj. **1.** shining brightly: brilliant jewels. **2.** extremely intelligent: a brilliant student. —'**bril•liance,** n. [noncount] —'**bril•liant•ly,** adv.

brim /brɪm/ n., v., **brimmed, brim•ming.** —n. [count] **1.** the upper edge of anything hollow, such as a glass. **2.** an edge that sticks out: the brim of a hat. —v. [no obj] **3.** to be full to the brim: Her eyes brimmed with tears.

brine /brayn/ n. [noncount] water containing salt, as for pickling food: pickles in brine.

bring /brɪŋ/ v. [~ + obj], **brought** /brɔt/, **bring• ing. 1.** to carry or cause (someone or something) to come toward the speaker: Bring the clock to me. **2.** to cause; produce: The medicine brought quick relief. **3.** to persuade or force (oneself) to do something: I couldn't bring myself to leave him. **4. bring about,** to cause: The recession will bring about higher unemployment. **5. bring in, a.** to yield, as profit or income: This new product will bring in lots of money. This will bring lots of money in. **b.** to introduce; cause to be part of (a job, work, or process): She brought in a new secretary. She wanted to bring minorities in. **6. bring out,** to make noticeable: That blue sweater brings out the color of your eyes. **7. bring up, a.** to care for and educate during childhood: They brought up their children with sound values. **b.** to introduce for consideration: Why don't you bring that idea up at the next meeting? We weren't allowed to bring up your new idea.

brink /brɪŋk/ n. [count; usually singular] **1.** the edge of any steep place: the brink of the cliff. **2.** a critical point after which something will happen: on the brink of disaster.

brisk /brɪsk/ adj., **-er, -est. 1.** quick and lively: to walk at a brisk pace. **2.** pleasantly cool and stimulating: brisk weather. —'**brisk•ly,** adv.: The wind blew briskly. —'**brisk•ness,** n. [noncount]

bris•tle /'brɪsəl/ n., v., **-tled, -tling.** —n. **1.** (a) short, stiff, rough hair: [count]: Hogs' bristles are used to make brushes. [noncount]: That brush is made of bristle. —v. [no obj] **2.** (of hair) to stand

B

or rise stiffly: *I could feel the hairs on the back of my neck bristle.* **3.** to become stiff because of anger: *He bristled at my suggestion.*

Brit., an abbreviation of: **1.** Britain. **2.** British.

Brit·ish /'brɪtɪʃ/ *adj.* **1.** of or relating to Great Britain. —*n.* [*plural; the* + ~; *used with a plural verb*] **2.** the citizens of Great Britain.

brit·tle /'brɪtl/ *adj.,* **-tler, -tlest.** hard but easily broken: *brittle fingernails.*

broach /browtʃ/ *v.* [~ + *obj*] to suggest for the first time: *I broached the subject of my raise.*

broad /brɔd/ *adj.,* **-er, -est. 1.** wide: *a broad river.* **2.** [*before a noun*] full; clear: *I was robbed in broad daylight.* **3.** not limited or narrow: *a broad range of interests.* **4.** [*before a noun*] general: *in the broad sense of the term.* —**broad·ly,** *adv.* —**broad·ness,** *n.* [*noncount*]

broad·cast /'brɔd,kæst/ *v.,* **-cast** or **-cast·ed, -cast·ing.** —*v.* **1.** to send out (radio or television programs): [~ + *obj*]: *Channel 5 broadcasts Russian-language programs.* [*no obj*]: *Channel 4 broadcasts 24 hours a day.* **2.** [~ + *obj*] to spread (news, etc.) widely; tell many people: *He broadcast lies all over town.* —*n.* [*count*] **3.** a single radio or television program: *We interrupt this broadcast to bring you a special warning.* —**broad·cast·er,** *n.* [*count*]

broad·en /'brɔdn/ *v.* to become or make broad or broader: [*no obj*]: *The road broadens here.* [~ + *obj*]: *Reading broadens the mind.*

'broad-'minded, *adj.* respecting the opinions of others.

bro·cade /brow'keyd/ *n.* [*noncount*] a heavy fabric with a raised design.

broc·co·li /'brɒkəliy/ *n.* [*noncount*] a vegetable whose green flower buds are eaten.

bro·chure /brow'ʃʊr/ *n.* [*count*] a leaflet: *an advertising brochure.*

brogue /browg/ *n.* [*count*] **1.** an Irish accent in the pronunciation of English. **2.** any strong regional accent.

broil /brɔyl/ *v.* **1.** to (cause to) be cooked by direct heat; grill: [~ + *obj*]: *Let's broil a couple of steaks.* [*no obj*]: *The meat needs to broil about ten minutes.* **2.** to (cause to) be very hot: [*no obj*]: *The oven is broiling.* [~ + *obj*]: *The August sun will broil you.*

broil·er /'brɔylər/ *n.* [*count*] **1.** a small oven in which food is broiled. **2.** a young chicken suitable for broiling.

broke /browk/ *v.* **1.** pt. of BREAK. —*adj.* [*be* + ~] **2.** without money: *I was broke last week.*

bro·ken /'browkən/ *v.* **1.** pp. of BREAK. —*adj.* **2.** interrupted or disconnected: *a broken line.* **3.** weakened by misfortune: *a broken heart.* **4.** [*before a noun*] (of language) imperfectly spoken: *broken English.* **5.** [*before a noun*] divided or disrupted: *broken families.*

bro·ken·heart·ed /'browkən'hɑrtɪd/ *adj.* suffering from great sorrow; heartbroken.

bro·ker /'browkər/ *n.* [*count*] **1.** an agent in business who buys or sells for another person: *an insurance broker.* **2.** a person who helps others arrange contracts, bargains, etc.: *a marriage broker.* **3.** STOCKBROKER.

bron·chi·tis /brɒŋ'kaytɪs/ *n.* [*noncount*] an illness of the lining of the windpipe.

bron·co /'brɒŋkow/ *n.* [*count*], *pl.* **bron·cos.** a wild horse of the western U.S.

bron·to·saur /'brɒntəˌsɔr/ *n.* [*count*] a huge, four-footed, plant-eating dinosaur.

bronze /brɒnz/ *n., v.,* **bronzed, bronz·ing.** —*n.* [*noncount*] **1.** a yellowish brown metal that is a mixture of copper and tin. —*v.* [~ + *obj*] **2.** to give the appearance or color of bronze to: *The sun bronzed his skin.*

brooch /browtʃ, bruwtʃ/ *n.* [*count*] a piece of jewelry pinned to clothing.

brood /bruwd/ *n.* [*count*] **1.** a number of young produced at one time: *The mother duck watched over her brood.* **2.** a family or group in a household: *How is the Jones brood?* —*v.* [*no obj*] **3.** to sit on eggs to hatch them. **4.** to think about a subject for a long time, often with anger or sadness: *He was brooding about his divorce.*

brook /brʊk/ *n.* [*count*] a small stream.

broom /bruwm, brʊm/ *n.* [*count*] a brush on a long handle for sweeping floors.

broom·stick /'bruwm,stɪk, 'brʊm-/ *n.* [*count*] the handle of a broom.

broth /brɔθ, brɒθ/ *n.* [*count*] [*noncount*] a thin soup.

broth·el /'brɒθəl, 'brɒð-, 'brɔθəl, -ðəl/ *n.* [*count*] a house of prostitution.

broth·er /'brʌðər/ *n.* [*count*] **1.** a male relative with the same parents: *She had only one brother.* **2.** [*often: Brother*] a man who devotes himself to the duties of a religious order without taking holy orders. —*interj.* **3.** (used to show disappointment, disgust, or surprise): *Oh, brother! I forgot my tickets.* —**broth·er·ly,** *adv.*

broth·er·hood /'brʌðər,hʊd/ *n.* **1.** [*noncount*] a feeling of friendship, loyalty, etc., toward another: *a strong sense of brotherhood.* **2.** [*count*] an organization of people working in a certain trade: *the brotherhood of firefighters.*

'brother-in-,law, *n.* [*count*], *pl.* **brothers-in-law. 1.** the brother of one's husband or wife. **2.** the husband of one's sister. **3.** the husband of one's wife's or husband's sister.

brought /brɔt/ *v.* pt. and pp. of BRING.

brow /braw/ *n.* [*count*] **1.** the forehead. **2.** eyebrow.

brow·beat /'braw,biyt/ *v.* [~ + *obj*], **-beat, -beat·en, -beat·ing.** to frighten (someone) into doing something: *She browbeat me into cleaning the apartment.*

brown /brawn/ *n., adj.,* **-er, -est,** *v.* —*n.* [*noncount*] **1.** the dark color of wood. —*adj.* **2.** of the color brown. —*v.* **3.** to make or become brown: [*no obj*]: *His skin browned during the summer.* [~ + *obj*]: *The sun browned his skin.* **4.** to fry, roast, etc., to a brown color: [*no obj*]: *The chicken is browning nicely.* [~ + *obj*]: *Brown the pieces of chicken.*

brown·ie /'brawniy/ *n.* [*count*] a piece of chewy cake, usually chocolate.

brown·stone /'brawn,stown/ *n.* [*count*] a house made of a reddish-brown stone.

browse /brawz/ *v.* [*no obj*], **browsed, brows·ing. 1.** to feed on plants, leaves, etc.: *The deer were browsing in the meadow.* **2.** to read parts of a book, magazine, etc., casually: *to browse through the newspaper.* **3.** to look in an unhurried way at goods in a store: *We browsed through the department store.* —**'brows·er,** *n.* [*count*]

bruise /bruwz/ *v.,* **bruised, bruis·ing,** *n.* —*v.* **1.** to injure without breaking the skin but causing a discolored spot: [~ + *obj*]: *She bruised her knee.* [*no obj*]: *He bruises easily.* —*n.* [*count*] **2.** an injury due to bruising.

brunch /brʌntʃ/ *n.* a meal that serves as both breakfast and lunch: [*noncount*]: *Let's have brunch on Sunday.* [*count*]: *What can you eat at these brunches?*

bru•net /bruw'nɛt/ adj. **1.** (of a white male) having dark hair and eyes. —n. [count] **2.** a man with dark hair and eyes.

bru•nette /bruw'nɛt/ adj. **1.** (of a white female) having dark hair and eyes. —n. [count] **2.** a woman with dark hair and eyes.

brunt /brʌnt/ n. [noncount] —Idiom. **bear the brunt of,** to suffer the main force of (an attack or blow): Our town bore the brunt of the storm.

brush[1] /brʌʃ/ n. [count] **1.** a small tool with bristles and a handle, used for painting, grooming, etc.: The painter cleaned his brushes. **2.** a close encounter, esp. with something undesirable: a brush with disaster. —v. [~ + obj] **3.** to paint, groom, etc., with a brush. **4.** to touch lightly in passing; pass lightly over: The plane just brushed the surface of the water. **5. brush aside** or **away,** to disregard; ignore: He brushed our objections aside. He brushed away our objections. **6. brush off,** to send (someone) away; to refuse to listen to: He brushed off his old girlfriend. She brushed him off. **7. brush up (on),** to revive or review (studies, a skill, etc.): He brushed up on his mathematics.

brush[2] /brʌʃ/ n. [noncount] a thick, heavy, dense growth of bushes, shrubs, etc.

brusque /brʌsk/ adj. quick and impolite: He was quite brusque with the students.

'Brus•sels 'sprout /'brʌsəlz/ n. [count] Usually, **Brussels sprouts.** a vegetable that looks like tiny cabbages.

bru•tal /'bruwtl̩/ adj. **1.** cruel; savage: a brutal attack. **2.** harsh; severe: a brutal storm. —**bru•tal•i•ty** /bruw'tælɪtiy/ n. [count] [noncount] —**'bru•tal•ly,** adv.

brute /bruwt/ n. [count] **1.** an animal; beast. **2.** a cruel person: Her husband is a brute. —adj. [before a noun] **3.** like an animal, as in strength or cruelty: brute force. —**'brut•ish,** adj.

B.S., an abbreviation of: Bachelor of Science.

B.Sc., an abbreviation of: Bachelor of Science.

bub•ble /'bʌbəl/ n., v., **-bled, -bling.** —n. [count] **1.** a round body of gas in a liquid: The bubbles rose to the top of the kettle as the water boiled. —v. [no obj] **2.** to form bubbles: The boiling water was bubbling. **3. bubble over,** to overflow with liveliness or happiness: She was bubbling over with joy.

bub•ble•gum /'bʌbəl,gʌm/ n. [noncount] chewing gum that can be blown into bubbles.

bub•bly /'bʌbliy/ adj., **-bli•er, -bli•est.** **1.** full of bubbles: bubbly champagne. **2.** lively; cheerful: a bubbly personality.

buck[1] /bʌk/ n. [count] the male of certain animals, as the deer.

buck[2] /bʌk/ v. **1.** [no obj] (of an animal) to jump up with the back arched: The donkey bucked when it saw the snake. **2.** [~ + obj] to throw off (a rider) by jumping this way: That wild bronco bucked its rider. **3.** to resist or oppose stubbornly: [~ + obj]: She bucked the system. [no obj]: He bucked at the suggestion to reduce his staff.

buck[3] /bʌk/ n. [noncount] **1.** final responsibility: The buck stops here. —Idiom. **2. pass the buck,** to shift responsibility or blame to another person: Quit passing the buck all the time!

buck[4] /bʌk/ n. [count] Slang. a dollar.

buck•et /'bʌkɪt/ n. [count] **1.** a round, open container with a handle: He put the mop in the bucket of water. **2.** an amount (of something) contained in a bucket: a bucket of sand. —Idiom. **3. a drop in the bucket,** a small, in-

adequate amount: That donation of fifty cents was just a drop in the bucket. **4. kick the bucket,** Slang. to die.

buck•le /'bʌkəl/ n., v., **-led, -ling.** —n. [count] **1.** a metal fastener for joining the two ends of a belt. —v. **2.** [~ + obj] to fasten with a buckle: Buckle your seat belt. **3.** to (cause to) bend or collapse: [no obj]: Suddenly my knees buckled. [~ + obj]: The intense heat buckled the road. **4. buckle down,** to set to work with strength and determination: Just buckle down and practice. **5. buckle up,** to fasten one's belt, seat belt, or buckles: Is everyone buckled up?

bud /bʌd/ n., v., **bud•ded, bud•ding.** —n. [count] **1.** a flower or leaf before it opens: The plants were showing a few buds. —v. [no obj] **2.** to produce buds: The plants began to bud in April. **3.** to begin to develop: His genius began to bud at an early age. —Idiom. **4. nip in the bud,** to stop (something) in the earliest stages: to nip a revolution in the bud.

Bud•dhism /'buwdɪzəm, 'bʊdɪz-/ n. [noncount] an Asian religion based on the teachings of Buddha (Gautama). —**'Bud•dhist,** n. [count], adj.

bud•dy /'bʌdiy/ n. [count], pl. **-dies.** Informal. a friend.

budge /bʌdʒ/ v., budged, budg•ing. (often used with a negative word) **1.** to (cause to) move slightly: [no obj]: The carton wouldn't budge. [~ + obj]: I couldn't budge the heavy carton. **2.** to (cause to) change an opinion or stated position; (cause to) give in: [no obj]: He refused to budge on the question. [~ + obj]: We couldn't budge her on the issue.

budg•et /'bʌdʒɪt/ n. [count] **1.** a plan of how much money will be received and spent in a particular period of time: a monthly budget. —adj. [before a noun] **2.** reasonably or cheaply priced: budget seats. —v. **3.** to plan an amount of (money, time, etc.): [~ + obj]: We budgeted our time carefully. [no obj]: We couldn't budget for every emergency.

buff /bʌf/ n. **1.** [noncount] a brownish yellow color. **2.** [count] one who knows a lot about a certain subject: an opera buff. —v. [~ + obj] **3.** to polish with a soft material: I buffed my shoes to a bright shine.

buf•fa•lo /'bʌfə,low/ n. [count], pl. **-loes, -los,** (esp. when thought of as a group) **-lo.** a large wild ox, such as the bison.

buff•er /'bʌfər/ n. [count] a person or thing that lessens the effect of a shock or other misfortune: investing money as a buffer against inflation.

buf•fet[1] /'bʌfɪt/ v. [~ + obj] to strike against or push repeatedly: The wind buffeted the house.

buf•fet[2] /bə'fey, bʊ-/ n. [count] a meal laid out so that guests may serve themselves.

buf•foon /bə'fuwn/ n. [count] a fool; clown. —**buf'foon•er•y,** n. [noncount]

bug /bʌg/ n., v., **bugged, bug•ging.** —n. [count] **1.** (loosely) any insect. **2.** Informal. a disease, or the germ causing the disease: I've got a flu bug. **3.** a defect, error, or mistake: Work out the bugs in that computer program. **4.** a small hidden microphone: They put the bug in the spy's room. —v. [~ + obj] **5.** to install a hidden microphone: The phone was bugged. **6.** Informal. to annoy: Quit bugging me!

bug•gy /'bʌgiy/ n. [count], pl. **-gies.** a light, four-wheeled, horse-drawn carriage with a single seat.

bu•gle /'byuwgəl/ n. [count] a brass wind instrument resembling a horn but usually without keys or valves.

build /bɪld/ v., built /bɪlt/, build•ing, n. —v. **1.** to make (a house, etc.) by putting together parts: [~ + obj]: to build a house. [no obj]: The town wants to build in that area. **2.** to start, increase, or strengthen: [~ + obj]: to build (up) the family business or to build the family business (up). [no obj]: The tension continued to build (up). **3.** **build on** or **upon,** to have as a basis: a relationship built on trust. —n. [count; singular] **4.** the shape of a person's body: She had a strong build. —'build•er, n. [count]

build•ing /'bɪldɪŋ/ n. [count] a structure with a roof and walls intended to be kept in one place.

bulb /bʌlb/ n. [count] **1.** a rounded underground stem of certain plants. **2.** the glass part of an electric light that lights up when electricity passes through it.

bulge /bʌldʒ/ n., v., bulged, bulg•ing. —n. [count] **1.** a rounded part that sticks out of something: She started to exercise to reduce the bulge at her waistline. —v. [no obj] **2.** to swell or stick out: His stomach bulged out over his belt.

bulk /bʌlk/ n. **1.** [noncount] great weight or size: mass: the great bulk of the aircraft carrier. **2.** [singular: the + ~ + of] the greater part or amount: The bulk of the debt was paid. —bulk•y, adj., -i•er, -i•est.

bull /bʊl/ n. [count] the male of the cow family or of certain other animals: the bull elephants.

bull•dog /'bʊl,dɔg, -,dɒg/ n. [count] a dog with a short neck and short, thick legs.

bull•doz•er /'bʊl,dowzər/ n. [count] a powerful tractor for moving large amounts of earth.

bul•let /'bʊlɪt/ n. [count] **1.** a small piece of metal fired from a gun. —**Idiom. 2. bite the bullet,** to force oneself to perform a painful task, or to endure an unpleasant situation: He bit the bullet and went on to complain to the boss.

bul•le•tin /'bʊlɪtn̩, -tɪn/ n. [count] **1.** a brief, official news report. **2.** a publication regularly issued by an organization, etc.: a church bulletin.

'bulletin ,board, n. [count] a board for putting up notices, etc.

bull•fight /'bʊl,fayt/ n. [count] a traditional Spanish entertainment in which a man fights a bull in a certain way. —'bull,fight•er, n. [count] —'bull,fight•ing, n. [noncount]

bull•frog /'bʊl,frɔg, -,frɑg/ n. [count] a large North American frog.

'bull's-,eye, n. [count], pl. -eyes. **1.** the circular spot at the center of a target. **2.** a shot that hits this.

bul•ly /'bʊliy/ n., pl. -lies, v., -lied, -ly•ing. —n. [count] **1.** one who bothers and hurts smaller or weaker people: the class bully. —v. [~ + obj] **2.** to use one's strength to bother (people): I was bullied into going along with the plan.

bum /bʌm/ n., v., bummed, bum•ming. —n. [count] **1.** a person who avoids work and lives off others. **2.** Informal. a person who is very interested in something: a beach bum. **3.** Informal. a worthless person. —v. [~ + obj] **4.** Informal. to borrow (something) without a promise to return: Can I bum a cigarette (off you)?

bum•ble•bee /'bʌmbəl,biy/ n. [count] a large, hairy bee.

bum•bling /'bʌmblɪŋ/ adj. [before a noun] tending to make awkward mistakes.

bump /bʌmp/ v. **1.** to (cause to) collide with: [~ + obj]: The car bumped a truck. I bumped my arm. [no obj]: The car bumped against a tree. She

bumped into me. **2. bump into,** to meet by chance: I bumped into her on the way home. **3. bump off,** Slang. to murder: planning to bump off the mobster; planning to bump him off. —n. [count] **4.** a blow or knock: We heard a bump on the ceiling. **5.** a swelling on the body from a blow: a bump on the head. **6.** a small, uneven area above the surface: many bumps on the road. —'bump•y, adj.

bump•er /'bʌmpər/ n. [count] **1.** a metal bar for protecting the front or rear of an automobile, truck, etc. —adj. [before a noun] **2.** unusually large: a bumper crop.

bun /bʌn/ n. [count] **1.** a round bread roll. **2.** hair tied into a round knot.

bunch /bʌntʃ/ n. **1.** [count] a number of things held together: a bunch of grapes. **2.** [count; singular; a + ~ + of] a group of people or things: a bunch of papers; a bunch of students. —v. [~ + obj] **3.** to group together: all bunched together in the crowded elevator.

bun•dle /'bʌndl̩/ n., v., -dled, -dling. —n. [count] **1.** a package: He brought in a few bundles from the car. **2.** several objects or a quantity of material fastened together: a bundle of wood. —v. **3.** [~ + obj] to wrap in a bundle: She bundled the packages together. **4. bundle up,** to dress warmly: Bundle up; it's cold outside. We bundled the kids up in layers of clothes.

bun•ga•low /'bʌŋgə,low/ n. [count] a small house or summer cottage.

bun•gle /'bʌŋgəl/ v., -gled, -gling. to do clumsily or badly: [~ + obj]: The electrician bungled the wiring job. [no obj]: If she keeps bungling, she'll lose the job.

bun•ion /'bʌnyən/ n. [count] a painful swelling at the base of the big toe.

bunk /bʌŋk/ n. [count] a bed built into the wall.

'bunk ,bed, n. [count] either of two single beds connected one above the other.

bun•ker /'bʌŋkər/ n. [count] **1.** a large storage container. **2.** a partially underground chamber, built as a bomb shelter.

bun•ny /'bʌniy/ n. [count], pl. -nies. a rabbit, esp. a young one.

bu•oy /'buwiy, bɔy/ n. [count] **1.** a floating object attached to the sea bottom, used as a marker for ships. —v. [~ + obj] **2. a.** to keep afloat. **b.** to encourage; cheer up: Her courage was buoyed by the doctor's assurances.

buoy•an•cy /'bɔyənsiy, 'buwyənsiy/ n. [noncount] **1.** the ability to float: That piece of wood has a lot of buoyancy. **2.** lightness of spirit; cheerfulness. —buoyant, adj.

bur•den /'bɜrdn̩/ n. [count] **1.** a heavy load: a burden of five hundred pounds. **2.** that which is difficult to bear: the burden of leadership. —v. [~ + obj] **3.** to load heavily: burdened with packages. **4.** to cause worry: burdened with problems.

bur•den•some /'bɜrdn̩səm/ adj. causing worry; hard to bear: burdensome debts.

bu•reau /'byʊrow/ n. [count], pl. bu•reaus, bu•reaux /'byʊrowz/. **1.** a chest of drawers: The keys are on top of the bureau. **2.** a division of a government department: the weather bureau. **3.** Chiefly Brit. a writing desk with drawers.

bu•reauc•ra•cy /byʊ'rɒkrəsiy/ n., pl. -cies. **1.** [noncount] government by a rigid, complex, and large number of bureaus and administrators: No one wants more bureaucracy. **2.** [noncount] rules, routines, and procedures of such a system. **3.**

B

[count] a body of officials and administrators, especially in a government.

bu•reau•crat /'byʊrə,kræt/ *n.* [count] an official of a bureaucracy. —,**bu•reau'crat•ic,** *adj.*

bur•geon /'bɜrdʒən/ *v.* [no obj] to grow quickly: *The town was burgeoning into a city.*

bur•gla•ry /'bɜrgləriy/ *n., pl.* **-ries.** the crime of entering a building by force in order to steal: [noncount]: *He was found guilty of burglary.* [count]: *There were more than fifty burglaries in three months.* —'**bur•glar,** *n.* [count] —**bur•glar•ize** /'bɜrglə,rayz/ *v.* [~ + *obj*], **-ized, -iz•ing.**

bur•i•al /'bɛriyəl/ *n.* [noncount] [count] the act or ceremony of burying a dead body.

bur•ly /'bɜrliy/ *adj.,* **-li•er, -li•est.** large in size; stout; sturdy: *a couple of burly cops.*

Bur•mese /bər'miyz, -'miys/ *n., pl.* **-mese. 1.** [count] a person born or living in Burma. **2.** [noncount] the language spoken by many of the people in Burma. —*adj.* **3.** of or relating to Burma or the language spoken there.

burn /bɜrn/ *v.,* **burned** or **burnt** /bɜrnt/, **burn•ing,** *n.* —*v.* **1.** to (cause to) be on fire: [no obj]: *The house is burning.* [~ + *obj*]: *The fire burned the house down.* **2.** to (cause to) use up fuel and give off energy: [no obj]: *The lights were burning all night.* [~ + *obj*]: *That plane burns a lot of fuel.* **3.** to (cause to) be hot: [no obj]: *She was burning with fever.* [~ + *obj*]: *The hot pavement burned my feet.* **4.** to (cause to) be damaged by fire or heat: [no obj]: *The steak is burning.* [~ + *obj*]: *She burned the steaks.* **5.** [no obj; usually: be + ~-ing] to feel strong emotion: *He was burning with anger.* **6. burn out, a.** to stop functioning because something has been burned up or worn out: *The rocket engine burned out. The firemen let the fire burn (itself) out.* **b.** to become exhausted or uninterested through overwork: *After twenty years at the same job, he had burned himself out and wanted a change.* **7. burn up, a.** to burn completely: *to burn up the letters* or *to burn the letters up.* **b.** *Informal.* to (cause to) become angry: *He's burned up because you're late. That kind of whining really burns me up!* —*n.* [count] **8.** an injury caused by heat or fire.

burn•er /'bɜrnər/ *n.* [count] the part of an appliance, as a stove, from which flame or heat comes out.

burnt /bɜrnt/ *v.* a pt. and pp. of BURN.

burp /bɜrp/ *Informal.* —*n.* [count] **1.** a belch. —*v.* **2.** to (cause to) belch: [no obj]: *In his culture it is polite to burp after a meal.* [~ + *obj*]: *She burped the baby.*

bur•ro /'bɜrow, 'bʊrow/ *n., pl.* **-ros.** a donkey, esp. a small one.

bur•row /'bɜrow, 'bʌrow/ *n.* [count] **1.** a hole or tunnel in the ground made by an animal: *The fox reached its burrow.* —*v.* **2.** to dig a burrow (into): [no obj]: *He burrowed into the ground.* [~ + *obj*]: *worms burrowing their way through the soil.* **3.** [no obj] to move as if by digging: *She burrowed under the blankets.*

burst /bɜrst/ *v.,* **burst** or, often, **burst•ed, burst•ing,** *n.* —*v.* **1.** to (cause to) break apart suddenly: [no obj]: *The balloon burst.* [~ + *obj*]: *The cold weather burst the pipes.* **2.** [no obj] to come forth suddenly and forcefully: *The police burst into the room.* **3.** to give sudden expression to a feeling: [~ + *into* + *obj*]: *to burst into tears.* [~ + *out*]: *to burst out laughing.* [~ + *with* + *obj*]: *to burst with pride.* —*n.* [count] **4.** an act or instance of bursting: *several bursts of machine gun fire.*

bur•y /'bɛriy/ *v.* [~ + *obj*], **bur•ied, bur•y•ing. 1.** to put (a dead body) in a grave: *They buried him yesterday.* **2.** to put into the ground: *They buried the treasure.* **3.** to cover with something: *He was buried in the rubble of the building.* **4.** [~ + *oneself*] to be occupied in: *He buried himself in his work.*

bus /bʌs/ *n., pl.* **bus•es, bus•ses,** *v.,* **bused** or **bussed, bus•ing** or **bus•sing.** —*n.* [count] **1.** a large, long motor vehicle that carries passengers. —*v.* **2.** to travel or transport by bus: [no obj]: *Let's see if we can bus back to the hotel.* [~ + *obj*]: *Some students are bused to schools very far from their homes.*

bus•boy /'bʌs,bɔy/ *n.* [count] a waiter's helper.

bush /bʊʃ/ *n.* **1.** [count] a low plant with many branches. **2.** [noncount; usually: the + ~] a large uncleared area covered with plant growth. —*Idiom.* **3. beat around** or **about the bush,** to avoid talking about a subject directly: *He beat around the bush before asking for a loan.*

bush•el /'bʊʃəl/ *n.* [count] **1.** a dry measure containing 2150.42 cubic inches in the U.S. or 2219.36 cubic inches in Great Britain. **2.** a large amount: *a bushel of kisses.*

bush•y /'bʊʃiy/ *adj.,* **-i•er, -i•est.** thick and shaggy: *bushy whiskers.*

busi•ness /'bɪznɪs/ *n.* **1.** [noncount] the buying and selling of goods for profit. **2.** [count] a corporation that buys and sells goods. **3.** [noncount] something with which a person is justly concerned: *Words are a writer's business.* —*Idiom.* **4. get down to business,** to apply oneself to serious matters: *That's enough small talk; let's get down to business.* **5. have no business,** to have no right: *You had no business using my car.* **6. (to) mean business,** to be completely serious: *I think the gunman means business.* **7. mind one's own business,** to keep from meddling in the affairs of others. —**busi•ness•man** /'bɪznɪs,mæn/ *n.* [count], *pl.* **-men** /-,mɛn/. —**busi•ness•per•son** /'bɪznɪs,pɜrsən/ *n.* [count] —**busi•ness•wom•an** /'bɪznɪs,wʊmən/ *n.* [count], *pl.* **-wom•en** /-,wɪmən/.

bus•ing or **bus•sing** /'bʌsɪŋ/ *n.* [noncount] the transporting of students by bus to schools outside their neighborhoods, esp. in an effort to achieve racial integration.

bus•ses /'bʌsɪz/ *n.* [plural] a pl. of BUS.

bust[1] /bʌst/ *n.* [count] **1.** a statue of the upper part of the human body. **2.** a woman's breasts.

bust[2] /bʌst/ *v.* [~ + *obj*] **1.** *Slang.* to place under arrest: *The police busted the drug dealer.* —*n.* [count] **2.** *Informal.* something unsuccessful; a failure: *The play turned out to be a real bust.* **3.** a sudden economic decline; depression. **4.** *Slang.* **a.** an arrest: *The rookie got credit for the bust of the Mafia boss.* **b.** a police raid.

bus•tle /'bʌsəl/ *v.,* **-tled, -tling,** *n.* —*v.* **1.** [~ + *about*] to move with great energy: *The chef bustled about in the kitchen.* **2.** [~ + *with* + *obj*] (of a place) to have a lot of (something): *The office bustled with activity.* —*n.* [noncount] **3.** excited, noisy activity: *much hustle and bustle.* —'**bus•tling,** *adj.*

bus•y /'bɪziy/ *adj.,* **bus•i•er, bus•i•est,** *v.,* **bus•ied, bus•y•ing.** —*adj.* **1.** having a lot of work to do: *He'll be busy all day.* **2.** full of activity: *a busy life.* **3.** (of a telephone line) in use: *Your phone was busy all night.* —*v.* [~ + *oneself* (+ *with* + *obj*)] **4.** to make or keep busy: *He busied himself with writing letters.* —'**bus•i•ly,** *adv.* —'**bus•y•ness,** *n.* [noncount]

bus·y·bod·y /ˈbɪziyˌbɒdiy/ *n.* [count], *pl.* **-bod·ies.** one who pries into the affairs of others.

but /bʌt/ *unstressed* bət/ *conj.* **1.** on the contrary: *My brother went, but I did not.* **2.** and yet; nevertheless: *The story is strange but true.* **3.** except: *She did nothing but complain. She is nothing but trouble.* —*adv.* **4.** only: *There is but one answer.* —*n.* **5.** buts, [*plural*] objections: *You'll do as you're told, no buts about it.*

butch·er /ˈbʊtʃər/ *n.* [count] **1.** one who kills animals for food or sells meat in a shop. **2.** a person guilty of brutal murder. —*v.* [~ + obj] **3.** to slaughter (animals) and prepare the meat for market: *He butchered the calf.* **4.** to kill (people) brutally or excessively.

but·ler /ˈbʌtlər/ *n.* [count] the chief male servant of a household.

butt¹ /bʌt/ *n.* [count] **1.** the end of anything: *a rifle butt; a cigar butt.* **2.** *Slang.* the buttocks.

butt² /bʌt/ *n.* [count; usually singular] a person that people make fun of: *He was the butt of all our jokes.*

butt³ /bʌt/ *v.* **1.** to strike or push (something) with the head or horns: [no obj]: *The rams were butting and pushing.* [~ + obj]: *He butted his head against the wall.* **2. butt in,** to interfere in the affairs of others: *He wished his mother-in-law would stop butting in.* —*n.* [count] **3.** a push or blow with the head or horns.

but·ter /ˈbʌtər/ *n.* [noncount] **1.** a yellowish fat made from cream, used as a spread and in cooking. —*v.* [~ + obj] **2.** to put butter on: *He buttered the toast.* **3. butter up,** to flatter or praise (someone) too much: *to butter up the boss or to butter the boss up.*

but·ter·cup /ˈbʌtərˌkʌp/ *n.* [count] a plant having yellow flowers and deeply cut leaves.

but·ter·fly /ˈbʌtərˌflay/ *n.* [count], *pl.* **-flies.** a flying insect that has a slender body and broad wings.

but·ter·scotch /ˈbʌtərˌskɒtʃ/ *n.* [noncount] **1.** a hard candy made of butter and brown sugar. **2.** the flavor of this candy, used in puddings, pastries, etc.

but·tock /ˈbʌtək/ *n.* [count] Usually, **buttocks.** [*plural*] either of the two fleshy parts of the body on which a person sits.

but·ton /ˈbʌtn̩/ *n.* [count] **1.** a small disk attached to clothing and serving as a fastener when passed through a hole: *He couldn't fasten the top button.* **2.** a badge with a name or slogan: *campaign buttons.* **3.** a small knob that is pressed to operate a machine: *an elevator button.* —*v.* **4.** [~ + obj] to fasten with buttons: *Button your coat (up)* or *Button (up) your coat.* **5.** [no obj] to be capable of being buttoned: *a blouse that buttons in the back.* —*Idiom.* **6. button up,** Also, **button (up) one's lip.** to keep silent, as to keep a secret: *Button up until the deal goes through.* **7. (right) on the button,** exactly at the desired time, goal, etc.: *She came at ten o'clock, right on the button.*

but·ton·hole /ˈbʌtn̩ˌhowl/ *n.* [count] the hole through which a button is passed and by which it is fastened.

but·tress /ˈbʌtrɪs/ *n.* [count] **1.** a support for a wall: *the buttresses of the cathedral.* **2.** any prop or support: *the buttresses of civilized society.* —*v.* [~ + obj] **3.** to support by means of a buttress. **4.** to support or strengthen: *Try to buttress your ideas with some details.*

bux·om /ˈbʌksəm/ *adj.* (of a woman) large in the bosom.

buy /bay/ *v.,* **bought** /bɔt/, **buy·ing,** *n.* —*v.* **1.** to get possession of (something) by paying money; purchase: [~ + obj]: *She bought a new computer.* [no obj]: *He buys at low prices.* **2.** [~ + obj] *Informal.* to accept or believe: *I don't buy that explanation.* —*n.* [count] **3.** a bargain: *The couch and the stereo are good buys.* —*Idiom.* **buy time,** *Informal.* to put off some action or decision: *trying to buy time by making conversation.* —ˈbuy·er, *n.* [count]

buzz /bʌz/ *n.* [count] **1.** a low, humming sound: *the buzz of machinery.* **2.** lively or excited activity: *the buzz in the classroom.* —*v.* **3.** [no obj] to make a low, humming sound: *The flies buzzed in the barnyard.* **4.** [no obj] to be filled with such a sound: *The dining hall buzzed with excitement.* **5.** [~ + obj] to call with a buzzer: *She buzzed her secretary.* **6.** [~ + obj] *Informal.* to make a phone call to: *I'll buzz you tonight.*

buz·zard /ˈbʌzərd/ *n.* [count] **1.** a broad-winged hawk of Europe and Asia. **2.** a vulture of the Americas, esp. the turkey vulture.

buzz·er /ˈbʌzər/ *n.* [count] something that buzzes: *My door buzzer is broken.*

buzz·word /ˈbʌzˌwɜrd/ *n.* [count] a word or phrase that is fashionable in popular culture or in a particular profession.

by /bay/ *prep.* **1.** near or next to: *a home by a lake.* **2.** using as a way of travel: *She came by air.* **3.** to and beyond a place: *We drove by the church.* **4.** to: *Come by my office.* **5.** during: *We drove by night.* **6.** not later than; before: *I'll be done by five o'clock.* **7.** to the extent or amount of: *He was taller by three inches.* **8.** (of a part of the body) holding onto: *He grabbed me by the arm.* **9.** according to: *a bad movie by any standards.* **10.** through the action of: *This book was written by experts.* **11.** through the means of: *Do you want to pay by cash or check?* **12.** as a result of: *We met by chance.* **13.** used before the second of two numbers to express the operations of multiplication or division, or to convey dimensions. **14.** in terms, groups, or amounts of: *Apples are sold by the bushel.* **15.** born of: *She had a son by her first husband.* —*adv.* **16.** near: *The school is close by.* **17.** to and beyond a point: *The car drove by.* **18.** to or at someone's home, office, etc.: *Can you stop by later?* **19.** past; over: *in times gone by.*

bye /bay/ *interj.* GOOD-BYE.

by·gone /ˈbayˌgɔn, -ˌgɒn/ *adj.* [before a noun] **1.** earlier; past: *bygone days.* —*Idiom.* **2. let bygones be bygones,** to put aside past disagreements.

by·pass /ˈbayˌpæs/ *n., v.,* **-passed, -passed** or **-past, -pass·ing.** —*n.* [count] **1.** a road allowing motorists to avoid heavy traffic points or to drive around an obstruction. **2.** a surgical operation in which the flow of blood through a diseased organ is redirected around the blockage: *a coronary bypass.* —*v.* [~ + obj] **3.** to avoid by going around: *We bypassed the city. I bypassed the manager and went straight to the owner.*

'by-ˌproduct, *n.* [count] something made during the manufacture of another product: *This acid is a by-product of fermentation.*

by·stand·er /ˈbayˌstændər/ *n.* [count] a person standing near, but not taking part in, something: *The police questioned bystanders about the accident.*

byte /bayt/ *n.* [count] a group of bits, usually eight, processed by a computer as a unit.

C

C, c /siy/ *n.* [*count*], *pl.* **Cs** or **C's, cs** or **c's.** the third letter of the English alphabet, a consonant.

C, *Symbol.* **1.** [*sometimes: c*] a grade or mark indicating fair or average quality. **2.** [*sometimes: c*] the Roman numeral for 100. **3.** Celsius: *The temperature is 10°C (said as "10 degrees Celsius").* **4.** centigrade.

c or **c.,** an abbreviation of: circa (used with a year): *c1775.*

CA, an abbreviation of: California.

ca or **ca.,** an abbreviation of: circa (used with a year): *ca 476 B.C.*

cab /kæb/ *n.* [*count*] **1.** a taxicab. **2.** the covered part of a truck or crane where the driver sits.

cab•a•ret /ˌkæbə'rey/ *n.* [*count*] a restaurant providing musical entertainment.

cab•bage /'kæbɪdʒ/ *n.* **1.** [*count*] a strong tasting vegetable with thick leaves that form into a rounded head. **2.** [*noncount*] the head or leaves of this plant, eaten cooked or raw: *I ate corned beef and cabbage.*

cab•in /'kæbɪn/ *n.* [*count*] **1.** a small, simple cottage. **2.** the enclosed space for the pilot or passengers in an airplane. **3.** a room in a ship.

cab•i•net /'kæbənɪt/ *n.* [*count*] **1.** a piece of furniture with shelves or drawers: *The dishes are in the kitchen cabinet.* **2.** [*often: Cabinet*] a group of persons who advise a president, king, etc.: *a meeting of the president's cabinet.*

ca•ble /'keybəl/ *n., v.,* **-bled, -bling. —n. 1.** [*noncount*] [*count*] a strong rope made of strands of metal wire, used to support bridges, etc. **2.** [*noncount*] [*count*] a cord of metal wire used to carry electrical power. **3.** [*count*] a telegram sent by underwater cable. —*v.* **4.** [*no obj*] [~ + *obj*] to send (a message) by cable.

'cable ,car, *n.* [*count*] a vehicle pulled along a track by a cable.

'cable 'television, *n.* [*noncount*] a system of broadcasting television programs to paying customers by means of special cable. Also called **cable TV.**

ca•boose /kə'buws/ *n.* [*count*] the last car on a freight train, used by the crew to eat and sleep.

ca•ca•o /kə'kaow/ *n.* [*count*], *pl.* **-os. 1.** a small tropical American evergreen tree grown for its seeds, the source of cocoa and chocolate. **2.** Also, **cocoa,** the seeds of this tree.

cack•le /'kækəl/ *v.,* **-led, -ling,** *n.* —*v.* [*no obj*] **1.** to utter a noisy cry, as a hen does. **2.** to laugh in this way. —*n.* [*count*] **3.** the act or sound of cackling.

cac•tus /'kæktəs/ *n.* [*count*], *pl.* **-ti** /-tay/, **-tus•es, -tus.** a plant of hot, dry regions, having thick, leafless stems usually with spines.

ca•det /kə'dɛt/ *n.* [*count*] a student who is training to be an officer in a police force or the armed forces.

Cae•sar•e•an /sɪ'zɛəriyən/ *n.* CESAREAN.

ca•fé /kæ'fey/ *n.* [*count*], *pl.* **-fés** or **-fes.** a small restaurant.

caf•e•te•ri•a /ˌkæfɪ'tɪəriyə/ *n.* [*count*], *pl.* **-as.** a restaurant in which diners select food at a counter and carry it to tables.

caf•feine /'kæfiyn/ *n.* [*noncount*] a chemical found in coffee or tea that acts as a stimulant.

cage /keydʒ/ *n., v.,* **caged, cag•ing.** —*n.* [*count*]

1. a boxlike enclosure with wires or bars forming the sides, for keeping birds or animals. —*v.* [~ + *obj*] **2.** to put in a cage.

cag•ey /'keydʒiy/ *adj.,* **-i•er, -i•est.** cautious, careful, or clever.

ca•jole /kə'dʒowl/ *v.* [~ + *obj*], **-joled, -jol•ing.** to persuade by promises, false praise, or humor: *We cajoled the ticket taker into letting us in free.*

cake /keyk/ *n., v.,* **caked, cak•ing.** —*n.* **1.** a sweet, baked, breadlike food: [*count*]: *birthday cakes.* [*noncount*]: *two pieces of cake.* **2.** [*count*] a shaped or molded mass of food: *a fish cake.* **3.** [*count*] a shaped block of something: *a cake of soap.* —*v.* [~ + *obj*] **4.** to coat thickly: *The window was caked with dirt.* —*Idiom.* **5. a piece of cake,** something that can be done easily, often with enjoyment. **6. take the cake,** to be an outstanding example: *That stupid idea takes the cake.*

ca•lam•i•ty /kə'læmɪtiy/ *n.* [*count*], *pl.* **-ties.** a great misfortune or disaster.

cal•ci•um /'kælsiyəm/ *n.* [*noncount*] a metallic element found in limestone and chalk and also in bone and shell: *Milk contains a lot of calcium.*

cal•cu•late /'kælkyə,leyt/ *v.,* **-lat•ed, -lat•ing.** to determine by using mathematical methods: [*no obj*]: *She calculated in her head for a moment.* [~ + *obj*]: *to calculate the speed of the train.*

cal•cu•lat•ing /'kælkyə,leytɪŋ/ *adj.* planning or plotting in a selfish way.

cal•cu•la•tion /ˌkælkyə'leyʃən/ *n.* **1.** the act or process of calculating; computation: [*noncount*]: *I did some rapid calculation in my head.* [*count*]: *The machine's calculations took only seconds.* **2.** [*count*] the result or product of calculating: *My calculations weren't correct.* **3.** [*count*] an estimate based on the known facts; forecast: *My calculation is that she won't want to continue the lawsuit.* **4.** [*noncount*] forethought; prior or careful planning: *They put a lot of calculation into this.* **5.** [*noncount*] scheming selfishness: *a look of cold calculation.*

cal•cu•la•tor /'kælkyə,leytər/ *n.* [*count*] a small electronic device that performs mathematical calculations: *He used a calculator to add the numbers.*

cal•en•dar /'kæləndər/ *n.* [*count*] **1.** a chart displaying the days of each month and week in a year. **2.** a list or record of appointments, meetings, etc.

calf¹ /kæf/ *n.* [*count*], *pl.* **calves** (kavz). **1.** the young of the cow or other cowlike animal. **2.** the young of certain other mammals, such as the elephant and whale.

calf² /kæf/ *n.* [*count*], *pl.* **calves** (kavz). the fleshy part of the back of the human leg below the knee.

cal•i•ber /'kæləbər/ *n.* **1.** [*count*] the measurement of the inside width of a gun barrel. **2.** [*noncount*] the degree of how good something is: *work of the highest caliber.* Also, *esp.* Brit., **cal'i•bre.**

cal•i•co /'kælɪ,kow/ *n.* [*noncount*], *pl.* **-coes, -cos.** a plain cotton cloth printed with a pattern.

Calif., an abbreviation of: California.

call /kɔl/ *v.* **1.** to cry out in a loud voice; shout: [~ + *obj*]: *to call someone's name.* [*no obj*]: *He called to his children.* **2.** [~ + *obj*] to ask to come: *Call a doctor, quick!* **3.** [~ + *obj*] [*no obj*] to telephone (someone). **4.** [~ + *obj*] to announce (a meeting, etc.) and invite people to attend: *He called a meeting of the new students.* **5.** [~ + *obj*] to name or address (someone) as (someone or something): *My friends call me Ray. We always called James by his nickname, Jim.* **6.** [~ + *obj*] to designate or describe (someone or something) as (someone or something): *She called me a liar. I'd call it crazy.* **7. call for, a.** to go or come to get: *I'll call for you at seven o'clock.* **b.** to demand or need: *An emergency calls for fast action.* **8. call off,** to cancel (something planned): *The teacher called off the test.* **9. call on** or **upon, a.** to ask; appeal to: *We called upon the president to aid the flood victims.* **b.** to visit for a short time. —*n.* [*count*] **10.** a cry or shout. **11.** the typical sound or cry of a bird or other animal. **12.** an act or instance of telephoning: *Give me a call when you're ready.* **13.** a short visit. —**'call•er,** *n.* [*count*]

'call ,girl, *n.* [*count*] a female prostitute who makes appointments by telephone.

cal•lig•ra•phy /kə'lɪgrəfiy/ *n.* [*noncount*] the art of beautiful handwriting. —**cal'lig•ra•pher,** *n.* [*count*]

call•ing /'kɔlɪŋ/ *n.* [*count; usually singular*] a profession or trade.

cal•lous /'kæləs/ *adj.* insensitive; uncaring.

cal•lus /'kæləs/ *n.* [*count*], *pl.* **-lus•es.** a hardened or thickened part of the skin, caused by rubbing.

calm /kɑm/ *adj.*, **-er, -est,** *n., v.* —*adj.* **1.** without rough motion; still: *a calm sea.* **2.** not windy: *a calm day.* **3.** free from excitement; peaceful: *a calm manner.* —*n.* [*noncount*] **4.** stillness of weather: *the calm before a storm.* **5.** freedom from excitement; peacefulness: *Calm returned to the city after the rioting.* —*v.* **6.** to (cause to) become calm: [*no obj*]: *The sea calmed (down) and the sun came out.* [~ + *obj*]: *Maybe this drink will calm you.* —**'calm•ly,** *adv.* —**'calm•ness,** *n.* [*noncount*]

cal•o•rie /'kæləriy/ *n.* [*count*], *pl.* **-ries.** a unit of measure of the amount of heat or energy that a certain food produces: *a diet of 2,000 calories a day.*

calve /kæv/ *v.* [*no obj*] [~ + *obj*], **calved, calv• ing.** to give birth to (a calf).

calves /kævz/ *n.* pl. of CALF.

ca•lyp•so /kə'lɪpsow/ *n.* [*noncount*] [*count*], *pl.* **-sos.** a musical style, or a song, of West Indian origin.

Cam•bo•di•an /kæm'bowdiyən/ *adj.* **1.** of or relating to Cambodia. —*n.* [*count*] **2.** a person born or living in Cambodia.

camcorder

cam•cord•er /'kæm,kɔrdər/ *n.* [*count*] a portable video camera and sound recorder.

came /keym/ *v.* pt. of COME.

cam•el /'kæməl/ *n.* [*count*] either of two large,

long-necked mammals with one or two humps on the back.

cam•e•o /'kæmiy,ow/ *n.* [*count*], *pl.* **-os, 1.** a piece of jewelry with a design or figure that is slightly raised from the background. **2.** a small but notable part, as in a film, played esp. by a well-known performer.

cam•er•a /'kæmərə/ *n.* [*count*], *pl.* **-as.** a device for taking photographs or films: *a TV camera.*

cam•ou•flage /'kæmə,flɑʒ/ *n., v.,* **-flaged, -flag•ing.** —*n.* [*noncount*] **1.** concealment by some means that hides the appearance: *The lizard changes color as camouflage.* —*v.* [~ + *obj*] **2.** to disguise or hide by means of camouflage: *We camouflaged our tanks and guns.*

camp /kæmp/ *n.* **1.** [*count*] a place where a group of people sleep in tents or other temporary shelters: *an army camp.* **2.** a recreation area in the country, with facilities for sports: [*count*]: *a boys' camp in the mountains.* [*noncount*]: *The children are going to summer camp.* —*v.* [*no obj*] **3.** to establish or put together a camp. **4. camp out,** to live or sleep in a tent or shelter temporarily: *They camped out by the stream.*

cam•paign /kæm'peyn/ *n.* [*count*] **1.** a series of military operations for a specific goal, esp. as part of a war. **2.** a course of planned activities designed for some specific purpose: *a sales campaign; a political campaign.* —*v.* [*no obj*] **3.** to engage in public activities that are intended to bring about a certain result: *She is campaigning for president. He campaigned for better schools.* —**cam'paign•er,** *n.* [*count*]

camp•er /'kæmpər/ *n.* [*count*] **1.** a person who stays or lives in a camp. **2.** a trucklike vehicle equipped for camping.

camp•fire /'kæmp,fayⁿr/ *n.* [*count*] an outdoor fire for warmth or cooking.

cam•pus /'kæmpəs/ *n.* [*count*] [*noncount*], *pl.* **-pus•es.** the grounds, often including the buildings, of a college or other school.

can¹ /kæn; *unstressed* kən/ *auxiliary (modal) verb. All present tense forms:* **can,** *past:* **could.** —*auxiliary verb* [~ + *root form of a verb*] **1.** to be able to: *She can solve the problem easily.* **2.** to know how to: *I can play chess, but not very well.* **3.** to have the right to: *He can change whatever he wants to in the script.* **4.** may; have permission to: *Can I speak to you for a moment?* **5.** to have the possibility to: *It can get very cold here in March.*

can² /kæn/ *n., v.,* **canned, can•ning.** —*n.* [*count*] **1.** a sealed metal container for food, liquid, etc.: *a can of soup.* **2.** a large container for garbage: *the trash can.* —*v.* [~ + *obj*] **3.** to preserve (food) by sealing in a can or jar: *She canned tomatoes for the winter.*

Ca•na•di•an /kə'neydiyən/ *adj.* **1.** of or relating to Canada. —*n.* [*count*] **2.** a person born or living in Canada.

ca•nal /kə'næl/ *n.* **1.** [*count*] [*noncount*] an artificial body of water for ships to travel along. **2.** [*count*] a tube-shaped passage in the body.

ca•nar•y /kə'nɛəriy/ *n.* [*count*], *pl.* **-ies.** a small, greenish yellow finch of the Canary Islands.

can•cel /'kænsəl/ *v.* [~ + *obj*], **-celed, -cel•ing** or (*esp. Brit.*) **-celled, -cel•ling. 1.** to make no longer valid: *to cancel a magazine subscription.* **2.** to decide or announce that (a planned event) will not take place: *She canceled the picnic.* **3. cancel out,** to balance or be equal: *The two opposing forces cancel out. One effect of the force*

(figure labels:) viewfinder, microphone, lens

cancels out the other. —**can•cel'la•tion,** *n.* [*noncount*] [*count*]

can•cer /'kænsər/ *n.* **1.** [*noncount*] very serious disease characterized by growths that occur when cells in the body increase without control: *cancer of the liver.* **2.** [*count*] an evil that spreads and brings destruction: *Racial hatred is a cancer in our society.* —**'can•cer•ous,** *adj.*

can•did /'kændɪd/ *adj.* **1.** open and sincere; honest: *a candid critic.* **2.** not posed; informal: *a candid photo.* —**'can•did•ly,** *adv.*

can•di•date /'kændɪ,deyt, -dɪt/ *n.* [*count*] **1.** a person who seeks a political office or other job: *presidential candidates.* **2.** a student studying for a degree: *a candidate for a doctoral degree.* —**can•di•da•cy** /'kændɪdəsiy/, *n.* [*noncount*]

can•died /'kændiyd/ *adj.* cooked or covered in sugar or syrup: *candied yams.*

can•dle /'kændl/ *n.* [*count*] a long, slender piece of wax with a wick in the middle, burned to give light.

can•dle•stick /'kændl,stɪk/ *n.* [*count*] a device having a cuplike opening for holding a candle.

can•dor /'kændər/ *n.* [*noncount*] the state or quality of being candid. Also, *esp. Brit.,* **can/dour.**

can•dy /'kændiy/ *n.* [*count*] [*noncount*], *pl.* **-dies.** a sweet food made mostly of sugar or syrup and usually cooked or baked.

cane /keyn/ *n., v.,* **caned, can•ing.** —*n.* [*count*] **1.** a short stick used to assist a person in walking. **2.** a long, hollow woody stem with joints, such as that of the bamboo plant. —*v.* [~ + *obj*] **3.** to hit with a cane.

ca•nine /'keynayn/ *adj.* [*before a noun*] **1.** of or like a dog. —*n.* [*count*] **2.** one of the four pointed teeth of the jaws.

can•is•ter /'kænəstər/ *n.* [*count*] a small box or jar for holding tea, coffee, etc.

can•ker /'kæŋkər/ *n.* [*count*] an inflamed or sore area, esp. in the mouth. Also called **'canker ,sore.**

can•ni•bal /'kænəbəl/ *n.* [*count*] a person who eats human flesh. —**'can•ni•bal•ism,** *n.* [*noncount*]

can•non /'kænən/ *n.* [*count*], *pl.* **-nons,** (*esp. when thought of as a group*) **-non.** a mounted gun for firing heavy metal balls: *The general moved his cannons into the field. Thirty cannon were used.*

can•not /'kænɒt, kæ'nɒt, kə-/ *auxiliary* (*modal*) *verb phrase.* [~ + *root form of a verb*] a form of can not.

ca•noe /kə'nuw/ *n., v.,* **-noed, -noe•ing.** —*n.* [*count*] **1.** a slender boat pointed at both ends. —*v.* [*no obj*] **2.** to go in a canoe.

can•o•py /'kænəpiy/ *n.* [*count*], *pl.* **-pies. 1.** a covering held up on poles or hung above a bed, throne, etc. **2.** a similar covering stretching from the doorway of a building to a curb. **3.** the cover formed by the leafy upper branches of the trees in a forest.

can't /kænt/ *contraction.* a shortened form of *cannot.*

can•ta•loupe /'kæntl,owp/ *n.* [*count*] [*noncount*] a melon with a hard green or yellow skin and pale orange flesh.

can•teen /kæn'tiyn/ *n.* [*count*] **1.** a small container for carrying water or other liquids. **2.** a small restaurant where simple foods or snacks are sold, as in a factory or school.

can•ter /'kæntər/ *n.* [*count*] **1.** an easy gallop:

The horses set off at a canter. —*v.* [*no obj*] [~ + *obj*] **2.** to (cause to) ride at a canter.

can•vas /'kænvəs/ *n.* [*noncount*] **1.** a closely woven, heavy cloth of cotton used esp. for tents. **2.** a piece of this or similar material on which a painting is made.

can•vass /'kænvəs/ *v.* [~ + *obj*] [*no obj*] to ask for votes or opinions from people. —**'can•vass•er,** *n.* [*count*]

can•yon /'kænyən/ *n.* [*count*] a deep valley with steep sides.

cap /kæp/ *n., v.,* **capped, cap•ping.** —*n.* [*count*] **1.** a close-fitting covering for the head, usually having no brim: *a woolen cap.* **2.** a hat that signals one's rank, occupation, or the like: *a nurse's cap.* **3.** a top, lid, or cover of a container or bottle: *a bottle cap.* —*v.* [~ + *obj*] **4.** to provide or cover with or as if with a cap: *Clouds capped the mountain.*

ca•pa•ble /'keypəbəl/ *adj.* **1.** having power and ability; skillful: *a capable instructor.* **2. be capable of,** to have the ability for; have the skill, motivation, etc., necessary for: *I'm sure she is capable of performing well.* —**ca•pa•bil•i•ty** /,keypə'bɪlɪtiy/, *n.* [*noncount*] [*count*] —**'ca•pa•bly,** *adv.*

ca•pac•i•ty /kə'pæsɪtiy/ *n., pl.* **-ties. 1.** the maximum amount or number that can be contained: [*count; usually singular*]: *a jug with a capacity of two quarts.* [*noncount*]: *The stadium was filled to capacity.* **2.** mental ability: [*noncount*]: *Those math problems were beyond my capacity.* [*count*]: *People bring different capacities to the language learning process.* **3.** [*count; usually singular*] power or ability: *a capacity to withstand pressure.* **4.** [*count*] position; function; role: *served in an advisory capacity.*

cape¹ /keyp/ *n.* [*count*] a piece of clothing without sleeves, fastened at the neck and falling loosely from the shoulders.

cape² /keyp/ *n.* [*count*] a piece of land extending out into the sea.

ca•per /'keypər/ *v.* [*no obj*] **1.** to skip about in a happy, lively manner. —*n.* [*count*] **2.** a prank or trick; silly act. **3.** *Slang.* a criminal act, as a robbery.

cap•il•lar•y /'kæpə,leriy/ *n.* [*count*], *pl.* **-ies.** one of the tiny, hairlike blood vessels between the arteries and the veins.

cap•i•tal /'kæpɪtl/ *n.* **1.** [*count*] the city that is the official center of government of a country or state. **2.** [*count*] a city thought of as being of special importance in some field of activity: *Hollywood, the entertainment capital.* **3.** CAPITAL LETTER. **4.** [*noncount*] money or property owned or used in business: *He needs capital to start his new business.* —*adj.* [*before a noun*] **5.** involving the loss of life: *capital punishment.*

cap•i•tal•ism /'kæpɪtl,ɪzəm/ *n.* [*noncount*] an economic system in which property and industry are owned by private individuals and not the government. —**'cap•i•tal•ist,** *n.* [*count*]

cap•i•tal•ize /'kæpɪtl,ayz/ *v.* [~ + *obj*], **-ized, -iz•ing. 1.** to write in capital letters. **2.** to supply (a business) with capital. **3. capitalize on,** to take advantage of: *to capitalize on one's opportunities.* —**cap•i•tal•i•za•tion** /,kæpɪtələ'zeyʃən/, *n.* [*noncount*]

'capital 'letter, *n.* [*count*] a letter of the alphabet that differs from its corresponding lowercase letter in form and height.

ca•pit•u•late /kə'pɪtʃə,leyt/ *v.* [*no obj*], **-lat•ed,**

C

car

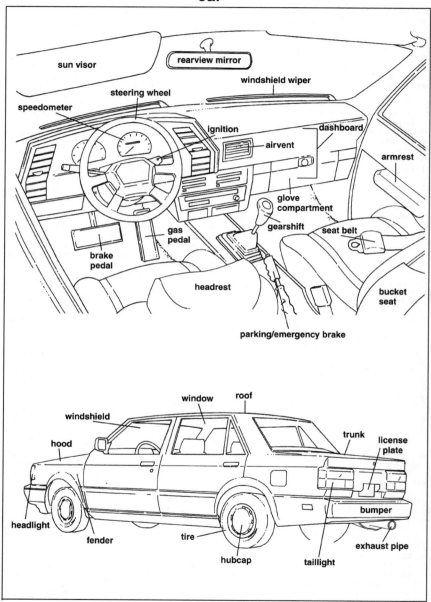

-lat•ing. to surrender usually after agreeing to certain terms.

cap•puc•ci•no /ˌkæpə'tʃiynow, ˌkɑpə-/ *n.* [*noncount*] [*count*] hot espresso coffee with foaming steamed milk added.

ca•price /kə'priys/ *n.* **1.** [*count*] a sudden, unpredictable change. **2.** [*noncount*] a tendency to change one's mind without reason. —**ca•pri•cious** /kə'prɪʃəs/, *adj.*

cap•size /'kæpsayz/ *v.* [*no obj*] [~ + *obj*], **-sized, -siz•ing.** to turn (a boat) bottom up; overturn.

cap•sule /'kæpsəl, -suwl/ *n.* **1.** a small, tube-shaped casing with a dose of medicine inside, designed to be swallowed. **2.** a sealed cabin in a spacecraft in which a person or animal can ride.

capt., an abbreviation of: captain.

cap•tain /'kæptən/ *n.* [*count*] **1.** a person in authority over others: *captain of the hockey team.* **2.** an officer in the armed forces.

cap•tion /'kæpʃən/ *n.* [*count*] a title or explanation printed near a picture.

cap•ti•vate /'kæptə,veyt/ *v.* [~ + *obj*], **-vat•ed, -vat•ing.** to charm or attract strongly.

cap•tive /'kæptɪv/ *n.* [*count*] **1.** a prisoner. —*adj.* [*before a noun*] **2.** kept in confinement: *captive animals.* —**cap'tiv•i•ty,** *n.* [*noncount*]

cap•tor /'kæptər/ *n.* [*count*] a person who has captured a person or animal.

cap•ture /'kæptʃər/ *v.,* **-tured, -tur•ing,** *n.* —*v.* [~ + *obj*] **1.** to take by force; take prisoner: *The patrol captured a dozen soldiers.* **2.** to gain control of; hold: *She captured my attention immediately.* **3.** to represent or record (a feeling, etc.): *a movie that captures life in Berlin in the 1930's.* —*n.* [*noncount*] **4.** the act of capturing.

car /kɑr/ *n.* **1.** an automobile: [*count*]: *three cars in the garage.* [*noncount*]: *to travel by car.* **2.** [*count*] a vehicle running on rails or tracks: *The train had eight cars.* **3.** [*count*] the part of an elevator that carries passengers or freight.

car•a•mel /'kærəməl/ *n.* **1.** [*noncount*] a liquid made by cooking sugar until it darkens, used for flavoring food. **2.** [*count*] a chewy candy made from sugar, butter, and milk.

car•at /'kærət/ *n.* [*count*] a unit of weight in gemstones, 200 milligrams.

car•a•van /'kærə,væn/ *n.* [*count*] **1.** a group of travelers journeying together for safety in passing through deserts, etc. **2.** a large covered vehicle for conveying passengers and goods.

car•bo•hy•drate /ˌkɑrbow'haydreyt/ *n.* [*count*] [*noncount*] any of a class of substances made of carbon, hydrogen, and oxygen, including starches and sugars: an important source of food for animals and people.

car•bon /'kɑrbən/ *n.* **1.** [*noncount*] an element combined with other elements in all living matter, and found in a pure form as diamond and coal. **2.** [*count*] a copy made by the use of carbon paper.

car•bon•at•ed /'kɑrbə,neytəd/ *adj.* containing carbon dioxide so as to produce bubbles: *carbonated drinks.* —**car•bon•a•tion** /ˌkɑrbə'neyʃən/, *n.* [*noncount*]

'carbon di'oxide /'day'ɒksayd/ *n.* [*noncount*] a colorless, odorless gas formed during respiration.

'carbon mon'oxide /mɒn'ɒksayd/ *n.* [*noncount*] a colorless, odorless, poisonous gas produced when carbon burns with insufficient air.

'carbon ,paper, *n.* [*noncount*] paper coated with carbon or other material, placed between two sheets of paper in order to reproduce on the lower sheet whatever is typed on the upper.

car•bu•re•tor /'kɑrbə,reytər, -byə-/ *n.* [*count*] a device in a car engine for mixing fuel and air to produce a mixture that can be exploded to provide power. Also, *esp. Brit.,* **car•bu•ret•tor** /'kɑrbyə,rɛtər/.

car•cass /'kɑrkəs/ *n.* [*count*] the dead body of an animal.

card /kɑrd/ *n.* **1.** [*count*] a piece of stiff paper used to record information: *an identification card.* **2.** [*count*] one of a set of thin pieces of cardboard, used in playing various games. **3. cards,** [*noncount; used with a singular verb*] game or games played with such a set. **4.** [*count*] a folded piece of thin cardboard printed with a holiday or other greeting: *a birthday card.* —*Idiom.* **5. in the cards,** destined or certain to occur. **6. put** or **lay one's cards on the table,** to be completely straightforward; conceal nothing.

card•board /'kɑrd,bɔrd/ *n.* [*noncount*] thick, stiff paper, posters, etc. used for boxes.

car•di•ac /'kɑrdiy,æk/ *adj.* [*before a noun*] of or relating to the heart.

car•di•gan /'kɑrdɪgən/ *n.* [*count*] a knitted sweater that opens down the front.

car•di•nal /'kɑrdn̩l/ *adj.* [*before a noun*] **1.** of the greatest importance. —*n.* [*count*] **2.** a high church official appointed by the pope. **3.** a songbird of North America, the male of which is bright red.

'cardinal 'number, *n.* [*count*] a number that expresses amount, as *two* or *three.*

car•di•ol•o•gy /ˌkɑrdiy'ɒlədʒiy/ *n.* [*noncount*] the study of the heart and its functions. —**,car•di•ol•o•gist,** *n.* [*count*]

care /kɛər/ *n., v.,* **cared, car•ing.** —*n.* **1.** [*count*] a worry or concern: *lots of cares.* **2.** [*noncount*] serious attention: *to devote care to one's work.* **3.** [*noncount*] protection: *We left our cat in the care of friends.* —*v.* **4.** to be concerned (about something): [*no obj*]: *Does the president really care about education?* [~ + *obj*]: *He cares what other people think.* **5.** [*no obj*] to look after someone; provide assistance: *Will you care for the children while I am in New York?* **6.** to desire; like: [~ + *obj*]: *Would you care to dance?* [*no obj*]: *Would you care for dessert?* —*Idiom.* **7. take care, a.** to be certain (to do something): *Take care not to burn yourself. He took care that everyone was paid on time.* **b.** (used as an expression of farewell): *I'll see you tomorrow; take care!* **8. take care of, a.** to watch over: *Who will take care of the children?* **b.** to deal with: *My wife takes care of the bills.*

ca•reer /kə'rɪər/ *n.* **1.** [*count*] a profession or series of jobs in the same field: *a career as a lawyer; a teaching career.* —*adj.* [*before a noun*] **2.** having as a career; professional: *He was a career diplomat.*

care•free /'kɛər,friy/ *adj.* being without worry.

care•ful /'kɛərfəl/ *adj.* **1.** cautious in one's actions: *a careful driver. He was careful not to make her angry.* **2.** done or performed with accuracy or caution: *He was a careful typist.* —**'care•ful•ly,** *adv.* —**'care•ful•ness,** *n.* [*noncount*]

care•giv•er /'kɛər,gɪvər/ *n.* [*count*] a person who cares for a child or for someone sick or disabled.

care•less /'kɛərlɪs/ *adj.* **1.** not paying enough attention to what one does: *He made a few careless mistakes.* **2.** not exact or accurate: *careless work.*

C

—**'care•less•ly,** *adv.* —**'care•less•ness,** *n.* [*noncount*]

ca•ress /kəˈrɛs/ *n.* [*count*] **1.** a light stroking gesture expressing affection or care. —*v.* [~ + *obj*] **2.** to touch or stroke lightly.

car•et /ˈkærɪt/ *n.* [*count*] a mark (^) made in written or printed matter to show the place where something is to be inserted.

care•tak•er /ˈkɛərˌteykər/ *n.* [*count*] a person in charge of the maintenance or upkeep of a building or grounds.

car•go /ˈkɑrgow/ *n.* [*noncount*] [*count*], *pl.* **-goes, -gos.** the load of goods carried by a ship, airplane, etc.

car•i•bou /ˈkærəˌbuw/ *n.* [*count*], *pl.* **-bous,** (*esp. when thought of as a group*) **-bou.** the reindeer of North America.

car•i•ca•ture /ˈkærɪkətʃər, -ˌtʃʊr/ *n.* [*count*] a picture exaggerating the special features of a person or thing.

car•nage /ˈkɑrnɪdʒ/ *n.* [*noncount*] the slaughter or killing of a great number of people, as in battle.

car•nal /ˈkɑrnl̩/ *adj.* relating to or characterized by the passions of the body; sexual.

car•na•tion /kɑrˈneyʃən/ *n.* [*count*] a fragrant flower occurring in a variety of colors.

car•ni•val /ˈkɑrnəvəl/ *n.* [*count*] **1.** a traveling amusement show having games, rides, etc. **2.** a festival: *a winter carnival.*

car•ni•vore /ˈkɑrnəˌvɔr/ *n.* [*count*] an animal that eats flesh. —**car•niv•o•rous** /kɑrˈnɪvərəs/, *adj.*

car•ol /ˈkærəl/ *n., v.,* **-oled, -ol•ing** or (*esp. Brit.*) **-olled, -ol•ling.** —*n.* [*count*] **1.** a song, esp. of joy. **2.** a Christmas song or hymn. —*v.* [*no obj*] **3.** to sing Christmas songs, esp. in a group outdoors: *They went caroling on Christmas Eve.* —**'car•ol•er,** *esp. Brit.,* **car'ol•ler,** *n.* [*count*]

car•ou•sel /ˌkærəˈsɛl, ˈkærəˌsɛl/ *n.* MERRY-GO-ROUND (def. 1).

carp[1] /kɑrp/ *v.* to find fault; complain without a good reason: [*no obj*]: *He's always carping at his employees.* [~ + *obj*]: *She is forever carping that we waste paper.*

carp[2] /kɑrp/ *n.* [*count*], *pl.* (*esp. when thought of as a group*) **carp,** (*esp. for kinds or species*) **carps.** a large freshwater fish widely used as food.

car•pen•ter /ˈkɑrpəntər/ *n.* [*count*] a person who practices carpentry.

car•pen•try /ˈkɑrpəntriy/ *n.* [*noncount*] the work or skill of making or building things of wood.

car•pet /ˈkɑrpɪt/ *n.* [*count*] **1.** a heavy, thick, woven fabric for covering floors. **2.** any surface or covering resembling a carpet: *a carpet of wildflowers in the meadow.* —*v.* [~ + *obj*] **3.** to cover with a carpet.

car•pool /ˈkɑrˌpuwl/ *n.* [*count*] an arrangement among automobile owners by which each in turn drives the others to and from a place.

car•riage /ˈkærɪdʒ/ *n.* **1.** [*count*] a wheeled vehicle pulled by horses. **2.** [*count*] a wheeled vehicle for a baby. **3.** [*noncount*] the manner in which a person's head and body are held when standing or walking.

car•ri•er /ˈkæriyər/ *n.* [*count*] a person, company, or thing that carries goods.

car•rot /ˈkærət/ *n.* [*count*] [*noncount*] a long, orange root vegetable.

car•ry /ˈkæriy/ *v.,* **-ried, -ry•ing. 1.** [~ + *obj*] to move while holding or supporting: *I'll carry the groceries home.* **2.** [~ + *obj*] to wear, hold, or have with one: *I always carry my driver's license.* **3.** [~ + *obj*] to serve as a way of sending from one place to another: *The pipes carry water.* **4.** [*no obj*] to be able to reach some distance: *Sounds carry well over water.* **5.** [~ + *obj*] to sing (a melody) on pitch. **6.** [~ + *oneself*] to hold (oneself) in a certain manner: *carries herself with dignity.* **7.** [~ + *obj*] to keep in a store for sale: *We don't carry that brand.* **8. carry away,** to stir strong emotions in: *Don't get carried away—it's only a movie.* **9. carry on, a.** to manage; conduct: *I don't know if we can carry on a conversation here.* **b.** to continue without stopping: *I carried on with my work while the kids were howling.* **c.** to be noisy, loud, or excited: *Stop carrying on like that or you'll be punished!* **10. carry out,** to put into operation; accomplish: *Can you carry out this plan?*

car•sick /ˈkɑrˌsɪk/ *adj.* ill with motion sickness during automobile travel.

cart /kɑrt/ *n.* [*count*] **1.** a two-wheeled vehicle pulled by horses, oxen, etc., and used to carry loads. **2.** any small vehicle pushed or pulled by hand: *a shopping cart.* —*v.* [~ + *obj*] **3.** to carry in a cart.

car•ti•lage /ˈkɑrtl̩ɪdʒ/ *n.* [*noncount*] a firm, elastic tissue in the body, such as the outside of the ear.

car•tog•ra•phy /kɑrˈtɒgrəfiy/ *n.* [*noncount*] the production of maps. —**car'tog•ra•pher,** *n.* [*count*]

car•ton /ˈkɑrtn̩/ *n.* [*count*] **1.** a cardboard or plastic box used for storage or shipping. **2.** a smaller container used for holding measured amounts of food or drink: *a carton of milk.*

car•toon /kɑrˈtuwn/ *n.* [*count*] **1.** a funny drawing in a newspaper, magazine, etc. **2.** COMIC STRIP. **3.** a television or motion-picture film in which the characters and background are pictures that are drawn and then animated.

car•tridge /ˈkɑrtrɪdʒ/ *n.* [*count*] **1.** a case that holds an explosive powder and a bullet for shooting from a gun. **2.** a small container filled with material to be inserted into a device: *a film cartridge for a camera; an ink cartridge for a laser printer.*

cart•wheel /ˈkɑrtˌhwiyl, -ˌwiyl/ *n.* [*count*] an acrobatic movement in which a standing person throws the body down and sideways, landing first on the hands and then on the feet.

carve /kɑrv/ *v.,* **carved, carv•ing. 1.** [~ + *obj*] to form from a solid material by cutting: *carving statues out of wood.* **2.** [~ + *obj*] [*no obj*] to cut a large piece of meat into slices.

cas•cade /kæsˈkeyd/ *n., v.,* **-cad•ed, -cad•ing.** —*n.* [*count*] **1.** a waterfall descending over a steep, rocky surface. **2.** anything that resembles a waterfall: *a cascade of hair falling over her shoulders.* —*v.* [*no obj*] **3.** to fall in or like a cascade.

case[1] /keys/ *n.* [*count*] **1.** one instance or an example of the occurrence of something: *a case of poor judgment.* **2.** the actual state of things: *If that's the case, you'd better get here sooner.* **3.** a suit or action before a judge: *a murder case.* —*Idiom.* **4. in any case,** regardless of circumstances; whatever happens: *In any case, I won't be home for dinner.* **5. in case,** if it should happen that; if: *Please walk the dog in case I don't come back on time.* **6. in case of,** in the event of; if there should be: *In case of fire, exit down the stairs.*

case² /keys/ *n.* [*count*] a container for carrying or holding something: *a jewel case.*

cash /kæʃ/ *n.* [*noncount*] **1.** money in the form of coins or bills. —*v.* [~ + *obj*] **2.** to give or obtain cash for (a check). **3. cash in on,** to profit from; use to one's advantage.

cash•ew /'kæʃuw, kə'ʃuw/ *n.* [*count*] the small, edible nut of an evergreen tree.

cash•ier /kæ'ʃɪər/ *n.* [*count*] an employee who collects payment from customers in a store.

'cash ma,chine, *n.* AUTOMATED-TELLER MACHINE.

cash•mere /'kæʒmɪər, 'kæʃ-/ *n.* [*noncount*] the fine, soft wool of a certain goat, or yarn made from this wool.

'cash ,register, *n.* [*count*] a business machine that indicates the amounts of individual sales and has a money drawer for making change.

cas•ing /'keysɪŋ/ *n.* [*count*] a protective case or covering.

ca•si•no /kə'siynow/ *n.* [*count*], *pl.* **-nos.** a building used for gambling or other entertainment.

cask /kæsk/ *n.* [*count*] a container like a barrel, for holding alcoholic drinks.

cas•ket /'kæskɪt/ *n.* [*count*] a coffin.

cas•se•role /'kæsə,rowl/ *n.* [*count*] **1.** a covered baking dish, as of glass or pottery. **2.** any food baked in such a dish: *tuna casseroles.*

cas•sette /kə'sɛt, kæ-/ *n.* [*count*] a plastic case in which audiotape or videotape runs between two reels for recording or playing back.

cast /kæst/ *v.*, **cast, cast•ing,** *n.* —*v.* [~ + *obj*] **1.** to throw or hurl; fling: *to cast dice.* **2.** to direct (the eye, etc.): *She kept casting glances at me.* **3.** to put or send forth: *This bulb casts a soft light.* **4.** to shed or drop: *The snake cast its skin.* **5.** to deposit or give (a ballot or vote). **6. a.** to select actors for (a play, etc.). **b.** to assign a role to (an actor): *They cast him as Hamlet in their production.* **7.** to form by pouring metal into a mold and letting it harden: *The statue was cast in bronze.* **8. cast away** or **aside,** to reject; discard. **9. cast off, a.** to throw away; reject: *We cast off our doubts and signed the contract.* **b.** to let go or let loose, as a ship from a mooring. —*n.* **10.** [*count*] the act of throwing. **11.** [*count*] a throw of dice. **12.** [*count; usually singular*] the group of performers in a play, film, etc. **13.** [*count*] something made by casting metal. **14.** [*count*] a rigid, hard covering used to protect and hold in place a broken bone: *Her leg is in a cast.*

cast•a•way /'kæstə,wey/ *n.* [*count*] a person whose ship has been wrecked and who has landed on a deserted island.

caste /kæst/ *n.* [*count*] any of the social divisions of Hindu society.

cas•ti•gate /'kæstɪ,geyt/ *v.* [~ + *obj*], **-gat•ed, -gat•ing.** to scold or criticize severely.

'cast 'iron, *n.* [*noncount*] a hard alloy of `iron, carbon, and other elements, cast in a mold.

'cast-'iron, *adj.* [*before a noun*] **1.** made of cast iron. **2.** strong; hardy: *a cast-iron stomach.*

cas•tle /'kæsəl/ *n.* [*count*] a fortified building, usually with a wall around it, owned by a noble, esp. in former times.

cas•trate /'kæstreyt/ *v.* [~ + *obj*], **-trat•ed, -trat•ing.** to remove the testes of. —**cas•tra• tion** /kæ'streyʃən/, *n.* [*noncount*] [*count*]

cas•u•al /'kæʒuwəl/ *adj.* **1.** happening by chance: *a casual meeting.* **2.** without serious in-

tention: *He made a casual remark about her glasses.* **3.** (of clothes, etc.) suitable to be worn on informal occasions. —**'cas•u•al•ly,** *adv.*

cas•u•al•ty /'kæʒuwəltiy/ *n.* [*count*], *pl.* **-ties.** one who is injured or killed in an accident or war.

cat /kæt/ *n.* [*count*] **1.** a small, furry animal often kept as a pet. **2.** a similar wild animal, such as the lion, tiger, leopard, and jaguar.

cat•a•clysm /'kætə,klɪzəm/ *n.* [*count*] a violent and sudden event, such as an earthquake. —,**cat• a'clys•mic,** *adj.*

cat•a•log /'kætl̩,ɔg, -,ɒg/ *n.* [*count*] **1.** a pamphlet that contains a list or record of items, often including descriptions or illustrations: *I ordered a dress from the store catalog. I bought a catalog of the art exhibit.* **2.** a list of the books or other materials in a library arranged according to a system. —*v.* [~ + *obj*] **3.** to enter (items) in a catalog.

cat•a•logue /'kætl̩,ɔg, -,ɒg/ *n., v.,* **-logued, -logu•ing.** CATALOG.

cat•a•lyst /'kætl̩ɪst/ *n.* [*count*] a substance that causes or speeds up a chemical reaction without itself being affected.

cat•a•pult /'kætə,pʌlt, -,pʊlt/ *n.* [*count*] **1.** an ancient military device for hurling heavy stones, etc. —*v.* [~ + *obj*] **2.** to hurl or be hurled from or as if from a catapult: *The crash catapulted her through the windshield.*

cat•a•ract /'kætə,rækt/ *n.* [*count*] **1.** a steep descent of water. **2.** an abnormal growth on the lens of the eye.

ca•tas•tro•phe /kə'tæstrəfiy/ *n.* [*count*] **1.** a sudden and widespread disaster. **2.** a great misfortune or failure: *Losing his job was a catastrophe.* —**cat•a•stroph•ic** /,kætə'strɒfɪk/, *adj.*

catch /kætʃ/ *v.,* **caught** /kɔt/, **catch•ing,** *n.* —*v.* [~ + *obj*] **1.** to seize or capture, esp. after chasing: *The police caught the thief.* **2.** to take and hold (something moving): *She caught the ball.* **3.** to surprise or notice, as in some action: *I caught them cheating.* **4.** to get (an) infectious disease): *caught a cold.* **5.** to be in time to get aboard: *We caught the train at Oslo.* **6.** to attract: *to catch our attention.* **7.** to understand: *I didn't catch the meaning of the joke.* **8.** to hear clearly: *I couldn't catch what he said.* **9. catch on, a.** to become popular. **b.** to understand: *I was slow but eventually I caught on.* **10. catch up, a.** to overtake someone or something moving: *I caught up with her and pulled her arm.* **b.** to overwhelm suddenly: *The truth caught up with him, and he realized what he had done.* **c.** to do enough so that one is no longer behind: *He was catching up on his work.* **d.** to be very involved or interested in: *He was caught up in his reading.* —*n.* **11.** [*count*] the act of catching. **12.** [*count*] anything that catches, esp. a device for fastening something: *Did you fasten the catch on the window.* **13.** [*count*] any tricky or concealed problem or difficulty: *There must be a catch in his plan.* **14.** [*count*] something caught, as a quantity of fish: *The fishermen brought in a large catch.* **15.** [*noncount*] a game in which a ball is thrown from one person to another.

catch•er /'kætʃər/ *n.* [*count*] **1.** a person or thing that catches. **2.** the baseball player stationed behind home plate to catch pitches not hit by the batter.

catch•y /'kætʃiy/ *adj.,* **-i•er, -i•est.** pleasing and easily remembered: *a catchy tune.*

C

cat•e•go•rize /'kætɪgə,rayz/ v. [~ + obj], **-rized, -riz•ing.** to arrange in categories.

cat•e•go•ry /'kætɪ,gɔriy/ n. [count], pl. **-ries.** any group or division in a system of classification; a class of things.

ca•ter /'keytər/ v. **1.** [no obj] [~ + obj] to provide food and drink for a party. **2.** [~ + to + obj] to provide or supply what is needed or gives pleasure: She caters to her children. —**'ca•ter•er,** n. [count]

cat•er•pil•lar /'kætə,pɪlər, 'kætər-/ n. [count] a small wormlike animal that becomes a butterfly or moth.

cat•fish /'kæt,fɪʃ/ n. [count], pl. (esp. when thought of as a group) **-fish,** (esp. for kinds or species) **-fish•es.** a fish having spines around the mouth that resemble a cat's whiskers.

ca•the•dral /kə'θiydrəl/ n. [count] any important or large church.

Cath•o•lic /'kæθəlɪk, 'kæθlɪk/ adj. **1.** of, relating to, or belonging to the Roman Catholic Church. —n. [count] **2.** a member of the Roman Catholic Church. —**Ca•thol•i•cism** /kə'θɒlə,sɪzəm/, n. [noncount]

cat•nap /'kæt,næp/ n. [count] a short, light nap.

cat•nip /'kætnɪp/ n. [noncount] a plant of the mint family, containing oils attractive to cats.

'CAT ,scan /kæt/ n. [count] an examination performed with a device that uses beams of x-rays at various angles to produce computerized images of a cross section of the body.

cat•sup /'kætsəp, 'kɛtʃəp, 'kætʃ-/ n. KETCHUP.

cat•tail /'kæt,teyl/ n. [count] a tall marsh plant resembling a reed.

cat•tle /'kætḷ/ n. [plural; used with a plural verb] large farm animals, as cows and steers, raised for their meat or milk.

cat•ty /'kætiy/ adj., **-ti•er, -ti•est.** mean in a sly way.

cau•cus /'kɔkəs/ n. [count] **1.** a meeting of the members of a political party to select candidates, determine policy, etc. **2.** a group organized to further a special interest or cause: The party caucus voted to introduce new rules.

caught /kɔt/ v. pt. and pp. of CATCH.

caul•dron /'kɔldrən/ n. [count] a large kettle or pot.

cau•li•flow•er /'kɔlɪ,flawər, 'kɒlɪ-/ n. [noncount] a vegetable with a large white head of flower buds.

caulk /kɔk/ v. [~ + obj] **1.** to use a waterproof material to seal the seams in (a window, ship's hull, etc.). —n. [noncount] **2.** Also, **caulk•ing.** a material used to caulk.

cause /kɔz/ n., v., **caused, caus•ing.** —n. **1.** [count] a person or thing that produces a result: What was the cause of the accident? **2.** [noncount] the reason or motive for some action: to complain without cause. **3.** [count] an ideal or goal to which a person or group is dedicated: the cause of human rights. —v. [~ + obj] **4.** to be the cause of; bring about: What caused the accident?

cause•way /'kɔz,wey/ n. [count] a raised road, as over a body of water.

caus•tic /'kɔstɪk/ adj. **1.** capable of burning, corroding, or destroying living tissue: Acid is caustic. **2.** severely critical or sarcastic: caustic remarks.

cau•tion /'kɔʃən/ n. [noncount] **1.** alertness in a dangerous situation; care: Proceed with caution. —v. **2.** to give a warning (to): [no obj]: I would caution against optimism. [~ + obj]: The referee cautioned him about his penalties. —**'cau•tion,ar•y,** adj.

cau•tious /'kɔʃəs/ adj. showing or using caution. —**'cau•tious•ly,** adv.

cav•al•cade /,kævəl'keyd/ n. [count] a procession of people riding on horses, in cars, etc.

cav•al•ry /'kævəlriy/ n. [count], pl. **-ries. 1.** a unit of troops on horseback. **2.** soldiers in motorized vehicles.

cave /keyv/ n., v., **caved, cav•ing.** —n. [count] **1.** a hollow place in the side of a hill. —v. [no obj] **2. cave in, a.** to collapse: The roof is caving in. **b.** to yield; surrender: At last I caved in and bought a new car.

'cave ,man, n. [count] a person who lived in a cave, esp. in prehistoric times.

cav•ern /'kævərn/ n. [count] a large cave, esp. one that is mostly underground.

cav•i•ar /'kæviy,ar/ n. [noncount] the eggs of various types of large fish, eaten esp. as an appetizer.

cav•i•ty /'kævɪtiy/ n. [count], pl. **-ties. 1.** any hollow place in a solid object. **2.** a pit in a tooth, produced by decay.

caw /kɔ/ n. [count] **1.** the loud, harsh call of the crow. —v. [no obj] **2.** to make this cry.

cay•enne /kay'ɛn, key-/ n. [noncount] a sharp-tasting powder used to flavor foods, made of the pods and seeds of a pepper plant. Also called **cay'enne 'pepper.**

CB, an abbreviation of: citizens band, a radio system used for short-distance communication.

cc, an abbreviation of: **1.** carbon copy. **2.** copies.

CD, an abbreviation of: compact disc.

CD player, n. [count] a device for playing compact discs.

cease /siys/ v., **ceased, ceas•ing.** to (cause to) stop or discontinue: [no obj]: The noise ceased when the teacher entered the room. [~ + obj]: We agreed to cease hostilities.

'cease-'fire, n. [count] a stopping of hostilities; truce.

ce•dar /'siydər/ n. **1.** [count] an evergreen tree having wide, spreading branches. **2.** [noncount] the sweet-smelling wood of this tree.

ceil•ing /'siylɪŋ/ n. [count] **1.** the upper inside surface of a room. **2.** an upper limit: a ceiling on spending.

cel•e•brate /'sɛlə,breyt/ v., **-brat•ed, -brat•ing. 1.** [~ + obj] [no obj] to show that (a day) is special by having ceremonies, parties, or other festivities. **2.** [~ + obj] to praise widely: Her music is celebrated all over the world.

cel•e•bra•tion /,sɛlə'breyʃən/ n. **1.** an event or occasion of celebrating: [count]: The postwar celebrations went on for days. [noncount]: a period of quiet celebration. **2.** [noncount] praise: Celebration for this fine author came only after her death.

ce•leb•ri•ty /sə'lɛbrɪtiy/ n., pl. **-ties. 1.** [count] a famous person. **2.** [noncount] fame: The pilot had gained celebrity for heroism.

cel•er•y /'sɛləriy/ n. [noncount] a plant whose stalks are eaten as a vegetable.

ce•les•tial /sə'lɛstʃəl/ adj. [before a noun] of or relating to the sky or heaven.

cell /sɛl/ n. [count] **1.** a small room, as in a prison. **2.** the basic structural unit of all organisms: blood cell; cancer cell. **3.** a device that converts chemical, heat, or light energy into electricity.

cel·lar /ˈsɛlər/ n. [count] an underground room, usually beneath a building.

cel·list /ˈtʃɛlɪst/ n. [count] one who plays the cello.

cel·lo /ˈtʃɛlow/ n. [count], pl. **-los.** a musical instrument that is the second largest member of the violin family.

cel·lo·phane /ˈsɛləˌfeyn/ n. [noncount] a transparent, flexible material like plastic, used for wrapping.

cel·lu·lar /ˈsɛlyələr/ adj. relating to, characterized by, or shaped like cells.

'cellular 'phone, n. [count] a portable telephone using a system of radio transmitters, each covering separate areas. Also called **'cell ˌphone.**

cel·lu·lose /ˈsɛlyəˌlows/ n. [noncount] the chief substance of the cell walls of plants, used to make cloth, paper, etc.

Cel·si·us /ˈsɛlsiyəs/ adj. relating to or measured according to a temperature scale **(Cel'sius scale')** in which 0° represents the point at which ice forms, and 100° represents the point at which steam forms: It was 10 degrees Celsius. Symbol: C.

ce·ment /sɪˈmɛnt/ n. [noncount] **1.** a mixture of clay and limestone, mixed with water and sand to form concrete. **2.** any sticky substance that acts as a glue. —v. [~ + obj] **3.** to join by or as if by cement.

cem·e·ter·y /ˈsɛmɪˌtɛriy/ n. [count], pl. **-ies.** a burial ground for dead people.

cen·sor /ˈsɛnsər/ n. [count] **1.** an official who examines books, television programs, etc., and removes parts judged to be immoral or offensive. —v. [~ + obj] **2.** to examine and remove (parts of a book, etc.) as a censor does.

cen·sor·ship /ˈsɛnsərˌʃɪp/ n. [noncount] the act or practice of censoring.

cen·sure /ˈsɛnʃər/ n., v., **-sured, -sur·ing.** —n. [noncount] **1.** strong expression of disapproval. —v. [~ + obj] **2.** show strong disapproval of.

cen·sus /ˈsɛnsəs/ n. [count], pl. **-sus·es.** an official count of the population of a country, state, etc., with details as to age, occupation, etc.

cent /sɛnt/ n. [count] **1.** a coin that is the smallest unit of money in the U.S., equal to ¹/₁₀₀ of a dollar. **2.** a unit of money in various other nations equal to ¹/₁₀₀ of the basic currency.

cen·taur /ˈsɛntɔr/ n. [count] a creature in Greek myth having the head, chest, and arms of a man, and the body and legs of a horse.

cen·ten·ar·y /sɛnˈtɛnəriy, ˈsɛntṇˌɛriy/ n. [count], pl. **-ies.** a centennial.

cen·ten·ni·al /sɛnˈtɛniyəl/ adj. **1.** of, relating to, or marking a 100th anniversary. **2.** lasting 100 years. —n. [count] **3.** a 100th anniversary or its celebration.

cen·ter /ˈsɛntər/ n. [count] **1.** the middle part or point of something. **2.** a focus, or place of interest or concern: She was the center of attention. **3.** a principal point, place, or object: a shipping center. —v. **4.** [~ + obj] to place in or on a center. **5.** to focus; concentrate: [~ + obj]: He centered his novel on the Civil War. [no obj]: His novel centers on the Civil War. Also, esp. Brit., **centre.**

Cen·ti·grade /ˈsɛntɪˌgreyd/ adj. CELSIUS: It was only 5 degrees Centigrade.

cen·ti·me·ter /ˈsɛntəˌmiytər/ n. [count] ¹/₁₀₀ of a meter. Also, esp. Brit., **cen'ti·me'tre.**

cen·ti·pede /ˈsɛntəˌpiyd/ n. [count] a small wormlike animal with a pair of legs on each of its segments.

cen·tral /ˈsɛntrəl/ adj. **1.** of, in, at, or near the center: Our home is in the central part of town. **2.** being the source from which all other related things proceed or are controlled: He reported to the central administration. **3.** most important; chief: He played a central role in settling the conflict. —'cen·tral·ly, adv.

cen·tral·ize /ˈsɛntrəˌlayz/ v. [~ + obj] [no obj], **-ized, -iz·ing.** to (cause to) come under one central control, esp. in government. —cen·tral·i·za·tion /ˌsɛntrələˈzeyʃən/, n. [noncount]

cen·tre /ˈsɛntər/ n., v., **-tred, -tring.** Chiefly Brit. CENTER.

cen·tu·ry /ˈsɛntʃəriy/ n. [count], pl. **-ries.** a period of 100 years.

CEO or **C.E.O.,** an abbreviation of: chief executive officer.

ce·ram·ics /səˈræmɪks/ n. **1.** [noncount; used with a singular verb] the art of making objects of clay and heating them to make them hard. **2.** [plural; used with a plural verb] articles or objects made from clay, etc. —ce·ram·ic, adj.

ce·re·al /ˈsɪəriyəl/ n. **1.** [count] a plant of the grass family, such as wheat, that produces grain that can be eaten. **2.** [noncount] [count] breakfast food made from this grain.

cer·e·mo·ny /ˈsɛrəˌmowniy/ n., pl. **-nies.** **1.** [count] the formal activities conducted on some solemn or important occasion: the marriage ceremony. **2.** [noncount] all the actions, words, or formal behavior on such an occasion. —ˌcer·e'mo·ni·al, adj.

cer·tain /ˈsɜrtṇ/ adj. **1.** free from doubt; sure; confident: I'm certain that I passed the test. **2.** destined; sure to happen: She is certain to be at the party. **3.** established as true or sure: It is certain that you tried. **4.** agreed upon; settled: For a certain amount I can get you across the border. —'cer·tain·ly, adv. —'cer·tain·ty, n. [noncount] [count], pl. **-ties.**

cer·tain·ly /ˈsɜrtṇliy/ adv. **1.** surely; without doubt; undoubtedly: You certainly have done a fine job. **2.** (used to show strong feeling about something, to show agreement, or to answer "yes" to a question): This is certainly a fine party, isn't it? May I have my pen back, please? —Certainly.

cer·tif·i·cate /sərˈtɪfɪkɪt/ n. [count] a written document that gives proof that something is true: a birth certificate.

cer·ti·fy /ˈsɜrtəˌfay/ v. [~ + obj], **-fied, -fy·ing. 1.** to declare that something is certain or true; confirm. **2.** to give a license to (someone), often by providing a certificate. —cer·ti·fi·ca·tion /ˌsɜrtəfɪˈkeyʃən/, n. [noncount]

cer·vix /ˈsɜrvɪks/ n. [count], pl. **-vix·es, -vi·ces** /-vəˌsiyz/ the opening part of the uterus.

Ce·sar·e·an /sɪˈzɛəriyən/ n. [count] an operation in which a baby is delivered by cutting open the woman's uterus. Also called Ce'sarean ˌsec·tion, C-section.

ces·sa·tion /sɛˈseyʃən/ n. [count; usually singular] a stopping; ceasing.

cess·pool /ˈsɛsˌpuwl/ n. [count] an underground container for receiving the waste from a house.

cf., an abbreviation of Latin confer: compare.

chafe /tʃeyf/ v. [~ + obj] [no obj], **chafed, chaf·ing.** to (cause to) become sore by rubbing.

cha·grin /ʃəˈgrɪn/ n. [noncount] a feeling of annoyance or humiliation: To my complete chagrin I realized I didn't have enough money to pay for dinner.

chain /tʃeyn/ n. **1.** [count] [noncount] a series of

C

metal rings passing through one another, used for hauling, for supporting, or as decoration. **2. chains, a.** [count; used with a plural verb] strong, usually metal rings attached to a prisoner's hands or feet. **b.** [noncount; usually, in + ~] the state of being a slave; bondage: to live one's life in chains. **3.** [count] a series of things connected one after the other: the chain of events leading up to the murder. **4.** [count] a range of mountains one after the other. **5.** [count] a number of businesses under one ownership or management: a hotel chain. —v. [~ + obj] **6.** to fasten or confine with a chain.

chair /tʃɛər/ n. [count] **1.** a seat for one person, usually having four legs for support and a rest for the back. **2.** a chairman or chairwoman. —v. [~ + obj] **3.** to be in charge of (a meeting).

chair•lift /'tʃɛər,lɪft/ n. [count] a series of chairs hanging from a cable, for carrying skiers up a slope.

chair•man /'tʃɛərmən/ n. [count], pl. **-men.** the officer in charge of a meeting, or the head of a board or department.

chair•per•son /'tʃɛər,pɜrsən/ n. [count] a person in charge of a meeting, or the head of a board or department.

chair•wom•an n. [count], pl. **-wom•en.** a woman who takes charge of a meeting, or heads a board or department.

cha•let /ʃæ'ley/ n. [count] a wooden house common in the Swiss Alps.

chalk /tʃɔk/ n. **1.** [noncount] a soft, white powder made of limestone. **2.** a solid piece of chalk or chalklike substance for writing on a blackboard. —v. [~ + obj] **3.** to write with chalk. **4. chalk up, a.** to score or earn. **b.** to give as a reason; attribute: Chalk it up to lack of experience. —'**chalk•y,** adj., **-i•er, -i•est.**

chalk•board /'tʃɔk,bɔrd/ n. [count] a blackboard.

chal•lenge /'tʃælɪndʒ/ n., v., **-lenged, -leng•ing.** —n. **1.** something that is difficult to accomplish and that tests a person's skill or ability, esp. in an interesting way: [count]: Space exploration is a challenge for humankind. [noncount]: I'd like a job that offers more challenge. **2.** [count] a call to compete in a contest or fight. **3.** [count] a demand, request, or question to explain or justify something: His speech was a challenge to the president's power. —v. [~ + obj] **4.** to summon (someone) to a contest or fight. **5.** to test (someone) because of its difficulty: The new job will challenge her. **6.** to demand or question whether (a person or thing) is correct or qualified: They challenged the dictator's authority. **7.** to halt and demand identification from: The guard challenged the reporter when she tried to enter the army base. —'**chal•leng•er,** n. [count]

cham•ber /'tʃeymbər/ n. [count] **1.** a private room in a house or apartment, esp. a bedroom. **2.** an enclosed space; cavity: a chamber of the heart.

'**chamber ,music,** n. [noncount] classical music played by a small group of instruments.

cha•me•le•on /kə'miyliyən/ n. [count] a slow-moving lizard having the ability to change color to match its surroundings.

champ¹ /tʃæmp, tʃɒmp/ also **chomp,** v. [~ + obj] [no obj] to bite upon or grind (something), esp. impatiently.

champ² /tʃæmp/ n. [count] Informal. a champion.

cham•pagne /ʃæm'peyn/ n. [noncount] [count] a sparkling dry white wine from France.

cham•pi•on /'tʃæmpiyən/ n. [count] **1.** a person or thing that defeats all opponents. **2.** a person who fights for or defends any person or cause: She became a champion of the poor. —v. [~ + obj] **3.** to defend; support: He championed the cause of liberty.

cham•pi•on•ship /'tʃæmpiyən,ʃɪp/ n. **1.** [count] the distinction or condition of being a champion. **2.** [noncount] support or defense: championship of human rights. **3.** [count] a contest to determine a champion.

chance /tʃæns/ n., v., **chanced, chanc•ing.** —n. **1.** [noncount] the unpredictable part of an event; luck. **2.** a possibility; likelihood: [count]: her chances of success. [noncount]: There is not much chance of changing his mind. **3.** [count] an opportunity: Now is your chance. **4.** [count] a risk or hazard. —v. **5.** [no obj] to happen accidentally or in an unplanned way: I chanced to see her last week. **6.** [~ + obj] to risk: Let's chance it. —**Idiom. 7. by chance,** unexpectedly; accidentally: I met her by chance. **8. on the (off) chance,** counting on the (slight) possibility.

chan•cel•lor /'tʃænsələr/ n. [count] **1.** the leader of some governments, as in Germany. **2.** a high-ranking officer in some American universities.

chanc•y /'tʃænsiy/ adj., **-i•er, -i•est.** risky; uncertain.

chan•de•lier /,ʃændl'ɪər/ n. [count] a branched holder for lights that is hung from a ceiling.

change /tʃeyndʒ/ v., **changed, chang•ing,** n. —v. **1.** to (cause to) become different: [~ + obj]: She decided to change her name. [no obj]: His kids thought he changed into a grouchy old man. **2.** [~ + obj] to exchange for another: I changed the light bulb. **3.** to transfer from one (bus, train, airplane, etc.) to another: [~ + obj]: I changed buses and went on to Sixth Street. [no obj]: You have to change in Paris to go to Brussels. **4.** [~ + obj (+ for + obj)] to give or get smaller money in exchange for: Can you change this twenty for two fives and a ten? **5.** [~ + obj + to/for + obj] to give or get foreign money in exchange for: I need to change these dollars to pounds. **6.** to remove and replace the clothes of: [~ + obj]: to change a baby. [no obj]: I changed out of work clothes into something more comfortable. —n. **7.** [count] [noncount] the act of changing or result of being changed. **8.** [count] a replacement or substitution. **9.** [noncount] the money returned when the amount paid is larger than the amount owed. **10.** [noncount] coins: rattling the change in his pocket. —**Idiom. 11. change one's mind,** to alter or modify one's opinion or plans. **12. for a change,** in order to do something differently from the usual way: Let's try a new restaurant for a change. —'**change•a•ble,** adj.

chan•nel /'tʃænl/ n. [count] **1.** the bottom or deeper part of a river or other body of water. **2.** a narrow body of water between a continent and an island: the English Channel. **3.** a course or way by which something is moved or directed: channels of trade. **4.** a frequency band or wavelength on which radio and television signals are broadcast: We usually watch the news on Channel 20.

chant /tʃænt/ n. [count] **1.** a short, simple melody or song, esp. a religious one. **2.** a phrase or slogan that is repeated, as by a crowd. —*v.* [~ + *obj*] [*no obj*] **3.** to say or say in a chant.

Cha·nu·kah /ˈxɑnəkə, ˈhɑ-/ *n.* HANUKKAH.

cha·os /ˈkeyɒs/ *n.* [*noncount*] a state of confusion or disorder. —**cha·ot·ic** /key'ɒtɪk/, *adj.*

chap¹ /tʃæp/ *v.* [~ + *obj*] [*no obj*], **chapped, chap·ping.** (of the lips or skin) to (cause to) become cracked, roughened, and reddened.

chap² /tʃæp/ *n.* [*count*] *Chiefly Brit.* fellow; guy.

chap·el /ˈtʃæpəl/ *n.* [*count*] **1.** a separate part of a church, or a small church. **2.** a room for worship that is part of another institution, such as a hospital.

chap·lain /ˈtʃæplɪn/ *n.* [*count*] a member of the clergy who serves with a military unit, or who works with the chapel of a college or hospital.

chap·ter /ˈtʃæptər/ *n.* [*count*] **1.** a main division of a book or the like, usually having a number or title. **2.** [*count*] an important part or division of anything: *He began a new chapter in his life at the new university.* **3.** [*count*] a local branch of a society, club, etc.: *our chapter of the honor society.*

char /tʃɑr/ *v.*, **charred, char·ring. 1.** [~ + *obj*] [*no obj*] to burn or reduce to charcoal: *The fire charred the paper.* **2.** [~ + *obj*] to burn slightly; scorch: *The flame charred the steak.*

char·ac·ter /ˈkærɪktər/ *n.* **1.** [*noncount*] the collection of qualities that form the individual nature of a person or thing, and that make it different from others: *The chief flaw in her character was impatience.* **2.** [*noncount*] one such feature or characteristic: *His letter was mostly positive in character.* **3.** [*noncount*] moral or ethical strength: *a woman of strong character.* **4.** [*noncount*] special, often interesting qualities: *an old hotel with a lot of character.* **5.** [*count*] a person, esp. with reference to behavior: *A suspicious character was standing in the hall.* **6.** [*count*] a person in a drama, story, etc.: *The play has only three characters.* **7.** [*count*] a symbol used in a system of writing.

char·ac·ter·is·tic /ˌkærɪktəˈrɪstɪk/ *adj.* **1.** showing the character of a person or thing; typical: *It was characteristic of her not to take all the credit.* —*n.* [*count*] **2.** a typical or special quality: *Curly hair is a characteristic of that family.*

char·ac·ter·ize /ˈkærɪktəˌrayz/ *v.* [~ + *obj*], **-ized, -iz·ing. 1.** to be a characteristic of. **2.** to describe the character of: *The president characterized the dictator as a scoundrel.*

cha·rade /ʃəˈreyd/ *n.* **1. charades,** [*noncount*; *used with a singular verb*] a game in which players act out, without speaking, a word or phrase for members of their team to guess. **2.** [*count*] an obvious lie or deception.

char·coal /ˈtʃɑrˌkowl/ *n.* [*noncount*] the black carbon material made by heating a substance, such as wood, in very little air.

charge /tʃɑrdʒ/ *v.*, **charged, charg·ing,** *n.* —*v.* **1.** [*no obj*] [~ + *obj*] to ask (money) for payment. **2.** [~ + *obj*] to record (a purchase) so that it can be paid for in the future: *He charged the coat on his credit card.* **3. a.** [~ + *obj*] to attack; rush forward against. **b.** [*no obj*] to rush suddenly or violently: *They charged up the hill after her.* **4.** [~ + *obj*] to accuse formally or in law: *They charged her with theft.* **5.** [~ + *obj*] to give an order or instruction to: *He charged his assistant with management of the budget.* **6.** [~ + *obj*] to put electrical energy into (a battery). **7.** [~ + *obj*; *usually: be* + ~*-ed* + *with* + *obj*] to fill with an emotion: *The air was charged with excitement.* —*n.* [*count*] **8.** a fee or price. **9.** an attack. **10.** someone or something given to one's

care: *The young children were her charges.* **11.** an accusation. **12.** electricity put into a battery. —*Idiom.* **13. in charge,** in command; having the care or responsibility: *Who's in charge here?* **14. take charge,** to assume control or responsibility: *Her boss expected her to take charge of the situation.*

'charge ac·count, *n.* [*count*] an account, esp. in a store, that permits a customer to buy goods and be billed at a later date.

'charge ,card, *n.* [*count*] an identification card used to make purchases on a charge account.

char·i·ot /ˈtʃæriyət/ *n.* [*count*] a light, horse-drawn vehicle, used in ancient battles, races, etc.

cha·ris·ma /kəˈrɪzmə/ *n.* [*noncount*] a quality of an individual to attract people, lead them, etc.: *a politician with great charisma.* —**char·is·mat·ic** /ˌkærɪzˈmætɪk/, *adj.*

char·i·ty /ˈtʃærɪtiy/ *n., pl.* **-ties. 1.** [*noncount*] gifts of money or things to aid the poor, ill, or helpless. **2.** [*noncount*] [*count*] a charitable fund, organization, or institution. **3.** [*noncount*] a generous feeling, esp. toward those in need: *to do something out of charity.* —**char·i·ta·ble** /ˈtʃærɪtəbəl/, *adj.*

charm /tʃɑrm/ *n.* **1.** [*noncount*] [*count*] a power of pleasing or attracting people, as through beauty. **2.** [*count*] a small ornament on a bracelet or necklace. **3.** [*count*] **a.** something worn or carried to bring good luck. **b.** words or chants believed to have magical power. —*v.* [~ + *obj*] **4.** to delight or please greatly.

chart /tʃɑrt/ *n.* [*count*] **1.** a sheet giving information in diagrams, such as graphs. **2.** a map, esp. a map of the sea. —*v.* [~ + *obj*] **3.** to make a chart of. **4.** to plan: *to chart a course of action.*

char·ter /ˈtʃɑrtər/ *n.* [*count*] **1.** a document defining the formal organization of an institution: *the Charter of the United Nations.* **2.** an arrangement by which a ship, airplane, etc., is hired for use at a particular time for a particular group. —*v.* [~ + *obj*] **3.** to issue a charter to. **4.** to hire for use for a specified time: *The school chartered a bus for the trip to the city.*

chase /tʃeys/ *v.*, **chased, chas·ing,** *n.* —*v.* [~ + *obj*] [*no obj*] **1.** to follow rapidly or closely in order to catch or drive away. —*n.* [*count*] **2.** the act of chasing; pursuit.

chasm /ˈkæzəm/ *n.* [*count*] a wide, deep crack in the earth's surface.

chas·sis /ˈtʃæsiy, ˈtʃæs-/ *n.* [*count*], *pl.* **chas·sis** /ˈtʃæsiyz, ˈtʃæs-/. the frame, wheels, and machinery of a motor vehicle.

chaste /tʃeyst/ *adj.*, **chast·er, chast·est. 1.** not engaging in sexual relations: *to remain chaste until marriage.* **2.** decent and modest: *a chaste kiss on the cheek.*

chas·tise /tʃæsˈtayz/ *v.* [~ + *obj*], **-tised, -tis·ing.** to punish or scold severely.

chas·ti·ty /ˈtʃæstɪtiy/ *n.* [*noncount*] the state or quality of being chaste.

chat /tʃæt/ *v.*, **chat·ted, chat·ting,** *n.* —*v.* [*no obj*] **1.** to talk in an informal way. —*n.* [*count*] **2.** an informal conversation.

chat·ter /ˈtʃætər/ *v.* [*no obj*] **1.** to talk rapidly and without purpose. **2.** to make rapid, speech-like sounds, such as a monkey or bird. **3.** to make a rapid noise caused by the striking together of separate parts: *His teeth were chattering from the cold.* —*n.* [*noncount*] **4.** rapid talk without a purpose. **5.** the act or sound of chattering.

chat·ter·box /ˈtʃætərˌbɒks/ *n.* [*count*] an overly talkative person.

C

chat·ty /'tʃætiy/ *adj.,* **-ti·er, -ti·est.** fond of chatting; eager to chat.

chauf·feur /'ʃowfər, ʃow'fɜr/ *n.* [*count*] **1.** a person hired to drive an automobile for the owner. —*v.* [~ + *obj*] **2.** to drive (a vehicle) as a chauffeur. **3.** to transport by car: *to chauffeur the kids to school.*

chau·vin·ism /'ʃowvə,nɪzəm/ *n.* [*noncount*] strong, unthinking devotion to one's country, or to any group or cause. —**chau·vin·ist** /'ʃowvənɪst/, *n.* [*count*]

cheap /tʃiyp/ *adj.,* **-er, -est,** *adv.* —*adj.* **1.** costing very little. **2.** charging low prices: *a cheap store.* **3.** poorly made; inferior. **4.** mean; cruel: *a cheap joke.* —*adv.* **5.** at a low price or small cost. —'**cheap·ly,** *adv.* —'**cheap·ness,** *n.* [*noncount*]

cheap·en /'tʃiypən/ *v.* [~ + *obj*] **1.** to make cheap or cheaper. **2.** to decrease the quality of; make inferior.

cheat /tʃiyt/ *v.* **1.** to lie (to) or behave dishonestly (with): [*no obj*]: *to cheat at cards.* [~ + *obj*]: *She cheated me out of my inheritance.* **2.** **cheat on,** to be sexually unfaithful to (someone). —*n.* [*count*] **3.** Also, '**cheat·er.** a person who cheats.

check /tʃɛk/ *v.* **1.** [~ + *obj*] to stop the motion of suddenly: *The pilot checked his speed.* **2.** [~ + *obj*] to test the correctness or condition of: *I checked the answers on the exam.* **3.** [~ + *obj*] to mark so as to indicate choice, completion, etc.: *Check the box next to the item you wish to order.* **4.** to search through; make an inquiry (into): [~ + *obj*]: *You'll have to check the files for the letter.* [*no obj*]: *You'll have to check into the matter.* **5.** [~ + *obj*] to leave (personal belongings) to be kept temporarily: *They checked their luggage before boarding the plane.* **6. check in,** to register or report one's arrival: *We checked in at the airport an hour before our flight left.* **7. check (up) on,** to investigate or inspect. **8. check out, a.** to leave a hotel or motel after settling one's account. **b.** to prove to be right or true. **c.** to find out if something is right or true. **d.** *Slang.* to examine carefully. —*n.* **9.** Also, *Brit.,* **cheque.** a written order directing a bank to pay money: [*count*]: *a check for $100.* [*noncount*]: *I'll pay for this by check.* **10.** [*count*] a slip of paper showing an amount owed, esp. at a restaurant: *The waiter brought us the check as soon as we finished eating.* **11.** [*count*] a mark, often indicated by (✓), to indicate that something has been noted, etc. **12.** [*count*] a search, inspection, or examination. **13.** [*count*] a pattern formed of squares: *pants with checks.*

check·book /'tʃɛk,bʊk/ *n.* [*count*] a pad of blank checks for paying money from an account.

check·er /'tʃɛkər/ *n.* **1.** [*count*] a small disk used in playing checkers. **2. checkers,** [*noncount; used with a singular verb*] a game played by two persons, each with 12 playing pieces, on a checkerboard.

check·er·board /'tʃɛkər,bɔrd/ *n.* [*count*] a board marked into 64 squares of two colors, on which checkers is played.

'**checking ac,count,** *n.* [*count*] a bank account against which checks can be written by the depositor.

check·out /'tʃɛk,awt/ *n.* **1.** [*noncount*] the time by which a guest at a hotel must leave a room. **2.** [*count*] Also called '**checkout ,counter.** a counter where customers pay for purchases, as in a supermarket.

check·up /'tʃɛk,ʌp/ *n.* [*count*] a physical examination by a physician.

ched·dar /'tʃɛdər/ *n.* [*noncount*] a hard cheese that varies in flavor from mild to sharp.

cheek /tʃiyk/ *n.* **1.** [*count*] either side of the face below the eye and above the jaw. **2.** [*noncount*] rude behavior.

cheep /tʃiyp/ *v.* [*no obj*] **1.** to chirp; peep. —*n.* [*count*] **2.** a chirp.

cheer /tʃɪər/ *n.* **1.** [*count*] a shout of encouragement or support. **2.** [*noncount*] gladness, gaiety, or liveliness: *The news of her recovery filled us with cheer.* —*interj.* **3. cheers,** (used as a greeting or toast): *They raised their glasses and said "Cheers!"* —*v.* **4.** [~ + *obj*] [*no obj*] to give shouts of approval or encouragement to (someone or something). **5.** [~ + *obj*] to gladden; raise the spirits of. **6. cheer up,** to become or make happier or more cheerful.

cheer·ful /'tʃɪərfəl/ *adj.* full of cheer; happy. —'**cheer·ful·ly,** *adv.* —'**cheer·ful·ness,** *n.* [*noncount*]

cheer·lead·er /'tʃɪər,liydər/ *n.* [*count*] one who leads spectators in cheering, esp. at an athletic event.

cheer·y /'tʃɪəriy/ *adj.,* **-i·er, -i·est.** cheerful; happy.

cheese /tʃiyz/ *n.* [*noncount*] [*count*] a food prepared from the curds of milk separated from the whey.

cheese·burg·er /'tʃiyz,bɜrgər/ *n.* [*count*] a hamburger topped with a melted slice of cheese.

cheese·cake /'tʃiyz,keyk/ *n.* [*noncount*] [*count*] a cake with a firm texture made with sweetened cream cheese.

chee·tah /'tʃiytə/ *n.* [*count*] a swift, black-spotted cat of SW Asia and Africa.

chef /ʃɛf/ *n.* [*count*] the chief cook, esp. in a restaurant.

chem·i·cal /'kɛmɪkəl/ *n.* [*count*] **1.** a substance produced by or used in chemistry. —*adj.* **2.** of, used in, or produced by chemistry or chemicals. —'**chem·i·cal·ly,** *adv.*

chem·ist /'kɛmɪst/ *n.* [*count*] **1.** a specialist in chemistry. **2.** *Chiefly Brit.* DRUGGIST.

chem·is·try /'kɛməstriy/ *n.* [*noncount*] **1.** the science that studies the composition, properties, and activity of substances and various elementary forms of matter. **2. a.** relationship between people in which there is mutual understanding. **b.** sexual attraction.

che·mo·ther·a·py /,kiymow'θɛrəpiy/ *n.* [*noncount*] Also, '**che·mo.** the use of chemicals to destroy cancerous tissue.

cheque /tʃɛk/ *n.* *Brit.* CHECK (def. 9).

cher·ish /'tʃɛrɪʃ/ *v.* [~ + *obj*] **1.** to regard as valuable or precious: *The early settlers cherished freedom.* **2.** to cling fondly to: *to cherish a memory.*

cher·ry /'tʃɛriy/ *n.* [*count*], *pl.* **-ries.** a small, soft, red, pulpy fruit that grows on a tree.

cher·ub /'tʃɛrəb/ *n.* [*count*], *pl.* **cher·u·bim** /'tʃɛrəbɪm, -yʊbɪm/ for 1, **cher·ubs** for 2. **1.** a kind of angel, often represented as a winged child. **2.** a child with a sweet, chubby, innocent face.

chess /tʃɛs/ *n.* [*noncount*] a game played on a board by two people who each move 16 pieces of six kinds.

chest /tʃɛst/ *n.* [*count*] **1.** the front portion of the body enclosed by the ribs. **2.** a box with a lid. **3.**

CHEST OF DRAWERS. **4.** a small cabinet, esp. one hung on a wall.

chest•nut /'tʃɛs,nʌt, -nət/ *n.* **1.** [*count*] any of several tall trees of the beech family, having nuts that can be eaten. **2.** [*count*] the nut of such a tree. **3.** [*noncount*] a reddish brown color.

'**chest of** '**drawers,** *n.* [*count*], *pl.* **chests of drawers.** a piece of furniture consisting of a set of drawers in a frame, for holding clothing, linens, etc.

chew /tʃuw/ *v.* **1.** [~ + *obj*] [*no obj*] to crush or grind (something) with the teeth. **2. chew out,** *Slang.* to scold harshly. —*n.* [*count*] **3.** an act or instance of chewing.

'**chewing** ,**gum** /'tʃuwɪŋ/ *n.* [*noncount*] a sweetened substance for chewing but not swallowing.

chew•y /'tʃuwiy/ *adj.,* -**i•er,** -**i•est.** (of food) not easily chewed, esp. because of toughness or stickiness.

chic /ʃiyk/ *adj.,* -**er,** -**est,** *n.* —*adj.* **1.** attractive and fashionable; stylish. —*n.* [*noncount*] **2.** elegance, esp. in dress design.

Chi•ca•na /tʃɪ'kɑnə/ *n.* [*count*], *pl.* -**nas.** a Mexican-American woman or girl.

Chi•ca•no /tʃɪ'kɑnow/ *n.* [*count*], *pl.* -**nos.** a Mexican-American, esp. a male.

chick /tʃɪk/ *n.* [*count*] **1.** a young chicken or other bird. **2.** *Slang* (*often offensive*). a young woman.

chick•a•dee /'tʃɪkə,diy/ *n.* [*count*] a small North American bird with white cheeks and a dark-colored throat and cap.

chick•en /'tʃɪkən/ *n.* **1.** [*count*] a bird developed in a number of breeds for its flesh, eggs, and feathers. **2.** [*noncount*] the flesh of the chicken used as food. **3.** [*count*] *Slang.* a cowardly or fearful person. —*adj.* **4.** *Informal.* cowardly; frightened: *He won't do it; he's chicken.* —*v.* [*no obj*] **5. chicken out,** *Informal.* to withdraw because of fear.

chick•en•pox /'tʃɪk,ənpɒks/ *n.* [*noncount*] a disease, commonly of children, marked by fever and red spots or blisters on the skin.

chick•pea /'tʃɪk,piy/ *n.* [*count*] the pealike seed of a widely grown plant, used as a food.

chic•o•ry /'tʃɪkəriy/ *n.* [*noncount*], *pl.* -**ries.** a plant whose leaves are used in salads and whose roots are ground and added to coffee.

chide /tʃayd/ *v.* [~ + *obj*], **chid•ed** or **chid** /tʃɪd/, **chid•ed** or **chid** or **chid•den** /'tʃɪdn̩/, **chid•ing.** to scold or reproach.

chief /tʃiyf/ *n.* [*count*] **1.** the head or leader of an organized group: *the chief of police.* **2.** the ruler of a tribe or clan: *an Indian chief.* —*adj.* **3.** highest in rank or authority: *the chief priest.* **4.** most important; principal: *the chief difficulty.* —*Idiom.* **5. in chief,** highest in rank: *commander in chief.*

chief•ly /'tʃiyfliy/ *adv.* **1.** most importantly; principally. **2.** for the most part; mainly.

chief•tain /'tʃiyftən/ *n.* [*count*] the chief of a clan or a tribe.

chif•fon /ʃɪ'fɒn/ *n.* [*noncount*] a soft, thin fabric of silk, nylon, or rayon.

chi•hua•hua /tʃɪ'wɑwə/ *n.* [*count*] one of a Mexican breed of very small dogs.

child /tʃayld/ *n.* [*count*], *pl.* **chil•dren** /'tʃɪldrən/. **1.** a young boy or girl. **2.** a son or daughter: *He has two children, a boy and a girl.* **3.** a person who has been strongly influenced by the ideas of another person or by having lived in a certain

time or place: *a child of the war years.* —'**child• less,** *adj.*

child•bear•ing /'tʃayld,bɛərɪŋ/ *n.* [*noncount*] the act of bringing forth children.

child•birth /'tʃayld,bɜrθ/ *n.* [*noncount*] [*count*] an act or instance of bringing forth a child.

child•hood /'tʃayldhʊd/ *n.* [*noncount*] [*count; usually singular*] the state or period of being a child.

child•ish /'tʃayldɪʃ/ *adj.* immature; babyish. —'**child•ish•ly,** *adv.*

chil•dren /'tʃɪldrən/ *n.* pl. of CHILD.

Chil•e•an /'tʃɪliyən/ *adj.* **1.** of or relating to Chile. —*n.* [*count*] **2.** a person born or living in Chile.

chil•i or **chil•e** /'tʃɪliy/ *n.,* *pl.* **chil•ies** or **chil• es. 1.** [*count*] Also called **chili pepper.** the hot-tasting pod of any of several species of pepper, used in cooking. **2.** [*noncount*] a spicy dish of chilis, tomatoes, and beans.

chill /tʃɪl/ *n.* [*count*] **1.** an uncomfortable coldness: *the chill of winter.* **2.** a sudden feeling of fear: *A chill went down her spine when she heard the news.* —*adj.* **3.** moderately cold; cool. —*v.* [*no obj*] [~ + *obj*] **4.** to (cause to) become cold. —'**chill•ing,** *adj.* —'**chill•y,** *adj.,* -**i•er,** -**i•est.**

chime /tʃaym/ *n.,* *v.,* **chimed, chim•ing.** —*n.* [*count*] **1.** Often, **chimes.** [*plural*] **a.** a set of bells producing musical tones when struck. **b.** a musical instrument consisting of such a set. **c.** the musical tone produced: *the chime of the clock.* —*v.* [*no obj*] **2.** to sound harmoniously or in chimes: *The church bells chimed at noon.* **3. chime in,** to enter a conversation, esp. to interrupt: *I was all set to chime in when the boss began to speak.*

chim•ney /'tʃɪmniy/ *n.* [*count*], *pl.* -**neys.** a structure containing a passage by which the smoke of a fire or furnace is carried off.

chimp /tʃɪmp/ *n.* [*count*] a chimpanzee.

chim•pan•zee /,tʃɪmpæn'ziy/ *n.* [*count*] a large humanlike ape of Africa, having a dark coat and a relatively bare face.

chin /tʃɪn/ *n.* [*count*] **1.** the lowest part of the face, below the mouth. —*Idiom.* **2. keep one's chin up,** to maintain one's courage.

chi•na /'tʃaynə/ *n.* [*noncount*] **1.** a delicate material made from baked clay and used for making plates, cups, etc. **2.** objects made of china.

Chi•nese /tʃay'niyz, -'niys/ *n.,* *pl.* -**nese,** *adj.* —*n.* **1.** [*noncount*] the standard language of China. **2.** [*noncount*] any of the other related languages spoken in China. **3.** [*count*] a person born or living in China. —*adj.* **4.** of or relating to China. **5.** of or relating to the languages spoken in China.

chink /tʃɪŋk/ *n.* [*count*] a narrow opening.

chi•no /'tʃiynow/ *n.,* *pl.* -**nos. 1.** [*noncount*] a cotton cloth used for trousers, uniforms, etc. **2.** Usually, **chinos.** [*plural*] trousers of this cloth.

chip /tʃɪp/ *n.,* *v.,* **chipped, chip•ping.** —*n.* [*count*] **1.** a small thin piece, as of wood, separated by chopping or breaking. **2.** a thin slice or small piece of food: *potato chips; chocolate chips.* **3.** a mark or flaw made by the breaking off of a small piece: *This glass has a chip.* **4.** Also called **microchip.** a tiny slice of semiconducting material on which a transistor or complex circuit is formed: *memory chips for computers.* **5. chips,** *Chiefly Brit.* FRENCH FRIES. —*v.* **6.** to break off or lose a small piece: [*no obj*]: *My tooth chipped.* [~ + *obj*]: *He chipped the paint off the wall.* **7. chip in,** to contribute money, time, etc.: *We each* chipped in five dollars. —*Idiom.* **8. chip off the old block,** a person who strongly resembles a parent: *His son is a chip off the old block.* **9. have a chip on one's shoulder,** to be constantly angry or ready to quarrel or fight. **10. when the chips are down,** when the need for support is greatest: *This is one guy who'll help you when the chips are down.*

chip•munk /'tʃɪpmʌŋk/ *n.* [*count*] a small, striped ground squirrel.

chi•ro•prac•tor /'kayrə,præktər/ *n.* [*count*] a person trained in a system of medicine for treatment of the back, based upon the interactions of the spine and nervous system.

chirp /tʃɜrp/ *n.* [*count*] **1.** the short, sharp sound made by small birds and some insects. —*v.* [*no obj*] **2.** to make the sound of a chirp.

chis•el /'tʃɪzəl/ *n.*, *v.*, **-eled, -el•ing** or (*esp. Brit.*) **-elled, -el•ling.** —*n.* [*count*] **1.** a metal tool with a cutting edge at the end of the blade, used for cutting or shaping wood, stone, etc. —*v.* [~ + *obj*] **2.** to shape or cut with a chisel.

chit•chat /'tʃɪt,tʃæt/ *n.* [*noncount*] light conversation; gossip.

chiv•al•ry /'ʃɪvəlriy/ *n.* [*noncount*] the qualities expected of a knight, including courage, generosity, and courtesy. —**chiv•al•rous** /'ʃɪvəlrəs/, *adj.*

chive /tʃayv/ *n.* [*count*] Usually, **chives.** [*plural*] a small bulb-shaped plant, related to the onion.

chlo•rine /'klɔriyn/ *n.* [*noncount*] a chemical element, a greenish yellow poisonous gas, used to purify water and to make bleaching powder.

chlo•ro•phyll /'klɔrəfɪl/ *n.* [*noncount*] the green substance in plant leaves that produces food by photosynthesis.

choc•o•hol•ic /,tʃɔkə'hɔlɪk, -'hɒlɪk, ,tʃɒkə-/ *n.* [*count*] a person who craves chocolate and eats a lot of it.

choc•o•late /'tʃɔkəlɪt, 'tʃɒkə-/ *n.* [*noncount*] **1.** a food made from cacao, often sweetened and flavored. **2.** [*count*] a piece of candy made from such a preparation: *a box of chocolates.* —*adj.* **3.** having the color of chocolate; dark-brown. —'**choc•o•lat•y, 'choc•o•lat•ey,** *adj.*

choice /tʃɔys/ *n.*, *adj.*, **choic•er, choic•est.** —*n.* **1.** [*count*] an act or instance of choosing; selection: *a wise choice of friends.* **2.** [*noncount*] the right, power, or opportunity to choose: *no choice but to go along.* **3.** [*count*] the person or thing chosen: *Blue is my choice for the rug.* **4.** [*count*] an abundance or variety from which to choose: *a wide choice of styles.* —*adj.* **5.** worthy of being chosen: *choice cuts of meat.* **6.** carefully selected: *a few choice words for his enemies.*

choir /kwayər/ *n.* [*count*] a group of singers, esp. those performing in a church service.

choke /tʃowk/ *v.*, **choked, chok•ing.** **1.** [~ + *obj*] [*no obj*] to stop the breath of (someone) by squeezing or blocking the windpipe; strangle. **2.** [~ + *obj*] to keep back or hold back: *She choked back her sobs.*

cho•les•ter•ol /kə'lɛstə,rowl, -,rɔl/ *n.* [*noncount*] a substance found in animal fats, meat, and eggs.

chomp /tʃɒmp/ *v.* CHAMP[1].

choose /tʃuwz/ *v.*, **chose** /tʃowz/, **cho•sen** /'tʃowzən/, **choos•ing. 1.** [~ + *obj*] [*no obj*] to pick from a number of possibilities. **2.** [~ + *to* + *verb*] to prefer or decide: *to choose to speak.*

choos•y /'tʃuwziy/ *adj.*, **-i•er, -i•est.** hard to please; very particular, esp. in making a choice.

chop /tʃɒp/ *v.*, **chopped, chop•ping,** *n.* —*v.* **1.** to cut or separate (something) with quick, heavy

blows, using a sharp tool like an ax: [~ + *obj*]: *They chopped down a tree. She chopped off a branch.* [*no obj*]: *He chopped at the tree.* **2.** [~ + *obj*] to cut into smaller pieces; mince: *to chop (up) celery.* —*n.* [*count*] **3.** an act or instance of chopping. **4.** an individual cut or portion of lamb, pork, or veal.

chop•py /'tʃɒpiy/ *adj.*, **-pi•er, -pi•est. 1.** (of the sea, a lake, etc.) forming short, irregular, broken waves. **2.** uneven in style: *short, choppy sentences.*

chop•stick /'tʃɒp,stɪk/ *n.* [*count*] one of a pair of thin sticks held between the thumb and fingers and used as an eating utensil.

cho•ral /'kɔrəl/ *adj.* [*before a noun*] of a chorus or a choir: *a choral hymn.*

chord[1] /kɔrd/ *n.* [*count*] the straight line between two points on a given curve.

chord[2] /kɔrd/ *n.* [*count*] a combination of two or more musical tones sounded at the same time.

chore /tʃɔr/ *n.* [*count*] a small, ordinary, or dull job.

cho•re•o•graph /'kɔriyə,græf/ *v.* [~ + *obj*] to provide the choreography for. —**cho•re•og•ra•pher** /,kɔriy'ɒgrəfər/, *n.* [*count*]

cho•re•og•ra•phy /,kɔriy'ɒgrəfiy/ *n.* [*noncount*] **1.** the art of composing ballets and other dances and planning the movements and patterns of dancers. **2.** the movements and patterns composed for a dance.

cho•rus /'kɔrəs/ *n.* [*count*], *pl.* **-rus•es. 1. a.** a group of persons singing together. **b.** a part of a song repeated at the end of each verse. **2.** singing or speaking something at the same time or with the same message: *a chorus of jeers.*

chose /tʃowz/ *v.* pt. of CHOOSE.

cho•sen /'tʃowzən/ *v.* pp. of CHOOSE.

chow•der /'tʃawdər/ *n.* [*noncount*] a thick soup usually made with seafood or vegetables and milk.

Christ /krayst/ *n.* Jesus of Nazareth, held by Christians to be the son of God and the Messiah.

chris•ten /'krɪsən/ *v.* [~ + *obj*], to receive into the Christian church by baptism; baptize. —'**chris•ten•ing,** *n.* [*count*]

Chris•tian /'krɪstʃən/ *adj.* **1.** of or relating to Jesus Christ or His teachings. **2.** of or relating to the religion based on the teachings of Jesus Christ: *a Christian church.* —*n.* [*count*] **3.** a person who believes in Jesus Christ.

Chris•ti•an•i•ty /,krɪstʃiy'ænɪtiy/ *n.* [*noncount*] the Christian religion, including the Catholic, Protestant, and Eastern Orthodox churches.

'Christian ,name, *n.* [*count*] the name given at baptism, as distinguished from the family name.

Christ•mas /'krɪsməs/ *n.* [*noncount*] [*count*] an annual Christian festival on December 25 that celebrates Jesus' birth.

chrome /krowm/ *n.* [*noncount*] chromium-plated trim, as on an automobile.

chro•mi•um /'krowmiyəm/ *n.* [*noncount*] a shiny metal element used in making alloy steels.

chro•mo•some /'krowmə,sowm/ *n.* [*count*] one of a set of threadlike structures in a cell that carry the genes determining an individual's inherited traits.

chron•ic /'krɒnɪk/ *adj.* **1.** being such by habit or for a long time: *a chronic liar.* **2.** (of a disease) lasting a long time; coming back again frequently. —'**chron•i•cal•ly,** *adv.*

chron•i•cle /'krɒnɪkəl/ *n.*, *v.*, **-cled, -cling.** —*n.* [*count*] **1.** a record of events in the order in which they occurred. —*v.* [~ + *obj*] **2.** to record in or as if in a chronicle.

chron•o•log•i•cal /ˌkrɒnlˈɒdʒɪkəl/ *adj.* of or relating to chronology.

chro•nol•o•gy /krəˈnɒlədʒiy/ *n.* [*noncount*] the science of arranging time in periods and figuring the dates and historical order of past events.

chrys•a•lis /ˈkrɪsəlɪs/ *n.* [*count*], *pl.* **chrys•a•lis•es.** a moth or butterfly in the stage between a larva and an adult.

chry•san•the•mum /krɪˈsænθəməm/ *n.* [*count*] a plant with showy flowers.

chub•by /ˈtʃʌbiy/ *adj.*, **-bi•er, -bi•est.** round and plump.

chuck /tʃʌk/ *v.* [~ + *obj*] **1.** to toss; throw: *Chuck the ball over here!* **2.** to throw away; throw out: *Can't we chuck these old boxes?*

chuck•le /ˈtʃʌkəl/ *v.*, **-led, -ling,** *n.* —*v.* [*no obj*] **1.** to laugh in a soft, quiet manner. —*n.* [*count*] **2.** a soft, quiet laugh.

chug /tʃʌg/ *n.*, *v.*, **chugged, chug•ging.** —*n.* [*count*] **1.** a short, dull, explosive sound: *the steady chug of an engine.* —*v.* [*no obj*] **2.** to make this sound.

chum /tʃʌm/ *n.* [*count*] a close companion or friend; pal.

chum•my /ˈtʃʌmiy/ *adj.*, **-mi•er, -mi•est.** friendly; sociable: *He was chummy with the boss.*

chunk /tʃʌŋk/ *n.* [*count*] **1.** a thick mass, lump, or piece: *a chunk of meat.* **2.** a large amount: *A chunk of my salary goes to pay the rent.*

chunk•y /ˈtʃʌŋkiy/ *adj.*, **-i•er, -i•est. 1.** (of people) thick or stout; stocky. **2.** full of chunks: *chunky soup.*

church /tʃɜrtʃ/ *n.* **1.** [*count*] a building for public Christian worship. **2.** [*noncount*] a religious service in such a building: *We were late for church again.* **3.** [*sometimes:* Church] **a.** [*count*] any major division of this body: *the Protestant Church.* **b.** [*noncount*] the clergy who have authority in decisions: *What is the church's position on this issue?*

churn /tʃɜrn/ *n.* [*count*] **1.** a machine in which cream is beaten to make butter. —*v.* **2.** [~ + *obj*] to shake, beat, or stir vigorously to make into butter: *to churn cream.* **3.** [~ + *obj*] [*no obj*] to shake or move about vigorously or violently: *The storm churned (up) the sea.*

chute /ʃuwt/ *n.* [*count*] a sloping channel for sending water, grain, etc., to a lower level.

CIA or **C.I.A.,** an abbreviation of: Central Intelligence Agency.

ci•der /ˈsaydər/ *n.* [*noncount*] the juice pressed from apples.

ci•gar /sɪˈgɑr/ *n.* [*count*] a thick roll of tobacco prepared for smoking.

cig•a•rette /ˌsɪgəˈrɛt/ *n.* [*count*] a narrow, short roll of finely cut tobacco wrapped in thin paper for smoking.

cinch /sɪntʃ/ *n.* **1.** [*count*] a strong rope for holding a pack or saddle. **2.** [*count; a* + ~] *Informal.* something sure or easy: *Fixing this leak was a cinch.*

cin•der /ˈsɪndər/ *n.* [*count*] a partially burned piece of coal, wood, etc.

cin•e•ma /ˈsɪnəmə/ *n.*, *pl.* **-mas. 1.** [*noncount*] motion pictures, as an art or industry. **2.** [*count*] a motion-picture theater.

cin•na•mon /ˈsɪnəmən/ *n.* [*noncount*] a sweet-smelling spice made from the inner bark of various Asian trees of the laurel family.

ci•pher /ˈsayfər/ *n.* [*count*] **1.** ZERO. **2.** the key to

a secret method of writing: *She uncovered the cipher after days of analysis.*

cir•ca /ˈsɜrkə/ *prep.*, *adv.* (used before a date) about; approximately: *The Vikings landed in North America circa 1000.*

cir•cle /ˈsɜrkəl/ *n.*, *v.*, **-cled, -cling.** —*n.* [*count*] **1.** a closed curve consisting of all the points at a given distance from the center. **2.** any ringlike object or arrangement: *a circle of dancers.* **3.** a number of persons joined by something in common: *a circle of friends.* —*v.* **4.** [~ + *obj*] to enclose in a circle: *Circle the correct answer.* **5.** [~ + *obj*] [*no obj*] to move in a circle around.

cir•cuit /ˈsɜrkɪt/ *n.* [*count*] **1.** a circular journey: *the earth's circuit around the sun.* **2.** a regular journey from place to place, as by sales representatives covering a route. **3.** the complete path of an electric current.

cir•cu•i•tous /sərˈkyuwɪtəs/ *adj.* going around instead of in a straight line; not direct: *She took a circuitous route back to her hotel.*

cir•cuit•ry /ˈsɜrkɪtriy/ *n.* [*noncount*] the parts or pieces of an electric circuit.

cir•cu•lar /ˈsɜrkyələr/ *adj.* **1.** having the form of a circle; round. **2.** moving in or forming a circle or a circuit: *a circular path.* —*n.* [*count*] **3.** a letter or notice intended for the public or for anyone to see.

cir•cu•late /ˈsɜrkyəˌleyt/ *v.*, **-lat•ed, -lat•ing. 1.** [*no obj*] [~ + *obj*] to move in a circle or circuit, such as blood in the body. **2.** [*no obj*] to pass from person to person: *I circulated among the guests during the party.* **3.** [~ + *obj*] [*no obj*] to (cause to) pass or be sold from place to place, etc.; distribute. —**cir•cu•la•tion** /ˌsɜrkyəˈleyʃən/, *n.* [*noncount*] [*count*] —**cir•cu•la•to•ry** /ˈsɜrkyələˌtɔriy/, *adj.*

circum-, a prefix meaning around or about (*circumference*).

cir•cum•cise /ˈsɜrkəmˌsayz/ *v.* [~ + *obj*], **-cised, -cis•ing.** to remove the foreskin of (a male). —**cir•cum•cis•ion** /ˌsɜrkəmˈsɪʒən/, *n.* [*count*] [*noncount*]

cir•cum•fer•ence /sərˈkʌmfərəns/ *n.* [*count*] the outer boundary, esp. of a circular area; perimeter.

cir•cum•flex /ˈsɜrkəmˌflɛks/ *n.* [*count*] a mark (ˆ or ˜) placed over a vowel in some languages to indicate how the vowel is to be pronounced.

cir•cum•stance /ˈsɜrkəmˌstæns/ *n.* **1.** Usually, **circumstances.** [*plural*] the conditions surrounding or affecting something: *What were the circumstances of his death?* **2. circumstances,** [*plural*] the condition or state of a person with respect to income: *a family in reduced circumstances.* —*Idiom.* **3. under no circumstances,** never, regardless of events or conditions. **4. under the circumstances,** because of conditions that exist at the moment.

cir•cus /ˈsɜrkəs/ *n.* [*count*], *pl.* **-cus•es.** a large public show featuring performing animals, clowns, etc.

cit•a•del /ˈsɪtədl̩, -əˌdɛl/ *n.* [*count*] a fortress for defending a city.

ci•ta•tion /sayˈteyʃən/ *n.* [*count*] a quotation from something written, used in support of a claim.

cite /sayt/ *v.* [~ + *obj*], **cit•ed, cit•ing. 1.** to quote (a book, author, etc.), esp. as an authority: *He cited Einstein's work as proof of this theory.* **2.** to refer to as an example: *He cited instances of abuse by the police.* **3.** to praise for outstanding service or devotion to duty.

C

cit•i•zen /'sɪtəzən, -sən/ n. [count] a member of a country who owes loyalty to its government and is entitled to its protection.

cit•i•zen•ship /'sɪtəzən,ʃɪp, -sən-/ n. [noncount] the state or condition of being a citizen.

'citric 'acid /'sɪtrɪk/ n. [noncount] a kind of acid found esp. in citrus fruits.

cit•rus /'sɪtrəs/ n. [count], pl. **-rus•es.** any of various trees or shrubs bearing fruit with shiny skin and tart-to-sweet juicy pulp, including the lemon, lime, and orange.

cit•y /'sɪtiy/ n. [count], pl. **cit•ies.** a large or important town.

civ•ic /'sɪvɪk/ adj. [before a noun] **1.** of or relating to a city. **2.** of or relating to citizenship.

civ•ics /'sɪvɪks/ n. [noncount; used with a singular verb] the study of the privileges and obligations of citizens.

civ•il /'sɪvəl/ adj. **1.** of, relating to, or consisting of citizens: civil unrest; civil duty. **2.** relating to the ordinary life and affairs of citizens rather than to military or religious affairs: They had a civil wedding ceremony at City Hall and then a religious one in a church. The civil authorities were able to stop the rioting without calling in the military. **3.** relating to the laws that regulate private matters rather than criminal ones: civil law; a civil trial. **4.** polite but not friendly. —**ci•vil•i•ty** /sɪ'vɪlɪtiy/, n. [noncount] [count]

ci•vil•ian /sɪ'vɪlyən/ n. [count] a person who is not on active duty with a military, naval, police, or firefighting organization.

civ•i•li•za•tion /,sɪvələ'zeyʃən/ n. [noncount] an advanced state of human society, in which a high level of culture has been reached.

civ•i•lize /'sɪvə,layz/ v. [~ + obj], **-lized, -liz•ing.** to bring out of a backward or uneducated state; make enlightened or refined.

'civil 'rights, n. [plural; often: Civil Rights] rights to personal liberty and equality.

'civil 'war, n. **1.** [noncount] [count] a war between political groups or regions within the same country. **2.** [usually: the Civil War] the war in the U.S. between the North and the South, 1861–65.

clad /klæd/ v. **1.** a pt. and pp. of CLOTHE. —adj. [usually used with a noun or adverb] **2.** dressed or clothed: poorly-clad beggars. **3.** provided with a protective coating of another metal: copper-clad pans.

claim /kleym/ v. [~ + obj] **1.** to ask for or demand by or as if by a right. **2.** to state (something) as true or as a fact: She claimed to be telling the truth. **3.** to take or expect to receive (credit, etc.): The terrorists claimed responsibility for the attack. **4.** to call for; collect (something missing or held for another): Has anyone claimed the lost wallet? **5.** to take (lives, casualties): The war claimed the lives of thousands of civilians. —n. [count] **6.** a demand for something due: to make unreasonable claims on a doctor's time. **7.** an assertion of something as a fact: I make no claims to originality. **8.** a right to claim or demand: His claim to the heavyweight title is disputed.

clam /klæm/ n., v., **clammed, clam•ming.** —n. [count] **1.** a soft-bodied shellfish with two shells that close tight around it. —v. [no obj] **2. clam up,** Informal. to refuse to talk or reply.

clam•my /'klæmiy/ adj., **-mi•er, -mi•est.** covered with a cold, sticky moisture: clammy hands.

clam•or /'klæmər/ n. [count] **1.** a loud noise or strong protest, as from a crowd of people. —v. **2.** to make a clamor: [no obj]: They clamored for a voice in the decision-making process. [~ + obj]: They clamored that their demands were not being listened to. Also, esp. Brit., **clam/our.**

clamp /klæmp/ n. [count] **1.** a device for holding or fastening objects together. —v. [~ + obj] **2.** to fasten with a clamp: He clamped the glued pieces of wood together for a stronger bond.

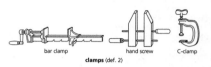
bar clamp   hand screw   C-clamp
clamps (def. 2)

clan /klæn/ n. [count] **1.** a group of families claiming descent from a common ancestor: Scottish clans. **2.** any family group or large family.

clan•des•tine /klæn'dɛstɪn/ adj. done in secrecy.

clap /klæp/ v., **clapped, clap•ping,** n. —v. [no obj] [~ + obj] **1.** to strike the palms of (one's hands) together. —n. [count] **2.** an act of clapping. **3.** a loud and quick or explosive noise, as of thunder.

clar•i•fy /'klærə,fay/ v. [~ + obj], **-fied, -fy•ing.** to make (an idea, etc.) clear or understandable. —**clar•i•fi•ca•tion** /,klærəfɪ'keyʃən/, n. [noncount] [count]

clar•i•net /,klærə'nɛt/ n. [count] a woodwind instrument in the form of a long tube. —**,clar•i'net•ist, ,clar•i'net•tist,** n. [count]

clar•i•ty /'klærɪtiy/ n. [noncount] the state or quality of being clear: the clarity of pure water; clarity of thought.

clash /klæʃ/ v. **1.** [no obj] [~ + obj] to strike with a loud, harsh noise. **2.** [no obj] to fight or disagree: The opponents frequently clashed on this issue. Your ideas often clash with mine. **3.** [no obj] (of colors or patterns) to not match. —n. [count] **4.** a loud, harsh noise, as of a collision: the clash of cymbals. **5.** a conflict, esp. of views or interests.

clasp /klæsp/ n. [count] **1.** a device for fastening together two or more things or parts: the clasp on a necklace. **2.** a firm grasp or grip of the hand. —v. [~ + obj] **3.** to fasten with or as if with a clasp. **4.** to grasp or grip with the hand. **5.** to hold in a tight embrace; hug.

class /klæs/ n. **1.** [count] a number of persons or things thought of as belonging together; kind; sort: the class of living things. **2.** [count] **a.** a group of students meeting regularly. **b.** the period in which they meet: The class is on Mondays and Wednesdays. **c.** a meeting of such a group: During our last class we talked about verb tenses in English. **3.** [count] a group of students graduated in the same year: the class of '92. **4.** a level of society sharing the same characteristics; social rank: [count]: the blue-collar class. [noncount]: socialists fighting against the concept of class. **5.** [noncount] a division of people or things according to rank, quality, etc.: a hotel of the highest class. **6.** [noncount] Informal. grace or dignity: She showed a lot of class during the interview. —v. [~ + obj] **7.** to place or arrange in a class; classify.

clas•sic /'klæsɪk/ adj. **1.** of the first or highest quality or rank. **2.** of or obeying an established set of standards or methods; typical: a classic example of fine writing. **3.** of long-lasting interest, quality, or style: a classic movie. —n. [count] **4.**

an author, book, etc., of long-lasting quality. **5.** an author or literary work of ancient Greece or Rome.

clas•si•cal /'klæsɪkəl/ adj. [before a noun] **1.** of or relating to ancient Greece and Rome, or to its culture. **2.** relating to or being music of the European tradition, such as opera, symphonies, and chamber music. **3.** accepted as having authority, as distinguished from experimental and unproven: classical physics.

'classified ,ad, n. [count] a brief advertisement in a newspaper or magazine, dealing with offers of or requests for jobs, houses, etc. Also called **'classified adver'tisement.**

clas•si•fy /'klæsə,faɪ/ v. [~ + obj], **-fied, -fy•ing. 1.** to arrange or organize by classes. **2.** to limit the availability of (information, etc.) to certain persons only: The government classified those documents. —**clas•si•fi•ca•tion** /,klæsəfɪ'keɪʃən/, n. [noncount] [count]

class•mate /'klæs,meɪt/ n. [count] a member of the same class at a school or college.

class•room /'klæs,ruwm, -,rʊm/ n. [count] a room, as in a school, in which classes are held.

class•y /'klæsiy/ adj., **-i•er, -i•est.** Informal. of high quality, rank, or grade; elegant.

clat•ter /'klætər/ v. [no obj] [~ + obj] **1.** to (cause to) make a loud, rattling sound, as that produced by hard objects striking one another. —n. [count; usually singular] **2.** a rattling noise.

clause /klɔz/ n. [count] **1.** (in grammar) a group of words containing a subject and predicate and forming either a part of a sentence or a whole sentence. **2.** a separate and particular section or provision in a contract or other legal document.

claus•tro•pho•bi•a /,klɔstrə'fowbiyə/ n. [noncount] an abnormal fear of being in enclosed or narrow places. —,**claus•tro'pho•bic,** adj.

claw /klɔ/ n. [count] **1.** a sharp, curved nail on the foot of an animal, such as on a cat. **2.** a similar curved limb of an insect. —v. [~ + obj] [no obj] **3.** to tear, scratch, etc., with or as if with claws: The kitten clawed at the door.

clay /kleɪ/ n. [noncount] a natural earthy material that is stiff and sticky when wet, and baked to make bricks, pottery, etc.

clean /kliyn/ adj. and adv., **-er, -est,** v. —adj. **1.** free from dirt; unsoiled: a clean dress. **2.** smooth, even, or regular: a clean cut with a scalpel. **3.** morally pure; not obscene: clean language. **4.** innocent of crime: He had a clean record. **5.** complete; total: a clean break with tradition. **6.** empty; bare: a clean sheet of paper. —adv. **7.** in a clean manner; so as to be clean: This shirt will never wash clean. **8.** Informal. completely: The bullet passed clean through the wall. —v. **9.** [no obj] [~ + obj] to perform or undergo a process of cleaning. **10.** [~ + obj] to dry-clean. **11. clean out, a.** to empty in order to straighten or clean: I had to clean out my desk. I cleaned it out before dinner. **b.** to empty or use up: The thief cleaned out the cash register. **12. clean up,** to make neat or clean. —**clean•li•ness** /'klɛnliynɪs/, n. [noncount]

'clean-'cut, adj. **1.** clearly outlined: a clean-cut design. **2.** neat and wholesome-looking: At least her boyfriend is smart and clean-cut.

clean•er /'kliynər/ n. [count] **1.** a person who cleans, esp. as an occupation. **2.** an apparatus for cleaning: a vacuum cleaner. **3.** Usually, **cleaners.** [plural] a dry-cleaning establishment.

cleanse /klɛnz/ v. [~ + obj], **cleansed, cleans•ing.** to make clean.

cleans•er /'klɛnzər/ n. [noncount] [count] a substance that cleanses.

clear /klɪər/ adj. and adv., **-er, -est,** v. —adj. **1.** free from darkness or cloudiness: a clear day. **2.** transparent: The water was clear. **3.** easily seen; sharply defined: a clear outline. **4.** easily heard: the clear sound of bells. **5.** easily understood: The choice is clear: fight or lose. **6.** evident; plain; obvious: a clear case of cheating. **7.** free from obstructions or obstacles: a clear path. —adv. **8.** in a clear or distinct manner; clearly: He could hear me loud and clear. **9.** so as not to be touching or near; away: Stand clear of the closing doors. —v. **10.** [~ + obj] to remove people or objects from (something): to clear the table of dishes. **11.** to (cause to) become clear, clean, or transparent: [no obj]: The sky cleared. [~ + obj]: This lotion will clear the blemishes from your skin. **12.** [~ + obj] to (cause to) become free of confusion, doubt, or uncertainty: Her mind cleared and she knew what she had to do. **13.** [~ + obj] to remove trees or other obstructions from (land), as for farming. **14.** [~ + obj] to make a dry, scraping noise in (the throat) by forcing air through, often to attract attention. **15.** [~ + obj] to free of anything suggesting disgrace: She fought to clear her name. **16.** [~ + obj] to pass by or over without contact: The ship cleared the reef. **17.** [~ + obj] to give clearance to; give official permission to: The control tower cleared the plane for takeoff. **18. clear away** or **off, a.** to (cause to) leave or disappear. **b.** to remove (something) from an area to make it clean: She cleared off the books from her desk. **19. clear out, a.** to remove the contents of. **b.** to go away, esp. quickly. **c.** to drive or force out. **20. clear up, a.** to make clear; explain. **b.** to put in order; tidy up: Can you clear up this mess? Can you clear it up? **c.** to cure: This medicine will clear up the infection. **d.** to become better or brighter, as the weather: I hope it clears up by noon.

clear•ance /'klɪərəns/ n. **1.** [noncount] [count] the act of clearing. **2.** [noncount] [count; usually singular] the distance between two objects; an amount of clear space: There isn't much clearance between the roof of this van and the bridge. **3.** [count] the selling of merchandise at reduced prices to make room for new goods.

clear•ing /'klɪərɪŋ/ n. [count] a piece of land that contains no trees or bushes: a clearing in the woods.

clear•ly /'klɪərliy/ adv. **1.** in a clear manner; distinctly: I could see clearly once I cleaned my glasses. Please speak clearly. **2.** obviously; without a doubt: Clearly, you've made him angry.

cleav•age /'kliyvɪdʒ/ n. **1.** [count] a division or split. **2.** [noncount] the area between a woman's breasts, esp. when revealed by a low neckline.

cleav•er /'kliyvər/ n. [count] a heavy knife or long-bladed hatchet, esp. one used by butchers.

clef /klɛf/ n. [count] a sign at the beginning of a musical staff to show the pitch of the notes.

cleft /klɛft/ n. [count] a space or opening made by cleavage; a split.

clem•en•cy /'klɛmənsiy/ n. [noncount] mercy or kind treatment.

clench /klɛntʃ/ v. [~ + obj] **1.** to close (the hands, teeth, etc.) tightly. **2.** to grasp firmly; grip: I clenched the cigar in my teeth.

cler•gy /'klɜrdʒiy/ n. [plural; used with a plural verb] the group of appointed leaders in a religion.

cler•gy•man /'klɜrdʒiymən/ n. [count], pl. **-men.** a member of the clergy.

C

cler·i·cal /'klɛrɪkəl/ adj. **1.** of, relating to, or for an office clerk: *made a clerical error in the report.* **2.** of, relating to, or for the clergy.

clerk /klɜrk/ n. [count] **1.** a person employed to keep records or perform general tasks in an office. **2.** a salesclerk.

clev·er /'klɛvər/ adj., **-er, -est. 1.** mentally bright; able to learn quickly. **2.** original or creative: *a clever idea.* —'**clev·er·ly,** adv. —'**clev·er· ness,** n. [noncount]

cli·ché /kliy'ʃey, klɪ-/ n. [count] a very common expression, idea, etc., that is used too often.

click /klɪk/ n. [count] **1.** a slight, sharp sound: *the click of the key in the lock.* —v. **2.** [no obj] [~ + obj] to (cause to) give off or make such a sound. **3.** [no obj] *Informal.* to become suddenly clear or understood: *The concept finally clicked in his mind.*

cli·ent /'klayənt/ n. [count] a person who uses the advice or services of a lawyer or other professional.

cli·en·tele /,klayən'tɛl/ n. [count; usually singular] clients or customers thought of as a group.

cliff /klɪf/ n. [count] a high, steep rock face.

cli·mac·tic /klay'mæktɪk/ adj. of, relating to, or being a climax: *the climactic scene of the movie.*

cli·mate /'klaymɪt/ n. [count] **1.** the general weather conditions of a region. **2.** the general attitudes or conditions of a group, period, or place: *a climate of political unrest.* —'**cli'mat·ic** /klay'mætɪk/ adj.

cli·max /'klaymæks/ n. [count] **1.** the most intense point in the development of something: *Being elected president was the climax of his career.* —v. [no obj] [~ + obj] **2.** to bring to or reach a climax.

climb /klaym/ v. **1.** to go up: [no obj]: *The sun climbed over the hill.* [~ + obj]: *to climb the stairs.* **2.** [no obj] to move using the hands and feet: *They all climbed into the car. He climbed along the ledge.* **3.** [no obj] (of numbers, etc.) to rise or increase in value: *Prices climbed by fifty cents a share today.* —n. [count] **4.** the act of climbing. —'**climb·er,** n. [count]

clinch /klɪntʃ/ v. [~ + obj] to settle (a matter) completely or decisively: *They clinched the deal in an hour.*

cling /klɪŋ/ v. [no obj], **clung** /klʌŋ/, **cling·ing. 1.** to stick to: *Wet paper clings to glass.* **2.** to hold tight, as by grasping or embracing: *The child clung to her mother.*

clin·ic /'klɪnɪk/ n. [count] a place for the medical treatment of patients who are not staying at a hospital.

clin·i·cal /'klɪnɪkəl/ adj. **1.** [before a noun] of or relating to a clinic or a hospital. **2.** not showing any feeling; cold and uncaring: *a clinical description of the accident.*

clink /klɪŋk/ v. [no obj] [~ + obj] **1.** to (cause to) make a light, sharp, ringing sound: *The coins clinked together.* —n. [count] **2.** a clinking sound.

clip¹ /klɪp/ v., **clipped, clipped** or **clipt** /klɪpt/, **clip·ping,** n. —v. [~ + obj] **1.** to cut off or out, as with scissors; to trim: *to clip a rose from a bush; to clip a hedge.* —n. [count] **2.** the act of clipping or something clipped off.

clip² /klɪp/ n., v., **clipped, clip·ping.** —n. [count] **1.** a device that grips tightly, esp. one for holding together papers. **2.** an article of jewelry clipped onto clothing. —v. **3.** to fasten with a clip: [no obj]: *This earring clips onto the ear.* [~ + obj]: *I clipped the reports together.*

clip·board /'klɪp,bɔrd/ n. [count] a small board

used to write on, with a clip at the top for holding papers.

clip·per /'klɪpər/ n. [count] Often, **clippers.** [plural; often used with a plural verb] a cutting tool: *a nail clipper; hedge clippers.*

clip·ping /'klɪpɪŋ/ n. [count] **1.** a piece of something that has been clipped: *lawn clippings.* **2.** an article clipped from a newspaper or magazine.

clique /kliyk, klɪk/ n. [count] a small group of people who keep others from joining them.

cloak /klowk/ n. [count] **1.** a loose outer garment, such as a cape. **2.** something that covers or conceals; disguise: *a cloak of secrecy.* —v. [~ + obj] **3.** to cover with a cloak. **4.** to hide; conceal.

clob·ber /'klɒbər/ v. [~ + obj] *Informal.* **1.** to hit or beat. **2.** to defeat completely.

clock /klɒk/ n. [count] **1.** a relatively large instrument for telling time. —v. [~ + obj] **2.** to time, test, or determine by means of a clock or watch: *The racehorse was clocked at two minutes thirty seconds.* —**Idiom. 3. around the clock,** for the entire 24-hour day without pause: *worked around the clock.*

clock·wise /'klɒk,wayz/ adv. **1.** in the same direction as the movement of the hands of a clock when viewed from the front or from above: *The handle turns clockwise.* —adj. **2.** directed clockwise.

clock·work /'klɒk,wɜrk/ n. [noncount] **1.** the mechanism of a clock. —**Idiom. 2. like clock- work,** with regularity; smoothly.

clod /klɒd/ n. [count] **1.** a lump of earth or clay. **2.** a very clumsy person.

clog /klɒg, klɔg/ v., **clogged, clog·ging,** n. —v. **1.** to (cause to) become blocked: [~ + obj]: *All that hair has clogged (up) the drain.* [no obj]: *The drain has clogged (up) again.* —n. [count] **2.** a shoe with a thick sole of wood, cork, etc.

clois·ter /'klɔystər/ n. [count] **1.** a covered walk, esp. in a church or other religious building. **2.** a place for religious people to live, such as a monastery.

clone /klown/ n., v., **cloned, clon·ing.** —n. [count] **1.** a living thing that is identical in its genes to the individual from which it was obtained. **2.** a person or thing that closely resembles another in appearance, use, etc.: *The new computers are clones of the original model.* —v. [~ + obj] **3.** to produce a clone of.

close /v., n. klowz; adj., adv. klows/ v., **closed, clos·ing,** adj., **clos·er, clos·est,** adv., n. —v. [no obj] [~ + obj] **1.** to (cause to) become shut. **2.** to (cause to) come to an end. **3. close down,** to end operation (of); discontinue; stop. **4. close in on** or **upon,** to approach quietly and secretly, as to capture or kill. —adj. **5.** near in space or time; nearby: *Our apartment is close to the train station.* **6.** similar: *Dark pink is close to red.* **7.** near in family relationship: *He was a close relative.* **8.** based on a strong feeling of respect, honor, or love; intimate: *She's a close friend.* **9.** careful; thorough: *close investigation.* **10.** nearly even or equal: *a close contest.* **11.** lacking fresh air. —adv. **12.** near: *I live fairly close to the train station.* —n. [count; usually singular] **13.** the act of closing. **14.** the end or conclusion. —'**close·ly,** adv. —'**close·ness,** n. [noncount]

closed /klowzd/ adj. **1.** not open for business: *The stores are closed on Sundays.* **2.** not open to the public: *a closed meeting.* **3.** not open to new ideas or arguments: *a closed mind.*

'**closed-'captioned,** adj. (of a television program) broadcast with captions visible with the use of a special device, for people who cannot hear well.

'close-'knit /klows-/ *adj.* tightly united or connected socially, religiously, etc.: *a close-knit family.*

clos•et /'klɒzɪt/ *n.* [*count*] **1.** a small room or cabinet for storing clothing, food, etc. —*Idiom.* **2. come out of the closet,** to reveal a fact about oneself previously kept hidden or unmentioned, as one's homosexuality.

close•up /'klows,ʌp/ *n.* [*count*] a photograph taken at close range.

clot /klɒt/ *n., v.,* **clot•ted, clot•ting.** —*n.* [*count*] **1.** a semisolid mass, such as of blood. —*v.* [*no obj*] [~ + *obj*] **2.** to (cause to) form into clots; coagulate.

cloth /klɔθ, klɒθ/ *n., pl.* **cloths** /klɔðz, klɒðz/. **1.** [*noncount*] material made by weaving or knitting from wool, silk, cotton, etc. **2.** [*count*] a piece of such a fabric used for clothing, upholstery, etc. —**Usage.** See CLOTHES.

clothe /klowð/ *v.* [~ + *obj*], **clothed** or **clad** /klæd/, **cloth•ing. 1.** to dress; cover: *clothed in elegant fur.* **2.** to provide with clothing: *to clothe the poor.*

clothes /klowz, klowðz/ *n.* [*plural*] things one wears to cover the body; garments. —**Usage.** The "th" sound in CLOTH "fabric" and its plural CLOTHS "pieces of fabric" are pronounced quite differently from CLOTHES "garments; things you wear." Notice too that the meanings are different, and that one's CLOTHES may or may not be made of CLOTH.

clothes•line /'klowz,layn, 'klowðz-/ *n.* [*count*] a line for hanging clothes, sheets, towels, etc., to dry, usually outdoors.

clothes•pin /'klowz,pɪn, 'klowðz-, 'klows-/ *n.* [*count*] a device made like a clip for fastening articles to a clothesline.

cloth•ing /'klowðɪŋ/ *n.* [*noncount*] clothes considered as a group; apparel: *to wear warm clothing.*

cloud /klawd/ *n.* [*count*] **1.** a white or gray mass of water or ice particles suspended in the sky. **2.** any similar mass, esp. of smoke or dust. **3.** anything that causes fear, suspicion, etc.: *The clouds of war were beginning to gather.* —*v.* **4.** [~ + *obj*] [*no obj*] to cover with clouds: [~ + *obj*] to make sad or gloomy. **5.** [~ + *obj*] to confuse: *Don't cloud the issue with unnecessary details.* —*Idiom.* **7. have one's head in the clouds, a.** to be lost in thought; be daydreaming. **b.** to be impractical. **8. on cloud nine,** very happy: *I was on cloud nine when she said she would marry me.*

cloud•y /'klawdiy/ *adj.,* **-i•er, -i•est. 1.** full of clouds. **2.** hard to see through; not clear: *cloudy windows.* —'**cloud•i•ness,** *n.* [*noncount*]

clout /klawt/ *n.* **1.** a blow or hit, esp. with the hand. **2.** [*noncount*] *Informal.* influence upon people who make decisions.

clove[1] /klowv/ *n.* [*count*] the dried flower bud of a tropical tree of the myrtle family, used as a spice.

clove[2] /klowv/ *n.* [*count*] one of the small bulbs formed in certain plants, as garlic.

clo•ver /'klowvər/ *n.* [*count*] [*noncount*], *pl.* **-vers,** (*esp. when thought of as a group*) **-ver.** a plant of the legume family, having three leaves joined together.

clown /klawn/ *n.* [*count*] **1.** a performer, esp. in a circus, who wears a funny costume and makeup, and acts to make people laugh. **2.** one who acts silly to make people laugh. —*v.* [*no obj*] **3.** to act silly: *The children were clowning (around) most of the night.* —'**clown•ish,** *adj.*

club /klʌb/ *n., v.,* **clubbed, club•bing.** —*n.* [*count*] **1.** a heavy stick that can be used as a weapon. **2.** a stick used to hit a ball in various games, such as golf. **3.** a group of people organized for a social purpose: *an athletic club.* **4.** an organization that offers its members certain benefits: *a book club.* **5.** a nightclub or cabaret. **6.** a playing card bearing a black figure that resembles a three-leafed clover. —*v.* [~ + *obj*] **7.** to beat with or as if with a club.

'club 'soda, *n.* SODA WATER (def. 1).

cluck /klʌk/ *v.* [*no obj*] **1.** to utter the noisy cry of a hen. —*n.* [*count*] **2.** a clucking sound.

clue /kluw/ *n.* [*count*] anything that guides or directs in the solution of a problem, game, puzzle, etc.: *I don't have a clue why he's so upset.*

clump /klʌmp/ *n.* [*count*] **1.** a small group or cluster, esp. of trees or plants. **2.** a lump or mass: *a clump of hair.* **3.** a heavy, thumping sound, as of footsteps. —*v.* [*no obj*] **4.** to walk heavily and clumsily.

clum•sy /'klʌmziy/ *adj.,* **-si•er, -si•est. 1.** awkward in movement or use: *a clumsy dancer.* **2.** awkwardly or poorly done: *a clumsy apology.* **3.** difficult to control or handle: *The motorcycle was clumsy on the road.* —'**clum•si•ly,** *adv.* —'**clum•si•ness,** *n.* [*noncount*]

clung /klʌŋ/ *v.* pt. and pp. of CLING.

clunk•y /'klʌŋkiy/ *adj.,* **-i•er, -i•est.** *Informal.* awkwardly heavy; clumsy: *clunky shoes.*

clus•ter /'klʌstər/ *n.* [*count*] **1.** a group of persons or things close together: *a cluster of stars.* —*v.* **2.** to form or gather in a cluster: [*no obj*]: *The students clustered together in the hall.* [~ + *obj*]: *The students were clustered around the professor.*

clutch /klʌtʃ/ *v.* **1.** [~ + *obj*] to seize with or as if with the hands; hold tightly. **2.** [*no obj*] to try to grasp or hold: *She clutched at my hand as I turned away.* —*n.* [*count*] **3.** Often, **clutches.** [*plural*] power or control, esp. when escape is impossible: *fell into the clutches of the enemy.* **4.** a tight grip or hold.

clut•ter /'klʌtər/ *v.* [~ + *obj*] **1.** to fill with things in a disorderly manner: *Newspapers cluttered (up) the living room.* —*n.* [*noncount*] **2.** things scattered in a disorderly heap.

cm or **cm.,** an abbreviation of: centimeter.

CO, an abbreviation of: Colorado.

co-, a prefix meaning: together (*cooperate*); joint or jointly (*coauthor*); helping (*copilot*).

Co. or **co.,** an abbreviation of: **1.** Company. **2.** County.

C/o or **c/o,** an abbreviation of: care of.

coach /kowtʃ/ *n.* **1.** [*count*] a large, horse-drawn, four-wheeled carriage, usually enclosed: *They traveled by coach.* **2.** [*count*] a bus. **3.** [*count*] an ordinary railroad car. **4.** [*noncount*] a class of airline travel less expensive than first class. **5.** [*count*] a person who trains an athlete or team. **6.** [*count*] a private instructor for a singer, actor, etc. —*v.* [~ + *obj*] [*no obj*] **7.** to instruct or work as a coach.

co•ag•u•late /kow'ægyə,leyt/ *v.* [*no obj*] [~ + *obj*], **-lat•ed, -lat•ing.** to change from a fluid into a thickened mass, as blood does when it forms a clot.

coal /kowl/ *n.* **1.** [*noncount*] a black mineral sub-

C

clothing

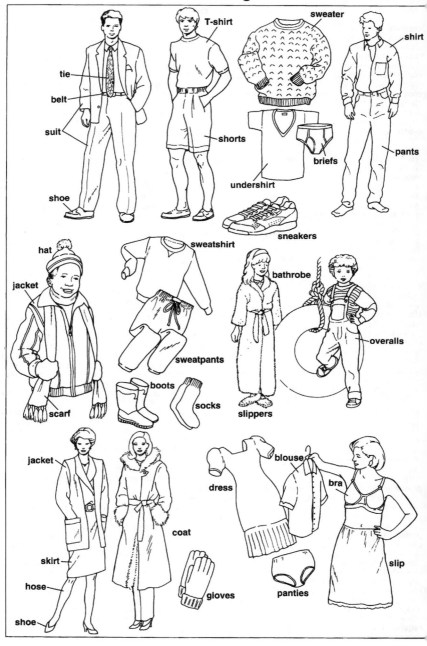

tie

belt

suit

shoe

T-shirt

shorts

undershirt

sweater

briefs

shirt

pants

sneakers

hat

jacket

scarf

sweatshirt

sweatpants

boots

socks

bathrobe

slippers

overalls

jacket

skirt

hose

shoe

coat

dress

gloves

blouse

panties

bra

slip

stance made of carbon, used as a fuel. **2.** [count] a piece of glowing or burned wood.

co•a•lesce /,kowə'lɛs/ v. [no obj], **-lesced, -lesc• ing.** to unite; join together.

co•a•li•tion /,kowə'lɪʃən/ n. [count] a combination, esp. a temporary one between different groups.

coarse /kɔrs/ adj., **coars•er, coars•est. 1.** made up of relatively large parts or particles. **2.** not delicate in texture: coarse fabric. **3.** vulgar; rude: coarse language. —**'coarse•ness,** n. [noncount]

coars•en /'kɔrsən/ v. [no obj] [~ + obj] to (cause to) become coarse.

coast /kowst/ n. [count] **1.** the land next to the sea; seashore. **2.** a slide down a hill or slope, as on a sled. —v. [no obj] **3.** to go downhill, as in a car or on a bicycle, without using power. **4.** to go forward or progress with little effort. —**Idiom. 5.** the coast is clear, nothing is present to interfere with one's progress. —**'coast•al,** adj.

coast•er /'kowstər/ n. [count] a small dish or mat, esp. for placing under a glass.

coast•line /'kowst,layn/ n. [count] the outline of a coast; shoreline: a rugged coastline.

coat /kowt/ n. [count] **1.** a warm outer garment covering at least the upper part of the body. **2.** a natural covering, such as hair or fur. **3.** a layer of anything that covers a surface: a coat of paint. —v. [~ + obj] **4.** to cover with a layer or coating.

coat•ing /'kowtɪŋ/ n. [count] a layer that covers a surface: a thick coating of dust.

'coat of 'arms, n. [count], pl. **'coats of 'arms.** a full display of the special designs, in the form of a shield, that represent a noble family.

coax /kowks/ v. [~ + obj] **1.** to attempt to influence by gentle persuasion: Maybe you can coax her to sing. See if you can coax them into giving us the recipe. **2.** to obtain or get (something) by coaxing: He coaxed the secret from her.

cob /kɒb/ n. CORNCOB (def. 1): We ate corn on the cob at the summer picnic.

co•balt /'kowbɔlt/ n. [noncount] a hard whitish metal element used to produce a blue coloring.

cob•ble•stone /'kɒbəl,stown/ n. [count] [noncount] a stone used in paving a road.

co•bra /'kowbrə/ n. [count], pl. **-bras.** a poisonous snake that can flatten its neck into the shape of a hood.

cob•web /'kɒb,wɛb/ n. [count] a web of threads produced by a spider.

co•caine /kow'keyn/ n. [noncount] a crystal-like substance used to kill pain and also used as an illegal drug.

cock[1] /kɒk/ n. [count] **1.** a male chicken; rooster. **2.** the male of any bird. **3.** a hand-operated valve or faucet that controls the flow of liquid or gas. —v. [~ + obj] **4.** to draw back the hammer of (a gun) before firing.

cock[2] /kɒk/ v. [~ + obj] to make (something) stand erect: The puppy cocked its ear at the sound.

'cocker 'spaniel, n. [count] one of a breed of small spaniels.

cock•eyed /'kɒk,ayd/ adj. Slang. **1.** tilted or slanted to one side; off-center. **2.** foolish; absurd; crazy.

cock•pit /'kɒk,pɪt/ n. [count] a space in the front of an airplane containing the flying controls and seat for the pilot.

cock•roach /'kɒk,rowtʃ/ n. [count] an insect that has a flattened body and is a common household pest. Also called **roach.**

cocks•comb /'kɒks,kowm/ n. [count] the red growth or comb that grows on the top of the head of a cock.

cock•tail /'kɒk,teyl/ n. [count] **1.** a chilled mixed drink of alcoholic liquor and juice or other liquid. **2.** a mixture of fruit or shellfish served as an appetizer.

cock•y /'kɒkiy/ adj., **-i•er, -i•est.** too sure of oneself; conceited.

co•coa /'kowkow/ n. [noncount] **1.** a powder made from cacao seeds. **2.** a beverage made by mixing cocoa powder with hot milk or water.

co•co•nut /'kowkə,nʌt/ n. [count] the large, hard-shelled seed of a palm tree, lined with a white edible meat and containing a milky liquid.

co•coon /kə'kuwn/ n. [count] the silky protective covering spun by caterpillars.

cod /kɒd/ n., pl. (esp. when thought of as a group) **cod,** (esp. for kinds or species) **cods. 1.** [count] a fish found in cool, N Atlantic waters. **2.** [noncount] its flesh, eaten as food.

C.O.D. or **c.o.d.,** an abbreviation of: cash, or collect, on delivery.

cod•dle /'kɒdl/ v. [~ + obj], **-dled, -dling. 1.** to treat too tenderly or too carefully; pamper. **2.** to cook (eggs, etc.) in water just below the boiling point.

code /kowd/ n., v., **cod•ed, cod•ing.** —n. **1.** [count] a system for communication by telegraph, etc., in which the letters are represented by long and short sounds or light flashes: Morse code. **2.** [count] [noncount] a system used to keep a message short or secret, with letters or symbols assigned definite meanings. **3.** [count] a collection of rules or regulations: a health code. —v. [~ + obj] **4.** to translate (a message) into a code.

cod•i•fy /'kɒdə,fay, 'kowdə-/ v. [~ + obj], **-fied, -fy•ing.** to arrange or put (laws, etc.) into a code.

co•ed or **co-ed** /'kow'ɛd, -,ɛd/ adj. **1.** serving both men and women alike: coed classes. —n. [count] **2.** a female student in a school for men and women.

co•erce /kow'ɜrs/ v. [~ + obj], **-erced, -erc• ing.** to compel by force or violence: She coerced him into signing the document. —**co•er•cion** /kow 'ɜrʃən/, n. [noncount]

co•ex•ist /,kowɪg'zɪst/ v. [no obj] **1.** to exist at the same time: The two empires coexisted on opposite sides of the globe. **2.** (esp. of nations) to exist together peacefully. —**,co•ex'ist•ence,** n. [noncount]

cof•fee /'kɔfiy, 'kɒfiy/ n. **1.** [noncount] [count] a beverage made from hot water poured over the roasted ground seeds (**'coffee ,beans**) of the coffee tree. **2.** [noncount] the powder made by grinding the seeds.

'coffee ,shop, n. [count] a small restaurant serving light meals.

'coffee ,table, n. [count] a low table, usually placed in front of a sofa.

cof•fin /'kɔfɪn, 'kɒfɪn/ n. [count] the box in which the body of a dead person is buried.

cog /kɒg, kɔg/ n. [count] a gear tooth that fits into the slot on a wheel with similar teeth, to transfer motion or power.

cog•ni•tion /kɒg'nɪʃən/ n. [noncount] the mental act of learning; understanding; perception. —**cog•ni•tive** /'kɒgnɪtɪv/, adj.

cog•wheel /'kɒg,hwiyl, -,wiyl/ n. [count] a

wheel having teeth or cogs that engage with another wheel.

co•her•ent /kow'hɪərənt, -'hɛr-/ *adj.* **1.** logically connected; consistent: *a coherent speech.* **2.** speaking, talking, or thinking clearly. **3.** having a natural agreement of parts; harmonious: *a coherent design.* —**co•her•ence** /kow'hɪərəns, -'hɛr-/, *n.* [*noncount*] —**co'her•ent•ly,** *adv.*

co•he•sive /kow'hiysɪv/ *adj.* fitting well together; working or relating well together.

coif /kwɑf/ *n., v.* COIFFURE.

coif•fure /kwɑ'fyʊr/ *n., pl.* **-fures,** *v.,* **-fured, -fur•ing.** —*n.* [*count*] **1.** a style of arranging the hair. —*v.* [~ + *obj*] **2.** to arrange (the hair) in a coiffure.

coil /kɔyl/ *v.* **1.** to wind (something) into rings one above the other or one around the other: [*no obj*]: *Smoke coiled up the chimney.* [~ + *obj*]: *She coiled her scarf around her neck.* **2.** [~ + *obj*] to gather (rope, etc.) into loops. —*n.* [*count*] **3.** a series of spirals or rings into which something is wound. **4.** a single such ring.

coin /kɔyn/ *n.* [*count*] **1.** a piece of metal stamped and issued by a government as money. —*v.* [~ + *obj*] **2.** to make (coins) by stamping metal. **3.** to invent: *to coin an expression.* —'**coin•age,** *n.* [*noncount*] [*count*]

co•in•cide /ˌkowɪn'sayd/ *v.* [*no obj*], **-cid•ed, -cid•ing. 1.** to happen at the same time: *Our vacations coincided this year. My vacation didn't coincide with my children's.* **2.** to agree: *Our opinions coincide more often than not.*

co•in•ci•dence /kow'ɪnsɪdəns/ *n.* [*noncount*] [*count*] a surprising chance occurrence of two or more events at once. —**co•in•ci•den•tal** /kow,ɪnsə'dɛntl̩/, *adj.*

co•i•tus /'kowɪtəs/ *n.* [*noncount*] sexual intercourse, esp. between a man and a woman.

col-, a form of the prefix COM-, used before roots beginning with the letter "l": (*collateral*).

Col., an abbreviation of: **1.** Colonel. **2.** Colorado.

col•an•der /'kʌləndər, 'kɒl-/ *n.* [*count*] a container with many small holes in the bottom and sides, used for draining and straining foods.

cold /kowld/ *adj.,* **-er, -est,** *n., adv.* —*adj.* **1.** having a relatively low temperature. **2.** feeling an uncomfortable lack of warmth; chilled: *I'm really cold today.* **3.** not affectionate or friendly: *a cold reply.* **4.** unconscious because of a severe blow, shock, etc.: *knocked him out cold.* —*n.* **5.** [*noncount*] the absence of heat or warmth. **6.** [*noncount; the* + ~] cold weather. **7.** [*count*] an illness of the lungs, throat, and nose, with sneezing, coughing, etc., caused by viruses. —*adv.* **8.** without preparation or prior notice: *He walked into the interview cold.* —*Idiom.* **9. catch (a) cold,** to become sick with a cold. **10. have** or **get cold feet,** to be afraid or unwilling to do something. **11. leave (someone) cold,** to fail to excite or interest (someone). **12. throw cold water on,** to dampen someone's enthusiasm about. —'**cold•ly,** *adv.* —'**cold•ness,** *n.* [*noncount*]

'**cold-'blooded,** *adj.* **1.** of or referring to animals, as fishes and reptiles, whose blood temperature changes with the temperature of the air or water surrounding them. **2.** done or acting without emotion: *a cold-blooded killer.*

'**cold ,cuts,** *n.* [*plural*] slices of prepared meats and cheeses served cold.

'**cold 'shoulder,** *n.* [*count*] deliberate indifference or other unfriendly treatment: *We gave her the cold shoulder whenever we saw her.*

'**cold ,sore,** *n.* [*count*] a cluster of blisters appearing in or around the mouth, caused by a virus.

cole•slaw /'kowl,slɔ/ *n.* [*noncount*] a salad of chopped raw cabbage and seasoned mayonnaise.

col•i•se•um /ˌkɒlɪ'siyəm/ *n.* [*count*] a stadium or large theater for sporting events, exhibitions, etc.

col•lab•o•rate /kə'læbəˌreyt/ *v.* [*no obj*], **-rat•ed, -rat•ing. 1.** to work together; cooperate: *The two writers collaborated on the script for the movie. He collaborated with his brother.* **2.** to cooperate with an enemy nation. —**col•lab•o•ra•tion** /kə,læbə'reyʃən/, *n.* [*noncount*]

col•lage /kə'lɑʒ/ *n.* [*count*] a work of art made by pasting materials such as newspaper clippings or parts of photographs onto a surface.

col•lapse /kə'læps/ *v.,* **-lapsed, -laps•ing,** *n.* —*v.* **1.** [*no obj*] [~ + *obj*] to fall or cave in; crumble suddenly. **2.** [*no obj*] to be made so that sections or parts can be folded up, as for storage: *The playpen collapses easily.* **3.** [*no obj*] to break down; fail utterly: *The peace talks have collapsed once again.* **4.** [*no obj*] to fall unconscious or fall down, such as from a heart attack. —*n.* **5.** [*noncount*] a falling in, down, or together: *the collapse of a tunnel.* **6.** [*count*] [*noncount*] a sudden, complete failure; breakdown.

col•lar /'kɒlər/ *n.* [*count*] **1.** the part of a shirt, blouse, etc., that goes around the neckline of the garment. **2.** a leather or metal band fastened around the neck of an animal. —*v.* [~ + *obj*] **3.** *Informal.* To place under arrest.

col•lat•er•al /kə'lætərəl/ *n.* [*noncount*] property or money promised to a bank or other lender if payment of a loan cannot be made.

col•league /'kɒliyg/ *n.* [*count*] a fellow member of a profession; a business associate.

col•lect /kə'lɛkt/ *v.* **1.** [*no obj*] [~ + *obj*] to gather together; assemble. **2.** [~ + *obj*] to obtain many examples of (something), or save (something), as a hobby: *He has been collecting stamps for many years.* **3.** [*no obj*] to receive payment that one is owed: *We finally collected from the insurance company on the damage to our house.* **4.** [~ + *obj*] to regain control of (oneself or one's thoughts or emotions). **5.** [*no obj*] to accumulate; gather in a layer. —*adj., adv.* **6.** requiring payment by the receiver: *a collect telephone call; to call collect.* —**col'lec•tor,** *n.* [*count*]

col•lec•tion /kə'lɛkʃən/ *n.* **1.** [*count*] a group of objects, etc., gathered together. **2.** [*noncount*] [*count*] the act of collecting. **3.** [*count*] an activity intended to raise money, as for charity.

col•lec•tive /kə'lɛktɪv/ *adj.* forming a whole; combined: *our collective assets.*

col•lege /'kɒlɪdʒ/ *n.* a school or institution of higher education that grants a bachelor's degree: [*count*]: *She chose a college that had a good business department.* [*noncount*]: *He was in college during the war.*

col•lide /kə'layd/ *v.* [*no obj*], **-lid•ed, -lid•ing. 1.** to strike each other forcefully; crash: *The two trains collided at a speed of over 50 mph. The car collided with a tree.* **2.** to clash; conflict. —**col•li•sion** /kə 'lɪʒən/, *n.* [*count*] [*noncount*]

col•lie /'kɒliy/ *n.* [*count*], *pl.* **-lies.** one of a breed of large Scottish dogs.

col•lo•qui•al /kə'lowkwiyəl/ *adj.* characteristic of or suitable to familiar conversation, rather than formal writing; informal: *colloquial style; colloquial expressions.*

Colo., an abbreviation of: Colorado.

Co•lom•bi•an /kə'lʌmbiyən/ adj. **1.** of or relating to Colombia. —n. [count] **2.** a person born or living in Colombia.

co•lon¹ /'kowlən/ n. [count] **1.** the sign (:) used to mark a major division in a sentence, indicating that what follows is further explanation of what precedes. **2.** the sign (:) used to separate groups of numbers, as hours from minutes in 5:30.

co•lon² /'kowlən/ n. [count], pl. **-lons, -la** (-lə). the lower part of the large intestine extending to the rectum.

colo•nel /'kɜrnl̩/ n. [count] an officer in the U.S. Army, Air Force, or Marine Corps.

co•lo•ni•al /kə'lowniyəl/ adj. **1.** [before a noun] of or relating to a colony or colonies. **2.** [often: Colonial] of or relating to the 13 British colonies that became the United States of America. —n. [count] **3.** an inhabitant of a colony.

co•lo•ni•al•ism /kə'lowniyə,lɪzəm/ n. [noncount] the policy by which a nation tries to extend its authority over other peoples or territories.

col•o•nist /'kɒlənɪst/ n. [count] an inhabitant of a colony.

col•o•nize /'kɒlə,nayz/ v. [~ + obj], **-nized, -niz•ing.** to establish a colony in; settle.

col•on•nade /,kɒlə'neyd/ n. [count] a series of regularly spaced columns holding up arches.

col•o•ny /'kɒləniy/ n. [count], pl. **-nies. 1.** a group of people who leave their native country to form a settlement in a new land that is to be connected with the parent nation. **2.** the country or district so settled.

col•or /'kʌlər/ n. [noncount] **1.** the quality of an object that gives it a certain appearance when light is reflected by it. **2.** (in people with white skin) a pinkish complexion, usually indicating good health. **3.** lively or interesting quality, as in a piece of writing. —v. **4.** [~ + obj] to give or apply color to; dye. **5.** [~ + obj] to give a special character to; affect: My experiences in that country color my judgment about it. **6.** [no obj] to flush; blush. —Idiom. **7. with flying colors,** very successfully: She passed the tests with flying colors. Also, esp. Brit., **colour.** —'col•or•less, adj.

'color-,blind, adj. unable to distinguish one or more colors, such as red and green.

col•ored /'kʌlərd/ adj. Often Offensive. belonging to a race other than the white, esp. to the black race.

col•or•fast /'kʌlər,fæst/ adj. keeping the original color without fading or running after washing.

col•or•ful /'kʌlərfəl/ adj. **1.** having many colors or a great deal of color. **2.** having lively, striking, or spirited parts: a colorful tale.

col•or•ing /'kʌlərɪŋ/ n. [noncount] **1.** appearance as to color: He has dark coloring like his mother. **2.** a substance used to color something: Add a few drops of food coloring to the icing for the cake.

co•los•sal /kə'lɒsəl/ adj. extremely great in size, extent, or degree; gigantic.

col•our /'kʌlər/ n., v. Chiefly Brit. COLOR.

colt /kowlt/ n. [count] a young male animal of the horse family.

col•umn /'kɒləm/ n. [count] **1.** a tall, slender pillar used for support or standing alone as a monument. **2.** any object, mass, or formation shaped like this: a column of smoke. **3.** a vertical row or list: Add this column of figures. **4.** a vertical arrangement of print on a page of a book: There are two columns on this page. **5.** an article that is a regular feature of a newspaper or magazine: a column on political affairs.

col•um•nist /'kɒləmnɪst/ n. [count] a person who writes a newspaper column.

com-, prefix. a prefix meaning with or together with: combine.

co•ma /'kowmə/ n. [count], pl. **-mas.** a state of deep unconsciousness, often caused by a serious head injury.

com•a•tose /'kɒmə,tows, 'kowmə-/ adj. affected with or suffering from a coma.

comb /kowm/ n. [count] **1.** a toothed strip of some hard material used to arrange or hold the hair. **2.** the fleshy growth on the head of roosters. —v. [~ + obj] **3.** to arrange (the hair) with a comb. **4.** to search everywhere in: to comb the files for a missing letter.

com•bat /v. kəm'bæt, 'kɒmbæt; n. 'kɒmbæt/ v., **-bat•ed, -bat•ing** or (esp. Brit.) **-bat•ted, -bat•ting,** n. —v. [~ + obj] **1.** to fight against; oppose vigorously: to combat crime; to combat disease with antibiotics. —n. **2.** [noncount] armed fighting with enemy forces. **3.** [count] a struggle or contest.

com•bi•na•tion /,kɒmbə'neyʃən/ n. **1.** [noncount] the act of combining or the state of being combined. **2.** [count] a number of things combined: a combination of ideas. **3.** [count] something formed by combining: A chord is a combination of notes. **4.** [count] the set of numbers or letters used to open a lock or a safe: He forgot the combination to his locker.

com•bine /kəm'bayn/ v., **-bined, -bin•ing. 1.** [~ + obj] [no obj] to join in a close union; unite to form one thing. **2.** to unite for a common purpose; join: [~ + obj]: Two groups combined efforts. [no obj]: Two groups combined to defeat the proposal.

com•bus•ti•ble /kəm'bʌstəbəl/ adj. capable of catching fire and burning; flammable.

com•bus•tion /kəm'bʌstʃən/ n. [noncount] the act or process of burning.

come /kʌm/ v. [no obj], **came** /keym/, **come, com•ing. 1.** to approach or move toward someone or something: Come a little closer. The tide came rushing in. **2.** to arrive: The train is coming. **3.** to move into view; appear: The light comes and goes. **4.** to extend; reach: The dress comes to her knees. **5.** to take place; happen: Her trumpet solo comes in the third act. **6.** to be available, be found, etc.: Toothpaste comes in a tube. **7.** to enter into a specified state: That word has come into popular use. **8.** to do or manage; progress: How are you coming with your term paper? **9.** Slang. to have an orgasm. **10. come about,** to happen: How did such a mess come about? **11. come across** or **upon,** to find or meet, esp. by chance. **12. come along, a.** to accompany a person or group: We're going to the mall; you can come along if you like. **b.** to proceed or advance: The project is coming along on schedule. **c.** to appear: An opportunity came along to invest in real estate. **13. come around, a.** Also, **come to.** to recover consciousness. **b.** to change one's opinion: She finally came around to our point of view. **14. come between,** [~ + between + obj] to separate; get in the way of: Nothing can come between us. **15. come down, a.** to fall down; collapse: The entire building came down on them. **b.** to lose wealth, rank, etc.: The senator has really come down in the world. **c.** to be passed along from a higher authority:

Our orders will come down tomorrow. **16. come down** on or **upon,** to scold; punish: *Why did you come down on her so hard?* **17. come down to,** to lead or point in a basic, important way: *It all comes down to a sense of pride.* **18. come down with,** to become sick from (an illness): *She came down with the flu.* **19. come into, a.** to inherit or get: *I came into a bit of money when my uncle died.* **b.** to get to be in (a state): *The president's car suddenly came into view.* **20. come off, a.** to happen; occur: *The invasion came off just before dawn.* **b.** to reach the end; conclude: *We want this project to come off without any delay.* **c.** to be effective or successful: *She didn't come off well in that interview.* **21. come out, a.** to appear or be seen: *Suddenly the sun came out.* **b.** to be published or made known: *The story came out in all the papers.* **22. come out for** (or **against**), to declare one's support for (or opposition to): *The president is expected to come out for a tax increase.* **23. come through, a.** to endure difficulty, illness, etc., successfully. **b.** to fulfill needs or meet demands. **24. come to, a.** to recover consciousness. **b.** to amount to. **c.** to be recalled in the mind or memory: *Suddenly it came to me; I had worked with her in Seoul.* **25. come up,** to be mentioned or referred to: *Your name came up in conversation.* **26. come up with,** to produce; supply.

come•back /ˈkʌm,bæk/ *n.* [count] **1.** a return to the success of an earlier time. **2.** a clever or effective answer.

co•me•di•an /kəˈmiydiyən/ *n.* [count] a professional entertainer who makes an audience laugh by telling jokes, funny stories, etc.

co•me•di•enne /kə,miydiyˈɛn/ *n.* [count] a woman who is a comic entertainer or actress.

com•e•dy /ˈkɒmɪdiy/ *n.* [count], *pl.* **-dies.** a play, movie, etc., of light and humorous character with a cheerful ending.

com•et /ˈkɒmɪt/ *n.* [count] a body in space that orbits the sun, made up of a central solid mass and a tail of dust and gas.

com•fort /ˈkʌmfərt/ *v.* [~ + obj] **1.** to soothe or reassure; bring cheer to. —*n.* **2.** [count] a person or thing that gives help or relief. **3.** [noncount] a state of ease and satisfaction of bodily wants.

com•fort•a•ble /ˈkʌmftəbəl, ˈkʌmfərtəbəl/ *adj.* **1.** (of clothing, furniture, etc.) producing or giving physical comfort. **2.** in a state of physical or mental comfort: *I was comfortable sitting in the old chair.* **3.** adequate or sufficient: *a comfortable salary.* —'**com•fort•a•bly,** *adv.*

com•ic /ˈkɒmɪk/ *adj.* **1.** [before a noun] **a.** relating to or characterized by comedy. **b.** performing in or writing comedy. **2.** causing laughter; funny. —*n.* [count] **3.** a comedian. **4. comics,** [plural; often: the + ~] a section of a newspaper featuring comic strips.

com•i•cal /ˈkɒmɪkəl/ *adj.* producing laughter; funny.

'**comic ‚book,** *n.* [count] a magazine made up of comic strips.

'**comic ‚strip,** *n.* [count] a sequence of drawings telling or showing a comic incident, an adventure, etc., often appearing in daily newspapers.

com•ma /ˈkɒmə/ *n.* [count], *pl.* **-mas.** the sign (,), a mark of punctuation used to separate words in a sentence or items in a list.

com•mand /kəˈmænd/ *v.* **1.** to direct with authority; order: [~ + obj]: *He commanded his troops to march.* [no obj]: *He commanded that*

they follow him. **2.** [~ + obj] to deserve and receive (respect, attention, etc.): *Her words command respect.* **3.** [~ + obj] to have authority or control over. —*n.* **4.** [noncount] the act of commanding or ordering with authority. **5.** [count] an order given by one in authority. **6.** expertise; mastery; strong ability: [count; usually singular]: *She has a command of four languages.* [noncount]: *His command of Russian was perfect.*

com•man•deer /,kɒmənˈdɪər/ *v.* [~ + obj] to seize (private property) for military or other public use.

com•mand•er /kəˈmændər/ *n.* [count] **1.** a person in authority; chief officer; leader. **2.** a military officer.

com•mand•ment /kəˈmændmənt/ *n.* [count] a command or mandate.

com•mem•o•rate /kəˈmɛmə,reyt/ *v.* [~ + obj], **-rat•ed, -rat•ing.** to serve as a memorial or reminder of. —**com•mem•o•ra•tion** /kə,mɛmə-'reyʃən/, *n.* [noncount] [count]

com•mence /kəˈmɛns/ *v.* [no obj] [~ + obj], **-menced, -menc•ing.** to begin; start.

com•mence•ment /kəˈmɛnsmənt/ *n.* **1.** [noncount] an act of commencing. **2.** [noncount] [count] the ceremony of awarding degrees at the end of the academic year.

com•mend /kəˈmɛnd/ *v.* [~ + obj] to single out or choose (someone) for special praise. —**com•men•da•tion** /,kɒmənˈdeyʃən/, *n.* [count]

com•ment /ˈkɒmɛnt/ *n.* **1.** a remark, observation, or criticism: *a comment about the weather.* —*v.* [no obj] **2.** to make remarks, observations, or criticisms: *The president refused to comment (on that issue).* —*Idiom.* **3. no comment,** [noncount] (used when the speaker wishes to say nothing in response to a question).

com•men•tar•y /ˈkɒmən,tɛriy/ *n.* [count], *pl.* **-ies.** an essay or other long writing that gives an explanation or interpretation.

com•men•ta•tor /ˈkɒmən,teytər/ *n.* [count] a person who discusses news or other topics on television or radio.

com•merce /ˈkɒmərs/ *n.* [noncount] an exchange of goods or commodities between different countries or between areas of the same country; trade.

com•mer•cial /kəˈmɜrʃəl/ *adj.* [usually: before a noun] **1.** of, relating to, or characteristic of commerce. **2.** made, produced, or marketed to be sold or to make a profit. —*n.* [count] **3.** a paid advertisement or announcement on radio or television.

com•mer•cial•ize /kəˈmɜrʃə,layz/ *v.* [~ + obj], **-ized, -iz•ing. 1.** to make profitable. **2.** to emphasize the money-making aspects of (something).

com•mis•er•ate /kəˈmɪzə,reyt/ *v.* [~ + with + obj], **-at•ed, -at•ing.** to feel, express, or share sorrow; sympathize: *I commiserated with him over the loss of his mother.*

com•mis•sion /kəˈmɪʃən/ *n.* **1.** [count] an order to perform a task, job, or duty. **2.** [count] the authority, position, or rank of an officer in the armed forces: *She resigned her commission.* **3.** [count] a group of persons given authority, as to investigate wrongdoing. **4.** [noncount] the act of committing a crime, error, etc. **5.** money paid to persons who make a sale, usually based on the value or price of what gets sold: [noncount]: *He works on commission.* [count]: *He gets a commission of 10% on all the products he sells.* —*v.* [~ + obj] **6.** to give a commission to: *The governor* *commissioned the panel to investigate the charges of bribery.* —***Idiom.*** **7. in** (or **out of**) **commission,** in (or not in) service or operating order.

com•mis•sion•er /kə'mɪʃənər/ *n.* [count] **1.** a member of a commission. **2.** a government official in charge of a department or district: *the police commissioner.*

com•mit /kə'mɪt/ *v.* [~ + *obj*], **-mit•ted, -mit•ting. 1.** to declare that one has a certain opinion or position: *The senator would not commit herself on the issue.* **2.** to obligate (oneself), as by a pledge or promise: *He committed himself to helping the poor. He was committed to attending the wedding.* **3.** to do; perform: *to commit murder.* **4.** to send (someone) to a prison or mental institution. —**com'mit•ment,** *n.* [noncount] [count]

com•mit•tee /kə'mɪtiy/ *n.* [count] a group of persons elected or appointed to perform some function or investigate a particular matter.

com•mod•i•ty /kə'mɒdɪtiy/ *n.* [count], *pl.* **-ties.** an article of trade or commerce, esp. a product that can be bought or sold.

com•mon /'kɒmən/ *adj.*, **-er, -est. 1.** belonging equally to, or shared alike by two or more people or things: *We all have a common goal.* **2.** widespread; general; universal: *There was a common understanding that he would be promoted.* **3.** of frequent occurrence; usual; familiar: *It was a common error.* **4.** lacking rank, station, etc.; ordinary; not special: *a common soldier.* —***Idiom.*** **5. in common,** in joint possession or use; shared equally: *We have much in common with people from other cultures.* —**'com•mon•ly,** *adv.*: *It's commonly understood that people say thank you when they receive a gift.*

'common 'noun, *n.* [count] a noun that notes any or all of a class of things and is not the name of a particular individual, as *man, city, horse, music.*

com•mon•place /'kɒmən,pleys/ *adj.* ordinary; uninteresting; usual.

'common 'sense, *n.* [noncount] sound practical judgment: *It's just common sense to look both ways before crossing a street.*

com•mon•wealth /'kɒmən,wɛlθ/ *n.* [count] **1.** the people of a nation or state, seen as a political unit. **2.** [Commonwealth] a group of self-governing nations associated by their own choice.

com•mo•tion /kə'mowʃən/ *n.* [count; singular] [noncount] violent, noisy action; disturbance; fuss.

com•mu•nal /kə'myuwnl/ *adj.* used or shared in common.

com•mune /'kɒmyuwn/ *n.* [count] a small group of persons living together, sharing possessions, work, income, etc.

com•mu•ni•ca•ble /kə'myuwnɪkəbəl/ *adj.* easily communicated or transmitted to another: *a communicable disease.*

com•mu•ni•cate /kə'myuwnɪ,keyt/ *v.*, **-cat•ed, -cat•ing. 1.** [~ + *obj*] to give to another; transmit: *to communicate a disease.* **2.** to give or exchange (thoughts, information, etc.): [no *obj*]: *They were trying to understand how dolphins communicate. We have to communicate with the chairman on this.* [~ + *obj*]: *You have to communicate your ideas clearly.*

com•mu•ni•ca•tion /kə,myuwnɪ'keyʃən/ *n.* **1.** [noncount] the act or process of communicating; fact of being communicated. **2.** [count] something communicated. **3. communications,** [plural; *used with a plural verb*] means of sending

messages, orders, etc., including telephone, telegraph, radio, and television.

com•mun•ion /kə'myuwnyən/ *n.* **1.** [noncount; often: Communion] Also called **Holy Communion. a.** the act of receiving the bread and wine at a Christian Eucharistic service. **b.** the bread and wine so received. **2.** [count] a group of people having a common religious faith; denomination: *the Anglican communion.* **3.** [noncount] the exchanging or sharing of thoughts or emotions: *communion with nature.*

com•mu•nism /'kɒmyə,nɪzəm/ *n.* [noncount; often: Communism] a theory or system of social organization based on the holding of all property in common, with ownership by the state. —**'com•mu•nist,** *n.* [count], *adj.*

com•mu•ni•ty /kə'myuwnɪtiy/ *n.* [count], *pl.* **-ties. 1.** a group of people who live in a specific location, share government, and often have a common cultural and historical heritage. **2.** a social, political, or other group sharing common characteristics or interests: *the business community.*

com•mute /kə'myuwt/ *v.*, **-mut•ed, -mut•ing,** *n.* —*v.* [no *obj*] **1.** to travel regularly over some distance, as from a suburb into a city and back again. —*n.* [count] **2.** a trip made by commuting. —**com'mut•er,** *n.* [count]

com•pact¹ /*adj.* kəm'pækt; *n.* 'kɒmpækt/ *adj.* **1.** joined or packed together; dense; solid: *compact soil.* **2.** designed to be small in size or economical in operation: *a compact kitchen.* —*n.* [count] **3.** a small case containing a mirror and face powder. —**com'pact•ness,** *n.* [noncount]

com•pact² /'kɒmpækt/ *n.* [count] a formal agreement between two or more parties, states, etc.; contract.

'compact 'disc, *n.* [count] a small disc on which digital sound, data, or images are recorded for playback by means of a laser. *Abbr.:* CD

com•pan•ion /kəm'pænyən/ *n.* [count] **1.** a person who frequently accompanies another. **2.** a person employed to accompany, assist, or live with another. —**com'pan•ion•ship,** *n.* [noncount]

com•pa•ny /'kʌmpəniy/ *n.*, *pl.* **-nies. 1.** [count] a number of individuals associated together. **2.** [noncount] a guest or guests: *We're having company tonight.* **3.** [noncount] companionship; association: *We always enjoy her company.* **4.** [count] a number of persons united for joint action, esp. for business: *a publishing company.*

com•pa•ra•ble /'kɒmpərəbəl/ *adj.* **1.** capable of being compared; permitting comparison: *Are the Roman and British empires comparable?* **2.** worthy of comparison: *shops comparable to those on Fifth Avenue in New York.*

com•par•a•tive /kəm'pærətɪv/ *adj.* **1.** [before a noun] measured, judged, or estimated by comparison: *He was a comparative stranger to the town.* **2.** of or naming a form of adjectives and adverbs used to show an increase in quality, quantity, or intensity: *The words* smaller *and* more *carefully are the comparative forms of* small *and* carefully. —*n.* [count] **3.** the comparative form of an adjective or adverb: *The comparative of* good *is the word* better. —**com'par•a•tive•ly,** *adv.*

com•pare /kəm'pɛər/ *v.*, **-pared, -par•ing,** *n.* —*v.* **1.** [~ + *obj*] to examine (things) to note similarities and differences: *to compare two restaurants; The pictures were compared with those of known spies. Compare the Chicago of today to* *that of the 1920's.* **2.** [~ + *obj*] to consider or describe as similar; liken. **3.** [*no obj*] to be worthy of comparison: *Whose plays can compare with Shakespeare's?* —*n.* [*noncount*] **4.** comparison: *a beauty beyond compare.*

com•par•i•son /kəm'pærəsən/ *n.* **1.** the act of comparing two people or things: [*count*]: *A comparison between our two countries shows some important differences.* [*noncount*]: *In comparison with some other countries, the cost of food in the U.S. is low.* **2.** [*noncount*] a likeness; similarity: *There is simply no comparison between your work and hers.*

com•part•ment /kəm'pɑrtmənt/ *n.* [*count*] a separate room, section, part, etc.

com•pass /'kʌmpəs, 'kɒm-/ *n.* [*count*] **1.** an instrument for determining directions. **2.** Often, **compasses.** [*plural*] a V-shaped instrument for drawing circles, measuring distances, etc. **3.** area; extent; scope: *the broad compass of the novel.*

com•pas•sion /kəm'pæʃən/ *n.* [*noncount*] a feeling of sympathy for another's misfortune. —**com'pas•sion•ate** /-ənɪt/, *adj.*

com•pat•i•ble /kəm'pætəbəl/ *adj.* **1.** capable of living or existing together in peace and harmony. **2.** able to exist with something else: *My blood type is not compatible with yours.* —**com•pat•i•bil•i•ty** /kəm,pætə'bɪlɪtiy/, *n.* [*noncount*]

com•pel /kəm'pɛl/ *v.* [~ + *obj*], **-pelled, -pel•ling.** to force or drive (someone) to do something; require: *We were compelled to work hard.*

com•pen•sate /'kɒmpən,seyt/ *v.*, **-sat•ed, -sat•ing.** **1.** to pay (someone) for something lost, damaged, or missing: [~ + *obj*]: *Let me compensate you for your trouble.* [*no obj*]: *Your apologies will not compensate for this damage.* **2.** to make up for: [~ + *obj*]: *He compensated for his lack of experience by his hard work.* [*no obj*]: *The good acting in the play compensated for its boring music.*

com•pen•sa•tion /,kɒmpən'seyʃən/ *n.* [*noncount*] **1.** money given to make up for a loss, damage, etc. **2.** salary. **3.** an action or adjustment that makes up for something unfortunate.

com•pete /kəm'piyt/ *v.* [*no obj*], **-pet•ed, -pet•ing.** to struggle to outdo another for acknowledgment, a prize, etc.; engage in a contest: *Birds compete for food with squirrels.* —**com•pet•i•tor** /kəm'pɛtɪtər/, *n.* [*count*]: *three competitors in the race.*

com•pe•tent /'kɒmpɪtənt/ *adj.* having suitable or sufficient skill, knowledge, experience, etc., for some purpose. —**com•pe•tence,** *n.* [*noncount*]

com•pe•ti•tion /,kɒmpɪ'tɪʃən/ *n.* **1.** [*noncount*] the act of competing; rivalry. **2.** [*count*] a contest for some prize, honor, or advantage: *an ice-skating competition.* **3.** [*noncount*] the rivalry offered by a competitor: *Small businesses are getting a lot of competition from the new, large stores that are moving into the neighborhood.*

com•pet•i•tive /kəm'pɛtɪtɪv/ *adj.* **1.** of or relating to competition. **2.** overly interested in competing. **3.** having the ability to compete: *Our prices are competitive when compared with those of the leading manufacturer.* —**com•pet•i•tive•ly,** *adv.* —**com•pet•i•tive•ness,** *n.* [*noncount*]

com•pile /kəm'payl/ *v.* [~ + *obj*], **-piled, -pil•ing.** to put together (a book, document, etc.) from materials taken from various sources. —**com•pi•la•tion** /,kɒmpə'leyʃən/ *n.* [*count*]

com•pla•cen•cy /kəm'pleysənsiy/ *n.* [*non-*

count] a feeling of security while unaware of unpleasant possibilities. —**com'pla•cent,** *adj.*

com•plain /kəm'pleyn/ *v.* [*no obj*] to express dissatisfaction, resentment, pain, grief, etc.: *always whining and complaining; complained of head pains; complaining about the weather.*

com•plaint /kəm'pleynt/ *n.* [*count*] [*noncount*] **1.** an expression of discontent, regret, pain, resentment, or grief. **2.** a cause of such discontent; reason for complaining.

com•ple•ment /*n.* 'kɒmpləmənt; *v.* 'kɒmplə,mɛnt/ *n.* [*count*] **1.** something that completes or makes perfect. —*v.* [~ + *obj*] **2.** to complete, as by adding good qualities to: *The excellent coffee complemented the brandy and dessert.*

com•plete /kəm'pliyt/ *adj.*, *v.*, **-plet•ed, -plet•ing.** —*adj.* **1.** having all parts or elements; lacking nothing: *I need complete instructions for using the computer.* **2.** finished; ended; concluded: *a complete orbit of the sun.* **3.** thorough; total: *a complete stranger.* —*v.* [~ + *obj*] **4.** to make whole, entire, or perfect. **5.** to bring to an end; finish. —**com'plete•ness,** **com•ple•tion** /kəm'pliyʃən/ *n.* [*noncount*]

com•plete•ly /kəm'pliytliy/ *adv.* totally; altogether: *I completely forgot about the meeting.*

com•plex /*adj.* kəm'plɛks; *n.* 'kɒmplɛks/ *adj.* **1.** composed of many related parts: *a complex system.* **2.** having a complicated arrangement of parts or pieces: *complex machinery.* —*n.* [*count*] **3.** a group, system, or assembly of related things that form a whole: *an apartment complex.* **4.** a group of related ideas, desires, and impulses that influence one's attitudes and behavior: *She had an inferiority complex.* —**com•plex•i•ty** /kəm'plɛksɪtiy/ *n.* [*count*] [*noncount*]

com•plex•ion /kəm'plɛkʃən/ *n.* [*count*] the natural color, texture, and appearance of the skin, esp. of the face.

com•pli•ance /kəm'playəns/ *n.* [*noncount*] the act of complying. —**com'pli•ant,** *adj.*

com•pli•cate /'kɒmplɪ,keyt/ *v.* [~ + *obj*], **-cat•ed, -cat•ing.** to make (something) complex or difficult. —**com•pli•ca•tion** /,kɒmplɪ'keyʃən/ *n.* [*count*]

com•pli•cat•ed /'kɒmplɪ,keytɪd/ *adj.* **1.** made up of connected parts; complex. **2.** difficult to analyze, understand, or explain.

com•plic•i•ty /kəm'plɪsɪtiy/ *n.* [*noncount*] the state of taking part with another person in a criminal act.

com•pli•ment /*n.* 'kɒmpləmənt; *v.* 'kɒmplə,mɛnt/ *n.* [*count*] **1.** an expression of praise or admiration: *He paid her a compliment on her dress.* —*v.* [~ + *obj*] **2.** to pay a compliment to; praise: *He complimented the hostess on the dinner.*

com•pli•men•ta•ry /,kɒmplə'mɛntəriy/ *adj.* **1.** expressing a compliment: *a complimentary remark.* **2.** given free as a gift or courtesy: *complimentary tickets to the game.*

com•ply /kəm'play/ *v.* [*no obj*] [~ + *with* + *obj*], **-plied, -ply•ing.** to act or be in accordance with wishes, requirements, or conditions; obey: *We cannot comply with your demands for the files.*

com•po•nent /kəm'pownənt/ *n.* [*count*] a basic or fundamental part from which something is made.

com•pose /kəm'powz/ *v.* [~ + *obj*], **-posed, -pos•ing.** **1.** to be or make up the parts of; form the basis of: *His spaghetti sauce was composed of many ingredients.* **2.** to create (a musical, literary, or dance work). **3.** to bring to a condition of calmness; settle down: *He took a moment to compose himself.*

com•pos•er /kəm'powzər/ *n.* [*count*] a person who composes music.

com•pos•ite /kəm'pɒzɪt/ *adj.* **1.** made up of different elements. —*n.* [*count*] **2.** something made up of different or separate parts; a blend.

com•po•si•tion /ˌkɒmpə'zɪʃən/ *n.* **1.** [*noncount*] the elements of which something is composed; makeup. **2.** [*noncount*] the act or process of producing a piece of writing. **3.** [*count*] something composed, such as a short essay or a piece of music.

com•post /'kɒmpowst/ *n.* [*noncount*] **1.** a mixture of decaying plant or animal matter used for fertilizing soil. —*v.* [~ + *obj*] **2.** to use in compost; make compost of.

com•po•sure /kəm'powʒər/ *n.* [*noncount*] self-controlled manner or state of mind; calmness.

com•pound¹ /*adj.*, *v.* 'kɒmpawnd, kəm'pawnd; *n.* 'kɒmpawnd/ *adj.* [*before a noun*] **1.** composed of two or more parts or ingredients. —*n.* [*count*] **2.** something formed by compounding or combining parts, elements, etc.: *Water is a compound of hydrogen and oxygen.* **3.** a compound word, esp. one composed of two or more words, as *raindrop.* —*v.* [~ + *obj*] **4.** to put together into a whole; combine. **5.** to increase or add to, esp. so as to worsen: *When he argued with the police officer it only compounded his problems.*

com•pound² /'kɒmpawnd/ *n.* [*count*] a separate area, usually fenced or walled, containing barracks or other structures.

com•pre•hend /ˌkɒmprɪ'hɛnd/ *v.* [~ + *obj*] to understand the nature or meaning of. —**com•pre•hen•sion** /ˌkɒmprɪ'hɛnʃən/ *n.* [*noncount*]

com•pre•hen•si•ble /ˌkɒmprɪ'hɛnsəbəl/ *adj.* capable of being comprehended.

com•pre•hen•sive /ˌkɒmprɪ'hɛnsɪv/ *adj.* wide in scope or in content.

com•press /*v.* kəm'prɛs; *n.* 'kɒmprɛs/ *v.* [~ + *obj*] **1.** to press or squeeze together; force into less space. **2.** to condense, shorten, or abbreviate. —*n.* [*count*] **3.** a soft pad held on the body to provide pressure or to supply moisture, cold, heat, or medication. —**com•pres•sion** /kəm'prɛʃən/ *n.* [*noncount*]

com•prise /kəm'prayz/ *v.* [~ + *obj*; *not: be* + ~*-ing*], **-prised, -pris•ing. 1.** to include or contain: *The Soviet Union comprised several republics.* **2.** to consist of; be composed of: *The United States comprises fifty states.* **3.** to form or constitute: *Seminars and lectures comprised the day's activities.* —***Idiom.* 4. be comprised of,** to consist of; be composed of: *The United States is comprised of fifty states.*

com•pro•mise /'kɒmprəˌmayz/ *n.*, *v.*, **-mised, -mis•ing.** —*n.* **1.** [*noncount*] the settlement of differences between two parties in which both sides give up something. **2.** [*count*] something intermediate or midway between two different things. —*v.* **3.** [*no obj*] to make a compromise or compromises. **4.** [~ + *obj*] to expose to danger, suspicion, scandal, etc.

comp•trol•ler /kən'trowlər/ *n.* CONTROLLER.

com•pul•sion /kəm'pʌlʃən/ *n.* **1.** [*noncount*] the act of compelling or the state of being compelled. **2.** [*count*] a strong impulse to perform an act, esp. one that is irrational or contrary to one's will.

com•pul•sive /kəm'pʌlsɪv/ *adj.* **1.** resulting from or caused by a compulsion: *compulsive*

overeating. **2.** not able to be resisted; having the power to compel.

com•pul•so•ry /kəm'pʌlsəriy/ *adj.* **1.** put into force by law or rules. **2.** using compulsion; compelling; forceful.

com•pute /kəm'pyuwt/ *v.*, **-put•ed, -put•ing. 1.** [~ + *obj*] to determine by calculation or by using a computer; calculate. **2.** [*no obj*] to use a computer. —**com•pu•ta•tion** /ˌkɒmpyʊ'teyʃən/ *n.* [*noncount*] [*count*]

com•put•er /kəm'pyuwtər/ *n.* [*count*] [*noncount*] an electronic device designed for performing operations on data at high speed.

com•put•er•ize /kəm'pyuwtəˌrayz/ *v.*, **-ized, -iz•ing. 1.** [~ + *obj*] to control, process, or store (data) by a computer. **2.** [~ + *obj*] [*no obj*] to equip (a business, etc.) with computers. —**com•put•er•i•za•tion** /kəmˌpyuwtərə'zeyʃən/, *n.* [*noncount*]

com•rade /'kɒmræd/ *n.* **1.** [*count*] a person who shares in one's activities, etc.; companion; friend. **2.** [*count*; *before a name*] a fellow member of a group, political party, etc., esp. of a Communist party.

con¹ /kɒn/ *adj.* **1.** against (a proposition, issue, etc.): *pro and con arguments.* —*adv.* **2.** against: *They argued pro and con.*

con² /kɒn/ *adj.*, *v.*, **conned, con•ning.** —*adj.* **1.** involving dishonesty and trickery; deceitful: *swindled by a con man.* —*v.* [~ + *obj*] **2.** to swindle; trick: *The crooks conned her out of her life savings.* **3.** to persuade by deception, threats, exaggeration, etc.

con-, a form of the prefix COM-, used before roots beginning with the letter "n": (*connection*).

con•cave /kɒn'keyv, 'kɒnkeyv/ *adj.* curved inward like the inside of a sphere: *a concave lens.*

con•ceal /kən'siyl/ *v.* [~ + *obj*] **1.** to hide; cover or keep from sight. **2.** to keep secret; avoid disclosing. —**con•ceal•ment,** *n.* [*noncount*]

con•cede /kən'siyd/ *v.*, **-ced•ed, -ced•ing. 1.** [~ + *obj*] to acknowledge as true, just, or proper; admit: *He finally conceded (that) she was right.* **2.** [~ + *obj*] [*no obj*] to acknowledge that one has lost (a contest, etc.) before it is officially established: *to concede an election.*

con•ceit /kən'siyt/ *n.* [*noncount*] an overly favorable opinion of one's own ability, importance, etc. —**con'ceit•ed,** *adj.*

con•ceive /kən'siyv/ *v.*, **-ceived, -ceiv•ing. 1.** to form (an idea, etc.) in the mind; imagine: [~ + *obj*]: *He conceived the project while on vacation.* [*no obj*]: *I can't conceive of living without a TV.* **2.** [~ + *obj*] [*no obj*] to become pregnant (with).

con•cen•trate /'kɒnsənˌtreyt/ *v.*, **-trat•ed, -trat•ing,** *n.* —*v.* **1.** [*no obj*] [~ + *obj*] to direct (one's attention or efforts) to a point of focus: *I concentrated on the problem.* **2.** [*no obj*] to be present in large numbers in a particular place, etc.: *The population was concentrated in the cities.* **3.** [~ + *obj*] to make stronger or purer, as by removing or reducing the amount of liquid: *Concentrate the gravy by boiling it.* —*n.* [*count*] **4.** a concentrated form of something; product of concentration: *Mix water with the orange juice concentrate.* —**con•cen•tra•tion** /ˌkɒnsən'treyʃən/ *n.* [*noncount*] [*count*]

concen'tration ˌcamp, *n.* [*count*] a guarded compound for the confinement of political prisoners, minorities, etc.

con•cen•tric /kən'sɛntrɪk/ *adj.* (esp. of circles or spheres) having a common center.

con•cept /'kɒnsɛpt/ *n.* [*count*] a general notion

C

or idea; conception: *They had no concept of how dangerous the storm was.*

con•cep•tion /kən'sɛpʃən/ *n.* **1.** [*noncount*] fertilization; the process in which there is union of sperm and egg. **2.** [*count*] a notion; general idea; concept. **3.** [*noncount*] the act or power of forming notions, ideas, or concepts in the mind.

con•cern /kən'sɜrn/ *v.* [~ + *obj*] **1.** to be of interest or importance to: *Drug abuse concerns us all.* **2.** to relate to; be about: *The magazine article concerns life in Bosnia.* **3.** to trouble, worry, or make unhappy: *Your headaches concern me.* —*n.* **4.** [*noncount*] something that relates to a person; one's business or affair: *That problem is of no concern to us.* **5.** [*noncount*] worry or anxiety: *to show concern for the homeless.* **6.** [*count*] a commercial or manufacturing company.

con•cerned /kən'sɜrnd/ *adj.* **1.** interested or affected: *concerned citizens.* **2.** troubled or anxious: *a concerned look on her face.* **3.** [*often: after a noun; sometimes:* be + ~] having a connection or involvement; participating: *All persons concerned will meet in the dean's office.* —**con•cern•ed•ly** /kən'sɜrnɪdliy/, *adv.*

con•cern•ing /kən'sɜrnɪŋ/ *prep.* relating to; regarding; about: *a dispute concerning a wage increase.*

con•cert /'kɒnsɜrt/ *n.* [*count*] **1.** a public performance of music or dancing. —*Idiom.* **2. in concert,** together; jointly: *to act in concert.*

con•cert•ed /kən'sɜrtɪd/ *adj.* [*before a noun*] **1.** determined; serious; sincere: *We made a concerted effort to get there on time.* **2.** performed, devised, or designed in cooperation: *a concerted attack.*

con•cer•to /kən'tʃɛrtow/ *n.* [*count*], *pl.* **-tos, -ti** /-tiy/. a musical composition for one or more instruments and orchestra.

con•ces•sion /kən'sɛʃən/ *n.* [*count*] **1. a.** the act of conceding something, such as a point in an argument. **b.** the point conceded: *They made a few concessions to the protesters.* **2.** the right to have a business or service in a place: *the refreshment concession at a theater.*

conch /kɒŋk, kɒntʃ/ *n.* [*count*], *pl.* **conchs** /kɒŋks/, **con•ches** /'kɒntʃɪz/. a marine shellfish having a thick pointed spiral shell with a wide outer lip.

con•cierge /ˌkɒnsiy'ɛərʒ/ *n.* [*count*], *pl.* **-cierges** /-siy'ɛərʒɪz, -siy'ɛərʒ/. a member of a hotel staff in charge of special services for guests.

con•cil•i•ate /kən'sɪliy,eyt/ *v.* [~ + *obj*], **-at•ed, -at•ing.** to overcome the distrust or hostility of. —**con•cil•i•a•tion** /kən,sɪliy'eyʃən/, *n.* [*noncount*]

con•cise /kən'says/ *adj.* expressing much in few words; succinct. —**con'cise•ly,** *adv.* —**con'cise•ness,** *n.* [*noncount*]

con•clude /kən'kluwd/ *v.,* **-clud•ed, -clud•ing.** **1.** [~ + *obj*] [*no obj*] to (cause to) come to an end; finish. **2.** [~ + *obj*] to determine by reasoning; infer: *From your smile I conclude that the news is good. What can you conclude from your data?*

con•clu•sion /kən'kluwʒən/ *n.* [*count*] **1.** the end or close; final part. **2.** a judgment or opinion resulting from reasoning. —*Idiom.* **3. in conclusion,** [*noncount*] lastly; to conclude: *The essay's last paragraph began "In conclusion..."* **4. jump to conclusions,** to arrive at or form a judgment too quickly.

con•coct /kən'kɒkt/ *v.* [~ + *obj*] **1.** to prepare by combining ingredients: *to concoct a meal from* simple ingredients. **2.** to make up; invent: *to concoct an excuse.* —**con•coc•tion** /kən'kɒkʃən/, *n.* [*count*]

con•cord /'kɒnkɔrd, 'kɒŋ-/ *n.* [*noncount; often:* in + ~] agreement or harmony between persons, groups, etc.

con•course /'kɒnkɔrs, 'kɒŋ-/ *n.* [*count*] **1.** a boulevard or other broad thoroughfare. **2.** a large open space for accommodating crowds, as at an airport.

con•crete /'kɒnkriyt, 'kɒŋ-, kɒn'kriyt, kɒŋ-;/ *adj.* **1.** [*often: before a noun*] being a real or actual thing; solid; substantial: *concrete proof.* **2.** relating to or concerned with real instances or things; specific: *some concrete proposals.* —*n.* [*noncount*] **3.** a stonelike building material made by mixing cement and sand with water and allowing the mixture to harden.

con•cur /kən'kɜr/ *v.* [*no obj*], **-curred, -cur•ring.** **1.** to agree in opinion: *Do you concur with that statement? The doctors concurred that her life was in danger.* **2.** to coincide; occur at the same time. —**con'cur•rence,** *n.* [*count*]

con•cus•sion /kən'kʌʃən/ *n.* [*count*] injury to the brain due to a blow or a fall.

con•demn /kən'dɛm/ *v.* [~ + *obj*] **1.** to express an unfavorable judgment or opinion of. **2.** to sentence to punishment, esp. a severe punishment: *to condemn a murderer to death; She was condemned to die.* **3.** to force into a specified, usually unhappy state: *His lack of education may condemn him to a life of poverty.* —**con•dem•na•tion** /ˌkɒndɛm'neyʃən/, *n.* [*noncount*] [*count*]

con•den•sa•tion /ˌkɒndən'seyʃən/ *n.* **1.** [*noncount*] drops of liquid formed by condensing. **2.** [*noncount*] [*count*] the act or state of condensing or shortening.

con•dense /kən'dɛns/ *v.,* **-densed, -dens•ing.** **1.** [~ + *obj*] to make more dense or compact; reduce to a shorter form: *She condensed the half-hour speech to a five-minute version.* **2.** [*no obj*] [~ + *obj*] to (cause to) change to a denser form, as by cooling: *The water vapor condensed into droplets.*

con•de•scend /ˌkɒndə'sɛnd/ *v.* [*no obj*] to behave as if one is better than someone else: *The boss which condescended to see you now.* —**con•des•cen•sion** /ˌkɒndə'sɛnʃən/, *n.* [*noncount*]

con•di•ment /'kɒndəmənt/ *n.* [*count*] something used to flavor food, such as salt or spices.

con•di•tion /kən'dɪʃən/ *n.* **1.** [*count*] a particular way of being; particular state of existing: *Your car is in poor condition.* **2.** [*noncount*] state of health: *He is in no condition to run in the race.* **3.** [*count*] an abnormal or diseased state of the body: *a heart condition.* **4.** Usually, **conditions.** [*plural*] existing circumstances: *poor living conditions.* **5.** [*count*] something demanded as a necessary or essential part of an agreement: *I'll go on the condition that you'll come too.* The conditions and terms of this contract are confusing. —*v.* [~ + *obj*] **6.** to put in a healthy, fit, or proper state: *Constant exercise conditioned him for the race.* —**con'di•tion•al,** *adj.*

con•di•tion•er /kən'dɪʃənər/ *n.* [*noncount*] [*count*] a thick liquid applied to the hair after a shampoo to make it easier to comb, etc.

con•do /'kɒndow/ *n.,* *pl.* **-dos.** CONDOMINIUM.

con•do•lence /kən'dowləns/ *n.* **1.** [*noncount*] sympathy or sorrow: *I sent her an expression of condolence when her mother died.* **2.** [*count; usually plural*] an expression of sympathy or sorrow:

We sent our condolences to our teacher on the death of her mother.

con•dom /'kɒndəm/ n. [count] a thin sheath, worn over the penis during intercourse to prevent conception or disease.

con•do•min•i•um /ˌkɒndə'mɪniyəm/ n. [count] **1.** an apartment house or office building in which the units are individually owned. **2.** a unit in such a building.

con•done /kən'down/ v. [~ + obj], **-doned, -don•ing.** to disregard, overlook, or approve of (something unacceptable, illegal, etc.).

con•dor /'kɒndɔr/ n. [count] a large vulture of North and South America.

con•duc•ive /kən'duwsɪv, -'dyuw-/ adj. leading, causing, or contributing to a result: *Exercise is conducive to good health.*

con•duct /n. 'kɒndʌkt; v. kən'dʌkt/ n. [noncount] **1.** personal behavior: *immature conduct during class.* **2.** the way something is organized or carried out; management: *the conduct of a business.* —v. **3.** [~ + oneself] to behave or manage (oneself): *conducted themselves well at the ceremonies.* **4.** [~ + obj] to direct in action or course; manage; carry on: *My sister conducted the family business.* **5.** [no obj] [~ + obj] to direct (an orchestra, etc.) as leader. **6.** [~ + obj] to serve as a channel for (heat, etc.); allow to pass through: *Copper conducts electricity.*

con•duc•tion /kən'dʌkʃən/ n. [noncount] the ability of a substance to allow energy to pass through it.

con•duc•tor /kən'dʌktər/ n. [count] **1.** a person who conducts; director or manager. **2.** an employee on a bus or train who is in charge of its movement and its passengers. **3.** a person who directs an orchestra, band, or chorus. **4.** a substance that conducts heat, etc.

cone /kown/ n. [count] **1.** a solid in which the bottom or base is a circle and the sides are smooth, curved lines narrowing to a point at the top. **2.** anything shaped like a cone: *the cone of a volcano.* **3.** the seed-bearing structure of certain trees, such as the pine.

con•fec•tion /kən'fɛkʃən/ n. [count] a sweet preparation, as a candy.

con•fed•er•a•cy /kən'fɛdərəsiy/ n. [count], pl. **-cies.** an alliance between persons, states, etc., to achieve some purpose.

con•fed•er•ate /n. kən'fɛdərɪt; v. kən'fɛdəˌreyt/ n., v., **-at•ed, -at•ing.** —n. [count] **1.** a person, nation, etc., united with others in a confederacy. **2.** someone working with another in an illegal or criminal act. —v. [no obj] [~ + obj] **3.** to unite in a league, alliance, or conspiracy.

con•fed•er•a•tion /kən,fɛdə'reyʃən/ n. [count] a league or alliance, esp. of states united for common purposes.

con•fer /kən'fɜr/ v., **-ferred, -fer•ring. 1.** [no obj] to discuss something together; compare ideas or opinions: *We conferred for a moment in private.* **2.** [~ + obj] to give as a gift, honor, etc., to someone: *to confer a degree on a graduate.*

con•fer•ence /'kɒnfərəns/ n. [count] a meeting for discussion or exchange of ideas.

con•fess /kən'fɛs/ v. **1.** to acknowledge or admit (a fault, etc.): [~ + obj]: *confessed his guilt to the police.* [no obj]: *confessed to the crime; confessed (that) he was the killer.* **2.** [~ + obj] to admit as true: *I must confess (that) I haven't read the book.* **3.** [~ + obj] [no obj] to declare or acknowledge (one's sins), esp. to God or to a

priest. —**con•fes•sion** /kən'fɛʃən/ n. [noncount] [count]

con•fes•sion•al /kən'fɛʃənl/ adj. **1.** of or characteristic of confession. —n. [count] **2.** a place for hearing confessions by a priest.

con•fet•ti /kən'fɛtiy/ n. [noncount] small bits of colored paper thrown or dropped from a height at festive events.

con•fi•dant /'kɒnfɪˌdænt, -ˌdɑnt/ n. [count] a person to whom another tells secrets: *Her secretary was her only confidant.*

con•fide /kən'fayd/ v., **-fid•ed, -fid•ing.** to tell (secrets) to another in trust: [no obj]: *She wouldn't confide in me.* [~ + obj]: *She was afraid to confide her plans to me. The paratrooper confided that he closed his .eyes whenever he jumped out of planes.*

con•fi•dence /'kɒnfɪdəns/ n. [noncount] **1.** belief in the reliability of a person or thing: *The bank manager had full confidence in his employees.* **2.** belief in oneself and one's powers or abilities: *He would be a better speaker if he had more confidence.* —**Idiom. 3. in confidence,** as a secret or private matter: *I'm telling you this in strictest confidence.*

con•fi•dent /'kɒnfɪdənt/ adj. **1.** [be + ~] sure; certain: *He was confident of success. He was confident (that) they would succeed.* **2.** sure of oneself; self-confident: *a confident performer.* —'con•fi•dent•ly, adv.: *I confidently expected him to do the job.*

con•fi•den•tial /ˌkɒnfɪ'dɛnʃəl/ adj. spoken, written, or acted on in secret. —**con•fi•den•ti•al•i•ty** /ˌkɒnfɪˌdɛnʃiy'ælɪtiy/, n. [noncount]

con•fig•u•ra•tion /kən,fɪɡyə'reyʃən/ n. [count] the arrangement of the parts or elements of a thing.

con•fine /v. kən'fayn; n. 'kɒnfayn/ v., **-fined, -fin•ing,** n. —v. [~ + obj (+ to + obj)] **1.** to enclose within bounds; limit or restrict: *He confined himself to a few remarks.* **2.** to keep in; prevent from leaving because of imprisonment, illness, etc.: *She is confined to a hospital.* —n. **3.** Usually, **confines.** [plural] a boundary or bound; limit; border: *He stayed within the confines of the hotel.* —**con•fine•ment, n.** [noncount]

con•firm /kən'fɜrm/ v. [~ + obj] **1.** to establish the truth of (something): *The secretary would not confirm the reports; She confirmed that my client was there at the time of the murder.* **2.** to acknowledge; make certain: *The hotel confirmed my reservation.* **3.** to make valid by formal or legal act: *Her appointment as Secretary of State was confirmed by the Senate.* **4.** to admit to full membership in a religious community: *He was confirmed when he was thirteen.* —**con•fir•ma•tion** /,kɒnfər'meyʃən/ n. [noncount] [count]

con•firmed /kən'fɜrmd/ adj. [before a noun] firmly established or settled in a habit or condition; unlikely to change: *a confirmed bachelor.*

con•fis•cate /'kɒnfəˌskeyt/ v. [~ + obj], **-cat•ed, -cat•ing.** to seize (something) by legal authority. —**con•fis•ca•tion** /ˌkɒnfə'skeyʃən/, n. [noncount]

con•fla•gra•tion /ˌkɒnflə'greyʃən/ n. [count] a destructive fire over a wide area.

con•flict /v. kən flikt'; n. kon'flikt/ v. [no obj] **1.** to disagree; be in opposition; clash. *Our views conflict. My views on learning conflict with yours.* —n. **2.** [noncount] [count] a fight, battle, or struggle. **3.** disagreement; quarrel; argument: [noncount]: *The department was in conflict over the hiring of professors.* [count]: *A conflict arose* *when the department tried to hire a famous pro-fessor.*

con•form /kən'fɔrm/ v. **1.** [no obj] to act in accordance or agreement; comply: *to conform to rules.* **2.** [no obj] to act in accordance with the standards or attitudes of a group. **3.** [~ + obj] to bring (something) into agreement or correspondence. —**con'form•ist,** n. [count] —**con'form•i•ty,** n. [noncount]

con•found /kən'fawnd/ v. [~ + obj] **1.** to amaze; confuse. **2.** to mix up by mistake: *The report confounded truth with errors and lies.*

con•front /kən'frʌnt/ v. [~ + obj] **1.** to face (someone) in hostility. **2.** to present facts or evidence to (someone). **3.** to occur or arise as something to be dealt with: *the difficulties that confronted us.* —**con•fron•ta•tion** /ˌkɒnfrən'teyʃən/ n. [noncount] [count]

con•fuse /kən'fyuwz/ v. [~ + obj], **-fused, -fus•ing. 1.** to cause to make a mistake; mix up. **2.** to make hard to understand or unclear: *Let's not confuse matters.* **3.** to fail to distinguish between (two things): *I always confuse the twins. I always confuse one twin with the other.*

con•fu•sion /kən'fyuwʒən/ n. [noncount] **1.** bewilderment; puzzlement: *Imagine our confusion when I started teaching in the wrong room.* **2.** disorder; chaos; upheaval: *The army retreated in confusion.*

con•geal /kən'dʒiyl/ v. [no obj] [~ + obj] to change from a soft or liquid state to a solid state, as by cooling; thicken.

con•gen•ial /kən'dʒiynyəl/ adj. **1.** agreeable, suitable, or pleasing. **2.** suited to each other in tastes, thinking, etc.; compatible: *a congenial couple.*

con•gen•i•tal /kən'dʒɛnɪtḷ/ adj. present or existing at the time of birth: *a congenital defect.*

con•ges•ted /kən'dʒɛstɪd/ adj. of, relating to, or marked by congestion.

con•ges•tion /kən'dʒɛstʃən/ n. [noncount] **1.** a condition of overcrowding: *Congestion on major roads is worse than usual.* **2.** a condition in the body in which there is an abnormal accumulation of fluid: *The congestion in his chest made it hard for him to breathe.*

con•glom•er•ate /n., kən'glɒmərɪt, kəŋ-; v. kən'glɒmə,reyt, kəŋ-/ n., v., **-at•ed, -at•ing.** —n. [count] **1.** a thing composed of unrelated elements mixed together. **2.** a business corporation made up of divisions that specialize in unrelated industries. —v. [~ + obj] **3.** to bring together into a mass. **4.** to gather into a rounded mass or close grouping. —**con•glom•er•a•tion** /kən,glɒmə'reyʃən, kəŋ-/ n. [count]

con•grat•u•late /kən'grætʃə,leyt/ v. [~ + obj], **-lat•ed, -lat•ing. 1.** to express pleasure to (a person) on a happy occasion: *congratulated her on her promotion.* **2.** to feel pride in (oneself) for an accomplishment or good fortune: *congratulated himself on his narrow escape.*

con•grat•u•la•tion /kən,grætʃə'leyʃən/ n. **1.** [noncount] the act of congratulating. **2. congratulations,** [plural] an expression of pleasure in the good fortune of another: *We sent our congratulations to the happy couple.* —interj. **3. congratulations.** (used to express pleasure in the good fortune of another): *Congratulations! You passed the test!*

con•gre•gate /'kɒŋgrɪ,geyt/ v. [no obj], **-gat•ed, -gat•ing.** to come together in a body; collect.

con•gre•ga•tion /ˌkɒŋgrɪ'geyʃən/ n. [count] an assembly of people who meet for worship.

con•gress /'kɒŋgrɪs/ n. **1.** [Congress] the national law-making body of the U.S.: [no article]: *Congress was not in session when we visited Washington.* [the + ~]: *The Congress won't agree to that plan.* **2.** [count] the national law-making body of a nation, esp. of a republic. —**con•gres•sion•al** /kən'grɛʃənḷ, kəŋ-/, adj.

con•gress•man /'kɒŋgrɪsmən/ n. [count; often: Congressman], pl. **-men.** a member of a congress.

con•gress•wom•an /'kɒŋgrɪs,wʊmən/ n. [count; often: Congresswoman], pl. **-wom•en.** a female member of a congress.

con•gru•ent /'kɒŋgruwənt, kən'gruw-, kəŋ-/ adj. **1.** agreeing; similar: *congruent opinions.* **2.** fitting; appropriate: *Is the punishment congruent with the crime?*

conj., an abbreviation of: conjunction.

con•jec•ture /kən'dʒɛktʃər/ n., v., **-tured, -tur•ing.** —n. **1.** [noncount] the forming or expressing of an opinion without sufficient proof: *Is that a fact or is it only conjecture?* **2.** [count] an opinion or theory so formed or expressed. —v. [~ + obj] **3.** to guess: *I conjectured that he was about fifty.*

con•ju•gal /'kɒndʒəgəl/ adj. [before a noun] **1.** of, relating to, or characteristic of marriage. **2.** of or relating to the relation of husband and wife, esp. the sexual relationship.

con•ju•gate /'kɒndʒə,geyt/ v. [~ + obj], **-gat•ed, -gat•ing.** to give the forms of (a verb) in a fixed order: *To conjugate the present tense of the verb* be *we gave the following:* am, is, are. —**con•ju•ga•tion** /ˌkɒndʒə'geyʃən/ n. [count] [noncount]

con•junc•tion /kən'dʒʌŋkʃən/ n. **1.** [count] one of a small class of words that connect words, phrases, clauses, or sentences, such as *and, because,* and *unless.* **2.** [noncount] the act of joining or the state of being joined: *The police worked in conjunction with the army.*

con•junc•ti•vi•tis /kən,dʒʌŋktə'vaytɪs/ n. [noncount] inflammation of the watery membrane surrounding the eye and the inside of the eyelids.

con•jure /'kɒndʒər, 'kʌn-/ v. [~ + obj], **-jured, -jur•ing. 1.** to make or cause to appear by or as if by magic: *to conjure (up) a miracle.* **2.** to bring to mind; imagine: *The island conjures (up) images of brightly colored flowers.*

conk[1] /kɒŋk, kɔŋk/ Slang. —v. [~ + obj] **1.** to strike on the head. —n. [count] **2.** a blow on the head.

conk[2] /kɒŋk, kɔŋk/ v. Slang. **conk out, 1.** (of a machine or engine) to break down or fail. **2.** to go to sleep.

Conn., an abbreviation of: Connecticut.

con•nect /kə'nɛkt/ v. **1.** [no obj] [~ + obj] (cause to) become linked together; join or unite. **2.** [~ + obj] to link to an electrical or telephone system; hook up. **3.** [~ + obj] to associate in the mind.

con•nec•tion /kə'nɛkʃən/ n. **1.** [noncount] the act or state of connecting or the state of being connected. **2.** [count] anything that connects; link: *an electrical connection.* **3.** association; relationship: [noncount]: *There is no connection with any other company.* [count]: *a connection between breathing polluted air and lung disease.* **4.** Usually, **connections.** [plural] associates, relatives, or friends, esp. when they are thought of as having influence. **5.** [*count*] a plane, train, etc., to which one transfers from an earlier plane, train, etc., in order to continue a trip: *I missed my connection in Tokyo.* —**Idiom. 6. in connection with,** concerning; relating to: *Her comment was in connection with the recent election.*

con•nive /kə'nayv/ *v.* [*no obj*], **-nived, -niv•ing.** to cooperate or work together secretly, esp. for something wrong or illegal: *He connived with his friends to get the job.*

con•nois•seur /ˌkɒnə'sɜr, -'sʊr/ *n.* [*count*] a person with good judgment, esp. in art or matters of taste: *a connoisseur of wine.*

con•no•ta•tion /ˌkɒnə'teyʃən/ *n.* [*count*] a secondary meaning of a word or expression that comes to mind or is suggested in addition to its primary meaning: *The word home often has the connotation "a place of warmth and affection."*

con•note /kə'nowt/ *v.* [~ + *obj*], **-not•ed, -not•ing.** to carry or suggest a connotation.

con•quer /'kɒŋkər/ *v.* [~ + *obj*] **1.** to overcome by force; defeat. **2.** to win by effort, personal appeal, etc. **3.** to gain control over (fear, a bad habit, etc.). —'**con•quer•or,** *n.* [*count*]

con•quest /'kɒŋkwɛst, 'kɒŋ-/ *n.* **1.** [*noncount*] the act or process of conquering. **2.** [*count*] anything taken or won by conquering.

con•science /'kɒnʃəns/ *n.* [*noncount*] [*count*] **1.** the sense of what is right or wrong in one's acts, thoughts, or motives. —**Idiom. 2. on one's conscience,** (of a wrongdoing) burdening one with guilt: *The crime had been on his conscience for years.*

con•sci•en•tious /ˌkɒnʃiy'ɛnʃəs/ *adj.* very careful; thorough.

con•scious /'kɒnʃəs/ *adj.* **1.** fully aware of something: *When he worked he was not conscious of the passage of time.* **2.** having the mind or mental processes fully active; awake: *He wanted to be conscious during the operation.* **3.** deliberate; intentional: *a conscious effort not to yawn.* —'**con•scious•ness,** *n.* [*noncount*]

con•se•crate /'kɒnsɪˌkreyt/ *v.* [~ + *obj*], **-crat•ed, -crat•ing. 1.** to make or declare (something) sacred; dedicate (something) to the service of a deity. **2.** to make (something) an object of honor; dedicate. —**con•se•cra•tion** /ˌkɒnsɪ'kreyʃən/, *n.* [*noncount*] [*count*]

con•sec•u•tive /kən'sɛkyətɪv/ *adj.* following one another in succession or order: *consecutive numbers such as 5, 6, 7, 8.* —**con'sec•u•tive•ly,** *adv.*

con•sen•sus /kən'sɛnsəs/ *n.,* pl. **-sus•es. 1.** [*count; often singular*] unanimous judgment or belief that a group comes to after discussion: *The consensus was that they should meet twice a month.* **2.** [*noncount*] general agreement; concord; harmony.

con•sent /kən'sɛnt/ *v.* [*no obj*] **1.** to permit, approve, or agree: *We asked our parents for permission to use the boat, but they wouldn't consent. He consented to the plan. She consented to marry him.* —*n.* [*noncount*] **2.** permission, approval, or agreement.

con•se•quence /'kɒnsɪˌkwɛns, -kwəns/ *n.* **1.** [*count*] the effect, result, or outcome of something occurring earlier. **2.** [*noncount*] importance or significance: *a matter of no consequence.* —**Idiom. 3. in consequence,** as a result; therefore: *In consequence, you'll have to be careful.* **4. take the consequences,** to suffer something unpleasant as a result of some other action, event, etc.

con•se•quent /'kɒnsɪˌkwɛnt, -kwənt/ *adj.* following as an effect; resulting. —'**con•se•quent•ly,** *adv.*: *I watched TV until after midnight and consequently I overslept.*

con•ser•va•tion /ˌkɒnsər'veyʃən/ *n.* [*noncount*] the controlled use of natural resources to preserve or protect them or to prevent waste. —ˌ**con•ser'va•tion•ist,** *n.* [*count*]

con•serv•a•tive /kən'sɜrvətɪv/ *adj.* **1.** tending to preserve existing conditions and to limit change. **2.** cautiously moderate; safe: *A conservative estimate shows an increase in inflation to 9%.* **3.** traditional in style or manner: *Wear a conservative suit to your interview.* —*n.* [*count*] **4.** a person who is conservative in principles, habits, etc.

con•serv•a•to•ry /kən'sɜrvəˌtɔriy/ *n.* [*count*], pl. **-ries. 1.** a school giving training in art, drama, or music. **2.** greenhouse.

con•serve /kən'sɜrv/ *v.* [~ + *obj*], **-served, -serv•ing. 1.** to prevent injury, waste, or loss of. **2.** to use or manage (natural resources) wisely.

con•sid•er /kən'sɪdər/ *v.* **1.** to think carefully or seriously about: [~ + *obj*]: *He considered taking the new job.* [*no obj*]: *The salesman gave us no time to consider.* **2.** [~ + *obj*] to think of in a certain way; have an opinion about: *I consider the matter (as) settled. I consider him (to be) an excellent mechanic.*

con•sid•er•a•ble /kən'sɪdərəbəl/ *adj.* rather large or great; substantial.

con•sid•er•ate /kən'sɪdərɪt/ *adj.* showing kind regard for the feelings of others; thoughtful.

con•sid•er•a•tion /kənˌsɪdə'reyʃən/ *n.* **1.** [*noncount*] the act of considering. **2.** [*count*] something kept in mind in making a decision: *Age could not be a consideration in the hiring process.* **3.** [*noncount*] sympathetic respect; thoughtfulness: *showed consideration for others' feelings.* —**Idiom. 4. of little** or **no consideration,** of little or no importance. **5. take into consideration,** to consider; take into account.

con•sid•er•ing /kən'sɪdərɪŋ/ *prep.* **1.** taking into consideration or account; in view of: *The campaign was a success, considering the lack of money.* —*conj.* **2.** (used before a clause): If one takes into consideration the fact that: *Considering they are newcomers, they've accomplished a lot.*

con•sign /kən'sayn/ *v.* [~ + *obj*] **1.** to hand over or deliver, esp. for sale: *to consign goods to a warehouse.* **2.** to transfer to another's custody or charge. —**con'sign•ment,** *n.* [*count*] [*noncount*]

con•sist / kən'sɪst / *v.* [*no obj*] to be made up, formed, or composed: *This cake consists mainly of sugar, flour, and butter.*

con•sist•en•cy /kən'sɪstənsiy/ *n.,* pl. **-en•cies 1.** degree of density, firmness, etc.: [*noncount*]: *a liquid with the consistency of cream.* [*count*]: *The milkshakes come in different consistencies.* **2.** [*noncount*] the state of staying constantly with the same principles, direction, etc.: *He shows no consistency in his behavior.* **3.** [*noncount*] agreement, harmony, or uniformity among the parts of a complex thing.

con•sist•ent /kən'sɪstənt/ *adj.* **1.** being the same as or agreeing with something else: *He took actions that were consistent with their views.* **2.** always having the same principles, course, form, etc.: *The governor has been a consistent opponent of capital punishment.* —**con'sist•ent•ly,** *adv.*: *He consistently opposed the war.*

con•sole¹ /kən'sowl/ *v.* [~ + *obj*], **-soled, -sol•**

C

ing. to lessen the grief, sorrow, or disappointment of; give comfort to. —**con•so•la•tion** /ˌkɒnsə'leyʃən/ n. [noncount]

con•sole[2] /'kɒnsowl/ n. [count] **1.** a television, phonograph, or radio cabinet designed to stand on the floor. **2.** the control unit of a computer, including the keyboard and monitor.

con•sol•i•date /kən'sɒlɪˌdeyt/ v. [no obj] [~ + obj] **-dat•ed, -dat•ing. 1.** to (cause to) unite; bring together (parts). **2.** to (cause to) be made solid, firm, or secure: The power had consolidated in the new dictator and his army. —**con•sol•i•da•tion** /kənˌsɒlɪ'deyʃən/, n. [noncount]

con•som•mé /ˌkɒnsə'mey/ n. [count] [noncount] a clear soup made from meat.

con•so•nant /'kɒnsənənt/ n. [count] **1.** a speech sound produced by stopping or changing the flow of air from the lungs. **2.** a letter or other symbol representing a consonant sound.

con•sort /n. 'kɒnsɔrt, v. kən'sɔrt/ n. [count] **1.** a husband or wife, esp. of a king or queen. —v. [~ + with + obj] **2.** to associate; keep company: to consort with criminals.

con•spic•u•ous /kən'spɪkyuwəs/ adj. easily seen or noticed; striking.

con•spir•a•cy /kən'spɪrəsiy/ n., pl. **-cies. 1.** [noncount] the act of conspiring. **2.** [count] a plan made in secret by two or more persons to commit an unlawful or treacherous act. **3.** [count] a group of conspirators.

con•spir•a•tor /kən'spɪrətər/ n. [count] a person involved in a conspiracy.

con•spire /kən'spayᵊr/ v. [no obj] **-spired, -spir•ing. 1.** to agree together, esp. secretly, to do something wrong, evil, or illegal: My brothers were conspiring against me. The army conspired to overthrow the government. **2.** to act or work together toward the same goal: A number of events conspired to keep me from finishing the assignment.

con•sta•ble /'kɒnstəbəl/ n. [count] **1.** a law-enforcement officer in a small town. **2.** Chiefly Brit. POLICE OFFICER.

con•stant /'kɒnstənt/ adj. **1.** not changing; staying the same: Driving at a constant speed saves gas. **2.** continuing without pause; not stopping: constant noise. **3.** faithful, as in love, devotion, or loyalty. —n. [count] **4.** something that does not change or vary. —'**con•stant•ly,** adv.

con•stel•la•tion /ˌkɒnstə'leyʃən/ n. [count] any of various groups of stars that have been named, such as the Big Dipper.

con•ster•na•tion /ˌkɒnstər'neyʃən/ n. [noncount] a sudden, alarming shock or fear that results in great confusion.

con•sti•pate /'kɒnstəˌpeyt/ v. [~ + obj], **-pat•ed, -pat•ing.** to cause to have infrequent or difficult bowel movements. —**con•sti•pa•tion** /ˌkɒnstə'peyʃən/ n. [noncount]

con•stit•u•en•cy /kən'stɪtʃuwənsiy/ n. [count], pl. **-cies. 1.** a body of constituents; the voters in an area who are represented by an elected official. **2.** the area itself.

con•stit•u•ent /kən'stɪtʃuwənt/ adj. **1.** serving to make up or form the basis of a thing: the constituent parts of a motor. —n. [count] **2.** an element, material, etc., that makes up a whole. **3.** a person who authorizes another to act in his or her behalf, esp. a voter in a district represented by an elected official.

con•sti•tute /'kɒnstɪˌtuwt/ v. [~ + obj], **-tut•ed, -tut•ing. 1.** to form (something) from parts: Carbohydrates and fats do not constitute a

balanced diet. **2.** to be the same as: Her behavior constitutes a direct threat to his power.

con•sti•tu•tion /ˌkɒnstɪ'tuwʃən, -'tyuw-/ n. **1.** [count; usually singular] the way in which a thing is formed or arranged; makeup or composition of a thing. **2.** [count; usually singular] the physical character of the body with regard to health, etc.: He had a strong constitution and seldom caught a cold. **3.** [the + Constitution] the fundamental law of the U.S., put into effect in 1789. **4.** [count] the system of fundamental principles according to which something is governed. —ˌcon•sti'tu•tion•al, adj.

con•strain /kən'streyn/ v. [~ + obj] to make (someone) do something; compel: He was constrained to admit what he had done.

con•straint /kən'streynt/ n. **1.** [count] a limitation; something that restricts one's actions or powers. **2.** [noncount] the condition of controlling one's natural feelings and desires.

con•strict /kən'strɪkt/ v. **1.** [no obj] [~ + obj] to (cause to) be tight, narrower, or smaller. This medicine will constrict the blood vessels. **2.** [~ + obj] to limit or restrain: The new constitution constricts the powers of the chairman. —**con•stric•tion** /kən'strɪkʃən/ n. [count] [noncount]

con•struct /kən'strʌkt/ v. [~ + obj] to build or form by putting together parts.

con•struc•tion /kən'strʌkʃən/ n. **1.** [noncount] the act, process, or art of constructing: a building under construction. **2.** [count] something constructed; structure. **3.** [noncount] the occupation or industry of building.

con•struc•tive /kən'strʌktɪv/ adj. causing or leading to development; helping to improve: The teacher's constructive criticism helped me write a better essay.

con•strue /kən'struw/ v. [~ + obj + as + obj], **-strued, -stru•ing.** to explain the meaning of; interpret: My comments were incorrectly construed as criticism.

con•sul /'kɒnsəl/ n. [count] an official appointed by a government to look after its interests and the welfare of its citizens in another country.

con•su•late /'kɒnsəlɪt/ n. [count] **1.** the place officially occupied by a consul. **2.** the position, authority, or term of service of a consul.

con•sult /kən'sʌlt/ v. **1.** to seek guidance or information from: [~ + obj]: Be sure to consult a lawyer. [no obj]: Be sure to consult with a lawyer before you do anything. **2.** [~ + obj] to refer to (a book, etc.) for information. —**con•sul•ta•tion** /ˌkɒnsəl'teyʃən/ n. [count] [noncount]

con•sult•ant /kən'sʌltnt/ n. [count] a person who gives professional or expert advice.

con•sume /kən'suwm/ v. [~ + obj], **-sumed, -sum•ing. 1.** to use up; expend: The minivan consumes a lot of gas. **2.** to eat or drink up. **3.** to destroy, as by burning: Fire consumed the forest.

con•sum•er /kən'suwmər/ n. [count] **1.** a person or thing that consumes. **2.** a person or organization that buys something or uses a service.

con•sum•mate /v. 'kɒnsəˌmeyt/; adj. kən'sʌmɪt, 'kɒnsəmɪt/ v., **-mat•ed, -mat•ing,** adj. —v. [~ + obj] **1.** to bring to a state of perfection; fulfill: Her joy was consummated by winning the gold medal. **2.** to complete (an arrangement, business agreement, etc.). **3.** to make a marriage complete by having sexual intercourse. —adj. **4.** complete or perfect; superb: She was a consummate violinist. —**con•sum•ma•tion** /ˌkɒnsə'meyʃən/, n. [noncount] [count]

con•sump•tion /kən'sʌmpʃən/ *n.* [*noncount*] **1.** the act of consuming. **2.** the amount consumed.

con•tact /'kɒntækt/ *n.* **1.** [*noncount*] the act or state of touching or of being near enough to touch: *The rear wheels lost contact with the road.* **2.** [*noncount*] the act or state of being in communication: *The pilot lost contact with the control tower. I'm still in contact with my high school friends.* **3.** [*count*] a person who can gain access to favors, influential people, etc. —*v.* [~ + *obj*] **4.** to communicate with; get in touch with: *We'll contact you by phone.*

'contact ,lens, *n.* [*count*] either of a pair of small plastic disks placed on the eye to correct vision defects.

con•ta•gious /kən'teydʒəs/ *adj.* **1.** (of a disease) able to be spread by bodily contact with an infected person or object. **2.** (of a person) carrying or spreading a contagious disease. **3.** tending to spread from person to person: *contagious laughter.*

con•tain /kən'teyn/ *v.* [~ + *obj*] **1.** to hold or include within its volume or area: *This glass contains water.* **2.** to have as contents or parts; include: *That food contains dangerous chemicals.* **3.** to keep under proper control; restrain: *He could not contain his amusement.*

con•tain•er /kən'teynər/ *n.* [*count*] anything that contains or can contain something, as a carton.

con•tam•i•nate /kən'tæmə,neyt/ *v.* [~ + *obj*], **-nat•ed, -nat•ing.** to make impure, harmful, or unusable by contact or mixture with something unclean: *The oil spill contaminated the sea.* —**con•tam•i•na•tion** /kən,tæmə'neyʃən/, *n.* [*noncount*]

contd., an abbreviation for: continued.

con•tem•plate /'kɒntəm,pleyt/ *v.* [~ + *obj*], **-plat•ed, -plat•ing. 1.** to look at with continued attention; observe thoughtfully. **2.** to consider thoroughly; think about fully or deeply. **3.** to have in view as a purpose; intend: *to contemplate bribery; We contemplated buying a new car.* —**con•tem•pla•tion** /,kɒntəm'pleyʃən/ *n.* [*noncount*]

con•tem•po•ra•ne•ous /kən,tɛmpə'reyniyəs/ *adj.* living or occurring during the same period of time.

con•tem•po•rar•y /kən'tɛmpə,rɛriy/ *adj., n., pl.* **-rar•ies.** —*adj.* **1.** existing, occurring, or living at the same time: *Hitler was contemporary with Mussolini.* **2.** of the present time; modern: *contemporary architecture.* —*n.* [*count*] **3.** a person or thing belonging to the same time or period as another: *Franklin Roosevelt and Winston Churchill were contemporaries.* **4.** a person of the same age as another: *a teenager and her contemporaries.*

con•tempt /kən'tɛmpt/ *n.* [*noncount*] **1.** a lack of respect; scorn; disregard: *She gave me a look of pure contempt. He was held in contempt by his employees.* **2.** deliberate disobedience to, or open disrespect for, the rules or orders of a court or legislative body: *charged with contempt of court.*

con•tempt•i•ble /kən'tɛmptəbəl/ *adj.* worthy of, or held in, contempt.

con•temp•tu•ous /kən'tɛmptʃuwəs/ *adj.* showing or expressing contempt; scornful: *contemptuous of those below him.* —**con'temp•tu•ous•ly,** *adv.* —**con'temp•tu•ous•ness,** *n.* [*noncount*]

con•tend /kən'tɛnd/ *v.* **1.** [*no obj*] to struggle in competition; compete: *to contend for first prize.*

2. [~ + *obj*] to declare; assert earnestly; claim: *She contended that taxes were too high.* —**con'tend•er,** *n.* [*count*]

con•tent[1] /'kɒntɛnt/ *n.* **1.** Usually, **contents.** [*plural*] **a.** something contained: *the contents of a box.* **b.** the chapters of a book or document: *a table of contents.* **2.** [*count; usually singular*] the amount of a substance contained: *a high calcium content.*

con•tent[2] /kən'tɛnt/ *adj.* **1.** satisfied with what one is or has: *He was content and settled back to enjoy his life.* **2.** willing or resigned, as to do or accept something: *He was not content with my answer. I am content to stay here.* —*v.* [~ + *obj*] **3.** to make content. —*n.* [*noncount*] **4.** the state or feeling of being content: *To her great content, the kids had cleaned up their rooms.* —**con'tent•ment,** *n.* [*noncount*]

con•ten•tion /kən'tɛnʃən/ *n.* **1.** [*noncount*] a struggling in opposition; conflict. **2.** [*noncount*] disagreement in debate; dispute: *The main point of contention was the school budget.* **3.** [*count*] an argument one puts forward; opinion or belief: *It's my contention that we must reduce spending.*

con•test /*n.* 'kɒntɛst; *v.* kən'tɛst/ *n.* [*count*] **1.** a competition between rivals. —*v.* [~ + *obj*] **2.** to struggle or fight for. **3.** to object to; challenge: *They contested his right to speak.*

con•test•ant /kən'tɛstənt/ *n.* [*count*] a person who takes part in a contest or competition.

con•text /'kɒntɛkst/ *n.* **1.** the parts of a statement that come before or follow a word or passage and influence its meaning or effect: [*count*]: *They tried to guess from the context what the message meant.* [*noncount*]: *What he said was taken out of context and was completely misunderstood.* **2.** [*count*] the facts that surround a particular event, etc.: *We have to understand these events in their historical context.*

con•tig•u•ous /kən'tɪgyuwəs/ *adj.* **1.** touching; in contact. **2.** being close without touching; near.

con•ti•nent /'kɒntn̩ənt/ *n.* [*count*] one of the seven main masses of land on the earth: Europe, Asia, Africa, North America, South America, Australia, and Antarctica.

con•tin•gen•cy /kən'tɪndʒənsiy/ *n.* [*count*], *pl.* **-cies.** a chance or possibility that might occur: *They were prepared with a plan for every contingency.*

con•tin•gent /kən'tɪndʒənt/ *adj.* **1.** dependent on something else; conditional: *The plans for an outdoor wedding were contingent on the weather.* —*n.* [*count*] **2.** any one of the groups that make up a larger group: *the New York contingent at the convention.*

con•tin•u•al /kən'tɪnyuwəl/ *adj.* happening regularly or frequently: *continual bus departures; the continual rain during April and May.* —**con'tin•u•al•ly,** *adv.*

con•tin•ue /kən'tɪnyuw/ *v.,* **-ued, -u•ing. 1.** to (cause to) go on without interruption: [*no obj*]: *The road continues for three miles.* [~ + *obj*]: *The army continued the battle for another three weeks.* **2.** to (cause to) go on after interrupting; resume: [*no obj*]: *He continued with his work after dinner.* [~ + *obj*]: *He continued his writing after making a phone call.* —**con,tin•u'a•tion,** *n.* [*noncount*] [*count*]

con•ti•nu•i•ty /,kɒntn̩'uwɪtiy, -'yuw-/ *n.* [*noncount*] the state or quality of being smoothly continuous and uninterrupted: *The U.S. has enjoyed political continuity since the Civil War.*

con•tin•u•ous /kən'tɪnyuwəs/ *adj.* **1.** uninter-

C

rupted in time; without stopping: *continuous noise during the movie.* **2.** being in immediate connection in space: *one continuous line of dancers.* —**con'tin•u•ous•ly,** *adv.* —**Usage.** See CONTINUAL.

con•tort /kən'tɔrt/ *v.* to (cause to) become twisted, bent, or strained: [*no obj*]: *His face contorted with rage.* [~ + *obj*]: *Anger contorted his face.* —**con•tor•tion** /kən'tɔrʃən/ *n.* [*count*] [*noncount*]

con•tour /'kɒntʊr/ *n.* [*count*] **1.** the outline of a figure or body. —*v.* [~ + *obj*] **2.** to mold or shape so as to fit a certain form: *The airplane seats were contoured for maximum comfort.*

contra-, a prefix meaning against, opposite, or opposing (*contradict*).

con•tra•band /'kɒntrə,bænd/ *n.* [*noncount*] anything prohibited by law from being imported or exported; goods imported or exported illegally.

con•tra•cep•tion /,kɒntrə'sɛpʃən/ *n.* [*noncount*] the prevention of pregnancy by various drugs, techniques, or devices; birth control. —,**con•tra'cep•tive** *n.* [*count*], *adj.*

con•tract /*n. and usually for v. 4* 'kɒntrækt; *otherwise v.* kən'trækt/ *v.* **1.** an agreement between two or more parties for the doing or not doing of something specified, or the written form of such an agreement: [*count*]: *The ballplayer signed a multimillion-dollar contract.* [*noncount*]: *I'm under contract to finish the work by June of next year.* —*v.* **2.** [*no obj*] [~ + *obj*] to (cause to) be smaller; draw the parts (of) together: *Her pupils contracted in the bright light.* **3.** [~ + *obj*] to get (an illness), as by exposure to something contagious. **4.** to enter into a contract or agreement (with): [*no obj*]: *We contracted with nonunion workers to do the job. We contracted to make the repairs.* [~ + *obj*]: *We contracted a freelancer to edit the book.*

con•trac•tion /kən'trækʃən/ *n.* **1.** [*count*] an act or instance of contracting. **2.** [*noncount*] the quality or state of being contracted. **3.** [*count*] a shortened form of a word or group of words, with the letters that were left out often replaced in written English by an apostrophe, such as *isn't* for *is not.*

con•tra•dict /,kɒntrə'dɪkt/ *v.* [~ + *obj*] **1.** to say the opposite of: *She always contradicted me.* **2.** to imply that the opposite of (something) is true: *His moral way of life contradicts his principles.* —**con•tra•dic•tion** /,kɒntrə'dɪkʃən/ *n.* [*noncount*] [*count*]

con•tra•dic•to•ry /,kɒntrə'dɪktəriy/ *adj.* involving contradiction; opposing or inconsistent.

con•trap•tion /kən'træpʃən/ *n.* [*count*] an odd or strange-looking machine: *That contraption looks like a sewing machine hooked up to a bicycle.*

con•trar•y /'kɒntrɛriy; *for 3 also* kən'trɛəriy/ *adj., n., pl.* **-ies,** *prep.* —*adj.* **1.** opposite in nature or character; opposed: *Those opinions are contrary to fact.* **2.** unreasonable; constantly disagreeing; stubbornly opposed: *Many two-year-olds enjoy being contrary.* —*n.* [*count*] **3.** something contrary or opposite; either of two contrary things. —*prep.* **4. contrary to,** in opposition; in an opposite manner or way: *to act contrary to one's principles.* —*Idiom.* **5. on the contrary,** in opposition to what has been stated: *"You'll be home at five." "On the contrary, I'll be lucky to get home by ten."* **6. to the contrary,** to the opposite effect: *I do care, whatever you may say to the contrary.*

con•trast /*v.* kən'træst, 'kɒntræst; *n.* 'kɒntræst/ *v.* **1.** [~ + *obj*] to compare in order to show differences: *Contrast your town's transportation system with that of a large city.* **2.** [*no obj*] to form a contrast: *The singer's soothing voice contrasts with her wild appearance.* —*n.* **3.** [*noncount*] the act of contrasting or the state of being contrasted: *In contrast with your views, the president believes we should sign the agreement.* **4.** [*count*] a striking difference between two things: *a contrast in views between the two opponents.* **5.** [*count*] a person or thing that is strikingly unlike another in comparison.

con•trib•ute /kən'trɪbyuwt/ *v.* [*no obj*] [~ + *obj*], **-ut•ed, -ut•ing. 1.** to give (money, etc.) with others, as to a common fund: *Many people contributed money to help the victims of the earthquake.* **2.** to provide (an article, etc.) for publication. —*Idiom.* **3. contribute to,** to be an important factor in; lead to: *There is no doubt that smoking contributes to cancer.* —,**con•tri'bu•tion,** *n.* [*count*] [*noncount*] —**con'trib•u•tor,** *n.* [*count*]

con•tri•bu•tion /,kɒntrə'byuwʃən/ *n.* [*count*] **1.** something contributed: *She made several valuable contributions to the discussion. Her family gave a contribution of one thousand dollars to the hospital.* **2.** a piece of writing that is published in a newspaper or magazine: *This issue of the magazine features contributions from two respected scientists.*

con•trite /kən'trayt/ *adj.* filled with, or showing, a sense of guilt and the desire to make up for some wrongdoing.

con•triv•ance /kən'trayvəns/ *n.* [*count*] something contrived, esp. a mechanical device.

con•trive /kən'trayv/ *v.* [~ + *obj*], **-trived, -triv•ing.** to plan with great cleverness; figure out; invent: *They managed to contrive a means of escape.* —**con'triv•er,** *n.* [*count*]

con•trol /kən'trowl/ *v.*, **-trolled, -trol•ling,** *n.* —*v.* [~ + *obj*] **1.** to regulate, govern, or command; manage: *The pilot controlled the plane from the cockpit.* **2.** to hold (something) back: *to control one's emotions.* —*n.* **3.** [*noncount*] the act or power of controlling. **4.** [*noncount*] check or restraint: *My anger was under control.* **5. controls,** [*plural*] an arrangement of devices, such as switches, for regulating or directing the operation of a machine.

con'trol ,freak, *n.* [*count*] a person having a strong need to control or manipulate situations, events, and other people.

con•trol•ler /kən'trowlər/ *n.* [*count*] a government official or an officer of a business firm in charge of financial accounts and transactions; comptroller.

'control ,tower, *n.* a tall structure at an airport from which planes are watched and guided as they take off and land.

con•tro•ver•sial /,kɒntrə'vɜrʃəl/ *adj.* of, characterized by, or subject to controversy.

con•tro•ver•sy /'kɒntrə,vɜrsiy/ *n.* [*noncount*], *pl.* **-sies.** a fierce and long public dispute concerning a matter of opinion; argument.

con•va•lesce /,kɒnvə'lɛs/ *v.* [*no obj*], **-lesced, -lesc•ing.** to recover health and strength after illness. —**con•va•les•cence** /,kɒnvə'lɛsəns/ *n.* [*noncount*] [*count*]

con•va•les•cent /,kɒnvə'lɛsənt/ *n.* [*count*] **1.** a person who is convalescing. —*adj.* [*before a noun*] **2.** of or relating to convalescence.

con•vene /kən'viyn/ *v.* [*no obj*] [~ + *obj*],

-vened, -ven•ing. to (cause to) assemble or come together for a meeting.

con•ven•ient /kən'viynyənt/ *adj.* **1.** suitable or agreeable to the purpose; useful; helpful: *Public transportation is convenient.* **2.** near or at hand; easily reached; accessible: *The homes are convenient to all transportation.* —**con•ven•ience** /kən'viynyəns/ *n.* [*noncount*] [*count*] —**con'ven•ient•ly,** *adv.*

con•vent /'kɒnvɛnt, -vənt/ *n.* [*count*] a place where nuns live.

con•ven•tion /kən'vɛnʃən/ *n.* [*count*] **1.** a formal meeting to discuss matters of concern. **2.** a practice established by usage; custom. —**con'ven•tion•al,** *adj.*

con•verge /kən'vɜrdʒ/ *v.* [*no obj*], **-verged, -verg•ing.** to come from different directions to meet at a point: *The train lines converge in Paris. The reporters converged on the movie star. Our political views were different at first, but began to converge.* —**con'ver•gence,** *n.* [*count*] [*noncount*]

con•ver•sa•tion /ˌkɒnvər'seyʃən/ *n.* **1.** [*noncount*] informal talk; oral communication between people. **2.** [*count*] an instance of this.

con•ver•sa•tion•al•ist /ˌkɒnvər'seyʃənlɪst/ *n.* [*count*] a person who enjoys and contributes to good conversation.

con•verse¹ /kən'vɜrs/ *v.* [*no obj*], **-versed, -vers•ing.** to engage in conversation: *The principal conversed with the students for over an hour.*

con•verse² /*adj.* kən'vɜrs; 'kɒnvɜrs; *n.* 'kɒnvɜrs/ *adj.* [*before a noun*] **1.** opposite or contrary in direction, action, sequence, etc. —*n.* [*count; singular; often: the + ~*] **2.** something opposite or contrary: *You say we'll win but I believe the converse is true.*

con•vert /*v.* kən'vɜrt; *n.* 'kɒnvɜrt/ *v.* **1.** to change into something of different form or properties; transform: [~ + *obj*]: *Electricity is converted into heat.* [*no obj*]: *The sofa converts to a bed.* **2.** to (cause to) adopt a different belief, etc.: [*no obj*]: *My Methodist father converted when he married my Catholic mother. She converted to Judaism.* [~ + *obj*]: *St. Patrick converted Ireland to Christianity.* **3.** [~ + *obj*] to turn to another use or purpose: *They converted the extra bedroom into a room for the baby.* **4.** [~ + *obj*] to obtain an equivalent value for in an exchange or calculation: *to convert yards into meters; to convert pounds to dollars.* —*n.* [*count*] **5.** a person who has been converted. —**con•ver•sion** /kən'vɜrʒən/ *n.* [*noncount*] [*count*] —**con'vert•i•ble,** *adj.*

con•vex /kɒn'vɛks/ *adj.* curved or rounded outward like the outside of a circle or sphere.

con•vey /kən'vey/ *v.* [~ + *obj*] **1.** to take from one place to another; transport: *They conveyed the supplies to the soldiers.* **2.** to communicate; tell; make known: *to convey a message.*

con•vey•ance /kən'veyəns/ *n.* **1.** [*noncount*] the act of conveying. **2.** [*count*] a means of transporting, esp. a vehicle.

con•vict /*v.* kən'vɪkt; *n.* 'kɒnvɪkt/ *v.* [~ + *obj*] **1.** to prove or declare (someone) guilty of an offense, esp. after a legal trial: *The defendant was convicted and sent to jail. The jury convicted him of murder.* —*n.* [*count*] **2.** a person found guilty of a crime and serving a sentence in prison.

con•vic•tion /kən'vɪkʃən/ *n.* **1. a.** [*noncount*] firm belief: *He spoke with conviction and sincerity.* **b.** [*count*] a fixed or firm belief: *He has strong religious convictions.* **2.** [*count*] the decla-

ration, as by a jury, that someone is guilty of breaking the law or committing a crime.

con•vince /kən'vɪns/ *v.* [~ + *obj*], **-vinced, -vinc•ing.** **1.** to cause (someone) to believe in or agree to something by using argument: *They could not convince the jurors of the defendant's guilt. We convinced the parents that the children were safe.* **2.** to persuade; coax: *We finally convinced them to stay.*

con•voke /kən'vowk/ *v.* [~ + *obj*], **-voked, -vok•ing.** to call together; summon to meet or assemble. —**con•vo•ca•tion** /ˌkɒnvə'keyʃən/ *n.* [*noncount*] [*count*]

con•voy /'kɒnvɔy; *v. also* kən'vɔy/ *n.* [*count*] **1.** a group of vehicles traveling together, esp. for protection. —*v.* [~ + *obj*] **2.** to accompany or escort (ships, etc.), for protection.

con•vul•sion /kən'vʌlʃən/ *n.* **1.** [*count*] a series of violent, involuntary muscle contractions. **2.** [*noncount*] violent agitation or disturbance. **3.** [*count*] an outburst of laughter.

coo /kuw/ *v.*, **cooed, coo•ing,** *n.* —*v.* [*no obj*] [~ + *obj*] **1.** to make or imitate the soft, murmuring sound of doves. —*n.* [*count*] **2.** a cooing sound.

cook /kʊk/ *v.* **1.** [~ + *obj*] [*no obj*] to prepare (food) by heat. **2.** [*no obj*] (of food) to undergo cooking. **3. cook up,** *Informal.* to make up (an excuse, etc.) in order to deceive. —*n.* [*count*] **4.** a person who cooks.

cook•book /'kʊk,bʊk/ *n.* [*count*] a book telling how to cook food.

cook•ie /'kʊkiy/ *n.* [*count*], *pl.* **-ies. 1.** a small, flat, sweetened cake. **2.** *Slang.* a person: *He's a smart cookie.*

cook•out /'kʊk,awt/ *n.* [*count*] **1.** an outdoor party at which food is cooked and eaten. **2.** a meal cooked and eaten in the open.

cool /kuwl/ *adj.,* **-er, -est,** *n.,* *v.* —*adj.* **1.** somewhat cold; neither warm nor cold. **2.** providing relief from heat: *a cool drink.* **3.** not excited; calm. **4.** lacking in interest, friendliness, or enthusiasm: *a cool reply to an invitation.* **5.** *Slang.* **a.** great; excellent: *What a cool play that was!* **b.** socially acceptable, right, or proper: *It's not cool to arrive at a party too early.* —*n.* [*noncount*] **6.** a cool part, place, or time. **7.** [*often: one's + ~*] calmness; composure; poise: *Keep your cool and don't get angry.* —*v.* [*no obj*] [~ + *obj*] **8.** to (cause to) become cool. **9.** to (cause to) become less excited, friendly, or interested. —*Idiom.* **10. cool down, a.** to (cause to) become cooler. **b.** to (cause to) become calm: *I hope he cools down before he does anything crazy.*

co-op /'kowɒp/ *n.* [*count*] a cooperative business, building, or apartment.

coop /kuwp, kʊp/ *n.* [*count*] **1.** a cage for poultry. —*v.* **2. coop up,** to place in or as if in a coop: *They cooped me up in this tiny cell.*

co•op•er•ate /kow'ɒpə,reyt/ *v.* [*no obj*], **-at•ed, -at•ing.** to work together for a common purpose: *The witness cooperated with the police.* —**co•op•er•a•tion** /kow,ɒpə'reyʃən/ *n.* [*noncount*]

co•op•er•a•tive /kow'ɒpərətɪv/ *adj.* **1.** of, relating to, or showing cooperation. —*n.* [*count*] **2.** a jointly owned business operated by its members: *an agricultural cooperative.* **3. a.** a building owned and managed by a corporation whose shareholders occupy individual units in the building. **b.** an apartment in such a building. —**co'op•er•a•tive•ly,** *adv.*

co•or•di•nate /kow'ɔrdn̩,eyt/ *v.* [~ + *obj*],

C

-nat•ed, -nat•ing. to cause to work or act together correctly and smoothly: *She coordinated the day's activities.*

co•or•di•na•tion /kow,ɔrdṇ'eyʃən/ *n.* [*noncount*] **1.** the act or state of coordinating or of being coordinated. **2.** correct interaction of functions or parts: *The drug causes you to lose muscular coordination.*

cop /kɒp/ *n.* [*count*] *Informal.* a police officer.

cope /kowp/ *v.*, **coped, cop•ing.** to deal successfully (with something): [~ + *with* + *obj*]: *I will try to cope with his rudeness.* [*no obj*]: *After his accident, he couldn't cope any longer.*

cop•i•er /'kɒpiyər/ *n.* [*count*] **1.** a person or thing that copies. **2.** a machine that makes copies of original documents.

co•pi•ous /'kowpiyəs/ *adj.* **1.** large in quantity or number. **2.** producing an abundant supply: *a copious harvest.*

cop•per /'kɒpər/ *n.* [*noncount*] a metal element having a reddish brown color, used as an electrical conductor and to make alloys.

cop•u•late /'kɒpyə,leyt/ *v.* [*no obj*], **-lat•ed, -lat•ing.** to have sexual intercourse. —**cop•u•la•tion** /,kɒpyə'leyʃən/, *n.* [*noncount*]

cop•y /'kɒpiy/ *n.*, *pl.* **cop•ies,** *v.,* **cop•ied, cop•y•ing.** —*n.* [*count*] **1.** an imitation or reproduction of an original: *a copy of a famous painting.* **2.** a single example of a book, newspaper, etc.: *I'll mail you a copy of my book.* —*v.* [~ + *obj*] **3.** to make a copy or copies (of). **4.** to follow as a pattern; imitate: *He was always copying his brother.*

cop•y•cat /'kɒpiy,kæt/ *n.* [*count*] a person or thing that imitates another exactly.

cop•y•right /'kɒpiy,rayt/ *n.* [*noncount*] [*count*] **1.** the legal ownership and control of a literary, musical, artistic, or other work: *Who holds the copyright on that book?* —*v.* [~ + *obj*] **2.** to protect by copyright.

cor-, a form of the prefix COM-, used before roots beginning with the letter "r": (*correlate*).

cor•al /'kɔrəl, 'kɒr-/ *n.* **1.** [*count*] the hard, often brightly colored skeleton of certain small sea animals. **2.** [*noncount*] such skeletons when thought of as a mass: *We dived down and examined the beautiful coral.*

cord /kɔrd/ *n.* **1.** [*noncount*] a string made of several strands braided, twisted, or woven together. **2.** [*count*] [*noncount*] a small, flexible, electrical wire covered with rubber for protection. **3.** [*count*] a cordlike structure of the body: *the spinal cord.*

cor•dial /'kɔrdʒəl/ *adj.* **1.** friendly and gracious; warm: *a cordial greeting.* —*n.* [*noncount*] [*count*] **2.** a strong, sweetened liqueur. —**'cor•dial•ly,** *adv.*

cor•du•roy /'kɔrdə,rɔy, ,kɔrdə'rɔy/ *n.* **1.** [*noncount*] a cotton fabric with rows of raised ridges or lines: *The jacket was made of gray corduroy.* **2.** corduroys, [*plural*] trousers made of this fabric.

core /kɔr/ *n., v.,* **cored, cor•ing.** —*n.* **1.** [*count*] the central part of a fleshy fruit, containing the seeds: *Remove the cores from the apples.* **2.** [*count; singular*] the central part of the earth. **3.** [*count*] the most important or essential part of anything: *the core of the problem.* —*v.* [~ + *obj*] **4.** to remove the core of (fruit). —*Idiom.* **5. to the core,** completely; thoroughly: *The villain was rotten to the core.*

cork /kɔrk/ *n.* **1.** [*noncount*] the thick outer bark of a Mediterranean oak tree, used for making

mats, stoppers for bottles, etc. **2.** [*count*] a piece of cork, rubber, or the like used as a stopper. —*v.* [~ + *obj*] **3.** to close up with a cork: *She corked (up) the bottle.*

cork•screw /'kɔrk,skruw/ *n.* [*count*] **1.** a tool consisting of a spiral-shaped metal piece with a point at one end, used for pulling corks from bottles. —*adj.* [*before a noun*] **2.** resembling a corkscrew; spiral: *a corkscrew curl.*

corn¹ /kɔrn/ *n.* [*noncount*] **1. a.** a tall cereal plant having kernels growing on large ears. **b.** the kernels of this plant, used for food. **c.** the ears of this plant. —*v.* [~ + *obj*] **2.** to preserve, season, or cook (food) with salty water: *corned beef.*

corn² /kɔrn/ *n.* [*count*] a hardened area of skin, esp. on the toes.

'corn ,bread or **'corn,bread,** *n.* [*noncount*] a bread made with cornmeal.

corn•cob /'kɔrn,kɒb/ *n.* [*count*] the long woody core on which the kernels of an ear of corn grow.

cor•ne•a /'kɔrniyə/ *n.* [*count*], *pl.* **-ne•as.** the clear part of the outer coat of the eye.

cor•ner /'kɔrnər/ *n.* **1.** [*count*] the place at which two lines, sides, edges, or surfaces meet; angle: *a chair in the corner of the room.* **2.** [*count*] an angle, end, side, or edge: *a table with sharp corners.* **3.** [*count*] the point where two streets meet. **4.** [*count; usually singular*] an awkward or difficult situation: *I was backed into a corner by the evidence.* **5.** [*count*] a region or part of the world: *The pilgrims came from every corner of the empire.* —*v.* [~ + *obj*] **6.** to force into an awkward or difficult situation; trap: *The policeman finally cornered the thief.* —*Idiom.* **7. cut corners,** to reduce costs, time, or effort in doing something. **8. just around the corner,** near in time or place: *The president predicted that an improvement in the economy was just around the corner.*

cor•net /kɔr'nɛt; *esp. Brit.* 'kɔrnɪt/ *n.* [*count*] **1.** a brass wind instrument, of the trumpet family. **2.** *Brit.* an ice-cream cone.

corn•meal /'kɔrn,miyl/ *n.* [*noncount*] meal made of corn.

corn•starch /'kɔrn,stɑrtʃ/ *n.* [*noncount*] a flour made from corn and used for thickening gravies, puddings, etc.

corn•y /'kɔrniy/ *adj.,* **-i•er, -i•est.** *Informal.* old-fashioned or overly sentimental. —**'corn•i•ness,** *n.* [*noncount*]

cor•o•nar•y /'kɔrə,nɛriy, 'kɒr-/ *adj., n., pl.* **-ies.** —*adj.* [*before a noun*] **1.** of or relating to the heart, or to the arteries near the heart. —*n.* [*count*] **2.** a heart attack.

cor•o•na•tion /,kɔrə'neyʃən, ,kɒr-/ *n.* [*count*] the act or ceremony of crowning a king or queen.

cor•o•ner /'kɔrənər, 'kɒr-/ *n.* [*count*] an official who investigates any death not clearly resulting from natural causes.

corp. or **Corp.,** an abbreviation of: **1.** corporal. **2.** corporation.

cor•po•ral¹ /'kɔrpərəl/ *adj.* bodily; physical: *corporal punishment.*

cor•po•ral² /'kɔrpərəl/ *n.* [*count*] an officer in the armed forces ranking below a sergeant.

cor•po•rate /'kɔrpərɪt/ *adj.* [*before a noun*] of, for, or belonging to a corporation or corporations.

cor•po•ra•tion /,kɔrpə'reyʃən/ *n.* [*count*] a business organization created by law and having powers similar to those given to individuals.

corps /kɔr/ *n.* [*count*], *pl.* **corps** /kɔrz/. **1.** a part of the armed forces, esp. a group assigned special duties: *the Marine Corps.* **2.** a group of persons associated or acting together: *the Moscow press corps.*

corpse /kɔrps/ *n.* [count] a dead body, esp. of a human being.

cor•pu•lence /'kɔrpyələns/ *n.* [noncount] fatness; largeness of body. —**'cor•pu•lent,** *adj.*

cor•pus•cle /'kɔrpəsəl, -pʌsəl/ *n.* [count] an unattached cell, esp. a blood cell.

cor•ral /kə'ræl/ *n., v.,* **-ralled, -ral•ling.** —*n.* [count] **1.** an enclosed area or pen for horses, etc. —*v.* [~ + *obj*] **2.** to confine in or as if in a corral: *She corralled me at the party and I couldn't get away.* **3.** *Informal.* to seize; capture: *The police corralled the fleeing suspects.*

cor•rect /kə'rɛkt/ *v.* [~ + *obj*] **1.** to make right; remove the errors or faults from: *The teacher corrected the essays. Her contact lenses correct her poor eyesight.* —*adj.* **2.** conforming to fact or truth; accurate: *Your answer was correct.* **3.** conforming to an accepted standard; proper: *correct behavior.* —**cor'rect•ly,** *adv.* —**cor'rect•ness,** *n.* [noncount] —**cor•rec•tion** /kə'rɛkʃən/ *n.* [noncount] [count]

cor•re•late /v. 'kɔrə,leyt, 'kɒr-; *n.* 'kɔrəlɪt, 'kɒr/ *v.,* **-lat•ed, -lat•ing,** *n.* —*v.* [~ + *obj*] to show or establish a connection between: *to correlate expenses and income.* **2.** [no obj] to have a relation or connection: *A person's weight usually correlates with eating habits.* —*n.* [count] **3.** either of two related things, esp. when one implies the other. —**cor•re•la•tion** /,kɔrə'leyʃən, ,kɒr-/ *n.* [noncount] [count]

cor•re•spond /,kɔrə'spɒnd, ,kɒr-/ *v.* [no obj] **1.** to be in agreement or conformity; match: *His actions don't correspond with his words.* **2.** to be similar: *The U.S. Congress corresponds to the British Parliament.* **3.** to communicate by exchange of letters: *She corresponded with her friends.*

cor•re•spond•ence /,kɔrə'spɒndəns, ,kɒr-/ *n.* **1.** [noncount] communication by exchange of letters. **2.** [count] [noncount] a letter or letters. **3.** [count] [noncount] agreement; similarity; conformity: *correspondence between a sound and a written letter.*

cor•re•spond•ent /,kɔrə'spɒndənt, ,kɒr-/ *n.* [count] **1.** a person who communicates by letters. **2.** a person who works for a newspaper, television network, etc., to gather and report news from a distant place.

cor•ri•dor /'kɔrɪdər, 'kɒr-/ *n.* [count] **1.** a passageway connecting rooms, apartments, etc.; hallway. **2.** a thickly populated part of a country with major land and air transportation routes: *Storms crippled air traffic along the Northeast corridor today.*

cor•rob•o•rate /kə'rɒbə,reyt/ *v.* [~ + *obj*], **-rat•ed, -rat•ing.** to support by giving proof; confirm: *The driver of the truck corroborated my account of the accident.* —**cor•rob•o•ra•tion** /kə,rɒbə'reyʃən/ *n.* [noncount]

cor•rode /kə'rowd/ *v.* [no obj] [~ + *obj*], **-rod•ed, -rod•ing.** to (cause to) become worn away gradually, esp. by chemical action: *The acid corroded the battery.* —**cor•ro•sion** /kə'rowʒən/ *n.* [noncount]

cor•ru•gat•ed /'kɔrə,geytɪd, 'kɒr-/ *adj.* bent into folds and ridges; wrinkled: *corrugated tin roofs.*

cor•rupt /kə'rʌpt/ *adj.* **1.** guilty of dishonest practices: *a corrupt judge.* **2.** immoral: *a corrupt society.* **3.** made inferior by errors or damage: *corrupt computer data.* —*v.* [~ + *obj*] **4.** to make corrupt. —**cor•rup•tion** /kə'rʌpʃən/ *n.*

[noncount] —**cor'rupt•ly,** *adv.* —**cor'rupt•ness,** *n.* [noncount]

cor•sage /kɔr'sɑʒ/ *n.* [count] a small decorative bouquet of flowers worn by a woman.

cor•set /'kɔrsɪt/ *n.* [count] a close-fitting, stiff undergarment, worn esp. to support the hips and waist.

cos•met•ic /kɒz'mɛtɪk/ *n.* [count] **1.** a powder, lotion, or other preparation to make the face, skin, etc., more beautiful. —*adj.* **2.** done to improve beauty, esp. of the face: *cosmetic surgery after the accident.* **3.** done to improve the appearance of something without really improving it: *a cosmetic attempt to hire more minorities.*

cos•mic /'kɒzmɪk/ *adj.* [before a noun] of, relating to, or characteristic of the cosmos.

cos•mo•naut /'kɒzmə,nɔt, -,nɒt/ *n.* [count] a Russian or Soviet astronaut.

cos•mo•pol•i•tan /,kɒzmə'pɒlɪtṇ/ *adj.* **1.** of or relating to the whole world, or to a great part of it: *the cosmopolitan nature of international agreements.* **2.** worldly; sophisticated: *the cosmopolitan customer who demands the very best.*

cos•mos /'kɒzməs, -mows/ *n.* [count; usually singular; the + ~], pl. **-mos, -mos•es.** the universe when it is thought of as an orderly, structured system.

cost /kɔst, kɒst/ *n., v.,* **cost** or **cost•ed, cost•ing.** —*n.* [count; usually singular] **1.** the price paid to buy, produce, or maintain anything: *The cost of the home is about $500,000.* **2.** a sacrifice or penalty: *The battle was won, but at a heavy cost in casualties.* —*v.* [~ + *obj*] **3.** to require the payment of; have (a sum of money) as the price of: *That camera costs $200. That camera cost us $200.* **4.** to result in the loss or injury of: *Carelessness costs lives. Drugs can cost you your life.* —**Idiom. 5. at all costs,** by any means necessary.

cost•ly /'kɔstliy, 'kɒst-/ *adj.,* **-li•er, -li•est. 1.** high in price. **2.** resulting in great loss. —**'cost•li•ness,** *n.* [noncount]

cos•tume /'kɒstuwm, -tyuwm/ *n., v.,* **-tumed, -tum•ing.** —*n.* **1.** [count] [noncount] style of dress typical of a particular nation, group, or historical period. **2.** [count] clothing of another period, place, etc., or for a particular occasion such as a party: *The clown put on his costume.* —*v.* [~ + *obj*] **3.** to provide with a costume; dress.

'costume ,jewelry, *n.* [noncount] inexpensive jewelry made of nonprecious metals and stones.

cot /kɒt/ *n.* [count] **1.** a light portable bed with a folding frame. **2.** *Brit.* a child's crib.

cot•tage /'kɒtɪdʒ/ *n.* [count] a small house, as at a lake or mountain resort.

'cottage ,cheese, *n.* [noncount] a soft, white, mild-flavored cheese made from skim milk.

cot•ton /'kɒtṇ/ *n.* [noncount] **1.** a soft, white substance made up of the fibers attached to seeds of a certain plant. **2.** cloth, thread, etc., made of cotton. —*v.* [~ + *obj*] **3.** cotton to or on to, *Informal.* to become fond of; begin to like: *The baby cottoned on to me immediately.*

cot•ton•tail /'kɒtṇ,teyl/ *n.* [count] a North American rabbit having a white tail.

couch /kawtʃ/ *n.* [count] **1.** a long piece of furniture for seating, typically having a back and arm supports; sofa. —*v.* [~ + *obj*] **2.** to arrange or express (words, etc.) in a certain way: *couching a threat in pleasant words.*

'couch po,tato, *n.* [count], pl. **couch potatoes.** *Informal.* a person whose leisure time is spent watching television.

cou•gar /'kuwgər/ n. [count], pl. **-gars**, (esp. when thought of as a group) **-gar**. a large, brownish-gray wild cat of North and South America.

cough /kɔf, kɒf/ v. **1. a.** [no obj] to push out air from the lungs suddenly with a harsh noise. **b.** [~ + obj] to expel (matter) from the lungs while coughing: He coughed (up) blood. **2.** [no obj] to make a noise like coughing: The plane's engine coughed and died. —n. [count] **3.** the act or sound of coughing. **4.** a sound similar to a cough.

could /kʊd; unstressed kəd/ auxiliary (modal) verb. [~ + root form of a verb] **1.** the past tense of CAN¹: Once I could run five miles a day. **2.** (used to express possibility): That could never be true. **3.** (used to express a possible condition): You could do it if you tried. **4.** (used to make polite requests): Could you open the door for me, please? **5.** (used to offer suggestions or give advice): You could ask for more information.

could•n't /'kʊdnt/ contraction of could not: Couldn't we get together next week?

could•'ve /'kʊdəv/ contraction of could have, when have appears before another verb: I wish I could've been there.

coun•cil /'kawnsəl/ n. [count] a body appointed or elected to give advice, to make rules, or to administer an organization.

coun•sel /'kawnsəl/ n., pl. **-sel** for 2, v., **-seled, -sel•ing** or (esp. Brit.) **-selled, -sel•ling.** —n. **1.** [noncount] advice. **2.** [count] [noncount] the lawyer or lawyers representing someone in court. —v. **3.** to give advice to or about; advise: [~ + obj]: We counseled him to accept the deal. [no obj]: "I would go straight for promotion," he counseled.

coun•se•lor /'kawnsələr, -slər/ n. [count] **1.** a person who counsels; adviser. **2.** a supervisor at a children's camp. **3.** a lawyer, esp. a trial lawyer.

count¹ /kawnt/ v. **1.** [~ + obj] to determine the total number of: We counted (up) all the towels in the room. **2.** [no obj] to list or name the numbers: Close your eyes and count (up) to ten. **3.** [no obj] to be worth something; have value; matter: Every bit of help counts. His twenty years of service should count for something. **4. count against,** to cause trouble for; work against: If I revealed my true feelings, it would count against me. **5. count on,** to depend or rely on: We're counting on you to be there. —n. **6.** [count] the act of counting. **7.** [count] [noncount] the number obtained by counting; the total. —'count•a•ble, adj.

count² /kawnt/ n. [count] a nobleman in France, Italy, etc.

count•down /'kawnt,dawn/ n. [count] the backward counting from the start of a rocket launching, with the moment of firing given as zero.

coun•te•nance /'kawntn̩əns/ n., v., **-nanced, -nanc•ing.** —n. [count] **1.** appearance, esp. the expression of the face: a sad countenance. **2.** the face itself. —v. [~ + obj] **3.** to permit.

count•er¹ /'kawntər/ n. [count] **1.** a table or surface at which customers can be waited on, as in a store or bank. **2.** a long, narrow table in a restaurant, behind which meals are prepared and served. **3.** a long, flat surface for the preparation of food in a kitchen. **4.** anything used to keep account, esp. a disk or other small object used in a game.

coun•ter² /'kawntər/ adv. **1.** in the reverse direction; contrary: His advice ran counter to what we expected. —adj. **2.** opposite; opposed; contrary: The attack was counter to our expectations. —v. [~ + obj] **3.** to oppose, esp. so as to weaken: I countered her arguments by pointing out the advantages of my plan.

counter-, a prefix meaning: against or in response to (counterattack); opposite (counterclockwise).

coun•ter•act /,kawntər'ækt/ v. [~ + obj] to act in opposition to; have an opposite effect: This medicine will counteract the effects of the disease.

coun•ter•clock•wise /,kawntər'klɒk,wayz/ adj., adv. in a direction opposite to that of the normal turning of the hands of a clock.

coun•ter•feit /'kawntər,fɪt/ adj. **1.** made in imitation of something genuine with the intention of deceiving; forged: counterfeit money. —n. [count] **2.** an imitation intended to be used as genuine; forgery. —v. [no obj] [~ + obj] **3.** to make a counterfeit (of); forge. —'coun•ter,feit•er, n. [count]

coun•ter•part /'kawntər,part/ n. [count] a person or thing closely resembling another, esp. in function: The new Russian president came to Washington to meet his counterpart.

count•ess /'kawntɪs/ n. [count] **1.** the wife or widow of a count. **2.** a woman having the rank of a count.

count•less /'kawntlɪs/ adj. so large a number as to be beyond counting: countless stars.

'count ,noun, n. [count] a noun, such as apple or birthday, that refers to a countable thing and that can be used in the singular and plural.

coun•try /'kʌntriy/ n., pl. **-tries.** —n. **1.** [count] a state or nation: European countries. **2.** [count; singular: the + ~] land that is outside of cities or towns: We both grew up in the country. **3.** COUNTRY MUSIC.

'country-and-'western, n. COUNTRY MUSIC.

'country ,club, n. [count] a club outside a city or town, with facilities for sports.

'country 'music, n. [noncount] music originally from the folk music of the Southeast and the cowboy music of the West.

coun•try•side /'kʌntriy,sayd/ n. [noncount] land that is outside of cities or towns: Beautiful countryside north of the city.

coun•ty /'kawntiy/ n. [count], pl. **-ties. 1.** the largest local division of government in most states of the U.S. **2.** a unit of local government in Great Britain, Canada, etc.

coup /kuw/ n. [count], pl. **coups** /kuwz/. **1.** a highly successful, unexpected act or move: It was quite a coup to get the Russian hockey star to play in New York. **2.** a sudden and forceful action that results in a change of government.

cou•ple /'kʌpəl/ n., v., **-pled, -pling.** —n. [count] **1.** a combination of two of a kind; a pair of things. **2.** a grouping of two persons, such as a husband and wife. **3. a couple of,** a few; several: a couple of miles. —v. [~ + obj] **4.** to fasten or associate together in a pair. **5.** to join; connect: The economic demands were coupled with cries for political freedom. —**Usage.** Do not confuse PAIR and COUPLE. Both words have the meaning "a group of two" but are used differently. PAIR is used when two things come as a set, with one not usually used without the other (a pair of socks; a pair of gloves), or when there is one item that has two parts (a pair of shorts; a pair of pliers). COUPLE is used for things of the same kind that happen to be two in number (*a couple of books; a couple of chairs*). Only COUPLE has the sense of "a few, several" (*a couple of miles away*). COUPLE therefore can mean "two (or more)"; PAIR will almost always mean "two (or less)."

cou•pon /'kuwpɒn, 'kyuw-/ *n.* [*count*] a ticket, label, or the like, entitling the holder to a gift or discount, or for use as an order blank.

cour•age /'kɜrɪdʒ, 'kʌr-/ *n.* [*noncount*] the quality of mind that enables a person to face difficulty, danger, etc., without fear; bravery. —**cou•ra•geous** /kə'reydʒəs/, *adj.* —**cou'ra•geous•ly,** *adv.*

cour•i•er /'kɜriyər, 'kʊr-/ *n.* [*count*] [*noncount*] a messenger.

course /kɔrs/ *n., v.,* **coursed** /kɔrst, kowrst/, **cours•ing.** —*n.* **1.** [*count*] [*noncount*] a direction or route to be taken. **2.** [*count*] the path along which anything moves: *the course of a stream.* **3.** [*count; usually singular*] the continuous passage through time or a series of stages: *in the course of a year.* **4.** [*count*] area, etc., on which a game is played, a race is run or sailed, etc.: *the downhill ski course.* **5.** [*count; usually singular*] a particular manner of proceeding: *planned a course of action.* **6.** [*count*] a program of instruction; class or number of classes: *an English course; a math course.* **7.** [*count*] a part of a meal served at one time: *The main course was roast beef.* —*v.* [*no obj*] **8.** to run, race, or move swiftly: *blood coursing through his veins.* —*Idiom.* **9.** in due course, in the proper order of events: *You'll get your promotion in due course.* **10.** of course, **a.** certainly; definitely: *"Of course you can go to the party."* **b.** in the usual order of things: *It would be better to have more time, but of course that's not possible.*

court /kɔrt/ *n.* **1. a.** [*count*] [*noncount*] a place where legal cases are heard and decided. **b.** [*count*] a group of people in a court, such as judges, lawyers, and a jury: *The court gasped in astonishment at the testimony.* **2.** [*count*] an open area surrounded by buildings, walls, etc. **3.** [*count*] a smooth, level, four-sided area marked with lines, on which to play tennis, etc. **4.** [*count*] the residence of a king or queen. —*v.* **5.** [~ + *obj*] to try to win the favor or goodwill of: *the president's tax plan to court the rich.* **6.** [~ + *obj*] [*no obj*] to seek the affections of; woo. **7.** [~ + *obj*] to act so as to cause: *courting disaster.*

cour•te•ous /'kɜrtiyəs/ *adj.* of, relating to, or showing courtesy: *a courteous note of thanks.* —**'cour•te•ous•ly,** *adv.* —**'cour•te•ous•ness,** *n.* [*noncount*]

cour•te•sy /'kɜrtəsiy/ *n., pl.* **-sies. 1.** [*noncount*] good manners or social conduct; polite behavior: *Treat everyone with courtesy.* **2.** [*count; usually plural*] a courteous, respectful act or expression. **3.** [*noncount*] favor, help, or generosity: *The actors appeared through the courtesy of their union.* —*prep.* **4. courtesy of,** thanks to; by the generosity of: *The prizes are courtesy of the mayor.*

court•ship /'kɔrtʃɪp/ *n.* [*noncount*] the act of trying to win the favorable attention of another, esp. by a man toward a woman.

court•yard /'kɔrt,yɑrd/ *n.* [*count*] a court open to the sky, esp. one enclosed on all sides.

cous•in /'kʌzən/ *n.* [*count*] the son or daughter of an uncle or aunt.

cove /kowv/ *n.* [*count*] a small opening in the shoreline of a sea, lake, or river; a small, sheltered bay.

cov•e•nant /'kʌvənənt/ *n.* [*count*] a formal agreement between two or more persons to do or not do something.

cov•er /'kʌvər/ *v.* [~ + *obj*] **1.** to be or serve as a covering for: *Snow covered the fields.* **2.** to place something on or over: *She covered (up) the baby with a blanket.* **3.** to spread on or over the surface of; coat: *to cover bread with honey.* **4.** to deal with; apply to: *The new rules cover all employees.* **5.** to report (a news event). **6.** to insure against risk or loss. **7.** [~ + *obj*] to aim a gun at: *Don't move; you're covered.* **8.** to travel over: *We covered about ten miles on our hike.* **9. cover up,** to keep (something) secret. —*n.* **10.** [*count*] something that covers: *a book cover.* **11.** [*plural; the* + ~] a blanket, quilt, or the like: *He threw off the covers.* **12.** [*noncount*] anything that hides; concealment: *under cover of darkness.* —*Idiom.* **13. cover all (the) bases,** to be prepared for anything that might happen. **14. take cover,** to seek shelter or safety.

cov•er•age /'kʌvərɪdʒ/ *n.* [*noncount*] **1.** protection against a risk as listed in an insurance policy: *coverage against fire and theft.* **2.** the reporting or broadcasting of news.

cov•er•ing /'kʌvərɪŋ/ *n.* [*count*] something laid over or wrapped around a thing, esp. for hiding or protection: *We used the blanket as a covering in the cold.*

co•vert /'kowvərt, 'kʌvərt/ *adj.* concealed; secret; disguised.

cov•et /'kʌvɪt/ *v.* [~ + *obj*] **1.** to desire improperly: *to covet another's property.* **2.** to wish for strongly or eagerly. —**'cov•et•ous,** *adj.*

cow[1] /kaw/ *n.* [*count*] **1.** the mature female of cattle. **2.** the female of various other large animals, such as the elephant.

cow[2] /kaw/ *v.* [~ + *obj*] to frighten with threats; intimidate: *I was cowed into agreeing with the boss.*

cow•ard /'kawərd/ *n.* [*count*] a person who shows a shameful lack of courage. —**'cow•ard•ly,** *adj.*

cow•ard•ice /'kawərdɪs/ *n.* [*noncount*] lack of courage.

cow•boy /'kaw,bɔy/ *n.* [*count*] a man on horseback who herds and tends cattle.

cow•er /'kawər/ *v.* [*no obj*] to pull back and away from, as in fear; cringe.

cow•girl /'kaw,gɜrl/ *n.* [*count*] a woman on horseback who herds and tends cattle.

cow•hide /'kaw,hayd/ *n.* **1.** [*count*] the skin or hide of a cow. **2.** [*noncount*] the leather made from it.

cowl /kawl/ *n.* [*count*] **1.** a hooded garment worn by monks. **2.** the hood itself.

coy /kɔy/ *adj.* shy or reserved. —**'coy•ly,** *adv.* —**'coy•ness,** *n.* [*noncount*]

coy•o•te /kay'owtiy, 'kayowt/ *n.* [*count*], *pl.* **-tes,** (*esp. when thought of as a group*) **-te.** a medium-sized North American animal resembling a wolf.

co•zy /'kowziy/ *adj.,* **-zi•er, -zi•est.** snugly warm and comfortable: *a cozy little house.* —**co•zi•ly** /'kowzəliy/ *adv.* —**'co•zi•ness,** *n.* [*noncount*]

CPA or **C.P.A.,** an abbreviation of: certified public accountant.

CPU, an abbreviation of: central processing unit, the basic part of a computer where most calculations take place.

crab[1] /kræb/ *n.* **1.** [*count*] a shellfish with a wide, flattened body and five pairs of legs. **2.** [*noncount*] the flesh of the crab.

C

crab² /kræb/ *n.* [*count*] a bad-tempered, unpleasant person. —'**crab•by,** *adj.*

'**crab ,apple,** *n.* [*count*] a small hard, sour apple, used for making jelly.

crack /kræk/ *v.* **1.** [*no obj*] [~ + *obj*] to break without separation of parts: *The window cracked when a rock hit it.* **2.** [~ + *obj*] [*no obj*] to break open or into many parts: *She cracked an egg into the bowl.* **3.** to (cause to) make a sudden, sharp sound: [*no obj*]: *The whip cracked and the lions roared.* [~ + *obj*]: *I cracked my knuckles nervously.* **4.** [*no obj*] (of the voice) to change to the wrong pitch. **5.** [~ + *obj*] to solve or reveal, esp. after much effort: *to crack a murder case.* **6. crack down,** to take severe action: *The mayor ordered the police to crack down on drug pushers.* **7. crack up,** *Informal.* **a.** to suffer a mental breakdown. **b.** to (cause to) crash: *cracked up his father's car.* **c.** to (cause to) laugh hard. —*n.* [*count*] **8.** a break without separation of parts. **9.** a slight opening, as between boards in a floor. **10.** a sudden, sharp noise. **11.** a sharp or funny remark. **12.** a break in the tone of the voice. **13.** a chance; try: *I'd like a crack at that.* —*Idiom.* **14. crack a smile,** *Informal.* to smile, esp. hesitantly. **15. get cracking,** to get moving; hurry up.

crack•er /'krækər/ *n.* [*count*] a thin, crisp biscuit.

crack•er•jack /'krækər,dʒæk/ *n.* [*count*] a person or thing that shows outstanding ability or excellence.

crack•le /'krækəl/ *v.,* **-led, -ling,** *n.* —*v.* [*no obj*] **1.** to make slight, sudden, sharp noises: *The campfire crackled in the night.* —*n.* [*count*] **2.** the act or sound of crackling: *the crackle of the fire.*

crack•pot /'kræk,pɒt/ *n.* [*count*] a person who is foolish or odd.

-cracy, a suffix meaning power, rule, or government (*democracy*).

cra•dle /'kreydl/ *n.,* *v.,* **-dled, -dling.** —*n.* [*count*] **1.** a small bed for an infant. **2.** a support for objects placed horizontally, as for the receiver of a telephone. —*v.* [~ + *obj*] **3.** to hold gently or protectively.

craft /kræft/ *n.,* *pl.* **crafts** or, for 2, **craft,** *v.* —*n.* **1.** [*count*] an art or trade requiring special skill, esp. with the hands. **2.** [*count*] a ship or other vessel. **3.** [*plural; used with a plural verb*] a number of ships, aircraft, etc., when thought of as a group. —*v.* [~ + *obj*] **4.** to make with great skill and care: *to craft a wooden horse.*

crafts•man /'kræftsmən/ *n.* [*count*], *pl.* **-men.** a person who is skilled in a craft. —'**crafts• man,ship,** *n.* [*noncount*]

craft•y /'kræftiy/ *adj.,* **-i•er, -i•est.** skillful in dishonest schemes; deceitful. —'**craft•i•ness,** *n.* [*noncount*]

crag /kræg/ *n.* [*count*] a steep, rugged rock, or part of a rock that sticks out.

crag•gy /'krægiy/ *adj.,* **-gi•er, -gi•est. 1.** full of crags. **2.** rugged; having deep lines: *a craggy face.*

cram /kræm/ *v.,* **crammed, cram•ming. 1.** [~ + *obj*] to fill (something) with more than it can easily hold: *The hall was crammed with people.* **2.** [~ + *obj*] to force or stuff (something): *He crammed his suitcases into the car.* **3.** [*no obj*] to study for an examination by memorizing facts at the last minute.

cramp¹ /kræmp/ *n.* [*count*] **1.** Often, **cramps.** [*plural*] a sudden and uncontrolled spasm of a muscle, as in the leg or stomach. —*v.* [*no obj*] [~ + *obj*] **2.** to (cause to) feel a cramp.

cramp² /kræmp/ *v.* [~ + *obj*] to restrict; confine narrowly: *I was cramped in the tiny room.*

cramped /kræmpt/ *adj.* severely limited in space.

cran•ber•ry /'kræn,beriy, -bəriy/ *n.* [*count*], *pl.* **-ries.** a small, sour red berry used esp. to make a sauce or juice.

crane /kreyn/ *n.,* *v.,* **craned, cran•ing.** —*n.* [*count*] **1.** a large wading bird with long legs, bill, and neck. **2.** a large device for lifting and moving very heavy objects. —*v.* [*no obj*] [~ + *obj*] **3.** to stretch (the neck), esp. to see better.

cra•ni•um /'kreyniyəm/ *n.* [*count*], *pl.* **-ni•ums, -ni•a** /-niyə/. the part of the skull that encloses the brain. —'**cra•ni•al,** *adj.*

crank /kræŋk/ *n.* [*count*] **1.** a handle for moving a rotating shaft or rod. **2.** *Informal.* a bad-tempered, grouchy person. —*v.* [~ + *obj*] **3.** to move by means of a crank: *I cranked the window open.* **4. crank out,** to produce in a mechanical way: *She cranked out two novels in a year.*

crank•y /'kræŋkiy/ *adj.,* **-i•er, -i•est.** ill-tempered; grouchy. —'**crank•i•ness,** *n.* [*noncount*]

crap /kræp/ *n.* [*noncount*] *Slang* (*sometimes vulgar*). **1.** nonsense; false statements. **2.** junk; litter.

crash /kræʃ/ *v.* **1.** [*no obj*] [~ + *obj*] to make a loud, clattering noise. **2.** [*no obj*] [~ + *obj*] to (cause to) break or fall to pieces with noise. **3.** [*no obj*] (of moving objects) to collide violently and noisily: *The cars crashed into a wall.* **4.** [*no obj*] (of a computer) to shut down because of something wrong with the hardware or software. **5.** [~ + *obj*] to enter or force one's way into (an event) without an invitation. —*n.* [*count*] **6.** an act or instance of crashing: *His son was killed in a car crash. The tree fell with a loud crash.* **7.** a sudden collapse of a business, the stock market, etc. —*adj.* [*before a noun*] **8.** marked by speed and great effort: *He went on a crash diet and lost ten pounds in two weeks. She took a crash course in English.*

crass /kræs/ *adj.,* **-er, -est.** without refinement; gross: *crass manners.*

crate /kreyt/ *n.,* *v.,* **crat•ed, crat•ing.** —*n.* [*count*] **1.** a wooden box made of slats, used for packing or shipping. —*v.* [~ + *obj*] **2.** to pack in a crate.

cra•ter /'kreytər/ *n.* [*count*] a bowl-shaped hole in the ground formed by volcanic action, a meteoroid, or the like: *the craters of the moon.*

crave /kreyv/ *v.* [~ + *obj*], **craved, crav•ing. 1.** to long for; desire eagerly. **2.** to require; need.

cra•ven /'kreyvən/ *adj.* showing a shameful lack of courage; cowardly.

crav•ing /'kreyvɪŋ/ *n.* [*count*] a strong or eager desire; yearning.

craw•fish /'krɔ,fɪʃ/ *n.,* *pl.* (*esp. when thought of as a group*) **-fish,** (*esp. for kinds or species*) **-fish•es.** CRAYFISH.

crawl /krɔl/ *v.* [*no obj*] **1.** to move with the head or face downward and the body close to the ground, or on the hands and knees: *Has the baby started crawling?* **2.** to move or progress slowly: *a line of cars crawling toward the beach.* **3.** to behave in a way that is an attempt to win favor: *He came crawling to the boss to ask for his job back.* **4.** to be full of: *The hut was crawling with insects.* —*n.* [*count*] **5.** the act of crawling; a crawling motion. **6.** a swimming stroke performed with one arm then the other rotating over the head.

cray•fish /'kreɪˌfɪʃ/ also **crawfish,** n. [count], pl. (esp. when thought of as a group) **-fish,** (esp. for kinds or species) **-fish•es.** a shellfish resembling a small lobster.

cray•on /'kreɪɒn, -ən/ n. [count] [noncount] **1.** a pointed stick of colored wax or chalk, used for drawing or coloring. —v. [no obj] [~ + obj] **2.** to draw or color with crayons.

craze /kreɪz/ v., **crazed, craz•ing,** n. —v. [~ + obj] **1.** to make insane or wildly excited: He was crazed with the desire for revenge. —n. [count] **2.** a person or object of great popular interest.

cra•zy /'kreɪziy/ adj. **1.** mentally unbalanced; insane. **2.** foolish; stupid: a crazy scheme; I thought she was crazy to get married. **3.** very enthusiastic: He's crazy about computers. **4.** very fond of: She's crazy about him. —Idiom. **5. like crazy,** Slang. with great enthusiasm or energy: We worked like crazy all morning.

creak /kriyk/ v. [no obj] [~ + obj] **1.** to (cause to) make a sharp, scraping, or squeaking sound. —n. [count] **2.** a creaking sound. —'creak•y, adj., -i•er, -i•est.

cream /kriym/ n. **1.** [noncount] the fatty, smooth, thick part of milk. **2.** [noncount] a substance like this, containing medicine or other ingredients, applied to the skin. **3.** [count] the best part of anything: the cream of society. **4.** [noncount] a yellowish white color. —v. [~ + obj] **5.** to mix (butter and sugar, etc.) thoroughly. —cream•y, adj., -i•er, -i•est.

'cream ˌcheese, n. [noncount] a soft, white cheese made of milk and sometimes cream.

crease /kriys/ n., v., **creased, creas•ing.** —n. [count] **1.** a line or groove on paper or cloth produced by folding, pressing, etc.: a single crease on slacks. **2.** a wrinkle, esp. on the face. —v. [no obj] [~ + obj] **3.** to (cause to) become creased.

cre•ate /kriy'eɪt/ v. [~ + obj], **-at•ed, -at•ing. 1.** to cause to come into being: the belief that God created the universe. **2.** to establish; set up: The government created several new agencies.

cre•a•tion /kriy'eɪʃən/ n. **1.** [noncount] the act of creating. **2. the Creation,** [noncount] the original bringing into existence of the universe by God. **3.** [noncount] the world; universe. **4.** [count] something created: Disney's creations brought joy to children everywhere.

cre•a•tive /kriy'eɪtɪv/ adj. **1.** having the quality or power of creating: a creative writer. **2.** resulting from original thought; imaginative: gave creative suggestions. —cre'a•tive•ly, adv.

cre•a•tiv•i•ty /ˌkriyey'tɪvɪtiy/ n. [noncount] the ability to produce original, imaginative ideas, solutions, or the like.

cre•a•tor /kriy'eɪtər/ n. **1.** [count] a person or thing that creates. **2. the Creator,** God.

crea•ture /'kriytʃər/ n. [count] **1.** an animal or other being. **2.** a person. **3.** a person under the control or influence of another person or thing: a creature of habit.

crèche /krɛʃ/ n. [count] a representation of Mary, Joseph, and others around the crib of Jesus in Bethlehem.

cre•dence /'kriydns/ n. [noncount] acceptance of the truth of something: to give credence to an advertiser's claims.

cre•den•tial /krɪ'dɛnʃəl/ n. [count] Usually, **credentials.** [plural] **1.** written evidence of a person's identity, position, etc. **2.** suitable qualifications: His credentials for the new job are impressive.

cred•i•ble /'krɛdəbəl/ adj. capable of being believed; trustworthy: The jury considered her testimony credible. —ˌcred•i'bil•i•ty, n. [noncount]

cred•it /'krɛdɪt/ n. **1.** [noncount] public praise given for some action, quality, etc. **2.** [count; usually singular] a source of pride or honor: Those Olympic athletes were a credit to our nation. **3.** [noncount] **a.** permission to pay for goods at a later date. **b.** one's reputation for paying bills on time: My credit is good. **4. a.** [noncount] official acceptance of the work of a student in a course of study. **b.** [count] one unit of such work: He took fifteen credits in English. **5.** [count] a sum of money due to a person: Your account shows a credit of $50. **6.** [count] an entry, or the total shown, on the credit side. —v. [~ + obj] **7.** to give responsibility for; attribute: Those herbs were credited with healing powers. **8.** to enter (a payment) in an account: He credited $50 to my account. —Idiom. **9. on credit,** by future payment: to buy a sofa on credit.

'credit ˌcard, n. [count] a card that entitles a person to make purchases on credit.

cred•i•tor /'krɛdɪtər/ n. [count] one to whom money is owed.

creed /kriyd/ n. [count] an accepted system of religious or other belief.

creek /kriyk, krɪk/ n. [count] **1.** a stream smaller than a river. —Idiom. **2. up the creek,** Slang. in a difficult or hopeless situation.

creep /kriyp/ v., **crept** /krɛpt/, **creep•ing,** n. —v. [no obj] **1.** to move slowly with the body close to the ground, on hands and knees. **2.** to approach slowly and quietly: He crept up to the door. **3.** to go forward slowly and often with difficulty: The car crept up the hill. —n. [count] **4.** Slang. an odd or disgusting person. **5. the creeps,** a feeling of fear or disgust: That movie gave me the creeps.

creep•y /'kriypiy/ adj., -i•er, -i•est. **1.** causing fear or disgust. **2.** Slang. (of a person) odd; weird.

cre•mate /'kriymeɪt/ v. [~ + obj], **-mat•ed, -mat•ing.** to burn (a dead body) to ashes. —cre•ma•tion /krɪ'meɪʃən/ n. [noncount] [count].

Cre•ole /'kriyowl/ n. [count] **1.** a French-speaking person of Louisiana. **2.** [usually: creole] a pidgin language that has become the native language of a speech community.

crepe /kreɪp; for 2 also krɛp/ n., pl. **crepes** /kreɪps; for 2 also krɛp/. —n. **1.** [noncount] a lightweight fabric of silk, cotton, or other fiber, with a wrinkled surface. **2.** [count] a thin pancake. **3.** [noncount] Also called **crepe paper.** paper with a wrinkled surface. Also, **crêpe** (for defs. 1, 2).

cres•cent /'krɛsənt/ n. [count] a shape resembling a half circle or the new moon.

crest /krɛst/ n. [count] **1.** the highest part of a hill or mountain range. **2.** the highest point or level: The president was riding the crest of his popularity. **3.** a tuft or other natural growth on the top of the head of an animal. —v. [no obj] **4.** to form or reach a crest, as a wave or river.

crev•ice /'krɛvɪs/ n. [count] a crack forming an opening.

crew /kruw/ n. [count] **1.** a group of people working together. **2.** the people who operate a ship, aircraft, or spacecraft.

crib /krɪb/ n., v., **cribbed, crib•bing.** —n. [count] **1.** a child's bed with enclosed sides. **2.** a bin for storing grain, salt, etc. **3.** Informal. a translation or list of correct answers, used dishonestly by students while taking exams. —*v.* [*no obj*] [~ + *obj*] **4.** *Informal.* to steal; plagiarize.

crick•et[1] /ˈkrɪkɪt/ *n.* [*count*] a jumping insect that produces noises by rubbing its wings together.

crick•et[2] /ˈkrɪkɪt/ *n.* [*noncount*] **1.** a game, popular esp. in England, for two teams of 11 members each. **2.** fair play; honorable conduct: *It's not cricket to ask such questions.*

cried /kraɪd/ *v.* pt. and pp. of CRY.

crime /kraɪm/ *n.* **1.** [*count*] an action considered harmful to the public good and legally prohibited: *the crime of murder.* **2.** [*noncount*] illegal activity: *a new plan to fight crime in the city.* **3.** [*count*] a foolish act or practice: *It's a crime to let that beautiful garden go to ruin.*

crim•i•nal /ˈkrɪmənəl/ *adj.* **1.** of the nature of or involving crime. **2.** senseless; foolish: *a criminal waste of food.* —*n.* [*count*] **3.** a person who is convicted of, or who commits, a crime.

crimp /krɪmp/ *v.* [~ + *obj*] **1.** to press into small regular folds; make wavy. **2.** to curl (hair).

crim•son /ˈkrɪmzən, -sən/ *adj.* **1.** deep purplish red. —*n.* [*noncount*] **2.** a crimson color.

cringe /krɪndʒ/ *v.* [*no obj*], **cringed, cring•ing. 1.** to move down and away, esp. in fear. **2.** to react toward something or someone with embarrassment, slight disgust, or reluctance: *I cringed at the thought of having to meet her again.*

crin•kle /ˈkrɪŋkəl/ *v.,* **-kled, -kling,** *n.* —*v.* **1.** [*no obj*] to wrinkle; ripple. **2.** [~ + *obj*] to bend or twist: *He crinkled the paper while he spoke.* —*n.* [*count*] **3.** a wrinkle.

crip•ple /ˈkrɪpəl/ *n., v.,* **-pled, -pling.** —*n.* [*count*] **1.** *Sometimes Offensive.* a lame or disabled person or animal. —*v.* [~ + *obj*] **2.** to make a cripple of; lame. **3.** to damage: *The snowstorm crippled the railway system.*

cri•sis /ˈkraɪsɪs/ *n., pl.* **-ses** /-siːz/. **1.** a point at which a situation might get better or worse: [*count*]: *a crisis in their marriage.* [*noncount*]: *a time of great crisis.* **2.** [*count*] a time of instability or danger, as in international relations, that leads to an important change.

crisp /krɪsp/ *adj.* **-er, -est,** *n.* —*adj.* Also, **crisp•y, -i•er, -i•est. 1.** hard but brittle: *crisp crackers.* **2.** firm and fresh: *crisp lettuce.* **3.** cold but giving a feeling of vigor: *crisp weather.* —*n.* **4.** *Brit.* POTATO CHIP.

criss•cross /ˈkrɪsˌkrɔs, -ˌkrɒs/ *v.* **1.** [~ + *obj*] to pass back and forth over: *The traveling salesman crisscrossed the country.* **2.** [*no obj*] to be arranged in a pattern of crossing lines. —*adj.* **3.** Also, **criss′crossed′.** having many crossing lines, paths, or the like.

cri•te•ri•on /kraɪˈtɪəriyən/ *n.* [*count*], *pl.* **-te•ri•a** /-ˈtɪəriyə/, **-te•ri•ons.** a standard by which to judge or criticize: *Which criterion is the most important when you grade essays?*

crit•ic /ˈkrɪtɪk/ *n.* [*count*] **1.** a person who judges or criticizes. **2.** a person who evaluates written or artistic works, as for a newspaper: *a film critic.*

crit•i•cal /ˈkrɪtɪkəl/ *adj.* **1.** tending to find fault or to judge severely. **2.** of greatest importance; crucial. **3.** dangerous or serious: *a critical shortage of food.* —**crit•i•cal•ly,** *adv.*

crit•i•cism /ˈkrɪtəˌsɪzəm/ *n.* **1.** [*noncount*] an act of criticizing. **2.** [*noncount*] an act of passing severe judgment. **3.** [*count*] an unfavorable judgment. **4.** [*noncount*] [*count*] the act or occupation of evaluating a literary or artistic work.

crit•i•cize /ˈkrɪtəˌsaɪz/ *v.* [~ + *obj*] [*no obj*], **-cized, -ciz•ing.** to find fault (with); judge unfavorably or harshly.

cri•tique /krɪˈtiːk/ *n.* [*count*] an article or essay judging a piece of writing or other work; review.

crit•ter /ˈkrɪtər/ *n.* [*count*] *Informal.* any creature, especially a small animal.

croak /krowk/ *v.* [*no obj*] **1.** to utter a low, harsh cry, such as the sound of a frog. —*n.* [*count*] **2.** the act or sound of croaking.

cro•chet /krowˈʃey/ *n., v.,* **-cheted** /-ˈʃeyd/, **-chet•ing** /-ˈʃeyɪŋ/. —*n.* [*noncount*] **1.** Also, **cro′chet•ing.** needlework done with a hooked needle for pulling a piece of thread or yarn through connected loops. —*v.* **2.** [*no obj*] to do this needlework. **3.** [~ + *obj*] to form or make by crocheting.

crock /krɒk/ *n.* [*count*] a clay pot, jar, or other container.

croc•o•dile /ˈkrɒkəˌdaɪl/ *n.* [*count*] a meat-eating reptile of warm waters, with a long, narrow snout and a large tail.

cro•cus /ˈkrowkəs/ *n.* [*count*], *pl.* **-cus•es.** a small bulb-shaped plant of the iris family, with showy flowers that bloom in spring.

crois•sant /krəˈsɑnt, kwɑ-/ *n.* [*count*], *pl.* **-sants** /-ˈsɑnts/. a crescent-shaped roll of rich, flaky pastry.

crook /krʊk/ *n.* [*count*] **1.** an instrument having a bent or curved part. **2.** a bend or curve: *Turn left at the crook in the road ahead.* **3.** a dishonest person, esp. a thief. —*v.* [~ + *obj*] [*no obj*] **4.** to bend; curve.

crook•ed /ˈkrʊkɪd/ *adj.* **1.** not straight; uneven: *a crooked line.* **2.** off balance; to one side: *a crooked smile.* **3.** dishonest or illegal: *a crooked deal.*

croon /kruwn/ *v.* [*no obj*] [~ + *obj*] **1.** to sing or hum softly. **2.** to sing in a smooth, slightly exaggerated manner.

crop /krɒp/ *n., v.,* **cropped, crop•ping.** —*n.* [*count*] **1.** the plant, or the product of a plant, produced while growing or when gathered: *the wheat crop.* **2.** a group of persons or things appearing or occurring together: *the new crop of students.* **3.** a pouch in the food passage of many birds, in which food is held for later digestion. **4.** a close cutting of something, such as the hair. —*v.* [~ + *obj*] **5.** to cut off the ends or a part of: *to crop the ears of a dog.* **6.** to cut short. **7. crop up,** to appear, esp. suddenly.

cro•quet /krowˈkey/ *n.* [*noncount*] a lawn game played by knocking wooden balls through hoops.

cross /krɔs, krɒs/ *n., v., adj.,* **-er, -est.** —*n.* [*count*] **1.** a figure made up of two lines drawn across each other usually at right angles. **2.** a figure of a cross, as a Christian emblem. **3.** a mixture of two animals, plants, things, etc.: *A mule is a cross between a horse and a donkey.* —*v.* **4.** [~ + *obj*] [*no obj*] to move from one side to the other side of (a street, room, etc.). **5.** [~ + *obj*] to cancel by marking with a cross or drawing a line through or across: *I crossed off the items on the shopping list. She crossed out my name on the list.* **6.** to intersect; meet: [*no obj*]: *The paths of our lives crossed again.* [~ + *obj*]: *Highway 50 crosses highway 80 right here.* **7.** [~ + *obj*] to go over and beyond. **8.** [~ + *obj*] to cause (members of two different species) to breed with each other. **9.** [~ + *obj*] to place across each other or on top of each other: *He crossed his legs.* **10.** [~ + *oneself*] to make the sign of the cross upon or over. —*adj.* **11.** angry and annoyed; ill-humored.

—**Idiom. 12. cross one's mind,** to occur to one: *The idea never crossed my mind.*

cross-coun•try /'krɔs,kʌntriy, 'krɒs-/ *adj.* [*before a noun*] **1.** proceeding over fields, through woods, etc., rather than on a road or track: *a cross-country race.* **2.** from one end of the country to the other.

'**cross-,eyed,** *adj.* having or showing a condition of the eyes in which one or both eyes turn inward.

cross-leg•ged /'krɔs,lɛgɪd, -,lɛgd/ *adj., adv.* **1.** having the knees wide apart and the ankles crossed. **2.** having one leg placed across the other.

'**cross 'reference,** *n.* [*count*] a reference from one part of a book, index, etc., to related material in another part.

'**cross ,section,** *n.* [*count*] **1.** a slice of something made by cutting across it: *This photo is a cross section of the brain.* **2.** a representative sample or example: *tried to determine what would appeal to a large cross section of voters.*

cross•walk /'krɔs,wɔk, 'krɒs-/ *n.* [*count*] a lane marked off for pedestrians to use when crossing a street.

'**crossword ,puzzle** /'krɔs,wɜrd, 'krɒs-/ *n.* [*count*] a puzzle in which words corresponding to numbered clues or definitions are fitted into a pattern of horizontal and vertical squares, one letter per square.

crotch /krɒtʃ/ *n.* [*count*] **1.** a place where something divides, such as the human body between the legs. **2.** the part of trousers, panties, etc., where the two legs or panels join.

crouch /krawtʃ/ *v.* [*no obj*] **1.** to stoop low with the knees bent. **2.** to bend close to the ground preparing to spring, as a cat does. —*n.* [*count*] **3.** the act of crouching.

crou•ton /'kruwtɒn, kruw'tɒn/ *n.* [*count*] a small cube of fried or toasted bread, used in salads, soups, etc.

crow[1] /krow/ *n.* [*count*] a large songbird typically black and found nearly worldwide.

crow[2] /krow/ *v.*, **crowed** or, for 1, (*esp. Brit.*), **crew** /kruw/, **crowed, crow•ing,** *n.* —*v.* [*no obj*] **1.** to utter the characteristic cry of a rooster. **2.** to boast or brag: *They were crowing over their victory.* —*n.* [*count*] **3.** the cry of a rooster. **4.** a cry of pleasure.

crow•bar /'krow,bɑr/ *n.* [*count*] a steel bar used as a lever.

crowd /krawd/ *n.* [*count*] **1.** a large number of people gathered together. —*v.* **2.** [*no obj*] to gather in large numbers: *They crowded around to watch the police give first aid.* **3.** [*~ + obj*] to fill (a space): *The protesters crowded the streets.*

crown /krawn/ *n.* [*count*] **1.** an ornament worn on the head, esp. by a king or queen. **2.** a championship title: *He won the batting crown for two years in a row.* **3.** the top or highest part of anything, such as of a hat or the head. —*v.* [*~ + obj*] **4.** to place a crown on. **5.** to honor or reward. **6.** to be at the top or highest part of: *The fog crowned the mountain.*

cru•cial /'kruwʃəl/ *adj.* of highest or greatest importance.

cru•ci•fix /'kruwsəfɪks/ *n.* [*count*] a cross with the figure of Jesus mounted on it.

cru•ci•fix•ion /,kruwsə'fɪkʃən/ *n.* **1.** [*noncount*] [*count*] the act of crucifying or the state of being crucified. **2.** [*Crucifixion; the + ~*] the death of Jesus on the Cross.

cru•ci•fy /'kruwsə,fay/ *v.* [*~ + obj*], **-fied, -fy•**

ing. to put to death by nailing or binding the hands and feet to a cross.

crude /kruwd/ *adj.*, **crud•er, crud•est. 1.** in a natural or unrefined state: *crude sugar; crude oil.* **2.** rough; undeveloped: *a crude shelter; a crude drawing.* **3.** lacking culture, refinement, etc.; vulgar: *crude behavior.* —'**crude•ly,** *adv.* —'**crude•ness,** *n.* [*noncount*]

cru•el /'kruwəl/ *adj.*, **-er, -est. 1.** willfully causing pain to others. **2.** severe; brutal: *a cruel winter.* —'**cru•el•ly,** *adv.* —'**cru•el•ty,** *n.* [*noncount*] [*count*], *pl.* **-ties.**

cruise /kruwz/ *v.*, **cruised, cruis•ing,** *n.* —*v.* **1.** [*no obj*] to sail about on a pleasure trip. **2.** to travel about (some place) slowly: [*no obj*]: *Taxis were cruising in the downtown area.* [*~ + obj*]: *The police were cruising the neighborhood.* —*n.* [*count*] **3.** a pleasure voyage on a ship.

cruis•er /'kruwzər/ *n.* [*count*] one of a class of warships of medium size, designed for high speed and long cruising radius.

crumb /krʌm/ *n.* [*count*] a small particle of bread, cake, etc.

crum•ble /'krʌmbəl/ *v.*, **-bled, -bling. 1.** [*no obj*] [*~ + obj*] to (cause to) break into small pieces. **2.** [*no obj*] to fall apart gradually; collapse; lose strength: *The empire was crumbling.* —'**crum•bly,** *adj.*, **-bli•er, -bli•est.**

crum•my /'krʌmiy/ *adj.*, **-mi•er, -mi•est.** *Informal.* **1.** of little value; worthless. **2.** miserable: *I had a really crummy evening.*

crum•ple /'krʌmpəl/ *v.*, **-pled, -pling.** to (cause to) be pressed into small wrinkles or creases: [*~ + obj*]: *I crumpled up the note in my hand.* [*no obj*]: *The front of the car had crumpled from the impact.*

crunch /krʌntʃ/ *v.* [*~ + obj*] [*no obj*] **1.** to chew with a sharp crushing noise: *crunching his cereal.* **2.** to crush or grind noisily: *Our boots crunched the snow as we walked over it.* —*n.* [*count*] **3.** an act or sound of crunching.

cru•sade /kruw'seyd/ *n.*, *v.*, **-sad•ed, -sad•ing.** —*n.* [*count*] **1.** [*often: Crusade*] any of the military activities undertaken by the Christians of Europe in the 11th, 12th, and 13th centuries to recapture the Holy Land. **2.** a strong movement or action on behalf of a cause. —*v.* [*no obj*] **3.** to go on or take part in a crusade. —**cru'sad•er,** *n.* [*count*]

crush /krʌʃ/ *v.* **1.** [*~ + obj*] to press with a force that destroys or changes the shape: *The women crushed the grapes to make wine.* **2.** [*~ + obj*] [*no obj*] to (cause to) wrinkle or collapse into tiny folds: *She crushed the paper and threw it away.* **3.** [*~ + obj*] to overwhelm; destroy completely. **4.** [*~ + obj*] to shock or upset. —*n.* **5.** [*noncount*] the act of crushing or the state of being crushed; force. **6.** [*count*] *Informal.* an intense, brief feeling of love or attraction for someone.

crust /krʌst/ *n.* **1.** [*count*] the brown, hard outer surface of a loaf of bread. **2.** [*count*] the pastry containing the filling of a pie. **3. a.** [*count*] any hard outer covering or coating, as of snow. **b.** [*count; usually singular*] the outer layer of the earth. —*v.* [*~ + obj*] **4.** to cover with a crust. —**crusty,** *adj.*

crus•ta•cean /krʌ'steyʃən/ *n.* [*count*] a shellfish, such as a lobster or crab.

crutch /krʌtʃ/ *n.* [*count*] **1.** a staff or stick to assist a person in walking, usually having a padded piece at one end to fit under the armpit. **2.** anything that serves as a temporary support or aid.

crux /krʌks/ *n.* [*count*], *pl.* **crux•es, cru•ces** /'kruwsiyz/. the central or most important point: *the crux of the matter.*

cry /kray/ *v.,* **cried, cry•ing,** *n., pl.* **cries.** —*v.* **1.** [*no obj*] to utter sounds, esp. of grief or suffering, usually with tears. **2.** to call loudly; shout: [*no obj*]: *She cried out in fear.* [~ + *obj*]: *He cried a warning as the wolf sprang at them.* —*n.* [*count*] **3.** the act or sound of crying. —*Idiom.* **4. a far cry,** completely different: *The small town was a far cry from the city he lived in.* **5. cry over spilled milk,** to regret what cannot be changed or undone: *There is no use crying over spilled milk.*

cry•ba•by /'kray,beybiy/ *n.* [*count*], *pl.* **-bies.** a person who cries or complains with little cause.

crypt /krɪpt/ *n.* [*count*] an underground chamber used as a burial place.

cryp•tic /'krɪptɪk/ *adj.* mysterious; puzzling.

crys•tal /'krɪstl/ *n.* **1.** [*noncount*] a clear, transparent mineral or glass resembling ice. **2.** [*count*] a single grain of a crystal-like substance: *a few crystals of sugar.* **3.** [*noncount*] glass of fine quality and a high degree of brilliance. —*adj.* **4.** made of crystal. **5.** resembling crystal; transparent.

crys•tal•line /'krɪstlɪn/ *adj.* **1.** of, like, containing, or in the form of crystals. **2.** clear, bright, or glittering like crystal.

crys•tal•lize /'krɪstl,ayz/ *v.* [*no obj*] [~ + *obj*], **-lized, -liz•ing. 1.** to (cause to) form into crystals. **2.** to (cause to) become definite or concrete in form.

C-sec•tion /'siy,sɛkʃən/ *n.* *Informal.* CESAREAN.

CT, an abbreviation of: Connecticut.

Ct., an abbreviation of: **1.** Connecticut. **2.** Count.

cub /kʌb/ *n.* [*count*] the young of certain animals, esp. the bear, wolf, or lion.

Cu•ban /'kyuwbən/ *adj.* **1.** of or relating to Cuba. —*n.* [*count*] **2.** a person born or living in Cuba.

cub•by•hole /'kʌbiy,howl/ *n.* [*count*] a small hole, usually one of several in a row, to store letters, papers, etc.

cube /kyuwb/ *n., v.,* **cubed, cub•ing.** —*n.* [*count*] **1.** a solid object with sides that are six equal squares. —*v.* [~ + *obj*] **2.** to make into a cube or cubes, as by cutting: *He cubed the potatoes.*

cu•bic /'kyuwbɪk/ *adj.* **1.** of or relating to the measurement of volume. **2.** relating to a unit of measure that is produced by multiplying length, width, and height: *a cubic foot.*

cu•bi•cle /'kyuwbɪkəl/ *n.* [*count*] a small space in a large room that is set off by a divider.

cuck•old /'kʌkəld/ *n.* [*count*] **1.** the husband of an unfaithful wife. —*v.* [~ + *obj*] **2.** to make a cuckold of (a husband).

cuck•oo /'kuwkuw, 'kʊkuw/ *n., pl.* **-oos,** *adj.* —*n.* [*count*] **1.** a slim, long-tailed bird. —*adj.* **2.** *Informal.* crazy; silly; foolish.

cu•cum•ber /'kyuwkʌmbər/ *n.* [*count*] [*noncount*] an edible, fleshy, green-skinned fruit.

cud /kʌd/ *n.* [*noncount*] the coarse food that a cow, goat, etc., brings back up from its first stomach to its mouth for further chewing.

cud•dle /'kʌdl/ *v.,* **-dled, -dling,** *n.* —*v.* [~ + *obj*] [*no obj*] **1.** to hold close in an affectionate manner. —*n.* [*count*] **2.** an act of cuddling; hug; embrace.

cudg•el /'kʌdʒəl/ *n.* [*count*] a short, thick stick used as a weapon; club.

cue[1] /kyuw/ *n., v.,* **cued, cu•ing.** —*n.* [*count*] **1.** anything that serves as a signal about what to do

or say. —*v.* [~ + *obj*] **2.** to give a cue to; prompt: *The announcer cued the audience to applaud.*

cue[2] /kyuw/ *n.* [*count*] a long wooden rod used to strike the ball in pool, billiards, etc.

cuff /kʌf/ *n.* [*count*] **1.** a fold or band at the end of a sleeve, serving as a trim. **2.** the turned-up fold at the bottom of a trouser leg. —*v.* [~ + *obj*] **3.** to make a cuff on. **4.** to handcuff. —*Idiom.* **5. off the cuff,** *Informal.* without preparing: *The speaker made a few remarks off the cuff.*

'cuff ,link or **'cuff,link,** *n.* [*count*] one of a pair of ornamental buttonlike devices for fastening a shirt cuff.

cui•sine /kwɪ'ziyn/ *n.* [*noncount*] a style or manner of cooking: *French cuisine.*

cul-de-sac /'kʌldə,sæk, 'kʊl-/ *n.* [*count*], *pl.* **culs-de-sac.** a street, lane, etc., closed at one end; dead-end street.

cu•li•nar•y /'kyuwlə,nɛriy, 'kʌlə-/ *adj.* of, relating to, or used in cooking or the kitchen.

cull /kʌl/ *v.* [~ + *obj*] to choose; select; pick.

cul•mi•nate /'kʌlmə,neyt/ *v.* [~ + *in* + *obj*], **-nat•ed, -nat•ing. 1.** to reach the highest development: *His career culminated in the winning of the Nobel prize.* **2.** to arrive at a final stage after a long development: *Their disagreement culminated in a quarrel.* —**cul•mi•na•tion** /,kʌlmə'neyʃən/, *n.* [*count*]

cu•lottes /kuw'lɒts, kyuw-/ also **cu'lotte,** *n.* [*plural*] women's trousers cut full to resemble a skirt.

cul•pa•ble /'kʌlpəbəl/ *adj.* [*be* + ~] deserving blame; guilty. —**cul•pa•bil•i•ty** /,kʌlpə'bɪlɪtiy/, *n.* [*noncount*]

cul•prit /'kʌlprɪt/ *n.* [*count*] **1.** a person accused or guilty of an offense or fault. **2.** a thing responsible for some bad effect.

cult /kʌlt/ *n.* [*count*] **1.** a system of worship, esp. with reference to its rites and ceremonies: *the cult of devil worship.* **2.** a system of devotion to a person, ideal, fad, etc.

cul•ti•vate /'kʌltə,veyt/ *v.* [~ + *obj*], **-vat•ed, -vat•ing. 1.** to prepare and work on (land or soil) in order to raise crops. **2.** to promote or improve the growth of (a crop). **3.** to develop or improve by education or training: *to cultivate a talent.* **4.** to advance the growth or development of (an art, etc.); foster. —**cul•ti•va•tion** /,kʌltə'veyʃən/, *n.* [*noncount*]

cul•tur•al /'kʌltʃərəl/ *adj.* **1.** of or relating to the way of life of a group of people: *the cultural traditions of the Japanese.* **2.** [*before a noun*] of or relating to music, art, and literature: *I had missed much of the cultural world.*

cul•ture /'kʌltʃər/ *n., v.,* **-tured, -tur•ing.** —*n.* **1.** [*noncount*] artistic and intellectual activities and products. **2.** [*noncount*] the sum total of ways of living built up by a group of people and handed down from one generation to another. **3. a.** [*noncount*] the growing or cultivation of microorganisms for scientific study, medicinal use, etc. **b.** [*count*] the cells or other products resulting from such cultivation: *a bacteria culture.* —*v.* [~ + *obj*] **4.** to grow (microorganisms, etc.) in or on a specially designed medium.

cum•ber•some /'kʌmbərsəm/ *adj.* **1.** heavy or bulky to carry, wear, etc. **2.** slow and inefficient; clumsy.

cu•mu•la•tive /'kyuwmyələtɪv, -,leytɪv/ *adj.* increasing steadily by successive additions: *the cumulative effect of lack of sleep.*

cun•ning /ˈkʌnɪŋ/ n. [noncount] **1.** skill used in a shrewd or sly manner to deceive. —adj. **2.** shrewd; crafty; sly.

cup /kʌp/ n., v., **cupped, cup•ping.** —n. [count] **1.** a small, open container used for drinking. **2.** a unit of capacity equal to 8 fluid ounces (237 milliliters): two cups of flour. **3.** an ornamental bowl, vase, etc., offered as a prize for a contest. —v. [~ + obj] **4.** to hold in or as if in a cup: He cupped the baby's face in his hands. **5.** to form into a cuplike shape: He cupped his hands and caught the ball. —**Idiom. 6. not one's cup of tea,** not something suited or attractive to one.

cup•board /ˈkʌbərd/ n. [count] a closet with shelves for dishes, cups, food, etc.

cup•cake /ˈkʌpˌkeɪk/ n. [count] a small cake, baked in a cup-shaped mold.

cup•ful /ˈkʌpfʊl/ n. [count], pl. **-fuls.** the amount a cup can hold.

cur /kɜr/ n. [count] a dog of mixed breed, esp. a worthless or unfriendly one.

cur•able /ˈkyʊrəbəl/ adj. able to be cured.

cu•ra•tor /kyʊˈreɪtər, ˈkyʊrey-/ n. [count] the person in charge of a museum, zoo, etc.

curb /kɜrb/ n. [count] **1.** a rim, esp. of concrete, forming an edge for a sidewalk. **2.** anything that restrains or controls: a curb on spending. —v. [~ + obj] **3.** to control; restrain.

curd /kɜrd/ n. [noncount] [count] a thick substance obtained from milk when it sours.

cur•dle /ˈkɜrdl/ v. [no obj] [~ + obj], **-dled, -dling.** to change into curd; turn sour. —**'cur•dler,** n. [count]

cure /kyʊr/ n., v., **cured, cur•ing.** —n. [count] **1.** a medicine or treatment to restore health; remedy. **2.** a means of correcting or relieving anything troublesome or harmful: a cure for inflation. —v. [~ + obj] **3.** to restore (someone) to health; heal. **4.** to relieve or rid of (an illness, problem, etc.). **5.** to prepare (meat, etc.) for preservation by smoking, salting, aging, etc.

cur•few /ˈkɜrfyuw/ n. [count] a regulation requiring a person to be home at a stated time, such as one imposed by a parent on a child.

cu•ri•o /ˈkyʊriyˌow/ n. [count], pl. **-ri•os.** a small article, object of art, etc., valued as a curiosity.

cu•ri•os•i•ty /ˌkyʊriyˈɒsɪtiy/ n., pl. **-ties. 1.** [noncount] the desire to learn or know about anything. **2.** [count] a curious or rare thing.

cu•ri•ous /ˈkyʊriyəs/ adj. **1.** eager to learn or know. **2.** taking an impolite or too great interest in others' affairs; prying. **3.** arousing attention or interest through being unusual or strange. —**'cu•ri•ous•ly,** adv.

curl /kɜrl/ v. [no obj] [~ + obj] **1.** to (cause to) grow in or form small rings, as the hair. **2.** to curve, twist, or coil: The sleeping cat's tail curled around its body. —n. [count] **3.** a coil or small ring of hair. **4.** anything of a spiral or curved shape. —**'curl•y,** adj. **-i•er, -i•est.**

curl•er /ˈkɜrlər/ n. [count] a small device used to curl the hair.

cur•rant /ˈkɜrənt, ˈkʌr-/ n. [count] **1.** a small seedless raisin used in cooking. **2.** the small, round, sour berry of certain shrubs.

cur•ren•cy /ˈkɜrənsiy, ˈkʌr-/ n., pl. **-cies. 1.** [noncount] [count] money in circulation as a medium of exchange. **2.** [noncount] general acceptance: The story gained currency as time went on.

cur•rent /ˈkɜrənt, ˈkʌr-/ adj. **1.** [before a noun] of the present time: the current rate of inflation. **2.** generally or commonly used or accepted: cur-

rent usage in English. **3.** most recent; most up-to-date: current events. **4.** publicly reported or known: a rumor current among the students. —n. [count] **5.** a portion of a large body of water or mass of air that moves in a certain direction. **6.** the movement or flow of electricity. **7.** a general course or trend, as of thinking or ideas. —**'cur•rent•ly,** adv.

cur•ric•u•lum /kəˈrɪkyələm/ n. [count], pl. **-la** (-lə), **-lums.** all the courses of study given in a school.

cur•ry[1] /ˈkɜriy, ˈkʌriy/ n. [count] [noncount], pl. **-ries.** a hot-tasting food cooked in a sauce with curry powder.

cur•ry[2] /ˈkɜriy, ˈkʌriy/ v. [~ + obj], **-ried, -ry•ing. 1.** to rub, clean, and brush (a horse) with a special comb. —**Idiom. 2.** curry favor, to seek to advance oneself by falsely praising another: She tried to curry favor with the boss.

'curry ˌpowder, n. [noncount] a hot-tasting mixture of spices, used esp. in Indian food.

curse /kɜrs/ n., v., **cursed** or **curst** /kɜrst/, **curs•ing.** —n. [count] **1.** the expression of a wish that misfortune happen to someone: The witch put a curse on the princess. **2.** an offensive, shocking, or obscene word or phrase, esp. one used in anger or for emphasis. —v. **3.** [~ + obj] to wish evil upon (someone or something). **4.** to swear (at): [~ + obj]: They cursed the pitcher. [no obj]: They cursed loudly at the pitcher.

cur•sive /ˈkɜrsɪv/ adj. (of handwriting) in flowing strokes with the letters joined together.

cur•sor /ˈkɜrsər/ n. [count] a symbol on a computer screen, used to indicate where text or commands may be typed.

cur•so•ry /ˈkɜrsəriy/ adj. going rapidly over something; superficial: a cursory glance.

curt /kɜrt/ adj., **-er, -est.** rudely brief in speech, or too quick in manner. —**'curt•ly,** adv. —**'curt•ness,** n. [noncount]

cur•tail /kərˈteyl/ v. [~ + obj] to cut short; reduce: The trip was curtailed because of bad weather. —**cur'tail•ment,** n. [noncount]

cur•tain /ˈkɜrtn/ n. [count] **1.** a hanging piece of fabric used to decorate a window or shut out the light. **2.** a piece of material that hangs in front of a stage and conceals it from the audience. **3.** anything that screens or conceals: a curtain of darkness.

curt•sy /ˈkɜrtsiy/ n., pl. **-sies,** v., **-sied, -sy•ing.** —n. [count] **1.** a respectful bow made by women and girls, consisting of bending the knees and lowering the body. —v. [no obj] **2.** to make a curtsy.

cur•va•ture /ˈkɜrvətʃər, -ˌtʃʊr/ n. [noncount] **1.** the act of curving or the state of being curved. **2.** a curved shape or condition, often abnormal: curvature of the spine.

curve /kɜrv/ n., v., **curved, curv•ing,** adj. —n. [count] **1.** a continuously bending line, without angles: a curve in the road. —v. [no obj] [~ + obj] **2.** to (cause to) bend in a curve. —**'curv•y,** adj. **-i•er, -i•est.**

cush•ion /ˈkʊʃən/ n. [count] **1.** a soft pad filled with feathers, air, etc., used to sit, lie, or lean on. —v. [~ + obj] **2.** to lessen or soften the effects of: to cushion a blow.

cush•y /ˈkʊʃiy/ adj., **-i•er, -i•est.** Informal. **1.** involving little effort and producing much profit: a cushy job. **2.** soft and comfortable. —**'cush•i•ness,** n. [noncount]

cusp /kʌsp/ n. [count] a point or pointed end, as on the crown of a tooth.

C

cus•tard /'kʌstərd/ n. [noncount] a dessert made with eggs, milk, and sugar, baked or boiled until thickened.

cus•to•di•an /kʌ'stowdiyən/ n. [count] **1.** a person who has custody. **2.** a person who guards or maintains a property; caretaker.

cus•to•dy /'kʌstədiy/ n. [noncount] **1. a.** guardianship; care. **b.** (in a divorce) the right of deciding where and how the children will live. **2.** the state of being imprisoned or guarded by the police: The suspect was taken into custody.

cus•tom /'kʌstəm/ n. **1.** [count] a habitual practice; the usual way of acting. **2.** [noncount] such ways of acting when thought of as a group; tradition. **3. customs,** [plural; used with a plural verb] fees imposed on imported or exported goods. —adj. **4.** making things for individual customers: a custom tailor.

cus•tom•ar•y /'kʌstə,mɛriy/ adj. according to or depending on custom: the customary weekly meeting; It is customary to send greeting cards around Christmas. —**cus•tom•ar•i•ly** /'kʌstə,mɛriliy; for emphasis, ,kʌstə'mɛərəliy/ adv.: She is customarily late for meetings.

cus•tom•er /'kʌstəmər/ n. [count] **1.** a person who purchases goods or services from another; buyer. **2.** Informal. a person one has dealings with: a tough customer.

cus•tom•ize /'kʌstə,mayz/ v. [~ + obj], -ized, -iz•ing. to modify or build (something) according to an individual's request.

'custom-'made, adj. made to individual order: custom-made shoes.

cut /kʌt/ v., cut, cut•ting, n. —v. **1.** [~ + obj] [no obj] to penetrate with or as if with a sharp-edged instrument: I cut my face while shaving. **2.** [~ + obj] to divide with a sharp-edged instrument: I cut the cake. **3.** [~ + obj] to trim by clipping: to cut hair. **4.** [~ + obj] to lower, reduce, or curtail: to cut prices. **5.** [no obj] to move or cross: to cut across an empty lot. **6.** [~ + obj] to grow (a tooth) through the gum. **7.** [~ + obj] to fail to attend: began to cut classes. **8. cut back,** to reduce or discontinue: to cut back steel production; We'll have to cut back on those expensive meals. **9. cut down on,** to lessen or decrease: to cut down on snacks. **10. cut in, a.** to thrust a vehicle or oneself suddenly between others. **b.** to interrupt: She would always cut in with some remark. **11. cut off, a.** to interrupt. **b.** to stop suddenly; discontinue. **12. cut out, a.** to omit, delete, or remove: Cut out a few paragraphs or Cut a few paragraphs out. **b.** to form by or as if by cutting: He cut circles out of colored paper. **13. cut up,** to cut into pieces or sections. —n. [count] **14.** the result of cutting: a deep cut in the wood. **15.** the act of cutting, as with a knife. **16.** the manner or fashion in which anything is cut: the cut of a dress. —**Idiom.** **17. a cut above,** somewhat superior to: Your work was a cut above the rest. **18. cut out for,** fitted for; capable of: He's just not cut out for the military. **19. cut short,** to end abruptly before completion.

'cut-and-'dried, adj. settled in advance; not needing much discussion.

cute /kyuwt/ adj., cut•er, cut•est. charmingly attractive, esp. in a dainty way. —**'cute•ness,** n. [noncount]

cute•sy /'kyuwtsiy/ adj., -si•er, -si•est. Informal. cute in a deliberate or forced way; coy.

cu•ti•cle /'kyuwtɪkəl/ n. [count] the hardened skin that surrounds the edges of a fingernail or toenail.

cut•ie /'kyuwtiy/ n. [count] Informal. a charmingly attractive person.

cut•ler•y /'kʌtləriy/ n. [noncount] cutting instruments when thought of as a group, esp. utensils used at the table for cutting and eating food.

cut•let /'kʌtlɪt/ n. [count] a slice of meat for broiling or frying.

'cut-'rate, adj. [before a noun] offering goods or services at reduced prices.

cut•throat /'kʌt,θrowt/ n. [count] **1.** a person who cuts throats; murderer. —adj. **2.** murderous. **3.** ruthless: cutthroat competition.

cut•ting /'kʌtɪŋ/ n. [count] **1.** a piece, such as a root or leaf, cut from a plant and used to start a new plant. —adj. **2.** sarcastic.

cyber-, a suffix meaning: computer (cyberspace); very modern (cyberfashion).

cy•ber•space /'saybər,speys/ n. [noncount] the worldwide system of computer networks in which electronic communication takes place.

cy•cle /'saykəl/ n., v., -cled, -cling. —n. [count] **1.** any complete round or repeating series of events: the cycle of the seasons. **2.** a bicycle, motorcycle, or the like. —v. [no obj] **3.** to ride or travel by cycle.

cy•clic /'sayklɪk, 'sɪklɪk/ also **'cy•clic•al,** adj. happening or occurring in cycles.

cy•clist /'sayklɪst/ n. [count] a person who rides or travels by bicycle, motorcycle, or the like.

cy•clone /'sayklown/ n. [count] a violent storm with circular wind motion.

cyl•in•der /'sɪlɪndər/ n. [count] **1.** a surface shape or solid having long straight sides and two flat round ends. **2.** any object or part shaped like a cylinder, as the part of a revolver holding the bullets.

cylinder (def. 1)

cy•lin•dri•cal /sə'lɪndrɪkəl/ adj. having the shape or form of a cylinder.

cym•bal /'sɪmbəl/ n. [count] a plate of brass or bronze that produces a sharp, ringing sound when struck.

cyn•ic /'sɪnɪk/ n. [count] **1.** a person who believes that only selfishness is the cause of all human actions. **2.** a person who shows a bitterly negative attitude, as by making hateful remarks about others. —**'cyn•i•cal,** adj. —**cyn•i•cism** /'sɪnɪ,sɪzəm/, n. [noncount]

cy•press /'sayprəs/ n. [count] an evergreen, cone-bearing tree.

cyst /sɪst/ n. [count] an abnormal saclike growth of the body.

czar /zɑr, tsɑr/ n. [count] **1.** an emperor or king. **2.** [often: Czar] the former emperor of Russia. **3.** any person exercising great authority or power: a czar of industry.

cza•ri•na /zɑ'riynə, tsɑ-/ n. [count], pl. -nas. the wife of a czar; a Russian empress.

Czech /tʃɛk/ adj. **1.** of or relating to the Czech Republic or to the language spoken there. —n. **2.** [count] a person born or living in the Czech Republic. **3.** [noncount] the language spoken by many of the people in the Czech Republic.

D

D, d /diy/ *n.* [*count*], *pl.* **Ds** or **D's, ds** or **d's. 1.** the fourth letter of the English alphabet, a consonant. **2.** [*sometimes:* d] (in some grading systems) a grade or mark indicating poor or barely acceptable quality.

'd, 1. contraction of *had: They'd already left.* **2.** contraction of *would: I'd like to see it.* **3.** contraction of *did: Where'd you go?* **4.** contraction of *-ed: She OK'd the plan.*

D, *Symbol.* [*sometimes:* d] the Roman numeral for 500.

d., an abbreviation of: **1.** date. **2.** daughter. **3.** day. **4.** deceased. **5.** diameter. **6.** died.

DA or **D.A.,** an abbreviation of: District Attorney.

dab /dæb/ *v.*, **dabbed, dab•bing,** *n.* —*v.* [~ + *obj*] **1.** to pat or tap gently: *I dabbed my eyes with a handkerchief. She dabbed at the stain on her dress.* **2.** to apply (a substance) by light strokes: *He dabbed some paint on the wall.* —*n.* [*count*] **3.** a light pat: *She applied her makeup with a few quick dabs.* **4.** a small quantity: *a dab of rouge.*

dab•ble /'dæbəl/ *v.*, **-bled, -bling. 1.** to play and splash in water: [*no obj*]: *The child was dabbling in the water.* [~ + *obj*]: *She was dabbling her toes in the bath water.* **2.** [*no obj*] to work without serious effort: *to dabble in literature.*

dachs•hund /'dɑks,hʊnt, -,hʊnd/ *n.* [*count*] a dog having very short legs and a long body and ears.

Da•cron /'deykrɒn, 'dækrɒn/ *Trademark.* a brand of polyester fiber.

dad /dæd/ *n.* [*count*] *Informal.* father.

dad•dy /'dædiy/ *n.* [*count*], *pl.* **-dies.** *Informal.* father.

'daddy-'longlegs or **'daddy 'longlegs** /'lɒŋ,legz, 'lɒŋ-/ *n.* [*count*], *pl.* **-long•legs.** a spiderlike insect having a rounded body and long legs.

daf•fo•dil /'dæfədɪl/ *n.* [*count*] a plant having a yellow flower with a trumpetlike top.

daffodil

dag•ger /'dægər/ *n.* [*count*] **1.** a short, swordlike weapon with a pointed blade. —*Idiom.* **2. look daggers at,** to look at (someone) with anger: *She looked daggers at me when I said it was fine for our guests to stay late.*

dahl•ia /'dælyə, 'dɑl-/ *n.* [*count*] a garden plant having showy flowers.

dai•ly /'deyliy/ *adj., adv., n., pl.* **-lies.** —*adj.* [*before a noun*] **1.** of, done, occurring, or coming out each day: *daily attendance.* —*adv.* **2.** every day: *The plane arrived daily from Paris.* —*n.* [*count*] **3.** a newspaper appearing every day.

dain•ty /'deyntiy/ *adj.*, **-ti•er, -ti•est. 1.** of delicate beauty: *a dainty lace handkerchief.* **2.** fussy; choosy: *a dainty eater.* —**'dain•ti•ly** /'deyntḷiy/, *adv.* —**'dain•ti•ness,** *n.* [*noncount*]

dair•y /'dɛəriy/ *n., pl.* **dair•ies,** *adj.* —*n.* [*count*] **1.** a place where milk and cream are kept and butter and cheese are made. **2.** a company or a store that sells such products. —*adj.* [*before a noun*] **3.** of or relating to milk, cream, butter, cheese, etc.: *dairy products.*

dai•sy /'deyziy/ *n.* [*count*], *pl.* **-sies.** a white flower with a yellow center.

dale /deyl/ *n.* [*count*] a valley, esp. a broad valley.

dal•ly /'dæliy/ *v.* [*no obj*], **-lied, -ly•ing. 1.** to waste time; delay: *Come straight home and don't dally.* **2.** to flirt: *She dallied with every handsome man.* —**dal•li•ance** /'dæliyəns/, *n.* [*noncount*] [*count*]

Dal•ma•tian /dæl'meyʃən/ *n.* [*count*] a medium-sized shorthaired dog having a white coat marked with black or brown spots.

dam¹ /dæm/ *n., v.*, **dammed, dam•ming.** —*n.* [*count*] **1.** a wall to control the flow of water, built across a stream or river. —*v.* [~ + *obj*] **2.** to confine with or as if with a dam: *to dam (up) a river; He had dammed up his feelings.*

dam² /dæm/ *n.* [*count*] a female parent of a domestic animal, such as a horse, goat, or sheep.

dam•age /'dæmɪdʒ/ *n., v.*, **-aged, -ag•ing.** —*n.* **1.** [*noncount*] harmful effect: *The earthquake caused great damage to the city.* **2. damages,** [*plural*] the money claimed for a loss or injury: *to pay $10,000 in damages.* —*v.* [~ + *obj*] **3.** to cause harm, injury, or destruction to: *The fire damaged our house.*

dame /deym/ *n.* [*count*] **1.** [*Dame*] (in Britain) the official title of a woman who holds a rank equivalent to that of a knight. **2.** *Slang* (*sometimes offensive*). a woman; female.

damn /dæm/ *v.* [~ + *obj*] **1.** to condemn as a failure: *The critics damned the new play.* **2.** to condemn to hell: *He was damned by his gambling debts.* —*interj.* **4.** (used to express anger, annoyance, disgust, etc.): *"Damn!" he swore as he stumbled into the coffee table.* —*n.* [*count; singular*] **5.** even a very small amount: *His promise is not worth a damn. I don't give a damn when you come home.*

dam•na•ble /'dæmnəbəl/ *adj.* **1.** deserving to be damned. **2.** very bad; hateful: *a damnable lie.* —**'dam•na•bly,** *adv.*

dam•na•tion /dæm'neyʃən/ *n.* [*noncount*] the act of damning or the state of being damned.

damned /dæmd/ *adj., superlative* **damned•est, damnd•est** /'dæmdɪst/, *adv.* —*adj.* **1.** condemned or doomed, esp. to eternal punishment: *damned souls.* **2.** [*before a noun*] awful: *Get that damned dog out of here!* —*adv.* **3.** extremely; very; absolutely: *a damned good singer; too damned lazy.*

damp /dæmp/ *adj.*, **-er, -est,** *n., v.* —*adj.* **1.** slightly wet; moist: *The towels were still damp.* —*n.* [*noncount*] **2.** moisture: *the damp of the morning.* —*v.* [~ + *obj*] **3.** to moisten. **4.** to extinguish: *to damp (down) a furnace.* —**'damp•ly,** *adv.* —**'damp•ness,** *n.* [*noncount*]

damp•en /'dæmpən/ *v.* **1.** to (cause to) become damp: [*no obj*]: *The clothes dampened in the humidity.* [~ + *obj*]: *He dampened the cloth.* **2.** to (cause to) become sad: [*no obj*]: *His spirits dampened at the thought.* [~ + *obj*]: *to dampen one's spirits.*

dance /dæns/ *v.*, **danced**, **danc•ing**, *n.* —*v.* **1.** to move following a rhythm and in a pattern of steps, esp. to the accompaniment of music: [*no obj*]: *She danced in the best Broadway shows.* [~ + *obj*]: *She danced every dance with him.* **2.** [*no obj*] to leap, skip, etc., as from excitement: *We danced for joy.* —*n.* **3.** [*count*] a series of steps or bodily motions following a rhythm and usually done to music. **4.** [*noncount*] the art of dancing: *to study dance.* **5.** [*count*] a party for dancing: *I met her at a high-school dance.* —**'danc•er,** *n.* [*count*]

dan•de•li•on /'dændḷ,ayən/ *n.* [*count*] a weedy plant having golden-yellow flowers and clusters of white, hairy seeds.

dan•druff /'dændrəf/ *n.* [*noncount*] small scales that form on and are shed from the scalp.

dan•dy /'dændiy/ *n.*, *pl.* **-dies**, *adj.*, **-di•er, -di• est.** —*n.* [*count*] **1.** a man overly concerned about his appearance. —*adj.* **2.** fine; excellent; first-rate; very good: *a dandy idea.*

Dane /deyn/ *n.* [*count*] a person born or living in Denmark.

dan•ger /'deyndʒər/ *n.* **1.** [*noncount*] the chance of harm or injury; risk: *a life full of danger.* **2.** [*count*] something that might cause harm, injury, or risk: *One of the dangers is risk of lightning.*

dan•ger•ous /'deyndʒərəs/ *adj.* **1.** full of danger: *The spy led a dangerous life.* **2.** able or likely to cause harm: *Smoking is dangerous.* —**'dan• ger•ous•ly,** *adv.*

dan•gle /'dæŋgəl/ *v.*, **-gled, -gling.** to (cause to) hang or swing loosely: [*no obj*]: *The rope dangled out the window.* [~ + *obj*]: *She dangled the rope out the window.*

Dan•ish /'deynɪʃ/ *adj.* **1.** of or relating to Denmark, the people living there, or the language spoken there. —*n.* **2.** [*noncount*] the language spoken in Denmark. **3.** [*sometimes: danish*] a type of flaky, rich pastry, often filled with cheese or fruit: [*noncount*]: *That store sells great Danish.* [*count*]: *A cheese danish and a coffee to go, please.*

dank /dæŋk/ *adj.*, **-er, -est.** damp and, often, chilly: *a dank cellar.* —**'dank•ness,** *n.* [*non-count*]

dap•pled /'dæpəld/ *adj.* marked with spots of a different color from the background; having patches of shade and light: *the dappled sea.*

dare /dɛər/ *v.*, **dared, dar•ing,** *pres. sing. 3rd pers.* **dares** or **dare,** *n.* —*v.* [~ + *obj*] **1.** to challenge (a person) to do something: *I dare you to climb that mountain.* **2.** to risk: *He will dare any test to prove his strength.* —*auxiliary or modal v.* **3.** As a verb that is like an AUXILIARY verb and like a MODAL verb, *dare* has the meaning "to have the courage or boldness to (do something):" *How dare you speak to me like that? The girl dares not take another step. Dare he mention the subject again? Dare I say it?* —*n.* [*count*] **4.** a challenge: *I took that stupid dare.*

dare•dev•il /'dɛər,dɛvəl/ *n.* [*count*] **1.** a reckless and daring person. —*adj.* [*before a noun*] **2.** recklessly daring: *daredevil feats.* —**'dare,dev•il• ry, dare•dev•il•try** /'dɛər,dɛvəltriy/, *n.* [*non-count*]

dar•ing /'dɛərɪŋ/ *n.* [*noncount*] **1.** adventurous courage; boldness; bravery: *a pilot of great daring.* —*adj.* **2.** bold or courageous; fearless: *a daring new economic plan.* —**'dar•ing•ly,** *adv.*

dark /dɑrk/ *adj.*, **-er, -est,** *n.* —*adj.* **1.** having very little or no light: *a dark room.* **2.** close to black in color: *a dark brown.* **3.** not pale: *She's dark but her children are blond.* **4.** gloomy; cheerless: *the dark days of the war.* —*n.* [*noncount*] **5.** the absence of light; darkness: *the dark and gloom of the forest.* **6.** night; nightfall: *to come home before dark.* —*Idiom.* **7. in the dark,** in ignorance; uninformed: *We were completely in the dark about his intentions.* —**'dark• en,** *v.* [~ + *obj*] [*no obj*] —**'dark•ly,** *adv.* —**'dark•ness,** *n.* [*noncount*]: *The electrical blackout threw the entire city into darkness.*

dark•room /'dɑrk,ruwm, -,rʊm/ *n.* [*count*] a totally darkened room in which film, photographic paper, etc., is handled or developed.

dar•ling /'dɑrlɪŋ/ *n.* [*count*] **1.** a person who is very dear to another: *My daughter is a little darling.* **2.** an affectionate term of address: *Darling, I'll always love you.* —*adj.* **3.** [*before a noun*] very dear; dearly loved: *my darling child.* **4.** charming; cute; lovable: *What a darling baby!*

darn¹ /dɑrn/ *v.* [~ + *obj*] **1.** to sew and mend with rows of stitches. —*n.* [*count*] **2.** a place or area that has been darned.

darn² /dɑrn/ *adj.* **1.** Also, **darned.** damned [*before a noun*]: *It's a darn shame.* —*adv.* **2.** damned: *You're darn right I'm angry.* —*v.* [~ + *obj*] **3.** to curse; damn: *Darn that pesky fly!*

dart /dɑrt/ *n.* [*count*] **1.** a small, slender object pointed at one end and usually feathered at the other: *A poisoned dart hit him in the neck.* **2.** a sudden, swift movement: *The squirrel made a quick dart across the street.* —*v.* **3.** [*no obj*] to move swiftly; dash: *The mice darted around the room.* **4.** [~ + *obj*] to move suddenly or rapidly: *She darted a quick glance at me.*

dash /dæʃ/ *v.* **1.** to (cause to) strike or smash violently, esp. so as to break to pieces: [~ + *obj*]: *The waves dashed the boat to pieces.* [*no obj*]: *The waves dashed against the shore.* **2.** [~ + *obj*] to ruin, destroy, or frustrate: *The rain dashed our hopes for a picnic.* **3.** [*no obj*] to move with great speed; rush: *to dash around the corner.* **4. dash off, a.** to hurry away; leave: *She dashed off before I could talk to her.* **b.** to write, make, do, etc., too quickly or hastily: *to dash off a letter; to dash it off in a hurry.* —*n.* [*count*] **5.** a small quantity of something: *a dash of salt.* **6.** a quick movement: *to make a mad dash for the door.* **7.** a short race: *the 100-yard dash.* **8.** a punctuation mark (—), used to note a break or pause.

dash•board /'dæʃ,bɔrd/ *n.* [*count*] the instrument panel of a car or truck.

dash•ing /'dæʃɪŋ/ *adj.* energetic and spirited; lively: *a dashing hero.* —**'dash•ing•ly,** *adv.*

da•ta /'deytə, 'dætə/ *n.* **1.** [*plural; used with a plural verb*] individual facts, statistics, or items of information: *Do your data support your conclusions?* **2.** [*noncount; used with a singular verb*] a body or collection of facts; information: *The data is not reliable.*

'data ,bank or **'data,bank,** *n.* DATABASE.

'data,base or **'data ,base,** *n.* [*count*] a collection of organized, related data, esp. one in electronic form that can be gathered and examined by a computer: *He made a database of the students in his class.*

'data ,processing, *n.* [*noncount*] the automated processing of information, esp. by computers. —**'data ,processor,** *n.* [*count*]: *worked as a data processor.*

date¹ /deyt/ *n.*, *v.*, **dat•ed, dat•ing.** —*n.* [*count*]

1. the month, day, or year of an event: *an important date in American history.* **2.** the time shown on a letter, document, coin, etc.: *a letter bearing the date January 16.* **3.** an appointment for a particular time, esp. a social meeting: *I took her out on a date. We made a date for next week.* **4.** a person with whom one has such an appointment: *Can I bring a date to the party?* —*v.* **5.** [*no obj*] to belong to a particular period: *The architecture dates as far back as 1830. The letter dates from 1873.* **6.** to go out socially on dates (with): [*no obj*]: *She's not old enough to be dating.* [~ + *obj*]: *He's dating his best friend's sister.* **7.** [~ + *obj*] to mark or furnish with a date: *The word processor dates your document automatically.* —*Idiom.* **8. to date,** up to the present time; until now: *We've seen nothing to date that would change our minds.* **9. up to date,** in accord with the latest styles, information, or technology: *fashion that is always up to date; Our new computers are up to date; the up-to-date office communication systems.* —'**dat•a•ble, 'date•a•ble,** *adj.* —'**dat•er,** *n.* [*count*]

date² /deyt/ *n.* [*count*] the oblong, brown, sweet, fleshy fruit of a palm tree growing in hot climates.

dat•ed /'deytɪd/ *adj.* **1.** having or showing a date: *a dated engraving by Rembrandt.* **2.** old-fashioned: *Some slang terms become dated quickly.*

'**date ,rape,** *n.* [*noncount*] sexual intercourse forced upon the person with whom one has a date.

daugh•ter /'dɔtər/ *n.* [*count*] the female child of a parent.

'**daughter-in-,law,** *n.* [*count*], *pl.* **daugh•ters-in-law.** the wife of one's son: *Do all their daughters-in-law live nearby?*

daunt /dɔnt, dɑnt/ *v.* [~ + *obj*] to discourage: *Don't be daunted by the remaining work.* —'**daunt•ing•ly,** *adv.*

daunt•less /'dɔntlɪs, 'dɑnt-/ *adj.* fearless; brave; bold: *a dauntless hero.* —'**daunt•less•ly,** *adv.* —'**daunt•less•ness,** *n.* [*noncount*]

dawn /dɔn/ *n.* **1.** [*count*] [*noncount*] daybreak; sunrise. **2.** [*count; usually singular*] the beginning of anything; advent: *the dawn of civilization.* —*v.* [*no obj*] **3.** to begin to grow light in the morning: *The day dawned without a cloud.* **4.** to begin to open or develop: *A new era of peace is dawning.* **5.** to begin to be known, seen, or understood: *The idea suddenly dawned upon her. It suddenly dawned on me that I was late.*

day /dey/ *n.* [*count*] **1.** the time between sunrise and sunset. **2.** a division of time equal to 24 hours, from one midnight to the next: *seven days in one week.* **3.** the portion of a day in which one works: *She put in an eight-hour day at the office.* **4.** Usually, **days.** period of life: *His days are numbered.* —*Idiom.* **5.** call it a day, to stop working for the rest of the day: *Let's call it a day; we've worked eighteen hours.* **6. make someone's day,** to make someone very happy: *Seeing my kids smile just makes my day.*

day•break /'dey,breyk/ *n.* [*noncount*] the first appearance of daylight in the morning; dawn.

'**day ,care,** *n.* [*noncount*] daytime care for children who are too young to go to school. —'**day-,care,** *adj.* [*before a noun*]: *a day-care center.*

day•dream /'dey,driym/ *n.* [*count*] **1.** a pleasant series of thoughts imagined while awake: *a daydream about life in the country.* —*v.* [*no obj*] **2.** to have daydreams. —'**day,dream•er,** *n.* [*count*]

day•light /'dey,layt/ *n.* [*noncount*] **1.** the period of light during a day: *In December in Sweden there is hardly any daylight.* **2.** dawn: *Attack at daylight.* —*adj.* [*before a noun*] **3.** taking place in daylight: *a daring, daylight robbery at the bank.*

'**daylight-'saving** (or '**daylight 'saving**) **,time,** *n.* [*noncount*] time in which clocks are set one hour ahead of standard time.

day•time /'dey,taym/ *n.* [*noncount*] **1.** the time between sunrise and sunset: *The sky grew dark even in the daytime.* —*adj.* [*before a noun*] **2.** of, occurring, or done during the day: *daytime classes.*

daze /deyz/ *v.,* **dazed, daz•ing,** *n.* —*v.* [~ + *obj*] **1.** to cause (someone) to be unable to think clearly. —*n.* [*count; singular*] **2.** a dazed condition: *He's still in a daze after the accident.*

daz•zle /'dæzəl/ *v.,* **-zled, -zling,** *n.* —*v.* [~ + *obj*] **1.** to blind temporarily with light: *The headlights dazzled the deer.* **2.** to astonish with delight: *The singer dazzled his audience.* —*n.* [*noncount*] **3.** brightness of light that prevents one from seeing properly: *the dazzle of the blue sea on a sunny day at the beach.* **4.** impressive or exciting quality: *She was lured to the city by the dazzle of an acting career.* —'**daz•zler,** *n.* [*count*] —'**daz•zling,** *adj.:* *a dazzling smile.*

dB or **db,** an abbreviation of: decibel.

DC or **D.C.,** an abbreviation of: District of Columbia.

D-day or **D-Day** /'diy,dey/ *n.* [*noncount*] a day set for beginning something, esp. June 6, 1944, the day of the invasion of W Europe by Allied forces in World War II.

DDT, *n.* [*noncount*] a poisonous chemical that was formerly widely used as an insecticide.

de-, a prefix meaning: away or off (*deplane*); down or lower (*degrade*); reverse (*deactivate*); remove (*decaffeinate*).

DE, an abbreviation of: Delaware.

dea•con /'diykən/ *n.* [*count*] a member of the Christian clergy below the rank of a priest, or a non-clerical officer having various duties.

de•ac•ti•vate /diy'æktə,veyt/ *v.* [~ + *obj*], **-vat•ed, -vat•ing.** to make inactive: *to deactivate a chemical.*

dead /dɛd/ *adj.,* **-er, -est,** *n., adv.* —*adj.* **1.** no longer living: *The victim was dead on arrival at the hospital.* **2.** having no sensation or feeling; numb: *My arm felt dead after I fell asleep on it.* **3.** not working: *a dead battery.* **4.** stale: *dead air.* **5.** dull or inactive: *a dead business day.* **6.** complete: *dead silence.* **7.** *Sports.* out of play: *a dead ball.* —*n.* **8.** [*noncount*] the period of greatest darkness, coldness, etc.: *the dead of night.* **9. the dead,** [*plural; used with a plural verb*] dead people; those who have died: *the souls of the dead.* —*adv.* **10.** absolutely; completely; very much: *dead tired.*

dead•en /'dɛdn̩/ *v.* [~ + *obj*] **1.** to make less sensitive, strong, or effective: *pills to deaden pain.* **2.** to make dull or lifeless: *The criticism deadened my enthusiasm.* —'**dead•en•ing,** *adj.*

'**dead 'end,** *n.* [*count*] **1.** an end of a street, corridor, etc., that has no exit: *Our apartment building stands on a dead end.* **2.** a position with no hope of progress: *That job was a dead end.* —'**dead-'end,** *adj.* [*before a noun*]

'**dead 'heat,** *n.* [*count*] a race in which two or more competitors finish in a tie.

dead•line /'dɛd,layn/ *n.* [*count*] the time by which something must be finished.

dead•lock /'dɛd,lɒk/ *n.* [*count*] **1.** a state in

which no agreement can be reached; stalemate: *Negotiations soon reached a deadlock.* **2.** (in sports) a tied score: *a 5-5 deadlock after six innings.* —*v.* **3.** to (cause to) come to a deadlock: [*no obj*]: *Negotiations deadlocked after two hours.* [~ + *obj*]: *A few stubborn people deadlocked the negotiations.*

dead•ly /'dɛdliy/ *adj.,* **-li•er, -li•est,** *adv.* —*adj.* **1.** causing or tending to cause death; lethal: *a deadly disease.* **2.** very great: *a deadly silence.* —*adv.* **3.** like death: *deadly pale.* **4.** completely: *deadly dull.* —'**dead•li•ness,** *n.* [*noncount*]

dead•wood /'dɛd,wʊd/ *n.* [*noncount*] **1.** dead branches or trees. **2.** useless or unprofitable persons or things: *The company wanted to get rid of its deadwood.*

deaf /dɛf/ *adj.,* **-er, -est. 1.** partly or completely without the sense of hearing: *She has been deaf from birth.* —*v.* **2.** refusing to listen or to pay attention to: *He was deaf to all the advice I gave him.* —'**deaf•ness,** *n.* [*noncount*]

deaf•en /'dɛfən/ *v.* [~ + *obj*] to make deaf. —'**deaf•en•ing,** *adj.*

deal /diyl/ *v.,* **dealt** /dɛlt/ **deal•ing,** *n.* —*v.* **1.** [*no obj*] [~ + *obj*] to give out or distribute something among a number of people. **2.** *Slang.* to buy and sell (drugs) illegally: [*no obj*]: *He was dealing when we arrested him.* [~ + *obj*]: *He was dealing all sorts of drugs.* **3. deal in,** to trade or do business: *to deal in used cars.* **4. deal with, a.** to be about; to be concerned with: *Botany deals with the study of plants.* **b.** to take necessary action with respect to a thing or person; to handle or see to: *Law courts deal with criminals.* —*n.* [*count*] **5.** a business agreement: *The company will make a deal with a Japanese firm.* **6.** an agreement in which both sides benefit: *the best deal in town.* **7.** an indefinite but large amount: *He earns a great deal of money.*

deal•er /'diylər/ *n.* [*count*] **1.** a person in a stated type of business: *a used-car dealer.* **2.** the person who gives out cards to players in a card game.

deal•ing /'diyliŋ/ *n.* **1.** Usually, **dealings.** [*plural*] interaction; business activity: *commercial dealings.* **2.** [*noncount*] conduct in relation to others: *a reputation for honest dealing.*

dean /diyn/ *n.* [*count*] **1.** an official in a college or one in charge of students, etc. **2.** an official in charge of a church or a diocese.

dear /dɪər/ *adj.,* **-er, -est,** *n., interj.* —*adj.* **1.** (used at the beginning of a letter as an expression of respect, friendship, etc.): *Dear Sir or Madam; My dear friends.* **2.** much loved: *The burglars had taken our dearest possessions.* —*n.* [*count*] **3.** a kind or generous person: *You're a dear to look after the children.* **4.** an affectionate term of address. —*interj.* **5.** (used as an exclamation of surprise, distress, etc.): *Oh dear, I've lost the phone number.*

dear•ly /'dɪərliy/ *adv.* **1.** greatly; deeply; with much feeling or emotion: *He loves his daughter dearly.* **2.** at a high or terrible cost; with much suffering: *He paid dearly for that victory.*

death /dɛθ/ *n.* **1.** [*count*] the act of dying; the end of life. **2.** [*noncount*] the state of being dead: *hands as cold as death.* **3.** [*count; usually singular*] end; destruction; extinction: *Democracy for that country meant the death of civilization as they knew it.* —*Idiom.* **4. at death's door,** in serious danger of dying; gravely ill: *at death's door from a heart attack.* **5. put to death,** to kill; execute: *They put him to death immediately. That*

government put to death over 1,000 dissidents. **6. to death,** to a degree that cannot be endured any longer: *sick to death of your complaining.* —'**death,like,** *adj.*

death•bed /'dɛθ,bɛd/ *n.* [*count*] **1.** the bed on which a person dies; the last hours before death: *confessed the crime on his deathbed.* —*adj.* [*before a noun*] **2.** of, relating to, or occurring at such a time: *a deathbed confession.*

death•blow /'dɛθ,blow/ *n.* [*count*] anything that causes death or destroys hopes or plans: *Those losses were the deathblow to his attempts to modernize the factory.*

death•ly /'dɛθliy/ *adj., adv.* like death: *a deathly paleness.*

'**death 'row,** *n.* [*noncount*] prison cells for prisoners awaiting execution.

death•trap /'dɛθ,træp/ *n.* [*count*] a building, place, or situation where there is risk of death.

de•base /dɪ'beys/ *v.* [~ + *obj*], **-based, -bas•ing. 1.** to lower in quality or value: *Inflation has debased the country's currency.* **2.** [~ + *oneself*] to disgrace (oneself): *You will debase yourself by accepting a bribe.* —**de'base•ment,** *n.* [*noncount*]

de•bate /dɪ'beyt/ *n., v.,* **-bat•ed, -bat•ing.** —*n.* **1.** [*count*] a discussion involving opposite viewpoints. **2.** [*count*] a formal contest in which two different points of view are argued by opposing speakers. **3.** [*noncount*] consideration: *After some debate they made their decision.* —*v.* **4.** [~ + *obj*] to think about; consider: *We debated (about) whether we should go or stay here.* **5.** [~ + *obj*] to argue or discuss (a question), as in a group: *We debated (about) the issue most of the night.* **6.** to have a formal debate (with): [*no obj*]: *When we left, the teams were still debating.* [~ + *obj*]: *I had to debate the best speaker in the district.* —**de'bat•a•ble,** *adj.* —**de'bat•er,** *n.* [*count*] —**de'bat•ing,** *n.* [*noncount*]

de•bil•i•tate /dɪ'bɪlɪ,teyt/ *v.* [~ + *obj*], **-tat•ed, -tat•ing.** to make (someone) weak. —**de'bil•i•tat•ing,** *adj.* —**de'bil•i•ty,** *n.* [*noncount*] [*count*]

deb•it /'dɛbɪt/ *n.* [*count*] **1.** a record of money owed or spent. **2.** a recorded item of debt. —*v.* [~ + *obj*] **3.** to charge with or as a debt: *They debited my account for the amount I owed.*

de•brief /diy'briyf/ *v.* [~ + *obj*] to ask (someone) questions in order to obtain useful information: *The pilots were debriefed after the last bombing run.*

de•bris or **dé•bris** /də'briy, 'deybriy/ *n.* [*noncount*] the remains of something destroyed; ruins: *They searched in the debris of the bombed building for survivors.*

debt /dɛt/ *n.* [*count*] **1.** something that is owed: *We owe him a great debt of gratitude for his help.* **2.** [*noncount*] an obligation to pay something: *He was in debt to the amount of $200,000.* —'**debt•or,** *n.* [*count*]

de•but or **dé•but** /dey'byuw, 'deybyuw/ *n.* [*count*] a first public appearance or presentation, as of a performer: *The hit TV show made its debut back in 1990.*

Dec or **Dec.,** an abbreviation of: December.

dec•ade /'dɛkeyd/ *n.* [*count*] a period of ten years: *the decade of the 1990's.*

dec•a•dence /'dɛkədəns/ *n.* [*noncount*] the act or process of falling into decay: *A long period of decadence came at the end of the empire.* —'**dec•a•dent,** *adj.*

de•caf•fein•ate /diy'kæfə,neyt/ *v.* [~ + *obj*],

-at•ed, -at•ing. to remove caffeine from: *They use plain water to decaffeinate the coffee beans.* —**de'caf•fein,at•ed,** *adj.*: *a cup of decaffeinated coffee.*

de•camp /dɪˈkæmp/ *v.* [*no obj*] to depart hastily and often secretly: *The treasurer decamped with all the money.* —**de'camp•ment,** *n.* [*noncount*]

de•cant /dɪˈkænt/ *v.* [~ + *obj*] to pour (a liquid) from one container to another.

de•cant•er /dɪˈkæntər/ *n.* [*count*] a decorative container for wine or the like.

de•cap•i•tate /dɪˈkæpɪˌteyt/ *v.* [~ + *obj*], **-tat•ed, -tat•ing.** to cut off the head of. —**de•cap•i•ta•tion** /dɪˌkæpɪˈteyʃən/, *n.* [*noncount*] *death by decapitation.*

de•cay /dɪˈkey/ *v.* **1.** to (cause to) rot: [*no obj*]: *The tree began to decay soon after it was cut down.* [~ + *obj*]: *Candy can decay your teeth.* **2.** [*no obj*] to decline in health or prosperity: *The transit system is rapidly decaying.* —*n.* [*noncount*] **3.** rot: *The house is in a state of decay.* **4.** a slow decline: *the decay of standards.* —**de'cayed,** *adj.*: *decayed timber.* —**de'cay•ing,** *adj.*: *the smell of decaying vegetation.*

de•cease /dɪˈsiys/ *n.* [*count; usually singular*] the act of dying; death: *at his decease.*

de•ceased /dɪˈsiyst/ *adj.* dead: *All the members of his family were deceased.*

de•ceit /dɪˈsiyt/ *n.* [*noncount*] being dishonest; cheating: *too much deceit practiced against consumers.* —**de'ceit•ful,** *adj.*

de•ceive /dɪˈsiyv/ *v.* [~ + *obj*], **-ceived, -ceiv•ing.** to mislead by a false appearance or statement: *I never thought she would deceive me. They deceived her into thinking she would be promoted.* —**de'ceiv•er,** *n.* [*count*] —**de'ceiv•ing•ly,** *adv.*

de•cel•er•ate /diyˈsɛləˌreyt/ *v.*, **-at•ed, -at•ing.** to (cause to) slow down or decrease the speed of: [*no obj*]: *The car decelerated to a stop.* [~ + *obj*]: *He decelerated the truck.*

De•cem•ber /dɪˈsɛmbər/ *n.* the 12th month of the year, containing 31 days.

de•cent /ˈdiysənt/ *adj.* **1.** acting or being in agreement with recognized and accepted standards. **2.** morally upright: *Although they may be hungry, decent people won't steal.* **3.** acceptable: *a decent room and dinner for a low price.* **4.** kind; courteous: *It was very decent of him to defend me.* —**'de•cen•cy,** *n.* [*noncount*] —**'de•cent•ly,** *adv.*: *He always acted decently toward me.*

de•cep•tion /dɪˈsɛpʃən/ *n.* **1.** [*noncount*] the act of deceiving or the state of being deceived: *We pointed out the deception in the salesperson's claims.* **2.** [*count*] something that deceives or is intended to deceive; a trick: *another obvious deception.*

de•cep•tive /dɪˈsɛptɪv/ *adj.* relating to or marked by deceit: *deceptive advertising.* —**de'cep•tive•ly,** *adv.*

deci-, a prefix meaning one-tenth: (*decimeter*).

dec•i•bel /ˈdɛsəˌbɛl, -bəl/ *n.* [*count*] a unit that is used to express differences in power, esp. in measuring the loudness of sound. *Abbr.*: dB

de•cide /dɪˈsayd/ *v.* [~ + *obj*], **-cid•ed, -cid•ing. 1.** to choose; make up one's mind: *He decided to learn how to type faster. She decided that she would stay.* **2.** to conclude (a dispute) by awarding victory to one side; settle: *to decide an argument;The judge decided in favor of the plaintiff.* **3.** to bring (a person) to a decision; persuade or convince: *What decided you to take the job?*

de•cid•ed /dɪˈsaydɪd/ *adj.* **1.** [*before a noun*]

clear and obvious: *a decided improvement.* **2.** determined: *She's dealing with her problems in a decided way.* —**de'cid•ed•ly,** *adv.*: *The economy has become decidedly worse.*

de•cid•u•ous /dɪˈsɪdʒuwəs/ *adj.* losing the leaves every year: *deciduous trees.*

dec•i•mal /ˈdɛsəməl, ˈdɛsməl/ *adj.* [*before a noun*] **1.** of or relating to tenths or to the number 10. **2.** proceeding by tens: *a decimal system.* —*n.* [*count*] **3.** a fraction expressed in tenths, hundredths, etc., such as 0.4 or 0.12.

dec•i•mate /ˈdɛsəˌmeyt/ *v.* [~ + *obj*], **-mat•ed, -mat•ing.** to destroy a great number or part of: *Disease decimated the population.* —**dec•i•ma•tion** /ˌdɛsəˈmeyʃən/, *n.* [*noncount*]

de•ci•pher /dɪˈsayfər/ *v.* [~ + *obj*] to make out the meaning of (something difficult to read): *I couldn't decipher his handwriting.* —**de'ci•pher•a•ble,** *adj.*

de•ci•sion /dɪˈsɪʒən/ *n.* **1.** [*count*] the act of deciding or something decided: *a difficult decision.* **2.** [*count*] a judgment, such as in a court: *The jury's decision was that he was guilty.* **3.** [*noncount*] the quality of being able to make a firm judgment: *He spoke with decision.*

de•ci•sive /dɪˈsaysɪv/ *adj.* **1.** resulting in a clear decision: *The decisive argument was the savings his plan would bring.* **2.** showing firmness: *a decisive manner.* **3.** indisputable; definite: *a decisive lead of 30-0 by halftime.* —**de'ci•sive•ly,** *adv.* —**de'ci•sive•ness,** *n.* [*noncount*]

deck /dɛk/ *n.* [*count*] **1.** a floorlike surface taking up one level of a hull of a vessel: *Our cabin was on the fifth deck down.* **2.** a surface suggesting the deck of a ship: *the upper deck of the sightseeing bus.* **3.** an open, unroofed porch extending from a house: *We relaxed outside on the wooden deck.* **4.** a pack of playing cards: *He shuffled the deck.* **5.** a cassette deck or tape deck. —*v.* [~ + *obj*] **6.** to decorate so as to look fancy or festive: *We decked (out) the room with streamers.* —*Idiom.* **7. clear the decks,** to prepare for work by removing all previous work: *Let's clear the decks and get started on this new project.*

dec•la•ra•tion /ˌdɛkləˈreyʃən/ *n.* [*count*] **1.** a firm statement: *The witness's declaration convicted the killer.* **2.** an official announcement or notification: *a declaration of war.*

de•clar•a•tive /dɪˈklærətɪv/ *adj.* serving to state or explain: *a declarative sentence.*

de•clare /dɪˈklɛər/ *v.* [~ + *obj*], **-clared, -clar•ing. 1.** to make known; state clearly; announce: *He declared his innocence. The police declared that the city was unsafe. The judges declared her the winner of the race.* **2.** to reveal; indicate: *Their appearance at the meeting declares their willingness to participate in the talks.* **3.** to make a statement of (goods being brought into a country, income for taxation, etc.): *You have to declare your earnings for the whole year.*

de•cline /dɪˈklayn/ *v.*, **-clined, -clin•ing,** *n.* —*v.* **1.** to deny consent (to do); refuse: [*no obj*]: *I asked her over, but she declined.* [~ + *obj*]: *He declined our invitation. He declined to say how he would vote.* **2.** [*no obj*] to slope downward: *The road declines sharply at this point.* **3.** [*no obj*] to fail in strength or health: *His health is declining.* **4.** [*no obj*] to become less; diminish: *to decline in popularity.* —*n.* [*count*] **5.** a downward movement, such as of prices or population: *a decline in the stock market.* **6.** a failing, such as in strength: *a sudden decline in his health.*

D

—**de•clin•ing,** *adj.* [*before a noun*]: *declining stock market prices.*

de•code /diy'kowd/ *v.* [~ + *obj*], **-cod•ed, -cod•ing.** to translate (data or a message) from a code or cipher into the original language or form.

de•com•pose /,diykəm'powz/ *v.* [*no obj*], **-posed, -pos•ing. 1.** to separate into the essential parts: *Salt decomposes into sodium and chlorine.* **2.** to rot; become decayed: *the smell of decomposing vegetation.* —**de•com•po•si•tion** /,diykɒmpə'zɪʃən/, *n.* [*noncount*]: *decomposition of leaves.*

de•con•ges•tant /,diykən'dʒɛstənt/ *adj.* [*before a noun*] **1.** relieving or clearing congestion of the nose and throat: *a decongestant cough syrup.* —*n.* [*count*] **2.** decongestant medicine.

de•con•tam•i•nate /,diykən'tæmə,neyt/ *v.* [~ + *obj*], **-nat•ed, -nat•ing.** to make (something) safe by removing dangerous substances: *to decontaminate the nuclear power plant where the leak took place.* —**de•con•tam•i•na•tion** /,diykən,tæmə'neyʃən/, *n.* [*noncount*]

dec•o•rate /'dɛkə,reyt/ *v.* [~ + *obj*], **-rat•ed, -rat•ing. 1.** to add something beautiful: *They decorate the streets with Christmas tree lights.* **2.** to honor (someone) with an award: *to decorate a soldier for bravery.* —'**dec•o,ra•tor,** *n.* [*count*]: *an interior decorator.*

dec•o•ra•tion /,dɛkə'reyʃən/ *n.* **1.** [*count*] something used for decorating. **2.** [*noncount*] the act of decorating: *The firm specialized in the decoration of private mansions.* **3.** [*count*] an award given and worn as a mark of honor: *Decorations covered the hero's chest.*

dec•o•ra•tive /'dɛkərətɪv/ *adj.* providing beauty; ornamenting: *some decorative woodwork and carvings.*

dec•o•rous /'dɛkərəs/ *adj.* proper and suitable; correct: *decorous behavior during the solemn occasion.* —'**dec•o•rous•ly,** *adv.*: *He behaved as decorously as he could.*

de•co•rum /dɪ'kɔrəm/ *n.* [*noncount*] dignified, proper conduct.

de•coy /*n.*'diykɔy; *v.* dɪ'kɔy, 'diykɔy/ *n.* [*count*] **1.** a person, thing, or action that lures another into danger or a trap: *The car the police were chasing was a decoy.* **2.** an artificial bird used to lure game into a trap or within gunshot: *a duck decoy.* —*v.* [~ + *obj*] **3.** to lure, trick, or trap by or as if by a decoy: *The fighter pilots were decoyed by the enemy into shooting at unarmed missiles.*

de•crease /*v.*dɪ'kriys; *n.* 'diykriys, dɪ'kriys/ *v.*, **-creased, -creas•ing,** *n.* —*v.* **1.** to (cause to) become less or smaller: [*no obj*]: *Water use had to decrease to avoid a drought.* [~ + *obj*]: *They told us to decrease spending.* —*n.* [*count*] **2.** the act or process of decreasing. **3.** the amount by which a thing becomes less: *a decrease of only 15%.* —**de'creas•ing,** *adj.* [*before a noun*]: *decreasing interest rates.* —**de'creas•ing•ly,** *adv.*

de•cree /dɪ'kriy/ *n.*, *v.*, **-creed, -cree•ing.** —*n.* [*count*] **1.** a formal order usually having the force of law: *a presidential decree.* —*v.* [~ + *obj*] **2.** to command, order, or decide by or as if by decree: *The king decreed an amnesty. The judge decreed that the parent could visit the children five times a year.*

de•crep•it /dɪ'krɛpɪt/ *adj.* weakened by old age or by long use. —**de•crep•i,tude,** *n.* [*noncount*]: *old buildings in various stages of decrepitude.*

de•cry /dɪ'kray/ *v.* [~ + *obj*], **-cried, -cry•ing.**

to condemn openly; denounce: *He decried the regime's ruthlessness.*

ded•i•cate /'dɛdɪ,keyt/ *v.*, **-cat•ed, -cat•ing.** [~ + *obj*] **1.** to devote or commit (something or someone) to some cause: *He dedicated himself to the clean-up of the river.* **2.** to offer (something) formally to a person or cause as a sign of respect: *I'd like to dedicate our first song to my mother.* **3.** to mark the official opening of (a public building or highway), by formal ceremonies: *The school dedicated the new building on Sunday.* —'**ded•i,cat•ed,** *adj.* —**ded•i•ca•tion** /,dɛdɪ'keyʃən/ *n.* [*count*] [*noncount*]

de•duce /dɪ'duws, -'dyuws/ *v.* [~ + *obj*], **-duced, -duc•ing.** to figure out (something) by reasoning: *to deduce the path of the hurricane; From her conversation I deduced that she had a large family.* —**de'duc•i•ble,** *adj.*

de•duct /dɪ'dʌkt/ *v.* [~ + *obj*] to take away from a total: *How much of this expense can you deduct from your taxes?* —**de'duct•i•ble,** *adj.*: *Is this income deductible?*

de•duc•tion /dɪ'dʌkʃən/ *n.* **1. a.** [*noncount*] the act or process of deducting. **b.** [*count*] something that is deducted: *a deduction of 10%.* **2. a.** [*noncount*] the act or process of deducing: *remarkable powers of deduction.* **b.** [*count*] something deduced from known facts: *It was the detective's deduction that the robbery was an inside job.* —**de•duc•tive** /dɪ'dʌktɪv/, *adj.*

deed /diyd/ *n.* [*count*] **1.** something that is done; an act: *a good deed.* **2.** an achievement; feat: *deeds of daring.* **3.** an official record of a sale, such as of a house: *Do you have the deed to the house in a safe place?* —*v.* [~ + *obj*] **4.** to transfer by deed: *He deeded the property to his sons.*

deep /diyp/ *adj.* and *adv.*, **-er, -est,** *n.* —*adj.* **1.** extending far down from the top or surface: *a deep well.* **2.** extending far in or back from the front: *a deep shelf.* **3.** coming from far down: *Now, take a deep breath.* **4.** difficult to understand: *a book too deep for young children.* **5.** serious: *deep thoughts.* **6.** sincere; great: *deep affections.* **7.** sound and heavy; undisturbed: *deep sleep.* **8.** strong, dark, and vivid in color: *a deep red.* **9.** low in pitch, such as sound: *a deep, rich voice.* **10.** [~ + *in*] giving one's full attention; absorbed: *He was deep in thought.* —*adv.* **11.** to or at a considerable or great depth: *We were about ten feet deep when our ears popped.* —*n.* [*noncount*] **12.** the midpoint or the part of greatest intensity: *the deep of winter; in the deep of the night.* —*Idiom.* **13. in deep,** involved: *He was in too deep with her and had to break off their relationship.* **14. in deep water,** in serious trouble: *The company is in deep water and can barely make ends meet.* —**deepen,** *v.* [~ + *obj*] [*no obj*] —'**deep•ly,** *adv.*: *She was deeply in love with him.* —'**deep•ness,** *n.* [*noncount*]

'**deep-'rooted,** *adj.* firmly implanted, fixed, or established: *a deep-rooted fear of strangers.*

'**deep-'sea,** *adj.* [*before a noun*] of or relating to the deeper parts of the sea: *deep-sea fishing.*

'**deep-'seated,** *adj.* firmly implanted, fixed, or established; unchanging: *a deep-seated loyalty.*

deer /dɪər/ *n.* [*count*], *pl.* **deer.** any of several cud-chewing animals, the males of which usually have antlers.

de•face /dɪ'feys/ *v.* [~ + *obj*], **-faced, -fac•ing.** to spoil the appearance of, such as by marking: *defacing all the posters.* —**de'face•ment,** *n.* [*noncount*]

de fac•to /diy'fæktow, dey/ *adj.*, *adv.* actually

existing, though not by law: *a situation of de facto segregation.*

de•fame /dɪˈfeym/ *v.* [~ + *obj*], **-famed, -fam•ing.** to attack the good name or reputation of: *The candidates seem to enjoy defaming each other.* —**deˈfam•a͵tor•y,** *adj.*

de•fault /dɪˈfɔlt/ *n.* [*noncount*] **1.** failure to act, esp. failure to pay one's debts: *to face financial default.* —*v.* [*no obj*] **2.** to fail to pay, perform a duty, etc.: *The bank had defaulted on that loan.* —**deˈfault•er,** *n.* [*count*]

de•feat /dɪˈfiyt/ *v.* [~ + *obj*], **1.** to overcome in a contest; beat: *He was defeated in the last election.* **2.** to cause to fail: *This kind of problem always defeats me.* —*n.* **3.** [*noncount*] the act of overcoming in a contest: *She didn't accept defeat well.* **4.** [*count*] an instance of defeat; setback: *He suffered several defeats in close elections.* —**deˈfeat•er,** *n.* [*count*]

de•fe•cate /ˈdɛfɪ͵keyt/ *v.* [*no obj*], **-cat•ed, -cat•ing.** to pass waste matter from the bowels. —**def•e•ca•tion** /͵dɛfɪˈkeyʃən/, *n.* [*noncount*]

de•fect /*n.* ˈdiyfɛkt, dɪˈfɛkt; *v.* dɪˈfɛkt/ *n.* [*count*] **1.** a fault or imperfection: *What defect in his character made him lie?* —*v.* [*no obj*] **2.** to desert a cause, country, etc., and go over to the opponent's side: *Would the spies want to defect to the West?* —**deˈfec•tion,** *n.* [*noncount*]: *the defection of several members of the ambassador's staff.* [*count*]: *Defections increased during the crisis.*

de•fec•tive /dɪˈfɛktɪv/ *adj.* faulty; imperfect; not working properly or effectively: *One of the tires was defective.*

de•fend /dɪˈfɛnd/ *v.* [~ + *obj*] **1.** ward off attack from; protect: *The armed forces defend our country.* **2.** to support by argument, evidence, etc.: *He defended the principle of freedom of the press.* **3.** to serve as a lawyer for someone accused of a crime: *defending her clients against the charge of conspiracy.* —**deˈfend•er,** *n.* [*count*]

de•fend•ant /dɪˈfɛndənt/ *n.* [*count*] one against whom a legal action is brought in a court: *The defendant had been accused by the manager of stealing.*

de•fense /dɪˈfɛns *or, esp. for 4,* ˈdiyfɛns/ *n.* **1.** [*count*] something that defends or protects: *We'll have to strengthen our border defenses.* **2.** [*noncount*] the arms production of a nation: *spending billions on defense.* **3.** [*count*] an argument defending some cause: *The speech was a brilliant defense of civil rights.* **4.** [*count*] the players or team attempting to resist the attack of a team having the ball, puck, etc. Also, *esp. Brit.,* **deˈfence.** —**deˈfense•less,** *adj.* —**deˈfen•si•ble,** *adj.*

de•fen•sive /dɪˈfɛnsɪv/ *adj.* **1.** [*before a noun*] of or relating to defense: *defensive weapons.* **2.** sensitive to criticism: *There's no need to be so defensive.* —*n.* [*noncount*] **3. on the defensive,** to be prepared to be attacked.

de•fer¹ /dɪˈfɜr/ *v.* [~ + *obj*], **-ferred, -fer•ring.** to postpone; delay; put off action on: *The pension is deferred until after age 65.* —**deˈfer•ment,** *n.* [*count*]

de•fer² /dɪˈfɜr/ *v.* [~ + *to* + *obj*], **-ferred, -fer•ring.** to yield to someone else's judgment or opinion: *I deferred to my father's authority.*

def•er•ence /ˈdɛfərəns/ *n.* [*noncount*] respectful or courteous behavior or attitude toward: *They treated her with deference.* —**def•er•en•tial** /͵dɛfəˈrɛnʃəl/, *adj.* —**͵def•er'en•tial•ly,** *adv.*

de•fi•ance /dɪˈfayəns/ *n.* [*noncount*] a bold resistance to authority; open disregard or contempt: *The strike was an act of open defiance.* —**deˈfi•ant,** *adj.*

de•fi•cien•cy /dɪˈfɪʃənsiy/ *n.* [*noncount*] [*count*], *pl.* **-cies.** a lack: *calcium deficiency.* —**deˈfi•cient,** *adj.*

def•i•cit /ˈdɛfəsɪt/ *n.* [*count*] **1.** the amount by which a sum of money is less than the required amount. **2.** the amount by which spending exceeds income: *the huge Federal deficit.*

de•file /dɪˈfayl/ *v.* [~ + *obj*], **-filed, -fil•ing.** to make foul, dirty, or unclean. —**deˈfile•ment,** *n.* [*noncount*] —**deˈfil•er,** *n.* [*count*]

de•fine /dɪˈfayn/ *v.* [~ + *obj*], **-fined, -fin•ing. 1.** to give the meaning of: *His job was to define new words.* **2.** to describe: *to define the problem.* —**deˈfin•er,** *n.* [*count*]

def•i•nite /ˈdɛfənɪt/ *adj.* **1.** clearly defined; precise: *a definite period of time.* **2.** positive; certain; sure: *He was definite about his feelings.* —**ˈdef•i•nite•ness,** *n.* [*noncount*]

ˈdefinite ˈarticle, *n.* [*count*] the English word *the.*

def•i•nite•ly /ˈdɛfənɪtliy/ *adv.* certainly; surely: *She will definitely have a place on the team next year.*

def•i•ni•tion /͵dɛfəˈnɪʃən/ *n.* **1.** [*count*] the act of defining. **2.** [*count*] the formal statement of the meaning of something: *She wrote definitions for "quark" and "atom."* **3.** [*noncount*] the sharpness of an image: *Adjust the definition on the TV monitor.*

de•fin•i•tive /dɪˈfɪnɪtɪv/ *adj.* final; unchanging: *a definitive answer.* —**deˈfin•i•tive•ly,** *adv.*

de•flate /dɪˈfleyt/ *v.* [~ + *obj*], **-flat•ed, -flat•ing. 1.** to release the air or gas from (something inflated): *They deflated the tire tubes and changed the outer walls.* **2.** to reduce (one's hopes); destroy: *The bad news really deflated our hopes for improvement.* **3.** to reduce (currency or prices) from an inflated condition: *The economy was badly deflated.* —**de•fla•tion** /dɪˈfleyʃən/ *n.* [*noncount*]

de•flect /dɪˈflɛkt/ *v.* to bend or turn aside: [*no obj*]: *The shot deflected into the net past the goalie.* [~ + *obj*]: *He deflected the shot past the goalie.* —**de•flec•tion** /dɪˈflɛkʃən/, *n.* [*count*] —**deˈflec•tor,** *n.* [*count*]

de•fo•li•ant /diyˈfowliyənt/ *n.* [*count*] a chemical preparation for defoliating plants.

de•fo•li•ate /diyˈfowliy͵eyt/ *v.* [~ + *obj*], **-at•ed, -at•ing.** to destroy leaves. —**de͵fo•li'a•tion,** *n.* [*noncount*]

de•form /dɪˈfɔrm/ *v.* [~ + *obj*] to spoil the natural form or beauty of; disfigure: *A body badly deformed by a birth defect.* —**de•for•ma•tion** /͵diyfɔrˈmeyʃən/, *n.* [*noncount*] [*count*] —**deˈformed,** *adj.*

de•form•i•ty /dɪˈfɔrmɪtiy/ *n.*, *pl.* **-ties. 1.** [*noncount*] the quality or state of being deformed: *the causes of birth deformity.* **2.** [*count*] an improperly formed part of the body: *a deformity that makes walking difficult.*

de•fraud /dɪˈfrɔd/ *v.* [~ + *obj* + *of* + *obj*] to take away someone's money or property by deceit: *He defrauded them of $500.* —**deˈfraud•er,** *n.* [*count*]

de•fray /dɪˈfrey/ *v.* [~ + *obj*], to pay all or part of: *to help defray some of the costs.*

de•frost /dɪˈfrɔst, -ˈfrɒst/ *v.* [~ + *obj*] [*no obj*] to (cause to) become free of ice or frost; to thaw. —**deˈfrost•er,** *n.* [*count*]

deft /dɛft/ *adj.*, **-er**, **-est**. skillful. —**'deft•ly**, *adv.*

de•fuse /diy'fyuwz/ *v.* [~ + *obj*], **-fused**, **-fus•ing**. **1.** to remove the fuse from (a bomb). **2.** to make less dangerous or tense: *She defused a tense situation.*

de•fy /dɪ'fay/ *v.* [~ + *obj*], **-fied**, **-fy•ing**. **1.** to resist boldly or openly: *They seemed to enjoy defying my authority.* **2.** to offer resistance to; withstand: *The problem defies all attempts to solve it.*

de•gen•er•ate /*v.* dɪ'dʒɛnəˌreyt; *adj., n.* -ərɪt/ *v.*, **-at•ed**, **-at•ing**, *adj., n.* —*v.* [*no obj*] **1.** to decline or get worse in personal qualities; deteriorate: *Idleness caused his character to degenerate.* —*adj.* **2.** having become worse; degraded; depraved: *a degenerate ruler.* —*n.* [*count*] **3.** a degenerate person. —**de•gen•er•a•cy** /dɪ'dʒɛnərəsiy/, *n.* [*noncount*] —**de•gen•er•a•tion** /dɪˌdʒɛnə'reyʃən/, *n.* [*noncount*]: *physical degeneration.* —**'de•gen•er•a•tive** /-ərətɪv, -əˌreytɪv/, *adj.*

de•grade /dɪ'greyd/ *v.*, **-grad•ed**, **-grad•ing**. **1.** [~ + *obj*] to lower in dignity or in respect; debase: *She wouldn't degrade herself by cheating.* **2.** [*no obj*] (esp. of an organic compound) to break down or decompose: *plastics that degrade for a thousand years.* —**deg•ra•da•tion** /ˌdɛgrə'deyʃən/, *n.* [*noncount*]: *facing the degradation of their liberty.* —**de'gra•ding**, *adj.*: *a degrading task.*

de•gree /dɪ'griy/ *n.* [*count*] **1.** any of a series of steps or stages; a point in any scale; level; grade: *He improved by degrees.* **2.** an academic title given upon the completion of studies: *a college degree.* **3.** a unit of measure, esp. of temperature, marked on the scale of a measuring instrument: *The thermometer said it was 26 degrees outside.* **4.** a unit of measure for angles, often represented by the sign °: *an angle of 45°.* **5.** the classification of a crime according to its seriousness: *murder in the first degree.* —***Idiom.* 6. by degrees,** by easy stages; gradually.

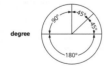

degree

de•hu•mid•i•fi•er /ˌdiyhyuw'mɪdəˌfayər/ *n.* [*count*] a device for removing moisture from indoor air. —**ˌde•hu'mid•i•fy,** *v.* [~ + *obj*], **-fied**, **-fy•ing.**

de•hy•drate /diy'haydreyt/ *v.* [~ + *obj*], **-drat•ed**, **-drat•ing.** to remove water from: *The vegetables were dehydrated and sealed in packages.* —**de•hy•dra•tion** /ˌdiyhay'dreyʃən/, *n.* [*noncount*]

de•i•fy /'diyəˌfay/ *v.* [~ + *obj*], **-fied**, **-fy•ing.** to make a god of; worship as a god: *to deify wealth.* —**de•i•fi•ca•tion** /ˌdiyəfɪ'keyʃən/, *n.* [*noncount*]: *deification of the Roman emperors.*

deign /deyn/ *v.* [*no obj.*] to consider to be fit or proper to one's dignity: *She would not deign to visit us.*

de•i•ty /'diyɪtiy/ *n.*, *pl.* **-ties. 1.** [*count*] a god or goddess. **2. the Deity,** God.

de•ject•ed /dɪ'dʒɛktɪd/ *adj.* sad; low-spirited: *He was dejected when she turned down his proposal.* —**de'ject•ed•ly,** *adv.*: *She answered dejectedly that she had failed.* —**de•jec•tion** /dɪ'dʒɛkʃən/, *n.* [*noncount*]: *feelings of dejection.*

Del., an abbreviation of: Delaware.

de•lay /dɪ'ley/ *v.* [~ + *obj*] **1.** to put off to a later time; postpone: *The committee delayed action on the matter.* **2.** to slow down; hold back: *The fog delayed the plane's landing.* —*n.* **3.** [*noncount*] the act of delaying: *Please finish your work without delay.* **4.** [*count*] an instance of being delayed: *The delay was caused by an accident.*

del•e•gate /*n.*'dɛlɪgɪt; *v.* -ˌgeyt/ *n., v.*, **-gat•ed**, **-gat•ing.** —*n.* [*count*] **1.** a person who acts for another; agent; representative: *delegates from a union.* —*v.* [~ + *obj*] **2.** to send or appoint (someone) as a representative: *We have delegated her to represent our city.* **3.** to give (power, etc.) to someone: *He delegated his authority to me.* —**del•e•ga•tion** /ˌdɛlɪ'geyʃən/ *n.*

de•lete /dɪ'liyt/ *v.* [~ + *obj*], **-let•ed**, **-let•ing.** to strike out or remove (something written or printed); cancel; erase. —**de•le•tion** /dɪ'liyʃən/, *n.* [*count*]: *deletions from the list.*

del•i /'dɛliy/ *n.* [*count*], *pl.* **del•is** /'dɛliyz/. delicatessen.

de•lib•er•ate /*adj.* dɪ'lɪbərɪt; *v.* -əˌreyt/ *adj., v.*, **-at•ed**, **-at•ing.** —*adj.* **1.** intentional; done on purpose: *a deliberate lie.* **2.** careful, slow, or unhurried: *a deliberate decision; deliberate speech.* —*v.* [~ + *obj*] [*no obj*] **3.** to consider carefully. —**de•lib•er•ate•ly** /dɪ'lɪbərɪtliy/, *adv.*: *They lied deliberately.*

de•lib•er•a•tion /dɪˌlɪbə'reyʃən/ *n.* [*noncount*] **1.** careful, unhurried consideration or discussion. **2.** deliberate quality; slowness of action: *He examined the painting with great deliberation.*

del•i•ca•cy /'dɛlɪkəsiy/ *n.*, *pl.* **-cies. 1.** [*noncount*] fineness of texture or quality: softness; daintiness: *the delicacy of lace.* **2.** [*count*] something delightful or pleasing, esp. a food: *delicacies that aroused the appetite.* **3.** [*noncount*] the quality of being easily broken; fragility: *the delicacy of his health.* **4.** [*noncount*] the quality of requiring or involving great care: *negotiations of great delicacy.*

del•i•cate /'dɛlɪkɪt/ *adj.* **1.** relating to or marked by delicacy. **2.** so fine as to be scarcely felt or sensed: *a light, delicate flavor.* **3.** requiring great care: *delicate negotiations; a delicate plant.* **4.** capable of noticing subtle differences; sensitive: *That instrument is so delicate it can detect earthquakes thousands of miles away.* **5.** easily disgusted: *a violent movie not for the delicate viewer.* —**'del•i•cate•ly,** *adv.* —**'del•i•cate•ness,** *n.* [*noncount*]

del•i•ca•tes•sen /ˌdɛlɪkə'tɛsən/ *n.* [*count*] a store selling ready-to-eat foods.

de•li•cious /dɪ'lɪʃəs/ *adj.* pleasing to the senses, esp. taste or smell: *delicious chocolate cake.* —**de'li•cious•ly,** *adv.*: *deliciously prepared foods.* —**de'li•cious•ness,** *n.* [*noncount*]

de•light /dɪ'layt/ *n.* **1.** [*noncount*] great enjoyment; joy; happiness: *I get a great deal of delight from watching my children.* **2.** [*count*] something that gives great pleasure: *The zoo is a delight to visit.* —*v.* **3.** [~ + *obj*] to give pleasure to: *The circus will delight young and old alike.* **4. delight in,** to take great pleasure in: *She delights in walking.* —**de'light•ed,** *adj.*: *I was delighted to see you.* —**de'light•ful,** *adj.*

de•lin•quent /dɪ'lɪŋkwənt/ *adj.* **1.** guilty of a misdeed or offense. —*n.* [*count*] **2.** a person who breaks a law. —**de'lin•quen•cy,** *n.* [*noncount*] [*count*], *pl.* **-cies.** —**de'lin•quent•ly,** *adv.*

de•lir•i•ous /dɪ'lɪəriyəs/ *adj.* **1.** relating to or

marked by delirium: *delirious with fever.* **2.** wild with excitement, enthusiasm, etc.: *The crowd at the concert became delirious.* —**de'lir•i•ous•ly,** *adv.*: *She was moaning deliriously through the night.* —**de'lir•i•ous•ness,** *n.* [*noncount*]

de•lir•i•um /dɪˈlɪəriyəm/ *n.* [*count*], *pl.* **-i•ums, -i•a** /-iyə/. a mental state marked by restlessness, excitement, and delusions.

de•liv•er /dɪˈlɪvər/ *v.* [~ + *obj*] **1.** to carry or take something to a person or place: *She delivered the letter last week.* **2.** to hand over; surrender: *to deliver a prisoner to the police.* **3.** to say, utter, or pronounce: *to deliver a speech.* **4.** to strike or throw: *to deliver a blow.* **5. deliver from,** to set free: *Moses delivered the Hebrews from bondage in Egypt.* **6.** to help at the birth of: *The doctor delivered the baby.*

de•liv•er•ance /dɪˈlɪvərəns/ *n.* [*noncount*] the act of being set free; salvation; liberation; rescue.

de•liv•er•y /dɪˈlɪvəriy/ *n., pl.* **-ies. 1.** [*count*] [*noncount*] the act of delivering. **2.** [*count*] something delivered: *Bring the deliveries to the back door.* **3.** [*noncount*] the manner of giving a speech: *the speaker's fine delivery.* **4.** [*count*] the act of giving birth to a child: *an easy delivery.*

del•ta /ˈdɛltə/ *n.* [*count*], *pl.* **-tas. 1.** the fourth letter of the Greek alphabet (Δ, δ). **2.** a flat, triangular area of land with rich soil lying between branches of the mouth of a river: *the Mississippi Delta.*

de•lude /dɪˈluwd/ *v.* [~ + *obj*], **-lud•ed, -lud• ing.** to mislead; deceive; fool; trick: *He deluded himself into thinking he'd lost weight.*

del•uge /ˈdɛlyuwdʒ/ *n., v.,* **-uged, -ug•ing.** —*n.* **1.** [*count*] a great flood of water. **2. the Deluge,** FLOOD (def. 3). **3.** [*count*] a drenching rain; downpour: *a deluge from the skies.* —*v.* [~ + *obj*] **4.** to flood: *The flooding river deluged the town.*

de•lu•sion /dɪˈluwʒən/ *n.* **1.** [*noncount*] the state of being deluded: *suffering from delusion.* **2.** [*count*] a false belief or opinion: *delusions of grandeur.* —**de•lu•sive** /dɪˈluwsɪv/, *adj.*

de•luxe or **de luxe** /dəˈlʌks, -ˈlʊks/ *adj.* [*before a noun*] splendid; luxurious: *a deluxe hotel.*

delve /dɛlv/ *v.* [*no obj*], **delved, delv•ing.** to dig into; make a deep and thorough search: *We delved into the files to find out when she was born.*

dem•a•gogue or **dem•a•gog** /ˈdɛməˌgɒg, -ˌgɔg/ *n.* [*count*] a political leader who gains power by appealing to people. —**dem•a•gog•ic** /ˌdɛməˈgɒgɪk, -ˈgɒdʒ-/, *adj.* —**dem•a•gogu•er• y, dem•a•go•gy** /ˈdɛməˌgowdʒiy, -ˌgɒdʒiy/, *n.* [*noncount*]

de•mand /dɪˈmænd/ *v.* [~ + *obj*] **1.** to ask for firmly; claim: *We demanded justice. I demanded to know what we had done wrong.* **2.** to call for, need, or require: *This task demands patience.* —*n.* **3.** [*count*] the act of demanding. **4.** [*count*] a necessary thing: *the conflicting demands of family and job.* **5.** [*noncount*] the state of being wanted or sought for: *an article in great demand.* —*Idiom.* **6. on demand, a.** upon request or presentation for payment: *The bill is payable on demand.* **b.** when requested: *abortion on demand.*

de•mand•ing /dɪˈmændɪŋ/ *adj.* calling for much effort or attention: *He has a very demanding job.* —**de'mand•ing•ly,** *adv.*

de•mean /dɪˈmiyn/ *v.* [~ + *obj*] to lower in dignity or standing; debase; degrade: *You demean the presidency by such conduct.* —**de'mean•ing,** *adj.*: *He said manual labor was demeaning.*

de•mean•or /dɪˈmiynər/ *n.* [*noncount*] conduct; behavior; manner: *His calm demeanor hides his tension.* Also, *esp. Brit.,* **de'mean•our.**

de•ment•ed /dɪˈmɛntɪd/ *adj.* crazy; insane; mad.

de•mer•it /dɪˈmɛrɪt/ *n.* [*count*] a mark against a person for doing something wrong: *He got a few demerits for his sloppy work.*

demi-, a combining form meaning half or lesser (*demigod*).

de•mil•i•ta•rize /diyˈmɪlɪtəˌrayz/ *v.* [~ + *obj*], **-rized, -riz•ing.** to remove the military from.

de•mise /dɪˈmayz/ *n.* [*count; usually singular*] death: *the demise of a hero.*

dem•i•tasse /ˈdɛmiˌtæs, -ˌtɑs, ˈdɛmiy-/ *n.* [*count*] a small cup for serving strong black coffee.

de•mo•bi•lize /diyˈmowbəˌlayz/ *v.* [~ + *obj*], **-lized, -liz•ing.** to send troops home: *The soldiers waited to be demobilized.* —**de•mo•bi•li•za•tion** /diyˌmowbələˈzeyʃən/, *n.* [*noncount*]

de•moc•ra•cy /dɪˈmɒkrəsiy/ *n., pl.* **-cies. 1.** [*noncount*] a form of government in which the people share the power through their elected representatives. **2.** [*count*] a country having such a form of government. **3.** [*noncount*] a state or condition in which there is equality of rights: *democracy in family relationships.*

dem•o•crat /ˈdɛməˌkræt/ *n.* [*count*] **1.** a supporter of democracy. **2.** [*Democrat*] a member of the Democratic Party.

dem•o•crat•ic /ˌdɛməˈkrætɪk/ *adj.* **1.** relating to or supporting democracy: *a democratic government.* **2.** relating to political or social equality: *democratic principles of electing delegates.* **3.** [*before a noun; Democratic*] of, relating to, or characteristic of the Democratic Party. —**,dem•o'crat• i•cal•ly,** *adv.*

'Demo'cratic 'Party, *n.* one of the two major political parties in the U.S.

de•moc•ra•tize /dɪˈmɒkrəˌtayz/ *v.* [~ + *obj*], **-tized, -tiz•ing.** to make democratic: *The union decided to democratize its voting procedures.* —**de•moc•ra•ti•za•tion** /dɪˌmɒkrətəˈzeyʃən/, *n.* [*noncount*]: *They called for the democratization of the labor unions.*

de•mol•ish /dɪˈmɒlɪʃ/ *v.* [~ + *obj*] **1.** to destroy or tear down (a building): *They are going to demolish the old apartment building.* **2.** to put an end to; destroy: *Those arguments will demolish anything his lawyer has to say.* —**demolition,** *n.* [*noncount*] [*count*]

de•mon /ˈdiymən/ *n.* [*count*] **1.** an evil spirit. **2.** a person with great energy: *a demon for work.* —**de•mon•ic** /dɪˈmɒnɪk/, *adj.*

de•mon•stra•ble /dɪˈmɒnstrəbəl/ *adj.* able to be demonstrated: *a demonstrable lie.* —**de'mon• stra•bly,** *adv.*: *a demonstrably false argument.*

dem•on•strate /ˈdɛmənˌstreyt/ *v.,* **-strat•ed, -strat•ing. 1.** [~ + *obj*] to describe or illustrate clearly; to show: *He demonstrated the proper method of fastening the parachute. He demonstrated great courage.* **2.** [*no obj*] to take part in a demonstration: *The protesters demonstrated against the new quotas.*

dem•on•stra•tion /ˌdɛmənˈstreyʃən/ *n.* [*count*] **1.** showing how something works: *a demonstration of the new manufacturing process.* **2.** a showing of emotion: *demonstrations of affection.* **3.** a public show of strong opinion: *a huge demonstration in the city's main square.*

de•mon•stra•tive /dəˈmɒnstrətɪv/ *adj.* **1.** showing openly one's emotions: *a demonstrative*

D

parent. **2.** pointing out the thing referred to: *The word this is a demonstrative pronoun and adjective.* —*n.* [count] **3.** a demonstrative word, as *this* or *there.*

dem•on•stra•tor /'dɛmən,streytər/ *n.* [count] **1.** a person or thing that demonstrates. **2.** a person who takes part in a public demonstration, as by marching or picketing.

de•mor•al•ize /dɪ'mɔrə,layz, -'mɒr-/ *v.* [~ + obj], **-ized, -iz•ing.** to destroy the spirit, courage, or discipline of: *The terrible defeat demoralized the army.* —**de•mor•al•i•za•tion** /dɪ,mɔrələ-'zeyʃən, -,mɒr-/, *n.* [noncount]: *nationwide demoralization.* —**de•mor•al•ized,** *adj.*: *The demoralized army trudged home after the defeat.* —**de•mor•al•iz•ing,** *adj.*: *The army suffered a demoralizing defeat.*

de•mote /dɪ'mowt/ *v.* [~ + obj], **-mot•ed, -mot•ing.** to reduce to a lower grade or rank: *He was demoted to the rank of private.* —**de•mo•tion** /dɪ'mowʃən/, *n.* [noncount] [count]

de•mur /dɪ'mɜr/ *v.*, **-murred, -mur•ring,** *n.* —*v.* [no obj] **1.** to object: *The majority were in favor, but a few demurred.* —*n.* [noncount] **2.** hesitation: *He followed any order without demur.* —**de'mur•ral,** *n.* [count]

de•mure /dɪ'myʊr/ *adj.*, **-mur•er, -mur•est.** characterized by shyness and modesty: *a demure smile.* —**de'mure•ly,** *adv.*

den /dɛn/ *n.* [count] **1.** the home or shelter of a wild animal: *the lion's den.* **2.** a quiet room in a home for reading, conversation, etc.

de•ni•al /dɪ'nayəl/ *n.* **1.** [count] a statement that something is false: *a denial of the story.* **2.** [noncount] denying; refusing a request: *denial of justice.*

den•im /'dɛnəm/ *n.* **1.** [noncount] a heavy cotton fabric, used esp. for jeans. **2. denims,** [plural; used with a plural verb] jeans: *The denims were hung on the line after they were washed.*

de•nom•i•na•tion /dɪ,nɒmə'neyʃən/ *n.* [count] **1.** a religious group: *To what denomination does he belong?* **2.** a unit in a series: *He had a few bills of various denominations in his wallet: singles, fives, and twenties.* **3.** a name, esp. one for a class of things. —**de,nom•i'na•tion•al,** *adj.*

de•nom•i•na•tor /dɪ'nɒmə,neytər/ *n.* [count] the number written under the line in a fraction: *In the fraction 3/4, 4 is the denominator.* Compare NUMERATOR.

de•note /dɪ'nowt/ *v.* [~ + obj], **-not•ed, -not•ing.** to indicate clearly; to mean: *A fever often denotes an infection.*

de•nounce /dɪ'nawns/ *v.* [~ + obj], **-nounced, -nounc•ing.** to condemn strongly, openly, or publicly: *She denounced the plan as a waste of money.*

dense /dɛns/ *adj.*, **dens•er, dens•est. 1.** having parts closely packed together; crowded: *a dense forest.* **2.** stupid: *He's too thick; hard to see through: a dense fog.* —'**dense•ly,** *adv.* —'**dense•ness,** *n.* [noncount] —'**dens•i•ty,** *n.* [noncount] [count]

dent /dɛnt/ *n.* [count] **1.** a hollow in a surface, such as from a blow: *The car had a few dents on the fender.* **2.** a noticeable effect, esp. of reduction: *a dent in one's pride.* —*v.* [~ + obj] **3.** to make a dent in or on: *She dented the front end of the car.*

den•tal /'dɛntl/ *adj.* [before a noun] of or relating to the teeth: *dental care.*

den•tist /'dɛntɪst/ *n.* [count] a doctor whose specialty is the care and treatment of teeth. —**den•tist•ry** /'dɛntɪstriy/, *n.* [noncount]

de•nun•ci•a•tion /dɪ,nʌnsiy'eyʃən, -ʃiy-/ *n.* [count] an act or instance of denouncing: *a denunciation of dishonest government.*

de•ny /dɪ'nay/ *v.* [~ + obj], **-nied, -ny•ing. 1.** to state that something is not true: *ready to deny any accusation.* **2.** to refuse to agree to: *The union decided to deny my petition.* **3.** to refuse to allow: *to deny access to information.* **4.** to refuse to recognize; disavow: *The traitor denied his country.* —**de'ni•a•ble,** *adj.* —**de•ni•a•bil•i•ty** /dɪ,nayə'bɪlɪtiy/, *n.* [noncount]

de•o•dor•ant /diy'owdərənt/ *n.* [noncount] [count] a substance for reducing odors.

de•o•dor•ize /diy'owdə,rayz/ *v.* [~ + obj], **-ized, -iz•ing.** to rid of an unpleasant smell: *a chemical that cleans and deodorizes rooms.* —**de'o•dor,iz•er,** *n.* [count]: *a room deodorizer.*

de•part /dɪ'pɑrt/ *v.* [no obj] **1.** to go away; leave: *The train never departs on time.* **2.** to be different; differ: *Our method departs from theirs in several respects.*

de•part•ed /dɪ'pɑrtɪd/ *adj.* **1.** [before a noun] dead: *our departed brother.* —*n.* **2. the departed,** [count] a dead person: *to mourn for the departed.*

de•part•ment /dɪ'pɑrtmənt/ *n.* [count] **1.** a division or branch, as of business: *He was assigned to a new department.* **2.** one's special area of activity or responsibility: *Tax questions are just not my department.* —**de•part•men•tal** /dɪ-pɑrt'mɛntl, ,diypɑrt-/, *adj.*

de'part•ment ,store, *n.* [count] a large store that sells a variety of goods organized by departments.

de•par•ture /dɪ'pɑrtʃər/ *n.* [count] [noncount] an act or instance of departing: *A bomb scare delayed the plane's departure. This new ceremony is a departure from tradition.*

de•pend /dɪ'pɛnd/ *v.* [no obj] **1.** to place trust in: *You may depend on our support.* **2.** to be determined by: *Our plans depend on the weather.*

de•pend•a•ble /dɪ'pɛndəbəl/ *adj.* worthy of trust: *a dependable employee.* —**de•pend•a•bil•i•ty** /dɪ,pɛndə'bɪlɪtiy/, *n.* [noncount] —**de'pend•a•bly,** *adv.*

de•pend•ence /dɪ'pɛndəns/ *n.* [noncount] **1.** the state of depending on someone or something: *the dependence on the West for luxury items.* **2.** trust: *dependence on religion.* **3.** the state of needing a drug: *the frightening dependence on drugs.*

de•pend•ent /dɪ'pɛndənt/ *adj.* **1.** needing someone or something else for aid or support: *dependent on her parents until she got a job.* **2. dependent on,** conditioned or determined by something else: *Our trip is dependent on the weather.* —*n.* [count] **3.** a person, such as a child, who depends on someone for aid or support: *Our children are no longer listed as dependents on our tax forms.* —**de'pend•ent•ly,** *adv.*

de•pict /dɪ'pɪkt/ *v.* [~ + obj] to represent by a picture or with words. —**de'pic•tion,** *n.* [count]

de•plete /dɪ'pliyt/ *v.* [~ + obj], **-plet•ed, -plet•ing.** to decrease badly; use up the supply of: *The drought has seriously depleted our water supply.* —**de•ple•tion** /dɪ'pliyʃən/, *n.* [noncount]: *We were faced with the depletion of our supplies just before the battle.*

de•plore /dɪ'plɔr/ *v.* [~ + obj], **-plored, -plor•ing. 1.** to regret deeply or strongly: *We deplore what our own soldiers have done.* **2.** to express strong disapproval of; condemn: *He deplored the*

action taken against his country. —de'plor•a•
ble, *adj.*

de•ploy /dɪ'plɔɪ/ *v.* [~ + *obj*] to arrange or
move into position, esp. for battle: *to deploy missiles.* —de'ploy•ment, *n.* [*noncount*] [*count*]

de•port /dɪ'pɔrt/ *v.* [~ + *obj*] to expel (an alien) from a country; banish: *The federal authorities deported him for illegal entry.* —de•por•ta•
tion /ˌdiypɔr'teyʃən/, *n.* [*noncount*]: *They were
faced with immediate deportation.* [*count*]: *increases in the number of deportations.*

de•pose /dɪ'powz/ *v.* [~ + *obj*], -posed, -pos•
ing. to remove from office or position, esp. high
office: *The nobles deposed the king.*

de•pos•it /dɪ'pɒzɪt/ *v.* [~ + *obj*] 1. to put or
place (something) for safekeeping: *He deposited
the fifty dollars in his savings account.* 2. to put
or set down, esp. carefully: *She deposited the
baby in the crib.* 3. to lay or throw down by a
natural process: *The river deposited soil at its
mouth.* 4. to give as security (for): *We deposited
$500 on the new car.* —*n.* [*count*] 5. money
placed in a bank account: *a deposit of over
$1,000.* 6. anything given as security or in partial
payment: *a bottle deposit of five cents.* 7. something left or thrown down, such as by a natural
process: *a deposit of rich soil left by the flood.*
—de'pos•i•tor, *n.* [*count*]: *Bank depositors will
use the new branch office.*

de•pot /'diypow/ *n.* [*count*] 1. a railroad or bus
station. 2. a place in which supplies are stored.

de•prave /dɪ'preyv/ *v.* [~ + *obj*], -praved,
-prav•ing. to make evil; corrupt. —de'praved,
adj. —de•prav•i•ty /dɪ'prævɪtiy/, *n.* [*noncount*]
[*count*] *pl.* -ties.

de•pre•ci•ate /dɪ'priyʃiy,eyt/ *v.*, -at•ed, -at•
ing. 1. [*no obj*] (of money, etc.) to decline or fall
in value: *The car depreciated in value.* 2. [~ +
obj] to reduce or lower the value of: *Inflation has
depreciated the country's currency.* —de•pre•ci•
a•tion /dɪ,priyʃiy'eyʃən/, *n.* [*noncount*]

de•press /dɪ'prɛs/ *v.* [~ + *obj*] 1. to make sad
or gloomy; sadden: *Her sad news depressed me.*
2. to lower in amount or value; lessen; weaken:
to depress the economy. 3. to press down: *Depress the brake pedal.* —de'pressed, *adj.*
—de'press•ing, *adj.* —de'press•ive, *adj.*

de•pres•sion /dɪ'prɛʃən/ *n.* 1. [*count*] a depressed or sunken place or part: *a depression in
the carpet where the lamp had stood.* 2. [*noncount*] a feeling of sadness and despair: *She suffered from long periods of depression.* 3. [*count*] a
period during which business, employment, and
stock-market values fall: *In the 1930's the world
experienced a severe depression.*

de•prive /dɪ'prayv/ *v.* [~ + *obj*], -prived, -priv•
ing. to keep (someone) from having or enjoying
something; keep or prevent (someone) from having or using: *to deprive a child of affection.*
—dep•ri•va•tion /ˌdɛprə'veyʃən/, *n.* [*noncount*]
a life of terrible hardship and deprivation.
[*count*]: *They suffered terrible deprivations during
the war.* —de'prived, *adj.*

dept., an abbreviation of: department.

depth /dɛpθ/ *n.* 1. [*noncount*] [*count*] a distance
measured from the surface of something downward, or from the front backward or inward. 2.
[*noncount*] the quality of being complex or difficult to understand: *a question of great depth.* 3.
[*noncount*] seriousness: *He explained the depth of
the crisis facing the state.* 4. [*noncount*] intensity,
such as of color or emotion: *a drawing with
depth of color; the depth of one's feelings.* 5.

depths, [*plural*] the deepest, farthest, or innermost part: *the depths of the forest.* —*Idiom.* 6.
in depth, extensively; thoroughly: *The committee
studied the problem in depth.* 7. out of or beyond one's depth, beyond one's knowledge or
ability: *He's out of his depth on that assignment.*

dep•u•ta•tion /ˌdɛpyə'teyʃən/ *n.* [*count*] a
body of persons appointed to represent another:
The president met the deputation at the door.

dep•u•tize /'dɛpyə,tayz/ *v.*, -tized, -tiz•ing. 1.
[~ + *obj*] to appoint as deputy: *The boss depu-
tized me to speak for her in her absence.* 2. [*no
obj*] to substitute for someone: *Can you deputize
for me tomorrow?*

dep•u•ty /'dɛpyətiy/ *n.* [*count*], *pl.* -ties. 1. a
person appointed to act as a substitute for another: *the boss's deputy.* 2. a person representing
a group of voters in certain law-making bodies.
—*adj.* [*before a noun*] 3. appointed, elected, or
serving as an assistant: *the deputy secretary of
foreign affairs.*

de•rail /diy'reyl/ *v.* [*no obj*] [~ + *obj*] (of a
train, etc.) to (cause to) run off the rails of a
track —de'rail•ment, *n.* [*count*]

de•ranged /dɪ'reyndʒd/ *adj.* made insane.
—de'range•ment, *n.* [*noncount*]

de•reg•u•late /diy'rɛgyə,leyt/ *v.* [~ + *obj*],
-lat•ed, -lat•ing. to remove government regulation of: *to deregulate the airline industry.* —de•
reg•u•la•tion /diy,rɛgyə'leyʃən/, *n.* [*noncount*]

der•e•lict /'dɛrəlɪkt/ *adj.* 1. neglecting duty; de-
linquent: *He was fired for being derelict in his duties.* —*n.* [*count*] 2. a person who has no home
or means of support; vagrant.

de•ride /dɪ'rayd/ *v.* [~ + *obj*], -rid•ed, -rid•
ing. to laugh at in contempt; mock: *They derided
his plan for saving money.* —de•ri•sion
/dɪ'rɪʒən/ *n.* [*noncount*]

der•i•va•tion /ˌdɛrə'veyʃən/ *n.* [*noncount*] 1.
the act of deriving or the state of being derived:
the derivation of new plastics from chemicals. 2.
source; origin: *a dance of German derivation.*

de•riv•a•tive /dɪ'rɪvətɪv/ *adj.* 1. not original;
coming from something earlier: *His music was
derivative.* —*n.* [*count*] 2. something derived or
developed from something else, such as a word
that has come from another.

de•rive /dɪ'rayv/ *v.* [~ + *obj*], -rived, -riv•ing.
1. to receive from another source; gain: *She derives great satisfaction from her children.* 2. to
come from or trace from a source or origin: *We
can derive the word deduct from Latin.*

der•ma•ti•tis /ˌdɜrmə'taytɪs/ *n.* [*noncount*] a
rash or inflammation of the skin.

der•ma•tol•o•gy /ˌdɜrmə'tɒlədʒiy/ *n.* [*noncount*] the branch of medicine dealing with the
skin and its diseases. —der•ma•to•log•i•cal
/ˌdɜrmətə'lɒdʒɪkəl/, *adj.* —der•ma•tol•o•gist
/ˌdɜrmə'tɒlədʒɪst/, *n.* [*count*]

de•rog•a•to•ry /dɪ'rɒgə,tɔriy/ *adj.* unfavorable;
disapproving: *a derogatory remark.*

der•rick /'dɛrɪk/ *n.* [*count*] 1. a crane for lifting
cargo, such as on a ship. 2. a framework like a
tower over an oil well.

de•scend /dɪ'sɛnd/ *v.* 1. to go from a higher to a
lower place, level, or series: [*no obj*]: *The elevator descended rapidly to the bottom floor.* [~ +
obj]: *She slowly descended the stairs.* 2. descend
from or be descended from, to be derived
from something in the past: *They are descended
from the early settlers.* 3. descend on or upon,
to attack or approach as if attacking: *A crowd de-*

D

scended on the scene of the crime. —**de'scend•ed**, adj.

de•scend•ant /dɪ'sɛndənt/ n. [count] one descended from someone: a descendant of the kings of Ireland. Compare ANCESTOR.

de•scent /dɪ'sɛnt/ n. **1.** [count] the act, process, or fact of going down: The spectators watched the descent of the balloon. **2.** [noncount] ancestry; the line tracing births to an ancestor: Greek descent.

de•scribe /dɪ'skrayb/ v. [~ + obj], **-scribed, -scrib•ing. 1.** to tell in words what something is like: to describe an accident in detail; Can you describe what he did next? **2.** to draw or trace the outline of: to describe an arc with a pencil.

de•scrip•tion /dɪ'skrɪpʃən/ n. **1.** describing; a statement that describes: [count]: He provided the police with a description of the killer. [noncount]: She has good powers of description. **2.** [count; usually singular] sort; kind; variety: She liked dogs of every description. —**de•scrip•tive** /dɪ'skrɪptɪv/, adj.: She wrote a descriptive essay of her favorite place. —**de'scrip•tive•ly**, adv.

des•e•crate /'dɛsɪˌkreyt/ v. [~ + obj], **-crat•ed, -crat•ing.** to violate by treating with disrespect; defile: They desecrated the building by scribbling on the walls. —**des•e•cra•tion** /ˌdɛsɪ'kreyʃən/, n. [noncount]

de•seg•re•gate /diy'sɛgrɪˌgeyt/ v., **-gat•ed, -gat•ing.** to eliminate racial or other segregation in: [~ + obj]: to desegregate schools. [no obj]: The governor had promised never to desegregate. —**de•seg•re•ga•tion** /diyˌsɛgrɪ'geyʃən/, n. [noncount]: fighting for desegregation of schools.

des•ert[1] /'dɛzərt/ n. [count] **1.** a hot, dry, sandy region with little or no rain or water: Some animals can survive in the desert on very little water. —adj. [before a noun] **2.** of, relating to, or like a desert: desert wilderness.

de•sert[2] /dɪ'zɜrt/ v. **1.** [~ + obj] to leave (a person, etc.) without intending to return: He deserted his wife and children. **2.** (of military personnel) to run away from (service, etc.) with the intention of never returning: [~ + obj]: He deserted his platoon and went over to the enemy. [no obj]: He deserted in the midst of battle. —**de'sert•er**, n. [count]

de•sert[3] /dɪ'zɜrt/ n. [count] Often, **deserts.** [plural] reward or punishment that is deserved: He got his just deserts when they discovered he'd lied to everyone.

de•serve /dɪ'zɜrv/ v. [~ + obj], **-served, -serv•ing.** to be worthy of, or have a claim to (reward, etc.) because of actions or qualities: The teachers deserve a pay raise. A hard worker deserves to succeed.

de•served /dɪ'zɜrvd/ adj. being worthy of reward, punishment, etc.: It was a well-deserved victory. —**de•serv•ed•ly** /dɪy'zɜrvɪdliy/, adv.: They won the race, and deservedly so.

de•serv•ing /dɪ'zɜrvɪŋ/ adj. worthy: He gave the prize money to a deserving charity.

de•sign /dɪ'zayn/ v. [~ + obj] **1.** to draw the plans for (work, clothing, etc.): The engineer designed a new bridge. He designed a new dress for the fashion show. **2.** to develop, set up, and plan for a purpose: That scholarship is designed for foreign students. —n. **3.** [count] an outline, sketch, or drawing of something to be done or constructed: designs for the new mall. **4.** the way in which something is composed, shaped, or made: [count]: I like the colors but not the overall design. [noncount]: to study art and design. **5.**

[count] a pattern: a little heart-shaped design on the bracelet. **6. designs on,** [plural] a hostile plan: He seems to have designs on my job.

des•ig•nate /'dɛzɪgˌneyt/ v. [~ + obj], **-nat•ed, -nat•ing. 1.** to mark or point out: He designated the place where we would meet. **2.** to select; assign: She was designated (as) the chairperson. She designated me to do the work. —**des•ig•na•tion** /ˌdɛzɪg'neyʃən/, n. [count]

'designated 'driver, n. [count] a person who does not drink alcoholic beverages at a gathering in order to be fit to drive companions home safely.

de•sign•er /dɪ'zaynər/ n. [count] **1.** a person who plans or creates designs, such as for works of art: a fashion designer. —adj. [before a noun] **2.** created by or as if by a famous designer: designer jeans.

de•sign•ing /dɪ'zaynɪŋ/ adj. scheming; crafty.

de•sir•a•ble /dɪ'zayᵊrəbəl/ adj. pleasing; suitable; attractive: a desirable apartment. —**de•sir•a•bil•i•ty** /dɪˌzayᵊrə'bɪlɪtiy/, n. [noncount] —**de•sir•a•bly**, adv.

de•sire /dɪ'zayᵊr/ v., **-sired, -sir•ing,** n. —v. [~ + obj] **1.** to wish for; want or long for: What he really desires is a raise. **2.** to want sexually. **3.** to ask for; request: The mayor desires your presence at the meeting. —n. **4.** [count] a longing or craving: an uncontrollable desire for chocolate. **5.** [noncount] a strong wish to have sexual relations.

de•sist /dɪ'zɪst, -'sɪst/ v. [~ (+ from + obj)] to stop: The company agreed to desist from false advertising.

desk /dɛsk/ n. [count] **1.** an article of furniture having a broad writing surface and drawers for papers, etc. **2.** a table or counter at which a certain job is performed or a service offered: Go to the information desk and see if they can help you.

desk•top /'dɛskˌtɒp/ adj. [before a noun] made to fit or be used on a desk or table: a desktop computer.

'desktop 'publishing, n. [noncount] the design and production of magazines and other publications by means of a computer and a printer.

des•o•late /adj. 'dɛsəlɪt; v. -ˌleyt/ adj., v., **-lat•ed, -lat•ing.** —adj. **1.** barren; empty; deserted: a treeless, desolate landscape. **2.** feeling lonely or hopeless; sad: She was desolate over the loss of her job. —v. [~ + obj] **3.** to make sad or distressed: They were desolated by the death of their good friend. —'**des•o•late•ly,** adv. —'**des•o•late•ness,** n. [noncount] —**des•o•la•tion** /ˌdɛsə'leyʃən/ n. [noncount]

de•spair /dɪ'spɛər/ n. **1.** [noncount] loss of hope; hopelessness: He sank into despair when his business failed. —v. [no obj] **2.** to lose, give up, or be without hope: Don't despair.

des•patch /dɪ'spætʃ/ v., n. DISPATCH.

des•per•ate /'dɛspərɪt/ adj. **1.** wild, reckless, or dangerous because of despair: a desperate killer. **2.** having an urgent need, desire, etc.: desperate for attention; desperate to succeed. **3.** very serious or dangerous: a desperate illness. **4.** making a final effort; giving all: a desperate attempt to save a life. —'**des•per•ate•ly,** adv. —**des•pe•ra•tion** /ˌdɛspə'reyʃən/ n. [noncount]

des•pi•ca•ble /'dɛspɪkəbəl, dɪ'spɪkə-/ adj. deserving to be despised: a despicable lie.

de•spise /dɪ'spayz/ v. [~ + obj], **-spised, -spis•ing.** to regard as very bad or worthless: I despised their actions.

de•spite /dɪ'spaɪt/ *prep.* in spite of: *I failed the test despite studying all night.*

de•spond•ent /dɪ'spɒndənt/ *adj.* greatly saddened and depressed: *It's easy to get despondent when your plans go wrong.* —**de'spond•en•cy,** *n.* [*noncount*] —**de'spond•ent•ly,** *adv.*

des•pot /'dɛspət, -pɒt/ *n.* [*count*] a ruler with absolute power. —**des•pot•ic** /dɪ'spɒtɪk/, *adj.*: *a despotic tyrant.* —**des'pot•i•cal•ly,** *adv.* —**des•pot•ism** /'dɛspə,tɪzəm/ *n.* [*noncount*]: *Fifty years of despotism ruined the country.*

des•sert /dɪ'zɜrt/ *n.* [*count*] [*noncount*] a sweet food, such as cake, served as the final course of a meal.

des•ti•na•tion /,dɛstə'neɪʃən/ *n.* [*count*] the place to which a person or thing travels or is sent: *The train's final destination is Chicago.*

des•tined /'dɛstɪnd/ *adj.* [*be* + ~] intended for a purpose decided in advance: *impractical ideas destined to fail.* [~ + *for*]: *He was destined for greatness as a musician.*

des•ti•ny /'dɛstəniy/ *n., pl.* **-nies. 1.** [*count; often singular*] one's future or fortune: *Her destiny was to be a surgeon.* **2.** [*noncount*] the course of events thought of as being impossible to resist and decided in advance; fate: *It's pure destiny that we met!*

des•ti•tute /'dɛstɪ,tuwt, -,tyuwt/ *adj.* without means to live: *money for destitute families.* —**des•ti•tu•tion** /,dɛstɪ'tuwʃən, -'tyuw-/, *n.* [*noncount*]

de•stroy /dɪ'strɔɪ/ *v.* [~ + *obj*] **1.** to ruin (a thing); injure beyond repair: *Fire destroyed several stores in the area.* **2.** to put an end to: *They destroyed communism from within.* **3.** to kill: *I had to destroy the injured animal.*

de•stroy•er /dɪ'strɔɪər/ *n.* [*count*] **1.** a person or thing that destroys. **2.** a fast, small warship: *Destroyers were good at hunting for submarines.*

de•struc•tion /dɪ'strʌkʃən/ *n.* [*noncount*] the act of destroying or the condition of being destroyed: *The fire caused the destruction of two famous landmarks in the area.* —**de'struc•tive,** *adj.*: *the destructive power of his angry words.* —**de'struc•tive•ly,** *adv.* —**de'struc•tive•ness,** *n.* [*noncount*]

de•tach /dɪ'tætʃ/ *v.* [~ + *obj*] to unfasten and separate; disconnect: *Detach the trailer from the car.* —**de'tach•a•ble,** *adj.*

de•tached /dɪ'tætʃt/ *adj.* **1.** not attached; separated: *a detached ticket stub.* **2.** not involved or concerned: *He felt detached from the problem.*

de•tach•ment /dɪ'tætʃmənt/ *n.* **1.** [*noncount*] the act of detaching or the condition of being detached. **2.** [*noncount*] distance in feeling; indifference: *His air of detachment caused him to lose a lot of friends.* **3.** [*noncount*] freedom from prejudice; objectivity: *The judge needs detachment to arrive at a fair verdict.* **4.** [*count*] a group of troops or ships sent on a special mission: *a special detachment to rescue the prisoners.*

de•tail /dɪ'teyl, 'diyteyl/ *n.* [*count*] **1.** a small piece or item: *The picture he drew was perfect in every detail.* **2.** an individual or group selected for a special task, or the task itself: *the kitchen detail.* —*v.* [~ + *obj*] **3.** to tell about one by one; list fully: *The employees were asked to detail their complaints.* **4.** to appoint or assign (soldiers) for duty: *A squad was detailed to find the deserters and bring them to the captain.* —**Idiom. 5. in detail,** item by item: *We discussed each complaint in detail.* —**de'tailed,** *adj.*: *a detailed explanation.*

de•tain /dɪ'teyn/ *v.* [~ + *obj*] to keep someone from leaving; delay: *I was detained at a meeting and missed the bus.* —**de'tain•ment,** *n.* [*noncount*]

de•tect /dɪ'tɛkt/ *v.* [~ + *obj*] to discover or notice the existence of; find or find out: *to detect the odor of gas.* —**de'tect•a•ble, de'tect•i•ble,** *adj.* —**de'tec•tion** /dɪ'tɛkʃən/, *n.* [*noncount*] —**de'tec•tor,** *n.* [*count*]

de•tec•tive /dɪ'tɛktɪv/ *n.* [*count*] **1.** a person whose job is to solve crimes: *detectives assigned to the case.* —*adj.* [*before a noun*] **2.** of or relating to detection or detectives: *detective novels.*

dé•tente or **de•tente** /dey'tɑnt/ *n.* [*noncount*] a relaxing of tension, esp. between nations.

de•ten•tion /dɪ'tɛnʃən/ *n.* **1.** [*noncount*] the act of detaining or the state of being detained. **2.** the keeping of a student after school hours as a punishment: [*noncount*]: *He got detention for two days in a row.* [*count*]: *The teacher gave out detentions to everyone in the French class.*

de•ter /dɪ'tɜr/ *v.* [~ + *obj*], **-terred, -ter•ring.** to discourage or prevent (someone) from acting: *The large dog deterred strangers from entering.* —**de'ter•rence,** *n.* [*noncount*]

de•ter•gent /dɪ'tɜrdʒənt/ *n.* [*count*] a cleaning agent that dissolves easily in water: *laundry detergent; dish detergent.*

de•te•ri•o•rate /dɪ'tɪəriyə,reyt/ *v.* [*no obj*], **-rat•ed, -rat•ing.** to become worse: *The patient's condition has deteriorated over the last few hours.* —**de•ter•i•o•ra•tion** /dɪ,tɪəriyə'reyʃən/, *n.* [*noncount*]: *The incident triggered the rapid deterioration of peaceful relations.*

de•ter•mi•na•tion /dɪ,tɜrmə'neyʃən/ *n.* **1.** [*count*] the act of determining: *a determination of the money owed to you.* **2.** [*count*] the settlement or decision of an argument, question, etc.: *The judge made a determination that everyone found satisfactory.* **3.** [*noncount*] firmness of purpose: *He showed great determination in finishing this book.*

de•ter•mine /dɪ'tɜrmɪn/ *v.* [~ + *obj*], **-mined, -min•ing. 1.** to decide firmly: *The date of the election has yet to be determined. They determined to leave the school at once. They determined that they would travel to Texas this summer.* **2.** to conclude or figure out: *I tried to determine the reasons for her actions.* **3.** to cause, affect, or control: *Demand usually determines supply.* —**de'ter•mi•na•ble,** *adj.*

de•ter•mined /dɪ'tɜrmɪnd/ *adj.* firm; unwilling to change; stubborn: *The kids made determined efforts to drive the babysitter crazy. She is determined to finish her book on time.*

de•ter•rent /dɪ'tɜrənt/ *adj.* **1.** serving or tending to prevent. —*n.* [*count*] **2.** something that prevents an action: *Is capital punishment a deterrent to crime?*

de•test /dɪ'tɛst/ *v.* [~ + *obj*] to feel great hatred for; hate: *They detest war. I detest jogging.* —**de'test•a•ble,** *adj.*: *Selfishness is a detestable quality.* —**de•tes•ta•tion** /,diyte'steyʃən/, *n.* [*noncount*]

det•o•nate /'dɛtn,eyt/ *v.*, **-nat•ed, -nat•ing.** to (cause to) explode: [*no obj*]: *The explosive detonated against the hull of the submarine.* [~ + *obj*]: *The soldiers detonated the explosives by remote control.* —**detonation,** *n.* [*noncount*] [*count*] —**'det•o,na•tor,** *n.* [*count*]: *Someone had removed the detonator, so the bomb wouldn't explode.*

de•tour /'diytʊr, dɪ'tʊr/ *n.* [*count*] **1.** a rounda-

D

bout way to travel, esp. one used temporarily when the main route is closed: *We took a detour around the scene of the accident.* —*v.* [*no obj*] [~ + *obj*] **2.** to (cause to) make a detour.

de•tract /dɪ'trækt/ *v.* [*no obj*] to lessen the value or reputation of: *That wild hairdo detracts from your appearance.* —**de•trac•tion** /dɪ'trækʃən/, *n.* [*noncount*] —**de'trac•tor,** *n.* [*count*]

det•ri•ment /'dɛtrəmənt/ *n.* loss, damage, or disadvantage: [*count*]: *Lack of education is often a detriment to a good career.* [*noncount*]: *He worked too hard, to the detriment of his health.*

det•ri•ment•al /,dɛtrə'mɛntl/ *adj.* harmful or damaging: *That mistake was detrimental to her career.*

de•val•ue /diy'vælyuw/ *v.* [~ + *obj*], **-val•ued, -val•u•ing.** to lower the value of: *He felt that his work was devalued at his old job. The dollar was devalued.* —**de,val•u'a•tion** *n.* [*count*] [*noncount*]

dev•as•tate /'dɛvə,steyt/ *v.* [~ + *obj*], **-tat•ed, -tat•ing.** to destroy completely; ruin: *The fire devastated the city.* —**dev•as•ta•tion** /,dɛvə'steyʃən/, *n.* [*noncount*]: *devastation caused by the earthquake.* —'**dev•as,tat•ed,** *adj.* —'**dev•as,tat•ing,** *adj.*

de•vel•op /dɪ'vɛləp/ *v.* **1.** to come or bring to a more advanced state: [*no obj*]: *Her reading skills were developing at a rapid pace.* [~ + *obj*]: *new plans to develop natural resources.* **2.** to (cause to) come into an active state: [*no obj*]: *Cancer developed rapidly in the lab mice.* [~ + *obj*]: *He had begun to develop an allergy.* **3.** [~ + *obj*] to build on or improve (a piece of land), esp. so as to make more profitable: *The builders are developing that part of town.* **4.** [*no obj*] to be made visible, clear, or easy to see: *The plot develops slowly.* **5.** to place (film) in chemicals so that an image becomes visible: [*no obj*]: *With this instant film, the picture develops in only one minute.* [~ + *obj*]: *How long will it take to develop these pictures?* —**de'vel•op•ment,** *n.* [*count*]: *Developments were proceeding so fast he could no longer keep up.* [*noncount*]: *the development of nuclear weapons.*

de•vel•oped /dɪ'vɛləpt/ *adj.* [*often: before a noun*] considered to be wealthy, industrialized, and modern: *the developed countries of the West.*

de•vel•op•er /dɪ'vɛləpər/ *n.* **1.** [*count*] a person or group of persons intending to build on or improve land so as to make a profit on it: *greedy land developers.* **2.** [*count*] a person bringing new products or methods into being: *Developers of the theory must now look elsewhere for data to confirm it.* **3.** [*noncount*] [*count*] a chemical used for developing photographic film.

de•vel•op•ing /dɪ'vɛləpɪŋ/ *adj.* [*often: before a noun*] considered to be lacking wealth or industry; poor: *The developing nations of the world were hit hardest by the rise in oil prices.*

de•vi•ate /'diyviy,eyt/ *v.* [*no obj*], **-at•ed, -at•ing,** to turn away from what is expected or usual: *The witness deviated from the truth.*

de•vi•a•tion /,diyviy'eyʃən/ *n.* **1.** [*noncount*] behavior that differs or departs from what is thought of as normal or standard. **2.** [*count*] an example of differing from what is expected; a change: *Some deviations from the regular readings on the compass were due to the presence of metal objects.*

de•vice /dɪ'vays/ *n.* [*count*] **1.** a thing made for a particular purpose: *She invented a device that*

automatically closes windows when it rains. **2.** a plan, scheme, or trick: *full of devices for arousing sympathy.*

dev•il /'dɛvəl/ *n.* **1.** the supreme spirit of evil; Satan: *The preacher warned that the devil would take their souls.* **2.** [*count*] *Informal.* a clever or mischievous person: *Those little devils poured a bucket of water on my head.* **3.** [*count*] an unlucky person: *That poor devil never knew what hit him.* —'**dev•il•ish,** *adj.*

de•vi•ous /'diyviyəs/ *adj.* **1.** departing or turning away from the most direct way; roundabout: *a devious course.* **2.** dishonest: *His devious business methods landed him in trouble.* —'**de•vi•ous•ly,** *adv.* —'**de•vi•ous•ness,** *n.* [*noncount*]: *the necessary deviousness to be a thief.*

de•vise /dɪ'vayz/ *v.* [~ + *obj*], **-vised, -vis•ing.** to plan, invent, or create: *to devise a method.*

de•void /dɪ'vɔyd/ *adj.* not possessing; totally lacking; empty of: *The judge was devoid of any sympathy.*

de•vote /dɪ'vowt/ *v.* [~ + *obj*], **-vot•ed, -vot•ing.** to apply (something) to a particular purpose; set apart or dedicate to: *to devote more of his time to study.*

de•vot•ed /dɪ'vowtɪd/ *adj.* **1.** relating to or marked by devotion: *a devoted friend.* **2.** [*before a noun*] involving great care or attention: *decades of devoted research.* —**de'vot•ed•ly,** *adv.*

dev•o•tee /,dɛvə'tiy, -'tey/ *n.* [*count*] one who is enthusiastic about something; a fan.

de•vo•tion /dɪ'vowʃən/ *n.* **1.** [*noncount*] serious attachment to a cause, person, religion, etc.: *His devotion to his children is plain to see.* **2.** Often, **devotions.** [*plural*] prayers. —**de'vo•tion•al,** *adj.* [*before a noun*]: *devotional candles.*

de•vour /dɪ'vawr/ *v.* [~ + *obj*] **1.** to swallow or eat up hungrily: *He devoured several helpings of stew.* **2.** to consume completely; demolish; destroy: *Fire devoured the museum.* **3.** to take in eagerly with the senses or mind: *He devoured one book after another.*

de•vout /dɪ'vawt/ *adj.*, **-er, -est. 1.** religious: *a devout Hindu.* **2.** [*before a noun*] serious; earnest; sincere: *a devout admirer of French painting.* —**de'vout•ly,** *adv.* —**de'vout•ness,** *n.* [*noncount*]

dew /duw, dyuw/ *n.* [*noncount*] moisture from the atmosphere, esp. at night, deposited in small drops upon a cool surface: *beads of dew on the grass.* —'**dew•y,** *adj.*, **-i•er, -i•est.**

'**dew ,point,** *n.* [*count*] temperature at which dew begins to form.

dex•ter•i•ty /dɛk'stɛrɪtiy/ *n.* [*noncount*] skill in using the body or mind, esp. the hands: *manual dexterity.*

dex•ter•ous /'dɛkstrəs, -stərəs/ *adj.* skillful or nimble in the use of the hands, body, or mind.

dex•trose /'dɛkstrows/ *n.* [*noncount*] a form of glucose or sugar occurring in fruits and in animal tissues.

di•a•be•tes /,dayə'biytɪs, -tiyz/ *n.* [*noncount*; *used with a singular verb*] a disorder in which there are high levels of glucose in the blood.

di•a•bet•ic /,dayə'bɛtɪk/ *n.* [*count*] **1.** a person suffering from diabetes. —*adj.* [*before a noun*] **2.** of or relating to diabetics or diabetes: *diabetic medicine.*

di•a•bol•ic /,dayə'bɒlɪk/ also ,**di•a'bol•i•cal,** *adj.* devilish; fiendish; extremely wicked: *a diabolic plot to kill the president.* —'**di•a'bol•i•cal•ly,** *adv.*

di•ag•nose /'dayəg,nows/ *v.* [~ + *obj*],

-nosed, -nos•ing. 1. to determine the identity of (a disease, etc.) by an examination: *His doctor diagnosed cancer of the liver.* **2.** to determine the cause or nature of (a problem) from the visible signs: *The car mechanic diagnosed the problem.*

di•ag•no•sis /ˌdayəg'nowsıs/ *n., pl.* **-ses** /-siyz/. [*noncount*] [*count*] an analysis of the cause or nature of a problem or disease: *A diagnosis would require a full-day examination; careful diagnosis of the problems in our schools.* —**di•ag•nos•tic** /ˌdayəg'nɒstık/, *adj.* —**di•ag•nos•ti•cian** /ˌdayəgnɒ'stıʃən/, *n.* [*count*]

di•ag•o•nal /day'ægənļ/ *adj.* **1.** connecting two angles that are not next to each other, such as at opposite corners of a square: *a diagonal line.* **2.** having a slanting direction: *diagonal stripes.* [*count*] **3.** a diagonal line or plane. —**di'ag•o•nal•ly,** *adv.*

di•a•gram /'dayəˌgræm/ *n., v.,* **-gramed** or **-grammed, -gram•ing** or **-gram•ming.** —*n.* [*count*] **1.** a drawing that outlines and explains the parts or operation of something: *a diagram of an engine.* **2.** a chart or plan: *The first diagram is a pie chart showing spending.* —*v.* [~ + *obj*] **3.** to represent by a diagram; make a diagram of.

di•al /'dayəl, dayl/ *n., v.,* **di•aled** or **di•alled, di•al•ing** or **di•al•ling.** —*n.* [*count*] **1.** a marked plate or disk on a clock or watch, upon which the time of day is indicated by hands or pointers. **2.** a plate with marks for indicating a measurement or number, usually by means of a pointer: *the dials on a gas meter.* **3.** a rotatable knob on a radio or television for tuning in stations. **4.** a rotatable disk on a telephone that is used in making calls. —*v.* [~ + *obj*] **5.** to select by means of a dial: *I dialed (in) a country-and-western station on the radio.* **6.** [~ + *obj*] to make a telephone call to: *I dialed your number but got a busy signal.*

di•a•lect /'dayəˌlɛkt/ *n.* a variety of a language spoken in a certain region. [*count*]: *Cockney is the colorful dialect spoken in the East End of London.* [*noncount*]: *He lapsed into dialect.* —**di•a•lect•al** /ˌdayə'lɛktļ/, *adj.: dialectal differences.*

di•a•logue or **di•a•log** /'dayəˌlɔg, -ˌlɒg/ *n.* [*count*] **1.** a conversation between two or more persons, or between two or more characters in a novel, drama, etc. **2.** an exchange of ideas or opinions.

di•am•e•ter /day'æmıtər/ *n.* [*count*] a straight line passing through the center of a circle or sphere.

di•a•met•ri•cal•ly /ˌdayə'mɛtrıkliy/ *adv.* in direct opposition; at opposite extremes: *diametrically opposed opinions.*

dia•mond /'daymənd, 'dayə-/ *n.* [*count*] **1.** a very hard, bright, precious gem. **2.** a four-sided figure with sides of equal length but with no right angles. **3.** a red figure shaped that way on a playing card. **4.** the infield or the entire playing field in baseball.

di•a•per /'daypər, 'dayəpər/ *n.* [*count*] **1.** a piece of folded cloth or other absorbent material worn as underpants by a baby: *disposable diapers.* —*v.* [~ + *obj*] **2.** to put a diaper on: *He diapered the baby.*

di•a•phragm /'dayəˌfræm/ *n.* [*count*] **1.** a wall of muscle separating the chest and abdomen: *When the diaphragm contracts uncontrollably, you get hiccups.* **2.** a thin vibrating disk, as in a telephone. **3.** a thin, dome-shaped, rubber contraceptive device that covers the cervix. **4.** a de-

vice in a camera that controls the amount of light entering the instrument.

di•ar•rhe•a or **di•ar•rhoe•a** /ˌdayə'riyə/ *n.* [*noncount*] an intestinal illness with frequent and loose bowel movements: *a bad case of diarrhea.*

di•a•ry /'dayəriy/ *n.* [*count*], *pl.* **-ries.** (a book for) a daily written record of events and feelings: *She wrote in her diary.* —**di•a•rist** /'dayərıst/, *n.* [*count*]

di•a•tribe /'dayəˌtrayb/ *n.* [*count*] a bitter criticism or act of denouncing: *In her diatribe, she gave full vent to all her resentments.*

dice /days/ *n. pl., sing.* **die,** **diced, dic•ing.** —*n.* [*plural*] **1.** small cubes, marked on each side with one to six spots, used in games or gambling: *We rolled the dice and I had a ten.* —*v.* [~ + *obj*] **2.** to cut into small cubes: *Dice the vegetables.*

dic•tate /*v.* 'dıkteyt, dık'teyt; *n.* 'dıkteyt/ *v.* **-tat•ed, -tat•ing,** *n.* —*v.* [~ + *obj*] **1.** to say or read out loud for another person to write down: *She dictated a memo to her secretary.* **2.** to order forcefully: *The victorious nations were able to dictate peace terms.* —*n.* [*count*] **3.** an order or direction: *Usually their dictates are to be obeyed.*

dic•ta•tion /dık'teyʃən/ *n.* **1.** the act of dictating: [*noncount*]: *She took a test in French dictation.* [*count*]: *Our teacher is always giving us dictations.* **2.** [*noncount*] the act of commanding: *There's no need for dictation from above.*

dic•ta•tor /'dıkteytər, dık'teytər/ *n.* [*count*] a ruler who has absolute power without the consent of the people. —**dic'ta•tor,ship,** *n.* [*noncount*] [*count*]

dic•ta•to•ri•al /ˌdıktə'tɔriyəl/ *adj.* **1.** of or relating to a dictator: *a president with no dictatorial powers.* **2.** overly demanding; controlling: *I resented his dictatorial manner.*

dic•tion /'dıkʃən/ *n.* [*noncount*] style of speaking or writing: *Her poor diction made her difficult to understand.*

dic•tion•ar•y /'dıkʃəˌneriy/ *n.* [*count*], *pl.* **-ies.** a book containing words, usually in alphabetical order, with information about their meanings, pronunciations, special forms, etc.

did /dıd/ *v.* pt. of DO[1].

didn't /'dıdnt/ contraction of *did not: He didn't go home until midnight.*

die[1] /day/ *v.* [*no obj*], **died, dy•ing. 1.** to cease to live; perish: *How many people died in the war? He died of thirst or starvation. He died from a gunshot wound.* **2.** to lose power: *The engine died.* **3.** *Informal.* to desire strongly or wish for keenly: *I'm dying for a cup of coffee. I'm dying to go back to the mountains.* **4. die away,** (of a sound) to become fainter and then cease altogether: *The laughter died away.* **5. die down,** to become calm or quiet: *The storm died down quickly.* **6. die off,** to die one after another until the number is greatly reduced: *All her old friends were dying off.* **7. die out, a.** to cease to exist; become extinct: *Little corner stores are in danger of dying out.* **b.** to die away; fade; subside: *Gradually the roar died out and the night became quiet.*

die[2] /day/ *n.* [*count*], *pl.* **dies** for 1, **dice** for 2. **1.** any of various devices for cutting or forming material in a press or a stamping machine. **2.** the singular form of DICE: *One die rolled right off the table.* —*Idiom.* **3. the die is cast,** a decision has been made and cannot be changed: *The die is cast—I just mailed my boyfriend a letter saying I want to break up.*

D

die•sel /'diyzəl, -səl/ *adj.* [*often: before a noun*] **1.** being or referring to a machine or vehicle powered by a diesel engine: *a diesel locomotive.* —*n.* **2.** [*count*] Also, **diesel engine.** an engine powered by heated oil, used by buses, trucks, and some cars. **3.** [*count*] a vehicle powered by a diesel engine: *Some diesels have trouble starting on cold days.* **4.** [*noncount*] Also, **diesel oil.** a type of heavy fuel oil used in a diesel engine.

di•et /'dayıt/ *n.* [*count*] **1.** the foods usually eaten by a person, animal, or group: *They live on a diet of roots, honey, and berries.* **2.** a limited list of food that one is allowed: *I'm going on a diet so I can lose 10 pounds. The doctor put her on a low-salt diet.* —*v.* [*no obj*] **3.** to select or limit the food one eats, esp. to lose weight: *No dessert for me, thanks, I'm dieting.* —**di•e•tar•y** /'dayı,tɛriy/ *adj.* —'**di•et•er,** *n.* [*count*]

di•e•ti•tian or **di•e•ti•cian** /,dayı'tıʃən/ *n.* [*count*] a person who is an expert in nutrition.

dif•fer /'dıfər/ *v.* [*no obj*] **1.** to be unlike: *The two candidates differ in style and substance. This candidate differed from the others.* **2.** to disagree: *They differed sharply in their approach to tax credits. I differ with my partner sometimes, but we usually agree.*

dif•fer•ence /'dıfərəns, 'dıfrəns/ *n.* **1.** [*noncount*] the state of being different. **2.** [*noncount*] a significant change in a situation: *It made no difference what I said.* **3.** the degree to which one person or thing differs from another: [*count; usually singular*]: *The difference in their ages is about six months.* [*noncount*]: *There isn't much difference between one convenience store and another.* **4.** [*count*] a disagreement: *a strong difference of opinion.*

dif•fer•ent /'dıfərənt, 'dıfrənt/ *adj.* **1.** not alike: *Her hat is different from yours.* **2.** separate: *three different answers.* **3.** [*before a plural noun*] various; several: *Different people told me the same story.* —'**dif•fer•ent•ly,** *adv.*: *They behaved differently when alone.* ——**Usage.** Although DIFFERENT FROM is more common today in introducing a phrase, DIFFERENT THAN is also used: *New York speech is different from/than that of Chicago.* DIFFERENT THAN is usually used when a clause follows, especially when the word "from" would create an awkward sentence: *The stream followed a different course than the map showed.*

dif•fer•en•tial /,dıfə'rɛnʃəl/ *adj.* **1.** of or relating to difference. —*n.* [*count*] **2.** the amount of difference between comparable things: *a wage differential between police and firefighters.*

dif•fer•en•ti•ate /,dıfə'rɛnʃiy,eyt/ *v.,* **-at•ed, -at•ing. 1.** [~ + *obj*] to form or mark differently from other such things; distinguish: *The chrome trim and tinted glass differentiate the high-price model from the standard one.* **2.** [*no obj*] to see, understand, or notice the difference in or between: *She learned to differentiate between French and German wines.* —**dif•fer•en•ti•a•tion** /,dıfə,rɛnʃiy'eyʃən/, *n.* [*noncount*]

dif•fi•cult /'dıfı,kʌlt, -kəlt/ *adj.* **1.** requiring special skill; not easy: *a difficult job; It was difficult (for her) to get a good job.* **2.** hard to deal with or get along with: *a difficult pupil.* —'**dif•fi,cult•ly,** *adv.*

dif•fi•cul•ty /'dıfı,kʌltiy/ *n., pl.* **-ties. 1.** [*noncount*] the fact or condition of being difficult: *The difficulty of the courses was too much for some students.* **2.** [*count*] Often, **difficulties.** [*plural*] an embarrassing situation, esp. of financial affairs: *We had difficulties paying our bills each month.*

dif•fi•dent /'dıfıdənt/ *adj.* lacking confidence in one's own ability: *He's diffident in saying what he thinks.* —'**dif•fi•dence,** *n.* [*noncount*]: *Their diffidence keeps them from making new friends.*

dif•fuse /*v.*dı'fyuwz; *adj.* -'fyuws/ *v.,* **-fused, -fusing,** *adj.* —*v.* **1.** to (cause to) spread or scatter widely: [*no obj*]: *The light diffused into the room.* [~ + *obj*]: *The printing press helped diffuse knowledge.* —*adj.* **2.** widely spread or scattered: *The room was bathed in soft, diffuse light.* **3.** using too many words in speech or writing: *I got lost in your rather diffuse essay.* —**dif'fuse•ly,** /dı'fyuwsliy/, *adv.* —**dif'fuse•ness,** *n.* [*noncount*] —**dif•fu•sion** /dı'fyuwʒən/, *n.* [*noncount*]: *diffusion of gases into the atmosphere.* —**dif•fu•sive** /dı'fyuwsıv/, *adj.*

dig /dıg/ *v.,* **dug** /dʌg/ **dig•ging,** *n.* —*v.* **1.** to break up and turn over earth, sand, etc., as with a shovel or spade: [*no obj*]: *We were digging in the tunnel most of the day.* [~ + *obj*]: *The little gopher digs a maze of tunnels underground.* **2.** [*no obj*] to work by or as if by removing or turning over material: *I'll have to dig through the old files.* **3. dig in, a.** to keep to one's opinion or position: *The negotiators dug in and refused to budge.* **b.** *Informal.* to start eating: *We dug in as soon as the food came out of the kitchen.* **4. dig out, a.** to hollow out by digging; free (something) by digging around: *We dug the car out of the snow. We dug out his car and got it going.* **b.** to find or discover by searching: *I dug out an old pair of shoes and a jacket from the 60's.* **5. dig up,** to discover in the course of digging and remove from the ground: *The rescue workers dug up nearly fifty bodies in the rubble. The coroner dug the body up and performed another autopsy.* —*n.* [*count*] **6.** a thrust; poke: *a quick dig in the ribs.* **7.** a cutting, sarcastic remark: *Someone had to get in a dig about my freckles.* **8.** an archaeological site being uncovered: *We visited the dig and saw the tools they had discovered.* —'**dig•ger,** *n.* [*count*]

dig•e•ra•ti /,dıdʒə'ratiy, -'rey-/ *n.* [*plural; used with a plural verb*] people who are skilled with or knowledgeable about computers.

di•gest /*v.*dı'dʒɛst, day-; *n.* 'daydʒɛst/ *v.* **1.** (of food) to (cause to) change or be changed into a form that the body can use: [*no obj*]: *Some foods don't digest easily.* [~ + *obj*]: *The baby had a hard time digesting such rich food.* **2.** [~ + *obj*] to obtain ideas or meaning from; think over; take into the mind: *I tried to digest this article on nuclear energy.* —*n.* [*count*] **3.** a collection of condensed writing; summary: *a thirty-page digest of the news.* —**di'gest•i•ble,** *adj.*: *The food was easily digestible.* —**di'ges•tion** /dı'dʒɛstʃən, day-/ *n.* [*noncount*] [*count; usually singular*] —**di'ges•tive,** *adj.*

dig•it /'dıdʒıt/ *n.* [*count*] **1.** any of the Arabic numerals of 1 through 9 and 0. **2.** a finger or toe.

dig•it•al /'dıdʒıtl/ *adj.* **1.** relating to or resembling a digit or finger. **2.** relating to or using data in the form of numerical digits: *a digital computer; a digital recording of the opera.* **3.** displaying the time by numerical digits rather than by hands on a dial: *a digital clock.* —'**dig•it•al•ly,** *adv.*

dig•ni•fied /'dıgnə,fayd/ *adj.* having or showing dignity.

dig•ni•fy /'dıgnə,fay/ *v.* [~ + *obj*], **-fied, -fy•ing.** to confer honor or dignity upon; honor.

dig•ni•tar•y /'dɪgnɪ,tɛriy/ n. [count], pl. **-tar•ies.** a person who holds a high rank or office.

dig•ni•ty /'dɪgnɪtiy/ n., pl. **-ties. 1.** [count; usually singular] appearance and conduct that show self-respect and formality: She maintained her dignity throughout the trial. **2.** [noncount] elevated rank, office, station, etc.: the dignity of the high court.

di•gress /dɪ'grɛs, day-/ v. [no obj] to wander away from the main topic: Let me digress for a moment and tell you a short story. —**di•gres•sion** /dɪ'grɛʃən, day-/, n. [noncount]: There's too much digression in your essay. [count]: a short digression from the topic. —**di•gres•sive,** adj.

dike or **dyke** /dayk/ n. [count] **1.** a thick wall for holding back the waters of the sea or a river. **2.** DITCH.

di•lap•i•dat•ed /dɪ'læpɪ,deytɪd/ adj. fallen into partial ruin or decay, such as from age, misuse, wear, or neglect: We bought a dilapidated old house. —**di•lap•i•da•tion** /dɪ,læpɪ'deyʃən/, n. [noncount]: a state of dilapidation.

di•late /day'leyt, 'dayleyt/ v., **-lat•ed, -lat•ing.** to (cause to) become wider, larger, or expanded: [no obj]: The cat's eyes dilated in the darkness. [~ + obj]: The medicine will dilate the blood vessels. —**di•la•tion** /day'leyʃən/, n. [noncount]

dil•a•to•ry /'dɪlə,tɔriy/ adj. tending to delay; intending to gain time: a dilatory strategy.

di•lem•ma /dɪ'lɛmə/ n. [count], pl. **-mas.** a difficult choice: I was in a dilemma: should I continue to work or go back to school?

dil•i•gence /'dɪlɪdʒəns/ n. [noncount] carefulness in work: We examined our accounting procedures with diligence.

dil•i•gent /'dɪlɪdʒənt/ adj. **1.** constant, careful, and serious in effort and work: a diligent student. **2.** done with careful attention: a diligent search. —**dil•i•gent•ly,** adv.

dill /dɪl/ n. **1.** [noncount] a plant of the parsley family having sweet-smelling seeds and finely divided leaves used as a flavoring. **2.** [count] Also, **dill pickle.** a kind of pickle prepared with vinegar, dill, and other spices.

di•lute /dɪ'luwt, day-/ v. [~ + obj], **-lut•ed, -lut•ing. 1.** to make (a liquid) thinner or weaker by the addition of water or other liquid: Dilute the ammonia with water before you use it. **2.** to reduce the strength of, as by adding or mixing something: The professor's proposals were diluted by the lack of support from his department. —**di•lu•tion** /dɪ'luwʃən, day-/, n. [noncount]

dim /dɪm/ adj., **dim•mer, dim•mest,** v., **dimmed, dim•ming.** —adj. **1.** not bright; lacking light: a dim room. **2.** not seen clearly, distinctly, or in detail; indistinct; faint: a dim outline. **3.** not seeing clearly: My eyes were dim with tears. **4.** not likely to happen, succeed, or be favorable: a dim chance of winning. —v. **5.** to (cause to) become or grow dim or dimmer: The lights dimmed and the show started. [~ + obj]: Would someone please dim the lights? —**Idiom. 6. take a dim view of,** to regard with disapproval or mild disbelief: She takes a dim view of my attempts to make changes. —**'dim•ly,** adv. —**'dim•ness,** n. [noncount]

dime /daym/ n. [count] **1.** a coin of the U.S. and Canada worth 10 cents. —**Idiom. 2. a dime a dozen,** common, abundant, and thus of little value: Such proposals are a dime a dozen.

di•men•sion /dɪ'mɛnʃən/ n. [count] **1.** a measurement of length, width, or thickness; size: **2.** Usually, **dimensions.** [plural] the scope or impor-

tance (of a problem or situation); magnitude; size: No one understood the dimensions of the problem. —**di'men•sion•al,** adj.

di•min•ish /dɪ'mɪnɪʃ/ v. to (cause to) seem smaller, decrease, or be reduced: [no obj]: Suddenly the wind diminished and the seas grew calm again. [~ + obj]: Time will not diminish our friendship. —**di'min•ished,** adj.: the diminished supply of firewood. —**di'min•ish•ing,** adj.: We now face the problem of diminishing returns.

di•min•u•tive /dɪ'mɪnyətɪv/ adj. smaller than the average; tiny: The Pygmies are a diminutive people.

dim•ple /'dɪmpəl/ n. [count] a small natural hollow formed in the cheek in smiling.

din /dɪn/ n. [count; usually singular] a loud, confused, continued noise: the din from the neighbor's party.

dine /dayn/ v. [no obj], **dined, din•ing.** to eat a meal, esp. the principal meal of the day; have dinner: We'll dine with our friends tonight at about eight.

din•er /'daynər/ n. [count] **1.** a person who dines, esp. in a restaurant. **2.** a railroad car in which food is served. **3.** an inexpensive restaurant.

din•gy /'dɪndʒiy/ adj., **-gi•er, -gi•est.** shabby; dirty-looking; dark: a dingy little hotel room. —**'din•gi•ness,** n. [noncount]: The darkness couldn't hide the dinginess of the room.

'dining ,room, n. [count] a room in which meals are eaten.

din•ner /'dɪnər/ n. **1.** the main meal of the day: [noncount]: We usually have dinner around six or six-thirty. [count]: We ate our dinners outside. **2.** [count] a formal meal in honor of some person or occasion.

di•no•saur /'daynə,sɔr/ n. [count] any of various plant- or flesh-eating reptiles of prehistoric times, most of which had long tails and were very large.

dint /dɪnt/ n. [noncount] —**Idiom. by dint of,** by the force of; through the power of: to achieve success by dint of hard work.

di•o•cese /'dayəsɪs, -,siyz, -,siys/ n. [count] a district under the rule of a bishop. —**di•oc•e•san** /day'ɒsəsən/, adj. [before a noun]: the diocesan newsletter.

dip /dɪp/ v., **dipped, dip•ping,** n. —v. **1.** [~ + obj] to plunge quickly into a liquid, so as to moisten, dye, or take up some of the liquid: She dipped the blouse into the hot water. **2. dip into, a.** to reach down into so as to remove something: They dipped into the pot and pulled out some lobsters. **b.** to remove something in small amounts: to dip into one's savings. **c.** to read briefly about a subject: to dip into astronomy. **3.** [no obj] to sink; go downward: The sun dipped below the horizon. **4.** [no obj] to go down slightly or briefly: Stock-market prices often dip on Fridays. —n. [count] **5.** the act of dipping. **6.** a small or brief decrease, such as in money, prices, etc. **7.** a downward slope or movement: a dip in the road. **8.** a tasty snack: a quick dip before lunch.

diph•the•ri•a /dɪf'θɪriyə, dɪp-/ n. [noncount] a serious infectious disease affecting the nose and throat.

diph•thong /'dɪfθɒŋ, -θɔŋ, 'dɪp-/ n. [count] a vowel sound that glides slightly from one sound to another but is considered to be a single sound, as the (oy) sound of toy or boil.

di•plo•ma /dɪ'plowmə/ n. [count], pl. **-mas.** a

D

document given by a school or college stating that one has completed a course of study.

di•plo•ma•cy /dɪ'ploʊməsiy/ *n.* [noncount] **1.** the management of relations between nations: *international diplomacy.* **2.** skill in managing people: *We'll need a lot of diplomacy to tell him he's fired.*

dip•lo•mat /'dɪplə,mæt/ *n.* [count] a person appointed by a national government to conduct official relations with other countries.

dip•lo•mat•ic /,dɪplə'mætɪk/ *adj.* **1.** [before a noun] of, relating to, or engaged in diplomacy: *a diplomatic post; the diplomatic corps.* **2.** skilled in dealing with sensitive matters or people: *He's diplomatic enough not to bring up such a private topic.* —,**dip•lo•mat•i•cal•ly,** *adv.*: *She handled the problem very diplomatically.*

dip•per /'dɪpər/ *n.* [count] **1.** a person or thing that dips. **2.** a cuplike container with a long handle, used for dipping.

dip•so•ma•ni•a /,dɪpsə'meyniyə, -sow-/ *n.* [noncount] an uncontrollable desire for alcoholic drink. —**dip•so'ma•ni,ac,** *n.* [count]

dire /dayⁿr/ *adj.,* **dir•er, dir•est. 1.** involving great fear or suffering; terrible: *dire consequences.* **2.** desperate: *in dire need of help.*

di•rect /dɪ'rɛkt, day-/ *v.* **1.** [~ + *obj*] to manage or guide by advice, instruction, etc.; supervise: *She directs the affairs of the estate.* **2.** [~ + *obj*] to give instructions to; order: *I directed him to leave the room.* **3.** to serve as a director in the production or performance of (a play, etc.): [~ + *obj*]: *He directed five movies.* [no *obj*]: *He directs with great skill.* **4.** [~ + *obj*] to tell or show (a person) the way to a place; guide: *Can you direct me to the center of town?* **5.** [~ + *obj*] to address (words, a speech, a letter, etc.) to a person or persons: *She directed her remarks to the chairman.* —*adj.* **6.** going in a straight line or by the shortest course; straight: *a direct route.* **7.** going in an unbroken line; with nothing in between: *a direct descendant; direct contact.* **8.** straightforward; honest: *I want you to be as direct as possible.* **9.** [before a noun] absolute; exact: *the direct opposite.* —*adv.* **10.** in a direct manner; directly; straight: *We flew direct to Moscow.* —**di'rect•ness,** *n.* [noncount]: *The directness of her answers startled me.*

di•rec•tion /dɪ'rɛkʃən, day-/ *n.* **1.** the point toward which anything lies, faces, or moves: [count]: *We wandered off in the wrong direction. The direction is north. We headed out in several directions at once.* [noncount]: *I have a bad sense of direction.* **2.** Usually, **directions.** [plural] instructions or guidance: *confusing directions for assembling the furniture.* **3.** [noncount] management; control; supervision: *Under his direction the company's profits soared.* —**di'rec•tion•al,** *adj.* [before a noun]: *I turned on the car's right directional signal.*

di•rec•tive /dɪ'rɛktɪv, day-/ *adj.* **1.** serving to direct; directing. —*n.* [count] **2.** an instruction or direction; an order: *He received a directive from headquarters.*

di•rect•ly /dɪ'rɛktliy, day-/ *adv.* **1.** in a direct line; straight: *She drove directly to school.* **2.** at once; without delay: *He left directly and didn't come back till later.* **3.** truthfully: *Don't be afraid to speak directly.*

di'rect 'object, *n.* [count] a word or group of words representing the person or thing on which the action of a verb is performed, or toward which it is directed: *The pronoun it in I saw it is the direct object.*

di•rec•tor /dɪ'rɛktər, day-/ *n.* [count] **1.** a person or thing that directs, esp. one of a group of persons chosen to govern the affairs of a company. **2.** one who supervises the development of a theater, film, television, or radio production. —**di'rec•tor,ship,** *n.* [noncount]

di•rec•to•rate /dɪ'rɛktərɪt, day-/ *n.* [count] **1.** the office of a director. **2.** a body of directors.

di•rec•to•ry /dɪ'rɛktəriy, day-/ *n.* [count], *pl.* **-ries.** a list of the names and addresses of persons in an area or organization: *the telephone directory.*

dirge /dɜrdʒ/ *n.* [count] a funeral song to mourn and honor the dead.

dirt /dɜrt/ *n.* [noncount] **1.** any foul or filthy substance, such as mud: *I couldn't get the dirt off my clothes.* **2.** earth or soil, esp. when loose: *good dirt for growing vegetables.* **3.** something or someone vile or worthless: *She treated me like dirt.* **4.** obscene talk.

'dirt-'cheap, *adj.* **1.** very cheap: *dirt-cheap prices.* —*adv.* **2.** very cheaply: *bought it dirt-cheap.*

dirt•y /'dɜrtiy/ *adj.,* **-i•er, -i•est,** *v.,* **-ied, -y•ing,** —*adj.* **1.** soiled with dirt: *He had to wash his dirty hands.* **2.** spreading dirt; soiling: *dirty smoke.* **3.** vile; mean; deserving contempt: *a dirty scoundrel.* **4.** obscene; pornographic: *a dirty joke; dirty pictures.* **5.** undesirable or unpleasant; disagreeable: *You left the dirty work for me.* **6.** not fair; dishonest; dishonorable: *a dirty fighter.* —*v.* **7.** to make or become dirty: [~ + *obj*]: *Try not to dirty your new white shoes.* [no *obj*]: *Those white socks dirty easily.* —**dirt•i•ly** /'dɜrtliy/, *adv.* —'**dirt•i•ness,** *n.* [noncount]

dis /dɪs/ *v.,* **dissed, dis•sing,** *n. Slang.* —*v.* [~ + *obj*] **1.** to show a lack of respect for (someone). **2.** to make (someone) feel unimportant; disparage. —*n.* [count] **3.** disparagement or criticism.

dis-, a prefix meaning: reverse or remove (*disconnect; dissolve*); opposite or lack of (*disagreement*); not (*dishonest*).

dis•a•bil•i•ty /,dɪsə'bɪlɪtiy/ *n.,* *pl.* **-ties. 1.** [noncount] lack of strength or ability: *a life of disability.* **2.** [count] a physical or mental handicap: *His disabilities were not going to stand in his way.*

dis•a•ble /dɪs'eybəl/ *v.* [~ + *obj*], **-bled, -bling.** to make unable or unfit; weaken or destroy the capability of; cripple: *That illness disabled him and left him unable to work.*

dis'a•bled, *adj.* **1.** handicapped: *He was disabled because of polio.* —*n.* [noncount; the + ~] **2.** disabled people: *It is now illegal to discriminate against the disabled in hiring practices.*

dis•a•buse /,dɪsə'byuwz/ *v.* [~ + *obj*], **-bused, -bus•ing.** to free (someone) from deception or error: *Let me disabuse you of that foolish idea.*

dis•ad•van•tage /,dɪsəd'væntɪdʒ/ *n.* [count; usually singular] an unfavorable position or condition. —**dis•ad•van•ta•geous** /dɪs,ædvən'teydʒəs/, *adj.*

dis•ad•van•taged /,dɪsəd'væntɪdʒd/ *adj.* **1.** lacking the necessities and comforts of life: *disadvantaged families.* —*n.* **the disadvantaged,** [plural; used with a plural verb] **2.** people who lack such necessities and comforts.

dis•af•fect•ed *adj.* discontented; not loyal: *the millions of disaffected voters.*

dis•a•gree /,dɪsə'griy/ *v.* **1.** [no *obj*] to fail to agree; differ: *I'm afraid our conclusions disagree.* **2. disagree with, a.** to differ in opinion; dissent: *Three of the judges disagreed with the verdict.* **b.** (of the weather, food, etc.) to cause physical discomfort; have ill effects on: *Oysters disagree with me.* —**dis•a'gree•ment,** *n.* [noncount]: *The two sides are in disagreement.* [count]: *We had a violent disagreement.*

dis•a•gree•a•ble /ˌdɪsə'griyəbəl/ *adj.* unpleasant. —**,dis•a'gree•a•bly,** *adv.*

dis•al•low /ˌdɪsə'law/ *v.* [~ + *obj*] to reject; refuse to allow or accept: *The judge disallowed our claim.*

dis•ap•pear /ˌdɪsə'pɪər/ *v.* [no *obj*] **1.** to go out of sight: *The sun disappeared beneath the horizon.* **2.** to cease to exist: *Dinosaurs disappeared millions of years ago.* —**,dis•ap'pear•ance,** *n.* [count] [noncount]

dis•ap•point /ˌdɪsə'pɔynt/ *v.* [~ + *obj*] **1.** to fail to reach the expectations, hopes, or wishes of: *That last job rejection disappointed me badly.* **2.** to defeat the fulfillment of: *to disappoint hopes.* —**,dis•ap'point•ed,** *adj.*: *The disappointed team went home after their loss.* —**,dis•ap'point•ing,** *adj.*: *It was a disappointing loss.* —**,dis•ap'point•ment,** *n.* [noncount]: *The actress learned to handle disappointment.* [count]: *His third novel was a big disappointment.*

dis•ap•prove /ˌdɪsə'pruwv/ *v.* [no *obj*], **-proved, -prov•ing.** to have or express an unfavorable opinion: *She wants to go away to college but her parents disapprove.* —**,dis•ap'prov•al,** *n.* [noncount]: *to give a frowning look of disapproval.* —**,dis•ap'prov•ing•ly,** *adv.*

dis•arm /dɪs'ɑrm/ *v.* **1.** [~ + *obj*] to take away weapons from (someone): *The police disarmed the remaining suspects.* **2.** [~ + *obj*] to take away anger, suspicion, etc.; charm: *She can always disarm me with one of her happy little smiles.* **3.** [no *obj*] (of a country) to reduce armed forces: *The superpowers never agreed to disarm.* —**dis'ar•ma•ment,** *n.* [noncount]

dis•ar•range /ˌdɪsə'reyndʒ/ *v.* [~ + *obj*], **-ranged, -rang•ing.** to disturb; unsettle: *The kids came in and disarranged the place.*

dis•ar•ray /ˌdɪsə'rey/ *n.* [noncount] disorder; confusion: *The unsupervised class was in total disarray.*

dis•as•so•ci•ate /ˌdɪsə'sowʃiy,eyt, -siy-/ *v.* [~ + *obj*], **-at•ed, -at•ing.** to dissociate.

dis•as•ter /dɪ'zæstər/ *n.* [count] **1.** a great calamity or catastrophe: *The earthquake was a terrible disaster for that town.* **2.** a great misfortune: *His defeat in the election was a disaster for his political career.* —**dis'as•trous,** *adj.*: *a disastrous earthquake.* —**dis'as•trous•ly,** *adv.*

dis•a•vow /ˌdɪsə'vaw/ *v.* [~ + *obj*] to deny knowledge of, connection with, or responsibility for: *The director disavowed any knowledge of my actions.* —**,dis•a'vow•al,** *n.* [noncount]: *disavowal of any knowledge.* [count]: *She issued a disavowal of that position.*

dis•band /dɪs'bænd/ *v.* to (cause to) break up or dissolve (an organization): [no *obj*]: *The organization disbanded when its leader was arrested.* [~ + *obj*]: *The government tried to disband his little organization.*

dis•bar /dɪs'bɑr/ *v.* [~ + *obj*], **-barred, -bar•ring.** to expel from the legal profession: *The lawyer was disbarred for his unethical behavior.* —**dis'bar•ment,** *n.* [noncount]: *She faced disbarment for perjury.*

dis•be•lief /ˌdɪsbɪ'liyf/ *n.* [noncount] refusing to believe: *My disbelief in his alibi was obvious.*

dis•be•lieve /ˌdɪsbɪ'liyv/ *v.* [~ + *obj*], **-lieved, -liev•ing.** to have no belief in; refuse or reject belief in: *I disbelieved him and his story.*

dis•burse /dɪs'bərs/ *v.* [~ + *obj*], **-bursed, -burs•ing.** to pay out (money), esp. for expenses. —**dis'burse•ment,** *n.* [noncount]

disc /dɪsk/ *n.* [count] **1.** a phonograph record. **2.** DISK.

dis•card /*v.*dɪ'skɑrd; *n.* 'dɪskɑrd/ *v.* [~ + *obj*] **1.** to throw away; get rid of: *We discarded some old clothes.* —*n.* [count] **2.** a person or thing that is cast out, rejected, or thrown out.

dis•cern /dɪ'sɜrn/ *v.* [~ + *obj*] to see or understand; recognize: *She could discern a faint light ahead in the forest; to discern right from wrong.* —**dis'cern•i•ble, dis'cern•a•ble,** *adj.*: *The light was barely discernible in the distance.* —**dis'cern•ment,** *n.* [noncount]

dis•cern•ing /dɪ'sɜrnɪŋ/ *adj.* showing good judgment and understanding: *The student was very discerning in his analysis of the problem.*

dis•charge /*v.*dɪs'tʃɑrdʒ; *n.* 'dɪstʃɑrdʒ, dɪs'tʃɑrdʒ/ *v.,* **-charged, -charg•ing,** *n.* —*v.* **1.** [~ + *obj*] to release or send away: *They discharged him from the hospital.* **2.** [~ + *obj*] to fulfill or do (a duty, etc.): *He was no longer able to discharge his duties faithfully.* **3.** [~ + *obj*] to take away the employment of; dismiss (someone) from service: *His boss discharged him because of his absences.* **4.** [~ + *obj*] to pay (a debt): *He discharged all his debts.* **5.** to (cause to) fire, go off, or shoot (a gun): [~ + *obj*]: *In crowded places the police should not discharge their weapons.* [no *obj*]: *The weapon discharged when it hit the ground.* **6.** to (cause to) lose or give up a charge of electricity: [no *obj*]: *The weakened battery was no longer discharging.* [~ + *obj*]: *It can't discharge electricity if it's not connected properly.* —*n.* **7.** [count] the act of firing a gun. **8.** a sending or coming forth: [noncount]: *to halt further discharge of waste into the river.* [count]: *a discharge of five million tons of crude oil.* **9.** [noncount] something sent forth: *a lot of discharge from the wound.* **10.** a release or dismissal: [count]: *an honorable discharge from the army.* [noncount]: *discharge of several employees.*

dis•ci•ple /dɪ'saypəl/ *n.* [count] **1.** one of the 12 apostles of Christ. **2.** a pupil or follower of another: *a disciple of Freud.*

dis•ci•pli•nar•i•an /ˌdɪsəplə'nɛəriyən/ *n.* [count] a person who enforces or favors the use of discipline: *a strict disciplinarian.*

dis•ci•pli•nar•y /'dɪsəplɪˌnɛəriy/ *adj.* [before a noun] of or relating to discipline: *a disciplinary teacher.*

dis•ci•pline /'dɪsəplɪn/ *n., v.,* **-plined, -plin•ing.** —*n.* **1.** [noncount] training to act in accordance with rules or to develop a skill; drill: *military discipline.* **2.** [noncount] behavior in accord with rules of conduct: *keeping good discipline in an army.* **3.** [noncount] punishment: *Discipline consisted of demerits for incorrect answers.* **4.** [count] a branch of learning: *the disciplines of history and economics.* —*v.* [~ + *obj*] **5.** to train by instruction and exercise; drill: *His dog was disciplined by a professional trainer.* **6.** to punish or penalize; correct: *Those teachers weren't afraid to discipline their students.* —**'dis•ci•plined,** *adj.*: *a strictly disciplined army.*

'disc ,jockey, *n.* [count] one who selects and

plays recordings on a radio program or at a discotheque. *Abbr.*: DJ

dis•claim /dɪsˈkleym/ v. [~ + obj] to deny connection with: *He disclaimed responsibility for the accident.* —**dis'claim•er,** n. [count]: *The company printed a disclaimer on the product.*

dis•close /dɪˈsklowz/ v. [~ + obj] **-closed, -clos•ing.** to make known; reveal: *to disclose a secret; The company disclosed that it had lost money on the deal.* —**dis•clo•sure** /dɪˈsklowʒər/ n. [count] [noncount]

dis•co /ˈdɪskow/ n., pl. **-cos,** v. —n. **1.** [count] a discotheque. **2.** [noncount] a style of popular dance music with a heavy, rhythmic beat. —v. [no obj] **3.** to dance to disco: *We were discoing all night.*

dis•col•or /dɪsˈkʌlər/ v. to (cause to) spoil the color (of); fade or stain: [no obj]: *The carpet had discolored over the years.* [~ + obj]: *Water discolored the carpet.* —**dis•col•or•a•tion** /dɪsˌkʌləˈreyʃən/, n. [noncount] [count]

dis•com•fit /dɪsˈkʌmfɪt/ v. [~ + obj] to confuse; upset; disconcert: *The reporter's question about his finances discomfited the mayor.* —**dis•com•fit•ure** /dɪsˈkʌmfɪtʃər/, n. [noncount]: *her discomfiture at the questions.*

dis•com•fort /dɪsˈkʌmfərt/ n. [count] **1.** an absence of comfort or ease: *a life of discomfort in a wheelchair.* **2.** anything disturbing to comfort: *the discomforts of waiting in the airport.*

dis•com•po•sure /ˌdɪskəmˈpowʒər/ n. [noncount] a condition of disorder and disturbance: *She showed obvious discomposure when questioned.*

dis•con•cert /ˌdɪskənˈsɜrt/ v. [~ + obj] to upset (a person's) self-confidence, as by distractions: *The students' constant whispering disconcerted the teacher.* —**dis•con'cert•ed,** adj. —**dis•con'cert•ing,** adj.

dis•con•nect /ˌdɪskəˈnɛkt/ v. [~ + obj] **1.** to interrupt the connection of (something) or between (two things): *I was talking on the phone and suddenly got disconnected.* **2.** to detach; separate: *Disconnect the power source from the computer before opening the back.* —**dis•con•nec•tion** /ˌdɪskəˈnɛkʃən/, n. [noncount]: *disconnection from reality.* [count]: *There was another disconnection before I could talk.*

dis•con•nect•ed /ˌdɪskəˈnɛktɪd/ adj. **1.** (of ideas) not holding together well: *a very disconnected essay.* **2.** (of a person) not coherent; seeming to be irrational: *The boy has seemed disconnected and strange ever since the incident.* —ˌ**dis•con'nect•ed•ly,** adv. —ˌ**dis•con'nect•ed•ness,** n. [noncount]

dis•con•so•late /dɪsˈkɒnsəlɪt/ adj. very depressed, downhearted, or unhappy: *She is disconsolate over the loss of her pet.* —**dis•con•so•late•ly,** adv.: *They sat disconsolately in the corner.*

dis•con•tent /ˌdɪskənˈtɛnt/ n. [noncount] Also, ˌ**dis•con'tent•ment.** lack of contentment; dissatisfaction: *a vague feeling of discontent.* —ˌ**dis•con'tent•ed,** adj.

dis•con•tin•ue /ˌdɪskənˈtɪnyuw/ v. [~ + obj] **-tin•ued, -tin•u•ing. 1.** to (cause to) come to an end or stop; cease: *I had to discontinue my class when I sprained my ankle. He discontinued running in the cold weather.* **2.** to stop using, producing, subscribing to, etc.: *The manufacturer discontinued that car back in 1989.* —**dis•con•tin•u•a•tion** /ˌdɪskənˌtɪnyuw'eyʃən/, n. [count]: *a discontinuation of business as usual.*

dis•con•ti•nu•i•ty /ˌdɪskɒntn̩'uwɪtiy, -'yuw-/ n. [noncount], pl. **-ties.** lack of continuity; irregular development or progress: *a time of discontinuity in the artist's life.*

dis•cord /ˈdɪskɔrd/ n. **1.** [noncount] lack of concord or harmony between persons or things: *The couple split up after years of discord.* **2.** [count] a lack of harmony between musical tones sounded together: *the discords in his music.* —**dis'cord•ant,** adj.

dis•co•theque or **dis•co•thèque** /ˈdɪskə,tɛk, ˌdɪskə'tɛk/ n. [count] a nightclub for dancing to live or recorded music. Also called **disco.**

dis•count /v.ˈdɪskawnt, dɪsˈkawnt; n., adj. ˈdɪskawnt/ v. [~ + obj] **1.** to take off a certain amount from (a bill, price, etc.): *They promise to discount prices.* **2.** to disregard: *I guess we shouldn't discount the possibility completely.* —n. [count] **3.** an amount taken off from the usual price; a reduction in price: *a discount of 25% on plane tickets.* —adj. [before a noun] **4.** selling at less than the usual price: *discount clothing.*

dis•cour•age /dɪˈskɜrɪdʒ, -ˈskʌr-/ v. [~ + obj] **-aged, -ag•ing. 1.** to take away courage or hope; dishearten: *Every job rejection discouraged him more.* **2.** to make (someone) less willing: *The broker discouraged him from buying stock.* —**dis'cour•aged,** adj.: *The discouraged team endured their fifth loss in a row.* —**discouragement,** n. [noncount] [count] —**dis'cour•ag•ing,** adj.: *a discouraging loss.* —**dis'cour•ag•ing•ly,** adv.

dis•course /n.ˈdɪskɔrs, v. dɪsˈkɔrs/ n., v., **-coursed, -cours•ing.** —n. **1.** [noncount] talk; conversation. **2.** [count] a formal discussion of a subject: *a long discourse on cultural differences.* —v. **3. discourse on,** to treat a subject formally in speech or writing: *The paper discourses on common mistakes made in learning English.*

dis•cour•te•ous /dɪsˈkɜrtiyəs/ adj. not courteous; impolite; rude: *I was hurt by the discourteous remarks.* —**dis•cour•te•sy** /dɪsˈkɜrtəsiy/ n. [noncount] [count]

dis•cov•er /dɪˈskʌvər/ v. [~ + obj] **1.** to gain knowledge of (something unknown): *Radioactivity was discovered by Marie Curie. He discovered that not all prehistoric apes were the same.* **2.** to notice or realize; find out about: *He discovered the treasure quite by accident.* —**dis'cov•er•er,** n. [count] —**Usage.** Do not confuse DISCOVER and INVENT, two words that deal with something new. DISCOVER is used when the object is an idea or place that existed before, but few people or no one knew about it. In the sentence *Columbus discovered the New World,* the New World clearly existed and was known to the people living there, but not to Columbus and the people of his time. INVENT is used when the object is a device or thing built. In the sentence *Edison invented the light bulb,* the light bulb did not exist before Edison invented it, and it was not known by anyone.

dis•cov•er•y n. **1.** [noncount] the act of discovering: *The discovery of oil on his farm made him rich.* **2.** [count] something discovered: *He made an important scientific discovery.*

dis•cred•it /dɪsˈkrɛdɪt/ v. [~ + obj] **1.** to cause a lack of confidence in: *She discredited my good name with gossip.* —n. [noncount] **2.** loss or lack of belief or confidence; distrust. —**dis'cred•it•a•ble,** adj.

dis•creet /dɪˈskriyt/ adj. careful in one's conduct or speech; diplomatic: *a few discreet inquiries about his credit rating.* —**dis'creet•ly,** *adv.*

dis•crep•an•cy /dɪˈskrɛpənsiy/ *n.* [*noncount*], *pl.* **-cies.** a lack of agreement; inconsistency: *discrepancy in the eyewitness accounts of the accident.*

dis•crete /dɪˈskriyt/ *adj.* apart or detached from others; separate; distinct: *The college was reorganized into six discrete departments.*

dis•cre•tion /dɪˈskrɛʃən/ *n.* [*noncount*] **1.** the power to decide or act according to one's own judgment: *The judge has discretion in the matter of sentencing.* **2.** the quality of being discreet: *I can count on your discretion to keep quiet about his drinking.* —*Idiom.* **3. at one's discretion, at the discretion of,** in accordance with (someone's) judgment or will: *They may withdraw the money at their discretion and use it to pay for college.* —**dis'cre•tion,ar•y,** *adj.*: *discretionary funds.*

dis•crim•i•nate /dɪˈskrɪməˌneyt / *v.* [*no obj*] **-nat•ed, -nat•ing. 1.** to treat a person differently on the basis of the group or class to which the person belongs: *No company should expect to discriminate today and get away with it. Those employers discriminated against women for higher-paying jobs. Is it acceptable to discriminate in favor of certain groups?* **2.** to notice a difference: *He has trouble discriminating between red and green.* —**dis'crim•i,nat•ing,** *adj.*

dis•crim•i•na•tion /dɪˌskrɪməˈneyʃən/ *n.* [*noncount*] **1.** the act or practice of discriminating: *job discrimination.* **2.** the ability to distinguish or judge among things: *fine discrimination in his choice of wine.*

dis•crim•i•na•to•ry /dɪˈskrɪmənəˌtɔriy/ *adj.* relating to or marked by discrimination: *She carefully monitored the company's discriminatory hiring practices for a future lawsuit.*

dis•cuss /dɪˈskʌs/ *v.* [~ + *obj*] to talk about: *He was happy to discuss anything with her.*

dis•cus•sion /dɪˈskʌʃən/ *n.* an act or instance of discussing: [*noncount*]: *I don't think his proposals leave much room for discussion.* [*count*]: *The students had many late-night discussions about the meaning of life.*

dis•dain /dɪsˈdeyn, dɪˈsteyn/ *v.* [~ + *obj*] **1.** to look upon or treat with contempt; despise; scorn: *He disdained all my offers of help.* —*n.* [*noncount*] **2.** a feeling of contempt for anything unworthy; scorn: *a look of disdain on her face.* —**dis'dain•ful,** *adj.*

dis•ease /dɪˈziyz/ *n.* **1.** illness; sickness: [*noncount*]: *Disease may result from infection, deficient nutrition, or environmental factors.* [*count*]: *Flu is a contagious disease.* **2.** [*count*] any harmful condition, as of society: *Poverty is a disease of the inner city.* —**dis'eased,** *adj.*: *the product of a diseased mind.*

dis•em•bark /ˌdɪsɛmˈbɑrk/ *v.* [*no obj*] **1.** to go ashore from a ship: *The troops disembarked on the beach just before dawn.* **2.** to leave an aircraft: *Passengers should disembark from the rear of the plane.* —**dis•em•bar•ka•tion** /ˌdɪsˌɛmbɑrˈkeyʃən/, **dis'em•bark'ment,** *n.* [*noncount*]

dis•en•chant•ed /ˌdɪsɛnˈtʃæntɪd/ *adj.* no longer pleased with: *I had become completely disenchanted with my job.* —**dis•en'chant•ment,** *n.* [*noncount*]

dis•en•fran•chise /ˌdɪsɛnˈfræntʃayz/ *v.* [~ + *obj*], **-chised, -chis•ing.** to take away the right of (a citizen) to vote.

dis•en•gage /ˌdɪsɛnˈgeydʒ/ *v.*, **-gaged, -gag•ing.** to (cause to) become free from connection: [*no obj*]: *Suddenly the clutch just disengaged.* [~ + *obj*]: *Disengage the clutch and let's see what happens.* —**dis•en'gage•ment,** *n.* [*noncount*]

dis•en•tan•gle /ˌdɪsɛnˈtæŋgəl/ *v.*, **-gled, -gling.** to (cause to) become free from tangles, knots, etc.: [~ + *obj*]: *They disentangled the ropes and threw them onto the ship.* [*no obj*]: *The wires disentangled and came loose.* —**dis•en'tan•gle•ment,** *n.* [*noncount*]

dis•fa•vor /dɪsˈfeyvər/ *n.* [*noncount*] disapproval; displeasure; dislike: *He feared the king's disfavor.* Also, *esp. Brit.,* **dis'fa•vour.**

dis•fig•ure /dɪsˈfɪgyər/ *v.* [~ + *obj*], **-ured, -ur•ing.** to spoil the appearance of; deform: *He was badly disfigured in the fire.* —**dis'fig•ure•ment,** *n.* [*count*] [*noncount*]

dis•gorge /dɪsˈgɔrdʒ/ *v.* [~ + *obj*], **-gorged, -gorg•ing.** to eject or throw out; empty out: *disgorging radioactive waste into the atmosphere.*

dis•grace /dɪsˈgreys/ *n., v.*, **-graced, -grac•ing.** —*n.* [*noncount*] **1.** the loss of respect or honor: *He had to resign in disgrace.* —*v.* [~ + *obj*] **2.** to bring or reflect shame or dishonor upon: *She disgraced herself by passing out at the party.* —**dis'grace•ful,** *adj.*: *disgraceful manners.* —**dis'grace•ful•ly,** *adv.*

dis•grun•tled /dɪsˈgrʌntld/ *adj.* discontented; irritated: *My father always became disgruntled if dinner was late.*

dis•guise /dɪsˈgayz, dɪˈskayz/ *v.* [~ + *obj*], **-guised, -guis•ing,** *n.* —*v.* **1.** to change the appearance of so as to deceive: *The army disguised the soldiers as ordinary villagers.* **2.** to conceal: *to disguise his true intentions.* —*n.* [*count*] **3.** something that conceals identity, character, or quality: *Dressing as palace guards was a clever disguise.*

dis•gust /dɪsˈgʌst, dɪˈskʌst/ *v.* [~ + *obj*] **1.** to cause a strong feeling of dislike or nausea in someone: *His terrible manners at the dinner table disgusted us.* —*n.* [*noncount*] **2.** strong dislike caused by bad behavior or something that offends one's senses: *He couldn't hide his disgust at the crime.* —**dis'gust•ed,** *adj.*: *The disgusted workers went home early.*

dis•gust•ing *adj.* causing disgust; offensive to one's physical or moral sense: *The movie was disgusting.*

dish /dɪʃ/ *n.* [*count*] **1.** a plate used esp. for holding, baking, or serving food: *Put the dishes on the table.* **2.** all the plates, bowls, cups, and utensils used at a meal: *Who will wash the dishes tonight?* **3.** a particular type of food or preparation of food: *This is an easy dish to make.* **4.** Also called **'dish ,anten•na.** a dish-shaped device used for receiving satellite and microwave signals. —*v.* **5. dish out,** *Informal.* **a.** to serve; distribute: *He dished out some food to the waiting customers.* **b.** to give out; inflict: *to dish out punishment.* **6. dish up,** to put (food) on plates; distribute: *He dished up meals for the homeless.*

dis•heart•en /dɪsˈhɑrtn/ *v.* [~ + *obj*] to lower or depress the hope, courage, or spirits of; discourage: *News of another job rejection disheartened him.* —**dis'heart•ened,** *adj.*: *disheartened job seekers.* —**dis'heart•en•ing,** *adj.*: *disheartening economic news.*

di•shev•el•ed /dɪˈʃɛvəld/ *adj.* or (*esp. Brit.*) **-elled.** untidy; messy: *their disheveled apartment; disheveled hair.* —**di'shev•el•ment,** *n.* [*noncount*]

dis•hon•est /dɪsˈɒnɪst/ *adj.* not honest; untrustworthy: *I wouldn't do business with such dishonest car dealers.* —**dis'hon•est•ly,** *adv.*: *He got most of his money dishonestly.*

dis•hon•es•ty /dɪs'ɒnɪstiy/ *n.* [*noncount*] a lack of honesty.

dis•hon•or /dɪs'ɒnər/ *n.* [*noncount*] **1.** lack or loss of honor; disgrace; shame. —*v.* [~ + *obj*] **2.** to deprive of honor; disgrace; bring shame on: *The senator's corruption dishonored both himself and his family.* —**dis'hon•or•a•ble,** *adj.*: *Treason is a dishonorable act.*

dish•wash•er /'dɪʃ,wɒʃər, -,wɔʃər/ *n.* [*count*] **1.** a person who washes dishes. **2.** a machine for washing dishes.

dis•il•lu•sion /,dɪsɪ'luwʒən/ *v.* [~ + *obj*] to free from an illusion or false belief: *I hate to disillusion you, but your chances of winning are practically zero.* —**dis•il'lu•sioned,** *adj.*: *disillusioned voters.* —**dis•il'lu•sion•ment,** *n.* [*noncount*]

dis•in•clined /,dɪsɪn'klaynd/ *adj.* unwilling; reluctant: *They are disinclined to fire someone without very good reason.*

dis•in•fect /,dɪsɪn'fɛkt/ *v.* [~ + *obj*] to cleanse of infection; destroy disease germs in: *to disinfect a wound.*

dis•in•fect•ant /,dɪsɪn'fɛktənt/ *n.* a substance that disinfects: [*noncount*]: *Pour some disinfectant on the wound.* [*count*]: *The bathroom spray has a disinfectant in it.*

dis•in•gen•u•ous /,dɪsɪn'dʒɛnyuwəs/ *adj.* lacking in honesty, truth, or sincerity; insincere: *She gave me a disingenuous answer.*

dis•in•her•it /,dɪsɪn'hɛrɪt/ *v.* [~ + *obj*] to exclude (an heir) from inheriting: *After the incident his father disinherited him.*

dis•in•te•grate /dɪs'ɪntə,greyt/ *v.*, **-grat•ed, -grat•ing.** to (cause to) break up or fall apart: [*no obj*]: *At that speed the plane began to disintegrate.* [~ + *obj*]: *The rain disintegrated our morning newspaper.* —**dis•in•te•gra•tion** /dɪs,ɪntə'greyʃən/, *n.* [*noncount*]

dis•in•ter•est•ed /dɪs'ɪntə,rɛstɪd, -trɪstɪd/ *adj.* **1.** able to act fairly because not influenced by personal interest or advantage: *We need a disinterested judge to settle the dispute.* **2.** not interested; indifferent: *becoming disinterested in his children.* —**Usage.** Do not confuse DISINTERESTED and UNINTERESTED. DISINTERESTED usually means "able to act fairly; not partial or biased," while UNINTERESTED means "not taking an interest." But the second meaning of DISINTERESTED listed here means the same as UNINTERESTED, and many users of English consider this use of DISINTERESTED incorrect.

dis•joint•ed /dɪs'dʒɔyntɪd/ *adj.* separated; disconnected; out of order; badly arranged: *The movie was too disjointed to make much sense.* —**dis'joint•ed•ly,** *adv.* —**dis'joint•ed•ness,** *n.* [*noncount*]

disk /dɪsk/ *n.* [*count*] **1.** any thin, flat, circular plate or object. **2.** any surface that is flat and round, or seemingly so: *the disk of the sun.* **3.** DISC (def. 1). **4.** any of several types of materials for storing electronic or computer data, consisting of thin round plates of plastic or metal. **5.** any of various roundish, flat anatomical structures, esp. between the bones of the backbone.

disk•ette /dɪ'skɛt/ *n.* a thin plastic disk for storing computer data and programs.

dis•like /dɪs'layk/ *v.*, **-liked, -lik•ing,** *n.* —*v.* [~ + *obj*] **1.** to not like: *I dislike selfish people. I dislike jogging early in the morning.* —*n.* [*noncount*] **2.** a feeling of not liking something or someone:

My feeling wasn't exactly one of hatred, but more of strong dislike.

dis•lo•cate /'dɪslow,keyt, dɪs'lowkeyt/ *v.* [~ + *obj*], **-cat•ed, -cat•ing. 1.** to put out of joint or out of position: *His shoulder was dislocated.* **2.** to throw out of order; upset: *Frequent strikes dislocated the economy.* —**dis•lo•ca•tion** /,dɪslow'keyʃən/, *n.* [*noncount*][*count*]

dis•lodge /dɪs'lɒdʒ/ *v.* [~ + *obj*], **-lodged, -lodg•ing.** to remove or force out of a particular place: *We needed a bulldozer to dislodge the rock.*

dis•loy•al /dɪs'lɔyəl/ *adj.* not loyal; faithless: *He was disloyal to his own department by telling the boss.* —**dis'loy•al•ty,** *n.* [*noncount*] [*count*]

dis•mal /'dɪzməl/ *adj.* causing gloom or sadness; cheerless: *a dismal little office.* —**'dis•mal•ly,** *adv.*: *a dismally dreary day.*

dis•man•tle /dɪs'mæntl/ *v.* [~ + *obj*], **-tled, -tling.** to take apart: *to dismantle a car's engine.*

dis•may /dɪs'mey/ *v.* [~ + *obj*] **1.** to take away the courage or hope of completely; surprise unpleasantly: *The child's failing grades dismayed his parents.* —*n.* [*noncount*] **2.** sudden or complete loss of courage or hope: *My heart sank with dismay as I realized what I had done.*

dis•mem•ber /dɪs'mɛmbər/ *v.* [~ + *obj*] to divide into parts; cut up: *a dismembered corpse.* —**dis'mem•ber•ment,** *n.* [*noncount*]

dis•miss /dɪs'mɪs/ *v.* [~ + *obj*] **1.** to direct or allow to leave: *The teacher dismissed the class early.* **2.** to fire; discharge from office or service: *to dismiss an employee.* **3.** to put aside from consideration: *At first the editor dismissed the story as a rumor.* —**dis'miss•al,** *n.* [*noncount*] [*count*]

dis•mount /*v.*dɪs'mawnt; *n. also* 'dɪs,mawnt/ *v.* [*no obj*] **1.** to get down or climb down from a horse or bicycle: *She dismounted from the motorcycle.* —*n.* [*count*] **2.** an act of dismounting, such as in gymnastics: *a dismount from the balance beam.*

dis•o•be•di•ence /,dɪsə'biydiyəns/ *n.* [*noncount*] lack of obedience; failure to obey: *Disobedience was punished quickly.*

dis•o•be•di•ent /,dɪsə'biydiyənt/ *adj.* refusing to obey: *Their disobedient children were never punished.*

dis•o•bey /,dɪsə'bey/ *v.* to fail or refuse to obey: [*no obj*]: *If you disobey, you'll just go to bed earlier.* [~ + *obj*]: *He was always disobeying his parents.*

dis•or•der /dɪs'ɔrdər/ *n.* **1.** [*noncount*] lack of order; confusion: *When the burglars left, the room was in complete disorder.* **2.** public disturbance; rioting: [*noncount*]: *The police could not cope with the disorder in the streets.* [*count*]: *There have been several disorders in the neighborhood in the last few months.* **3.** [*count*] sickness: *a mild stomach disorder.* —*v.* [~ + *obj*] **4.** to destroy the order of; disarrange: *The room was disordered when we arrived at the scene of the burglary.*

dis•or•der•ly /dɪs'ɔrdərliy/ *adj.* **1.** characterized by disorder; untidy: *a disorderly living room.* **2.** unruly; behaving in an uncontrolled way: *disorderly conduct.* —**dis'or•der•li•ness,** *n.* [*noncount*]

dis•or•gan•ize /dɪs'ɔrgə,nayz/ *v.* [~ + *obj*], **-ized, -iz•ing.** to destroy the organization of; throw into confusion: *The secretary's sudden departure disorganized the whole company.* —**dis•or•gan•i•za•tion** /dɪs,ɔrgənə'zeyʃən/, *n.* [*noncount*]

dis•o•ri•ent /dɪs'ɔriy,ɛnt/ *v.* [~ + *obj*] to confuse, esp. so that one loses the sense of time, place, or one's personal identity: *When she regained consciousness she was disoriented.* —**dis•o•ri•en•ta•tion** /dɪs,ɔriyɛn'teyʃən, -,owr-/, *n.* [*noncount*]

dis•own /dɪs'own/ *v.* [~ + *obj*] to refuse to admit connection with: *They disowned their daughter after she eloped.*

dis•par•age /dɪ'spærɪdʒ/ *v.* [~ + *obj*], **-aged, -ag•ing.** to belittle, ridicule, or discredit: *Don't disparage his attempts to become a doctor.* —**dis'par•age•ment,** *n.* [*noncount*] —**dis'par•ag•ing,** *adj.*: *disparaging remarks.*

dis•pa•rate /'dɪspərɪt, dɪ'spær-/ *adj.* differing greatly: *It was surprising to hear such disparate views from members of the same family.*

dis•par•i•ty /dɪ'spærɪtiy/ *n.* clear or obvious difference: [*noncount*]: *We were shocked by the disparity in wages.* [*count*]: *Too often there is a great disparity between campaign promises and what the candidate does when elected.*

dis•pas•sion•ate /dɪs'pæʃənɪt/ *adj.* free from or unaffected by personal feeling or bias: *He described the accident in a dispassionate and objective way.* —**dis'pas•sion•ate•ly,** *adv.*

dis•patch /*v.* dɪ'spætʃ; *n. also* 'dɪspætʃ/ *v.* [~ + *obj*] **1.** to send off or away with speed: *He dispatched his best troops to the borders.* **2.** to put to death; kill: *The injured horse was dispatched painlessly by its owner.* **3.** to settle (a matter) promptly: *The negotiations were dispatched almost as soon as the two sides sat down to talk.* —*n.* **4.** [*count; usually singular*] the sending off of a messenger, letter, troops, etc.: *the dispatch of a special brigade to the troubled region.* **5.** [*noncount*] prompt or speedy action: *done with dispatch.* **6.** [*count*] an official communication or a news story. —**dis'patch•er,** *n.* [*count*]: *The police dispatcher sent several squad cars to the area.*

dis•pel /dɪ'spɛl/ *v.* [~ + *obj*], **-pelled, -pel•ling.** to drive off or cause to disappear: *That fine performance dispelled any doubts about her abilities.*

dis•pen•sa•ble /dɪ'spɛnsəbəl/ *adj.* not necessary or essential: *There are lots of dispensable items in the budget.*

dis•pen•sa•ry /dɪ'spɛnsəriy/ *n.* [*count*], *pl.* **-ries.** a public facility where medical care and medicines are given out.

dis•pen•sa•tion /,dɪspən'seyʃən, -pɛn-/ *n.* **1.** [*noncount*] an act or instance of dispensing: *the fair dispensation of justice.* **2.** [*count*] doing away with a general rule or law in a particular instance: *She needed a special dispensation to marry outside the parish.*

dis•pense /dɪ'spɛns/ *v.* [~ + *obj*], **-pensed, -pens•ing. 1.** to deal out; distribute: *They dispensed the money to charity.* **2.** to administer: *to dispense the law without bias.* **3.** to make up and distribute (medicine), esp. on prescription: *a license to dispense drugs.* **4. dispense with,** to do away with; get rid of: *Can we dispense with the rules?*

dis•pens•er /dɪ'spɛnsər/ *n.* [*count*] a container from which something may be poured, etc: *They filled the soap dispensers in the bathroom.*

dis•perse /dɪ'spɜrs/ *v.*, **-persed, -pers•ing.** to (cause to) separate and move in different directions; (cause to) become scattered: [*no obj*]: *The crowd dispersed when the police arrived.* [~ + *obj*]: *The riot police dispersed the crowd.* —**dis'per•sal,** *n.* [*noncount*] —**dis'per•sion** /-ʒən, -ʃən/, *n.* [*noncount*]

dis•pir•it /dɪ'spɪrɪt/ *v.* [~ + *obj*] to deprive of spirit or hope; discourage; dishearten. —**dis'pir•it•ed,** *adj.*: *a dispirited team.*

dis•place /dɪs'pleys/ *v.* [~ + *obj*], **-placed, -plac•ing. 1.** to move or put out of place: *to displace a joint.* **2.** to take the place of; replace: *He is trying to displace me in my job.*

dis'placed 'person, *n.* [*count*] a person driven or expelled from a homeland by war, famine, etc.

dis•place•ment /dɪs'pleysmənt/ *n.* **1.** [*noncount*] the act of displacing; the state of being displaced: *the displacement of different scientific theories by new ones.* **2.** [*count*] the weight or the volume of liquid displaced by a body, such as a ship: *The ship had a displacement of 50,000 tons.*

dis•play /dɪ'spley/ *v.* [~ + *obj*] **1.** to show or exhibit; make visible: *The vendors displayed their fruit.* —*n.* **2.** an act or instance of displaying; exhibition: [*count*]: *fireworks displays on the Fourth of July.* [*noncount*]: *There was a fair amount on display but nothing worth buying.*

dis•please /dɪs'pliyz/ *v.* [~ + *obj*], **-pleased, -pleas•ing.** to annoy or make angry: *Rude behavior displeases her greatly.*

dis•pleas•ure /dɪs'plɛʒər/ *n.* [*noncount*] dissatisfaction; disapproval.

dis•pos•a•ble /dɪ'spowzəbəl/ *adj.* **1.** designed for or capable of being thrown away after use: *disposable diapers.* **2.** [*often: before a noun*] free for use; available: *Your disposable income is what is left after paying taxes and other essentials.* —**dis•pos•a•bil•i•ty** /dɪ,spowzə'bɪlɪtiy/, *n.* [*noncount*]

dis•pos•al /dɪ'spowzəl/ *n.* [*noncount*] **1.** a disposing of or getting rid of something: *disposal of hazardous wastes.* **2.** power or right to use or have use of a thing; control: *The car was left at my disposal.*

dis•pose /dɪ'spowz/ *v.*, **-posed, -pos•ing. dis•pose of,** **1.** to deal with finally; settle: *Let's dispose of this matter once and for all.* **2.** to get rid of: *Dispose of the waste papers in this bin.* **3.** to give away or sell: *His property holdings will be disposed of in his will.*

dis•posed /dɪ'spowzd/ *adj.* inclined, willing, or motivated to (do something): *The committee was not disposed to hold another meeting.*

dis•po•si•tion /,dɪspə'zɪʃən/ *n.* [*count*] **1.** the predominant or prevailing tendency of one's spirits; characteristic attitude: *a cheerful disposition.* **2.** arrangement or placing, such as of troops: *the careful disposition of the remaining troops.* **3.** final settlement of a matter: *What was the disposition of the case?*

dis•pos•sess /,dɪspə'zɛs/ *v.* [~ + *obj*] to force a person to give up a dwelling place: *If you pay your rent, you can't be dispossessed.*

dis•prove /dɪs'pruwv/ *v.* [~ + *obj*], **-proved, -prov•ing.** to prove a statement to be false or wrong: *The latest evidence disproves the theory.* —**dis'prov•a•ble,** *adj.*

dis•pute /dɪ'spyuwt/ *v.*, **-put•ed, -put•ing,** *n.* —*v.* **1.** [*no obj*] to be in an argument or debate; argue: *The school board members spend their time disputing and getting nothing done.* **2.** [~ + *obj*] to argue against; to question the truth of: *The accountant disputes the figures you gave her. The administration does not dispute that the cuts in personnel will hurt good service.* —*n.* [*count*] **3.** debate, controversy, or difference of opinion: *The dispute concerns capital punishment.* **4.** a quarrel; a fight: *a loud dispute in the middle of the night.* —**dis'put•a•ble,** *adj.*

D

dis•qual•i•fy /dɪs'kwɒlə,faɪ/ v. [~ + obj], **-fied, -fy•ing.** to make unfit or unqualified: *The lack of a good education might disqualify you from some jobs.* —**dis•qual•i•fi•ca•tion** /dɪs,kwɒləfɪ'keɪʃən/, n. [count] [noncount]

dis•qui•et /dɪs'kwaɪɪt/ n. [noncount] **1.** lack of calm or peace; anxiety. —v. [~ + obj] **2.** to upset or make anxious: *The news about the layoffs disquieted a lot of workers.* —**dis'qui•et•ed,** adj. —**dis'qui•et•ing,** adj.: *disquieting news about the war.*

dis•re•gard /,dɪsrɪ'gɑrd/ v. [~ + obj] **1.** to pay no attention to; ignore: *Please disregard the mess and sit right here.* —n. [noncount] **2.** lack of attention; neglect: *his complete disregard of orders.*

dis•re•pair /,dɪsrɪ'pɛər/ n. [noncount] the condition of needing repair; a neglected state: *The house had fallen into total disrepair.*

dis•rep•u•ta•ble /dɪs'rɛpyətəbəl/ adj. having a bad reputation: *a disreputable part of town.*

dis•re•pute /,dɪsrɪ'pyuwt/ n. [noncount] disfavor; the state of having lost a good reputation: *The secret service had fallen into disrepute with one scandal after another.*

dis•re•spect /,dɪsrɪ'spɛkt/ n. [noncount] lack of respect; rudeness: *The disrespect she shows her parents is shocking.* —,**dis•re'spect•ful,** adj.: *a disrespectful student.* —,**dis•re'spect•ful•ly,** adv.: *behaving disrespectfully.*

dis•rupt /dɪs'rʌpt/ v. [~ + obj] **1.** to cause disorder or turmoil in: *The war disrupted the lives of millions.* **2.** to interrupt the normal operation of: *The tornado disrupted broadcasting along the entire coast.*

dis•rup•tion /dɪs'rʌpʃən/ n. **1.** [noncount] the act of disrupting: *the cruel disruption of lives during the war.* **2.** temporary interruption of something: [noncount]: *disruption of the phone lines.* [count]: *a few more disruptions of the broadcasts during the hurricane.*

dis•rup•tive /dɪs'rʌptɪv/ adj. causing disorder: *disruptive behavior in class.*

dis•sat•is•fac•tion /,dɪssætɪs'fækʃən, dɪs,sæt-/ n. [noncount] the state or attitude of not being satisfied: *a lot of dissatisfaction on the job.*

dis•sat•is•fy /dɪs'sætɪs,faɪ/ v. [~ + obj], **-fied, -fy•ing.** to fail to satisfy; disappoint; displease: *This new plan dissatisfies everyone.* —**dis'sat•is,fied,** adj.: *dissatisfied with her examination results.*

dis•sect /dɪ'sɛkt, daɪ-/ v. [~ + obj] to cut apart (an animal body, a plant, etc.) to examine the structure and relation of parts: *In biology class we had to dissect a frog.* —**dis•sec•tion** /dɪ'sɛkʃən, daɪ-/, n. [count]: *The students performed several frog dissections.* [noncount]: *to subject the frog to dissection.*

dis•sem•i•nate /dɪ'sɛmə,neɪt/ v. [~ + obj], **-nat•ed, -nat•ing.** to scatter or spread widely; distribute: *The embassy disseminated information about its new programs.* —**dis•sem•i•na•tion** /dɪ,sɛmə'neɪʃən/, n. [noncount]: *the dissemination of information.*

dis•sen•sion /dɪ'sɛnʃən/ n. [noncount] strong disagreement; discord: *a lot of dissension among the ordinary soldiers.*

dis•sent /dɪ'sɛnt/ v. [no obj] **1.** to differ in thinking or opinion: *If enough of us dissent, the new regulation won't be passed.* —n. [noncount] **2.** difference of opinion; disagreement: *Dissent about the matter kept us from reaching an agreement.* —**dis'sent•er,** n. [count]

dis•ser•ta•tion /,dɪsər'teɪʃən/ n. [count] a long piece of writing, esp. one done by a candidate for a doctoral degree: *He wrote a dissertation on economic policy.*

dis•serv•ice /dɪs'sɜrvɪs/ n. [count; usually singular] an instance of hurting; an injustice: *He did you a disservice by not helping.*

dis•si•dent /'dɪsɪdənt/ n. [count] **1.** a person who dissents: *The dissidents marched in protest against the war.* —adj. [before a noun] **2.** disagreeing: *The dissident members kept the issue from coming to a vote.* —'**dis•si•dence,** n. [noncount]

dis•sim•i•lar /dɪ'sɪmələr/ adj. not similar; unlike; different: *dissimilar ways of doing things.* —**dis•sim•i•lar•i•ty** /dɪ,sɪmə'lærɪtiy/, n., pl. **-ties.** [noncount]: *great dissimilarity in the way they conduct elections.* [count]: *Write about the similarities and dissimilarities of the characters in the novel.*

dis•si•pate /'dɪsə,peyt/ v., **-pat•ed, -pat•ing. 1.** to (cause to) become scattered in different directions; disperse: [no obj]: *The fog dissipated when the sun rose.* [~ + obj]: *The police managed to dissipate the mob in minutes.* **2.** [~ + obj] to spend wastefully: *He dissipated his large inheritance.* —'**dis•si,pat•ed,** adj.

dis•si•pa•tion /,dɪsə'peyʃən/ n. [noncount] **1.** the act of wasting one's life in foolish or harmful pleasure: *Decades of dissipation had a powerful impact on his health.* **2.** the act of scattering or of being scattered: *the dissipation of the fog.*

dis•so•ci•ate /dɪ'sowʃiy,eyt, -siy-/ v. [~ + obj], **-at•ed, -at•ing.** to cut off or separate from; disconnect: *He tried to dissociate himself from his past.* —**dis•so•ci•a•tion** /dɪ,sowʃiy'eyʃən, -siy-/, n. [noncount]

dis•so•lute /'dɪsə,luwt/ adj. immoral; corrupt; dissipated: *He led a dissolute life, thinking only of his own pleasure.* —'**dis•so,lute•ly,** adv. —'**dis•so,lute•ness,** n. [noncount]

dis•so•lu•tion /,dɪsə'luwʃən/ n. [noncount] the breaking up of a partnership, marriage, organization, etc.

dis•solve /dɪ'zɒlv/ v., **-solved, -solv•ing. 1.** to (cause to) become a mixture or solution of: [no obj]: *The sugar will dissolve in your coffee.* [~ + obj]: *to dissolve salt in water.* **2.** to (cause to) become undone; (cause to) come to an end: [~ + obj]: *They dissolved their business partnership.* [no obj]: *He helplessly watched his marriage dissolve.*

dis•so•nance /'dɪsənəns/ n. [noncount] **1.** harsh sound; discord: *the dissonance of the untuned violins.* **2.** lack of agreement: *no way to reconcile such dissonance of opinion.* —'**dis•so•nant,** adj.: *dissonant colors.*

dis•suade /dɪ'sweyd/ v. [~ + obj] **-suad•ed, -suad•ing.** to advise (someone) against doing something: *Nothing could dissuade him. My teacher dissuaded me from going into business.*

dis•tance /'dɪstəns/ n. **1.** the amount of space between two things: [count]: *The distance between my school and the house is only one half mile.* [noncount]: *The train I take to work is within walking distance of our apartment.* **2.** [noncount] the state or fact of being apart in space: *Distance from the city isn't a factor in our search for a new home.* **3.** [noncount] a distant point or place: *Can you see the house in the distance?* —**Idiom. 4. keep one's distance,** to remain apart and reserved: *I kept my distance and never told her about my love for her.*

dis•tant /'dɪstənt/ adj. **1.** far off in space or

time; remote: *He enjoyed traveling to distant lands.* **2.** not closely related: *a distant relative.* **3.** reserved; not friendly: *In a cold and distant voice he told me to pack and leave.* —**dis•tant•ly,** *adv.*

dis•taste /dɪs'teyst/ *n.* dislike; a desire to avoid: [*count; usually singular*]: *a distaste for household chores.* [*noncount*]: *a look of distaste on his face.* —**dis'taste•ful,** *adj.*

dis•tem•per /dɪs'tɛmpər/ *n.* [*noncount*] an infectious disease, esp. of dogs and cats.

dis•tend /dɪ'stɛnd/ *v.* to swell: [~ + *obj*]: *Air distends a balloon.* [*no obj*]: *The balloon distended to about five inches in length.* —**dis•ten•tion** /dɪ'stɛnʃən/, *n.* [*noncount*]: *suffering from distention of the stomach.* [*count*]: *a distention of several inches.*

dis•till /dɪ'stɪl/ *v.* **1.** to heat (a liquid) hot enough to evaporate, then allow it to cool: [~ + *obj*]: *They distilled the salt water and made it into drinking water.* [*no obj*]: *The liquid distills when heated.* **2.** [~ + *obj*] to get the most important elements of an experience: *She has distilled a number of wonderful stories from her experiences as a crime lab technician.* —**dis'till•er,** *n.* [*count*]

dis•tinct /dɪ'stɪŋkt/ *adj.* **1.** not the same; separate; dissimilar: *The two books are clearly distinct and written for different audiences. Her business life is distinct from her social life.* **2.** clear; plain; unmistakable: *a distinct shape.* —**dis'tinct•ly,** *adv.*: *Hanging out on a beach is distinctly more fun than working.*

dis•tinc•tion /dɪ'stɪŋkʃən/ *n.* **1.** [*count*] [*noncount*] difference. **2.** [*count*] a distinguishing quality or characteristic: *It has the distinction of being the oldest house in town.* **3.** [*noncount*] marked superiority; excellence: *He passed all his exams with distinction.*

dis•tinc•tive /dɪ'stɪŋktɪv/ *adj.* serving to distinguish: *the zebra's distinctive stripes.* —**dis'tinc•tive•ly,** *adv.*: *his distinctively New England accent.* —**dis'tinc•tive•ness,** *n.* [*noncount*]

dis•tin•guish /dɪ'stɪŋgwɪʃ/ *v.* [~ + *obj*] **1.** to mark off as different; show a difference: *His height distinguishes him from the other boys.* **2.** to recognize as distinct or different: *Can you distinguish right from wrong?* **3.** to see, hear, or recognize clearly: *Without my glasses I can't distinguish certain signs on the road.* **4.** **distinguish oneself,** to make prominent or eminent: *He distinguished himself in the arts.* —**dis'tin•guish•a•ble,** *adj.*

dis•tin•guished /dɪ'stɪŋgwɪʃt/ *adj.* made well-known by excellence or success: *a distinguished scientist.*

dis•tort /dɪ'stɔrt/ *v.* [~ + *obj*] **1.** to twist out of shape: *Pain had distorted his face.* **2.** to give a false meaning to; misrepresent: *That journalist distorted the candidate's remarks.* —**dis•tor•tion** /dɪ'stɔrʃən/ *n.* [*noncount*] [*count*]

dis•tract /dɪ'strækt/ *v.* [~ + *obj*] to draw one's attention away: *The music distracted us from our work.* —**dis'tract•ing,** *adj.*

dis•trac•tion /dɪ'strækʃən/ *n.* **1.** [*count*] the act of distracting or the state of being distracted: *It's just a distraction to keep us from thinking about the real problem.* **2.** [*noncount*] mental distress: *You are driving me to distraction with that music.* **3.** a person or thing that prevents concentration: [*count*]: *The talking in the hallway was a distraction for the students.* [*noncount*]: *There was too much distraction at the office.*

dis•traught /dɪ'strɔt/ *adj.* very anxious; deeply agitated: *The distraught mother waited for news of her child.*

dis•tress /dɪ'strɛs/ *n.* [*noncount*] **1.** sharp or strong anxiety, pain, or sorrow: *Obvious signs of distress showed up during the crisis.* **2.** a state of extreme necessity, trouble, or misfortune: *a time of poverty and distress.* —*v.* [~ + *obj*] **3.** to cause pain, anxiety, or sorrow: *The tragic news distressed us all.* —**dis'tress•ing,** *adj.*

dis•trib•ute /dɪ'strɪbyuwt/ *v.* [~ + *obj*], **-ut•ed, -ut•ing.** **1.** to divide and give out in shares: *The relief agency will distribute the food among several countries; distributing political pamphlets on the streets.* **2.** to spread over an area; scatter: *to distribute seeds.*

dis•tri•bu•tion /ˌdɪstrə'byuwʃən/ *n.* [*count; usually singular*] an act or instance of distributing: *a more equitable distribution of wealth among rich and poor nations.*

dis•trib•u•tor /dɪ'strɪbyətər/ *n.* [*count*] **1.** a person or thing that distributes. **2.** a device in an engine that distributes the electricity to the spark plugs.

dis•trict /'dɪstrɪkt/ *n.* [*count*] a division of territory marked off for administrative, voting, or other purposes: *the Wall Street district.*

'district at'torney, *n.* an attorney who acts for the people or government within a specified district.

dis•trust /dɪs'trʌst/ *v.* [~ + *obj*] **1.** to look at or consider (someone) with suspicion; have no trust in: *I have distrusted him ever since he cheated me.* —*n.* [*noncount*] **2.** lack of trust; doubt; suspicion: *Their feelings of distrust about him have affected me, too.* —**dis'trust•ful,** *adj.*

dis•turb /dɪ'stɜrb/ *v.* [~ + *obj*] to interrupt the quiet, rest, peace, or order of; bother: *She'll be angry if you disturb her while she's in conference.* —**dis'turb•ing,** *adj.*

dis•turb•ance /dɪ'stɜrbəns/ *n.* **1.** [*noncount*] an act of disturbing or the state of being disturbed: *You can work here without disturbance.* **2.** [*count*] a riot, outbreak of public disorder, or fighting: *There were disturbances in that region before full-scale fighting broke out.*

dis•turbed /dɪ'stɜrbd/ *adj.* mentally or emotionally unsettled or upset: *The emotionally disturbed child needs special care.*

dis•use /*n.* dɪs'yuws/ *n.* [*noncount*] a state of no longer being used or practiced: *Happily such weapons have fallen into disuse.* —**dis'used,** *adj.*: *old disused factories that were rotting away.*

ditch /dɪtʃ/ *n.* [*count*] **1.** a long, narrow channel dug in the ground, such as for drainage or irrigation; trench. —*v.* **2.** [~ + *obj*] *Slang.* to get rid of; abandon: *The robbers ditched the stolen car. He ditched his girlfriend.*

dit•to /'dɪtow/ *n., pl.* **-tos,** *adv.* —*n.* [*noncount*] **1.** what has just been said or mentioned earlier; the above; the same (used in lists, etc.): *We bought two books at $45.00 each, ditto at $65.* —*adv.* **2.** (used after another phrase or sentence) just as already stated; likewise; the same: *"I'll have a beer." — "Ditto." (= I'll have one, too.)*

'ditto ,mark, *n.* [*count*] Often, **ditto marks.** two small marks (") indicating the repetition of something, usually placed beneath the thing repeated.

div., an abbreviation of: **1.** divine. **2.** divinity. **3.** division. **4.** divorced.

dive /dayv/ *v.,* **dived** or **dove** /dowv/, **dived, div•ing,** *n.* —*v.* [*no obj*] **1.** to plunge into water,

D

esp. headfirst: *He dove straight into the pool.* **2.** to plunge, fall, or descend through the air: *The acrobats dived into nets.* **3.** to jump or move quickly; dart: *The spy dived quickly into a doorway.* **4.** to enter deeply or plunge into a subject, activity, etc.: *She dove straight into the new book and read all night.* —*n.* [*count*] **5.** an act or instance of diving. **6.** *Informal.* a dirty, cheap, disreputable bar or nightclub. —**'div•er,** *n.* [*count*]

di•verge /dɪ'vɜrdʒ, day-/ *v.* [*no obj*], **-verged,** **-verg•ing. 1.** to move or lie in different directions from a common point: *The path diverges just after the cabin.* **2.** to differ in opinion, character, or form: *Our views on that matter diverge.*

di•ver•gence /dɪ'vɜrdʒəns, day-/ *n.* difference of opinion, character, or form: [*noncount*]: *I think too much divergence keeps us from ever agreeing.* [*count*]: *a divergence of opinion.*

di•ver•gent /dɪ'vɜrdʒənt, day-/ *adj.* **1.** different; conflicting: *I tried to combine their divergent views.* **2.** splitting off; separating: *The two roads run parallel for a while, then become divergent.*

di•verse /dɪ'vɜrs, day-/ *adj.* of a different kind, form, or character: *diverse ideas on how to raise children.* —**di•'verse•ly,** *adv.*

di•ver•si•fy /dɪ'vɜrsə,faɪ, day-/ *v.,* **-fied, -fy•ing.** to give or increase variety or diversity to: [*~ + obj*]: *to diversify the campus by hiring people with unusual interests.* [*no obj*]: *The college had already diversified greatly by hiring people with wider interests.* —**di•ver•si•fi•ca•tion** /dɪ,vɜrsəfɪ'keɪʃən, day-/ *n.* [*noncount*]

di•ver•sion /dɪ'vɜrʒən, day-/ *n.* **1.** the act of diverting: [*count*]: *a diversion of industry into the war effort.* [*noncount*]: *They urged diversion of resources toward the poor and middle classes.* **2.** [*count*] something that amuses and draws one's attention away from care or routine. **3.** [*count*] a false attack intended to draw off attention from the point of main attack. —**di•'ver•sion,ar•y,** *adj.*

di•ver•si•ty /dɪ'vɜrsɪtiy, day-/ *n.* [*noncount*], *pl.* **-ties.** the state or fact of being diverse; variety: *Diversity of opinion makes for a more interesting discussion.*

di•vert /dɪ'vɜrt, day-/ *v.* [*~ + obj*] **1.** to turn aside or from a path or course: *We diverted our funds to paying for college.* **2.** to distract (the attention): *My attention was diverted for a moment by the accident.*

di•vest /dɪ'vɛst, day-/ *v.* [*~ + obj*] to take away, deprive, or strip (someone or something), esp. of property or rights: *The family was divested of its home.* —**di•'vest•i•ture,** *n.* [*noncount*] [*count*]

di•vide /dɪ'vaɪd/ *v.,* **-vid•ed, -vid•ing. 1.** to (cause to) become separated into parts: [*~ + obj*]: *I divided the class and took one section to the library and left the other to write an essay.* [*no obj*]: *The group divided and headed off in different directions.* **2.** [*~ + obj*] to separate and classify, arrange, or put in order: *She divided the pencils by color.* **3.** [*~ + obj*] to separate in opinion or feeling; cause to disagree: *The issue divided the senators.* **4.** [*~ + obj*] to separate (a number) into equal parts by division: *Divide 50 by 5.*

div•i•dend /'dɪvɪ,dɛnd/ *n.* [*count*] **1.** money paid to someone, esp. a sum paid to people who own shares in a company: *a dividend of $50.* **2.** anything received that is more than one had expected; bonus: *Making two friends was an unexpected dividend of taking the history course.*

di•vid•er /dɪ'vaɪdər/ *n.* [*count*] a person or thing that divides: *a room divider.*

di•vine /dɪ'vaɪn/ *adj.,* **-vin•er, -vin•est,** *n.* —*adj.* **1.** of, like, or from a god: *The altar was a place of divine worship.* —*n.* **2. the Divine, a.** God. **b.** [*noncount*] the spiritual aspect in humans regarded as godly or godlike. —**di•'vine•ly,** *adv.*

di•vin•i•ty /dɪ'vɪnɪtiy/ *n.,* *pl.* **-ties. 1.** [*noncount*] the quality of being divine: *questions about the divinity of Christ.* **2.** [*count*] a divine being; God. **3.** [*noncount*] the study of religion.

di•vis•i•ble /dɪ'vɪzəbəl/ *adj.* able to be divided. —**di•vis•i•bil•i•ty** /dɪ,vɪzə'bɪlɪtiy/, *n.* [*noncount*]

di•vi•sion /dɪ'vɪʒən/ *n.* **1.** [*noncount*] the act of dividing; state of being divided. **2.** [*noncount*] the process of dividing one number into another: *We had fifteen problems in division for homework.* **3.** [*count*] something that divides or separates: *The mountains form the division between the two countries.* **4.** [*count*] one of the parts into which an organization is divided; section: *the upper division of the university.* **5.** [*count*] [*noncount*] disagreement; dissension. —**di•'vi•sion•al,** *adj.* [*before a noun*]

di•vi•sive /dɪ'vaɪsɪv/ *adj.* creating feelings of disagreement: *His tactics were divisive, trying to make everyone mad at one another.* —**di•'vi•sive•ly,** *adv.* —**di•'vi•sive•ness,** *n.* [*noncount*]

di•vorce /dɪ'vɔrs/ *n.,* *v.,* **-vorced, -vorc•ing.** —*n.* [*count*] **1.** a legal ending of a marriage: *She told him she wanted a divorce.* —*v.* **2.** [*~ + obj*] to separate by divorce. **3.** to separate; cut off: [*no obj*]: *Life and art cannot be divorced.* [*~ + obj*]: *Can you divorce life from art?* —**di•'vorced,** *adj.*: *divorced couples.*

di•vor•cée or **di•vor•cee** /dɪvɔr'seɪ, -ɪ'siy, -ɪ'vɔrseɪ/ *n.* [*count*], *pl.* **-cées** or **-cees.** a divorced woman.

di•vulge /dɪ'vʌldʒ, day-/ *v.* [*~ + obj*], **-vulged, -vulg•ing.** to tell (something secret): *He promised not to divulge their hiding place. He wouldn't divulge that he knew the facts.*

Dix•ie /'dɪksiy/ *n.* the southern states of the United States, esp. those that were part of the Confederacy.

diz•zy /'dɪziy/ *adj.,* **-zi•er, -zi•est,** *v.,* **-zied, -zy•ing.** —*adj.* **1.** feeling that things are going round and round: *I always feel dizzy after riding the merry-go-round.* **2.** confused: *I came out of the lecture a little dizzy from all those facts and figures.* —*v.* [*~ + obj*] **3.** to make dizzy: *We drove at speeds that dizzied me.* —**diz•zi•ly** /'dɪzəliy/, *adv.*: *I staggered dizzily.* —**'diz•zi•ness,** *n.* [*noncount*] —**'diz•zy•ing,** *adj.*: *He drove at dizzying speed.*

DJ, an abbreviation of: disc jockey.

DMZ, an abbreviation of: demilitarized zone.

DNA, an abbreviation of: deoxyribonucleic acid: the part of a cell that contains genetic information.

do /duw/ *unstressed* dʊ, də/ *v.* and *auxiliary v.,* *pres. sing. 1st* and *2nd pers.* **do,** *3rd* **does** /dʌz/ *pres. pl.* **do;** *past sing.* and *pl.* **did** /dɪd/; *past part.* **done** /dʌn/; *pres. part.* **do•ing;** *n.,* *pl.* **dos, do's.** —*v.* **1.** [*~ + obj*] to perform (an act, duty, role, etc.): *He does a great comedy act.* **2.** [*~ + obj*] to finish: *He has already done it.* **3.** [*~ + obj*] to put forth; exert: *Do your best.* **4.** [*~ + obj*] to cause (good, harm, etc.): *Drugs can do harm to you. Drugs can do you a lot of harm.* **5.** [*~ + obj*] to fix, clean, arrange, etc. (anything): *I did the windows and the laundry.* **6.** [*~ + obj* to make or prepare: *I'll do the salad.* **7.** [~ + *obj*] to study or work at: *I have to do my math tonight.* **8.** [*no obj*] to act or behave: *Do as I say, not as I do.* **9.** [*no obj*] to get along; fare; manage: *How are you doing at work?* —*auxiliary v.* [~ + *root form of a verb*] **10. a.** (used in questions before the subject): *Do you like music? When did he leave?* **b.** (used in negative sentences): *I do not like you. I don't care. I didn't see you last night.* **c.** (used to stand for, or repeat, another verb): *I think as you do (= I think as you think).* *I enjoy jogging and John does, too (= and John enjoys jogging, too). John enjoys jogging, doesn't he?* **11. do away with, a.** to put an end to: *We did away with that old custom years ago.* **b.** to kill: *He did away with most of his rivals.* **12. do in, a.** to kill; murder: *They did him in with a knife.* **b.** to tire out: *All that hard work really did me in.* **13. do out of,** *Informal.* to cheat: *They did him out of his life savings.* **14. do over, a.** to redecorate: *They did the room over.* **b.** to do again: *Do the work over; it's a mess.* **15. do up, a.** to wrap and tie up: *They did up the package and mailed it for me.* **b.** to fasten: *Do up your coat.* **16. do without,** to manage or exist without: *We'll just have to do without a car until they fix it. We'll just have to do without for a while.* —*Idiom.* **17. dos and don'ts,** customs, rules, or regulations. —'**do•a•ble,** *adj.*: *He assured me my project was doable.*

doc•ile /'dɒsɪl/ *adj.* easily managed; tame. —**do'cil•i•ty** /-'sɪlɪtiy/, *n.* [*noncount*]

dock¹ /dɒk/ *n.* [*count*] **1.** a place for loading and unloading ships. **2.** a platform for loading and unloading trucks, etc.: *a loading dock.* —*v.* **3.** to (cause to) come or go into a dock: [*no obj*]: *The ship docked and the passengers filed off.* [~ + *obj*]: *The pilot docked the ship.*

dock² /dɒk/ *v.* [~ + *obj*] to take away a part from (wages): *Their employer docked their pay.*

dock³ /dɒk/ *n.* [*count*] the place in a courtroom where a prisoner stands during trial.

doc•tor /'dɒktər/ *n.* [*count*] **1.** a person trained in medicine. **2.** a person who has received the highest degree that can be offered by a university. —*v.* [~ + *obj*] **3.** to give medical treatment (to): *She doctored him back to health.* **4.** to change falsely; tamper with; falsify: *to doctor information on a passport.* —'**doc•tor•al,** *adj.* [*before a noun*]: *a doctoral candidate in linguistics.*

doc•tor•ate /'dɒktərɪt/ *n.* DOCTOR'S DEGREE.

'**doctor's de,gree,** *n.* [*count*] the highest degree awarded by universities.

doc•tri•naire /,dɒktrə'nɛər/ *adj.* strict and rigid about one's ideas: *a doctrinaire preacher.*

doc•trine /'dɒktrɪn/ *n.* a particular belief or group of teachings: [*count*]: *The church teaches the doctrine of free will.* [*noncount*]: *He is critical of church doctrine.* —'**doc•tri•nal,** *adj.* [*before a noun*]: *shifts in doctrinal policies.*

doc•u•ment /*n.*'dɒkyəmənt; *v.* -,mɛnt/ *n.* [*count*] **1.** a written paper providing proof or evidence, such as a passport, etc.; a legal or official paper. —*v.* [~ + *obj*] **2.** to support by written evidence: *The lawyers worked to document their case.* —**doc•u•men•ta•tion** /,dɒkyəmən'teyʃən/, *n.* [*noncount*]: *Do you have documentation that proves you paid these bills?*

doc•u•men•ta•ry /,dɒkyə'mɛntəriy, -triy/ *adj., n., pl.* **-ries.** —*adj.* **1.** relating to, made up of, or taken from documents: *documentary evidence.* **2.** showing an actual event: *a documentary film.*

—*n.* [*count*] **3.** a documentary film, television program, etc.: *We saw a documentary on the war.*

dodge /dɒdʒ/ *v.,* **dodged, dodg•ing,** *n.* —*v.* **1.** to move aside suddenly: [*no obj*]: *She threw a rock at me but I dodged out of the way.* [~ + *obj*]: *to dodge a blow.* **2.** [~ + *obj*] to avoid, esp. by dishonest means: *dodging his taxes.* —*n.* [*count*] **3.** a quick movement to avoid something. **4.** a clever scheme to deceive: *She found a new dodge to keep from paying taxes.* —'**dodg•er,** *n.* [*count*]

doe /dow/ *n.* [*count*], *pl.* **does,** (*esp. when thought of as a group*) **doe.** the female of the deer, antelope, goat, rabbit, and certain other animals.

does /dʌz/ *v.* 3rd pers. sing. pres. indic. of DO¹: *She does not want to go.* See DO.

does•n't /'dʌzənt/ *v.* contraction of *does not*: *She doesn't really want to go with you.* See DO.

dog /dɔg, dɒg/ *n.* [*count*] **1.** a common four-legged animal kept as a pet, often used for protection. **2.** *Slang.* an unattractive person: *My date last night was a real dog.* —*Idiom.* **3. go to the dogs,** to go to a worse state or condition. **4. lead a dog's life,** to have an unhappy existence: *He leads a dog's life, commuting three hours each way to a terrible job.*

dog

'**dog-,ear** or '**dog,ear,** *n.* [*count*] **1.** (in a book) a corner of a page folded over to mark a place. —*v.* [~ + *obj*] **2.** to fold down the corner of (a page in a book). —'**dog,eared,** *adj.*

dog•ged /'dɔgɪd, 'dɒgɪd/ *adj.* [*before a noun*] refusing to give up: *his dogged determination.* —'**dog•ged•ly,** *adv.*: *He doggedly insisted he was innocent.*

dog•gy or **dog•gie** /'dɔgiy, 'dɒgiy/ *n.* [*count*], *pl.* **-gies. 1.** a small dog or a puppy. **2.** a name for any dog.

'**doggy ,bag,** *n.* [*count*] a small bag provided by a restaurant for a customer to take home uneaten food.

dog•house /'dɔg,haws, 'dɒg-/ *n.* [*count*] **1.** a small shelter for a dog. —*Idiom.* **2. in the doghouse,** in disfavor or disgrace.

dog•ma /'dɔgmə, 'dɒg-/ *n.* [*noncount*] [*count*], *pl.* **-mas.** a set of beliefs to be accepted without question.

dog•mat•ic /dɔg'mætɪk, dɒg-/ *adj.* putting forward opinions in a rigid, forceful manner. —**dog'mat•i•cal•ly,** *adv.*

dog•wood /'dɔg,wʊd, 'dɒg-/ *n.* [*count*] a tree or shrub of Europe and America with pink or white blossoms.

dole /dowl/ *n., v.,* **doled, dol•ing.** —*n.* [*count; usually singular*] **1.** an amount of money given to the needy by a charity or government: *A dole is given to them every two weeks or so.* —*v.* [~ + *obj*] **2.** to give out (something) in small quantities: *to dole (out) water.*

D

dole•ful /'dowlfəl/ adj. sad; sorrowful: a doleful sigh. —'**dole•ful•ly,** adv.

doll /dɒl/ n. [count] **1.** a small figure that looks like a baby or other human being, used esp. as a child's toy. **2.** Slang. **a.** a physically attractive person. My date last night was a real doll. **b.** a generous or helpful person: You're a real doll for giving me a ride home.

dol•lar /'dɒlər/ n. [count] the basic monetary unit of various countries, including the U.S. and Canada.

dol•ly /'dɒliy/ n. [count], pl. -lies. **1.** Informal. a doll. **2.** a low cart with small wheels for moving heavy loads.

dol•phin /'dɒlfɪn, 'dɔl-/ n. [count] a small-toothed mammal of the sea having a beaklike nose and mouth. Compare PORPOISE.

-dom, a suffix meaning: area ruled (kingdom); group of persons (officialdom); rank (earldom); general condition (freedom).

do•main /dow'meyn/ n. [count] **1.** an area of thought, interest, etc.; subject: He works in the domain of public health. **2.** the area governed by a ruler: His domains stretched for hundreds of miles in every direction.

dome /dowm/ n. [count] a roof or ceiling that is rounded. —**domed,** adj.: the domed roof of the Capitol building in Washington, D.C.

do•mes•tic /də'mɛstɪk/ adj. **1.** of or relating to the home or home life: domestic as opposed to industrial uses of natural gas. **2.** tame: Cats are domestic animals. **3.** produced in one's own country: domestic cheese. —n. [count] **4.** a household servant. —**do'mes•ti•cal•ly,** adv.

do•mes•ti•cate /də'mɛstɪˌkeyt/ v. [~ + obj], -cat•ed, -cat•ing. **1.** to tame (an animal): If you domesticate that raccoon, it will have trouble living in the wild. **2.** to make (someone) become used to life in a household. —**do•mes•ti•ca•tion** /dəˌmɛstɪ'keyʃən/, n. [noncount]

do•mes•tic•i•ty /ˌdowmɛ'stɪsɪtiy/ n. [noncount] the state of being domestic or of liking home life: a blissful view of domesticity.

dom•i•nant /'dɒmənənt/ adj. most important or powerful: The dominant powers took control of the conference. —'**dom•i•nance,** n. [noncount] —'**dom•i•nant•ly,** adv.

dom•i•nate /'dɒməˌneyt/ v. [~ + obj], -nat•ed, -nat•ing. **1.** to rule over; control: She completely dominates the family. **2.** to tower above: The church dominates the entire village. **3.** to be the most important factor in: The issue of gun control will dominate the next election. —**dom•i•na•tion** /ˌdɒmə'neyʃən/, n. [noncount]

dom•i•neer•ing /ˌdɒmə'nɪərɪŋ/ adj. using or having great control; ruling strongly: a domineering personality.

Do•min•i•can /də'mɪnɪkən for 1, 3; ˌdɒmə'niykən for 2, 4 / adj. **1.** of or relating to the Dominican Republic. **2.** of or relating to Dominica. —n. [count] **3.** a person born or living in the Dominican Republic. **4.** a person born or living in Dominica.

do•min•ion /də'mɪnyən/ n. **1.** [noncount] the power to govern: The king declared he had sole dominion over this land. **2.** [count] the area subject to the control of a ruler or government: The law was put into effect throughout the dominion.

dom•i•no /'dɒməˌnow/ n., pl. -noes. **1.** [count] a small, flat block having two squares, each either blank or painted with dots. **2.** dominoes. [noncount; used with a singular verb] a game played with dominoes.

do•nate /'downeyt, dow'neyt/ v., -nat•ed, -nat•ing. to present (something) as a gift: [~ + obj]: She donated a pint of blood last year. The millionaire donated money to charity. [no obj]: I've already donated, please don't ask again.

do•na•tion /dow'neyʃən/ n. **1.** [noncount] the act of donating something: donation of his time and energy. **2.** [count] something given, presented, or donated as a gift: My donation was fifty dollars.

done /dʌn/ v. **1.** pp. of DO[1]: I've already done the dishes. —adj. **2.** finished; completed. **3.** cooked enough: Is the meat done yet? **4.** acceptable: That sort of thing simply isn't done. —**Idiom. 5.** be or have done with, to break off relations with. **6. done in,** very tired; exhausted: I'm all done in after that five-mile walk.

don•key /'dɒŋkiy, 'dɒŋ-, 'dʌŋ-/ n. [count], pl. -keys. **1.** a long-eared domesticated mammal related to the horse. **2.** a stupid, silly, or stubborn person.

do•nor /'downər/ n. [count] **1.** a person who gives or donates. **2.** a provider of blood or an organ for transfusion or transplantation: She is waiting for a kidney donor. —adj. [before a noun] **3.** of or relating to the biological tissue of a donor: a donor organ. **4.** relating to a giver of a donation: a donor card.

don't /downt/ v. contraction of do not: Don't come in.

do•nut /'downət, -ˌnʌt/ n. DOUGHNUT.

doo•dle /'duwdl/ v. [no obj] [~ + obj], -dled, -dling. to draw or scribble idly.

doom /duwm/ n. [noncount] **1.** terrible or evil fate. —v. [~ + obj; usually: be + ~ -ed] **2.** to be destined to a bad fate: They were doomed to a life of poverty.

dooms•day /'duwmzˌdey/ n. [noncount] the end of the world.

door /dɔr/ n. [count] **1.** a movable object of wood, glass, or metal for closing an entrance. **2.** DOORWAY (def. 1). **3.** a house or building, as represented by its entrance: My brother lives just two doors away. **4.** any means of getting to something: the door to learning. —**Idiom. 5. at death's door,** near death; dying. **6. next door,** at the next house, building, or apartment: He fell in love with the girl next door. **7. show someone the door,** to order someone to leave: The bodyguard showed me the door.

door•bell /'dɔrˌbɛl/ n. [count] a bell or buzzer rung by persons wanting to come in.

door•man /'dɔrˌmæn, -mən/ n. [count], pl. -men. a person who is on duty at the door of a large building.

door•mat /'dɔrˌmæt/ n. [count] a mat placed before a door for people to wipe their shoes.

door•step /'dɔrˌstɛp/ n. [count] a step in front of a door.

'door-to-'door, adj. [before a noun] going from one house to another: a door-to-door salesman.

door•way /'dɔrˌwey/ n. [count] **1.** the way of entering a building, room, etc. **2.** a means of gaining something: the doorway to success.

dope /dowp/ n., v., doped, dop•ing. —n. **1.** [noncount] Slang. an illegal drug. **2.** [count] Informal. a stupid person. —v. [~ + obj] **3.** to give dope to or put dope in: She doped his drink.

dop•ey or **dop•y** /'dowpiy/ adj., -i•er, -i•est. Informal. **1.** stupid; foolish. **2.** sleepy, as if from drugs or alcohol.

dorm /dɔrm/ n. [count] a dormitory.

dor•mant /'dɔrmənt/ adj. **1.** not active: dormant

plants and animals; a dormant volcano. **2.** not developed; held back: *She had talents that lay dormant.* —**dor•man•cy** /'dɔrmənsiy/, *n.* [*noncount*]

dor•mi•to•ry /'dɔrmɪˌtɔriy/ *n.* [*count*], *pl.* **-ries,** **1.** a building, such as at a college, in which students live. **2.** a large room containing a number of beds for a group of people: *the barracks dormitory.*

DOS /dɔs, dɒs/ *n.* [*noncount*] an operating system for microcomputers: *DOS is an abbreviation for disk operating system.*

dos•age /'dowsədʒ/ *n.* [*count; usually singular*] the amount of medicine to be taken at one time: *The dosage is two tablets every four hours.*

dose /dows/ *n., v.,* **dosed, dos•ing.** —*n.* [*count*] **1.** an amount of medicine to be taken at one time: *an hourly dose of medicine.* **2.** an unpleasant experience: *a dose of bad luck.* —*v.* [~ + *obj*] **3.** to give a dose of medicine to: *We dosed her with aspirin to reduce the fever.*

dos•si•er /'dɔsiyˌey, 'dɒsiyˌey/ *n.* [*count*] a set of papers containing information about a person or thing.

dot /dɒt/ *n., v.,* **dot•ted, dot•ting.** —*n.* [*count*] **1.** a small, round mark: *She forgot the dot on the letter* i. —*v.* [~ + *obj*] **2.** to mark with or as if with a dot or dots: *to dot the letter* i. **3.** to cover with or as if with dots: *From above we could see the trees dotting the landscape.* —*Idiom.* **4.** on **the dot,** exactly at the time said: *We arrived at 6:00 on the dot.*

dot•age /'dowtɪdʒ/ *n.* [*noncount*] **1.** a decline or weakening of the mind, esp. as associated with old age: *In his dotage he didn't recognize me.* **2.** foolish affection: *his dotage on his grandchildren.*

dote /dowt/ *v.* [*no obj*], **dot•ed, dot•ing.** to show too much fondness or love for: *Grandparents love to dote on their grandchildren.* —'**dot• ing•ly,** *adv.*

dot•ted /'dɒtɪd/ *adj.* [*usually: before a noun*] made up of a row of dots: *Sign on the dotted line below.*

dot•ty /'dɒtiy/ *adj.,* **-ti•er, -ti•est.** *Chiefly Brit.* **1.** a little bit crazy: *She was a dotty old woman.* **2.** [*be* + ~ + *about*] eager about (something): *She was dotty about horse-racing.*

dou•ble /'dʌbəl/ *adj., n., v.,* **-bled, -bling,** *adv.* —*adj.* **1.** twice as large; twice as many: *The workers receive double pay for working on Sundays. He ordered a double whiskey.* **2.** [*before a noun*] made up of two similar parts: *a double sink.* **3.** [*usually: before a noun*] for two persons: *We rented a double room.* **4.** having two meanings: *His comment had a double meaning.* **5.** folded in two layers. —*n.* **6.** anything that is twice the usual size, amount, etc.: [*noncount*]: *She offered me double for the computer.* [*count*]: *He ordered a double of Scotch.* **7.** [*count*] a person who closely resembles another: *She is the double of her mother.* **8.** [*count*] a hotel room for two people. **9. doubles,** [*noncount; used with a singular verb*] a game or match, as in tennis, in which there are two players on each side: *a doubles match.* —*v.* **10.** to (cause to) become twice as great: [*no obj*]: *Our taxes doubled.* [~ + *obj*]: *The landlord doubled our rent.* **11.** [~ + *obj*] to fold or bend with one part over another: *He doubled the blankets to keep warm.* **12. double as,** to do a second job: *The director doubles as an actor.* **13. double back,** to turn back: *I doubled back to find the missing earring.* **14. double up, a.** to share space planned for only one person: *You can stay*

with us; we'll all just double up. **b.** Also, **double over.** to (cause to) bend over, as from pain: *As the next wave of pain hit, he doubled over.* —*adv.* **15.** up to twice the amount: *We paid double for that room.* **16.** two together: *to sleep double.* —*Idiom.* **17. on the double,** without delay; rapidly: *Get up there on the double.*

dou•bly /'dʌbliy/ *adv.* twice as: *to be doubly careful.*

doubt /dawt/ *v.* [~ + *obj*] **1.** to be uncertain about; wonder: *I doubt his honesty.* **2.** [~ + *obj*] to consider unlikely: *I doubt that she will help.* —*n.* [*noncount*] [*count*] **3.** a feeling of uncertainty. —*Idiom.* **4. beyond (a** or **the shadow of) a doubt,** with certainty; definitely: *guilty beyond a shadow of a doubt.* **5. in doubt,** in a state of uncertainty: *The outcome of the election was in doubt.* **6. no doubt,** probably: *No doubt you'll be in school tomorrow.* **7. without doubt,** certainly: *She is, without doubt, the finest teacher in the school.* —'**doubt•er,** *n.* [*count*] —'**doubt• ing•ly,** *adv.*

doubt•ful /'dawtfəl/ *adj.* **1.** uncertain: *a doubtful future.* **2.** undecided: *I'm doubtful about my choice.* —'**doubt•ful•ly,** *adv.*

doubt•less /'dawtlɪs/ *adv.* Also, **doubt′less•ly.** **1.** without doubt; certainly: *Doubtless he'll be here on time.* **2.** very probably: *She'll doubtless- (ly) accept the job.* —*adj.* **3.** sure; free from doubt.

dough /dow/ *n.* [*noncount*] **1.** flour combined with water, milk, etc., for baking: *We made our own pizza dough.* **2.** *Slang.* money: *Can you lend me some dough?*

dough•nut or **do•nut** /'downət, -ˌnʌt/ *n.* [*count*] a small, ring-shaped cake of fried sweetened dough.

douse /daws/ *v.* [~ + *obj*], **doused, dous•ing.** **1.** to throw water on: *We doused the children with the hose.* **2.** to put out: *to douse a candle.*

dove[1] /dʌv/ *n.* [*count*] **1.** a bird of the pigeon family. **2.** a person who calls for peace.

dove[2] /dowv/ *v.* a pt. of DIVE.

dove•tail /'dʌvˌteyl/ *n.* [*count*] **1.** a joint in the shape of a wedge that fits tightly into a gap in another piece of wood. —*v.* [*no obj*] **2.** (of ideas, figures, etc.) to fit together neatly: *My figures dovetailed nicely with theirs.*

dow•el /'dawəl/ *n.* [*count*] a small, round wooden rod.

down[1] /dawn/ *adv.* **1.** from higher to lower: *Tell him to come down.* **2.** to or in a sitting or lying position: *Please sit down.* **3.** to a lower value, level, or rate: *Slow down.* **4.** to a lower volume: *Turn down the radio.* **5.** in or to a less active state: *The wind died down.* **6.** from a greater to a lesser strength, amount, etc.: *to water down a drink.* **7.** to the point of defeat: *They shouted down the opposition.* **8.** on paper: *Write this down.* **9.** in a low place: *down at the bottom of the ocean.* **10.** toward or in the south: *He went from New York down to Washington.* **11.** into a condition of bad health: *He came down with the flu.* —*prep.* **12.** to or at a lower level: *They ran down the stairs.* **13.** along: *They ran down the street.* —*adj.* **14.** [*before a noun*] directed downward; going down: *Take the down escalator.* **15.** [*be/seem* + ~] sad; gloomy: *You seem down to- day.* **16.** [*be* + ~] sick and in bed: *He's down with a bad cold.* —*v.* [~ + *obj*] **17.** to knock, throw, or bring down: *He downed his opponent.* **18.** to drink quickly: *I downed the vodka in one gulp.* —*Idiom.* **19. down cold** or **pat,** learned

D

perfectly: *He always has his facts down cold.* **20.** **down in the mouth,** discouraged; sad; depressed: *He looks down in the mouth today.* **21.** **down on,** hostile to: *They were down on his candidacy.* **22. down with,** (used in a command or a wish, without a subject) to do away with: *Down with the king!*

down² /dawn/ *n.* [*noncount*] the short, soft feathers of some birds. —'**down•y** *adj.*, **-i•er, -i•est.**

down•fall /'dawn,fɔl/ *n.* [*noncount*] fall from power: *the downfall of the dictator.*

down•grade /'dawn,greyd/ *v.*, **-grad•ed, -grad•ing,** *n.* —*v.* [~ + *obj*] **1.** to reduce to a lower level of importance. —*n.* [*count*] **2.** a downward slope, esp. of a road. **3.** a lowering in importance.

down•heart•ed /'dawn'hɑrtɪd/ *adj.* sad; depressed: *She was downhearted because she failed again.*

down•hill /*adv.*'dawn'hɪl; *adj.* -,hɪl/ *adv.* **1.** down the slope of a hill: *to ski downhill.* **2.** into a worse condition: *Things have gone downhill again.* —*adj.* **3.** going downward on or as if on a hill: *a downhill trail.*

'**down 'payment,** *n.* [*count*] an amount of money given as partial payment at the time one buys something.

down•pour /'dawn,pɔr/ *n.* [*count*] a very heavy rain.

down•right /'dawn,rayt/ *adv.* **1.** completely; thoroughly: *downright angry.* —*adj.* [*before a noun*] **2.** complete: *a downright lie.*

down•size /'dawn,sayz/ *v.*, **-sized, siz•ing.** to reduce the number of; cut back: [~ + *obj*]: *The plant downsized its staff.* [*no obj*]: *The company will have to downsize to cut costs.*

down•stairs /*adv.*, *n.* 'dawn'stɛrz; *adj.* -,stɛrz/ *adv.* **1.** down the stairs; to or on a lower floor: *Come downstairs for breakfast now!* —*adj.* **2.** Also, '**down,stair.** [*before a noun*] relating to or on a lower floor: *my downstairs neighbor.* —*n.* [*noncount; used with a singular verb*] **3.** the lower floors of a building: *Downstairs is locked.*

down•stream /'dawn'striym/ *adv.* in the direction of the current of a river.

down•town /'dawn'tawn/ *adv.* **1.** to or in the main business section of a city: *This train goes downtown.* —*adj.* [*before a noun*] **2.** in, or relating to, the downtown section of a city: *the downtown area.* —*n.* [*noncount*] **3.** the downtown section of a city: *trying to rebuild the downtown.*

down•trod•den /'dawn,trɒdn/ *adj.* treated harshly by those in power; oppressed: *trying to help the downtrodden masses.*

down•ward /'dawnwərd/ *adv.* **1.** Also, '**down•wards.** from a higher to a lower level: *The car sank downward in the muddy river.* —*adj.* [*before a noun*] **2.** moving to a lower level or condition: *a downward trend in the economy.*

dow•ry /'dawriy/ *n.* [*count*], *pl.* **-ries.** the money, goods, etc., that a wife brings to her husband at marriage.

dowse /daws/ *v.*, **dowsed, dows•ing.** DOUSE.

doz., an abbreviation of: *dozen.*

doze /dowz/ *v.* [*no obj*], **dozed, doz•ing.** to sleep lightly and briefly; nap: *She was dozing in the hammock.*

doz•en /'dʌzən/ *n.* [*count*], *pl.* **doz•ens,** (*as after a numeral*) **doz•en** a group of 12: *I'll have a dozen eggs.*

Dr., an abbreviation of: **1.** Doctor. **2.** Drive (used in street names).

drab /dræb/ *adj.*, **drab•ber, drab•best.** not bright; dull: *a drab, cheerless office.* —'**drab•ness,** *n.* [*noncount*]

draft /dræft/ *n.* **1.** [*count*] a drawing, sketch, or design. **2.** [*count*] a first plan of something written: *The first draft of the paper had some mistakes.* **3.** [*count*] a current of air: *I felt a draft on my neck.* **4.** [*count*] a written order for payment of money: *He wrote a draft for $100 for his cousin.* **5.** [*count; usually singular*] a selection of persons for military service, an athletic team, etc. —*v.* [~ + *obj*] **6.** to sketch: *She drafted her plans for the park.* **7.** to write a first version: *I drafted my speech last night.* **8.** to select by draft, such as for military service: *He was drafted early in the war.* —*Idiom.* **9. on draft,** drawn from a keg: *beer on draft.*

drafts•man /'dræftsmən/ *n.* [*count*], *pl.* **-men.** **1.** a person employed in making mechanical drawings. **2.** an artist skilled in drawing: *Matisse was a superb draftsman.* —'**drafts•man,ship,** *n.* [*noncount*]

draft•y /'dræftiy/ *adj.*, **-i•er, -i•est.** with uncomfortable currents of air: *We had to work in a cold, drafty room.* —'**draft•i•ness,** *n.* [*noncount*]

drag /dræg/ *v.*, **dragged, drag•ging,** *n.* —*v.* **1.** [~ + *obj*] to pull slowly and with effort; haul: *He dragged his injured foot behind him.* **2.** [*no obj*] to be pulled along: *The dress dragged on the ground.* **3.** [~ + *obj*] to search (a lake, etc.) with a net or hook: *They began to drag the lake for bodies.* **4.** to (cause to) go on for too long a time: [*no obj*]: *The discussion dragged on for hours.* [~ + *obj*]: *They dragged the discussion out for three hours; to drag out a discussion.* **5.** [*no obj*] to feel very tired; to move in such a manner: *This heat has everyone dragging around.* —*n.* **6.** [*count*] someone or something that keeps one from moving forward: *a drag on his career.* **7.** [*count; usually: a + ~*] *Slang.* someone or something boring: *This party's a drag.* **8.** [*noncount*] *Slang.* clothing usually worn by the opposite sex: *He went to the dance in drag.*

drag•on /'drægən/ *n.* [*count*] **1.** an imaginary winged monster that breathed fire. **2.** a fierce person.

drain /dreyn/ *v.* **1.** to empty by removing liquid: [~ + *obj*]: *to drain a swimming pool.* [*no obj*]: *The water drained away.* **2.** [~ + *obj*] to use up money or strength: *He drained his parents of every cent.* —*n.* [*count*] **3.** a pipe or other device that allows a liquid to drain. **4.** something that causes a weakening of loss: *These bills are a drain on our finances.* —*Idiom.* **5. go down the drain,** to be wasted: *All my work went down the drain because I didn't have time to finish.* —'**drain•er,** *n.* [*count*]

drain•age /'dreynɪdʒ/ *n.* [*noncount*] **1.** the act or process of draining. **2.** a system of drains.

drain•pipe /'dreyn,payp/ *n.* [*count*] a large pipe that carries away waste.

drake /dreyk/ *n.* [*count*] a male duck. Compare DUCK[1] (def. 2).

dra•ma /'drɑmə, 'dræmə/ *n.*, *pl.* **-mas. 1.** [*count*] a theatrical play: *historical dramas.* **2.** [*noncount*] an exciting event or series of events: *the drama of the election year.*

dra•mat•ic /drə'mætɪk/ *adj.* **1.** [*before a noun*] of or relating to the drama. **2.** exciting and interesting. —**dra'mat•i•cal•ly,** *adv.*

dra•mat•ics /drə'mætɪks/ *n.* [*plural; used with a plural verb*] **1.** dramatic productions. **2.** behavior that is too emotional: *Then the tears and the dramatics started.*

dram•a•tist /'dræmətɪst, 'drɑmə-/ *n.* [*count*] a writer of dramas; playwright.

dram•a•tize /'dræmə,tayz, 'drɑmə-/ *v.*, **-tized,** **-tiz•ing.** **1.** [~ + *obj*] to make a story into a play to be acted. **2.** [*no obj*] [~ + *obj*] to express (something) in a dramatic or exciting way. —**dram•a•ti•za•tion** /,dræmətə'zeyʃən, ,drɑmə-/, *n.* [*count*]: *They performed the dramatization of his novel.*

drank /dræŋk/ *v.* a pt. and pp. of DRINK.

drape /dreyp/ *v.*, **draped, drap•ing,** *n.* —*v.* [~ + *obj*] **1.** to cover or hang with cloth: *She carefully draped the fabric over the table.* —*n.* [*count*] **2.** a curtain, usually of heavy fabric and long length, esp. one hung across a window.

dra•per•y /'dreypəriy/ *n.*, *pl.* **-per•ies.** **1.** [*noncount*] coverings of fabric, esp. as arranged in loose, graceful folds. **2.** Usually, **draperies.** [*plural*] long curtains, often of heavy fabric.

dras•tic /'dræstɪk/ *adj.* extreme; very great: *We keep facing drastic cuts in spending.* —**dras•ti•cal•ly,** *adv.*: *They kept cutting the budget drastically.*

draw /drɔ/ *v.*, **drew** /druw/ **drawn, draw•ing,** *n.* —*v.* **1.** [*no obj*] to (cause to) move in a certain direction: *The car drew slowly along the street. She drew away from me.* **2.** [~ + *obj*] to move by or as if by pulling: *The horses drew the cart along. I drew her away from the crowd.* **3.** [~ + *obj*] to bring, take, or pull out from a source: *to draw water from a well.* **4.** [~ + *obj*] to attract: *The sale drew large crowds.* **5.** to make or create a picture: [~ + *obj*]: *to draw a portrait.* [*no obj*]: *I really can't draw.* **6.** [~ + *obj*] to suck in; take (a breath) in: *to draw liquid through a straw; I drew a deep breath.* **7.** [~ + *obj*] to produce; bring in: *The deposits draw interest.* **8.** [~ + *obj*] (of a ship) to need (a certain depth of water) to float: *The boat draws six feet.* **9.** to finish (a game) with neither side winning; tie: [~ + *obj*]: *They drew the game at 37-37.* [*no obj*]: *They drew at 37-37.* **10. draw off,** to cause to move back or away: *He drew off the enemy. He drew the enemy off.* **11. draw on, a.** to come nearer; approach: *Winter was drawing on.* **b.** to put (clothing) on: *to draw on one's gloves; He drew his gloves on.* **c.** to use, esp. as a source: *The newspaper article draws heavily on gossip.* **12. draw out, a.** to make longer: *I drew out the discussion for as long as I could.* **b.** to persuade someone to speak: *The police carefully drew the child out.* **c.** to take (money) from a place of deposit: *We drew out $5,000 as the down payment. We drew some money out of our savings.* **13. draw up, a.** to write in legal form: *to draw up a contract; We drew the agreement up quickly.* **b.** to make (oneself) stand as straight or as tall as one can: *He drew himself up to his full height.* **c.** to bring or come to a stop; halt: *The bus drew up to the curb. The driver drew the bus up to the curb.* —*n.* [*count*] **14.** an act of drawing. **15.** something that attracts customers, etc.: *That famous movie star is a big draw.* **16.** something chosen by a lot or chance: *a lottery draw.* **17.** a contest that ends in a tie: *The game ended in a draw.*

draw•back /'drɔ,bæk/ *n.* [*count*] something that is not desirable: *The cost was one of the drawbacks.*

draw•bridge /'drɔ,brɪdʒ/ *n.* [*count*] a bridge in which a section may be raised or drawn aside, to leave a passage open for boats, barges, etc.

draw•er /drɔr/ *n.* [*count*] a sliding horizontal container, such as in a desk, that may be pulled out or pushed back in: *He opened the drawer of his desk and took out the papers.*

draw•ing /'drɔɪŋ/ [*count*] *n.* **1.** the act of a person or thing that draws. **2.** [*count*] a picture, esp. one made with pen, pencil, or crayon. **3.** [*noncount*] the art of making pictures: *She is very good at drawing.*

drawl /drɔl/ *v.* **1.** to speak in a slow manner: [*no obj*]: *She drawled in that slow, lazy style of hers.* [~ + *obj*]: *She drawled a greeting to me.* —*n.* [*count*] **2.** speaking by drawling: *She had that drawl of the deep South.*

drawn /drɔn/ *v.* **1.** pp. of DRAW. —*adj.* **2.** looking tired, thin, or unhappy.

draw•string or **draw string** /'drɔ,strɪŋ/ *n.* [*count*] a cord that is used to close something or to make something tighter.

dread /drɛd/ *v.* [~ + *obj*] **1.** to fear greatly: *to dread death.* —*n.* [*noncount*] **2.** terror or fear about something in the future: *filled with horror and dread.* **3.** a person or thing dreaded: *the dread of being late for the exam.* —*adj.* [*before a noun*] **4.** greatly feared; terrible: *a dread disease.* —**'dread•ed,** *adj.*

dread•ful /'drɛdfəl/ *adj.* **1.** causing great dread, fear, or terror: *a dreadful storm.* **2.** very bad or unpleasant: *a dreadful scandal; a dreadful smell.*

dread•ful•ly /'drɛdfəliy/ *adv.* **1.** very; extremely: *It was a dreadfully bad day.* **2.** in a dreadful manner or way: *He drove dreadfully.*

dream /driym/ *n.*, *v.*, **dreamed** or **dreamt** /drɛmt/, **dream•ing.** —*n.* **1.** [*count*] a series of images passing through the mind during sleep: *I had another dream about living in Europe.* **2.** [*usually: singular;* ɑ̨ + ~] a state of the mind in which one does not pay attention to one's surroundings: *He's walking around in a dream these days.* **3.** [*count*] a hope: *It had always been our dream to take the children to Europe.* **4.** [*count*] something of great beauty, charm, or excellence: *His new apartment is a dream.* —*v.* **5.** [*no obj*] to have a dream. **6.** [~ + *obj*] to see or imagine in sleep or in the imagination: *I dream of quitting my job. I dreamed that a monster was chasing me.* **7.** [*no obj*] to pass (time) in dreaming: *Stop dreaming and get back to work.* **8. dream up,** to create or form in the imagination: *He dreamed up a new plan.* —**'dream•er,** *n.* [*count*] —**'dream•less,** *adj.* —**'dream,like,** *adj.*

dream•y /'driymiy/ *adj.*, **-i•er, -i•est.** **1.** vague; dim: *a dreamy memory of what had happened.* **2.** causing dreams or a dreamlike mood, esp. pleasantly: *dreamy music.* —**dream•i•ly** /'driyməliy/, *adv.*

drear•y /'drɪəriy/ *adj.*, **-i•er, -i•est.** gloomy; depressing: *a cold, dreary winter day.* —**drear•i•ly** /'drɪərəliy/, *adv.* —**'drear•i•ness,** *n.* [*noncount*]

dredge /drɛdʒ/ *n.*, *v.*, **dredged, dredg•ing.** —*n.* [*count*] **1.** a powerful machine for removing earth, as by a scoop. —*v.* [~ + *obj*] **2.** to clear out with a dredge: *to dredge a river.* **3. dredge up,** to discover and make known: *She dredged up yet another scandal.* —**'dredg•er,** *n.* [*count*]

dreg /drɛg/ *n.* [*count*] **1. dregs,** [*plural*] the last part of liquid left in a container; grounds: *He drank the dregs of his coffee.* **2.** Usually, **dregs.** [*plural*] the least valuable part of anything: *the dregs of society.*

drench /drɛntʃ/ *v.* [~ + *obj*] **1.** to wet thoroughly; soak: *I was drenched after the walk in the rain.* **2.** to cover or fill completely: *Sunlight*

D

drenched the trees. —'**drench•ing,** *adj.*: *a drenching rainfall.*

dress /drɛs/ *n.* **1.** [*count*] an outer garment for women and girls, made up of an upper part and a skirt. **2.** [*noncount*] clothing: *Do we have to wear evening dress to the opera? The folk dancers appeared in the national dress of their country.* —*adj.* [*before a noun*] **3.** of or for a formal occasion: *a full dress uniform.* **4.** requiring formal dress: *a dress reception.* —*v.* **5.** to put clothing on: [*no obj*]: *I was dressing when the phone rang.* [~ + *obj*]: *Let's dress the kids.* **6.** [*no obj*] to put on or wear clothes of a certain kind: *They dressed in their best clothes. He said he'd go to the ballet if he didn't have to dress.* **7.** [~ + *obj*] to comb out and do up (hair). **8.** [~ + *obj*] to pour a dressing on: *to dress a salad with oil and vinegar.* **9.** [~ + *obj*] to apply medication or a dressing to (a wound): *The nurse dressed the wound.* **10. dress up, a.** to put on one's best or fanciest clothing: *I'll go to church if I don't have to dress up.* **b.** to dress in costume: *They dressed him up as a ghost. She likes to dress up in her mother's hat and heels.*

dressed /drɛst/ *adj.* **1.** [*be* + ~] wearing clothes: *You can come in now; I'm dressed.* **2.** [*be* + ~ + *in*] wearing the clothes mentioned: *They were dressed in their Sunday best.* **3.** having put on clothes: *She was dressed and ready to go.*

dress•er[1] /'drɛsər/ *n.* [*count*] a person who dresses in a certain manner: *a fancy dresser.*

dress•er[2] /'drɛsər/ *n.* [*count*] a chest of drawers; bureau.

dress•ing /'drɛsɪŋ/ *n.* **1.** a sauce, esp. for salad or other cold foods: [*noncount*]: *Do you like dressing on your salad?* [*count*]: *I'd like a blue cheese dressing.* **2.** [*noncount*] stuffing for a turkey, chicken, or other fowl: *turkey dressing.* **3.** [*count*] material used to dress or cover a wound while it heals: *The doctor will change the dressing.*

drew /druw/ *v.* pt. of DRAW.

drib•ble /'drɪbəl/ *v.,* **-bled, -bling,** *n.* —*v.* **1.** to (cause to) flow in drops; trickle: [*no obj*]: *A little milk dribbled onto the floor.* [~ + *obj*]: *He dribbled some milk onto the cereal.* **2.** to (cause to) move a ball, by bouncing it: [*no obj*]: *She dribbled down the court, then rushed to the basket and shot.* [~ + *obj*]: *He dribbled the ball down the court.* —*n.* [*count*] **3.** a small quantity of anything: *a dribble of revenue.* **4.** an act or instance of dribbling a ball or puck. —'**drib•bler,** *n.* [*count*]

dried /drayd/ *v.* pt. and pp. of DRY.

dri•er[1] /'drayər/ *n.* **1.** one that dries. **2.** DRYER (def. 1).

dri•er[2] /'drayər/ *adj.* comparative of DRY.

dri•est /'drayɪst/ *adj.* superlative of DRY.

drift /drɪft/ *v.* [*no obj*] **1.** to move along, by or as if by currents of water: *The boat drifted out to sea.* **2.** to wander without purpose: *Some people just drift through life.* **3.** to be driven into heaps: *The snow drifted into huge mounds overnight.* —*n.* **4.** [*count*] a drifting movement, as of a current of water: *a drift of some 10 to 15 miles a day.* **5.** [*count*] the course along which something moves: *a drift toward the political right.* **6.** [*count; usually singular*] a meaning; intent: *I get your drift (= I understand your meaning or intent).* **7.** [*count*] a heap of snow driven together.

drift•er /'drɪftər/ *n.* [*count*] a person who goes from one place, job, etc., to another but stays in each only briefly.

drift•wood /'drɪft,wʊd/ *n.* [*noncount*] wood floating in water or washed ashore.

drill /drɪl/ *n.* **1.** [*count*] a tool with a cutting edge for making holes in firm materials: *an electric drill.* **2.** [*noncount*] military training in marching or other movements. **3.** [*count*] any practice or exercise: *We had a spelling drill in school today.* —*v.* **4.** [~ + *obj*] to make a hole in (something) with a drill: *The dentist drilled the cavity and filled it.* **5.** [~ + *obj*] [*no obj*] to instruct and exercise soldiers in marching, etc. **6.** [~ + *obj*] to teach by strict repetition: *The teacher drilled grammar and the multiplication tables every day.* —'**drill•er,** *n.* [*count*]

drink /drɪŋk/ *v.,* **drank** /dræŋk/, **drunk** /drʌŋk/, **drink•ing,** *n.* —*v.* **1.** to take liquid into the mouth and swallow it: [~ + *obj*]: *She drank some wine with dinner.* [*no obj*]: *He wasn't drinking that night.* **2. drink in,** to take something in through the senses, esp. with eagerness and pleasure: *I drank in his every sentence; drinking the mountain scenery in.* —*n.* [*count*] **3.** a liquid that is swallowed; beverage: *a drink of soda.* **4.** liquor; alcoholic beverage: *Let's have a drink after work.* —'**drink•a•ble,** *adj.* —'**drink•er,** *n.* [*count*]

drip /drɪp/ *v.,* **dripped, drip•ping,** *n.* —*v.* **1.** [*no obj*] to let drops fall: *This faucet drips.* **2.** to (cause to) fall in drops: [*no obj*]: *The milk dripped out of the bottle.* [~ + *obj*]: *He dripped some water on her face.* —*n.* **3.** [*noncount*] an act of dripping: *the drip of the rain.* **4.** [*count; usually singular*] the sound made by falling drops: *the annoying drip of a faucet.*

drive /drayv/ *v.,* **drove** /drowv/, **driv•en** /'drɪvən/, **driv•ing,** *n.* —*v.* **1.** [~ + *obj*] to send or cause to move by force: *to drive away the flies; to drive back an attacking army; to drive a person to despair.* **2.** to operate and control the movement of (a car, etc.): [~ + *obj*]: *He learned to drive a car at the age of fifteen.* [*no obj*]: *Where did you learn how to drive?* **3.** to (cause to) go or be carried in a car: [~ + *obj*]: *Let me drive you home.* [*no obj*]: *We drove to the beach.* **4.** [~ + *obj*] to force to work, do, or act: *He drove the workers until they collapsed. Pride drove him to finish the work on time.* **5.** [~ + *obj*] to keep (machinery) going: *The engine drives the propellers.* **6.** [~ + *obj*] to hit or kick (a ball, etc.) with much force: *The batter drove the next pitch over the fence.* **7.** [*no obj*] to rush or dash violently: *The rain was driving in our faces.* **8. drive at,** to intend to convey (a meaning): *What are you driving at?* **9. drive off,** to push or send back; stop an attack of: *We managed to drive off the next attack. Somehow we drove them off.* —*n.* **10.** [*count*] the act of driving. **11.** [*count*] a trip in a car, esp. for pleasure: *Let's take a drive upstate.* **12.** [*count*] a road for vehicles, such as to a private house. **13.** [*count*] a basic, instinctive need: *one's hunger drive.* **14.** [*count*] a vigorous action or course that leads toward an objective: *her drive for the presidency.* **15.** [*count*] a united effort: *a drive to raise money for the hospital.* **16.** [*noncount*] energy; motivation: *That student had a lot of drive.* **17.** [*noncount*] a driving mechanism: *His new car has four-wheel drive.* —*Idiom.* **18. drive home,** to make (something) understood: *I tried to drive home the importance of hard work. I tried to drive the point home that we could not afford college.* —'**driv•ing,** *adj.*: *We ran through the driving rain.*

'**drive-,in,** *adj.* **1.** designed for customers in their cars: *a drive-in restaurant.* —*n.* [*count*] **2.** such a business.

driv•el /'drɪvəl/ *n.*, *v.*, **-eled** or **-elled, -el•ing** or **-el•ling.** —*n.* [*noncount*] **1.** childish, silly, or meaningless thinking: *I had to listen to his drivel for hours.* —*v.* [*no obj*] **2.** to talk childishly or foolishly: *She was driveling on about her friends at school.*

driv•er /'drayvər/ *n.* [*count*] a person who drives a vehicle.

drive•way /'drayv,wey/ *n.* [*count*] a road leading from a street to a building.

driz•zle /'drɪzəl/ *v.*, **-zled, -zling,** *n.* —*v.* [*no obj*] **1.** to rain gently and steadily; sprinkle: *It was drizzling all day.* —*n.* [*noncount*] **2.** a very light rain. —'**driz•zly,** *adj.*: *drizzly weather.*

drone[1] /'droʊn/ *n.* [*count*] **1.** the male of the honeybee and other bees. **2.** a person who lives on the work of others.

drone[2] /'droʊn/ *v.*, **droned, dron•ing,** *n.* —*v.* [*no obj*] **1.** to make a continued, low sound. **2.** to speak in or proceed in a dull manner: *The meeting droned (on) for hours.* —*n.* [*count*] **3.** a low humming tone: *the steady drone of the airplane.*

drool /druwl/ *v.* [*no obj*] **1.** to water at the mouth: *The baby was drooling with his thumb in his mouth.* **2.** to show feelings of pleasure: *I was drooling at the thought of debating him. The staff was drooling over having a day off.*

droop /druwp/ *v.* **1.** to (cause to) sag, sink, or hang down, such as from exhaustion: [*no obj*]: *The flowers drooped in the heat.* [~ + *obj*]: *an eagle drooping its wings.* **2.** [*no obj*] to fall into a weakened state: *Our spirits drooped.* —*n.* [*count*] **3.** a sinking or bending as from lack of support. —'**droop•i•ness,** *n.* [*noncount*] —'**droop•y,** *adj.*, **-i•er, -i•est:** *The plants are droopy and need to be watered.*

drop /drɒp/ *n.*, *v.*, **dropped, drop•ping.** —*n.* [*count*] **1.** a very small amount of liquid. **2.** a very small quantity of anything: *not even a drop of mercy.* **3.** Usually, **drops.** [*plural*] liquid medicine given from a medicine dropper, such as a solution for the eyes. **4.** an act or instance of dropping; fall: *The sudden drop startled the airplane's passengers.* **5.** the distance or depth to which anything drops: *a drop of ten feet.* **6.** a steep slope: *It's a short drop to the lake.* **7.** a decline in amount: *The stock market saw a drop of about fifty points.* **8.** a small, round piece of candy or medication: *chocolate drops; cough drops.* —*v.* **9.** to (cause to) fall: [*no obj*]: *The fruit dropped off the tree.* [~ + *obj*]: *He dropped a few coconuts down to us.* **10.** to (cause to) become less: [*no obj*]: *Prices dropped in the spring.* [~ + *obj*]: *The store dropped its prices, but sales didn't increase.* **11.** to (cause to) come to an end; stop: [*no obj*]: *There the matter dropped.* [~ + *obj*]: *We dropped the matter.* **12.** [~ + *obj*] to utter or express casually or incidentally: *to drop a hint.* **13.** to set down or unload, such as from a car: [~ + *obj*]: *Drop us at the corner.* [~ + *obj* + *off*]: *Can you drop us off at the corner?* [~ + *off* + *obj*]: *We dropped off the family at the train station.* **14.** [~ + *obj*] to leave out or omit (a letter) in speaking: *Drop your final r's.* **15.** to (cause to) lower (the voice) in pitch or loudness: [*no obj*]: *His voice dropped as he approached.* [~ + *obj*]: *He dropped his voice to a whisper.* **16.** **drop behind,** to fail to keep up: *With all her other activities she was dropping behind at school.* **17. drop in** or **drop by,** to make an unexpected visit: *We were in the neighborhood, so we*

dropped in to see you. **18. drop off, a.** to fall asleep: *She drops off at about eleven each night.* **b.** to decrease; decline: *Prices began to drop off significantly.* **19. drop out,** to stop attending school or college: *I haven't seen her lately; do you think she's dropped out?* —**Idiom. 20. at the drop of a hat,** for the smallest reason and without delay: *to argue at the drop of a hat.* **21. drop in the bucket,** a very small, insignificant amount: *What's a few million dollars in the national budget? A drop in the bucket.*

drop•let /'drɒplɪt/ *n.* [*count*] a little drop.

drop•out or **drop-out** /'drɒp,awt/ *n.* [*count*] a student who stops going to school.

drought /drawt/ *n.* [*count*] a long period of dry weather: *The drought lasted for months.*

drove /droʊv/ *v.* pt. of DRIVE.

drown /drawn/ *v.* **1.** to (cause to) die from being put under water: [*no obj*]: *Several hundred people drowned in the flood.* [~ + *obj*]: *The flood drowned several hundred people.* **2.** [~ + *obj*] to destroy by or as if by flooding: *She drowned her sorrow in drinking.* **3.** [~ + *obj*] to overwhelm (with sounds, etc.) so as to make (someone or something) impossible to hear: *The roar of the plane drowned (out) the pilot's announcements. They drowned me out during my talk.*

drowse /drawz/ *v.* [*no obj*], **drowsed, drows•ing.** to be sleepy or half-asleep: *I was drowsing in the garden.*

drow•sy /'drawziy/ *adj.*, **-si•er, -si•est.** half-asleep; sleepy: *The medicine made me drowsy.* —'**drow•si•ness,** *n.* [*noncount*]: *His drowsiness was caused by medication.*

drudge /drʌdʒ/ *n.* [*count*] **1.** a person who does dull work. **2.** a person who works in a routine way.

drudg•er•y /'drʌdʒəriy/ *n.* [*noncount*] dull work: *taking the drudgery out of some of those household tasks.*

drug /drʌg/ *n.*, *v.*, **drugged, drug•ging.** —*n.* [*count*] **1.** a chemical used in medicines for the treatment of disease, or to improve physical or mental well-being: *Some drugs are useful in preventing disease.* **2.** a habit-forming or illegal substance, esp. a narcotic: *He was dealing in drugs.* —*v.* [~ + *obj*] **3.** to administer a medicinal drug to: *She drugged him with sedatives.* **4.** to make unconscious or poison (someone) with a drug: *They drugged him and smuggled him across the border.*

drug•gist /'drʌgɪst/ *n.* [*count*] **1.** PHARMACIST. **2.** the owner or operator of a drugstore.

drug•store or **drug store** /'drʌg,stɔr/ *n.* [*count*] the place of business of a druggist, where medicines are sold, usually also selling cosmetics, stationery, etc.

drum /drʌm/ *n.*, *v.*, **drummed, drum•ming.** —*n.* [*count*] **1.** a musical instrument made of a hollow body covered at one or both ends with a tightly stretched skin which is struck to produce sound. **2.** a rounded box or container: *They were rolling the oil drums off the ramp.* —*v.* **3.** [*no obj*] to beat or play a drum: *He drums for the school band.* **4.** to beat on anything: [~ + *obj*]: *He drummed his fingers on the table.* [*no obj*]: *The rain was drumming on the tin roof.* **5. drum into,** to drive or force into, as by constant repetition: *He tried to drum the idea of success into her head. He tried to drum into her that education was important.* **6. drum up,** to obtain or create (trade, interest, etc.) through strong effort: *He was trying to drum up new business.*

D

drum•mer /'drʌmər/ *n.* [*count*] a person who plays a drum.

drum•stick /'drʌm,stɪk/ *n.* [*count*] **1.** a stick for beating a drum. **2.** the meaty leg of a chicken or turkey.

drunk /drʌŋk/ *adj.* **1.** [*often:* be + ~] being in a temporary state in which one's abilities are affected by alcohol; intoxicated. **2.** [*often:* be + ~ + *with*] overcome by a strong feeling: *He was drunk with success and power.* —*n.* [*count*] **3.** a person who is drunk. —*v.* **4.** pp. and nonstandard pt. of DRINK.

drunk•ard /'drʌŋkərd/ *n.* [*count*] a person who is often drunk.

drunk•en /'drʌŋkən/ *adj.* [*before a noun*] **1.** intoxicated; drunk: *the drunken man.* **2.** often or frequently drunk. **3.** relating to or caused by drinking too much liquor: *a drunken quarrel.* —'**drunk•en•ly,** *adv.* —'**drunk•en•ness,** *n.* [*noncount*]

dry /draɪ/ *adj.,* **dri•er, dri•est,** *v.,* **dried, dry•ing.** —*adj.* **1.** free from moisture; not wet: *dry branches.* **2.** having little or no rain: *This dry weather is bad for the crops.* **3.** [be + ~] thirsty: *I'm so dry; let's stop for a soda.* **4.** (of bread, etc.) stale: *The bread was dry.* **5.** [*before a noun*] of or relating to nonliquid substances: *A peck is a unit of dry measure.* **6.** (esp. of wines) not sweet: *a dry white wine.* **7.** prohibiting the sale of alcoholic liquors: *Iowa was a dry state.* **8.** dull; uninteresting: *a dry subject.* **9.** not producing anything: *Even the greatest artists sometimes have dry years.* —*v.* **10.** to (cause to) become dry or to lose moisture: [~ + *obj*]: *She dried her hair with a towel.* [*no obj*]: *The paint will dry in two hours. Leave the dishes to dry.* **11. dry up,** **a.** to cease to exist; evaporate: *The river bed dried up. The heat had dried up the lake. The heat had dried it up.* **b.** *Informal.* to stop talking: *Oh, dry up and leave us alone!* —'**dry•ly,** *adv.* —'**dry•ness,** *n.* [*noncount*]

'**dry 'cleaning,** *n.* [*noncount*] **1.** the cleaning of garments, items, etc., with chemicals: *Dry cleaning is recommended for that sweater.* **2.** garments and other items for such cleaning: *Please pick up the dry cleaning.* —'**dry-'clean,** *v.* [~ + *obj*] —'**dry 'cleaner,** *n.* [*count*]

dry•er /'draɪər/ *n.* [*count*] **1.** Also, **drier.** a machine for removing moisture, as by forced heat: *a clothes dryer; a hair dryer.* **2.** DRIER[1] (def. 1).

'**dry 'run,** *n.* [*count*] a practice or exercise: *We staged a dry run to see if our plan would work.*

DST or **D.S.T.,** an abbreviation of: daylight-saving time.

du•al /'duwəl, 'dyuw-/ *adj.* [*before a noun*] of, relating to, or meaning two; made up of two people, items, parts, etc., together: *dual ownership.* —'**du•al•ism,** *n.* [*noncount*]: *the dualism of good and evil.* —**du•al•i•ty** /duw'ælɪtiy, dyuw-/, *n.* [*noncount*]

dub[1] /dʌb/ *v.* [~ + *obj* + *obj*], **dubbed, dub•bing,** to give a name, nickname, or title: *He was dubbed a hero.* —'**dub•ber,** *n.* [*count*]

dub[2] /dʌb/ *v.* [~ + *obj*], **dubbed, dub•bing. 1.** to furnish (a film or tape) with a new soundtrack: *The movie was poorly dubbed.* **2.** to add (music, etc.) to a recording: *He dubbed in the music.* —'**dub•ber,** *n.* [*count*]

du•bi•ous /'duwbiyəs, 'dyuw-/ *adj.* **1.** of doubtful quality; questionable: *dubious friends.* **2.** unsure; uncertain in opinion; hesitant: *I'm dubious about our chances of success.* —'**du•bi•ous•ly,** *adv.*

duch•ess /'dʌtʃɪs/ *n.* [*count*] **1.** the wife or widow of a duke. **2.** a woman who holds the rank of a duke.

duck[1] /dʌk/ *n.* [*count*], *pl.* **ducks,** (*esp. when thought of as a group*) **duck. 1.** a small, short-necked, web-footed swimming bird. **2.** the female of this bird. Compare DRAKE.

duck[2] /dʌk/ *v.* **1.** to (cause to) bend suddenly, esp. in order to avoid something: [*no obj*]: *When the shooting started, we ducked behind a car.* [~ + *obj*]: *He ducked his head (down) as the shots rang out.* **2.** [~ + *obj*] to avoid, or try to escape from (an unpleasant task, etc.); dodge: *He's trying to duck responsibility for his actions.* **3.** to plunge (the whole body or the head) under water: [*no obj*]: *I ducked under the hose and washed my face.* [~ + *obj*]: *She ducked her head under the hose and washed off.*

duck•ling /'dʌklɪŋ/ *n.* [*count*] a young duck.

duct /dʌkt/ *n.* [*count*] **1.** a tube, canal, or pipe by which a substance is conducted or carried: *The hero escapes by climbing through the air ducts and out of the building.* **2.** a tube carrying bodily liquids: *tear ducts.* —'**duct•less,** *adj.*

dud /dʌd/ *n.* [*count*] something that is a failure: *His new play was a dud.*

due /duw, dyuw/ *adj.* **1.** [be + ~] **a.** owing or owed: *This bill is due next month.* **b.** owed immediately: *The electric bill is due.* **2.** [be + ~] owing or deserved as a moral or natural right: *She is entitled to all the respect due (to) a scholar.* **3.** [be + ~] expected to be ready, be present, or arrive: *The plane is due at noon. The committee is due to meet at twelve-thirty.* —*n.* **4.** [*noncount; usually: one's* + ~] that which belongs to someone: *He gave them their due.* **5.** Usually, **dues.** [*plural*] a regular fee to be paid to an organization: *yearly membership dues.* —*adv.* **6.** directly or exactly: *due east.* —*Idiom.* **7. due to, a.** caused by: *The delay was due to an accident.* **b.** because of; owing to: *absence from school due to illness.* **8. in due course** or **time,** in the natural order of events; eventually: *In due course you'll get your refund.* **9. pay one's dues,** to earn respect by working hard.

du•el /'duwəl, 'dyuw-/ *n., v.,* **-eled** or **-elled, -el•ing** or **-el•ling.** —*n.* [*count*] **1.** a formal fight between two persons with deadly weapons. **2.** a contest between two persons or teams: *The football game promises to be a real duel.* —*v.* [*no obj*] **3.** to fight in a duel. —'**du•el•er, 'du•el•ist,** *n.* [*count*]

du•et /duw'ɛt, dyuw-/ *n.* [*count*] a piece of music for two voices or instruments.

dug /dʌg/ *v.* a pt. and pp. of DIG.

dug•out /'dʌg,awt/ *n.* [*count*] a roofed structure in which baseball players sit when not on the field.

du jour /də 'ʒʊr, duw/ *adj.* [*after a noun*] as prepared or served on a certain day: *soup du jour.*

duke /duwk, dyuwk/ *n.* [*count*] a nobleman holding the highest rank.

dul•cet /'dʌlsɪt/ *adj.* pleasant to the ear; having a pleasing melody; gentle: *dulcet tones.*

dull /dʌl/ *adj.,* **-er, -est,** *v.* —*adj.* **1.** not sharp; blunt: *a dull knife.* **2.** boring: *She almost fell asleep during his dull sermon.* **3.** not lively: *She always feels dull in hot weather.* **4.** not bright or clear: *a dull, cloudy day.* **5.** mentally slow; somewhat stupid. —*v.* **6.** [*no obj*] [~ + *obj*] to (cause to) become dull. —'**dull•ness,** *n.* [*noncount*]

—**'dul•ly,** *adv.*: *He answered dully that he didn't really care.*

dumb /dʌm/ *adj.*, **-er, -est. 1.** stupid: *He was dumb to try a stunt like that. What a dumb idea!* **2.** unable to speak (often considered offensive when applied to humans): *a dumb animal.* **3.** speechless: *in a dumb, furious rage.* —**'dumb•ly,** *adv.* —**'dumb•ness,** *n.* [*noncount*]

dumb•found /dʌmˈfawnd, 'dʌmˌfawnd/ *v.* [~ + *obj*] to make speechless with amazement: *He was dumbfounded by all the damage done by the storm.*

dum•my /ˈdʌmiy/ *n., pl.* **-mies,** *adj.* —*n.* [*count*] **1.** an object resembling a human figure, such as for showing clothes: *the dummy in the shop window.* **2.** something made to look like something else: *The gun used in the play was a dummy.* **3.** *Informal.* a stupid person; fool: *Some dummy gave us wrong information.* —*adj.* [*before a noun*] **4.** noting or relating to a copy: *dummy shells in the gun.*

dump /dʌmp/ *v.* **1.** [~ + *obj*] to drop or let fall heavily or suddenly: *Dump the topsoil here.* **2.** to throw away (garbage, etc.): [~ + *obj*]: *The company dumped the toxic wastes into this canal.* [*no obj*]: *a sewage pipe that dumps into the ocean.* **3.** [~ + *obj*] to rid oneself of (someone or something) suddenly and rudely: *Don't dump your troubles on me! He dumped her after 20 years of marriage.* **4. dump on,** to criticize harshly; abuse; insult: *They were always dumping on him.* —*n.* [*count*] **5.** a place where garbage, etc., is dumped. **6.** *Informal.* a place, area, house, or town that is run-down, dirty, or a mess: *He lived in a dump, with no kitchen or bathroom.*

dump•ling /ˈdʌmpliŋ/ *n.* [*count*] **1.** a rounded mass of steamed and seasoned dough. **2.** a wrapping of dough enclosing fruit or some tasty filling.

dumps /dʌmps/ *n.* [*plural*] —**Idiom. (down) in the dumps,** in a depressed or sad state of mind: *She's really (down) in the dumps about leaving home.*

dump•y /ˈdʌmpiy/ *adj.*, **-i•er, -i•est.** short and stout: *a dumpy figure.*

dun /dʌn/ *v.* [~ + *obj*], **dunned, dun•ning.** to make repeated demands upon, esp. for the payment of a debt: *The landlord kept dunning us about the overdue rent.*

dunce /dʌns/ *n.* [*count*] a stupid person.

dune /duwn, dyuwn/ *n.* [*count*] a sand hill formed by the wind, usually in the desert or near the ocean.

dung /dʌŋ/ *n.* [*noncount*] waste matter from animals; manure.

dun•ga•rees /ˌdʌŋgəˈriyz/ *n.* [*plural*] **1.** work clothes, overalls, etc., of blue denim. **2.** BLUE JEANS.

dun•geon /ˈdʌndʒən/ *n.* [*count*] a strong, dark prison or cell, such as in a medieval castle.

dunk /dʌŋk/ *v.* [~ + *obj*] **1.** to dip (a cookie, etc.) into a beverage, before eating. **2.** to put (someone or something) briefly under the surface of a liquid: *She dunked the shirt in some detergent.*

du•o /ˈduwow, 'dyuwow/ *n.* [*count*], *pl.* **du•os. 1.** DUET. **2.** two persons associated with each other; couple. **3.** a pair.

dupe /duwp, dyuwp/ *n., v.,* **duped, dup•ing.** —*n.* [*count*] **1.** a person who is easily tricked: *He was the dupe of the criminals.* —*v.* [~ + *obj*] **2.** to deceive; trick: *The agency duped her. They had duped me into the sale.* —**'dup•er,** *n.* [*count*]

du•plex /ˈduwplɛks, 'dyuw-/ *n.* [*count*] **1.** an apartment for one family but having two levels. Also called **duplex apartment. 2.** a house built for two families.

du•pli•cate /*n., adj.*ˈduwplɪkɪt, 'dyuw-; *v.* -ˌkeyt/ *n., v.,* **-cat•ed, -cat•ing,** *adj.* —*n.* [*count*] **1.** an exact copy: *He made a duplicate and handed me the original.* —*v.* [~ + *obj*] **2.** to make an exact copy of: *She duplicated my letter.* **3.** to do or perform again; repeat: *You'll just have to duplicate your performance.* —*adj.* [*before a noun*] **4.** exactly like something else: *a duplicate key.* —**Idiom. 5. in duplicate,** in two identical copies: *I'll need your letter, in duplicate, on my desk by morning.* —**du•pli•ca•tion** /ˌduwplɪˈkeyʃən, ˌdyuw-/, *n.* [*noncount*]: *illegal duplication of material.*

du•pli•ca•tor /ˈduwplɪˌkeytər, 'dyuw-/ *n.* [*count*] a machine for making duplicates. Also called **'duplicating ma,chine.**

du•plic•i•ty /duwˈplɪsɪtiy, dyuw-/ *n.* [*noncount*] deception or dishonesty in speech or behavior.

du•ra•ble /ˈdʊrəbəl, 'dyʊr-/ *adj.* very strong; capable of enduring: *The raincoat is made of durable material.* —**du•ra•bil•i•ty** /ˌdʊrəˈbɪlɪtiy, ˌdyʊr-/, *n.* [*noncount*]: *That car is noted for its exceptional durability.* —**'du•ra•bly,** *adv.*

du•ra•tion /dʊˈreyʃən, dyʊ-/ *n.* [*noncount*] **1.** the length of time something exists: *Luckily these viruses are of short duration.* **2. for the duration,** for as long as (something) lasts or continues: *He was drafted for the duration of the war.*

du•ress /dʊˈrɛs, dyʊ-/ *n.* [*noncount*] threat or force: *He had signed the confession under duress.*

dur•ing /ˈdʊrɪŋ, 'dyʊr-/ *prep.* **1.** throughout the duration of: *He lived in Florida during the winter.* **2.** at some time or point in the course of: *They departed during the night.*

dusk /dʌsk/ *n.* [*noncount*] the period of partial darkness between day and night; twilight: *We met at dusk and traveled through the night.*

dusk•y /ˈdʌskiy/ *adj.*, **-i•er, -i•est. 1.** somewhat dark; dim: *a dusky evening.* **2.** having a dark color: *dusky complexions.*

dust /dʌst/ *n.* [*noncount*] **1.** matter in fine, powdery, dry particles: *a layer of dust on the books.* **2.** finely powdered earth: *The car sped off in a cloud of dust.* —*v.* **3.** to wipe the dust from (furniture, etc.): [*no obj*]: *On Fridays we dust and vacuum.* [~ + *obj*]: *We dusted the bookshelves.* **4.** [~ + *obj*] to sprinkle (crops, etc.) with a powder or dust: *to dust crops with insecticide.* **5. dust off,** to prepare to use again: *I dusted off those old speeches and got them ready to use again.* —**'dust•less,** *adj.* —**'dust•y,** *adj.*, **-i•er, -i•est.**

dust•er /ˈdʌstər/ *n.* [*count*] **1.** a cloth, etc., for removing dust. **2.** a device for sprinkling dust, powder, or the like.

dust•pan /ˈdʌstˌpæn/ *n.* [*count*] a short-handled shovellike utensil into which dust is swept.

Dutch /dʌtʃ/ *adj.* **1.** of or relating to the Netherlands. **2.** of or relating to the language spoken in the Netherlands. —*n.* **3.** [*plural; the + ~; takes a plural verb*] the people born or living in the Netherlands. **4.** [*noncount*] the language spoken in the Netherlands. —**Idiom. 5. go Dutch,** to pay one's own expenses, as on a date: *Let's go Dutch for dinner.*

'Dutch 'oven, *n.* [*count*] a large heavy pot with a close-fitting lid, used for stews, etc.

du•ty /ˈduwtiy, 'dyuw-/ *n., pl.* **-ties. 1.** [*noncount*] something that one is expected to do: *He*

D

had a strong sense of duty. **2.** an action or task required by a person's position: [count]: *The duties of a clergyman involve performing marriages.* [noncount]: *I reported for duty at twelve o'clock sharp.* **3.** a tax imposed by law on the import or export of goods; tariff: [noncount]: *How much duty did you have to pay on the watch?* [count]: *Where do they collect customs duties?* —*Idiom.* **4. off** (or **on**) **duty,** not at (or at) one's post or work: *The guard will be off duty tomorrow. The nurse is on duty until midnight.* —**'du•ti•ful,** adj.

du•vet /duw'vey, dyuw-/ n. [count] a quilt, often with a removable cover.

dwarf /dwɔrf/ n., pl. **dwarfs, dwarves** /dwɔrvz/, adj., v. —n. [count] **1.** a person of unusually small size. **2.** an animal or plant much smaller than the average. **3.** a small, imaginary being, often represented as a tiny old man, who is skilled as a worker and has magical powers. —adj. [before a noun] **4.** of unusually small size: *dwarf marigolds.* —v. [~ + obj] **5.** to cause to seem small in size, etc., as by being much larger: *This current budget crisis dwarfs all our previous troubles.* —'**dwarf•ish,** adj. —'**dwarf•ism,** n. [noncount]

dweeb /dwiyb/ n. [count] *Slang.* a person who is considered to be unfashionable, socially awkward, or unpopular.

dwell /dwɛl/ v. [no obj], **dwelt** /dwɛlt/ or **dwelled, dwell•ing. 1.** to live or stay as a permanent resident; reside: *He dwells in the country for most of the year.* **2. dwell on,** or **upon,** to think, speak, or write about for a long time or often: *She dwelt at length on the similarities between the two paintings.* —'**dwell•er,** n. [count]

dwell•ing /'dwɛlɪŋ/ n. [count] a building or other place to live in: *a comfortable two-story dwelling.*

DWI, an abbreviation of: driving while intoxicated.

dwin•dle /'dwɪndl̩/ v. [no obj], **-dled, -dling.** to become smaller: *Our food supply began to dwindle.*

dye /day/ n., v., **dyed, dye•ing.** —n. [noncount] [count] **1.** a coloring material. —v. [~ + obj] **2.** to color (cloth, etc.) with or as if with a dye: *to dye a dress green.* —'**dy•er,** n. [count]

dy•ing /'dayɪŋ/ adj. [before a noun] **1.** about to die: *a dying patient.* **2.** of or associated with death: *his dying hour.* **3.** drawing to a close: *the dying year.* —n. **4. the dying,** [plural; used with a plural verb] people who are approaching death.

dyke /dayk/ n. DIKE (def. 1).

dy•nam•ic /day'næmɪk/ adj. Also, **dy•nam'i•cal. 1.** very active or forceful; energetic: *a dynamic person.* **2.** producing change or progress: *It's a dynamic process, not a static one.* **3.** of or relating to the science of dynamics. —**dy'nam•i•cal•ly,** adv.

dy•nam•ics /day'næmɪks/ n. [noncount; used with a singular verb] the branch of physics that deals with motion: *Dynamics tells us how underwater forces work on the movement of submarines.*

dy•na•mite /'daynə,mayt/ n., v., **-mit•ed, -mit•ing,** —n. [noncount] **1.** a powerful explosive. —v. [~ + obj] **2.** to blow up, shatter, or destroy with dynamite: *The soldiers dynamited the bridge.*

dy•na•mo /'daynə,mow/ n. [count], pl. **-mos. 1.** an electric generator, esp. for direct current. **2.** an energetic, forceful person: *She's a real dynamo.*

dy•nas•ty /'daynəstiy/ n. [count] pl. **-ties.** a series of rulers from the same family: *the Ming dynasty.* —**dy•nas•tic** /day'næstɪk/, adj.

dys-, a combining form meaning ill or bad (*dyslexia*).

dys•en•ter•y /'dɪsən,tɛriy/ n. [noncount] an infectious disease of the large intestines.

dys•lex•i•a /dɪs'lɛksiyə/ n. [noncount] a reading disorder in which the person has difficulty in reading and spelling. —**dys'lex•ic,** adj., n. [count]

dz., an abbreviation of: dozen.

E

E, e /iy/ *n.* [*count*], *pl.* **Es** or **E's, es** or **e's.** the fifth letter of the English alphabet, a vowel.

E., an abbreviation of: **1.** Earth. **2.** east. **3.** eastern.

ea., an abbreviation of: each.

each /iytʃ/ *adj.* **1.** every one of a group of two or more persons or things, considered separately: [*before a singular noun*]: *Each student has a different solution.* [*after a plural noun or pronoun*]: *The students each have a different solution.* —*pron.* **2.** every one individually; each one: *Each has a different solution. Each of these students has a different solution.* —*adv.* **3.** to, from, or for each; apiece: *The pens cost a dollar each.*

each 'other, *pron.* [*used as an object to refer to the subject*] (each person or thing does something or is connected in some way to the other): *Those two love each other.*

ea·ger /'iygər/ *adj.* having or showing strong desire or interest: *an eager student; eager for success; eager to try it.* —'**ea·ger·ly,** *adv.* —'**ea·ger·ness,** *n.* [*noncount*]

ea·gle /'iygəl/ *n.* [*count*] a large, powerful, broad-winged bird having claws to catch its prey.

'eagle-,eyed, *adj.* having unusually sharp ability to watch or observe: *She is an eagle-eyed teacher who catches my slightest mistakes.*

ear¹ /ɪər/ *n.* **1.** [*count*] the organ of hearing, including the outer part on either side of the head. **2.** [*noncount*] the sense of hearing: *sounds that are pleasing to the ear.* **3.** [*noncount*] good recognition of sounds, esp. in music and languages: *She has no ear for music.* —*Idiom.* **4.** **be all ears,** to listen with great interest: *Tell me about it; I'm all ears.* **5. by ear,** without reference to written music: *He could play any tune by ear.*

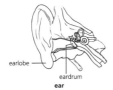

earlobe
eardrum
ear

ear² /ɪər/ *n.* [*count*] the top part of a cereal plant, containing the seed grains: *an ear of corn.*

ear·ache /'ɪər,eyk/ *n.* [*count*] a pain or ache in the ear.

ear·drum /'ɪər,drʌm/ *n.* [*count*] a thin tissue stretched across the inside of the ear that vibrates when sound waves hit it.

'ear,lobe or **'ear ,lobe,** *n.* [*count*] the soft, hanging lower part of the outer ear.

ear·ly /'ɜrliy/ *adv.* and *adj.,* **-li·er, -li·est.** —*adv.* **1.** in or during the beginning: *early in the year.* **2.** before the usual or expected time; ahead of time: *The train arrived early.* —*adj.* **3.** [*before a noun*] occurring in the beginning: *an early hour of the day.* **4.** occurring before the usual or expected time: *an early dinner; an early warning.* —*Idiom.* **5. early on,** not long after the beginning.

earmuffs, *n.* [*plural*] a pair of connected coverings worn over the ears in cold weather.

earn /ɜrn/ *v.* [~ + *obj*] **1.** to receive in return for one's work or service: *to earn $50,000 a year.* **2.** to deserve; to merit (something) as a result of work or behavior: *He earned a reputation for honesty.*

ear·nest /'ɜrnɪst/ *adj.* **1.** very serious: *The earnest young man had no time for jokes.* —*Idiom.* **2. in earnest,** in full seriousness: *Work began in earnest as the deadline approached.* —'**ear·nest·ly,** *adv.* —'**ear·nest·ness,** *n.* [*noncount*]

earn·ings /'ɜrnɪŋz/ *n.* [*plural*] money earned; wages; profits: *I can buy fewer things with my earnings as inflation rises.*

ear·phone /'ɪər,fown/ *n.* [*count*] **1.** a sound receiver, as of a radio or telephone, that fits in or over the ear. **2.** Usually, **earphones.** [*plural*] a headset.

ear·ring /'ɪərɪŋ/ *n.* [*count*] a piece of jewelry worn on or hanging from the earlobe.

ear·shot /'ɪər,ʃɒt/ *n.* [*noncount*] the distance within which a sound, voice, etc., can be heard: *I was out of earshot but could see them waving.*

earth /ɜrθ/ *n.* **1.** [*singular*] the planet on which human beings live, third in order from the sun. **2.** [*singular*] the surface of this planet: *to fall to earth.* **3.** [*noncount*] soil and dirt, as distinguished from rock and sand.

earth·ly /'ɜrθliy/ *adj.,* **-li·er, -li·est.** of or relating to the earth or world, esp. as opposed to heaven: *We were warned about being too occupied by earthly pleasures.*

earth·quake /'ɜrθ,kweyk/ *n.* [*count*] vibrations in the earth's crust causing the ground to shake.

earth·shak·ing /'ɜrθ,ʃeykɪŋ/ *adj.* challenging or affecting basic beliefs, attitudes, or relationships: *earthshaking changes in our culture.*

earth·worm /'ɜrθ,wɜrm/ *n.* [*count*] a long worm that lives in soil.

earth·y /'ɜrθiy/ *adj.,* **-i·er, -i·est. 1.** of, like, or consisting of earth or soil: *an earthy smell.* **2.** direct; frank: *an earthy sense of humor.* —'**earth·i·ness,** *n.* [*noncount*]

ease /iyz/ *n., v.,* **eased, eas·ing.** —*n.* [*noncount*] **1.** freedom from concern, worry, or difficulty. —*v.* **2.** [~ + *obj*] to free from worry or care: *Her calm voice eased my mind.* **3.** to (cause to) become less painful or severe: [~ + *obj*]: *The aspirin eased his headache.* [*no obj*]: *As the aspirin took effect, his headache eased.* **4.** [~ + *obj*] to move or shift with great care: *The pilot eased the plane down the runway.*

ea·sel /'iyzəl/ *n.* [*count*] a stand or frame for supporting or displaying a painting, blackboard, etc.

eas·i·ly /'iyzəliy, 'iyzliy/ *adv.* **1.** in an easy manner; without trouble: *She easily swam across the river.* **2.** without doubt: *This drawing is easily the best.* **3.** likely: *He may easily change his mind.*

east /iyst/ *n.* [*noncount; usually: the* + ~] **1.** one of the four main points of the compass, the direction from which the sun rises. **2.** [*usually: East*] a region or territory lying in this direction. —*adj.* **3.** toward the east: *an east window.* **4.** coming from the east: *an east wind.* —*adv.* **5.** to, toward, or in the east: *heading east.* —'**east·er·ly,** *adj., adv.* —**east·ward** /'iystwərd/, *adj., adv.* —'**east·wards,** *adv.*

Eas·ter /'iystər/ *n.* [*noncount*] [*count*] a yearly

Christian festival to celebrate the resurrection of Jesus Christ.

east•ern /'iystərn/ adj. **1.** lying toward or in the east. **2.** directed or proceeding toward the east. **3.** coming from the east.

eas•y /'iyziy/ adj. and adv., **-i•er, -i•est.** —adj. **1.** requiring no great work or effort: The teacher gave us an easy assignment. The assignment was easy to do. **2.** free from pain or care: an easy mind. **3.** [before a noun] easygoing; rela.xed: an easy manner. —adv. **4.** in an easy manner; easily. —Idiom. **5. easy does it,** be careful: Easy does it when you lift the refrigerator. **6. take it easy** or **go easy,** to not work too hard: The doctor advised me to take it easy. —'eas•i•ness, n. [noncount]

'**easy ,chair,** n. [count] a usually large, comfortable armchair.

eas•y•go•ing /'iyziy'gowɪŋ/ adj. relaxed and casual; calm.

eat /iyt/ v., **ate** /eyt/ esp. Brit. ɛt/ **eat•en** /'iytn̩/ **eat•ing, 1.** to take (food) into the mouth and swallow: [~ + obj]: We ate dinner early. [no obj]: We haven't eaten all day. **2.** [no obj] to have a meal: When do we eat today? **3.** [~ + obj] to use up, esp. wastefully: Unexpected expenses ate up their savings. **4.** [no obj] to damage something by wearing away or chemical action: The acid ate through the metal. —'eat•er, n. [count]

eat•er•y /'iytəriy/ n. [count], pl. **-er•ies.** Informal. a restaurant.

eave /iyv/ n. [count] Usually, **eaves.** [plural] the overhanging lower edge of a roof.

eaves•drop /'iyvz,drɒp/ v. [no obj], **-dropped, -drop•ping.** to listen secretly to a private conversation. —'eaves,drop•per, n. [count]

ebb /ɛb/ n. [noncount] **1.** the flowing back of the tide as the water returns to the sea. —v. [no obj] **2.** to flow back or away, such as the tide. **3.** to decline or decay; fade away: His strength began to ebb.

eb•on•y /'ɛbəniy/ n., pl. **-on•ies. 1.** [noncount] a hard, dark wood from tropical Africa and Asia. **2.** [count] any tree providing such wood. **3.** [noncount] a deep black color.

ec•cen•tric /ɪk'sɛntrɪk/ adj. **1.** odd; strange: eccentric behavior. —n. [count] **2.** an eccentric person. —ec'cen•tri•cal•ly, adv.

ec•cen•tric•i•ty /,ɛksɛn'trɪsɪtiy/ n., pl. **-ties. 1.** [noncount] odd or strange behavior. **2.** [count] an action, habit, or attitude that is odd or strange.

ec•cle•si•as•tic /ɪ,kliyziy'æstɪk/ n. [count] a member of the clergy, especially in the Christian church.

ec•cle•si•as•ti•cal /ɪ,kliyziy'æstɪkəl/ adj. of or relating to the church or the clergy.

ech•o /'ɛkow/ n., pl. **ech•oes,** v., **-oed, -o•ing.** —n. [count] **1.** a repetition of sound produced by the reflection of sound waves from a surface. —v. **2.** [no obj] (of a place) to give out the sound of an echo: The hall echoed with cheers. **3.** to repeat or be repeated by an echo: [no obj]: Cheers echoed in the hall. [~ + obj]: The hall echoes the faintest sounds. **4.** [~ + obj] to repeat, copy, or imitate (words, sentiments, etc.): He echoed my call for caution.

e•clipse /ɪ'klɪps/ n., v., **e•clipsed** /ɪ'klɪpst/ **e•clips•ing.** —n. [count] **1.** the covering or cutting off of the light of one heavenly body by another: lunar eclipse; solar eclipse. —v. [~ + obj] **2.** to cause to undergo eclipse: The moon eclipsed the sun. **3.** to make less outstanding or important

by comparison: This eclipses all his former achievements.

e•col•o•gy /ɪ'kɒlədʒiy/ n. [noncount] **1.** the branch of biology dealing with the relations between living things and their environment. **2.** the set of relationships between organisms and their environment. —ec•o•log•i•cal /,ɛkə'lɒdʒɪkəl, ,iykə-/ adj. —e'col•o•gist, n. [count]

ec•o•nom•ic /,ɛkə'nɒmɪk, ,iykə-/ adj. [before a noun] of or relating to trade, industry, wealth, or the science of economics.

ec•o•nom•i•cal /,ɛkə'nɒmɪkəl, ,iykə-/ adj. avoiding waste; thrifty: an economical meal. —,ec•o'nom•i•cal•ly, adv.

ec•o•nom•ics /,ɛkə'nɒmɪks, ,iykə-/ n. [noncount; used with a singular verb] the science that deals with the production, distribution, and use of goods and services. —e•con•o•mist /ɪ'kɒnəmɪst/, n. [count]

e•con•o•mize /ɪ'kɒnə,mayz/ v. [no obj] [~ + on + obj], **-mized, -miz•ing.** to spend carefully in order to save money.

e•con•o•my /ɪ'kɒnəmiy/ n., pl. **-mies. 1.** [noncount] thrifty management of money, materials, etc. **2.** [count] the management of the resources of a community, country, etc., esp. with a view to its productivity.

ec•o•sys•tem /'ɛkow,sɪstəm, 'iykow-/ n. [count] a system formed by a community of living things, their environment, and the relationship between them.

ec•sta•sy /'ɛkstəsiy/ n., pl. **-sies. 1.** [noncount] extreme joyfulness or happiness. **2.** [count] any overpowering emotion; sudden, intense feeling or excitement. —ec•stat•ic /ɛk'stætɪk/, adj. —ec'stat•i•cal•ly, adv.

-ed, 1. a. a suffix forming the past tense of regular verbs (He waited). For most regular verbs that end in a consonant, -ed is added directly afterwards: cross + -ed → crossed. When the verb ends in -y, the -y changes to -i- and -ed is added: ready + -ed → readied. If the word ends in -e, an e is dropped: save + -ed → saved. **b.** a suffix forming the past participle of regular verbs (He has crossed the river) and also forming verbs that function as adjectives (inflated balloons). **2.** a suffix forming adjectives from nouns and meaning having or characterized by (diseased; bearded).

edge /ɛdʒ/ n., v., **edged, edg•ing.** —n. [count] **1.** a line or border at which a surface ends: Grass grew along the edge of the road. **2.** the sharp side of the blade of a cutting instrument or weapon. **3.** an improved position; advantage: an edge on our competitors. —v. **4.** [~ + obj] to provide with an edge or border. **5.** to move sideways slowly or gradually: [no obj]: They edged toward the door. [~ + obj]: She edged the car up to the curb. —Idiom. **6. on edge,** tense; nervous.

edg•y /'ɛdʒiy/ adj., **-i•er, -i•est.** nervous.

ed•i•ble /'ɛdəbəl/ adj. **1.** fit or safe to be eaten. —n. [count] **2.** Usually, **edibles.** [plural] edible substances; food.

ed•it /'ɛdɪt/ v. [~ + obj] **1.** to supervise the preparation of (a publication): Who edits the newspaper? **2.** to collect and arrange (materials) for publication: She edited the president's speeches. **3.** to revise or correct, such as a manuscript. **4.** to prepare (film or tape) by deleting, arranging, and changing parts.

e•di•tion /ɪ'dɪʃən/ n. [count] **1.** one of a series of printings of a book, newspaper, etc., each produced at a different time. **2.** the total number of copies of a book, newspaper, etc., printed at one time.

ed•i•tor /ɛdɪtər/ n. [count] a person who edits.

ed•i•to•ri•al /ˌɛdɪˈtɔriyəl/ n. [count] **1.** an article in a newspaper, magazine, etc., that presents the opinion of the publishers or editors. —adj. [before a noun] **2.** of or relating to an editor or editing.

ed•u•cate /ˈɛdʒʊˌkeyt/ v. [~ + obj], **-cat•ed, -cat•ing. 1.** to teach (a person) by instruction or schooling: He was educated at Harvard. **2.** to send to school: They raised and educated their two daughters.

ed•u•ca•tion /ˌɛdʒʊˈkeyʃən/ n. **1.** [noncount] the act or process of educating. **2.** [count; usually singular] a degree, level, or kind of schooling: a college education. —**ed•u'ca•tion•al,** adj.: He enjoys watching educational TV programs.

-ee, a suffix meaning a person who is the object, receiver, or performer of an action (addressee; es-capee).

eel /iyl/ n. [count], pl. (esp. when thought of as a group) **eel,** (esp. for kinds or species) **eels.** a snakelike fish.

e'er /ɛər/ adv. Chiefly Literary. ever.

-eer, a suffix meaning a person who produces, handles, or is associated with something (engineer).

ee•rie /ˈɪəriy/ adj., **-ri•er, -ri•est.** strange and mysterious, so as to be frightening. —**'ee•ri•ly** /ˈɪəriliy/, adv.

ef-, a form of the prefix EX-, used before roots beginning with the letter "f": efficient.

ef•fect /ɪˈfɛkt/ n. **1.** [count] something produced; result; consequence. **2.** [noncount] the state of being in use or operation: to bring a plan into effect. —v. [~ + obj] **3.** to produce as an effect; bring about; accomplish: to effect a change. —**Idiom. 4. in effect, a.** essentially; basically: in effect, a whole new way of rewarding workers. **b.** operating or functioning: The new law is in effect. **5. take effect,** to begin to function; start to produce a result: I could feel the whiskey begin to take effect. —**Usage.** See AFFECT[1].

ef•fec•tive /ɪˈfɛktɪv/ adj. **1.** able to accomplish a purpose: effective teaching methods. **2.** [before a noun] real; actual: The militia was the effective government at the time. —**ef'fec•tive•ly,** adv.: The new president governed very effectively —**ef'fec•tive•ness,** n. [noncount]

ef•fects /ɪˈfɛkts/ n. [plural] personal property. He took all his personal effects with him when he left his wife.

ef•fem•i•nate /ɪˈfɛmənɪt/ adj. (of a man or boy) having traits, tastes, or habits traditionally considered feminine.

ef•fer•vesce /ˌɛfərˈvɛs/ v. [no obj], **-vesced, -vesc•ing. 1.** to give off bubbles of gas, such as a carbonated liquid. **2.** to show enthusiasm or liveliness. —**ˌef•fer'ves•cence,** n. [noncount] —**ˌef•fer'ves•cent,** adj.

ef•fi•cient /ɪˈfɪʃənt/ adj. performing or functioning effectively with the least waste of time and effort: She was an efficient manager. —**ef•fi•cien•cy** /ɪˈfɪʃənsiy/, n. [noncount]: He was promoted quickly in his job because of his efficiency. —**ef'fi•cient•ly,** adv.

ef•fort /ˈɛfərt/ n. **1.** [noncount] the use of physical or mental power. **2.** [count] a try; an attempt. **3.** [count] something done by hard work.

EFL, an abbreviation of: English as a foreign language.

e.g., an abbreviation of Latin exempli gratia: for example; such as.

egg[1] /ɛg/ n. **1.** [count] a round or oval object from which a baby bird, reptile, fish, or insect hatches. **2.** [count] [noncount] the contents of an egg used for food. **3.** [count] a cell produced by the female that joins with a male cell to form a baby.

egg[2] /ɛg/ v. [~ + obj + on] to urge or encourage; incite: He egged his opponent on to make the tennis match more exciting.

egg•nog /ˈɛgˌnɒg/ n. [noncount] a thick drink made of eggs, cream, sugar, and often liquor.

egg•plant /ˈɛgˌplænt/ n. [count] [noncount] a dark-purple vegetable shaped like a large pear.

egg•shell /ˈɛgˌʃɛl/ n. [count] the shell of a bird's egg.

e•go /ˈiygow/ n., pl. **e•gos. 1.** [count] the "I" or self of a person that experiences and reacts to the outside world. **2.** [noncount] egotism; self-importance.

e•go•cen•tric /ˌiygowˈsɛntrɪk/ adj. having little or no thoughts about interests or feelings other than one's own; self-centered.

e•go•ism /ˈiygowˌɪzəm/ n. [noncount] excessive care of or concern with oneself; selfishness. —**ˌe•go•ist,** n. [count]

e•go•tism /ˈiygəˌtɪzəm/ n. [noncount] too much reference to oneself in conversation or writing; conceit. —**ˈe•go•tist,** n. [count]

E•gyp•tian /ɪˈdʒɪpʃən/ adj. **1.** of or relating to Egypt. —n. [count] **2.** a person born or living in Egypt.

eight /eyt/ n. [count] a number, seven plus one, written as 8. —**eighth** /eytθ, eyθ/ adj.

eight•een /ˈeyˈtiyn/ n. [count] a number, ten plus eight, written as 18. —**ˈeight'eenth,** adj.

eight•y /ˈeytiy/ n. [count], pl. **eight•ies.** a number, ten times eight, written as 80. —**ˈeight•i•eth,** adj.

ei•ther /ˈiyðər, ˈayðər/ adj. [~ + singular count noun] **1.** one or the other of two: You may sit at either end of the table. **2.** each of two; the one and the other: There are trees on either side of the river. —pron. **3.** one or the other: Either will do. —conj. **4.** (used with or to indicate a series of choices): Either call or write.

e•jac•u•late /ɪˈdʒækyəˌleyt/ v., **-lat•ed, -lat•ing. 1.** [~ + obj] [no obj] to send out or discharge, esp. semen, from the body. **2.** [~ + obj] to utter suddenly and briefly; exclaim. —**e,jac•u'la•tion,** n. [count] [noncount]

e•ject /ɪˈdʒɛkt/ v. [~ + obj] to drive or force out: The police ejected the noisy demonstrators from the mayor's office. —**e•jec•tion** /ɪˈdʒɛkʃən/, n. [count] [noncount]

e•lab•o•rate /adj. ɪˈlæbərɪt; v. -əˌreyt/ adj., v., **-rat•ed, -rat•ing. —adj. 1.** having many parts; complex: an elaborate lighting system. —v. [no obj] **2.** to work out in great detail: Please elaborate on your idea. —**e'lab•o•rate•ly,** adv. —**e,lab•o•ra'tion** /ɪˌlæbəˈreyʃən/, n. [noncount]

e•lapse /ɪˈlæps/ v. [no obj], **e•lapsed, e•laps•ing.** (of time) to slip or pass by: Three months elapsed before she responded to his letter.

e•las•tic /ɪˈlæstɪk/ adj. **1.** capable of returning to its original length or shape after being stretched. **2.** flexible; adaptable: elastic rules. —n. [noncount] **3.** fabric or material that is made elastic, as with strips of rubber.

e•lat•ed /ɪˈleytɪd/ adj. extremely happy; overjoyed. —**e•la•tion** /ɪˈleyʃən/, n. [noncount]

el•bow /ˈɛlbow/ n. [count] **1.** the bend or joint

E

of the arm between the upper arm and forearm. —*v.* [~ + *obj*] **2.** to push aside with or as if with the elbow; jostle.

eld•er[1] /ˈɛldər/ *adj. a compar. of* **old** *with* **eldest** *as superl.* [*before a noun; used only of people*] **1.** of greater age; older: *my elder sister.* —*n.* [*count*] **2.** an older person.

el•der[2] /ˈɛldər/ *n.* [*count*] a shrub or tree having clusters of berries.

eld•er•ly /ˈɛldərliy/ *adj.* **1.** approaching old age. —*n.* **2. the elderly,** [*plural; used with a plural verb*] elderly persons when they are thought of as a group.

eld•est /ˈɛldɪst/ *adj. a superlative of* **old** *with* **elder** *as comparative.* oldest; of greatest age.

e•lect /ɪˈlɛkt/ *v.* [~ + *obj*] **1.** to choose or select by vote. **2.** to choose: *I elected not to take the job because it involved too much traveling.* —*adj.* **3.** [*after a noun*] selected for an office, but not yet at work: *the governor-elect.* —**e'lec•tion,** *n.* [*noncount*]: *Senators are chosen by election.* [*count*]: *He won the election for class president.*

e•lec•tor•ate /ɪˈlɛktərɪt/ *n.* [*count*] the people who are entitled to vote in an election.

e•lec•tric /ɪˈlɛktrɪk/ *adj.* **1.** [*before a noun*] produced or operated by electricity. **2.** thrilling; exciting: *The singer had an electric effect on the crowd at the concert.*

e•lec•tri•cal /ɪˈlɛktrɪkəl/ *adj.* concerned with electricity: *The fire was caused by an electrical fault.* —**e'lec•tri•cal•ly,** *adv.*

e'lectric 'chair, *n.* [*count*] a chair used to electrocute criminals who are sentenced to death.

e•lec•tri•cian /ɪlɛkˈtrɪʃən, ˌiylɛk-/ *n.* [*count*] a person who installs or repairs electrical wiring or devices.

e•lec•tric•i•ty /ɪlɛkˈtrɪsɪtiy, ˌiylɛk-/ *n.* [*noncount*] energy or power produced by the motion of electrons and protons; electric current.

e•lec•tri•fy /ɪˈlɛktrəˌfay/ *v.* [~ + *obj*], **-fied, -fy•ing. 1.** to provide with electricity. **2.** to thrill or excite. —**e•lec•tri•fi•ca•tion** /ɪˌlɛktrɪfɪˈkeyʃən/, *n.* [*noncount*]

e•lec•tro•cute /ɪˈlɛktrəˌkyuwt/ *v.* [~ + *obj*], **-cut•ed, -cut•ing.** to kill by electricity. —**e•lec•tro•cu•tion** /ɪˌlɛktrəˈkyuwʃən/, *n.* [*noncount*] [*count*]

e•lec•trode /ɪˈlɛktrowd/ *n.* [*count*] a point, or terminal, through which an electric current enters or leaves a battery or other electrical device.

e•lec•tro•mag•net•ism /ɛˌlɛktrowˈmægnɪˌtɪzəm/ *n.* [*noncount*] **1.** the actions associated with electric and magnetic fields, and with electric charges and currents. **2.** the science that studies these things. —**e•lec•tro•mag•net•ic** /ɛˌlɛktrowmægˈnɛtɪk/ *adj.*

e•lec•tron /ɪˈlɛktrɒn/ *n.* [*count*] a tiny particle that has a negative electric charge and moves around the nucleus of an atom.

e•lec•tron•ic /ɪlɛkˈtrɒnɪk, ˌiylɛk-/ *adj.* **1.** [*usually: before a noun*] of or relating to devices, such as televisions and radios, that work by the principles of electronics. **2.** of, relating to, or controlled by computers: *electronic mail.* —**e•lec•tron•i•cal•ly,** *adv.*

e•lec•tron•ics /ɪlɪkˈtrɒnɪks, ˌiylɛk-/ *n.* **1.** [*noncount; used with a singular verb*] the science dealing with devices that use electric current produced by electrons in motion. **2.** [*plural; used with a plural verb*] such devices or systems.

el•e•gant /ˈɛlɪgənt/ *adj.* graceful; very stylish; fine: *an elegant lady dressed in a gown.* —**el•e•gance** /ˈɛlɪgəns/, *n.* [*noncount*] —**'el•e•gant•ly,** *adv.*

el•e•ment /ˈɛləmənt/ *n.* [*count*] **1.** one of the parts of a whole: *Cells are the basic elements of the human body.* **2.** one of a class of substances that cannot be chemically separated into simpler substances: *Hydrogen and oxygen are the elements that make up water.* **3.** a small amount: *There was an element of truth in his explanation.* **4. elements,** [*plural*] **a.** the forces of nature, such as wind and rain. **b.** the basic principles of a subject. —*Idiom.* **5. in** (or **out of**) **one's element,** in a situation that is (not) familiar, enjoyable, or suitable: *She was in her element on the stage.*

el•e•men•ta•ry /ˌɛləˈmɛntəriy/ *adj.* of or relating to the elements or basic principles; simple: *elementary arithmetic.*

ele'mentary ˌschool, *n.* [*count*] [*noncount*] a school giving instruction in basic subjects, often starting with kindergarten and continuing through sixth or eighth grade.

el•e•phant /ˈɛləfənt/ *n.* [*count*], *pl.* **-phants,** (*esp. when thought of as a group*) **-phant.** a very large mammal having a long trunk and large tusks living in Africa and in India.

el•e•vate /ˈɛləˌveyt/ *v.* [~ + *obj*], **-vat•ed, -vat•ing. 1.** to raise to a higher place or position: *We need to elevate the platform.* **2.** to raise to a higher state or rank; promote: *The vice president was elevated to president.*

el•e•va•tion /ˌɛləˈveyʃən/ *n.* [*count*] **1.** the act of elevating or the state of being elevated. **2.** the height of a place above sea level or ground level: *a cliff at an elevation of two hundred feet.* **3.** an elevated place: *We picnicked on an elevation overlooking a lake.*

el•e•va•tor /ˈɛləˌveytər/ *n.* [*count*] **1.** a moving platform or cage for carrying passengers or freight from one level to another in a building. **2.** a building in which grain is stored and handled.

e•lev•en /ɪˈlɛvən/ *n.* [*count*] **1.** a number, ten plus one, written as 11. —*adj.* **2.** amounting to eleven in number. —**e'lev•enth,** *adj.*

elf /ɛlf/ *n.* [*count*], *pl.* **elves** /ɛlvz/. a small imaginary creature who enjoys interfering in human affairs.

el•i•gi•ble /ˈɛlɪdʒəbəl/ *adj.* **1.** being a proper or worthy choice: *an eligible mate.* **2.** meeting the requirements; qualified: *Anyone over 21 is eligible to play this game.* —**el•i•gi•bil•i•ty** /ˌɛlɪdʒəˈbɪlɪtiy/, *n.* [*noncount*]

e•lim•i•nate /ɪˈlɪməˌneyt/ *v.* [~ + *obj*], **-nat•ed, -nat•ing.** to get rid of or leave out: *to eliminate errors.* —**e•lim•i•na•tion** /ɪˌlɪməˈneyʃən/, *n.* [*noncount*]

e•lite or **é•lite** /ɪˈliyt/ *n.* **1.** [*count; often used with a plural verb*] the best or most important members of a group. —*adj.* [*before a noun*] **2.** relating to or forming an elite: *an elite group of authors.*

elk /ɛlk/ *n.* [*count*], *pl.* **elks,** (*esp. when thought of as a group*) **elk. 1.** a large North American deer. **2.** a moose.

el•lipse /ɪˈlɪps/ *n.* [*count*] a curved figure shaped like an oval.

elm /ɛlm/ *n.* [*count*] a tall tree having spreading branches.

e•lon•gate /ɪˈlɔŋgeyt, ɪˈlɒŋ-/ *v.* [~ + *obj*] [*no obj*], **-gat•ed, -gat•ing.** to (cause to) lengthen or stretch out. —**e•lon•ga•tion** /ˌiylɔŋˈgeyʃən, ˌiylɒŋ-/, *n.* [*count*] [*noncount*]

e•lope /ɪˈlowp/ *v.* [*no obj*], **e•loped, e•lop•ing.**

to run off secretly to be married. —**e'lope•ment,** *n.* [*noncount*] [*count*]

el•o•quent /'ɛləkwənt/ *adj.* skilled in effective and appropriate speech: *an eloquent teacher.* —**el•o•quence** /'ɛləkwəns/, *n.* [*noncount*] —**'el•o•quent•ly,** *adv.*

else /ɛls/ *adj.* **1.** other; different: *What else could I do?* **2.** in addition to persons or things mentioned; more: *Who else was there?* —*adv.* **3.** otherwise; if not: *Walk carefully, or else you'll slip.* **4.** in some other way: *How else could I have acted?*

else•where /'ɛls,hwɛər, -,wɛər/ *adv.* somewhere else; in or to some other place: *You will have to look elsewhere for the information.*

e•lude /ɪ'luwd/ *v.* [~ + *obj*], **e•lud•ed, e•lud•ing. 1.** to avoid capture by; escape from: *The thief eluded the police.* **2.** to escape the understanding of: *His popularity eludes me.* —**Usage.** See ESCAPE.

e•lu•sive /ɪ'luwsɪv/ *adj.* **1.** hard to express or understand: *elusive concepts.* **2.** difficult to catch: *an elusive criminal.*

elves /ɛlvz/ *n.* pl. of ELF.

em-, a form of the prefix EN-, used before roots beginning with the letters "b," "p," and sometimes "m" (*emphasis*).

e-mail or **email** /'iy,meyl/ *n.* **1.** [*noncount*] electronic mail: *a system of sending messages from one computer to another or others.* **2.** [*count*] a message sent by e-mail.

e•man•ci•pate /ɪ'mænsə,peyt/ *v.* [~ + *obj*], **-pat•ed, -pat•ing.** to free (someone) from restrictions or slavery. —**e•man•ci•pa•tion** /ɪ,mænsə'peyʃən/, *n.* [*noncount*] —**e'man•ci,pa•tor,** *n.* [*count*]

em•bank•ment /ɛm'bæŋkmənt/ *n.* [*count*] a mound, as of earth or stone, built up to hold back water, support a road, etc.

em•bar•go /ɛm'bargow/ *n.* [*count*], pl. **-goes.** a restriction on trade, esp. a government order preventing the movement of ships into or out of its ports.

em•bark /ɛm'bark/ *v.* [*no obj*] **1.** to board a ship or aircraft. **2.** to start a difficult activity or project: *to embark on a long journey.*

em•bar•rass /ɛm'bærəs/ *v.* to (cause to) become ashamed, uncomfortable, or awkward: [*no obj*]: *She embarrasses so easily.* [~ + *obj*]: *The child's crying embarrassed her parents.* —**em'bar•rass•ing,** *adj.* —**em'bar•rass•ment,** *n.* [*noncount*] [*count*]

em•bas•sy /'ɛmbəsiy/ *n.* [*count*], pl. **-sies. 1.** the official headquarters of an ambassador in a foreign country. **2.** an ambassador and staff.

em•bel•lish /ɛm'bɛlɪʃ/ *v.* [~ + *obj*] to make more beautiful by decorating or ornamenting: *a dress embellished with pearls.*

em•ber /'ɛmbər/ *n.* [*count*] Often, **embers.** [*plural*] a small, still burning piece of coal, wood, etc., in the ashes of a fire.

em•bez•zle /ɛm'bɛzəl/ *v.* [~ + *obj*], **-zled, -zling.** to steal (money) that has been placed in one's care: *He embezzled thousands of dollars from the insurance company.* —**em'bez•zle•ment,** *n.* [*noncount*]

em•blem /'ɛmbləm/ *n.* [*count*] an object that symbolizes a quality or state; a symbol: *The olive branch is an emblem of peace.*

em•brace /ɛm'breys/ *v.*, **-braced, -brac•ing,** *n.* —*v.* **1.** [~ + *obj*] [*no obj*] to clasp in the arms; hug. **2.** [~ + *obj*] to accept willingly: *I don't know whether they'll embrace your idea.* **3.** to in-

clude or contain: *The report embraced many topics.* —*n.* [*count*] **4.** an encircling hug with the arms.

em•broi•der /ɛm'brɔydər/ *v.* [~ + *obj*] **1.** to decorate with embroidery. **2.** to add extra or imaginary details: *She embroidered her story to make it more exciting.*

em•broi•der•y /ɛm'brɔydəriy, -driy/ *n.* [*noncount*] **1.** the sewing of decorative designs on cloth with a needle and thread. **2.** such embroidered work or decoration.

em•bry•o /'ɛmbriy,ow/ *n.* [*count*], pl. **-os.** an animal in the early stages of development in the womb or egg.

em•er•ald /'ɛmərəld/ *n.* **1.** [*count*] a green gem. **2.** [*noncount*] a bright green color. —*adj.* **3.** having a clear, deep green color.

e•merge /ɪ'mɜrdʒ/ *v.* [*no obj*] [~ + *from* + *obj*], **e•merged, e•merg•ing. 1.** to come forth into view, as from hiding: *Two rabbits emerged from the bushes.* **2.** to come into existence or become known: *New evidence emerged from her investigation.* —**e'mer•gence,** *n.* [*noncount*]

e•mer•gen•cy /ɪ'mɜrdʒənsiy/ *n.* [*count*], pl. **-cies.** a sudden, usually unexpected event or happening requiring immediate action.

em•i•grate /'ɛmɪ,greyt/ *v.* [*no obj*], **-grat•ed, -grat•ing.** to leave one country or region to settle in another; migrate: *My grandmother emigrated from Russia in 1930.* —**em•i•grant** /'ɛmɪgrənt/, *n.* [*count*] —**e•mi•gra•tion** /,ɛmɪ'greyʃən/, *n.* [*count*] [*noncount*]

em•i•nent /'ɛmənənt/ *adj.* **1.** high in rank or reputation: *an eminent scholar.* **2.** greatest; outstanding: *I was treated with eminent fairness.* —**'em•i•nence,** *n.* [*count*] [*noncount*]

e•mit /ɪ'mɪt/ *v.* [~ + *obj*], **e•mit•ted, e•mit•ting. 1.** to send forth (liquid, light, particles, etc.); discharge: *The fireplace emitted a pleasant warmth.* **2.** to utter (a sound). —**e•mis•sion** /ɪ'mɪʃən/, *n.* [*count*] [*noncount*]

e•mo•tion /ɪ'mowʃən/ *n.* [*count*] any of the feelings of joy, sorrow, fear, hate, love, etc.

e•mo•tion•al *adj.* **1.** concerning or involving the emotions: *Her son has emotional problems.* **2.** easily affected by emotions: *She cries easily because she's very emotional.* **3.** showing or causing strong feelings: *The lawyer made a strong emotional plea for her client* —**e'mo•tion•al•ly,** *adv.*

em•pa•thize /'ɛmpə,θayz/ *v.* [~ + *with* + *obj*], **-thized, -thiz•ing.** to experience empathy.

em•pa•thy /'ɛmpəθiy/ *n.* [*noncount*] the power or ability to identify with another's feelings, thoughts, etc., as if they were one's own.

em•per•or /'ɛmpərər/ *n.* [*count*] the male supreme ruler of an empire.

em•pha•sis /'ɛmfəsɪs/ *n.*, pl. **-ses** /-,siyz/. **1.** [*noncount*] special stress or importance attached to something: *Her teacher puts emphasis on neatness.* **2.** [*count*] something given special stress or importance: *The main emphasis of his speech was the budget.*

em•pha•size /'ɛmfə,sayz/ *v.* [~ + *obj*], **-sized, -siz•ing.** to give emphasis to; stress.

em•pire /'ɛmpayər/ *n.* [*count*] **1.** a group of nations, states, or peoples ruled over by an emperor, empress, or other powerful sovereign: *The Roman Empire.* **2.** a large and powerful group of businesses headed by one person or group: *He built a communications empire.*

em•ploy /ɛm'plɔy/ *v.* [~ + *obj*] **1.** to hire the services of (a person or persons). **2.** to make use of for a specific task: *They employed computers to*

E

produce the catalog. —*n.* [*noncount*] **3.** employment; service.

em•ploy•ee /ɛm'plɔyiy, ɛmplɔy'iy/ *n.* [*count*] a person who has been hired to work for another.

em•ploy•er *n.* [*count*] a person or group that employs others.

em•ploy•ment /ɛm'plɔymənt/ *n.* [*noncount*] **1.** the state of being employed: *He has had steady employment since he left school.* **2.** the act of employing: *The employment of force by the police was not necessary.*

em•pow•er /ɛm'pawər/ *v.* [~ + *obj* + *to* + *verb*] to give official or legal power or authority to.

em•press /'ɛmprɪs/ *n.* [*count*] **1.** a female ruler of an empire. **2.** the wife of an emperor.

emp•ty /'ɛmptiy/ *adj.,* **-ti•er, -ti•est,** *v.,* **-tied, -ty•ing.** —*adj.* **1.** containing nothing: *an empty box; an empty house.* **2.** meaningless: *empty promises.* —*v.* [*no obj*] [~ + *obj*] **3.** to (cause to) become empty. —'**emp•ti•ness,** *n.* [*noncount*]

'**emp•ty-'hand•ed,** *adj.* **1.** having nothing in the hands. **2.** having achieved nothing: *I came back from the meeting empty-handed.*

em•u•late /'ɛmyə,leyt/ *v.* [~ + *obj*], **-lat•ed, -lat•ing.** to imitate (someone or something) in an effort to do as well as or better than.

en-, a prefix meaning: to put into or on (*entomb; enthrone*); to cover or surround with (*encircle*); to make or cause to be (*enlarge*).

-en¹, a suffix meaning: to make or become (*harden*); to cause or come to have (*strengthen*).

-en², a suffix meaning made of or resembling (*woolen*).

en•a•ble /ɛn'eybəl/ *v.* [~ + *obj* + *to* + *verb*], **-bled, -bling.** to make able; give power or ability: *The money will enable us to hire more workers.*

en•act /ɛn'ækt/ *v.* [~ + *obj*], **1.** to make into law. **2.** to represent in a play: *He enacted the role of the villain.* —**en•act•ment,** *n.* [*count*]

e•nam•el /ɪ'næməl/ *n.* [*noncount*] **1.** a glassy substance that is applied by heat to the surface of metal, pottery, etc., as a decoration or for protection. **2.** a paint that dries to a hard, shiny finish. **3.** the hard covering of a tooth.

en•am•ored /ɪ'næmərd/ *adj.* filled with admiration or love: *They are enamored of each other.* Also, *esp. Brit.,* **en•am'oured.**

en•case /ɛn'keys/ *v.* [~ + *obj*], **-cased, -cas•ing.** to enclose in or as if in a case: *a jewel encased in satin.*

-ence, a suffix meaning: act or fact (*abhorrence*); state or quality (*absence*).

en•chant /ɛn'tʃænt/ *v.* [~ + *obj*] **1.** to place (someone) under a magical spell. **2.** to delight: *The new baby enchanted her parents.* —**enchantment,** *n.* [*noncount*] [*count*]

en•cir•cle /ɛn'sɜrkəl/ *v.* [~ + *obj*], **-cled, -cling.** to form a circle around; surround: *Trees encircled the park.*

en•close /ɛn'klowz/ *v.* [~ + *obj*], **-closed, -clos•ing. 1.** to close in on all sides; surround: *A high wall enclosed the estate.* **2.** to put in the same envelope with something else: *I am enclosing a check with this letter.*

en•clo•sure /ɛn'klowʒər/ *n.* [*count*] **1.** an enclosed area of land. **2.** something put in the same envelope with something else.

en•code /ɛn'kowd/ *v.* [~ + *obj*], **-cod•ed, -cod•ing.** to convert (information, a message, etc.) into code.

en•com•pass /ɛn'kʌmpəs/ *v.* [~ + *obj*] **1.** to encircle; surround: *High mountains encompass the lake.* **2.** to include completely: *The reorganization plan encompasses all employees.*

en•core /'ɑŋkɔr, 'ɑn-/ *interj.* **1.** (used by an audience in demanding a repeated or an additional performance) —*n.* [*count*] **2.** a performance given in response to such a demand.

en•coun•ter /ɛn'kawntər/ *v.* [~ + *obj*] **1.** to come upon or meet with: *She encountered an old friend on the street. They encountered problems with the new computer system.* **2.** to meet in conflict: *The pilots soon encountered the enemy planes.* —*n.* [*count*] **3.** a meeting with a person or thing. **4.** a meeting of people or groups in conflict.

en•cour•age /ɛn'kɜrɪdʒ, -'kʌr-/ *v.* [~ + *obj*], **-aged, -ag•ing.** to give (someone) the courage or confidence to do something: *She encouraged him with praise.* —**en'cour•age•ment,** *n.* [*noncount*] —**en'cour•ag•ing,** *adj.:* *He gave his daughter an encouraging hug before her piano recital.*

en•croach /ɛn'krowtʃ/ *v.* [~ + *on/upon* + *obj*] to intrude upon the property or rights of another, esp. gradually or secretly. —**en'croach•ment,** *n.* [*noncount*] [*count*]

en•cum•ber /ɛn'kʌmbər/ *v.* [~ + *obj*] to weigh down; burden. —**en'cum•brance,** *n.* [*count*]

en•cy•clo•pe•di•a /ɛn,sayklə'piydiyə/ *n.* [*count*], *pl.* **-dias.** a book or set of books containing articles on one subject or all subjects, usually in alphabetical order. —**en•cy•clo'pe•dic,** *adj.*

end /ɛnd/ *n.* [*count*] **1.** the last part; the point where something stops: *the two ends of a rope; the west end of town; the end of winter.* **2.** a purpose or aim: *to achieve one's ends.* **3.** a piece or part left over; remnant. —*v.* **4.** to (cause to) come to an end; conclude: [*no obj*] *The semester ends in June.* [~ + *obj*] *Those remarks ended her speech.* **5. end in,** to result: *The battle ended in a victory.* **6. end up,** to reach a final state or condition: *We ended up parking many blocks away.* —*adj.* [*before a noun*] **7.** final or ultimate: *the end result.* —**Idiom. 8. at the end of one's rope,** at the end of one's resources, patience, or strength. **9. end to end,** in a row with ends touching: *to line up playing cards end to end.* **10. in the end,** finally; after all. **11. make (both) ends meet,** to manage to live on one's income. **12. no end,** very much or many: *We were pleased no end by the enthusiastic response.* **13. on end, a.** with one end down; upright: *to stand a box on end.* **b.** continuously: *to talk for hours on end.* **14. put an end to,** to stop; finish: *Let's put an end to this constant arguing.*

en•dan•ger /ɛn'deyndʒər/ *v.* [~ + *obj*] **1.** to expose to danger. **2.** to threaten (an animal or plant species) with extinction. —**en'dan•ger•ment,** *n.* [*noncount*]

en•deav•or /ɛn'dɛvər/ *v.* [~ + *to* + *verb*] **1.** to try hard to do something. —*n.* **2.** a strong effort or attempt: [*noncount*]: *a new field of endeavor.* [*count*]: *The boy made an honest endeavor to do the right thing.* Also, *esp. Brit.,* **en•deav'our.**

end•less /'ɛndlɪs/ *adj.* having or seeming to have no end. —**'end•less•ly,** *adv.*

en•dorse /ɛn'dɔrs/ *v.* [~ + *obj*], **-dorsed, -dors•ing. 1.** to express approval or support of, esp. publicly: *to endorse a candidate.* **2.** to make (a check) payable to oneself by signing one's name on the back. —**en'dorse•ment,** *n.* [*count*] [*noncount*]

en•dow /ɛn'daw/ *v.* [~ + *obj*] **1.** to provide

with a permanent source of income: *The graduate endowed her college with a million dollars.* **2.** to furnish, as with some talent or quality: *Nature endowed him with a beautiful voice.* —**en'dow•ment,** *n.* [count] [noncount]

en•dure /ɛn'dʊr, -'dyʊr/ *v.,* **-dured, -dur•ing. 1.** [~ + obj] to bear patiently or without complaint; undergo: *I could hardly endure the heat.* **2.** [no obj] to continue to exist; last: *The music of Bach has endured through the ages.* —**en'dur•ing,** *adj.*: *deep and enduring affection.* —**en'dur•ance,** *n.* [noncount]

en•e•my /'ɛnəmiy/ *n.* [count], *pl.* **-mies. 1.** a person who hates or wishes harm to another. **2.** one who opposes someone or something; opponent: *enemies of the state.*

en•er•get•ic /ˌɛnər'dʒɛtɪk/ *adj.* possessing or showing energy; active. —**ˌen•er'get•i•cal•ly,** *adv.*

en•er•gize /'ɛnər,dʒayz/ *v.* [~ + obj], **-gized, -giz•ing.** to give energy to.

en•er•gy /'ɛnərdʒiy/ *n.* [noncount] **1.** the capacity or power to work hard or be very active: *I had enough energy to jog home.* **2.** *Physics.* the capacity to do work. **3.** any source of usable power, as electricity or solar radiation.

en•fold /ɛn'fowld/ *v.* [~ + obj] to wrap up; envelop; surround: *The baby was enfolded in a blanket.*

en•force /ɛn'fɔrs/ *v.* [~ + obj], **-forced** /-'fɔrst/, **-forc•ing.** to make sure (a rule or law) is carried out or obeyed: *The police tried to enforce the new law.* —**en'force•ment,** *n.* [noncount]

en•gage /ɛn'geydʒ/ *v.,* **-gaged, -gag•ing. 1.** to occupy the attention or efforts of; involve: [~ + obj]: *He engaged his daughter in conversation.* [no obj]: *He engaged in politics.* **2.** [~ + obj] to hire; employ. **3.** [~ + obj] to enter into conflict with: *The army engaged the enemy.* **4.** [~ + obj] [no obj] (of gears or the like) to interlock or cause to become interlocked.

en•gaged /ɛn'geydʒd/ *adj.* pledged to be married: *an engaged couple.*

en•gage•ment /ɛn'geydʒmənt/ *n.* [count] **1.** the act of engaging or the state of being engaged. **2.** an appointment or arrangement to be somewhere or do something at a particular time: *a dinner engagement.* **3.** an agreement to marry: *They announced their engagement in the newspaper.*

en•gen•der /ɛn'dʒɛndər/ *v.* [~ + obj] to produce, cause, or give rise to: *Heavy rains engender floods.*

en•gine /'ɛndʒən/ *n.* [count] **1.** a machine for converting heat energy into force and motion. **2.** a railroad locomotive.

en•gi•neer /ˌɛndʒə'nɪər/ *n.* [count] **1.** a person who is trained in engineering: *a civil engineer; an electrical engineer.* **2.** a person who operates a railroad locomotive. —*v.* [~ + obj] **3.** to plan, build, or manage using the methods of engineering: *This bridge is engineered for heavy traffic.* **4.** to arrange or manage by clever means: *He engineered the election of his friend.*

en•gi•neer•ing /ˌɛndʒə'nɪərɪŋ/ *n.* [noncount] **1.** the practical application of science and mathematics, as in the design and construction of machines, vehicles, structures, and roads. **2.** the work or profession of an engineer.

Eng•lish /'ɪŋglɪʃ, -lɪʃ/ *adj.* **1.** of or relating to England. **2.** of or relating to the language spoken in England, the United States, Canada, Australia,

and other countries. —*n.* **3.** [plural; the + ~; used with a plural verb] the people born or living in England. **4.** [noncount] the language spoken in England, the United States, Canada, Australia, and other countries.

Eng•lish•man /'ɪŋglɪʃmən, -lɪʃ-/ *n.* [count], *pl.* **-men.** a person born or living in England, esp. a man.

Eng•lish•wom•an /'ɪŋglɪʃ,wʊmən, -lɪʃ-/ *n.* [count], *pl.* **-wom•en.** a woman born or living in England.

en•grave /ɛn'greyv/ *v.* [~ + obj], **-graved, -grav•ing. 1.** to cut (letters, designs, etc.) into a hard surface, as of metal or wood. **2.** to mark or ornament with cut letters, designs, etc.

en•grav•ing /ɛn'greyvɪŋ/ *n.* **1.** [noncount] the act or art of a person who engraves. **2.** [count] an engraved design, impression, or print.

en•gross /ɛn'grows/ *v.* [~ + obj] to occupy the mind or one's attention completely; absorb: *He was engrossed by the crossword puzzle.*

en•gulf /ɛn'gʌlf/ *v.* [~ + obj] to overwhelm or surround completely: *The stormy sea engulfed the ship.*

en•hance /ɛn'hæns/ *v.* [~ + obj], **-hanced, -hanc•ing.** to increase the value, attractiveness, or quality of; improve: *A fine wine will enhance a delicious meal.* —**en'hance•ment,** *n.* [noncount] [count]

e•nig•ma /ə'nɪgmə/ *n.* [count], *pl.* **-mas.** a puzzling event, situation, or person.

en•joy /ɛn'dʒɔy/ *v.* [~ + obj] **1.** to take pleasure in; experience with joy: *I enjoy walking to school.* **2.** to have and use with satisfaction: *They enjoy a high standard of living.* —**Idiom. 3. enjoy oneself,** to experience pleasure; have a good time: *Did you enjoy yourself at the party?* —**en'joy•a•ble,** *adj.*: *an enjoyable movie.* —**en'joy•ment,** *n.* [noncount] [count]

en•large /ɛn'lɑrdʒ/ *v.,* **-larged, -larg•ing. 1.** to (cause to) become larger; add (to): [no obj]: *That photograph will not enlarge well.* [~ + obj]: *to enlarge a business.* **2.** [no obj] to add more information: *The lecturer enlarged upon her topic.* —**en'large•ment,** *n.* [noncount] [count]

en•light•en /ɛn'laytn/ *v.* [~ + obj] to give understanding or knowledge to; instruct. —**en'light•en•ment,** *n.* [noncount]

en•list /ɛn'lɪst/ *v.* **1.** [no obj] to join the armed forces. **2.** [~ + obj] to persuade (someone) to sign up for military service. **3.** [~ + obj] to obtain (someone's services, help, or aid, etc.) for a cause or activity. —**en'list•ment,** *n.* [noncount] [count]

en•liv•en /ɛn'layvən/ *v.* [~ + obj] to make active or lively.

en•mesh /ɛn'mɛʃ/ *v.* [~ + obj] to catch in or as if in a net; entangle: *He was enmeshed in financial difficulties.*

en•mi•ty /'ɛnmɪtiy/ *n.* [noncount] [count], *pl.* **-ties.** a feeling of bitter hostility or hatred.

e•nor•mi•ty /ɪ'nɔrmɪtiy/ *n.,* *pl.* **-ties. 1.** [noncount] outrageous or evil character: *the enormity of the crime.* **2.** [count] something outrageous or evil, as an offense. **3.** [noncount] greatness of size or extent: *the enormity of the task.*

e•nor•mous /ɪ'nɔrməs/ *adj.* much greater or larger than the usual. —**e'nor•mous•ly,** *adv.*: *We are enormously proud of you.*

e•nough /ɪ'nʌf/ *adj.* **1.** adequate or sufficient for the purpose: [before a noncount noun]: *Do we have enough water for the trip?* [before a plural noun]: *There are enough seats for everyone.*

E

—*pron.* **2.** an adequate or sufficient quantity, amount, or number: *Do you think $50 is enough? We still have enough of the wine to last for a week. Enough of us are here to begin the meeting.* —*adv.* [*after a verb, adverb, or adjective*] **3.** in a quantity or degree that is sufficient for a purpose or need: *You've worked enough; rest for a while. She studied hard enough to pass the test.* —*interj.* **4.** (used to express impatience or annoyance): *Enough! Stop fighting!*

en•quir•y /ɛn'kwayᵊriy, 'ɛnkwəriy/ *n., pl.* **-quir• ies.** INQUIRY.

en•rage /ɛn'reydʒ/ *v.* [~ + *obj*], **-raged, -rag• ing.** to make extremely angry.

en•rich /ɛn'rɪtʃ/ *v.* [~ + *obj*] **1.** to supply with riches or wealth. **2.** to improve in quality, as by adding desirable or useful ingredients: *to enrich soil.* —**en'rich•ment,** *n.* [*noncount*]

en•roll /ɛn'rowl/ *v.,* **-rolled, -roll•ing.** to (cause to) become a member of a group, school, or course: [*no obj*]: *She enrolled in business school.* [~ + *obj*]: *They enrolled me in the club when I paid the fee.*

en•roll•ment /ɛn'rowlmənt/ *n.* **1.** [*noncount*] the act or state of enrolling or being enrolled. **2.** [*count*] the number of people who are registered or enrolled.

en route /ɑn'ruwt, ɛn, ɑ̃/ *adv.* on or along the way: *We met them en route to the party.*

en•sem•ble /ɑn'sɑmbəl, -'sɑmb, ɑ̃-/ *n.* [*count*] **1.** all the parts of a thing taken together as a whole: *The living room furniture is a striking ensemble.* **2.** a group of singers, musicians, etc., performing together.

en•shrine /ɛn'ʃrayn/ *v.* [~ + *obj*] **-shrined, -shrin•ing.** to keep, hold, and protect as sacred.

en•sign /'ɛnsən / *n.* [*count*] **1.** a flag or banner. **2.** a low-ranking officer in the navy or coast guard.

en•slave /ɛn'sleyv/ *v.* [~ + *obj*], **-slaved, -slav• ing.** to put into slavery. —**en'slave•ment,** *n.* [*noncount*]

en•sure /ɛn'ʃʊr, -'ʃɜr/ *v.* [~ + *obj*], **-sured, -sur•ing.** to guarantee; make sure: *They are taking measures to ensure success. Come early to ensure that you get a seat.*

-ent, a suffix meaning: a person or thing that performs or promotes (*president; student*); performing or being (*insistent; different*).

en•tan•gle /ɛn'tæŋgəl/ *v.* [~ + *obj*], **-gled, -gl• ing.** **1.** to make tangled; intertwine. **2.** to involve in difficulties. —**en'tan•gle•ment,** *n.* [*noncount*] [*count*]

en•ter /'ɛntər/ *v.* **1.** to come or go into: [~ + *obj*]: *to enter a room; The thought never entered my mind.* [*no obj*]: *Please knock before you enter.* **2.** [~ + *obj*] to become a member of; join. **3.** [~ + *obj*] to cause to be admitted: *to enter a horse in a race.* **4. enter into, a.** to participate in: *They entered into negotiations.* **b.** to form an important part or ingredient of: *Money doesn't enter into the decision.*

en•ter•prise /'ɛntər,prayz/ *n.* **1.** [*count*] an important, complicated, or difficult plan or project. **2.** [*count*] a business company. **3.** [*noncount*] boldness; adventurous spirit: *He built up his business through hard work and enterprise.*

en•ter•pris•ing /'ɛntər,prayzɪŋ/ *adj.* having or showing imagination and energy.

en•ter•tain /,ɛntər'teyn/ *v.* **1.** [~ + *obj*] [*no obj*] to hold the attention of (someone) pleasantly; amuse. **2.** [~ + *obj*] [*no obj*] to invite (guests) to one's house. **3.** [~ + *obj*] to con-

sider: *to entertain an idea.* —,**en•ter'tain•er,** *n.* [*count*]

en•ter•tain•ment /,ɛntər'teynmənt/ *n.* **1.** [*noncount*] the act of entertaining, as by providing food to guests. **2.** [*noncount*] amusement; distraction from one's regular thoughts: *What do you do for entertainment?* **3.** [*count*] something giving pleasure or amusement: *plays and other entertainments.*

en•thrall /ɛn'θrɔl/ *v.* [~ + *obj*], **-thralled, -thrall•ing.** to capture one's interest; captivate. —**en'thrall•ing,** *adj.*

en•thu•si•asm /ɛn'θuwziy,æzəm/ *n.* **1.** [*noncount*] lively interest; eager involvement: *We are looking forward to your visit with enthusiasm. Her enthusiasm for the plan was obvious.* **2.** [*count*] something in which lively interest is shown; passion: *Rock climbing is one of his enthusiasms.* —**en•thu•si•ast** /ɛn'θuwziy,æst, -ɪst/, *n.* [*count*]

en•thu•si•as•tic /ɛn,θuwziy'æstɪk/ *adj.* greatly interested in or deeply involved: *an enthusiastic hockey fan.* —**en,thu•si'as•tic•al•ly,** *adv.*

en•tice /ɛn'tays/ *v.* [~ + *obj*], **-ticed, -tic•ing.** to tempt or persuade (someone); lure: *How can we entice him to come?* —**en'tice•ment,** *n.* [*count*] [*noncount*]

en•tire /ɛn'tayᵊr/ *adj.* [*before a noun*] having all the parts or elements; complete: *His entire career was spent in the army.* —**en•tire•ly,** *adv.: I agree with you entirely.* —**en•tire•ty** /ɛn'tayᵊrtiy -'tayrɪ-/ *n.* [*noncount*]

en•ti•tle /ɛn'taytl/ *v.* [~ + *obj*], **-tled, -tling.** **1.** to give a right or claim; qualify: *The position of president entitles her to a large office.* **2.** to call by a particular title or name: *Her article was entitled "The Operas of Mozart."*

en•ti•ty /'ɛntɪtiy/ *n.* [*count*], *pl.* **-ties.** something that exists as a separate or independent unit: *Germany became two entities after World War II.*

en•trance /'ɛntrəns/ *n.* **1.** [*count*] the act of entering: *She made a dramatic entrance into the hall.* **2.** [*count*] a point or place of entering, as a doorway. **3.** [*noncount*] the right or permission to enter: *exams for entrance into college.*

en•trant /'ɛntrənt/ *n.* [*count*] a person who takes part in a competition or contest.

en•treat /ɛn'triyt/ *v.* [~ + *obj*] to ask (a person) with deep feeling; beg: *to entreat the judge to show mercy.*

en•treat•y /ɛn'triytiy/ *n.* [*count*], *pl.* **-treat•ies.** an act of entreating; plea.

en•trée /'ɑntrey/ *n.* [*count*] a dish served as the main course of a meal.

en•tre•pre•neur /,ɑntrəprə'nɜr, -'nʊr/ *n.* [*count*] a person who organizes and manages a business, usually with considerable skill and financial risk. —,**en•tre•pre'neur•ship,** *n.* [*noncount*]

en•trust /ɛn'trʌst/ *v.* [~ + *obj*] to give something to someone to take care of: *She entrusted me with the money. She entrusted the child to me.*

en•try /'ɛntriy/ *n.* [*count*], *pl.* **-tries. 1.** the act of entering; entrance. **2.** a place of entrance. **3.** a statement or item recorded in a book, list, or account: *the entries in her diary.* **4.** a person or thing entered in a contest or competition.

en•twine /ɛn'twayn/ *v.* [*no obj*] [~ + *obj*], **-twined, -twin•ing.** to twine about, around, or together.

e•nu•mer•ate /ɪ'nuwmə,reyt, ɪ'nyuw-/ *v.* [~ + *obj*], **-at•ed, -at•ing.** to name one by one;

list. —**e•nu•mer•a•tion** /ɪˌnuwməˈreyʃən/, *n.* [*noncount*]

e•nun•ci•ate /ɪˈnʌnsiyˌeyt/ *v.* [~ + *obj*] [*no obj*], **-at•ed, -at•ing.** to utter or pronounce. —**e•nun•ci•a•tion** /ɛˌnʌnsiyˈeyʃən/, *n.* [*noncount*]

en•vel•op /ɛnˈvɛləp/ *v.* [~ + *obj*] to wrap up in or as if in a covering: *She enveloped me in her arms.*

en•ve•lope /ˈɛnvəˌlowp, ˈɑn-/ *n.* [*count*] a flat paper container, as for a letter.

en•vi•a•ble /ˈɛnviyəbəl/ *adj.* worthy of envy.

en•vi•ous /ˈɛnviyəs/ *adj.* full of, feeling, or expressing envy: *She was envious of her friend's good luck.* —**'en•vi•ous•ly,** *adv.* —**'en•vi•ous• ness,** *n.* [*noncount*]

en•vi•ron•ment /ɛnˈvayrənmənt, -ˈvayərn-/ *n.* **1.** [*count*] social and cultural surroundings: *bringing up children in a safe environment.* **2.** [*count*] [*noncount*] the external factors and forces surrounding and affecting an organism, person, or population. —**en•vi•ron•men•tal** /ɛnˌvayrən- ˈmɛntəl, -ˌvayərn-/ *adj.: Poverty may be one environmental cause of crime.* —**en,vi•ron'men•tal• ist,** *n.* [*count*]

en•vi•sion /ɛnˈvɪʒən/ *v.* [~ + *obj*] to picture in the mind, esp. some future event: *He envisioned a shopping mall bringing over the park.*

en•voy /ˈɛnvɔy, ˈɑn-/ *n.* [*count*] an official messenger or representative.

en•vy /ˈɛnviy/ *n. v.,* **-vied, -vy•ing.** —*n.* [*noncount*] **1.** a feeling of discontent caused by a desire for another's advantages or achievements; jealousy. **2.** [*the* + ~ + *of*] an object of envy: *Her excellent grades made her the envy of her classmates.* —*v.* [~ + *obj*] **3.** to look at with envy; be jealous of.

en•zyme /ˈɛnzaym/ *n.* [*count*] a protein substance from living cells that is capable of producing chemical changes in plants and animals, as in digestion.

e•on /ˈiyən, ˈiyɒn/ *n.* [*count*] an extremely long period of time.

ep•ic /ˈɛpɪk/ *adj.* **1.** of unusually great size or extent. —*n.* [*count*] **2.** a long poem in a formal style, usually about heroic events.

ep•i•dem•ic /ˌɛpɪˈdɛmɪk/ *n.* [*count*] **1.** an occurrence of a disease affecting many people and spreading from person to person quickly. **2.** a rapid increase in the occurrence of something: *an epidemic of robberies.*

ˌep•i'der•mis, *n.* [*noncount*] the outermost layer of the skin.

ep•i•lep•sy /ˈɛpəˌlɛpsiy/ *n.* [*noncount*] a disorder of the nervous system that causes convulsions or loss of consciousness. —**ˌep•i'lep•tic,** *adj., n.* [*count*]

ep•i•logue /ˈɛpəˌlɔg, -ˌlɒg/ *n.* [*count*] a concluding part added to a book, story, or play.

E•pis•co•pa•lian /ɪˌpɪskəˈpeylyən/ *adj.* **1.** of or relating to the Protestant Episcopal Church of the United States, descended from the Church of England. —*n.* [*count*] **2.** a member of the Episcopal Church.

ep•i•sode /ˈɛpəˌsowd/ *n.* [*count*] **1.** one incident or event, as in a person's life. **2.** an incident, scene, etc., within a story. **3.** an individual program in a radio or television series.

ep•i•taph /ˈɛpɪˌtæf/ *n.* [*count*] words carved on a tomb or monument.

ep•i•thet /ˈɛpəˌθɛt/ *n.* [*count*] a descriptive word or phrase added to or used in place of a name.

e•pit•o•me /ɪˈpɪtəmiy/ *n.* [*count; the* + ~ + *of*] a person or thing that is typical of a whole class of things: *She is the epitome of kindness.*

ep•och /ˈɛpək; *esp. Brit.* ˈiypɒk/ *n.* [*count*] a period of time marked by noteworthy features or events: *an epoch of peace.*

e•qual /ˈiykwəl/ *adj., n., v.,* **e•qualed, e•qual• ing** or (*esp. Brit.*) **e•qualled, e•qual•ling.** —*adj.* **1.** the same or alike in quantity, degree, value, etc.: *The two men were of equal height. Two plus two is equal to four.* **2.** having adequate ability or means; suited: *I'm sure you will be equal to the task.* —*n.* [*count*] **3.** a person or thing that is equal: *We always considered each other equals.* —*v.* [~ + *obj*] **4.** to be or become equal to: *Two plus two equals four. I cannot equal him in intelligence.* —**e•qual•i•ty** /ɪˈkwɑlɪtiy/ *n.* [*noncount*] —**'e•qual•ly,** *adv.*

e•qual•ize /ˈiykwəˌlayz/ *v.* [~ + *obj*], **-ized, -iz•ing.** to make equal.

e•qual•ly /ˈiykwəliy/ *adv.* **1.** in the same manner: *to treat the rich and poor equally.* **2.** to the same degree: *They are equally beautiful.*

'equal ˌsign or **'equals ˌsign,** *n.* [*count*] the symbol (=) used, esp. in a mathematical expression, to indicate that the terms it separates are equal.

e•quate /ɪˈkweyt/ *v.* [~ + *obj*], **e•quat•ed, e•quat•ing.** to consider or treat as equivalent: *Some people equate experience with wisdom.*

e•qua•tion /ɪˈkweyʒən/ *n.* [*count*] an expression in mathematics, stating that two quantities are equal.

e•qua•tor /ɪˈkweytər/ *n.* [*count*] an imaginary line that circles the earth and is the same distance from the North Pole and South Pole. —**e• qua•to•ri•al** /ˌiykwəˈtɔriyəl, -ˈtowr-, ˌɛkwə-/ *adj.*

e•ques•tri•an /ɪˈkwɛstriyən/ *adj.* [*before a noun*] of or relating to horseback riding or horseback riders.

e•qui•dis•tant /ˌiykwɪˈdɪstənt, ˌɛkwɪ-/ *adj.* equally distant: *The two cities are equidistant from here.*

e•qui•lat•er•al /ˌiykwəˈlætərəl, ˌɛkwə-/ *adj.* having all the sides equal: *an equilateral triangle.*

e•qui•lib•ri•um /ˌiykwəˈlɪbriyəm, ˌɛkwə-/ *n.* [*noncount*] **1.** a state of rest or balance between opposing forces, powers, or influences. **2.** mental or emotional balance.

e•qui•nox /ˈiykwəˌnɒks, ˈɛkwə-/ *n.* [*count*] one of the times when the sun crosses the earth's equator, making night and day of approximately equal length all over the earth.

e•quip /ɪˈkwɪp/ *v.* [~ + *obj*], **e•quipped, e•quip•ping.** to provide with what is needed for use or for an activity: *The computer is equipped with a modem. They are not properly equipped for a long climb.*

e•quip•ment /ɪˈkwɪpmənt/ *n.* [*noncount*] the tools, machines, etc., used or needed for a certain purpose or activity: *office equipment.*

eq•ui•ta•ble /ˈɛkwɪtəbəl/ *adj.* fair or just.

eq•ui•ty /ˈɛkwɪtiy/ *n.* [*noncount*] the quality of being fair or impartial; fairness.

e•quiv•a•lent /ɪˈkwɪvələnt/ *adj.* **1.** equal in value, measure, or force. —*n.* [*count*] **2.** something equivalent: *That car cost the equivalent of a year's salary.* —**e'quiv•a•lence,** *n.* [*noncount*] [*count*] —**e'quiv•a•lent•ly,** *adv.*

-er¹, a suffix meaning: a person who is occupied with or works at something (*teacher*); a native or resident of a place (*New Yorker; southerner*); a person or thing associated with a particular char-

E

acteristic or circumstance (*teenager*); a person or thing that performs or is used in performing an action (*fertilizer*).

-er², a suffix forming the comparative of adjectives (*smaller*) and adverbs (*faster*).

e•ra /'ɪərə, 'ɛrə/ n. [count], pl. **e•ras**. a period of time marked by special character, events, etc.; the period of time to which anything belongs.

e•rad•i•cate /ɪ'rædɪˌkeyt/ v. [~ + obj], **-cat•ed, -cat•ing**. to remove or destroy completely. —**e•rad•i•ca•tion** /ɪˌrædɪ'keyʃən/, n. [noncount]

e•rase /ɪ'reys/ v. [~ + obj], **e•rased, e•ras•ing**. 1. to rub out (written marks): *She erased her name from the blackboard.* 2. to remove; eliminate: *She couldn't erase the scene from her memory.*

e•ras•er /ɪ'reysər/ n. [count] a device, as a piece of rubber, for erasing marks of pencil, chalk, etc.

e•rect /ɪ'rɛkt/ adj. 1. upright and straight in position or posture: *to sit erect.* —v. [~ + obj] 2. to build; construct. —**e•rec•tion** /ɪ'rɛkʃən/, n. [noncount] [count]

e•rode /ɪ'rowd/ v., **e•rod•ed, e•rod•ing**. to (cause to) be worn away; to (cause to) be destroyed slowly: [no obj]: *The bridge was eroding from the salt spray.* [~ + obj]: *Wind eroded the loose soil.* —**e•ro•sion** /ɪ'rowʒən/ n. [noncount]

e•rot•ic /ɪ'rɒtɪk/ adj. of, relating to, or about sexual love.

err /ɜr, ɛr/ v. [no obj] to be incorrect; make an error.

er•rand /'ɛrənd/ n. [count] a short trip to accomplish a certain purpose: *I have to do a few errands for my mother.*

er•rat•ic /ɪ'rætɪk/ adj. changeable in behavior or style; unpredictable.

er•ro•ne•ous /ə'rowniyəs, ɛ'row-/ adj. containing error; mistaken; incorrect.

er•ror /'ɛrər/ n. 1. [count] a mistake. 2. [noncount] the condition of being wrong: *I was in error about the date of the party.*

e•rupt /ɪ'rʌpt/ v. 1. [no obj] [~ + obj] (of a volcano, etc.) to throw out matter violently. 2. [no obj] to break out in a sudden and violent manner; burst forth: *Words of anger erupted from her.* —**e•rup•tion**, n. [noncount] [count]

-ery, a suffix meaning: things as a group (*machinery*); people as a group (*peasantry*); occupation, activity, or condition (*archery*); a place for (*winery*); characteristic conduct (*prudery*).

-es¹, a variant form of -s¹: (*pitches; studies*).

-es², a variant form of -s²: (*riches; losses; babies*).

es•ca•late /'ɛskəˌleyt/ v. [no obj] [~ + obj], **-lat•ed, -lat•ing**. to (cause to) increase in intensity, degree, or amount. —**es•ca•la•tion** /ˌɛskə'leyʃən/, n. [noncount]

es•ca•la•tor /'ɛskəˌleytər/ n. [count] a continuously moving stairway on an endless loop for carrying passengers up or down.

es•cape /ɪ'skeyp/ v., **-caped, -cap•ing**, n. —v. 1. [no obj] to get away, as from confinement or jail: *How did the mice escape from their cage?* 2. to avoid (capture, punishment, injury, or the like): [~ + obj]: *The town escaped the worst of the storm.* [no obj]: *He managed to escape with only cuts and bruises.* 3. [~ + obj] to be unnoticed or forgotten: *His name escapes me.* —n. 4. [count] an act or instance of escaping. 5. [count] [noncount] a way or means of escaping. —**Usage**. ESCAPE, ELUDE, EVADE mean to keep away from something. To ESCAPE is to manage to keep away from danger, pursuit, observation,

etc.: *to escape punishment*. To ELUDE is to slip through an apparently tight net, and implies using skill or cleverness: *The fox eluded the hounds*. To EVADE is to turn aside from or go out of reach of a person or thing, usually by moving or directing attention elsewhere: *to evade the police*.

es•cort /n. 'ɛskɔrt; v. ɪ'skɔrt/ n. [count] 1. a person or group accompanying another for protection or guidance. 2. an armed or protective guard, as a body of soldiers or ships. 3. a man or woman who accompanies another person to a public event. —v. [~ + obj] 4. to accompany as an escort.

-ese, a suffix meaning: the inhabitants of a place or their language (*Japanese*); a characteristic jargon, style, or accent (*Brooklynese; legalese*).

Es•ki•mo /'ɛskəˌmow/ n., pl. **-mo, -mos** for 1. 1. *Sometimes Offensive*. [count] a member of a people living in regions from Greenland through Canada and Alaska to NE Siberia. 2. [noncount] the group of languages spoken by the Eskimos.

ESL, an abbreviation of: English as a second language.

e•soph•a•gus /ɪ'sɒfəgəs/ n. [count] a tube that allows food to pass from the back of the mouth to the stomach.

esp., an abbreviation of: especially.

es•pe•cial•ly /ɪ'spɛʃəliy/ adv. 1. to an exceptional degree; particularly: *Be especially watchful.* 2. for a particular purpose; specifically: *These clothes were designed especially for you.*

es•pres•so /ɛ'sprɛsow/ n., pl. **-sos** for 2. 1. [noncount] a strong coffee prepared by forcing steam through finely ground coffee beans. 2. [count] a cup of espresso.

-esque, a suffix meaning: resembling (*picturesque; Lincolnesque*); in the style or manner of (*Kafkaesque*).

-ess, a suffix forming feminine nouns (*countess; goddess; lioness*).

es•say /'ɛsey or, for 2, ɛ'sey/ n. [count] 1. a short piece of writing on a particular theme or subject. 2. an effort to perform or accomplish something; attempt.

es•say•ist /'ɛseyɪst/ n. [count] a writer of essays.

es•sence /'ɛsəns/ n. 1. [noncount] the basic, unchanging nature or meaning of a thing: *The essence of civilized behavior is courtesy.* 2. [count] [noncount] a concentrated substance made from a plant, drug, or the like. —**Idiom**. 3. **in es•sence**, essentially; basically: *What she said, in essence, is that everything is all right.*

es•sen•tial /ə'sɛnʃəl/ adj. 1. absolutely necessary: *essential vitamins; It is essential that you be at the meeting.* 2. [before a noun] relating to the essence of a thing: *The essential purpose of a vacation is to relax.* —n. [count] 3. a basic or necessary item or thing.

es•sen•tial•ly adv. in reality, basically: *He's essentially intelligent.*

-est, a suffix forming the superlative of adjectives (*warmest*) and adverbs (*fastest*).

es•tab•lish /ɪ'stæblɪʃ/ v. [~ + obj] 1. to bring into being on a firm or permanent basis: *to establish a university.* 2. [~ + oneself] to put or settle in a position, place, business, etc.: *They established themselves as founders of the organization.* 3. to figure out; determine: *The doctor was able to establish the cause of death.*

es•tab•lish•ment /ɪ'stæblɪʃmənt/ n. 1. [noncount] the act of establishing or the state of being established. 2. [count] a place of business: *That* *flour mill is the oldest establishment in town.* **3. the Establishment,** [*noncount*] the people and institutions that make up the power structure in society. **4.** (*often: Establishment;*) [*count*] the controlling group in a specific field: *the scientific Establishment.*

es•tate /ɪˈsteyt/ *n.* **1.** [*count*] a large piece of land as property, esp. one with a large house on it. **2.** [*noncount*] property or possessions, as the property of someone who has died.

es•teem /ɪˈstiym/ *v.* [~ + *obj*] **1.** to have high regard for: *She is esteemed for her fine qualities.* —*n.* [*noncount*] **2.** favorable opinion; respect or regard: *to hold a person in high esteem.*

es•ti•mate /*v.* ˈɛstəˌmeyt; *n.* -mɪt/ *v.*, **-mat•ed, -mat•ing,** *n.* —*v.* [~ + *obj*] **1.** to form a judgment regarding the worth, amount, size, etc. of: *He estimated the cost at about $5,000.* —*n.* [*count*] **2.** an approximate judgment or calculation. **3.** a judgment or opinion: *My estimate of his character was incorrect.*

et al. /ˈɛt æl, ˈɑl, ˈɔl/ a Latin abbreviation meaning: and others.

etc., (et setˈər ə, seˈtrə) an abbreviation of: et cetera (used after a list of things to show that similar things have been left out of the list): *cows, sheep, pigs, etc.*

etch /ɛtʃ/ *v.* **1.** [*no obj*] [~ + *obj*] to cut into (metal or glass) with an acid, knife, or the like, to form a design that can be transferred to paper. **2.** [~ + *obj*] to outline clearly or sharply: *The old man's face was etched with lines.* —ˈetch•er, *n.* [*count*]

etch•ing /ˈɛtʃɪŋ/ *n.* **1.** [*noncount*] the act or process of making designs on a metal plate or glass. **2.** [*count*] a design made from an etched plate.

e•ter•nal /ɪˈtɜrnl/ *adj.* **1.** having no beginning or end; lasting forever: *the eternal movement of the planets.* **2.** constant: *This eternal chatter is driving me crazy.* —e'ter•nal•ly, *adv.*

e•ter•ni•ty /ɪˈtɜrnɪtiy/ *n., pl.* **-ties.** **1.** [*noncount*] time without beginning or end. **2.** [*count; usually singular*] a period of time that seems endless: *I waited an eternity for a bus.*

eth•ic /ˈɛθɪk/ *n.* [*count; singular*] all the moral principles or values of a culture, group, etc. See ETHICS.

eth•i•cal /ˈɛθɪkəl/ *adj.* relating to morality or ethics. —ˈeth•i•cal•ly, *adv.*

eth•ics /ˈɛθɪks/ *n.* [*plural; used with a plural verb*] a system or set of moral principles.

eth•nic /ˈɛθnɪk/ *adj.* [*before a noun*] relating to or characteristic of a group of people, esp. a group (**ˈethnic ˈgroup**) sharing a common and distinctive culture. —ˈeth•ni•cal•ly, *adv.*

et•i•quette /ˈɛtɪkɪt, -ˌkɛt/ *n.* [*noncount*] the rules of proper social or professional behavior; manners.

-ette, a suffix meaning: little (*kitchenette*).

et•y•mol•o•gy /ˌɛtəˈmɒlədʒiy/ *n.* [*count*], *pl.* **-gies.** the history of words or word elements.

eu•ca•lyp•tus /ˌyuwkəˈlɪptəs/ *n.* [*count*], *pl.* **-ti** /-tay/, **-tus•es.** a tree chiefly from Australia and nearby islands having sweet-smelling evergreen leaves.

Eu•cha•rist /ˈyuwkərɪst/ *n.* [*often: the* + ~] **1.** Holy Communion. **2.** the bread and wine taken at Holy Communion. —ˌEu•chaˈris•tic, *adj.*

eu•lo•gy /ˈyuwlədʒiy/ *n.* [*count*], *pl.* **-gies.** a speech in praise of a person who has died.

eu•phe•mism /ˈyuwfəˌmɪzəm/ *n.* [*count*] a mild or vague expression substituted for one

thought to be offensive or harsh. —ˌeu•pheˈmis•tic, *adj.*

eu•pho•ri•a /yuwˈfɔriyə/ *n.* [*noncount*] a strong feeling of happiness, confidence, or well-being. —euˈphor•ic, *adj.*

Eu•ro•pe•an /ˌyʊrəˈpiyən/ *adj.* **1.** of or relating to Europe. —*n.* [*count*] **2.** a person born or living in Europe.

eu•tha•na•sia /ˌyuwθəˈneyʒə/ *n.* [*noncount*] painless killing of a person or animal suffering from an incurable condition.

e•vac•u•ate /ɪˈvækyuˌweyt/ *v.* [~ + *obj*], **-at•ed, -at•ing.** to remove (persons or things) from a place, esp. for safety. —e•vac•u•a•tion /ɪˌvækyuwˈeyʃən/, *n.* [*count*] [*noncount*]

e•vade /ɪˈveyd/ *v.* [~ + *obj*], **e•vad•ed, e•vad•ing.** to escape or avoid, esp. by cleverness or trickery. —**Usage.** See ESCAPE.

e•val•u•ate /ɪˈvælyuˌweyt/ *v.* [~ + *obj*], **-at•ed, -at•ing.** to determine the value, quality, or importance of. —e•val•u•a•tion /ɪˌvælyuwˈeyʃən/, *n.* [*count*] [*noncount*]

e•van•gel•i•cal /ˌiyvænˈdʒɛlɪkəl, ˌɛvən-/ *adj.* belonging or referring to the Christian churches that emphasize the authority of the Scriptures and faith in Christ.

e•van•ge•lism /ɪˈvændʒəˌlɪzəm/ *n.* [*noncount*] the preaching of the Christian gospel. —eˈvan•ge•list, *n.* [*count*] —e•van•ge•lize /ɪˈvændʒəˌlayz/ *v.* [~ + *obj*], **-lized, -liz•ing.**

e•vap•o•rate /ɪˈvæpəˌreyt/ *v.*, **-rat•ed, -rat•ing. 1.** [*no obj*] [~ + *obj*] to change from a liquid or solid state into vapor or gas. **2.** [*no obj*] to disappear; vanish: *His hopes evaporated.* —e•vap•o•ra•tion /ɪˌvæpəˈreyʃən/, *n.* [*noncount*]

e•va•sion /ɪˈveyʒən/ *n.* [*count*] [*noncount*] an act or instance of evading.

e•va•sive /ɪˈveysɪv/ *adj.* using evasion: *evasive answers.*

eve /iyv/ *n.* [*count*] the evening or the day before an event, esp. a holiday.

e•ven /ˈiyvən/ *adj.* **1.** without bumps on the surface; smooth: *an even road.* **2.** on the same level: *even with the ground.* **3.** free from sudden changes; uniform: *even motion.* **4.** (of a number) that can be divided by two. **5.** equal in measure or quantity: *even amounts of oil and vinegar.* **6.** equally balanced or divided: *the scales are even.* **7.** calm: *an even temper.* —*adv.* **8.** in an even manner; smoothly: *The road ran even over the fields.* **9.** still; yet: *even more suitable.* **10.** fully or quite: *ready to fight even unto death.* **11.** (used to stress or emphasize the truth of something): *He is willing, even eager.* —*v.* **12. even out,** to make or become level, smooth, or equal: *The wrinkles will even out when the suit dries.* —*Idiom.* **13. break even,** to have one's profits equal one's losses: *The company was managing only to break even.* —ˈe•ven•ly, *adv.* —ˈe•ven•ness, *n.* [*count*] [*noncount*]

eve•ning /ˈiyvnɪŋ/ *n.* the last part of the day and early part of the night.

e•vent /ɪˈvɛnt/ *n.* [*count*] **1.** something that happens in a certain place during a particular time. —*Idiom.* **2. in any event,** regardless of what happens: *In any event, I'll call you tomorrow.*

e•vent•ful /ɪˈvɛntfəl/ *adj.* full of interesting or important events or incidents.

e•ven•tu•al /ɪˈvɛntʃuwəl/ *adj.* [*before a noun*] happening at some time in the future; resulting: *His mistakes led to his eventual dismissal.*

E

—e'ven•tu•al•ly, *adv.*: *After a long search, I eventually found my keys.*

ev•er /'ɛvər/ *adv.* **1.** at any time: *Did you ever go skiing? I hardly ever drink soda. If you ever see him, tell him to call me. I doubt that I'll ever see her again. She looks better than ever now.* **2.** at all times; always: *an ever-present danger.* **3.** starting in the past and going on up to now: *Ever since then we've been best friends.*

ev•er•green /'ɛvər,griyn/ *adj.* **1.** (of trees, shrubs, etc.) having green leaves throughout the year. —*n.* [*count*] **2.** an evergreen plant.

ev•er•last•ing /,ɛvər'læstɪŋ, -'lɑstɪŋ/ *adj.* lasting forever; eternal: *everlasting life.*

eve•ry /'ɛvriy/ *adj.* **1.** being one of a group taken together; each (of a group): *We go to the office every day.* **2.** all possible; the greatest possible degree of: *We wished him every chance of success.* —*Idiom.* **3. every now and then** or **every so often,** on occasion; from time to time: *I see him every now and then.* **4. every other,** every second; every alternate: *every other day.*

eve•ry•bod•y /'ɛvriy,bɒdiy, -,bʌdiy/ *pron.* [*used with a singular verb*] every person: *Everybody wants another drink.*

eve•ry•day /'ɛvriy,dey; -'dey/ *adj.* [*before a noun*] **1.** of or relating to every day; daily: *an everyday occurrence.* **2.** ordinary; common: *These are my everyday dishes, not my good china.*

eve•ry•one /'ɛvriy,wʌn, -wən/ *pron.* [*used with a singular verb*] every person; everybody: *Everyone wants to get ahead.*

eve•ry•thing /'ɛvriy,θɪŋ/ *pron.* **1.** every single thing; all: *Put away everything on the floor.* **2.** all that matters: *Love is everything.*

eve•ry•where /'ɛvriy,hwɛər, -,wɛər/ *adv.* in every place or part; in all places: *She takes her baby with her everywhere.*

e•vict /ɪ'vɪkt/ *v.* [~ + *obj*] to force out (a tenant) from land, a building, etc., by legal action. —e•vic•tion /ɪ'vɪkʃən/ *n.* [*count*] [*noncount*]

ev•i•dence /'ɛvɪdəns/ *n.* [*noncount*] **1.** information or objects that tend to prove something: *The play's large audiences are evidence of its popularity.* **2.** something that makes plain or clear: *His flushed face was evidence of his fever.*

ev•i•dent /'ɛvɪdənt/ *adj.* plain or clear: *his evident surprise at not being hired.* —'ev•i•dent•ly, *adv.*

e•vil /'iyvəl/ *adj.* **1.** morally wrong or bad; wicked. —*n.* [*count*] **2.** something evil; evil quality or conduct. —'e•vil•ly, *adv.* —'e•vil•ness, *n.* [*noncount*]

e•voc•a•tive /ɪ'vɒkətɪv, ɪ'vowkə-/ *adj.* tending to call up memories or feelings.

e•voke /ɪ'vowk/ *v.* [~ + *obj*], e•voked, e•vok•ing. to call up (memories, feelings, etc.): *The book evoked memories of her childhood.*

ev•o•lu•tion /,ɛvə'luwʃən/ *esp. Brit.* ,iyvə-/ *n.* [*noncount*] **1.** any process of formation or growth: *the evolution of language.* **2.** the theory that all existing organisms developed from earlier forms. —ev•o'lu•tion,ar•y, *adj.*

e•volve /ɪ'vɒlv/ *v.,* e•volved, e•volv•ing. **1.** to (cause to) come forth gradually into being; develop: [*no obj*]: *The whole idea evolved from a casual remark.* [~ + *obj*]: *to evolve a scheme.* **2.** [*no obj*] (of a species or population) to develop by a process of evolution.

ewe /yuw/ *n.* [*count*] a female sheep, esp. when it is mature.

ex-, a prefix meaning: out of, from, away, or forth (*export; exhale*); former (*ex-governor*).

ex., an abbreviation of: **1.** examination. **2.** example. **3.** except. **4.** exception. **5.** exchange.

ex•ac•er•bate /ɪg'zæsər,beyt, ɛk'sæs-/ *v.* [~ + *obj*] -bat•ed, -bat•ing. to make (something) worse. —ex•ac•er•ba•tion /ɪg,zæsər'beyʃən, ɛk,sæs-/, *n.* [*noncount*]

ex•act /ɪg'zækt/ *adj.* very accurate; correct; precise: *an exact thinker.* —ex'act•ness, *n.* [*noncount*]

ex•act•ing /ɪg'zæktɪŋ/ *adj.* demanding or expecting much effort or care.

ex•act•ly /ɪg'zæktliy/ *adv.* **1.** accurately; correctly; precisely: *Follow my directions exactly.* **2.** (used to add force to an expression) really; quite: *This dress is exactly what I wanted.*

ex•ag•ger•ate /ɪg'zædʒə,reyt/ *v.,* -at•ed, -at•ing. to make (something) greater, harder, etc., than it really is: [~ + *obj*]: *to exaggerate the difficulties of a situation.* [*no obj*]: *I was exaggerating when I said he is as tall as a tree.* —ex•ag•ger•a•tion /ɪg,zædʒə'reyʃən/, *n.* [*count*] [*noncount*]

ex•alt /ɪg'zɔlt/ *v.* [~ + *obj*] **1.** to raise in rank, power, or character; elevate. **2.** to praise highly. —ex•al•ta•tion /,ɛgzɔl'teyʃən, ,ɛksɔl-/ *n.* [*noncount*]

ex•am /ɪg'zæm/ *n.* [*count*] *Informal.* an examination.

ex•am•i•na•tion /ɪg,zæmə'neyʃən/ *n.* **1.** [*noncount*] [*count*] the act or process of examining. **2.** [*count*] a test for knowledge of a subject.

ex•am•ine /ɪg'zæmɪn/ *v.* [~ + *obj*], -ined, -in•ing. **1.** to look at carefully in order to judge or discover something: *to examine merchandise.* **2.** to test the knowledge or qualifications of (a pupil, candidate, etc.), as by questions.

ex•am•ple /ɪg'zæmpəl/ *n.* [*count*] **1.** one of a number of things, or a part of something, that represents the whole: *This painting is an example of his early work.* **2.** a pattern or model: *Parents should set a good example for their children.* **3. for example,** (used before an instance or instances of what has just been mentioned): *The train I take is always late. For example, this morning it was half an hour late.*

ex•as•per•ate /ɪg'zæspə,reyt/ *v.* [~ + *obj*], -at•ed, -at•ing. to irritate or annoy extremely: *Constant interruptions exasperate me.* —ex'as•per,at•ing, *adj.*

ex•ca•vate /'ɛkskə,veyt/ *v.* [~ + *obj*], -vat•ed, -vat•ing. **1.** to make a hole in: *The ground was excavated for the new building.* **2.** to expose by digging: *The archaeologist excavated the ruins of ancient Troy.* —ex•ca•va•tion /,ɛkskə'veyʃən/, *n.* [*count*] [*noncount*]

ex•ceed /ɪk'siyd/ *v.* [~ + *obj*] **1.** to be greater than, as in quantity or degree: *The price of the house exceeded $200,000.* **2.** to do more than (what is expected, necessary, etc.): *She exceeded her family's expectations when she graduated from law school.* —ex'ceed•ing•ly, *adv.*

ex•cel /ɪk'sɛl/ *v.* [*no obj*] -celled, -cel•ling. to do better than others or be superior in some way: *She excels in math.*

ex•cel•lent /'ɛksələnt/ *adj.* having outstanding quality or superior merit; very good. —'ex•cel•lence, *n.* [*noncount*] —'ex•cel•lent•ly, *adv.*

ex•cept¹ /ɪk'sɛpt/ *prep.* **1.** not including; other than: *They were all there except me.* —*conj.* **2.** only; with the exception of: *They are similar except (that) one is younger than the other.* **3.** otherwise than; but: *The city is well fortified except in that area.* —*Idiom.* **4. except for,** if it were not for:

They would travel except for lack of money.
—Usage. See ACCEPT.

ex•cept² /ɪk'sɛpt/ v. [~ + obj] to exclude; leave out: *The A students were excepted from taking the exam.* **—Usage.** See ACCEPT.

ex•cep•tion /ɪk'sɛpʃən/ n. **1.** [noncount] the act of leaving out or the fact of being left out: *Fill in every line in this form without exception.* **2.** [count] something that is not included in a group or general rule: *I'll make an exception in your case.* **—Idiom. 3. take exception to,** to be made angry (by): *I took exception to her rude comments.*

ex•cep•tion•al /ɪk'sɛpʃənl/ adj. **1.** forming an exception or rare instance; unusual. **2.** unusually excellent; superior. **—ex'cep•tion•al•ly,** adv.

ex•cerpt /'ɛksɜrpt/ n. [count] a passage taken from a book, document, film, or the like.

ex•cess /ɪk'sɛs, 'ɛksɛs/ n. **1.** [noncount] the fact of exceeding in amount or degree: *The cost was in excess of our estimate.* **2.** [count] the amount or degree by which one thing exceeds another: *an excess of several dollars.* **3.** [count] more than a reasonable amount: *He drank to excess.* —adj. [before a noun] **4.** more than what is necessary or usual: *excess baggage.* **—ex'ces•sive,** adj. **—ex'ces•sive•ly,** adv.

ex•change /ɪks'tʃeyndʒ/ v., **-changed, -chang•ing,** n. —v. [~ + obj] **1.** to give up (something) for a replacement or substitute: *I exchanged the broken radio for a new one.* **2.** to give and receive; interchange: *We exchange gifts on the holiday.* —n. **3.** an act or instance of exchanging: [count]: *an exchange of prisoners.* [noncount]: *The trapper got some coffee and gunpowder in exchange for his furs.* **4.** [count] something exchanged. **5.** [count] a place for buying and selling goods, stock, etc.

ex•cise¹ /'ɛksayz/ n. [noncount] a tax on certain goods placed on their manufacture, sale, or use within the country.

ex•cise² /ɪk'sayz/ v. [~ + obj] **-cised, -cis•ing.** to remove by or as if by cutting out or off: *The surgeons excised the tumor.*

ex•cit•a•ble /ɪk'saytəbəl/ adj. easily excited. **—ex,cit•a'bil•i•ty,** n. [noncount]

ex•cite /ɪk'sayt/ v. [~ + obj], **-cit•ed, -cit•ing.** to stir up the emotions or feelings of: *The coming of Christmas excites the children.*

ex•cit•ed /ɪk'saytɪd/ adj. full of strong emotions or feelings. **—ex•cit'ed•ly,** adv.

ex•cite•ment /ɪk'saytmənt/ n. [count] [noncount] (something that causes) an excited state or condition.

ex•cit•ing /ɪk'saytɪŋ/ adj. producing or causing excitement.

ex•claim /ɪk'skleym/ v. [no obj] to cry out or speak suddenly and loudly.

ex•cla•ma•tion /ˌɛksklə'meyʃən/ n. [count] the act of exclaiming.

excla'mation ,point, n. [count] the sign (!) used in writing after an exclamation or interjection expressing strong emotion or astonishment. Also called **excla'mation ,mark.**

ex•clude /ɪk'skluwd/ v. [~ + obj], **-clud•ed, -clud•ing. 1.** to shut up or keep out; prevent the entrance of: *That club excludes women.* **2.** to shut out from consideration: *The doctor excluded food poisoning as the cause of illness.* **—ex'clu•sion,** n. [noncount]

ex•clu•sive /ɪk'skluwsɪv, -zɪv/ adj. **1.** not fitting with another; unable to be used or held at the same time as: *mutually exclusive plans of action.*

2. omitting from consideration or account; excluding: *It was a profit of ten percent, exclusive of taxes.* **3.** expensive or fashionable. **4.** not allowing outsiders to be admitted: *an exclusive circle of friends.* —n. [count] **5.** a news story obtained by a newspaper along with the right to use it first. **—ex'clu•sive•ly,** adv.

ex•com•mu•ni•cate /ˌɛkskə'myuwnɪˌkeyt/ v. [~ + obj], **-cat•ed, -cat•ing.** to cut off from the rites of a church. **—ex•com•mu•ni•ca•tion** /ˌɛkskə,myuwnɪ'keyʃən/, n. [count] [noncount]

ex•cre•ment /'ɛkskrəmənt/ n. [noncount] waste matter discharged from the body, esp. solid waste.

ex•crete /ɪk'skriyt/ v. [~ + obj], **-cret•ed, -cret•ing.** to eliminate from the body: *excreting urine.* **—ex•cre•tion** /ɪk'skriyʃən/, n. [noncount]

ex•cru•ci•at•ing /ɪk'skruwʃiy,eytɪŋ/ adj. causing intense suffering: *excruciating pain.*

ex•cur•sion /ɪk'skɜrʒən/ n. [count] a short trip or outing.

ex•cus•a•ble /ɪk'skyuwzəbəl/ adj. that may be forgiven or excused.

ex•cuse /ɪk'skyuwz; n. -'skyuws/ v., **-cused, -cus•ing,** n. —v. [~ + obj] **1.** to pardon or forgive; overlook: *Please excuse my child's rude behavior.* **2.** to offer an apology for: *She excused her son's absence by saying that he was ill.* **3.** to free from an obligation or duty: *to be excused from a class.* —n. [count] **4.** an act or instance of excusing. **5.** a reason for excusing or being excused: *Ignorance of the law is no excuse.* **—Idiom. 6. excuse me,** (used as a polite way to interrupt or disturb someone): *Excuse me, but may I talk to you for a moment?*

ex•e•cute /'ɛksɪ,kyuwt/ v. [~ + obj], **-cut•ed, -cut•ing. 1.** to carry out; accomplish: *to execute a plan.* **2.** to put to death. **—ex•e•cu•tion** /ˌɛksɪ'kyuwʃən/, n. [count] [noncount] **—,ex•e'cu•tion•er,** n. [count]

ex•ec•u•tive /ɪg'zɛkyətɪv/ n. [count] **1.** a person or group having administrative or supervisory authority in an organization or government. —adj. [before a noun] **2.** of or related to an executive.

ex•em•pli•fy /ɪg'zɛmplə,fay/ v. [~ + obj], **-fied, -fy•ing. 1.** to show or illustrate by example. **2.** to serve as an example of.

ex•empt /ɪg'zɛmpt/ v. [~ + obj] **1.** to free from an obligation, rule, or duty. —adj. **2.** released from, or not subject to, an obligation, rule, or duty: *Charitable organizations are usually exempt from taxes.* **—ex•emp•tion** /ɪg'zɛmpʃən/, n. [count] [noncount]

ex•er•cise /'ɛksər,sayz/ n., v., **-cised, -cis•ing.** —n. **1.** activity or exertion, esp. for the sake of practice, training, or improvement: [noncount]: *Walking is good exercise.* [count]: *leg exercises.* **2.** [count] something done as practice or training: *arithmetic exercises; naval exercises.* **3.** [noncount] a putting into action, use, or effect: *the exercise of caution when driving.* —v. **4.** [~ + obj] [no obj] to (cause to) go through exercises. **5.** [~ + obj] to put into action, practice, or use: *They exercised their right to vote.*

ex•ert /ɪg'zɜrt/ v. [~ + obj] **1.** to put into use; exercise: *a president exerting his authority.* **2.** to put (oneself) into vigorous action or effort: *If you exert yourself, you can finish the task on time.* **—ex•er•tion** /ɪg'zɜrʃən/, n. [noncount] [count]

ex•hale /ɛks'heyl, ɛk'seyl/ v., **-haled, -hal•ing.** to breathe out; send out (air, vapor, sound, etc.): [no obj]: *He exhaled through his mouth.* [~ +

E

obj]: *She exhaled smoke in his face.* —**ex•ha•la•tion** /ˌɛkshəˈleɪʃən/, *n.* [*noncount*] [*count*]

ex•haust /ɪgˈzɔst/ *v.* [~ + *obj*] **1.** to drain of strength or energy: *The children exhausted their babysitter.* **2.** to use up completely: *The soldiers exhausted their supply of ammunition.* —*n.* [*noncount*] **3.** the steam or gases that escape or are sent out of an engine. **4.** the parts of an engine through which the exhaust is sent out. —**ex•haus•tion** /ɪgˈzɔstʃən/, *n.* [*noncount*]

ex•hib•it /ɪgˈzɪbɪt/ *v.* [~ + *obj*] **1.** to offer or expose to public view: *to exhibit Van Gogh's paintings; to exhibit ignorance.* —*n.* [*count*] **2.** something exhibited.

ex•hi•bi•tion /ˌɛksəˈbɪʃən/ *n.* [*count*] **1.** an act of exhibiting: *an exhibition of ignorance; an exhibition of temper.* **2.** a public display, as of artistic works: *a Picasso exhibition.*

ex•hil•a•rate /ɪgˈzɪləˌreɪt/ *v.* [~ + *obj*], -rat•ed, -rat•ing. to make cheerful or merry.

ex•ile /ˈɛgzayl, ˈɛksayl/ *n., v.,* -iled, -il•ing. —*n.* **1.** [*noncount*] being forced out of one's native land; banishment. **2.** [*count*] a person who is forced out of his or her country. —*v.* [~ + *obj*] **3.** to force out (a person) from his or her country.

ex•ist /ɪgˈzɪst/ *v.* [*no obj*] **1.** to have actual being; be: *The world has existed for a very long time.* **2.** to have life; live: *Human beings could not exist without water.* **3.** to continue to be or live: *Belief in magic still exists.* **4.** be found; occur: *A life that is free from all worry doesn't exist.*

ex•ist•ence /ɪgˈzɪstəns/ *n.* **1.** [*noncount*] [*count*] the state or fact of existing; being. **2.** [*noncount*] continuing in being or life; life: *It was a constant struggle for existence.*

ex•ist•ing /ɛgˈzɪstɪŋ/ *adj.* [*before a noun*] being in use or in operation at the time of writing or speaking: *under the existing economic conditions.*

ex•it /ˈɛgzɪt, ˈɛksɪt/ *n.* [*count*] **1.** a way or passage out, as a door or stairs. **2.** a going out or away; departure: *He made a polite exit.* —*v.* **3.** to go out (of); leave (from): [*no obj*]: *They exited from the room.* [~ + *obj*]: *To exit the building, follow these directions.*

ex•o•dus /ˈɛksədəs/ *n.* [*count; usually singular*] a mass departure or emigration: *the Israelite exodus from Egypt; the summer exodus to the shore.*

ex•ot•ic /ɪgˈzɒtɪk/ *adj.* **1.** coming from outside a country; foreign: *The city has many restaurants with exotic foods.* **2.** very unusual or strange in appearance or nature.

ex•pand /ɪkˈspænd/ *v.* to increase in extent, size, scope, or volume: [*no obj*]: *The balloon expanded until it burst.* [~ + *obj*]: *The heat expanded the metal.* —**ex•pan•sion,** *n.* [*noncount*]: *The house is designed to allow for future expansion.*

ex•panse /ɪkˈspæns/ *n.* [*count*] an uninterrupted space or area: *an expanse of water.*

ex•pect /ɪkˈspɛkt/ *v.* [~ + *obj*] **1.** to look forward to; regard as likely to happen: *We are expecting fifty guests.* —**Idiom. 2. be expecting,** to be pregnant. —**ex'pect•ed,** *adj.*: *He is the expected winner in the election.*

ex•pect•an•cy /ɪkˈspɛktənsiy/ *n.* [*noncount*] the quality or state of expecting.

ex•pect•ant /ɪkˈspɛktənt/ *adj.* **1.** looking forward to something; expecting: *an expectant audience.* **2.** [*before a noun*] pregnant: *an expectant mother.* —**ex'pect•ant•ly,** *adv.*

ex•pec•ta•tion /ˌɛkspɛkˈteɪʃən/ *n.* **1.** [*noncount*] the act or state of expecting; anticipation.

2. [*count*] something expected. **3.** Often, **expectations.** [*plural*] good reasons to expect future benefit or fortune: *to have great expectations.*

ex•pe•di•tion /ˌɛkspɪˈdɪʃən/ *n.* [*count*] a journey made for a specific purpose, as to explore.

ex•pel /ɪkˈspɛl/ *v.* [~ + *obj*], -pelled, -pel•ling. to drive or force out or away: *The army expelled the rebels from the region.*

ex•pend /ɪkˈspɛnd/ *v.* [~ + *obj*] to use up or spend: *to expend money; expended much time and energy.*

ex•pend•a•ble /ɪkˈspɛndəbəl/ *adj.* not worth keeping or maintaining: *Lives must be saved, but the equipment is expendable.*

ex•pend•i•ture /ɪkˈspɛndɪtʃər/ *n.* [*count*] something expended: *Government expenditures are expected to rise next year.*

ex•pense /ɪkˈspɛns/ *n.* **1.** [*noncount*] cost; charge: *the expense of a good meal.* **2.** [*count*] a cause or occasion of spending: *A home is a necessary expense.* **3. expenses,** [*plural*] charges and costs related to a particular purpose: *business expenses.* —**Idiom. 4. at the expense of,** at the sacrifice of; to the harm of: *The restaurant served large portions at the expense of quality.*

ex•pen•sive /ɪkˈspɛnsɪv/ *adj.* requiring great expense; costing a lot of money. —**ex'pen•sive•ly,** *adv.*

ex•pe•ri•ence /ɪkˈspɪəriyəns/ *n., v.,* -enced, -enc•ing. —*n.* **1.** [*count*] something observed, lived through, or undergone: *That car crash was a frightening experience.* **2.** [*noncount*] the observing, living through, or undergoing of things in the course of time: *to learn from experience.* —*v.* [~ + *obj*] **3.** to have experience of; live through; undergo: *to experience pleasure.*

ex•pe•ri•enced /ɪkˈspɪəriyənst/ *adj.* wise or skillful in a particular field through experience: *an experienced teacher.*

ex•per•i•ment /*n.* ɪkˈspɛrəmənt; *v.* -ˌmɛnt/ *n.* [*count*] [*noncount*] **1.** a test for the purpose of discovering something unknown, or of testing a principle, law, or theory: *a laboratory experiment.* —*v.* [*no obj*] **2.** to do an experiment: *The scientists experimented on two groups of subjects.* —**ex,per•i'men•tal,** *adj.* —**ex,per•i'men•tal•ly,** *adv.* —**ex•per•i•men•ta•tion** /ɪkˌspɛrə-mɛnˈteɪʃən/, *n.* [*noncount*]

ex•pert /ˈɛkspɜrt; *adj. also* ɪkˈspɜrt/ *n.* [*count*] **1.** a person who has special skill or knowledge in a particular field. —*adj.* **2.** having special skill or knowledge; trained by practice: *She is an expert horseback rider.* —**'expert•ly,** *adv.*

ex•per•tise /ˌɛkspərˈtiyz/ *n.* [*noncount*] expert skill or knowledge.

ex•pire /ɪkˈspayᵊr/ *v.,* -pired, -pir•ing. **1.** [*no obj*] to come to an end: *The contract expired at the end of the month.* **2.** [*no obj*] to give out the last breath; die: *In the novel the hero expired after an illness.* **3.** [*no obj*] [~ + *obj*] to breathe out (air) from the lungs. —**ex•pi•ra•tion** /ˌɛkspəˈreɪʃən/ *n.* [*noncount*]

ex•plain /ɪkˈspleyn/ *v.* [~ + *obj*] **1.** to make clear or understandable: *Please explain your plan.* **2.** to give or be the reason for: *He explained why he was late.* —**explanation,** *n.* [*noncount*] [*count*]

ex•pla•na•tion /ˌɛkspləˈneyʃən/ *n.* **1.** [*noncount*] the act or process of explaining. **2.** [*count*] something that explains: *one of many explanations.*

ex•plan•a•to•ry /ɪkˈsplænəˌtɔriy/ *adj.* serving to explain.

ex•plic•it /ɪkˈsplɪsɪt/ *adj.* fully and clearly expressed or shown: *explicit instructions.* —**ex'plic•it•ly,** *adv.*

ex•plode /ɪkˈsplowd/ *v.,* **-plod•ed, -plod•ing.** to (cause to) burst or blow up forcefully: [~ + *obj]* The terrorists exploded the bomb. [no *obj]: to explode in laughter.

ex•ploit¹ /ˈɛksplɔyt/ *n.* [*count*] a brave deed; feat.

ex•ploit² /ɪkˈsplɔyt/ *v.* [~ + *obj*] **1.** to use for profit or advantage: *to exploit a business opportunity.* **2.** to use selfishly or unfairly: *The owner exploited her workers by paying very low wages.* —**ex•ploi•ta•tion** /ˌɛksplɔyˈteyʃən/, *n.* [*noncount*]

ex•plore /ɪkˈsplɔr/ *v.,* **-plored, -plor•ing. 1.** [~ + *obj*] [no *obj*] to travel over (a region, area, etc.) for the purpose of discovery. **2.** [~ + *obj*] to look into closely; investigate: *We have to explore that idea.* —**ex•plor•a•tion** /ˌɛksplɔˈreyʃən/, *n.* [*noncount*] [*count*] —**ex'plor•er,** *n.* [*count*]

ex•plo•sion /ɪkˈsplowʒən/ *n.* [*count*] **1.** an act or instance of exploding. **2.** the noise of an explosion.

ex•plo•sive /ɪkˈsplowsɪv/ *adj.* **1.** tending or serving to explode: *an explosive gas; an explosive temper.* **2.** likely to lead to violence, anger, or hostility: *That is an explosive issue for many people.* —*n.* [*count*] [*noncount*] **3.** an explosive agent or substance.

ex•po•nent /ɪkˈspownənt/ *n.* [*count*] a person or thing that supports or explains a cause: *The congressman is a leading exponent of free trade.*

ex•port /v. ɪkˈspɔrt, ˈɛkspɔrt, *n.,* adj. ˈɛkspɔrt/ *v.* [~ + *obj*] **1.** to ship (goods) to other countries. —*n.* **2.** [*noncount*] the act or business of exporting. **3.** [*count*] something exported. —**ex•por•ta•tion** /ˌɛkspɔrˈteyʃən/, *n.* [*noncount*] —**ex'port•er,** *n.* [*count*]

ex•pose /ɪkˈspowz/ *v.* [~ + *obj*], **-posed, -pos•ing. 1.** to lay open to danger, attack, or harm: *to expose people to disease.* **2.** to uncover; bare: *to expose one's head to the rain.* **3.** to make known; reveal (the truth of): *He exposed his true feelings.*

ex•po•si•tion /ˌɛkspəˈzɪʃən/ *n.* [*count*] **1.** a large public exhibition. **2.** a detailed explanation.

ex•po•sure /ɪkˈspowʒər/ *n.* **1.** [*noncount*] the act of exposing or state of being exposed: *exposure to the effects of radiation.* **2. a.** [*noncount*] the act of subjecting a film to light. **b.** [*count*] a photographic image that is produced: *A few of the exposures were blurred.*

ex•press /ɪkˈsprɛs/ *v.* [~ + *obj*] **1.** to put into words: *to express an idea.* **2.** to show; reveal: *She expressed her anger.* —*adj.* [before a noun] **3.** clearly indicated; explicit: *an express command.* **4.** direct or fast, esp. making few or no stops: *an express train.* —*n.* [*count*] **5.** an express vehicle. —*adv.* **6.** by express: *to travel express.*

ex•pres•sion /ɪkˈsprɛʃən/ *n.* **1.** [*noncount*] the act of expressing: *the free expression of opinions.* **2.** [*count*] a particular word or phrase. **3.** [*noncount*] the manner or form in which a thing is expressed: *clarity of expression.* **4.** [*count*] a look on a person's face: *a joyful expression.*

ex•pres•sive /ɪkˈsprɛsɪv/ *adj.* showing one's thoughts or feelings: *an expressive shrug.* —**ex'pres•sive•ly,** *adv.*

ex•press•ly /ɪkˈsprɛsliy/ *adv.* for the specific purpose; specially: *I came expressly to see you.*

ex•press•way /ɪkˈsprɛsˌwey/ *n.* [*count*] a highway for high-speed traffic.

ex•pul•sion /ɪkˈspʌlʃən/ *n.* [*noncount*] [*count*] the act of expelling; the state of being expelled.

ex•quis•ite /ɪkˈskwɪzɪt, ˈɛkskwɪzɪt/ *adj.* of special beauty and appealing excellence. —**ex'quis•ite•ly,** *adv.*

ex•tend /ɪkˈstɛnd/ *v.* **1.** [~ + *obj*] to stretch or draw out: *I extended my leg.* **2.** [~ + *obj*] to make longer; lengthen: *to extend a highway.* **3.** [no *obj*] to reach or stretch: *Their visit extended another hour.* **4.** [~ + *obj*] to give (help, etc.) to someone: *They extended a warm welcome to him.*

ex•ten•sion /ɪkˈstɛnʃən/ *n.* [*count*] **1.** an addition: *built an extension to the house.* **2.** an increase in length of time, area, or scope: *an extension for filing our taxes.* **3.** an additional telephone that operates on a principal line.

ex•ten•sive /ɪkˈstɛnsɪv/ *adj.* of great extent; wide; broad. —**ex'ten•sive•ly,** *adv.*

ex•tent /ɪkˈstɛnt/ *n.* [*noncount*] the space or degree to which a thing extends: *the extent of their property; I agree with you to some extent.*

ex•te•ri•or /ɪkˈstɪriyər/ *adj.* **1.** being on the outer side or the outside: *exterior surfaces.* —*n.* [*count*] **2.** the outer surface or part; outside: *the exterior of the house.*

ex•ter•mi•nate /ɪkˈstɜrməˌneyt/ *v.* [~ + *obj*], **-nat•ed, -nat•ing.** to kill large numbers of (insects, animals, or people). —**ex•ter•mi•na•tion** /ɪkˌstɜrməˈneyʃən/, *n.* [*noncount*]

ex•ter•nal /ɪkˈstɜrnl/ *adj.* **1.** of or relating to the outside or outer part; outer. **2.** to be applied to the outside of the body: *The medicine is for external use only.* —**ex'ter•nal•ly,** *adv.*

ex•tinct /ɪkˈstɪŋkt/ *adj.* **1.** no longer in existence: *an extinct species.* **2.** no longer in use; obsolete: *an extinct custom.* **3.** no longer active: *an extinct volcano.* —**ex•tinc•tion** /ɪkˈstɪŋkʃən/, *n.* [*noncount*]

ex•tin•guish /ɪkˈstɪŋgwɪʃ/ *v.* [~ + *obj*] **1.** to cause to stop burning; put out: *They extinguished the fire.* **2.** to put an end to or bring to an end: *His business failures extinguished his hopes.* —**ex•tin•guish•er,** *n.* [*count*]

ex•tol /ɪkˈstowl, -ˈstɒl/ *v.* [~ + *obj*], **-tolled, -tol•ling.** to praise highly.

ex•tort /ɪkˈstɔrt/ *v.* [~ + *obj*] to get (money) from a person by force, threats, violence, etc. —**ex•tor•tion** /ɪkˈstɔrʃən/, *n.* [*noncount*]

ex•tra /ˈɛkstrə/ *adj., n., pl.* **-tras,** *adv.* —*adj.* [before a noun] **1.** beyond, more, or better than what is usual: *Make an extra copy.* —*n.* [*count*] **2.** a special edition of a newspaper. **3.** an additional feature. —*adv.* **4.** beyond the usual amount, size, or degree: *extra large boots.*

extra-, a prefix meaning outside or beyond (*extrasensory*).

ex•tract /v. ɪkˈstrækt; *n.* ˈɛkstrækt/ *v.* [~ + *obj*] **1.** to pull or draw out, esp. with effort: *The dentist extracted my tooth.* **2.** to take out (a substance) from another substance: *to extract oil from olives.* —*n.* **3.** [*count*] something extracted. **4.** [*count*] a passage taken from a written work; excerpt. **5.** [*noncount*] a substance in concentrated form: *vanilla extract.* —**ex•trac•tion** /ɪkˈstrækʃən/ *n.* [*noncount*] [*count*]

ex•tra•cur•ric•u•lar /ˌɛkstrəkəˈrɪkyələr/ *adj.* outside the regular program of courses at a school: *extracurricular activities.*

ex•tra•mar•i•tal /ˌɛkstrəˈmærɪtl/ *adj.* relating to sexual relations with someone other than one's spouse: *an extramarital affair.*

E

ex•traor•di•nar•y /ɪk'strɔrdn̩ˌɛriy, ˌɛkstrə'ɔr-/ *adj.* being beyond what is usual; exceptional; remarkable: *extraordinary speed; an extraordinary idea.* —**ex,traor•di'nar•i•ly,** *adv.*

ex•tra•sen•so•ry /ˌɛkstrə'sɛnsəriy/ *adj.* beyond one's normal sense perception.

ex•tra•ter•res•tri•al /ˌɛkstrətə'rɛstriyəl/ *adj.* **1.** existing, involving, or coming from outside the limits of the earth: *extraterrestrial biology.* —*n.* [*count*] **2.** an imagined extraterrestrial creature.

ex•trav•a•gant /ɪk'strævəgənt/ *adj.* **1.** spending much more than is necessary or wise. **2.** beyond what is reasonable; excessive: *extravagant demands.* —**ex'trav•a•gance,** *n.* [*noncount*] [*count*] —**ex'trav•a•gant•ly,** *adv.*

ex•trav•a•gan•za /ɪkˌstrævə'gænzə/ *n.* [*count*], *pl.* **-zas.** a fancy or elaborate show or entertainment.

ex•treme /ɪk'striym/ *adj.,* **-trem•er, -trem•est,** *n.* —*adj.* **1.** going beyond the ordinary or average: *extreme cold.* **2.** [*before a noun*] very great in degree: *extreme joy.* **3.** [*before a noun*] farthest from the center or middle: *the extreme limit of the city.* —*n.* [*count*] **4.** one of two things that are as different from each other as possible: *She experienced the extremes of joy and grief.* —**ex'treme•ly,** *adv.*: *The music of Mozart is extremely beautiful.*

ex•trem•ism /ɪk'striymɪzəm/ *n.* [*noncount*] a tendency to go to extremes, esp. in politics. —**ex'trem•ist,** *n.* [*count*]

ex•trem•i•ty /ɪk'strɛmɪtiy/ *n.,* *pl.* **-ties. 1.** [*count*] the end or furthest point, limit, or part of something. **2.** Usually, **extremities.** [*plural*] the hands or feet.

ex•tro•vert /'ɛkstrəˌvɜrt/ *n.* [*count*] an outgoing, talkative, cheerful person. —**'ex•tro,vert•ed,** *adj.*

ex•u•ber•ant /ɪg'zuwbərənt/ *adj.* overflowing with enthusiasm, excitement, or cheerfulness: *an exuberant welcome.* —**ex'u•ber•ance,** *n.* [*noncount*] —**ex'u•ber•ant•ly,** *adv.*

ex•ult /ɪg'zʌlt/ *v.* [*no obj*] to show or feel a lively or triumphant joy: *The players exulted over their victory.* —**ex'ult•ant,** *adj.* —**ex•ul•ta•tion** /ˌɛgzəl'teyʃən, ˌɛksəl-/, *n.* [*noncount*]

eye /ay/ *n., v.,* **eyed, ey•ing** *or* **ey•ing.** —*n.* **1.** [*count*] the organ of sight. **2.** [*count; usually singular*] sight; vision: *The hunter had a sharp eye.* **3.** [*count; usually singular*] the power of seeing and appreciating something through vision: *an artistic eye.* **4.** [*count; usually singular*] an attentive look; observation: *under the watchful eye of the guard.* **5.** [*count*] point of view; intention:

through the eyes of a ten-year-old. **6.** [*count*] something suggesting the eye in appearance, such as the hole in a needle. —*v.* [~ + *obj*] **7.** to look at; view; watch: *He eyed the strangers with suspicion.* —*Idiom.* **8. catch someone's eye,** to attract someone's attention: *She caught my eye as I moved toward the door.* **9. have an eye for,** have good judgment about or appreciation for: *He has an eye for bargains.* **10. have eyes for,** to be attracted to: *She only has eyes for you.* **11. keep one's eyes open,** to be especially alert or observant: *The guards were told to keep their eyes open for a possible escape.* **12. see eye to eye,** to agree: *We finally see eye to eye after our misunderstanding.*

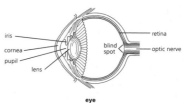

eye

eye•ball /'ay,bɔl/ *n.* [*count*] the rounded part of the eye.

eye•brow, *n.* [*count*] the fringe of hair growing above the eye.

eye•glass•es /'ay,glæsɪz/, *n.* [*plural*] GLASS (def. 3).

eye•lash /'ay,læʃ/ *n.* [*count*] any of the short hairs growing in a fringe on the edge of an eyelid.

eye•let /'aylɪt/ *n.* [*count*] a small hole for a cord or lace to pass through.

eye•lid /'ay,lɪd/ *n.* [*count*] the movable lid of skin that covers and uncovers the eyeball.

eye•lin•er /'ay,laynər/ *n.* [*count*] a cosmetic applied in a line along the edge of the eyelids.

'eye ,shadow, *n.* [*noncount*] a cosmetic coloring material applied to the eyelids.

eye•sight /'ay,sayt/ *n.* SIGHT (def. 1).

eye•sore /'ay,sɔr/ *n.* [*count*] something unpleasant to look at.

eye•strain /'ay,streyn/ *n.* [*noncount*] discomfort in the eyes produced by excessive or improper use.

eye•wit•ness /'ay'wɪtnɪs/ *n.* [*count*] a person who sees some act or event and can give a description of it.

F

F, f /ɛf/ *n.* [*count*], *pl.* **F's** or **Fs, f's** or **fs.** the sixth letter of the English alphabet, a consonant.

F, an abbreviation of: **1.** female. **2.** franc.

F, *Symbol.* **1.** a grade indicating academic work of the lowest quality. **2.** Fahrenheit: *Water turns to ice at 32°F (said as "32 degrees Fahrenheit").*

F., an abbreviation of: **1.** Fahrenheit. **2.** Friday.

fa•ble /ˈfeybəl/ *n.* [*count*] **1.** a short tale used to teach a moral lesson, often with animals as characters. **2.** a story not based on fact, such as a myth. —**fabled,** *adj.*

fab•ric /ˈfæbrɪk/ *n.* **1.** [*count*] a cloth made by weaving or knitting threads or fibers: *clothes made with modern fabrics.* **2.** [*noncount*] framework; structure: *the fabric of family life.*

fab•ri•cate /ˈfæbrɪˌkeyt/ *v.* [~ + *obj*], **-cat•ed, -cat•ing.** **1.** to build, esp. by putting together parts; make. **2.** to invent; make up. —**fab•ri•ca•tion** /ˌfæbrəˈkeyʃən/ *n.* [*noncount*] [*count*]

fab•u•lous /ˈfæbyələs/ *adj.* **1.** almost impossible to believe: *fabulous adventures.* **2.** excellent: *That was a fabulous concert.* —**'fab•u•lous•ly,** *adv.*

fa•cade or **fa•çade** /fəˈsɑd, fæ-/ *n.* [*count*] **1.** the front of a building. **2.** a false appearance: *a facade of self-confidence.*

face /feys/ *n., v.,* **faced, fac•ing.** —*n.* **1.** [*count*] the front part of the head: *He has a handsome face.* **2.** [*count*] an expression on the face: *a sad face.* **3.** [*count; usually singular*] the surface of something: *He seemed to disappear from the face of the earth.* —*v.* **4.** to have the front toward: [~ + *obj*]: *The barn faces the field.* [*no obj*]: *The building faced south.* **5.** [~ + *obj*] to meet boldly: *You have to face facts.* **6. face up to, a.** to admit: *You have to face up to your mistake.* **b.** to meet with courage: *He must face up to the possibility of losing his job.* —**Idiom. 7. face to face,** opposite or confronting one another; facing: *The dancers stood face to face with their partners. The candidates finally met face to face.* **8. in the face of,** in spite of: *He succeeded in the face of great difficulty.* **9. lose** (or **save**) **face,** to suffer (or escape from) embarrassment: *It was impos*

face•less /ˈfeyslɪs/ *adj.* lacking personality or identity: *a faceless mob.* —**'face•less•ness,** *n.* [*noncount*]

fac•et /ˈfæsɪt/ *n.* [*count*] **1.** one of the small polished flat surfaces of a gem. **2.** aspect; side; part: *all facets of the business.*

fa•ce•tious /fəˈsiyʃəs/ *adj.* not serious; joking in a silly way: *a facetious comment.* —**fa'ce•tious•ly,** *adv.* —**fa'ce•tious•ness,** *n.* [*noncount*]

fa•cial /ˈfeyʃəl/ *adj.* having to do with the face: *a facial expression.* —**'fa•cial•ly,** *adv.*

fac•ile /ˈfæsɪl/ *adj.* **1.** quick in understanding or action: *a facile mind in learning languages.* **2.** too easy; not deep: *facile answers to hard questions.* —**'fac•ile•ly,** *adv.*

fa•cil•i•tate /fəˈsɪlɪˌteyt/ *v.* [~ + *obj*], **-tat•ed, -tat•ing.** to make easier or less difficult. —**fa•cil•i•ta•tion** /fəsɪlɪˈteyʃən/ *n.* [*noncount*] —**fa'cil•i,ta•tor,** *n.* [*count*]

fa•cil•i•ty /fəˈsɪlɪtiy/ *n., pl.* **-ties. 1.** Often, **fa•cilities.** [*count*] something designed or built to provide a specific service: *a new research facility.* **2.** [*noncount*] the ability to do something with ease: *Mozart composed music with great facility.*

3. Usually, **facilities.** [*plural*] a public bathroom; rest room: *There are no facilities on this highway.*

fac•sim•i•le /fækˈsɪməliy/ *n.* [*count*] **1.** an exact copy: *a facsimile of the Declaration of Independence.* **2.** FAX.

fact /fækt/ *n.* **1.** [*noncount*] reality; truth: *no basis in fact.* **2.** [*count*] something known to exist or to have happened: *It is a fact that an eclipse took place.* —**Idiom. 3. in fact,** in truth; in reality: *They are, in fact, great patriots.* Also, **as a matter of fact.**

fac•tion /ˈfækʃən/ *n.* [*count*] a group within a larger group: *several factions of the Liberal Party.* —**'fac•tion•al,** *adj.* —**'fac•tion•al•ism,** *n.* [*noncount*]

'fact of 'life, *n.* [*count*] **1.** something that exists and must be accepted. —**Idiom. 2. facts of life, a.** information about sex and birth. **b.** the way things really are.

fac•toid /ˈfæktɔyd/ *n.* [*count*] **1.** something that is untrue or unproven but is presented as fact and believed to be true because of constant repetition. **2.** an insignificant or unimportant fact.

fac•tor /ˈfæktər/ *n.* [*count*] **1.** one of the elements contributing to a particular result: *Various factors could be the cause of the disease.* **2.** one of two or more numbers, that when multiplied together produce a given product: *6 and 3 are factors of 18.*

fac•to•ry /ˈfæktəriy/ *n.* [*count*], *pl.* **-ries.** a building where things are manufactured.

fac•tu•al /ˈfæktʃuwəl/ *adj.* of or relating to facts: *factual accuracy.* —**'fac•tu•al•ly,** *adv.*

fac•ul•ty /ˈfækəltiy/ *n.* [*count*], *pl.* **-ties. 1.** one of the powers of the mind, such as memory or speech: *He is 90 years old but still has most of his faculties.* **2.** the people who teach at a school or college: [*plural*]: *The faculty met as a group.* [*singular*]: *The faculty is paid well.*

fad /fæd/ *n.* [*count*] a temporary fashion, interest, etc. —**'fad•dish,** *adj.* —**'fad•dist,** *n.* [*count*]

fade /feyd/ *v.,* **fad•ed, fad•ing. 1.** to (cause to) lose brightness of color: [*no obj*]: *The green dress faded in the sun.* [~ + *obj*]: *The sun faded her green dress.* **2.** [*no obj*] to disappear slowly: *The sunlight gradually faded. Her memory faded with age. Hopes of peace are fading away.*

fae•ces /ˈfiysiyz/ *n.* [*plural*] *Chiefly Brit.* FECES.

Fahr•en•heit /ˈfærənˌhayt/ *adj.* relating to a temperature scale (**'Fahrenheit ,scale**) in which water freezes at 32° and boils at 212°. *Symbol:* F Compare CELSIUS.

fail /feyl/ *v.* **1.** [*no obj*] to be unsuccessful: *The experiment failed.* **2.** [~ + *obj*] to be of no help to; to disappoint: *His friends failed him.* **3.** [~ + *obj*] to receive less than the passing grade or mark in (an examination, class, or course of study): *You are failing the course.* **4.** [*no obj*] to become weak: *The runner's strength failed.* —**'fail•ing,** *n.* [*count*]

fail•ure /ˈfeylyər/ *n.* **1.** [*noncount*] lack of success: *a life of failure.* **2.** [*count*] a person or thing that is unsuccessful: *The meeting was a failure.* **3.** an instance of not doing something required or expected: [*count*]: *a failure to appear.* [*noncount*]: *failure to pay.*

faint /feynt/ *adj.,* **-er, -est,** *v., n.* —*adj.* **1.** lacking brightness, clearness, loudness, strength, etc.:

a faint voice. —*v. [no obj]* **2.** to lose consciousness temporarily. —*n. [count]* **3.** a temporary loss of consciousness. —'**faint•ly,** *adv.* —'**faint•ness,** *n. [noncount]*

fair¹ /fɛər/ *adj. and adv.,* **-er, -est.** —*adj.* **1.** honest; just: *a fair trial; a fair wage.* **2.** neither excellent nor poor: *fair health.* **3.** (of the sky or the weather) bright; sunny: *fair skies.* **4.** of a light color; not dark: *fair skin.* **5.** attractive: *a fair young face.* **6.** likely; promising: *a fair chance of success.* —*adv.* **7.** in a fair manner: *He doesn't play fair.* —'**fair•ness,** *n. [noncount]*

fair² /fɛər/ *n. [count]* **1.** a show of farm products and animals, etc., held annually by a county or state. **2.** a gathering of buyers and sellers: *a book fair.*

fair•ground /'fɛər,grawnd/ *n. [count]* Often, **fairgrounds.** *[plural]* an area set aside by a county, city, or state for an annual fair.

fair•ly /'fɛərliy/ *adv.* **1.** in a fair manner; justly: *We want you to judge fairly.* **2.** moderately; to a large extent: *a fairly heavy rain.*

fair•y /'fɛəriy/ *n. [count],* pl. **-ies.** a tiny imaginary being that possesses magical powers.

'**fairy ,tale,** *n. [count]* **1.** a story, usually for children, about magical beings and creatures. **2.** an untrue story; lie.

faith /feyθ/ *n.* **1.** *[noncount]* trust in a person or thing: *I have faith that she'll do the right thing.* **2.** *[noncount]* belief in God or in the teachings of religion: *It was a question of faith.* **3.** *[count]* a system of religious belief; religion: *the Jewish faith.*

faith•ful /'feyθfəl/ *adj.* **1.** loyal; constant: *faithful friends.* **2.** trusted or believed: *faithful assurances of help.* —'**faith•ful•ly,** *adv.* —'**faith•ful•ness,** *n. [noncount]* —'**faith•less,** *adj.*

fa•ji•tas /fɑ'hiytəz, fə-/ *n. [count; used with a singular or plural verb]* a Mexican dish consisting of thin strips of grilled beef or chicken with sliced peppers and onions, usually wrapped in tortillas.

fake /feyk/ *v.,* **faked, fak•ing,** *n., adj.* —*v. [~ + obj]* **1.** to make or prepare (something) so as to deceive or cheat: *The employee faked the report.* **2.** to pretend: *to fake illness.* —*n. [count]* **3.** anything that deceives, cheats, or fools by seeming to be what it is not: *The diamond was a fake.* —*adj.* **4.** designed to deceive or cheat; counterfeit: *a fake signature.* —'**fak•er,** *n. [count]*

fal•con /'fɔlkən, 'fæl-/ *n. [count]* a bird of prey having long pointed wings.

fall /fɔl/ *v.,* **fell** /fɛl/ **fall•en, fall•ing,** *n.* —*v. [no obj]* **1.** to come down under the force of gravity: *The apple fell from the tree.* **2.** to come down from a standing position, esp. suddenly: *I fell to my knees.* **3.** to become less or lower: *The temperature fell rapidly.* **4.** to grow less powerful: *The wind fell.* **5.** to hang down: *Her hair fell to her waist.* **6.** to lose to an attack: *The city fell to the enemy.* **7.** *[no obj]* to be killed: *to fall in battle.* **8.** to pass into some physical or mental state: *to fall into a coma.* **9. fall back,** to retreat: *The troops fell back to their fortified positions.* **10. fall back on** or **upon,** to use when other things have failed: *We had no savings to fall back on.* **11. fall behind, a.** to fail to keep level with: *to fall behind in their studies.* **b.** to fail to pay one's debts on time. **12. fall for,** *Slang.* **a.** to be deceived by: *Don't fall for an old trick like that.* **b.** to fall in love with: *He had fallen for her pretty badly.* **13. fall through,** to fail to succeed: *My plans kept falling through.* —*n.* **14.** *[count]* an act or instance of dropping from a higher to a lower

place or position: *a rapid fall in prices.* **15.** *[noncount]* the season of the year that comes after summer and before winter; autumn. **16.** *[count]* the distance through which anything falls: *a long fall to the ground.* **17.** Usually, **falls.** *[plural]* a waterfall.

fal•la•cy /'fæləsiy/ *n.,* pl. **-cies.** **1.** *[count]* a false idea: *It's a fallacy to think that government will solve all our problems.* **2.** *[noncount]* faulty reasoning: *The statement was based on fallacy.*

'**falling 'star,** *n. [count]* a meteor; shooting star.

fall•out or **fall-out** /'fɔl,awt/ *n. [noncount]* **1.** the settling to the ground of dust thrown into the atmosphere by a nuclear explosion. **2.** the results or outcome of some occurrence, esp. when unexpected or unwanted: *The fallout of the scandal embarrassed his family.*

false /fɔls/ *adj.,* **fals•er, fals•est.** **1.** not true or correct; wrong: *a false statement.* **2.** not faithful or loyal: *a false friend.* **3.** *[before a noun]* not real: *false teeth.* —'**false•ly,** *adv.* —'**false•ness,** *n. [noncount]*

false•hood /'fɔlshʊd/ *n. [count]* an untrue statement or lie.

fal•si•fy /'fɔlsəfay/ *v. [~ + obj],* **-fied, -fy•ing.** to make false or incorrect, esp. so as to deceive: *to falsify income-tax reports.* —**fal•si•fi•ca•tion** /'fɔlsəfɪ'keyʃən/, *n. [count] [noncount]*

fame /feym/ *n. [noncount]* the state or condition of being well or widely known. —'**fa•mous,** *adj.*: *a famous writer.*

fa•mil•iar /fə'mɪlyər/ *adj.* **1.** commonly known or seen: *a familiar landmark.* **2.** having a thorough knowledge of something: *She is familiar with mathematical symbols.* —**fa•mil•i•ar•i•ty** /fə,mɪliy'ærɪtiy/, *n. [noncount]* —**fa'mil•iar,ize** *v.,* **-ized, -iz•ing.** —fa'mil•iar•ly, *adv.*

fam•i•ly /'fæməliy, 'fæmliy/ *n.,* pl. **-lies,** *adj.* —*n. [count]* **1.** parents and their children made up of as a group: *How many people are in your family?* **2.** a group of persons sharing the same ancestors, as parents, children, uncles, aunts, and cousins. **3.** a group of related things or animals: *the mint family; the cat family.* —*adj. [before a noun]* **4.** of, relating to, or characteristic of a family: *a family trait.*

'**family 'planning,** *n. [noncount]* planning the size of families through contraception.

'**family 'tree,** *n. [count]* a chart showing the relationships within a family.

fam•ine /'fæmɪn/ *n.* great and widespread shortage of food, esp. within a large geographical area: *[noncount]: widespread famine. [count]: a famine that killed thousands of people.*

fam•ished /'fæmɪʃt/ *adj.* very hungry.

fan¹ /fæn/ *n., v.,* **fanned, fan•ning.** —*n. [count]* **1.** a device for producing a current of air: *an electric fan.* **2.** a flat object of plastic, paper, wood, etc., for waving lightly to create a cooling current of air: *a beautiful Chinese fan.* —*v.* **3.** *[~ + obj]* to move (the air) with a fan. **4.** to spread out like a fan: *[no obj]: The soldiers fanned out around the enemy. [~ + obj]: The magician fanned the cards expertly.*

fan² /fæn/ *n. [count]* an enthusiastic admirer of a team, sport, celebrity, etc.: *hockey fans; rock fans.*

fa•nat•ic /fə'nætɪk/ *n. [count]* **1.** a person with extreme enthusiasm, such as in religion or politics. —*adj.* Also, **fa'nat•i•cal. 2.** having extreme enthusiasm. —**fa'nat•i•cal•ly,** *adv.*

fan•ci•ful /'fænsɪfəl/ *adj.* **1.** showing imagination: *fanciful ideas.* **2.** imaginary; unreal: *the fan-*

ciful characters in his books for children. —**'fan•ci•ful•ly,** *adv.*

fan•cy /'fænsiy/ *n., pl.* **-cies,** *adj.,* **-ci•er, -ci•est,** *v.,* **-cied, -cy•ing.** —*n.* **1.** imagination or fantasy: [*noncount*]: *in a flight of fancy.* [*count*]: *happy fancies of being famous.* —*adj.* **2.** decorative; not plain: *a cake with a fancy icing.* —*v.* [~ + *obj*] **3.** to imagine: *Fancy her living with him.* **4.** to like: *She fancies chocolates.*

fan•fare /'fænfɛər/ *n.* [*count*] a short piece of music played on trumpets.

fang /fæŋ/ *n.* [*count*] a long sharp projecting tooth.

fan•ta•size /'fæntə,sayz/ *v.* [*no obj*], **-sized, -siz•ing.** to daydream; imagine.

fan•tas•tic /fæn'tæstɪk/ *adj.* **1.** very strange: *fantastic rock formations.* **2.** imaginary; fanciful: *fantastic fears.* **3.** wonderful: *a fantastic musical.* —**fan'tas•ti•cal•ly,** *adv.*

fan•ta•sy /'fæntəsiy, -ziy/ *n.* [*noncount*] [*count*], *pl.* **-sies.** a creation of the imagination; illusion.

far /fɑr/ *adv., adj.,* **far•ther** or **fur•ther, far•thest** or **fur•thest.** —*adv.* **1.** at or to a great distance; a long way off: *How far is it from here?* **2.** at or to a great extent or degree: *far behind.* **3.** much or many: *I need far more time.* —*adj.* **4.** being at a great distance; remote in time or place: *the far future.* —**Idiom. 5. by far,** by a great deal; very much: *too expensive by far.* **6. far and wide,** over great distances: *to search far and wide.* **7. go far,** to achieve a great deal: *I'm sure she'll go far.* **8. how far,** to what distance, extent, or degree: *How far can we go with this plan?* **9. so far,** until now: *So far the budget cuts haven't hit us too badly.* **10. the far side,** the farther or opposite side: *the far side of the moon.* **11. thus far,** so far: *Thus far we've been spared any crises.*

far•a•way /'fɑrə'wey/ *adj.* [*before a noun*] **1.** distant: *faraway lands.* **2.** dreamy: *a faraway look in his eyes.*

farce /fɑrs/ *n.* [*count*] **1.** a funny play based on unlikely situations: *the latest farce on Broadway.* **2.** a foolish, false, or meaningless show: *dishonest politicians who make a farce of good government.*

fare /fɛər/ *n., v.,* **fared, far•ing.** —*n.* **1.** [*count*] the price of traveling in a bus, airplane, taxi, etc.: *special fares for senior citizens.* **2.** [*noncount*] food: *The restaurant serves hearty fare.* —*v.* [*no obj*] **3.** to progress; get on: *He didn't fare too well on his own.*

fare•well /,fɛər'wɛl/ *interj.* **1.** good-bye. —*n.* [*count*] **2.** goodbye: *a friendly farewell.* —*adj.* [*before a noun*] **3.** final: *a farewell performance.*

farm /fɑrm/ *n.* [*count*] **1.** a piece of land on which crops and animals are raised. —*v.* **2.** to use land to grow things: [*no obj*]: *The peasants have been farming on this land for many generations.* [~ + *obj*]: *peasants farming the land.*

farmer *n.* [*count*] a person who owns or works on a farm.

farm•house /'fɑrm,haws/ *n.* [*count*] a house on a farm.

farm•land /'fɑrm,lænd/ *n.* [*noncount*] land used to grow crops.

'far-'off, *adj.* distant: *far-off lands.*

'far-'reaching, *adj.* having a wide influence, effect, etc.: *the far-reaching effect of the economic crisis.*

far•sight•ed /'fɑr'saytɪd, -,saytɪd/ *adj.* **1.** seeing objects at a distance more clearly than those nearby. **2.** wise, as in foreseeing the future and planning for it. —**'far'sight•ed•ness,** *n.* [*noncount*]

far•ther /'fɑrðər/ *adv., comparative of* **far** *with* **farthest** *as superlative.* **1.** at or to a greater distance: *farther down the road.* *adj., comparative of* **far** *with* **farthest** *as superlative.* **2.** more distant: *the farther side of the mountain.* —**Usage.** FARTHER is used to indicate physical distance: *Is it much farther to the hotel?* FURTHER is used to refer to additional time, amount, or abstract ideas: *I would rather not talk about this further.* But both FARTHER and FURTHER are often used for distance of any kind: *Look no farther* (or *further*); *here is the solution. His study of the novel reaches farther* (or *further*) *than any earlier one.*

far•thest /'fɑrðɪst/ *adj., superlative of* **far** *with* **farther** *as comparative.* **1.** most distant: *Who came the farthest?* —*adv., superlative. of* **far** *with* **farther** *as comparative.* **2.** at or to the greatest distance: *This is the farthest I've been from home.*

fas•ci•nate /'fæsə,neyt/ *v.* [~ + *obj*], **-nat•ed, -nat•ing.** to attract and hold the attention or interest of: *Ancient Egypt has always fascinated me.* —**'fas•ci•nated,** *adj.* —**'fas•ci•nat•ing,** *adj.* —**fas•ci•na•tion** /,fæsə'neyʃən/, *n.* [*noncount*]

fas•cism /'fæʃɪzəm/ *n.* [*noncount*; *sometimes:* *Fascism*] a political system that is led by a dictator and emphasizes nationalism, militarism, and often racism. —**'fas•cist,** *n.* [*count*], *adj.*

fash•ion /'fæʃən/ *n.* **1.** [*count*] [*noncount*] a popular style of dress, behavior, etc. **2.** [*count*] manner; way: *to behave in a warlike fashion.* —*v.* [~ + *obj*] **3.** to make or form: *fashioned a necklace from paper clips.*

fash•ion•a•ble /'fæʃənəbəl/ *adj.* conforming to the latest fashion: *fashionable clothes.* —**'fash•ion•a•bly,** *adv.*

fast¹ /fæst/ *adj.* and *adv.,* **-er, -est.** —*adj.* **1.** quick; swift; rapid: *a fast horse.* **2.** (of a clock or watch) showing a time later than the correct time: *My watch is fast.* **3.** permanent: *a fast color.* **4.** loyal; devoted: *fast friends.* —*adv.* **5.** quickly: *She drove very fast.* **6.** tightly; firmly: *She held on fast to my hand.* **7.** ahead of the correct time: *My alarm clock is running fast.*

fast² /fæst/ *v.* [*no obj*] **1.** to eat no food, esp. for religious reasons. —*n.* [*count*] **2.** a period of not eating.

fas•ten /'fæsən/ *v.* [~ + *obj*] to attach firmly in place or to something else: *She fastened a pin to her dress.* —**'fas•ten•er,** *n.* [*count*]

fas•ten•ing /'fæsənɪŋ/ *n.* [*count*] something that fastens, such as a lock or clasp.

'fast 'food, *n.* [*count*] [*noncount*] restaurant food that is prepared and served quickly. —**fast-food,** *adj:* *McDonald's and other fast-food restaurants.*

fas•tid•i•ous /fæ'stɪdiyəs/ *adj.* fussy; hard to please; a fastidious eater. —**fas'tid•i•ous•ly,** *adv.* —**fas'tid•i•ous•ness,** *n.* [*noncount*]

fat /fæt/ *n., adj.,* **fat•ter, fat•test.** —*n.* **1.** an oily substance found in certain animal tissue and plant seeds, and used in cooking and in making soaps and other products: [*noncount*]: *His diet was too rich in fat.* [*count*]: *Different fats are used in the preparation of this cooking oil.* —*adj.* **2.** plump; well-fed: *a fat chicken.* **3.** made up of or containing fat. **4.** providing a lot of money: *a fat job in government.*

fa•tal /'feytl/ *adj.* causing death: *a fatal accident.* —**'fa•tal•ly,** *adv.*

fa•tal•ism /'feytl,ɪzəm/ *n.* [*noncount*] a belief

F

that all events are determined by fate. —'fa•tal•ist, *n.* [*count*] —,fa•tal'is•tic, *adj.*

fa•tal•i•ty /fey'tælɪtiy/ *n.* [*count*], *pl.* -ties. a death caused by a disaster: *highway fatalities.*

fate /feyt/ *n.* 1. [*count; usually singular*] something that unavoidably happens to a person; one's fortune: *The judge decided her fate.* 2. [*noncount*] the power by which events are thought to be decided; destiny: *By a strange twist of fate, Thomas Jefferson and John Adams both died on July 4, 1826.* —'fat•ed, *adj.* —'fate•ful, *adj.*

fa•ther /'faðər/ *n.* 1. [*count*] a male parent. 2. [*count; sometimes: Father*] a priest or a title for a priest. 3. [*Father*] God. —*v.* [~ + *obj*] 4. to become the father of. —'fa•ther,hood, *n.* [*noncount*] —'fa•ther•less, *adj.* —'fa•ther•ly, *adj.*

'father-in-,law, *n.* [*count*], *pl.* fa•thers-in-law. the father of one's husband or wife.

fa•ther•land /'faðər,lænd/ *n.* [*count*] 1. one's native country. 2. the land of one's ancestors.

fath•om /'fæðəm/ *n., pl.* -oms, (*esp. when thought of as a group*) -om, *v.* —*n.* [*count*] 1. a nautical unit of length equal to 6 feet (1.8 m). —*v.* [~ + *obj*] 2. to understand: *I couldn't fathom his motives.* —'fath•om•a•ble, *adj.*

fa•tigue /fə'tiyg/ *n., v.,* -tigued, -ti•guing. —*n.* [*noncount*] 1. tiredness: *a feeling of great fatigue after that long trip.* —*v.* [~ + *obj*] 2. to cause to be tired; exhaust: *Climbing the mountain fatigued the whole group.*

fat•ten /'fætn/ *v.* [~ + *obj*] to cause to grow fat: *fatten livestock.*

fat•ty /'fætiy/ *adj.,* -ti•er, -ti•est. [*before a noun*] made up of, containing, or resembling fat: *fatty tissue.* —'fat•ti•ness, *n.* [*noncount*]

fau•cet /'fɔsɪt/ *n.* [*count*] a device for controlling the flow of water from a pipe; tap.

fault /fɔlt/ *n.* 1. [*count*] a mistake or imperfection; flaw: *His only fault is that he lacks ambition.* 2. [*count; usually singular*] responsibility for a wrongful act: *Whose fault was it?* 3. [*count*] a crack in a body of rock or in the earth's surface: *Faults in southern California sometimes cause earthquakes.* —*v.* [~ + *obj*] 4. to accuse of a mistake; criticize: *The boss can't fault you on inaccuracy.* —*Idiom.* 5. at fault, deserving blame or criticism; responsible: *She was at fault for lying.* 6. find fault, to be critical: *She always found fault with him.* —'fault•less, *adj.* —'fault•less•ly, *adv.* —'fault•y, *adj.,* -i•er, -i•est.

fau•na /'fɔnə/ *n.* the animals of a given area or time period.

fa•vor /'feyvər/ *n.* 1. [*count*] a kind act: *to ask a favor of me.* 2. [*noncount*] approval: *I wanted to win her favor.* —*v.* [~ + *obj*] 3. to regard with favor; approve: *How many favor Smith's proposal?* 4. to prefer: *She thought her father favored her sister.* 5. to make easier: *The wind favored their journey.* —*Idiom.* 6. find favor with, to be liked by: *The play found favor with the critics.* 7. in favor of, in support of: *in favor of aid to education.* 8. in one's favor, to one's advantage: *comments made in your favor.* 9. out of favor, no longer liked: *fashions now out of favor.* Also, *esp. Brit.,* favour.

fa•vor•a•ble /'feyvərəbəl, 'feyvrə-/ *adj.* 1. giving approval or support: *a favorable report.* 2. creating or winning favor; pleasing: *a favorable impression.* 3. providing advantage, opportunity, or convenience: *a favorable rate of interest.* 4. promising; hopeful: *conditions favorable for employment.* —'fa•vor•a•bly, *adv.*

fa•vor•ite /'feyvərɪt, 'feyvrɪt/ *n.* [*count*] 1. a person or thing regarded with special preference or approval: *Vanilla is my favorite.* 2. a horse, etc., considered likely to win: *the favorite in the race.* —*adj.* 3. most liked: *my favorite movie star.*

fa•vor•it•ism /'feyvərɪ,tɪzəm, 'feyvrɪ-/ *n.* [*noncount*] the unfair favoring of one person or group over others.

fawn /fɔn/ *n.* [*count*] a young deer.

fax /fæks/ *n.* 1. a. [*noncount*] a method for sending documents, drawings, photographs, or the like by telephone lines for exact reproduction elsewhere: *Our office has a fax.* b. [*count*] a machine ('fax ma,chine) for doing this: *Our office has a fax.* 2. [*count*] a copy sent by fax. —*v.* [~ + *obj*] 3. to send by fax: *I'll fax the documents to you. I'll fax you the documents.*

faze /feyz/ *v.* [~ + *obj*], fazed, faz•ing. to cause to be upset: *The roof could fall in and it wouldn't faze her.*

FBI, an abbreviation of: Federal Bureau of Investigation.

FCC, an abbreviation of: Federal Communications Commission.

FDA, an abbreviation of: Food and Drug Administration.

FDIC, an abbreviation of: Federal Deposit Insurance Corporation.

fear /fɪər/ *n.* 1. [*noncount*] a feeling caused by danger, evil, pain, etc.: *shaking in fear.* 2. [*count*] a specific instance of such a feeling: *a fear of heights.* —*v.* [~ + *obj*] 3. to be afraid of: *She fears no one.* —'fear•less, *adj.* —'fear•less•ly, *adv.* —'fear•less•ness, *n.* [*noncount*]

fear•ful /'fɪərfəl/ *adj.* causing or feeling fear. —'fear•ful•ly, *adv.*

fea•si•ble /'fiyzəbəl/ *adj.* able to be done: *a feasible plan.* —fea•si•bil•i•ty /,fiyzə'bɪlɪtiy/ *n.* [*noncount*] —'fea•si•bly, *adv.*

feast /fiyst/ *n.* 1. [*count*] any rich or large meal. 2. something very pleasing: *a feast for the eyes.* 3. Also, feast day. a religious celebration. —*v.* [*no obj*] 4. to eat a large meal: *They feasted for days.*

feat /fiyt/ *n.* [*count*] a difficult act or achievement: *an athletic feat that is hard to match.*

feath•er /'fɛðər/ *n.* [*count*] 1. one of the light, horny structures that form the principal covering of birds. —*Idiom.* 2. a feather in one's cap, an honor: *It was a feather in his cap to be named to the town council.* 3. feather one's nest, to make oneself rich by using one's position: *She feathered her own nest instead of helping her clients.* —'feath•ered, *adj.* —'feath•er•y, *adj.,* -i•er, -i•est.

fea•ture /'fiytʃər/ *n., v.,* -tured, -tur•ing. —*n.* [*count*] 1. an important or noticeable part: *an attractive feature of the house.* 2. any of the parts of the face, such as the nose or chin: *The veil hid her features.* 3. a column, cartoon, etc., appearing regularly in a newspaper or magazine. —*v.* [~ + *obj*] 4. to give importance to: *The magazine featured a story on the hurricane.*

Feb or Feb., an abbreviation of: February.

Feb•ru•ar•y /'fɛbruw,ɛriy, 'fɛbyuw-/ *n., pl.* -ar•ies. the second month of the year, ordinarily containing 28 days, but containing 29 days in leap years.

fe•ces /'fiysiyz/ *n.* [*plural*] waste matter from the bowels. Also, *esp. Brit.,* faeces. —fe•cal /'fiykəl/ *adj.*

fed /fɛd/ *v.* 1. pt. and pp. of FEED. —*Idiom.* 2.

fed up, impatient; disgusted: *I was fed up with his excuses.*

fed., an abbreviation of: **1.** federal. **2.** federation.

fed·er·al /'fɛdərəl/ *adj.* [*before a noun*] **1.** of, relating to, or of the nature of a union of states under a central government: *the federal government of the U.S.* **2.** of or involving such a central government: *federal laws.* —**'fed·er·al·ly,** *adv.*

fed·er·al·ism /'fɛdərə,lɪzəm/ *n.* [*noncount*] **1.** the federal principle of government. **2.** belief in this principle. —**'fed·er·al·ist,** *n.* [*count*], *adj.*

fed·er·a·tion /,fɛdə'reyʃən/ *n.* **1.** [*noncount*] the act of uniting or forming a union of states, societies, etc., each of which keeps control of its own internal affairs: *the parties opposing federation.* **2.** [*count*] a union of states, societies, etc., formed in this way: *The United States is a federation.*

fee /fiy/ *n.* [*count*] a sum charged or paid, as for professional services: *a doctor's fee.*

fee·ble /'fiybəl/ *adj.*, **-bler, -blest.** weak; frail. —**'fee·ble·ness,** *n.* [*noncount*] —**'fee·bly,** *adv.*

'feeble-'minded, *adj.* mentally weak.

feed /fiyd/ *v.*, **fed** /fɛd/ **feed·ing,** *n.* —*v.* **1.** [~ + *obj*] to give food to: *to feed pigeons.* **2.** [*no obj*] (esp. of animals) to take food; eat: *The cows were feeding.* —*n.* [*noncount*] **3.** food, esp. for farm animals: *grain feed.* —**'feed·er,** *n.* [*count*]

feed·back /'fiyd,bæk/ *n.* [*noncount*] a reaction or response to a process or activity: *feedback from a speech.*

feel /fiyl/ *v.*, **felt** /fɛlt/ **feel·ing,** *n.* —*v.* **1.** [~ + *obj*] to learn about (something) by touching: *I could feel a slight breeze.* **2.** [~ + *obj*] to find (one's way) by touching: *I felt my way through the darkened room.* **3.** [~ + *obj*] to think or believe: *I feel (that) the book was very good.* **4.** to experience a state of mind or a condition of body; to become conscious of: [~ + *obj*]: *She felt pride in her accomplishments.* [~ + *adjective*]: *I'm feeling fine. She feels happy.* **5.** [~ + *adjective*] to make itself felt or noticed; seem: *Her head feels cold.* —*n.* [*count; usually singular*] **6.** a sensation of something felt: *a feel of sadness in the air.* **7.** the sense of touch: *soft to the feel.* —*Idiom.* **8. feel like, a.** to have a desire for: *I felt like screaming at them.* **b.** to appear or seem like: *It feels like rain.* **9. feel (like) oneself,** to be in one's normal healthy and happy state: *You'll feel like yourself again tomorrow.* **10. feel up to,** to feel strong enough to: *He's not feeling up to running today.*

feel·ing /'fiylɪŋ/ *n.* **1.** [*noncount*] the sensation of touch: *He has no feeling in his left hand.* **2.** [*count*] a particular sensation of this kind: *a feeling of warmth.* **3.** [*count*] an emotion: *a feeling of joy.* **4.** [*noncount*] a belief or opinion: *I have a feeling (that) I forgot something.* **5. feelings,** [*plural*] emotions: *They hurt her feelings.* **6.** [*noncount*] sympathy. —**'feel·ing·ly,** *adv.*

feet /fiyt/ *n.* **1.** pl. of FOOT. —*Idiom.* **2. drag one's feet,** to act slowly: *They were dragging their feet when it came to refunding our money.* **3. get one's feet wet,** to take the first step in an activity, etc. **4. have one's feet on the ground,** to have a sensible attitude. **5. stand on one's own (two) feet,** to be independent. **6. sweep off one's feet,** to impress or overwhelm by ability, enthusiasm, or charm.

feign /feyn/ *v.* [~ + *obj*] to pretend: *to feign sickness.*

fe·line /'fiylayn/ *adj.* **1.** belonging or relating to

the cat family; catlike: *feline agility.* —*n.* [*count*] **2.** cat.

fell¹ /fɛl/ *v.* pt. of FALL.

fell² /fɛl/ *v.* [~ + *obj*] to cause to fall: *to fell a tree.*

fel·la /'fɛlə/ *n. Informal.* FELLOW (defs. 1-3).

fel·low /'fɛlow/ *n.* [*count*] **1.** a man or boy: *a handsome fellow.* **2.** *Informal.* a person; one: *They don't treat a fellow very well here.* **3.** a companion; associate: *his fellows at work.* **4.** a graduate student to whom an allowance is granted for special study. —*adj.* [*before a noun*] **5.** belonging to the same class or group: *fellow students.*

fel·low·ship /'fɛlow,ʃɪp/ *n.* **1.** [*noncount*] companionship: *fellowship among old friends.* **2.** [*count*] an association or society: *a member of the youth fellowship.* **3.** [*count*] the position of, or the money given to, a fellow of a college or university: *a small fellowship for expenses and some tuition.*

fel·on /'fɛlən/ *n.* [*count*] a person who has committed a felony.

fel·o·ny /'fɛləniy/ *n.* [*count*], *pl.* **-nies.** a serious crime, such as murder or burglary. —**fe·lo·ni·ous** /fə'lowniyəs/, *adj.*

felt¹ /fɛlt/ *v.* pt. and pp. of FEEL.

felt² /fɛlt/ *n.* [*noncount*] a thick cloth made of pressed wool, fur, or hair.

fem., an abbreviation of: **1.** female. **2.** feminine.

fe·male /'fiymeyl/ *n.* [*count*] **1.** a person or animal of the sex that bears young. **2.** a plant that produces fruit. —*adj.* **3.** of, relating to, or being a female: *a female mammal.*

fem·i·nine /'fɛmənɪn/ *adj.* relating to or characteristic of women or girls: *feminine clothes.* —,**fem·i'nin·i·ty,** *n.* [*noncount*]

fem·i·nism /'fɛmə,nɪzəm/ *n.* [*noncount*] the belief that women should have the same social, political, and economic rights as men.

fem·i·nist /'fɛmə,nɪst/ *n.* [*count*] **1.** one who believes in feminism. —*adj.* **2.** of or relating to feminism.

fence /fɛns/ *n.*, *v.*, **fenced, fenc·ing.** —*n.* [*count*] **1.** a barrier around a field, yard, etc. **2.** a person who receives and disposes of stolen goods. —*v.* **3.** [~ + *obj*] to separate by or as if by a fence: *to fence (off) a corner of a garden.* **4.** [*no obj*] to practice the art or sport of fencing.

fenc·ing /'fɛnsɪŋ/ *n.* [*noncount*] the sport of fighting with a special sword.

fend /fɛnd/ *v.* **1. fend off,** to keep or push away: *He used a stick to fend off his attackers.* —*Idiom.* **2. fend for oneself,** to provide for oneself; support oneself: *He had to fend for himself after his father died.*

fend·er /'fɛndər/ *n.* [*count*] the part that covers the wheels of an automobile, bicycle, etc.

fer·ment /*n.* 'fɜrmɛnt; *v.* fər'mɛnt/ *n.* [*noncount*] **1.** excitement or disturbance: *political ferment.* —*v.* **2.** to (cause to) undergo fermentation: [*no obj*]: *When wine ferments, it changes sugar to alcohol.* [~ + *obj*]: *This enzyme ferments the wine faster.*

fer·men·ta·tion /,fɜrmɛn'teyʃən/ *n.* [*noncount*] a chemical change, such as the conversion of grape sugar into alcohol.

fern /fɜrn/ *n.* [*count*], *pl.* **ferns** or **fern.** a nonflowering plant having feathery leaves.

fe·ro·cious /fə'rowʃəs/ *adj.* **1.** fierce; brutal: *ferocious animals.* **2.** extreme or intense: *a ferocious thirst.* —**fe'ro·cious·ly,** *adv.* —**fe'ro·cious·ness, fe·roc·i·ty** /fə'rɒsitiy/, *n.* [*noncount*]

F

fer•ret /'fɛrɪt/ n. [count] **1.** a small tame variety of the polecat. —v. [~ + obj] **2.** to drive out by or as if by using a ferret: to ferret rabbits from their burrows; to ferret out enemies; to ferret them out.

'Ferris ,wheel /'fɛrɪs/ n. [count] an amusement ride made of a large upright wheel rotating on a fixed stand and having seats suspended freely from its rim.

Ferris wheel

fer•ry /'fɛriy/ n., pl. **-ries,** v., **-ried, -ry•ing.** —n. [count] **1.** a boat used to carry people and cars across a river, lake, etc. —v. [~ + obj] **2.** to carry back and forth over a fixed route in a boat or plane: They ferried the passengers across the lake.

fer•tile /'fɜrtl̩/ adj. **1.** able to produce healthy plants; productive: fertile soil. **2.** able to bear offspring. **3.** [usually: before a noun] imaginative; creative: a fertile imagination. —**fer•til•i•ty** /fər'tɪlɪtiy/, n. [noncount]

fer•ti•lize /'fɜrtl̩ˌayz/ v. [~ + obj], **-lized, -liz•ing.** to make fertile. —**fer•ti•li•za•tion** /ˌfɜrtl̩ə'zeyʃən/, n. [noncount]

fer•ti•liz•er /'fɜrtl̩ˌayzər/ n. [count] any substance used to make the soil more fertile.

fer•vent /'fɜrvənt/ adj. having or showing feeling; strong: a fervent admirer. —**'fer•vent•ly,** adv.

fer•vor /'fɜrvər/ n. [noncount] great strength of feeling; passion. Also, esp. Brit., **'fer•vour.**

fes•ter /'fɛstər/ v. [no obj] **1.** to become infected: a festering wound. **2.** (of hatred, anger, jealousy, etc.) to grow stronger or worse slowly: The desire for revenge festered in her heart.

fes•ti•val /'fɛstəvəl/ n. [count] **1.** a religious or other celebration: the May festival. **2.** a program of cultural events or entertainment: a music and art festival.

fes•tive /'fɛstɪv/ adj. relating to a feast or festival; joyous; merry: festive decorations; a festive mood. —**'fes•tive•ly,** adv.

fes•tiv•i•ty /fɛ'stɪvɪtiy/ n. [count], pl. **-ties.** a festive celebration, event, or occasion: the Christmas festivities.

fe•tal /'fiytl̩/ adj. of or relating to a fetus: The doctor monitored the fetal heartbeat during the mother's labor.

fetch /fɛtʃ/ v. **1.** to go and bring back; get: [~ + obj]: to fetch a glass of water. [no obj]: She taught the dog to fetch. **2.** [~ + obj] to sell for or bring (a price, amount of money, etc.): The horse fetched more money than it cost.

fete or **fête** /feyt, fɛt/ n., pl. **fetes** or **fêtes,** v., **fet•ed** or **fêt•ed, fet•ing** or **fêt•ing.** —n. [count] **1.** a festive celebration. —v. [~ + obj] **2.** to entertain at or honor with a fete: The Nobel prize winner was feted at a gala luncheon.

fet•ish /'fɛtɪʃ, 'fiytɪʃ/ n. [count] an object regarded as having magical power.

fet•ter /'fɛtər/ n. [count] **1.** a chain placed on the feet of a prisoner. **2.** Usually, **fetters.** [plural] anything that confines or restrains: Education is supposed to remove fetters from the mind. —v. [~ + obj] **3.** to put fetters upon: The pirates fettered their captives.

fet•tle /'fɛtl̩/ n. [noncount] state; condition: They felt in fine fettle.

fet•tuc•ci•ne or **fet•tuc•ci•ni** /ˌfɛtə'tʃiyniy/ n. [noncount; used with a singular verb] pasta cut in flat narrow strips.

fe•tus /'fiytəs/ n. [count], pl. **-tus•es.** unborn or unhatched young in the womb or egg.

feud /fyuwd/ n. [count] **1.** a long, bitter quarrel or argument. —v. [no obj] **2.** to have a feud: The two groups had been feuding for years.

feu•dal•ism /'fyuwdl̩ˌɪzəm/ n. [noncount] the political, military, and social system of the Middle Ages in Western Europe, based on the work done by peasants for a landowner who gave protection in return. —**'feu•dal,** adj.

fe•ver /'fiyvər/ n. **1.** a very high body temperature: [noncount]: Fever and chills are often symptoms of the flu. [count]: I was worried because she had a high fever. **2.** [count; usually singular] a state of great excitement: in a fever of anticipation. —**'fe•ver•ish,** adj. —**'fe•ver•ish•ly,** adv.

few /fyuw/ adj., **-er, -est,** n., pron. —adj. [before a plural noun] **1.** not many but more than one: Few artists are rich. —n. [plural; used with a plural verb] **2.** [a + ~] a small number or amount: Did everyone go home? No, a few were still waiting. —pron. [plural] **3.** a small number of persons or things: Few of us are going to his party. —Idiom. **4. few and far between,** not frequent or plentiful: Chances like this are few and far between. **5. quite a few,** a fairly large number of; many: He had quite a few friends. —Usage. See LESS.

fi•an•cé /ˌfiyɑn'sey, fiy'ɑnsey/ n. [count] pl., **-cés.** a man who is engaged to be married.

fi•an•cée /ˌfiyɑn'sey, fiy'ɑnsey/ n. [count] pl., **-cées.** a woman who is engaged to be married.

fib /fɪb/ n., v., **fibbed, fib•bing.** —n. [count] **1.** a small lie. —v. [no obj] **2.** to tell a fib: Stop fibbing and tell me the truth. —**'fib•ber,** n. [count]

fi•ber /'faybər/ n. **1.** [count] a fine, threadlike plant or animal growth. **2.** [noncount] a basic character or quality: people of strong moral fiber. **3.** [noncount] Also called **bulk, roughage.** parts of fruits and vegetables that aid in digestion: a diet rich in fiber. Also, esp. Brit., **'fi•bre.** —**'fi•brous** /'faybrəs/ adj.

fi•ber•glass or **fi•ber glass** /'faybər glæs/ n. [noncount] a material made up of fine threadlike pieces of glass.

fick•le /'fɪkəl/ adj. not steady or loyal. —**'fick•le•ness,** n. [noncount]

fic•tion /'fɪkʃən/ n. [noncount] literature about people and events that are imagined: I like to read fiction. —**'fic•tion•al,** adj. —**'fic•tion•al,ize,** v., **-ized, -iz•ing.** [~ + obj]

fic•ti•tious /fɪk'tɪʃəs/ adj. made up; false: fictitious names. —**fic'ti•tious•ly,** adv.

fid•dle /'fɪdl̩/ n., v., **-dled, -dling.** —n. [count] **1.** a violin. —v. [no obj] [~ + obj] to play (a tune) on a fiddle. **3. fiddle with,** to touch something, as to adjust it: I fiddled with the wires to the battery. —**'fid•dler,** n. [count]

fi•del•i•ty /fɪ'dɛlɪtiy, fay-/ n. [noncount] **1.** faithfulness. **2.** exactness.

fidg•et /ˈfɪdʒɪt/ v. [no obj] to move about restlessly, nervously, or impatiently: She was fidgeting anxiously before being interviewed.

field /fiyld/ n. [count] **1.** a piece of open land, esp. one used for pasture or growing plants: The cows were grazing in the fields. **2.** a piece of ground used for playing sports. **3.** a particular kind of activity or interest: the field of mathematics; the medical field. **4.** a large area of anything: a field of ice. **5.** any region or area characterized by a particular feature or resource: an oil field. —v. [~ + obj] **6.** (in baseball and cricket) to catch or pick up (the ball) in play. **7.** to answer skillfully: The president fielded the question. —'field•er, n. [count]

'**field ,day,** n. [count] **1.** a day devoted to outdoor sports or athletic contests, such as at a school. **2.** an occasion to enjoy oneself completely: The children had a field day playing with their new toys.

'**field ,hock•ey,** n. [noncount] a field game in which two teams of 11 players each use curved sticks to try to drive a ball into a netted goal.

fiend /fiynd/ n. [count] **1.** any evil spirit; demon. **2.** a very cruel or wicked person. —'fiend•ish, adj. —'fiend•ish•ly, adv.

fierce /fɪərs/ adj., fierc•er, fierc•est. **1.** wild or savage: fierce beasts. **2.** violent: a fierce hurricane. —'fierce•ly, adv. —'fierce•ness, n. [noncount]

fier•y /ˈfayˈriy/ adj., -i•er, -i•est. **1.** made up of fire; very hot: the fiery pits of hell. **2.** like fire: a fiery chili sauce. **3.** passionate: a fiery speech. **4.** easily angered: a fiery temper. —'fier•i•ness, n. [noncount]

fi•es•ta /fiyˈɛstə/ n. [count], pl. -tas. a festival or festive celebration.

fif•teen /ˈfɪfˈtiyn/ n. [count] **1.** a number, ten plus five, written as 15. —adj. [before a noun] **2.** amounting to 15 in number. —'fif'teenth, adj.

fifth /fɪfθ/ adj. **1.** next after the fourth: the fifth door on the right. **2.** being one of five equal parts. —n. [count] **3.** a fifth part, esp. of one (⅕). —adv. **4.** in the fifth place.

fif•ty /ˈfɪftiy/ n., pl. -ties, adj. —n. [count] **1.** a number, ten times five, written as 50. —adj. [before a noun] **2.** amounting to 50 in number. —'fif•ti•eth, adj.

fif•ty-fif•ty or **50-50** /ˈfɪftiyˈfɪftiy/ adj. **1.** equally good and bad, favorable and unfavorable, etc.: a fifty-fifty chance of success. —adv. **2.** in an equally divided way: The money was divided fifty-fifty.

fig /fɪg/ n. [count] a sweet fruit with small seeds.

fig., an abbreviation of: **1.** figurative. **2.** figuratively. **3.** figure.

fight /fayt/ n., v., fought /fɔt/, fight•ing. —n. **1.** [count] a battle. **2.** [count] any struggle: a tough fight for reelection. **3.** [count] an angry argument: a fight over who would use the car. **4.** [noncount] ability or will to keep trying or to resist: She still had some fight left in her. —v. **5.** to take part in battle or in any struggle: [~ + obj]: The armies fought each other. [no obj]: They fought hard to win their case. They fought for their rights. **6.** [no obj] to have an angry argument: He always fights with his brother.

fight•er /ˈfaytər/ n. [count] **1.** a military aircraft. **2.** a person who fights, struggles, etc.

fig•ment /ˈfɪgmənt/ n. [count] something not real: The noises were just a figment of his imagination.

fig•ur•a•tive /ˈfɪgyərətɪv/ adj. (of words) used in an imaginative way rather than in the usual, literal sense: She used the word "dead" in a figurative sense to mean "tired." —'fig•ur•a•tive•ly, adv.

fig•ure /ˈfɪgyər/ n., v., -ured, -ur•ing. —n. [count] **1.** a symbol for a number. **2.** an amount expressed in numbers: a figure that was more than we could afford. **3.** the shape of something: a dim figure in the dark room. **4.** the human form: a graceful figure. **5.** an important person: Abraham Lincoln was an important historical figure. **6.** a diagram. —v. **7.** [~ + obj] to calculate: Let's figure (up) the total and split the bill. **8.** [~ + obj] Informal. to think: I figured that you wanted me to stay. **9.** [no obj] to be or appear in something: Your name figures in my report. **10.** **figure out,** to understand; solve: I can't figure out the directions. I can't figure them out.

fig•ure•head /ˈfɪgyərˌhɛd/ n. [count] **1.** a person who is head of a group, country, etc., but has little or no power: The queen of England is a figurehead. **2.** a carved figure on the front of a ship.

'**figure of 'speech,** n. [count] an expression in which words are used in a figurative way: When I said she was growing like a weed it was just a figure of speech.

fil•a•ment /ˈfɪləmənt/ n. [count] a very fine thread or threadlike structure: filaments of gold. —fil•a•men•tous /ˌfɪləˈmɛntəs/, adj.

file¹ /fayl/ n., v., filed, fil•ing. —n. [count] **1.** a folder, cabinet, or other container in which papers, letters, etc., are arranged in order. **2.** a collection of papers, records, etc., arranged in order. the patient's medical file. **3.** a collection of related computer records stored by name, such as on a disk. —v. [~ + obj] **4.** to arrange (papers, records, etc.) in order for storage or reference: He asked his secretary to file the forms. **5.** to begin (legal proceedings): to file charges against the driver. —Idiom. **6.** **on file,** held in a file or record: They promised to keep my application on file.

file² /fayl/ n., v., filed, fil•ing. —n. [count] **1.** a metal tool having rough surfaces for reducing or smoothing metal, wood, etc. **2.** NAIL FILE. —v. [~ + obj] **3.** to reduce, smooth, or remove with a file: She filed her nails.

fill /fɪl/ v. **1.** to (cause to) become full: [~ + obj]: to fill a jar with water. [no obj]: Her eyes filled with tears. **2.** [~ + obj] to put someone into or to hold a job or position: The company has filled the position. **3.** [~ + obj] to stop up or close (a cavity, hole, etc.): to fill a tooth. **4.** **fill in, a.** to tell (missing information): The spy filled in the names of the missing scientists. **b.** to take someone's place: I filled in for him while he was on vacation. **5.** **fill out,** to complete (a document or form) by writing the needed information: He filled out the form and signed it. He filled it out. **6.** **fill up,** to (cause to) become full to the top: The tank filled up in no time. He filled up the tank with gas. He filled it up. —n. [noncount] **7.** enough to satisfy want or need: to eat one's fill. **8.** material such as earth or stones. —'fill•er, n.

fil•let /fɪˈley/ n., v., fil•leted /fɪˈleyd/, fil•let•ing. —n. **1.** a boneless cut or slice of meat or fish. [noncount]: Fillet is usually very tender and very expensive. [count]: two fillets of beef. —v. [~ + obj] **2.** to cut or prepare (meat or fish) as a fillet.

fill•ing /ˈfɪlɪŋ/ n. [count] **1.** an act or instance of

F

filling. **2.** a substance used to fill a hole in a tooth: *The dentist put in a temporary filling.*

film /fɪlm/ *n.* **1.** [*count*] a thin layer or coating: *a film of grease.* **2.** [*noncount*] a thin strip of coated plastic for taking photographs: *a roll of film.* **3.** a motion picture; movie. —*v.* [~ + *obj*] **4.** to make a motion picture: *The cast and crew have been filming this movie for a year.*

fil•ter /'fɪltər/ *n.* [*count*] **1.** any device or a substance through which liquid or gas is passed to remove impurities or to trap solids: *Pour boiling water into the coffee filter.* **2.** colored glass used in photography to control the color or to reduce the intensity of light. —*v.* [~ + *obj*] **3.** to remove by the action of a filter: *This device filters germs out of the drinking water.* **4.** to act as a filter for: *The air conditioner filters the air.* —'fil•ter•a•ble, fil•tra•ble /'fɪltrəbəl/, *adj.* —'fil•ter•er, *n.* [*count*] —fil•tra•tion /fɪl'treyʃən/ *n.* [*noncount*]

filth /fɪlθ/ *n.* [*noncount*] **1.** disgusting dirt: *sidewalks covered with filth.* **2.** moral impurity or obscenity: *How can you read such filth?* —**filth•y,** *adj.,* -i•er, -i•est: *Your hands are filthy!*

fin /fɪn/ *n.* [*count*] **1.** a winglike or paddlelike part on the body of fishes and certain other water animals. **2.** any part resembling a fin, such as part of a boat or an aircraft.

fin., an abbreviation of: **1.** finance. **2.** financial. **3.** finish.

fi•nal /'faynļ/ *adj.* **1.** [*before a noun*] coming at the end; last in place, order, or time: *the final meeting of the season.* **2.** unchangeable: *That's my final offer.* —*n.* [*count*] **3. a.** Often, **finals.** [*plural*] the last game in a series: *Our team made it to the finals.* **b.** the last examination in a course of study: *Do you have a final in history?*

fi•na•le /fɪ'næliy, -'nɑliy/ *n.* [*count*], *pl.* -les. the last part of something; end.

fi•nal•ist /'faynļɪst/ *n.* [*count*] a person who is taking part in the final round of a contest.

fi•nal•ly /'faynļiy/ *adv.* **1.** after a long delay; at last: *The concert finally started.* **2.** definitely or decisively: *The terms of the contract are not finally settled.*

fi•nance /fɪ'næns, 'faynæns/ *n., v.,* -nanced, -nanc•ing. —*n.* **1.** [*noncount*] the management of money, as in banking and investment. **2. finances,** [*plural*] the money available for use by a company, individual, or government: *Our finances are in good shape.* —*v.* [~ + *obj*] **3.** to supply with money; obtain money or credit for; fund: *How will we finance this building project?*

fi•nan•cial /fɪ'nænʃəl, fay-/ *adj.* relating to money: *the candidate's financial affairs.* —fi'nan•cial•ly, *adv.*

fin•an•cier /ˌfɪnən'sɪər, ˌfaynən-/ *n.* [*count*] a person skilled in managing large financial operations: *Wall Street financiers.*

finch /fɪntʃ/ *n.* [*count*] a small songbird having a short cone-shaped bill.

find /faynd/ *v.,* found /fawnd/, find•ing, *n.* —*v.* [~ + *obj*] **1.** to come upon by chance: *to find a dime in the street.* **2.** to locate or get by search or effort: *to find her an apartment.* **3.** to discover (something) after thinking about it or experiencing it: *to find something to be true. I found it hard to believe. I found that money can't buy happiness.* **4.** [~ + *obj*] to decide after a trial: *to find a person guilty.* **5. find out, a.** to discover: *The detective couldn't find out anything about that suspect.* **b.** to uncover the true nature of

(someone): *You will be found out if you steal money.* —'find•er, *n.* [*count*]

find•ing /'fayndɪŋ/ *n.* [*count*] **1.** a decision made by a judge or jury. **2.** something learned in an official inquiry: *The findings of the committee were reported in the newspaper.*

fine[1] /fayn/ *adj.,* fin•er, fin•est, *adv.* —*adj.* **1.** [*often: before a noun*] of very good quality; excellent: *fine wine; a fine musician.* **2.** made up of tiny pieces: *fine sand.* **3.** very thin: *fine thread.* **4.** delicate; subtle: *He missed some of the fine parts of my argument.* **5.** healthy; well: *She looks fine.* —*adv.* **6.** *Informal.* excellently; very well: *You did fine on the test.* —'fine•ly, *adv.*

fine[2] /fayn/ *n., v.,* fined, fin•ing. —*n.* [*count*] **1.** an amount of money paid as punishment for breaking a law: *a parking fine.* —*v.* [~ + *obj*] **2.** to punish by a fine: *The judge fined him fifty dollars for littering.*

'fine 'arts /fayn/ *n.* [*plural*] painting, sculpture, music, etc.

fin•er•y /'faynəriy/ *n.* [*noncount*] beautiful dress, ornaments, etc.

fi•nesse /fɪ'nɛss/ *n.* [*noncount*] extreme skill in handling a difficult situation: *She handled his emotional outburst with finesse.*

fin•ger /'fɪŋgər/ *n.* [*count*] **1.** any of the jointed end members of the hand. —*v.* [~ + *obj*] **2.** to touch with the fingers: *He fingered the gun.* **3.** to identify, esp. as a criminal: *He fingered his neighbor as the thief.* —**Idiom. 4. have a finger in the pie,** to be involved in something. **5. keep one's fingers crossed,** to wish for good luck or success. **6. lay or put one's finger on, a.** to remember precisely. **b.** to locate exactly.

fin•ger•nail /'fɪŋgərˌneyl/ *n.* [*count*] the nail at the end of a finger.

fin•ger•print /'fɪŋgərˌprɪnt/ *n.* [*count*] **1.** the mark made on a surface by the tip of the thumb or other finger. —*v.* [~ + *obj*] **2.** to take the fingerprints of: *The police fingerprinted the suspect.*

fin•ger•tip /'fɪŋgərˌtɪp/ *n.* [*count*] the tip or end of a finger: *His fingertips were dirty from the ink.*

fin•ick•y /'fɪnɪkiy/ *adj.* very particular; difficult to please; fussy: *a finicky eater.*

fin•ish /'fɪnɪʃ/ *v.* **1.** to bring or come to an end; to complete: [~ + *obj*]: *We finished dinner at about 9 o'clock.* [*no obj*]: *When does school finish this year?* **2.** [~ + *obj*] to put a finish on (wood, metal, etc.): *He finished the chair with a glossy varnish.* —*n.* **3.** [*count*] the end; the final part: *We're getting close to the finish now.* **4.** [*count; usually singular*] the surface coating of wood, metal, etc.: *This old table has a beautiful hand-rubbed finish.*

fi•nite /'faynayt/ *adj.* having limits; measurable. —'fi•nite•ly, *adv.*

fir /fɜr/ *n.* [*count*] an evergreen tree of the pine family, having flat needles and erect cones.

fire /fayᵊr/ *n., v.,* fired, fir•ing. —*n.* **1.** [*noncount*] light, heat, and flame due to burning. **2.** [*count*] a burning mass of fuel, such as on a hearth. **3.** [*noncount*] excitement: *a speech that was full of fire.* **4.** [*noncount*] the shooting of firearms: *The enemy returned fire.* —*v.* **5.** [~ + *obj*] to set on fire: *It took several matches to fire the wood.* **6.** [~ + *obj*] to arouse: *fired my interest in astronomy.* **7.** to shoot (a gun): [~ + *obj*]: *The police fired their pistols at the suspect.* [*no obj*]: *Fire when ready.* **8.** [~ + *obj*] to dismiss from a job: *The boss fired her.* —**Idiom. 9. catch (on) fire,** to burn: *The wet logs just* *wouldn't catch (on) fire.* **10. under fire,** under attack.

fire•arm /'fayᵊr,ɑrm/ *n.* [*count*] a gun.

fire•ball /'fayᵊr,bɔl/ *n.* [*count*] a ball of fire, such as a large burst of flame from an explosive.

fire•bomb /'fayᵊr,bɒm/ *n.* [*count*] **1.** an explosive device that burns things near it. —*v.* [~ + *obj*] **2.** to attack with firebombs: *The terrorists firebombed the enemy.*

fire•crack•er /'fayᵊr,krækər/ *n.* [*count*] a paper or cardboard tube filled with an explosive and discharged to make a noise, as during a celebration.

'fire ,engine, *n.* [*count*] a truck equipped for firefighting.

'fire es,cape, *n.* [*count*] an outside stairway for escaping from a burning building.

'fire ex,tinguisher, *n.* [*count*] a portable container filled with chemicals for putting out a fire.

fire•fight•er or **fire fight•er** /'fayᵊr,faytər/ *n.* [*count*] a person who fights fires: *The firefighters arrived at the scene.* —**'fire,fight•ing,** *n.* [*noncount*], *adj.*

fire•fly /'fayᵊr,flay/ *n.* [*count*], *pl.* **-flies.** a beetle that comes out at night, having a light-producing organ at the rear of the abdomen. Also called **lightning bug.**

fire•house /'fayᵊr,haws/ *n.* FIRE STATION.

'fire 'hydrant, *n.* HYDRANT.

fire•man /'fayᵊrmən/ *n.* [*count*], *pl.* **-men.** a firefighter.

fire•place /'fayᵊr,pleys/ *n.* [*count*] the part of a chimney that opens into a room and in which fuel is burned.

fire•proof /'fayᵊr,pruwf/ *adj.* **1.** not able to be damaged by fire: *fireproof gloves.* —*v.* [~ + *obj*] **2.** to make fireproof: *to fireproof the school.*

fire•side /'fayᵊr,sayd/ *n.* [*count; usually: the* + ~] the space around a fire: *to sit around the fireside and swap stories.*

'fire ,station, *n.* [*count*] a building in which firefighting apparatus and usually fire department personnel are housed; firehouse.

fire•trap /'fayᵊr,træp/ *n.* [*count*] a building that is esp. dangerous in case of fire.

fire•wood /'fayᵊr,wʊd/ *n.* [*noncount*] wood suitable for fuel.

fire•work /'fayᵊr,wɜrk/ *n.* [*count*] Often, **fireworks.** [*plural*] an explosive device for producing a display of light or a loud noise, used for signaling or as part of a celebration.

'firing ,squad, *n.* [*count*] a group of soldiers assigned to execute a condemned person by shooting.

firm¹ /fɜrm/ *adj.* **-er, -est,** *v.* —*adj.* **1.** not soft: *a firm mattress.* **2.** securely in place; steady; fixed: *Is that chair firm enough to sit on?.* **3.** unyielding to change: *a firm belief in God.* —*v.* [*no obj*] **4.** to become firm: *The pudding firmed (up) in the freezer.* —**'firm•ly,** *adv.* —**'firm•ness,** *n.* [*noncount*]

firm² /fɜrm/ *n.* [*count*] a business: *She started her own firm.*

first /fɜrst/ *adj.* **1.** being before all others in time, order, rank, importance, etc.: *I was the first guest to arrive.* —*adv.* **2.** before all others or anything else in time, order, rank, etc.: *We arrived first.* **3.** before some other thing, event, etc.: *Clean up your room first.* **4.** for the first time: *We first met in the library stacks.* —*n.* **5.** [*count; singular: the* + ~] the person or thing that is first in time, order, rank, etc.: *I was the first to arrive.*

'first 'aid, *n.* [*noncount*] emergency treatment given to the sick or injured. —**'first-'aid,** *adj.* [*before a noun*]: *a first-aid worker.*

'first 'class, *n.* [*noncount*] the best, finest, or highest class, grade, or rank. —**'first-'class,** *adj., adv.*

first•hand or **first-hand** /'fɜrst,hænd/ *adv.* **1.** from the source; directly: *I learned firsthand not to disagree.* —*adj.* [*before a noun*] **2.** direct from the source: *firsthand knowledge.*

'first 'lady, *n.* [*count; often: First Lady*] the wife of the president of the U.S. or of the governor of a state.

first•ly /'fɜrstliy/ *adv.* in the first place; first.

'first 'person, *n.* [*count; singular; usually: the* + ~] the form of a pronoun or verb that refers to the speaker, such as *I, we,* or *am.*

'first-'rate, *adj.* excellent: *a first-rate job.*

fis•cal /'fɪskəl/ *adj.* [*before a noun*] relating to financial matters: *fiscal policies.* —**'fis•cal•ly,** *adv.*

fish /fɪʃ/ *n., pl.* (*esp. when thought of as a group*) **fish,** (*esp. for kinds or species*) **fish•es,** *v.* —*n.* **1.** [*count*] a cold-blooded animal living in water, having gills, fins, and usually a long body covered with scales. **2.** [*noncount*] the flesh of a fish used as food. —*v.* **3.** to go fishing (for): [~ + *obj*]: *to fish trout.* [*no obj*]: *I was fishing all day; fishing for salmon.* —*Idiom.* **4. fish out of water,** a person who feels out of place: *She felt like a fish out of water in the big city.* —**'fish•er•man,** *n., pl.* **-men.** [*count*]

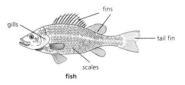

fish

fish•er•man /'fɪʃərmən/ *n.* [*count*], *pl.* **-men.** a person who fishes for profit or pleasure.

fish•ing /'fɪʃɪŋ/ *n.* [*noncount*] the occupation or sport of catching fish: *to go fishing.*

fish•y /'fɪʃiy/ *adj.*, **-i•er, -i•est. 1.** like a fish: *a fishy odor.* **2.** questionable: *That excuse sounds fishy.*

fis•sion /'fɪʃən/ *n.* [*noncount*] the splitting of the nucleus of an atom.

fis•sure /'fɪʃər/ *n.* [*count*] a narrow opening or groove: *a fissure in the earth.*

fist /fɪst/ *n.* [*count*] the hand closed tightly with the fingers doubled into the palm.

fit¹ /fɪt/ *adj.,* **fit•ter, fit•test,** *v.,* **fit•ted** or **fit, fit•ting,** —*adj.* **1.** [*be* + ~] adapted or suited: *The water is not fit to drink.* **2.** in good physical condition; in good health: *She looked fit and trim.* —*v.* **3.** to be adapted to or suitable for (a purpose, object, occasion, etc.): [*no obj*]: *The house fits nicely in that wooded area.* [~ + *obj*]: *Does lunch at noon fit your schedule?* **4.** to be the right size or shape. [~ + *obj*]: *The sweater fits him well.* [*no obj*]: *This dress doesn't fit.* —**'fit•ness,** *n.* [*noncount*] —**'fit•ter,** *n.* [*count*]

fit² /fɪt/ *n.* [*count*] **1.** a sudden attack of a disease, esp. one with unconsciousness: *a fit of epilepsy.* **2.** a period of emotion, activity, etc.: *a fit of weeping.*

fit•ful /'fɪtfəl/ *adj.* having an irregular pattern of activity: *fitful sleep.* —**'fit•ful•ly,** *adv.*

fit•ting /'fɪtɪŋ/ *adj.* **1.** suitable or proper: *a fitting role in the new company.* —*n.* [*count*] **2.** try-

F

ing on clothes that are being made: *Suits are made to order with only a few fittings.* —'**fit•ting•ly**, *adv.*

five /fayv/ *n.* [*count*] **1.** a number, four plus one, written as 5. **2.** a five-dollar bill. —*adj.* [*before a noun*] **3.** amounting to five in number.

fix /fɪks/ *v.* [~ + *obj*] **1.** to repair; mend; adjust: *The plumber fixed the broken sink.* **2.** to attach: *She fixed a poster on the wall.* **3.** to direct steadily: *His eyes fixed themselves on the distant ship.* **4.** to arrange action of, esp. dishonestly: *to fix the election.* —*n.* [*count*] **5.** a position from which it is difficult to escape: *I'm in a bad fix.*

fixed /fɪkst/ *adj.* not moveable or changeable: *The wedding date is fixed. He has very fixed ideas.*

fix•ture /'fɪkstʃər/ *n.* [*count*] **1.** something securely attached: *a light fixture.* **2.** a person or thing long established in the same place: *She was a fixture at the license bureau for many years.*

fizz /fɪz/ *v.* [*no obj*] to make a hissing sound: *The soda fizzed in the glass.*

fjord or **fiord** /fyord/ *n.* [*count*] a long narrow branch of the sea bordered by steep cliffs.

FL, an abbreviation of: Florida.

fl., an abbreviation of: **1.** floor. **2.** fluid.

Fla., an abbreviation of: Florida.

flab•by /'flæbiy/ *adj.,* **-bi•er, -bi•est.** lacking firmness: *flabby muscles.* —'**flab•bi•ness,** *n.* [*noncount*]

flac•cid /'flæksɪd, 'flæsɪd/ *adj.* soft and limp: *flaccid skin.*

flag¹ /flæg/ *n., v.,* **flagged, flag•ging.** —*n.* [*count*] **1.** a piece of cloth marked with special colors or designs and used as a symbol or as a means of signaling: *The American flag has both stars and stripes.* —*v.* [~ + *obj*] **2.** to signal with or as if with a flag: *to flag (down) a taxi; to flag a taxi (down).*

flag² /flæg/ *v.* [*no obj*], **flagged, flag•ging.** to lose energy or interest: *Attendance flagged after the team lost.*

flag•pole /'flæg,powl/ *n.* [*count*] a pole on which a flag is displayed.

fla•grant /'fleygrənt/ *adj.* [*before a noun*] very noticeable or evident; obvious; glaring: *a flagrant error.* —'**fla•grant•ly,** *adv.*

flag•ship /'flæg,ʃɪp/ *n.* [*count*] **1.** a ship carrying the commander of a fleet. **2.** the most important one of a group: *The largest store is the flagship of the chain.*

flag•stone /'flæg,stown/ *n.* [*count*] a flat stone slab used esp. for paving.

flair /flɛər/ *n.* **1.** [*count*] a natural talent or ability: *a flair for comedy.* **2.** [*noncount*] a sense of style: *She dresses with flair.*

flake /fleyk/ *n.* [*count*] a small, flat, thin piece: *a few flakes of snow.* —'**flak•y,** *adj.,* **-i•er, -i•est.**

flam•boy•ant /flæm'bɔyənt/ *adj.* very bold or brilliant; showy: *flamboyant clothes; flamboyant behavior.* —**flam'boy•ance,** *n.* [*noncount*] —**flam'boy•ant•ly,** *adv.*

flame /fleym/ *n., v.,* **flamed, flam•ing.** —*n.* [*count*] **1.** burning gas: *the flame of a match.* **2.** Often, **flames.** [*plural*] the state or condition of burning: *a house in flames.* —*v.* [*no obj*] **3.** to burn with or burst into flames: *The gasoline flamed suddenly.* —**flaming,** *adj.*

fla•min•go /flə'mɪŋgow/ *n.* [*count*], *pl.* **-gos, -goes.** a wading bird having pinkish feathers.

flam•ma•ble /'flæməbəl/ *adj.* easily set on fire:

flammable rags. —**flam•ma•bil•i•ty** /ˌflæmə'bɪlɪtiy/, *n.* [*noncount*]

flank /flæŋk/ *n.* [*count*] **1.** the side of an animal or a person between the ribs and hip. —*v.* [~ + *obj*] **2.** to stand at the side of: *Two policemen flanked the mayor.*

flan•nel /'flænl/ *n.* [*noncount*] a warm, soft fabric of wool or cotton.

flap /flæp/ *v.,* **flapped, flap•ping,** *n.* —*v.* **1.** to (cause to) swing back and forth or to move up and down: [*no obj*]: *A loose shutter flapped noisily.* [~ + *obj*]: *The bird flapped its wings.* —*n.* [*count*] **2.** something flat and broad that is attached at one side only and covers an opening: *the flap on a jacket pocket.* **3.** a flapping motion or sound: *the flap of wings.*

flare /flɛər/ *n., v.,* **flared, flar•ing,** *n.* —*v.* [*no obj*] **1.** to blaze with a burst of flame: *The fire flared (up) suddenly.* **2.** to burst out in sudden activity or emotion: *Tempers flared (up).* —*n.* **3.** [*noncount*] a sudden burst of flame. **4.** [*count*] a bright light used as a signal: *flares at the scene of the crash.*

flash /flæʃ/ *n.* [*count*] **1.** a brief, sudden burst of bright light or flame: *a flash of lightning.* **2.** a sudden, brief outburst: *a flash of humor; a flash of anger.* **3.** a sudden thought or vision: *a flash of inspiration.* —*v.* **4.** to (cause to) shine briefly or irregularly: [*no obj*]: *The light on the police car was flashing.* [~ + *obj*]: *The police car flashed its lights.* **5.** [*no obj*] to appear suddenly: *The answer flashed into his mind.* **6.** [~ + *obj*] to send a message, as by radio or telegraph: *They flashed the news report to London.* —*adj.* **7.** [*before a noun*] sudden and brief: *a flash fire; a flash flood.*

flash•back /'flæʃ,bæk/ *n.* [*noncount*] a scene in a novel, film, etc., which shows something that happened at an earlier time.

flash•bulb or **flash bulb** /'flæʃ,bʌlb/ *n.* [*count*] a glass bulb that provides light for taking a photograph.

flash•light /'flæʃ,layt/ *n.* [*count*] Also called, esp. *Brit.,* **torch.** a small portable electric lamp powered by batteries.

flash•y /'flæʃiy/ *adj.,* **-i•er, -i•est. 1.** briefly and superficially brilliant: *a flashy performance.* **2.** overly showy and tasteless: *flashy clothes.*

flask /flæsk/ *n.* [*count*] **1.** a bottle having a rounded body and a narrow neck. **2.** a flat bottle for carrying in the pocket: *a brandy flask.*

flat¹ /flæt/ *adj.,* **flat•ter, flat•test,** *adv., n.* —*adj.* **1.** horizontally level: *a flat roof.* **2.** not deep, high, or thick: *flat boxes.* **3.** with the air out; collapsed: *a flat tire.* **4.** (of a carbonated beverage) having lost its bubbles: *The soda is flat.* **5.** [*after a letter indicating tone*] (in music) lowered a half step in tone: *B flat.* —*adv.* **6.** in a flat position: *The trees had been laid flat by the hurricane.* **7.** (in music) below the true tone: *to sing flat.* —*n.* [*count*] **8.** a woman's shoe with a very low heel. **9.** a flat surface, side, or part of anything: *She held the stone in the flat of her hand.* **10.** (in music) a tone that is one half step below another. **11.** an automobile tire that has lost the air. —'**flat•ly,** *adv.* —'**flat•ness,** *n.* [*noncount*] —'**flat•ten,** *v.* [~ + *obj*]

flat² /flæt/ *n.* [*count*] a residential apartment: *He rented a flat in the city.*

flat•ter /'flætər/ *v.* **1.** [~ + *obj*] to praise too much or insincerely. **2.** [~ + *obj*; *usually*: *be + ~ -ed*] to please by compliments or attentions: *I* *was flattered by the invitation.* —'**flat•ter•ing,** *adj.* —'**flat•ter•y,** *n.*

flaunt /flɔnt/ *v.* [~ + *obj*] to show too much: *to flaunt her wealth.*

fla•vor /'fleyvər/ *n.* **1.** [*count*] a particular taste: *The shop sells ice cream in eight flavors.* **2.** [*noncount*] the taste of food: *This stew has no flavor.* **3.** [*noncount*] the special quality of a thing: *the true flavor of your experience in the jungle.* —*v.* [~ + *obj*] **4.** to give flavor to (something): *She flavored the icing with vanilla.* Also, *esp. Brit.,* **flavour.** —'**fla•vor•ful,** *adj.* —'**fla•vor•ing,** *n.* [*noncount*] —'**fla•vor•less,** *adj.*

flaw /flɔ/ *n.* [*count*] an imperfection; blemish: *a flaw in the diamond.* —**flawed,** *adj.* —'**flaw•less,** *adj.* —'**flaw•less•ly,** *adv.*

flax /flæks/ *n.* [*noncount*] a plant with blue flowers that is grown for its fiber, used for making linen yarn. —'**flax•en,** *adj.*

flea /fliy/ *n.* [*count*] a small, wingless, blood-sucking insect, noted for its ability to leap.

'**flea ,market,** *n.* [*count*] a market, often outdoors, with a number of stalls selling old or used articles.

fleck /flɛk/ *n.* [*count*] **1.** a small bit: *a fleck of dirt.* —*v.* [~ + *obj; usually: be* + *~ -ed*] **2.** to mark with flecks: *The leaves were flecked with sunlight.*

fledg•ling /'flɛdʒlɪŋ/ *n.* [*count*] **1.** a young bird that has recently grown its feathers. **2.** an inexperienced person. Also, *esp. Brit.,* '**fledge•ling.**

flee /fliy/ *v.,* **fled** /flɛd/, **flee•ing.** to run away (from), as from danger; escape: [*no obj*]: *They fled from their home.* [~ + *obj*]: *They fled the country.*

fleece /fliys/ *n., v.,* **fleeced, fleec•ing.** —*n.* [*noncount*] **1.** the coat of wool that covers a sheep. —*v.* [~ + *obj* (+ *of*)] **2.** to take money by deception; swindle: *The con artists fleeced the elderly couple of their savings.* —'**fleec•y,** *adj.,* -**i•er, -i•est:** *a blue sky with white, fleecy clouds.*

fleet[1] /fliyt/ *n.* [*count*] **1.** all the naval ships of a nation; navy: *the American fleet.* **2.** a group of vehicles under one management: *a fleet of cabs.*

fleet[2] /fliyt/ *adj.,* -**er, -est.** swift; rapid: *a fleet horse.* —'**fleet•ness,** *n.* [*noncount*]

fleet•ing /'fliytɪŋ/ *adj.* passing swiftly: *a fleeting glance.* —'**fleet•ing•ly,** *adv.*

flesh /flɛʃ/ *n.* [*noncount*] **1.** the soft substance of an animal body between the skin and the skeleton. **2.** [*the* + *~*] the body, esp. as distinguished from the spirit: *The spirit is willing but the flesh is weak.* —*v.* **3. flesh out,** to develop: *Flesh out your essay with more details. Flesh the essay out.* —*Idiom.* **4. in the flesh,** in person: *She is even more beautiful in the flesh.*

flesh•y /'flɛʃiy/ *adj.,* -**i•er, -i•est.** plump: *fleshy cheeks.*

flew /fluw/ *v.* a pt. of FLY[1].

flex /flɛks/ *v.* to bend, as a part of the body: [~ + *obj*]: *I needed to flex my legs.* [*no obj*]: *My fingers wouldn't flex.*

flex•i•ble /'flɛksəbəl/ *adj.* **1.** able to be bent without breaking: *That hose is flexible.* **2.** that can be changed: *a flexible schedule.* —**flex•i•bil•i•ty** /,flɛksə'bɪlitiy/, *n.* [*noncount*]

flick /flɪk/ *n.* [*count*] **1.** a light and rapid movement: *a flick of the wrist.* —*v.* [~ + *obj*] **2.** to cause to move rapidly or suddenly: *a bird flicking its tail.*

flick•er /'flɪkər/ *v.* [*no obj*] **1.** to burn unsteadily: *The candle flickered in the wind.* **2.** to appear quickly and briefly: *A smile flickered on his face.*

—*n.* [*count*] **3.** an unsteady light. **4.** a brief appearance: *I saw a flicker of interest in her eyes.*

flied /flayd/ *v.* a pt. and pp. of FLY[1].

fli•er or **fly•er** /'flayər/ *n.* [*count*] **1.** a person, animal, or thing that flies. **2.** a small piece of paper that gives information.

flight[1] /flayt/ *n.* **1.** [*noncount*] the act, manner, or power of flying. **2.** [*count*] a trip by airplane. **3.** [*count*] a series of steps between two floors of a building.

flight[2] /flayt/ *n.* [*count*] **1.** fleeing or running away: *flight from persecution.* —*Idiom.* **2. take flight,** to run away; flee.

'**flight at,tendant,** *n.* [*count*] an airline employee who attends to passengers' comfort and safety.

flight•less /'flaytlɪs/ *adj.* incapable of flying: *Penguins are flightless birds.*

flight•y /'flaytiy/ *adj.,* -**i•er, -i•est.** unstable: *He's too flighty to deal with this problem.* —'**flight•i•ness,** *n.* [*noncount*]

flim•sy /'flɪmziy/ *adj.,* -**si•er, -si•est. 1.** not strong: *a flimsy fabric.* **2.** not convincing: *a flimsy excuse.* —**flim•si•ly** /'flɪmzəliy/, *adv.* —'**flim•si•ness,** *n.* [*noncount*]

flinch /flɪntʃ/ *v.* [*no obj*] to draw back, as from something dangerous or painful.

fling /flɪŋ/ *v.,* **flung** /flʌŋ/, **fling•ing,** *n.* —*v.* [~ + *obj*] **1.** to throw violently: *She flung the dishes to the floor.* —*n.* [*count*] **2.** a short period of fun.

flint /flɪnt/ *n.* [*noncount*] [*count*] a hard gray stone used for making a fire.

flip /flɪp/ *v.,* **flipped, flip•ping,** *adj.,* **flip•per, flip•pest.** —*v.* [~ + *obj*] **1.** to turn over by tossing: *to flip a coin.* **2.** to move with a sudden stroke: *to flip a switch.* —*adj.* **3.** flippant: *a flip answer.*

flip•pant /'flɪpənt/ *adj.* lacking respect or seriousness: *a flippant answer.* —'**flip•pant•ly,** *adv.*

flip•per /'flɪpər/ *n.* [*count*] **1.** a broad flat limb, such as of a seal or whale, adapted for swimming. **2.** a large flat rubber shoe worn in scuba diving and swimming.

flirt /flɜrt/ *v.* [*no obj*] **1.** to behave romantically toward someone in a playful manner. **2.** to think about without seriousness: *He flirted with the idea of singing professionally* —*n.* [*count*] **3.** a person who flirts. —**flir'ta•tion,** *n.* [*noncount*] [*count*] —**flir•ta•tious** /flɜr'teyʃəs/ *adj.* —**flir'ta•tious•ly,** *adv.*

flit /flɪt/ *v.* [*no obj*], **flit•ted, flit•ting.** to fly or move swiftly and lightly: *A smile flitted across his face.*

float /flowt/ *v.* **1.** to (cause to) rest on the surface of a liquid, in the air, etc.: [*no obj*]: *I don't think that raft will float.* [~ + *obj*]: *Float the whipped cream on the coffee.* **2.** [*no obj*] to move lightly and gracefully: *She floated down the stairs.*

flock /flɒk/ *n.* [*count*] **1.** a group of animals, esp. sheep, goats, or birds. **2.** a large group of people or things: *flocks of tourists.* —*v.* [*no obj*] **3.** to gather in a flock: *They flocked around the hero.*

floe /flow/ *n.* [*count*] a large sheet of floating ice on the surface of the sea.

flog /flɒg, flɔg/ *v.* [~ + *obj*], **flogged, flog•ging.** to beat: *The guard flogged the prisoners.*

flood /flʌd/ *n.* **1.** [*count*] a great flowing of water, esp. over land. **2.** [*count*] any great flowing stream: *a flood of tears.* —*v.* **3.** to cover with a flood: [~ + *obj*]: *The river flooded the town.* [*no obj*]: *The basement flooded with water.* **4.** to arrive (at) in large numbers: [~ + *obj*]: *Telegrams*

F

flooded the senator's office. [*no obj*]: *Tourists flooded into the city.*

flood•gate /ˈflʌdˌgeyt/ *n.* [*count*] **1.** a gate regulating the flow of water. **2.** anything that controls the passage of something: *opened (or closed) the floodgates to immigration.*

flood•light /ˈflʌdˌlayt/ *n., v.,* **-light•ed** or **-lit,** **-light•ing.** —*n.* [*count*] **1.** a lamp that produces a light directed over a wide area. —*v.* [~ + *obj*] **2.** to light with a floodlight: *to floodlight buildings.*

floor /flɔr/ *n.* **1.** [*count*] the surface of a room on which one stands and walks: *The floor had a soft rug on it.* **2.** [*count*] a surface extending horizontally throughout a building and making up one level or stage in the structure: *Our apartment is on the fifth floor.* **3.** [*singular*] the right of a member of a legislative body to speak officially to other members in the legislative chamber: *The senator from Alaska has the floor.* —*v.* [~ + *obj*] **4.** to cover or furnish with a floor. **5.** to knock down: *He floored the bully with one punch.*

floor•board /ˈflɔrˌbɔrd/ *n.* [*count*] a board making up a wooden floor.

flop /flɒp/ *v.,* **flopped, flop•ping,** *n.* —*v.* [*no obj*] **1.** to move, drop, or fall in a heavy or clumsy manner: *He flopped down on the couch.* **2.** to be a complete failure: *The play flopped.* —*n.* [*count*] **3.** an act or sound of flopping. **4.** a complete failure: *The surprise party was a flop.*

flop•py /ˈflɒpiy/ *adj.,* **-pi•er, -pi•est,** *n., pl.* **-pies.** —*adj.* **1.** tending to flop: *a dog with floppy ears.* —*n.* [*count*] **2.** FLOPPY DISK. —**flop•pi•ly** /ˈflɒpəliy/, *adv.* —**flop•pi•ness,** *n.* [*noncount*]

ˈfloppy ˈdisk, *n.* [*count*] DISKETTE.

flo•ra /ˈflɔrə/ *n.* [*noncount*] the plants of a particular region or time period: *He studies the flora of the desert.*

flo•ral /ˈflɔrəl/ *adj.* [*before a noun*] relating to or made up of flowers: *a floral wreath.*

flor•id /ˈflɔrɪd, ˈflɒr-/ *adj.* **1.** red: *a florid complexion.* **2.** decorated excessively; showy: *florid writing.*

flo•rist /ˈflɔrɪst, ˈflɒr-/ *n.* [*count*] a person who sells flowers and plants.

floss /flɔs, flɒs/ *n.* [*noncount*] **1.** strong thread used to clean between the teeth. —*v.* **2.** to use dental floss on (the teeth): [*no obj*]: *to floss regularly.* [~ + *obj*]: *She flosses her teeth.*

flo•til•la /flowˈtɪlə/ *n.* [*count*] a group of small ships.

flounce /flawns/ *v.* [*no obj*], **flounced, flounc•ing.** to move in an impatient, angry way: *to flounce out of the room in a rage.*

floun•der¹ /ˈflawndər/ *v.* [*no obj*] to struggle wildly to gain one's balance or move: *to flounder in the mud.*

floun•der² /ˈflawndər/ *n.* [*count*], *pl.* (*esp. when thought of as a group*) **-der,** (*esp. for kinds or species*) **-ders.** any of various fishes with a flattened body, valued as food.

flour /flawˀr, ˈflawər/ *n.* [*noncount*] **1.** the finely ground meal of grain used in baking and cooking: *whole-wheat flour.* —*v.* [~ + *obj*] **2.** to sprinkle or coat with flour.

flour•ish /ˈflɜrɪʃ, ˈflʌr-/ *v.* **1.** [*no obj*] to do well; thrive: *a period in which art flourished.* **2.** [~ + *obj*] to hold (something) dramatically for all to see: *He flourished the trophy.* —*n.* [*count*] **3.** a dramatic gesture: *With a flourish he placed the document in her hands.*

flow /flow/ *v.* [*no obj*] **1.** to move in a stream: *The river flows to the sea.* **2.** to move continu-

ously and easily: *The words flowed from his pen.* —*n.* [*count; usually singular*] **3.** an act of flowing. **4.** movement in a stream: *the flow of traffic.*

flow•er /ˈflawər/ *n.* **1.** [*count*] the blossom of a plant; bloom. **2.** [*count*] a plant grown for its beauty: **3.** [*singular; the* + ~] the best or finest member, product, or example: *the flower of American youth.* —*v.* [*no obj*] **4.** to produce flowers; blossom: *These plants flower in the shade.* **5.** to flourish: *Her talent for writing flowered.* —ˈflow•ered, *adj.*

flow•er•pot /ˈflawərˌpɒt/ *n.* [*count*] a pot in which to grow plants.

flow•er•y /ˈflawəriy/ *adj.,* **-i•er, -i•est. 1.** covered with or having many flowers; decorated with floral designs: *a flowery dress.* **2.** elaborate in speech or writing: *a speech with flowery language.*

flown /flown/ *v.* a pp. of FLY¹.

fl. oz., an abbreviation of: fluid ounce.

flu /fluw/ *n.* [*noncount; often: the* + ~] influenza.

fluc•tu•ate /ˈflʌktʃuˌeyt/ *v.* [*no obj*], **-at•ed, -at•ing.** to shift back and forth or up and down: *Prices fluctuated wildly.* —**fluc•tu•a•tion** /ˌflʌktʃuˈeyʃən/, *n.* [*count*]

flue /fluw/ *n.* [*count*] a passage for smoke to escape from a chimney.

flu•ent /ˈfluwənt/ *adj.* **1.** spoken or written with ease: *He spoke fluent French.* **2.** able to speak or write smoothly, easily, or readily: *She is fluent in three languages.* —ˈflu•en•cy, *n.* [*noncount*] —ˈflu•ent•ly, *adv.*

fluff /flʌf/ *n.* [*noncount*] **1.** light downy particles. **2.** something light or frivolous: *The book is pure fluff but fun to read.* —*v.* [~ + *up* + *obj*] **3.** to make fluffy: *He fluffed up his thinning hair.*

fluff•y /ˈflʌfiy/ *adj.,* **-i•er, -i•est. 1.** of, resembling, or covered with fluff; downy: *a fluffy little chick.* **2.** light or airy: *a fluffy cake.* —ˈfluff•i•ness, *n.* [*noncount*]

flu•id /ˈfluwɪd/ *n.* **1.** a liquid: [*noncount*]: *Fluid dripped from the tank.* [*count*]: *to drink fluids.* —*adj.* **2.** capable of flowing: *a fluid substance.* **3.** smooth: *fluid gestures.* —**flu•id•i•ty** /fluwˈɪdɪtiy/, *n.* [*noncount*] —ˈflu•id•ly, *adv.*

ˈfluid ˈounce, *n.* [*count*] a measure of capacity equal to ¹⁄₁₆ pint.

flung /flʌŋ/ *v.* pt. and pp. of FLING.

flunk /flʌŋk/ *v.* **1.** to fail (in) a course or examination: [*no obj*]: *You are in danger of flunking.* [~ + *obj*]: *He flunked math.* **2.** [~ + *obj*] to give a failing grade to: *The professor flunked half the class.* **3. flunk out,** to (cause to) leave a school because of failing grades: *She is in danger of flunking out.*

fluo•res•cence /fluˈrɛsəns, flɔ-, flow-/ *n.* [*noncount*] the giving off of visible light by a substance exposed to another light or to x-rays. —fluoˈres•cent, *adj.*

fluor•i•date /ˈflʊrɪˌdeyt/ *v.* [~ + *obj*], **-dat•ed, -dat•ing.** to add fluorides to (a water supply) to reduce tooth decay. —ˌfluor•i•ˈda•tion, *n.* [*noncount*]

fluor•ide /ˈflʊrayd, ˈflɔr-/ *n.* [*noncount*] a chemical compound that prevents tooth decay.

flur•ry /ˈflɜriy, ˈflʌriy/ *n., pl.* **-ries. 1.** [*count*] a brief shower of snow. **2.** [*count; usually singular*] sudden burst of activity.

flush¹ /flʌʃ/ *n.* [*count*] **1.** a reddening of the skin. —*v.* [*no obj*] to redden: [*no obj*]: *Her face flushed.* [~ + *obj*]: *Happiness flushed her face.* **3.** [~ (+ *out*) + *obj*] to flood or spray thoroughly with water: *to flush a pipe clean; flushed out the stables.*

flush² /flʌʃ/ *adj.* **1.** level with a surface: *The window frame is flush with the wall.* —*adv.* **2.** on the same level or plane: *The door shuts flush with the wall.*

flus•ter /'flʌstər/ *v.* to (cause to) become confused: [~ + *obj*]: *I was flustered by my unexpected visitor.* [*no obj*]: *He flusters too easily.*

flute /fluwt/ *n.* [*count*] a wind instrument with a high range, made of a tube with fingerholes or keys.

flut•ist /'fluwtɪst/ *n.* [*count*] a flute player.

flut•ter /'flʌtər/ *v.* [*no obj*] **1.** to (cause to) wave or flap about: *Banners fluttered in the breeze.* **2.** to flap the wings rapidly: *The pigeons fluttered away.* —*n.* **3.** [*count*] a fluttering movement: *a flutter of wings.* **4.** [*count; usually singular*] a state of nervous excitement: *in a flutter of anticipation.* —'flut•ter•y, *adj.*, -i•er, -i•est.

fly¹ /flay/ *v.*, **flew** /fluw/ or **flied**, **flown** /flown/, **fly•ing**, *n.*, *pl.* **flies.** —*v.* **1.** [*no obj*] to move through the air using wings. **2.** [*no obj*] to travel in an airplane. **3.** to (cause to) float in the air: [*no obj*]: *The king's banner flew over his tent.* [~ + *obj*]: *He tried to fly his kite.* **4.** [*no obj*] to pass swiftly: *How time flies!* —*n.* [*count*] **5.** a covered front opening on a pair of pants. —*Idiom.* **6. fly in the face** or **teeth of,** to defy: *to fly in the face of tradition.* **7. fly off the handle,** *Informal.* to become very angry. —'fly•ing, *adj.*

fly² /flay/ *n.* [*count*], *pl.* **flies.** a two-winged insect, such as the common housefly.

fly•er /'flayər/ *n.* FLIER.

'flying 'saucer, *n.* [*count*] a spacecraft believed to come from another planet.

FM, an abbreviation of: **1.** frequency modulation, a method of broadcasting a signal on a radio wave. **2.** a system of radio broadcasting using this method. Compare AM.

foal /fowl/ *n.* [*count*] a young horse.

foam /fowm/ *n.* [*noncount*] **1.** a mass of tiny bubbles. —*v.* [*no obj*] **2.** to form foam: *The boiling milk foamed.* —'foam•y, *adj.*, -i•er, -i•est.

'foam 'rubber, *n.* [*noncount*] a light, spongy rubber used for mattresses, cushions, etc.

'focal ,point, *n.* [*count*] the center of activity or attention: *The focal point of our discussion was the budget.*

fo•cus /'fowkəs/ *n.*, *pl.* **-cus•es**, **-ci** /-say, -kay/, *v.*, **-cused**, **-cus•ing** or (*esp. Brit.*) **-cussed**, **-cus•sing.** —*n.* **1.** [*count*] a central point, such as of attraction, attention, or activity: *His focus was on earning a living.* **2.** [*noncount*] the adjustment of a camera, telescope, etc., that is necessary to produce a clear image: *The picture is in focus.* —*v.* **3.** to (cause to) come to a focus or into focus: [~ + *obj*]: *to focus the lens of a camera.* [*no obj*]: *For a few moments my eyes wouldn't focus.* **4.** to concentrate: [~ + *obj*]: *I tried to focus my thoughts.* [*no obj*]: *I tried to focus on the project.*

fod•der /'fɒdər/ *n.* [*noncount*] coarse food for livestock.

foe /fow/ *n.* [*count*] an enemy; opponent: *a bitter foe.*

foe•tus /'fiytəs/ *n.*, *pl.* **-tus•es.** FETUS.

fog /fɒg, fɔg/ *n.*, *v.*, **fogged**, **fog•ging.** —*n.* [*noncount*] **1.** a cloudlike mass of water drops near the surface of the earth: *We drove through heavy fog.* —*v.* **2.** to (cause to) become covered with fog: [~ + *obj*]: *The steam fogged his glasses.* [*no obj*]: *The windshield has fogged.* —'fog•gy, *adj.*, -gi•er, -gi•est.

fog•horn /'fɒg,hɔrn, 'fɔg-/ *n.* [*count*] a deep, loud horn for sounding warnings to ships in foggy weather.

foil¹ /fɔyl/ *v.* [~ + *obj*] to prevent the success of: *Loyal troops foiled the revolt.*

foil² /fɔyl/ *n.* **1.** [*noncount*] metal in very thin sheets: *aluminum foil.* **2.** [*count*] a person or thing that contrasts with another.

foil³ /fɔyl/ *n.* [*count*] a thin sword used for fencing.

fol., an abbreviation of: **1.** followed. **2.** following.

fold¹ /fowld/ *v.* **1.** to bend the parts of something and lay them together: [~ + *obj*]: *I always have trouble folding (up) highway maps. Sometimes I can't fold them (up) neatly.* [*no obj*]: *The bed folds (up) to save space.* **2.** [~ + *obj*] to bring together and cross: *He folded his arms.* —*n.* [*count*] **3.** a part that is folded: *folds of cloth.* **4.** a line made by folding.

fold² /fowld/ *n.* [*count*] an enclosure for sheep.

-fold, a combining form meaning: having a specific number of parts (*a fourfold plan*); multiplied a specific number of times (*to increase tenfold*).

fold•er /'fowldər/ *n.* [*count*] a folded sheet of light cardboard for holding papers.

fo•li•age /'fowliyɪdʒ/ *n.* [*noncount*] leaves: *beautiful autumn foliage.*

folk /fowk/ *n.* **1.** Usually, **folks.** [*plural; used with a plural verb*] people in general: *Some folks simply won't take "no" for an answer.* **2.** Often, **folks.** [*plural; used with a plural verb*] people of a specified group: *Country folk are usually friendly.* **3. folks,** [*plural*] *Informal.* one's parents: *My folks won't let me go to the dance.* —*adj.* [*before a noun*] **4.** of or coming from the common people: *folk music.*

folk•lore /'fowk,lɔr/ *n.* [*noncount*] the traditional beliefs, legends, customs, etc., of a people. —'folk,lor•ic, *adj.* —'folk,lor•ist, *n.* [*count*]

fol•low /'fɒlow/ *v.* **1.** to go or come after: [~ + *obj*]: *Night follows day.* [*no obj*]: *Drive ahead and I'll follow.* **2.** [~ + *obj*] to act according to: *to follow orders; to follow his example.* **3.** [~ + *obj*] to move forward along: *Follow this path to the lake.* **4.** to understand (an argument, story, etc.): [~ + *obj*]: *I can't follow your argument.* [*no obj*]: *That's the explanation; can you follow?* **5.** [~ + *obj*] to result from: *Higher prices usually follow wage increases.* —'fol•low•er, *n.* [*count*]

fol•low•ing /'fɒlowɪŋ/ *n.* [*count*] **1.** a group of admirers: *That television show has a large following.* —*adj.* [*before a noun*] **2.** coming next in order or time: *the following day.*

'follow-,up, *n.* [*count*] **1.** an action that continues something previously done: *Come back to the doctor's office for a follow-up.* **2.** a news story providing more information about an earlier story: *She wanted to do a follow-up but her editor said not to.* —*adj.* [*before a noun*] **3.** serving to follow up: *a follow-up interview.*

fol•ly /'fɒliy/ *n.*, *pl.* **-lies. 1.** [*noncount*] foolishness: *to travel without money would be folly.* **2.** [*count*] a foolish action, idea, etc.

fond /fɒnd/ *adj.*, **-er**, **-est.** [*be* + ~ + *of*] having a liking for: *fond of animals.* —'fond•ly, *adv.* —'fond•ness, *n.* [*noncount*]

fon•dle /'fɒndl/ *v.* [~ + *obj*], **-dled**, **-dling. 1.** to touch lovingly. **2.** to touch or stroke sexually.

font¹ /fɒnt/ *n.* [*count*] **1.** a basin for the water used in baptism. **2.** someone or something providing useful information: *The book is a font of useful tips.*

F

font² /fɒnt/ n. [count] all of the letters and numbers of one style and size of printing type.

food /fuwd/ n. [noncount] **1.** anything that can be eaten. **2. food for thought,** something to think about carefully.

'food ,court, n. [count] a space, usually in a shopping mall, with a variety of fast-food stalls and a common eating area.

'food ,processor, n. [count] an electric appliance with a container and blades that can slice, chop, shred, or purée food.

'food ,stamp, n. [count] a coupon given by the government to needy persons and used to buy food. Also called **'food ,coupon.**

fool /fuwl/ n. [count] **1.** a silly or stupid person. —v. [~ + obj] **2.** to trick: They tried to fool us.

fool•har•dy /'fuwl,hɑrdiy/ adj., **-di•er, -di•est.** foolishly bold: Driving in the blizzard was a foolhardy thing to do.

fool•ish /'fuwlɪʃ/ adj. silly: a foolish prank. —'**fool•ish•ly,** adv. —'**fool•ish•ness,** n. [noncount]

fool•proof /'fuwl,pruwf/ adj. easy to understand: a foolproof VCR.

foot /fʊt/ n., pl. **feet** /fiyt/. **1.** [count] the bottom of the leg, below the ankle joint. **2.** [count] a unit of length equal to 12 inches or 30.48 centimeters. **3.** [count] the lowest part, or bottom, such as of a hill, ladder, or page: the foot of the mountain. **4.** [count; usually singular] the part of anything opposite the top or head: Her cat slept at the foot of her bed. —v. [~ + obj] **5.** to pay: Who will foot the bill? —adj. —Idiom. **6. drag one's feet,** to delay. **7. get off on the right (or wrong) foot,** to begin well (or badly): I got off on the wrong foot by arriving late. **8. on foot,** by walking: to travel on foot. **9. put one's foot down,** to be firm: She put her foot down and didn't allow the children to watch television.

foot•ball /'fʊt,bɔl/ n. **1.** [noncount] a game in which two teams of 11 players each defend goals at opposite ends of a field. **2.** [count] the inflated oval ball used in this game. **3.** [noncount] Chiefly Brit. SOCCER.

-footed, a combining form attached to nouns to form adjectives meaning "having a certain number or kind of feet": a four-footed animal.

foot•hill /'fʊt,hɪl/ n. [count] a low hill at the base of a mountain range.

foot•hold /'fʊt,howld/ n. [count] **1.** a place where a person may stand or walk securely. **2.** a secure position that is a firm basis for further progress.

foot•ing /'fʊtɪŋ/ n. **1.** [noncount] a firm placing of the feet: to regain one's footing. **2.** [count; usually singular] the basis on which anything is established: firm economic footing.

foot•light /'fʊt,layt/ n. [count] Usually, **footlights.** [plural] the lights at the front of a stage.

foot•note /'fʊt,nowt/ n. [count] a note at the bottom of a page.

foot•path /'fʊt,pæθ/ n. [count] a path for people going on foot.

foot•print /'fʊt,prɪnt/ n. [count] a mark left by a foot: They found footprints leading from the house.

foot•step /'fʊt,stɛp/ n. [count] the setting down of a foot, or the sound so produced: He heard footsteps behind him.

foot•wear /'fʊt,wɛər/ n. [noncount] shoes, slippers, or boots.

for /fɔr; unstressed fər/ prep. **1.** with the purpose of: She likes to run for exercise. **2.** intended to be used by: books for the school. **3.** in payment of; in return for; in exchange for: The tomatoes cost three for a dollar. **4.** in order to obtain: I had to work for decent wages. **5.** sensitive to: The art critic has an eye for beauty. **6.** with regard to: pressed for time; bad for your health. **7.** during a period of or at a time: waiting for days; We have dinner reservations for 6 o'clock. **8.** over a distance: to walk for a mile. **9.** in favor of: My kids are all for saving the environment. **10.** meaning: What is the Swahili word for "head"? **11.** in punishment of: payment for the crime. **12.** in honor of: a dinner for our guest. **13.** as compared to others of: tall for his age. **14.** because of: to shout for joy. —conj. **15.** since; because: I couldn't see them, for it was almost dark.

for•age /'fɔrɪdʒ, 'fɒr-/ v., **-aged, -ag•ing.** to wander or go in search of something: [no obj]: They were foraging through the countryside for food. [~ + obj]: They foraged the countryside for food. —'**for•ag•er,** n. [count]

for•bade /fər'bæd/ v. a pt. of FORBID.

for•bear /fɔr'bɛər/ v. [no obj], **-bore, -borne, -bear•ing.** to hold oneself back from: I wanted to argue but decided to forbear.

for•bear•ance /fɔr'bɛərəns/ n. [noncount] patience or self-control.

for•bid /fər'bɪd, fɔr-/ v. [~ + obj], **-bade** or **-bid, -bid•den** or **-bid, -bid•ding.** to command (a person) not to do something: I forbid you entry to this house.

for•bid•ding /fər'bɪdɪŋ, fɔr-/ adj. threatening: a forbidding frown. —for'**bid•ding•ly,** adv.

force /fɔrs/ n., v., **forced, forc•ing.** —n. **1.** [noncount] strength; power: the force of the waves. **2.** [noncount] power to influence: the force of an argument. **3.** Often, **forces.** [plural] the military or fighting strength, esp. of a nation: armed forces. **4.** [count] an organized group: sales force; police force. **5.** [noncount] a power producing a change in movement: the measurement of the amount of force used. —v. [~ + obj] **6.** to make (someone) do something: The police forced him to confess. **7.** to drive against resistance: to force one's way through a crowd. —'**force•ful,** adj.

force•ful /'fɔrsfəl, 'fowrs-/ adj. powerful; vigorous: a forceful blow; a forceful speech. —'**force•ful•ly,** adv.

for•ceps /'fɔrsəps, -sɛps/ n. [plural] an instrument for holding objects firmly, as in surgical operations.

for•ci•ble /'fɔrsəbəl/ adj. done by physical force: forcible entry. —'**for•ci•bly,** adv.

ford /fɔrd/ n. [count] **1.** a place where a river can be crossed by wading. —v. [~ + obj] **2.** to cross (a river, stream, etc.) at a ford: The wagons forded the stream.

fore /fɔr/ adj. [before a noun] **1.** front: the fore part of a boat. —Idiom. **2. to the fore,** into a noticeable place or position.

fore-, a prefix meaning: before (forewarn); front (forehead); preceding (forefather); superior (foreman).

fore•arm /'fɔr,ɑrm/ n. [count] the part of the arm between the elbow and the wrist.

fore•bear or **for•bear** /'fɔr,bɛər/ n. [count] ancestor.

fore•bod•ing /fɔr'bowdɪŋ/ n. a strong feeling of future misfortune or evil: [noncount]: It was a sense of foreboding. [count]: He felt forebodings all day.

fore•cast /'fɔr,kæst/ v., **-cast** or **-cast•ed, -cast•**

ing, *n.* —*v.* [~ + *obj*] **1.** to tell (a future condition or event): *to forecast a heavy snowfall.* —*n.* [*count*] **2.** a statement as to something in the future: *weather forecast; economic forecasts.* —'**fore,cast•er,** *n.* [*count*]

fore•close /fɔr'klowz/ *v.,* **-closed, -clos•ing.** (of a bank) to take back (property or holdings bought with a mortgage): [*no obj*]: *The bank foreclosed on them.* [~ + *obj*]: *to foreclose a mortgage.* —**fore•clo•sure** /fɔr'klowʒər/ *n.* [*noncount*] [*count*]

fore•fa•ther /'fɔr,faðər/ *n.* [*count*] an ancestor.

fore•fin•ger /'fɔr,fɪŋgər/ *n.* [*count*] the finger next to the thumb.

fore•front /'fɔr,frʌnt/ *n.* [*count; usually singular*] the most forward part or place: *the forefront of a literary movement.*

'**fore'gone con'clusion,** *n.* [*count*] a result that will occur under any circumstances: *It's a foregone conclusion that you won't be hired.*

fore•ground /'fɔr,grawnd/ *n.* [*count; usually singular*] **1.** the part of a scene nearest to the viewer. **2.** an important position.

fore•hand /'fɔr,hænd/ *adj.* **1.** (in tennis, squash, etc.) relating to a stroke made with the palm of the hand turned forward. —*n.* [*count*] **2.** (in tennis, squash, etc.) a forehand stroke.

fore•head /'fɔrɪd, -,hɛd, 'fɒr-/ *n.* [*count*] the part of the face above the eyebrows.

for•eign /'fɔrɪn, 'fɒr-/ *adj.* of, relating to, or coming from another country or nation.

for•eign•er /'fɔrənər, 'fɒr-/ *n.* [*count*] a person from a foreign country.

'**foreign ex'change,** *n.* [*noncount*] the system under which the money of one country is exchanged for money from another.

fore•leg /'fɔr,lɛg/ *n.* [*count*] either of the front legs of a four-legged animal.

fore•man /'fɔrmən/ or **-wom•an** /-,wʊmən/ or **-per•son** /-,pərsən/ *n.* [*count*], *pl.* **-men** or **-wom•en** or **-per•sons. 1.** a person in charge of a group of workers. **2.** the leader of a jury.

fore•most /'fɔr,mowst, -məst/ *adj., adv.* first in place, rank, or importance: *to bring in the foremost surgeons; to put one's studies foremost.*

fo•ren•sic /fə'rɛnsɪk, -zɪk/ *adj.* relating to or used in courts of law: *forensic medicine.* —**fo'ren•si•cal•ly,** *adv.*

fore•play /'fɔr,pley/ *n.* [*noncount*] sexual activity preceding intercourse.

fore•run•ner /'fɔr,rʌnər, fɔr'rʌnər/ *n.* [*count*] person or thing that prepares the way for something that comes or happens after.

fore•see /fɔr'siy/ *v.* [~ + *obj*], **-saw, -seen, -see•ing.** to sense or know in advance: *He foresaw no problems.* —**fore'see•a•ble,** *adj.*

fore•shad•ow /fɔr'ʃædow/ *v.* [~ + *obj*] to be a sign of something that will happen: *work that foreshadowed later inventions.*

fore•sight /'fɔr,sayt/ *n.* [*noncount*] **1.** knowledge of the future. **2.** planning for the future: *Through lack of foresight I had run out of money.*

fore•skin /'fɔr,skɪn/ *n.* [*noncount*] the skin covering the tip of the penis.

for•est /'fɔrɪst, 'fɒr-/ *n.* [*count*] a large area of land covered with trees and underbrush; woods. —'**for•est•ed,** *adj.*

for•est•ry /'fɔrəstriy, 'fɒr-/ *n.* [*noncount*] the science of planting and taking care of trees and forests. —'**for•est•er,** *n.* [*count*]

fore•taste /'fɔr,teyst/ *n.* [*count; usually singular*] a sample of something to come in the future.

fore•tell /fɔr'tɛl/ *v.* [~ + *obj*], **-told, -tell•ing.** to tell of beforehand; predict: *Who can foretell the future?*

fore•thought /'fɔr,θɔt/ *n.* [*noncount*] planning for the future: *an escape plan prepared with forethought.*

for•ev•er /fɔr'ɛvər, fər-/ *adv.* **1.** for all time; eternally: *She's gone forever.* —*n.* [*noncount*] **2.** a seemingly endless period of time: *Don't spend forever on the phone.*

fore•warn /fɔr'wɔrn/ *v.* [~ + *obj*] to warn in advance: *Thunder forewarned us of the coming storm.*

fore•word /'fɔr,wərd, -wərd/ *n.* [*count*] an introductory statement in a book.

for•feit /'fɔrfɪt/ *n.* [*count*] **1.** an act of forfeiting. —*v.* **2.** to (cause to) lose, because of a failure to do something: [~ + *obj*]: *They forfeited the game because they arrived late.* [*no obj*]: *She had to forfeit because she couldn't continue the game.* —**for•fei•ture** /'fɔrfɪtʃər/ *n.* [*noncount*]

for•gave /fər'geyv/ *v.* pt. of FORGIVE.

forge¹ /fɔrdʒ/ *v.,* **forged, forg•ing,** *n.* —*v.* [~ + *obj*] **1.** to form by heating and hammering: *The blacksmith forged the horseshoe.* **2.** to form or make: *The two sides managed to forge a treaty.* **3.** to make a forgery of: *He forged our signatures.* —*n.* [*count*] **4.** a furnace in which metal is heated before shaping. —'**forg•er,** *n.* [*count*]

forge² /fɔrdʒ/ *v.* [*no obj*], **forged, forg•ing.** to move ahead slowly and steadily: *We forged ahead and finished the work.*

for•ger•y /'fɔrdʒəriy/ *n., pl.* **-ger•ies. 1.** [*noncount*] the crime of falsely making or changing writing or a signature: *She was convicted of forgery.* **2.** [*count*] a piece of writing so made: *That signature is an obvious forgery.*

for•get /fər'gɛt/ *v.,* **-got** /-'gɒt/, **got•ten** /-'gɒtn/, or **-got, -get•ting. 1.** to fail to remember: [~ + *obj*]: *I have forgotten your name.* **2.** to stop thinking of: [~ + *obj*]: *I tried to forget the past.* [~ + *about* + *obj*]: *I tried to forget all about her.*

for•get•ful /fər'gɛtfəl/ *adj.* apt to forget: *He got forgetful in old age.* —**for'get•ful•ly,** *adv.* —**for'get•ful•ness,** *n.* [*noncount*]

for'get-me-,not, *n.* [*count*] a plant having small light-blue flowers.

for•give /fər'gɪv/ *v.,* **-gave** /-'geyv/, **-giv•en, -giv•ing. 1.** to stop blaming (someone) for (an offense): [~ + *obj*]: *to forgive a sin.* [*no obj*]: *Forgive and go forward.* **2.** [~ + *obj*] to cancel (a debt, obligation, etc.): *to forgive the interest owed on a loan.* —**for'give•ness,** *n.* [*noncount*] —**for'giv•ing,** *adj.*

for•go or **fore•go** /fɔr'gow/ *v.* [~ + *obj*], **-went, -gone, -go•ing.** to give up: *I agreed to forgo a raise for this year for a larger one next year.*

fork /fɔrk/ *n.* [*count*] **1.** an instrument having two or more points for holding, lifting, etc.: *knives, forks, and spoons.* **2.** the point at which a thing, such as a river or a road, divides into two parts. **3.** either of the parts into which a thing divides: *When the road splits, take the left fork.* —*v.* [*no obj*] **4.** to divide into two parts: *The road forks up ahead.* —**forked,** *adj.* —'**fork•ful** /-fʊl/, *n.* [*count*], *pl.* **-fuls.**

for•lorn /fɔr'lɔrn/ *adj.* sad and lonely. —**for'lorn•ly,** *adv.*

form /fɔrm/ *n.* [*count*] **1.** the shape or appearance of a thing or person: *He could make out a dim form in the distance.* **2.** a particular condi-

F

tion in which something appears: *Ice is water in another form.* **3.** a printed paper with blank spaces to be filled in: *a tax form.* **4.** a word with a particular ending or other change: *The word goes is a form of go.* —*v.* **5.** [~ + *obj*] to make; put together: *Form the clay into a bowl.* **6.** [*no obj*] to take or assume form: *Ice began to form on the window.* **7.** [~ + *obj*] to give form or shape to: *Form the dough into squares.* **8.** [~ + *obj*] to develop; establish: *He formed the habit of looking over the tops of his glasses.*

for•mal /ˈfɔrməl/ *adj.* **1.** [*before a noun*] being in accordance with accepted customs: *He offered his sword as a formal act of surrender.* **2.** marked by form or ceremony: *The reception was a formal occasion.* **3.** requiring dress suitable for formal social events: *a formal dance.* **4.** of or relating to language used in official situations: *formal English.* —**for•mal•i•ty** /fɔrˈmælɪti/ *n.* [*noncount*] [*count*], *pl.* **-ties.** —**ˈfor•mal•ly,** *adv.*

for•mat /ˈfɔrmæt/ *n.* [*count*] the organization, plan, or style of something, such as the general appearance of a book, magazine, or newspaper.

for•ma•tion /fɔrˈmeyʃən/ *n.* **1.** [*noncount*] the act or process of forming or the state of being formed: *the formation of ice.* **2.** [*count*] [*noncount*] the arrangement of people, ships, etc. **3.** [*count*] a thing that is formed: *a cloud formation.* **4.** [*noncount*] development; creation: *The Pilgrims' goal was the formation of a colony in the New World.*

form•a•tive /ˈfɔrmətɪv/ *adj.* [*before a noun*] **1.** giving form or shape: *a formative process in manufacturing.* **2.** relating to growth or development: *a child's formative years.*

for•mer /ˈfɔrmər/ *adj.* [*before a noun*] **1.** preceding in time; earlier: *We had met on a former occasion.* **2.** being the first mentioned of two (distinguished from *latter*): *The former suggestion was better than the latter.* —*n.* [*noncount*; the + ~] **3.** the one first mentioned: *We have two dogs, a collie and a beagle; the former is the older.* —**ˈfor•mer•ly,** *adv.*

for•mi•da•ble /ˈfɔrmɪdəbəl/ *adj.* **1.** causing fear or awe: *a formidable opponent.* **2.** very difficult: *a formidable problem.* —**ˈfor•mi•da•bly,** *adv.*

for•mu•la /ˈfɔrmyələ/ *n.,* *pl.* **-las, -lae** /-ˌliy/. **1.** [*count*] a set group of words. **2.** [*count*] a fixed method: *She produced her popular novels by a formula.* **3.** [*count*] a mathematical rule, frequently expressed in symbols: $E = mc^2$ *is a formula expressing the relationship between matter and energy.* **4.** [*count*] a recipe or prescription: *The formula for making that new plastic is a closely kept secret.* **5.** [*noncount*] a special mixture of milk or milk substitute for feeding a baby. —**for•mu•la•ic** /ˌfɔrmyəˈleyɪk/, *adj.*

for•mu•late /ˈfɔrmyəˌleyt/ *v.* [~ + *obj*], **-lat•ed, -lat•ing.** **1.** to express as a formula. **2.** to develop: *They managed to formulate a peace plan acceptable to both sides.* —**for•mu•la•tion** /ˌfɔrmyæˈleyʃən/, *n.* [*noncount*] [*count*] —**ˈfor•mu,la•tor,** *n.* [*count*]

for•sake /fɔrˈseyk/ *v.* [~ + *obj*], **-sook, -sak•en, -sak•ing.** **1.** to quit or leave entirely; abandon: *to forsake one's family.* **2.** to give up: *I persuaded him to forsake smoking.*

for•syth•i•a /fɔrˈsɪθiyə, fər-/ *n.* [*count*], *pl.* **-as.** a shrub having yellow flowers that blossom in early spring.

fort /fɔrt/ *n.* [*count*] a location occupied by troops and equipped for defense.

for•te /ˈfɔrtey/ *Music.* —*adj.* **1.** loud (opposed to *piano*). —*adv.* **2.** loudly.

forth /fɔrθ/ *adv.* **1.** onward or outward; forward or away: *She rode forth to do battle.* **2.** out; into view: *Decency shines forth in his every action.*

for•ti•fy /ˈfɔrtəˌfay/ *v.* [~ + *obj*], **-fied, -fy•ing.** **1.** to increase the defenses of: *They fortified the town.* **2.** to make stronger: *I had fortified myself with a good breakfast.* —**for•ti•fi•ca•tion** /ˌfɔrtəfɪˈkeyʃən/ *n.* [*noncount*] [*count*]

for•tis•si•mo /fɔrˈtɪsəˌmow/ *Music.* —*adj.* **1.** very loud. —*adv.* **2.** very loudly.

for•ti•tude /ˈfɔrtɪˌtuwd, -ˌtyuwd/ *n.* [*noncount*] mental and emotional strength: *It took fortitude to live on the frontier.*

fort•night /ˈfɔrtˌnayt/ *n.* [*count*] a period of two weeks. —**ˈfortˌnight•ly,** *adj., adv.*

for•tress /ˈfɔrtrɪs/ *n.* [*count*] fort or stronghold.

for•tu•nate /ˈfɔrtʃənɪt/ *adj.* lucky: *You were very fortunate to escape from that explosion.* —**ˈfor•tu•nate•ly,** *adv.*

for•tune /ˈfɔrtʃən/ *n.* **1.** [*count*] wealth; riches: *She inherited a fortune.* **2.** [*noncount*] chance; luck: *They had the bad fortune to go bankrupt.* **3.** [*count*] fate: *She told his fortune by reading his palm.*

for•ty /ˈfɔrtiy/ *n., pl.* **-ties,** *adj.* —*n.* [*count*] **1.** a number, ten times four, written as 40. —*adj.* [*before a noun*] **2.** amounting to 40 in number. —**ˈfor•ti•eth,** *adj., n.* [*count*]

fo•rum /ˈfɔrəm/ *n.* [*count*] a public place for discussion: *The magazine is a forum for various political views.*

for•ward /ˈfɔrwərd/ *adv.* Also, **forwards. 1.** toward what is in front or in the future: *from this day forward.* **2.** into view: *She brought forward a good suggestion.* —*adj.* **3.** [*before a noun*] directed toward the front or the future: *a forward motion; forward planning.* **4.** too bold: *a rude, forward child.* —*n.* [*count*] **5.** a player stationed in front of others on a team, as in basketball. —*v.* [~ + *obj*] **6.** to send to a new address: *The post office forwarded our letters.* **7.** to promote: *forwarding one's career.* **8.** to cause to advance: *to forward a tape on a VCR.*

for•went /fɔrˈwɛnt/ *v.* pt. of FORGO.

fos•sil /ˈfɒsəl/ *n.* [*count*] the preserved remains, or an imprint, of an organism from a former age. —**ˈfos•silˌize,** *v.* [~ + *obj*] [*no obj*]

fos•ter /ˈfɒstər, ˈfɔstər/ *v.* [~ + *obj*] **1.** to promote the growth of: *to foster new ideas.* **2.** to bring up: *to foster an abandoned child.* —*adj.* [*before a noun*] **3.** providing or receiving parental care without any relationship by blood or law: *a foster home; foster children.*

fought /fɔt/ *v.* pt. and pp. of FIGHT.

foul /fawl/ *adj.* **1.** offensive; disgusting: *a foul smell; a foul crime.* **2.** stormy; inclement: *foul weather.* **3.** irritable: *in a foul temper.* **4.** against the rules, as in a game. —*adv.* **5.** in a foul manner. —*n.* [*count*] **6.** an act that is against the rules of a sport or game: *He was disqualified for too many fouls.* —*v.* **7.** [~ + *obj*] to make dirty: *a river fouled with pollution.* **8.** [*no obj*] to commit a foul in a sport or game. —**ˈfoul•ly,** *adv.* —**ˈfoul•ness,** *n.* [*noncount*]

foul-mouthed /ˈfawlˈmawðd, -ˈmawθt/ *adj.* using obscene or profane language.

ˈfoul ˈplay, *n.* [*noncount*] a violent crime, esp. murder.

found¹ /fawnd/ *v.* pt. and pp. of FIND.

found² /fawnd/ *v.* [~ + *obj*] to establish on a

firm or long-lasting basis: *She went on to found a new company.*

foun•da•tion /fawn'deyʃən/ *n.* **1.** the basis of anything: [*noncount*]: *The criminal charges were without foundation.* [*count*]: *We need a foundation of trust.* **2.** [*count*] the base on which a structure rests: *They poured the concrete for the building foundation.* **3.** [*noncount*] the act of founding: *the events marking the foundation of the republic.* **4.** [*count*] an organization that gives out money, as to aid research or the arts.

foun•der¹ /'fawndər/ *v.* [*no obj*] **1.** to fill with water and sink: *The ship foundered during the typhoon.* **2.** to fail: *The project foundered when its supporters quit.*

foun•der² /'fawndər/ *n.* [*count*] a person who founds: *the founders of the republic.*

found•ling /'fawndlɪŋ/ *n.* [*count*] an infant who is found abandoned.

found•ry /'fawndriy/ *n.* [*count*], *pl.* **-ries.** a place where metal is melted and shaped.

fount /fawnt/ *n.* [*count*] a spring of water; fountain.

foun•tain /'fawntn/ *n.* [*count*] **1.** the source or origin of anything: *a fountain of wisdom.* **2.** an artificial stream of water that spouts from an opening.

'fountain ,pen, *n.* [*count*] a pen that is refill able.

four /fɔr/ *n.* [*count*] **1.** a number, three plus one, written as 4. —*adj.* [*before a noun*] **2.** amounting to four in number. —*Idiom.* **3. on all fours,** on one's hands and knees.

four•score /'fɔr'skɔr/ *adj.* four times twenty; eighty.

four•teen /'fɔr'tiyn/ *n.* [*count*] **1.** a number, ten plus four, written as 14. —*adj.* [*before a noun*] **2.** amounting to 14 in number. —**'four'teenth,** *adj., n.* [*count*]

fourth /fɔrθ/ *adj.* **1.** next after the third. **2.** being one of four equal parts. —*n.* [*count*] **3.** a fourth part, esp. of one (¼); quarter. **4.** the fourth member of a series. —*adv.* **5.** in the fourth place. —**'fourth•ly,** *adv.*

'Fourth of Ju'ly, *n.* [*the* + ~] INDEPENDENCE DAY.

'four-,wheel also **'four-'wheeled,** *adj.* [*before a noun*] **1.** having four wheels. **2.** powered by four wheels: *four-wheel drive.*

fowl /fawl/ *n.* [*count*], *pl.* **fowls,** (*esp. when thought of as a group*) **fowl.** **1.** a domestic hen or rooster; chicken. **2.** any of several other similar birds, such as turkeys or pheasants.

fox /fɒks/ *n.* [*count*], *pl.* **fox•es,** (*esp. when thought of as a group*) **fox.** a small member of the dog family having a sharply pointed nose and face and a long bushy tail.

foy•er /'fɔyər, 'fɔyey/ *n.* [*count*] **1.** the lobby of a theater, hotel, or apartment house. **2.** an entrance hall in a house or apartment.

frac•tion /'frækʃən/ *n.* [*count*] **1.** a number usually expressed in the form *a/b.* **2.** a very small part: *a fraction of the original cost.* —'**frac•tion•al,** *adj.*

frac•ture /'fræktʃər/ *n., v.,* **-tured, -tur•ing.** —*n.* [*count*] **1.** the breaking of a bone: *a fracture of the wrist.* **2.** a break; split: *a fracture in relations between the two countries.* —*v.* **3.** to (cause to) become broken; to (cause to) suffer a fracture in: [*no obj*]: *The arm fractured when she fell.* [~ + *obj*]: *The bullet fractured his arm.*

frag•ile /'frædʒəl/ *adj.* **1.** easily broken or damaged: *a fragile vase.* **2.** delicate in appearance:

fragile beauty. —**fra•gil•i•ty** /frə'dʒɪlɪtiy/, *n.* [*noncount*]

frag•ment /*n.*'frægmənt; *v.* 'frægment, fræg'ment/ *n.* [*count*] **1.** a part broken off: *fragments of shattered glass.* —*v.* **2.** to (cause to) break into pieces: [*no obj*]: *The parchment is likely to fragment if you touch it.* [~ + *obj*]: *Outside influences fragmented that culture.* —**frag•men•tar•y** /'frægmən,teriy/ *adj.* —,**frag•men'ta•tion,** *n.* [*noncount*]

frag•men•tar•y /'frægmən,teriy/ *adj.* incomplete: *Only fragmentary evidence remained.*

fra•grance /'freygrəns/ *n.* [*count*] **1.** a pleasing scent: *the fragrance of roses.* **2.** a perfume.

fra•grant /'freygrənt/ *adj.* having a pleasing scent: *a fragrant rose.* —'**fra•grant•ly,** *adv.*

frail /freyl/ *adj.,* **-er, -est.** easily broken; fragile: *The climber dangled by one frail rope.* —**frail•ty** /'freyltiy, 'freyəl-/ *n.* [*noncount*] [*count*]

frame /freym/ *n., v.,* **framed, fram•ing.** —*n.* [*count*] **1.** a border for enclosing a picture, mirror, etc. **2.** a rigid structure formed of joined pieces and used as a major support: *The frame of the car was rusting.* **3.** a body, esp. with reference to its size or build: *a woman with a delicate frame.* —*v.* [~ + *obj*] **4.** to construct; shape; develop: *to frame a new constitution.* **5.** to put into a frame: *to frame the portrait.* —'**fram•er,** *n.* [*count*]

frame•work /'freym,wɜrk/ *n.* [*count*] a structure designed to support or enclose something.

frank¹ /fræŋk/ *adj.,* **-er, -est.** direct; honest: *frank criticism.* —'**frank•ly,** *adv.:* *They spoke freely and frankly.* —'**frank•ness,** *n.* [*noncount*]

frank² /fræŋk/ *n.* [*count*] a frankfurter.

frank•furt•er or **frank•fort•er** /'fræŋkfərtər/ *n.* [*count*] a cooked and smoked sausage.

fran•tic /'fræntɪk/ *adj.* **1.** desperate or wild with emotion: *a mother frantic with worry.* **2.** marked by desperate urgency: *a frantic effort to rescue the mountain climbers.* —'**fran•ti•cal•ly,** *adv.*

fra•ter•nal /frə'tɜrnl/ *adj.* of or befitting a brother; brotherly. —**fra'ter•nal•ly,** *adv.*

fra•ter•ni•ty /frə'tɜrnɪtiy/ *n.* [*count*], *pl.* **-ties.** a social organization of male college students.

frat•er•nize /'frætər,nayz/ *v.* [*no obj*], **-nized, -niz•ing.** to associate in a friendly way. —**frat•er•ni•za•tion** /,frætərnə'zeyʃən/, *n.* [*noncount*]

frat•ri•cide /'frætrɪ,sayd, 'frey-/ *n.* [*noncount*] the act of killing one's brother. —,**frat•ri'cid•al,** *adj.*

fraud /frɔd/ *n.* [*noncount*] criminal trickery carried out for profit: *mail fraud.* —**fraud•u•lent** /'frɔdʒələnt/ *adj.*

fray /frey/ *v.* to (cause to) become worn into loose threads at the edge or end: [*no obj*]: *Sweaters often fray at the elbows.* [~ + *obj*]: *All that traffic frayed the carpet.*

freak /friyk/ *n.* [*count*] **1.** an unusual or strange person, animal, or thing. —*adj.* [*before a noun*] **2.** unusual; odd: *a freak storm.* —'**freak•ish,** '**freak•y,** *adj.,* **-i•er, -i•est.**

freck•le /'frɛkəl/ *n., v.,* **-led, -ling.** —*n.* [*count*] **1.** a small brownish spot on the skin. —*v.* **2.** to (cause to) be covered with freckles: [*no obj*]: *She freckles easily.* [~ + *obj*]: *The sun freckled his skin.* —'**freck•led,** *adj.*

free /friy/ *adj.,* **fre•er, fre•est,** *adv., v.,* **freed, free•ing.** —*adj.* **1.** enjoying personal rights or liberty: *free from bondage.* **2.** having civil and political liberties: *the free nations of the world.* **3.** not blocked: *a free flow of water.* **4.** not busy: *I have free time after class.* **5.** not in use: *The room is free now.* **6.** without cost: *free parking.* —*adv.*

F

7. in a free manner; freely. **8.** loose: *The button came free and fell off.* —*v.* [~ + *obj*] **9.** to set at liberty: *The enemy freed the hostages.* **10.** to release: *They freed the trapped victims from the wreckage.* —*Idiom.* **11. free and clear,** without any debt or restriction: *He paid off the mortgage free and clear.* **12. with a free hand,** generously: *He donated money with a free hand.*

free•dom /'friydəm/ *n.* **1.** the state of being free or at liberty: [*noncount*]: *freedom of the press.* [*count*]: *They believe in the same freedoms as we do.* **2.** [*noncount*] political or national independence: *fighting for freedom.* **3.** [*count*] a liberty taken: *You're taking some freedoms with the truth* (= *You're not really telling the truth*).

'**free 'enterprise,** *n.* [*noncount*] the doctrine that a capitalist economy can regulate itself without governmental regulation.

'**free 'hand,** *n.* [*singular*] unrestricted freedom or authority: *a free hand to cut the budget.*

free•hand /'friy,hænd/ *adj.* **1.** drawn by hand without instruments: *a freehand map.* —*adv.* **2.** in a freehand manner: *to draw freehand.*

free•lance or **free-lance** /'friy,læns/ *n.*, *v.*, **-lanced, -lanc•ing,** *adj.*, *adv.* —*n.* **1.** Also, '**free,lanc•er.** a person who sells work or services to employers as needed. —*v.* [*no obj*] **2.** to act or work as a freelance. —*adj.* **3.** of or relating to a freelance or to freelancing: *freelance writing.* —*adv.* **4.** as a freelance: *She works freelance.*

free•ly /'friyliy/ *adv.* without limiting or restraining: *He spent freely on the project.*

free•stand•ing /'friy'stændɪŋ/ *adj.* standing alone.

'**free 'trade,** *n.* [*noncount*] international trade that is free from protective duties and quotas.

free•way /'friy,wey/ *n.* [*count*] an express highway with no intersections.

free•wheel•ing /'friy'hwiylɪŋ, -'wiy-/ *adj.* [*before a noun*] not held back by rules: *a freewheeling lifestyle.*

'**free 'will,** *n.* [*noncount*] free and independent choice.

free•will /'friy'wɪl/ *adj.* voluntary: *a freewill choice.*

freeze /friyz/ *v.,* **froze** /frowz/, **fro•zen** /'frowzən/, **freez•ing,** *n.* —*v.* **1.** to (cause to) become hardened into ice: [*no obj*]: *Salt water freezes at a lower temperature than fresh water.* [~ + *obj*]: *The cold will freeze the pond.* **2.** to (cause to) feel very cold: [*no obj*]: *We froze until the heat came on.* [~ + *obj*]: *Those cold winter nights froze us.* **3.** [*no obj*] to become unable to move or speak, as through fear: *When he got up in front of the huge audience, he froze.* **4.** to (cause to) become blocked by the formation of ice: [*no obj*]: *The water pipes froze.* [~ + *obj*]: *The cold froze the pipes.* **5.** [~ + *obj*] to hold wages, prices, etc. at a certain level. **6. freeze over,** to become coated with ice: *The highway froze over.* —*n.* [*count; usually singular*] **7.** an act or instance of freezing. **8.** a period of very cold weather: *A freeze set in.*

'**freeze-'dry,** *v.* [~ + *obj*], **-dried, -dry•ing.** to preserve by freezing and then drying in a vacuum: *to freeze-dry coffee.*

freez•er /'friyzər/ *n.* [*count*] a refrigerator held at or below 32°F (0°C).

'**freezing ,point,** *n.* [*count*] the temperature at which a liquid freezes: *The freezing point of water is 32°F, or 0°C.*

freight /freyt/ *n.* [*noncount*] **1.** goods transported for pay: *huge trucks carrying many tons of*

freight. **2.** the charges for such transportation: *having to pay the freight.*

freight•er /'freytər/ *n.* [*count*] a large ship used for carrying goods.

French /frɛntʃ/ *adj.* **1.** of or relating to France. **2.** of or relating to the language spoken in France. —*n.* **3.** [*plural; the* + ~; *used with a plural verb*] the people born or living in France. **4.** [*noncount*] the language spoken in France.

'**French 'fry,** *n.* [*count*], *pl.* '**French 'fries.** a strip of potato that has been deep-fried. Also called '**French-,fried po'tato.**

'**French 'horn,** *n.* [*count*] a brass wind instrument with a long coiled tube and an end that flares out.

'**French 'toast,** *n.* [*noncount*] bread dipped in a batter of egg and milk and sautéed until brown.

fren•zy /'frɛnziy/ *n.* [*count*], *pl.* **-zies.** wild or violent excitement: *In a sudden frenzy he hurled the chair through the window.* —'**fren•zied,** *adj.*

fre•quen•cy /'friykwənsiy/ *n.*, *pl.* **-cies.** **1.** [*noncount*] the state or fact of being frequent. **2.** [*noncount*] rate at which something happens: *Similar crimes had decreased in frequency.* **3.** [*count*] the number of cycles per second of an electromagnetic wave, such as a radio or sound wave: [*noncount*]: *They played back the message at high frequency.* [*count*]: *sounds at high frequencies that can't be heard by humans.*

fre•quent /*adj.*'friykwənt; *v.* frɪ'kwɛnt, 'friykwənt/ *adj.* **1.** happening often: *She made frequent trips to Japan.* **2.** regular: *He was a frequent guest at our house.* —*v.* [~ + *obj*] **3.** to visit often: *They frequented their neighborhood restaurant.* —'**fre•quent•ly,** *adv.*: *They go to the opera frequently.*

fres•co /'frɛskow/ *n.* [*count*], *pl.* **-coes, -cos.** a picture painted on a moist plaster surface.

fresh /frɛʃ/ *adj.,* **-er, -est,** *adv.* —*adj.* **1.** newly made: *fresh footprints in the snow.* **2.** not previously known, met with, etc.; new: *to uncover fresh evidence.* **3.** [*often: before a noun*] (of water) not salty. **4.** not stale or spoiled: *fresh bread; fresh milk.* **5.** recently harvested: *fresh vegetables.* **6.** not tired: *I felt fresh after that long walk.* **7.** looking healthy: *a fresh complexion.* **8.** pure or cool, such as air: *to breathe fresh air.* **9.** *Informal.* too bold: *Don't get fresh with my sister!* —'**fresh•ly,** *adv.* —'**fresh•ness,** *n.* [*noncount*]

fresh•en /'frɛʃən/ *v.* [*no obj*] [~ + *obj*] to (cause to) become or grow fresh or refreshed.

fresh•man /'frɛʃmən/ *n.* [*count*], *pl.* **-men.** **1.** a student in the first year at a university, college, or high school. **2.** a beginner: *a freshman in politics.*

fresh•wa•ter or **fresh-wa•ter** /'frɛʃ,wɔtər, -,wɒtər/ *adj.* [*before a noun*] of or living in water that is not salty: *freshwater fish.*

fret /frɛt/ *v.* [*no obj*], **fret•ted, fret•ting.** to feel worry or annoyance: *Don't fret; things will get better.*

Fri., an abbreviation of: Friday.

fric•tion /'frɪkʃən/ *n.* [*noncount*] **1.** the rubbing of one surface against another: *friction on a rope.* **2.** disagreement; conflict: *friction between nations.*

Fri•day /'fraydey, -diy/ *n.* [*count*] the sixth day of the week, following Thursday.

fridge /frɪdʒ/ *n.* [*count*] a refrigerator.

friend /frɛnd/ *n.* [*count*] **1.** a person whom one knows and likes: *She was my best friend.* **2.** a person who gives help: *He is a friend of the poor.* —'**friend•less,** *adj.*

friend•ly /'frɛndliy/ *adj.*, **-li•er, -li•est. 1.** characteristic of a friend: *a friendly greeting.* **2.** kind; helpful: *a friendly passerby.* **3.** not hostile: *a friendly game of softball.* —**'friend•li•ness,** *n.* [*noncount*]

friend•ship /'frɛndʃɪp/ *n.* **1.** [*noncount*] the state of being friends. **2.** [*count*] a friendly relationship: *friendships with people from her own culture.*

frieze /friyz/ *n.* [*count*] a decorative band around the top of a wall.

fright /frayt/ *n.* sudden fear: [*noncount*]: *a feeling of fright.* [*count; usually singular*]: *You gave me quite a fright.*

fright•en /'fraytn̩/ *v.* [~ + *obj*] to (cause to) become afraid: *Your story frightened me.* —**'fright•en•ing,** *adj.*

frightened *adj.* afraid: *The frightened child ran to her mother.*

fright•ful /'fraytfəl/ *adj.* **1.** causing fright: *a frightful explosion.* **2.** horrible or shocking: *The storm did frightful damage.* —**'fright•ful•ly,** *adv.*

frig•id /'frɪdʒɪd/ *adj.* very cold in temperature: *a frigid climate.*

frill /frɪl/ *n.* [*count*] **1.** a trimming, such as a strip of cloth or lace, gathered at one edge; ruffle. **2.** something desirable but not necessary: *a car with frills like a CD player.* —**'frill•y,** *adj.*, **-i•er, -i•est.**

fringe /frɪndʒ/ *n.* [*count*] **1.** a decorative border of short threads: *fringe at the bottom edge of the curtain.* **2.** something resembling a fringe: *a fringe of grass.* **3.** the outer edge: *society's fringes.*

'fringe ,benefit, *n.* [*count*] a benefit, such as health insurance or a pension, received by an employee in addition to regular pay.

frisk /frɪsk/ *v.* **1.** [*no obj*] to dance, leap, or skip: *The children frisked about.* **2.** [~ + *obj*] to search (a person) for concealed weapons, illegal possessions, etc.

frisk•y /'frɪskiy/ *adj.*, **-i•er, -i•est.** lively; playful: *a frisky kitten.* —**frisk•i•ly** /'frɪskəliy/, *adv.* —**'frisk•i•ness,** *n.* [*noncount*]

frit•ter¹ /'frɪtɚ/ *v.* **fritter away,** to (cause to) go to waste little by little: *to fritter away his money; to fritter money away.*

frit•ter² /'frɪtɚ/ *n.* [*count*] a small cake of fried batter containing corn, fruit, etc.

friv•o•lous /'frɪvələs/ *adj.* not serious: *frivolous conduct.* —**'friv•o•lous•ly,** *adv.*

frizz /frɪz/ *v.* to (cause to) form into small crisp curls: [*no obj*]: *Her hair frizzed when it rained.* [~ + *obj*]: *The hairdresser frizzed her hair.* —**'frizz•y,** *adj.*, **-i•er, -i•est:** *frizzy hair.*

fro /frow/ *adv.* from; back: *to and fro.*

frog /frɒg, frɔg/ *n.* [*count*] a small tailless animal that lives in water and on land and has long hind legs for jumping.

frog•man /'frɒg,mæn, -mən, 'frɔg-/ *n.* [*count*], *pl.* **-men.** a swimmer who is equipped with air tanks, wet suit, diving mask, etc., for underwater activity.

frol•ic /'frɒlɪk/ *n.*, *v.*, **-icked, -ick•ing.** —*n.* [*count*] **1.** fun; playful behavior or action: *a frolic in the park.* —*v.* [*no obj*] **2.** to play in a frisky, light-spirited manner: *The family was frolicking in the snow.* —**'frol•ic•some,** *adj.*

from /frʌm, frɒm; *unstressed* frəm/ *prep.* **1.** (used to show a starting point in space or time): *a train running west from Chicago; from six o'clock to ten o'clock.* **2.** (used to show the lower point in expressing limits or amounts): *The num-* ber will be increased from 25 to 30. **3.** (used to express the idea of being separated): *The house is two miles from the shore.* **4.** (used to show the source): *My wife comes from the Midwest.* **5.** (used to show cause or reason): *Death was from starvation.*

front /frʌnt/ *n.* [*count*] **1.** [*the* + ~] the forward part of anything: *the front of the airplane.* **2.** an area of activity: *news from the business front.* **3.** a person or thing that serves as a disguise for an illegal activity: *The store was a front for gamblers.* **4.** a line between two different air masses: *a cold front coming from the north.* —*adj.* [*before a noun*] **5.** of or relating to the front; situated in or at the front: *front seats.* —*v.* [~ + *obj*] **6.** to have the front toward; face: *Our house fronts the lake.* —**Idiom. 7. in front,** in a forward place or position: *My family was sitting in front, but I stayed in back.* **8. in front of, a.** ahead of: *They were sitting in front of me.* **b.** outside the entrance of: *We met in front of the hotel.* **c.** in the presence of: *Don't talk like that in front of the children.* **9. out front, a.** outside the entrance: *Let's meet out front.* **b.** ahead of others: *The runner from Kenya was out front for most of the race.*

front•age /'frʌntɪdʒ/ *n.* [*count*] the space between a building and the street, a body of water, etc.

fron•tier /frʌn'tɪɚr/ *n.* [*count*] **1.** the border between two countries: *the frontier crossing.* **2.** the furthest regions of a country. **3.** Often, **frontiers.** the limit of knowledge or the most advanced achievement: *the frontier(s) of medical research.*

'front-'runner or **'front'runner,** *n.* [*count*] a person who leads in any competition: *That candidate quickly established himself as the front-runner.*

frost /frɔst, frɒst/ *n.* **1.** a state of coldness that is enough to cause the freezing of water: [*noncount*]: *We're expecting frost tonight over most of the region.* [*count*]: *A slight frost will kill this plant.* **2.** [*noncount*] a covering of tiny ice crystals. —*v.* **3.** to (cause to) become covered with frost: [*no obj*]: *The high school track frosted over last night.* [~ + *obj*]: *The cold weather frosted up the track last night.* **4.** [~ + *obj*] to give a frostlike surface to (glass, metal, etc.).

frost•bite /'frɔst,bayt, 'frɒst-/ *n.*, *v.*, **-bit, -bit•ten, -bit•ing.** —*n.* [*noncount*] **1.** injury to the body caused by extreme cold. —*v.* [~ + *obj*] **2.** to injure by frost or extreme cold: *My toes were frostbitten from skating too long.*

frost•ed /'frɔstɪd, 'frɒstɪd/ *adj.* **1.** covered with frost. **2.** (of glass, metal, etc.) having a frostlike appearance.

frost•ing /'frɔstɪŋ, 'frɒstɪŋ/ *n.* [*noncount*] a sweet, creamy mixture for coating or filling cakes; icing.

frost•y /'frɔstiy, 'frɒstiy/ *adj.*, **-i•er, -i•est. 1.** very cold; covered with frost: *frosty weather.* **2.** unfriendly: *She gave a frosty reply to my request.* —**frost•i•ly** /'frɔstəliy, 'frɒsti-/, *adv.*

froth /frɔθ, frɒθ/ *n.* [*noncount*] a mass of small bubbles, such as on a liquid that has been shaken hard.

frown /frawn/ *v.* [*no obj*] **1.** to wrinkle the forehead, such as when one is displeased or in deep thought: *She frowned when I gave the wrong answer.* **2. frown on** or **upon,** to look on with disapproval: *The boss frowned on my idea to buy new computers.* —*n.* [*count*] **3.** a disapproving look or expression on the face; scowl.

froze /frowz/ *v.* pt. of FREEZE.

fruits and vegetables

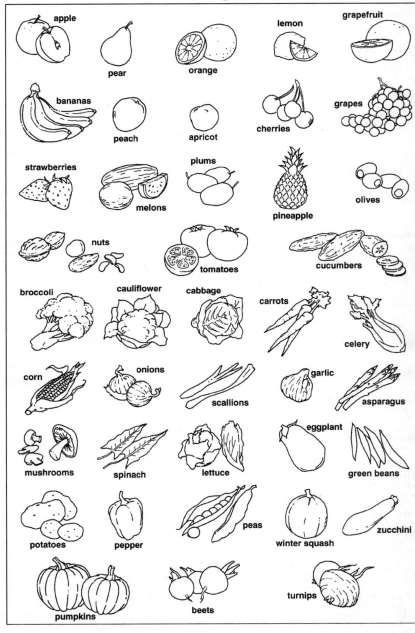

fro•zen /'frowzən/ *v.* **1.** pp. of FREEZE. —*adj.* **2.** turned into ice. **3.** very cold: *Let me in; I'm frozen.* **4.** not permitted to be changed; fixed: *frozen rents.*

fru•gal /'fruwgəl/ *adj.* **1.** economical; not wasteful: *a frugal manager.* **2.** requiring little expense or few resources: *a frugal meal.* —**fru•gal•i•ty** /fruw'gælɪtiy/, *n.* [*noncount*] —'**fru•gal•ly**, *adv.*

fruit /fruwt/ *n., pl.* **fruits,** (*esp. when thought of as a group*) **fruit.** **1.** the part of a plant that is used as food: [*noncount*]: *Fruit provides vitamins.* [*count*]: *Apples and oranges are fruits.* **2.** [*count*] a product or result: *the fruits of one's labors.* —*Idiom.* **3. bear fruit,** to produce a result or profit: *The effort bore fruit.*

'**fruit ,fly,** *n.* [*count*] a very small fly whose eggs are laid in fruit.

fruit•ful /'fruwtfəl/ *adj.* producing good results: *a fruitful meeting.*

fruit•less /'fruwtlɪs/ *adj.* not producing results: *a fruitless search.* —'**fruit•less•ly,** *adv.*

frus•trate /'frʌstreyt/ *v.* [~ + *obj*], **-trat•ed, -trat•ing.** **1.** to prevent (plans, efforts, etc.) from being carried out: *The steady rains frustrated our plans.* **2.** to disappoint; discourage: *If you give a child problems that are hard to solve, you may frustrate him.* —**frus'tra•tion,** *n.* [*noncount*]: *feelings of frustration.* [*count*]: *He took his frustrations out on his staff.*

fry /fray/ *v.,* **fried, fry•ing,** *n., pl.* **fries.** —*v.* [~ + *obj*] **1.** to cook in fat or oil: *Let's fry some bacon and eggs.* —*n.* [*count*] **2.** a French fry. —**fried,** *adj.*

ft., an abbreviation of: **1.** feet. **2.** foot. **3.** fort.

FTC, an abbreviation of: Federal Trade Commission.

fuch•sia /'fyuwʃə/ *n.* [*count*], *pl.* **-sias.** **1.** a plant with pink to purplish drooping flowers. **2.** a bright purplish red color. —*adj.* **3.** of the color fuchsia.

fudge /fʌdʒ/ *n.* [*noncount*] a soft candy made with sugar, butter, milk, and flavoring.

fu•el /'fyuwəl/ *n., v.,* **-eled, -el•ing** or (*esp. Brit.*) **-elled, -el•ling.** —*n.* **1.** matter that can be burned to create heat or power, such as coal, wood, oil, or gas: [*noncount*]: *We ran out of fuel.* [*count*]: *Kerosene and gas are fuels.* —*v.* [~ + *obj*] **2.** to supply with fuel: *to fuel the plane.* **3.** to encourage: *to fuel suspicion.*

fu•gi•tive /'fyuwdʒɪtɪv/ *n.* [*count*] **1.** a person who is fleeing: *a fugitive from justice.* —*adj.* [*before a noun*] **2.** running away: *a fugitive convict.*

fugue /fyuwg/ *n.* [*count*] a musical composition with two or more voices. —'**fu•gal,** *adj.*

-ful, a suffix meaning: full of or characterized by (*beautiful*); tending to or able to (*harmful*); as much as will fill (*spoonful*).

ful•fill or **ful•fil** /fʊl'fɪl/ *v.* [~ + *obj*], **-filled, -fill•ing** or **-fil•ling.** **1.** to carry out: *The dream of a world without war is yet to be fulfilled.* **2.** to perform or do, such as duty; obey or follow, such as commands: *ability to fulfill the job.* **3.** to satisfy (a need, demand, etc.): *to fulfill a lifelong dream.* **4.** to develop the full potential of (oneself): *He fulfilled himself as a musician.* —**ful'fill•ment,** *n.* [*noncount*]

full /fʊl/ *adj.,* **-er, -est. 1.** completely filled: *a full cup; He is full of his own problems.* **2.** [*before a noun*] complete; entire: *a full supply of food; at full speed.* **3.** well-supplied: *a cabinet full of medicine.* **4.** (of a garment) wide; fitting loosely: *a full skirt.* **5.** (of a shape) rounded: *a full face; a full moon.* **6.** having eaten as much as one can:

feeling full from dinner. —'**full•ness,** *n.* [*noncount*] —'**ful•ly,** *adv.*

full-fledged /'fʊl'flɛdʒd/ *adj.* [*before a noun*] **1.** of full rank: *a full-fledged ambassador.* **2.** fully developed: *full-fledged adulthood.*

'**full 'moon,** *n.* [*count; singular*] the moon when the whole of its disk is showing.

'**full-'scale,** *adj.* [*before a noun*] **1.** having the exact size of the original: *a full-scale replica of the submarine.* **2.** complete: *a full-scale attack.*

'**full-'time,** *adj.* **1.** working the usual number of hours: *a full-time employee.* Compare PART-TIME. —*adv.* **2.** on a full-time basis: *to work full-time.*

ful•ly *adv.* entirely; completely: *Her children are fully grown.*

fum•ble /'fʌmbəl/ *v.* [*no obj*], **-bled, -bling.** to feel about awkwardly: *He fumbled in his pocket for the keys.*

fume /fyuwm/ *n., v.,* **fumed, fum•ing.** —*n.* [*count*] **1.** Often, **fumes.** [*plural*] smoke, gas, or vapor: *tobacco fumes.* —*v.* [*no obj*] **2.** to give off fumes or vapor. **3.** to be irritated: *She always fumes when the mail is late.*

fun /fʌn/ *n.* [*noncount*] **1.** something that provides amusement: *A picnic would be fun.* **2.** enjoyment: *She's full of fun.* —*adj.* **3.** *Informal.* enjoyable: *He's a fun person* —*Idiom.* **4. for** or **in fun,** as a joke: *We played that prank on him for fun.* **5. make fun of,** to make the object of jokes: *She likes to make fun of the neighbors.*

func•tion /'fʌŋkʃən/ *n.* [*count*] **1.** the purpose of a person, thing, or institution: *The function of the kidneys is to purify the blood.* **2.** a formal social occasion: *a charity function.* —*v.* [*no obj*] **3.** to serve: *Let me function as your guide.*

func•tion•al /'fʌŋkʃənl/ *adj.* **1.** able to function: *When will the ventilating system be functional again?* **2.** having a useful purpose: *This screen is functional as well as decorative.*

fund /fʌnd/ *n.* [*count*] **1.** a sum of money set aside for a special purpose: *a retirement fund.* **2.** supply: *a fund of knowledge.* **3. funds,** [*plural*] money available: *Do we have enough funds for the project?* —*v.* [~ + *obj*] **4.** to provide funds for (a program, project, etc.): *The government funded his research.*

fun•da•men•tal /,fʌndə'mɛntl/ *adj.* **1.** very important: *a fundamental review of a theory.* —*n.* [*count*] **2.** a basic principle, rule, or the like: *the fundamentals of engineering.* —,**fun•da'men•tal•ly,** *adv.*

fu•ner•al /'fyuwnərəl/ *n.* [*count*] **1.** the ceremonies for a dead person before the body is buried or burned. —*adj.* [*before a noun*] **2.** of or relating to a funeral: *funeral expenses.*

fu•ne•re•al /fyuw'nɪəriyəl/ *adj.* mournful; sad: *a funereal atmosphere of gloom.* —**fu'ne•re•al•ly,** *adv.*

fun•gus /'fʌŋgəs/ *n.* [*count*], *pl.* **fun•gi** /'fʌndʒay, 'fʌŋgay/, **fun•gus•es.** a plant without leaves that lives on the organic material in which it grows: *Fungi include the mushrooms and molds.* —'**fun•gal,** '**fun•gous,** *adj.*

fun•nel /'fʌnl/ *n., v.,* **-neled, -nel•ing** or (*esp. Brit.*) **-nelled, -nel•ling.** —*n.* [*count*] **1.** a cone-shaped utensil with a tube at the point for pouring a liquid through a small opening. —*v.* **2.** to (cause to) pass through a funnel or narrow space: [*no obj*]: *The group funneled out of the stadium.* [~ + *obj*]: *The police funneled the traffic around the accident.*

fun•ny /'fʌniy/ *adj.,* **-ni•er, -ni•est. 1.** causing

F

laughter: *a funny movie.* **2.** strange: *The car is making a funny noise.*

fur /fɜr/ *n.* [*noncount*] **1.** the soft, hairy coat of a mammal. —*adj.* [*before a noun*] **2.** of or relating to fur or animal skins: *a fur coat.* —**'fur•ry,** *adj.,* **–ri•er, –ri•est.**

fu•ri•ous /ˈfyʊriyəs/ *adj.* **1.** very angry: *a furious argument.* **2.** wild: *a furious hurricane.* —**'fu•ri•ous•ly,** *adv.*

fur•long /ˈfɜrlɔŋ, -lɒŋ/ *n.* [*count*] a distance equal to 220 yards (201 m).

fur•nace /ˈfɜrnɪs/ *n.* [*count*] a structure in which heat is generated, such as for heating houses, melting metals, etc.

fur•nish /ˈfɜrnɪʃ/ *v.* [~ + *obj*] **1.** to supply (a house, etc.) with what is needed, esp. with furniture: *to furnish an apartment.* **2.** to provide: *The delay furnished me with the time I needed.*

fur•ni•ture /ˈfɜrnɪtʃər/ *n.* [*noncount*] movable articles such as tables, chairs, or cabinets, for use in a house, office, etc.

fu•ror /ˈfyʊrɔr, -ər/ *n.* [*count; usually singular*] an outburst of excitement or disagreement: *a public furor over political corruption.*

fur•row /ˈfɜrow, ˈfʌrow/ *n.* [*count*] **1.** a long mark cut into the ground, esp. by a plow. **2.** a wrinkle: *the furrows of a wrinkled face.* —*v.* **3.** to (cause to) have wrinkles in (the face): [~ + *obj*]: *to furrow one's brow.* [*no obj*]: *His face furrowed in worry.*

fur•ther /ˈfɜrðər/ *comparative adv. and adj.* of **far** *with superlative* **fur•thest,** *v.* —*adv.* **1.** at or to a greater distance; farther: *too tired to go further.* **2.** in addition: *Further, he should be here any minute.* —*adj.* **3.** more distant: *The map shows it to be further than I thought.* **4.** [*before a noun*] additional; more: *Further meetings seem pointless.* —*v.* [~ + *obj*] **5.** to help forward (a work, etc.); advance: *We counted on her to further our cause.* —**Usage.** See FARTHER.

fur•ther•more /ˈfɜrðər,mɔr/ *adv.* besides; in addition.

fur•ther•most /ˈfɜrðər,mowst/ *adj.* [*before a noun*] most distant.

fur•thest /ˈfɜrðɪst/ *adj., adv., superlative of* **far** *with* **fur•ther** *as comparative.* FARTHEST.

fur•tive /ˈfɜrtɪv/ *adj.* stealthy; secret: *a furtive glance.* —**'fur•tive•ly,** *adv.*

fu•ry /ˈfyʊriy/ *n., pl.* **-ries.** **1.** violent rage: [*noncount*]: *The soldiers were filled with fury.* [*count; usually singular*]: *I felt a sudden fury.* **2.** [*non-*

count] violence; fierceness: *the fury of a hurricane.*

fuse¹ /fyuwz/ *n.* [*count*] **1.** a tube, cord, etc., filled with matter that burns easily, used for exploding a bomb. **2.** a device for causing an explosion. —**—Idiom. 3. have a short fuse,** *Informal.* to get angry easily. —**'fuse•less,** *adj.*

fuse² /fyuwz/ *n., v.,* **fused, fus•ing.** —*n.* [*count*] **1.** a safety device containing a wire that will melt when too much current runs through an electric circuit. —*v.* **2.** to (cause to) combine by melting together: [*no obj*]: *The metal fused under the extreme heat.* [~ + *obj*]: *The extreme heat will fuse these elements together.*

fu•se•lage /ˈfyuwsə,lɑʒ, -lɪdʒ/ *n.* [*count*] the central part of an airplane.

fu•sion /ˈfyuwʒən/ *n.* **1.** [*noncount*] the act or process of combining different things into one. **2.** [*count*] the result of such combining: *a fusion of the major political parties.*

fuss /fʌs/ *n.* [*count*] **1.** an unnecessary display of attention or activity: *She made a fuss over a little accident.* —*v.* [*no obj*] **2.** to care too much about unimportant things: *to fuss over details.* **3.** to behave in a busy or nervous manner: *mothers fussing over their children.*

fuss•y /ˈfʌsiy/ *adj.,* **-i•er, -i•est. 1.** too busy with small, unimportant things. **2.** hard to please: *a fussy eater who did not like anything on the menu.* **3.** with too much decoration: *a fussy hat.* —**'fuss•i•ly,** *adv.* —**'fuss•i•ness,** *n.* [*noncount*]

fu•tile /ˈfyuwtl̩, ˈfyuwtayl/ *adj.* **1.** not producing any result: *Attempts to reach her by telephone were futile.* **2.** of little value: *futile remarks.* —**'fu•tile•ly,** *adv.* —**fu•til•i•ty** /fyuwˈtɪlɪtiy/, *n.* [*noncount*]

fu•ton /ˈfuwtɒn/ *n.* [*count*] a quiltlike mattress placed on a floor or a frame for sleeping.

fu•ture /ˈfyuwtʃər/ *n.* [*count; singular; the* + ~] **1.** time that will come later: *some day in the future.* **2.** something that will exist or happen in time to come. —*adj.* [*before a noun*] **3.** being or coming after the present: *future events.*

fuzz /fʌz/ *n.* [*noncount*] loose, light, fluffy matter; bits of thread.

fuzz•y /ˈfʌziy/ *adj.,* **-i•er, -i•est. 1.** resembling or covered with fuzz: *a fuzzy blanket.* **2.** not clear: *a fuzzy photograph.* **3.** not logical: *a fuzzy thinker.* —**fuzz•i•ly** /ˈfʌzəliy/, *adv.* —**'fuzz•i•ness,** *n.* [*noncount*]

-fy, a suffix meaning: to make, become, or cause to be (*purify; simplify*).

G

G, g /dʒiy/ n. [count], pl. **Gs** or **G's, gs** or **g's.** the seventh letter of the English alphabet, a consonant.

G, an abbreviation of: general: a motion-picture rating advising that the film is suitable for general audiences, or for children as well as adults.

g, an abbreviation of: gram.

GA or **Ga.,** an abbreviation of: Georgia.

ga•ble /'geybəl/ n. [count] the three-sided part of the wall of a building between the sides of a sloping roof. —**'ga•bled,** adj.

gad /gæd/ v. [no obj], **gad•ded, gad•ding.** to go from one place to another in search of pleasure or amusement: to gad about town.

gadg•et /'gædʒɪt/ n. [count] a small tool or electronic device: a gadget for peeling garlic. —**gad•get•ry** /'gædʒɪtriy/ n. [noncount]: computer gadgetry.

gaffe /gæf/ n. [count] a mistake or awkward remark or act in public that offends others.

gag /gæg/ v., **gagged, gag•ging,** n. —v. **1.** [~ + obj] to stop up the mouth of (a person) by inserting a gag: They gagged their prisoner. **2.** [no obj] to (cause to) choke: She gagged on the strong whiskey. —n. [count] **3.** something put into a person's mouth to prevent speech, shouting, etc.

gage /geydʒ/ n., v., **gaged, gag•ing.** GAUGE. —**'gag•er,** n. [count]

gai•e•ty /'geyɪtiy/ n. [noncount] the quality or state of being cheerful; merriment.

gai•ly /'geyliy/ adv. cheerfully: They waved gaily from the window.

gain /geyn/ v. **1.** [~ + obj] to get (something desired), esp. as a result of one's efforts: to gain possession of land. **2.** [~ + obj] to increase in: He gained weight. —n. **3.** [noncount] profit or advantage: I see no gain in this plan. **4.** [count] an increase: He showed a small gain in weight.

gain•ful /'geynfəl/ adj. [before a noun] profitable: He is looking for gainful employment. —**'gain•ful•ly,** adv.

gait /geyt/ n. [count] **1.** a manner of walking or running: a slow gait. **2.** any of the ways in which a horse moves, as a trot or gallop.

ga•la /'geylə, 'gælə/ n. [count] **1.** a celebration, often with entertainment: a gala held at the concert hall. —adj. [usually: before a noun] **2.** festive: a gala affair.

gal•ax•y /'gæləksiy/ n., pl. **-ax•ies. 1. a.** [count] a large system of stars separated from similar systems by vast regions of space. **b.** MILKY WAY. **2.** [count] any large and brilliant or impressive group: a galaxy of opera stars. —**ga'lac•tic,** adj.

gale /geyl/ n. [count] **1.** a very strong wind. **2.** a noisy outburst: a gale of laughter.

gall¹ /gɔl/ n. [noncount] **1.** rude boldness; nerve: He has a lot of gall expecting me to finish his work. **2.** BILE (def. 1).

gall² /gɔl/ v. to annoy greatly: [~ + obj]: His arrogant manner galls me. [It + ~ + obj + (that) clause]: It galls me that we can't fire him. —**'gall•ing,** adj.

gal•lant /'gælənt for 1, gə'lænt, -'lɑnt, 'gælənt for 2 / adj. **1.** brave or heroic: a gallant knight. **2.** very polite and attentive to women. —**'gal•lant•ly,** adv. —**'gal•lan•try,** n. [noncount]

gal•ler•y /'gæləriy, 'gælriy/ n. [count], pl. **-ler-**

ies. 1. a raised area in a theater, church, or other public building, used as a place for spectators, exhibits, etc. **2.** a place for showing works of art. **3.** a long covered area, narrow and open at one or both sides, used esp. as a walkway.

gal•ley /'gæliy/ n. [count], pl. **-leys.** the kitchen area of a ship.

gal•lon /'gælən/ n. [count] a unit of liquid measurement equal to four quarts, the U.S. standard gallon being equal to 231 cubic inches (3.7853 liters) and the British imperial gallon to 277.42 cubic inches (4.546 liters). Abbr.: gal.

gal•lop /'gæləp/ v. **1.** to ride (a horse) at full speed: [no obj]: The rider galloped away. [~ + obj]: The cavalry galloped their horses for hours. **2.** [no obj] to run at a gallop: The horses galloped away. —n. [count] **3.** the fastest pace for a horse.

ga•lore /gə'lɔr/ adj. [after a noun] in great amounts: food galore at the party.

ga•losh or **ga•loshe** /gə'lɒʃ/ n. [count; usually plural] a waterproof boot or shoe, esp. a high one.

gal•va•nize /'gælvə,nayz/ v. [~ + obj], **-nized, -niz•ing. 1.** to startle into sudden activity: The news of the riots galvanized the police. **2.** to coat (iron or steel) with zinc.

gam•ble /'gæmbəl/ v., **-bled, -bling,** n. —v. **1.** [no obj] to play at a game of chance for money: to gamble at cards. **2.** [~ + obj] to risk something of value on the outcome of something: I'll gamble my life on his honesty. —n. [count] **3.** any matter or thing involving risk: We took a gamble in hiring him. —**'gam•bler,** n. [count]

game /geym/ n., adj., **gam•er, gam•est.** —n. **1.** [count] an amusement or pastime: card games. **2.** [count] an activity in which players compete against others. **3.** [noncount] wild animals, including birds and fishes, that are hunted for food or for sport or profit. **4.** [noncount] any object of attack, abuse, etc.: Any new student is fair game for the school bully. —adj. **5.** [before a noun] relating to animals viewed as game: game laws. **6.** brave: a game fighter. **7.** [be + ~] having the required spirit or will: Who's game for a hike? —Idiom. **8. give the game away,** to reveal the truth about something.

gan•der /'gændər/ n. [count] the male of the goose. Compare GOOSE (def. 2).

gang /gæŋ/ n. [count] **1.** a group or band: a gang of tourists. **2.** a group of criminals: terrorist gangs. **3.** a group of people with similar tastes or interests: the gang I bowl with.

gan•gling /'gæŋglɪŋ/ also **gan•gly,** adj., **-gli-er, -gli-est.** awkwardly and loosely built; lanky: a tall, gangling youth.

gang•plank /'gæŋ,plæŋk/ n. [count] a small movable bridge used for boarding or leaving a ship at a pier. Also called **gangway.**

gan•grene /'gæŋgriyn, gæŋ'griyn/ n. [noncount] the death of body tissue due to blocked blood flow, usually followed by decay. —**gan•gre•nous** /'gæŋgrənəs/, adj.

gang•ster /'gæŋstər/ n. [count] a member of a gang of criminals; mobster.

gang•way /'gæŋ,wey / n. [count] **1.** a passageway, esp. a narrow walkway. **2.** GANGPLANK.

gap /gæp/ n. [count] **1.** a break or opening: The animals escaped through a gap in the fence. **2.** a great difference in ways of thinking or seeing: *a communications gap.*

gape /geyp, gæp/ *v.,* **gaped** /geypt, gæpt/, **gap•ing.** **1.** [~ + *at* + *obj*] to stare with the mouth wide open, as in shock, wonder, or surprise: *The tourists gaped at the tall buildings.* **2.** [*no obj*] to open or spread widely; split: *The canyon gaped before them.* —**'gap•ing,** *adj.* [*before a noun*]

ga•rage /gə'rɑʒ, -'rɑdʒ/ *n., v.,* **-raged, -rag•ing.** —*n.* [*count*] **1.** a building or indoor area for parking motor vehicles. **2.** a business for repairing motor vehicles. —*v.* [~ + *obj*] **3.** to put or keep in a garage: *They garaged their car.*

gar•bage /'gɑrbɪdʒ/ *n.* [*noncount*] **1.** matter that has been thrown away, esp. food waste. **2.** worthless talk; lies; foolishness.

'garbage ,can, *n.* [*count*] a container for the disposal of waste.

gar•ble /'gɑrbəl/ *v.* [~ + *obj*], **-bled, -bling.** to distort: *to garble instructions.*

gar•den /'gɑrdṇ/ *n.* [*count*] **1.** a plot of ground where flowers, vegetables, etc., are grown. **2.** a public park. —*v.* [*no obj*] **3.** to work in a garden: *She loves to garden.* —*Idiom.* **4. lead (someone) down** or **up the garden path,** to mislead through false hopes or promises of reward. —'gar•den•er, *n.*

gar•de•nia /gɑr'diynyə, -niyə/ *n.* [*count*], *pl.* **-nias.** an evergreen shrub having shiny leaves and fragrant white flowers.

gar•gle /'gɑrgəl/ *v.,* [*no obj*] **-gled, -gling.** to wash the throat or mouth by blowing through a liquid held in the throat.

gar•goyle /'gɑrgɔyl/ *n.* [*count*] a water spout in the form of an ugly human or animal figure.

gar•ish /'geərɪʃ, 'gær-/ *adj.* overly or tastelessly colorful, showy, or elaborate: *garish Christmas decorations.*

gar•land /'gɑrlənd/ *n.* [*count*] a wreath of flowers or leaves worn as a decoration.

gar•lic /'gɑrlɪk/ *n.* [*noncount*] a plant having a strong-smelling and strong-tasting bulb which is used in cooking.

gar•ment /'gɑrmənt/ *n.* [*count*] any article of clothing: *flowing garments.*

gar•net /'gɑrnɪt/ *n.* **1.** [*count*] a hard, deep red, glass-like mineral used as a gem. **2.** [*noncount*] a deep red color.

gar•nish /'gɑrnɪʃ/ *v.* [~ + *obj*] **1.** to decorate. —*n.* **2.** [*noncount*] decoration.

gar•ri•son /'gærəsən/ *n.* [*count*] **1.** a body of troops stationed in a fort or town. **2.** any military post. —*v.* [~ + *obj*] **3.** to provide (a fort, town, etc.) with a garrison.

gar•ru•lous /'gærələs, 'gæryə-/ *adj.* endlessly talkative, esp. about unimportant matters: *a garrulous gossip.* —**gar•ru•li•ty** /gə'ruwlɪtiy/, **'gar•ru•lous•ness,** *n.* [*noncount*] —'gar•ru•lous•ly, *adv.*

gar•ter /'gɑrtər/ *n.* [*count*] an elastic band worn around the leg for holding up a stocking.

'garter ,snake, *n.* [*count*] a harmless snake common in North and Central America, usually with three long stripes on the back.

gas /gæs/ *n., pl.* **gas•es,** *v.,* **gassed, gas•sing.** —*n.* **1.** a fluid substance that can expand without limit, as opposed to a solid or a liquid: [*noncount*]: *huge clouds of gas in outer space.* [*count*]: *Some gases are lighter than air.* **2.** [*noncount*] gasoline: *gas for a car.* **3.** gas used for cooking, heating, etc. **4.** [*noncount*] intestinal gas. —*v.* [~ + *obj*] **5.** to overcome or poison with gas or fumes: *Entire villages were gassed in the war.*

—*Idiom.* **6. step on the gas,** *Informal.* to increase one's speed: *You'll have to step on the gas to finish the book in time.*

'gas ,chamber, *n.* [*count*] a room used for executing prisoners by means of poison gas.

gas•e•ous /'gæsiyəs, 'gæʃəs/ *adj.* having the form or characteristics of gas: *a gaseous smell.*

gash /gæʃ/ *n.* [*count*] **1.** a long, deep wound or cut. —*v.* [~ + *obj*] **2.** to make a gash in: *The wire gashed my leg.*

gas•ket /'gæskɪt/ *n.* [*count*] a rubber or metal ring for placing around an opening to make it close tight.

'gas ,mask, *n.* [*count*] a masklike device that filters air to protect the wearer against harmful gases.

gas•o•line /ˌgæsə'liyn, 'gæsəˌliyn/ *n.* [*noncount*] a liquid obtained from petroleum that burns rapidly and easily, used as a fuel for motor vehicles.

gasp /gæsp/ *n.* [*count*] **1.** a sudden, short intake of breath, as in shock or surprise: *a gasp of horror.* **2.** a struggling effort to breathe: *gave a gasp for air.* —*v.* [*no obj*] **3.** to catch one's breath: *The audience gasped in horror.* **4.** to struggle for breath: *He came out of the water and stood there gasping.*

'gas ,station, *n.* SERVICE STATION (def. 1).

gas•tric /'gæstrɪk/ *adj.* [*before a noun*] relating to the stomach: *a gastric ulcer.*

gas•tro•en•ter•i•tis /ˌgæstrowˌɛntə'raytɪs/ *n.* [*noncount*] a painful inflammation of the stomach and intestines.

gas•tro•in•tes•ti•nal /ˌgæstrowɪn'tɛstənḷ/ *adj.* of, relating to, or affecting the stomach and intestines.

gate /geyt/ *n.* [*count*] **1.** a movable barrier closing an opening in a fence, wall, or other enclosure. **2.** any movable barrier, as at a railroad crossing. **3.** [*usually singular; the* + ~] the number of persons who pay to attend a sporting event, performance, etc.

gate•way /'geytˌwey/ *n.* [*count*] an entrance that may be closed by a gate.

gath•er /'gæðər/ *v.* **1.** to bring or come together into one place; collect: [~ + *obj*]: *to gather firewood.* [*no obj*]: *A crowd gathered.* **2.** [~ + *obj*] to pick or harvest: *to gather vegetables from the garden.* **3.** [~ + *obj*] to increase: *The car quickly gathered speed.* **4.** [~ + *obj*] to assemble or collect, as for an effort: *I gathered my energy for one last try.* **5.** [~ + *obj*] to understand: *I gather (that) she is the real leader.* **6.** [~ + *obj*] to wrap around: *He gathered his scarf around his neck.* —'gath•er•ing, *n.* [*count*]

gauche /gowʃ/ *adj.* lacking social grace; awkward; tactless: *a gauche remark.* —**'gauche•ly,** *adv.* —'gauche•ness, *n.* [*noncount*]

gaud•y /'gɔdiy/ *adj.,* **-i•er, -i•est.** showy in a tasteless way; flashy: *a gaudy display of wealth.* —**gaud•i•ly** /'gɔdḷiy/, *adv.* —'gaud•i•ness, *n.* [*noncount*]

gauge /geydʒ/ *v.,* **gauged, gaug•ing,** *n.* —*v.* [~ + *obj*] **1.** to figure out the exact size or quantity of; measure: *to gauge the thickness of a wall.* —*n.* [*count*] **2.** an instrument for measuring or testing something: *a pressure gauge.* Also, *esp. in technical use,* **gage.**

gaunt /gɔnt/ *adj.,* **-er, -est.** extremely thin and bony: *He looked gaunt after his illness.* —'gaunt•ness, *n.* [*noncount*]

gaunt•let /'gɔntlɪt, 'gɑnt-/ *n.* [*count*] **1.** a heavy glove with an extended, long cuff: *a police offi-*

cer's motorcycle gauntlets. —**Idiom. 2. take up the gauntlet,** to accept a challenge to fight. **3. throw down the gauntlet,** to challenge someone to fight.

gauze /gɔz/ *n.* [*noncount*] a thin, loosely woven transparent fabric used esp. as a dressing for wounds or surgery. —**'gauz•y,** *adj.,* **-i•er, -i•est.**

gave /geyv/ *v.* pt. of GIVE.

gav•el /'gævəl/ *n.* [*count*] a small hammer used esp. by the officer leading a meeting or by a judge, to signal for attention.

gawk /gɔk/ *v.* [~ + *at*] to stare stupidly or with astonishment: *Onlookers gawked at the car accident.*

gawk•y /'gɔkiy/ *adj.,* **-i•er, -i•est.** awkward; ungainly; clumsy. —**'gawk•i•ly,** *adv.*

gay /gey/ *adj.,* **-er, -est,** *n.* —*adj.* **1.** having or showing a merry, lively mood: *in gay spirits.* **2.** homosexual. —*n.* [*count*] **3.** a homosexual person, esp. a male.

gaze /geyz/ *v.,* **gazed, gaz•ing,** *n.* —*v.* [*no obj*] **1.** to look steadily, as with great interest or wonder: *He gazed out the window at the sunset.* —*n.* [*count*] **2.** a steady look.

ga•zelle /gə'zɛl/ *n.* [*count*], *pl.* **-zelles,** (*esp. when thought of as a group*) **-zelle.** any of various small graceful antelopes of Africa and Asia.

ga•zette /gə'zɛt/ *n.* [*count*] a newspaper (now used chiefly in names): *The Phoenix Gazette.*

gear /gɪər/ *n.* **1.** [*count*] a wheel having teeth that mesh with teeth in another part of a machine. **2.** [*noncount*] equipment used for a particular purpose: *fishing gear.* —*v.* [~ + *obj*] **3.** to adjust or adapt to a situation in order to bring about satisfactory results: *They geared their output to consumer demands.* —**Idiom. 4. in** or **into high gear,** in or into a state of the highest speed and efficiency: *They went into high gear in an effort to finish.* **5. shift** or **switch gears,** to change one's thinking in a significant way.

gear

gear•shift /'gɪər,ʃɪft/ *n.* [*count*] a lever for shifting gears, esp. in a motor vehicle.

gee /dʒiy/ *interj.* This word is used to express surprise, disappointment, enthusiasm, or simple emphasis: *Gee, what a beautiful day it is!*

geese /giys/ *n.* a pl. of GOOSE.

'Geiger ,counter /'gaygər/ *n.* [*count*] an instrument for detecting radiation.

gel /dʒɛl/ *n., v.,* **gelled, gel•ling.** —*n.* **1.** a partly solid, partly liquid substance, as jelly or glue, sometimes used in hair styling: [*noncount*]: *She uses gel to style her hair.* [*count*]: *There are a number of gels on the market.* —*v.* [*no obj*] **2.** to form or become a gel. **3.** JELL (def. 2).: *Most of my ideas need time to gel.*

gel•a•tin or **gel•a•tine** /'dʒɛlətn̩/ *n.* [*noncount*] a nearly transparent, oily substance used in making jellies, glues, and the like. —**ge•lat•i• nous** /dʒə'lætn̩əs/ *adj.*

gel•ig•nite /'dʒɛlɪg,nayt/ *n.* [*noncount*] a powerful explosive substance.

gem /dʒɛm/ *n.* [*count*] a mineral, pearl, or other natural substance valued for its rarity and beauty and used in jewelry: *diamonds and other gems.*

gem•stone /'dʒɛm,stown/ *n.* [*count*] a mineral or crystal that can be cut and polished for use as a gem.

gen•der /'dʒɛndər/ *n.* **1. a.** [*noncount*] a grouping of nouns and pronouns into the categories masculine, feminine, and neuter. **b.** [*count*] one of the categories in such a set. **2. sex:** [*noncount*]: *discrimination on the grounds of gender.* [*count*]: *the feminine and masculine genders.*

gene /dʒiyn/ *n.* [*count*] the basic physical unit of heredity.

ge•ne•al•o•gy /ˌdʒiyniy'ɒlədʒiy, -'æl-, ˌdʒɛniy-/ *n.* [*noncount*], *pl.* **-gies.** the record or the study of family ancestries and histories. —**ge• ne•a•log•i•cal** /ˌdʒiyniyə'lɒdʒɪkəl, ˌdʒɛniy-/, *adj.* —,**ge•ne'al•o•gist,** *n.* [*count*]

gen•er•al /'dʒɛnərəl/ *adj.* **1.** [*before a noun*] of, relating to, or true of most persons or things: *the general mood of the people.* **2.** dealing with broad, universal, or important aspects: *The state issued general guidelines.* —*n.* [*count*] **3.** an army, air force, or Marine Corps officer of high rank. —**Idiom. 4. in general, a.** as a whole; for the most part: *He likes people in general.* **b.** as a rule; usually: *In general, the bus is on time.*

gen•er•al•i•ty /ˌdʒɛnə'rælɪtiy/ *n.* [*count*], *pl.* **-ties. 1.** an indefinite statement, one lacking details: *talking in generalities.* **2.** something usually true: *It's a generality that people want to improve their lives.*

gen•er•al•i•za•tion /ˌdʒɛnərələ'zeyʃən/ *n.* **1.** [*noncount*] the act or process of generalizing. **2.** [*count*] a statement that is a general idea or principle.

gen•er•al•ize /'dʒɛnərə,layz/ *v.* [*no obj*], **-ized, -iz•ing.** to form (a general opinion or conclusion) from only a few facts: *We can't generalize from so little evidence.*

gen•er•al•ly /'dʒɛnərəliy/ *adv.* **1.** usually; ordinarily: *He generally comes home at noon.* **2.** for the most part; widely: *a generally true statement.* **3.** without reference to details or specific things: *I generally agree with you.*

'general prac'titioner, *n.* [*count*] a physician whose practice is not limited to any specialty. *Abbr.:* G.P.

'general 'store, *n.* [*count*] a store, usually in a country area, that sells a wide variety of merchandise.

gen•er•ate /'dʒɛnə,reyt/ *v.* [~ + *obj*], **-at•ed, -at•ing. 1.** to bring into existence; produce: *to generate ideas.* **2.** to create by a natural or chemical process: *They used the waterfalls to generate power.*

gen•er•a•tion /ˌdʒɛnə'reyʃən/ *n.* **1.** [*count*] the entire group of individuals born and living at about the same time: *the postwar generation.* **2.** [*count*] the term of years accepted as the average period between the birth of parents and the birth of their offspring. **3.** [*noncount*] the act or action of generating: *the generation of electricity.* —,**gen•er'a•tion•al,** *adj.*

gen•er•a•tor /'dʒɛnə,reytər/ *n.* [*count*] a machine that converts one form of energy into another, esp. mechanical energy into electrical energy: *a car's generator.*

ge•ner•ic /dʒə'nɛrɪk/ *adj.* **1.** shared by all the members of a class, group, or kind: *a trait that is generic to humanity.* **2.** not protected by trademark registration: *The doctor prescribed a generic drug.* —**ge'ner•i•cal•ly,** *adv.*

G

gen•er•ous /'dʒɛnərəs/ *adj.* **1.** free in giving or sharing; unselfish: *He is generous with his money.* **2.** large; abundant; ample: *a generous portion of pie.* —**gen•er•os•i•ty** /,dʒɛnə'rɒsɪtiy/ *n.* [*noncount*] —'**gen•er•ous•ly,** *adv.*

gen•e•sis /'dʒɛnəsɪs/ *n.* [*count*], *pl.* **-ses** /-,siyz/. an origin; creation: *the genesis of an idea.*

Genesis *n.* [*noncount*] the first book of the Bible.

ge•net•ic /dʒə'nɛtɪk/ *adj.* of or relating to genes: *genetic differences between species.* —**ge•net•i•cal•ly,** *adv.* —**ge•net•i•cist** /dʒə'nɛtəsɪst/, *n.* [*count*]

ge•net•ics /dʒə'nɛtɪks/ *n.* [*noncount; used with a singular verb*] the branch of biology that deals with the way genes contribute to differences and similarities: *Genetics is a science that combines biology and statistics.*

gen•ial /'dʒiynyəl, 'dʒiyniyəl/ *adj.* warmly and pleasantly cheerful: *a genial disposition.* —**ge•ni•al•i•ty** /,dʒiyniy'ælɪtiy/, *n.* [*noncount*] —'**gen•ial•ly,** *adv.*

gen•i•tal /'dʒɛnɪtl/ *adj.* [*before a noun*] **1.** of or relating to reproduction. **2.** of or relating to the sexual organs.

gen•i•ta•li•a /,dʒɛnɪ'teyliyə, -'teylyə/ *n.* [*plural*] the organs of reproduction, esp. the external organs.

gen•i•tals /'dʒɛnɪtlz/ *n.* GENITALIA.

gen•ius /'dʒiynyəs/ *n.*, *pl.* **-ius•es. 1.** very great capacity of intellect or ability: [*noncount*]: *Mozart's genius.* [*count; usually singular*]: *a genius for leadership.* **2.** [*count*] a person having such capacity: *Einstein was a scientific genius.*

gen•o•cide /'dʒɛnə,sayd/ *n.* [*noncount*] the deliberate and systematic killing of a national, racial, political, or cultural group.

gen•re /'ʒɑnrə/ *n.* [*count*] a class or category.

gen•tile /'dʒɛntayl/ *adj.* (*sometimes:* Gentile) **1.** of or relating to any people not Jewish. —*n.* [*count*] **2.** a person who is not Jewish, esp. a Christian.

gen•tle /'dʒɛntl/ *adj.*, **-tler, -tlest. 1.** kindly; calm: *She had a soothing, gentle manner.* **2.** not rough or violent: *a gentle tap on the arm.* —**gen•tle•ness,** *n.* [*noncount*] —**gen•tly** /'dʒɛntliy/, *adv.*: *She stroked the baby gently.*

gen•tle•man /'dʒɛntlmən/ *n.* [*count*], *pl.* **-men 1.** a man of good family or social position. **2.** (used as a polite term) a man: *Do you know that gentleman in the tweed suit?* **3. gentlemen,** (used as a form of address): *Gentlemen, please come this way.* **4.** a polite, well-mannered man: *He is always a perfect gentleman.* —'**gen•tle•man•ly,** *adj.*

gen•try /'dʒɛntriy/ *n.* [*plural*] people of a good or noble family, esp. an aristocracy.

gen•u•ine /'dʒɛnyuwɪn *or, sometimes,* -,ayn/ *adj.* authentic; real; not counterfeit: *genuine leather; genuine emotions.* —'**gen•u•ine•ly,** *adv.*

ge•nus /'dʒiynəs/ *n.* [*count*], *pl.* **gen•e•ra** /'dʒɛnərə/, **ge•nus•es. 1.** the major division of a biological family in the scientific system of classifying living things.

ge•og•ra•phy /dʒiy'ɒgrəfiy/ *n.*, *pl.* **-phies. 1.** [*noncount*] the science dealing with the areas of the earth's surface, climate, elevation, vegetation, population, and land use. **2.** [*count*] the features of a given area on the earth: *the geography of a region.* —**ge'og•ra•pher,** *n.* [*count*] —**ge•o•graph•i•cal** /,dʒiyə'græfɪkəl/, **ge•o'graph•ic,** *adj.* —,**ge•o'graph•i•cal•ly,** *adv.*

ge•ol•o•gy /dʒiy'ɒlədʒiy/ *n.*, *pl.* **-gies. 1.** [*non-*

count] the science that deals with the physical history of the earth and the rocks of which it is made up. **2.** [*count*] the rocks found in a given region: *the geology of the Andes.* —**ge•o•log•ic** /,dʒiyə'lɒdʒɪk/, ,**ge•o'log•i•cal,** *adj.* —,**ge•o'log•i•cal•ly,** *adv.* —**ge'ol•o•gist,** *n.* [*count*]

ge•om•e•try /dʒiy'ɒmɪtriy/ *n.* [*noncount*] the branch of mathematics that deals with points, lines, angles, and shapes and their relationship to each other. —**ge•o•met•ric** /,dʒiyə'mɛtrɪk/, ,**ge•o'met•ri•cal,** *adj.* —,**ge•o'met•ri•cal•ly,** *adv.*

ge•ra•ni•um /dʒɪ'reyniyəm/ *n.* [*count*] a common garden plant with small white, pink, or red flowers and rounded leaves.

ger•bil /'dʒɜrbəl/ *n.* [*count*] a small rodent with long hind legs that is popular as a pet.

ger•i•at•rics /,dʒɛriy'ætrɪks, ,dʒɪər-/ *n.* [*noncount; used with a singular verb*] the branch of medicine dealing with the diseases and care of aged persons. —,**ger•i'at•ric,** *adj.*

germ /dʒɜrm/ *n.* [*count*] **1.** a very small living thing that produces disease. **2.** origin; seed: *the germ of an idea.*

Ger•man /'dʒɜrmən/ *adj.* **1.** of or relating to Germany. **2.** of or relating to the language spoken in Germany. —*n.* **3.** [*count*] a person born or living in Germany. **4.** [*noncount*] the language spoken in Germany.

'**German 'measles,** *n.* [*noncount; used with a singular verb*] RUBELLA.

'**German 'shepherd,** *n.* [*count*] one of a breed of large dogs often used in police work and as a guide dog.

ger•mi•nate /'dʒɜrmə,neyt/ *v.*, **-nat•ed, -nat•ing.** to (cause to) begin to grow or develop, as a seed into a plant: [*no obj*]: *The seeds germinated in the soil.* [~ + *obj*]: *She germinated the seeds.* —**ger•mi•na•tion** /,dʒɜrmə'neyʃən/, *n.* [*noncount*]

ger•on•tol•o•gy /,dʒɛrən'tɒlədʒiy, ,dʒɪər-/ *n.* [*noncount*] the study of aging and the problems of aged people. —**ge•ron•to•log•i•cal** /dʒə,rɒntl'ɒdʒɪkəl/, *adj.* —,**ger•on'tol•o•gist,** *n.* [*count*]

ges•ta•tion /dʒɛ'steyʃən/ *n.* [*noncount*] the process or period of time in which the female carries an unborn offspring in the womb: *Human gestation takes nine months.* —**ges'ta•tion•al,** *adj.*

ges•tic•u•late /dʒɛ'stɪkyə,leyt/ *v.* [*no obj*], **-lat•ed, -lat•ing.** to make or use gestures, esp. in an excited manner: *He gesticulated wildly.* —**ges•tic•u•la•tion** /dʒɛ,stɪkyə'leyʃən/, *n.* [*count*] [*noncount*]

ges•ture /'dʒɛstʃər/ *n.*, *v.*, **-tured, -tur•ing.** —*n.* [*count*] **1.** a movement of the hand, arm, body, head, or face that expresses an idea, opinion, emotion, etc.: *He made a threatening gesture.* **2.** any action intended to show how one feels: *The donation was a gesture of friendship.* —*v.* [*no obj*] **3.** to make or use a gesture or gestures (to express something): *She gestured to me.*

get /gɛt/ *v.*, **got** /gɒt/ *or* **got•ten** /'gɒtn/, **get•ting. 1.** [~ + *obj*] to receive: *She got a lovely gift for her birthday.* **2.** [~ + *obj*] to bring (something) for oneself or another; fetch: *Please get me a cup of coffee.* **3.** to (cause to) become, to do, to move, etc.: [~ + *obj*]: *We couldn't get the car into the garage. We couldn't get the car started.* [*no obj*]: *She'd like to get away for a while.* **4.** [~ + *obj*] to catch (a disease or sickness) or feel the bad effects of: *I got a headache from the noise.* **5.** [~ + *obj*] to understand: *I* didn't get the joke. **6.** [~ + obj] to catch: *Get him before he escapes!* **7.** [~ + obj] to prepare; make ready: *to get dinner.* **8.** [~ + obj] to hit, strike, wound, or kill: *The bullet got him in the leg.* **9.** [*no obj*] to come to a place; arrive; reach: *to get home late.* **10.** The verb *get* may be used as an auxiliary verb (like BE) and be followed by a past participle to form the passive; it means almost the same as "become": *She got married when she was twenty-five.* **11. get ahead,** to be successful, as in business or society: *She wants to get ahead in her job.* **12. get along, a.** to survive or continue to go on: *I can't get along without her.* **b.** to agree: *He couldn't get along with his in-laws.* **13. get around, a.** to overcome; outwit: *She found a way to get around the law.* **b.** to travel from place to place: *I don't get around much anymore.* **14. get away, a.** to escape; flee: *The thieves got away.* **b.** to start out; leave: *Can you get away from the office by five o'clock?* **15. get away with,** to do something without punishment: *She got away with a lot of mistakes.* **16. get by, a.** to escape the notice (of): *Somehow these errors got by.* These errors got by our accountants.* **b.** to survive or manage to live or continue: *I couldn't get by on that low salary.* **17. get off, a.** to (help someone to) escape punishment, esp. by providing legal assistance: *He got off with a very light sentence. The lawyer got his client off.* **b.** to finish, as one's day at work: *We get off at five o'clock.* **18. get on, a.** to make progress: *How are you getting on with your work?* **b.** to continue: *Let's get on with the trial, please.* **19. get out,** to (cause to) leave: *Get out of this room. Get them out of this room.* **20. get over, a.** to recover from: *to get over an illness.* **b.** to overcome: *I got over that problem.* **21. get through, a.** to finish: *I hope I can get through all this work.* **b.** to reach someone, as by telephone: *I tried calling you, but I couldn't get through.* **c.** to make oneself clearly understood: *Am I getting through (to you)?* **d.** to survive: *They managed to get through the worst of the winter.* **22. get to-gether,** to (cause to) meet or gather together: *We got together at the church. The minister got them together for a meeting.* **23. get up, a.** to (cause to) sit up or stand: *The child got up from the floor. Get her up.* **b.** to (cause to) rise from bed: *The radio got me up at six o'clock. I was so tired I couldn't get up on time.*

get•a•way /ˈgɛtəˌweɪ/ *n.* [*count*] **1.** an escape: *The thieves made a clean getaway.* **2.** a short vacation. **3.** a place for a vacation: *The shore is their favorite getaway.*

'get-to,gether, *n.* [*count*] an informal, usually small social gathering or meeting.

ghast•ly /ˈgæstliy/ *adj.*, **-li•er, -li•est. 1.** dreadful; horrible: *a ghastly murder.* **2.** resembling a ghost: *a ghastly pallor.* **3.** very bad: *a ghastly error.* —ˈghast•li•ness, *n.* [*noncount*]

ghet•to /ˈgɛtow/ *n.* [*count*], *pl.* **-tos, -toes.** a section of a city, in which mostly members of a minority group live. —ˈghet•to,ize, *v.*, **-ized, -iz-ing.** [~ + *obj*]

ghost /gowst/ *n.* [*count*] **1.** the spirit of a dead person, imagined as wandering among the living. **2.** a weak or weakened version: *She's a ghost of her former self.* —*Idiom.* **3. give up the ghost,** to die. —ˈghost•ly, *adj.*, **-li•er, -li•est.**

gi•ant /ˈdʒayənt/ *n.* [*count*] **1.** a person or thing of very great size or power. —*adj.* [*before a noun*] **2.** very large: *a giant dinosaur.*

gib•ber•ish /ˈdʒɪbərɪʃ, ˈgɪb-/ *n.* [*noncount*] meaningless talk or writing; nonsense.

gibe /dʒayb/ *n.* [*count*] an insulting, taunting, or sarcastic remark.

gid•dy /ˈgɪdiy/ *adj.*, **-di•er, -di•est.** dizzy; feeling that everything is spinning and that one might fall: *She felt a little giddy at such a height.* —ˈgid•di•ness, *n.* [*noncount*]

gift /gɪft/ *n.* [*count*] **1.** something given to another; a present: *birthday gifts.* **2.** a special ability; natural talent: *a gift for music.*

gift•ed /ˈgɪftɪd/ *adj.* having special talent or ability: *She is a gifted storyteller.*

gig /gɪg/ *n.* [*count*] *Slang.* a single job, as by jazz or rock musicians.

gi•gan•tic /dʒayˈgæntɪk, dʒɪ-/ *adj.* very large; huge: *We got lost in that gigantic airport.*

gig•gle /ˈgɪgəl/ *v.*, **-gled, -gling,** *n.* —*v.* [*no obj*] **1.** to laugh in a high, silly way. —*n.* [*count*] **2.** a high, silly laugh. —ˈgig•gly, *adj.*, **-gli•er, -gli•est.**

gild /gɪld/ *v.* [~ + *obj*], **gild•ed** or **gilt** /gɪlt/, **gild•ing. 1.** to coat with gold, gold leaf, or a gold-colored substance. —*Idiom.* **2. gild the lily,** to add unnecessary decoration to something that is already beautiful. —ˈgild•ing, *n.* [*noncount*]

gill /gɪl/ *n.* [*count*] **1.** the breathing organ of fish. —*Idiom.* **2. green around the gills,** somewhat pale, as from sickness: *He was a little green around the gills after the boat ride.*

gilt /gɪlt/ *v.* **1.** a pt. and pp. of GILD. —*adj.* **2.** coated with or as if with gold; gilded; gold in color; golden. —*n.* [*noncount*] **3.** the thin layer of gold or other material applied in gilding.

gin¹ /dʒɪn/ *n.* [*noncount*] [*count*] a clear, colorless alcoholic liquor.

gin² /dʒɪn/ *n.* [*noncount*] Also called **gin rummy.** a card game, a variety of rummy for two players.

gin•ger /ˈdʒɪndʒər/ *n.* [*noncount*] **1.** a reedlike plant having a spicy root used in cooking and in medicine. —*adj.* [*before a noun*] **2.** flavored or made with ginger. —ˈgin•ger•y, *adj.*

'ginger 'ale, *n.* [*noncount*] [*count*] a bubbling soft drink flavored with ginger.

gin•ger•bread /ˈdʒɪndʒər,brɛd/ *n.* [*noncount*] a cake or cookie flavored with ginger and molasses.

gin•ger•ly /ˈdʒɪndʒərliy/ *adv.* **1.** with great care: *I stepped gingerly over the broken glass.* —*adj.* **2.** careful: *to walk in a gingerly manner.*

'gin 'rummy, *n.* GIN²

gi•raffe /dʒəˈræf/ *n.* [*count*] a tall, long-necked, spotted animal of Africa, the tallest living four-legged animal.

gird•er /ˈgɜrdər/ *n.* [*count*] a large steel or wooden beam used for supporting buildings.

gir•dle /ˈgɜrdl/ *n.* [*count*] **1.** an undergarment worn to shape the abdomen, hips, and buttocks. **2.** a belt, cord, sash, or the like, worn about the waist.

girl /gɜrl/ *n.* [*count*] **1.** a female child, from birth to full growth. **2.** girlfriend; sweetheart: *He had a girl in every port.* —ˈgirl,hood, *n.* [*noncount*] —ˈgirl•ish, *adj.*

girl•friend /ˈgɜrl,frɛnd/ *n.* [*count*] **1.** a frequent or favorite female companion or lover. **2.** a female friend.

girth /gɜrθ/ also **girt,** *n.* the measure around a body or object: [*count*]: *The girth of that huge tree was several yards.* [*noncount*]: *The tree was several yards in girth.*

gist /dʒɪst/ *n.* [*noncount; the* + ~] the main point of a matter: *the gist of a story.*

give /gɪv/ v., **gave** /geyv/, **giv•en**, **giv•ing. 1.** to present freely and without expecting something in return; make a gift of: [~ + obj]: *to give a birthday present to my wife* or *to give my wife a birthday present.* [no obj]: *The charity asked us to give generously.* **2.** [~ + obj] to place in someone's care: *I gave the folders to your assistant.* **3.** [~ + obj] to express in words: *I gave her my phone number.* **4.** [~ + obj] to set forth or show; present; offer: *to give a reason for his actions.* **5.** [~ + obj] to provide as an entertainment: *to give a party.* **6.** [~ + obj] to produce or cause: *The beer gave me a headache.* **7.** [no obj] to yield a little, as to persuasion: *Each side in the dispute must give on some points.* **8. give away, a.** to offer as a present: *He gave away all his money* or *He gave all his money away.* **b.** to let out, tell, or expose: *Would we be giving any secrets away?* **9. give back,** to return (something), as to the owner: *I gave back the book* or *I gave the book back.* **10. give in,** to admit defeat; surrender; yield: *She gave in to despair.* **11. give out, a.** to hand out: *I gave out the test booklets* or *I gave the test booklets out.* **b.** to become exhausted or used up: *The battery gave out.* **12. give up, a.** to abandon hope: *After a while I just gave up.* **b.** to stop doing something: *After searching for ten hours, we gave up; to give up smoking.* **c.** to surrender: *The police told the escaped convict to give (himself) up.* **—Idiom. 13. give or take,** plus or minus a certain amount: *I'll be ready in an hour, give or take five minutes.* **—'giv•er,** n. [count]

'give-and-'take, n. [noncount] willingness to compromise; cooperation.

giv•en /'gɪvən/ v. **1.** pp. of GIVE. **—adj. 2.** [before a noun] stated or certain: *a payment to be made at a given time.* **3.** [be + ~ + to] inclined; disposed: *He was given to making nasty remarks.* **4.** This word is used to mean the same thing as "if (something) is true," followed by a conclusion: *Given A and B, C follows (= If A and B are true, then so is C).* **—n.** [count; usually singular] **5.** a known fact, condition, factor, etc.: *It was a given that the meetings were always late.*

'given 'name, n. [count] the name given to one, as distinguished from an inherited family name; first name: *Her given name was Nancy.*

gla•cial /'gleyʃəl/ adj. **1.** of or relating to ice or glaciers: *glacial terrain.* **2.** bitterly cold; icy: *a glacial winter wind.* **—'gla•cial•ly,** adv.

gla•cier /'gleyʃər/ n. [count] a large mass of ice formed from snow falling and gathering over the years and moving very slowly.

glad /glæd/ adj., **glad•der, glad•dest.** [be + ~] feeling joy or pleasure; delighted; pleased: *She was glad about the good news. He was glad to get a job. We were glad that he finally got remarried.* **—'glad•den,** v. [~ + obj] **—'glad•ly,** adv. **—'glad•ness,** n. [noncount]

glade /gleyd/ n. [count] an open space in a forest.

glam•our or **glam•or** /'glæmər/ n. [noncount] **1.** the quality of fascinating or attracting, esp. by a combination of mysterious charm and good looks. **2.** excitement and adventure: *the glamour of being an astronaut.* **—'glam•or•ous,** adj.

glance /glæns/ v., **glanced, glanc•ing,** n. **—v.** [no obj] **1.** to look quickly or briefly at: *She glanced at the TV screen.* **2.** to strike something indirectly, esp. so as to bounce off at an angle: *The arrow glanced off his shield.* **—n.** [count] **3.** a quick look: *loving glances.*

glanc•ing /'glænsɪŋ/ adj. [before a noun] striking at an angle: *a glancing blow.*

gland /glænd/ n. [count] an organ or group of cells that produces liquid substances that are used by or released from the body: *sweat glands.* **—glan•du•lar** /'glændʒələr/, adj.

glare /glɛər/ n., v., **glared, glar•ing. —n. 1.** [noncount] a very harsh, bright light: *the glare of sunlight.* **2.** [count] an angry stare. **—v.** [no obj] **3.** to shine with a very harsh, bright light: *Headlights glared in the night.* **4.** to stare with an angry look: *She glared angrily. She glared at him.*

glar•ing /'glɛərɪŋ/ adj. **1.** shining with a very bright light. **2.** obviously bad: *a glaring error.* **—'glar•ing•ly,** adv.

glass /glæs/ n. **1.** [noncount] a hard, brittle substance, usually produced by heating and melting sand, soda, and lime, as in the ordinary kind used for windows. **2.** [count] a drinking container made of glass: *a drinking glass.* **3. glasses,** Also called **eyeglasses.** [plural] two glass or plastic lenses set in a frame to help someone see better or to protect the eyes. **—adj. 4.** made of glass: *a glass bead.* **—'glass•y,** adj.

glass•ware /'glæs,wɛər/ n. [noncount] articles of glass, esp. drinking glasses.

glaze /gleyz/ v., **glazed, glaz•ing,** n. **—v.** [~ + obj] **1.** to give a shiny coating to. **—n. 2.** [count] a smooth, shiny surface or coating. **3.** [noncount] the substance for making such a coating. **—glazed,** adj.

gla•zier /'gleyʒər/ n. [count] a person who fits glass into window frames.

gleam /gliym/ n. [count] **1.** a flash or beam of light: *the gleam of a lantern.* **—v.** [no obj] **2.** to send forth a gleam: *She polished the silver until it gleamed.*

glee /gliy/ n. [noncount] delight; great joy: *The children were full of glee.* **—'glee•ful,** adj. **—'glee•ful•ly,** adv.

glib /glɪb/ adj., **glib•ber, glib•best.** able to speak easily and often insincerely: *a glib salesman.* **—'glib•ly,** adv. **—'glib•ness,** n. [noncount]

glide /glayd/ v., **glid•ed, glid•ing,** n. **—v.** [no obj] **1.** to move smoothly, as if without effort: *Skaters glided over the ice.* **—n.** [count] **2.** an act or instance of gliding.

glid•er /'glaydər/ n. [count] an aircraft without a motor, launched by towing.

glim•mer /'glɪmər/ n. [count] **1.** a faint or unsteady light; gleam: *I saw a glimmer in the woods.* **2.** a faint sign: *a glimmer of hope.* **—v.** [no obj] **3.** to shine faintly or unsteadily; twinkle: *The lights glimmered in the distance.* **—'glim•mer•ing,** n. [count]: *faint glimmerings of hope.*

glimpse /glɪmps/ n., v., **glimpsed, glimps•ing. —n.** [count] **1.** a very brief look, sight, or view: *a quick glimpse of the gunmen.* **—v.** [~ + obj] **2.** to look briefly at: *He barely glimpsed the thief.*

glint /glɪnt/ n. [count] a quick flash of light: *a glint from the shiny knife.*

glis•ten /'glɪsən/ v. [no obj] to reflect a sparkling light or a faint, flickering glow; shine: *The black street glistened in the rain.*

glitch /glɪtʃ/ n. [count] *Informal.* a small fault: *a computer glitch.*

glit•ter /'glɪtər/ v. [no obj] **1.** to shine brightly; sparkle: *The gold on her necklace glittered.* **—n. 2.** [count; usually singular] a sparkling brightness: *the glitter of sunlight on the ocean.* **3.** [noncount] false, showy splendor: *the glitter of fame.* **—'glit•ter•ing,** adj. **—'glit•ter•y,** adj.

gloat /glowt/ v. [no obj] to be happy about another's misfortune: *Our opponents gloated over our bad luck.*

glob /glɒb/ *n.* [*count*] a lump of some soft substance: *a glob of whipped cream.*

glob•al /ˈglowbəl/ *adj.* **1.** relating to or involving the whole world: *global weather.* **2.** wide-ranging: *a global analysis of the problem.* —**ˈglob•al•ly,** *adv.*

globe /glowb/ *n.* **1.** [*count; singular; the* + ~] the planet Earth. **2.** [*count*] a round ball on which is shown a map of the earth. **3.** [*count*] a round shape.

glob•ule /ˈglɒbyuwl/ *n.* [*count*] a small drop: *a globule of sweat.*

gloom /gluwm/ *n.* [*noncount*] **1.** darkness: *I couldn't see in the gloom.* **2.** sadness: *I was filled with gloom.*

gloom•y /ˈgluwmiy/ *adj.,* **-i•er, -i•est. 1.** dark. **2.** causing sadness: *a gloomy situation.* —**ˈgloom•i•ly,** *adv.* —**ˈgloom•i•ness,** *n.* [*noncount*]

glo•ri•fy /ˈglɔrəˌfay/ *v.* [~ + *obj*], **-fied, -fy•ing. 1.** to cause to be or treat as being more splendid, excellent, etc., than it is: *to glorify military life.* **2.** to praise the glory of (God), esp. as an act of worship. —**glo•ri•fi•ca•tion** /ˌglɔrəfɪˈkeyʃən/, *n.* [*noncount*] —**ˈglo•ri•ˌfied,** *adj.*

glo•ri•ous /ˈglɔriyəs/ *adj.* **1.** wonderful: *a glorious vacation; a glorious summer day.* **2.** full of glory: *a glorious hero.* —**ˈglo•ri•ous•ly,** *adv.*

glo•ry /ˈglɔriy/ *n., pl.* **-ries,** *v.,* **-ried, -ry•ing.** —*n.* **1.** [*noncount*] very great praise, honor, or fame: *He won great glory.* **2.** [*noncount*] wonderful beauty or splendor: *the glory of autumn.* **3.** [*count*] something that is a source of honor, fame, or admiration: *the glories of ancient Greece.* —*v.* [~ + *in*] **4.** to rejoice proudly: *They gloried in their children's success.*

gloss /glɒs, glɔs/ *n.* [*noncount*] **1.** a luster or shine on the surface of something; glaze: *the gloss of satin.* —*v.* [~ + *obj*] **2.** to put a gloss on: *She glossed her lips.* **3. gloss over,** to give a falsely good appearance to: *to gloss over someone's mistakes.* —**ˈglos•sy,** *adj.*

glos•sa•ry /ˈglɒsəriy, ˈglɔsə-/ *n.* [*count*], *pl.* **-ries.** a list of terms in a special subject, field, or area of usage, with definitions, esp. at the back of a book.

glove /glʌv/ *n.* [*count*] a covering for the hand made with a separate part for each finger and for the thumb. —**gloved,** *adj.*

glow /glow/ *n.* [*count; usually singular*] **1.** a light given off by a heated substance: *the glow of hot coals.* **2.** a feeling of bodily heat: *a warm glow after exercising.* **3.** a warm, usually reddish color of the cheeks. **4.** warmth of emotion or passion; ardor: *She felt the glow of love.* —*v.* [*no obj*] **5.** to give off a glow: *The coals glowed for hours.* **6.** to have a healthy, reddish color: *Her face glowed.* **7.** to show happiness: *to glow with pride.* —**ˈglow•ing,** *adj.*

glow•er /ˈglawər/ *v.* [*no obj;* (~ + *at* + *obj*)] to look or stare with dislike, discontent, or anger; to glare.

glu•cose /ˈgluwkows/ *n.* [*noncount*] a simple sugar found in fruit.

glue /gluw/ *n., v.,* **glued, glu•ing.** —*n.* [*noncount*] **1.** a thick, sticky substance, used to hold things together. —*v.* [~ + *obj*] **2.** to join or attach firmly with or as if with glue: *to glue a label on a package; The kids' eyes were glued to the TV screen.* —**ˈglue•y,** *adj.,* **-i•er, -i•est.**

glum /glʌm/ *adj.,* **glum•mer, glum•mest. 1.** sad: *feeling glum.* **2.** depressing: *a glum prospect for victory.* —**ˈglum•ly,** *adv.* —**ˈglum•ness,** *n.* [*noncount*]

glut /glʌt/ *v.,* **glut•ted, glut•ting,** *n.* —*v.* [~ + *obj*] **1.** to feed or fill too much: *to glut oneself with candy.* **2.** to flood (a market) with a particular item so that the supply greatly exceeds the demand: *The market was glutted with luxury cars.* —*n.* [*count*] **3.** an overly large supply or amount.

glu•ti•nous /ˈgluwtṇəs/ *adj.* sticky. —**ˈglu•ti•nous•ly,** *adv.*

glut•ton /ˈglʌtṇ/ *n.* [*count*] a person who eats and drinks too much. —**ˈglut•ton•ous,** *adj.* —**ˈglut•ton•y,** *n.* [*noncount*]

glyc•er•in /ˈglɪsərɪn/ also **glyc•er•ine** /ˈglɪsərɪn, -əˌriyn/ *n.* GLYCEROL.

glyc•er•ol /ˈglɪsəˌrɔl, -ˌrɒl/ *n.* [*noncount*] a colorless liquid used as a sweetener and preservative.

gnarled /nɑrld/ *adj.* twisted or knotted: *gnarled tree roots; gnarled hands.*

gnat /næt/ *n.* [*count*] a very small fly that bites.

gnaw /nɔ/ *v.,* **gnawed, gnawed** or **gnawn, gnaw•ing. 1.** to bite or chew on: [~ + *obj*]: *The dog gnawed the bone.* [*no obj*]: *The dog gnawed at the bone.* **2.** [*no obj*] to trouble: *Her mistake gnawed at her conscience.*

GNP or **G.N.P.,** an abbreviation of: gross national product.

go /gow/ *v.,* [*no obj*] **went** /wɛnt/, **gone** /gɔn, gɒn/, **go•ing,** *n., pl.* **goes** —*v.* **1.** to move or proceed, from one place to another: *to go home; We went to see her last week.* **2.** to leave a place; depart: *Please go now.* **3.** to be in motion; function; work: *I hear the engine going.* **4.** to become: *He went mad.* **5.** to be in a certain state: *to go barefoot.* **6.** to act as stated: *to go full speed ahead.* **7.** to come into a certain state or condition: *Let's go to sleep.* **8.** to reach: *This road goes to the beach.* **9.** to pass by: *The time went fast.* **10.** [~ + *to* + *verb*] to tend: *This only goes to prove the point.* **11.** to belong; have a place: *This book goes here.* **12.** to fit: *This belt won't go around my waist.* **13.** to be used up: *The cake went fast.* **14.** to be thrown away or dismissed: *That awful jacket has got to go.* **15.** to end: *How did the game go?* **16.** to move with great speed: *Look at that airplane go!* **17.** to make a certain sound: *The gun goes bang.* **18.** to fail or give way: *His eyesight is beginning to go.* **19.** to die: *She went peacefully in her sleep last night.* **20.** to intend or plan: *We're going to leave soon* (= *We will leave soon*). *Their daughter is going to be a doctor* (= *Their daughter's goal is to be a doctor*). **21. go along,** to agree: *She'll go along with your decision.* **22. go by,** to pass: *Don't let this chance go by. Several months went by.* **23. go for,** to make an attempt at: *to go for a win.* **24. go off, a.** to explode: *The bomb went off.* **b.** to make a loud noise: *What time will the alarm go off?* **25. go on, a.** to happen: *What's going on at the office?* **b.** to continue: *Go on working.* **c.** to behave; act: *If you go on like that, they'll fire you.* **d.** to talk without stopping. **26. go out, a.** to stop working: *The lights went out.* **b.** to take part in social activities: *to go out on weekends.* **27. go over,** to review: *Let's go over the examples one more time.* **28. go under, a.** to fail: *Yet another business went under.* **b.** (of a ship) to sink. **29. go with,** to match: *That hat goes with your dress.* —*n.* **30.** [*noncount*] energy or spirit: *She's got a lot of go.* **31.** [*count*] an attempt: *to have a go at the puz-*

G

zle. **—Idiom. 32. go all out,** to give the great-est possible effort: *He went all out to succeed.* **33. go it alone,** to act without help. **34. go (out) with,** to have a relationship with; to date: *He went out with her a few times.* **35. let go, a.** to free; release: *Let go of my hand.* **b.** to dismiss: *The company let go a hundred workers. They let a hundred of them go.* **c.** to leave behind one's doubts or inhibitions: *Sometimes you just have to let (yourself) go.* **36. on the go, a.** very busy; active: *on the go from morning to night.* **b.** while traveling: *luggage for the traveler (who is) on the go.*

goad /gowd/ *n.* [*count*] **1.** anything that urges; a stimulus to action. **—***v.* [~ + *obj* (+ *into*)] **2.** to urge by irritating: *actions meant to goad us into war.*

'go-a,head, *n.* [*count; often singular*] permission to proceed: *They got the go-ahead on the building project.*

goal /gowl/ *n.* [*count*] **1.** purpose; aim: *His goal was to become a famous statesman.* **2.** (in soccer, football, etc.) an area into which the ball must go in order for the team to score. **3.** the point scored by doing this.

goal•ie /'gowliy/ *n.* GOALKEEPER.

goal•keep•er /'gowl,kiypər/ *n.* [*count*] (in hockey, soccer, etc.) a player who stands at the goal and whose chief duty is to prevent the other team from scoring. —**'goal,keep•ing,** *n.* [*non-count*]

goat /gowt/ *n.* [*count*] **1.** a small animal with hollow horns, closely related to sheep. **—Idiom. 2. get someone's goat,** *Informal.* to anger or annoy someone.

gob /gɒb/ *n.* [*count*] **1.** a mass or lump: *He smeared a gob of plaster in the hole.* **2. gobs,** [*plural*] *Informal.* a large amount: *gobs of money.*

gob•ble /'gɒbəl/ *v.* [~ + *obj*], **-bled, -bling.** to swallow or eat quickly or hungrily in large pieces; gulp: *We gobbled (up) our lunch.*

'go-be,tween, *n.* [*count*] a person who acts as a messenger between persons who cannot meet.

gob•let /'gɒblɪt/ *n.* [*count*] a drinking glass with a base and stem.

gob•lin /'gɒblɪn/ *n.* [*count*] an evil spirit that is mischievous or harmful.

God /gɒd/ *n.* **1.** the creator and ruler of the universe in certain religions, as Judaism, Christianity, or Islam; the Supreme Being. **2.** [*god; count*] one of several beings thought to live forever, having power over worldly affairs; deity: *the Greek and Roman gods.* —**'god,like,** *adj.*

god•child /'gɒd,tʃayld/ *n.* [*count*], *pl.* **-chil•dren.** a child for whom someone serves as a godparent.

god•dess /'gɒdɪs/ *n.* [*count*] a female god: *the Greek and Roman goddesses.*

'god-,fearing, *adj.* religious; devout; godly.

god•less /'gɒdlɪs/ *adj.* **1.** acknowledging no god or deity: *a godless society.* **2.** evil; sinful.

god•ly /'gɒdliy/ *adj.*, **-li•er, -li•est. 1.** obeying God or the rules of one's religion; devout. **2.** coming from God; divine. —**'god•li•ness,** *n.* [*noncount*]

god•par•ent /'gɒd,pɛərənt, -,pær-/ *n.* [*count*] a person who takes responsibility for a child's religious upbringing.

go•fer or **go-fer** /'gowfər/ *n.* [*count*] *Slang.* an employee whose chief duty is running errands.

'go-,getter, *n.* [*count*] *Informal.* an active, ener-getic person who works hard to succeed. —**'go-'getting,** *adj.*

gog•gle /'gɒgəl/ *n.* **goggles,** [*plural*] large glasses worn to protect the eyes from strong wind, flying objects, blinding light, etc.

go•ing /'gowɪŋ/ *n.* **1.** [*count*] the act or fact of leaving: *comings and goings.* **2.** [*noncount*] the condition or speed of doing something: *It was rough going.* —*adj.* [*before a noun*] **3.** current; usual: *What is the going rate for baby-sitting nowadays?* **4.** working; thriving: *a going business.*

gold /gowld/ *n.* [*noncount*] **1.** a precious yellow metal element. **2.** jewelry, etc. made of gold. **3.** a bright yellow color. —*adj.* [*before a noun*] **4.** made of, relating to, or like gold.

gold•en /'gowldən/ *adj.* **1.** of the color of gold: *golden hair.* **2.** made of gold: *golden earrings.* **3.** excellent: *a golden opportunity.*

'golden 'rule, *n.* [*count; usually singular; the +* ~] a rule of moral conduct, usually phrased "Do unto others as you would have others do unto you."

gold•finch /'gowld,fɪntʃ/ *n.* [*count*] a small bird, the male of which has yellow colors in the summer.

gold•fish /'gowld,fɪʃ/ *n.* [*count*], *pl.* (*esp. when thought of as a group*) **-fish,** (*esp. for kinds or species*) **-fish•es.** a small, usually yellow or orange fish, kept as a pet in glass bowls or garden ponds.

'gold 'medal, *n.* [*count*] a medal awarded to the person who wins a race or other competition.

gold•smith /'gowld,smɪθ/ *n.* [*count*] a person who makes gold jewelry, etc.

golf /gɒlf, gɔlf/ *n.* [*noncount*] **1.** a game in which a small, hard, white ball is hit into a series of holes, usually 9 or 18, situated on a course. —*v.* [*no obj*] **2.** to play golf. —**'golf•er,** *n.* [*count*]

'golf ,club, *n.* [*count*] **1.** a long stick, usually made of metal, used to strike a golf ball. **2.** a place where golf is played.

-gon, a combining form meaning having a specific number or sort of angles (*polygon*).

gone /gɔn/ *adj.; v.* pp. of GO.

gong /gɔŋ, gɒŋ/ *n.* [*count*] a round piece of metal that produces a loud, hollow tone when struck.

gon•or•rhe•a /,gɒnə'riyə/ *n.* [*noncount*] a sexually transmitted disease. Also, *esp. Brit.,* ,gon•or'rhoe•a. —,gon•or'rhe•al, *adj.*

good /gʊd/ *adj.,* **bet•ter** /'bɛtər/, **best** /bɛst/, *n., interj.* —*adj.* **1.** morally excellent; virtuous: *a wise and good man.* **2.** satisfactory: *a good teacher.* **3.** well-behaved. **4.** honorable or worthy: *the company's good name.* **5.** sensible: *to use good judgment.* **6.** healthful: *Fresh fruit is good for you.* **7.** favorable: *good news.* **8.** [*before a noun*] cheerful: *in good spirits.* **9.** [*before a noun*] enjoyable: *Have a good time.* **10.** skillful: *He's good at arithmetic.* **11.** correct: *He writes very good English.* **12.** socially proper: *good manners.* **13.** fairly large: *a good amount.* **14.** loyal: *a good friend.* —*n.* [*noncount*] **15.** [*used with negative words, or in questions*] profit or advantage; benefit: *What good will that do?* **16.** kindness: *to do good.* **17.** that which is morally right; virtue: *to be a power for good.* —*interj.* **18.** This word is used to express approval or satisfaction: *Good! Now we can all go home.* —**Idiom. 19. a good deal of,** quite a lot: *a good deal of money.* See DEAL. **20. come to no good,** to end in failure: *She'll come to no good if she hangs around with* *that crowd.* **21. for good,** forever: *We left that country for good.* **22. no good,** without value or merit: *Face it, that car is no good.* —'**good•ness,** *n.* [noncount]

good-by or **good•by** or **good-bye** /ˌgʊd'bay/ *interj., n., pl.* **-bys** or **-byes.** —*interj.* **1.** This word is used when the speaker is leaving someone, or being left by someone: *"Good-bye! See you tomorrow."* —*n.* [count] **2.** an act of saying "good-bye": *They made their good-byes.*

'**good-for-'nothing,** *adj., n., pl.* **good-for-nothings.** —*adj.* **1.** worthless: *that good-for-nothing loafer.* —*n.* [count] **2.** a worthless or useless person.

'**good-'hearted** or '**good'hearted,** *adj.* kind or generous; benevolent. —'**good-'heartedly,** *adv.* —'**good-'heartedness,** *n.* [noncount]

'**good-'hu•mored,** *adj.* cheerful; pleasant: *good-humored joking.*

good morning, *interj.* This expression is used when meeting someone in the morning.

'**good-'natured,** *adj.* friendly and kind. —'**good-'naturedly,** *adv.*

good•ness /'gʊdnɪs/ *n.* [noncount] **1.** the state or quality of being good. **2.** the best or most valuable part of anything. —*interj.* **3.** This word is used to express surprise, alarm, etc.: *Goodness! I didn't see you behind the couch.*

good night *interj.* This expression is used when leaving, or being left by, someone at night, esp. when going to bed.

goods *n. pl.* **1.** possessions, esp. movable property. **2.** articles for sale: *linen goods.*

good•will or **good will** /'gʊd'wɪl/ *n.* [noncount] **1.** friendly behavior; kindness. **2.** the good reputation of a business, considered as part of its value.

good•y or **good•ie** /'gʊdiy/ *n.* [count], *pl.* **good•ies.** Usually, **goodies.** [plural] **1.** something pleasing to eat. **2.** something esp. desirable: *all sorts of goodies.*

goose /guws/ *n.* [count], *pl.* **geese. 1.** a water bird, larger and with a longer neck and legs than a duck. **2.** the female of this bird. Compare GANDER. **3.** a silly person.

'**goose ‚flesh** or '**goose‚flesh,** *n.* [noncount] small, raised spots on the skin, as from cold or fear. Also called '**goose ‚pimples,** '**goose ‚bumps.** [count; plural]

GOP or **G.O.P.,** an abbreviation of: Grand Old Party, a nickname for the Republican Party.

go•pher /'gowfər/ *n.* [count] a burrowing rodent having a stout body and a short tail.

gore[1] /gɔr/ *n.* [noncount] **1.** blood that is shed. **2.** bloodshed: *a movie full of gore.*

gore[2] /gɔr/ *v.* [~ + *obj*], **gored, gor•ing.** to pierce with a horn or tusk: *The bull gored the bullfighter.*

gorge /gɔrdʒ/ *n., v.,* **gorged, gorg•ing.** —*n.* [count] **1.** a narrow valley with steep, rocky walls. —*v.* **2.** to stuff with food: [~ + *obj*]: *to gorge oneself.* [no obj]: *They gorged on food.*

gor•geous /'gɔrdʒəs/ *adj.* splendid; beautiful: *gorgeous weather.* —'**gor•geous•ly,** *adv.*

go•ril•la /gə'rɪlə/ *n.* [count], *pl.* **-las.** the largest manlike ape.

gor•y /'gɔriy/ *adj.,* **-i•er, -i•est.** having much bloodshed and violence: *a gory movie.* —'**gor•i•ness,** *n.* [noncount]

gosh /gɒʃ/ *interj.* This word is used to express surprise: *Gosh, I didn't expect to see you here.*

gos•pel /'gɒspəl/ *n.* **1.** [often: *Gospel; noncount;*

often: the + ~] the story of Jesus' life and teachings. **2.** the first four books of the New Testament, namely Matthew, Mark, Luke, and John. **3.** [count] a very important doctrine: *political gospel.* —*adj.* [before a noun] **4.** of or relating to the gospel; evangelical.

gos•sip /'gɒsəp/ *n., v.,* **-siped** or **-sipped, -sip•ing** or **-sip•ping.** —*n.* **1.** [noncount] idle talk or rumor, esp. about others. **2.** [count] a person who enjoys gossip. —*v.* [no obj] **3.** to talk gossip. —'**gos•sip•y,** *adj.*

got /gɒt/ *v.* a pt. and pp. of GET.

got•ten /'gɒtṇ/ *v.* a pp. of GET.

gouge /gawdʒ/ *v.* [~ + *obj*], **gouged, goug•ing. 1.** to make a hole in (something) with a pointed tool: *The hammer gouged the wall.* **2. gouge out,** to dig out with a pointed object: *to gouge out a piece of wood.*

gourd /gɔrd, gʊrd/ *n.* [count] the hard-shelled fruit of a climbing plant, made into bowls, ladles, etc.

gour•met /gʊr'mey, 'gʊrmey/ *n.* [count] **1.** one who is fond of fine food and drink. —*adj.* [usually: before a noun] **2.** of or for gourmets: *gourmet cooking.*

gov. or **Gov.,** an abbreviation of: **1.** government. **2.** governor.

gov•ern /'gʌvərn/ *v.* **1.** to rule: [~ + *obj*]: *to govern a nation.* [no obj]: *to govern fairly.* **2.** [~ + *obj*] to influence; control: *the motives that govern a decision.* —'**gov•ern•a•ble,** *adj.* —**gov•ern•ance** /'gʌvərnəns/, *n.* [noncount]

gov•ern•ment /'gʌvərnmənt, -ərmənt/ *n.* **1.** [noncount] the political system by which a community, society, state, etc., is governed. **2.** [count; usually singular; *the* + ~] the governing body in a state, community, etc. —**gov•ern•men•tal** /ˌgʌvərn'mɛntḷ, ˌgʌvər-/, *adj.*

gov•er•nor /'gʌvərnər, -ənər/ *n.* [count] **1.** the executive head of a state in the U.S. **2.** a person who directs an institution, society, etc.: *the governor of a prison.* —'**gov•er•nor‚ship,** *n.* [noncount]

Govt. or **govt.,** government.

gown /gawn/ *n.* [count] **1.** a woman's dress, esp. one that is full-length: *wedding gowns; evening gowns.* **2.** a loose, flowing outer garment.

GP or **G.P.,** an abbreviation of: general practitioner.

GPO or **G.P.O.,** an abbreviation of: **1.** general post office. **2.** Government Printing Office.

gr., an abbreviation of: **1.** grade. **2.** grain. **3.** gram. **4.** gravity. **5.** gross.

grab /græb/ *v.,* **grabbed, grab•bing,** *n.* —*v.* [~ + *obj*] **1.** to take suddenly, eagerly, or roughly: *He grabbed his hat and dashed off. She grabbed (at) the railing.* —*n.* [count] **2.** a sudden, eager grasp: *I made a grab for my hat.* —'**grab•ber,** *n.* [count]

grace /greys/ *n., v.,* **graced, grac•ing.** —*n.* **1.** [noncount] elegance or beauty of form, manner, or movement: *She moves with elegance and grace.* **2.** Also, **grace period.** extra time given someone to pay a debt: [noncount]: *30 days' grace.* [count]: *a grace period of 30 days.* **3.** [noncount] favor or goodwill. **4.** [noncount] the favor and love of God. **5.** [noncount] a short prayer before or after a meal: *Let's say grace.* —*v.* [~ + *obj*] **6.** to decorate: *paintings graced the walls.* **7.** to honor: *Will you grace us with your presence?* —*Idiom.* **8. fall from grace, a.** to sin. **b.** to lose favor with those in power. **9. in someone's good (** or **bad) graces,** thought of with favor (or disfavor) by someone. **10. with good (or bad) grace,** willingly (or unwillingly): *He congratulated the winner with good grace.* —**'grace•less,** *adj.* —**'grace•less•ly,** *adv.* —**'grace•less•ness,** *n.* [*noncount*]

grace•ful /'greysfəl/ *adj.* having grace of form, movement, or speech. —**'grace•ful•ly,** *adv.* —**'grace•ful•ness,** *n.* [*noncount*]

gra•cious /'greyʃəs/ *adj.* **1.** pleasantly kind; polite: *a gracious host.* **2.** characterized by good taste, comfort, ease, or luxury: *gracious suburban living.* —**'gra•cious•ly,** *adv.* —**'gra•cious•ness,** *n.* [*noncount*]

grad /græd/ *n.* [*count*] *Informal.* a graduate of a school.

grade /greyd/ *n., v.,* **grad•ed, grad•ing.** —*n.* [*count*] **1.** a degree or step in quality, rank, or value: *several grades of wool.* **2.** a class of persons or things of the same relative rank, quality, etc. **3.** a class in a school: *students in seventh and eighth grades.* **4.** a mark given for a student's work. —*v.* [~ + *obj*] **5.** to arrange in grades; sort: *a machine that grades eggs.* **6.** to give a grade to a student's work; mark.

gra•di•ent /'greydiyənt/ *n.* [*count*] the degree at which a highway, railroad, etc., slopes up or down: *a steep gradient.*

grad•u•al /'grædʒuwəl/ *adj.* taking place, changing, etc., slowly: *His health showed gradual improvement.* —**'grad•u•al•ly,** *adv.*

grad•u•ate /*n., adj.* 'grædʒuwɪt, -,eyt; *v.* -,eyt/ *n., adj., v.,* **-at•ed, -at•ing.** —*n.* [*count*] **1.** a person who has received a degree or diploma from a university, college, or school. —*adj.* [*before a noun*] **2.** of, relating to, or involved in academic study beyond a bachelor's or first professional degree: *graduate studies.* —*v.* **3. graduate from,** to receive a grade or diploma: *to graduate from college.*

grad•u•at•ed /'grædʒuw,eytɪd/ *adj.* arranged in steps, as the scale of a thermometer.

'graduate ,school /'grædʒuwɪt/ *n.* [*count*] a division of a university offering courses leading to advanced degrees.

grad•u•a•tion /,grædʒuw'eyʃən/ *n.* [*noncount*] **1.** an act of graduating from a college or school. **2.** the ceremony of graduating, as at a college or school: *Graduation is next week.*

graf•fi•ti /grə'fiytiy/ *n.* [*noncount*] drawings or writings made on walls.

graft¹ /græft/ *n.* [*count*] **1.** a small shoot cut from a plant and placed into a slit in a stem of another plant in which it continues to grow. **2.** a piece of living tissue transplanted from one part of a person's body to another, or from one person to another. —*v.* [~ + *obj*] **3.** to insert (a graft) into a tree or other plant. **4.** to transplant (a piece of living tissue) as a graft.

graft² /græft/ *n.* [*noncount*] getting money or advantage by dishonest means.

grain /greyn/ *n.* **1.** [*count*] a small, hard seed. **2.** [*noncount*] the gathered seed of plants such as wheat, rye, etc.: *They shipped tons of grain.* **3.** [*noncount*] the pattern of the fibers in wood, meat, etc.: *the beautiful grain of walnut.* —**grainy,** *adj.*

gram /græm/ *n.* [*count*] a unit of mass or weight in the metric system, equal to 15.432 grains; ¹⁄₁₀₀₀ of a kilogram. *Abbr.:* g, gr. Also, *esp. Brit.,* **gramme.**

-gram, a combining form meaning something written or drawn, either by hand or machine (*diagram; mammogram*).

gram•mar /'græmər/ *n.* **1.** [*noncount*] rules according to which the sentences or words of a language are constructed. **2.** [*count*] a book that teaches these rules. —**gram•mar•i•an** /grə'mɛəriyən/ *n.* [*count*]

gram•mat•i•cal /grə'mætɪkəl/ *adj.* **1.** obeying the rules of grammar of a language: *a grammatical sentence.* **2.** of or relating to the study of grammar or grammatical rules: *grammatical rules.* —**gram'mat•i•cal•ly,** *adv.*

gra•na•ry /'greynəriy, 'grænə-/ *n.* [*count*], *pl.* **-ries.** a storehouse for grain.

grand /grænd/ *adj.,* **-er, -est,** *n.* —*adj.* **1.** impressive in size, appearance, or general effect: *grand mountain scenery.* **2.** dignified: *a grand and regal manner.* **3.** respected: *a grand old man.* **4.** [*before a noun*] complete: *the grand total.* **5.** wonderful: *We had a grand time.* —*n.* **6.** GRAND PIANO. **7.** [*count; singular*] *Informal.* a thousand dollars. —**'grand•ly,** *adv.*

grand•child /'græn,tʃayld/ *n.* [*count*], *pl.* **-chil•dren.** a child of one's son or daughter.

grand•daugh•ter /'græn,dɔtər/ *n.* [*count*] a daughter of one's son or daughter.

gran•deur /'grændʒər/ *n.* [*noncount*] the quality of being grand, magnificent, or impressive: *the grandeur of the universe.*

grand•fa•ther /'græn,faðər, 'grænd-/ *n.* [*count*] the father of one's father or mother.

'grandfather (or **'grandfather's**) **,clock,** *n.* [*count*] a large floor clock as tall as or taller than a person.

gran•di•ose /'grændiy,ows/ *adj.* falsely or foolishly grand: *grandiose words; grandiose schemes.*

grand•ma /'græn,ma, -,mɔ, 'grænd-, 'græm-/ *n., pl.* **-mas.** *Informal.* GRANDMOTHER.

grand•moth•er /'græn,mʌðər, 'grænd-, 'græm-/ *n.* [*count*] the mother of one's father or mother.

grand•pa /'græn,pa, -,pɔ, 'grænd-, 'græm-/ *n., pl.* **-pas.** *Informal.* GRANDFATHER.

grand•par•ent /'græn,pɛərənt, -,pær-, 'grænd-/ *n.* [*count*] a parent of a parent; a grandmother or grandfather.

'grand pi'ano, *n.* [*count*] a large piano having horizontal strings and a frame supported on three legs.

grand•son /'græn,sʌn, 'grænd-/ *n.* [*count*] a son of one's son or daughter.

grand•stand /'græn,stænd, 'grænd-/ *n.* [*count*] **1.** a main seating area, as of a stadium or racetrack. —*v.* [*no obj*] **2.** to conduct oneself or perform so as to impress onlookers.

gran•ite /'grænɪt/ *n.* [*noncount*] a coarse-grained stone, used chiefly in roads and in building. —**gra•nit•ic** /grə'nɪtɪk/, *adj.*

gran•ny or **gran•nie** /'græniy/ *n., pl.* **-nies.** *Informal.* GRANDMOTHER.

gra•no•la /grə'nowlə/ *n.* [*noncount*] a breakfast food of rolled oats, nuts, dried fruit, brown sugar, etc.

grant /grænt/ *v.* [~ + *obj*] **1.** to give: *The teacher granted permission to leave.* **2.** to agree to: *to grant a request.* **3.** to admit (to) the truth of (something): *I grant that you're right in this case.* —*n.* [*count*] **4.** something given, as a privilege, a sum of money, or a tract of land. —*Idiom.* **5. take for granted, a.** to assume without question: *I take his honesty for granted.* **b.** to treat carelessly: *You'll regret it if you take her for granted.* —**'grant•er, 'gran•tor,** *n.* [*count*]

gran•u•lar /'grænyələr/ *adj.* **1.** of the nature of

granules; grainy. **2.** showing a grainy structure or surface: *a granular surface.* —**gran•u•lar•i•ty** /ˌɡrænyəˈlærɪtiy/, *n.* [*noncount*]

gran•u•lat•ed /ˈɡrænyəˌleytɪd/ *adj.* made like or resembling grains: *granulated sugar.* —**gran•u•la•tion** /ˌɡrænyəˈleyʃən/, *n.* [*noncount*]

gran•ule /ˈɡrænyuwl/ *n.* [*count*] a little grain: *granules of sand.*

grape /ɡreyp/ *n.* [*count*] the smooth-skinned, green or purple fruit that grows in clusters on vines and is used to make wine.

grape•fruit /ˈɡreypˌfruwt/ *n.* [*count*] [*noncount*] a large, roundish, yellow-skinned citrus fruit that has a juicy, acid inside that may be eaten.

grape•vine /ˈɡreypˌvayn/ *n.* [*count*] **1.** a vine that bears grapes. **2.** an informal means of spreading information: *I heard it through the grapevine.*

graph /ɡræf/ *n.* [*count*] **1.** a diagram showing the connections or relations among two or more things. —*v.* [~ + *obj*] **2.** to represent by a graph: *She graphed the current trends.*

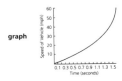

graph

graph•ic /ˈɡræfɪk/ *adj.* Also, **'graph•i•cal. 1.** giving a clear description or picture: *a graphic account of the riots.* **2.** relating to the use of diagrams, graphs, pictures, or the like. —**'graph•i•cal•ly,** *adv.*

'graphic 'arts, *n.* [*plural*] **1.** the means by which copies of a design are printed. **2.** the arts of drawing, painting, and printmaking.

graph•ics /ˈɡræfɪks/ *n.* **1.** [*noncount; used with a singular verb*] the art of drawing. **2.** GRAPHIC ARTS (def. 1). **3.** [*noncount; used with a plural verb*] pictures and designs produced by means of a computer software program.

graph•ite /ˈɡræfayt/ *n.* [*noncount*] a soft form of carbon, used for pencil leads and as a lubricant.

grap•ple /ˈɡræpəl/ *v.* [*no obj*], **-pled, -pling.** to struggle with by or as by wrestling: *The two wrestlers grappled in the ring. He grappled with his conscience.*

grasp /ɡræsp/ *v.* [~ + *obj*] **1.** to seize and hold: *He grasped my arm.* **2.** to understand: *I grasp your meaning.* —*n.* [*count; usually singular*] **3.** the act of grasping. **4.** reach: *The new job was within his grasp.* **5.** power to understand: *She has a good grasp of math.*

grasp•ing /ˈɡræspɪŋ/ *adj.* greedy.

grass /ɡræs/ *n.* **1.** [*count*] a plant that has blade-like leaves and is grown for lawns, used as pasture, or cut for hay. **2.** [*noncount*] grass-covered ground: *a picnic on the grass.* **3.** *Slang.* MARIJUANA.

grass•hop•per /ˈɡræsˌhɒpər/ *n.* [*count*] a plant-eating insect having large hind legs used for leaping.

'grass 'roots, *n.* [*plural; used with a plural verb but sometimes used with a singular verb*] **1.** ordinary citizens, esp. as contrasted with a leadership. —*adj.* [*grass-roots; before a noun*] **2.** of, from, or aimed at the grass roots: *grass-roots support.*

gras•sy /ˈɡræsiy/ *adj.*, **-si•er, -si•est.** covered with grass.

grate¹ /ɡreyt/ *n.* [*count*] **1.** a frame of metal bars for holding fuel when burning, as in a fireplace, furnace, or stove. **2.** a framework of bars used as a guard, as over a window.

grate² /ɡreyt/ *v.*, **grat•ed, grat•ing. 1.** [~ + *on*] to have an irritating effect: *His constant chatter grates on my nerves.* **2.** [*no obj*] to (cause to) make a sound of rough scraping: *The wheels grated against the fence.* **3.** [~ + *obj*] to make into small pieces by rubbing against a rough surface: *to grate a carrot.* —**'grat•er,** *n.* [*count*]

grate•ful /ˈɡreytfəl/ *adj.* feeling or expressing gratitude: *a grateful letter.* —**'grate•ful•ly,** *adv.* —**'grate•ful•ness,** *n.* [*noncount*]

grat•i•fy /ˈɡrætəˌfay/ *v.* [~ + *obj*], **-fied, -fy•ing. 1.** to give pleasure to (a person or persons): *Her praise gratified us all. It gratified us that we were going home soon.* **2.** to satisfy: *always wanted to gratify her desires instantly.* —**grat•i•fi•ca•tion** /ˌɡrætəfɪˈkeyʃən/, *n.* [*noncount*] —**'grat•i•fy•ing,** *adj.*

grat•ing¹ /ˈɡreytɪŋ/ *n.* [*count*] a fixed frame of bars covering an opening, to keep things out while letting in light or air.

grat•ing² /ˈɡreytɪŋ/ *adj.* irritating; annoying: *a grating personality.*

grat•is /ˈɡrætɪs, ˈɡrɑtɪs/ *adj., adv.* free: [*adj.; be* + ~]: *The books are gratis.* [*adverb*]: *The teachers got the books gratis.*

grat•i•tude /ˈɡrætɪˌtuwd, -ˌtyuwd/ *n.* [*noncount*] the feeling of being grateful.

gra•tu•i•tous /ɡrəˈtuwɪtəs, -ˈtyuw-/ *adj.* **1.** free or voluntary: *gratuitous help.* **2.** being without apparent reason or cause; completely unnecessary: *a gratuitous insult.*

gra•tu•i•ty /ɡrəˈtuwɪtiy, -ˈtyuw-/ *n.* [*count*], *pl.* **-ties.** money given for a service done; a tip.

grave¹ /ɡreyv/ *n.* [*count*] a place in the ground in which to bury a dead body.

grave² /ɡreyv/ *adj.*, **grav•er, grav•est. 1.** serious or solemn: *grave thoughts.* **2.** dangerous: *a grave international crisis.* —**'grave•ly,** *adv.* —**'grave•ness,** *n.* [*noncount*]

grav•el /ˈɡrævəl/ *n.* [*noncount*] small stones and pebbles or a mixture of these with sand.

grav•el•ly /ˈɡrævəliy/ *adj.* **1.** covered with gravel; like gravel in texture: *a gravelly road.* **2.** sounding rough or harsh: *a gravelly voice.*

grav•en /ˈɡreyvən/ *adj.* (of an image) carved.

grave•stone /ˈɡreyvˌstown/ *n.* [*count*] a stone marking the place where a person is buried.

grave•yard /ˈɡreyvˌyɑrd/ *n.* CEMETERY.

grav•i•tate /ˈɡrævɪˌteyt/ *v.* [*no obj*], **-tat•ed, -tat•ing.** to be strongly attracted: *The press gravitated toward the celebrities.*

grav•i•ta•tion /ˌɡrævɪˈteyʃən/ *n.* [*noncount*] **1.** the force of attraction between any two masses. **2.** a movement toward something or someone: *the gravitation of people toward the suburbs.* —ˌ**grav•i•ta•tion•al,** *adj.*

grav•i•ty /ˈɡrævɪtiy/ *n.* [*noncount*] **1.** the force by which objects tend to fall toward the center of the earth. **2.** seriousness: *an illness of considerable gravity.*

gra•vy /ˈɡreyviy/ *n.* [*noncount*], *pl.* **-vies.** the juices of cooked meat. *She served gravy with the roast.*

gray or **grey** /ɡrey/ *adj.*, **gray•er, gray•est** or **grey•er, grey•est,** *n.* —*adj.* **1.** of a color between white and black. **2.** dull and dreary: *a gray*

G

day. **3.** having gray hair: *He was gray by his early thirties.* **4.** vague or intermediate: *a gray area between right and wrong.* —*n.* **5.** [*noncount*] [*count*] a color between white and black. —'**gray•ish,** *adj.* —'**gray•ness,** *n.* [*noncount*]

'**gray ,matter,** *n.* [*noncount*] **1.** nerve tissue of the brain and spinal cord. **2.** *Informal.* intelligence.

graze¹ /greyz/ *v.* [*no obj*], **grazed, graz•ing.** to feed on growing grass, as cattle, sheep, etc., do: *grazing in the field.*

graze² /greyz/ *v.,* **grazed, graz•ing,** *n.* —*v.* **1.** to touch lightly in passing: [~ + *obj*]: *His knee grazed the chair.* [*no obj*]: *His knee grazed against the rough wall.* **2.** [~ + *obj*] to scrape the skin from: *The bullet just grazed his shoulder.* —*n.* [*count*] **3.** a slight scratch.

grease /*n.*griys; *v.* griys, griyz/ *n., v.,* **greased, greasing.** —*n.* [*noncount*] **1.** the soft melted fat of animals. **2.** fatty or oily matter in general: *grease for the axle of the car.* —*v.* [~ + *obj*] **3.** to put grease on: *to grease the axle of a car.* —'**greas•y,** *adj.,* **-i•er, -i•est.**

great /greyt/ *adj.,* **-er, -est,** *adv.* —*adj.* **1.** very large in size, number, degree, or power: *great herds of buffalo; great pain.* **2.** wonderful; excellent: *to have a great time.* **3.** healthy; well: *feeling great.* **4.** [*before a noun*] special: *a great occasion.* **5.** [*before a noun*] excellent; important; famous: *a great inventor.* **6.** [*before a noun*] being of one generation older or younger (used in combination): *a great-grandson.* —*adv.* **7.** *Informal.* very well: *Things are going great.* **8.** very: *a great big hole.* —'**great•ness,** *n.* [*noncount*]

great•ly /'greytliy/ *adv.* very much; to a great degree: *His health has greatly improved.*

greed /griyd/ *n.* [*noncount*] overly strong desire for wealth, profit, or possessions. —'**greed•y,** *adj.,* **-i•er, -i•est.** —'**greed•i•ly,** *adv.* —'**greed•i•ness,** *n.* [*noncount*]

Greek /griyk/ *adj.* **1.** of or relating to Greece. **2.** of or relating to the language spoken in Greece. —*n.* **3.** [*count*] a person born or living in Greece. **4.** [*noncount*] the language spoken in ancient or modern Greece. **5.** [*noncount*] something difficult to understand: *This contract is Greek to me.*

green /griyn/ *adj.,* **-er, -est,** *n.* —*adj.* **1.** of the color of growing plants: *green leaves.* **2.** immature; inexperienced: *green troops.* —*n.* **3.** the color of most grasses and leaves while growing: [*noncount*]: *The room was painted green.* [*count*]: *The room was painted a pale green.* **4.** **greens,** [*plural*] the leaves and stems of certain plants, as spinach or lettuce, eaten as a vegetable. **5.** [*count*] a plot of grassy ground, esp. in the center of a town. —*Idiom.* **6. green with envy,** very jealous.

green•er•y /'griynəriy/ *n.* [*noncount*], *pl.* **-er•ies.** **1.** green leaves. **2.** greens used for decoration.

'**green-,eyed,** *adj.* jealous; envious.

green•house /'griyn,haws/ *n.* [*count*] a glass building used for growing plants.

'**green 'thumb,** *n.* [*count; usually singular; a +* ~] skill in growing plants.

greet /griyt/ *v.* [~ + *obj*] **1.** to welcome: *She greeted us at the door.* **2.** to receive: *He greeted my suggestion with applause.*

greet•ing /'griytɪŋ/ *n.* **1.** an act or words of welcoming: [*noncount*]: *She lifted her hand in greeting.* [*count*]: *a friendly greeting.* **2.** **greetings,** [*plural*] an expression of friendly wishes: *sending our greetings.*

gre•gar•i•ous /grɪ'gɛəriyəs/ *adj.* liking the company of others: *A politician must be friendly and gregarious.* —**gre'gar•i•ous•ly,** *adv.* —**gre'gar•i•ous•ness,** *n.* [*noncount*]

gre•nade /grɪ'neyd/ *n.* [*count*] a small bomb thrown by hand.

grew /gruw/ *v.* pt. of GROW.

grey /grey/ *adj.,* **-er, -est,** *n., v.* GRAY.

grey•hound /'grey,hawnd/ *n.* [*count*] one of a breed of tall, slender shorthaired dogs noted for their keen sight and speed.

grid /grɪd/ *n.* [*count*] **1.** a framework of crossed bars. **2.** a network of crossed lines for locating points on a map, chart, etc. **3.** any network like this. **4.** a system of wires for electrical distribution: *a power grid.*

grid•dle /'grɪdl/ *n.* [*count*] a flat pan for cooking pancakes, bacon, etc.

grid•i•ron /'grɪd,ayərn/ *n.* [*count*] **1.** a football field. **2.** a utensil consisting of parallel metal bars on which to broil food.

grid•lock /'grɪd,lɒk/ *n.* **1.** [*noncount*] a traffic jam in which all movement stops because intersections are blocked by traffic. **2.** [*count*] a complete stoppage of normal activity: *financial gridlock.*

grief /griyf/ *n.* **1.** [*noncount*] great sorrow over a loss or disappointment. **2.** [*count; usually singular*] a cause of great sorrow: *His leaving was a great grief to her.* —*Idiom.* **3. come to grief,** to suffer misfortune: *All his great ideas came to grief.*

griev•ance /'griyvəns/ *n.* **1.** [*count*] a cause for complaint. **2.** [*noncount*] a complaint: *She filed a grievance with her union.*

grieve /griyv/ *v.,* **grieved, griev•ing.** to (cause to) feel grief, distress, or great sorrow: [*no obj*]: *She grieved for her dog.* [~ + *obj*]: *Her loss grieved me.*

griev•ous /'griyvəs/ *adj.* **1.** causing grief or great sorrow: *a grievous loss.* **2.** causing great harm: *a grievous offense.* —'**griev•ous•ly,** *adv.*

grill¹ /grɪl/ *n.* [*count*] **1.** a metal grate for cooking food over a fire. —*v.* [~ + *obj*] **2.** to cook on a grill: *We'll grill a steak.*

grill² /grɪl/ *n.* GRILLE.

grille or **grill** /grɪl/ *n.* [*count*] a metal grating or barrier, as for a gate.

grim /grɪm/ *adj.,* **grim•mer, grim•mest.** **1.** stern; serious; not yielding: *grim determination; a grim look.* **2.** terrible: *War is a grim undertaking.* —'**grim•ly,** *adv.* —'**grim•ness,** *n.* [*noncount*]

grim•ace /'grɪməs, grɪ'meys/ *n., v.,* **-aced, -ac•ing.** —*n.* [*count*] **1.** a facial expression, often ugly or twisted, that indicates disapproval, pain, etc. —*v.* [*no obj*] **2.** to make grimaces: *She grimaced from the pain.*

grime /graym/ *n.* [*noncount*] dirt or soot stuck to a surface. —'**grim•y,** *adj.,* **-i•er, -i•est.**

grin /grɪn/ *v.,* **grinned, grin•ning,** *n.* —*v.* [*no obj*] **1.** to smile broadly: *He grinned with delight.* —*n.* [*count*] **2.** a broad smile. —*Idiom.* **3. grin and bear it,** to endure something unpleasant without complaining.

grind /graynd/ *v.,* **ground** /grawnd/, **grind•ing,** *n.* —*v.* [~ + *obj*] **1.** to wear down, make smooth, or sharpen (something) by rubbing: *to grind a lens; to grind knives.* **2.** to crush (something) into small particles, as by pounding: *The glass bottles were ground (up) for recycling.* **3. grind down,** to oppress, torment, or crush: *to be ground down by poverty.* —*n.* **4.** [*count*] the size of ground particles: *That coffee is available in* *various grinds.* **5.** [*count; usually singular*] hard, dull work: *the daily grind.* **6.** [*count*] *Informal.* a student who works and studies hard.

grip /grɪp/ *n., v.,* **gripped, grip•ping.** —*n.* [*count*] **1.** a seizing and holding tightly; firm grasp: *He held the hammer securely in his grip.* **2.** mental control: *a good grip on the problem.* —*v.* [~ + *obj*] **3.** to grasp or seize firmly; hold tightly: *I gripped the pole on the subway car.* **4.** to hold the interest of: *to grip the mind.* —*Idiom.* **5. come to grips with,** to face and cope with: *to come to grips with a problem.*

gripe /graɪp/ *v.,* **griped, grip•ing,** *n.* —*v.* [*no obj*] **1.** *Informal.* to complain or grumble: *soldiers griping about army food.* —*n.* [*count*] **2.** *Informal.* a nagging complaint: *I've got a few gripes.* —*grip•er, n.* [*count*]

grip•ping /ˈgrɪpɪŋ/ *adj.* holding one's interest: *a gripping novel.*

gris•ly /ˈgrɪzliy/ *adj.,* **-li•er, -li•est.** causing a feeling of horror: *a grisly murder.*

gris•tle /ˈgrɪsəl/ *n.* [*noncount*] tough tissue, esp. in meat. —**gris•tly,** *adj.,* **-tli•er, -tli•est:** *gristly beef.*

grit /grɪt/ *n., v.,* **grit•ted, grit•ting.** —*n.* [*noncount*] **1.** hard, rough particles, as of sand, stone, or gravel. **2.** firmness of character: *He showed grit in the face of danger.* —**'grit•ty,** *adj.,* **-ti•er, -ti•est.**

griz•zled /ˈgrɪzəld/ *adj.* having gray hair.

'griz•zly ˌbear /ˈgrɪzliy/ *n.* [*count*] a large North American brown bear with rough, gray-tipped fur.

groan /grown/ *n.* [*count*] **1.** a low, mournful sound made in response to pain or grief. **2.** a deep creaking sound due to a continued strain: *The groan of the timbers in the wind.* —*v.* [*no obj*] **3.** to utter a deep, mournful sound that expresses pain or grief. **4.** to make a sound resembling a groan: *The steps of the old house groaned under my weight.*

gro•cer /ˈgrowsər/ *n.* [*count*] the owner of a store that sells food.

gro•cer•y /ˈgrowsəriy, ˈgrowsriy/ *n.* [*count*], *pl.* **-cer•ies. 1.** Also called **'gro•cery ˌstore.** a grocer's store. **2.** Usually, **groceries.** [*plural*] things sold by a grocer.

grog•gy /ˈgrɒgiy/ *adj.,* **-gi•er, -gi•est.** unsteady and weak, as from lack of sleep or illness. —**'grog•gi•ly,** *adv.* —**'grog•gi•ness,** *n.* [*noncount*]

groin /grɔyn/ *n.* [*count*] the place where the thigh joins the abdomen.

groom /gruwm, grʊm/ *n.* **1.** BRIDEGROOM. **2.** [*count*] a person in charge of horses. —*v.* [~ + *obj*] **3.** to make (oneself or one's clothing) neat or tidy. **4.** to clean or brush (a horse, dog, etc.). **5.** to prepare for a position, etc.: *being groomed for higher office.*

groove /gruwv/ *n.* **1.** [*count*] a long, narrow cut in a surface. **2.** [*count; usually singular*] a fixed routine: *to get into a groove.*

grope /growp/ *v.,* **groped, grop•ing. 1.** [*no obj*] to feel about with the hands: *to grope around in the darkness.* **2.** [~ + *obj*] *Slang.* to touch or handle (someone) sexually; fondle.

gross /grows/ *adj.,* **-er, -est,** *v.* —*adj.* **1.** total (opposed to *net*): *gross earnings.* **2.** [*before a noun*] inexcusable: *gross injustice.* **3.** vulgar: *gross language.* **4.** *Slang.* disgusting: *a really gross habit.* **5.** very fat. —*v.* [~ + *obj*] **6.** to earn as a total amount: *He grossed over three million*

dollars last year. —**'gross•ly,** *adv.* —**'gross•ness,** *n.* [*noncount*]

'gross 'national 'product, *n.* [*count*] the total value of all goods and services produced in a country during one year. *Abbr.:* GNP

gro•tesque /grow'tɛsk/ *adj.* strange, unnatural, and ugly in shape, appearance, or character. —**gro'tesque•ly,** *adv.*

grouch /grawtʃ/ *n.* [*count*] a complaining and continually unhappy person: *an old grouch.* —**'grouch•i•ness,** *n.* [*noncount*] —**'grouch•y,** *adj.,* **-i•er, -i•est.**

ground¹ /grawnd/ *n.* **1.** [*noncount; the* + ~] the solid surface of the earth; firm or dry land. **2.** [*count*] Often, **grounds.** [*plural*] an area of land put to a special use: *picnic grounds; hunting grounds.* **3.** [*count*] Often, **grounds.** [*plural*] reason or cause: *grounds for divorce.* **4.** [*noncount*] the main surface or background, as in a painting. **5. grounds,** [*plural*] the gardens, lawn, etc., around a building. —*v.* **6.** [~ + *obj*] to place (an idea or argument) on a firm or logical basis: *an argument firmly grounded in logic.* **7.** [~ + *obj*] to force (an aircraft or pilot) to stay on the ground; prevent from flying: *If the pilot used drugs, he was grounded.* **8.** [~ + *obj*] to restrict the activities of as a punishment: *His parents grounded him for coming home late.* —*Idiom.* **9. gain ground,** to make progress. **10. hold** or **stand one's ground,** to maintain one's position. **11. lose ground,** to fail to advance. **12. off the ground,** into action or well under way: *The plan never got off the ground.*

ground² /grawnd/ *v.* **1.** a pt. and pp. of GRIND. —*adj.* **2.** reduced to very small pieces by grinding: *ground beef.*

'ground 'floor, *n.* [*count; often: the* + ~] the floor of a building at or nearest to ground level.

ground•hog /ˈgrawndˌhɔg, -ˌhɒg/ *n.* [*count*] a North American animal that burrows in holes and hibernates in the winter.

ground•less /ˈgrawndlɪs/ *adj.* without reasonable basis: *groundless fears.*

'ground ˌrule, *n.* [*count*] a basic principle of conduct in a situation: *the ground rules of the debate.*

group /gruwp/ *n.* [*count*] **1.** any collection of persons or things that are related in some way: *a group of students.* **2.** musicians who play together: *a rock group.* —*v.* **3.** to (cause to) form together in a group: [~ + *obj*]: *We grouped the students by age.* [*no obj*]: *The workers grouped together to protest.*

grouse¹ /graws/ *n.* [*count*], *pl.* **grouse, grous•es.** a plump bird of the pheasant family.

grouse² /graws/ *v.,* **groused, grous•ing.** *Informal.* to grumble; complain: [*no obj*]: *grousing about his job.* [~ + *obj*]: *grousing that he hated his job.*

grove /growv/ *n.* [*count*] a small group of trees.

grow /grow/ *v.,* **grew** /gruw/, **grown, grow•ing. 1.** [*no obj*] to increase in size: *The children have grown tall.* **2.** to (cause to) come into being and develop: [*no obj*]: *Plants grow wild here.* [~ + *obj*]: *The farmers grow corn in that region.* **3.** [*no obj*] to utter a deep, mournful [*sic*] **grow into, a.** to become large enough to wear (an item of clothing): *She grew into her sister's clothes.* **b.** to become experienced enough to do: *He eventually grew into his job.* **4. grow out of, a.** to become too large for: *She's grown out of her baby clothes.* **b.** to develop from: *The program grew out of a simple idea.* **5. grow up, a.** to be-

G

come fully grown. **b.** to arise: *New cities grew up in the desert.* —**'grow•er,** *n.* [*count*]

growl /graul/ *v.* **1.** to utter a deep, throaty sound of anger or hostility: [*no obj*]: *The dog growled.* [~ + *obj*]: *The dog growled a warning.* —*n.* [*count*] **2.** the act or sound of growling: *a loud growl.*

grown /groun/ *adj.* **1.** adult: *a grown man.* —*v.* **2.** pp. of GROW.

'grown-'up, *adj.* adult; mature.

grown•up /'groun,ʌp/ *n.* [*count*] an adult.

growth /grouθ/ *n.* **1.** [*noncount*] the act or process or a manner of growing; development: *the growth of one's children; the growth of a business.* **2.** [*noncount*] size or stage of development: *full growth.* **3.** [*count*] an abnormal increase in a mass of tissue, as a tumor.

grub /grʌb/ *n.*, *v.*, **grubbed, grub•bing.** —*n.* **1.** [*count*] the thick-bodied, sluggish young of certain insects, esp. the beetle. **2.** [*noncount*] *Slang.* food: *How's the grub in that place?* —*v.* **3.** to dig out of the ground: [~ + *obj*]: *The birds grubbed worms.* [*no obj*]: *They were grubbing for worms.* —**'grub•ber,** *n.* [*count*]

grub•by /'grʌbiy/ *adj.*, **-bi•er, -bi•est.** dirty: *grubby work clothes.* —**'grub•bi•ness,** *n.* [*noncount*]

grudge /grʌdʒ/ *n.*, *v.*, **grudged, grudg•ing.** —*n.* [*count*] **1.** a feeling of ill will or resentment: *She can really hold a grudge.* —*v.* [~ + *obj*] **2.** to give or permit unwillingly: *They grudged us every day we were away.* —**'grudg•ing,** *adj.*

gru•el•ing /'gruwəlɪŋ, 'gruwlɪŋ/ *adj.* very tiring: *a grueling day at work.* Also, *esp. Brit.*, **'gru•el•ling.**

grue•some /'gruwsəm/ *adj.* causing horror and disgust: *a gruesome murder.* —**'grue•some•ly,** *adv.* —**'grue•some•ness,** *n.* [*noncount*]

gruff /grʌf/ *adj.*, **-er, -est. 1.** low and harsh: *a gruff voice.* **2.** not friendly: *a gruff manner.* —**'gruff•ly,** *adv.* —**'gruff•ness,** *n.* [*noncount*]

grum•ble /'grʌmbəl/ *v.*, **-bled, -bling,** *n.* —*v.* [*no obj*] **1.** to complain unhappily: *All he did was grumble.* —*n.* [*count*] **2.** a complaint. —**'grum•bler,** *n.* [*count*]

grump•y /'grʌmpiy/ *adj.*, **-i•er, -i•est.** bad-tempered: *She's always a little grumpy when she wakes up.* —**'grump•i•ness,** *n.* [*noncount*]

grunt /grʌnt/ *v.* [*no obj*] **1.** to make the deep, throaty sound that a pig makes. —*n.* [*count*] **2.** a sound of grunting.

guar•an•tee /,gærən'tiy/ *n.*, *pl.* **-tees,** *v.*, **-teed, -tee•ing.** —*n.* [*count*] **1.** a formal assurance that something is of specified quality, content, benefit, etc: *The VCR has a two-year guarantee.* **2.** something that assures a particular outcome: *Wealth is not a guarantee of happiness.* —*v.* [~ + *obj*] **3.** to offer a guarantee for: *The company guarantees its machines for ten years.* **4.** to assure that a stated outcome is certain: *I guarantee that I'll be there.*

guar•an•tor /'gærən,tɔr, -tər/ *n.* [*count*] one that makes or gives a guarantee.

guard /gard/ *v.* [~ + *obj*] **1.** to keep safe from harm or danger; protect: *The dog guarded the house.* **2.** to keep under close watch: *He guarded the prisoner.* **3. guard against,** to provide with protection: *This ingredient guards your teeth against decay.* —*n.* **4.** [*count*] a person or group that guards. **5.** [*noncount*] a close watch: *under armed guard.* **6.** [*count*] a device that prevents injury, loss, etc.: *a guard for a goalie in hockey.* —*Idiom.* **7. off (one's) guard,** unprepared: *I*

was caught off guard. **8. on (one's) guard,** watching; vigilant; wary. **9. stand guard over,** to protect: *They stood guard over their wounded friend.* —**'guard•ed,** *adj.*

guard•i•an /'gardiyən/ *n.* [*count*] **1.** a person who guards: *the guardians of democracy.* **2.** a person legally entrusted with the care of a child. —*adj.* [*before a noun*] **3.** guarding; protecting: *a guardian angel.* —**'guard•i•an,ship,** *n.* [*noncount*]

gu•ber•na•to•ri•al /,guwbərnə'tɔriyəl,gyuw-/ *adj.* of or relating to a state governor or the office of state governor: *a gubernatorial election.*

guer•ril•la or **gue•ril•la** /gə'rɪlə/ *n.* [*count*], *pl.* **-las.** a member of a band of unofficial soldiers that attacks an enemy in small groups.

guess /gɛs/ *v.* [~ + *obj*] **1.** to give an opinion about (something) without knowing for certain if it is true: *to guess (at) a person's weight.* **2.** to think, believe, or suppose: *I guess that I can find time to help you.* —*n.* [*count*] **3.** an opinion that one reaches without enough evidence. **4.** the act of forming such an opinion.

guest /gɛst/ *n.* [*count*] **1.** a person who spends some time at another's home or in a hotel. **2.** a person who is invited to and paid for at a restaurant, etc., by another. **3.** a person invited to appear in a television or other program. —*adj.* [*before a noun*] **4.** provided for a guest: *a guest towel.* **5.** taking part or performing as a guest: *a guest conductor for the orchestra.*

guid•ance /'gaydns/ *n.* [*noncount*] **1.** the act or function of guiding; leadership. **2.** advice or counseling, esp. for students.

guide /gayd/ *v.*, **guid•ed, guid•ing,** *n.* —*v.* [~ + *obj*] **1.** to assist (a person) to travel through, or reach a destination in, an unfamiliar area: *He guided us to the town.* **2.** to direct the course of: *The pilot guided the plane to a safe landing.* **3.** to give advice to (a person). —*n.* [*count*] **4.** a person who guides, esp. one hired to guide travelers, tourists, etc. **5.** a book, pamphlet, or the like with information, instructions, or advice; guidebook or handbook.

guide•book /'gayd,bʊk/ *n.* [*count*] a book of directions and information for travelers: *a guidebook to downtown Copenhagen.*

guide•line /'gayd,layn/ *n.* [*count*] any guide or indication of a future course of action, or of some course or set of steps to follow: *guidelines on tax reform.*

guile /gayl/ *n.* [*noncount*] deception. —**'guile•ful,** *adj.* —**'guile•less,** *adj.*

guil•lo•tine /'gɪlə,tiyn, 'giyə-/ *n.*, *v.*, **-tined, -tin•ing.** —*n.* [*count*] **1.** a device for cutting off a person's head. —*v.* [~ + *obj*] **2.** to cut the head off (someone) by the guillotine.

guilt /gɪlt/ *n.* [*noncount*] **1.** the fact or state of having committed a crime or wrong, esp. against the law: *to admit one's guilt in a robbery.* **2.** a feeling of shame for some act of wrongdoing: *feelings of guilt.* —**'guilt•less,** *adj.*

guilt•y /'gɪltiy/ *adj.*, **-i•er, -i•est. 1.** having committed a crime or wrong: *The jury found the defendant guilty of murder.* **2.** [*before a noun*] having or showing a feeling of guilt: *a guilty conscience.* —**guilt•i•ly** /'gɪltļiy/, *adv.* —**'guilt•i•ness,** *n.* [*noncount*]

'guinea ,pig, *n.* [*count*] **1.** a small, mildly fat, furry animal without a tail, often raised as a pet. **2.** the subject of any sort of test or experiment.

gui•tar /gɪ'tar/ *n.* [*count*] a stringed musical instrument with a long neck; a flat, somewhat violinlike body; and usually six strings. —**gui'tar•ist,** *n.* [*count*]

gulch /gʌltʃ/ *n.* [*count*] a deep, narrow valley, esp. one marking the course of a stream.

gulf /gʌlf/ *n.* [*count*] **1.** a portion of an ocean or sea partly enclosed by land. **2.** any wide difference between two or more things, as in opinion.

gull /gʌl/ *n.* [*count*] a long-winged water-dwelling bird.

gul•let /ˈgʌlɪt/ *n.* [*count*] the tube that goes from the mouth to the stomach; esophagus.

gul•li•ble /ˈgʌləbəl/ *adj.* too willing to believe everything: *selling junk to gullible consumers.* Sometimes, **'gul•la•ble.** —**gul•li•bil•i•ty** /ˌgʌləˈbɪlɪtiy/, *n.* [*noncount*]

gul•ly /ˈgʌliy/ *n.* [*count*], *pl.* -**lies.** a small valley originally worn away by running water; a ditch.

gulp /gʌlp/ *v.* [*no obj*] [~ + *obj*] **1.** to swallow quickly. —*n.* [*count*] **2.** the act of gulping. **3.** the amount swallowed at one time.

gum¹ /gʌm/ *n., v.,* **gummed, gum•ming.** —*n.* [*count*] **1.** a sticky substance that comes from plants. **2.** chewing gum. —*v.* [~ + *obj*] **3.** to stick together with gum. **4.** to clog: *The engine was gummed (up) and wouldn't start.* —**'gum•my,** *adj.,* -**mi•er,** -**mi•est.**

gum² /gʌm/ *n.* [*count*] Often, **gums.** [*plural*] the firm, fleshy tissue around the teeth.

gun /gʌn/ *n.* [*count*] **1.** a weapon consisting of a metal tube from which bullets or shells are shot. —*Idiom.* **2. stick to** or **stand by one's guns,** to keep firmly to one's position. **3. under the gun,** under pressure, as to meet a deadline or solve a problem. —**'gun•ner,** *n.* [*count*]

gun•fire /ˈgʌnˌfayᵊr/ *n.* [*noncount*] the firing of guns.

gun•man /ˈgʌnmən/ *n.* [*count*], *pl.* -**men.** a person who uses a gun unlawfully.

gun•point /ˈgʌnˌpɔynt/ —*Idiom.* **at gunpoint,** under threat of being shot: *He held them up at gunpoint.*

gun•pow•der /ˈgʌnˌpawdər/ *n.* [*noncount*] an explosive mixture used in shells and cartridges, in fireworks, and for blasting.

gun•shot /ˈgʌnˌʃɒt/ *n.* [*count*] the shooting of a gun or the sound made by this.

gur•gle /ˈgərgəl/ *v.,* -**gled,** -**gling,** *n.* —*v.* [*no obj*] **1.** to flow in a broken, irregular, noisy current: *The water gurgled down the drain.* —*n.* [*count*] **2.** the act or noise of gurgling.

gush /gʌʃ/ *v.* **1.** to (cause to) flow out suddenly, in great amounts, or forcefully: [*no obj*]: *Oil gushed from the crippled tanker.* [~ + *obj*]: *The crippled tanker gushed oil.* —*n.* [*count; usually singular*] **2.** a sudden great outflow of a fluid: *a gush of blood.* —**'gush•er,** *n.* [*count*]

gust /gʌst/ *n.* [*count*] **1.** a sudden strong blast of wind. **2.** a sudden burst of strong feeling: *a gust of anger.* —*v.* [*no obj*] **3.** to blow in gusts: *The wind was gusting up to fifty miles per hour.* —**'gust•y,** *adj.,* -**i•er,** -**i•est:** *a cold, gusty March day.*

gus•to /ˈgʌstow/ *n.* [*noncount*] strong, hearty, or eager enjoyment.

gut /gʌt/ *n., v.,* **gut•ted, gut•ting,** *adj.* —*n.* **1.** [*count*] the part of the body that carries food and digests it. **2. guts, a.** [*plural*] the bowels. **b.** [*noncount*] courage: *He didn't have the guts to defend them.* —*v.* [~ + *obj*] **3.** to take out the inner organs of: *to gut a fish.* **4.** to destroy the inside of: *Fire gutted the building.* —*adj.* [*before a noun*] **5. a.** basic: *gut issues.* **b.** based on instincts or emotions: *a gut reaction.* —**'gut•less,** *adj.*

guts•y /ˈgʌtsiy/ *adj.,* -**i•er,** -**i•est.** daring or courageous: *a gutsy decision.*

gut•ter /ˈgʌtər/ *n.* [*count*] **1.** a channel at the side of a road for carrying off surface water. **2.** a channel on the roof of a building, for carrying off rainwater.

guy /gay/ *n.* [*count*] **1.** a man or boy. **2. guys,** [*plural*] *Informal.* persons of either sex; people.

guz•zle /ˈgʌzəl/ *v.,* -**zled,** -**zling. 1.** to drink greedily or excessively: [*no obj*]: *She had been guzzling all evening.* [~ + *obj*]: *She guzzled beer.* **2.** [~ + *obj*] to use in large amounts: *This car guzzles gas.* —**'guz•zler,** *n.* [*count*]

gym /dʒɪm/ *n.* **1.** [*count*] a gymnasium: *The dance was held in the gym.* **2.** PHYSICAL EDUCATION: *a course in gym.* —*adj.* [*before a noun*] **3.** of, relating to, or used for athletics or physical education: *gym clothes.*

gym•na•si•um /dʒɪmˈneyziyəm/ *n.* [*count*], *pl.* -**si•ums,** -**si•a** /-ziyə, -zə/. a building or room equipped for indoor sports, exercise, or physical education.

gym•nast /ˈdʒɪmnæst, -nəst/ *n.* [*count*] one who is trained in gymnastics.

gym•nas•tics /dʒɪmˈnæstɪks/ *n.* [*plural; used with a plural verb*] physical exercises that develop strength and balance. —**gym'nas•tic,** *adj.*

gy•ne•col•o•gy /ˌgaynɪˈkɒlədʒiy, ˌdʒɪnɪ-/ *n.* [*noncount*] the branch of medicine that deals with the health and diseases of women, esp. of the reproductive organs. —**gy•ne•co•log•ic** /ˌgaynɪkəˈlɒdʒɪk, ˌdʒɪnɪ-/, **gy/ne•co•log/i•cal,** *adj.* [*before a noun*] —**,gyn•e'col•o•gist,** *n.* [*count*]

gyp /dʒɪp/ *v.,* **gypped, gyp•ping,** *n.* —*v.* [~ + *obj* (+ *out of*)] **1.** to cheat or rob by deceit: *He gypped us out of our money.* —*n.* [*count*] **2.** *Informal.* a trick, swindle, or fraud.

gyp•sum /ˈdʒɪpsəm/ *n.* [*noncount*] a soft white mineral used to make plaster of Paris and as a fertilizer.

Gyp•sy /ˈdʒɪpsiy/ *n., pl.* -**sies,** *adj.* —*n.* [*count*] **1.** a member of a people who traditionally traveled in covered carts carrying their possessions, but who now live mostly in permanent communities. **2.** [*gypsy*] a person who is like a Gypsy in appearance or way of life. —*adj.* [*before a noun*] **3.** of or relating to the Gypsies.

gy•rate /ˈdʒayreyt, dʒayˈreyt/ *v.,* -**rat•ed,** -**rat•ing.** to move in a circle; whirl; revolve; rotate: [*no obj*]: *They gyrated to the music.* [~ + *obj*]: *She gyrated her hips to the music.* —**gy•ra•tion** /dʒayˈreyʃən/, *n.* [*count*]

G

H

H, h /eytʃ/ n. [count], pl. **Hs** or **H's, hs** or **h's.** the eighth letter of the English alphabet, a consonant.

ha or **hah** /hɑ/ interj. This word is used to express surprise, victory, etc.

hab•it /'hæbɪt/ n. **1.** usual or customary behavior: [noncount]: I got up at 6 a.m. out of habit. [count]: Smoking had become a habit. **2.** [count] the long garment worn by a monk or nun.

hab•it•a•ble /'hæbɪtəbəl/ adj. (of a place) that can be lived in. —**hab•it•a•bil•i•ty** /ˌhæbɪtə-'bɪlɪtiy/, n. [noncount]

hab•i•tat /'hæbɪˌtæt/ n. [count] the natural environment of an animal or plant.

hab•i•ta•tion /ˌhæbɪ'teyʃən/ n. [noncount] the act of living in a place: buildings unfit for human habitation.

ha•bit•u•al /hə'bɪtʃuwəl/ adj. **1.** [before a noun] done by habit: a habitual smoker. **2.** usual; customary: their habitual lateness. —**ha'bit•u•al•ly**, adv.

hack¹ /hæk/ v. **1.** [~ + obj] to cut or chop with rough blows: They hacked down the trees. **2.** to clear by cutting away vines, trees, etc.: [~ + obj]: They hacked their way through the jungle. [no obj]: They hacked through the jungle.

hack² /hæk/ n. [count] **1.** a person willing to do hard or boring work for pay. **2.** a person, esp. a writer, who produces low-quality work. —adj. [before a noun] **3.** working as a hack: a hack writer. **4.** suitable to or typical of a hack: hack work.

hack•er /'hækər/ n. [count] Slang. **1.** a person who is excellent at computer programming. **2.** a person who uses computer systems illegally.

hack•neyed /'hækniyd/ adj. not interesting because used too often: a hackneyed saying.

hack•saw or **hack saw** /'hæk,sɔ/ n. [count] a saw with a fine-toothed blade.

had /hæd/ v. pt. and pp. of HAVE.

had•dock /'hædək/ n. [count], pl. (esp. when thought of as a group) **-dock,** (esp. for kinds or species) **-docks.** a food fish of the cod family.

had•n't /'hædnt/ contraction of had not.

hag /hæg/ n. [count] an ugly old woman, esp. an evil or bad-tempered one.

hag•gard /'hægərd/ adj. looking very tired: a haggard, worried face. —**'hag•gard•ly**, adv. —**'hag•gard•ness**, n. [noncount]

hag•gle /'hægəl/ v. [no obj], **-gled, -gling.** to bargain about the cost of something. —**hag•gler** /'hæglər/, n. [count]

hah /hɑ/ interj. HA.

ha-ha /'hɑˈhɑ, ˌhɑ'hɑ/ interj. This word is used to express laughter, amusement, etc.

hail¹ /heyl/ v. [~ + obj] **1.** to greet or welcome: to hail an old friend. **2.** to call out or signal to: to hail a cab. **3.** to approve of publicly: He hailed the new law as a victory. **4. hail from,** to have as one's home or place of birth or residence: She hails from Indiana.

hail² /heyl/ n. **1.** [noncount] a shower or storm of small balls of ice. **2.** [count; usually singular] a shower of anything: a hail of bullets. —v. **3.** [it + ~; (no obj)] to pour down hail: It hailed all afternoon. **4.** [no obj] [~ + obj] to (cause to) fall like hail.

hail•stone /'heyl,stown/ n. [count] a small ball of hail.

hail•storm /'heyl,stɔrm/ n. [count] a storm with hail.

hair /hɛər/ n. **1.** [count] any of many small, threadlike pieces growing from the skin of people and animals. **2.** [noncount] a mass of such pieces, such as that covering the human head. —**Idiom. 3. let one's hair down,** to behave in a relaxed, informal manner. **4. make someone's hair stand on end,** to shock or frighten. —**'hair•less,** adj. —**'hair•y,** adj., **-i•er, -i•est.**

hair•brush /'hɛər,brʌʃ/ n. [count] a brush for arranging the hair.

hair•cut /'hɛər,kʌt/ n. [count] **1.** an act or instance of cutting the hair. **2.** the style in which the hair is cut: a short haircut.

hair•do /'hɛər,duw/ n. [count], pl. **-dos.** a way of arranging the hair.

hair•dress•er /'hɛər,drɛsər/ n. [count] a person who cuts or arranges hair. —**'hair•dress•ing,** n. [noncount]

hair•line /'hɛər,layn/ n. [count] **1.** a very thin line. **2.** the border on the forehead where the hair starts to grow. —adj. [before a noun] **3.** narrow or fine as a hair: a hairline crack in the wall.

hair•piece /'hɛər,piys/ n. [count] a covering of false hair for the head.

hair•pin /'hɛər,pɪn/ n. [count] **1.** a slender U-shaped pin used to fasten the hair. —adj. [before a noun] **2.** (of a road, etc.) curved like a hairpin.

'hair-,raising, adj. very frightening or exciting: hair-raising adventures.

hair•split•ting /'hɛər,splɪtɪŋ/ n. [noncount] the stressing of unimportant details. —**'hair,split•ter,** n. [count]

hair•style or **hair style** /'hɛər,stayl/ n. HAIRDO. —**'hair,styl•ist,** n. [count]

Hai•tian /'heyʃən/ adj. **1.** of or relating to Haiti. **2.** of or relating to the language spoken by many of the people in Haiti. —n. **3.** [count] a person born or living in Haiti. **4.** [noncount] the language spoken by many of the people living in Haiti, also called Haitian Creole.

hale /heyl/ adj., **hal•er, hal•est.** strong and well; healthy: hale and hearty feeling.

half /hæf/ n., pl. **halves** (havz), pron., adj., adv. —n. [count] **1.** one of two equal parts of something: two halves of an apple. **2.** a quantity or amount equal to one half of something (½): half a loaf; half the class. —pron. **3.** a quantity or amount equal to one half of (some group or thing): Half of the passengers are ill. —adj. [before a noun] **4.** being one of two equal parts of a whole: a half quart. **5.** being half in degree, amount, length, etc.: to travel at half speed. —adv. **6.** in or to the extent of a half: The glass was half empty. **7.** not completely; partly: He was half awake.

'half ,brother, n. [count] a male having only one parent in common with another person.

'half-,caste, n. [count] a person whose parents are of different races.

half•heart•ed /'hæf'hɑrtɪd/ adj. having or showing little enthusiasm: a halfhearted attempt to cook. —**'half'heart•ed•ly,** adv. —**'half'heart•ed•ness,** n. [noncount]

'half-'mast, *n.* [*noncount*] a position halfway between the top of a mast, staff, etc., and its base: *a flag flown at half-mast.*

'half ,sister, *n.* [*count*] a female having only one parent in common with another person.

half•time or **half-time** /'hæf,taym/ *n.* [*noncount*] [*count*] the period of time between the two halves of a sports contest.

'half-,truth, *n.* [*count*] a statement that is only partly true, esp. one intended to deceive.

half•way /'hæf'wey/ *adv.* **1.** to half of the distance: *to run halfway to town.* **2.** nearly; almost: *He halfway agreed to their demands.* —*adj.* [*before a noun*] **3.** midway, as between two points. **4.** partial: *halfway measures.*

'halfway ,house, *n.* [*count*] a house in which persons newly released from mental hospitals, prisons, etc., can live temporarily.

'half-,wit, *n.* [*count*] a stupid or foolish person. —**'half-'witted,** *adj.*: *a half-witted idea.*

hal•i•but /'hæləbət, 'hɒl-/ *n.* [*count*], *pl.* (*esp. when thought of as a group*) **-but,** (*esp. for kinds or species*) **-buts.** any of various large fish with flattened bodies, used for food.

hall /hɔl/ *n.* [*count*] **1.** a passageway in a building. **2.** a large room or building for public gatherings: *a concert hall.* **3.** a large building for living in, for instruction, etc., at a college or university.

hal•le•lu•jah or **hal•le•lu•iah** /,hælə'luwyə/ *interj.* This word is used to express joy, praise, or thanks to God.

hal•low /'hælow/ *v.* [~ + *obj*] to make or honor as holy: *to hallow the name of the Lord.* —**'hal•lowed,** *adj.*

Hal•low•een or **Hal•low•e'en** /,hælə'wiyn, ,hɒl-/ *n.* [*noncount*] [*count*] the evening of Oct. 31, esp. celebrated by children, who dress up in costumes.

hal•lu•ci•na•tion /hə,luwsə'neyʃən/ *n.* [*count*] seeing something that is not really present, esp. as a result of drugs or illness. —**hal'lu•ci,nate,** *v.*, **-nat•ed, -nat•ing.** [*no obj*] [~ + *obj*]

hall•way /'hɔl,wey/ *n.* [*count*] a hall or passageway.

ha•lo /'heylow/ *n.* [*count*], *pl.* **-los, -loes. 1.** a golden ring of light above or around the head of a holy person in a painting. **2.** a bright circle surrounding the sun or moon.

halt /hɔlt/ *v.* **1.** to (cause to) stop: [*no obj*]: *The car halted in front of the house.* [~ + *obj*]: *He halted the car.* —*n.* [*count*] **2.** a temporary or permanent stop: *Work came to a halt.* —*interj.* **3.** This word is used to command someone to stop.

hal•ter /'hɔltər/ *n.* [*count*] **1.** a rope or strap that fits round the head of a horse for leading or tying it. **2.** a garment tied or fastened behind the neck and across the back, leaving the arms and upper back bare.

halt•ing /'hɔltɪŋ/ *adj.* slow and uncertain, esp. in speech: *a halting voice.* —**'halt•ing•ly,** *adv.*

halve /hæv/ *v.* [~ + *obj*], **halved, halv•ing. 1.** to divide into two equal parts: *Halve the apple so we can both eat it.* **2.** to reduce to half: *to halve a recipe.*

halves /hævz/ *n.* **1.** pl. of HALF. —*Idiom.* **2. go halves,** to share equally; divide evenly: *We went halves on the dinner bill.*

ham[1] /hæm/ *n.* [*noncount*] [*count*] a cut of meat from the back leg or shoulder of a pig.

ham[2] /hæm/ *n.* [*count*] **1.** an actor or performer who overacts; a bad actor. **2.** an amateur radio operator.

ham•burg•er /'hæm,bɜrgər/ *n.* [*count*] a round, flat patty of ground beef, esp. in a bun.

ham•let /'hæmlɪt/ *n.* [*count*] a small village.

ham•mer /'hæmər/ *n.* [*count*] **1.** a tool with a heavy metal head on a handle, used for driving nails, beating metals, etc. **2.** something that is shaped or used like a hammer. —*v.* **3.** to hit over and over: [~ + *obj*]: *He hammered the nails in.* [*no obj*]: *They hammered at the door with their fists.* **4.** [~ + *obj*] to shape (metal or a metal object) by hammering: *He hammered the metal into a horseshoe.*

ham•mock /'hæmək/ *n.* [*count*] a bed of canvas or net that hangs between two supports.

ham•per[1] /'hæmpər/ *v.* [~ + *obj*] to get in the way of: *Heavy rain hampered traffic.*

ham•per[2] /'hæmpər/ *n.* [*count*] a large covered basket: *a picnic hamper; a hamper for dirty clothes.*

ham•ster /'hæmstər/ *n.* [*count*] a small, short-tailed animal with large cheek pouches, often kept as a pet.

ham•string /'hæm,strɪŋ/ *n., v.,* **-strung** /-,strʌŋ/, **-string•ing.** —*n.* [*count*] **1.** a tendon behind the knee that connects a muscle to a bone. —*v.* [~ + *obj*] **2.** to disable by cutting the hamstring. **3.** to make powerless.

hand /hænd/ *n.* **1.** [*count*] the end part of the arm in humans and some animals. **2.** [*count*] the pointer on a clock, meter, etc.: *The hands of the clock pointed to twelve.* **3.** [*count*] a worker, as on a ranch or ship. **4.** [*count*] a person with experience: *an old hand at fund-raising.* **5.** [*count*] skill: *The painting shows a master's hand.* **6.** [*count; singular*] help; aid: *Give me a hand with this ladder.* **7.** [*count*] style of handwriting: *a clear hand.* **8.** [*count; singular*] a round of applause for a performer: *Let's give the singer a big hand.* **9.** [*count*] a promise of marriage. **10.** [*count*] **a.** the playing cards held by each player at one time. **b.** one round of a card game. —*v.* **11.** [~ + *obj*] to give or pass with the hand; offer: *I handed the note to the teacher.* **12.** [~ + *obj*] to provide: *He handed us a golden opportunity.* **13. hand down, a.** to deliver; pronounce: *The judge handed down the decision* or *The judge handed the decision down.* **b.** to pass along in turn: *to hand down the family traditions* or *to hand the traditions down.* **14. hand in,** to present for acceptance: *He handed in his paper. He handed his paper in.* **15. hand out,** to give or pass out: *She handed out the tests* or *She handed the tests out.* **16. hand over,** to deliver to another: *The kidnappers handed over the hostages* or *The kidnappers handed the hostages over.* —*Idiom.* **17. at hand, a.** within reach: *He picked up the first pencil at hand.* **b.** about to happen: *Their wedding day was at hand.* **c.** under consideration: *a discussion of the matter at hand.* **18. by hand,** by using the hands instead of a machine. **19. change hands,** to pass from one owner to another. **20. hand it to,** to give approval to; praise: *You've got to hand it to her, she tried hard.* **21. have a hand in,** to take part in: *She had a hand in raising the money.* **22. in hand, a.** under control: *He has the situation well in hand.* **b.** in one's possession: *He's got enough cash in hand.* **23. in someone's hands,** in someone's possession, control, or care: *My fate is in your hands.* **24. keep one's hand in,** to continue to work at or practice: *Although retired, he kept his hand in his former business.* **25. on hand, a.** ready for use: *We don't have enough cash on*

H

hand. **b.** present: *How many staff members are on hand?* **26. on one's hands,** as one's responsibility: *They had a big problem on their hands.* **27. on the one hand/on the other (hand),** an expression used for comparing two opposite opinions, ideas, etc.: *On the one hand he likes to travel, but on the other (hand) he can't afford it.* **28. out of hand,** out of control: *The crowd got completely out of hand.*

hand•bag /'hænd,bæg/ n. [count] a small bag for carrying money and personal articles, used esp. by women.

hand•ball /'hænd,bɔl/ n. [noncount] a game played by two or four persons who strike a ball against a wall with the hand.

hand•bill /'hænd,bɪl/ n. [count] a small printed advertisement usually for giving out by hand.

hand•book /'hænd,bʊk/ n. [count] a book of instruction or guidance; manual.

hand•cuff /'hænd,kʌf/ n. [count] **1.** one of a pair of metal rings that can be locked around a prisoner's wrist. —v. [~ + obj] **2.** to put handcuffs on.

hand•ful /'hændfʊl/ n., pl. **-fuls. 1.** [count] the amount that the hand can hold: *A handful of sand.* **2.** [count; singular] a small quantity: *A handful of people attended.* **3.** [count; singular] a person or animal that is hard to control: *That dog is a handful.*

hand•gun /'hænd,gʌn/ n. [count] a small gun held and fired with one hand.

hand•i•cap /'hændiy,kæp/ n., v., **-capped, -cap•ping.** —n. [count] **1.** a disability or disadvantage: *He was born with a physical handicap.* *She thought being poor was a handicap.* **2.** an advantage or disadvantage in a sports contest. —v. [~ + obj] **3.** to place at a disadvantage. —'hand•i,capped, adj.

hand•i•craft /'hændiy,kræft/ n. [count; usually plural] an art, craft, or trade needing skilled use of the hands.

hand•i•work /'hændiy,wɜrk/ n. [noncount] **1.** work done by hand. **2.** work showing some sign of the person who has done it: *You can tell from the colors that this painting is my brother's handiwork.*

hand•ker•chief /'hæŋkərtʃɪf, -,tʃiyf/ n. [count] a small piece of cloth for wiping the nose, eyes, etc.

han•dle /'hændl/ n., v., **-dled, -dling.** —n. [count] **1.** a part of an object made to be picked up or held by the hand. —v. [~ + obj] **2.** to touch or hold with the hands: *Handle the painting carefully.* **3.** to manage or deal with: *She handled that angry customer with tact.* **4.** to trade in: *That store doesn't handle computer software.* —*Idiom.* **5. fly off the handle,** to lose one's temper; become angry.

han•dle•bars /'hændl,bɑrz/ n. [plural] the curved bar on a bicycle or motorcycle gripped by the hands for steering.

han•dler /'hændlər/ n. [count] a person who trains a boxer or controls an animal, esp. a dog.

hand•made /'hænd'meyd/ adj. made by hand.

hand•shake /'hænd,ʃeyk/ n. [count] a gripping and shaking of each other's right hand, as when saying hello or goodbye.

hand•some /'hænsəm/ adj., **-som•er, -som•est. 1.** having a pleasing appearance: *a handsome man.* **2.** generous: *a handsome reward.* —'hand•some•ly, adv. —'hand•some•ness, n. [noncount]

'**hands-'on,** adj. involving active personal participation: *hands-on experience with computers.*

hand•stand /'hænd,stænd/ n. [count] an act of supporting the body upside down by balancing on the palms of the hands.

'**hand-to-'hand,** adj. close to one's enemy or opponent: *hand-to-hand combat.*

'**hand-to-'mouth,** adj., adv. offering or providing barely enough to live on: *He made a hand-to-mouth living. She was always living hand-to-mouth.*

hand•writ•ing /'hænd,raytɪŋ/ n. [noncount] a style or manner of writing by hand: *Her handwriting is difficult to read.* —**hand•writ•ten** /'hænd,rɪtn/, adj.

hand•y /'hændiy/ adj., **-i•er, -i•est. 1.** within easy reach: *He kept supplies handy.* **2.** skillful with the hands: *He's handy with most tools.* **3.** useful and easy to use: *This is a handy dictionary.* —'hand•i•ness, n. [noncount]

hand•y•man /'hændiy,mæn/ n. [count], pl. **-men.** a person skillful at small repair jobs.

hang /hæŋ/ v., **hung** /hʌŋ/ or (esp. for 2) **hanged, hang•ing,** n. —v. [~ + obj] **1.** to fasten or be supported only from above: *to hang a few pictures on the wall.* **2.** to kill by hanging with a rope around the neck: *to hang a murderer.* **3. hang around,** Informal. to spend time: *He's been hanging around with older kids.* **4. hang on, a.** to keep hold of: *She hung on to the rope.* **b.** to be dependent on: *The future of our company may hang on this one deal.* **c.** to wait briefly: *"Hang on, we're almost home," he shouted.* **d.** to listen carefully to: *They hung on his every word.* **5. hang out,** Informal. to spend time informally: *We hang out at the mall on weekends.* **6. hang up,** to end a telephone call by breaking the connection: *She was so angry that she hung up on him.* —n. [count; usually singular] **7.** the way in which a thing hangs: *the hang of a jacket.* **8.** Informal. the way of doing or using something: *I've finally got the hang of using this computer.*

hang•ar /'hæŋər/ n. [count] a large building for keeping aircraft.

hang•er /'hæŋər/ n. [count] a shoulder-shaped frame with a hook at the top, used for hanging up clothing.

'**hanger-'on,** n. [count], pl. **hang•ers-on.** a person who hangs around another in the hope of personal gain.

hang•ing /'hæŋɪŋ/ n. **1.** [noncount] [count] an act or instance of death by hanging. **2.** [count] something for hanging on a wall.

hang•nail /'hæŋ,neyl/ n. [count] a small, loose piece of skin next to a fingernail.

hang•out /'hæŋ,awt/ n. [count] Informal. a place where a person often spends time, esp. for pleasure.

hang•o•ver /'hæŋ,owvər/ n. [count] **1.** an unpleasant feeling the day after drinking too much alcohol. **2.** something remaining from a former time.

'**hang-,up** or '**hang,up,** n. [count] Slang. something that a person worries about often or fears greatly: *She had a hang-up about meeting new people.*

han•ky or **han•kie** /'hæŋkiy/ n. [count], pl. **-kies.** a handkerchief.

Ha•nuk•kah or **Cha•nu•kah** /'hɑnəkə, 'xɑ-/ n. [noncount] [count] an eight-day Jewish festival in December, celebrated esp. by lighting candles.

hap•haz•ard /ˈhæpˈhæzərd/ *adj.* lacking order or planning. —**hap'haz•ard•ly,** *adv.*

hap•pen /ˈhæpən/ *v.* [*no obj*] **1.** to take place: *What happened after the accident?* **2.** to be or do by chance: *I happened to see him today.* **3.** to come as injury or harm: *Nothing happened to her.*

hap•pen•ing /ˈhæpənɪŋ/ *n.* [*count*] something that happens; an event.

hap•py /ˈhæpiy/ *adj.,* **-pi•er, -pi•est. 1.** very pleased; glad: *I'm happy to hear the good news.* **2.** satisfied with one's condition: *a happy baby.* **3.** fortunate; lucky: *Being seated next to you at dinner was a happy coincidence.* —**hap•pi•ly** /ˈhæpəliy/, *adv.* —**'hap•pi•ness,** *n.* [*noncount*]

'happy-go-'lucky, *adj.* without worries.

ha•rangue /həˈræŋ/ *n., v.,* **-rangued, -rangu•ing.** —*n.* [*count*] **1.** a long, loud, and forceful speech, esp. in public. —*v.* [~ + *obj*] **2.** to address or speak to (someone) in a harangue.

ha•rass /həˈræs, ˈhærəs/ *v.* [~ + *obj*] to annoy or trouble repeatedly. —**ha'rass•er,** *n.* [*count*] —**ha'rass•ment,** *n.* [*noncount*]

har•bor /ˈhɑrbər/ *n.* [*count*] **1.** a sheltered body of water for ships. —*v.* [~ + *obj*] **2.** to give shelter or protection to: *to harbor a criminal.* **3.** to keep in the mind: *to harbor suspicions.* Also, *esp. Brit.,* **'har•bour.**

hard /hɑrd/ *adj. and adv.,* **-er, -est.** —*adj.* **1.** not soft; solid and firm: *Rocks are hard.* **2.** difficult; troublesome: *a hard task; You are hard to please.* **3.** needing or using great effort: *a hard worker.* **4.** full of pain, trouble, etc.: *a hard life.* **5.** showing no kindness: *a hard face.* **6.** severe: *a hard winter.* **7.** [*before a noun*] resentful; bitter: *hard feelings.* **8.** (of water) containing mineral salts that prevent soap from working well. —*adv.* **9.** with great effort: *to work hard.* **10.** with great force: *It was snowing hard.* **11.** badly or severely: *The workers were hit hard by the pay cuts.* **12.** so as to be solid, tight, or firm: *The ice was frozen hard.* **13.** with great pain or sorrow: *He took the bad news very hard.* —**'hard•ness,** *n.* [*noncount*]

'hard-and-'fast, *adj.* strict; not changing: *hard-and-fast rules.*

'hard-'boiled, *adj.* (of an egg) boiled in the shell until the yolk and white are solid.

'hard 'copy, *n.* [*noncount*] computer information printed out on paper.

'hard 'disk, *n.* [*count*] a stiff disk built into a personal computer for storing computer programs and large amounts of data.

hard•en /ˈhɑrdn/ *v.* **1.** to (cause to) become hard or harder: [*no obj*]: *The ice cream hardened in the freezer.* [~ + *obj*]: *The freezer will harden the ice cream.* **2.** to (cause to) become less sensitive or kind: [*no obj*]: *His heart hardened with anger.* [~ + *obj*]: *His cruel life had hardened his heart.*

hard•head•ed or **hard-head•ed** /ˈhɑrdˌhɛdɪd/ *adj.* **1.** practical and tough. **2.** stubborn.

hard•heart•ed /ˈhɑrdˈhɑrtɪd/ *adj.* showing no kindness.

'hard-'line or **'hard,line,** *adj.* unwilling to change: *hard-line union demands.* —**'hard-'liner,** *n.* [*count*]

hard•ly /ˈhɑrdliy/ *adv.* **1.** only just; almost not: *I could hardly walk.* **2.** or never: *She hardly ever laughs.* **3.** not at all: *It's hardly surprising.*

'hard of 'hearing, *adj.* [*be* + ~] unable to hear well; almost deaf.

hard•press•ed /ˈhɑrdˈprɛst/ *adj.* in great difficulty: *He was hardpressed for money.*

hard•ship /ˈhɑrdʃɪp/ *n.* [*noncount*] something that causes suffering or difficulty.

'hard 'up, *adj. Informal.* in need of money.

hard•ware /ˈhɑrdˌwɛər/ *n.* [*noncount*] **1.** articles made of metal, such as tools, locks, or machine parts. **2.** the mechanical and electronic parts of a computer system.

hard•wood /ˈhɑrdˌwʊd/ *n.* [*noncount*] the hard, strong wood of trees with broad leaves: *furniture made of hardwood.*

har•dy /ˈhɑrdiy/ *adj.,* **-di•er, -di•est.** capable of bearing hardship; strong. —**har•di•ly** /ˈhɑrdḷiy/, *adv.* —**har•di•ness,** *n.* [*noncount*]

hare /hɛər/ *n.* [*count*], *pl.* **hares,** (*esp. when thought of as a group*) **hare.** a long-eared animal similar to a rabbit but usually larger.

hark /hɑrk/ *v.* [*no obj*] **1.** to listen attentively. **2.** **hark back,** to talk often about the past.

harm /hɑrm/ *n.* [*noncount*] **1.** injury or damage: *to do someone bodily harm.* —*v.* [~ + *obj*] **2.** to do or cause harm to. —**'harm•ful,** *adj.* —**'harm•less,** *adj.*

har•mon•i•ca /hɑrˈmɒnɪkə/ *n.* [*count*], *pl.* **-cas.** a small musical wind instrument containing a set of metal reeds.

har•mo•nize /ˈhɑrməˌnayz/ *v.,* **-nized, -niz•ing. 1.** to (cause to) be in harmony: [~ + *obj*]: *to harmonize colors with each other.* [*no obj*]: *The colors harmonize nicely.* **2.** [*no obj*] to sing or play in musical harmony.

har•mo•ny /ˈhɑrməniy/ *n., pl.* **-nies. 1.** [*noncount*] agreement of feelings, action, etc.: *They lived in perfect harmony.* **2.** [*noncount*] a pleasing arrangement of related parts: *the harmony of color in a painting.* **3.** [*noncount*] [*count*] a pleasing arrangement of musical sounds. —**har•mo•ni•ous,** *adj.* —**har'mo•ni•ous•ly,** *adv.*

har•ness /ˈhɑrnɪs/ *n.* [*count*] **1.** the straps and bands used to attach a horse to a cart, etc. —*v.* [~ + *obj*] **2.** to put a harness on. **3.** to control (a natural force) for use: *to harness water power.*

harp /hɑrp/ *n.* [*count*] a musical instrument having a triangular frame and strings plucked with the fingers. —**'harp•ist,** *n.* [*count*]

har•poon /hɑrˈpuwn/ *n.* [*count*] **1.** a spear with a rope attached, used in hunting whales and large fish. —*v.* [~ + *obj*] **2.** to spear with a harpoon.

harp•si•chord /ˈhɑrpsɪˌkɔrd/ *n.* [*count*] a musical instrument like a piano whose strings are plucked by leather points. —**'harp•si,chord•ist,** *n.* [*count*]

har•ried /ˈhæriyd/ *adj.* worried.

har•row•ing /ˈhærowɪŋ/ *adj.* causing fright, upset, or pain: *a harrowing storm.*

harsh /hɑrʃ/ *adj.,* **-er, -est. 1.** cruel; severe: *He received harsh treatment.* **2.** unpleasant to the senses: *harsh soap; a harsh voice.* —**'harsh•ly,** *adv.* —**'harsh•ness,** *n.* [*noncount*]

har•vest /ˈhɑrvɪst/ *n.* **1.** Also, **'har•vest•ing.** the gathering of crops: *They helped with the harvest.* **2.** the season when ripened crops are gathered. **3.** the crop that is gathered: *a harvest of wheat.* —*v.* [~ + *obj*] **4.** to gather (a crop): *The farmer harvested the grain.*

has /hæz; *unstressed* həz, əz/ *v.* a 3rd pers. sing. pres. indic. of HAVE.

'has-,been, *n.* [*count*] a person or thing that is no longer effective, successful, or popular.

hash¹ /hæʃ/ *n.* **1.** [*noncount*] [*count*] cooked chopped meat and potatoes re-cooked together. **2.** [*count; usually singular*] a confused mess: *He made a hash of his first job.*

H

hash² /hæʃ/ *n.* [*noncount*] *Slang.* hashish.

hash•ish /ˈhæʃiyʃ, haˈʃiyʃ/ *n.* [*noncount*] a drug made from the hemp plant.

has•n't /ˈhæzənt/ contraction of *has not.*

has•sle /ˈhæsəl/ *n., v.,* **-sled, -sling.** *Informal.* —*n.* [*count*] **1.** a difficult or annoying situation. —*v.* [~ + *obj*] **2.** to annoy or harass: *Stop hassling me!*

haste /heyst/ *n.* [*noncount*] **1.** quick action or movement; speed. —*Idiom.* **2.** **make haste,** to hurry. —**has•ten** /ˈheysən/ *v.* [~ + *obj*] [*no obj*]

hast•y /ˈheystiy/ *adj.,* **-i•er, -i•est. 1.** moving, acting, or done with speed or haste: *a hasty visit.* **2.** too quick; rash: *He regretted his hasty decision.* —**hast•i•ly** /ˈheystʃiy/ *adv.*

hat /hæt/ *n.* [*count*] **1.** a covering for the head. —*Idiom.* **2. old hat,** old fashioned. **3. pass the hat,** to collect money for a special cause. **4. under one's hat,** secret: *Keep this information under your hat.* —**'hat•less,** *adj.*

hatch¹ /hætʃ/ *v.* **1.** [*no obj*] [~ + *obj*] (of young birds) to (cause to) break out of an egg. **2.** [*no obj*] (of eggs) to break open and allow a young bird to come out: *When will the eggs hatch?* **3.** [~ + *obj*] to invent, esp. in secret: *They hatched a clever plan.*

hatch² /hætʃ/ *n.* [*count*] **1. a.** Also called **hatch•way** /ˈhætʃˌwey/. an opening in the deck of a ship, used as a passageway. **b.** the cover over such an opening. **2.** a door in an aircraft: *an escape hatch.*

hatch•back /ˈhætʃˌbæk/ *n.* [*count*] a car whose rear door and rear window lift and open together.

hatch•et /ˈhætʃɪt/ *n.* [*count*] a small, short-handled ax.

hate /heyt/ *v.,* **hat•ed, hat•ing,** *n.* —*v.* [~ + *obj*] **1.** to dislike intensely: *They hate violence. I hate getting up early.* —*n.* [*noncount*] **2.** intense dislike: *enemies who are full of hate.* —**'hat•ed,** *adj.* —**'hate•ful,** *adj.* —**'hat•er,** *n.* [*count*]

ha•tred /ˈheytrɪd/ *n.* [*noncount*] hate.

haugh•ty /ˈhɔtiy/ *adj.,* **-ti•er, -ti•est.** having or showing too much pride. —**haugh•ti•ly** /ˈhɔtliy/ *adv.* —**'haugh•ti•ness,** *n.* [*noncount*]

haul /hɔl/ *v.* **1.** to pull hard: [~ + *obj*]: *They hauled the boat onto the beach.* [*no obj*]: *The sailors hauled on the ropes.* **2.** [~ + *obj*] to transport; carry: *to haul freight.* —*n.* [*count*] **3.** an act of hauling. **4.** an amount gained: *a big haul of fish.* **5.** the distance something is hauled: *a long haul.* —**'haul•er,** *n.* [*count*]

haunch /hɔntʃ, hɑntʃ/ *n.* [*count, usually plural*] the hip and upper thigh of a person or animal: *the dog sat on its haunches.*

haunt /hɔnt, hɑnt/ *v.* [~ + *obj*] **1.** to visit or live in as a ghost: *to haunt a house.* **2.** to return often to the mind: *Old memories haunted me.* —*n.* [*count*] **3.** Often, **haunts.** [*plural*] a place visited often: *He returned to his old haunts.* —**'haunt•ing,** *adj.*

have /hæv; *unstressed* həv, əv; *for 13 usually* hæf/ *v. and auxiliary v., pres. sing. 1st and 2nd pers.* **have,** *3rd pers.* **has;** *pres. pl.* **have;** *past and past part.* **had;** *pres. part.* **hav•ing,** —*v.* [~ + *obj*] **1.** to possess; own: *I have a house. She has green eyes.* **2.** to receive or get: *I had some good news today.* **3.** to experience: *to have a good time; to have a bad cold.* **4.** to cause something to be done: *I had my hair cut.* **5.** to hold in the mind: *I have some doubts about it.* **6.** to carry on: *to have a conversation.* **7.** to eat or drink: *We had cake for dessert.* **8.** to permit; allow: *I will not have any talking during class.* **9.** to give birth to: *She's*

going to have a baby. **10.** to hold an advantage over: *He has you there.* **11.** to deceive; cheat: *We'd been had by a con artist.* —*auxiliary verb.* **12.** The verb *have* is used as a helping verb with a past participle of another verb to form: **a.** the present perfect tense, which shows that an action happened in the past or its effects are still felt: *I have just eaten. I've known her ever since she came to the United States.* **b.** the past perfect tense, which shows that the action of that verb happened earlier in time than another verb: *By the time the police came to the house, the thief had already left.* **13.** The verb *have* is used with *to* and the root form of a main verb to mean "must": *I have to leave now.* —*Idiom.* **14.** **have had it, a.** to have experienced enough: *I've had it with your excuses.* **b.** to be no longer useful: *These old computers have had it.* **15. have to do with,** to be concerned with: *Her work has to do with the law.*

ha•ven /ˈheyvən/ *n.* [*count*] a place of shelter and safety.

have•n't /ˈhævənt/ contraction of *have not.*

hav•oc /ˈhævək/ *n.* [*noncount*] **1.** great destruction or confusion: *havoc caused by the bombing.* —*Idiom.* **2. play havoc with** or **wreak havoc on, a.** to create confusion in. **b.** to destroy; ruin.

hawk¹ /hɔk/ *n.* [*count*] **1.** a bird that catches animals for food, having a short, hooked beak, broad wings, and curved claws. **2.** a person who calls for forceful military action. —**'hawk•ish,** *adj.*

hawk² /hɔk/ *v.* [~ + *obj*] to offer (goods) for sale, esp. by calling out loud in public. —**'hawk•er,** *n.* [*count*]

'hawk-,eyed, *adj.* having very keen sight.

haw•thorn /ˈhɔˌθɔrn/ *n.* [*count*] a small tree of the rose family, with stiff thorns, white or red flowers, and bright-colored fruit.

hay /hey/ *n.* [*noncount*] grass cut and dried for use as food for animals.

'hay ,fever, *n.* [*noncount*] an illness of the nose, eyes, throat, and lungs, caused by breathing pollen from plants.

hay•stack /ˈheyˌstæk/ *n.* [*count*] **1.** a large pile of hay built up outdoors. —*Idiom.* **2. a needle in a haystack,** something difficult to find.

haz•ard /ˈhæzərd/ *n.* [*count*] **1.** something causing danger or risk: *Smoking is a hazard to one's health.* —*v.* [~ + *obj*] **2.** to offer: *I'd hazard a guess that the loss is in the millions.* **3.** to risk: *He hazarded all his savings.* —**'haz•ard•ous,** *adj.*

haze /heyz/ *n.* **1.** a thin, whitish mist or smoke in the air: [*count; usually singular*]: *a haze of cigarette smoke.* [*noncount*]: *The mountain was hidden in the haze.* **2.** [*count; singular*] a confused state of mind.

ha•zel /ˈheyzəl/ *n.* [*count*] **1.** a small tree that bears nuts that can be eaten. —*adj.* **2.** of a light golden- or greenish-brown color: *hazel eyes.*

ha•zel•nut /ˈheyzəlˌnʌt/ *n.* [*count*] the nut of the hazel.

ha•zy /ˈheyziy/ *adj.,* **-zi•er, -zi•est. 1.** misty: *a hazy sky.* **2.** unclear; confused: *a few hazy ideas.* —**ha•zi•ly** /ˈheyzəliy/ *adv.* —**'ha•zi•ness,** *n.* [*noncount*]

H-bomb /ˈeytʃˌbɒm/ *n.* HYDROGEN BOMB.

HDTV, an abbreviation of: high-definition television.

he /hiy; *unstressed* iy/ *pron., nom.* **he,** *poss.* **his,** *obj.* **him;** *pl. nom.* **they,** *poss.* **their** or **theirs,** *obj.* **them;** *n., pl.* **hes;** *adj.* —*pron.* **1.** the male person or animal last mentioned; that male:

Where did that man go? He's in the back of the room. **2.** anyone; that person: *Anyone can succeed if he tries.* —*n.* [count] **3.** any male person or animal: *Is that cat a he or a she?* —*adj.* **4.** male: *a he-goat.*

head /hɛd/ *n.* **1.** [count] the top part of the body, containing the mouth, eyes, ears, nose, and brain. **2.** [count] mental ability; the mind: *a good head for mathematics.* **3.** [count] a position of leadership or honor: *at the head of her class.* **4.** [count] a person in charge of others; chief: *the head of the household; the head of the government.* **5.** [count] the top or upper end of something: *the head of a pin.* **6.** [count] the front end of something: *at the head of the line.* **7.** [count; singular] a person or animal considered as one of a number, herd, or group: *ten head of cattle.* **8.** [count] a dense cluster of leaves or flowers on a plant: *a head of cabbage.* **9.** HEADLAND. **10.** [count] Also, **heads.** the side of a coin that has a head or other main figure (opposed to TAIL). **11.** [count] pressure: *a head of steam.* —*adj.* [before a noun] **12.** first in rank or position: *head cook.* —*v.* **13.** [~ + obj] to go at the head of or in front of: *She headed the parade.* **14.** [~ + obj] to be in charge of: *to head (up) a school.* **15.** to (cause to) move in a certain direction: [no obj]: *The bus headed out of town.* [~ + obj]: *I'll head the boat for shore.* **16. head for,** to move toward (something): *heading for trouble.* **17. head off,** to get ahead of and cause to stop or turn aside: *to head off the robbers at the pass* or *to head the robbers off at the pass.* —*Idiom.* **18. come to a head,** to reach a critical point. **19. go to one's head, a.** to make a person feel drunk: *The wine went straight to her head.* **b.** to make a person too proud: *Don't let your recent success go to your head.* **20. hang** or **hide one's head,** to show a feeling of shame. **21. head over heels, a.** with the head going first: *He fell head over heels into the pool.* **b.** completely: *head over heels in love.* **22. keep one's head,** to remain calm and effective: *She kept her head in the emergency.* **23. keep one's head above water,** to have enough money to live. **24. lose one's head,** to become uncontrolled. **25. over one's head,** beyond one's understanding or ability. —**head•ed,** *adj.*

head•ache /'hɛd,eyk/ *n.* [count] **1.** a pain in the head. **2.** an annoying person, situation, etc.

head•band /'hɛd,bænd/ *n.* [count] a band worn around the head.

head•dress /'hɛd,drɛs/ *n.* [count] a covering or decoration for the head.

head•first /'hɛd'fɚst/ *adv.* with the head going in front or bent forward: *to dive headfirst into the sea.*

head•gear /'hɛd,gɪɚr/ *n.* [noncount] a covering for the head, as a hat or a helmet.

head•ing /'hɛdɪŋ/ *n.* [count] a title for a page or chapter.

head•land /'hɛdlənd/ *n.* [count] a high piece of land that sticks out into a large body of water.

head•light /'hɛd,layt/ *n.* [count] a bright light on the front of a vehicle.

head•line /'hɛd,layn/ *n.* [count] **1.** a statement printed in large letters above a newspaper article. **2. headlines,** [plural] the most important news stories: *The peace conference has been in the headlines all week.*

head•long /'hɛd,lɔŋ, -,lɒŋ/ *adv.* **1.** with the head going first; headfirst: *to dive headlong into the water.* **2.** quickly and carelessly: *to rush headlong into marriage.* —*adj.* **3.** hurried: *a headlong*

flight. **4.** done or going with the head first: *a headlong dive.*

head•mas•ter or **-mis•tress** /'hɛd,mæstər/ or /-'mɪstrɪs/ *n.* [count] the person in charge of a private school.

'head-'on, *adj., adv.* with the head or front parts first: *a head-on car crash; The two cars crashed head-on.*

head•phone /'hɛd,fown/ *n.* [count] Usually, **headphones.** [plural] a headset for use with a stereo system.

head•quar•ter /'hɛd,kwɔrtər, -,kwɔ-/ *v.* [~ + obj] to have headquarters in or at: *The company is headquartered in Dallas.*

head•quar•ters /'hɛd,kwɔrtɚz, -,kwɔ-/ *n.* [count], *pl.* **head•quar•ters.** a center of operations, as of a military commander or a business: *Their headquarters is in New York City.*

head•room /'hɛd,ruwm, -,rʊm/ *n.* [noncount] clear space overhead, as in a vehicle.

head•set /'hɛd,sɛt/ *n.* [count] a device consisting of one or two earphones, and sometimes a microphone, attached to a headband: *a portable stereo with headset.*

'head 'start, *n.* [count] **1.** an early start or other advantage given in a competition, race, etc. **2.** an early start: *He got a head start on the work.*

head•strong /'hɛd,strɔŋ, -,strɒŋ/ *adj.* determined to have one's own way.

head•wait•er /'hɛd'weytər/ *n.* [count] the waiter in charge, as in a restaurant.

head•way /'hɛd,wey/ *n.* [noncount] forward movement or progress.

head•wind /'hɛd,wɪnd/ *n.* [count] a wind blowing against a moving ship, aircraft, etc.

heal /hiyl/ *v.* to (cause to) become healthy or well again: [~ + obj]: *This medicine should heal that sore on your leg.* [no obj]: *When will my leg heal?* —**heal•er,** *n.* [count]

health /hɛlθ/ *n.* [noncount] **1.** the general condition of the body or mind: *She's in poor health.* **2.** the state of being free from illness or injury: *to lose one's health.*

health•ful /'hɛlθfəl/ *adj.* good for one's health; wholesome: *a healthful diet.*

health•y /'hɛlθiy/ *adj.*, **-i•er, -i•est. 1.** having or showing good health: *He looked so healthy after a week in the country.* **2.** encouraging good health: *a healthy climate.* —**health•i•ly** /'hɛlθəliy/, *adv.* —**health•i•ness,** *n.* [noncount]

heap /hiyp/ *n.* [count] **1.** a pile or mass of something: *a heap of stones.* —*v.* [~ + obj] **2.** to gather in large amounts: *to heap up riches.*

hear /hɪər/ *v.* [~ + obj], **heard, hear•ing. 1.** to become aware of (sounds, noises, etc.) by the ear: *I hear music.* **2.** to learn by hearing: *I hear you have a new job.* **3.** to give a formal hearing to (something): *to hear a legal case.* **4. hear of, a.** to know of: *I have heard of someone who can help us.* **b.** to listen with favor or agreement: *I will not hear of your going!*

hear•ing /'hɪərɪŋ/ *n.* **1.** [noncount] the sense making it possible to hear: *good hearing.* **2.** [noncount] the distance within which one can hear something: *loud enough to be within hearing.* **3.** [count] the chance to be heard: *to get a fair hearing.* **4.** [count] a legal case before a judge.

hearing aid, *n.* [count] a small device worn to improve one's hearing.

hear•say /'hɪər,sey/ *n.* [noncount] information heard from another that is not yet proved; rumor.

H

hearse /hɜrs/ n. [count] a vehicle for carrying the body of a dead person.

heart /hɑrt/ n. [count] **1.** a muscular organ in humans and many animals that pumps blood through the body. **2.** the center of a person's feelings: *He's very kind at heart.* **3.** the central part: *Let's get to the heart of the matter.* **4.** a figure shaped like the heart. **5.** a playing card with red, heart-shaped figures. —**Idiom. 6. break someone's heart,** to make someone very unhappy. **7. by heart,** from or by memory: *She learned the poem by heart.* **8. take heart,** to gain courage or confidence. **9. take to heart, a.** to consider seriously: *He took to heart her advice* or *He took her advice to heart.* **b.** to grieve over: *He took the loss to heart* or *He took to heart the loss.*

heart•ache /ˈhɑrtˌeyk/ n. [count] [noncount] great sorrow and pain.

'**heart at,tack,** n. [count] a serious condition in which the heart suddenly fails to beat regularly.

heart•beat /ˈhɑrtˌbiyt/ n. [count] one complete movement of the heart.

heart•break /ˈhɑrtˌbreyk/ n. [noncount] great sorrow. —'**heart,break•ing,** adj.

heart•bro•ken /ˈhɑrtˌbrowkən/ adj. filled with deep sorrow or grief.

heart•burn /ˈhɑrtˌbɜrn/ n. [noncount] an unpleasant burning feeling in the upper chest, usually caused by indigestion.

heart•en /ˈhɑrtn/ v. [~ + obj] to give courage or confidence to; encourage. —'**heart•en•ing,** adj.

heart•felt /ˈhɑrtˌfɛlt/ adj. sincere: *heartfelt sympathy.*

hearth /hɑrθ/ n. [count] the floor of a fireplace or the area around it.

heart•less /ˈhɑrtlɪs/ adj. unkind; cruel: *a heartless employer.* —'**heart•less•ly,** adv. —'**heart•less•ness,** n. [noncount]

heart•rend•ing /ˈhɑrtˌrɛndɪŋ/ adj. causing or expressing deep pain or sorrow: *a heartrending scream.* —'**heart,rend•ing•ly,** adv.

heart•strings /ˈhɑrtˌstrɪŋz/ n. [plural] one's deepest feelings of love, sympathy, etc.

'**heart-to-'heart,** adj. honest and open: *a heart-to-heart talk.*

heart•warm•ing /ˈhɑrtˌwɔrmɪŋ/ adj. warmly pleasing: *a heartwarming story.*

heart•y /ˈhɑrtiy/ adj., **-i•er, -i•est. 1.** [before a noun] heartfelt; sincere: *a hearty welcome.* **2.** loud and merry: *hearty laughter.* **3.** strong and well; healthy: *You look hale and hearty.* **4.** [before a noun] large and satisfying: *a hearty meal.* —'**heart•i•ly,** /ˈhɑrtliy/ adv. —'**heart•i•ness,** n. [noncount]

heat /hiyt/ n. [noncount] **1.** the condition or quality of being hot: *Heat rises.* **2.** degree of hotness; temperature: *high heat.* **3.** warmth or strength of feeling: *the heat of anger.* —v. **4.** (cause to) become hot or warm: [no obj]: *The house is heating up in the sun.* [~ + obj]: *Heat the soup. The sun is heating up the house.*

heat•ed /ˈhiytɪd/ adj. excited or angry: *a heated argument.* —'**heat•ed•ly,** adv.: *to argue heatedly.*

heat•er /ˈhiytər/ n. [count] a device for heating water or air: *a gas heater.*

heath /hiyθ/ n. [count] an area of open land covered with low bushes.

hea•then /ˈhiyðən/ n., pl. **-thens, -then,** adj. —n. [count] **1.** a person who does not belong to one of the major religions. **2.** an uncivilized person. —adj. **3.** of or relating to heathens. **4.** uncultured or uncivilized.

heath•er /ˈhɛðər/ n. [noncount] a heath plant having small pink or purple flowers.

heat•ing /ˈhiytɪŋ/ n. [noncount] a system or the machines involved in keeping a building warm.

heat•stroke /ˈhiytˌstrowk/ n. [noncount] a condition of headache, fever, hot and dry skin, etc., caused by exposure to too much heat.

heave /hiyv/ v., **heaved** or (esp. Nautical) **hove** /howv/, **heav•ing,** n. —v. **1.** [~ + obj] to lift or pull with effort: *He heaved her to her feet.* [~ + obj] to throw: *She heaved a rock.* **3.** [~ + obj] to let out (a breath): *I heaved a sigh of relief.* **4.** to (cause to) rise and fall regularly: [no obj]: *His chest was heaving after the race.* [~ + obj]: *The rough seas heaved the boat about.* —n. [count] **5.** an act or effort of heaving.

heav•en /ˈhɛvən/ n. **1.** [noncount] the place where God, the angels, and the spirits of good people are believed to live after death. **2.** Usually, **heavens.** [plural] the sky: *admiring the heavens at night.* **3.** [noncount] a place or state of great happiness. —'**heav•en•ly,** adj., **-li•er, -li•est.** —**heav•en•ward** /ˈhɛvənwərd/, adv., adj.

heav•y /ˈhɛviy/ adj., **-i•er, -i•est. 1.** of great weight; hard to lift or carry: *a heavy load.* **2.** of great amount, quantity, or size: *heavy traffic.* **3.** of a degree greater than usual: *a heavy blanket; a heavy drinker; a heavy sleeper.* **4.** serious: *a heavy punishment.* **5.** troubled; sad: *a heavy heart.* **6.** threatening bad weather: *a heavy sky.* **7.** difficult and boring: *heavy reading.* **8.** (of food) not easily digested: *a heavy meal.* **9.** Slang. very serious or important. —**heav•i•ly** /ˈhɛvəliy/, adv.: *It rained heavily yesterday.* —'**heav•i•ness,** n. [noncount]

'**heavy-'duty,** adj. [usually: before a noun] **1.** made to withstand great strain or use: *heavy-duty machinery.* **2.** very important or intense: *heavy-duty competition.*

He•brew /ˈhiybruw/ n. **1.** [count] a member of one of the Jewish tribes of ancient times. **2.** [noncount] the language of the ancient Hebrews, also spoken today by the people of Israel. —adj. **3.** of the Hebrews or their language.

heck•le /ˈhɛkəl/ v. [~ + obj], **-led, -ling.** to interrupt with questions, insults, etc.: *The audience began to heckle the speaker.* —**heck•ler** /ˈhɛklər/, n. [count]

hec•tic /ˈhɛktɪk/ adj. full of excitement or hurried activity: *a hectic day.* —'**hec•ti•cal•ly,** adv.

he'd /hiyd/ unstressed iyd/ contraction. **1.** a shortened form of he had: *He'd been here before.* **2.** a shortened form of he would: *He'd be a great doctor.*

hedge /hɛdʒ/ n., v., **hedged, hedg•ing.** —n. [count] **1.** a row of bushes or small trees forming a fence. —v. **2.** [~ + obj] to enclose with or separate by a hedge. **3.** [no obj] to avoid answering a question directly. —'**hedg•er,** n. [count]

hedge•hog /ˈhɛdʒˌhɒg, -ˌhɔg/ n. [count] an insect-eating animal with needle-like hairs on the back and sides.

heed /hiyd/ v. [~ + obj] **1.** to give careful attention to: *to heed a warning.* —n. [noncount] **2.** careful attention: *Take heed of my warning.* —'**heed•ful,** adj. —'**heed•less,** adj.

heel /hiyl/ n. [count] **1.** the back part of the human foot below the ankle. **2.** the part of a sock or shoe covering this. **3.** a solid raised base attached to the back part of the sole of a shoe. **4.** the end part of a loaf of bread. —v. **5.** [~ + obj] to provide (shoes) with heels. **6.** [no obj] (of a dog) to follow at one's heels on command.

—Idiom. 7. down at heel, poorly dressed. **8. kick up one's heels,** to have an unusually lively, entertaining time. **9. on** or **upon the heels of,** closely following: *The police were on the heels of the criminals.*

heft•y /'hɛftiy/ *adj.,* **-i•er, -i•est. 1.** heavy; weighty: *a hefty dictionary.* **2.** powerful: *a hefty line of football players.* **3.** large: *a hefty increase in pay.* —**'heft•i•ness,** *n.* [*noncount*]

heif•er /'hɛfər/ *n.* [*count*] a young cow that has not produced a calf.

height /hayt/ *n.* **1.** [*noncount*] extent or distance upward: *The plane gained height rapidly.* **2.** [*count*] distance from bottom to top: *His height was about six feet.* **3.** [*count; usually singular*] the quality or degree of being high or tall: *She felt proud of her height.* **4.** Often, **heights.** [*plural*] a high place: *I'm afraid of heights.* **5.** [*count; usually singular; often: the* + ∼] the highest point or degree: *the height of pleasure.*

height•en /'haytn/ *v.* to increase (the degree of): [∼ + *obj*]: *to heighten one's appreciation.* [*no obj*]: *Their excitement heightened.*

heir /ɛər/ *n.* [*count*] a person who has the legal right to the property or title of a person who dies: *sole heir to the fortune; an heir to the throne.*

heir•ess /'ɛərɪs/ *n.* [*count*] a woman who is an heir.

heir•loom /'ɛər,luwm/ *n.* [*count*] a family possession handed down from generation to generation.

held /hɛld/ *v.* pt. and pp. of HOLD[1].

hel•i•cop•ter /'hɛlɪ,kɑptər, 'hiylɪ-/ *n.* [*count*] an aircraft that is kept in the air by horizontal rotating blades attached to its top.

hel•i•port /'hɛlə,pɔrt/ *n.* [*count*] a takeoff and landing place for helicopters.

he•li•um /'hiyliyəm/ *n.* [*noncount*] a light colorless gas used esp. in balloons.

hell /hɛl/ *n.* [*noncount*] **1.** the place or state of punishment where wicked people are believed to go after death. **2.** any place or state of great suffering. **3.** extreme disorder or confusion: *All hell broke loose.* —*interj.* **4.** This word is used alone in swearing to express anger, disgust, surprise, etc., or for emphasis: *Hell! I've lost my wallet. What the hell was that?*

he'll /hiyl; *unstressed* iyl, hɪl, ɪl/ *contraction.* a shortened form of *he will: He'll be home later.*

hell•hole /'hɛl,howl/ *n.* [*count*] an extremely unpleasant place.

hell•ish /'hɛlɪʃ/ *adj.* extremely unpleasant; terrible. —**'hell•ish•ly,** *adv.*

hel•lo /hɛ'low, hə-, 'hɛlow/ *interj., n., pl.* **-los.** —*interj.* **1.** This word is used to express a greeting, answer a telephone, or attract attention: *Hello, how are you?* —*n.* [*count*] **2.** an act or instance of saying "hello": *a shy hello.*

helm /hɛlm/ *n.* [*count*] **1.** a wheel or handle by which a ship is steered. **2. at the helm,** in the position of control.

hel•met /'hɛlmɪt/ *n.* [*count*] a usually strong and hard covering worn on the head for protection. —**'hel•met•ed,** *adj.*

help /hɛlp/ *v.* **1.** to give or do something useful or needed: [∼ + *obj*]: *She helped me with my work. We helped him (to) get settled in. I helped (to) carry the bags.* [*no obj*]: *I hope this money will help.* **2.** [∼ + *obj*] to save from danger or harm: *Help me, I'm falling!* **3.** [∼ + *obj*] to be useful or profitable to: *Your knowledge of languages will help you in your career.* —*n.* **4.** [*non-*

count] the act of helping: *Do you need help?* **5.** [*count*] a person or thing that helps: *You were a big help after the fire.* **6.** [*noncount*] one or more employees: *He hired new help at the shop.* **7.** [*noncount*] a means of dealing with something: *There is no help for the problem now.* —*interj.* **8.** This word is used by someone in difficulty: *"Help!" she called, "I can't swim."* —*Idiom.* **9. cannot** or **can't help (but),** to be unable to avoid: *I can't help laughing about it. You can't help but admire her.* **10. help oneself (to), a.** to serve oneself with: *Help yourself to some pie.* **b.** to take without asking permission: *He just helped himself to the money on the table.* **11. so help me (God),** I am speaking the truth. —**'help•er,** *n.* [*count*] —**'help•less,** *adj.* —**'help•less•ly** *adv.* —**'help•less•ness** *n.* [*noncount*]

help•ful /'hɛlpfəl/ *adj.* giving aid or assistance: *helpful comments; a helpful person.* —**'help•ful•ly,** *adv.* —**'help•ful•ness,** *n.* [*noncount*]

help•ing /'hɛlpɪŋ/ *n.* [*count*] an amount of food for one person.

'help,mate /-,meyt/ or **-meet** /-,miyt/ *n.* [*count*] **1.** a companion and helper. **2.** a wife or husband.

hem /hɛm/ *n., v.,* **hemmed, hem•ming,** —*n.* [*count*] **1.** the bottom edge or border of a garment or piece of cloth, made by folding back an edge and sewing it down. —*v.* **2.** [∼ + *obj*] to form or sew a hem on: *She hemmed the skirt.* **3. hem in,** to enclose; surround: *a fence to hem in the sheep* or *a fence to hem the sheep in.*

hem•i•sphere /'hɛmɪ,sfɪər/ *n.* [*count*] **1.** [*often: Hemisphere*] half of the earth: *the Western Hemisphere; the Northern Hemisphere.* **2.** a half of a sphere. —**hem•i•spher•ic** /,hɛmɪ'sfɛrɪk/, **hem•i'spher•i•cal,** *adj.*

hem•line /'hɛm,layn/ *n.* [*count*] the bottom edge of a coat, skirt, etc.

hem•lock /'hɛm,lɒk/ *n.* **1.** [*count*] a poisonous plant of the parsley family. **2.** [*noncount*] a poisonous drink made from this plant.

he•mo•glo•bin /'hiymə,glowbɪn, 'hɛmə-/ *n.* [*noncount*] a protein in red blood cells that contains iron and carries oxygen.

he•mo•phil•i•a /,hiymə'fɪliyə, -'fiylyə/ *n.* [*noncount*] a condition that shows its effects only in males, in which there is too much bleeding from minor injuries. —**he•mo•phil•i•ac** /,hiymə'fɪli-y,æk/, *n.* [*count*]

hem•or•rhage /'hɛmərɪdʒ, 'hɛmrɪdʒ/ *n., v.,* **-rhaged, -rhag•ing.** —*n.* [*noncount*] [*count*] **1.** a flow of blood, esp. in large amounts. —*v.* [*no obj*] **2.** to bleed a great deal: *The patient was hemorrhaging.*

H

helmets

medieval   modern

hem•or•rhoid /'hɛmə,rɔyd, 'hɛmrɔyd/ *n.* Usually, **hemorrhoids.** [*plural*] a swollen blood vessel in or near the anus. Also called **pile.**

hemp /hɛmp/ *n.* [*noncount*] a tall plant whose strong fibers are used for making rope and cloth.

hen /hɛn/ *n.* [*count*] **1.** an adult female chicken. **2.** the female of any bird.

hence /hɛns/ *adv.* **1.** for this reason; therefore:

The clerk was caught stealing and hence must be fired. **2.** from this time or place: *in a month hence.*

hence•forth /ˌhɛnsˈfɔrθ/ also **hence•for•ward** /-ˈfɔrwərd/ *adv.* from now on.

hench•man /ˈhɛntʃmən/ *n.* [count], *pl.* **-men.** **1.** a person hired by another to do dishonest or illegal acts. **2.** a trusted supporter or follower, esp. in politics.

hep•a•ti•tis /ˌhɛpəˈtaytɪs/ *n.* [noncount] inflammation of the liver.

her /hər; *unstressed* hər, ər/ *pron.* **1.** the form of the pronoun SHE, used as a direct or indirect object, or sometimes after the verb *be*: *We saw her this morning. I gave her the message. It's her.* **2.** the form of the pronoun SHE used to show possession or some relation: *Her coat is on the chair.* Compare HERS. **3.** of that female already mentioned: *Sally sat down in her chair.*

her•ald /ˈhɛrəld/ *n.* [count] **1.** a royal or official messenger. **2.** a person or thing that comes before: *The robins are heralds of spring.* —*v.* [~ + obj] **3.** to signal the coming of: *Robins herald the spring.*

her•ald•ry /ˈhɛrəldriy/ *n.* [noncount] the study of coats of arms.

herb /ɜrb/ *n.* [count] a plant used for flavoring, in medicines, or for its pleasant smell. —**her•ba•ceous** /hərˈbeyʃəs, ɜr-/, *adj.*

herb•al /ˈɜrbəl, ˈhɜr-/ *adj.* [before a noun] of or relating to herbs: *herbal tea.*

herb•al•ist /ˈhɜrbəlɪst, ˈɜr-/ *n.* [count] a person who collects or deals in medicinal herbs, or uses them in healing.

herb•i•cide /ˈhɜrbəˌsayd, ˈɜr-/ *n.* a substance or chemical for killing plants, esp. weeds. —**her•bi•cid•al** /ˌhɜrbəˈsaydl, ˌɜr-/, *adj.*

her•bi•vore /ˈhɜrbəˌvɔr/ *n.* [count] an animal that eats only plants. —**her•biv•o•rous** /hɜrˈbɪvərəs/ *adj.*

herd /hɜrd/ *n.* [count] **1.** a number of animals living or traveling together: *a herd of cattle.* **2.** a group of people; crowd: *a herd of tourists.* —*v.* **3.** to (cause to) move in a herd: *The students all herded into the classroom.* [~ + obj]: *The guide herded us into the hotel.* —**'herd•er,** *n.* [count]

herds•man /ˈhɜrdzmən/ *n.* [count], *pl.* **-men.** the keeper of a herd, esp. of cattle or sheep; herder.

here /hɪər/ *adv.* **1.** in, at, or to this place: *Put the pen here. Come here.* **2.** at this point in an action, speech, etc.: *Here the speaker paused.* **3.** The word *here* is used as the first word in a sentence to call attention to some person or thing. It is the subject that decides which form of the verb is used, singular or plural, should be used: [~ + verb + subject]: *Here comes the bride. Here is your newspaper. Here come the boys. Here are the tickets.* [~ + pronoun subject + verb]: *Here she is! Here they are.* —*interj.* **4.** The word *here* is used to attract attention, call an animal, answer a roll call, etc. —*Idiom.* **5. here and there,** in or to various places; scattered about. **6. neither here nor there,** not related to the present subject.

here•a•bout /ˈhɪərəˌbawt/ also **'here•a,bouts,** *adv.* near here.

here•af•ter /hɪərˈæftər/ *adv.* **1.** in the future; from now on: *Hereafter you must be on time.* —*n.* [count; singular; the + ~] **2.** a life after death.

here•by /hɪərˈbay, ˈhɪərˌbay/ *adv.* by this action,

document, etc.: *I hereby resign (= By saying or writing this, I resign).*

he•red•i•tar•y /həˈrɛdɪˌtɛriy/ *adj.* **1.** passed on naturally from parent to child: *a hereditary disease; a hereditary skill.* **2.** passed on to an heir: *a hereditary title.*

he•red•i•ty /həˈrɛdɪtiy/ *n.* [noncount] the passing on of qualities, characteristics, or traits from parents to their children.

her•e•sy /ˈhɛrəsiy/ *n.* [count] [noncount], *pl.* **-sies.** **1.** religious belief that is completely different from the accepted one. **2.** any belief strongly different from established beliefs, customs, etc.

her•e•tic /ˈhɛrɪtɪk/ *n.* [count] a person who is guilty of heresy. —**he•ret•i•cal** /həˈrɛtɪkəl/, *adj.*

her•it•age /ˈhɛrɪtɪdʒ/ *n.* [count; usually singular] the traditions and ways of life handed down within a family or country.

her•met•ic /hɜrˈmɛtɪk/ also **her'met•i•cal,** *adj.* closed so tightly that no air can escape. —**her'met•i•cal•ly,** *adv.*

her•mit /ˈhɜrmɪt/ *n.* [count] a person who lives alone, esp. for religious reasons.

her•mit•age /ˈhɜrmɪtɪdʒ/ *n.* [count] the place where a hermit lives.

her•ni•a /ˈhɜrniyə/ *n.* [count], *pl.* **-ni•as, -ni•ae** /-niyˌiy/. the pushing of a body organ or tissue through an opening in its surrounding walls.

he•ro /ˈhɪərow/ *n.* [count], *pl.* **1.** a man who is admired for his courage, brave deeds, and noble qualities. **2.** the principal male character in a story, play, film, etc. —**her•o•ism** /ˈhɛrowˌɪzəm/ *n.* [noncount]

he•ro•ic /hɪˈrowɪk/ *adj.* Also, **he'ro•i•cal.** **1.** very brave; courageous: *a heroic attempt to save the child's life.* **2.** concerned with the deeds of heroes: *a heroic poem.* —*n.* **3. heroics,** [plural] language or behavior that is meant to attract attention. —**he'ro•i•cal•ly,** *adv.*

her•o•in /ˈhɛrowɪn/ *n.* [noncount] an illegal drug made from morphine that is addictive.

her•o•ine /ˈhɛrowɪn/ *n.* [count] **1.** a woman who is admired for her courage, brave deeds, and noble qualities. **2.** the principal female character in a story, play, film, etc.

her•on /ˈhɛrən/ *n.* [count] a long-necked bird that lives near water.

her•pes /ˈhɜrpiyz/ *n.* [noncount] a viral disease in which blisters appear on the skin.

her•ring /ˈhɛrɪŋ/ *n.* [count], *pl.* (*esp. when thought of as a group*) **-ring,** (*esp. for kinds or species*) **-rings.** a small, saltwater food fish.

hers /hɜrz/ *pron.* a form of the pronoun SHE used to show possession, or to mean "that or those belonging to her": *Are you a friend of hers?* [be + ~]: *The red umbrella is hers.*

her•self /hərˈsɛlf/ *pron.* **1.** the form of the pronoun SHE, a reflexive pronoun, used to show that the subject of the sentence and this pronoun refer to the same person: *Anne supports herself (= Anne supports Anne).* **2.** (used to give emphasis): *She herself told me.* **3.** her usual or customary self: *After her illness she was herself again.*

he's /hiyz; *unstressed* iyz/ *contraction.* **1.** a shortened form of *he is: He's late again.* **2.** a shortened form of *he has: He's already gone to bed.*

hes•i•tant /ˈhɛzɪtənt/ *adj.* doubtful; uncertain: *I'm hesitant about leaving early.* —**hes•i•tan•cy,** *n.* [noncount] —**'hes•i•tant•ly,** *adv.*

hes•i•tate /ˈhɛzɪˌteyt/ *v.* [no obj], **-tat•ed, -tat•ing.** **1.** to wait or pause because of doubt, fear, or uncertainty: *She hesitated before taking the* *job.* **2.** to be unwilling: *He hesitated to break to law.* —'**hes•i,tat•ing•ly,** *adv.* —**hes•i•ta•tion** /ˌhɛzɪˈteyʃən/ *n.* [*noncount*] [*count*]

het•er•o•ge•ne•ous /ˌhɛtərəˈdʒiyniyəs, -ˈdʒiynyəs/ *adj.* made up of different kinds; mixed. —ˌ**het•er•o'ge•ne•ous•ly,** *adv.*

het•er•o•sex•u•al /ˌhɛtərəˈsɛkʃuwəl/ *adj.* **1.** attracted sexually to the opposite sex. **2.** of or relating to the opposite sex or to both sexes: *a heterosexual relationship.* —*n.* [*count*] **3.** a person attracted to the opposite sex. —**het•er•o•sex•u•al•i•ty** /ˌhɛtərəˌsɛkʃuwˈælɪtiy/, *n.* [*noncount*]

hew /hyuw/ *v.* [~ + *obj*], **hewed, hewed** or **hewn, hew•ing.** to strike or cut with an ax or other tool.

hex•a•gon /ˈhɛksəˌgɒn, -gən/ *n.* [*count*] a figure having six angles and six sides. —**hex•ag•o•nal** /hɛkˈsægənl/, *adj.*

hey /hey/ *interj.* This word is used to call attention or to express pleasure, surprise, interest, etc.: *Hey, come back here, you!*

hey•day /ˈhey,dey/ *n.* [*count; usually singular*] the stage or period of greatest success: *the heyday of the silent films.*

hgt., an abbreviation of: height.

hi /hay/ *interj.* This word is used as an informal greeting: *Hi, how are you?*

HI, an abbreviation of: Hawaii.

hi•ber•nate /ˈhaybər,neyt/ *v.* [*no obj*], **-nat•ed, -nat•ing.** to spend the winter in a sleep-like state, as bears do. —**hi•ber•na•tion** /ˌhaybərˈneyʃən/, *n.* [*noncount*]

hic•cup or **hic•cough** /ˈhɪkʌp, -əp/ *n.,* *v.,* **hic•cuped** or **hic•cupped** or **hic•coughed** /ˈhɪkʌpt, -əpt/, **-cup•ing** or **-cup•ping** or **-cough•ing.** —*n.* [*count*] **1.** a sharp sound in the throat caused by a sudden, brief stopping of the breath. **2.** Usually, **hiccups.** [*plural*] an attack of hiccups. —*v.* [*no obj*] **3.** to make a hiccup.

hick /hɪk/ *n.* [*count*] a person from the country who lacks experience in city living.

hick•o•ry /ˈhɪkəriy, ˈhɪkriy/ *n.* [*count*], *pl.* **-ries.** a North American tree of the walnut family.

hid /hɪd/ *v.* pt. or pp. of HIDE.

hide¹ /hayd/ *v.,* **hid, hid•den** /ˈhɪdn̩/ or **hid, hid•ing.** **1.** to put or keep out of sight: [~ + *obj*]: *Where did you hide the money?* [*no obj*]: *to hide under the bed.* **2.** [~ + *obj*] to keep secret: *He couldn't hide his true feelings.* **3. hide out,** to go into or remain in hiding: *The criminals were hiding out in the woods.*

hide² /hayd/ *n.* [*count*] the skin of a large animal, as a cow.

'**hide-and-'seek,** *n.* [*noncount*] a children's game in which one player gives the other players a chance to hide and then tries to find them.

hide•a•way /ˈhaydəˌwey/ *n.* [*count*] a place where a person can be alone.

hid•e•ous /ˈhɪdiyəs/ *adj.* very ugly; horrible: *a hideous monster.* —'**hid•e•ous•ly,** *adv.*

hide-out or **hide-out** /ˈhayd,awt/ *n.* [*count*] a safe place for hiding, esp. from the law.

hid•ing¹ /ˈhaydɪŋ/ *n.* [*noncount*] the state of being hidden: *to go into hiding.*

hid•ing² /ˈhaydɪŋ/ *n.* [*count*] a beating.

hi•er•ar•chy /ˈhayə,rɑrkiy, ˈhayrɑr-/ *n.* [*count*], *pl.* **-chies.** **1.** a system of persons or things ranked one above another. **2.** the persons in authority: *the church hierarchy.* —**hi•er•ar•chic** /ˌhayəˈrɑrkɪk/, **hi•er'ar•chi•cal,** *adj.*

hi•er•o•glyph•ic /ˌhayərəˈglɪfɪk, ˌhayrə-/ *adj.* Also, ˌ**hi•er•o'glyph•i•cal.** **1.** of a type of writing

in which pictures or symbols represent ideas: *The ancient Egyptians used a hieroglyphic system of writing.* —*n.* [*count*] **2.** Also, '**hi•er•o,glyph.** a hieroglyphic symbol. **3.** Usually, **hieroglyphics.** [*plural*] hieroglyphic writing.

hieroglyphics

hi-fi /ˈhay'fay/ *n.,* *pl.* **-fis,** *adj.* —*n.* **1.** HIGH FIDELITY. **2.** [*count*] a stereo, radio, tape recorder, etc., that produces high-quality sound: *She bought an expensive hi-fi.* —*adj.* [*before a noun*] **3.** of, relating to, or characteristic of hi-fi.

high /hay/ *adj.* and *adv.,* **-er, -est,** *n.* —*adj.* **1.** (of things) having much height; tall: *a high wall.* **2.** (of things) having a given height: *The tree is 20 feet high.* **3.** greater than the usual degree, measure, or amount: *high speed; high prices; high adventure.* **4.** important: *a high official.* **5.** above other sounds: *high notes.* **6.** morally good; noble: *high ideals.* **7.** favorable: *He has a high opinion of her.* **8.** [*before a noun*] luxurious: *living the high life.* **9.** merry; happy: *They were in high spirits.* **10.** [*be* + ~] under the influence of alcohol or drugs. **11.** (of a gear) giving the greatest speed. —*adv.* **12.** at or to a high point, place, or level: *flying high.* **13.** luxuriously: *to live high.* —*n.* **14.** [*noncount*] the high gear of a vehicle. **15.** [*count*] a high or the highest point, place, or level: *a record high for unemployment.* **16.** [*count*] a state or feeling of extreme pleasure: *on a high.* —*Idiom.* **17. high and dry,** alone and helpless: *She was left high and dry without money or friends.* **18. high and low,** everywhere: *to search high and low.*

high•brow /ˈhay,braw/ *n.* [*count*] a person who is knowledgeable about art, music, etc.

high•chair /ˈhay,tʃɛər/ *n.* [*count*] a tall chair with long legs and a tray for food, for use by a very young child during meals.

'**high-defi'nition 'television,** *n.* [*noncount*] a television system that produces a sharper image and greater picture detail. *Abbr.:* HDTV

'**higher edu'cation,** *n.* [*noncount*] education at a college or university.

'**higher-'up,** *n.* [*count*] a person of high authority in an organization.

'**high fi'delity,** *n.* [*noncount*] high-quality reproduction of recorded sound. Also called **hi-fi.**

'**high-'flown,** *adj.* **1.** not reasonable: *high-flown ideas.* **2.** (of language) sounding too grand.

'**high-'handed,** *adj.* using one's power unfairly or carelessly. —'**high-'hand•ed•ly,** *adv.* —'**high-'hand•ed•ness,** *n.* [*noncount*]

'**high ,jinks,** *n.* [*plural; used with a plural verb*] wild fun.

'**high ,jump,** *n.* [*noncount*] the sport of jumping over a high bar set between two poles.

high•land /ˈhayləndz/ *n.* **highlands,** [*plural*] a high or mountainous part of a country.

H

'high-'level, *adj.* [*before a noun*] **1.** of or involving important people: *a high-level meeting.* **2.** having importance: *high-level executives.*

high•light /'haɪ,laɪt/ *v.* [~ + *obj*] **1.** to emphasize: *The paper highlights the difficulties of the working poor.* —*n.* **2.** Also, **'high ,light.** [*count*] the most important part of something.

high•ly /'haɪliy/ *adv.* **1.** extremely: *highly amusing.* **2.** with favor: *They spoke highly of you.* **3.** generously: *a highly paid employee.*

'high-'minded, *adj.* having a high standard of behavior. —**'high-'mind•ed•ly**, *adv.* —**'high-'mind•ed•ness**, *n.* [*noncount*]

High•ness /'haɪnɪs/ *n.* [*count*] a title of honor for members of a royal family, usually used with *His, Her, Your,* or *Their: His Royal Highness, the Prince of Wales.*

high-pow•ered /'haɪ'paʊərd/ *adj.* **1.** very forceful: *a high-powered sales talk.* **2.** very powerful: *a high-powered telescope.*

'high-,rise or **'high,rise**, *adj.* [*before a noun*] **1.** (of a building) very tall. —*n.* [*count*] **2.** Also, **'high ,rise, high-riser.** a high-rise building.

'high ,school, *n.* [*count*] [*noncount*] a school that usually has grades 9 or 10 through 12.

'high 'seas, *n.* [*plural*] the open sea that is not controlled by any country.

'high-'spirited, *adj.* full of life and energy.

'high-'strung, *adj.* being highly sensitive or nervous.

'high 'tide, *n.* [*count*] [*noncount*] the tide when the ocean is at its highest level.

high•way /'haɪ,weɪ/ *n.* [*count*] a main road, esp. one between towns or cities.

hi•jack /'haɪ,dʒæk/ *v.* [~ + *obj*] to seize (an airplane or other vehicle) by force, esp. for political aims: *The terrorists hijacked the plane.* —**'hi,jack•er**, *n.* [*count*]

hike /haɪk/ *n., v.,* **hiked, hik•ing,** —*n.* [*count*] **1.** a long walk. **2.** an increase: *a hike in wages.* —*v.* **3.** [*no obj*] to go on a hike: *to hike through the woods.* **4.** [~ + *obj*] to increase, often sharply and suddenly: *to hike prices.* —**'hik•er**, *n.* [*count*]

hi•lar•i•ous /hɪˈlɛəriyəs, -'lær-/ *adj.* extremely funny: *a hilarious joke.* —**hi'lar•i•ous•ly**, *adv.*

hi•lar•i•ty /hɪˈlɛərɪtiy, -'lær-/ *n.* [*noncount*] merry laughter.

hill /hɪl/ *n.* [*count*] **1.** a raised part of the earth's surface, smaller than a mountain. **2.** a slope on a road, etc. —*Idiom.* **3. over the hill,** advanced in age or no longer at one's best.

hill•side /'hɪl,saɪd/ *n.* [*count*] the side of a hill.

hill•top /'hɪl,tɑp/ *n.* [*count*] the top of a hill.

hill•y /'hɪliy/ *adj.,* **-i•er, -i•est.** full of hills.

hilt /hɪlt/ *n.* [*count*] **1.** the handle of a sword, knife, or dagger. —*Idiom.* **2. to the hilt,** completely; fully: *He played the movie role to the hilt.*

him /hɪm/ *pron.* the form of the pronoun HE, used as a direct or indirect object: *I'll see him tomorrow. Give him the message.*

him•self /hɪmˈsɛlf/ *pron.* **1.** the form of the pronoun HE, a reflexive pronoun, used to show that the subject of the sentence and this pronoun refer to the same male person: *John cut himself (= John cut him). He wrote himself a note.* **2.** (used to give emphasis): *He himself told me.* **3.** his usual or customary self: *After his illness he was himself again.*

hind /haɪnd/ *adj.* [*before a noun*] at the back: *the hind legs of an animal.*

hin•der /'hɪndər/ *v.* [~ + *obj*] to delay the progress of: *Lack of money hindered the project.*

hind•quar•ter /'haɪnd,kwɔrtər, -,kwɔ-/ *n.* hindquarters, [*plural*] the back part of a four-legged animal.

hin•drance /'hɪndrəns/ *n.* **1.** [*noncount*] the act of hindering; the state of being hindered. **2.** [*count*] a person or thing that hinders.

hind•sight /'haɪnd,saɪt/ *n.* [*noncount*] the ability to understand something after it has happened: *We saw our mistake in hindsight.*

Hin•du /'hɪnduw/ *n., pl.* **-dus,** *adj.* —*n.* [*count*] **1.** a person who believes in Hinduism. —*adj.* **2.** of or relating to Hindus or Hinduism.

Hin•du•ism /'hɪnduw,ɪzəm/ *n.* [*noncount*] the chief religion of India, noted esp. for the belief that one returns after death in another form.

hinge /hɪndʒ/ *n., v.,* **hinged, hing•ing.** —*n.* [*count*] **1.** a metal joint on which a door or gate swings. —*v.* [~ + *obj*] **2.** to put hinges on. **3. hinge on,** depend on: *Everything hinges on her decision.*

hint /hɪnt/ *n.* [*count*] **1.** an indirect, partly hidden, or helpful suggestion; clue: *Give me a hint about my gift.* —*v.* **2.** [~ + *obj*] to give a hint of: *The gray skies hinted snow.* **3.** [*no obj*] to make a hint. **4. hint at,** to suggest indirectly: *He hinted at a solution to the problem.*

hin•ter•land /'hɪntər,lænd/ *n.* [*count*] **1.** Often, **hinterlands.** [*plural*] the distant inner or back parts of a country. **2.** the land behind a coast.

hip /hɪp/ *n.* [*count*] **1.** the part on each side of the body just below the waist. **2.** the joint at this part. —**hipped,** *adj.: wide-hipped.*

hip•pie or **hip•py** /'hɪpiy/ *n.* [*count*], *pl.* **-pies.** a young person of the 1960's who rejected established social values and often wore long hair and unusual clothes.

hip•po /'hɪpow/ *n.* HIPPOPOTAMUS.

hip•po•pot•a•mus /,hɪpə'pɒtəməs/ *n.* [*count*], *pl.* **-mus•es, -mi** /-,maɪ/. a large African mammal with a hairless, thick body, living in and near rivers.

hire /haɪˀr/ *v.,* **hired, hir•ing.** [~ + *obj*] **1.** to employ (someone) for wages: *to hire a clerk.* **2.** to pay for the temporary use of (something); rent: *She hired a boat.*

hire•ling /'haɪˀrlɪŋ/ *n.* [*count*] a person who works merely for pay.

his /hɪz; *unstressed* ɪz/ *pron.* **1.** the form of the pronoun HE used to show possession or some relation: *His coat is the brown one. Do you mind his speaking first.* **2.** the form of the pronoun HE used to show possession, or to mean "that or those belonging to him": *His was the best idea of all.* [*be* + ~]: *I borrowed a tie of his. I thought it was his.* **3.** of that male person or animal already mentioned: *John sat down in his chair.*

His•pan•ic /hɪ'spænɪk/ *adj.* **1.** of Spain or Spanish-speaking countries. **2.** of Hispanics. —*n.* [*count*] **3.** a U.S. citizen or resident of Spanish or Latin-American descent.

hiss /hɪs/ *v.* **1.** [*no obj*] to make or give off a sharp sound like that of the letter *s: The snake hissed.* **2.** to express disapproval (of) by making this sound: [*no obj*]: *As the play got worse, the audience began to hiss and boo.* [~ + *obj*]: *The audience hissed the actor off the stage.* —*n.* [*count*] **3.** a hissing sound.

his•to•ri•an /hɪ'stɔriyən/ *n.* [*count*] a writer of history.

his•tor•ic /hɪ'stɔrɪk, -'stɑr-/ *adj.* [*before a noun*]

1. well-known or important in history: *a historic building.* **2.** HISTORICAL.

his·tor·i·cal /hɪˈstɔrɪkəl, -ˈstɒr-/ *adj.* [*before a noun*] **1.** of, relating to, or treating history or past events: *historical records.* **2.** based on or suggested by history: *a historical novel.* **3.** HISTORIC (def. 1).: *It was a historical event.* —**his'tor·i·cal·ly,** *adv.* —**his'tor·i·cal·ness,** *n.* [*noncount*]

his·to·ry /ˈhɪstəriy, ˈhɪstriy/ *n.,* *pl.* **-ries.** **1.** [*noncount*] the branch of knowledge dealing with past events: *majoring in history.* **2.** [*count*] a telling of past events: *a short history of the war.* **3.** [*count*] a record of past events and times, esp. of a particular person: *the patient's medical history.*

hit /hɪt/ *v.,* **hit, hit·ting,** *n.* —*v.* **1.** [~ + *obj*] to deal a blow or stroke to: *Hit the nail with the hammer.* **2.** to come against with force: [~ + *obj*]: *The wheel of the car hit the curb. The car hit against the railing.* **3.** [~ + *obj*] to reach; strike: *Did the arrow hit the target?* **4.** [~ + *obj*] to drive or propel by a stroke: *to hit a ball onto the green.* **5.** [~ + *obj*] to affect severely: *families hit hard by inflation.* **6.** *Informal.* [~ + *obj*] to request of: *He hit me for a loan.* **7.** [~ + *obj*] to reach or attain (a level or amount): *Prices hit a new high.* **8.** to come (upon) by accident or search: [~ + *obj*]: *to hit the right answer.* [~ + *on/upon* + *obj*]: *He finally hit on a solution to the problem.* —*n.* [*count*] **9.** a strike; collision: *a sudden hit against a window.* **10.** a blow: *a direct hit.* **11.** critical comment: *The candidate took several hits from the press.* **12.** BASE HIT. **13.** a success: *The play is a big hit.* —*Idiom.* **14. hit it off,** to become friendly: *The two hit it off immediately.* **15. hit the books,** *Slang.* to study hard. **16. hit the bottle,** to drink too much alcohol. **17. hit the ceiling** or **roof,** *Informal.* to become angry. **18. hit the hay** or **sack,** *Slang.* to go to bed. **19. hit the nail on the head,** to say or do exactly the right thing. **20. hit the road,** to leave. —**'hit·ter,** *n.* [*count*]

'hit-and-'run, *adj.* [*before a noun*] being or involving a driver who is guilty of leaving the scene of an accident he or she has caused.

hitch¹ /hɪtʃ/ *v.* [~ + *obj*] **1.** to fasten or tie with a rope or strap: *to hitch a horse to a post.* **2.** to harness (an animal) to a vehicle: *He hitched the horse to the carriage.* —*n.* [*count*] **3.** an unexpected problem: *The rain was a hitch in our plans.*

hitch² /hɪtʃ/ *v. Informal.* to hitchhike.

hitch·hike /ˈhɪtʃˌhayk/ *v.,* **-hiked, -hik·ing.** [*no obj*] [~ + *obj*] to travel by standing on the side of the road seeking free rides from passing vehicles: *He hitchhiked from St. Louis to Chicago.* —**'hitch,hik·er,** *n.* [*count*]

HIV, an abbreviation of: human immunodeficiency virus, a virus that is a cause of AIDS.

hive /hayv/ *n.* [*count*] **1.** a shelter for honeybees; beehive. **2.** a colony of bees. **3.** a very busy place: *a hive of activity.*

hives /hayvz/ *n.* a rash of itchy bumps on the skin, usually caused by an allergy: [*noncount*]: *Hives is sometimes a serious condition.* [*plural; used with a plural verb*]: *The hives on her skin were itchy.*

h'm or **hmm** /hmm/ *interj.* This sound is used to express a pause, doubt, or dissatisfaction.

HMO, an abbreviation of: health maintenance organization.

hoard /hɔrd/ *n.* [*count*] **1.** a supply of something saved and hidden for future use: *a hoard of*

money. —*v.* [*no obj*] [~ + *obj*] **2.** to save and store a supply (of). —**'hoard·er,** *n.* [*count*]

hoarse /hɔrs/ *adj.,* **hoars·er, hoars·est.** (of a voice or person) sounding harsh or rough. —**'hoarse·ly,** *adv.* —**'hoarse·ness,** *n.* [*noncount*]

hoar·y /ˈhɔriy/ *adj.,* **-i·er, -i·est.** **1.** gray or white with age: *hoary hair.* **2.** ancient. —**'hoar·i·ness,** *n.* [*noncount*]

hoax /howks/ *n.* [*count*] **1.** something intended to deceive: *Was the bomb threat real or just another hoax?* —*v.* [~ + *obj*] **2.** to deceive by a hoax. —**'hoax·er,** *n.* [*count*]

hob·ble /ˈhɒbəl/ *v.,* **-bled, -bling.** **1.** [*no obj*] to walk lamely; limp. **2.** [~ + *obj*] to tie together the legs of (a horse) to prevent free motion. **3.** [~ + *obj*] to get in the way of; hamper. —**'hob·bler,** *n.* [*count*]

hob·by /ˈhɒbiy/ *n.* [*count*], *pl.* **-bies.** an activity engaged in for pleasure. —**'hob·by·ist,** *n.* [*count*]

ho·bo /ˈhowbow/ *n.* [*count*], *pl.* **-bos, -boes.** a person who wanders from place to place.

hock¹ /hɒk/ *n.* [*count*] a joint above the foot in the hind leg of a horse, cow, etc.

hock² /hɒk/ *v.* [~ + *obj*] **1.** to pawn: *He had hocked his wife's jewelry to raise money.* —*n.* [*noncount*] **2.** the state of being held as security; pawn: *the jewelry was in hock.* **3.** the condition of owing; debt.

hock·ey /ˈhɒkiy/ *n.* **1.** ICE HOCKEY. **2.** FIELD HOCKEY.

hodge·podge /ˈhɒdʒˌpɒdʒ/ *n.* [*count*] a confused mixture.

hoe /how/ *n.,* *v.,* **hoed, hoe·ing.** —*n.* [*count*] **1.** a long-handled tool with a flat, square blade, used esp. in breaking up soil and in weeding. —*v.* [~ + *obj*] [*no obj*] **2.** to dig with a hoe.

hog /hɔg, hɒg/ *n.,* *v.,* **hogged, hog·ging.** —*n.* [*count*] **1.** a large pig, esp. one grown for eating. **2.** a selfish or dirty person. —*v.* [~ + *obj*] **3.** to take more than one's share of: *He hogged all the food.* —**'hog·gish,** *adj.*

hoist /hɔyst/ *v.* [~ + *obj*] **1.** to raise or lift, esp. by a mechanical device: *to hoist the sails on a boat.* —*n.* [*count*] **2.** an apparatus for hoisting. **3.** the act of hoisting.

hold¹ /howld/ *v.,* **held** /hɛld/ **hold·ing,** *n.* —*v.* **1.** [~ + *obj*] to keep in the hand: *I held her hand as we crossed the street.* **2.** [~ + *obj*] to support: *I held the baby gently.* **3.** [*no obj*] to remain attached or fastened: *The glue held.* **4.** to (cause to) be, stay, or remain in a certain state: [~ + *obj*]: *The teacher held the students' attention.* [*no obj*]: *I hope our luck holds.* **5.** [~ + *obj*] to carry on: *to hold a meeting.* **6.** [~ + *obj*] to prevent from leaving: *The police held her for questioning.* **7.** [~ + *obj*] to keep in control: *Please hold your applause.* **8.** [~ + *obj*] to own: *to hold shares of stock.* **9.** [~ + *obj*] to be able to contain: *This bottle holds a quart.* **10.** [~ + *obj*] to keep in the mind; believe: *I held an opposing view.* **11.** [~ + *obj*] to make responsible: *We will hold you to your word.* **12.** [*no obj*] to remain valid: *The argument still holds.* **13.** [~ + *obj*] to have the position of: *He holds the office of president.* **14.** [~ + *obj*] to keep (a telephone call) from reaching someone. **15. hold back, a.** to keep in control: *She tried to hold back her tears* or *She tried to hold her tears back.* **b.** to keep secret: *to hold back information* or *to hold information back.* **16. hold down, a.** to keep at a low level: *to hold down interest rates* or *to hold interest rates down.*

H

b. to continue in: *to hold down a job.* **17. hold forth,** to speak at great length. **18. hold off, a.** to keep away; resist: *The troops held off the enemy* or *They held the enemy off.* **b.** to delay action: *Let's hold off on that decision for now.* **19. hold on, a.** to continue: *The troops can hold on for another week.* **b.** to wait, esp. while on the telephone: *Can you hold on a moment?* **20. hold out, a.** to offer: *They held out their hands in greeting.* **b.** [*no obj*] to last: *Will the food hold out?* **c.** to refuse to give in: *We are holding out for higher wages.* **21. hold over, a.** to keep for a later date: *We'll hold that discussion over for later* or *We'll hold over that discussion for later.* **b.** to keep beyond the arranged period: *They held the movie over for an extra week* or *The movie was held over for an extra week.* **22. hold up, a.** to delay: *Something is holding up the work* or *Something is holding the work up.* **b.** to continue in spite of difficulties: *How are you holding up under the strain?* **c.** to present for attention: *to hold up the child as a good example* or *to hold the child up as a good example.* **d.** to rob at gunpoint: *A thief held up the store.* —*n.* [*count*] **23.** an act of holding with the hand or other physical means: *a good hold on the rope.* **24.** something to hold a thing by, as in climbing. **25.** a controlling force or influence: *Drugs had a powerful hold on them.* —*Idiom.* **26. on hold,** into a state of waiting or delay: *The plans were put on hold.*

hold² /howld/ *n.* [*count*] a space for cargo in a ship or aircraft.

holder *n.* [*count*] something that holds: *a pencil holder.*

-holder, a person who owns or possesses something: *landholder; officeholder.*

hold•ing /'howldɪŋ/ *n.* [*count*] **1.** a section of land leased esp. for farming purposes. **2.** Often, **holdings.** [*plural*] legally owned property, as shares of stock.

hold•o•ver /'howld,owvər/ *n.* [*count*] something remaining from a former time.

hold•up /'howld,ʌp/ *n.* [*count*] **1.** a robbery at gunpoint. **2.** a delay.

hole /howl/ *n., v.,* **holed, hol•ing.** —*n.* [*count*] **1.** an opening through something: *a hole in the roof.* **2.** a hollow place in a solid mass: *a hole in the ground.* **3.** the burrow of an animal: *a rabbit hole.* **4.** a small, unpleasant place to live in. **5.** an embarrassing situation: *to be in a hole.* **6.** a fault; flaw: *There are holes in your argument.* —*v.* **7. hole up,** to hide in order to escape: *They holed up in the old hotel. They were holed up in the old hotel.*

hol•i•day /'hɒlɪ,dey/ *n.* [*count*] **1.** a day set aside to honor the memory of an event or person. **2.** any day of relaxation from work. **3.** Sometimes, **holidays.** *Chiefly Brit.* VACATION. —*adj.* [*before a noun*] **4.** of or suitable for a holiday; joyous: *in a holiday mood.*

ho•li•ness /'howliynɪs/ *n.* **1.** [*noncount*] the quality or state of being holy. **2.** [*His/Your + Holiness*] a title of the pope.

hol•low /'hɒlow/ *adj.,* **-er, -est,** *v.* —*adj.* **1.** having a space inside; empty: *a hollow sphere.* **2.** (of a surface) curving inward or downward: *hollow cheeks.* **3.** (of a sound) dull, deep, or echoing. —*n.* [*count*] **4.** a hole or empty space. **5.** a valley. —'**hol•low•ness,** *n.* [*noncount*]

hol•ly /'hɒliy/ *n.* [*count*], *pl.* **-lies.** a tree with shiny leaves and red berries.

hol•o•caust /'hɒlə,kɔst, 'howlə-/ *n.* **1.** [*count*] a great or complete destruction, esp. by fire. **2. the**

Holocaust, the mass killing of European Jews in Nazi concentration camps during World War II.

hol•ster /'howlstər/ *n.* [*count*] a leather holder for a gun, often worn on a belt.

ho•ly /'howliy/ *adj.,* **-li•er, -li•est. 1.** relating to religion and the worship of God; sacred. **2.** devoted to God: *a holy life.*

'Holy Com'munion, *n.* COMMUNION (def. 1).

'Holy 'Ghost, *n.* the third person of the Trinity. Also called **Holy Spirit.**

'Holy 'Spirit, *n.* **1.** the spirit of God. **2.** HOLY GHOST.

hom•age /'hɒmɪdʒ, 'ɒm-/ *n.* [*noncount*] great respect.

home /howm/ *n., adj., adv., v.,* **homed, hom•ing.** —*n.* **1.** [*count*] [*noncount*] the usual place where one lives, esp. with one's family. **2.** [*noncount*] the place that a person comes from. **3.** [*count*] the place or region where something comes from: *Australia is the home of kangaroos.* **4.** [*count*] a place for the care of people with special needs: *a nursing home.* —*adj.* [*before a noun*] **5.** of, relating to, or done or made in one's home or country; domestic: *home products.* **6.** played in a team's own area: *a home game.* —*adv.* **7.** to, toward, or at home: *I want to go home.* **8.** deep; to the heart: *The truth struck home.* **9.** to the point aimed at: *He drove the nail home.* —*v.* **10. home in (on),** to go or move exactly toward: *The missile homed in on the target.* —*Idiom.* **11. at home, a.** in one's own house. **b.** comfortable; at ease: *Make yourself at home.* —'**home,like,** *adj.*

home•com•ing /'howm,kʌmɪŋ/ *n.* [*count*] **1.** a return to one's home. **2.** an annual event held by a college, university, or high school for visiting alumni.

home•grown /'howm'grown/ *adj.* grown or produced at home or locally: *homegrown tomatoes.*

home•land /'howm,lænd, -lənd/ *n.* [*count*] **1.** one's native land. **2.** a region created or considered as a state by or for a particular ethnic group: *the Palestinian homeland.*

home•less /'howmlɪs/ *adj.* **1.** having no home: *homeless people.* **2.** of or serving people having no home: *homeless shelters.* —'**home•less•ness,** *n.* [*noncount*]

home•ly /'howmliy/ *adj.,* **-li•er, -li•est. 1.** not attractive: *a homely face.* **2.** simple and plain: *homely food.* —'**home•li•ness,** *n.* [*noncount*]

home•made /'howm'meyd/ *adj.* made at home or by hand: *homemade cookies.*

home•mak•er /'howm,meykər/ *n.* [*count*] a person who manages the family household. —'**home,-mak•ing,** *n.* [*noncount*], *adj.*

home•room /'howm'ruwm, -'rʊm/ *n.* [*count*] a classroom in which a group of students in the same grade meet at the beginning of the day.

'home 'run, *n.* [*count*] a hit in baseball allowing the batter to circle the bases and score a run.

home•sick /'howm,sɪk/ *adj.* sad because of being away from home or family. —'**home,sick•ness,** *n.* [*noncount*]

home•stead /'howmstɛd, -stɪd/ *n.* [*count*] **1.** a farm with its land and other buildings. **2.** an area of land given by the government to a settler for farming. —'**home,stead•er,** *n.* [*count*]

home•stretch /'howm'strɛtʃ/ *n.* [*count*] **1.** the straight part of a racetrack from the last turn to the finish line. **2.** the final stage: *the homestretch of the election.*

home•ward /'howmwərd/ *adv.* **1.** Also, '**home•**

wards. toward home: *heading homeward.* —*adj.*
2. going toward home: *a homeward journey.*

home•work /'howm,wɜrk/ *n.* [noncount] schoolwork to be done away from school.

hom•ey or **hom•y** /'howmiy/ *adj.*, **-i•er, -i•est.** comfortably informal; cozy: *a homey inn.* —'hom•ey•ness, 'hom•i•ness, *n.* [noncount]

hom•i•cide /'hɒmə,sayd, 'howmə-/ *n.* **1.** [noncount] [count] the killing of one human being by another. **2.** [count] a person who kills another. —,hom•i'cid•al, *adj.*

hom•i•ly /'hɒməliy/ *n.* [count], *pl.* **-lies. 1.** a sermon. **2.** a long talk about how to behave.

'**homing ,pigeon,** *n.* [count] a pigeon trained to carry messages and return home.

ho•mo•ge•ne•ous /,howmə'dʒiyniyəs, -'dʒiynyəs, ,hɒmə-/ *adj.* made up of parts or elements that are all alike: *Japan has a largely homogeneous population.* —,ho•mo'ge•ne•ous•ly, *adv.*

ho•mog•e•nize /hə'mɒdʒə,nayz/ *v.* [~ + *obj*], **-nized, -niz•ing. 1.** to make homogeneous. **2.** to break up the fat in (milk or cream), causing it to be evenly distributed throughout.

hom•o•nym /'hɒmənɪm/ *n.* [count] a word that is the same as another in sound and spelling but different in meaning, such as *bear* "to carry" and *bear* "large, brown or black furry animal."

ho•mo•pho•bi•a /,howmə'fowbiyə/ *n.* [noncount] fear of or hatred toward homosexuals and homosexuality.

hom•o•phone /'hɒmə,fown, 'howmə-/ *n.* [count] a word that sounds the same as another but is different in meaning or spelling, such as *heir* and *air.*

ho•mo•sex•u•al /,howmə'sɛkʃuwəl/ *adj.* **1.** attracted sexually to members of one's own sex. **2.** of or relating to homosexuality. —*n.* [count] **3.** a homosexual person. —ho•mo•sex•u•al•i•ty /,howmə,sɛkʃuw'ælɪtiy/, *n.* [noncount]

hom•y /'howmiy/ *adj.*, **hom•i•er, hom•i•est.** HOMEY.

Hon., an abbreviation of: **1.** Honorable. **2.** Honorary.

Hon•du•ran /hɒn'dʊrən, -'dyʊr-/ *adj.* **1.** of or relating to Honduras. —*n.* [count] **2.** a person born or living in Honduras.

hone /hown/ *v.* [~ + *obj*], **honed, hon•ing. 1.** to sharpen (a knife or sword). **2.** to make more effective: *She honed her skills.*

hon•est /'ɒnɪst/ *adj.* **1.** truthful; trustworthy: *an honest person.* **2.** sincere; open: *an honest face.* **3.** gotten fairly: *an honest living.* —'hon•es•ty, *n.* [noncount]

hon•est•ly /'ɒnɪstliy/ *adv.* **1.** in an honest manner. **2.** really; truly: *I honestly don't know.* —*interj.* **3.** This word is used to express mild disbelief, disapproval, etc.: *Honestly! You're always on the phone.*

hon•ey /'hʌniy/ *n.*, *pl.* **hon•eys,** *adj.* —*n.* **1.** [noncount] a sweet, sticky fluid produced by bees from nectar. **2.** [count] *Informal.* sweetheart; darling. —*adj.* [before a noun] **3.** of, like, relating to, or containing honey.

hon•ey•bee /'hʌn,iy biy/ *n.* [count] any bee that collects and stores honey.

hon•ey•comb /'hʌniy,kowm/ *n.* [count] **1.** a wax structure of six-sided cells made by bees in their hive for storing honey, pollen, and their eggs. —*v.* [~ + *obj*] **2.** to cause to be full of holes.

hon•ey•dew /'hʌniy,duw, -,dyuw/ *n.* [non-count] [count] a melon having a smooth, greenish rind and sweet, light green flesh.

hon•ey•moon /'hʌniy,muwn/ *n.* [count] **1.** a vacation taken by a newly married couple. —*v.* [no obj] **2.** to go on a honeymoon: *They honeymooned in Paris.* —'hon•ey,moon•er, *n.* [count]

hon•ey•suck•le /'hʌniy,sʌkəl/ *n.* [noncount] a climbing plant with sweet-smelling, tube-like flowers.

honk /hɒŋk, hɔŋk/ *n.* [count] **1.** the cry of a goose. **2.** the sound of a car horn. —*v.* **3.** to (cause to) give off a honk: [no obj]: *geese honking in flight.* [~ + obj]: *The driver honked his horn impatiently.*

hon•or /'ɒnər/ *n.* **1.** [noncount] high moral standards: *a person of honor.* **2.** [noncount] good reputation: *to defend one's honor.* **3.** [count; usually singular] a source of great respect: *to be an honor to one's country.* **4.** [noncount] high public respect: *a ceremony in honor of the dead.* **5.** [count] something that brings pride: *an honor to be chosen.* **6.** [His/Her/Your + ~] a title of respect for judges and mayors. **7. honors,** [plural] special recognition given by a school to an outstanding student: *He graduated with honors.* —*v.* [~ + obj] **8.** to show or feel high respect for: *to honor one's parents.* **9.** to keep to the terms of (an agreement). Also, *esp. Brit.,* '**hon•our.** —,hon•or'ee, *n.* [count], *pl.* **-ees.**

hon•or•a•ble /'ɒnərəbəl/ *adj.* **1.** showing principles of honor: *an honorable leader.* **2.** bringing or deserving honor: *honorable mention in the competition.* **3.** [Honorable; often: the + ~ + name] a title of respect for certain government officials or certain British nobility. *Abbr.:* Hon. —'hon•or•a•bly, *adv.*

hon•or•ar•y /'ɒnə,reriy/ *adj.* [usually: before a noun] **1.** given as an honor: *an honorary degree from a university.* **2.** serving without payment: *an honorary president.*

hood¹ /hʊd/ *n.* [count] **1.** a covering for the head and neck, attached to a garment. **2.** the hinged movable part covering the engine of a vehicle. —'hood•ed, *adj.*

hood² /hʊd/ *n.* [count] *Slang.* a hoodlum.

-hood, a suffix meaning: state or condition (*childhood*); character or nature (*likelihood*); a group of persons of a particular character or class (*priesthood*).

hood•lum /'huwdləm, 'hʊd-/ *n.* [count] **1.** a violent criminal. **2.** a young criminal, esp. one belonging to a gang.

hood•wink /'hʊd,wɪŋk/ *v.* [~ + obj] to trick or deceive.

hoof /hʊf, huwf/ *n.* [count], *pl.* **hoofs** or **hooves** /hʊvz, huwvz/. **1.** the hard, horny covering protecting the ends of the foot in certain animals, such as the ox and horse. **2.** the entire foot of a horse, donkey, etc. —**hoofed,** *adj.:* hoofed animals.

hook /hʊk/ *n.* [count] **1.** a curved piece of metal, wood, etc., for catching or holding something: *I hung my coat up on the hook.* **2.** a curved piece of metal with a sharp point, used for catching fish. **3.** something that attracts attention: *a sales hook.* **4.** (in boxing) a blow with the elbow bent. —*v.* **5.** [~ + obj] [no obj] to fasten or catch hold of with or as if with a hook: **6.** [~ + obj] to catch (fish) with a hook. **7.** [no obj] to curve or bend like a hook: *The road hooked to the left.* **8. hook up,** to connect to a power supply: *I hooked up the computer* or *I hooked the computer up.* —*Idiom.* **9. by hook or by crook,** by any

H

hospital

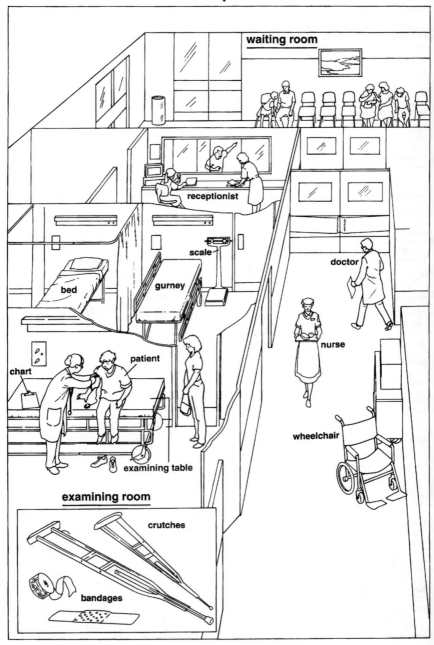

waiting room

receptionist

scale

bed

gurney

doctor

nurse

chart

patient

wheelchair

examining table

examining room

crutches

bandages

means. **10. off the hook, a.** out of trouble: *You're off the hook, so if things go wrong, you won't be blamed.* **b.** (of a telephone receiver) not resting on the main part.

hooked /hʊkt/ *adj.* **1.** shaped like a hook. **2.** *Informal.* [*be* + ~ (+ *on*)] **a.** dependent on drugs: *She was hooked on cocaine.* **b.** very enthusiastic about something: *He is hooked on computers.*

hook·y or **hook·ey** /'hʊkiy/ *n.* ——*Idiom.* **play hooky** or **hookey,** to be absent from school or work without permission.

hoop /huwp, hʊp/ *n.* [*count*] a circular band or ring, as one of metal or wood.

hoo·ray /hʊ'rey/ also **hoo·rah** /-'rɑ/ *interj., v., n.* HURRAH.

hoot /huwt/ *v.* **1.** to show disapproval (of) by shouting: [*no obj*]: *The fans hooted at the umpire.* [~ + *obj*]: *The fans hooted the umpire.* **2.** [*no obj*] to make the cry of an owl, or a similar sound. ——*n.* [*count*] **3.** the cry of an owl. **4.** any similar sound: *the hoot of the train in the distance.* **5.** a shout, esp. of disapproval.

hooves /hʊvz, huwvz/ *n.* a pl. of HOOF.

hop¹ /hɒp/ *v.,* **hopped, hop·ping,** *n.* ——*v.* **1.** [*no obj*] to make a short jump on one foot. **2.** [*no obj*] to jump with all feet at once: *Rabbits hop.* **3.** [~ + *obj*] to jump over: *He hopped the fence and was gone.* **4.** to board or get onto (a vehicle): [~ + *obj*]: *to hop a train.* [*no obj*]: *He hopped into his car.* **5.** [*no obj*] to move frequently from one place to another: *to party-hop* (= *to go from one party to another*). ——*n.* [*count*] **6.** a short leap on one foot. **7.** a bounce. **8.** a short trip.

hop² /hɒp/ *n.* [*count*] **1.** a climbing plant of the hemp family. **2. hops,** [*plural*] its dried ripe cones, used esp. in brewing beer.

hope /howp/ *n., v.,* **hoped, hop·ing.** ——*n.* **1.** [*noncount*] a belief or desire that events will turn out well: *They lost all hope of success.* **2.** [*count*] something desired: *the hope of winning.* **3.** [*noncount*] a person or thing that provides a reason for hope: *The medicine is her last hope.* ——*v.* **4.** to look forward (to) with desire and reasonable confidence: [*no obj*]: *We can only wait and hope.* [~ + *obj*]: *I hope to see you soon.*

hope·ful /'howpfəl/ *adj.* **1.** full of hope: *I'm hopeful about getting into college.* **2.** causing a feeling of hope: *The new pitcher is a hopeful prospect.* —'**hope·ful·ness,** *n.* [*noncount*]

hope·ful·ly /'howpfəliy/ *adv.* **1.** in a hopeful manner. **2.** it is hoped: *Hopefully, we won't be late.*

hope·less /'howplɪs/ *adj.* **1.** without hope or beyond help: *a hopeless situation.* **2.** useless: *He's hopeless at the computer.* —'**hope·less·ly,** *adv.* —'**hope·less·ness,** *n.* [*noncount*]

hop·ping /'hɒpɪŋ/ *adj.* **1.** busy: *He kept his staff hopping.* ——*Idiom.* **2. hopping mad,** very angry.

hop·scotch /'hɒp,skɒtʃ/ *n.* [*noncount*] a game in which a child hops around a diagram drawn on the pavement to pick up a small object, as a stone or stick.

horde /hɔrd/ *n.* [*count*] a large crowd: *hordes of grasshoppers; hordes of shoppers.*

ho·ri·zon /hə'rayzən/ *n.* [*count*] **1.** the line where the earth and sky seem to meet. **2.** the limit of one's experience.

hor·i·zon·tal /,hɔrə'zɒntl, ,hɒr-/ *adj.* flat or level: *a horizontal position.* —,**hor·i·zon·tal·ly,** *adv.*

hor·mone /'hɔrmown/ *n.* [*count*] a chemical produced in the body that helps control growth, digestion, etc. —**hor·mo·nal** /hɔr'mownl/, *adj.*

horn /hɔrn/ *n.* **1.** [*count*] one of the hard, pointed, and usually curved growths that stick out from the heads of cows, goats, sheep, etc. **2.** [*noncount*] the hard substance of which horn growths are made: *a handle made of horn.* **3.** [*count*] a wind instrument in music, as a trumpet. **4.** [*count*] a device for sounding a warning signal: *a car horn.* ——*v.* **5. horn in,** *Informal.* to intrude: *He was always horning in when I tried to talk to her.* ——*adj.* [*before a noun*] **6.** made of horn: *a horn handle.* —**horned,** *adj.*: *a great horned owl.* —'**horn·y,** *adj.*

hor·net /'hɔrnɪt/ *n.* [*count*] a large stinging wasp.

hor·o·scope /'hɔrə,skowp, 'hɒr-/ *n.* [*count*] a description of a person's character, or a prediction about his or her future, based on the position of the stars and planets at the moment of birth.

hor·ren·dous /hə'rɛndəs/ *adj.* very shocking; terrible: *a horrendous crime.* —**hor'ren·dous·ly,** *adv.*

hor·ri·ble /'hɔrəbəl, 'hɒr-/ *adj.* **1.** causing horror: *a horrible accident.* **2.** extremely unpleasant: *a horrible smell.* —'**hor·ri·bly,** *adv.*

hor·rid /'hɔrɪd, 'hɒr-/ *adj.* **1.** causing horror. **2.** extremely unpleasant; nasty: *a horrid taste.* —'**hor·rid·ly,** *adv.*

hor·ri·fy /'hɔrə,fay, 'hɒr-/ *v.* [~ + *obj*], **-fied, -fy·ing.** to cause to feel horror; shock: *The accident horrified us.*

hor·ror /'hɔrər, 'hɒr-/ *n.* [*noncount*] **1.** a feeling of intense fear, shock, or dislike. ——*adj.* [*before a noun*] **2.** inspiring fear: *a horror movie.*

hors d'oeuvre /'ɔr dɜrv/ *n.* [*count*], *pl.* **hors d'oeuvre** /'ɔr dɜrv/, **hors d'oeuvres** /'ɔr dɜrvz, 'dɜrv/. food served before a meal.

horse /hɔrs/ *n.* [*count*], *pl.* **hors·es,** (*esp. when thought of as a group*) **horse. 1.** a large mammal with solid hooves, used for carrying or pulling loads and for riding. **2.** a wooden apparatus for exercising or performing gymnastics. ——*Idiom.* **3. eat like a horse,** to eat a great deal. **4. hold one's horses,** *Informal.* to be patient: *Hold your horses, we're almost there.* **5. look a gift horse in the mouth,** to be critical of a gift.

H

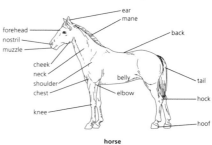

horse

horse·back /'hɔrs,bæk/ *n.* [*noncount*] **1.** the back of a horse: *riders on horseback.* ——*adv., adj.* **2.** on the back of a horse: *to ride horseback; horseback riding.*

'**horse ,chestnut,** *n.* [*count*] a tree with large leaves and white flowers.

'**horse ,fly** or '**horse,fly,** *n.* [*count*] a large fly that bites animals and people.

hotel

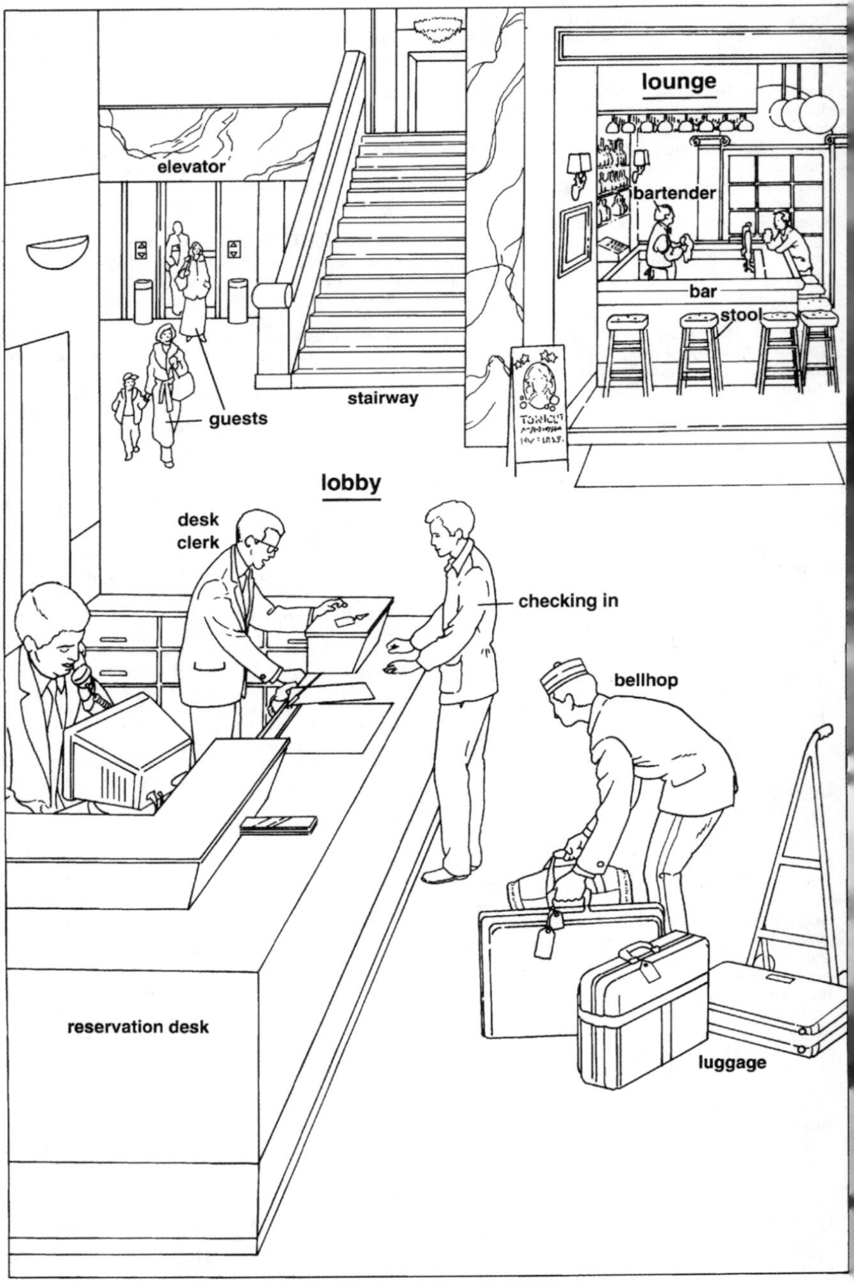

lounge

elevator

bartender

bar

stool

guests

stairway

lobby

desk clerk

checking in

bellhop

reservation desk

luggage

horse•man or **-wo•man** /'hɔrsmən/ or /-,wʊmən/ n. [count], pl. **-men** or **-wo•men. 1.** a person who is skilled in managing or riding a horse. **2.** a person who rides on horseback.

horse•play /'hɔrs,pleɪ/ n. [noncount] rough, noisy play.

horse•pow•er /'hɔrs,paʊər/ n. [noncount] a unit for measuring the power of an engine.

horse•rad•ish /'hɔrs,rædɪʃ/ n. [noncount] a plant whose root is used to flavor food.

horse•shoe /'hɔrs,ʃuw, 'hɔrʃ-/ n. **1.** [count] a U-shaped metal plate nailed to a horse's hoof to protect it. **2. horseshoes,** [noncount; used with a singular verb] a game in which horseshoes or other U-shaped objects are tossed at an iron post.

hor•ti•cul•ture /'hɔrtɪ,kʌltʃər/ n. [noncount] the science or art of growing flowers, fruits, and vegetables. —**,hor•ti'cul•tur•al,** adj. —,**hor•** ti'cul•tur•ist,** n. [count]

ho•san•na /hoʊ'zænə/ interj. This word is used to express praise of God.

hose /hoʊz/ n., pl. **hos•es** for 1; **hose** for 2, v., **hosed, hos•ing.** —n. [count] **1.** a flexible tube for carrying a liquid, such as water, to a desired point: a garden hose. **2.** [plural; used with a plural verb] stockings or socks. —v. [~ + obj] **3.** to pour water on with a hose: He hosed the sidewalk. He hosed off the car. He hosed down the lawn.

ho•sier•y /'hoʊʒəriy/ n. [noncount] stockings and socks.

hos•pice /'hɒspɪs/ n. [count] a special place, or a system of home visits and care, for people who are dying.

hos•pi•ta•ble /'hɒspɪtəbəl, hɒ'spɪtəbəl/ adj. **1.** treating guests or strangers warmly: a hospitable family. **2.** favorable toward: hospitable to new ideas. —'**hos•pi•ta•bly,** adv.

hos•pi•tal /'hɒspɪtl/ n. [count] a place for the care of sick and injured people.

hos•pi•tal•i•ty /,hɒspɪ'tælɪtiy/ n. [noncount] a friendly welcome and treatment of guests or strangers.

hos•pi•tal•ize /'hɒspɪtl,aɪz/ v. [~ + obj], **-ized, -iz•ing.** to place in a hospital for medical care. —**hos•pi•tal•i•za•tion** /,hɒspɪtl'zeyʃən/, n. [noncount] [count]

host¹ /howst/ n. [count] **1.** a person who welcomes or entertains guests. **2.** a person who introduces or interviews guests on a television or radio show. —v. [~ + obj] **3.** to be the host at: She hosted the party.

host² /howst/ n. [count; usually: ~ + of] a great number: a host of details.

hos•tage /'hɒstɪdʒ/ n. [count] a person held prisoner by another so that certain terms will be met by the person's family, etc.

hos•tel /'hɒstl/ n. [count] a simple, cheap lodging, esp. for young travelers: a youth hostel.

host•ess /'howstɪs/ n. [count] **1.** a woman who is a host. **2.** a woman who is employed in a restaurant to take guests to their seats.

hos•tile /'hɒstl/ adj. **1.** of or relating to an enemy: hostile forces. **2.** unfriendly.

hos•til•i•ty /hɒ'stɪlɪtiy/ n., pl. **-ties. 1.** [noncount] unfriendliness: Hostility between the two countries eased. **2. hostilities.** [plural] a hostile act, as of war.

hot /hɒt/ adj., **hot•ter, hot•test,** adv. —adj. **1.** having or giving off much heat: hot coffee. **2.** [be + ~] having or causing a feeling of great bodily heat: He was hot with fever. **3.** spicy: Is this mustard hot? **4.** [usually: before a noun] showing

strong or violent feeling: He has a hot temper. **5.** new; fresh: news hot off the press. **6.** [usually: be + ~] following closely: The search party was hot on their trail. **7.** Informal. very good: The movie was not so hot. **8.** Informal. currently popular: the hottest new styles. **9.** Slang. stolen recently. **10.** Informal. eager: She was hot to get started. —adv. **11.** while hot: Serve the fish hot from the oven. —**Idiom. 12. hot under the collar,** angry.

'**hot 'air,** n. [noncount] Informal. empty talk.

hot•bed /'hɒt,bɛd/ n. [count] an environment that favors rapid growth, esp. of something unwanted.

'**hot-'blooded,** adj. quick to get excited.

'**hot-'button,** adj. arousing strong feelings; very emotional: abortion and other hot-button issues.

'**hot ,cake** or '**hot,cake,** n. [count] **1.** a pancake. —**Idiom. 2. sell** or **go like hot cakes,** to be bought, taken, or used up very quickly.

'**hot ,dog,** n. [count] a frankfurter.

ho•tel /how'tɛl/ n. [count] a building that offers a temporary place to stay for travelers.

hot•head /'hɒt,hɛd/ n. [count] a person who acts without thinking, or one who is quick to anger. —'**hot,head•ed,** adj.

hot•house /'hɒt,haws/ n. [count] **1.** a heated building, esp. a greenhouse, for the growing of tender plants. —adj. [before a noun] **2.** grown in a hothouse: hothouse tomatoes.

'**hot ,line,** n. [count] **1.** a direct telephone connection between heads of state. **2.** Also, '**hot,line.** a telephone number providing direct service for people needing information, advice, etc.

hot•ly /'hɒtliy/ adv. **1.** forcefully: They were arguing hotly. **2.** closely: The thief was hotly pursued.

'**hot ,plate,** n. [count] a portable appliance having an electrical unit for cooking.

hot•shot /'hɒt,ʃɒt/ Slang. —adj. [before a noun] **1.** showily successful: a hotshot sales manager. —n. [count] **2.** Also, '**hot ,shot.** a showily successful person.

'**hot ,tub,** n. [count] a big, usually wooden tub filled with hot water and used for relaxation.

'**hot 'water,** n. [noncount] a difficult situation; trouble: He was in hot water with the police.

hound /hawnd/ n. [count] **1.** a breed of dog used in hunting. —v. [~ + obj] **2.** to trouble or annoy continually: She hounded him to get the work done.

hour /awʳ, 'awər/ n. [count] **1.** a period of time equal to 60 minutes. **2.** a particular time: At what hour do you open? **3.** a customary or usual time: the dinner hour. **4. hours,** [plural] a fixed or certain period of time: office hours; He likes to keep late hours. **5.** the distance that can be traveled in an hour: We live about an hour from the city. —**Idiom. 6. on the hour,** at the start of each hour.

hour•ly /'awʳliy, 'awər-/ adj. [before a noun] **1.** done or happening each hour: hourly news reports. **2.** calculated by the hour: hourly wages. —adv. **3.** every hour or once an hour.

house /n., adj. haws; v. hawz/ n., pl. **hous•es** /'hawzɪz/, v., **housed, hous•ing,** adj. —n. **2.** [count] **1.** a building in which people live. **2.** household: The whole house was asleep. **3.** [often: House] a royal or noble family. **4. a.** [often: House] a law-making body or branch of government: the House of Representatives. **b.** the building in which such a body meets. **5.** the audience

H

house

in a theater, concert hall, etc.: *The whole house applauded.* —*v.* [~ + *obj*] **6.** to provide with a place to live: *to house students in a dorm.* —*adj.* [*before a noun*] **7.** suitable for or customarily kept in a house: *house paint; house cats.* **8.** served by a restaurant as its customary brand: *the house wine.* —*Idiom.* **9. keep house,** to maintain a home. **10. on the house,** as a gift from the management; free: *drinks on the house.* —**house•ful** /ˈhawsfəl/, *n.* [*count*], *pl.* **-fuls.**

house•boat /ˈhawsˌbowt/ *n.* [*count*] a flat-bottomed boat fitted for use as a place to live.

house•break /ˈhawsˌbreyk/ *v.* [~ + *obj*], **-broke, -bro•ken, -break•ing.** to train (a pet) to excrete outdoors or in a specific place.

house•break•er /ˈhawsˌbreykər/ *n.* [*count*] a person who breaks into and enters a house with the intention to rob or steal.

house•fly or **house fly** /ˈhawsˌflay/ *n.* [*count*], *pl.* **-flies.** a medium-sized fly common wherever humans live.

house•hold /ˈhawsˌhowld, -ˌowld/ *n.* [*count*] **1.** a house and all the people living in it. —*adj.* [*before a noun*] **2.** of or concerning the home: *household chores; household bleach.*

ˈhousehold ˈword, *n.* [*count*] a familiar name, phrase, or saying.

house•keep•er /ˈhawsˌkiypər/ *n.* [*count*] a person whose job is managing a household. —ˈhouseˌkeep•ing, *n.* [*noncount*]

house•plant /ˈhawsˌplænt/ *n.* [*count*] a plant grown indoors.

house•sit or **house-sit** /ˈhawsˌsɪt/ *v.* [*no obj*], **-sat, -sit•ting.** to take care of a home while the owner is away. —ˈhouse ˌsitter, ˈhouse-ˌsitter, *n.* [*count*]

house•warm•ing /ˈhawsˌwɔrmɪŋ/ *n.* [*count*] a party to celebrate a move to a new home.

house•wife /ˈhawsˌwayf/ *n.* [*count*], *pl.* **-wives.** a married woman who manages her own household, esp. one who does not work outside the home.

house•work /ˈhawsˌwɜrk/ *n.* [*noncount*] the work of cleaning, cooking, etc., to be done in the home.

hous•ing /ˈhawzɪŋ/ *n.* **1.** [*noncount*] houses thought of as a group. **2.** [*noncount*] the providing of houses or shelter: *housing of the poor.* **3.** [*count*] a covering that protects a machine.

hove /howv/ *v.* a pt. and pp. of HEAVE.

hov•el /ˈhʌvəl, ˈhɒv-/ *n.* [*count*] a small house in poor condition.

hov•er /ˈhʌvər, ˈhɒv-/ *v.* [*no obj*] **1.** to remain in the air: *a kite hovering over the yard.* **2.** to remain close by: *He kept hovering outside my office.*

hov•er•craft /ˈhʌvərˌkræft, ˈhɒv-/ *n.* [*count; sometimes:* Hovercraft], *pl.* **-craft.** a passenger craft that moves over land or water and is kept in the air by fans.

how /haw/ *adv.* **1.** [*used in questions*] **a.** in what way: *How did the fire start?* **b.** to what extent, degree, etc.: *How difficult was the test?* **c.** at what amount or rate: *How much is this?* **d.** in what state or condition: *How is the baby?* **e.** for what reason; why: *How can you say that?* **2.** This word is used to express strong feeling: *How nice of you to come.* —*conj.* **3.** the manner or way in which: *I couldn't figure out how to solve the problem.* **4.** about the manner or condition in which: *Be careful how you act.* —*Idiom.* **5. and how!** *Informal.* certainly: *Am I happy? And how!* **6. how about?** This phrase is used to mean "What do

you think about?": *If they don't have pumpkin pie, how about apple?* **7. how are you?** This phrase is used as a greeting to someone already known to the speaker: *I haven't seen you lately; how are you?* **8. how come?** *Informal.* This phrase introduces a question meaning "how is it that? why?": *How come you don't visit us anymore?* **9. how do you do?** This expression is used when one is introduced to someone in a formal situation: *"This is my husband, Mr. Smith."— "How do you do, Mr. Smith?"*

how•ev•er /hawˈɛvər/ *adv.* **1.** in spite of that; but: *We have not yet won; however, we shall keep trying.* **2.** to whatever extent or degree: *However much you spend, I will repay you.* **3.** in whatever way: *He can dress however he likes.*

howl /hawl/ *v.* [*no obj*] **1.** to make a loud, long, wailing cry: *The dog was howling at the moon.* —*n.* [*count*] **2.** a loud, long cry or a similar sound: *the howl of the wind.*

H.P. or **h.p.** or **HP,** an abbreviation of: horsepower.

H.Q. or **h.q.** or **HQ,** an abbreviation of: headquarters.

hr., an abbreviation of: hour.

H.S., an abbreviation of: high school.

ht., an abbreviation of: height.

hub /hʌb/ *n.* [*count*] **1.** the central part of a wheel. **2.** a center of activity or interest: *The city was the manufacturing hub.*

hub•cap /ˈhʌbˌkæp/ *n.* [*count*] a round, removable cover for the hub of a car wheel.

huck•le•ber•ry /ˈhʌkəlˌbɛriy/ *n.* [*count*], *pl.* **-ries.** a dark blue or black berry that may be eaten.

huck•ster /ˈhʌkstər/ *n.* [*count*] **1.** a person who uses showy methods of selling things. **2.** a person who sells small items.

hud•dle /ˈhʌdl/ *v.,* **-dled, -dling,** *n.* —*v.* **1.** to (cause to) gather or crowd together: [*no obj*]: *They huddled around the stove to get warm.* [~ + *obj*]: *They huddled the children round the campfire.* —*n.* [*count*] **2.** a group gathered close together: *football players in a huddle.*

hue /hyuw/ *n.* [*count*] **1.** a shade of a color; tint: *pale hues.* **2.** color: *all the hues of the rainbow.* —**hued,** *adj.*

ˈhue and ˈcry, *n.* [*count; usually singular*] noisy public protest or alarm.

huff /hʌf/ *n.* [*count; usually singular*] **1.** a fit of anger or resentment. —*v.* [*no obj*] **2.** to show or express anger. **3.** to breathe heavily.

huff•y /ˈhʌfiy/ *adj.,* **-fi•er, -fi•est.** annoyed; offended. —**huf•fi•ly** /ˈhʌfəliy/, *adv.*

hug /hʌg/ *v.,* **hugged, hug•ging,** *n.* —*v.* **1.** to hold tightly in the arms: [~ + *obj*]: *to hug one's child.* [*no obj*]: *They were hugging and crying.* **2.** [~ + *obj*] to keep close to: *The biker hugged the curb.* —*n.* [*count*] **3.** the act of hugging.

huge /hyuwdʒ/ *adj.,* **hug•er, hug•est. 1.** extremely large in size or amount: *a huge ship.* **2.** very great: *The book was a huge success.*

huh /hʌ/ *interj.* This word is used to express surprise, disapproval, etc., or to ask a question: *Huh! Look at that! You're OK, huh?*

hulk /hʌlk/ *n.* [*count*] **1.** the shell of something wrecked or abandoned, as a ship. **2.** a large, awkward person.

hulk•ing /ˈhʌlkɪŋ/ *adj.* [*before a noun*] large, heavy, and awkward.

hull¹ /hʌl/ *n.* [*count*] **1.** the outer covering of a

H

seed or fruit. —v. [~ + obj] **2.** to remove the hull of: *to hull corn.*

hull² /hʌl/ n. [count] the sides and bottom of a ship.

hum /hʌm/ v., **hummed, hum•ming,** n. —v. **1.** [no obj] to make a low, continuous sound: *bees humming in the garden.* **2.** to sing with closed lips: [no obj]: *He was humming quietly.* [~ + obj]: *He hummed a tune.* **3.** [no obj] to be in a state of busy activity: *The household was humming.* —n. [count] **4.** the act or sound of humming.

hu•man /ˈhyuwmən/ adj. **1.** of people: *the human race; human nature.* **2.** sympathetic; humane. —n. [count] **3.** Also called **'human 'be•ing.** a person.

hu•mane /hyuwˈmeyn/ adj. sympathetic and kind: *He was humane in his treatment of the prisoners.* —**hu'mane•ly,** adv.

hu•man•ism /ˈhyuwmə,nɪzəm/ n. [count; often: Humanism] a system of beliefs in which human interests and values are most important, not a belief in God or in religion. —**'hu•man•ist,** n. [count], adj. —,**hu•man'is•tic,** adj.

hu•man•i•tar•i•an /hyuw,mænɪˈtɛəriyən/ adj. **1.** having concern for or helping to improve people's lives. —n. [count] **2.** a person who promotes humanitarian causes. —**hu,man•i'tar•i•an•ism,** n. [noncount]

hu•man•i•ty /hyuwˈmænɪtiy/ n. [noncount], pl. **-ties. 1.** all human beings thought of as a group. **2.** the quality of being humane; kindness.

hu•man•kind /ˈhyuwmən,kaynd/ n. [noncount] human beings thought of as a group.

hu•man•ly /ˈhyuwmənliy/ adv. within the limits of human ability: *It's not humanly possible to do that.*

hum•ble /ˈhʌmbəl/ adj., **-bler, -blest,** v., **-bled, -bling.** —adj. **1.** not proud; modest. **2.** low in importance or condition: *humble work; a humble home.* —v. [~ + obj] **3.** to make humble: *She was humbled by defeat.* —**'hum•bly,** adv.

hum•drum /ˈhʌm,drʌm/ adj. lacking variety; boring; dull.

hu•mid /ˈhyuwmɪd/ adj. containing a high amount of water vapor: *humid air.*

hu•mid•i•fy /hyuwˈmɪdə,fay/ v. [~ + obj], **-fied, -fy•ing.** to make humid. —**hu'mid•i,fi•er,** n. [count]

hu•mid•i•ty /hyuwˈmɪdɪtiy/ n. [noncount] the amount of water vapor in the air.

hu•mil•i•ate /hyuwˈmɪliy,eyt/ v. [~ + obj], **-at•ed, -at•ing.** to cause (a person) a painful loss of pride; embarrass. —**hu,mil•i'a•tion,** n. [noncount] [count]

hu•mil•i•ty /hyuwˈmɪlɪtiy/ n. [noncount] the quality or state of being humble (def.1).

hum•ming•bird /ˈhʌmɪŋ,bɜrd/ n. [count] a tiny, usually colorful bird with a long bill.

hu•mor /ˈhyuwmɜr/ n. [noncount] **1.** a quality causing amusement: *the humor in a play.* **2.** the ability to amuse or be amused: *a keen sense of humor.* **3.** a temporary mood: *He's in a good humor.* —v. [~ + obj] **4.** to go along with the mood of (someone) in order to please: *to humor a child.* Also, esp. Brit., **'hu•mour.** —**'hu•mor•ist,** n. [count] —**'hu•mor•less,** adj.

hu•mor•ous /ˈhyuwmərəs/ adj. having humor; funny; amusing: *a humorous story; a humorous person.* —**'hu•mor•ous•ly,** adv.

hump /hʌmp/ n. [count] **1.** a rounded lump, as on the back of a camel. —*Idiom.* **2. over the hump,** past the worst part of something.

hump•back /ˈhʌmp,bæk/ n. [count] **1.** a back that has a hump. **2.** a whale noted for the way it arches its back as it dives. —**'hump,backed,** adj.

hu•mus /ˈhyuwməs/ n. [noncount] dark, rich soil made by the decay of plant or animal matter.

hunch /hʌntʃ/ v. [~ + obj] **1.** to draw up in a rounded shape: *He hunched his shoulders.* —n. [count] **2.** a feeling or guess, esp. about the future: *I had a hunch you'd be late.*

hunch•back /ˈhʌntʃ,bæk/ n. [count] a person whose back has a rounded hump. —**'hunch,backed,** adj.

hun•dred /ˈhʌndrɪd/ n., pl. **-dreds,** (as after a numeral) **-dred,** adj. —n. [count] **1.** ten times ten; 100. **2. hundreds,** [plural] a generally large number or amount: *Hundreds came to the funeral.* —adj. [after a number and before a noun] **3.** amounting to 100 in number: *two hundred dollars.* —**'hun•dredth,** adj., n. [count]

hun•dred•weight /ˈhʌndrɪd,weyt/ n. [count], pl. **-weights,** (as after a numeral) **-weight.** a unit of weight equal to 100 pounds (45.359 kilograms) in the U.S. Abbr.: cwt

hung /hʌŋ/ v. **1.** pt. and pp. of HANG. —*Idiom.* **2. hung over,** suffering the effects of a hangover: *He was hung over from the vodka.* **3. hung up,** Slang. **a.** delayed: *We were hung up by the traffic jam.* **b.** confused by a problem: *He was hung up on how to end his novel.* **c.** Also, **hung-up.** having emotional problems.

Hun•gar•i•an /hʌŋˈgɛəriyən/ adj. **1.** of or relating to Hungary. **2.** of or relating to the language spoken in Hungary. —n. **3.** [count] a person born or living in Hungary. **4.** [noncount] the language spoken in Hungary.

hun•ger /ˈhʌŋgɜr/ n. [noncount] **1.** a strong need or desire for food. **2.** a shortage of food; famine: *the fight against hunger.* **3.** a strong desire for anything: *his hunger for power.* —v. [no obj] **4.** to have a strong desire: *They hungered for justice. He hungered after power.*

hun•gry /ˈhʌŋgriy/ adj., **-gri•er, -gri•est. 1.** having a desire or need for food. **2.** [be + ~ + for + obj] eager: *She was hungry for success.* **3. go hungry,** to lack enough food. —**hun•gri•ly** /ˈhʌŋgrəliy/, adv.

hunk /hʌŋk/ n. [count] **1.** a large piece: *a hunk of meat.* **2.** Slang. a handsome man with a well-developed body.

hunt /hʌnt/ v. **1.** [~ + obj] [no obj] to chase or search for (game or other wild animals) for the purpose of catching or killing. **2.** [~ + obj] to chase (a person) in order to capture: *to hunt down a kidnapper.* —n. [count] **3.** the act or practice of hunting. **4.** a search.

hunt•er /ˈhʌntɜr/ n. [count] a person or animal that hunts.

hur•dle /ˈhɜrdl/ n., v., **-dled, -dling.** —n. [count] **1.** a fencelike barrier or frame over which racers or horses must jump in certain races. **2.** a difficulty to be overcome. —v. [~ + obj] **3.** to jump over while running.

hurl /hɜrl/ v. [~ + obj] **1.** to throw with force: *He hurled a brick through the window.* **2.** to say with force: *hurling insults.*

hur•rah /həˈrɑ, -ˈrɔ/ also **hur•ray** /-ˈrey/ interj. This word is used to express joy, approval, or encouragement.

hur•ri•cane /ˈhɜrɪ,keyn, ˈhʌr-/ n. [count] a violent storm with very strong winds.

hur•ried /ˈhɜriyd, ˈhʌriyd/ adj. done quickly: *She had a hurried meal.* —**'hur•ried•ly,** adv.

hur•ry /ˈhɜriy, ˈhʌriy/ v., **-ried, -ry•ing,** n. —v.

1. to (cause to) act quickly: [*no obj*]: *He hurried into town. She hurried to help him. Please hurry up!* [~ + *obj*]: *She hurried the children along.* —*n.* [*noncount*] **2.** a need to act quickly: *There's no hurry; take your time.* —*Idiom.* **3. in a hurry, a.** quickly: *She finished in a hurry.* **b.** wanting to act quickly: *I was in a hurry to go home.*

hurt /hɜrt/ *v.*, **hurt, hurt•ing,** *n., adj.* —*v.* **1.** [~ + *obj*] to cause bodily injury to; injure: *That fall hurt his leg.* **2.** to cause a feeling of bodily pain to or in: [~ + *obj*]: *The old wound still hurts him.* [~ + *oneself*]: *He hurt himself long ago.* [*no obj*]: *The old wound still hurts.* **3.** [~ + *obj*] to affect in a bad way; harm: *Those lies hurt his reputation.* **4.** [*no obj*] to suffer from a lack of something: *The farmers are still hurting from the crop failure.* —*n.* **5.** [*noncount*] mental pain: *feelings of hurt.* **6.** [*count*] a bodily wound or injury. —*adj.* **7.** physically injured: *a badly hurt leg.* **8.** offended: *hurt pride.*

hurt•ful /ˈhɜrtfəl/ *adj.* causing hurt.

hur•tle /ˈhɜrtl/ *v.* [*no obj*], **-tled, -tling.** to move with great speed: *A car hurtled by.*

hus•band /ˈhʌzbənd/ *n.* [*count*] a married man.

hush /hʌʃ/ *interj.* **1.** This word is used as a command to be quiet. —*v.* [~ + *obj*] **2.** to cause to become silent or quiet: *We hushed the children when the show began.* **3. hush up,** to keep secret: *to hush up a scandal* or *to hush a scandal up.* —*n.* [*count*; *usually singular*] **4.** silence or quiet: *A hush fell over the crowd.*

'hush-'hush, *adj.* highly secret.

husk /hʌsk/ *n.* [*count*] **1.** the dry outer covering of certain fruits or seeds. —*v.* [~ + *obj*] **2.** to remove the husk from: *husking corn.*

husk•y¹ /ˈhʌskiy/ *adj.*, **-i•er, -i•est. 1.** big and strong: *husky football players.* **2.** (of the voice) dry and rough. —**husk•i•ly** /ˈhʌskəliy/ *adv.* —ˈhusk•i•ness, *n.* [*noncount*]

husk•y² /ˈhʌskiy/ *n.* [*count*], *pl.* **husk•ies.** a furry, strong dog used to pull sleds over snow.

hus•tle /ˈhʌsəl/ *v.*, **-tled, -tling,** *n.* —*v.* **1.** to (cause to) move quickly: *She hustled off to work.* [~ + *obj*]: *He hustled the kids to school.* **2.** [~ + *obj*] to persuade (a person) forcefully: *The salesman hustled us into buying the car.* **3.** *Slang.* to earn one's living by illegal means: [*no obj*]: *hustling on the streets.* [~ + *obj*]: *hustling drugs.* —*n.* [*noncount*] **4.** energetic or hurried activity. —**hus•tler** /ˈhʌslər/ *n.* [*count*]

hut /hʌt/ *n.* [*count*] a small, simple house or shelter.

hutch /hʌtʃ/ *n.* [*count*] a chest with doors or drawers.

hy•a•cinth /ˈhayəsɪnθ/ *n.* [*count*] a plant grown from a bulb with sweet-smelling, colorful flowers.

hy•brid /ˈhaybrɪd/ *n.* [*count*] **1.** the offspring of two different kinds of animals or plants. —*adj.* [*before a noun*] **2.** relating to or being a hybrid.

hy•drant /ˈhaydrənt/ *n.* [*count*] a wide pipe connected underground to a water supply and used esp. for fighting fires.

hy•drau•lic /hayˈdrɔlɪk, -ˈdrɒlɪk/ *adj.* operated by or relating to the pressure of a moving liquid, esp. water: *hydraulic brakes.*

hy•dro•e•lec•tric /ˌhaydrowɪˈlɛktrɪk/ *adj.* of or relating to electricity produced from the energy of falling water: *a hydroelectric power station.*

hy•dro•gen /ˈhaydrədʒən/ *n.* [*noncount*] a col-

orless, odorless gas that burns easily and combines with oxygen to form water.

'hydrogen ˌbomb, *n.* [*count*] a bomb that takes its explosive energy from the fusion of hydrogen atoms. Also called **H-bomb.**

hy•e•na /hayˈiynə/ *n.* [*count*], *pl.* **-nas.** a doglike wild animal with a laughing cry.

hy•giene /ˈhaydʒiyn/ *n.* [*noncount*] **1.** the study of how to preserve health and prevent disease through cleanliness. **2.** cleanliness in general. —**hy•gi•en•ic** /ˌhaydʒiyˈɛnɪk, hayˈdʒɛn-/, *adj.*

hymn /hɪm/ *n.* [*count*] a song of praise to God.

hym•nal /ˈhɪmnl/ *n.* [*count*] a book of hymns.

hy•per•ac•tive /ˌhaypərˈæktɪv/ *adj.* unusually active: *a hyperactive child.*

hy•per•bo•le /hayˈpɜrbəliy/ *n.* [*noncount*] obvious and intentional exaggeration: *an example of hyperbole, such as "I've read billions of books."*

hy•per•ten•sion /ˌhaypərˈtɛnʃən/ *n.* [*noncount*] high blood pressure.

hy•phen /ˈhayfən/ *n.* [*count*] a short line (-) used to connect two words or the parts of a divided word.

hy•phen•ate /ˈhayfəˌneyt/ *v.*, **-at•ed, -at•ing.** [~ + *obj*] **1.** to join by a hyphen. **2.** to write or divide with a hyphen. —**hy•phen•a•tion** /ˌhayfəˈneyʃən/, *n.* [*noncount*]

hyp•no•sis /hɪpˈnowsɪs/ *n.* [*noncount*], *pl.* **-ses** /-siyz/. a sleep-like state in which a person is more likely to take suggestions from someone else than when fully awake and aware. —**hyp•not•ic,** *adj.* —**hyp•not•i•cal•ly,** *adv.*

hyp•no•tism /ˈhɪpnəˌtɪzəm/ *n.* [*noncount*] the study or practice of causing hypnosis. —ˈhyp•no•tist, *n.* [*count*] —**hyp•no•tize** /ˈhɪpnəˌtayz/ *v.*, [~ + *obj*] **-tized, -tiz•ing.**

hy•po•chon•dri•a /ˌhaypəˈkɒndriyə/ *n.* [*noncount*] unnecessary worry about one's health. —**hy•po•chon•dri•ac** /ˌhaypəˈkɒndriyˌæk/, *n.* [*count*]

hy•poc•ri•sy /hɪˈpɒkrəsiy/ *n.* [*noncount*] [*count*], *pl.* **-sies.** an act or instance of pretending to have desirable qualities or views that one does not really possess.

hyp•o•crite /ˈhɪpəkrɪt/ *n.* [*count*] a person who practices hypocrisy. —**hyp•o'crit•i•cal,** *adj.*

hy•po•der•mic /ˌhaypəˈdɜrmɪk/ *adj.* **1.** of or relating to the process of injecting drugs under the skin. —*n.* [*count*] **2.** an injection under the skin. **3.** a syringe or needle used for this.

hy•pot•e•nuse /hayˈpɒtnˌuws, -ˌyuws/, *n.* [*count*] the longest side of a right triangle, opposite the right angle.

hy•poth•e•sis /hayˈpɒθəsɪs, hɪ-/ *n.* [*count*], *pl.* **-ses** /-ˌsiyz/. an idea that is suggested to explain something.

hy•po•thet•i•cal /ˌhaypəˈθɛtɪkəl/ *adj.* supposed to exist but not yet shown to be real: *a hypothetical situation.* —ˌhy•po'thet•i•cal•ly, *adv.*

hys•ter•ec•to•my /ˌhɪstəˈrɛktəmiy/ *n.* [*count*], *pl.* **-mies.** removal of the womb by a medical operation.

hys•te•ri•a /hɪˈstɛriyə, -ˈstɪər-/ *n.* [*noncount*] **1.** wild excitement. **2.** uncontrollable emotional behavior, as from fear or grief.

hys•ter•i•cal /hɪˈstɛrɪkəl/ *adj.* uncontrollably emotional or upset. —**hys'ter•i•cal•ly,** *adv.*

hys•ter•ics /hɪˈstɛrɪks/ *n.* [*plural*] an attack of uncontrollable laughing or weeping.

H

I

I, i /ay/ *n.* [*count*], *pl.* **I's** or **Is, i's** or **is.** the ninth letter of the English alphabet, a vowel.

I /ay/ *pron., nom.* **I,** *poss.* **my** or **mine,** *obj.* **me;** *pl. nom.* **we,** *poss.* **our** or **ours,** *obj.* **us;** *n., pl.* **I's.** —*pron.* (used as the singular subject pronoun by a speaker or writer in referring to himself or herself): *I am happy to see you.*

I, an abbreviation of: interstate (used with a number to designate an interstate highway): *I-95.*

IA or **Ia.,** an abbreviation of: Iowa.

-ial, a variant form of the suffix -AL¹: (*editorial*).

-ian, a variant form of the suffix -AN¹: (*Washingtonian; Bostonian*).

-ibility, a variant form of the suffix -ABILITY: (*flexibility*).

-ible, a variant form of the suffix -ABLE: (*visible; horrible*).

i•bu•pro•fen /ˌaybyuw'prowfən/ *n.* [*noncount*] a non-aspirin drug used esp. for reducing pain and swelling.

-ic¹, an adjective suffix meaning: of or relating to (*metallic; poetic*); like or characteristic of (*idyllic*); containing or made of (*alcoholic*); produced by or suggestive of (*Homeric*).

-ic², a noun suffix meaning: a person having (*arthritic*); an agent or drug (*cosmetic*); a follower or supporter (*Socratic*).

-ical, a suffix that is a combination of -ic and -AL¹, used in forming adjectives from nouns (*rhetorical*). Originally it provided synonyms for adjectives ending in -ic (*poetic-poetical*). But some of these word pairs are now different in meaning (*economic-economical; historic-historical*).

ice /ays/ *n., v.,* **iced, ic•ing.** —*n.* **1.** [*noncount*] the solid form of water; frozen water. **2.** [*count*] a frozen dessert made of sweetened water and fruit juice. **3.** [*count*] *Brit.* a portion of ice cream. —*v.* **4. ice up** or **over,** to cover or to become covered with ice: *The airport runway iced over. The cold has iced the windshield up* or *The cold has iced up the windshield.* **5.** [~ + *obj*] to make cold with or as if with ice: *to ice a drink.* **6.** [~ + *obj*] to cover with icing; frost: *to ice a cake.* —*Idiom.* **7. break the ice,** to make an awkward social situation easier: *His joke broke the ice.*

ice•berg /'aysbɜrg/ *n.* [*count*] **1.** a large floating mass of ice. —*Idiom.* **2. tip of the iceberg,** the first hint of something larger or more complicated.

ice•box /'ays,bɒks/ *n.* [*count*] a refrigerator.

ice•break•er /'ays,breykər/ *n.* [*count*] **1.** a ship for breaking through ice and making passages. **2.** something that eases tension: *His joke was an icebreaker at the party.*

ice•cap /'ays,kæp/ *n.* [*count*] a thick cover of ice over an area, sloping downward in all directions.

'ice ,cream, *n.* [*noncount*] a frozen mixture made with cream or milk, sugar, and flavoring.

iced /ayst/ *adj.* **1.** made cold: *iced tea.* **2.** covered with icing: *iced cupcakes.*

'ice ,hockey, *n.* [*noncount*] a game played on ice between two teams of six skaters each.

'ice ,skate, *n.* [*count*] a shoe fitted with a metal blade for skating on ice.

'ice-,skate, *v.* [*no obj*], **-skat•ed, -skat•ing.** to skate on ice. —**'ice ,skater,** *n.* [*count*]

-ician, a suffix meaning a person having a certain occupation (*physician; politician*).

i•ci•cle /'aysɪkəl/ *n.* [*count*] a hanging, pointed mass of ice formed by the freezing of dripping water.

ic•ing /'aysɪŋ/ *n.* [*noncount*] a sweet mixture of sugar, butter, and flavoring, used as a coating on cakes, cookies, etc.; frosting.

-ics, a suffix meaning: an art, science, or field of knowledge (*physics*); activities or practices of a certain kind (*acrobatics*).

ICU, an abbreviation of: intensive care unit.

i•cy /'aysiy/ *adj.,* **i•ci•er, i•ci•est. 1.** made of or covered with ice: *an icy sidewalk.* **2.** very cold: *icy hands.* **3.** very unfriendly: *an icy stare.*

ID /'ay'diy/ *n.* [*noncount*] [*count*], *pl.* **ID's, IDs.** a document proving who a person is. Also, **I.D.**

ID or **Id.,** an abbreviation of: Idaho.

I'd /ayd/ **1.** contraction of *I would: I'd like a nap.* **2.** contraction of *I had: I'd been there before.*

I.D., an abbreviation of: **1.** identification. **2.** identity.

i•de•a /ay'diyə, ay'diyə/ *n.* **1.** [*count*] a thought that comes as a result of mental activity. **2.** [*count; usually singular*] an opinion, view, or belief: *His idea of a good time is relaxing at home.*

i•de•al /ay'diyəl, ay'diyl/ *n.* **1.** [*count*] a perfect example: *He's my ideal of a good father.* **2.** [*count; usually plural*] a standard of excellence: *a person with high ideals.* **3.** [*count*] something that exists only in the imagination. —*adj.* **4.** perfect: *an ideal childhood.*

i•de•al•ism /ay'diyə,lɪzəm/ *n.* [*noncount*] the belief that one should follow or try to achieve ideals: *youthful idealism.* —**i'de•al•ist,** *n.* [*count*] —**i,de•al'is•tic,** *adj.*

i•de•al•ize /ay'diyə,layz/ *v.* [~ + *obj*], **-ized, -iz•ing.** to think of (someone or something) as perfect. —**i•de•al•i•za•tion** /ay,diyəlɪ'zeyʃən/, *n.* [*noncount*]

i•de•al•ly /ay'diyəliy/ *adv.* **1.** perfectly: *ideally suited for the job.* **2.** in theory: *Ideally we should finish by noon.*

i•den•ti•cal /ay'dɛntɪkəl, ɪ'dɛn-/ *adj.* **1.** the very same. **2.** exactly alike: *identical twins.* —**i'den•ti•cal•ly,** *adv.*

i•den•ti•fi•ca•tion /ay,dɛntəfɪ'keyʃən, ɪ,dɛn-/ *n.* [*noncount*] **1.** an act of identifying or the state of being identified: *Positive identification of the accident victim was impossible.* **2.** something, as a birth certificate or driver's license, that proves who a person is.

i•den•ti•fy /ay'dɛntə,fay, ɪ'dɛn-/ *v.* [~ + *obj*], **-fied, -fy•ing. 1.** to prove or recognize exactly who a person is or what a thing is: *The eyewitness identified the robber.* **2.** to associate or connect closely: *He identifies owning an expensive car with success.* **3. identify with,** to feel that one shares (something); to feel sympathy: *I identified with one of the characters in the novel.*

i•den•ti•ty /ay'dɛntɪtiy, ɪ'dɛn-/ *n., pl.* **-ties. 1.** condition or character as to who a person is or what a thing is: [*noncount*]: *a case of mistaken identity.* [*count*]: *the identity of the victim.* **2.** [*noncount*] the sense of self.

i•de•ol•o•gy /ˌaydiy'ɒlədʒiy, ˌɪdiy-/ *n., pl.* **-gies.** the body of belief, doctrine, or thought that guides a person, movement, or group: [*noncount*]: *communist ideology.* [*count*]: *many ideologies of social behavior.* —**i•de•o•log•i•cal** /ˌaydiyə'lɒdʒɪkəl, ˌɪdiy-/, *adj.*

id•i•o•cy /'ɪdiyəsiy/ *n., pl.* **-cies. 1.** [*noncount*] stupidity. **2.** [*count*] something stupid.

id•i•om /'ɪdiyəm/ *n.* [*count*] an expression or phrase whose meaning cannot be understood from the meaning of its separate parts: *The expression* kick the bucket, *meaning "to die," is an idiom in English.*

id•i•o•mat•ic /ˌɪdiyə'mætɪk/ *adj.* that sounds natural and correct to a native speaker of a language. —**id•i•o'mat•i•cal•ly,** *adv.*

id•i•o•syn•cra•sy /ˌɪdiyə'sɪŋkrəsiy, -'sɪn-/ *n.* [*count*], *pl.* **-sies.** a characteristic behavior of a person. —**id•i•o•syn•crat•ic** /ˌɪdiyowsɪn'krætɪk, -sɪŋ-/, *adj.*: *her idiosyncratic ways.*

id•i•ot /'ɪdiyət/ *n.* [*count*] a completely stupid or foolish person. —**id•i•ot•ic** /ˌɪdiy'ɒtɪk/ *adj.*

i•dle /'aydl/ *adj.,* **i•dler, i•dlest,** *v.,* **i•dled, i•dling.** —*adj.* **1.** not working or active: *idle employees; idle machinery.* **2.** not filled with activity: *idle hours.* **3.** [*usually: before a noun*] of no real worth or purpose: *idle threats.* —*v.* **4.** [*no obj*] to pass time doing nothing: *just idling around the house.* **5. idle away,** to waste (time): *He idled the day away* or *He idled away the day.* **6.** to (cause to) run slowly and out of gear: [*no obj*]: *The car idled at the red light.* [~ + *obj*]: *He idled his car's engine.* —**i•dle•ness,** *n.* [*noncount*] —**i'dly,** *adv.*: *chatted idly.*

i•dol /'aydl/ *n.* [*count*] **1.** an image worshiped as a god. **2.** a person or thing greatly admired or loved: *a movie idol.*

i•dol•ize /'aydl,ayz/ *v.* [~ + *obj*], **-ized, -iz•ing.** to treat as an idol: *She idolizes her father.*

i•dyll or **i•dyl** /'aydl/ *n.* [*count*] a simple charming scene. —**i•dyl•lic** /ay'dɪlɪk/, *adj.*: *an idyllic scene of country life.*

i.e., an abbreviation of: Latin *id est* that is.

-ier, a form of the suffix **-EER** (*financier*).

if /ɪf/ *conj.* **1.** on condition that: *We'll go if it doesn't rain.* **2.** supposing that: *If I were you, I wouldn't worry. If I had lots of money I would travel.* **3.** even though: *It was an enthusiastic, if small, audience.* **4.** whether: *I wonder if she will be able to come with us.* **5.** (used for expressing a wish): *If I had only known, I would have helped.* **6.** (used after words expressing feelings): *I'm sorry if you don't agree.* —*Idiom.* **7. no ifs, ands, or buts,** no reasons or excuses given: *You'd better have this finished on time, no ifs, ands, or buts about it.*

if•fy /'ɪfiy/ *adj.,* **-fi•er, -fi•est.** uncertain: *an iffy situation.*

igloo

ig•loo /'ɪgluw/ *n.* [*count*], *pl.* **-loos.** a dome-shaped Eskimo dwelling of blocks of hard snow.

ig•nite /ɪg'nayt/ *v.* [*no obj*] [~ + *obj*], **-nit•ed, -nit•ing.** to (cause to) catch fire; (cause to) begin to burn.

ig•ni•tion /ɪg'nɪʃən/ *n.* **1.** [*noncount*] the act of igniting or the state of being ignited. **2.** [*count;*

usually singular] (in an engine) the process, spark, or switch that ignites the fuel.

ig•no•rance /'ɪgnərəns/ *n.* [*noncount*] lack of knowledge about something.

ig•no•rant /'ɪgnərənt/ *adj.* **1.** lacking knowledge. **2.** [*be* + ~ + *of*] not informed or unaware: *He was ignorant of the law.* —'**ig•no•rant•ly,** *adv.*

ig•nore /ɪg'nɔr/ *v.* [~ + *obj*], **-nored, -nor•ing.** to keep oneself from noticing: *I just ignored their rudeness.*

IL, an abbreviation of: Illinois.

il-¹, a form of the prefix IN-², used before roots beginning with the letter "l" (*illegible*).

il-², a form of the prefix IN-¹, attached to roots beginning with the letter "l" (*illuminate*).

ill /ɪl/ *adj.,* **worse** /wɜrs/, **worst** /wɜrst/, *n., adv.* —*adj.* **1.** [*be* + ~] sick: *She's ill with a cold.* **2.** [*before a noun*] unkind: *ill feeling between them.* **3.** [*before a noun*] not favorable: *ill fortune.* —*n.* **4.** [*noncount*] harm or injury: *His remarks did much ill.* **5.** [*count*] trouble; misfortune: *the many ills of humanity.* —*adv.* **6.** poorly; badly: *Things went ill with us.* **7.** unkindly: *to speak or think ill of someone.* **8.** The word *ill* can be used in combination with other adjectives or participles to mean "badly, improperly; inadequately." —*Idiom.* **9. ill at ease,** uncomfortable; uneasy.

I'll /ayl/ contraction of *I will; I shall: I'll see you soon.*

Ill., an abbreviation of: Illinois.

'ill-ad'vised, *adj.* unwise: *an ill-advised remark.*

'ill-'bred, *adj.* showing lack of good manners.

il•le•gal /ɪ'liygəl/ *adj.* against the law; not legal. —**il'le•gal•ly,** *adv.*

il•le•gal•i•ty /ˌɪliy'gælɪtiy/ *n.* **1.** [*noncount*] the act or state of being illegal. **2.** [*count*] an illegal action.

il•leg•i•ble /ɪ'lɛdʒəbəl/ *adj.* impossible or hard to read: *illegible handwriting.* —**il•leg•i•bil•i•ty** /ɪˌlɛdʒə'bɪlɪtiy/, *n.* [*noncount*] —**il'leg•i•bly,** *adv.*

il•le•git•i•mate /ˌɪlɪ'dʒɪtəmɪt/ *adj.* **1.** born of parents who are not married to each other. **2.** not allowed by law. —**il•le'git•i•mate•ly,** *adv.*

'ill-'humor, *n.* [*noncount*] an unpleasant mood.

il•lic•it /ɪ'lɪsɪt/ *adj.* not allowed by law or custom: *illicit drugs; an illicit love affair.* —**il'lic•it•ly,** *adv.*

il•lit•er•ate /ɪ'lɪtərɪt/ *adj.* **1.** unable to read and write: *Many adults in this country are still illiterate.* —*n.* [*count*] **2.** an illiterate person. —**il'lit•er•a•cy,** *n.* [*noncount*]

ill•ness /'ɪlnɪs/ *n.* [*noncount*] [*count*] poor health; sickness.

il•log•i•cal /ɪ'lɒdʒɪkəl/ *adj.* unreasonable.

'ill-'treat, *v.* [~ + *obj*] to treat badly; abuse. —**'ill-'treatment,** *n.*

il•lu•mi•nate /ɪ'luwmə,neyt/ *v.* [~ + *obj*], **-nat•ed, -nat•ing. 1.** to supply with light; light up: *The streets were well illuminated.* **2.** to make clear; explain: *The professor illuminated many difficult points.* —**il,lu•mi'na•tion,** *n.* [*noncount*]

il•lu•mi•nat•ing /ɪ'luwmə,neytɪŋ/ *adj.* helping to make clear or understandable: *an illuminating lecture on mathematics.*

il•lu•sion /ɪ'luwʒən/ *n.* **1.** [*count*] something that deceives a person by seeming to be real: *The puddle of water on the dry road ahead was just an optical illusion.* **2.** [*noncount*] a false belief in something not true or real: *I was under the illusion that she was rich.*

I

il·lu·so·ry /ɪˈluwsəriy, -zə-/ adj. causing or based on an illusion: illusory hopes of success.

il·lus·trate /ˈɪləˌstreyt, ɪˈlʌstreyt/ v. [~ + obj], -trat·ed, -trat·ing. **1.** to provide with pictures: to illustrate a book. **2.** to explain by providing examples: He illustrated his point with a little story. —ˈil·lusˌtra·tor, n. [count]

il·lus·tra·tion /ˌɪləˈstreyʃən/ n. **1.** [count] something that illustrates; a picture or drawing. **2.** [count] an example given to explain something.

il·lus·tra·tive /ɪˈlʌstrətɪv/ adj. serving to illustrate: illustrative examples.

il·lus·tri·ous /ɪˈlʌstriyəs/ adj. famous.

'ill 'will, n. [noncount] unfriendly feeling.

I'm, contraction of I am: I'm here. I'm hungry.

im-¹, a form of the prefix IN-², used before roots beginning with the letters "b", "m", or "p": (immigrate).

im-², a form of the prefix IN-¹, used before roots beginning with the letters "b", "m", or " p": (impossible).

im·age /ˈɪmɪdʒ/ n. [count] **1.** a picture formed in the mind. **2.** a representation of a person, animal, or thing. **3.** a picture of an object formed by a mirror or a camera lens. **4.** a person or thing very much like another. **5.** the general idea of a person, product, etc., held by the public. **6.** a figure of speech used to describe something.

im·age·ry /ˈɪmɪdʒriy/ n. [noncount] the use of figurative language to produce mental images.

im·ag·i·na·ble /ɪˈmædʒənəbəl/ adj. that can be imagined.

im·ag·i·nar·y /ɪˈmædʒəˌnɛriy/ adj. existing only in the imagination; not real.

im·ag·i·na·tion /ɪˌmædʒəˈneyʃən/ n. **1.** the ability to form mental images of things that are elsewhere, not part of one's experience, or not real: [count]: Fairy tales help develop children's imaginations. [noncount]: She has lots of imagination. **2.** [noncount] creative talent: a job that requires imagination. —im'ag·i·na·tive, adj. —im'ag·i·na·tive·ly, adv.

im·ag·ine /ɪˈmædʒɪn/ v., -ined, -in·ing. **1.** to form an image (of) in the mind: [~ + obj]: I tried to imagine a clear mountain stream. [no obj]: He's just imagining. **2.** [~ + (that) clause] to believe; suppose: I imagined (that) the house was haunted.

im·bal·ance /ɪmˈbæləns/ n. [count] the state or condition of lacking balance.

im·be·cile /ˈɪmbəsɪl, -səl/ n. [count] a stupid or foolish person.

im·i·tate /ˈɪmɪˌteyt/ v. [~ + obj], -tat·ed, -tat·ing. to look, speak, or act the same as; copy. —ˈim·iˌta·tor, n. [count]

im·i·ta·tion /ˌɪmɪˈteyʃən/ n. **1.** [noncount] the act of imitating. **2.** [count] a result of imitating; a copy. **3.** [count] an impersonation: He does imitations of famous people. —adj. [before a noun] **4.** not real; artificial: imitation leather.

im·mac·u·late /ɪˈmækyəlɪt/ adj. **1.** clean and neat: immaculate clothes. **2.** free from errors; perfect. —im'mac·u·late·ly, adv.

im·ma·te·ri·al /ˌɪməˈtɪəriyəl/ adj. **1.** unimportant: What I think is immaterial. **2.** not in the physical world; spiritual.

im·ma·ture /ˌɪməˈtʃʊr, -ˈtʊr/ adj. **1.** not mature or ripe: immature fruit. **2.** not developed emotionally; childish: immature behavior. —ˌim·ma'ture·ly, adv. —ˌim·ma'tur·i·ty, n. [noncount]

im·meas·ur·a·ble /ɪˈmɛʒərəbəl/ adj. too large or great to be measured. —im'meas·ur·a·bly, adv.

im·me·di·ate /ɪˈmiydiyɪt/ adj. [before a noun] **1.** happening or done without delay: an immediate reply. **2.** very close in time, space, or relationship: the immediate future; just the immediate family.

im·me·di·ate·ly /ɪˈmiydiyɪtliy/ adv. **1.** at once: Telephone your mother immediately. **2.** with no object or space in between: He sits immediately beside me in class.

im·mense /ɪˈmɛns/ adj. extremely large: an immense country. —im'mense·ly, adv.: We enjoyed the party immensely. —im'men·si·ty, n. [noncount]: the immensity of the universe.

im·merse /ɪˈmɜrs/ v. [~ + obj], -mersed, -mers·ing. **1.** to place under a liquid. **2.** to involve completely: She's deeply immersed in her work. —im'mers·i·ble, adj.: That electric coffeepot is not immersible. —im'mer·sion /-ʒən, -ʃən/ n. [noncount]

im·mi·grant /ˈɪmɪɡrənt/ n. [count] a person who comes from one country to settle in another.

im·mi·grate /ˈɪmɪˌɡreyt/ v. [~ + to + obj], -grat·ed, -grat·ing. to come into a country of which one is not a native, usually to live there permanently: They immigrated to the United States in the 1850's. —ˌim·mi'gra·tion, n. [noncount]

im·mi·nent /ˈɪmənənt/ adj. likely to happen at any moment. —ˈim·mi·nent·ly, adv.

im·mo·bile /ɪˈmowbəl, -biyl/ adj. **1.** unable to move or be moved. **2.** not moving; motionless. —im·mo·bil·i·ty /ˌɪmowˈbɪlɪtiy/, n. [noncount]

im·mo·bi·lize /ɪˈmowbəlayz/ v. [~ + obj], -lized, -liz·ing. to cause to be immobile.

im·mod·er·ate /ɪˈmɒdərɪt/ adj. not sensible: immoderate eating. —im'mod·er·ate·ly, adv.

im·mod·est /ɪˈmɒdɪst/ adj. not modest in behavior, speech, etc.: an immodest bathing suit.

im·mor·al /ɪˈmɔrəl, ɪˈmɒr-/ adj. going against moral principles; wrong.

im·mo·ral·i·ty /ˌɪməˈrælɪtiy, ˌɪmɔ-/ n. [noncount], pl. -ties. **1.** immoral quality or conduct: the immorality of the war. **2.** immoral sexual behavior.

im·mor·tal /ɪˈmɔrtl/ adj. **1.** living or lasting forever. —n. [count] **2.** an immortal being.

im·mor·tal·i·ty /ˌɪmɔrˈtælɪtiy/ n. [noncount] **1.** immortal condition or quality. **2.** long-lasting fame.

im·mor·tal·ize /ɪˈmɔrtlˌayz/ v. [~ + obj], -ized, -iz·ing. to give lasting fame to: She was immortalized in the movies.

im·mune /ɪˈmyuwn/ adj. **1.** [be/become + ~ + to] protected from a disease, as by an injection: immune to the flu. **2.** [before a noun] of or relating to the production of special cells in the body that fight disease. **3.** [be + ~ + from] protected: immune from punishment. **4.** [be + ~ + to] not affected by something: He was immune to criticism in his job. —im'mu·ni·ty, n. [noncount]

im·mu·nize /ˈɪmyəˌnayz, ɪˈmyuwnayz/ v. [~ + obj], -nized, -niz·ing. to make immune: The vaccine immunized her against measles. —im·mu·ni·za·tion /ˌɪmyənɪˈzeyʃən, ɪˌmyuw-/, n. [noncount]

imp /ɪmp/ n. [count] **1.** a small devil. **2.** a mischievous child.

im·pact /n. ˈɪmpækt; v. ɪmˈpækt/ n. **1.** the striking of one thing against another: [noncount]: The cars crashed on impact. [count]: The bullet struck with a great impact. **2.** [*noncount*] a strong influence or effect: *the impact of Einstein on modern physics.* —*v.* [~ + *obj*] **3.** to press firmly into something. **4.** to hit against. **5.** to have an effect on; influence.

im•pair /ɪm'pɛər/ *v.* [~ + *obj*] to weaken or damage: *Smoking impairs your health.* —**im'pair•ment,** *n.* [*noncount*]: *impairment of the learning process.* [*count*]: *a hearing impairment.*

im•pale /ɪm'peyl/ *v.* [~ + *obj*], **-paled, -pal•ing.** to pierce with something pointed, as a spear.

im•part /ɪm'pɑrt/ *v.* [~ + *obj* (+ *to* + *obj*)] to give (information, qualities, etc.).

im•par•tial /ɪm'pɑrʃəl/ *adj.* fair; just: *Judges must be impartial.* —**im•par•ti•al•i•ty** /ɪm,pɑrʃiy'ælɪtiy/, *n.* [*noncount*] —**im'par•tial•ly,** *adv.*

im•pass•a•ble /ɪm'pæsəbəl/ *adj.* (of a road, etc.) not allowing passage.

im•passe /'ɪmpæs/ *n.* [*count; usually singular*] a situation in which further movement is impossible: *The discussions reached an impasse.*

im•pas•sioned /ɪm'pæʃənd/ *adj.* filled with intense feeling: *an impassioned plea for forgiveness.*

im•pas•sive /ɪm'pæsɪv/ *adj.* showing no feelings. —**im'pas•sive•ly,** *adv.*

im•pa•tience /ɪm'peyʃəns/ *n.* [*noncount*] inability to wait calmly for something.

im•pa•tient /ɪm'peyʃənt/ *adj.* **1.** showing a lack of patience. **2.** restless or eager: *impatient to begin.* —**im'pa•tient•ly,** *adv.*

im•peach /ɪm'piytʃ/ *v.* [~ + *obj*] to bring formal charges of wrongdoing against (a public official). —**im'peach•ment,** *n.* [*noncount*] [*count*]

im•pec•ca•ble /ɪm'pɛkəbəl/ *adj.* perfect; faultless: *impeccable manners.* —**im•pec•ca•bly,** *adv.: The children behaved impeccably.*

im•pede /ɪm'piyd/ *v.* [~ + *obj*], **-ped•ed, -ped•ing.** to cause to slow down in movement or progress.

im•ped•i•ment /ɪm'pɛdəmənt/ *n.* [*count*] **1.** something that delays progress. **2.** a physical defect involving speech: *a speech impediment.*

im•pel /ɪm'pɛl/ *v.* [~ + *obj*], **-pelled, -pel•ling.** to urge forward; force: *Financial problems impelled the company to dismiss employees.*

im•pend•ing /ɪm'pɛndɪŋ/ *adj.* about to happen: *the impending birth.*

im•pen•e•tra•ble /ɪm'pɛnɪtrəbəl/ *adj.* **1.** that cannot be passed through: *an impenetrable forest.* **2.** that cannot be understood: *an impenetrable mystery.*

im•per•a•tive /ɪm'pɛrətɪv/ *adj.* **1.** absolutely necessary: *It is imperative that we leave.* **2.** of or naming a grammatical mood used in commands, as in *Listen! Go!* —*n.* **3.** [*count*] a command; order. **4.** [*noncount; usually: the* + ~] the imperative mood; a verb in this mood. —**im'per•a•tive•ly,** *adv.*

im•per•fect /ɪm'pɜrfɪkt/ *adj.* **1.** not perfect: *imperfect vision; imperfect knowledge.* **2.** of or naming a verb tense or form that shows a repeated, habitual, or continuing action or state in the past: *"They were speaking" is in imperfect tense.* —*n.* [*noncount; usually: the* + ~] **3.** the imperfect tense; a verb form in this tense. —**im'per•fect•ly,** *adv.: I spoke English imperfectly at first.*

im•per•fec•tion /,ɪmpər'fɛkʃən/ *n.* **1.** [*count*] a fault: *a few minor imperfections.* **2.** [*noncount*] the quality or state of being imperfect.

im•pe•ri•al /ɪm'pɪəriyəl/ *adj.* [*before a noun*] of,

relating to, or characteristic of an empire, emperor, or empress. —**im'pe•ri•al•ly,** *adv.*

im•pe•ri•al•ism /ɪm'pɪəriyə,lɪzəm/ *n.* [*noncount*] the policy of trying to control the political or economic affairs of other countries. —**im'pe•ri•al•ist,** *n.* [*count*], *adj.*

im•per•il /ɪm'pɛrəl/ *v.* [~ + *obj*], **-iled, -il•ing** or (*esp. Brit.*) **-illed, -il•ling.** to put in danger.

im•per•son•al /ɪm'pɜrsənḷ/ *adj.* **1.** lacking reference to a particular person: *impersonal remarks.* **2.** lacking human feeling or warmth: *a cold, impersonal letter.* **3.** [*before a noun*] (of a verb) having only third person singular forms, usually with the pronoun *it* as the subject, as in *It is raining.*

im•per•son•ate /ɪm'pɜrsə,neyt/ *v.* [~ + *obj*], **-at•ed, -at•ing.** to pretend to be (another person) in order to deceive or amuse. —**im•per•son•a•tion** /ɪm,pɜrsə'neyʃən/, *n.* [*noncount*] [*count*] —**im'per•son,a•tor,** *n.* [*count*]

im•per•ti•nent /ɪm'pɜrtṇənt/ *adj.* rude; not respectful: *an impertinent reply.* —**im'per•ti•nence,** *n.* [*noncount*] —**im'per•ti•nent•ly,** *adv.*

im•pet•u•ous /ɪm'pɛtʃuwəs/ *adj.* acting or done too quickly, with little thought. —**im'pet•u•ous•ly,** *adv.*

im•pe•tus /'ɪmpɪtəs/ *n.,* pl. **-tus•es. 1.** [*count*] a force that moves one to action: *Some children need an impetus to study.* **2.** [*noncount*] the force of a moving body: *The car rolled down the hill under its own impetus.*

im•pinge /ɪm'pɪndʒ/ *v.* [~ + *on/upon*], **-pinged, -ping•ing. 1.** to go beyond a limit: *to impinge on another's rights.* **2.** to have an effect: *an idea that impinges on the mind.* —**im'pinge•ment,** *n.* [*noncount*]

imp•ish /'ɪmpɪʃ/ *adj.* mischievous.

im•plac•a•ble /ɪm'plækəbəl, -'pleykə-/ *adj.* impossible to satisfy or stop: *an implacable enemy.* —**im'plac•a•bly,** *adv.: The enemy advanced implacably.*

im•plant /*v.*ɪm'plænt; *n.* 'ɪm,plænt/ *v.* [~ + *obj*] **1.** to fix firmly in the mind: *to implant a new idea.* **2.** to put (tissue, an organ, etc.) into the body: *The doctors implanted the new heart in the patient.* —*n.* [*count*] **3.** a device or material implanted in the body: *an organ implant.*

im•ple•ment /*n.*'ɪmpləmənt; *v. also* -,mɛnt/ *n.* [*count*] **1.** a tool or utensil for doing work. —*v.* [~ + *obj*] **2.** to carry out: *to implement a plan.* —**im•ple•men•ta•tion** /,ɪmpləmən'teyʃən/, *n.* [*noncount*]

im•pli•cate /'ɪmplɪ,keyt/ *v.* [~ + *obj*], **-cat•ed, -cat•ing.** to show or declare (someone else) to be involved, usually in a crime.

im•pli•ca•tion /,ɪmplɪ'keyʃən/ *n.* **1.** [*count*] something implied: *the implications of the president's speech.* **2.** [*noncount*] the state of being implicated: *his implication in the crime.*

im•plic•it /ɪm'plɪsɪt/ *adj.* **1.** not stated directly; implied: *an implicit agreement.* **2.** [*usually: before a noun*] complete: *implicit trust.* —**im'plic•it•ly,** *adv.: We agreed implicitly on most of the issues.*

im•plore /ɪm'plɔr/ *v.* [~ + *obj*], **-plored, -plor•ing.** to beg urgently (for): *He implored her help. They implored him not to go.* —**im'plor•ing,** *adj.: an imploring look.* —**im'plor•ing•ly,** *adv.*

im•ply /ɪm'play/ *v.* [~ + *obj*], **-plied, -ply•ing.** to suggest (something) without its being stated in words: *The doctor's frown implied that something was wrong.*

im•po•lite /,ɪmpə'layt/ *adj.* not polite; rude. —,**im•po'lite•ly,** *adv.*

I

im•port /v.ɪm'pɔrt; n. 'ɪmpɔrt/ v. [~ + obj] **1.** to bring in from a foreign country: *to import cars and computer parts.* —n. **2.** [count] something imported: *Imports rose again.* **3.** [noncount] the act of importing: *the import of cars.* **4.** [noncount] importance: *matters of great import.* —**im'port•er,** n. [count]

im•por•tance /ɪm'pɔrtns/ n. [noncount] the quality or state of being important.

im•por•tant /ɪm'pɔrtnt/ adj. **1.** having great value or meaning: *an important event in history.* **2.** having great authority or power: *an important person.* —**im'por•tant•ly,** adv.

im•pose /ɪm'powz/ v., **-posed, -pos•ing. 1.** [~ + obj] to force the acceptance of: *to impose taxes.* **2.** to push (oneself) impolitely upon others: [no obj]: *Are you sure I'm not imposing?* [~ + oneself]: *to impose oneself on others.* **3. impose on,** to take unfair advantage of: *They imposed on his good nature.* —**,im•po'si•tion,** n. [noncount] [count]

im•pos•ing /ɪm'powzɪŋ/ adj. impressive because of size, appearance, etc.

im•pos•si•ble /ɪm'pɒsəbəl/ adj. **1.** not possible. **2.** extremely difficult: *in an impossible situation.* —**im•pos•si•bil•i•ty** /ɪm,pɒsə'bɪlɪtiy/, n. [noncount] [count] —**im'pos•si•bly,** adv. [before an adjective or adverb]: *moving impossibly fast.*

im•pos•tor or **im•post•er** /ɪm'pɒstər/ n. [count] one who pretends to be another in order to deceive someone.

im•po•tent /'ɪmpətənt/ adj. **1.** lacking power; helpless or ineffective. **2.** (of a male) unable to make or keep the penis erect during sex. —**'im•po•tence,** n. [noncount] —**'im•po•ten•cy,** n. [noncount] —**'im•po•tent•ly,** adv.

im•pound /ɪm'pawnd/ v. [~ + obj] to take and keep (possessions, property, etc.) by law.

im•pov•er•ish /ɪm'pɒvərɪʃ, -'pɒvrɪʃ/ v. [~ + obj] to make poor. —**im'pov•er•ished,** adj.: *an impoverished family; impoverished soil.*

im•prac•ti•ca•ble /ɪm'præktɪkəbəl/ adj. not capable of being put into practice or use. —**im'prac•ti•ca•bly,** adv.

im•prac•ti•cal /ɪm'præktɪkəl/ adj. **1.** not practical or useful. **2.** not sensible or realistic. —**im•prac•ti•cal•i•ty** /ɪm,præktɪ'kælɪtiy/, n. [noncount]

im•pre•cise /,ɪmprə'says/ adj. not exact: *an imprecise measurement.* —**,im•pre'cise•ly,** adv.

im•preg•na•ble /ɪm'prɛgnəbəl/ adj. strong enough to withstand attack: *an impregnable fort.*

im•preg•nate /ɪm'prɛgneyt/ v. [~ + obj], **-nat•ed, -nat•ing. 1.** to make pregnant. **2.** to cause to enter and be spread throughout: *to impregnate a handkerchief with perfume.*

im•press /ɪm'prɛs/ v. **1.** [~ + obj] to have a strong effect on the mind or feelings of: *Her excellent work impressed me.* **2.** [~ + on + obj + obj] to establish firmly in the mind: *We impressed on her the importance of being honest.* **3.** [~ + obj] to produce (a mark) by pressure; imprint.

im•pres•sion /ɪm'prɛʃən/ n. [count] **1.** a strong effect produced on the mind or feelings: *His behavior made a bad impression on me* **2.** an uncertain feeling or idea: *I had a general impression of distant voices.* **3.** a mark produced by pressure. **4.** a funny imitation of someone.

im•pres•sion•a•ble /ɪm'prɛʃənəbəl, -'prɛʃnə-/ adj. easily influenced; sensitive.

im•pres•sion•ism /ɪm'prɛʃə,nɪzəm/ n. [noncount; usually: *Impressionism*] a style of late 19th-century painting with short brush strokes of bright colors next to each other to represent the effect of light on objects. —**im'pres•sion•ist,** n. [count]

im•pres•sion•is•tic /ɪm,prɛʃə'nɪstɪk/ adj. **1.** of or relating to impressionism. **2.** based on feelings rather than on facts.

im•pres•sive /ɪm'prɛsɪv/ adj. causing admiration because of size, appearance, etc.: *the impressive castles of France.* —**im'pres•sive•ly,** adv.

im•print /n.'ɪmprɪnt; v. ɪm'prɪnt/ n. [count] **1.** a mark made by pressing. **2.** a long-lasting effect: *His difficult childhood left a strong imprint on him.* —v. [~ + obj] **3.** to mark by or as if by pressure: *to imprint a book with a mark.* **4.** to fix firmly in the mind: *That day is imprinted on his memory forever.* —**im'print•er,** n. [count]

im•pris•on /ɪm'prɪzən/ v. [~ + obj] to put or keep in a prison. —**im'pris•on•ment,** n. [noncount] [count]

im•prob•a•ble /ɪm'prɒbəbəl/ adj. unlikely to be true or to happen: *an improbable ending to a story.* —**im•prob•a•bil•i•ty** /ɪm,prɒbə'bɪlɪtiy/, n. [count] —**im'prob•a•bly,** adv.

im•promp•tu /ɪm'prɒmptuw, -tyuw/ adj. **1.** done without preparation: *an impromptu party.* —adv. **2.** without preparation: *to deliver a speech impromptu.*

im•prop•er /ɪm'prɒpər/ adj. **1.** not suitable: *improper dress for the occasion.* **2.** socially unacceptable: *improper remarks.* **3.** not correct; wrong: *improper methods.* —**im'prop•er•ly,** adv.

im•prove /ɪm'pruwv/ v., **-proved, -prov•ing.** to make or become better: [~ + obj]: *Exercise improves one's health.* [no obj]: *His health seems to be improving.* —**im'prov•a•ble,** adj.

im•prove•ment /ɪm'pruwvmənt/ n. **1.** [noncount] an act of improving or the state of being improved: *signs of economic improvement.* **2.** [count] a change or addition by which a thing is improved: *home improvements.*

im•pro•vise /'ɪmprə,vayz/ v., **-vised, -vis•ing. 1.** to perform without preparation: [~ + obj]: *The teacher improvised a lecture.* [no obj]: *Good jazz musicians can improvise for hours.* **2.** [~ + obj] [no obj] to make, provide, or arrange (something) from available materials. —**im,prov•i'sa•tion** /-,prɒvə'zeyʃ ən/, n. [noncount] [count] —**'im•pro,vis•er, im'pro•vi'sor,** n. [count]

im•pru•dent /ɪm'pruwdnt/ adj. not careful and sensible: *imprudent behavior.* —**im'pru•dence,** n. [noncount]

im•pu•dent /'ɪmpyədənt/ adj. rude; not respectful: *an impudent child.* —**'im•pu•dence,** n. [noncount] —**'im•pu•dent•ly,** adv.

im•pulse /'ɪmpʌls/ n. **1.** sudden desire leading to action: [count]: *He had a generous impulse.* [noncount]: *I called my friend on impulse.* **2.** [count] a sudden force that causes motion: *an electrical impulse.*

im•pul•sive /ɪm'pʌlsɪv/ adj. acting or done because of a sudden urge and without thought. —**im'pul•sive•ly,** adv. —**im'pul•sive•ness,** n. [noncount]

im•pu•ni•ty /ɪm'pyuwnɪtiy/ n. [noncount] avoidance of punishment: *to steal money with impunity.*

im•pure /ɪm'pyur/ adj. **1.** mixed with something else, esp. a harmful substance. **2.** morally wrong. —**im'pure•ly,** adv. —**im'pu•ri•ty,** n. [count] [noncount], pl. **-ties.**

in /ɪn/ prep. **1.** contained or enclosed by; inside; within: *walking in the park; I held the cat in my* *arms.* **2.** having the activity, occupation, or function of: *the hero in the story; He is in banking. She worked in politics.* **3.** to or at a situation or condition of: *She's always in debt. He smiled in amusement.* **4.** forming the whole or part of: *There are 12 months in a year.* **5.** (of a period of time) during or after: *They lived in ancient times. We'll be there in an hour.* **6.** with the form or arrangement of: *a play in three acts.* **7.** as part of; belonging to: *It isn't in him to cheat.* **8.** by the means or use of: *written in French; paid in cash.* **9.** with the aim or purpose of: *speaking in honor of the event.* **10.** into: *He got in the car.* **11.** wearing: *the woman in the hat.* **12.** with reference to: *belief in God; to vary in size.* **13.** showing a ratio: *One in ten will succeed.* —*adv.* **14.** in or into some place, position, state, relation, etc.: *Please come in.* **15.** having arrived: *Her plane isn't in yet.* **16.** in one's house or office: *I wasn't in all day.* **17.** in office or power: *They voted the Democrats in.* **18.** in season: *Strawberries aren't in now.* —*adj.* **19. a.** fashionable; popular: *the in place to go.* **b.** [*before a noun*] understood only by a special group: *an in joke.* **20.** [*before a noun*] included in a favored group: *She was never part of the in crowd.* **21.** being in power: *the in party during the war.* —*n.* [*count*] **22.** pull or influence: *He's got an in with the boss.* —**Idiom.** **23. in for,** certain to undergo (an unpleasant experience): *It looks as if we're in for stormy weather.* **24. in for it,** *Slang.* about to suffer punishment. **25. in that,** because: *The house is attractive in that we can afford it.* **26. the ins and outs,** all the details or parts of: *a book on the ins and outs of photography.*

IN, an abbreviation of: Indiana.

in-¹, a prefix meaning in, into, within, or toward (*incarcerate*).

in-², a prefix meaning not or lack of (*inexperience*).

-in, a combining form meaning any organized protest or social activity (*sit-in*).

in., an abbreviation of: inch.

in•a•bil•i•ty /ˌɪnəˈbɪlɪtiy/ *n.* lack of ability: [*noncount*]: *He failed through obvious inability.* [*count; usually singular*]: *an inability to deal with the facts.*

in•ac•ces•sible /ˌɪnəkˈsɛsəbl/ *adj.* that cannot be reached: *an inaccessible mountain hideaway.* —**in•ac•ces•si•bil•i•ty** /ˌɪnək,sɛsəˈbɪlɪtiy/, *n.* [*noncount*]

in•ac•cu•rate /ɪnˈækyərɪt/ *adj.* not correct. —**in'ac•cu•ra•cy,** *n.* [*noncount*] [*count*], *pl.,* **-cies.** —**in'ac•cu•rate•ly,** *adv.*

in•ad•e•quate /ɪnˈædɪkwɪt/ *adj.* not equal to what is needed. —**in'ad•e•qua•cy,** *n.* [*noncount*] [*count*], *pl.* **-cies.** —**in'ad•e•quate•ly,** *adv.*

in•ad•vert•ent /ˌɪnədˈvɜrtnt/ *adj.* not intentional: *an inadvertent insult.* —ˌin•ad'vert•ent•ly, *adv.*

in•al•ien•a•ble /ɪnˈeylyənəbl, -ˈeyliyə-/ *adj.* that cannot be taken away: *inalienable rights.*

in•ane /ɪˈneyn/ *adj.* lacking sense; silly: *inane questions.*

in•an•i•mate /ɪnˈænəmɪt/ *adj.* not living: *A stone is an inanimate object.*

in•ap•pli•ca•ble /ɪnˈæplɪkəbl, ˌɪnəˈplɪkəbl/ *adj.* unable to be used: *Your idea is exciting but inapplicable.*

in•ap•pro•pri•ate /ˌɪnəˈprowpriyɪt/ *adj.* not suitable or correct.

in•ar•tic•u•late /ˌɪnɑrˈtɪkyəlɪt/ *adj.* **1.** lacking the ability to express oneself clearly. **2.** unclear in expression: *inarticulate speech.*

in•as•much as /ˌɪnəzˈmʌtʃ əz, ˌæz/ *conj.* **1.** in view of the fact that; since. **2.** to the extent that: *She'll help us, inasmuch as she is able.*

in•aud•i•ble /ɪnˈɔdəbl/ *adj.* that cannot be heard. —**in'au•dib•ly,** *adv.*

in•au•gu•ral /ɪnˈɔgyərəl, -gərəl/ *adj.* [*before a noun*] of or relating to an inauguration: *the President's inaugural address.*

in•au•gu•rate /ɪnˈɔgyə,reyt, -gə-/ *v.* [~ + *obj*], **-rat•ed, -rat•ing.** **1.** to put (a new official) into office with formal ceremonies: *The President was inaugurated in January.* **2.** to open or begin to use formally: *to inaugurate a new bridge.* **3.** to introduce or cause to begin: *Airmail service was inaugurated in 1918.* —**in•au•gu•ra•tion** /ɪn,ɔgyəˈreyʃən, -gə-/, *n.* [*noncount*] [*count*]

in•born /ˈɪnˈbɔrn/ *adj.* naturally present at birth: *the inborn ability to learn.*

in•bound /ˈɪnˈbawnd/ *adj.* inward bound: *inbound ships.*

in•bred /ˈɪnˈbrɛd/ *adj.* **1.** inborn: *an inbred talent.* **2.** resulting from or involved in inbreeding.

in•breed•ing /ˈɪn,briydɪŋ/ *n.* [*noncount*] the breeding or mating of closely related people or animals.

inc., an abbreviation of: incorporated.

in•ca•pa•ble /ɪnˈkeypəbl/ *adj.* [*be* ~ + *of*] not able to do something: *incapable of harming anyone.* —**in•ca•pa•bil•i•ty** /ɪn,keypəˈbɪlɪtiy/, *n.* [*noncount*]

in•ca•pac•i•tate /ˌɪnkəˈpæsɪ,teyt/ *v.* [~ + *obj*], **-tat•ed, -tat•ing.** to make unable to do something: *He was incapacitated as a result of his accident.*

in•ca•pac•i•ty /ˌɪnkəˈpæsɪtiy/ *n.* [*noncount*] lack of skill or power.

in•car•cer•ate /ɪnˈkɑrsə,reyt/ *v.* [~ + *obj*], **-at•ed, -at•ing.** to put in prison. —**in,car•cer'a•tion,** *n.* [*noncount*]

in•car•na•tion /ˌɪnkɑrˈneyʃən/ *n.* **1.** [*count; usually singular; usually: the* + ~] a person or thing that is a good example of a given quality. **2.** [*count*] the state of being given a bodily form.

in•cen•di•ar•y /ɪnˈsɛndiy,ɛriy/ *adj.* [*before a noun*] **1.** used for setting property on fire: *incendiary bombs.* **2.** causing anger or violence: *incendiary speeches.*

in•cense¹ /ˈɪnsɛns/ *n.* [*noncount*] a substance producing a sweet odor when burned.

in•cense² /ɪnˈsɛns/ *v.* [~ + *obj*], **-censed, -cens•ing.** to make angry.

in•cen•tive /ɪnˈsɛntɪv/ *n.* something that urges someone on: [*noncount*]: *She had very little incentive to work.* [*count*]: *The government gave incentives to the farmers.*

in•ces•sant /ɪnˈsɛsənt/ *adj.* not ending: *incessant noise.* —**in'ces•sant•ly,** *adv.*

in•cest /ˈɪnsɛst/ *n.* [*noncount*] sexual relations between persons so closely related that they are forbidden to marry. —**in'ces•tu•ous** /ɪnˈsɛstʃuwəs/, *adj.*

inch /ɪntʃ/ *n.* [*count*] **1.** a unit of length, ¹/₁₂ of a foot or 2.54 centimeters. —*v.* **2.** to move by small degrees: [*no obj*]: *We inched slowly through the traffic.* [~ + *obj*]: *We inched our way along.* —**Idiom.** **3. every inch,** completely: *She's every inch a lady.* **4. within an inch of,** very close to: *We came within an inch of being drowned.*

in•ci•dence /ˈɪnsɪdəns/ *n.* [*count; usually singu-*

lar] the rate or range of happening of something: *a high incidence of flu.*

in•ci•dent /'ɪnsɪdənt/ *n.* [*count*] an event: *an unpleasant incident at the office.*

in•ci•den•tal /ˌɪnsɪ'dɛntļ/ *adj.* happening in connection with something more important: *incidental expenses.*

in•ci•den•tal•ly /ˌɪnsɪ'dɛntļiy -'dɛntļiy/ *adv.* apart or aside from the main subject; by the way.

in•cin•er•ate /ɪn'sɪnəˌreyt/ *v.* [~ + *obj*], **-at•ed, -at•ing.** to burn to ashes: *He incinerated the rubbish.* —**in•cin•er•a•tion** /ɪnˌsɪnə'reyʃən/, *n.* [*noncount*]

in•cin•er•a•tor /ɪn'sɪnəˌreytər/ *n.* [*count*] a furnace or device for burning materials.

in•cip•i•ent /ɪn'sɪpiyənt/ *adj.* [*before a noun*] just beginning: *an incipient cold.*

in•ci•sion /ɪn'sɪʒən/ *n.* [*count*] **1.** a cut. **2.** a surgical cut into tissue.

in•ci•sive /ɪn'saysɪv/ *adj.* clear and direct; keen: *an incisive criticism.* —**in•ci•sive•ly,** *adv.* —**in•ci•sive•ness,** *n.* [*noncount*]

in•ci•sor /ɪn'sayzər/ *n.* [*count*] any of the four front teeth, used for cutting.

in•cite /ɪn'sayt/ *v.* [~ + *obj*], **-cit•ed, -cit•ing. 1.** to encourage: *The union incited the workers to strike.* **2.** to cause: *They were put in jail for inciting a riot.* —**in•cite•ment,** *n.* [*noncount*] [*count*]

in•clem•ent /ɪn'klɛmənt/ *adj.* stormy; bad: *inclement weather.*

in•cli•na•tion /ˌɪnklə'neyʃən/ *n.* [*count*] **1.** a special liking for something: *no inclination to travel.* **2.** a movement downward. **3.** a slope.

in•cline /v. ɪn'klayn;n. 'ɪnklayn, ɪn'klayn/ *v.,* **-clined, -clin•ing,** *n.* —*v.* **1.** [*no obj*] [~ + *obj*] to (cause to) lean or slope. **2.** [~ + *obj*] to bend (the head or body) forward. **3.** [*no obj*] to have a tendency or preference: *She inclines toward cheerfulness.* —*n.* [*count*] **4.** a slope.

in•clined /ɪn'klaynd/ *adj.* **1.** [*be* + ~ + *to* + *verb*] wanting to: *I'm inclined to believe you.* **2.** [*be* + ~ + *to* + *verb*] likely; having a tendency: *She's inclined to be very active.* **3.** [*be* + *adverb* + ~] naturally skilled: *He's athletically inclined.* **4.** sloping: *an inclined roof.*

in•clude /ɪn'kluwd/ *v.* [~ + *obj*], **-clud•ed, -clud•ing. 1.** to contain or have as part of a whole: *The meal includes dessert and coffee.* **2.** to put in with something else: *Include us in your plans.* —**in•clu•sion** /ɪn'kluwʒən/, *n.* [*noncount*]

in•clud•ed /ɪn'kluwdɪd/ *adj.* [*after a noun*] being part of the whole; including: *It costs $100, tax included.*

in•clud•ing /ɪn'kluwdɪŋ/ *prep.* having as part of a whole; containing: *It costs $50, including tax.*

in•clu•sive /ɪn'kluwsɪv/ *adj.* including everything: *an inclusive fee.*

in•cog•ni•to /ˌɪnkɒg'niytow, ɪn'kɒgniˌtow/ *adj., adv.* with one's identity hidden: *traveling incognito.*

in•co•her•ent /ˌɪnkow'hɪərənt, -'hɛr-/ *adj.* not organized; unclear: *incoherent thoughts.* —**in•co'her•ence,** *n.* [*noncount*] —**in•co'her•ent•ly,** *adv.*

in•come /'ɪnkʌm/ *n.* payment received for goods or for services, or from rents or investments: [*count*]: *an annual income of $25,000.* [*noncount*]: *low income.*

'income ˌtax, *n.* [*noncount*] [*count*] a tax on one's income.

in•com•ing /'ɪnˌkʌmɪŋ/ *adj.* [*before a noun*] **1.**

coming in: *the incoming tide; incoming mail.* **2.** about to take office: *the incoming mayor.*

in•com•pa•ra•ble /ɪn'kɒmpərəbəl, -prəbəl/ *adj.* too good or fine for comparison: *incomparable beauty.*

in•com•pat•i•ble /ˌɪnkəm'pætəbəl/ *adj.* **1.** unable to exist together in harmony: *incompatible roommates.* **2.** unable to be used with another: *That computer is incompatible with mine.* —**in•com•pat•i•bil•i•ty** /ˌɪnkəmˌpætə'bɪlɪtiy/, *n.* [*noncount*]

in•com•pe•tent /ɪn'kɒmpɪtənt/ *adj.* lacking ability; incapable: *She's incompetent to do the work.* —**in'com•pet•ence,** *n.* [*noncount*] —**in'com•pe•tent•ly,** *adv.*

in•com•plete /ˌɪnkəm'pliyt/ *adj.* lacking some part; not complete.

in•com•pre•hen•si•ble /ˌɪnkɒmprɪ'hɛnsəbəl, ɪnˌkɒm-/ *adj.* impossible to understand.

in•con•ceiv•a•ble /ˌɪnkən'siyvəbəl/ *adj.* impossible to imagine or believe. —**ˌin•con'ceiv•ab•ly,** *adv.*

in•con•clu•sive /ˌɪnkən'kluwsɪv/ *adj.* not proving something beyond doubt: *The results of the tests were inconclusive.*

in•con•gru•ous /ɪn'kɒŋgruwəs/ *adj.* out of place; inappropriate. —**in•con•gru•i•ty** /ˌɪnkən'gruwɪtiy/, *n.* [*noncount*] [*count*] —**in'con•gru•ous•ly,** *adv.*

in•con•sid•er•ate /ˌɪnkən'sɪdərɪt/ *adj.* not thinking of other people's feelings. —**ˌin•con'sid•er•ate•ly,** *adv.*

in•con•sist•ent /ˌɪnkən'sɪstənt/ *adj.* **1.** not in agreement with something. **2.** changeable. —**ˌin•con'sist•en•cy,** *n.* [*noncount*] [*count*] —**ˌin•con'sist•ent•ly,** *adv.*

in•con•sol•a•ble /ˌɪnkən'sowləbəl/ *adj.* not to be comforted: *She was inconsolable after his death.*

in•con•spic•u•ous /ˌɪnkən'spɪkyuwəs/ *adj.* not easily seen or noticed. —**ˌin•con'spic•u•ous•ly,** *adv.*

in•con•ti•nent /ɪn'kɒntṇənt/ *adj.* unable to control a bodily discharge, as of urine. —**in'con•ti•nence,** *n.* [*noncount*]

in•con•ven•ience /ˌɪnkən'viynyəns/ *n., v.,* **-ienced, -ienc•ing.** —*n.* **1.** [*noncount*] lack of comfort or ease. **2.** [*count*] trouble or annoyance. —*v.* [~ + *obj*] **3.** to cause inconvenience to.

in•con•ven•ient /ˌɪnkən'viynyənt/ *adj.* causing inconvenience. —**ˌin•con'ven•ient•ly,** *adv.*

in•cor•po•rate /ɪn'kɔrpəˌreyt/ *v.,* **-rat•ed, -rat•ing. 1.** [*no obj*] [~ + *obj*] to form (into) a corporation. **2.** [~ + *obj*] to include as a part: *His book incorporates his earlier work.* —**in•cor•po'ra•tion,** *n.* [*noncount*]

in•cor•po•rat•ed /ɪn'kɔrpəˌreytɪd/ *adj.* formed into a legal corporation: *an incorporated business.* [*after a noun*]: usually part of the name of the corporation, in abbreviated form: *Whitehall Industries, Inc.*

in•cor•rect /ˌɪnkə'rɛkt/ *adj.* not correct; wrong: *an incorrect answer; incorrect English.* —**ˌin•cor'rect•ly,** *adv.*

in•crease /v.ɪn'kriys; n. 'ɪnkriys/ *v.,* **-creased, -creas•ing,** *n.* —*v.* **1.** to (cause to) become greater: [*no obj*]: *Her knowledge increased daily.* [~ + *obj*]: *He wanted to increase his knowledge of business.* —*n.* **2.** [*noncount*] growth in size, strength, or quality: *The economy is on the increase.* **3.** [*count*] an amount by which something is increased: *an increase of 12%.* —**in'creased,** *adj.*: *increased output.*

in•creas•ing /ɪnˈkriysɪŋ/ adj. [often: before a noun] growing larger or greater: the increasing use of computers in the schools. —**in'creas•ing•ly**, adv.: increasingly difficult.

in•cred•i•ble /ɪnˈkrɛdəbəl/ adj. **1.** impossible or hard to believe: incredible distances between the stars. **2.** very surprising; amazing: incredible skill. —**in'cred•i•bly**, adv.: incredibly huge.

in•cred•u•lous /ɪnˈkrɛdʒələs/ adj. not believing; showing doubt: He's incredulous about the claims of budget cuts. —**in•cre•du•li•ty** /ɪnˌkrɪˈduwlɪtiy, -ˈdyuw- /, n. [noncount] —**in'cred•u•lous•ly**, adv.

in•cre•ment /ˈɪnkrəmənt, ˈɪŋ-/ [count] **1.** something added or gained, as in money or value. **2.** one of a series of regular additions: bank deposits in increments of $500.

in•crim•i•nate /ɪnˈkrɪməˌneyt/ v. [~ + obj], -nat•ed, -nat•ing. to make (someone) seem guilty of a crime. —**in'crim•i,nat•ing**, adj.: incriminating evidence.

in•cu•bate /ˈɪnkyəˌbeyt, ˈɪŋ-/ v., -bat•ed, -bat•ing. **1.** [~ + obj] to sit on (eggs) for hatching: The bird incubated its eggs. **2.** [~ + obj] [no obj] to (cause eggs to) hatch, as by artificial heat. **3.** [~ + obj] to develop: to incubate an idea. —**in•cu•ba•tion** /ˌɪnkyəˈbeyʃən, ˌɪŋ-/, n. [noncount]

in•cu•ba•tor /ˈɪnkyəˌbeytər, ˈɪŋ-/ n. [count] **1.** an artificially heated apparatus for incubation. **2.** an apparatus for the care of very small or sick babies.

in•cum•bent /ɪnˈkʌmbənt/ adj. **1.** currently holding an office: the incumbent president. **2.** [be + ~ + upon/on] morally necessary: a duty that was incumbent upon me. —n. [count] **3.** the holder of an office. —**in'cum•ben•cy**, n. [noncount] [count]

in•cur /ɪnˈkɜr/ v. [~ + obj], -curred, -cur•ring. **1.** to become liable for: to incur debts. **2.** to bring upon oneself: We incurred her displeasure.

in•cur•a•ble /ɪnˈkyʊrəbəl/ adj. **1.** not curable: an incurable disease. **2.** not likely to change: incurable pessimism. —**in'cur•a•bly**, adv.: incurably optimistic.

in•cur•sion /ɪnˈkɜrʒən, -ʃən/ n. [count] a sudden attack on or entrance into a place that belongs to other people.

Ind., an abbreviation of: Indiana.

in•debt•ed /ɪnˈdɛtɪd/ adj. **1.** [be + ~ + to] owing money; in debt: He is indebted to the bank. **2.** very grateful: He feels indebted to his teachers.

in•de•cent /ɪnˈdiysənt/ adj. offending standards of what is right or proper, esp. in matters dealing with sex: an indecent joke. —**in'de•cen•cy**, n. [noncount] [count] —**in'de•cent•ly**, adv.

in•de•ci•sion /ˌɪndɪˈsɪʒən/ n. [noncount] lack of ability to decide.

in•de•ci•sive /ˌɪndɪˈsaysɪv/ adj. **1.** unable to decide: She's indecisive about what to do next. **2.** not clear as to result: an indecisive battle. —**in•de'ci•sive•ness**, n. [noncount]

in•deed /ɪnˈdiyd/ adv. **1.** really; truly: It did indeed rain. **2.** (used after very to show emphasis): very good indeed. —interj. **3.** (used to show surprise or disbelief): That's a fine excuse indeed.

in•de•fen•si•ble /ˌɪndɪˈfɛnsəbəl/ adj. not capable of being defended or excused: indefensible behavior.

in•de•fin•a•ble /ˌɪndɪˈfaynəbəl/ adj. not easily described: The music had an indefinable quality.

in•def•i•nite /ɪnˈdɛfənɪt/ adj. **1.** having no

fixed limit: an indefinite number of days. **2.** not clear; uncertain: Our plans are still indefinite. —**in'def•i•nite•ly**, adv.

in'definite 'article, n. [count] either of the articles a or an.

in•del•i•ble /ɪnˈdɛləbəl/ adj. not removable: indelible stains. —**in'del•i•bly**, adv.

in•dem•ni•ty /ɪnˈdɛmnɪtiy/ n., pl. -ties. **1.** [noncount] protection against damage or loss. **2.** [count] money as payment for loss.

in•dent /ɪnˈdɛnt/ v. to set in from the margin: [~ + obj]: Indent the first line of a paragraph. [no obj]: You forgot to indent. —,in•den'ta•tion, n. [count]

Inde'pendence 'Day, n. July 4, a U.S. holiday celebrating the adoption of the Declaration of Independence in 1776.

in•de•pend•ent /ˌɪndɪˈpɛndənt/ adj. **1.** not ruled by another country; self-governing. **2.** not influenced or controlled by others: an independent inquiry. **3.** not depending upon something or someone else: a decision independent of the facts; independent of her parents. **4.** not belonging to a political party: independent voters. —n. [count; sometimes: Independent] **5.** a person who does not belong to a particular political party. —,in•de'pend•ence, n. [noncount] —,in•de'pend•ent•ly, adv.: He worked independently.

'in-'depth, adj. thorough: an in-depth study.

in•de•scrib•a•ble /ˌɪndɪˈskraybəbəl/ adj. being beyond description: indescribable joy. —,in•de'scrib•a•bly, adv.

in•de•struct•i•ble /ˌɪndɪˈstrʌktəbəl/ adj. that cannot be destroyed. —,in•de'struct•i•bly, adv.

in•dex /ˈɪndɛks/ n., pl. -dex•es, -di•ces /-dəˌsiyz/, v. —n. [count] **1.** an alphabetical list at the back of a book, of names and subjects with their page numbers. **2.** an ordered arrangement of material, as in a library card catalog. **3.** a number used to measure change in prices, wages, etc.: the cost-of-living index. —v. [~ + obj] **4.** to provide with or enter in an index. —'in•dex•er, n. [count]

'index ,finger, n. FOREFINGER.

In•di•an /ˈɪndiyən/ n. [count] **1.** Also called **Native American**. a member of any of the original peoples of North and South America. **2.** a person born or living in India. —adj. **3.** of or relating to American Indians, or to any of the languages spoken by them. **4.** of or relating to India.

'Indian ,corn, n. [noncount] **1.** CORN¹ (def. 1). **2.** any corn with kernels of different colors.

'Indian 'summer, n. [noncount] [count] a period of mild, dry weather in late autumn.

in•di•cate /ˈɪndɪˌkeyt/ v. [~ + obj], -cat•ed, -cat•ing. **1.** to be a sign of; show: A fever indicates that a person is ill. **2.** to point out or point to: to indicate a place on a map. —**in•di•ca•tion** /ˌɪndɪˈkeyʃən/ n. [count]: Fever is an indication of illness. [noncount]: They gave no indication of their willingness to help.

in•dic•a•tive /ɪnˈdɪkətɪv/ adj. [be + ~ (+ of)] **1.** showing or suggesting: Her smile was indicative of her approval. **2.** of or naming the grammatical mood used for ordinary statements and questions, as the mood of the verb plays in She plays tennis. —n. [count; usually singular; usually: the + ~] **3.** the indicative mood; a verb in this mood: The verb was is in the indicative in the sentence: He was at home.

in•di•ca•tor /ˈɪndɪˌkeytər/ n. [count] **1.** a pointing device, as a needle on the dial of a measuring

I

instrument. **2.** a light on a car that flashes to show which way the car will turn.

in•dict /ɪn'daɪt/ v. [~ + obj] **1.** to charge formally with a crime: *The state indicted him for murder.* **2.** to accuse of wrongdoing, etc.: *He indicted the administration as being unsympathetic to the needs of the cities.* —**in'dict•a•ble,** adj.

in•dict•ment /ɪn'daɪtmənt/ n. a formal charge of a crime: [count]: *The judge handed down an indictment.* [noncount]: *The criminal is now under indictment.*

in•dif•fer•ence /ɪn'dɪfərəns/ n. [noncount] lack of interest or concern. —**in'dif•fer•ent,** adj. —**in'dif•fer•ent•ly,** adv.

in•dig•e•nous /ɪn'dɪdʒənəs/ adj. coming from a particular area or country: *the indigenous peoples of southern Africa.* [be + ~ + to]: *plants that are indigenous to Canada.*

in•di•gest•i•ble /ˌɪndɪ'dʒɛstəbəl, -daɪ-/ adj. not easily digested.

in•di•ges•tion /ˌɪndɪ'dʒɛstʃən, -daɪ-/ n. [noncount] discomfort from difficulty in digesting food.

in•dig•nant /ɪn'dɪgnənt/ adj. showing anger, esp. at something unfair or offensive. —**in'dig•nant•ly,** adv. —**ˌin•dig'na•tion,** n. [noncount]

in•dig•ni•ty /ɪn'dɪgnɪtiy/ n. [noncount] [count], pl. **-ties.** an injury or insult causing shame or loss of self-respect.

in•di•rect /ˌɪndə'rɛkt, -daɪ-/ adj. **1.** not following a straight line: *an indirect route.* **2.** not going straight to the point: *indirect answers.* **3.** not directly connected: *indirect evidence.* —**ˌin•di'rect•ly,** adv. —**ˌin•di'rect•ness,** n. [noncount]

'indirect 'object, n. [count] a word or group of words representing the person or thing to which or for which the action of a verb is performed: *In the sentence* She gave the boy the book, *the noun* boy *is the indirect object.*

'indirect 'tax, n. [count] a tax on something that is included as part of the market price.

in•dis•creet /ˌɪndɪ'skriyt/ adj. lacking good judgment about what one says or does. —**ˌin•dis'creet•ly,** adv.

in•dis•cre•tion /ˌɪndɪ'skrɛʃən/ n. **1.** [noncount] lack of good judgment: *indiscretion in dealing with people.* **2.** [count] an indiscreet act, remark, etc.

in•dis•crim•i•nate /ˌɪndɪ'skrɪmənɪt/ adj. lacking in care or judgment: *an indiscriminate buyer.* —**ˌin•dis'crim•i•nate•ly,** adv.

in•dis•pen•sa•ble /ˌɪndɪ'spɛnsəbəl/ adj. completely necessary.

in•dis•posed /ˌɪndɪ'spowzd/ adj. **1.** [be + ~] slightly sick or ill. **2.** [~ + to + verb] not willing (to do something). —**in•dis•po•si•tion** /ˌɪndɪspə'zɪʃən/, n. [noncount]

in•dis•put•a•ble /ˌɪndɪ'spyuwtəbəl, ɪn'dɪspyə-/ adj. that cannot be questioned or denied: *indisputable evidence.* —**ˌin•dis'put•a•bly,** adv.

in•dis•tinct /ˌɪndɪ'stɪŋkt/ adj. not clear to the mind or the senses: *indistinct markings.* —**ˌin•dis'tinct•ly,** adv.

in•dis•tin•guish•a•ble adj. that cannot be recognized as different.

in•di•vid•u•al /ˌɪndə'vɪdʒuwəl/ n. [count] **1.** a single human being. **2.** a person: *He's a friendly individual.* —adj. [before a noun] **3.** single; particular; separate. **4.** of or for one person. —**ˌin•di'vid•u•al•ly,** adv.

in•di•vid•u•al•i•ty /ˌɪndə,vɪdʒuw'ælɪtiy/ n. [noncount] the qualities that make one person or thing different from others.

in•di•vis•i•ble /ˌɪndə'vɪzəbəl/ adj. that cannot be divided or separated.

in•doc•tri•nate /ɪn'dɒktrə,neyt/ v. [~ + obj], **-nat•ed, -nat•ing.** to instruct (someone) in a fixed set of beliefs. —**in•doc•tri•na•tion** /ɪn,dɒktrə'neyʃən/, n. [noncount]

in•do•lent /'ɪndələnt/ adj. lazy. —**'in•do•lence,** n. [noncount] —**'in•do•lent•ly,** adv.

in•dom•i•ta•ble /ɪn'dɒmɪtəbəl/ adj. that cannot be easily discouraged: *an indomitable fighter.* —**in'dom•i•ta•bly,** adv.

In•do•ne•sian /ˌɪndə'niyʒən, -ʃən/ n. **1.** [count] a person born or living in Indonesia. **2.** [noncount] the language spoken by many of the people in Indonesia. —adj. **3.** of or relating to Indonesia. **4.** of or relating to the language spoken by many of the people in Indonesia.

in•door /'ɪn,dɔr/ adj. located, used, or done inside a building.

in•doors /ɪn'dɔrz/ adv. in or into a building: *Let's go indoors.*

in•duce /ɪn'duws, -'dyuws/ v. [~ + obj], **-duced, -duc•ing. 1.** to persuade: *See if you can induce him to stay.* **2.** to cause: *to induce sleep.* —**in'duce•ment,** n. [count] [noncount]

in•duc•tion /ɪn'dʌkʃən/ n. **1.** [noncount] [count] formal introduction of a person to a new job, organization, etc. **2.** [noncount] a process of reasoning in which individual facts are used to arrive at a general statement or conclusion. —**in'duc•tive,** adj.: *inductive reasoning.*

in•dulge /ɪn'dʌldʒ/ v., **-dulged, -dulg•ing. 1.** [no obj] to allow oneself to enjoy something: *He indulged in a nap.* **2.** [~ + obj] to give in to the wishes of: *He indulges his children.* **3.** [~ + obj] to fulfill: *She indulged her passion for dancing.*

in•dul•gence /ɪn'dʌldʒəns/ n. **1.** [noncount] the act or practice of indulging. **2.** [count] something indulged in: *Rich desserts are an indulgence.* —**in'dul•gent,** adj.: *an indulgent parent.*

in•dus•tri•al /ɪn'dʌstriyəl/ adj. [before a noun] **1.** of or relating to industry: *industrial pollution.* **2.** having many industries; industrialized: *a well-developed, industrial country.*

in•dus•tri•al•ist /ɪn'dʌstriyəlɪst/ n. [count] the owner of a factory or large industrial company.

in•dus•tri•al•ize /ɪn'dʌstriyə,layz/ v. [~ + obj], **-ized, -iz•ing.** to develop (an area or country) with many industries. —**in•dus•tri•al•i•za•tion** /ɪn,dʌstriyəlɪ'zeyʃən/, n. [noncount]

in'dustrial-'strength, adj. [usually: before a noun] unusually strong or effective: *industrial-strength soap.*

in•dus•tri•ous /ɪn'dʌstriyəs/ adj. hard-working: *an industrious student.* —**in'dus•tri•ous•ly,** adv. —**in'dus•tri•ous•ness,** n. [noncount]

in•dus•try /'ɪndəstriy/ n., pl. **-tries. 1.** [count] the group of manufacturing businesses in a particular field: *the steel industry.* **2.** [count] any general business activity: *the tourist industry.* **3.** [noncount] energetic activity at a task.

-ine[1], an adjective suffix meaning: of or characteristic of (*Alpine*); made of or like (*crystalline*).

-ine[2], a noun suffix indicating a chemical substance or element (*caffeine; chlorine*).

in•e•bri•at•ed /ɪn'iybriy,eytɪd/ adj. drunk. —**in•e•bri•a•tion** /ɪn,iybriy'eyʃən/, n. [noncount]

in•ed•i•ble /ɪn'ɛdəbəl/ adj. not fit to be eaten.

in•ef•fec•tive /ˌɪnɪ'fɛktɪv/ adj. **1.** not effective: *an ineffective air conditioner.* **2.** inefficient or incompetent: *an ineffective manager.*

in•ef•fec•tu•al /ˌɪnɪ'fɛktʃuwəl/ *adj.* producing no satisfactory results: *an ineffectual effort.*

in•ef•fi•cient /ˌɪnɪ'fɪʃənt/ *adj.* not efficient: *an old, inefficient heating system.* —ˌin•ef'fi•cien•cy, *n.* [*count*], *pl.* -cies. —ˌin•ef'fi•cient•ly, *adv.*

in•el•i•gi•ble /ɪn'ɛlɪdʒəbəl/ *adj.* not having the right qualifications: *ineligible for citizenship.* —in•el•i•gi•bil•i•ty /ɪn,ɛlɪdʒə'bɪlɪtiy/, *n.* [*noncount*]

in•ept /ɪn'ɛpt/ *adj.* lacking skill or ability; incompetent: *inept handling of the problem.* —in•ept•i•tude, *n.* [*noncount*] —in'ept•ly, *adv.* —in'ept•ness, *n.* [*noncount*]

in•e•qual•i•ty /ˌɪnɪ'kwɒlɪtiy/ *n.,* *pl.* -ties. 1. [*noncount*] the condition of not being equal. 2. [*count*] an instance of not being equal: *the many inequalities women face in business.*

in•ert /ɪn'ɜrt/ *adj.* 1. having no power of action: *inert matter.* 2. (of chemical substances) having little or no ability to react: *Nitrogen is an inert gas.* 3. slow to think or move.

in•er•tia /ɪn'ɜrʃə/ *n.* [*noncount*] 1. a desire to remain still. 2. the property of matter by which it keeps still or moving so long as it is not acted upon by an outside force: *to overcome the inertia of such a huge mass.*

in•es•cap•a•ble /ˌɪnə'skeypəbəl/ *adj.* that cannot be avoided. —ˌin•es'cap•a•bly, *adv.*

in•ev•i•ta•ble /ɪn'ɛvɪtəbəl/ *adj.* 1. unable to be avoided; certain to happen: *It was inevitable that we would lose.* 2. usual and expected: *smoking his inevitable cigarette.* —in•ev•i•ta•bil•i•ty /ɪn,ɛvɪtə'bɪlɪtiy/, *n.* [*noncount*]: *the inevitability of death.* —in'ev•i•ta•bly, *adv.*: *She is inevitably late.*

in•ex•cus•a•ble /ˌɪnɪk'skyuwzəbəl/ *adj.* that may not be excused: *inexcusable behavior.* —ˌin•ex'cus•a•bly, *adv.*

in•ex•haust•i•ble /ˌɪnɪg'zɔstəbəl/ *adj.* 1. that cannot be used up: *an inexhaustible supply of energy.* 2. not tiring easily: *an inexhaustible runner.* —ˌin•ex'haust•i•bly, *adv.*

in•ex•o•ra•ble /ɪn'ɛksərəbəl/ *adj.* 1. not able to be changed: *the inexorable passage of time.* 2. not to be affected by requests; merciless: *The judge was inexorable and passed the maximum sentence.* —in'ex•o•ra•bly, *adv.*

in•ex•pen•sive /ˌɪnɪk'spɛnsɪv/ *adj.* not high in price.

in•ex•pe•ri•ence /ˌɪnɪk'spɪəriyəns/ *n.* [*noncount*] lack of experience. —ˌin•ex'pe•ri•enced, *adj.*

in•ex•pli•ca•ble /ɪn'ɛksplɪkəbəl, ˌɪnɪk'splɪkə-/ *adj.* incapable of being explained: *an inexplicable delay.* —in'ex•pli•ca•bly, *adv.*: *inexplicably delayed.*

in•ex•press•i•ble /ˌɪnɪk'sprɛsəbəl/ *adj.* that cannot be described in words: *inexpressible joy.*

in•ex•tri•ca•ble /ɪn'ɛkstrɪkəbəl, ˌɪnɪk'strɪkə-/ *adj.* that cannot be escaped from, untied, or solved. —in'ex•tri•ca•bly, *adv.*

in•fal•li•ble /ɪn'fæləbəl/ *adj.* 1. never failing; certain: *an infallible remedy for a cold.* 2. never wrong: *He thought he was infallible.* —in•fal•li•bil•i•ty /ɪn,fælə'bɪlɪtiy/, *n.* [*noncount*] —in'fal•li•bly, *adv.*

in•fa•mous /'ɪnfəməs/ *adj.* having or deserving of an evil reputation.

in•fa•my /'ɪnfəmiy/ *n.,* *pl.* -mies. 1. [*noncount*] evil reputation; dishonor. 2. [*noncount*] great wickedness. 3. [*count*] an evil act.

in•fan•cy /'ɪnfənsiy/ *n.* [*noncount*] 1. the state

or period of being a baby. 2. a very early stage: *Space science is still in its infancy.*

in•fant /'ɪnfənt/ *n.* [*count*] 1. a baby. —*adj.* [*before a noun*] 2. of or relating to infants or infancy: *an infant car seat.*

in•fan•tile /'ɪnfən,tayl, -tɪl/ *adj.* 1. characteristic of or behaving like an infant; childish. 2. of infants or infancy.

in•fan•try /'ɪnfəntriy/ *n.,* *pl.* -tries. [*noncount*] [*count*] soldiers or military units that fight on foot. —'in•fan•try•man, *n.* [*count*], *pl.* -men.

in•fat•u•ated /ɪn'fætʃuw,eytɪd/ *adj.* having a foolish or unreasonable love for someone. —in•fat•u•a•tion, *n.* [*noncount*] [*count*]

in•fect /ɪn'fɛkt/ *v.* [~ + *obj*] 1. to give a disease to, as by means of bacteria. 2. to influence the mind or feelings of: *His courage infected the other soldiers.*

in•fec•tion /ɪn'fɛkʃən/ *n.* 1. [*noncount*] the state of being infected. 2. [*count*] an infectious disease: *an ear infection.*

in•fec•tious /ɪn'fɛkʃəs/ *adj.* 1. (of a disease) spread by infection, as from one person to another. 2. spreading quickly: *infectious laughter.*

in•fer /ɪn'fɜr/ *v.* [~ + *obj*] -ferred, -fer•ring. to come to believe by reasoning: *From the tone of his voice I inferred that he was angry.* —'in•fer•ence, *n.* [*count*] [*noncount*]

in•fe•ri•or /ɪn'fɪəriyər/ *adj.* 1. low or lower in quality, importance, or value: *He felt inferior to his co-workers.* 2. poor in quality: *inferior goods.* —*n.* [*count*] 3. an inferior person. —in•fe•ri•or•i•ty /ɪn,fɪəriy'ɔrɪtiy, -'ɒr-/, *n.* [*noncount*]

in•fer•nal /ɪn'fɜrnl/ *adj.* 1. very bad: *infernal wickedness.* 2. of hell. 3. very annoying: *infernal noise.*

in•fer•no /ɪn'fɜrnow/ *n.* [*count*], *pl.* -nos. 1. hell. 2. a place or state of great heat, flames, etc.

in•fer•tile /ɪn'fɜrtl/ *adj.* not fertile; barren: *infertile soil.* —in•fer•til•i•ty /ˌɪnfər'tɪlɪtiy/, *n.* [*noncount*]

in•fest /ɪn'fɛst/ *v.* [~ + *obj*] to live in or on in great numbers: *The mice infested the farmhouse. Our dog was infested with fleas.* —in•fes•ta•tion /ˌɪnfɛ'steyʃən/, *n.* [*count*] [*noncount*]

in•fi•del•i•ty /ˌɪnfɪ'dɛlɪtiy/ *n.* [*noncount*] [*count*], *pl.* -ties. disloyal or unfaithful behavior, esp. toward one's marriage partner.

in•fight•ing /'ɪn,faytɪŋ/ *n.* [*noncount*] 1. fighting at close range. 2. fighting between people closely associated: *political infighting.* —'in,fight•er, *n.* [*count*]

in•fil•trate /ɪn'fɪltreyt, 'ɪnfɪl,treyt/ *v.* [~ + *obj*] [*no obj*], -trat•ed, -trat•ing. to move into (an enemy country, etc.) secretly to do harm. —in•fil•tra•tion /ˌɪnfɪl'treyʃən/, *n.* [*noncount*] —in'fil,tra•tor, *n.* [*count*]

in•fi•nite /'ɪnfənɪt/ *adj.* 1. without limits or an end: *The universe seems infinite.* 2. very great: *infinite kindness.* —'in•fi•nite•ly, *adv.*: *It's infinitely easier to do it this way.*

in•fin•i•tes•i•mal /ˌɪnfɪnɪ'tɛsəməl/ *adj.* extremely small.

in•fin•i•tive /ɪn'fɪnɪtɪv/ *n.* [*count*] a simple form of a verb that is not inflected for person, number, or tense, and in English can be used with *to* and after other verbs, such as: *I need to eat; to sleep for eight hours.*

in•fin•i•ty /ɪn'fɪnɪtiy/ *n.* [*noncount*] endless space, time, distance, or amount.

in•firm /ɪn'fɜrm/ *adj.* feeble or weak esp. be-

I

cause of old age. —**in'fir•mi•ty,** *n.* [count] [non-count]

in•fir•ma•ry /ɪnˈfɜrməriy/ *n.* [count], *pl.* **-ries.** a place for the care of people who are infirm, sick, or injured.

in•flame /ɪnˈfleym/ *v.* [~ + *obj*], **-flamed, -flam•ing. 1.** to excite greatly: *The speaker inflamed the crowd with his angry words.* **2.** (of a bodily part) to affect with inflammation. —**in'flamed,** *adj.: eyes inflamed from crying.*

in•flam•ma•ble /ɪnˈflæməbəl/ *adj.* **1.** easily set on fire: *inflammable liquids.* **2.** easily excited, esp. to anger. —**in•flam•ma•bil•i•ty** /ɪnˌflæməˈbɪlɪtiy/, *n.* [noncount]

in•flam•ma•tion /ˌɪnfləˈmeyʃən/ *n.* [noncount] [count] redness, swelling, and fever in an area of the body, in reaction to an infection or injury.

in•flam•ma•to•ry /ɪnˈflæməˌtɔriy/ *adj.* likely to cause anger, violence, etc.: *inflammatory speeches.*

in•flate /ɪnˈfleyt/ *v.,* **-flat•ed, -flat•ing. 1.** [~ + *obj*] [no *obj*] (of tires, balloons, etc.) to (cause to) swell with air or gas. **2.** [~ + *obj*] to fill with too much pride: *The praise inflated her ego.* **3.** [~ + *obj*] to increase too much, such as the level of prices. —**in'flat•a•ble,** *adj.: an inflatable life raft.*

in•fla•tion /ɪnˈfleyʃən/ *n.* [noncount] **1.** the act or process of inflating. **2.** a steady rise in prices. —**in•fla•tion•ar•y** /ɪnˈfleyʃəˌneriy/, *adj.*

in•flect /ɪnˈflɛkt/ *v.* [~ + *obj*] **1.** to change (the pitch or the tone of the voice) in speaking. **2.** to change the form of a word by inflection.

in•flec•tion /ɪnˈflɛkʃən/ *n.* [noncount] **1.** change in the level of the voice in speaking. **2.** change in the form of a word to show a past tense, as *liked* from *like,* a plural, as *feet* from *foot,* etc. Also, *esp. Brit.,* **in'flex•ion.**

in•flex•i•ble /ɪnˈflɛksəbəl/ *adj.* **1.** that cannot be bent; stiff. **2.** (of people) not easily influenced; strong-willed. **3.** not changing; strict: *inflexible rules.* —**in•flex•i•bil•i•ty** /ɪnˌflɛksəˈbɪlɪtiy/, *n.* [noncount] —**in'flex•i•bly,** *adv.*

in•flict /ɪnˈflɪkt/ *v.* [~ + *obj*] to force (something unpleasant) on someone or something: *to inflict punishment (on a thief); The storm inflicted severe damage (on the crops).*

in•flu•ence /ˈɪnfluwəns/ *n., v.,* **-enced, -enc•ing.** —*n.* **1.** [noncount] the power to produce effects by indirect means: *the influence of religion in politics.* **2.** [count] a person or thing that has this power: *Is he a good influence on her behavior?* **3.** [noncount] the ability to persuade, or to obtain advantages from, someone: *Thanks to his uncle's influence, he was able to get a job.* —*v.* [~ + *obj*] **4.** to have an influence on.

in•flu•en•tial /ˌɪnfluwˈɛnʃəl/ *adj.* having great influence; powerful.

in•flu•en•za /ˌɪnfluwˈɛnzə/ *n.* [noncount] a serious, easily spread disease caused by different viruses and marked by coughing, fever, and muscle aches; the flu.

in•flux /ˈɪnflʌks/ *n.* [count] the arrival of people or things, esp. in large numbers: *an influx of tourists.*

in•fo /ˈɪnfow/ *n.* [noncount] *Informal.* information.

in•fo•mer•cial /ˌɪnfowˈmɜrʃəl/ *n.* [count] a very long television commercial that is made to seem as a regular program.

in•form /ɪnˈfɔrm/ *v.* **1.** [~ + *obj*] to give information to; tell: *We informed them of our arrival.* **2.** [~ + *on/against* + *obj*] to give information about someone, as to the police: *He informed on the other members of the gang.*

in•for•mal /ɪnˈfɔrməl/ *adj.* **1.** without formality; casual: *an informal visit.* **2.** not according to the official manner: *informal proceedings.* —**in'for•mal•ly,** *adv.: She dressed informally for the party.* —**in•for•mal•i•ty** /ˌɪnfɔrˈmælɪtiy/ *n.* [noncount] [count]

in•form•ant /ɪnˈfɔrmənt/ *n.* [count] a person who gives information, esp. secretly.

in•for•ma•tion /ˌɪnfɔrˈmeyʃən/ *n.* [noncount] facts or knowledge about something.

in•form•a•tive /ɪnˈfɔrmətɪv/ *adj.* giving information; educational. —**in'form•a•tive•ly,** *adv.*

informed *adj.* having or based on knowledge: *an informed choice.*

in•form•er /ɪnˈfɔrmər/ *n.* [count] one who gives information, esp. secretly, as to the police.

in•fra•red /ˌɪnfrəˈrɛd/ *n.* [noncount] **1.** light that is invisible, near the red end of the spectrum. —*adj.* **2.** of, relating to, or using infrared rays: *infrared radiation.* Compare ULTRAVIOLET.

in•fra•struc•ture /ˈɪnfrəˌstrʌktʃər/ *n.* [noncount] **1.** the basic structure of a system or organization. **2.** basic facilities, such as transportation and communication systems.

in•fre•quent /ɪnˈfriykwənt/ *adj.* not frequent; occasional: *infrequent visits; an infrequent visitor.* —**in'fre•quent•ly,** *adv.*

in•fringe /ɪnˈfrɪndʒ/ *v.,* **-fringed, -fring•ing. 1.** [~ + *obj*] to break (a law, rule, etc.). **2. infringe on** or **upon,** to break in on (another's rights): *They infringed on her privacy.* —**in'fringe•ment,** *n.* [count] [noncount]

in•fu•ri•ate /ɪnˈfyʊriyˌeyt/ *v.* [~ + *obj*], **-at•ed, -at•ing.** to make very angry. —**in'fu•ri,at•ed,** *adj.: infuriated passengers.* —**in'fu•ri,at•ing,** *adj.: an infuriating delay.* —**in'fu•ri,at•ing•ly,** *adv.*

in•fuse /ɪnˈfyuwz/ *v.* [~ + *obj*], **-fused, -fus•ing. 1.** to introduce, as if by pouring: *to infuse new life into industry.* **2.** to fill (someone) with a quality, feeling, etc.: *The coach infused the team with enthusiasm.* **3.** to soak (tea leaves, herbs, etc.) in hot water to obtain a drink. —**in•fu•sion** /ɪnˈfyuwʒən/, *n.* [count] [noncount]

-ing[1], a suffix meaning: an action or process (*building*); an instance or result of such action (*listing*); material used in an action (*padding*); something that performs or receives an action (*covering*).

-ing[2], a suffix forming the present participle of verbs (*thinking*). These participles are often used as adjectives: *warring factions.*

in•gen•ious /ɪnˈdʒiynyəs/ *adj.* clever and original: *an ingenious person; an ingenious invention.* —**in'gen•ious•ly,** *adv.*

in•ge•nu•i•ty /ˌɪndʒəˈnuwɪtiy, -ˈnyuw-/ *n.* [noncount] the quality of being ingenious: *a device of great ingenuity.*

in•gen•u•ous /ɪnˈdʒɛnyuwəs/ *adj.* simple and honest; without deceit. —**in'gen•u•ous•ly,** *adv.* —**in'gen•u•ous•ness,** *n.* [noncount]

in•gest /ɪnˈdʒɛst/ *v.* [~ + *obj*] to take into the body, as food or liquid. —**in•ges•tion** *n.* [noncount]

in•got /ˈɪŋgət/ *n.* [count] a mass of metal that is often shaped like a brick or bar: *a gold ingot.*

in•grained /ɪnˈgreynd, ˈɪnˌgreynd/ also **en•grained,** *adj.* deeply or firmly fixed: *an ingrained habit.*

in•gra•ti•ate /ɪnˈgreyʃiyˌeyt/ *v.* [~ + *oneself*], **-at•ed, -at•ing.** to make (oneself) favored by others, esp. by falsely acting pleasant: *He's trying to ingratiate himself with the boss.* —in'gra•ti,a•ting, *adj.*

in•grat•i•tude /ɪn'grætɪ,tuwd, -,tyuwd/ *n.* [*noncount*] lack of gratitude: *She showed her ingratitude by not thanking us.*

in•gre•di•ent /ɪn'griydiyənt/ *n.* [*count*] **1.** something that is an element of a mixture: *the ingredients of a cake.* **2.** an important part of anything: *the ingredients of a good marriage.*

in•hab•it /ɪn'hæbɪt/ *v.* [~ + *obj*] to live in (a place), as people or animals do. —in'hab•it•a•ble, *adj.*

in•hab•it•ant /ɪn'hæbɪtənt/ *n.* [*count*] a person or animal living in a place.

in•hale /ɪn'heyl/ *v.*, -haled, -hal•ing. to breathe in (smoke, air, etc.): [~ + *obj*]: *to inhale fresh air.* [*no obj*]: *She inhaled deeply on her cigarette.*

in•hal•er /ɪn'heylər/ *n.* [*count*] an apparatus or device used in inhaling medicine.

in•her•ent /ɪn'hɪərənt, -'hɛr-/ *adj.* existing as a permanent, natural part or quality of someone or something. —in'her•ent•ly, *adv.*: *inherently lazy.*

in•her•it /ɪn'hɛrɪt/ *v.* **1.** [~ + *obj*] [*no obj*] to receive (money,property, etc.) after the owner has died. **2.** [~ + *obj*] to receive (a genetic trait, quality, etc.) from a parent or ancestor: *She inherited her beauty from her grandmother.* —in'her•i•tor, *n.* [*count*]

in•her•it•ance /ɪn'hɛrɪtəns/ *n.* **1.** [*noncount*] the act of inheriting. **2.** [*count*] something that is inherited. **3.** [*noncount*] the receiving of a genetic trait, quality, etc.: *the inheritance of blue eyes.*

in•hib•it /ɪn'hɪbɪt/ *v.* [~ + *obj*] to hold back or keep from some action, feeling, etc.: *Her constant presence inhibits me.*

in•hib•it•ed /ɪn'hɪbɪtɪd/ *adj.* unable to feel at ease and behave naturally.

in•hi•bi•tion /,ɪnɪ'bɪʃən, ,ɪnhɪ-/ *n.* **1.** [*noncount*] the act of inhibiting; the state of being inhibited: *a life of inhibition.* **2.** [*count*] a feeling of being inhibited.

in•hu•man /ɪn'hyuwmən/ *adj.* lacking kindness and pity; cruel.

in•hu•mane /,ɪnhyuw'meyn/ *adj.* showing no kindness; cruel: *inhumane treatment of animals.* —,in•hu'mane•ly, *adv.*

in•hu•man•i•ty /,ɪnhyuw'mænɪtiy/ *n.* [*noncount*] the state or quality of being inhuman or inhumane; cruelty.

in•im•i•ta•ble /ɪ'nɪmɪtəbəl/ *adj.* too good to be equaled. —in'im•i•ta•bly, *adv.*

in•i•tial /ɪ'nɪʃəl/ *adj., n., v.*, -tialed, -tial•ing or (*esp. Brit.*) -tialled, -tial•ling. —*adj.* [*usually: before a noun*] **1.** of or at the beginning; first: *the initial step in a process.* —*n.* [*count*] **2.** the first letter of a word or name —*v.* [~ + *obj*] **3.** to mark or sign with one's initials. —in'i•tial•ly, *adv.*: *Initially they didn't like each other.*

in•i•ti•ate /v.ɪ'nɪʃiy,eyt; n. -ɪt, -,eyt/ *v.*, -at•ed, -at•ing, *n.* —*v.* [~ + *obj*] **1.** to begin: *The countries initiated trade relations.* **2.** to introduce into a group, club, etc. —*n.* [*count*] **3.** a person who has recently been initiated. —in•i•ti•a•tion /ɪ,nɪʃiy'eyʃən/, *n.* [*noncount*] [*count*]

in•i•ti•a•tive /ɪ'nɪʃiyətɪv, ɪ'nɪʃə-/ *n.* **1.** [*count*] a first act or step in a process: *to take the initiative in making friends.* **2.** [*noncount*] the ability to act independently: *to lack initiative.*

in•ject /ɪn'dʒɛkt/ *v.* [~ + *obj*] **1.** to force (a fluid) into a part of the body with a special needle: *The nurse injected the drug into his arm. She*

injected the patient with the drug. **2.** to introduce: *He tried to inject some humor into the situation.*

in•jec•tion /ɪn'dʒɛkʃən/ *n.* [*noncount*] [*count*] the act of injecting or the amount injected.

in•junc•tion /ɪn'dʒʌŋkʃən/ *n.* [*count*] an official order from a court of law.

in•jure /'ɪndʒər/ *v.* [~ + *obj*], -jured, -jur•ing. to cause harm to; hurt or damage: *He injured his hand. She injured her friend's feelings.*

in•ju•ry /'ɪndʒəriy/ *n., pl.* -ries. [*noncount*] [*count*] harm, damage, or wrong done or suffered. —in•ju•ri•ous /ɪn'dʒʊriyəs/, *adj.*

in•jus•tice /ɪn'dʒʌstɪs/ *n.* **1.** [*noncount*] the lack of justice; unfairness: *fighting against injustice.* **2.** [*count*] an unfair act; a wrong.

ink /ɪŋk/ *n.* [*noncount*] [*count*] a colored liquid used for writing or drawing.

ink•ling /'ɪŋklɪŋ/ *n.* [*count*] a slight suggestion; hint: *He had no inkling of the danger.*

in•laid /'ɪn,leyd, ɪn'leyd/ *adj.* decorated with a design set into the surface: *an inlaid table.*

in•land /'ɪnlənd/*adj.* [*before a noun*] **1.** of or in the inner part of a region: *inland cities.* —*adv.* **2.** in or toward the middle of a country or region: *We traveled inland.*

'in-,law, *n.* [*count*] a relative by marriage.

in•lay /v.'ɪn,ley, ,ɪn'ley; n. 'ɪn,ley/ *v.*, -laid, -lay•ing, *n.* —*v.* [~ + *obj*] **1.** to put (pieces of wood, ivory, etc.) in the surface of an object. **2.** to decorate with such pieces. —*n.* [*count*] **3.** inlaid work. **4.** a hard, pre-shaped tooth filling, as of gold.

in•let /'ɪnlɛt, -lɪt/ *n.* [*count*] a narrow body of water reaching into the land.

'in-,line 'skate, *n.* [*count*] a roller skate with four rubber wheels in a straight line. —'in-line 'skating, *n.* [*noncount*]

in•mate /'ɪn,meyt/ *n.* [*count*] a person who is kept in a prison, hospital, etc.

inn /ɪn/ *n.* [*count*] a small hotel; lodge.

in•nards /'ɪnərdz/ *n.* [*plural*] **1.** the inside parts of the body, esp. of an animal. **2.** the inner parts of something: *the engine's innards.*

in•nate /ɪ'neyt/ *adj.* existing from birth; inborn: *innate talents.* —in'nate•ly, *adv.*

in•ner /'ɪnər/ *adj.* [*before a noun*] **1.** farther inside: *an inner room.* **2.** more private or secret: *inner feelings.*

'inner 'city, *n.* [*count*] a central part of a city, inhabited mainly by poor people. —'inner-'city, *adj.* [*before a noun*]: *inner-city crime.*

in•ner•most /'ɪnər,mowst/ *adj.* **1.** farthest inward: *the innermost reaches of the jungle.* **2.** most private or secret: *my innermost thoughts.*

in•ning /'ɪnɪŋ/ *n.* [*count*] a division of a baseball game during which each team has an opportunity to score.

inn•keep•er /'ɪn,kiypər/ *n.* [*count*] a person who owns or manages an inn.

in•no•cent /'ɪnəsənt/ *adj.* **1.** free from moral wrong; not recognizing evil: *the innocent children.* **2.** free from legal wrong: *innocent until proven guilty.* **3.** harmless: *an innocent mistake.* —'in•no•cence, *n.* [*noncount*] —'in•no•cent•ly, *adv.*

in•noc•u•ous /ɪ'nɒkyuwəs/ *adj.* **1.** not harmful. **2.** not likely to offend. —in'noc•u•ous•ly, *adv.*

in•no•vate /'ɪnə,veyt/ *v.*, -vat•ed, -vat•ing. **1.** [*no obj*] to introduce something new; make changes. **2.** [~ + *obj*] to bring in as something new: *to innovate a computer operating system.* —,in•no'va•tion, *n.* [*count*]: *Medical innovations*

I

have saved many lives. [noncount]: *The history of science has been marked by innovation.* —**'in•no,va•tive,** *adj.* —**'in•no,va•tor,** *n.* [count]

in•nu•en•do /ˌɪnyuwˈɛndow/ *n.* [noncount] [count] *pl.* **-dos, -does.** an indirect hint, esp. of an offensive nature.

in•nu•mer•a•ble /ɪˈnuwmərəbəl, ɪˈnyuw-/ *adj.* too many to be counted: *innumerable stars.*

in•oc•u•late /ɪˈnɒkyəˌleyt/ *v.* [~ + *obj*], **-lat•ed, -lat•ing.** to inject with a vaccine in order to protect against a disease: *The doctor inoculated me against yellow fever.* —**in•oc•u•la•tion** /ɪˌnɒkyəˈleyʃən/, *n.* [count] [noncount]

in•of•fen•sive /ˌɪnəˈfɛnsɪv/ *adj.* not offensive; harmless.

in•op•por•tune /ɪnˌɒpərˈtuwn, -ˈtyuwn/ *adj.* not suitable; inconvenient: *It's an inopportune time to talk to him.*

in•or•di•nate /ɪnˈɔrdnɪt/ *adj.* not within proper limits: *to drink an inordinate amount of wine.* —**in'or•di•nate•ly,** *adv.*

in•or•gan•ic /ˌɪnɔrˈgænɪk/ *adj.* not having the characteristics of living things: *inorganic rocks.*

in•put /ˈɪnˌpʊt/ *n., v.,* **-put•ted** or **-put, -put•ting.** —*n.* **1.** [count] something put in, such as information into a computer. **2.** [noncount] the act or process of putting in. **3.** [noncount] contribution of information, ideas, etc.: *Before making a decision we need your input.* —*v.* [~ + *obj*] **4.** to enter (information) into a computer.

in•quest /ˈɪnkwɛst/ *n.* [count] a legal inquiry to find out the cause of death.

in•quire /ɪnˈkwayᵊr/ also **enquire,** *v.,* **-quired, -quir•ing.** to try to get information by questioning; ask: [*no obj*]: *to inquire about a person.* [~ + *obj*]: *to inquire a person's name.* —**in'quir•er,** *n.* [count]

in•quir•ing /ɪnˈkwayᵊrɪŋ/ *adj.* [before a noun] showing a desire to learn: *an inquiring mind.*

in•quir•y /ɪnˈkwayᵊriy, ˈɪnkwəriy/ also **en•quiry,** *n., pl.* **-quir•ies. 1.** [noncount] [count] a looking for information. **2.** [count] a question: *He made inquiries as to her name and address.*

in•qui•si•tion /ˌɪnkwəˈzɪʃən, ˌɪŋ-/ *n.* [count] a long, severe, and very thorough investigation.

in•quis•i•tive /ɪnˈkwɪzɪtɪv/ *adj.* **1.** eager for knowledge; curious: *an inquisitive mind.* **2.** too eager for details; prying. —**in'quis•i•tive•ly,** *adv.* —**in'quis•i•tive•ness,** *n.* [noncount]

in•roads *n.* [plural] —*Idiom.* **make inroads into** or **on,** to use up or take away gradually: *His bad diet made inroads on his health.*

in•sane /ɪnˈseyn/ *adj.* **1.** mentally ill. **2.** very foolish: *an insane idea.* —**in'sane•ly,** *adv.* —**in•san•i•ty** /ɪnˈsænɪtiy/, *n.* [noncount]

in•sa•tia•ble /ɪnˈseyʃəbəl, -ʃiyə-/ *adj.* that cannot be satisfied: *an insatiable appetite.* —**in'sa•tia•bly,** *adv.*

in•scribe /ɪnˈskrayb/ *v.* [~ + *obj*], **-scribed, -scrib•ing. 1.** to write in or on: *The author inscribed the boy's book.* **2.** to mark (a surface) permanently with words or letters: *The ring was inscribed with initials.* —**in•scrip•tion** /ɪnˈskrɪpʃən/ *n.* [count]

in•sect /ˈɪnsɛkt/ *n.* [count] a very small, winged animal having a body divided into three parts and three pairs of legs: *insects such as beetles, ants, and flies.*

in•sec•ti•cide /ɪnˈsɛktəˌsayd/ *n.* [noncount] [count] a chemical for killing insects.

in•se•cure /ˌɪnsɪˈkyʊr/ *adj.* **1.** not confident: *an insecure person.* **2.** not safe: *an insecure fort.* **3.** not firmly fixed: *an insecure fastening.* —**in•**

se•cure•ly, *adv.* —**in•se•cu•ri•ty** /ˌɪnsɪˈkyʊrɪtiy/, *n., pl.* **-ties.** [noncount] [count]

in•sen•si•ble /ɪnˈsɛnsəbəl/ *adj.* **1.** unconscious. **2.** not aware of something: *insensible of the danger.* **3.** unable to feel something: *insensible to pain.* —**in•sen•si•bil•i•ty** /ɪnˌsɛnsəˈbɪlɪtiy/, *n.* [noncount]

in•sen•si•tive /ɪnˈsɛnsɪtɪv/ *adj.* not sensitive: *an insensitive nature; insensitive skin.* —**in'sen•si•tive•ly,** *adv.* —**in•sen•si•tiv•i•ty** /ɪnˌsɛnsəˈtɪvɪtiy/, *n.* [noncount]

in•sep•a•ra•ble /ɪnˈsɛpərəbəl, -ˈsɛprə-/ *adj.* that cannot be separated or parted: *inseparable friends.*

in•sert /*v.*ɪnˈsɜrt; *n.* ˈɪnsɜrt/ *v.* [~ + *obj*] **1.** to put or place in: *to insert a key in a lock.* —*n.* [count] **2.** something inserted for advertising: *a sales insert.* —**in'ser•tion,** *n.* [noncount] [count]

in•set /*n.* ˈɪnˌsɛt; *v.* ɪnˈsɛt/ *n.* [count] something inserted, such as a small map within the border of a larger one: *The inset shows a close-up of the city streets.*

in•side /ˌɪnˈsayd, ˈɪnˌsayd/ *prep.* **1.** on the inner side or part of: *She stepped inside the circle.* —*adv.* **2.** in or into the inner part: *Look inside.* **3.** indoors: *to play inside on rainy days.* —*n.* [count] **4.** the inner part; interior: *the inside of the house.* **5.** the inner side or surface: *the inside of the hand.* **6. insides,** [plural] *Informal.* the inner parts of the body, esp. the stomach and bowels. **7.** a position of special power or knowledge. —*adj.* [before a noun] **8.** on or in the inside: *an inside seat on the airplane.* **9.** close to the middle of the road: *The car tried to pass on the inside lane.* **10.** private or special: *inside information.* —*Idiom.* **11. inside of,** in less than; before: *We'll be there inside of twenty minutes.* **12. inside out, a.** with the inner side on the outside: *to turn a shirt inside out.* **b.** completely: *to know a subject inside out.*

in•sid•er /ˌɪnˈsaydər/ *n.* [count] a member of a group who knows or can find out special information: *insiders in the White House.*

in•sid•i•ous /ɪnˈsɪdiyəs/ *adj.* doing harm gradually and secretly: *an insidious disease.* —**in'sid•i•ous•ly,** *adv.*

in•sight /ˈɪnˌsayt/ *n.* [noncount] [count] an act or instance of understanding the true nature of a thing. —**in'sight•ful,** *adj.*: *an insightful article on marriage.*

in•sig•ni•a /ɪnˈsɪgniyə/ *n.* [count], *pl.* **-ni•a** or **-ni•as.** a badge or other official symbol that shows office or rank: *military insignia.*

in•sig•nif•i•cant /ˌɪnsɪgˈnɪfɪkənt/ *adj.* unimportant. —**,in•sig'nif•i•cance,** *n.* [noncount] —**,in•sig'nif•i•cant•ly,** *adv.*

in•sin•cere /ˌɪnsɪnˈsɪər/ *adj.* not sincere; dishonest. —**,in•sin'cere•ly,** *adv.* —**in•sin•cer•i•ty** /ˌɪnsɪnˈsɛrɪtiy/, *n.* [noncount]

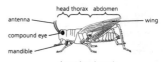

insect (grasshopper)

in•sin•u•ate /ɪnˈsɪnyuwˌeyt/ *v.* [~ + *obj*], **-at•ed, -at•ing. 1.** to suggest (something unpleasant) indirectly: *He insinuated that they weren't telling the truth.* **2.** to put or introduce (doubt, etc.), as into the mind. —**in•sin•u•a•tion** /ˌɪnˌsɪnyuw'eyʃən/ n. [noncount] [count]

in•sip•id /ɪn'sɪpɪd/ adj. uninteresting: insipid food; an insipid personality.

in•sist /ɪn'sɪst/ v. to demand or declare (something) in a strong, firm way: [~ + on/upon + obj]: She insists on coming with us. [~ + (that) clause]: He insisted that we stay home. I insisted I was right. —**in'sist•ence**, n. [noncount]

in•sist•ent /ɪn'sɪstənt/ adj. **1.** demanding something firmly: He's insistent about visiting us. **2.** urgent: the insistent ringing of the telephone. —**in'sist•ent•ly**, adv.

insofar as conj. to the degree that: I will do the work insofar as I am able.

in•so•lent /'ɪnsələnt/ adj. rude or disrespectful; insulting. —**'in•so•lence**, n. [noncount] —'**in•so•lent•ly**, adv.

in•sol•u•ble /ɪn'sɒlyəbəl/ adj. **1.** (of a substance) that cannot be dissolved: insoluble salts. **2.** (of a problem, crime, etc.) that cannot be solved: an insoluble mystery.

in•sol•vent /ɪn'sɒlvənt/ adj. unable to pay one's debts. —**in'sol•ven•cy**, n. [noncount]

in•som•ni•a /ɪn'sɒmniyə/ n. [noncount] habitual difficulty in falling or staying asleep. —**in•som•ni•ac** /ɪn'sɒmniy,æk/, n. [count], adj.

in•spect /ɪn'spɛkt/ v. [~ + obj] **1.** to look carefully at or over: to inspect every part of a motor. **2.** to examine officially: The general inspected the troops. —**in'spec•tion**, n. [noncount]: The general went on a tour of inspection. [count]: There were several inspections of the crashed airplane. —**in'spec•tor**, n. [count]

in•spi•ra•tion /ˌɪnspə'reyʃən/ n. **1.** [noncount] an influence to do or make something, esp. of lasting value. **2.** [count] a person or thing that inspires. **3.** [count] a sudden good idea. —**in•spi'ra•tion•al**, adj.

in•spire /ɪn'spayᵊr/ v. [~ + obj], -**spired**, -**spiring. 1.** to fill (someone) with strong feelings: Her courage inspired her followers. **2.** to influence (someone to do something): Her criticisms inspired him to try harder. —**inspiring**, adj.: an inspiring leader.

in•spir•ed /ɪn'spayᵊrd/ adj. filled with or showing inspiration.

in•sta•bil•i•ty /ˌɪnstə'bɪlɪtiy/ n. [noncount] lack of stability: Political instability led to a revolution.

in•stall or **in•stal** /ɪn'stɔl/ v. [~ + obj], -**stalled**, -**stall•ing. 1.** to place in position for use: to install a heating system. **2.** to establish (someone) in a place: They installed their son in his new apartment. **3.** to bring (someone) into an office with ceremonies: He was installed as the club president. —**installation**, n. [count] [noncount]

in•stall•ment or **in•stal•ment** /ɪn'stɔlmənt/ n. [count] **1.** any of several parts into which a debt is divided for regular payment. **2.** a single part of a story that appears in parts at fixed times, as in a magazine or on TV.

in'stallment ,plan, n. [count] a system for paying for an item in installments.

in•stance /'ɪnstəns/ n. [count] **1.** an example supporting a general idea: I mentioned several instances of unfairness. —**Idiom. 2. for instance**, as an example.

in•stant /'ɪnstənt/ n. **1.** [count] a very short space of time; moment: In an instant they were gone. **2.** [count] a particular moment: Stop that this instant! —adj. **3.** happening immediately: an instant reaction; instant relief. **4.** (of a food or

drink) needing very little time and effort to prepare: Just add boiling water to the instant coffee.

in•stan•ta•ne•ous /ˌɪnstən'teyniyəs/ adj. happening immediately. —**ˌin•stan'ta•ne•ous•ly**, adv.

in•stant•ly /'ɪnstəntliy/ adv. immediately: He died instantly in the crash.

in•stead /ɪn'stɛd/ adv. **1.** in place of another person or thing: The bus is late so we'll walk instead. —**Idiom. 2. instead of**, in place of: Instead of meat, how about fish?

in•step /'ɪn,stɛp/ n. [count] the arched upper surface of the human foot.

in•sti•gate /'ɪnstɪ,geyt/ v., -**gat•ed**, -**gat•ing.** [~ + obj] to cause (something) to happen by urging: to instigate a quarrel. —**in•sti•ga•tion** /ˌɪnstɪ'geyʃən/, n. [noncount] —'**in•sti,ga•tor**, n. [count]

in•still or **in•stil** /ɪn'stɪl/ v. [~ + obj (+ in/into + obj)], -**stilled**, -**still•ing** or -**stil•ling.** to introduce little by little: He instilled a love of learning into his children.

in•stinct /'ɪnstɪŋkt/ n. [count] [noncount] a way of behaving that comes naturally and does not have to be learned. —**in•stinc•tu•al** /ɪn'stɪŋktʃuwəl/, adj.

in•stinc•tive /ɪn'stɪŋktɪv/ adj. based on instinct: Babies have an instinctive fear of falling.

in•sti•tute /'ɪnstɪ,tuwt, -,tyuwt/ v., -**tut•ed**, -**tut•ing**, n. —v. [~ + obj] **1.** to set up; establish: to institute new rules. —n. [count] **2.** an organization set up for a special purpose: a medical research institute.

in•sti•tu•tion /ˌɪnstɪ'tuwʃən, -'tyuw-/ n. **1.** [count] an organization set up for a social or public purpose: institutions such as schools and hospitals. **2.** [count] an established custom or practice: the institution of marriage. **3.** [noncount] the act of instituting: the institution of new laws. —**ˌin•sti'tu•tion•al**, adj.

in•sti•tu•tion•al•ize /ˌɪnstɪ'tuwʃənl,ayz, -'tyuw-/ v. [~ + obj], -**ized**, -**iz•ing. 1.** to make (something) into an institution (def. 2). **2.** to place (someone) in an institution, as for treatment. —**ˌin•sti•tu•tion•al•i•za•tion** /ˌɪnstɪ,tuwʃənlɪ'zeyʃən, -,tyuw-/, n. [noncount]

in•struct /ɪn'strʌkt/ v. [~ + obj] **1.** to teach, esp. by a systematic method: The teacher instructed her students in mathematics. **2.** to give orders to: She instructed us to leave one by one.

in•struc•tion /ɪn'strʌkʃən/ n. **1.** [noncount] the act of teaching. **2.** [count] an order to a person or machine. **3.** [count] Usually, **instructions.** [plural] an explanation of how to do something; directions. —**in'struc•tion•al**, adj.: instructional materials for the classroom.

in•struc•tor /ɪn'strʌktər/ n. [count] a person who instructs; teacher.

in•stru•ment /'ɪnstrəmənt/ n. [count] **1.** a device or tool, esp. one used for delicate work: medical instruments. **2.** a device for producing musical sounds: Her instrument is the piano.

in•stru•men•tal /ˌɪnstrə'mɛntl/ adj. **1.** helping to do or cause something: Your friend was instrumental in getting me that job. **2.** of or for musical instruments.

in•sub•or•di•nate /ˌɪnsə'bɔrdnɪt/ adj. not obeying orders; disobedient. —**in•sub•or•di•na•tion** /ˌɪnsə,bɔrdn'eyʃən/, n. [noncount]

in•suf•fer•a•ble /ɪn'sʌfərəbəl/ adj. not bearable: insufferable behavior. —**in'suf•fer•a•bly**, adv.

in•suf•fi•cient /ˌɪnsə'fɪʃənt/ adj. not enough:

insufficient food. —,**in•suf'fi•cien•cy,** *n.* [*non-count*] —,**in•suf'fi•cient•ly,** *adv.*

in•su•lar /'ınsələr, 'ınsyə-/ *adj.* **1.** of or relating to an island. **2.** narrow-minded. —**in•su•lar•i•ty** /,ınsə'lærıtiy, ,ınsyə-/, *n.* [*noncount*]

in•su•late /'ınsə,leyt, 'ınsyə-/ *v.* [~ + *obj*], **-lat•ed, -lat•ing. 1.** to cover or surround with a material that prevents or reduces the passage of heat, electricity, or sound: *They insulated the house for warmth.* **2.** to place (a person) in a protected situation. —'**in•su,la•tor,** *n.* [*count*]

in•su•la•tion /,ınsə'leyʃən, ,ınsyə-/ *n.* [*non-count*] **1.** the act of insulating or the state of being insulated. **2.** material used for insulating.

in•sult /v.ın'sʌlt; *n.* 'ınsʌlt/ *v.* [~ + *obj*] **1.** to be rude to; offend. —*n.* [*count*] **2.** a rude action or remark. —**in'sult•ing,** *adj.*: *insulting remarks.*

in•sur•ance /ın'ʃurəns, -'ʃɜr-/ *n.* [*noncount*] **1.** the act, system, or business of insuring property, life, etc., against loss or harm in return for regular payment. **2.** money paid under a contract by or to a company for a loss. **3.** any means of protection against loss or harm: *He takes vitamin C as insurance against colds.*

in•sure /ın'ʃur, -'ʃɜr/ *v.* [~ + *obj*], **-sured, -sur•ing. 1.** to promise to protect (someone or something) against death, loss, or damage by insurance: *The car was insured against accident or theft.* **2.** ENSURE.

in•sur•gent /ın'sɜrdʒənt/ *n.* [*count*] **1.** a person who takes part in armed resistance to an established government; a rebel. —*adj.* [*before a noun*] **2.** rising in revolt; rebellious. —**in'sur•gence,** *n.* [*count*] [*noncount*]

in•sur•mount•a•ble /,ınsər'mawntəbəl/ *adj.* that cannot be solved or overcome: *insurmountable problems.*

in•sur•rec•tion /,ınsə'rεkʃən/ *n.* [*noncount*] [*count*] an act or instance of rising in rebellion against an established government. —,**in•sur'rec•tion•ist,** *n.* [*count*]

in•tact /ın'tækt/ *adj.* not damaged.

in•take /'ın,teyk/ *n.* [*count; usually singular*] a quantity taken in.

in•tan•gi•ble /ın'tændʒəbəl/ *adj.* **1.** not definite or clear to the mind: *an intangible presence in the room.* **2.** having no material existence: *Praise is an intangible reward.* —*n.* [*count*] **3.** something intangible, esp. a business asset: *Goodwill is an intangible.*

in•te•ger /'ıntıdʒər/ *n.* [*count*] a whole number, as 1, 2, 3, etc.

in•te•gral /'ıntıgrəl, ın'tεgrəl/ *adj.* [*usually: before a noun*] necessary to completeness: *an integral part of the process.*

in•te•grate /'ıntı,greyt/ *v.* [~ + *obj*], **-grat•ed, -grat•ing. 1.** to bring together into a whole or into a larger unit: *He integrated several ideas from that novelist into his writing.* **2.** to make (a school, etc.) open or available to people of all races. —'**in•te,gra•ted,** *adj.*: *a fully integrated school.* —**in•te•gra•tion** /,ıntı'greyʃən/, *n.* [*noncount*]

in•teg•ri•ty /ın'tεgrıtiy/ *n.* [*noncount*] **1.** honesty. **2.** the state of being whole or entire.

in•tel•lect /'ıntḷ,εkt/ *n.* [*count*] the power to reason, esp. when highly developed.

in•tel•lec•tu•al /,ıntḷ'εktʃuwəl/ *adj.* **1.** appealing or relating to the intellect: *intellectual interests.* **2.** having or showing a well-developed intellect. —*n.* [*count*] **3.** an intellectual person. —,**in•tel'lec•tu•al•ly,** *adv.*

in•tel•li•gence /ın'tεlıdʒəns/ *n.* [*noncount*] **1.** the ability to learn, reason, and understand. **2.** mental quickness of understanding: *He writes with intelligence and humor.* **3.** information, esp. about an enemy.

in•tel•li•gent /ın'tεlıdʒənt/ *adj.* having good understanding or a high mental ability. —**in'tel•li•gent•ly,** *adv.*

in•tel•li•gi•ble /ın'tεlıdʒəbəl/ *adj.* that can be understood: *intelligible speech.* —**in•tel•li•gi•bil•i•ty** /ın,tεlıdʒə'bılıt iy/, *n.* [*noncount*] —**in'tel•li•gi•bly,** *adv.*

in•tend /ın'tεnd/ *v.* [~ + *obj*] **1.** to have in mind as something to be done; plan: *We intend to leave in a month.* **2.** to mean for a particular person or purpose: *The money was intended for emergencies.*

in•tense /ın'tεns/ *adj.* very great or strong; extreme: *intense heat; intense sorrow.* —**in'tense•ly,** *adv.*

in•ten•si•fy /ın'tεnsə,fay/ *v.*, **-fied, -fy•ing.** [*no obj*] [~ + *obj*] to (cause to) become intense or more intense. —**in•ten•si•fi•ca•tion** /ın,tεnsəfı'keyʃən/, *n.* [*noncount*]

in•ten•si•ty /ın'tεnsıtiy/ *n.*, *pl.* **-ties.** [*noncount*] great energy, strength, or force, as of activity or feeling.

in•ten•sive /ın'tεnsıv/ *adj.* marked by full attention to the work at hand: *intensive questioning of the witness.* —**in'ten•sive•ly,** *adv.*

in'tensive 'care, *n.* [*noncount*] specialized care for a person who is critically ill, usually in a special area in a hospital (an **in'tensive 'care ,unit**).

in•tent¹ /ın'tεnt/ *n.* **1.** [*count; usually singular*] purpose; intention: *My intent was to learn English.* **2.** [*noncount*] meaning; basic idea. —*Idiom.* **3.** to or **for all intents and purposes,** in nearly every way.

in•tent² /ın'tεnt/ *adj.* [*be* + ~] **1.** having the attention firmly fixed on something: *She was intent on her work.* **2.** strongly determined: *He is intent on going.* —**in'tent•ly,** *adv.*

in•ten•tion /ın'tεnʃən/ *n.* [*noncount*] aim; purpose; plan: *His intention was to buy a house. She's full of good intentions.*

in•ten•tion•al /ın'tεnʃənḷ/ *adj.* done deliberately: *an intentional insult.* —**in'ten•tion•al•ly,** *adv.*

in•ter /ın'tɜr/ *v.* [~ + *obj*], **-terred, -ter•ring.** to bury (a dead body). —**in'ter•ment,** *n.* [*noncount*]

inter-, a prefix meaning: between or among (*intercity*); mutually (*interdependent*).

in•ter•act /,ıntər'ækt/ *v.* **1.** to act upon one another: [*no obj*]: *When the two chemicals interact they form a gas. One chemical interacts with the other.* **2.** to talk, work, or socialize together. —,**in•ter'ac•tion,** *n.* [*noncount*]: *social interaction.* [*count*]: *day-to-day interactions.* —,**in•ter'ac•tive,** *adj.*: *Interactive video lets the user decide what to see on the screen.*

in•ter•cede /,ıntər'siyd/ *v.* [*no obj*], **-ced•ed, -ced•ing.** to speak in behalf of someone, esp. so as to gain a favor or save from harm. —,**in•ter'ces•sion,** *n.* [*count*]

in•ter•cept /,ıntər'sεpt/ *v.* [~ + *obj*] to stop (someone or something on the way from one place to another): *to intercept a messenger.* —,**in•ter'cep•tion,** *n.* [*noncount*] [*count*]

in•ter•change /*v.* ,ıntər'tʃeyndʒ; *n.* 'ıntər,tʃeyndʒ/ *v.*, **-changed, -chang•ing,** *n.* —*v.* [~ + *obj*] [*no obj*] **1.** to cause (one thing) to change places with another. —*n.* [*count*] **2.** an act or instance of interchanging: *the free inter-*

change of ideas. **3.** a highway intersection in which vehicles may move from one road to another without crossing traffic. —,**in•ter'change• a•ble,** *adj.*

in•ter•com /'ɪntərˌkɒm/ *n.* [*count*] a communication system, as within a building, with a loudspeaker and a microphone at each of two or more points.

in•ter•con•ti•nen•tal /ˌɪntərˌkɒntn̩'ɛntl̩/ *adj.* between continents: *intercontinental travel.*

in•ter•course /'ɪntərˌkɔrs/ *n.* [*noncount*] **1.** dealings or communication between individuals, groups, etc.: *social intercourse.* **2.** sexual relations.

in•ter•est /'ɪntərɪst, -trɪst/ *n.* **1.** a feeling of having one's attention attracted by something: [*count*]: *an interest in art.* [*noncount*]: *I lost interest in the movie.* **2.** [*count*] something that causes such feelings: *Music is his only interest.* **3.** [*noncount*] the power to cause concern or curiosity: *a matter of great interest.* **4.** [*count; often plural*] advantage; benefit. **5.** [*count*] a legal share, right, or title, as in the ownership of property. **6.** [*count*] Often, **interests.** [*plural*] a group having influence on and often financially involved in a business. **7.** [*noncount*] money paid or charged for a loan: *I borrowed at 8 percent interest.* —*v.* [*~ + obj*] **8.** to excite the attention of: *Nothing interests her anymore.* **9.** to involve: *Can I interest you in a walk?* —*Idiom.* **10. in the interest(s) of,** for the sake of: *acting in the interests of good government.*

in•ter•est•ed /'ɪntrəstɪd, -tə,rɛstɪd/ *adj.* **1.** having an interest in something: *to be interested in sports.* **2.** [*usually: before a noun*] influenced by personal interest; biased: *an interested witness.*

in•ter•est•ing /'ɪntərəstɪŋ, -trəstɪŋ/ *adj.* exciting or holding one's attention: *an interesting book.*

in•ter•fere /ˌɪntər'fɪər/ *v.* [*no obj*], **-fered, -fer• ing. 1.** to prevent the progress of someone or something: *The television interferes with his studying.* **2.** to concern oneself with the affairs of others without being asked. **3.** to cause interference.

in•ter•fer•ence /ˌɪntər'fɪərəns/ *n.* [*noncount*] **1.** the act of interfering. **2.** noise or unwanted signals that prevent good radio or television reception.

in•ter•im /'ɪntərəm/ *n.* [*noncount*] **1. in the interim,** in the time between two events. —*adj.* [*before a noun*] **2.** lasting for a short time; temporary.

in•te•ri•or /ɪn'tɪəriyər/ *adj.* [*before a noun*] **1.** inside; inner: *the interior walls of a house.* —*n.* [*count*] **2.** the inner part; inside: *the interior of a house.* **3.** [*usually singular; usually: the + ~*] the inland part of a region, country, etc.

in'terior deco'ration, *n.* [*noncount*] the art or profession of designing and furnishing the interior of a house, office, etc. —**in'terior 'decora• tor,** *n.* [*count*]

in•ter•ject /ˌɪntər'dʒɛkt/ *v.* [*~ + obj*] [*no obj*] to put in or insert (a remark), often suddenly.

in•ter•jec•tion /ˌɪntər'dʒɛkʃən/ *n.* [*count*] a word or short phrase used to express a feeling, such as *Hey! Oh! Ouch! Good grief! Indeed!*

in•ter•lock /ˌɪntər'lɒk/ *v.* [*no obj*] [*~ + obj*] to fit into each other, as in machinery, so that various parts work together.

in•ter•lude /'ɪntərˌluwd/ *n.* [*count*] **1.** a period of time that comes between others: *a quiet inter*-

lude. **2.** a short musical piece between the acts of a play.

in•ter•mar•ry /ˌɪntər'mæriy/ *v.* [*no obj*], **-ried, -ry•ing.** to become connected by marriage, as two families, tribes, or religions. —**in•ter•mar• riage** /ˌɪntər'mærɪdʒ/, *n.* [*noncount*]

in•ter•me•di•ar•y /ˌɪntər'miydiyˌɛriy/ *n.,* pl. **-ies,** *adj.* —*n.* [*count*] **1.** a person who comes between two quarreling groups and acts to bring them into agreement. —*adj.* **2.** being between: *an intermediary stage.*

in•ter•me•di•ate /ˌɪntər'miydiyɪt/ *adj.* **1.** between two points or stages; in the middle. **2.** between the levels of beginner and advanced: *a class for intermediate students.*

in•ter•mi•na•ble /ɪn'tɜrmənəbəl/ *adj.* lasting too long; seeming to be endless: *an interminable wait.* —**in'ter•mi•na•bly,** *adv.*

in•ter•mis•sion /ˌɪntər'mɪʃən/ *n.* [*count*] [*noncount*] an interval, as between acts of a play or periods of play in a sport.

in•ter•mit•tent /ˌɪntər'mɪtnt/ *adj.* stopping for a time, then starting again: *intermittent pain.* —,**in•ter•mit•tent•ly,** *adv.*

in•tern[1] /ɪn'tɜrn/ *v.* [*~ + obj*] to imprison or keep within certain limits, as prisoners of war. —**in'tern•ment,** *n.* [*noncount*]

in•tern[2] /'ɪntɜrn/ *n.* [*count*] **1.** a recent medical school graduate serving under supervision in a hospital. **2.** someone working as a trainee to gain practical job experience. —*v.* [*no obj*] **3.** to serve as an intern. —'**in•tern,ship,** *n.* [*count*]

in•ter•nal /ɪn'tɜrnl̩/ *adj.* **1.** of or relating to the inside or inner part: *the internal organs of the body.* **2.** [*before a noun*] of or relating to the domestic affairs of a country. —**in'ter•nal•ly,** *adv.*

in'ternal-com'bustion ,engine, *n.* [*count*] an engine in which the burning of fuel takes place within the engine's cylinders.

in•ter•na•tion•al /ˌɪntər'næʃənl̩/ *adj.* of or involving two or more nations: *international trade.* —,**in•ter'na•tion•al•ly,** *adv.*

In•ter•net /'ɪntərˌnɛt/ *n.* [*noncount; usually: the + ~*] a large computer network linking smaller computer networks worldwide.

in•ter•per•son•al /ˌɪntər'pɜrsənl̩/ *adj.* between persons.

in•ter•play /'ɪntərˌpley/ *n.* [*noncount*] action, effect, or influence on each other.

in•ter•pose /ˌɪntər'powz/ *v.* [*~ + obj*], **-posed, -pos•ing. 1.** to place (something) between two things. **2.** to put in (a remark, question, etc.) as an interruption. —**in•ter•po•si•tion** /ˌɪntərpə'zɪʃən/, *n.* [*noncount*]

in•ter•pret /ɪn'tɜrprɪt/ *v.* **1.** [*~ + obj*] to explain the meaning of: *to interpret a poem.* **2.** [*~ + obj*] to understand in a particular way: *We chose to interpret the reply as favorable.* **3.** [*no obj*] [*~ + obj*] to translate what is said in a foreign language. —**in'ter•pret•er,** *n.* [*count*]

in•ter•pre•ta•tion /ɪnˌtɜrprɪ'teyʃən/ *n.* [*noncount*] [*count*] the act of interpreting; explanation.

in•ter•ro•gate /ɪn'tɛrəˌgeyt/ *v.* [*~ + obj*], **-gat•ed, -gat•ing.** to question (a person), esp. formally and thoroughly: *The police interrogated them for hours.* —**in•ter•ro•ga•tion** /ɪnˌtɛrə'geyʃən/, *n.* [*count*] [*noncount*] —**in'ter• ro,ga•tor,** *n.* [*count*]

in•ter•rog•a•tive /ˌɪntə'rɒgətɪv/ *adj.* **1.** relating to, used in, or forming a question: *an interrogative sentence.* —*n.* [*count*] **2.** an interrogative word, as *who, what, which.*

I

in•ter•rupt /ˌɪntəˈrʌpt/ v. **1.** [~ + obj] to make a break in the continuity of: *The flow of the river is interrupted by a waterfall.* **2.** [no obj] [~ + obj] to stop (a person) while speaking or working, esp. by a remark added in. —ˌin•ter•rup•tion, n. [count] [noncount]

in•ter•sect /ˌɪntərˈsɛkt/ v. **1.** [~ + obj] to divide by passing through or across: *The highway intersects the town.* **2.** [no obj] to meet and cross: *The two streets intersect at the red light.*

in•ter•sec•tion /ˌɪntərˈsɛkʃən/ n. **1.** [count] a place where two or more roads meet. **2.** [noncount] the act or fact of intersecting.

in•ter•sperse /ˌɪntərˈspɜrs/ v. [~ + obj], -spersed, -spers•ing. to scatter among other things: *to intersperse flowers among the vegetables.*

in•ter•state /adj.,ˌɪntərˈsteɪt/ n. ˈɪntərˌsteɪt/ adj. [before a noun] connecting or involving different states: *an interstate highway; interstate trade.* —n. [count; sometimes: Interstate] **2.** a highway that is part of a nationwide U.S. system of highways connecting major cities.

in•ter•val /ˈɪntərvəl/ n. [count] **1.** a period of time between two events. **2.** a space between two things: *an interval of ten feet between each sign.*

in•ter•vene /ˌɪntərˈviyn/ v. [no obj], -vened, -ven•ing. **1.** to come between quarreling people: *His daughters would keep fighting until he intervened.* **2.** to happen between points of time or events: *A few years intervened before they met again.* **3.** to interfere with force or a threat of force: *to intervene in the affairs of another country.* —in•ter•ven•tion /ˌɪntərˈvɛnʃən/ n. [noncount]: *Police intervention prevented the angry mob from rioting.*

in•ter•view /ˈɪntərˌvyuw/ n. [count] **1.** a formal meeting in which a person is asked questions: *an interview for a job.* **2.** a meeting in which a writer, reporter, or television host obtains information for a news story, broadcast, etc. —v. [~ + obj] [no obj] **3.** to ask (a person) questions in an interview. —ˈin•ter,view•er, n. [count]

in•tes•tate /ɪnˈtɛsteyt, -tɪt/ adj. not having made a will: *to die intestate.* —in•tes•ta•cy /ɪnˈtɛstəsiy/, n. [noncount]

in•tes•tine /ɪnˈtɛstɪn/ n. [count] Usually, **intestines.** [plural] the long tube from the stomach to the anus that carries and digests food and stores waste. —in•tes•ti•nal, adj.

in•ti•ma•cy /ˈɪntəməsiy/ n., pl. -cies. **1.** [noncount] the state of being intimate. **2.** [count; usually plural] an act that shows close feeling.

in•ti•mate¹ /ˈɪntəmɪt/ adj. **1.** having a close personal relationship: *intimate friends.* **2.** very private and personal: *one's intimate thoughts.* **3.** [before a noun] coming from close study or familiar experience: *intimate knowledge of a subject.* —ˈin•ti•mate•ly, adv.

in•ti•mate² /ˈɪntəˌmeyt/ v. [~ + obj], -mat•ed, -mat•ing. to make known indirectly; suggest: *He intimated his dislike.* —ˌin•ti•ma•tion, n. [count]

in•tim•i•date /ɪnˈtɪmɪˌdeyt/ v. [~ + obj], -dat•ed, -dat•ing. to make fearful, esp. by threats of violence: *The bullies intimidated the new kids at school.* —in•tim•i•da•tion /ɪnˌtɪmɪˈdeyʃən/, n. [noncount]

in•to /ˈɪntuw; unstressed -tʊ, -tə/ prep. **1.** to the inside of; in toward: *He walked into the room.* **2.** toward or in the direction of: *Are you going into town?* **3.** to a point of contact with; against: *He backed his truck into a tree.* **4.** so as to be in or

included in: *I put the key into the lock. We welcomed her into the family.* **5.** to a certain condition or form: *The water turned into ice. I got into debt.* **6.** to the work, activity, etc., of: *She went into banking.* **7.** until a point during: *The party lasted well into the night.* **8.** (used between two numbers to be divided): *2 into 20 equals 10.* —Idiom. **9. be into something,** to be very interested in: *He's into acting.*

in•tol•er•a•ble /ɪnˈtɒlərəbəl/ adj. unbearable: *intolerable pain.* —in•tol•er•a•bly, adv.

in•tol•er•ant /ɪnˈtɒlərənt/ adj. not respecting beliefs, opinions, behavior, etc. different from one's own. —in•tol•er•ance, n. [noncount]

in•to•na•tion /ˌɪntowˈneyʃən, -tə-/ n. [noncount] [count] the rising or falling changes in the voice in speaking.

in•tox•i•cate /ɪnˈtɒksɪˌkeyt/ v., -cat•ed, -cat•ing. **1.** [~ + obj] [no obj] to make drunk. **2.** [~ + obj] to make enthusiastic; delight: *The beauty of the summer night intoxicated her.* —in•tox•i,cat•ed, adj. —in•tox•i,cat•ing, adj. —in•tox•i•ca•tion /ɪnˌtɒksɪˈkeyʃən/, n. [noncount]

intra-, a prefix meaning within (*intraspecies*).

in•tran•si•tive /ɪnˈtrænsɪtɪv/ adj. of or being a verb that is used without a direct object, as *sits* in *The dog sits.* In this book the symbol for an intransitive verb is: [no obj]. —in•tran•si•tive•ly, adv.

in•trep•id /ɪnˈtrɛpɪd/ adj. fearless: *an intrepid explorer.* —in•trep•id•ly, adv.

in•tri•cate /ˈɪntrɪkɪt/ adj. very involved or complicated: *a story with an intricate plot.* —intricacy, n. [noncount] [count], pl. -cies.

in•trigue /v. ɪnˈtriyg; n. also ˈɪntriyg/ v., -trigued, -tri•guing, n. —v. **1.** [~ + obj] to make curious or interested: *Your unusual idea intrigues me.* **2.** [no obj] to plan something bad in secret. —n. [count] **3.** a secret plan: *political intrigues.*

in•tri•guing /ɪnˈtriygɪŋ/ adj. very interesting: *an intriguing mystery.*

in•trin•sic /ɪnˈtrɪnsɪk, -zɪk/ adj. being part of a thing by its very nature: *A good education has intrinsic value.* —in•trin•si•cal•ly, adv.

intro-, a prefix meaning: inside or within (*introspection*).

in•tro•duce /ˌɪntrəˈduws, -ˈdyuws/ v. [~ + obj], -duced, -duc•ing. **1.** to present (a person) to another by name: *I would like to introduce you to my father.* **2.** to give knowledge or experience of: *He introduced me to skiing.* **3.** to bring into notice or use for the first time: *to introduce a new system; a plant introduced into America from Africa.* **4.** to begin: *She introduced her talk with a funny story.* **5.** to present (a speaker, performer, etc.) to an audience.

in•tro•duc•tion /ˌɪntrəˈdʌkʃən/ n. **1.** [noncount] the act of introducing or the state of being introduced. **2.** [count] the introducing of one person to another. **3.** [count] a beginning part before the main part, as of a book, speech, musical piece, etc.

in•tro•duc•to•ry /ˌɪntrəˈdʌktəriy/ adj. relating to or providing general or basic information: *an introductory course; introductory remarks.*

in•tro•spec•tion /ˌɪntrəˈspɛkʃən/ n. [noncount] the act of studying one's own thoughts and feelings. —in•tro•spec•tive /ˌɪntrəˈspɛktɪv/, adj.

in•tro•vert /ˈɪntrəˌvɜrt/ n. [count] a shy, quiet person. —ˈin•tro,vert•ed, adj.

in•trude /ɪnˈtruwd/ v., -trud•ed, -trud•ing. to enter or bring in when not wanted: [no obj]: *I* *don't want to intrude on you if you're busy. I hope I'm not intruding.* [~ + *obj*]: *The judge intruded her prejudices into the case.*

in•trud•er /ɪnˈtruwdər/ *n.* [*count*] a person who enters a place secretly or illegally.

in•tru•sion /ɪnˈtruwʒən/ *n.* [*noncount*] [*count*] an act or instance of intruding. —**in•tru•sive** /ɪnˈtruwsɪv/, *adj.*: *an intrusive question.* —**in•tru•sive•ly,** *adv.*

in•tu•i•tion /ˌɪntuwˈɪʃən, -tyuw-/ *n.* **1.** [*noncount*] the power of understanding something quickly and without conscious reasoning. **2.** [*count*] knowledge resulting from this power. —**intuitive,** *adj.* —**intuitively,** *adv.*

In•u•it /ˈɪnuwˈɪt/ *n.* [*count*], *pl.* **-it, -its. 1.** a member of any of the Eskimo groups inhabiting an area from Greenland to W arctic Canada. **2.** Eskimo (def. 1).

in•un•date /ˈɪnənˌdeyt/ *v.* [~ + *obj*], **-dat•ed, -dat•ing. 1.** to flood: *Heavy rains inundated the town.* **2.** to overwhelm: *inundated with questions.*

in•vade /ɪnˈveyd/ *v.,* **-vad•ed, -vad•ing. 1.** [~ + *obj*] [*no obj*] to enter forcefully as an enemy. **2.** [~ + *obj*] to enter and do harm to: *viruses that invade the bloodstream.* **3.** [~ + *obj*] to crowd into: *Tourists invaded the town.* **4.** [~ + *obj*] to intrude upon: *to invade someone's privacy.* —**in'vad•er,** *n.* [*count*]

in•va•lid¹ /ˈɪnvəlɪd/ *n.* [*count*] a person who is weakened or disabled by illness.

in•val•id² /ɪnˈvælɪd/ *adj.* not valid; without force: *an invalid contract; an invalid argument.* —**in•va•lid•i•ty** /ˌɪnvəˈlɪdɪtiy/, *n.* [*noncount*]

in•val•u•a•ble /ɪnˈvælyuwəbəl/ *adj.* of great worth; priceless: *Your help was invaluable.*

in•var•i•a•ble /ɪnˈvɛəriyəbəl/ *adj.* **1.** not able to be changed; staying the same. —*n.* [*count*] **2.** something invariable; a constant. —**in'var•i•a•bly,** *adv.*: *She was invariably late to class.*

in•va•sion /ɪnˈveyʒən/ *n.* [*count*] **1.** an act or instance of invading, esp. by an army. **2.** the entrance or coming or spread of anything usually troublesome or harmful, as disease. **3.** entrance so as to overrun: *the annual invasion of tourists.* —**in'va•sive,** *adj.*

in•vec•tive /ɪnˈvɛktɪv/ *n.* [*noncount*] a very forceful attack in words.

in•vent /ɪnˈvɛnt/ *v.* [~ + *obj*] **1.** to create (something that did not exist before): *Who invented the light bulb?* **2.** to make up (something false): *He was quick at inventing excuses.* —**in'ven•tor,** *n.* [*count*] —**Usage.** See discover.

in•ven•tion /ɪnˈvɛnʃən/ *n.* **1.** [*noncount*] the act of inventing: *the invention of the computer chip.* **2.** [*count*] anything invented.

in•ven•tive /ɪnˈvɛntɪv/ *adj.* skilled at inventing things; creative. —**in'ven•tive•ness,** *n.* [*noncount*]

in•ven•to•ry /ˈɪnvənˌtɔriy/ *n.* [*count*], *pl.* **-ries,** *v.,* **-ried, -ry•ing. 1.** a complete listing of goods on hand, as in a store. —*v.* [~ + *obj*] **2.** to make an inventory of.

in•verse /ɪnˈvɜrs, ˈɪnvɜrs/ *adj.* **1.** reversed in position, order, direction, or tendency; opposite: *Read the numbers in inverse order.* —*n.* [*noncount*] **2.** the direct opposite. —**in'verse•ly,** *adv.*

in•vert /ɪnˈvɜrt/ *v.* [~ + *obj*] **1.** to turn upside down. **2.** to put in the opposite order. —**in'ver•sion,** *n.* [*noncount*]

in•vest /ɪnˈvɛst/ *v.* **1.** to put up or spend (money) in hopes of making a profit: [~ + *obj*]: *They invested their money in stocks and bonds.*

[*no obj*]: *They decided to invest in stocks and bonds.* **2.** [*no obj*] to buy something of value: *He invested in a computer.* **3.** [~ + *obj*] to give (time or effort) to a piece of work: *She invested days in planning the trip.* —**in'ves•tor,** *n.* [*count*]: *Many investors lost money when the company went bankrupt.*

in•ves•ti•gate /ɪnˈvɛstɪˌgeyt/ *v.,* **-gat•ed, -gat•ing.** to examine (the details of something) carefully so as to find out the truth: [*no obj*]: *The police were called in to investigate.* [~ + *obj*]: *The police were investigating the murder.* —**in,ves•ti'ga•tion,** *n.* [*noncount*]: *Investigation of the robbery showed he was innocent.* [*count*]: *There were many newspaper investigations of the senator's private life.* —**investigative,** *adj.*: *an investigative reporter.* —**in'ves•ti,ga•tor,** *n.* [*count*]

in•vest•ment /ɪnˈvɛstmənt/ *n.* **1.** [*noncount*] the investing of money in order to make a profit. **2.** [*count*] a thing invested in, as a business or a product. **3.** [*count*] a sum of money invested.

in•vet•er•ate /ɪnˈvɛtərɪt/ *adj.* habitual: *an inveterate smoker.*

in•vig•or•ate /ɪnˈvɪgəˌreyt/ *v.* [~ + *obj*], **-at•ed, -at•ing.** to fill with strength and energy: *I was invigorated by a quick walk.*

in•vin•ci•ble /ɪnˈvɪnsəbəl/ *adj.* that cannot be defeated: *an invincible army.*

in•vi•o•la•ble /ɪnˈvayələbəl/ *adj.* that must not be violated: *an inviolable promise.* —**in,vi•o•la'bil•i•ty,** *n.* [*noncount*]

in•vi•o•late /ɪnˈvayəlɪt, -ˌleyt/ *adj.* free from harm; not disturbed: *The castle remained inviolate.*

in•vis•i•ble /ɪnˈvɪzəbəl/ *adj.* not able to be seen; not visible. —**in•vis•i•bil•i•ty** /ɪnˌvɪzə-ˈbɪlɪtiy/, *n.* [*noncount*] —**in'vis•i•bly,** *adv.*

in•vi•ta•tion /ˌɪnvɪˈteyʃən/ *n.* **1.** [*noncount*] the act of inviting. **2.** [*count*] an often written request to take part in something: *a wedding invitation.*

in•vite /ɪnˈvayt/ *v.* [~ + *obj*], **-vit•ed, -vit•ing. 1.** to ask (someone) to do something: *to invite friends to dinner.* **2.** to ask for: *The speaker invited questions.* **3.** to act so as to make likely: *to invite trouble.*

in•vit•ing /ɪnˈvaytɪŋ/ *adj.* attractive: *an inviting job offer.*

in•vo•ca•tion /ˌɪnvəˈkeyʃən/ *n.* **1.** [*noncount*] the act of praying to a power, esp. God, for help. **2.** [*count*] a prayer at the beginning of a ceremony or public occasion.

in•voice /ˈɪnvɔys/ *n.,* *v.,* **-voiced, -voic•ing.** —*n.* [*count*] **1.** a bill listing the goods sold and prices charged. —*v.* [~ + *obj*] **2.** to present an invoice to or for: *They invoiced the company for the delivery.*

in•voke /ɪnˈvowk/ *v.* [~ + *obj*], **-voked, -vok•ing. 1.** to call out to (God) for help. **2.** to declare to be in effect: *to invoke the law.* **3.** to call forth; cause: *The poem invoked sad feelings.* **4.** to request or beg for: *to invoke aid.*

in•vol•un•tar•y /ɪnˈvɒlənˌtɛriy/ *adj.* unintentional: *an involuntary cry of pain.* **2.** automatic: *Breathing is involuntary.* —**in•vol•un•tar•i•ly** /ɪnˈvɒlənˌtɛrəliy, -ˌvɒlənˈtɛər-/, *adv.*

in•volve /ɪnˈvɒlv/ *v.* [~ + *obj*], **-volved, -volv•ing. 1.** to have as a necessary part: *This job involves long hours.* **2.** to cause (someone) to take part in something: *Don't involve me in your quarrel.* **3.** to include or have an effect on: *Many workers were involved in the strike.* —**in'volve•ment,** *n.* [*noncount*]: *His involvement in the rob-*

I

bery was not proved. [*count*]: *She had had many romantic involvements.*

in•volved /ɪn'vɒlvd/ *adj.* **1.** [*be/become* + ~] associated in a close personal relationship. **2.** [*be* + ~] completely taken up with something: *He was very involved in his work.* **3.** complicated.

in•vul•ner•a•ble /ɪn'vʌlnərəbəl/ *adj.* that cannot be hurt or damaged: *an invulnerable fortress.* —**in•vul•ner•a•bil•i•ty** /ɪn,vʌlnərə'bɪlɪtiy/, *n.* [*noncount*]

in•ward /'ɪnwərd/ *adv.* Also, **in′wards. 1.** toward the inside, as of a place. **2.** toward the mind or spirit. —*adj.* **3.** directed toward the inside. **4.** relating to the inside; inner. —'**in•ward•ly,** *adv.*: *inwardly frightened.*

'**in-,your-'face,** *adj. Informal.* marked by or being bold and aggressive; provocative: *in-your-face journalism.*

Io., an abbreviation of: Iowa.

i•o•dine /'ayə,dayn, -dɪn/ *in Chemistry also* -,diyn/ also **i•o•din** /-dɪn/ *n.* [*noncount*] **1.** a chemical element used in medicine and photography. **2.** a medicine containing iodine, used on cuts to prevent infection.

i•on /'ayən, 'aynn/ *n.* [*count*] an atom or atom group that is electrically charged.

-ion, a suffix meaning: action or process (*inspection*); state or condition (*depression*). Compare -TION.

i•o•ta /ay'owtə/ *n.* [*count*], *pl.* **-tas.** [*used with a negative word, or in questions*] a very small amount: *Why should I care an iota about that?*

IOU or **I.O.U.,** *n.* [*count*], *pl.* **IOUs, IOU's,** or **I. O.U.'s.** a note saying one owes money and consisting of the letters *IOU,* the sum owed, and the signature of the person who owes the money: *The letters IOU are from the pronunciation of the phrase "I owe you".*

-ious, a variant form of the suffix -ous: (*hilarious*).

IQ, an abbreviation of: intelligence quotient, a measure of a person's intelligence.

ir-1, a form of the prefix IN-1, used before roots beginning with the letter "r": (*irradiate*).

ir-2, a form of the prefix IN-2, used before roots beginning with "r": (*irreducible*).

I•ra•ni•an /ɪ'reyniyən, ɪ 'rɑ-, ay'rey-/ *adj.* **1.** of or relating to Iran. —*n.* [*count*] **2.** a person born or living in Iran.

I•ra•qi /ɪ'ræckiy, ɪ'rɑkiy/ *n., pl.* **-qis. 1.** [*count*] a person born or living in Iraq. **2.** [*noncount*] the language spoken by many of the people living in Iraq. —*adj.* **3.** of or relating to Iraq. **4.** of or relating to the language spoken by many of the people in Iraq.

i•rate /ay'reyt, 'ayreyt/ *adj.* angry. —**i'rate•ly,** *adv.*

ir•i•des•cent /,ɪrɪ'dɛsənt/ *adj.* displaying bright, strong, shifting colors: *iridescent soap bubbles.* —,**ir•i'des•cence,** *n.* [*noncount*]

i•ris /'ayrɪs/ *n.* [*count*] **1.** the round, colored, front part of the eye that contains an opening, the pupil, in its center. **2.** a tall plant with showy, colorful flowers.

I•rish /'ayrɪʃ/ *adj.* **1.** of or relating to Ireland. **2.** of or relating to the language spoken by many of the people in Ireland. —*n.* **3.** [*plural; the* + ~ ; *used with a plural verb*] the people born or living in Ireland. **4.** [*noncount*] a language spoken by many of the people in Ireland.

irk /ɜrk/ *v.* [~ + *obj*] to annoy: *I was irked by the delay.*

irk•some /'ɜrksəm/ *adj.* annoying.

i•ron /'ayərn/ *n.* **1.** [*noncount*] a common metallic element needed by all plants and animals, and also used for making steel, tools, machinery, etc. **2.** [*count*] an electrical appliance with a flat metal bottom, used when heated to press cloth. **3.** **irons,** [*plural*] heavy chains for a prisoner. —*adj.* [*before a noun*] **4.** made of iron: *an iron gate.* **5.** like iron in firmness, strength, etc.: *She has an iron will.* —*v.* **6.** [~ + *obj*] [*no obj*] to press with a heated iron (clothes, etc.). **7. iron out,** to clear away (difficulties): *They tried to iron out their differences; They tried to iron them out.* —*Idiom.* **8. have plenty of/several/some irons in the fire,** to be involved in a number of activities.

'**iron 'curtain,** *n.* [*the* + ~; *sometimes: Iron Curtain*] a barrier to the exchange of information and ideas, esp. the barrier that existed between the former Soviet Union or its allies and other countries.

i•ron•ic /ay'rɒnɪk/ also **i'ron•i•cal,** *adj.* using or showing irony. —**i'ron•i•cal•ly,** *adv.*

i•ro•ny /'ayrəniy, 'ayər-/ *n., pl.* **-nies. 1.** [*noncount*] saying or writing the opposite of one's actual meaning. **2.** [*noncount*] [*count*] an effect or result opposite to what was expected.

ir•ra•tion•al /ɪ'ræʃənl/ *adj.* not controlled or influenced by reason: *irrational fears.* —**ir'ra•tion•al•ly,** *adv.*

ir•rec•on•cil•a•ble /ɪ'rɛkən,sayləbəl, ɪ,rɛkən-'say-/ *adj.* that cannot be brought into agreement: *irreconcilable differences.*

ir•reg•u•lar /ɪ'rɛgyələr/ *adj.* **1.** uneven: *an irregular surface.* **2.** varied in timing; unequal: *He worked very irregular hours.* **3.** not according to established rules, standards, etc.; unusual. **4.** not following the usual grammatical pattern: *irregular verbs.* —**ir•reg•u•lar•i•ty** /ɪ,rɛgyə'lærɪtiy/, *n.* [*count*] [*noncount*] —**ir'reg•u,lar•ly,** *adv.*

ir•rel•e•vant /ɪ'rɛləvənt/ *adj.* not relevant; not to the point. —**ir'rel•e•vance,** *n.* [*noncount*]

ir•rep•a•ra•ble /ɪ'rɛpərəbəl/ *adj.* that cannot be repaired or made good: *irreparable damage.*

ir•re•place•a•ble /,ɪrɪ'pleysəbəl/ *adj.* too special to be replaced: *an irreplaceable vase.*

ir•re•press•i•ble /,ɪrɪ'prɛsəbəl/ *adj.* that cannot be held back; uncontrollable: *irrepressible laughter.* —,**ir•re'press•i•bly,** *adv.*

ir•re•proach•a•ble /,ɪrɪ'prowtʃəbəl/ *adj.* that cannot be criticized.

ir•re•sist•i•ble /,ɪrɪ'zɪstəbəl/ *adj.* **1.** too strong to be resisted: *an irresistible force.* **2.** very desirable: *The cake was irresistible.* —,**ir•re'sist•i•bly,** *adv.*

ir•re•spon•si•ble /,ɪrɪ'spɒnsəbəl/ *adj.* lacking a sense of responsibility. —**ir•re•spon•si•bil•i•ty** /,ɪrɪ,spɒnsə'bɪlɪtiy/, *n.* [*noncount*] —,**ir•re'spon•si•bly,** *adv.*

ir•rev•er•ent /ɪ'rɛvərənt/ *adj.* not showing respect, esp. for religion. —**ir'rev•er•ence,** *n.* [*noncount*] —,**ir'rev•er•ent•ly,** *adv.*

ir•rev•o•ca•ble /ɪ'rɛvəkəbəl/ *adj.* that cannot be changed or taken back: *an irrevocable decision.* —**ir'rev•o•ca•bly,** *adv.*

ir•ri•gate /'ɪrɪ,geyt/ *v.* [~ + *obj*], **-gat•ed, -gat•ing.** to supply (land) with water by artificial means. —**ir•ri•ga•tion** /,ɪrɪ'geyʃən/, *n.* [*noncount*]

ir•ri•ta•ble /'ɪrɪtəbəl/ *adj.* easily annoyed. —**ir•ri•ta•bil•i•ty** /,ɪrɪtə'bɪlɪtiy/, *n.* [*noncount*] —'**ir•ri•ta•bly,** *adv.*

ir•ri•tant /'ɪrɪtənt/ *n.* [*count*] **1.** anyone or anything that causes annoyance. **2.** a substance that irritates the skin, eyes, etc.

ir•ri•tate /'ɪrɪ,teyt/ v. [~ + obj], **-tat•ed, -tat• ing. 1.** to annoy: *Her complaining really irritates me.* **2.** to make (a bodily part) sore or sensitive: *The strong soap irritates my skin.* —,ir•ri'ta•tion, n. [noncount] [count] —'ir•ri,tat•ed, adj. —'ir• ri,tat•ing, adj.

IRS, an abbreviation for: Internal Revenue Service.

is /ɪz/ v. 3rd pers. sing. pres. indic. of BE.

-ise, Chiefly Brit. a variant form of the suffix -IZE (organise).

-ish, a suffix meaning: of or belonging to a particular nation or people (British); like or having the characteristics of (babyish); near or about (fiftyish); somewhat (reddish).

Is•lam /ɪs'lɑm, 'ɪslɑm, -ləm, 'ɪz-/ n. [noncount] **1.** the religion of the Muslims, which teaches that there is only one God, Allah, and that Muhammad is His prophet. **2.** the whole body of Muslim believers and countries. —**Is'lam•ic,** adj.

is•land /'aylənd/ n. [count] an area of land completely surrounded by water.

is•land•er /'ayləndər/ n. [count] someone who lives on an island.

isle /ayl/ n. [count] an island, esp. a small one.

-ism, a suffix meaning: action or practice (baptism); state or condition (alcoholism); doctrine or principle (Marxism); distinctive feature or usage (witticism; Americanism).

isn't /'ɪzənt/ contraction of is not: *She isn't sick.*

i•so•late /'aysə,leyt/ v. [~ + obj], **-lat•ed, -lat• ing.** to set or place apart; separate from others. —**i•so•la•tion** /,aysə'leyʃən/, n. [noncount]

i•so•lat•ed /'aysə,leytɪd/ adj. **1.** happening alone or once: *an isolated event.* **2.** far from others: *an isolated cabin.*

Is•rae•li /ɪz'reyliy/ n. [count], pl. **-lis** or **-li. 1.** a person born or living in Israel. —adj. **2.** of or relating to Israel.

is•sue /'ɪʃuw/ n., v., **-sued, -su•ing.** —n. **1.** [count] the act of sending or giving out. **2.** [count] something that is sent or given out: *a magazine issue.* **3.** [count] a subject for discussion: *His age isn't the issue.* **4.** [noncount; used with a singular or plural verb] children: *to die without issue.* —v. **5.** [~ + obj] to bring out to the public. **6.** [~ + obj] to supply: *The school issued books to the students.* **7.** [~ + obj] to send out, as a statement. **8.** to (cause to) come out: [no obj]: *to issue forth into battle.* [~ + obj]: *The factory issued pollutants into the river.*

-ist, a suffix meaning: one who makes or produces (novelist); one who operates or practices (machinist); one skilled in (cellist); follower or supporter (socialist).

isth•mus /'ɪsməs/ n. [count], pl. **-mus•es, -mi** /-may/. a narrow strip of land, bordered on both sides by water, connecting two larger bodies of land: *the isthmus of Panama.*

it /ɪt/ pron., nom. **it,** poss. **its,** obj. **it,** pl. nom. **they,** poss. **their** or **theirs,** obj. **them,** n. —pron. **1.** that person, animal, object, etc., just mentioned: *I don't know who it is. I found my watch but it was broken.* **2.** (used of a baby or animal whose sex is unknown): *Is it a boy or a girl?* **3.** (used with the verb to be to refer to time, distance, or the weather): *It is six o'clock. It's four miles to town. It was foggy.* **4.** (used when the subject or object comes later): *It's too bad you didn't win. It is said that love is blind.* **5.** (used in referring to life in general): *How's it going with*

you? **6.** (used to give emphasis): *It was a gun that he was carrying. I didn't like it that she had tricked us.* —n. [noncount] **7.** (in children's games) the player who is to perform some task, as the one who must catch the others in tag.

I•tal•ian /ɪ'tælyən/ adj. **1.** of or relating to Italy. **2.** of or relating to the language spoken in Italy. —n. **3.** [count] a person born or living in Italy. **4.** [noncount] the language spoken in Italy.

i•tal•ic /ɪ'tælɪk, ay'tæl-/ adj. **1.** of a style of printing type in which the letters slope to the right: *This sentence is in italic type.* —n. **2.** Often, **italics.** [plural] italic type.

itch /ɪtʃ/ v. [no obj] **1.** to feel an irritation of the skin that causes a desire to scratch: *My skin itches.* **2.** to cause such a feeling: *This shirt itches.* —n. [count] **3.** the feeling of itching: *a bad itch.* **4.** a strong desire: *an itch for excitement.* —'**itch•y,** adj., **-i•er, -i•est.**

it'd /'ɪtəd/ **1.** contraction of it would: *It'd be great to see you again.* **2.** contraction of it had: *It'd been cloudy all day.*

-ite, a suffix meaning: inhabitant (Tokyoite); follower (Laborite); mineral or fossil (anthracite); commercial product (dynamite).

i•tem /'aytəm/ n. [count] **1.** a single thing in a group or list. **2.** a single piece of news. **3.** Slang. a topic of gossip: *The director and the actress have become an item.*

i•tem•ize /'aytə,mayz/ v. [~ + obj], **-ized, -iz• ing.** to list by items: *to itemize one's expenses.*

i•tin•er•ant /ay'tɪnərənt, ɪ'tɪn-/ adj. [before a noun] traveling from place to place: *itinerant workers.*

i•tin•er•ar•y /ay'tɪnə'rɛriy, ɪ'tɪn-/ n. [count], pl. **-ar•ies.** a detailed plan for a journey, esp. a list of places to visit.

-itis, a suffix meaning inflammation of a specified body part (appendicitis).

it'll /'ɪtl/ contraction of it will: *Do you think it'll rain?*

its /ɪts/ adj. of that object or animal just mentioned: *The tree shed its leaves. The dog hurt its paw.*

it's /ɪts/ **1.** contraction of it is: *It's starting to rain.* **2.** contraction of it has: *It's been raining all day.*

it•self /ɪt'sɛlf/ pron. **1.** (used as the direct or indirect object of a verb or the object of a preposition to refer to the same thing as the subject): *The machine somehow fixed itself. The bird built a nest for itself.* **2.** (used to give emphasis): *The land itself was not for sale.*

I've /ayv/ contraction of I have: *I've been busy.*

-ive, a suffix meaning: tending to (destructive); of the nature of (festive).

i•vo•ry /'ayvəriy, 'ayvriy/ n., pl. **-ries,** adj. —n. **1.** [noncount] the hard white substance that makes up the main part of the tusks, esp. of the elephant and walrus. **2. ivories,** [plural] Slang. the keys of a piano. **3.** [noncount] a creamy or yellowish white. —adj. **4.** [before a noun] consisting or made of ivory. **5.** of the color ivory.

'**ivory 'tower,** n. [count] a place kept apart from practical or unpleasant matters.

i•vy /'ayviy/ n. [noncount] a climbing evergreen plant with smooth, shiny leaves.

-ize, a suffix meaning: to practice or engage in (economize); to treat in a certain way (idolize); to become or form into (unionize); to make or cause to be (civilize).

I

J

J, j /dʒey/ *n., pl.* **Js** or **J's, js** or **j's.** the tenth letter of the English alphabet, a consonant.

jab /dʒæb/ *v.,* **jabbed, jab•bing,** *n.* —*v.* **1.** to poke quickly, as with an end or point: [~ + *obj*]: *He jabbed his elbow into my side.* [*no obj*]: *to jab at a fire with a stick.* —*n.* [*count*] **2.** a sudden strong push or blow.

jab•ber /ˈdʒæbər/ *v.* [*no obj*] [~ + *obj*] to speak (something) quickly and unclearly. —**ˈjab•ber•er,** *n.* [*count*]

jack /dʒæk/ *n.* [*count*] **1.** a device for lifting a heavy object, as a car, off the ground. **2.** a playing card with the picture of a soldier or servant: *a pair of jacks.* **3.** —*v.* **jack up, 4.** to lift (something) with a jack: *to jack up a car* or *to jack a car up.* **5.** to increase (prices, wages, speed, etc.): *They jacked up oil prices* or *They jacked oil prices up.*

jack•al /ˈdʒækəl, -ɔl/ *n.* [*count*] a wild dog of Asia and Africa that hunts in packs.

jack•ass /ˈdʒækˌæs/ *n.* [*count*] **1.** a male donkey. **2.** a very foolish or stupid person.

jack•et /ˈdʒækɪt/ *n.* [*count*] **1.** a short coat with sleeves. **2.** the skin of a baked potato. **3.** a protective outer covering, as the plastic around a wire, a casing for a bullet, or a wrapper for a book.

'Jack 'Frost, *n.* frost or freezing cold thought of as a person.

'jack-in-the-ˌbox or **'jack-in-a-ˌbox,** *n.* [*count*], *pl.* **-box•es.** a toy made up of a box from which an enclosed doll jumps up when the lid is opened.

jack•knife /ˈdʒækˌnayf/ *n., pl.* **-knives,** *v.,* **-knifed, -knif•ing.** —*n.* [*count*] **1.** a large pocketknife. —*v.* [*no obj*] [~ + *obj*] **2.** (of a trailer truck) to have the cab and trailer turn at the point where they meet until they form a V shape, as in an accident.

ˌjack-of-'all-'trades, *n.* [*count*], *pl.* **jacks-of-all-trades.** a person who is skilled at many different kinds of work.

jack-o'-lan•tern /ˈdʒækəˌlæntərn/ *n.* [*count*] a pumpkin that has been cleaned out and cut with openings to look like a face, traditionally displayed at Halloween.

jack•pot /ˈdʒækˌpɒt/ *n.* [*count; usually singular; often: the + ~*] **1.** the largest money prize in a game, contest, etc. —*Idiom.* **2. hit the jackpot, a.** to achieve sudden great success. **b.** to win a jackpot.

'jack ˌrabbit, *n.* [*count*] a large hare of W North America, having long hind legs and long ears.

Ja•cuz•zi /dʒəˈkuwziy/ [*count*] *pl.* **-zis.** *Trademark.* a brand name for a device for a whirlpool bath and related products.

jade /dʒeyd/ *n.* [*noncount*] **1.** a hard, usually green mineral from which jewelry and carvings are made. **2.** Also called **'jade 'green.** a color varying from bluish green to yellowish green.

jad•ed /ˈdʒeydɪd/ *adj.* tired and bored, usually after overdoing something.

jag•ged /ˈdʒægɪd/ *adj.* roughly uneven on the edges: *jagged cliffs.*

jag•uar /ˈdʒægwɑr, -yuwˌɑr/ *n.* [*count*] a large spotted wild cat of central America.

jail /dʒeyl/ *n.* [*count*] [*noncount*] **1.** a prison, esp. one for holding persons who are awaiting trial or who have been found guilty of breaking the law. —*v.* [~ + *obj*] **2.** to put in jail; imprison.

jail•er or **jail•or** /ˈdʒeylər/ *n.* [*count*] a person in charge of a jail.

ja•la•pe•ño or **ja•la•pe•no** /ˌhɑləˈpeynyow/ *n.* [*noncount*] [*count*], *pl.* **-ños** or **-nos.** a hot-tasting, green or orange-red pepper used esp. in Mexican cooking. Also called **'jala'peño 'pepper.**

jam¹ /dʒæm/ *v.,* **jammed, jam•ming,** *n.* —*v.* **1.** to squeeze or push into a space; fill tightly: [~ + *obj*]: *He jammed his socks into a drawer.* [*no obj*]: *People jammed into the elevator.* **2.** [~ + *obj*] to push hard: *I jammed my foot on the brake.* **3.** [~ + *obj*] to crush by squeezing: *I jammed my hand in the car door.* **4.** [~ + *obj*] to block up completely: *Crowds jammed the doors.* **5.** (of a machine, part, etc.) to (cause to) become stuck and not to work: [*no obj*]: *The lock jammed and I couldn't open it.* [~ + *obj*]: *I jammed the lock.* **6.** [~ + *obj*] to block (a radio broadcast) by sending out noise. **7. jam on,** to push down on (the brakes of a vehicle) suddenly and hard: *jamming on the brakes* or *jamming the brakes on.* —*n.* [*count*] **8.** the act of jamming or the state of being jammed: *a huge jam of people; a traffic jam.* **9.** *Informal.* a difficult situation: *to be in a jam.*

jam² /dʒæm/ *n.* [*noncount*] [*count*] a food made from crushed fruit boiled with sugar.

Ja•mai•can /dʒəˈmeykən/ *adj.* **1.** of or relating to Jamaica. —*n.* [*count*] **2.** a person born or living in Jamaica.

jamb /dʒæm/ *n.* [*count*] either of the sides of a door or window: *a door jamb.*

jam•bo•ree /ˌdʒæmbəˈriy/ *n.* [*count*], *pl.* **-rees.** a large party or other social gathering.

'jam-'packed, *adj.* very crowded.

Jan or **Jan.,** an abbreviation of: January.

jan•gle /ˈdʒæŋgəl/ *v.,* **-gled, -gling.** —*v.* **1.** to (cause to) make a harsh ringing or metallic sound: [*no obj*]: *Suddenly the fire alarm jangled.* [~ + *obj*]: *He jangled a bunch of keys.* **2.** [~ + *obj*] to irritate or upset: *a loud noise that jangles the nerves.* —*n.* [*count*] **3.** a harsh ringing or metallic sound.

jan•i•tor /ˈdʒænɪtər/ *n.* [*count*] a person who is employed to take care of a building: *the school janitor.*

Jan•u•ar•y /ˈdʒænyuˌɛriy/ *n., pl.* **-ar•ies.** the first month of the year, containing 31 days.

Jap•a•nese /ˌdʒæpəˈniyz, -ˈniys/ *adj., n., pl.* **-nese.** —*adj.* **1.** of or relating to Japan. **2.** of or relating to the language spoken in Japan. —*n.* **3.** [*count*] a person born or living in Japan. **4.** [*noncount*] the language of Japan.

jar¹ /dʒɑr/ *n.* [*count*] a wide-mouthed container often made of glass.

jar² /dʒɑr/ *v.,* **jarred, jar•ring,** *n.* —*v.* **1.** to have a sudden and unpleasant effect on (one's nerves, feelings, etc.): [~ + *obj*]: *The loud bang jarred my nerves.* [*no obj*]: *Her voice soon jarred on me.* **2.** [~ + *obj*] to cause to vibrate or shake: *The explosion jarred several buildings.* —*n.* [*count*] **3.** a jolt or shake. **4.** a sudden unpleasant effect; shock. —**'jar•ring,** *adj.*: *a jarring noise.* —**'jar•ring•ly,** *adv.*

jar•gon /ˈdʒɑrgən/ *n.* [*noncount*] the specialized language used by a particular profession or group of people: *medical jargon; legal jargon.*

jaun•dice /ˈdʒɔndɪs, ˈdʒɑn-/ *n.* [*noncount*] a disease in which the skin and the whites of the eyes become yellow.

jaun•diced /ˈdʒɔndɪst, ˈdʒɑn-/ *adj.* **1.** affected with or colored by or as if by jaundice: *jaundiced skin.* **2.** showing doubt or dislike: *He has a jaundiced view of politics.*

jaunt /dʒɔnt, dʒɑnt/ *n.* [*count*] a short journey, esp. for pleasure.

jaun•ty /ˈdʒɔntiy, ˈdʒɑn-/ *adj.*, **-ti•er, -ti•est.** lively and confident: *to walk with a jaunty step.* —**jaun•ti•ly** /ˈdʒɔntl̩iy, ˈdʒɑn-/, *adv.* —**ˈjaun•ti•ness,** *n.* [*noncount*]

jave•lin /ˈdʒævlɪn, ˈdʒævə-/ *n.* [*count*] a light spear for throwing, esp. in a sport.

jaw /dʒɔ/ *n.* [*count*] **1.** either of the bony structures that frame the mouth and hold the teeth: *the upper and lower jaws.* **2.** the lower part of the face. **3.** jaws, [*plural*] two hinged parts in a mechanical device that hold something tightly.

jaw•bone /ˈdʒɔˌbown/ *n.* [*count*] either of the two bones forming the lower jaw.

jay /dʒey/ *n.* [*count*] a noisy, brightly colored bird of the crow family.

jay•walk /ˈdʒeyˌwɔk/ *v.* [*no obj*] to cross a street without obeying traffic lights or rules. —**ˈjayˌwalk•er,** *n.* [*count*]

jazz /dʒæz/ *n.* [*noncount*] **1.** music originating from black songs in New Orleans around the beginning of the 20th century and over time developing many styles, characterized by strong rhythms and improvisation. —*v.* **2.** jazz up, *Slang.* to make something exciting or interesting: *She tried to jazz up the party* or *She tried to jazz the party up.*

jazz•y /ˈdʒæziy/ *adj.*, **-i•er, -i•est. 1.** of or like jazz. **2.** *Slang.* fancy or bright: *a jazzy sweater.*

jeal•ous /ˈdʒɛləs/ *adj.* **1.** [*be ~ of + obj*] feeling bitterness or anger about someone's success, advantages, etc.: *to be jealous of a rich brother.* **2.** fearful of losing someone to another: *a jealous husband.* **3.** protective of what one has: *jealous of one's freedom.* —**ˈjeal•ous•ly,** *adv.* —**ˈjeal•ous•y,** *n.* [*noncount*] [*count*], *pl.* **-ies.**

jeans /dʒiynz/ [*plural; used with a plural verb*] pants made of strong cotton cloth for informal wear.

Jeep /dʒiyp/ *Trademark.* [*count*] a small, powerful vehicle for traveling over rough areas.

jeer /dʒɪər/ *v.* **1.** to shout or laugh rudely (at): [*no obj*]: *The crowd began to jeer at the speaker.* [*~ + obj*]: *The crowd jeered the speaker.* —*n.* [*count*] a jeering remark or noise.

jell /dʒɛl/ *v.* **1.** to (cause to) become firmer, like jelly; gel: [*no obj*]: *The pudding had begun to jell.* [*~ + obj*]: *The cold refrigerator will jell the dessert.* **2.** to (cause to) take a clear shape: [*no obj*]: *My ideas began to jell.* [*~ + obj*]: *Talking with you helped jell my ideas.*

jel•ly /ˈdʒɛliy/ *n.* [*noncount*] [*count*], *pl.* **-lies.** a sweet, soft food spread on bread, etc., made of fruit juice boiled with sugar. —**ˈjel•ly,like,** *adj.*

jel•ly•bean /ˈdʒɛliyˌbiyn/ *n.* [*count*] a small, bean-shaped, chewy candy.

jel•ly•fish /ˈdʒɛliyˌfɪʃ/ *n.* [*count*], *pl.* (*esp. when thought of as a group*) **-fish,** (*esp. for kinds or species*) **-fish•es.** a stinging, jellylike sea creature.

jeop•ard•y /ˈdʒɛpərdiy/ *n.* [*noncount*] risk of loss, harm, death, or injury; danger: *to put one's life in jeopardy.* —**ˈjeop•ard,ize,** *v.* [*~ + obj*], **-ized, -iz/ing.**

jerk /dʒɜrk/ *n.* [*count*] **1.** a sharp, sudden pull or movement: *The train started with a jerk.* **2.** *Slang.* a foolish, stupid person. —*v.* **3.** to pull or move with a sharp, sudden motion: [*~ + obj*]: *She jerked the child by the hand.* [*no obj*]: *The car jerked to a stop.*

jerk•y /ˈdʒɜrkiy/ *adj.*, **-i•er, -i•est.** marked by sudden starts and stops.

jer•sey /ˈdʒɜrziy/ *n.*, *pl.* **-seys. 1.** [*noncount*] a plain-knit, machine-made fabric of wool, silk, nylon, etc., that is usually soft and elastic, used for garments. **2.** [*count*] a close-fitting knitted sweater or shirt.

jest /dʒɛst/ *n.* **1.** [*count*] a joke or funny remark. **2.** [*noncount*] fun; joking: *to speak in jest.* —*v.* [*no obj*] **3.** to joke.

jest•er /ˈdʒɛstər/ *n.* [*count*] a man in former times whose job was to amuse the king or queen.

Je•sus /ˈdʒiyzəs, -zəz/ *n.* Also called **ˈJesus ˈChrist, ˈJesus of ˈNazareth.** born 4? B.C., died A.D. 29?, the founder of the Christian religion.

jet¹ /dʒɛt/ *n.*, *v.*, **jet•ted, jet•ting.** —*n.* [*count*] **1.** a stream of a liquid, gas, etc., forcefully shooting out from a small opening. **2.** a narrow opening that lets out liquid or gas: *a gas jet on a stove.* **3.** Also, **jet plane.** an aircraft moved by a jet engine. **4.** JET ENGINE. —*v.* [*no obj*] [*~ + obj*] **5.** to travel or transport by jet. **6.** to shoot (something) forth in a stream.

jet² /dʒɛt/ *n.* [*noncount*] **1.** a hard black coal that can be highly polished, sometimes used in jewelry. **2.** a deep black. —*adj.* [*before a noun*] **3.** of the color jet: *jet black hair.*

ˈjet ˈengine, *n.* [*count*] an engine, such as of an aircraft, that produces forward motion by pushing out backwards a jet of fluid or heated air and gases.

ˈjet ˌlag or **ˈjetˌlag,** *n.* [*noncount*] a feeling of tiredness or confusion after a long flight through several time zones.

ˈjet proˈpulsion, *n.* [*noncount*] movement of an aircraft, rocket, etc., by a stream of hot gas forced out in the opposite direction. —**ˈjet-proˈpelled,** *adj.*

jet•ti•son /ˈdʒɛtəsən, -zən/ *v.* [*~ + obj*] to throw away as useless.

jet•ty /ˈdʒɛtiy/ *n.* [*count*], *pl.* **-ties. 1.** a wall built out into a body of water, as to protect a harbor. **2.** a landing place for boats.

Jew /dʒuw/ *n.* [*count*] **1.** a person who is descended from the ancient Hebrews. **2.** a person whose religion is Judaism. —**ˈJew•ish,** *adj.*

jew•el /ˈdʒuwəl/ *n.* [*count*] **1.** a cut and polished precious stone. **2.** an ornament that is decorated with precious stones. **3.** a person or thing that is highly valued. —**jeweled,** *adj.*

jew•el•er /ˈdʒuwələr/ *n.* [*count*] a person who makes, sells, or repairs jewelry, watches, etc. Also, *esp. Brit.,* **ˈjew•el•ler.**

jew•el•ry /ˈdʒuwəlriy/ *n.* [*noncount*] ornaments, as necklaces, rings, etc., esp. when made of precious metals, jewels, or pearls. Also, *esp. Brit.,* **ˈjew•el•ler•y.**

jibe¹ /dʒayb/ *n.* GIBE.

jibe² /dʒayb/ *v.* [*no obj*], **jibed, jib•ing.** to be in agreement: *These measurements don't jibe.*

jif•fy /ˈdʒɪfiy/ *n.* [*count; usually singular*], *pl.* **-fies.** *Informal.* a very short time: *She got dressed in a jiffy.*

jig /dʒɪg/ *n.*, *v.*, **jigged, jig•ging.** —*n.* [*count*] **1.** a fast, lively dance. **2.** the music for this dance.

J

—v. **3.** [no obj] to dance a jig. **4.** [no obj] [~ + obj] to move with a quick up-and-down motion.

jig•gle /'dʒɪgəl/ v., **-gled, -gling.** to move lightly and quickly up and down or back and forth: [~ + obj]: You have to jiggle the handle to get the machine started. [no obj]: His fat stomach jiggled as he walked.

'jigsaw ,puzzle, n. [count] a puzzle made up of small irregular pieces that can be fitted together to make a picture.

jilt /dʒɪlt/ v. [~ + obj] to suddenly leave (a lover or sweetheart).

jim•my /'dʒɪmiy/ n., pl. **-mies,** v., **-mied, -my•ing.** —n. [count] **1.** a metal bar used to open something closed or locked, as a door or window. —v. [~ + obj] **2.** to force open with or as if with a jimmy: The thief must have jimmied the door.

jin•gle /'dʒɪŋgəl/ v., **-gled, -gling,** n. —v. [no obj] [~ + obj] **1.** to (cause to) make a light ringing sound, as of small bells; tinkle. —n. [count] **2.** a light ringing sound: the jingle of her keys. **3.** a short, light tune or rhyme, used esp. for advertising.

jinx /dʒɪŋks/ n. [count] **1.** a person or thing that is thought to bring bad luck. **2.** a spell of bad luck. —v. [~ + obj] **3.** to bring bad luck to: Acting too hastily might jinx the deal.

jit•ters /'dʒɪtərz/ n. [plural; usually the + ~] a feeling of fright or uneasiness. —**'jit•ter•y,** adj., **-i•er, -i•est.**

jive /dʒayv/ n., v., **jived, jiv•ing,** adj. —n. [noncount] **1.** swing music. **2.** Slang. deceiving or foolish talk. —v. [~ + obj] [no obj] **3.** Slang. to fool or kid (someone). —adj. **4.** Slang. intended to deceive: jive talk.

job /dʒɒb/ n. [count] **1.** a piece of work to do: He had the job of mowing the lawn every Saturday. **2.** a position of work; occupation or employment. **3.** the performance of a task: to do a good job. **4.** a difficult task: We had quite a job getting him to agree. **5.** Slang. a theft or similar crime: The thief was caught after a bank job. —adj. [before a noun] **6.** of or relating to employment: job security. —**Idiom. 7. on the job,** while working; at work: He got that injury on the job. —**'job•less,** adj. —**'job•less•ness,** n. [noncount]

jock¹ /dʒɒk/ n. [count] **1.** a jockstrap. **2.** Informal. a person who is good at sports; athlete.

jock² /dʒɒk/ n. [count] a jockey.

jock•ey /'dʒɒkiy/ n., pl. **-eys,** v., **-eyed, -ey•ing.** —n. [count] **1.** a person who rides horses professionally in races. —v. [~ + obj] **2.** Informal. to operate or guide the movement of: He jockeyed the sofa through the door. **3. jockey for position,** to try hard to get an advantage.

jock•strap /'dʒɒk,stræp/ n. [count] an undergarment consisting of an elastic belt with a supporting pocket, worn by men esp. during sports. Also called **athletic supporter.**

joc•u•lar /'dʒɒkyələr/ adj. joking. —**joc•u•lar•i•ty** /,dʒɒkyə'lærɪtiy/, n. [noncount]

jog /dʒɒg/ v., **jogged, jog•ging,** n. —v. **1.** [~ + obj] to push or knock slightly: to jog someone's elbow. **2.** [~ + obj] to help (the memory) to operate: Hearing the name jogged his memory of an earlier time. **3.** [no obj] to run slowly, esp. for exercise. —n. [count] **4.** a slight push. **5.** a reminder: a jog to the memory. **6.** a slow, steady run. —**'jog•ger,** n. [count]

john /dʒɒn/ n. [count] Informal. a toilet or bathroom.

'John 'Doe /dow/ n. [count] a name used in le-

gal actions for a male person whose true name is not known: the defendant known as John Doe.

join /dʒɔyn/ v. **1.** to (cause to) bring together; connect: [~ + obj]: They all joined hands. [no obj]: Their hands joined and they formed a circle. **2.** to (cause to) come together: [no obj]: The two streams join here. [~ + obj]: Here the river joins the sea. **3.** [~ + obj] to come into the company of: Can you join us for a drink? **4.** [~ + obj] to become a member of: to join a club. **5.** [~ + obj] to bring into close relationship: The minister joined them in marriage. **6. join in,** to take part in (something): He was too shy to join in. Wouldn't you like to join in the fun?

joint /dʒɔynt/ n. [count] **1.** the place at which two things or parts are joined. **2.** the place where two bones meet: the joint of the elbow. **3.** a large piece of meat. **4.** Slang. a marijuana cigarette. **5.** Slang. a cheap bar, nightclub, etc. —adj. [before a noun] **6.** shared by two or more people: joint owners; a joint effort. —**'joint•ly,** adv.: They worked jointly on the task.

joist /dʒɔyst/ n. [count] one of a number of small parallel beams of wood, steel, or reinforced concrete that support a floor or ceiling.

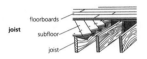

joke /dʒowk/ n., v., **joked, jok•ing.** —n. [count] **1.** a short, humorous story with an ending that causes laughter. **2.** anything said or done to cause amusement or laughter. **3.** something not taken seriously: That law is just a joke: no one obeys it. **4. no joke,** a serious matter: Waiting in the cold was no joke. —v. [no obj] **5.** to make or tell jokes. **6.** to say something in fun or teasing: I was only joking. —**'jok•ing•ly,** adv.

jok•er /'dʒowkər/ n. [count] **1.** a person who jokes. **2.** an extra playing card used in some games. **3.** Informal. a person; fellow.

jol•ly /'dʒɒliy/ adj., **-li•er, -li•est,** adv. —adj. **1.** merry and cheerful. —adv. **2.** Brit. very: jolly good. —**'jol•li•ness,** n. [noncount]

jolt /dʒowlt/ v. **1.** to (cause to) move roughly; bump or jerk: [no obj]: The bus jolted along the bumpy road. [~ + obj]: The driver jolted the bus along. **2.** [~ + obj] to shock or surprise: We were jolted by the news of her sudden death. —n. [count] **3.** a jolting movement or blow. **4.** a surprise or shock.

jon•quil /'dʒɒŋkwɪl, 'dʒɒn-/ n. [count] a plant having long, narrow leaves and yellow or white flowers.

Jor•da•ni•an /dʒɔr'deyniyən/ n. [count] **1.** a person born or living in Jordan. —adj. **2.** of or relating to Jordan.

jos•tle /'dʒɒsəl/ v., **-tled, -tling,** n. —v. **1.** to push roughly against (someone): [~ + obj]: The crowd jostled her. [no obj]: Many people jostled against her. —n. [count] **2.** a rough bump or push.

jot /dʒɒt/ v., **jot•ted, jot•ting,** n. —v. **1.** [~ + obj] to write quickly or briefly: to jot a note to a friend. **2. jot down,** to make a short, quick note of something: to jot down a number or to jot a number down. —n. [count; singular] **3.** a little bit: I don't care a jot.

jour•nal /'dʒɜrnl̩/ n. [count] **1.** a daily record of events: to keep a journal. **2.** a daily newspaper.

3. a magazine, esp. one devoted to a special interest: *a business journal.*

jour•nal•ism /'dʒɜrnl,ɪzəm/ *n.* [*noncount*] the work of writing and publishing or broadcasting news. —'**jour•nal•ist,** *n.* [*count*] —,**jour•nal'is•tic,** *adj.*

jour•ney /'dʒɜrniy/ *n., pl.* **-neys,** *v.,* **-neyed, -ney•ing.** —*n.* [*count*] **1.** a long trip: *a journey to China.* **2.** a distance or period of time traveled: *It's an hour's journey from here.* —*v.* [*no obj*] **3.** to make a trip; travel.

jo•vi•al /'dʒoʊviyəl/ *adj.* friendly and cheerful: *a jovial smile.* —'**jo•vi•al•ly,** *adv.*: *He greeted her jovially.*

jowl /dʒaʊl/ *n.* [*count; usually plural*] a fold of flesh hanging from the jaw. —**jowled,** *adj:* *heavily jowled.* —'**jowl•y,** *adj.,* **-i•er, -i•est.**

joy /dʒɔɪ/ *n.* **1.** [*noncount*] great happiness: *He was filled with joy at the birth of his daughter.* **2.** [*count*] a cause of great pleasure: *a book that was a joy to read.* —'**joy•ful,** *adj.* —'**joy•ful•ly,** *adv.*

joy•ous /'dʒɔɪəs/ *adj.* joyful; happy: *a joyous occasion.* —'**joy•ous•ly,** *adv.*

joy•ride /'dʒɔɪ,raɪd/ *n., v.,* **-rode, -rid•den, -rid•ing.** —*n.* [*count*] **1.** a pleasure ride, esp. in a stolen or carelessly driven vehicle. —*v.* [*no obj*] **2.** to go on a joyride.

JP or **J.P.,** an abbreviation of: Justice of the Peace.

Jr. or **jr.,** an abbreviation of: Junior.

ju•bi•lant /'dʒuwbələnt/ *adj.* showing great joy: *He was jubilant over his victory.* —'**ju•bi•lant•ly,** *adv.*

ju•bi•la•tion /,dʒuwbə'leɪʃən/ *n.* [*noncount*] great happiness or joy.

ju•bi•lee /'dʒuwbə,liy, ,dʒuwbə'liy/ *n.* [*count*], *pl.* **-lees.** the celebration of an anniversary, esp. a 50th anniversary.

Ju•da•ism /'dʒuwdiy,ɪzəm, -də-/ *n.* [*noncount*] the religion and culture of the Jews.

judge /dʒʌdʒ/ *n., v.,* **judged, judg•ing.** —*n.* [*count*] **1.** a public officer with the authority to decide cases in a court of law. **2.** a person who decides the winner in a competition. **3.** a person qualified to give an opinion: *a good judge of horses.* —*v.* **4.** [~ + *obj*] to pass legal judgment on: *The court judged him to be the guilty party.* **5.** to act as a judge in (something): [~ + *obj*]: *to judge a tennis match.* [*no obj*]: *You're not in a position to judge in the matter.* **6.** [~ + *obj*] to form an opinion of: *I judged the distance to be about two miles.*

judg•ment /'dʒʌdʒmənt/ *n.* **1.** [*noncount*] the ability to decide or judge wisely: *He showed good judgment in choosing friends.* **2.** [*count*] an opinion: *It was the reviewer's judgment that the play would not be a success.* **3.** [*count*] a decision given by a judge or court. Also, *esp. Brit.,* '**judge•ment.**

judg•men•tal /dʒʌdʒ'mɛntl/ *adj.* tending to make moral judgments.

ju•di•cial /dʒuw'dɪʃəl/ *adj.* [*before a noun*] relating to courts of law or to judges. —**ju'di•cial•ly,** *adv.*

ju•di•ci•ar•y /dʒuw'dɪʃiy,ɛriy, -'dɪʃəriy/ *n.* [*count; usually singular; often: the* + ~], *pl.* **-ar•ies. 1.** the judicial branch of government. **2.** the system of courts in a country. **3.** judges thought of as a group.

ju•di•cious /dʒuw'dɪʃəs/ *adj.* having or marked by good judgment: *He made judicious use of his money.* —**ju'di•cious•ly,** *adv.*

ju•do /'dʒuwdoʊ/ *n.* [*noncount*] a Japanese

sport of fighting and defending oneself without weapons.

jug /dʒʌg/ *n.* [*count*] a large container for liquids that has a handle and a narrow neck.

jug•gle /'dʒʌgəl/ *v.,* **-gled, -gling. 1.** to keep (several objects, esp. balls) in continuous motion in the air at the same time by skillful throwing and catching: [*no obj*]: *The clown learned how to juggle.* [~ + *obj*]: *He juggled oranges and apples.* **2.** [~ + *obj*] to change (accounts, business figures, etc.) in order to deceive: *to juggle the firm's accounts to hide the theft.* —'**jug•gler,** *n.* [*count*]

juice /dʒuws/ *n., v.,* **juiced, juic•ing.** —*n.* **1.** [*noncount*] [*count*] the natural liquid from fruits, vegetables, or meat. **2.** [*count*] the liquid part or contents of a plant or animal substance: *Use the juice from the roast to make gravy.* **3.** [*noncount*] *Informal.* power, esp. electricity. —*v.* [~ + *obj*] **4.** to remove the juice from: *to juice oranges.*

juic•y /'dʒuwsiy/ *adj.,* **-i•er, -i•est. 1.** full of juice: *a juicy pear.* **2.** very interesting esp. when slightly scandalous: *juicy gossip; juicy details.*

juke•box /'dʒuwk,bɒks/ *n.* [*count*] a large coin-operated phonograph having records selected by pushing a button.

Jul or **Jul.,** an abbreviation of: July.

Ju•ly /dʒʊ'laɪ/ *n., pl.* **-lies.** the seventh month of the year, containing 31 days.

jum•ble /'dʒʌmbəl/ *v.,* **-bled, -bling,** *n.* —*v.* **1.** to mix in disorder: [~ + *obj*]: *The clothes were all jumbled together. Someone jumbled (up) the files.* —*n.* [*count*] **2.** a confused mixture or condition.

jum•bo /'dʒʌmboʊ/ *n., pl.* **-bos,** *adj.* —*n.* [*count*] **1.** one that is very large of its kind, as a very large jet airplane. —*adj.* [*usually: before a noun*] **2.** very large: *a jumbo box of cereal.*

jump /dʒʌmp/ *v.* **1.** [*no obj*] to use the force of the legs and feet to move quickly into the air. **2.** [~ + *obj*] to pass over through the air: *to jump a stream.* **3.** [*no obj*] to move suddenly, as from shock: *I jumped when the firecracker exploded.* **4.** [*no obj*] *Informal.* to be full of activity: *The town is jumping with excitement.* **5.** [*no obj*] to rise or increase suddenly in amount: *Oil prices jumped last month.* **6.** [~ + *obj*] to attack suddenly: *The gang jumped him in a dark alley.* **7. jump at,** to accept quickly and eagerly: *We jumped at the offer.* —*n.* [*count*] **8.** an act or instance of jumping; leap. **9.** something to be jumped over. **10.** a sudden rise in amount, price, etc.: *last year's jump in oil prices.* —*Idiom.* **11. jump the gun,** to do something too soon. **12. jump to conclusions,** to decide about something too quickly.

jump•er[1] /'dʒʌmpər/ *n.* [*count*] **1.** a person or thing that jumps. **2.** a shot in basketball made while jumping.

jump•er[2] /'dʒʌmpər/ *n.* [*count*] **1.** a sleeveless dress usually worn over a blouse or sweater. **2.** *Brit.* a pullover sweater.

jump•y /'dʒʌmpiy/ *adj.,* **-i•er, -i•est.** nervous or anxious. —'**jump•i•ness,** *n.* [*noncount*]

Jun or **Jun.,** an abbreviation of: June.

junc•tion /'dʒʌŋkʃən/ *n.* [*count*] a place where roads or railroad lines meet or cross.

junc•ture /'dʒʌŋktʃər/ *n.* [*count*] a point of time or state of affairs: *At this juncture, we must decide whether to continue negotiations.*

June /dʒuwn/ *n.* the sixth month of the year, containing 30 days.

jun•gle /'dʒʌŋgəl/ *n.* [*noncount*] [*count*] land in

J

tropical regions that is covered with thick, dense plant life.

jun·ior /'dʒuwnyər/ adj. **1. a.** younger: *your junior brother.* **b.** This word is used to name a son after his father; it is often written as *Jr.* following the name: *Edward Hansen, Jr.* **2.** of lower rank or position: *a junior law partner.* **3.** of or relating to juniors in high school or college: *junior year.* —*n.* [count] **4.** a person who is younger than another: *She is two years my junior.* **5.** a person of lower rank: *a junior in the firm.* **6.** a student in the next to the last year at a high school or college.

'junior 'college, *n.* [count] [noncount] an institution offering courses only through the first two years of college instruction.

'junior 'high ,school, *n.* [count] [noncount] a school between elementary school and high school, usually for grades seven through nine.

ju·ni·per /'dʒuwnəpər/ *n.* [count] an evergreen shrub or tree having berrylike purple cones.

junk /dʒʌŋk/ *n.* [noncount] things that are old and useless or no longer wanted. —**junk·y,** *adj.,* **-i·er, -i·est.**

jun·ket /'dʒʌŋkɪt/ *v.* [no obj] to go on a pleasure trip or excursion.

'junk ,food, *n.* [noncount] food that is high in sugar or fat, thought to be bad for one's health.

junk·ie or **junk·y** /'dʒʌŋkiy/ *n.* [count], *pl.* **junk·ies.** *Informal.* a drug addict.

'junk ,mail, *n.* [noncount] advertisements and requests for donations, mailed in bulk.

ju·ris·dic·tion /,dʒʊrɪs'dɪkʃən/ *n.* [noncount] **1.** the right, power, or authority to administer justice. **2.** the range of legal authority: *a case under local jurisdiction.* —**ju·ris'dic·tion·al,** *adj.*

ju·ris·pru·dence /,dʒʊrɪs'pruwdns/ *n.* [noncount] **1.** the science or philosophy of law. **2.** a system of laws. **3.** a branch of law: *medical jurisprudence.*

ju·rist /'dʒʊrɪst/ *n.* [count] a person who knows a lot about the law, esp. a judge.

ju·ror /'dʒʊrər, -ɔr/ *n.* [count] a member of a jury.

ju·ry /'dʒʊriy/ *n.* [count], *pl.* **-ries. 1.** a group of people in a court of law who decide if a person is guilty of a crime. **2.** a group of people who choose the winners in a competition.

just /dʒʌst/ *adv.* **1.** only a moment before: *The sun just came out.* **2.** at this moment: *The movie is just ending.* **3.** exactly or precisely: *That's just what I mean.* **4.** by a narrow margin; barely: *She's just over six feet tall.* **5.** only or merely: *I was just a child.* **6.** quite; really: *I'm feeling just fine.* —*adj.* **7.** guided by reason, justice, and fairness: *a just society.* **8.** lawful: *a just claim to the land.* **9.** given or awarded rightly; deserved: *The criminal received a just punishment.* —**'just·ly,** *adv..*

jus·tice /'dʒʌstɪs/ *n.* **1.** [noncount] the quality of being fair or morally right. **2.** [noncount] legal power or action: *The courts administer justice.* **3.** [count] a judge in a court of law. —*Idiom.* **4. do justice, a.** to appreciate properly. **b.** to treat fairly or satisfactorily.

'justice of the 'peace, *n.* [count] a local public officer having authority to decide lesser cases in court, to perform marriages, etc.

jus·ti·fi·a·ble /'dʒʌstə,fayəbəl, ,dʒʌstə'fay-/ *adj.* that can be justified as right. —**'jus·ti,fi·a·bly,** *adv.*

jus·ti·fi·ca·tion /,dʒʌstəfɪ'keyʃən/ *n.* [noncount] [count] a reasonable excuse.

jus·ti·fy /'dʒʌstə,fay/ *v.* [~ + obj], **-fied, -fy·ing. 1.** to show to be fair or reasonable: *The pleasure these paintings give justifies their high cost.* **2.** to give a good reason for; excuse: *I can't justify my actions.*

jut /dʒʌt/ *v.* [no obj], **jut·ted, jut·ting.** to stick out beyond the main body or line: *a strip of land jutting (out) into the sea.*

ju·ve·nile /'dʒuwvənḷ, -,nayl/ *adj.* **1.** of or suitable for children or young people: *juvenile books.* **2.** childish: *juvenile behavior.* —*n.* [count] **3.** a young person.

'juvenile de'linquency, *n.* [noncount] illegal or criminal behavior by a young person not yet an adult. —**'juvenile de'linquent,** *n.* [count]

jux·ta·pose /'dʒʌkstə,powz, ,dʒʌkstə'powz/ *v.* [~ + obj], **-posed, -pos·ing.** to place close together or side by side, as for comparison. —**jux·ta·po·si·tion** /,dʒʌkstəpə'zɪʃən/, *n.* [noncount]

K

K, k /key/ *n.* [*count*], *pl.* **Ks** or **K's, ks** or **k's.** the 11th letter of the English alphabet, a consonant.

K, an abbreviation of: **1.** the number 1000: *a $20K salary.* **2.** kindergarten.

k. or **k,** an abbreviation of: kilogram.

ka•bob /kə'bɒb/ *n.* KEBAB.

ka•lei•do•scope /kə'laydə,skowp/ *n.* [*count*] a tube-shaped instrument in which loose bits of colored glass at the end of the tube are reflected in mirrors so as to display changing patterns as the tube is turned.

kan•ga•roo /,kæŋgə'ruw/ *n.* [*count*], *pl.* **-roos,** (*esp. when thought of as a group*) **-roo.** an Australian animal that jumps with powerful hind legs and carries its young in its pouch.

Kans., an abbreviation of: Kansas.

ka•put /kɑ'pʊt, -'puwt, kə-/ *adj.* [*be* + ~] *Slang.* broken: *The TV is kaput.*

ka•ra•o•ke /,kæriy'owkiy/ *n.* [*count*] a device that allows a person to sing along to the music of a song and record his or her voice, the original singing having been electronically eliminated.

ka•ra•te /kə'rɑtiy/ *n.* [*noncount*] a Japanese method of self-defense using fast, hard blows with the hands, elbows, knees, or feet.

ka•ty•did /'keytiydɪd/ *n.* [*count*] a large, green insect that looks like a grasshopper.

kay•ak /'kayæk/ *n.* [*count*] **1.** a narrow covered boat with a center opening, used by Eskimos. **2.** a small boat resembling this. —*v.* [*no obj*] **3.** to go or travel by kayak.

ke•bab or **ka•bob** /kə'bɒb/ *n.* [*count*] small pieces of meat cooked on a metal stick, often with vegetables.

keel /kiyl/ *n.* [*count*] **1.** a wood or metal bar along the bottom of a boat, from which the sides are built. —*v.* **2. keel over, a.** (of a boat) to turn over; capsize: *The sailboat keeled over in the storm.* **b.** to fall over suddenly: *He keeled over from the heat.* —*Idiom.* **3. on an even keel,** in a steady or calm state.

keen /kiyn/ *adj.,* **-er, -est. 1.** very sharp: *a keen knife.* **2.** very sensitive, strong, or quick: *a keen sense of hearing; a keen mind.* **3.** extreme: *keen competition for the job.* **4.** [*usually: be* + ~] enthusiastic: *He was very keen on football.* —'**keen•ly,** *adv.: She felt the loss keenly.*

keep /kiyp/ *v.,* **kept, keep•ing,** *n.* —*v.* **1.** [~ + *obj*] to have or hold in one's possession: *I kept the change from a ten-dollar bill.* **2.** [~ + *obj*] to put or store: *I keep the car in the garage.* **3.** to (cause to) continue or stay in a certain position, condition, action, or place: [~ + *obj*]: *to keep a light burning; Keep the children quiet during the ceremony.* [*no obj*]: *She keeps on annoying me. Keep off the grass.* **4.** to maintain in good condition: [~ + *obj*]: *to keep meat by freezing it.* [*no obj*]: *How long will this meat keep?* **5.** [~ + *obj*] to maintain for one's use: *She keeps a car and a driver.* **6.** [~ + *obj*] to reserve; save: *to keep the best wine for guests.* **7.** [~ + *obj*] to prevent, as from an action: *to keep someone from leaving.* **8.** [~ + *obj*] to delay: *He's late; what could be keeping him?* **9.** [~ + *obj*] to not tell: *to keep a secret.* **10.** [~ + *obj*] to write or make entries in: *to keep a diary.* **11.** [~ + *obj*] to fulfill: *She always keeps her promises.* **12.** [~ + *obj*] to own or manage: *to keep a small grocery store.* **13.** [~

+ *obj*] to guard; protect: *He kept her from harm.* **14.** [~ + *obj*] to take care of; maintain or support: *Can you keep a family on those wages?* **15.** [*no obj*] to continue to follow a path, course, etc.: *Keep on this road. Keep left.* **16. keep back,** to withhold; not tell: *Don't keep any information back* or *Don't keep back any information.* **17. keep down, a.** to control the level of: *Keep the music down* or *Keep down the music.* **b.** to prevent from advancing: *They shouldn't keep the good workers down.* or *They shouldn't keep down the good workers.* **18. keep up, a.** to move at the same speed as others: *She easily kept up with the rest of the runners.* **b.** to continue: *She kept up (with) the payments. He told her to keep up the good work. The rain kept up all night.* **c.** to maintain in good condition or repair: *He liked to keep up old cars.* **d.** to stay informed: *He kept up with all the latest sports events.* —*n.* [*count; usually singular*] **19.** the cost of food and a place to live or stay: *He had to work for his keep.* —*Idiom.* **20. keep to oneself, a.** to remain apart from others. **b.** to hold (something) as secret or private.

keep•er /'kiypər/ *n.* [*count*] **1.** a person who guards or watches, as a prison warden. **2.** a person who has the charge or care of something: *hotelkeeper; zookeeper.*

keep•ing /'kiypɪŋ/ *n.* [*noncount*] **1.** care or charge: *in safe keeping.* **2. in keeping with,** in agreement with: *Her actions were not in keeping with her words.*

keg /kɛg/ *n.* [*count*] a small barrel.

kelp /kɛlp/ *n.* [*noncount*] a large brown seaweed used as food and in manufacturing.

ken•nel /'kɛnl/ *n.* [*count*] **1.** a shelter for a dog or cat. **2.** a place for dogs or cats while their owners are away.

Ken•yan /'kɛnyən, 'kiyn-/ *adj.* **1.** of or relating to Kenya. —*n.* [*count*] **2.** a person born or living in Kenya.

kept /kɛpt/ *v.* pt. and pp. of KEEP.

kerb /kɜrb/ *n. Brit.* CURB (def. 1).

ker•chief /'kɜrtʃɪf, -tʃiyf/ *n.* [*count*] a piece of cloth worn over the head or around the neck.

ker•nel /'kɜrnl/ *n.* [*count*] **1.** a grain or seed, as of corn, wheat, etc. **2.** the inner part of a nut or seed. **3.** the essential part of a subject: *There's not a kernel of truth in his story.*

ker•o•sene /'kɛrə,siyn/ *n.* [*noncount*] a liquid made from petroleum, used esp. as a fuel.

ketch•up /'kɛtʃəp, 'kætʃ-/ *n.* [*noncount*] a thick sauce made of tomatoes, onions, vinegar, sugar, and spices.

ket•tle /'kɛtl/ *n.* [*count*] **1.** a pot for boiling liquid or cooking food. **2.** a pot with a spout, used for boiling water.

ket•tle•drum /'kɛtl,drʌm/ *n.* [*count*] a large drum consisting of a hollow curved bottom over which is stretched a skin.

key¹ /kiy/ *n., pl.* **keys,** *adj., v.,* **keyed, key•ing.** —*n.* [*count*] **1.** a small metal instrument that locks or unlocks a door, starts a car, etc. **2.** something that solves or explains: *the key to a secret code; a pronunciation key.* **3.** a means of getting something: *the key to happiness.* **4.** one of the buttons or levers to be pressed on the keyboard of a typewriter, computer, piano, etc. **5.** a

set of related musical notes: *a song in the key of C.* —*adj.* [*before a noun*] **6.** very important; essential: *a key industry.* —*v.* **7.** [~ + *obj*] to adjust: *The ads should be keyed to the viewing audience.* **8.** [~ + *obj*] to regulate the musical pitch of. **9. key in,** to type (data) into a computer: *He keyed in all the data* or *He keyed all the data in.*
key² /kiy/ *n.* [*count*], *pl.* **keys.** a reef or low island.
key•board /'kiy,bɔrd/ *n.* [*count*] **1.** the row or set of keys on a piano, typewriter, computer, etc. —*v.* [~ + *obj*] **2.** to enter (data) into a computer by means of a keyboard. —**'key,board•er,** *n.* [*count*]
'keyed 'up, *adj.* very nervous or excited.
key•hole /'kiy,howl/ *n.* [*count*] a hole for inserting a key in a lock.
key•note /'kiy,nowt/ *n.* [*count*] the central idea, as of a speech or political campaign.
key•stone /'kiy,stown/ *n.* [*count*] **1.** the top stone in the middle of an arch. **2.** the main part or principle of something.
kg, an abbreviation of: kilogram.
khak•i /'kækiy/ *n., pl.* **khak•is. 1.** [*noncount*] dull yellowish brown. **2.** [*noncount*] a strong cotton cloth of this color. **3.** Usually, **khakis.** [*plural*] a military uniform or other clothing made of khaki.
kib•butz /kɪ'bʊts, -'bʊwts/ *n.* [*count*], *pl.* **-but•zim** /-bʊt'siym/. (in Israel) a community settlement or farm.
kick /kɪk/ *v.* **1.** [~ + *obj*] to hit with the foot: *to kick a ball.* **2.** [*no obj*] to make a sudden or forceful movement with the feet: *The baby was laughing and kicking.* **3.** [~ + *obj*] to drive, force, etc., by or as if by kicks: *He kicked a hole in the door.* **4.** [~ + *obj*] *Football.* to score (a field goal) by kicking the ball. **5.** [*no obj*] (of a gun) to move back quickly on firing; recoil. **6. kick in, a.** to contribute one's share: *We kicked in a few dollars for the tip* or *We kicked a few dollars in for the tip.* **b.** to go into effect: *Next year the new tax law kicks in.* **7. kick out,** to force to leave: *They kicked him out of school for fighting.* —*n.* [*count*] **8.** the act of kicking. **9. a.** a strong feeling of excitement: *He gets a kick out of sailing.* **b.** a strong but temporary interest: *Photography is his latest kick.* **10.** a recoil, as of a gun. —*Idiom.* **11. kick the bucket,** to die. **12. kick the habit,** to give up smoking, drinking alcohol, etc. —**'kick•er,** *n.* [*count*]
kick•back /'kɪk,bæk/ *n.* [*count*] a portion of one's income or profit given to someone as payment for having made the income possible.
kick•off or **kick-off** /'kɪk,ɔf, -,ɒf/ *n.* [*count*] **1.** a kick that puts the ball into play in football or soccer. **2.** start; beginning.
kid¹ /kɪd/ *n.* **1.** [*count*] *Informal.* a child or young person. **2. a.** [*count*] a young goat. **b.** [*noncount*] leather made from its skin. —*adj.* [*before a noun*] **3.** *Informal.* younger: *my kid sister.*
kid² /kɪd/ *v.,* **kid•ded, kid•ding.** *Informal.* **1.** to tease: [*no obj*]: *We were just kidding; we didn't mean to hurt you.* [~ + *obj*]: *We were just kidding you about your clothes.* **2.** [~ + *obj*] [*no obj*] to deceive us as a joke. —**'kid•der,** *n.* [*count*]
kid•die or **kid•dy** /'kɪdiy/ *n.* [*count*], *pl.* **-dies.** *Informal.* a child.
kid•nap /'kɪdnæp/ *v.* [~ + *obj*], **-napped** or **-naped, -nap•ping** or **-nap•ing.** to take away (a person) by force and illegally, esp. in order to demand ransom money. —**'kid•nap•per, kid'•nap•er,** *n.* [*count*]

kid•ney /'kɪdniy/ *n., pl.* **-neys. 1.** [*count*] one of a pair of organs that remove waste from the blood and produce urine. **2.** [*count*] [*noncount*] the kidney of an animal used as food.
'kidney ,bean, *n.* [*count*] the dark red, eatable kidney-shaped seed of a bean plant.
kill /kɪl/ *v.* **1. a.** [*no obj*] to cause death. **b.** [~ + *obj*] to cause to die. **2.** [~ + *obj*] (of time) to use up: *She killed time by watching TV.* **3.** [~ + *obj*] *Informal.* to consume completely: *They killed a bottle of wine.* **4.** [~ + *obj*] to bring to an end; destroy: *to kill someone's hopes.* **5.** [~ + *obj*] *Informal.* to hurt: *My feet are killing me!* **6.** [~ + *obj*] *Informal.* to be very angry with: *He'll kill me when he finds out I wrecked the car.* —*n.* [*count*; *usually singular*] **7.** the act of killing, esp. game. **8.** an animal or animals killed. —**'kill•er,** *n.* [*count*]
'killer 'whale, *n.* [*count*] a large, black-and-white whale that feeds chiefly on fish.
kill•ing /'kɪlɪŋ/ *n.* [*noncount*] [*count*] **1.** the act of one that kills. —*Idiom.* **2. make a killing,** to make a quick and unusually large profit.
'kill•joy or **'kill,joy,** *n.* [*count*] a person who spoils the pleasure of others.
kiln /kɪl, kɪln/ *n.* [*count*] an oven for baking or drying something, esp. pottery or bricks.
ki•lo /'kiylow/ *n.* [*count*], *pl.* **-los.** a kilogram.
kilo-, a combining form meaning thousand (*kilowatt*).
kil•o•gram /'kɪlə,græm/ *n.* [*count*] a metric unit of weight equal to 1000 grams or about 2.2 pounds. *Abbr.:* kg Also, *esp. Brit.,* **'kil•o,gramme.**
kil•o•me•ter /kɪ'lɒmɪtər, 'kɪlə,miy-/ *n.* [*count*] a metric unit of length equal to 1000 meters or about 0.62 mile. *Abbr.:* km Also, *esp. Brit.,* **'kil•o,me•tre.**
kil•o•watt /'kɪlə,wɒt/ *n.* [*count*] a unit of electrical power equal to 1000 watts. *Abbr.:* kW, kw
ki•mo•no /kə'mownə, -now/ *n.* [*count*], *pl.* **-nos.** a loose, wide-sleeved Japanese robe, fastened with a broad sash.
kin /kɪn/ *n.* [*plural*] all of a person's relatives.
kind¹ /kaynd/ *adj.,* **-er, -est.** friendly and helpful to others: *a kind, generous person; It was kind of you to help me.* —**'kind•ness,** *n.* [*noncount*] [*count*]
kind² /kaynd/ *n.* **1.** [*count*] a class or group of animals, people, objects, etc., that are the same in some way. **2.** [*count*] a particular variety; sort: *What kind of dog is that?* **3.** [*count; a* + ~ + *of* + *noun*] a doubtful example of something: *The branches formed a kind of shelter.* —*Idiom.* **4. in kind, a.** in the same way: *She answered his insults in kind.* **b.** in goods or services rather than money: *payment in kind.* **5. kind of,** *Informal.* somewhat; rather: *I'm kind of tired.*
kin•der•gar•ten /'kɪndər,gɑrtn, -dṇ/ *n.* [*count*] [*noncount*] a class or school for young children, usually five-year-olds.
kind•heart•ed /'kaynd'hɑrtɪd/ *adj.* having or showing sympathy or kindness. —**'kind'heart•ed•ness,** *n.* [*noncount*]
kin•dle /'kɪndḷ/ *v.,* **-dled, -dling. 1.** to (cause to) begin burning: [~ + *obj*]: *to kindle a fire.* [*no obj*]: *The wood did not kindle easily.* **2.** to (cause to) become aroused or excited: [~ + *obj*]: *The promise of money kindled their interest.* [*no obj*]: *Their interest kindled and grew.*
kin•dling /'kɪndlɪŋ/ *n.* [*noncount*] materials used in lighting a fire.
kind•ly /'kayndliy/ *adj.,* **-li•er, -li•est,** *adv.*

—*adj.* **1.** kind. —*adv.* **2.** in a kind manner. **3.** please: *Kindly close the door.* **4.** very much: *Thank you kindly.* **5.** with liking: *He didn't take kindly to the idea.* —'**kind•li•ness,** *n.* [*noncount*]

kin•dred /'kındrıd/ *n.* [*noncount*] **1.** a person's relatives thought of as a group; kin. **2.** family relationship. —*adj.* **3.** closely similar: *She and I are kindred spirits.*

ki•net•ic /kı'nɛtık, kay-/ *adj.* of, related to, or caused by motion: *kinetic energy.*

kin•folk /'kın,fowk/ *n.* [*plural; used with a plural verb*] relatives; kin. Sometimes, '**kin,folks.**

king /kıŋ/ *n.* [*count*] **1.** the male ruler of a country, usually the son of the previous ruler: *the king of England.* [*used as a title*]: *King Henry VIII.* **2.** a person or thing best in its class. **3.** a playing card with a picture of a king. **4.** an important piece in a game of chess or checkers. —'**king•ship,** *n.* [*noncount*]

king•dom /'kıŋdəm/ *n.* [*count*] **1.** a country ruled by a king or queen. **2.** one of the three main divisions of natural objects: *the animal, vegetable, and mineral kingdoms.*

king•fish•er /'kıŋ,fıʃər/ *n.* [*count*] a brightly colored bird with a long beak for catching fish.

kink /kıŋk/ *n.* [*count*] **1.** a twist or curl, as in a thread, rope, wire, or hair. **2.** stiffness or soreness in a muscle. **3.** difficulty: *a few kinks in the plan.* **4.** something odd in a person's character. —*v.* [*no obj*] [~ + *obj*] **5.** to (cause to) form a kink or kinks. —'**kink•y,** *adj.* **-i•er, -i•est.**

kin•ship /'kınʃıp/ *n.* [*noncount*] **1.** the state of being kin. **2.** [*singular*] relationship because of likeness: *He felt a kinship with fellow sufferers.*

ki•osk /'kiyɒsk, kiy'ɒsk/ *n.* [*count*] a small, open structure used as a newsstand, refreshment stand, etc.

kiss /kıs/ *v.* [~ + *obj*] [*no obj*] **1.** to touch with the lips to show affection, greeting, etc. —*n.* [*count*] **2.** a touch given with the lips. —*Idiom.* **3. kiss of death,** something that causes harm. —'**kiss•a•ble,** *adj.*

kit /kıt/ *n.* [*count*] **1.** a set of tools, supplies, or materials used for a specific purpose: *a first-aid kit.* **2.** a set of parts or materials to be put together: *a model airplane kit.*

kitch•en /'kıtʃən/ *n.* [*count*] a room or place equipped for cooking or preparing food.

kite /kayt/ *n.* [*count*] **1.** a light frame covered with paper, cloth, etc., and having a long string for flying in the wind. **2.** a hawk with long, narrow wings and a hooked bill.

kit•ten /'kıtn/ *n.* [*count*] a young cat. —'**kit•ten•ish,** *adj.*

kit•ty¹ /'kıtiy/ *n., pl.* **-ties. 1.** [*count*] a kitten or a cat. **2.** a pet name for a cat.

kit•ty² /'kıtiy/ *n.* [*count*], *pl.* **-ties.** a sum of money collected from a number of people and meant for a particular purpose.

ki•wi /'kiywiy/ *n.* [*count*], *pl.* **-wis. 1.** a New Zealand bird that cannot fly. **2.** Also called '**ki•wi,fruit** /-,fruwt/. a small, round fruit with brown skin and green flesh.

Kleen•ex /'kliynɛks/ *n.* [*noncount*] [*count*], *pl.* **-ex•es.** *Trademark.* thin soft paper used for blowing the nose, wiping the eyes, etc.

klep•to•ma•ni•a /,klɛptə'meyniyə, -'meynyə/ *n.* [*noncount*] an uncontrollable desire to steal things. —**klep•to•ma•ni•ac** /,klɛptə'meyniy,æk/, *n.* [*count*], *adj.*

klutz /klʌts/ *n.* [*count*] *Slang.* an awkward person. —'**klutz•y,** *adj.,* **-i•er, -i•est.**

km, an abbreviation of: kilometer.

knack /næk/ *n.* [*count; usually singular*] a special skill, talent, or ability: *a knack for sewing.*

knap•sack /'næp,sæk/ *n.* [*count*] a bag with straps for carrying clothing or supplies on the back.

knead /niyd/ *v.* [~ + *obj*] **1.** to press and stretch with the hands: *to knead bread dough.* **2.** to press and rub (muscles); massage.

knee /niy/ *n.* [*count*] **1.** the joint of the leg between the thigh and the lower leg. **2.** the part of a garment covering the knee. —*Idiom.* **3. bring someone to his** or **her knees,** to force someone to do one's will.

knee•cap /'niy,kæp/ *n.* [*count*] the small, flat, protective bone in front of the knee.

'**knee-'deep,** *adj.* **1.** reaching the knees: *knee-deep mud.* **2.** [*be* + ~] covered up to the knees: *We were knee-deep in the river.* **3.** [*be* + ~] deeply involved: *She was knee-deep in debt.*

kneel /niyl/ *v.* [*no obj*], **knelt** /nɛlt/ or **kneeled, kneel•ing.** to go down on the bent knees: *to kneel in prayer.*

knell /nɛl/ *n.* [*count*] the sound of a bell rung esp. for a death or a funeral.

knelt /nɛlt/ *v.* a pt. and pp. of KNEEL.

knew /nuw, nyuw/ *v.* pt. of KNOW.

knick•knack /'nık,næk/ *n.* [*count*] a small item used mostly for decoration.

knife /nayf/ *n., pl.* **knives** /nayvz/, *v.,* **knifed, knif•ing.** —*n.* [*count*] **1.** an instrument for cutting, made of a sharp-edged metal blade fitted with a handle. —*v.* [~ + *obj*] **2.** to cut or stab with a knife.

knight /nayt/ *n.* [*count*] **1.** (in the Middle Ages) a noble soldier serving under a lord or king. **2.** (in Great Britain) a man who is given the honorary title of "Sir." **3.** a chess piece shaped like a horse's head. —*v.* [~ + *obj*] **4.** to make (someone) a knight.

knight•hood /'nayt,huwd/ *n.* [*count*] [*noncount*] the rank of a knight.

knit /nıt/ *v.,* **knit•ted** or **knit, knit•ting,** *n.* —*v.* **1.** [~ + *obj*] [*no obj*] to make (cloth or clothing) by joining loops of yarn by hand with knitting needles or by machine. **2.** to (cause to) become closely and firmly joined together: [*no obj*]: *The broken bones would knit in about a month.* [~ + *obj*]: *a closely knit family.* —*n.* [*count*] **3.** a fabric or garment produced by knitting. —'**knit•ting,** *n.* [*noncount*]

knob /nɒb/ *n.* [*count*] **1.** a rounded handle or control button. **2.** a rounded lump. —'**knob•by,** *adj.,* **-bi•er, -bi•est:** *knobby knees.*

knock /nɒk/ *v.* **1.** [*no obj*] to make a noise by hitting something: *She knocked loudly at the door.* **2.** to hit with force: [*no obj*]: *He knocked against the table and fell.* [~ + *obj*]: *He knocked his head when he fell.* **3.** [*no obj*] to make a banging noise: *The car's engine is knocking.* **4.** [~ + *obj*] *Informal.* to criticize or find fault with: *Don't knock it until you've tried it.* **5. knock down, a.** to cause to fall by hitting: *Lightning knocked the tree down* or *Lightning knocked down the tree.* **b.** to lower the price of: *to knock the price down by $500* or *to knock down the price by $500.* **6. knock off, a.** to stop an activity, esp. the day's work: *The boss let us knock off a little early today. We knocked off work a little early today.* **b.** to reduce a price by the amount of: *Knock off $500* or *Knock $500 off.* **7. knock out,** to make unconscious, as by a hard blow or a drug: *The fighter knocked out his opponent.*

K

—n. 8. [count] a sharp, hard blow: *a knock on the head.* **9.** [noncount] the banging noise made by an engine. **—Idiom. 10. knock it off,** to stop doing or saying something.

knock•er /'nɒkər/ *n.* [count] a hinged knob, bar, etc., on a door, to use for knocking.

knock•out /'nɒk,awt/ *n.* [count] **1.** an act or instance of knocking out. **2.** the state or fact of being knocked out. **3.** *Informal.* a very attractive or impressive person or thing.

knoll /nowl/ *n.* [count] a small, rounded hill.

knot /nɒt/ *n.*, *v.*, **knot•ted, knot•ting. —n.** [count] **1.** a fastening made by tying together the ends of pieces of thread, rope, etc. **2.** a twisted mass: *She combed out the knots in the dog's fur.* **3.** a small group of persons or things. **4.** the hard, round mass in a board, showing where a branch joined the tree trunk. **5.** a cramping, as of a muscle. **6.** a unit of speed used on ships equal to one nautical mile (6,076 feet) per hour. **—v. 7.** to (cause to) become tied or tangled in a knot: [~ + *obj*]: *He knotted the rope.* [*no obj*]: *The rope is too wet to knot easily.*

knot•ty /'nɒtiy/ *adj.*, **-ti•er, -ti•est. 1.** having or full of knots: *knotty wood.* **2.** difficult to solve: *a knotty problem.*

know /now/ *v.*, **knew** /nuw, nyuw/, **known** /nown/, **know•ing,** *n.* **—v. 1.** to understand clearly and with certainty: [~ + *obj*]: *She knows that he is the thief.* [*no obj*]: *She knows about your bad habits.* **2.** [~ + *obj*] to have (something) fixed in the mind or memory: *to know a poem by heart.* **3.** [~ + *obj*] to be acquainted or familiar with: *I know the neighbors and the neighborhood well.* **4.** [~ + *obj*] to recognize: *He was so changed I hardly knew him.* **5.** [~ + *obj*] to have skill or experience with: *She knows German. He knows how to swim.* **6.** [~ + *obj*] to have direct experience of: *to have known sorrow.* **7. know of,** to have heard about: *Do you know of any computer stores around here?* **—Idiom. 8. in the know,** having special knowledge or information; well-informed.

'know-,how, *n.* [noncount] knowledge of how to do something: *financial know-how.*

know•ing /'nowɪŋ/ *adj.* **1.** showing knowledge of secret information: *a knowing look.* **2.** intentional: *a knowing lie.* **—'know•ing•ly,** *adv.*

'know-it-,all, *n.* [count] a person who acts as though he or she knows everything.

knowl•edge /'nɒlɪdʒ/ *n.* **1.** [noncount] understanding. **2.** [count; singular; often: a + ~] all that someone has learned about a subject: *a knowledge of music.* **3.** [noncount] everything that is known; information: *Knowledge of the situation is limited.* **—'knowl•edge•a•ble,** *adj.*: *He is very knowledgeable about history.*

knuck•le /'nʌkəl/ *n.*, *v.*, **-led, -ling. —n.** [count] **1.** a joint of a finger. **—v. 2. knuckle down,** to work hard: *You must knuckle down if you want to succeed.* **3. knuckle under,** to admit defeat; yield: *He won't ever knuckle under to your threats.*

ko•a•la /kow'ɑlə/ *n.* [count], *pl.* **-las.** a gray-furred, tree-dwelling Australian animal like a small bear.

Ko•ran /kə'rɑn, -'ræn, kɔ-, kow-/ *n.* the holy book of the Muslims.

Ko•re•an /kə'riyən, kɔ-, kow-/ *adj.* **1.** of or relating to either North Korea or South Korea or to the language spoken there. **—n. 2.** [count] a person born or living in North Korea or South Korea. **3.** [noncount] the language spoken in North Korea or South Korea.

ko•sher /'kowʃər/ *adj.* **1. a.** prepared according to certain laws of Judaism: *kosher food.* **b.** selling or preparing kosher food: *a kosher restaurant.* **2.** *Informal.* proper: *Cheating them wouldn't be kosher.*

kow•tow /'kaw'taw, -,taw/ *v.* [*no obj*] to act too respectfully: *kowtowing to the manager.*

KS, an abbreviation of: Kansas.

ku•dos /'kuwdowz, -dows, -dɒs, 'kyuw-/ *n.* [noncount; used with a singular verb] praise: *kudos for a job well done.*

kung fu /'kʌŋ' fuw, 'kʊŋ/ *n.* [noncount] a Chinese style of fighting or self-defense related to karate.

Kwan•zaa or **Kwan•za** /'kwɑnzə/ *n.* [count; noncount], *pl.* **-zaas** or **-zas.** a harvest festival celebrated from December 26 until January 1 in some African-American communities.

KY or **Ky.,** an abbreviation of: Kentucky.

L

L, l /ɛl/ n. [count], pl. **Ls** or **L's**, **ls** or **l's**. the 12th letter of the English alphabet, a consonant.

L, Symbol. (sometimes l.c.) the Roman numeral for 50.

l, an abbreviation of: liter.

l., an abbreviation of: **1.** pl. **ll.** line. **2.** liter.

LA, an abbreviation of: Louisiana.

lab /læb/ n. [count] laboratory.

la•bel /'leybəl/ n., v., **-beled, -bel•ing** or (esp. Brit.) **-belled, -bel•ling.** —n. [count] **1.** a piece of paper, cloth, etc., fastened to something to describe what it is, who made or owns it, etc. **2.** a descriptive word or phrase. —v. [~ + obj] **3.** to mark with a label. **4.** to describe as: He was labeled a fool.

la•bor /'leybər/ n. **1.** [noncount] hard physical or mental work; toil. **2.** [noncount] workers as a group: a meeting between labor and management to avoid a strike. **3.** [count; usually plural] a job or task. **4.** the process of giving birth: [count]: a difficult labor. [noncount]: Labor can take hours. —v. **5.** [no obj] to do hard work. **6.** [~ + for] to work hard for: She labored for peace all her life. **7.** [no obj] to move slowly and with effort: The truck labored up the hill. **8.** [~ + obj] to develop in too much detail: Don't labor the point. —adj. [usually before a noun] **9.** of or relating to workers. Also, esp. Brit., **la'bour.** —**'la•bor•er,** n. [count] —**la'bo•ri•ous** /lə'bɔriyəs/ adj.

lab•o•ra•to•ry /'læbrə,tɔriy, 'læbərə-/ n. [count], pl. **-ries.** a room or building for doing scientific experiments or manufacturing drugs.

'Labor ,Day, n. a legal holiday in the U.S. and Canada observed on the first Monday in September in honor of workers.

'labor ,union, n. [count] an organization of workers for support and protection, and for dealing as a group with employers.

lab•y•rinth /'læbərɪnθ/ n. [count] a complicated combination of paths or passages in which it is difficult to find one's way.

lace /leys/ n., v., **laced, lac•ing.** —n. **1.** [noncount] a netlike decorative cloth of fine threads that form fancy designs. **2.** [count] a cord or string for holding or drawing together, esp., a shoelace. —v. [~ + obj] **3.** to pull or fasten together with a lace: She laced (up) her skates. **4.** to add a small amount of alcohol to (coffee, tea, etc.) —**'lac•y,** adj., **-i•er, -i•est.**

lac•er•ate /'læsə,reyt/ v. [~ + obj], **-at•ed, -at•ing.** to cut or tear (flesh) roughly. —**lac•er•a•tion** /,læsə'reyʃən/, n. [noncount] [count]

lack /læk/ n. **1.** the fact or state of not enough or not enough of something needed or desired: [noncount]: There is no lack of talent on this team. [count; usually singular]: The team has a lack of skill. —v. [~ + obj] **2.** to be without; have need of: You lack common sense.

lack•ing /'lækɪŋ/ adj. [be + ~] **1.** not having enough of something: He was lacking in courage. —prep. **2.** being without: Lacking water, the plants died.

lac•quer /'lækər/ n. [noncount] **1.** a transparent liquid put on wood or metal to form a hard, shiny, protective surface. —v. [~ + obj] **2.** to cover with lacquer.

la•crosse /lə'krɔs, -'krɒs/ n. [noncount] a game in which two 10-member teams attempt to send a small ball into each other's netted goal, each player carrying a stick at the end of which is a netted pocket for catching, carrying, or throwing the ball.

lad /læd/ n. [count] a boy or young man.

lad•der /'lædər/ n. [count] **1.** a structure of wood, metal, or rope having two side pieces between which a series of steps or rungs are set for climbing. **2.** a series of stages or levels: the social ladder. **3.** Chiefly Brit. a run in a stocking.

lad•en /'leydn/ adj. [usually: be + ~ + with + obj] heavily loaded: trees laden with apples.

'ladies' ,room, n. [count] a public bathroom for women.

la•dle /'leydl/ n., v., **-dled, -dling.** —n. [count] **1.** a long-handled utensil with a cup-shaped bowl at the end, used for dipping and pouring liquids. —v. [~ + obj] **2.** to serve with or as if with a ladle: to ladle soup into bowls.

la•dy /'leydiy/ n., pl. **-dies,** adj. —n. [count] **1.** a woman who has good manners. **2.** any woman: the lady who answered the phone. **3.** a woman of high social position. **4.** [Lady] (in Great Britain) the title of a woman of noble rank. **5.** [usually: Lady] a quality or idea thought of as a female person: Lady Luck. —adj. [before a noun] **6.** Sometimes Offensive. female: a lady cab driver.

la•dy•bug /'leydiy,bʌg/ n. [count] a small, round, bright red or orange beetle with black dots. Also, **la•dy•bird** /'leydiy,bɜrd/.

la•dy•like /'leydiy,layk/ adj. of or suitable for a lady; proper.

lag /læg/ v., **lagged, lag•ging,** n. —v. [no obj] **1.** to fail to maintain a desired pace or speed: to lag behind in production. —n. [count] **2.** a lagging behind: a lag in production. **3.** a period of time between events: a lag of ten minutes.

la•ger /'lɑgər, 'lɔ-/ n. [noncount] [count] a light beer.

la•goon /lə'guwn/ n. [count] an area of shallow water separated from the sea by banks of sand or coral reefs.

laid /leyd/ v. pt. and pp. of LAY¹.

'laid-'back, adj. Informal. relaxed; easygoing.

lain /leyn/ v. pp. of LIE².

lair /lɛər/ n. [count] the home or resting place of a wild animal.

la•i•ty /'leyɪtiy/ n. [plural; used with a plural verb; usually: the + ~] **1.** the body of religious worshipers that are not members of the clergy. **2.** the people outside of a particular profession.

lake /leyk/ n. [count] a body of fresh or salt water of considerable size, surrounded by land.

lamb /læm/ n. **1.** [count] a young sheep. **2.** [noncount] the meat of a young sheep. **3.** [count] a gentle or innocent person.

lame /leym/ adj., **lam•er, lam•est,** v., **lamed, lam•ing.** —adj. **1.** unable to walk properly; limping. **2.** being stiff and sore: a lame arm from tennis. **3.** not effective; weak: a lame excuse. —v. [~ + obj] **4.** to make lame: The bullet lamed him for life. —**'lame•ly,** adv. —**'lame•ness,** n. [noncount]

'lame 'duck, n. [count] an elected official whose period in office is nearly over. —**'lame-,duck,** adj.: a lame-duck president.

landscape

mountain

hill

forest

valley

field

river

cliff

highway

car

farmhouse

barn

silo

chicken coop

__farm__

fence

shed

truck

pond

large

la•ment /lə'mɛnt/ v. [~ + obj] [no obj] **1.** to express grief or regret (for or over). —n. [count] **2.** a crying out in sorrow. **3.** a song or poem expressing grief. —,lam•en'ta•tion, n. [noncount] [count]

la•men•ta•ble /'læməntəbəl, lə'mɛntəbəl/ adj. regrettable: a lamentable decision. —la'men•tab•ly, adv.

lam•i•nat•ed /'læmə,neytɪd/ adj. **1.** made from thin layers of material joined together: laminated wood. **2.** covered over with a layer, usually of plastic: a laminated ID card.

lamp /læmp/ n. [count] a device that provides artificial light, as by electricity or gas.

lamp•post /'læmp,powst/ n. [count] a pole supporting a lamp that lights a street or other outdoor area.

lamp•shade /'læmp,ʃeyd/ n. [count] a cover for a lamp.

lance /læns/ n., v., **lanced, lanc•ing.** —n. [count] **1.** a long spearlike weapon, esp. one used by a knight on horseback. —v. [~ + obj] **2.** to cut open with a sharp instrument: The nurse lanced the boil.

land /lænd/ n. **1.** [noncount] any part of the earth's surface not covered by a body of water. **2.** [noncount] an area of ground: land good for farming. **3.** [noncount] land owned as property. **4.** [count] a region or country: Immigrants came from many lands. —v. **5.** to (cause to) come or go ashore: [no obj]: The boat lands at Cherbourg. [~ + obj]: She landed the boat at the shoreline. **6.** [~ + obj] Informal. to obtain: to land a job. **7.** to (cause to) come down upon a surface: [no obj]: The plane landed on time. [~ + obj]: The pilot landed the plane smoothly. **8.** to (cause to) arrive at a certain place or condition: [~ + obj]: His behavior will land him in jail. [no obj]: to land in trouble.

land•ed /'lændɪd/ adj. [before a noun] **1.** owning a large amount of land. **2.** consisting of land: landed property.

land•ing /'lændɪŋ/ n. [count] **1.** the act or process of coming to land: The plane made an emergency landing. **2.** a place where persons or goods are landed: a boat landing. **3.** the level place at the end of a set of stairs.

'landing ,gear, n. [noncount] the wheels, floats, etc., of an aircraft, upon which it lands and moves on ground or water.

'land,la•dy, n. [count], pl. **-dies.** a woman from whom one rents a room, apartment, etc.

land•locked /'lænd,lɒkt/ adj. entirely or almost entirely surrounded by land, as a bay or country.

land•lord /'lænd,lɔrd/ n. [count] **1.** a person or organization that owns and rents apartments, a building, land, etc. **2.** an innkeeper.

land•mark /'lænd,mɑrk/ n. [count] **1.** an object that is easily noticed or that serves as a guide: The tower is a local landmark. **2.** an important building, structure, or place. **3.** a very important event.

land•scape /'lænd,skeyp/ n., v., **-scaped, -scap•ing.** —n. [count] **1.** an area of land that can be seen from a place; view. **2.** a picture of such a view. —v. [~ + obj] **3.** to improve the appearance of (an area of land) by planting trees, flowers, etc. —'land,scap•er, n. [count]

land•slide /'lænd,slayd/ n. [count] **1.** the sliding of a mass of soil or rock on or from a steep slope. **2.** a very great victory in an election: He won by a landslide.

lane /leyn/ n. [count] **1.** a narrow country road or city street. **2.** a part of a highway or road wide enough for one vehicle. **3.** a regular route for ships or aircraft.

lan•guage /'læŋgwɪdʒ/ n. **1.** [noncount] the system of human communication by means of spoken or written words. **2.** [count] the speech of a particular group or country: the English language. **3.** [noncount] form or style of expression: legal language; informal language. **4.** [count] any set or system of special symbols, signs, etc.: sign language; computer language.

lan•guid /'læŋgwɪd/ adj. lacking in strength or energy; dull and slow: I'm feeling languid from the heat.

lan•guish /'læŋgwɪʃ/ v. [no obj] **1.** to be or become weak: languishing from the heat. **2.** to continue in a state of suffering: He languished in his dull job.

lan•guor /'læŋgər/ n. [noncount] **1.** lack of energy or strength. **2.** pleasant laziness or relaxation. —'lan•guor•ous, adj.

lank /læŋk/ adj., **-er, -est.** (of hair) straight and limp; without curl.

lank•y /'læŋkiy/ adj., **-i•er, -i•est.** ungracefully tall and thin: a lanky teenager. —'lank•i•ness, n. [noncount]

lan•o•lin /'lænlɪn/ n. [noncount] a fatty substance taken from wool and used in ointments, cosmetics, etc.

lan•tern /'læntərn/ n. [count] a portable case for enclosing a light and protecting it from the weather.

lap[1] /læp/ n. [count] the front part of a seated person from the waist to the knees: He held the baby in his lap.

lap[2] /læp/ n. [count] **1.** one stage of a long trip, task, etc. **2.** one complete time around a racetrack.

lap[3] /læp/ v., **lapped, lap•ping,** n. —v. **1.** (of water) to wash or move gently against (something): [no obj]: The water lapped gently. [~ + obj]: The waves lapped the shore. **2.** [~ + obj] to drink (liquid) by lifting it up with the tongue: The cat lapped the milk. **3. lap up, a.** to take up (liquid) with the tongue: The cat lapped up its milk or The cat lapped its milk up. **b.** to receive enthusiastically: The actress lapped up the applause. She just lapped it up. —n. [count] **4.** the lapping of water against something.

la•pel /lə'pɛl/ n. [count] the front part of the collar of a coat or jacket that is folded back.

lapse /læps/ n., v., **lapsed, laps•ing.** —n. [count] **1.** a small mistake or failure: a lapse of memory. **2.** a passing of time; interval: a lapse of several weeks. —v. [no obj] **3.** to fail to maintain a normal or expected level: She often lapsed into carelessness. **4.** to come to an end; stop: We let our magazine subscription lapse. **5.** to fall, slip, or sink gradually: to lapse into silence. **6.** to turn away from or abandon principles, beliefs, etc.: a lapsed Catholic.

lap•top /'læp,tɒp/ n. [count] a portable microcomputer small enough to rest on the lap.

lar•ce•ny /'lɑrsəniy/ n. [noncount] [count], pl. **-nies.** Law. the wrongful taking of the personal goods of another. —'lar•ce•nous, adj.

lard /lɑrd/ n. [noncount] the fat of pigs, used in cooking.

lar•der /'lɑrdər/ n. [count] a room or place where food is kept; pantry.

large /lɑrdʒ/ adj., **larg•er, larg•est,** n. —adj. **1.** of more than average size, quantity, degree, etc.; big: a large house; a large number; a large shirt.

L

—Idiom. 2. at large, a. [be + ~] free: *The criminals were still at large.* **b.** as a whole; in general: *society at large.*

large•ly /ˈlɑrdʒliy/ *adv.* to a great extent; mostly: *He owes his success largely to hard work.*

lar•gess or **lar•gesse** /lɑrˈʒɛs, -ˈdʒɛs/ *n.* [noncount] generous giving of gifts; generosity.

lark¹ /lɑrk/ *n.* [count] a small songbird.

lark² /lɑrk/ *n.* [count] something done for fun.

lar•va /ˈlɑrvə/ *n.* [count], *pl.* **-vae** /-viy/. the early stage of an insect in which it looks like a short worm. **—'lar•val,** *adj.*: *the larval stage.*

lar•yn•gi•tis /ˌlærənˈdʒaytɪs/ *n.* [noncount] redness and soreness of the larynx, often with hoarseness or loss of voice.

lar•ynx /ˈlærɪŋks/ *n.* [count], *pl.* **la•ryn•ges** /ləˈrɪndʒiyz/, **lar•ynx•es.** a box-shaped structure at the upper part of the throat, containing the vocal cords.

las•civ•i•ous /ləˈsɪviyəs/ *adj.* feeling, showing, or causing strong sexual desire.

la•ser /ˈleyzər/ *n.* [count] a device that produces a narrow but very powerful beam of light.

'laser ,disc, *n.* [count] OPTICAL DISC.

lash¹ /læʃ/ *n.* [count] **1.** the end part of a whip, used for striking. **2.** a blow with a whip. **3.** a sudden or forceful movement. **4.** an eyelash. —*v.* **5.** [~ + obj] to strike with or as if with a whip. **6.** [~ + obj] to beat violently or sharply against: *The high waves lashed the rocks.* **7.** [~ + obj] [no obj] (esp. of an animal's tail) to (cause to) move back and forth quickly. **8. lash out,** to attack with blows or harsh words: *She lashed out at her opponent.*

lash² /læʃ/ *v.* [~ + obj] to fasten tightly with a rope, etc.: *They lashed their tent to a tree during the storm.*

las•so /ˈlæsow, læˈsuw/ *n.*, *pl.* **-sos, -soes,** *v.*, **-soed, -so•ing.** —*n.* [count] **1.** a long rope with a knotted loop, used for catching horses, cattle, etc. —*v.* [~ + obj] **2.** to catch with a lasso.

last¹ /læst/ *adj.*, a superlative of **late** with **later** as comparative. **1.** coming after all others: *the last line on a page.* **2.** [before a noun indicating time] coming just before this; most recent: *I saw her last week.* **3.** [before a noun] being the only one remaining: *It's my last dollar.* **4.** most unlikely: *He's the last person I'd ask for help.* —*adv.* **5.** after all others; latest: *Do this last.* **6.** most recently: *He was alone when last seen.* —*n.* **7.** [count; singular: the + ~] a person or thing that is last: *He drank the last of the brandy.* **8.** [noncount; the + ~] a final appearance or mention: *That's the last we'll hear of it.* —*Idiom.* **9. at (long) last,** after a lot of delay; finally: *At long last we had finished the job.*

last² /læst/ *v.* [no obj] **1.** to continue in time: *The party lasted all night.* **2.** to be enough: *Will the money last?* **3.** to stay in good condition: *She hoped the shoes would last.*

last•ing /ˈlæstɪŋ/ *adj.* [before a noun] continuing for a long time: *our lasting friendship.* **—'last•ing•ly,** *adv.*

last•ly /ˈlæstliy/ *adv.* in conclusion; finally: *Lastly, I'd like to thank my wife.*

'last 'straw, *n.* [count; singular; usually: the + ~] the last of a number of troubles coming one after the other, that leads to a loss of patience, to a misfortune, etc.

latch /lætʃ/ *n.* [count] **1.** a small wood or metal device for holding a door, gate, or window closed. —*v.* [~ + obj] [no obj] **2.** to close or fasten (with a latch).

late /leyt/ *adj.*, **lat•er** or **lat•est** or **last** /læst/, *adv.*, **lat•er, lat•est.** —*adj.* **1.** coming after the usual or proper time: *a late spring.* **2.** near or at the end: *late evening; in his late twenties; late summer.* **3.** recent: *a late news bulletin.* **4.** [before a noun] recently dead: *his late wife.* —*adv.* **5.** after the usual or proper time: *to arrive an hour late.* **6.** near or toward the end: *late in the year.* **—'late•ness,** *n.* [noncount] [count]

late•ly /ˈleytliy/ *adv.* recently.

la•tent /ˈleytnt/ *adj.* existing but not yet appearing or developing: *a latent talent.* **—'la•ten•cy,** *n.* [noncount]

lat•er /ˈleytər/ *adj.* **1.** a comparative of LATE: *She was later than expected.* —*adv.* **2.** at a later time; afterwards: *I'll speak to you later.*

lat•er•al /ˈlætərəl/ *adj.* of, at, from, or toward the side: *a lateral pass in football.* **—'lat•er•al•ly,** *adv.*

lat•est /ˈleytɪst/ *adj.* **1.** most recent; current: *the latest fashions.* **2.** last. —*adv.* **3. at the latest,** not any later than (a time mentioned). —*n.* [noncount; the + ~] **4.** the most recent news, development, etc.: *Here's the latest from our news bureau.*

lathe /leyð/ *n.* [count] a machine used in cutting or forming a piece of wood, metal, etc., by holding and turning it against a tool that shapes it.

lath•er /ˈlæðər/ *n.* [noncount] [count; singular] **1.** foam made by mixing soap and water. **2.** foam caused by sweating, as a horse does. —*v.* **3.** [no obj] to form a lather. **4.** [~ + obj] to cover with lather.

Lat•in /ˈlætn/ *n.* **1.** [noncount] the language of the ancient Romans. **2.** [count] **a.** a member of any people speaking a language descended from Latin, as French, Spanish, Italian, or Portuguese. **b.** a native or inhabitant of any country in Latin America; Latin American. —*adj.* **3.** of or relating to Latin. **4.** of or relating to the people or countries that use languages descended from Latin.

'Latin A'merica, *n.* the parts of Central or South America where Spanish or Portuguese is spoken. **—'Latin A'merican,** *n.* [count], *adj.*

La•ti•no /ləˈtiynow, læ-/ *n.*, *pl.* **-nos.** HISPANIC.

lat•i•tude /ˈlætɪˌtuwd, -ˌtyuwd/ *n.* **1.** [noncount] [count; usually singular] the distance, measured north or south from the equator, of a point on the earth's surface, expressed in degrees. **2.** [noncount] freedom of action, opinion, etc.

lat•te /ˈlɑtey/ *n.* [count] hot espresso served mixed with hot milk.

lat•ter /ˈlætər/ *adj.* **1.** being the second of two things mentioned: *Of red and blue, I prefer the latter color.* **2.** nearer to the end: *the latter part of the century.* —*n.* [noncount; the + ~] **3.** the second thing mentioned of two: *Of your two examples, I prefer the latter.*

lat•tice /ˈlætɪs/ *n.* [count] a framework of crossed wooden or metal strips.

laud /lɔd/ *v.* [~ + obj] to praise.

laud•a•ble /ˈlɔdəbəl/ *adj.* deserving praise: *a laudable effort.* **—'laud•a•bly,** *adv.*

laugh /læf/ *v.* **1.** [no obj] to make the sounds and facial movements that show amusement, happiness, ridicule, etc. **2. laugh off,** to dismiss as unimportant: *He laughed the threats off or He laughed off the threats.* —*n.* [count] **3.** the act or sound of laughing; laughter. **4.** *Informal.* an amusing person or situation. **—Idiom. 5. have the last laugh,** to prove successful despite the doubts of others. **6. no laughing matter,** something serious. —'**laugh•ing•ly,** *adv.*

laugh•a•ble /'læfəbəl/ *adj.* amusing or ridiculous. —'**laugh•a•bly,** *adv.*

laugh•ing•stock /'læfɪŋˌstɒk/ *n.* [count] an object of ridicule.

laugh•ter /'læftər/ *n.* [noncount] the action or sound of laughing.

launch[1] /lɔntʃ, lɑntʃ/ *v.* **1.** [~ + obj] to set (a boat or ship) afloat: *to launch a new ship.* **2.** [~ + obj] to send into the sky: *to launch a space-craft.* **3.** [~ + obj] to start: *to launch a business.* **4.** [no obj] to begin something energetically: *She launched into her speech.* —*n.* [count] **5.** the act of launching. —'**launch•er,** *n.* [count]

launch[2] /lɔntʃ, lɑntʃ/ *n.* [count] a heavy, open motorboat used to carry people.

'**launch** (or '**launching**) ˌ**pad** or '**launchˌpad,** *n.* [count] the platform from which a rocket, missile, etc., is launched.

laun•der /'lɔndər, 'lɑn-/ *v.* [~ + obj] [no obj] to wash or wash and iron (clothes, sheets, etc.).

laun•der•ette /ˌlɔndə'rɛt, ˌlɑn-/ also **laun•drette** /lɔn'drɛt, lɑn-/ *n.* [count] a place with coin-operated machines for washing and drying clothes.

laun•dry /'lɔndri, 'lɑn-/ *n.,* pl. **-dries. 1.** [noncount] clothes, sheets, etc., that have been or are to be washed. **2.** [count] a room or business establishment where clothes are laundered.

lau•rel /'lɔrəl, 'lɒr-/ *n.* [count] Also called **bay.** a small European evergreen tree, having dark, glossy green leaves.

la•va /'lɑvə, 'lævə/ *n.* [noncount] **1.** the hot, liquid rock that comes out of a volcano. **2.** the rock formed when this becomes solid and cools.

lav•a•to•ry /'lævəˌtɔriy/ *n.* [count], pl. **-ries. 1.** a washbowl. **2.** a room with washbowls and toilets.

lav•en•der /'lævəndər/ *n.* **1.** [noncount] a pale purple color. **2.** [count] a plant with sweet-smelling, pale purple flowers.

lav•ish /'lævɪʃ/ *adj.* **1.** generous. **2.** given or produced in great amounts: *a lavish meal; lavish praise.* —*v.* [~ + obj] **3.** to give generously: *to lavish gifts on one's children.* —'**lav•ish•ly,** *adv.*

law /lɔ/ *n.* **1.** [count] a rule made by authority, esp. a government, for all the people of a group. **2.** [noncount] a set or system of such rules: *Stealing is against the law.* **3.** [noncount] the profession of a lawyer: *to practice law.* **4.** [count; the + ~] the police. **5.** [count] any rule or principle to be obeyed: *the laws of English grammar.* **6.** [count] a statement describing a set of related events that always happen the same under certain conditions: *the laws of nature.* —'**law•less,** *adj.* —'**law•less•ness,** *n.* [noncount]

'**law-aˌbiding,** *adj.* obeying the law.

'**law and 'order,** *n.* [noncount] the rule of law as accepted and obeyed by citizens.

law•break•er /'lɔˌbreykər/ *n.* [count] one who breaks the law. —'**law,break•ing,** *n.* [noncount], *adj.*

law•ful /'lɔfəl/ *adj.* allowed or recognized by law. —'**law•ful•ly,** *adv.*

law•mak•er /'lɔˌmeykər/ *n.* [count] a person who makes laws; a legislator.

lawn /lɔn/ *n.* [count] an area with grass that is kept closely cut.

'**lawn ˌmower,** *n.* [count] a machine for cutting the grass of a lawn.

law•suit /'lɔˌsuwt/ *n.* [count] a non-criminal case brought before a court.

law•yer /'lɔyər, 'lɔyər/ *n.* [count] a person who is qualified to give legal advice and represent people in a court of law.

lax /læks/ *adj.,* **-er, -est. 1.** not strict; careless: *lax morals.* **2.** not tense; loose: *a lax rope.* **3.** not exact; vague: *lax thinking.*

lax•a•tive /'læksətɪv/ *n.* [count] **1.** a medicine that helps the bowels to move. —*adj.* [before a noun] **2.** of or being a laxative.

lay[1] /ley/ *v.,* **laid, lay•ing,** *n.* —*v.* **1.** [~ + obj] to put down, esp. in a flat position; set down: *Lay the book on the desk.* **2.** [~ + obj] to place or apply: *Don't you lay a hand on her.* **3.** [~ + obj] to place in proper order or position: *to lay bricks.* **4.** [~ + obj] to establish as a basis: *The president laid the foundations for the peace talks.* **5.** to produce (an egg or eggs): [~ + obj]: *The hens laid an egg every day.* [no obj]: *The hens weren't laying.* **6.** [~ + obj] to devise or arrange: *They laid their plans carefully.* **7.** [~ + obj] to bet (money): *He laid $10 on the horse.* **8.** [~ + obj] to put forward (a charge, claim, etc.): *She laid the blame on her parents.* **9. lay aside,** to save for later use: *to lay aside some money* or *to lay some money aside.* **10. lay away, a.** to lay aside. **b.** to hold merchandise until final payment or request for delivery: *to lay away a winter coat.* **11. lay down, a.** to give up: *The police laid down their guns.* **b.** to state with authority: *Their parents laid down the rules.* **12. lay into,** *Informal.* to attack with blows or words: *He laid into his opponent.* **13. lay off, a.** to dismiss from work, often temporarily: *The boss laid ten workers off* or *The boss laid off ten workers.* **b.** *Informal.* to stop work: *Let's lay off early.* **c.** to stop doing something harmful: *Lay off drinking.* **14. lay on,** to cover with: *to lay on a coat of wax.* **15. lay out, a.** to spread out in order: *She laid out her tools* or *She laid her tools out.* **b.** to plan or design: *to lay out the garden nicely; to lay it out nicely.* **c.** *Informal.* to spend (money): *He laid out $50 for each ticket.* **d.** *Slang.* to knock (someone) down or unconscious: *He laid him out with one blow.* **16. lay up,** to cause to be indoors or in bed: *I was laid up with the flu.* —*Idiom.* **17. lay bare,** to reveal something hidden. **18. lay of the land,** the conditions or situation: *Let's get the lay of the land before going ahead.* —**Usage.** For many speakers, the verbs LAY and LIE[2] are confused because both have the meaning of "in a flat position." LAY means "to put down" or "to place, especially in a flat position." A general rule to remember is that if the word "put" or "place" can be substituted in a sentence, then LAY is the verb to use: *Lay (= put, place) the books on the table. She laid (= put, placed) the baby in the cradle.* But the verb LIE[2] means "to be in a flat position" or "to be situated": *Lie down and rest a moment. The baby is lying down.* For many speakers, the problem comes in the past tense for these two verbs, because the past tense of LIE[2] is *lay,* which looks like, but is not, the present tense of LAY: *The dog will want to lie in the shade; yesterday it lay in the grass.* Note that we can *lay* a baby down on a bed; he or she will *lie* there until picked up.

lay[2] /ley/ *v.* pt. of LIE[2].

lay[3] /ley/ *adj.* [before a noun] **1.** of or by someone not a member of the clergy: *a lay sermon.* **2.** not of or from a profession, esp. the law or medicine: *a lay opinion.*

lay•er /'leyər/ *n.* [count] **1.** a thickness of some

L

material, often one of several, on a surface: *a layer of dust; She wore clothing in layers.* **2.** a hen kept for egg production. —*v.* [~ + *obj*] **3.** to form, put down, or arrange in layers.

lay•man /'leymən/ *n.* [*count*], *pl.* **-men. 1.** a person who is not a member of the clergy. **2.** a person who is not a member of a given profession, as law or medicine.

lay•off /'ley,ɔf, -,ɒf/ *n.* [*count*] the act of dismissing employees, esp. temporarily.

lay•out /'ley,awt/ *n.* [*count*] an arrangement or plan: *the layout of a house; the layout of a magazine page.*

laze /leyz/ *v.* [*no obj*], **lazed, laz•ing. 1.** to relax or lounge lazily. **2. laze away,** to pass (time, life, etc.) lazily: *He's just been lazing his days away; to laze away the days.*

la•zy /'leyziy/ *adj.*, **-zi•er, -zi•est. 1.** unwilling to work or be active. **2.** encouraging inactivity: *a lazy afternoon.* **3.** slow-moving: *a lazy stream.* —**la•zi•ly** /'leyzəliy/ *adv.* —**'la•zi•ness,** *n.* [*noncount*]

lb., an abbreviation of Latin *libra:* pound.

lead¹ /liyd/ *v.*, **led** /lɛd/, **lead•ing,** *n., adj.* —*v.* **1.** [~ + *obj*] [*no obj*] to go before or with to show the way; guide. **2.** [~ + *obj*] to influence (the thoughts); cause: *What led her to change her mind?* **3.** [~ + *obj*] to go through or pass (time, life, etc.): *to lead a full and happy life.* **4.** [*no obj*] to have as a result: *a mistake that led to trouble.* **5.** (of a road, passage, etc.) to be or mark a way (for): [~ + *obj*]: *The next street will lead you to the post office.* [~ + *to* + *obj*]: *That path leads directly to the house.* **6.** [~ + *obj*] to go at the head of: *The mayor will lead the parade.* **7.** to be or go ahead of (someone or something): [~ + *obj*]: *Iowa leads the nation in corn production.* [*no obj*]: *Our team was leading at the half.* **8.** [~ + *obj*] to direct or control: *to lead a discussion.* **9. lead on,** to mislead: *He led the customer on; He led on dozens of them.* —*n.* [*count*] **10.** the first place or position: *to take the lead in the race.* **11.** the distance by which one is ahead: *a lead of several yards.* **12.** a piece of useful information: *The police have several leads.* **13.** a guiding example; leadership: *to follow someone's lead.* **14. a.** the principal part in a play. **b.** the person who plays it. **15.** an insulated single wire carrying electrical current. —*adj.* [*before a noun*] **16.** most important: *a lead editorial.* —**'lead•er,** *n.* [*count*]

lead² /lɛd/ *n.* [*noncount*] **1.** a heavy, soft, bluish-gray metal that can be shaped easily. **2.** the soft black substance in a pencil.

lead•en /'lɛdn/ *adj.* **1.** very heavy, dull, or slow. **2.** of a dull gray color.

lead•er /'liydər/ *n.* [*count*] a person or thing that leads: *the leader in the race; political leaders.*

lead•er•ship /'liydər,ʃɪp/ *n.* **1.** [*noncount*] ability to lead. **2.** [*count; usually singular*] the leaders of a group.

lead•ing /'liydɪŋ/ *adj.* [*before a noun*] most important: *a leading authority.*

'leading 'question, *n.* [*count*] a question asked in a way that suggests the desired answer.

leaf /liyf/ *n., pl.* **leaves** /liyvz/, *v.* —*n.* **1.** [*count*] one of the usually green, flat parts at the end of a stem on a plant. **2.** [*count*] a sheet of paper. **3.** [*noncount*] a very thin sheet of metal: *gold or silver leaf.* **4.** [*count*] a movable flat part of a tabletop. —*v.* **5. leaf through,** to turn pages of: *leafing through a book.* —*Idiom.* **6. turn over a**

new leaf, to make a fresh start. —**'leaf•less,** *adj.* —**'leaf•y,** *adj.*

leaf•let /'liyflɪt/ *n.* [*count*] a small sheet of printed matter, as an advertisement or notice.

league /liyg/ *n.* [*count*] **1.** a group of people, organizations, or countries joined together for a common purpose. **2.** a group of athletic teams that compete mainly against each other: *a bowling league.* **3.** group; class: *As a pianist he simply isn't in your league.* —*Idiom.* **4. in league (with),** working together, esp. secretly.

leak /liyk/ *n.* [*count*] **1.** an unintentional hole, crack, etc., through which something enters or escapes: *a leak in the roof.* **2.** a substance that enters or escapes: *a gas leak.* **3.** a spreading or release of secret information to the public. —*v.* **4.** [*no obj*] to have a leak: *The boat leaks.* **5.** to (cause to) pass through a hole, etc.: [*no obj*]: *Gas was leaking from a pipe.* [~ + *obj*]: *The brakes are leaking fluid.* **6.** to (cause or allow to) become known: [*no obj*]: *The news leaked to the public.* [~ + *obj*]: *Who leaked that story to the press?*

leak•age /'liykɪdʒ/ *n.* [*noncount*] [*count*] an act of leaking; an amount that leaks.

lean¹ /liyn/ *v.*, **leaned** or (*esp. Brit.*) **leant** /lɛnt/, **lean•ing. 1.** to bend from a vertical position: [*no obj*]: *She leaned out the window.* [~ + *obj*]: *He leaned his head forward.* **2.** [*no obj*] to be in a sloping position: *The post leans to the left.* **3.** to (cause to) rest on or against something: [*no obj*]: *She leaned against a wall.* [~ + *obj*]: *He leaned the bike against the tree.* **4.** [*no obj*] to tend to agree with or be in favor of: *They're leaning toward our point of view.* **5. lean on** or **upon,** to depend on: *to lean on one's friends.*

lean² /liyn/ *adj.*, **-er, -est. 1.** (of persons or animals) without much flesh or fat; thin. **2.** (of meat) containing little or no fat. **3.** not productive; poor: *a lean year for crops.* —**'lean•ness,** *n.* [*noncount*]

lean•ing /'liynɪŋ/ *n.* [*count*] a tendency; inclination: *artistic leanings.*

leap /liyp/ *v.*, **leaped** or **leapt** /lɛpt, liypt/, **leap•ing,** *n.* —*v.* **1.** to jump (over): [*no obj*]: *to leap over a ditch.* [~ + *obj*]: *to leap a fence.* **2.** [*no obj*] to move or act quickly or suddenly: *to leap aside.* —*n.* [*count*] **3.** a jumping movement. **4.** the distance covered in a leap. **5.** a sudden change, usually for the better: *a leap in profits.* —*Idiom.* **6. by leaps and bounds,** very quickly: *The baby grew by leaps and bounds.* —**'leap•er,** *n.* [*count*]

'leap ,year, *n.* [*count*] a year that has an extra day, February 29, happening every four years.

learn /lɜrn/ *v.*, **learned** /lɜrnd/ or **learnt** /lɜrnt/, **learn•ing. 1.** to gain knowledge of or skill in (something) by study, instruction, or experience: [~ + *obj*]: *to learn a new language.* [~ + (*how*) *to* + *verb*]: *Where did you learn (how) to throw a ball like that?* [*no obj*]: *She learns quickly.* **2.** [~ + *obj*] to memorize, as a poem. **3.** to become informed of (something); find out: [~ + *obj*]: *to learn the truth.* [*no obj*]: *When did you learn about his past?* —**'learn•er,** *n.* [*count*]

learn•ed /'lɜrnɪd for 1 lɜrnd for 2/ *adj.* **1.** having much knowledge. **2.** obtained by experience, study, etc.: *learned behavior.*

learn•ing /'lɜrnɪŋ/ *n.* [*noncount*] knowledge obtained by careful study.

lease /liys/ *n., v.*, **leased, leas•ing.** —*n.* [*count*] **1.** a contract allowing the use of land, a building, etc., in exchange for rent or other payment. —*v.*

[~ + *obj*] **2.** to rent: *to lease one's apartment to a friend.* —*Idiom.* **3. a new lease on life,** a chance to improve one's situation or to live more happily.

leash /liyʃ/ *n.* [*count*] **1.** a chain, strap, etc., for controlling a dog or other animal. —*v.* [~ + *obj*] **2.** to fasten to a leash: *Leash your dog.*

least /liyst/ *adj., a superlative of* **little** *with* **less** *or* **lesser** *as comparative.* **1.** smallest in size, amount, degree, etc.: *She has the least amount of money.* —*n.* [*noncount; the* + ~] **2.** something that is least: *That is the least of my worries.* —*adv.* **3.** *superlative of* **little** *with* **less** *as comparative in or to the smallest extent, amount, or degree: the least important problem.* —*Idiom.* **4. at least, a.** at the lowest figure: *We'll have to pay $500 at least.* **b.** if nothing else: *At least she wasn't hurt.*

leath·er /'lɛðər/ *n.* [*noncount*] a soft, strong material made from treated animal skin, used for shoes, belts, etc. —**'leath·er·y,** *adj.*

leave¹ /liyv/ *v.,* **left** /lɛft/, **leav·ing. 1.** to go out of or away from (a place): [~ + *obj*]: *to leave the house.* [*no obj*]: *We left for the airport.* **2.** [~ + *obj*] to let remain behind: *The bear left tracks in the snow.* **3.** [~ + *obj*] to let stay or be in the condition stated: *Leave the motor running.* **4.** [~ + *obj*] to let (a thing) remain for another's responsibility: *We left the details to the lawyer.* **5.** [~ + *obj*] to give in charge: *Leave the package with my neighbor.* **6.** [~ + *obj*] to give through a will: *She left him a lot of money.* **7.** [~ + *obj*] to have remaining: *4 from 7 leaves 3.* **8. leave out,** to omit: *She left out the best part* or *She left out the best part.*

leave² /liyv/ *n.* [*noncount*] **1.** permission to be absent, as from work or military duty. **2.** permission to do something. —*Idiom.* **3. on leave,** away from one's duty with permission. **4. take one's leave,** to depart; go.

leav·en /'lɛvən/ *n.* [*noncount*] **1.** a substance, as yeast or baking powder, that causes fermentation and expansion of dough or batter. —*v.* [~ + *obj*] **2.** to add leaven to (dough or batter).

leaves /liyvz/ *n.* pl. of LEAF.

Leb·a·nese /ˌlɛbə'niyz, -'niys/ *adj., n., pl.* **-nese.** —*adj.* **1.** of or relating to Lebanon. —*n.* [*count*] **2.** a person born or living in Lebanon.

lech·er·ous /'lɛtʃərəs/ *adj.* having or showing a strong interest in sexual activity. —'**lech·er,** *n.* [*count*] —'**lech·er·ous·ly,** *adv.* —**lech·er·y,** *n.* [*noncount*]

lec·tern /'lɛktərn/ *n.* [*count*] a high stand with a sloping top, used to hold a speaker's book, speech, etc.

lectern

lec·ture /'lɛktʃər/ *n., v.,* **-tured, -tur·ing.** —*n.* [*count*] **1.** an educational talk delivered before an audience or a class. **2.** a scolding or warning. —*v.* **3.** [*no obj*] to give a lecture. **4.** [~ + *obj*] to scold or warn. —'**lec·tur·er,** *n.* [*count*]

led /lɛd/ *v.* pt. and pp. of LEAD¹.

ledge /lɛdʒ/ *n.* [*count*] a narrow shelf sticking out from a wall, cliff, etc.

ledg·er /'lɛdʒər/ *n.* [*count*] an account book in which money amounts coming into and going out of a business are recorded.

leech /liytʃ/ *n.* [*count*] **1.** a small bloodsucking worm. **2.** a person who uses another for personal gain.

leek /liyk/ *n.* [*count*] a vegetable with long, thick leaves and a bulb like an onion.

leer /lɪər/ *n.* [*count*] **1.** an unpleasant sideways look that suggests sexual interest or evil intention. —*v.* [*no obj*] **2.** to look with a leer.

leer·y /'lɪəriy/ *adj.* **-i·er, -i·est.** [*be* + ~ + *of*] careful and not trusting: *I'm leery of his advice.*

lee·way /'liy,wey/ *n.* [*noncount*] a degree of freedom of action or thought.

left¹ /lɛft/ *adj.* **1.** of, on, or near the side of the body that is turned toward the west when the person is facing north: *He writes with his left hand.* **2.** (*often: Left*) of or belonging to the left wing of a political party; liberal or radical. —*n.* **3.** [*noncount*] the left side. **4.** [*count*] a turn toward the left. —*adv.* **5.** toward the left.

left² /lɛft/ *v.* **1.** pt. and pp. of LEAVE¹. —*adj.* [*be* + ~] **2.** remaining; not used: *Only one piece is left.*

'**left-'hand,** *adj.* [*before a noun*] **1.** on or to the left. **2.** of, for, or with the left hand.

'**left-'handed,** *adj.* **1.** using the left hand more easily than the right. **2.** done with the left hand. **3.** made to be used by the left hand: *a left-handed tool.* **4.** having more than one meaning; doubtful: *a left-handed compliment.* —*adv.* **5.** with the left hand: *to write left-handed.*

left·ist /'lɛftɪst/ *n.* [*count; sometimes: Leftist*] **1.** a member of the political Left. —*adj.* **2.** of, relating to, or called for by the political Left.

left·o·ver /'lɛft,owvər/ *n.* [*count*] **1.** Usually, **leftovers.** [*plural*] food remaining after a meal, esp. when saved for later use. —*adj.* [*before a noun*] **2.** remaining: *leftover meat loaf.*

'**left 'wing,** *n.* [*count; usually: the* + ~] the liberal or radical element in a political party. —'**left-'wing,** *adj.*: *left-wing politics.* —'**left-'winger,** *n.* [*count*]

leg /lɛg/ *n.* [*count*] **1.** one of the parts of the body of a person or animal that support and move the body. **2.** the part of a garment that covers the leg. **3.** a support for a piece of furniture. **4.** one part of a journey. —*Idiom.* **5. not have a leg to stand on,** to not have facts or proof to support one's claims or arguments: *With such skimpy evidence against us the police don't have a leg to stand on.* **6. on one's** or **its last legs,** nearly failing. **7. pull someone's leg,** to deceive playfully.

leg·a·cy /'lɛgəsiy/ *n.* [*count*], *pl.* **-cies. 1.** (in a will) a gift of money or personal property to someone. **2.** something left as a result: *He left a legacy of debt.*

le·gal /'liygəl/ *adj.* **1.** permitted by law; lawful. **2.** [*before a noun*] of or relating to law or lawyers: *the legal system.* —'**le·gal·ly,** *adv.*

'**legal 'age,** *n.* [*count*] [*noncount*] the age, 18 in most states, at which a person is legally responsible and may enter into contracts.

'**legal 'holiday,** *n.* [*count*] a public holiday established by law.

le·gal·i·ty /liy'gælɪtiy/ *n.* [*noncount*] the state of being legal.

le·gal·ize /'liygə,layz/ *v.* [~ + *obj*], **-ized, -iz·**

L

ing. to make legal. **—le•gal•i•za•tion** /ˌliygəlɪ'zeyʃən/, n. [noncount]

leg•end /'lɛdʒənd/ n. [count] **1.** a story handed down by tradition from earlier times that may not be entirely true. **2.** a list on a map, chart, etc., explaining the symbols used. **3.** a famous person or event: a legend in his own time.

leg•end•ar•y /'lɛdʒənˌdɛriy/ adj. of or relating to a legend: a legendary hero.

leg•ged /'lɛgɪd, lɛgd/ adj. having a certain number or kind of legs: two-legged; long-legged.

leg•ging /'lɛgɪŋ/ n. [count] **1.** a covering for the leg. **2. leggings,** [plural] close-fitting leg coverings worn outdoors in the winter.

leg•i•ble /'lɛdʒəbəl/ adj. neat and clear, as writing or printing. **—leg•i•bil•i•ty** /ˌlɛdʒə'bɪlɪtiy/, n. [noncount] **—'leg•i•bly,** adv.

le•gion /'liydʒən/ n. [count] **1.** a military unit, esp. in ancient Rome. **2.** any great number of persons or things. —adj. [be + ~] **3.** very many: His followers were legion.

leg•is•late /'lɛdʒɪsˌleyt/ v., **-lat•ed, -lat•ing. 1.** [no obj] to make laws. **2.** [~ + obj] to create or control by legislation: attempts to legislate morality. **—'leg•is•la•tor,** n. [count]

leg•is•la•tion /ˌlɛdʒɪs'leyʃən/ n. [noncount] **1.** the act of making laws. **2.** the laws made.

leg•is•la•tive /'lɛdʒɪsˌleytɪv/ adj. **1.** having the power to make laws: the legislative branch of government. **2.** of or relating to the making of laws.

leg•is•la•ture /'lɛdʒɪsˌleytʃər/ n. [count] a body of persons that has the power to make and change laws.

le•git•i•mate /lɪ'dʒɪtəmɪt/ adj. **1.** according to law; lawful: the property's legitimate owner. **2.** born of legally married parents. **3.** reasonable: I had a legitimate complaint. **—le•git•i•ma•cy** /lɪ'dʒɪtəməsiy/, n. [noncount] **—le•git•i•mate•ly,** adv.

leg•ume /'lɛgyuwm, lɪ'gyuwm/ n. [count] a plant whose seeds grow in pods, such as peas, beans, and peanuts.

lei•sure /'liyʒər, 'lɛʒər/ n. [noncount] **1.** freedom from work or duty: a life of leisure. —adj. **2.** of or relating to free time: leisure hours. **—Idiom. 3. at leisure, a.** with free time: Do it when you're at leisure. **b.** without hurrying: He finished the book at leisure. **—'lei•sure•ly,** adj.: a leisurely walk.

lem•on /'lɛmən/ n. **1.** [noncount] [count] the oval, yellow, acid fruit of a citrus tree. **2.** [noncount] a pale yellow color. **3.** [count] Informal. something that is faulty: Our new car turned out to be a lemon. —adj. [before a noun] **4.** made of or with lemon: lemon pie.

lem•on•ade /ˌlɛmə'neyd, 'lɛməˌneyd/ n. [noncount] a drink made from lemon juice, sugar, and water.

lend /lɛnd/ v. [~ + obj], **lent** /lɛnt/, **lend•ing. 1.** to give the use of (something) to someone temporarily: He lent his car to me. He lent me his car. **2.** to give (money) on condition that it is returned and that interest is paid for its temporary use: Will the bank lend money to you? Will the bank lend you the money? **3.** to add: The flowers lend color to the room. **—Idiom. 4. lend a hand,** to give help: Can you lend a hand with this job? **—'lend•er,** n. [count] **—Usage.** See BORROW.

length /lɛŋkθ, lɛnθ/ n. **1.** [noncount] the distance of anything as measured from end to end: The length of the yard was three hundred feet. **2.** [noncount] the amount or extent from beginning to end: a novel 300 pages in length; the length of a visit. **3.** [count] a distance figured by the extent of something given: Hold the picture at arm's length. **4.** [count] a piece of something: a length of rope. **—Idiom. 5. at length, a.** after a considerable time; finally. **b.** in great detail. **6. go to great/any/some lengths,** to be ready to do whatever is necessary.

length•en /'lɛŋkθən, 'lɛn-/ v. to (cause to) become longer: [no obj]: Her hair lengthened gradually. [~ + obj]: They lengthened the road.

length•wise /'lɛŋkθˌwayz, 'lɛnθ-/ adj., adv. in the direction of the length of something.

length•y /'lɛŋkθiy, 'lɛn-/ adj., **-i•er, -i•est.** very long.

le•ni•ent /'liyniyənt, 'liynyənt/ adj. not strict or severe; kind: to be lenient toward the children. **—'le•ni•en•cy,** n. [noncount] **—'le•ni•ent•ly,** adv.

lens /lɛnz/ n. [count], pl. **lens•es. 1.** a piece of glass, curved on one or both surfaces, used in eyeglasses, microscopes, etc., to make things appear clearer, closer, or larger. **2.** a part of the eye behind the pupil that focuses light on the retina. **3.** CONTACT LENS.

lent /lɛnt/ v. pt. and pp. of LEND.

Lent /lɛnt/ n. (in many Christian churches) the forty weekdays before Easter. **—Lent•en, lent•en** /'lɛntṇ/, adj.: the Lenten season.

len•til /'lɛntɪl, -tḷ/ n. [count] a flat, round seed resembling a bean, dried and used for food.

leop•ard /'lɛpərd/ n. [count] a large, powerful animal of the cat family, usually yellowish brown with black spots.

le•o•tard /'liyəˌtard/ n. [count] a close-fitting single piece of clothing worn by acrobats, dancers, etc.

lep•er /'lɛpər/ n. [count] **1.** a person who has leprosy. **2.** a person who is not accepted by others; an outcast.

lep•ro•sy /'lɛprəsiy/ n. [noncount] an infectious disease in which the skin and tissue of the body are destroyed and there is a loss of sensation. **—'lep•rous,** adj.

les•bi•an /'lɛzbiyən/ n. [count] a homosexual woman. **—'les•bi•an•ism,** n. [noncount]

less /lɛs/ adv., a comparative of **little** with **least** as superlative. **1.** to a smaller extent or degree: a less-developed country. —adj., a compar. of **little** with **least** as superl. **2.** not as much: He has less money than before. **3.** lower in importance: She complained to no less a person than the mayor. —n. [noncount] **4.** a smaller amount: She eats less every day. —prep. **5.** minus; subtracting: a year less two days. **—Idiom. 6. less and less,** to a decreasing degree. **—Usage.** FEWER is the comparative form of FEW. It is properly used before plural nouns that refer to individuals or things that can be counted (fewer words; no fewer than 31 states). LESS is the comparative form of LITTLE. It should modify only singular mass nouns that refer to things that are abstract or cannot be counted (less sugar; less doubt). LESS may be used before plural nouns only when they suggest combination into a unit or group (less than $50; less than three miles).

-less, a suffix meaning: without (childless); not able to (sleepless); not able to be (useless).

less•en /'lɛsən/ v. to (cause to) become less: [no obj]: Soon the pain lessened. [~ + obj]: Cold lessens feeling.

less•er /'lɛsər/ adj., a comparative of **little** with **least** as superlative. **1.** smaller: a lesser evil.

—*adv., a compar. of* **little** *with* **least** *as superl.* **2.** less: *lesser-known.*

les•son /ˈlɛsən/ *n.* [*count*] **1.** a period of time given to instruction: *to take driving lessons.* **2.** something to be learned, taught, or studied. **3.** something useful learned through experience: *The accident taught him a lesson.*

lest /lɛst/ *conj.* for fear that: *We worried lest the secret become known.*

let /lɛt/ *v.,* **let, let•ting,** *n.* —*v.* [~ + *obj*] **1.** to allow or permit: *I let him borrow my car.* **2.** to allow to pass or go: *She let the dog out.* **3.** to cause to; make: *Let her know the truth.* **4.** (used to express a command, request, warning, etc.): *Let's go. Let me see your book. Let them try.* **5.** to rent: *to let rooms.* **6. let down, a.** to disappoint: *He let the whole team down* or *He let down the whole team.* **b.** to make (a garment) longer: *He let down the dress a few inches* or *He let the dress down a few inches.* **7. let in on,** to allow to share in: *I'll let you in on a secret.* **8. let off, a.** to release like an explosion: *to let off steam.* **b.** to excuse from (work, a duty, etc.): *The boss let us off early.* **c.** to punish lightly: *The judge let him off with a fine.* **9. let on,** to tell (a secret): *He didn't let on that he knew about the party. She knew about the party, but she never let on.* **10. let out, a.** to express: *let out a scream.* **b.** to make (a garment) larger: *She let out her jeans* or *She let her jeans out.* **11. let up,** to lessen or stop: *At last, the rain is letting up.* —*n.* [*count; usually singular*] **12.** *Brit.* a housing rental. —*Idiom.* **13. let go, a.** to allow to escape: *She let the fish go.* **b.** to stop holding on to: *She let go of the rope and fell. Hold on, don't let go.* **14. let (someone) have it,** *Informal.* to attack.

-let, a suffix meaning: small (*booklet*); an ornament or article of clothing worn on (*anklet*).

let•down /ˈlɛtˌdawn/ *n.* [*count*] a disappointment.

le•thal /ˈliyθəl/ *adj.* causing death: *a lethal weapon; a lethal drug.*

leth•ar•gy /ˈlɛθərdʒiy/ *n.* [*noncount*] the quality or state of being tired, lazy, or dull. —**le•thar•gic** /ləˈθɑrdʒɪk/ *adj.*

let's /lɛts/ contraction of *let us: Let's go.*

let•ter /ˈlɛtər/ *n.* [*count*] **1.** a written message sent to someone. **2.** a sign used in writing and printing to represent a speech sound. —*Idiom.* **3. to the letter,** exactly: *I followed your instructions to the letter.*

'letter ,carrier, *n.* MAIL CARRIER.

let•ter•ing /ˈlɛtərɪŋ/ *n.* [*noncount*] letters or words, esp. with regard to their style.

let•tuce /ˈlɛtɪs/ *n.* [*noncount*] [*count*] a plant with large crisp green leaves used in salads.

let•up /ˈlɛtˌʌp/ *n.* [*count*] [*count*] a lessening or stopping of activity.

leu•ke•mi•a /luwˈkiymiyə/ *n.* [*noncount*] a serious disease in which the blood-forming organs produce too many white blood cells.

lev•ee /ˈlɛviy/ *n.* [*count*], *pl.* **-ees. 1.** a raised area designed to prevent the flooding of a river. **2.** a landing place for ships.

lev•el /ˈlɛvəl/ *adj., n., v.,* **-eled, -el•ing** or (*esp. Brit.*) **-elled, -el•ling.** —*adj.* **1.** having a flat or even surface: *level land.* **2.** equal, as in height, condition, etc.: *His shoulders are level with mine.* **3.** steady; not changing: *to speak in a level voice.* —*n.* **4.** height: [*noncount*]: *a shelf built at eye level.* [*count*]: *The water rose to a level of 30 feet.* **5.** [*count*] a position on a scale of value, quality, or quantity: *an average level of skill.* **6.** [*count*]

rank or status: *the top levels of government.* **7.** [*count*] a floor or story of a structure. **8.** [*count*] a device used to determine if a surface is flat or even. —*v.* [~ + *obj*] **9.** to make (a surface) level: *They leveled the ground before planting corn.* **10.** to pull down or destroy: *to level trees.* **11.** to aim (a weapon or criticism) at someone: *Charges have been leveled against you.* **12. level off, a.** (of an aircraft) to (cause to) become horizontal: *The plane leveled off. The pilot leveled the plane off.* **b.** to become steady after rising and falling: *Unemployment hasn't leveled off.* **c.** to make even or smooth: *He leveled off the ground* or *He leveled the ground off.* **13. level with,** to speak truthfully and openly with: *Level with me; how much will it cost?* —*Idiom.* **14. on the level,** honest; sincere: *Is this offer on the level?*

lev•el•head•ed /ˈlɛvəlˈhɛdɪd/ *adj.* sensible. —'lev•el'head•ed•ness, *n.* [*noncount*]

lev•er /ˈlɛvər, ˈliyvər/ *n.* [*count*] **1.** a handle used to operate something, as a piece of machinery. **2.** a bar used to pry things open or to lift something heavy. **3.** a means of influence. —*v.* [~ + *obj*] **4.** to move with a lever.

lev•er•age /ˈlɛvərɪdʒ, ˈlɛvrɪdʒ, ˈliyvərɪdʒ, -vrɪdʒ/ *n.* [*noncount*] **1.** the power of a lever. **2.** power to influence people: *He has leverage with the police.*

Le•vi's /ˈliyvayz/ *Trademark.* [*plural; used with a plural verb*] a brand of jeans.

lev•i•ty /ˈlɛvɪtiy/ *n.* [*noncount*] lack of proper seriousness.

lev•y /ˈlɛviy/ *n., pl.* **lev•ies,** *v.,* **lev•ied, lev•y•ing.** —*n.* [*count*] **1.** a collecting of a tax by authority or force. **2.** the tax itself. —*v.* [~ + *obj*] **3.** to impose (a tax, fine, etc.): *to levy a duty on imports.*

lewd /luwd/ *adj.,* **-er, -est.** dealing with sex in an offensive way: *lewd behavior; lewd jokes.* —'lewd•ness, *n.* [*noncount*]

li•a•bil•i•ty /ˌlayəˈbɪlɪtiy/ *n., pl.* **-ties. 1.** liabilities, [*plural*] money owed; debts. **2.** [*count*] something that is a disadvantage: *His lack of education is a liability.* **3.** [*noncount*] the state of being liable.

li•a•ble /ˈlayəbəl/ *adj.* [*be* + ~] **1.** legally responsible: *You are liable for the damage.* **2.** likely: *She's liable to get angry.*

li•ai•son /liyˈeyzən, ˈliyəˌzɒn/ *n.* **1.** [*noncount*] a working connection between military units or different groups of people. **2.** [*count*] a love affair between people not married to each other.

li•ar /ˈlayər/ *n.* [*count*] a person who tells lies.

li•bel /ˈlaybəl/ *n., v.,* **-beled, -bel•ing** or (*esp. Brit.*) **-belled, -bel•ling.** —*n.* [*noncount*] [*count*] **1.** damage to a person's reputation by means of published statements, pictures, etc. —*v.* [~ + *obj*] **2.** to publish a libel against. —'li•bel•er, *n.* [*count*] —'li•bel•ous, *adj.*

lib•er•al /ˈlɪbərəl, ˈlɪbrəl/ *adj.* **1.** favorable to progress, change, or reform, as in political or religious affairs. **2.** generous: *a liberal donation.* **3.** giving a broad general knowledge; not specialized: *a liberal education.* **4.** not narrow-minded; tolerant of others. —*n.* [*count*] **5.** a person who is liberal. —'lib•er•al•ism, *n.* [*noncount*] —'lib•er•al•ly, *adv.*

lib•er•al•ize /ˈlɪbərəˌlayz, ˈlɪbrə-/ *v.* [~ + *obj*], **-ized, -iz•ing.** to free from limitations: *to liberalize government policies.* —**lib•er•al•i•za•tion** /ˌlɪbərəlɪˈzeyʃən, ˌlɪbrə-/, *n.* [*noncount*]

lib•er•ate /ˈlɪbəˌreyt/ *v.* [~ + *obj*], **-at•ed, -at•ing.** to set free, as from prison, unfair control,

L

etc. —**lib•er•a•tion** /ˌlɪbəˈreyʃən/, n. [noncount]
—**ˈlib•er,a•tor,** n. [count]

Li•be•ri•an /layˈbɪəriyən/ adj. **1.** of or relating to Liberia. —n. [count] **2.** a person born or living in Liberia.

lib•er•ty /ˈlɪbərtiy/ n. [noncount] [count], pl. **-ties. 1.** freedom from another's control or rule. **2.** power or right to act according to choice. —**Idiom. 3. at liberty,** free: You are at liberty to leave.

li•bi•do /lɪˈbiydow/ n. [noncount] the sexual urge.

li•brar•i•an /layˈbrɛəriyən/ n. [count] a person who is in charge of a library.

li•brar•y /ˈlay,brɛriy/ n. [count], pl. **-brar•ies. 1.** a collection of books, magazines, recordings, etc. **2.** a room or building for such a collection.

Lib•y•an /ˈlɪbiyən/ adj. **1.** of or relating to Libya. —n. [count] **2.** a person born or living in Libya.

lice /lays/ n. [plural] a pl. of LOUSE.

li•cense /ˈlaysəns/ n., v., **-censed, -cens•ing.** —n. **1.** [count] an official paper, card, etc., giving proof of permission to do or own something: a driver's license. **2.** [noncount] excessive or undue freedom or liberty: My parents think there is too much sexual license today. —v. [~ + obj] **3.** to give a license to or for. —**ˈli•censed,** adj.

lick /lɪk/ v. **1.** [~ + obj] to pass the tongue over the surface of: to lick a postage stamp. **2.** [~ + obj] to take into the mouth with the tongue: The cat licked up the milk. **3.** (of waves, flames, etc.) to touch lightly: [~ + obj]: The waves licked the shore. [no obj]: The flames licked at the roof. **4.** [~ + obj] Informal. to defeat: Our team licked their team. —n. [count] **5.** the act of licking. **6.** Informal. a small amount: I haven't done a lick of work. —**Idiom. 7. lick one's lips,** to show eager expectation. **8. lick one's wounds,** to attempt to comfort oneself after injury or defeat.

lic•o•rice /ˈlɪkərɪʃ, ˈlɪkrɪʃ, ˈlɪkərɪs/ n. **1.** [noncount] a plant whose sweet-tasting root is used in medicine and candy. **2.** [noncount] [count] a candy flavored with licorice.

lid /lɪd/ n. [count] **1.** a movable cover for a pot, jar, or other container. **2.** an eyelid.

lie¹ /lay/ n., v., **lied, ly•ing.** —n. [count] **1.** a false statement made knowingly and on purpose. —v. **2.** to tell a lie: [no obj]: He lied about his age. [~ + obj]: He lied his way out of difficulty.

lie² /lay/ v., **lay** /ley/, **lain** /leyn/, **ly•ing,** n. —v. [no obj] **1.** to be in a flat or horizontal position, as on a bed or the ground: I had to lie down after work. The book lies on the table. **2.** to be or remain in the state that is mentioned: The money lay hidden for years. **3.** to be situated: the land lying along the coast. **4.** to stretch out; extend: The road lay before us. **5.** to be found; exist: The problem lies here. **6. lie behind,** to be the real reason for something: What lies behind her decision to quit? **7. lie with,** to be the duty or responsibility of: The blame lies with the parents. —n. [count] **8.** the way something lies. —**Usage.** See LAY¹.

lieu /luw/ n. [noncount] —**Idiom. in lieu of,** instead of: gave us an IOU in lieu of cash.

lieu•ten•ant /luwˈtɛnənt/ n. [count] **1.** a rank in the armed forces above a sergeant and below a captain. **2.** a commissioned officer in the U.S. Navy or Coast Guard.

life /layf/ n., pl. **lives** /layvz/. **1.** [noncount] the quality that makes animals and plants able to grow, reproduce, and change in response to the environment: There are many forms of life on

earth. **2.** [count] the period between birth and death: She led a long life. **3.** [noncount] the state of human existence: Life is full of surprises. **4.** [count] a person: Doctors try to save lives. **5.** [noncount] living things: insect life. **6.** [count] a biography: a life of Mark Twain. **7.** [noncount] energy; spirit: The party was full of life. **8.** [noncount] a way of living: city life. **9.** [count] the period during which something lasts or works: the life of a camera. —**Idiom. 10. come to life,** to become active or lively. **11. not on your life,** certainly not. **12. take one's life in one's hands,** to risk death by knowingly doing something very dangerous. **13. take (someone's) life,** to kill. —**ˈlife•less,** adj. —**ˈlife•like,** adj.

life•blood /ˈlayf,blʌd/ n. [noncount] a necessary force or resource: Farming is the lifeblood of that country.

life•boat /ˈlayf,bowt/ n. [count] a ship's boat used for saving lives at sea.

life•guard /ˈlayf,gard/ n. [count] a person employed to protect swimmers at a beach or pool.

ˈlife ,jacket, n. [count] a life preserver in the form of a sleeveless jacket. Also called **ˈlife ,vest.**

life•line /ˈlayf,layn/ n. [count] **1.** a line or rope for saving life, as at sea. **2.** something considered absolutely necessary.

life•long /ˈlayf,lɔŋ, -,lɒŋ/ adj. [before a noun] lasting throughout one's life: lifelong regret.

ˈlife pre,server, n. [count] a jacket, belt, or other device that keeps a person afloat in water.

ˈlife-ˈsize or **ˈlife-ˈsized,** adj. of the natural size of a person or object: a life-size statue.

ˈlife,style or **ˈlife-,style,** n. [count] the typical way of living of an individual or group.

life•time /ˈlayf,taym/ n. [count] the time that the life of someone or something continues.

lift /lɪft/ v. **1.** [~ + obj] to raise to a higher level: She lifted the child onto the chair. **2.** [no obj] to rise and disappear, as fog. **3.** [~ + obj] to stop or put an end to: Congress lifted the blockade. **4.** [~ + obj] to raise in mood, condition, etc.: The news lifted my spirits. **5.** [~ + obj] Informal. to steal: He was caught trying to lift someone's wallet. **6. lift off,** (of a spacecraft) to rise into the air. —n. [count] **7.** the act of lifting. **8.** a free ride in a vehicle. **9.** a feeling of happiness or encouragement. **10.** a device for lifting something. **11.** Brit. ELEVATOR (def. 2). —**Idiom. 12. not lift a finger,** to not exert any effort: They won't lift a finger to help you.

lift•off or **lift-off** /ˈlɪft,ɔf, -,ɒf/ n. [count] the rising of a spacecraft into the air from its launch pad.

lig•a•ment /ˈlɪgəmənt/ n. [count] a band of strong tissue that connects bones or holds organs in place.

light¹ /layt/ n., adj., **light•er, light•est,** v., **light•ed** or **lit** /lɪt/, **light•ing.** —n. **1.** [noncount] the brightness that makes things able to be seen: The sun gives off light. **2.** [count] something giving off such brightness, as the sun or a lamp. **3.** [count] a device for starting or means of starting a fire, a spark, flame, or match. **4.** [count] a traffic light: He went through a red light. **5.** [count; usually singular] the way in which a thing appears or is looked at: He saw things in a new light. **6.** [count] a gleam or sparkle: a fierce light in her eyes. —adj. **7.** having light; bright: The room was light enough to read in. **8.** pale in color: a light blue. —v. **9.** to (cause to) burn: [~ + obj]: They lit the fire. She lit (up) a cigarette. [no obj]: These wet logs won't light (up). **10.** to (cause to) become bright: [*no obj*]: *The sky lights up at sunrise.* [~ + *obj*]: *to light (up) a room.* [~ + *up* + *obj*]: *The car's headlights lit up the area ahead.* —***Idiom.*** **11. bring to light,** to discover or make known: *She brought to light new facts about the case.* **12. come to light,** to be discovered or made known: *New facts came to light.* **13. in (the) light of,** because of; considering. **14. light at the end of the tunnel,** a future possibility of success or relief. **15. see the light,** to understand something at last.

light² /layt/ *adj.* and *adv.*, **-er, -est.** —*adj.* **1.** of little weight; not heavy: *a light load.* **2.** of small amount, force, etc.: *a light rain.* **3.** easy to do or bear: *light duties.* **4.** gentle: *a light touch.* **5.** not very serious; entertaining: *light reading.* **6.** unimportant: *light conversation.* **7.** easily digested: *a light meal.* **8.** (of drinks) low in alcohol. **9.** moving easily: *to be light on one's feet.* **10.** cheerful; carefree: *a light heart.* **11.** dizzy: *I felt light in the head.* **12.** (of sleep) not deep. —*adv.* **13.** without many possessions: *He prefers to travel light.* —'**light•ly,** *adv.* —'**light•ness,** *n.*

light³ /layt/ *v.* [*no obj*], **light•ed** or **lit** /lɪt/, **light• ing. 1.** to come down to rest: *The bird lighted on the branch.* **2.** to come by chance; happen: *to light on a clue.* **3. light into,** to attack with blows or words: *He lit into the next speaker with criticism.*

light•en¹ /'laytṇ/ *v.* to (cause to) become brighter: [*no obj*]: *The sky lightened at dawn.* [~ + *obj*]: *The sun lightened her hair.*

light•en² /'laytṇ/ *v.* **1.** [~ + *obj*] to make lighter in weight: *to lighten a heavy load.* **2.** to (cause to) become less severe: [~ + *obj*]: *to lighten taxes.* [*no obj*]: *Our responsibilities have begun to lighten.*

light•er /'laytər/ *n.* [*count*] a mechanical device used in lighting cigarettes, cigars, or pipes.

light•head•ed /'layt'hɛdɪd/ *adj.* dizzy.

light•heart•ed /'layt'hɑrtɪd/ *adj.* carefree; cheerful. —'**light'heart•ed•ly,** *adv.* —'**light'heart•ed•ness,** *n.* [*noncount*]

light•house /'layt,haws/ *n.* [*count*] a tower with a bright light on top to guide ships.

lighthouse

light•ing /'laytɪŋ/ *n.* [*noncount*] **1.** the act of making something give light or start burning. **2.** the arrangement of lights for a particular effect or the effect produced.

light•ning /'laytnɪŋ/ *n.* [*noncount*] **1.** a brilliant flash in the sky, caused by an electric spark in the atmosphere. —*adj.* [*before a noun*] **2.** very quick or sudden: *moved with lightning speed.*

'**lightning ,bug,** *n.* FIREFLY.

light•weight /'layt,weyt/ *adj.* **1.** light in weight. **2.** unimportant. —*n.* [*count*] **3.** a boxer weighing up to 135 lb. **4.** *Informal.* a person who is of little importance.

'**light-,year,** *n.* [*count*] the distance that light can travel in one year, about 5.88 trillion mi. (9.46 trillion km).

lik•a•ble or **like•a•ble** /'laykəbəl/ *adj.* easily liked; pleasing: *a likeable fellow.* —'**lik•a•ble• ness, lik•a•bil•i•ty** /,lɪkə'bɪlɪtiy/, *n.* [*noncount*]

like¹ /layk/ *adj.* [*before a noun*] **1.** similar: *The sisters wore like dresses.* —*prep.* **2.** in a similar way as: *She works like a beaver.* **3.** similar to: *Your hat is like mine.* **4.** likely to: *It looks like rain.* **5.** typical of: *It's just like them to be late.* **6.** inclined to: *I didn't feel like studying.* **7.** such as: *She enjoys sports like golf and tennis.* —*adv.* **8.** nearly: *The house is more like 40 years old.* —*conj.* **9.** in the same way as: *It happened like you said it would.* —*n.* **10.** a similar person or thing; equal: *No one has seen her like in a long time.* **11. the like,** something of a similar nature: *They grow oranges, lemons, and the like.* —***Idiom.*** **12. like anything, blazes, crazy, hell,** or **mad,** *Informal.* to the greatest extent or degree possible: *I ran like crazy.* **13. the like** or **likes of,** the equal of: *I have never seen the like(s) of her since.*

like² /layk/ *v.,* **liked, lik•ing,** *n.* —*v.* **1.** [~ + *obj*] to be fond of; enjoy: *to like opera; She likes playing baseball.* **2.** [~ + *obj*] to feel toward; to regard: *I like you as a friend.* **3.** [~ + *obj*] to wish or want: *Would you like a glass of wine?* **4.** [*no obj*] to be inclined; choose: *Go whenever you like.* —*n.* [*count*] **5.** Usually, **likes.** [*plural*] the things a person likes: *Find out about his likes and dislikes.*

-like, a suffix meaning: like or characteristic of (*childlike*).

like•li•hood /'laykliy,hʊd/ also '**like•li•ness,** *n.* [*noncount*] [*count*] probability.

like•ly /'laykliy/ *adj.,* **-li•er, -li•est,** *adv.* —*adj.* **1.** probable; expected: *It's likely she will win.* **2.** [*before a noun*] believable: *a likely enough excuse.* **3.** [*before a noun*] suitable: *a likely place to stay.* —*adv.* **4.** probably: *We will most likely stay home.*

'**like-'minded,** *adj.* having the same or a similar opinion, way of thinking or acting, etc.

lik•en /'laykən/ *v.* [~ + *obj*] to compare (someone or something) to (another): *He likened her to a rose.*

like•ness /'layknɪs/ *n.* **1.** [*count*] a portrait: *He drew a beautiful likeness of her.* **2.** [*noncount*] the condition of looking alike.

like•wise /'layk,wayz/ *adv.* **1.** also; too. **2.** in the same way; similarly.

lik•ing /'laykɪŋ/ *n.* [*count; usually singular*] **1.** fondness: *a liking for sweets.* **2.** preference; taste: *Rock music is not to my liking.*

li•lac /'laylək, -lɑk, -læk/ *n.* **1.** [*noncount*] [*count*] a shrub with sweet-smelling purple or white flowers. **2.** [*noncount*] a pale pinkish purple color.

lilt /lɪlt/ *n.* [*count*] rhythmic rising or falling in the voice. —'**lilt•ing,** *adj.*

lil•y /'lɪliy/ *n.* [*count*], *pl.* **lil•ies.** a plant that grows from a bulb and has large, showy white flowers.

'**lima ,bean** /'laymə/ *n.* [*count*] a bean having a broad, flat seed that can be eaten.

limb /lɪm/ *n.* [*count*] **1.** a leg, arm, or wing. **2.** a large branch of a tree. —***Idiom.*** **3. out on a limb,** in a risky or dangerous situation.

lim•ber /'lɪmbər/ *adj.* **1.** able to bend easily; supple: *a limber athlete.* —*v.* **2. limber up,** to exercise one's muscles: *to limber up before a game.*

L

lim•bo /'lɪmbow/ *n.* [*noncount*] a place or state of uncertainty.

lime[1] /laym/ *n.* [*noncount*] a whitish substance used in making plaster and cement.

lime[2] /laym/ *n.* [*count*] [*noncount*] the small, greenish yellow, acid fruit of a citrus tree related to the lemon.

lime•light /'laym,layt/ *n.* [*noncount; the* + ~] a position at the center of public attention.

lime•stone /'laym,stown/ *n.* [*noncount*] a hard rock used for building and for making lime.

lim•it /'lɪmɪt/ *n.* [*count*] **1.** the point at which something ends: *the speed limit; I had reached the limit of my patience.* **2.** the greatest amount possible: *to catch the limit of fish.* —*v.* [~ + *obj*] **3.** to set a limit to: *to limit spending.* —'**lim•it•less,** *adj.*

lim•i•ta•tion /,lɪmɪ'teyʃən/ *n.* **1.** [*count*] a lack of power or ability; weakness: *He's aware of his own limitations.* **2.** [*noncount*] the act of limiting; the state of being limited.

lim•it•ed /'lɪmɪtɪd/ *adj.* confined within limits; restricted: *a train making limited stops.*

lim•ou•sine /'lɪmə,ziyn, ,lɪmə'ziyn/ *n.* [*count*] **1.** a large, luxurious car, esp. one driven by a chauffeur. **2.** a large sedan or small bus for transporting passengers to and from an airport, train station, etc.

limp[1] /lɪmp/ *v.* [*no obj*] **1.** to walk unevenly or with difficulty. —*n.* [*count*] **2.** a lame or uneven walk.

limp[2] /lɪmp/ *adj.*, **-er, -est. 1.** not stiff or firm. **2.** lacking strength. —'**limp•ly,** *adv.* —'**limp•ness,** *n.* [*noncount*]

lim•pid /'lɪmpɪd/ *adj.* clear or transparent, as water.

line[1] /layn/ *n., v.,* **lined, lin•ing.** —*n.* [*count*] **1.** a long thin mark on a surface: *notebook paper with blue lines.* **2.** a row of people or things: *He hid behind a line of trees.* **3.** a number of persons standing one behind the other: *a long line for tickets.* **4.** a boundary; limit: *lines on a football field.* **5.** a unit in the structure of a poem: *a line of poetry.* **6.** Usually, **lines.** [*plural*] the words of an actor's part in a play. **7.** a short written message. **8.** a system of transportation: *a bus line.* **9.** a course or direction; path: *the line of flight.* **10.** a series of people, esp. of the same family: *a line of kings.* **11.** [*usually singular*] a person's occupation: *He's in the selling line.* **12.** Informal. a statement made for effect: *He handed us a line about his rich relatives.* **13.** outline or shape: *That ship has fine lines.* **14. lines,** [*plural*] a plan of doing or making: *stories written along the same lines.* **15.** a length of thread, rope, wire, etc.: *a fishing line.* **16.** a telephone connection: *Please hold the line.* **17.** a type of goods: *a new line of beauty products.* **18.** a series of military defenses: *behind enemy lines.* —*v.* [~ + *obj*] **19.** to mark with a line or lines. **20.** to form a line along: *Rocks lined the driveway.* **21. line up, a.** to obtain: *We lined up a singer* or *We lined a singer up.* **b.** to (cause to) get in a line: *We lined up at the ticket office. The sergeant lined up his troops* or *The sergeant lined his troops up.* —**Idiom. 22. draw the line,** to establish a limit: *They draw the line at drinking before noon.* **23. hold the line,** to maintain the current situation: *to hold the line on price increases.* **24. in line, a.** in alignment; straight: *The tires are in line.* **b.** in agreement: *Your ideas are in line with mine.* **c.** under control: *He kept the children in line during dinner.* **d.** in a line or row: *waiting in line for an hour.* **25. on line,** actively linked to a computer. **26. on the line,** in a risky position: *He had put his reputation on the line.* **27. out of line, a.** not in a straight line: *The tires were out of line.* **b.** behaving unacceptably: *You're way out of line with your criticism.*

line[2] /layn/ *v.* [~ + *obj*], **lined, lin•ing.** to cover the inside of: *to line a coat with blue silk.*

lin•e•ar /'lɪniyər/ *adj.* **1.** of or using lines: *linear design.* **2.** arranged in a line: *a linear series.* **3.** of length: *linear measurements.* —'**lin•e•ar•ly,** *adv.*

lin•en /'lɪnən/ *n.* **1.** [*noncount*] cloth woven from flax yarns. **2.** Often, **linens.** [*plural*] [*noncount*] sheets, towels, tablecloths, etc., made of linen or a similar cloth, as cotton. —*adj.* **3.** made of linen: *a linen jacket.*

lin•er /'laynər/ *n.* [*count*] **1.** a ship or airplane operated by a transportation line. **2.** EYELINER.

lines•man /'laynzmən/ *n.* [*count*], *pl.* **-men.** an official in tennis, soccer, football, or ice hockey who decides on limits or distances.

line•up /'layn,ʌp/ *n.* [*count*] **1.** an orderly arrangement of persons or things: *the fall lineup of TV programs.* **2.** a group of persons lined up for inspection, etc.

-ling, a suffix meaning: a person concerned or connected (in a negative way) with (*hireling*); little (*duckling*).

lin•ger /'lɪŋgər/ *v.* [*no obj*] **1.** to remain longer than is usual or expected: *They lingered over their coffee.* **2.** to be slow to disappear: *Old prejudices lingered after the war.* —'**lin•ger•ing,** *adj.*: *a lingering illness.*

lin•ge•rie /,lɑnʒə'rey, 'lænʒə,riy/ *n.* [*noncount*] underwear or sleepwear for women.

lin•guist /'lɪŋgwɪst/ *n.* [*count*] **1.** a specialist in linguistics. **2.** a person who is skilled in several languages. —**lin'guis•tic,** *adj.*: *linguistic knowledge.*

lin•guis•tics /lɪŋ'gwɪstɪks/ *n.* [*noncount; used with a singular verb*] the study of language.

lin•i•ment /'lɪnəmənt/ *n.* [*count*] [*noncount*] a liquid for rubbing on the skin, esp. to relieve soreness.

lin•ing /'laynɪŋ/ *n.* [*count*] a layer of material that covers the inside of something, as a garment.

link /lɪŋk/ *n.* [*count*] **1.** one of the rings or loops of a chain. **2.** a connection: *The locket was a link with her past.* —*v.* **3.** to join; connect: [~ + *obj*]: *The new bridge will link (up) the island and the mainland.* [*no obj*]: *The company will soon link (up) with a hotel chain.* —'**link•age,** *n.* [*noncount*] [*count*]

li•no•le•um /lɪ'nowliyəm/ *n.* [*noncount*] a hard, shiny floor covering.

'linseed ,oil, *n.* [*noncount*] an oil made by pressing seeds from flax, used in making paints, printing inks, linoleum, etc.

lint /lɪnt/ *n.* [*noncount*] bits of thread.

li•on /'layən/ *n.* [*count*] a large, strong, usually yellowish-brown member of the cat family.

li•on•ess /'layənɪs/ *n.* [*count*] a female lion.

li•on•heart•ed /'layən,hɑrtɪd/ *adj.* very brave.

'lion's ,share, *n.* [*count; usually singular*] the largest part or share.

lip /lɪp/ *n.* **1.** [*count*] either of the two fleshy outside edges of the mouth. **2.** [*count*] the edge of an opening. **3.** [*noncount*] Slang. rude or disrespectful talk: *Don't give me any lip.* —**Idiom. 4. keep a stiff upper lip,** to maintain a determined attitude when facing difficulty. —**lipped,** *adj.: thin-lipped.*

lip•read•ing /'lɪp,riydɪŋ/ *n.* [*noncount*] a method of understanding spoken words by watching the movements of a speaker's lips. —**'lip,read,** *v.,* -**read** /-,rɛd/, -**read•ing:** [*no obj*]: *learning to lipread.* [~ + *obj*]: *She could lipread his words.* —**'lip,read•er,** *n.* [*count*]

lip•stick /'lɪp,stɪk/ *n.* [*noncount*] [*count*] a stick of coloring material for the lips.

liq•ue•fy /'lɪkwə,fay/ *v.* [*no obj*] [~ + *obj*], -**fied,** -**fy•ing.** to (cause to) become liquid.

li•queur /lɪ'kɜr, -'kyʊr/ *n.* [*noncount*] [*count*] a strong, usually sweet alcoholic liquor.

liq•uid /'lɪkwɪd/ *n.* [*count*] [*noncount*] **1.** a form of matter that is not a solid or a gas but that flows freely: *Water and oil are liquids.* —*adj.* **2.** of or made up of liquids: *a liquid diet.* **3.** in cash or easily changed into cash: *liquid assets.*

liq•ui•date /'lɪkwɪ,deyt/ *v.* [~ + *obj*], -**dat•ed,** -**dat•ing. 1.** to settle or pay (a debt). **2.** to change (property or other assets) into cash. **3.** *Informal.* to get rid of, esp. by killing. —**liq•ui•da•tion** /,lɪkwɪ'deyʃən/ *n.* [*noncount*]

liq•uor /'lɪkər/ *n.* [*noncount*] a strong alcoholic drink, such as whiskey or gin.

lisp /lɪsp/ *n.* [*count*] **1.** a speech defect in which *s* and *z* are pronounced like the *th-* sounds of *thin* and *this,* in that order. —*v.* [*no obj*] [~ + *obj*] **2.** to pronounce or speak with a lisp.

list¹ /lɪst/ *n.* [*count*] **1.** a series of items written down together: *a shopping list.* —*v.* [~ + *obj*] **2.** to set down or enter in a list. —**'list•ing,** *n.* [*count*]

list² /lɪst/ *n.* [*count*] **1.** a leaning to one side, as of a ship. —*v.* [*no obj*] **2.** to lean to one side: *The ship listed in the storm.*

lis•ten /'lɪsən/ *v.* **1.** to pay attention for the purpose of hearing: [~ + *to* + *obj*]: *He listened to every word.* [*no obj*]: *I wasn't listening.* **2. listen in,** to listen to a conversation, esp. secretly: *He sat in the back, listening in; I wanted to listen in on the talks.* —**'lis•ten•er,** *n.* [*count*]

list•less /'lɪstlɪs/ *adj.* lacking energy or spirit. —**'list•less•ly,** *adv.* —**'list•less•ness,** *n.* [*noncount*]

lit /lɪt/ *v.* a pt. and pp. of LIGHT¹.

li•ter /'liytər/ *n.* [*count*] a metric unit of measure for liquids, slightly more than a quart. *Abbr.:* l Also, *esp. Brit.,* **litre.**

lit•er•a•cy /'lɪtərəsiy/ *n.* [*noncount*] the ability to read and write.

lit•er•al /'lɪtərəl/ *adj.* **1.** being in accordance with the basic or usual meaning of a word; not figurative. **2.** following the words of the original exactly: *a literal translation.* —**'lit•er•al•ness,** *n.* [*noncount*]

lit•er•al•ly /'lɪtərəliy/ *adv.* **1.** word for word: *to translate literally.* **2.** really; actually: *The town was literally destroyed.* **3.** (used to give emphasis): *I was literally drowning in debt.*

lit•er•ar•y /'lɪtə,reriy/ *adj.* of books or authors.

lit•er•ate /'lɪtərɪt/ *adj.* **1.** able to read and write. **2.** educated; well-read.

lit•er•a•ture /'lɪtərətʃər, 'lɪtrə-/ *n.* [*noncount*] **1.** writing that has lasting value or excellence: *English literature.* **2.** writing on a particular subject: *the medical literature.* **3.** informative printed material.

lithe /layð/ *adj.,* **lith•er, lith•est.** able to bend or move easily: *a lithe dancer.*

lit•i•gant /'lɪtɪgənt/ *n.* [*count*] a person engaged in a lawsuit.

lit•i•gate /'lɪtɪ,geyt/ *v.* [*no obj*], -**gat•ed,** -**gat•ing.** to carry on a lawsuit. —**lit•i•ga•tion** /,lɪtɪ'geyʃən/ *n.* [*noncount*] [*count*] —**'lit•i,ga•tor,** *n.* [*count*]

lit•mus /'lɪtməs/ *n.* [*noncount*] coloring matter that turns blue in alkaline solution and red in acid solution, used as a chemical indicator.

li•tre /'liytər/ *n. Chiefly Brit.* LITER.

lit•ter /'lɪtər/ *n.* **1.** [*noncount*] rubbish scattered about: *streets full of litter.* **2.** [*count*] the group of young born to an animal at one birth: *a litter of six kittens.* **3.** [*count*] a stretcher for carrying a sick or wounded person. —*v.* **4.** to make (a place) dirty or untidy with litter: [~ + *obj*]: *to be fined for littering the sidewalk.* [*no obj*]: *He was fined for littering.* **5.** [~ + *obj*] to scatter (objects) in disorder: *Papers littered the floor.*

lit•ter•bug /'lɪtər,bʌg/ *n.* [*count*] a person who litters public places.

lit•tle /'lɪtl/ *adj.,* **lit•tler** or **less** /lɛs/ or **less•er,** **lit•tlest** or **least** /liyst/, *adv.,* **less, least,** *n.* —*adj.* **1.** [*before a noun*] small: *a little desk; a little voice.* **2.** [*before a noun*] short in time or distance: *We'll be home in a little while.* **3.** [*before a noun*] small in number: *a little group of scientists.* **4.** [*before a noun,* also *a* + ~ + *noun*] of a certain amount; some: *I have a little money left. We're having a little difficulty.* **5.** [*before a noun*] younger: *her little brother.* **6.** unimportant: *life's little pleasures.* —*adv.* **7.** [*before a verb*] not at all: *He little knows what awaits him.* **8.** not much; slightly: *a little known work of art; She's little better than she was before.* —*n.* **9.** [*noncount*] a small amount, quantity, or degree: *They did little to make us comfortable. Save a little for me.* **10.** [*count; singular; a* + ~] a short time or distance: *Stay here for a little. Step back a little.* —*Idiom.* **11. little by little,** gradually.

'little 'finger, *n.* [*count*] the smallest finger on the hand.

liv•a•ble or **live•a•ble** /'lɪvəbəl/ *adj.* **1.** suitable for living in: *They made the old house livable.* **2.** worth living: *making life more livable.*

live¹ /lɪv/ *v.* [*no obj*], **lived, liv•ing. 1.** to be alive; to have life. **2.** to stay alive: *so ill he might not live.* **3.** to have enough for one's existence: *He can't live on his salary.* **4.** to feed on: *She lived on fruit.* **5.** to have one's home: *to live in a cottage.* **6. live down,** to live so as to cause (a past action) to be forgotten or forgiven: *She'll never live down her failure* or *She'll never live her failure down.* **7. live together,** to live as if married: *They lived together before getting married.* **8. live up to,** to satisfy (ideals, standards, etc.): *He tried to live up to his father's high standards.* **9. live with, a.** to dwell in the same place with: *She lived with him before they got married.* **b.** to endure: *We'll just have to live with that noise.*

live² /layv/ *adj.,* **liv•er, liv•est** for 2, 5, *adv.* —*adj.* **1.** [*before a noun*] being alive; living: *live animals.* **2.** burning or glowing: *live coals.* **3.** loaded but unexploded: *live ammunition.* **4.** broadcast while happening or being performed: *a live television show.* **5.** of current interest: *a live issue.* **6.** connected to a source of electricity: *a live outlet.*

live•li•hood /'layvliy,hʊd/ *n.* [*count; usually singular*] a means of earning one's money.

live•ly /'layvliy/ *adj.,* -**li•er, -li•est. 1.** full of life or energy; spirited: *a lively discussion; a lively tune.* **2.** bright and strong: *lively colors.* **3.** keen:

L

They took a lively interest in us. —**'live•li•ness,** *n.* [*noncount*]

liv•en /'layvən/ *v.* to (cause to) become more lively: [~ + *obj*]: *Can we liven (up) the party?* [*no obj*]: *The party livened up.*

liv•er /'lɪvər/ *n.* **1.** [*count*] a large organ in the body that makes bile and cleans the blood. **2.** [*noncount*] the liver of an animal, used as food.

lives /layvz/ *n.* pl. of LIFE.

live•stock /'layv,stɒk/ *n.* the animals raised on a farm or ranch: [*noncount*]: *The livestock is valuable.* [*plural*]: *The livestock are in the barn.*

liv•id /'lɪvɪd/ *adj.* **1.** of a bluish gray color, as a bruise. **2.** extremely angry.

liv•ing /'lɪvɪŋ/ *adj.* **1.** having life; being alive. **2.** still in use: *a living language.* **3.** [*before a noun*] of or for human life: *not enough living space.* **4.** [*before a noun*] true to life; exact: *The statue is the living image of the general.* —*n.* **5.** [*noncount*] the state of being alive. **6.** [*count*] a manner of life: *a poor standard of living.* **7.** [*count; singular*] livelihood: *to earn a living.* **8. the living,** [*plural*] people who are alive.

'living,room, *n.* [*count*] a room in a home for general use.

liz•ard /'lɪzərd/ *n.* [*count*] a small, rough-skinned reptile with four legs and a long tail.

lla•ma /'lɑmə, 'yɑ-/ *n.* [*count*], pl. **-mas.** a woolly-haired South American animal related to the camel.

load /lowd/ *n.* [*count*] **1.** something carried: *a truck with a load of wood.* **2.** the amount or number that can be carried, used esp. in combination: *a busload of tourists.* **3.** the amount of work required of a person, machine, etc. **4.** burden: *That's a load off my mind.* **5. loads of** or **a load of,** *Informal.* a great quantity or number: *loads of people.* —*v.* **6.** [~ + *obj*] to put a load on or in; fill: *to load a ship.* **7.** [*no obj*] to take on a load, as of passengers or goods: *All buses load at the platform.* **8.** [~ + *obj* + *down*] to weigh down: *to load oneself down with duties.* **9.** [~ + *obj*] [*no obj*] to put a bullet into (a gun). **10.** [~ + *obj*] to place (film, tape, etc.) into (a camera or other device): *He loaded the camera with film.* —**'load•er,** *n.* [*count*]

load•ed /'lowdɪd/ *adj.* **1.** carrying a load. **2.** filled with hidden meaning: *a loaded question.* **3.** *Slang.* **a.** very rich. **b.** drunk.

loaf¹ /lowf/ *n.* [*count*] pl. **loaves** /lowvz/. a shaped mass of bread or other food.

loaf² /lowf/ *v.* to pass time lazily: [*no obj*]: *He loafed during the summer.* [~ + *obj*]: *to loaf the afternoon away.* —**'loaf•er,** *n.* [*count*]

loan /lown/ *n.* [*count*] **1.** the act of lending: *the loan of a book.* **2.** something lent, esp. a sum of money lent at interest: *a loan of $25,000.* —*v.* [~ + *obj*] **3.** to lend: *Can you loan me a dollar? She loaned her car to us.* —*Idiom.* **4. on loan,** borrowed: *The books are on loan.*

loath /lowθ, lowð/ *adj.* [*be* + ~ + *to* + *verb*] unwilling: *She is loath to go.*

loathe /lowð/ *v.* [~ + *obj*], **loathed, loath•ing.** to dislike strongly: *He loathes going to the dentist.* —**'loath•ing,** *n.* [*noncount*] [*count*]

loath•some /'lowðsəm, 'lowθ-/ *adj.* disgusting.

loaves /lowvz/ *n.* pl. of LOAF¹.

lob•by /'lɒbiy/ *n.*, pl. **-bies,** *v.*, **-bied, -by•ing.** —*n.* [*count*] **1.** a hall or room at the entrance to a building. **2.** a group of persons who try to influence legislators to vote in a certain way. —*v.* **3.** to try to influence the actions or votes of (legislators): [~ + *obj*]: *He lobbied a few key senators.*

[*no obj*]: *He lobbied for the bill.* —**'lob•by•ist,** *n.* [*count*]

lobe /lowb/ *n.* [*count*] **1.** a rounded division, as of an organ or a leaf. **2.** an earlobe.

lob•ster /'lɒbstər/ *n.,* pl. (*esp. when thought of as a group*) **-ster,** (*esp. for kinds or species*) **-sters. 1.** [*count*] a shellfish with eight legs and two large claws. **2.** [*noncount*] the edible flesh of the lobster.

lo•cal /'lowkəl/ *adj.* **1.** of a particular place: *a local custom; a local hospital.* **2.** stopping at most or all stations: *a local train.* **3.** affecting only a part of the body: *The dentist gave the patient a local anesthetic.* —*n.* [*count*] **4.** a local train, bus, etc. **5.** a local anesthetic. **6.** Often, **locals.** [*plural*] a person who lives in a particular place. —**'lo•cal•ly,** *adv.*: *locally grown apples.*

lo•cal•i•ty /low'kælɪtiy/ *n.* [*count*], pl. **-ties.** a specific place or area; location.

lo•cate /'lowkeyt, low'keyt/ *v.,* **-cat•ed, -cat•ing. 1.** [~ + *obj*] to find the place or position of: *to locate a missing book.* **2.** to establish in a place; settle: [~ + *obj*]: *They located their offices downtown.* [*no obj*]: *They decided to locate in New Mexico.* —**'lo•cat•er, 'lo•ca•tor,** *n.* [*count*]

lo•ca•tion /low'keyʃən/ *n.* [*count*] **1.** a place or position: *a house in a fine location.* —*Idiom.* **2. on location,** in a particular place to make a movie, TV show, etc.

lock¹ /lɒk/ *n.* [*count*] **1.** a fastener for a door, window, drawer, etc. **2.** an enclosed section of a canal, dam, etc., for raising or lowering ships by changing the water level. —*v.* **3.** to fasten with a lock: [~ + *obj*]: *I locked the car doors.* [*no obj*]: *The car doors lock automatically.* **4.** [~ + *obj*] to shut in or out of a place. *We locked the animals in the barn. We locked ourselves out of the house.* **5.** [~ + *obj*] [*no obj*] to (cause to) become fixed or stuck. **6. lock up, a.** to imprison for a crime: *to lock the thief up* or *to lock up the thief.* **b.** to make secure with a lock: *He locked up the money in his safe* or *He locked the money up in his safe. The watchman locked up for the night.*

lock² /lɒk/ *n.* [*count*] **1.** a piece of hair. **2. locks,** [*plural*] the hair of the head: *curly locks.*

lock•er /'lɒkər/ *n.* [*count*] a small chest, cabinet, or closet in which clothing and valuables may be locked.

lock•et /'lɒkɪt/ *n.* [*count*] a small case for a picture, lock of hair, etc., worn on a chain around the neck.

lock•jaw /'lɒk,dʒɔ/ *n.* [*noncount*] a condition in which the jaws become locked together, caused by tetanus.

lock•smith /'lɒk,smɪθ/ *n.* [*count*] a person who makes, repairs, and installs locks.

lo•co•mo•tion /,lowkə'mowʃən/ *n.* [*noncount*] the act or power of moving from place to place.

lo•co•mo•tive /,lowkə'mowtɪv/ *n.* [*count*] a self-propelled railroad engine for pulling or pushing railroad cars.

lo•cust /'lowkəst/ *n.* [*count*] a large grasshopper that travels in huge groups and destroys crops.

lodge /lɒdʒ/ *n., v.,* **lodged, lodg•ing.** —*n.* [*count*] **1.** a country house or cabin, as for hunters or skiers. —*v.* **2.** [*no obj*] to stay in a place, esp. temporarily: *We lodged in a guest house for the night.* **3.** [*no obj*] to live in rented rooms in another's house. **4.** [~ + *obj*] to provide with a place to live: *to lodge a foreign student.* **5.** to (cause to) settle or fix firmly in a place; stick: [*no obj*]: *The bullet lodged in the wall.* [~ + *obj*]: *He lodged the stick in the ground.* **6.** [~ + *obj*] to bring to someone in authority: *She lodged a complaint with the union.* —**'lodg•er,** *n.* [*count*]

lodg•ing /'lɒdʒɪŋ/ *n.* **1.** [*noncount*] a place to stay: *to provide lodging.* **2. lodgings,** [*plural*] a room or rooms rented for living in.

loft /lɔft, lɒft/ *n.* [*count*] **1.** an upper room or storage area beneath a sloping roof. **2.** a large, open room in a building.

loft•y /'lɔftiy, 'lɒf-/ *adj.,* **-i•er, -i•est. 1.** very high: *lofty mountains.* **2.** noble: *lofty sentiments.* **3.** too proud: *a lofty manner.* —**'loft•i•ness,** *n.* [*noncount*]

log /lɔg, lɒg/ *n., v.,* **logged, log•ging.** —*n.* [*count*] **1.** a length of wood cut from a tree trunk. **2.** an official record, esp. of the journey of a ship or aircraft. —*v.* **3.** [~ + *obj*] [*no obj*] to cut down the trees on (land). **4.** [~ + *obj*] to enter in a log: *The captain logged the ship's position.* **5. log in** or **on,** to start using a computer system or on-line service by keying in a name or number. **6. log off** or **out,** to stop using such a system or service. —**'log•ger,** *n.* [*count*]

lo•gan•ber•ry /'lowgən,bɛriy/ *n.* [*count*], *pl.* **-ries.** a dark red, sharp-tasting, long berry of a kind of blackberry bush.

log•ic /'lɒdʒɪk/ *n.* [*noncount*] **1.** the science or method of reasoning by formal rules. **2.** sound and sensible reasoning: *There's much logic in her argument.* —**'log•i•cal,** *adj.: a logical argument.* —**'log•i•cal•ly,** *adv.*

-logy, a combining form meaning field of study (*astrology; biology*).

loin /lɔyn/ *n.* **1.** Usually, **loins.** [*plural*] the part of an animal between the ribs and the hipbones. **2.** [*count*] a cut of meat from this region. **3. loins,** [*plural*] the parts of the human body between the hips and the upper thighs.

loi•ter /'lɔytər/ *v.* [*no obj*] **1.** to stand around idly. **2.** to move along slowly. —**'loi•ter•er,** *n.* [*count*]

loll /lɒl/ *v.* [*no obj*] **1.** to lie or sit in a relaxed manner: *to loll on a sofa.* **2.** to hang loosely: *The dog's tongue lolled out.*

lol•li•pop or **lol•ly•pop** /'lɒliy,pɒp/ *n.* [*count*] a piece of hard candy on the end of a small stick.

lone /lown/ *adj.* [*before a noun*] away from others; alone: *a lone tree in the field.*

lone•ly /'lownliy/ *adj.,* **-li•er, -li•est. 1.** unhappy from being alone; lonesome. **2.** not often visited or used: *a lonely road.* —**'lone•li•ness,** *n.* [*noncount*]

lon•er /'lownər/ *n.* [*count*] a person who is or prefers to be alone.

lone•some /'lownsəm/ *adj.* lonely.

long¹ /lɔŋ, lɒŋ/ *adj.,* **long•er** /'lɔŋgər, 'lɒŋ-/, **long•est** /'lɒŋgɪst, 'lɒŋ-/, *n., adv.* —*adj.* **1.** having a great extent in space or time: *a long table; a long trip.* **2.** covering a certain time or distance: *How long was your class? The river was eight miles long.* **3.** (of a speech sound) lasting a relatively long time: *long vowels.* —*n.* [*noncount*] **4.** a long time: *They haven't been gone for long.* —*adv.* **5.** for a long time: *I didn't stay long.* **6.** at a distant time: *It happened long ago.* **7.** throughout: *all night long.* —*Idiom.* **8. as long as,** provided that; if: *You can watch television as long as you have finished your homework.* **9. before long,** soon.

long² /lɔŋ, lɒŋ/ *v.* [*no obj*] to want very much: *to long for spring; He longed to return home.*

'long-'distance, *adj.* going between distant places: *a long-distance phone call.* —**'long-'distance,** *adv.: to call long-distance.*

lon•gev•i•ty /lɒn'dʒɛvɪtiy, lɔn-/ *n.* [*noncount*] long life: *a family known for longevity.*

long•hand /'lɔŋ,hænd, 'lɒŋ-/ *n.* [*noncount*] writing that is done by hand.

long•ing /'lɔŋɪŋ, 'lɒŋ-/ *n.* **1.** [*count*] a strong desire: *She was filled with longing for the past.* —*adj.* **2.** showing a strong desire: *a longing look.* —**'long•ing•ly,** *adv.*

lon•gi•tude /'lɒndʒɪ,tuwd, -,tyuwd/ *n.* [*noncount*] [*count*] the distance east or west on the earth's surface, as measured in degrees from the meridian of some particular place to the prime meridian at Greenwich, England. —**,lon•gi'tu•di•nal,** *adj.*

'long ,jump, *n.* [*count; singular; usually: the* + ~] an athletic field event featuring competition in a jump from a running start.

'long-'range, *adj.* [*before a noun*] covering a long period of time or distance: *a long-range weather forecast; long-range rockets.*

'long ,shot, *n.* [*count*] **1.** a horse in a race, or a team, etc., that has little chance of winning. **2.** something unlikely to be successful.

long•stand•ing /'lɔŋ'stændɪŋ, 'lɒŋ-/ *adj.* that has existed for a long time: *a longstanding quarrel.*

'long-'suffering, *adj.* patiently bearing injury, trouble, or pain.

'long-,term, *adj.* of or for a long period of time: *long-term effects of a drug.*

'long-'winded /'wɪndɪd/ *adj.* talking or writing too long; tiresome.

look /lʊk/ *v.* **1.** [*no obj*] to use one's eyes in order to see: *I'm looking at this book. She looked out the window.* **2.** [~ + *adjective*] to appear; seem: *You look pale. See LOOK LIKE below.* **3.** [*no obj*] to face or give a view: *The room looks on the garden.* **4.** to pay attention to: [~ + *obj*]: *Now look what you've done!* [*no obj*]: *Look at what's happened.* **5. look after,** to take care of: *Who will look after the kids?* **6. look ahead,** to think about or plan for the future: *Our leaders have to look ahead.* **7. look back,** to review past events: *looking back to his childhood.* **8. look down on** or **upon,** to consider oneself better than: *She looked down on her neighbors.* **9. look for,** to try to find: *I've been looking for you.* **10. look forward to,** to wait for eagerly: *She's looking forward to working here.* **11. look into,** to investigate or examine: *The detective was looking into the kidnapping.* **12. look like, a.** to resemble: *He looks just like his father.* **b.** to seem to be: *looks like he's working.* **c.** to be probable that: *It looks like we'll be late.* **13. look out,** be careful: *Look out; here comes a car.* **14. look over,** to examine, esp. briefly: *I looked over your term paper. I looked it over.* **15. look to,** to depend on: *to look to the president for leadership.* **16. look up, a.** to become better; improve: *The business is looking up.* **b.** to search for in a reference book or the like: *looking words up in the dictionary* or *looking up words in the dictionary.* **c.** to find the home of, esp. to visit: *to look up an old friend; We looked her up.* **17. look up to,** to respect: *He looks up to his father.* —*n.* [*count*] **18.** the act of looking: *Have a look at this.* **19.** appearance: *He has the look of an honest man.* **20. looks,** [*plural*] **a.** outward appearance: *We didn't like the looks of the place.* **b.** physical appearance, esp. when attractive: *good looks.*

look•out /'lʊk,awt/ *n.* [*count*] **1.** a careful watch for someone or something. **2.** a person who keeps a careful watch. **3.** a place from which a

L

watch is kept. **4.** a matter of care or concern: *That problem's not my lookout.*

loom[1] /luwm/ *n.* [count] a hand-operated or motor-driven device for weaving cloth.

loom[2] /luwm/ *v.* [no obj] to appear as large and often threatening: *Suddenly the mountain loomed over them. His problems loomed large in his mind.*

loon /luwn/ *n.* [count] a large, ducklike diving bird with a loud, laughing call.

loon•y or **loon•ey** /'luwniy/ *adj.*, **-i•er, -i•est.** *Informal.* **1.** insane. **2.** foolish.

loop /luwp/ *n.* [count] **1.** a portion of a cord, ribbon, etc., folded or doubled upon itself so as to leave an opening between the parts. **2.** anything shaped like a loop. **—v. 3.** to make or form a loop: [no obj]: *The river loops around the two towns.* [~ + obj]: *The pilot looped her plane.*

loop•hole /'luwp,howl/ *n.* [count] a way of avoiding a legal requirement, esp. because of a fault in it: *loopholes in the tax code.*

loose /luws/ *adj.*, **loos•er, loos•est,** *adv., v.,* **loosed, loos•ing.** **—adj. 1.** not fastened or attached firmly: *a loose rope; a loose tooth.* **2.** free: *We set the dog loose.* **3.** not fitting tightly: *a loose sweater.* **4.** not fastened together: *loose keys.* **5.** not exact: *a loose translation.* **—adv. 6.** in a loose manner: *loose-fitting.* **—v.** [~ + obj] **7.** to set free. **8.** to (cause to) become less tight. **—Idiom. 9. break loose,** to escape: *The circus animals broke loose.* **10. on the loose,** free: *escaped prisoners still on the loose.* **—'loose•ly,** *adv.*

'loose 'end, *n.* [count] **1.** Usually, **loose ends.** [plural] an unfinished detail. **—Idiom. 2. at loose ends,** in an uncertain state: *She felt at loose ends with the family away.*

'loose-,leaf, *adj.* [before a noun] having sheets of paper or pages that can be easily put in or taken out: *a loose-leaf notebook.*

loos•en /'luwsən/ *v.* **1.** to (cause to) become less tight: [~ + obj]: *to loosen a belt.* [no obj]: *His hold loosened.* **2.** [~ + obj] to set free. **3. loosen up,** to relax: *They had a drink to loosen up.*

loot /luwt/ *n.* [noncount] **1.** goods taken in war or by thieves. **2.** *Slang.* money or gifts. **—v. 3.** to take loot (from): [~ + obj]: *The rioters looted several stores.* [no obj]: *Rioters were looting all night.* **—'loot•er,** *n.* [count]

lop•sid•ed /'lɒp'saydɪd/ *adj.* higher on one side than the other; unevenly balanced. **—'lop'sid•ed•ly,** *adv.* **—'lop'sid•ed•ness,** *n.* [noncount]

lo•qua•cious /low'kweyʃəs/ *adj.* talking a lot. **—lo•quac•i•ty** /low'kwæsɪtiy/, *n.* [noncount]

lord /lɔrd/ *n.* **1.** [count] a master or ruler. **2.** [count] a nobleman. **3.** God. **—interj. 4.** [often: Lord] This word is used to express surprise, worry, etc.: *Good Lord!*

lore /lɔr/ *n.* [noncount] the body of knowledge, esp. of a traditional or popular nature, on a particular subject: *nature lore.*

lor•ry /'lɔriy, 'lɒriy/ *n.* [count], *pl.* **-ries.** *Chiefly Brit.* a large motor truck.

lose /luwz/ *v.*, **lost** /lɔst, lɒst/, **los•ing. —v. 1.** [~ + obj] to come to be without; be unable to find: *I lost my hat. We lost our way.* **2.** [~ + obj] to fail to keep: *She lost her balance. He lost interest in life.* **3.** [~ + obj] to suffer the taking away of: *to lose one's job.* **4.** [~ + obj] (of a timepiece) to run slower by: *The watch loses three minutes a day.* **5.** [~ + obj] to get rid of: *to lose weight.* **6.** [~ + obj] to (cause to) fail to understand: *I'm afraid you've lost me.* **7.** to fail to win: [~ + obj]: *Our team lost the game.* [no obj]: *Our team lost again.* **8.** [~ + obj] to waste: *She lost no time in leaving.* **9. lose out,** to suffer defeat or loss: *Our company lost out on the deal.* **—Idiom. 10. lose it,** to become upset.

los•er /'luwzər/ *n.* [count] **1.** a person who has been defeated: *a poor loser.* **2.** a person who is a failure. **—Idiom. 3. born loser,** a person who is always unsuccessful.

loss /lɔs, lɒs/ *n.* **1.** [noncount] the act or fact of losing something: *the loss of property.* **2.** [count] someone or something that is lost: *They suffered great losses in the fire.* **3.** [count] money lost in business. **—Idiom. 4. at a loss,** uncertain or confused.

lost /lɔst, lɒst/ *adj.* **1.** [before a noun] no longer possessed: *lost friendships.* **2.** no longer to be found: *lost keys.* **3.** unable to find one's way: *a lost driver.* **4.** destroyed: *ships lost at sea.* **5.** [be + ~] preoccupied: *He was lost in thought.* **—v. 6.** pt. and pp. of LOSE. **—Idiom. 7. get lost,** *Slang.* to stop annoying someone.

lot /lɒt/ *n.* **1.** [count] one of a set of objects, as straws or pebbles, used to decide a question or choice by chance. **2.** [count; *usually singular*] fate: *Her lot was not a happy one.* **3.** [count] a piece of land: *a building lot.* **4.** [count] a set or group of people or things: *a poor lot of fruit.* **5.** [count] an item to be sold at an auction. **6.** [count] a large number or amount: *She had a lot of books. She had lots of money.* **—Idiom. 7. a lot,** to a great degree; much: *I feel a lot better.* **8. draw** or **cast lots,** to settle a question by the use of lots: *They drew lots to decide.*

lo•tion /'lowʃən/ *n.* [noncount] [count] a liquid preparation used for medicines and for protecting and soothing the skin.

lot•ter•y /'lɒtəriy/ *n.* [count], *pl.* **-ter•ies.** a gambling game or method of raising money in which a large number of tickets are sold and a drawing is held for prizes.

lo•tus /'lowtəs/ *n.* [count], *pl.* **-tus•es.** a plant with large pink, yellow, or white flowers growing on the water.

loud /lawd/ *adj.*, **-er, -est,** *adv.* **—adj. 1.** marked by strong sound: *a loud noise.* **2.** too bright or showy: *loud colors; a loud tie.* **—adv. 3.** in a loud manner: *Don't talk so loud.* **—'loud•ly,** *adv.* **—'loud•ness,** *n.* [noncount]

loud•speak•er /'lawd,spiykər/ *n.* [count] a device that changes electrical signals into sound.

lounge /lawndʒ/ *v.*, **lounged, loung•ing,** *n.* **—v.** [no obj] **1.** to pass time lazily: *I'm just lounging around.* **—n.** [count] **2.** a room for relaxing or waiting, as at an airport or hotel.

louse /laws/ *n.* [count], *pl.* **lice** /lays/ for 1 **lous•es** for 2. **1.** a small insect that lives on humans and animals. **2.** *Slang.* a mean, worthless person.

lous•y /'lawziy/ *adj.*, **-i•er, -i•est. 1.** covered with lice. **2.** *Informal.* very bad: *That was a lousy thing to do; lousy weather.*

lout /lawt/ *n.* [count] a rough, bad-mannered boy or man. **—'lout•ish,** *adj.*

love /lʌv/ *n.*, **loved, lov•ing. —n. 1.** [noncount] deep affection and sexual attraction for another person. **2.** [noncount] a strong fondness or affection: *a mother's love for her child; love of one's country.* **3.** [count] a person toward whom love is felt: *He is the love of my life.* **4.** [count] a strong liking: *a love of books.* **5.** [count] the object of such liking: *The theater was her first love.* **—v. 6.** [~ + obj] to have love for: *He loves her* *dearly.* **7.** to like very much: *He loves to read.* **—Idiom. 8. in love (with),** feeling love (for): *I'm glad you're in love. She's in love with me.* **9. make love,** to have sexual relations. —**'lov•a•ble,** *adj.* —**'love•less,** *adj.*

love affair, *n.* [count] a romantic, sexual relationship between two people.

love•ly /'lʌvliy/ *adj.,* **-li•er, •-li•est. 1.** beautiful: *a lovely woman.* **2.** very pleasing: *We had a lovely time.* —**'love•li•ness,** *n.* [noncount]

lov•er /'lʌvər/ *n.* [count] **1.** a person who has a romantic, sexual relationship with another. **2.** a person who is fond of something: *a music lover.*

lov•ing /'lʌvɪŋ/ *adj.* feeling or showing love. —**'lov•ing•ly,** *adv.*

low /low/ *adj. and adv.,* **-er, -est,** *n.* —*adj.* **1.** not high or tall: *a low wall; a low fence.* **2.** below the usual level: *low ground; low prices.* **3.** below average in quality: *a low grade of meat.* **4.** vulgar or immoral: *low company.* **5.** of or having only a small number, amount, degree, etc.: *low on gas; a low-fat diet.* **6.** not loud: *a low voice.* **7.** (of a musical note) deep in pitch. **8.** not favorable: *I had a low opinion of the book.* **9.** not well or happy: *feeling low.* **10.** or or for the slowest speed: *Put the car in low gear.* —*adv.* **11.** at or to a low place or level: *The plane flew low. We're running low on fuel.* —*n.* **12.** [count] a low point, place, or level: *recent lows in temperature.* **13.** [noncount] the gear giving the slowest speed: *Put the car in low.* —**Idiom. 14. lie low,** to hide oneself.

low•er /'lowər/ *v.* **1.** to (cause to) move to a lower position: [~ + *obj*]: *to lower a flag.* [no *obj*]: *The sun lowered in the west.* **2.** to (cause to) become less in amount or degree: [~ + *obj*]: *They lowered the price.* [no *obj*]: *Her voice suddenly lowered.* —*adj.* **3.** at or being the bottom part of something: *the lower leg.* —**Idiom. 4. lower oneself,** to make oneself less deserving of respect: *She wouldn't lower herself to cheat.* —**'low•er,most,** *adj.*

low•er•case /'lowər'keys/ *adj.* **1.** (of an alphabetical letter) printed in its small form, as a, b, q, r. —*n.* [noncount] **2.** a lowercase letter.

'lower 'class /'lowər/ *n.* [count] a class of people below the middle class in social standing and usually having low income and lacking education. —**'low'er-class,** *adj.*

'low-'key or **'low-'keyed,** *adj.* calm and controlled: *a low-key meeting.*

low•land /'lowlənd/ *n.* [noncount] **1.** land that is lower than the surrounding land. —*adj.* [before *a noun*] **2.** of, in, or from a lowland.

low•ly /'lowliy/ *adj.,* **-li•er, -li•est,** *adv.* —*adj.* **1.** humble. —*adv.* **2.** in a low position, manner, or degree. —**'low•li•ness,** *n.* [noncount]

'low 'profile, *n.* [count] a way of behaving that makes one less noticeable: *to keep a low profile.*

'low 'tide, *n.* [noncount] the tide when the level of the sea is at its lowest.

lox /lɒks/ *n.* [noncount] smoked salmon.

loy•al /'lɔyəl/ *adj.* faithful: *a loyal friend; loyal to one's country.* —**'loy•al•ly,** *adv.* —**'loy•al•ty,** *n.* [noncount] [count]

loz•enge /'lɒzɪndʒ/ *n.* [count] a small, sweet tablet often containing medication: *throat lozenges.*

LSD, *n.* [noncount] a strong drug that produces temporary hallucinations.

Lt., an abbreviation of: lieutenant.

lu•bri•cant /'luwbrɪkənt/ *n.* [count] [noncount]

a substance, as oil or grease, that helps mechanical parts to move easily.

lu•bri•cate /'luwbrɪ,keyt/ *v.* [~ + *obj*], **-cat•ed, -cat•ing.** to put oil or grease on or in (a mechanical part) to help it work smoothly. —**lu•bri•ca•tion** /,luwbrɪ'keyʃən/, *n.* [noncount]

lu•cid /'luwsɪd/ *adj.* **1.** easily understood: *a lucid explanation.* **2.** not confused in one's thoughts or speech. —**lu•cid•i•ty** /luw'sɪdɪtiy/, **'lu•cid•ness,** *n.* [noncount] —**'lu•cid•ly,** *adv.*

Lu•cite /'luwsayt/ *Trademark.* [noncount] a strong transparent plastic.

luck /lʌk/ *n.* [noncount] **1.** the force that seems to operate for good or ill in a person's life: *good/ bad luck.* **2.** good fortune: *Wish me luck!* **3. luck out,** to have an occasion of very good luck. —**Idiom. 4. in/out of luck,** fortunate/ unfortunate.

luck•y /'lʌkiy/ *adj.,* **-i•er, -i•est.** having, bringing, or caused by good luck. —**luck•i•ly** /'lʌkəliy/, *adv.*: *Luckily, she wasn't hurt.*

lu•cra•tive /'luwkrətɪv/ *adj.* profitable.

lu•di•crous /'luwdɪkrəs/ *adj.* causing laughter because of being ridiculous: *a ludicrous hat; a ludicrous idea.* —**'lu•di•crous•ly,** *adv.*

lug¹ /lʌg/ *v.* [~ + *obj*], **lugged, lug•ging.** to pull or carry with great effort: *lugging heavy rocks.*

lug² /lʌg/ *n.* [count] a projecting piece by which anything is held or supported.

lug•gage /'lʌgɪdʒ/ *n.* [noncount] the suitcases, bags, etc., of a traveler; baggage.

luke•warm /'luwk'wɔrm/ *adj.* **1.** slightly warm: *lukewarm water.* **2.** not enthusiastic: *a lukewarm greeting.*

lull /lʌl/ *v.* **1.** to (cause to) become calm: [~ + *obj*]: *He lulled the baby to sleep.* [no *obj*]: *The storm finally lulled.* —*n.* [count; usually singular] **2.** a temporary calm: *a lull in a storm.*

lull•a•by /'lʌlə,bay/ *n.* [count], *pl.* **-bies.** a song used to lull a child to sleep.

lum•ba•go /lʌm'beygow/ *n.* [noncount] pain in the lower, side region of the back.

lum•ber¹ /'lʌmbər/ *n.* [noncount] boards made from logs.

lum•ber² /'lʌmbər/ *v.* [no *obj*] to move in a heavy, awkward way.

lum•ber•jack /'lʌmbər,dʒæk/ *n.* [count] a person whose job is to cut down trees.

lu•mi•nous /'luwmənəs/ *adj.* shining; bright: *luminous eyes.*

lump /lʌmp/ *n.* [count] **1.** a hard piece or mass, esp. without regular shape: *a lump of coal.* **2.** a swelling: *A blow to his head raised a lump.* **3.** a small block of sugar, for sweetening hot coffee, tea, etc. —*adj.* [before *a noun*] **4.** not divided or separated: *to pay a debt in a lump sum.* —*v.* [no *obj*] **5.** to form lumps. **6. lump together,** to put together: *We lumped all our debts together.* —**'lump•y,** *adj.,* **-i•er, -i•est.**

lu•na•cy /'luwnəsiy/ *n.,* *pl.* **-cies. 1.** [noncount] madness. **2.** [noncount] [count] extreme foolishness.

lu•nar /'luwnər/ *adj.* [before *a noun*] of the moon: *lunar orbit; a lunar month.*

lu•na•tic /'luwnətɪk/ *n.* [count] **1.** an insane person. —*adj.* **2.** insane; crazy. **3.** wildly foolish.

lunch /lʌntʃ/ *n.* [count] [noncount] **1.** a meal eaten between breakfast and dinner. —*v.* [no *obj*] **2.** to eat lunch.

lunch•eon /'lʌntʃən/ *n.* [count] lunch, esp. one that is formal.

L

lunch•eon•ette /ˌlʌntʃəˈnɛt/ n. [count] a place where light meals are served.

lunchtime n. [noncount] the time at which lunch is eaten.

lung /lʌŋ/ n. [count] either of the two organs used for breathing in the chest of humans and air-breathing animals.

lunge /lʌndʒ/ n., v., **lunged, lung•ing. —n.** [count] **1.** a sudden movement forward. —v. [no obj] **2.** to make a lunge: He lunged for the ball but missed it.

lurch /lɜrtʃ/ n. [count] **1.** a sudden movement esp. to one side, as of a ship or of a person losing his or her balance. —v. [no obj] **2.** to move with a lurch.

lure /lʊr/ n., v., **lured, lur•ing. —n.** [count] **1.** a strong attraction: the lure of the big city. —v. [~ + obj] **2.** to attract or tempt: He was lured by the promise of wealth.

lu•rid /ˈlʊrɪd/ adj. **1.** shocking: the lurid details of the accident. **2.** shining with an unnatural, fiery glow: a lurid sunset. —**ˈlu•rid•ly,** adv. —**ˈlu•rid•ness,** n. [noncount]

lurk /lɜrk/ v. [no obj] **1.** to wait in hiding, esp. in order to attack. **2.** to exist without being seen, suspected, or detected.

lus•cious /ˈlʌʃəs/ adj. having a very pleasant taste, smell, or appearance: sweet, luscious peaches.

lush /lʌʃ/ adj., -er, -est. **1.** (of plants, grass, and trees) growing thickly and well. **2.** rich and comfortable: a lush life. —**ˈlush•ness,** n. [noncount]

lust /lʌst/ n. **1.** [noncount] strong sexual desire. **2.** [noncount] a strong desire for something: lust for power. **3.** [count] strong enthusiasm: a lust for life. —v. [~ + for/after + obj] **4.** to have a strong desire for someone or something. —**ˈlust• ful,** adj. —**ˈlust•ful•ly,** adv.

lus•ter /ˈlʌstər/ n. [noncount] **1.** soft, glowing brightness: the luster in her eyes. **2.** glory. Also, esp. Brit., **ˈlus•tre.** —**ˈlus•ter•less,** adj. —**ˈlus• trous,** adj.: lustrous hair.

lust•y /ˈlʌstiy/ adj., -i•er, -i•est. strong and energetic. —**lust•i•ly** /ˈlʌstɪliy/, adv.: singing lustily. —**ˈlust•i•ness,** n. [noncount]

lute /luwt/ n. [count] a musical instrument with strings, a long neck, and a hollow, pear-shaped body.

lux•u•ri•ant /lʌgˈʒʊriyənt, lʌkˈʃʊr-/ adj. **1.** growing thickly; lush. **2.** rich or great in amount; abundant. —**luxˈu•ri•ance,** n. [noncount] —**luxˈu•ri•ant•ly,** adv.

lux•u•ri•ate /lʌgˈʒʊriyˌeyt, lʌkˈʃʊr-/ v. [no obj], -at•ed, -at•ing. to enjoy oneself fully: to luxuriate in a bath.

lux•u•ry /ˈlʌkʃəriy, ˈlʌgʒə-/ n., pl. -ries. **1.** [count] something costly and pleasurable but not necessary. **2.** [noncount] comfort and pleasure provided by wealth: a life of luxury. —**lux•ur•i• ous** /lʌgˈʒʊriyəs, lʌkˈʃʊr-/ adj.

-ly, a suffix meaning: in a specified manner (loudly); in or according to (theoretically); to or from a specified direction (inwardly); like or characteristic of (saintly); every (hourly).

lye /lay/ n. [noncount] a strong substance used for washing and for making soap.

ly•ing[1] /ˈlayɪŋ/ n. [noncount] the telling of lies.

ly•ing[2] /ˈlayɪŋ/ v. pres. part. of LIE[2].

lymph /lɪmf/ n. [noncount] a clear, yellowish liquid in the blood that contains special blood cells that fight infection. —**lymˈphat•ic,** adj.

lynch /lɪntʃ/ v. [~ + obj] to put to death, esp. by hanging, without legal authority.

lynx /lɪŋks/ n. [count], pl. **lynx•es,** (esp. when thought of as a group) **lynx.** a wild animal of the cat family.

lyr•ic /ˈlɪrɪk/ adj. **1.** (of a poem) expressing strong, personal feelings. —n. [count] **2.** a lyric poem. **3.** Usually, **lyrics.** [plural] the words of a song.

lyr•i•cal, adj. **1.** lyric. **2.** enthusiastic. —**ˈlyr•i• cal•ly,** adv.

M

M, m /ɛm/ n. [count], pl. **Ms** or **M's, ms** or **m's.** the 13th letter of the English alphabet, a consonant.

M, Symbol. the Roman numeral for 1000.

m, an abbreviation of: 1. mass. 2. meter.

ma /mɑ/ n. [count], pl. **mas.** mother.

MA, an abbreviation of: Massachusetts.

M.A., an abbreviation of: Master of Arts.

ma'am /mæm, mɑm; unstressed məm/ n. [often: Ma'am] MADAM (def. 1).

ma•ca•bre /məˈkɑbrə, -ˈkɑb/ adj. strange or frightening; horrible.

mac•a•ro•ni /ˌmækəˈrowniy/ n. [noncount], pl. **-nis, -nies.** a kind of tube-shaped pasta made of wheat flour.

mac•a•roon /ˌmækəˈruwn/ n. [count] a cookie made of beaten egg whites, sugar, and almond paste.

Mace /meys/ Trademark. [noncount] a chemical spray that causes severe eye irritation, used against rioters or an attacker.

mach•i•na•tion /ˌmækəˈneyʃən/ n. [count] Usually, **machinations.** [plural] a clever course of action to gain power: his machinations to win the election.

ma•chine /məˈʃiyn/ n. [count] 1. an apparatus made of connected parts having separate functions, used to accomplish work: a sewing machine. 2. a group of persons that controls a political party: the Democratic machine.

ma'chine ˌgun, n. [count] a firearm capable of shooting a continuous stream of bullets.

ma•chin•er•y /məˈʃiynəriy/ n. [noncount] 1. a collection of machines: the machinery in the factory. 2. the parts of a machine thought of as a group. 3. a system that achieves results: the criminal justice machinery.

ma•chin•ist /məˈʃiynɪst/ n. [count] one who operates, makes, or repairs machines.

ma•cho /ˈmɑtʃow/ adj. having or showing an exaggerated sense of manliness: The teenage gang member needed to display a macho attitude.

mack•er•el /ˈmækərəl, ˈmækrəl/ n. [count], pl. (esp. when thought of as a group) **-el,** (esp. for kinds or species) **-els.** a food fish of the N Atlantic.

mack•in•tosh or **mac•in•tosh** /ˈmækɪnˌtɒʃ/ n. Chiefly Brit. RAINCOAT.

macro-, a combining form meaning large (macrocosm).

mac•ro•bi•ot•ic /ˌmækrowbayˈɒtɪk/ adj. of or relating to a dietary philosophy that emphasizes achieving good health by eating a carefully balanced diet of whole grains and vegetables.

mac•ro•cosm /ˈmækrəˌkɒzəm/ n. [count] the universe, or any system, considered as a whole or a single unit.

mad /mæd/ adj., **mad•der, mad•dest.** 1. mentally disturbed or mentally ill. 2. [be + ~] angry; enraged: He's really mad at his daughter. 3. affected with rabies: a mad dog. 4. [be + ~] full of enthusiasm: He's mad about opera. —*Idiom.* 5. drive someone mad, to cause someone to be furious or greatly irritated: Slow service always drives her mad. 6. like mad, at a very fast pace: rushing around like mad. —ˈmad•ly, adv.: madly in love with her. —ˈmad•ness, n. [noncount]

mad•am /ˈmædəm/ n. [count], pl. **mes•dames** /meyˈdæm, -ˈdɑm/ for 1, **mad•ams** for 2. 1. [often: Madam] a respectful term of address to a woman: Please step this way, Madam. 2. a woman in charge of a brothel.

mad•den /ˈmædn̩/ v. [~ + obj] to make very angry. —ˈmad•den•ing, adj.

made /meyd/ v. 1. pt. and pp. of MAKE. —adj. 2. This word is often used in combination with another word to mean "produced, made (in a particular place or way)": machine-made clothes. —*Idiom.* 3. have it made, Informal. to be assured of success: Now that he's president, he has it made.

ˈmade-to-ˈorder, adj. made to fit an individual's particular measurements or the like: made-to-order shoes.

ˈmade-ˈup, adj. 1. fabricated; invented: a made-up story. 2. [usually: be + ~] wearing facial makeup: She was heavily made-up.

mad•house /ˈmædˌhaws/ n. [count], pl. **-houses** /-ˌhawzɪz/. 1. a hospital for the mentally disturbed. 2. a disorderly, noisy place: The train station was a madhouse.

mad•man or **-wom•an** /ˈmædˌmæn, -mən/ or /-ˈwˌʊmən/ n. [count], pl. **-men** or **-wom•en.** one who is or appears to be insane.

Ma•don•na /məˈdɒnə/ n. 1. Mary, the mother of Jesus; the Virgin Mary. 2. [count] an image of the Virgin Mary.

maes•tro /ˈmaystrow/ n. [count], pl. **-tros.** a famous composer or conductor of music.

Ma•fi•a /ˈmɑfiyə, ˈmæfiyə/ n. 1. [count; usually: the + ~] a secret organization engaged in criminal activities, esp. in certain U.S. cities. 2. [mafia; count] any powerful, controlling group: the Hollywood mafia.

mag•a•zine /ˌmægəˈziyn, ˈmægəˌziyn/ n. [count] 1. a publication published regularly, containing articles and often illustrations: a news magazine. 2. a receptacle in a gun for holding cartridges.

ma•gen•ta /məˈdʒɛntə/ n. [noncount] a purplish red color.

mag•got /ˈmægət/ n. [count] a soft-bodied, wormlike creature that grows into certain flies.

mag•ic /ˈmædʒɪk/ n. [noncount] 1. the art of producing illusions or tricks that fool or deceive an audience. —adj. [before a noun] 2. done by or used in magic: a magic trick. 3. mysteriously enchanting or effective. —ˈmag•i•cal, adj. —ˈmag•i•cal•ly, adv.

ma•gi•cian /məˈdʒɪʃən/ n. [count] an entertainer who performs illusions that fool an audience.

mag•is•trate /ˈmædʒəˌstreyt, -strɪt/ n. [count] 1. a civil officer who administers the law. 2. a judicial officer, as a justice of the peace.

mag•nan•i•mous /mægˈnænəməs/ adj. generous and gracious in forgiving an insult or injury. —magˈnan•i•mous•ly, adv. —mag•na•nim•i•ty, n. [noncount]

mag•nate /ˈmægneyt, -nɪt/ n. [count] a person of great influence or importance in a particular industry: an oil magnate.

mag•ne•sia /mægˈniyʒə, -ʃə/ n. [noncount] a

white, tasteless substance used to reduce stomach acids and as a laxative.

mag•ne•si•um /mæg'niyziyəm, -ʒəm, -ʃiyəm/ *n.* [*noncount*] a light, silver-white element that burns with a dazzling light, used in fireworks and flashbulbs.

mag•net /'mægnɪt/ *n.* [*count*] **1.** a body, as a piece of iron or steel, that has the property of attracting certain substances, as iron. **2.** a person or thing that attracts: *He's a magnet to women.* —**mag•net•ic** /mæg'nɛtɪk/ *adj.*

mag'netic 'field, *n.* [*count*] a region of space in which a magnetic force acts.

mag•net•ism /'mægnɪ,tɪzəm/ *n.* [*noncount*] **1.** the properties of attraction that magnets possess. **2.** strong attractive power or charm.

mag•net•ize /'mægnɪ,tayz/ *v.* [~ + *obj*], **-ized, -iz•ing.** to make a magnet of: *Rubbing the nail with a magnet will magnetize it.*

mag•nif•i•cent /mæg'nɪfəsənt/ *adj.* **1.** splendid or impressive in appearance: *a magnificent palace.* **2.** very fine; superb: *magnificent weather.* —**mag'nif•i•cence,** *n.* [*noncount*] —**mag'nif•i•cent•ly,** *adv.*

mag•ni•fy /'mægnə,fay/ *v.* [~ + *obj*], **-fied, -fy•ing. 1.** to increase the apparent size of: *Binoculars magnify images.* **2.** to exaggerate; overstate: *to magnify one's difficulties.* —**mag•ni•fi•ca•tion** /,mægnəfɪ'keyʃən/ *n.* [*noncount*] [*count*]

'magnifying ,glass, *n.* [*count*] a lens that makes an object appear larger.

mag•ni•tude /'mægnɪ,tuwd/ *n.* [*noncount*] **1.** greatness of size or amount. **2.** great importance or consequence: *an event of great magnitude.* —*Idiom.* **3. of the first magnitude,** of greatest significance.

mag•no•lia /mæg'nowlyə, -'nowliyə/ *n.* [*count*], *pl.* **-lias.** a shrub or tree having large, usually fragrant flowers, grown for ornament.

mag•pie /'mæg,pay/ *n.* [*count*] a bird of the jay family, having long, black-and-white feathers and noisy habits.

ma•hog•a•ny /mə'hɒgəniy/ *n.* [*noncount*], *pl.* **-nies.** the hard, reddish brown wood of a tropical American tree.

maid /meyd/ *n.* [*count*] **1.** a female servant. **2.** a girl or young unmarried woman.

maid•en /'meydn̩/ *n.* [*count*] **1.** a girl or young unmarried woman; maid. —*adj.* [*before a noun*] **2.** unmarried: *a maiden aunt.* **3.** first: *a maiden flight.* —**'maid•en,hood,** *n.* [*noncount*]

'maiden 'name, *n.* [*count*] a woman's family name before marriage.

'maid of 'honor, *n.* [*count*] an unmarried woman who is the chief attendant of a bride.

mail /meyl/ *n.* [*noncount*] **1.** letters, etc., sent or delivered by the postal service. —*v.* [~ + *obj*] **2.** to send by mail: *Mail the package tomorrow. Mail me the proposal.*

mail•box /'meyl,bɒks/ *n.* [*count*] **1.** a public box in which mail is placed for pickup. **2.** a private box into which mail is delivered. **3.** a file in a computer for the storage of electronic mail.

'mail 'carrier, *n.* [*count*] one employed to deliver the mail.

mail•man /'meyl,mæn/ *n., pl.* **-men.** MAIL CARRIER.

maim /meym/ *v.* [~ + *obj*] to injure (someone) so that part of the body can no longer be used: *The explosion maimed her for life. He was maimed in the fire.*

main /meyn/ *adj.* [*before a noun*] **1.** chief in size, extent, or importance: *He had the main part in the play.* —*n.* [*count*] **2.** a principal pipe in a system used to carry and send water, gas, etc. —*Idiom.* **3. in the main,** for the most part. —**'main•ly,** *adv.*: *He got rich mainly from government contracts.*

main•frame /'meyn,freym/ *n.* [*count*] a large computer, often the center of a system serving many users.

main•land /'meyn,lænd, -lənd/ *n.* [*count; usually singular; usually: the + ~*] the principal land of a region, etc., as distinguished from nearby islands: *We took a ferry back to the mainland.*

main•line /'meyn,layn, -'layn/ *v.*, **-lined, -lin•ing,** *adj.* —*v.* [~ + *obj*] [*no obj*] **1.** *Slang.* to inject a narcotic directly into a vein. —*adj.* **2.** having a principal or established position: *mainline churches.*

main•spring /'meyn,sprɪŋ/ *n.* [*count*] the principal spring in a mechanism, as in a watch.

main•stay /'meyn,stey/ *n.* [*count*] a person or thing that acts as a chief support or part: *She's the mainstay of the company.*

main•stream /'meyn,striym/ *n.* [*count*] **1.** the principal or most usual course of action, way of thinking, or cultural trend: *the mainstream of American culture.* —*adj.* [*before a noun*] **2.** of or relating to a principal or widely accepted group, style, etc.: *The candidate appealed to mainstream America.*

main•tain /meyn'teyn/ *v.* [~ + *obj*] **1.** to keep in existence; preserve: *They maintained their friendship for over forty years.* **2.** to keep in a certain condition or state; provide for the upkeep or support of: *to maintain an even temperature; Is that salary enough to maintain a family?* **3.** to state or declare: *He maintained that he had been home all night.* —**'main•te•nance** /'meyntənəns/, *n.* [*noncount*]

ma•jes•tic /mə'dʒɛstɪk/ *adj.* impressive; grand: *majestic mountains.* —**ma'jes•ti•cal•ly,** *adv.*

maj•es•ty /'mædʒəstiy/ *n., pl.* **-ties. 1.** [*noncount*] high and noble dignity; grandeur: *the majesty of the Blue Ridge Mountains.* **2.** [*count; usually Majesty; often: Your/His/Her + ~*] a title of a king, queen, or sovereign: *Her Majesty, the Queen.*

ma•jor /'meydʒər/ *n.* [*count*] **1.** a military officer ranking below a lieutenant colonel and above a captain. **2. a.** a field of study in which a student specializes: *a major in botany.* **b.** a student specializing in such a field: *a history major.* —*adj.* [*before a noun*] **3.** great in size, extent, or importance: *a major part in the play; a major operation.* —*v.* [*no obj*] **4.** to follow an academic major: *I majored in physics.*

ma•jor•i•ty /mə'dʒɔrɪtiy, -'dʒɑr-/ *n., pl.* **-ties. 1.** [*count*] a number, part, or amount forming more than half of the whole or total: *He got a majority of the votes in the election.* **2.** [*noncount*] the amount by which the greater number, as of votes, exceeds the remainder. **3.** [*noncount*] the state or time of being of full legal age: *to attain one's majority.*

make /meyk/ *v.*, **made** /meyd/, **mak•ing,** *n.* —*v.* [~ + *obj*] **1.** to bring into existence by combining material; produce: *to make a dress; I'll make the kids some breakfast.* **2.** to cause to exist or happen; engage in; produce: *to make war; Why is he always making trouble?* **3.** to cause to be or become; transform: *This news will make her*

happy. *The evidence makes you the chief suspect.*
4. to force or cause (someone to do something):
The pain made her cry out. **5.** to put in the
proper condition or state; prepare: *to make a bed.*
6. to establish; enact: *to make laws; Her last book
really made her reputation as a scholar.* **7.** to
form in the mind: *to make a decision.* **8.** to
amount to; total: *Two plus two makes four.* **9.** to
serve as; have the (often desirable) qualities of:
*That book makes good reading. That would make
a good title.* **10.** to arrive in time for; catch: *I just
made the plane.* **11.** to attain a position in or on:
The novel made the bestseller list. **12.** to earn or
acquire: *trying to make friends; making a good
living.* **13. make of,** to explain; interpret: *What
do you make of his remark?* **14. make off with,**
to carry away; steal: *The robbers made off with a
million dollars in cash.* **15. make out, a.** to write
out or complete: *I made out the check* or *I made
the check out.* **b.** to see clearly enough so as to
be able to read: *I can't make out his handwriting*
or *I can't make his handwriting out.* **c.** to manage; succeed: *How are you making out in school?*
d. *Slang.* to engage in kissing and caressing:
making out in the back seat. **16. make over, to**
remodel; change or alter: *The carpenters made
over the room* or *The carpenters made the room
over.* **17. make up, a.** to form; be the components of: *Immigrants make up a large part of our
school's population. Two guitarists and a drummer made up the band.* **b.** to prepare by putting
together; compile: *Make up a list of what you'll
need* or *Make a list up of what you'll need.* **c.** to
invent; imagine: *She made up the whole story* or
She made the whole story up. **d.** to lead or propel
to a decision or conclusion: *Make up your mind*
or *Make your mind up.* **e.** to become friends
again after a quarrel or disagreement: *We finally
made up after years of fighting.* **f.** to provide
enough so that (something) is no longer lacking:
*The college will make up the difference between
your loan and your tuition.* **18. make up for,** to
repay; compensate for: *Perhaps $50 will make up
for your trouble.* —*n.* [*count*] **19.** brand: *a foreign
make of car.* —**Idiom. 20. make believe,** to
imagine; pretend: *Kids like to make believe. She
made believe (that) he had won the lottery.* **21.
make do,** to manage with whatever is available:
*If these are the only tools we have, we'll just have
to make do.* **22. make ends meet,** to pay all of
one's living expenses out of one's income: *How
do part-time workers make ends meet?* **23. make
good, a.** to succeed: *These graduates will make
good.* **b. make good on,** to fulfill, as a promise.
24. make it, a. to achieve success: *He really
seems to have made it: big house, good job.* **b.** to
arrive on time: *I just made it to that meeting!* **25.
make light of,** to treat as unimportant. **26.
make love,** to have sexual relations (with). **27.
make much of,** to treat as important: *The press
tried to make much of his past.* —'**mak•er,** *n.*
[*count*]

'**make-be,lieve,** *n.* [*noncount*] **1.** a state of innocent pretending: *a world of make-believe.*
—*adj.* [*before a noun*] **2.** pretended; imaginary.

make•shift /'meyk,ʃɪft/ *adj.* used temporarily
because nothing better is available: *a makeshift
classroom.*

make•up or **make-up** /'meyk,ʌp/ *n.* [*noncount*] cosmetics, esp. for the face or some part
of it: *wearing a lot of eye makeup.*

mak•ing /'meykɪŋ/ *n.* [*noncount*] the act of a
person or thing that makes, produces, etc.: *the
making of dresses.* **2.** Usually, **makings.** [*plural*]

the qualities necessary to develop into or become
something: *has the makings of a first-rate officer.*
—**Idiom. 3. in the making,** in the process or
having the potential of developing; unfinished;
incomplete: *a writer in the making.*

mal-, a combining form meaning bad, wrongful,
or ill (*malfunction*).

mal•ad•just•ed /,mælə'dʒʌstɪd/ *adj.* badly or
poorly adjusted, esp. to one's social
circumstances, etc. —,**mal•ad'just•ment,** *n.*
[*noncount*]

mal•a•dy /'mælədiy/ *n.* [*count*], *pl.* **-dies.** a disorder or disease of the body.

ma•laise /mæ'leyz, -'lɛz, mə-/ *n.* [*noncount*] a
condition of general bodily weakness or unease.

ma•lar•i•a /mə'lɛəriyə/ *n.* [*noncount*] a disease
characterized by chills, fever, and sweating,
caused by microorganisms that enter the bloodstream from the bite of a certain mosquito.
—ma'lar•i•al, *adj.*

male /meyl/ *n.* [*count*] **1.** an individual or organism of the sex or sexual phase that normally produces sperm cells that fertilize female eggs.
—*adj.* [*usually: before a noun*] **2.** relating to or
consisting of boys or men: *the male ego; a male
choir.* —'**male•ness,** *n.* [*noncount*]

ma•lev•o•lent /mə'lɛvələnt/ *adj.* wishing evil
or harm to others. —**ma'lev•o•lence,** *n.* [*noncount*] —**ma'lev•o•lent•ly,** *adv.*

mal•func•tion /mæl'fʌŋkʃən/ *n.* [*count*] **1.** failure to function properly: *They canceled the mission because of a malfunction in the torpedo.* —*v.*
[*no obj*] **2.** to fail to function properly.

mal•ice /'mælɪs/ *n.* [*noncount*] a desire to inflict
harm or suffering on another: *His malice toward
his opponent did not stop after the election.* —**ma•
li•cious** /mə'lɪʃəs/, *adj.*: *his malicious lies.*
—**ma'li•cious•ly,** *adv.*

ma•lign /mə'layn/ *v.* [~ + *obj*] to speak harmful lies about; to slander; defame: *She maligned
her friend whenever she could.*

ma•lig•nant /mə'lɪgnənt/ *adj.* **1.** inclined to
cause harm, suffering, or distress: *malignant remarks.* **2.** very dangerous or harmful; tending to
produce death: *a malignant tumor.* —**ma'lig•
nan•cy,** *n.* [*count*], *pl.* **-cies** [*noncount*]

ma•lin•ger /mə'lɪŋgər/ *v.* [*no obj*] to pretend illness, esp. in order to avoid duty or work.
—**ma'lin•ger•er,** *n.* [*count*]

mall /mɔl/ *n.* [*count*] **1.** a large area with many
shops and restaurants in nearby buildings or in a
single large building. **2.** a city street lined with
shops and closed off to motor vehicles.

mal•lard /'mælərd/ *n.* [*count*], *pl.* **-lards,** (*esp.
when thought of as a group*) **-lard.** a common
wild duck from which the domestic ducks are descended.

mal•le•a•ble /'mæliyəbəl/ *adj.* **1.** capable of being shaped by hammering or by pressure from
rollers. **2.** adaptable; able to change or adjust:
Young children have malleable personalities.
—**mal•le•a•bil•i•ty** /,mæliyə'bɪlitiy/, *n.* [*noncount*]

mal•let /'mælɪt/ *n.* [*count*] **1.** a hammerlike tool
with an enlarged head, typically of wood, used
for driving another tool. **2.** the wooden implement used to strike a ball in croquet or polo.

mal•nu•tri•tion /,mælnuw'trɪʃən, -nyuw-/ *n.*
[*noncount*] lack of proper nutrition; inadequate
or unbalanced nutrition.

mal•prac•tice /mæl'præktɪs/ *n.* [*noncount*] behavior by a professional, as a doctor or lawyer,

that is against the rules of that profession, or that causes injury or loss.

malt /mɔlt/ *n.* **1.** [*noncount*] grain prepared by boiling and drying, used in brewing beer. **2.** [*count*] an alcoholic beverage, as beer, brewed from malt. **3.** [*count*] MALTED MILK (def. 2).

'malted 'milk, *n.* **1.** [*noncount*] a powder made of dried milk and cereals that can be added to water and dissolved. **2.** [*count*] Also called **malt, malted.** a beverage made from malted milk, ice cream, and flavoring.

mal·treat /mæl'triyt/ *v.* [~ + *obj*] to treat or handle badly or roughly; abuse. —**mal'treat·ment,** *n.* [*noncount*]

ma·ma or **mam·ma** /'mɑmə, mə'mɑ/ *n., pl.* **-mas.** MOTHER.

mam·mal /'mæməl/ *n.* [*count*] a warm-blooded animal with a backbone, having a covering of hair on some or most of the body and a heart with four chambers, nourishing its newborn with its milk. —**mam·ma·li·an** /mə'meyliyən, -'meylyən/, *adj.*

mam·ma·ry /'mæməriy/ *adj.* [*before a noun*] of or relating to the breasts, or the glands that a female mammal uses to feed her young with milk.

mam·mo·gram /'mæmə,græm/ *n.* [*count*] an x-ray photograph obtained by mammography.

mam·mog·ra·phy /mæ'mɒgrəfiy/ *n.* [*noncount*] x-ray photography of a breast, esp. to detect tumors.

mam·moth /'mæməθ/ *n.* [*count*] **1.** an extinct elephant with long hair and tusks. —*adj.* **2.** very large; enormous: *a mammoth budget.*

man /mæn/ *n., pl.* **men** /mɛn/, *interj., v.,* **manned, man·ning.** —*n.* **1.** [*count*] an adult male person, as distinguished from a boy or a woman. **2.** [*count*] a human being, or a person without regard to sex: *All men are equal in the eyes of the law.* **3.** [*noncount*] the human individual as representing the species, without reference to sex; the human race; humankind: *Man does not live by bread alone.* **4.** [*count*] *Slang.* (used as a term of familiar address): *Hey, man, take it easy.* **5.** [*count*] a playing piece used in certain games, as chess or checkers. —*interj.* **6.** used to express astonishment, delight, or other strong emotion: *Man, what a car!* —*v.* [~ + *obj*] **7.** to supply with people, as for service or operation: *to man the ship.* —**'man·ly,** *adj.*

-man, a combining form of MAN: (*mailman*).

man·a·cle /'mænəkəl/ *n., v.,* **-cled, -cling.** —*n.* [*count*] **1.** a handcuff. —*v.* [~ + *obj*] **2.** to handcuff; fetter. **3.** to keep held back; restrain.

man·age /'mænɪdʒ/ *v.* [~ + *obj*], **-aged, -ag·ing. 1. a.** to take charge of; supervise; control: *to manage a business.* **b.** to handle the career of: *to manage a performer.* **2.** to succeed in accomplishing or dealing with; bring about: *They managed to see the governor. I don't know how, but he managed it.* —**'man·age·a·ble,** *adj.* —**'man·age·ment,** *n.* [*noncount*] [*count*]

man·ag·er /'mænɪdʒər/ *n.* [*count*] **1.** one who manages a business or one of its parts. **2.** one who directs the activities of an athlete or team. **3.** a person who manages another's career: *the rock star's manager.* —**man·a·ge·ri·al** /,mænə'dʒɪəriyəl/ *adj.*

man·date /'mændeyt/ *n., v.,* **-dat·ed, -dat·ing.** —*n.* [*count*] **1.** authorization to act in a particular way given by the people to an elected representative: *The president received a clear mandate to end the war.* **2.** any authoritative order or command: *a royal mandate.* —*v.* [~ + *obj*] **3.** to au-

thorize (a particular action); to order or require: *The principal mandated the new dress code.*

man·da·to·ry /'mændə,tɔriy/ *adj.* ordered by an authority: *mandatory budget cuts.*

man·di·ble /'mændəbəl/ *n.* [*count*] the bone part of the lower jaw of animals with backbones.

man·do·lin /'mændlɪn, ,mændl'ɪn/ *n.* [*count*] an eight-stringed musical instrument with a pear-shaped wooden body.

mane /meyn/ *n.* [*count*] the long, thick hair around or at the back of the neck of some animals, as the horse or lion.

ma·neu·ver /mə'nuwvər/ *n.* [*count*] **1.** a planned movement of troops, warships, etc. **2. maneuvers,** [*plural*] a series of military exercises used as practice for war: *The troops are out on maneuvers.* **3.** a clever or skillful movement or action: *another maneuver to gain control of the company.* —*v.* **4.** to move or change the position of by a maneuver: [~ + *obj*]: *She maneuvered the truck around the fallen tree.* [*no obj*]: *He maneuvered out of the way of the fallen tree.* **5.** [*no obj*] to scheme; plot; intrigue: *He maneuvered for the job for a year.* —**ma'neu·ver·a·ble,** *adj.*

man·ger /'meyndʒər/ *n.* [*count*] a box or open container in a stable or barn from which animals eat.

man·gle /'mæŋgəl/ *v.* [~ + *obj*; *usually: be* + ~], **-gled, -gling.** to damage or injure severely by cutting, tearing, or crushing: *The coat sleeve was mangled in the machine.*

man·go /'mæŋgow/ *n.* [*count*], *pl.* **-goes, -gos.** the sweet yellow or orange fruit of a tree that grows in hot climates.

man·gy /'meyndʒiy/ *adj.,* **-gi·er, -gi·est.** dirty and run-down; shabby; unclean.

man·han·dle /'mæn,hændl, mæn'hændl/ *v.* [~ + *obj*], **-dled, -dling.** to handle roughly.

man·hole /'mæn,howl/ *n.* [*count*] a hole, usually with a cover, giving access to a sewer, drain, etc.

man·hunt /'mæn,hʌnt/ *n.* [*count*] an intensive search for a person, esp. a criminal.

ma·ni·a /'meyniyə, 'meynyə/ *n., pl.* **-ni·as. 1.** excitement for something; craze: [*count*]: *a mania for rock stars.* [*noncount*]: *car mania.* **2.** [*noncount*] a mental illness in which the victim suffers from overexcitedness, too much activity, and confused judgment.

ma·ni·ac /'meyniy,æk/ *n.* [*count*] **1.** an insane person; lunatic. **2.** a person who is very enthusiastic or overly excited (about something): *a maniac about neatness.* —**ma·ni·a·cal** /mə'nayəkəl/, *adj.*

man·ic /'mænɪk/ *adj.* **1.** relating to or affected by mania: *manic behavior during a crisis.* **2.** overly excited or enthusiastic: *a manic person when it comes to details.*

man·i·cure /'mænɪ,kyʊr/ *n., v.,* **-cured, -cur·ing.** —*n.* [*count*] **1.** a cosmetic treatment of the hands or fingernails. —*v.* [~ + *obj*] **2.** to apply manicure treatment to. **3.** to trim or cut very carefully: *to manicure a lawn.* —**'man·i,cur·ist,** *n.* [*count*]

man·i·fest /'mænə,fɛst/ *adj.* **1.** readily and easily seen; evident; plain: *a manifest error.* —*v.* [~ + *obj*] **2.** to make clear or evident: *Hepatitis manifests itself with yellowed eyes and skin.* —**man·i·fes·ta·tion** /,mænəfə'steyʃən, -fɛ-/ *n.* [*noncount*] [*count*] —**'man·i,fest·ly,** *adv.*

man·i·fes·to /,mænə'fɛstow/ *n.* [*count*], *pl.* **-tos, -toes.** a public statement of one's intentions

M

or purposes: *The political party manifesto called for increased military spending.*

ma•nil•a /məˈnɪlə/ *adj.* [*before a noun*] made of strong, often light brownish-yellow paper or fiber: *Put the report in a manila folder.*

'man in the 'street, *n.* [*count*] an ordinary person; average citizen.

ma•nip•u•late /məˈnɪpyəˌleyt/ *v.* [~ + *obj*], **-lat•ed, -lat•ing. 1.** to handle or use, esp. with skill: *to manipulate a large tractor easily.* **2.** to manage or influence skillfully and often unfairly: *He could manipulate people's feelings to get his way.* —**ma•nip•u•la•tion** /məˌnɪpyəˈleyʃən/, *n.* [*noncount*] [*count*] —**ma•nip•u•la•tive** /məˈnɪpyəˌleytɪv, -lətɪv/, *adj.* —**maˈnip•uˌla•tor,** *n.* [*count*]

man•kind /ˈmænˈkaynd/ *n.* [*noncount*] **1.** human beings thought of as a group without reference to sex; humankind: *Mankind is not ready to explore the stars.* **2.** men as distinguished from women.

'man-'made, *adj.* produced by humans; not resulting from natural processes: *man-made pollution.*

manned /mænd/ *adj.* carrying or operated by (one or more) human beings: *a manned spacecraft.*

man•ne•quin /ˈmænɪkɪn/ *n.* [*count*] **1.** a solid representation of the human form used in window displays, etc.; a dummy. **2.** one employed to model clothing.

man•ner /ˈmænər/ *n.* **1.** [*count*] a way of doing, being done, or happening: *In what manner were you notified?* **2. manners,** [*plural*] **a.** the ways of living characteristic of a people, class, or period: *Victorian manners.* **b.** ways of behaving with reference to polite standards: *She has such good manners.* **3.** [*count*] a characteristic or customary style or fashion: *built in the 19th-century manner.* **4.** [*count; singular; but used with a singular or plural verb*] kind; sort: *What manner of man is he? All manner of things were happening.*

man•nered /ˈmænərd/ *adj.* **1.** having manners of a specific kind (usually used in combination): *ill-mannered.* **2.** affected; having a false appearance: *a mannered walk.*

man•ner•ism /ˈmænəˌrɪzəm/ *n.* [*count*] a habitual or characteristic manner or way of doing something: *his annoying mannerism of picking at his teeth while talking.*

man•nish /ˈmænɪʃ/ *adj.* being typical or suggestive of a man rather than a woman. —**'man•nish•ly,** *adv.*: *She was dressed mannishly in a suit and tie.*

man•or /ˈmænər/ *n.* [*count*] the main house on an estate. —**ma•nor•i•al** /məˈnɔriyəl/, *adj.*

man•pow•er /ˈmænˌpawər/ *n.* [*noncount*] power in terms of the number of people available for work or military service.

man•sion /ˈmænʃən/ *n.* [*count*] a very large or stately house.

man•slaugh•ter /ˈmænˌslɔtər/ *n.* [*noncount*] the unlawful killing of a human being when there is no prior intent to kill.

man•tel or **man•tle** /ˈmæntl/ *n.* [*count*] **1.** a construction that frames the opening of a fireplace. **2.** a shelf above a fireplace opening. Also called **man•tel•piece,** **man•tle•piece** /ˈmæntlˌpiys/.

man•tis /ˈmæntɪs/ *n.* [*count*], *pl.* **-tis•es, -tes** /-tiyz/. an insect having a long body and typically holding the front legs in an upraised position as if in prayer.

man•tle /ˈmæntl/ *n.* [*count*] **1.** a cloak without sleeves. **2.** something that covers, surrounds, or conceals: *the mantle of darkness.* **3.** MANTEL.

man•u•al /ˈmænyuwəl/ *adj.* **1.** [*before a noun*] operated by hand rather than mechanically: *a manual gearshift.* **2.** involving or requiring human effort; physical: *manual labor.* —*n.* [*count*] **3.** a book giving instructions on how something works or on how to do something: *a computer manual.* —**'man•u•al•ly,** *adv.*: *When the automatic devices failed, he tried to land the plane manually.*

man•u•fac•ture /ˌmænyəˈfæktʃər/ *v.*, **-tured, -tur•ing,** *n.* —*v.* [~ + *obj*] **1.** to make or produce by hand or machinery, esp. on a large scale: *The company manufactures handguns.* **2.** to make up (something untrue): *to manufacture an excuse.* —*n.* [*noncount*] **3.** the making of goods or products by manual labor or by machinery, esp. on a large scale: *the manufacture of cars.* —**,man•u'fac•tur•er,** *n.* [*count*]

ma•nure /məˈnʊr, -ˈnyʊr/ *n.* [*noncount*] solid waste material from animals, used as a substance to fertilize soil.

man•u•script /ˈmænyəˌskrɪpt/ *n.* [*count*] **1.** a written or typed piece of writing before being set in type. **2.** a piece of writing on parchment or paper before books were invented: *ancient manuscripts.*

man•y /ˈmeniy/ *adj.,* **more** /mɔr/, **most** /mowst/, *n., pron.* —*adj.* [*before a plural noun*] **1.** forming a large number; numerous: *many people.* —*n.* [*count*] **2. the many,** [*plural; used with a plural verb*] the greater part of humankind, or of a given group: *The needs of the many outweighed the needs of the few.* —*pron.* [*used with a plural verb*] **3.** many persons or things: *Many were unable to attend. Many of us dislike your new policies.* —*Idiom.* **4. a good** or **great many,** a large number of persons or things: *A good many of the students were absent.* **5. many a time,** again and again; frequently.

map /mæp/ *n., v.,* **mapped, map•ping.** —*n.* [*count*] **1.** a drawing on a flat surface of parts or features of a place, as of the earth. —*v.* **2.** [~ + *obj*] to represent or draw on or as if on a map: *He mapped the tourist attractions in the region.* **3. map out,** to sketch or plan out in detail: *to map out a new career* or *to map a new career out.* —**'map•mak•er,** *n.* [*count*]

ma•ple /ˈmeypəl/ *n.* **1.** [*count*] any of numerous trees or shrubs grown for ornament, for timber, or for sap. **2.** [*noncount*] the flavor of maple syrup or maple sugar.

'maple 'sugar, *n.* [*noncount*] a yellowish brown sugar produced by boiling down maple syrup.

'maple 'syrup, *n.* [*noncount*] a syrup produced by partially boiling down the sap of the sugar maple.

mar /mɑr/ *v.* [~ + *obj*], **marred, mar•ring.** to damage the attractiveness of; spoil: *The litter marred the beauty of the mountain trail.*

mar•a•thon /ˈmærəˌθɑn, -θən/ *n.* [*count*] a foot race over a course measuring 26 mi. 385 yd. (42 km 352 m). —**'mar•a,thon•er,** *n.* [*count*]

mar•ble /ˈmɑrbəl/ *n.* **1.** [*noncount*] limestone that has been changed into a hard rock, used in sculpture and in buildings: *columns of beautiful marble.* **2.** [*count*] a little ball, usually made of glass, for use in games. **3. marbles,** [*noncount; used with a singular verb*] a game for children played with marbles in a marked area on the ground.

mar•bled /'marbəld/ *adj.* having a pattern of, or colored like, the grainy or streaked colors of marble.

march /martʃ/ *v.* [*no obj*] **1.** to walk with regular steps, esp. in step with others: *The soldiers marched down the street.* **2.** to go forward or advance: *Time marches on.* **3.** to take part in an organized demonstration: *They marched for civil rights.* —*n.* **4.** [*count*] the act of marching: *daily marches in the Army.* **5.** [*count*] the distance covered in a single period of marching: *a day's march.* **6.** [*count; usually singular*] advance; progress: *the march of science.* **7.** [*count*] a piece of music with a steady rhythm, suitable for marching to. **8.** [*count*] a procession organized as a protest or demonstration: *a march on Washington.* —'**march•er,** *n.* [*count*]

March /martʃ/ *n.* the third month of the year, containing 31 days.

mare /mɛər/ *n.* [*count*] a female horse or donkey.

mar•ga•rine /'mardʒərɪn, -dʒə,riyn/ *n.* [*noncount*] a butterlike product made of vegetable oils.

mar•gin /'mardʒɪn/ *n.* [*count*] **1.** the blank space around the printed matter on a page: *Leave a margin of one inch on each side of your essay.* **2.** an amount allowed beyond what is necessary: *no margin for error.* **3.** an amount or degree of difference: *She won by a margin of three votes.*

mar•gin•al /'mardʒənəl/ *adj.* **1.** of, relating to, or located in a margin: *marginal notes.* **2.** barely adequate: *a marginal student.* —'**mar•gin•al•ly,** *adv.*: *He improved only marginally.*

mar•i•gold /'mæri,gowld/ *n.* [*count*] a plant having golden or orange flowers and strong-scented leaves.

ma•ri•jua•na /,mærə'wanə/ *n.* [*noncount*] **1.** the dried leaves and flowers of the hemp plant, used esp. as a drug. **2.** HEMP (def. 1).

ma•ri•na /mə'riynə/ *n.* [*count*], *pl.* **-nas.** a boat basin where small boats can dock and be serviced.

mar•i•nate /'mærə,neyt/ *v.,* **-nat•ed, -nat•ing.** (of food) to (cause to) be soaked in a mixture of herbs, spices, wine or vinegar, etc., for flavoring before cooking: [*~* + *obj*]: *Marinate the chicken overnight.* [*no obj*]: *Allow the meat to marinate overnight.* —**mar•i•na•tion** /,mærə'neyʃən/, *n.* [*noncount*]

ma•rine /mə'riyn/ *adj.* [*before a noun*] **1.** of or relating to the sea: *marine vegetation.* **2.** of or relating to shipping by sea. —*n.* [*count; sometimes: Marine*] **3.** a member of the U.S. Marine Corps.

Ma'rine ,Corps, *n.* a branch of the U.S. Navy trained to make sea-launched assaults on land targets.

mar•i•ner /'mærənər/ *n.* [*count*] a person who directs or assists in the sailing of a ship; a sailor.

mar•i•on•ette /,mæriyə'nɛt/ *n.* [*count*] a puppet moved by strings attached to its limbs.

mar•i•tal /'mærɪtl̩/ *adj.* [*before a noun*] of or relating to marriage: *marital vows.* —'**mar•i•tal•ly,** *adv.*

mar•i•time /'mærɪ,taym/ *adj.* [*before a noun*] **1.** of or relating to navigation. **2.** of or relating to the sea: *maritime weather.*

mark /mark/ *n.* [*count*] **1.** a visible impression on a surface, as a line or spot: *She had a mark on her face from the scratch.* **2.** a symbol used in writing or printing: *a punctuation mark.* **3.** some-

thing that indicates something else; a sign: *to bow as a mark of respect.* **4.** something typical or characteristic of something else; a trait: *a mark of nobility.* **5. a.** a symbol used in rating a student's achievement; grade: *Her mark was an A.* **b.** Often, **marks.** [*plural*] any rating: *We gave him high marks for trying so hard.* **6.** an object or sign serving to indicate position, as a point reached on a scale: *I finally reached the halfway mark of the book.* **7.** a target; goal: *to miss the mark.* **8.** the starting line in a race: *"On your mark...get set...go!"* —*v.* [*~* + *obj*] **9.** to be a distinguishing feature of: *a day marked by sadness.* **10.** to make or put a mark or marks (on): *She marked the wall with her greasy glove.* **11.** to assign a grade to: *When will you mark the exams?* **12.** to serve as a sign or signal of; to indicate: *That day marked the end of a career.* **13.** to designate by or as if by marks: *He marked the sections that he wanted to delete.* **14. mark down, a.** to reduce the price of: *They had marked down the prices* or *They had marked the prices down.* **b.** to make a note of in writing: *We'd better mark down the sizes. We'd better mark them down.* **15. mark off,** to mark the dimensions or boundaries of: *They marked off the area with tape* or *They marked the area off with tape.* **16. mark up, a.** to mar or ruin the appearance of with marks: *Don't mark up the wall!* **b.** to mark with notations or symbols, as of comments or corrections: *The teacher marked up the student's paper.* **c.** to add an amount or percentage to a seller's cost to arrive at a selling price: *The store manager marked up the dresses 50%.* —*Idiom.* **17. make one's mark,** to achieve success: *to make one's mark in show business.* **18. wide of the mark,** far from the target or one's aim: *comments wide of the mark.*

mark•down /'mark,dawn/ *n.* [*count*] **1.** a reduction in the price of an item: *a markdown on sofas.* **2.** the amount by which a price is reduced: *a markdown of 30%.*

marked /markt/ *adj.* **1.** striking; conspicuous: *She showed marked improvement in all subject areas.* **2.** singled out as someone suspected of something, or as the object of revenge: *The accountant is a marked man.* **3.** having a mark or marks. —**mark•ed•ly** /'markɪdliy/, *adv.*: *His grades improved markedly after tutoring.*

mark•er /'markər/ *n.* [*count*] **1.** a thing that indicates a place or shows the position of something: *I left a piece of paper in the book as a marker.* **2.** a tool for making marks: *He used a yellow marker to highlight the misspelled words.*

mar•ket /'markɪt/ *n.* [*count*] **1.** a place where buyers and sellers meet for the sale of goods. **2.** a store for selling food. **3.** a geographical region viewed as an area in which goods or services can be sold: *manufactured for the New England market.* **4.** demand for an item or a product: *The health-food market is expanding.* **5.** [*usually: the + ~*] STOCK MARKET. —*v.* **6.** [*no obj*] to buy food or other provisions for the home: *They went marketing on Saturdays.* **7.** [*~* + *obj*] to offer in a market for sale; to sell: *to market computers.* —'**mar•ket•a•ble,** *adj.* —'**mar•ket•ing,** *n.* [*noncount*]

mar•ket•place /'markɪt,pleys/ *n.* [*count*] **1.** an area in a town where a market is held. **2.** the world of business and trade: *In a free, open marketplace our goods can compete.* **3.** any sphere in which people or things compete: *a marketplace of ideas.*

marks•man /'marksmən/ *n.* [*count*], *pl.* **-men.**

M

one who is skilled in shooting at a target. —'**marks•man**,**ship,** *n.* [*noncount*]

mark•up /'mɑrk,ʌp/ *n.* [*count*] the amount by which a seller's cost is increased to establish a selling price: *a 50% markup on dresses.*

mar•ma•lade /'mɑrmə,leyd, ,mɑrmə'leyd/ *n.* [*noncount*] a jelly made from boiled fruit, containing pieces of citrus fruit.

ma•roon[1] /mə'ruwn/ *n.* [*noncount*] a dark brownish red color.

ma•roon[2] /mə'ruwn/ *v.* [~ + *obj; usually: be* + ~ *-ed*] to put ashore and abandon on an isolated island or coast: *He was marooned on an island.*

mar•quee /mɑr'kiy/ *n.* [*count*], *pl.* **-quees.** a canopy-like structure that sticks out over the entrance to a building.

mar•riage /'mærɪdʒ/ *n.* **1.** [*noncount*] the institution under which a man and woman live as husband and wife under law. **2.** [*count*] the state or relationship of being married: *Her first two marriages were unhappy.* **3.** [*count*] the ceremony by which such a union is legally accomplished; wedding. —'**mar•riage•a•ble,** *adj.* —**mar•ried** /'mæriyd/ *adj.*

mar•row /'mærow/ *n.* [*noncount*] the soft fatty tissue in the cavities of bones where blood cells are produced.

mar•ry /'mæriy/ *v.,* **-ried, -ry•ing. 1.** to take (someone) as a husband or wife: [~ + *obj*]: *He married her when he was eighteen.* [*no obj*]: *In some countries girls can marry when they are fourteen.* **2.** [~ + *obj*] to perform the marriage ceremony for (a couple): *The priest married them in the old church.* **3.** [~ + *obj*] to join or unite closely: *marrying the two musical forms to produce a new style.*

marsh /mɑrʃ/ *n.* [*count*] an area of waterlogged soil covered with tall grasses. —'**marsh•y,** *adj.,* **-i•er, -i•est.**

mar•shal /'mɑrʃəl/ *n., v.,* **-shaled, -shal•ing.** —*n.* [*count*] **1.** an administrative officer of a U.S. court with duties similar to a sheriff's. **2.** the chief of a police or fire department. **3.** an official who leads special ceremonies, as a parade. —*v.* [~ + *obj*] **4.** to arrange in proper or effective order: *to marshal the facts.*

marsh•mal•low /'mɑrʃ,mɛlow, -,mælow/ *n.* a spongy candy made from gelatin, corn syrup, and flavoring: [*count*] *toasting marshmallows around the campfire.* [*noncount*]: *cookies filled with marshmallow.*

mar•su•pi•al /mɑr'suwpiyəl/ *n.* [*count*] an animal, as a kangaroo, that gives birth to immature young that complete their development in a pouch on the mother's abdomen.

mart /mɑrt/ *n.* [*count*] market; trading center.

mar•tial /'mɑrʃəl/ *adj.* [*before a noun*] relating to or suitable for war: *martial music.* —'**mar•tial•ly,** *adv.*

'martial 'art, *n.* [*count*] Often, **martial arts.** [*plural*] a traditional form of East Asian self-defense, as karate or judo.

'martial 'law, *n.* [*noncount*] law or control temporarily imposed upon an area by military forces.

mar•tyr /'mɑrtər/ *n.* [*count*] **1.** one who willingly suffers death rather than give up his or her religion: *early Christian martyrs.* **2.** one who suffers for a cause. —**mar•tyr•dom** /'mɑrtərdəm/, *n.* [*noncount*]

mar•vel /'mɑrvəl/ *n., v.,* **-veled, -vel•ing.** —*n.* [*count*] **1.** something that causes wonder or astonishment: *an engineering marvel.* —*v.* **2.** to be filled with wonder (at): [*no obj*]: *I marveled at*

her ability to charm. [~ + *obj*]: *They marveled that you won.*

mar•vel•ous /'mɑrvələs/ *adj.* superbly fine; wonderful: *a marvelous show.* —'**mar•vel•ous•ly,** *adv.*

Marx•ism /'mɑrksɪzəm/ *n.* [*noncount*] the system of thought developed by Karl Marx and Friedrich Engels, esp. the doctrine that struggle among the social classes has been the main force of historical change. —'**Marx•ist,** *n.* [*count*], *adj.*

mar•zi•pan /'mɑrzə,pæn/ *n.* [*noncount*] a molded candy made of almond paste.

masc., an abbreviation for: masculine.

mas•car•a /mæ'skærə/ *n.* [*noncount*] a cosmetic applied to the eyelashes.

mas•cot /'mæskɒt, -kət/ *n.* [*count*] something adopted by a group as its symbol to bring good luck: *The team took in the stray dog and made it their mascot.*

mas•cu•line /'mæskyəlɪn/ *adj.* **1.** of or relating to a man or men. **2.** of or relating to the grammatical gender that has among its members most nouns referring to males as well as other nouns. —**mas•cu•lin•i•ty** /,mæskyə'lɪnɪtiy/, *n.* [*noncount*]

mash /mæʃ/ *v.* [~ + *obj*] **1.** to change (something) into a soft, pulpy mass by beating: *I mashed the carrots.* **2.** to crush: *He mashed his fingers when the door closed on them.* —**mashed,** *adj.*: *mashed potatoes.*

mask /mæsk/ *n.* [*count*] **1.** a covering for the face, worn to hide one's identity, to frighten, or to cause laughter. **2.** a covering, as of wire or gauze, worn over all or part of the face, for protection, etc.: *a catcher's mask.* —*v.* [~ + *obj*] **3.** to cover, hide, or shield with or as if with a mask: *eyes masked by sunglasses.* —**masked,** *adj.*: *a masked robber.*

mas•och•ism /'mæsə,kɪzəm, 'mæz-/ *n.* [*noncount*] **1.** a psychological disorder in which sexual pleasure is derived from pain. **2.** the tendency to find pleasure in submissiveness, etc. —'**mas•och•ist,** *n.* [*count*] —,**mas•och'is•tic,** *adj.*

ma•son /'meysən/ *n.* [*count*] one whose trade is building with stones or bricks.

ma•son•ry /'meysənriy/ *n.* [*noncount*] work built by a mason.

mas•quer•ade /,mæskə'reyd/ *n., v.,* **-ad•ed, -ad•ing.** —*n.* [*count*] **1.** a party of people wearing masks and costumes. **2.** false, outward show; pretense: *a masquerade of his true feelings.* —*v.* [*no obj*] **3.** to represent oneself falsely: *masquerading as a surgeon.*

mass[1] /mæs/ *n.* **1.** [*count*] a body of matter, usually of indefinite shape: *took a mass of dough and spread it on the pan.* **2.** [*count*] a large number; a great deal of: *a mass of errors.* **3.** [*noncount*] *Physics.* the quantity of matter in a body. **4. the masses,** [*plural*] ordinary people thought of as a whole: *an appeal to the masses.* —*adj.* [*before a noun*] **5.** of, relating to, or affecting a large number of people: *mass unemployment; the mass media.* **6.** on a large scale: *weapons of mass destruction.* —*v.* [~ + *obj*] [*no obj*] **7.** to (cause to) come together in or form a mass.

mass[2] /mæs/ *n.* [*often: Mass*] the ceremony of the Eucharist: [*noncount*]: *Mass is held on Sunday.* [*count*]: *The priest performed two Masses each Sunday.*

Mass., an abbreviation for: Massachusetts.

mas•sa•cre /'mæsəkər/ *n., v.,* **-cred, -cring.** —*n.* [*count*] **1.** the violent killing of a large number of esp. helpless human beings. —*v.* [~ + *obj*] **2.** to kill in a massacre; slaughter.

mas•sage /mə'sɑʒ/ *n.*, *v.*, **-saged, -sag•ing.** —*n.* **1.** the skill of treating the body by rubbing, squeezing, etc., so as to stimulate circulation or take away pain: [*count*]: *He went to the trainer's room for a massage.* [*noncount*]: *treatment with massage.* —*v.* [~ + *obj*] **2.** to treat by massage: *She massaged his stiff neck.*

mas'sage ˌparlor, *n.* [*count*] **1.** an es*t*ablishment providing massages. **2.** a similar establishment that also provides sexual services.

mas•seur /mə'sɜr, -'sʊr/ *n.* [*count*] a man who provides massages as a profession.

mas•seuse /mə'suws, -'suwz/ *n.* [*count*] a woman who provides massages as a profession.

mas•sive /'mæsɪv/ *adj.* **1.** made up of or forming a large mass: *the massive columns of the ancient temple.* **2.** large in amount or degree: *a massive dose of medicine.*

'mass 'noun, *n.* [*count*] a noun that refers to an abstract idea, or to a quantity or mass of things regarded as a whole or collection. A mass noun does not normally have a plural, unless we refer to a measure or type of such a thing. The noncount meaning of "sugar" is shown in the sentence "I like sugar." The count meaning of "sugar" is shown in the sentence "How many sugars (= spoonfuls or packets of sugar) do you want in your coffee?" Abstract ideas, such as "happiness" and "love," are examples of mass nouns.

'mass-pro'duce, *v.* [~ + *obj*] **-duced, -duc•ing.** to produce (goods) in large amounts, esp. by machinery. —**'mass pro'duction,** *n.* [*noncount*]

mast /mæst/ *n.* [*count*] **1.** a polelike structure rising above a ship to hold the sails. **2.** any upright pole, as a support for a flag.

mas•tec•to•my /mæ'stɛktəmiy/ *n.* [*count*], *pl.* **-mies.** the surgical removal of all or part of the breast.

mas•ter /'mæstər/ *n.* [*count*] **1.** a person with the ability or power to control: *She wanted to be the master of her fate.* **2.** an owner of a slave or animal: *The dog followed its master everywhere.* **3.** a person very skilled or famous in a discipline, as an art or science: *one of the great masters of modern art.* **4.** *Chiefly Brit.* a male teacher. **5.** an original document, tape, disk, etc., from which copies are made. —*adj.* [*before a noun*] **6.** chief; principal: *a master list; The house has a large master bedroom.* **7.** controlling others of its type: *a master switch.* **8.** being a master from which copies can be made: *a master tape.* **9.** very skilled: *a master designer.* —*v.* [~ + *obj*] **10.** to make oneself master of; to learn to use or control: *to master a foreign language.*

mas•ter•ful /'mæstərfəl/ *adj.* **1.** having or showing the qualities of a master; authoritative. **2.** done well; showing mastery: *a masterful performance.* —**'mas•ter•ful•ly,** *adv.*

'master ˌkey, *n.* [*count*] a key that will open a number of different locks.

mas•ter•mind /'mæstər,maynd/ *v.* [~ + *obj*] **1.** to plan and direct skillfully: *to mastermind a robbery.* —*n.* [*count*] **2.** one who is responsible for the performance of a project: *the mastermind behind the plot.*

'master of 'ceremonies, *n.* [*count*] one who presides at an event, as a formal dinner or television broadcast, acting as host and introducing the speakers. *Abbr.:* MC

mas•ter•piece /'mæstər,piys/ *n.* [*count*] **1.** a person's greatest piece of work, as in an art form. **2.** a fine example of excellence: *That speech was a masterpiece.*

mas•ter•stroke /'mæstər,strowk/ *n.* [*count*] an extremely skillful or effective action: *a masterstroke of cunning.*

mas•ter•y /'mæstəriy/ *n.* [*noncount*] knowledge or skill: *His mastery of Italian was obvious.*

mas•tiff /'mæstɪf/ *n.* [*count*] a breed of large, powerful, shorthaired dogs having a spotted coat and a dark muzzle.

mas•tur•bate /'mæstər,beyt/ *v.*, **-bat•ed, -bat•ing.** to stimulate the genitals of (oneself or someone else) for sexual pleasure: [*no obj*]: *Masturbating is normal.* [~ + *obj*]: *masturbating one another.* —**mas•tur•ba•tion** /ˌmæstər'beyʃən/, *n.* [*noncount*]

mat /mæt/ *n.*, *v.*, **mat•ted, mat•ting.** —*n.* [*count*] **1.** a piece of fabric used on a floor as a covering: *a floor mat.* **2.** a piece of material set under an object, as a dish: *a place mat.* **3.** a thick tangled mass, as of weeds or hair. —*v.* [*no obj*] [~ + *obj*] **4.** to form into a tangled mass.

match¹ /mætʃ/ *n.* [*count*] a slender piece of wood or cardboard with a tip having a chemical substance that produces fire when rubbed on a rough or chemically prepared surface.

match² /mætʃ/ *n.* [*count*] **1.** a person or thing that equals or resembles another in some respect. **2.** a pair of persons or things that go together well: *They are a perfect match.* **3.** a game or competition in which two or more contestants oppose each other: *a tennis match.* —*v.* **4.** [~ + *obj*] to equal: *He couldn't match his earlier score.* **5.** to go harmoniously or suitably with because of color or design: [~ + *obj*]: *The skirt matches the jacket perfectly.* [*no obj*]: *The skirt and jacket match perfectly.*

match•book /'mætʃ,bʊk/ *n.* [*count*] a small folder into which matches are stapled or glued.

match•mak•er /'mætʃ,meykər/ *n.* [*count*] one who arranges marriages by introducing possible mates.

mate /meyt/ *n.*, *v.*, **mat•ed, mat•ing.** —*n.* [*count*] **1.** a husband or wife; spouse. **2.** a sexual partner of an animal. **3.** *Chiefly Brit.* friend; buddy; chum (often used as a friendly term of address). **4.** an officer on a merchant ship below the rank of captain. **5.** This word is used after a root or word with the meaning "a person who shares": *an office-mate* (= *someone sharing an office*); *a teammate* (= *someone on the same team*). —*v.* **6.** to (cause to) have sexual relations in order to breed, as animals: [*no obj*]: *Those animals mate in the fall.* [~ + *obj*]: *Researchers tried to mate the female with the male.* —**'mat•ing,** *adj.* [*before a noun*]: *the mating season.*

ma•te•ri•al /mə'tɪəriyəl/ *n.* **1.** [*noncount*] the substances or components of which something is made: *raw materials.* **2. materials,** [*plural*] the apparatus or implements needed to make or do something: *writing materials.* **3.** a textile fabric, as cloth: [*noncount*]: *She bought some material to make a dress.* [*count*]: *She used light materials to make her dress.* **4.** [*noncount*] ideas or experiences that can provide the basis for some work: *material for a book.* —*adj.* [*before a noun*] **5.** formed of matter; physical: *the material world.* **6.** relating to the physical as opposed to the spiritual or intellectual: *material comforts.* **7.** substantially important; relevant: *Your work made a material difference in the success of our program.*

ma•te•ri•al•ism /mə'tɪəriyə,lɪzəm/ n. [noncount] too much emphasis on material objects, comforts, and considerations as opposed to spiritual or intellectual values: the materialism of the 1970's and 1980's. —**ma,ter•i•a'list•ic,** adj.

ma•te•ri•al•ize /mə'tɪəriyə,layz/ v. [no obj], -**ized, -iz•ing. 1.** to become real: Our ideas never materialized. **2.** to assume material form: A tall man suddenly materialized from the shadows.

ma•ter•nal /mə'tɜrnl/ adj. **1.** of or relating to a mother: maternal instincts. **2.** [before a noun] related through a mother's side of the family: a maternal uncle. —**ma'ter•nal•ly,** adv.

ma•ter•ni•ty /mə'tɜrnɪtiy/ n. [noncount] **1.** the state of being a mother; motherhood. —adj. [before a noun] **2.** applying to mothers before, during, and after childbirth: maternity clothes; maternity leave.

math /mæθ/ n. [noncount] mathematics.

math•e•ma•ti•cian /,mæθəmə'tɪʃən/ n. [count] a specialist in mathematics.

math•e•mat•ics /,mæθə'mætɪks/ n. [noncount; used with a singular verb] the systematic study of numbers and the relations between quantities expressed by symbols. —**,math•e'mat•i•cal,** adj.

mat•i•née or **mat•i•nee** /,mætn'ey/ n. [count] a performance, as of a play, held in the daytime, usually in the afternoon.

ma•tri•arch /'meytriy,ɑrk/ n. [count] **1.** the female head of a family or tribal line. **2.** a woman who is the founder or most important member of a group. —**,ma•tri'ar•chal,** adj.

ma•tri•ar•chy /'meytriy,ɑrkiy/ n., pl. -**chies. 1.** a family, society, or state governed by women. **2.** a form of social organization in which the mother is head of the family and women have considerable power and property.

mat•ri•cide /'mætrɪ,sayd, 'mey-/ n. [noncount] [count] the act of killing one's mother. —**mat•ri•cid•al,** /,mætrɪ'saydl, ,mey-/, adj.

ma•tric•u•late /mə'trɪkyə,leyt/ v., -**lat•ed, -lat•ing.** to (cause to) be enrolled as a student in a college or university as a candidate for a degree: [~ + obj]: The college matriculated over 1200 new students. [no obj]: He took enough courses to matriculate. —**ma•tric•u•la•tion** /mə,trɪkyə'leyʃən/, n. [noncount]

mat•ri•mo•ny /'mætrə,mowniy/ n. [noncount] the state of being married; marriage. —**mat•ri•mo•ni•al** /,mætrə'mowniyəl/, adj. [before a noun]: matrimonial bliss.

ma•tron /'meytrən/ n. [count] **1.** a married woman, esp. one who is mature and dignified. **2.** a female officer, as in a prison for women. —**'ma•tron•ly,** adj.

'matron of 'honor, n. [count] a married woman who is the principal attendant of the bride at a wedding.

matte /mæt/ adj. having a dull surface; not shiny or glossy: matte paint.

mat•ter /'mætər/ n. **1.** [noncount] the material of which any physical object is composed; physical substance, as distinguished from parts of the mind. **2.** [count] a situation; affair; circumstance; event: a trivial matter. **3.** [count; singular; a + ~ + of] an amount counted approximately: It's only a matter of time before the police get us. **4. the matter,** [count; singular; the + ~] the trouble: Is something the matter? What's the matter? **5.** [noncount] something written or printed: reading matter. —v. [no obj] **6.** to be of importance: The cost doesn't matter to him. It doesn't matter that your hair is too long. —**Idiom. 7. a**

matter of opinion, a topic on which there may be different opinions: It's a matter of opinion which of the two dogs is cuter. **8. as a matter of fact,** in reality; actually: As a matter of fact, I don't care.

'matter-of-'fact, adj. concerned with facts alone rather than emotions; nonchalant: I tried to be very matter-of-fact, but my heart was breaking. —**'matter-of-'factly,** adv.

mat•tress /'mætrɪs/ n. [count] a large pad used on a bed for support.

ma•ture /mə'tʊr, -'tyʊr, -'tʃʊr/ adj., -**tur•er, -tur•est,** v., -**tured, -tur•ing.** —adj. **1.** fully developed in body or mind: mature enough to take care of herself when she came home from school. **2.** complete in natural growth or development: The wine is fully mature. **3.** [before a noun] intended for or composed of adults: mature subjects; a movie for mature audiences. **4.** payable; due: a mature bond. —v. **5.** to (cause to) become mature: [no obj]: The wine had matured beautifully. [~ + obj]: Experience has matured him. **6.** [no obj] to become due: The bond had matured and was worth $50. —**mat•u•ra•tion** /,mætʃə'reyʃən/, n. [noncount] —**ma'ture•ly,** adv. —**ma'tu•ri•ty,** n. [noncount]

maud•lin /'mɔdlɪn/ adj. embarrassingly sentimental or foolishly sad: a maudlin story about a lost dog.

maul /mɔl/ v. [~ + obj] to handle or use roughly; injure by rough treatment: The lion tamer was suddenly mauled by one of the lions.

mau•so•le•um /,mɔsə'liyəm, -zə-/ n. [count], pl. -**le•ums, -le•a** /-'liyə/. a large, impressive tomb.

mauve /mowv, mɔv/ n. [noncount] a pale purple.

mav•er•ick /'mævərɪk, 'mævrɪk/ n. [count] one who thinks and acts independently: a political maverick.

max•i /'mæksiy/ n. [count], pl. **max•is.** an ankle-length coat or skirt.

max•im /'mæksɪm/ n. [count] a proverb.

max•i•mal /'mæksəməl/ adj. [usually before a noun] greatest possible; highest: making maximal use of his time. —**'max•i•mal•ly,** adv.

max•i•mize /'mæksə,mayz/ v. [~ + obj], -**mized, -miz•ing. 1.** to increase to the greatest possible amount: to maximize profits. **2.** to make fullest use of: to maximize one's potential.

max•i•mum /'mæksəməm/ n. [count] **1.** the highest amount, value, or degree that can be reached; an upper limit allowed by regulation: At a maximum, we have twenty students in each class. —adj. [before a noun] **2.** being the greatest, largest, or highest that can be reached: a maximum prison sentence of 50 years.

may /mey/ auxiliary (modal) v. [~ + root form of a verb], pres. **may;** past **might;** imperative, infinitive, and participles lacking. **1. a.** (used to express possibility): It may rain. You may have been right. He might have been here before us. **b.** (used to express permission or opportunity): You may see the doctor now. May we have a word with you? **2.** (used to express that one thing follows another, esp. in clauses that convey condition, limitation, purpose, or result): Let's agree on this so that we may go home early. He may be unpleasant, but he's harmless. I'll stand by you, come what may. **3.** (used to express a wish or prayer): Long may you live! May the couple always be happy and healthy. See CAN.

May /mey/ *n.* the fifth month of the year, containing 31 days.

may•be /'meybiy/ *adv., n., pl.* **-bes.** —*adv.* **1.** perhaps; possibly: *Maybe I'll go too.* —*n.* [*count*] **2.** a possibility or uncertainty: *There are too many maybes in his plan.*

may•hem /'meyhɛm, 'meyəm/ *n.* [*noncount*] random or deliberate violence or damage.

may•o /'meyow/ *n.* MAYONNAISE.

may•on•naise /ˌmeyə'neyz, 'meyə,neyz/ *n.* [*noncount*] a thick sauce made of egg yolks, lemon juice, oil, and seasonings.

may•or /'meyər, mɛər/ *n.* [*count*] the chief executive of a city or town. —'**may•or•al,** *adj.* [*before a noun*]: *a mayoral candidate.* —'**may•or•al•ty,** *n.* [*noncount*]

maze /meyz/ *n.* [*count*] **1.** a confusing network of paths; labyrinth: *a maze of corridors.* **2.** a complicated, perplexing system: *a maze of rules.*

MBA or **M.B.A.,** *n.* [*count*], *pl.* **MBA's** or **M.B. A.'s. 1.** an academic degree, Master of Business Administration: *has an MBA from a good school.* **2.** one who has earned this degree: *a lot of MBA's looking for jobs.*

MC, an abbreviation of: master of ceremonies.

MD, an abbreviation of: **1.** Doctor of Medicine. **2.** Maryland.

Md., an abbreviation of: Maryland.

me /miy/ *pron.* **1.** This pronoun is used as the direct or indirect object of the pronoun *I*: *They asked me to the party. Give me your hand.* **2.** This pronoun is used instead of the pronoun *I* after the verb *to be* in many non-formal instances: *Who is it? –It's me.* **3.** This pronoun is used instead of the pronoun *I* after the words *as* and *than* and in certain constructions in non-formal instances: *She's a lot smarter than me (= than I am). He's as smart as me.* **4.** This pronoun is used instead of the pronoun *my* before an *-ing* form of a verb in many non-formal instances: *Did you hear about me getting promoted?*

ME, an abbreviation of: Maine.

Me., an abbreviation of: Maine.

mead•ow /'mɛdow/ *n.* [*count*] a grassy, flat area.

mead•ow•lark /'mɛdow,lɑrk/ *n.* [*count*] a North American songbird having a brown-streaked back.

mea•ger /'miygər/ *adj.* not enough in quantity or quality; insufficient: *a meager salary.* —'**mea•ger•ly,** *adv.*

meal[1] /miyl/ *n.* [*count*] **1.** the food served and eaten at one time or occasion: *The children were served a hot meal.* **2.** one such regular time or occasion for eating.

meal[2] /miyl/ *n.* [*noncount*] a coarse powder ground from the seeds of any grain: *barley meal.* —'**meal•y,** *adj.,* **-i•er, -i•est:** *a mealy taste.*

meal•time /'miyl,taym/ *n.* [*count*] the usual time for a meal.

mean[1] /miyn/ *v.,* **meant** /mɛnt/, **mean•ing. 1.** [~ + *obj*] to have as its meaning or its sense; to signify: *The word "klock" in Swedish means "smart; wise." That gesture means that she hates you.* **2.** to have in mind as one's purpose or intention; intend: [~ + *obj*]: *She meant no harm. I've been meaning to call you, but things got too busy. What did you mean by that?* [*no obj*]: *I'm sure they meant well, but they didn't finish the job.* **3.** [*be* + *meant*] to be expected to happen in a certain way; have as a particular destiny: *The couple were meant for each other.* **4.** [~ + *obj*] to indicate that something exists as a cause: *A flickering screen could mean that your computer cables are not connected tightly.* **5.** [~ + *obj*] to have the value of; to have the importance of: *Money means everything to them.*

mean[2] /miyn/ *adj.,* **-er, -est. 1.** having evil or unkind intentions; malicious: *a mean remark.* **2.** stingy; miserly. **3.** low in status: *of mean and humble birth.* —'**mean•ly,** *adv.* —'**mean•ness,** *n.* [*noncount*]

mean[3] /miyn/ *n.* [*count*], *pl.* **means. 1.** Usually, **means.** [*plural*] an instrument, thing, or method used to achieve something: *They have the means, but do they have the will?* [*count; singular; used with a singular verb*]: *The quickest means of travel into the jungle is by canoe.* [*plural; used with a plural verb*]: *The means of winning that election are bribery and threats.* **2. means,** [*plural*] available resources, esp. money: *We don't have sufficient means to send our children to college.* **3.** something located in the middle between two extremes: *to seek a mean between doubt and certainty.* —*adj.* [*before a noun*] **4.** occupying a middle position: *the mean amount of rainfall for that region.* —*Idiom.* **5. by all means,** certainly: *By all means help yourself to the cookies, but save some for me.* **6. by means of,** by the way or method of; by the use of or by using: *accomplished by means of new technology.* **7. by no means** or **not by any means,** not at all; definitely not: *By no means is he ready to retire.*

me•an•der /miy'ændər/ *v.* [*no obj*] **1.** to proceed by a winding course: *a stream meandering through the valley.* **2.** to wander aimlessly.

mean•ing /'miynɪŋ/ *n.* **1.** what is intended to be or is expressed: [*count*]: *Most meanings of a word are given in the dictionary.* [*noncount*]: *What is the meaning of this interruption?* **2.** [*noncount*] the end, purpose, or significance of something: *His life no longer had any meaning for him after his wife died.* —'**mean•ing•ful,** *adj.* —'**mean•ing•less,** *adj.*

meant /mɛnt/ *v.* pt. and pp. of MEAN[1].

mean•time /'miyn,taym/ *n.* [*noncount*] **1.** the time between two events: *We have to leave at seven; in the meantime, let's have a drink.* —*adv.* **2.** MEANWHILE.

mean•while /'miyn,hwayl, -,wayl/ *n.* [*noncount*] **1.** MEANTIME. —*adv.* **2.** in the time between: *The meeting's in forty minutes; meanwhile, I have to get some lunch.* **3.** at the same time: *Meanwhile, I was enjoying myself.*

mea•sles /'miyzəlz/ *n.* [*noncount; used with a singular verb*] a disease characterized by small red spots on the skin, fever, and coldlike symptoms.

mea•sly /'miyzliy/ *adj.,* **-sli•er, -sli•est.** so little or small as to be inadequate: *a measly salary.*

meas•ur•a•ble /'mɛʒərəbəl/ *adj.* **1.** that can be measured. **2.** large or significant enough to be measured: *a measurable difference between the two experiments.* —'**meas•ur•a•bly,** *adv.*

meas•ure /'mɛʒər/ *n., v.,* **-ured, -ur•ing.** —*n.* **1.** [*count*] a unit or standard of measurement: *A second is a measure of time.* **2.** [*count*] an instrument, as a container, that holds a certain amount or various amounts and has marks indicating one or more amounts: *a one-cup measure.* **3.** [*count; singular*] the extent, dimensions, etc., of something, figured by comparison with a standard or by judging against others: *to take the measure of a room.* **4.** [*count*] a known amount measured out: *a measure of brandy.* **5.** Usually, **measures.** [*plural*] actions to achieve an end: *took several* *measures to avoid suspicion.* —*v.* [~ + *obj*] **6.** to figure out the size, dimensions, etc., of (something): *to measure the floor with a tape measure.* **7.** to be of a certain size, amount, etc.: *The yard measured 100 feet by 200 feet.* **8. measure up, a.** to reach a certain level or standard: *The exhibition didn't measure up to last year's.* **b.** to have the right qualifications: *He didn't quite measure up, so we didn't hire him.* —*Idiom.* **9. for good measure,** as an extra: *In addition to dessert, they served chocolates for good measure.*

meas•ured /ˈmɛʒərd/ *adj.* slow, careful, and deliberate: *He spoke in soft, measured tones.*

meas•ure•ment /ˈmɛʒərmənt/ *n.* **1.** [*noncount*] the act of measuring. **2.** [*count*] the number representing the extent, size, etc., determined by measuring: *The measurements of the house are 100 feet by 200 feet.* **3.** [*noncount*] a system of measuring: *liquid measurement.*

meas•ur•ing /ˈmɛʒərɪŋ/ *adj.* [*before a noun*] used for making a measurement: *a measuring spoon.*

meat /miyt/ *n.* **1.** the flesh of animals used for food: [*noncount*]: *Is the meat fresh?* [*count*]: *Different meats were displayed behind the counter.* **2.** [*count*] the part of something that can be eaten, as a nut. **3.** [*noncount*] important or valuable content, points, or part (of something): *Her article had some clever phrases but not much meat.* —**meat•y,** *adj.,* -**i•er,** -**i•est.**

meat•ball /ˈmiyt,bɔl/ *n.* [*count*] a small ball of seasoned ground meat.

mec•ca /ˈmɛkə/ *n.* [*count*] a place that attracts many people with some interest in common: *a mecca for the film industry.*

me•chan•ic /məˈkænɪk/ *n.* [*count*] one who repairs machinery, or who is skilled in the use of tools and equipment: *an auto mechanic.*

me•chan•i•cal /məˈkænɪkəl/ *adj.* **1.** of, relating to, or operated by machinery: *He has no mechanical skills; a mechanical toy.* **2.** lacking freshness; dull or done by habit: *a mechanical job that required no thinking.* **3.** of or relating to the study of mechanics. —**me'chan•i•cal•ly,** *adv.*

me•chan•ics /məˈkænɪks/ *n.* **1.** [*noncount; used with a singular verb*] the branch of physics that deals with the action of forces on bodies and with motion. **2.** [*plural; the* + ~ + *of; used with a plural verb*] the practical procedures or techniques involved in an activity: *the mechanics of running a household.*

mech•an•ism /ˈmɛkə,nɪzəm/ *n.* [*count*] **1.** an assembly of moving parts performing a function: *The alarm mechanism is jammed.* **2.** the way or means by which an effect is produced: *the language-learning mechanism in the human brain.*

mech•a•nize /ˈmɛkə,nayz/ *v.* [~ + *obj*], -**nized,** -**niz•ing.** to make mechanical; to operate by machinery. —**mech•a•ni•za•tion** /ˌmɛkənɪˈzeyʃən/, *n.* [*noncount*]: *Will mechanization in the industry result in a loss of jobs?*

med•al /ˈmɛdl/ *n.* [*count*] a flat piece of metal with a design on it, awarded as a sign of victory or for bravery, merit, or the like.

me•dal•lion /məˈdælyən/ *n.* [*count*] an ornament resembling a medal.

med•dle /ˈmɛdl/ *v.* [*no obj*], -**dled,** -**dling.** to involve oneself in a matter without right or invitation: *Stop meddling in our affairs and leave us alone!* —**med•dler,** *n.* [*count*] —**med•dle•some** /ˈmɛdlsəm/, *adj.*

me•di•a /ˈmiydiyə/ *n.* **1.** [*plural*] a pl. of MEDIUM. **2.** [*the* + ~] [*used with a plural or singular*

verb] the means of mass communication, as radio, television, and magazines, with wide reach and influence: *The media is surely not to blame for the defeat of our candidate. The media have a responsibility to be accurate and fair.*

me•di•an /ˈmiydiyən/ *adj.* [*usually: before a noun*] **1.** situated in or relating to the middle: *a low median income.* —*n.* [*count*] **2.** the middle number in a sequence of numbers, or the average of the middle two numbers of an even-numbered sequence: *4 is the median of 1, 3, 4, 8, 9; 7 is the median of 1, 3, 5, 9, 26, 55.* **3.** a straight line from an angle of a triangle to the midpoint of the opposite side. **4.** Also called **'median 'strip.** a strip in the middle of a highway designed to separate opposite lanes of traffic.

me•di•ate /ˈmiydiy,eyt/ *v.,* -**at•ed,** -**at•ing.** to attempt to settle (a dispute) between two opposing sides: [*no obj*]: *The UN president agreed to mediate.* [~ + *obj*]: *She agreed to mediate the dispute.* —**me•di•a•tion** /ˌmiydiyˈeyʃən/, *n.* [*noncount*] —**'me•di,a•tor,** *n.* [*count*]

Med•i•caid /ˈmɛdɪ,keyd/ *n.* a government program of medical insurance for the poor.

med•i•cal /ˈmɛdɪkəl/ *adj.* [*before a noun*] of or relating to medicine. —**'med•i•cal•ly,** *adv.*

Med•i•care /ˈmɛdɪ,kɛər/ *n.* a government program of medical insurance for the aged or disabled.

med•i•cate /ˈmɛdɪ,keyt/ *v.* [~ + *obj*], -**cat•ed,** -**cat•ing.** to treat with medicine or put medicine in: *The cough drops are medicated.*

med•i•ca•tion /ˌmɛdɪˈkeyʃən/ *n.* a medicine: [*noncount*]: *The doctor prescribed medication for the pain.* [*count*]: *Her medications were very costly.*

me•dic•i•nal /məˈdɪsənəl/ *adj.* of or relating to a medicine: *That soda has a medicinal taste.* —**me'dic•i•nal•ly,** *adv.*

med•i•cine /ˈmɛdəsɪn/ *n.* **1.** [*count*] a substance used in treating disease or illness. **2.** [*noncount*] the art or science of preserving health and treating disease.

me•di•e•val /ˌmiydiyˈiyvəl, ˌmɛdiy-, ˌmɪdiy-, mɪdˈiyvəl/ *adj.* of, relating to, or characteristic of the Middle Ages: *medieval architecture.* —**,me•di'e•val•ist,** *n.* [*count*]

me•di•o•cre /ˌmiydiyˈowkər/ *adj.* of ordinary quality; barely adequate. —**me•di•oc•ri•ty** /ˌmiydiyˈɒkrɪtiy/, *n.* [*noncount*]

med•i•tate /ˈmɛdɪ,teyt/ *v.* [*no obj*], -**tat•ed,** -**tat•ing.** **1.** to think calmly, carefully, and thoroughly about something. **2.** to try to achieve a calm, relaxed state of mind, as by deep breathing: *He meditates as part of his yoga training.* —**med•i•ta•tion** /ˌmɛdɪˈteyʃən/ *n.* [*noncount*] [*count*] —**'med•i,ta•tive,** *adj.*

me•di•um /ˈmiydiyəm/ *n., pl.* -**di•a** /-diyə/ for 1–4, -**di•ums** for 5, *adj.* —*n.* [*count*] **1.** a middle state or condition: *He had reached a happy medium: not too rich, not too poor.* **2.** a substance, as air, through which a force acts or is carried: *the medium of air, through which sound waves travel.* **3.** a means by which something is accomplished or created: *Words are a medium of expression.* **4.** one of the means of general communication or entertainment in society, as newspapers or television. **5.** a person through whom the spirits of the dead are supposedly able to contact the living. —*adj.* [*usually: before a noun*] **6.** halfway between extremes in degree, quantity, position, or quality: *He was of medium build.*

med•ley /'mɛdliy/ n. [count], pl. **-leys.** a piece of music combining passages from various sources: a medley of songs from the 1950's.

meek /miyk/ adj., **-er, -est. 1.** humbly patient. **2.** timid; spiritless; tame. —**'meek•ly,** adv. —**'meek•ness,** n. [noncount]

meet /miyt/ v., **met** /mɛt/, **meet•ing,** n. —v. **1.** to come into the presence of or encounter; to come together at an agreed place or time: [~ + obj]: I met him on the street yesterday. Meet me at noon at the usual place. [no obj]: We met at the reunion. The directors will meet on Tuesday. **2.** to be introduced to or become acquainted (with): [~ + obj]: I've never met your cousin. [no obj]: "Yes, we've already met," she said. **3.** [~ + obj] to come to the notice of: A strange sight met my eyes. **4.** to form a connection: [no obj]: The two streets meet in front of our house. [~ + obj]: His eyes met hers. **5.** [~ + obj] to comply with: to meet a deadline. **6. meet with,** to receive; experience: Your proposal met with a lot of opposition. —n. [count] **7.** an assembly for athletic or sports competition, as for racing: a track meet.

meet•ing /'miytɪŋ/ n. [count] **1.** the act of encountering or coming together: Our meeting was a complete accident. **2.** a scheduled assembly or conference: the last meeting of the parents' group. **3.** a point of contact: the meeting of two roads.

mega-, a combining form meaning: large or great (megavitamin); 1,000,000 times a given unit of measure (megaton).

meg•a•hertz /'mɛgə,hɜrts/ n. [count], pl. **-hertz, -hertz•es.** a unit of frequency equal to one million cycles per second.

meg•a•phone /'mɛgə,fown/ n. [count] a cone-shaped device for making the voice louder.

meg•a•ton /'mɛgə,tʌn/ n. [count] **1.** one million tons. **2.** an explosive force equal to that of one million tons of TNT.

mel•an•chol•y /'mɛlən,kɒliy/ n. [noncount] **1.** a gloomy state of mind. —adj. **2.** affected with or causing melancholy: a melancholy mood; a melancholy song.

me•lee or **mê•lée** /'meyley, mey'ley, 'mɛley/ n. [count] a state of confusion: a wild melee of shouting and screaming.

mel•low /'mɛlow/ adj., **-er, -est,** v. —adj. **1.** sweet and full-flavored from ripeness. **2.** soft and rich, as sound or colors: the mellow sound of the muted trumpet. **3.** made gentle by age or maturity: He became mellow after his retirement. —v. **4.** to (cause to) become mellow: [no obj]: The music mellowed as the band settled into a quiet mood. [~ + obj]: The years have mellowed her.

mel•o•dra•ma /'mɛlə,drɑmə, -,dræmə/ n. [count], pl. **-mas.** a play, film, etc., that exaggerates emotion and emphasizes plot or action. —**mel•o•dra•mat•ic** /,mɛlədrə'mætɪk/ adj.

mel•o•dy /'mɛlədiy/ n. [count], pl. **-dies.** a pleasing sequence of musical notes; a tune. —**me•lod•ic** /mə'lɒdɪk/, **me•lo•di•ous** /mə'lowdiyəs/ adj.

mel•on /'mɛlən/ n. the fruit of any of various plants of the gourd family, as the watermelon: [noncount]: I had some melon for breakfast. [count]: Melons were unavailable at that time of year.

melt /mɛlt/ v. **1.** to (cause to) become liquid by heat: [no obj]: In just a few hours the snow melted. [~ + obj]: The hot sun melted the snow. **2.** [no obj] to dissolve: candies melting in your mouth. **3.** to become softened in feel-ing: [no obj]: Her heart melted in response to his letter. [~ + obj]: a story to melt your heart. **4.** [no obj] to (cause to) become less or nothing: His fortune slowly melted away.

melt•down /'mɛlt,dawn/ n. [count] **1.** the melting of the core of a nuclear reactor, due to inadequate cooling of the fuel elements. **2.** any quickly developing breakdown or accident.

'melting ,pot, n. [count] a country or situation in which a blending of races, peoples, etc., takes place: the traditional description of the United States as a melting pot.

mem•ber /'mɛmbər/ n. [count] **1.** an individual forming part of a group: a member of the House of Representatives. **2.** a limb, as a leg, arm, or wing.

mem•ber•ship /'mɛmbər,ʃɪp/ n. **1.** [noncount] the state of being a member: Membership entitles you to free parking. **2.** [count; usually singular] the total number of members belonging to an organization: The membership of the group has declined recently.

mem•brane /'mɛmbreyn/ n. [count] a thin layer of tissue that covers an organ, etc. —**mem•bra•nous** /'mɛmbrənəs/, adj.

me•men•to /mə'mɛntow/ n. [count], pl. **-tos, -toes.** something that serves as a reminder of what is past or gone; a souvenir: mementos of her trip.

mem•o /'mɛmow/ n. [count], pl. **mem•os.** a memorandum.

mem•oir /'mɛmwɑr, -wɔr/ n. [count] a record of events based on the writer's personal observation and experience.

mem•o•ra•bil•i•a /,mɛmərə'bɪliyə, -'bɪlyə/ n. [plural] mementos or souvenirs that are collected and kept.

mem•o•ra•ble /'mɛmərəbəl/ adj. worth remembering; outstanding: a memorable performance. —**'mem•o•ra•bly,** adv.

mem•o•ran•dum /,mɛmə'rændəm/ n. [count], pl. **-dums, -da** /-də/. a written message, esp. one between employees of a company; memo.

me•mo•ri•al /mə'mɔriyəl/ n. [count] **1.** something designed to preserve the memory of a person, etc., as a monument: a memorial to the war dead. —adj. **2.** serving to preserve the memory: memorial services.

mem•o•rize /'mɛmə,rayz/ v. [~ + obj], **-rized, -riz•ing.** to learn (something) completely so that it can be repeated exactly: to memorize a poem. —**mem•o•ri•za•tion** /,mɛmərɪ'zeyʃən/, n. [noncount]

mem•o•ry /'mɛməriy/ n., pl. **-ries. 1.** the mental ability to keep and recall facts, events, or experiences: [noncount]: short-term memory. He recited it from memory (= without written notes). [count]: Both of them have excellent memories. **2.** [noncount] the length of time over which remembering extends: within living memory (= within the memory of persons now alive). **3.** [count] a mental picture kept in the mind; a recollection: memories of summer at the beach. **4.** [noncount] Also called **storage. a.** the capacity of a computer to store information. **b.** the components of the computer in which such information is stored: He bought extra memory and installed it in his computer. —**Idiom. 5. in memory of,** in honor of a fondly remembered person.

men /mɛn/ n. pl. of MAN.

men•ace /'mɛnɪs/ n., v., **-aced, -ac•ing.** —n. [count] **1.** someone or something that threatens to cause evil, etc.; a threat: He is a menace to soci-

ety and should be locked away. —*v.* [~ + *obj*] **2.** to threaten; put in danger: *A gang menaced the students.* —'**men•ac•ing,** *adj.*

me•nag•er•ie /mə'nædʒəriy, -'næʒ-/ *n.* [*count*] **1.** a collection of animals, esp. for displaying. **2.** an unusual group of people.

mend /mɛnd/ *v.* [~ + *obj*] **1.** to make (something damaged) better by repairing: *to mend torn clothes.* **2.** to set right; improve: *See if you can mend matters between them.* —*n.* [*count*] **3.** a mended part. —*Idiom.* **4. mend one's ways,** to improve one's behavior: *He mended his ways and became a useful citizen.* **5. on the mend,** improving, esp. in health: *The patient was on the mend.*

me•ni•al /'miyniyəl, 'miynyəl/ *adj.* of or suitable for servants; humble; lowly: *menial work.* —'**me•ni•al•ly,** *adv.*

men•o•pause /'mɛnə,pɔz/ *n.* [*noncount*] the time when a woman's menstruation naturally stops. —,**men•o'pau•sal,** *adj.*

me•nor•ah /mə'nɔrə/ *n.* [*count*] a special candleholder used during the Jewish festival of Hanukkah.

'**men's room,** *n.* [*count*] a public bathroom for men.

men•stru•al /'mɛnstruwəl/ *adj.* [*before a noun*] of or relating to menstruation: *menstrual flow.*

men•stru•a•tion /,mɛnstruw'eyʃən, -'strey-/ *n.* [*noncount*] the periodic flow of blood and tissue from a woman's uterus. —'**men•stru,ate,** *v.* [*no obj*], **-ated, -ating.**

-ment, a suffix meaning: an action or resulting state (*government; abridgment*); a product (*fragment*); a means (*ornament*).

men•tal /'mɛntl/ *adj.* [*before a noun*] **1.** of or relating to the mind: *mental capacity.* **2.** of or relating to a disorder of the mind: *a mental patient.* —'**men•tal•ly,** *adv.: mentally ill.*

men•tal•i•ty /mɛn'tælɪtiy/ *n., pl.* **-ties. 1.** [*noncount*] mental capacity; the ability of the mind: *superior mentality.* **2.** [*count*] a person's mental outlook: *a bossy mentality.*

'**mental retar'dation,** *n.* [*noncount*] a developmental disorder impairing the ability of a person to learn and to mature in other ways.

men•tion /'mɛnʃən/ *v.* [~ + *obj*] **1.** to refer briefly to; speak of: *Did she mention my name? Did I mention that we're leaving in five minutes?* —*n.* [*noncount*] **2.** an incidental reference: *The dog barked at the mention of its master's name.* **3.** formal recognition for a noteworthy act: *He received honorable mention for his essay.* —*Idiom.* **4. Don't mention it.** This phrase is used as a polite answer to someone who has thanked you for your help: *"Thanks for everything." "-Don't mention it; I was glad to help."*

men•tor /'mɛntɔr, -tər/ *n.* [*count*] **1.** a trusted counselor or teacher. —*v.* [~ + *obj*] [*no obj*] **2.** to act as a mentor to.

men•u /'mɛnyuw/ *n.* [*count*], *pl.* **men•us. 1.** a list of the items served at a meal or available for ordering, as at a restaurant. **2.** a list of items from which to choose, as of options available to a computer user.

mer•ce•nar•y /'mɜrsə,nɛriy/ *adj., n., pl.* **-nar• ies.** —*adj.* **1.** working for money and not for ideals: *She'd become mercenary and no longer cared about the quality of her work.* **2.** hired to serve in a foreign army: *mercenary forces.* —*n.* [*count*] **3.** a professional soldier hired to serve in a foreign army.

mer•chan•dise /*n.* 'mɜrtʃən,dayz, -,days; *v.*

-,dayz/ *n., v.,* **-dised, -dis•ing.** —*n.* [*noncount*] **1.** goods bought and sold. —*v.* [*no obj*] **2.** to carry on trade.

mer•chant /'mɜrtʃənt/ *n.* [*count*] **1.** a storekeeper; retailer. —*adj.* [*before a noun*] **2.** used for trade or commerce: *a merchant ship.*

'**merchant ma'rine,** *n.* [*noncount*] **1.** the ships of a nation that work in commerce. **2.** the officers and crews of such ships.

mer•ci•ful /'mɜrsɪfəl/ *adj.* **1.** showing mercy to another: *a merciful judge.* **2.** fortunate: *a merciful release from the pain.* —'**mer•ci,ful•ly,** *adv.*

mer•ci•less /'mɜrsɪlɪs/ *adj.* **1.** having or showing no mercy: *merciless to his enemies.* **2.** harsh; difficult: *merciless snowstorms.* —'**mer•ci•less•ly,** *adv.*

mer•cu•ry /'mɜrkyəriy/ *n.* [*noncount*] a heavy, silver-white element, liquid at room temperature: *Mercury is used in thermometers.*

mer•cy /'mɜrsiy/ *n.* [*noncount*] **1.** compassion or kindness shown toward an offender or an enemy: *to show no mercy toward enemies.* —*Idiom.* **2. at the mercy of,** entirely in the power of; dependent on the kindness of.

'**mercy ,killing,** *n.* EUTHANASIA.

mere•ly /'mɪərliy/ *adv.* only (and nothing more); just; simply: *Instead of making a fuss, he merely said he was sorry.*

merge /mɜrdʒ/ *v.,* **merged, merg•ing.** to (cause to) become combined; (cause to) lose identity by blending: [*no obj*]: *The two rivers merge at that city.* [~ + *obj*]: *We merged the two branch offices.*

merg•er /'mɜrdʒər/ *n.* [*count*] a combining of corporations by transferring the two properties into one corporation.

me•rid•i•an /mə'rɪdiyən/ *n.* [*count*] **1.** a great circle of the earth passing from one pole to another. **2.** the half of such a circle between the poles.

me•ringue /mə'ræŋ/ *n.* [*count*] a dessert made of stiffly beaten egg whites sweetened with sugar.

mer•it /'mɛrɪt/ *n.* **1.** [*noncount*] claim to respect and praise; excellence; worth: *She received a pay raise on the basis of merit.* **2.** [*count*] something that deserves praise; desirable quality: *Its chief merit is simplicity.* —*v.* [~ + *obj*] **3.** to be worthy of; deserve: *Do you think this case merits further discussion?*

mer•ri•ment /'mɛrɪmənt/ *n.* [*noncount*] cheerful or joyful behavior; enjoyment; mirth.

mer•ry /'mɛriy/ *adj.,* **-ri•er, -ri•est.** full of cheerfulness or joy; joyous in spirit. —'**mer•ri•ly,** *adv.*

'**merry-go-,round,** *n.* [*count*] a revolving circular platform with wooden horses, benches, etc., on which people ride, as at an amusement park.

mer•ry•mak•ing /'mɛriy,meykɪŋ/ *n.* [*noncount*] the act of taking part gaily or joyfully in some festivity. —'**mer•ry,mak•er,** *n.* [*count*]

me•sa /'meysə/ *n.* [*count*], *pl.* **-sas.** a land formation having steep sides and a relatively flat top, common in the southwestern U.S.

mesh /mɛʃ/ *n.* [*noncount*] **1.** an arrangement of interlocking metal links used in jewelry, sieves, etc. **2.** any fabric of open texture resembling a net: *stockings of mesh.* —*v.* **3.** [*no obj*] [~ + *obj*] to (cause to) become or be engaged, as the teeth of gears. **4.** [*no obj*] to match, coordinate, or fit together: *Her ideas meshed with mine.*

mes•mer•ize /'mɛzmə,rayz, 'mɛs-/ *v.* [~ + *obj*], **-ized, -iz•ing.** to keep the attention of; fascinate or spellbind: *Television mesmerizes the children.*

mess /mɛs/ n. **1.** [count; singular] a dirty or disorderly state: Things are in a mess here. **2.** [count; usually singular] an unpleasant situation; trouble: Look at the mess you've gotten us into now. **3.** [count] a meal regularly eaten together by a group of people, as soldiers. —v. **4.** [~ + obj] to make dirty or untidy: Please, you're messing (up) my hair. **5. mess around** or **about, a.** to busy oneself without purpose; waste time: He was just messing around. **b.** to involve oneself, esp. for unlawful purposes or in some dangerous way: to mess around with gamblers. **c.** to have sexual affairs: to mess around with other women. **6. mess up,** to perform something poorly; spoil or ruin: It's your big chance, so don't mess up. They messed up our plans. **7. mess with,** to become involved with (someone or something dangerous): Don't mess with drugs. —'mess•y, adj., -i•er, -i•est.

mes•sage /ˈmɛsɪdʒ/ n. [count] **1.** a communication delivered in writing, speech, etc.: There was a message at the hotel for me. **2.** the main point of something, as of a speech or book: The message of the movie was clear: war is horrible. —*Idiom.* **3. get the message,** to understand a warning sent: She doesn't get the message that her work is not satisfactory.

mes•sen•ger /ˈmɛsəndʒər/ n. [count] a person who carries messages or parcels.

Mes•si•ah /mɪˈsaɪə/ n. **1.** the promised deliverer of the Jewish people. **2.** [usually: the + ~] Jesus, regarded by Christians as fulfilling this promise. —**Mes•si•an•ic** /ˌmɛsiˈænɪk/, adj. [before a noun]

Messrs. /ˈmɛsərz/ pl. of Mr.

met /mɛt/ v. pt. and pp. of MEET¹.

meta-, a prefix meaning: after (metaphysics); beyond (metalinguistics); change (metamorphosis).

me•tab•o•lism /məˈtæbəˌlɪzəm/ n. the physical and chemical processes in a living body by which it is maintained: [noncount]: studying the metabolism of dolphins. [count]: He has a very active metabolism. —**met•a•bol•ic** /ˌmɛtəˈbɒlɪk/ adj.

met•al /ˈmɛtl/ n. [noncount] [count] **1.** a usually solid, shiny, basic substance, as gold, silver, or copper, that can be used to conduct electricity or heat. **2.** an alloy or mixture of such substances, as brass. —**me•tal•lic** /məˈtælɪk/ adj.

met•al•lur•gy /ˈmɛtlˌɜrdʒiy/ n. [noncount] the science of metals, including their properties and uses. —**met•al,lur•gist,** n. [count]

met•a•mor•pho•sis /ˌmɛtəˈmɔrfəsɪs/ n., pl. -ses /-ˌsiyz/. **1.** [noncount] [count] a significant change in form from one stage to the next in the life history of a living thing, as from the caterpillar to the pupa to the butterfly. **2.** [count] any complete change in appearance, character, etc.: Professional baseball is undergoing a complete metamorphosis.

met•a•phor /ˈmɛtəˌfɔr, -fər/ n. [count] a way of describing another object or thing by suggesting a comparison of it to something else, but without using the word "like" or "as": The rose is often a metaphor for love in poetry. —,met•a'phor•i•cal, adj.

mete /miyt/ v. [~ + obj], **met•ed, met•ing.** to distribute by measure; allot: to mete out punishment.

me•te•or /ˈmiytiyər, -ˌɔr/ n. [count] **1.** a meteoroid that has entered the earth's atmosphere. **2.** a fiery streak in the sky produced by a meteoroid passing through the earth's atmosphere.

me•te•or•ic /ˌmiytiyˈɔrɪk, -ˈɒr-/ adj. resembling

a meteor in quick brilliance, suddenness of appearance, etc.: a meteoric rise to fame.

me•te•or•ite /ˈmiytiyəˌrayt/ n. [count] **1.** the remains of a meteoroid that has reached the earth from outer space. **2.** a meteoroid.

me•te•or•oid /ˈmiytiyəˌrɔyd/ n. [count] a small body of rock or metal traveling through space that, upon entering the earth's atmosphere, is heated to glowing and becomes a meteor.

me•te•or•ol•o•gy /ˌmiytiyəˈrɒlədʒiy/ n. [noncount] the science dealing with the atmosphere, weather, and climate. —,me•te•or'ol•o•gist, n. [count]

me•ter¹ /ˈmiytər/ n. [count] a unit of length, equivalent to 39.37 inches.

me•ter² /ˈmiytər/ n. [noncount] the rhythmic element, defined by patterns of beats and accents, in music or poetry.

me•ter³ /ˈmiytər/ n. [count] an instrument for measuring and recording the quantity of something, as of water, miles, or time: an electric meter.

meth•a•done /ˈmɛθəˌdown/ n. [noncount] an artificially produced narcotic similar to morphine but taken orally: Methadone is used as a heroin substitute.

meth•ane /ˈmɛθeyn/ n. [noncount] a colorless, odorless gas that can be burned.

meth•od /ˈmɛθəd/ n. **1.** [count] a procedure, technique, or planned way of doing something: There are several methods we could use to recover your lost data. **2.** [noncount] order or system in doing anything: There's no method to your work. —**meth•od•i•cal** /məˈθɒdɪkəl/ adj.

Meth•od•ist /ˈmɛθədɪst/ n. [count] a member of a Christian group founded by John Wesley.

me•tic•u•lous /məˈtɪkyələs/ adj. taking or showing extreme care about small details. —**me•tic•u•lous•ly,** adv. —**me•tic•u•lous•ness,** n. [noncount]

me•tre /ˈmiytər/ n. Chiefly Brit. METER.

met•ric /ˈmɛtrɪk/ adj. [before a noun] relating to the meter or to the metric system.

met•ri•cal /ˈmɛtrɪkəl/ also **metric,** adj. **1.** relating to or composed in meter. **2.** relating to measurement. —**'met•ri•cal•ly,** adv.

'metric ,system, n. [count] a decimal system of weights and measures, universally used in science and the official system of measurement in many countries.

'metric 'ton, n. [count] a unit of 1000 kilograms, equivalent to 2204.62 pounds.

met•ro /ˈmɛtrow/ n. [count] [noncount], pl. -ros. [often: Metro] the underground railway of certain cities, as Washington, D.C., and Paris, France.

met•ro•nome /ˈmɛtrəˌnowm/ n. [count] an instrument used to mark rhythm in practicing music by means of repeated clicking sounds at an adjustable pace.

me•trop•o•lis /mɪˈtrɒpəlɪs/ n. [count], pl. -lis•es. the chief city of a country or region.

met•ro•pol•i•tan /ˌmɛtrəˈpɒlɪtn/ adj. **1.** of or relating to a metropolis: Storms are expected in the metropolitan area tonight. **2.** of or like a metropolis in being sophisticated: a metropolitan outlook.

met•tle /ˈmɛtl/ n. [noncount] **1.** courage or willingness to do a task: a man of mettle. **2.** disposition or temperament: of fine mettle.

mew /myuw/ n. [count] **1.** the high-pitched cry

of a cat. —*v.* [*no obj*] **2.** to make a mew or similar sound.

Mex•i•can /ˈmɛksɪkən/ *adj.* **1.** of or relating to Mexico. —*n.* [*count*] **2.** a person born or living in Mexico.

mez•za•nine /ˈmɛzəˌniyn, ˌmɛzəˈniyn/ *n.* [*count*] **1.** the lowest balcony in a theater: *seats in the mezzanine.* **2.** a low-ceilinged story between two other stories, usually immediately above the ground floor.

mfg., an abbreviation of: manufacturing.

mfr., an abbreviation of: **1.** manufacture. **2.** *pl.* **mfrs.** manufacturer.

mg, an abbreviation of: milligram.

MHz, an abbreviation of: megahertz.

MI, an abbreviation of: Michigan.

mi., an abbreviation of: **1.** mile. **2.** mill.

mice /mays/ *n.* pl. of MOUSE.

Mich., an abbreviation of: Michigan.

micro-, a prefix meaning: very small (*microfilm*); microscopic (*microorganism*); one millionth (*micron*).

mi•crobe /ˈmaykrowb/ *n.* [*count*] a microorganism, esp. a disease-causing bacterium.

mi•cro•brew•er•y /ˈmaykrowˌbruwəriy, -ˌbruriy/ *n.* [*count*], *pl.* **-er•ies.** a small brewery usually producing unique or high quality beer.

mi•cro•chip /ˈmaykrowˌtʃɪp/ *n.* CHIP¹ (def. 5).

mi•cro•com•put•er /ˈmaykrowkəmˌpyuwtər/ *n.* [*count*] a compact computer having less power than a minicomputer.

mi•cro•cosm /ˈmaykrəˌkɒzəm/ *n.* [*count*] a world in miniature that has all the features of a larger world: *The problems in our community are a microcosm of what is happening around the country.*

mi•cro•fiche /ˈmaykrəˌfiyʃ/ *n.,* *pl.* **-fiche, -fich•es.** a flat sheet of microfilm: [*noncount*]: *documents available on microfiche.* [*count*]: *a machine to read microfiches.*

mi•cro•film /ˈmaykrəˌfɪlm/ *n.* [*noncount*] [*count*] **1.** a film bearing a miniature photographic copy of printed matter, as of newspaper pages. —*v.* [~ + *obj*] **2.** to make a microfilm of.

mi•cron /ˈmaykrɒn/ *n.* [*count*], *pl.* **-crons, -cra** /-krə/. the millionth part of a meter.

mi•cro•or•gan•ism /ˌmaykrowˈɔrgəˌnɪzəm/ *n.* [*count*] any organism too small to be viewed by the unaided eye, as bacteria.

mi•cro•phone /ˈmaykrəˌfown/ *n.* [*count*] an instrument that changes sound waves into electric currents, used in recording or transmitting sound.

mi•cro•proc•es•sor /ˈmaykrowˌprɒsɛsər, -əsər/ *n.* [*count*] a small computer circuit that performs all the functions of a CPU.

mi•cro•scope /ˈmaykrəˌskowp/ *n.* [*count*] an instrument having a magnifying lens, used for viewing objects too small to be seen by the unaided eye.

mi•cro•scop•ic /ˌmaykrəˈskɒpɪk/ *adj.* **1.** very small; tiny: *a microscopic organism.* **2.** using a microscope: *a microscopic examination.* —**mi•cro'scop•i•cal•ly,** *adv.*

mi•cro•sur•ger•y /ˈmaykrowˌsɜrdʒəriy, ˌmaykrowˈsɜr-/ *n.* [*noncount*] a surgical procedure performed under magnification and with specialized instruments.

mi•cro•wave /ˈmaykrowˌweyv/ *n., v.,* **-waved, -wav•ing.** —*n.* [*count*] **1.** an electromagnetic wave of extremely high frequency. **2.** a microwave oven. —*v.* [~ + *obj*] **3.** to cook or heat in a microwave oven. —**mi•cro•wav•a•ble,** *adj.*

¹microwave ˌoven, *n.* [*count*] an electrically operated oven that uses microwaves to generate heat.

mid¹ /mɪd/ *adj.* [*before a noun*] being at or near the middle point of: *in mid autumn.*

mid² or **'mid** /mɪd/ *prep.* AMID.

mid-, a combining form meaning at or near the middle point of: (*midday; mid-Victorian; mid-twentieth century*).

mid•air /ˈmɪdˈɛər/ *n.* [*noncount*] **1.** any point in the air not touching the earth: *The helicopter hovered in midair.* —*adj.* [*before a noun*] **2.** occurring in midair: *a midair collision.*

mid•day /*n.*ˈmɪdˈdey, -ˌdey; *adj.* -ˌdey/ *n.* [*noncount*] **1.** the middle of the day: *The sun is highest at midday.* —*adj.* [*before a noun*] **2.** of, relating to, or occurring at the middle part of the day: *a midday news broadcast.*

mid•dle /ˈmɪdl/ *adj.* [*before a noun*] **1.** in or near the center; central: *the middle part of a room.* —*n.* [*count; usually singular*] **2.** the point, part, time, etc., that is at an equal distance from extremes, limits, or starting and ending points: *in the middle of the pool.*

'middle 'age, *n.* [*noncount*] the period of human life between youth and old age, usually considered as the years between 45 and 65. —**'middle-'aged,** *adj.*

'Middle 'Ages, *n.* [*plural; the* + ~] the time in European history from the late fifth century to about 1500.

'middle 'class, *n.* [*count*] a class of people intermediate between those of higher and lower economic or social standing. —**'middle-'class,** *adj.*

mid•dle•man /ˈmɪdlˌmæn/ *n.* [*count*], *pl.* **-men. 1.** one who buys goods from a producer and resells them to retailers or consumers. **2.** a person who communicates with disputing parties to try to settle a conflict.

'middle-of-the-'road, *adj.* favoring an intermediate position between two extremes, esp. in politics.

'middle ˌschool, *n.* [*count*] [*noncount*] a school for grades five or six through eight.

midg•et /ˈmɪdʒɪt/ *n.* [*count*] **1.** a very small person. **2.** any animal or thing that is very small for its kind. —*adj.* [*before a noun*] **3.** very small or of a class below the usual size; miniature.

mid•i /ˈmɪdiy/ *n.* [*count*], *pl.* **mid•is.** a garment, as a coat, extending to the middle of the calf.

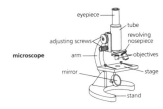

microscope — eyepiece, tube, revolving nosepiece, adjusting screws, arm, objectives, mirror, stage, stand

mid•land /ˈmɪdlənd/ *n.* [*count; usually: the* + ~] **1.** the middle or interior part of a country. —*adj.* [*before a noun*] **2.** in or of the midland; inland.

mid•night /ˈmɪdˌnayt/ *n.* [*noncount; usually: no article*] **1.** twelve o'clock at night: *to stay up past midnight.* —*adj.* [*before a noun*] **2.** of or relating to midnight: *a midnight swim.*

'midnight 'sun, *n.* [*noncount; the* + ~] the

sun that is visible at midnight during the summer in the Arctic and Antarctic.

mid•point /'mɪd,pɔynt/ n. [count] a point at or near the middle of something, as a line: *the midpoint of the trip.*

mid•riff /'mɪdrɪf/ n. [count] the middle portion of the human body, between the chest and the waist.

midst /mɪdst/ n. [noncount] **1.** the position of being among other things or parts: *in the midst of the crowd.* **2.** the state of being engaged in: *He was in the midst of work when the phone rang.*

mid•stream /'mɪd'striym/ n. [noncount] the middle of a stream.

mid•term /'mɪd,tɜrm/ n. **1.** [noncount] the halfway point of a term, as a term of office. **2.** [count] an examination given halfway through a school term. —*adj.* [before a noun] **3.** relating to, at, or near the middle of a term: *a midterm vacation.*

mid•town /'mɪd,tawn, -,tawn/ n. [noncount] **1.** the central part of a city, between uptown and downtown. —*adj.* [before a noun] **2.** of, relating to, or located in this part: *a midtown café.*

mid•way /'mɪd'wey/ adj., adv. in the middle of the way; halfway: [adjective; before a noun]: *the midway point of the project.* [adverb]: *positioned midway between the two warring sides.*

mid•week /'mɪd,wiyk/ adj. [before a noun] relating to or occurring in the middle of the week: *a midweek conference.*

mid•wife /'mɪd,wayf/ n. [count], pl. **-wives.** a woman who assists women during childbirth.

might[1] /mayt/ auxiliary (modal) v. [~ + root form of a verb], pres. sing. and pl. **might;** past **might. 1. a.** (used to express an uncertain possibility): *It might rain. You might be right.* **b.** (used with regard to something that did not happen, but for which there was a strong possibility): *I can't believe he did that; he might have been killed!* **c.** (used to express that some action is or would have been a good idea): *They might at least have tried to get there on time.* **d.** (used to suggest some action): *You might begin by apologizing to her.* **e.** (used to politely ask for something or for permission): *Might I speak to you for a moment?* **2.** pt. of MAY[1]: *I asked if we might borrow their car.* **3.** (used to express that one thing follows another, esp. in clauses that convey condition, limitation, purpose, or result): *Let's agree on this so that we might go home early. Difficult as it might be, we managed to do it.*

might[2] /mayt/ n. [noncount] superior strength; force: *He didn't believe that might makes right.*

might•y /'maytiy/ adj., **-i•er, -i•est,** n. —*adj.* **1.** having or showing might: *mighty rulers.* **2.** great in amount, extent, or importance: *a mighty accomplishment.* —*n.* [noncount] **3.** mighty persons considered as a group: *How the mighty have fallen!* —**might•i•ly** /'maytḷiy/, adv.

mi•graine /'maygreyn/ n. [count] [noncount] a severe, repeated headache, with pressure or throbbing.

mi•grant /'maygrənt/ adj. [before a noun] **1.** migrating: *migrant workers.* —*n.* [count] **2.** a person or animal that migrates. **3.** Also called **'mi•grant ,worker.** one who moves from place to place to get work.

mi•grate /'maygreyt/ v. [no obj], **-grat•ed, -grat•ing. 1.** to move from one country, region, or place to another: *migrating from the farms to the cities.* **2.** to pass at regular periods from one region to another, as certain birds: *The birds mi-*

grated south for the winter. —**mi•gra•tion** /may'greyʃən/, n. [count] [noncount] —**mi•gra•to•ry** /'maygrə,tɔriy/, adj.

mike /mayk/ n., v., **miked, mik•ing.** —*n.* [count] **1.** a microphone. —*v.* [~ + obj] **2.** to supply or amplify with a microphone, as a singer.

mild /mayld/ adj., **-er, -est. 1.** gentle or soft in feeling, manner, etc.: *a mild disposition.* **2.** not severe or extreme; temperate: *a mild winter.* **3.** moderate in strength, degree, or force: *a mild drug; a mild fever.* —**'mild•ly,** adv.: *He spoke mildly to us.* —**'mild•ness,** n. [noncount]

mil•dew /'mɪl,duw, -,dyuw/ n. [noncount] **1.** a cottony coating on plants, fabrics, etc., caused by fungi: *mildew on the pages of the old diary.* —*v.* **2.** to (cause to) become affected with mildew: [no obj]: *The book had mildewed over the years.* [~ + obj]: *The book had been mildewed by moisture.*

mile /mayl/ n. [count] **1.** a unit of distance on land in English-speaking countries equal to 5280 feet, or 1760 yards (1.609 kilometers). **2.** NAUTICAL MILE.

mile•age /'maylɪdʒ/ n. [noncount] **1.** the total number of miles traveled in a given time: *The mileage for our trip was over 2000.* **2.** the number of miles or average distance that a vehicle can travel on a quantity of fuel: *This van's mileage is about 20 miles per gallon.*

mile•post /'mayl,powst/ n. [count] any one of a series of posts set up to mark distance by miles, as along a highway.

mile•stone /'mayl,stown/ n. [count] **1.** a stone that functions as a milepost. **2.** a significant or important event in history: *The fall of Communism was one of the milestones of the twentieth century.*

mi•lieu /mɪl'yu/ n. [count], pl. **mi•lieus** /mɪl'yuz, miyl-/, **mi•lieux** /Fr. miy'lyœ/. surroundings; environment: *an exciting social milieu.*

mil•i•tant /'mɪlɪtənt/ adj. **1.** strongly aggressive, esp. in support of a cause: *militant reformers.* —*n.* [count] **2.** a militant person: *Militants staged violent demonstrations.* —**'mil•i•tan•cy,** n. [noncount] —**'mil•i•tant•ly,** adv.

mil•i•ta•rism /'mɪlɪtə,rɪzəm/ n. [noncount] a strong military spirit or policy; commitment to the maintenance of a large military establishment. —,**mil•i•ta'ris•tic,** adj.

mil•i•tar•y /'mɪlɪ,teriy/ adj., n., pl. **-tar•y,** sometimes **-tar•ies.** —*adj.* [before a noun] **1.** of or relating to the army, the armed forces, soldiers, or war-making. —*n.* **2. the military, a.** [noncount; used with a singular verb] the armed forces of a nation; the military establishment: *The military does not want him to become president.* **b.** [plural; used with a plural verb] military personnel: *The military were not treating civilians kindly.*

mi•li•tia /mɪ'lɪʃə/ n. [count] a body of citizens enrolled for military service, serving full time only in emergencies. —**mi'li•tia•man,** n. [count], pl. **-men.**

milk /mɪlk/ n. [noncount] **1.** a white liquid produced by the mammary glands of female mammals, serving to nourish their young. **2.** this liquid from cows and other animals, used by humans for food or to make butter, cheese, etc.: *a glass of milk.* —*v.* [~ + obj] **3.** to draw milk from the udder or breast of: *He milked the cows twice every day.* —*Idiom.* **4. cry over spilled milk,** to regret past actions or events that cannot be changed or corrected. —'**milk•y**, *adj.*, **-i•er, -i•est.**

milk•man /'mɪlk,mæn/ *n.* [*count*], *pl.* **-men.** a person who sells or delivers milk.

'**milk of mag'nesia**, *n.* [*noncount*] a milky white liquid to control stomach acids or as a laxative.

'**milk ,shake** or '**milk,shake**, *n.* [*count*] a beverage blended of milk, flavoring, and ice cream.

milk•weed /'mɪlk,wiyd/ *n.* [*count*] a plant having a milky juice and clusters of white-to-purple flowers.

'**Milky 'Way**, *n.* the spiral-shaped galaxy containing our solar system.

mill /mɪl/ *n.* [*count*] **1.** a factory for certain kinds of manufacture, as steel or textiles. **2.** a building with machinery for grinding grain into flour. —*v.* **3.** [~ + *obj*] to grind, work, or shape in or with a mill: *The men milled the wheat into flour.* **4.** [*no obj*] to move slowly around without aim or purpose, or in confusion: *After the accident the crowd milled around.*

mil•len•ni•um /mɪ'lɛniyəm/ *n.* [*count*], *pl.* **-ni•ums, -ni•a** /-niyə/. **1.** a period of 1000 years: *to view history through the millennia.* **2.** a thousandth anniversary. —**mil'len•ni•al**, *adj.*

mill•er /'mɪlər/ *n.* [*count*] a person who owns or operates a mill, esp. a mill that grinds grain.

milli-, a combining form meaning: thousand (*millipede*); thousandth (*millimeter*).

mil•li•gram /'mɪlɪ,græm/ *n.* [*count*] a unit of mass or weight equal to ¹/₁₀₀₀ of a gram.

mil•li•li•ter /'mɪlə,liytər/ *n.* [*count*] a unit of volume equal to ¹/₁₀₀₀ of a liter, equivalent to 0. 033815 fluid ounce.

mil•li•me•ter /'mɪlə,miytər/ *n.* [*count*] a unit of length equal to ¹/₁₀₀₀ of a meter, equivalent to 0. 03937 inch.

mil•lion /'mɪlyən/ *n.*, *pl.* **-lions,** (*as after a numeral*) **-lion,** *adj.* —*n.* [*count*] **1.** a number, 1000 times 1000. **2.** a very great number or amount: *Thanks a million; millions of things to do.* —*adj.* **3.** amounting to one million in number: *Two million dollars is a lot to pay.* —'**mil•lionth**, *adj.*, *n.* [*count*]

mil•lion•aire or **mil•lion•naire** /,mɪlyə'nɛər, 'mɪlyə,nɛər/ *n.* [*count*] one whose wealth amounts to a million or more in some unit of currency, as dollars.

mil•li•pede or **mil•le•pede** /'mɪlə,piyd/ *n.* [*count*] a small creature having a long, rounded body of many segments, each with two pairs of legs.

mime /maym/ *n.*, *v.*, **mimed, mim•ing.** —*n.* **1.** [*noncount*] the art or technique of portraying a character, mood, or story by body movements without words; pantomime. **2.** [*count*] an actor who specializes in this art. —*v.* **3.** [~ + *obj*] to mimic; show one's meaning by actions: *I mimed turning a steering wheel to indicate that I wanted to rent a car.* **4.** [*no obj*] to act in mime.

mim•ic /'mɪmɪk/ *v.*, **-icked, -ick•ing,** *n.* —*v.* [~ + *obj*] **1.** to imitate or copy in action, speech, etc., often playfully, sometimes to insult another: *He mimicked the teacher's scolding.* —*n.* [*count*] **2.** a person or thing that mimics, esp. a performer.

mi•mo•sa /mɪ'mowsə, -zə/ *n.* [*count*], *pl.* **-sas.** a plant, shrub, or tree of warm regions, having small flowers in rounded heads.

min., an abbreviation of: **1.** minimum. **2.** minor. **3.** minute.

mince /mɪns/ *v.*, **minced, minc•ing. 1.** [~ + *obj*] to chop into very small pieces: *meat that has been minced.* **2.** [~ + *obj*] to soften or moderate, esp. for the sake of politeness: *He was angry and didn't mince words.* **3.** to move with short, unnaturally dainty steps: [*no obj*]: *He minced across the room.* [~ + *obj*]: *He minced his way across the room.*

mind /maynd/ *n.* **1.** [*count*] the part in a conscious being that reasons, thinks, feels, wills, perceives, judges, etc. **2.** intellectual power or ability: *a first-class mind.* **3.** a person considered with reference to intellectual ability: *the greatest minds of the century.* **4.** [*count*] sanity or a sound, healthy mental condition: *losing his mind.* **5.** [*count*] opinion, view, or sentiments: *I've changed my mind.* **6.** [*noncount*] remembrance or recollection; memory: *to call to mind.* **7.** [*count*] attention; thoughts: *He can't keep his mind on his studies.* —*v.* **8.** [~ + *obj*] to pay attention to: *Don't mind me; just pretend I'm not here.* **9.** to be careful about: *Mind your manners.* **10.** [~ + *obj*] to look after; take care of; attend to: *Who's minding the children? Mind your own business.* **11.** [~ + *obj*; often with a negative word or phrase, or in questions] to feel concern at; care about; object to: *I wouldn't mind a drink right about now.* (= *I would like to have a drink.*) *I wouldn't mind having that drink now. Do you mind if I smoke?* **12.** [~ + *obj*] to obey: *Mind your parents.* —*Idiom.* **13.** **bear** or **keep (something) in mind,** to hold in one's memory; remember: *Bear in mind that your taxes are due. Keep that fact in mind.* **14.** **never mind,** This phrase is used to express: **a.** comfort to another after something unfortunate has happened: *Never mind about that broken window.* **b.** the attitude that something is not important. **15.** **on one's mind,** in one's thoughts; of concern to one: *You've been on my mind lately.* **16.** **out of one's mind, a.** insane; mad. **b.** emotionally overwhelmed; frantic: *out of my mind with worry.*

mind•ed /'mayndɪd/ *adj.* having a certain kind of mind (usually used in combination): *strong-minded; sports-minded.*

mind•ful /'mayndfəl/ *adj.* [*usually:* be + ~ + *of*] attentive; aware: *Be mindful of the consequences.* —'**mind•ful•ly**, *adv.* —'**mind•ful•ness**, *n.* [*noncount*]

mind•less /'mayndlɪs/ *adj.* **1.** using or requiring no intelligence: *a boring, mindless job.* **2.** [be + ~ + *of*] refusing to worry or think about; heedless: *He was mindless of all the dangers.* **3.** stupid; thoughtless: *mindless violence.*

mine[1] /mayn/ *pron.* **1.** the form of the pronoun *I* used to show possession after the verb *be*: *The yellow sweater is mine.* **2.** the form of the pronoun *I* used to refer to a thing or things that belong to the speaker: *Mine is on the left. He was a good friend of mine.*

mine[2] /mayn/ *n.*, *v.*, **mined, min•ing.** —*n.* [*count*] **1.** an area dug up for minerals, as ore, coal, or precious stones. **2.** an abundant source; store: *a mine of information.* **3.** an explosive device placed in the ground or in the water. —*v.* **4.** to dig in (the earth) for extracting a mineral substance: [*no obj*]: *They mined for a year before striking gold.* [~ + *obj*]: *to mine an area for years.* **5.** [~ + *obj*] to place mines, as in military or naval operations: *to mine the entrance to the harbor.* —'**min•er**, *n.* [*count*]

mine•field /'maynfiyld/ *n.* [*count*] an area of land or water throughout which explosive mines have been laid.

min•er•al /'mɪnərəl, 'mɪnrəl/ n. [count] **1.** a substance occurring in nature, of definite chemical composition and usually of definite crystal structure: *Coal, iron, salt, and tin are minerals.* **2.** an inorganic element, as calcium, etc., essential to the functioning of the human body: *vitamins and minerals.* **3.** a substance that is neither animal nor vegetable.

min•er•al•o•gy /ˌmɪnəˈrɒlədʒiy, -ˈrælə-/ n. [noncount] the study of minerals. —ˌmin•er'al•o•gist, n. [count]

'mineral ˌoil, n. [noncount] a colorless, oily, almost tasteless oil obtained from petroleum.

'mineral ˌwater, n. [noncount] water containing dissolved mineral salts or gases.

min•e•stro•ne /ˌmɪnəˈstrowniy/ n. [noncount] a thick vegetable soup.

min•gle /'mɪŋgəl/ v., **-gled, -gling.** to mix or combine; put together in a mixture; blend: [no obj]: *His shouts mingled with those of other survivors.* [~ + obj]: *His account mingled truth with exaggerations.*

min•i /'mɪniy/ n. [count], pl. **min•is. 1.** MINISKIRT. **2.** anything small of its kind.

mini-, a combining form meaning: smaller than others of its kind (*minibike*); very short (*miniskirt*).

min•i•a•ture /'mɪniyətʃər, 'mɪnətʃər/ n. [count] **1.** a representation or image of something on a small or reduced scale. **2.** something small of its class or kind. —adj. [before a noun] **3.** represented on a small scale; reduced: *a miniature poodle.*

min•i•bus /'mɪniyˌbʌs/ n. [count] a small bus typically used for transporting people short distances.

min•i•com•put•er /'mɪniykəmˌpyuwtər/ n. [count] a computer with processing and storage capabilities smaller than those of a mainframe but larger than those of a microcomputer.

min•i•mal /'mɪnəməl/ adj. making up or being a minimum; barely adequate or the least possible: *a minimal weight loss of two pounds a week.* —'min•i•mal•ly, adv.

min•i•mize /'mɪnəˌmayz/ v. [~ + obj], **-mized, -miz•ing. 1.** to reduce to the smallest possible amount or degree: *to minimize their losses.* **2.** to make something seem of low value; belittle: *My father kept minimizing my accomplishments.*

min•i•mum /'mɪnəməm/ n. [count] **1.** the least amount possible, allowable, or needed: *to work a minimum of six hours a day.* —adj. [before a noun] **2.** of or relating to a minimum: *a minimum stay of five days.*

min•i•se•ries /'mɪniyˌsɪəriyz/ n. [count], pl. **-ries.** a television program broadcast in parts over several days.

min•i•skirt /'mɪniyˌskɜrt/ n. [count] a short skirt ending several inches above the knee.

min•is•ter /'mɪnəstər/ n. [count] **1.** a person with authority to conduct religious worship. **2.** a person appointed to a high office of state, esp. as head of an administrative department: *a foreign minister.* **3.** a diplomatic representative ranking below an ambassador. —v. **4. minister to,** to give service, care, or aid: *to minister to the needs of the hungry.*

min•is•try /'mɪnəstriy/ n., pl. **-tries. 1.** [count; usually singular; the + ~] the body or class of ministers of religion; clergy. **2.** [count] an administrative department headed by a government minister: *the ministry of defense.*

min•i•van /'mɪniyˌvæn/ n. [count] a small passenger van, usually seating six or more people.

mink /mɪŋk/ n., pl. **minks,** (esp. when thought of as a group) **mink. 1.** [count] a weasel of North America and of Europe and Asia. **2.** [noncount] the soft, shiny fur of this animal: *a coat of mink.*

Minn., an abbreviation of: Minnesota.

min•now /'mɪnow/ n. [count], pl. (esp. for kinds or species) **-nows,** (esp. when thought of as a group; rare) **-now.** a small freshwater fish.

mi•nor /'maynər/ adj. **1.** lesser, as in size, extent, or rank: *a minor role.* **2.** under full legal age. **3.** of or relating to a student's academic minor: *minor subjects.* —n. [count] **4.** a person under full legal age. **5. a.** a subject or course of knowledge studied secondarily to a major subject or course. **b.** a student studying such a subject. —v. [no obj] **6.** to choose or study as a secondary academic subject: *to minor in biology.*

mi•nor•i•ty /mɪˈnɔrɪtiy, -ˈnɒr-, may-/ n., pl. **-ties,** adj. —n. [count] **1.** a number, part, or amount forming less than half of the whole: *He got a minority of the votes in his first election.* **2.** a smaller group opposed to a majority: *a minority of the stockholders.* **3.** Also called **mi'nority ˌgroup.** a group differing, esp. in race, religion, or ethnic background, from the majority of a population. —adj. **4.** [before a noun] of or relating to a minority: *a minority opinion.*

mint¹ /mɪnt/ n. **1.** [noncount] a sweet-smelling herb, such as the peppermint. **2.** [count] a mint-flavored candy. —adj. [before a noun] **3.** flavored with mint: *mint tea.*

mint² /mɪnt/ n. [count] **1.** a place where coins, etc., are produced under government authority. —adj. **2.** being in its original condition, as if newly made: *an old car in mint condition.* —v. [~ + obj] **3.** to make (money) by stamping metal: *to mint coins.*

min•u•et /ˌmɪnyuwˈɛt/ n. [count] **1.** a slow, stately dance in triple meter. **2.** a piece of music for such a dance.

mi•nus /'maynəs/ prep. **1.** less by the subtraction of: *Ten minus six is four.* **2.** lacking or without: *What you have is a play minus a last act.* —adj. **3.** indicating subtraction: *a minus sign.* **4.** algebraically negative: *a minus quantity.* **5.** [after a noun] (of school grades) less than; just below: *to get a C minus on a test* (= to get a grade just below C). **6.** [before a number] (in stating a temperature) the number of degrees below zero: *a temperature of minus 40* (= a temperature of 40 degrees below zero). —n. [count] **7.** MINUS SIGN. **8.** a minus quantity. **9.** a deficiency or loss.

mi•nus•cule /'mɪnəˌskyuwl, mɪˈnʌskyuwl/ adj. very small.

'minus ˌsign, n. [count] the symbol (−) that indicates subtraction or a negative quantity.

min•ute¹ /'mɪnɪt/ n. [count] **1.** the sixtieth part (¹/₆₀) of an hour; 60 seconds. **2.** any short space of time: *Give me a few minutes; I'll be right there.* **3. minutes,** [plural] the official record of the proceedings of a meeting: *The minutes have several errors.* **4.** Geometry. the sixtieth part of a degree in measuring angles, often represented by the sign '. —Idiom. **5.** the last minute, the last moment of time: *waited until the last minute before handing in her test.* **6. up to the minute,** modern; up-to-date: *His clothes were always up to the minute.*

mi•nute² /may'nuwt, -'nyuwt, mɪ-/ adj., **-nut•er, -nut•est.** extremely small, as in size or degree: *minute differences.*

mir•a•cle /ˈmɪrəkəl/ n. [count] **1.** a supernatural or divine event or happening: Jesus was said to have performed a number of miracles. **2.** a superb or extraordinary example of something; a marvel: It was a miracle that the pilot landed the plane in that snowstorm. —**mi•rac•u•lous** /mɪˈrækyələs/ adj.

mi•rage /mɪˈrɑʒ/ n. [count] an image one sees, esp. in the desert, of an object that is not present; an illusion: so thirsty that they saw mirages of lakes.

mir•ror /ˈmɪrər/ n. [count] **1.** a reflecting surface, usually of glass with a silvery backing: She looked in the mirror to comb her hair. **2.** something that gives a faithful reflection or mental picture of something else: Gershwin's music was a mirror of its time. —v. [~ + obj] **3.** to reflect as if in a mirror: The gray sea mirrored the rainy sky. **4.** to be or give a good reflection or representation of: His editorial columns mirror the opinions of many Americans.

mirth /mɜrθ/ n. [noncount] amusement, esp. with laughter: the mirth of the holiday season.

mis-, a prefix meaning: wrong (misconduct); wrongly (misjudge); lack of (mistrust).

mis•ad•ven•ture /ˌmɪsədˈvɛntʃər/ n. [noncount] [count] misfortune; mishap.

mis•an•dry /ˈmɪsændriy/ n. [noncount] hatred of or hostility toward men.

mis•an•thrope /ˈmɪsənˌθrowp, ˈmɪz-/ also **mis•an•thro•pist** /mɪsˈænθrəpɪst, mɪz-/ n. [count] one who hates all human beings. —**mis•an•throp•ic** /ˌmɪsənˈθrɒpɪk, ˌmɪz-/, adj. —**mis•an•thro•py** /mɪsˈænθrəpiy/, n. [noncount]

mis•ap•pre•hend /ˌmɪsæprɪˈhɛnd/ v. [~ + obj] to misunderstand. —**mis•ap•pre•hen•sion** /ˌmɪsæprɪˈhɛnʃən/, n. [count]: under a grave misapprehension that things were proceeding smoothly. [noncount]: blaming mistakes on misapprehension.

mis•ap•pro•pri•ate /ˌmɪsəˈprowpriy,eyt/ v. [~ + obj], **-at•ed, -at•ing.** to apply wrongfully or dishonestly, as funds that were placed in one's care: The dishonest manager misappropriated funds. —**mis•ap•pro•pri•a•tion** /ˌmɪsəˌprowpriyˈeyʃən/, n. [noncount] [count]

mis•be•have /ˌmɪsbɪˈheyv/ v., **-haved, -hav•ing.** to behave badly or improperly: [no obj]: misbehaving in church. [~ + oneself]: misbehaving himself at parties. —, **mis•be•hav•ior,** n. [noncount]

mis•cal•cu•late /mɪsˈkælkyəˌleyt/ v., **-lated, -lat•ing.** to make a mistake in counting: [no obj]: I miscalculated when adding the figures. [~ + obj]: He miscalculated the total. **2.** to make an error in judging: [no obj]: The candidate miscalculated badly. [~ + obj]: She miscalculated the opposition to her proposal. —**mis•cal•cu•la•tion** /ˌmɪskælkyəˈleyʃən/, n. [count] [noncount]

mis•car•riage /ˌmɪsˈkærɪdʒ, ˈmɪsˌkær-/ n. [count] **1.** the birth of a dead offspring: She suffered a miscarriage during her last pregnancy. **2.** a failure to attain a desirable or appropriate result: a miscarriage of justice.

mis•car•ry /mɪsˈkæriy/ v. [no obj], **-ried, -ry•ing. 1.** to have a miscarriage of a fetus. **2.** to fail to attain the right or desirable end; be unsuccessful: The plan miscarried.

mis•cast /mɪsˈkæst/ v. [~ + obj], **-cast, -cast•ing.** to cast (an actor) in an unsuitable role.

mis•cel•la•ne•ous /ˌmɪsəˈleyniyəs/ adj. made up of parts of different kinds; of or having mixed character, kinds, etc.: The party attracted a miscellaneous group of people.

mis•cel•la•ny /ˈmɪsəˌleyniy/ n. [count], pl. **-nies.** a collection or mixture of various items or parts.

mis•chief /ˈmɪstʃɪf/ n. [noncount] **1.** conduct or activity that causes slight annoyance: The children were always getting into mischief. **2.** harm or injury; damage.

mis•chie•vous /ˈmɪstʃəvəs/ adj. **1.** maliciously or playfully annoying: The mischievous boys stole apples from the neighbor's tree. **2.** harmful; causing damage or trouble. —ˈmis•chie•vous•ly, adv. —ˈmis•chie•vous•ness, n. [noncount]

mis•con•ceived /ˌmɪskənˈsiyvd/ adj. poorly planned; not carefully or properly thought through: the government's misconceived foreign policy.

mis•con•cep•tion /ˌmɪskənˈsɛpʃən/ n. [count] a mistaken or erroneous idea: a major misconception about AIDS.

mis•con•duct /mɪsˈkɒndʌkt/ n. [noncount] improper behavior, esp. by an official in office, or in the administration of justice: official misconduct as mayor.

mis•con•strue /ˌmɪskənˈstruw/ v. [~ + obj], **-strued, -stru•ing.** to misunderstand the meaning of; misinterpret: I don't want my words to be misconstrued. —**mis•con•struc•tion** /ˌmɪskənˈstrʌkʃən/, n. [noncount] [count]

mis•count /v.mɪsˈkawnt; n. ˈmɪsˌkawnt/ v. [no obj] [~ + obj] **1.** to count incorrectly. —n. [count] **2.** an incorrect counting: a miscount in the last census.

mis•deed /mɪsˈdiyd/ n. [count] an immoral deed.

mis•de•mean•or /ˌmɪsdɪˈmiynər/ n. [count] **1.** a criminal offense less serious than a felony. **2.** an instance of misbehavior.

mis•di•al v. [~ + obj] [no obj] to dial (a phone number) incorrectly.

mis•di•rect /ˌmɪsdɪˈrɛkt/ v. [~ + obj] **1.** to direct, instruct, or address wrongly: to misdirect a person to the wrong office. **2.** to make use of wrongly or unwisely: He misdirected all his energy.

mi•ser /ˈmayzər/ n. [count] a person who saves his or her money and doesn't like to spend it. —ˈmi•ser•ly, adj.

mis•er•a•ble /ˈmɪzərəbəl, ˈmɪzrə-/ adj. unfortunate, unhappy, or uncomfortable: Her illness made her miserable. —ˈmis•er•a•bly, adv.: He failed miserably in his last few games.

mis•er•y /ˈmɪzəriy/ n., pl. **-er•ies.** extreme unhappiness; great suffering: [noncount]: the misery he felt after his defeat. [count]: home and job miseries.

mis•fire /mɪsˈfɪʳr/ v. [no obj], **-fired, -fir•ing. 1.** to fail to fire or ignite properly: The engine was sputtering and misfiring. **2.** to fail to achieve the desired result or have the desired effect: His criticisms misfired completely.

mis•fit / mɪsˈfɪt, ˈmɪsˌfɪt/ n. [count] one not suited or able to adjust to his or her circumstances or situation: a social misfit; a misfit in his new job.

mis•for•tune /mɪsˈfɔrtʃən/ n. [noncount] bad fortune; bad luck.

mis•giv•ing /mɪsˈgɪvɪŋ/ n. [count] Often, misgivings. [plural] a feeling of doubt: He had a few misgivings about the plan.

mis•guid•ed /mɪsˈgaydɪd/ adj. wrong because

of bad judgment: *a few misguided attempts to take over the business.*

mis•hap /'mɪshæp, mɪs'hæp/ *n.* an unfortunate event; an accident: [count]: *We had a little mishap on the way over here.* [noncount]: *They flew through the snowstorm without mishap.*

mish•mash /'mɪʃ,mɑʃ, -,mæʃ/ also **mish•mosh** /'mɪʃ,mɒʃ/ *n.* [noncount] a confused mess; hodgepodge.

mis•in•form /,mɪsɪn'fɔrm/ *v.* [~ + obj] to give false or misleading information to. —**mis•in•for•ma•tion** /,mɪsɪnfər'meyʃən/ *n.* [noncount]

mis•in•ter•pret /,mɪsɪn'tɜrprɪt/ *v.* [~ + obj] to interpret incorrectly: *to misinterpret her quiet anger as agreement.* —**mis•in•ter•pre•ta•tion** /,mɪsɪn,tɜr'prɪteyʃən/, *n.* [noncount]: *a speech open to misinterpretation.* [count]: *numerous misinterpretations to be cleared up.*

mis•judge /mɪs'dʒʌdʒ/ *v.* [~ + obj], **-judged, -judg•ing.** to judge or form an opinion incorrectly or unjustly: *If I misjudged you, I'm sorry.* —**mis'judg•ment,** *n.* [count] [noncount]

mis•lay /mɪs'ley/ *v.* [~ + obj], **-laid, -lay•ing.** to lose temporarily; misplace.

mis•lead /mɪs'liyd/ *v.* [~ + obj], **-led, -lead•ing.** to lead (someone) into error; lead astray: *I was misled into believing he was honest.*

mis•lead•ing /,mɪs'liydɪŋ/ *adj.* intended to deceive: *We gave the spy misleading information.*

mis•man•age /mɪs'mænɪdʒ/ *v.* [~ + obj], **-aged, -ag•ing.** to manage poorly or dishonestly: *She had mismanaged the funds.* —**mis'man'age•ment,** *n.* [noncount]

mis•no•mer /mɪs'nowmər/ *n.* [count] a misapplied or inappropriate name or designation: *To call him a professional is a misnomer.*

mi•sog•y•ny /mɪ'sɒdʒəniy, may-/ *n.* [noncount] hatred of or hostility toward women. —**mi'sog•y•nist,** *n.* [count]

mis•place /mɪs'pleys/ *v.* [~ + obj], **-placed, -plac•ing. 1.** to put in a wrong place. **2.** to place or bestow improperly or unwisely: *He misplaced his trust in her.* —**mis'placed,** *adj.*: *misplaced loyalties.*

mis•play /n. mɪs'pley, 'mɪs,pley/ *v.* mɪs'pley/ *n.* [count] **1.** a wrong or bad play. —*v.* [~ + obj] **2.** to make an error or incorrect play with: *The catcher misplayed the ball.*

mis•print /n. 'mɪs,prɪnt, mɪs'prɪnt/ *v.* mɪs'prɪnt/ *n.* [count] **1.** a mistake in printing: *The misprints in the headline were pretty obvious.* —*v.* [~ + obj] **2.** to print incorrectly: *They misprinted the sign.*

mis•pro•nounce /,mɪsprə'nawns/ *v.* [~ + obj], **-nounced, -nounc•ing.** to pronounce incorrectly. —**mis•pro•nun•ci•a•tion** /,mɪsprə,nʌnsiy'eyʃən/, *n.* [noncount]: *mispronunciation of the French vowels.* [count]: *a list of common mispronunciations.*

mis•quote /mɪs'kwowt/ *v.*, **-quot•ed, -quot•ing,** *n.* —*v.* [~ + obj] **1.** to quote incorrectly. —*n.* [count] **2.** Also, **mis•quo•ta•tion** /,mɪskwow'teyʃən/. an incorrect quotation.

mis•read /mɪs'riyd/ *v.* [~ + obj], **-read** /-rɛd/, **-read•ing. 1.** to read wrongly: *I misread the date.* **2.** to misunderstand: *We misread the dictator's intentions.*

mis•rep•re•sent /,mɪsrɛprɪ'zɛnt/ *v.* [~ + obj] to represent incorrectly or falsely: *The candidate's position was misrepresented in her opponent's TV ads.* —**mis•rep•re•sen•ta•tion** /,mɪsrɛprɪzən'teyʃən/, *n.* [noncount] [count]

miss¹ /mɪs/ *v.* **1.** to fail to hit: [~ + obj]: *The batter missed the first pitch.* [no obj]: *He swung and missed.* **2.** [~ + obj] to fail to meet, catch, etc.: *to miss a train.* **3.** [~ + obj] to fail to take advantage of: *I missed a chance to meet him.* **4.** [~ + obj] to notice the absence or loss of: *When did you first miss your wallet?* **5.** [~ + obj] to regret the absence or loss of: *I miss you all. He missed watching the African sunsets.* **6.** [~ + obj] to fail to understand: *to miss the point of a remark.* **7. miss out,** to fail to experience or take advantage of something: *They missed out on an opportunity to improve their financial situation.* —*n.* [count] **8.** a failure of any kind, esp. a failure to hit something: *a couple of swings and misses and the game is over.*

miss² /mɪs/ *n.,* pl. **miss•es. 1.** [*Miss*] This word is used as a title of respect before the name of an unmarried woman: *Miss Mary Jones.* **2.** [*Miss*] This word is used as a polite form of address to a young woman: *Miss, please bring me some ketchup.* **3.** [*Miss*] This word is used as a title before the name of a place, or a quality, that a young woman has been selected to represent: *Miss America; Miss Politeness.* **4.** ms. (def. 2). **5.** [count] a young unmarried woman; girl.

Miss., an abbreviation of: Mississippi.

mis•shape /mɪs'ʃeyp, mɪʃ-/ *v.* [~ + obj], **-shaped, -shaped** or **-shap•en, -shap•ing.** to shape badly or wrongly; deform. —**mis'shap•en,** *adj.*

mis•sile /'mɪsəl/ *n.* [count] **1.** an object or weapon propelled at a target, as a stone, bullet, etc. **2.** a rocket-propelled weapon.

miss•ing /'mɪsɪŋ/ *adj.* lacking, absent, or not found: *the missing murder weapon.*

mis•sion /'mɪʃən/ *n.* [count] **1.** a committee sent to a foreign country to conduct negotiations, establish relations, etc.: *a fact-finding mission to the Caribbean.* **2.** a group of people sent by a church to carry on religious and other work in other countries. **3.** a specific task that one is sent to perform: *on a mission of mercy.* **4.** one's chosen duty or task: *His mission in life was to educate the illiterate.* **5.** a place providing charity, as food or shelter, for the poor.

mis•sion•ar•y /'mɪʃə,nɛriy/ *n.* [count], pl. **-ar•ies,** /'mɪʃənər/. a person sent by a church into an area to carry on religious or humanitarian work: *a missionary in Africa.*

mis•spell /mɪs'spɛl/ *v.* [~ + obj], **-spelled** or **-spelt, -spell•ing.** to spell incorrectly: *misspelling simple words.* —**mis'spell•ing,** *n.* [count]: *Many of his misspellings involved simple words.* [noncount]: *too much misspelling.*

mis•spend /mɪs'spɛnd/ *v.* [~ + obj], **-spent, -spend•ing.** to spend wrongly or unwisely: *My brother misspent his inheritance.*

mis•state /mɪs'steyt/ *v.* [~ + obj], **-stat•ed, -stat•ing.** to state wrongly or misleadingly; make a wrong statement about: *You misstated your true intentions.* —**mis'state•ment,** *n.* [count]

mis•step /mɪs'stɛp/ *n.* [count] **1.** a wrong step: *One misstep and you'll fall down the mountain.* **2.** an error in conduct: *some missteps during his interview.*

mist /mɪst/ *n.* **1.** a mass of tiny drops of water, resembling fog: [noncount]: *driving through mist.* [count]: *heavy mists.* **2.** [count] a cloud of particles resembling this: *a mist of perfume.* —*v.* **3.** to (cause to) become covered with tiny drops of water: [no obj]: *His eyes misted (over) when he told us about his missing dog.* [~ + obj]: *The humidity misted the car window.* **4.** [no obj; it ~ ~] to

M

rain in very fine drops; drizzle: *It was misting, not quite raining.* —'**mist•y,** *adj.,* -**i•er,** -**i•est.**

mis•take /mɪˈsteyk/ *n., v.,* -**took,** -**tak•en,** -**tak•ing.** —*n.* [*count*] **1.** an error in action or judgment caused by poor reasoning, carelessness, etc.: *too many mistakes in grammar.* —*v.* [~ + *obj*] **2.** to identify wrongly as something or someone else: *I mistook her for the mayor.* **3.** to understand or interpret wrongly: *I must have mistaken the date.* —*Idiom.* **4. by mistake,** accidentally: *to set off the alarm by mistake.*

mis•tak•en /mɪˈsteykən/ *adj.* **1.** wrongly thought or done: *a mistaken notion; a mistaken strategy.* **2.** being in error; wrong: *If you think you'll get away with this, you are mistaken.* —**mis'tak•en•ly,** *adv.: I mistakenly assumed that you would be here.*

mis•ter /ˈmɪstər/ *n.* **1.** [*Mister*] This word is used as a title of respect before a man's name or position, and is usually written as *Mr.: Mr. Jones. "Mr. Mayor, what is your opinion?" they shouted.* **2.** [*singular*] This word is used as an informal term of address to a man: *Watch out, mister!*

mis•treat /mɪsˈtriyt/ *v.* [~ + *obj*] to treat badly or harmfully: *That dog's owner mistreats him terribly.* —**mis'treat•ment,** *n.* [*noncount*]

mis•tress /ˈmɪstrɪs/ *n.* [*count*] **1.** a woman who has authority, esp. the female head of a household: *The servant did whatever the mistress of the house ordered.* **2.** a woman who has a continuing sexual relationship with a man not married to her: *He had mistresses in several cities.*

mis•tri•al /ˈmɪsˌtrayl, ˈmɪstrayl/ *n.* [*count*] a trial forced to end without a decision, esp. because of an error in the proceedings or because the jury cannot agree: *The judge declared a mistrial.*

mis•trust /mɪsˈtrʌst/ *n.* [*noncount*] **1.** lack of trust or confidence; distrust: *eyes full of mistrust.* —*v.* [~ + *obj*] **2.** to regard or think about (someone) with doubt or suspicion; distrust: *I mistrust anyone who uses an initial for his first name.* —**mis'trust•ful,** *adj.: staring with mistrustful eyes.*

mis•un•der•stand /ˌmɪsʌndərˈstænd/ *v.,* -**stood,** -**stand•ing.** to interpret incorrectly; attach a wrong meaning to: [~ + *obj*]: *The radar operators misunderstood his orders.* [*no obj*]: *I think you misunderstood; please repeat the instructions.*

mis•un•der•stand•ing /ˌmɪsʌndərˈstændɪŋ/ *n.* **1.** a failure to understand: [*noncount*]: *The memo was a source of misunderstanding.* [*count*]: *a major misunderstanding during the peace talks.* **2.** [*count*] a disagreement or quarrel: *We had a misunderstanding, but now we're friends again.*

mis•use /*n.* mɪsˈyuws; *v.* -ˈyuwz/ *n., v.,* -**used,** -**us•ing.** —*n.* **1.** wrong or improper use: [*noncount*]: *The principal was dismissed for misuse of school funds.* [*count*]: *a misuse of the word "appropriately."* —*v.* [~ + *obj*] **2.** to use incorrectly: *to misuse a word.*

mite /mayt/ *n.* **1.** [*count; usually singular; a* ~ + *of*] a very small amount: *a mite of difficulty.* **2.** [*count*] a very small creature, person, or thing. —*Idiom.* **3. a mite,** somewhat; a bit: *could be a mite mean if he hasn't slept well.*

mit•i•gate /ˈmɪtɪˌgeyt/ *v.* [~ + *obj*], -**gat•ed,** -**gat•ing.** to lessen in force or intensity; make less severe: *to mitigate the harshness of a punishment.* —**mit•i•ga•tion** /ˌmɪtɪˈgeyʃən/, *n.* [*noncount*]

mitt /mɪt/ *n.* [*count*] **1.** a rounded, thickly pad-ded, mittenlike glove used by catchers in baseball. **2.** a mitten for a particular use: *an oven mitt.*

mit•ten /ˈmɪtn̩/ *n.* [*count*] a hand covering that surrounds the four fingers together and the thumb separately.

mix /mɪks/ *v.* **1.** to (cause to) become combined into one mass: [*no obj*]: *a paint that mixes with water.* [~ + *obj*]: *You can mix this paint with water.* **2.** [~ + *obj*] to combine or unite: *to mix business and pleasure.* **3.** [~ + *obj*] to form or make by combining ingredients: *to mix mortar.* **4. mix up, a.** to confuse completely: *He's all mixed up and doesn't know which way to go. He mixed me up by calling the meeting for today.* **b.** to mistake (one thing) for another: *He's always mixing the two of us up* or *He's always mixing up the two of us.* **c.** to rearrange the order of: *She mixed up the cards* or *She mixed the cards up.* —*n.* [*count*] **5.** a product of mixing; mixture: *a mix of concrete; an odd mix of people.* **6.** a commercial preparation to which usually only a liquid must be added before cooking or baking: *a cake mix.* —'**mix•a•ble,** *adj.* —'**mix•er,** *n.* [*count*]

mixed /mɪkst/ *adj.* [*before a noun*] **1.** made up of things that are different but of the same general type: *I ate some mixed nuts.* **2.** of or relating to persons of different religions or races: *a mixed marriage.* **3.** including contrasting, sometimes opposite elements or parts: *mixed emotions about going abroad.*

'**mixed-'up,** *adj.* confused or unstable: *a mixed-up kid.*

mix•er /ˈmɪksər/ *n.* [*count*] an electrical machine used for mixing things together.

mix•ture /ˈmɪkstʃər/ *n.* [*count*] **1.** a product of mixing: *Pour the mixture into the mold.* **2.** any blend of different elements: *a mixture of rock and classical music.*

mix-up /ˈmɪksˌʌp/ *n.* [*count*] a state of confusion or disorder; a mistake: *There must be a mix-up; we were told we didn't need reservations.*

ml, an abbreviation of: milliliter.

mm, an abbreviation of: millimeter.

MN, an abbreviation of: Minnesota.

mne•mon•ic /nɪˈmɒnɪk/ *adj.* **1.** assisting the memory: *He used a mnemonic device—a song—to memorize the names of the chemical elements.* —*n.* [*count*] **2.** something intended to assist the memory, as a song or formula.

MO, an abbreviation of: **1.** method or mode of operation. **2.** Missouri.

Mo., an abbreviation of: **1.** Missouri. **2.** Monday.

mo., *pl.* **mos.** an abbreviation of: month.

moan /mown/ *n.* [*count*] **1.** a low, sad, or miserable sound expressing suffering or complaint: *more moans about low pay.* —*v.* [*no obj*] **2.** to utter moans: *He moaned softly with pain.* **3.** to complain; grumble: *He's always moaning about being too busy.*

mob /mɒb/ *n., adj., v.,* **mobbed, mob•bing.** —*n.* [*count*] **1.** a disorderly crowd of people: *angry mobs of protesters.* **2.** *Informal.* a criminal gang involved in organized crime. —*adj.* [*before a noun*] **3.** of or by a disorderly crowd: *mob rule.* —*v.* [~ + *obj*] **4.** to crowd around noisily, as from curiosity or hostility: *Fans mobbed the actor.* **5.** to fill with people; crowd: *The theater was mobbed with people trying to get in.*

mo•bile /ˈmowbəl, -biyl/ *adj.* **1.** capable of moving or being moved easily or quickly: *My grandmother was still mobile when she was 99.* **2.** using a motor vehicle for easy movement from place to place: *a mobile x-ray unit.* —*n.* [count] **3.** a sculpture or other hanging device, usually having delicately balanced parts that can move independently, as when stirred by a breeze. —**mo·bil·i·ty** /mow'bɪlɪti/, *n.* [noncount]

'mobile 'home, *n.* [count] a large house trailer, designed for year-round living in one place.

'mobile 'phone, *n.* [count] any wireless telephone that operates over a relatively large area, as a cellular phone.

mo·bi·lize /'mowbə,layz/ *v.,* **-lized, -liz·ing.** to (cause to) assemble and prepare for war, action, or some other purpose: [~ + *obj*]: *She mobilized all her resources. Would the president mobilize troops?* [*no obj*]: *The whole country mobilized for war.* —**mo·bi·li·za·tion** /,mowbəlɪ'zeyʃən/, *n.* [noncount] [count]

mob·ster /'mɒbstər/ *n.* [count] a member of a criminal mob.

moc·ca·sin /'mɒkəsɪn, -zən/ *n.* [count] a shoe without a heel, made entirely of soft leather, as deerskin, worn originally by American Indians.

mo·cha /'mowkə/ *n.* [noncount] **1.** a variety of coffee, originally grown in Arabia. **2.** a flavoring obtained by blending coffee with chocolate.

mock /mɒk/ *v.* [~ + *obj*] **1.** to make fun of; to treat with ridicule or contempt: *They mocked him and called him a coward.* **2.** to imitate or mimic: *He mocked the way his teacher spoke.* —*adj.* [before a noun] **3.** deliberately faked, as for demonstration purposes; imitation: *a mock examination.* —**'mock·ing·ly,** *adv.*

mock·er·y /'mɒkəriy/ *n., pl.* **-er·ies. 1.** [noncount] the act of laughing at or making fun of something: *a target of mockery.* **2.** [count] something done poorly or badly: *The trial was a mockery of justice.*

mock·ing·bird /'mɒkɪŋ,bɜrd/ *n.* [count] a songbird that uses the calls of other bird species.

'mock-,up or **'mock,up,** *n.* [count] a model, often full-size, for study, testing, or teaching: *They strapped the pilot into a mock-up of the experimental aircraft.*

mod·al /'mowdl/ *adj.* A *modal verb* is used before an auxiliary or a main verb to indicate the speaker's attitude toward the action expressed by the main verb. Modal verbs in English are: CAN, COULD, MAY, MIGHT, MUST, OUGHT, SHALL, SHOULD, WILL and WOULD. Some characteristics of these verbs are: **1.** Modal verbs do not change in the present tense, third-person singular form: *I can run. He can run (He runs).* **2.** Modal verbs are followed by the root form of the next verb: *I can swim. She could have walked. He might be staying.* **3.** Modal verbs come before the word NOT in negative sentences: *I will not see you today. She won't be home.* **4.** Modal verbs come before the subject in questions: *Can I see you in your office? Will you be home tomorrow?* **5.** Modal verbs can stand alone when another main verb is understood but has been left out: *I'd like to talk with you now but I can't* (= *can't talk with you now*). *He'll be there, won't he?* (= *won't he be there?*) **6.** Modal verbs express different attitudes toward the action of the main verb. Some of these feelings include: possibility: *It might rain tomorrow;* ability: *He could lift a hundred pounds;* permission: *May I go home now?;* necessity: *It must be here somewhere!;* a suggestion: *We could have pizza tonight, I guess.* See each verb for more details.

mode¹ /mowd/ *n.* [count] a manner of acting or doing; method: *modes of transportation.*

mode² /mowd/ *n.* [count] fashion or style in manners, dress, etc.

mod·el /'mɒdl/ *n., adj., v.,* **-eled, -el·ing** or (*esp. Brit.*) **-elled, -el·ling.** —*n.* [count] **1.** a standard or example of something that can be used for imitation or comparison: *He is a model of hard work.* **2.** a copy, usually in miniature, to show the appearance of something: *a model of an airplane.* **3.** a person or thing that serves as a subject for an artist, etc.: *the model for the art class.* **4.** a style of a particular product, as a car, machine, etc.: *a new model every year.* **5.** a simplified representation of a system or of some event or action, proposed by scientists to explain or describe the event or action: *a model of the universe.* —*adj.* [before a noun] **6.** serving as an example or model: *They went through the model home.* **7.** worthy to serve as a model: *a model student.* **8.** being a miniature version of something: *model ships.* —*v.* **9.** [~ + *obj*] to make a model of: *to model airplanes out of wood.* **10.** [~ + *obj*] to display to other persons, esp. by wearing: *She modeled expensive dresses.* **11.** [no *obj*] to serve or be employed as a model: *I've modeled for several companies.* **12.** [~ + *obj*] to copy the qualities or character of another: *The scientists modeled the robots on a science-fiction story.*

mo·dem /'mowdəm, -dɛm/ *n.* [count] an electronic device that makes possible the transmission of data to or from a computer through telephone lines.

mod·er·ate /*adj., n.* 'mɒdərɪt, 'mɒdrɪt; *v.* -ə,reyt/ *adj., n., v.,* **-at·ed, -at·ing.** —*adj.* **1.** keeping within reasonable or proper limits: *moderate prices.* **2.** of medium quantity, extent, or amount: *a moderate income.* **3.** of or relating to moderates, as in politics or religion: *the moderate wing of the party.* —*n.* [count] **4.** one who is moderate in opinion or who is opposed to extreme views, as in politics. —*v.* **5.** to be at the head of or preside over (a public forum, etc.): [~ + *obj*]: *He moderated the last town meeting.* [no *obj*]: *He's good at moderating: he keeps the discussion moving.* —**'mod·er·ate·ly,** *adv.*

mod·er·a·tion /,mɒdə'reyʃən/ *n.* [noncount] **1.** restraint, esp. with respect to one's behavior or emotions: *Moderation in eating should keep your weight down.* **2.** reduction or reducing; lessening: *The drug brought some moderation of the pain.* —*Idiom.* **3. in moderation,** within reasonable or sensible limits: *Drinking in moderation will not damage his health.*

mod·er·a·tor /'mɒdə,reytər/ *n.* [count] a person presiding over a group event or meeting: *As the moderator, he decides who speaks and for how long.*

mod·ern /'mɒdərn/ *adj.* **1.** of or relating to present and recent time; contemporary. **2.** [before a noun] of or relating to certain styles of art, literature, etc., that reject older, traditional forms: *modern art.* —**mo·der·ni·ty** /mɒ'dɜrnɪtiy/, *n.* [noncount]

mod·ern·ize /'mɒdər,nayz/ *v.,* **-ized, -iz·ing.** to (cause to) become modern: [~ + *obj*]: *Our competitors modernized their equipment.* [no *obj*]: *If we hope to compete today we have to modernize.* —**mod·ern·i·za·tion** /,mɒdərnɪ'zeyʃən/, *n.* [noncount]

mod·est /'mɒdɪst/ *adj.* **1.** having or showing a moderate opinion of one's merits, importance, etc.; not boasting: *She was very modest about re-*

ceiving the award. **2.** free from obvious displays of showiness: *a modest house.* **3.** showing regard for the decencies of behavior, dress, etc.: *She was too modest to wear a bikini.* **4.** limited in amount, extent, etc.: *a modest salary.* —'**mod•est•ly,** *adv.* —'**mod•es•ty,** *n.* [*noncount*]

mod•i•fy /'mɒdə,faɪ/ *v.* [~ + *obj*], **-fied, -fy•ing. 1.** to change somewhat the form or qualities of; amend: *to modify a contract.* **2.** (of a word, phrase, or clause) to describe, limit, or qualify (another word, phrase, or clause): *In the phrase a good cook, the word good modifies the word cook.* —**mod•i•fi•ca•tion** /,mɒdəfɪ'keɪʃən/, *n.* [*noncount*]: *to accept a contract without modification.* [*count*]: *The modifications were completed in a week.* —'**mod•i,fi•er,** *n.* [*count*]: *When the word* model *is used as a modifier, it goes before the noun it modifies, as in the phrase* a model home.

mod•u•lar /'mɒdʒələr/ *adj.* made up of standardized units that enable easy construction or arrangement: *a series of modular boxes that fit into each other.*

mod•u•late /'mɒdʒə,leɪt/ *v.* [~ + *obj*], **-lat•ed, -lat•ing.** to regulate by or adjust to a certain measure or amount; to soften or tone down, as the voice. —**mod•u•la•tion** /,mɒdʒə'leɪʃən/, *n.* [*noncount*]

mod•ule /'mɒdʒuwl/ *n.* [*count*] a part that can be separated from the rest, frequently one that may be exchanged with or used in place of others: *The kit contained modules that could be put together to form various toys.*

Mo•ham•med /mʊ'hæmɪd, -'hɑmɪd, mow-/ *n.* MUHAMMAD.

moist /mɔɪst/ *adj.* **-er, -est.** slightly wet; damp: *a moist rag.* —'**moist•ness,** *n.* [*noncount*]

mois•ten /'mɔɪsən/ *v.* to make or become moist: [~ + *obj*]: *She moistened her lips before speaking.* [*no obj*]: *Her eyes moistened.* —'**moist•en•er,** *n.* [*count*]

mois•ture /'mɔɪstʃər/ *n.* [*noncount*] liquid, esp. water, that has turned into steam or a fine mist.

mois•tur•ize /'mɔɪstʃə,raɪz/ *v.* [~ + *obj*], **-ized, -iz•ing.** to add or restore moisture to: *some lotion to moisturize the skin.* —'**mois•tur,iz•er,** *n.* [*noncount*]: *Rub some moisturizer on the skin.* [*count*]: *many moisturizers to choose from.* —'**mois•tur,iz•ing,** *adj.*

mo•lar /'mowlər/ *n.* [*count*] Also called '**mo•lar ,tooth.** a tooth having a broad biting surface for grinding.

mo•las•ses /mə'læsɪz/ *n.* [*noncount*] a thick syrup produced during the refining of sugar.

mold[1] /mowld/ *n.* [*count*] **1.** a hollow form for giving a particular shape to a liquid: *pouring the concrete into a mold.* —*v.* [~ + *obj*] **2.** to work into a required shape or form; shape: *to mold a figure in clay.* **3.** to have influence in forming, as the character of someone or something: *Parents mold their children more by example than by preaching.*

mold[2] /mowld/ *n.* **1.** [*noncount*] a growth of very small fungi on vegetable or animal matter. **2.** any of the fungi that produce such a growth; mildew: [*noncount*]: *Mold grows rapidly in damp places.* [*count*]: *The molds grow rapidly in the dark.* —'**mold•y,** *adj.,* **-i•er, -i•est.**

mold•ing /'mowldɪŋ/ *n.* [*noncount*] [*count*] something molded, esp. a long, narrow ornamental strip, as of wood, for decoration on furniture and buildings.

mole[1] /mowl/ *n.* [*count*] **1.** a small, insect-eating

mammal living chiefly underground. **2.** a spy who becomes part of and works from within the ranks of an enemy intelligence agency.

mole[2] /mowl/ *n.* [*count*] a small spot or blemish on the human skin, present from birth, usually of a dark color.

mol•e•cule /'mɒlə,kyuwl/ *n.* [*count*] **1.** the smallest physical unit of an element or compound, made up of one or more similar atoms in an element and two or more different atoms in a compound. **2.** any very small particle. —**mo•lec•u•lar** /mə'lɛkyələr/ *adj.*

mole•hill /'mowl,hɪl/ *n.* [*count*] **1.** a small ridge of earth raised up by a mole burrowing under the ground. —**Idiom. 2. make a mountain out of a molehill,** to exaggerate a minor difficulty.

mo•lest /mə'lɛst/ *v.* [~ + *obj*] to attack or harm in a sexual way: *molesting children.* —**mo•les•ta•tion** /,mowlɛ'steɪʃən, ,mɒlɛ-/, *n.* [*noncount*] —**mo'lest•er,** *n.* [*count*]

mol•li•fy /'mɒlə,faɪ/ *v.* [~ + *obj*], **-fied, -fy•ing. 1.** to cause to calm down: *The lollipop seemed to mollify the crying child.* **2.** to reduce: *to mollify one's demands.* —**mol•li•fi•ca•tion** /,mɒləfɪ'keɪʃən/, *n.* [*noncount*]

mol•lusk /'mɒləsk/ *n.* [*count*] an animal without a backbone, having a soft body enclosed by a shell: *Mollusks include snails and octopuses.*

molt /mowlt/ *v.* [*no obj*] [~ + *obj*] **1.** (of an animal) to cast off or shed skin, etc., in the process of growth. —*n.* [*noncount*] **2.** an act or instance of molting. **3.** something dropped in molting.

mol•ten /'mowltn/ *adj.* **1.** liquefied by heat: *molten rock pouring from the volcano.* **2.** produced by melting and casting: *a molten image.*

mom /mɒm/ *n.* [*count*] *Informal.* mother.

mo•ment /'mowmənt/ *n.* **1.** [*count*] an indefinitely short period of time; instant: *I'll be with you in a moment.* **2.** [*count*] the particular time when something happens: *The moment he began speaking, cheers filled the room.* **3.** [*noncount*] importance or consequence: *a decision of great moment.*

mo•men•tar•i•ly /,mowmən'tɛərəliy, 'mowmən,tɛr-/ *adv.* **1.** for a moment; briefly: *Flames escaped from the capsule momentarily.* **2.** at any moment; soon: *He'll be here momentarily.*

mo•men•tar•y /'mowmən,tɛriy/ *adj.* **1.** lasting only a moment; very brief: *a momentary lull in the fighting.* **2.** that might occur at any moment: *momentary disaster.*

mo•men•tous /mow'mɛntəs/ *adj.* of great importance: *The fall of Rome was a momentous event.*

mo•men•tum /mow'mɛntəm/ *n.* [*noncount*] force or speed of movement; impetus, as of physical objects or of events: *The car gained momentum as it hurtled down the street. Her career has lost momentum.*

mom•my or **mom•mie** /'mɒmiy/ *n., pl.* **-mies.** *Informal.* MOTHER (def. 1).

Mon., an abbreviation of: Monday.

mon•arch /'mɒnərk, -ɑrk/ *n.* [*count*] a ruler, as a king, queen, or emperor; the sole ruler of a state or nation. —**mo•nar•chic** /mə'nɑrkɪk/, **mo'nar•chi•cal,** *adj.* —'**mon•ar•chy** /mɑ'nɑrkiy/, *n.* [*count*], *pl.* **-chies** [*noncount*]

mon•as•ter•y /'mɒnə,stɛriy/ *n.* [*count*], *pl.* **-ter•ies.** a place where a community of monks lives.

mo•nas•tic /mə'næstɪk/ *adj.* Also, **mo'nas•ti•cal.** of or relating to monks or monasteries: *monastic vows.* —**mo'nas•ti•cism,** *n.* [*noncount*]

M

Mon•day /'mʌndey, -diy/ n. [count] the second day of the week, following Sunday.

mon•e•tar•y /'mɒnɪˌteriy, 'mʌn-/ adj. of or relating to the coinage or money supply of a country: *monetary policy.* —**mon•e•tar•i•ly** /ˌmɒnɪ'teərəliy, ˌmʌn-/, adv.

mon•ey /'mʌniy/ n. [noncount] **1.** the coins and bills issued by a country to buy something: *He doesn't have a lot of money with him.* **2.** wealth: *Money can't buy your youth when you're old.* —*Idiom.* **3. for my money,** in my opinion: *For my money, she'd make a perfect president.* **4. in the money,** wealthy. **5. make money,** to get money by earning it: *She makes good money as an accountant.* **6. one's money's worth,** a value equal to what one spends or has paid for something: *We got our money's worth on that car.* **7. on the money,** accurate; exact; precise.

'money ˌorder, n. [count] an order for the payment of money, as one issued by one bank or post office and payable at another.

mon•grel /'mʌŋgrəl, 'mɒŋ-/ n. [count] an animal, esp. a dog, of mixed breed.

mon•i•ker or **mon•ick•er** /'mɒnɪkər/ n. [count] *Slang.* name; nickname: *His teammates gave him the moniker "Smilin' Jack."*

mon•i•tor /'mɒnɪtər/ n. [count] **1.** a device for observing or recording the operation of a machine or system, esp. an automatically controlled system: *a heart monitor.* **2.** a large television receiver used in a control room or studio for monitoring transmissions. **3.** a component with a display screen for viewing computer data, etc.: *The monitor wasn't hooked up correctly to the computer.* —v. [~ + obj] **4.** to observe or detect (an operation) with instruments: *to monitor the patient's heartbeat.* **5.** to supervise or watch closely; keep track of: *to monitor the progress of the committee.*

monk /mʌŋk/ n. [count] a man who is a member of a religious order, usually living in a monastery and often bound by restrictive vows.

mon•key /'mʌŋkiy/ n., pl. **-keys,** v. —n. [count] **1.** a primate usually having a long tail. —v. **2. monkey (around) with,** to tamper or meddle: *Quit monkeying (around) with the antenna.*

'monkey ˌwrench, n. [count] a wrench having a movable opening that can be adjusted for grasping nuts of different sizes.

mon•o /'mɒnow/ n. mononucleosis.

mono-, a combining form meaning one, single, or lone (*monorail; monosyllable*).

mon•o•chro•mat•ic /ˌmɒnəkrow'mætɪk/ adj. **1.** of or having one color. **2.** of or relating to light of one color or to radiation of a single wavelength.

mo•nog•a•my /mə'nɒgəmiy/ n. [noncount] the having of only one spouse at a time. —**mo'nog•a•mous,** adj. —**mo'nog•a•mous•ly,** adv.

mon•o•gram /'mɒnəˌgræm/ n., v., **-grammed, -gram•ming.** —n. [count] **1.** a design made up of combined alphabetical letters, commonly one's initials. —v. [~ + obj] **2.** to decorate with a monogram: *a shirt that was monogrammed.*

mon•o•graph /'mɒnəˌgræf/ n. [count] a learned piece of writing or detailed study, usually on a single topic or subject.

mon•o•logue or **mon•o•log** /'mɒnəˌlɔg, -ˌlɒg/ n. [count] **1.** a dramatic piece spoken by a single performer. **2.** a long speech by a single speaker.

mon•o•nu•cle•o•sis /ˌmɒnəˌnuwkliy'owsɪs, -ˌnyuw-/ n. [noncount] a disease with a high,

sudden fever and fatigue, that is easily transmitted to others.

mo•nop•o•lize /mə'nɒpəˌlayz/ v. [~ + obj], **-lized, -liz•ing. 1.** to have sole power over: *A few large companies have monopolized the oil industry.* **2.** to take over completely; dominate: *to monopolize the conversation.*

mo•nop•o•ly /mə'nɒpəliy/ n., pl. **-lies.** the exclusive and complete control of a product, service, or invention that makes it possible to control prices: [noncount]: *their former monopoly on phone services.* [count]: *a virtual monopoly of machinery.* —**mo•nop•o•li•za•tion** /məˌnɒpəli'zeyʃən/, n. [noncount]

mon•o•rail /'mɒnəˌreyl/ n. [count] a single rail functioning as a track for wheeled vehicles, such as railroad cars, balanced upon or hanging from it.

mon•o•so•di•um glu•ta•mate /ˌmɒnə'sowdiyəm gluwtəˌmeyt/ n. [noncount] a white, crystal-like powder used to intensify the flavor of food. Also called **MSG.**

mon•o•syl•la•ble /'mɒnəˌsɪləbəl/ n. [count] a word of one syllable: *The words yes and no are monosyllables.* —**mon•o•syl•lab•ic** /ˌmɒnəsɪ'læbɪk/, adj.

mon•o•the•ism /'mɒnəθiyˌɪzəm/ n. [noncount] the belief that there is only one God. —**'mon•o,the•ist,** n. [count] —**mon•o•the•is•tic,** /ˌmɒnəθiy'ɪstɪk/, adj.

mon•o•tone /'mɒnəˌtown/ n. [count; usually singular] a sound of one unchanging tone or pitch: *speaking in a boring monotone.*

mo•not•o•nous /mə'nɒtnəs/ adj. lacking in variety: *a boring, monotonous job.* —**mo'not•o•nous•ly,** adv. —**mo•not•o•ny** /mə'nɒtˌniy/, n. [noncount]

mon•si•gnor /mɒn'siynyər, ˌmɒnsiy'nyɔr/ n., pl. **mon•si•gnors, mon•si•gno•ri** /ˌmɒnsiy'nyɔriy/. **1.** [*Monsignor*] a title for certain Roman Catholic priests: *Will Monsignor Kelly please step forward?* **2.** [count] a person bearing this title: *a monsignor from Rome.*

mon•soon /mɒn'suwn/ n. [count] **1.** a seasonal wind of the Indian Ocean and southern Asia. **2.** the rainy season during which the southwest monsoon blows.

mon•ster /'mɒnstər/ n. [count] any animal or human that does not have a normal shape or character; any creature ugly enough to frighten people: *monsters of myth and legend.*

mon•stros•i•ty /mɒn'strɒsɪtiy/ n. [count], pl. **-ties.** something monstrous: *That monstrosity blocks our view of the river.*

mon•strous /'mɒnstrəs/ adj. **1.** of or relating to a monster: *the monstrous creature.* **2.** large; huge; gigantic: *The huge ship cast a monstrous shadow.* **3.** horribly wicked or cruel: *monstrous acts of murder.*

Mont., an abbreviation of: Montana.

month /mʌnθ/ n. [count] **1.** any of the 12 parts, as January or February, into which the calendar year is divided. **2.** the time from any day of one calendar month to the corresponding day of the next, or a period of four weeks or 30 days. —'**month•ly,** adj.

mon•u•ment /'mɒnyəmənt/ n. [count] **1.** something erected in memory of a person, event, etc., as a pillar or statue: *The arch in St. Louis is a monument to the pioneers.* **2.** anything that has lasted a long time and is evidence of something noteworthy: *The canal remains a monument to*

M

human skill. —**mon•u•men•tal** /ˌmɒnyə'mɛntl/ *adj.*

moo /muw/ *n., pl.* **moos,** *v.,* **mooed, moo•ing.** —*n.* [*count*] **1.** the deep, low sound a cow makes. —*v.* [*no obj*] **2.** to make such a sound.

mood¹ /muwd/ *n.* [*count*] **1.** a person's emotional state at a particular time: *What kind of mood is she in now?* **2.** a feeling or emotion held by a large number of people at a time: *the country's distrustful mood.*

mood² /muwd/ *n.* [*count*] a category or set of categories of the verb that indicates whether the verb expresses a fact, a question, a possibility, a wish, or a command: *the indicative mood.*

mood•y /'muwdiy/ *adj.,* **-i•er, -i•est. 1.** (of a person) changing one's moods. **2.** unhappy; gloomy or sullen; depressed: *He's been moody since he lost his job.* —**mood•i•ly** /'muwdļiy/, *adv.: She answered moodily that she didn't care one way or the other.* —'**mood•i•ness,** *n.* [*noncount*]

moon /muwn/ *n.* **1.** [*count; singular; the + ~*] the earth's natural satellite. **2.** [*count*] a natural satellite that goes around any planet: *the moons of Jupiter.* —**Idiom. 3. once in a blue moon,** rarely.

moon•light /'muwn,layt/ *n.* [*noncount*] **1.** the light of the moon. —*adj.* [*before a noun*] **2.** occurring by moonlight, or at night: *a moonlight swim.* —*v.* [*no obj*] **3.** to work at an additional job after one's regular employment, as at night: *As a firefighter he was not supposed to moonlight.* —'**moon,light•er,** *n.* [*count*] —**moon•lit** /'muwn,lɪt/, *adj.*

moor¹ /mʊr/ *n.* [*count*] an area of open wasteland, often overgrown with grass and heath.

moor² /mʊr/ *v.* [*~ + obj*] [*no obj*] to hold and attach (a ship, etc.) in a particular place, as by ropes or anchors.

moor•ing /'mʊrɪŋ/ *n.* [*count*] **1.** Usually, **moorings.** [*plural*] the means by which a ship, boat, or aircraft is moored: *Ships were torn from their moorings.* **2. moorings,** [*plural*] a place where something may be moored: *The safest moorings were on the mainland.*

moose /muws/ *n.* [*count*], *pl.* **moose.** a large, long-headed deer of the Northern Hemisphere, the male of which has enormous, flat antlers.

mop /mɒp/ *n., v.,* **mopped, mop•ping.** —*n.* [*count*] **1.** a device consisting of absorbent material, as a sponge, fastened to a handle and used esp. for washing floors. **2.** a thick mass of hair. —*v.* **3.** to wipe with or as if with a mop: [*~ + obj*]: *He mopped his brow with a handkerchief. They mopped up the water. They mopped the water up.* [*no obj*]: *You vacuum while I mop (up).*

mo•ped /'mow,pɛd/ *n.* [*count*] a motorized bicycle with pedals, designed for low-speed operation.

mor•al /'mɔrəl, 'mɒr-/ *adj.* **1.** [*before a noun*] of or relating to the principles of right conduct, or to the distinction between right and wrong; ethical: *Abortion presents a difficult moral problem.* **2.** [*before a noun*] based on principles of right conduct, rather than on law, custom, etc.: *She made the decision on moral grounds. He has a moral obligation to care for his family.* **3.** adhering to high standards of right conduct; virtuous: *a highly moral person.* —*n.* [*count*] **4.** the lesson contained in a fable, etc.: *The moral of the story was to do what you can today and not put it off until tomorrow.* **5. morals,** [*plural*] principles, standards, or habits with respect to right or

wrong conduct: *He acts without morals.* —'**mor•al•ly,** *adv.*

mo•rale /mə'ræl/ *n.* [*noncount*] emotional or mental condition with respect to cheerfulness, confidence, etc., esp. in the face of opposition, etc.: *The morale of the troops was high.*

mor•al•ist /'mɔrəlɪst, 'mɒr-/ *n.* [*count*] **1.** one who practices or teaches morality. **2.** a person concerned with regulating the morals of others, as by censorship. —,**mor•al'is•tic,** *adj.*

mo•ral•i•ty /mə'rælitiy, mɔ-/ *n.* [*noncount*] agreement with the rules of conduct; moral conduct: *the decline of morality on TV shows.*

mor•al•ize /'mɔrə,layz, 'mɒr-/ *v.* [*no obj*], **-ized, -iz•ing.** to express opinions about matters of right and wrong, esp. in a tiresome way or when intolerant of other's views: *moralizing about what TV shows our children should watch.*

mo•rass /mə'ræs/ *n.* [*count*] **1.** a tract of low, soft, wet ground; marsh; bog; swamp. **2.** any confusing or troublesome situation, esp. one from which it is difficult to escape.

mor•a•to•ri•um /ˌmɔrə'tɔriyəm, mɒr-/ *n.* [*count*], *pl.* **-to•ri•a** /-'tɔriyə/, **-to•ri•ums.** a stopping, usually temporary, of some activity: *a moratorium on rent increases.*

mor•bid /'mɔrbɪd/ *adj.* suggesting an unhealthy mental state because of too much gloominess, gruesomeness, etc.: *a morbid interest in horror movies.* —'**mor•bid•ly,** *adv.* —'**mor•bid•ness,** *n.* [*noncount*]

more /mɔr/ *adj., comparative of* **much** or **many** *with* **most** *as superlative.* **1.** in greater quantity, amount, or number: *I need more money. Do you need more time?* **2.** additional or further: *More discussion seems pointless.* —*n.* [*noncount*] **3.** an additional quantity, amount, or number: *Would you like more?* **4.** a greater quantity, amount, or degree; something of greater importance: *The price is more than I thought. Your essay is more than just a review.* —*pron.* **5.** [*used with a plural verb*] a greater number of persons or of a specified class: *More have been injured in automobile accidents this year than ever before.* —*adv.,* *comparative of* **much** *with* **most** *as superlative.* **6.** [*often used before adjectives and adverbs, and regularly before those of more than two syllables*] in or to a greater extent or degree: *Things have become more interesting. The car moved more slowly.* **7.** in addition; further, again: *Let's talk more tomorrow.* —**Idiom. 8. more or less,** to some extent; somewhat: *We came to more or less the same conclusion.*

more•o•ver /mɔr'owvər, 'mɔr,owvər/ *adv.* in addition to what has been said; further; besides: *He didn't finish the work on time; moreover, it was poorly done.*

mo•res /'mɔreyz, -iyz/ *n.* [*plural*] customs considered to be of central importance and to indicate the fundamental moral values of a group.

morgue /mɔrg/ *n.* [*count*] **1.** a place in which dead bodies are kept until they have been identified or disposed of. **2.** a reference file of old clippings, etc., esp. in a newspaper office.

Mor•mon /'mɔrmən/ *n.* [*count*] a member of the Church of Jesus Christ of Latter-day Saints (**'Mormon 'Church**), founded in the U.S. in 1830 by Joseph Smith.

morn•ing /'mɔrnɪŋ/ *n.* the first period of the day, usually from dawn, but sometimes considered from midnight, up to noon: [*noncount*]: *On Monday morning we arrived at work.* [*count*]: *On Monday mornings she usually comes to work late.*

'morning ,glory or **'morning-,glory,** *n.* [*count*] a twining plant having funnel-shaped flowers of various colors, often opening only in the morning.

'morning ,sickness, *n.* [*noncount*] nausea occurring esp. in the early part of the day during the first months of pregnancy.

mo•ron /'mɔrɒn/ *n.* [*count*] a person who is stupid or lacking in good judgment.

mo•rose /məˈrows/ *adj.* angrily gloomy, often in a quiet way: *a morose and grouchy mood.* —**mo'rose•ly,** *adv.*: *He looked at us morosely.* —**mo'rose•ness,** *n.* [*noncount*]

mor•phine /'mɔrfiyn/ *n.* [*noncount*] a drug made from opium and used chiefly in medicine as a pain reliever.

morph•ing /'mɔrfɪŋ/ *n.* [*noncount*] a technique in which one image is gradually and smoothly changed into another by means of a computer, as in a motion picture or video: *My favorite part of the cartoon was the morphing of the hero into a wild animal.*

'Morse 'code /mɔrs/ *n.* [*noncount*] either of two systems of clicks and spaces, short and long sounds, or flashes of light, used to represent letters, numerals, etc.

mor•sel /'mɔrsəl/ *n.* [*count*] a small piece or amount of anything, esp. food; scrap; bit.

mor•tal /'mɔrtl̩/ *adj.* **1.** that will suffer death: *All humans are mortal.* **2.** causing or liable to cause death; fatal: *a mortal wound.* **3.** [*before a noun*] never giving up or surrendering: *a mortal enemy.* **4.** severe; extreme: *in mortal danger.* —*n.* [*count*] **5.** a human being. —**mor•tal•i•ty** /mɔrˈtælɪtiy/ *n.* [*noncount*] —**'mor•tal•ly,** *adv.*: *He fell, mortally wounded.*

mor•tar¹ /'mɔrtər/ *n.* [*count*] **1.** a bowl-shaped container in which substances can be pounded or ground with a pestle. **2.** a very short cannon for throwing shells at high angles.

mor•tar² /'mɔrtər/ *n.* [*noncount*] a mixture of lime or cement with sand and water, used to hold stones, etc., together.

mor•tar•board /'mɔrtərˌbɔrd/ *n.* [*count*] a close-fitting cap with a square, flat top and a tassel, worn at formal academic ceremonies by graduates or faculty.

mort•gage /'mɔrgɪdʒ/ *n., v.,* **-gaged, -gag•ing.** —*n.* [*count*] **1.** an amount of money loaned to buy a house. **2.** an agreement to give up property if one is unable to pay back the money loaned. —*v.* [~ + *obj*] **3.** to place (property) under such an agreement: *They had to mortgage their house to pay the bills.*

mor•ti•cian /mɔrˈtɪʃən/ *n.* [*count*] one who oversees the preparation of a dead person's body for burial and directs funeral services.

mor•ti•fy /'mɔrtəˌfay/ *v.* [~ + *obj*], **-fied, -fy•ing.** to humiliate (someone), as by an injury to self-respect: *He was mortified when he forgot his speech.* —**mor•ti•fi•ca•tion** /ˌmɔrtəfɪˈkeyʃən/, *n.* [*noncount*]

mor•tu•ar•y /'mɔrtʃuwˌɛriy/ *n.* [*count*], *pl.* **-ar•ies.** a building or business where the bodies of the dead are prepared for burial or cremation and for viewing, and where services are often held.

mo•sa•ic /mow'zeyɪk/ *n.* [*count*] **1.** a picture made of small colored pieces of stone, etc., fitted together in a flat surface: *a handmade mosaic.* **2.** something resembling a mosaic, esp. in being made up of many distinct, different elements: *This city has become a cultural mosaic.*

mosque /mɒsk, mɔsk/ *n.* [*count*] a Muslim place of public worship.

mos•qui•to /məˈskiytow/ *n.* [*count*], *pl.* **-toes, -tos.** a two-winged insect, the female of which sucks the blood of animals and humans.

moss /mɔs, mɒs/ *n.* [*noncount*] a tiny, leafy-stemmed plant that grows in a thick mass on moist ground, tree trunks, rocks, etc. —'moss•y, *adj.,* -i•er, -i•est.

most /mowst/ *adj., superlative of* **much** *or* **many** *with* **more** *as comparative.* **1.** [*the* + ~] in the greatest number, amount, or degree: [*before a plural noun*]: *He received the most votes.* [*before a noncount noun*]: *She has the most talent.* **2.** [*before a plural noun*] in the majority of instances; more than half: *Most operations are successful.* —*n.* **3.** [*noncount; the* + ~] the greatest quantity, amount, or degree: *The most I can hope for is a passing grade.* **4.** [*noncount;* ~ + *of*] the greatest number or greater part of what is specified: *Most of his writing is rubbish.* **5.** [*noncount*] the majority of persons: *to be happier than most.* —*adv., superlative of* **much** *with* **more** *as comparative.* **6.** [*often used before adjectives and adverbs, and regularly before those of more than two syllables*] in or to the greatest extent or degree: *the most popular kid in the class.* **7.** very: *a most interesting case.* —**Idiom.** **8. at (the) most,** at the maximum: *Jog for one hour at (the) most.* **9. for the most part,** on the whole; generally; usually: *For the most part we walked, but occasionally we ran.* **10. make the most of,** to use to greatest advantage: *Make the most of your opportunities.*

most•ly /'mowstliy/ *adv.* for the most part; chiefly; generally: *The guests are mostly friends of the bride. The train is mostly on time. We mostly hiked on unpaved roads.*

mo•tel /mow'tɛl/ *n.* [*count*] a hotel designed for people traveling by car.

moth /mɔθ, mɒθ/ *n.* [*count*], *pl.* **moths** /mɔðz, mɒðz/. an insect that resembles a butterfly and is active mostly at night.

moth•ball /'mɔθ,bɔl, 'mɒθ-/ *n.* [*count*] a small ball of a strong-smelling chemical, for placing in storage areas to repel moths.

moth•er /'mʌðər/ *n.* [*count*] **1.** a female parent. **2.** something that gives rise to something else: *Necessity is the mother of invention.* —*adj.* [*before a noun*] **3.** relating to or characteristic of a mother: *mother love.* **4.** derived from or as if from one's mother; native: *Swedish is his mother tongue.* —*v.* [~ + *obj*] **5.** to care for or protect like a mother: *She mothered her children wisely.* —'moth•er•hood, *n.* [*noncount*]

'mother-in-,law, *n.* [*count*], *pl.* **mothers-in-law.** the mother of one's husband or wife.

moth•er•land /'mʌðərˌlænd/ *n.* [*count; usually: the/one's* + ~] one's native land.

'mother-of-'pearl, *n.* [*noncount*] a hard, shiny substance that forms the inner layer of certain shells, used for making buttons, beads, etc.

mo•tif /mow'tiyf/ *n.* [*count*] a subject, theme, etc., that repeats in a literary, artistic, or musical work: *a flower motif in the wallpaper pattern.*

mo•tion /'mowʃən/ *n.* **1.** [*noncount*] the action or process of moving; movement: *the effects of energy on motion.* **2.** [*count*] the manner of moving the body while walking; gait: *walking with a swaying motion.* **3.** [*count*] a bodily movement or change of posture; gesture: *She made motions to indicate she was ready to leave.* **4.** [*count*] a formal proposal, esp. one made to a group deciding

M

an issue: *My motion was defeated.* —*v.* [*no obj*] **5.** to make a motion or gesture, as with the hand: *He motioned to us to come forward.* —**Idiom. 6. go through the motions,** to do something half-heartedly, without enthusiasm or conviction. —'**mo•tion•less,** *adj.*

'**motion 'picture,** *n.* [*count*] **1.** a series of photographs projected on a screen in such rapid succession as to give the illusion of movement. **2.** a narrative, documentary, etc., presented in this form; movie.

'**motion ˌsickness,** *n.* [*noncount*] nausea resulting from the effect of motion, as during car or plane travel.

mo•ti•vate /'mowtə,veyt/ *v.* [~ + *obj*], **-vat•ed, -vat•ing.** to provide (someone) with a motive or motives; impel: *A good teacher will motivate the students. Her betrayal motivated him to seek revenge.*

mo•ti•va•tion /ˌmowtə'veyʃən/ *n.* [*noncount*] the state or condition of being motivated; desire: *Motivation was a key to their success.* —ˌ**mo•ti'va•tion•al,** *adj.*: *a motivational seminar.*

mo•tive /'mowtɪv/ *n.* [*count*] something that causes a person to act in a certain way; incentive: *What could possibly be the motive for such a crime?*

mo•tor /'mowtər/ *n.* [*count*] **1.** a small and powerful engine, esp. in an automobile or boat. **2.** a machine that changes electrical energy into mechanical energy: *an electric motor.* —*adj.* [*before a noun*] **3.** of or relating to muscular movement: *a motor response.*

mo•tor•boat /'mowtər,bowt/ *n.* [*count*] a boat powered by a motor.

mo•tor•cade /'mowtər,keyd/ *n.* [*count*] a parade of automobiles: *the president's motorcade.*

mo•tor•cy•cle /'mowtər,saykəl/ *n.* [*count*] a motor vehicle similar to a bicycle but usually larger and heavier. —'**mo•tor,cy•clist,** *n.* [*count*]

'**motor ˌhome,** *n.* [*count*] a vehicle with living quarters, used for camping or taking long trips.

mo•tor•ist /'mowtərɪst/ *n.* [*count*] a person who drives a privately owned automobile.

mo•tor•ize /'mowtə,rayz/ *v.* [~ + *obj*], **-ized, -iz•ing.** to furnish with a motor.

mo•tor•man /'mowtərmən/ *n.* [*count*], *pl.* **-men.** one who drives an electrically operated vehicle, as a subway train.

'**motor ˌscooter,** *n.* SCOOTER (def. 2).

'**motor ˌvehicle,** *n.* [*count*] an automobile, truck, bus, or similar motor-driven vehicle.

mot•tled /'mɒtld/ *adj.* marked with blotches of different colors: *a mottled face.*

mot•to /'mɒtow/ *n.* [*count*], *pl.* **-toes, -tos.** a word, phrase, or sentence adopted as an expression of a guiding principle: *"Be prepared, that's my motto,"* she declared.

mould /mowld/ *n., v.* Chiefly Brit. MOLD.

mound /mawnd/ *n.* [*count*] **1.** an elevation of earth: *Native Americans raised special burial mounds in southern Illinois.* **2.** a heap or raised mass: *two mounds of mashed potatoes.*

mount[1] /mawnt/ *v.* **1.** to go up; climb; ascend: [~ + *obj*]: *She mounted the stairs.* [*no obj*]: *I approached the stairs and mounted carefully.* **2.** [~ + *obj*] to get up on (a horse, a platform, etc.); to set (a person) on horseback: *He mounted the excited horse uneasily. She mounted her daughter on the horse.* **3.** [~ + *obj*] to set or place at a higher position: *The Greeks mounted their wooden horse on a platform.* **4.** [~ + *obj*] to organize and launch (an attack, etc.): *A search was*

mounted the next day. **5.** [~ + *obj*] to fix on or in a frame, etc.: *to mount a photograph on cardboard.* **6.** [~ + *obj*] (of an animal) to climb upon (another animal) for sexual relations. **7.** [*no obj*] to increase in amount or intensity: *The tension mounted as the two old enemies began their debate.* —*n.* [*count*] **8.** an animal, esp. a horse, used for riding. **9.** a support, backing, etc., on or in which something is mounted.

mount[2] /mawnt/ *n.* [*count; often: Mount; no article; part of the name of a mountain*] a mountain: *climbing Mount Kilimanjaro.*

moun•tain /'mawntn̩/ *n.* [*count*] **1.** a natural high piece of land rising more or less quickly to a high point: *We climbed up the mountain.* **2.** a large mass or heap; pile: *a mountain of papers on my desk.*

'**mountain ˌbike,** *n.* [*count*] a sturdy bicycle with thick tires.

moun•tain•eer /ˌmawntn̩'ɪər/ *n.* [*count*] **1.** a climber of mountains, esp. for sport. —*v.* [*no obj*] **2.** to climb mountains: *They enjoy mountaineering.*

'**mountain ˌlion,** *n.* COUGAR.

moun•tain•ous /'mawntnəs/ *adj.* (of a region) having many mountains.

moun•tain•top /'mawntn̩,tɒp/ *n.* [*count*] the top of a mountain.

mount•ed /'mawntɪd/ *adj.* [*before a noun*] riding on horses or motorcycles: *mounted police.*

mourn /mɔrn/ *v.* to grieve or express sadness, esp. over the death of (someone): [*no obj*]: *She still mourns for her son.* [~ + *obj*]: *We barely had time to mourn our dead.* —'**mourn•er,** *n.* [*count*]

mourn•ful /'mɔrnfəl/ *adj.* feeling or expressing grief; sad: *mournful visitors to the funeral home.* —'**mourn•ful•ly,** *adv.* —'**mourn•ful•ness,** *n.* [*noncount*]

mourn•ing /'mɔrnɪŋ/ *n.* [*noncount*] **1.** the act of a person who mourns: *an occasion for mourning.* **2.** the period during which a person grieves or formally expresses grief. **3. in mourning,** said of a person during this period: *She's still in mourning for her father.*

mouse /maws/ *n.* [*count*], *pl.* **mice** /mays/. **1.** a small rodent having a long, thin tail. **2.** a quiet, timid person: *"Are you a man or a mouse?"* she yelled. **3.** a palm-sized device equipped with one or more buttons, used to select items on a computer display screen and to control the movement of the cursor.

mouse•trap /'maws,træp/ *n.* [*count*] **1.** a trap for mice, esp. a wooden one with a metal spring. **2.** a device or trick for trapping someone.

mousse /muws/ *n.* **1.** [*noncount*] [*count*] a sweetened dessert usually made with gelatin and whipped cream or beaten egg whites and chilled in a mold. **2.** [*noncount*] a foamy preparation used to set or style the hair.

mous•tache /'mʌstæʃ, mə'stæʃ/ *n.* MUSTACHE.

mous•y or **mous•ey** /'mawsiy, -ziy/ *adj.*, **-i•er, -i•est.** resembling a mouse, as in being drab and colorless or meek and timid: *mousy brown hair; a mousy little man.* —'**mous•i•ness,** *n.* [*noncount*]

mouth /*n.* mawθ; *v.* mawð/ *n.*, *pl.* **mouths** /mawðz/, *v.* —*n.* [*count*] **1.** the opening through which a person or animal takes in food. **2.** the opening in the face thought of as the source of speaking: *Secrets came tumbling out of his mouth.* **3.** an opening leading out of or into a hole or hollow thing: *the mouth of the jar.* **4.** the lower end of a river or stream, where flowing water is discharged. —*v.* [~ + *obj*] **5.** to say (something) without believing or understanding: *He mouthed the usual empty promises for reform.* **6.** [~ + *obj*] to form (words) with the lips without making a sound: *He mouthed his answer so as not to wake the sleeping child.* **7. mouth off,** *Slang.* to express one's opinions forcefully or without holding oneself back: *He's always mouthing off at our meetings.* —*Idiom.* **8. down in** or **at the mouth,** sad; depressed. **9. put words into someone's mouth,** to falsely state or imply that someone has said something. **10. take the words out of someone's mouth,** to say something that someone else was about to say.

mouth•ful /'mawθ₁fʊl/ *n., pl.* **-fuls. 1.** [*count*] the amount a mouth can hold; the amount taken into the mouth at one time. **2.** [*singular; a + ~*] a long word or phrase, esp. one hard to pronounce.

mouth•piece /'mawθ₁piys/ *n.* [*count*] **1.** a piece placed at or forming the mouth, as of a telephone, etc. **2.** a piece or part, as of a musical instrument, applied to or held in the mouth. **3.** a person, newspaper, etc., that expresses the opinions of others: *That newspaper is a mouthpiece for the publisher.*

mouth•wash /'mawθ₁wɔʃ, -₁wɒʃ/ *n.* [*noncount*] [*count*] a liquid solution for cleaning or refreshing the mouth.

'mouth-₁watering, *adj.* very appetizing in appearance, aroma, or description: *a mouthwatering chocolate cake.*

move /muwv/ *v.,* **moved, mov•ing,** *n.* —*v.* **1.** to (cause to) pass from one position to another; to change one's position: *He fell down and didn't move.* [~ + *obj*]: *Can you move some books off your desk?* **2.** to (cause to) change the place where one lives or does business; relocate: [*no obj*]: *She moved to Illinois.* [~ + *obj*]: *The company moved him to Texas.* **3.** to (cause to) progress: [*no obj*]: *Work on the project is moving well.* [~ + *obj*]: *The coach really moved his team ahead.* **4.** [*no obj*] [~ + *obj*] to transfer a piece in a game, as chess. **5.** (of the bowels) to (cause to) discharge the feces: [*no obj*]: *His bowels wouldn't move unless he took a laxative.* [~ + *obj*]: *He couldn't move his bowels.* **6.** [~ + *obj*] to affect (someone) with strong emotion or feeling: *I was moved by your troubles. Her words moved me to anger.* **7.** to propose (a motion, etc.) formally, as to a court or judge: [~ + *obj*]: *I move (that) we all get big raises.* [*no obj*]: *He moved for adjournment.* **8. move in,** to begin to occupy a place, esp. by bringing in one's possessions: *You can move in any time after September 1st.* **9. move on,** to turn one's attention in a new direction or towards a new activity: *We've debated this for hours; it's time to move on. He moved on to another job.* **10. move up,** to advance to a higher level: *She moved up quickly in the company.* —*n.* [*count*] **11.** an act or instance of moving; movement: *The child stood still and didn't make a move.* **12.** a change of location or residence: *a move to Los Angeles.* **13.** (in chess, etc.) an act of moving a piece in a game, or a player's right or turn to make a play: *It's your move.* —*Idiom.* **14. get a move on,** to get going; to act, esp. hastily. —'**mov•a•ble, 'move•a•ble,** *adj.*

move•ment /'muwvmənt/ *n.* **1.** the act or result of moving: [*noncount*]: *The patient explained that any movement was painful.* [*count*]: *nervous movements of his hands.* **2.** Usually, **movements.** [*plural*] actions or activities, as of a

person, or a change of position or location, as of troops or ships. **3.** the direction, course, or trend of affairs in a field: [*noncount*]: *movement in education toward more computer use.* [*count*]: *a movement away from established traditions.* **4.** [*count*] a loosely organized group favoring a common goal: *the women's movement.* **5.** [*count*] BOWEL MOVEMENT. **6.** [*count*] the working parts of a mechanism, as of a watch. **7.** [*count*] a principal division or section of a symphony.

mov•ie /'muwviy/ *n.* [*count*] **1.** MOTION PICTURE: *They stayed up to watch a late-night movie.* **2.** Usually, **the movies.** [*plural*] a motion-picture theater: *We went to the movies last night.* **3. the movies,** [*plural*] the business of making motion pictures; the motion-picture industry: *a producer who made his fortune in the movies.*

mov•ing /'muwvɪŋ/ *adj.* **1.** [*before a noun*] capable of or having motion: *a moving object.* **2.** causing or stirring strong emotions or feelings: *a moving performance in the play.* —'**mov•ing•ly,** *adv.*: *She spoke movingly about the refugees.*

mow /mow/ *v.,* **mowed, mowed** or **mown** /mown/, **mow•ing. 1.** to cut down (grass, etc.), esp. with a machine: [~ + *obj*]: *He earned money mowing lawns.* [*no obj*]: *She was out mowing all morning.* **2. mow down,** to destroy or kill in great numbers, as in a battle: *He mowed them down with the machine gun. We mowed down the advancing troops.* —'**mow•er,** *n.* [*count*]

moz•za•rel•la /₁mɒtsə'rɛllə, ₁mowt-/ *n.* [*noncount*] a mild, white, semisoft Italian cheese.

MP, an abbreviation of: **1.** Member of Parliament. **2.** Military Police.

mpg or **m.p.g.,** an abbreviation of: miles per gallon.

mph or **m.p.h.,** an abbreviation of: miles per hour.

Mr. /'mɪstər/ *pl.* **Messrs.** /'mɛsərz/. **1.** mister; a title of respect used before a man's name, or sometimes before a position: *Mr. Jones is here. Mr. President, what are your views on the situation?* **2.** (used before an imagined name to express the opinion that the man so named possesses a particular quality, characteristic, identity, etc.): *She's waiting for Mr. Right.*

Mrs. /'mɪsɪz, 'mɪzɪz/ *pl.* **Mmes.** /mey'dɑm, -'dæm/. a title of respect used before the name of a married woman: *Mrs. Jones.*

MS, an abbreviation of: Mississippi.

Ms. /mɪz/ *pl.* **Mses.** /'mɪzəz/. a title of respect used before a woman's name: unlike *Miss* or *Mrs.,* it does not indicate whether or not she is married.

MS., *pl.* **MSS.** an abbreviation of: manuscript.

ms., *pl.* **mss.** an abbreviation of: manuscript.

M.S., Master of Science.

MSG, an abbreviation of: monosodium glutamate.

MT, an abbreviation of: **1.** Montana. **2.** Mountain Time.

Mt. or **mt.,** an abbreviation of: **1.** mount. **2.** mountain.

much /mʌtʃ/ *adj.,* **more** /mɔr/, **most** /mowst/, *n., pron., adv.,* **more, most.** —*adj.* [*before a noncount noun*] **1.** great in amount, measure, or degree: *much wasted effort.* —*n.* [*noncount*], *pron.* **2.** a great quantity, measure, or degree: *not much to do; He owed much of his success to his family.* **3.** an amount or degree of something: *How much does it cost?* —*adv.* **4.** to a great extent or degree: *to talk too much.* —*Idiom.* **5. make**

much of, to treat or consider (something) as being important: *Her opponent tried to make much of the fact that she had tried marijuana in college.* **6. not much of a,** not a very good or enjoyable example of (something): *We didn't have much of a vacation: rain and cold weather.*

muck /mʌk/ *n.* [*noncount*] **1.** mud, filth, dirt, or slime. —*v.* **2. muck up,** *Informal.* to make a mess of; fail badly at; bungle: *He mucked up the whole report. He mucked it all up.*

mu•cous /'myuwkəs/ *adj.* [*before a noun*] **1.** of or resembling mucus. **2.** containing or releasing mucus: *a mucous membrane.*

mu•cus /'myuwkəs/ *n.* [*noncount*] a watery, slippery substance produced in the body that serves to protect and moisten certain surfaces, as the lining of the nose.

mud /mʌd/ *n.* [*noncount*] **1.** wet, soft dirt: *He slipped in the mud.* **2.** scandalous or false and harmful claims or information. —'**mud•dy,** *adj.,* **-i•er, -i•est.**

mud•dle /'mʌdl/ *v.* [*no obj*], **-dled, -dling.** to think or act in a confused manner: *She muddled along, waiting for a good opportunity.*

mud•sling•ing /'mʌd,slɪŋɪŋ/ *n.* [*noncount*] efforts or actions to damage one's opponent, as in a political campaign, by harmful, false, or scandalous attacks. —'**mud,sling•er,** *n.* [*count*]

muen•ster /'mʌnstər, 'mʊn-/ *n.* [*noncount; often Muenster*] a semisoft cheese made from whole milk.

muff /mʌf/ *n.* [*count*] **1.** a thick, tube-shaped cover, as of fur, to keep the hands warm. —*v.* [~ + *obj*] **2.** to handle badly; miss: *He muffed the throw to first base.*

muf•fin /'mʌfɪn/ *n.* [*count*] a small, round bread made with flour or cornmeal, eggs, milk, etc., and baked in a pan containing a series of cuplike molds.

muf•fle /'mʌfəl/ *v.* [~ + *obj*], **-fled, -fling.** to deaden (sound) by or as if by wrappings: *to muffle the drums; His voice was muffled over the phone.*

muf•fler /'mʌflər/ *n.* [*count*] **1.** a scarf worn around the neck for warmth. **2.** a device for deadening sound: *With the muffler loose, the car rumbled noisily down the street.*

mug /mʌg/ *n., v.,* **mugged, mug•ging.** —*n.* [*count*] **1.** a rounded drinking cup with a handle: *a coffee mug.* —*v.* [~ + *obj*] **2.** to assault or attack, usually in order to rob: *He was mugged in a dark street.* —'**mug•ger,** *n.* [*count*] —'**mug•ging,** *n.* [*count*]: *a savage mugging on a deserted street.* [*noncount*]: *a short prison term for mugging.*

mug•gy /'mʌgiy/ *adj.,* **-gi•er, -gi•est.** (of the weather, etc.) uncomfortably humid; damp and close: *a hot, muggy day.* —'**mug•gi•ness,** *n.* [*noncount*]

Mu•ham•mad /mʊ'hæməd, -'hɑməd/ *n.* Also, **Mohammed.** A.D. 570–632, an Arab prophet and the founder of Islam.

mu•lat•to /mə'lætow, -'lɑtow, myuw-/ *n.* [*count*], *pl.* **-toes.** the offspring of one white parent and one black parent.

mul•ber•ry /'mʌl,bɛriy, -bəriy/ *n.* [*count*], *pl.* **-ries.** a purplish, berrylike fruit that can be eaten.

mulch /mʌltʃ/ *n.* [*noncount*] **1.** a covering, as of straw, spread on the ground around plants to prevent loss of water or soil. —*v.* [~ + *obj*] **2.** to cover with mulch.

mule /myuwl/ *n.* [*count*] **1.** an animal produced by a female horse and a male donkey: *A mule is* sterile and cannot produce offspring. **2.** a stubborn person.

mull /mʌl/ *v.* **mull over,** to think about carefully: *I mulled over the idea or I mulled the idea over.*

multi-, a combining form meaning: many or many times (*multivitamin; multimillionaire*).

mul•ti•cul•tur•al /,mʌltiy'kʌltʃərəl, ,mʌltay-/ *adj.* of, relating to, or incorporating aspects of different cultures: *multicultural studies.* —,**mul•ti'cul•tur•al•ism,** *n.* [*noncount*]

mul•ti•lat•er•al /,mʌltiy'lætərəl, ,mʌltay-/ *adj.* **1.** having several or many sides. **2.** involving more than two opposing nations, parties, etc.: *multilateral agreements to stop the spread of nuclear arms.*

mul•ti•lin•gual /,mʌltiy'lɪŋgwəl, ,mʌltay-/ *adj.* **1.** using or able to speak several languages with some ease or ability. **2.** of or involving several different languages: *a multilingual dictionary.*

mul•ti•me•di•a /,mʌltiy'miydiyə, ,mʌltay-/ *adj.* of or relating to the use of several media simultaneously: *a multimedia presentation with slides, music, and videos.*

mul•ti•na•tion•al /,mʌltiy'næʃənl, ,mʌltay-/ *n.* [*count*] **1.** a large corporation with operations and branches in several countries. —*adj.* **2.** of, relating to, or involving several nations: *multinational peacekeeping forces in the region.*

mul•ti•ple /'mʌltəpəl/ *adj.* [*before a noun*] **1.** consisting of, having, or involving several individuals, parts, etc.: *suffered multiple injuries in the car wreck.* —*n.* [*count*] **2.** a number that contains another, smaller number an exact number of times without a remainder: *12 is a multiple of 3.*

'**multiple-'choice,** *adj.* providing several possible answers from which the correct one must be selected: *a multiple-choice question.*

mul•ti•pli•ca•tion /,mʌltəplɪ'keyʃən/ *n.* [*noncount*] **1.** the act or process of multiplying. **2.** a mathematical operation, symbolized by × or ·.

mul•ti•plic•i•ty /,mʌltə'plɪsɪtiy/ *n.* [*count*], *pl.* **-ties.** a large number: *a multiplicity of new problems.*

mul•ti•ply /'mʌltə,play/ *v.,* **-plied, -ply•ing. 1.** to determine the product (of numbers) by multiplication: [~ + *obj*]: *Multiply the length by the width to get the area.* [*no obj*]: *You made a mistake when you multiplied; you should have divided.* **2.** [*no obj*] to increase in number by giving birth to offspring: *Soon the insects multiplied and destroyed the crops.* **3.** [*no obj*] [~ + *obj*] to (cause to) grow in number, etc.; increase.

mul•ti•tude /'mʌltɪ,tuwd, -,tyuwd/ *n.* [*count*] **1.** a great number: *a multitude of problems.* **2.** a great number of people gathered together; a crowd; throng: *the multitudes who tried to see him.*

mul•ti•vi•ta•min /,mʌltɪ'vaytəmɪn, 'mʌltɪ,vay-/ *adj.* **1.** containing or made up of several vitamins: *a multivitamin supplement.* —*n.* [*count*] **2.** a compound of several vitamins.

mum /mʌm/ *n.* CHRYSANTHEMUM.

mum•ble /'mʌmbəl/ *v.,* **-bled, -bling,** *n.* —*v.* to say or speak in a soft manner that is hard to understand: [*no obj*]: *He tended to mumble.* [~ + *obj*]: *He mumbled a few words that I couldn't understand.* [*used with quotations*]: *"I'm sorry,"* he mumbled. —*n.* [*count*] **2.** a soft, indistinct utterance or sound.

mum•mi•fy /'mʌmə,fay/ *v.* [~ + *obj*], **-fied, -fy•ing.** to make (a dead body) into a mummy.

musical instruments

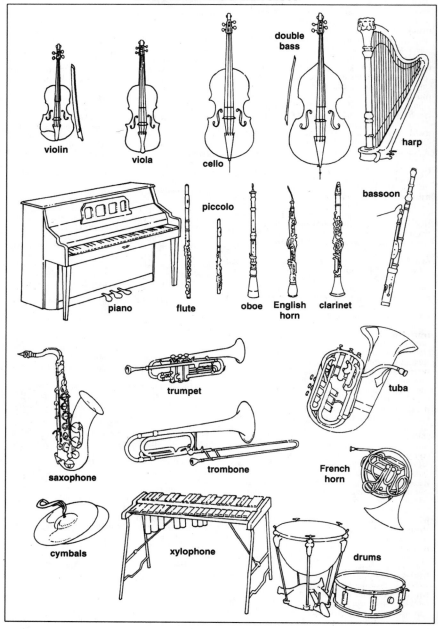

M

—mum•mi•fi•ca•tion /ˌmʌməfɪ'keyʃən/, n. [noncount]

mum•my /'mʌmiy/ n. [count], pl. **-mies.** the dead body of a human being or animal that has been preserved from decay by an ancient Egyptian process or some similar method.

mumps /mʌmps/ n. [noncount; often: the + ~; used with a singular verb] an infectious disease in which certain glands in the throat, neck, and mouth swell: The mumps is sometimes a serious disease.

munch /mʌntʃ/ v. to chew steadily or strongly and often loudly enough to be heard: [no obj]: He munched on an apple. [~ + obj]: He munched his cereal.

mun•dane /mʌn'deyn, 'mʌndeyn/ adj. common; ordinary; uninteresting: to bring some excitement to our mundane lives. —**mun'dane•ly,** adv.

mu•nic•i•pal /myuw'nɪsəpəl/ adj. [before a noun] of or relating to a municipality or its local government: municipal elections.

mu•nic•i•pal•i•ty /myuwˌnɪsə'pælɪtiy/ n. [count], pl. **-ties.** a city, town, or borough having its own government.

mu•ral /'myʊrəl/ n. [count] a large picture painted directly on a wall or ceiling. —**'mu•ral•ist,** n. [count]

mur•der /'mɜrdər/ n. **1.** the unlawful killing of a person, esp. when done deliberately: [noncount]: guilty of murder. [count]: a decrease in the number of murders. **2.** [noncount] any very difficult or unpleasant experience or situation: That final exam was murder! —v. **3.** [~ + obj] [no obj] to kill (a person) unlawfully and deliberately. **4.** [~ + obj] Informal. to defeat thoroughly: The home team murdered their opponents, 60-0. **5.** [~ + obj] to spoil by bad performance or execution: She murdered the song. —**Idiom. 6. get away with murder,** to do something very harmful, damaging, immoral, etc., and not to be punished: Just because she's famous, she thinks that she can get away with murder. —**'mur•der•er,** n. [count] —**'mur•der•ous,** adj.

murk•y /'mɜrkiy/ adj., **-i•er, -i•est. 1.** dark, gloomy, and cheerless: a murky, dark cave. **2.** muddy; hard to see through: Fish were dying in the murky ponds. **3.** vague; unclear: a murky statement. —**'murk•i•ness,** n. [noncount]

mur•mur /'mɜrmər/ n. [count] **1.** a low, soft, continuous sound, as of a brook or of distant voices. **2.** a mumbled, low, soft sound made by a person, as in complaining: She went to bed without a murmur of protest. **3.** an abnormal sound heard within the body, esp. one coming from the heart valves: a heart murmur. —v. **4.** [no obj] to make a low, soft, continuous sound: A brook murmured in the distance. **5.** to express in murmurs: [no obj]: The villagers murmured among themselves. [~ + obj]: He murmured his approval.

mus•cle /'mʌsəl/ n. **1.** a tissue in the body made up of long cells that can contract, causing movement of the body: [count]: His leg muscles had grown weak. [noncount]: to cut through muscle to get to the diseased organ. **2.** [noncount] muscular strength. **3.** [noncount] effective power or influence. —v. [~ + obj] **4.** to force or compel, as by exercising influence: She muscled the bill through Congress. —**Idiom. 5. muscle in (on),** to impose one's presence or participation, as with respect to an existing activity, business, etc.

mus•cle•bound /'mʌsəlˌbawnd/ adj. having enlarged muscles, as from too much exercise.

mus•cu•lar /'mʌskyələr/ adj. **1.** of or relating to muscle or the muscles. **2.** having well-developed muscles; brawny: muscular lifeguards.

muse¹ /myuwz/ v. [no obj], **mused, mus•ing.** to think about or ponder quietly: He sat by the window, musing about the world.

muse² /myuwz/ n. [count; sometimes: Muse] the imaginary or spiritual force regarded as inspiring poets, writers, artists, etc., or any source of creative inspiration, esp. another person.

mu•se•um /myuw'ziyəm/ n. [count] a building where works of art or other objects of value are kept and displayed.

mush /mʌʃ or, esp. for 2, 3 mʊʃ/ n. [noncount] **1.** a thick mixture made by boiling meal, esp. cornmeal, in water or milk. **2.** anything that is overly emotional or sentimental. —v. [~ + obj] **3.** to squeeze or crush; crunch.

mush•room /'mʌʃruwm, -rʊm/ n. [count] **1.** a fungus with a stem and rounded top: Some mushrooms are poisonous. —v. [no obj] **2.** to spread, grow, or develop quickly: Sales began to mushroom.

mush•y /'mʌʃiy, 'mʊʃiy/ adj., **-i•er, -i•est. 1.** resembling mush; pulpy: mushy oatmeal. **2.** overly emotional or sentimental: mushy love letters. —**'mush•i•ness,** n. [noncount]

mu•sic /'myuwzɪk/ n. [noncount] **1.** sounds arranged to have pleasing or otherwise expressive melody, rhythm, or harmony: music to soothe the soul; The music (of the song) was (composed) by Oscar Hammerstein II. **2.** the written or printed set of musical notes for a composition: She tried to play from memory, but found that she needed the music.

mu•si•cal /'myuwzɪkəl/ adj. **1.** [before a noun] of, relating to, or resembling music: a musical instrument. **2.** fond of or skilled in music: My daughters are both very musical. —n. [count] **3.** Also called **'musical 'comedy.** a play or motion picture in which the story is told by songs, dances, etc. —**'mu•si•cal•ly,** adv.

mu•si•cian /myuw'zɪʃən/ n. [count] one who performs music, esp. professionally. —**mu'si•cian,ship,** n. [noncount]

musk /mʌsk/ n. [noncount] **1.** a strong-smelling substance obtained from a certain deer and used to make perfumes. **2.** an artificial imitation of this substance. —**'musk•y,** adj., **-i•er, -i•est.**

musk•rat /'mʌskˌræt/ n. [count], pl. **-rats,** (esp. when thought of as a group) **-rat.** a large North American rodent that lives in water.

Mus•lim /'mʌzlɪm, 'mʊz-, 'mʊs-/ also **Mos•lem** /'mɒzləm, 'mɒs-/ adj., n., pl. **-lims, -lim.** —adj. **1.** of or relating to the religion, law, or civilization of Islam. —n. [count] **2.** a follower of Islam.

mus•lin /'mʌzlɪn/ n. [noncount] a cotton fabric made in various degrees of fineness, used esp. for sheets.

muss /mʌs/ v. [~ + obj] to put into disorder; make messy: She mussed his hair a little. She mussed up his hair. She mussed her hair up.

mus•sel /'mʌsəl/ n. [count] a two-shelled water creature, a mollusk, the soft body of which can be eaten.

must /mʌst/ auxiliary v., pres. sing. and pl. 1st, 2nd, and 3rd pers. **must,** past **must,** n. —auxiliary (modal) verb. [~ + root form of a verb] **1.** (used to express that the action of the next verb is something that is morally or otherwise obligatory): *I must keep my promise. You must keep your word.* **2.** (used to express that the action of the next verb is a requirement of law or of social, religious, etc., convention or rule): *The rules must be obeyed. You must not smoke inside public buildings.* **3.** (used to express that the action of the next verb cannot be avoided, or that it is necessary because of natural law or the way the universe is): *All good things must come to an end. One must eat to live.* **4.** (used to express that the action of the next verb is necessary in order to achieve some result): *We must hurry if we're to arrive on time.* **5.** (used to express feeling strongly motivated, though not really required, to do the action of the next verb): *I must buy that book.* **6.** (used to express that the action of the next verb is very likely to happen or to be true, or that it is reasonable to expect that action to happen or to be true): *You must be joking. He must be at least 70 years old.* **7.** (used in clauses with "if," and in certain questions, to express annoyance): *If you must know, I was late. Must you repeat everything I say?* —*n.* [*count; singular; a* + ~] **8.** something necessary or required: *Getting enough sleep is a must.*

mus•tache /ˈmʌstæʃ, məˈstæʃ/ *n.* [*count*] the hair growing on the upper lip. —**'mus•tached,** *adj.*

mus•tang /ˈmʌstæŋ/ *n.* [*count*] a small, strong horse of the American plains.

mus•tard /ˈmʌstərd/ *n.* [*noncount*] a strong-smelling and strong-tasting condiment prepared from the seed of a plant, used esp. as a food seasoning.

mus•ter /ˈmʌstər/ *v.* **1.** to assemble (troops, etc.), as for battle or inspection: [~ + *obj*]: *The ship's company was mustered on the main deck.* [*no obj*]: *The ship's company mustered on the main deck.* **2.** [~ + *obj*] to gather or summon: *He mustered all his courage.*

must•n't /ˈmʌsənt/ a contraction of *must not.*

mus•ty /ˈmʌstiy/ *adj.,* **-ti•er, -ti•est.** having an odor or flavor that suggests mold: *a musty old library.* —**'mus•ti•ness,** *n.* [*noncount*]

mu•tate /ˈmyuwteyt/ *v.,* **-tat•ed, -tat•ing.** to (cause to) undergo mutation: [*no obj*]: *The plant must have mutated.* [~ + *obj*]: *Radiation can mutate plant life by affecting the genes.*

mu•ta•tion /myuwˈteyʃən/ *n.* **1. a.** [*noncount*] [*count*] sudden departure or change from the parent type, seen in offspring in one or more characteristics that have been inherited, caused by a change in a gene or chromosome. **b.** [*count*] an individual, species, or the like resulting from such a change. **2.** [*count*] [*noncount*] a change or alteration, as in form or nature.

mute /myuwt/ *adj.,* **mut•er, mut•est** *n., v.,* **mut•ed, mut•ing.** —*adj.* **1.** silent; not having or giving off any sound: *They were mute when questioned.* **2.** incapable of speech: *mute from birth.* —*n.* [*count*] **3.** a person incapable of speech. **4.** a mechanical device for muffling the tone of a musical instrument. —*v.* [~ + *obj*] **5.** to deaden or muffle the sound of a (musical instrument, etc.) **6.** to reduce the intensity of (a color) by the addition of another color. —**'mute•ly,** *adv.*

mu•ti•late /ˈmyuwtᵊleyt/ *v.* [~ + *obj*], **-lat•ed, -lat•ing.** to injure the appearance of, by damaging its parts: *to mutilate a painting.* —**mu•ti•la•tion** /ˌmyuwtᵊˈleyʃən/, *n.* [*noncount*]

mu•ti•ny /ˈmyuwtᵊniy/ *n., pl.* **-nies,** *v.,* **-nied, -ny•ing.** —*n.* **1.** rebellion against legal authority, esp. by sailors or soldiers against their officers:

[*noncount*]: *guilty of mutiny.* [*count*]: *a mutiny on board the ship.* —*v.* [*no obj*] **2.** to commit mutiny. —**'mu•ti•nous,** *adj.: a mutinous crew.*

mutt /mʌt/ *n.* [*count*] *Slang.* a dog of mixed breeds; a mongrel.

mut•ter /ˈmʌtər/ *v.* to say words or make sounds in a low tone that is hard to hear or understand; murmur: [*no obj*]: *He sat, muttering quietly to himself.* [~ + *obj*]: *He muttered a few words of greeting.* —**'mut•ter•er,** *n.* [*count*]

mut•ton /ˈmʌtn̩/ *n.* [*noncount*] the flesh of a mature sheep, used as food.

mu•tu•al /ˈmyuwtʃuwəl/ *adj.* **1.** felt or performed by each of two with respect to the other; reciprocal: *The couple showed mutual respect.* **2.** having the same relation each toward the other: *mutual enemies.* —**'mu•tu•al•ly,** *adv.*

'mutual ˌfund, *n.* [*count*] an investment company that constantly sells its stock, which it must repurchase from its shareholders when asked to do so.

muz•zle /ˈmʌzəl/ *n., v.,* **-zled, -zling.** —*n.* [*count*] **1.** the part of the head of an animal that comprises the jaws, mouth, and nose. **2.** the mouth of the barrel of a gun, etc. **3.** a device, usually an arrangement of straps or wires, placed over an animal's mouth to prevent the animal from biting, eating, etc. —*v.* [~ + *obj*] **4.** to put a muzzle on (an animal). **5.** to restrain from or prevent speech or the expression of opinion: *The censors muzzled the press.*

my /may/ *pron.* **1.** a form of the possessive case of the pronoun I, used as an adjective before a noun: *My soup is cold.* **2.** (used in formal or polite forms of address before titles, names, etc.): *Yes, my lord, I'll see to it right away. My dear Mrs. Adams, how nice to see you.* —*interj.* **3.** an exclamation of mild surprise or dismay: *My, what a mess!*

my•o•pi•a /mayˈowpiyə/ *n.* [*noncount*] a condition of the eye in which objects can be seen clearly only when near to the eye; nearsightedness. —**my•op•ic** /mayˈɒpɪk/, *adj.*

myr•i•ad /ˈmɪriyəd/ *n.* [*count*] **1.** a great number of persons or things: *a myriad of problems.* —*adj.* [*before a noun*] **2.** of a great number.

myr•tle /ˈmɜrtl/ *n.* [*count*] a shrub of S Europe, having evergreen leaves, fragrant white flowers, and sweet-smelling berries.

my•self /mayˈself/ *pron.* **1.** a form of the pronoun ME, a reflexive pronoun, used as the direct or indirect object of a verb or as the object of a preposition, when the subject is *I: I excused myself from the table. I gave myself a treat. I was pretty happy with myself.* **2.** (used to add emphasis to the pronouns I or ME): *I myself don't like it. I did it all myself.* **3.** my normal, healthy, or customary self: *I wasn't myself when I said that.*

mys•ter•y /ˈmɪstəriy, -triy/ *n., pl.* **-er•ies.** **1.** [*count*] anything that is kept secret or remains unexplained or unknown: *the mysteries of nature.* **2.** [*count*] a novel, film, or the like with a plot involving the solving of a puzzle, esp. a crime. **3.** [*noncount*] the quality of being hidden, hard to understand, or puzzling: *The place has an air of mystery about it.* —**my•ste•ri•ous** /mɪˈstɪəriyəs/ *adj.* —**mys'te•ri•ous•ly,** *adv.*

mys•tic /ˈmɪstɪk/ *adj.* [*before a noun*] **1.** mystical. —*n.* [*count*] **2.** one who claims to have insight into ultimate reality or mysteries beyond ordinary human knowledge.

mys•ti•cal /ˈmɪstɪkəl/ *adj.* **1.** [*before a noun*] occult; of spiritual or mysterious character or significance. **2.** of or relating to mystics or mysticism: *mystical writings.* —'**mys•ti•cal•ly,** *adv.*

mys•ti•cism /'mɪstə,sɪzəm/ *n.* [*noncount*] the belief that it is possible to gain knowledge of spiritual truths beyond ordinary human understanding, through a direct union with God that occurs after fasting, praying, meditating, or the like.

mys•ti•fy /'mɪstə,faɪ/ *v.* [~ + *obj*], **-fied, -fy• ing.** to cause confusion; to perplex or bewilder: *We were completely mystified by his decision not to take such a good job.* —**mys•ti•fi•ca•tion** /,mɪstəfɪ'keɪʃən/, *n.* [*noncount*]

mys•tique /mɪ'stiyk/ *n.* [*noncount*] a feeling or aura of mystery surrounding a particular person, institution, activity, etc.: *the mystique of appearing in a Broadway show.*

myth /mɪθ/ *n.* **1.** [*count*] a traditional story, esp. one that involves gods and heroes and explains a practice or some natural or historical phenomenon: *Greek, Roman, and African myths.* **2.** [*noncount*] stories of this kind thought of as a group; mythology. **3.** an invented story, fictitious person, etc.: [*noncount*]: *His account of the event is pure myth.* [*count*]: *Her wealthy lover is just a myth.* **4.** [*count*] a belief or set of beliefs that surround a person, phenomenon, or institution: *myths of racial superiority.* —'**myth•i•cal,** *adj.*

my•thol•o•gy /mɪ'θɒlədʒiy/ *n., pl.* **-gies. 1.** [*count*] a body of myths, as that of a particular people. **2.** [*noncount*] the science or study of myths. **3.** [*count*] a set of stories, traditions, or beliefs associated with a particular person, event, or institution: *An entire mythology has grown around the dead movie star.* —**myth•o•log•i•cal** /,mɪθə'lɒdʒɪkəl/, *adj.*

N

N, n /ɛn/ *n.* [*count*], *pl.* **Ns** or **N's, ns** or **n's.** the 14th letter of the English alphabet, a consonant.

N., an abbreviation of: **1.** north. **2.** northern. **3.** November.

n., an abbreviation of: **1.** name. **2.** neuter. **3.** new. **4.** north. **5.** northern. **6.** noun. **7.** number.

N.A., an abbreviation of: **1.** North America. **2.** not applicable.

nab /næb/ *v.* [~ + *obj*], **nabbed, nab•bing.** *Informal.* **1.** to arrest or capture: *The police nabbed the crooks.* **2.** to catch or seize, esp. suddenly: *The kidnappers nabbed him as he got into his car.*

nag /næg/ *v.*, **nagged, nag•ging,** *n.* —*v.* [~ + *obj*] [*no obj*] **1.** to annoy by continuously finding fault or making demands. **2.** to be a constant source of worry or irritation to: *a nagging backache; The debt kept nagging at his conscience.* —*n.* [*count*] **3.** a person who nags.

nail /neyl/ *n.* [*count*] **1.** a thin, rod-shaped piece of metal with a pointed tip, hammered into wood as a fastener. **2.** a thin, hard covering at the end of a finger or toe. —*v.* [~ + *obj*] **3.** to fasten with a nail: *to nail a picture to the wall; to nail (up) a sign on the wall.* **4.** *Informal.* to catch; seize: *The police nailed him as he was trying to escape.* **5. nail down,** to make final; settle: *to nail down an agreement; Nail it down before you sign anything.*

'nail ,file, *n.* [*count*] a bar of metal or plastic with a rough surface, used for shaping the fingernails.

na•ive or **na•ïve** /nɑˈiyv/ *adj.* **1.** childlike and innocent. **2.** showing a lack of experience, wisdom, or judgment. —**na'ive•ly,** *adv.*

na•ive•té or **na•ïve•té** /nɑiyvˈtey, -ˌiyvəˈtey, -ˈiyvtey, -ˈiyvə-/ *n.* [*noncount*] the quality or state of being naive.

na•ked /ˈneykɪd/ *adj.* **1.** being without clothing; nude. **2.** [*before a noun*] lacking the usual covering or protection: *naked light bulbs.* **3.** [*before a noun*] not assisted by the use of a microscope, telescope, or other instrument: *a planet barely visible to the naked eye.* **4.** [*before a noun*] plain; simple: *the naked truth.* —**'na•ked•ly,** *adv.* —**'na•ked•ness,** *n.* [*noncount*]

name /neym/ *n.*, *v.*, **named, nam•ing,** *adj.* —*n.* **1.** [*count*] a word or phrase by which a person or thing is identified or known. **2.** [*count*] an insulting description: *He called her names.* **3.** [*count; usually singular*] a reputation: *His dishonesty gave him a bad name.* **b.** a famous reputation: *made a name for herself in politics.* —*v.* [~ + *obj*] **4.** to give a name to; call: *to name a baby; They named their baby Frederick.* **5.** to identify by name: *Name all the state capitals.* **6.** to appoint or nominate for duty or office: *They named him (as) campaign manager.* **7.** to specify; say what something should be: *Name your price.* —*adj.* [*before a noun*] **8.** famous; well-known: *a (big) name author.* **9.** designed for or bearing a name: *name tags.* —**Idiom.** **10. by name,** using the name of someone directly: *I mentioned you by name.* **11. in name only,** having a title or position but not the power to go with it: *a king in name only.*

name•ly /ˈneymliy/ *adv.* that is to say; specifi-

cally: *a new item of legislation, namely, the housing bill.*

name•sake /ˈneym,seyk/ *n.* [*count*] **1.** a person named after another. **2.** a person having the same name as another.

nan•ny /ˈnæniy/ *n.* [*count*], *pl.* **-nies.** a person hired to care for children in a household.

nap /næp/ *v.*, **napped, nap•ping,** *n.* —*v.* [*no obj*] **1.** to sleep for a short time; doze. —*n.* [*count*] **2.** a brief period of sleep, esp. one taken during daytime. —**'nap•per,** *n.* [*count*]

nape /neyp, næp/ *n.* [*count*] the back of the neck.

nap•kin /ˈnæpkɪn/ *n.* [*count*] **1.** a piece of cloth or paper for use in wiping the lips and fingers and to protect the clothes while eating. **2.** *Chiefly Brit.* DIAPER.

nap•py /ˈnæpiy/ *n.* [*count*], *pl.* **-pies.** *Brit.* a diaper.

nar•cis•sus /nɑrˈsɪsəs/ *n.* [*count*], *pl.* **-cis•sus,** **-cis•sus•es, -cis•si** /-ˈsɪsiy, -ˈsɪsay/. a plant that grows from a bulb and has yellow or white flowers.

nar•cot•ic /nɑrˈkɒtɪk/ *n.* [*count*] an often addictive substance that causes sleep or relief from pain.

nar•rate /ˈnæreyt, næˈreyt/ *v.* [~ + *obj*], **-rat•ed, -rat•ing.** to give an account of (events, experiences, etc.). —**nar•ra•tion** /næˈreyʃən/, *n.* [*noncount*] [*count*] —**'nar•ra•tor,** *n.* [*count*]

nar•ra•tive /ˈnærətɪv/ *n.* [*count*] a story or account of events, experiences, or the like, whether true or fictional.

nar•row /ˈnærow/ *adj.*, **-er, -est,** *v.* —*adj.* **1.** of little width; not wide or broad: *a narrow alley.* **2.** limited in range or scope: *a narrow view of right and wrong.* **3.** barely successful: *a narrow escape.* —*v.* [*no obj*] [~ + *obj*] **4.** to (cause to) become narrow. —**'nar•row•ness,** *n.* [*noncount*]

nar•row•ly /ˈnærowliy/ *adv.* **1.** nearly; only just: *narrowly avoided capture.* **2.** closely; with close attention: *She watched them narrowly.*

'narrow-'minded, *adj.* having a mind that is unwilling to accept or consider new ideas. —**'narrow-'mindedness,** *n.* [*noncount*]

NASA /ˈnæsə/ *n.* National Aeronautics and Space Administration.

na•sal /ˈneyzəl/ *adj.* of or relating to the nose.

nas•tur•tium /nəˈstɜrʃəm, næ-/ *n.* [*count*], *pl.* **-tiums.** a garden plant having shield-shaped leaves and colorful flowers.

nas•ty /ˈnæstiy/ *adj.*, **-ti•er, -ti•est.** **1.** offensive to taste, smell, or the senses in general: *a nasty smell of garbage.* **2.** unpleasant; mean: *a nasty temper.* **3.** very bad: *a nasty accident.* —**nas•ti•ly** /ˈnæstḷiy/, *adv.* —**'nas•ti•ness,** *n.* [*noncount*]

na•tal /ˈneytḷ/ *adj.* of or relating to birth.

na•tion /ˈneyʃən/ *n.* [*count*] a body of people living in a particular territory, unified by culture, language, customs, and government. —**'na•tion,hood,** *n.* [*noncount*]

na•tion•al /ˈnæʃənḷ, ˈnæʃnəl/ *adj.* of, relating to, or belonging to a nation: *a national anthem.* —**'na•tion•al•ly,** *adv.*

na•tion•al•ism /ˈnæʃənḷ,ɪzəm, ˈnæʃnə,lɪz-/ *n.* [*noncount*] devotion and loyalty to one's own nation; patriotism. —**'na•tion•al•ist,** adj., n. [count]

na•tion•al•i•ty /,næʃ ə'nælɪtiy/ n., pl. **-ties. 1.** [noncount] the condition of belonging to a particular nation, whether by birth or by becoming a citizen. **2.** [count] a particular people: Many different nationalities came to the U.S.

na•tion•al•ize /'næʃənļ,ayz, 'næʃnə,layz/ v. [~ + obj], **-ized, -iz•ing.** to bring (a private industry) under the ownership or control of a government. —**na•tion•al•i•za•tion** /,næʃənļɪ'zeyʃən/, n. [noncount]

na•tion•wide /'neyʃən'wayd/ adj. extending throughout a nation.

na•tive /'neytɪv/ adj. **1.** [before a noun] being the place or environment in which a person was born or in which a thing came into being: returned to his native land. **2.** [before a noun] belonging to a person by birth or to a thing by nature: the desert's native beauty. **3.** belonging to or originating in a certain place: The dancers wore their native dress. —n. [count] **4.** a person who lived in a place originally or has lived there a long time. **5.** an animal or plant originating in a particular region.

'Native A'merican, n. AMERICAN INDIAN.

na•tiv•i•ty /nə'tɪvɪtiy, ney-/ n., pl. **-ties. 1.** [count] a birth. **2.** [the Nativity] the birth of Christ.

NATO /'neytow/ n. North American Treaty Organization.

nat•u•ral /'nætʃərəl, 'nætʃrəl/ adj. **1.** existing in, relating to, or formed by nature and not by humans. **2.** [before a noun] being such because of one's nature; innate: natural athletes. **3.** normal; to be expected: a natural result; It's natural that parents should miss their children. **4.** sincere; not faked: a natural manner. —n. [count] **5.** a person with a natural skill: Watch him race. He's a natural! —**'nat•u•ral•ness,** n. [noncount]

'natural 'gas, n. [noncount] a gas that is found underground and under the sea, and is used for heating and cooking.

'natural 'history, n. [noncount] the study of plants, animals, rocks, and other natural objects.

nat•u•ral•ist /'nætʃərəlɪst, 'nætʃrə-/ n. [count] a person who studies plants or animals.

nat•u•ral•ize /'nætʃərə,layz, 'nætʃrə-/ v. [~ + obj], **-ized, -iz•ing.** to make (someone) a citizen. —**nat•u•ral•i•za•tion** /,nætʃərəlɪ'zeyʃən/, n. [noncount]

nat•u•ral•ly /'nætʃərəliy, 'nætʃrəliy, / adv. **1.** in a natural manner: Just smile naturally. **2.** being in a certain way by nature: She has naturally curly hair. **3.** of course; as would be expected: Naturally, you'll have to pay in advance. —Idiom. **4. come naturally,** to be easy for someone to do or learn: Playing the violin comes naturally to her.

na•ture /'neytʃər/ n. **1.** [noncount] the natural world as it exists without human beings or civilization; the elements of the natural world, as trees, animals, or rivers. **2.** [count] the typical character of someone or something: It is a cat's nature to keep itself clean. **3.** character or type: [count; usually singular]: What is the nature of the problem? [noncount]: The problems are economic in nature.

naught /nɔt/ n. [noncount] **1.** nothing. **2.** zero: a score of ten to naught. —Idiom. **3. come to naught,** to end in failure: His plans came to naught.

naugh•ty /'nɔtiy/ adj., **-ti•er, -ti•est. 1.** disobe-

dient; mischievous. **2.** improper or offensive: a naughty word. —**naugh•ti•ly** /'nɔtliy/, adv. —**'naugh•ti•ness,** n. [noncount]

nau•se•a /'nɔziyə, -ʒə, -siyə, -ʃə/ n. [noncount] sickness in the stomach, esp. when accompanied by a desire to vomit.

nau•se•ate /'nɔziy,eyt, -ʒiy-, -siy-, -ʃiy-/ v. [~ + obj], **-at•ed, -at•ing. 1.** to cause (someone) to feel nausea: The rolling of the ship nauseated him. **2.** to cause to feel great disgust: I was nauseated by such cruelty.

nau•se•at•ing /'nɔziy,eytɪŋ, -ʒiy-, -siy-, -ʃiy-/ adj. causing a feeling of nausea: a nauseating smell. —**'nau•se,at•ing•ly,** adv.

nau•seous /'nɔʃəs, -ziyəs/ adj. **1.** affected with nausea or disgust: I feel nauseous. **2.** causing nausea or disgust: a nauseous smell. —**'nau•seous•ness,** n. [noncount]

nau•ti•cal /'nɔtɪkəl, 'nɒtɪ-/ adj. of or relating to sailors, ships, or navigation.

'nautical 'mile, n. [count] a unit of distance at sea, equal to 1.852 kilometers.

na•val /'neyvəl/ adj. [before a noun] of or relating to ships or to a navy.

nave /neyv/ n. [count] the long central area of a church from the main entrance to the space around the altar.

na•vel /'neyvəl/ n. [count] the hollow part of the abdomen where the umbilical cord was connected with the fetus.

nav•i•ga•ble /'nævɪgəbəl/ adj. deep and wide enough for ships to pass through: a navigable river.

nav•i•gate /'nævɪ,geyt/ v., **-gat•ed, -gat•ing. 1.** [~ + obj] [no obj] to move on, over, or through (water, air, or land) in a ship or aircraft. **2.** [~ + obj] [no obj] to direct or manage (a ship, aircraft, spacecraft, etc.) on its course. **3.** to walk or find one's way on, in, or across: [~ + obj]: It was hard to navigate the stairs in the dark. [no obj]: Can you navigate through the downtown area safely? —**nav•i•ga•tion** /,nævɪ'geyʃən/ n. [noncount] —**nav•i•ga•tor** /'nævɪ,geytər/ n. [count]

na•vy /'neyviy/ n., pl. **-vies. 1.** [count] the warships and supplies used by a country for fighting at sea. **2.** [noncount] Also, **navy blue.** a dark blue color.

nay /ney/ n. [count] **1.** a denial or refusal. **2.** a negative vote or voter.

Na•zi /'nɑtsiy, 'næt-/ n. [count], pl. **-zis. 1.** a member of the German fascist party that controlled Germany from 1933 to 1945 under Adolf Hitler. **2.** [often: nazi] a person with racist or fascist views. —**'Na•zism** /'nɑtsɪzəm, 'næt-/, **'Na•zi•ism,** n. [noncount]

NB or **N.B.,** an abbreviation of Latin nota bene: note well; take careful notice of what has been said or written.

n/c, an abbreviation of: no charge.

NC or **N.C.,** an abbreviation of: North Carolina.

ND or **N.D.,** an abbreviation of: North Dakota.

N.Dak., an abbreviation of: North Dakota.

NE, an abbreviation of: Nebraska.

near /nɪər/ adv. and adj., **-er, -est,** prep., v. —adv. **1.** close in space or time: Come nearer. The wedding day was drawing near. **2.** almost: a near-fatal accident. —adj. **3.** being close in space or time: the nearest city; the near future. **4.** closely related or connected: near relatives. **5.** narrow or close: That was a near miss. —prep. **6.** at, to, or within a short distance from: regions near (to) the equator. **7.** close to in time: Let's *meet again near the beginning of the year.* **8.** close to a condition, action, or amount: *She came near to hitting him.* —*v.* [~ + *obj*] [*no obj*] **9.** to come or draw near; approach. —**'near•ness,** *n.* [*noncount*]

near•by /'nɪər'bay/ *adj.* **1.** close at hand; next to; neighboring; adjacent: *This drug can be bought at your nearby pharmacy.* —*adv.* **2.** in the area close by: *The race was held nearby.*

near•ly /'nɪərliy/ *adv.* very close to; almost: *a plan nearly like our own.*

near•sight•ed /'nɪər,saytɪd, -'say-/ *adj.* able to see clearly at a short distance only. —'**near,sight•ed•ness,** *n.* [*noncount*]

neat /niyt/ *adj.,* **-er, -est. 1.** in a pleasingly orderly and clean condition: *a neat room.* **2.** cleverly effective: *a neat solution to the problem.* **3.** *Slang.* great; wonderful; fine. —'**neat•ly,** *adv.* —'**neat•ness,** *n.* [*noncount*]

Neb. or **Nebr.,** an abbreviation of: Nebraska.

neb•u•lous /'nɛbyələs/ *adj.* hazy, vague, unclear, or confused: *his nebulous theories.*

nec•es•sar•i•ly /,nɛsə'sɛrəliy, -'sɛr-/ *adv.* as a necessary or logical result: *That conclusion doesn't necessarily follow.*

nec•es•sar•y /'nɛsə,sɛriy/ *adj.* essential; needed: *a necessary change in our plans; It is necessary that you stay until Sunday. It isn't necessary (for you) to stay.*

ne•ces•si•tate /nə'sɛsɪ,teyt/ *v.* [~ + *obj*], **-tat•ed, -tat•ing.** to make necessary: *These comments don't necessitate a response. The extra guests necessitated our taking two cars.*

ne•ces•si•ty /nə'sɛsɪtiy/ *n., pl.* **-ties. 1.** [*count*] something necessary: *The poor lacked food, shelter, and other necessities of life.* **2.** [*noncount*] the fact of something being necessary or needed: *the necessity of having safe housing.* —*Idiom.* **3. of necessity,** unavoidably; necessarily: *The report we wrote was of necessity rushed and full of errors.*

neck /nɛk/ *n.* [*count*] **1.** the part of the body that connects the head and the trunk. **2.** the part of a garment closest to the neck. **3.** a slender part that resembles a neck: *a bottle with a narrow neck.* —*v.* [*no obj*] **4.** *Informal.* to engage in kissing and caressing. —*Idiom.* **5. neck and neck,** just even or very close in a race. **6. stick one's neck out,** *Informal.* to take a risk: *willing to stick his neck out to help his friends.*

neck•lace /'nɛklɪs/ *n.* [*count*] a piece of jewelry worn around the neck.

neck•line /'nɛk,layn/ *n.* [*count*] the opening at the neck of a garment.

neck•tie /'nɛk,tay/ *n.* [*count*] a band of decorative fabric worn around the neck under the collar and knotted in front with the ends hanging down.

nec•tar /'nɛktər/ *n.* [*noncount*] the sweet liquid of a plant that attracts bees or birds.

nec•tar•ine /,nɛktə'riyn, 'nɛktə,riyn/ *n.* [*count*] a variety of peach having a smooth, shiny skin.

need /niyd/ *v.* **1.** [*count*] a lack of something wanted or necessary: *the needs of the poor.* **2.** [*noncount*] urgent want: *They have need of your help.* **3.** [*count*] a necessary duty or obligation: *There is no need to go there.* —*v.* [~ + *obj*] **4.** to have need of; require: *Fish need water. The lawn needed mowing. Do you need me to help with the dishes?* —*auxiliary v.* [~ + *root form of a verb*] **5.** [*with a negative word or phrase, or in a question*] to have to: *Need I say more? You need not drive so fast.*

nee•dle /'niydl/ *n., v.,* **-dled, -dling.** —*n.* [*count*] **1.** a thin, pointed piece of metal with a hole for thread, used in sewing. **2.** a needle used to give an injection under the skin. **3.** a needle-shaped leaf of a pine tree. —*v.* [~ + *obj*] **4.** *Informal.* to tease; make fun of.

need•less /'niydlɪs/ *adj.* **1.** unnecessary: *a needless waste of food.* —*Idiom.* **2. needless to say,** (used to emphasize that what is about to be said is clear and obvious): *We played the champions and, needless to say, we lost again.* —'**need•less•ly,** *adv.*

nee•dle•work /'niydl,wɜrk/ *n.* [*noncount*] the art, process, or product of working with a needle, esp. in embroidery and sewing.

need•n't /'niydnt/ a contraction of *need not: You needn't worry.*

need•y /'niydiy/ *adj.,* **-i•er, -i•est,** *n.* —*adj.* **1.** poor or in need. —*n.* **2. the needy,** [*plural*] needy persons thought of as a group. —'**need•i•ness,** *n.* [*noncount*]

ne•gate /nɪ'geyt, 'nɛgeyt/ *v.* [~ + *obj*], **-gat•ed, -gat•ing. 1.** to deny or refuse: *negated our beliefs.* **2.** to cause to be ineffective or useless: *The judge's decision negated the other court's ruling.* —**ne'ga•tion,** *n.* [*noncount*] [*count*]

neg•a•tive /'nɛgətɪv/ *adj.* **1.** containing or suggesting the word "no" or "not;" expressing denial or refusal. **2.** not helpful or willing: *a negative attitude.* **3.** *Math.* **a.** involving subtraction; minus. **b.** less than zero. **4.** being a photographic image in which the lightest areas are shown as the darkest. **5.** of or relating to the electric charge of a body that has an excess of electrons. **6.** showing that a disease or condition is not present: *The test was negative.* —*n.* [*count*] **7.** a negative statement, answer, word, gesture, etc. **8.** a negative quality or characteristic. **9.** a negative photographic image. —*Idiom.* **10. in the negative,** in the form of a negative response: *to answer in the negative.* —'**neg•a•tive•ly,** *adv.*

ne•glect /nɪ'glɛkt/ *v.* [~ + *obj*] **1.** to fail to give enough care to: *She neglected her health.* **2.** to fail to do something: *to neglect to do the household chores; He neglected to answer your invitation.* —*n.* [*noncount*] **3.** an act or instance of neglecting: *neglect of the property.* **4.** the fact or state of being neglected: *a house left in total neglect.* —**ne'glect•ful,** *adj.*

neg•li•gent /'nɛglɪdʒənt/ *adj.* not attentive or careful; characterized by neglect: *a negligent driver.* —'**neg•li•gence,** *n.* [*noncount*] —'**neg•li•gent•ly,** *adv.*

neg•li•gi•ble /'nɛglɪdʒəbəl/ *adj.* so small or unimportant as to be safely ignored: *negligible expenses.*

ne•go•ti•a•ble /nɪ'gowʃiyəbəl, -ʃəbəl/ *adj.* **1.** capable of being discussed or negotiated: *Most of their demands are not negotiable.* **2.** that can be transferred or exchanged for money: *negotiable stocks and bonds.*

ne•go•ti•ate /nɪ'gowʃiy,eyt/ *v.,* **-at•ed, -at•ing. 1.** [*no obj*] [~ + *obj*] to deal or bargain with another or others, as in working out the terms of a contract. **2.** [~ + *obj*] to move through or over in an effective or safe way: *The car had trouble negotiating sharp curves.* —**ne,go•ti'a•tion,** *n.* [*noncount*] [*count*] —**ne'go•ti,a•tor,** *n.* [*count*]

Ne•gro /'niygrow/ *adj., n., pl.* **-groes.** *Sometimes Offensive.* —*adj.* **1.** of or being one of the traditional racial divisions of human beings, the people of which have brown to black skin and dark eyes and come originally from central and southern Africa. —*n.* [*count*] **2.** a member of the Negro race; black person.

neigh /ney/ *n.* [*count*] **1.** the high-pitched, snorting sound of a horse. —*v.* [*no obj*] **2.** to make such a sound.

neigh•bor /'neybər/ *n.* [*count*] **1.** a person who lives near another. **2.** a person or thing that is near another: *Canada, America's neighbor to the North.* Also, *esp. Brit.,* '**neigh•bour.** —'**neigh•bor•ing,** *adj.*: *neighboring villages.*

neigh•bor•hood /'neybər,hʊd/ *n.* [*count*] **1.** an area within a larger place: *the kids in the neighborhood; the safest neighborhood in the city.* —*Idiom.* **2. in the neighborhood of,** approximately; about: *The job will pay in the neighborhood of $60,000.*

neigh•bor•ly /'neybərliy/ *adj.* friendly and helpful to neighbors. —'**neigh•bor•li•ness,** *n.* [*noncount*]

nei•ther /'niyðər, 'nay-/ *conj.* **1.** [~ + *phrase* + *nor* + *phrase*] not either: *Neither John nor Betty is at home.* **2.** (used after a negative phrase or clause; the subject and verb after it are reversed) nor: *He can't be there; neither can I.* —*adj.* [*before a noun*] **3.** not either; not the one or the other: *We'll take neither path; instead, we'll rest under this tree.* —*pron.* [*usually considered singular and used with a singular verb*] **4.** not either; not one person or thing or the other: *Neither is to be trusted. Neither of the keys fits the lock.*

neo-, a prefix meaning new, recent, or revived (*neoclassic; neocolonialism*).

ne•on /'niyɒn/ *n.* [*noncount*] **1.** a colorless, odorless gas used in a type of electrical lamp. **2.** an advertising sign formed from a type of electrical lamp containing neon.

neph•ew /'nɛfyuw/ *n.* [*count*] **1.** a son of one's brother or sister. **2.** a son of one's spouse's brother or sister.

nerd /nɜrd/ *n.* [*count*] *Slang.* a socially awkward person, esp. one interested in intellectual subjects or technology: *a computer nerd.* —'**nerd•y,** *adj.,* **-i•er, -i•est.**

nerve /nɜrv/ *n.* **1.** [*count*] one or more bundles of fibers that carry messages of feeling or motion between the brain and other parts of the body. **2.** [*noncount*] courage: *It took nerve to enter the burning building.* **3.** [*noncount*] boldness; rude behavior. **4. nerves,** [*plural*] nervousness: *a bad attack of nerves.* —*Idiom.* **5. get on someone's nerves,** to irritate or annoy someone.

'**nerve ,cell,** *n.* NEURON.

'**nerve-,racking** or '**nerve-,wracking,** *adj.* producing great worry, tension, or irritation.

nerv•ous /'nɜrvəs/ *adj.* **1.** [*be* + ~] very uneasy or worried; fearful; tense: *He's nervous about the results of the election.* **2.** [*before a noun*] of, relating to, or affecting the nerves: *a nervous disease.* —'**nerv•ous•ly,** *adv.* —'**nerv•ous•ness,** *n.* [*noncount*]

'**nervous 'breakdown,** *n.* [*count*] a severe but unspecific mental or emotional disorder.

'**nervous 'system,** *n.* [*count*] the system in humans and animals that receives messages from outside the body and sends messages that result in movement and other responses; in vertebrates, it includes the brain, spinal cord, and nerves.

nerv•y /'nɜrviy/ *adj.,* **-i•er, -i•est. 1.** bold; pushy: *a nervy request for a free ticket.* **2.** having or showing courage.

-ness, a suffix meaning quality or state (*goodness; darkness*).

nest /nɛst/ *n.* [*count*] **1.** a home or shelter prepared by a bird, insect, or other animal for holding eggs and caring for young. **2.** a set of items that fit close together or one within another: *a nest of tables.* —*v.* [*no obj*] **3.** to build or have a nest: *Many birds nest in trees.*

nes•tle /'nɛsəl/ *v.,* **-tled, -tling.** to lie close and snug; snuggle; cuddle: [*no obj*]: *They were nestling in bed.* [~ + *obj*]: *She nestled herself in the chair.*

nest•ling /'nɛstlɪŋ, 'nɛslɪŋ/ *n.* [*count*] a bird too young to leave the nest.

net¹ /nɛt/ *n., v.,* **net•ted, net•ting.** —*n.* **1.** [*noncount*] a fabric made from strings or rope knotted together with holes in between. **2.** [*count*] a bag or other piece of such fabric, for catching fish, butterflies, etc. **3.** [*count*] a piece of net used to divide a court in racket games. **4.** [*the Net*] the Internet. —*v.* [~ + *obj*] **5.** to catch with a net: *to net fish.*

net² /nɛt/ *adj., n., v.,* **net•ted, net•ting.** —*adj.* **1.** (of an amount of money) remaining after no further expenses or taxes need to be subtracted: *net price; net earnings; earned $200 net.* **2.** final; ultimate: *a net result.* **3.** (of weight) after deducting the weight of the container or wrapping: *The net weight is six grams. It weighs six grams net.* —*n.* [*count; usually singular*] **4.** net income, profit, etc. —*v.* [~ + *obj*] **5.** to gain or produce as profit: *The company netted over $150 million.*

net•tle /'nɛtl/ *n., v.,* **-tled, -tling.** —*n.* [*count*] **1.** a plant covered with stinging hairs. —*v.* [~ + *obj*] **2.** to irritate; annoy.

net•work /'nɛt,wɜrk/ *n.* [*count*] **1.** any combination of crossing pieces, lines, passages, etc.: *a network of veins.* **2.** a group of radio or television stations linked by wire or microwaves. **3.** any group of related or linked elements esp. over a large area: *a network of hospitals.* **4.** a group of computers that are linked to each other to permit exchange of information. **5.** a group of people who have a common interest and share information and services. —*v.* [~ + *obj*] **6.** to link (computers) in a network.

neu•ral /'nʊrəl, 'nyʊr-/ *adj.* [*before a noun*] of or relating to a nerve or the nervous system.

neu•rol•o•gy /nʊ'rɒlədʒiy, nyʊ-/ *n.* [*noncount*] the branch of medicine dealing with the nervous system. —**neu•ro•log•i•cal** /ˌnʊrə'lɒdʒɪkəl, ˌnyʊr-/, *adj.* —**neu'rol•o•gist,** *n.* [*count*]

neu•ron /'nʊrɒn, 'nyʊr-/ *n.* [*count*] a special cell in the body that sends along messages that represent feelings, commands to muscles, etc.

neu•ro•sis /nʊ'rowsɪs, nyʊ-/ *n.* [*count*], *pl.* **-ses** /-siyz/. a disorder of the mind in which anxiety, fears, obsessions, etc., control the personality. —**neu•rot•ic** /nʊ'rɒtɪk, nyʊ-/ *adj., n.* [*count*]

neu•ter /'nuwtər, 'nyuw-/ *adj.* **1.** of or being a grammatical gender that refers to things that are neither masculine nor feminine. —*v.* [*count*] **2.** a neuter word or word form. —*v.* [~ + *obj*] **3.** to remove the organs of reproduction of (a dog, cat, etc.) so it cannot produce babies.

neu•tral /'nuwtrəl, 'nyuw-/ *adj.* **1.** not taking part or giving assistance in a dispute or war between others: *a neutral nation.* **2.** being black, gray, beige, or white in color. —*n.* [*noncount*] **3.** the gear position in a car in which no power is transmitted from the engine to the wheels. —**neu'tral•i•ty,** *n.* [*noncount*] —'**neu•tral•ly,** *adv.*

neu·tral·ize /'nuwtrə,layz, 'nyuw-/ v. [~ + obj], -ized, -iz·ing. 1. to make neutral. 2. to make (something) have little or no effect; counteract: *His campaign team tried to neutralize the bad effects of the scandal.* —**neu·tral·i·za·tion** /,nuwtrəlɪ'zeyʃən, ,nyu-/, n. [*noncount*]

neu·tron /'nuwtrɒn, 'nyuw-/ n. [*count*] a tiny particle found in the nucleus of most atoms, having no electrical charge.

Nev., an abbreviation of: Nevada.

nev·er /'nɛvər/ adv. 1. not ever; at no time: *It never happened.* —**Idiom.** 2. **never mind,** don't bother; don't concern yourself: *Never mind about your mistake.*

nev·er·more /,nɛvər'mɔr/ adv. never again.

nev·er·the·less /,nɛvərðə'lɛs/ adv. however; in spite of that: *a small but nevertheless important improvement.*

new /nuw, nyuw/ adj., -er, -est, adv. —adj. 1. recently created, made, bought, etc.: *a new book.* 2. of a kind now existing or appearing for the first time: *a new concept of the universe.* 3. having only lately become known, discovered, or invented: *a new comet.* 4. unfamiliar (with something); just recently come to a place or position: *She is new to this town; a new student in our class.* —adv. 5. (used with an adjective or participle of a verb) recently: *a new-found friend.* —'**new·ness,** n. [*noncount*]

new·bie /'nuwbiy, 'nyuw-/ n. [*count*] a beginner, esp. an inexperienced user of the Internet or of computers in general.

new·born /'nuw'bɔrn, 'nyuw-/ adj., n., pl. -born, -borns. —adj. 1. recently or only just born. —n. [*count*] 2. a newborn infant.

new·com·er /'nuw,kʌmər, 'nyuw-/ n. [*count*] a person or thing that has recently arrived.

new·ly /'nuwliy, 'nyuw-/ adv. very recently: *newly married.*

new·ly·wed /'nuwliy,wɛd, 'nyuw-/ n. [*count*] a person who has recently married.

'new 'moon, n. [*count; usually singular*] the moon when it is almost invisible or visible only as a slender crescent.

news /nuwz, nyuwz/ n. [*noncount; used with a singular verb*] 1. a report of a recent event; information: *to hear news of a relative.* 2. [*the* + ~] a report on recent events in a newspaper or magazine, or on radio or television.

news·boy /'nuwz,bɔy, 'nyuwz-/ n. [*count*] a person, typically a boy, who sells or delivers newspapers.

news·cast /'nuwz,kæst, 'nyuwz-/ n. [*count*] a broadcast of news on radio or television. —'**news,cast·er,** n. [*count*]

news·let·ter /'nuwz,lɛtər, 'nyuwz-/ n. [*count*] an informational report issued regularly by an organization to employees, contributors, or the public.

news·pa·per /'nuwz,peypər, 'nyuwz-, 'nuws-, 'nyuws-/ n. [*count*] a publication, usually issued daily or weekly, containing news, articles of general interest, and advertising.

news·stand /'nuwz,stænd, 'nyuwz-/ n. [*count*] a stall or other place at which newspapers, magazines, and sometimes candy and other items are sold.

news·wor·thy /'nuwz,wɜrðiy, 'nyuwz-/ adj. of enough interest to be presented as news.

news·y /'nuwziy, 'nyuw-/ adj., -i·er, -i·est. full of news: *wrote a long, newsy letter.*

newt /nuwt, nyuwt/ n. [*count*] a brightly colored salamander that can live on land and in water.

'New 'Testament, n. the portion of the Christian Bible that records the life and teachings of Christ and his disciples.

'new 'year, n. [*count; singular; often: New Year*] the year approaching or newly begun: *Happy New Year!*

'New ,Year's 'Day, n. January 1, a day celebrated as a holiday in many countries.

'New ,Year's 'Eve, n. the night of December 31.

next /nɛkst/ adj. 1. immediately following in time, order, importance, etc.: *the next day; the next flight for the Bahamas.* 2. [*before a noun; usually: the* + ~] nearest or closest in place or position: *She lives in the next house.* —adv. 3. in the place, time, order, etc., nearest or immediately following: *We're going to London next.* —**Idiom.** 4. **next to, a.** near or close to: *Sit next to me.* **b.** almost; nearly: *Climbing that mountain was next to impossible.* **c.** aside from: *Next to me, you're the best.*

next-door /adv.'nɛks'dɔr, 'nɛkst-; adj. -,dɔr/ adv. 1. Also, **'next 'door.** to, at, or in the next house, apartment, etc.: *They live next door.* —adj. [*before a noun*] 2. located or living in the next house, apartment, etc.: *next-door neighbors.*

NH or **N.H.,** an abbreviation of: New Hampshire.

nib /nɪb/ n. [*count*] the point of a pen.

nib·ble /'nɪbəl/ v., -bled, -bling, n. —v. 1. to take small bites (of): [*no obj*]: *to nibble on a cracker.* [~ + obj]: *nibbling a cracker.* 2. to bite lightly or gently: [*no obj*]: *The puppy nibbled at his ear.* [~ + obj]: *She nibbled his ear.* —n. [*count*] 3. a small piece bitten off; a bite.

nice /nays/ adj., nic·er, nic·est. 1. pleasing; agreeable; delightful: *We had a nice visit. It was nice to see you again.* 2. kind; thoughtful: *Be nice to guests.* 3. polite in manners, speech, etc.: *It isn't nice to make noise in the library.* —**Idiom.** 4. **nice and,** (used with an adjective to express stronger pleasure, comfort, or the like): *It's nice and warm in here.* —'**nice·ly,** adv. —'**nice·ness,** n. [*noncount*]

ni·ce·ty /'naysɪtiy/ n. [*count*], pl. -ties. a delicate or fine point; a detail: *observing the niceties of polite behavior.*

niche /nɪtʃ/ n. [*count*] 1. a hollow place in a wall, as for a statue or other decorative object. 2. a suitable place or position: *trying to find his niche in the business world.*

nick /nɪk/ n. [*count*] 1. a small dent or cut: *a couple of nicks on his face from shaving.* —v. [~ + obj] 2. to make a nick in: *The rocks must have nicked the car door.*

nick·el /'nɪkəl/ n. 1. [*noncount*] a hard, silvery white metallic element, used in combinations of metals. 2. [*count*] a coin of the U.S., equal to five cents.

nick·name /'nɪk,neym/ n., v., -named, -naming. —n. [*count*] 1. a familiar, informal form of a proper name, as *Jim* for *James.* —v. [~ + obj] 2. to give a nickname to; call by a nickname.

nic·o·tine /'nɪkə,tiyn, -tɪn, ,nɪkə'tiyn/ n. [*noncount*] a poisonous and addictive substance found in tobacco.

niece /niys/ n. [*count*] 1. a daughter of one's brother or sister. 2. a daughter of one's spouse's brother or sister.

nif·ty /'nɪftiy/ adj., -ti·er, -ti·est. *Informal.* 1. very good; fine; excellent: *a nifty idea.* 2. attractively stylish: *a nifty new suit.*

nig·gard·ly /'nɪgərdliy/ adj. very stingy.

nigh /nay/ *adv.* near in space, time, or relation: *The ship drew nigh to the dock.*

night /nayt/ *n.* **1.** [*count*] [*noncount*] the period of darkness between sunset and sunrise. **2.** [*count*] evening: *Last night we saw a movie.* —*Idiom.* **3. night and day,** without stopping; continually: *worked night and day on the problem.*

night•club /'nayt,klʌb/ *n.* [*count*] an establishment open at night, offering food, drink, shows, dancing, etc.

night•fall /'nayt,fɔl/ *n.* [*noncount*] the coming of night; dusk.

night•gown /'nayt,gawn/ *n.* [*count*] a loose gown, worn in bed esp. by women or children.

night•ie /'naytiy/ *n.*, *pl.* **-ies.** *Informal.* NIGHT-GOWN.

night•in•gale /'naytn̩,geyl, 'naytɪŋ-/ *n.* [*count*] a small European wild bird known for its beautiful song, often heard at night.

night•ly /'naytliy/ *adj.* [*often: before a noun*] **1.** coming or occurring each night or at night. **2.** appearing or active at night. —*adv.* **3.** on every night: *Performances are given nightly.* **4.** at or by night.

night•mare /'nayt,mɛər/ *n.* [*count*] **1.** a frightening dream. **2.** an unpleasant condition, thought, or experience: *Driving in heavy traffic is a nightmare.*

night•shirt /'nayt,ʃɜrt/ *n.* [*count*] a nightgown cut like a long shirt.

night•spot /'nayt,spɒt/ *n.* NIGHTCLUB.

'night ,stick, *n.* [*count*] a police officer's club.

'night ,table, *n.* [*count*] a small table next to a bed.

night•time /'nayt,taym/ *n.* [*noncount*] the time between evening and morning.

nil /nɪl/ *n.* [*noncount*] nothing; zero: *Our profits were nil.*

nim•ble /'nɪmbəl/ *adj.*, **-bler, -blest. 1.** quick and light in movement; agile: *nimble feet.* **2.** quick to understand, think, etc.: *a nimble mind.* —'**nim•ble•ness,** *n.* [*noncount*] —'**nim•bly,** *adv.*

nine /nayn/ *n.* [*count*] **1.** a number, equal to eight plus one, written as 9. —*adj.* [*before a noun*] **2.** amounting to nine in number.

nine•teen /'nayn'tiyn/ *n.* [*count*] **1.** a number, equal to ten plus nine, written as 19. —*adj.* [*before a noun*] **2.** amounting to 19 in number. —'**nine'teenth,** *adj.*, *n.* [*count*]

nine•ty /'naytiy/ *n.*, *pl.* **-ties,** *adj.* —*n.* [*count*] **1.** a number, equal to ten times nine, written as 90. —*adj.* [*before a noun*] **2.** amounting to 90 in number. —'**nine•ti•eth,** *adj.*, *n.* [*count*]

ninth /naynθ/ *adj.* **1.** next after the eighth. —*n.* [*count*] **2.** a ninth part, esp. of one; 1/9.

nip /nɪp/ *v.*, **nipped, nip•ping,** *n.* —*v.* **1.** to squeeze tightly between two fingers or the teeth; pinch; bite: [~ + *obj*]: *The dog nipped my leg.* [*no obj*]: *The dog nipped at her heels.* **2.** [~ + *obj*] to check in growth or development: *He nipped that rumor quickly.* **3.** [~ + *obj*] to affect sharply and painfully, as extreme cold does: *The wind nipped our faces.* —*n.* [*count*] **4.** an act of nipping. **5.** sharp coldness: *quite a nip in the air tonight.*

nip•ple /'nɪpəl/ *n.* [*count*] **1.** the dark part at the center of the breast where, in the female, milk is sucked by a baby. **2.** something resembling it, such as the mouthpiece of a baby's bottle.

nip•py /'nɪpiy/ *adj.*, **-pi•er, -pi•est.** chilly; cold: *a nippy wind.*

ni•tro•gen /'naytrədʒən/ *n.* [*noncount*] a colorless, odorless, gaseous element that makes up about four-fifths of the earth's atmosphere and is found in animal and vegetable tissues.

nit•ty-grit•ty /'nɪtiy'grɪtiy/ *n.* [*count*], *pl.* **-grit•ties.** the essential or fundamental parts or details of a matter.

nit•wit /'nɪt,wɪt/ *n.* [*count*] a forgetful, stupid, or foolish person.

NJ or **N.J.,** an abbreviation of: New Jersey.

NM or **N.M.,** an abbreviation of: New Mexico.

N. Mex., an abbreviation of: New Mexico.

no¹ /now/ *adv.*, *n.*, *pl.* **noes, nos.** —*adv.* **1.** (used to express disagreement, denial, or refusal, as in response to a question or request, or in giving a command): *"Can we leave now?"—"No, stay here."* **2.** (used to emphasize or introduce a negative statement): *No, not one of them came.* **3.** not in any degree or manner; not at all: *She's no better today than she was yesterday.* —*n.* [*count*] **4.** an instance of saying the word "no." **5.** a denial or refusal: *a definite no to our request.* **6.** a negative vote or voter.

no² /now/ *adj.* **1.** not any: *He had no money. I had no books. I had no way of knowing who would be there.* **2.** (used before a noun to suggest the opposite of that noun) not at all; far from being: *He is no genius.*

no. or **No.,** an abbreviation of: **1.** north. **2.** number.

no•bil•i•ty /now'bɪlɪtiy/ *n.* [*noncount*] **1.** the noble class in a country. **2.** the state or quality of being noble.

no•ble /'nowbəl/ *adj.*, **-bler, -blest,** *n.* —*adj.* **1.** of or belonging to a social class with high rank or status given by birth. **2.** of a high moral character: *It was noble of him to accept the blame.* **3.** grand in appearance; magnificent: *a noble mansion.* —*n.* [*count*] **4.** a nobleman or noblewoman. —'**no•bly,** *adv.*

no•ble•man or **-wom•an** /'nowbəlmən/ or /-,wʊmən/ *n.* [*count*], *pl.* **-men** or **-wom•en.** a person of noble rank; a noble.

no•bod•y /'now,bɒdiy, -,bʌdiy, -bədiy/ *pron.*, *n.*, *pl.* **-bod•ies.** —*pron.* **1.** no person; not anyone; no one: *Nobody is home.* —*n.* [*count*] **2.** a person of no importance: *treated their part-time staff like nobodies.*

no-brain•er /'now'breynər/ *n.* [*count*] *Informal.* something that is easy or simple to understand or do.

noc•tur•nal /nɒk'tɜrnl̩/ *adj.* **1.** of or relating to the night. **2.** active at night: *nocturnal animals.* —**noc'tur•nal•ly,** *adv.*

nod /nɒd/ *v.*, **nod•ded, nod•ding,** *n.* —*v.* **1.** to make a slight bending movement of the head, as in agreement, greeting, or command: [*no obj*]: *She nodded at us and we stood up.* [~ + *obj*]: *He nodded his head in approval.* **2.** [*no obj*] to let the head fall slightly forward with a sudden movement, as from sleepiness. —*n.* [*count*] **3.** a short, quick, up and down movement of the head.

node /nowd/ *n.* [*count*] **1.** something that sticks up or out; a swelling. **2.** a part of a stem from which a leaf or branch grows.

nod•ule /'nɒdʒuwl/ *n.* [*count*] a small node.

No•el /now'ɛl/ *n.* CHRISTMAS.

no-good /'now'gʊd/ *adj.* lacking worth or value; useless; bad: *He's a no-good cheater.*

noise /nɔyz/ *n.* **1.** [*noncount*] loud, harsh, or confused sound. **2.** [*count*] a sound of any kind: *strange noises coming from the engine.*

N

nois•y /ˈnɔyziy/ adj., -i•er, -i•est. **1.** making much noise: *noisy children.* **2.** full of noise: *a noisy party.* —**nois•i•ly** /ˈnɔyzəliy/, adv. —**nois•i•ness,** n. [noncount]

nom., an abbreviation of: nominative.

no•mad /ˈnowmæd/ n. [count] **1.** a member of a people who have no permanent home but move from place to place, usually within an established area. **2.** any wanderer. —**no'mad•ic,** adj.: *nomadic tribes.*

nom•i•nal /ˈnɒmənl̩/ adj. **1.** being such in name only; so-called: *He was only the nominal head of the country.* **2.** small or low: *He offered them the house for a nominal price.* —'**nom•i•nal•ly,** adv.

nom•i•nate /ˈnɒmə,neyt/ v. [~ + obj], -nat•ed, -nat•ing. to propose that (someone) be appointed or elected to an office or duty: *The party nominated her for vice-president. She nominated him (as) her representative.* —**nom•i•na•tion** /,nɒməˈneyʃən/, n. [noncount] [count]

nom•i•na•tive /ˈnɒmənətɪv, ˈnɒmnə-/ adj. **1.** of, relating to, or being a grammatical case that shows the subject of a verb: *The pronoun "he" is in the nominative case.* —n. [count] **2.** the nominative case. **3.** a word or phrase in the nominative case.

nom•i•nee /,nɒməˈniy/ n. [count] a person who has been nominated.

non-, a prefix meaning not (*nonviolent; nonpayment*).

non•al•co•hol•ic /,nɒnælkəˈhɔlɪk, -ˈhɒlɪk/ adj. not being or containing alcohol.

non•cha•lant /,nɒnʃəˈlɑnt, ˈnɒnʃə,lɑnt, -lənt/ adj. showing calmness or lack of interest. —,**non•cha'lance,** n. [noncount] —,**non•cha'lant•ly,** adv.

non•com•mit•tal /,nɒnkəˈmɪtl̩/ adj. having or giving no particular view, feeling, character, or the like: *a noncommittal answer.*

non•con•form•ist /,nɒnkənˈfɔrmɪst/ n. [count] **1.** a person who refuses to accept established customs, attitudes, or ideas. —adj. [before a noun] **2.** of or relating to this kind of person or behavior. —,**non•con'form•i•ty,** n. [noncount]

non•de•script /,nɒndɪˈskrɪpt/ adj. dull; without interest or character; not easily noticed: *nondescript clothes.*

none /nʌn/ pron. **1.** no one; not one: *None of the members is going.* **2.** not any: *That is none of your business.* **3.** no part; nothing: *I'll have none of that nonsense.* **4.** [used with a plural verb] not any persons or things: *There were many and now there are none.* —adv. **5.** **none but,** only: *He had none but the best wishes for her.* **6.** **none the,** to no extent; not at all: *We are none the worse after all we've been through.*

non•en•ti•ty /nɒnˈɛntɪtiy/ n. [count], pl. -ties. a person or thing of no importance.

none•the•less /,nʌnðəˈlɛs/ adv. nevertheless; in spite of that: *He had a learning disability but became a great scientist nonetheless.*

non•ex•is•tent /,nɒnɪgˈzɪstənt/ adj. not existing: *Basic services were nonexistent in the poorer parts of the country.*

non•fat /ˈnɒnˈfæt/ adj. having the fat or fat solids removed: *nonfat milk.*

non•fic•tion /nɒnˈfɪkʃən/ n. [noncount] writing that is not fictional.

non•flam•mable /,nɒnˈflæməbəl/ adj. not burning or catching fire easily. Compare INFLAM-MABLE.

'**no-,no,** n. [count], pl. -nos, -no's. Informal. something forbidden or unacceptable.

'**no-'nonsense,** adj. [before a noun] serious; businesslike: *He gave a no-nonsense explanation.*

non•par•ti•san /nɒnˈpɑrtəzən/ adj. **1.** not supporting or controlled by one particular political party or other group. —n. [count] **2.** a person who is nonpartisan.

non•pay•ment /,nɒnˈpeymənt/ n. [noncount] failure to pay an amount of money owed.

non•pre•scrip•tion /,nɒnprɪˈskrɪpʃən/ adj. [before a noun] (of drugs, medication, etc.) that may be obtained legally without a doctor's prescription.

non•prof•it /nɒnˈprɒfɪt/ adj. not established for the purpose of making a profit: *a nonprofit organization.*

non•pro•lif•er•a•tion /,nɒnprə,lɪfəˈreyʃən/ n. [noncount] **1.** the action or practice of slowing or stopping the spread of nuclear weapons. —adj. [before a noun] **2.** of or relating to this practice: *a nonproliferation treaty.*

non•sec•tar•i•an /,nɒnsɛkˈtɛəriyən/ adj. not associated with or limited to a certain religion or sect.

non•sense /ˈnɒnsɛns, -səns/ n. [noncount] **1.** words that have no meaning; gibberish. **2.** talk or actions that are foolish or ridiculous: *a lot of nonsense about how women can't do the job.*

non•sex•ist /nɒnˈsɛksɪst/ adj. not showing, calling for, promoting, or involving sexism: *nonsexist language.*

non•stand•ard /nɒnˈstændərd/ adj. **1.** not standard. **2.** not conforming to the pronunciation, grammar, or vocabulary considered acceptable by educated native speakers: *nonstandard English.*

non•stick /nɒnˈstɪk/ adj. having a type of surface designed to prevent food from sticking during cooking: *a nonstick pan.*

non•stop /ˈnɒnˈstɒp/ adj. **1.** being without a single stop on the way: *a nonstop flight from New York to Dallas.* **2.** happening without a pause: *held nonstop meetings.* —adv. **3.** without a single stop: *flew nonstop from San Diego to New York.* **4.** without interruption: *talking nonstop.*

non•vi•o•lence /nɒnˈvayələns/ n. [noncount] **1.** absence or lack of violence. **2.** the policy or practice of deliberately avoiding or opposing the use of violence. —**non'vi•o•lent,** adj.

non•white /nɒnˈhwayt, -ˈwayt/ adj. **1.** not belonging to the white race. —n. [count] **2.** a person not belonging to the white race.

noo•dle /ˈnuwdl̩/ n. [count] a dried strip of dough made from flour, water, and eggs, boiled and served as a side dish or in soups.

nook /nʊk/ n. [count] **1.** a corner, as in a room: *a breakfast nook.* **2.** a sheltered spot: *a shady nook.*

noon /nuwn/ n. [noncount] midday; twelve o'clock in the daytime.

'**no ,one,** pron. no person: *No one is at home.*

noose /nuws/ n. [count] a loop in a rope that tightens as part of it is pulled, as in a lasso or a rope to hang someone.

nope /nowp/ adv. Informal. no.

nor /nɔr; unstressed nər/ conj. **1.** (used in negative phrases, esp. after *neither*, to introduce new items in a list or series): *Neither he nor I will be there.* **2.** (used to continue force of a negative word coming before it): *I never saw him again, nor did I care. She couldn't make it to the party, nor could we. She had no way of knowing, nor did we.*

norm /nɔrm/ n. [count] **1.** a standard, model, or pattern, esp. a standard of behavior. **2.** the expected or usual number, level, amount, or average: *It is the norm to finish college in four years.*

nor•mal /'nɔrməl/ *adj.* **1.** conforming to or agreeing with the standard or common type; usual: *a normal height for his age.* **2.** nearly average in one's mental or emotional state. —*n.* [*noncount*] **3.** the normal form or state: *Things returned to normal after the war.* —**nor•mal•i•ty** /nɔr'mæltiy/ *n.* [*noncount*]

nor•mal•ize /'nɔrməlayz/ *v.*, **-ized, -iz•ing.** to (cause to) become normal; to (cause to) return to a previous state, esp. of friendliness: [~ + *obj*]: *to normalize relations between the two countries.* [*no obj*]: *The situation seems to have normalized.* —**nor•mal•i•za•tion** /ˌnɔrmli'zeyʃən/, *n.* [*noncount*]

nor•mal•ly /'nɔrməliy/ *adv.* **1.** in a normal manner or a normal way: *breathing normally.* **2.** in a usual manner or usual way; usually: *Normally we wouldn't ask such a question.*

north /nɔrθ/ *n.* [*noncount; usually: the* + ~] **1.** one of the four main points of the compass, to the left of a person facing the rising sun. **2.** [*noncount; usually: the* + ~] the direction in which this point lies: *Look to the north.* **3.** [*noncount; usually: the North*] a region or territory in this direction. **4. the North,** the northern area of the United States. —*adj.* **5.** in, toward, or facing the north: *the north gate.* **6.** directed or going toward the north: *The tanks were taking a north course.* **7.** coming from the north: *a north wind.* —*adv.* **8.** to, toward, or in the north: *sailing north.*

north•bound /'nɔrθ,bawnd/ *adj.* moving or going in a north direction: *a northbound train.*

north•east /ˌnɔrθ'iyst; *Nautical.* ˌnɔr-/ *n.* **1.** [*noncount*] a point on the compass midway between north and east. **2.** [*noncount*] a region in this direction. **3. the Northeast,** the northeastern part of the United States. —*adj.* **4.** in, toward, or facing the northeast. **5.** coming from the northeast. —*adv.* **6.** toward the northeast. —ˌnorth'east•er•ly, *adv.* —ˌnorth'east•ern, *adj.*

north•er•ly /'nɔrðərliy/ *adj., adv.* —*adj.* **1.** moving, directed, or located toward the north. **2.** (esp. of a wind) coming from the north. —*adv.* **3.** toward the north. **4.** from the north.

north•ern /'nɔrðərn/ *adj.* **1.** lying toward or located in the north. **2.** directed or going toward the north. **3.** coming from the north, as a wind. **4.** [*often: Northern*] of or relating to the North.

north•ern•er /'nɔrðərnər/ *n.* [*count; often: Northerner*] someone born or living in the north, esp. the northern U.S.

'northern 'lights, *n.* [*plural*] the aurora of the Northern Hemisphere.

'North 'Pole, *n.* [*the* + ~] the northern end of the earth's axis; the northernmost point on earth.

north•ward /'nɔrθwərd; *Nautical.* 'nɔrðərd/ *adv.* Also, **'north'wards.** toward the north. —*adj.* **2.** moving, facing, or located toward the north.

north•west /ˌnɔrθ'wɛst; *Nautical.* ˌnɔr-/ *n.* **1.** [*noncount*] a point on the compass midway between north and west. **2.** [*noncount*] a region in this direction. **3. the Northwest, a.** the northwestern part of the United States when its western boundary was the Mississippi River. **b.** the northwestern part of Canada. —*adj.* **4.** in, toward, or facing the northwest. **5.** coming from the northwest. —*adv.* **6.** toward the northwest. —ˌnorth'west•er•ly, *adv.* —ˌnorth'west•ern, *adj.*

Nor•we•gian /nɔr'wiydʒən/ *adj.* **1.** of or relat-

ing to Norway. **2.** of or relating to the language spoken in Norway. —*n.* **3.** [*count*] a person born or living in Norway. **4.** [*noncount*] the language spoken in Norway.

nos. or **Nos.,** an abbreviation of: numbers.

nose /nowz/ *n., v.,* **nosed, nos•ing.** —*n.* [*count*] **1.** the part of the face above the mouth that contains the nostrils and organs of smell and through which a person breathes. **2.** the sense of smell: *Certain breeds of dog have a good nose.* **3.** anything that resembles a nose: *the nose of a plane.* —*v.* **4.** to move forward with or as if with the nose: [~ + *obj*]: *The boat nosed its way toward shore.* [*no obj*]: *The plane nosed forward cautiously.* **5.** [*no obj*] to meddle or pry: *nosing around asking questions.* —**Idiom. 6. on the nose,** precisely; exactly: *We arrived at 3 o'clock on the nose.* **7. turn up one's nose at,** to reject (something) with scorn: *turned up his nose at the low salary.* **8. under someone's nose,** plainly visible: *It was right under my nose all the time.*

nose•bleed /'nowz,bliyd/ *n.* [*count*] bleeding from the nostrils.

nose•dive /'nowz,dayv/ *n., v.,* **-dived** or **-dove, -dived, -div•ing.** —*n.* [*count*] **1.** a fast downward motion of an aircraft with the forward part pointing downward. **2.** a sudden sharp drop or rapid decline: *Stock prices took a nosedive.* —*v.* [*no obj*] **3.** to go into a nosedive.

nosh /nɒʃ/ *Informal.* —*v.* [*no obj*] [~ + *obj*] **1.** to snack or eat (something) between meals. —*n.* [*count*] **2.** a snack.

nos•tal•gia /nɒ'stældʒə, nə-/ *n.* [*noncount*] a sentimental longing for places, things, friends, or conditions belonging to the past. —**nos'tal•gic,** *adj.*

nos•tril /'nɒstrəl/ *n.* [*count*] either of the two outer openings of the nose.

nos•y or **nos•ey** /'nowziy/ *adj.,* **-i•er, -i•est.** overly curious about the affairs of others; prying. —**nos•i•ly** /'nowziy/, *adv.* —'**nos•i•ness,** *n.* [*noncount*]

not /nɒt/ *adv.* **1.** (used to express the opposite of the main verb, and also to express denial, refusal, prohibition, etc.): *I do not remember the answer. You must not think about it. It's not far from here. They are not coming.* **2.** (used before a singular count noun) not even one: *Not a single missile got through the defense system.* —**Idiom. 3. not at all, a.** (used as an answer to someone else's thanks): *"I appreciate your help."* —*"Not at all."* **b.** (used to emphasize an answer of "no"): *"Did you like the show?"* —*"Not at all!"*

no•ta•ble /'nowtəbəl/ *adj.* **1.** worthy of notice; important; remarkable: *a notable success.* —*n.* [*count*] **2.** an important, distinguished, or remarkable person.

not•a•bly /'nowtəbliy/ *adv.* **1.** in a way that is worthy of being noticed: *The audience was notably small.* **2.** especially; particularly: *a notably fine meal.*

no•ta•rize /'nowtə,rayz/ *v.* [~ + *obj*], **-rized, -riz•ing.** to make (a contract, document, etc.) legal by signing it before a notary. —**no•ta•ri•za•tion** /ˌnowtəri'zeyʃən/, *n.* [*noncount*]

no•ta•ry /'nowtəriy/ *n.* [*count*], *pl.* **-ries.** a person authorized to witness the signing of documents. Also called **'notary 'public.**

no•ta•tion /now'teyʃən/ *n.* [*noncount*] a system of special symbols or signs for a particular use: *musical notation.*

notch /nɒtʃ/ *n.* [*count*] **1.** a V-shaped cut in the edge or top of something. **2.** an amount within a

scale; degree: *She's a notch above the average.* —*v.* [~ + *obj*] **3.** to make a notch or notches in.
note /noʊt/ *n., v.,* **not•ed, not•ing.** —*n.* [*count*] **1.** a brief written record to help remember something: *She took notes in her English class.* **2.** a brief written statement giving information: *I left you a note on the refrigerator door.* **3.** a short letter: *a note of thanks.* **4.** a quality or tone indicating an emotion: *a note of fear in his voice.* **5.** a musical tone of a certain pitch, or a sign used to represent it in a piece of music. **6.** a piece of paper money. —*v.* [~ + *obj*] **7.** to make a note of so as to remember later: *He noted the professor's comments in his notebook. Note (down) this name.* **8.** to make special mention of: *noted the heroic efforts of her staff; noted that her staff had done a fine job.* —*Idiom.* **9. compare notes (on),** to share information about: *They compared notes on the experience.* **10. make a mental note (of),** to try to remember: *You should make a mental note of just who voted for you in that last election.* **11. of note,** having fame or importance: *writers of note.* **12. take note (of),** to notice: *The sign warned trespassers to take note. He failed to take note of the warning lights.*
note•book /'noʊt,bʊk/ *n.* [*count*] **1.** a book of or for notes. **2.** a small, lightweight laptop computer.

notebook (def. 2)

not•ed /'noʊtɪd/ *adj.* well-known; famous: *a noted scholar; The town is noted for its hills.*
note•pa•per /'noʊt,peɪpər/ *n.* [*noncount*] writing paper suitable for notes.
note•wor•thy /'noʊt,wɜrðiy/ *adj.* worthy of notice; notable.
noth•ing /'nʌθɪŋ/ *pron.* **1.** not anything: *He was warned to say nothing.* **2.** something of no importance or value: *Money means nothing to him.* —*n.* **3.** [*count*] a person of no importance. **4.** [*noncount*] zero. —*adv.* **5.** not at all: *It was nothing like that.* —*Idiom.* **6. for nothing, a.** free of charge: *He fixed the car for nothing.* **b.** for no apparent reason: *We went to all that trouble for nothing.* **7. nothing but,** only; just: *I saw nothing but corn everywhere I looked.* **8. think nothing of,** to regard as unimportant or easy: *thought nothing of running ten miles a day.*
no•tice /'noʊtɪs/ *n., v.,* **-ticed, -tic•ing.** —*n.* **1.** [*noncount*] information or warning of something about to happen: *to give notice of a change in plans.* **2.** [*noncount*] a notification that an agreement will end at a certain time: *She decided to leave her job and gave her employer two-weeks' notice.* **3.** [*count*] a written statement with information or a warning: *She posted a notice about a meeting of all the students.* **4.** [*noncount*] observation or attention: *to take notice of one's surroundings.* —*v.* [~ + *obj*] **5.** to become aware of or pay attention to; observe: *I suddenly noticed her at the door. She noticed that I was frowning.* —'**no•tice•a•ble,** *adj.*
no•ti•fy /'noʊtə,faɪ/ *v.* [~ + *obj*], **-fied, -fy•ing.** to inform; give notice to; tell: *to notify the* police of a crime; *You'll have to notify him that there's been an accident.* —**no•ti•fi•ca•tion** /,noʊtəfɪ'keɪʃən/, *n.* [*count*] [*noncount*]
no•tion /'noʊʃən/ *n.* [*count*] **1.** an idea or view, esp. one's own view. **2. notions,** [*plural*] small articles, as buttons or ribbon, displayed together for sale.
no•to•ri•e•ty /,noʊtə'raɪətiy/ *n.* [*noncount*] the state of being widely known, esp. for something unfavorable.
no•to•ri•ous /noʊ'tɔriyəs, nə-/ *adj.* widely known, esp. for something unfavorable. —**no'to•ri•ous•ly,** *adv.*
not•with•stand•ing /,nɒtwɪð'stændɪŋ, -wɪθ-/ *prep.* **1.** in spite of: *Notwithstanding a brilliant defense, he was found guilty.* [*after a noun*]: *The doctor's orders notwithstanding, she returned to work.* —*adv.* **2.** nevertheless; anyway.
nought /nɔt/ *n.* NAUGHT.
noun /naʊn/ *n.* [*count*] a word that can function as the subject or object in a sentence or phrase, and typically refers to a person, place, animal, thing, state, or quality.
nour•ish /'nɜrɪʃ, 'nʌr-/ *v.* [~ + *obj*] **1.** to supply with what is necessary for life, health, and growth: *This food will nourish them.* **2.** to keep alive; cause to grow: *still nourished the hope of peace.* —'**nour•ish•ing,** *adj.*: *It's important to eat a nourishing breakfast.* —'**nour•ish•ment,** *n.* [*noncount*]
Nov or **Nov.,** an abbreviation of: November.
nov•el¹ /'nɒvəl/ *n.* [*count*] a long written story about characters and events that have been invented by the writer.
nov•el² /'nɒvəl/ *adj.* of a new kind; different from anything seen or known before.
nov•el•ist /'nɒvəlɪst/ *n.* [*count*] a person who writes novels.
nov•el•ty /'nɒvəltiy/ *n., pl.* **-ties. 1.** [*noncount*] the state or quality of being novel: *brought novelty to the old way of doing business.* **2.** [*count*] a novel event, experience, etc. **3.** [*count*] a small, cheap, decorative or amusing object.
No•vem•ber /noʊ'vɛmbər/ *n.* the 11th month of the year, containing 30 days.
nov•ice /'nɒvɪs/ *n.* [*count*] **1.** a person who is new to the circumstances, work, etc., in which he or she is placed; beginner. **2.** a person admitted into a religious order for a period of testing before taking vows.
now /naʊ/ *adv.* **1.** at the present time or moment: *I am now reading this definition.* **2.** without further delay; immediately: *Do it now.* **3.** in the very recent past: *I saw them just now.* **4.** (used to introduce a statement, question, or command): *Now, may I ask you something? Now stop that!* **5.** (used to hesitate while the speaker thinks of something): *Now, let me think.* —*conj.* **6.** Also, **now that.** since: *Now that you're here, why not stay for dinner.* —*n.* [*noncount; no article*] **7.** the present time or moment: *Up to now no one has volunteered.*
now•a•days /'naʊə,deɪz/ *adv.* at the present time; these days: *Nowadays I hardly ever see her.*
'**no 'way,** *adv. Informal.* absolutely not; no: *No way will I be there.*
no•way /'noʊ,weɪ/ also **no•ways** /'noʊ,weɪz/ *adv. Informal.* in no way; not at all: *He was noway responsible.*
no•where /'noʊ,hwɛər, -,wɛər/ *adv.* **1.** in or at no place; not anywhere; to no place: *We went nowhere last weekend.* —*n.* [*noncount*] **2.** a state or

place of nonexistence: *Thieves appeared from nowhere.*

'no-'win, *adj.* not likely to yield benefit, success, or victory: *a no-win situation.*

nox•ious /ˈnɒkʃəs/ *adj.* harmful to the health.

noz•zle /ˈnɒzəl/ *n.* [count] a spout of a pipe, hose, or the like, used to direct the flow of liquid.

nt. wt., an abbreviation of: net weight.

nu•ance /ˈnuwɑns, ˈnyuw-, nyuwˈɑns, nyuw-/ *n.* [count] a slight difference or distinction, as in expression, meaning, or color: *nuances of feeling in a poem.*

nu•cle•ar /ˈnuwkliyər, ˈnyuw-/ *adj.* **1.** relating to or involving atomic weapons: *a nuclear war.* **2.** operated or powered by atomic energy: *a nuclear submarine.*

'nuclear 'energy, *n.* [noncount] energy released by reactions within atomic nuclei; atomic energy.

'nuclear re'actor, *n.* REACTOR.

nu•cle•us /ˈnuwkliyəs, ˈnyuw-/ *n.* [count], *pl.* **-cle•i** /-kliy,ay/, **-cle•us•es.** **1.** a central part around which other parts are grouped: *A few loyal friends formed the nucleus of the club.* **2.** a mass of material in a cell that directs its growth and reproduction and contains the genetic information. **3.** the central, positively charged mass within an atom, made up of neutrons and protons.

nude /nuwd, nyuwd/ *adj., n.* **nud•er, nud•est,** *n.* —*adj.* **1.** being without clothing or covering; naked. —*n.* **2.** [count] a sculpture, painting, etc., of a nude human figure. **3.** [noncount] the condition of being unclothed: *to sleep in the nude.* —ˈnu•di•ty, *n.* [noncount]

nudge /nʌdʒ/ *v.,* **nudged, nudg•ing,** *n.* —*v.* [~ + *obj*] **1.** to push slightly or gently, esp. with the elbow to get someone's attention. —*n.* [count] **2.** a slight or gentle push.

nud•ism /ˈnuwdɪzəm, ˈnyuw-/ *n.* [noncount] the practice of going nude in public, esp. in special secluded places. —ˈnud•ist, *n.* [count], *adj.*

nug•get /ˈnʌgɪt/ *n.* [count] **1.** a lump, esp. of gold or other precious metal. **2.** anything small but of great value: *nuggets of wisdom.*

nui•sance /ˈnuwsəns, ˈnyuw-/ *n.* [count] a person, animal, or thing that is unpleasant, inconvenient, or annoying.

null /nʌl/ *adj.* **1.** lacking value or significance. —*Idiom.* **2. null and void,** without force or effect; not valid: *The contract is now null and void.*

nul•li•fy /ˈnʌləˌfay/ *v.* [~ + *obj*], **-fied, -fy•ing.** to declare (something) to have no effect: *The budget proposal nullified our plans; to nullify a contract.* —**nul•li•fi•ca•tion** /ˌnʌləfɪˈkeyʃən/, *n.* [noncount]

numb /nʌm/ *adj.,* **-er, -est,** *v.* —*adj.* **1.** incapable of feeling sensations: *fingers that were numb with cold.* **2.** empty of emotion; stunned: *felt numb with grief.* —*v.* [~ + *obj*] **3.** to make numb. —ˈnumb•ing, *adj.* —ˈnumb•ly, *adv.* —ˈnumb•ness, *n.* [noncount]

num•ber /ˈnʌmbər/ *n.* **1.** [count] a mathematical figure or unit used to count or express an amount, quantity, etc.: *Six is an even number.* **2.** the total of a group of persons or things: [noncount]: *What is the number of people with tickets?* [noncount]: *Rivers are few in number in that state.* **3.** [count] a written figure assigned to an object to identify or distinguish it: *a telephone number.* **4. numbers,** [plural] **a.** a considerable amount or quantity: *arrived in large numbers.* **b.** a

greater amount: *There is strength in numbers.* **5.** [count] a tune for singing or dancing; a piece of music. —*v.* **6.** [~ + *obj*] to mark with or distinguish by numbers. **7.** [~ + *obj*] [no *obj*] to amount to or reach in number; total. **8.** [~ + *obj*] to figure out the amount or quantity of; count: *We numbered the days until we could go home again.* —**Usage.** See AMOUNT.

nu•mer•al /ˈnuwmərəl, ˈnyuw-; ˈnuwmrəl, ˈnyuwm-/ *n.* [count] a word, letter, or symbol representing a number: *the Roman numeral X for 10.*

nu•mer•a•tor /ˈnuwməˌreytər, ˈnyuw-/ *n.* [count] the term written above or before the line in a fraction. Compare DENOMINATOR.

nu•mer•i•cal /nuwˈmɛrɪkəl, nyuw-/ also **nuˈmer•ic,** *adj.* **1.** of or relating to numbers; of the nature of a number: *Put the pages in numerical order.* **2.** expressed in numbers: *numerical equations.* —**nuˈmer•i•cal•ly,** *adv.*

nu•mer•ous /ˈnuwmərəs, ˈnyuw-/ *adj.* very many; existing in great quantity: *We have been there on numerous occasions.*

nun /nʌn/ *n.* [count] a woman who is a member of a religious order, esp. one who observes vows of poverty, chastity, and obedience.

nun•ner•y /ˈnʌnəriy/ *n.* [count], *pl.* **-ner•ies.** a residence for nuns; convent.

nup•tial /ˈnʌpʃəl, -tʃəl/ *adj.* **1.** of or relating to marriage or the marriage ceremony: *nuptial vows.* —*n.* **2.** Usually, **nuptials.** [plural] a wedding or marriage.

nurse /nɜrs/ *n., v.,* **nursed, nurs•ing.** —*n.* [count] **1.** a person trained in the care of the sick. **2.** a person hired to care for a child or children. —*v.* **3.** [~ + *obj*] to tend to or take care of (someone) in sickness: *She nursed him back to health.* **4.** [~ + *obj*] [no *obj*] (of a woman) to feed (an infant) at the breast. **5.** [no *obj*] (of an infant) to feed at the breast.

nurse•maid /ˈnɜrsˌmeyd/ *n.* [count] a woman whose job is to care for children.

nurs•er•y /ˈnɜrsəriy/ *n.* [count], *pl.* **-er•ies.** **1.** a room or place set apart for infants or very young children. **2.** a place where young plants are raised.

'nursery ˌrhyme, *n.* [count] a short, simple poem or song for very young children.

'nursery ˌschool, *n.* [count] [noncount] a school for children before they attend kindergarten.

'nursing ˌhome, *n.* [count] a residence where older or sick people are cared for.

nur•ture /ˈnɜrtʃər/ *v.,* **-tured, -tur•ing,** *n.* —*v.* [~ + *obj*] **1.** to feed; supply with nourishment. **2.** to bring up; train; educate. —*n.* [noncount] **3.** upbringing; training; education: *providing for the nurture of young artists.* **4.** something that nourishes; nourishment; food.

nut /nʌt/ *n.* [count] **1.** a dry fruit made up of a kernel that may be eaten, and enclosed in a woody or leathery shell. **2.** the kernel itself. **3.** a hard, one-seeded fruit, as the chestnut or the acorn. **4.** a metal piece with a hole so that it can be screwed onto a bolt. **5.** *Slang.* a person who is very interested in or enthusiastic about something: *She's a sports nut.* **6.** *Slang.* **a.** a foolish, silly, or odd person. **b.** an insane person.

nut•crack•er /ˈnʌtˌkrækər/ *n.* [count] an instrument for cracking the shells of nuts.

nut•meg /ˈnʌtmɛg/ *n.* [noncount] the powder made from the seed of an East Indian tree, used as a spice.

N

nu•tri•ent /'nuwtriyənt, 'nyuw-/ adj. [before a noun] **1.** nourishing; providing nourishment. —n. [count] **2.** a nutrient substance.

nu•tri•ment /'nuwtrəmənt, 'nyuw-/ n. [count] any substance that when taken into a living organism serves to keep it alive.

nu•tri•tion /nuw'trɪʃən, nyuw-/ n. [noncount] **1.** the study or science of the food and diet requirements of humans and animals for proper health and development. **2.** the process by which living things take in and use food. **3.** food; nutriment. —nu'tri•tion•al, adj.

nu•tri•tious /nuw'trɪʃəs, nyuw-/ adj. providing nourishment; nourishing: Vegetables and grains are nutritious foods. —nu'tri•tious•ly, adv.

nut•shell /'nʌt,ʃɛl/ n. [count] **1.** the shell of a nut. —Idiom. **2.** in a nutshell, briefly; in a few words.

nut•ty /'nʌtiy/ adj., -ti•er, -ti•est. **1.** nutlike, esp. in flavor. **2.** Slang. foolish, silly, or odd. —'nut•ti•ness, n. [noncount]

nuz•zle /'nʌzəl/ v., -zled, -zling, n. —v. **1.** [~ + obj] to touch or rub with the nose, snout, muzzle, etc. **2.** [no obj] [~ + obj] to lie very close (to); cuddle or snuggle up (to). —n. [count] **3.** an affectionate embrace or cuddle.

NV, an abbreviation of: Nevada.

NY or **N.Y.,** an abbreviation of: New York.

ny•lon /'naylɒn/ n. **1.** [noncount] a strong synthetic fiber used esp. for yarn, fabrics, and bristles. **2. nylons,** [plural] stockings made of nylon.

nymph /nɪmf/ n. [count] **1.** any of various female deities in mythology living in waters or forests. **2.** a beautiful young woman. **3.** the young of an insect.

nym•pho•ma•ni•a /,nɪmfə'meyniyə, -'meynyə/ n. [noncount] overwhelmingly strong sexual desire in a female. —**nym•pho•ma•ni•ac** /,nɪmfə'meyniy,æk/, n. [count], adj.

O

O, o /ow/ *n.* [*count*], *pl.* **O's** or **Os; o's** or **os** or **oes.** the 15th letter of the English alphabet, a vowel.

O /ow/ *interj., n., pl.* **O's.** —*interj.* **1.** (used esp. in solemn or poetic language): *Hear, O Israel!* **2.** OH.

O, *Symbol.* **1.** the Arabic numeral zero; cipher. **2.** oxygen.

oak /owk/ *n.* [*count*] a tree that bears the acorn as its fruit; the hard wood of this tree.

oar /ɔr/ *n.* [*count*] a long pole with a broad, wide blade at one end, used for rowing or steering a boat. —'**oars•man,** *n.* [*count*], *pl.* **-men.**

o•a•sis /ow'eysɪs/ *n.* [*count*], *pl.* **-ses** /-siyz/. **1.** an area in a desert region where plants and trees can grow. **2.** a safe, quiet, or welcoming place.

oat /owt/ *n.* **1.** [*noncount*] a cereal grass grown for its grain. **2.** Usually, **oats.** [*plural*] the grain of this plant, used for food.

oath /owθ/ *n.* [*count*], *pl.* **oaths** /owðz, owθs/. **1.** a solemn declaration that one will speak the truth or keep one's promises. **2.** a disrespectful use of the name of God. **3.** a curse word. —*Idiom.* **4. under oath,** solemnly bound by the obligations of an oath.

oat•meal /'owt,miyl/ *n.* [*noncount*] a cooked breakfast food made from crushed oats.

ob-, a prefix meaning: toward or to (*object*); on or over (*obscure*); against (*obstruct*).

o•be•di•ent /ow'biydiyənt/ *adj.* willing to obey: *an obedient child; She is obedient to her parents.* —o'**be•di•ence,** *n.* [*noncount*]

o•bese /ow'biys/ *adj.* extremely fat. —o•be•si•ty /ow'biysɪtiy/, *n.* [*noncount*]

o•bey /ow'bey/ *v.* **1.** to do or follow the wishes or instructions of (someone): [~ + *obj*]: *She always obeyed her parents.* [*no obj*] *Teach your dog to obey.* **2.** [~ + *obj*] to conform to; be subject to: *All objects obey the law of gravity.*

o•bit•u•ar•y /ow'bɪtʃuw,ɛriy/ *n.* [*count*], *pl.* **-ar•ies.** a written notice of the death of a person, as in a newspaper.

obj., an abbreviation of: **1.** object. **2.** objective.

ob•ject /*n.* 'ɒbdʒɪkt, -dʒɛkt; *v.* əb'dʒɛkt/ *n.* **1.** [*count*] anything that can be seen or touched and is usually not alive. **2.** [*count*] a thing or person to which thought or action is directed: *the object of her desires.* **3.** [*count*] a noun, noun phrase, or pronoun that represents the goal or the thing receiving the action of a verb, or that represents the goal of a preposition: *The word* ball *in the sentence* I hit the ball *is an object. The word* table *in the phrase* under the table *is also an object.* **4.** [*noncount*] a cause for worry or restraint: *Money is no object, so spend all you want.* —*v.* [*no obj*] **5.** to express or feel disapproval, dislike, or opposition: *They objected to my plan.*

ob•jec•tion /əb'dʒɛkʃən/ *n.* [*count*] a reason or argument offered in opposition to some plan or idea: *Despite her family's objection, she married him.*

ob•jec•tion•a•ble /əb'dʒɛkʃənəbəl/ *adj.* causing a feeling of disapproval; offensive; unacceptable: *objectionable behavior.*

ob•jec•tive /əb'dʒɛktɪv/ *n.* [*count*] **1.** a purpose; aim; goal. —*adj.* **2.** not influenced by personal feelings or prejudice: *an objective opinion.* **3.** of, relating to, or being a grammatical case

that typically indicates the object of a transitive verb or of a preposition. —**ob'jec•tive•ly,** *adv.* —**ob•jec•tiv•i•ty** /,ɒbdʒɪk'tɪvɪtiy, -dʒɛk-/, *n.* [*noncount*]

ob•li•gate /'ɒblɪ,geyt/ *v.* [~ + *obj*], **-gat•ed, -gat•ing.** to make (someone) feel or understand that some action is morally or legally necessary: *The contract obligates you to pay on time.*

ob•li•ga•tion /,ɒblɪ'geyʃən/ *n.* something that a person feels morally or legally bound to do: [*count*]: *to feel an obligation to help one's parents.* [*noncount*]: *a strong sense of family obligation.*

ob•blig•a•to•ry /ə'blɪgə,tɔriy, 'ɒblɪgə-/ *adj.* required; necessary.

o•blige /ə'blaydʒ/ *v.* [~ + *obj*], **o•bliged, o•blig•ing.** to require, as by law, conscience, or force: *We were obliged to invite them to our party. The will obliges the heirs to live in the family mansion.*

o•blique /ə'bliyk, ow'bliyk/ *adj.* **1.** slanting; sloping; sideways: *an oblique line.* **2.** indirectly expressed: *an oblique reference to the queen.*

ob•lit•er•ate /ə'blɪtə,reyt/ *v.* [~ + *obj*], **-at•ed, -at•ing.** to remove or destroy completely: *The bombing obliterated the village.* —**ob,lit•er'a•tion,** *n.* [*noncount*]

ob•liv•i•on /ə'blɪviyən/ *n.* [*noncount*] **1.** the state of being completely forgotten: *All their plans have faded into oblivion.* **2.** the state of forgetting or of being not aware: *the oblivion of sleep.*

ob•liv•i•ous /ə'blɪviyəs/ *adj.* unaware of what is around oneself: *They were oblivious to the danger.* —**ob'liv•i•ous•ness,** *n.* [*noncount*]

ob•long /'ɒb,lɔŋ, -,lɒŋ/ *adj.* **1.** in the form of a rectangle one of whose dimensions is much greater than the other. —*n.* [*count*] **2.** an oblong figure.

ob•nox•ious /əb'nɒkʃəs/ *adj.* very objectionable or offensive.

o•boe /'owbow/ *n.* [*count*] a woodwind instrument having a slender, cone-shaped body. —'**o•bo•ist,** *n.* [*count*]

ob•scene /əb'siyn/ *adj.* **1.** offensive to people's feelings about what is moral or decent: *obscene language.* **2.** terrible; disgusting: *obscene cruelty.* —**ob•scen•i•ty** /əb'sɛnɪtiy/ *n.* [*count*] [*noncount*]

ob•scure /əb'skyʊr/ *adj.*, **-scur•er, -scur•est,** *v.,* **-scured, -scur•ing,** —*adj.* **1.** not clear or plain; uncertain: *an obscure message; obscure motives.* **2.** unknown: *an obscure artist.* **3.** hard to see, as if hidden by darkness: *an obscure figure in the shadows.* —*v.* [~ + *obj*] **4.** to conceal; cover; mask. —**ob'scure•ly,** *adv.* —**ob'scu•ri•ty,** *n.* [*noncount*]

ob•serv•ance /əb'zɜrvəns/ *n.* [*noncount*] **1.** the action of following or obeying a law, custom, etc. **2.** a celebration by ceremonies, special practices, etc.: *the observance of the Sabbath.*

ob•serv•ant /əb'zɜrvənt/ *adj.* **1.** quick to notice; alert: *Be observant for signs of danger.* **2.** careful in the observing of a law, religious ritual, custom, or the like: *an observant Catholic.*

ob•ser•va•tion /,ɒbzɜr'veyʃən/ *n.* **1.** [*count*] an act or instance of watching attentively or noting something. **2.** [*noncount*] the ability or habit of observing or noticing things: *good powers of ob-*

servation. **3.** [count] a judgment made on the basis of what one has observed: *He shared her observations on how people behaved.* **4.** [count] a remark; comment.

ob•serv•a•to•ry /əb'zɜrvə,tɔriy/ n. [count], pl. **-ries.** a building equipped for studying the heavens or other natural phenomena.

ob•serve /əb'zɜrv/ v., **-served, -serv•ing.** [~ + obj] **1.** to see, watch, or notice: *I observed a person dashing across the field.* **2.** to keep or maintain in one's action, conduct, etc.: *to observe silence.* **3.** to obey or conform to: *to observe the law.* **4.** to celebrate, as a holiday, in a customary way. —**ob'serv•er,** n. [count]

ob•sess /əb'sɛs/ v. **1.** [~ + obj] to dominate the thoughts of: *Revenge obsessed him.* **2.** [no obj] to think about something without stopping: *He obsessed about his old girlfriend for years.*

ob•ses•sion /əb'sɛʃən/ n. **1.** [noncount] the intense domination of one's thoughts by a single idea or feeling; the state of being obsessed. **2.** [count] the idea, image, desire, etc., itself.

ob•sess•ive /əb'sɛsɪv/ adj. **1.** of, being, or resembling an obsession: *an obsessive fear of disease.* **2.** tending to have obsessions: *an obsessive personality.* —**ob'sess•ive•ly,** adv.

ob•so•lete /,ɒbsə'liyt, 'ɒbsə,liyt/ adj. no longer in general use: *obsolete customs.*

ob•sta•cle /'ɒbstəkəl/ n. [count] something that prevents or slows progress; an obstruction.

ob•stet•rics /əb'stɛtrɪks/ n. [noncount; used with a singular verb] the branch of medicine dealing with pregnancy and childbirth. —**ob'stet•ri•cal, ob'stet•ric,** adj. —**ob•ste•tri•cian** /,ɒbstɪ'trɪʃən/ n. [count]

ob•sti•nate /'ɒbstənɪt/ adj. firmly or stubbornly unwilling to change one's purpose, opinion, or course of action. —**'ob•sti•na•cy,** n. [noncount]

ob•struct /əb'strʌkt/ v. [~ + obj] **1.** to block or close up, as by being in the way: *The fallen rocks obstructed the road.* **2.** to interrupt, slow down, or prevent the progress of: *to face charges of obstructing justice.* —**ob'struc•tion,** n. [noncount] [count] —**ob'struc•tive,** adj.

ob•tain /əb'teyn/ v. [~ + obj] to come into possession of; acquire; get: *to obtain a driver's license.* —**ob'tain•a•ble,** adj.

ob•tru•sive /ɒb'truwsɪv/ adj. causing attention in an unpleasant way: *obtrusive gold decoration.* —**ob'tru•sive•ly,** adv. —**ob'tru•sive•ness,** n. [noncount]

ob•tuse /əb'tuws, -'tyuws/ adj. **1.** not quick or alert in the ability to understand or feel; dull. **2.** (of an angle) greater than 90° but less than 180°. —**ob'tuse•ness,** n. [noncount]

ob•vi•ous /'ɒbviyəs/ adj. easily or clearly understood or seen; evident: *an obvious solution to a problem; It was obvious to everyone that he was lying.*

ob•vi•ous•ly /'ɒbviyəsliy/ adv. used to express the opinion that what follows is, or should be, clearly understood or recognized: *Obviously we'll have to finish this part of the course first. They had obviously not slept well.*

oc•ca•sion /ə'keyʒən/ n. [count] **1.** a particular time, esp. when certain events or circumstances take place: *On several occasions he was seen leaving the spy's apartment.* **2.** a special or important time, event, ceremony, etc.: *The party was quite an occasion.* —v. [~ + obj] **3.** to cause; bring about: *Those actions occasioned hostility and eventually war.* —**Idiom.** **4. on occasion,** once in a while; occasionally: *to drink on occasion.*

oc•ca•sion•al /ə'keyʒənḷ/ adj. [before a noun] occurring or appearing at irregular times or not very often: *an occasional headache.* —**oc'ca•sion•al•ly,** adv.

oc•cult /ə'kʌlt, 'ɒkʌlt/ adj. **1.** of or relating to any system claiming use or knowledge of secret, magical, or supernatural powers. —n. [noncount; the + ~] **2.** supernatural, secret, or magical powers or affairs.

oc•cu•pan•cy /'ɒkyəpənsiy/ n. [noncount] the condition, state, or fact of occupying something or of having living quarters in some place: *Occupancy by more than 250 persons is dangerous.*

oc•cu•pant /'ɒkyəpənt/ n. [count] a person or group that occupies something.

oc•cu•pa•tion /,ɒkyə'peyʃən/ n. [count] **1.** a person's usual or principal work, esp. in earning a living. **2.** the act of entering and taking control of an area, esp. by military forces. —,**oc'cu'pa•tion•al,** adj.

oc•cu•py /'ɒkyə,pay/ v. [~ + obj], **-pied, -py•ing. 1.** to have, hold, or take as a separate space: *The orchard occupies half the farm.* **2.** to be a resident or tenant of: *Our company occupies the three top floors of that building.* **3.** to fill up with some activity; spend: *to occupy time reading.* **4.** to take possession and control of (a place), as by military invasion.

oc•cur /ə'kɜr/ v. [no obj], **-curred, -cur•ring. 1.** to happen; take place; come to pass: *The accident occurred last night.* **2.** to exist: *Crime and disease occur in all countries of the world.* **3.** to come to mind: *An idea just occurred to me. It never occurred to me (that) we would not have enough money.* —**oc'cur•rence,** n. [count] [noncount]

o•cean /'owʃən/ n. **1.** [noncount; the + ~] the vast body of salt water that covers almost three-fourths of the earth's surface. **2.** [count] any of the divisions of this body, commonly known as the Atlantic, the Pacific, the Indian, the Arctic, and the Antarctic oceans. —**o•ce•an•ic** /,owʃiy'ænɪk/ adj.

o•cea•nog•ra•phy /,owʃə'nɒgrəfiy, ,owʃiyə-/ n. [noncount] the science that deals with the ocean. —,**o•cea'nog•ra•pher,** n. [count]

o'clock /ə'klɒk/ adv. (used after a number, from 1 to 12, to specify the hour of the day): *11 o'clock in the morning.*

Oct or **Oct.,** an abbreviation of: October.

oc•ta•gon /'ɒktə,gɒn, -gən/ n. [count] a flat, geometrical shape or figure having eight angles and eight sides. —**oc•tag•o•nal** /ɒk'tægənḷ/, adj.

oc•tane /'ɒkteyn/ n. [noncount] a chemical substance found in petroleum and used to indicate the level of quality of gasoline.

oc•tave /'ɒktɪv, -teyv/ n. [count] **1. a.** a tone on the eighth degree from a given musical tone. **b.** the interval between such tones. **2.** a series or group of eight.

Oc•to•ber /ɒk'towbər/ n. the tenth month of the year, containing 31 days.

oc•to•pus /'ɒktəpəs/ n. [count], pl. **-pus•es, -pi** /-,pay/. a sea creature having a soft, oval body and eight tentacles.

oc•u•lar /'ɒkyələr/ adj. **1.** of, relating to, or for the eyes. **2.** performed or seen by the eye or eyesight.

OD /'ow'diy/ n., pl. **ODs** or **OD's,** v., **OD'd** or **ODed, OD'•ing.** —n. [count] **1.** an overdose of a drug, esp. a fatal one. —v. [no obj] **2.** to take or die from a drug overdose.

odd /ɒd/ adj., **-er, -est. 1.** strange; unusual: *Those boys are very odd. It's odd that she hasn't* come home yet. *He's an odd choice for ambassador.* **2.** leaving a remainder when divided by 2: *3 and 5 are odd numbers.* **3.** being part of a pair, set, or series of which the rest is lacking: *an odd glove.* **4.** not regular or full-time; occasional: *He did odd jobs.* —'**odd•ly,** *adv.*

odd•ball /ˈɒd,bɔl/ *Informal.* —*n.* [*count*] **1.** an odd person. —*adj.* [*before a noun*] **2.** odd; strange: *oddball behavior.*

odd•i•ty /ˈɒdɪtiy/ *n.* [*count*], *pl.* **-ties. 1.** an odd person, thing, or event. **2.** an odd characteristic or trait.

odds /ɒdz/ *n.* [*plural*] **1.** the probability that something is more likely to occur than something else: *The odds are that it will rain today.* **2.** probability, expressed as a number: *The odds are two-to-one that it will rain today.* —*Idiom.* **3. at odds,** in disagreement: *They were at odds (with each other) over politics.* —**oddly,** *adv.*

'**odds and 'ends,** *n.* [*plural*] small, unimportant things, matters, etc.

'**odds-'on,** *adj.* [*usually: before a noun*] being the one more or most likely to achieve something: *an odds-on favorite to win.*

o•di•ous /ˈowdiyəs/ *adj.* deserving or causing hatred; hateful.

o•dom•e•ter /owˈdɒmɪtər/ *n.* [*count*] an instrument for measuring distance traveled, as by an automobile.

o•dor /ˈowdər/ *n.* [*count*] [*noncount*] a smell, esp. an unpleasant one. Also, *esp. Brit.,* **odour.**

o•dor•ous /ˈowdərəs/ *adj.* giving off a strong odor.

o'er /ɔr/ *prep., adv.* (in literary use) OVER.

of /ʌv, ɒv; *unstressed* əv *or, esp. before consonants,* ə/ *prep.* **1.** (used to indicate distance or direction from something, separation from something, or the condition of being left without something): *within a mile of the house; robbed of all his money.* **2.** by; coming from: *the songs of Gershwin.* **3.** concerning; about: *talk of peace; a book of mythology.* **4.** resulting from or in connection with: *He died of cancer.* **5.** owned by or belonging to: *the cover of a container; the property of the church.* **6.** (used to indicate that a noun is included, or to show a part of an amount): *You are now one of us. Three-fifths of a cup is enough.* **7.** (used to indicate that the following noun is the object or receiver of the action): *the bombing of the city.* **8.** before the hour of; until: *at ten minutes of one.* **9.** (used to indicate a certain time): *It was the autumn of 1941.* **10.** on the part of: *It was nice of you to come.* **11.** set aside for: *a moment of prayer.* **12.** containing or consisting of: *a dress of silk.*

off /ɔf, ɒf/ *adv.* **1.** so as to be no longer supported or attached: *This button is about to come off.* **2.** so as to be no longer covering: *Pull the wrapping off.* **3.** in a direction that is away from a place: *The mountains are off toward the west.* **4.** away from what is considered normal, standard, or the like: *He's always going off on some strange topic.* **5.** so as to go from one condition to another: *drifted off to sleep.* **6.** from a price: *took 10 percent off.* **7.** at a distance in space or future time: *Summer is only a week off.* **8.** out of operation: *Turn the lights off.* **9.** in absence from work, service, etc.: *got a day off.* **10.** completely: *Finish off that last piece of meat.* —*prep.* **11.** so as no longer to be supported by, resting on, etc.: *Wipe the dirt off your shoes.* **12.** away from: *The ship is 50 miles off course.* **13.** below the usual level or standard: *20 percent off the marked price.*

14. free from: *He's off duty on Tuesdays.* **15.** not wanting or requiring: *off drugs.* **16.** leading away from: *an alley off 12th Street.* —*adj.* [*be + ~*] wrong: *You are off on that point.* **18.** [*before a noun*] not up to the usual or expected standard: *The play has its off moments.* **19.** [*be + ~*] no longer in effect: *The deal is off.* **20.** free from work or duty: *He's off tomorrow.* **21.** [*before a noun*] of less than the ordinary activity: *the off season at the beach.* **22.** [*be + ~*] starting on one's way: *I'm off to Europe on Monday.* **23.** [*be + ~*] lower in price or value: *Stock prices were off this morning.* —*Idiom.* **24. off and on,** with periods of time in between: *to work off and on.* Also, **on and off.**

off•beat /ˈɔf,biyt, ˈɒf-/ *adj.* not usual or ordinary: *an offbeat restaurant.*

'**off-'color,** *adj.* containing slightly offensive language, actions, etc.: *off-color jokes.*

of•fend /əˈfɛnd/ *v.* [*~ + obj*] **1.** to irritate, annoy, or anger: *His impolite remarks offended the audience.* **2.** to affect (the senses) in an unpleasant or disagreeable way: *a horrible color that offends the eye.* —**of'fend•er,** *n.* [*count*]

of•fense /əˈfɛns *or, esp. in sports,* ˈɔfɛns, ˈɒfɛns/ *n.* **1.** [*count*] a crime or act of breaking the law: *a traffic offense.* **2.** an act or cause of annoying or angering someone: [*noncount*]: *to avoid giving offense; takes offense easily.* [*count*]: *an offense against decency.* **3.** attack or assault: [*noncount*]: *weapons of offense.* [*count*]: *a strong offense.* **4.** [*count*] the team or unit responsible for scoring points in a game. Also, *esp. Brit.,* **of'fence.**

of•fen•sive /əˈfɛnsɪv *or, for 3* ˈɔfɛn-, ˈɒfɛn-/ *adj.* **1.** irritating; causing anger. **2.** unpleasant or disagreeable to the senses; disgusting: *offensive odors.* **3.** of or relating to offense or attack: *a good offensive strategy.* —*n.* **4.** [*noncount; usually: the + ~*] the position or strategy of attacking: *to take the offensive; to go on the offensive.* **5.** [*count*] an attack: *launching an offensive against the enemy.*

of•fer /ˈɔfər, ˈɒfər/ *v.* [*~ + obj*] **1.** to present (something) for acceptance or rejection: *He offered a drink to his guests.* **2.** to show willingness (to do something): *I offered to go first.* **3.** to present as an act of worship: *Let us offer thanks. They offered the gods sacrifices.* **4.** to present for sale or propose as a price: *They offered $100,000 for the house. Their car is being offered for sale.* **5.** to put forth; do or perform: *to offer resistance.* —*n.* [*count*] **6.** an act or instance of offering. **7.** a proposal to give or pay something.

of•fer•ing /ˈɔfərɪŋ, ˈɒfər-/ *n.* [*count*] **1.** something offered in devotion to a deity or a church. **2.** something presented for inspection or sale.

off•hand /ˈɔfˈhænd, ˈɒf-/ *adj.* unplanned; casual: *offhand remarks.*

of•fice /ˈɔfɪs, ˈɒfɪs/ *n.* **1.** [*count*] a place where business, work, or one's job is conducted or accomplished. **2.** [*count*] a business or professional organization: *a law office.* **3.** [*noncount*] a position of duty, trust, or authority: *the office of president; How long has he been in office?*

of•fice•hold•er /ˈɔfɪs,howldər, ˈɒfɪs-/ *n.* [*count*] a government official.

of•fi•cer /ˈɔfəsər, ˈɒfə-/ *n.* [*count*] **1.** a person who holds a position of authority in an organization or in the armed forces. **2.** a member of a police department.

of•fi•cial /əˈfɪʃəl/ *n.* [*count*] **1.** a person appointed or elected to an office: *a court official.*

0

office

clock

bookcase

file cabinet

file drawer

bulletin board

copier

calendar

telephone

desk

drawer

swivel chair

file folders

stapler

monitor

computer

mouse

fax

mouse pad

keyboard

—*adj.* **2.** appointed, authorized, or approved by a government or organization: *an official flag; official powers.* —**of·fi·cial·ly,** *adv.*

of·fi·ci·ate /ə'fɪʃiy,eyt/ *v.* [*no obj*], **-at·ed, -at·ing.** to perform the duties or function of some office or position.

of·fi·cious /ə'fɪʃəs/ *adj.* offering help or advice that is not asked for and not wanted; meddlesome.

'off-'key, *adj., adv.* out of tune: *an off-key song; She sang off-key.*

'off-'limits, *adj.* [*be* + ~] forbidden to be visited, used, etc., by certain persons: *The downtown area was off-limits to enlisted men.*

'off-,line or **'off,line,** *adj.* operating independently of, or no longer connected to, another computer. Compare ON-LINE.

off-peak /'ɔf'piyk, 'ɒf-/ *adj.* of or relating to a time of day or a period of time other than the regular or busiest time: *Hotel rooms are cheaper during the off-peak tourist season.*

'off-'season, *n.* [*count*] **1.** a time of year other than the regular or busiest one for a particular activity. —*adj.* **2.** of, relating to, or during the off-season. —*adv.* **3.** in or during the off-season: *They always traveled off-season.*

off·shoot /'ɔf,ʃuwt, 'ɒf-/ *n.* [*count*] **1.** a branch growing from a main stem. **2.** anything thought of as developing from a main source: *an offshoot of medical science.*

off·shore /'ɔf'ʃɔr, 'ɒf-/ *adv.* **1.** off or away from the shore: *drifting offshore.* —*adj.* **2.** moving away from the shore: *an offshore wind.* **3.** located or operating at some distance from the shore: *offshore oil wells.*

off·spring /'ɔf,sprɪŋ, 'ɒf-/ *n.* [*count*], *pl.* **-spring.** children or young of a particular parent; descendants.

'off-the-'wall, *adj.* very unusual; bizarre.

of·ten /'ɔfən, 'ɒfən; 'ɔftən, 'ɒf-/ *adv.* many times; frequently: *I've been to their home often.*

o·gre /'owgər/ *n.* [*count*] **1.** a monster or giant in fairy tales. **2.** a frightening or cruel person.

oh /ow/ *interj.* **1.** (used to express surprise, pain, disapproval, sympathy, agreement, and other emotions): *Oh! What's that noise?* **2.** (used to attract a person's attention): *Oh, waiter!* **3.** (used when the speaker is thinking, guessing, etc.): *The fish must have weighed, oh, six or seven pounds.*

OH, an abbreviation of: Ohio.

ohm /owm/ *n.* [*count*] the international unit or measure of electrical resistance.

-oid, a suffix meaning resembling or like (*humanoid*).

oil /ɔyl/ *n.* **1.** any of various liquid substances that are thick and sticky, taken from the ground, from the fat of animals, or from plants, and used for cooking, heating, providing power in engines, and making machine parts run smoother: [*noncount*]: *motor oil.* [*count*]: *vegetable oils.* **2.** [*noncount*] a paint made by mixing pigment with oil. —*v.* [~ + *obj*] **3.** to rub, cover, or supply with oil. —*adj.* [*before a noun*] **4.** of, relating to, or using oil: *oil heat.* —**oily, -lier, -liest,** *adj.*

'oil ,painting, *n.* [*count*] a painting made in oils.

'oil ,slick, *n.* [*count*] a layer of oil on the surface of a body of water.

'oil ,well, *n.* [*count*] a well drilled to obtain petroleum.

oink /ɔyŋk/ *n.* [*count*] **1.** the grunting sound

made by a hog. —*v.* [*no obj*] **2.** to make such a sound.

oint·ment /'ɔyntmənt/ *n.* [*noncount*] [*count*] a soft, oily preparation for soothing or healing the skin.

OK or **O.K.** or **o·kay** /'ow'key, ,ow'key, 'ow,key/ *adj., adv., n., pl.* **OKs** or **OK's** or **O.K.'s** or **o·kays,** *v.,* **OK'd** or **O.K.'ed** or **o·kayed, OK'·ing** or **O.K.'·ing** or **o·kay·ing,** *interj.* —*adj.* **1.** all right; satisfactory: *Is everything OK?* **2.** feeling well: *The patient's OK now.* **3.** safe: *Stay behind me and you'll be OK.* **4.** good enough; adequate: *an OK speech; The play was just OK.* —*adv.* **5.** all right; well enough: *We got along OK.* —*n.* [*count*] an approval: *Do you have an OK to do this?* —*v.* [~ + *obj*] **7.** to approve; authorize: *O.K.'ed the plan.* —*interj.* **8.** (used to express agreement): *OK, I'll come to the party.* **9.** (used to find out if a person understands what has been said): *Start running when I signal, OK?*

OK, an abbreviation of: Oklahoma.

Okla., an abbreviation of: Oklahoma.

old /owld/ *adj.,* **old·er, old·est** or **eld·er, eld·est,** *n.* —*adj.* **1.** having lived or existed for a long time: *an old man; an old building.* **2.** of or relating to the later part of life or existence: *old age.* **3.** having lived or existed for a certain time: *a six-month-old company.* **4.** known or in use for a long time: *an old friend; the same old excuses.* **5.** having been replaced by something newer or more recent: *We sold our old house.* **6.** sensible, mature, or wise: *old beyond her years.* —*n.* **7.** **the old,** [*plural; used with a plural verb*] old persons thought of as a group. **8.** [*count*] a person or animal of a specified age or age group: *a program for six-year-olds.*

'old-'fashioned, *adj.* **1.** of a kind that is no longer in style; out-of-date. **2.** having or choosing the conservative behavior, beliefs, or tastes of earlier times: *old-fashioned ideas.*

'old 'hand, *n.* [*count*] a person with long experience in a subject or area: *an old hand at politics.*

old·ie /'owldiy/ *n.* [*count*] *Informal.* a song, joke, movie, etc., that was popular at a time in the past.

'Old 'Testament, *n.* [*the* + ~] the complete Bible of the Jews, being the first of the two main divisions of the Christian Bible.

'old-'time, *adj.* [*before a noun*] **1.** belonging to old or former times, methods, ideas, etc. **2.** being long established: *old-time residents.*

'old-'timer, *n.* [*count*] **1.** a person who has lived in a place, belonged to an organization, or worked at something for a long time. **2.** an elderly person.

ol·ive /'ɒlɪv/ *n.* **1.** [*count*] an evergreen tree of warm regions. **2.** [*count*] the small, oval-shaped fruit of this tree, eaten as a food and used as a source of oil. **3.** [*noncount*] the green color of the unripe olive.

O'lympic 'Games, /ə'lɪmpɪk, ow'lɪm-/ *n.* [*plural; usually: the* + ~] an international sports competition traditionally held every four years but after 1992 with Summer Games and Winter Games alternating every two years. Also, **Olympics.** —**O'lym·pic,** *adj.*

om·e·let or **om·e·lette** /'ɒmlɪt, 'ɒmə-/ *n.* [*count*] beaten eggs cooked until set and often served folded around a filling, as of cheese.

o·men /'owmən/ *n.* [*count*] any event believed to signal the coming of something good or evil.

om·i·nous /'ɒmənəs/ *adj.* being an omen of something bad; threatening: *ominous black*

O

clouds. —'**om•i•nous•ly,** adv. —'**om•i•nous•ness,** n. [noncount]

o•mit /ow'mɪt/ v. [~ + obj], **o•mit•ted, o•mit•ting.** to leave out; fail to include: omitted a few details from the report. —o'**mis•sion,** n. [noncount] [count]

omni-, a combining form meaning all (omnipotent).

om•nip•o•tent /ɒm'nɪpətənt/ adj. infinite in power, such as God. —om'**nip•o•tence,** n. [noncount]

om•ni•pres•ent /ˌɒmnə'prɛzənt/ adj. being everywhere at the same time. —ˌom•ni'**pres•ence,** n. [noncount]

om•nis•cient /ɒm'nɪʃənt/ adj. knowing everything. —om'**nis•cience,** n. [noncount]

om•niv•o•rous /ɒm'nɪvərəs/ adj. **1.** feeding on both animals and plants. **2.** taking in everything, as with the mind: an omnivorous reader. —om•ni•vore /'ɒmnə,vɔr/, n. [count]

on /ɒn, ɔn/ prep. **1.** so as to be supported by: Put the package on the table. **2.** so as to be attached to: a label on the jar. **3.** so as to be a covering for: Put the blanket on the baby. **4.** connected or associated with: to serve on a jury. **5.** (used to show location, situation, etc.): a scar on the face. **6.** very close to; at the edge of: a house on the lake. **7.** (used to show a means of transporting, supporting, or providing movement): arrived on the noon plane. **8.** by the agency or means of: drunk on wine. **9.** having as a subject; being about (something): a book on dogs. **10.** in a condition or process of: The workers are on strike. **11.** subject to: The doctor is on call all weekend. **12.** having as a source or agent: depended on his friends. **13.** having as a basis or ground: on my word of honor. **14.** assigned to or working at: Who's on duty today? **15.** at the time or occasion of: on Sunday. **16.** having as the goal of action, thought, desire, etc.: to gaze on a scene. **17.** paid for by: Dinner is on me. **18.** taking or using to improve one's health, energy, etc.: He's on a low-salt diet. —adv. **19.** in, into, or onto a position of being supported or attached: Sew the buttons on. **20.** in, into, or onto a position of covering: Put your raincoat on. **21.** tightly attached to a thing, as for support: Hold on! **22.** toward a place, point, activity, or object: to look on while others work. **23.** forward, onward, or along: further on. **24.** into or in active operation: Turn the gas on. —adj. [be + ~] **25.** operating or in use: Is the radio on? **26.** taking place; occurring: Don't you know there's a war on? **27.** being broadcast: What's on tonight? **28.** scheduled or planned: Do you have anything on for tomorrow? —**Idiom. 29. on and off,** with periods of time in between. Also, **off and on. 30. on and on,** without stopping: to chatter on and on. —**Usage.** See ABOUT.

once /wʌns/ adv. **1.** formerly: a once powerful nation. **2.** a single time: We eat out once a week. **3.** at any time; ever: If the facts once became known, we'd be in trouble. **4.** by a single step or degree: She's my first cousin once removed. —conj. **5.** whenever; as soon as: Once you're finished, you can leave. —**Idiom. 6. at once, a.** immediately; promptly: left at once. **b.** at the same time; simultaneously: They all sprang up at once. **7. once in a while,** sometimes; occasionally.

on•col•o•gy /ɒŋ'kɒlədʒiy/ n. [noncount] the study of tumors, including cancers. —on'**col•o•gist,** n. [count]

on•com•ing /'ɒn,kʌmɪŋ, 'ɔn-/ adj. [before a noun] approaching; nearing: an oncoming train.

one /wʌn/ adj. **1.** being or amounting to a single unit or individual: one child; only one piece of cake left. **2.** of the same kind, nature, or condition: We are of one mind. **3.** (used to refer to an unspecified day or time): one evening last week. **4.** being a particular individual or item: She's the one person I can trust. —n. [count] **5.** the first and lowest whole number, written as 1. **6.** a single person or thing: Let's do one at a time. —pron. **7.** (used to stand for a person or thing of a number or kind): He is one of the medieval poets. **8.** (used to stand for a person or thing that has just been mentioned): The portraits are good ones. **9.** a person or being: Satan, the evil one. **10.** any person or thing; people in general: One shouldn't insult the boss. —**Idiom. 11. one and all,** everyone. **12. one by one,** singly and following after another.

'one an'other, pron. EACH OTHER.

'one-di'mensional, adj. **1.** having one dimension only: A line is one-dimensional. **2.** having no depth, scope, or interesting qualities: a novel with one-dimensional characters.

'one-'liner, n. [count] a brief joke or witty remark.

one•self /wʌn'sɛlf, wʌnz-/ pron. **1.** (used when the subject of a sentence is ONE and the object of the verb or a preposition refers to the same individual): One should be able to laugh at oneself. **2.** (used when the subject or object of a sentence is ONE and the speaker wishes to emphasize that subject or object): To do something oneself brings great satisfaction. —**Idiom. 3. be oneself, a.** to be in one's normal state of mind or physical condition: He was himself again after a nap. **b.** to be sincere: Just be yourself during the interview. **4. by oneself, a.** without a companion; alone. **b.** without help: Did you draw this picture by yourself?

'one-'sided, adj. **1.** partial; unfair: a one-sided judgment. **2.** with one side much better than the other; unequal: a one-sided fight.

'one-,time, adj. [before a noun] **1.** former: a one-time ski instructor. **2.** occurring, done, etc., only once: a one-time offer.

'one-,track, adj. [before a noun] unable or unwilling to deal or work with more than one idea, subject, etc., at one time: a one-track mind.

'one-'way, adj. [before a noun] **1.** moving or allowing movement in one direction only: a one-way street. **2.** used for travel in one direction only: a one-way ticket.

on•go•ing /'ɒn,gowɪŋ, 'ɔn-/ adj. continuing without ending or without interruption: ongoing research.

on•ion /'ʌnyən/ n. [count] a round vegetable with a strong smell and taste.

'on-'line, or 'on,line, adj. **1.** operating under the direct control of, or connected to, a computer: an on-line printer. **2.** connected by computer to one or more other computers, esp. on the Internet.

on•look•er /'ɒn,lʊkər, 'ɔn-/ n. [count] a spectator: onlookers to an accident.

on•ly /'ownliy/ adv. **1.** without others or anything further; exclusively: This information is for your eyes only. **2.** no more than; just: We get away from the city only on weekends. **3.** as recently as: I read that article only yesterday. **4.** in the final outcome or decision: That will only make matters worse. —adj. **5.** being the single one of a kind: *Is this the only seat left?* —*conj.* **6.** but; except: *I would have gone, only you objected.*

on•slaught /'ɒn,slɔt, 'ɔn-/ *n.* [*count*] a fierce attack.

on•to /'ɒntuw, 'ɔn-; *unstressed* 'ɒntə, 'ɔn-/ *prep.* **1.** to a place or position on; upon; on: *They pulled him onto his feet.* **2.** *Informal.* aware of the true nature, motive, or meaning of: *I'm onto your tricks.*

on•ward /'ɒnwərd, 'ɔn-/ *adv.* Also, **on′wards.** **1.** toward a point ahead or in front; forward, as in space or time: *The army marched onward.* —*adj.* [*before a noun*] **2.** directed or moving onward: *the onward flight to freedom.*

on•yx /'ɒnɪks/ *n.* [*count*] [*noncount*] a mineral stone, a form of quartz, having parallel bands of alternating colors.

oo•dles /'uwdlz/ *n.* [*plural; sometimes used with a singular verb*] *Informal.* a large quantity: *oodles of fun.*

ooze /uwz/ *v.* **1.** [*no obj*] (of liquid) to flow slowly or gradually: *Water was oozing from her sneakers.* **2.** [~ + *obj*] to allow to flow gradually: *The wound began to ooze blood.*

o•pal /'owpəl/ *n.* [*count*] [*noncount*] a mineral made into a gemstone with many shining colors in it.

o•paque /ow'peyk/ *adj.* **1.** not allowing light to pass through; difficult to see through. **2.** hard to understand: *opaque arguments.*

op. cit. /'ɒp' sɪt/ an abbreviation of Latin *opere citato*: in the work cited.

o•pen /'owpən/ *adj.* **1.** not closed or barred: *She left the windows open at night.* **2.** mostly free of things that block or that prevent movement through: *an open floor plan.* **3.** built or designed so as not to be fully enclosed: *an open staircase.* **4.** not covered or closed: *His eyes were open.* **5.** extended, unfolded, or arranged: *an open newspaper; The book was open on the desk.* **6.** without restrictions or limits as to who may participate: *open enrollment.* **7.** available: *Which job is open?* **8.** ready for or carrying on normal trade or business: *The new store is now open.* **9.** so clear that all can see or know: *open disregard of the rules.* **10.** truthful; honest; candid: *always open and fair in his dealings with others.* **11.** generous: *to give with an open hand.* **12.** likely to receive: *His actions left him open to criticism.* **13.** undecided; unsettled: *several open questions.* —*v.* **14.** to (cause to) be moved from a shut or closed position, such as a door, window, etc.: [~ + *obj*]: *He opened the door.* [*no obj*]: *The door slowly opened.* **15.** [~ + *obj*] to remove a blockage or barrier from: *to open the road after a snowstorm.* **16.** to (cause to) be not covered or closed: [~ + *obj*]: *He opened his mouth to speak.* [*no obj*]: *His eyes opened suddenly.* **17.** [~ + *obj*] to make available: *to open a port for trade.* **18.** to (cause to) be made ready for customers or normal work activity: [~ + *obj*]: *They open the store at nine o'clock.* [*no obj*]: *They open at nine o'clock.* **19.** to (cause to) be set in action, begun, or started: [~ + *obj*]: *opened the meeting with a short speech.* [*no obj*]: *The meeting opened with a short speech.* **20.** to (cause to) be expanded, unfolded, spread out; (cause to) be turned or arranged to be read: [~ + *obj*]: *to open a map.* [*no obj*]: *The map opened easily.* **21.** [*no obj*] to provide a way of approaching a place: *The door opens into the garden.* **22.** [*no obj*] to part or seem to part: *The clouds opened.* **23.** to (cause to) spread or expand: [*no obj*]: *The*

flower opened in the sunlight. [~ + *obj*]: *The fisherman opened the oysters with a sharp knife.* **24. open up, a.** to make or become open: *The flower opened up in the sun. They opened up their shops. It was too early to open them up.* **b.** to share or become willing to share one's feelings, etc.: *She had to learn to open up to others.* —*n.* **25.** [*noncount; the* + ~] the open air; outdoors: *They slept out in the open.* **26.** [*noncount; the* + ~] open water, as of the sea. —'**o•pen•ness,** *n.* [*noncount*]

'**open** '**air,** *n.* [*noncount*] the outdoors. —,**open-**'**air,** *adj.* [*before a noun*]: *an open-air market.*

'**open-**'**ended,** *adj.* **1.** not having fixed limits: *an open-ended discussion.* **2.** having no fixed answer: *an open-ended test question.*

o•pen•er /'owpənər/ *n.* [*count*] **1.** a person or thing that opens. **2.** a device for opening sealed containers or cans: *a can opener.*

o•pen•hand•ed /'owpən'hændɪd/ *adj.* generous.

'**open-**'**hearted,** *adj.* **1.** candid or frank. **2.** kindly; wishing for good.

o•pen•ing /'owpənɪŋ/ *n.* [*count*] **1.** an unoccupied space or place: *an opening in the woods.* **2.** a hole in something solid. **3.** a vacancy for a job. **4.** a formal or official beginning: *The mayor was present for the opening of the new highway.* —*adj.* [*before a noun*] **5.** coming first; beginning: *opening remarks.*

o•pen•ly /'owpənliy/ *adv.* without hiding or trying to deceive; clearly: *They discussed their problems openly.*

'**open-**'**minded,** *adj.* **1.** willing to consider new ideas or arguments. **2.** not having or showing prejudice.

op•er•a /'ɒpərə, 'ɒprə/ *n.* [*count*] [*noncount*], *pl.* **-er•as.** a long dramatic musical work in which the parts are sung.

op•er•a•ble /'ɒpərəbəl, 'ɒprə-/ *adj.* able to be treated by a surgical operation.

op•er•ate /'ɒpə,reyt/ *v.,* **-at•ed, -at•ing. 1.** to (cause to) work or function: [*no obj*]: *This coffee machine is not operating properly.* [~ + *obj*]: *Can you operate farm machinery?* **2.** [*no obj*] to carry on business: *The company operates in southern California.* **3.** [*no obj*] to perform a medical procedure in which the body is cut open and a part is removed or repaired: *The surgeon operated on several patients.*

op•er•at•ic /,ɒpə'rætɪk/ *adj.* of or relating to opera.

op•er•a•tion /,ɒpə'reyʃən/ *n.* **1.** [*count*] an act, instance, or manner of working. **2.** [*noncount*] the state of working or being in force: *a rule no longer in operation.* **3.** [*count*] a mechanical process: *a delicate operation in watchmaking.* **4.** [*count*] a business, esp. a large one. **5.** [*count*] a medical procedure of cutting open the body to remove or repair a damaged part. —,**op•er′a•tion•al,** *adj.*

op•er•a•tive /'ɒpərətɪv, 'ɒprətɪv, 'ɒpə,reytɪv/ *adj.* **1.** working or functioning; in use: *The plant was fully operative.* **2.** being in force: *The regulation became operative last month.*

op•er•a•tor /'ɒpə,reytər/ *n.* [*count*] **1.** a person who operates a machine or apparatus, esp. a telephone switchboard. **2.** a person who manages a business: *a hotel operator.*

op•er•et•ta /,ɒpə'retə/ *n.* [*count*], *pl.* **-tas.** a light and amusing opera.

oph•thal•mol•o•gy /,ɒfθəl'mɒlədʒiy, -θə-,

O

,ɒp-/ n. [noncount] the branch of medicine dealing with the functions and diseases of the eye. —,**oph•thal'mol•o•gist,** n. [count]

o•pin•ion /ə'pɪnyən/ n. [count] **1.** a personal view or belief. **2.** the formal expression of a professional judgment: She got a second medical opinion.

o•pin•ion•at•ed /ə'pɪnyə,neytɪd/ adj. stubbornly believing in one's own opinions.

o•pi•um /'owpiyəm/ n. [noncount] a narcotic drug made from the juice of poppy seeds.

o•pos•sum /ə'pɒsəm, 'pɒsəm/ n. [count], pl. **-sums,** (esp. when thought of as a group) **-sum.** a small animal that carries its young in a pouch and is noted for pretending to be dead when it is in danger.

op•po•nent /ə'pownənt/ n. [count] a person who is on an opposing side in a game, argument, etc.

op•por•tune /,ɒpər'tuwn, -'tyuwn/ adj. **1.** suitable; apt: an opportune comment. **2.** happening at a suitable time: an opportune meeting.

op•por•tun•ism /,ɒpər'tuwnɪzəm, -'tyuw-/ [noncount] the practice of taking action based on chance of success and gain, without regard to moral principles. —,**op•por'tun•ist,** n. [count] —,**op•por'tun•is•tic,** adj.

op•por•tu•ni•ty /,ɒpər'tuwnɪtiy, -'tyuw-/ n., pl. **-ties. 1.** [count] a favorable occasion or time (to do something): an opportunity to apologize. **2.** [noncount] a situation that provides a good chance for success: a land of opportunity.

op•pose /ə'powz/ v. [~ + obj], **-posed, -pos•ing. 1.** to be strongly against something: Several senators opposed the project. —**Idiom. 2. as opposed to,** in contrast to; instead of: I'd rather have a small computer as opposed to a big one.

op•pos•ing /ə'powzɪŋ/ adj. opposite; contrary: The two speakers took opposing viewpoints.

op•po•site /'ɒpəzɪt, -sɪt/ adj. **1.** located directly across from: They sat at opposite ends of the room. **2.** totally different: opposite opinions. —n. [count] **3.** a person or thing that is opposite in character. —prep. **4.** across from; facing: He sat opposite me on the train. —adv. **5.** on or to the opposite side: I was at one end and she sat opposite.

op•po•si•tion /,ɒpə'zɪʃən/ n. **1.** [noncount] the action of opposing. **2.** [count; usually singular; usually: the + ~] a person or group of people opposing something or someone.

op•press /ə'prɛs/ v. [~ + obj] **1.** to use harsh authority or power over (others): The dictator oppressed his people. **2.** to weigh heavily on (the mind, a person, etc.): She's oppressed by worry. —**op'pres•sion,** n. [noncount] —**op'pres•sive,** adj. —**op'pres•sor,** n. [count]

opt /ɒpt/ v. [no obj] to make a choice; choose: They opted to retire early.

op•tic /'ɒptɪk/ adj. [before a noun] of or relating to the eye or eyesight.

op•ti•cal /'ɒptɪkəl/ adj. [before a noun] **1.** of or relating to the science of optics: A telescope is an optical instrument. **2.** of or relating to the eye or eyesight.

'optical 'disc, n. [count] **1.** Also called **laser disc.** a plastic disk on which digital data, as music or pictures, are stored as tiny pits in the surface and read by a laser. **2.** VIDEODISC. Compare COMPACT DISC.

op•ti•cian /ɒp'tɪʃən/ n. [count] a person who makes or sells eyeglasses and contact lenses.

op•tics /'ɒptɪks/ n. [noncount; used with a singu-

lar verb] the science dealing with the properties and actions of both visible and invisible light and with vision.

op•ti•mism /'ɒptə,mɪzəm/ n. [noncount] a tendency to look on the more favorable side or to expect the most favorable outcome or result of events or conditions. —'**op•ti•mist,** n. [count] —,**op•ti'mis•tic,** adj. —,**op•ti'mis•ti•cal•ly,** adv.

op•ti•mum /'ɒptəməm/ n., pl. **-ma** /-mə/, **-mums,** adj. —n. [count] **1.** the most favorable point, degree, or amount of something for obtaining a certain result. —adj. [before a noun] **2.** most favorable or desirable; best: optimum conditions for growth. —'**op•ti•mal,** adj.

op•tion /'ɒpʃən/ n. **1.** [noncount] the power or right of choosing: to have no option but to stay. **2.** [count] something that may be chosen; choice: Your options are law school or taking a job. —'**op•tion•al,** adj.

op•tom•e•try /ɒp'tɒmɪtriy/ n. [noncount] the profession of examining the eyes for defects of vision and for eye disorders. —**op'tom•e•trist,** n. [count]

op•u•lence /'ɒpyələns/ n. [noncount] the state of being or appearing very wealthy. —'**op•u•lent,** adj.

o•pus /'owpəs/ n. [count], pl. **o•pus•es.** a literary, musical, or artistic work.

or /ɔr; unstressed ər/ conj. **1.** (used to connect words, phrases, or clauses that represent choices): Do you want vanilla or chocolate? **2.** (used to connect different words or names that refer to the same thing): the Hawaiian, or Sandwich, Islands. **3.** (used with the word EITHER to connect two clauses showing one choice followed by another): Either we go now or we wait till tomorrow. **4.** (used to correct or rephrase what was previously said): His autobiography, or rather his memoirs, will be published soon. **5.** otherwise; else: Be here on time, or we'll leave without you.

OR, an abbreviation of: Oregon.

-or, a suffix meaning a person or thing that does something (orator; tractor).

o•ral /'ɔrəl/ adj. **1.** made or expressed by the mouth; spoken: oral testimony. **2.** of, using, or carried by speech: oral teaching methods. **3.** involving the mouth: oral hygiene. —'**o•ral•ly,** adv.

or•ange /'ɔrɪndʒ, 'ɒr-/ n. **1.** [count] a rounded, reddish yellow citrus fruit. **2.** [count] a white-flowered evergreen tree bearing such fruit. **3.** [noncount] a reddish yellow color. —adj. **4.** of, relating to, or containing the orange or its juice or flavor. **5.** of the color orange.

o•rang•u•tan /ɔ'ræŋʊ,tæn, ow'ræŋ-, ə'ræŋ-/ also **o'rang•u,tang** /-,tæŋ/ n. [count] a large, mostly tree-dwelling, humanlike ape of Borneo and Sumatra.

o•ra•tion /ɔ'reyʃən, ow'rey-/ n. [count] a formal public speech, esp. for a special occasion.

or•a•tor /'ɔrətər, 'ɒr-/ n. [count] a person noted for giving public speeches.

or•a•to•ry /'ɔrə,tɔriy, 'ɒr-/ n. [noncount] skill or ability in public speaking; the art of public speaking.

orb /ɔrb/ n. [count] a round object, as a sphere or globe.

or•bit /'ɔrbɪt/ n. **1.** the curved path that a planet, satellite, spaceship, etc., follows around a heavenly body: [count]: a comet with a very irregular orbit. [noncount]: a spacecraft in orbit. —v. **2.** to travel in an orbit around: [~ + obj]: The satellite orbited the earth. [no obj]: The moon orbited above the horizon. —**or•bit•al** /'ɔrbɪtl/, adj.

or•chard /'ɔrtʃərd/ n. [count] **1.** an area of land used for the growing of fruit or nut trees. **2.** a group of such trees.

or•ches•tra /'ɔrkəstrə, -kɛs trə/ n. [count], pl. **-tras.** a group of musicians who play string, wind, and other instruments together. —**or•ches•tral** /ɔr'kɛstrəl/, adj.

or•ches•trate /'ɔrkə,streyt/ v. [~ + obj], **-trat•ed, -trat•ing. 1.** to compose or arrange (music) for an orchestra. **2.** to arrange, coordinate, or organize the elements of (something): to orchestrate negotiations. —**or•ches•tra•tion** /,ɔrkə'streyʃən/, n. [count]

or•chid /'ɔrkɪd/ n. [count] a plant having unusually shaped, very showy flowers.

or•dain /ɔr'deyn/ v. [~ + obj] **1.** to make (someone) a priest, minister, or rabbi. **2.** to order or establish by law, command, etc.: The king ordained that everyone should pay tax. —**or•di•na•tion** /,ɔrdn'eyʃən/ n. [count] [noncount]

or•deal /ɔr'diyl, -'diyəl/ n. [count] any very severe or difficult test, experience, or trial.

or•der /'ɔrdər/ n. **1.** a command or instruction given by someone in authority: [count]: gave orders not to be disturbed. [noncount]: We're here to arrest you by order of the queen. **2.** [noncount] the way of arranging things to follow one after another: words in alphabetical order. **3.** [noncount] proper, satisfactory, or working condition: a motorcycle in working order. **4.** [noncount] obedience to law and respect for authority: to keep order in the classroom. **5.** [count] a direction or request to make or provide something: sent in an order for shirts. **6.** [count] an amount of goods purchased or sold: Your order hasn't been delivered yet. **7.** [count] a portion of food requested or served in a restaurant: an order of French fries. —v. **8.** [~ + obj] to give an order or command to: She ordered them to leave at once. **9.** to ask for (something) to be done, made, or provided: [~ + obj]: to order a book; She ordered the flags to be lowered. [no obj]: "Are you ready to order?" the waiter asked. **10.** [~ + obj] to arrange in a suitable way: to order one's schedule. **11. order around,** to give orders to (someone) in an unpleasant, rude, or bossy way. —**Idiom. 12. call to order,** to begin (a meeting): They called the meeting to order. **13. in order, a.** right and proper; appropriate: An apology is certainly in order. **b.** properly arranged or prepared: Everything's in order, so we can go now. **14. in order to,** (used to introduce a phrase that explains the reason for something): The students are studying in order to get better grades. **15. out of order, a.** not arranged correctly: These pages are out of order. **b.** not suitable: Your remarks are out of order. **c.** not working: The elevators are out of order.

or•der•ly /'ɔrdərliy/ adj., n., pl. **-lies.** —adj. **1.** arranged or organized in a neat manner: orderly closets. **2.** observing or obeying laws, rules, or discipline: an orderly crowd. —n. [count] **3.** a hospital attendant having general, nonmedical duties.

'ordinal 'number, n. [count] a number that expresses position in a series, as first or second.

or•di•nance /'ɔrdnəns/ n. [count] a public regulation, rule, or law: a city ordinance.

or•di•nar•i•ly /,ɔrdn'ɛərəliy, 'ɔrdn,ɛrəliy/ adv. **1.** most of the time; generally; usually: Ordinarily this train is on time. **2.** in an ordinary manner or fashion: dressed ordinarily.

or•di•nar•y /'ɔrdn,ɛriy/ adj. **1.** of no special

quality or interest; commonplace: not a hero but an ordinary man. **2.** customary; usual; normal: wore their ordinary clothes. —n. [noncount; the + ~] **3.** customary or average condition, degree, etc.: ability far above the ordinary. —**Idiom. 4. out of the ordinary, a.** unusual. **b.** unusually good. —'**or•di,nar•i•ness,** n. [noncount]

ore /ɔr/ n. a metal-bearing mineral or rock that can be mined: [noncount]: iron ore. [count]: profitable ores.

Ore., an abbreviation of: Oregon.

Oreg., an abbreviation of: Oregon.

o•reg•a•no /ə'rɛgə,now, ɔ'rɛg-/ n. [noncount] a sweet-smelling herb.

or•gan /'ɔrgən/ n. [count] **1. a.** a musical instrument played by a keyboard that controls the flow of air through a set of pipes. **b.** a similar musical instrument having the tones produced electronically. **2.** a plant or animal structure that performs a special task.

or•gan•ic /ɔr'gænɪk/ adj. **1.** [before a noun] of or relating to a class of chemical compounds that contain carbon. **2.** [before a noun] relating to, characteristic of, or coming from living things. **3.** raised or grown without artificial or synthetic fertilizers, pesticides, or drugs. **4.** organized; systematic: a view of language as an organic whole. —**or'gan•i•cal•ly,** adv.

or•gan•ism /'ɔrgə,nɪzəm/ n. [count] any individual life form thought of as a single unit; an animal or plant.

or•gan•ist /'ɔrgənɪst/ n. [count] a person who plays the organ.

or•gan•i•za•tion /,ɔrgənə'zeyʃən/ n. **1.** [noncount] the act or process of organizing: the organization of a banquet. **2.** [noncount] the state or manner of being organized. **3.** [count] a group of persons joined for some purpose or work: a national organization devoted to women's rights. —**or•gan•i•za•tion•al** /,ɔrgənə'zeyʃənl/, adj.

or•gan•ize /'ɔrgə,nayz/ v. [~ + obj], **-ized, -iz•ing. 1.** to form as or into a whole, esp. for united action: to organize a committee. **2.** to arrange or plan something: She organized her notes before the test. Who is organizing the party? —'**or•gan,iz•er,** n. [count]

or•gan•ized /'ɔrgə,nayzd/ adj. **1.** grouped or associated with an organization, esp. with a union: organized labor. **2.** having a structure for directing many activities over a wide area: organized crime.

or•gasm /'ɔrgæzəm/ n. [count] [noncount] the intense physical and emotional feeling experienced at the peak of sexual excitement.

or•gy /'ɔrdʒiy/ n. [count], pl. **-gies. 1.** a party with drinking and sexual activity. **2.** any actions that are uncontrolled or wild: an orgy of killing.

o•ri•ent /n.'ɔriyənt, -iy,ɛnt, v. 'ɔriy,ɛnt/ n. **1. Orient,** [the + ~] the countries of East Asia, such as China, Japan, and India. —v. [~ + obj] **2.** to familiarize (oneself or another person) with new surroundings, circumstances, facts, etc.: lectures to orient the new students. **3.** to place (something) in a position that relates to the points of the compass: to orient a building north and south. —,**o•ri•en'ta•tion,** n. [noncount] [count]

O•ri•en•tal /,ɔriy'ɛntl/ adj. **1.** [sometimes: oriental] of, relating to, or characteristic of the Orient. —n. [count] **2.** Usually Offensive. a native or inhabitant of East Asia, or a person of East Asian descent.

o•ri•ent•ed /'ɔriyəntɪd, -ɛn-/ adj. interested in,

aimed at, or believing in: *a child-oriented business; businesses oriented toward children; socially oriented agencies.*

or•i•fice /'ɔrəfɪs, 'ɒr-/ *n.* [count] a mouthlike opening, as of a tube or pipe.

or•i•gin /'ɔrɪdʒɪn, 'ɒr-/ *n.* [count; usually singular] a source from which anything arises or derives; the beginning of something.

o•rig•i•nal /ə'rɪdʒənl/ *adj.* **1.** [before a noun] belonging or relating to the beginning of something; earliest: *the original owner of the house.* **2.** new; inventive: *an original idea.* **3.** thinking or acting in an independent and creative manner: *an original thinker.* **4.** [before a noun] created, undertaken, or presented for the first time: *the original performance of a play.* —*n.* [count] **5.** a primary form or type from which other, different types come. **6.** an original work, document, or the like, as opposed to a copy or imitation. —**o•rig•i•nal•i•ty** /ə,rɪdʒə'nælɪtiy/, *n.* [noncount]

o•rig•i•nal•ly /ə'rɪdʒənliy/ *adv.* at first; in the beginning: *My husband's family came originally from Italy. Originally the book was going to be much longer.*

o•rig•i•nate /ə'rɪdʒə,neyt/ *v.,* **-nat•ed, -nat•ing.** to (cause to) arise or begin: [no obj]: *Where did this idea originate?* [~ + obj]: *Who originated this scheme?* —**o•rig•i•na•tion** /ə,rɪdʒə'neyʃən/, *n.* [noncount] —**o'rig•i,na•tor,** *n.* [count]

o•ri•ole /'ɔriy,owl/ *n.* [count] a songbird, the male of which is black and orange.

or•na•ment /n.'ɔrnəmənt; v. -,mɛnt, -mənt/ *n.* **1.** [count] an object or feature that adds beauty to the appearance of something; decoration. **2.** [noncount] a group or style of such objects or features. —*v.* [~ + obj] **3.** to add ornaments to; decorate. —**or•na•men•tal** /,ɔrnə'mɛntl/, *adj.* —**or•na•men•ta•tion** /,ɔrnəmən'teyʃən, -mɛn-/, *n.* [noncount]

or•nate /ɔr'neyt/ *adj.* overly decorated; too showy. —**or'nate•ly,** *adv.*

or•ni•thol•o•gy /,ɔrnə'θɒlədʒiy/ *n.* [noncount] the study of birds. —**,or•ni'thol•o•gist,** *n.* [count]

or•phan /'ɔrfən/ *n.* [count] **1.** a child who has lost both parents through death. —*v.* [~ + obj] **2.** to cause to become an orphan.

or•phan•age /'ɔrfənɪdʒ/ *n.* [count] a place or institution for the housing and care of orphans.

or•tho•don•tia /,ɔrθə'dɒnʃə/ *n.* [noncount] **1.** ORTHODONTICS. **2.** treatment for the correction of crooked teeth.

or•tho•don•tics /,ɔrθə'dɒntɪks/ *n.* [noncount; used with a singular verb] the branch of dentistry dealing with the prevention and correction of crooked teeth. —**,or•tho'don•tist,** *n.* [count]

or•tho•dox /'ɔrθə,dɒks/ *adj.* **1.** agreeing with or following the officially accepted form of any belief, religion, philosophy, etc., esp. the older, more traditional form. **2.** customary or normal; generally accepted: *an orthodox viewpoint.* —'**or•tho,dox•y,** *n.* [count], *pl.* **-doxies** [noncount]

or•thog•ra•phy /ɔr'θɒgrəfiy/ *n., pl.* **-phies.** **1.** [noncount] correct spelling. **2.** [count] a method or system of spelling, as by the use of an alphabet. —**or•tho•graph•ic** /,ɔrθə'græfɪk/, *adj.*

or•tho•pe•dics /,ɔrθə'piydɪks/ *n.* [noncount; used with a singular verb] the branch of medicine dealing with the bones. —**,or•tho'pe•dic,** *adj.* —**,or•tho'pe•dist,** *n.* [count]

-ory¹, an adjective suffix meaning of, character-

ized by, or serving to (excretory; sensory; satisfactory).

-ory², a noun suffix meaning a place or instrument for (observatory).

os•cil•late /'ɒsə,leyt/ *v.* [no obj], **-lat•ed, -lat•ing.** **1.** to move to and fro, forward and back, or side to side: *The pendulum oscillated.* **2.** to vary, change, or switch between differing or opposite beliefs or feelings. —**,os•cil'la•tion,** *n.* [noncount] [count]

-ose¹, an adjective suffix meaning given to, abounding in, or like (verbose).

-ose², a noun suffix forming the name of sugars and other carbohydrates (glucose).

os•ten•si•ble /ɒ'stɛnsəbəl/ *adj.* [before a noun] outwardly appearing a certain way; pretended: *an ostensible reason.* —**os'ten•si•bly,** *adv.*

os•ten•ta•tious /,ɒstɛn'teyʃəs, -tən-/ *adj.* **1.** marked by a false or overly grand display of wealth: *ostentatious jewelry.* **2.** done in an exaggerated way that draws attention to oneself: *an ostentatious bow.* —**,os•ten'ta•tion,** *n.* [noncount] —**,os•ten'ta•tious•ly,** *adv.*

os•te•o•po•ro•sis /,ɒstiyowpə'rowsɪs/ *n.* [noncount] a disorder in which the bones break easily because of loss of calcium and other minerals.

os•tra•cize /'ɒstrə,sayz/ *v.* [~ + obj], **-cized, -ciz•ing.** to exclude (someone) from society, privileges, membership, etc. —'**os•tra•cism,** *n.* [noncount]

os•trich /'ɔstrɪtʃ, 'ɒstrɪtʃ/ *n.* [count] a two-toed, swift-footed bird that cannot fly.

oth•er /'ʌðər/ *adj.* [before a noun] **1.** additional: *I made one other purchase.* **2.** different from the one mentioned: *Some other player might be better at the game.* **3.** being the remaining ones of a number: *Some other countries may join the boycott.* **4.** [the + ~] not long past: *I saw her the other night.* —*n.* [count] **5.** the other one: *Each praises the other.* —*pron.* **6.** Usually, **others.** [plural] other persons or things: *Others in the medical profession may not like this.* —*adv.* **7.** other than, otherwise; differently: *We can't collect the rent other than by suing the tenant.* —*Idiom.* **8. every other,** the first or the second of two: *We have a meeting every other week.*

oth•er•wise /'ʌðər,wayz/ *adv.* **1.** under other circumstances: *With this chip the computer runs faster than it would otherwise.* **2.** in another manner or way; differently: *Could he do otherwise than smile?* **3.** in every other way: *an otherwise happy and uneventful life.*

ot•ter /'ɒtər/ *n.* [count], *pl.* **-ters,** (esp. when thought of as a group) **-ter.** a furry, water-dwelling mammal.

ouch /awtʃ/ *interj.* (used to express sudden pain or dismay): *Ouch, that needle hurt!*

ought /ɔt/ *auxiliary (modal) verb.* [~ + to + root form of a verb] **1.** (used to express duty or moral obligation): *Every citizen ought to help.* **2.** (used to express justice or moral rightness): *He ought to be punished.* **3.** (used to express correctness or appropriateness for the situation): *We ought to bring her flowers.* **4.** (used to express that an action is probable or expected): *That ought to be our train now.*

ounce /awns/ *n.* [count] **1.** a unit of weight equal to ¹/₁₆ of a pound. **2.** FLUID OUNCE.

our /aw³r, 'awər; unstressed ɑr/ *pron.* [before a noun] a form of the pronoun WE used to show possession: *Our team won.* Compare OURS.

-our, Chiefly Brit. a variant form of the suffix -OR (colour).

ours /aw^ərz, 'awərz *or, often,* ɑrz/ *pron.* **1.** [*be* + ~] a form of the pronoun WE used to show possession: *Which house is ours?* **2.** that or those belonging to us: *Ours are the pink ones. She's a cousin of ours.*

our•selves /ɑr'sɛlvz, aw^ər-, ˌawər-/ *pron. pl.* **1.** a form of the pronoun WE, a reflexive pronoun used as the direct or indirect object of a verb or the direct object of a preposition when the subject is WE: *We may be deceiving ourselves. We don't have enough money for ourselves.* **2.** (used to add emphasis to the pronouns WE and US): *We ourselves would never say such a thing.* **3.** (used in place of WE or US in certain phrases with "and" and "than"): *The children and ourselves want to thank you. No one is more fortunate than ourselves.*

-ous, a suffix meaning full of, characterized by, or having (*glorious*).

oust /awst/ *v.* [~ + *obj*] to remove or force (someone) from a place or position.

oust•er /'awstər/ *n.* [*count*] the removal or forcing of someone from a place or position: *an ouster from political office.*

out /awt/ *adv.* **1.** not in the usual place, position, etc.: *Those books are out of alphabetical order.* **2.** away from one's home, work, etc., as specified: *to go out of town.* **3.** in or into the outdoors: *to go out for a walk; Take the dog out.* **4.** to a state in which everything is totally used up: *to pump a well out.* **5.** to a point or state of dying out or fading away: *That practice is on the way out.* **6.** not burning or lit: *The lights went out. Put that cigarette out.* **7.** so as not to be in the normal position: *Her back went out when she fell.* **8.** in or into public notice or knowledge: *Her story has come out at last.* **9.** from a certain source or material: *made out of scraps.* **10.** aloud or loudly: *to cry out.* —*adj.* **11.** [*be* + ~] not at one's home or place of work: *will be out all week.* **12.** [*be* + ~] lacking; without: *We had some tickets but now we're out.* **13.** [*be* + ~ + *of*] no longer holding a job: *to be out of work.* **14.** [*be* + ~] unconscious: *A few drinks and he's out.* **15.** *Baseball.* [*be* + ~] (of a batter) not succeeding in getting on base: *Two men are out.* **16.** [*be* + ~] outside of official limits, as in a game on a marked court. —*prep.* **17.** (used to indicate movement or direction from the inside to the outside of something): *She ran out the door.* **18.** (used to indicate location): *The car is out back.* —*interj.* **19.** Go away!: *Out! And don't come back!* —*n.* [*count*] **20.** *Baseball.* an instance of putting out a batter or base runner. —*v.* [*no obj*] **21.** to come out; become public: *The truth will out.* —*Idiom.* **22. all out,** with the highest or greatest effort: *They went all out to finish by Friday.* **23. out for,** strongly or eagerly determined to get, achieve, etc.: *He was out for money.* **24. out of, a.** not within: *They ran out of the house.* **b.** beyond the reach of: *out of sight.* **c.** not in a condition of: *out of danger.* **d.** without; lacking: *We're out of milk.* **e.** from within or among: *Take the jokers out of the pack of cards.* **f.** because of: *They did that out of spite.* **25. out of it,** *Informal.* **a.** not participating: *I'm out of it these days; tell me what's going on.* **b.** not conscious. **c.** confused: *too out of it to remember his own name.* **26. out of place, a.** not in the correct position or order. **b.** not suitable to the circumstances or surroundings.

out-, a prefix meaning: outward or outside (*outburst*); at a distance from (*outpost*); to surpass (*outlast; outdo*).

out•age /'awtɪdʒ/ *n.* [*count*] an interruption or failure in the supply of power, esp. electricity.

'out-and-'out, *adj.* [*before a noun*] complete; absolute: *an out-and-out lie.*

out•board /'awt,bɔrd/ *adj.* located on the outside of a boat or aircraft: *an outboard motor.*

out•bound /'awt'bawnd/ *adj.* headed, sailing, or going outward.

out•break /'awt,breyk/ *n.* [*count*] a sudden occurrence or appearance; eruption: *the outbreak of disease.*

out•build•ing /'awt,bɪldɪŋ/ *n.* [*count*] a building apart from a main building.

out•burst /'awt,bɜrst/ *n.* [*count*] a sudden and often violent release, outpouring, or eruption: *an outburst of tears.*

out•cast /'awt,kæst/ *n.* [*count*] a person who is rejected or cast out, as from home or society.

out•come /'awt,kʌm/ *n.* [*count*] a final product or result: *What was the outcome of your interview?*

out•cry /'awt,kray/ *n.* [*count*], *pl.* **-cries. 1.** a strong and usually public expression of protest or anger. **2.** a loud cry.

out•dat•ed /ˌawt'deytɪd/ *adj.* out-of-date; not modern; outmoded.

out•dis•tance /ˌawt'dɪstəns/ *v.* [~ + *obj*], **-tanced, -tanc•ing.** to go far ahead of, as in running.

out•do /ˌawt'duw/ *v.* [~ + *obj*], **-did, -done, -do•ing.** to perform better than; do better than.

out•door /'awt,dɔr/ *adj.* [*before a noun*] located, occurring, or belonging outdoors: *outdoor activities.*

out•doors /ˌawt'dɔrz/ *adv.* **1.** outside; in the open air: *They stood outdoors in the rain.* —*n.* [*noncount; used with a singular verb; usually: the* + ~] **2.** the world outside of or away from houses; open air: *to live in the outdoors.*

out•er /'awtər/ *adj.* [*before a noun*] **1.** located on or toward the outside; exterior: *an outer wall.* **2.** located farther out or farther from the center: *the outer planets of the solar system.*

out•er•most /'awtər,mowst/ *adj.* [*before a noun*] farthest out; farthest from the inside or center: *the outermost limits of the galaxy.*

'outer 'space, *n.* [*noncount*] **1.** space beyond the atmosphere of the earth. **2.** space beyond the solar system.

out•fit /'awt,fɪt/ *n., v.,* **-fit•ted, -fit•ting.** —*n.* [*count*] **1.** clothes and equipment used for a particular task or role: *a cowboy's outfit.* **2.** a business organization or military unit. —*v.* [~ + *obj*] **3.** to furnish; supply: *They outfitted him with a gun.*

out•go•ing /'awt,gowɪŋ/ *adj.* **1.** going out; departing: *outgoing trains.* **2.** [*before a noun*] leaving or retiring from a position or office: *the outgoing mayor.* **3.** friendly; sociable.

out•grow /ˌawt'grow/ *v.* [~ + *obj*], **-grew, -grown, -grow•ing. 1.** to grow too large for: *had outgrown last year's boots.* **2.** to grow too old for; grow out of: *to outgrow a fear of the dark.*

out•growth /'awt,growθ/ *n.* [*count*] a natural development or result: *Success was an outgrowth of their hard work.*

out•house /'awt,haws/ *n.* [*count*], *pl.* **-hous•es. 1.** an outbuilding serving as a toilet. **2.** OUTBUILDING.

out•ing /'awtɪŋ/ *n.* [*count*] a pleasure trip, picnic, etc.

O

out·land·ish /awt'lændɪʃ/ *adj.* strange or odd, esp. in a way that is displeasing.

out·last /ˌawt'læst/ *v.* [~ + *obj*] to endure or last longer than.

out·law /'awt,lɔ/ *n.* [*count*] **1.** a criminal, esp. one who is running away and hiding to avoid being captured. —*v.* [~ + *obj*] **2.** to prohibit: *to outlaw smoking.*

out·let /'awtlet, -lɪt/ *n.* [*count*] **1.** an opening or passage by which anything is let out; vent; exit. **2.** a point on a wiring system at which current may be taken to supply electric devices: *Plug the lamp into the outlet.*

out·line /'awt,layn/ *n.*, *v.*, **-lined, -lin·ing.** —*n.* [*count*] **1.** a line that shows the shape or edge of a figure or object: *We could see an outline of the shore in the distance.* **2.** a description or report indicating the main features of a subject: *an outline of a book.* —*v.* [~ + *obj*] **3.** to draw the outline of (something), or draw (something) in outline. **4.** to indicate the main features of: *outlined his strategy.*

out·live /ˌawt'lɪv/ *v.* [~ + *obj*], **-lived, -liv·ing. 1.** to live longer than; survive: *She outlived all her friends.* **2.** to outlast; live through: *He outlived the war.*

out·look /'awt,lʊk/ *n.* **1.** mental attitude or view; point of view: [*count*]: *a gloomy outlook.* [*noncount*]: *optimistic in outlook.* **2.** [*count*] prospect for the future: *The political outlook is grim.*

out·ly·ing /'awt,layɪŋ/ *adj.* [*before a noun*] lying or located at a distance from the center or the main area: *the outlying districts of the town.*

out·mod·ed /ˌawt'mowdɪd/ *adj.* **1.** no longer fashionable. **2.** no longer acceptable or usable: *outmoded teaching methods.*

out·num·ber /ˌawt'nʌmbər/ *v.* [~ + *obj*] to be greater than in number.

'out-of-date' *adj.* outmoded; obsolete: *out-of-date technology.*

out·pa·tient /'awt,peyʃənt/ *n.* [*count*] a person who receives treatment at a hospital but does not stay there overnight.

out·post /'awt,powst/ *n.* [*count*] a post or settlement in a foreign place or in foreign surroundings.

out·put /'awt,pʊt/ *n.*, *v.*, **-put·ted** or **-put, -put·ting.** —*n.* **1.** the quantity or amount of something produced, esp. in a specified period: [*count; usually singular*]: *an output of over 500 computers a day.* [*noncount*]: *Output has increased.* **2.** [*noncount*] the material produced; product; yield. **3.** [*noncount*] [*count; usually singular*] information made available by computer, as on a printout, display screen, or disk. —*v.* [~ + *obj*] **4.** to transfer (computer output): *Output the data to the printer.* **5.** to produce; yield.

out·rage /'awtreydʒ/ *n.*, *v.*, **-raged, -rag·ing.** —*n.* **1.** [*count*] an act of great cruelty or violence that strongly offends the feelings. **2.** [*count*] any act that strongly offends the feelings: *It's an outrage that she was fired.* **3.** [*noncount*] a strong feeling of resentment or anger aroused by an injury, insult, or injustice. —*v.* [~ + *obj*] **4.** to anger or offend; shock. —**out'ra·geous,** *adj.*

out·rank /ˌawt'ræŋk/ *v.* [~ + *obj*] to have a higher rank than.

out·right [*adj.*'awt,rayt; *adv.* 'awt'rayt, -,rayt/ *adj.* [*before a noun*] **1.** complete; total: *an outright victory.* **2.** not hiding or holding something back: *an outright denial.* —*adv.* **3.** completely; entirely: *We own the house outright.* **4.** without holding anything back: *Ask her outright for a* raise. **5.** at once; instantly: *Three were killed outright.*

out·run /ˌawt'rʌn/ *v.* [~ + *obj*], **-ran, -run, -run·ning. 1.** to run faster or farther than. **2.** to grow faster than; exceed: *Production is outrunning sales.*

out·set /'awt,set/ *n.* [*count; usually singular; usually: the* + ~] beginning; start: *at the outset of the war.*

out·shine /ˌawt'ʃayn/ *v.* [~ + *obj*], **-shone** or **-shined, -shin·ing. 1.** to shine more brightly than. **2.** to go beyond (another) in excellence, achievement, etc.

out·side /*n.*'awt'sayd, -,sayd; *adj.* ˌawt'sayd, 'awt-; *adv.* ˌawt'sayd; *prep.* ˌawt'sayd, 'awt,sayd/ *n.* [*count*] **1.** the outer side, surface, or part; exterior: *painted the outside of the house.* **2.** the space beyond a boundary or enclosure: *The prisoner had no idea of life on the outside.* —*adj.* [*before a noun*] **3.** of, situated in, or coming from the outside: *news from the outside world; the outside walls.* **4.** situated away from the inside or center: *the outside lane on a highway.* **5.** not belonging to a specified group: *outside influences.* —*adv.* **6.** on or to the outside: *Take the dog outside.* —*prep.* **7.** on the outside of: *a noise outside the door.* **8.** beyond the limits or borders of: *visitors from outside the country.* **9.** aside from: *She has no interests outside her work.*

out·sid·er /ˌawt'saydər/ *n.* [*count*] a person who is not part of a particular group.

out·smart /ˌawt'smɑrt/ *v.* [~ + *obj*] to defeat or gain an advantage over (someone) by being more clever.

out·spo·ken /'awt'spowkən/ *adj.* **1.** said or expressed with honesty and openness. **2.** unafraid to say what one believes. —'out'spo·ken·ness, *n.* [*noncount*]

out·stand·ing /ˌawt'stændɪŋ/ *adj.* **1.** superior; excellent; distinguished. **2.** not taken care of or solved: *outstanding debts; Several questions are still outstanding.* —**out'stand·ing·ly,** *adv.*: *an outstandingly fine restaurant.*

out·strip /ˌawt'strɪp/ *v.* [~ + *obj*], **-stripped, -strip·ping.** to outdo; surpass: *He has outstripped his competition.*

out·ward /'awtwərd/ *adj.* [*before a noun*] **1.** moving or directed toward the outside or away from a center: *the outward flow of water.* **2.** relating to apparent or visible qualities only; superficial: *an outward show of grief.* —*adv.* Also, 'out·wards. **3.** toward the outside; out: *The door opened outward.* —'out'ward·ly, *adv.*

out·weigh /ˌawt'wey/ *v.* [~ + *obj*] to be greater than in value or importance: *Safety outweighed all other considerations.*

out·wit /ˌawt'wɪt/ *v.* [~ + *obj*], **-wit·ted, -wit·ting.** to outsmart.

out·worn /'awt'wɔrn/ *adj.* out-of-date; no longer modern or useful: *outworn theories.*

o·val /'owvəl/ *adj.* **1.** having the general form or outline of an egg; egg-shaped. —*n.* [*count*] **2.** something oval in shape or outline.

o·va·ry /'owvəriy/ *n.* [*count*], *pl.* **-ries.** a female reproductive organ in which the eggs develop. —o·var·i·an /ow'veəriyən/, *adj.*

o·va·tion /ow'veyʃən/ *n.* [*count*] long, loud applause or other expression of great approval.

ov·en /'ʌvən/ *n.* [*count*] a small box-shaped area with a door, usually part of a stove, for baking, roasting, or heating.

o·ver /'owvər/ *prep.* **1.** above in place or position: *the roof over one's head.* **2.** above and to the other side of: *The car went over the guard rail.* **3.** above in authority, rank, etc.: *They have control over the news media.* **4.** so as to rest on or cover: *She pulled the blankets over her head.* **5.** across; throughout: *They traveled all over Europe.* **6.** on or to the other side of; across: *to go over the bridge.* **7.** more than: *read over twenty books.* **8.** in preference to: *He was chosen over another applicant.* **9.** throughout the length of; during: *We wrote to each other over a long period of years.* **10.** concerning or about: *to quarrel over a matter.* **11.** via; by means of: *I heard it over the radio.* —*adv.* **12.** beyond the top or rim of something: *The soup boiled over.* **13.** so as to cover or affect the whole surface: *The furniture was covered over with dust.* **14.** through a region or area: *He is known the world over.* **15.** from one side or place to another: *Toss the ball over, will you?* **16.** from one person to another: *He handed the property over to his brother.* **17.** from a standing or straight position: *to knock over a glass; to fall over.* **18.** a reversed position: *The dog rolled over.* **19.** once more; again: *Do the work over.* **20.** in addition: *to pay the full sum and something over.* —*adj.* [*be* + ~] **21.** ended; past: *They became friends when the war was over.* —*Idiom.* **22.** all over, **a.** throughout; everywhere: *They traveled all over when they visited Australia.* **b.** ended; finished: *The season was all over when they lost that game.* **23. over and above,** in addition to: *These expenses are over and above our estimates.* **24. over and over,** many times: *We thanked him over and over.* **25. over the hill,** past one's prime: *That actor is over the hill.*

over-, a prefix meaning: too or too much (*overact*); over or above (*overflow*); higher in authority or rank (*overlord*).

o•ver•a•chieve /ˌowvərə'tʃiyv/ *v.* [*no obj*], **-chieved, -chiev•ing.** to perform better or achieve more than is usual or expected. —**o•ver•a'chiev•er,** *n.* [*count*]

o•ver•act /ˌowvər'ækt/ *v.* [~ + *obj*] [*no obj*] to perform (a role) in an exaggerated manner.

o•ver•all /*adv.*'owvər'ɔl; *adj., n.* 'owvər,ɔl/ *adj., adv.* **1.** from one end or limit to the other: *The overall length is 15 feet.* —*n.* **2. overalls,** [*plural*] loose, sturdy trousers, usually having a bib with attached shoulder straps.

o•ver•bear•ing /ˌowvər'bɛərɪŋ/ *adj.* very rude in the way one gives orders or demands.

o•ver•blown /'owvər'blown/ *adj.* overdone or excessive: *overblown praise.*

o•ver•board /'owvər,bɔrd/ *adv.* **1.** over the side of a ship or boat: *His canoe rocked suddenly and he fell overboard.* —*Idiom.* **2. go overboard,** to be excessive: *Don't go overboard with the decorations.*

o•ver•cast /'owvər'kæst, -,kæst / *adj.* cloudy.

o•ver•charge /ˌowvər'tʃɑrdʒ/ *v.* [~ + *obj*] [*no obj*], **-charged, -charg•ing.** to charge (a purchaser) too high a price.

o•ver•coat /'owvər,kowt/ *n.* [*count*] a coat worn over one's ordinary indoor clothing, as in cold weather.

o•ver•come /ˌowvər'kʌm/ *v.,* **-came, -come, -com•ing.** **1.** [~ + *obj*] [*no obj*] to defeat or gain an advantage over (someone or something) in a struggle or conflict; conquer. **2.** [~ + *obj*] to succeed in controlling: *to overcome a fear.* **3.** [~ + *obj*] to overpower or overwhelm in body or mind: *The firefighters were overcome by smoke.*

o•ver•crowd /ˌowvər'krawd/ *v.* [~ + *obj*] to crowd or fill too much.

o•ver•do /ˌowvər'duw/ *v.* [~ + *obj*], **-did, -done, -do•ing.** **1.** to do too much: *to overdo dieting.* **2.** to exaggerate: *The scene was funny but a bit overdone.*

o•ver•dose /*n.*'owvər,dows, *v.* 'owvərdows, ˌowvər'dows/ *n., v.,* **-dosed, -dos•ing.** —*n.* [*count*] **1.** a dose of a drug that is too great. —*v.* [*no obj*] **2.** to take or die from a drug overdose: *He overdosed on cocaine.*

o•ver•draw /ˌowvər'drɔ/ *v.* [*no obj*] [~ + *obj*], **-drew, -drawn, -draw•ing.** to spend an amount from one's bank account that is greater than the money available.

o•ver•dress /ˌowvər'drɛs/ *v.* [*no obj*] [~ + *obj*] **1.** to dress too formally for the occasion. **2.** to dress with too much clothing.

o•ver•due /ˌowvər'duw, -'dyuw/ *adj.* having passed the time when due or expected: *overdue library books.*

o•ver•es•ti•mate /ˌowvər'ɛstə,meyt/ *v.* [~ + *obj*], **-mated, -mat•ing.** to estimate at too high an amount, value, etc.: *overestimated the cost; to overestimate an employee's ability.*

o•ver•flow /*v.*ˌowvər'flow; *n.* 'owvər,flow/ *v.* **1.** [*no obj*] [~ + *obj*] to flow or run over, such as water. **2.** to pass from one part to another as if flowing from a place that is too full: [*no obj*]: *The crowd overflowed into the street.* [~ + *obj*]: *The crowd overflowed the auditorium.* **3.** [*no obj*] to be supplied with something in great amount: *His heart was overflowing with gratitude.* —*n.* [*count*] **4.** something that overflows. **5.** too great an amount or quantity: *an overflow of applicants for the job.*

o•ver•grown /ˌowvər'grown, 'owvər,grown/ *adj.* **1.** covered with a growth of something: *overgrown with moss.* **2.** having grown too much: *overgrown weeds.*

o•ver•hand /'owvər,hænd/ *adj.* **1.** thrown or performed with the arm raised over the shoulder: *an overhand serve in tennis.* —*adv.* **2.** with the hand raised above the shoulder: *to pitch overhand.*

o•ver•hang /*v.*ˌowvər'hæŋ; *n.* 'owvər,hæŋ/ *v.,* **-hung, -hang•ing,** *n.* —*v.* **1.** to hang over (something); stick out over (something below): [*no obj*]: *pools of water where trees overhang.* [~ + *obj*]: *The tree branches overhang the water.* —*n.* [*count*] **2.** something that overhangs.

o•ver•haul /*v.*ˌowvər'hɔl, 'owvər,hɔl/ *n.* 'owvər,hɔl/ *v.* [~ + *obj*] **1.** to make necessary repairs on: *to overhaul an engine.* **2.** to examine completely and revise: *to overhaul a school curriculum.* —*n.* **3.** a complete examination and repair: [*noncount*]: *The engines were in need of overhaul.* [*count*]: *a simple overhaul of procedures.*

o•ver•head /*adv.*'owvər'hɛd; *adj., n.* 'owvər,hɛd/ *adv.* **1.** up in the air or sky, esp. high in the sky: *The planes circled overhead.* —*adj.* **2.** located, operating, or passing above or over the head. —*n.* [*noncount*] **3.** the general, steady costs of running a business, as rent and heating expenses.

o•ver•hear /ˌowvər'hɪər/ *v.* [~ + *obj*] [*no obj*], **-heard, -hear•ing.** to hear (speech or a speaker) without the speaker's intention or knowledge.

o•ver•heat /ˌowvər'hiyt/ *v.* [~ + *obj*] [*no obj*] to (cause to) become too hot or be heated too much.

o•ver•joy /ˌowvər'dʒɔy/ *v.* [~ + *obj*] to cause to feel great joy or delight.

o•ver•lap /*v.*ˌowvər'læp; *n.* 'owvər,læp/ *v.,* **-lapped, -lap•ping,** *n.* —*v.* **1.** [~ + *obj*] [*no*

O

obj] to stretch over and cover a part of (something else). **2.** to have some part in common: [~ + *obj*]: *My work schedule overlapped his.* [*no obj*]: *Our schedules overlapped.* —*n.* **3.** [*noncount*] an act or instance of overlapping: *an overlap between two theories.* **4.** [*count*] an overlapping part.

o•ver•load /,owvər'lowd / *v.* **1.** [~ + *obj*] to load too much: *The bus was overloaded.* **2.** to (cause to) use too much electricity: [*no obj*]: *The circuits overloaded.* [~ + *obj*]: *You overloaded the circuits.*

o•ver•look /*v.*,owvər'lʊk; *n.* 'owvər,lʊk/ *v.* [~ + *obj*] **1.** to fail to notice or think about: *overlooked several facts.* **2.** to disregard in a kind way; excuse: *I'll overlook your mistake this time.* **3.** to look over, as from a higher position: *a room that overlooks the ocean.* —*n.* [*count*] **4.** a piece of land that provides a good view below.

o•ver•ly /'owvərliy/ *adv.* excessively; very: *overly curious.*

o•ver•night /*adv.*'owvər'nayt; *adj., n.* 'owvər,nayt/ *adv.* **1.** for or during the night: *We'll stay overnight.* **2.** very quickly: *New suburbs sprang up overnight.* —*adj.* [*before a noun*] **3.** done or continuing during the night: *an overnight flight.* —*n.* [*count*] **4.** an overnight stay or trip.

o•ver•pass / 'owvər,pæs / *n.* [*count*] a road or bridge that provides a means of travel above another route.

o•ver•pop•u•late /,owvər'pɒpyə,leyt/ *v.* [~ + *obj*], **-lat•ed, -lat•ing.** to fill with too many people or inhabitants and thus cause a strain on resources. —**o•ver•pop•u•la•tion** /'owvər,pɒpyə'leyʃən/, *n.* [*noncount*]

o•ver•pow•er /,owvər'pawər/ *v.* [~ + *obj*] to overcome (someone or something) by superior force: *She overpowered her attacker.* —,**o•ver'pow•er•ing,** *adj.*: *an overpowering smell.*

o•ver•price /,owvər'prays/ *v.* [~ + *obj*], **-priced, -pric•ing.** to put too high a price on: *That dress is overpriced.*

o•ver•qual•i•fied /'owvər'kwɒlə,fayd/ *adj.* having more education, training, or experience than is required for a job.

o•ver•rate /,owvər'reyt/ *v.* [~ + *obj*], **-rat•ed, -rat•ing.** to rate or classify too highly or favorably.

o•ver•re•act /,owvərriy'ækt/ *v.* [*no obj*] to react or respond to something more strongly than is necessary.

o•ver•ride /,owvər'rayd/ *v.* [~ + *obj*], **-rode, -rid•den, -rid•ing.** **1.** to give a command that cancels the effect of something: *She overrode our objections and went ahead with the plan.* **2.** to be more important than (something): *The need for food and shelter overrides most other concerns.*

o•ver•rid•ing /,owvər'raydɪŋ/ *adj.* [*before a noun*] most important; principal: *The overriding concern is the safety of the children.*

o•ver•rule /,owvər'ruwl/ *v.* [~ + *obj*], **-ruled, -rul•ing.** to rule against (a person, argument, etc.) by using higher authority: *The judge overruled the lawyer.*

o•ver•run /,owvər'rʌn / *v.* [~ + *obj*], **-ran, -run, -run•ning.** **1.** to spread over (an area) quickly and in great numbers: *Weeds are overrunning the garden.* **2.** to go beyond: *to overrun the budget.* **3.** to overflow: *The stream overran its banks.*

o•ver•seas /*adv.*,owvər'siyz; *adj.* 'owvər'siyz/ *adv.* **1.** over, across, or beyond the sea; abroad: *lived overseas.* —*adj.* **2.** across or over the sea: *overseas shipments.* **3.** of, from, or located in places across the sea; foreign: *overseas competition.*

o•ver•see /,owvər'siy/ *v.* [~ + *obj*], **-saw, -seen, -see•ing.** to supervise; manage: *He oversaw the project.* —'**o•ver,se•er,** *n.* [*count*]

o•ver•shad•ow /,owvər'ʃædow/ *v.* [~ + *obj*] **1.** to be greater than in importance or interest: *She was overshadowed by her famous sister.* **2.** to cast a shadow over.

o•ver•shoot /,owvər'ʃuwt/ *v.* [~ + *obj*], **-shot, -shoot•ing.** to pass or go by or beyond (a landing or stopping place) unintentionally: *The plane overshot the runway.*

o•ver•sight /'owvər,sayt/ *n.* **1.** [*noncount*] failure to notice or consider something: *guilty of oversight.* **2.** [*count*] a careless mistake. **3.** [*noncount*] the act of watching over; supervision.

o•ver•sim•pli•fy /,owvər'sɪmplə,fay/ *v.* [~ + *obj*] [*no obj*], **-fied, -fy•ing.** to make (something) seem simpler than it really is and therefore represent it incorrectly.

o•ver•sleep /,owvər'sliyp/ *v.* [*no obj*], **-slept, -sleep•ing.** to sleep beyond the proper or intended time of waking up.

o•ver•state /,owvər'steyt/ *v.* [~ + *obj*], **-stat•ed, -stat•ing.** to state too strongly; exaggerate.

o•ver•step /,owvər'stɛp/ *v.* [~ + *obj*], **-stepped, -step•ping.** to go beyond: *The officer overstepped his authority.*

o•vert /ow'vɜrt, 'owvɜrt/ *adj.* open to view or knowledge; not hidden or secret. —**o'vert•ly,** *adv.*

o•ver•take /,owvər'teyk/ *v.* [~ + *obj*], **-took, -tak•en, -tak•ing.** **1.** to catch up with and pass: *We overtook that slow truck.* **2.** to happen to (someone) suddenly: *Bad luck overtook them.*

'**over-the-'counter,** *adj.* sold legally without a prescription: *over-the-counter drugs.*

o•ver•throw /*v.*,owvər'θrow; *n.* 'owvər,θrow/ *v.*, **-threw, -thrown, -throw•ing,** *n.* —*v.* [~ + *obj*] **1.** to remove (a dictator, king, etc.) from a position of power. **2.** to put an end to by force: *to overthrow tyranny.* —*n.* [*count*] **3.** an act or instance of overthrowing or of being overthrown.

o•ver•time /'owvər,taym/ *n.* [*noncount*] **1.** time spent working that is before or after one's regularly scheduled working hours. **2.** pay for such time: *got overtime for working on the weekend.* —*adv.* **3.** during overtime. —*adj.* [*before a noun*] **4.** of or for overtime: *overtime pay.*

o•ver•tone /'owvər,town/ *n.* [*count*] a meaning or quality, as in speech or behavior, that is not expressed but is understood or felt by others.

o•ver•ture /'owvərtʃər, -,tʃʊr/ *n.* [*count*] **1.** Often, **overtures.** [*plural*] a first move in a negotiation or relationship. **2.** a piece of music that introduces an opera or other musical work.

o•ver•turn / ,owvər't3rn / *v.* **1.** [*no obj*] [~ + *obj*] to (cause to) turn over on the side, face, or back. **2.** [~ + *obj*] to destroy the power of; overthrow.

o•ver•view /'owvər,vyuw/ *n.* [*count*] a general outline of a subject or situation; summary.

o•ver•weight / 'owvər'weyt / *adj.* weighing too much.

o•ver•whelm /,owvər'hwɛlm, -'wɛlm/ *v.* [~ + *obj*] **1.** to overpower or overcome: *overwhelmed the enemy.* **2.** to burden: *He was overwhelmed with family problems.*

o•ver•whelm•ing /,owvər'hwɛlmɪŋ, -'wɛl-

adj. very large, as in amount or size; very great: *an overwhelming victory.* —**o•ver'whelm•ing•ly,** *adv.*

o•ver•work /*v.*ˌowvər'wɜrk, *n.* 'owvərˌwɜrk/ *v.* [~ + *obj*] [*no obj*] **1.** to (cause to) work too hard, too much, or too long. —*n.* [*noncount*] **2.** a condition of overworking.

o•ver•wrought /'owvər'rɔt, ˌowvər-/ *adj.* extremely excited, nervous, or upset.

ov•u•late /'ɒvyəˌleyt, 'owvyə-/ *v.* [*no obj*], **-lat•ed, -lat•ing.** to produce and discharge eggs from an ovary. —**ov•u•la•tion** /ˌɒvyə'leyʃən, ˌowvyə-/, *n.* [*noncount*]

ow /aw/ *interj.* (used esp. to express sharp or sudden pain): *Ow! I stepped on a nail.*

owe /ow/ *v.,* **owed, ow•ing. 1.** to be obligated to pay, repay, or give (something): [~ + *obj*]: *They still owe a hundred thousand dollars on their house. I owe him a dollar.* [*no obj*]: *Do you still owe on that boat?* **2.** [~ + *obj*] to be grateful to someone or something for making (something) possible: *owed his success to his wife.*

ow•ing /'owɪŋ/ *adj.* [*be* + ~] **1.** owed, unpaid, or due for payment: *to pay what is owing.* —*Idiom.* **2. owing to,** because of; as a result of: *delayed owing to the bad weather.*

owl /awl/ *n.* [*count*] a bird that hunts small animals for food and is mainly active at night.

own /own/ *adj.* **1.** of or belonging to oneself or itself: *He spent only his own money.* **2.** (used after a possessive pronoun when the subject is the only performer of an action): *She insists on being her own doctor.* —*pron.* **3.** something that belongs to oneself: *He thought the office computer was his own.* —*v.* **4.** [~ + *obj*] to have or hold as one's own; possess: *She owns several cars.* **5.** to acknowledge or admit; confess: [~ + *obj*]: *He owned that he might have been at fault.* [*no obj*]: *He owned (up) to stealing the car.* —*Idiom.* **6. of one's own,** belonging to oneself: *They wanted a home of their own.* **7. on one's own, a.** through one's own efforts: *did the job on her own.* **b.** living independently: *was on her own at the age of 17.* —**'own•er,** *n.* [*count*] —**'own•er,ship,** *n.* [*noncount*]

ox /ɒks/ *n.* [*count*], *pl.* **ox•en.** a large animal belonging to the same family as domestic cows, esp. an adult male with its sex organs removed, used as a work animal.

ox•ide /'ɒksayd, -sɪd/ *n.* [*count*] a chemical compound in which oxygen is bonded to one or more atoms.

ox•y•gen /'ɒksɪdʒən/ *n.* [*noncount*] a colorless, odorless gas, an element that is about one-fifth of the volume of the atmosphere and is present in a combined state in nature.

ox•y•gen•ate /'ɒksɪdʒəˌneyt/ *v.* [~ + *obj*], **-at•ed, -at•ing.** to treat, combine, or enrich with oxygen: *to oxygenate blood.*

oys•ter /'ɔystər/ *n.* [*count*] a sea animal that may be eaten, having two shells that enclose it.

oz., an abbreviation of Italian *onza:* ounce.

o•zone /'owzown, ow'zown/ *n.* [*noncount*] **1.** a form of oxygen, O₃, produced when ultraviolet light passes through air or oxygen. **2.** OZONE LAYER.

'ozone ,layer, *n.* [*count; usually: the* + ~] the layer of the upper atmosphere where most of the ozone is concentrated.

O

P

P, p /piy/ *n.* [*count*], *pl.* **Ps** or **P's, ps** or **p's.** the 16th letter of the English alphabet, a consonant.
p., an abbreviation of: **1.** page. **2.** penny; pence.
PA, an abbreviation of: **1.** Pennsylvania. **2.** public-address system.
Pa., an abbreviation of: Pennsylvania.
pace /peys/ *n., v.,* **paced, pac•ing.** —*n.* **1.** [*count; usually singular*] a rate of movement, esp. in walking or running: *a rapid pace.* **2.** [*count*] a single step. **3.** [*count*] the distance covered in a step: *standing only a few paces apart.* —*v.* **4.** to cross with regular or slow steps: [~ + *obj*]: *We paced the floor nervously.* [*no obj*]: *We paced up and down the hall.* —*Idiom.* **5. keep pace,** to do or work at the same rate (as): *Newspapers could hardly keep pace with developments during the war.* **6. set the pace,** to act as an example for others to equal: *We want our company to set the pace for sales in the whole region.*
pac•i•fi•er /'pæsəˌfayər/ *n.* [*count*] a device, often shaped like a nipple, for a baby to suck on.
pac•i•fism /'pæsəˌfɪzəm/ *n.* [*noncount*] the belief that war or violence should never be used to settle disputes. —'**pac•i•fist,** *n.* [*count*]
pac•i•fy /'pæsəˌfay/ *v.* [~ + *obj*], **-fied, -fy•ing.** to bring or restore to a state of peace or calmness.
pack /pæk/ *n.* [*count*] **1.** a number of things wrapped together for easy handling. **2.** a definite amount of something sold, along with its package: *a pack of cigarettes.* **3.** a group of things: *a pack of lies.* **4.** a group of wild animals: *a pack of wolves.* **5.** a set of playing cards; a deck. —*v.* **6.** [~ + *obj*] to make into a pack. **7.** [*no obj*] to be easily made into a pack or any small, tight mass: *Wet snow packs easily.* **8.** [~ + *obj*] to fill (something) with suitable objects: *to pack a trunk with clothes.* **9.** [~ + *obj*] [*no obj*] to put (clothes, etc.) into a case, etc., as for traveling or storage. **10.** to crowd into; cram: [~ + *obj*]: *The crowd packed the gallery.* [*no obj*]: *Thousands packed into the stadium.* **11. pack off** or **away,** to send away, often with speed or eagerness: *to pack the kids off to camp* or *to pack off the kids to camp.*
pack•age /'pækɪdʒ/ *n., v.,* **-aged, -ag•ing,** *adj.* —*n.* [*count*] **1.** a bundle packed and wrapped or put in a box. **2.** a combination of related parts offered as a unit: *The president vetoed the new tax package.* —*v.* [~ + *obj*] **3.** to make or put into a package. —*adj.* [*before a noun*] **4.** offered as a unit combining a number of goods or services: *a package tour, including hotels and meals.*
packed /pækt/ *adj.* very full; crowded to overflowing: *a packed auditorium.*
pack•et /'pækɪt/ *n.* [*count*] a small package or parcel: *a packet of letters.*
pact /pækt/ *n.* [*count*] an agreement or treaty.
pad¹ /pæd/ *n., v.,* **pad•ded, pad•ding.** —*n.* [*count*] **1.** a mass of soft material used for comfort or protection, for applying medicine, or for stuffing: *The skaters wore knee pads.* **2.** a number of sheets of paper glued together at one edge. **3.** the fleshy, cushionlike mass of tissue on the bottom of an animal's foot. **4.** *Slang.* one's living quarters. —*v.* [~ + *obj*] **5.** to provide with a pad or padding. **6.** to expand or add to without need

or in a dishonest way: *The repairman padded his bill.*
pad² /pæd/ *n., v.,* **pad•ded, pad•ding.** —*n.* [*count*] **1.** a dull, soft sound. —*v.* [*no obj*] **2.** to walk so that one's footsteps make a dull, soft sound: *He padded softly behind her.*
pad•ding /'pædɪŋ/ *n.* [*noncount*] material, as cotton or straw, used to pad something.
pad•dle /'pædl/ *n., v.,* **-dled, -dling.** —*n.* [*count*] **1.** a short, flat-bladed oar. **2.** any similar tool used for mixing, stirring, or beating. **3.** a racket with a short handle, used in table tennis. —*v.* **4.** [*no obj*] [~ + *obj*] to (cause to) move in a canoe or the like by using a paddle. **5.** [~ + *obj*] to spank with or as if with a paddle.
pad•dock /'pædək/ *n.* [*count*] an enclosed field, used for letting animals out to pasture or to exercise.
pad•dy /'pædiy/ *n.* [*count*], *pl.* **-dies.** a rice field.
pad•lock /'pædˌlɒk/ *n.* [*count*] a small lock made of a U-shaped bar that can be opened.
pa•gan /'peygən/ *n.* [*count*] **1.** a person who is not a member of the Christian, Jewish, or Muslim religion. —*adj.* **2.** of or relating to pagans or their religion.
page¹ /peydʒ/ *n., v.,* **paged, pag•ing.** —*n.* [*count*] **1.** one side, or both sides, of a sheet of something printed or written, as a book or letter. —*v.* **2. page through,** to turn pages of (a book).
page² /peydʒ/ *n., v.,* **paged, pag•ing.** —*n.* [*count*] **1.** a boy servant or attendant. —*v.* [~ + *obj*] **2.** to summon (a person) by calling out or announcing his or her name, or by using an electronic pager.
pag•eant /'pædʒənt/ *n.* [*count*] a parade in which the participants wear decorative costumes.
pag•eant•ry /'pædʒəntriy/ *n.* [*noncount*] spectacular display: *the pageantry of the Olympics.*
pag•er /'peydʒər/ *n.* [*count*] a pocket-sized electronic device that notifies the person carrying it of telephone calls.
pa•go•da /pə'gowdə/ *n.* [*count*], *pl.* **-das.** a temple or sacred building of the Far East, usually a tower.

pagoda (Chinese, 11th century)

paid /peyd/ *v.* a pt. and pp. of PAY¹.
pail /peyl/ *n.* [*count*] a container with a handle; bucket.
pain /peyn/ *n.* **1.** [*noncount*] physical suffering; great discomfort. **2.** [*count*] an instance of such suffering: *a back pain.* **3.** [*noncount*] severe mental or emotional distress. **4. pains,** [*plural*] **a.** great care: *Take pains with your work.* **b.** the contractions in the uterus during childbirth. **5.** [*count*] Also called **pain in the neck.** an annoying person or thing. —*v.* [~ + *obj*] **6.** to cause

pain to. —*Idiom.* **7. go to great pains,** to make a great effort to do something: *He went to great pains to avoid the test.*

pain•ful /ˈpeynfəl/ *adj.* causing or characterized by pain. —**ˈpain•ful•ly,** *adv.*

pain•kill•er /ˈpeynˌkɪlər/ *n.* [*count*] a drug or treatment that relieves pain.

pain•less /ˈpeynləs/ *adj.* **1.** not causing or involving pain. **2.** simple; not demanding effort: *a painless way of learning a language.* —**ˈpain•less•ly,** *adv.*

pains•tak•ing /ˈpeynzˌteykɪŋ, ˈpeynˌstey-/ *adj.* taking pains; careful.

paint /peynt/ *n.* [*noncount*] [*count*] **1.** a liquid substance applied to a surface for color or decoration. —*v.* **2.** to cover or decorate with paint: [~ + *obj*]: *She paints houses for a living.* [*no obj*]: *They painted all day.* **3.** [~ + *obj*] [*no obj*] to produce (a picture, etc.) with paint. **4.** [~ + *obj*] to describe vividly in words: *The ads painted the resort as a paradise.*

paint•brush /ˈpeyntˌbrʌʃ/ *n.* [*count*] a brush for applying paint.

paint•er /ˈpeyntər/ *n.* [*count*] **1.** a person who paints pictures. **2.** a person who paints houses, rooms, etc.

paint•ing /ˈpeyntɪŋ/ *n.* **1.** [*count*] a picture, design, or piece of art done in paints. **2.** [*noncount*] the act, art, or work of one who paints.

pair /pɛər/ *n., pl.* **pairs, pair,** *v.,* **paired, pair•ing.** —*n.* [*count*] **1.** two things that are the same or similar, or that are matched together: *a pair of bookends.* **2.** something made of two parts joined together: *a pair of scissors.* **3.** two similar or associated individuals: *a pair of oxen.* —*v.* **4.** to arrange in pairs or groups of two: [~ + *obj*]: *to pair socks.* [*no obj*]: *to pair off for a dance.* —**Usage.** See COUPLE.

pa•ja•mas /pəˈdʒɑməz, -ˈdʒæməz/ *n.* [*plural*] clothing worn for sleeping, made of loose-fitting trousers and a top. Also, *esp. Brit.,* **pyjamas.**

Pa•ki•sta•ni /ˌpækəˈstæniy, ˌpɑkəˈstɑniy/ *n.* [*count*], *pl.* **-nis, -ni. 1.** a person born or living in Pakistan. —*adj.* **2.** of or relating to Pakistan.

pal /pæl/ *n.* [*count*] *Informal.* a close friend.

pal•ace /ˈpælɪs/ *n.* [*count*] the official home of a king, queen, or other high-ranking person.

pal•at•a•ble /ˈpælətəbəl/ *adj.* **1.** acceptable or agreeable to the taste. **2.** agreeable to the mind or feelings: *Is the revised plan more palatable to him?*

pal•ate /ˈpælɪt/ *n.* [*count*] **1.** the inside top part, or roof, of the mouth in mammals. **2.** the sense of taste: *a dinner to delight the palate.*

pa•la•tial /pəˈleyʃəl/ *adj.* of, relating to, or resembling a palace.

pale /peyl/ *adj.,* **pal•er, pal•est,** *v.,* **paled, pal•ing.** —*adj.* **1.** lacking strong or natural color: *a pale complexion.* **2.** not bright; dim: *the pale moon.* —*v.* [*no obj*] **3.** to become pale. **4.** to become or seem less important: *My problems pale in comparison to hers.* —**ˈpale•ness,** *n.* [*noncount*]

pa•le•on•tol•o•gy /ˌpeyliyənˈtɒlədʒiy/ *n.* [*noncount*] the science that deals with the forms of life existing long ago, as represented by fossils. —ˌpa•le•onˈtol•o•gist, *n.* [*count*]

pal•ette /ˈpælɪt/ *n.* [*count*] a thin board used by painters for holding and mixing colors.

pal•i•sade /ˌpæləˈseyd/ *n.* [*count*] **1.** a fence or stakes set firmly in the ground to defend an area. **2. palisades,** [*plural*] a line of cliffs.

pall /pɔl/ *n.* **1.** [*count; usually singular*] a heavy or dark covering: *a pall of smoke; a pall of gloom.* **2.** [*count*] a cloth for spreading over a coffin.

pal•lid /ˈpælɪd/ *adj.* pale: *a pallid complexion.*

pal•lor /ˈpælər/ *n.* [*noncount*] paleness in a person's face.

palm[1] /pɑm/ *n.* [*count*] **1.** the part of the inner surface of the hand that reaches from the wrist to the bases of the fingers. —*v.* [~ + *obj*] **2.** to hide in the palm, as in doing a magic trick. **3. palm off,** to get rid of something by falsely describing it: *He palmed off the cheap jewelry as genuine* or *He palmed the cheap jewelry off as genuine.*

palm[2] /pɑm/ *n.* [*count*] a tall tree without branches, with a mass of leaves at the top.

pal•o•mi•no /ˌpæləˈmiynow/ *n.* [*count*], *pl.* **-nos.** a horse with a golden coat and a white mane and tail.

pal•pa•ble /ˈpælpəbəl/ *adj.* plainly seen or felt; obvious.

pal•pi•tate /ˈpælpɪˌteyt/ *v.* [*no obj*] [~ + *obj*], **-tat•ed, -tat•ing.** to (cause to) beat very fast, as the heart; flutter. —**pal•pi•ta•tion** /ˌpælpɪˈteyʃən/, *n.* [*count*] [*noncount*]

pam•per /ˈpæmpər/ *v.* [~ + *obj*] to treat with too much kindness or care: *to pamper a child.*

pam•phlet /ˈpæmflɪt/ *n.* [*count*] a very short publication, usually about a matter of public interest.

pan[1] /pæn/ *n., v.,* **panned, pan•ning.** —*n.* [*count*] **1.** a shallow metal container used for frying, baking, soaking, etc. —*v.* **2.** [~ + *obj*] *Informal.* to criticize harshly, as in a review. **3.** [*no obj*] [~ + *obj*] to wash (gravel, etc.) in a pan to separate gold. **4. pan out,** *Informal.* to have an end or outcome: *Things did not pan out well at his new job.*

pan[2] /pæn/ *v.* [*no obj*] [~ + *obj*], **panned, pan•ning.** to move a camera from one side to another to follow a moving subject.

pan•cake /ˈpænˌkeyk/ *n.* [*count*] a thin, flat cake of flour, eggs, and milk, fried on both sides.

pan•cre•as /ˈpænkriyəs, ˈpæŋ-/ *n.* [*count*] a large gland located near the stomach, which releases digestive enzymes.

pan•da /ˈpændə/ *n.* [*count*], *pl.* **-das.** a white-and-black bearlike mammal.

pan•de•mo•ni•um /ˌpændəˈmowniyəm/ *n.* [*noncount*] wild or noisy uproar or disorder.

pane /peyn/ *n.* [*count*] a single plate of glass in a window frame.

pan•el /ˈpænl/ *n.* [*count*] **1.** a section of a wall or door sunk below or raised above the surface. **2.** a group conducting a public discussion, judging a contest, etc. **3.** a surface on which dials and controls are mounted.

pan•el•ist /ˈpænlɪst/ *n.* [*count*] a member of a panel.

pang /pæŋ/ *n.* [*count*] a sudden feeling of pain, guilt, etc.

pan•han•dle /ˈpænˌhændl/ *v.* [*no obj*], **-dled, -dling.** to approach people and beg from them.

pan•ic /ˈpænɪk/ *n., v.,* **-icked, -ick•ing.** —*n.* **1.** [*noncount*] a sudden, great fear. **2.** [*count*] an instance, outbreak, or period of such fear: *A sudden panic seized him.* —*v.* [*no obj*] [~ + *obj*] **3.** to (cause to) have a feeling of panic. —**ˈpan•ick•y,** *adj.*

pan•o•ram•a /ˌpænəˈræmə, -ˈrɑmə/ *n.* [*count*], *pl.* **-ram•as.** a wide view of a large area. —**pan•o•ram•ic** /ˌpænəˈræmɪk/, *adj.*

P

pan•sy /'pænziy/ n. [count], pl. **-sies. 1.** a violet grown in many kinds, having flowers in many different, rich colors. **2.** Slang (offensive). an effeminate man.

pant /pænt/ v. [no obj] **1.** to breathe hard and quickly, as after hard work. —n. [count] **2.** a short, quick effort to breathe; gasp.

pan•ther /'pænθər/ n. [count], pl. **-thers,** (esp. when thought of as a group) **-ther. 1.** COUGAR. **2.** a leopard, esp. a black leopard.

pant•ies /'pæntiyz/ n. [plural] short underpants for women and children.

pan•to•mime /'pæntə,maym/ n., v., **-mimed, -mim•ing.** —n. [noncount] **1.** the art of conveying actions and thoughts by movements without speech. —v. [~ + obj] [no obj] **2.** to represent or express in pantomime. —**pan•to•mim•ist** /'pæntə,maymɪst/, n. [count]

pan•try /'pæntriy/ n. [count], pl. **-tries.** a small room near a kitchen, in which food, dishes, etc., are kept.

pants /pænts/ n. [plural] **1.** a piece of clothing reaching from the waist to the ankles, with a separate section for each leg: His pants were too tight. **2.** underpants; panties.

pant•y•hose /'pæntiy,howz/ n. [plural; used with a plural verb] a one-piece garment for women, combining panties and stockings.

pa•pa /'pɑpə, pə'pɑ/ n. [count], pl. **-pas.** Informal. father.

pa•pal /'peypəl/ adj. [before a noun] of or relating to the pope.

pa•pa•ya /pə'pɑyə/ n. [count] [noncount], pl. **-yas.** a yellow, melonlike fruit of a tropical tree.

pa•per /'peypər/ n. **1.** [noncount] a substance made from wood pulp, rags, or other fiber, used to write or print on, or for wrapping. **2.** [count] a piece or sheet of this. **3.** [count] a newspaper or journal. **4.** [count] a written piece of schoolwork. —v. [~ + obj] **5.** to cover with wallpaper.

pa•per•back /'peypər,bæk/ n. [count] [noncount] a book bound in a flexible paper cover.

'paper ,clip, n. [count] a flat clip that holds sheets of paper between two loops.

pa•per•weight /'peypər,weyt/ n. [count] a small, heavy object placed on papers to keep them in place.

pa•per•work /'peypər,wɜrk/ n. [noncount] writing letters, keeping records, and other clerical work.

pa•pier-mâ•ché /,peypərmə'ʃey, pɑ,pyey-/ n. [noncount] paper pulp mixed with glue, made into shapes that harden when dry.

pa•poose /pæ'puws, pə-/ n. [count] a North American Indian baby or young child.

pap•ri•ka /pæ'priykə, pə-, pɑ-, 'pæprɪkə/ n. [noncount] a red powder made from dried, ripe sweet peppers, used as a spice.

par /pɑr/ n. **1.** [count; usually singular] an equality in value; a level of equality: Her ability is on a par with yours. **2.** [noncount] an average or normal amount, degree, etc.: He doesn't look up to par these days; maybe he's tired. **3.** [noncount] the number of golf strokes set as a standard for a certain hole or a complete course. —**Idiom. 4. par for the course,** exactly what one might expect: His nasty behavior is par for the course in that company.

para-, a prefix meaning: at or to one side of; beside (paragraph); beyond (parapsychology); helping (paralegal).

par•a•ble /'pærəbəl/ n. [count] a short story that illustrates some truth or lesson.

par•a•chute /'pærə,ʃuwt/ n. [count] a circular fabric device with cords, used to allow people or loads to descend slowly from an aircraft.

pa•rade /pə'reyd/ n., v., **-rad•ed, -rad•ing.** —n. [count] **1.** a public procession in honor of an event, person, etc., or to celebrate something. —v. **2.** [no obj] [~ + obj] (to cause to) march in a procession. **3.** [~ + obj] to show in an obvious way, as to gain attention: She likes to parade her wealth to make her friends jealous.

par•a•dise /'pærə,days, -,dayz/ n. **1.** [noncount] heaven, the final resting place of good people when they die. **2.** [count] a place of great beauty or happiness. **3.** [noncount] a state of supreme happiness.

par•a•dox /'pærə,dɒks/ n. [count] **1.** a seemingly contradictory statement that may be true. **2.** a person or thing that seems to be contradictory: the paradox of American society, where enough food is grown to feed the world but people still go hungry. —,**par•a'dox•i•cal,** adj.

par•af•fin /'pærəfɪn/ n. [noncount] a colorless waxy substance, used esp. in candles.

par•a•graph /'pærə,græf/ n. [count] a division of a piece of writing that deals with a single idea, beginning on a new line.

par•a•keet /'pærə,kiyt/ n. [count] a small parrot having a long tail.

par•al•lel /'pærə,lɛl, -ləl/ adj., n., v., **-leled, -lel•ing** or (esp. Brit.) **-lelled, -lel•ling.** —adj. **1.** (of two or more lines or rows) extending in the same direction, never meeting or spreading apart: The highway was parallel to the country road for a few miles. **2.** having a similar direction, nature, or course: parallel situations. —n. **3.** [count] a parallel line or plane. **4.** [count] anything parallel or comparable to something else. **5.** [count] any of the imaginary lines on the earth's surface, parallel to the equator, that mark latitude. —v. [~ + obj] **6.** to provide a parallel for: The rate of inflation paralleled the price of oil. **7.** to be in a parallel course to: The road parallels the river.

par•al•lel•o•gram /,pærə'lɛlə,græm/ n. [count] a four-sided figure having both pairs of opposite sides parallel to each other.

pa•ral•y•sis /pə'ræləsɪs/ n., pl. **-ses** /-,siyz/. **1.** [count] a loss of the ability to move or to feel a sensation in a body part. **2.** [noncount] a state of helpless inability to act: The strike caused a paralysis of all shipping.

par•a•lyze /'pærə,layz/ v. [~ + obj], **-lyzed, -lyz•ing.** to affect with paralysis. Also, esp. Brit., **'par•a,lyse.**

par•a•med•ic /,pærə'mɛdɪk/ n. [count] one who is trained to assist a doctor or to give medical care in the absence of a doctor.

par•a•mount /'pærə,mawnt/ adj. chief in importance, rank, etc.

par•a•noi•a /,pærə'nɔyə/ n. [noncount] **1.** a mental disorder in which a person believes that the actions of others are hostile to him or her. **2.** too much distrust of others, without reason.

par•a•noid /'pærə,nɔyd/ adj. **1.** of or relating to paranoia. —n. [count] **2.** a person suffering from paranoia.

par•a•pher•na•lia /,pærəfər'neylyə, -fə'neyl-/ n. equipment or items, esp. personal belongings, necessary for a particular activity: [plural; used with a plural verb]: All the maps and travel paraphernalia were stored in the car. [noncount; used with a singular verb]: Is all this paraphernalia necessary to take a simple photograph?

par·a·phrase /'pærə,freyz/ *n.*, *v.*, **-phrased, -phras·ing. —n.** [*count*] **1.** a restatement of something written or spoken, using different words. **—v.** [~ + *obj*] **2.** to restate in a paraphrase.

par·a·ple·gi·a /,pærə'pliydʒiyə, -dʒə/ *n.* [*noncount*] paralysis of both legs due to spinal disease or injury. **—par·a·ple·gic** /,pærə'pliydʒɪk/, *adj.*, *n.* [*count*]

par·a·site /'pærə,sayt/ *n.* [*count*] **1.** a living being that lives on or within a different plant or animal, from which it gets food. **2.** one who receives support from another without giving anything in return. **—par·a·sit·ic** /,pærə'sɪtɪk/, *adj.*

par·a·sol /'pærə,sɔl, -,sɒl/ *n.* [*count*] a lightweight umbrella used to shade oneself from the sun.

par·a·troop·er /'pærə,truwpər/ *n.* [*count*] a soldier who is trained to land in combat areas by parachute.

par·cel /'pɑrsəl/ *n.*, *v.*, **-celed, -cel·ing** or (*esp. Brit.*) **-celled, -cel·ling. —n.** [*count*] **1.** an object wrapped up to form a small bundle; a package. **2.** a distinct, continuous piece of land. **—v.** [~ + *obj*] **3.** to divide into or give out in portions: *He parceled (out) the land among his three sons.*

parch /pɑrtʃ/ *v.* [~ + *obj*] **1.** to make (something) too dry, as heat, sun, and wind do. **2.** to make thirsty.

parch·ment /'pɑrtʃmənt/ *n.* **1.** [*noncount*] the skin of sheep, goats, etc., prepared so as to be written on. **2.** [*count*] something written, as a manuscript, on such material.

par·don /'pɑrdn/ *n.* [*count*] **1.** forgiveness, as for an offense or inconvenience: *I beg your pardon.* **2.** a legal release from punishment for an unlawful act, given by a government official. **—v.** [~ + *obj*] **3.** (used without a subject as a polite command) to excuse; forgive: *Pardon me for interfering.* **4.** to release (a person) from punishment.

pare /pɛər/ *v.* [~ + *obj*], **pared, par·ing. 1.** to cut off or trim the outer coating or layer of: *to pare an apple.* **2.** to reduce or remove by or as if by cutting: *to pare (down) expenses.*

par·ent /'pɛərənt, 'pær-/ *n.* [*count*] **1.** a father or a mother. **2.** any living thing that produces another. **—v.** [~ + *obj*] **3.** to be or act as a parent of. **—pa·ren·tal** /pə'rɛntl/ *adj.* **—'par·ent,hood,** *n.* [*noncount*]

pa·ren·the·sis /pə'rɛnθəsɪs/ *n.* [*count*], *pl.* **-ses** /-,siyz/. either or both of a pair of signs () used to mark off an additional remark that interrupts or explains.

par·ish /'pærɪʃ/ *n.* [*count*] a local church and the area assigned to it.

pa·rish·ion·er /pə'rɪʃənər/ *n.* [*count*] a member or inhabitant of a parish.

par·i·ty /'pærɪtiy/ *n.* [*noncount*] equality.

park /pɑrk/ *n.* [*count*] **1.** a public area of land having trees, benches, and sometimes facilities for sports. **—v.** [~ + *obj*] [*no obj*] **2.** to leave (a vehicle) in a certain place for a period of time.

par·ka /'pɑrkə/ *n.* [*count*], *pl.* **-kas.** a hooded coat for very cold weather.

'parking ,meter, *n.* [*count*] a device for receiving payment for the length of time that a vehicle is to occupy a parking space.

park·way /'pɑrk,wey/ *n.* [*count*] a wide road with a dividing strip planted with grass, trees, etc.

par·lia·ment /'pɑrləmənt; *sometimes* 'pɑrlyə-/

n. [*count*] the national law-making body of certain countries, such as Great Britain. **—par·lia·men·ta·ry** /,pɑrlə'mɛntəriy/ *adj.*

par·lor /'pɑrlər/ *n.* [*count*] **1.** a room in a home for receiving visitors. **2.** a shop or business establishment: *a funeral parlor; a beauty parlor.* Also, *esp. Brit.,* **parlour.**

pa·ro·chi·al /pə'rowkiyəl/ *adj.* **1.** of or relating to parishes. **2.** very limited or narrow in opinions, scope, or outlook: *the teacher's parochial attitudes toward foreign students.*

pa'rochial ,school, *n.* [*noncount*] [*count*] a primary or secondary school run by a religious organization.

par·o·dy /'pærədiy/ *n.*, *pl.* **-dies,** *v.*, **-died, -dy·ing. —n.** [*count*] **1.** a humorous imitation of a serious piece of literature or music. **—v.** [~ + *obj*] **2.** to make a parody of.

pa·role /pə'rowl/ *n.*, *v.*, **-roled, -rol·ing. —n.** [*noncount*] **1.** the release of a person from prison before the end of the sentence, usually for good behavior. **—v.** [~ + *obj*] **2.** to release on parole.

par·rot /'pærət/ *n.* [*count*] **1.** a noisy, often brightly colored tropical bird. **—v.** [~ + *obj*] **2.** to repeat without thought or understanding.

parse /pɑrs, pɑrz/ *v.* [~ + *obj*], **parsed, pars·ing.** to analyze (a sentence) in terms of its grammatical parts.

pars·ley /'pɑrsliy/ *n.* [*noncount*] an herb used as a flavoring or to decorate food.

pars·nip /'pɑrsnɪp/ *n.* [*count*] [*noncount*] a plant with a yellow root eaten as a vegetable.

par·son /'pɑrsən/ *n.* [*count*] a member of the clergy, esp. a Protestant minister.

par·son·age /'pɑrsənɪdʒ/ *n.* [*count*] the house of a parson.

part /pɑrt/ *n.* **1.** a separate or distinct portion of a whole: [*count*]: *the front part of the house.* [*noncount*]: *That is only part of the problem.* **2.** [*count*] the dividing line formed in separating the hair when combing it. **3.** [*count*] a basic piece of a machine or tool, esp. a replacement for the original piece. **4.** [*count*] the written section of a piece of music for one of the singers or instruments. **5.** a person's participation or concern in something: [*noncount*]: *I had no part in hiring her.* [*count; usually singular*]: *Is there a useful part I can play in helping you move?* **6.** [*count*] a role in a play. **—v. 7.** [*no obj*] to divide or become divided into parts. **8.** to separate: [~ + *obj*]: *The teacher parted the rowdy boys.* [*no obj*]: *We parted as friends.* **9.** [~ + *obj*] to comb (the hair) away from a dividing line. **10. part with,** to give up: *She couldn't bear to part with her toy.* **—adv. 11.** in part; partly: *He's crazy, part mean.* **—Idiom. 12. in part,** in some degree. **13. on the part of,** as done by: *too much noise on the part of the class.* **14. take part,** to participate: *He refused to take part in the festivities.*

par·take /pɑr'teyk/ *v.* [*no obj*], **-took, -tak·en, -tak·ing. 1.** to take part in something with others: *to partake in a celebration.* **2.** to have a portion: *to partake of a meal.*

par·tial /'pɑrʃəl/ *adj.* **1.** being in part only; incomplete: *partial payment.* **2.** biased in favor of one person: *The judge was partial.* **—Idiom. 3. partial to,** favoring; especially fond of: *She is partial to vanilla ice cream.* **—'par·tial·ly,** *adv.*

par·tic·i·pant /pɑr'tɪsəpənt/ *n.* [*count*] a person or group who participates in something.

par·tic·i·pate /pɑr'tɪsə,peyt/ *v.* [*no obj*], **-pat·ed, -pat·ing.** to have a share or join with others: *to participate in a conversation.* **—par•tic•i•pa•tion** /pɑr,tɪsə'peyʃən/, *n.* [*noncount*]

par•ti•ci•ple /'pɑrtə,sɪpəl, -səpəl/ *n.* [*count*] a verb form that can function as an adjective or be used with auxiliary verbs to make compound verb forms, as *burning* in *a burning candle* or *running* in *She was running.* In English, participles are the *-ing* or *-ed/-en* forms of verbs. Compare PAST PARTICIPLE, PRESENT PARTICIPLE.

par•ti•cle /'pɑrtɪkəl/ *n.* [*count*] **1.** a tiny portion or amount; a small bit: *a particle of dust.* **2.** one of the extremely small, most basic pieces of matter, as an atom or proton.

par•tic•u•lar /pər'tɪkyələr, pə'tɪk-/ *adj.* **1.** [*before a noun*] relating to a single or specific person, thing, group, etc.; not general: *one's particular interests.* **2.** [*before a noun*] greater or stronger than usual: *Take particular care.* **3.** [*be + ~*] fussy; hard to please: *He is very particular about his food.* **—n.** [*count*] **4.** Usually, **particulars.** [*plural*] specific points, details, or circumstances: *the particulars of a case.* **—Idiom. 5. in particular,** especially: *Are you doing anything in particular at the moment?* **—par'tic•u•lar•ly,** *adv.*

par•ti•san /'pɑrtəzən, -sən/ *n.* [*count*] a supporter or follower of a person or cause.

par•ti•tion /pɑr'tɪʃən, pər-/ *n.* **1.** [*noncount*] a division into portions or parts: *the partition of the empire.* **2.** [*count*] a wall or barrier that divides a space into separate areas. **—v.** [*~ + obj*] **3.** to divide into parts. **4.** to separate by a partition: *to partition (off) a dining area.*

part•ly /'pɑrtliy/ *adv.* in part; not wholly or completely: *partly made of iron.*

part•ner /'pɑrtnər/ *n.* [*count*] **1.** one who is associated with another, esp. in a business. **2.** either of two people who dance together, play tennis together, etc. **—'part•ner,ship,** *n.* [*noncount*] [*count*]

'part of 'speech, *n.* [*count*], *pl.* **parts of speech.** a class of words in a language, grouped on the basis of their meaning, form, or use in a sentence: *In English, noun, verb, and adjective are parts of speech.*

par•tridge /'pɑrtrɪdʒ/ *n.* [*count*], *pl.* **-tridg•es,** (*esp. when thought of as a group*) **-tridge.** a plump bird of the pheasant family.

part-time /*adj.*'pɑrt,taym; *adv.* 'pɑrt'taym/ *adj.* **1.** working or attending school on less than a full-time schedule. **—adv. 2.** on a part-time basis: *was working part-time.*

par•ty /'pɑrtiy/ *n.,* *pl.* **-ties,** *v.,* **-tied, -ty•ing.** **—n.** [*count*] **1.** a social gathering for conversation, refreshments, etc. **2.** a group gathered for some special purpose or task: *a search party to find the missing child.* **3.** a political group seeking political power in elections: *two main parties in the United States.* **—v.** [*no obj*] **4.** to go to or give parties.

pass /pæs/ *v.* **1.** to move past: [*~ + obj*]: *to pass the house.* [*no obj*]: *Several cars passed.* **2.** to go forward, through, or across: [*no obj*]: *The car could not pass through.* [*~ + obj*]: *to pass a barrier.* **3.** (of time) to go by or cause to go by: [*~ + obj*]: *How did you pass the time in Finland?* [*no obj*]: *The days passed quickly.* **4.** [*no obj*] to come to an end: *The crisis soon passed.* **5.** to undergo or complete successfully: [*~ + obj*]: *to pass an examination.* [*no obj*]: *Two students passed.* **6.** [*~ + obj*] to permit (a person) to complete an examination, course, etc., successfully: *The teacher passed all of her students.* **7.**

[*no obj*] to be not very good but still acceptable: *This copy is hard to read, but it will pass.* **8.** [*~ + obj*] to give or transfer: *Please pass the salt.* **9.** [*no obj*] to be exchanged or conveyed, as between two persons: *Angry words passed between them.* **10.** [*~ + obj*] to approve, esp. by vote: *Congress passed the bill.* **11. pass away** or **on,** to die: *She passed away in her sleep.* **12. pass down,** to tell or teach to one's descendants; hand down: *passing down traditions to the next generation.* **13. pass off,** to present or sell deceptively: *She passed herself off as an experienced writer.* **14. pass out,** to faint: *He passed out from all the drinking.* **15. pass up,** to refuse or neglect to take advantage of: *When he turned down that job offer, he passed up a good opportunity. The offer was so good she just couldn't pass it up.* **—n.** [*count*] **16.** an act of passing. **17.** a narrow route across a low area in a mountain range. **18.** a permission to pass or enter. **19.** a gesture, action, or remark intended to be sexually inviting: *He made a pass at her.* **—Idiom. 20. come to pass,** to happen; occur: *It came to pass that a handsome prince was looking for a princess to marry.*

pass•a•ble /'pæsəbəl/ *adj.* **1.** that can be traveled through or crossed: *The road is barely passable.* **2.** barely acceptable; adequate: *a passable knowledge of English.*

pas•sage /'pæsɪdʒ/ *n.* **1.** [*count*] a section of a written, spoken, or musical work: *a passage of Scripture.* **2.** [*noncount*] the act or process of passing: *the passage of time.* **3.** [*count*] an opening or entrance into, through, or out of something: *the nasal passages.*

pas•sage•way /'pæsɪdʒ,wey/ *n.* [*count*] a hall, alley, etc., that provides passage.

pas•sen•ger /'pæsəndʒər/ *n.* [*count*] a person traveling in an automobile, train, etc., esp. one who is not the operator.

pass•er•by or **pass•er-by** /'pæsər'bay, -,bay/ *n.* [*count*], *pl.* **pass•ers•by** or **pass•ers-by** /'pæsərz'bay, -,bay/. a person passing by.

pass•ing /'pæsɪŋ/ *adj.* [*before a noun*] **1.** going past, as in time: *Each passing day her love grew stronger.* **2.** brief; not lasting long: *a passing thought.* **—n.** [*noncount*] **3.** the act of going by: *the passing of time.* **4.** death. **—Idiom. 5. in passing,** by the way; incidentally: *Let me mention, in passing, the help I received from the police.*

pas•sion /'pæʃən/ *n.* **1.** [*noncount*] [*count*] (an instance or an experience of) strong feeling, such as love or hatred. **2.** [*noncount*] (an instance or feeling of) strong sexual desire; lust. **3.** [*count; usually singular*] a strong fondness or desire: *a passion for music.*

pas•sion•ate /'pæʃənɪt/ *adj.* showing passion. **—'pas•sion•ate•ly,** *adv.*

pas•sive /'pæsɪv/ *adj.* **1.** not acting or participating much; inactive: *a passive member of a committee.* **2.** of, relating to, or being a verb form or construction that has a subject that undergoes the action of the verb: *In the passive sentence* The letter was written last week, *the subject* letter *receives the action of writing.* **—n.** [*count*] **3.** a passive verb form or construction. **—'pas•sive•ly,** *adv.* **—pas•siv•i•ty** /pæ'sɪvɪtiy/ *n.* [*noncount*]

'passive 'smoking, *n.* [*noncount*] the inhaling of the cigarette, cigar, or pipe smoke of others.

Pass•o•ver /'pæs,owvər/ *n.* [*noncount*] [*count*] a Jewish festival celebrated in March or April in memory of the Exodus of the Israelites from Egypt.

pass•port /'pæspɔrt/ *n.* [count] an official document that proves citizenship and gives the right to travel to other countries.

pass•word /'pæs,wɜrd/ *n.* [count] a secret word or expression used to gain entrance or access, as to a computer system.

past /pæst/ *adj.* **1.** gone by in time: *The bad times are all past now.* **2.** [before a noun] gone by just before the present time: *during the past year.* **3.** [before a noun] having once been; having formerly served as: *three past presidents of the club.* **4.** [before a noun] of or relating to a verb tense or form indicating to events or states in times gone by: *The past tense of "come" is "came".* —*n.* [noncount] **5.** [the + ~] time gone by: *That happened in the distant past.* **6.** the history of a person, nation, etc. **7.** [the + ~] the past tense. —*adv.* **8.** so as to pass by or beyond; by: *The troops marched past.* —*prep.* **9.** beyond; after: *It's already past noon.*

pas•ta /'pɑstə/ *n., pl.* **-tas.** a food made of thin dough in a variety of shapes, as spaghetti or macaroni: [noncount]: *a serving of pasta.* [count]: *The restaurant serves various pastas.*

paste /peyst/ *n., v.,* **past•ed, past•ing.** —*n.* [noncount] **1.** a mixture of flour and water, used for causing material to stick to something. **2.** a soft mixture of food and a liquid: *almond paste.* **3.** a mixture of powder and a liquid. —*v.* [~ + obj] **4.** to fasten or stick with paste: *I pasted the children's pictures on the wall.*

pas•tel /pæ'stɛl/ *n.* **1.** [count] a color having a soft, pale shade. **2.** [noncount] the art of drawing with chalky crayons. **3.** [count] a drawing so made. —*adj.* [before a noun] **4.** having a soft, pale color or shade.

pas•teur•ize /'pæstʃə,rayz/ *v.* [~ + obj], **-ized, -iz•ing.** to heat (a food, as milk, beer, or wine) to a high temperature to destroy bacteria without changing taste or quality. —**pas•teur•i•za•tion** /,pæstʃərı'zeyʃən/, *n.* [noncount]

pas•time /'pæs,taym/ *n.* [count] something, as a game or hobby, that serves to make time pass agreeably.

pas•tor /'pæstər/ *n.* [count] a minister or priest in charge of a church.

pas•to•ral /'pæstərəl/ *adj.* **1.** relating to the country or to life in the country; rural; rustic. **2.** of or relating to a pastor.

'past 'participle, *n.* [count] a participle used to express a past action or state, to form the passive, or as an adjective: *fallen, sung, and defeated are past participles.*

pas•tra•mi /pə'strɑmiy/ *n.* [noncount] beef left in a mixture of seasonings and smoked before cooking.

pas•try /'peystriy/ *n., pl.* **-tries. 1.** [noncount] [count] a sweet baked food made of dough. **2.** [noncount] dough used to enclose food.

pas•ture /'pæstʃər/ *n.* [noncount] [count] an area of ground covered with grass for cattle to eat.

past•y /'peystiy/ *adj.,* **-i•er, -i•est.** of or like paste, as in texture or color: *a pasty complexion.*

pat¹ /pæt/ *v.,* **pat•ted, pat•ting,** *n.* —*v.* [~ + obj] **1.** to stroke or tap lightly with the hand: *She patted her hair.* —*n.* [count] **2.** a light stroke, tap, or blow. **3.** a small piece, usually flat and square, formed by patting, cutting, etc.: *a pat of butter.* —**Idiom. 4.** **pat on the back, a.** praise, congratulations, or encouragement: *She needed a*

pat on the back. **b.** to praise, congratulate, or encourage: *The boss patted him on the back for his fine work.*

pat² /pæt/ *adj.* unconvincing because it seems to have been rehearsed, practiced, or memorized: *He gave his usual pat answers.*

patch /pætʃ/ *n.* [count] **1.** a small piece of material used to repair a tear, cover a hole, or strengthen a weak place. **2.** a small piece, scrap, or area of anything: *a patch of ice on the sidewalk.* —*v.* [~ + obj] **3.** to mend or strengthen with a patch: *He patched the pants with some scraps of denim.* **4. patch up,** to settle or smooth over (a quarrel): *They tried to patch up their differences. They tried to patch things up.*

patch•work /'pætʃ,wɜrk/ *n.* [noncount] sewn work made of pieces of material in many different colors or shapes.

patch•y /'pætʃiy/ *adj.,* **-i•er, -i•est.** not regular in quality, texture, or distribution: *patchy fog.*

pat•ent /'pætnt/ *n.* [count] **1.** the right granted to an inventor to be the only manufacturer or seller of an invention for a specified number of years. —*v.* [~ + obj] **2.** to obtain a patent on (an invention).

'patent 'leather /'pætnt, 'pætṇ; *esp. Brit.* 'peytnt/ *n.* [noncount] hard, shiny, smooth leather used esp. for shoes and handbags.

pa•ter•nal /pə'tɜrnḷ/ *adj.* **1.** relating to or characteristic of a father. **2.** related on the father's side: *his paternal grandfather.*

pa•ter•ni•ty /pə'tɜrnɪtiy/ *n.* [noncount] the state of being a father; fatherhood.

path /pæθ/ *n.* [count], *pl.* **paths** /pæðz/. **1.** a way, track, or trail made by human or animal feet: *a path through the woods.* **2.** a narrow walk or way: *a bicycle path.* **3.** a route or course along which something moves: *the path of a hurricane.*

pa•thet•ic /pə'θɛtɪk/ *adj.* causing sympathy or pity.

pa•thol•o•gy /pə'θɒlədʒiy/ *n.* [noncount], *pl.* **-gies.** the study of diseases. —**pa'thol•o•gist,** *n.* [count]

pa•tient /'peyʃənt/ *n.* [count] **1.** a person under medical care or treatment. —*adj.* **2.** able to control one's feelings in spite of annoyance or misfortune, without complaining. **3.** continuing to work steadily. —**'pa•tience,** *n.* [noncount] —**'pa•tient•ly,** *adv.*

pat•i•o /'pætiy,ow/ *n.* [count], *pl.* **-i•os.** a paved area connected to a house and used for outdoor relaxation.

pat. pend., an abbreviation of: patent pending.

pa•tri•arch /'peytriy,ɑrk/ *n.* [count] the male head of a family or tribe. —**'pa•tri,arch•y,** *n.* [noncount] [count]

pa•tri•ot /'peytriyət, -,ɒt/ *n.* [count] one who loves and defends his or her country. —**,pa•tri'ot•ic,** *adj.* —**'pa•tri•ot•ism,** *n.* [noncount]

pa•trol /pə'trowl/ *v.,* **-trolled, -trol•ling,** *n.* —*v.* [~ + obj] [no obj] **1.** (of a police officer, etc.) to pass regularly along (a route) or through (an area) to maintain order and security. —*n.* **2.** [count] a person or group that patrols. **3.** [noncount] the act of patrolling.

pa•trol•man *or* **-wom•an** /pə'trowlmən/ *or* /-,wʊmən/ *n.* [count], *pl.* **-men** *or* **-wom•en.** a police officer assigned to patrol.

pa•tron /'peytrən/ *n.* [count] **1.** a regular customer of a store, etc. **2.** a person who supports an artist, charity, etc., by giving money.

pa•tron•age /'peytrənɪdʒ, 'pæ-/ *n.* [noncount] **1.** the financial support or business given to a store, hotel, etc., by customers or paying guests. **2.** the power of public officials to appoint their supporters to government jobs.

pa•tron•ize /'peytrə,nayz, 'pæ-/ v. [~ + obj], **-ized, -iz•ing. 1.** to give (a store, hotel, etc.) one's regular business. **2.** to behave toward (someone) as if superior or more important: *He tends to patronize his coworkers.*

pat•ter¹ /'pætər/ v. [no obj] **1.** to make a sound of many quick, light taps: *The rain pattered on the tin roof.* —n. [count] **2.** a rapid series of light tapping sounds.

pat•ter² /'pætər/ n. [noncount] rapid talk used to attract attention, etc.

pat•tern /'pætərn/ n. [count] **1.** a decorative design, as for wallpaper, made up of elements in a regular arrangement. **2.** a combination of actions, qualities, etc., characteristic of a particular person or group: *the behavior patterns of teenagers.* **3.** an original used as a guide: *The U.S. Constitution has been a pattern for many other countries.* —v. [~ + obj] **4.** to make or design according to a pattern: *He patterned his writing on his favorite author.*

pat•ty /'pætiy/ n. [count], pl. **-ties.** a thin, round piece of ground-up food, as of meat: *hamburger patties.*

paunch /pɔntʃ, pantʃ/ n. [count] a large belly, or one that sticks out.

pau•per /'pɔpər/ n. [count] a person without any means of support; a poor person.

pause /pɔz/ n., v., **paused, paus•ing.** —n. [count] **1.** a temporary stop or rest: *After a brief pause, he resumed his speech.* —v. [no obj] **2.** to make a brief stop or delay.

pave /peyv/ v. [~ + obj], **paved, pav•ing. 1.** to cover or lay (a road, etc.) with concrete, stones, etc., to make a firm, level surface. —**Idiom. 2. pave the way for,** to prepare the way for; make possible: *The agreements paved the way for increased trade between the two countries.*

pave•ment /'peyvmənt/ n. [noncount] a paved surface or floor.

pa•vil•ion /pə'vɪlyən/ n. [count] **1.** a light, usually open building, used for concerts, etc. **2.** any of a number of buildings forming a hospital or the like.

paw /pɔ/ n. [count] **1.** the foot of an animal that has claws or nails. —v. **2.** to strike or scrape with the paws or feet: [~ + obj]: *The cat pawed the door.* [no obj]: *The dog pawed at the door, trying to get in.*

pawn¹ /pɔn/ v. [~ + obj] to leave (something valuable) with a pawnbroker.

pawn² /pɔn/ n. [count] **1.** one of eight chess pieces of the lowest value. **2.** a person used to further another person's purposes.

pawn•bro•ker /'pɔn,browkər/ n. [count] a person who lends money at interest in exchange for personal property left and claimed later.

pay /pey/ v., **paid, pay•ing,** n., adj. —v. **1.** [~ + obj] [no obj] to settle (a debt, bill, etc.) by handing over money or goods, or by doing something. **2.** to give (money) to (someone) in exchange for something: [~ + obj]: *She paid him fifty dollars to clean up the yard.* [no obj]: *Teaching pays poorly.* **3.** [no obj] to be worthwhile: *Crime does not pay. Sometimes it pays to be courteous.* **4.** [~ + obj] to give (attention, etc.), when it is proper to do so: *The class was not paying attention to the teacher. She paid him a nice compliment.* **5.** [~ + obj] to make (a call, visit, etc.). **6.** to suffer in punishment: [~ + obj]: *to*

pay the penalty for his crimes. [no obj]: *I'll make him pay for his treachery.* **7. pay back, a.** to repay or return: *He paid back every cent he owed. I lent him money but he hasn't paid me back.* **b.** to punish in return for some hurt or offense: *She paid him back for lying to her.* **8. pay off, a.** to pay in full: *He paid off the debt* or *He paid the debt off.* **b.** *Informal.* to bribe: *to pay off a cop* or *to pay a cop off.* —n. [noncount] **9.** the act of paying or being paid; payment. **10.** wages or salary paid for work. —adj. **11.** operated by depositing coins: *a pay phone.* —**'pay•ment,** n. [count] [noncount]

pay•a•ble /'peyəbəl/ adj. [be + ~] that should or must be paid; due: *The dentist's bill is payable on the first of the month.*

pay•ee /pey'iy/ n. [count], pl. **-ees.** one to whom money is paid.

pay•roll /'pey,rowl/ n. [count] a list of employees to be paid, with the amount owed to each.

PC, an abbreviation of: **1.** pl. **PCs** or **PC's.** personal computer. **2.** politically correct.

PCS, an abbreviation of: Personal Communications Service, a system for mobile phones, which often includes many special features.

pea /piy/ n. [count], pl. **peas.** a round, green seed eaten as a vegetable.

peace /piys/ n. **1.** [noncount] freedom from war; absence of fighting between nations. **2.** [noncount] a state of harmony between people. **3.** [noncount; the + ~] public order and security: *The police keep the peace.* **4.** [noncount] freedom from worry or annoyance: *peace of mind.* **5.** [noncount] a state of calmness. **6.** [noncount] silence; stillness. **7.** [count] a treaty that ends a war or fighting. —**Idiom. 8. at peace, a.** not at war: *a nation once again at peace.* **b.** untroubled; calm. **9. hold** or **keep one's peace,** to keep silent. **10. make one's peace with,** to stop arguing with (someone). —**'peace•ful,** adj. —**'peace•ful•ly,** adv.

peach /piytʃ/ n. [count] [noncount] the round, pink-to-yellow, fuzzy-skinned fruit of a tree of the rose family.

pea•cock /'piy,kɒk/ n. [count], pl. **-cocks,** (esp. when thought of as a group) **-cock.** a bird with bright tail feathers that can be spread in a fan.

peak /piyk/ n. [count] **1.** the pointed top of a mountain or ridge. **2.** a mountain with a pointed top. **3.** the most important or maximum level: *at the peak of her career.* **4.** the front piece of a cap that sticks out over the eyes. —v. [no obj] **5.** to reach a peak: *His popularity peaked after the election.* —adj. [before a noun] **6.** of or being the time when traffic, use, or demand is greatest: *Hotel prices are high during the peak travel season.*

peal /piyl/ n. [count] **1.** a loud, long ringing of bells. **2.** any loud, long sound: *peals of laughter.* —v. [no obj] [~ + obj] **3.** to (cause to) make a loud, ringing sound.

pea•nut /'piy,nʌt, -nət/ n. [count] a nutlike seed that grows underground.

'peanut ,butter, n. [noncount] a paste made from ground, roasted peanuts.

pear /pɛər/ n. [count] [noncount] a juicy fruit that is rounded at one end and smaller toward the stem.

pearl /pɜrl/ n. [count] a smooth, rounded bead, formed within the shells of oysters, valued as a gem. —**'pearl•y,** adj., **-i•er, -i•est.**

peas•ant /'pɛzənt/ n. [count] a member of a class of farmers of low social rank, as in Europe.

peb•ble /'pɛbəl/ n. [count] a small, rounded stone. —'**peb•bly**, adj., -**bli•er**, -**bli•est**.

pe•can /pɪ'kɑn, -'kæn, 'piykæn/ n. [count] a sweet nut with a thin shell.

peck[1] /pɛk/ n. [count] a unit of measurement for dry goods, equal to 8 quarts.

peck[2] /pɛk/ v. **1.** [~ + obj] [no obj] to strike or pierce with the beak, as a bird does. **2.** [~ + obj] to kiss (someone) lightly on the cheek. **3. peck at**, to nibble at without much interest: The boy sat there pecking at his meal. —n. [count] **4.** a quick stroke, as in pecking. **5.** a quick, light kiss.

pe•cu•liar /pɪ'kyuwlyər/ adj. **1.** strange; odd. **2.** characteristic of some person, group, or thing: the peculiar properties of that drug; an expression peculiar to Canadians. —**pe'cu•liar•ly**, adv.

pe•cu•li•ar•i•ty /pɪ,kyuwliy'ærɪtiy/ n., pl. -**ties**. **1.** [noncount] the quality or condition of being peculiar. **2.** [count] a strange manner or way of thinking. **3.** [count] a quality distinctive to only one group or thing: the peculiarities of her dialect.

ped•al /'pɛdl; for also 'piydl/ n., v., -**aled**, -**al•ing** or (esp. Brit.) -**alled**, -**al•ling**. —n. [count] **1.** a foot-operated lever, as on a bicycle, piano, or sewing machine. —v. [no obj] [~ + obj] **2.** to work or use pedals.

ped•dle /'pɛdl/ v. [~ + obj] [no obj], -**dled**, -**dling**. to carry (small articles) from place to place for sale. —'**ped•dler**, n. [count]

ped•es•tal /'pɛdəstl/ n. [count] a supporting base for a column, statue, etc.

pe•des•tri•an /pə'dɛstriyən/ n. [count] one who travels on foot.

pe•di•at•rics /,piydiy'ætrɪks/ n. [noncount; used with a singular verb] the branch of medicine concerned with the development, care, and diseases of babies and children. —,**pe•di'at•ric**, adj. —**pe•di•a•tri•cian** /,piydiyə'trɪʃən/, n. [count]

ped•i•gree /'pɛdɪ,griy/ n. [noncount] [count] **1.** one's line of ancestors; ancestry. —adj. Also, '**ped•i,greed**. **2.** having established ancestry from a recognized breed: a pedigree collie.

pee /piy/ v., **peed**, **pee•ing**, n. Slang (sometimes vulgar). —v. [no obj] **1.** to urinate. —n. **2.** [noncount] urine. **3.** [count] an act of urinating.

peek /piyk/ v. [no obj] **1.** to glance quickly or secretly. —n. [count] **2.** a quick or secret look or glance.

peel /piyl/ v. **1.** [~ + obj] to strip (something) of its skin, rind, etc.: to peel some potatoes. **2.** [no obj] to come off in pieces: My skin peeled after the sunburn. **3.** [~ + obj] to strip away from something: to peel paint from a car. —n. [noncount] **4.** the skin or rind of a fruit or vegetable: grated lemon peel.

peep[1] /piyp/ v. [no obj] **1.** to look through a small opening or from a hidden or secret location: peeping through the curtains. —n. [count] **2.** a quick or secret look.

peep[2] /piyp/ n. [count] a short, high-pitched cry or sound, as of a young bird.

peep•hole /'piyp,howl/ n. [count] a small hole, as in a door, through which to look.

peer[1] /pɪər/ n. [count] one who is the equal of another as in age, ability, or social status.

peer[2] /pɪər/ v. [no obj] **1.** to look carefully, as in making an effort to see clearly: He peered at the computer screen, wondering what his mistake was. **2.** to appear slightly; come into view: The sun peered briefly from behind the clouds.

pee•vish /'piyvɪʃ/ adj. irritable, grouchy, or cranky.

pee•wee /'piy,wiy/ n. [count], pl. -**wees**. Informal. a person or thing that is unusually small.

peg /pɛg/ n. [count] a short, thin piece of wood, metal, etc., driven into something as a fastening, support, etc.: hung his coat on the peg by the door.

Pe•king•ese or **Pe•kin•ese** /,piykə'niyz, -'niys/ n. [count], pl. -**ese**. one of a Chinese breed of small dogs having a flat, wrinkled muzzle.

pel•i•can /'pɛlɪkən/ n. [count] a large bird having a throat pouch that expands.

pel•let /'pɛlɪt/ n. [count] **1.** a small ball of food or medicine. **2.** a small metal ball shot from a gun.

pell-mell or **pell•mell** /'pɛl'mɛl/ adv. done too fast and without enough care or thinking: The man ran pell-mell into the crowd.

pelt[1] /pɛlt/ v. **1.** [~ + obj] to attack (someone) with repeated blows. **2.** [no obj] to beat or pound without stopping: rain pelting down.

pelt[2] /pɛlt/ n. [noncount] the untanned hide or skin of an animal.

pel•vis /'pɛlvɪs/ n. [count] the bones forming the cavity in the lower trunk of the body. —'**pel•vic**, adj.

pen[1] /pɛn/ n. [count] an instrument for writing or drawing with ink.

pen[2] /pɛn/ n., v., **penned**, **pen•ning**. —n. [count] **1.** a small fenced-in area for farm animals. —v. [~ + obj] **2.** to confine in or as if in a pen.

pe•nal /'piynl/ adj. of or relating to punishment for crimes: a penal system.

pe•nal•ize /'piynl,ayz, 'pɛn-/ v. [~ + obj], -**ized**, -**iz•ing**. to punish (someone) with a penalty.

pen•al•ty /'pɛnltiy/ n. [count], pl. -**ties**. a punishment for breaking a law or violating a rule: penalties for littering.

pence /pɛns/ n. [plural] Brit. a pl. of PENNY (used after a number in referring to a sum of money rather than to the coins themselves): sixpence.

pen•cil /'pɛnsəl/ n., v., -**ciled**, -**cil•ing** or (esp. Brit.) -**cilled**, -**cil•ling**. —n. [count] [noncount] **1.** a slender tube of wood containing a piece of graphite used for writing or drawing. —v. [~ + obj] **2.** to write, draw, or mark with a pencil.

pend•ant /'pɛndənt/ n. [count] a hanging ornament on a necklace.

pend•ing /'pɛndɪŋ/ prep. **1.** while awaiting; until: We'll do this work pending his return. **2.** during: pending the trial. —adj. **3.** awaiting decision or settlement: That case is still pending. **4.** about to happen: Dad knew the driving test was pending; why was he late?

pen•du•lum /'pɛndʒələm, 'pɛndyə-, -də-/ n. [count] a weight hanging from a fixed point so as to move back and forth freely, used esp. to control a clock.

pen•e•trate /'pɛnɪ,treyt/ v., -**trat•ed**, -**trat•ing**. **1.** to pierce or pass into or through: [~ + obj]: The nail penetrated my shoe. [no obj]: Maybe the bullet didn't penetrate. **2.** [~ + obj] to understand something difficult: to penetrate Einstein's theories. —**pen•e•tra•tion** /,pɛnɪ'treyʃən/ n. [count] [noncount]

pen•guin /'pɛŋgwɪn, 'pɛn-/ n. [count] a bird of the Southern Hemisphere that swims but cannot fly.

P

pen•i•cil•lin /ˌpɛnəˈsɪlɪn/ *n.* [*noncount*] an antibiotic produced from molds.

pen•in•su•la /pəˈnɪnsələ, -ˈnɪnsyələ/ *n.* [*count*], *pl.* **-las.** an area of land almost surrounded by water.

pe•nis /ˈpiynɪs/ *n.* [*count*], *pl.* **-nis•es, -nes** /-niyz/. the male sex organ, and, in mammals, the organ through which urine is released.

pen•i•tent /ˈpɛnɪtənt/ *adj.* expressing sorrow for wrongdoing and desiring to make up for the wrong. —**ˈpen•i•tence,** *n.* [*noncount*]

pen•i•ten•tia•ry /ˌpɛnɪˈtɛnʃəriy/ *n.* [*count*], *pl.* **-ries.** a place for imprisonment or punishment.

pen•knife /ˈpɛnˌnayf/ *n.* [*count*], *pl.* **-knives.** a small pocketknife.

pen•man•ship /ˈpɛnmənˌʃɪp/ *n.* [*noncount*] **1.** the art of handwriting; use of the pen in writing. **2.** a person's style or manner of handwriting.

Penn. or **Penna.,** an abbreviation of: Pennsylvania.

ˈpen ˌname, *n.* [*count*] a name used by a writer that is not his or her real name.

pen•nant /ˈpɛnənt/ *n.* [*count*] **1.** a long flag that narrows toward one end. **2.** a flag that symbolizes victory or championship, esp. in baseball.

pen•ni•less /ˈpɛnɪlɪs/ *adj.* totally without money.

pen•ny /ˈpɛniy/ *n.* [*count*], *pl.* **pen•nies,** (*esp.* for 2) **pence. 1.** a unit of money of the U.S., Canada, and other countries, equal to ¹/₁₀₀ of a dollar; one cent. **2.** a unit of money of the United Kingdom, equal to ¹/₁₀₀ of a pound. **3.** a sum of money: *He spends every penny he earns. He hasn't got a penny to spend.*

ˈpenny ˌpincher, *n.* [*count*] a stingy person.

ˈpen ˌpal, *n.* [*count*] a person with whom one keeps up an exchange of letters, usually someone far away.

pen•sion /ˈpɛnʃən; *Fr.* pãˈsyɔ̃ for / *n.* [*count*], *pl.* **-sions** /-ʃənz; *Fr.* ˈsyɔ̃ for /. a fixed amount of money paid regularly to one who has retired from a company. —**ˈpen•sion•er,** *n.* [*count*]

pen•sive /ˈpɛnsɪv/ *adj.* dreamily thoughtful; thinking deeply or sadly.

pen•ta•gon /ˈpɛntəˌgɒn/ *n.* **1.** [*count*] a flat figure having five angles and five sides. **2. the Pentagon,** a building in Arlington, Va., headquarters of the U.S. Department of Defense.

pent•house /ˈpɛntˌhaws/ *n.* [*count*], *pl.* **-hous•es.** an apartment on the roof of a building.

ˈpent-ˈup, *adj.* not let out or expressed; curbed: *pent-up rage.*

pe•o•ny /ˈpiyəniy/ *n.* [*count*], *pl.* **-nies.** a plant having large pink or white showy flowers.

peo•ple /ˈpiypəl/ *n.,* *pl.* **-ples.** —*n.* **1.** [*plural*] persons as a group; persons in general: *There were too many people in the room.* **2.** [*count*] the entire body of persons who make up a community, tribe, etc., having a common culture, religion, or the like: *a hard-working, industrious people; the Jewish people.* **3.** [*plural*] a person's family or relatives.

pep /pɛp/ *n., v.,* **pepped, pep•ping.** —*n.* [*noncount*] **1.** lively spirits or energy: *After her coffee she felt full of pep again.* —*v.* **2. pep up,** to make or become spirited: *pepped up the students* or *pepped the students up.* —**ˈpep•py,** *adj.,* **-pi•er, -pi•est.**

pep•per /ˈpɛpər/ *n.* **1.** [*noncount*] the hot-tasting dried berries of a tropical shrub, used as a spice. **2.** [*count*] a hollow vegetable ranging from mild to very strong in flavor. —*v.* [~ + *obj*] **3.** to sea-

son with pepper. **4.** to pelt with small objects: *The side of the ship was peppered with gunshots.* —**ˈpep•per•y,** *adj.*

pep•per•corn /ˈpɛpərˌkɔrn/ *n.* [*count*] the dried berry of the pepper plant.

pep•per•mint /ˈpɛpərˌmɪnt, -mənt/ *n.* **1.** [*noncount*] an herb of the mint family. **2.** [*noncount*] the strong-smelling oil of this plant, used as a flavoring. **3.** [*count*] a candy flavored with peppermint.

ˈpep ˌtalk, *n.* [*count*] a lively, emotional talk intended to inspire enthusiasm.

per /pər; *unstressed* pər/ *prep.* for each or in each: *Membership costs $100 per year.*

per•ceive /pərˈsiyv/ *v.,* **-ceived, -ceiv•ing.** [~ + *obj*] **1.** to become aware of or identify by the senses: *to perceive differences in shade and tone.* **2.** to recognize or understand: *He perceived that there would be difficulties.*

per•cent /pərˈsɛnt/ *n.* **1.** [*noncount; usually after a number*] one one-hundredth part; ¹/₁₀₀: *Our supervisor has reduced our work by fifty percent.* **2.** PERCENTAGE.

per•cent•age /pərˈsɛntɪdʒ/ *n.* [*count*] **1.** a rate per hundred: *A high percentage of our students go on to college.* **2.** a part in general; portion: *increasing percentages of happy campers every year.*

per•cep•ti•ble /pərˈsɛptəbəl/ *adj.* capable of being perceived: *a perceptible change in behavior.*

per•cep•tion /pərˈsɛpʃən/ *n.* [*noncount*] [*count*] the act of perceiving or ability to perceive.

per•cep•tive /pərˈsɛptɪv/ *adj.* having or showing perception; quick to recognize or understand.

perch¹ /pɜrtʃ/ *n.* [*count*] **1.** any high place or platform for a bird, animal, or person to land on or rest on. —*v.* **2.** [*no obj*] to land on or rest on a perch: *The birds perched on the telephone wires.* **3.** to (cause to) settle or rest in some high position: [~ + *obj*]: *He was perched on his throne.* [*no obj*]: *The prince perched on his throne.*

perch² /pɜrtʃ/ *n.* [*count*], *pl.* (*esp. when thought of as a group*) **perch,** (*esp. for kinds or species*) **perch•es.** a small freshwater fish.

per•co•late /ˈpɜrkəˌleyt/ *v.* [*no obj*] [~ + *obj*], **-lat•ed, -lat•ing.** (of ground coffee) to pass or cause to pass through something that traps solid materials.

per•co•la•tor /ˈpɜrkəˌleytər/ *n.* [*count*] a coffeepot in which boiling water is forced up a hollow stem and filters down through ground coffee.

perˈcussion ˌinstrument, *n.* [*count*] a musical instrument, as the drum or cymbal, that is struck to produce a sound.

per•en•ni•al /pəˈrɛniyəl/ *adj.* **1.** lasting for an indefinitely long time: *perennial problems.* **2.** (of plants) having a life cycle of more than two years. —*n.* [*count*] **3.** a perennial plant.

per•fect /*adj.*ˈpɜrfɪkt; *v.* pərˈfɛkt/ *adj.* **1.** excellent beyond improvement; of the very best kind, degree, etc.: *a perfect score on the test.* **2.** exactly fitting a particular need: *The director found the perfect actor for the part.* **3.** complete: *a perfect stranger.* —*v.* [~ + *obj*] **4.** to make perfect. —**per•fec•tion** /pərˈfɛkʃən/ *n.* [*noncount*] —**ˈper•fect•ly,** *adv.*

per•fo•rate /ˈpɜrfəˌreyt/ *v.* [~ + *obj*], **-rat•ed, -rat•ing. 1.** to make holes in by piercing or punching. **2.** to pierce through; penetrate. —**per•fo•ra•tion** /ˌpɜrfəˈreyʃən/ *n.* [*noncount*] [*count*]

per•form /pərˈfɔrm/ *v.* **1.** [~ + *obj*] to carry out; execute; do: *to perform surgery.* **2.** [~ + *obj*] [*no obj*] to act (a play, etc.), as on the stage;

to play or sing a piece of music. —**per'form•er,**
n. [*count*]

per•for•mance /pər'fɔrməns/ *n.* **1.** [*count*] an
entertainment presented before an audience. **2.**
[*noncount*] the act of performing. **3.** [*noncount*]
a. the capacity to perform; effectiveness: *good
performance under pressure.* **b.** the manner in
which something fulfills its purpose: *poor engine
performance in hot weather.*

per•fume /n.'pɜrfyuwm, pər'fyuwm; *v.*
pər'fyuwm, 'pɜrfyuwm/ *n., v.,* **-fumed, -fum•**
ing. —*n.* **1.** [*noncount*] [*count*] a substance that
gives off an agreeable smell, esp. a fluid extracted from flowers. **2.** [*noncount*] the scent of
substances that have an agreeable smell: *flowers
with a lovely perfume.* —*v.* [~ + *obj*] **3.** to give
a pleasant fragrance to: *Roses perfumed the air.*

per•haps /pər'hæps/ *adv.* **1.** maybe; possibly:
Perhaps I misunderstood you. **2.** (used to make
requests more polite): *Perhaps we could meet
again next week?*

per•il /'pɛrəl/ *n.* **1.** [*noncount*] great risk; danger;
jeopardy: *The ship was in peril.* **2.** [*count*] something that causes risk or danger.

per•il•ous /'pɛrələs/ *adj.* of or relating to peril:
a perilous sea voyage. —**'per•il•ous•ly,** *adv.*

pe•rim•e•ter /pə'rɪmɪtər/ *n.* [*count*] **1.** the border of a two-dimensional figure: *the perimeter of
a square.* **2.** the length of such a boundary: *The
perimeter is 20 inches.*

pe•ri•od /'pɪəriyəd/ *n.* [*count*] **1.** an extent of
time in the life of a person, in history, etc.: *a period of illness.* **2.** a round of time marked by
some repeating event or action: *the rainy period.*
3. any of the parts into which something, as a
school day, is divided. **4.** the point or character
(.) used to mark the end of a declarative sentence
or to indicate an abbreviation. **5.** an occurrence
of menstruation.

pe•ri•od•ic /,pɪəriy'ɒdɪk/ occurring again and
again, usually at regular intervals of time: *periodic outbreaks of violence.* —,**pe•ri'od•i•cal•ly,**
adv.

pe•ri•od•i•cal /,pɪəriy'ɒdɪkəl/ *n.* [*count*] a publication issued under the same title at regular periods.

'peri'odic 'table /'pɪəriy'ɒdɪk/ *n.* [*count*] a table in which the chemical elements are arranged
according to their atomic numbers in related
groups.

pe•riph•er•al /pə'rɪfərəl/ *adj.* **1.** of or relating
to the periphery: *the peripheral boundaries.* —*n.*
[*count*] **2.** a device, as a keyboard or printer, that
is connected to a computer.

pe•riph•er•y /pə'rɪfəriy/ *n.* [*count*], *pl.* **-er•ies.**
1. the outside boundary of a surface or area; the
outer limits. **2.** the less central parts or aspects of
a question or problem.

per•i•scope /'pɛrə,skowp/ *n.* [*count*] an instrument for viewing objects at a higher level, used
esp. in submarines.

per•ish /'pɛrɪʃ/ *v.* [*no obj*] to die as a result of
violence or natural disaster.

per•ish•a•ble /'pɛrɪʃəbəl/ *adj.* **1.** that may decay or be destroyed: *Perishable foods need to be
refrigerated.* —*n.* [*count*] **2.** Usually, **perishables.**
[*plural*] something perishable, esp. food.

per•ju•ry /'pɜrdʒəriy/ *n.* [*noncount*] the willful
telling of a lie after having sworn under oath not
to do so.

perk¹ /pɜrk/ *v.* Usually, **perk up. 1.** to (cause to)
become lively or cheerful again: *She perked up
when I told her we could get a dog. The party*

perked up the students or *The party perked the
students up.* **2.** to (cause to) rise quickly or
briskly: *The dog's ears perked up. The dog perked
up its ears* or *The dog perked its ears up.*

perk² /pɜrk/ *v.* [*no obj*] [~ + *obj*] to percolate.

perk³ /pɜrk/ *n.* [*count*] an extra payment, benefit, or privilege at one's job.

perk•y /'pɜrkiy/ *adj.,* **-i•er, -i•est.** lively or
cheerful.

perm /pɜrm/ *n. Informal.* **1.** PERMANENT (def. 3).
—*v.* [~ + *obj*] **2.** to give a permanent to: *She
permed her hair.*

per•ma•nent /'pɜrmənənt/ *adj.* **1.** existing forever; not stopping. **2.** intended to serve, function,
etc., for a long period: *a member of the permanent faculty.* —*n.* [*count*] **3.** a wave or curl set
into the hair by treating it with chemicals or
heat. —**'per•ma•nence,** *n.* [*noncount*] —**'per•
ma•nent•ly,** *adv.*

per•me•ate /'pɜrmiy,eyt/ *v.,* **-at•ed, -at•ing.** to
pass into or through every part of: [~ + *obj*]:
Sunshine permeated the room. [*no obj*]: *Water
permeated through the wood.*

per•mis•si•ble /pər'mɪsəbəl/ *adj.* allowed or
permitted: *Running is not permissible in a classroom.*

per•mis•sion /pər'mɪʃən/ *n.* [*noncount*] the act
of permitting: *to ask permission to leave the
room.*

per•mis•sive /pər'mɪsɪv/ *adj.* too willing to permit something that others might disapprove of or
forbid: *permissive parents who allowed their son
to stay up late.*

per•mit /v.pər'mɪt; n. 'pɜrmɪt, pər'mɪt/ *v.,* **-mit•**
ted, -mit•ting, *n.* —*v.* [~ + *obj*] **1.** to allow to
be done or occur; to allow to do: *laws that permit the sale of certain drugs; Permit me to explain.* —*n.* [*count*] **2.** an official certificate of permission; license: *a work permit.*

per•pen•dic•u•lar /,pɜrpən'dɪkyələr/ *adj.* **1.**
vertical; straight up and down; upright. **2.** meeting at right angles: *Forty-second Street is perpendicular to Fifth Avenue.*

per•pe•trate /'pɜrpɪ,treyt/ *v.* [~ + *obj*],
-trat•ed, -trat•ing. to carry out; do; commit: *to
perpetrate a crime.* —**'per•pe,tra•tor,** *n.* [*count*]

per•pet•u•al /pər'pɛtʃuwəl/ *adj.* **1.** continuing
or lasting forever; everlasting. **2.** lasting for a
very long time. —**per'pet•u•al•ly,** *adv.: The
child was perpetually whining.*

per•pet•u•ate /pər'pɛtʃuw,eyt/ *v.* [~ + *obj*],
-at•ed, -at•ing. to make (something) continue:
to perpetuate a myth. —**per•pet•u•a•tion**
/pər,pɛtʃuw'eyʃən/, *n.* [*noncount*]

per•plex /pər'plɛks/ *v.* [~ + *obj*] to cause to be
confused over what is not understood or certain:
Her strange behavior perplexed me. —**per'plex•**
ing, *adj.: a perplexing problem.*

per•plex•i•ty /pər'plɛksɪtiy/ *n.,* *pl.* **-ties. 1.**
[*noncount*] the state or condition of being perplexed. **2.** [*count*] something that is perplexing.

per•se•cute /'pɜrsɪ,kyuwt/ *v.* [~ + *obj*],
-cut•ed, -cut•ing. to treat (someone) cruelly or
unfairly, esp. because of religion, race, etc.
—**per•se•cu•tion** /,pɜrsɪ'kyuwʃən/ *n.* [*noncount*]
[*count*] —**'per•se,cu•tor,** *n.* [*count*]

per•se•vere /,pɜrsə'vɪər/ *v.* [*no obj*], **-vered,
-ver•ing.** to continue to pursue something in
spite of obstacles, problems, or opposition: *to per-
severe and finish college.* —,**per•se'ver•ance,** *n.*
[*noncount*]

per•sist /pər'sɪst, -'zɪst/ *v.* [*no obj*] **1.** to continue to do something in spite of difficulty or op-

P

position: *The student persisted in breaking the rules.* **2.** to last a long time: *That legend has persisted for fifteen centuries.* —**per'sist•ence,** *n.* [*noncount*] —**per'sist•ent,** *adj.*

per•son /'pɜrsən/ *n.* [*count*] **1.** a human being; a man, woman, or child: *How many persons are there in the United States?* **2.** a grammatical category for pronouns and verbs that distinguishes between the speaker (the first person), the person spoken to (the second person), and other people or things spoken about (the third person). —*Idiom.* **3. in person,** directly and personally present (at a place): *Applicants for this job must apply in person.*

-person, a combining form of PERSON, replacing such paired, sex-specific forms as -MAN and -WOMAN: (*salesperson*).

per•son•a•ble /'pɜrsənəbəl/ *adj.* having an agreeable or pleasing personality.

per•son•age /'pɜrsənɪdʒ/ *n.* [*count*] a person of distinction or importance.

per•son•al /'pɜrsənl/ *adj.* **1.** [*before a noun*] of or relating to a person; individual: *He gave his personal opinion.* **2.** private: *My feelings for her are too personal for me to discuss.* **3.** [*before a noun*] directed to or intended for a particular person: *a personal favor.* —*n.* [*count*] **4.** a notice placed in a newspaper by a person seeking friendship, marriage, etc.

'personal com'puter, *n.* [*count*] a small desktop computer designed for individual use.

per•son•al•i•ty /ˌpɜrsə'nælɪtiy/ *n.*, *pl.* **-ties.** **1.** all the distinguishing qualities or characteristics that an individual possesses: [*count*]: *a charming personality.* [*noncount*]: *Personality is shaped early in life.* **2.** [*count*] a famous or well-known person.

per•son•al•ly /'pɜrsənliy/ *adv.* **1.** in person; directly: *I thanked them personally.* **2.** as if directed at oneself: *Don't take the boss's comments personally.* **3.** giving one's opinion: *Personally, I don't care to go.* **4.** as a person: *I like her personally, but not as a boss.*

per•son•i•fy /pər'sɒnəˌfay/ *v.* [~ + *obj*], **-fied, -fy•ing. 1.** to show that (a thing) has a human nature: *The Greek goddess Demeter personifies the richness of mother earth.* **2.** to be a typical example of: *That businessman personifies ruthless ambition.* —**per•son•i•fi•ca•tion** /pərˌsɒnəfɪ'keyʃən/, *n.* [*noncount*]: *He was the personification of evil.*

per•son•nel /ˌpɜrsə'nɛl/ *n.* **1.** [*plural; used with a plural verb*] all the persons working in an organization. **2.** [*noncount; used with a singular verb*] a department of an organization that deals with employees and their rights, benefits, etc.

per•spec•tive /pər'spɛktɪv/ *n.* **1.** [*noncount*] a technique of drawing objects to show their relative distance, size, etc. **2.** [*count*] one's opinion or way of thinking: *an interesting perspective on the situation.* **3.** [*noncount*] the ability to see the importance of something in relation to something else: *Can't you put this minor defeat into perspective?*

per•spire /pər'spayᵊr/ *v.* [*no obj*], **-spired, -spir•ing.** to release a salty fluid from glands of the skin; to sweat. —**per•spi•ra•tion** /ˌpɜrspə'reyʃən/, *n.* [*noncount*]

per•suade /pər'sweyd/ *v.* [~ + *obj*], **-suad•ed, -suad•ing.** to convince (someone); cause (someone) to do or believe something: *They persuaded the judge of her innocence. They persuaded the judge that she was innocent.*

per•sua•sion /pər'sweyʒən/ *n.* **1.** [*noncount*] the act of persuading or seeking to persuade. **2.** [*count*] a form or system of belief: *those of the liberal persuasion.*

per•sua•sive /pər'sweysɪv, -zɪv/ *adj.* able or intended to persuade: *a persuasive argument.* —**per'sua•sive•ly,** *adv.*

pert /pɜrt/ *adj.*, **-er, -est. 1.** bold or impolite in speech or behavior. **2.** neat and stylish.

per•tain /pər'teyn/ *v.* [~ + *to* + *obj*] to have reference or relation to (something); relate: *documents pertaining to the lawsuit.*

per•ti•nent /'pɜrtn̩ənt/ *adj.* pertaining or relating to the matter being considered; relevant: *pertinent details.* —**'per•ti•nence,** *n.* [*noncount*]

per•turb /pər'tɜrb/ *v.* [~ + *obj*] to disturb (someone) greatly; worry.

Pe•ru•vi•an /pə'ruwviyən/ *adj.* **1.** of or relating to Peru. —*n.* [*count*] **2.** a person born or living in Peru.

per•vade /pər'veyd/ *v.* [~ + *obj*], **-vad•ed, -vad•ing.** to become spread throughout all parts of: *The smell of coffee pervaded the air.*

per•va•sive /pər'veysɪv/ *adj.* tending to pervade: *a pervasive sense of fear.*

per•verse /pər'vɜrs/ *adj.* willfully determined not to do what is expected or desired; contrary: *a perverse child.* —**per'verse•ness,** *n.* [*noncount*] —**per•ver•si•ty** /pər'vɜrsɪtiy/, *n.* [*noncount*]

per•ver•sion /pər'vɜrʒən, -ʃən/ *n.* **1.** [*count*] the act of perverting. **2.** [*noncount*] the state of being perverted. **3.** [*count*] any of various abnormal sexual practices.

per•vert /*v.*pər'vɜrt; *n.* 'pɜrvərt/ *v.* [~ + *obj*] **1.** to lead (someone) away from what is right or moral: *perverting children with pornography.* —*n.* [*count*] **2.** one who practices a sexual perversion.

pe•se•ta /pə'seytə/ *n.* [*count*], *pl.* **-tas** (-təz). the basic monetary unit of Spain.

pes•ky /'pɛskiy/ *adj.*, **-ki•er, -ki•est.** annoying; troublesome.

pe•so /'peysow/ *n.* [*count*], *pl.* **-sos.** the basic monetary unit of Mexico, the Philippines, and several other countries in South and Central America.

pes•si•mism /'pɛsəˌmɪzəm/ *n.* [*noncount*] the tendency to see only what is gloomy, or to expect the worst possible outcome. —**'pes•si•mist,** *n.* [*count*] —**pes•si'mis•tic,** *adj.*

pest /pɛst/ *n.* [*count*] **1.** an annoying or troublesome person, animal, or thing; nuisance. **2.** an insect or other small animal that harms or destroys garden plants, trees, etc.

pes•ter /'pɛstər/ *v.* [~ + *obj*] to be a pest; annoy.

pes•ti•cide /'pɛstəˌsayd/ *n.* [*noncount*] [*count*] a chemical preparation for destroying plant or animal pests.

pes•tle /'pɛsəl, 'pɛstl̩/ *n.* [*count*] a tool for grinding substances in a mortar.

pet /pɛt/ *n.*, *adj.*, *v.*, **pet•ted, pet•ting.** —*n.* [*count*] **1.** an animal kept as a companion in the home. **2.** a person who is especially well cared for or favored: *a teacher's pet.* —*adj.* [*before a noun*] **3.** favorite; preferred: *a pet theory.* **4.** showing fondness or affection: *pet names.* —*v.* **5.** [~ + *obj*] to stroke or touch kindly with the hand: *She petted the dog.* **6.** [*no obj*] to kiss and caress in a way expressing sexual attraction.

pet•al /'pɛtl̩/ *n.* [*count*] one of the often colored parts of the main base of a flower.

pe•ter /'piytər/ *v.* **peter out, 1.** to tire; become

exhausted: *In the last part of the race she just petered out.* **2.** to grow less gradually and stop: *The hot water petered out.*

pe•tite /pə'tiyt/ *adj.* (of a woman) short and having a slim figure.

pe•ti•tion /pə'tıʃən/ *n.* [*count*] **1.** a formal written request or document, addressed to those in authority, asking for some favor, right, or benefit. —*v.* [~ + *obj*] **2.** to address a petition to.

pet•ri•fy /'pɛtrə,fay/ *v.*, **-fied, -fy•ing.** **1.** [*no obj*] [~ + *obj*] to (cause to) become changed into stone or a stony substance. **2.** [~ + *obj*] to cause to be in a state of shock, as from fear.

pet•rol /'pɛtrəl/ *n.* Brit. GASOLINE.

pe•tro•le•um /pə'trowliyəm/ *n.* [*noncount*] an oily, thick, easily burned liquid, used as fuel or made into gasoline, kerosene, etc.

pet•ti•coat /'pɛtiy,kowt/ *n.* [*count*] a garment worn under a skirt or dress.

pet•ty /'pɛtiy/ *adj.,* **-ti•er, -ti•est.** **1.** of little or no importance. **2.** showing meanness of spirit: *petty revenge.* —'**pet•ti•ness,** *n.* [*noncount*]

pet•u•lant /'pɛtʃələnt/ *adj.* showing sudden irritation over an unimportant matter. —'**pet•u•lance,** *n.* [*noncount*] —'**pet•u•lant•ly,** *adv.*

pe•tu•nia /pı'tuwnyə, -niyə, -'tyuw-/ *n.* [*count*], *pl.* **-nias.** a garden plant having funnel-shaped flowers.

pew /pyuw/ *n.* [*count*] (in a church) one of a number of benches arranged in rows for use by the congregation.

pew•ter /'pyuwtər/ *n.* [*noncount*] a kind of metal in which tin is mixed with lead or copper.

pg., an abbreviation of: page.

pH, a symbol used to measure a chemical solution on a scale of 0 (more acidic) to 14 (more alkaline).

phal•lus /'fæləs/ *n.* [*count*] a representation of the penis, usually as a symbol of male sexual power. —'**phal•lic** /'fælık/, *adj.*

phan•tom /'fæntəm/ *n.* [*count*] an appearance of something that is not really there or does not exist, esp. a ghost.

phar•aoh /'fɛərow, 'færow, 'feyrow/ *n.* [*count*] an ancient Egyptian king.

phar•ma•ceu•ti•cal /,farmə'suwtıkəl/ *adj.* relating to drugs or medicine.

phar•ma•cist /'farməsıst/ *n.* [*count*] a person licensed to prepare and give out drugs.

phar•ma•cy /'farməsiy/ *n.* [*count*], *pl.* **-cies.** a drugstore.

phase /feyz/ *n., v.,* **phased, phas•ing.** —*n.* [*count*] **1.** a stage in a process of change or development: *Her tantrums are just part of the phase she's going through.* **2.** the particular, usually repeated appearance presented by the moon or a planet at a given time. —*v.* **3. phase in,** to put or come into use gradually: *phased in some changes* or *phased some changes in.* **4. phase out,** to bring or come to an end gradually; ease out of service: *phased out the weapons* or *phased the weapons out.*

Ph.D., an abbreviation of: Doctor of Philosophy.

pheas•ant /'fɛzənt/ *n.* **1.** [*count*] a large, long-tailed bird. **2.** [*noncount*] the meat of this bird.

phe•nom•e•nal /fı'nɒmənəl/ *adj.* very remarkable, wonderful, or extraordinary.

phe•nom•e•non /fı'nɒmə,nɒn, -nən/ *n.* [*count*], *pl.* **-na** /-nə/ or **-nons. 1.** a fact or circumstance observed or observable: *the phenomena of nature.* **2.** someone or something remarkable.

phi•lan•thro•py /fı'lænθrəpiy/ *n.* [*noncount*], *pl.* **-pies.** unselfish concern for human beings, esp. as shown by voluntary service or donations of money. —**phil•an•throp•ic** /,fılən'θrɒpık/, *adj.* —phi'lan•thro•pist, *n.* [*count*]

-phile, a combining form meaning a person who loves or has a strong enthusiasm for (*audiophile*).

phil•o•den•dron /,fılə'dɛndrən/ *n.* [*count*], *pl.* **-drons, -dra** /-drə/. a climbing plant with shiny, evergreen leaves.

phil•o•soph•i•cal /,fılə'sɒfıkəl/ *adj.* **1.** of or relating to philosophy. **2.** remaining calm after disappointment: *She was philosophical about her loss.*

phi•los•o•phy /fı'lɒsəfiy/ *n., pl.* **-phies. 1.** [*noncount*] the study of the truths and principles of existence, knowledge, and conduct. **2.** [*count*] a particular system of such study or beliefs: *the philosophy of Plato.* **3.** [*count*] a system of principles for guidance in one's everyday affairs: *a simple philosophy of life.* —phi'los•o•pher, *n.* [*count*]

phlegm /flɛm/ *n.* [*noncount*] the mucus in the nose, mouth, and throat, esp. when a person has a cold.

-phobe, a combining form meaning a person who hates or fears (*computerphobe*).

pho•bi•a /'fowbiyə/ *n.* [*count*], *pl.* **-bi•as.** a continuous, irrational fear of something that leads to an overwhelming desire to avoid it.

-phobia, a combining form meaning fear or dread of (*claustrophobia*).

phone /fown/ *n., v.,* **phoned, phon•ing.** —*n.* [*count*] **1.** a telephone. —*v.* [~ + *obj*] [*no obj*] **2.** to use a telephone to call (someone).

'**phone ,tag,** *n.* [*noncount*] many unsuccessful attempts by two persons to connect with one another by telephone.

pho•net•ic /fə'nɛtık, fow-/ *adj.* **1.** [*before a noun*] of or relating to phonetics, or to the sound system of a language. **2.** of or relating to a system of spelling in which one sound is represented by one letter, and one letter represents only one sound.

pho•net•ics /fə'nɛtıks, fow-/ *n.* [*noncount; used with a singular verb*] the study of speech sounds and how they are made, transmitted, and heard.

phon•ics /'fɒnıks/ *n.* [*noncount; used with a singular verb*] a method of teaching reading and spelling based upon the study of how sounds are related to ordinary spelling.

pho•no•graph /'fownə,græf/ *n.* [*count*] a machine that reproduces sound using records in the form of grooved disks.

pho•ny or **pho•ney** /'fowniy/ *adj.,* **-ni•er, -ni•est,** *n., pl.* **-nies** or **-neys.** —*adj.* **1.** not real or genuine; fake; false: *phony diamonds.* —*n.* [*count*] **2.** a phony person or thing. —'**pho•ni•ness,** *n.* [*noncount*]

phos•pho•res•cence /,fɒsfə'rɛsəns/ *n.* [*noncount*] the property of giving off light at temperatures below burning, as after exposure to light or other radiation. —,**phos•pho'res•cent,** *adj.*

phos•pho•rus /'fɒsfərəs/ *n.* [*noncount*] a nonmetallic chemical element and a basic part of plant and animal tissue.

pho•to /'fowtow/ *n.* [*count*], *pl.* **-tos.** a photograph.

photo-, a combining form meaning: light (*photograph*); photograph or photographic (*photocopy*).

pho•to•cop•i•er /'fowtə,kɒpiyər/ *n.* [*count*]

P

any electrically operated machine that makes photocopies.

pho·to·cop·y /'fowtə,kɒpiy/ n., pl. **-cop·ies,** v., **-cop·ied, -cop·y·ing.** —n. [count] **1.** an instant copy of written or printed material made by a photographic method. —v. [~ + obj] **2.** to make a photocopy of.

pho·to·gen·ic /,fowtə'dʒɛnɪk/ adj. forming an attractive subject for photography.

pho·to·graph /'fowtə,græf/ n. [count] **1.** a picture produced by photography. —v. **2.** [~ + obj] to take a photograph of. **3.** [no obj] to be photographed, esp. in some specified way: The children photographed well.

pho·tog·ra·phy /fə'tɒɡrəfiy/ n. [noncount] the process of producing images of objects on special paper by the chemical action of light. —pho'tog·ra·pher, n. [count] —pho·to·graph·ic /,fowtə'græfɪk/ adj.

pho·to·syn·the·sis /,fowtə'sɪnθəsɪs/ n. [noncount] the process by which green plants make food from carbon dioxide and water, using sunlight as energy.

phrase /freyz/ n., v., phrased, phras·ing. —n. [count] **1.** a group of two or more words that make up a meaningful grammatical unit but lack a verb or a subject and verb. —v. [~ + obj] **2.** to express or say (something) in a particular way. —'phras·al, adj.

phra·se·ol·o·gy /,freyziy'ɒlədʒiy/ n. [noncount] manner or style of verbal expression: legal phraseology.

phys·i·cal /'fɪzɪkəl/ adj. **1.** [before a noun] of or relating to the body: physical growth. **2.** [before a noun] of or relating to that which can be seen or touched: the physical universe. **3.** sexual: a physical attraction. —n. [count] **4.** an examination of the body by a doctor. —'phys·i·cal·ly, adv.

'physical edu'cation, n. [noncount] instruction in sports, exercise, and hygiene, esp. as part of a school program.

'physical 'therapy, n. [noncount] the treatment or management of physical injuries or pain by exercise, massage, etc. —'physical 'therapist, n. [count]

phy·si·cian /fɪ'zɪʃən/ n. [count] one licensed to practice medicine; a doctor of medicine.

phys·ics /'fɪzɪks/ n. [noncount; used with a singular verb] the science that deals with matter, energy, motion, and force. —phys·i·cist /'fɪzəsɪst/, n. [count]

phy·sique /fɪ'ziyk/ n. [count] the structure, shape, or appearance of the human body or of a person's body: the muscular physique of an athlete.

pi·an·ist /piy'ænɪst, 'pyæn-, 'piyənɪst/ n. [count] one who plays the piano, esp. as a profession.

pi·an·o /piy'ænow, 'pyænow/ n. [count], pl. **-an·os.** a musical instrument in which felt-covered hammers, operated from a keyboard, strike metal strings.

pic·co·lo /'pɪkə,low/ n. [count], pl. **-los.** a small flute with a higher pitch than an ordinary flute.

pick[1] /pɪk/ v. [~ + obj] **1.** to choose or select, esp. with care. **2.** to provoke: to pick a fight. **3.** to steal the contents of: to pick a pocket. **4.** to open (a lock) with a device other than a key, esp. for the purpose of burglary. **5.** to pull out and gather one by one: to pick flowers. **6.** to play (a stringed instrument) by plucking with the fingers: picking his guitar. **7. pick apart,** to criticize severely or in great detail: picked apart his argu-

ments or picked his arguments apart. **8. pick at,** to eat only a small amount: For days she only picked at her meals. **9. pick on, a.** to tease; bother greatly: The other kids picked on her because she was poor. **b.** to single out; choose: The teacher tended to pick on her often. **10. pick out,** to choose; select: We picked out the best tomatoes or We picked the best tomatoes out. **11. pick up, a.** to lift or take up: to pick up a stone or to pick a stone up. **b.** to obtain or learn casually or as a result of occasional opportunity: He picked up English fairly quickly or He picked English up fairly quickly. **c.** to take on casually as a passenger: They picked up some guy on Interstate 40 or They picked some guy up on Interstate 40. **d.** to accelerate; gain (speed): The car picked up speed. **e.** to improve or recover: Business is picking up. **f.** to become acquainted with casually, often in hope of a sexual relationship: Let's try to pick up those girls or Let's try to pick those girls up. **12. pick up on,** Informal. to become aware of; notice: I picked up on his hostility right away. —n. **13.** [noncount] the act of selecting; choice: Take your pick. **14.** [count] a person or thing selected. **15.** [noncount] the best or most desirable part or example: This horse is the pick of the stable.

pick[2] /pɪk/ n. [count] **1.** a heavy tool coming to a point at one or both ends, used for breaking up soil, rock, etc. **2.** any pointed tool or instrument for picking: an ice pick. **3.** PLECTRUM.

pick·ax or **pick·axe** /'pɪk,æks/ n., pl. **-ax·es.** PICK[2] (def. 1).

pick·et /'pɪkɪt/ n. [count] **1.** a post driven into the ground for use in a fence or to fasten down a tent. **2.** a person stationed outside a store, etc., to persuade others not to enter it during a strike. —v. **3.** to be or place a picket (at): [~ + obj] The workers were picketing the shop. [no obj]: The employees were picketing for better working conditions.

pick·le /'pɪkəl/ n., v., **-led, -ling.** —n. **1.** [count] [noncount] a vegetable, esp. a cucumber, preserved and flavored in brine or vinegar. **2.** [noncount] a liquid prepared with salt or vinegar, for preserving or flavoring meat, etc. **3.** [count; usually singular; usually: a + ~] a troublesome situation; a difficulty: We're in a pickle now, surrounded by woods. —v. [~ + obj] **4.** to preserve or soak in brine or other liquid.

pick·pock·et /'pɪk,pɒkɪt/ n. [count] one who steals from the pockets of people, as in a crowded public place.

pick·up /'pɪk,ʌp/ n. **1.** [noncount] acceleration, or the ability to accelerate: not much pickup with such a small engine. **2.** [count] Also called **'pickup ,truck.** a small truck with an open back, used for hauling.

pick·y /'pɪkiy/ adj., **-i·er, -i·est.** fussy; too particular: a picky eater.

pic·nic /'pɪknɪk/ n., v., **-nicked, -nick·ing.** —n. [count] **1.** a trip or social gathering in which food is brought and a meal is shared in the open air. **2.** [used with negative words or phrases] Informal. an enjoyable experience, task, etc.: Three years in the Army was no picnic. —v. **3.** to go on or take part in a picnic. —'pic·nick·er, n. [count]

pic·to·ri·al /pɪk'tɔriyəl/ adj. of or relating to a picture; illustrated by or containing pictures: a pictorial biography.

pic·ture /'pɪktʃr/ n., v., **-tured, -tur·ing.** —n. [count] **1.** a representation of a person, object, or scene, as a painting, drawing, or photograph. **2.**

a mental image: *a picture in his mind of that beautiful mountain in Norway.* **3.** MOTION PICTURE (def. 2). **4.** [*the* + *~*] the image or perfect likeness of someone else: *She is the picture of her father.* **5.** the image on a television screen, motion-picture screen, or computer monitor. —*v.* [*~* + *obj*] **6.** to represent by or in a picture: *The artist pictured her as a young, pretty woman.* **7.** to form a mental picture of; imagine: *I can't picture him as president.*

pic•tur•esque /ˌpɪktʃə'rɛsk/ *adj.* charming or pleasing to the eye: *a picturesque village.*

pidg•in /'pɪdʒən/ *n.* [*count*] [*noncount*] a language that has developed from the need of speakers of two different languages to communicate and is primarily a simplified form of one of the languages.

pie /pay/ *n.* [*count*] [*noncount*] **1.** a crust of baked dough, filled with fruit, pudding, meat, etc. —*Idiom.* **2. easy as pie,** extremely easy or simple.

piece /piys/ *n., v.,* **pieced, piec•ing.** —*n.* [*count*] **1.** a portion or quantity of something: *a piece of land.* **2.** a portion of a whole: *a piece of apple pie.* **3.** an individual thing of a particular class or set: *a piece of furniture.* **4.** a created work of art, music, or writing: *He wrote a very funny piece for that magazine.* **5.** one of the figures, disks, or the like used in playing a board game: *a chess piece.* **6.** a coin: *a five-cent piece.* —*v.* **7. piece together,** to join together, as pieces or parts: *I pieced together the broken fragments* or *I pieced the broken fragments together.* —*Idiom.* **8. a piece of one's mind,** a sharp scolding or criticism: *He gave his daughter a piece of his mind when she came home so late.* **9. go to pieces,** to lose control of oneself: *After her son's death she simply went to pieces.* **10. in pieces,** destroyed; in ruins; not effective: *Careful plans of conquest lay in pieces.* **11. piece of cake,** *Informal.* something easily done: *Robbing the store was a piece of cake.*

piece•meal /'piys,miyl/ *adv.* **1.** one piece or stage at a time: *to work piecemeal.* —*adj.* **2.** done piecemeal.

pier /pɪər/ *n.* [*count*] a structure built on posts extending from land out over water, used as a landing place for ships and boats.

pierce /pɪərs/ *v.,* **pierced, pierc•ing. 1.** [*~* + *obj*] [*no obj*] to penetrate or go through (something), as a pointed object does. **2.** [*~* + *obj*] to make a hole or opening in: *She got her ears pierced.* **3.** [*~* + *obj*] to sound sharply through (the air, etc.): *A scream pierced the silence of the night.*

pi•e•ty /'payɪtiy/ *n.* [*noncount*] **1.** reverence for or devotion to God, or deep respect for religion. **2.** the quality or state of being pious.

pig /pɪg/ *n., v.,* **pigged, pig•ging.** —*n.* [*count*] **1.** a short, fat mammal with hooves and a curly tail, esp. one kept on a farm. **2.** one who eats too much, is greedy, or is very sloppy. —*v.* **3. pig out,** *Slang.* to eat too much food: *We pigged out on pizza last night.*

pi•geon /'pɪdʒən/ *n.* [*count*] a bird having a plump body and small head.

pi•geon•hole /'pɪdʒən,howl/ *n., v.,* **-holed, -hol•ing.** —*n.* [*count*] **1.** one of a series of small, open compartments in a desk or cabinet. —*v.* [*~* + *obj*] **2.** to assign to a definite place in an orderly system: *to pigeonhole the demonstrators as radicals.*

pigeon-,toed, *adj.* having the toes or feet turned inward.

pig•gish /'pɪgɪʃ/ *adj.* **1.** greedy; eating too much. **2.** stubborn.

pig•gy /'pɪgiy/ *n.* [*count*], *pl.* **-gies.** a small or young pig.

pig•gy•back /'pɪgiy,bæk/ *adv.* **1.** on the back or shoulders: *The child rode piggyback on her father.* —*adj.* [*before a noun*] **2.** on the back or shoulders: *a piggyback ride.* —*n.* [*count*] **3.** a piggyback ride.

'piggy ,bank, *n.* [*count*] a small bank, usually in the shape of a pig, with a slot to receive coins.

pig•head•ed /'pɪg,hɛdɪd/ *adj.* stupidly stubborn.

pig•let /'pɪglɪt/ *n.* [*count*] a little pig.

pig•ment /'pɪgmənt/ *n.* **1.** [*noncount*] [*count*] a dry substance that when mixed in liquid becomes a paint or dye. **2.** [*noncount*] any natural coloring substance, as chlorophyll or hemoglobin, that produces color in living things.

pig•men•ta•tion /ˌpɪgmən'teyʃən/ *n.* [*noncount*] coloring, esp. of the skin: *dark pigmentation.*

pig•pen /'pɪg,pɛn/ *n.* [*count*] a pen for keeping pigs.

pig•tail /'pɪg,teyl/ *n.* [*count*] a braid of hair hanging down the sides or the back of the head.

pike¹ /payk/ *n.* [*count*], *pl.* (*esp. when thought of as a group*) **pike,** (*esp. for kinds or species*) **pikes.** a large, slender, freshwater fish.

pike² /payk/ *n.* [*count*] a long weapon having a pointed head, formerly used by soldiers.

pile¹ /payl/ *n., v.,* **piled, pil•ing.** —*n.* [*count*] **1.** a group of things lying one upon the other: *a huge pile of papers.* **2.** a large number or amount of anything: *a pile of work.* —*v.* **3.** [*~* + *obj*] to put or lay in a pile: *to pile leaves.* **4.** to (cause to) be accumulated, gathered, or stored: [*~* + *obj*]: *to pile up money; The teacher really enjoys piling on the homework.* [*no obj*]: *His debts kept piling up.* **5.** [*~* + *obj*] to cover or load with a pile: *The back of the car was piled high with firewood.* **6.** [*no obj*] to move as a group in a more or less confused, disorderly manner: *They piled off the train.*

pile² /payl/ *n.* [*count*] a long piece of wood, concrete, etc., hammered upright into soil to form part of a foundation.

pile³ /payl/ *n.* [*noncount*] **1.** a surface or thickness of soft hair, down, etc. **2.** a soft surface on fabric, as velvet, formed by upright yarns.

pil•fer /'pɪlfər/ *v.* [*~* + *obj*] [*no obj*] to steal, esp. in small quantities.

pil•grim /'pɪlgrɪm, -grəm/ *n.* [*count*] **1.** a person on a pilgrimage. **2.** a traveler or wanderer, esp. in a foreign place.

pil•grim•age /'pɪlgrəmɪdʒ/ *n.* [*count*] [*noncount*] a journey, esp. a long one, made to some sacred or holy place as an act of religious devotion.

pill /pɪl/ *n.* **1.** [*count*] a small tablet or capsule of medicine. **2.** [*count*] *Slang.* a disagreeable person. **3. the pill,** an oral contraceptive for women.

pil•lage /'pɪlɪdʒ/ *v.* [*no obj*] [*~* + *obj*], **-laged, -lag•ing.** to steal goods by open violence and force, as in war; plunder.

pil•lar /'pɪlər/ *n.* [*count*] **1.** a tall, narrow column used as a building support, or standing alone, as for a monument. **2.** anything resembling this in shape: *a pillar of smoke.* **3.** a person important to a town, organization, etc.: *a pillar of the community.*

P

pil•low /ˈpɪloʊ/ n. [count] **1.** a cloth bag or case filled with feathers or other soft material, used to cushion the head during sleep. **2.** a small cushion used for decoration, as on a sofa.

pil•low•case /ˈpɪloʊˌkeɪs/ n. [count] a removable sacklike covering, usually of cotton, fitted over a pillow. Also called **pil•low•slip** /ˈpɪloʊˌslɪp/.

pi•lot /ˈpaɪlət/ n. [count] **1.** a person qualified to operate an airplane, balloon, or other aircraft. **2.** a person qualified to steer ships. **3.** a preliminary trial or test. —v. [~ + obj] **4.** to act as pilot on, in, or over.

pi•men•to /pɪˈmɛntoʊ/ n. [count], pl. **-tos.** the red, mild-flavored fruit of a sweet pepper used esp. as a stuffing for olives.

pimp /pɪmp/ n. [count] **1.** a man who finds customers for a prostitute. —v. [no obj] **2.** to act as a pimp.

pim•ple /ˈpɪmpəl/ n. [count] a small, usually inflamed swelling of the skin. —**pim•ply,** adj., **-pli•er, -pli•est.**

pin /pɪn/ n., v., **pinned, pin•ning.** —n. [count] **1.** a small, slender, pointed piece of metal, used esp. to fasten material together. **2.** any of many different badges or ornaments fastened to clothing with a pin: a fraternity pin; a tiepin; a diamond pin on her dress. **3.** any of the rounded wooden clubs set up as the target in bowling. —v. [~ + obj] **4.** to fasten or attach with pins: I pinned the pages together. **5.** to hold (something) still in a spot or position: He was pinned under the wreckage during the earthquake. **6. pin down,** to force (someone) to deal with a situation, answer a question directly, or come to a decision: I can't pin down the boss or I can't pin the boss down.

PIN /pɪn/ n. [count] personal identification number: a number assigned to a person so that he or she can use an ATM or other computerized service.

pin•a•fore /ˈpɪnəˌfɔr/ n. [count] a sleeveless, apronlike piece of clothing worn over a dress.

pin•cers /ˈpɪnsərz/ n. [plural] **1.** a gripping tool made of two joined and crossed parts forming a pair of jaws and a pair of handles. **2.** a pair of claws, as of a lobster.

pinch /pɪntʃ/ v. **1.** [~ + obj] to squeeze between the finger and thumb, the jaws of an instrument, or the like: She pinched the child's cheek. **2.** [~ + obj] [no obj] to squeeze painfully or tightly, as a tight shoe does. —n. [count] **3.** the act of pinching. **4.** as much of something as can be taken up between the finger and thumb: a pinch of salt for flavor. —**Idiom. 5. in a pinch,** if absolutely necessary, as in an emergency: In a pinch we could cut our meals down to two a day. **6. pinch pennies,** to spend very little money.

pin•cush•ion /ˈpɪnˌkʊʃən/ n. [count] a small cushion into which pins are stuck until needed.

pine[1] /paɪn/ n. [count] an evergreen tree having needlelike leaves and woody cones.

pine[2] /paɪn/ v. [no obj], **pined, pin•ing. 1.** to wish for or want deeply; long (for): pining for his family; pining to live in a free country. **2.** to fail gradually in health or strength because of grief or longing: After his wife's death he pined away.

pine•ap•ple /ˈpaɪnˌæpəl/ n. [count] [noncount] a juicy tropical fruit with a prickly skin.

pink /pɪŋk/ n. [noncount] **1.** a pale red color, a mixture of red and white. **2. in the pink,** in the highest form or degree of health: The economy is in the pink again.

pink•eye /ˈpɪŋkˌaɪ/ n. CONJUNCTIVITIS.

pink•ie or **pink•y** /ˈpɪŋkiy/ n. [count], pl. **-ies.** Informal. the little finger.

pin•na•cle /ˈpɪnəkəl/ n. [count] **1.** a high peak of a mountain, esp. one that is pointed. **2.** [often: the + ~] the highest point one can reach, as of success or power.

pin•point /ˈpɪnˌpɔɪnt/ v. [~ + obj] to locate or describe exactly or precisely: The pilot pinpointed the target.

'pins and 'needles, n. [plural] **1.** a tingly, prickly sensation in an arm, hand, foot, or leg that is recovering from numbness. —**Idiom. 2. on pins and needles,** in a state of nervous or anxious waiting.

pin•stripe /ˈpɪnˌstraɪp/ n. [count] a very thin stripe on a fabric, esp. a white stripe on a dark background.

pint /paɪnt/ n. [count] a liquid and dry measure of capacity, equal to one half of a quart.

pin•up /ˈpɪnˌʌp/ n. [count] a large photograph of a sexually attractive person, suitable for pinning on a wall.

pin•wheel /ˈpɪnˌhwiyl, -ˌwiyl/ n. [count] a toy consisting of a small wheel with vanes attached by a pin to a stick, designed to spin when blown.

pi•o•neer /ˌpaɪəˈnɪər/ n. [count] **1.** one of the first people to enter or settle a region: the early pioneers of the American West. **2.** one who is among the earliest in a field of study: a pioneer in using computers to teach language. —v. [~ + obj] [no obj] **3.** to be a pioneer (in).

pi•ous /ˈpaɪəs/ adj. having or showing strong belief in God or religion.

pipe /paɪp/ n., v., **piped, pip•ing.** —n. [count] **1.** a tube or cylinder of metal or other material, used for carrying water, gas, etc. **2.** a tube of wood, clay, or other material, with a bowl at one end, used for smoking tobacco. **3. a.** a musical wind instrument, as a flute, made of a single tube. **b.** one of the tubes through which air is forced and from which the tones of an organ are produced. **c.** pipes, [plural] BAGPIPE. —v. **4.** [~ + obj] [no obj] to play on a pipe. **5.** [~ + obj] to carry or send by or as if by pipes: to pipe music into the room. **6. pipe down,** Slang. to stop talking; be quiet: Tell the kids to pipe down. **7. pipe up,** to make oneself heard; speak up suddenly: She piped up with a good suggestion.

pipe•line /ˈpaɪpˌlaɪn/ n. [count] **1.** a series of pipes used to carry crude oil, water, etc., over great distances. **2.** a route or channel along which supplies or information pass.

pip•ing /ˈpaɪpɪŋ/ n. [noncount] **1.** a system of pipes. **2.** material formed into pipes. —**Idiom. 3. piping hot,** (of food or drink) very hot.

pip•squeak /ˈpɪpˌskwiyk/ n. [count] Informal. a small or unimportant person.

pi•quant /ˈpiykənt, -kɑnt, piyˈkɑnt/ adj. **1.** agreeably strong or sharp in taste. **2.** of an interesting and lively character: a piquant wit. —'pi•quan•cy /-ˈkænsiy/ n. [noncount]

pique /piyk/ v., **piqued, piqu•ing,** n. —v. [~ + obj] **1.** to cause anger in (someone) by an insult: He was piqued by nasty references to his teaching ability. **2.** to excite or arouse; provoke: The report piqued my curiosity. —n. [noncount] **3.** a feeling of irritation or resentment: He left the room in a fit of pique.

pi•ra•cy /ˈpaɪrəsiy/ n. [noncount] the practice of pirating.

pi•rate /ˈpaɪrət/ n., v., **-rat•ed, -rat•ing.** —n. [count] **1.** one who robs or commits illegal violence at sea. —*v.* [~ + *obj*] **2.** to steal from (ships) at sea. **3.** to use or copy (a book, an invention, etc.) without permission or legal right.

pir•ou•ette /ˌpɪruw'ɛt/ *n., v.,* **-et•ted, -et•ting.** —*n.* [*count*] **1.** a whirling about on one foot or on the points of the toes, as in ballet. —*v.* [*no obj*] **2.** to perform a pirouette.

pis•tach•i•o /pɪ'stæʃiy,ow, -'staʃiy,ow/ *n.* [*count*], *pl.* **-chi•os.** the nut of a tree of the cashew family, containing a greenish kernel.

pis•til /'pɪstl/ *n.* [*count*] the part of a flower carrying the seed.

pis•tol /'pɪstl/ *n.* [*count*] a short firearm intended to be held and fired with one hand.

pis•ton /'pɪstən/ *n.* [*count*] a disk or tube-shaped piece moving up and down inside a longer tube, used in engines.

pit¹ /pɪt/ *n., v.,* **pit•ted, pit•ting.** —*n.* [*count*] **1.** a hole or cavity in the ground. **2.** a natural hollow in the body or a small hollow mark on the skin. **3. the pits,** [*be* + ~] *Slang.* an extremely unpleasant or depressing place or condition: *Living there was the pits.* —*v.* [~ + *obj*] **4.** to mark or indent with pits. **5.** to set (two opponents) in combat: *The candidates were pitted against each other.*

pit² /pɪt/ *n., v.,* **pit•ted, pit•ting.** —*n.* [*count*] **1.** the stone of a fruit, as of a cherry or plum. —*v.* [~ + *obj*] **2.** to remove the pit from.

pi•ta /'piytə/ *n.* [*noncount*] a round, flat Middle Eastern bread having a pocket that can be filled to make a sandwich.

pitch¹ /pɪtʃ/ *v.* **1.** [~ + *obj*] to erect or set up (a tent, camp, etc.). **2.** *Baseball.* [~ + *obj*] [*no obj*] **a.** to throw (the ball) to the batter. **b.** to serve as pitcher of (a game). **3.** [*no obj*] [~ + *obj*] to (cause to) plunge with alternate fall and rise of bow and stern, as a ship. **4. pitch in,** *Informal.* to contribute to a common cause: *If everybody pitches in, we can finish this job.* —*n.* **5.** [*count; usually singular*] relative point, level, or degree: *a high pitch of excitement.* **6.** [*count*] the degree of tilt or slope of something: *The roof was at a steep pitch.* **7.** (in music or speech) the degree of height or depth of a sound: [*noncount*]: *a change in pitch.* [*count*]: *differences in the pitch of their voices.* **8.** [*count*] the act or manner of pitching, as in baseball. **9.** [*count*] *Informal.* a sales talk in which a salesperson tries to convince someone to buy something.

pitch² /pɪtʃ/ *n.* [*noncount*] a dark, sticky, thick substance used for repairing holes in ships or for paving roads.

'pitch-'black, *adj.* extremely black or dark.

pitch•er¹ /'pɪtʃər/ *n.* [*count*] a container for liquids, usually with a handle and spout.

pitch•er² /'pɪtʃər/ *n.* [*count*] a baseball player who throws the ball to the opposing batter.

pitch•fork /'pɪtʃ,fɔrk/ *n.* [*count*] a large, long-handled fork for lifting and pitching hay, etc.

pit•fall /'pɪt,fɔl/ *n.* [*count*] any trap, danger, or mistake that puts someone in danger.

pith /pɪθ/ *n.* [*noncount*] **1.** the soft, spongy tissue in the stems of certain plants and trees. **2.** the important or essential part: *the pith of the matter.*

pith•y /'pɪθiy/ *adj.,* **-i•er, -i•est.** brief, forceful, and to the point: *a pithy observation.*

pit•i•a•ble /'pɪtiyəbəl/ *adj.* **1.** arousing a feeling of pity. **2.** deserving contempt or scorn.

pit•i•ful /'pɪtɪfəl/ *adj.* **1.** arousing a feeling of pity; deserving pity: *a pitiful fate.* **2.** arousing contempt or scorn: *pitiful attempts to hide the truth.* —**'pit•i•ful•ly,** *adv.*

pit•i•less /'pɪtɪlɪs, 'pɪtiy-/ *adj.* feeling or showing no pity; merciless. —**'pit•i•less•ly,** *adv.*

pit•tance /'pɪtns/ *n.* [*count*] a small amount, esp. a very small amount of money: *working for a pittance.*

pit•y /'pɪtiy/ *n., pl.* **pit•ies,** *v.,* **pit•ied, pit•y•ing.** —*n.* **1.** [*noncount*] a feeling of sorrow or sympathy for another's suffering, distress, or misfortune. **2.** [*count; usually singular*] a cause or reason for pity, sorrow, or regret: *What a pity you couldn't go! It's a pity (that) you can't come to the party.* —*v.* [~ + *obj*] **3.** to feel pity for; be sorry for. —*Idiom.* **4. have** or **take pity on,** to have compassion for, or show mercy to: *He begged her to have pity on the prisoners.*

piv•ot /'pɪvət/ *n.* [*count*] **1.** a pin or point supporting something that turns on it: *a pivot on a gear mechanism.* **2.** a person or thing on which something else turns or depends: *She was the pivot of the campaign's success.* —*v.* [*no obj*] **3.** to turn on or as if on a pivot: *He pivoted on his heel and left the room.*

piv•ot•al /'pɪvətl/ *adj.* crucial; affecting the success of something: *a pivotal event.*

pix•ie or **pix•y** /'pɪksiy/ *n.* [*count*], *pl.* **pix•ies.** **1.** a fairy, esp. one who enjoys playing tricks. **2.** a playful person.

piz•za /'piytsə/ *n.* [*noncount*] [*count*], *pl.* **-zas.** a baked pie consisting of a thin layer of dough topped with tomato sauce, cheese, and often other toppings.

piz•ze•ri•a /ˌpiytsə'riyə/ *n.* [*count*], *pl.* **-ri•as.** a restaurant or bakery where pizzas are made and sold.

pj's or **p.j.'s** or **P.J.'s** /'piy,dʒeyz/ *n.* [*plural*] *Informal.* pajamas.

pkg., an abbreviation of: package.

pkwy., an abbreviation of: parkway.

pl., an abbreviation of: **1.** place. **2.** plural.

plac•ard /'plækard, -ərd/ *n.* [*count*] a sign or notice posted or carried in a public place.

pla•cate /'pleykeyt, 'plækeyt/ *v.* [~ + *obj*], **-cat•ed, -cat•ing.** to cause (someone) to stop being angry, resentful, etc., as by giving in to demands.

place /pleys/ *n., v.,* **placed, plac•ing.** —*n.* **1.** [*count*] a particular portion of space: *We visited a lot of places in Scotland.* **2.** [*count*] any part of a body, surface, or building; spot: *the places on her arm where she had been bitten.* **3.** [*count*] a space or seat for a person: *She saved my place on line.* **4.** [*count*] position or circumstances: *I would complain if I were in your place.* **5.** [*count; usually singular*] a function or duty: *It is not your place to offer criticism.* **6.** [*count*] a region or area: *to travel to distant places.* **7.** [*count; singular: in* + *the* + *a word indicating number or rank* + ~] (used to introduce each one of a series of examples, details, etc.; preceded by a word indicating number or rank): *We're not voting for him for two reasons: in the first place, there's too much unemployment; in the second place, we don't trust him.* —*v.* [~ + *obj*] **8.** to put in the proper position or order; arrange: *Place the silverware on the table.* **9.** to find a home, place, etc., for: *The foster home placed the orphan with a family.* **10.** to give (an order) to a store or company. **11.** to assign a certain position or rank to: *I would place him among the top five mathematicians in the world.* —*Idiom.* **12. go places,** to advance in one's career; succeed: *He was really going places until the scandal was made public.* **13. in place, a.** in the correct posi-

plant and tree

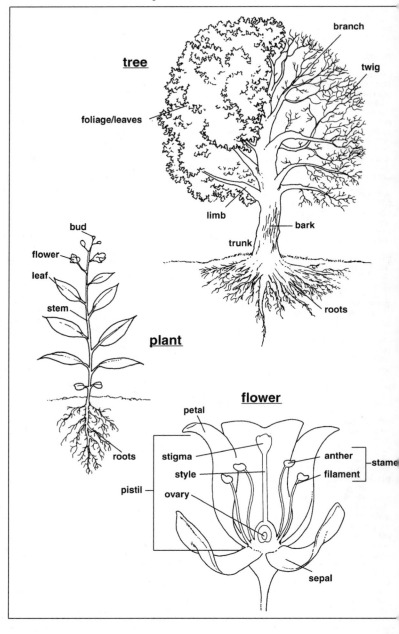

tree

branch

twig

foliage/leaves

limb

bark

trunk

roots

plant

bud

flower

leaf

stem

roots

flower

petal

stigma

style

ovary

pistil

anther

filament

stamen

sepal

tion or order: *Everything's back in place now that you've returned.* **b.** in the same spot, without advancing or retreating: *to jog in place.* **14. in place of,** instead of: *Use yogurt in place of sour cream.* **15. out of place, a.** not in the correct position or order: *These files are all out of place.* **b.** unsuitable; inappropriate: *Your remarks were out of place.* **16. put someone in his** or **her place,** to scold someone or remind someone of his or her position: *That clever answer really put the reporter in his place.* **17. take place,** to happen; occur: *A lot of things took place during your absence.* —'**place•ment,** *n.* [*noncount*] [*count*]

plac•id /'plæsɪd/ *adj.* pleasantly calm or peaceful.

pla•gia•rism /'pleydʒəˌrɪzəm/ *n.* [*noncount*] the act of stealing another's ideas, written passages, concepts, etc., and using them as one's own.

pla•gia•rize /'pleydʒəˌrayz/ *v.* [~ + *obj*] [*no obj*], **-rized, -riz•ing.** to steal by plagiarism. —'**pla•gia•rist,** *n.* [*count*]

plague /pleyg/ *n., v.,* **plagued, pla•guing.** —*n.* [*noncount*] [*count*] **1.** a widespread disease that causes a great number of deaths. —*v.* [~ + *obj*] **2.** to trouble, annoy, or torment in any manner.

plaid /plæd/ *n.* **1.** [*noncount*] a fabric woven of differently colored yarns in a pattern of squares. **2.** [*count*] a pattern of this kind.

plain /pleyn/ *adj.,* **-er, -est,** *adv., n.* —*adj.* **1.** easy to see or hear: *in plain view.* **2.** clear to the mind; evident: *He made his meaning plain.* **3.** [*before a noun*] complete; utter: *plain stupidity.* **4.** not beautiful; unattractive: *a plain face.* **5.** simple; not fancy: *a plain blue suit.* —*adv.* **6.** clearly and simply: *They're just plain stupid.* —*n.* [*count*] **7.** a large, flat area of land not higher than nearby areas. —'**plain•ly,** *adv.*

plain•tiff /'pleyntɪf/ *n.* [*count*] one who starts a legal action in a court.

plain•tive /'pleyntɪv/ *adj.* expressing sorrow or sadness; mournful: *a plaintive melody.* —'**plain• tive•ly,** *adv.*

plait /pleyt, plæt/ *n.* [*count*] **1.** a knot formed by twisting three or more lengths of rope, hair, etc., together; a braid. —*v.* [~ + *obj*] **2.** to form a plait; to braid.

plan /plæn/ *n., v.,* **planned, plan•ning.** —*n.* [*count*] **1.** a way, idea, or method of acting, proceeding, etc., developed in advance: *a battle plan.* **2.** an outline, diagram, or sketch that shows how things are arranged: *a building plan.* —*v.* [~ + *obj*] **3.** to put together a plan for: *The city wants to plan a new park.* **4.** to have in mind as an intention: *What are you planning for her retirement party? I planned to be there on time. I hadn't planned on seeing you today.*

plane¹ /pleyn/ *n.* [*count*] **1.** a flat or level surface. **2.** a level of dignity or character: *The candidates kept the debate on a high moral plane.* **3.** an airplane.

plane² /pleyn/ *n., v.,* **planed, plan•ing.** —*n.* [*count*] **1.** a tool for cutting or smoothing wood by means of a tilted blade. —*v.* [~ + *obj*] **2.** to smooth with or as if with a plane.

plan•et /'plænɪt/ *n.* [*count*] any of the nine large heavenly bodies revolving around the sun and shining by reflected light. —'**plan•e•tar•y** /'plænɪˌteriy/ *adj.*

plan•e•tar•i•um /ˌplænɪˈtɛəriyəm/ *n.* [*count*], *pl.* **-tar•i•ums, -tar•i•a** /-ˈtɛəriyə/. a building or room with equipment for projecting images of the movements of stars and planets.

plank /plæŋk/ *n.* [*count*] a long, flat piece of

wood, thicker than a board: *They used a couple of planks to walk across the stream.*

plank•ton /'plæŋktən/ *n.* [*noncount*] a mass of tiny animals or plants drifting in water.

plant /plænt/ *n.* [*count*] **1.** a living thing that usually has stems, leaves, and roots, and grows in the ground. **2.** a factory where a product is manufactured: *a steel plant.* —*v.* **3.** [~ + *obj*] [*no obj*] to put or set in the ground for growth, as seeds or young trees. **4.** [~ + *obj*] to stock with plants: *They planted a few acres with corn.* **5.** [~ + *obj*] to establish (ideas, etc.) in the mind; cause someone to believe (something): *Who planted that ridiculous idea in his head?* **6.** [~ + *obj*] to put in or set firmly in or on the ground: *to plant fence posts.* **7.** [~ + *obj*] to place (a spy) secretly in a group or organization.

plan•ta•tion /plæn'teyʃən/ *n.* [*count*] a usually large farm or land area, maintained by workers who live there: *a coffee plantation.*

plaque /plæk/ *n.* **1.** [*count*] a flat plate of metal, porcelain, etc., inscribed with words to honor someone, usually placed on a wall. **2.** [*noncount*] an abnormal, hardened deposit on the wall of an artery. **3.** [*noncount*] a sticky, whitish film that forms on tooth surfaces.

plas•ma /'plæzmə/ *n.* [*noncount*] the fluid part of blood, in which the cells are carried.

plas•ter /'plæstər/ *n.* [*noncount*] **1.** a pasty mixture of lime, sand, and water, applied to walls and ceilings and allowed to harden and dry. **2.** a solid preparation spread on cloth to form a case, then applied to the body, esp. to hold a broken limb in place. —*v.* [~ + *obj*] **3.** to cover or fill with plaster. **4.** to cause to lay flat: *He plastered his hair down with a greasy gel.* **5.** to spread or cover with something, esp. too much: *The students plastered the walls with posters.*

'**plaster of 'Paris** /'pærɪs/ *n.* [*noncount*] a white powdery substance used in making plasters and decorative casts.

plas•tic /'plæstɪk/ *n.* **1.** [*noncount*] [*count*] a substance made from oil or coal that may be shaped when soft and then hardened to a strong, lightweight material. —*adj.* **2.** made of plastic. **3.** capable of being shaped or molded.

'**plastic 'surgery,** *n.* [*noncount*] surgery that repairs or reshapes parts of the body or face. —'**plastic 'surgeon,** *n.* [*count*]

plate /pleyt/ *n., v.,* **plat•ed, plat•ing.** —*n.* **1.** [*count*] a flat, usually round dish from which food is eaten. **2.** [*noncount*] household dishes, utensils, etc., of metal covered with a thin layer of gold or silver. **3.** [*count*] a thin, flat sheet of metal or glass. **4.** [*count*] a sheet on which something has been engraved, to be inked and used in a printing press. —*v.* [~ + *obj*] **5.** to coat (metal) with a thin film of gold, silver, etc. **6.** to cover with metal plates for protection: *The tank was plated with thick armor.* —'**plat•ed,** *adj.*: *gold-plated silverware.*

pla•teau /plæ'tow/ *n.* [*count*], *pl.* **-teaus, -teaux** /-'towz, -towz/. **1.** a land area having a level surface raised much higher above nearby land. **2.** a state of little growth, esp. one in which progress stops: *He felt he'd reached a plateau in his career.*

plat•form /'plætfɔrm/ *n.* [*count*] **1.** a horizontal surface, usually raised above the level of the surrounding area. **2.** the raised area along the tracks of a railroad station, from which the train is entered. **3.** a public statement of the principles, aims, goals, etc., esp. of a political party.

P

plat•i•num /'plætṇəm, 'plætnəm/ *n.* [*noncount*] a grayish-white metal used esp. for jewelry.

pla•toon /plə'tuwn/ *n.* [*count*] a military unit consisting of two or more squads and a headquarters.

plat•ter /'plætər/ *n.* [*count*] a large, shallow dish for serving food.

plat•y•pus /'plætɪpəs/ *n.* [*count*], *pl.* **-pus•es,** **-pi** /-,pay/. an egg-laying animal of Australia and Tasmania, having a ducklike bill.

plau•si•ble /'plɔzəbəl/ *adj.* having an appearance of truth or reason; believable: *a plausible excuse.* —**plau•si•bil•i•ty** /,plɔzə'bɪlɪtiy/, *n.* [*noncount*]: *The story lacks plausibility.*

play /pley/ *n.* **1.** [*count*] a dramatic composition or performance; drama: *the plays of Shakespeare.* **2.** [*noncount*] activity done for recreation or amusement, as by children. **3.** [*count*] an act or instance of playing: *That one careless play may have cost us the match.* **4.** [*noncount*] manner or style of playing, or of behavior generally: *a believer in fair play.* **5.** [*count; usually singular*] quick, light, or changing movement: *the play of a water fountain.* **6.** [*noncount*] freedom for activity or movement: *to allow full play of the imagination.* **7.** [*noncount*] attention; coverage: *All those blunders got a lot of play in the newspapers.* —*v.* **8.** to portray; act the part of: [~ + *obj*]: *to play Macbeth.* [*no obj*]: *to play in several Broadway shows.* **9.** to (cause to) be performed or shown: [~ + *obj*]: *They're playing my favorite movie.* [*no obj*]: *What's playing on TV tonight?* **10.** to take part in (a game, sport, etc.); occupy oneself in some kind of recreation: [~ + *obj*]: *They played chess.* [*no obj*]: *playing with blocks.* **11.** to take part in a game against: [~ + *obj*]: *The girls' basketball team plays their rivals tonight.* [*no obj*]: *They play against their rivals for the championship.* **12.** [~ + *obj*] to perform in (a certain position or role) in a game or competition: *to play center field.* **13.** to perform on (a musical instrument): [~ + *obj*]: *She plays the trumpet.* [*no obj*]: *She doesn't play very well.* **14.** [~ + *obj*] to perform (music) on an instrument: *They played my favorite song.* **15.** to (cause to) produce sound or pictures: [~ + *obj*]: *They played the VCR.* [*no obj*]: *His radio was playing all night long.* **16.** [~ + *obj*] to carry out, esp. as a sly or dishonest action: *to play tricks.* **17.** [*no obj*] to joke around: *We were just playing; nobody meant to insult you.* **18.** [*no obj*] to act in a certain way: *to play fair.* **19.** **play along,** to pretend to agree to do something: *just playing along in order to get him to admit to his crime.* **20. a.** to pretend to do or be: *The kids were playing at being soldiers.* **b.** to do without being serious: *He was just playing at politics.* **21.** **play back,** to play (a recording, esp. one newly made): *The police played back the recording of him admitting his crimes. They played it back in the courtroom.* **22.** **play down,** to treat (something) as being of little importance; belittle: *The senator kept playing down the state of the economy. He tried to play it down.* **23.** **play on** or **upon,** to use the weaknesses of (another) for one's own gain; take advantage of: *to play on someone's generosity.* **24.** **play up,** to treat (something) as important; publicize: *In your job interview, try to play up your good points. Play your good points up during the interview.* **25.** **play up to,** to attempt to impress in order to gain the favor of: *playing up to the boss.* —*Idiom.* **26.** **make a play for,** to use maneuvers to attract, esp. sexually: *making a play for his pal's girlfriend.* **27.** **play a part,** to

have an effect on; contribute to: *Politics played an important part in the decision to fire him.*

play•boy or **-girl** /'pley,bɔy/ or /-,gɜrl/ *n.* [*count*] one who leads a life of pleasure without responsibility or attachments.

play•er /'pleyər/ *n.* [*count*] **1.** one who takes part in some game or sport. **2.** a performer on a musical instrument: *a horn player.*

play•ful /'pleyfəl/ *adj.* **1.** full of play or fun: *a playful puppy.* **2.** pleasantly humorous; meant to tease: *a playful remark.* —**'play•ful•ly,** *adv.* —**'play•ful•ness,** *n.* [*noncount*]

play•ground /'pley,grawnd/ *n.* [*count*] an area used by children for outdoor play activities.

play•mate /'pley,meyt/ *n.* [*count*] a companion, esp. of a child, in play or recreation.

'play on 'words, *n.* [*count*] a pun.

play•pen /'pley,pɛn/ *n.* [*count*] a small closed-in structure in which a baby can play.

play•wright /'pley,rayt/ *n.* [*count*] a writer of plays.

pla•za /'plɑzə, 'plæzə/ *n.* [*count*], *pl.* **-zas.** **1.** a public square in a city or town. **2.** a group of stores, banks, etc.; shopping center.

plea /pliy/ *n.* [*count*], *pl.* **pleas.** **1.** an appeal or request: *a plea for mercy.* **2.** a defendant's answer to a legal charge: *a plea of not guilty.*

plead /pliyd/ *v.*, **plead•ed** or **pled** /plɛd/, **plead•ing.** **1.** [*no obj*] to request sincerely; beg: *to plead for more time.* **2.** [~ + *obj*] to use as an excuse or defense: *He pleaded ignorance of the law.* **3. a.** [~ + *obj*] to argue (a case) before a court. **b.** to answer a charge (with a response): [*no obj*]: *How do you plead?* [~ + *obj*]: *He pled guilty.*

pleas•ant /'plɛzənt/ *adj.* **1.** pleasing, agreeable, or enjoyable: *the pleasant news of her promotion.* **2.** (of persons, manners, etc.) socially acceptable; polite: *a pleasant personality.* —**'pleas•ant•ly,** *adv.*: *She greeted me pleasantly.*

please /pliyz/ *adv.*, *v.*, **pleased,** **pleas•ing.** —*adv.* **1.** (used as a polite addition to a request) if you would be so willing; kindly: *Please come here. A cup of coffee, please.* —*v.* **2.** [~ + *obj*] to give pleasure, happiness, or gratification to: *You can't please everyone.* **3.** [*no obj*] to like, wish, or feel inclined; choose: *Go wherever you please. Ask anyone you please. Do as you please.*

pleas•ur•a•ble /'plɛʒərəbəl/ *adj.* that gives or causes pleasure: *a pleasurable experience.*

pleas•ure /'plɛʒər/ *n.* **1.** [*noncount*] enjoyment from something that one likes: *They get a lot of pleasure from their grandchildren.* **2.** [*count*] a cause or source of enjoyment or delight: *the pleasures of having children.* —**Idiom.** **3.** **with pleasure** or **my pleasure,** (used to express polite willingness to do what has been asked, or gracious satisfaction at having been helpful): *"Can you come tonight?" —"With pleasure." "Thanks for your help." —"My pleasure."*

pleat /pliyt/ *n.* [*count*] **1.** a fold in clothing made by doubling cloth or material upon itself. —*v.* [~ + *obj*] **2.** to arrange in pleats: *The skirt is pleated.*

plec•trum /'plɛktrəm/ *n.* [*count*], *pl.* **-tra** /-trə/, **-trums.** a small piece of plastic or metal used to pluck the strings of a guitar, banjo, etc.

pled /plɛd/ *v.* a pt. and pp. of PLEAD.

pledge /plɛdʒ/ *n.*, *v.*, **pledged,** **pledg•ing.** —*n.* [*count*] **1.** a solemn promise to do or stop doing something: *a pledge of economic aid.* —*v.* [~ + *obj*] **2.** to bind (someone) by or as if by a pledge: *pledged everyone to secrecy.* **3.** to promise solemnly: *to pledge support; She pledged to support him. He pledged that he would never be disloyal.*

plen•ti•ful /'plɛntɪfəl/ *adj.* providing or yielding an amount or quantity that is more than enough: *a plentiful harvest.* —**'plen•ti•ful•ly,** *adv.*

plen•ty /'plɛntiy/ *n.* **1.** a full supply or amount that is more than enough: [*used with a singular verb*]: *There is plenty of time.* [*used with a plural verb*]: *There are plenty of chairs.* **2.** [*noncount*] the state or quality of being plentiful; abundance: *the land's plenty.* —*adj.* **3.** more than enough: *This portion is plenty for me.*

pli•a•ble /'playəbəl/ *adj.* **1.** easily bent; flexible: *pliable leather.* **2.** easily influenced or persuaded.

pli•ant /'playənt/ *adj.* pliable. —**pli•an•cy** /'playənsiy/ *n.* [*noncount*]

pli•ers /'playərz/ *n.* small pincers, used for bending wire, holding small objects, etc.: [*plural; used with a plural verb*]: *The pliers are on the table.* [*a pair of + ~; used with a singular verb*]: *A pair of pliers is what I need.*

plight /playt/ *n.* [*singular*] a distressing situation: *in a sorry plight.*

plod /plɒd/ *v.* [*no obj*], **plod•ded, plod•ding. 1.** to walk heavily or with difficulty; trudge. **2.** to work or proceed with steady but slow or difficult progress: *He plodded along at his job.*

plop /plɒp/ *v.* [*no obj*] [*~ + obj*] **1.** to (cause to) fall and make a sound like that of something falling or dropping into water: *Big raindrops plopped against the window. The fisherman plopped the bait into the river.* **2.** to (cause to) drop or fall with full force or direct impact: *She plopped into her chair. He plopped the heavy bags down on the chair.* —*n.* [*count*] **3.** a plopping sound or fall. **4.** the act of plopping.

plot /plɒt/ *n., v.,* **plot•ted, plot•ting.** —*n.* [*count*] **1.** a secret plan to accomplish some purpose, esp. to do something wrong or illegal. **2.** the main events in a story: *the plot of a novel.* **3.** a small piece of ground: *a garden plot.* —*v.* **4.** [*~ + obj*] [*no obj*] to plan secretly. **5.** [*~ + obj*] to mark on a plan, chart, or graph, as the course of a ship or aircraft. —**'plot•ter,** *n.* [*count*]

plow /plaw/ *n.* [*count*] **1.** a large tool used in farming for turning over and breaking up soil. **2.** a tool resembling this, as a large shovel used to clear away snow from a road. —*v.* **3.** [*~ + obj*] [*no obj*] to turn up (soil) with a plow. **4.** to cut into or move through (a surface) as if with a plow: [*~ + obj*]: *The tornado plowed up an acre of trees.* [*no obj*]: *A bicycle plowed into the side of the car.* **5.** [*~ + obj*] [*no obj*] to clear (an area) by the use of a plow, esp. a snowplow. **6.** [*no obj*] to move along or proceed slowly and with great effort: *I still have to plow through a pile of reports.*

ploy /plɔy/ *n.* [*count*] an act or statement, usually a trick, to gain an advantage.

pluck /plʌk/ *v.* **1.** [*~ + obj*] to pull off from the place of growth, as fruit, flowers, or feathers. **2.** [*~ + obj*] to remove feathers or hair from by pulling: *to pluck a chicken.* **3.** to grasp or grab: [*~ + obj*]: *He plucked her sleeve to get her attention.* [*no obj*]: *He kept plucking at her sleeve.* **4.** [*~ + obj*] to sound (the strings of a musical instrument) by pulling at them with the fingers or a plectrum. —*n.* **5.** [*count*] the act of plucking; a tug. **6.** [*noncount*] courage; a desire not to give up or surrender: *He showed a lot of pluck by staying in the game.*

plug /plʌg/ *n., v.,* **plugged, plug•ging.** —*n.*

[*count*] **1.** a piece of wood or other material used to block a hole or opening: *He put plugs in his ears to keep out the noise.* **2.** an attachment at the end of an electrical cord, inserted into an electrical outlet. **3.** the favorable mention of a product, etc., as in a television interview. —*v.* **4.** [*~ + obj*] to block or fill up with or as if with a plug: *to plug a leak.* **5.** [*~ + obj*] to mention (a product) favorably: *He kept plugging his new book on the radio.* **6.** [*no obj*] to work with persistence on something: *She plugged away at her novel.* **7. plug in,** to connect to an electrical power source: *Plug in the TV* or *Plug the TV in.*

plum /plʌm/ *n., adj.,* **plum•mer, plum•mest.** —*n.* **1.** [*count*] a sweet, round fruit, usually red or purple. **2.** [*noncount*] a deep purple, between blue and red. —*adj.* [*before a noun*] **3.** desirable or rewarding: *a plum job.*

plum•age /'pluwmɪdʒ/ *n.* [*noncount*] the entire feathery covering of a bird.

plumb•er /'plʌmər/ *n.* [*count*] one who installs and repairs plumbing.

plumb•ing /'plʌmɪŋ/ *n.* [*noncount*] the system of pipes, drains, etc., for carrying water, liquid wastes, etc., as in a building.

plume /pluwm/ *n.* [*count*] a large, long feather, often used as an ornament.

plum•met /'plʌmɪt/ *v.* [*no obj*] to fall straight down; plunge.

plump /plʌmp/ *adj.,* **-er, -est.** well filled out or rounded in form; fleshy or fat. —**'plump•ness,** *n.* [*noncount*]

plun•der /'plʌndər/ *v.* **1.** to rob of valuables by force, as in war: [*~ + obj*]: *to plunder a town.* [*no obj*]: *The Vikings raided and plundered all along this coast.* —*n.* [*noncount*] **2.** that which is taken in plundering; loot.

plunge /plʌndʒ/ *v.,* **plunged, plung•ing,** *n.* —*v.* **1.** [*~ + obj*] to push (something) into something else with force: *He plunged a sword into his enemy's chest.* **2.** to (cause to) fall suddenly from a great height: [*no obj*]: *The car plunged into the sea.* [*~ + obj*]: *to plunge the car off the cliff.* **3.** to (cause to) be brought into some condition suddenly: [*~ + obj*]: *When the storm damaged the electrical wires, every house was plunged into darkness.* [*no obj*]: *to plunge into debt.* —*n.* [*count*] **4.** the act of plunging. —**Idiom. 5. take the plunge,** to enter upon a course of action, esp. after being uncertain: *They should take the plunge and get married.*

plu•ral /'plʊrəl/ *adj.* **1.** of or belonging to the form of a word used when referring to more than one person or thing: *The word* children *is the plural form of* child. —*n.* **2.** [*noncount*] the plural form. **3.** [*count*] a word in the plural.

plu•ral•ize /'plʊrə,layz/ *v.* [*~ + obj*], **-ized, -iz•ing.** to make plural in form.

plus /plʌs/ *prep., adj., n., pl.* **plus•es** or **plus•ses,** *conj.* —*prep.* **1.** increased by: *Ten plus two is twelve.* **2.** in addition to: *a salary plus benefits.* —*adj.* [*before a noun*] **3.** involving or naming the process of addition or adding: *Use a plus sign,* +, *between the numbers you are adding.* **4.** positive: *On the plus side, you'll have a wonderful house if you move there.* —*n.* [*count*] **5.** Also called **'plus ,sign.** the symbol (+) indicating addition or a positive amount. **6.** an advantage or gain: *It would be a tremendous plus for us to hire her.* —*conj.* **7.** also; furthermore: *It's safe, plus it's economical.*

plush /plʌʃ/ *adj.,* **-er, -est.** expensive and luxurious, in a showy way: *a plush hotel.*

P

plu•to•ni•um /pluw'towniyəm/ n. [noncount] a radioactive, metallic element used in nuclear reactors and weapons.

ply¹ /play/ v., **plied, ply•ing. 1.** [~ + obj] to carry on or continue doing steadily: to ply a trade. **2.** [~ + obj] to keep supplying or offering something to: He plied her with questions. She plied him with drink. **3.** to pass over or along steadily: [~ + obj]: boats plying the Mississippi. [no obj]: ships plying between Europe and America.

ply² /play/ n. [noncount] **1.** a measure of the thickness or layer of something: two-ply toilet paper. **2.** a unit of yarn: single ply.

ply•wood /'play,wʊd/ n. [noncount] a building material consisting of layers of wood glued over each other.

p.m. or **P.M.,** an abbreviation of Latin post meridiem: **1.** after noon (used with hours of a day). **2.** the period between noon and midnight.

pneu•mo•nia /nu'mownyə, nyu-/ n. [noncount] infection of the lungs caused by bacteria.

P.O., an abbreviation of: **1.** postal (money) order. **2.** post office.

poach¹ /powtʃ/ v. [no obj] [~ + obj] to hunt for (game or fish) illegally. —**'poach•er,** n. [count]

poach² /powtʃ/ v. [~ + obj] to cook (eggs, fish, etc.) in a hot liquid just below the boiling point.

pock•et /'pɒkɪt/ n. [count] **1.** a shaped piece of fabric attached to a garment and forming a pouch, used esp. for carrying small articles. **2.** a group or element that is different from whatever surrounds it: the few remaining pockets of resistance. —adj. [before a noun] **3.** small enough for carrying in the pocket: a pocket calculator. —v. [~ + obj] **4.** to put into one's pocket. **5.** to take as one's own, often dishonestly: to pocket public funds. —**Idiom. 6. out of pocket,** from one's own financial resources: out-of-pocket expenses.

poc•ket•book /'pɒkɪt,bʊk/ n. [count] a woman's purse or handbag.

pock•et•knife /'pɒkɪt,nayf/ n. [count], pl. **-knives.** a very small knife with one or more blades that fold into the handle.

pock•mark /'pɒk,mɑrk/ n. [count] a small pit on the skin, caused by chickenpox, acne, etc.

pod /pɒd/ n. [count] a long container or covering for a seed, as of the pea or bean.

po•di•a•try /pə'dayətriy, pow-/ n. [noncount] the care of the human foot, esp. the treatment of foot disorders. —**po'di•a•trist,** n. [count]

po•di•um /'powdiyəm/ n. [count], pl. **-di•ums, -di•a** /-diyə/. a small platform for an orchestra conductor, speaker, etc.

po•em /'powəm/ n. [count] a piece of writing in verse, esp. one offering an imaginative interpretation of the subject.

po•et /'powɪt/ n. [count] one who writes poetry.

po•et•ic /pow'ɛtɪk/ adj. **1.** of the nature of or resembling poetry. **2.** of, relating to, or characteristic of a poet or of poetry.

po•et•ry /'powɪtriy/ n. [noncount] poetic works; poems; verse.

poign•ant /'pɔynyənt, 'pɔynənt/ adj. **1.** distressing to the feelings; causing sadness. **2.** affecting the emotions: a poignant scene in the movie. —**'poign•an•cy,** n. [noncount] —**'poign•ant•ly,** adv.

poin•set•ti•a /pɔyn'sɛtiyə, -'sɛtə/ n. [count], pl. **-ti•as.** a plant having very bright red, pink, or white leaves.

point /pɔynt/ n. **1.** [count] a sharp, thin or narrow end, as of a knife. **2.** [count] a dot used in writing or printing, as in decimals. **3.** [count] a particular place; a spot: At several points along the highway, construction is in progress. **4.** [count] a degree or stage: the boiling point. **5.** [count] a particular instant of time: At that point, so late in the day, we were all very tired. **6.** the essential thing or idea; one's purpose: [count]: The speaker made three interesting points. [count; usually singular]: Please stop being vague and get to the point. What's the point of going on? [noncount]: There's no point in continuing the discussion. **7.** [count] a particular mark that distinguishes someone or something from another: His best point is his ability to work alone. **8.** [count] a unit of counting in the score of a game: Our team scored thirteen points. —v. **9.** to aim or direct (the finger, a weapon, etc.) toward something: [~ + obj]: He pointed the gun at the target. [no obj]: In some cultures it is rude to point at a person. **10.** [~ + obj] to stretch or extend (the fingers, toes, etc.). **11. point out, a.** to show the presence or position of (something), as by moving the finger in the direction of it: She pointed out her friend or She pointed her friend out. **b.** to direct or call attention to: pointed out several advantages; pointed them out; pointed out that there was still a chance to win. **12. point to** or **toward,** to direct the mind in some direction; be a sign or signal of: The evidence points to their guilt. —**Idiom. 13. beside the point,** not important to, or related to, what is being discussed: Her comments about his money are beside the point. **14. make a point of,** to be sure to (do something): Make a point of checking your work. **15. to the point,** important to (the thing being discussed); relevant: His answers were brief but to the point. —**'point•y,** adj., **-i•er, -i•est.**

'point-'blank, adj. **1.** aimed or fired close to or near the target: a point-blank shot. **2.** straightforward; plain; direct: a point-blank denial. —adv. **3.** with a direct aim; directly; straight. **4.** in a blunt way; frankly.

point•er /'pɔyntər/ n. [count] **1.** a long stick used in pointing things out on a map, blackboard, or the like. **2.** the hand on a watch, clock, etc. **3.** a piece of advice, esp. on how to succeed.

point•less /'pɔyntlɪs/ adj. meaningless; useless: This whole discussion is pointless.

'point of 'view, n. [count; usually singular] **1.** a way of looking or thinking about something: We need a fresh point of view. **2.** an opinion or judgment: He refuses to change his point of view.

poise /pɔyz/ n., v., **poised, pois•ing.** —n. [noncount] **1.** a dignified, calm, and confident manner: She showed great poise in giving her speech. —v. [~ + obj] **2.** to put in a balanced position, as for use: The hunter poised the spear.

poised /pɔyzd/ adj. **1.** having poise: a poised speaker. **2.** close to or ready for (something): The armies were poised for attack. He was poised to win the championship.

poi•son /'pɔyzən/ n. [noncount] [count] **1.** a substance that taken into the body can cause illness or death. —v. [~ + obj] **2.** to kill or injure with or as if with poison. **3.** to put poison into or upon: The drink was poisoned. **4.** to ruin or corrupt: Hatred had poisoned their minds.

'poison 'ivy, n. [noncount] **1.** a vine with groups of three leaves and whitish berries. **2.** the rash caused by touching poison ivy.

poi•son•ous /'pɔyzənəs/ adj. full of or containing poison.

poke /powk/ v., **poked, pok•ing,** n. —v. **1.** [~ + obj] to push, esp. with something pointed: She poked him in the ribs with her elbow. **2.** [~ + obj] [no obj] to make (a hole, etc.) by or as if by pushing. **3.** to push (out) or extend: [~ + obj]: She poked her head out of the window. [no obj]: a handkerchief poking out of his pocket. **4.** to push (oneself) into the affairs of others: [~ + obj]: always poking himself into our affairs. [no obj]: They poked into her private life. **5. poke around,** to search impolitely into the affairs of another: She was poking around on my desk, looking for the letter. **6.** [no obj] to proceed slowly: The horse was just poking along the road. —n. [count] **7.** a push. —**Idiom. 8. poke fun at,** to make fun of; mock: The kids poked fun at him for his clothes. **9. poke one's nose into,** to interfere in; pry into: He poked his nose into everyone's business.

pok•er[1] /'powkər/ n. [count] a metal rod for poking or stirring a fire.

pok•er[2] /'powkər/ n. [noncount] a card game in which the players bet on the value of their hands.

pok•y /'powkiy/ adj., **-i•er, -i•est.** slow in an annoying way.

po•lar /'powlər/ adj. [before a noun] **1.** of or relating to any pole, as of the earth. **2.** opposite in character or action: There were polar differences between the candidates.

'polar ,bear, n. [count] a large white bear of arctic regions.

po•lar•ize /'powlə,rayz/ v. [~ + obj], **-ized, -iz•ing.** to divide into sharply opposing groups: an issue that polarized the city's voters. —**po•lar•i•za•tion,** n. [noncount]

pole[1] /powl/ n. [count] a long, rounded, narrow piece of wood, metal, etc.: telephone poles.

pole[2] /powl/ n. [count] **1.** each of the ends of the axis of the earth or of any rounded body. **2.** one of two opposite principles, of interest, etc. **3.** either of the two regions of an electric battery or magnet that are opposite in charge.

Pole /powl/ n. [count] a person born or living in Poland.

pole•cat /'powl,kæt/ n. [count], pl. **-cats,** (esp. when thought of as a group) **-cat. 1.** a European weasel that sends out a bad-smelling fluid when it is attacked. **2.** a North American skunk.

po•lice /pə'liys/ n., v., **-liced, -lic•ing.** —n. [plural; used with a plural verb; often: the + ~] **1.** an organized, nonmilitary force for maintaining order, detecting crime, and enforcing the laws. —v. [~ + obj] **2.** to regulate or keep in order by or as if by means of police: Squad cars policed the area.

po•lice•man or **-wom•an** /pə'liysmən/ or /,wumən/ n. [count], pl. **-men** or **-wom•en.** a member of a police force.

po'lice 'officer, n. [count] a member of a police force.

pol•i•cy[1] /'pɒləsiy/ n., pl. **-cies.** a definite course of action followed by a business, government, etc: [count]: a new company policy. [noncount]: U.S. trade policy.

pol•i•cy[2] /'pɒləsiy/ n. [count], pl. **-cies.** a document stating the terms of a contract or agreement for insurance.

pol•i•cy•hold•er /'pɒləsiy,howldər/ n. [count] the individual or business in whose name an insurance policy is written.

po•li•o•my•e•li•tis /,powliyow,mayə'laytɪs/ also **po•li•o** /'powliyow/ n. [noncount] a disease

of the spinal cord and brain, often causing paralysis.

pol•ish /'pɒlɪʃ/ v. [~ + obj] **1.** to make smooth, shiny, and glossy, esp. by rubbing: She polished her shoes. **2.** to make (something) complete or perfect: She stayed up late to polish her speech. **3. polish off,** to finish or dispose of quickly: We polished off the cake in one day or We polished the cake off in one day. —n. **4.** a substance used to give smoothness or gloss: [noncount]: silver polish. [count]: the polishes and waxes. **5.** [count] the act of polishing. **6.** [noncount] smoothness of a surface. **7.** [noncount] perfection; refinement; elegance: He behaves with such polish and good manners.

Po•lish /'powlɪʃ/ adj. **1.** of or relating to Poland, its people, or their language. —n. [noncount] **2.** the language spoken in Poland.

po•lite /pə'layt/ adj., **-lit•er, -lit•est. 1.** showing good manners; courteous: a polite reply. **2.** refined or cultured: polite society. —**po'lite•ly,** adv. —**po'lite•ness,** n. [noncount]

po•lit•i•cal /pə'lɪtɪkəl/ adj. of, relating to, or concerned with government or politics. —**po'lit•i•cal•ly,** adv.: politically involved.

po'litically cor'rect, adj. conforming to language, behavior, or attitudes that do not offend minority groups, disabled people, homosexuals, etc.

po'litical 'science, n. [noncount] a social science dealing with political institutions and government.

pol•i•ti•cian /,pɒlɪ'tɪʃən/ n. [count] one who is active in politics, esp. as a career.

pol•i•tics /'pɒlɪtɪks/ n. **1.** [noncount; used with a singular verb] the science or art of government. **2.** [plural; used with a plural verb] political principles or opinions: His politics are quite conservative. **3.** [plural; used with a plural verb] the use of schemes and secrecy to obtain power or control: Office politics are getting worse these days.

pol•ka /'powlkə, 'powkə/ n. [count], pl. **-kas.** a lively dance for couples.

'polka ,dot, n. [count] **1.** a dot repeated to form a pattern on a fabric. **2.** a pattern of such dots.

poll /powl/ n. [count] **1.** a survey of opinions by asking the same questions to a group of people. **2.** Usually, **polls.** [plural] the place where votes are cast: Polls are open until nine o'clock. —v. [~ + obj] **3.** to ask (someone) for his or her opinions: Students were polled on their food preferences.

pol•len /'pɒlən/ n. [noncount] the powdery, yellowish grains on flowering plants that fertilize other plants.

pol•li•nate /'pɒlə,neyt/ v. [~ + obj], **-nat•ed, -nat•ing.** to make (a flower) produce seeds by carrying pollen to it. —**pol•li•na•tion** /,pɒlə'neyʃən/, n. [noncount]

poll•ster /'powlstər/ n. [count] one whose occupation is the taking of public-opinion polls.

pol•lu•tant /pə'luwtnt/ n. [count] something that pollutes or contaminates.

pol•lute /pə'luwt/ v. [~ + obj], **-lut•ed, -lut•ing. 1.** to make foul or unclean, esp. with harmful chemical or waste products; contaminate: to pollute the air with smoke. **2.** to make morally unclean: to pollute the mind with bigotry. —**pol'lut•er,** n. [count] —**pol'lu•tion,** n. [noncount]

po•lo /'powlow/ n. [noncount] a game played on

horseback between two teams, who score points by driving a ball with a mallet.

poly-, a combining form meaning much or many (*polygamy*).

pol•y•es•ter /'pɒliy,ɛstər/ n. [noncount] a synthetic fabric used esp. for clothes.

po•lyg•a•my /pə'lɪgəmiy/ n. [noncount] the practice of having more than one spouse, esp. more than one wife, at one time.

pol•y•gon /'pɒliy,gɒn/ n. [count] a closed flat figure, having three or more straight sides.

pol•yp /'pɒlɪp/ n. **1.** [count] [noncount] the rounded body form in the life cycle of a jellyfish or similar animal, having stinging tentacles around the mouth. **2.** [count] a growth on a mucous surface of the body, as the inside of the nose.

pol•y•sty•rene /,pɒliy'stayriyn, -'stɪəriyn/ n. [noncount] a stiff, light plastic used for making disposable containers, etc.

pol•y•un•sat•u•rat•ed /,pɒliyʌn'sætʃə,reytɪd/ adj. (of a food) made from vegetable fats and associated with a low cholesterol content of the blood.

pomp /pɒmp/ n. [noncount] grand display; splendor; magnificence.

pom•pom or **pom-pom** /'pɒm,pɒm/ n. [count] an ornamental ball of strips or streamers. Also, **pom•pon** /'pɒmpɒn/.

pomp•ous /'pɒmpəs/ adj. having or showing too much self-importance. —**pom•pos•i•ty** /pɒm'pɒsɪtiy/, n. [noncount] —'**pomp•ous•ly,** adv.

pon•cho /'pɒntʃow/ n. [count], pl. **-chos. 1.** a blanketlike cloak with an opening in the center for the head, originally worn in South America. **2.** a waterproof garment styled like this.

pond /pɒnd/ n. [count] a body of water smaller than a lake, sometimes artificially formed.

pon•der /'pɒndər/ v. [no obj] [~ + obj] to consider something deeply, thoughtfully, and thoroughly.

pon•der•ous /'pɒndərəs/ adj. **1.** of great weight; heavy; massive. **2.** dull.

pon•tiff /'pɒntɪf/ n. [count; usually: the + ~] the Roman Catholic pope.

po•ny /'powniy/ n. [count], pl. **-nies.** a small horse of any of several breeds.

po•ny•tail /'powniy,teyl/ n. [count] hair gathered at the back of the head and fastened so as to hang down.

pooch /puwtʃ/ n. [count] Informal. a dog.

poo•dle /'puwdl̩/ n. [count] a dog with long, thick, frizzy or curly hair.

pool¹ /puwl/ n. [count] **1.** a small body of standing water; a small pond. **2.** any small collection of liquid on a surface; puddle: a pool of blood. **3.** a large, artificial basin filled with water for swimming.

pool² /puwl/ n. **1.** [noncount] a game in which a stick is used to drive balls into pockets on a table. **2.** [count] a combination of resources, funds, etc., dedicated to some common purpose. **3.** [count] a facility or service shared by a group of people: I joined a car pool to get to and from work. —v. [~ + obj] **4.** to put (resources, etc.) into a common fund, as for a business.

poop /puwp/ v. [~ + obj] Informal. to cause to become out of breath or exhausted: I was pooped after the long hike.

poor /pʊr/ adj., **-er, -est,** n. —adj. **1.** having little or no money or resources: He came from a poor

family. **2.** low in quality; inferior: poor workmanship. **3.** [before a noun] wretched; unfortunate: That poor cat looks so skinny. **4.** not much in amount; scanty or meager: poor attendance. —n. **5. the poor,** [plural; used with a plural verb] poor persons thought of as a group: aid for the poor.

poor•ly /'pʊrliy/ adv. not well; badly: poorly paid workers.

pop¹ /pɒp/ v., **popped, pop•ping,** n., adv. —v. **1.** to (cause to) make a short, quick, explosive sound: [no obj]: The cork popped. [~ + obj]: He popped the cork off the bottle. **2.** to burst open with such a sound: [no obj]: The popcorn has finished popping. [~ + obj]: Someone was popping all the balloons. **3.** [no obj] to come or go quickly, suddenly, or when not expected: She just popped by and said hello. **4.** [~ + obj] to put or thrust quickly: Pop the muffins into the oven. **5. pop up,** to appear or show up suddenly: She pops up at the oddest times. —n. [count] **6.** a short, quick, explosive sound. **7.** a popping. **8.** SODA POP.

pop² /pɒp/ n. [noncount] modern popular music with a strong beat. Also called '**pop 'music.**

pop., an abbreviation for: population.

pop•corn /'pɒp,kɔrn/ n. [noncount] any of several varieties of corn whose kernels burst open and puff out when heated.

Pope /powp/ n. [sometimes: pope] the head of the Roman Catholic Church.

pop•lar /'pɒplər/ n. [count] a rapidly growing tree of the willow family.

pop•py /'pɒpiy/ n. [count], pl. **-pies.** a plant having showy, usually red flowers.

pop•u•lace /'pɒpyələs/ n. [count] the people living in a place; population.

pop•u•lar /'pɒpyələr/ adj. **1.** looked on or thought of with approval or affection by people in general; well-liked; admired: a popular preacher. **2.** [before a noun] of or relating to the common people or the people as a whole: popular government. —,**pop•u'lar•i•ty,** n. [noncount] —'**pop•u•lar•ly,** adv.

pop•u•late /'pɒpyə,leyt/ v. [~ + obj], **-lat•ed, -lat•ing.** to inhabit; live in: The region was populated by immigrants.

pop•u•la•tion /,pɒpyə'leyʃən/ n. the total number of persons, animals, or other living things living in a country, city, etc.: [count]: a population of over two billion people. [noncount]: a decrease in population.

pop•u•lous /'pɒpyələs/ adj. containing many people; heavily populated: a populous area.

por•ce•lain /'pɔrsəlɪn, pɔrslɪn/ n. [noncount] a hard, shiny substance made by baking clay, used to make dishes.

porch /pɔrtʃ/ n. [count] an outside addition to a building with a roof but no walls.

por•cu•pine /'pɔrkyə,payn/ n. [count] a large rodent having stiff, sharp quills.

pore¹ /pɔr/ v., **pored, por•ing. pore over,** to read or study with great attention, concentration, or hard work: poring over old manuscripts in the library.

pore² /pɔr/ n. [count] a very small opening, as in the skin or a leaf, for perspiration, absorption, etc.

pork /pɔrk/ n. [noncount] the flesh of a hog or pig used as food.

porn /pɔrn/ n. [noncount] Informal. pornography.

por•nog•ra•phy /pɔr'nɒgrəfiy/ n. [noncount]

writings, photographs, etc., intended to arouse sexual desire. —**por•no'graph•ic,** *adj.*

po•rous /'pɔrəs/ *adj.* allowing water, air, etc., to pass through.

por•poise /'pɔrpəs/ *n.* [count], *pl.* (*esp. when thought of as a group*) **-poise,** (*esp. for kinds or species*) **-pois•es.** a marine mammal resembling a dolphin.

por•ridge /'pɔrɪdʒ, 'pɒr-/ *n.* [noncount] a thick cereal made esp. of oatmeal boiled in water or milk.

port¹ /pɔrt/ *n.* [count] **1.** a city or town where ships load or unload. **2.** a place where ships may be safe from storms; harbor.

port² /pɔrt/ *n.* [noncount] the left-hand side of a ship or aircraft, facing forward.

port³ /pɔrt/ *n.* [noncount] a very sweet, dark red wine, originally from Portugal.

port•a•ble /'pɔrtəbəl/ *adj.* **1.** that can be transported: *a portable stage.* **2.** easily carried by hand: *a portable radio.* —**port•a•bil•i•ty** /ˌpɔrtə'bɪlɪtiy/, *n.* [noncount]

por•ter /'pɔrtər/ *n.* [count] **1.** one hired to carry baggage, as at a hotel. **2.** one who does cleaning, repairs, etc., in a building, store, etc.

port•fo•li•o /pɔrt'fowliyˌow/ *n.* [count], *pl.* **-li•os. 1.** a flat, thin, portable case for carrying loose papers, etc. **2.** the stocks, bonds, etc., held by an investor.

port•hole /'pɔrtˌhowl/ *n.* [count] a round, windowlike opening in the side of a ship.

por•tion /'pɔrʃən/ *n.* [count] **1.** a part or share of a whole; a segment: *a portion of the work.* **2.** an amount of food served to one person; serving; helping.

port•ly /'pɔrtliy/ *adj.*, **-li•er, -li•est.** rather heavy or fat.

por•trait /'pɔrtrɪt, -treyt/ *n.* [count] **1.** a drawing or painting of a person, esp. of the face. **2.** a description of a person, in words or writing: *The book gives an interesting portrait of the movie star.*

por•tray /pɔr'trey/ *v.* [~ + *obj*] **1.** to make a portrait. **2.** to describe in words, esp. in a certain way: *In that TV program the father is portrayed as lovable but foolish.* **3.** to represent dramatically, as on the stage: *the actor who portrayed Napoleon.* —**por'tray•al,** *n.* [count]

Por•tu•guese /ˌpɔrtʃə'giyz, -'giys, pɔrtʃəˌgiyz, -ˌgiys/ *adj., n., pl.* **-guese.** —*adj.* **1.** of or relating to Portugal. **2.** of or relating to the language spoken in Portugal and Brazil. —*n.* **3.** [*plural*] **the Portuguese,** the people of Portugal. **4.** [noncount] the language spoken in Portugal and Brazil.

pose /powz/ *v.*, **posed, pos•ing,** *n.* —*v.* **1.** to (cause to) get into or hold a physical position, as for an artistic purpose: [no obj]: *to pose for a painter.* [~ + *obj*]: *The photographer posed the group.* **2.** [no obj] to pretend to be what one is not: *The thieves posed as police officers.* **3.** [~ + *obj*] to state for others to consider; to present: *Let me pose a question to you.* **4.** [~ + *obj*] to cause (something) to exist; create: *Her odd behavior poses problems.* —*n.* [count] **5.** a way of holding the body in a certain position, esp. for an artistic purpose.

posh /pɒʃ/ *adj.*, **-er, -est.** stylishly elegant; grand; luxurious.

po•si•tion /pə'zɪʃən/ *n.* **1.** [count] location; situation; condition with regard to place: *the position of the moon in the sky.* **2.** [count] a place occupied or to be occupied; site: *The headquarters*

was a well-fortified position. **3.** [count; usually singular] situation or condition, esp. in relation to circumstances: *Her absence put us in an awkward position.* **4.** [count] status or standing; rank. **5.** [count] a job. **6.** [count] an attitude, opinion, or belief. —*v.* [~ + *obj*] **7.** to put (something) in a particular, proper, or correct position: *He positioned himself next to the president.*

pos•i•tive /'pɒzɪtɪv/ *adj.* **1.** confident in belief or in what one says; sure: *He is positive that he'll win.* **2.** expressing agreement; favorable: *a positive reaction to his speech.* **3.** expressing a statement that indicates or means "yes": *a positive answer.* **4.** emphasizing what is hopeful about a situation: *Be more positive in your outlook on life.* **5.** clear; definite: *a positive denial.* **6.** relating to the electricity in a body lacking in electrons: *a positive charge.* **7.** (of a medical test) indicating the presence of the disease, condition, etc., tested for.

pos•i•tive•ly /'pɒzɪtɪvliy *or, esp. for 2,* ˌpɒzɪ'tɪvliy/ *adv.* **1.** with certainty; absolutely: *It's better to think positively instead of negatively.* **2.** definitely; without question: *Her behavior was positively disgusting!*

pos•se /'pɒsiy/ *n.* [count] a group of people brought together to assist a sheriff.

pos•sess /pə'zɛs/ *v.* [~ + *obj*] **1.** to have (something) as belonging to one; own: *Everything they possessed was lost in the war.* **2.** (of a spirit or a feeling) to control (a person) from within: *She was possessed by demons.*

pos•ses•sion /pə'zɛʃən/ *n.* **1.** [noncount] the act or fact of possessing: *She took possession of the house.* **2.** [noncount] ownership. **3.** [count] a thing possessed or owned: *her favorite possession, a teddy bear.*

pos•ses•sive /pə'zɛsɪv/ *adj.* **1.** desiring to dominate and be the controlling influence on someone: *a jealous, possessive husband.* **2.** unwilling to share with other people; selfish. **3.** (of a word, construction, or grammatical case) showing possession, ownership, origin, etc., as *Jane's* in *Jane's coat.*

pos•si•bil•i•ty /ˌpɒsə'bɪlɪtiy/ *n., pl.* **-ties. 1.** [noncount] the state or fact of being possible: *the possibility of error.* **2.** [count] something possible: *had tried every possibility but one.*

pos•si•ble /'pɒsəbəl/ *adj.* **1.** that may or can exist, happen, be done, be used, etc.: *a possible cure.* **2.** that may be true or may be the case: *It is possible that she has already gone.*

pos•sib•ly /'pɒsəbliy/ *adv.* **1.** perhaps; maybe: *It may possibly rain today.* **2.** by any possibility; reasonably: *She has all the money she can possibly use.*

pos•sum /'pɒsəm/ *n.* [count], *pl.* **-sums,** (*esp. when thought of as a group*) **-sum. 1.** OPOSSUM. —*Idiom.* **2. play possum,** to pretend to be asleep or dead.

post¹ /powst/ *n.* [count] **1.** a piece of wood or metal fixed into the ground and used as a support, to mark off something, etc. —*v.* [~ + *obj*] **2.** to put up (a public notice).

post² /powst/ *n.* [count] **1.** a position of duty or trust to which one is assigned: *a responsible post in government.* **2.** a permanent military station. —*v.* [~ + *obj*] **3.** to place or station at a post.

post³ /powst/ *n.* [noncount] **1.** Chiefly Brit. **a.** a single collection or delivery of mail. **b.** a mail system. —*v.* [~ + *obj*] **1.** to supply with up-to-date information: *Keep me posted on your activities.* **3.** Chiefly Brit. to send by mail.

P

post-, a prefix meaning: following, after, or behind (*postwar*).

post•age /'powstɪdʒ/ n. [noncount] the charge for sending something by mail.

post•al /'powstl/ adj. of or relating to the post office or mail service.

post•card /'powst,kɑrd/ n. [count] a small printed card for mailing a message without an envelope.

post•er /'powstər/ n. [count] a large, stiff piece of paper with a message on it, posted in a public place.

pos•te•ri•or /pɒ'stɪəriyər, pow-/ adj. **1.** [before a noun] located behind or at the rear of. **2.** coming after (something) in order or in time; later.

pos•ter•i•ty /pɒ'stɛrɪtiy/ n. [noncount] future generations; one's descendants: He hoped that posterity would view him as a hero.

post•man /'powstmən/ n., pl. -men. MAIL CARRIER.

post•mark /'powst,mɑrk/ n. [count] **1.** an official mark stamped on mail, showing the place and date of sending or receipt. —v. [~ + obj] **2.** to stamp with a postmark.

'**post ,office,** n. [count] a government office at which mail is received and sorted and from which it is delivered.

post•pone /powst'pown, pows-/ v. [~ + obj], -poned, -pon•ing. to put (something) off to a later time: We have postponed our departure until tomorrow. —post'pone•ment, n. [count] [noncount]

post•script /'powst,skrɪpt, 'pows-/ n. [count] a paragraph, sentence, etc., added to a letter already finished and signed by the writer. Abbr.: P.S.

pos•ture /'pɒstʃər/ n. [noncount] [count] the position of the arms, legs, etc., or the way the body is held by a person when standing or walking.

pot¹ /pɒt/ n., v., pot•ted, pot•ting. —n. [count] **1.** a container made of baked clay, metal, etc., used for cooking, serving, and other purposes. **2.** FLOWERPOT. —v. [~ + obj] **3.** to put into a pot: to pot a plant.

pot² /pɒt/ n. [noncount] Slang. marijuana.

po•tas•si•um /pə'tæsiyəm/ n. [noncount] a silvery white metallic chemical element, used in making fertilizer and found in bananas and other foods.

po•ta•to /pə'teytow, -tə/ n. [count] [noncount], pl. -toes. a white vegetable with a brown or reddish skin that grows underground.

po'tato ,chip, n. [count] a thin slice of potato fried until crisp and usually salted.

pot•bel•ly /'pɒt,bɛliy/ n. [count], pl. -lies. a rounded belly or stomach that sticks out.

po•tent /'powtnt/ adj. **1.** powerful; mighty: a potent air force. **2.** (of a male) capable of having sexual relations. —'po•ten•cy, n. [noncount]

po•ten•tial /pə'tɛnʃəl/ adj. [before a noun] **1.** possible, as opposed to actual; that might or could be true but is not yet so: the potential uses of nuclear energy. **2.** capable of being or becoming: a potential danger. —n. [noncount] **3.** possibility: That investment has little growth potential. **4.** a talent or ability that is present but not yet developed: She had great potential as a gymnast.

pot•hold•er /'pɒt,howldər/ n. [count] a thick piece of material used to protect hands from hot pots.

pot•hole /'pɒt,howl/ n. [count] a hole formed in pavement, caused by traffic or weather.

po•tion /'powʃən/ n. [count] a drink having healing, poisonous, or magical powers.

pot•luck /'pɒt,lʌk, -'lʌk/ n. [count] a meal, esp. for a large group, to which guests bring food to be shared.

'**pot ,roast,** n. [count] [noncount] a cut of beef stewed in one piece in a covered pot and served in its own gravy.

pot•ter /'pɒtər/ n. [count] one who makes pottery.

pot•ter•y /'pɒtəriy/ n. [noncount] pots, bowls, or other utensils made from baked clay or ceramic material.

pot•ty /'pɒtiy/ n. [count], pl. -ties. a seat of reduced size fitting over a toilet seat, for use by a small child.

pouch /pawtʃ/ n. [count] **1.** a bag or sack, esp. a small one: a tobacco pouch. **2.** a baglike structure on kangaroos, for carrying the young.

poul•try /'powltriy/ n. **1.** [plural; used with a plural verb] birds raised for their meat and eggs, as chickens, turkeys, etc. **2.** [noncount; used with a singular verb] the meat of these birds: Poultry is as expensive as beef.

pounce /pawns/ v., pounced, pounc•ing, n. —v. [no obj] **1.** to swoop down or spring suddenly, as an animal in seizing its prey: The cat pounced on the mouse. **2.** to seize suddenly: We pounced on the opportunity. —n. [count] **3.** a sudden swoop.

pound¹ /pawnd/ v. **1.** to strike repeatedly with force: [~ + obj]: The boxer pounded his opponent. [no obj]: The waves were pounding on the shore. **2.** [no obj] to beat heavily or quickly, as the heart. —n. [count] **3.** the act of pounding.

pound² /pawnd/ n. [count], pl. pounds, (when thought of as a group) pound. **1.** (in English-speaking countries) a unit of weight equal to 16 ounces (0.453 kg). **2.** Also called '**pound 'sterling.** the basic monetary unit of the United Kingdom equal to 100 pence. **3.** the basic monetary unit of various other countries, as Egypt, Ireland, etc.

pound³ /pawnd/ n. [count] a place kept by public authorities for sheltering stray animals.

pour /pɔr/ v. **1.** to (cause to) flow, as from one container to another, or into, over, or on something: [~ + obj]: She poured milk into her coffee. [no obj]: Grain poured into the bin. **2.** [no obj] to move in great amount or number: Crowds poured from the stadium after the game. **3.** [no obj; It + ~] to rain heavily: It poured all day. **4. pour out,** to produce or speak in or as if in a flood: She poured out her troubles or She poured her troubles out.

pout /pawt/ v. [no obj] **1.** to push out the lips, esp. to show displeasure, unhappiness, or anger. —n. [count] **2.** the act of pouting.

pov•er•ty /'pɒvərtiy/ n. [noncount] the state of having little or no money, goods, or means of support.

'**poverty-,stricken,** adj. extremely poor.

pow•der /'pawdər/ n. **1.** a substance pounded, crushed, or ground into tiny, loose particles; a preparation in this form: [noncount]: some baking powder. [count]: tried various face powders. —v. [~ + obj] **2.** to make into powder: powdered milk. **3.** to apply powder to (the face, skin, etc.) as a cosmetic. —'pow•der•y, adj.

'**powder ,room,** n. LADIES' ROOM.

pow•er /'pawər/ n. **1.** ability to do or act: [non-

count]: *lost the power to speak after his stroke.* [*count*]: *at the height of his powers as a pitcher.* **2.** [*noncount*] great ability to do or act: *the power of nature.* **3.** [*noncount*] control over others: *holding power over people's minds.* **4.** [*count*] a person, group, or nation having authority or influence: *the major world powers.* **5.** [*noncount*] mechanical or electrical energy: *hydroelectric power.* —*v.* [~ + *obj*] **6.** to supply power to (a machine): *Electricity powers the trains.*

pow•er•ful /ˈpaʊərfəl/ *adj.* of or relating to power: *a powerful political leader; a powerful drug.* —**ˈpow•er•ful•ly,** *adv.*

pow•er•less /ˈpaʊərlɪs/ *adj.* lacking power to act; helpless.

pp., an abbreviation of: **1.** pages. **2.** past participle.

ppr. or **p.pr.,** an abbreviation of: present participle.

PR, an abbreviation of: public relations.

prac•ti•ca•ble /ˈpræktɪkəbəl/ *adj.* **1.** capable of being done or put into practice: *Our plan is not practicable at the moment.* **2.** capable of being used.

prac•ti•cal /ˈpræktɪkəl/ *adj.* **1.** of or relating to practice or action rather than theory: *practical mathematics.* **2.** useful: *a practical car for a family.* **3.** having good judgment; sensible.

prac•ti•cal•i•ty /ˌpræktɪˈkælɪtiy/ *n.* the practical events or real facts of a situation, as opposed to theory: [*noncount*]: *a sense of practicality in dealing with problems.* [*count*]: *You can't ignore the practicalities, such as time and expense.*

ˈ**practical** ˈ**joke,** *n.* [*count*] a playful trick in which the victim is placed in an embarrassing position.

prac•ti•cal•ly /ˈpræktɪkliy/ *adv.* **1.** in a practical manner: *to think practically.* **2.** from a practical point of view. **3.** almost; nearly: *practically certain that he'll run for office.*

prac•tice /ˈpræktɪs/ *n., v.,* **-ticed, -tic•ing.** —*n.* **1.** [*noncount*] a normal or customary way of doing something: *office practice.* **2.** [*count*] a habit; custom: *to make a practice of borrowing money.* **3.** [*noncount*] the act of doing something repeatedly, for the purpose of learning it well: *Throwing a good pitch takes practice.* **4.** [*noncount*] the action or process of carrying something out: *to put a scheme into practice.* **5.** [*count*] the business of a doctor, lawyer, or other professional: *a law practice.* —*v.* **6.** [~ + *obj*] to perform or do (something) by habit or usually: *to practice a routine of exercise.* **7.** to follow or observe by custom: [~ + *obj*]: *to practice one's religion.* [*no obj*]: *He's a Catholic but he's no longer practicing.* **8.** to do as a profession: [~ + *obj*]: *He practices law.* [*no obj*]: *He's no longer practicing as a doctor.* **9.** to do something repeatedly in order to gain skill or ability: [~ + *obj*]: *practiced the trumpet every day.* [*no obj*]: *practices on the trombone every day.* Also, *Brit.,* ˈ**prac•tise.**

prag•mat•ic /prægˈmætɪk/ *adj.* concerned with practical actions and results; sensible. —ˈ**prag•ma•tism,** *n.* [*noncount*]

prai•rie /ˈprɛəriy/ *n.* [*count*] a large, level or slightly hilly area of land, mostly without trees, originally covered with grasses.

praise /preyz/ *n., v.,* **praised, prais•ing.** —*n.* [*noncount*] **1.** the act of expressing approval or admiration: *Children need praise.* —*v.* [~ + *obj*] **2.** to express admiration of; commend: *praised her for her good work.* **3.** to worship (a deity), as

in words or song: *Let us join together and praise God.*

praise•wor•thy /ˈpreyzˌwɜrðiy/ *adj.* deserving of praise.

prance /præns/ *v.,* **pranced, pranc•ing. 1.** [*no obj*] to walk in a proud manner and try to get attention, as by moving with exaggerated steps. **2.** [*no obj*] [~ + *obj*] to (cause a horse to) spring from the hind legs, or move by springing.

prank /præŋk/ *n.* [*count*] an amusing or playful trick. —ˈ**prank•ster,** *n.* [*count*]

prawn /prɔn/ *n.* [*count*] a sea animal like a large shrimp.

pray /prey/ *v.* [*no obj*] [~ + *obj*] **1.** to offer praise or thanks to God, or ask God for something: *to pray for her recovery.* **2.** to hope for: *We prayed that it wouldn't rain.*

prayer /prɛər/ *n.* **1.** [*count*] an established formula used in praying: *the Lord's Prayer.* **2.** [*noncount*] the act or practice of praying. **3.** [*count*] something prayed for.

ˈ**praying** ˈ**mantis,** *n.* MANTIS.

pre-, a prefix meaning: before or earlier than (*precook*); in front or ahead of (*preface*); above or surpassing (*preeminent*).

preach /priytʃ/ *v.* **1.** [*no obj*] [~ + *obj*] to deliver or give (a talk about religion). **2.** [*no obj*] to give moral advice, esp. in an annoying manner: *always preaching to me about being more helpful to my parents.*

preach•er /ˈpriytʃər/ *n.* [*count*] a member of the clergy, as a priest.

pre•car•i•ous /prɪˈkɛəriyəs/ *adj.* dangerous because insecure or unsteady; uncertain: *a precarious hold on the rope.*

pre•cau•tion /prɪˈkɔʃən/ *n.* [*count*] an action taken in advance to avoid harm: *took precautions against theft.*

pre•cede /prɪˈsiyd/ *v.* [~ + *obj*], **-ced•ed, -ced•ing.** to go before, as in place, position, or rank: *He preceded me into the room.*

prec•e•dence /ˈprɛsɪdəns, prɪˈsiydns/ *n.* [*noncount*] the right to be dealt with or placed before others because of order, rank, or importance: *This problem takes precedence over all the others.*

prec•e•dent /ˈprɛsɪdənt/ *n.* [*count*] an act, decision, or case that may serve as an example or guide in similar situations in the future.

pre•ced•ing /prɪˈsiydɪŋ/ *adj.* [*before a noun*] that precedes; coming before; previous: *In the preceding lesson we discussed verb tense.*

pre•cept /ˈpriysɛpt/ *n.* [*count*] a direction given as a rule of behavior, esp. moral behavior.

pre•cinct /ˈpriysɪŋkt/ *n.* [*count*] a district, as of a city, marked out for election purposes or for police protection.

pre•cious /ˈprɛʃəs/ *adj.* **1.** of high price or great value: *precious metals.* **2.** considered valuable or special: *precious memories.* —*adv.* **3.** extremely; very: *We have precious little time.*

prec•i•pice /ˈprɛsəpɪs/ *n.* [*count*] a cliff with a steep or overhanging face.

pre•cip•i•tate /prɪˈsɪpɪˌteyt/ *adj.* **-tit, -ˌteyt**/ *v.,* **-tat•ed, -tat•ing,** *adj.* —*v.* **1.** [~ + *obj*] to speed up (an event); to bring about too soon: *to precipitate a crisis.* **2.** [*no obj*] to rain, snow, etc. —*adj.* **3.** too sudden or hurried: *a precipitate marriage.*

pre•cip•i•ta•tion /prɪˌsɪpɪˈteyʃən/ *n.* [*noncount*] falling water that has been condensed in the atmosphere, as rain, snow, or hail.

P

pre•cip•i•tous /prɪ'sɪpɪtəs/ *adj.* like a precipice; very steep: *precipitous mountain trails.*

pre•cise /prɪ'says/ *adj.* **1.** definitely stated, defined, or fixed: *precise directions.* **2.** [*before a noun*] being that one and no other: *I bought the precise dress I wanted.* **3.** exact in measuring, recording, etc.: *a precise instrument.* —**pre'ci•sion,** *n.* [*noncount*]

pre•cise•ly /prɪ'saysliy/ *adv.* **1.** exactly; done in an accurate manner: *Measure as precisely as possible.* **2.** (used to express exact or intensified agreement or confirmation): *That's precisely why I want to see you.*

pre•co•cious /prɪ'kowʃəs/ *adj.* unusually advanced or mature: *a precocious child.*

pre•con•ceived /ˌpriykən'siyvd/ *adj.* (of an opinion or idea) formed beforehand, esp. from bias.

pre•con•cep•tion /ˌpriykən'sɛpʃən/ *n.* [*count*] an opinion or idea based on bias, with no allowance made for knowledge or evidence.

pre•cur•sor /prɪ'kɜrsər, 'priykɜr-/ *n.* [*count*] a person, animal, or thing that comes before something else: *large machines that were the precursors of the personal computer.*

pred•a•tor /'prɛdətər, -ˌtɔr/ *n.* [*count*] any organism that exists by preying on another: *The hawk is a predator.* —**'pred•a,tor•y,** *adj.*

pred•e•ces•sor /'prɛdəˌsɛsər/ *n.* [*count*] one who comes before another in an office or job.

pre•des•tine /prɪ'dɛstɪn/ *v.* [~ + *obj*], **-tined, -tin•ing.** to decide or determine in advance: *According to some religions, God has predestined everything that will happen to you.*

pre•dic•a•ment /prɪ'dɪkəmənt/ *n.* [*count*] an unpleasantly difficult situation.

pred•i•cate /'prɛdɪˌkɪt/ *n.* [*count*] a unit that is one of the two main parts of a sentence, the other being the subject, and that consists of a verb and any words belonging with the verb, as objects, complements, or adverbs: *The predicate of the sentence* The package is here *is the phrase* is here.

'predicate 'adjective /'prɛdɪkɪt/ *n.* [*count*] an adjective that comes after a verb, esp. after the verb *be: In "He is ill," "ill" is a predicate adjective.*

pre•dict /prɪ'dɪkt/ *v.* [~ + *obj*] to declare in advance; foretell: *She predicted that you would be elected.* —**pre'dict•a•ble,** *adj.* —**pre'dic•tion,** *n.* [*noncount*] [*count*]

pre•dis•pose /ˌpriydɪ'spowz/ *v.* [~ + *obj*], **-posed, -pos•ing. 1.** to make likely to have a particular health problem: *genetic factors predisposing me to diabetes.* **2.** to influence (someone) in a particular way: *His unhappy childhood predisposed him to act cruelly toward others.*

pre•dom•i•nant /prɪ'dɒmənənt/ *adj.* **1.** having authority or influence over others: *a predominant ethnic group.* **2.** greater in number or amount: *the predominant color of a painting.* —**pre'dom•i•nance,** *n.* [*noncount*] —**pre'dom•i•nant•ly,** *adv.*: *Their student population is predominantly middle-class.*

pre•dom•i•nate /prɪ'dɒməˌneyt/ *v.* [*no obj*], **-nat•ed, -nat•ing. 1.** to be the stronger or leading element or force: *Blues and greens predominated in the painting.* **2.** to have or exert controlling power: *Good sense predominated over anger.*

pre•em•i•nent or **pre-em•i•nent** /priy'ɛmənənt/ *adj.* above or before others in some quality; superior.

preen /priyn/ *v.* **1.** [~ + *obj*] (of a bird) to clean or dress (its feathers, etc.) with the beak or tongue. **2.** [*no obj*] [~ + *oneself*] to dress (oneself) carefully or smartly.

pref•ace /'prɛfɪs/ *n., v.,* **-aced, -ac•ing.** —*n.* [*count*] **1.** a statement in the front of a book, setting forth the book's purpose. **2.** an introductory part, as of a speech. —*v.* [~ + *obj*] **3.** to provide with a preface.

pre•fer /prɪ'fɜr/ *v.* [~ + *obj*], **-ferred, -fer•ring.** to like better than someone or something else: *She prefers cheese, if you have some. She prefers running to walking. I'd prefer to leave now.*

pref•er•a•ble /'prɛfərəbəl, 'prɛfrə-* or, *often,* prɪ'fɜr-/ *adj.* more desirable or suitable: *Driving there is preferable to walking.* —**'pref•er•a•bly,** *adv.*: *They're looking for a new car, preferably one that is not very expensive.*

pref•er•ence /'prɛfərəns/ *n.* **1.** [*noncount*] the act of preferring; the state of being preferred: *showing preference in hiring practices.* **2.** [*count*] something preferred: *My preference would be for a vegetarian meal.*

pre•fix /'priyfɪks/ *n.* [*count*] an affix placed before a base or another prefix, as *un-* in *unkind,* and *un-* and *re-* in *unrewarding.*

preg•nant /'prɛgnənt/ *adj.* having a child or offspring developing in the body, as a woman or female mammal: *pregnant with her fourth child.* —**'preg•nan•cy,** *n.* [*noncount*] [*count*]

pre•his•tor•ic /ˌpriyhɪ'stɔrɪk, -'stɒr-, ˌpriyɪ-/ *adj.* of or relating to the time before history was recorded: *prehistoric cave paintings.*

prej•u•dice /'prɛdʒədɪs/ *n., v.,* **-diced, -dic•ing.** —*n.* **1.** an opinion or set of attitudes formed beforehand or without knowledge or thought, esp. about a racial, religious, or national group: [*noncount*]: *showing his prejudice against women drivers; prejudice against foreigners.* [*count*]: *the prejudices of his parents.* —*v.* [~ + *obj*] **2.** to affect (someone) with a prejudice.

pre•lim•i•nar•y /prɪ'lɪməˌnɛriy/ *adj., n., pl.* **-nar•ies.** —*adj.* **1.** going before and leading up to the main part; preparatory: *The preliminary details had been worked out.* —*n.* [*count*] **2.** something that goes before and leads up to something else, as an introductory step or stage: *Once the social preliminaries were over, the two leaders began a serious discussion.*

prel•ude /'prɛlyuwd, 'preyl-, 'preyluwd, 'priy-/ *n.* [*count*] **1.** an action that comes before another action: *The bombing of headquarters was just a prelude to the full-scale attack that began the next day.* **2.** a relatively short piece of music serving to introduce another.

pre•mar•i•tal /priy'mærɪtl/ *adj.* coming before marriage: *premarital sex.*

pre•ma•ture /ˌpriymə'tʃʊr, -'tʊr, -'tyʊr/ *adj.* **1.** occurring, coming, or done too soon: *made a premature announcement that he had won the election.* **2.** born before the normal amount of time of full development: *premature babies.* —,**pre•ma'ture•ly,** *adv.*

pre•med•i•tat•ed /priy'mɛdɪˌteytɪd/ *adj.* considered or planned before doing: *premeditated murder.*

pre•mier /prɪ'mɪər, -'myɪər, 'priymɪər/ *n.* [*count*] **1.** the head of the cabinet in France and other countries; prime minister. —*adj.* [*before a noun*] **2.** first in rank; chief; leading: *the premier writer of this decade.*

pre•miere /prɪ'mɪər, -'myɛər/ *n., v.,* **-miered, -mier•ing.** —*n.* [*count*] **1.** a first public performance or showing of a play, etc. —*v.* **2.** to (cause to) be presented publicly for the first time: [~ + *obj*]: *premiering a new film.* [*no obj*]: *The act premiered in Boston.*

prem•ise /'prɛmɪs/ *n.* [*count*] **1.** **premises,** [*plural*] an area of land including its buildings: *You'll have to leave the premises at once.* **2.** an assumed idea or principle on which further reasoning is based: *I was acting on the premise that I had your support.*

pre•mi•um /'priymiyəm/ *n.* [*count*] **1.** a prize or bonus given as a way of increasing sales of a product. **2.** the amount paid in installments by a policyholder for insurance coverage. **3.** great value: *puts a high premium on loyalty.*

pre•mo•ni•tion /,priymə'nɪʃən, ,prɛmə-/ *n.* [*count*] a feeling of worry over a future event: *a premonition of danger.*

pre•na•tal /priy'neytl̩/ *adj.* before birth or before giving birth: *costs of prenatal care.*

pre•oc•cu•py /priy'ɒkyə,pay/ *v.* [~ + *obj*], **-pied, -py•ing.** to take all the attention of (someone): *She was preoccupied by fears about her mother's health.* —**pre•oc•cu•pa•tion,** *n.* [*count*] [*noncount*]

prep., an abbreviation of: **1.** preparation. **2.** preparatory. **3.** prepare. **4.** preposition.

prep•a•ra•tion /,prɛpə'reyʃən/ *n.* **1.** [*count; usually plural*] an act or step by which one prepares for something: *last-minute preparations for their journey.* **2.** [*noncount*] the act of preparing: *the student's lack of preparation for the exam.* **3.** [*count*] something prepared: *She applied a soothing preparation to the burns.*

pre•par•a•to•ry /prɪ'pærə,tɔriy, -'pɛər-, 'prɛpərə-/ *adj.* [*before a noun*] serving or designed to prepare: *preparatory arrangements.*

pre'paratory ,school, *n.* **1.** [*count*] [*noncount*] a private secondary school designed to prepare students for college. **2.** [*count*] *Brit.* a private elementary school. Also called **prep school.**

pre•pare /prɪ'pɛər/ *v.,* **-pared, -par•ing. 1.** to put in proper condition or readiness; to get ready: [~ + *obj*]: *The general prepared his troops for the attack. The troops were preparing to cross the river.* [*no obj*]: *She prepared for the debate.* **2.** [~ + *obj*] to get (a meal) ready for eating, as by cooking, etc. **3.** [~ + *obj*] to manufacture or compose: *to prepare a cough syrup; to prepare a report.*

prep•o•si•tion /,prɛpə'zɪʃən/ *n.* [*count*] a word used before a noun or pronoun to form a phrase that expresses a relationship of time, place, or the like: *Some prepositions in English are* on, by, to, with, *and* since. —,**prep•o'si•tion•al,** *adj.* [*before a noun*]

pre•pos•ter•ous /prɪ'pɒstərəs, -trəs/ *adj.* completely senseless or foolish.

prep•py /'prɛpiy/ *n., pl.* **-pies,** *adj.,* **-pi•er, -pi•est.** —*n.* [*count*] **1.** a student at, or a graduate of, a preparatory school. **2.** one whose clothing or behavior is associated with students of preparatory schools. —*adj.* **3.** of, relating to, or characteristic of a preppy.

pre•req•ui•site /prɪ'rɛkwəzɪt, priy-/ *n.* [*count*] something required before something else; a condition: *A course on grammar is a prerequisite to the advanced writing course.*

pre•rog•a•tive /prɪ'rɒgətɪv, pə'rɒg-/ *n.* [*count*] a special right, privilege, etc., limited to a particular person or group.

pres., an abbreviation of: **1.** present. **2.** presidency. **3.** president.

Pres•by•te•ri•an /,prɛzbɪ'tɪəriyən, ,prɛs-/ *adj.* **1.** of or relating to Protestant churches governed by officials of equal rank. —*n.* [*count*] **2.** a member of a Presbyterian church.

pre•school /*adj.*'priy'skuwl; *n.* 'priy,skuwl/ *adj.* **1.** of or relating to a child between infancy and kindergarten age. —*n.* [*count*] [*noncount*] **2.** a school or nursery for preschool children. —'**pre'school•er,** *n.* [*count*]

pre•scribe /prɪ'skrayb/ *v.* [~ + *obj*], **-scribed, -scrib•ing. 1.** to order as a rule or course of action to be followed: *the punishment that the law prescribes.* **2.** to name or order the use of (a medicine, etc.): *The doctor prescribed a painkiller.*

pre•scrip•tion /prɪ'skrɪpʃən/ *n.* **1.** [*count*] a written direction by a physician for the preparation and use of a medicine. **2.** [*noncount*] the act of prescribing. **3.** [*count*] something prescribed: *a prescription for success.*

pres•ence /'prɛzəns/ *n.* [*noncount*] **1.** the state or fact of being present: *Her presence at the party created some excitement.* **2.** the ability to give off a sense of ease, dignity, or self-assurance: *an attorney with definite presence.*

pres•ent[1] /'prɛzənt/ *adj.* **1.** [*before a noun*] being, existing, or occurring now: *the present economic situation.* **2.** [*before a noun*] of or relating to a verb tense or form used to refer to an action or state existing or happening now, or to a habitual event, such as *He* knows *the answer* or *He* drives *to work.* **3.** [*be* + ~] being in the place mentioned or understood: *Carbon is present in many minerals.* —*n.* [*count; singular; usually: the* + ~] **4.** the present time: *If there's work to be done, there's no time like the present.* **5. a.** the present tense. **b.** a verb form in the present tense, such as *knows.* —*Idiom.* **6. at present,** at the present time or moment; now: *We don't know at present who will win.* **7. for the present,** for now; temporarily: *For the present you'll have to stay in this hotel.*

pre•sent[2] /*v.*prɪ'zɛnt; *n.* 'prɛzənt/ *v.* [~ + *obj*] **1.** to give a gift or the like, esp. by formal act: *The committee presented the winner's trophy to her. The committee presented her with the winner's trophy.* **2.** to offer or give in a formal way: *The ambassador presented his credentials to the king.* **3.** to furnish or provide (an opportunity, problem, etc.): *The test presented no difficulties.* **4.** to bring before or introduce to the public: *to present a new play.* —*n.* **pres•ent** [*count*] **5.** a gift.

pre•sent•a•ble /prɪ'zɛntəbəl/ *adj.* capable of being presented; of good appearance.

pres•en•ta•tion /,prɛzən'teyʃən, ,priyzɛn-/ *n.* [*noncount*] **1.** an act of presenting; the state of being presented: *the presentation of news.* **2.** the way in which something is presented.

pres•ent•ly /'prɛzəntliy/ *adv.* **1.** in a little while; soon: *We'll be arriving presently.* **2.** at the present time; now: *Presently we have only three teachers.*

'**present 'participle,** *n.* [*count*] a participle formed from the root of a verb plus the suffix *-ing,* used to indicate that the action or event repeats or lasts for some time, as in *The weeds are* growing, *or used as an adjective, as in the* growing *weeds.*

pre•serv•a•tive /prɪ'zɜrvətɪv/ *n.* [*count*] something that preserves, esp. a chemical used to preserve foods.

pre•serve /prɪ'zɜrv/ *v.,* **-served, -serv•ing,** *n.* —*v.* [~ + *obj*] **1.** to keep (something) alive or in existence; make (something) lasting: *to preserve our liberties.* **2.** to keep up; maintain: *to preserve historical monuments.* **3.** to keep possession of; retain: *He managed to preserve his composure during the debates.* **4.** to prepare (food) so as to prevent or slow down its decay. —*n.* [count] **5.** Usually, **preserves.** [*plural*] fruit prepared by cooking with sugar. **6.** a place set apart for protection of game or fish, esp. for sport: *a forest preserve.* —**,pres•er'va•tion,** *n.* [noncount] —**pre'serv•er,** *n.* [count]

pre•side /prɪ'zayd/ *v.* [*no obj*], **-sid•ed, -sid•ing.** **1.** to have or hold the place of authority or control, as in a meeting: *The judge presided at the trial.* **2. preside over,** to exercise management or control over: *The chairman presided over the meeting.*

pres•i•den•cy /'prɛzɪdənsiy/ *n.* [count] **1.** the office of a president: *never elected to the presidency.* **2.** the time of a president's holding office: *the last three Republican presidencies.*

pres•i•dent /'prɛzɪdənt/ *n.* [count] **1.** [*often: President*] the chief of state and often the chief executive officer of a modern republic, as the United States: *He wondered if he would make a good president. Will the President be reelected? President Lincoln.* **2.** the chief officer of a college, corporation, etc. —**,pres•i'den•tial,** *adj.*

press /prɛs/ *v.* **1.** to act upon or move (something) with steady force; to push: [~ + *obj*]: *He pressed the elevator button.* [*no obj*]: *He pressed on the gas pedal but nothing happened.* **2.** to put pressure on (something) to change its shape or size: [~ + *obj*]: *He pressed the clay into a ball.* [*no obj*]: *She pressed down on the dough.* **3.** [~ + *obj*] to flatten or make smooth by ironing: *He pressed his slacks.* **4.** to urge in an annoying way: [~ + *obj*]: *Don't press your kids so hard.* [*no obj*]: *The media kept pressing for an explanation.* **5.** to push forward or onward: [*no obj*]: *The army pressed on.* —*n.* [count] **6.** an act of pressing. **7.** [count] a machine for printing books, newspapers, etc. **8.** [noncount; usually: *the* + ~] printed publications or news organizations thought of as a group. **9.** [plural; used with a plural verb; usually: *the* + ~] a group of people from the news media, as reporters and photographers. **10.** [count] any of various devices or machines for squeezing, stamping, or crushing: *a wine press.*

pressed /prɛst/ *adj.* [*be* + ~ + *for*] not having enough of: *I was pressed for time.*

press•ing /'prɛsɪŋ/ *adj.* urgent; needing attention: *a pressing need for food supplies.*

pres•sure /'prɛʃər/ *n., v.,* **-sured, -sur•ing.** —*n.* **1.** [noncount] the action of force upon a surface by an object, fluid, etc., in contact with it: *air pressure.* **2.** [count] the strength or amount of this force: *At high pressures the wings could fall off.* **3.** stress; a burden or strain: [count]: *the pressures of daily life.* [noncount]: *works well under pressure.* **4.** [noncount] a force or influence that causes some action: *Social pressure from his friends made him start smoking.* —*v.* [~ + *obj*] **5.** to force (someone) to do a particular thing or action: *She pressured him to accept that job.*

pres•sur•ize /'prɛʃə,rayz/ *v.* [~ + *obj*], **-ized, -iz•ing.** to produce or maintain normal air pressure in (an airplane cabin, etc.), esp. at high altitudes or in space.

pres•tige /prɛ'stiyʒ, -'stiydʒ/ *n.* [noncount] respect or admiration resulting from success, achievement, etc. —**pres'tig•ious,** *adj.*

pre•sum•a•bly /prɪ'zuwməbliy/ *adv.* probably.

pre•sume /prɪ'zuwm/ *v.* [~ + *obj*], **-sumed, -sum•ing.** **1.** to assume as true because there is no evidence that suggests the opposite: *We presume his innocence. We presume him (to be) innocent. I presume you're coming with us, aren't you?* **2.** to dare (to do something) with too much boldness: *How can she presume to talk like that to the teacher?*

pre•sump•tion /prɪ'zʌmpʃən/ *n.* **1.** [noncount] the act of presuming: *presumption of innocence.* **2.** [count] something presumed: *a presumption that he will accept our offer.* **3.** [noncount] too much boldness.

pre•sump•tu•ous /prɪ'zʌmptʃuwəs/ *adj.* too bold: *presumptuous of her to assume I'd be paying for dinner.*

pre•teen /priy'tiyn/ *n.* [count] a boy or girl under the age of 13, esp. one between the ages of 10 and 13.

pre•tend /prɪ'tɛnd/ *v.* to give a false show of; make believe; claim falsely: [~ + *obj*]: *to pretend illness; She pretended to sleep whenever I came in. The children pretended they were cowboys.* [*no obj*]: *The kids were only pretending.*

pre•tense /prɪ'tɛns, 'priytɛns/ *n.* an act or instance of pretending: [count]: *a pretense of friendship.* [noncount]: *It's all pretense; he has no intention of cutting our budget.*

pre•ten•sion /prɪ'tɛnʃən/ *n.* **1.** Often, **pretensions.** [*plural*] a claim made to some quality, merit, or importance. **2.** [noncount] [count] the act of claiming to be something one is not.

pre•ten•tious /prɪ'tɛnʃəs/ *adj.* full of pretension; giving a show of importance that one does not really have.

pre•text /'priytɛkst/ *n.* [count] a reason given to hide a true purpose; an excuse: *She came into my office on the pretext of borrowing a stapler.*

pret•ty /'prɪtiy/ *adj.,* **-ti•er, -ti•est,** *adv.* —*adj.* **1.** pleasing or attractive, esp. in a delicate or graceful way: *a pretty face.* —*adv.* **2.** fairly or moderately; somewhat: *We had a pretty good time.* **3.** quite; very: *The wind blew pretty hard.* —**'pret•ti•ness,** *n.* [noncount]

pret•zel /'prɛtsəl/ *n.* [count] a usually crisp, dry biscuit, typically in the form of a knot or stick.

pre•vail /prɪ'veyl/ *v.* [*no obj*] **1.** to be widespread or current; be found in many places: *The opinion that he is a loser still prevails.* **2.** to be or prove superior in strength, power, or influence: *Greed has prevailed once again; to prevail over one's enemies.* **3.** to persuade successfully: *Can you prevail on him to go?*

prev•a•lent /'prɛvələnt/ *adj.* **1.** widespread; generally used or accepted: *the prevalent point of view.* **2.** having greater power; dominant. —**'prev•a•lence,** *n.* [noncount]

pre•vent /prɪ'vɛnt/ *v.* [~ + *obj*] **1.** to keep from occurring; stop: *She took some pills to prevent seasickness.* **2.** to stop (someone) from doing something: *Nothing will prevent us from going.* —**pre'ven•tion,** *n.* [noncount]

pre•view /'priy,vyuw/ *n.* [count] **1.** an advance showing of a motion picture, etc., before its public opening. **2.** anything that gives an advance impression of something: *Living together gave them a preview of marriage.* —*v.* [~ + *obj*] **3.** to view or show beforehand: *We previewed the video before we let our kids watch it.*

pre•vi•ous /'priyviyəs/ *adj.* [before a noun] **1.** occurring before something else; prior: *The previous owner of this car was an old lady.* —*Idiom.*

2. previous to, before; prior to: *Previous to moving here she lived in Chicago.* —**'pre•vi•ous•ly,** *adv.*

prey /pray/ *n., v.,* **preyed, prey•ing.** —*n.* [*noncount*] **1.** an animal hunted for food, esp. by a meat-eating animal. **2.** a person or thing that is the victim of an enemy, disease, etc. —*v.* **prey on** or **upon, 3.** to seize and eat animals for food: *Foxes prey on rabbits.* **4.** to make raids or attacks in order to steal or destroy: *The Vikings preyed on coastal England.* **5.** to take dishonest advantage of another: *merchants who prey upon the poor.*

price /prays/ *n., v.,* **priced, pric•ing.** —*n.* [*count*] **1.** the sum of money for which anything is bought, sold, or offered for sale: *Our prices will beat the competition's.* **2.** that which must be given, done, or experienced in order to obtain something: *We won the battle, but at a heavy price: 3,000 dead.* —*v.* [~ + *obj*] **3.** to fix the price of: *He priced the painting at $3,000.* **4.** to ask or find out the price of: *He went around pricing the dishwasher at different stores.*

price•less /'prayslɪs/ *adj.* extremely valuable: *priceless artwork.*

pric•ey /'praysiy/ also **pricy,** *adj.,* **-i•er, -i•est.** too expensive.

prick /prɪk/ *n.* [*count*] **1.** a puncture made by a needle, thorn, or the like. **2.** the act of pricking: *felt the prick of the needle.* —*v.* **3.** [~ + *obj*] to make a hole in with a sharp point; pierce: *I pricked my finger.* **4.** to (cause to) feel sharp pain, as from piercing [*no obj*]: *The thorns prick if you touch them.* [~ + *obj*]: *The tall grass pricked her legs.* —**Idiom. 5. prick up one's ears, a.** to become very alert; listen attentively: *She pricked up her ears when she overheard the boss talking about her.* **b.** to cause its ears to point upward: *The dog pricked up its ears when it heard the call.*

prick•le /'prɪkəl/ *n., v.,* **-led, -ling.** —*n.* [*count*] **1.** a small, sharp thorn that sticks out, as on a plant. **2.** a pricking sensation. —*v.* [*no obj*] **3.** to cause a pricking sensation. —**'prick•ly,** *adj.*

pride /prayd/ *n., v.,* **prid•ed, prid•ing.** —*n.* [*noncount*] **1.** the feeling of being properly proud about something good that one has or has done; self-respect: *He pointed with pride at the fine books in his library.* **2.** too high an opinion of oneself; conceit: *His pride kept him from admitting he was wrong.* **3.** something that causes one to be proud: *Her paintings were the pride of the family.* —*v.* **4. pride oneself on,** to have a feeling of pride about: *She prides herself on being a good mother.*

priest /priyst/ *n.* [*count*] **1.** (in Christian use) a member of the clergy; minister. **2.** one whose job is to perform religious ceremonies, etc.: *Hindu priests.*

priest•hood /'priyst,hʊd/ *n.* [*noncount*] **1.** the office of a priest. **2.** priests thought of as a group.

prim /prɪm/ *adj.,* **prim•mer, prim•mest. 1.** precise or proper in a very formal way. **2.** stiffly neat.

pri•ma•ri•ly /pray'mɛrəliy, -'mɛr-/ *adv.* essentially; chiefly: *Their income is primarily from farming.*

pri•ma•ry /'praymɛriy, -məriy/ *adj., n., pl.* **-ries.** —*adj.* **1.** first in rank or importance; chief: *one's primary goal.* **2.** [*before a noun*] first in order; first in time; earliest. —*n.* [*count*] **3.** an election in which voters of each political party nomi-

nate candidates who then run for office in a later election.

'primary ,school, *n.* [*count*] [*noncount*] an elementary school, esp. one covering the first three or four grades and sometimes kindergarten.

pri•mate /'praymeyt, -mɪt/ *n.* [*count*] a mammal of a group that includes humans, apes, and monkeys.

prime /praym/ *adj., n., v.,* **primed, prim•ing.** —*adj.* **1.** of the first importance: *a prime consideration.* **2.** of the best quality: *prime ribs of beef.* —*n.* [*count; singular*] **3.** the choicest or best part. —*v.* [~ + *obj*] **4.** to prepare for a particular purpose, as by supplying with information: *He primed himself for the meeting by reviewing his figures.* **5.** to pour liquid into (a pump) so as to push out air and prepare it for action. **6.** to cover (a wall or other surface) with an undercoat of paint or the like.

,prime 'minister, *n.* [*count*] the head of government and the head of the cabinet in parliamentary governments.

prim•er /'prɪmər/ *n.* [*count*] an elementary book for teaching children to read.

pri•me•val /pray'miyvəl/ *adj.* of or relating to the first or earliest age or ages, esp. of the world: *primeval forms of life.*

prim•i•tive /'prɪmɪtɪv/ *adj.* **1.** [*before a noun*] being the first or earliest of its kind or in existence: *primitive forms of life.* **2.** not showing the effects of civilization; simple or crude: *primitive customs.*

primp /prɪmp/ *v.* [*no obj*] [~ + *oneself*] to dress or groom (oneself) with care.

prince /prɪns/ *n.* [*count*] **1.** a male member of a royal family who is not ruling. **2.** (in Great Britain) a son of the king or queen, or a son of the son of a king or queen. —**'prince•ly,** *adj.*

prin•cess /'prɪnsɪs, -sɛs, prɪn'sɛs/ *n.* [*count*] **1.** a female member of a royal family who is not ruling. **2.** the wife of a prince. **3.** (in Great Britain) a daughter of the king or queen; the daughter of a son of the king or queen.

prin•ci•pal /'prɪnsəpəl/ *adj.* [*before a noun*] **1.** first in rank, value, etc.; chief; foremost. —*n.* **2.** [*count*] a chief or head. **3.** [*count*] the head of a school or, esp. in England, a college. **4.** [*noncount*] [*count; usually singular*] a sum of money, not counting interest or profit on it.

prin•ci•pal•i•ty /,prɪnsə'pælɪtiy/ *n.* [*count*], *pl.* **-ties.** a country or state ruled by a prince.

prin•ci•pal•ly /'prɪnsəpəliy, -sɪpliy/ *adv.* chiefly; mainly; especially: *principally interested in progress.*

prin•ci•ple /'prɪnsəpəl/ *n.* **1.** [*count*] a fundamental law that describes how a thing moves, works, or acts: *the principles of physics.* **2.** a basic rule by which one lives: [*count*]: *Stick to your principles and be honest.* [*noncount*]: *a man of principle.* —**Idiom. 3. in principle,** basically; fundamentally: *He favors the plan in principle.* **4. on principle,** according to rules for right conduct: *I refused to support her candidacy on principle.*

print /prɪnt/ *v.* **1.** to produce (marks, etc.) by pressing plates, blocks, etc., to paper or other material: [~ + *obj*]: *This computer printer prints 100 characters per second.* [*no obj*]: *Can it print in color?* **2.** [~ + *obj*] to publish in printed form: *The newspaper refused to print the story.* **3.** to write in letters like those commonly used in print: [~ + *obj*]: *Please print your name at the top.* [*no obj*]: *Please print clearly.* **4.** [~ + *obj*] to produce (a pattern, etc.), as by pressure on cloth: *a printed Japanese kimono.* **5. print out,** *Computers.* to produce (data) in printed form: *Print out the spreadsheet and hand it in. Print the essay out and hand it in with your disk.* —*n.* **6.** [*noncount*] printed material: *There they were, right in print, his very words for all to see.* **7.** [*count*] a picture, etc., printed from an engraved block, plate, etc.: *Several of the artist's best prints were hung on the wall.* **8.** [*count*] a fingerprint: *Your prints were found on the weapon.* **9.** [*count*] a design or pattern on cloth made by dyeing, weaving, or printing with engraved rollers, etc. **10.** [*count*] a photograph, esp. a positive made from a negative: *The prints had come out blurry.* —*Idiom.* **11. in** (or **out of**) **print,** (of a book or the like) still available (or no longer available) for purchase from the publisher.

print•er /ˈprɪntər/ *n.* [*count*] **1.** a person or company in the business of printing. **2.** a machine used for printing. **3.** a computer output device that produces a paper copy of data or graphics.

print•ing /ˈprɪntɪŋ/ *n.* **1.** [*noncount*] the skill, process, or business of producing books and other printed material. **2.** [*count; usually singular*] the total number of copies of a publication printed at one time: *a first printing of 3000 copies.* **3.** [*noncount*] writing in which the letters resemble printed ones.

print•out /ˈprɪntˌaʊt/ *n.* [*count*] [*noncount*] computer output produced by a printer.

pri•or /ˈpraɪər/ *adj.* [*before a noun*] **1.** coming before another; earlier: *a prior commitment.* **2.** greater in importance: *a prior claim on his time.* —*Idiom.* **3. prior to,** coming before; preceding; before: *Prior to this job she worked in Austria.*

pri•or•i•ty /praɪˈɔrɪtiy, -ˈɒr-/ *n., pl.* **-ties. 1.** [*noncount*] the right to come before or precede in order, rank, etc.: *Soldiers who are badly wounded have priority over those with minor wounds.* **2.** [*count*] something given or meriting special or prior attention: *Balancing the budget is a top priority.*

prism /ˈprɪzəm/ *n.* [*count*] a transparent solid object used for breaking up light into a spectrum of colors.

pris•on /ˈprɪzən/ *n.* **1.** [*count*] a place for keeping people accused or convicted of a crime. **2.** [*noncount*] imprisonment: *thirty years in prison.* **3.** [*count*] any place or state of confinement. —ˈpris•on•er, *n.* [*count*]

pri•vate /ˈpraɪvɪt/ *adj.* **1.** [*before a noun*] belonging to some particular person or persons: *private property.* **2.** intended only for the person or persons concerned; personal: *a private memo.* **3.** [*before a noun*] not holding public office or employment: *private citizens.* **4.** [*before a noun*] working as an independent agent: *a private detective.* **5.** [*before a noun*] not funded by public sources or agencies: *a private Catholic school.* —*n.* [*count*] **6.** a soldier of the lowest enlisted ranks. **7. privates,** PRIVATE PARTS. —*Idiom.* **8. in private,** not publicly; secretly: *We met in private.* —ˈpri•va•cy, *n.* [*noncount*] —ˈpri•vate•ly, *adv.*

ˈprivate ˈparts, *n.* [*plural*] the sex organs.

priv•i•lege /ˈprɪvəlɪdʒ, ˈprɪvlɪdʒ/ *n.* **1.** a special right or advantage granted to particular persons that frees them from certain obligations: [*noncount*]: *The president claimed executive privilege.* [*count*]: *Employees have parking privileges.* **2.** [*count*] an opportunity for pleasure: *It's my privilege to be here.*

priv•i•leged /ˈprɪvəlɪdʒd, ˈprɪvlɪdʒd/ *adj.* **1.** belonging to a class that enjoys privileges. **2.** restricted to a select group or an individual: *privileged information.*

priv•y /ˈprɪviy/ *adj.*, **-i•er, -i•est,** *n., pl.* **priv•ies.** —*adj.* [*be* + ~ + *to*] **1.** having the knowledge of something private or secret: *Many people were privy to the plot.* —*n.* **2.** OUTHOUSE.

prize¹ /praɪz/ *n.* **1.** a reward for victory, as in a contest or competition: [*count*]: *She won a prize.* [*noncount*]: *She won first prize in the science exhibit.* —*adj.* [*before a noun*] **2.** having won a prize: *a prize play.* **3.** worthy of a prize: *his prize stamp collection.*

prize² /praɪz/ *v.* [~ + *obj*], **prized, priz•ing.** to value (something) highly.

pro¹ /proʊ/ *n.* [*count*] the argument, position, or person who votes in favor of something: *aware of the pros and cons of taking the new job.* Compare CON¹.

pro² /proʊ/ *n.* [*count*], *pl.* **pros.** a professional.

pro-¹, a prefix meaning: favoring or supporting (*prowar*); forth or forward (*proceed*); in place of (*pronoun*).

pro-², a prefix meaning: before, beforehand, or in front of (*prognosis*).

prob., an abbreviation of: **1.** probable. **2.** probably.

prob•a•bil•i•ty /ˌprɒbəˈbɪlɪtiy/ *n., pl.* **-ties. 1.** [*noncount*] the quality or fact of being probable: *little probability of success.* **2.** [*count*] a probable event, circumstance, etc.: *It's a real probability that he'll be reelected.* —*Idiom.* **3. in all probability,** very probably; quite likely: *The factory will in all probability be shut down.*

prob•a•ble /ˈprɒbəbəl/ *adj.* likely to occur or prove true: *a probable defeat.* —ˈprob•a•bly, *adv.*

pro•ba•tion /proʊˈbeɪʃən/ *n.* [*noncount*] **1.** the status or period of trial for a student who has failing marks or bad behavior: *He was put on probation.* **2.** the status of a convicted offender who has been allowed to go free under supervision: *The courts released him on probation.*

probe /proʊb/ *v.*, **probed, prob•ing,** *n.* —*v.* [~ + *obj*] [*no obj*] **1.** to examine with or as if with a probe: *The doctor probed the wound. She probed carefully into the wound.* **2.** to search into or examine thoroughly: *He probed his conscience to figure out what he should do. The economist probed into the problem.* —*n.* [*count*] **3.** a slender surgical instrument for exploring a wound, sinus, or the like. **4.** any slender device inserted into something in order to explore or examine: *a heat probe.* **5.** an investigation of suspected illegal activity.

prob•lem /ˈprɒbləm/ *n.* [*count*] **1.** any question or matter involving doubt or difficulty: *has financial problems.* **2.** a statement requiring a solution, usually by means of mathematics: *simple problems in addition.* —*adj.* [*before a noun*] **3.** unwilling to cooperate; unruly: *a problem child.*

prob•lem•at•ic /ˌprɒbləˈmætɪk/ also **ˌprob•lem•at•i•cal,** *adj.* of the nature of a problem; doubtful: *a problematic rise in unemployment.*

pro•ce•dure /prəˈsiydʒər/ *n.* [*count*] [*noncount*] any established way for doing something, or for conducting business. —**pro•ce•dur•al,** *adj.*

pro•ceed /*v.* prəˈsiyd; *n.* ˈproʊsiyd/ *v.* [*no obj*] **1.** to move or go forward or onward, esp. after stopping. **2.** to carry on or continue any action already started: *Proceed with your meeting.* —*n.*

proceeds, [*plural*] **3.** the total amount or profit made from a sale or other business activity.

pro•ceed•ings /prə'siydɪŋz/ *n.* [*plural*] **1.** a series of activities or events. **2.** a record of the business discussed at a meeting. **3.** legal action, esp. as carried on in a court of law.

proc•ess /'prɒsɛs/ *n., pl.* **proc•ess•es** /'prɒsɛsɪz, -əsɪz, -ə,siyz/ *v.* —*n.* [*count*] **1.** a series of actions aimed at making something or accomplishing some result: *a process for homogenizing milk.* **2.** a continuous action, operation, or series of changes taking place in a definite manner: *the process of decay.* —*v.* [~ + *obj*] **3.** to treat or prepare (raw materials or the like) by some process, as in manufacturing. **4.** to handle (persons, papers, etc.) according to a regular procedure: *to process an application.* —*Idiom.* **5. in the process of,** doing something right now: *She is in the process of packing the boxes.*

pro•ces•sion /prə'sɛʃən/ *n.* **1.** the act of moving along or proceeding in an orderly manner, and in a formal and ceremonial way: [*count*]: *a bridal procession.* [*noncount*]: *marching in procession.* **2.** [*count*] a group of persons, vehicles, etc., moving along in such a manner: *a funeral procession.*

proc•es•sor /'prɒsɛsər/ *n.* [*count*] **1.** a person or thing that processes: *a food processor.* **2.** a computer.

pro-choice /prow'tʃɔys/ *adj.* supporting the right to legalized abortion.

pro•claim /prow'kleym, prə-/ *v.* [~ + *obj*] to declare in an official public manner: *proclaimed victory.*

proc•la•ma•tion /,prɒklə'meyʃən/ *n.* **1.** [*noncount*] the act of proclaiming: *approved by proclamation.* **2.** [*count*] something proclaimed: *a proclamation of independence.*

pro•cras•ti•nate /prow'kræstə,neyt, prə-/ *v.* [*no obj*], **-nat•ed, -nat•ing.** to put off action until some later time. —**pro•cras•ti•na•tion** /prow,kræstə'neyʃən, prə-/, *n.* [*noncount*] —**pro'cras•ti,na•tor,** *n.* [*count*]

proc•tor /'prɒktər/ *n.* [*count*] **1.** one whose job is to keep watch over students during examinations. —*v.* [~ + *obj*] [*no obj*] **2.** to supervise or monitor.

pro•cure /prow'kyʊr, prə-/ *v.,* **-cured, -cur•ing. 1.** [~ + *obj*] to obtain (something) by care or effort: *to procure secret documents.* **2.** [~ + *obj*] [*no obj*] to obtain (a person) for prostitution.

prod /prɒd/ *v.,* **prod•ded, prod•ding,** *n.* —*v.* [~ + *obj*] **1.** to jab with something pointed. **2.** to urge (someone) to do something: *Let's prod him to get a job.* —*n.* [*count*] **3.** the act of prodding. **4.** a pointed instrument used to force a person or animal to move along: *a cattle prod.*

pro•di•gious /prə'dɪdʒəs/ *adj.* **1.** extraordinary in size, amount, etc. **2.** causing admiration: *a prodigious feat.*

prod•i•gy /'prɒdɪdʒiy/ *n.* [*count*], *pl.* **-gies.** a person, esp. a child, having extraordinary talent.

pro•duce /*v.*prə'duws, -'dyuws; *n.* 'prɒduws, -yuws, 'prowduws, -dyuws/ *v.,* **-duced, -duc•ing,** *n.* —*v.* **1.** to make or manufacture: [~ + *obj*]: *to produce automobiles for export.* [*no obj*]: *The new auto plant is not ready to produce yet.* **2.** [~ + *obj*] to present; exhibit: *He produced his passport.* **3.** [~ + *obj*] to bring (a play, etc.) before the public: *He has produced several TV shows.* —*n.* **prod•uce,** [*noncount*] **4.** agricultural products thought of as a group, esp. vegetables and fruits. —**pro'duc•er,** *n.* [*count*]

prod•uct /'prɒdəkt, -ʌkt/ *n.* [*count*] **1.** a thing produced by labor: *farm products.* **2.** a person or thing thought of as resulting from a process: *She was a product of a good private school.* **3.** *Math.* the result of multiplying two or more numbers together.

pro•duc•tion /prə'dʌkʃən/ *n.* **1.** [*noncount*] the act of producing: *improved methods of production.* **2.** [*count*] something produced; a product. **3.** [*count*] a situation or activity that has been made complicated or difficult for no good reason: *That child makes a big production out of going to bed.*

pro•duc•tive /prə'dʌktɪv/ *adj.* **1.** that produces a large amount: *a productive writer.* **2.** producing a useful result: *a productive meeting.*

pro•duc•tiv•i•ty /,prowdʌk'tɪvɪtiy, ,prɒdək-/ *n.* [*noncount*] the degree to which a person, company, etc., is able to produce efficiently: *Decreases in productivity lead to declining profits.*

Prof., an abbreviation of: Professor.

pro•fane /prə'feyn, prow-/ *adj.* **1.** showing disrespect toward God or sacred things. **2.** not devoted to holy purposes.

pro•fan•i•ty /prə'fænɪtiy, prow-/ *n., pl.* **-ties. 1.** [*noncount*] the quality of being profane. **2.** [*noncount*] [*count*] disrespectful speech.

pro•fess /prə'fɛs/ *v.* [~ + *obj*] **1.** to claim to have, be, or feel (something), often insincerely: *professed regret; professed to respect human rights.* **2.** to declare openly: *He professed his complete satisfaction.*

pro•fes•sion /prə'fɛʃən/ *n.* **1.** [*count*] an occupation requiring a great deal of education or training. **2.** any occupation or form of employment: [*count*]: *an interesting profession.* [*noncount*]: *a teacher by profession.* **3.** [*count*] the act of professing or declaring something.

pro•fes•sion•al /prə'fɛʃənl/ *adj.* **1.** [*before a noun*] engaged in an occupation as a means of earning a livelihood: *a professional musician.* **2.** relating or appropriate to a profession: *a professional license.* —*n.* [*count*] **3.** a member of a profession. **4.** a person who earns a living in a sport or other occupation that is engaged in by amateurs: *a tennis professional.* —**pro'fes•sion•al•ly,** *adv.*

pro•fes•sor /prə'fɛsər/ *n.* [*count*] a college or university teacher of the highest academic rank.

pro•fi•cient /prə'fɪʃənt/ *adj.* fully skilled; competent. —**pro'fi•cien•cy** /prə'fɪʃənsiy/, *n.* [*noncount*] —**pro'fi•cient•ly,** *adv.*

pro•file /'prowfayl/ *n.* [*count*] **1.** the outline of the human face as viewed from one side. **2.** a short, informal piece of writing about someone.

prof•it /'prɒfɪt/ *n.* **1.** [*count*] [*noncount*] Often, **profits.** [*plural*] money gained, as from a business or sale, after deducting costs. **2.** [*noncount*] advantage; benefit; gain: *What profit is there in honesty?* —*v.* [~ + *obj*] **3.** to gain a profit. —**prof•it•a•ble,** *adj.*

pro•found /prə'fawnd/ *adj.,* **-er, -est. 1.** showing deep insight or understanding. **2.** coming from the deepest part of one's feelings or being: *his profound grief.* **3.** [*before a noun*] complete and total: *a profound silence.* —**pro'found•ly,** *adv.*

pro•fuse /prə'fyuws/ *adj.* generous; abundant: *profuse in their praise.* —**pro'fuse•ly,** *adv.* —**pro'fu•sion** /-'fyuwʒən/, *n.* [*noncount*]

prog•no•sis /prɒg'nowsɪs/ *n.* [*count*], *pl.* **-ses** /-siyz/. a forecasting of the probable course and outcome of a disease.

P

pro•gram /'prowgræm, -grəm/ *n.*, *v.*, **-grammed** or **-gramed**, **-gram•ming** or **-gram•ing**. —*n.* [*count*] **1.** a plan of action to accomplish a certain goal: *a drug rehabilitation program.* **2.** a planned schedule of activities. **3.** a radio or television performance or production. **4.** a list of selections, performers, etc., included in a musical, theatrical, or other entertainment, or the selections themselves. **5.** a piece of computer software. —*v.* **6.** [~ + *obj*] to schedule or establish as part of a program: *The bells are programmed to go off at noon.* **7.** [~ + *obj*] [*no obj*] to provide a computer program for. Also, *esp. Brit.*, **'pro•gramme.**

pro•gram•mer /'prowgræmər/ *n.* [*count*] a person who writes computer programs.

prog•ress /*n.* 'progrɛs, -rəs; *v.* prə'grɛs/ *n.* [*noncount*] **1.** advancement toward a goal or to a further or higher stage: *to make progress in the peace talks.* **2.** forward or onward movement: *the progress of the planets around the sun.* —*v.* **pro•gress** [*no obj*] **3.** to go forward or onward in space or time: *The years are progressing.* —*Idiom.* **4. in progress,** going on; under way: *His long novel is a work in progress.* —**pro'gres•sion,** *n.* [*noncount*] [*count*]

pro•gres•sive /prə'grɛsɪv/ *adj.* **1.** calling for or favoring progress or reform, esp. in political and social matters. **2.** continuously increasing in extent or severity: *a progressive worsening of the disease.* —*n.* [*count*] **3.** a person who favors progress or reform. —**pro'gres•sive•ly,** *adv.*

pro•hib•it /prow'hɪbɪt/ *v.* [~ + *obj*] **1.** to forbid by authority, rule, or law: *Smoking is prohibited in this building.* **2.** to prevent; make impossible: *Lack of funds prohibited her from taking classes.* —,**pro•hi'bi•tion,** *n.* [*noncount*] [*count*]

proj•ect /*n.* 'prɒdʒɛkt, -ɪkt; *v.* prə'dʒɛkt/ *n.* [*count*] **1.** a specific plan; scheme. **2.** a large or important undertaking: *a project to widen the streets of the city.* —*v.* **pro•ject 3.** [~ + *obj*] to propose or plan: *The campaign was projected to include all 50 states.* **4.** [~ + *obj*] to throw or force forward or outward. **5.** [~ + *obj*] to calculate or estimate (some future cost, amount, etc.): *Inflation is projected to increase next year.* **6.** [~ + *obj*] to throw (a ray of light or an image) onto a surface or screen: *The light projected his shadow onto the wall behind him.* **7.** [*no obj*] to stick out beyond an edge or surface: *His ears projected from the sides of his head.*

pro•jec•tile /prə'dʒɛktɪl, -tayl/ *n.* [*count*] an object fired from a gun, as a bullet.

pro•jec•tion /prə'dʒɛkʃən/ *n.* **1.** [*noncount*] the act of projecting. **2.** [*count*] something that sticks out beyond an edge or surface. **3.** [*count*] an estimate of some future cost, amount, or the like: *sales projections for next year.*

pro•jec•tor /prə'dʒɛktər/ *n.* [*count*] a machine for throwing an image, films, photographs, etc., onto a screen.

pro-'life, *adj.* opposed to legalized abortion.

pro•lif•er•ate /prə'lɪfə,reyt/ *v.* [*no obj*], **-at•ed,** **-at•ing.** to increase in number; spread rapidly: *Fish proliferated in the warm seas.* —**pro•lif•er•a•tion** /prəlɪfə'reyʃən/, *n.* [*noncount*]

pro•lif•ic /prə'lɪfɪk/ *adj.* highly productive: *a prolific writer.*

pro•logue /'prowlɔg, -lɒg/ *n.* [*count*] an introductory part of a story, poem, novel, speech, etc.

pro•long /prə'lɔŋ, -'lɒŋ/ *v.* [~ + *obj*] to extend the amount of time for; cause (something) to

continue longer: *prolonged their visit.* —**pro•lon•ga•tion** /,prowlɒŋ'geyʃən/, *n.* [*noncount*]

prom /prɒm/ *n.* [*count*] a formal dance held by a high school or college class.

prom•e•nade /,prɒmə'neyd, -'nɑd/ *n.* [*count*] **1.** a stroll or walk, esp. in a public place. **2.** an area used for such walking.

prom•i•nent /'prɒmənənt/ *adj.* **1.** standing out so as to be seen easily; conspicuous: *a prominent bruise.* **2.** leading; very important: *prominent business leaders.* —**'prom•i•nence,** *n.* [*noncount*] —**'prom•i•nent•ly,** *adv.*

pro•mis•cu•ous /prə'mɪskyuwəs/ *adj.* having numerous sexual partners. —**prom•is•cu•i•ty,** *n.* [*noncount*] —**pro'mis•cu•ous•ly,** *adv.*

prom•ise /'prɒmɪs/ *n.*, *v.*, **-ised, -is•ing.** —*n.* **1.** [*count*] a statement or declaration that something will or will not be done, given, etc: *He kept his promise to write regularly.* **2.** [*noncount*] an indication or a sign of future excellence or achievement: *a young writer who shows great promise.* —*v.* **3.** to make a promise of something: [~ + *obj*]: *to promise eternal love; She promised to help with the decorating. She promised (me) that she would help.* [*no obj*]: *I'll be there; I promise.*

prom•is•ing /'prɒməsɪŋ/ *adj.* giving favorable promise; likely to turn out well: *The future looks promising.*

prom•on•to•ry /'prɒmən,tɔriy/ *n.* [*count*], *pl.* **-ries.** a high point of land or rock that sticks out into a body of water.

pro•mote /prə'mowt/ *v.* [~ + *obj*], **-mot•ed,** **-mot•ing.** **1.** to help or encourage the growth or progress of: *to promote world peace.* **2.** to advance in rank or position: *promoted him to sales manager.* **3.** to encourage the sales or public recognition of: *promoted the new car with advertising.* —**pro'mo•tion,** *n.* [*noncount*] [*count*]

prompt /prɒmpt/ *adj.*, **-er, -est,** *v.* —*adj.* **1.** done or acting at once or without delay: *a prompt reply.* —*v.* [~ + *obj*] **2.** to assist (a speaker or performer) by giving a cue: *The teacher prompted the student with the next word of the poem.* —**'prompt•ly,** *adv.* —**'prompt•ness,** *n.* [*noncount*]

pron., an abbreviation of: **1.** pronoun. **2.** pronunciation.

prone /prown/ *adj.* **1.** having a natural tendency toward something; disposed: *The teacher is prone to anger.* **2.** having the front of the body downward; lying with the face down.

prong /prɔŋ, prɒŋ/ *n.* [*count*] one of the long, pointed ends of a fork.

pro•noun /'prow,nawn/ *n.* [*count*] a word used as a substitute for a noun or a noun phrase. *Pronouns in English include* I, you, he, she, it, we, they, them, this, who, *and* what.

pro•nounce /prə'nawns/ *v.* [~ + *obj*], **-nounced, -nounc•ing.** **1.** to make or utter (sounds, words, etc.): *In the word* came, *the letter* "e" *is not pronounced.* **2.** to declare (a person or thing) to be as specified, esp. officially: *I now pronounce you husband and wife. He pronounced the meal fit for a king.* —**pro'nounce•a•ble,** *adj.* —**pro'nounce•ment,** *n.* [*count*]

pro•nun•ci•a•tion /prə,nʌnsiy'eyʃən/ *n.* [*count*] [*noncount*] the way in which a sound, word or language is pronounced: *making fun of my pronunciation.*

proof /pruwf/ *n.* **1.** [*noncount*] evidence or facts that are enough to establish a thing as true or believable. **2.** [*count*] an early copy, as of a manuscript, that is printed for correction or changes. —*v.* [~ + *obj*] **3.** to proofread.

-proof, a combining form meaning: resistant to (*waterproof*); protected against (*bulletproof*).

proof•read /'pruwf,riyd/ *v.,* **-read** /-,rɛd/, **-read•ing.** to read in order to find and mark errors to be corrected: [~ + *obj*]: *proofreading the document.* [*no obj*]: *He enjoys proofreading.* —'**proof,read•er,** *n.* [*count*]

prop¹ /prɒp/ *v.,* **propped, prop•ping,** *n.* —*v.* [~ + *obj*] **1.** to support, or prevent from falling: *to prop an old fence; to prop (up) an unpopular government.* **2.** to rest (a thing) against a support: *He propped the ladder against the wall.* —*n.* [*count*] **3.** something that props; support.

prop² /prɒp/ *n.* [*count*] a movable item used by an actor or entertainer to enliven and enrich the performance.

prop•a•gan•da /,prɒpə'gændə/ *n.* [*noncount*] information or ideas, whether true or false, that are spread about a government, policy, etc.

prop•a•gate /'prɒpə,geyt/ *v.,* **-gat•ed, -gat•ing. 1.** to (cause to) multiply or increase by any process of natural reproduction from the parent stock: [~ + *obj*]: *to propagate seeds.* [*no obj*]: *The insects propagated in great numbers.* **2.** [~ + *obj*] to spread (a report, practice, etc.) from person to person. —**prop•a•ga•tion** /,prɒpə'geyʃən/ *n.* [*noncount*]

pro•pel /prə'pɛl/ *v.* [~ + *obj*], **-pelled, -pel•ling.** to drive forward or onward: *to propel a boat with oars.*

pro•pel•ler /prə'pɛlər/ *n.* [*count*] a device with rotating blades, attached to an engine for propelling an airplane, ship, etc.

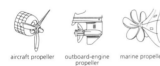

aircraft propeller   outboard-engine   marine propeller
propeller

propellers

pro•pen•si•ty /prə'pɛnsɪtiy/ *n.* [*count*], *pl.* **-ties.** a natural tendency or preference: *a propensity for lying.*

prop•er /'prɒpər/ *adj.* **1.** [*before a noun*] most suitable; right; correct: *Is this the proper time to plant strawberries?* **2.** agreeing with established or accepted standards: *proper behavior; It's not proper to come so late.* —'**prop•er•ly,** *adv.*

'**proper 'noun,** *n.* [*count*] a noun that is the name of a particular person, place, or thing and is usually capitalized in English, as *Lincoln, Beth, Boston.* Also called '**proper 'name.**

prop•er•ty /'prɒpərtiy/ *n.,* *pl.* **-ties. 1.** [*noncount*] the possession or possessions of a particular owner; things owned. **2.** [*noncount*] [*count*] land or buildings, or both together: *They own property upstate.* **3.** [*count*] a basic, essential, or special quality of a thing: *the chemical properties of alcohol.*

proph•e•cy /'prɒfəsiy/ *n.,* *pl.* **-cies. 1.** [*noncount*] the predicting of what is to happen in the future, or the ability to do this: *The magician had the gift of prophecy.* **2.** [*count*] any prediction or forecast: *a prophecy about the election.*

proph•e•sy /'prɒfə,say/ *v.* [~ + *obj*] [*no obj*], **-sied, -sy•ing.** to foretell or predict.

proph•et /'prɒfɪt/ *n.* [*count*] **1.** a person who speaks for God or a god, so as to lead or warn

people. **2.** a person who predicts the future. —**pro'phet•ic,** *adj.*

pro•po•nent /prə'pownənt/ *n.* [*count*] a person who argues in favor of something; advocate.

pro•por•tion /prə'pɔrʃən/ *n.* **1.** [*count*] a relation between things when compared to one another in regard to size, quantity, number, etc.: *A large proportion of the students came from China.* **2.** [*noncount*] proper relation between things or parts: *to have a sense of proportion.* **3. proportions,** [*plural*] dimensions or size: *a man of large proportions.* —**pro'por•tion•al,** *adj.*

pro•pose /prə'powz/ *v.,* **-posed, -pos•ing. 1.** [~ + *obj*] to offer for consideration, acceptance, or action; suggest: *to propose a new method; I propose that we do away with that tax.* **2.** [~ + *obj*] to plan; intend: *He proposes to leave by five.* **3.** [~ + *obj*] [*no obj*] to make an offer, esp. of marriage. —**pro'pos•al,** *n.* [*noncount*] [*count*]

prop•o•si•tion /,prɒpə'zɪʃən/ *n.* [*count*] **1.** the act of proposing. **2.** a plan or scheme proposed; anything put forward for discussion. **3.** a thing, matter, or person considered as something to be dealt with or encountered: *Climbing that mountain is a tough proposition.* —*v.* [~ + *obj*] **4.** to propose having sexual relations with.

pro•pound /prə'pawnd/ *v.* [~ + *obj*] to put forward for discussion; propose.

pro•pri•e•tar•y /prə'prayɪ,tɛriy/ *adj.* made or sold only by the owner of the patent or trademark: *a proprietary medicine.*

pro•pri•e•tor /prə'prayɪtər/ *n.* [*count*] the owner of a business.

pro•pri•e•ty /prə'prayɪtiy/ *n.* [*noncount*], *pl.* **-ties.** agreement with established standards of good or proper behavior or manners: *behaving with the utmost propriety.*

pro•pul•sion /prə'pʌlʃən/ *n.* [*noncount*] the act of propelling; the state of being propelled: *jet propulsion.*

pro•sa•ic /prow'zeyɪk/ *adj.* commonplace or dull.

pro•scribe /prow'skrayb/ *v.* [~ + *obj*], **-scribed, -scrib•ing.** to condemn (a thing) as harmful or illegal; prohibit.

prose /prowz/ *n.* [*noncount*] the ordinary form of spoken or written language, as distinguished from poetry or verse.

pros•e•cute /'prɒsɪ,kyuwt/ *v.* [~ + *obj*] [*no obj*], **-cut•ed, -cut•ing.** to conduct legal proceedings against (a person), as in a court of law. —,**pros•e'cu•tion,** *n.* [*noncount*] [*count*]

pros•e•cu•tor /'prɒsɪ,kyuwtər/ *n.* [*count*] an attorney who conducts legal proceedings against a person.

pros•e•lyt•ize /'prɒsəlɪ,tayz/ *v.* [*no obj*] [~ + *obj*], **-ized, -iz•ing.** to attempt to convert (someone) to one's own faith or cause.

pros•pect /'prɒspɛkt/ *n.* **1.** Usually, **prospects.** [*plural*] a person's chances of advancement, success, profit, etc.: *chosen for his good prospects as a leader.* **2.** anticipation; expectation: [*noncount*]: *the prospect of facing yet another day without hope.* [*count*]: *Prospects for peace have improved.* **3.** [*count*] a possible or likely customer, candidate, etc. —*v.* [*no obj*] [~ + *obj*] **4.** to search or explore (a region), as for precious minerals.

pro•spec•tive /prə'spɛktɪv/ *adj.* [*before a noun*] possible, likely, or expected; potential: *a prospective customer.*

pros•pec•tor /'prɒspɛktər/ *n.* [*count*] one who prospects for minerals.

pros•per /'prɒspər/ *v.* [*no obj*] to be successful

or fortunate, esp. financially. —**pros•per•ous,** *adj.*

pros•per•i•ty /prɒ'spɛrɪtiy/ *n.* [*noncount*] a successful, flourishing, or thriving condition, esp. in financial respects.

'prostate ,gland /'prɒsteyt/ *n.* [*count*] a gland at the base of the bladder in males. Also, **'pros•tate.**

pros•ti•tute /'prɒstɪ,tuwt, -,tyuwt/ *n.* [*count*] a woman or man who engages in sexual acts for money. —,**pros•ti'tu•tion,** *n.* [*noncount*]

pros•trate /'prɒstreyt/ *v.,* **-trat•ed, -trat•ing,** *adj.* —*v.* [~ + *oneself*] **1.** to throw (oneself) flat on the ground with the face down, as to show submission or adoration. —*adj.* **2.** lying with the face down. —**pros•tra•tion** /prɒstreyʃən/, *n.* [*noncount*]

pro•tag•o•nist /prow'tægənɪst/ *n.* [*count*] the leading character of a drama or other piece of writing.

pro•tect /prə'tɛkt/ *v.* to defend or guard from attack, invasion, loss, insult, etc.: [~ + *obj*]: *The turtle's shell protects it from injury.* [*no obj*]: *The police are there to protect.* —**pro'tec•tion,** *n.* [*noncount*] [*count*] —**pro'tec•tor,** *n.* [*count*]

pro•tec•tive /prə'tɛktɪv/ *adj.* **1.** [*before a noun*] having the quality or function of protecting: *a protective helmet.* **2.** tending strongly to protect: *She had very protective parents. A mother robin is very protective of her young.*

pro•té•gé /'prowtə,ʒey, ,prowtə'ʒey/ *n.* [*count*], *pl.* **-gés.** a person who receives support or guidance from someone older or more experienced.

pro•tein /'prowtiyn, -tiyɪn/ *n.* **1.** [*count*] a molecule that makes up a large portion of the mass of every life form, and is necessary to the diet of all animals. plant or animal tissue rich in such molecules: [*noncount*]: *Meat is a source of protein.* [*count*]: *various animal proteins.*

pro•test /*n.* 'prowtɛst; *v.* prə'tɛst, 'prowtɛst/ *n.* [*noncount*] [*count*] **1.** an act of declaring one's objection to, disapproval of, or disagreement with some act or action. —*v.* **2.** to make a protest (against): [*no obj*]: *They protested against the war.* [~ + *obj*]: *The students protested the bombing.* **3.** [~ + *obj*] to affirm or declare in protest: *They protested their innocence. They protested that they were innocent.* —,**protes'ta•tion,** *n.* [*count*] —**pro'test•er,** *n.* [*count*]

Prot•es•tant /'prɒtəstənt/ *n.* [*count*] any Western Christian who is not a Roman Catholic.

proto-, a combining form meaning: earliest or original (*prototype*); foremost or essential (*protoplasm*).

pro•to•col /'prowtə,kɔl, -,kɒl/ *n.* [*noncount*] the customs, rules, and regulations dealing with formal courtesies, good manners, or diplomatic relations between countries.

pro•ton /'prowtɒn/ *n.* [*count*] a positively charged particle found in all atomic nuclei.

pro•to•plasm /'prowtə,plæzəm/ *n.* [*noncount*] the liquid substance of which cells are formed.

pro•to•type /'prowtə,tayp/ *n.* [*count*] a model or first version of a product to be manufactured on a large scale.

pro•to•zo•an /,prowtə'zowən/ *n.* [*count*], *pl.* **-zo•ans,** (*esp. when thought of as a group*) **-zo•a** /-'zowə/. a one-celled organism.

pro•tract•ed /prow'træktɪd, prə-/ *adj.* drawn out, esp. in time; prolonged: *a protracted discus--sion.*

pro•trac•tor /prow'træktər, prə-/ *n.* [*count*] an instrument used for measuring or drawing angles.

pro•trude /prow'truwd, prə-/ *v.,* **-trud•ed, -trud•ing.** to (cause to) stick out: [*no obj*]: *His belly protruded over his belt.* [~ + *obj*]: *The snake protruded its tongue.* —**pro'tru•sion,** *n.* [*noncount*] [*count*]

pro•tu•ber•ance /prow'tuwbərəns, -'tyuw-, prə-/ *n.* **1.** [*count*] a part or thing that sticks out or bulges out. **2.** [*noncount*] the state or quality of protruding. —**pro'tu•ber•ant,** *adj.*

proud /prawd/ *adj.,* **-er, -est, 1.** feeling satisfaction over something thought of as bringing credit or honor to oneself: *the proud parents of a new baby; We are proud of our country. She is proud to accept the honor. She is proud that she is an American.* **2.** having too high an opinion of oneself: *too proud to admit she's wrong.* **3.** having or showing self-respect: *too proud to accept a loan.* —'**proud•ly,** *adv.*

prove /pruwv/ *v.,* **proved, proved** or **prov•en** /'pruwvən/, **prov•ing. 1.** [~ + *obj*] to establish the truth of something, as by evidence or argument: *He was able to prove his innocence by producing a witness. She proved to me that she was not the one spreading gossip.* **2.** [~ + *oneself*] to show (oneself) to be worthy or capable: *This job will give you a chance to prove yourself.* **3.** [~ + *obj*] to demonstrate as having a particular quality: *The medicine proved (to be) effective.*

prov•e•nance /'prɒvənəns, -,nɑns/ *n.* [*noncount*] a place or source of origin: *a manuscript of unknown provenance.*

prov•erb /'prɒvərb/ *n.* [*count*] a short popular saying that expresses some commonplace truth or useful thought.

pro•vide /prə'vayd/ *v.,* **-vid•ed, -vid•ing. 1.** [~ + *obj*] to make available; furnish or supply: *to provide benefits for employees; to provide employees with benefits.* **2.** [*no obj*] to supply means of support: *They worked hard to provide for their children.* **3.** [~ + *obj*] to require, as by a provision: *The contract provides that the writer will receive $10,000.* —**pro'vid•er,** *n.* [*count*]

pro•vid•ed /prə'vaydɪd/ *conj.* on the condition or understanding (that); if: *She'll talk to you provided (that) you listen.*

prov•i•dence /'prɒvɪdəns/ *n.* [*noncount; often: Providence*] the care and guidance of God or nature, esp. in controlling human lives.

prov•i•dent /'prɒvɪdənt/ *adj.* having or showing careful thought for the future, as by saving money.

pro•vid•ing /prə'vaydɪŋ/ *conj.* provided: *You can stay, providing (that) you help with the housework.*

prov•ince /'prɒvɪns/ *n.* **1.** [*count*] a division or unit of a country that has its own government: *the provinces of Canada.* **2.** [*count; usually singular*] an area or field of activity, study, or knowledge.

pro•vin•cial /prə'vɪnʃəl/ *adj.* **1.** of or relating to the provinces. **2.** narrow-minded in outlook; unsophisticated.

pro•vi•sion /prə'vɪʒən/ *n.* **1.** [*noncount*] the act of providing or supplying: *the provision of electricity to the region.* **2.** [*noncount*] an arrangement or preparation for the future: *Did they make provision for the possibility that costs would increase?* **3.** **provisions,** [*plural*] supplies of food. **4.** [*count*] a legal or formal requirement or condition.

pro•vi•sion•al /prə'vɪʒənļ/ *adj.* serving for the

time being only; temporary: *a provisional government.*

prov•o•ca•tion /ˌprɒvəˈkeyʃən/ *n.* the act of provoking or causing a violent or strong reaction: [*noncount*]: *The animal attacked without provocation.* [*count*]: *Numerous provocations led to a full-scale war.*

pro•voc•a•tive /prəˈvɒkətɪv/ *adj.* **1.** tending or serving to provoke. **2.** intending to arouse sexual desire: *a provocative dress.* —**pro'voc•a•tive•ly**, *adv.*

pro•voke /prəˈvowk/ *v.* [~ + *obj*], **-voked, -vok•ing. 1.** to anger or annoy: *Stop provoking them with your negative comments.* **2.** to stir up, arouse, or call forth (feelings, desires, or actions): *She provoked anger in a lot of people.*

prow /praw/ *n.* [*count*] the front part of a ship or boat; bow.

prow•ess /ˈprawɪs/ *n.* [*noncount*] great or exceptional ability, skill, or strength.

prowl /prawl/ *v.* to go about or move around in a quiet, sneaky way, as in search of something to steal or capture: [*no obj*]: *The neighbor's cat prowls around all night.* [~ + *obj*]: *The gang was out prowling the streets.* —**'prowl•er,** *n.* [*count*]

prox•im•i•ty /prɒkˈsɪmɪtiy/ *n.* [*noncount*] nearness in place, time, relation, etc.

prude /pruwd/ *n.* [*count*] a person who is overly proper or modest and is easily shocked, esp. in matters involving sex. —**prud•er•y** /ˈpruwdəriy/, *n.* [*noncount*] —**'prud•ish,** *adj.*

pru•dent /ˈpruwdnt/ *adj.* **1.** wise in practical affairs; thinking carefully before acting; sensible. **2.** careful in providing for the future: *prudent saving.* —**'pru•dence,** *n.* [*noncount*] —**'pru•dent•ly,** *adv.*

prune[1] /pruwn/ *n.* [*count*] a dried plum.

prune[2] /pruwn/ *v.* [~ + *obj*], **pruned, prun•ing.** to cut or chop off extra or unwanted twigs, branches, or roots from; trim: *She pruned the trees in her garden.* —**'prun•er,** *n.* [*count*]

pry[1] /pray/ *v.* [*no obj*], **pried, pry•ing.** to ask rude or impolite questions about something private: *He pried into her personal life.*

pry[2] /pray/ *v.* [~ + *obj*], **pried, pry•ing.** to move, raise, or open, with or as if with a lever: *pried off the lid of the jar.*

P.S., an abbreviation of: **1.** Also, **p.s.** postscript. **2.** Public School.

psalm /sɑm/ *n.* [*count*] a sacred song or hymn.

pseudo-, a combining form meaning false or pretended (*pseudonym*).

pseu•do•nym /ˈsuwdn̩ɪm/ *n.* [*count*] a false name used by an author to conceal identity.

psy•che /ˈsaykiy/ *n.* [*count*] the human soul, spirit, or mind.

psy•che•del•ic /ˌsaykɪˈdɛlɪk/ *adj.* **1.** (of certain drugs) causing a person to see things that are not really present. **2.** resembling or characteristic of images or sounds experienced while in such a state: *a psychedelic painting.*

psy•chi•a•try /sɪˈkayətriy, say-/ *n.* [*noncount*] the branch of medicine concerned with the study and treatment of mental disorders. —**psy•chi'at•ric,** *adj.* —**psy'chi•a•trist,** *n.* [*count*]

psy•chic /ˈsaykɪk/ *adj.* **1.** of or relating to the human psyche. **2.** of or relating to some force that is outside natural or scientific knowledge: *psychic power to tell what people are thinking.* —*n.* [*count*] **3.** a person with psychic powers.

psy•cho•a•nal•y•sis /ˌsaykowəˈnæləsɪs/ *n.*

[*noncount*] a method for studying the hidden or unconscious processes of the mind as a way of treating mental illness. —**psy•cho•an•a•lyst** /ˌsaykowˈænl̩ɪst/, *n.* [*count*]

psy•chol•o•gy /sayˈkɒlədʒiy/ *n.* [*noncount*], *pl.* **-gies. 1.** the science of the mind or of mental states and processes. **2.** mental ploys or strategy: *He used psychology on his boss to get a promotion.* —ˌ**psy•cho'log•i•cal,** *adj.* —**psy'chol•o•gist,** *n.* [*count*]

psy•cho•ther•a•py /ˌsaykowˈθɛrəpiy/ *n.* [*noncount*] [*count*], *pl.* **-pies.** the psychological treatment of mental or emotional disorders. —**psy•cho'ther•a•pist,** *n.* [*count*]

pt., an abbreviation of: pint.

pub /pʌb/ *n.* [*count*] a bar or tavern.

pu•ber•ty /ˈpyuwbərtiy/ *n.* [*noncount*] the period of life during which the sex organs mature.

pu•bic /ˈpyuwbɪk/ *adj.* [*before a noun*] of or near the genital organs: *pubic hair.*

pub•lic /ˈpʌblɪk/ *adj.* **1.** of, for, or affecting a population or community as a whole: *the public welfare.* **2.** relating to a government or its services: *a public official.* **3.** generally known to most people of a community: *The information became public.* —*n.* [*noncount*; the + ~] **4.** the people who make up a community, state, or nation. —*Idiom.* **5. in public,** in a situation open to public notice: *She doesn't like to sing in public.* —**'pub•lic•ly,** *adv.*

pub•li•ca•tion /ˌpʌblɪˈkeyʃən/ *n.* **1.** [*noncount*] the act of publishing something. **2.** [*count*] something published.

pub•lic•i•ty /pʌˈblɪsɪtiy/ *n.* [*noncount*] widespread mention about a person or thing in the newspapers, on TV, etc.: *publicity for his new book.*

pub•li•cize /ˈpʌbləˌsayz/ *v.* [~ + *obj*], **-cized, -ciz•ing.** to give publicity to: *Can you publicize the school play?*

'public ˌschool, *n.* [*count*] [*noncount*] **1.** (in the U.S.) a school, usually for primary or secondary grades, that is paid for by public taxes. **2.** (in England) any of a number of secondary boarding schools that prepare students for the universities or public service.

pub•lish /ˈpʌblɪʃ/ *v.* **1.** [~ + *obj*] [*no obj*] to issue (newspapers, books, software, etc.) for sale or distribution to the public. **2.** [~ + *obj*] to issue publicly (the work of): *They publish (the plays of) William Shakespeare.* —**'pub•lish•er,** *n.* [*count*]

puck /pʌk/ *n.* [*count*] a hard rubber disk that is hit into the goal in ice hockey.

puck•er /ˈpʌkər/ *v.* to draw or gather into wrinkles or folds: [*no obj*]: *His face puckered when he bit into the sour candy.* [~ + *obj*]: *She puckered her lips, expecting a kiss.*

pud•ding /ˈpʊdɪŋ/ *n.* [*noncount*] [*count*] a soft, thickened dessert, made with milk, sugar, flour, and flavoring.

pud•dle /ˈpʌdl̩/ *n.* [*count*] a small pool of water or other liquid.

pudg•y /ˈpʌdʒiy/ *adj.*, **-i•er, -i•est.** short and fat or thick: *an infant's pudgy fingers.*

pueb•lo /ˈpwɛblow/ *n.* [*count*], *pl.* **-los.** a dwelling of certain Native Americans of the southwestern U.S., usually made of sun-dried clay bricks.

puff /pʌf/ *n.* **1.** a short, quick blast of air, smoke, etc. **2.** an act of inhaling and exhaling, as on a cigarette. **3.** a ball of light pastry filled with whipped cream, jam, etc. —*v.* **4.** [~ + *obj*] [*no obj*] to (cause to) be let out or given out in a puff. **5.** [*no obj*] to breathe quickly and with difficulty. **6.** [*no obj*] to go or move with puffs: *The train puffed into the station.* **7.** to (cause to) become inflated or fluffy: [*no obj*]: *Her face puffed (up) in reaction to the poison ivy.* [~ + *obj*]: *The bird puffed (up) its feathers.*

puf•fy /ˈpʌfiy/ *adj.,* **-fi•er, -fi•est.** swollen in appearance.

pug /pʌg/ *n.* [*count*] one of a breed of small, squarely built dogs with a deeply wrinkled face.

pug•na•cious /pʌgˈneyʃəs/ *adj.* too ready or eager to quarrel or fight.

'pug 'nose, *n.* [*count*] a short, broad, somewhat turned-up nose.

puke /pyuwk/ *v.,* **puked, puk•ing,** *n. Slang.* —*v.* [*no obj*] [~ + *obj*] **1.** to vomit. —*n.* [*noncount*] **2.** vomit.

pull /pʊl/ *v.* **1.** to draw or move something toward oneself or in a particular direction: [~ + *obj*]: *He pulled the sled up the hill.* [*no obj*]: *He pulled at the sled.* **2.** [~ + *obj*] to draw or pluck away from a place of growth, attachment, etc.: *The dentist pulled four of her teeth.* **3.** [~ + *obj*] to strain (a muscle). **4.** [*no obj*] to move or go: *The train pulled away from the station.* **5. pull in,** to arrive: *The train just pulled in.* **6. pull off,** *Informal.* to perform successfully, esp. something difficult: *His team pulled off a victory. I don't know how you pulled it off, but you got the job!* **7. pull out, a.** to depart: *The train pulled out about three hours later.* **b.** to abandon abruptly: *to pull out of an agreement.* **8. pull over,** to direct one's automobile or other vehicle to the curb: *The police officer told me to pull over. He told me to pull the car over.* **9. pull through,** to (cause to) come safely through (a crisis, illness, etc.): *If we stay together, we'll pull through. I'm sure we'll pull through this crisis.* **10. pull up, a.** to bring or draw closer: *She ran faster and finally pulled up to me.* **b.** to remove by the roots: *He pulled up some weeds* or *He pulled some weeds up.* —*n.* **11.** [*count*] the act of pulling: *signaled them with two pulls on the rope.* **12.** [*count*] a part or thing to be pulled, as a handle on a drawer. **13.** [*noncount*] influence, as with persons able to grant favors: *has a lot of pull with the mayor.*

pul•let /ˈpʊlɪt/ *n.* [*count*] a young hen.

pul•ley /ˈpʊliy/ *n.* [*count*], *pl.* **-leys.** a device consisting of a wheel with a grooved edge in which a rope or cable can move, used for lifting heavy things.

pull•o•ver /ˈpʊlˌowvər/ *n.* [*count*] a garment, esp. a sweater, that is drawn over the head.

pul•mo•nar•y /ˈpʌlməˌnɛriy, ˈpʊl-/ *adj.* of or affecting the lungs.

pulp /pʌlp/ *n.* [*noncount*] **1.** the soft, juicy part of a fruit that can be eaten. **2.** the inner substance of the tooth. **3.** a soft, moist, slightly sticky mass of wood or rags, used to make paper. —**'pulp•y,** *adj.,* **-i•er, -i•est.**

pul•pit /ˈpʊlpɪt, ˈpʌl-/ *n.* [*count*] a platform in a church, from which the service is conducted.

pul•sate /ˈpʌlseyt/ *v.* [*no obj*], **-sat•ed, -sat•ing.** **1.** to beat; throb: *The blood was pulsating through his veins.* **2.** to vibrate.

pulse /pʌls/ *n.,* *v.,* **pulsed, puls•ing.** —*n.* [*count*] **1.** the regular beating or throbbing of the arteries, caused by the contractions of the heart: *The doctor felt his wrist for a pulse.* **2.** a stroke, vibration, or regular series of beats: *a pulse of drums.* —*v.* [*no obj*] **3.** to beat or throb; pulsate: *The blood pulsed through his veins.*

pul•ver•ize /ˈpʌlvəˌrayz/ *v.,* **-ized, -iz•ing.** to

(cause to) be turned into dust or powder, as by pounding or grinding: [~ + *obj*]: *The workers pulverized the rocks.* [*no obj*]: *Over time the mineral slowly pulverized.*

pu•ma /ˈpyuwmə, ˈpuw-/ *n.,* *pl.* **-mas.** COUGAR.

pum•ice /ˈpʌmɪs/ *n.* [*noncount*] a rough or sometimes spongy rock, a form of volcanic glass, used to clean or smooth objects.

pum•mel /ˈpʌməl/ *v.* [~ + *obj*], **-meled, -mel•ing** or (*esp. Brit.*) **-melled, -mel•ling.** to beat or punch with or as if with the fists.

pump[1] /pʌmp/ *n.* [*count*] **1.** a machine for forcing fluids or gases into or out of a place or container: *an air pump; gas pumps.* —*v.* **2.** to raise or drive with a pump: [~ + *obj*]: *to pump water from the well.* [*no obj*]: *His heart was still pumping.* **3.** [~ + *obj*] to free from water or other liquid by means of a pump: *After the flood they tried to pump (out) the basement.* **4.** [~ + *obj*] to question (someone) cleverly or persistently: *tried to pump me for information.* **5. pump up, a.** to inflate by pumping: *to pump up a tire* or *to pump a tire up.* **b.** to cause to have enthusiasm, competitive spirit, etc.: *The coach pumped up the team* or *The coach pumped the team up.*

pump[2] /pʌmp/ *n.* [*count*] a woman's shoe that slips on the foot without fastening.

pum•per•nick•el /ˈpʌmpərˌnɪkəl/ *n.* [*noncount*] a dark, slightly sour bread made from rye flour.

pump•kin /ˈpʌmpkɪn or, commonly, ˈpʌŋkɪn/ *n.* a large, orange-yellow fruit that grows on a vine that lies on the ground: [*count*]: *to carve pumpkins on Halloween.* [*noncount*]: *a pie filled with pumpkin.*

pun /pʌn/ *n.,* *v.,* **punned, pun•ning.** —*n.* [*count*] **1.** a joke based on a word that has more than one meaning, or two words that sound alike but have different meanings. —*v.* [*no obj*] **2.** to make puns.

punch[1] /pʌntʃ/ *n.* **1.** [*count*] a blow, esp. with the fist. **2.** [*noncount*] forcefulness or effectiveness; power: *Your writing lacks punch.* —*v.* [~ + *obj*] [*no obj*] **3.** to give a sharp thrust or blow to, esp. with the fist: *punched him right in the nose; They started punching and wrestling.* **4.** to strike or hit in operating: *to punch an elevator button; punching at the computer keyboard.* **5. punch in** or **out,** to record one's time of arrival at work (or departure from work) by inserting a card in a machine.

punch[2] /pʌntʃ/ *n.* [*count*] **1.** a tool or machine for making holes in paper or metal. —*v.* [~ + *obj*] **2.** to make holes in with a punch.

punch[3] /pʌntʃ/ *n.* [*noncount*] a drink consisting of liquor mixed with fruit juice, soda, etc.

'punch ,line, *n.* [*count*] the final phrase or sentence in a joke or humorous story that conveys the point and is the source of humor.

punc•tu•al /ˈpʌŋktʃuwəl/ *adj.* being on time; prompt: *He was always punctual for meetings.* —**punc•tu•al•i•ty** /ˌpʌŋktʃuwˈælɪtiy/ *n.* [*noncount*]

punc•tu•ate /ˈpʌŋktʃuwˌeyt/ *v.* [~ + *obj*] [*no obj*], **-at•ed, -at•ing.** to mark or divide (something written) with punctuation.

punc•tu•a•tion /ˌpʌŋktʃuwˈeyʃən/ *n.* [*noncount*] **1.** the use of certain marks or characters in writing or printing to separate the elements of sentences and make the meaning clear: *correct punctuation, such as ending a sentence with a period.* **2.** punctuation marks, thought of as a group: *Use punctuation to signal a pause.*

punc•ture /ˈpʌŋktʃər/ *n.,* *v.,* **-tured, -tur•ing.**

—*n.* [*count*] **1.** the act of piercing or making a hole in something, as with a pointed instrument or object. **2.** a hole or mark so made: *punctures from the needle.* —*v.* [~ + *obj*] [*no obj*] **3.** to make or get a hole in something.

pun•gent /ˈpʌndʒənt/ *adj.* sharply affecting the sense of taste or smell: *the pungent aroma of garlic.* —**'pun•gen•cy,** *n.* [*noncount*]

pun•ish /ˈpʌnɪʃ/ *v.* [~ + *obj*] **1.** to cause (someone) to suffer pain, loss, etc., as a penalty for some offense or fault. **2.** to inflict such a penalty for (an offense or fault): *to punish theft.* —**'pun•ish•ment,** *n.* [*noncount*] [*count*]

pu•ni•tive /ˈpyuwnɪtɪv/ *adj.* serving as, concerned with, or giving punishment.

punk /pʌŋk/ *n.* **1.** [*count*] *Slang.* a young hoodlum. **2.** [*noncount*] a style of the 1970's characterized by mostly black clothing and brightly colored hair.

'punk 'rock, *n.* [*noncount*] loud rock music having aggressive, often violent lyrics.

punt /pʌnt/ *n.* [*count*] **1.** a kick, as in football or Rugby, in which the ball is dropped and kicked before it touches the ground. —*v.* [~ + *obj*] [*no obj*] **2.** to kick (a dropped ball) before it touches the ground.

pu•ny /ˈpyuwniy/ *adj.,* **-ni•er, -ni•est. 1.** of less than normal size and strength; weak: *a puny body.* **2.** unimportant; insignificant: *a puny threat.*

pup /pʌp/ *n.* [*count*] **1.** a young dog; puppy. **2.** the young of certain other animals, as the rat or fur seal.

pu•pa /ˈpyuwpə/ *n.* [*count*], *pl.* **-pae** /-piy/, **-pas.** an insect in the nonfeeding, usually nonmoving, stage between the larva and the adult. —**'pu•pal,** *adj.*

pu•pil¹ /ˈpyuwpəl/ *n.* [*count*] a person, usually young, who is being taught by a teacher; student.

pu•pil² /ˈpyuwpəl/ *n.* [*count*] the opening in the iris of the eye that narrows and widens as more or less light passes through.

pup•pet /ˈpʌpɪt/ *n.* [*count*] a usually small figure representing a human being or an animal, moved by the hands or by rods, wires, etc. —**pup•pet•ry** /ˈpʌpɪtriy/, *n.* [*noncount*]

pup•pet•eer /ˌpʌpɪ'tɪər/ *n.* [*count*] a person who moves or handles puppets, as in a puppet show.

pup•py /ˈpʌpiy/ *n.* [*count*], *pl.* **-pies.** a young dog.

pur•chase /ˈpɜrtʃəs/ *v.,* **-chased, -chas•ing,** *n.* —*v.* [~ + *obj*] **1.** to get by the payment of money or its equivalent; buy: *to purchase a house.* —*n.* **2.** [*noncount*] the act of getting something by the payment of money or its equivalent: *Mail in a proof of purchase.* **3.** [*count*] something purchased or bought. —**'pur•chas•er,** *n.* [*count*]

pure /pyor/ *adj.,* **pur•er, pur•est. 1.** free from any extra matter or material: *water pure enough to drink.* **2.** not changed by mixing; clear: *pure white.* **3.** [*before a noun*] complete; absolute: *a pure accident.* **4.** of unmixed ancestry: *The dog was a pure German shepherd.* **5.** free from blemishes: *pure skin.* **6.** free from evil: *a pure heart.* **7.** chaste; virgin: *a pure maiden.* —**'pure•ness,** *n.* [*noncount*]

pu•rée or **pu•ree** /pyʊ'rey, -'riy/ *n., v.,* **-réed, -rée•ing.** —*n.* [*noncount*] [*count*] **1.** a thick liquid prepared from cooked vegetables, fruit, etc., put through a sieve or in a blender. —*v.* [~ + *obj*] **2.** to make a purée of: *puréed the tomatoes.*

pure•ly /ˈpyʊrliy/ *adv.* completely; utterly; absolutely: *It was purely coincidental.*

pur•ga•to•ry /ˈpɜrgəˌtɔriy/ *n.* [*noncount*], *pl.* **-ries.** (esp. in Roman Catholic belief) a place or state following death in which souls are purified of lesser sins and are made ready for heaven.

purge /pɜrdʒ/ *v.,* **purged, purg•ing,** *n.* —*v.* [~ + *obj*] **1.** to rid of impurities; cleanse; purify. **2.** to get rid of or remove (undesirable members) from a government, political organization, etc. —*n.* [*count*] **3.** the act or process of purging.

pu•ri•fy /ˈpyʊrəˌfay/ *v.* [~ + *obj*], **-fied, -fy•ing. 1.** to make pure; free from anything that pollutes or contaminates. **2.** to free from extra or undesirable elements. —**pu•ri•fi•ca•tion** /ˌpyʊrəfɪ'keyʃən/, *n.* [*noncount*] —**'pu•ri,fi•er,** *n.* [*count*]

Pu•ri•tan /ˈpyʊrɪtn̩/ *n.* [*count*] **1.** a member of a group of Protestants of 16th-century England who sought to simplify worship. **2.** [*puritan*] a person who is strict in moral or religious matters, often to an excessive degree. —,**pur•i'tan•i•cal,** *adj.*

pu•ri•ty /ˈpyʊrɪtiy/ *n.* [*noncount*] the quality or state of being pure.

purl /pɜrl/ *n.* [*count*] **1.** a basic stitch in knitting, the reverse of the knit. —*v.* [~ + *obj*] [*no obj*] **2.** to knit with a purl stitch.

pur•ple /ˈpɜrpəl/ *n.* [*noncount*] [*count*] any color having both red and blue, esp. one deep in tone.

pur•pose /ˈpɜrpəs/ *n.* **1.** [*count*] the reason for which something exists or is done, made, etc.: *For what purpose are we meeting today?* **2.** [*noncount*] willingness to accomplish or achieve some goal: *A good student has to have a sense of purpose.* —**Idiom. 3. on purpose,** intentionally: *She spilled the paint on purpose.*

purr /pɜr/ *n.* [*count*] **1.** the low, continuous, vibrating sound a cat makes, as when contented. —*v.* [*no obj*] [~ + *obj*] **2.** to utter such a sound.

purse /pɜrs/ *n., v.,* **pursed, purs•ing.** —*n.* [*count*] **1.** a woman's handbag. **2.** a small bag or case for carrying money. —*v.* [~ + *obj*] **3.** to pucker: *to purse one's lips.*

pur•sue /pər'suw/ *v.* [~ + *obj*], **-sued, -su•ing. 1.** to follow in order to overtake, capture, kill, etc.; chase: *The army pursued the retreating enemy.* **2.** to carry on or continue (a course of action, inquiry, etc.), esp. in order to accomplish some goal: *She pursued a degree in business.* —**pur'su•er,** *n.* [*count*]

pur•suit /pər'suwt/ *n.* **1.** [*noncount*] the act of pursuing: *raced down the street in pursuit of the thief.* **2.** [*count*] an occupation or pastime that one regularly engages in: *literary pursuits.*

pus /pʌs/ *n.* [*noncount*] a yellow-white, liquidlike substance produced by the body in an infected wound, in sores, etc.

push /pʊʃ/ *v.* **1.** to press against with force in order to move: [~ + *obj*]: *He rudely pushed them aside.* [*no obj*]: *They were pushing and shoving.* **2.** to move (something) in a certain way, as by exerting force: [~ + *obj*]: *pushed the door open.* [*no obj*]: *He pushed past me.* **3.** to urge (someone) to some action, or to some course of action: [*no obj*]: *He's pushing to get a promotion.* [~ + *obj*]: *He's pushing himself too hard at his new job. His parents pushed him to get a job.* **4.** [*no obj*] to urge the use, acceptance, or sale of something; promote: *still pushing for reform.* **5.** [~ + *obj*] *Slang.* to sell (illegal drugs): *He was arrested for pushing cocaine.* **6. push around,** to bully or boss around: *pushed around the younger boys* or *pushed the younger boys around.* —*n.* [*count*] **7.**

the act of pushing; a shove or thrust. **8.** a strong effort, campaign, military attack, etc.

'push ,button, *n.* [*count*] a button that opens or closes an electric circuit when it is pressed or released.

push•er /'pʊʃər/ *n.* [*count*] a person who sells illegal drugs.

'push-,up, *n.* [*count*] an exercise in which a person lies with the face down and raises and lowers the body using only the arms.

push•y /'pʊʃiy/ *adj.*, **-i•er, -i•est.** annoyingly bold or self-assertive.

puss /pʊs/ *n.* [*count*] a cat.

puss•y /'pʊsiy/ *n.* [*count*], *pl.* **puss•ies.** a cat, esp. a kitten.

'pussy 'willow /'pʊsiy/ *n.* [*count*] a small willow having silky, furry flowers.

put /pʊt/ *v.*, **put, put•ting,** *n.* —*v.* [~ + *obj*] **1.** to move (anything) into a specific location or position; place: *Put your clothes back in your closet.* **2.** to bring into some condition, relation, etc.: *putting one's affairs in order.* **3.** to force (someone) to undergo something or set (someone) to a duty, task, or action: *They put me to work chopping wood.* **4.** to assign; to place (something) in connection with something else in the mind: *to put the blame on others.* **5.** to estimate: *I'd put the distance at about fifty miles.* **6.** to express or state: *To put it honestly, I don't care.* **7.** to apply to a use or purpose: *She put her knowledge to good use.* **8.** to impose: *to put a tax on beverages.* **9. put aside** or **by,** to store up; save: *She managed to put some money aside* or *She managed to put aside some money.* **10. put down, a.** to write down; record: *Put down your name on the list* or *Put your name down on the list.* **b.** to crush; defeat: *The army put down the rebellion* or *The army put the rebellion down.* **c.** to embarrass; insult: *She always puts me down.* **d.** to pay (money) as a deposit: *putting fifty dollars down* or *putting down fifty dollars.* **11. put in,** to spend (time) as indicated: *He put in twenty-five years at that job.* **12. put off, a.** to postpone: *He put the meeting off* or *He put off the meeting.* **b.** to get rid of by avoiding or delaying: *Put that salesman off until next week* or *Put off that salesman until next week.* **13. put on, a.** to clothe oneself in: *Put your clothes on* or *Put on your clothes.* **b.** to produce or stage: *Put on a show* or *Put a show on.* **c.** *Informal.* to deceive (someone) as a joke; tease: *You're putting me on—there really isn't a*

day off. **14. put through,** to cause (someone) to suffer or endure (something): *She put us through misery.* **15. put up, a.** to construct; erect: *to put up a tent* or *to put a tent up.* **b.** to provide or stake (money), as in gambling or business: *Put up the cash* or *Put the cash up.* **c.** to provide with a place to sleep: *We can put up a few guests* or *We can put a few guests up.* **16. put up with,** to tolerate: *How can you put up with such pain?* —*n.* [*count*] **17.** a throw, esp. with a forward motion of the hand. —*Idiom.* **18. put one's best foot forward,** to try to make as good an impression as possible. **19. put oneself out,** to go to trouble or expense. **20. put something over on,** to deceive.

pu•trid /'pyuwtrɪd/ *adj.* **1.** being in a state of foul decay. **2.** of very low quality; rotten.

putt /pʌt/ *v.* [~ + *obj*] [*no obj*] **1.** to strike (a golf ball) gently so as to make it roll into the hole. —*n.* [*count*] **2.** a stroke made in putting.

put•ter /'pʌtər/ *v.* [*no obj*] to busy or occupy oneself in a leisurely or ineffective manner: *puttering around the house.*

put•ty /'pʌtiy/ *n.* [*noncount*], *pl.* **-ties.** a paste used to hold windowpanes in place, patch woodwork, seal the joints of pipes, etc.

puz•zle /'pʌzəl/ *n.*, *v.*, **-zled, -zling.** —*n.* **1.** [*count*] a toy or other game that presents difficulties to be solved by clever thinking or patient effort. **2.** [*count; usually singular*] a matter or person that is difficult to understand or explain. —*v.* **3.** [~ + *obj*] to confuse; baffle: *My symptoms puzzled the doctor.* **4.** [*no obj*] to think over some confusing or perplexing matter. —**'puz•zle•ment,** *n.* [*noncount*]

Pyg•my /'pɪgmiy/ *n.* [*count*], *pl.* **-mies. 1.** a member of any of several small or short peoples of central Africa. **2.** [*pygmy*] a small or dwarfish person or thing.

py•jam•as /pə'dʒɑməz, -'dʒæməz/ *n.* *Chiefly Brit.* PAJAMAS.

pyr•a•mid /'pɪrəmɪd/ *n.* [*count*] **1.** a very large, four-sided structure with faces that are triangular, such as a tomb of ancient Egypt. **2.** any object or arrangement of objects shaped like a pyramid.

pyre /pay³r/ *n.* [*count*] a pile for burning a dead body, esp. as part of a funeral rite.

py•thon /'payθɒn, -θən/ *n.* [*count*] a snake that kills its prey by crushing or squeezing it to death.

Q

Q, q /kyuw/ *n.* [*count*], *pl.* **Qs** or **Q's, qs** or **q's.** the 17th letter of the English alphabet, a consonant.

qt., qt., qts. an abbreviation of: quart.

quack /kwæk/ *n.,* [*count*] **1.** the harsh, throaty cry of a duck, or any similar sound. —*v.* [*no obj*] **2.** to utter a quack.

quad¹ /kwɒd/ *n.* QUADRANGLE (def. 2).

quad² /kwɒd/ *n.* [*count*] *Informal.* a quadruplet.

quad•ran•gle /ˈkwɒdˌræŋgəl/ *n.* [*count*] **1.** a flat figure having four angles and four sides, such as a square. **2.** a four-sided space surrounded by a building or buildings, as on a college campus.

quad•rant /ˈkwɒdrənt/ *n.* [*count*] **1.** a quarter of a circle; an arc of 90°. **2.** an instrument used in astronomy, navigation, etc., for measuring heights and angles.

quad•ri•lat•er•al /ˌkwɒdrəˈlætərəl/ *adj.* **1.** having four sides. —*n.* [*count*] **2.** a geometric figure with four sides.

quad•ri•ple•gi•a /ˌkwɒdrəˈpliydʒiyə, -dʒə/ *n.* [*noncount*] paralysis of all four limbs or of the entire body below the neck. —**quad•ri'ple•gic,** *n.* [*count*], *adj.*

quad•ru•ped /ˈkwɒdrʊˌpɛd/ *adj.* **1.** four-footed. —*n.* [*count*] **2.** an animal that has four feet.

quad•ru•ple /kwɒˈdruwpəl, -ˈdrʌpəl, ˈkwɒdrʊpəl/ *adj., n., v.,* **-pled, -pling.** —*adj.* **1.** made up of four parts: *a quadruple alliance.* **2.** four times as great. —*n.* [*count*] **3.** a number, amount, etc., four times as great as another. —*v.* [*no obj*] [~ + *obj*] **4.** to make or become four times as great.

quad•ru•plet /kwɒˈdrʌplɪt, -ˈdruwplɪt, ˈkwɒd-drʊplɪt/ *n.* [*count*] one of four children or offspring born of the same mother at the same time.

quag•mire /ˈkwæɡˌmayᵊr, ˈkwɒɡ-/ *n.* [*count*] **1.** a very muddy or boggy area of ground. **2.** a difficult situation.

quail¹ /kweyl/ *n.* [*count*], *pl.* **quails,** (*esp. when thought of as a group*) **quail.** a small, plump bird of the pheasant family.

quail² /kweyl/ *v.* [*no obj*] to lose courage; be very afraid.

quaint /kweynt/ *adj.,* **-er, -est.** having an old-fashioned charm: *a quaint old house.* —**'quaint•ness,** *n.* [*noncount*]

quake /kweyk/ *v.,* **quaked, quak•ing,** *n.* —*v.* [*no obj*] **1.** to shudder or quiver, as from cold or fear. **2.** to shake or tremble, as from shock: *The earth quaked.* —*n.* [*count*] **3.** an act or instance of quaking, esp. an earthquake.

qual•i•fi•ca•tion /ˌkwɒləfɪˈkeyʃən/ *n.* **1.** [*count*] a quality or accomplishment that fits a person for some job, function, or the like. **2.** [*noncount*] the act of qualifying or state of being qualified. **3.** limitation or restriction: [*noncount*]: *to agree without qualification.* [*count*]: *raised some qualifications concerning her candidacy.*

qual•i•fied /ˈkwɒləˌfayd/ *adj.* **1.** having the necessary qualifications: *She's qualified to take over in my absence.* **2.** restricted or limited: *The new design was only a qualified success.*

qual•i•fy /ˈkwɒləˌfay/ *v.,* **-fied, -fy•ing. 1.** [~ + *obj*] to provide with proper or necessary skills, knowledge, etc.: *The training program qualified her for the job.* **2.** [*no obj*] to show that one has the ability for something: *She clearly qualifies for*

the job. **3.** [~ + *obj*] to make less strong or positive; modify or limit: *He qualified his earlier praise of the candidate.*

qual•i•ta•tive /ˈkwɒlɪˌteytɪv/ *adj.* relating to or concerned with quality or qualities. —**'qual•i,ta•tive•ly,** *adv.*

qual•i•ty /ˈkwɒlɪtiy/ *n., pl.* **-ties,** *adj.* —*n.* **1.** [*count*] an essential or basic characteristic or feature: *What are some of the qualities found in great writing?* **2.** [*noncount*] character with respect to how excellent or good something is: *materials of poor quality.* **3.** [*noncount*] superiority; excellence: *The company has a reputation for quality.* **4.** [*count*] something typical of one's personality or character: *Kindness is one of her many good qualities.* —*adj.* [*before a noun*] **5.** of or having superior quality: *quality paper.*

qualm /kwɑm, kwɔm/ *n.* [*count*] **1.** an uneasy feeling regarding one's conduct: *He has no qualms about lying.* **2.** a sudden feeling of nervousness or fear.

quan•da•ry /ˈkwɒndəriy, -driy/ *n.* [*count*], *pl.* **-ries.** a state of uncertainty, esp. as to what to do: *He was in a quandary about marrying.*

quan•ti•fy /ˈkwɒntəˌfay/ *v.* [~ + *obj*], **-fied, -fy•ing.** to figure out, show, or express the quantity of: *to quantify the results.*

quan•ti•ta•tive /ˈkwɒntɪˌteytɪv/ *adj.* of or relating to quantity.

quan•ti•ty /ˈkwɒntɪtiy/ *n., pl.* **-ties. 1.** [*count*] an amount that is indefinite or in a collection: *a quantity of sugar; vast quantities of oil.* **2.** [*count*] an exact or specified amount or measure: *in the quantities called for.* **3.** [*noncount*] a great amount: *to buy food in quantity.*

quar•an•tine /ˈkwɔrənˌtiyn, ˈkwɒr-, ˌkwɔrən-ˈtiyn, ˌkwɒr-/ *n., v.,* **-tined, -tin•ing.** —*n.* **1.** a period during which a person or animal is kept apart from others to ensure that disease will not be spread: [*noncount*]: *kept in quarantine.* [*count; usually singular*]: *imposing a quarantine.* —*v.* [~ + *obj*] **2.** to put in or place under quarantine.

quark /kwɔrk, kwɑrk/ *n.* [*count*] any of a group of particles smaller than an atom, thought to form the basis of all matter.

quar•rel /ˈkwɔrəl, ˈkwɒr-/ *n., v.,* **-reled, -rel•ing** or (*esp. Brit.*) **-relled, -rel•ling.** —*n.* [*count*] **1.** an angry dispute or argument. —*v.* [*no obj*] **2.** to disagree angrily; argue.

quar•rel•some /ˈkwɔrəlsəm, ˈkwɑr-/ *adj.* tending to quarrel.

quar•ry¹ /ˈkwɔriy, ˈkwɒriy/ *n., pl.* **-ries,** *v.,* **-ried, -ry•ing.** —*n.* [*count*] **1.** an open hole or pit in the ground, from which stone, slate, etc., is dug. —*v.* [~ + *obj*] **2.** to obtain from a quarry.

quar•ry² /ˈkwɔriy, ˈkwɒriy/ *n.* [*count*], *pl.* **-ries.** any object of search, pursuit, or attack: *The soldiers finally located their quarry.*

quart /kwɔrt/ *n.* [*count*] a unit of liquid measure, equal to one fourth of a gallon. *Abbr.:* qt.

quar•ter /ˈkwɔrtər/ *n.* [*count*] **1.** one of the four equal or approximately equal parts into which something is divided: *a quarter of a pound.* **2.** a coin equal to one fourth of a U.S. or Canadian dollar, equivalent to 25 cents. **3.** one fourth of an hour: *It's a quarter to six.* **4.** one fourth of a year. **5.** any of the four equal periods of play in certain games, such as basketball. **6.** a region occupied by a particular group: *the student quarter of Paris.* **7.** Usually, **quarters.** [*plural*] housing accommodations; a place to live or stay. —*v.* [~ + *obj*] **8.** to divide into four equal or approximately equal parts. **9.** to provide (someone) with a place to stay: *soldiers quartered in barracks.*

quar•ter•ly /'kwɔrtərliy/ *adj., n., pl.* **-lies,** *adv.* —*adj.* **1.** occurring, done, issued, etc., at the end of every quarter of a year, or four times a year: *a quarterly report.* —*n.* [*count*] **2.** a magazine issued every three months. —*adv.* **3.** once each quarter of a year: *to pay interest quarterly.*

quar•tet /kwɔr'tɛt/ *n.* [*count*] **1.** an organized group of four singers or players. **2.** a musical composition for four voices or instruments.

quartz /kwɔrts/ *n.* [*noncount*] a hard mineral that is the chief part of sand.

qua•sar /'kweyzɑr, -sɑr/ *n.* [*count*] a starlike object that is extremely distant from the earth and extremely bright.

qua•ver /'kweyvər/ *v.* [*no obj*] **1.** to shake, quiver, or tremble: *Her voice quavered because she was afraid.* —*n.* [*count*] **2.** a quivering or trembling.

quay /kiy, key, kwey/ *n.* [*count*] a landing place built near the edge of a body of water.

quea•sy /'kwiyziy/ *adj.,* **-si•er, -si•est.** feeling sick or slightly dizzy; nauseated. —'**quea•si•ness,** *n.* [*noncount*]

queen /kwiyn/ *n.* [*count*] **1.** a female ruler or monarch. **2.** the wife of a king. **3.** a woman considered to be important in some way: *a beauty queen.* **4.** a playing card with a picture of a queen. **5.** the most powerful chess piece of either color. **6.** a female ant, bee, or wasp capable of laying eggs. —'**queen•ly,** *adj.,* **-li•er, -li•est.**

queer /kwɪər/ *adj.,* **-er, -est.** strange or odd; unusually different: *A queer old man suddenly emerged from the corner of the bookshop.* —'**queer•ly,** *adv.*

quell /kwɛl/ *v.* [~ + *obj*] **1.** to put down; suppress: *The army quelled the uprising.* **2.** to quiet; free from: *to quell a child's fear.*

quench /kwɛntʃ/ *v.* [~ + *obj*] **1.** to satisfy: *I had a drink to quench my thirst.* **2.** to put out; extinguish (fire, flames, etc.).

que•ry /'kwɪəriy, 'kwɛriy/ *n., pl.* **-ries,** *v.,* **-ried, -ry•ing.** —*n.* [*count*] **1.** a question; an inquiry. —*v.* [~ + *obj*] **2.** to question as doubtful: *to query a statement.* **3.** to ask questions of: *They queried her on their future plans.*

quest /kwɛst/ *n.* [*count*] **1.** a long search: *a quest for truth.* —*Idiom.* **2. in quest of,** in search of.

ques•tion /'kwɛstʃən/ *n.* [*count*] **1.** a sentence in a form that is intended to get information in reply: *Please answer my question.* **2.** a problem or proposal being discussed; issue: *The question of aid is being considered by the committee.* **3.** a problem or question given as part of an examination. —*v.* [~ + *obj*] **4.** to ask questions of. **5.** to make a question of; doubt: *They questioned our sincerity. I question if you are ready for success.*

ques•tion•a•ble /'kwɛstʃənəbəl/ *adj.* not completely honest, moral, or proper: *accused of questionable activities.*

'**question ,mark,** *n.* [*count*] a mark indicating a question: usually, as in English, the mark (?) placed after a question.

ques•tion•naire /,kwɛstʃə'nɛər/ *n.* [*count*] a list of questions given out to a number of people

so that replies can be analyzed for usable information.

queue /kyuw/ *n., v.,* **queued, queu•ing.** —*n.* [*count*] **1.** a line of people waiting their turn. **2.** a number of items waiting in order for electronic action in a computer system. —*v.* **3.** [*no obj*] to form in a line while waiting: *People had queued (up) to buy tickets.* **4.** [~ + *obj*] to arrange or organize (electronic data) into a queue.

quib•ble /'kwɪbəl/ *n., v.,* **-bled, -bling.** —*n.* [*count*] **1.** a criticism about something unimportant. —*v.* [*no obj*] **2.** to complain about small and unimportant matters. —'**quib•bler,** *n.* [*count*]

quiche /kiyʃ/ *n.* [*noncount*] [*count*] a pie of unsweetened custard baked with other ingredients, as cheese or onions.

quick /kwɪk/ *adj. and adv.,* **-er, -est.** —*adj.* **1.** done, moving, or occurring fast; rapid: *a quick response.* **2.** easily aroused: *a quick temper.* —*adv.* **3.** in a quick manner; quickly: *Come quick!* —'**quick•ly,** *adv.* —'**quick•ness,** *n.* [*noncount*]

quick•en /'kwɪkən/ *v.* **1.** to make or become quicker: [~ + *obj*]: *She quickened her pace.* [*no obj*]: *Her pulse quickened.* **2.** [~ + *obj*] to give liveliness to; stimulate: *to quicken the imagination.*

quick•sand /'kwɪk,sænd/ *n.* [*noncount*] deep loose sand mixed with water, that tends to cause an object on its surface to sink.

'**quick-'witted,** *adj.* having an alert mind.

qui•et /'kwayɪt/ *adj.,* **-er, -est,** *n., v.* —*adj.* **1.** making little or no noise or sound: *quiet neighbors.* **2.** free from noise: *a quiet street.* **3.** [*be* + ~] silent: *Be quiet!* **4.** shy; not talking much. **5.** free from excitement; calm: *a quiet life in the country.* **6.** still or barely moving: *quiet waters.* —*n.* [*noncount*] **7.** the state of being quiet. —*v.* [~ + *obj*] [*no obj*] **8.** to make or become quiet. —'**qui•et•ly,** *adv.* —'**qui•et•ness,** *n.* [*noncount*]

quill /kwɪl/ *n.* [*count*] **1.** one of the large feathers of a bird's wing or tail. **2.** a feather, as that of a goose, used as a pen for writing. **3.** one of the spines on a porcupine.

quilt /kwɪlt/ *n.* [*count*] **1.** a padded covering for a bed made of two layers of fabric. —*v.* **2.** [~ + *obj*] to stitch together (two pieces of cloth and a soft lining), usually in an ornamental pattern. **3.** [*no obj*] to make quilts or quilted work. —'**quilt•ed,** *adj.: a quilted down comforter.* —'**quilt•er,** *n.* [*count*] —'**quilt•ing,** *n.* [*noncount*]

qui•nine /'kwaynayn, 'kwɪnayn/ *n.* [*noncount*] a white substance from the bark of certain trees, used for treating malaria.

quint /kwɪnt/ *n.* [*count*] *Informal.* a quintuplet.

quin•tes•sen•tial /,kwɪntə'sɛnʃəl/ *adj.* [*before a noun*] being or representing the most perfect type or example of something.

quin•tet /kwɪn'tɛt/ *n.* [*count*] **1.** a group of five singers or players. **2.** a piece of music written for five voices or instruments.

quin•tu•plet /kwɪn'tʌplɪt, -'tuwplɪt, -'tyuw-/ *n.* [*count*] one of five children or offspring born of the same mother at the same time.

quip /kwɪp/ *n., v.,* **quipped, quip•ping.** —*n.* [*count*] **1.** a clever or witty remark or comment. —*v.* [*no obj*] **2.** to make or utter a quip.

quirk /kwɜrk/ *n.* [*count*] **1.** an odd habit, trait, or example of behavior. **2.** an accident; strange event: *a cruel quirk of fate.* —'**quirk•i•ness,** *n.* [*noncount*] —'**quirk•y,** *adj.*

quit /kwɪt/ *v.,* **quit** or **quit•ted, quit•ting. 1.** to

stop or discontinue: [~ + *obj*]: *to quit smoking.*
[*no obj*]: *Will that noise ever quit?* **2.** to give up
or resign: [~ + *obj*]: *She quit her job.* [*no obj*]:
decided to quit.

quite /kwayt/ *adv.* **1.** completely or entirely: *not
quite finished.* **2.** actually, really, or truly: *This is
quite a sudden change.* **3.** to a considerable extent: *He is quite young to be walking.*

quiv•er /'kwɪvər/ *v.* [*no obj*] **1.** to shake with a
slight but rapid motion; tremble: *The dog quiv-
ered with excitement.* —*n.* [*count*] **2.** the act or
state of quivering.

quix•ot•ic /kwɪk'sɒtɪk/ *adj.* foolishly romantic
or impractical: *a quixotic attempt to save the
world.*

quiz /kwɪz/ *n.*, *pl.* **quiz•zes**, *v.*, **quizzed, quiz•
zing.** —*n.* [*count*] **1.** an informal or short test.
—*v.* [~ + *obj*] **2.** to test informally: *quizzed her
students on irregular verbs.* **3.** to question (someone) closely: *The reporters quizzed the president.*

quiz•zi•cal /'kwɪzɪkəl/ *adj.* puzzled; uncertain: *a
quizzical expression on her face.*

quo•rum /'kwɔrəm/ *n.* [*count*] the number of
members of a group, usually a majority, that
must be present in order to have a meeting or
transact business.

quo•ta /'kwowtə/ *n.* [*count*] the share, number,
or amount that is required or allowed: *The government set quotas to limit the number of immigrants. The police officers issued their quota of
speeding tickets.*

quo•ta•tion /kwow'teyʃən/ *n.* [*count*] **1.** a
word, phrase, or passage taken from a book,
speech, etc., and repeated. **2.** an estimate of a
cost for doing some work: *The quotation for the
repairs was too high.*

quo'tation ,mark, *n.* [*count*] one of the marks
used at the beginning and end of a quotation; in
English usually shown as (") at the beginning
and (") at the end.

quote /kwowt/ *v.*, **quot•ed, quot•ing,** *n.* —*v.* **1.**
to repeat (a passage, phrase, etc.) from a book,
speech, or the like: [*no obj*]: *In his book he
quoted from speeches of Churchill.* [~ + *obj*]: *He
quotes you in his article.* **2.** [~ + *obj*] to refer to
as evidence or support: *He quoted the contract as
the basis for the lawsuit.* **3.** [~ + *obj*] to offer as
a price or amount: *The salesman quoted a low
figure for the house.* —*n.* **4.** QUOTATION. **5.** QUOTA-
TION MARK.

quo•tient /'kwowʃənt/ *n.* [*count*] the result of
division: *When you divide 12 by 6 the quotient
is 2.*

R

R, r /ɑr/ *n., pl.* **Rs** or **R's, rs** or **r's.** the 18th letter of the English alphabet, a consonant.

rab•bi /'ræbay/ *n.* [*count*], *pl.* **-bis.** the chief religious official of a synagogue who performs rituals and teaches.

rab•bit /'ræbɪt/ *n.* [*count*], *pl.* **-bits,** (*esp. when thought of as a group*) **-bit.** a large-eared, hopping animal, living in holes in the ground.

rab•ble /'ræbəl/ *n.* [*count*] a disorderly crowd; mob.

rab•id /'ræbɪd/ *adj.* **1.** [*before a noun*] irrational, unreasonable, or extreme: *a rabid revolutionary.* **2.** affected with rabies.

ra•bies /'reybiyz/ *n.* [*noncount; used with a singular verb*] a usually fatal disease of dogs, cats, and other warm-blooded animals, passed on to humans by the bite of an infected animal.

rac•coon /ræ'kuwn/ *n.* [*count*], *pl.* **-coons,** (*esp. when thought of as a group*) **-coon.** a small animal active at night, having a masklike black stripe across the eyes.

race¹ /reys/ *n., v.,* **raced, rac•ing.** —*n.* [*count*] **1.** a contest of speed, such as in running. **2.** any contest or competition: *a Senate race.* —*v.* [*no obj*] [~ + *obj*] **3.** to run in a race against (someone). **4.** to (cause to) run or move swiftly: *He raced back to the house. They raced the injured boy to the hospital.* —'**rac•er,** *n.* [*count*]

race² /reys/ *n.* **1.** [*count*] [*noncount*] any of several classifications of human beings, formerly based on physical characteristics, as skin color or eye shape, and now frequently based on genetic differences. **2.** [*count*] any people united by common history, language, etc.: *the Dutch race.* **3.** [*count*] any class or kind of creatures: *the human race.* —*adj.* [*before a noun*] **4.** of or relating to race: *race relations.* —'**ra•cial,** *adj.*

race•horse /'reys,hɔrs/ *n.* [*count*] a horse trained for racing.

race•track /'reys,træk/ *n.* [*count*] an area of ground used for racing.

rac•ism /'reysɪzəm/ *n.* [*noncount*] **1.** a belief that one's own race is superior. **2.** hatred or intolerance of other races. —'**rac•ist,** *n.* [*count*], *adj.*

rack¹ /ræk/ *n.* [*count*] **1.** a framework of bars, pegs, etc., for holding or hanging things: *a clothes rack; a ski rack.* **2.** a shelf, often attached to something: *a luggage rack.* —*v.* [~ + *obj*] **3.** to cause great pain to. **4.** to strain or struggle in mental effort: *He racked his brains trying to come up with an answer.*

rack² /ræk/ *n.* [*noncount*] wreckage or destruction: *to go to rack and ruin.*

rack•et¹ /'rækɪt/ *n.* **1.** [*count; usually singular*] a loud noise, esp. of a disturbing or confusing kind. **2.** [*count*] an organized illegal or dishonest activity.

rack•et² or **rac•quet** /'rækɪt/ *n.* [*count*] a light bat with netting stretched in an oval frame, used in tennis, badminton, etc.

rac•y /'reysiy/ *adj.,* **-i•er, -i•est.** slightly improper, as by containing sexual references.

ra•dar /'reydɑr/ *n.* [*noncount*] a system for figuring out the location or speed of an object by using radio waves.

ra•di•al /'reydiyəl/ *adj.* having parts arranged like lines coming out of the center of a circle.

ra•di•ant /'reydiyənt/ *adj.* **1.** [*before a noun*] giving off rays of light. **2.** bright with joy, hope, etc.: *a radiant smile.* —'**ra•di•ance,** *n.* [*noncount*] —'**ra•di•ant•ly,** *adv.*

ra•di•ate /v.'reydiy,eyt / *v.,* **-at•ed, -at•ing.** **1.** [*no obj*] to spread out from a center point: *The main avenues in Paris radiate from the center.* **2.** [*no obj*] [~ + *obj*] to give off rays, as of light or heat. **3.** [~ + *obj*] to send forth strongly: *She radiated confidence.*

ra•di•a•tion /ˌreydiy'eyʃən/ *n.* [*noncount*] **1.** the process in which energy is sent out, transmitted, and absorbed. **2.** radioactivity: *nuclear radiation.*

ra•di•a•tor /'reydiy,eytər/ *n.* [*count*] **1.** a heating device, as a series of pipes through which steam or hot water passes. **2.** a device used for cooling circulating water, as in an automobile engine.

rad•i•cal /'rædɪkəl/ *adj.* **1.** complete or extreme: *a radical change in policy.* **2.** favoring extreme political or social change. **3.** basic; fundamental. —*n.* [*count*] **4.** a person with extreme beliefs or principles. —'**rad•i•cal•ly,** *adv.*

ra•di•i /'reydiy,ay/ *n.* [*plural*] a pl. of RADIUS.

ra•di•o /'reydiy,ow/ *n., pl.* **-di•os,** *v.,* **-di•oed, -di•o•ing.** —*n.* **1.** [*noncount*] a system of communicating speech or other sounds by sending electromagnetic waves over long distances. **2.** [*count*] a device for receiving or sending radio broadcasts. —*v.* [*no obj*] [~ + *obj*] **3.** to send (a message, music, etc.) by radio.

ra•di•o•ac•tiv•i•ty /ˌreydiyowæk'tɪvɪtiy/ *n.* [*noncount*] the property of certain elements, as radium and uranium, by which they release harmful particles or rays because of changes in the nuclei of their atoms. —ˌ**ra•di•o•'ac•tive,** *adj.*

ra•di•ol•o•gy /reydiy'ɒlədʒiy/ *n.* [*noncount*] the branch of medicine dealing with x-rays and other radiation. —ˌ**ra•di•'ol•o•gist,** *n.* [*count*]

rad•ish /'rædɪʃ/ *n.* [*count*] a crisp, sharp-tasting white or red root vegetable.

tennis   court tennis   squash   squash tennis

badminton   paddle tennis   table tennis

racket²

ra•di•um /'reydiyəm/ *n.* [*noncount*] a radioactive metallic element that has been used to treat cancer.

ra•di•us /'reydiyəs/ *n.* [*count*], *pl.* **-di•i** /-diy,ay/, **-di•us•es.** **1.** a straight line from the center of a circle to the circumference. **2.** a circular area measured by the length of a given radius: *They searched every house within a radius of 50 miles.*

ra•don /'reydɒn/ *n.* [*noncount*] a radioactive chemical element produced by the decay of radium.

raf•fle /'ræfəl/ *n., v.,* **-fled, -fling.** —*n.* [*count*] **1.** a form of lottery in which people buy chances to win a prize. —*v.* [~ + *obj*] **2.** to give away (something) in a raffle: *The club raffled (off) two movie tickets.*

raft /ræft/ *n.* [*count*] **1.** a floating platform made of logs, rubber, etc. —*v.* [*no obj*] [~ + *obj*] **2.** to travel or carry on a raft.

raf•ter /'ræftər/ *n.* [*count*] any of a series of sloped, large pieces of wood, used for holding up a roof.

rag¹ /ræg/ *n.* **1.** [*count*] [*noncount*] a piece of cloth, esp. one that is torn or worn. **2. rags,** [*plural*] tattered clothing: *dressed in rags.* —*Idiom.* **3. from rags to riches,** from a state of poverty to that of wealth.

rag² /ræg/ *v.* [~ + *obj*], **ragged, rag•ging.** *Informal.* **1.** to scold. **2.** to tease.

rag³ /ræg/ *n.* [*count*] a piece of music in ragtime.

rage /reydʒ/ *n., v.,* **raged, rag•ing.** —*n.* **1.** [*noncount*] [*count*] (a fit of) violent anger. **2.** [*count; usually singular; usually: the* + ~] *Informal.* an object of current popularity or fashion: *I remember when long hair was all the rage.* —*v.* [*no obj*] **3.** to act or speak with violent anger. **4.** to move violently and noisily: *He raged around the room.*

rag•ged /'rægɪd/ *adj.* **1.** wearing old or worn-out clothing: *ragged beggars.* **2.** worn to rags; torn: *ragged pants.* **3.** rough and uneven: *a ragged hole where the bullet had gone through.* —'**rag•ged•y,** *adj.*

rag•time /'ræg,taym/ *n.* [*noncount*] a type of jazz marked by a strong beat.

rag•weed /'ræg,wiyd/ *n.* [*noncount*] a plant that in autumn releases pollen into the air, causing hay fever.

raid /reyd/ *n.* [*count*] **1.** a sudden assault, attack, or other act of entering: *a police raid on a narcotics dealer; an enemy raid.* —*v.* [*no obj*] [~ + *obj*] **2.** to make a raid (on). —'**raid•er,** *n.* [*count*]

rail /reyl/ *n.* **1.** [*count*] a horizontal bar attached to posts and used for a fence or railing. **2.** [*count*] one of a pair of parallel steel bars on which the wheels of trains run. **3.** [*noncount*] railroad: *to travel by rail.*

rail•ing /'reylɪŋ/ *n.* [*count*] a fencelike barrier alongside a stairway, walkway, etc., made of horizontal rails.

rail•road /'reyl,rowd/ *n.* [*count*] **1.** a permanent road made of rails forming a track on which locomotives and cars are run. **2.** an entire system of such roads together with its engines, cars, buildings, etc. —*v.* [~ + *obj*] **3.** to transport by railroad. **4.** to force into an action or decision too quickly: *We were railroaded into signing a bad deal.*

rail•way /'reyl,wey/ *n.* [*count*] **1.** a railroad operating over short distances. **2.** RAILROAD.

rain /reyn/ *n.* **1.** [*noncount*] water that falls in drops from the clouds. **2.** [*count; usually singular*] a heavy and continuous fall of something unwelcome: *a rain of blows.* —*v.* **3.** [*no obj; it* + ~] (of rain) to fall: *It rained all night.* **4.** to (cause to) come down like rain: [*no obj*]: *Tears rained from their eyes.* [~ + *obj*]: *The jets rained bombs down on the enemy.* **5. rain out,** to cancel or postpone because of rain: *The last game was rained out.*

rain•bow /'reyn,bow/ *n.* [*count*] **1.** an arch of colors appearing in the sky, caused by the sun's rays passing through drops of rain. —*adj.* [*before a noun*] **2.** of many colors; multicolored.

'**rain ,check,** *n.* [*count*] **1.** a postponement of an invitation until a more convenient time. **2.** a ticket allowing a customer to buy at a later date and for the same price a sale item that is temporarily unavailable.

rain•coat /'reyn,kowt/ *n.* [*count*] a waterproof or water-repellent coat worn in the rain.

rain•drop /'reyn,drɒp/ *n.* [*count*] a drop of rain.

rain•fall /'reyn,fɔl/ *n.* the amount of rain falling within a given time and area: [*count*]: *a rainfall of 70 inches a year.* [*noncount*]: *areas where rainfall is slight.*

'**rain ,forest,** *n.* [*count*] a tropical forest where much rainfall occurs.

rain•y /'reyniy/ *adj.,* **-i•er, -i•est.** having great amounts of rain: *the rainy season.*

raise /reyz/ *v.,* **raised, rais•ing,** *n.* —*v.* [~ + *obj*] **1.** to move to a higher position; lift up: *She raised her head and looked around.* **2.** to increase in amount, degree, loudness, or force: *He raised his voice so they could hear him. The news raised his spirits.* **3.** to grow or breed: *to raise corn.* **4.** to bring up; rear: *to raise a child.* **5.** to present for consideration: *I'd like to raise a question.* **6.** to advance in rank or position: *to raise her to the rank of colonel.* **7.** to assemble or collect: *to raise money.* —*n.* [*count*] **8.** an increase in amount, as of wages.

rai•sin /'reyzɪn/ *n.* [*count*] a grape that has been dried in the sun or by artificial means.

rake /reyk/ *n., v.,* **raked, rak•ing.** —*n.* [*count*] **1.** a farming or gardening tool with metal teeth, as for gathering dead leaves. —*v.* **2.** [*no obj*] [~ + *obj*] to clear, smooth, or gather with a rake. **3. rake in,** to gather or collect a great deal: *to rake in money* or *to rake money in.*

'**rake-,off,** *n.* [*count; singular*] a share or amount taken or received esp. illegally.

ral•ly /'ræliy/ *v.,* **-lied, -ly•ing,** *n., pl.* **-lies.** —*v.* **1.** to gather and organize: [~ + *obj*]: *The general rallied the scattered troops.* [*no obj*]: *The scattered troops rallied.* **2.** [*no obj*] to come to the assistance of a person or cause: *rallied around the president.* **3.** [*no obj*] to revive or recover, as from illness. —*n.* [*count*] **4.** a renewal or recovery of strength, activity, etc. **5.** a mass meeting to promote a common cause: *a political rally.*

ram /ræm/ *n., v.,* **rammed, ram•ming.** —*n.* [*count*] **1.** a male sheep. **2.** BATTERING RAM. —*v.* **3.** [*no obj*] [~ + *obj*] to strike with great force. **4.** [~ + *obj*] to push firmly; force: *to ram a bill through the Senate.*

ram•ble /'ræmbəl/ *v.,* **-bled, -bling,** *n.* —*v.* [*no obj*] **1.** to wander around; stroll. **2.** to have a winding course or direction, as a stream or path. **3.** to talk or write in a wandering or confused way. —*n.* [*count*] **4.** a leisurely walk without a definite route.

ram•bling /'ræmblɪŋ/ *adj.* **1.** growing or spread out in a random way: *a rambling old farmhouse.* **2.** aimless; wandering: *a long, rambling answer.*

ram•i•fi•ca•tion /,ræməfɪ'key∫ən/ *n.* [*count*] a consequence; outgrowth: *The new tax law has many ramifications for small businesses.*

ramp /ræmp/ *n.* [*count*] **1.** any long, sloping walk or passageway. **2.** a road leading on or off a highway: *an exit ramp.*

ram•page /'ræmpeydʒ; *v. also* ræm'peydʒ/ *n., v.,* **-paged, -pag•ing.** —*n.* [*count*] **1.** a sudden

R

occurrence of reckless or destructive behavior: *The crowd went on a rampage.* —*v.* [*no obj*] **2.** to rush or behave furiously or violently: *The gangs rampaged through the towns.*

ramp•ant /ˈræmpənt/ *adj.* growing or spreading steadily and without stopping: *a rampant rumor; rampant disease.* —**ˈramp•ant•ly,** *adv.*

ram•part /ˈræmpɑrt, -pərt/ *n.* [*count*] a mound of earth or rubble built around a castle or fort for protection.

ram•shack•le /ˈræmˌʃækəl/ *adj.* loosely made or held together; shaky: *a ramshackle house.*

ran /ræn/ *v.* pt. of RUN.

ranch /ræntʃ/ *n.* [*count*] **1.** a place for raising horses, cattle, and sheep, usually a very large farm in which there is enough land for grazing. —*v.* [*no obj*] **2.** to own, manage, or work on a ranch. —**ˈranch•er,** *n.* [*count*]

ran•cid /ˈrænsɪd/ *adj.* having an unpleasant smell or taste, usually because of decay: *rancid butter.*

ran•dom /ˈrændəm/ *adj.* **1.** occurring or done without definite aim, reason, plan, or pattern: *a few random examples; random killings.* —*Idiom.* **2. at random,** in a random way: *to choose colors at random.* —**ˈran•dom•ly,** *adv.*

rang /ræŋ/ *v.* pt. of RING[2].

range /reɪndʒ/ *n., adj., v.,* **ranged, rang•ing.** —*n.* **1.** [*count*] the extent to which, or the limits between which, something can change or vary: *a price range between $500 and $1,000.* **2.** the extent or scope in which something operates or is effective: [*noncount*]: *one's range of vision.* [*count; usually singular*]: *His singing voice has a range of one octave.* **3.** the distance of the target from the weapon: [*noncount*]: *The man was shot at close range.* [*count*]: *The officer fired from a range of three feet.* **4.** [*count*] an area equipped with targets for practice in shooting: *a rifle range.* **5.** [*count*] a row or series of similar products: *a wide range of computer equipment.* **6.** [*count*] the region in which a population or species of animal or plant is found. **7.** a chain of mountains forming a single system: [*count*]: *an important mountain range.* [*often: the* + ~]: *the Cascade Range.* —*adj.* [*before a noun*] **8.** working or grazing on a range: *range animals.* —*v.* **9.** [*no obj*] to vary or be within certain limits: *Her emotions ranged from joy to despair.* **10.** [*no obj*] to extend or wander over, so as to include or cover: *Their talks ranged over a variety of subjects.* **11.** [~ + *obj*] to classify.

rang•er /ˈreɪndʒər/ *n.* [*count*] a person who patrols a region, as a forest.

rank[1] /ræŋk/ *n.* **1.** [*count*] a social or official position, as in the armed forces: *the rank of captain.* **2.** [*noncount*] high position or station: *a person of rank.* **3.** [*count*] a row or series of things or persons. **4. ranks,** [*plural*] ordinary soldiers, rather than officers. —*v.* **5.** to (cause to) be assigned to a particular position: [~ + *obj*]: *They ranked him as one of the best pitchers in the world.* [*no obj*]: *Their work ranked well above that of the other students.*

rank[2] /ræŋk/ *adj.,* **-er, -est. 1.** growing thickly: *rank foliage.* **2.** having a very unpleasant smell or taste. **3.** [*before a noun*] complete; utter; absolute: *a rank amateur.* —**ˈrank•ness,** *n.* [*noncount*]

rank•ing /ˈræŋkɪŋ/ *adj.* [*before a noun*] **1.** being superior in rank, position, etc.: *a ranking diplomat.* **2.** highly regarded: *a ranking authority.* **3.**

of or having a certain rank: *a low-ranking executive.*

ran•sack /ˈrænsæk/ *v.* [~ + *obj*] to search thoroughly and vigorously through: *We ransacked the drawers for the lost money.*

ran•som /ˈrænsəm/ *n.* **1.** [*noncount*] the release of a prisoner, kidnapped person, etc., for a demanded price. **2.** [*count*] the price paid or demanded. —*v.* [~ + *obj*] **3.** to free or release someone by paying a demanded price.

rant /rænt/ *v.* [*no obj*] to speak or talk in a wild or violent way; rave.

rap /ræp/ *v.,* **rapped, rap•ping,** *n.* —*v.* **1.** to strike, esp. with a quick, light blow: [~ + *obj*]: *His father rapped him on the knuckles.* [*no obj*]: *Somebody rapped on the door.* **2.** [~ + *obj*] to say or shout sharply: *to rap (out) orders.* —*n.* **3.** [*count*] a quick, light blow. **4.** [*count*] the sound produced by such a blow. **5.** [*noncount*] *Slang.* blame or punishment: *I'm not going to take the rap for your mistakes.* **6.** [*count*] *Slang.* a criminal charge: *a murder rap.* **7.** [*noncount*] a kind of music with a steady beat and rhymed words that follow the beat. —*Idiom.* **8. beat the rap,** *Slang.* to avoid punishment, as for a crime.

rape /reɪp/ *n., v.,* **raped, rap•ing.** —*n.* [*noncount*] [*count*] **1.** the unlawful act of forcing (someone) to have sexual relations. —*v.* [~ + *obj*] [*no obj*] **2.** to force (someone) to have sexual relations. —**ˈrap•ist,** *n.* [*count*]

rap•id /ˈræpɪd/ *adj.,* **-er, -est,** *n.* —*adj.* **1.** fast; swift: *rapid motion; rapid growth.* —*n.* **2.** Usually, **rapids.** [*plural*] a part of a river where the current runs very swiftly. —**ra•pid•i•ty** /rəˈpɪdɪti/, **ˈrap•id•ness,** *n.* [*noncount*] —**ˈrap•id•ly,** *adv.*

ra•pi•er /ˈreɪpiyər/ *n.* [*count*] a narrow sword having a double-edged blade.

rap•port /ræˈpɔr, rə-/ *n.* a sympathetic and understanding relationship: [*count; usually singular*]: *a close rapport between teacher and students.* [*noncount*]: *a feeling of rapport.*

rapt /ræpt/ *adj.* deeply interested in or absorbed in something: *a rapt listener.* —**ˈrapt•ly,** *adv.* —**ˈrapt•ness,** *n.* [*noncount*]

rap•ture /ˈræptʃər/ *n.* [*noncount*] overwhelming joy or delight; ecstasy. —**ˈrap•tur•ous,** *adj.*

rare[1] /rɛər/ *adj.,* **rar•er, rar•est.** not happening or found very often; very uncommon. —**ˈrare•ly,** *adv.*: *I'm rarely late for appointments.* —**ˈrare•ness,** *n.* [*noncount*]

rare[2] /rɛər/ *adj.,* **rar•er, rar•est.** cooked so as to be still red on the inside: *rare steak.* —**ˈrare•ness,** *n.* [*noncount*]

rar•e•fied /ˈrɛərəˌfaɪd/ *adj.* **1.** lofty; grand: *rarefied language.* **2.** thin: *a rarefied atmosphere.*

rar•ing /ˈrɛərɪŋ/ *adj.* very eager or anxious; enthusiastic: *They were raring to go.*

rar•i•ty /ˈrɛərɪtiy/ *n., pl.* **-ties. 1.** [*noncount*] the state or quality of being rare. **2.** [*count*] something rare: *Earthquakes are a rarity in this area.*

ras•cal /ˈræskəl/ *n.* [*count*] **1.** a dishonest person. **2.** a mischievous person or animal.

rash[1] /ræʃ/ *adj.,* **-er, -est.** acting or done quickly or without careful thought. —**ˈrash•ly,** *adv.* —**ˈrash•ness,** *n.* [*noncount*]

rash[2] /ræʃ/ *n.* [*count*] **1.** an area of spots or redness on the skin resulting from an irritation or illness. **2.** many occurrences of something at about the same time: *a rash of robberies.*

rasp /ræsp/ *v.* **1.** [~ + *obj*] [*no obj*] to scrape or grate with a rough instrument. **2.** [~ + *obj*] to irritate: *The sound rasped (on) his nerves.* **3.** [~

+ *obj*] to say with a grating sound. —*n.* [*count*] **4.** a rasping sound. **5.** a coarse file used for smoothing wood or metal. —'**rasp•ing,** '**rasp•y,** *adj.*, -**i•er,** -**i•est.**

rasp•ber•ry /'ræz,bɛriy, -bəriy/ *n.* [*count*], *pl.* -**ries. 1.** the red or black berry of a prickly shrub. **2.** a noise made with the lips and tongue to express disapproval.

rat /ræt/ *n., interj., v.,* **rat•ted, rat•ting.** —*n.* [*count*] **1.** a rodent that resembles a mouse but is larger. **2.** *Slang.* a disloyal or untrustworthy person. —*interj.* **3. rats,** (used to show disgust or disappointment). —*v.* [*no obj*] **4.** *Slang.* to betray one's associates: *She ratted on us when the cops caught her.*

rate /reyt/ *n., v.,* **rat•ed, rat•ing.** —*n.* [*count*] **1.** the amount of a charge or payment: *a high rate of interest on loans.* **2.** a certain amount of one thing considered in relation to a unit of another thing: *a rate of 60 miles an hour.* **3.** degree of speed or progress: *to work at a rapid rate.* —*v.* [~ + *obj*] **4.** to estimate the value or worth of; consider: *She is highly rated as a teacher. I would rate him (as) a fine teacher.* **5.** to deserve or merit: *That event doesn't rate a mention in my book.* —*Idiom.* **6. at any rate,** in any event; at least: *Traffic was heavy, but at any rate they arrived on time.*

rath•er /'ræðər/ *adv.* **1.** quite; to some degree: *He's rather good at baseball.* **2.** preferably; more willingly: *to die rather than yield.* **3.** more truly or correctly: *I'll finish late Monday, or, rather, Tuesday morning.* —*Idiom.* **4. would rather,** to prefer that or to: *I would rather be fishing.*

rat•i•fy /'rætə,fay/ *v.* [~ + *obj*], -**fied, -fy•ing.** to formally approve or agree to: *to ratify an amendment to the Constitution.* —,**rat•i•fi'ca•tion,** *n.* [*noncount*]

rat•ing /'reytɪŋ/ *n.* [*count*] **1.** position or level given to something in comparison to others: *a good credit rating.* **2.** a percentage indicating the number of listeners to or viewers of a radio or television broadcast.

ra•tio /'reyʃow, -ʃiy,ow/ *n.* [*count*], *pl.* -**tios.** the relation between two numbers or amounts, with respect to the number of times the first contains the second: *The ratio of 3 to 9 is the same as the ratio of 1 to 3.*

ra•tion /'ræʃən, 'reyʃən/ *n.* [*count*] **1.** a fixed allowance, esp. of food. —*v.* [~ + *obj*] **2.** to limit to a ration: *They rationed the child to one television program a day.* **3.** to restrict the use or distribution of: *to ration meat.*

ra•tion•al /'ræʃənl, 'ræʃnl/ *adj.* **1.** logical; sensible: *a rational decision.* **2.** able to think or speak clearly and logically: *The patient seems perfectly rational.* —'**ra•tion•al•ly,** *adv.*

ra•tion•ale /,ræʃə'næl/ *n.* [*count*] the basic reason or reasons for something: *There is no rationale for such behavior.*

ra•tion•al•ize /'ræʃənl,ayz, 'ræʃnl-/ *v.*, -**ized,** -**iz•ing.** to regard (one's actions) as resulting from causes that seem reasonable but are not true causes: [~ + *obj*]: *He tried to rationalize his use of drugs by saying that they helped him relax.* [*no obj*]: *Don't rationalize; be honest about your true motives.* —**ra•tion•al•i•za•tion** /,ræʃənli-'zeyʃən, ,ræʃnl-/, *n.* [*count*] [*noncount*]

'**rat** ,**race,** *n.* [*count*] exhausting, highly competitive activity, esp. one aimed at success in business.

rat•tle /'ræṭl/ *v.*, -**tled, -tling,** *n.* —*v.* **1.** (cause to) make a rapid series of short, sharp

sounds: [*no obj*]: *The doors rattled in the storm.* [~ + *obj*]: *I rattled the keys.* **2. rattle off,** to say or do in a rapid or lively manner: *He rattled off the answers or He rattled the answers off.* **3.** [~ + *obj*] to confuse; make nervous. —*n.* [*count*] **4.** a rapid series of short, sharp sounds. **5.** a baby's toy filled with small pellets that rattle when shaken.

rat•tle•snake /'ræṭl,sneyk/ *n.* [*count*] a snake having a rattle at the end of the tail.

rau•cous /'rɔkəs/ *adj.* harsh; rough; unpleasant in sound. —'**rau•cous•ly,** *adv.*

raun•chy /'rɔntʃiy, 'rɑn-/ *adj.*, -**chi•er, -chi•est. 1.** dirty. **2.** obscene. —'**raun•chi•ness,** *n.* [*noncount*]

rav•age /'rævɪdʒ/ *v.*, -**aged, -ag•ing,** *n.* —*v.* [~ + *obj*] **1.** to damage or injure severely: *The storm ravaged the coastline.* —*n.* **ravages,** [*plural*] **2.** great damage, destruction, or ruin: *the ravages of war.*

rave /reyv/ *v.*, **raved, rav•ing,** *n., adj.* —*v.* [*no obj*] **1.** to talk wildly or irrationally. **2.** to talk or write with great enthusiasm about something: *They raved about the movie.* —*n.* [*count*] **3.** an enthusiastic review. —*adj.* [*before a noun*] **4.** enthusiastic.

ra•ven /'reyvən/ *n.* [*count*] **1.** a very large black bird having a loud, harsh call. —*adj.* **2.** shining black: *raven hair.*

rav•en•ous /'rævənəs/ *adj.* extremely hungry. —'**rav•en•ous•ly,** *adv.*

ra•vine /rə'viyn/ *n.* [*count*] a narrow, steep-sided valley.

rav•ing /'reyvɪŋ/ *adj.* **1.** talking wildly. **2.** extraordinary in degree: *a raving beauty.* —*adv.* **3.** completely: *raving mad.* —*n.* **4.** Usually, **ravings.** [*plural*] talk that is wild or without reason.

ra•vi•o•li /,ræviy'owliy/ *n.* [*noncount*; *used with a singular verb*] square pockets of pasta, filled with cheese, ground meat, etc.

rav•ish•ing /'rævɪʃɪŋ/ *adj.* extremely beautiful or attractive.

raw /rɔ/ *adj.*, -**er, -est. 1.** uncooked. **2.** [*before a noun*] not processed, treated, or refined: *raw cotton.* **3.** painfully open or exposed: *raw wounds.* **4.** inexperienced; untrained: *a raw recruit.* **5.** harsh or unfair: *We got a raw deal when we were fired.* **6.** cold and wet: *a raw day.*

ray[1] /rey/ *n.* [*count*] **1.** a narrow beam of light. **2.** a slight sign or indication: *a ray of hope.*

ray[2] /rey/ *n.* [*count*] a kind of fish having a flattened body.

ray•on /'reyɒn/ *n.* [*noncount*] a smooth, silklike material manufactured from cellulose, cotton, or wood chips.

raze /reyz/ *v.* [~ + *obj*], **razed, raz•ing.** to level to the ground; tear down: *The bulldozer razed the buildings.*

ra•zor /'reyzər/ *n.* [*count*] a sharp-edged instrument used for shaving hair from the skin.

rd., an abbreviation of: road.

R.D., an abbreviation of: rural delivery.

re /riy, rey/ *prep.* with reference to; regarding: *Re your question, the answer is as follows.*

'**re** /ər/ contraction of *are: They're leaving.*

re-, a prefix meaning: back or backward (*repay*); again or once more (*recapture*).

reach /riytʃ/ *v.* **1.** [~ + *obj*] to arrive at: *The boat reached the shore.* **2.** [~ + *obj*] to succeed in touching or seizing, as with a hand or a pole: *to reach a book on a high shelf.* **3.** to stretch or extend so as to touch or meet: [~ + *obj*]: *The*

R

bookcase reaches the ceiling. [no obj]: Her dress reached to the floor. **4.** [~ + obj] to establish communication with: I called but couldn't reach you. —n. [noncount] **5.** the extent or distance of reaching: If you are within reach of my voice, please answer. The medicine was kept out of reach of the children.

re•act /riy'ækt/ v. [no obj] **1.** to act in response: I reacted to the dust by sneezing. **2.** to act in opposition: taxpayers reacting against the new law. **3.** to undergo a chemical change.

re•ac•tion /riy'ækʃən/ n. **1.** [count] an action in a reverse direction or manner. **2.** action in response to some influence, event, etc.: [noncount]: the nation's reaction to the president's speech. [count]: Their reactions were mostly favorable. **3.** [count] the action of chemical agents upon each other.

re•ac•tion•ar•y /riy'ækʃə'nɛriy/ adj., n., pl. -ar•ies. —adj. **1.** relating to or calling for a return to an earlier system or order. —n. [count] **2.** a reactionary person.

re'ac•tor /riy'æktər/ n. [count] a large machine that produces nuclear energy or power.

read /riyd/ v., read /rɛd/, read•ing /'riydɪŋ/, n. —v. **1.** to look at so as to understand the meaning of (something written or printed): [~ + obj]: reading the newspaper; could read music. [no obj]: When did she start reading? **2.** to say aloud (something written or printed): [~ + obj]: to read a story to a child. [no obj]: The instructor read aloud to the class. **3.** [~ + obj] to figure out or understand by observing outward appearances: to read someone's mind. **4.** [~ + obj] to register or indicate: The thermometer reads seventy-two degrees. **5.** [~ + obj] Brit. to study (a subject) at a university. **6.** [no obj] to be readable in a certain way: The essay reads well. **7. read up on,** to learn about by reading: I've been reading up on the subject. —n. [count] **8.** an act or instance of reading. **9.** something read: Her new novel is a good read. —**Idiom. 10. read between the lines,** to understand more than is directly stated. —'**read•a•ble,** adj. —'**read•er,** n. [count]

read•i•ly /'rɛdʝiy/ adv. **1.** promptly; quickly; easily: The information was readily available. **2.** willingly: He readily agreed to help us out.

read•ing /'riydɪŋ/ n. **1.** [noncount] [count] something read or for reading. **2.** [count] an interpretation given to anything: What is your reading of the situation? **3.** [count] the indication of an instrument that measures something: temperature readings.

read•y /'rɛdiy/ adj., -i•er, -i•est, v., read•ied, read•y•ing. —adj. **1.** completely prepared or in fit condition for action or use: The troops were ready for battle. The team was ready to play. **2.** [be + ~ + to + verb] willing; not hesitating: He was always ready to criticize. **3.** [before a noun] immediately available for use: ready money. —v. [~ + obj] **4.** to make ready; prepare. —**Idiom. 5. at the ready,** ready for use: holding their weapons at the ready. —'**read•i•ness,** n. [noncount]

'**ready-'made,** adj. made in advance for sale to any purchaser; not custom-made.

re•al /'riyəl, riyl/ adj. **1.** [before a noun] true; not just apparent or visible: the real reason for his actions. **2.** actual rather than imaginary, ideal, or pretended: real events; a story taken from real life. **3.** genuine; authentic: real pearls. **4.** [before a noun] Informal. absolute; complete; utter: She's

a real brain. That's a real mess. —adv. **5.** Informal. very or extremely: You did a real nice job.

'**real es₁tate,** n. [noncount] **1.** property, esp. in land. **2.** houses and the land on which they are built.

re•al•is•tic /,riyə'lɪstɪk/ adj. interested in, concerned with, or based on what is real or practical: a realistic estimate of costs. —,**re•al'is•ti•cal•ly,** adv.

re•al•i•ty /riy'ælɪtiy/ n., pl. -ties. **1.** [count] a real thing or fact: We had to face some harsh realities about ourselves. **2.** [noncount] real things, facts, or events thought of as a whole: reading fantasy books to escape from reality.

re•al•ize /'riyə₁layz/ v. [~ + obj], -ized, -iz•ing. **1.** to become aware of; understand clearly: At last he realized the truth. Suddenly he realized what had happened. **2.** to make real: He realized his dream and became a teacher. **3.** to obtain for oneself by labor or investment: We realized a net profit of $100. —,**re•al•i'za•tion,** n. [noncount]

re•al•ly /'riyəliy, 'riyliy/ adv. **1.** actually: sees things as they really are. **2.** genuinely; truly: a really hot day. **3.** indeed: Really, this is too much. —interj. **4.** (used to express surprise, scolding, disapproval, etc.): Really, be serious!

realm /rɛlm/ n. [count] any area of thought or activity: within the realm of possibility; the realm of science fiction.

re•al•ty /'riyəltiy, 'riyl-/ n. [noncount] real estate.

reap /riyp/ v. **1.** [~ + obj] [no obj] to gather or cut (a crop, esp. grain). **2.** [~ + obj] to get as a return or result: The company reaped large profits.

reap•er /'riypər/ n. [count] **1.** a machine for cutting standing grain. **2.** a person who reaps.

re•ap•pear /,riyə'pɪər/ v. [no obj] to appear again: The problems keep reappearing. —,**re•ap'pear•ance,** n. [count] [noncount]

rear /rɪər/ v. **1.** [~ + obj] to take care of and support (a young person) up to the age of maturity. **2.** [no obj] to rise on the hind legs: The horse reared (up) and threw off its rider.

rear•most /'rɪər₁mowst/ adj. farthest in the rear; last.

rear•ward /'rɪərwərd/ adv. **1.** Also, '**rear•wards.** toward or in the rear. —adj. [before a noun] **2.** located in or toward the rear. **3.** directed toward the rear.

rea•son /'riyzən/ n. **1.** [count] a basis or cause, as for some belief, action, or event: a good reason for declaring war. **2.** [noncount] the mental powers concerned with forming conclusions and judgments: Animals do not possess reason. **3.** [noncount] sound judgment; good sense: He won't listen to reason. —v. **4.** [no obj] [~ + obj] to think or argue in a logical manner. **5.** [~ + obj] to form conclusions or judgments from facts: I reasoned that he must have fallen and hit his head. —**Idiom. 6. within reason,** within reasonable or sensible limits: We'll pay if the cost is within reason.

rea•son•a•ble /'riyzənəbəl, 'riyznə-/ adj. **1.** sensible or logical: a reasonable conclusion from the facts. **2.** not too expensive; fair: a reasonable price for the new car.

rea•son•a•bly /'riyzənəbliy, 'riyznə-/ adv. **1.** sensibly; with fairness: No one could reasonably expect him to agree. **2.** somewhat; fairly: The house is in reasonably good condition.

rea•son•ing /'riyzənɪŋ/ n. [noncount] the process of using reason in making a judgment or arriving at a conclusion.

re•as•sure /ˌriyə'ʃʊr, -'ʃɜr/ v. [~ + obj], **-sured, -sur•ing.** to give a feeling of confidence to. —,re•as'sur•ance, n. [noncount]

re•bate /'riybeyt/ n. [count] a return of part of the original payment for something bought or for some service: a $500 cash rebate on the new car.

reb•el /n.'rɛbəl; v. rɪ'bɛl/ n., v., **-belled, -bel•ling.** —n. [count] **1.** a person who refuses to obey or fights against a government or ruler. **2.** a person who resists any authority, control, or tradition. —v. [no obj] re•bel **3.** to show strong opposition: Some children rebel to test their parents' patience. —re•bel•lion /rɪ'bɛlyən/ n. [noncount] [count] —re'bel•lious, adj.

re•birth /riy'bɜrθ, 'riy,bɜrθ/ n. [count; usually singular] a renewed existence or activity; revival.

re•bound /v.rɪ'bawnd, 'riy'bawnd/ n. 'riy,bawnd, rɪ'bawnd/ v. [no obj] **1.** to bounce or spring back from the force of hitting something: The ball rebounded off the wall. **2.** to recover, as from ill health or discouragement. **3.** to have a bad effect on someone, as if springing back: His dishonesty rebounded on him when they discovered his lies. —n. [count] **4.** the act of rebounding.

re•buff /n.rɪ'bʌf, 'riybʌf; v. rɪ'bʌf/ n. [count] **1.** a sudden or quick rejection or refusal, as of a person making a request. —v. [~ + obj] **2.** to give a rebuff to.

re•buke /rɪ'byuwk/ v., **-buked, -buk•ing,** n. —v. [~ + obj] **1.** to express sharp, stern disapproval of; scold. —n. [count] **2.** a scolding.

re•but /rɪ'bʌt/ v. [~ + obj], **-but•ted, -but•ting.** to prove to be false by evidence or argument. —re'but•tal, n. [count]

re•call /v.rɪ'kɔl; n. rɪ'kɔl, 'riykɔl for 3; 'riykɔl for 4 / v. **1.** [~ + obj] to remember: I can't recall her name. **2.** [~ + obj] to call or order back to a place of origin: The car was recalled because of faulty brakes. —n. **3.** [noncount] ability to remember: has recall of every detail. **4.** [count] a summons by a manufacturer for the return of a faulty product.

re•cap•ture /riy'kæptʃər/ v. [~ + obj], **-tured, -tur•ing. 1.** to capture again. **2.** to remember or experience again: to recapture those happy moments of youth.

recd. or **rec'd.,** an abbreviation of: received.

re•cede /rɪ'siyd/ v. [no obj], **-ced•ed, -ced•ing. 1.** to move back; withdraw: The waters finally receded. **2.** to become more distant: The painful memory began to recede. **3.** to slope backward: a chin that recedes.

re•ceipt /rɪ'siyt/ n. **1.** [count] a note that states that someone has received money or goods. **2.** receipts, [plural] money, goods, etc., received. **3.** [noncount] the act of receiving or the state of being received.

re•ceive /rɪ'siyv/ v. [~ + obj], **-ceived, -ceiv•ing. 1.** to get or have delivered to one: to receive a letter. **2.** to obtain or take into one's possession: to receive gifts. **3.** to meet with; experience: That baby receives a lot of attention. **4.** to admit (a person) to a place, into an organization or membership, etc.

re•ceiv•er /rɪ'siyvər/ n. [count] a device or apparatus, as a television set, that receives electrical signals, waves, or the like and makes them into images or sounds.

re•cent /'riysənt/ adj. occurring, appearing, or starting a short while ago. —'re•cent•ly, adv.

re•cep•ta•cle /rɪ'sɛptəkəl/ n. [count] a container, device, etc., that receives or holds something.

re•cep•tion /rɪ'sɛpʃən/ n. **1.** [count] a way of reacting to something; a manner of being received: The book had a favorable reception. **2.** [count] a party or occasion when persons are formally received: a wedding reception. **3.** [noncount] the measure of the quality obtained in receiving radio or television broadcasts: poor TV reception.

re•cep•tion•ist /rɪ'sɛpʃənɪst/ n. [count] a person whose job is to receive and assist callers, clients, etc., as in an office.

re•cep•tive /rɪ'sɛptɪv/ adj. willing to receive, as new or different offers or ideas.

re•cess /rɪ'sɛs, 'riysɛs/ n. [count] **1.** a temporary stopping of the usual work or activity; a break. **2.** a part of a room built back or in from the main area. —v. **3.** [~ + obj] to place in a recess. **4.** [~ + obj] [no obj] to stop temporarily or take a recess.

re•ces•sion /rɪ'sɛʃən/ n. **1.** [count] [noncount] a period of economic decline. **2.** [noncount] the act of receding.

rec•i•pe /'rɛsəpiy/ n. [count], pl. **-pes. 1.** a set of instructions for making or preparing something, esp. food. **2.** a method to achieve a desired result: a recipe for happiness.

re•cip•i•ent /rɪ'sɪpiyənt/ n. [count] a person who receives.

re•cip•ro•cal /rɪ'sɪprəkəl/ adj. given, received, performed, felt, etc., in return: reciprocal respect; reciprocal aid.

re•cip•ro•cate /rɪ'sɪprə,keyt/ v., **-cat•ed, -cat•ing.** to give, receive, feel, etc., in return: [no obj]: They gave us a gift so we reciprocated. [~ + obj]: to reciprocate favors.

re•cit•al /rɪ'saytl/ n. [count] a musical or dance entertainment given by one or more performers.

re•cite /rɪ'sayt/ v., **-cit•ed, -cit•ing. 1.** [~ + obj] [no obj] to repeat the words of (a poem, story, etc.) sometimes from memory, esp. in a formal manner. **2.** [~ + obj] to describe; provide details of: He recited a long list of complaints. —rec•i•ta•tion /ˌrɛsɪ'teyʃən/ n. [noncount] [count]

reck•less /'rɛklɪs/ adj. completely unconcerned about the results of one's actions; careless. —'reck•less•ly, adv. —'reck•less•ness, n. [noncount]

reck•on /'rɛkən/ v. [~ + obj] **1.** to count or calculate: to reckon profits. **2.** to consider: They reckoned her (as) an expert. She is reckoned among the experts in that field. **3.** reckon with, **a.** to consider or anticipate: He hadn't reckoned with bad weather. **b.** to deal with: She has to reckon with this kind of complaint all day long. **c.** to consider seriously: a sales force to be reckoned with.

reck•on•ing /'rɛkənɪŋ/ n. [noncount] **1.** computation; calculation: By her reckoning we still owe money. **2.** judgment: a day of reckoning.

re•claim /rɪ'kleym/ v. [~ + obj] to bring (uncultivated land or wasteland) into a condition for farming or other use.

re•cline /rɪ'klayn/ v., **-clined, -clin•ing.** to (cause to) lean back or lie back: [no obj]: He reclined on the sofa. [~ + obj]: to recline a car seat.

rec•luse /'rɛkluws, rɪ'kluws/ n. [count] a person who deliberately lives apart from society. —re•clu•sive /rɪ'kluwsɪv/, adj.

R

rec•og•ni•tion /ˌrɛkəg'nɪʃən/ *n.* [*noncount*] **1.** identification of a person or thing as having previously been seen or known. **2.** perception of something as existing, true, or right: *recognition that students need encouragement.* **3.** the acknowledgment of achievement, ability, status, etc.

rec•og•nize /'rɛkəgˌnayz/ *v.* [~ + *obj*], **-nized, -niz•ing. 1.** to identify as previously seen or known: *I recognized my old classmate.* **2.** to perceive or accept as existing, true, or right: *She recognized the problem.* **3.** to accept as entitled to treatment as a political unit: *The UN formally recognized the territory.* **4.** to show appreciation of: *Today we recognize your great achievements.* —**rec•og•niz•a•ble** /ˌrɛkəg'nayzəbəl/, *adj.*

re•coil /*v.*rɪ'kɔyl; *n.* 'riyˌkɔyl, rɪ'kɔyl/ *v.* [*no obj*] **1.** to jump or shrink back suddenly, as in alarm or disgust. **2.** to spring or fly back because of impact or because of the discharge of a bullet: *The rifle recoiled.* —*n.* [*noncount*] [*count*] **3.** an act or instance of recoiling.

rec•ol•lect /ˌrɛkə'lɛkt/ *v.* [~ + *obj*] [*no obj*] to remember; recall. —ˌ**rec•ol'lec•tion,** *n.* [*noncount*] [*count*]

rec•om•mend /ˌrɛkə'mɛnd/ *v.* [~ + *obj*] **1.** to present (someone or something) as suitable, worthy, or good. **2.** to suggest or advise: *to recommend a special diet.* —ˌ**rec•om•men'da•tion,** *n.* [*count*]: *The club made a recommendation to change the rule.* [*noncount*]: *We chose the restaurant on our neighbor's recommendation.*

rec•om•pense /'rɛkəmˌpɛns/ *v.*, **-pensed, -pens•ing,** *n.* —*v.* [~ + *obj*] **1.** to give something to as payment for work done, injury suffered, or favors received. —*n.* [*noncount*] **2.** a repayment or reward.

rec•on•cile /'rɛkənˌsayl/ *v.*, **-ciled, -cil•ing. 1.** [~ + *obj*] to cause (a person) to accept something undesirable: *He was reconciled to his fate.* **2.** to (cause to) become friendly again, as by settling a quarrel: [~ + *obj*]: *to reconcile hostile persons.* [*no obj*]: *The husband and wife reconciled last week.* **3.** [~ + *obj*] to settle (a quarrel, dispute, etc.): *They have reconciled their differences.* —ˌ**rec•on•cil•i'a•tion,** *n.* [*count*] [*noncount*]

re•con•nais•sance /rɪ'kɒnəsəns, -zəns/ *n.* [*noncount*] [*count*] the act of reconnoitering.

re•con•noi•ter /ˌriykə'nɔytər, ˌrɛkə-/ *v.* [~ + *obj*] [*no obj*] to observe or survey (an enemy position) in order to gain information for military purposes.

re•con•struct /ˌriykən'strʌkt/ *v.* [~ + *obj*] **1.** to construct again; rebuild. **2.** to re-create in the mind from available information. —ˌ**re•con'struc•tion,** *n.* [*count*] [*noncount*]

re•cord /*v.*rɪ'kɔrd; *n., adj.* 'rɛkərd/ *v.* **1.** [~ + *obj*] to set down in writing for future reference: *to record the dates of battles.* **2.** [~ + *obj*] to indicate on a scale: *The instruments recorded the earthquake.* **3.** to preserve sounds, images, or other signals by copying them electronically so that they can be heard or seen later: [~ + *obj*]: *She recorded several songs.* [*no obj*]: *This video camera can record and play back.* —*n.* [*count*] **rec•ord 4.** a written account that preserves the memory or knowledge of certain facts or events. **5.** an official file of someone's criminal activity. **6.** the standing of a team or individual with respect to contests won, lost, and tied. **7.** the highest or best rate, amount, etc., ever achieved, esp. in sports. **8.** something on which sound or images have been electronically recorded, esp. a grooved disk played on a phonograph. —*adj.* [*before a noun*] **rec•ord 9.** superior to all others: *a record year for sales.* —*Idiom.* **10. off the record,** not for publication; unofficial. **11. on record, a.** existing as a matter of public knowledge. **b.** officially noted or stated.

re•cord•er /rɪ'kɔrdər/ *n.* [*count*] **1.** a device for recording sound, images, or data. **2.** a flute with a mouthpiece like a whistle.

re•cord•ing /rɪ'kɔrdɪŋ/ *n.* [*count*] sound or images recorded on a disk or tape.

'record ˌplayer, *n.* PHONOGRAPH.

re-count /*v.*riy'kawnt; *n.* 'riyˌkawnt, riy'kawnt/ *v.* [~ + *obj*] **1.** to count again. —*n.* [*count*] **2.** a second or additional count: *demanded a re-count of the votes.*

re•count /rɪ'kawnt/ *v.* [~ + *obj*] to relate or narrate; tell in detail.

re•coup /rɪ'kuwp/ *v.* [~ + *obj*] to get back what one has lost or spent.

re•course /'riykɔrs, rɪ'kɔrs/ *n.* [*noncount*] the act of going to a person or thing for help, protection, or the like: *Without recourse to a map, how will you know where you are?*

re•cov•er /rɪ'kʌvər/ *v.* **1.** [~ + *obj*] to get back (something lost or taken away): *The police helped us recover our money.* **2.** to get back one's strength or emotional well-being: [*no obj*]: *I'm recovering from a bad cold.* [~ + *obj*]: *He recovered his composure.* —**re'cov•er•y,** *n.* [*noncount*] [*count*], *pl.* **-er•ies.**

rec•re•a•tion /ˌrɛkriy'eyʃən/ *n.* [*noncount*] [*count*] refreshment by means of a hobby or the like, as a way of relaxing. —ˌ**rec•re'a•tion•al,** *adj.*

re•crim•i•na•tion /rɪˌkrɪmə'neyʃən/ *n.* [*count*] [*noncount*] accusing another of bad conduct or of other charges.

re•cruit /rɪ'kruwt/ *n.* [*count*] **1.** a new member of the armed forces. **2.** a new member of any group or organization. —*v.* [~ + *obj*] [*no obj*] **3.** to seek to hire, enroll, or enlist as a recruit. —**re'cruit•er,** *n.* [*count*] —**re'cruit•ment,** *n.* [*noncount*]

rec•tan•gle /'rɛkˌtæŋgəl/ *n.* [*count*] a four-sided figure with parallel sides, having four right angles. —**rec•tang•u•lar** /rɛk'tæŋgyələr/, *adj.*

rec•ti•fy /'rɛktəˌfay/ *v.* [~ + *obj*], **-fied, -fy•ing.** to make, put, or set right; correct.

rec•tor /'rɛktər/ *n.* [*count*] a member of the Christian clergy in charge of a parish.

rec•to•ry /'rɛktəriy/ *n.* [*count*], *pl.* **-ries.** a rector's house.

rec•tum /'rɛktəm/ *n.* [*count*], *pl.* **-tums, -ta** /-tə/. the straight, final part of the large intestine, ending in the anus.

re•cu•per•ate /rɪ'kuwpəˌreyt, -'kyuw-/ *v.* [*no obj*], **-at•ed, -at•ing.** to regain health or strength. —**re,cu•per'a•tion,** *n.* [*noncount*]

re•cur /rɪ'kɜr/ *v.* [*no obj*], **-curred, -cur•ring. 1.** to happen again. **2.** to return to the mind: *The idea kept recurring.* —**re•cur•rence,** *n.* [*count*] [*noncount*] —**re'cur•rent,** *adj.*

re•cy•cle /riy'saykəl/ *v.* [~ + *obj*], **-cled, -cling.** to treat (used or waste materials) so as to make suitable for reuse: *to recycle newspapers.*

red /rɛd/ *n., adj.,* **red•der, red•dest.** —*n.* [*noncount*] [*count*] **1.** a color resembling the color of blood. —*adj.* **2.** of the color red. **3.** (of hair) brownish orange. **4.** (of the face) flushed, esp. from anger or embarrassment. —*Idiom.* **5. in**

the red, operating at a loss or being in debt. —**'red•dish,** *adj.* —**'red•ness,** *n.* [*noncount*]

red•den /'rɛdn̩/ *v.* [*no obj*] [~ + *obj*] (to make or cause) to become red.

re•deem /rɪ'diym/ *v.* [~ + *obj*] **1.** to recover (something pledged or mortgaged) by payment. **2.** to exchange for money or goods: *to redeem a coupon for a free box of cereal.* **3.** to fulfill (a pledge, promise, etc.). **4.** to set free from captivity by paying a penalty. **5.** to make up for; offset: *After making that blunder, how will you redeem yourself?* —**re'demp•tion,** *n.* [*noncount*]

'red-'hot, *adj.* red with heat; very hot.

re•dou•ble /riy'dʌbəl/ *v.* [~ + *obj*], **-bled, -bling.** to increase greatly or by twice as much: *They redoubled their efforts to finish on time.*

'red 'pepper, *n.* **1.** CAYENNE. **2.** [*count*] the mild, ripe fruit of the sweet pepper, used as a vegetable.

re•dress / *n.* 'riydrɛs, rɪ'drɛs; *v.* rɪ'drɛs/ *n.* [*noncount*] **1.** the setting right of what is morally wrong. **2.** relief from wrong or injury, as in the form of payment. —*v.* [~ + *obj*] **3.** to remedy or make right: *to redress a grievance.*

'red 'tape, *n.* [*noncount*] the procedure or routine of a bureaucracy that delays or prevents action.

re•duce /rɪ'duws, -'dyuws/ *v.* [~ + *obj*], **-duced, -duc•ing. 1.** to make smaller, less, cheaper, etc. **2.** to act in a destructive manner upon: *Their house was reduced to ashes by the fire.* —**re•duc•tion** /rɪ'dʌkʃən/ *n.* [*count*]: *a reduction in costs.* [*noncount*]: *reduction of the number of workers.*

re•dun•dant /rɪ'dʌndənt/ *adj.* **1.** exceeding what is usual or necessary: *It is redundant to say "The giant is big."* **2.** Chiefly Brit. being laid off from employment. —**re'dun•dan•cy,** *n.* [*count*] [*noncount*]

red•wood /'rɛd,wʊd/ *n.* [*count*] a cone-bearing tree of the cypress family, native to California.

reed /riyd/ *n.* [*count*] **1.** the straight stalk of a type of tall grass. **2.** a flexible, vibrating piece of wood or metal in the mouthpiece of various wind instruments.

reed•y /'riydiy/ *adj.,* **-i•er, -i•est. 1.** full of reeds. **2.** (of a voice) thin in quality.

reef /riyf/ *n.* [*count*] a ridge of rocks, coral, or sand near the surface of the water.

reek /riyk/ *v.* [*no obj*] **1.** to smell strongly and unpleasantly: *The room reeked of pesticide.* **2.** to contain or seem to contain a potent atmosphere of something: *a suburb that reeks of money.* —*n.* [*count; usually singular*] **3.** a strong, unpleasant smell.

reel[1] /riyl/ *n.* [*count*] **1.** a rounded cylinder that spins and is used to wind up or let out wire, rope, film, etc. **2.** an amount of something wound on a reel: *a reel of film.* **3.** Brit. a spool of thread. —*v.* [~ + *obj*] **4.** to wind on a reel. **5.** to pull by winding a line on a reel: *to reel in a fish.*

reel[2] /riyl/ *v.* [*no obj*] to sway in standing or walking, as from dizziness or drunkenness.

ref /rɛf/ *n.* [*count*] *Informal.* a referee.

re•fer /rɪ'fɜr/ *v.,* **-ferred, -fer•ring. 1.** [~ + *obj*] to direct (someone) to a person, place, or thing for information or assistance. **2.** [~ + *obj*] to send (something) to someone for decision, information, etc.: *Please refer your questions to the supervisor.* **3.** [*no obj*] to apply or relate: *This regulation does not really refer to your company.* **4.** [*no obj*] to turn to for information or help: *to refer to a dictionary for spelling.* **5.** [*no obj*] to men-

tion someone or something; make reference: *The author referred to his mother in his article.*

ref•er•ee /,rɛfə'riy/ *n., pl.* **-ees,** *v.,* **-eed, -ee•ing.** —*n.* [*count*] **1.** a judge in charge of certain games and sports. —*v.* [~ + *obj*] [*no obj*] **2.** to act as a referee for (a game).

ref•er•ence /'rɛfərəns, 'rɛfrəns/ *n., v.,* **-enced, -enc•ing.** —*n.* **1.** [*count*] a mention; allusion: *In her complaint she made references to him as a witness.* **2.** [*noncount*] [*count*] a direction of the attention, as in a book, to some other book or passage. **3.** [*count*] a book or other source of useful information. **4.** [*count*] a person who can provide a statement about another's character or abilities. **5.** [*noncount*] regard or connection; relation: *without reference to age.* —*adj.* [*before a noun*] **6.** of or for materials used for finding information: *dictionaries and other reference books.*

ref•er•en•dum /,rɛfə'rɛndəm/ *n.* [*count*], *pl.* **-dums, -da** /-də/. a vote by the people on whether to approve or reject some proposal or policy.

re•fer•ral /rɪ'fɜrəl/ *n.* **1.** [*count*] an act or instance of referring. **2.** [*count*] a person referred or recommended. **3.** [*noncount*] the state of being referred.

re•fill /*v.* riy'fɪl; *n.* 'riy,fɪl/ *v.* [~ + *obj*] [*no obj*] **1.** to fill again. —*n.* [*count*] **2.** a material or supply to replace something that has been used up: *a refill for a fountain pen.* **3.** a drink after one has finished a previous one: *a refill of coffee.*

re•fine /rɪ'fayn/ *v.* [~ + *obj*], **-fined, -fin•ing. 1.** to remove impure substances from: *to refine oil.* **2.** to make more polished, precise, or fine: *to refine a theory.*

re•fined /rɪ'faynd/ *adj.* **1.** having or showing good manners or taste. **2.** freed from impurities. **3.** very exact: *refined measurements.*

re•fine•ment /rɪ'faynmənt/ *n.* **1.** [*noncount*] fineness or elegance of feeling, taste, manners, language, etc. **2.** [*noncount*] the act or process of refining; the state of being refined. **3.** [*count*] an improved form of something.

re•fin•er•y /rɪ'faynəriy/ *n.* [*count*], *pl.* **-er•ies.** a factory for refining something, such as metal, sugar, or oil.

re•flect /rɪ'flɛkt/ *v.* **1.** to throw back (light, heat, sound, etc.) from a surface: [~ + *obj*]: *The mirror reflected his image perfectly.* [*no obj*]: *This dull surface doesn't reflect.* **2.** [~ + *obj*] to express; show: *The party seems to reflect the views of its leader.* **3.** [*no obj*] to think over: *We took time to reflect on what had gone wrong.* **4. reflect on, a.** to bring blame or discredit: *His crimes reflected on the whole community.* **b.** to give a particular impression: *That accomplishment reflects well on your abilities.* —**re'flec•tive,** *adj.*

re•flec•tion /rɪ'flɛkʃən/ *n.* **1.** [*noncount*] the act of reflecting or the state of being reflected. **2.** [*count*] something reflected, as an image. **3.** [*noncount*] careful consideration. Also, *esp. Brit.,* **re'flex•ion.**

re•flex /'riyflɛks/ *n.* any automatic, habitual behavior or response: [*count*]: *Sneezing is a reflex.* [*noncount*]: *He smiles at other people almost by reflex.*

re•flex•ive /rɪ'flɛksɪv/ *adj.* **1. a.** (of a verb) taking an object that refers to the same subject, such as *cut* in *I cut myself.* **b.** (of a pronoun) used as an object referring to the same subject, such as *myself* in *I cut myself.* **2.** responding by way of a

R

reflex: *a reflexive act of self-preservation.* —*n.* [*count*] **3.** a reflexive verb or pronoun.

re•form /rɪ'fɔrm/ *n.* [*noncount*] [*count*] **1.** the improvement, changing, or removing of what is wrong, evil, unsatisfactory, etc.: *social reform.* —*v.* **2.** [~ + *obj*] to change to a better state, form, etc. **3.** [*no obj*] [~ + *obj*] to (cause a person to) abandon wrong or evil ways. —**ref•or•ma•tion** /ˌrɛfər'meyʃən/ *n.* [*noncount*] [*count*] —**re'form•er,** *n.* [*count*]

re•form•a•to•ry /rɪ'fɔrməˌtɔriy/ *n.* [*count*], *pl.* **-ries.** Also called **reform school.** a jail or similar institution for young offenders.

re•fract /rɪ'frækt/ *v.* [~ + *obj*] to cause (a ray of light) to change direction as it passes through different substances, as glass or water, at an angle. —**re•frac•tion** /rɪ'frækʃən/ *n.* [*noncount*]

re•frain[1] /rɪ'freyn/ *v.* [*no obj*] to keep oneself from doing or saying something: *Please refrain from laughing.*

re•frain[2] /rɪ'freyn/ *n.* [*count*] a phrase or verse that is repeated in a song or poem.

re•fresh /rɪ'frɛʃ/ *v.* [~ + *obj*] **1.** to provide new strength and energy by rest, food, etc. **2.** to stimulate: *Let me refresh your memory.*

re•fresh•ing /rɪ'frɛʃɪŋ/ *adj.* bringing a feeling of refreshment: *a refreshing dip in the pool.*

re•fresh•ment /rɪ'frɛʃmənt/ *n.* **1.** **refreshments,** [*plural*] food and drink, esp. for a snack or light meal. **2.** [*noncount*] the act of refreshing or the state of being refreshed.

re•frig•er•ate /rɪ'frɪdʒəˌreyt/ *v.* [~ + *obj*], **-at•ed, -at•ing.** to make or keep (food or drinks) cold or cool in order to keep them fresh. —**re•frig•er•a•tion** /rɪˌfrɪdʒə'reyʃən/, *n.* [*noncount*]

re•frig•er•a•tor /rɪ'frɪdʒəˌreytər/ *n.* [*count*] a large appliance in which food and drinks are kept cool.

re•fu•el /riy'fyuwəl/ *v.* **1.** [~ + *obj*] to supply (an airplane, car, etc.) with fuel. **2.** [*no obj*] (of an airplane) to take on a supply of fuel.

ref•uge /'rɛfyuwdʒ/ *n.* **1.** [*noncount*] shelter or protection from danger, trouble, etc. **2.** [*count*] a place of shelter, protection, or safety: *a refuge from the storm; a wildlife refuge.*

ref•u•gee /ˌrɛfyu'dʒiy, 'rɛfyuˌdʒiy/ *n.* [*count*], *pl.* **-gees.** a person who flees for refuge or safety, esp. to a foreign country.

re•fund /*v.*rɪ'fʌnd, 'riyfʌnd; *n.* 'riyfʌnd/ *v.* [~ + *obj*] **1.** to give back or restore (esp. money); repay. —*n.* **2.** [*noncount*] [*count*] an act or instance of refunding. **3.** [*count*] an amount refunded.

re•fur•bish /riy'fɜrbɪʃ/ *v.* [~ + *obj*] to clean, decorate, or renovate.

re•fuse[1] /rɪ'fyuwz/ *v.*, **-fused, -fus•ing.** to deny or not accept (a request, offer, etc.): [~ + *obj*]: *to refuse an award.* [*no obj*]: *She asked him to go but he refused.* —**re'fus•al,** *n.* [*noncount*] [*count*]

ref•use[2] /'rɛfyuws/ *n.* [*noncount*] something thrown away as worthless or useless; rubbish.

re•fute /rɪ'fyuwt/ *v.* [~ + *obj*], **-fut•ed, -fut•ing.** to prove to be false or to be in error: *We refuted his accusations.*

re•gain /riy'geyn/ *v.* [~ + *obj*] **1.** to get again; recover: *He regained his health at last.* **2.** to succeed in reaching again: *to regain the shore.*

re•gal /'riygəl/ *adj.* fitting, worthy of, or resembling a king or queen.

re•ga•li•a /rɪ'geyliyə, -'geylyə/ *n.* [*plural*] the ceremonial clothes or emblems of royalty.

re•gard /rɪ'gɑrd/ *v.* [~ + *obj*] **1.** to look at or

think of in a certain way; consider: *to regard a person with favor. I have always regarded you as a friend.* —*n.* **2.** [*noncount*] an aspect or area of concern: *The new machine is quite satisfactory in this regard.* **3.** [*noncount*] thought; attention; concern: *He had no regard for my feelings.* **4.** **regards,** [*plural*] expressions of respect or affection: *Give them my regards.* —**Idiom. 5. with** or **in regard to,** with reference to; concerning: *We have some questions with regard to the contract.*

re•gard•ing /rɪ'gɑrdɪŋ/ *prep.* with regard to; about; concerning: *Regarding payment, send us a check.*

re•gard•less /rɪ'gɑrdlɪs/ *adv.* **1.** without concern as to advice, circumstances, etc.; anyway: *Do as she says, regardless.* —**Idiom. 2. regardless of,** in spite of; without regard for: *I like them regardless of your opinion.*

re•gen•cy /'riydʒənsiy/ *n.*, *pl.* **-cies. 1.** [*noncount*] the government of a regent. **2.** [*count*] the term of office of a regent.

re•gen•er•ate /rɪ'dʒɛnəˌreyt / *v.* [~ + *obj*], **-at•ed, -at•ing.** to revive or produce again: *to regenerate the economy.* —**re•gen•er•a•tion** /rɪˌdʒɛnə'reyʃən/, *n.* [*noncount*]

re•gent /'riydʒənt/ *n.* [*count*] a person who rules when the king or queen is too young or is disabled.

reg•gae /'rɛgey/ *n.* [*noncount*] a style of Jamaican music blending blues, calypso, and rock.

re•gime or **ré•gime** /rə'ʒiym, rey-/ *n.* [*count*] a government in power, or the period of time in which it is in power.

reg•i•men /'rɛdʒəmən, -ˌmɛn/ *n.* [*count*] a regulated course, as of diet or exercise, to gain a result.

reg•i•ment /*n.*'rɛdʒəmənt; *v.* -ˌmɛnt/ *n.* [*count*] **1.** a military unit made up of two or more battalions. —*v.* [~ + *obj*] **2.** to manage or treat according to strict discipline. —ˌ**re•gi•men'ta•tion,** *n.* [*noncount*]

re•gion /'riydʒən/ *n.* [*count*] **1.** a large area of a surface, space, or body: *a region of the earth; pains in the shoulder region.* **2.** a district of a certain kind: *an industrial region.* —**Idiom. 3. in the region of,** approximately. —'**re•gion•al,** *adj.*

reg•is•ter /'rɛdʒəstər/ *n.* [*count*] **1.** a list or record of events, names, etc. **2.** the range of a voice or of a musical instrument. **3.** CASH REGISTER. —*v.* **4.** [*no obj*] [~ + *obj*] to enter or cause to be entered in a register. **5.** [~ + *obj*] to cause (mail) to be recorded upon delivery to a post office for safeguarding against loss or damage. **6.** [*no obj*] [~ + *obj*] to enroll (a student, voter, etc.). **7.** [~ + *obj*] [*no obj*] to show (surprise, anger, etc.), as by facial expression or by actions. **8.** [*no obj*] to have some effect; make some impression: *I don't know if the danger has registered on him yet.* —**reg•is•tra•tion** /ˌrɛdʒə'streyʃən/ *n.* [*noncount*] [*count*]

registered 'nurse, *n.* [*count*] a nurse who has passed a state examination and is licensed to practice nursing.

reg•is•trar /'rɛdʒəˌstrɑr/ *n.* [*count*] a person who keeps records, esp. a school or college official who maintains students' records.

re•gress /rɪ'grɛs / *v.* [*no obj*] to go back, esp. to an earlier, worse, or less advanced state or form: *The patient was making progress, but now he seems to be regressing.* —**re•gres•sion** /rɪ'grɛʃən/, *n.* [*noncount*]

re•gret /rɪ'grɛt/ v., **-gret•ted, -gret•ting,** n. —v. [~ + obj] **1.** to feel sorry about something said or done: He said he did not regret his decision to retire. The thief said he regretted stealing the money. **2.** (used in the present tense to express sorrow): We regret to inform you that the train will be late. —n. **3.** [noncount] [count] a feeling of sorrow, unhappiness, or guilt. **4.** **regrets,** [plural] a polite, usually formal refusal of an invitation. —**re'gret•ful,** adj. —**re'gret•ful•ly,** adv. —**re'gret•ta•ble,** adj.

reg•u•lar /'rɛgyələr/ adj. **1.** usual; normal; customary: Put the book in its regular place. **2.** evenly arranged; balanced; symmetrical: regular facial features. **3.** steady and even; not changing: a regular heartbeat. —n. [count] **4.** a habitual customer or client. —**reg•u•lar•i•ty** /,rɛgyə-'lærɪtiy/, n. [noncount] —**'reg•u•lar•ly,** adv.

reg•u•lar•ize /'rɛgyələ,rayz/ v. [~ + obj], **-ized, -iz•ing.** to make regular.

reg•u•late /'rɛgyə,leyt/ v. [~ + obj], **-lat•ed, -lat•ing. 1.** to control or direct by a rule, principle, or method. **2.** to adjust to some standard or requirement: to regulate the temperature. —**'reg•u,la•tor,** n. [count] —**reg•u•la•to•ry** /'rɛgyələ,tɔriy, /, adj.

reg•u•la•tion /,rɛgyə'leyʃən/ n. **1.** [count] a law, rule, or other order given by authority. **2.** [noncount] the act of regulating or the state of being regulated.

re•ha•bil•i•tate /,riyhə'bɪlɪ,teyt, ,riyə-/ v. [~ + obj], **-tat•ed, -tat•ing. 1.** to restore (something) to good condition or functioning: exercises for rehabilitating damaged knees. **2.** to restore (someone) to former rights, standing, etc.: to rehabilitate criminals. —**,re•ha,bil•i'ta•tion,** n. [noncount]

re•hash /riy'hæʃ/ v. [~ + obj] to reuse (old material) without significant or important changes.

re•hearse /rɪ'hɜrs/ v. [~ + obj] [no obj], **-hearsed, -hears•ing.** to practice (a play, speech, musical piece, etc.) before performing in public. —**re'hears•al,** n. [noncount] [count]

reign /reyn/ n. [count] **1.** the period during which a ruler occupies the throne. —v. [no obj] **2.** to possess or use the power or authority of a ruler.

re•im•burse /,riyɪm'bɜrs/ v. [~ + obj], **-bursed, -burs•ing.** to pay back; refund. —**,re•im'burse•ment,** n. [noncount]

rein /reyn/ n. [count] **1.** a leather strap fastened to a bridle, by which a rider controls a horse. —Idiom. **2.** **give (free) rein to,** to give complete freedom to. **3.** **keep a tight rein on,** to control or restrain tightly.

re•in•car•na•tion /,riyɪnkar'neyʃən/ n. [noncount] the belief that the soul, after the death of the body, comes back to earth in another body or form.

rein•deer /'reyn,dɪər/ n. [count], pl. **-deer,** (occasionally) **-deers.** a large deer of northern and arctic regions of the world.

re•in•force /,riyɪn'fɔrs/ v. [~ + obj], **-forced, -forc•ing. 1.** to strengthen with some added piece or material: to reinforce a wall with concrete. **2.** to make more forceful or effective; strengthen: to reinforce the law. —**,re•in'force•ment,** n. [noncount] [count]

re•in•state /,riyɪn'steyt/ v. [~ + obj], **-stat•ed, -stat•ing.** to put back or establish again: to reinstate the ousted president. —**,re•in'state•ment,** n. [noncount]

re•it•er•ate /riy'ɪtə,reyt/ v. [~ + obj] [no obj],

-at•ed, -at•ing. to say or do over again or repeatedly. —**re•it•er•a•tion** /riy,ɪtə'reyʃən/, n. [noncount] [count]

re•ject / v. rɪ'dʒɛkt;n. 'riydʒɛkt/ v. [~ + obj] **1.** to refuse to grant (a request, demand, etc.); deny. **2.** to refuse to accept or admit: The other children rejected him. —n. [count] **3.** one that is rejected. —**re'jec•tion,** n. [noncount] [count]

re•joice /rɪ'dʒɔys/ v. [no obj] [~ + obj], **-joiced, -joic•ing.** to feel or cause to feel joy or gladness.

re•ju•ve•nate /rɪ'dʒuwvə,neyt/ v. [~ + obj], **-nat•ed, -nat•ing. 1.** to restore to a feeling of being or looking young: The vacation rejuvenated him. **2.** to make fresh or new again: to rejuvenate an old sofa. —**re•ju•ve•na•tion** /rɪ,dʒuwvə'neyʃən/, n. [noncount]

re•lapse / v. rɪ'læps; n. ælsə 'riylæps/ v., **-lapsed, -laps•ing.** —v. [no obj] **1.** to fall or slip back into a former state or practice: to relapse into silence. —n. [count] **2.** an act or instance of relapsing. **3.** a return of a disease after one has partly recovered from it.

re•late /rɪ'leyt/ v., **-lat•ed, -lat•ing. 1.** [~ + obj] to tell (the story of something); describe (an event or events). **2.** [~ + obj] to show an association or connection between things: to relate events to probable causes. **3.** [no obj] to have a connection: Those two ideas do not relate.

re•lat•ed /rɪ'leytɪd/ adj. **1.** associated; connected. **2.** associated or connected by family, marriage, or common origin: related languages; She is distantly related to me.

re'lating to, prep. concerned with: issues relating to education.

re•la•tion /rɪ'leyʃən/ n. **1.** [noncount] association between or among things; connection; relationship: the relation between cause and effect. **2.** **relations,** [plural] **a.** the different connections or dealings between peoples, countries, etc.: business relations. **b.** sexual intercourse. —Idiom. **3.** **in** or **with relation to,** with reference to; concerning. —**re'la•tion•al,** adj.

re•la•tion•ship /rɪ'leyʃən,ʃɪp/ n. **1.** [count] a connection, association, or involvement. **2.** [count; usually singular] connection between persons by blood or marriage; kinship. **3.** [count] a sexual involvement; affair.

rel•a•tive /'rɛlətɪv/ n. [count] **1.** a member of one's family. **2.** something having, or standing in, some relation to something else: English is a close relative to Dutch. —adj. [before a noun] **3.** considered or measured in relation to something else: the relative merits of gas and electric heating. —Idiom. **4.** **relative to,** when compared with: Our profits were up, relative to costs.

rel•a•tive•ly /'rɛlətɪvliy/ adv. somewhat; comparatively: It was relatively easy to see.

re•lax /rɪ'læks/ v. to (cause to) be made less tense, rigid, or firm: [no obj]: I'm too busy to relax. [~ + obj]: Watching television relaxes me. —**re•lax•a•tion** /,riylæk'seyʃən/ n. [noncount] [count]

re•lay /'riyley; v. also rɪ'ley/ n., pl. **-lays,** v., **-layed, -lay•ing.** —n. [count] **1.** a series of persons who take turns helping one another; a shift. **2.** a race in which each member of a team runs part of the way. —v. [~ + obj] **3.** to carry or send by or as if by relays: relaying a message.

re•lease /rɪ'liys/ v., **-leased, -leas•ing,** n. —v. [~ + obj] **1.** to free from jail, burdens, debt, pain, etc.: The guard was released from some of his duties. **2.** to allow to be known, issued,

R

broadcast, or exhibited: *The police released information about the suspect.* —*n.* [count] **3.** the act of releasing. **4.** something that releases. **5.** a film, book, statement, etc., that is released.

rel•e•gate /'rɛlɪ,geyt/ *v.* [~ + *obj* (+ *to* + *obj*)], **-gat•ed, -gat•ing.** to send (someone or something) to a lower-ranking or worse position, place, or condition: *The team relegated him to the minor leagues.* —**rel•e•ga•tion** /,rɛlɪ'geyʃən/, *n.* [noncount]

re•lent /rɪ'lɛnt/ *v.* [no obj] to soften in one's feeling or determination; become more mild or forgiving. —**re'lent•less,** *adj.*

rel•e•vant /'rɛləvənt/ *adj.* connected with the matter at hand; pertinent: *Your comment isn't relevant to the discussion.* —**'rel•e•vance, 'rel•e•van•cy,** *n.* [noncount]

re•li•a•ble /rɪ'layəbəl/ *adj.* capable of being relied on; dependable in character, judgment, performance, or result. —**re•li•a•bil•i•ty** /rɪ,layə'bɪlɪtiy/, *n.* [noncount] —**re'li•a•bly,** *adv.*

re•li•ance /rɪ'layəns/ *n.* [noncount] dependence: *a child's reliance on his mother.*

re•li•ant /rɪ'layənt/ *adj.* dependent on someone or something: *was reliant on his parents.*

rel•ic /'rɛlɪk/ *n.* [count] **1.** something having interest because of its age or its connection with the past. **2.** a body part or personal object that belonged to a saint.

re•lief¹ /rɪ'liyf/ *n.* **1.** [noncount] the ending or lessening of pain, worry, fear, etc. **2.** a feeling of comfort or ease caused by the ending of pain or distress: [count; usually singular]: *What a relief it was to get home.* [noncount]: *breathed a sigh of relief.* **3.** [noncount] money, food, or other help given to people in need.

re•lief² /rɪ'liyf/ *n.* **1.** [noncount] the standing out of a design from the surface where it is formed, as in sculpture. **2.** [count] a carving with a design that stands out from the surface.

re•lieve /rɪ'liyv/ *v.* [~ + *obj*], **-lieved, -liev•ing. 1.** to ease, lessen, or make less unpleasant: *Aspirin may relieve the pain.* **2.** to release (a person on duty) by being or providing a replacement: *The manager relieved his best pitcher.* —**reliev•er,** *n.* [count]

re•lieved /rɪ'liyvd/ *adj.* having a feeling of relief; glad: *We were relieved to hear the news.*

re•li•gion /rɪ'lɪdʒən/ *n.* **1.** [noncount] a set of beliefs concerning the nature and purpose of the universe, esp. when the universe is believed to have been created by a deity. **2.** [count] a certain set of such beliefs and practices accepted by a number of persons: *the religions of the world.*

re•li•gious /rɪ'lɪdʒəs/ *adj.* **1.** [before a noun] of or relating to religion: *a religious holiday.* **2.** practicing a religion; devout.

re•lin•quish /rɪ'lɪŋkwɪʃ/ *v.* [~ + *obj*] to surrender (a possession, right, etc.); abandon: *to relinquish a throne.* —**re'lin•quish•ment,** *n.* [noncount]

rel•ish /'rɛlɪʃ/ *n.* **1.** great enjoyment: [count; usually singular]: *a relish for fast driving.* [noncount]: *I listened with relish to the gossip.* **2.** [noncount] [count] something tasty or appetizing added to a meal, as olives or pickles. —*v.* [~ + *obj*] **3.** to enjoy greatly: *He relishes arguments.*

re•luc•tant /rɪ'lʌktənt/ *adj.* unwilling; not inclined to do something: *a reluctant candidate.* —**re'luc•tance,** *n.* [noncount] —**re'luc•tant•ly,** *adv.*

re•ly /rɪ'lay/ *v.* [no obj], **-lied, -ly•ing.** to put trust in: *Can I rely on your support?*

re•main /rɪ'meyn/ *v.* **1.** to continue to be as specified: [~ + *adjective*]: *He remained loyal to his friends.* [~ + *obj*]: *He remained a bachelor.* **2.** [no obj] to stay behind or in the same place: *He remained at home while the others left.* **3.** [no obj] to be left to be done, told, etc.: *Two questions remain.* —*n.* **remains,** [plural] **4. a.** a dead body; corpse. **b.** parts or substances remaining from animal or plant life: *fossil remains.*

re•main•der /rɪ'meyndər/ *n.* [count] a remaining part: *the remainder of the day.*

re•mark /rɪ'mɑrk/ *v.* **1.** to say casually, as in making a comment: [~ + *obj*]: *He remarked that she was his best student.* [no obj]: *A few folks remarked on her absence.* —*n.* [count] **2.** a casual comment.

re•mark•a•ble /rɪ'mɑrkəbəl/ *adj.* unusual; noteworthy: *a remarkable hat; an ability that is remarkable.* —**re'mark•a•bly,** *adv.*

re•me•di•al /rɪ'miydiyəl/ *adj.* intended to improve anything: *a remedial math program.*

rem•e•dy /'rɛmɪdiy/ *n.*, *pl.* **-dies,** *v.*, **-died, -dy•ing.** —*n.* [count] **1.** something, as a medicine, that cures or relieves a disease or anything wrong with the body. **2.** something that corrects or removes an error or undesirable condition: *punishment as a remedy for bad behavior.* —*v.* [~ + *obj*] **3.** to restore to the proper condition; put right: *to remedy a problem.*

re•mem•ber /rɪ'mɛmbər/ *v.* **1.** to bring back to mind; think of again; recall: [~ + *obj*]: *I can remember my old phone number. I remember giving you the keys.* [no obj]: *I'm having trouble remembering.* **2.** to keep in mind; have in one's memory: [~ + *obj*]: *She remembered to bring her umbrella.* [no obj]: *Remember, I'll see you at 2:00.*

re•mem•brance /rɪ'mɛmbrəns/ *n.* **1.** [noncount] the act of remembering or the state of being remembered. **2.** [count] a memento.

re•mind /rɪ'maynd/ *v.* [~ + *obj*] **1.** to cause (a person) to remember: *Remind me to call home.* **2.** to cause (a person) to think (of someone or something): *She reminds me of my mother.* —**re'mind•er,** *n.* [count]

rem•i•nisce /,rɛmə'nɪs/ *v.* [no obj], **-nisced, -nisc•ing.** to recall or talk about past experiences, events, etc. —**,rem•i'nis•cent,** *adj.*

rem•i•nis•cence /,rɛmə'nɪsəns/ *n.* **1.** [noncount] [count] the act of recalling past experiences, events, etc. **2.** Often, **reminiscences.** [plural] an account of memorable experiences.

re•mis•sion /rɪ'mɪʃən/ *n.* **1.** [noncount] [count] forgiveness, as of sins. **2.** [noncount] a temporary or permanent decrease in the symptoms of a disease, as cancer.

re•mit /rɪ'mɪt/ *v.* [~ + *obj*], **-mit•ted, -mit•ting.** to send (money, a check, etc.), usually in payment. —**re'mit•tance,** *n.* [count]

rem•nant /'rɛmnənt/ *n.* [count] a remaining, usually small part or amount of something.

re•morse /rɪ'mɔrs/ *n.* [noncount] deep regret for having done something wrong: *The killer seemed to have no remorse.* —**re'morse•ful,** *adj.* —**re'morse•ful•ly,** *adv.*

re•mote /rɪ'mowt/ *adj.*, **-mot•er, -mot•est. 1.** not near well-populated areas; secluded: *a remote village.* **2.** distant in space, time, relationship, etc.: *a remote ancestor.* **3.** slight; unlikely: *a remote chance they might hear our signals.* **4.** operating or controlled from a distance, as by remote control. —**re'mote•ly,** *adv.* —**re'mote•ness,** *n.* [noncount]

re•mote con•trol, *n.* **1.** [noncount] control of

an apparatus from a distance, as the control of a guided missile by radio signals. **2.** [*count*] a device used to control an apparatus or machine, as a television set, from a distance.

re•move /rɪ'muwv/ v. [~ + *obj*], **-moved, -mov•ing. 1.** to move or shift from a place or position: *She removed her hands from the steering wheel.* **2.** to dismiss from a position; discharge. **3.** to eliminate; put an end to: *to remove the threat of danger.* —**re'mov•a•ble,** *adj.* —**re'mov•al,** *n.* [*noncount*]

re•moved /rɪ'muwvd/ *adj.* [*be* + ~] distant or greatly different from: *Her policies are far removed from mine.*

Ren•ais•sance /ˌrɛnə'sɑns, 'rɛnəˌsɑns/ *n.* **1.** [*the* + ~] the great revival of art, literature, and learning in Europe between the 14th and 17th centuries. **2.** [*count; usually: renaissance*] any similar revival.

re•nal /'riynl̩/ *adj.* of or relating to the kidneys.

ren•der /'rɛndər/ v. [~ + *obj*] **1.** to cause to be or become; make: *The blow to the head rendered him unconscious.* **2.** to give; provide: *to render aid.* **3.** to represent or interpret in drawing, painting, or performing: *to render a song.*

ren•dez•vous /'rɑndəˌvuw, -dey-/ *n., pl.* **-vous** /-ˌvuwz/, *v.,* **-voused** /-ˌvuwd/, **-vous•ing** /-ˌvuwɪŋ/. —*n.* [*count*] **1.** a place designated for a meeting or assembling. **2.** the meeting itself. —*v.* [*no obj*] **3.** to assemble at a rendezvous.

ren•di•tion /rɛn'dɪʃən/ *n.* [*count*] an interpretation or performance, as of a role in a play.

ren•e•gade /'rɛnɪˌgeyd/ *n.* [*count*] a person who deserts one country, cause, belief, etc., for another.

re•new /rɪ'nuw, -'nyuw/ v. [~ + *obj*] **1.** to begin or take up again; resume: *to renew a friendship.* **2.** to make (a license, passport, etc.) effective for an additional period. **3.** to make, say, or do again: *The army renewed its attacks.* **4.** to restore to a former state, esp. so as to be used again: *We need to renew our strength.* —**re'new•al,** *n.* [*noncount*] [*count*]

re•nounce /rɪ'nawns/ v. [~ + *obj*], **-nounced, -nounc•ing.** to give up or put aside (a title, claim, belief, etc.).

ren•o•vate /'rɛnəˌveyt/ v. [~ + *obj*], **-vat•ed, -vat•ing.** to restore to good condition; to make like new: *They bought an old house and renovated it.* —**ren•o•va•tion** /ˌrɛnə'veyʃən/, *n.* [*noncount*] [*count*]

re•nown /rɪ'nawn/ *n.* [*noncount*] widespread fame: *a scholar of great renown.* —**re'nowned,** *adj.: a renowned musician; renowned for his paintings.*

rent /rɛnt/ *n.* [*noncount*] [*count*] **1.** a regular payment to the owner of land or other property, for the right to live in or use the property. —*v.* [~ + *obj*] **2.** to pay money for the use of (property): *I rented a small apartment.* **3.** to allow the possession and use of (real estate, machinery, etc.) in return for rent: *The lodge will rent skis for the day. The company will not rent cars (out) to anyone under 18 years old.* —**Idiom. 4. for rent,** available to be rented. —'**rent•er,** *n.* [*count*]

rent•al /'rɛntl̩/ *n.* [*count*] **1.** an amount received or paid as rent. **2.** something offered or given for rent. —*adj.* [*before a noun*] **3.** of, relating to, or available for rent: *rental property.*

re•nun•ci•a•tion /rɪˌnʌnsiy'eyʃən, -ʃiy-/ *n.* [*noncount*] an act or instance of renouncing something, as a right or title.

rep¹ /rɛp/ *n.* [*count*] *Informal.* a representative of a company, esp. a salesperson.

rep² /rɛp/ *n.* [*count*] a repertory theater or company.

re•pair /rɪ'pɛər/ v. [~ + *obj*] **1.** to restore to a good condition after damage or decay; fix: *Can you repair this computer?* —*n.* **2.** the act or result of repairing: [*plural*]: *The brakes need repairs.* [*noncount*]: *in need of repair.* **3.** [*noncount*] condition with respect to soundness and usability: *a house in good* (or *bad*) *repair.*

rep•a•ra•tion /ˌrɛpə'reyʃən/ *n.* **1.** [*noncount*] the act of repaying or of making up for losses or injuries. **2.** Usually, **reparations.** [*plural*] payment made by a defeated nation to the victor for loss suffered during war.

re•pay /rɪ'pey/ v. [~ + *obj*], **-paid, -pay•ing. 1.** to pay back or refund. **2.** to make return for or to: *to repay a compliment with a smile.* —**re'pay•ment,** *n.* [*noncount*] [*count*]

re•peal /rɪ'piyl/ v. [~ + *obj*] **1.** to do away with officially or formally; cancel: *The county repealed the law.* —*n.* [*count*] **2.** the act of repealing.

re•peat /rɪ'piyt/ v. [~ + *obj*] **1.** to say or do again: *Repeat the exercise three times.* **2.** to tell (something heard) to another: *I asked her not to repeat what I was about to tell her.* **3.** to undergo again: *History seems to repeat itself.* —*n.* [*count*] **4.** the act of repeating. **5.** something repeated, as a television program broadcast at least once before. —**re'peat•er,** *n.* [*count*]

re•peat•ed /rɪ'piytɪd/ *adj.* [*before a noun*] done or said again and again: *repeated attempts.* —**re'peat•ed•ly,** *adv.: She warned us repeatedly.*

re•pel /rɪ'pɛl/ v. [~ + *obj*], **-pelled, -pel•ling. 1.** to drive or force back: *The army repelled the invasion.* **2.** to cause a feeling of distaste or dislike: *She was repelled by his bad manners.*

re•pel•lent /rɪ'pɛlənt/ *adj.* **1.** causing distaste or dislike; repulsive. **2.** resistant to something (often used in combination): *a water-repellent raincoat.* —*n.* [*count*] [*noncount*] **3.** something that repels insects or other pests.

re•pent /rɪ'pɛnt/ v. to feel regretful or sorry for (something one has done): [*no obj*]: *to repent of an unkind act.* [~ + *obj*]: *He repented his angry words.* —**re'pent•ance** /rɪ'pɛntns/, *n.* [*noncount*] —**re'pent•ant,** *adj.*

re•per•cus•sion /ˌriypər'kʌʃən, ˌrɛpər-/ *n.* [*count*] an effect or result of some previous action or event: *The assassination had far-reaching political repercussions.*

rep•er•toire /'rɛpərˌtwɑr, -ˌtwɔr, 'rɛpə-/ *n.* [*count*] all the works that a performing company or an artist is prepared to present.

rep•er•to•ry /'rɛpərˌtɔriy/ *n.* [*count*], *pl.* **-ries.** the practice in which a theatrical company performs several different works during one season: *a repertory company.*

rep•e•ti•tion /ˌrɛpɪ'tɪʃən/ *n.* [*noncount*] [*count*] the act of repeating; a repeated action or performance.

rep•e•ti•tious /ˌrɛpɪ'tɪʃəs/ *adj.* full of repetition.

re•pet•i•tive /rɪ'pɛtɪtɪv/ *adj.* having or showing repetition.

re•phrase /riy'freyz/ v. [~ + *obj*], **-phrased, -phras•ing.** to ask, say, or put into words differently.

re•place /rɪ'pleys/ v. [~ + *obj*], **-placed, -plac•ing. 1.** to take the place of: *Computers have replaced typewriters in most offices.* **2.** to provide a substitute for: *to replace a broken dish.* **3.** to re-

R

store to or put back in the proper place: *He re-placed the book on the shelf.* —**re'place•a•ble,** *adj.* —**re'place•ment,** *n.* [*noncount*] [*count*]

re•play /*v.*riy'pley; *n.* 'riy,pley/ *v.* [~ + *obj*] **1.** to play again, as a tape. **2.** to play again, as a game. —*n.* [*count*] **3.** an act or instance of re-playing.

re•plen•ish /rɪ'plɛnɪʃ/ *v.* [~ + *obj*] to make full or complete again; fill again: *They replenished the refrigerator with food.* —**re'plen•ish•ment,** *n.* [*noncount*]

rep•li•ca /'rɛplɪkə/ *n.* [*count*], *pl.* **-cas.** a close copy or reproduction, as of a work of art.

re•ply /rɪ'play/ *v.*, **-plied, -ply•ing,** *n.*, *pl.* **-plies.** —*v.* **1.** to give an answer in words or action; re-spond: [*no obj*]: *to reply to a question.* [~ + *obj*]: *He replied that no one would go.* —*n.* [*count*] **2.** a response in words or action.

re•port /rɪ'pɔrt/ *n.* [*count*] **1.** a detailed account of an event, situation, etc., usually based on what one has observed or asked questions about. **2.** an item of news; rumor; gossip. **3.** a loud noise, as from an explosion. —*v.* **4.** to give a for-mal account or statement of: [~ + *obj*]: *to report a profit for the year.* [*no obj*]: *to report on the ef-fects of pollution.* **5.** [~ + *obj*] to make a charge against (a person), usually to a supervisor: *She reported him to the dean for cheating.* **6.** [~ + *obj*] [*no obj*] to write an account for publication in a newspaper or magazine. **7.** [*no obj*] to pres-ent oneself as ordered: *The officer reported for duty.*

re•port•er /rɪ'pɔrtər/ *n.* [*count*] a person whose job is to gather and report news, such as for a newspaper.

re•pose /rɪ'powz/ *n.*, *v.*, **-posed, -pos•ing.** —*n.* [*noncount*] **1.** the state of being at rest; sleep. —*v.* [*no obj*] **2.** to lie down or be at rest.

re•pos•i•tor•y /rɪ'pɒzɪ,tɔriy/ *n.* [*count*], *pl.* **-tor•ies.** **1.** a container or place where things are deposited and stored. **2.** an abundant source or supply: *She is a repository of interesting stories.*

rep•re•hen•si•ble /,rɛprɪ'hɛnsəbəl/ *adj.* bad or evil enough to deserve blame.

rep•re•sent /,rɛprɪ'zɛnt/ *v.* [~ + *obj*] **1.** to ex-press by some symbol, character, or the like: *to represent musical sounds by notes.* **2.** to stand or act in place of, as an agent or substitute. **3.** to be the equivalent of; serve as an example of: *His policies represent a bold program for the future.* —**,rep•re•sen'ta•tion,** *n.* [*count*] [*noncount*]

rep•re•sent•a•tive /,rɛprɪ'zɛntətɪv/ *n.* [*count*] **1.** a person or thing that represents another or others. **2.** a person who represents a certain com-munity in a law-making body, esp. a member of the U.S. House of Representatives. **3.** a typical example of something. —*adj.* **4.** serving to repre-sent; typical: *Those opinions are representative of our neighborhood.* **5.** [*before a noun*] of or based on government by chosen representatives: *a rep-resentative democracy.*

re•press /rɪ'prɛs/ *v.* [~ + *obj*] **1.** to hold back (actions or desires): *repressed a sneeze.* **2.** to hold down and control (persons) unfairly or evilly: *to repress citizens.* —**re•pres•sion** /rɪ'prɛʃən/ *n.* [*noncount*] —**re'pres•sive,** *adj.*

re•prieve /rɪ'priyv/ *v.*, **-prieved, -priev•ing,** *n.* —*v.* [~ + *obj*] **1.** to delay punishment of (a con-demned person). —*n.* [*count*] **2.** an official order to delay or cancel punishment, esp. execution. **3.** any temporary relief from something bad.

rep•ri•mand /'rɛprə,mænd; *v.* also ,rɛprə'mænd/ *n.* [*count*] **1.** a severe scolding.

—*v.* [~ + *obj*] **2.** to scold or blame (someone) severely.

re•pris•al /rɪ'prayzəl/ *n.* [*count*] [*noncount*] the act of causing equal or greater injuries to one's enemy as a reaction to the injuries done to one-self.

re•proach /rɪ'prowtʃ/ *v.* [~ + *obj*] **1.** to find fault with (a person, group, etc.). —*n.* **2.** [*non-count*] blame; disapproval: *a term of reproach.* **3.** [*count*] an expression of, or words that express, such blame. —**re'proach•ful,** *adj.*

re•pro•duce /,riyprə'duws, -'dyuws/ *v.*, **-duced, -duc•ing.** **1.** to make a copy or close imitation of: [~ + *obj*]: *The tape reproduced the sound of the conversation fairly well.* [*no obj*]: *That copier re-produces badly.* **2.** to produce offspring of (one-self): [~ + *obj*]: *Some animals reproduce them-selves by laying eggs.* [*no obj*]: *If an animal can't reproduce, its species will not survive.* —**,re•pro'duc•tion,** *n.* [*count*] [*noncount*] —**re•pro•duc•tive** /,riyprə'dʌktɪv/, *adj.*

re•proof /rɪ'pruwf/ *n.* [*count*] an expression of criticism, blame, or correction.

re•prove /rɪ'pruwv/ *v.* [~ + *obj*], **-proved, -prov•ing.** to express strong disapproval of; blame; criticize sharply.

rep•tile /'rɛptɪl, -tayl/ *n.* [*count*] any air-breathing animal having a backbone, a com-pletely bony skeleton, and a covering of dry scales or horny plates: *Reptiles include snakes, lizards, turtles, and crocodiles.* —**rep•til•i•an** /rɛp'tɪliyən/, *adj.*

re•pub•lic /rɪ'pʌblɪk/ *n.* [*count*] **1.** a state which is governed by representatives elected by citi-zens. **2.** a state in which the head of government is not a monarch and is usually an elected presi-dent.

re•pub•li•can /rɪ'pʌblɪkən/ *adj.* **1.** of or sup-porting the principles of a republic. **2.** [*Republi-can*] of or relating to the Republican Party. —*n.* [*count*] **3.** a person who favors a republican form of government. **4.** [*Republican*] a member of the Republican Party.

Re'publican 'Party, *n.* one of the two major political parties in the U.S.

re•pu•di•ate /rɪ'pyuwdiy,eyt/ *v.* [~ + *obj*], **-at•ed, -at•ing.** **1.** to refuse to have any connec-tion with (a person). **2.** to reject and disapprove, condemn, or deny: *to repudiate an accusation.* —**re•pu•di•a•tion** /rɪ'pyuwdiy'eyʃən/, *n.* [*non-count*]

re•pug•nant /rɪ'pʌgnənt/ *adj.* causing a feeling of strong dislike; repellent. —**re'pug•nance,** *n.* [*noncount*]

re•pulse /rɪ'pʌls/ *v.* [~ + *obj*], **-pulsed, -puls•ing.** **1.** to drive back; repel: *The squadron re-pulsed the next assault.* **2.** to refuse or reject: *She repulsed his attempts at friendliness.*

re•pul•sion /rɪ'pʌlʃən/ *n.* [*noncount*] **1.** the feel-ing of being disgusted, as by the presence of something disliked. **2.** the force that tends to sep-arate bodies of similar electric charge or magnet-ism.

re•pul•sive /rɪ'pʌlsɪv/ *adj.* causing a feeling of strong dislike.

rep•u•ta•ble /'rɛpyətəbəl/ *adj.* honorable; re-spectable: *a reputable bank.*

rep•u•ta•tion /,rɛpyə'teyʃən/ *n.* [*count*] the opinion that others have about a person or thing: *That college has a good reputation.*

re•pute /rɪ'pyuwt/ *n.*, *v.*, **-put•ed, -put•ing.** —*n.* [*noncount*] **1.** opinion in the view of others; reputation: *persons of good repute.* **2.** favorable reputation. —*v.* [~ + *obj*] **3.** to consider or believe (a person or thing) to be as described: *He was reputed to be a millionaire.*

re•put•ed /rɪˈpyuwtɪd/ *adj.* [*before a noun*] reported or supposed to be such: *the reputed author of a book.* —**re'put•ed•ly,** *adv.*

re•quest /rɪˈkwɛst/ *n.* [*count*] **1.** the act of asking for something to be given or done: *a request for silence.* **2.** something asked for: *Please grant our request.* —*v.* [~ + *obj*] **3.** to ask for, esp. formally or politely.

re•quire /rɪˈkwayᵊr/ *v.,* **-quired, -quir•ing. 1.** [~ + *obj*] to have need of; need: *He requires medical care.* **2.** to order (someone) to do something: [~ + *obj*]: *The judge required the witness to testify.* [*no obj*]: *to do as the law requires.* —**re'quire•ment,** *n.* [*count*]

req•ui•site /ˈrɛkwəzɪt/ *adj.* [*before a noun*] **1.** required; necessary: *the requisite skills for a job.* —*n.* [*count*] **2.** something required.

res•cue /ˈrɛskyuw/ *v.,* **-cued, -cu•ing,** *n.* —*v.* [~ + *obj*] **1.** to free from danger; save from harm: *a plan to rescue the hostages.* —*n.* [*count*] **2.** the act of rescuing. —**'res•cu•er,** *n.* [*count*]

re•search /rɪˈsɜrtʃ, ˈriysɜrtʃ/ *n.* **1.** [*noncount*] careful study of a subject in order to discover or revise facts, theories, principles, etc. **2.** [*count*] a particular piece of research. —*v.* [~ + *obj*] [*no obj*] **3.** to investigate or look into something carefully; to do research on. —**re'search•er,** *n.* [*count*]

re•sem•ble /rɪˈzɛmbəl/ *v.* [~ + *obj*], **-bled, -bling.** to be like or similar to: *That girl closely resembles her mother.* —**re'sem•blance,** *n.* [*noncount*]

re•sent /rɪˈzɛnt/ *v.* [~ + *obj*] to feel or show displeasure or anger toward (something or someone), because of a feeling of being insulted or wronged: *The older brother resented his younger sister's success.* —**re'sent•ful,** *adj.* —**re'sent•ment,** *n.* [*noncount*] [*count*]

res•er•va•tion /ˌrɛzərˈveyʃən/ *n.* [*count*] **1.** a doubt in one's mind or an exception in one's thinking: *I accept what he says, but with some reservations.* **2.** an area of public land set apart for a special purpose, esp. for the use of Native Americans. **3.** an arrangement to set aside something for use at a later time, as a room in a hotel or a table at a restaurant.

re•serve /rɪˈzɜrv/ *v.,* **-served, -serv•ing,** *n.* —*v.* [~ + *obj*] **1.** to keep back or save for future use, handling, etc.: *He reserved his strength for the last half mile of the race.* **2.** to set apart for a particular use, purpose, etc.: *Those seats are reserved for the elderly.* —*n.* **3.** [*count*] cash held aside to meet unexpected expenses. **4.** [*count*] something stored or saved for use when needed: *a reserve of food.* **5.** [*count*] an area of public land set apart for a special purpose: *a forest reserve.* **6. reserves,** [*plural*] part of a military force held in readiness to assist the main force. **7.** [*noncount*] caution or formality in one's words or actions. —*Idiom.* **8. in reserve,** put aside for a future need: *money held in reserve.*

re•served /rɪˈzɜrvd/ *adj.* cautious or formal in dealing with others.

res•er•voir /ˈrɛzər،vwɑr, ˈrɛzə-/ *n.* [*count*] a natural or artificial place where water is collected for use, supplying a community or region.

re•side /rɪˈzayd/ *v.* [*no obj*], **-sid•ed, -sid•ing. 1.** to live; dwell: *residing at 15 Maple Lane; residing in Paris.* **2.** (of things, qualities, etc.) to be

present or to be found normally in something: *Power resided in the monarchy.*

res•i•dence /ˈrɛzɪdəns/ *n.* **1.** [*count*] the place, esp. the house, in which a person lives or resides. **2.** [*noncount*] the act or fact of residing.

res•i•den•cy /ˈrɛzɪdənsiy/ *n.* [*noncount*] [*count*], *pl.* **-cies.** the position of a medical resident.

res•i•dent /ˈrɛzɪdənt/ *n.* [*count*] **1.** a person who lives in a place: *a resident of the Czech Republic.* **2.** a physician working in a hospital while receiving specialized training there. —*adj.* [*before a noun*] **3.** residing; dwelling in a place.

res•i•den•tial /ˌrɛzɪˈdɛnʃəl/ *adj.* (of a place or area) consisting mainly of private homes rather than businesses.

res•i•due /ˈrɛzɪˌduw, -ˌdyuw/ *n.* [*count*] something that remains after a part is removed, disposed of, or used.

re•sign /rɪˈzayn/ *v.* **1.** to give up an office or position: [*no obj*]: *He was forced to resign from the job.* [~ + *obj*]: *The officer resigned his commission.* **2. resign oneself,** to accept something without struggle or resistance: *He resigned himself to failure.* —**res•ig•na•tion** /ˌrɛzɪgˈneyʃən/ *n.* [*count*] [*noncount*]

re•sil•ient /rɪˈzɪlyənt/ *adj.* **1.** flexible: *a resilient rubber ball.* **2.** recovering quickly and easily from illness, troubles, or the like. —**re'sil•ience, re'sil•ien•cy,** *n.* [*noncount*]

res•in /ˈrɛzɪn/ *n.* [*noncount*] a sticky substance that comes from pine, used in medicine and in varnishes and plastics. —**'res•in•ous,** *adj.*

re•sist /rɪˈzɪst/ *v.* **1.** to withstand or fight against; oppose: [~ + *obj*]: *The management resisted the workers' demands.* [*no obj*]: *The army was ordered to resist.* **2.** to keep or stop oneself from doing or accepting: [~ + *obj*]: *The kids couldn't resist the chocolates. They couldn't resist peeking under the curtain.*

re•sist•ance /rɪˈzɪstəns/ *n.* [*noncount*] **1.** the act or power of resisting or opposing: *The plans met with a great deal of resistance.* **2.** opposing force: *wind resistance that slows the car down.* **3.** the ability of the human body to resist infection or illness. —**re'sist•ant,** *adj.*

re•sis•tor /rɪˈzɪstər/ *n.* [*count*] a device designed to reduce the current in an electric circuit.

res•o•lute /ˈrɛzə،luwt/ *adj.* set in purpose or opinion; resolved; determined. —**'res•o،lute•ly,** *adv.*

res•o•lu•tion /ˌrɛzəˈluwʃən/ *n.* **1.** [*count*] a formal expression by a group of its opinion: *The legislature passed a resolution condemning the invasion.* **2.** [*count*] the act of deciding on a course of action, or the thing decided on: *made a New Year's resolution.* **3.** [*noncount*] the mental state of being resolute or determined: *He went forward with renewed resolution.* **4.** [*noncount*] [*count*] a solution of a problem.

re•solve /rɪˈzɒlv/ *v.,* **-solved, -solv•ing,** *n.* —*v.* [~ + *obj*] **1.** to make a resolution: *I resolved to work harder.* **2.** to state in a formal resolution: *It was resolved that the committee approve her promotion.* **3.** to settle or solve (a problem, dispute, etc.). —*n.* **4.** [*count*] a firm decision; a resolution. **5.** [*noncount*] firmness of purpose; determination: *They began the project with great resolve.*

res•o•nate /ˈrɛzə،neyt/ *v.* [*no obj*], **-nat•ed, -nat•ing.** to make a deep, clear, echoing or continuing sound: *His booming voice resonated in the church.* —**res•o•nance** /ˈrɛzənəns/ *n.* [*noncount*] [*count*] —**'res•o•nant,** *adj.*

R

restaurant

re•sort /rɪ'zɔrt/ *n.* **1.** [*count*] a place with facilities for vacationers: *a beach resort.* **2.** [*noncount*] the action of turning to someone for help; resource: *The Supreme Court was the court of last resort for his case.* —*v.* [*no obj*] **3.** to turn to for help, often as a final option: *to resort to war to accomplish our aims.*

re•sound /rɪ'zawnd/ *v.* [*no obj*] **1.** to echo or ring with sound: *The room resounded with applause.* **2.** to make an echoing sound; sound loudly: *The cheers resounded through the room.*

re•sound•ing /rɪ'zawndɪŋ/ *adj.* [*before a noun*] **1.** loud, clear, and echoing: *a resounding cheer.* **2.** very great: *resounding successes.*

re•source /'riysɔrs/ *n.* [*count*] **1.** a source of supply, support, or aid, esp. one held in reserve: *Religion is a resource for many families.* **2.** a source of wealth of a country: *minerals and other natural resources.* **3.** Usually, **resources.** [*plural*] money or assets.

re•source•ful /rɪ'sɔrsfəl/ *adj.* able to deal with difficulties or new situations: *Teachers need to be resourceful and creative.*

re•spect /rɪ'spɛkt/ *n.* **1.** [*noncount*] honor or high regard: *to be held in respect.* **2.** [*count*] a detail or feature: *The two plans differ in some respects.* **3.** [*noncount*] proper courtesy: *respect for the flag.* **4. respects,** [*plural*] a formal gesture of greeting or sympathy: *Give my respects to your parents.* —*v.* [~ + *obj*] **5.** to hold in honor: *Do the students respect the flag?* —**re'spect•ful,** *adj.* —**re'spect•ful•ly,** *adv.*

re•spect•a•ble /rɪ'spɛktəbəl/ *adj.* **1.** worthy of respect: *a respectable citizen.* **2.** fairly large in size or amount. —**re•spect•a•bil•i•ty** /rɪ,spɛktə'bɪlɪtiy/, *n.* [*noncount*]

re•spec•tive /rɪ'spɛktɪv/ *adj.* relating individually to each; particular: *We need to judge the respective merits of each of the candidates.*

re•spec•tive•ly /rɪ'spɛktɪvliy/ *adv.* (of several subjects) in the order given: *Joe and Bob escorted Betty and Alice, respectively.*

res•pi•ra•tion /,rɛspə'reyʃən/ *n.* [*noncount*] the process of breathing. —**res•pi•ra•to•ry** /'rɛspərə,tɔriy/ *adj.*: *respiratory ailments.*

res•pite /'rɛspɪt/ *n.* [*count*] [*noncount*] a delay; a period of relief.

re•splend•ent /rɪ'splɛndənt/ *adj.* shining brilliantly; radiant. —**re'splend•ence,** *n.* [*noncount*]

re•spond /rɪ'spɒnd/ *v.* [*no obj*] **1.** to answer in words: *How do you respond to that question?* **2.** to return by an action: *to respond to a charity drive with donations.* **3.** to react favorably: *The patient didn't respond to the treatment.*

re•sponse /rɪ'spɒns/ *n.* **1.** [*count*] an answer; reply. **2.** an action done as an answer to another action: [*count*]: *a friendly response to his greeting.* [*noncount*]: *She nodded in response to his greeting.*

re•spon•si•bil•i•ty /rɪ,spɒnsə'bɪlɪtiy/ *n.*, *pl.* **-ties. 1.** [*noncount*] the state or fact of being responsible: *Will anyone assume responsibility for this damage?* **2.** [*count*] a person or thing for which one is responsible: *the responsibilities of being a father.*

re•spon•si•ble /rɪ'spɒnsəbəl/ *adj.* **1.** expected to do or care for something: *The children are responsible for setting the table.* **2.** involving duties or obligations: *a responsible job.* **3.** being the source or cause of something: *Who is responsible for this mess?* **4.** reliable or dependable; trustworthy: *a mature, responsible young adult.* —**re'spon•si•bly,** *adv.*

re•spon•sive /rɪ'spɒnsɪv/ *adj.* responding quickly and with sympathy.

rest[1] /rɛst/ *n.* **1.** [*count*] a period of time of sleep, ease, etc. **2.** the stopping or absence of motion: [*count; usually singular*]: *The ball rolled and then came to a rest.* [*noncount*]: *a state of rest.* **3.** [*count*] *Music.* a sign indicating a period of silence between tones. —*v.* **4.** [*no obj*] [~ + *obj*] to refresh oneself, as by sleeping, lying down, or being at ease. **5.** [*no obj*] to stop moving: *The ball rested a few inches from the hole.* **6.** [*no obj*] to remain without further notice: *Why don't you let the matter rest?* **7.** to (cause to) lie, sit, lean, or be set: [*no obj*]: *His arm rested on the table.* [~ + *obj*]: *He rested his arm on her shoulder.* **8.** to (cause to) be based: [*no obj*]: *His whole argument rests on false assumptions.* [~ + *obj*]: *He rested his arguments on false assumptions.* **9.** [*no obj*] to be found; belong: *The blame rests with them.* —*Idiom.* **10. at rest, a.** not active; not in motion. **b.** free from worry; calm. **11. lay to rest, a.** to bury (a dead body). **b.** to relieve: *They laid most of my fears to rest.*

rest[2] /rɛst/ *n.* [*the* + ~; *used with a singular verb*] the part that remains; remainder: *The first part was hard, but the rest was easy.* **2.** [*the* + ~; *used with a plural verb*] the others: *All the rest are going.* —*v.* [~ + *adj*] **3.** to continue to be: *Rest assured that all is well.*

res•tau•rant /'rɛstərənt, -tə,rɑnt, -trɑnt/ *n.* [*count*] a place of business where meals are served.

rest•ful /'rɛstfəl/ *adj.* **1.** giving rest: *a restful vacation.* **2.** at rest; peaceful.

'rest ,home, *n.* [*count*] a nursing home.

res•ti•tu•tion /,rɛstɪ'tuwʃən, -'tyuw-/ *n.* [*noncount*] **1.** payment for loss, damage, or injury. **2.** the restoration of property taken away.

rest•less /'rɛstlɪs/ *adj.* **1.** unable to rest or characterized by an inability to remain at rest: *a restless mood.* —**'rest•less•ly,** *adv.* —**'rest•less•ness,** *n.* [*noncount*]

re•stor•a•tive /rɪ'stɔrətɪv/ *adj.* **1.** capable of renewing health or strength. —*n.* [*count*] **2.** a restorative food or medicine.

re•store /rɪ'stɔr/ *v.* [~ + *obj*], **-stored, -stor•ing. 1.** to bring back into existence, use, etc.; reestablish: *to restore order.* **2.** to bring back to a former condition: *to restore a painting.* **3.** to bring back to a state of health or strength: *The treatments restored him to health.* —**res•to•ra•tion** /,rɛstə'reyʃən/ *n.* [*noncount*] [*count*]

re•strain /rɪ'streyn/ *v.* [~ + *obj*] to hold back from action; check; repress: *He was so mad he could hardly restrain himself.*

re•straint /rɪ'streynt/ *n.* **1.** [*noncount*] a restraining influence. **2.** [*count*] a means of restraining: *the restraints of society.*

re•strict /rɪ'strɪkt/ *v.* [~ + *obj*] to keep within limits, as of space, action, or amount: *His diet was restricted because of a heart condition.* —**re'stric•tion,** *n.* [*count*] [*noncount*]

re•stric•tive /rɪ'strɪktɪv/ *adj.* tending or serving to restrict. —**re'stric•tive•ness,** *n.* [*noncount*]

'rest ,room, *n.* [*count*] a bathroom in a public building.

re•sult /rɪ'zʌlt/ *v.* [*no obj*] **1.** to arise or proceed from previous actions, circumstances, or events: *poverty resulting from unemployment.* **2.** to end in a particular way: *efforts that resulted in failure.* —*n.* [*count*] **3.** something that happens because of something else; an effect or outcome: *What was the result of your discussion?*

R

re•sume /rɪˈzuwm/ v., -sumed, -sum•ing. **1.** to begin again after stopping: [~ + obj]: The soldiers resumed marching. [no obj]: The voices ceased when she arrived, then quickly resumed. **2.** [~ + obj] to take or occupy again: Ladies and gentlemen, please resume your seats. —re'sump•tion, n. [noncount] [count]

ré•su•mé or **re•su•me** /ˈrɛzʊˌmey, ˌrɛzʊˈmey/ n. [count] **1.** a summary. **2.** a brief written account of educational and professional qualifications and experience.

res•ur•rect /ˌrɛzəˈrɛkt/ v. [~ + obj] **1.** to raise from the dead; bring to life again. **2.** to bring back into use, attention, etc.: to resurrect an old theory.

res•ur•rec•tion /ˌrɛzəˈrɛkʃən/ n. **1.** [noncount] [count] the act of resurrecting. **2.** [Resurrection] **a.** the rising of Christ after His death and burial. **b.** the rising of the dead at the end of the world.

re•sus•ci•tate /rɪˈsʌsɪˌteyt/ v. [~ + obj], -tat•ed, -tat•ing. to revive from unconsciousness: to resuscitate the drowning victim. —re•sus•ci•ta•tion /rɪˌsʌsɪˈteyʃən/, n. [noncount]

re•tail /ˈriyteyl/ n. [noncount] **1.** the sale of goods to individual consumers. —adv. **2.** by retail: These jackets sell at $50 retail. —v. **3.** to (cause to) be sold directly to the consumer: [~ + obj]: to retail hardware goods. [no obj]: These shoes retail at $50 a pair. —'re•tail•er, n. [count]

re•tain /rɪˈteyn/ v. [~ + obj] **1.** to continue to hold or have: clothing that retains its color. **2.** to hire, esp. by payment of a fee: to retain a lawyer.

re•tal•i•ate /rɪˈtæliyˌeyt/ v. [no obj], -at•ed, -at•ing. to strike back for an injury or wrong. —re•tal•i•a•tion, n. [noncount] —re•tal•i•a•to•ry /rɪˈtæliyəˌtɔriy/, adj.

re•tard /rɪˈtɑrd/ v. [~ + obj] to delay the development or progress of: Cold retards the growth of bacteria. —re•tar•da•tion /ˌriytɑrˈdeyʃən/, n. [noncount]

re•tard•ed /rɪˈtɑrdɪd/ adj. **1.** less developed mentally than others; lacking normal intelligence: a retarded child. —n. **2. the retarded,** [plural; used with a plural verb] mentally retarded people thought of as a group: education of the retarded.

retch /rɛtʃ/ v. [no obj] to make efforts to vomit.

re•ten•tion /rɪˈtɛnʃən/ n. [noncount] the act of retaining, or the state of being retained.

re•ten•tive /rɪˈtɛntɪv/ adj. **1.** tending to retain. **2.** able to remember well: a retentive memory.

ret•i•na /ˈrɛtnə, ˈrɛtnə/ n. [count], pl. ret•i•nas. the innermost coat of the back part of the eyeball that receives the image produced by the lens.

re•tire /rɪˈtayᵊr/ v., -tired, -tir•ing. **1.** [no obj] to withdraw, esp. to a place of privacy: She retired to her study. **2.** [no obj] to go to bed. **3.** to (cause to) give up or withdraw from a job or career, usually because of age: [no obj]: Dad retired from the fire department. [~ + obj]: The navy decided to retire the old battleship. —re'tire•ment, n. [noncount]

re•tir•ing /rɪˈtayᵊrɪŋ/ adj. withdrawing from contact with others; shy.

re•tort /rɪˈtɔrt/ v. **1.** to reply in a sharp or clever way: [~ + obj]: He retorted that he would have nothing to do with her. [no obj]: quick to retort. —n. [count] **2.** a sharp or clever reply.

re•tract[1] /rɪˈtrækt/ v. to draw back or in: [~ + obj]: A snake can retract its fangs. [no obj]: The wheels on the airplane don't retract.

re•tract[2] /rɪˈtrækt/ v. [~ + obj] to formally

withdraw (a statement, etc.) as wrong or unfair. —re'trac•tion, n. [count]

re•tread /v.riyˈtrɛd; n. ˈriyˌtrɛd/ v. [~ + obj] **1.** to put a new tread on (a worn tire). —n. [count] **2.** a retreaded tire.

re•treat /rɪˈtriyt/ n. **1.** [count] [noncount] the withdrawal of a military force before an enemy. **2.** [count] a place for quiet thinking or privacy. —v. [no obj] **3.** to draw back from an earlier position: The Senator began to retreat from his strong stand on civil rights.

ret•ri•bu•tion /ˌrɛtrəˈbyuwʃən/ n. [noncount] punishment for some evil.

re•trieve /rɪˈtriyv/ v. [~ + obj], -trieved, -triev•ing. **1.** to find and bring back: The dog retrieved the bone. **2.** to locate and read (data) from computer storage, as for display on a monitor. —re'triev•al, n. [noncount]

re•triev•er /rɪˈtriyvər/ n. [count] **1.** a person or thing that retrieves. **2.** a breed of dog used esp. to retrieve game.

ret•ro /ˈrɛtrow/ adj. of or being the style of an earlier time: retro clothes.

retro-, a prefix meaning back or backward (retroactive).

ret•ro•ac•tive /ˌrɛtrowˈæktɪv/ adj. **1.** having effect back in the past, as a new law. **2.** effective as of a past date: a February pay raise retroactive to January 1st. —ˌret•ro'ac•tive•ly, adv.

ret•ro•spect /ˈrɛtrəˌspɛkt/ n. ——**Idiom.** in retrospect, on evaluating the past; upon reflection: He knew in retrospect that he should have married her. —ˌret•ro'spec•tion, n. [noncount]

ret•ro•spec•tive /ˌrɛtrəˈspɛktɪv/ adj. **1.** looking or directed backward. —n. [count] **2.** an exhibit showing all of an artist's work.

re•turn /rɪˈtɜrn/ v. **1.** [no obj] to go or come back, as to a former place or state: to return from abroad. **2.** [~ + obj] to put, bring, take, or give back: He returned the book to the shelf. **3.** [~ + obj] to report officially: The jury returned a verdict of guilty. **4.** [~ + obj] to yield (a profit, etc.). —n. **5.** [count] a recurrence; a happening again: the return of winter. **6.** [noncount] repayment or exchange: We gave her a gift in return for her kindness. **7.** Often, **returns.** [plural] a profit or gain, as from work. **8.** [count] an official form showing income, deductions, and taxes due. **9.** Usually, **returns.** [plural] a report on a count of votes: election returns. —adj. [before a noun] **10.** of or relating to a return or returning: a return address. —re'turn•a•ble, adj., n. [count]

re•un•ion /riyˈyuwnyən/ n. **1.** [noncount] the state of being together again. **2.** [count] a gathering of relatives, friends, etc., at regular times.

rev /rɛv/ v. [~ + obj], revved, rev•ving. Informal. to make (an engine) go faster: I revved (up) the motor and began the race.

re•veal /rɪˈviyl/ v. [~ + obj] to make known or allow to be seen; disclose: to reveal the secret.

re•veal•ing /rɪˈviylɪŋ/ adj. allowing something to be seen or known: She wore a short dress that was too revealing.

rev•el /ˈrɛvəl/ v., -eled, -el•ing or (esp. Brit.) -elled, -el•ling, n. —v. [no obj] **1.** to take great pleasure in; enjoy greatly: to revel in luxury. —n. **2.** Often, **revels.** [plural] an occasion of parties, feasting, etc. —ˈrev•el•er; esp. Brit., rev'el•ler, n. [count]

rev•e•la•tion /ˌrɛvəˈleyʃən/ n. **1.** [noncount] the act of revealing. **2.** [count] something revealed, esp. a surprising fact: It came as a revelation that he was adopted as a child.

re•venge /rɪ'vɛndʒ/ v., **-venged, -veng•ing,** n.
—v. [~ + obj] **1.** to punish or hurt someone in
return for harm suffered: *to revenge a brother's
murder.* —n. [noncount] **2.** the act of revenging:
his big chance for revenge. —**re'venge•ful,** adj.

rev•e•nue /'rɛvən,yuw, -ə,nuw/ n. [noncount]
[plural] **1.** the income of a government from taxation, used for public expenses. **2.** money regularly coming in; a source of income: *business revenue; revenues from airline tickets.*

re•ver•ber•ate /rɪ'vɜrbə,reyt/ v. [no obj],
-at•ed, -at•ing. to echo again and again: *Her
singing reverberated through the house.* —re,ver•
ber'a•tion, n. [noncount] [count]

re•vere /rɪ'vɪər/ v. [~ + obj], **-vered, -ver•ing.**
to look upon (someone or something) with reverence: *to revere the beauty of nature.*

rev•er•ence /'rɛvərəns/ n. [noncount] a feeling
of deep respect and awe. —**'rev•er•ent,** adj.

rev•er•end /'rɛvərənd, 'rɛvrənd/ n. **1.** [Rever-
end; sometimes: the + ~] (used, usually before
a proper name, as a title of respect for a member
of the clergy: *the Reverend Timothy Schade; Reverend Mother.* **2.** [count; usually singular] a member of the clergy, esp. a Protestant minister: *Perhaps the good reverend would stand over here.*

re•ver•sal /rɪ'vɜrsəl/ n. **1.** [noncount] an act or
instance of reversing; a state of being reversed.
2. [count] a change of one's fortune or luck for
the worse.

re•verse /rɪ'vɜrs/ adj., n., v., **-versed, -vers•ing.**
—adj. [before a noun] **1.** opposite or contrary in
position, direction, order, etc.: *to arrange the
names in reverse order.* **2.** with the back toward
the observer: *the reverse side of a fabric.* —n. **3.**
[noncount; the + ~] the opposite or contrary of
something: *His answer was the reverse of what we
expected.* **4.** [noncount; the + ~] the back or
rear of anything: *Can't you button this on the reverse?* **5.** [count] a change of fortune for the
worse. **6.** [noncount] the condition of being reversed: *to put an engine into reverse.* —v. **7.** [~
+ obj] [no obj] to turn in an opposite position,
direction, or order. **8.** [~ + obj] to change to the
opposite: *to reverse the policy of racial discrimination.* —*Idiom.* **9. reverse (the) charges,** to
have the charges for a telephone call billed to the
person receiving the call. —**'revers•i•ble,** adj.

re•vert /rɪ'vɜrt/ v. [no obj] **1.** to return to a former habit, belief, etc.: *He's reverted to smoking
again.* **2.** to return to the former owner or that
person's heirs: *The property reverts to his two
sons.* —**re•ver•sion** /rɪ'vɜrʒən/, n. [noncount]

re•view /rɪ'vyuw/ n. **1.** [count] an article in a
newspaper or magazine that gives an opinion
about a book, play, etc. **2.** the process of going
over a subject again to keep it in the memory:
[count]: *He made a quick review of his notes just
before his presentation.* [noncount]: *He left no
time for review before the test.* **3.** a formal inspection of a military force: [count]: *a review of the
troops.* [noncount]: *The troops were on review.* **4.**
a second examination of something: [noncount]:
The case is under review by the Supreme Court.
[count]: *The case was sent to a higher court for
review.* —v. **5.** [~ + obj] [no obj] to go over
(lessons, etc.) in review. **6.** [~ + obj] to examine again, esp. with a thought of changing: *to review the way government aides are appointed.* **7.**
[~ + obj] to inspect, esp. formally. **8.** [~ +
obj] to write a critical review of. —**re'view•er,**
n. [count]: *The reviewers criticized the play.*

re•vile /rɪ'vayl/ v. [~ + obj], **-viled, -vil•ing.** to

address (someone) or speak of (someone) with
contempt or insulting language.

re•vise /rɪ'vayz/ v. [~ + obj], **-vised, -vis•ing.**
1. to change or alter, esp. after thinking about
(something): *She revised her opinion of him when
she saw his work.* **2.** to change or alter in order
to make corrections or improve: *to revise a manuscript.* —**re•vi•sion** /rɪ'vɪʒən/ n. [noncount]
[count]

re•vi•tal•ize /riy'vaytl,ayz/ v. [~ + obj], **-ized,
-iz•ing.** to give new life, vitality, or strength to: *to
revitalize the steel industry.*

re•vive /rɪ'vayv/ v., **-vived, -viv•ing. 1.** to
(cause to) be brought back or used again; (cause
to) be renewed: [~ + obj]: *Don't revive those old
prejudices.* [no obj]: *Her interest in playing the
trumpet revived.* **2.** to restore to life or consciousness: [~ + obj]: *to revive the drowning victim.*
[no obj]: *Somehow she revived after a few
minutes.* **3.** [~ + obj] to put on or produce
again: *to revive a play.* —**re'viv•al,** n. [noncount]
[count]

re•voke /rɪ'vowk/ v. [~ + obj], **-voked, -vok•
ing.** to take back or withdraw; cancel: *His driver's license was revoked.*

re•volt /rɪ'vowlt/ v. **1.** [no obj] to engage in a
revolution; rebel. **2.** to (cause to) have a feeling
of disgust or horror: [~ + obj]: *The violence in
that movie revolted her.* [no obj]: *One's mind re-
volts at the thought of killing.* —n. **3.** an act of re-
volting; rebellion: [count]: *an open revolt against
the dean's power.* [noncount]: *peasants in revolt
against the government.*

re•volt•ing /rɪ'vowltɪŋ/ adj. disgusting.

rev•o•lu•tion /,rɛvə'luwʃən/ n. **1.** [noncount]
[count] a complete overthrow and replacement of
an established government by force. **2.** [count] a
sudden, complete change in something: *a revolution caused by computerization.* **3.** [count] **a.** a
circular movement around a fixed point: *The engine was racing at over 50,000 revolutions per
minute.* **b.** a circular movement around a central
point: *one complete revolution around the racetrack.* **4.** [count] the orbiting of one heavenly
body around another: *The earth's revolution
around the sun takes one year.*

rev•o•lu•tion•ar•y /,rɛvə'luwʃə,nɛriy/ adj., n.,
pl. **-ar•ies.** —adj. **1.** [before a noun] of or relating
to a revolution: *a revolutionary leader.* **2.** new or
different; causing great change: *a revolutionary
discovery.* —n. [count] **3.** a person participating
in or calling for a revolution.

rev•o•lu•tion•ize /,rɛvə'luwʃə,nayz/ v. [~ +
obj], **-ized, -iz•ing.** to bring about a revolution
in.

re•volve /rɪ'vɒlv/ v. [no obj], **-volved, -volv•
ing. 1.** to move in a circular course: *The earth revolves around the sun.* **2.** to focus or center on:
*The discussion revolved around a plan to increase
profits.*

re•volv•er /rɪ'vɒlvər/ n. [count] a pistol having
a revolving chamber for holding bullets.

re•vue /rɪ'vyuw/ n. [count] a form of theatrical
entertainment in which recent events, popular
fads, etc., are made fun of.

re•vul•sion /rɪ'vʌlʃən/ n. [noncount] a strong
feeling of disgust, distaste, or dislike.

re•ward /rɪ'wɔrd/ n. **1.** something given or received for services done or for merit: [count]:
*Seeing his children succeed was the most impor-
tant reward in his life.* [noncount]: *There is not
much financial reward in teaching.* —v. [~ +

R

obj] **2.** to give a reward to (a person or animal) for service, merit, etc.

re•ward•ing /rɪ'wɔrdɪŋ/ *adj.* giving or providing a reward or satisfaction: *a rewarding occupation.*

RFD or **R.F.D.,** an abbreviation of: rural free delivery.

rhap•so•dy /'ræpsədiy/ *n.* [*count*], *pl.* **-dies. 1.** a piece of music that is highly emotional. **2.** an expression of great passion.

rhet•o•ric /'rɛtərɪk/ *n.* [*noncount*] **1. a.** the art of effectively using language in speech or writing. **b.** language skillfully used. **2.** exaggerated language that is empty and meaningless. —**rhe•tor•i•cal** /rɪ'tɔrɪkəl, -'tɒr-/, *adj.* [*before a noun*]

rhe'torical 'question, *n.* [*count*] a question asked only for effect and not to obtain a reply.

rheu•ma•tism /'ruwmə,tɪzəm/ *n.* [*noncount*] any of several medical disorders affecting the joints or muscles.

rhi•no /'raynow/ *n.* [*count*], *pl.* **-nos,** (*esp. when thought of as a group*) **-no.** a rhinoceros.

rhi•noc•er•os /ray'nɒsərəs/ *n.* [*count*], *pl.* **-os•es,** (*esp. when thought of as a group*) **-os.** a large, thick-skinned mammal of Africa and Asia, with one or two horns on the snout.

rho•do•den•dron /,rowdə'dɛndrən/ *n.* [*count*] a shrub having rounded clusters of bright flowers and oval leaves.

rhu•barb /'ruwbɑrb/ *n.* [*noncount*] the fleshy leafstalks of a plant, used in making pies, preserves, etc.

rhyme /raym/ *n., v.,* **rhymed, rhym•ing.** —*n.* **1.** [*noncount*] sameness in the final sound of words or lines of verse. **2.** [*count*] a word that ends with the same sound as another word. **3.** [*count*] a rhyming poem. —*v.* **4.** [*no obj*] to form a rhyme; end with the same sound: *The word "find" rhymes with "kind." The last two lines of your poem don't rhyme.* —'**rhym•er,** *n.* [*count*]

rhythm /'rɪðəm/ *n.* a regular pattern of repeated beats, accents, or movements: [*count*]: *the even rhythms of her heartbeat.* [*noncount*]: *the use of rhythm in music and dance.*

'**rhythm and 'blues,** *n.* [*noncount*] a folk-based form of black popular music.

rhyth•mic /'rɪðmɪk/ *adj.* Also, '**rhyth•mical.** of or relating to rhythm: *the rhythmic sound of raindrops on the tin roof.* —'**rhyth•mi•cal•ly,** *adv.*

RI, an abbreviation of: Rhode Island.

rib /rɪb/ *n.* [*count*] **1.** one of a series of curved bones that enclose the chest. **2.** a cut of meat, as beef, containing a rib. **3.** something resembling a rib in form or use: *the ribs of an umbrella.*

rib•bon /'rɪbən/ *n.* [*count*] **1.** a band of fine material, used for decoration, tying the hair, etc. **2.** a band of inked material used in a typewriter, printer, etc.

rice /rays/ *n.* [*noncount*] the starchy seeds of a tall grass of marshy areas, used for food.

rich /rɪtʃ/ *adj.,* **-er, -est. 1.** having wealth or great possessions. **2.** having many natural resources: *a rich region.* **3.** having a great amount of something: *fruits rich in vitamin C.* **4.** containing a large amount of cream, butter, sugar, or the like: *a rich gravy.* **5.** (of color, etc.) deep or strong. —'**rich•ly,** *adv.* —'**rich•ness,** *n.* [*noncount*]

rich•es /'rɪtʃɪz/ *n.* [*plural*] a great many valuable possessions; wealth.

rick•et•y /'rɪkɪtiy/ *adj.,* **-i•er, -i•est.** likely to fall or collapse; shaky.

ric•o•chet /,rɪkə'ʃey, 'rɪkə,ʃey/ *n., v.,* **-cheted** /-'ʃeyd, -,ʃeyd/, **-chet•ing** /-'ʃeyɪŋ, -,ʃeyɪŋ/ or (*esp. Brit.*) **-chet•ted** /-,ʃetɪd/, **-chet•ting** /-,ʃetɪŋ/. —*n.* [*count*] **1.** the bouncing back of an object after it hits a surface at an angle. —*v.* [*no obj*] **2.** to move in this way: *bullets ricocheting off the walls.*

ri•cot•ta /rɪ'kɒtə, -'kɔtə/ *n.* [*noncount*] a soft Italian cheese that resembles cottage cheese.

rid /rɪd/ *v.* [~ + *obj* + *of* + *obj*], **rid** or **rid•ded, rid•ding. 1.** to free or relieve of something unwanted: *to rid the house of mice.* —*Idiom.* **2. be** or **get rid of,** to be or become free of: *Please get rid of this trash.*

rid•dance /'rɪdns/ *n.* —*Idiom.* **good rid•dance,** (used to express relief that someone or something has gone: *They're gone, and good riddance!*

rid•den /'rɪdn/ *v.* a pp. of RIDE.

rid•dle[1] /'rɪdl/ *n.* [*count*] **1.** a puzzling question that has a clever or amusing answer: *A childhood riddle is "What kind of dog has no tail?" —The answer: a hot dog.* **2.** a puzzling problem, matter, or person.

rid•dle[2] /'rɪdl/ *v.* [~ + *obj*], **-dled, -dling.** to pierce with many holes: *Bullets riddled the target.*

ride /rayd/ *v.,* **rode** /rowd/, **rid•den** /'rɪdn/, **rid•ing,** *n.* —*v.* **1.** to sit on and manage an animal in motion: [*no obj*]: *He rode on a white horse.* [~ + *obj*]: *He rode the elephant all around the circus ring.* **2.** to (cause to) be carried along in or on a vehicle: [~ + *obj*]: *She rides a bicycle to school.* [*no obj*]: *He rode on the subway to work.* **3.** [*no obj*] to have a specified character for riding purposes: *The car rides smoothly.* **4.** [*no obj*] to depend: *Her hopes were riding on a promotion.* **5.** [*no obj*] to continue without interference: *Let the matter ride.* **6.** [~ + *obj*] to sit or move along on: *The ship rode the waves.* **7.** to ride over, along, or through: [*no obj*]: *They rode along the highways.* [~ + *obj*]: *They rode the back roads.* **8. ride up,** to move up from the proper place or position: *This skirt always rides up.* —*n.* [*count*] **9.** a journey on a horse or other animal, or on or in a vehicle. **10.** a vehicle, such as a roller coaster, on which people ride for amusement. —'**rid•er,** *n.* [*count*]

ridge /rɪdʒ/ *n.* [*count*] **1.** a long, narrow elevation of land. **2.** the long and narrow upper edge of something, as a wave. **3.** any raised, narrow strip, as on cloth.

ridged /rɪdʒd/ *adj.* having, formed into, or showing ridges: *a ridged fabric.*

rid•i•cule /'rɪdɪ,kyuwl/ *n., v.,* **-culed, -cul•ing.** —*n.* [*noncount*] **1.** insulting speech or action intended to cause others to laugh unkindly: *His foolish comments were met with ridicule.* —*v.* [~ + *obj*] **2.** to make fun of: *He ridiculed his rivals whenever he could.*

ri•dic•u•lous /rɪ'dɪkyələs/ *adj.* of or deserving ridicule; foolish: *What a ridiculous idea!* —**ri'dic•u•lous•ly,** *adv.* —**ri'dic•u•lous•ness,** *n.* [*noncount*]

rife /rayf/ *adj.* common or plentiful: *Crime is rife in the city.* —'**rife•ness,** *n.* [*noncount*]

ri•fle[1] /'rayfəl/ *n.* [*count*] a shoulder firearm with a long barrel.

ri•fle[2] /'rayfəl/ *v.* [~ + *obj*], **-fled, -fling.** to search through and steal or rob: *The burglars rifled (through) our dresser drawers.*

rift /rɪft/ *n.* [*count*] **1.** a narrow crack or hole. **2.** a break in friendly relations.

rig /rɪg/ *v.,* **rigged, rig•ging,** *n.* —*v.* [~ + *obj*]

1. to fit (a ship, etc.) with ropes, chains, etc. **2.** to furnish with equipment: *The truck was rigged with a roof rack.* **3.** to assemble, install, or prepare: *The campers rigged (up) a shelter from tree branches.* **4.** to arrange in a dishonest way; fix: *to rig prices.* —*n.* [*count*] **5.** the arrangement of the masts, sails, etc., on a ship. **6.** a device or apparatus designed for some purpose: *an oil rig.*

right /rayt/ *adj.*, **-er, -est,** *n.*, *adv.*, *v.* —*adj.* **1.** morally good, proper, or just: *Is it ever right to kill someone?* **2.** correct in one's judgment or action: *You were right; the movie was terrible.* **3.** correct in fact: *Is that the right answer?* **4.** suitable; desirable: *the right clothes for the occasion.* **5.** [*before a noun*] of or relating to the side of a person or thing that is toward the east when that person or thing is facing north. **6.** sound; sane: *in one's right mind.* —*n.* **7.** [*count*] a moral or legal claim to something: *the right to free speech.* **8.** [*noncount*] that which is morally or legally proper: *the difference between right and wrong.* **9.** [*noncount*] the right side or direction. **10. the Right,** [*noncount*] individuals or groups holding conservative political and social views. —*adv.* **11.** quite; completely: *My hat was knocked right off.* **12.** immediately; promptly: *I turned on the TV right after dinner.* **13.** exactly; precisely: *Put it down right here on the table.* **14.** correctly or accurately: *You guessed right.* **15.** to one's benefit or advantage: *Everything turned out right.* **16.** on or to the right: *to turn right.* —*v.* [~ + *obj*] **17.** to make upright: *to right a fallen lamp.* **18.** to make right: *The king would right the wrongs done by the prince.* —**Idiom. 19. by rights,** in fairness; justly: *We should by rights have gotten our money by this time.* **20. in the right,** having the support of reason or law. **21. right away** or **off,** without hesitation; immediately: *Right off, you could tell he disliked her.* —**'right•ness,** *n.* [*noncount*]

'right 'angle, *n.* [*count*] the angle formed by two perpendicular lines; an angle of 90°.

right•eous /'raytʃəs/ *adj.* **1.** having just cause for something; justifiable: *righteous anger at being accused falsely.* **2.** of or relating to a proper or moral way of life; virtuous. —**'right•eous•ly,** *adv.* —**'right•eous•ness,** *n.* [*noncount*]

'right-'hand, *adj.* **1.** on or to the right. **2.** of, for, or with the right hand. **3.** trusted; being of great assistance: *the governor's right-hand man.*

'right-'handed, *adj.* **1.** preferring to use the right hand: *a right-handed pitcher.* **2.** adapted to or performed by the right hand: *a car with a right-handed steering wheel.* —*adv.* **3.** with the right hand.

'right of 'way, *n.*, *pl.* **rights of way, right of ways. 1.** [*noncount*] the right to proceed ahead of another vehicle: *At the stop sign she had the right of way.* **2.** [*count*] a path or area of land that may lawfully be used or crossed.

right•size /'rayt,sayz/ *v.* [~ + *obj*], **-sized, -siz•ing.** to adjust to an appropriate size: *We will have to fire about 50 workers in order to rightsize our staff.*

'right 'triangle, *n.* [*count*] a triangle having a right angle.

'right 'wing, *n.* [*count*] **1.** the conservative members in a political party. —*adj.* **'right-'wing. 2.** of or relating to the right wing.

rig•id /'rɪdʒɪd/ *adj.* **1.** stiff; not easily moved: *a rigid strip of metal.* **2.** strict or severe: *The rules are too rigid.* —**ri'gid•i•ty,** *n.* [*noncount*] —**'rig•id•ly,** *adv.*

rig•or /'rɪgər/ *n.* **1.** [*noncount*] the quality of being strict or severe. **2.** [*count*] hardship of some kind: *the rigors of winter.* Also, *esp.* *Brit.,* **'rig•our.** —**'rig•or•ous,** *adj.*

rim /rɪm/ *n.* [*count*] **1.** the outer edge or border of something: *a chip on the rim of the glass.* **2.** the outer circle of a wheel, attached to the hub by spokes.

rind /raynd/ *n.* a thick outer coat: [*noncount*]: *orange rind.* [*count*]: *a few bacon rinds.*

ring¹ /rɪŋ/ *n.*, *v.*, **ringed, ring•ing.** —*n.* [*count*] **1.** a circular band, as of silver or gold, worn on the finger as an ornament. **2.** anything having the form of such a band: *a smoke ring.* **3.** a circular line or mark: *dark rings around the eyes.* **4.** a number of persons or things arranged in a circle: *a ring of hills.* **5.** a closed area for a contest or exhibition: *a boxing ring; a circus ring.* **6.** a group working together for illegal purposes: *a ring of drug dealers.* —*v.* [~ + *obj*] **7.** to surround with a ring; encircle: *The police ringed the theater to prevent riots.*

ring² /rɪŋ/ *v.*, **rang** /ræŋ/, **rung** /rʌŋ/, **ring•ing,** *n.* —*v.* **1.** [*no obj*] to give forth a clear, echoing sound: *The phone is ringing.* **2.** to cause a bell, telephone, etc., to give off a sound: [*no obj*]: *Just ring for service.* [~ + *obj*]: *Ring the doorbell.* **3.** to telephone: [~ + *obj*]: *Ring us (up) when you get home.* [*no obj*]: *Ring when you get a chance.* **4.** [~ + *obj*] to announce by the sound of a bell: *The bell rang the hour.* **5. ring off,** *Chiefly Brit.* to end a telephone conversation: *to ring off and get back to work.* **6. ring up,** to register (the amount of a sale) on a cash register: *He rang up the sale. I just rang it up.* —*n.* **7.** [*count*] a ringing sound: *the ring of sleigh bells.* **8.** [*count*] *Informal.* a telephone call: *Give me a ring.* **9.** [*count*; *usually singular*] a characteristic sound or quality: *This story has a ring of truth to it.*

ring•worm /'rɪŋ,wɜrm/ *n.* [*noncount*] a skin disease caused by fungi.

rink /rɪŋk/ *n.* [*count*] **1.** a smooth area of ice for ice-skating. **2.** a smooth floor for roller-skating.

rinse /rɪns/ *v.*, **rinsed, rins•ing,** *n.* —*v.* [~ + *obj*] **1.** to wash lightly in clean water without soap: *I rinsed the dishes.* —*n.* **2.** [*count*] an act or instance of rinsing. **3.** [*noncount*] [*count*] a liquid used on the hair after washing, esp. to color or condition it.

ri•ot /'rayət/ *n.* [*count*] **1.** a noisy, violent public disorder: *The arrest caused a riot in the city.* **2.** a wild mix or confusion: *a riot of colors.* —*v.* [*no obj*] **3.** to take part in a riot: *thousands of people rioting in the streets.* —**Idiom. 4. run riot,** to behave wildly: *The townspeople ran riot after the verdict.* —**'ri•ot•er,** *n.* [*count*] —**'ri•ot•ous,** *adj.*

rip /rɪp/ *v.*, **ripped, rip•ping,** *n.* —*v.* **1.** to tear apart roughly or forcefully: [~ + *obj*]: *to rip open a seam; to rip up the newspaper; to rip a cloth.* [*no obj*]: *Her slacks ripped when she fell.* **2. rip into,** *Informal.* to attack strongly: *The president really ripped into the proposal.* **3. rip off,** *Slang.* **a.** to steal: *Someone ripped off my new umbrella.* **b.** to cheat or take from dishonestly: *trying to rip us off; trying to rip off the tourists.* —*n.* [*count*] **4.** a tear made by ripping.

ripe /rayp/ *adj.*, **rip•er, rip•est. 1.** completely matured, such as grain or fruit that is ready to be picked and eaten: *ripe, juicy oranges.* **2.** old enough to be used, as cheese. **3.** characterized by full development; mature. —**'ripe•ly,** *adv.* —**'ripe•ness,** *n.* [*noncount*]

R

rip•en /'raypən/ v. [~ + obj] [no obj] to (cause to) become ripe.

rip-off /'rɪp,ɔf, -,ɒf-/ n. [count] Slang. an act of stealing or cheating.

rip•ple /'rɪpəl/ v., **-pled, -pling,** n. —v. **1.** to form small waves (on): [no obj]: The water rippled in the sunlight. [~ + obj]: The breeze rippled the water. **2.** to (cause to) have a wavelike shape or movement: [no obj]: His muscles rippled as he lifted the load. [~ + obj]: rippling his muscles. **3.** [no obj] (of sound) to move along with a rising and falling sound: Laughter rippled through the crowd. —n. [count] **4.** a small wave. **5.** a movement, form, or sound similar to this: a ripple of laughter.

rise /rayz/ v., **rose** /rowz/, **ris•en** /'rɪzən/, **ris•ing,** n. —v. [no obj] **1.** to get up from a lying, sitting, or kneeling position: She rose and walked over to greet me. **2.** to rebel or resist someone: The people rose up against the dictator. **3.** to move from a lower to a higher position: The smoke rose into the sky. **4.** to appear above the horizon, as the sun. **5.** to extend directly upward: The building rises about 40 stories. **6.** to increase, as in height, amount, value, or force: The river is rising three feet an hour. **7.** to swell or puff up, as dough from the action of yeast. **8.** to become louder or higher in pitch, as the voice. **9.** to return from the dead. **10. rise above,** to ignore and overcome: She rose above the insults and teasing. **11. rise to the occasion,** to prove that one can handle a demand, emergency, etc.: He rose to the occasion by being a strong leader. —n. **12.** [count] an act or instance of rising. **13.** [noncount] increase in rank, fortune, etc.: the rise and fall of Rome. **14.** [count] an increase, as in height, amount, or value; the amount of such increase: a rise in unemployment. **15.** [count] the measured height of a roof or a stair step. **16.** [noncount] the beginning: the rise of dictatorship. **17.** [count] a piece of rising or high ground.

risk /rɪsk/ n. **1.** a dangerous chance: [noncount]: Investing money is worth the risk. [count]: He takes too many risks. **2.** Insurance. **a.** [noncount] the probability of a loss or injury. **b.** [count] a person or thing that is insured against loss: She was a poor risk because she had so many accidents. —v. [~ + obj] **3.** to put (someone or something) in danger: to risk one's life. **4.** to take the chance of; to hazard: You risk a fall walking on icy stairs. —Idiom. **5. at risk,** in danger: Young children are at risk of injury. **6. at the risk of,** in spite of the danger of: At the risk of looking foolish, may I ask what you mean? —'risk•y, adj., **-i•er, -i•est.**

rite /rayt/ n. [count] **1.** a ceremony in religious or other solemn use: funeral rites. **2.** a customary practice or tradition: the rites of spring.

rit•u•al /'rɪtʃuwəl/ n. **1. a.** [count] an established procedure for a religious or other rite: rituals for the dead. **b.** [noncount] a system of such rites: the comfort of ritual during a time of loss. **2.** [count] a practice regularly performed in a definite manner: Another ritual was the annual tea party. —'rit•u•al•ly, adv.

ri•val /'rayvəl/ n., v., **-valed, -val•ing** or (esp. Brit.) **-valled, -val•ling.** —n. [count] **1.** one who seeks to achieve the same goal as another; a competitor: They were rivals for the job. **2.** a person or thing that is almost equal to another: This car has no rival in its class. —v. [~ + obj] **3.** to prove to be a worthy rival of: One contestant rivaled the others in skill. **4.** to equal (something); to be as good as: The speed of this computer ri-

vals that of more expensive brands. —'ri•val•ry, n. [count] [noncount]

riv•er /'rɪvər/ n. [count] **1.** a natural stream of water flowing in a definite course. **2.** a similar stream: rivers of tears.

riv•et /'rɪvɪt/ n., v., **-et•ed, -et•ing** or (esp. Brit.) **-et•ted, -et•ting.** —n. [count] **1.** a metal pin for passing through holes in plates to hold them together. —v. [~ + obj] **2.** to fasten with or as if with a rivet: riveting the wings to the body of the plane. **3.** to hold (someone's attention) firmly: Her attention was riveted on the magician.

RN or **R.N.,** an abbreviation of: registered nurse.

roach /rowtʃ/ n. [count] a cockroach.

road /rowd/ n. [count] **1.** a stretch of land with a leveled surface along which vehicles or people can travel. **2.** a way or course: the road to peace. —Idiom. **3. on the road, a.** traveling or touring: The band has been on the road for two months. **b.** changing, as from one condition to another: on the road to recovery.

road•block /'rowd,blɒk/ n. [count] a barrier placed across a road to halt or slow traffic.

road•run•ner /'rowd,rʌnər/ n. [count] a fast-running cuckoo, found mainly in dry regions of the western U.S.

road•side /'rowd,sayd/ n. [count] **1.** the side or border of the road. —adj. [before a noun] **2.** on or near the roadside: a roadside café.

roam /rowm/ v. to travel without purpose; wander: [no obj]: He roamed around the world for a few years. [~ + obj]: She roamed the countryside.

roar /rɔr/ v. **1.** to make or express in a loud, deep sound: [no obj]: The crowd roared when she scored the winning basket. The lion roared at the children. [~ + obj]: The crowd roared its approval. **2.** [no obj] to laugh loudly or noisily. **3.** [no obj] to make a loud noise, as thunder or cannon. —n. [count] **4.** a roaring sound.

roar•ing /'rɔrɪŋ/ adj. [before a noun] **1.** very active: a roaring business. **2.** complete; utter: a roaring success. —adv. **3.** very; completely: roaring drunk.

roast /rowst/ v. **1.** to cook (food) by direct, dry heat, as in an oven: [~ + obj]: We roasted chicken at the party. [no obj]: The turkey is still roasting. **2.** to dry and cause to turn brown by heating: [~ + obj]: to roast coffee beans. [no obj]: You could smell the peanuts roasting. —n. [count] **3.** roasted meat. —adj. [before a noun] **4.** roasted: roast beef.

rob /rɒb/ v., **robbed, rob•bing. 1.** [~ + obj] [no obj] to steal from (a person or place). **2.** [~ + obj] to take away a right, opportunity, etc., from (someone): Her sisters robbed her of her inheritance. —'rob•ber, n. [count] —'rob•ber•y, n. [noncount] [count], pl. **-ies.**

robe /rowb/ n., v., **robed, rob•ing.** —n. [count] **1.** a long, loose or flowing gown. **2.** a bathrobe. —v. [~ + obj] [no obj] **3.** to put on a robe.

rob•in /'rɒbɪn/ n. [count] a large North American bird, having a reddish breast.

ro•bot /'rowbɒt, -bɒt/ n. [count] **1.** a machine that looks something like a human and does mechanical tasks. **2.** a machine that performs such tasks automatically. **3.** a person who acts and responds in a mechanical, routine manner.

ro•bust /row'bʌst, 'rowbʌst/ adj. **1.** strong and healthy. **2.** stoutly built: the robust police officer. **3.** rich and strong in flavor.

rock¹ /rɒk/ n. **1.** [noncount] a large mass of stone forming a hill, cliff, etc. **2.** [count] a stone of any size. —*Idiom*. **3. on the rocks, a.** *Informal*. ruined or about to be ruined: *They worried that their marriage was on the rocks.* **b.** (of an alcoholic beverage) served over ice cubes: *Scotch on the rocks.*

rock² /rɒk/ *v.* **1.** to move to and fro gently: [~ + *obj*]: *He rocked his child in his arms.* [*no obj*]: *She rocked quietly in her chair.* **2.** [~ + *obj*] to shake violently: *An explosion rocked the building.* —*n.* **3.** [*count*] a rocking movement. **4.** [*noncount*] a musical style coming originally from blues and folk music, having a strong beat and repeating phrases. —*adj.* [*before a noun*] **5.** of or relating to rock music: *a rock band.*

'**rock and 'roll** or '**rock 'n' 'roll,** *n.* ROCK² (def. 4).

rock•er /'rɒkər/ *n.* [*count*] a chair mounted on two curved pieces that allow it to rock back and forth. Also called '**rocking ,chair.**

rock•et /'rɒkɪt/ *n.* [*count*] **1.** a tubelike device containing material that burns rapidly and propels the tube through the air. **2.** a space capsule or vehicle put into orbit by such a device. —*v.* **3.** [~ + *obj*] to move by a rocket: *The capsule was rocketed into space.* **4.** [*no obj*] to move like a rocket: *The plane rocketed ahead.*

'**rocket ,science,** *n.* [*noncount*] **1.** the science of rocket design and flight; rocketry. **2.** something requiring great intelligence, esp. mathematical ability.

'**rocket ,scientist,** *n.* [*count*] **1.** a specialist in rocket design. **2.** a highly intelligent person, esp. one with mathematical ability.

rock•y¹ /'rɒkiy/ *adj.*, **-i•er, -i•est. 1.** full of rocks. **2.** made up of rock; rocklike.

rock•y² /'rɒkiy/ *adj.*, **-i•er, -i•est. 1.** full of troubles or difficulties: *a rocky marriage.* **2.** physically unsteady or weak.

rod /rɒd/ *n.* [*count*] a long straight stick or pole: *a fishing rod.*

rode /rowd/ *v.* a pt. of RIDE.

ro•dent /'rowdnt/ *n.* [*count*] a mammal belonging to a family of animals that has sharp teeth that grow continually: *Rodents include mice, squirrels, and rats.*

ro•de•o /'rowdiy,ow, row'deyow/ *n.* [*count*], *pl.* **-de•os.** a public exhibition of cowboy skills, such as riding wild horses.

roe /row/ *n.* [*noncount*] the mass of eggs in the bodies of certain fish, eaten as food.

rogue /rowg/ *n.* [*count*] a dishonest person; scoundrel. —'**ro•guish,** *adj.*

role /rowl/ *n.* [*count*] **1.** a part played by an actor or singer: *the role of the villain in the play.* **2.** the proper function of a person or thing: *the role of computers in teaching math.*

roll /rowl/ *v.* **1.** to move along a surface by turning over and over: [*no obj*]: *A huge stone rolled down the hill.* [~ + *obj*]: *They rolled a barrel out the door.* **2.** to move or be moved on wheels: [~ + *obj*]: *He rolled the wagon down the street.* [*no obj*]: *The car rolled to a stop.* **3.** [*no obj*] to move with a continuous, steady, or swaying motion: *Tears rolled down her face. The ship rolled in the waves. The years rolled by quickly.* **4.** [*no obj*] [~ + *obj*] (of the eyes) to turn around in different directions. **5.** to curl, cover, or fold up so as to form a rounded object: [~ + *obj*]: *She rolled the string into a ball.* [*no obj*]: *The map rolls (up) easily.* **6.** [~ + *obj*] to spread out flat, as with a rolling pin: *She rolled (out) the pastry dough.* **7.** [~ + *obj*] [*no obj*] to throw (dice). **8. roll up, a.** to fold the edges of: *Roll up your pants or Roll*

your pants up. **b.** to arrive in a car, etc.: *She rolled up in a white limousine.* —*n.* [*count*] **9.** a register or list, as of names: *The teacher called the roll.* **10.** anything rolled up in a tubelike shape: *a roll of tape.* **11.** a rounded mass: *rolls of fat on his stomach.* **12.** a small cake of bread sometimes folded over before baking. **13.** an act or instance of rolling or swaying. **14.** a deep, long sound, as of thunder or drums.

roll•er /'rowlər/ *n.* [*count*] **1.** a cylinder, wheel, etc., around which something is rolled, such as a window shade. **2.** a tubelike object used for spreading, crushing, or flattening something: *a paint roller.*

Roll•er•blade /'rowlər,bleyd/ **1.** [*count*] *Trademark.* a brand of in-line skates. —*v.* [~ + *obj*], **-blad•ed, -blad•ing. 2.** (*often: rollerblade*) to skate on in-line skates. —'**roll•er,blad•er,** *n.* [*count*]

'**roller ,coaster,** *n.* [*count*] a train of open cars that moves along sharply winding tracks, found in amusement parks.

'**roller ,skate,** *n.* [*count*] a form of skate with wheels, for use on a smooth surface.

'**roller-,skate,** *v.* [*no obj*], **-skat•ed, -skat•ing.** to move by using roller skates.

roll•ing /'rowlɪŋ/ *adj.* **1.** [*before a noun*] rising and falling in gentle waves into the distance: *rolling hills.* **2.** [*be* + ~ + *in*] having a great deal of: *He's rolling in money.*

ROM /rɒm/ *n.* [*noncount*] read-only memory: computer memory that is not usually changed by the user, holding programmed instructions to the system.

Ro•man /'rowmən/ *adj.* **1.** of or relating to the city of Rome, or to its inhabitants. **2.** of or relating to the Roman Catholic Church. —*n.* [*count*] **3.** a native, inhabitant, or citizen of Rome.

'**Roman 'Catholic,** *adj.* **1.** of or relating to the Roman Catholic Church. —*n.* [*count*] **2.** a member of the Roman Catholic Church. —'**Roman Ca'tholicism,** *n.* [*noncount*]

'**Roman 'Catholic 'Church,** *n.* [*usually: the* + ~] the Christian church of which the pope is the supreme head.

ro•mance /row'mæns/ *n.* **1.** [*count*] a story of love, heroic deeds, great adventures, etc. **2.** [*noncount*] a feeling or quality of passionate love: *no romance in their marriage.* **3.** [*count*] a love affair.

'**Roman 'numeral,** *n.* [*count*] any of the numerals in an ancient Roman system, still used occasionally. The basic symbols are **I** (=1), **V** (=5), **X** (=10), **L** (=50), **C** (=100), **D** (=500), and **M** (=1000).

ro•man•tic /row'mæntɪk/ *adj.* **1.** of or relating to romance: *a romantic relationship.* **2.** not practical or realistic. —*n.* [*count*] **3.** a romantic person. —**ro'man•ti•cal•ly,** *adv.*

ro•man•ti•cize /row'mæntə,sayz/ *v.*, **-cized, -ciz•ing.** to describe as more exciting or romantic than it really is: [~ + *obj*]: *He's romanticizing his trip around the world.* [*no obj*]: *romanticizing about the past.*

romp /rɒmp/ *v.* [*no obj*] **1.** to play in a lively, active way. —*n.* [*count*] **2.** a lively, noisy, active time.

roof /ruwf, rʊf/ *n.* [*count*] **1.** the outside, upper covering of a building. **2.** something that covers like a roof, such as the top of a car. —*v.* [~ + *obj*] **3.** to provide or cover with a roof. —*Idiom*. **4. go through the roof, a.** (esp. of costs) to in-

R

crease quickly and surprisingly. **b.** Also, **hit the roof.** to lose one's temper.

roof•ing /'ruwfɪŋ, 'rʊfɪŋ/ *n.* [*noncount*] material for roofs.

rook•ie /'rʊkiy/ *n.* [*count*] an inexperienced newcomer, esp. an athlete.

room /ruwm, rʊm/ *n.* **1.** [*count*] a portion of space within a building enclosed by walls from other parts: *five rooms in the apartment.* **2.** [*noncount*] extent of space available for something: *The desk will take up more room.* **3.** [*noncount*] opportunity for something: *room for improvement.* —*v.* [*no obj*] **4.** to occupy a room or rooms; lodge: *He roomed with a nice couple.*

'**room and 'board,** *n.* [*noncount*] rented room or rooms, plus meals, usually available for one fixed price.

room•mate /'ruwm,meyt, 'rʊm-/ *n.* [*count*] one who shares a room or apartment with another.

room•y /'ruwmiy/ *adj.*, **-i•er, -i•est.** having or giving plenty of room or space.

roost /ruwst/ *n.* [*count*] **1.** a perch upon which birds rest. —*v.* [*no obj*] **2.** to sit on a perch.

roost•er /'ruwstər/ *n.* [*count*] an adult male chicken.

root¹ /ruwt, rʊt/ *n.* **1.** a part of a plant that develops downward into the soil. **2.** the part of a hair, tooth, etc., holding it to the main part of the body. **3.** the fundamental part; the source or origin: *the root of all evil.* **4. roots,** [*plural*] the original home and culture of a person or of a person's ancestors. **5.** a part of a word, or the word itself, present in other forms of that word: *"Dance" is the root in "danced" and "dancer"; the root of the word "extend" is Latin "-tend-".* —*v.* **6.** [*no obj*] to form roots: *Will these plants root well?* **7.** [~ + *obj*] to fix by or as if by roots: *I was rooted to the spot in amazement.* **8. root out,** to remove completely: *to root out crime* or *to root crime out.* —*Idiom.* **9. take root, a.** to send out roots; begin to grow. **b.** to become established: *prejudices that took root in our country.*

root² /ruwt, rʊt/ *v.* [*no obj*] [~ + *obj*] **1.** to turn up the soil with the nose, as pigs do. **2.** [*no obj*] to poke, pry, or search: *He rooted around in the drawer for a key.*

root³ /ruwt/ *v.* [*no obj*] **1.** to support a team or player by cheering strongly: *We rooted for the team.* **2.** to lend support: *We're all rooting for you.*

rope /rowp/ *n.*, *v.*, **roped, rop•ing.** —*n.* **1.** [*noncount*] [*count*] a strong, thick line or cord, made of twisted fibers. **2. ropes,** [*plural*] the operations of a business: *to learn the ropes at a new job.* —*v.* [~ + *obj*] **3.** to tie or fasten with a rope. **4. rope in,** to persuade to do something, esp. by trickery: *Let's rope the students in to help* or *Let's rope in the students to help.* **5. rope off,** to enclose or mark off with a rope: *We roped off part of the room* or *We roped part of the room off.* —*Idiom.* **6. at the end of one's rope,** at the end of one's patience, strength, or will to go on.

ro•sa•ry /'rowzəriy/ *n.* [*count*], *pl.* **-ries. 1.** a series of prayers said by Roman Catholics. **2.** a string of beads used in counting these prayers.

rose¹ /rowz/ *n.* **1.** [*count*] a shrub usually with prickly stems and showy flowers. **2.** [*count*] the flower of any such shrub: *He sent her a dozen roses.* **3.** [*noncount*] a pinkish red or purplish pink color.

rose² /rowz/ *v.* pt. of RISE.

ros•ter /'rɒstər/ *n.* [*count*] a list of persons or groups, as of military units.

ros•trum /'rɒstrəm/ *n.* [*count*], *pl.* **-trums, -tra** /-trə/. any platform, stage, or the like, for public speaking.

ros•y /'rowziy/ *adj.*, **-i•er, -i•est. 1.** pink or pinkish red: *rosy cheeks.* **2.** bright or promising: *a rosy future.*

rot /rɒt/ *v.*, **rot•ted, rot•ting,** *n.* —*v.* **1.** to (cause to) undergo decay: [*no obj*]: *The dead leaves rotted in the soil.* [~ + *obj*]: *Overwatering will rot the plants.* —*n.* [*noncount*] **2.** the state of being rotten; decay.

ro•ta•ry /'rowtəriy/ *adj.* turning on one point or an axis, such as a wheel.

ro•tate /'rowteyt/ *v.*, **-tat•ed, -tat•ing. 1.** to (cause to) turn on an axis; revolve: [*no obj*]: *The earth rotates once every twenty-four hours.* [~ + *obj*]: *rotating the coin on his finger.* **2.** to (cause to) proceed in a fixed routine, as in a cycle: [*no obj*]: *The guards rotated in keeping watch.* [~ + *obj*]: *to rotate crops.* —**ro'ta•tion,** *n.* [*count*] [*noncount*]

rote /rowt/ *n.* [*noncount*] **1.** a habitual or mechanical procedure. —*Idiom.* **2. by rote,** from memory, without thought of the meaning: *to learn by rote.*

rot•ten /'rɒtn/ *adj.*, **-er, -est. 1.** spoiled, as from decay: *rotten eggs.* **2.** very bad; unpleasant: *a rotten trick; a rotten day.*

ro•tund /row'tʌnd/ *adj.* rounded and fat or plump.

rouge /ruwʒ/ *n.* [*noncount*] a reddish powder used as a cosmetic.

rough /rʌf/ *adj.*, **-er, -est,** *n.*, *adv.*, *v.* —*adj.* **1.** having a coarse or uneven surface; not smooth: *rough skin.* **2.** lacking in gentleness, care, or consideration: *rough handling.* **3.** difficult or unpleasant: *a rough year for consumers.* **4.** dangerous because of violence or crime: *a rough neighborhood.* **5.** not perfected; unpolished: *a rough draft.* —*n.* [*noncount*] **6.** something rough, esp. ground. **7.** anything in its unfinished or early form, as a drawing. —*adv.* **8.** in a rough manner; roughly. —*v.* **9. rough up,** to treat (someone) with physical violence: *The muggers roughed up their victim* or *The muggers roughed their victim up.* —*Idiom.* **10. rough it,** *Informal.* to live without comforts or conveniences: *The family roughed it in the country for two years.* —'**rough•ly,** *adv.* —'**rough•ness,** *n.* [*noncount*]

rough•en /'rʌfən/ *v.* [~ + *obj*] [*no obj*] to (cause to) become rough or rougher.

rou•lette /ruw'lɛt/ *n.* [*noncount*] a game of chance in which a small ball is spun on a dishlike device.

round /rawnd/ *adj.*, **-er, -est,** *n.*, *adv.*, *prep.*, *v.* —*adj.* **1.** shaped like a ball or circle: *The earth is round.* **2.** made of or having full, curved lines: *He had a round face.* **3.** [*before a noun*] expressed to the nearest ten, hundred, etc.: *In round numbers, the house cost $350,000.* —*n.* [*count*] **4.** a complete course or series, one following the other: *the next round of peace talks.* **5.** Often, **rounds.** [*plural*] a going around from place to place, as in a definite direction: *The doctor made her rounds in the hospital.* **6.** a completed game or stage of a game: *a round of bridge.* **7.** a single outburst: *a round of applause.* **8.** a piece of ammunition: *The soldier fired a few rounds at the enemy.* **9.** a single serving of drink to everyone present: *My boss bought the next round of drinks.* **10.** a short piece of music in which different voices or instruments begin melody at different times. —*adv.* **11.** from the beginning to the end of a period of time: *open all year round.* **12.** Also, **'round.** around. —*prep.* **13.** throughout: *a resort visited round the year.* **14.** around: *It happened round noon.* —*v.* **15.** [~ + *obj*] to travel or pass around. **16.** to (cause to) become round: [~ + *obj*]: *He rounded his lips and tried to whistle.* [*no obj*]: *Her eyes rounded in amazement.* **17.** [~ + *obj*] to express (an amount) as a round number: *You can round (off) 15,837 to 15,840.* **18. round up,** to drive or bring together: *to round up the cattle* or *to round the cattle up.* —**'round•ness,** *n.* [*noncount*]

round•a•bout /*adj.*,rawndə'bawt, 'rawndə-,bawt; *n.* 'rawndə,bawt/ *adj.* **1.** not straight or direct: *a roundabout way.* —*n.* [*count*] *Brit.* **2.** a traffic circle. **3.** a merry-go-round.

round•ly /'rawndliy/ *adv.* **1.** in an outspoken way; severely: *He criticized her roundly.* **2.** completely or fully: *roundly defeated.*

'round 'trip, *n.* [*count*] a trip to a certain place and back again.

rouse /rawz/ *v.*, **roused, rous•ing.** **1.** [~ + *obj*] [*no obj*] to (cause to) come out of a state of sleep, unconsciousness, etc. **2.** [~ + *obj*] to cause excitement or anger in: *His speech roused the crowd to action.*

rout /rawt/ *n.* **1.** a defeat, followed by disorderly retreat: [*noncount*]: *to put an army to rout.* [*count*]: *The last game was a rout.* —*v.* [~ + *obj*] **2.** to defeat completely, causing a disorderly retreat.

route /ruwt, rawt/ *n.*, *v.*, **rout•ed, rout•ing.** —*n.* [*count*] **1.** a course, way, or road for travel. **2.** a customary line of travel, often with stops regularly made: *a bus route; a newspaper route.* —*v.* [~ + *obj*] **3.** to fix the path or route of: *to route a tour.* **4.** to send by a particular route: *Calls were routed through the switchboard.*

rou•tine /ruw'tiyn/ *n.* **1.** a regular course of procedure: [*noncount*]: *office routine.* [*count*]: *the baby's routines of waking, eating, playing, and sleeping.* **2.** [*noncount*] boring procedure done without thinking: *the dull routine of the assembly line.* —*adj.* **3.** of the nature of routine: *routine work.* —**rou'tine•ly,** *adv.*: *He routinely brought his lunch.*

rove /rowv/ *v.*, **roved, rov•ing.** to move here and there at random: [~ + *obj*]: *to rove the subways.* [*no obj*]: *to rove in the woods.* —**'rov•er,** *n.* [*count*]

row[1] /row/ *n.* [*count*] **1.** a number of people or things in a line: *the rows of customers.* **2.** a line of seats facing the same way, as in a theater. —*Idiom.* **3. in a row, a.** lined up one after the other or side by side: *six children, all in a row.* **b.** happening one after the other without interruption: *The team lost seven games in a row.*

row[2] /row/ *v.* [*no obj*] [~ + *obj*] to move a boat by the use of oars. —**'row•er,** *n.* [*count*]

row[3] /raw/ *n.* [*count*] a noisy argument.

row•dy /'rawdiy/ *adj.*, **-di•er, -di•est.** rough and disorderly: *rowdy behavior.* —**'row•di•ness,** *n.* [*noncount*]

roy•al /'rɔyəl/ *adj.* [*before a noun*] **1.** fit for or relating to a king or queen: *a royal banquet.* **2.** *Informal.* extreme: *He's a royal pain in the neck.* —*n.* [*count*] **3.** *Informal.* a member of the royal family. —**'roy•al•ly,** *adv.*

roy•al•ty /'rɔyəltiy/ *n.*, *pl.* **-ties.** **1.** [*noncount*] royal persons thought of as a group. **2.** [*noncount*] royal rank, dignity, or power. **3.** [*count*] an agreed portion of the money earned from a

piece of writing or music paid to its author or composer.

RR or **R.R.,** an abbreviation of: **1.** railroad. **2.** rural route.

RSVP, an abbreviation used on an invitation to indicate that a reply is requested.

rub /rʌb/ *v.*, **rubbed, rub•bing,** *n.* —*v.* **1.** to move something back and forth on a surface with pressure, as in polishing or massaging: [~ + *obj*]: *He rubbed the silver teapot with a cloth and some polish.* [*no obj*]: *He rubbed until the silver shone. The noise you hear is the mechanism rubbing against something.* **2.** [~ + *obj*] to spread or apply with pressure: *to rub lotion on chapped hands.* **3. rub down,** to smooth, polish, or clean by rubbing: *to rub down the door* or *to rub the door down.* **4. rub off on,** to pass along to: *Her interest in biology rubbed off on her daughters.* **5. rub out,** to erase: *rubbed out the error* or *rubbed the error out.* —*n.* [*count*] **6.** an act or instance of rubbing: *an alcohol rub.* —*Idiom.* **7. rub elbows** or **shoulders with,** to associate or mix socially with: *rubbing shoulders with the important people in Washington.* **8. rub it in,** to repeat something unpleasant to tease or annoy: *kept rubbing it in about how I tripped on the stage.* **9. rub (someone) the wrong way,** to irritate; offend; annoy.

rub•ber /'rʌbər/ *n.* **1.** [*noncount*] a highly elastic solid from the milky juice of rubber trees. **2.** [*noncount*] a similar substance and material made synthetically. **3.** [*count; usually plural*] a low boot of this material, worn in the rain. **4.** RUBBER BAND. **5.** [*count*] *Slang.* a condom. —**'rub•ber•y,** *adj.*

'rubber 'band, *n.* [*count*] a narrow circular band of rubber, used for holding things together.

rub•bish /'rʌbɪʃ/ *n.* [*noncount*] **1.** worthless material that is thrown out; trash. **2.** nonsense, as in writing or art.

rub•ble /'rʌbəl/ *n.* [*noncount*] broken bits and pieces of bricks, rocks, etc.: *Bombing reduced the town to rubble.*

rub•down /'rʌb,dawn/ *n.* [*count*] a massage.

ru•bel•la /ruw'bɛlə/ *n.* [*noncount*] an infection with a fever, cough, and a red rash. Also called **German measles.**

ru•by /'ruwbiy/ *n.*, *pl.* **-bies.** **1.** [*count*] a red stone used as a gem. **2.** [*noncount*] a deep red.

ruck•sack /'rʌk,sæk, 'rʊk-/ *n.* [*count*] a type of knapsack carried by hikers, bicyclists, etc.

rud•der /'rʌdər/ *n.* [*count*] a vertical blade at the rear of a ship or plane that can be turned to control direction.

rud•dy /'rʌdiy/ *adj.*, **-di•er, -di•est.** **1.** having a healthy red color: *a ruddy complexion.* **2.** red or reddish.

rude /ruwd/ *adj.*, **rud•er, rud•est.** **1.** impolite, esp. deliberately so: *a rude reply.* **2.** [*before a noun*] rough, harsh, or ungentle: *a rude shock.* —**'rude•ly,** *adv.* —**'rude•ness,** *n.* [*noncount*]

ru•di•ment /'ruwdəmənt/ *n.* Usually, **rudiments.** [*plural*] **1.** the elements of a subject: *the rudiments of grammar.* **2.** an undeveloped or imperfect form of something: *the rudiments of a plan.* —**,ru•di'men•ta•ry,** *adj.*

ruf•fi•an /'rʌfiyən, 'rʌfyən/ *n.* [*count*] a tough, violent person; a bully.

ruf•fle /'rʌfəl/ *v.*, **-fled, -fling,** *n.* —*v.* [~ + *obj*] **1.** to interfere with the smoothness of: *The wind ruffled the calm surface of the sea.* **2.** to disturb or irritate: *The speaker was ruffled from all the interruptions.* —*n.* [*count*] **3.** a break in the

R

smoothness or evenness of a surface. **4.** a strip of material gathered along one edge and used as a trimming. —*Idiom.* **5. ruffle someone's feathers,** to upset or annoy someone.

rug /rʌg/ *n.* [*count*] a piece of thick fabric for covering part of a floor.

Rug•by /'rʌgbiy/ *n.* [*noncount*] a form of football played between two teams of 13 or 15 members each. Also called **'Rug•by 'foot•ball.**

rug•ged /'rʌgɪd/ *adj.* **1.** roughly irregular or uneven, as by having wrinkles: *a man's rugged features.* **2.** rough, harsh, or severe: *a rugged life.* **3.** capable of lasting through hardship, wear, etc.: *a rugged car.* —'**rug•ged•ly,** *adv.*: *ruggedly handsome.* —'**rug•ged•ness,** *n.* [*noncount*]

ru•in /'ruwɪn/ *n.* **1. ruins,** [*plural*] the remains of a building, etc., destroyed or in decay. **2.** [*count*] a destroyed or decayed building, etc. **3.** [*noncount*] a wrecked or decayed condition: *The house fell into ruin.* —*v.* [~ + *obj*] **4.** to reduce to ruin; destroy: *Her smoking is ruining her health.* —'**ru•in•ous,** *adj.*

rule /ruwl/ *n., v.,* **ruled, rul•ing.** —*n.* **1.** [*count*] a principle guiding how one behaves, the way things are done, etc.: *a rule against running in the halls.* **2.** [*count*] the customary way something is done: *In this office long meetings are the rule.* **3.** [*noncount*] control or government: *under foreign rule.* **4.** RULER (def. 2). —*v.* **5.** [~ + *obj*] [*no obj*] to use authority or influence over. **6.** to make an official decision: [*no obj*]: *The court will rule on the matter at its next session.* [~ + *obj*]: *The committee ruled that he could not continue as president.* **7.** [~ + *obj*] to mark with lines, with the aid of a ruler: *to rule a sheet of paper.* **8. rule out,** to decide to ignore: *We haven't ruled out the possibility of error.* —*Idiom.* **9. as a rule,** generally; usually.

rul•er /'ruwlər/ *n.* [*count*] **1.** one who rules or governs, as a king. **2.** a strip of wood or other material that has a straight edge and is marked off in inches or centimeters, used for drawing lines and measuring.

rul•ing /'ruwlɪŋ/ *n.* [*count*] a decision, as one by a judge.

rum /rʌm/ *n.* [*noncount*] an alcoholic liquor made from molasses.

rum•ble /'rʌmbəl/ *v.,* **-bled, -bling,** *n.* —*v.* [*no obj*] **1.** to make a deep, rolling and continuous sound, such as thunder. —*n.* [*count*] **2.** a rumbling sound.

rum•bling /'rʌmblɪŋ/ *n.* [*count*] Often, **rumblings.** [*plural*] the first signs of dissatisfaction: *rumblings from the employees.*

rum•mage /'rʌmɪdʒ/ *v.,* **-maged, -mag•ing,** *n.* —*v.* [*no obj*] [~ + *obj*] **1.** to search thoroughly, esp. by moving around, turning over, or looking through contents. —*n.* [*noncount*] **2.** a jumble of things; odds and ends.

rum•my /'rʌmiy/ *n.* [*noncount*] any of various card games for several players, in which the object is to match cards into sets and sequences.

ru•mor /'ruwmər/ *n.* [*count*] **1.** a story or statement that has no solid basis and is not known to be true. —*v.* [~ + *obj; usually: be* + ~*-ed*] **2.** to report, circulate, or claim by a rumor: *It's been rumored that he will leave.* Also, *esp. Brit.,* '**ru•mour.**

rump /rʌmp/ *n.* [*count*] the hind or back part of an animal, above the hind legs.

rum•pus /'rʌmpəs/ *n.* [*count*] a noisy or violent uproar or argument.

run /rʌn/ *v.,* **ran** /ræn/, **run, run•ning,** *n.* —*v.* **1.** [*no obj*] to go quickly by moving the legs more rapidly than at a walk: *He ran down the street.* **2.** [~ + *obj*] to perform by or as if by running: *She ran an errand.* **3.** [~ + *obj*] to go (a distance) in running: *He ran the mile in four minutes.* **4.** [~ + *obj*] to pass over or through quickly: *He ran his fingers over the keyboard.* **5.** [*no obj*] to make a quick trip: *to run to the supermarket.* **6.** [~ + *obj*] to transport: *I'll run you home in my car.* **7.** to (cause to) be a candidate for election: [*no obj*]: *She's running for president.* [~ + *obj*]: *The party ran a woman for president.* **8.** to (cause to) turn away from a proper or given route: [*no obj*]: *The ship ran aground.* [~ + *obj*]: *The driver ran the car up onto the curb.* **9.** to (cause to) travel along a certain route: [*no obj*]: *The bus runs between New Haven and Hartford.* [~ + *obj*]: *The company runs ferries between New York and Hoboken.* **10.** to (cause to) unravel: [*no obj*]: *Her stockings ran when she knelt down.* [~ + *obj*]: *to run a stocking.* **11.** to (cause to) flow in or as if in a stream: [*no obj*]: *Tears ran from her eyes. Her nose was running.* [~ + *obj*]: *He ran water into the tub.* **12.** [*no obj*] (of colors) to spread to other things: *The colors in your blouse will run if you use hot water.* **13.** to (cause to) operate or function: [*no obj*]: *How is the office running these days?* [~ + *obj*]: *Run the dishwasher again.* **14.** [~ + *obj*] to manage or conduct: *to run a business.* **15.** [~ + *obj*] to cost (an amount): *This watch runs about $30.* **16.** [~ + *obj*] to cost (a person) an amount: *The repair will run you $90.* **17.** [*no obj*] to continue: *The story runs for eight pages.* **18.** [~ + *obj*] to extend in a particular direction: *to run the cable under the road.* **19.** to (cause to) appear in print: [*no obj*]: *The story ran in all the papers.* [~ + *obj*]: *The newspaper ran the story on page one.* **20.** to (cause to) be performed: [*no obj*]: *The play ran for two years.* [~ + *obj*]: *The movie was run in ten theaters.* **21.** [*no obj*] to occur again through time: *Musical ability runs in my family.* **22.** [~ + *obj*] to process (the instructions in a program) by computer. **23.** [~ + *obj*] to expose oneself to: *running a big risk.* **24.** [~ + *obj*] to drive, force, or thrust: *The hero ran the sword through his rival.* **25. run around,** to have more than one romantic involvement: *running around with another man.* **26. run away,** to flee, esp. with no intent to return: *The child said she was going to run away.* **27. run away with, a.** to go away with, esp. to marry: *Her husband ran away with another woman.* **b.** to steal: *to run away with the money.* **c.** to overwhelm: *Sometimes his enthusiasm runs away with him.* **28. run down, a.** to strike and overturn, esp. with a vehicle: *ran the child down* or *ran down the child.* **b.** to chase after and seize: *to run down criminals* or *to run criminals down.* **c.** to stop: *The battery ran down in just a few hours.* **29. run into, a.** to collide with: *We ran into each other and fell.* **b.** to meet accidentally: *I ran into an old friend.* **c.** to total: *This project could run into the millions.* **30. run off,** to leave quickly; run away: *She ran off before I could thank her.* **31. run off with, a.** to steal: *running off with the money.* **b.** to leave suddenly with, so as to have an affair with: *He ran off with the mayor's wife.* **32. run on,** to continue without relief or interruption: *He ran on about his good luck.* **33. run out, a.** to come to an end: *My visa has run out.* **b.** to become used up: *The fuel has run out.* **34. run out of,** to use up a supply of: *We've run out of wood.* **35. run over, a.** to hit with a vehicle: *to run over a child* or *to run a* *child over.* **b.** to go beyond: *His speech ran over the time limit.* **36. run through, a.** to use up wastefully: *He ran through all their money.* **b.** to practice or rehearse: *Let's run through that tune one more time.* **37. run up,** to gather or accumulate: *running up huge debts.* —*n.* [count] **38.** a fleeing; flight. **39.** the distance covered, as by running. **40.** a quick trip. **41.** a routine or regular trip: *the deliveryman's run.* **42.** a place in a stocking where a series of stitches have come undone. **43.** a course, trend, or tendency: *the normal run of events.* **44.** any extensive and continued demand: *a sudden run on umbrellas.* **45.** a series of demands for payment: *a run on the banks.* **46.** *Baseball.* the score made by running around all the bases and reaching home plate. —*Idiom.* **47. in the long run,** in the course of long experience. **48. in the short run,** in the near future. **49. on the run, a.** rushing about to perform one's activities: *on the run all day.* **b.** while rushing to get somewhere: *eating breakfast on the run.* **c.** moving from place to place so as to hide from the police. **50. run for it,** *Informal.* to flee quickly. **51. run short,** to have too little of something: *My patience is running short.*

run•a•way /ˈrʌnəˌwey/ *n.* [count] **1.** one who runs away. —*adj.* [before a noun] **2.** escaped; fugitive. **3.** not held back or restrained: *runaway prices.*

'run'-down, *adj.* **1.** very tired; exhausted. **2.** in poor health: *He's severely run-down and really should see a doctor.* **3.** in neglected condition: *a run-down neighborhood.*

rung¹ /rʌŋ/ *v.* pt. and pp. of RING².

rung² /rʌŋ/ *n.* [count] **1.** one of the steps of a ladder. **2.** a piece attached horizontally to add strength, as between the legs of a chair. **3.** a level or degree, as in an organization.

'run-,in, *n.* [count] a quarrel; argument: *He had a run-in with his boss.*

run•ner /ˈrʌnər/ *n.* [count] **1.** a person, animal, or thing that runs. **2.** a strip of metal or wood on which a sled or ice skate slides.

'runner-'up, *n.* [count], *pl.* **run•ners-up.** the player, team, or competitor finishing in second place.

run•ning /ˈrʌnɪŋ/ *n.* [noncount] **1.** the act of a person, animal, or thing that runs. **2.** management; direction: *the running of a business.* —*adj.* [before a noun] **3.** flowing: *running water.* **4.** continuous: *a running commentary.* **5.** performed with or done with a run: *a running leap and off he went.* **6.** moving or proceeding smoothly: *They got off to a running start.*

'running 'mate, *n.* [count] a candidate for a political office, linked with a more important office or position: *the presidential candidate and his running mate.*

run•off /ˈrʌnˌɔf, -ˌɒf/ *n.* **1.** [noncount] something that flows off, such as rain water. **2.** [count] a contest held to break a tie.

'run-,on, *adj.* **1.** (of a sentence) having a thought that carries over to what should be another sentence or clause. —*n.* [count] **2.** a run-on sentence.

run•way /ˈrʌnˌwey/ *n.* [count] a strip on which planes land and take off.

rup•ture /ˈrʌptʃər/ *n., v.,* **-tured, -tur•ing.** —*n.* **1.** [count] the act of bursting. **2.** [noncount] the state of being burst. **3.** [count] a break from once-friendly relations. —*v.* [no obj] [~ + obj] **4.** to break or burst.

ru•ral /ˈrʊrəl/ *adj.* of or like the country, country life, or country people.

ruse /ruwz/ *n.* [count] a trick.

rush¹ /rʌʃ/ *v.* **1.** to (cause to) move with great or too much speed: [no obj]: *He rushed ahead with the plan.* [~ + obj]: *He rushed the nomination through the committee.* **2.** to (cause to) appear, go, etc., rapidly or suddenly: [no obj]: *The train rushed by.* [~ + obj]: *Rush him to a hospital.* —*n.* **3.** [count] the act of rushing. **4.** [noncount] hurried activity: *There's no rush; we have plenty of time.* **5.** [count] period of hurried activity: *the mid-morning rush.* **6.** [count] a rushing of many people to some region: *the California gold rush.* —*adj.* [before a noun] **7.** requiring or done in haste: *a rush job.*

rush² /rʌʃ/ *n.* [count] a grasslike plant found in wet or marshy places, having a long, thin stem.

'rush ,hour, *n.* [count] a time of day in which large numbers of people are traveling to or from work.

Rus•sian /ˈrʌʃən/ *adj.* **1.** of or relating to Russia. **2.** of or relating to the language spoken in Russia. —*n.* **3.** [count] a person born or living in Russia. **4.** [noncount] the language spoken in Russia.

rust /rʌst/ *n.* [noncount] **1.** the red coating that forms on iron when exposed to air and moisture. **2.** reddish yellow or reddish brown. —*v.* **3.** [no obj] [~ + obj] to (cause to) become covered by rust. **4.** [no obj] to decline in quality: *He could feel his pitching abilities rusting away.* —'rust•y, *adj.*

rus•tic /ˈrʌstɪk/ *adj.* **1.** of or relating to the country; rural. —*n.* [count] **2.** a country person.

rus•tle /ˈrʌsəl/ *v.,* **-tled, -tling,** *n.* —*v.* [no obj] [~ + obj] **1.** to make the slight, soft sounds of gentle rubbing, as leaves. **2. rustle up,** *Informal.* to put together by effort or search: *to rustle up some lunch; to rustle something up for lunch.* —*n.* [count] **3.** the sound made by anything that rustles.

rut /rʌt/ *n.* [count] **1.** a narrow, deep track in the ground, esp. one made by vehicles. **2.** a fixed way of proceeding, usually dull or unpromising: *to fall into a rut at his job.*

ruth•less /ˈruwθlɪs/ *adj.* without pity or compassion; cruel; merciless. —'ruth•less•ly, *adv.* —'ruth•less•ness, *n.* [noncount]

RV, an abbreviation of: recreational vehicle, a large vehicle used by a family, esp. for camping.

Rx, an abbreviation of: **1.** (medical) prescription. **2.** (used in prescriptions) take.

-ry, a variant form of the suffix -ERY: (*jewelry*).

rye /ray/ *n.* [noncount] **1.** a cereal grass. **2.** the seeds or grain of this plant, used for making flour and whiskey. **3.** bread made from this grain. **4.** Also called **'rye 'whiskey.** a whiskey made from rye grain.

R

S

S, s /ɛs/ *n.* [*count*], *pl.* **Ss** or **S's, ss** or **s's.** the 19th letter of the English alphabet, a consonant.

S, an abbreviation of: **1.** satisfactory. **2.** small. **3.** Also, **s** south. **4.** southern.

's¹ /s, z, ɪz/ an ending that is added to nouns or noun phrases to indicate possession by: *man's; women's; children's; James's; witness's; attorney general's; king of England's; anyone's.*

's² /s, z, ɪz/ a contraction that appears at the end of a noun or pronoun that is the subject of a verb, and is a shortened form of **1.** the verb *is: She's here* (= *She is here*). **2.** the verb *has: He's been there* (= *He has been there*). **3.** the verb *does: What's he do for a living?* (= *What does he do for a living?*).

's³ /s/ a contraction that appears at the end of the verb *let* and is a shortened form of *us: Let's go* (= *Let us go*).

-s¹ or **-es,** /s, z, ɪz/ an ending marking the third person singular present indicative of verbs: *He walks.*

-s² or **-es,** an ending marking nouns as plural: *two weeks.*

Sab•bath /ˈsæbəθ/ *n.* [*noncount; usually: the +* ~] **1.** the seventh day of the week, Saturday, the day of rest devoted to worship among Jews and some Christians. **2.** the first day of the week, Sunday, devoted to worship by most Christians.

sa•ber /ˈseybər/ *n.* [*count*] a one-edged sword, usually slightly curved.

sa•ble /ˈseybəl/ *n., pl.* **-bles,** (*esp. when thought of as a group* for 1) **-ble. 1.** [*count*] a small dark-colored animal valued for its fur. **2.** [*noncount*] the fur of the sable.

sab•o•tage /ˈsæbəˌtɑʒ/ *n., v.,* **-taged, -tag•ing.** —*n.* [*noncount*] **1.** deliberate damage of equipment, etc., as by employees during a dispute with their company. —*v.* [~ + *obj*] **2.** to damage or spoil by sabotage: *to sabotage the communications facilities.*

sac•cha•rin /ˈsækərɪn/ *n.* [*noncount*] an artificial sugar substitute.

sack¹ /sæk/ *n.* **1.** [*count*] a large strong bag, as for potatoes. **2.** [*noncount; usually: the +* ~] *Slang.* dismissal from a job: *She got the sack for always being late for work.* —*v.* [~ + *obj*] **3.** *Slang.* to dismiss from a job; fire. —*Idiom.* **4. hit the sack,** to go to bed: *Time to hit the sack!*

sack² /sæk/ *v.* [~ + *obj*] **1.** to steal property from a captured place. —*n.* [*count*] **2.** stealing from a captured place: *the sack of Troy.*

sac•ra•ment /ˈsækrəmənt/ *n.* [*count*] a ceremony of the Christian churches, as baptism.

sa•cred /ˈseykrɪd/ *adj.* **1.** worthy of religious respect because of association with God: *the sacred relics of the saints.* **2.** very important: *an hour sacred to study.* **3.** worthy of great respect: *the sacred memory of the dead.*

sac•ri•fice /ˈsækrəˌfays/ *n., v.,* **-ficed, -fic•ing.** —*n.* **1.** [*noncount*] the offering of animal or human life or of some object to a god as part of a ceremony. **2.** the giving up of something important for the sake of something else: [*count*]: *making many sacrifices for his children.* [*noncount*]: *the sacrifice of leisure time to pursue a career.* **3.** [*count*] the thing that is offered or given up. —*v.* [~ + *obj*] **4.** to make a sacrifice of. —,**sac•ri'fi•cial** /-ˈfɪʃəl/, *adj.*

sac•ri•lege /ˈsækrəlɪdʒ/ *n.* [*count*] the act of mistreating something sacred. —**sac•ri•le•gious** /ˌsækrəˈlɪdʒəs/, *adj.*

sad /sæd/ *adj.,* **sad•der, sad•dest. 1.** unhappy: *to feel sad.* **2.** expressing or causing sorrow: *a sad song.* —'**sad•ly,** *adv.* —'**sad•ness,** *n.* [*noncount*]

sad•den /ˈsædṇ/ *v.* to make sad: [~ + *obj*]: *The news of their teammate's injury saddened the team.* [*It +* ~ + *obj*]: *It saddened me that she wouldn't trust me.*

sad•dle /ˈsædl/ *n., v.,* **-dled, -dling.** —*n.* [*count*] **1.** a seat for a rider on the back of a horse or other animal. —*v.* [~ + *obj*] **2.** to put a saddle on (an animal): *They saddled their horses and rode off.* **3.** to give to (someone), as a responsibility: *The boss saddled our staff with extra work.*

sa•dism /ˈseydɪzəm, ˈsædɪz-/ *n.* [*noncount*] **1.** (sexual pleasure from) causing pain to others. **2.** pleasure in being cruel. —'**sa•dist,** *n.* [*count*], *adj.* —**sa•dis•tic** /səˈdɪstɪk/, *adj.*

sa•fa•ri /səˈfɑriy/ *n.* [*count*], *pl.* **-ris.** a trip for hunting, adventure, etc.

safe /seyf/ *adj.,* **saf•er, saf•est,** *n.* —*adj.* **1.** giving protection from danger: *a safe neighborhood.* **2.** free from injury: *They arrived home safe.* **3.** reasonably correct: *a safe estimate.* **4.** careful: *a safe driver.* —*n.* [*count*] **5.** a strong box for valuables. —*Idiom.* **6. play (it) safe,** to avoid taking unnecessary risks: *He played it safe and didn't drive fast in the snow.* —'**safe•ly,** *adv.*

safe•guard /ˈseyf,gɑrd/ *n.* [*count*] **1.** something that serves as a protection: *stricter safeguards on nuclear fuels.* —*v.* **2.** to prevent (someone or something) from being harmed: [*no obj*]: *to safeguard against attack.* [~ + *obj*]: *You can safeguard your home from burglars.*

safe•keep•ing /ˈseyfˈkiypɪŋ/ *n.* [*noncount*] the act of keeping safe or the state of being kept safe: *money in the bank for safekeeping.*

'safe 'sex, *n.* [*noncount*] sexual activity in which precautions are taken to prevent diseases spread through sexual contact.

safe•ty /ˈseyftiy/ *n.* [*noncount*] the state of being safe from injury, loss, etc.

'safety ,pin, *n.* [*count*] a pin bent back on itself to form a spring, with a guard to cover the point.

sag /sæg/ *v.* [*no obj*], **sagged, sag•ging. 1.** to sink downward by or as if by weight: *The old couch sagged in the middle.* **2.** to become less in strength or intensity: *Our spirits began to sag.*

sa•ga /ˈsɑgə/ *n.* [*count*], *pl.* **-gas.** any piece of writing that tells of heroic events or deeds.

sa•ga•cious /səˈgeyʃəs/ *adj.* wise: *a sagacious lawyer.* —**sa•gac•i•ty** /səˈgæsɪtiy/, *n.* [*noncount*]

sage¹ /seydʒ/ *n., adj.,* **sag•er, sag•est.** —*n.* [*count*] **1.** a very wise person. —*adj.* **2.** wise: *sage advice.*

sage² /seydʒ/ *n.* [*noncount*] an herb belonging to the mint family, used in cooking.

said /sɛd/ *v.* pt. and pp. of SAY.

sail /seyl/ *n.* [*count*] **1.** a piece of canvas on a ship to catch the wind and propel the vessel. **2.** a trip in a boat or ship. —*v.* **3.** [~ + *obj*] **a.** to travel in a ship. **b.** to pilot a ship. **4.** to control a sailboat, esp. for sport: [*no obj*]: *She likes to sail on weekends.* [~ + *obj*]: *They sailed their boat*

sandal

into the harbor. **5.** [no obj] to begin a journey by water: *We sail at dawn.* —*Idiom.* **6. set sail,** to start a voyage.

sail•boat /'seyl,bowt/ *n.* [count] a boat using sails.

sail•or /'seylər/ *n.* [count] one whose job is sailing; a member of the navy.

saint /seynt/ *n.* [count] a person of great holiness, formally recognized by the Christian Church.

saint•ly /'seyntliy/ *adj.*, **-li•er, -li•est.** of or like a saint: *the teacher's saintly patience.*

sake /seyk/ *n.* [noncount] **1.** benefit or well-being: *She worked hard for the sake of her family.* **2.** purpose: *You're just talking for the sake of talking.*

sal•ad /'sæləd/ *n.* **1.** a cold dish of raw vegetables, served with a dressing: [noncount]: *We had salad with dinner.* [count]: *many different salads at the restaurant.* **2.** a dish of raw or cold foods, mixed with mayonnaise or other dressing: [noncount]: *potato salad.* [count]: *delicious pasta salads.*

sal•a•man•der /'sælə,mændər/ *n.* [count] a small animal able to live in water or on land, having a moist, scaleless skin.

sa•la•mi /sə'lɑmiy/ *n.*, [noncount] [count], *pl.* **-mis.** a spicy, garlic-flavored sausage.

sal•a•ry /'sæləriy/ *n.* [count], *pl.* **-ries.** a fixed amount of money paid regularly to a person for work. —**'sal•a,ried,** *adj.*: *a salaried worker.*

sale /seyl/ *n.* [count] **1.** an act of selling. **2.** a special offering of goods at reduced prices. **3. sales,** [plural] total receipts from selling. —*Idiom.* **4. for sale,** available for purchase: *This house is for sale.* **5. on sale,** to be bought at reduced prices: *The store has coats on sale for 50% off.* —**'sal•a•ble, 'sale•a•ble,** *adj.*

sales•clerk /'seylz,klɑrk/ *n.* [count] one who sells goods in a store.

sales•man or **-wom•an** /'seylzmən/ or /-,wumən/ *n.* [count], *pl.* **-men** or **-wom•en.** a man or woman who sells goods, services, etc.

sales•per•son /'seylz,pɑrsən/ *n.* [count] one who sells goods, services, etc.

sa•line /'seyliyn, -layn/ *adj.* salty: *saline soil.*

sa•li•va /sə'layvə/ *n.* [noncount] a watery fluid in the mouth. —**sal•i•var•y** /'sælə,vɛriy/, *adj.*

sal•low /'sælow/ *adj.*, **-er, -est.** of a sickly, yellowish color: *a sallow complexion.*

salm•on /'sæmən/ *n.*, *pl.* **-ons,** (*esp. when thought of as a group*) **-on. 1.** [count] a fish having edible, pink flesh. **2.** [noncount] a light yellowish pink.

sal•mo•nel•la /,sælmə'nɛlə/ *n.* [count], *pl.* **-nel•lae** /-'nɛliy/, **-nel•las.** a bacterium that causes food poisoning.

sa•loon /sə'luwn/ *n.* [count] a place where alcoholic drinks are sold and drunk.

sal•sa /'sɑlsə, -sɑ/ *n.* [noncount], *pl.* **-sas.** a sauce, esp. a spicy sauce containing hot chilies.

salt /sɔlt/ *n.* **1.** [noncount] a white, crystal-like substance, used for flavoring food. **2.** [count] a chemical compound formed by combining an acid and a base. —*v.* [~ + obj] **3.** to put salt in or on. —*Idiom.* **4. take (something) with a grain** or **pinch of salt,** to be somewhat doubtful about: *The company claimed to have made a million dollars in profits, but I'd take that figure with a grain of salt.* —**'salt•y,** *adj.*, **-i•er, -i•est.**

salt•cel•lar /'sɔlt,sɛlər/ *n.* [count] a small container from which the salt can be shaken.

sal•tine /sɔl'tiyn/ *n.* [count] a crisp, salted cracker.

'salt,shak•er /'sɔlt,ʃeykər/ *n.* [count] a small container for salt, as at the table, from which the salt can be shaken.

salt•wa•ter /'sɔlt,wɔtər, -,wɒtər/ *adj.* [before a noun] of or relating to salt water: *saltwater fish.*

sa•lute /sə'luwt/ *n.*, *v.*, **-lut•ed, -lut•ing.** —*n.* [count] **1.** a formal gesture of respect, as raising the hand to the forehead. —*v.* **2.** to give a salute to (someone or something): [no obj]: *The soldiers saluted smartly.* [~ + obj]: *They saluted the flag.* **3.** [~ + obj] to express respect or praise for: *We salute the dead of our past wars.*

sal•vage /'sælvɪdʒ/ *n.*, *v.*, **-vaged, -vag•ing.** —*n.* [noncount] **1.** the saving of a ship or its cargo from the sea. **2.** the saving of anything from danger or destruction. **3.** the property, etc., saved this way. —*v.* [~ + obj] **4.** to save from shipwreck, fire, or other danger.

sal•va•tion /sæl'veyʃən/ *n.* [noncount] **1.** the act of saving or the state of being saved from harm, loss, or sin. **2.** a cause or means of being saved: *That loan was my salvation.*

salve /sæv, sɑv/ *n.*, *v.*, **salved, salv•ing.** —*n.* **1.** a paste containing medicine for treating wounds: [count]: *greasy, soothing salves.* [noncount]: *Rub salve on the wound.* —*v.* [~ + obj] **2.** to soothe: *to salve one's conscience.*

same /seym/ *adj.* [before a noun] **1.** identical with the thing mentioned: *This street is the same one we were on yesterday.* **2.** exactly alike: *two boxes of the same dimensions.* **3.** unchanged: *It's the same town after all these years.* —*pron.* [the + ~] **4.** the same person, thing, or kind of thing: *She wants a computer, and I want the same.* —*Idiom.* **5. all the same, a.** anyway; nevertheless: *I know you're tired, but all the same, I wish you'd stay.* **b.** of no difference: *It's all the same to me whether you go or not.* **6. just the same, a.** in the same way. **b.** nevertheless; all the same. **7. the same,** in an identical or similar way: *I see the same through your glasses as through mine.*

sam•ple /'sæmpəl/ *n.*, *v.*, **-pled, -pling.** —*n.* [count] **1.** a small part from a larger whole that shows what the whole is like: *a paint sample.* —*v.* [~ + obj] **2.** to take a sample of: *I sampled the food before serving it.*

san•a•to•ri•um /,sænə'tɔriyəm/ *n.* [count], *pl.* **-to•ri•ums, -to•ri•a** /-'tɔriyə/. a hospital for the treatment of long-lasting illnesses.

sanc•tion /'sæŋkʃən/ *n.* **1.** [noncount] official approval from an authority. **2.** [count] action by a state to force another state to follow rules, etc.: *to impose sanctions against a hostile nation.* —*v.* [~ + obj] **3.** to allow officially: *No one will sanction such violence.*

sanc•tu•ar•y /'sæŋktʃuw,ɛriy/ *n.*, *pl.* **-ar•ies. 1.** [count] a sacred or holy place. **2.** [count] a place that provides refuge, esp. (formerly) freedom from being arrested. **3.** [noncount] the protection provided by such a place; asylum: *The thief claimed that the chapel provided sanctuary.* **4.** [count] an area where wildlife live and breed in safety.

sand /sænd/ *n.* **1.** [noncount] the powdery, loose grains made from rocks rubbing against each other: *a beach of white sand.* —*v.* [~ + obj] **2.** to make smooth with sandpaper. —**'sand•er,** *n.* [count] —**'sand•y,** *adj.*

san•dal /'sændl/ *n.* [count] a shoe made up of a

bottom and straps by which it is fastened to the foot.

sand•bag /ˈsænd,bæg/ *n., v.,* **-bagged, -bag•ging.** **1.** [count] a bag filled with sand, used to protect against the water, etc.: *We built a wall of sandbags against the flood.* —*v.* [~ + obj] **2.** to furnish with sandbags, so as to protect.

'sand ,bar, *n.* [count] a bar of sand formed by the action of tides or currents.

sand•box /ˈsænd,bɒks/ *n.* [count] a box for holding sand, esp. one for children to play in.

sand•pa•per /ˈsænd,peypər/ *n.* [noncount] paper coated with a layer of sand, used for smoothing or polishing.

sand•wich /ˈsændwɪtʃ, ˈsæn-/ *n.* [count] **1.** two slices of bread with other food between them. —*v.* [~ + obj] **2.** to put (something or someone) between two other persons or things: *a suspected thief sandwiched between two police officers.*

sane /seyn/ *adj.,* **san•er, san•est. 1.** having a healthy mind. **2.** having good sense. —**'sane•ly,** *adv.*

sang /sæŋ/ *v.* pt. of SING.

san•i•tar•y /ˈsænɪ,tɛriy/ *adj.* **1.** of or relating to health, esp. cleanliness, prevention of disease, etc.: *sanitary regulations.* **2.** free from dirt, bacteria, etc.

'sanitary 'napkin, *n.* [count] a pad of soft, absorbent material, such as cotton, worn by women during their menstrual period to absorb the flow.

san•i•ta•tion /,sænɪˈteyʃən/ *n.* [noncount] systems for disposal of sewage and solid waste: *the department of sanitation.*

san•i•tize /ˈsænɪ,tayz/ *v.* [~ + obj], **-tized, -tiz•ing.** to make sanitary, as by cleaning or sterilizing.

san•i•ty /ˈsænɪtiy/ *n.* [noncount] the state of being sane: *The court did not question the sanity of the witness.*

sank /sæŋk/ *v.* a pt. of SINK.

sap¹ /sæp/ *n.* [noncount] a watery juice that passes through the tissues of a plant.

sap² /sæp/ *v.* [~ + obj], **sapped, sap•ping.** to weaken slowly: *Over time the disease sapped his strength.*

sap•ling /ˈsæplɪŋ/ *n.* [count] a young tree.

sap•phire /ˈsæfayᵊr/ *n.* [noncount] [count] a bright blue precious gem.

sar•casm /ˈsɑrkæzəm/ *n.* [noncount] bitter statements that mean the opposite of what is said: *"Oh, this is very good work," he said with obvious sarcasm, staring at the low test grade.* —**sar'cas•tic,** *adj.*

sar•dine /sɑrˈdiyn/ *n.* [count], pl. *(esp. when thought of as a group)* **-dine,** *(esp. for kinds or species)* **-dines.** a small fish used as food.

sa•ri /ˈsɑriy/ *n.* [count], pl. **-ris.** a type of dress made of a long cloth wrapped around the body, worn chiefly in India.

sash¹ /sæʃ/ *n.* [count] a long band or scarf worn over one shoulder or around the waist.

sash² /sæʃ/ *n.* [count] a framework, as in a window, in which panes of glass are set.

sat /sæt/ *v.* a pt. and pp. of SIT.

Sat., an abbreviation of: Saturday.

Sa•tan /ˈseytṇ/ *n.* the devil.

satch•el /ˈsætʃəl/ *n.* [count] a small bag.

sat•el•lite /ˈsætḷ,ayt/ *n.* [count] **1.** a natural body in space, as a moon, that revolves around a planet. **2.** a device launched into orbit around the earth, another planet, the sun, etc.: *a satellite that takes photographs of the earth.* **3.** a country under the control or influence of another.

sat•in /ˈsætṇ/ *n.* [noncount] a fabric that is smooth and shiny.

sat•ire /ˈsætayᵊr/ *n.* **1.** [noncount] the use of ridicule to make a person or thing look foolish or evil. **2.** [count] a piece of writing or a performance doing this. —**sa•tir•i•cal** /səˈtɪrɪkəl/, *adj.*

sat•i•rize /ˈsætə,rayz/ *v.* [~ + obj], **-rized, -riz•ing.** to make fun of by using satire: *The actors satirized several presidents.*

sat•is•fac•tion /,sætɪsˈfækʃən/ *n.* **1.** [noncount] the feeling of being satisfied: *satisfaction at a job well done.* **2.** [count] a means of fulfilling a need. **3.** [noncount] money or action to pay for a wrong: *They demanded satisfaction for the damage done to their house.*

sat•is•fac•to•ry /,sætɪsˈfæktəriy, -ˈfæktriy/ *adj.* good enough: *I gave him a satisfactory answer.* —**sat•is•fac•to•ri•ly** /,sætɪsˈfæktərəliy/, *adv.*

sat•is•fy /ˈsætɪs,fay/ *v.* [~ + obj], **-fied, -fy•ing.** **1.** to fulfill the desires or demands of: *Only a full apology will satisfy me.* **2.** to fulfill (a desire or need): *This food will satisfy her hunger.* **3.** to give (someone) proof; convince: *to satisfy oneself by investigation of the facts.* **4.** to fulfill (a demand or condition); meet: *He can't become a member unless certain requirements are satisfied.*

sat•u•rate /ˈvˈsætʃə,reyt/ *adj.* -ərɪt, -ə,reyt/ *v.* [~ + obj], **-rat•ed, -rat•ing.** **1.** to fill as much as possible: *The smell of roses saturated the air.* **2.** to cause to become very wet: *The rain saturated the fields.* —**sat•u•ra•tion** /,sætʃəˈreyʃən/, *n.* [noncount]

Sat•ur•day /ˈsætər,dey, -diy/ *n.* [count] the seventh day of the week, following Friday.

sauce /sɔs/ *n.* **1.** a liquid put on food to flavor it: [noncount]: *spaghetti sauce.* [count]: *some spicy sauces.* **2.** [noncount] stewed fruit: *cranberry sauce.*

sauce•pan /ˈsɔs,pæn/ *n.* [count] a cooking pan of medium depth, usually with a long handle.

sau•cer /ˈsɔsər/ *n.* [count] a small, shallow dish for holding a cup.

sau•na /ˈsɔnə, ˈsaw-/ *n.* [count], pl. **-nas.** a very hot room for a steam bath.

saun•ter /ˈsɔntər, ˈsɑn-/ *v.* [no obj] to walk in an unhurried way.

sau•sage /ˈsɔsɪdʒ/ *n.* [count] [noncount] finely chopped, seasoned meat stuffed into a casing.

sav•age /ˈsævɪdʒ/ *adj.* **1.** fierce; wild: *savage beasts.* **2.** cruel; vicious: *savage criticism of her book.* **3.** uncivilized. —*n.* [count] **4.** an uncivilized human being. —**'sav•age•ly,** *adv.*

sav•age•ry /ˈsævədʒriy/ *n.* [noncount] savage behavior.

sa•van•na or **sa•van•nah** /səˈvænə/ *n.* [count], pl. **-nas** or **-nahs.** a mostly flat area of coarse grass and scattered tree growth.

save /seyv/ *v.,* **saved, sav•ing. 1.** [~ + obj] to rescue from danger or harm. **2.** [~ + obj] to keep safe: *"God save the queen," they shouted.* **3.** [~ + obj] to avoid the using up of (some resource): *to save fuel by driving at 55 mph.* **4.** to set (money) aside for future use: [~ + obj]: *to save (up) money for college; to save money (up).* [no obj] *We'll just have to save for college.* **5.** [~ + obj] to copy (computer data) onto a hard or floppy disk, etc.: *Save your file before turning off the computer.*

sav•ing /ˈseyvɪŋ/ *n.* [count] **1.** a lessening of spending, or something saved: *a saving of over*

$50,000 a year. **2. savings,** [*plural*] money saved and put in a safe place.

sav•ior or **sav•iour** /'seyvyər/ *n.* **1.** [*count*] one who rescues: *the savior of the country.* **2.** a title of Jesus: *our Savior.*

sa•vor /'seyvər/ *v.* [~ + *obj*] **1.** to sense (something) by taste or smell, esp. with enjoyment: *savoring the chocolate.* **2.** to enjoy: *She savored her victory.* Also, *esp. Brit.,* **'sa•vour.**

sa•vor•y /'seyvəriy/ *adj.,* **-i•er, -i•est. 1.** pleasant in taste or smell. **2.** pleasing or attractive. **3.** morally respectable. Also, *esp. Brit.,* **'sa•vour•y.**

saw¹ /sɔ/ *n., v.,* **sawed, sawed** or **sawn, saw•ing. —n.** [*count*] **1.** a thin blade of metal with sharp teeth for cutting. —*v.* [*no obj*] [~ + *obj*] **2.** to cut with a saw.

saw² /sɔ/ *v.* pt. of SEE¹.

saw•dust /'sɔ,dʌst/ *n.* [*noncount*] tiny pieces of wood produced when sawing.

saw•mill /'sɔ,mɪl/ *n.* [*count*] a building in which wood is sawed into planks, etc., by machinery.

sax•o•phone /'sæksə,fown/ *n.* a musical wind instrument having a cone-shaped tube with keys or valves: [*count*]: *a brand-new saxophone.* [*noncount*]: *He played saxophone with the jazz band.* —'**sax•o**,**phon•ist,** *n.* [*count*]

say /sey/ *v.,* said /sɛd/, **say•ing,** *n., interj.* —*v.* **1.** [~ + *obj*] to speak: *Don't say a word.* **2.** to express (something) in words: [*used with quotations*]: *"I'll be there," he said.* [~ + *obj*]: *I wrote and said (that) I wanted to see her again.* **3.** [~ + *obj*] to show: *The clock says ten-thirty.* —*n.* [*noncount*] **4.** the chance to state an opinion: *to have one's say in a decision.* —*interj.* **5.** (used to express surprise): *Say! That's great news!* —*Idiom.* **6. go without saying,** to be obvious: *It goes without saying (that) you must write a thank-you note for a gift.* **7. that is to say,** in other words; meaning that: *She lost the bet; that is to say, she had to pay us $100.* —Usage. The verbs SAY and TELL are sometimes confused. The verb SAY is not followed by a person as its object: *He said a few words and sat down.* If a person is mentioned after SAY, the word *to* must be used before it: *He said to her that he was ready.* The verb TELL may be followed by a person as an object: *He told him he was ready.* See also SPEAK.

say•ing /'seyɪŋ/ *n.* [*count*] something said, esp. a proverb: *the old saying, "A stitch in time saves nine."*

SC, an abbreviation of: South Carolina.

scab /skæb/ *n.* [*count*] the crusty, dry patch that forms over a wound.

scaf•fold /'skæfəld, -owld/ *n.* [*count*] **1.** a raised platform for workers and materials. **2.** a raised platform on which a criminal is executed by hanging.

scaf•fold•ing /'skæfəldɪŋ, -owl-/ *n.* [*noncount*] **1.** a scaffold or system of scaffolds. **2.** materials for scaffolds.

scald /skɔld/ *v.* [~ + *obj*] **1.** to burn with hot liquid or steam. **2.** to heat to a temperature just below the boiling point: *to scald milk.* —*n.* [*count*] **3.** a burn caused by scalding.

scale¹ /skeyl/ *n., v.,* **scaled, scal•ing. —n.** [*count*] **1.** one of the thin, flat plates that cover fish, snakes, or lizards. —*v.* [~ + *obj*] **2.** to remove the scales from: *to scale a fish.* —'**scal•y,** *adj.,* **-i•er, -i•est.**

scale² /skeyl/ *n.* [*count*] Often, **scales.** [*plural*] a device for weighing.

scale³ /skeyl/ *n., v.,* **scaled, scal•ing. —n.** [*count*] **1.** a series of marks at certain distances,

such as along a line, for measuring, adding, etc.: *the scale of a thermometer.* **2.** the ratio between the measurements on a map or model and the actual size: *a model on a scale of one inch to one foot.* **3.** relative size or extent: *planning done on a grand scale.* **4.** a series of musical tones arranged in order of pitch. —*v.* [~ + *obj*] **5.** to climb by or as if by a ladder: *He scaled the wall.* **6. scale down** (or **up**), to decrease (or increase) in amount: *to scale down wages.*

scal•lion /'skælyən/ *n.* [*count*] a kind of onion.

scal•lop /'skɒləp, 'skæl-/ *n.* [*count*] a sea animal with two wavy-edged shells.

scalp /skælp/ *n.* [*count*] **1.** the skin of the upper part of the head. —*v.* [~ + *obj*] **2.** to cut or tear the scalp from: *They scalped their victims.*

scal•pel /'skælpəl/ *n.* [*count*] a small, light, usually straight knife used in surgery, laboratory work, etc.

scam /skæm/ *n.* [*count*] an illegal scheme to make money: *One of his scams was to pose as a police officer.*

scamp•er /'skæmpər/ *v.* [*no obj*] **1.** to run or go hastily: *The dog scampered out of the room.* —*n.* [*count*] **2.** an act or instance of scampering.

scan /skæn/ *v.,* **scanned, scan•ning,** *n.* —*v.* [~ + *obj*] **1.** to examine (something) carefully: *scanning the crowd for his parents' faces.* **2.** to read quickly: *to scan the newspaper.* **3.** to examine (a body part) with a scanner: *to scan the kidneys.* —*n.* [*count*] **4.** an act or instance of scanning.

scan•dal /'skændḷ/ *n.* **1.** [*count*] an offensive or shocking action or situation: *Several scandals rocked the government.* **2.** [*noncount*] talk intended to harm others: *spreading scandal all over town.* —'**scan•dal•ous,** *adj.*

scan•dal•ize /'skændḷ,ayz/ *v.* [~ + *obj*], **-ized, -iz•ing.** to shock by something disgraceful or immoral: *behavior that scandalized the neighbors.*

scan•ner /'skænər/ *n.* [*count*] **1.** a device that scans, such as one that uses radar to detect or examine distant objects. **2.** a device for examining a body, organ, or tissue.

scant /skænt/ *adj.,* **-er, -est.** barely enough: *Her new book received scant attention in the press.*

scant•y /'skæntiy/ *adj.,* **-i•er, -i•est.** not enough in amount or size. —**scant•i•ly** /'skæntḷiy/, *adv.:* *scantily dressed.*

scape•goat /'skeyp,gowt/ *n.* [*count*] a person who is forced to take the blame for others.

scar /skɑr/ *n., v.,* **scarred, scar•ring.** —*n.* [*count*] **1.** a mark left by a healed wound. **2.** a lasting effect after a bad experience: *The trial left emotional scars.* —*v.* [~ + *obj*] **3.** to leave a scar on (someone or something).

scarce /skɛərs/ *adj.* [*often:* be + ~], **scarc•er, scarc•est.** hard to find: *Jobs are scarce in difficult times.* —**scar•ci•ty,** *n.* [*count*] [*noncount*], *pl.* **-ties.**

scarce•ly /'skɛərsliy/ *adv.* **1.** barely; not quite: *I can scarcely see.* **2.** definitely not: *This is scarcely the time to argue.*

scare /skɛər/ *v.,* **scared, scar•ing,** *n.* —*v.* **1.** [~ + *obj*] to frighten: *Something scared her.* **2.** [*no obj*] to become frightened: *She doesn't scare easily.* **3. scare off** or **away,** to frighten (someone) enough to cause him or her to run away: *We scared off the thief. They scared the thief away.* —*n.* [*count*] **4.** a sudden fright: *We got quite a scare when she stopped breathing.* —**scar•y,** *adj.,* **-i•er, -i•est.**

scare•crow /'skɛər,krow/ *n.* [*count*] a figure in

S

school

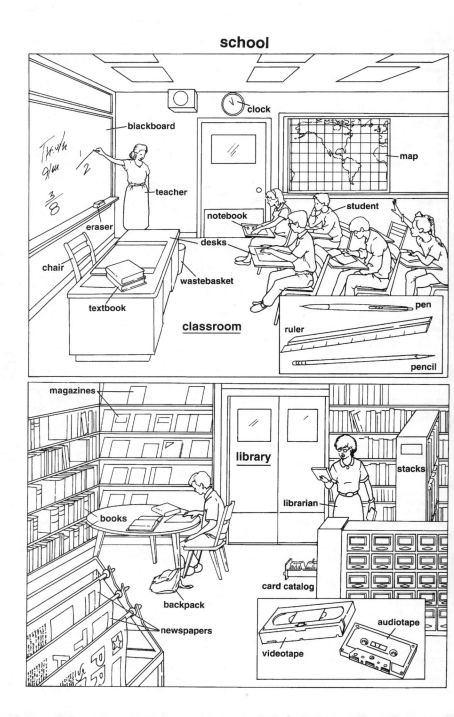

clock

blackboard

map

teacher

student

notebook

eraser

desks

chair

wastebasket

pen

textbook

ruler

classroom

pencil

magazines

library

stacks

librarian

books

card catalog

backpack

audiotape

newspapers

videotape

the shape of a person in old clothes, set up to frighten birds away from crops.

scarf /skɑrf/ n. [count], pl. **scarfs, scarves** /skɑrvz/ a long strip of cloth worn about the neck.

scar•let /'skɑrlɪt/ n. [noncount] a bright red color.

'**scarlet** '**fever,** n. [noncount] a disease, esp. of children, that produces a high fever and a red rash.

scath•ing /'skeyðɪŋ/ adj. harsh; cruel: a scathing remark. —'**scath•ing•ly,** adv.

scat•ter /'skætər/ v. **1.** [~ + obj] to toss loosely about: to scatter seeds. **2.** to (cause to) separate: [~ + obj]: The police scattered the crowd. [no obj]: The crowd quickly scattered.

scat•ter•brain /'skætər,breyn/ n. [count] a foolish, forgetful person. —'**scat•ter,brained,** adj.

scav•enge /'skævɪndʒ/ v., **-enged, -eng•ing.** to gather (something usable) by searching through discarded food or rubbish: [no obj]: The vultures scavenged for food. [~ + obj]: He scavenged some automobile parts from the dump. —'**scav•en•ger,** n. [count]

sce•nar•i•o /sɪ'nɛəriy,ow, -'nɑr-/ n. [count], pl. **-i•os. 1.** an outline of a plot, describing the scenes, etc. **2.** an outline of possible events.

scene /siyn/ n. [count] **1.** the place where some action occurs or has occurred: the scene of the accident. **2.** a view: an artist who paints scenes of the South. **3.** an embarrassing display of emotion: Don't make a scene. **4.** a part of a play, etc., that represents a single episode: In the first scene the characters are introduced.

scen•er•y /'siynəriy/ n. [noncount] **1.** the general appearance of a place: beautiful scenery in the Alps. **2.** hangings, curtains, etc., used as background on a stage.

sce•nic /'siynɪk/ adj. having beautiful or pleasant scenery: a scenic park.

scent /sɛnt/ n. **1.** [count] a special smell, esp. when pleasant. **2.** [count] a smell by which an animal or person may be traced. **3.** [noncount] perfume. **4.** [noncount] the sense of smell: animals with keen scent. —v. [~ + obj] **5.** to recognize by or as if by the sense of smell: to scent trouble. **6.** to fill with an odor or smell: a room heavily scented with pine. —'**scent•ed,** adj.

scep•ter /'sɛptər/ n. [count] a rod held in the hand as a sign of royal power. Also, esp. Brit., '**scep•tre.**

sched•ule /'skɛdʒuwl, -ʊl, -uwəl/ n., v., **-uled, -ul•ing.** —n. [count] **1.** a list of events, times of performances, etc. **2.** a timetable: a train schedule for next year. —v. [~ + obj] **3.** to make a schedule of or enter in a schedule: a flight scheduled for six o'clock.

scheme /skiym/ n., v., **schemed, schem•ing.** —n. [count] **1.** a plan of action: a clever scheme to speed up production. **2.** a dishonest, usually secret plot. —v. [no obj] **3.** to create (something) as a scheme; plot: He schemed to avoid doing the work. —'**schem•er,** n. [count]

schiz•o•phre•ni•a /,skɪtsə'friyniyə, -'friynyə/ n. [noncount] a severe mental disorder. —,**schiz•o'phren•ic,** adj., n. [count]

schol•ar /'skɒlər/ n. [count] **1.** a person of great learning. **2.** a student. —'**schol•ar•ly,** adj.

schol•ar•ship /'skɒlər,ʃɪp/ n. **1.** [count] a gift of money to help a student with his or her studies: awarded a full scholarship. **2.** [noncount] the qualities or accomplishments of a scholar.

scho•las•tic /skə'læstɪk/ adj. [before a noun] of or relating to schools or education.

school[1] /skuwl/ n. **1.** a place for teaching people: [count]: His children went to a private school. Did she go to driving school? [noncount]: Are your children old enough to go to school? **2.** [count] a college or university. **3.** [count] an academic department for instruction in a particular field: the school of engineering. **4.** [noncount] the activity of teaching or of learning: School doesn't start until September. **5.** [count] a group of pupils or followers of a certain master, system, etc.: the Platonic school of philosophy. —v. [~ + obj] **6.** to educate in or as if in a school; teach: He was schooled in magic and sorcery.

school[2] /skuwl/ n. [count] a large number of fish, porpoises, etc., feeding or traveling together.

school•mas•ter /'skuwl,mæstər/ n. [count] a man who teaches in a school.

schoon•er /'skuwnər/ n. [count] a kind of sailing vessel having a mast in front and a main mast.

sci•ence /'sayəns/ n. **1.** [noncount] a system of knowledge about the physical world, obtained by observing and experimenting and explained in general laws. **2.** [noncount] the study that yields this knowledge. **3.** a branch of this study, such as physics or chemistry: [count]: the social sciences. [noncount]: You need one more course in science to graduate.

'**science** '**fiction,** n. [noncount] fiction that is based on scientific knowledge but describes imaginary societies, inventions, etc., of the future.

sci•en•tif•ic /,sayən'tɪfɪk/ adj. [before a noun] of or relating to science or the sciences: scientific studies.

sci•en•tist /'sayəntɪst/ n. [count] an expert in science.

sci-fi /'say'fay/ n., adj. Informal. science fiction.

scin•til•lat•ing /'sɪntl,eytɪŋ/ adj. clever or witty: a scintillating conversation. —**scin•til•la•tion** /,sɪntl'eyʃən/, n. [noncount]

scis•sors /'sɪzərz/ n. a cutting instrument for paper, cloth, etc., made of two blades: [plural; used with a plural verb]: The scissors are on the table; could you hand them to me? [count; used with a singular verb; a pair of + ~]: I need a pair of scissors.

scoff /skɔf, skɒf/ v. [no obj] to mock; jeer: He scoffed at her fears.

scold /skowld/ v. [~ + obj] to find fault with someone in an angry way.

scoop /skuwp/ n. [count] **1.** a short-handled utensil shaped like a shovel, used for measuring flour, etc. **2.** a utensil made of a small bowl and a handle, for dishing out ice cream, etc. **3.** a news item appearing in one newspaper, etc., before all others. —v. [~ + obj] **4.** to take up or out with or as if with a scoop: She scooped some ice cream. **5. scoop up,** to gather by a sweeping motion of one's arms or hands: She scooped up her books or She scooped her books up.

scoot /skuwt/ v. [no obj] to go swiftly.

scoot•er /'skuwtər/ n. [count] **1.** a child's vehicle that has two wheels and is made to move by pushing one foot against the ground. **2.** Also called **motor scooter.** a similar but larger and heavier vehicle for adults, propelled by a motor.

scope /skowp/ n. [noncount] **1.** range of view, outlook, etc.: a question beyond the scope of this paper. **2.** chance for activity: to give one's imagination full scope.

scorch /skɔrtʃ/ v. **1.** to burn slightly: [~ + obj]:

S

The hot iron *scorched* the shirt. [*no obj*]: *The shirt will scorch if your iron is too hot.* **2.** [~ + *obj*] to dry up with heat: *The sun scorched the grass.*

score /skɔr/ *n., pl.* **scores; score** for 4; *v.,* **scored, scor•ing.** —*n.* [*count*] **1.** the number of points made by the players in a game or contest: *The score was 4-3.* **2.** performance on an examination: *Her score on the test was 99%.* **3.** a scratch: *scores on the table.* **4.** twenty: *a score of victims.* **5.** a written copy of a piece of music. —*v.* **6.** to earn in a game, as points: [~ + *obj*]: *Our team scored 3 runs in the first inning.* [*no obj*]: *We failed to score in the first half.* **7.** to get a score of: [~ + *obj*]: *I scored 98 on the test.* [*no obj*]: *How well did you score on the last test?* **8.** to keep score, as of a game: [*no obj*]: *He scored for us as we bowled.* [~ + *obj*]: *Someone has to score the game for us.* **9.** [~ + *obj*] **a.** to arrange music for certain instruments. **b.** to compose the music for (a movie, play, etc.). **10.** [~ + *obj*] to cut shallow ridges or lines on something. **11.** to achieve a success: [~ + *obj*]: *The author scored another triumph with his new book.* [*no obj*]: *The director scored again with his third major film this year.*

scorn /skɔrn/ *n.* [*noncount*] **1.** open contempt. —*v.* [~ + *obj*] **2.** to refuse with contempt: *She scorned my help.*

scorn•ful /ˈskɔrnfəl/ *adj.* of or relating to scorn: *scornful remarks; a scornful attitude.* [*be* + ~ + *of*]: *He was scornful of people who didn't earn a lot of money.* —**ˈscorn•ful•ly,** *adv.*

scor•pi•on /ˈskɔrpiyən/ *n.* [*count*] a small animal that has front claws and a poisonous stinger in its tail.

Scot /skɒt/ *n.* [*count*] a person born or living in Scotland. Also, **ˈScots•man, ˈScots,wom•an.**

Scotch /skɒtʃ/ *n.* [*noncount*][*count*] whiskey made in Scotland.

ˈScotch ˈtape, *Trademark.* [*noncount*] a brand name for tapes made of clear plastic.

ˈscot-ˈfree, *adv.* free from harm or punishment: *He went off scot-free after the murder.*

Scot•tish /ˈskɒtɪʃ/ *adj.* Also, **Scots. 1.** of or relating to Scotland or its inhabitants. **2.** [*plural; the* + ~; *used with a plural verb*] the people born or living in Scotland.

scoun•drel /ˈskawndrəl/ *n.* [*count*] a dishonest, wicked, selfish, or dishonorable person.

scour¹ /skawᵊr, ˈskawər/ *v.* [~ + *obj*] to cleanse by hard rubbing: *to scour a dirty frying pan.*

scour² /skawᵊr, ˈskawər/ *v.* [~ + *obj*] to search (an area) carefully: *to scour the countryside for a lost child.*

scourge /skɜrdʒ/ *n.* [*count*] a cause of great trouble: *the scourge of famine.*

scout /skawt/ *n.* [*count*] **1.** a person sent out to obtain information. **2.** [*sometimes: Scout*] a member of the Boy Scouts or Girl Scouts. —*v.* [*no obj*] **3.** to make a search: *scouting around for a good restaurant.*

scowl /skawl/ *v.* [*no obj*] **1.** to frown deeply. —*n.* [*count*] **2.** a deep frown on one's face.

scrag•gly /ˈskræɡliy/ *adj.,* **-gli•er, -gli•est. 1.** irregular; uneven. **2.** not neat in appearance: *a scraggly beard.*

scram /skræm/ *v.* [*no obj*], **scrammed, scram•ming.** *Informal.* to go away quickly.

scram•ble /ˈskræmbəl/ *v.,* **-bled, -bling,** *n.* —*v.* **1.** [*no obj*] to climb using one's hands and feet: *The hikers scrambled quickly up the hill.* **2.** [*no obj*] to compete with others to gain something: *to scramble for a new job.* **3.** [~ + *obj*] to mix

something up: *He scrambled his words.* **4.** [~ + *obj*] to fry (eggs) while constantly stirring them. —*n.* [*count*] **5.** a quick climb or movement over rough, irregular ground. **6.** any disorderly rush.

scrap¹ /skræp/ *n., v.,* **scrapped, scrap•ping.** —*n.* **1.** [*count*] a small piece: *a scrap of paper.* **2.** **scraps,** [*plural*] bits of leftover food. **3.** [*noncount*] material that has been thrown away and can be reused. —*v.* [~ + *obj*] **4.** to throw away as useless: *We scrapped our plans.*

scrap² /skræp/ *n., v.,* **scrapped, scrap•ping.** *Informal.* —*n.* [*count*] **1.** a fight. —*v.* [*no obj*] **2.** fight.

scrap•book /ˈskræp,bʊk/ *n.* [*count*] a book in which pictures, newspaper articles, etc., may be pasted.

scrape /skreyp/ *v.,* **scraped, scrap•ing,** *n.* —*v.* **1.** [~ + *obj*] to rub (a surface) with something rough: *to scrape a table to remove paint.* **2.** [~ + *obj*] to remove (paint, etc.) by rubbing with something rough or sharp: *to scrape the paint from the table.* **3.** [~ + *obj*] to injure by brushing against something rough or sharp: *I scraped my knee when I fell.* **4.** to rub roughly on (something): [~ + *obj*]: *He scraped the floor with his chair.* [*no obj*]: *The chair scraped on the floor.* **5. scrape up** or **together,** to collect with difficulty: *Can you scrape up enough money for college? She scraped enough money together for college.* —*n.* [*count*] **6.** an act or sound of scraping. **7.** a scraped place: *a bad scrape on the arm.* **8.** a difficult situation. —**ˈscrap•er,** *n.* [*count*]

scratch /skrætʃ/ *v.* **1.** to mark the surface of by scraping with something rough: [~ + *obj*]: *The cat scratched her.* [*no obj*]: *The cat scratched at the door.* **2.** [~ + *obj*] [*no obj*] to scrape slightly, as with the fingernails, to relieve itching. **3.** [~ + *obj*] to reject (an idea, etc.). —*n.* [*count*] **4.** a slight injury or mark caused by scratching. **5.** the act or sound of scratching. —*Idiom.* **6. from scratch, a.** from the beginning: *Let's start from scratch.* **b.** using basic pieces or ingredients rather than prepared or processed ones: *to bake a cake from scratch.*

scrawl /skrɔl/ *v.* [~ + *obj*] **1.** to write or draw in a careless manner: *He scrawled his name on the form.* —*n.* [*count; usually singular*] **2.** careless handwriting: *Nobody could read his scrawl.*

scrawn•y /ˈskrɔniy/ *adj.,* **-i•er, -i•est.** very thin; lean: *scrawny kids.*

scream /skriym/ *v.* **1.** to make a loud, sharp cry: [*no obj*]: *I screamed with fright.* [~ + *obj*]: *to scream an answer.* [*used with quotations*]: *"Get out of here!" she screamed.* **2.** [*no obj*] to give off a loud, high sound: *The sirens screamed.* —*n.* [*count*] **3.** a shrill, piercing sound: *the scream of the jet planes.* —**ˈscream•er,** *n.* [*count*]

screech /skriytʃ/ *v.* **1.** to make a harsh, shrill sound: [*no obj*]: *The car's tires screeched.* [~ + *obj*]: *to scream an answer.* [*used with quotations*]: *"Get out of here!" she screeched.* —*n.* [*count*] **2.** a harsh, shrill sound: *the screech of tires.*

screen /skriyn/ *n.* [*count*] **1.** a device, usually a covered frame, that provides shelter, separates parts of a room, etc.: *The doctor placed a screen around the patient's bed.* **2.** a surface on which motion pictures may be shown. **3.** the part of a television or computer on which a picture is formed or information is displayed. **4.** anything that shelters or hides: *a screen of trees.* **5.** a frame holding a mesh of wire, for placing in a window, etc. —*v.* [~ + *obj*] **6.** to hide with or as if with a screen: *The tall trees screened the house from view.* **7.** to examine and accept or reject: *We screened several applicants for the job.* **8.** to provide with a screen or screens: *to screen in the porch.* **9.** to show (a motion picture) on a screen.

screen•play /'skriyn,pley/ *n.* [count] the outline or full script of a motion picture.

screw /skruw/ *n.* [count] **1.** a nail-like metal fastener, having a thin end with a spiral groove and a head with a slot. —*v.* **2.** [~ + *obj*] to turn (a screw). **3.** to (cause to) be fastened with or as if with a screw: [~ + *obj*]: *He screwed the seats into the floor.* [*no obj*]: *The seats screw into the floor.* **4.** to tighten or loosen (a threaded part) by twisting: [~ + *obj*]: *Screw the top of the bottle back on. Screw on the lid.* [*no obj*]: *The lid screws off.* **5. screw up,** *Slang.* to make a mess (of): *He screwed up every job we gave him. He screwed the job up. He's always screwing up.* —*Idiom.* **6. have a screw loose,** *Slang.* to behave or think oddly.

screw•driv•er /'skruw,drayvər/ *n.* [count] a hand tool for tightening or loosening a screw.

scrib•ble /'skrɪbəl/ *v.,* **-bled, -bling,** *n.* —*v.* **1.** to write quickly and carelessly: [~ + *obj*]: *to scribble a letter.* [*no obj*]: *scribbling in his notebook.* —*n.* **2.** [count] a hasty drawing or piece of writing. **3.** [*noncount*] handwriting that is hard to read.

scribe /skrayb/ *n.* [count] one who wrote copies of written things before the invention of printing.

script /skrɪpt/ *n.* **1.** [*noncount*] handwriting, esp. writing in which the letters are joined together. **2.** [count] the written words of a play, movie, etc. **3.** any system of writing: [*noncount*]: *Persian script.* [count]: *an ancient script.*

Scrip•ture /'skrɪptʃər/ *n.* Often, **Scriptures.** Also called **Holy Scripture.** the sacred writings of the Bible: [*plural*]: *The Scriptures tell us it is wrong to kill.* [*noncount*]: *Scripture tells us little about Jesus' early life.* —**'scrip•tur•al,** *adj.*

scroll /skrowl/ *n.* [count] **1.** a roll of paper used for writing: *the ancient scrolls found near the Dead Sea.* —*v.* [*no obj*] **2.** (on a computer display) to move a cursor smoothly, causing new data to replace old on the monitor: *As you type, your old data will scroll up.*

scrounge /skrawndʒ/ *v.,* **scrounged, scroung•ing.** to borrow without expecting to repay: [*no obj*]: *to scrounge off his friends.* [~ + *obj*]: *to scrounge a cigarette.* —**'scroung•er,** *n.*

scrub¹ /skrʌb/ *v.,* **scrubbed, scrub•bing,** *n.* —*v.* **1.** [~ + *obj*] [*no obj*] to rub hard with a brush, cloth, etc., in washing. **2.** [~ + *obj*] to remove (dirt, etc.) from something by hard rubbing while washing: *to scrub grime from the walls.* —*n.* [count] **3.** an act or instance of scrubbing.

scrub² /skrʌb/ *n.* [*noncount*] low trees or shrubs.

scruff /skrʌf/ *n.* [count] the back of the neck.

scruff•y /'skrʌfiy/ *adj.,* **-i•er, -i•est.** untidy; wearing worn clothes; shabby.

scrump•tious /'skrʌmpʃəs/ *adj.* extremely pleasing to the taste: *a scrumptious dinner.*

scrunch•y or **scrunch•ie** /'skrʌntʃiy/ *n.* [count], *pl.* **scrunch•ies.** an elastic fabric band, used to fasten the hair.

scru•ple /'skruwpəl/ *n.* a moral belief that prevents a person from doing certain actions: [count]: *His scruples kept him from stealing.* [*noncount*]: *killing without scruple.*

scru•pu•lous /'skruwpyələs/ *adj.* **1.** of or relating to scruples. **2.** strictly exact: *scrupulous honesty.* —**'scru•pu•lous•ly,** *adv.*

scru•ti•nize /'skruwtṇ,ayz/ *v.* [~ + *obj*], **-nized, -niz•ing.** to examine carefully: *He scrutinized the report.*

scru•ti•ny /'skruwtṇiy/ *n.* [*noncount*] a careful examination.

scu•ba /'skuwbə/ *n., pl.* **-bas. 1.** [count] a breathing device strapped on the back of a diver. **2.** [*noncount*] the act of swimming underwater with such a device.

scuff /skʌf/ *v.* [~ + *obj*] **1.** to make a mark on (something) by hard use, such as shoes. **2.** to drag (one's foot or feet) over something.

scuf•fle /'skʌfəl/ *v.,* **-fled, -fling,** *n.* —*v.* [*no obj*] **1.** to struggle in a rough, disorderly manner: *scuffling with the mugger.* —*n.* [count] **2.** a rough, confused fight.

sculpt /skʌlpt/ *v.* to carve, model, or make by sculpture: [*no obj*]: *The artist sculpts in wood.* [~ + *obj*]: *to sculpt figures of marble.*

sculp•tor /'skʌlptər/ *n.* [count] one who makes sculptures.

sculp•ture /'skʌlptʃər/ *n., v.,* **-tured, -tur•ing.** —*n.* **1.** [*noncount*] the art of making figures from marble, metal, wood, etc. **2.** [*noncount*] such works of art thought of as a group. **3.** [count] a piece of such work: *a sculpture by Rodin.* —*v.* [~ + *obj*] **4.** to carve or make (a piece of sculpture).

scum /skʌm/ *n.* [*noncount*] **1.** a layer of matter on the surface of a liquid: *pond scum.* **2.** low, worthless people.

scur•ry /'skɜriy, 'skʌriy/ *v.* [*no obj*], **-ried, -ry•ing.** to move in a great hurry: *We scurried around trying to get ready for the wedding.*

scuzz•y /'skʌziy/ *adj.,* **-i•er, -i•est.** *Slang.* dirty; disgusting.

scythe /sayð/ *n.* [count] a tool that has a long, curving blade for cutting grass, grain, etc., by hand.

SD, an abbreviation of: South Dakota.

sea /siy/ *n.* **1.** the salt waters that cover most of the earth's surface; ocean: [count]: *the seven seas.* [*noncount*]: *The early settlers traveled great distances by sea.* **2.** [count; usually: the + ~] an area of these waters, marked off by land boundaries: *The Dead Sea is between Israel and Jordan.* **3.** [count] a large amount: *a sea of faces.* —*Idiom.* **4. at sea, a.** on the ocean. **b.** confused; uncertain: *was totally at sea in his new job.*

sea•board /'siy,bɔrd/ *n.* [count] **1.** the line where land and sea meet. **2.** a region or area of land bordering a coast: *the eastern seaboard.*

sea•coast /'siy,kowst/ *n.* [count] the land next to the sea.

sea•far•er /'siy,fɛərər/ *n.* [count] **1.** a sailor. **2.** a traveler on the sea. —**'sea,far•ing,** *adj.*: *The Vikings were a seafaring people.*

sea•food /'siy,fuwd/ *n.* [*noncount*] any fish or shellfish from the sea used for food.

'sea ,gull, *n.* [count] a gull living near the sea.

'sea ,horse or **'sea,horse,** *n.* [count] a fish having a head and neck resembling that of a horse.

seal¹ /siyl/ *n.* [count] **1.** an emblem, symbol, etc., placed on something to show that it is genuine: *the president's seal of office on the stationery.* **2.** a metal stamp engraved with such an emblem. **3.** a piece of wax or similar material stuck on to a document, envelope, etc., that must be broken when the object is opened. **4.** anything that

S

closes or fastens a thing: *a seal on the bottle.* **5.** anything that serves as a sign to give assurance or confirmation: *the seal of approval.* —*v.* [~ + *obj*] **6.** to place a seal on (something): *to seal the document.* **7.** to close with a fastening that must be broken to open: *to seal a letter in the envelope.* **8.** to fasten by or as if by a seal: *My lips are sealed; I won't tell anyone.* **9.** to decide: *His mistake sealed his fate.*

seal² /siyl/ *n.* [*count*], *pl.* **seals,** (*esp. when thought of as a group*) **seal.** a fish-eating mammal with flippers, that lives in or near the sea.

'sea ˌlevel, *n.* [*noncount*] the average level of the surface of the sea between high and low tide.

'sea ˌlion, *n.* [*count*] a large-eared seal having a blunt nose.

seam /siym/ *n.* [*count*] **1.** the line formed by sewing together pieces of cloth, etc. **2.** a thin layer of a mineral between other rocks.

sea•man /'siymən/ *n.* [*count*], *pl.* **-men.** a sailor.

sea•plane /'siy,pleyn/ *n.* [*count*] an airplane with floats for water takeoffs and landings.

sea•port /'siy,pɔrt/ *n.* [*count*] **1.** a port or harbor that can take in boats or ships. **2.** a town or city at such a place.

search /sɜrtʃ/ *v.* **1.** to examine or look through (a place, etc.) to find something: [~ + *obj*]: *I searched the house for my keys.* [*no obj*]: *I searched for my keys.* —*n.* [*count*] **2.** an act or instance of searching. —*Idiom.* **3.** **in search of,** looking for; trying to find: *early explorers in search of gold.*

search•ing /'sɜrtʃɪŋ/ *adj.* [*usually: before a noun*] **1.** sharply observing: *He gave me a searching look.* **2.** examining carefully: *a searching inspection.*

search•light /'sɜrtʃ,layt/ *n.* [*count*] a device for throwing a powerful beam of light.

sear•ing /'sɪərɪŋ/ *adj.* causing a sharp burning: *searing pain.*

sea•shell or **sea shell** /'siy,ʃɛl/ *n.* [*count*] the shell of an oyster, clam, etc.

sea•shore /'siy,ʃɔr/ *n.* [*noncount*] land along the sea.

sea•sick /'siy,sɪk/ *adj.* feeling sick to one's stomach as the result of the motion of a vessel at sea. —'**sea,sick•ness,** *n.* [*noncount*]

sea•side /'siy,sayd/ *n.* [*count; singular; usually: the* + ~] the land along the sea; seacoast.

sea•son /'siyzən/ *n.* [*count*] **1.** one of the four main periods of the year. **2.** a period of the year when something happens: *the tourist season.* —*v.* [~ + *obj*] **3.** to give flavor to (food) by adding salt, pepper, etc. **4.** to prepare for use, as by drying: *to season timber.* —*Idiom.* **5.** **in season,** available: *Asparagus is now in season.* **6. out of season,** not available: *Peaches are out of season.*

sea•son•a•ble /'siyzənəbəl/ *adj.* usual for the season: *seasonable temperatures.*

sea•son•al /'siyzənḷ/ *adj.* of or relating to a particular season: *seasonal work picking grapes.*

sea•son•ing /'siyzənɪŋ/ *n.* [*noncount*] [*count*] something, such as salt, an herb, or a spice, for flavoring food.

seat /siyt/ *n.* [*count*] **1.** something on which one sits, as a chair. **2.** the part of something on which one sits: *a chair seat.* **3.** the buttocks, or the part of the garment covering the buttocks: *the seat of his pants.* **4.** a place in which something occurs: *a college as a seat of learning.* **5.** a right to sit as a member, as in a legislative or financial body: *a seat on the stock exchange.* —*v.* [~ + *obj*] **6.** to place on a seat: *He seated himself by*

the window. **7.** to guide to a seat: *The ushers seated her in the front row.* **8.** to provide with seats: *a theater that seats 1200 people.*

'seat ˌbelt, *n.* [*count*] a strap to keep a passenger in a car, airplane, etc., firmly secure.

seat•ing /'siytɪŋ/ *n.* [*noncount*] the arrangement or providing of seats, as in a theater.

sea•weed /'siy,wiyd/ *n.* [*noncount*] any of various green plants that grow in the sea.

sec, an abbreviation of: second.

se•cede /sɪ'siyd/ *v.* [*no obj*], **-ced•ed, -ced•ing.** to withdraw from a group, organization, etc.: *The Confederate States claimed the right to secede from the Union.* —**se'ces•sion,** *n.* [*noncount*]

se•clude /sɪ'kluwd/ *v.* [~ + *obj*], **-clud•ed, -clud•ing. 1.** to remove from contact with other people: *He secluded himself in his room.* **2.** to shut off; keep apart: *They secluded the garden from the rest of the property.* —**se'clu•sion,** *n.* [*noncount*]

sec•ond¹ /'sɛkənd/ *adj.* **1.** next after the first: *the second person in command.* **2.** [*before a noun*] alternate: *every second week.* **3.** [*before a noun*] other; another: *a second pair of stockings.* —*n.* [*count*] **4.** a person or thing next after the first. **5.** Usually, **seconds.** [*plural*] an additional helping of food: *Can we have seconds on dessert?* **6.** Usually, **seconds.** [*plural*] goods of less than the highest quality. —*v.* [~ + *obj*] **7.** (in a meeting or debate) to express formal support of (a motion, etc.): *I second the motion.* —*adv.* **8.** in the second place: *The catcher is batting second.* —'**sec•ond•ly,** *adv.*

sec•ond² /'sɛkənd/ *n.* [*count*] **1.** the sixtieth part of a minute of time. **2.** a very short period of time: *It takes only a second to phone.*

sec•ond•ar•y /'sɛkən,dɛriy/ *adj.* **1.** next after the first in order, rank, or time. **2.** not original: *secondary sources.* **3.** of lesser importance: *For some employees, a high salary is secondary.* —'**sec•ond,ar•i•ly** /'sɛkən,dɛrəliy, ,sɛkən'dɛər-/ *adv.*

'secondary ˌschool, *n.* [*count*] a high school.

'second ˌhand, *n.* [*count*] **1.** the hand that indicates the seconds on a clock. —*adj.,* **sec•ond•hand** /'sɛkənd'hænd/. **2.** not directly experienced: *secondhand knowledge.* **3.** owned by someone else first: *secondhand clothes.* —*adv.* **4.** after another user or owner: *He bought it secondhand.* **5.** indirectly: *I heard the news secondhand.*

'second-'rate, *adj.* of lower quality: *a second-rate college.*

'second 'thought, *n.* [*count*] Often, **second thoughts.** [*plural*] considering a previous action, position, etc., again because one doubts its correctness: *We had second thoughts about firing her.*

se•cret /'siykrɪt/ *adj.* **1.** done without the knowledge of others: *a secret meeting.* **2.** kept from general knowledge: *a secret password.* —*n.* [*count*] **3.** something hidden: *She kept several secrets from her husband.* **4.** a reason not easily understood: *What is the secret of her success?* —*Idiom.* **5.** **in secret,** so as to remain hidden: *They met in secret.* —**'se•cre•cy,** *n.* [*noncount*] —'**se•cret•ly,** *adv.*

sec•re•tar•y /'sɛkrɪ,tɛriy/ *n.* [*count*], *pl.* **-tar• ies. 1.** one whose job is to do work in a business office, such as typing, filing, and answering phones. **2.** a person in charge of records, letters, etc., as for a company, club, etc. **3.** [*often: Secretary*] an officer of a government whose job is management of a department: *the Secretary of the Treasury.* —,**sec•re'tar•i•al**, *adj.*

se•crete¹ /sɪ'kriyt/ *v.* [~ + *obj*], **-cret•ed, -cret•ing.** to give off or produce (a chemical substance): *The pancreas secretes a digestive fluid.* —**se'cre•tion,** *n.* [*noncount*] [*count*]

se•crete² /sɪ'kriyt/ *v.* [~ + *obj*], **-cret•ed, -cret•ing.** to hide: *He quickly secreted the letter in his desk drawer.*

se•cre•tive /'siykrɪtɪv, sɪ'kriy-/ *adj.* having a desire for secrecy: *He was pretty secretive about his new assignment.* —'**se•cre•tive•ly,** *adv.*

sect /sɛkt/ *n.* [*count*] a group of people following a particular religious faith.

sec•tion /'sɛkʃən/ *n.* [*count*] **1.** a distinct, separate part of anything, such as a community: *one of the nicer sections of town.* —*v.* [~ + *obj*] **2.** to divide into sections.

sec•tor /'sɛktər/ *n.* [*count*] a distinct part, esp. of society: *the business sector.*

sec•u•lar /'sɛkyələr/ *adj.* not relating to or concerned with religion.

se•cure /sɪ'kyʊr/ *adj., v.,* **-cured, -cur•ing.** —*adj.* **1.** safe; protected: *They kept the jewels secure in the bank.* **2.** not likely to fail, give way, etc.: *He had a secure grip on the rope.* **3.** free from anxiety: *emotionally secure.* —*v.* [~ + *obj*] **4.** to obtain: *to secure a new job.* **5.** to make safe: *to secure the town from flooding.* **6.** to make tight: *to secure a rope.* —**se'cure•ly,** *adv.*: *Be sure your seatbelt is fastened securely.*

se•cu•ri•ty /sɪ'kyʊrɪtiy/ *n.* [*noncount*] **1.** freedom from danger, risk, etc.: *Job security was an important issue.* **2.** freedom from care or anxiety. **3.** prevention of crime, sabotage, etc.: *in charge of plant security.* **4.** something given as a guarantee for paying back a loan.

se•dan /sɪ'dæn/ *n.* [*count*] an automobile having two or four doors and seating four or more persons.

se•date /sɪ'deyt/ *adj., v.,* **-dat•ed, -dat•ing.** —*adj.* **1.** calm: *a sedate personality.* —*v.* [~ + *obj*] **2.** to cause to become sleepy or calm: *The nurse sedated the patient before the operation.* —**se•da•tion** /sɪ'deyʃən/, *n.* [*noncount*]: *The patient is under sedation.*

sed•a•tive /'sɛdətɪv/ *adj.* **1.** causing a feeling of calm: *a sedative drug.* —*n.* [*count*] **2.** a drug that calms or causes sleepiness.

sed•en•tar•y /'sɛdn̩ˌtɛriy/ *adj.* **1.** done while sitting: *a sedentary occupation.* **2.** not active: *The desk clerk led a sedentary life.*

sed•i•ment /'sɛdəmənt/ *n.* [*noncount*] [*count*] the matter that settles to the bottom of a liquid.

se•duce /sɪ'duws, -'dyuws/ *v.* [~ + *obj*], **-duced, -duc•ing. 1.** to tempt (someone) into having sexual intercourse. **2.** to win over: *The warm spring day seduced her from her work.* —**se'duc•er,** *n.* [*count*] —**se'duc•tion,** *n.* [*noncount*] [*count*]

se•duc•tive /sɪ'dʌktɪv/ *adj.* tending to seduce; attractive: *a seductive offer to switch companies; a seductive smile.*

see /siy/ *v.,* **saw** /sɔ/, **seen** /siyn/, **see•ing. 1.** [~ + *obj*] to view (something) with the eyes; look at: *I saw her in the park. I saw him shoot the police officer.* **2.** [*no obj*] to have the power of sight: *He can't see; he's been blind from birth.* **3.** to understand: [~ + *obj*]: *I see your point.* [*no obj*]: *Don't you see; we want to help you!* **4.** [~ + *obj*] to form a mental image of: *I can't see him as president.* **5.** [~ + *obj*] to imagine or believe that one sees something: *You must be seeing*

things; there's nothing here. **6.** [*no obj*] (used as a polite request to draw the attention of someone to something): *See, here it comes.* **7.** to find out: [~ + *obj*]: *See who is at the door.* [*no obj*]: *See for yourself.* **8.** [~ + *obj*] to make sure: *See that the door is locked.* **9.** [~ + *obj*] to visit: *Why don't you come and see me?* **10.** [~ + *obj*] to go with (someone): *It's late; I'll see you home.* **11.** [*no obj*] (used with the subject pronouns *I* and *we*, or after LET and the object pronouns *me* or *us*, to indicate a pause) to think: *Let me see, what was his name?* **12. see off,** to go with (someone about to go on a trip) to the place of departure: *We went to the airport to see off my aunt and uncle; to see them off.* **13. see through, a.** to discover a lie: *I saw right through his excuses.* **b.** to continue until something is completed: *Don't quit now; let's see this job through.* **14. see to,** to take care of: *I'll see to all the travel arrangements.*

seed /siyd/ *n., pl.* **seeds,** (*esp. when thought of as a group*) **seed,** *v.* —*n.* [*count*] **1.** the small, hard part of a plant that grows into a new plant. **2.** the beginning of something: *the seeds of discord.* —*v.* **3.** [~ + *obj*] to sow (a field, etc.) with seed. **4.** [*no obj*] to produce seed. **5.** [~ + *obj*] to remove the seeds from (fruit). —'**seed•less,** *adj.*: *seedless oranges.*

seed•ling /'siydlɪŋ/ *n.* [*count*] a plant grown from a seed.

seed•y /'siydiy/ *adj.,* **-i•er, -i•est. 1.** containing many seeds. **2.** shabby: *a seedy neighborhood.* —'**seed•i•ness,** *n.* [*noncount*]

seek /siyk/ *v.* [~ + *obj*], **sought** /sɔt/, **seek•ing. 1.** to look for: *to seek (out) a new life; to seek her (out), wherever she was.* **2.** to ask for: *to seek advice from a lawyer.* **3.** to try: *to seek to win the election.* —'**seek•er,** *n.* [*count*]

seem /siym/ *v.* [*no obj*] to appear to be (such): *He seemed friendly until I mentioned money. The trip seemed long.*

seem•ing /'siymɪŋ/ *adj.* [*usually: before a noun*] appearing so: *Their team had a seeming advantage.*

'**seem•ing•ly** /'siymɪŋliy/ *adv.* apparently; evidently: *a seemingly endless supply of soldiers.*

seem•ly /'siymliy/ *adj.,* **-li•er, -li•est.** fitting; suitable: *seemly behavior in church.* —'**seem•li•ness,** *n.* [*noncount*]

seen /siyn/ *v.* pp. of SEE¹.

seep /siyp/ *v.* [*no obj*] to flow very slowly. —'**seep•age,** *n.* [*noncount*]

see•saw /'siyˌsɔ/ *n.* [*count*] **1.** a long plank balanced at the middle, on which two children ride up and down while seated at opposite ends. —*v.* [*no obj*] **2.** to ride on a seesaw. **3.** to move up and down: *Stock prices seesawed all day.*

seethe /siyð/ *v.* [*no obj*], **seethed, seeth•ing. 1.** (of a liquid) to bubble as if boiling. **2.** to be angry.

'**see-,through,** *adj.* Also, '**see-,thru.** transparent: *a see-through blouse.*

seg•ment /'sɛgmənt/ *n.* [*count*] one of the parts into which something is divided: *the segments of an orange.*

seg•re•gate / 'sɛgrɪˌgeyt / *v.,* **-gat•ed, -gat•ing. 1.** [~ + *obj*] to set apart from others: *The hospital segregates patients with contagious diseases.* **2.** to separate (a certain group) from the rest of society: [~ + *obj*]: *It is illegal to segregate blacks and whites.* [*no obj*]: *a society that segregates on the basis of religion.* —,**seg•re'ga•tion,** *n.* [*noncount*]

S

seis•mic /'sayzmɪk/ *adj.* relating to earthquakes.

seize /siyz/ *v.* [~ + *obj*], **seized, seiz•ing. 1.** to take hold of with force: *He seized a knife.* **2.** to take advantage of promptly: *to seize an opportunity.*

sei•zure /'siyʒər/ *n.* [*noncount*] [*count*] an act of seizing. **2.** [*count*] a sudden attack, as of some disease: *an epileptic seizure.*

sel•dom /'sɛldəm/ *adv.* not often: *We seldom see them anymore.*

se•lect /sɪ'lɛkt/ *v.* [~ + *obj*] **1.** to choose: *Only the best students were selected for admission.* —*adj.* **2.** limited to only a few: *a select group of skaters.*

se•lec•tion /sɪ'lɛkʃən/ *n.* **1.** [*noncount*] an act of selecting, or the state of being selected: *The selection of a president takes place every four years.* **2.** [*count*] a thing or things selected.

se•lec•tive /sɪ'lɛktɪv/ *adj.* **1.** choosing carefully: *a selective shopper.* **2.** relating to a few chosen items: *selective enforcement of the laws.*

self /sɛlf/ *n.* [*count*] and *pron.*, *pl.* **selves. 1.** one's usual nature, etc.: *his better self.* **2.** one's own pleasure, wants, etc.: *always thinking of self.*

self-, a combining form meaning: of the self (*self-image*); by oneself or itself (*self-imposed*); to, with, toward, for, on, or in oneself or itself (*self-absorbed*); independent (*self-government*); automatic (*self-winding*).

'self-as'surance, *n.* [*noncount*] self-confidence.

'self-'centered, *adj.* thinking about oneself only.

,self-'confidence, *n.* [*noncount*] faith in one's own ability, etc. —**,self-'confident,** *adj.*

'self-'conscious, *adj.* too uncomfortable about being looked at by others: *self-conscious about speaking in the meeting.* —**'self-'consciously,** *adv.* —**'self-'consciousness,** *n.* [*noncount*]

'self-con'trol, *n.* [*noncount*] the ability to control one's actions, feelings, etc.

'self-de'fense, *n.* [*noncount*] the act of defending one's person or interests: *The police officer shot the robber in self-defense.*

'self-es'teem, *n.* [*noncount*] self-respect.

,self-'evident, *adj.* obvious in itself without needing to be proved: *It is self-evident that day follows night.*

'self-ex'planatory, *adj.* needing no explanation; obvious.

'self-'image, *n.* [*count*] the mental image one has of oneself.

,self-'interest, *n.* [*noncount*] **1.** regard for one's own interest, esp. with disregard for others. **2.** personal advantage: *It's in his self-interest to learn English.* —**,self'in•terest•ed,** *adj.*

self•ish /'sɛlfɪʃ/ *adj.* caring chiefly for oneself: *a selfish child; selfish motives.* —**'self•ish•ly,** *adv.* —**'self•ish•ness,** *n.* [*noncount*]

'self-re'spect, *n.* [*noncount*] proper regard for one's character, abilities, etc.: *He lost all his self-respect.*

,self-'righteous, *adj.* too confident that one's character, beliefs, etc., are better than other people's.

,self-'sacrifice, *n.* [*noncount*] sacrifice of oneself or one's interests. —**,self-'sacrificing,** *adj.*

'self-'satisfied, *adj.* feeling too much satisfaction with oneself.

'self-'service, *n.* [*noncount*] the system of serving oneself in a shop, restaurant, etc.

'self-suf'ficient, *adj.* able to supply one's or its

own needs without help. —**'self-suf'ficiency,** *n.* [*noncount*]

sell /sɛl/ *v.*, **sold** /sowld/, **sell•ing. 1.** to give something to someone in exchange for money: [~ + *obj*]: *He sold his car. She sold her car to her sister. She sold her sister her old car.* [*no obj*]: *He said he wasn't selling because he wanted to wait until spring.* **2.** [~ + *obj*] to keep or offer for sale: *to sell insurance.* **3.** [~ + *obj*] to total sales of: *The record sold a million copies.* **4.** [*no obj*] to be offered for sale at the price stated: *This TV sells for $200.* **5.** [*no obj*] to be in demand by buyers: *On a rainy day, umbrellas really sell.* **6.** to (cause to) be accepted: [~ + *obj*]: *to sell an idea to the public.* [*no obj*]: *Now there's an idea that will really sell!* **7. sell out, a.** to sell everything: *The store is sold out of that toy. The store sold out before we even got there!* **b.** to betray one's principles: *He committed suicide rather than sell out to the enemy.*

sell•er /'sɛlər/ *n.* [*count*] **1.** a person who sells, esp. as an occupation. **2.** a thing sold: *a poor seller.*

selt•zer /'sɛltsər/ *n.* [*noncount*] **1.** bubbling mineral water. **2.** carbonated tap water. Also called **'seltzer ,water.**

selves /sɛlvz/ *n.* pl. of SELF.

sem•a•phore /'sɛmə,fɔr/ *n.*, *v.*, **-phored, -phor•ing.** —*n.* [*noncount*] **1.** a system of signaling by flags or lights. —*v.* [~ + *obj*] [*no obj*] **2.** to signal by semaphore.

sem•blance /'sɛmbləns/ *n.* [*noncount*] outward appearance: *I won't continue until there is some semblance of order in here.*

se•men /'siymən/ *n.* [*noncount*] a slightly thick, whitish fluid containing sperm produced in the male reproductive organs.

se•mes•ter /sɪ'mɛstər/ *n.* [*count*] one of two terms into which the school year is divided.

semi-, a combining form meaning: half (*semiannual*); partially or somewhat (*semiautomatic*).

sem•i•cir•cle /'sɛmɪ,sɜrkəl/ *n.* [*count*] half of a circle.

sem•i•co•lon /'sɛmɪ,kowlən/ *n.* [*count*] the punctuation mark (;) used to separate parts of a sentence. Semicolons indicate a break that is longer than a comma but shorter than a period: *We were late for the party; however, the hostess didn't mind.*

sem•i•con•duc•tor /'sɛmiykən,dʌktər, 'sɛmay-/ *n.* [*count*] a substance that can conduct electricity with less efficiency than a true conductor. —**'sem•i•con,duc•ting,** *adj.*

sem•i•fi•nal /,sɛmiy'faynl, ,sɛmay-/ *n.* [*count*] the next to last round in a tournament. —**,sem•i'fi•nal•ist,** *n.* [*count*]

sem•i•nar /'sɛmə,nɑr/ *n.* [*count*] a small group of advanced students studying together.

sem•i•nar•y /'sɛmə,nɛriy/ *n.* [*count*], *pl.* **-nar•ies.** a school that prepares students to be priests, ministers, or rabbis.

sen•ate /'sɛnɪt/ *n.* [*count*; *sometimes:* Senate; *sometimes:* the + ~] **1.** an assembly having the highest law-making powers in a government. **2.** a governing body, as at some universities.

sen•a•tor /'sɛnətər/ *n.* [*count*; *sometimes:* Senator] a member of a senate: *Several senators were interviewed. Senator Smith will answer your questions now.*

send /sɛnd/ *v.* [~ + *obj*], **sent** /sɛnt/, **send•ing. 1.** to cause to go: *sending troops to battle.* **2.** to cause to be brought to a destination: *to send money; to send a letter to him; to send him a let-*

serene

ter. **3.** to cause to move quickly: *The blast sent pieces of concrete flying.* **4. send away for,** to order (goods) to be delivered by mail: *I sent away for tulip bulbs.* **5. send for,** to ask that somebody come: *Someone send for a doctor!* **6. send in,** to mail to a point of collection: *to send in one's taxes* or *to send one's taxes in.* **7. send out, a.** to order delivery: *We sent out for coffee and donuts.* **b.** to cause to go out: *to send invitations out* or *to send out invitations.* —**'send•er,** *n.* [count]

'send-,off, *n.* [count] an expression of good wishes for a person who is leaving: *The office gave their coworker a fine send-off at a nearby restaurant.*

se•nile /'siynaɪl, 'sɛnaɪl/ *adj.* showing a weakening of physical strength or mental functioning as a result of old age. —**se•nil•i•ty** /sɪ'nɪlɪtiy/, *n.* [noncount]

sen•ior /'siynyər/ *adj.* **1.** [after a noun] older (identifying a father whose son is named after him; often abbreviated as Sr.): *John Doe, Sr.* **2.** of higher rank: [be + ~ + to]: *The captain was senior to him by only a few months.* [before a noun]: *the senior officers present.* **3.** [before a noun] of or relating to seniors in high school or college: *her senior year.* —*n.* [count] **4.** one who is older or of higher rank than another: *The captain was his senior by several months.* **5.** a student in the final year at a high school or college. **6.** a senior citizen.

'senior 'citizen, *n.* [count] a person over the age of 60 or 65, esp. one who is retired.

sen•ior•i•ty /siyn'yɔrɪtiy, -'yɒr-/ *n.* [noncount] the state of being senior.

sen•sa•tion /sɛn'seyʃən/ *n.* **1.** the ability to feel something; feeling: [noncount]: *He lost all sensation in his legs as a result of the accident.* [count]: *sensations of heat and cold.* **2.** [count; usually singular] widespread excitement: *The divorce caused a sensation.*

sen•sa•tion•al /sɛn'seyʃənl/ *adj.* **1.** causing a sensation: *a sensational scandal.* **2.** very good: *a sensational performer.*

sense /sɛns/ *n., v.,* **sensed, sens•ing.** —*n.* **1.** [count] any of the powers such as sight, hearing, smell, taste, or touch, by which humans and animals are aware of things: *the five senses; Dogs have a better sense of hearing than humans do.* **2.** [count] a vague feeling: *a sense of security.* **3.** [count] any special mental capacity or understanding: *a sense of values; a great sense of humor.* **4.** Usually, **senses.** [plural] sanity: *Have you taken leave of your senses?* **5.** [noncount] good practical intelligence or judgment: *to have the sense to stop talking and just listen.* **6.** meaning: [noncount]: *You missed the sense of his statement.* [count]: *One of the senses of the word "bachelor" is "unmarried male."* —*v.* [~ + obj] **7.** to take notice of: *I sensed a large object in the darkness.* **8.** to have a feeling of: *to sense danger.*

sense•less /'sɛnslɪs/ *adj.* **1.** unconscious. **2.** stupid; foolish: *senseless chattering.*

sen•si•bil•i•ty /,sɛnsə'bɪlɪtiy/ *n.* [count], pl. **-ties.** Often, **sensibilities.** [plural] capacity for delicate feeling.

sen•si•ble /'sɛnsəbəl/ *adj.* **1.** having, using, or showing good sense: *a sensible woman.* **2.** knowing; aware: *He was sensible of his fault.* **3.** practical: *sensible shoes for camping.* —**'sen•si•bly,** *adv.*: *dressed sensibly for the hike.*

sen•si•tive /'sɛnsɪtɪv/ *adj.* **1.** responsive to the feelings of others: *sensitive to your needs.* **2.** easily hurt or affected (by something): *very sensitive*

to heat; *a sensitive young child.* **3.** highly secret or delicate: *sensitive diplomatic issues.* —**sen•si•tiv•i•ty** /,sɛnsɪ'tɪvɪtiy/, *n.* [noncount]

sen•si•tize /'sɛnsɪ,tayz/ *v.* [~ + obj], **-tized, -tiz•ing.** to make sensitive.

sen•so•ry /'sɛnsəriy/ *adj.* of or relating to the senses or sensation.

sen•su•al /'sɛnʃuwəl/ *adj.* enjoying physical pleasure, esp. sexual satisfaction: *a lazy, sensual person.* —**sen•su•al•i•ty** /,sɛnʃuw'ælɪtiy/, *n.* [noncount]

sen•su•ous /'sɛnʃuwəs/ *adj.* affecting the senses, esp. pleasantly: *a sensuous bath.* —**'sen•su•ous•ly,** *adv.* —**'sen•su•ous•ness,** *n.* [noncount]

sent /sɛnt/ *v.* pt. and pp. of SEND.

sen•tence /'sɛntns/ *n., v.,* **-tenced, -tenc•ing.** —*n.* **1.** [count] a group of words that states something or asks a question: *A sentence in English typically consists of a subject and a predicate containing a verb.* **2.** a court decision stating punishment for a crime: [count]: *to get the maximum sentence.* [noncount]: *to pass sentence on criminals.* —*v.* [~ + obj] **3.** to condemn to punishment: *He sentenced the murderer to life imprisonment.*

sen•ti•ment /'sɛntəmənt/ *n.* **1.** a feeling toward something; opinion: [noncount]: *Public sentiment is against taxes.* [count]: *I agree; those are my sentiments exactly.* **2.** [noncount] emotional feeling: *You can't allow sentiment to get in the way of business.*

sen•ti•men•tal /,sɛntə'mɛntl/ *adj.* **1.** of or relating to the emotions or feelings: *sentimental dreams of love and romance.* **2.** embarrassingly emotional: *Let's not get too sentimental about our relationship.* —**sen•ti•men•tal•i•ty** /,sɛntəmən'tælɪtiy/, *n.* [noncount] —**,sen•ti'men•tal•ly,** *adv.*

sen•ti•nel /'sɛntnl, -tənl/ *n.* [count] a guard.

sen•try /'sɛntriy/ *n.* [count], pl. **-tries.** a guard soldier who is on duty.

sep•a•rate / *v.* 'sɛpə,reyt; *adj.* -ərɪt/ *v.,* **-rat•ed, -rat•ing,** *adj.* —*v.* **1.** to (cause to) come apart; divide: [~ + obj]: *to separate two fighting boys; The school separates the boys from the girls.* [no obj]: *The two fighters separated.* **2.** [no obj] (of a married couple) to stop living together. —*adj.* **3.** not connected: *a garage separate from the house.* **4.** different: *five separate meanings.* —**'sep•a•rate•ly,** *adv.*

sep•a•ra•tion /,sɛpə'reyʃən/ *n.* **1.** [noncount] separating or being separated: *the separation of two fields by a fence.* **2.** [count] a formal act of separating by a married couple.

Sept., an abbreviation of: September.

Sep•tem•ber /sɛp'tɛmbər/ *n.* the ninth month of the year, containing 30 days.

sep•tic /'sɛptɪk/ *adj.* infected with germs.

se•quel /'siykwəl/ *n.* [count] a book, play, etc., that continues the story from an earlier work.

se•quence /'siykwəns/ *n.* **1.** [noncount] the following of one thing after another: *to arrange the cards in sequence.* **2.** [count] a series of things: *a computer programming sequence.* —**se'quen•tial,** *adj.*

ser•e•nade /,sɛrə'neyd, 'sɛrə,neyd/ *n., v.,* **-nad•ed, -nad•ing.** —*n.* [count] **1.** a piece of music written to be performed outdoors at night. —*v.* [~ + obj] **2.** to entertain with a serenade.

se•rene /sə'riyn/ *adj.* calm: *a serene temperament.* —**se'rene•ly,** *adv.* —**se'ren•i•ty,** *n.* [noncount]

S

ser•geant /ˈsɑrdʒənt/ n. [count] **1.** an officer in the armed forces ranking above a corporal. **2.** a police officer ranking below a captain or a lieutenant.

se•ri•al /ˈsɪəriyəl/ n. [count] **1.** anything published, broadcast, etc., in parts. —adj. [usually: before a noun] **2.** of or relating to a series: the serial numbers on the checks.

se•ries /ˈsɪəriyz/ n. [count], pl. **se•ries. 1.** a number of related things, events, etc., occurring one after another: a series of murders. **2.** a number of games, etc., with the same teams or players: a championship series.

se•ri•ous /ˈsɪəriyəs/ adj. **1.** involving much thought: a serious study of inner-city violence. **2.** not cheerful: He was very serious and didn't even smile. **3.** sincere: a serious offer to buy the house. **4.** important: Marriage is a serious matter. **5.** giving cause for worry or fear: a serious illness. —'se•ri•ous•ly, adv. —'se•ri•ous•ness, n. [noncount]

ser•mon /ˈsɜrmən/ n. [count] a talk given for religious or moral instruction.

ser•pent /ˈsɜrpənt/ n. [count] a snake.

ser•rat•ed /ˈsɛreytɪd, səˈrey-/ adj. having sawlike teeth for cutting: a serrated knife.

se•rum /ˈsɪərəm/ n. [noncount] [count] a liquid that contains disease-fighting substances.

serv•ant /ˈsɜrvənt/ n. [count] one who works for another.

serve /sɜrv/ v., served, serv•ing, n. —v. **1.** to act as a servant to (another); work for: [no obj]: The maid served in the kitchen. [~ + obj]: He served his young master well. **2.** to give (food or drink) to (a person at a table): [~ + obj]: He served the food. [no obj]: She served at the church reception. **3.** to be suitable for (a purpose): [no obj]: That cup will serve as a sugar bowl. [~ + obj]: These supplies will serve our needs. **4.** to carry out the duties of a soldier, senator, etc.: [no obj]: My father served in the armed forces. [~ + obj]: She served her country in the Gulf War. **5.** [~ + obj] to spend time in prison. **6.** [~ + obj] [no obj] (in tennis, etc.) to put (the ball) in play with a stroke. —n. [count] **7.** the act or right of serving, as in tennis: Whose serve is it? —Idiom. **8. serve (someone) right,** to be someone's just punishment, as for improper behavior: It served her right to get caught; she was cheating all the time. —'serv•er, n. [count]

serv•ice /ˈsɜrvɪs/ n., v., -iced, -ic•ing. —n. **1.** [noncount] the serving of customers in a restaurant: The restaurant has terrible service. **2.** (an act of) helpful activity: [count]: to do someone a service. [noncount]: Let me know if I can be of service. **3.** [noncount] the supplying of a public need, such as water, electricity, etc.: improved bus service. **4.** the providing of care required by the public, such as repair: [noncount]: to bring the air conditioner in for service. [count]: a television repair service. **5.** the armed forces: [noncount]: He was in the service during the war. [count]: Which one of the services were you in? **6.** [count] a form of public religious worship: Sunday morning services. —v. [~ + obj] **7.** to make fit for use: to service a car.

serv•ice•man /ˈsɜrvɪsˌmæn, -mən/ n. [count], pl. -men. a member of the armed forces.

'service ˌstation, n. [count] a place for servicing automobiles. Also called **gas station.**

serv•ing /ˈsɜrvɪŋ/ n. [count] a portion of food: two servings of cherry pie.

ses•sion /ˈsɛʃən/ n. **1.** [noncount; often: in +

~] the meeting or series of meetings of a court, council, etc., for its business: The court is now in session. **2.** [count] a period of time in which instruction is given at a school, college, etc. **3.** [count] a period of time used for a specific purpose: a study session.

set /sɛt/ v., set, set•ting, n., adj. —v. **1.** [~ + obj] to put (something) in a particular place: to set a vase on a table. **2.** [~ + obj] to cause something to be in a certain condition: to set a house on fire. **3.** [~ + obj] to decide upon: to set a wedding date. **4.** [~ + obj] to place firmly: to set a flagpole in concrete. **5.** [~ + obj] to establish (an example, etc.) for others to follow: to set a fast pace. **6.** [~ + obj] to place china, silver, etc., for use on (a table): Set the table for dinner. **7.** [~ + obj] to adjust (a mechanism) so that it works correctly: to set one's watch. **8.** [~ + obj] to cause to sit: to set a child in a highchair. **9.** [~ + obj] to put (a broken bone) in position to mend. **10.** to become or cause to become hard: [no obj]: Has the glue set yet? [~ + obj]: The cold air will set the cement faster. **11.** [~ + obj] to write music for words to be sung. **12.** [~ + obj] to arrange (type) for printing. **13.** [no obj] to go down: The sun sets early in winter. **14. set back, a.** to slow down progress of: Bad weather set back the rescue attempts. **b.** Informal. to cost: The house set them back $200,000. **15. set forth, a.** to describe: The physicist set forth her ideas. **b.** to begin a journey: They set forth on the expedition. **16. set off, a.** to cause to explode: to set off fireworks or to set fireworks off. **b.** to cause to begin: The TV show set off a rush of phone calls. **17. set on,** Also, **set upon.** to attack: He was set upon by a gang. **18. set out, a.** to begin a journey: The explorers set out long before dawn. **b.** to undertake: We set out to reform the system. **c.** to describe: He set out his main ideas or He set his main ideas out. **19. set up, a.** to put in a ready position: to set up a roadblock or to set a roadblock up. **b.** to start: to set up a business or to set a business up. —n. [count] **20.** a collection of articles for use together: a set of carving knives. **21.** a number of similar things: a set of ideas. **22.** a receiver for radio or television programs: My TV set is broken. **23.** scenery for a play, film, etc. —adj. **24.** [before a noun] customary: a few set phrases in the same old speech. **25.** [before a noun] fixed; not moving: a set smile. **26.** [be + ~] ready: Is everyone set?

set•back /ˈsɛtˌbæk/ n. [count] a stopping or delay in one's progress.

set•ter /ˈsɛtər/ n. [count] a breed of long-haired hunting dogs.

set•ting /ˈsɛtɪŋ/ n. [count] **1.** the level to which something, such as a thermostat, has been set. **2.** surroundings: one's home setting. **3.** the place or time in which a novel, play, etc., takes place: The setting was a spooky old castle.

set•tle /ˈsɛtl/ v., -tled, -tling. **1.** [~ + obj] to decide on: We have settled the matter; we'll buy the house. **2.** to make comfortable: [~ + obj]: The child settled himself on her lap. [no obj]: He settled in the chair. **3.** [~ + obj] to pay, as a bill. **4.** to make a home in (a place): [no obj]: Many Norwegian immigrants settled in Minnesota. [~ + obj]: Many Norwegians settled the Minnesota region. **5.** to (cause to) become calm: [~ + obj]: took a deep breath to settle his nerves. [no obj]: My upset stomach finally settled. **6.** [no obj] to (cause to) sink: The sugar settled in the bottom of the cup. **7.** [no obj] to come to rest: a *bird settling on a tree branch.* **8. settle down,** to become calm or quiet: *I sang to the baby until he settled down.* **9. settle for,** to be satisfied with: *You shouldn't have to settle for second best.* **10. settle on** or **upon,** to decide or agree: *to settle on a plan.* —'**set•tler,** *n.* [*count*]

set•tle•ment /'sɛt̬lmənt/ *n.* **1.** [*noncount*] the act of settling in a place, or the state of being settled. **2.** [*count*] a colony: *a small settlement in Jamestown, Virginia.* **3.** [*count*] a small community. **4.** [*count*] an agreement that settles an argument: *to reach a settlement before the workers went on strike.*

set•up /'sɛt̬,ʌp/ *n.* [*count*] organization: *an efficient setup at work.*

sev•en /'sɛvən/ *n.* [*count*] **1.** a number, 6 plus 1, written as 7. —*adj.* [*before a noun*] **2.** amounting to seven in number: *my seven sisters.* —'**sev• enth,** *adj., n.* [*count*]

sev•en•teen /'sɛvən'tiyn/ *n.* [*count*] **1.** a number, 10 plus 7, written as 17. —*adj.* [*before a noun*] **2.** amounting to 17 in number: *seventeen summers ago.* —,**sev•en'teenth,** *adj., n.* [*count*]

sev•en•ty /'sɛvəntiy/ *n., pl.* **-ties,** *adj.* —*n.* [*count*] **1.** a number, 10 times 7, written as 70. —*adj.* [*before a noun*] **2.** amounting to 70 in number. —'**sev•en•ti•eth,** *adj., n.* [*count*]

sev•er /'sɛvər/ *v.* [~ + *obj*] **1.** to separate (a part) from the whole, as by cutting: *His leg had been severed in an accident.* **2.** to break off or end: *The government has severed all diplomatic relations.*

sev•er•al /'sɛvərəl, 'sɛvrəl/ *adj.* [~ + *plural noun*] **1.** being more than two but fewer than many: *There are several ways to do the same thing.* —*n.* [*plural; used with a plural verb*] **2.** a few; some: *Several have already signed up.*

se•vere /sə'vɪər/ *adj.,* **-ver•er, -ver•est. 1.** harsh: *severe criticism.* **2.** very bad: *a severe illness.* **3.** difficult: *a severe test of strength.* —se'vere•ly, *adv.* —se•ver•i•ty /sə'vɛrɪt̬iy/, *n.* [*noncount*]

sew /sow/ *v.,* **sewed, sewn** /sown/ or **sewed, sew•ing.** **1.** to fasten; to make stitches with a needle and thread: [~ + *obj*]: *He sewed a button on his shirt.* [*no obj*]: *I learned how to sew at an early age.* —'**sew•er,** *n.* [*count*]

sew•age /'suwɪdʒ/ also **sew•er•age** /'suwərɪdʒ/ *n.* [*noncount*] the waste matter that passes through sewers.

sew•er /'suwər/ *n.* [*count*] an underground pipe for carrying off waste from sinks, toilets, etc.

'**sewing ma,chine,** *n.* [*count*] a machine for sewing.

sex /sɛks/ *n.* **1.** [*count*] either the female or male division of a species: *What sex is your kitten?* **2.** [*noncount*] all the differences by which the female and the male are distinguished: *discrimination on the basis of sex.* **3.** SEXUAL INTERCOURSE: *premarital sex.*

sex•ism /'sɛksɪzəm/ *n.* [*noncount*] prejudice based on a person's sex, esp. against women. —'**sex•ist,** *adj.: a sexist attitude.* —*n.* [*count*]: *sexists in the workplace.*

sex•u•al /'sɛkʃuwəl/ *adj.* [*usually: before a noun*] **1.** of or relating to sex: *sexual pleasure.* **2.** having sexual organs: *sexual reproduction in the animal world.* —**sex•u•al•i•ty** /,sɛkʃuw'ælɪt̬iy/, *n.* [*noncount*] —'**sex•u•al•ly,** *adv.*

'**sexual 'intercourse,** *n.* [*noncount*] genital contact between individuals, esp. penetration of the penis into the vagina.

sex•y /'sɛksiy/ *adj.,* **-i•er, -i•est.** sexually inter-

esting, attractive, or exciting. —'**sex•i•ness,** *n.* [*noncount*]

Sgt., an abbreviation of: Sergeant.

shab•by /'ʃæbiy/ *adj.,* **-bi•er, -bi•est. 1.** showing signs of wear: *a shabby old overcoat.* **2.** mean; unfair: *shabby behavior.*

shack /ʃæk/ *n.* [*count*] a small, poorly built house.

shack•le /'ʃækəl/ *n., v.,* **-led, -ling.** —*n.* [*count*] **1.** a fastening, as of iron, for placing around the wrist or ankle of a prisoner. **2.** Often, **shackles.** [*plural*] anything that serves to reduce freedom, thought, etc.: *shackles of prejudice.* —*v.* [~ + *obj*] **3.** to restrict the freedom of: *to shackle the press.*

shade /ʃeyd/ *n., v.,* **shad•ed, shad•ing.** —*n.* **1.** [*noncount*] the darkness caused by the screening of sunlight from an area: *to stand in the shade of a big tree.* **2.** [*count*] a cover that reduces light, as on a window or a lamp. **3.** [*count*] the degree of darkness of a color: *a shade of blue.* **4.** [*count*] a slight amount: *a shade of difference.* —*v.* [~ + *obj*] **5.** to produce shade in, on, or over: *The house is well shaded by the tall trees.* **6.** to introduce degrees of darkness into (a drawing or painting): *to shade (in) the figures of the sketch with pencil.*

shad•ow /'ʃædow/ *n.* **1.** [*count*] a dark image cast on a surface by something that blocks light: *watching her shadow grow longer.* **2.** [*noncount*] shade or some darkness: *standing in shadow.* **3.** [*count*] a slight trace: *innocent beyond the shadow of a doubt.* —*v.* [~ + *obj*] **4.** to follow the movements of (a person) secretly: *Agents shadowed the suspected spy.*

shad•y /'ʃeydiy/ *adj.,* **-i•er, -i•est. 1.** shaded: *a shady park.* **2.** of untrustworthy character: *a shady deal.*

shaft /ʃæft/ *n.* [*count*] **1.** a long stick: *the shaft of the arrow.* **2.** a beam: *shafts of sunlight.* **3.** a vertical passage, as in a building: *an elevator shaft.*

shag•gy /'ʃægiy/ *adj.,* **-gi•er, -gi•est. 1.** covered with long, rough hair: *a shaggy dog.* **2.** forming a bushy mass, such as hair: *a shaggy beard.* **3.** untidy; messy. —'**shag•gi•ness,** *n.* [*noncount*]

shake /ʃeyk/ *v.,* **shook** /ʃʊk/, **shak•en** /'ʃeykən/, **shak•ing,** *n.* —*v.* **1.** to (cause to) move quickly from side to side or up and down: [*no obj*]: *The car shook when the engine started.* [~ + *obj*]: *The earthquake shook the house.* **2.** [*no obj*] to tremble: *His voice shook with rage.* **3.** to take hold of (usually the right hand of another person) as a greeting: [~ + *obj*]: *They shook hands.* [*no obj*]: *Let's shake on it.* **4.** [~ + *obj*] to upset (someone) greatly: *He was badly shaken by her death.* **5. shake off,** to get rid of: *She can't shake off a feeling of despair. I can't shake this flu off.* —*n.* [*count*] **6.** an act or instance of shaking: *a slight shake of the head.* —**shak•y,** *adj.,* **-i•er, -i• est.**

shale /ʃeyl/ *n.* [*noncount*] a kind of rock formed from clay.

shall /ʃæl; unstressed ʃəl/ *auxiliary (modal) v., pres.* **shall;** *past* **should;** *imperative, infinitive, and participles lacking.* [~ + *root form of a verb*] **1.** (used to express the future tense): *I shall go later.* **2.** (used to express that the action of the main verb must be carried out): *Council meetings shall be held in public.* **3.** (used in question forms to make an offer or suggestion): *Shall I help you, or do you want to do it yourself? Shall I apologize to her?*

S

shal·lot /'ʃælət, ʃə'lɒt/ n. [count] a plant related to the onion.

shal·low /'ʃælow/ adj., **-er, -est. 1.** not deep: shallow water. **2.** lacking seriousness: a shallow mind.

sham /ʃæm/ n. [count] **1.** a person or thing pretending to be someone or something else: Her illness was a sham to gain sympathy. —adj. [before a noun] **2.** pretended: sham sorrow.

sham·bles /'ʃæmbəlz/ n. [count; singular; used with a singular verb; usually: a/the + ~] a condition of great disorder: Her desk is a shambles.

shame /ʃeym/ n., v., **shamed, sham·ing.** —n. **1.** [noncount] the painful feeling of having done something wrong. **2.** [noncount] the ability to experience this feeling: to be without shame. **3.** [noncount] disgrace: His dishonesty brings shame to the whole team. **4.** [count; singular; usually: a + ~] a cause for regret: It was a shame you weren't there. —v. [~ + obj] **5.** to cause to suffer disgrace: Her actions shamed her entire family. **6.** to cause (someone) to do something because of a feeling of shame: She shamed me into going. —Idiom. **7.** **put (someone or something) to shame,** to be better than: Their beautiful house puts mine to shame. —'**shame·ful,** adj.

shame·faced /'ʃeym,feyst/ adj. showing shame: shamefaced apologies.

sham·poo /ʃæm'puw/ n. **1.** [noncount] [count] a liquid soap for washing the hair. **2.** [count] the act of washing the hair with such a preparation: had a shampoo and haircut. —v. [~ + obj] **3.** to wash with a shampoo: She shampoos her hair every day. —**sham'poo·er,** n. [count]

sham·rock /'ʃæmrɒk/ n. [count] [noncount] a small, three-leaved clover.

shape /ʃeyp/ n., v., **shaped, shap·ing.** —n. **1.** [count] the form of an object: Italy has the shape of a boot when you see it on a map. **2.** [noncount] condition: The old house was in bad shape. —v. [~ + obj] **3.** to give a shape to: to shape the ground beef into meatballs. **4.** to direct (one's course, etc.): The events of his youth shaped his thinking. **5. shape up,** to change, esp. favorably: Things are finally beginning to shape up in the economy. —Idiom. **6. take shape,** to become defined: Her ideas began to take shape.

shard /ʃɑrd/ n. [count] a piece that is broken off, esp. a piece of pottery.

share /ʃɛər/ n., v., **shared, shar·ing.** —n. [count] **1.** a part of a whole divided among a group of people. **2.** one of the equal parts into which the capital stock of a corporation is divided: He bought shares in IBM. —v. **3.** to divide and give out (something) in shares: [~ + obj]: The two sisters shared their toys. [no obj]: Children must learn to share. **4.** [~ + obj] to use, receive, etc., jointly: The two chemists shared the Nobel prize. **5. share in,** to have a share or part in: We shared in their triumphs.

shark¹ /ʃɑrk/ n. [count] a large fish that has many sharp teeth.

shark² /ʃɑrk/ n. [count] one who cheats others.

sharp /ʃɑrp/ adj., **-er, -est,** adv., n. —adj. **1.** having a thin cutting edge or a fine point: a sharp knife. **2.** changing direction suddenly: a sharp curve in the road. **3.** clearly defined: a sharp contrast between black and white. **4.** biting in taste: a sharp cheese. **5.** piercing in sound: a sharp cry. **6.** intense: a sharp pain in his arm. **7.** quick and angry: some sharp words about your behavior. **8.** mentally quick; clever: a sharp lad.

9. Music. **a.** (of a tone) raised a half step in pitch: F sharp. **b.** above an intended pitch, as a note; too high (opposed to flat). **10.** Informal. very stylish: a sharp dresser. —adv. **11.** carefully or alertly: to look sharp. **12.** suddenly: The thief turned sharp and ran. **13.** exactly at (a certain time): one o'clock sharp. **14.** Music. above the true pitch: to sing sharp. —n. [count] **15.** Music. a sharp note. —'**sharp·ly,** adv.: He spoke sharply to the dog. —'**sharp·ness,** n. [noncount]

sharp·en /'ʃɑrpən/ v. [~ + obj] to make sharp or sharper: to sharpen a knife. —'**sharp·en·er,** n. [count]: a pencil sharpener.

shat·ter /'ʃætər/ v. **1.** to (cause to) break into many pieces: [no obj]: The glass shattered when it hit the floor. [~ + obj]: The looters shattered the shop windows. **2.** [~ + obj] to weaken or destroy: His nerves were shattered by that experience.

shave /ʃeyv/ v., **shaved, shaved** or (esp. in combination) **shav·en, shav·ing.** —v. **1.** [~ + obj] [no obj] to remove hair from (the face, etc.) by cutting it off close to the skin with a razor. **2.** [~ + obj] to scrape away the surface of (something) with a sharp-edged tool: to use a scraper to shave the bottom of the door. —n. [count] **3.** the act of shaving or being shaved. —Idiom. **4. close shave,** a narrow escape from disaster.

shav·er /'ʃeyvər/ n. [count] an electric razor.

shav·ing /'ʃeyvɪŋ/ n. [count] Often, **shavings.** [plural] a very thin piece or slice, esp. of wood.

shawl /ʃɔl/ n. [count] a large piece of fabric worn about a woman's shoulders.

she /ʃiy/ pron., sing. nom. **she,** poss. **her** or **hers,** obj. **her,** pl. nom. **they,** poss. **their** or **theirs,** obj. **them,** n., pl. **shes,** adj. —pron. **1.** the female person or animal mentioned: "How is your mother?" —"She's fine, thanks." **2.** the woman: She who listens learns. **3.** anything considered to be feminine: She's a great-looking car, and economical, too. —n. [count] **4.** a female person or animal: Is your dog a she? —adj. **5.** female (usually used in combination with a noun): a she-goat.

sheaf /ʃiyf/ n. [count], pl. **sheaves** /ʃiyvz/. **1.** a bundle into which cereal plants are tied up after being gathered. **2.** any bundle or collection: a thick sheaf of papers.

shear /ʃɪər/ v., **sheared, sheared** or **shorn** /ʃɔrn/, **shear·ing,** n. —v. [~ + obj] **1.** to cut the wool from a sheep. —n. [count] **2.** Usually, **shears.** [plural] a large cutting instrument with two blades like scissors.

sheath /ʃiyθ/ n. [count], pl. **sheaths** /ʃiyðz/. a close-fitting covering: He put his knife back in its sheath.

sheathe /ʃiyð/ v. [~ + obj], **sheathed, sheath·ing.** to put into a sheath.

shed¹ /ʃɛd/ n. [count] a small, roughly built structure for storage, etc.

shed² /ʃɛd/ v., **shed, shed·ding. 1.** [~ + obj] to let fall: to shed tears. **2.** [~ + obj] to send forth (light, influence, etc.): The detective can shed light on what happened. **3.** to drop off (hair, skin, etc.) naturally: [no obj]: The dog is shedding all over the rug. [~ + obj]: The trees were shedding their leaves.

she'd /ʃiyd/ contraction of **1.** she had: She'd seen him and could identify him. **2.** she would: She'd have to come in.

sheen /ʃiyn/ n. [noncount] brightness: the sheen of the newly polished floor.

sheep /ʃiyp/ n. [count], pl. **sheep.** a mammal that eats grass and grows a woolly fleece.

sheep•dog /'ʃiyp,dɔg, -,dɒg/ n. [count] a dog trained to herd and guard sheep.

sheep•ish /'ʃiypɪʃ/ adj. embarrassed at having done something foolish: He gave a sheepish grin after tripping on the steps.

sheer /ʃɪər/ adj., **-er, -est,** adv. —adj. **1.** very thin and light in weight: sheer stockings. **2.** [before a noun] total: sheer luck; sheer nonsense. **3.** extending down or up very steeply: a sheer descent. —adv. **4.** vertically: cliffs rising sheer from the sea.

sheet /ʃiyt/ n. [count] **1.** a large rectangular piece of cotton used for bedding. **2.** a thin, rectangular piece of glass, tin, etc. **3.** a piece of paper on which to write. **4.** a wide extent or expanse: sheets of ice; sheets of flame; sheets of rain.

sheik /ʃiyk; also ʃeyk/ n. [count] Also, **sheikh.** (in Arab countries) the male leader of a tribe or family. —'**sheik•dom,** n. [count]

shelf /ʃɛlf/ n. [count], pl. **shelves** (shɛlvz). **1.** a thin, flat piece of wood, metal, etc., attached horizontally to a wall, etc., for supporting objects. **2.** a surface like this, such as rock.

shell /ʃɛl/ n. [count] **1.** a hard outer covering of an animal, such as of a clam, snail, or turtle. **2.** the hard outer covering of an egg. **3.** the hard outer covering of a seed, fruit, etc.: peanut shells; coconut shells. **4.** a hollow container filled with explosive and fired from a gun, etc.: mortar shells bursting in the air. **5.** the framework of a building. —v. [~ + obj] **6.** to remove the shell of: to shell some peanuts. **7.** to fire shells at: The rebels shelled the town. **8. shell out,** Informal. to pay (money): I've shelled out enough money; to shell it out again.

she'll /ʃiyl; unstressed ʃɪl/ contraction of she will: The doctor is in; she'll see you now.

shell•fish /'ʃɛl,fɪʃ/ n. [count], pl. (esp. when thought of as a group) **-fish,** (esp. for kinds or species) **-fish•es.** an animal living in water and having a shell, such as the oyster, clam, etc.

shel•ter /'ʃɛltər/ n. **1.** [count] something that provides protection, as from storms, cold, danger, etc. **2.** [noncount] the protection or safety given by such a thing: We found shelter in a nearby barn. **3.** [count] a temporary place to live, as for the homeless or unwanted animals. —v. [~ + obj] **4.** to provide with a shelter.

shelve /ʃɛlv/ v. [~ + obj], **shelved, shelv•ing. 1.** to place on a shelf: to shelve the books. **2.** to put aside: to shelve a question.

shelves /ʃɛlvz/ n. pl. of SHELF.

shep•herd /'ʃɛpərd/ n. [count] **1.** one who takes care of sheep. —v. [~ + obj] **2.** to lead like a shepherd: to shepherd the children.

sher•bet /'ʃɜrbɪt/ n. Also, **sher•bert** /'ʃɜrbərt/. [noncount] [count] a frozen, fruit-flavored ice.

sher•iff /'ʃɛrɪf/ n. the law-enforcement officer of a county: [count]: The sheriff got out of his car and approached the speeders. [before a name]: Sheriff Jones got out of his car.

sher•ry /'ʃɛriy/ n. [noncount] [count] pl. **-ries.** an amber-colored wine of S Spain.

she's /ʃiyz/ contraction of **1.** she is: She's a fool. **2.** she has: She's got big problems.

shied /ʃayd/ v. pt. and pp. of SHY.

shield /ʃiyld/ n. [count] **1.** a device used as a defense against blows, esp. a broad piece of metal carried on the arm. **2.** something that protects, as from injury: the heat shield on the space capsule.

3. something shaped like a shield, such as the badge of a police officer. —v. [~ + obj] **4.** to protect: to shield her children from the truth.

shift /ʃɪft/ v. **1.** to move from one place, person, etc., to another: [~ + obj]: Let's shift the load to the other side. [no obj]: If the weight they are lifting shifts, it could fall. **2.** to change or exchange: [~ + obj]: to shift ideas. [no obj]: to shift in one's thinking. **3.** [~ + obj] [no obj] to change (gears) in driving a motor vehicle. —n. [count] **4.** a change from one place, position, etc., to another: a shift in the wind. **5.** the period of time when someone works: the night shift, from eleven at night until eight in the morning. **6.** a group of people who work during a specific shift.

shift•y /'ʃɪftiy/ adj., **-i•er, -i•est.** avoiding looking at someone directly: He gave me a shifty glance. —'**shift•i•ness,** n. [noncount]

shim•mer /'ʃɪmər/ v. [no obj] to shine with a soft light: The ocean waves shimmered in the sunlight. —'**shim•mer•y,** adj.

shin /ʃɪn/ n., v., **shinned, shin•ning.** —n. [count] **1.** the front part of the leg from the knee to the ankle. —v. **2.** to climb (a pole or the like) by holding fast with the legs after pulling oneself up with the hands: [no obj]: to shin up a tree. [~ + obj]: They liked to shin the trees in their backyard.

shine /ʃayn/ v., **shone** /ʃown/ or, esp. for 4 **shined; shin•ing;** n. —v. **1.** [no obj] to glow with or to reflect light: The sun shone brightly. **2.** [~ + obj] to direct the light of (a lamp, etc.): He shone his flashlight on my face. **3.** [no obj] to do very well: to shine in algebra. **4.** [~ + obj] to polish (shoes, etc.). —n. [count; usually singular] **5.** brightness caused by light shining off an object: a beautiful shine on the floor. **6.** a polish given to shoes. —'**shin•y,** adj., **-i•er, -i•est.**

shin•gle /'ʃɪŋgəl/ n., v., **-gled, -gling.** —n. [count] **1.** a thin piece of wood, slate, etc., used to cover the roofs and sides of buildings. —v. [~ + obj] **2.** to cover with shingles.

ship /ʃɪp/ n., v., **shipped, ship•ping.** —n. [count] **1.** a large boat. **2.** an airplane or spacecraft. —v. [~ + obj] **3.** to send or transport by ship, rail, etc.

-ship, a suffix meaning: state or quality (friendship); office or position (governorship); rank or title (lordship); skill or art (horsemanship); all people involved (ridership).

ship•mate /'ʃɪp,meyt/ n. [count] a person who serves with another on the same ship.

ship•ment /'ʃɪpmənt/ n. **1.** [noncount] an act of shipping cargo: shipment by sea. **2.** [count] cargo shipped: a shipment of supplies.

ship•shape /'ʃɪp,ʃeyp/ adj. neat or tidy: Their room was finally shipshape.

ship•wreck /'ʃɪp,rɛk/ n. **1.** [noncount] [count] the destruction of a ship, as by sinking, or an occurrence of such a loss. —v. [~ + obj] **2.** to cause to suffer shipwreck: The crew were shipwrecked on a deserted island.

ship•yard /'ʃɪp,yɑrd/ n. [count] an area in which ships are built or repaired.

shirk /ʃɜrk/ v. to try to keep from doing (work, duty, etc.): [~ + obj]: to shirk one's duty. [no obj]: He always shirks from doing what he must.

shirt /ʃɜrt/ n. [count] a garment for the upper part of the body.

shiv•er /'ʃɪvər/ v. [no obj] **1.** to shake with cold, fear, etc. —n. [count] **2.** a shaking motion: a shiver of fear.

S

shoal¹ /ʃowl/ n. [count] a place where a sea or river is shallow.

shoal² /ʃowl/ n. [count] a school of fish.

shock /ʃɒk/ n. **1.** the feeling caused by something unpleasant and unexpected: [count]: Her death came as a shock. [noncount]: a reaction of shock. **2.** [count] a sudden blow or impact: the shocks from an earthquake. **3.** [count] the effect on the body produced by an electric current. —v. [~ + obj] **4.** to have an effect on (someone) of strong surprise, horror, etc. **5.** to give an electric shock to.

shock•ing /ʃɒkɪŋ/ adj. **1.** causing great surprise, horror, etc.: the shocking news of her death. **2.** very bad: shocking table manners.

'shock ,jock, n. [count] a radio disc jockey who features offensive or controversial material.

shod /ʃɒd/ v. a pt. and pp. of SHOE.

shod•dy /ʃɒdiy/ adj., **-di•er, -di•est.** of poor quality: shoddy products that fall apart.

shoe /ʃuw/ n., v., **shod** /ʃɒd/ or **shoed, shoe•ing. —n.** [count] **1.** an outer covering for the foot, with an upper part ending at or below the ankle. **2.** a horseshoe. —v. [~ + obj] **3.** to provide with shoes: to shoe a horse. —**Idiom. 4. fill someone's shoes,** to take the place of another in an acceptable way: I'll never fill the boss's shoes. **5. in someone's shoes,** in the position of another: If you were in my shoes, you would know how difficult this job is.

shoe•lace /ʃuw,leys/ n. [count] a string or lace for fastening a shoe.

shoe•mak•er /ʃuw'meykər/ n. [count] one who makes or mends shoes.

shoe•string /ʃuw,strɪŋ/ n. [count] **1.** SHOELACE. **2.** a very small amount of money.

shone /ʃown/ v. a pt. and pp. of SHINE.

shoo /ʃuw/ interj. **1.** (used as a noise to drive away birds, animals, etc.). —v. [~ + obj] **2.** to drive away by saying "shoo": He shooed the animals into the barn.

shook /ʃʊk/ v. pt. of SHAKE.

shoot /ʃuwt/ v., **shot** /ʃɒt/, **shoot•ing,** n. —v. **1.** to send forth (a bullet, arrow, etc.) from a weapon: [no obj]: Stop or I'll shoot! [~ + obj]: He shot an arrow into the air. **2.** [~ + obj] to hit, wound, or kill with a bullet, shell, etc., fired from a weapon: The bank robbers shot five police officers. **3.** [~ + obj] to send forth quickly or suddenly: The reporters shot questions at the general. **4.** [no obj] to (cause to) move suddenly: The car shot down the road. **5.** [~ + obj] to photograph: shooting one picture after another. **6. shoot for,** to try to accomplish: If we shoot for the best, we may get it. **7. shoot up, a.** to grow or increase suddenly: Prices have shot up since last year. You've shot up several inches since I last saw you. **b.** to wound or damage by shooting: to shoot up several parked cars; to shoot them up. —n. [count] **8.** a shooting trip or contest. **9.** the new growth from a plant. —**Idiom. 10. shoot off one's mouth,** Slang. to make foolish or indiscreet remarks. **11. shoot the breeze,** Informal. to talk pleasantly about things that are not serious. —**shoot•er,** n. [count]

'shooting 'star, n. [count] a meteor.

shoot•out /ʃuwt,awt/ n. [count] a fight between two or more persons armed with guns.

shop /ʃɒp/ n., v., **shopped, shop•ping. —n.** [count] **1.** a small store. **2.** a place for doing skilled work: a carpenter's shop. —v. [no obj] **3.** to visit shops for buying goods: My parents went out to shop. —**'shop•per,** n. [count]

shop•lift•er /ʃɒp,lɪftər/ n. [count] one who steals goods from a store while pretending to shop. —**'shop,lift,** v. [no obj]: arrested for shoplifting. [~ + obj]: arrested for trying to shoplift some expensive jewelry.

'shopping ,center, n. [count] a group of stores, restaurants, etc., within a specially designed area.

shore¹ /ʃɔr/ n. [count] the land along the edge of a sea, lake, etc.

shore² /ʃɔr/ v. [~ + obj], **shored, shor•ing.** to support or strengthen: The workers shored (up) the walls with timbers.

shore•line /ʃɔr,layn/ n. [count] the line where shore and water meet.

shorn /ʃɔrn/ v. a pp. of SHEAR.

short /ʃɔrt/ adj., **-er, -est,** adv., n., v. —adj. **1.** having little length or height: the shortest boy in class. **2.** extending only a little way: a short path. **3.** brief: a short time. **4.** abrupt: surprised by his short reply. **5.** not reaching the required amount: The pound of apples was short by several ounces. **6.** not having enough of: always short on money. —adv. **7.** suddenly: to stop short. **8.** briefly; curtly. **9.** on the near side of a point: The arrow landed short. —n. [count] **10. shorts,** [plural] trousers, knee-length or shorter. **11.** SHORT CIRCUIT. —v. **12.** to form a short circuit (in): [~ + obj]: The frayed wire shorted the connection. [no obj]: The car kept shorting. —**Idiom. 13. come** or **fall short, a.** to fail to reach a standard, level, etc.: The arrow fell short of the target. **b.** to be lacking: The walls with timbers. **14. cut short,** to end abruptly. **15. in short,** stated briefly: In short, you're fired. —**'short•ness,** n. [noncount]

short•age /ʃɔrtɪdʒ/ n. [count] **1.** the state of not having enough: a shortage of cash. **2.** the amount of such a lack: a shortage of fifty dollars.

short•change /ʃɔrt'tʃeyndʒ/ v. [~ + obj], **-changed, -chang•ing.** to cheat, esp. to give less than the correct change to: to shortchange a customer.

'short 'circuit, n. [count] a bad electrical connection that allows too much current to flow into a circuit: The short circuit resulted in a blown fuse.

'short-'circuit, v. **1.** [~ + obj] to cause to have a short circuit: The bad connection short-circuited the electric mixer. **2.** [no obj] (of an appliance, switch, etc.) to have a short circuit: The mixer has short-circuited again.

short•com•ing /ʃɔrt,kʌmɪŋ/ n. [count] a failure or lack, as in conduct, condition, etc.

short•cut /ʃɔrt,kʌt/ n. [count] a shorter way to get somewhere: a shortcut between the buildings.

short•en /ʃɔrtn/ v. [~ + obj] to cause to become short or shorter: to shorten a dress.

short•hand /ʃɔrt,hænd/ n. [noncount] a method of fast handwriting using simple strokes, abbreviations, etc.

'short-'handed, adj. not having the necessary number of workers, etc.

'short-'lived /layvd, lɪvd/ adj. lasting only a little while: Their happiness was short-lived.

short•ly /ʃɔrtliy/ adv. **1.** in a short time; soon: He said he would be with us shortly. **2.** abruptly; rudely: answered shortly.

short•sight•ed /ʃɔrt'saytɪd/ adj. **1.** unable to see far; nearsighted. **2.** thinking only of the present: It's shortsighted to fire those employees now because you'll need them again later.

'short 'story, n. [count] a piece of prose fiction, usually under 10,000 words.

'short-'tempered, *adj.* easily angered, excited, or irritated.

'short-'term, *adj.* covering or involving a short period of time: *short-term memory.*

short•wave /'ʃɔrt'weyv/ *n.* **1.** [*noncount*] radio transmission or receiving that uses radio waves shorter than those used in AM broadcasting. **2.** [*count*] **a.** a radio wave of this type. **b.** a radio that receives or transmits such waves.

shot¹ /ʃɒt/ *n.* [*count*] **1.** an act or instance of shooting a gun, bow, etc. **2.** one who shoots: *Are you a good shot?* **3.** anything like a shot, esp. in being sudden and forceful: *a sudden shot to the jaw.* **4.** an aimed stroke, throw, etc., as in certain games: *The center's shot went into the net.* **5.** an attempt or try: *Let me take a shot at the question.* **6.** an injection, as of a drug: *to get a flu shot.* **7.** a photograph, esp. a snapshot.

shot² /ʃɒt/ *v.* pt. and pp. of SHOOT.

'shot ,put, *n.* [*count; singular*] a contest in which a heavy metal ball, or shot, is thrown for distance.

should /ʃʊd/ *auxiliary (modal) v.* [~ + *root form of a verb*] **1.** (used to express the idea of obligation): *You should respect your mother and your father.* **2.** (used to express a condition): *If he were to arrive, I should be pleased.* **3.** (used to make a statement less direct): *I should think you'll want to apologize.* **4.** (used to express the idea of expectation): *He should be here any minute.* **5.** pt. of SHALL.

shoul•der /'ʃowldər/ *n.* [*count*] **1.** the part on either side of the body where the arm joins the rest of the body. **2.** Usually, **shoulders.** [*plural*] the upper part of the back: *The backpack rested on his shoulders.* **3.** a corresponding part in animals. **4.** the part of a garment that fits over the shoulder. **5.** a border alongside a road. —*v.* **6.** to push (something or someone) with the shoulder: [~ + *obj*]: *He shouldered his way through the crowd.* [*no obj*]: *to shoulder through the crowd.* **7.** [~ + *obj*] to take on as a responsibility: *We shouldered the expense.* —***Idiom.*** **8.** **shoulder to shoulder,** side by side: *We worked shoulder to shoulder.*

'shoulder ,blade, *n.* [*count*] one of the two flat bones on the upper part of the back.

should•n't /'ʃʊdnt/ contraction of *should not: One shouldn't lie.*

shout /ʃawt/ *v.* **1.** to call loudly: [*no obj*]: *She shouted to him from the window.* [~ + *obj*]: *She shouted a warning.* **2. shout down,** to prevent (someone) from being heard by talking in a loud voice: *The crowd shouted the speaker down. The crowd shouted down the student leaders.* —*n.* [*count*] **3.** a loud cry: *a shout for help.*

shove /ʃʌv/ *v.*, **shoved, shov•ing,** *n.* —*v.* [~ + *obj*] [*no obj*] **1.** to push roughly. —*n.* [*count*] **2.** an act of shoving: *She gave him a shove.*

shov•el /'ʃʌvəl/ *n.*, *v.*, **-eled, -el•ing** or (*esp. Brit.*) **-elled, -el•ling.** —*n.* [*count*] **1.** a hand tool made of a broad blade attached to a handle, used for taking up dirt, snow, etc. **2.** any machine with a broad scoop having a similar purpose: *a steam shovel.* —*v.* [~ + *obj*] **3.** to move with a shovel: *We shoveled the snow off the driveway.*

show /ʃow/ *v.*, **showed, shown** /ʃown/ or **showed, show•ing,** *n.* —*v.* **1.** to (cause or allow to) appear, be seen, etc.: [~ + *obj*]: *The photograph shows our new house. Show the photograph to the jury.* [*no obj*]: *Is my slip showing?* [~ + *obj*] to point out: *to show the way; The polls show (that) he is losing popularity. The man showed us*

the entrance to the museum. **3.** [~ + *obj*] to guide: *Show her in.* **4.** [~ + *obj*] to make known: *She showed us an easier way to solve the problem.* **5.** [~ + *obj*] to make clear: *Your work shows promise. They showed that the idea wouldn't work.* **6.** [~ + *obj*] to grant or express: *to show mercy to his enemies; to show his enemies mercy.* **7. show off,** to seek attention: *a child showing off in front of guests.* **8. show up, a.** to be seen: *White shows up well against the blue.* **b.** to arrive at a place: *When did he show up?* —*n.* **9.** [*count*] a theatrical production, etc.: *a Broadway show.* **10.** [*count*] a radio or television program: *a morning radio show.* **11.** [*count*] a group of things to be displayed to the public: *a show of paintings by Renoir.* **12.** [*noncount*] overly dramatic display: *His apology was all show.* **13.** [*count*] a display or demonstration: *a show of courage.*

'show ,business, *n.* [*noncount*] the entertainment industry, as theater, motion pictures, etc.

show•down /'ʃow,dawn/ *n.* [*count*] a face-to-face meeting to settle an argument.

show•er /'ʃawər/ *n.* [*count*] **1.** a brief fall of rain, hail, or snow. **2.** a bath in which water is sprayed on the body from above. **3.** something falling like a shower: *a shower of sparks.* —*v.* **4.** [~ + *obj*] to give a great deal of (something) to someone: *to shower his employees with praise; to shower praise on his employees.* **5.** [*no obj*] to rain in a shower: *It showered all day.* **6.** [*no obj*] to bathe in a shower: *He showered before dinner.*

shown /ʃown/ *v.* a pp. of SHOW.

'show-,off, *n.* [*count*] one who tries to get attention and praise.

show•room /'ʃow,ruwm, -,rʊm/ *n.* [*count*] a room used for the display of goods.

show•y /'ʃowiy/ *adj.*, **-i•er, -i•est.** making a good display: *showy flowers.* —**'show•i•ly** /'ʃowəliy/ *adv.* —**'show•i•ness,** *n.* [*noncount*]

shrank /ʃræŋk/ *v.* a pt. of SHRINK.

shrap•nel /'ʃræpnl/ *n.* [*noncount*] fragments from an exploding artillery shell: *soldiers wounded by shrapnel.*

shred /ʃrɛd/ *n.*, *v.*, **shred•ded** or **shred, shred•ding.** —*n.* [*count*] **1.** a piece cut or torn off. **2.** a very small amount: *not a shred of evidence.* —*v.* [~ + *obj*] **3.** to cut or tear into small pieces. —**'shred•der,** *n.* [*count*]

shrewd /ʃruwd/ *adj.*, **-er, -est.** clever in practical matters: *a shrewd politician.* —**'shrewd•ly,** *adv.*

shriek /ʃriyk/ *n.* [*count*] **1.** a loud, shrill cry: *shrieks of laughter.* —*v.* [*no obj*] **2.** to make such a sound: *The children shrieked with laughter.*

shrill /ʃrɪl/ *adj.* high-pitched and piercing: *a shrill cry.* —**'shrill•ness,** *n.* [*noncount*]

shrimp /ʃrɪmp/ *n.* [*count*] [*noncount*] pl. **shrimps,** (*esp. when thought of as a group*) **shrimp.** a small, edible shellfish.

shrine /ʃrayn/ *n.* [*count*] **1.** a place devoted to some saint or deity. **2.** any place associated with a historic event or person.

shrink /ʃrɪŋk/ *v.*, **shrank** /ʃræŋk/ or, often, **shrunk** /ʃrʌŋk/, **shrunk** or **shrunk•en** /'ʃrʌŋkən/, **shrink•ing. 1.** to (cause to) become smaller: [*no obj*]: *clothes that shrink if washed in hot water.* [~ + *obj*]: *Hot water will shrink some of those clothes.* **2.** [*no obj*] to move back suddenly, as in horror: *to shrink from danger.*

shrink•age /'ʃrɪŋkɪdʒ/ *n.* [*noncount*] the process or the amount of shrinking: *to avoid shrinkage of the fabric.*

shriv•el /'ʃrɪvəl/ *v.*, **-eled, -el•ing** or (*esp. Brit.*)

S

-elled, -el·ling. to (cause to) become smaller and wrinkled, as from great heat: [*no obj*]: *The plants shriveled in the heat.* [~ + *obj*]: *The heat shriveled the plants.*

shroud /ʃrawd/ *n.* [*count*] **1.** a sheet in which a dead body is wrapped for burial. **2.** something that covers: *a shroud of darkness.* —*v.* [~ + *obj*] **3.** to wrap or clothe (a body) for burial. **4.** to cover; hide: *an enemy camp shrouded by night.*

shrub /ʃrʌb/ *n.* [*count*] a woody plant smaller than a tree.

shrub·ber·y /'ʃrʌbəriy/ *n.* [*noncount*] [*count*] *pl.* **-ber·ies.** a planting of shrubs.

shrug /ʃrʌg/ *v.,* **shrugged, shrug·ging,** *n.* —*v.* **1.** to raise and contract the (shoulders) to indicate lack of interest or knowledge: [~ + *obj*]: *He shrugged his shoulders and said, "I don't care."* [*no obj*]: *When we asked him where the dog was, he just shrugged.* **2. shrug off,** to treat (something) as unimportant: *to shrug off an insult; to shrug it off.* —*n.* [*count*] **3.** the movement of raising the shoulders.

shrunk /ʃrʌŋk/ *v.* a pp. and pt. of SHRINK.

shrunk·en /'ʃrʌŋkən/ *v.* a pp. of SHRINK.

shud·der /'ʃʌdər/ *v.* [*no obj*] **1.** to tremble with a sudden movement, as from horror. —*n.* [*count*] **2.** a trembling, as from horror or cold.

shuf·fle /'ʃʌfəl/ *v.,* **-fled, -fling,** *n.* —*v.* **1.** [*no obj*] to walk without lifting the feet: *He shuffled around the room.* **2.** [~ + *obj*] to move (one's feet) along the ground without lifting them: *She shuffled her feet to the music.* **3.** to mix up (objects, cards, etc.) randomly: [~ + *obj*]: *shuffling papers on his desk.* [*no obj*]: *Whose turn is it to shuffle?* —*n.* [*count*] **4.** a dragging walk. **5.** an instance of shuffling or of changing something: *He lost his job in an office shuffle.*

shun /ʃʌn/ *v.* [~ + *obj*], **shunned, shun·ning.** to keep away from: *She shunned her family.*

shut /ʃʌt/ *v.,* **shut, shut·ting. 1.** to (cause to) become closed: [~ + *obj*]: *Shut the door.* [*no obj*]: *The doors shut quickly behind him.* **2.** [~ + *obj*] to close by bringing together the parts of: *Shut your book.* **3.** to (cause to) stop operating for a given period of time: [~ + *obj*]: *shutting the office for two weeks.* [*no obj*]: *The stores shut at noon.* **4. shut down,** to stop operating indefinitely: *The automobile plant shut down last year. They shut down the plant* or *They shut the plant down.* **5. shut off, a.** to stop the supply of: *He shut off the electricity* or *He shut the electricity off.* **b.** to separate: *The storm shut the island off from the mainland.* **6. shut out,** to keep from entering: *to shut someone out of the club.* **7. shut up, a.** to imprison: *They shut the prisoners up in a tiny room* or *They shut up the prisoners in a tiny room.* **b.** to close entirely: *They shut up their store for vacation; to shut the old house up until it was sold.* **c.** to stop talking: *After nearly twenty minutes he finally shut up.* **d.** to stop (someone) from talking: *Will somebody please shut her up?*

shut·ter /'ʃʌtər/ *n.* [*count*] **1.** a solid, movable cover for a window. **2.** a movable cover, such as over the opening of a camera lens. —*v.* [~ + *obj*] **3.** to close with shutters: *to shutter a window.*

shut·tle /'ʃʌtəl/ *n., v.,* **-tled, -tling.** —*n.* [*count*] **1.** a device in a loom for passing the thread from one side to the other. **2.** a train, bus, etc., that travels back and forth at regular times. —*v.* **3.** to (cause to) move back and forth: [~ + *obj*]: *to shuttle the troop trains back and forth.* [*no obj*]: *He shuttled between the two countries.*

shy /ʃay/ *adj.,* **shy·er** or **shi·er, shy·est** or **shi·est,** *v.,* **shied, shy·ing.** —*adj.* **1.** timid when among people: *a shy smile.* —*v.* [*no obj*] **2.** (esp. of a horse) to make a sudden movement in fear or alarm. **3. shy away from,** to hesitate to do: *They shied away from that deal because they didn't trust the salesman.* —**'shy·ly,** *adv.* —**'shy·ness,** *n.* [*noncount*]

sib·ling /'sɪblɪŋ/ *n.* [*count*] a brother or sister.

sick /sɪk/ *adj.,* **-er, -est,** *n.* —*adj.* **1.** having ill health. **2.** [*be* + ~] ready to vomit: *I feel sick.* **3.** [*be* + ~] very upset: *was sick at heart.* **4.** [*be* + ~] annoyed with or tired of: *She's sick and tired of your complaints.* **5.** cruel or offensive: *sick jokes.* —*n.* [*plural; used with a plural verb*] **6. the sick,** sick people.

sick·en /'sɪkən/ *v.* to (cause to) become sick: [*no obj*]: *Eventually she sickened and died.* [~ + *obj*]: *You sicken me with your disgusting jokes.*

sick·en·ing /'sɪkənɪŋ/ *adj.* causing a feeling of nausea or disgust: *a sickening smell.*

sick·le /'sɪkəl/ *n.* [*count*] a tool with a hooklike blade for cutting grain, etc.

sick·ly /'sɪkliy/ *adj.,* **-li·er, -li·est. 1.** not strong; unhealthy: *The baby was still sickly.* **2.** caused by ill health: *a sickly complexion.* **3.** causing a feeling of nausea or disgust: *What is that sickly smell?*

sick·ness /'sɪknɪs/ *n.* **1.** [*count*] a particular illness. **2.** [*noncount*] the state of being sick. **3.** [*noncount*] nausea.

side /sayd/ *n., v.,* **sid·ed, sid·ing.** —*n.* [*count*] **1.** one of the surfaces forming the outside of something: *the side of a building.* **2.** either of the two surfaces of a door, a sheet of paper, etc. **3.** a surface that is not the front, back, top, or bottom: *The side of the box had been crushed.* **4.** either the right or left part of a thing, esp. of the body. **5.** position with reference to a central line or point: *the east side of a city.* **6.** a part or phase of something: *We need to examine all sides of the crime problem.* **7.** a competing team: *Our side won the baseball game.* —*v.* **8. side with** (or **against**), to support (or oppose), as in an argument: *Her parents always sided with her brother.* —*Idiom.* **9. on the side,** in addition to some primary thing: *He ordered some French fries on the side.* **10. side by side, a.** next to one another: *The friends stood side by side.* **b.** closely associated: *working side by side for peace.* **11. take sides,** to support one person in an argument.

'side ef·fect, *n.* [*count*] an indirect, often harmful effect, as of a drug.

side·kick /'sayd,kɪk/ *n.* [*count*] **1.** a close friend. **2.** an assistant.

side·line /'sayd,layn/ *n.* [*count*] **1.** an activity done in addition to one's regular job. **2.** a line that marks the side boundary of an athletic field or court.

side·long /'sayd,lɔŋ, -,lɑŋ/ *adj.* [*before a noun*] directed to one side: *a sidelong glance.*

side·show /'sayd,ʃow/ *n.* [*count*] a minor show in connection with a principal one, as at a circus.

side·step /'sayd,stɛp/ *v.* [~ + *obj*] [*no obj*], **-stepped, -step·ping. 1.** to step to one side and avoid (a blow, etc.). **2.** to try to avoid (a question or problem).

side·track /'sayd,træk/ *v.* [~ + *obj*] to move from the main subject or course: *We can't afford to get sidetracked.*

side·walk /'sayd,wɔk/ *n.* [*count*] a paved path at the side of a road.

side•ways /'sayd,weyz/ *adv.* **1.** to or from one side. —*adj.* **2.** directed toward one side: *a sideways glance.*

siege /siydʒ/ *n.* [*count*] **1.** the act of surrounding a city in such a way as to force its surrender. —*Idiom.* **2. lay siege to,** to surround and attack (a place).

sieve /sɪv/ *n.*, *v.*, **sieved, siev•ing.** —*n.* [*count*] **1.** a utensil with a wire net used for separating larger pieces from smaller, or for straining liquids to remove solid pieces. —*v.* [~ + *obj*] **2.** to put through a sieve.

sift /sɪft/ *v.* [~ + *obj*] **1.** to put (flour, etc.) through a sieve: *to sift the flour.* **2.** to examine closely: *The detectives are sifting (through) the evidence.*

sigh /say/ *v.* **1.** [*no obj*] to take and let out a deep breath expressing sorrow, relief, etc.: *He sighed in despair.* **2.** [~ + *obj; used with quotations*] to express with a sigh: *"Yes, I suppose so," she sighed.* —*n.* [*count*] **3.** the act or sound of sighing.

sight /sayt/ *n.* **1.** [*noncount*] the ability to see. **2.** [*count*] the act or fact of seeing; a view or quick look: *to catch sight of the thief.* **3.** [*noncount*] the range within which one can see: *Don't let them out of your sight.* **4.** [*count*] something seen or worth seeing: *to see all the sights of London.* **5.** [*count; usually singular; a* + ~] something that looks bad, strange, silly, etc.: *He was quite a sight after the fight.* **6.** [*count; often plural*] a device, as on a firearm, for aiding the eye in aiming. —*v.* [~ + *obj*] **7.** to observe: *to sight a rare bird.* —*Idiom.* **8. at first sight,** after only one brief look: *When they met, it was love at first sight.* **9. lose sight of,** to fail to keep in mind: *Let's not lose sight of our main goal.* **10. out of sight, a.** beyond one's range of vision: *Soon the runner was out of sight.* **b.** *Informal.* too much: *The price is out of sight.* **11. sight unseen,** without previous examination: *We bought it sight unseen.*

sight•see•ing /'sayt,siyɪŋ/ *n.* [*noncount*] the act of visiting places and things of interest. —**'sight,se•er,** *n.* [*count*]

sign /sayn/ *n.* [*count*] **1.** a mark or symbol used to represent something, as in music, mathematics, etc.: *a dollar sign.* **2.** a board, etc., with writing or a drawing that gives a warning, advertisement, or other information: *a traffic sign.* **3.** something that means something else: *Bowing is a sign of respect.* **4.** something that shows the existence of something else: *There wasn't a sign of the crooks.* —*v.* **5.** to write (one's name) on (something): [~ + *obj*]: *to sign a letter.* [*no obj*]: *Where should I sign?* **6. sign away,** to give something by putting one's name on a document: *She signed away all her property* or *She signed all the property away.* **7. sign off, a.** to stop broadcasting: *The station signed off at three in the morning.* **b.** to give one's approval: *The boss signed off on my plan.* **8. sign on, a.** to hire: *He signed on several good players.* **b.** to agree to do something: *I signed on to help.* **9. sign up, a.** to join a group: *to sign up for the navy.* **b.** to hire: *Sign him up if he can pitch tomorrow; to sign up some good players.* —**'sign•er,** *n.* [*count*]

sig•nal /'sɪgnl/ *n.*, *v.*, **-naled, -nal•ing** or (*esp. Brit.*) **-nalled, -nal•ling.** —*n.* [*count*] **1.** anything that serves to direct, warn, etc., such as a light, a gesture, or an act: *a traffic signal.* **2.** an act or event that causes an action: *The dictator's speech was a signal for revolt.* **3.** a message sent by radio waves: *a TV signal.* —*v.* **4.** to make a signal to (someone or something): [*no obj*]: *The police officer stood there signaling.* [~ + *obj*]: *The captain wanted to signal his ship.*

sig•na•ture /'sɪgnətʃər/ *n.* [*count*] a person's name signed on a letter, check, etc.

sig•nif•i•cant /sɪg'nɪfɪkənt/ *adj.* **1.** important: *a significant event in world history.* **2.** having a special meaning: *She gave him a significant look.* —**sig'nif•i•cance,** *n.* [*noncount*] —**sig'nif•i•cant•ly,** *adv.*

sig•ni•fy /'sɪgnə,fay/ *v.* [~ + *obj*], **-fied, -fy•ing. 1.** to make known: *He signified his agreement with a smile.* **2.** to have the meaning of: *A sign showing a cigarette with a red line through it signifies "No smoking."*

'sign ,language, *n.* [*count*] any of several systems of communication employing manual gestures, as used among deaf people.

sign•post /'sayn,powst/ *n.* [*count*] a post with a sign that gives information.

si•lence /'sayləns/ *n.*, *v.*, **-lenced, -lenc•ing.** —*n.* [*noncount*] **1.** the state or fact of being silent: *He received the news with silence.* **2.** absence of comment, as for keeping something secret: *governmental silence about the scandal.* —*v.* [~ + *obj*] **3.** to make silent: *The teacher could silence the class with just one stern look.*

si•lent /'saylənt/ *adj.* **1.** making no sound; quiet: *the silent desert.* **2.** not speaking: *silent observers.* **3.** (of a letter) not pronounced, as the *b* in *doubt.* —**'si•lent•ly,** *adv.*

sil•hou•ette /,sɪluw'ɛt/ *n.*, *v.*, **-et•ted, -et•ting.** —*n.* [*count*] **1.** a picture of the outline of an object, filled in with black. —*v.* [~ + *obj*] **2.** to show in or as if in a silhouette.

silhouette

S

sil•i•con /'sɪlɪkən, -,kɒn/ *n.* [*noncount*] a nonmetallic element occurring in minerals and rocks: used in computer chips, etc.

silk /sɪlk/ *n.* [*noncount*] **1.** the thread from the cocoon of the silkworm. **2.** cloth made from this fiber. —**'silk•y,** *adj.*, **-i•er, -i•est.**

silk•en /'sɪlkən/ *adj.* **1.** made of silk. **2.** like silk in smoothness or softness.

silk•worm /'sɪlk,wɜrm/ *n.* [*count*] a caterpillar that spins a silken cocoon.

sill /sɪl/ *n.* [*count*] a flat ledge beneath a window, door, or other opening.

sil•ly /'sɪliy/ *adj.*, **-li•er, -li•est.** lacking good sense. —**'sil•li•ness,** *n.* [*noncount*]

silt /sɪlt/ *n.* [*noncount*] earth left behind by moving water.

sil•ver /'sɪlvər/ *n.* **1.** [*noncount*] a shiny white metallic element, used for making jewelry, coins, etc. **2.** [*noncount; used with a singular verb*] coins made of this metal: *a handful of silver.* **3.** [*noncount; used with a singular verb*] table articles, such as knives, forks, and spoons, made of silver. **4.** [*noncount*] a bright, grayish white color. —*adj.* [*before a noun*] **5.** made of or like silver. —**'sil•ver•y,** *adj.*

sil•ver•smith /'sɪlvər,smɪθ/ *n.* [*count*] one who makes and repairs articles of silver.

sil•ver•ware /'sɪlvər,wɛər/ *n.* [*noncount; used with a singular verb*] eating and serving utensils made of silver, silver-plated metals, stainless steel, etc.

sim•i•lar /'sɪmələr/ *adj.* having a likeness or resemblance: *two similar houses.* [*be* + ~ (+ *to*)]: *The houses are similar to each other.* —**sim•i'lar• i•ty** /ˌsɪməˈlærɪtiy/, *n.* [noncount] [count], *pl.* -**ties.** —**sim•i•lar•ly,** *adv.*

sim•i•le /'sɪməliy/ *n.* [noncount] a comparison using "like" or "as," such as in "She is like a rose."

sim•mer /'sɪmər/ *v.* **1.** to cook just below the boiling point: [no obj]: *The sauce is simmering.* [~ + obj]: *Simmer the sauce.* **2.** [no obj] to be in a state in which a strong feeling is present but not expressed: *He was simmering with anger.* **3. simmer down,** to become calm or quiet. —*n.* [count; usually singular] **4.** the state of simmering.

sim•ple /'sɪmpəl/ *adj.,* -**pler,** -**plest. 1.** easy to understand or do: *a simple problem; It was simple to solve her problems.* **2.** not complicated: *a simple design.* **3.** sincere: *He's a simple man.* **4.** lacking mental sharpness.

sim•plic•i•ty /sɪmˈplɪsɪtiy/ *n.* [noncount] the state or quality of being simple.

sim•pli•fy /'sɪmpləˌfay/ *v.* [~ + obj], -**fied,** -**fy• ing.** to make simple: *to simplify the problem.* —**sim•pli•fi•ca•tion** /ˌsɪmpləfɪˈkeyʃən/, *n.* [noncount] [count]

sim•ply /'sɪmpliy/ *adv.* **1.** in a simple manner: *He spoke simply and directly.* **2.** only: *It is simply a cold.* **3.** absolutely: *simply delicious.*

sim•u•late /'sɪmyəˌleyt/ *v.* [~ + obj], -**lat•ed,** -**lat•ing. 1.** to create a model of: *During the drill we will simulate emergency conditions.* **2.** to pretend to do or have: *to simulate illness.* —**,sim• u'la•tion,** *n.* [noncount] [count]

si•mul•ta•ne•ous /ˌsaymɔlˈteyniyəs, ˌsɪmɔl-/ *adj.* existing, occurring, or operating at the same time: *simultaneous translation of all speeches at the United Nations.* —**,si•mul'ta•ne•ous•ly,** *adv.*

sin /sɪn/ *n., v.,* **sinned, sin•ning.** —*n.* **1.** [noncount] breaking divine or moral law: *a life full of sin.* **2.** [count] any act regarded as breaking such a law: *He asked for forgiveness of his sins.* —*v.* [no obj] **3.** to commit a sin: *He had sinned and so he begged God for forgiveness.* —**'sin•ner,** *n.* [count]

since /sɪns/ *adv.* **1.** from then till now (often preceded by *ever*): *Those elected in 1990 have been on the committee ever since.* **2.** between a certain past time and the present: *She at first refused, but has since agreed.* **3.** before now: *She has long since left him.* —*prep.* **4.** between a past time and the present: *There have been many changes since the war.* —*conj.* **5.** from the time when: *He has written once since he left.* **6.** because: *Since it was raining, we didn't go.*

sin•cere /sɪnˈsɪər/ *adj.,* -**cer•er,** -**cer•est. 1.** honest: *a sincere apology.* **2.** genuine; real: *a sincere effort to improve.* —**sin'cere•ly,** *adv.* —**sin•cer• i•ty** /sɪnˈsɛrɪtiy/, *n.* [noncount]

sin•ew /'sɪnyuw/ *n.* [count] a tendon.

sing /sɪŋ/ *v.,* **sang** /sæŋ/ or, often, **sung** /sʌŋ/, **sung, sing•ing. 1.** [no obj] to make words or sounds with musical changes in the tone of the voice. **2.** to perform (songs or music) with the voice: [no obj]: *Once she sang on national TV.* [~ + obj]: *They sang some old tunes around the campfire.* **3.** [no obj] to make a whizzing sound: *The bullet sang past his ear.* —**'sing•er,** *n.* [count]

sing., an abbreviation of: singular.

singe /sɪndʒ/ *v.,* **singed, singe•ing,** *n.* —*v.* [~ + obj] **1.** to burn slightly: *The hot iron singed the shirt.* —*n.* [count] **2.** a slight burn.

sin•gle /'sɪŋgəl/ *adj., v.,* -**gled,** -**gling.** —*adj.* **1.** [before a noun] one only: *a single example.* **2.** [before a noun] relating to or suitable for one person only: *a single room.* **3.** unmarried: *a single man.* —*v.* **4. single out,** to choose (one) from others: *to single someone out for special mention; to single out a hardworking employee.* —*n.* [count] **5.** one person or thing. **6.** a room in a hotel, a bed, etc., for one person only. **7.** an unmarried person: *The bar is for singles only.* **8.** a one-dollar bill: *Give me change in singles, please.* **9. singles,** [plural] a game with one player on each side, as a tennis match.

'single 'file, *n.* [noncount] a line of persons or things arranged one behind the other: *The class lined up in single file.*

'single-'handed, *adj.* **1.** done by one person alone. —*adv.* **2.** by oneself: *She built the garage single-handed.*

'single-'minded, *adj.* having great determination: *a single-minded desire to succeed.*

sin•gly /'sɪŋgliy/ *adv.* one at a time: *Some guests arrived singly, and others came in pairs.*

sin•gu•lar /'sɪŋgyələr/ *adj.* **1.** of or belonging to the grammatical category indicating that a word refers to one person, place, or thing, such as *child, it,* or *goes.* **2.** remarkable; exceptional: *a singular success.* **3.** unusual or strange: *singular behavior.* —*n.* [count] **4.** a word in the singular: *What is the singular for the plural word addenda?*

sin•gu•lar•ly /'sɪŋgyələrliy/ *adv.* remarkably; very: *singularly good taste.*

sin•is•ter /'sɪnəstər/ *adj.* suggesting evil, harm, or trouble: *a sinister face.*

sink /sɪŋk/ *v.,* **sank** /sæŋk/ or, often, **sunk** /sʌŋk/, **sunk** or **sunk•en, sink•ing,** *n.* —*v.* **1.** to (cause to) fall to a lower level: [no obj]: *The ship sank to the bottom of the sea.* [~ + obj]: *The submarine sank two ships.* **2.** [no obj] to become discouraged or depressed: *My heart sank when I heard the news.* **3. sink in,** to become understood: *I repeated "You're safe" until I was sure the words had sunk in.* —*n.* [count] **4.** a basin for washing: *the kitchen sink.*

sin•u•ous /'sɪnyuwəs/ *adj.* having many curves or turns; winding: *a sinuous path.*

si•nus /'saynəs/ *n.* [count], *pl.* -**nus•es.** one of the hollow spaces in the skull connecting with the nose: *a sinus headache.*

sip /sɪp/ *v.,* **sipped, sip•ping,** *n.* —*v.* [~ + obj] **1.** to drink (a liquid) a little at a time. —*n.* [count] **2.** a small quantity taken by sipping.

si•phon /'sayfən/ *n.* [count] **1.** a U-shaped pipe that uses natural pressure to draw liquid from one place to another. —*v.* [~ + obj] **2.** to carry through a siphon: *We siphoned (off) some gasoline from the car's gas tank; to siphon some gas off.*

sir /sɜr/ *n.* [count] **1.** a formal term of address used to a man: *"Dear Sir," the letter began.* **2.** [*Sir*] the title of a knight: *Sir Walter Scott.*

sire /say°r/ *n., v.,* **sired, sir•ing.** —*n.* [count] **1.** the male parent of a four-legged animal. —*v.* [~ + obj] **2.** to father (offspring): *He had sired two fine sons.*

si•ren /'sayrən/ *n.* [count] a warning device that produces a loud, piercing sound.

sir•loin /'sɜrlɔyn/ *n.* [noncount] [count] the portion of the loin of beef in front of the rump.

sis•ter /'sɪstər/ *n.* [*count*] **1.** a female relative having the same parents. **2.** a female member of the same nationality, etc., as another. **3.** a woman member of a religious order. —'**sis•ter•ly,** *adj.*: *a sisterly kiss on the cheek.*

sis•ter-in-law /'sɪstərɪn,lɔ/ *n.* [*count*], *pl.* **sis•ters-in-law. 1.** the sister of one's husband or wife. **2.** the wife of one's brother. **3.** the wife of the brother of one's husband or wife.

sit /sɪt/ *v.,* **sat** /sæt/, **sat, sit•ting. 1.** [*no obj*] to rest with the body supported by one's buttocks or thighs. **2.** to (cause to) lower the body into a position of rest supported by one's buttocks or thighs: [*no obj*]: *Please sit (down); I'll be back in a minute.* [~ + *obj*]: *His mother sat the child (down) on the sofa.* **3.** [*no obj*] to be located: *The house sits on a cliff.* **4.** [*no obj*] to hold a session: *The court sits in judgment.* **5.** [*no obj*] to baby-sit. **6. sit around,** to do nothing: *The workers were sitting around.* **7. sit in (on),** to be a spectator at (some event or circumstance): *I'd like permission to sit in on your class.* **8. sit up,** to (cause to) rise from a lying position to a sitting position: *Sit up straight and answer me. The nurse sat him up in his bed.*

site /saɪt/ *n.* [*count*] the location of something: *the site of the battle.*

sit•u•ate /'sɪtʃuw,eyt/ *v.* [~ + *obj; often: be* + ~ *-ed*], **-at•ed, -at•ing.** to put in or on a particular site or place: *situated herself near the exit door.*

sit•u•a•tion /,sɪtʃuw'eyʃən/ *n.* [*count*] **1.** combination of circumstances: *The international situation is grave.* **2.** location with reference to what is around: *a city in a beautiful situation.*

six /sɪks/ *n.* [*count*] **1.** a number, five plus one, written as 6. —*adj.* [*before a noun*] **2.** amounting to six in number. —**sixth,** *adj., n.* [*count*]

six•teen /'sɪks'tiyn/ *n.* [*count*] **1.** a number, ten plus six, written as 16. —*adj.* [*before a noun*] **2.** amounting to 16 in number. —'**six'teenth,** *adj., n.* [*count*]

six•ty /'sɪkstiy/ *n., pl.* **-ties,** *adj.* —*n.* [*count*] **1.** a number, ten times six, written as 60. —*adj.* [*before a noun*] **2.** amounting to 60 in number. —'**six•ti•eth,** *adj., n.* [*count*]

siz•a•ble or **size•a•ble** /'sayzəbəl/ *adj.* fairly large.

size /sayz/ *n., v.,* **sized, siz•ing.** —*n.* [*count*] **1.** the physical largeness of anything: *the size of a farm.* **2.** one of a series of measures for manufactured articles: *shoe sizes.* —*v.* [~ + *obj*] **3.** to sort according to size. **4. size up,** to form an opinion of: *The lawyer sized up his opponent; to size him up and dismiss him.*

siz•zle /'sɪzəl/ *v.,* **-zled, -zling,** *n.* —*v.* [*no obj*] **1.** to make a hissing sound, as in frying: *The bacon sizzled in the frying pan.* —*n.* [*count*] **2.** a sizzling sound.

skate¹ /skeyt/ *n., v.,* **skat•ed, skat•ing.** —*n.* **1.** ICE SKATE (def. 1). **2.** ROLLER SKATE. —*v.* [*no obj*] **3.** to move oneself on skates: *skating at the ice rink.* —'**skat•er,** *n.* [*count*]

skate² /skeyt/ *n.* [*count*], *pl.* (*esp. when thought of as a group*) **skate,** (*esp. for kinds or species*) **skates.** a fish with winglike fins.

skate•board /'skeyt,bɔrd/ *n.* [*count*] **1.** a device made of a board mounted on large roller-skate wheels and supporting a rider. —*v.* [*no obj*] **2.** to ride a skateboard.

skel•e•ton /'skɛlɪtn/ *n.* [*count*] **1.** the bones of a human or animal that form the inner framework of the body. **2.** a supporting framework, as

of a leaf, building, or ship. **3.** an outline, as of a piece of writing: *Can you describe the skeleton of the plot?*

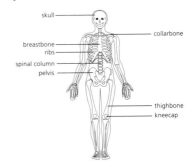

skeleton (human)

skep•tic /'skɛptɪk/ *n.* [*count*] one who questions the truth of something that others believe. —'**skep•ti•cal,** *adj.* —'**skep•ti•cism,** *n.* [*noncount*]

sketch /skɛtʃ/ *n.* [*count*] **1.** a simply made drawing. **2.** a brief description: *a quick sketch of what had happened.* **3.** a short comic piece or routine. —*v.* **4.** to make a sketch or sketches of (something or someone): [~ + *obj*]: *He sketched a quick drawing of the skyline.* [*no obj*]: *artists sketching along the river.*

sketch•y /'skɛtʃiy/ *adj.,* **-i•er, -i•est.** giving only outlines and not details: *He could only give us a sketchy account of what had happened.*

skew•er /'skyuwər/ *n.* [*count*] **1.** a long pin for inserting through meat or other food to hold it while it is cooking. —*v.* [~ + *obj*] **2.** to fasten by piercing with a skewer.

ski /skiy/ *n., v.,* **skis, ski,** *v.,* **skied, ski•ing.** —*n.* [*count*] **1.** one of a pair of long, slender pieces of wood, plastic, or metal used in gliding over snow. **2.** WATER SKI. —*v.* [*no obj*] **3.** to travel on skis, as for sport: *He skied in Colorado.* —'**ski•er,** *n.* [*count*]

skid /skɪd/ *n., v.,* **skid•ded, skid•ding.** —*n.* [*count*] **1.** an unexpected slide on a smooth surface: *The car went into a skid on the ice.* —*v.* **2.** to (cause to) slip or slide: [*no obj*]: *Her feet were skidding on the icy pavement.* [~ + *obj*]: *He skidded the car into a fence.*

skill /skɪl/ *n.* **1.** the ability to do something well: [*noncount*]: *She showed great skill in handling difficult problems.* [*count*]: *the skills of reading and writing in a foreign language.* **2.** [*count*] a job requiring special training: *to learn a skill.* —'**skill•ful,** *adj.*: *a skillful way of dealing with people.* —'**skill•ful•ly,** *adv.*

skilled /skɪld/ *adj.* having, needing, or showing skill or ability: *a skilled craftsman.* [*be* + ~ + *in/at* + *obj*]: *She was skilled in dealing with all sorts of people.*

skil•let /'skɪlɪt/ *n.* [*count*] a frying pan.

skim /skɪm/ *v.,* **skimmed, skim•ming. 1.** [~ + *obj*] to remove (floating matter) from the surface of a liquid: *to skim the fat off the soup.* **2.** [~ + *obj*] to clear (liquid) in this way: *to skim milk.* **3.** [*no obj*] to glide lightly over (a surface, as of water): *The seaplane skimmed over the water and then landed.* [~ + *obj*]: *The plane skimmed the water barely a few feet from the surface.* **4.** to

S

skull

collarbone

breastbone

ribs

spinal column

pelvis

thighbone

kneecap

read quickly but not carefully: [~ + obj]: to skim the chapters for the main idea. [no obj]: teaching her students to skim.

'skim 'milk or **'skimmed 'milk,** n. [noncount] milk from which the cream has been skimmed.

skimp•y /'skɪmpiy/ adj., -i•er, -i•est. lacking in size, quantity, etc.; scanty: a skimpy bathing suit.

skin /skɪn/ n., v., skinned, skin•ning. —n. 1. the outer covering of a human or animal body: [noncount]: the smell of her clean skin after a shower. [count]: a fair skin that is easily sunburned. 2. the outer covering taken from the body of an animal: [count]: a beaver skin. [noncount]: a coat of beaver skin. 3. a covering of a fruit, vegetable, etc.: [noncount]: the skin of sausage. [count]: potato skins. —v. [~ + obj] 4. to remove the skin of: to skin the fruit. —Idiom. 5. by the skin of one's teeth, just barely: She won the election by the skin of her teeth. 6. get under one's skin, a. to irritate someone: All those rude comments really get under my skin. b. to affect someone deeply. 7. have a thick skin, to be insensitive to criticism. 8. have a thin skin, to be easily offended.

skin•ny /'skɪniy/ adj., -ni•er, -ni•est. very thin: a tall, skinny guy.

skin•tight /'skɪn'tayt/ adj. fitting almost as tightly as skin: skintight jeans.

skip /skɪp/ v., skipped, skip•ping, n. —v. 1. [no obj] to move in a light, springy manner by hopping forward on first one foot then the other. 2. [~ + obj] to jump lightly over: to skip rope. 3. to move quickly or pass over: [no obj]: The speaker skipped from one subject to another. [~ + obj]: The teacher skipped chapter five. 4. to go away quickly and secretly from (some place): [~ + obj]: The criminals skipped town. [no obj]: They've already skipped. 5. [~ + obj] to be absent from: Your son skipped class again. —n. [count] 6. a skipping movement.

skip•per /'skɪpər/ n. [count] the captain of a small vessel.

skirt /skɜrt/ n. [count] 1. a woman's garment hanging downward from the waist. —v. [~ + obj] 2. to lie along the edge of: The hills skirt the town. 3. to keep distant from (something risky, etc.): trying to skirt the issue.

skit /skɪt/ n. [count] a short theatrical scene.

skulk /skʌlk/ v. [no obj] to move while trying to avoid being seen.

skull /skʌl/ n. [count] the bony framework of the head.

skunk /skʌŋk/ n. [count], pl. skunks, (esp. when thought of as a group) skunk. an animal having a bushy tail and a black coat with white markings and spraying a foul-smelling fluid as a defense.

sky /skay/ n. [count; often: the + ~; often: skies] [noncount], pl. skies. the region of the clouds or the upper air.

'sky-'high, adj., adv. very high: sky-high prices.

sky•jack /'skay,dʒæk/ v. [~ + obj] to hijack (an airliner). —'sky,jack•er, n. [count]

sky•lark /'skay,lɑrk/ n. [count] a brown-speckled lark famous for its beautiful song.

sky•light /'skay,layt/ n. [count] an opening in a roof for admitting daylight.

sky•line /'skay,layn/ n. [count] the outline of the buildings of a city against the sky.

sky•rock•et /'skay,rɒkɪt/ n. [count] 1. a firework that explodes high in the air. —v. [no obj]

2. to increase rapidly: Prices skyrocketed overnight.

sky•scrap•er /'skay,skreypər/ n. [count] a tall building of many stories.

slab /slæb/ n. [count] a broad, flat, thick piece of stone, wood, etc.

slack /slæk/ adj., -er, -est, adv., n., v. —adj. 1. loose: a slack rope. 2. careless: slack in answering letters. 3. not active or busy: the slack season in an industry. —n. [noncount] 4. a slack condition or part, esp. of a rope, sail, or the like, that hangs loose, without strain upon it: too much slack in the sails. —v. 5. slack off, a. to be lazy: often slacking off at work. b. Also, slack up. to become less active or intense: At last some of the work slacked off and he could relax. —'slack•ness, n. [noncount]

slack•en /'slækən/ v. 1. to (cause to) become less active, busy, etc.: [no obj]: At last the work slackened a bit. [~ + obj]: He never slackened his efforts to improve. 2. to (cause to) become looser: [no obj]: The sails slackened as the wind died down. [~ + obj]: to slacken the sails.

slacks /slæks/ n. [plural] trousers for casual wear: The slacks were too tight.

slain /sleyn/ v. pp. of SLAY.

slam /slæm/ v., slammed, slam•ming, n. —v. 1. [~ + obj] to shut with force and noise: to slam the door. 2. [~ + obj] to strike or throw with force and noise on impact: She slammed the book on the table. 3. [no obj] to stop with force and noise: The truck slammed into the wall. 4. [~ + obj] to criticize harshly: She slammed her opponent. —n. [count] 5. the noise made by something being slammed.

slan•der /'slændər/ n. 1. [noncount] the act of knowingly making a false statement to ruin someone's reputation. 2. [count] such a false statement. —v. [~ + obj] 3. to make a false statement about (someone) to ruin his or her reputation. —'slan•der•ous, adj.

slang /slæŋ/ n. [noncount] very informal words and phrases not normally used in formal situations. —'slang•y, adj., -i•er, -i•est: He used some slangy expressions in his term paper.

slant /slænt/ v. 1. to (cause to) lean in a certain way; slope: [no obj]: The roof slants upward sharply. [~ + obj]: to slant a roof upward. 2. [~ + obj] to distort (information): The article was slanted in favor of the president. —n. 3. [noncount] slanting direction; slope: the slant of a roof. 4. [count] a slanting line, surface, etc. 5. [count] a particular viewpoint: a story with a humorous slant.

slap /slæp/ n., v., slapped, slap•ping, adv. —n. [count] 1. a sharp blow with the open hand. —v. [~ + obj] 2. to strike sharply with the open hand. —adv. 3. directly; straight: to fall slap into the river.

slap•dash /'slæp,dæʃ/ adj. too quick and careless: a slapdash answer.

slap•stick /'slæp,stɪk/ n. [noncount] comedy characterized by silly, noisy, and physically violent action.

slash /slæʃ/ v. 1. to cut with a violent sweeping stroke: [~ + obj]: She had slashed her wrists. [no obj]: to slash at the weeds with a sickle. 2. [~ + obj] to reduce: to slash salaries. —n. [count] 3. the act of slashing. 4. a cut or mark made with such a stroke. 5. a short diagonal stroke (/) between two words indicating that either one may be chosen to complete the sense of the text.

slat /slæt/ n. [count] a long, narrow strip of wood, metal, etc.

slate /sleyt/ n. **1.** [noncount] a blue-gray rock that tends to split into thin plates. **2.** [count] a thin piece of this rock used for roofing.

slaugh•ter /'slɔtər/ n. [noncount] **1.** the killing of cattle, sheep, etc. **2.** a brutal or violent killing. —v. [~ + obj] **3.** to defeat completely. **4.** to kill in a brutal or violent manner.

slave /sleyv/ n., v., **slaved, slav•ing.** —n. [count] **1.** one who is owned by and forced to work for another. **2.** one who is under the control of another person or power: a slave to his desires. —v. [no obj] **3.** to work like a slave: He slaved away all last night. I slaved over the hot stove to prepare the meal.

slav•er•y /'sleyvəriy, 'sleyvriy/ n. [noncount] **1.** the condition of a slave; bondage: kept in slavery. **2.** the keeping of slaves: outlawing slavery in most countries.

slav•ish /'sleyvɪʃ/ adj. imitating closely: a slavish reproduction of the book in movie form.

slay /sley/ v. [~ + obj], **slew** /sluw/, **slain** /sleyn/, **slay•ing.** to kill by violence: to slay the enemy. —'**slay•er,** n. [count]

slea•zy /'sliyziy/ adj., **-zi•er, -zi•est.** disgustingly low, cheap, or vulgar: printing sleazy stories.

sled /slɛd/ n., v., **sled•ded, sled•ding.** —n. [count] **1.** a platform mounted on runners for traveling over snow or ice. —v. [no obj] **2.** to ride on a sled.

sledge•ham•mer /'slɛdʒˌhæmər/ n. [count] a large heavy hammer used with both hands.

sleek /sliyk/ adj., **-er, -est. 1.** smooth or glossy: sleek, combed-back hair. **2.** finely shaped: a sleek sports car.

sleep /sliyp/ v., **slept** /slɛpt/, **sleep•ing,** n. —v. **1.** [no obj] to be in the condition of rest that comes when the body suspends certain functions and is in a state of unconsciousness. **2.** [~ + obj] to have enough beds for (people): This trailer sleeps three people. **3. sleep around,** to have sexual relationships with many different partners: She accused her husband of sleeping around. **4. sleep off,** to get rid of (a headache, etc.) by sleeping: to sleep off a bad hangover; to sleep it off. **5. sleep on,** to postpone making a decision about (something) for at least a day: I'll sleep on the idea and call you tomorrow. **6. sleep over,** to sleep in another person's home: My daughters want to sleep over (at) their cousin's. **7. sleep through,** to sleep in spite of (noise or the like): There was a loud party in the next room but somehow we slept through it. **8. sleep together,** to be sexual partners. **9. sleep with,** to have sexual relations with: He said he had never slept with anyone but his wife. —n. **10.** [noncount] the state of a person, animal, or plant that sleeps. **11.** [count; usually singular] a period of sleeping: a good sleep. —**Idiom. 12. go to sleep, a.** to fall asleep: Every time the baby went to sleep, the phone rang. **b.** to become numb: My foot's gone to sleep and I can't stand on it. **13. put to sleep,** to kill in a painless way: They had to put their sick dog to sleep. —'**sleep•less,** adj. —'**sleep•er,** n.

'**sleeping ˌbag,** n. [count] a warm body-length bag in which one can sleep outdoors.

'**sleeping ˌpill,** n. [count] a pill containing a drug that causes sleep.

sleep•walk•ing /'sliypˌwɔkɪŋ/ n. [noncount]

the act of walking while asleep. —'**sleepˌwalk•er,** n. [count]

sleep•y /'sliypiy/ adj., **-i•er, -i•est. 1.** ready to sleep. **2.** inactive: a sleepy, quiet village. —'**sleep•i•ness,** n. [noncount]

sleet /sliyt/ n. [noncount] **1.** rain in the form of ice pellets. —v. [no obj] **2.** to send down sleet: It's sleeting hard.

sleeve /sliyv/ n. [count] the part of a garment that covers the arm. —'**sleeve•less,** adj.

sleigh /sley/ n. [count] a light vehicle on runners, usually open and generally horse-drawn, used for transporting people over snow.

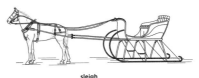

sleigh

slen•der /'slɛndər/ adj., **-er, -est. 1.** long and narrow: a slender post. **2.** thin or slim: slender youths. **3.** small: The chances of winning were slender. —'**slen•der•ness,** n. [noncount]

slept /slɛpt/ v. pt. and pp. of SLEEP.

sleuth /sluwθ/ n. [count] a detective.

slew¹ /sluw/ v. pt. of SLAY.

slew² /sluw/ n. [count] Informal. a large number: A whole slew of people showed up.

slice /slays/ n., v., **sliced, slic•ing.** —n. [count] **1.** a thin, flat piece cut from something: a slice of bread. **2.** a portion: a slice of land. —v. [~ + obj] **3.** to cut into slices: to slice the meat into strips. **4.** to cut through (something) with a knife: to slice (off) a piece of cake. —'**slic•er,** n. [count]

slick /slɪk/ adj., **-er, -est. 1.** smooth or slippery: his slick black hair. **2.** so smooth in manners, speech, etc., as to seem untrustworthy. **3.** well done but shallow in content: slick writing.

slick•er /'slɪkər/ n. [count] a long, loose raincoat.

slide /slayd/ v., **slid** (slid), **slid•ing,** n. —v. **1.** to (cause to) move smoothly across a surface: [no obj]: He slid down the hill. [~ + obj]: The bartender slid a glass of beer along the bar. **2.** to (cause to) move easily or without being noticed: [no obj]: Tears slid down her face. [~ + obj]: He slid the child into the car seat. **3.** [no obj] to fall gradually into a specified state, etc.: to slide into depression. **4. let (something) slide,** to neglect or ignore (something): to let a matter slide. —n. [count] **5.** an act or instance of sliding. **6.** a smooth surface for sliding down. **7.** a small frame of film for projection on a screen: slides from our trip to Africa. **8.** a plate of glass on which objects are placed for examination under a microscope.

slight /slayt/ adj., **-er, -est,** v., n. —adj. **1.** small in amount, degree, etc.: I heard a slight noise. **2.** of little importance, etc.: His influence is very slight. **3.** slender or slim: She was slight and had delicate features. —v. [~ + obj] **4.** to treat (someone) as if he or she were unimportant: I didn't mean to slight the dinner guest. —n. [count] **5.** an instance of treating someone as unimportant: a deliberate slight. —'**slight•ly,** adv.: slightly overweight.

slim /slɪm/ adj., **slim•mer, slim•mest. 1.** slender,

as in the width around one's body or in form: *a slim figure*. **2.** poor: *a slim chance of success*.

slime /slaym/ *n*. [*noncount*] any sticky, mostly liquid matter, esp. of a foul kind. —**'slim•y,** *adj.,* **-i•er, -i•est.**

sling /slɪŋ/ *n., v.,* **slung** /slʌŋ/, **sling•ing.** —*n.* [*count*] **1.** a strap or band forming a loop by which something is suspended or carried, such as a bandage for an injured arm. —*v.* [~ + *obj*] **2.** to throw: *The bully slung a rock at him.*

slink /slɪŋk/ *v.* [*no obj*], **slunk** /slʌŋk/, **slink•ing.** to move in a sneaky manner, as from shame: *After those insulting remarks he slunk quietly away.*

slip[1] /slɪp/ *v.,* **slipped, slip•ping,** *n.* —*v.* **1.** [*no obj*] to slide suddenly and accidentally: *He slipped on the icy ground.* **2.** [*no obj; usually:* ~ + *by/away*] to pass quickly: *Another opportunity to catch him slipped by.* **3.** [*no obj*] to move quietly or without being noticed: *to slip out of a room.* **4.** to put on or take off (a piece of clothing) quickly: [~ + *on/off* + *obj*]: *He slipped off his jacket.* [~ + *obj* + *on/off*]: *He slipped it on.* **5.** [*no obj*] to make a mistake: *Someone in the office must have slipped (up).* **6.** [~ + *obj*] to put quickly or while trying not to be noticed: *to slip a note into a person's pocket.* **7.** [~ + *obj*] to pass from (one's memory, etc.): *The date for our meeting has slipped my mind.* —*n.* [*count*] **8.** an act or instance of slipping. **9.** a sudden slide: *a slip on the ice.* **10.** a mistake, as in speaking or writing, esp. a small, careless one: *a slip of the tongue.* **11.** a woman's skirted undergarment.

slip[2] /slɪp/ *n.* [*count*] a small piece of paper on which information is noted: *a bank withdrawal slip.*

slip•per /'slɪpər/ *n.* [*count*] a light, soft shoe intended to be worn in the house.

slip•per•y /'slɪpəriy, 'slɪpriy/ *adj.,* **-i•er, -i•est.** **1.** causing slipping: *a slippery road.* **2.** not trustworthy: *a slippery scoundrel.*

slip•shod /'slɪpˌʃɑd/ *adj.* careless or sloppy: *slipshod work.*

'slip-,up, *n.* [*count*] a mistake.

slit /slɪt/ *v.,* **slit, slit•ting,** *n.* —*v.* [~ + *obj*] **1.** to make a long cut in: *to slit the envelope open.* —*n.* [*count*] **2.** a straight, narrow opening: *a slit in the skirt.*

slith•er /'slɪðər/ *v.* [*no obj*] to move or walk with a sliding motion, as a snake.

sliv•er /'slɪvər/ *n.* [*count*] a small, thin, often sharp piece, as of wood or glass.

slob /slɑb/ *n.* [*count*] a very sloppy or bad-mannered person.

slo•gan /'slowgən/ *n.* [*count*] a phrase identified with a particular political party, product, etc.: *a campaign slogan.*

slop /slɑp/ *v.,* **slopped, slop•ping.** to (cause to) spill (liquid): [~ + *obj*]: *They were slopping water all over the place.* [*no obj*]: *The liquid slopped onto the floor.*

slope /slowp/ *v.,* **sloped, slop•ing,** *n.* —*v.* **1.** to (cause to) have an angle that is between flat and upright; slant: [*no obj*]: *The roof sloped sharply upward.* [~ + *obj*]: *The builder sloped the roof sharply upward.* —*n.* **2.** [*count*] ground that is not level, such as the side of a hill: *the sharp slopes of the hills.* **3.** [*noncount*] slant, esp. downward or upward.

slop•py /'slɑpiy/ *adj.,* **-pi•er, -pi•est. 1.** muddy, slushy, or very wet: *sloppy ground.* **2.** untidy; messy: *a sloppy eater.* **3.** careless: *His sloppy writing was due to his sloppy thinking.* —**'slop•pi•ness,** *n.* [*noncount*]

slosh /slɑʃ/ *v.* **1.** [*no obj*] to splash through water, mud, etc. **2.** (of a liquid) to (cause to) move about actively: [*no obj*]: *The water sloshed over the sides.* [~ + *obj*]: *to slosh the gasoline in the tank.*

slot /slɑt/ *n., v.,* **slot•ted, slot•ting.** —*n.* [*count*] **1.** a narrow opening, esp. one for receiving something, such as a letter. **2.** a position, as in a series: *Her TV show is in the eight o'clock slot on Thursdays.* —*v.* [~ + *obj*] **3.** to place or fit into a slot: *You've been slotted for a four o'clock meeting.*

sloth /slɔθ *or, esp. for 2,* slowθ/ *n.* **1.** [*noncount*] laziness. **2.** [*count*] a slow-moving, tree-dwelling tropical American animal. —**'sloth•ful,** *adj.*

slouch /slawtʃ/ *v.* [*no obj*] **1.** to sit, stand, or walk in a drooping way: *to slouch around all day.* —*n.* **2.** [*count; usually singular*] an awkward, drooping way of standing or walking. **3.** [*count*] a lazy or incapable person: *He's no slouch.*

slov•en•ly /'slʌvənliy/ *adj.,* **-li•er, -li•est.** unclean in appearance: *a slovenly room in a cheap hotel.*

slow /slow/ *adj. and adv.,* **-er, -est,** *v.* —*adj.* **1.** moving with little speed; not fast: *a slow train.* **2.** mentally dull: *a slow child.* **3.** dull or boring: *a slow party.* —*adv.* **4.** in a slow manner; slowly: *Drive slow.* —*v.* **5.** to (cause to) be slow or slower: [*no obj*]: *The car slowed (up) and then came to a stop.* [~ + *obj*]: *He slowed the train (down) but couldn't avoid the collision.* —**'slow•ly,** *adv.*: *Drink this slowly.* —**'slow•ness,** *n.* [*noncount*]

slug[1] /slʌg/ *n.* [*count*] **1.** a slow-moving animal, similar to a snail. **2.** a bullet.

slug[2] /slʌg/ *v.* [~ + *obj*], **slugged, slug•ging.** to hit hard: *The two fighters slugged each other.*

slug•gish /'slʌgɪʃ/ *adj.* working or moving slowly: *a sluggish heartbeat.*

slum /slʌm/ *n.* [*count*] a run-down part of a city.

slum•ber /'slʌmbər/ *v.* [*no obj*] **1.** to sleep. —*n.* [*noncount*] **2.** sleep.

slump /slʌmp/ *v.* [*no obj*] **1.** to fall heavily: *He slumped to the floor.* **2.** to decrease suddenly: *His health slumped.* —*n.* [*count*] **3.** an act or instance of slumping: *The economy is in a slump.*

slung /slʌŋ/ *v.* pt. and pp. of SLING[1].

slunk /slʌŋk/ *v.* a pt. and pp. of SLINK.

slur[1] /slɜr/ *v.,* **slurred, slur•ring.** to pronounce (a syllable, word, etc.) unclearly by combining sounds: [*no obj*]: *His voice slurred because he wasn't yet awake.* [~ + *obj*]: *a habit of slurring her speech.*

slur[2] /slɜr/ *v.,* **slurred, slur•ring,** *n.* —*v.* [~ + *obj*] **1.** to insult: *to slur someone's reputation.* —*n.* [*count*] **2.** an insulting remark.

slurp /slɜrp/ *v.* **1.** to eat or drink with loud sucking noises: [~ + *obj*]: *to slurp one's soup.* [*no obj*]: *The kids were slurping as they drank their sodas.* —*n.* [*count*] **2.** an act or sound of slurping.

slush /slʌʃ/ *n.* [*noncount*] partly melted snow. —**'slush•y,** *adj.,* **-i•er, -i•est.**

sly /slay/ *adj.,* **sly•er** *or* **sli•er, sly•est** *or* **sli•est,** *n.* —*adj.* **1.** sneaky; tricky: *The sly old fox was able to outsmart us once again.* —*n.* **Idiom. 2. on the sly,** secretly. —**'sly•ly,** *adv.* —**'sly•ness,** *n.* [*noncount*]

smack[1] /smæk/ *v.* **smack of,** to have a flavor or trace of something: *His words smack of flattery.*

smack[2] /smæk/ *v.* [~ + *obj*] **1.** to strike sharply with the open hand; slap. **2.** to close and open (the lips) noisily as a sign of enjoyment or anticipation: *They smacked their lips when she brought in the cake.* —*n.* [count] **3.** a sharp, loud-sounding blow; slap. **4.** a loud kiss. —*adv.* **5.** suddenly and violently: *He drove smack up against the side of the house.*

small /smɔl/ *adj.* and *adv.,* **-er, -est.** —*adj.* **1.** not large; little: *a small box.* **2.** [*before a noun*] carrying on some activity on a limited scale: *a small business.* **3.** not important: *We have a small problem.* **4.** very young: *When he was just a small boy, his mother took him to New York.* —*adv.* **5.** in a small manner: *to write small.*

'small-'minded, *adj.* selfish and mean: *small-minded attitudes.*

'small ,talk, *n.* [noncount] light conversation about subjects that are not serious.

smart /smɑrt/ *v., adj.,* **-er, -est,** *adv.* —*v.* [no obj] **1.** to be a cause of sharp, stinging pain: *The cut on his arm still smarted.* —*adj.* **2.** having quick intelligence; clever: *a smart student.* [*It + be + ~ + to + verb*]: *It wasn't very smart of you to try to cheat.* **3.** neat in appearance, as a person or garment: *a very smart outfit.* **4.** sophisticated or fashionable: *the smart crowd.* **5.** sharp: *a smart pain; a smart slap on the arm.* —*adv.* **6.** in a smart manner; smartly. —'**smart•ly,** *adv.:* *to dress smartly; She rapped smartly on the door.* —'**smart•ness,** *n.* [noncount]

smart•en /'smɑrtn/ *v.* **smarten up,** to (cause to) become smarter: *When will you smarten up; you're being made a fool of! Can anything smarten her up? Nothing can smarten up that loser.*

smash /smæʃ/ *v.* **1.** to (cause to) break into pieces; shatter: [no obj]: *The vase smashed when I dropped it.* [~ + obj]: *He smashed the vase.* **2.** to hit or drive with force: [no obj]: *The car smashed into the wall.* [~ + obj]: *He smashed the car into the wall.* —*n.* [count] **3.** an act or sound of smashing. **4.** *Informal.* something that achieves great success: *Their new movie was a huge smash.* —*adj.* [before a noun] **5.** *Informal.* relating to a great success: *a smash hit on Broadway.*

smear /smɪər/ *v.* **1.** [~ + obj] to spread (an oily, greasy, or wet substance) on something: *to smear butter on bread.* **2.** to (cause to) be blurred, as by rubbing: [~ + obj]: *The signature was smeared.* [no obj]: *The ink will smear if it gets wet.* **3.** [~ + obj] to ruin a reputation, etc.: *He tried to smear his opponent during the campaign.* —*n.* [count] **4.** an oily or wet substance. **5.** a stain or mark made by such a substance. **6.** an attempt to ruin the good name of someone, as by spreading lies.

smell /smɛl/ *v.,* **smelled** or **smelt** /smɛlt/, **smell•ing,** *n.* —*v.* **1.** to detect the odor of (something) through the nose: [~ + obj]: *He smelled the flowers in the garden.* [no obj]: *Because he had a bad cold, he could hardly smell.* **2.** [no obj] to have an odor: *These flowers don't smell at all.* **3.** [no obj] to have a bad odor: *That fish really smells!* **4.** [~ + obj] to test by the sense of smell: *He smelled the meat to see if it was fresh.* —*n.* **5.** [noncount] the ability to detect something with the nose: *the sense of smell.* **6.** [count] that quality of a thing that is smelled: *The fish has a pretty strong smell.* **7.** [count] an act or instance of smelling.

smell•y /'smɛliy/ *adj.,* **-i•er, -i•est.** having a bad odor.

smelt /smɛlt/ *v.* a pt. and pp. of SMELL.

smile /smayl/ *v.,* **smiled, smil•ing,** *n.* —*v.* **1.** to

put on a facial expression that involves an up-turning of the corners of the mouth, usually indicating pleasure or amusement: [no obj]: *He smiled happily when he heard the news.* [~ + obj]: *She smiled a happy smile at the news.* —*n.* [count] **2.** a smiling expression of the face: *A broad smile crossed his face.*

smirk /smɜrk/ *v.* [no obj] **1.** to smile in an offensive way: *They smirked behind the teacher's back.* —*n.* [count] **2.** the facial expression of a person who smirks.

smock /smɒk/ *n.* [count] a loose, lightweight piece of clothing worn over the outer clothes to protect them while working.

smog /smɒg, smɔg/ *n.* [noncount] smoke combined with fog.

smoke /smowk/ *n., v.,* **smoked, smok•ing.** —*n.* **1.** [noncount] the visible gases given off by a burning substance. **2.** [count] an act of smoking something, esp. tobacco. —*v.* **3.** [no obj] to give off smoke. **4.** to breathe the smoke of a cigarette, etc.: [no obj]: *She doesn't like to smoke.* [~ + obj]: *He smoked a pack of cigarettes a day.* **5.** [~ + obj] to dry and flavor meat, fish, etc., with smoke. **6. smoke out,** to drive from a place by the use of smoke: *to smoke out the raccoons* or *to smoke the raccoons out.* —*Idiom.* **7. go up in smoke,** to be unsuccessful: *All his plans for promotion went up in smoke.* —'**smok•er,** *n.* [count]: *Is he a smoker?* —'**smok•y,** *adj.,* **-i•er, -i•est.**

'smoke de,tector, *n.* [count] an electronic fire alarm that gives out a loud signal in the presence of smoke. Also called **'smoke ,alarm.**

smol•der /'smowldər/ *v.* [no obj] to burn slowly without flame: *The campfire was still smoldering.*

smooth /smuwð/ *adj.,* **-er, -est,** *adv., v.* —*adj.* **1.** not rough; having an even surface: *a smooth road.* **2.** free from lumps, as a sauce: *smooth gravy.* **3.** having an even, uninterrupted movement: *a smooth ride.* **4.** free from problems or difficulties: *a smooth day at the office.* **5.** too polite: *a smooth talker.* —*adv.* [often: used before another word to form an adjective] **6.** in a smooth manner: *a smooth-running car.* —*v.* [~ + obj] **7.** to make the surface of (something) smooth: *to smooth the boards with sandpaper before polishing them; He smoothed his jacket.* **8. smooth over,** to make seem less severe or disagreeable: *The chairman smoothed over the difficulties and got the two sides talking again.* —'**smooth•ly,** *adv.* —'**smooth•ness,** *n.* [noncount]

smoth•er /'smʌðər/ *v.* **1.** to (cause to) die, as by smoke or lack of air: [~ + obj]: *He was smothered by the smoke.* [no obj]: *He'll smother under those blankets.* **2.** [~ + obj] to put out (fire, etc.) by covering: *to smother the fire with blankets.* **3.** [~ + obj] to cover thickly: *to smother a steak with mushrooms.*

smudge /smʌdʒ/ *n., v.,* **smudged, smudg•ing.** —*n.* [count] **1.** a dirty mark: *a few smudges on his face.* —*v.* [~ + obj] **2.** to mark with dirty streaks: *His face was smudged with mud.* **3.** to rub so as to smear: *She didn't want to smudge her lipstick.*

smug /smʌg/ *adj.,* **smug•ger, smug•gest.** too self-satisfied: *He was very smug when he walked into the interview.* —'**smug•ly,** *adv.* —'**smug•ness,** *n.* [noncount]

smug•gle /'smʌgəl/ *v.* [~ + obj], **-gled, -gling.** to take (goods or people) secretly and illegally into or out of a place or a country: *to smuggle heroin.* —'**smug•gler,** *n.* [count]

S

smut /smʌt/ *n.* [*noncount*] **1.** sooty matter. **2.** indecent language or writing. —**'smut•ty,** *adj.*, **-ti•er, -ti•est.**

snack /snæk/ *n.* [*count*] **1.** a small portion of food or drink eaten between regular meals. —*v.* [*no obj*] **2.** to have a snack: *It's not wise to snack before bedtime; to snack on too many sweets.*

snag /snæg/ *n., v.*, **snagged, snag•ging.** —*n.* [*count*] **1.** something that is sharp and sticks out. **2.** a tear in a fabric, caused by catching on something that sticks out. **3.** anything that gets in the way of progress. —*v.* [~ + *obj*] **4.** to catch on a snag: *She snagged her sweater on the branches.*

snail /sneyl/ *n.* [*count*] a soft-bodied, slow-moving animal that lives in a spiral-shaped shell.

'snail ‚mail, *n.* [*noncount*] standard postal service, as contrasted with electronic mail.

snake /sneyk/ *n., v.*, **snaked, snak•ing.** —*n.* [*count*] **1.** a scaly reptile with a long thin body that has no legs. **2.** a treacherous person. —*v.* [*no obj*] **3.** to twist in the manner of a snake: *The road snakes through the mountains.*

snap /snæp/ *v.*, **snapped, snap•ping,** *n., adj.* —*v.* **1.** to open or close with a sharp sound, as a door or lid: [*no obj*]: *The door snapped shut.* [~ + *obj*]: *She snapped the lid shut.* **2.** to (cause to) break suddenly with a cracking sound: [~ + *obj*]: *He snapped a piece of wood in half.* [*no obj*]: *The wood snapped in half.* **3.** [~ + *obj*] to take (photographs): *tourists snapping pictures of the cathedral.* **4.** to speak quickly and sharply: [*no obj*]: *The captain snapped at the first mate.* [*used with quotations*]: *"Mind your own business!" he snapped.* **5. snap out of,** to recover from: *Will the economy snap out of the recession?* **6. snap up,** to seize quickly: *They snapped up the best bargains* or *They snapped the best bargains up.* —*n.* **7.** [*count*] a quick, sudden action or sound, as the breaking of a twig. **8.** [*count*] a fastener that snaps when it closes. **9.** [*count*] a short period, as of cold weather: *a cold snap.* **10.** [*count; usually singular; usually: a + ~*] *Informal.* an easy task, duty, etc.: *Fixing the toaster was a snap.* —*adj.* [*before a noun*] **11.** done suddenly: *a snap judgment.*

snap•py /'snæpiy/ *adj.*, **-pi•er, -pi•est. 1.** quick in action: *a snappy answer.* **2.** irritable. **3.** *Informal.* smart, lively, etc.: *a snappy dresser.*

snap•shot /'snæp‚ʃɒt/ *n.* [*count*] an informal photograph.

snare /snɛər/ *n., v.*, **snared, snar•ing.** —*n.* [*count*] **1.** a device made up of a rope with a loop, for capturing small animals. **2.** anything serving to trap someone. —*v.* [~ + *obj*] **3.** to catch with a snare; trap.

snarl¹ /snɑrl/ *v.* **1.** [*no obj*] to growl angrily with the teeth bared, as a dog: *The dog snarled at the child.* **2.** to speak in a sharp, angry voice: [*no obj*]: *He was snarling (at his family) all day.* [~ + *obj*]: *to snarl a threat.* [*used with quotations*]: *"Get back, all of you!" he snarled.* —*n.* [*count*] **3.** the act of snarling.

snarl² /snɑrl/ *n.* [*count*] **1.** a tangle, as of thread or hair. **2.** a confused condition: *a traffic snarl.* —*v.* **3.** [~ + *obj*] [*no obj*] to (cause to) become tangled, as thread or hair. **4.** to (cause to) become confused: [~ + *obj*]: *Traffic was badly snarled at the bridge.* [*no obj*]: *Traffic snarled at the entrance ramp.*

snatch /snætʃ/ *v.* **1.** to make a sudden move to seize (something): [~ + *at* + *obj*]: *He snatched at her purse.* [~ + *obj*]: *He snatched the woman's purse.* —*n.* [*count*] **2.** an act or instance

of snatching. **3.** a small piece of something: *I heard snatches of their conversation.*

sneak /sniyk/ *v.*, **sneaked** or **snuck** /snʌk/, **sneak•ing,** *n.* —*v.* **1.** [*no obj*] to go in a secretive way: *Let's sneak out the back door.* **2.** [~ + *obj*] to move, put, etc., in a sly or dishonest manner: *He sneaked the gun into his pocket.* —*n.* [*count*] **3.** a person who should not be trusted. —**'sneak•i•ness,** *n.* [*noncount*] —**'sneak•y,** *adj.*, **-i•er, -i•est.**

sneak•er /'sniykər/ *n.* [*count*] a shoe of canvas with a flat rubber sole.

sneer /snɪər/ *v.* **1.** to act, speak, or write in a way that shows ridicule or scorn: [*no obj*]: *They sneered at her beliefs.* [*used with quotations*]: *"Just try it," he sneered.* —*n.* [*count*] **2.** a look, action, or remark of ridicule or scorn.

sneeze /sniyz/ *v.*, **sneezed, sneez•ing,** *n.* —*v.* [*no obj*] **1.** to produce air suddenly, forcibly, and loudly through the nose and mouth involuntarily. —*n.* [*count*] **2.** an act or sound of sneezing.

snick•er /'snɪkər/ *v.* [*no obj*] **1.** to laugh quietly and disrespectfully: *The children snickered when the teacher turned his back. They snickered at his attempt to roller-skate.* —*n.* [*count*] **2.** a snickering laugh.

snide /snayd/ *adj.*, **snid•er, snid•est.** insulting in a nasty, sly manner: *snide remarks about her dress.*

sniff /snɪf/ *v.* **1.** [*no obj*] to draw air through the nose in a short, somewhat noisy way. **2.** to smell by doing this: [~ + *obj*]: *to sniff the flowers.* [*no obj*]: *The bloodhounds sniffed at the ground.* —*n.* [*count*] **3.** an act or sound of sniffing.

snip /snɪp/ *v.*, **snipped, snip•ping,** *n.* —*v.* [~ + *obj*] **1.** to cut or remove with a small, quick stroke with scissors: *to snip a rose.* —*n.* [*count*] **2.** the act of snipping.

snip•py /'snɪpiy/ *adj.*, **-pi•er, -pi•est.** sharp or curt, esp. in a nasty way: *a snippy answer.*

snob /snɒb/ *n.* [*count*] one who admires or imitates people of high social rank. —**'snob•ber•y, 'snob•bish•ness,** *n.* [*noncount*] —**'snob•bish,** *adj.* —**'snob•by,** *adj.*, **-bi•er, -bi•est.**

snoop /snuwp/ *Informal.* —*v.* [*no obj*] **1.** to go about in a sneaky way while trying to gain information: *always snooping around the office.* —*n.* [*count*] **2.** Also, **'snoop•er.** one who snoops.

snooze /snuwz/ *v.*, **snoozed, snooz•ing,** *n.* —*v.* [*no obj*] **1.** to doze; nap: *snoozing on the couch.* —*n.* [*count*] **2.** a short nap.

snore /snɔr/ *v.*, **snored, snor•ing,** *n.* —*v.* [*no obj*] **1.** to breathe during sleep with loud, harsh sounds: *snoring so loudly he woke her up.* —*n.* [*count*] **2.** the act of snoring. —**'snor•er,** *n.* [*count*]

snor•kel /'snɔrkəl/ *n.* [*count*] **1.** a tube with which a swimmer can breathe while moving just below the surface of the water. —*v.* [*no obj*] **2.** to swim while breathing with a snorkel. —**'snor•kel•er,** *n.* [*count*]

snort /snɔrt/ *v.* **1.** [*no obj*] to force the breath loudly through the nose. **2.** to express (contempt, anger, etc.) by a snort: [*no obj*]: *I snorted in disbelief.* [*used with quotations*]: *"Ridiculous!" he snorted, "It'll never work."* —*n.* [*count*] **3.** the act or sound of snorting.

snout /snawt/ *n.* [*count*] the part of an animal's head that contains the nose and jaws.

snow /snow/ *n.* [*noncount*] **1. a.** frozen water in the form of white flakes. **b.** these flakes as forming a layer on the ground. —*v.* **2.** [*no obj; it* + ~] (of snow) to fall: *It snowed heavily last night.*

3. snow in, to cover, block, etc., with snow: *We were snowed in for two days.* **4. snow under,** to cause to have too much of something: *I've been snowed under with all this work.* —'**snow•y,** *adj.,* **-i•er, -i•est.**

snow•ball /'snow,bɔl/ *n.* [*count*] **1.** a ball of snow pressed together, as for throwing. —*v.* [*no obj*] **2.** to (cause to) become larger at an increasing rate: *Soon a few small lies had snowballed into a huge scandal.*

snow•board /'snow,bɔrd, -,bowrd/ *n.* [*count*] a board that resembles a wide ski, used for gliding on snow while in a standing position.

snow•drift /'snow,drɪft/ *n.* [*count*] a mound of snow blown together by the wind.

snow•flake /'snow,fleyk/ *n.* [*count*] one of the small crystals in which snow falls.

snow•man /'snow,mæn/ *n.* [*count*], *pl.* **-men.** a figure of a person made out of packed snow.

snow•mo•bile /'snowmə,biyl/ *n.* [*count*] a motor vehicle with a revolving tread in the rear and steerable skis in the front, for traveling over snow.

snow•plow /'snow,plaw/ *n.* [*count*] a vehicle or machine for clearing away snow from highways, etc.

snow•shoe /'snow,ʃuw/ *n.* [*count*] a frame shaped like a racket and attached to the shoe for walking on deep snow without sinking.

snow•storm /'snow,stɔrm/ *n.* [*count*] a storm with a heavy fall of snow.

snub /snʌb/ *v.,* **snubbed, snub•bing,** *n.* —*v.* [~ + *obj*] **1.** to treat rudely; ignore: *He waved at her but she snubbed him.* —*n.* [*count*] **2.** an act or instance of snubbing.

snuck /snʌk/ *v.* a pp. and pt. of SNEAK.

snuff /snʌf/ *v.* **snuff out, 1.** to put out (a flame), as by pressing with the fingers: *to snuff out the candles* or *to snuff the candles out.* **2.** to suppress: *The dictator snuffed out all opposition; to snuff opposition out.*

snug /snʌg/ *adj.,* **snug•ger, snug•gest. 1.** warmly comfortable or cozy: *a snug little house.* **2.** fitting tightly: *a snug sweater.* —'**snug•ly,** *adv.: That dress fits too snugly.*

snug•gle /'snʌgəl/ *v.,* **-gled, -gling.** to lie close, as for comfort or from affection: [*no obj*]: *They snuggled under the covers.* [~ + *up*]: *The child snuggled up to his mother.*

so /sow/ *adv.* **1.** in the manner shown: *Do it so.* **2.** to such a degree or amount: *Don't walk so fast.* **3.** very: *I'm so happy.* **4.** to such a degree or extent; as: *So far as I know, she has always been trustworthy.* **5.** therefore; for that reason: *She was ill, so she stayed home.* **6.** indeed; truly; too: *"You weren't at the party last night." —"I was so!"* **7.** also; likewise; too: *If he is going, then so am I.* —*conj.* **8.** [~ (+ *that*)] in order that: *He wore warm clothes so he wouldn't be cold in the winter snows.* **9.** therefore: *He wasn't feeling well so he went to lie down on the couch.* —*interj.* **10.** (used to show surprise, shock, indifference, etc., according to the situation). —*adj.* [*be* + ~] **11.** true as stated or reported: *Say it isn't so!*

soak /sowk/ *v.* **1.** to (cause to) become thoroughly wet by being in a liquid: [*no obj*]: *The clothes were left to soak in the soapy water.* [~ + *obj*]: *I soaked my foot in warm water.* **2.** [~ + *obj*] to wet thoroughly: *The floods soaked the rug and ruined it.* —*n.* [*count*] **3.** the act or state of soaking, or the state of being soaked.

soap /sowp/ *n.* [*noncount*] **1.** a substance used

for washing, made of fat or oil. —*v.* [~ + *obj*] **2.** to rub with soap. —'**soap•y,** *adj.,* **-i•er, -i•est.**

'**soap ,opera** /'ppərə, 'ppra/ *n.* [*count*] a radio or television series presenting the daily lives and problems of many characters.

soar /sɔr/ *v.* [*no obj*] **1.** to fly upward, such as a bird. **2.** to rise to a more or higher or more exalted level: *His hopes soared.*

sob /spb/ *v.,* **sobbed, sob•bing,** *n.* —*v.* [*no obj*] **1.** to weep with a catching of the breath or in sudden, short gasps: *She sobbed at the news.* —*n.* [*count*] **2.** the act of sobbing, or a sound suggesting this.

so•ber /'sowbər/ *adj.,* **-er, -est,** *v.* —*adj.* **1.** not drunk: *I stayed sober at the party.* **2.** serious or solemn: *a sober expression.* **3.** not flashy or showy, such as clothes. —*v.* **4. sober up,** to (cause to) become free of the effects of too much liquor: *A cup of coffee will sober him up; coffee to sober up the guests; He tried to sober up.* —'**so•ber•ly,** *adv.*

'**so-'called,** *adj.* [*before a noun*] **1.** called thus: *the so-called "Kid's Club."* **2.** incorrectly called thus: *Her so-called friends are the ones who tempted her to use drugs.*

soc•cer /'spkər/ *n.* [*noncount*] a form of football played by two 11-member teams, in which the ball may be kicked or bounced off any part of the body but the arms and hands.

'**soccer ,mom,** *n.* [*count*] a typical American suburban woman with school-age children.

so•cia•ble /'sowʃəbəl/ *adj.* glad to associate with others: *a sociable couple who enjoy parties.* —**so•cia•bil•i•ty** /,sowʃə'bɪlɪtiy/ *n.* [*noncount*] —'**so•cia•bly,** *adv.*

so•cial /'sowʃəl/ *adj.* **1.** of or relating to friendly companionship or relations: *a social club.* **2.** living with others: *Humans are social animals.* **3.** [*often: before a noun*] of or relating to human society: *the social classes of the Middle Ages in Europe.* —'**so•cial•ly,** *adv.*

so•cial•ism /'sowʃə,lɪzəm/ *n.* [*noncount*] a system of social organization in which the means of production and distribution of goods are owned and controlled by groups or by the government. —'**so•cial•ist,** *adj., n.* [*count*]

so•cial•ize /'sowʃə,layz/ *v.,* **-ized, -iz•ing. 1.** [~ + *obj*] to make fit for life in companionship with others: *to socialize a child.* **2.** [*no obj*] to associate sociably with others: *some friends to socialize with.* —**so•cial•i•za•tion** /,sowʃəlɪ'zeyʃən/ *n.* [*noncount*]

'**social 'science,** *n.* [*count*] a field of study, such as sociology or economics, dealing with society or social activity.

'**social se'curity,** *n.* [*noncount*; *often: Social Security*] a U.S. government program of old age, unemployment, health, disability, and survivors' insurance.

'**social ,work,** *n.* [*noncount*] any organized service or activity to improve social conditions in a community, such as assistance to troubled families. —'**social ,worker,** *n.* [*count*]

so•ci•e•ty /sə'sayɪtiy/ *n., pl.* **-ties. 1.** [*noncount*] human beings thought of as a group and viewed as members of a community. **2.** a highly structured system of human organization: [*noncount*]: *American society.* [*count*]: *They studied societies of ancient Egypt and Greece.* **3.** [*count*] a group of people who have a common interest: *an Irish-American cultural society.* **4.** [*noncount*] wealthy, fashionable persons: *people in high society.*

S

so•ci•ol•o•gy /ˌsowsiy'ɒlədʒiy, ˌsowʃiy-/ n. [noncount] the science or study of human society. —**so•ci•o•log•i•cal** /ˌsowsiyə'lɒdʒɪkəl, ˌsowʃiy-/ adj. —**so•ci'ol•o•gist,** n. [count]

sock[1] /sɒk/ n. [count], pl. **socks** or sometimes, **sox.** a short stocking usually reaching to the calf.

sock[2] /sɒk/ v. [~ + obj] **1.** to hit hard: She socked him in the jaw. —n. [count] **2.** a hard blow.

sock•et /'sɒkɪt/ n. [count] a hollow part that contains or fits into another part: a socket for a light bulb.

sod /sɒd/ n., v., **sod•ded, sod•ding.** —n. [count] [noncount] **1.** a section cut or torn from the surface of grass, containing the matted roots. —v. [~ + obj] **2.** to cover with sod.

so•da /'sowdə/ n., pl. **-das. 1.** SODA POP: [noncount]: doesn't drink soda. [count]: How many sodas did you drink? **2.** SODA WATER. **3.** [count] a drink made with soda water and flavored syrup: an ice-cream soda. **4.** [count] a compound containing sodium.

'soda ,pop, n. [noncount] a carbonated, flavored, and sweetened soft drink: some cherry soda pop.

'soda ,water, n. [noncount] water charged with carbon dioxide.

sod•den /'sɒdn̩/ adj. very wet.

so•di•um /'sowdiyəm/ n. [noncount] a soft, silver-white, chemically active metallic element.

'sodium bi'carbonate, n. [noncount] a white powder used to control stomach acid, to extinguish fires, and to make dough rise in baking. Also called **bicarbonate of soda, baking soda.**

so•fa /'sowfə/ n. [count], pl. **-fas.** a long upholstered couch with a back and raised ends.

'sofa ,bed or **'so•fa,bed,** n. [count] a sofa that can be converted into a bed.

soft /sɔft, sɒft/ adj., **-er, -est. 1.** not hard or firm: a soft pillow. **2.** easy to bend, crush, or cut: soft wood. **3.** smooth and pleasing to the touch: soft skin. **4.** not harsh to the eye or ear: soft light. **5.** gentle; kind: You're too soft with those students. **6.** easy: He has a soft job. —**'soft•ly,** adv.: She spoke softly. —**'soft•ness,** n. [noncount]

soft•ball /'sɔftˌbɔl, 'sɒft-/ n. **1.** [noncount] a form of baseball played on a smaller playing field with a larger and softer ball. **2.** [count] the ball itself.

'soft-'boiled, adj. (of an egg) boiled in the shell until the yolk and white are only partially set.

'soft 'drink, n. [count] a beverage that is not alcoholic and is usually carbonated, such as ginger ale.

soft•en /'sɔfən, 'sɒfən/ v. to (cause to) become soft or softer: [~ + obj]: cream to soften the skin. [no obj]: His voice softened when he saw that the child was afraid. —**'soft•en•er,** n. [count]

'soft 'palate, n. PALATE (def. 1).

soft•ware /'sɔftˌwɛər, 'sɒft-/ n. [noncount; used with a singular verb] programs or instructions for directing a computer or processing electronic data. Compare HARDWARE.

sog•gy /'sɒgiy/ adj., **-gi•er, -gi•est.** thoroughly wet. —**sog•gi•ness,** n. [noncount]

soil[1] /sɔyl/ n. [noncount] the top portion of the earth's surface in which plants grow.

soil[2] /sɔyl/ v. to (cause to) become dirty: [~ + obj]: The baby had soiled her diapers. [no obj]: These white clothes soil too easily.

sol•ace /'sɒlɪs/ n. **1.** [noncount] comfort in sorrow or misfortune. **2.** [count] a source of comfort.

so•lar /'sowlər/ adj. of or relating to the sun: solar energy.

'solar ,system, n. [count; usually: the + ~] the sun and all the planets and other bodies that revolve around it.

sold /sowld/ v. pt. and pp. of SELL.

sol•der /'sɒdər/ n. [noncount] **1.** a soft metal that is melted and used to join objects made of other metals. —v. [~ + obj] **2.** to join (metal objects) with solder.

sol•dier /'sowldʒər/ n. [count] one who works in military service.

sole[1] /sowl/ adj. [before a noun] **1.** being the only one: the sole living relative. **2.** belonging to one individual or group only: sole right to the estate. —**'sole•ly,** adv.: He did it solely through his own efforts.

sole[2] /sowl/ n., v., **soled, sol•ing.** —n. [count] **1.** the bottom surface of a foot. **2.** the corresponding under part of a shoe. —v. [~ + obj] **3.** to furnish with a sole.

sole[3] /sowl/ n. [count], pl. (esp. when thought of as a group) **sole,** (esp. for kinds or species) **soles.** a kind of fish having a flattened body and a hooklike snout, used for food.

sol•emn /'sɒləm/ adj. **1.** grave; not funny: solemn remarks. **2.** serious or formal: solemn assurance that he would keep his word. —**so•lem•ni•ty** /sə'lɛmnɪtiy/, n. [noncount] —**'sol•emn•ly,** adv.

so•lic•it /sə'lɪsɪt/ v. **1.** [~ + obj] to make a request for: to solicit aid from the United Nations. **2.** [~ + obj] to ask (someone) for something: to solicit the committee for funds. **3.** [no obj] to ask for business, as by selling or trading: No soliciting is allowed in this building. —**so•lic•i•ta•tion** /səˌlɪsɪ'teyʃən/, n. [noncount]

sol•id /'sɒlɪd/ adj. **1.** not hollow: a piece of solid rock. **2.** having the three dimensions of length, breadth, and thickness: A cube is a solid figure. **3.** firm: standing on solid ground. **4.** serious: solid scholarship. **5.** [before a noun] made up entirely of one substance: That ring is solid gold. **6.** fully dependable: a solid citizen. —n. [count] **7.** something solid. **8.** a substance that is not a liquid or a gas. —**so•lid•i•ty** /sə'lɪdɪtiy/, n. [noncount] —**'sol•id•ly,** adv. —**'sol•id•ness,** n. [noncount]

sol•i•dar•i•ty /ˌsɒlɪ'dærɪtiy/ n. [noncount] agreement in attitude or purpose, as between members of a group: Our union went on strike in solidarity with the others.

so•lid•i•fy /sə'lɪdɪˌfay/ v., **-fied, -fy•ing.** to (cause to) become solid or firm: [no obj]: Water solidifies and becomes ice. [~ + obj]: Let's solidify the procedures.

sol•i•tar•y /'sɒlɪˌtɛriy/ adj. **1.** [before a noun] without companions: a solitary passerby. **2.** [before a noun] being the only one: a solitary exception. **3.** far away from others; secluded: a solitary cabin in the woods.

sol•i•tude /'sɒlɪˌtuwd, -ˌtyuwd/ n. [noncount] the state of being or living alone.

so•lo /'sowlow/ n., pl. **-los,** adj., adv. —n. [count] **1.** a musical composition, dance, etc., for one performer. —adj. **2.** of, relating to, or being a solo. —adv. **3.** on one's own; alone: She's flying solo. —**'so•lo•ist,** n. [count]

sol•u•ble /'sɒlyəbəl/ adj. capable of being dissolved in a liquid: a soluble powder.

so·lu·tion /sə'luwʃən/ n. **1.** [noncount] the act or process of solving a problem, or the state of being solved: No solution is possible for that problem. **2.** [count] an answer to a problem. **3. a.** [noncount] the process by which a solid is dissolved in a liquid: in solution. **b.** [count] a liquid resulting from this process.

solve /sɒlv/ v. [~ + obj], **solved, solv·ing.** to find the answer or solution to: to solve a puzzle. —'**solv·a·ble,** adj.

sol·vent /'sɒlvənt/ adj. **1.** able to pay all one's debts. —n. [count] **2.** a substance that dissolves another to form a solution: Water is a solvent for sugar. —'**sol·ven·cy,** n. [noncount]

som·ber /'sɒmbər/ adj. **1.** dull in color or tone: a somber dress. **2.** serious; grave: a somber expression on one's face. Also, esp. Brit., '**som·bre.** —'**som·ber·ly,** adv.

some /sʌm; unstressed səm/ adj. **1.** [~ + singular count noun] unknown or not specified: Some people may object. We asked if there would be some adult present in the class. **2.** [~ + noncount noun] being an unspecified amount or part of, but not all of: I agree with you to some extent. Will you spend some time with your friends? —pron. **3. a.** certain persons not specified: [used in place of a plural noun]: Some think he is dead. [~ + of + plural noun]: Some of the people think he is dead. **b.** a certain part or amount not specified: [used in place of a noncount noun]: Some is spoiled, but some is still good. [~ + of the + noncount noun]: Some of the food is spoiled. —adv. **4.** [before a number] approximately; about: The building was some fifty stories high. **5.** to some degree or extent: I like baseball some. —**Usage.** SOME is used in sentences that are affirmative: I'd like some milk. ANY is used instead of SOME with negative phrases or in questions: I don't want any milk. I never see any of my friends these days. Do you have any milk? But SOME can be used in questions when the answer is expected to be "yes": Can I have some milk, please?

-some[1], a suffix meaning: like (burdensome); tending to (quarrelsome).

-some[2], a suffix meaning a group of a certain number (threesome).

some·bod·y /'sʌm,bɒdiy, -,bʌdiy, -bədiy/ pron., n., pl. **-bod·ies.** —pron. **1.** someone not known or specified: Maybe somebody will think of a better solution. There's somebody at the door. —n. **2.** This word may be used as a pronoun (with no article) or as a count noun (with an article if singular) to mean "a person of some importance:" Right now he may not seem special, but one day he'll be somebody.

some·day /'sʌm,dey/ adv. at an indefinite time in the future: Someday she'll be president.

some·how /'sʌm,haw/ adv. in some way not specified or known: They knew that somehow they would meet again.

some·one /'sʌm,wʌn, -wən/ pron. some person; somebody: Our hosts arranged for someone to meet us at the airport.

som·er·sault /'sʌmər,sɔlt/ n. [count] **1.** an acrobatic movement, either forward or backward, in which the body rolls end over end. —v. [no obj] **2.** to perform a somersault.

some·thing /'sʌm,θɪŋ/ pron. **1.** a certain thing not determined or specified: Something is wrong there. Tell me something; what do you think about this? **2.** (used to express that an idea or comment is not exact or complete): I was think-

ing of joining a health club or something. —n. [noncount] **3.** a thing of some importance: There's something to what you say. —adv. **4.** to some extent: I saw a bird that was something like a crow.

some·time /'sʌm,taym/ adv. at some indefinite time: Our friends arrived sometime last week.

some·times /'sʌm,taymz/ adv. on some occasions; now and then: Sometimes I walk to work.

some·what /'sʌm,hwʌt, -,hwɒt, -,wʌt, -,wɒt/ adv. to some extent: The defeat was somewhat surprising.

some·where /'sʌm,hwɛər, -,wɛər/ adv. in, at, or to some place unspecified or unknown: I've left the book somewhere.

son /sʌn/ n. [count] **1.** a male child or person in relation to his parents by birth or adoption. **2.** (used by an older person to address a younger male): "Well, son, here's the choice: jail or a fine," the sheriff said.

song /sɔŋ, sɒŋ/ n. [count] **1.** a short piece of music for singing. **2.** a patterned vocal sound produced by an animal, as by male birds, frogs, etc. —**Idiom. 3. for a song,** at a very low price: I bought the rug for a song.

song·bird /'sɔŋ,bɜrd, 'sɒŋ-/ n. [count] a bird that sings.

son·ic /'sɒnɪk/ adj. of or relating to sound or to the speed of sound.

'son-in-,law, n. [count], pl. **sons-in-law.** the husband of one's daughter.

soon /suwn/ adv., **-er, -est. 1.** within a short period; before long: I'll be back soon. **2.** quickly: Finish as soon as you can. **3.** readily or willingly: I would as soon walk as ride. —**Idiom. 4. sooner or later,** sometime; eventually: Sooner or later you must face the truth.

soot /sʊt, suwt/ n. [noncount] a black substance produced during incomplete burning of coal, etc.: Black soot was shooting out of the chimneys. —'**soot·y,** adj., **-i·er, ·-i·est:** sooty fireplaces.

soothe /suwð/ v., **soothed, sooth·ing. 1.** [~ + obj] to cause to be calm: to soothe someone with kind words. **2.** to relieve the pain in or of (something): [~ + obj]: a lotion to soothe sunburned skin. [no obj]: The lotion soothes as it heals. —'**sooth·ing,** adj.

so·phis·ti·cat·ed /sə'fɪstɪ,keytɪd/ adj. **1.** having or showing knowledge of the world: sophisticated travelers. **2.** complex: a sophisticated electronic control system. —**so·phis·ti·ca·tion** /sə,fɪstɪ'keyʃən/, n. [noncount]: The sophistication of the child's drawing amazed everyone.

soph·o·more /'sɒfə,mɔr, 'sɒfmɔr/ n. [count] a student in the second year at a high school, college, or university.

sop·ping /'sɒpɪŋ/ adj. very wet.

so·pran·o /sə'prænow, -'prɑnow/ n. [count], pl. **-pran·os. 1.** the highest singing voice in women and boys. **2.** a singer with such a voice.

sor·cer·y /'sɔrsəriy/ n. [noncount] black magic; witchcraft. —'**sor·cer·er,** n. [count] —'**sor·cer·ess,** n. [count]

sor·did /'sɔrdɪd/ adj. **1.** morally low; corrupt: a sordid life; a sordid business deal. **2.** filthy; badly cared for: a sordid slum. —'**sor·did·ly,** adv. —'**sor·did·ness,** n. [noncount]

sore /sɔr/ adj., **sor·er, sor·est.** —adj. **1.** physically painful or sensitive, such as a wound: a sore arm. **2.** [before a noun] causing very great misery or hardship: The team is in sore need of a new pitcher. **3.** [be + ~ (+ at + obj)] annoyed; angered: The boss is sore (at me) because I lost

S

her report. **4.** causing annoyance or irritation: *Her parking ticket is a sore subject right now.* —*n.* [*count*] **5.** a painfully irritated or infected spot on the body. —**'sore•ly,** *adv.*: *The injured star pitcher will be sorely missed by his teammates.* —**'sore•ness,** *n.* [*noncount*]

so•ror•i•ty /səˈrɔrɪtiy, -ˈrɒr-/ *n.* [*count*], *pl.* **-ties.** a society of women or girls, esp. in a college.

sor•row /ˈsɒrow, ˈsɔrow/ *n.* **1.** [*noncount*] distress caused by loss, disappointment, etc.; grief. **2.** [*count*] a cause of grief: *Too many sorrows crushed her spirit.* —**'sor•row•ful,** *adj.* —**'sor•row•ful•ly,** *adv.*

sor•ry /ˈsɒriy, ˈsɔriy/ *adj.*, **-ri•er, -ri•est. 1.** [*be* + ~] feeling regret, sadness, pity, etc.: *We are sorry to leave our friends. We are sorry (that) we have to leave. He felt sorry for her.* **2.** [*before a noun*] causing pity: *This family is in a sorry situation.* **3.** (used to apologize): *Did I bump into you? Sorry.* **4.** (used to ask someone to repeat what was said): *"Sorry, I didn't hear what you said."*

sort /sɔrt/ *n.* [*count*] **1.** a particular kind; type: *There are many sorts of people.* **2.** character or quality: *friends of a nice sort.* —*v.* **3.** [~ + *obj*] to separate according to kind: *to sort socks into matching pairs.* **4. sort out,** to put in order; to make clear: *trying to sort things out at home; to sort out one's problems.* —**Idiom. 5. out of sorts, a.** annoyed, irritable, or depressed: *feeling out of sorts.* **b.** sick; ill. **6. sort of,** rather: *The book was sort of interesting, wasn't it?*

SOS /ˈɛsˌowˈɛs/ *n.* [*count*], *pl.* **SOSs, SOS's.** an internationally recognized distress signal, consisting of the letters SOS in Morse code.

'so-,so or **'so ,so,** *adj.* **1.** neither very good nor very bad: *a so-so day at work.* —*adv.* **2.** neither very well nor very badly: *Things were going so-so at the time.*

sought /sɔt/ *v.* pt. and pp. of SEEK.

soul /sowl/ *n.* **1.** [*count*] the spiritual part of humans: *to have an immortal soul.* **2.** [*count*] a person: *brave souls.* **3.** [*count; usually: the* + ~ + *of* + *obj*] an excellent example of some quality: *He was the very soul of tact.* **4.** [*noncount*] deeply or strongly felt emotion: *The painting was soul.* **5.** SOUL MUSIC.

'soul 'music, *n.* [*noncount*] music with roots in African-American gospel music.

sound¹ /sawnd/ *n.* **1.** something that can be heard: [*noncount*]: *Sound travels at speeds slower than light.* [*count*]: *the sound of fire engines.* **2.** [*count; usually singular; usually: the* + ~ + *of* + *obj*] the idea produced by something one has heard or read: *I don't like the sound of that report.* —*v.* **3.** to (cause to) give off sound: [~ + *obj*]: *Sound the alarm.* [*no obj*]: *The alarm sounded.* **4.** [~ + *adjective*] to give a certain impression when heard or read: *His voice sounded strange. The engine backfire sounded like a gunshot. That idea sounds as if it will work.* **5. sound off,** *Informal.* to speak frankly or too angrily: *Quit sounding off about everything.*

sound² /sawnd/ *adj.,* **-er, -est,** *adv.* —*adj.* **1.** in good condition; healthy: *a sound body.* **2.** sensible; valid: *sound judgment.* **3.** honorable: *sound values.* **4.** uninterrupted and untroubled: *She woke up from a sound sleep.* **5.** severe: *a sound beating.* —*adv.* **6.** deeply: *She was sound asleep.* —**'sound•ly,** *adv.*: *The team was soundly defeated.* —**'sound•ness,** *n.* [*noncount*]

sound³ /sawnd/ *v.* **1.** [~ + *obj*] to measure the

depth of (water, a deep hole, etc.) by letting down a lead weight at the end of a line. **2. sound out,** to ask (someone) for an opinion in an indirect way: *Let's sound him out about the new plan. Always sound out your spouse before buying something expensive.*

sound⁴ /sawnd/ *n.* a narrow passage of water between the mainland and an island: [*count*]: *long sounds along the coast.* [*used as part of a proper noun*]: *Long Island Sound.*

sound•proof /ˈsawndˌpruwf/ *adj.* **1.** not allowing sound to pass through: *a soundproof room.* —*v.* [~ + *obj*] **2.** to make (a room, etc.) soundproof.

sound•track /ˈsawndˌtræk/ *n.* [*count*] the sound recorded on a film, esp. music or voices.

soup /suwp/ *n.* a liquid food made by cooking together vegetables, seasonings, and often meat or fish: [*noncount*]: *a bowl of hot chicken soup.* [*count*]: *The restaurant offers three soups daily.*

sour /sawᵊr, ˈsawər/ *adj.,* **-er, -est,** *v.* —*adj.* **1.** having an acid taste resembling that of vinegar: *Lemons taste sour.* **2.** spoiled: *sour milk.* —*v.* **3.** to (cause to) become sour: [*no obj*]: *The milk soured in a few hours.* [~ + *obj*]: *Poor refrigeration will sour milk.* —**Idiom. 4. go sour,** to become unsatisfactory; fail: *Their marriage has gone sour.* —**'sour•ly,** *adv.* —**'sour•ness,** *n.* [*noncount*]

source /sɔrs/ *n.* [*count*] any thing or place from which something comes; origin: *the source of a river.*

south /sawθ/ *n.* [*count; singular; often: the* + ~] **1.** the point of the compass lying directly opposite north, to the right of a person facing the rising sun. **2.** a region situated in this direction. **3. the South,** (in the United States) the general area south of Pennsylvania and the Ohio River and east of the Mississippi River. —*adj.* **4.** lying toward or situated in the south. **5.** coming from the south: *a south wind.* —*adv.* **6.** to, toward, or in the south: *The plane headed south.*

south•east /ˌsawθˈiyst; *Nautical.* ˌsaw-/ *n.* [*count; singular; often: the* + ~] **1.** the direction midway between south and east. —*adj.* **2.** in, toward, or facing the southeast. **3.** (of a wind) coming from the southeast. —*adv.* **4.** toward the southeast: *sailing southeast.* —**,south'east•ern,** *adj.*

south•ern /ˈsʌðərn/ *adj.* of or relating to the south.

south•ern•er /ˈsʌðərnər/ *n.* [*count*] **1.** a native or inhabitant of the south. **2.** [*Southerner*] a native or inhabitant of the southern U.S.

'South 'Pole, *n.* [*the* + ~] the southern end of the earth's axis.

south•ward /ˈsawθwərd; *Nautical.* ˈsʌðərd/ *adj.* **1.** moving, facing, or situated toward the south. —*adv.* **2.** Also, **'south•wards.** toward the south; south.

south•west /ˌsawθˈwɛst; *Nautical.* ˌsaw-/ *n.* [*count; singular; often: the* + ~] **1.** the direction midway between south and west. —*adj.* **2.** in, toward, or facing the southwest. **3.** (of a wind) coming from the southwest. —*adv.* **4.** toward the southwest: *sailing southwest.* —**,south'west•ern,** *adj.*

sou•ve•nir /ˌsuwvəˈnɪər, ˈsuwvəˌnɪər/ *n.* [*count*] a small, inexpensive article that is a reminder of a place one has visited, a special occasion, etc.

sov•er•eign /ˈsɒvrɪn, ˈsɒvərɪn, ˈsʌv-/ *n.* [*count*] **1.** a monarch. —*adj.* [*before a noun*] **2.** having unlimited power: *the sovereign lord of the king-dom.* **3.** independent: *a sovereign nation.*

sov•er•eign•ty /'sɒvrɪntiy, 'sʌv-/ *n.* [*noncount*] the quality or state of being sovereign.

sow¹ /sow/ *v.*, **sowed, sown** or **sowed, sow•ing. 1.** to scatter (seed) over or on (land, etc.), for growth; plant: [~ + *obj*]: *to sow seeds on the farm; to sow the field with seeds.* [*no obj*]: *It was not quite time for sowing.* **2.** [~ + *obj*] to introduce or spread: *sowing distrust among his co-workers.*

sow² /saw/ *n.* [*count*] an adult female pig.

soy•bean /'sɔy,biyn/ *n.* [*count*] a type of bean used for food and for its oil.

spa /spɑ/ *n.* [*count*], *pl.* **spas. 1.** a mineral spring. **2.** a luxurious resort.

space /speys/ *n.*, *v.*, **spaced, spac•ing. —n. 1.** [*noncount*] the area in which all objects are located: *Events happen in time and space.* **2.** extent or area between objects: [*noncount*]: *We need more space to set up our equipment.* [*count*]: *wide spaces between the teeth.* **3.** [*noncount*] the place beyond the earth's atmosphere. **4.** [*count; usually singular*] a period of time: *a space of two hours.* **—v. 5.** [~ + *obj*] to set (items) some distance apart from each other: *Space (out) the desks evenly; to space the desks (out) to prevent cheating.*

space•craft /'speys,kræft/ *n.* [*count*], *pl.* **-crafts, -craft.** a vehicle for travel beyond the earth's atmosphere.

space•ship /'speys,ʃɪp/ *n.* [*count*] a spacecraft, esp. one that has a pilot or a crew.

spa•cious /'speyʃəs/ *adj.* containing much space; roomy. —**'spa•cious•ness,** *n.* [*noncount*]

spade¹ /speyd/ *n.* [*count*] a tool for digging, having a long handle and a narrow metal blade.

spade² /speyd/ *n.* **1.** [*count*] a black figure shaped like an upside-down heart with a short stem, used on playing cards. **2.** a card of the suit bearing spades.

spa•ghet•ti /spə'gɛtiy/ *n.* [*noncount*] pasta in the form of long strings.

spam /spæm/ *n.* [*count*] **1.** an unwanted or inappropriate message, such as an advertisement, that appears on a computer network. —*v.* [~ + *obj*] [*no obj*] **2.** to send spam.

span /spæn/ *n.*, *v.*, **spanned, span•ning. —n.** [*count*] **1.** the full extent of something: *We explored the entire span of the island.* **2.** a period of time during which something continues: *The span of human life is short.* **3.** the distance or space between two supports of a structure, such as a bridge. **—v.** [~ + *obj*] **4.** to extend across (space or time): *Their friendship spanned a lifetime.* **5.** to provide with something that extends across: *to span a river with a bridge.*

span•iel /'spænyəl/ *n.* [*count*] a breed of small or medium-sized dogs usually having long, drooping ears and a long, silky coat.

Span•ish /'spænɪʃ/ *adj.* **1.** of or relating to Spain. **2.** of or relating to the language spoken in Spain, Mexico, and most of Central and South America. —*n.* **3.** [*plural; the* + ~; *used with a plural verb*] the people born or living in Spain. **4.** [*noncount*] the language spoken in Spain, Mexico, and most of Central and South America.

spank /spæŋk/ *v.* [~ + *obj*] **1.** to strike with the open hand esp. on the buttocks, as in punishment: *to spank a child.* —*n.* [*count*] **2.** a blow given in spanking; slap: *a quick spank.*

spar /spɑr/ *v.* [*no obj*], **sparred, spar•ring. 1.** (of a boxer) to make the motions of attack and de-fense as a part of training. **2.** to argue, esp. in a friendly manner.

spare /spɛər/ *v.*, **spared, spar•ing,** *adj.*, **spar•er, spar•est,** *n.* **—v. 1.** [~ + *obj*] to refrain from harming or killing: *to spare the condemned man.* **2.** [~ *(+ obj)* + *obj*] to omit: *Spare (me) the gory details.* **3.** [~ + *obj*] to give without inconvenience: *Can you spare a dollar?* —*adj.* **4.** kept in reserve for possible use: *a spare part.* **5.** not taken up with work, etc.: *spare time.* **6.** thin, such as a person: *a short, spare man.* —*n.* [*count*] **7.** a spare thing or part, as an extra tire for emergency use. ——***Idiom.*** **8. to spare,** remaining; left over: *We finished early, with time to spare.*

spark /spɑrk/ *n.* [*count*] **1.** a fiery particle thrown off by something burning: *Sparks flew into the air when the firewood burned.* **2.** the light produced by a sudden discharge of electricity through air: *There was a spark when he plugged in the hairdryer.* **3.** anything, esp. something small, that activates or stimulates: *His question produced the spark that started a lively debate.* —*v.* **4.** [*no obj*] to give out sparks: *The wires sparked briefly and the lights went out.* **5.** [~ + *obj*] to stimulate: *to spark some enthusiasm.*

spar•kle /'spɑrkəl/ *v.*, **-kled, -kling,** *n.* —*v.* [*no obj*] **1.** to shine with gleams of light, such as a gem: *The diamond sparkled in the bright light.* **2.** to be lively or merry: *Her eyes sparkled.* **3.** (of wine, soda water, etc.) to give off small bubbles of gas. —*n.* **4.** [*count*] a sparkling appearance. [*noncount*] brilliance or liveliness.

'spark ,plug, *n.* [*count*] a device that sets on fire the fuel mixture in a cylinder of an engine.

spar•row /'spærow/ *n.* [*count*] any of a group of small songbirds, usually dull gray-brown.

sparse (spärs), *adj.*, **spars•er, spars•est.** not thick or dense: *sparse gray hairs on his head.* —'**sparse•ly,** *adv.* —'**sparse•ness,** *n.* [*noncount*]

spasm /'spæzəm/ *n.* [*count*] **1.** a sudden, uncontrolled movement of a muscle. **2.** any sudden, brief spell of great energy, activity, etc.: *spasms of anger.*

spat /spæt/ *v.* a pt. and pp. of SPIT¹.

spa•tial /'speyʃəl/ *adj.* of or relating to space.

spat•ter /'spætər/ *v.* **1.** [*no obj*] to send out small particles: *The bacon grease spattered on the kitchen wall.* **2.** [~ + *obj*] to splash with drops, esp. so as to soil: *The mud from the puddles spattered us.*

spat•u•la /'spætʃələ/ *n.* [*count*], *pl.* **-las.** a tool with a wide, flat, usually flexible blade, used for mixing, spreading, etc.

spawn /spɒn/ *n.* [*noncount*] **1.** the eggs of fish and other creatures that live in the water. —*v.* **2.** [*no obj*] to produce spawn. **3.** [~ + *obj*] to produce: *His disappearance spawned many rumors.*

spay /spey/ *v.* [~ + *obj*] to remove the ovaries of (an animal): *Her female cats were spayed.*

speak /spiyk/ *v.*, **spoke** /spowk/, **spo•ken** /'spowkən/, **speak•ing. 1.** to say words; talk: [*no obj*]: *He was too frightened to even speak.* [~ + *obj*]: *He spoke a few words.* **2.** [~ + *obj*] to make known: *to speak the truth.* **3.** [*no obj*] to converse: *They're so mad at each other they're not even speaking anymore.* **4.** [*no obj*] to deliver a speech: *She spoke to our group about the concerns of women.* **5.** to use (a language) as a way of communicating: [~ + *obj*]: *We tried to speak Russian.* [*no obj*]: *Try speaking in German.* **6. speak for,** to speak in behalf of: *I'd like to speak* for our partner, who can't be here today. **—Idiom. 7. to speak of,** (used with a negative word or phrase) hardly at all: *They have no debts to speak of.* **—Usage.** Do not confuse SPEAK, SAY, and TALK. We use SPEAK before the name of a language (*She speaks good Russian*) and to express a more formal sense than TALK: *May I speak with the owner?* The word SAY is used most often to describe the words one uses in communicating: *I didn't say much, just a few words.* The word TALK suggests communicating with another, so that there is an exchange: *At last the two enemies sat down and began to talk to each other. We talked with him about our problem.*

speak•er /'spiykər/ n. [count] **1.** one who speaks: *a native speaker of English.* **2.** a device that changes electric signals into sound.

spear /spɪər/ n. [count] **1.** a long wooden shaft with a sharp-pointed head of metal or stone. *—v.* [~ + obj] **2.** to pierce with or as if with a spear: *to spear a slice of fruit from the plate.*

spe•cial /'spɛʃəl/ adj. **1.** of a particular kind: *a special key.* **2.** having a specific purpose: *a special messenger to greet the ambassador.* **3.** remarkable; exceptional: *a document of special importance.*

spe•cial•ist /'spɛʃəlɪst/ n. [count] one who specializes: *a heart specialist; a computer specialist.*

spe•cial•ize /'spɛʃə,layz/ v. [no obj], **-ized, -iz•ing.** to become expert in some special area of study, work, etc.: *The doctor specializes in eye surgery.* **—spe•cial•i•za•tion** /ˌspɛʃələ'zeyʃən/, n. [noncount]

spe•cial•ly /'spɛʃə liy/ adv. for a certain, specific purpose: *The plane was waiting specially for the high-ranking diplomat.*

spe•cial•ty /'spɛʃəltiy/ n. [count], pl. **-ties. 1.** a special subject of study, area of work, skill, or the like. **2.** an article or service for which a person, business, etc., is known.

spe•cies /'spiyʃiyz, -siyz/ n. [count], pl. **-cies.** a distinct group, sort, or kind of animals or plants having some common characteristics and that can breed among themselves.

spe•cif•ic /spɪ'sɪfɪk/ adj. **1.** definite, precise, or exact: *What is the specific problem?* **2.** [be + ~ + to + obj] relating to only certain persons or things: *This symptom is specific to those who have high blood pressure.* **—spe•cif•i•cal•ly,** adv.

spec•i•fi•ca•tion /ˌspɛsəfɪ'keyʃən/ n. [count] Usually, **specifications.** [plural] a detailed description of requirements, materials, etc., as in a plan for a building.

spec•i•fy /'spɛsə,fay/ v. [~ + obj], **-fied, -fy•ing.** to state in an exact way: *He specified the times of arrival and departure of the flights.*

spec•i•men /'spɛsəmən/ n. [count] **1.** a part or an individual taken as an example of a class of things; typical animal, mineral, etc.: *The archaeologists dug up several specimens of dinosaurs.* **2.** a sample of a material to be tested: *To do the test we'll need a specimen of your blood.*

speck /spɛk/ n. [count] **1.** a small spot. **2.** a very small bit, or something appearing small: *They were just specks in the distance at first, but soon we could make out a flock of geese.*

speck•le /'spɛkəl/ n., v., **-led, -ling. —n.** [count] **1.** a small colored speck, spot, or mark. **—v.** [~ + obj] **2.** to mark with or as if with speckles.

spec•ta•cle /'spɛktəkəl/ n. [count] **1.** a striking or impressive sight. **2.** a grand public show or display. **3. spectacles,** [plural] eyeglasses.

spec•tac•u•lar /spɛk'tækyələr/ adj. of or like a

spectacle; impressive: *The wedding was a spectacular affair.*

spec•ta•tor /'spɛkteytər, spɛk'tey-/ n. [count] a member of the audience at a public performance, athletic event, etc.

spec•trum /'spɛktrəm/ n. [count], pl. **-tra** /-trə/, **-trums.** a broad range of different but related ideas, objects, etc.: *the full spectrum of political beliefs, from conservative to liberal.*

spec•u•late /'spɛkyə,leyt/ v., **-lat•ed, -lat•ing.** to wonder or think curiously about (something): [no obj]: *The audience is left to speculate on what might happen when the hero returns.* [~ + obj]: *to speculate that an agreement will be reached.* **—,spec•u'la•tion,** n. [noncount] [count]

speech /spiytʃ/ n. **1.** [noncount] the ability to speak or the act of speaking. **2.** [count] a communication in spoken language, made before an audience: *The mayor gave five speeches.* **3.** [noncount] manner of speaking of a certain person: *slurred speech.*

speech•less /'spiytʃlɪs/ adj. temporarily unable to speak: *She was speechless with anger.*

speed /spiyd/ n., v., **sped** /spɛd/ or **speed•ed, speed•ing. —n. 1.** [noncount] quickness in moving, performing, etc.: *His speed and strength helped him win the race.* **2.** [count] rate of movement: *the speed of light.* **—v. 3.** to (cause to) go fast: [no obj]: *The car sped away before we could read the license plate.* [~ + obj]: *The security guards sped the witness out of the courtroom.* **4.** [no obj] to drive at a rate faster than allowed by law: *I was ticketed for speeding.* **5. speed up, a.** to increase the speed of (something or someone): *to speed up production* or *to speed production up.* **b.** to go faster: *Can't we speed up a little?* **—'speed•er,** n. [count]: *Convicted speeders will pay high fines.*

speed•om•e•ter /spiy'dɒmɪtər, spɪ-/ n. [count] an instrument on a vehicle that shows how fast it is going.

speed•y /'spiydiy/ adj., **-i•er, -i•est.** quick: *a speedy process.* **—'speed•i•ly,** adv.

spell¹ /spɛl/ v., **spelled** or **spelt** /spɛlt/, **spell•ing. 1.** to name or write the letters of (a word, syllable, etc.): [~ + obj]: *Did you spell your name right?* [no obj]: *How did you learn to spell so well?* **2.** [~ + obj] (of letters) to form (a word, syllable, etc.): *Y-e-s spells yes.* **3.** [~ + obj] to mean: *This delay spells disaster for the business.* **4. spell out,** to explain something clearly: *Must I spell it out for you? Would someone spell out for me just what this crisis means?*

spell² /spɛl/ n. **1.** [count] a word or phrase believed to have magic power: *uttering charms and spells.* **2.** [count] a state of enchantment caused by magic power: *living under a spell.* **3.** [count; usually singular] any strong influence: *under the spell of music.*

spell³ /spɛl/ n. [count] **1.** a continuous period of activity: *Let someone else take a spell at the wheel.* **2.** an attack: *a coughing spell.* **3.** an indefinite period of time: *Come visit us for a spell.*

spell•bind /'spɛl,baynd/ v. [~ + obj], **-bound, -bind•ing.** to hold by or as if by a spell; enchant: *They were spellbound by her performance.*

spell•ing /'spɛlɪŋ/ n. **1.** the way in which words are spelled: [noncount]: *mistakes in spelling.* [count]: *There are two spellings for the word "center": center and centre.* **2.** [noncount] the process of spelling: *He's very good at spelling.*

spend /spɛnd/ v., **spent** /spɛnt/, **spend•ing. 1.** to pay out (money, resources, etc.): [~ + obj]:

We had spent too much money. [no obj]: All we do is spend. **2.** [~ + obj] to pass (time, labor, etc.) on some work, in some place, etc.: spending the day fishing. **3.** [~ + obj] to use up: The storm had spent its fury.

spent /spɛnt/ v. pt. and pp. of SPEND.

sperm /spɜrm/ n. [count], pl. **sperm, sperms.** a male reproductive cell.

spew /spyuw/ v. **1.** [no obj] to gush or pour out, esp. quickly and violently: Oil spewed from the broken pipes. **2.** [~ + obj] to pour out violently: The broken pipes spewed oil.

sphere /sfɪər/ n. [count] **1.** a solid, round figure or body. **2.** an area of activity, interest, etc.

spher•i•cal /'sfɛrɪkəl, 'sfɪər-/ adj. having the shape of a sphere; rounded.

spice /spays/ n., v., **spiced, spic•ing.** —n. **1.** [count] [noncount] a substance, such as pepper or cinnamon, used to season food. **2.** [noncount] something that gives liveliness or interest: The jokes added spice to the mayor's speech. —v. [~ + obj] **3.** to add spice to.

spic•y /'spaysiy/ adj., **-i•er, -i•est. 1.** having or containing spice: spicy Mexican food. **2.** exciting and slightly improper: some spicy gossip.

spi•der /'spaydər/ n. [count] a small eight-legged creature that produces a silky web for trapping insects.

spike /spayk/ n. [count] **1.** a naillike fastener. **2.** something resembling such a nail, as a metal point attached to the sole of an athletic shoe.

spill /spɪl/ v., **spilled** or **spilt** /spɪlt/, **spill•ing,** n. —v. **1.** to (cause or allow liquid to) run or fall from a container, esp. accidentally: [~ + obj]: to spill milk. [no obj]: The milk spilled on the floor. **2.** [~ + obj] to let (a secret) become known. —n. [count] **3.** a spilling, as of liquid: an oil spill. **4.** a fall from a horse, bicycle, etc.

spin /spɪn/ v., **spun** /spʌn/, **spin•ning,** n. —v. **1.** [~ + obj] [no obj] to form wool, cotton, etc. into thread or yarn. **2.** [~ + obj] to produce a thread, web, etc.: The spider spun its web. **3.** to (cause to) go round and round rapidly: [~ + obj]: to spin a coin on a table. [no obj]: The coin spun on the table. **4.** [~ + obj] to invent in a manner like spinning thread: He spun a fantastic tale about his childhood. **5.** [no obj] to have a sensation of going round and round: My head began to spin. —n. [count] **6.** the act of causing a spinning or whirling motion: She gave the coin a quick spin. **7.** a spinning motion: We never notice the spin of the earth. **8.** a short drive for pleasure. —'spin•ner, n. [count]

spin•ach /'spɪnɪtʃ/ n. [noncount] a plant with dark green leaves that can be eaten as a vegetable.

spi•nal /'spaynl/ adj. of or relating to the spine.

'**spinal ,column,** n. [count] the series of bones forming the central structure of the skeleton in animals that have a backbone.

'**spinal ,cord,** n. [count] the cord of nerve tissue extending through the spinal column.

spin•dly /'spɪndliy/ adj., **-dli•er, -dli•est.** long and thin: spindly legs.

spine /spayn/ n. **1.** [count] the backbone. **2.** [count] **a.** a hard, sharp-pointed outgrowth on a plant. **b.** a stiff-pointed part of an animal, such as the quill of a porcupine. **3.** [noncount] courage. **4.** [count] the back of a book binding. —'spin•y, adj., **-i•er, -i•est:** the fish's spiny fins.

'**spin-,off** or '**spin,off,** n. [count] something that results from something that already exists.

spi•ral /'spayrəl/ n., adj., v., **-raled, -ral•ing** or

(esp. Brit.) **-ralled, -ral•ling.** —n. [count] **1.** a curve that moves around a fixed point. **2.** a continuous increase or decrease. —adj. [before a noun] **3.** of or of the nature of a spiral or coil: a spiral staircase. —v. [no obj] **4.** to take a spiral course: The plane exploded and spiraled down to earth. **5.** to rise or fall steadily: Wages have spiraled down once again.

spirals

spire /spayᵊr/ n. [count] a tall, sharply pointed tower, esp. on a church.

spir•it /'spɪrɪt/ n. **1.** [count; usually singular] the feelings and thoughts of a human; the soul: They believe that the spirit cannot die. **2.** [count] a being without a body: evil spirits. **3.** [count] a feeling or principle that stirs one to action, etc.: the spirit of reform. **4. spirits,** [plural] the state of someone's mind: in high spirits. **5.** [count; usually singular] the real meaning or intent of a law: The judge ruled that he had violated the spirit of the law. **6.** Often, **spirits.** [plural] a strong alcoholic liquor. —v. [~ + obj (+ off/away)] **7.** to carry off mysteriously or secretly: The child was spirited away by kidnappers.

spir•it•ed /'spɪrɪtɪd/ adj. **1.** having or showing courage, liveliness, etc.: The villagers put up a spirited defense. **2.** (used after an adjective) having the mood of the adjective stated: a high-spirited girl.

spir•it•u•al /'spɪrɪtʃuwəl/ adj. **1.** of or relating to the spirit or soul. **2.** religious. —n. [count] **3.** a religious song of a type originating among African-Americans in the southern U.S. —**spir•it•u•al•i•ty** /,spɪrɪtʃuw'ælɪtiy/, n. [noncount] —'**spir•it•u•al•ly,** adv.

spit¹ /spɪt/ v., **spit** or **spat** /spæt/, **spit•ting,** n. —v. **1.** [no obj] to expel saliva from the mouth. **2.** [~ + obj] to expel (something) from the mouth: to spit watermelon seeds. —n. [noncount] **3.** saliva. **4.** the act of spitting. —Idiom. **5. spit and image,** exact likeness. Also, **spitting image.**

spit² /spɪt/ n. [count] **1.** a pointed rod for holding meat over a fire. **2.** a narrow point of land sticking out into the water.

spite /spayt/ n., v., **spit•ed, spit•ing.** —n. [noncount] **1.** a mean, narrow-minded desire to harm another person: He was mean to her just from spite. —v. [~ + obj] **2.** to treat with spite: I'm sure they turned her down just to spite me. —Idiom. **3. in spite of,** in disregard of: In spite of repeated warnings, she continued to smoke. —'**spite•ful,** adj.

splash /splæʃ/ v. **1.** [no obj] (of water, mud, etc.) to fly or be thrown out in scattered drops: Mud splashed from the bus tires. **2.** to throw (a liquid) about in drops: [no obj]: The kids were splashing happily in the bathtub. [~ + obj]: They were splashing water on each other. —n. [count] **3.** the act or sound of splashing. **4.** a great impression: The news of their engagement made quite a splash.

splat•ter /'splætər/ v. [~ + obj] **1.** to splash on or against in drops that scatter: Rain splattered the windows. —n. [count] **2.** an act or instance of splattering.

splen•did /'splɛndɪd/ adj. **1.** magnificent; beautiful: splendid jewels. **2.** excellent or very good: We

S

had a splendid time at the party. —'**splen•did•ly,** *adv.*

splen•dor /'splɛndər/ *n.* [*noncount*] brilliant or beautiful appearance, coloring, etc.: *the splendor of the rising sun.* Also, *esp. Brit.,* '**splen•dour.**

splice /splays/ *v.* [~ + *obj*], **spliced, splic•ing.** to join (two pieces of rope, film, etc.) together.

splint /splɪnt/ *n.* [*count*] a thin piece of rigid material used to prevent a broken bone from moving.

splin•ter /'splɪntər/ *n.* [*count*] **1.** a small, thin, sharp piece of wood, bone, etc. —*v.* **2.** to (cause to) be split into splinters: [*no obj*]: *The wooden guard rail splintered as the truck drove through it.* [~ + *obj*]: *The truck splintered the guard rail.*

split /splɪt/ *v.,* **split, split•ting,** *n., adj.* —*v.* **1.** to divide from end to end: [~ + *obj*]: *She took an ax and split a log in two.* [*no obj*]: *The log split nicely in two when she cut it.* **2.** to divide into separate parts: [~ + *obj*]: *The book is split (up) into five major divisions.* [*no obj*]: *We'll split (up) here and continue the search separately.* **3.** to (cause to) part or separate: [*no obj*]: *They split (up) after several years of marriage.* [~ + *obj*]: *That issue split the Republican Party.* **4.** [~ + *obj*] to share: *They split the money they had won.* —*n.* [*count*] **5.** the act of splitting. **6.** a crack caused by splitting. —*adj.* **7.** divided: *a split opinion.*

split•ting /'splɪtɪŋ/ *adj.* (of a headache) very painful.

splut•ter /'splʌtər/ *v.* **1.** [*no obj*] [~ + *obj*] to speak rapidly and unclearly. **2.** [*no obj*] to make a sputtering sound.

spoil /spɔyl/ *v.,* **spoiled** or **spoilt** /spɔylt/, **spoil•ing. 1.** [*no obj*] [~ + *obj*] to (cause to) become bad or unfit for use, such as food that does not last long unless kept cold. **2.** [~ + *obj*] to damage or harm severely; ruin: *The rip spoiled the delicate fabric.* **3.** [~ + *obj*] to affect in a bad or unfortunate way: *Bad weather spoiled our vacation.* **4.** [~ + *obj*] to treat (someone) too well, as by giving too much, and thus affect his or her character in a bad way.

spoke[1] /spowk/ *v.* a pt. of SPEAK.

spoke[2] /spowk/ *n.* [*count*] one of the bars that connects the center of a wheel to the rim.

spo•ken /'spowkən/ *v.* a pp. of SPEAK.

spokes•man or **-wom•an** or **-per•son** /'spowksmən/ or /-,wʊmən/ or /-,pɜrsən/ *n.* [*count*], *pl.* **-men** or **-wom•en** or **-persons.** one who speaks for another or for a group.

sponge /spʌndʒ/ *n., v.,* **sponged, spong•ing.** —*n.* **1.** [*count*] a sea creature that has a rubbery body full of holes that absorbs water easily. **2.** [*count*] the skeleton of one of these creatures or a piece of any of various absorbent materials that are soft when wet: [*count*]: *He used a sponge to wipe up the spilled soda.* [*noncount*]: *cushions of sponge filling.* —*v.* **3.** [~ + *obj*] to wipe with a sponge: *I'll sponge up the milk. Please sponge the table (down).* **4.** [*no obj*] to get something free by taking advantage of another's kindness: *He sponged off his relatives for a few months before he finally got a job.* —'**spong•er,** *n.* [*count*] —'**spong•y,** *adj.,* **-i•er, -i•est.**

spon•sor /'spɒnsər/ *n.* [*count*] **1.** one who is responsible for a person. **2.** a person or group that pays for an event: *the corporate sponsors of a race.* —*v.* [~ + *obj*] **3.** to act as sponsor for. —'**spon•sor,ship,** *n.* [*noncount*]

spon•ta•ne•ous /spɒn'teyniyəs/ *adj.* happening naturally; not planned: *spontaneous applause*

during the performance. —**spon•ta•ne•i•ty** /,spɒntə'niyɪtiy, -'ney-/, *n.* [*noncount*] —**spon'ta•ne•ous•ly,** *adv.*

spoof /spuwf/ *n.* [*count*] **1.** a humorous imitation: *a spoof of a film classic.* —*v.* **2.** to mock (something or someone) lightly and with good humor: [~ + *obj*]: *They spoofed a famous love scene from the film.* [*no obj*]: *The school newspaper was always spoofing about the regulations.*

spook•y /'spuwkiy/ *adj.,* **-i•er, -i•est.** causing fear: *a dark, spooky old house.*

spool /spuwl/ *n.* [*count*] a rounded object on which something is wound: *a spool of thread.*

spoon /spuwn/ *n.* [*count*] **1.** an object used in eating, stirring, measuring, etc., made up of a small, shallow bowl with a handle. —*v.* [~ + *obj*] **2.** to eat with a spoon: *He spooned some ice cream into his mouth.*

spo•rad•ic /spə'rædɪk/ *adj.* happening occasionally: *sporadic interruptions.* —**spo'rad•i•cal•ly,** *adv.*

spore /spɔr/ *n.* [*count*] a small cell like a seed: *the spores of a mushroom.*

sport /spɔrt/ *n.* **1.** [*count*] an athletic activity requiring skill or physical ability: *interested in several sports: gymnastics, baseball, and soccer.* **2.** [*noncount*] such activities thought of as a group: *news from the world of sport.* **3.** [*count*] one who behaves in a fair way: *We hope he'll be a (good) sport and give us the raise we deserve.* —*v.* [~ + *obj*] **4.** to wear or display: *She sported a diamond ring.*

'**sports ,car,** *n.* [*count*] a small, high-powered automobile.

sports•man /'spɔrtsmən/ *n.* [*count*], *pl.* **-men.** one who takes part in sports. —'**sports•man,ship,** *n.* [*noncount*]

'**sport-u,tility ,vehicle,** *n.* [*count*] a sturdy passenger vehicle with a trucklike frame.

sport•y /'spɔrtiy/ *adj.,* **-i•er, -i•est. 1.** flashy; showy: *a fast, sporty car.* **2.** suitable for sport.

spot /spɒt/ *n., v.,* **spot•ted, spot•ting.** —*n.* [*count*] **1.** a dirty mark. **2.** a small blemish on the skin. **3.** a small mark differing from the rest of a surface in color, appearance, or character: *a bald spot.* **4.** a place: *This is the spot where I found it.* **5.** [*usually singular*] a difficult position: *We're in a bit of a spot.* —*v.* **6.** to make a spot on (something); stain: [*no obj*]: *Ink can spot badly.* [~ + *obj*]: *The blood spotted his shirt.* **7.** [~ + *obj*] to identify by seeing: *to spot an error.* —**Idiom. 8. on the spot. a.** at once; instantly: *He was there on the spot.* **b.** at the very place in question: *She is always on the spot when we need her.* —'**spot•less,** *adj.*

spot•light /'spɒt,layt/ *n., v.,* **-light•ed** or **-lit, -light•ing.** —*n.* **1.** [*count*] a very strong light focused on a certain place, or the lamp producing this light. **2.** [*count; usually singular*] the area of public attention: *Asia is in the spotlight now.* —*v.* [~ + *obj*] **3.** to direct the beam of a spotlight upon. **4.** to call attention to: *to spotlight a problem.*

spouse /spaws, spawz/ *n.* [*count*] one's husband or wife.

spout /spawt/ *v.* **1.** to (cause to) shoot out forcefully or violently: [*no obj*]: *Ash and lava spouted from the volcano.* [~ + *obj*]: *The faucet was spouting hot water.* **2.** to say in a showy or pompous manner: [~ + *obj*]: *spouting his theories on foreign policy.* [*no obj*]: *He's always spouting (off) about his wonderful job.* —*n.* [*count*] **3.**

a pipe or tube through which a liquid is poured: *the spout of the teapot.*

sprain /spreyn/ *v.* [~ + *obj*] **1.** to twist (a joint) so as to injure without a break: *He sprained his knee when he fell.* —*n.* [*count*] **2.** an injury to a joint.

sprang /spræŋ/ *v.* a pt. of SPRING.

sprawl /sprɔl/ *v.* [*no obj*] **1.** to spread out (the legs) when sitting or lying: *She sprawled on the couch.* **2.** to be spread out over a distance: *The city sprawls for miles.* —*n.* [*noncount*] **3.** an act or instance of sprawling.

spray /sprey/ *n.* **1.** [*noncount*] liquid broken up into very tiny droplets and blown through the air: *salt spray from the ocean.* **2.** liquid forced into the air from a special device: [*noncount*]: *a can of bug spray.* [*count*]: *Those bug sprays smell awful.* —*v.* **3.** [*no obj*] (of liquid) to scatter in the form of very tiny particles: *The water sprayed into our eyes.* **4.** [~ + *obj*] to apply a spray: *spraying paint on the wall.* **5.** [~ + *obj*] to cover or treat with a spray: *to spray a table with polish.* —'**spray•er,** *n.* [*count*]

spread /spred/ *v.,* **spread, spread•ing,** *n.* —*v.* **1.** [~ + *obj*] to stretch out over a flat surface: *Spread the blanket under the tree.* **2.** [~ + *obj*] to extend out: *The bird spread its wings and flew.* **3.** to (cause to) be distributed over an area: [~ + *obj*]: *to spread seed on the ground.* [*no obj*]: *The fire spread quickly in the high winds.* **4.** [~ + *obj*] to apply in a thin layer: *to spread jam on the bread.* **5.** [*no obj*] to be able to be applied in a layer or coating: *The butter spreads easily.* **6.** to (cause to) become widely known: [~ + *obj*]: *Someone is spreading rumors.* [*no obj*]: *How do such rumors spread?* —*n.* **7.** [*count; usually: singular*] an act or instance of spreading: *the rapid spread of malaria.* **8.** [*count; usually: singular*] extent: *to measure the spread of branches.* **9.** [*count*] a cloth covering for a bed. **10.** [*count*] a food that is spread on bread, such as jam or peanut butter. —'**spread•a•ble,** *adj.* —'**spread•er,** *n.* [*count*]

spread•sheet /'spred,ʃiyt/ *n.* [*count*] **1.** a very large, wide ledger sheet used by accountants. **2.** such a sheet when it is represented electronically by computer software, used esp. for financial planning.

spright•ly /'spraytliy/ *adj.,* **-li•er, -li•est.** full of life; bouncy; lively. —'**spright•li•ness,** *n.* [*noncount*]

spring /spriŋ/ *v.,* **sprang** /spræŋ/ or, often, **sprung** /sprʌŋ/, **sprung, spring•ing,** *n.* —*v.* **1.** [*no obj*] to jump or move suddenly and swiftly: *The tiger stood ready to spring on its victim. The door sprang open.* **2.** to (cause to) happen suddenly: [~ + *obj*]: *He sprung a joke on us.* [*no obj*]: *An objection sprang to mind.* **3.** [*no obj*] to come into being: *This rude behavior springs from selfishness.* **4.** **spring for,** *Informal.* to treat someone to: *He sprang for dinner.* —*n.* **5.** [*count*] a sudden leap or bound. **6.** [*count*] the place where water comes up from the ground: *mineral springs.* **7.** [*count*] an elastic quality: *He had a spring in his walk.* [*noncount*]: *There's not much spring in her steps because of her arthritis.* **8.** [*count*] a coil of wire that returns to its shape after being pulled or pushed. **9.** [*count; usually: singular*] the season between winter and summer. —'**spring•y,** *adj.,* **-i•er, -i•est.**

sprin•kle /'spriŋkəl/ *v.,* **-kled, -kling,** *n.* —*v.* [~ + *obj*] **1.** to scatter a liquid in drops: *sprinkling*

water on the flowers. —*n.* [*count*] **2.** a light rain. —'**sprin•kler,** *n.* [*count*]: *a lawn sprinkler.*

sprint /sprint/ *v.* **1.** to run at full speed for a short distance: *At the last minute he sprinted (ahead) to win the race.* —*n.* [*count*] **2.** a short, fast run. —'**sprint•er,** *n.* [*count*]

sprout /sprawt/ *v.* [*no obj*] **1.** to begin to grow. —*n.* [*count*] **2.** a shoot of a plant. **3.** a new growth from a seed.

spruce /spruws/ *n.* [*count*] a tree of the pine family, having short, needle-shaped leaves.

sprung /sprʌŋ/ *v.* a pt. and pp. of SPRING.

spun /spʌn/ *v.* pt. and pp. of SPIN.

spunk /spʌŋk/ *n.* [*noncount*] courage. —'**spunk•y,** *adj.,* **-i•er, -i•est.**

spur /spɜr/ *n.,* *v.,* **spurred, spur•ring.** —*n.* [*count*] **1.** a sharp U-shaped device attached to the heel of a boot, used by a rider to urge a horse forward. **2.** something that forces one to action. —*v.* [~ + *obj*] **3.** to prick with a spur to urge (a horse) to go faster: *The sheriff spurred his horse (on) and rode quickly after the bandit.* **4.** to encourage (one) to take action: *The insult spurred him to fight back.* —*Idiom.* **5.** **on the spur of the moment,** suddenly; without planning: *On the spur of the moment he sent her flowers.*

spurn /spɜrn/ *v.* [~ + *obj*] to reject (something); scorn: *She spurned his offer of marriage.*

spurt /spɜrt/ *v.* **1.** [*no obj*] to gush out of something in a stream: *Blood spurted from the wound.* **2.** [~ + *obj*] to discharge quickly and forcefully: *The wound was spurting blood.* **3.** [*no obj*] to show a sudden brief increase in activity, etc.: *The economy spurted last month.* —*n.* [*count*] **4.** a sudden, forceful jet: *a spurt of blood.* **5.** a sudden increase of activity or effort.

sput•ter /'spʌtər/ *v.* [*no obj*] to make explosive popping or sizzling sounds: *When the water hose broke, the car sputtered and stopped.*

spy /spay/ *n.,* *pl.* **spies,** *v.,* **spied, spy•ing.** —*n.* [*count*] **1.** a person employed by a government to obtain secret information about another country, usually an enemy. **2.** one who keeps close and secret watch on another. —*v.* **3.** [~ + *obj*] to catch sight of: *to spy a rare bird.* **4.** **spy on,** to watch secretively: *He was spying on everyone.*

sq., an abbreviation of: **1.** sequence. **2.** square.

squab•ble /'skwɒbəl/ *v.,* **-bled, -bling,** *n.* —*v.* [~ + *over* + *obj*] **1.** to quarrel about something unimportant. —*n.* [*count*] **2.** a quarrel about a small detail.

squad /skwɒd/ *n.* [*count*] a small group of persons engaged in a common activity or job: *a squad of cheerleaders; police officers in the bomb squad.*

squad•ron /'skwɒdrən/ *n.* [*count*] an army cavalry unit, a part of a naval fleet, or a group of war planes.

squal•id /'skwɒlɪd, 'skwɔlɪd/ *adj.* filthy and disgusting: *a squalid prison cell.* —'**squal•id•ness,** *n.* [*noncount*]

squall¹ /skwɔl/ *n.* [*count*] a sudden, violent wind, often accompanied by rain, snow, or sleet.

squall² /skwɔl/ *v.* [*no obj*] to cry loudly: *The baby was squalling.*

squal•or /'skwɒlər, 'skwɔlər/ *n.* [*noncount*] the condition of being squalid; filth and misery.

squan•der /'skwɒndər/ *v.* [~ + *obj*] to spend wastefully: *He had squandered the family fortune on gambling.*

square /skwɛər/ *n.,* *v.,* **squared, squar•ing,** *adj.,* **squar•er, squar•est,** *adv.* —*n.* [*count*] **1.** a

S

rectangle having all four sides of equal length. **2.** something having or resembling this form, such as a city block, an area on a game board, etc. **3.** an open area formed at the place where two or more streets meet: *The concert was held in the village square.* **4. a.** the second power of a number, expressed as $a^2 = a \times a$, where *a* is the number. **b.** a number that is the second power of another: *Four is the square of two.* **5.** *Slang.* a person who is old-fashioned, boring, conventional, or conservative. —*v.* **6.** [~ + *obj*] to make square: *to square an uneven piece of cut wood.* **7.** [~ + *obj*] to multiply (a quantity) by itself. **8.** [~ + *obj*] to make straight, level, or even: *Square the cloth on the table.* **9.** [*no obj*] to agree; match: *That theory does not square with the facts.* **10. square off,** to hold oneself in a position showing one is ready to fight: *The two teams square off tonight to decide the city championship.* **11. square up,** to settle an account: *I'll pay the bill now, and we can square up later.* —*adj.* **12.** forming a right angle: *a square corner.* **13.** having four sides and four right angles: *a square box.* **14.** [*after a number; before a noun*] having the form of a square: *one square foot.* **15.** fair; honest; straightforward: *We got a square deal on the car.* —*adv.* **16.** in square or rectangular form. **17.** at right angles: *The carpenter lined up the door frame square with the floor and walls.* **18.** fairly; honestly: *He treated us fair and square.* **19.** firmly: *She looked him square in the eye.* —**'square•ly,** *adv.* —**'square•ness,** *n.* [*noncount*]

squash[1] /skwɒʃ, skwɔʃ/ *v.* **1.** [~ + *obj*] to crush: *to squash a bug.* **2.** to press into a small space; squeeze: [*no obj*]: *Six of us squashed into the tiny car.* [~ + *obj*]: *They squashed us into the tiny room.* —*n.* **3.** [*noncount*] a game played on a four-walled court with rackets and a rubber ball.

squash[2] /skwɒʃ, skwɔʃ/ *n.*, *pl.* **squash•es,** (*esp. when thought of as a group*) **squash.** the fruit of a plant of the gourd family, eaten as a vegetable: [*count*]: *Buy two squashes at the store.* [*noncount*]: *some cooked squash.*

squat /skwɒt/ *v.*, **squat•ted, squat•ting,** *adj.*, **squat•ter, squat•test,** *n.* —*v.* [*no obj*] **1.** to sit in a crouching position with the legs drawn up closely beneath or in front of the body. **2.** to occupy property without permission: *The migrant workers squatted on the unused farm.* —*adj.* **3.** very short and thickset: *a heavy, squat man.* —*n.* [*count*] **4.** the act, position, or posture of squatting. —**'squat•ter,** *n.* [*count*]

squawk /skwɔk/ *v.* **1.** to utter (a loud, harsh cry): [*no obj*]: *The ducks squawked as they flew overhead.* [~ + *obj*]: *The duck squawked a warning.* **2.** to express (a complaint, etc.) loudly and strongly: *Quit squawking about your grade!* [~ + *obj*]: *They squawked their disapproval.* —*n.* [*count*] **3.** a loud, harsh cry or sound. **4.** a loud, strong complaint.

squeak /skwiyk/ *n.* [*count*] **1.** a sharp, shrill cry or sound: *Her voice rose to a squeak.* —*v.* **2.** [*no obj*] to make a sound like a squeak: *The door squeaks every time you open it.* **3. squeak by** or **through,** to succeed, survive, etc., by a very narrow margin: *We managed to squeak by even though our budget had been cut.* —**'squeak•y,** *adj.*, **-i•er, -i•est.**

squeal /skwiyl/ *n.* [*count*] **1.** a long, sharp cry, as of pain, fear, pleasure, or surprise. —*v.* [*no obj*] **2.** to make a squeal: *The teenagers squealed*

with delight. **3.** *Slang.* to give information to the police about one's fellow criminals.

squeam•ish /'skwiymɪʃ/ *adj.* easily made sick to the stomach: *I'm too squeamish for horror movies.*

squeeze /skwiyz/ *v.*, **squeezed, squeez•ing,** *n.* —*v.* **1.** [~ + *obj*] to press together with force: *The crowd almost squeezed me flat!* **2.** [~ + *obj*] to apply pressure to (something) in order to force out juice, sap, or the like: *to squeeze juice out of an orange.* **3.** to fit into a small space or time span: [~ + *obj*]: *I squeezed the car into the parking space.* [*no obj*]: *I squeezed into the crowded bus.* —*n.* [*count*] **4.** an act or instance of squeezing: *a tight squeeze on the elevator.* **5.** the fact or state of being squeezed or crowded.

squelch /skweltʃ/ *v.* [~ + *obj*] to suppress: *The dictator squelched all opposition.*

squid /skwɪd/ *n.* [*count*], *pl.* (*esp. when thought of as a group*) **squid,** (*esp. for kinds or species*) **squids.** a ten-armed sea creature with a slender body.

squint /skwɪnt/ *v.* [*no obj*] **1.** to look with the eyes partly closed: *She squinted through the microscope.* —*n.* [*count*] **2.** an act or instance of squinting.

squirm /skwɜrm/ *v.* [*no obj*] to twist the body in discomfort, distress, etc.: *He squirmed in his seat during the lecture.*

squir•rel /'skwɜrəl, 'skwʌr-/ *n.* [*count*], *pl.* **-rels,** (*esp. when thought of as a group*) **-rel.** a small, bushy-tailed rodent that lives in trees and eats nuts.

squirt /skwɜrt/ *v.* **1.** to send out (liquid) in a quick, sudden stream: [*no obj*]: *The lemon squirted in my eye.* [~ + *obj*]: *The hose squirted water.* —*n.* [*count*] **2.** the act of squirting. **3.** a small quantity of liquid that has been squirted: *a squirt of chocolate sauce.*

Sr., an abbreviation of: Senior.

St., an abbreviation of: **1.** Saint. **2.** Street.

stab /stæb/ *v.*, **stabbed, stab•bing,** *n.* —*v.* [~ + *obj*] **1.** to pierce with a pointed weapon. —*n.* [*count*] **2.** an act of stabbing. **3.** an attempt: *to make a stab at an answer.* —*Idiom.* **4. stab in the back,** to betray (someone trusting).

sta•bi•lize /'steybə,layz/ *v.*, [~ + *obj*] [*no obj*] **-lized, -liz•ing.** to make or hold stable. —**sta•bi•li•za•tion** /,steybələ'zeyʃən/, *n.* [*noncount*]

sta•ble[1] /'steybəl/ *n.*, *v.*, **-bled, -bling.** —*n.* [*count*] **1.** a building with stalls where horses or cows are kept and fed. —*v.* [~ + *obj*] **2.** to put in a stable.

sta•ble[2] /'steybəl/ *adj.*, **-bler, -blest. 1.** not likely to fall; firm; steady: *The building has a stable foundation.* **2.** not likely to change quickly: *a stable currency.* —**sta'bil•i•ty,** *n.* [*noncount*]

stack /stæk/ *n.* [*count*] **1.** a neat pile: *a stack of cards.* **2.** a large pile of hay, straw, or the like. **3. stacks,** [*plural*] a set of shelves for books in a library. **4.** a large amount. —*v.* [~ + *obj*] **5.** to place in a stack: *She stacked the suitcases on the roof rack.*

sta•di•um /'steydiyəm/ *n.* [*count*], *pl.* **-di•ums, -di•a** /-diyə/. a sports arena with rising rows of seats for viewers.

staff /stæf/ *n.*, *pl.* **staffs** for 1, **staves** /steyvzɒsl or **staffs** for 2, 3, 4; *v.* —*n.* **1.** [*count*] [*noncount*] a group of people who carry out the work of an organization. **2.** [*count*] a stick for aid in walking. **3.** [*count*] a pole on which a flag is displayed. **4.** [*count*] a set of five lines on which music is written. —*v.* [~ + *obj*] **5.** to provide with a staff of assistants or workers.

stag /stæg/ *n.* [*count*] a male deer.

stage /steydʒ/ *n.*, *v.*, **staged, stag•ing.** —*n.* [*count*] **1.** a step in a development or series: *in the early stages of his career.* **2.** the platform on which the actors perform in a theater. **3. the stage,** [*usually singular*] the acting profession. —*v.* [~ + *obj*] **4.** to produce on a stage: *to stage a play.*

stage•coach /'steydʒ,kowtʃ/ *n.* [*count*] a horse-drawn coach that was formerly used to carry passengers, parcels, etc.

'**stage** '**fright,** *n.* [*noncount*] nervousness felt by a performer in front of an audience.

stag•ger /'stægər/ *v.* **1.** to (cause to) walk unsteadily: [*no obj*]: *He staggered from the force of the blow.* **2.** [~ + *obj*] to astonish: *a fact that staggers the mind.* **3.** [~ + *obj*] to arrange so that things do not happen at the same time: *to stagger our lunch hours.* —*n.* [*count*] **4.** an unsteady, reeling movement.

stag•ger•ing /'stægərɪŋ/ *adj.* causing shock, disbelief, or astonishment: *staggering rates of inflation.*

stag•nant /'stægnənt/ *adj.* **1.** not flowing or moving, as water or air. **2.** inactive; sluggish: *a stagnant economy.*

stag•nate /'stægneyt/ *v.* [*no obj*], **-nat•ed, -nat•ing. 1.** to stop flowing, as water or air. **2.** to become bad-smelling from standing, as a pool of water. **3.** to stop progressing: *was just stagnating in his job.* —**stag•na•tion** /stæg'neyʃən/, *n.* [*noncount*]

staid /steyd/ *adj.* too serious, dull, or settled in one's ways. —'**staid•ly,** *adv.*

stain /steyn/ *n.* **1.** [*count*] a discolored mark on a material. **2.** [*count*] a cause of disgrace. **3.** a liquid for coloring woods, textiles, etc.: [*noncount*]: *Try using stain on the rocking chair.* [*count*]: *several wood stains to choose from: red, dark brown, or light brown.* —*v.* **4.** to (cause to) become discolored: [~ + *obj*]: *The blood stained his shirt.* [*no obj*]: *The white rug will stain too easily.* **5.** [~ + *obj*] to color (wood, cloth, etc.). **6.** [~ + *obj*] to bring disgrace or dishonor upon: *to stain someone's reputation.* —'**stain•less,** *adj.*

'**stainless** '**steel,** *n.* [*noncount*] steel that resists rust.

stair /stɛər/ *n.* [*count*] **1.** one of a series of steps for going from one level to another. **2. stairs,** [*plural*] a series of steps going from one level to another.

stair•case /'stɛər,keys/ *n.* [*count*] a series of stairs.

stair•way /'stɛər,wey/ *n.* [*count*] a passageway from one level to another by a series of stairs.

stake¹ /steyk/ *n.*, *v.*, **staked, stak•ing.** —*n.* [*count*] **1.** a stick pointed at one end for driving into the ground. —*v.* **2. stake out,** (of the police) to keep (a place) under watch: *The police staked out the bank; to stake it out for a week.*

stake² /steyk/ *n.*, *v.*, **staked, stak•ing.** —*n.* [*count*] **1.** an investment in business: *a big stake in the company.* **2.** a personal interest: *I had a stake in the decision.* **3.** Often, **stakes.** [*plural*] a sum of money bet in a game. —*v.* **4.** [~ + *obj*] to risk (something) upon the outcome of an event, business venture, etc.: *He staked a lot of money on the deal.* —*Idiom.* **5. at stake,** in danger of being lost: *There's a great deal at stake in the upcoming election.*

stale /steyl/ *adj.*, **stal•er, stal•est. 1.** not fresh: *stale bread.* **2.** overly familiar: *a stale joke.*

stale•mate /'steyl,meyt/ *n.* [*count*] a situation in which no action can be taken: *The discussion had reached a stalemate.*

stalk¹ /stɔk/ *n.* [*count*] the stem of a plant.

stalk² /stɔk/ *v.* **1.** [~ + *obj*] **a.** to pursue quietly for the purpose of capturing: *hunters stalking a deer.* **b.** to follow (a person) continually: *Her ex-husband was stalking her.* **2.** [*no obj*] to walk with stiff or proud strides: *They stalked angrily out of the room.*

stall¹ /stɔl/ *n.* [*count*] **1.** a compartment for an animal in a stable. **2.** a booth in which goods are displayed for sale. —*v.* **3.** [*no obj*] (of a motor or vehicle) to stop: *The car started but then immediately stalled.* **4.** [~ + *obj*] to cause (a vehicle or motor) to stop functioning suddenly.

stall² /stɔl/ *v.* **1.** to delay: [~ + *obj*]: *Management tried to stall the talks so that we wouldn't get a raise.* [*no obj*]: *You're stalling; just give us an answer.* **2.** [*no obj*] to be delayed: *Once again contract talks have stalled.*

stal•lion /'stælyən/ *n.* [*count*] an uncastrated adult male horse, esp. one used for breeding.

stam•i•na /'stæmənə/ *n.* [*noncount*] strength to go on in spite of fatigue, stress, etc.; endurance.

stam•mer /'stæmər/ *v.* [*no obj*] **1.** to speak with breaks and pauses or to repeat sound rapidly: *He stammered nervously.* —*n.* [*count*] **2.** a stammering way of speaking.

stamp /stæmp/ *v.* **1.** to bring (the foot) down forcibly on the ground, floor, etc.: [~ + *obj*]: *stamping their feet to keep warm.* [*no obj*]: *She stamped on my foot.* **2. stamp out,** to extinguish: *He quickly stamped out the small fire; to stamp it out before it spreads.* **3.** [~ + *obj*] to put a mark on (something) to indicate that it is genuine or that it has approval: *The immigration officials stamped my passport.* **4.** [~ + *obj*] to stick a postage stamp to (a letter, etc.). —*n.* [*count*] **5.** Also, **postage stamp.** a small label for sticking on an envelope to show that postage has been paid. **6.** a small block of wood or metal with a design that can be used to make a mark. **7.** a mark printed by such a block. **8.** a strong impression: *The president had left his stamp on the country.* **9.** an act of stamping: *He gave an impatient stamp of his foot.*

stam•pede /stæm'piyd/ *n.*, *v.*, **-ped•ed, -ped•ing.** —*n.* [*count*] **1.** a sudden, uncontrolled rush of a herd of frightened animals. **2.** any uncontrolled rush: *The fuel shortage caused a stampede to the gas stations.* —*v.* [*no obj*] **3.** to scatter or flee in a stampede.

stance /stæns/ *n.* [*count*] **1.** the position of the body while standing, esp. in sports: *He assumed a karate stance.* **2.** a position or opinion taken with respect to something: *the governor's stance on the education issue.*

stand /stænd/ *v.*, **stood** /stʊd/, **stand•ing,** *n.* —*v.* **1.** [*no obj*] to be or get in an upright position on the feet. **2.** [~ + *a noun showing measurement*] to have a certain height: *He stands six feet tall.* **3.** [~ + *obj*] to place in an upright position: *He stood the broom in the corner.* **4.** [*no obj*] to be located: *The building stands upon the hill.* **5.** [*no obj*] to remain unchanged: *The score stands (at) 18 to 14.* **6.** [~ + *obj*] to be able to tolerate: *My eyes can't stand the glare.* **7.** [~ + *obj*] to perform one's duty as: *He stood guard over the prisoners.* **8. stand by, a.** to support: *to stand by a friend in need.* **b.** to remain firm about (something): *I stand by my original statement.* **c.** to wait: *Please stand by, we're having technical difficulties.* **9. stand for, a.** to represent: *P.S. stands for "postscript."* **b.** to allow: *"I won't stand for any nonsense," the teacher said.* **10. stand in,** to take the place of: *I'm standing in for the manager.* **11. stand out,** to be noticed easily: *She stands out in a crowd.* **12. stand up, a.** to be convincing: *That evidence won't stand up in court.* **b.** to last in spite of hard use: *Wool stands up better than silk.* **c.** to fail to keep an appointment with: *She stood up several of my friends. She stood him up.* —*n.* [*count*] **13.** the act of standing. **14.** a resistance to attack. **15.** an opinion, etc., with respect to an issue. **16. stands,** [*plural*] a raised section of seats for spectators at a sports event. **17.** a small open building where articles are displayed for sale: *a fruit stand.* —*Idiom.* **18. stand to reason,** to be logical or reasonable: *It stands to reason that he'll choose her.*

stand·ard /'stændərd/ *n.* [*count*] **1.** something considered to be a basis for comparison: *an official standard for weight.* **2.** an average or normal quality or level: *The work isn't up to his usual standard.* **3.** a special flag or emblem. —*adj.* **4.** serving as a basis for comparison of weight, measure, or value. **5.** usual or customary: *Air conditioning is a standard feature of this car.*

stand·ard·ize /'stændər,dayz/ *v.* [~ + *obj*], **-ized, -iz·ing.** to cause to conform to a standard. —**stand·ard·i·za·tion** /,stændərdə'zeyʃən/, *n.* [*noncount*]

stand·by /'stænd,bay/ *n.* [*count*], *pl.* **-bys.** something kept ready to use: *We have an emergency generator as a standby.*

stand·ing /'stændɪŋ/ *n.* [*noncount*] **1.** rank or status: *a person of little standing in the community.* **2.** length of continuing, living, or staying in a place: *friends of long standing.* —*adj.* [*before a noun*] **3.** performed in an upright position: *a standing jump.* **4.** lasting or permanent: *a strong standing army.*

stand·still /'stænd,stɪl/ *n.* [*count; usually singular*] a state in which action has stopped; stop: *The work had come to a standstill.*

stank /stæŋk/ *v.* a pt. of STINK.

sta·ple¹ /'steypəl/ *n.*, *v.*, **-pled, -pling.** —*n.* [*count*] **1.** a short piece of wire put through sheets of paper and bent to hold them together. —*v.* [~ + *obj*] **2.** to fasten by a staple: *Staple the pages together.* —**'sta·pler,** *n.* [*count*]

sta·ple² /'steypəl/ *n.* [*count*] a basic or necessary item of food: *flour, salt, and other staples.*

star /stɑr/ *n.*, *v.*, **starred, star·ring.** —*n.* [*count*] **1.** a large, burning ball of gas in the sky, such as the sun. **2.** a figure having five or six points, sometimes used as an ornament, badge, award, etc.: *The restaurant was awarded five stars.* **3.** a famous actor, singer, etc. —*v.* **4.** [~ + *obj*] to have as a star: *That old movie starred Rudolf Valentino.* **5.** [*no obj*] (of a performer) to appear as a star: *Rudolf Valentino starred in that movie.* —**'star·ry,** *adj.*, **-ri·er, -ri·est:** *a brilliant starry sky.*

starch /stɑrtʃ/ *n.* **1.** [*noncount*] [*count*] a white, tasteless food substance found in rice, corn, wheat, and many other vegetable foods. **2.** [*noncount*] this substance used to stiffen fabrics in laundering. —*v.* [~ + *obj*] **3.** to stiffen with starch: *to starch the shirts.* —**'starch·y,** *adj.*, **-i·er, -i·est.**

stare /stɛər/ *v.*, **stared, star·ing,** *n.* —*v.* [*no obj*]

1. to look at intently for a long time: *He kept staring at her. Don't stare; it's rude.* —*n.* [*count*] **2.** a staring look.

star·fish /'stɑr,fɪʃ/ *n.* [*count*], *pl.* (*esp. when thought of as a group*) **-fish,** (*esp. for kinds or species*) **-fish·es.** a sea creature having the shape of a star.

stark /stɑrk/ *adj.*, **-er, -est,** *adv.* —*adj.* **1.** [*before a noun*] complete; clear: *a stark difference.* **2.** harsh, grim, or severe in appearance: *The room was simple and stark.* —*adv.* **3.** completely: *stark raving mad.* —**'stark·ness,** *n.* [*noncount*]

star·ling /'stɑrlɪŋ/ *n.* [*count*] a medium-sized songbird with shiny black coloring.

start /stɑrt/ *v.* **1.** to (cause to) begin: [*no obj*]: *We'll start at dawn.* [~ + *obj*]: *I started my current job in 1992. The fir trees started to lose their needles. She started running when she saw him.* —*n.* [*count*] **2.** a beginning of an action, journey, etc.: *Our business got off to a slow start.* **3.** a place or time from which something begins: *It's the start of the new season.* **4.** a sudden, involuntary jerk of the body: *I awoke with a start.* **5.** a lead, as over competitors.

star·tle /'stɑrtl/ *v.* [~ + *obj*], **-tled, -tling.** to surprise: *You startled me when you slammed the door so loudly.*

starve /stɑrv/ *v.*, **starved, starv·ing.** **1.** to (cause to) weaken or die from lack of food: [*no obj*]: *He nearly starved.* [~ + *obj*]: *He tried to starve his enemy.* **2.** [*no obj*] to be very hungry: *When do we eat? I'm starved/starving.* **3.** to (cause to) feel a strong need: [*no obj*]: *The child is starving for affection.* [~ + *obj*]: *The children were being starved of affection.* —**star'va·tion,** *n.* [*noncount*]

state /steyt/ *n.*, *adj.*, *v.*, **stat·ed, stat·ing.** —*n.* **1.** [*count; usually singular*] the condition of a person or thing: *the state of one's health.* **2.** [*count; sometimes: State*] a nation: *the State of Israel.* **3.** [*count; sometimes: State*] any of the political units that together make up a country. —*adj.* [*before a noun*] **4.** of or relating to the state. **5.** very formal: *a state dinner.* —*v.* [~ + *obj*] **6.** to declare or say, as in speech or writing: *Please state your name and address.* —**'state,hood,** *n.* [*noncount*]

state·ly /'steytliy/ *adj.*, **-li·er, -li·est.** impressive or imposing.

state·ment /'steytmənt/ *n.* [*count*] **1.** something stated in speech or writing: *I disagree with your last statement.* **2.** a financial report: *a bank statement.*

states·man /'steytsmən/ *n.* [*count*], *pl.* **-men.** a person who has an important role in government.

stat·ic /'stætɪk/ *adj.* Also, **stat'i·cal.** **1.** not moving or changing. **2.** [*before a noun*] (of electricity) not flowing or moving through a substance: *His hair stood on end from the static electricity.* —*n.* [*noncount*] **3.** static or atmospheric electricity.

sta·tion /'steyʃən/ *n.* [*count*] **1.** a stopping place for trains, buses, etc.: *a subway station.* **2.** a place for some particular kind of work or service: *a police station.* **3.** a building from which radio, television, cable, etc., broadcasts are sent. —*v.* [~ + *obj*] **4.** to place (someone) in a station or position: *He was stationed by the door to act as a lookout.*

sta·tion·ar·y /'steyʃə,nɛriy/ *adj.* not moving.

sta·tion·er·y /'steyʃə,nɛriy/ *n.* [*noncount*] **1.** paper used for writing letters. **2.** writing materials, such as pens, pencils, etc.

'station ˌwagon, *n.* [*count*] an automobile with an area behind the seats into which suitcases, parcels, etc., can be loaded through a door at the back.

sta•tis•tic /stə'tɪstɪk/ *n.* [*count*] a numerical fact: *Here's an alarming statistic: A car is stolen every three minutes.* **—sta'tis•ti•cal,** *adj.*

sta•tis•tics /stə'tɪstɪks/ *n.* **1.** [*noncount; used with a singular verb*] the science of collecting and interpreting information in the form of numbers. **2.** [*plural; used with a plural verb*] the information itself: *Statistics prove that you are safer in an airplane than in a car.*

stat•ue /'stætʃuw/ *n.* [*count*] a figure of a person or animal carved in stone, wood, etc.

stat•ure /'stætʃər/ *n.* [*noncount*] **1.** the height of a person: *He's tall in stature.* **2.** importance based on one's good qualities or achievements: *a person of stature in the community.*

sta•tus /'steytəs, 'stætəs/ *n.* [*noncount*] **1.** the position of an individual in relation to others: *a job of low status.* **2.** state of affairs: *What is the status of the contract negotiations?*

stat•ute /'stætʃuwt/ *n.* a law passed by a legislature: [*count*]: *a statute against littering.* [*noncount*]: *Working conditions are regulated by statute.*

staunch /stɔntʃ, stɑntʃ/, *adj.,* **-er, -est.** firm; dependable, loyal, etc.: *a staunch Democrat.* **—'staunch•ly,** *adv.*

stave /steyv/ *v.,* **staved, stav•ing. stave off,** to keep off, as by force: *to stave off an attack; to stave it off.*

staves /steyvz/ *n.* [*plural*] a pl. of STAFF.

stay /stey/ *v.,* **stayed,** or **staid, stay•ing,** *n.* —*v.* [*no obj*] **1.** to remain in a place, situation, or condition: *The children wanted to stay up late.* **2.** to live in a place for a while: *to stay at a friend's apartment.* —*n.* [*count*] **3.** the act of stopping or being stopped. **4.** a period of living somewhere: *a week's stay in Miami.* **—Idiom. 5. stay put,** to remain in the same position or place: *Now stay put until I come back.*

stead•fast /'stɛd,fæst/ *adj.* firm; not changing: *a steadfast friend.*

stead•y /'stɛdiy/ *adj.,* **stead•i•er, stead•i•est,** *v.,* **stead•ied, stead•y•ing.** —*adj.* **1.** firmly placed; not moving or shaking: *a steady ladder.* **2.** regular in movement: *a steady rhythm.* **3.** unchanging: *a steady diet of rice and beans.* **4.** [*usually: before a noun*] constant or regular: *a steady customer.* **5.** calm: *steady nerves.* —*v.* **6.** to (cause to) become firm or steady, as in position or movement: [*no obj*]: *The boat lurched in the rough water, then steadied again.* [~ + *obj*]: *The pilot steadied the plane.* **—stead•i•ly** /'stɛdəliy/, *adv.*: *It rained steadily all night.* **—'stead•i•ness,** *n.* [*noncount*]

steak /steyk/ *n.* [*noncount*] [*count*] a slice of meat or fish.

steal /stiyl/ *v.,* **stole** /stowl/, **sto•len, steal•ing.** **1.** to take something belonging to someone else, esp. secretly or by force: [~ + *obj*]: *Someone stole my dad's car last night.* [*no obj*]: *The two brothers were always stealing from each other.* **2.** [*no obj*] to move or (cause to) go secretly or quietly: *He stole away into the night.* **—Idiom. 3. steal the show, a.** to take credit for something unfairly. **b.** to perform better than anyone else.

stealth /stɛlθ/ *n.* [*noncount*] secret action or movement. **—'stealth•y,** *adj.,* **-i•er, -i•est.**

steam /stiym/ *n.* [*noncount*] **1.** water in the form of an invisible gas. **2.** the mist that rises from

boiling water. —*v.* **3.** [*no obj*] to give off steam or vapor: *pipes steaming in the cold air.* **4.** to (cause to) become misty with steam, as a car window: [*no obj*]: *To prevent the window from steaming (up), use the defroster.* [~ + *obj*]: *His hot breath steamed (up) the window.* **5.** [*no obj*] to move by the power of steam: *The ship steamed out to sea.* **6.** [~ + *obj*] to cook with steam: *to steam the vegetables.* **—'steam•y,** *adj.,* **-i•er, -i•est.**

'steam ˌengine, *n.* [*count*] an engine powered by steam.

steam•er /'stiymər/ *n.* [*count*] **1.** something propelled or operated by steam. **2.** a container in which food is steamed.

steam•roll•er /'stiym,rowlər/ *n.* [*count*] a heavy steam-powered vehicle having a roller for leveling materials used in building a road.

steel /stiyl/ *n.* [*noncount*] **1.** a form of iron made with carbon. —*v.* [~ + *oneself*] **2.** to make (oneself) determined: *She steeled herself against the pain she knew was coming.*

steep[1] /stiyp/ *adj.,* **-er, -est. 1.** having an almost vertical slope: *a steep hill.* **2.** (of a price) too high: *$50,000 is a little steep for a new car.* **—'steep•ly,** *adv.*: *The mountain rose steeply in front of us.* **—'steep•ness,** *n.* [*noncount*]

steep[2] /stiyp/ *v.* **1.** [*no obj*] to be soaked in water: *The tea is steeping in the pot.* **2. steep in,** to be filled with (knowledge, a quality, etc.): *The incident was steeped in mystery.*

stee•ple /'stiypəl/ *n.* [*count*] a tower having a spire, built on a church.

steer /stɪər/ *v.* **1.** to guide the course of (something): [~ + *obj*]: *He steered the car around the wreck.* [*no obj*]: *He steered around the wreck.* **—Idiom. 2. steer clear of,** to stay away from: *to steer clear of trouble.* **—'steer•a•ble,** *adj.*

stem[1] /stɛm/ *n., v.,* **stemmed, stem•ming.** —*n.* [*count*] **1.** the part of a plant that grows upward from the root and that supports a leaf, flower, or fruit. **2.** a long, slender, supporting part, as of a wine glass or a tobacco pipe. —*v.* **3. stem from,** to come from: *Most of our problems stem from a lack of funds.*

stem[2] /stɛm/ *v.* [~ + *obj*], **stemmed, stem•ming.** to slow down, esp. the flow of something: *to stem the flow of blood from a wound.*

stench /stɛntʃ/ *n.* [*count; usually singular*] an offensive, strong smell: *a stench of rotting garbage.*

sten•cil /'stɛnsəl/ *n., v.,* **-ciled, -cil•ing** or (*esp. Brit.*) **-cilled, -cil•ling.** —*n.* [*count*] **1.** a thin sheet of material in which letters, numbers, etc., have been cut. —*v.* [~ + *obj*] **2.** to mark, print, or copy by means of a stencil: *She stenciled her name on the poster.*

step /stɛp/ *n., v.,* **stepped, step•ping.** —*n.* [*count*] **1.** a movement made by the foot in walking. **2.** the distance covered by one such movement. **3.** the sound made by the foot in making such a movement: *I heard steps outside the door.* **4.** a way of stepping: *She has a heavy step.* **5.** any of a series of stages in a process: *the five steps to success.* **6.** a support for the foot in going up or down: *the steps of a ladder; We sat on the porch steps.* —*v.* **7.** [*no obj*] to move in steps: *She stepped lightly out the door.* **8.** [*no obj*] to walk, esp. for a short distance: *Step over to my office.* **9.** [*no obj*] to put the foot down: *Don't step on the grass.* **10. step down,** to give up one's authority: *He had to step down because of illness.* **11. step in,** to become involved: *The United Nations was asked to step in.* **12. step out,** to leave

S

a place, esp. for a short time: *Ms. Jones has stepped out of the office for a moment.* **13. step up, a.** to raise by degrees: *to step up one's efforts.* **b.** to be promoted: *He stepped up quickly through the ranks.* —*Idiom.* **14. step by step,** gradually; by stages: *We made progress step by step.* **15. take steps,** to do what is necessary: *What steps have you taken to prevent future catastrophes?* **16. watch one's step,** to act, speak, or walk carefully: *You'd better watch your step in that part of town.*

-ster, a suffix meaning: a person who is (*youngster*); a person who is associated with (*gangster*); a person who makes or does (*trickster*).

ster•e•o /'stɛriy,ow, 'stɪər-/ *n., pl.* **ster•e•os. 1.** [count] a system or piece of equipment for producing sound that comes from different speakers. **2.** [noncount] the producing of this kind of sound; the sound itself.

ster•e•o•type /'stɛriyə,tayp, 'stɪər-/ *n., v.,* **-typed, -typ•ing.** —*n.* [count] **1.** a fixed idea about a person, group, etc. —*v.* [~ + obj] **2.** to make a stereotype of: *a tendency to stereotype ethnic groups.*

ster•ile /'stɛrɪl/ *adj.* **1.** free from germs: *a sterile bandage.* **2.** not able to produce young. **3.** not producing vegetation: *sterile soil.* —**ste•ril•i•ty** /stə'rɪlɪtiy/, *n.* [noncount]

ster•i•lize /'stɛrə,layz/ *v.* [~ + obj], **-lized, -liz•ing.** to make sterile: *to sterilize surgical instruments.* —**ster•i•li•za•tion** /,stɛrələ'zeyʃən/, *n.* [noncount] [count]

ster•ling /'stɜrlɪŋ/ *adj.* **1.** excellent: *a person of sterling character.* —*n.* [noncount] **2.** British money. **3.** articles made with a standard amount of silver in them.

stern¹ /stɜrn/ *adj.,* **-er, -est.** serious, strict, or severe: *a stern reprimand.* —'**stern•ly,** *adv.:* *The judge spoke sternly to the lawyer.* —'**stern•ness,** *n.* [noncount]

stern² /stɜrn/ *n.* [count] the rear part of a boat.

stew /stuw, styuw/ *v.* **1.** [no obj] [~ + obj] to (cause food to) cook slowly in liquid. **2.** [no obj] to worry. —*n.* **3.** [noncount] [count] food cooked by stewing, esp. a mixture of meat and vegetables. **4.** [count; singular] a state of nervous excitement or worry: *She's in a stew about finishing her term paper on time.*

stew•ard /'stuwərd, 'styuw-/ *n.* [count] a person who waits on the passengers on a ship, plane, etc.

stick¹ /stɪk/ *n.* [count] **1.** a long, thin piece of wood. **2.** a long, thin piece or part of anything: *a stick of celery.* **3.** an implement used to strike and drive a ball or puck, as a hockey stick.

stick² /stɪk/ *v.,* **stuck** /stʌk/, **stick•ing. 1.** [~ + obj] to pierce with something pointed: *He stuck the watermelon with a knife.* **2.** [~ + obj] to push (something pointed) into: *sticking pins into the pincushion.* **3.** [~ + obj] to put in a specified position: *Stick the chair in the corner.* **4.** to (cause to) be fastened: [~ + obj]: *to stick a stamp on a letter.* [no obj]: *The stamp won't stick.* **5.** [no obj] to be unable to move: *As soon as I put on my pants, the zipper stuck.* **6.** [no obj] to remain for a long time: *a fact that sticks in the mind.* **7. stick around,** *Informal.* to wait in the same place: *Stick around; I'll be right back.* **8. stick by,** to remain loyal: *Her husband stuck by her during her illness.* **9. stick out, a.** to (cause to) be pushed out: *His ears stuck out. She stuck her tongue out at the teacher* or *She stuck out her tongue at the teacher.* **b.** to be easily noticed, as

by being unusual: *She sticks out in a crowd because of her purple hair.* **10. stick to, a.** to remain firm in one's opinion, keep steadily to a task, etc.: *He stuck to it and eventually finished the job.* **b.** Also, **stick with.** to continue with something: *Stick to your original plans.* **11. stick together, a.** to (cause to) be attached: *After you glue them, the pieces will stick together. He stuck the pieces together with glue.* **b.** to stay loyal to one another: *The two Army buddies stuck together after the war.* **12. stick up for,** to speak in favor of; support: *He always stuck up for his sister.* —*Idiom.* **13. stick it out,** to endure something patiently to the end: *The part-time student stuck it out and finished college.*

stick•er /'stɪkər/ *n.* [count] an adhesive label.

stick•y /'stɪkiy/ *adj.,* **-i•er, -i•est. 1.** being able to stick to other things, as glue. **2.** covered with matter that sticks easily. **3.** requiring careful treatment: *a sticky problem.* —'**stick•i•ness,** *n.* [noncount]

stiff /stɪf/ *adj.,* **-er, -est,** *adv.* —*adj.* **1.** rigid or firm: *a stiff collar.* **2.** not moving easily: *The garage door handle gets stiff in the cold.* **3.** (of a person or animal) moving with difficulty, as from cold, age, etc.: *He was stiff from back pain.* **4.** strong; forceful: *stiff winds.* **5.** not very friendly: *She gave me a stiff, cold smile.* —*adv.* **6.** completely or extremely: *scared stiff; bored stiff.* —'**stiff•ly,** *adv.* —'**stiff•ness,** *n.* [noncount]

stiff•en /'stɪfən/ *v.* to (cause to) become stiff: [no obj]: *Whip the cream until it stiffens.* [~ + obj]: *The cold stiffened the lock.*

sti•fle /'stayfəl/ *v.* [~ + obj], **-fled, -fling.** to hold back: *I tried to stifle my laughter.*

sti•fling /'stayflɪŋ/ *adj.* **1.** causing difficulty in breathing: *a stifling room.* **2.** having difficulty in breathing: *I'm stifling in this overheated car.*

stig•ma /'stɪgmə/ *n.* [count], *pl.* **stig•ma•ta** /'stɪgmətə, stɪg'mɑtə/, **stig•mas.** a mark of shame: *no stigma attached to losing the election.*

stig•ma•tize /'stɪgmə,tayz/ *v.* [~ + obj], **-tized, -tiz•ing.** to put some mark of shame upon (someone): *The father's crime stigmatized the whole family.*

still /stɪl/ *adj.,* **-er, -est,** *adv., conj., v.* —*adj.* **1.** remaining at rest: *He stayed perfectly still.* **2.** quiet: *The empty house was still.* **3.** not flowing, as water: *The surface of the lake was still.* —*adv.* **4.** up to this time: *We are still waiting for your answer.* **5.** (used with comparative adjectives for emphasis) even (greater): *He was after still greater riches.* **6.** nevertheless: *He is rich and he still desires more.* **7.** without sound or movement; quietly: *Sit still!* —*conj.* **8.** nevertheless: *It was hopeless; still they fought.* —*v.* [~ + obj] **9.** to make calm or quiet: *to still one's fears.* —'**still•ness,** *n.* [noncount]: *the stillness of the night.*

stilt /stɪlt/ *n.* [count] one of two poles, each with a support for the foot, enabling the wearer to walk above the ground.

stim•u•lant /'stɪmyələnt/ *n.* [count] an agent that temporarily quickens some bodily activity: *a heart stimulant.*

stim•u•late /'stɪmyə,leyt/ *v.* [~ + obj], **-lat•ed, -lat•ing.** to encourage to start or to do some action: *Talking to her stimulates my mind.* —**stim•u•la•tion** /,stɪmyə'leyʃən/, *n.* [noncount] [count]

stim•u•lat•ing /'stɪmyə,leytɪŋ/ *adj.* bringing a feeling of enthusiasm; inspiring: *a stimulating conversation.*

stim•u•lus /'stɪmyələs/ *n.* [count], *pl.* **-li** /-,lay/.

something that stimulates: *Fear or excitement is a stimulus.*

sting /stɪŋ/ *v.*, **stung** /stʌŋ/, **sting•ing**, *n.* —*v.* **1.** to wound (a person or animal) with a sharp-pointed part of the body that often contains poison or venom: [~ + *obj*]: *The bee stung her on the foot.* [*no obj*]: *Dogs bite and bees sting.* **2.** to (cause to) feel a sharp pain: [~ + *obj*]: *The shot stung his arm.* [*no obj*]: *His eyes stung from the smoke.* **3.** to cause (someone) to feel anger, resentment, insult, etc.: [~ + *obj*]: *Those remarks stung her deeply.* [*no obj*]: *The memory of that insult still stings.* —*n.* [*count*] **4.** a wound or pain caused by stinging. **5.** any sharp physical or mental wound, hurt, or pain. —**'sting•er,** *n.* [*count*]

stin•gy /ˈstɪndʒiy/ *adj.*, **-gi•er, -gi•est.** unwilling to give or spend; not generous. —**'stin•gi•ness,** *n.* [*noncount*]

stink /stɪŋk/ *v.*, **stank** /stæŋk/ or, often, **stunk** /stʌŋk/, **stunk, stink•ing,** *n.* —*v.* [*no obj*] **1.** to give off a strong, bad smell: *The kitchen stinks; what are you cooking in there?* **2.** *Informal.* to be very bad, unpleasant, or inferior: *This job stinks!* —*n.* [*count; usually singular*] **3.** a very strong, powerfully disgusting smell. **4.** *Informal.* an unpleasant fuss.

stint /stɪnt/ *v.* **1. stint on,** to provide only a small amount: *Don't stint on the food.* —*n.* [*count*] **2.** a period of time spent doing something: *a stint in the army.*

stip•u•late /ˈstɪpyə,leyt/ *v.* [~ + *obj*], **-lat•ed, -lat•ing.** to require as a condition for agreement: *She stipulated that her daughter would have to receive money for school.* —**,stip•u'la•tion,** *n.* [*count*]

stir /stɜr/ *v.*, **stirred, stir•ring,** *n.* —*v.* **1.** [~ + *obj*] to mix (a liquid or other substance) with a continuous movement of a spoon, etc. **2.** to move, esp. in a slight way: [~ + *obj*]: *He didn't stir a finger to help.* [*no obj*]: *She was sleeping so soundly she didn't stir when I came in.* **3.** [~ + *obj*] to arouse (people or their feelings): *to stir pity.* **4. stir up,** to excite: *stirring up trouble; stirring them up to revolt.* —*n.* **5.** [*count*] the act of stirring or moving. **6.** [*count; usually singular*] general excitement or commotion: *What's all the stir?*

stir•rup /ˈstɜrəp, ˈstɪr-/ *n.* [*count*] a loop hung from the saddle of a horse to support the rider's foot.

stitch /stɪtʃ/ *n.* [*count*] **1.** one complete movement of a threaded needle through a material such as to leave behind a single loop of thread. **2.** the portion of thread so left. **3.** [*used with a negative word or phrase*] the least bit of anything: *They wouldn't do a stitch of work.* **4.** a sudden, sharp pain, esp. in the side of the body. —*v.* **5.** to fasten with stitches: [~ + *obj*]: *The doctor stitched the wound.* [*no obj*]: *She enjoys stitching.* —*Idiom.* **6. in stitches,** laughing uncontrollably: *Soon the comedian had the audience in stitches.*

stock /stɒk/ *n.* **1.** [*count*] goods kept on hand by a merchant, etc., for sale to customers. **2.** [*count*] a supply of something kept for future use: *a good stock of cans in the cupboard.* **3.** [*noncount*] livestock; farm animals. **4.** shares of a company: [*noncount*]: *He owns stock in a few computer software companies.* [*count*]: *investing in stocks and bonds.* **5.** [*noncount*] the liquid from boiled meat, fish, etc. —*adj.* [*before a noun*] **6.** of the usual type: *He gave his stock answer when asked about his plans for the future.*

—*v.* **7.** [~ + *obj*] to provide with a supply for future use: *They stocked the cupboard with food.* **8. stock up,** to get supplies: *You had better stock up now on cooking oil.* **9.** [~ + *obj*] to have in a store, as for sale. —*Idiom.* **10. put stock in,** to put confidence in: *I wouldn't put much stock in his promises.* **11. take stock,** to examine or evaluate what one possesses, what one needs, etc.: *It's time to take stock of our progress.*

stock•brok•er /ˈstɒk,browkər/ *n.* [*count*] a person who buys and sells stocks for customers.

'stock ex,change, *n.* [*count*] a place where stocks are bought and sold.

stock•ing /ˈstɒkɪŋ/ *n.* [*count*] a close-fitting covering for the foot and part of the leg, made of cotton, nylon, etc.

'stock ,market, *n.* [*count; usually: the + ~*] a market where stocks and bonds are traded; stock exchange.

stock•pile /ˈstɒk,payl/ *n.*, *v.*, **-piled, -pil•ing.** —*n.* [*count*] **1.** a supply of a material held in reserve. —*v.* [~ + *obj*] **2.** to put or store in a stockpile: *to stockpile goods in case of emergency.*

stock•y /ˈstɒkiy/ *adj.*, **-i•er, -i•est.** of sturdy form or build; thickset.

sto•ic /ˈstowɪk/ *adj.* **1.** stoical. —*n.* [*count*] **2.** a stoical person. —**sto•i•cism** /ˈstowə,sɪzəm/, *n.* [*noncount*]

sto•i•cal /ˈstowɪkəl/ *adj.* showing a calm, patient acceptance of difficulty. —**'sto•i•cal•ly,** *adv.*

stoke /stowk/ *v.* [~ + *obj*], **stoked, stok•ing.** to tend a fire. —**'stok•er,** *n.* [*count*]

stole[1] /stowl/ *v.* pt. of STEAL.

stole[2] /stowl/ *n.* [*count*] a piece of clothing worn over the shoulders.

sto•len /ˈstowlən/ *v.* pp. of STEAL.

stom•ach /ˈstʌmək/ *n.* [*count*] **1.** a saclike part of the body where food is digested. **2.** the lower front part of the body: *has a fat stomach.* **3.** [*used with a negative word or phrase, or in questions*] liking or desire: *They have no stomach for an expensive party.* —*v.* [~ + *obj*; *used with a negative word or phrase, or in questions*] **4.** to endure or tolerate; bear: *She can't stomach violence.*

stomp /stɒmp/ *v.* **1.** to walk on or step on heavily: [~ + *obj*]: *He stomped the floor with his heavy boots.* [*no obj*]: *He stomped back and forth.* —*n.* [*count*] **2.** the act of stomping.

stone /stown/ *n.*, *pl.* **stones,** *v.*, **stoned, ston•ing.** —*n.* **1.** [*noncount*] the hard substance, formed of mineral matter, of which rocks are made. **2.** [*count*] a piece of rock made into a specific size and shape for a particular purpose: *paving stones.* **3.** [*count*] a gem used in jewelry. **4.** [*count*] any small, hard seed, as of a cherry or a date; a pit. —*v.* [~ + *obj*] **5.** to throw stones at: *The angry mob stoned the embassy.*

ston•y /ˈstowniy/ *adj.*, **-i•er, -i•est. 1.** full of stones or rocks. **2.** unfeeling: *a stony stare.* —**ston•i•ly** /ˈstownliy/, *adv.*: *He stared stonily at his rival.*

stood /stʊd/ *v.* pt. and pp. of STAND.

stool /stuwl/ *n.* [*count*] **1.** a simple armless and backless seat. **2.** a short, low support on which to step, kneel, or rest the feet.

stoop[1] /stuwp/ *v.* **1.** to bend the head and shoulders forward and downward: [*no obj*]: *The basketball player had to stoop when climbing into the bus.* [~ + *obj*]: *He stooped his head a little when he climbed on the bus.* **2. stoop to,** to lower oneself from one's normal level of dignity and do something considered dishonest, etc.: *You wouldn't think he would stoop to such treachery.*

S

department store

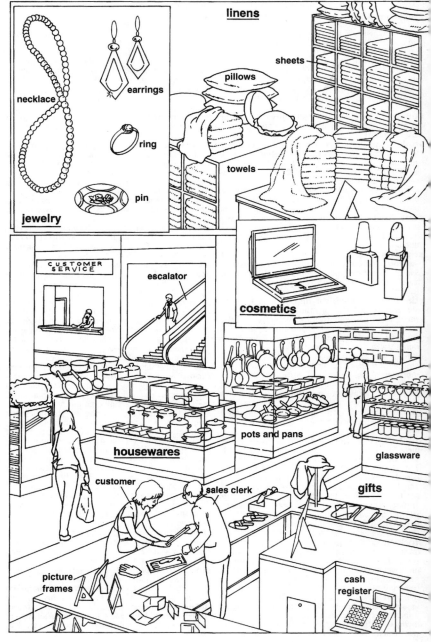

jewelry
- necklace
- earrings
- ring
- pin

linens
- sheets
- pillows
- towels

cosmetics

CUSTOMER SERVICE

escalator

housewares
- pots and pans
- glassware

gifts

- customer
- sales clerk
- picture frames
- cash register

Would he stoop to stealing money from his own children? —*n.* [*count*] **3.** a stooping position of the body: *to walk with a stoop.*

stoop² /stuwp/ *n.* [*count*] a small porch with steps at the entrance of a house.

stop /stɒp/ *v.,* **stopped, stop•ping,** *n.* —*v.* **1.** [~ + *obj*] to cease from doing; finish (an activity): *I couldn't stop laughing at the joke.* **2.** to (cause to) come to an end: [~ + *obj*]: *to stop crime.* [*no obj*]: *The music stopped.* **3.** [*no obj*] to come to a halt, as in a course or journey: *He stopped at the side of the road.* **4.** [*no obj*] to halt for a stay or visit: *They're stopping at a nice hotel.* **5.** [~ + *obj*] to prevent: *I couldn't stop him (from going).* **6.** to (cause to) be prevented from proceeding, acting, or operating: [~ + *obj*]: *to stop a car.* [*no obj*]: *The car stopped when it ran out of gas.* **7. stop by** or **in,** to make a brief visit: *We stopped by to say hello. We stopped by their house on the way.* **8. stop off,** to halt for a brief stay at some point on the way elsewhere: *Let's stop off in Chicago for a few days.* —*n.* [*count*] **9.** the act of stopping. **10.** a bringing to an end of an activity: *Put a stop to that!* **11.** a stay made at a place, as in the course of a journey: *We had a brief stop in Oslo.* **12.** a place where vehicles halt to take on and let off passengers: *a bus stop.*

stop•page /'stɒpɪdʒ/ *n.* [*count*] a stopping of activity: *a work stoppage.*

stop•per /'stɒpər/ *n.* [*count*] a plug, cork, or other piece for closing a bottle, tube, drain, etc.

stor•age /'stɔrɪdʒ/ *n.* [*noncount*] **1.** the act of storing; the state or fact of being stored. **2.** space for storing: *We had our belongings in storage.*

store /stɔr/ *n., v.,* **stored, stor•ing,** *adj.* —*n.* [*count*] **1.** a place where goods are sold: *a department store; a hardware store.* **2.** a supply of something for future use. —*v.* [~ + *obj*] **3.** to put away for future use: *Squirrels store nuts for the winter.* **4.** to put (data) in a computer memory unit. —*Idiom.* **5. in store,** about to happen: *You don't know what's in store for you.*

stork /stɔrk/ *n.* [*count*], *pl.* **storks,** (*esp. when thought of as a group*) **stork.** a wading bird having long legs and a long neck and bill.

storm /stɔrm/ *n.* [*count*] **1.** a weather condition with strong winds, rain, thunder and lightning, etc. **2.** a sudden outburst of feelings, etc.: *a storm of tears.* —*v.* **3.** [*no obj*] to move or speak angrily: *He stormed out of the room.* **4.** [~ + *obj*] to attack: *The army stormed the fortress.* —'**storm•y,** *adj.,* -i•er, -i•est.

sto•ry¹ /'stɔriy/ *n.* [*count*], *pl.* -ries. **1.** a telling of imaginary events; a tale. **2.** an article in a newspaper. **3.** a lie.

sto•ry² /'stɔriy/ *n.* [*count*], *pl.* -ries. one floor of a building. Also, *esp. Brit.,* **storey.**

stout /stawt/ *adj.,* -er, -est. **1.** overweight. **2.** [*before a noun*] brave: *stout warriors.* **3.** firm; forceful: *The army met stout resistance.* —'**stout•ly,** *adv.* —'**stout•ness,** *n.* [*noncount*]

stove /stowv/ *n.* [*count*] an apparatus that furnishes heat for warmth or cooking.

stow /stow/ *v.* [~ + *obj*] to put away in an orderly fashion: *The sailors stowed their gear below.*

stow•a•way /'stowə,wey/ *n.* [*count*] one who hides aboard a boat, airplane, etc., as a way of getting free transportation.

strad•dle /'strædl/ *v.* [~ + *obj*], -dled, -dling. to stand or sit on (something) with the legs on either side of: *to straddle a horse.*

strag•gle /'strægəl/ *v.* [*no obj*], -gled, -gling. to lag behind a group walking or working: *He's*

straggling behind the group and may get lost. —'**strag•gler,** *n.* [*count*]

strag•gly /'strægliy/ *adj.,* -gli•er, -gli•est. growing in an untidy way: *a straggly beard.*

straight /streyt/ *adj.,* -er, -est, *adv.* —*adj.* **1.** without a bend or curve: *a straight path.* **2.** level: *straight shoulders.* **3.** honest; truthful: *a straight answer.* **4.** *Informal.* **a.** heterosexual. **b.** traditional; conventional: *He's too straight to try anything that unusual.* **5.** not mixed with water: *straight whiskey.* —*adv.* **6.** in a straight line: *to walk straight.* **7.** in an erect posture: *Stand straight.* **8.** directly: *Go straight home.* —'**straight•ness,** *n.* [*noncount*]

straight•en /'streytn/ *v.* **1.** to (cause to) become straight, orderly, or neat: [*no obj*]: *Her curls straightened in the rain. Let's straighten (up) a bit before Grandpa comes over.* [~ + *obj*]: *Straighten your tie. Let's straighten (up) your room a bit.* **2. straighten out,** to (cause to) become free of confusion or difficulties: *Let's see if we can straighten this problem out. The police tried to straighten out the mess.*

straight•for•ward /,streyt'fɔrwərd/ *adj.* honest.

strain¹ /streyn/ *v.* [~ + *obj*] **1.** to use one's efforts or strength as much as possible: *straining every muscle to lift the box.* **2.** to injure (a muscle, etc.) by stretching too hard: *He strained his leg muscle on that last jump.* **3.** to force beyond the usual limit: *straining the budget.* **4.** to pour or press through a strainer: *to strain the broth.* —*n.* **5.** any force tending to alter shape, cause a break, etc.: [*noncount*]: *The cord broke under the strain.* [*count*]: *strains on the airplane caused by high winds.* **6.** [*noncount*] [*count*] an injury to a muscle caused by stretching too much. **7.** the condition of being strained: [*noncount*]: *The strain on the economy was great.* [*count*]: *Strains in the relationship were beginning to show.* **8.** worry or distress: [*noncount*]: *the strain of hard work.* [*count*]: *the strains of immigrating to a new country.*

strain² /streyn/ *n.* [*count*] a variety of bacteria, virus, etc.

strain•er /'streynər/ *n.* [*count*] a sieve for separating liquids from solids.

strait /streyt/ *n.* [*count*] **1.** Often, **straits.** [*plural form may be used with a singular verb*] a narrow passage of water connecting two large bodies of water: *the Strait(s) of Gibraltar.* **2.** Often, **straits.** [*plural*] difficulty or distress: *At the moment she is in dire straits, with no money and no job.*

strand¹ /strænd/ *v.* [~ + *obj*] to leave in a helpless position, unable to leave a place, etc.: *tourists stranded by the airline strike.*

strand² /strænd/ *n.* [*count*] **1.** a single piece or fiber that is twisted together to form a rope. **2.** a ropelike length of anything: *a strand of hair.* **3.** any of the parts that make up a whole: *the strands of a plot.*

strange /streyndʒ/ *adj.,* **strang•er, strang•est.** **1.** odd; unusual: *puzzled by her strange behavior.* **2.** unfamiliar: *It was hard for them to move to a strange place.* —'**strange•ly,** *adv.:* *The machine is acting strangely.* —'**strange•ness,** *n.* [*noncount*]

stran•ger /'streyndʒər/ *n.* [*count*] **1.** a person whom one does not know. **2.** a newcomer in a place: *a stranger in town.*

stran•gle /'stræŋgəl/ *v.* [~ + *obj*], -gled, -gling. to kill by squeezing the throat and preventing air from coming in.

S

city street

skyscraper

office building

traffic light

street sign

THIRD AVENUE

lamppost

DRY CLEANERS

PHARMACY

taxi

fire hydrant

sidewalk

street

crosswalk

bus

subway entrance

mailbox

MAIL

pedestrian

strap /stræp/ *n., v.,* **strapped, strap·ping.** —*n.* [count] **1.** a narrow strip of material, esp. leather, used for holding things together or for carrying something: *The strap on my sandal broke.* —*v.* [~ + obj] **2.** to fasten with a strap: *He strapped his snowshoes on.*

strap·ping /'stræpɪŋ/ *adj.* [before a noun] strong; large: *a strapping young fellow.*

stra·te·gic /strə'tiydʒɪk/ *adj.* of or relating to any strategy to achieve a goal: *making strategic plans to increase sales.* —**stra'te·gi·cal·ly,** *adv.*

strat·e·gy /'strætɪdʒiy/ *n., pl.* **-gies. 1.** [noncount] the science of planning and directing military operations. **2.** a plan or method for achieving a goal: [count]: *a strategy for winning at bridge.* [noncount]: *At our next sales meeting we'll discuss strategy.* —**'strat·e·gist,** *n.* [count]

straw /strɔ/ *n.* **1.** [count] a single stalk or stem, esp. of wheat, oats, etc. **2.** [noncount] a mass of such stalks, used for feeding animals. **3.** [count] a narrow tube for sucking up a beverage. —*Idiom.* **4. (the) last straw,** something intolerable that is the latest in a series of bad events. **5. straw in the wind,** a piece of information that seems to indicate future events.

straw·ber·ry /'strɔ,bɛriy, -bəriy/ *n.* [count], *pl.* **-ries.** the juicy red fruit of a stemless plant that grows close to the ground.

stray /strey/ *v.* [no obj] **1.** to move away from the right way: *to stray from the main road.* —*n.* [count] **2.** a domestic animal found wandering or without an owner. —*adj.* [before a noun] **3.** having strayed: *a stray cat.* **4.** found apart from others: *a few stray hairs.*

streak /striyk/ *n.* [count] **1.** a long, narrow mark, smear, etc.: *streaks of paint.* **2.** a quality in someone's behavior or personality: *a wild streak.* **3.** a number of occurrences, as in a series: *a streak of good luck.* —*v.* **4.** to form streaks (on): [no obj]: *The windows streak if you don't wash them.* [~ + obj]: *The windows were streaked with dirt.* **5.** [no obj] to go rapidly: *The jets streaked across the sky.*

stream /striym/ *n.* [count] **1.** a body of water flowing in a channel, as a brook. **2.** any flow or current of liquid, fluid, or gas: *a stream of gas escaping.* **3.** a series of things: *a stream of words.* —*v.* [no obj] **4.** to flow in a stream: *The river streamed past the house.* **5.** to proceed without stopping: *The traffic streamed past.* **6.** to float: *The runner's hair was streaming behind her.*

stream·er /'striymər/ *n.* [count] any long narrow piece or thing, as a paper ribbon.

stream·line /'striym,layn/ *v.* [~ + obj], **-lined, -lin·ing. 1.** to give something a smooth, narrow shape so that it moves more rapidly: *to streamline the shape of the car.* **2.** to make something more efficient or simple: *to streamline the procedures.*

street /striyt/ *n.* [count] a paved public road in a town or city.

street·car /'striyt,kɑr/ *n.* [count] a public vehicle on rails running along city streets.

strength /strɛŋθ, strɛnθ/ *n.* **1.** [noncount] the quality of being strong: *It took a lot of strength to lift the rock. It took strength of character to get through that ordeal.* **2.** [count] a strong quality or characteristic: *He was asked to list his strengths and weaknesses on the interview form.* —*Idiom.* **3. on the strength of,** on the basis of: *We decided to hire him on the strength of your recommendation.*

strength·en /'strɛŋkθən, 'strɛn-/ *v.* to (cause

to) grow stronger: [no obj]: *The storm strengthened.* [~ + obj]: *We'll have to strengthen our skills.*

stren·u·ous /'strɛnyuwəs/ *adj.* using or needing strong, vigorous activity: *strenuous exercise.* —'**stren·u·ous·ly,** *adv.*: *She objected strenuously to the remarks by the witness.* —'**stren·u·ous·ness,** *n.* [noncount]

stress /strɛs/ *n.* **1.** [noncount] importance attached to a thing; emphasis: *to lay stress upon good manners.* **2.** [noncount] [count] force expressed in pronouncing a speech sound, syllable, or word. **3.** [noncount] [count] physical, mental, or emotional strain. —*v.* [~ + obj] **4.** to emphasize; give importance to something: *He stressed the need for higher education.* —'**stress·ful,** *adj.*: *a long, stressful workday.*

stretch /strɛtʃ/ *v.* **1.** to spread out fully: [~ + obj]: *She stretched herself out on the ground.* [no obj]: *He yawned and stretched.* **2.** to (cause to) extend from one place to another: [~ + obj]: *The crew stretched a rope across the road.* [no obj]: *The forest stretches for miles.* **3.** [no obj] to extend in time: *His memory stretches back to his early childhood.* **4.** to (cause to) be drawn tight, without breaking or snapping: [~ + obj]: *to stretch the strings of a violin.* [no obj]: *Will this nylon stretch?* —*n.* **5.** [count] an act of stretching. **6.** [noncount] ability to be stretched: *These socks have lost their stretch.* **7.** [count] a continuous length: *a stretch of meadow.* **8.** [count] an amount of time: *gone for a stretch of ten years.*

stretch·er /'strɛtʃər/ *n.* [count] a framework covered with canvas, used to carry a sick or dead person.

strick·en /'strɪkən/ *v.* **1.** a pp. of STRIKE. —*adj.* **2.** affected by disease, trouble, or sorrow: *stricken with cancer.*

strict /strɪkt/ *adj.,* **-er, -est. 1.** demanding obedience to requirements or principles: *a strict observance of rituals.* **2.** exact; precise: *in the strict sense of the word.* **3.** absolute; complete: *strict silence.* —'**strict·ly,** *adv.* —'**strict·ness,** *n.* [noncount]

stride /strayd/ *v.,* **strode** /strowd/, **strid·den** /'strɪdn/, **strid·ing,** *n.* —*v.* [no obj] **1.** to walk with long steps. —*n.* [count] **2.** a long step in walking. **3.** a step forward in development or progress: *The student has made great strides in learning English.* —*Idiom.* **4. take (something) in stride,** to deal with (something) calmly: *He took the defeat in stride.*

strike /strayk/ *v.,* **struck** /strʌk/, **struck** or **strick·en, strik·ing,** *n.* —*v.* **1.** [~ + obj] to hit (someone), as with the fist, a weapon, or a hammer. **2.** to attack suddenly: [no obj]: *The bombers struck at dawn.* [~ + obj]: *The bombers struck the oil refineries.* **3.** to crash into: [~ + obj]: *The ship struck a rock.* [no obj]: *Will lightning strike in the same place twice?* **4.** [~ + obj] to cause to light: *He struck a match.* **5.** [~ + obj] to impress in a particular manner: *It strikes me as a ridiculous idea.* **6.** [~ + obj] to find; discover: *The drilling crew struck oil.* **7.** [~ + obj] to arrive at; achieve: *The two sides struck a compromise.* **8.** [~ + obj] to cross out; remove: *to strike a sentence from his speech.* **9.** to mark (the time) by chimes, bells, or the like: [no obj]: *The clock struck at midnight.* [~ + obj]: *The clock struck 12.* **10.** to stop working as a protest: [~ + obj]: *The workers struck the packing plant.* [no obj]: *The packing plant workers went on strike for higher wages.* **11. strike off,** to remove: *to strike*

S

names off a list; to strike off his name from our list. —n. [count] **12.** an act or instance of striking. **13.** a stoppage of work as a protest. **14.** the discovery of a rich mineral deposit: a gold strike. —'**strik•er**, n. [count]

strik•ing /ˈstraykɪŋ/ adj. obviously attractive or impressive: a striking photo.

string /strɪŋ/ n., v., **strung** /strʌŋ/, **string•ing.** —n. **1.** [noncount] [count] a thin cord used for binding, connecting, or tying. **2.** [count] a collection of objects on a string: She wore a beautiful string of pearls. **3.** [count] a series of things: a string of questions. **4.** [count] the tightly stretched cord or wire of a musical instrument: a violin string. **5. strings,** [plural] **a.** stringed instruments, esp. those played with a bow. **b.** players of such instruments in an orchestra or band. **6.** Usually, **strings.** [plural] limitations on a proposal: a generous offer with no strings attached. —v. [~ + obj] **7.** to provide (something) with a string or strings: to string a banjo. **8.** to hang or tie on a string: stringing (up) a line of lights on the Christmas tree. **9.** to thread on a string: to string beads. **10.** to arrange in a series: stringing words together.

strin•gent /ˈstrɪndʒənt/ adj. very demanding, strict, or severe: stringent traffic laws.

string•y /ˈstrɪŋiy/ adj., **-i•er, -i•est.** of or like string: stringy hair.

strip¹ /strɪp/ v., **stripped** or **stript, strip•ping,** n. —v. **1.** to take off covering, clothes, etc.: [~ + obj]: to strip sheets from a bed. [no obj]: He stripped and jumped into the lake. **2.** [~ + obj] to remove paint, etc., from. **3. strip of,** to take (something) away from someone: He was stripped of his rights.

strip² /strɪp/ n. [count] **1.** a long narrow piece of material. **2.** a narrow piece of land. **3.** an area of commercial development along a road.

stripe /strayp/ n., v., **striped, strip•ing.** —n. [count] **1.** a narrow band differing in color, material, or texture from the background: the stripes of a zebra. —v. [~ + obj] **2.** to mark or furnish with stripes.

strive /strayv/ v. [no obj], **strove** /strowv/ or **strived, striv•en** /ˈstrɪvən/ or **strived, striv•ing. 1.** to try hard: to strive for success; to strive to do well. **2.** to oppose in battle or conflict; compete: to strive against foes.

strode /strowd/ v. pt. of STRIDE.

stroke¹ /strowk/ n., v., **stroked, strok•ing.** —n. [count] **1.** an act of striking or hitting. **2.** a sound made by a bell: at the stroke of midnight. **3.** a blockage or breaking of a blood vessel in the brain. **4.** a sudden, strong action or movement that is like a blow in its effect: a stroke of lightning. **5.** a single complete movement that is repeated: a swimming stroke. **6.** a movement of a pen, pencil, brush, etc.; a mark made by such a movement: a few strokes of the brush. **7.** a sudden, chance happening: a stroke of luck. —v. [~ + obj] **8.** to mark with a stroke or strokes; cancel, as by a stroke of a pen.

stroke² /strowk/ v., **stroked, strok•ing,** n. —v. [~ + obj] **1.** to pass the hand over gently: He stroked his cat. —n. [count] **2.** an act or instance of stroking: a gentle stroke on the arm.

stroll /strowl/ v. [no obj] **1.** to walk slowly for pleasure: to stroll along the beach. —n. [count] **2.** a slow, leisurely walk.

stroll•er /ˈstrowlər/ n. [count] **1.** one who strolls. **2.** a four-wheeled, chairlike carriage in which small children are pushed.

strong /strɔŋ, strɒŋ/ adj., **strong•er** /ˈstrɔŋgər, ˈstrɒŋ-/, **strong•est** /ˈstrɔŋgɪst, ˈstrɒŋ-/. **1.** having, showing, or involving great power: strong enough to lift a hundred pounds. **2.** very able in a specific field or respect: She is strong in mathematics. **3.** of great force, effectiveness, or power: strong reasons for abandoning the project. **4.** able to resist strain, force, wear, etc.: strong cloth. **5.** firm; not giving in: strong faith. **6.** moving or acting with force or power: strong winds. **7.** clear or marked, as an impression or a resemblance: a strong similarity in their political positions. **8.** intense or concentrated: a strong tea. **9.** [after a noun or number] having the stated number: an army 20,000 strong. —'**strong•ly,** adv.: She strongly disagrees with you.

strong•hold /ˈstrɔŋ,howld, ˈstrɒŋ-/ n. [count] a fort or fortress.

struck /strʌk/ v. pt. and a pp. of STRIKE.

struc•ture /ˈstrʌktʃər/ n., v., **-tured, -tur•ing.** —n. **1.** [noncount] the way in which something is put together: the structure of the building. **2.** [count] something constructed, as a building or bridge. —v. [~ + obj] **3.** to give a structure to; organize: to structure a company. —'**struc•tur•al,** adj.

strug•gle /ˈstrʌgəl/ v., **-gled, -gling,** n. —v. [no obj] **1.** to fight hard against an attacker: He struggled and broke free. **2.** to make great efforts: struggling to succeed. —n. [count] **3.** an act or instance of struggling.

strum /strʌm/ v., **strummed, strum•ming.** to play on (a stringed musical instrument) by running the fingers lightly across the strings: [no obj]: to strum on the guitar. [~ + obj]: softly strumming my guitar.

strung /strʌŋ/ v. pt. and pp. of STRING.

strut /strʌt/ v., **strut•ted, strut•ting,** n. —v. [no obj] **1.** to walk in an overly proud or self-important way. —n. [count] **2.** the act of strutting.

stub /stʌb/ n., v., **stubbed, stub•bing.** —n. [count] **1.** a short remaining piece, as of a pencil or cigar. **2.** (in a checkbook, receipt book, etc.) the inner end of each page that is kept in the book as a record. **3.** the returned part of a ticket: You'll need your ticket stub if you want to get back inside the theater. —v. **4.** [~ + obj] to strike (one's toe) against some object. **5. stub out,** to put out the burning end of (a cigarette or cigar) by crushing it: He stubbed out his cigar or He stubbed his cigar out.

stub•ble /ˈstʌbəl/ n. [noncount] a short, rough growth, as of a beard. —'**stub•bly,** adj., **-bli•er, -bli•est.**

stub•born /ˈstʌbərn/ adj. **1.** unreasonably unwilling to change; determined: a stubborn refusal. **2.** difficult to handle, treat, do away with, etc.: a stubborn pain. —'**stub•born•ly,** adv. —'**stub•born•ness,** n. [noncount]

stub•by /ˈstʌbiy/ adj., **-bi•er, -bi•est.** short and thick: the baby's stubby little fingers.

stuck /stʌk/ v. pt. and pp. of STICK².

stud /stʌd/ n., v., **stud•ded, stud•ding.** —n. [count] **1.** a head of a nail that sticks out from a surface as an ornament: a wooden chest with brass studs. **2.** a buttonlike object mounted on a pin that is passed through an article of clothing to fasten it: a collar stud. —v. [~ + obj] **3.** to set with or as if with studs: Stars studded the sky.

stu•dent /ˈstuwdnt, ˈstyuwd-/ n. [count] **1.** one who is studying, learning, or training at a school.

2. one who studies an art, science, etc., thoughtfully: *a student of Chinese pottery.*

stu•di•o /'stuwdiy,ow, 'styuw-/ *n.* [*count*], *pl.* -di•os. **1.** the workroom of an artist. **2.** a place for instruction in a performing art: *a dance studio.* **3.** a place where radio or television programs, movies, etc., are made. **4.** Also, **studio apartment.** an apartment consisting of one main room that is a combination kitchen, bedroom, and living room.

stud•y /'stʌdiy/ *n.,* *pl.* stud•ies, *v.,* stud•ied, stud•y•ing. —*n.* **1.** [*noncount*] the process of learning, as by reading, investigation, etc.: *the study of law.* **2.** Often, **studies.** a student's work at school or college: [*plural*]: *to pursue one's studies.* [*noncount*]: *After years of study he got his diploma.* **3.** [*count*] a complete investigation and analysis of a subject, etc.: *Studies show that smoking causes cancer.* **4.** [*count*] a room set apart for private study. —*v.* **5.** to apply oneself to learning: [*no obj*]: *She spends much time studying.* [~ + *obj*]: *He's been studying chemistry.* **6.** to take a course of study, as at a college: [*no obj*]: *He's studying at Harvard.* [~ + *obj*]: *She's studying architecture at Yale.* **7.** [~ + *obj*] to examine carefully and in detail: *The police officer studied the accident scene.*

stuff /stʌf/ *n.* [*noncount*] **1.** the material of which anything is made: *Kerosene is oily black stuff.* **2.** objects of some kind not specified: *What is all that stuff on the floor?* **3.** property, such as personal belongings: *I left some of my stuff in Dad's attic.* —*v.* [~ + *obj*] **4.** to push (something) into something else: *I stuffed my clothes into the suitcase.* **5.** to fill (a container), esp. by packing the contents closely together: *He stuffed his suitcase with old clothes.*

stuff•ing /'stʌfɪŋ/ *n.* [*noncount*] a material used to stuff something.

stuff•y /'stʌfiy/ *adj.,* -i•er, -i•est. **1.** uncomfortable because of a lack of fresh air: *stuffy air; a stuffy room.* **2.** blocked: *He had a stuffy nose.* **3.** dull or boring. —'stuff•i•ness, *n.* [*noncount*]

stum•ble /'stʌmbəl/ *v.,* -bled, -bling, *n.* —*v.* [*no obj*] **1.** to strike the foot against something, so that one almost falls. **2.** to walk unsteadily. **3.** to make a mistake: *The scientists stumbled in their search for a cure.* **4. stumble on** or **across,** to discover or come upon, accidentally or unexpectedly: *They stumbled on a little village and stayed there.* —*n.* [*count*] **5.** the act of stumbling. **6.** a slip or blunder.

stump /stʌmp/ *n.* [*count*] **1.** the lower end of a tree trunk left standing after the upper part is cut off. **2.** the part of a limb of the body remaining after the rest has been cut off. —*v.* [~ + *obj*] **3.** to confuse (someone): *The question stumped me.*

stun /stʌn/ *v.* [~ + *obj*], stunned, stun•ning. **1.** to cause (someone) to lose consciousness by a blow, fall, etc. **2.** to astonish; shock: *We were completely stunned by her hostile reaction.*

stung /stʌŋ/ *v.* a pt. and pp. of STING.

stunk /stʌŋk/ *v.* a pt. and pp. of STINK.

stun•ning /'stʌnɪŋ/ *adj.* of striking beauty: *a stunning redhead.*

stunt[1] /stʌnt/ *v.* [~ + *obj*] to slow down or prevent the growth of: *The roses had been stunted by the frost.*

stunt[2] /stʌnt/ *n.* [*count*] **1.** a performance displaying a person's skill or daring: *performing some gymnastic stunts, such as somersaults.* **2.**

something foolish or dangerous that is done to attract attention: *a publicity stunt.*

stu•pid /'stuwpɪd, 'styuw-/ *adj.,* -er, -est. not intelligent: *a stupid person; a stupid question.* —**stu•pid•i•ty** /stuw'pɪdɪtiy/ *n.* [*noncount*] [*count*] —'**stu•pid•ly,** *adv.*

stu•por /'stuwpər, 'styuw-/ *n.* [*count; usually singular*] a state of near unconsciousness, as caused by disease, narcotics, etc.

stur•dy /'stɜrdiy/ *adj.,* -di•er, -di•est. strongly built; strong; hardy: *a sturdy young fellow.* —'**stur•di•ness,** *n.* [*noncount*]

stut•ter /'stʌtər/ *v.* **1.** to speak with the rhythm interrupted by repetitions or blocks of sounds or syllables: [*no obj*]: *He stuttered when he spoke.* [*used with quotations*]: *"Wha-..wha-..what do you mean?" he stuttered.* —*n.* [*count*] **2.** an act or instance of stuttering. **3.** stuttering speech. —'**stut•ter•er,** *n.* [*count*]

sty[1] /stay/ *n.* [*count*], *pl.* sties. a pigpen.

sty[2] /stay/ *n.* [*count*], *pl.* sties. an infected area on the edge of the eyelid.

style /stayl/ *n.,* *v.,* styled, styl•ing. —*n.* **1.** [*count*] a particular form, appearance, or type: *different styles of houses.* **2.** [*count*] a particular way of behaving, speaking, etc.: *to do things in a grand style.* **3.** [*noncount*] current fashion in clothes: *clothes that are never out of style.* **4.** [*noncount*] an elegant way of living: *to live in style.* —*v.* [~ + *obj*] **5.** to design in a given style: *She styled my hair beautifully.*

styl•ish /'staylɪʃ/ *adj.* agreeing with the current style: *stylish clothes.* —'**styl•ish•ly,** *adv.*

styl•ist /'staylɪst/ *n.* [*count*] a designer or consultant on style, esp. in hairdressing or clothing.

suave /swɑv/ *adj.,* suav•er, suav•est. smoothly polite in manner. —'**suave•ly,** *adv.* —**suav•i•ty** /'swɑvɪtiy/ *n.* [*noncount*]

S

sub /sʌb/ *n.,* *v.,* subbed, sub•bing. —*n.* [*count*] **1.** a submarine. **2.** a substitute: *We hired a sub to teach her class.* —*v.* [*no obj*] **3.** to act as a substitute for another.

sub-, a prefix meaning: under, below, or beneath (*subway*); just outside of or near (*subtropical*); less than or not quite (*subteen*); secondary or below in rank (*subcommittee*).

sub•con•scious /sʌb'kɒnʃəs/ *adj.* **1.** existing in the mind beneath the thoughts and feelings of which one is aware: *subconscious feelings of love.* —*n.* [*noncount*] **2.** that part of one's mind that is hidden to an individual and yet has an influence or effect on that person: *Somewhere in your subconscious you know she is right.* —**sub'con•scious•ly,** *adv.*

sub•di•vide /sʌbdɪ,vayd/ *v.,* -vid•ed, -vid•ing. (of something already divided) to (cause to) become divided into smaller parts: [*no obj*]: *The recently formed egg cells subdivided.* [~ + *obj*]: *to subdivide the land.*

sub•due /səb'duw, -'dyuw/ *v.* [~ + *obj*], -dued, -du•ing. **1.** to overcome or overpower by force. **2.** to hold back or keep in control (feelings, etc.): *His soothing words subdued her fears.*

sub•dued /səb'duwd, -'dyuw/ *adj.* **1.** quiet; very calm: *a subdued voice.* **2.** (of colors) reduced in brightness.

sub•ject /*n., adj.* 'sʌbdʒɪkt; *v.* səb'dʒɛkt/ *n.* [*count*] **1.** that which forms a basic matter of thought, discussion, etc.: *He keeps changing the subject.* **2.** a branch of knowledge: *Which subjects are you taking this semester?* **3.** something or someone written about or represented in writing, art, or music. **4.** in a sentence, a noun or phrase that is the one performing the action or being in the state expressed by the verb: *The subject of the sentence Jesse shot the sheriff is Jesse.* —*adj.* **5.** being under the rule, control, or influence of something: *We are subject to the rules and regulations in effect.* **6.** [*be* + ~ + *to*] likely to get: *I am subject to colds.* —*v.* **7.** [~ + *obj*] to bring under rule, control, or influence: *The weaker tribes were subjected by a warlike people.* **8. subject to, a.** to expose to: *to subject metal to intense heat.* **b.** to expose to attack by (something): *to subject yourself to ridicule.* —**sub'jec•tion,** *n.* [*noncount*]

sub•jec•tive /səb'dʒɛktɪv/ *adj.* **1.** existing in the mind and not necessarily in reality: *a subjective impression that the building was leaning to the right.* **2.** relating to or influenced by personal feelings: *a subjective judgment.* —**sub'jec•tive•ly,** *adv.* —**sub•jec•tiv•i•ty** /ˌsʌbdʒɛk'tɪvɪti/, *n.* [*noncount*]

sub•junc•tive /səb'dʒʌŋktɪv/ *adj.* **1.** of or being a grammatical mood used for statements or questions that are doubtful, possible, or contrary to fact, as the mood of the verb *be* in *if I were a rich man.* —*n.* [*count*] **2.** the subjunctive mood. **3.** a verb form in the subjunctive mood.

sub•let / *v.* sʌb'lɛt, 'sʌbˌlɛt;*n.* 'sʌbˌlɛt/ *v.,* **-let, -let•ting,** *n.* —*v.* [~ + *obj*] **1.** to rent (an apartment or house) to another person: *We sublet our apartment (to John). John sublet our apartment (from us).* —*n.* [*count*] **2.** an act or instance of subletting.

sub•ma•rine /ˌsʌbmə'riyn, 'sʌbməˌriyn/ *n.* [*count*] a ship that can move under water.

sub•merge /səb'mɜrdʒ/ *v.,* **-merged, -merg•ing. 1.** to put or sink below the surface of water: [*no obj*]: *The submarine submerged.* [~ + *obj*]: *The boat was submerged in thirty fathoms of water.* **2.** [~ + *obj*] to cover with water; immerse: *Do not submerge this electric skillet in water.* **3.** [~ + *obj*] to cover; hide: *Certain facts were submerged by the witness.* —**sub•mer•sion** /səb'mɜrʒən, -ʃən/, *n.* [*noncount*]

sub•mis•sion /səb'mɪʃən/ *n.* **1.** [*noncount*] the act or an instance of submitting: *their submission to the wishes of their children.* **2.** [*count*] something presented, as an application, manuscript, etc., for consideration.

sub•mis•sive /səb'nɪsɪv/ *adj.* showing a willingness to give in to the power or wishes of another.

sub•mit /səb'mɪt/ *v.,* **-mit•ted, -mit•ting. 1.** to surrender or yield to the power or authority of another: [~ + *obj*]: *We submitted ourselves to their wishes.* [*no obj*]: *At last the exhausted army submitted.* **2.** [~ + *obj*] to present for consideration: *He submitted his plans for the new town square.*

sub•or•di•nate /*adj.,* *n.* sə'bɔrdṇɪt; *v.* -dṇˌeyt/ *adj., n., v.,* **-nat•ed, -nat•ing.** —*adj.* **1.** being in a lower rank: *He had to accept a subordinate post in the new administration.* **2.** of less importance: *In some colleges teaching is considered subordinate to research.* —*n.* [*count*] **3.** a subordinate person or thing: *He's a subordinate to the district attorney.* —*v.* [~ + *obj* (+ *to*)] **4.** to make less important: *to make work subordinate to pleasure.*

sub•scribe /səb'skrayb/ *v.,* **-scribed, -scrib•ing. 1.** to pay or pledge (a sum of money) as a contribution, gift, or investment: [~ + *obj*]: *to subscribe fifty dollars to the animal shelter fund.* [*no obj*]: *to subscribe to the animal shelter fund.* **2. subcribe to, a.** to agree to receive and pay for:

to subscribe to a magazine. **b.** to agree to: *They don't subscribe to the notion that everyone is equal under the law.* —**sub'scrib•er,** *n.* [*count*]

sub•scrip•tion /səb'skrɪpʃən/ *n.* [*count*] **1.** a sum of money given as a contribution, investment, etc. **2.** the right to have a newspaper or magazine delivered, attend a series of concerts or plays, etc., in exchange for a sum paid.

sub•se•quent /'sʌbsɪkwənt/ *adj.* following or happening after; succeeding: *In subsequent lessons the teacher made clearer what she had said at the beginning.* —**'sub•se•quent•ly,** *adv.*

sub•side /səb'sayd/ *v.* [*no obj*], **-sid•ed, -sid•ing. 1.** to sink to a lower level: *The water in the sink subsided slowly.* **2.** to become quiet, less active, or less violent: *By dawn the storm had subsided.*

sub•sid•i•ar•y /səb'sɪdiˌɛriy/ *adj., n., pl.* **-ar•ies.** —*adj.* **1.** less important: *subsidiary issues that are not our main concern.* —*n.* [*count*] **2.** a company controlled by another company.

sub•si•dize /'sʌbsɪˌdayz/ *v.* [~ + *obj*], **-dized, -diz•ing.** to give a subsidy to: *subsidized housing for those unable to afford high rents.*

sub•si•dy /'sʌbsɪdiy/ *n.* [*count*], *pl.* **-dies.** a direct payment of money made by a government to a private business, an individual, or another government: *The subsidy paid to the theater keeps the ticket prices low.*

sub•sist /səb'sɪst/ *v.* [*no obj*] to have just enough of something, as of food, resources, etc., to live on: *The survivors of the plane crash subsisted on nuts and berries.* —**sub'sist•ence,** *n.* [*noncount*]

sub•stance /'sʌbstəns/ *n.* **1.** [*noncount*] the physical matter that makes up some thing, object, etc.: *form and substance.* **2.** [*count*] a particular kind of material: *a metallic substance.* **3.** [*noncount*] importance: *Those claims lack substance.* **4.** [*noncount*] the meaning, as of speech or writing: *The substance of his speech was that we have to raise money.*

sub•stan•tial /səb'stænʃəl/ *adj.* **1.** of large amount, quantity, etc.: *a substantial amount of money.* **2.** that can be felt or touched: *a substantial fabric.* **3.** strong: *a substantial charge.*

sub•stan•tial•ly /səb'stænʃəliy/ *adv.* **1.** to a great degree; a lot: *Our ESL program has improved substantially in the last ten years.* **2.** in an important way: *Has the situation changed substantially since last year?*

sub•stan•ti•ate /səb'stænʃiyˌeyt/ *v.* [~ + *obj*], **-at•ed, -at•ing.** to show (a claim, opinion, etc.) by proof: *to substantiate a charge.*

sub•sti•tute /'sʌbstɪˌtuwt, -ˌtyuwt/ *n., v.,* **-tut•ed, -tut•ing.** —*n.* **1.** a person or thing serving in place of another: [*count*]: *The coach sent in a substitute.* [*noncount*]: *There is simply no substitute for hard work.* —*v.* **2.** [~ + *obj*] to put (a person or thing) in the place of another: *We substituted fish for meat several times a week.* **3.** [*no obj*] to act as a substitute: *substituting when the regular teachers were sick.* —**sub•sti'tu•tion,** *n.* [*noncount*] [*count*]

sub•ter•fuge /'sʌbtərˌfyuwdʒ/ *n.* [*noncount*] [*count*] a dishonest or illegal action.

sub•ter•ra•ne•an /ˌsʌbtə'reyniyən/ *adj.* underground: *a subterranean silver mine.*

sub•ti•tle /'sʌbˌtaytḷ/ *n., v.,* **-tled, -tling.** —*n.* [*count*] **1.** a secondary title of a book, etc. **2.** (in motion pictures and television) the text of dialog translated into another language and shown on the bottom of the screen: *a French film with Eng-*

lish subtitles. —*v.* [~ + *obj*] **3.** to give a subtitle or subtitles to.

sub•tle /'sʌtl/ *adj.*, **-tler, -tlest.** difficult to notice, perceive, or describe: *a subtle perfume; subtle humor.* —'**sub•tle•ty,** *n.* [*noncount*] [*count*], *pl.* **-ties.** —'**sub•tly,** *adv.*

sub•tract /səb'trækt/ *v.* [~ + *obj*] [*no obj*] to take away, as a part from a whole, or one number from another. —**sub'trac•tion,** *n.* [*noncount*] [*count*]

sub•urb /'sʌbɜrb/ *n.* [*count*] **1.** a residential area lying immediately outside a city or town. **2. the suburbs,** [*plural*] an area composed of such communities. —**sub•ur•ban** /sə'bɜrbən/, *adj.*

sub•ur•bi•a /sə'bɜrbiyə/ *n.* [*noncount*] the social and cultural aspects of life in the suburbs.

sub•ver•sion /səb'vɜrʒən, -ʃən/ *n.* [*noncount*] the act of overthrowing or attempting to overthrow some power or authority. —**sub'ver•sive,** *adj., n.* [*count*]

sub•vert /səb'vɜrt/ *v.* [~ + *obj*] to engage in or attempt subversion: *Instead of cooperating, he worked to subvert her authority.*

sub•way /'sʌb,wey/ *n.* **1.** an underground electric railroad: [*count*]: *no delays this morning on the subways.* [*noncount*]: *to travel by subway.* **2.** [*count*] Chiefly Brit. a short tunnel.

suc•ceed /sək'siyd/ *v.* **1.** [*no obj*] to end as one wished: *Our efforts succeeded.* **2.** [*no obj*] to accomplish what is intended: *We succeeded in our efforts to start the car.* **3.** [~ + *obj*] to follow or replace another in some office, etc.: *He succeeded his mother to the throne.* **4.** [~ + *obj*] to follow: *one movement succeeding another.*

suc•cess /sək'sɛs/ *n.* **1.** [*noncount*] the favorable result of something attempted: *success in learning a new language.* **2.** [*count*] a successful person or thing: *Was the party a success?* —**suc'cess•ful,** *adj.* —**suc'cess•ful•ly,** *adv.*

suc•ces•sion /sək'sɛʃən/ *n.* **1.** [*noncount*] the coming of one person or thing after another: *He fired his secretaries in quick succession.* **2.** [*count*] a number of persons or things following one another: *a succession of secretaries.*

suc•ces•sive /sək'sɛsɪv/ *adj.* following in succession: *three successive days of rain.*

suc•ces•sor /sək'sɛsər/ *n.* [*count*] a person who succeeds another, as in an office.

suc•cinct /sək'sɪŋkt/ *adj.* expressed well in few words: *succinct and direct answers.* —**suc'cinct•ly,** *adv.* —**suc'cinct•ness,** *n.* [*noncount*]

suc•cu•lent /'sʌkyələnt/ *adj.* **1.** juicy. **2.** (of a plant) having fleshy, juicy tissues. —'**suc•cu•lence,** *n.* [*noncount*]

suc•cumb /sə'kʌm/ *v.* [*no obj*] **1.** to give way to superior force; yield: *She succumbed to his charms.* **2.** to be unable to resist disease, wounds, etc.: *He succumbed to his wounds and died in the night.*

such /sʌtʃ/ *adj.* **1.** of the kind, character, degree, etc., indicated: *Drop out of school? Such talk is foolish.* **2.** like or similar: *tea, coffee, and other such beverages.* **3.** to a certain degree: *He is such a liar. That is such nonsense.* **4.** being as stated or indicated: *Such is the case.* —*adv.* **5.** so; to such a degree: *They are such nice people.* **6.** in such a way or manner. —*pron.* **7.** such a person or thing or such persons or things: *kings, princes, and such.* **8.** someone or something indicated: *She claims to be a friend but is not such.* —*Idiom.* **9. such as, a.** of the kind specified: *a*

plan such as you propose. **b.** for example: *pastimes, such as reading and chess.*

'such and ,such, *adj.* **1.** definite or particular but not named or specified: *Let's imagine we meet at such and such a place.* —*pron.* **2.** something or someone not specified: *if such and such should happen.*

suck /sʌk/ *v.* **1.** to draw into the mouth by using the lips and tongue: [~ + *obj*]: *to suck lemonade through a straw.* [*no obj*]: *The baby was sucking at his mother's breast.* **2.** [~ + *obj*] to draw (water, air, etc.) out of something: *Plants suck moisture from the air.* **3.** to put into the mouth and lick with the tongue: [~ + *obj*]: *to suck a piece of candy.* [*no obj*]: *sucking on a cough drop.* —*n.* [*count*] **4.** an act or instance of sucking.

suck•er /'sʌkər/ *n.* [*count*] **1.** a body part of an animal used for sucking or clinging by suction. **2.** *Informal.* a person easily deceived.

suck•le /'sʌkəl/ *v.*, **-led, -ling.** to (cause to or provide the means to) feed with milk at the breast: [*no obj*]: *The newborn colt suckled at its mother's udder.* [~ + *obj*]: *to suckle a baby.*

suc•tion /'sʌkʃən/ *n.* [*noncount*] the force that attracts a fluid or solid to where the pressure is lowest.

sud•den /'sʌdn/ *adj.* **1.** happening, coming, made, or done quickly or unexpectedly: *a sudden storm.* —*Idiom.* **2. all of a sudden,** without warning; unexpectedly: *All of a sudden we were surrounded.* —'**sud•den•ly,** *adv.* —'**sud•den•ness,** *n.* [*noncount*]

suds /sʌdz/ *n.* [*plural*] water containing soap and having bubbles on the surface. —'**suds•y,** *adj.,* **-i•er, -i•est.**

sue /suw/ *v.*, **sued, su•ing.** to bring legal action against: [~ + *obj*]: *to sue someone for damages.* [*no obj*]: *I threatened to sue if an accident happened.*

suede or **suède** /sweyd/ *n.* [*noncount*] leather finished with a soft, slightly rough surface.

su•et /'suwɪt/ *n.* [*noncount*] hard, fatty animal tissue used in cooking and for making candles.

suf-, a form of the prefix SUB-, used before roots beginning with the letter "f": (*suffer*).

suf•fer /'sʌfər/ *v.* **1.** to feel pain or great distress: [*no obj*]: *She suffered greatly as a child.* [~ + *obj*]: *She suffered poverty as a child.* **2.** [*no obj*] to become worse: *My work suffers when I'm distracted.* **3.** to experience something, such as a disease, injury, or loss: [*no obj*]: *to suffer from heart disease.* [~ + *obj*]: *He suffered a broken leg.* **4.** [~ + *obj*] to tolerate or allow: *I do not suffer fools gladly.* —'**suf•fer•er,** *n.* [*count*]

suf•fer•ing /'sʌfərɪŋ, 'sʌfrɪŋ/ *n.* **1.** [*noncount*] the state of a person or thing that suffers. **2.** Often, **sufferings.** [*plural*] something suffered; pain.

suf•fice /sə'fays/ *v.* [*no obj*], **-ficed, -fic•ing.** to be enough: *A few payments will suffice.*

suf•fi•cient /sə'fɪʃənt/ *adj.* enough: *There are barely sufficient funds for the project.* —**suf'fi•cien•cy,** *n.* [*noncount*] —**suf'fi•cient•ly,** *adv.*

suf•fix /'sʌfɪks/ *n.* [*count*] a syllable that is added to a word and changes its meaning, as *-ment* in *entertainment*.

suf•fo•cate /'sʌfə,keyt/ *v.*, **-cat•ed, -cat•ing. 1.** [~ + *obj*] to kill by preventing from breathing. **2.** [*no obj*] to die in this manner. **3.** to (cause to) be uncomfortable because of a lack of fresh air: [~ + *obj*]: *This hot classroom is suffocating in this students.* [*no obj*]: *We're all suffocating in this*

S

hot room. —**suf•fo•ca•tion** /ˌsʌfəˈkeyʃən/, *n.* [*noncount*]

suf•frage /ˈsʌfrɪdʒ/ *n.* [*noncount*] the right to vote.

sug•ar /ˈʃʊgər/ *n.* a sweet, crystalline substance made from various plants: [*noncount*]: *two cups of sugar.* [*count*]: *I'd like two sugars for my coffee, please.* —**'sug•ar•y,** *adj.*

sug•gest /səgˈdʒɛst, sə-/ *v.* [~ + *obj*] **1.** to mention, introduce, or propose (an idea, plan, etc.) for consideration, possible action, etc.: *The teacher suggested several different reference books. I suggested that we meet for lunch.* **2.** to hint at indirectly; imply: *Your question suggests that you doubt my sincerity.* **3.** to call (something) up in the mind through association of ideas: *The music suggests a still night.*

sug•ges•tion /səgˈdʒɛstʃən, sə-/ *n.* **1.** [*noncount*] the act of suggesting. **2.** [*count*] something suggested: *a suggestion for better communication.* **3.** [*count*] a hint, slight trace, or sign: *a suggestion of tears in his eyes.* **4.** [*noncount*] the calling up in the mind of one idea by another.

sug•ges•tive /səgˈdʒɛstɪv, sə-/ *adj.* implying, suggesting, or hinting at something improper, esp. sexual matters: *suggestive remarks.*

su•i•cid•al /ˌsuwəˈsaydəl/ *adj.* **1.** of or relating to suicide: *his suicidal tendencies.* **2.** likely to cause disaster: *politically suicidal acts.*

su•i•cide /ˈsuwəˌsayd/ *n.* **1.** killing oneself intentionally: [*noncount*]: *to commit suicide.* [*count*]: *The number of suicides increases in the winter.* **2.** [*noncount*] destruction of one's own interests or chances: *financial suicide.* **3.** [*count*] one who intentionally kills himself or herself.

suit /suwt/ *n.* [*count*] **1.** a set of garments of the same color, material, or fabric, typically trousers or a skirt and a jacket. **2.** any costume or outfit worn for some special activity: *a bathing suit.* **3.** *Law.* an act or instance of suing in a court of law; a lawsuit. **4.** one of the classes into which cards are divided, as spades, clubs, diamonds, and hearts. —*v.* [~ + *obj*] **5.** to make (something) right for: *to suit the punishment to the crime.* **6.** to look attractive on: *The color blue suits you very well.* **7.** to be acceptable or agreeable to: *The arrangements suit me just fine. You can go or stay; suit yourself.*

suit•a•ble /ˈsuwtəbəl/ *adj.* acceptable; fitting: *Is she suitable for this mission?* —**suit•a•bil•i•ty** /ˌsuwtəˈbɪlɪtiy/, *n.* [*noncount*] —**'suit•a•bly,** *adv.*: *We were suitably impressed with her performance.*

suit•case /ˈsuwtˌkeys/ *n.* [*count*] a flat bag for carrying clothes while traveling.

suite /swiyt/ *for 2 often* suwt/ *n.* [*count*] **1.** a connected series of rooms to be used together: *a hotel suite.* **2.** a set of matching furniture: *a bedroom suite.* **3.** an ordered series of pieces of music.

suit•or /ˈsuwtər/ *n.* [*count*] a man who tries to gain the affection of a woman.

sul•fur /ˈsʌlfər/ *n.* [*noncount*] Also, *esp. Brit.,* **sulphur.** a yellow element that can be burned, used esp. in making fertilizer and matches, and in medicine.

sulk /sʌlk/ *v.* [*no obj*] to keep silent because one is angry or displeased. —**'sulk•y,** *adj.,* **-i•er, -i•est.**

sul•len /ˈsʌlən/ *adj.* showing irritation or anger by a gloomy silence. —**'sul•len•ly,** *adv.* —**'sul•len•ness,** *n.* [*noncount*]

sul•ly /ˈsʌliy/ *v.* [~ + *obj*], **-lied, -ly•ing.** to make dirty or to spoil.

sul•try /ˈsʌltriy/ *adj.,* **-tri•er, -tri•est.** uncomfortably hot and humid: *a sultry day.*

sum /sʌm/ *n., v.,* **summed, sum•ming.** —*n.* [*count*] **1.** the total of two or more numbers, determined by addition: *The sum of 6 and 8 is 14.* **2.** an amount of money: *to lend small sums.* **3.** the full amount, or the whole: *the sum of our knowledge.* —*v.* **4.** [~ + *obj*] to figure out the sum of, as by addition. **5. sum up, a.** to express in a brief yet complete statement: *He summed up the main points of the speech; ready to sum up at last after a long speech. Can you sum it up in just a few words?* **b.** to form a quick judgment of: *summing up the situation; She summed him up after meeting him just once.* —**Idiom. 6. in sum,** in brief but complete form: *In sum, the government believes it knows what it is doing.*

sum•ma•rize /ˈsʌməˌrayz/ *v.* [~ + *obj*], **-rized, -riz•ing.** to make a summary of; to state or express in a brief but complete form.

sum•ma•ry /ˈsʌməriy/ *n.* [*count*], *pl.* **-ries.** a complete yet brief account of something.

sum•mer /ˈsʌmər/ *n.* [*count*] [*noncount*] **1.** the warm season between spring and autumn. —*v.* [*no obj*] **2.** to spend the summer: *She summers in Maine.* —**'sum•mer•y,** *adj.*: *summery weather.*

sum•mit /ˈsʌmɪt/ *n.* [*count*] **1.** the highest point: *the summit of the mountain.* **2.** the highest point of attaining or gaining something: *the summit of her ambition.* **3.** a conference between heads of state or other important government officials.

sum•mon /ˈsʌmən/ *v.* [~ + *obj*] **1.** to order to come: *The king summoned a servant.* **2.** to call forth (from oneself): *He summoned all his courage (up). Suffering from the flu, I could hardly summon (up) the strength to whisper.*

sum•mons /ˈsʌmənz/ *n.* [*count*], *pl.* **-mons•es.** a demand to appear before a court.

sump•tu•ous /ˈsʌmptʃuwəs/ *adj.* lavish; splendid: *a sumptuous feast.*

sun /sʌn/ *n., v.,* **sunned, sun•ning.** —*n.* **1.** [*often: Sun; usually: the* + ~] the star that is the central body of the solar system. **2.** the heat and light from the sun; sunshine: [*count; usually: singular; usually: the* + ~]: *to be exposed to the sun.* [*noncount*]: *You'll get too much sun and have a bad sunburn tonight.* **3.** [*count*] any star: *Many of the stars could be suns of their own solar systems.* —*v.* **4.** to expose (oneself) or be exposed to the sun's rays: [~ + *obj*]: *sunning themselves in the park.* [*no obj*]: *They were sunning for hours.* —**Idiom. 5. under the sun,** on earth; anywhere: *There's nothing like this under the sun.*

Sun., an abbreviation of: Sunday.

sun•bathe /ˈsʌnˌbeyð/ *v.* [*no obj*], **-bathed, -bath•ing.** to expose one's body to the sun. —**sun•bath•er** /ˈsʌnˌbeyðər/, *n.* [*count*]

sun•beam /ˈsʌnˌbiym/ *n.* [*count*] a ray of sunlight.

'sun,block *n.* [*count*] [*noncount*] a lotion that protects the skin against sunburn, often preventing tanning.

sun•burn /ˈsʌnˌbɜrn/ *n., v.,* **-burned** or **-burnt, -burn•ing.** —*n.* **1.** reddened, sore skin caused by too much exposure to the sun: [*count*]: *a bad sunburn.* [*noncount*]: *lotion for sunburn.* —*v.* **2.** (of the skin) to (cause to) become reddened and sore from too much exposure to the sun: [*no obj*]: *Her fair skin sunburns easily.* [~ + *obj*]: *The African summer will sunburn you quickly.*

sun•dae /'sʌndey, -diy/ n. [count] a dish of ice cream topped with syrup, nuts, whipped cream, etc.

Sun•day /'sʌndey, -diy/ n. [count] the first day of the week, observed as the Sabbath by most Christian denominations.

sun•flow•er /'sʌn,flawər/ n. [count] a plant having showy, yellow flower heads and edible seeds.

sung /sʌŋ/ v. a pt. and pp. of SING.

sun•glass•es /'sʌn,glæsɪz/ n. [plural] eyeglasses with colored lenses that protect the eyes from sunlight.

sunk /sʌŋk/ v. a pt. and pp. of SINK.

sunk•en /'sʌŋkən/ adj. **1.** having sunk or been sunk beneath the surface: The divers explored the sunken ocean liner. **2.** on a lower level: a sunken living room. **3.** hollow: sunken cheeks.

sun•light /'sʌn,layt/ n. [noncount] the light of the sun; sunshine.

sun•lit /'sʌn,lɪt/ adj. lighted by the sun.

sun•ny /'sʌniy/ adj., **-ni•er, -ni•est. 1.** having much sunshine: a warm, sunny room. **2.** cheerful: a sunny disposition. **3.** of or resembling the sun.

sun•rise /'sʌn,rayz/ n. [count] [noncount] the rise of the sun above the horizon in the morning.

sun•screen /'sʌn,skriyn/ n. [noncount] [count] a lotion containing a substance that protects the skin from the sun.

sun•set /'sʌn,sɛt/ n. [count] [noncount] the setting or descent of the sun below the horizon in the evening.

sun•shine /'sʌn,ʃayn/ n. [noncount] **1.** the shining of the sun. **2.** a place where the direct rays of the sun fall: out in the sunshine.

sun•tan /'sʌn,tæn/ n. [count] a darkening of the skin caused by exposure to sunlight.

sup-, a form of the prefix SUB-, used before the letter "p": (suppose).

su•per /'suwpər/ n. [count] **1.** a superintendent, esp. of an apartment house. —adj. **2.** very good; excellent: a super job.

super-, a prefix meaning: above or over (superimpose; superstructure); going beyond a customary amount or level (superpower; superhighway).

su•perb /su'pərb/ adj. admirably fine or excellent; wonderful: The dinner was superb. —su'perb•ly, adv.

su•per•fi•cial /,suwpər'fɪʃəl/ adj. **1.** being at, on, or near the surface: a superficial wound. **2.** concerned with only what is obvious: a superficial analysis of the problem. —su•per•fi•ci•al•i•ty /,suwpər,fɪʃiy'ælɪtiy/, n. [noncount] —,su•per'fi•cial•ly, adv.

su•per•flu•ous /su'pərfluwəs/ adj. being more than enough; too much: superfluous words.

su•per•im•pose /,suwpərɪm'powz/ v. [~ + obj (+ on/upon)], **-posed, -pos•ing.** to put, place, or set over or on something else: He superimposed one of his photos on top of another.

su•per•in•tend•ent /,suwpərɪn'tɛndənt, ,suwprɪn-/ n. [count] **1.** one who directs some work, establishment, etc.: the superintendent of schools. **2.** one who is in charge of maintenance and repairs for an apartment house.

su•pe•ri•or /sə'pɪəriyər, su-/ adj. **1.** higher in rank, degree, class, etc.: a superior officer. **2.** above the average: a superior student. **3.** showing a feeling of being better than others: He had a superior attitude toward everyone. —n. [count] **4.** one who is superior to another in rank, as in a

job: She's my superior at work. —su•pe•ri•or•i•ty /sə,pɪəriy'ɔrɪtiy, -'ɒr-, su-/, n. [noncount]

su•per•la•tive /sə'pərlətɪv, su-/ adj. **1.** of the highest kind above all others: The performance was superlative. **2.** of or naming a form of adjectives and adverbs used to show the greatest in quality, quantity, or intensity, as in smallest, best, and most carefully, the superlative forms of small, good, and carefully. —n. [count] **3.** the superlative form of an adjective or adverb: The word best is a superlative.

su•per•mar•ket /'suwpər,mɑrkɪt/ n. [count] a large self-service store that sells food and other household goods.

su•per•nat•u•ral /,suwpər'nætʃərəl, -'nætʃrəl/ adj. relating to that which cannot be explained by science: supernatural powers.

su•per•pow•er /'suwpər,pawər/ n. [count] a very powerful nation.

su•per•sede /,suwpər'siyd/ v. [~ + obj], **-sed•ed, -sed•ing.** to take the place of (another): The new law supersedes the old one.

su•per•son•ic /,suwpər'sɒnɪk/ adj. greater than the speed of sound.

su•per•star /'suwpər,stɑr/ n. [count] a very famous performer or athlete.

su•per•sti•tion /,suwpər'stɪʃən/ n. **1.** [count] belief based on luck or magic. **2.** [noncount] a collection of such beliefs: Baseball players place a lot of emphasis on superstition. —,su•per'sti•tious, adj.

su•per•store /'suwpər,stɔr, -,stowr/ n. [count] a very large store, esp. one selling a wide variety of goods.

su•per•vise /'suwpər,vayz/ v. [~ + obj], **-vised, -vis•ing.** to watch over and direct (a process, work, etc.): She supervised the ESL program at the college. —,su•per'vi•sion, n. [noncount] —,su•per'vi•sor, n. [count] —,su•per'vi•so•ry adj.

sup•per /'sʌpər/ n. the evening meal: [count]: delicious meatless suppers. [noncount]: Come over for supper next Monday.

sup•plant /sə'plænt/ v. [~ + obj] to take the place of (another): to supplant the liberal leader with a military man.

sup•ple /'sʌpəl/ adj., **-pler, -plest.** bending easily: supple branches; supple dancers.

sup•ple•ment /n.'sʌpləmənt; v. -,mɛnt/ n. [count] **1.** something added to complete a thing or extend something: The supplies were a supplement to what they already had. **2.** something added to a publication that supplies further information, etc.: a supplement to the newspaper. —v. [~ + obj] **3.** to add to: The computer can supplement what has been taught in a classroom. —,sup•ple'men•tal, adj. —,sup•ple'men•ta•ry, adj.

sup•ply /sə'play/ v., **-plied, -ply•ing,** n., pl. **-plies.** —v. [~ + obj] **1.** to furnish (a person, thing, etc.) with what is needed: These foods supply the body with necessary vitamins and minerals. **2.** to furnish or provide (something needed): The dam supplied water to the region. —n. **3.** [noncount] the act of supplying, furnishing, satisfying, etc. **4.** [count] something supplied: the city's water supply. **5.** [count] a quantity or amount of something available: The store carries a large supply of software. **6.** Usually, **supplies.** [plural] an amount or store of food or other necessary things: supplies for the camping trip. —sup'pli•er, n. [count]

sup•port /sə'pɔrt/ v. [~ + obj] **1.** to hold up:

S

supermarket

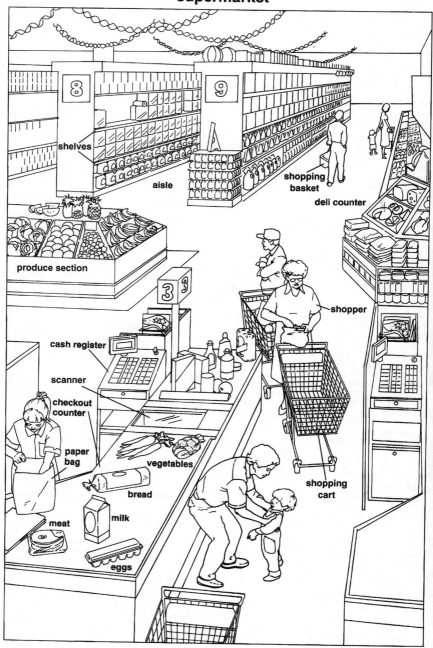

shelves

aisle

shopping basket

deli counter

produce section

shopper

cash register

scanner

checkout counter

paper bag

vegetables

bread

milk

meat

eggs

shopping cart

He supported himself by holding on to the wall. **2.** to provide the necessities of existence for a person, family, etc.: *Is that enough money to support yourself?* **3.** to give help, comfort, etc., to (a person, one's spirits, etc.)in a time of trouble: *Her brother supported her during the tragedy.* **4.** to show one's agreement with (a person, cause, etc.): *I support his nomination for president.* **5.** to show to be true: confirm: *His testimony will support her plea of innocence.* —*n.* **6.** [*noncount*] the providing of necessary means for someone to live: *He provides child support for his kids.* **7.** [*noncount*] an act or instance of supporting: *to show support for our fired coworkers.* **8.** [*count*] something that serves as a foundation to hold something up: *The explosives ripped the cable car's two supports from the wire.* —**sup'port•er,** *n.* [*count*] —**sup'port•ive,** *adj.*: *a supportive teacher.*

sup•pose /sə'powz/ *v.,* **-posed, -pos•ing,** *conj.* —*v.* **1.** [~ + *obj*] to assume (something), as for the sake of argument: *Suppose (that) you won a million dollars in the lottery.* **2.** [~ + *obj*] to think or hold as an opinion; believe: *What do you suppose (that) he will do?* **3. be supposed to,** to be expected to: *The machine is not supposed to make noise.* —*conj.* **4.** Also, **supposing.** (used to put forward something to be considered): *Suppose (supposing) we do wait until tomorrow; what then?*

sup•posed /sə'powzd, sə'powzɪd/ *adj.* **1.** assumed as true: *the supposed site of Atlantis.* **2.** imagined: *The supposed gains would be outweighed by the costs.* —**sup'pos•ed•ly,** *adv.*: *He was supposedly the best in the business.*

sup•po•si•tion /ˌsʌpə'zɪʃən/ *n.* **1.** [*noncount*] an act of supposing: *Their accusation is pure supposition.* **2.** [*count*] something that is supposed: *suppositions about how the money was spent.*

sup•press /sə'prɛs/ *v.* [~ + *obj*] **1.** to put an end to: *to suppress a revolt.* **2.** to hold back (a thought or action): *He had a hard time suppressing his anger.* **3.** to keep back from public knowledge: *The president's office suppressed the report.* **4.** to stop: *to suppress a cough.* —**sup•pres•sion** /sə'prɛʃən/, *n.* [*noncount*]

su•prem•a•cy /sə'prɛməsiy, su-/ *n.* [*noncount*] the state of being supreme.

su•preme /sə'priym, su-/ *adj.* [*before a noun*] **1.** highest in rank or authority: *the supreme commander.* **2.** greatest: *the supreme sacrifice: giving up her life for another.* —**su'preme•ly,** *adv.*

Supt. or **supt.,** an abbreviation of: superintendent.

sur-, a prefix meaning: over or above (*surcharge*); in addition (*surtax*).

sur•charge / 'sɜr,tʃɑrdʒ/ *n.* [*count*] a cost added on to the usual charge: *a surcharge on imported oil.*

sure /ʃʊr/ *adj.,* **sur•er, sur•est,** *adv.* —*adj.* **1.** (of a person) free from doubt as to the reliability, character, action, etc., of something: *Are you sure?—Well, I'm pretty sure. She was very sure of her facts. She was sure (that) she had told him.* **2.** confident, as of something expected: *They felt sure of success. He was sure (that) he wouldn't fail again.* **3.** [*before a noun*] certain beyond question: *a sure victory.* **4.** [*before a noun*] unfailing: *This investment is a sure thing.* **5.** certain: *It is sure to happen.* —*adv.* **6.** certainly; surely: *She sure acts funny sometimes.* —**Idiom. 7. be** or **make sure,** to take care (to be or do as specified): *Be sure to set your alarm clock. Could you*

make sure (that) the door is locked? **8. for sure,** without a doubt: *We'd like to know for sure if you're on our side.*

sure•ly /'ʃʊrliy, 'ʃɜr-/ *adv.* **1.** undoubtedly or certainly: *Surely she knows what she's doing.* **2.** (used for emphasis): *Surely you are mistaken.* **3.** (used to answer a question) yes; indeed: *"May I wait inside?"—"Surely."*

surf /sɜrf/ *n.* [*noncount*] **1.** the white waves breaking upon a shore: *rough surf during the hurricane.* —*v.* [*no obj*] **2.** to go surfing. —**'surf•er,** *n.* [*count*]

sur•face /'sɜrfɪs/ *n., adj., v.,* **-faced, -fac•ing.** —*n.* **1.** [*count*] the outside of a thing: *the surface of the earth.* **2.** [*count; usually singular; often: the* + ~] the outward appearance of something: *On the surface it looked like a simple murder case.* **3.** [*count*] the top part of a liquid or body of water: *The submarine rose to the surface.* —*adj.* [*before a noun*] **4.** of, on, or relating to the surface. **5.** apparent rather than real. **6.** of, relating to, or by land or sea rather than air: *Send that parcel home by surface mail.* —*v.* **7.** [~ + *obj*] to give a particular kind of surface to by covering: *to surface the road with asphalt.* **8.** [*no obj*] to rise to the surface: *The submarine surfaced.* **9.** [*no obj*] to appear or emerge; turn up: *New evidence has surfaced.*

surf•board /'sɜrf,bɔrd/ *n.* [*count*] **1.** a long, narrow board on which a person rides the crest of a breaking wave toward the shore in surfing. —*v.* [*no obj*] **2.** to ride a surfboard.

sur•feit /'sɜrfɪt/ *n.* [*count; usually singular*] too much of something; excess: *a surfeit of speeches.*

surge /sɜrdʒ/ *n., v.,* **surged, surg•ing.** —*n.* [*count*] **1.** a strong, forward movement like a wave: *the surge of the crowd toward the stadium.* **2.** a sudden, strong rush or burst: *a surge of energy.* —*v.* [*no obj*] **3.** to rise, roll, or move forward in waves. **4.** to rise as if by a swelling force, as of strong feeling: *She could feel anger surging through her body.*

sur•geon /'sɜrdʒən/ *n.* [*count*] a physician who specializes in surgery.

sur•ger•y /'sɜrdʒəriy/ *n.* [*noncount*] **1.** the treatment of diseases, injuries, etc., by performing medical operations or procedures, or the branch of medicine dealing with such treatment: *medical school courses in surgery.* **2.** an operation performed by a surgeon: *You may not need surgery after all.*

sur•gi•cal /'sɜrdʒɪkəl/ *adj.* [*before a noun*] of or relating to surgery or surgeons: *surgical procedures.* —**'sur•gi•cal•ly,** *adv.*

sur•ly /'sɜrliy/ *adj.,* **-li•er, -li•est.** rude, unfriendly, or bad-tempered.

sur•mount /sər'mawnt/ *v.* [~ + *obj*] to overcome: *to surmount great difficulties.*

sur•name /'sɜr,neym / *n.* [*count*] the name that a person shares with other family members; family name.

sur•pass /sər'pæs/ *v.* [~ + *obj*] to go beyond in amount, excellence, or degree: *She surpassed all the others in skill.*

sur•plus /'sɜrplʌs, -pləs/ *n.* [*count*] the amount of something that remains beyond what is used or needed: *a surplus of wheat.*

sur•prise /sər'prayz, sə-/ *v.,* **-prised, -pris•ing,** *n.* —*v.* [~ + *obj*] **1.** to cause to feel wonder or astonishment, esp. by being unexpected: *Those sales figures surprised me!* **2.** to come upon suddenly and unexpectedly: *We surprised a deer in the yard.* —*n.* **3.** [*noncount*] the state of being

S

surprised, esp. at something unexpected: *I was filled with surprise.* **4.** [*count*] something that surprises: *She likes surprises for her birthday.* **5.** [*noncount*] an act of surprising: *Perhaps the element of surprise gave us the victory.* —*Idiom.* **6. take (someone) by surprise,** to surprise someone by happening unexpectedly: *Her sudden arrival took us by surprise.*

sur·prised /sər'prayzd, sə-/ *adj.* affected by a feeling of surprise: *The surprised soldiers surrendered meekly. I was surprised (that) she would do such a crazy thing. I was surprised to hear such anger in your voice.*

sur·pris·ing /sər'prayzɪŋ, sə-/ *adj.* causing a feeling of surprise: *A surprising number of students showed up for the lecture. It was surprising that so many students showed up for the lecture.* —**sur'pris·ing·ly,** *adv.*

sur·ren·der /sə'rɛndər/ *v.* **1.** [*no obj*] to give oneself up, as by agreeing to stop fighting because of defeat: *The enemy formally surrendered to the Allies.* **2.** [~ + *obj*] to give up (something) to the possession of another, as after defeat: *to surrender the fort to the enemy.* **3.** [*no obj*] to give (oneself) up to some influence, course, etc.: *to surrender (oneself) to greed.* —*n.* **4.** an act of surrendering: [*noncount*]: *to starve the country into surrender.* [*count*]: *The government signed a formal surrender.*

sur·round /sə'rawnd/ *v.* [~ + *obj*] to enclose on all sides: *The presidential candidate was surrounded by admirers.*

sur·round·ing /sə'rawndɪŋ/ *n.* **1. surroundings,** [*plural*] the things that are all around a person: *peaceful surroundings.* —*adj.* [*before a noun*] **2.** enclosing or encircling: *snow in the city and the surrounding suburbs.*

sur·veil·lance /sər'veyləns/ *n.* [*noncount*] a watch kept over someone or something: *police surveillance.*

sur·vey / *v.* sər'vey; *n.* 'sɜrvey/ *v., n., pl.* **-veys.** —*v.* [~ + *obj*] **1.** to consider or study in a general way: *to survey a situation.* **2.** to view in detail, esp. in order to know the condition or value of something: *The inspector surveyed the building.* **3.** to conduct a study of the opinions of (a group of people): *to survey TV viewers.* **4.** to determine the exact dimensions and position of (an area of land) by measuring it: *to survey the land for the public park.* —*n.* [*count*] **5.** a general view, description, course of study, etc.: *a survey of Italian painting.* **6.** a sampling of opinions: *Their survey of smokers suggests that many would like to quit.* —**sur'vey·or,** *n.* [*count*]

sur·viv·al /sər'vayvəl/ *n.* **1.** [*noncount*] the act or fact of surviving: *survival of the fittest.* **2.** [*count*] something that continues to exist, as from an earlier time: *Some of our customs are survivals from an earlier era.*

sur·vive /sər'vayv/ *v.,* **-vived, -viv·ing. 1.** to remain alive, as after the death of another or the occurrence of some event; continue to exist: [*no obj*]: *A few were killed but most survived.* [~ + *obj*]: *Most survived the explosion.* **2.** [~ + *obj*] to continue to live or exist after the death of: *She survived three husbands.* **3.** to continue to function or manage in spite of difficult circumstances or hardship; endure: [*no obj*]: *Our company will survive, no matter what.* [~ + *obj*]: *I've survived two divorces.* —**sur'vi·vor,** *n.* [*count*]

sus·cep·ti·ble /sə'sɛptəbəl/ *adj.* **1.** responding to some specified treatment: *Is the disease susceptible to treatment with drugs?* **2.** easily affected

by: *She's very susceptible to colds.* —**sus·cep·ti·bil·i·ty** /sə,sɛptə'bɪlɪtiy/, *n.* [*noncount*]

sus·pect /*v.* sə'spɛkt; *n.* 'sʌspɛkt; *adj.* 'sʌspɛkt, sə'spɛkt/ *v.* [~ + *obj*] **1.** to believe (something) to be possible or true: *I suspected (that) he might have left already. I only suspected it.* **2.** to believe to be guilty, with little or no proof: *to suspect a person of murder.* **3.** to mistrust: *I suspect his motives.* —*n.* [*count*] **4.** one who is suspected, esp. of a crime. —*adj.* **5.** not to be trusted: *His behavior was suspect.*

sus·pend /sə'spɛnd/ *v.* [~ + *obj*] **1.** to hang: *Suspend the swing from the tree branch.* **2.** to delay: *I'll suspend judgment until all the facts are in.* **3.** to bring to a stop, usually for a time: *He suspended payments on the car until it was fixed.* —**sus'pen·sion,** *n.* [*noncount*] [*count*]

sus·pend·er /sə'spɛndər/ *n.* [*count*] **1.** Usually, **suspenders.** Also called, *esp. Brit.,* **braces.** [*plural*] adjustable straps worn over the shoulders with the ends secured to the waistband of a skirt or a pair of trousers. **2.** *Brit.* a garter.

sus·pense /sə'spɛns/ *n.* [*noncount*] a state of mental anxiety and uncertainty, as in awaiting the outcome of something. —**sus'pense·ful,** *adj.*

sus·pi·cion /sə'spɪʃən/ *n.* **1.** [*noncount*] the act of suspecting. **2.** [*count*] an instance of suspecting something or someone: *I have my suspicions about who did it.* **3.** [*noncount*] the state of being suspected: *We had you under suspicion for a while.* **4.** [*count*] a slight trace, hint, or suggestion: *a suspicion of a smile.*

sus·pi·cious /sə'spɪʃəs/ *adj.* **1.** tending to cause suspicion: *suspicious behavior.* **2.** feeling or showing suspicion: *He was suspicious of strangers.*

sus·tain /sə'steyn/ *v.* [~ + *obj*] **1.** to bear the weight of: *Can the bridge sustain the weight of all these trucks?* **2.** to suffer (injury, loss, etc.): *The army sustained heavy losses.* **3.** to keep (a person) alive: *The thought of seeing his family again sustained him.* **4.** to keep going, as an action or process: *to sustain a conversation.*

sus·te·nance /'sʌstənəns/ *n.* [*noncount*] **1.** food or drink as the means of sustaining life. **2.** the process of sustaining; the state of being sustained.

swab /swɒb/ *n., v.,* **swabbed, swab·bing.** —*n.* [*count*] **1.** a bit of cotton, etc., often fixed to a stick, for applying medicine, etc. —*v.* [~ + *obj*] **2.** to take up or apply (moisture, etc.) with a swab on (a wound): *to swab antiseptic on the wound.*

swag·ger /'swægər/ *v.* [*no obj*] **1.** to walk in a proud, boastful way. —*n.* [*count*] **2.** a swaggering walk or manner.

swal·low¹ /'swɒlow/ *v.* **1.** to cause (food or liquid) to go down the throat with a muscular action: [~ + *obj*]: *He couldn't swallow the meat.* [*no obj*]: *I tried to swallow.* **2.** [~ + *obj*] to take in so as to cause to disappear: *She was swallowed (up) in the crowd.* **3.** [~ + *obj*] to accept without question: *He swallowed her lies.* **4.** [~ + *obj*] to keep in or suppress (emotion, etc.): *He swallowed his anger.* —*n.* [*count*] **5.** an act or instance of swallowing. **6.** an amount swallowed at one time: *one more swallow of this medicine.*

swal·low² /'swɒlow/ *n.* [*count*] a small, long-winged, fork-tailed songbird noted for its swift, graceful flight.

swam /swæm/ *v.* pt. of SWIM.

swamp /swɒmp/ *n.* [*count*] **1.** an area of wet, spongy land. —*v.* [~ + *obj*] **2.** to flood with water. **3.** to overwhelm: *swamped with work.* —'**swamp•y,** *adj.*, **-i•er, -i•est.**

swan /swɒn/ *n.* [*count*] a large water bird, having a long, slender neck and usually pure-white feathers.

swap /swɒp/ *v.*, **swapped, swap•ping,** *n.* —*v.* **1.** to trade; make an exchange: [~ + *obj*]: *I'll swap my orange for your apple.* [*no obj*]: *You like my cookies and I like yours; let's swap.* —*n.* [*count*] **2.** an exchange: *He got the radio in a swap.*

swarm /swɔrm/ *n.* [*count*] **1.** a large group of insects that fly together. **2.** a great number of things or persons moving together: *a swarm of reporters.* —*v.* [*no obj*] **3.** to move about together in great numbers: *The crowd swarmed around the winner.*

swarth•y /'swɔrðiy, -θiy/ *adj.*, **-i•er, -i•est.** (of skin color, complexion, etc.) dark or darkish.

swat /swɒt/ *v.*, **swat•ted, swat•ting,** *n.* —*v.* [~ + *obj*] **1.** to hit sharply with a flat object or the hand; slap or smack: *to swat a fly.* —*n.* [*count*] **2.** a sharp blow. —'**swat•ter,** *n.* [*count*]

swatch /swɒtʃ/ *n.* [*count*] a sample of cloth or other material.

sway /swey/ *v.* **1.** to (cause to) move or swing from side to side: [*no obj*]: *swaying to the music.* [~ + *obj*]: *The wind swayed the trees.* **2.** [~ + *obj*] to influence: *The jurors were swayed by the lawyer's appeal.* —*n.* [*noncount*] **3.** swaying movement: *the unsteady sway of the ferry.* **4.** influence; control: *He still holds sway over a large bureaucracy.*

swear /swɛər/ *v.*, **swore** /swɔr/, **sworn** /swɔrn/, **swear•ing. 1.** to make a solemn statement or promise: [*no obj*]: *He swore on the Bible.* [~ + *obj*]: *You swore to tell the truth. He swore (that) he would tell the truth.* **2.** [*no obj*] to use obscene or profane language: *He swore when the driver cut him off. He swore at the driver who cut him off.* **3.** [~ + *obj*] to make (someone) promise by an oath: *They swore her to secrecy.* **4. swear by,** to have great confidence in; trust in: *He swears by this mixture of tea, lemon juice, and honey for a cold.* **5. swear in,** to admit to office by administering an oath: *The Chief Justice swore in the President; to swear him in.* —'**swear•er,** *n.* [*count*]

sweat /swɛt/ *v.*, **sweat** or **sweat•ed, sweat•ing,** *n.* —*v.* [*no obj*] **1.** to give off moisture from the skin when one is sick, hot, nervous, etc. **2.** to gather moisture from the surrounding air: *The cold glass was sweating in the hot room.* **3.** *Informal.* **a.** to work hard. **b.** to be anxious or distressed. —*n.* **4.** [*noncount*] the moisture released from the skin: *Sweat was pouring down his face.* **5.** [*noncount*] hard work: *Blood, sweat, and tears went into this house.* **6.** [*count; usually singular*] *Informal.* a state of anxiety or impatience: *in a sweat awaiting the results.* **7. sweats,** [*plural*] sweatpants, sweatshirts, sweat suits, or the like.

sweat•er /'swɛtər/ *n.* [*count*] a knitted piece of clothing, often like a shirt or jacket.

sweat•pants /'swɛt,pænts/ *n.* [*plural*] loose-fitting pants of soft, absorbent fabric.

sweat•shirt /'swɛt,ʃərt/ *n.* [*count*] a loose, long-sleeved shirt of soft, absorbent fabric.

sweat•shop /'swɛt,ʃɒp/ *n.* [*count*] a shop where workers are paid low wages and work for long hours under poor conditions.

'**sweat ,suit,** *n.* [*count*] an outfit consisting of sweatpants and a sweatshirt or matching jacket.

sweat•y /'swɛtiy/ *adj.*, **-i•er, -i•est. 1.** giving off

sweat: *his hot, sweaty face.* **2.** causing sweat, as from being hard or difficult: *It was hot, sweaty work.*

Swed•ish /'swiydɪʃ/ *adj.* **1.** of or relating to Sweden. **2.** of or relating to the language spoken in Sweden. —*n.* **3.** [*plural; the* + ~; *used with a plural verb*] the people born or living in Sweden. **4.** [*noncount*] the language spoken in Sweden.

sweep /swiyp/ *v.*, **swept** /swɛpt/, **sweep•ing,** *n.* —*v.* **1.** [~ + *obj*] [*no obj*] to remove or clear (dust, dirt, etc.) with a broom, brush, etc., from (a room, floor, etc.). **2.** to (cause to) move by some steady force, as a wind or wave: [~ + *obj*]: *The storm swept the boat out to sea.* [*no obj*]: *She swept into the room.* **3.** to spread quickly over (an area): [~ + *obj*]: *The fashion was sweeping the country.* [*no obj*]: *Those fashions swept through the country.* **4.** [~ + *obj*] to clear (a surface, place, etc.): *to sweep the sea of enemy ships.* **5.** [~ + *obj*] to pass over a surface with a continuous stroke or movement: *The painter swept a brush over his canvas.* **6.** [*no obj*] to move in a wide curve or circuit: *His glance swept around the room.* —*n.* [*count*] **7.** the act of sweeping with a broom. **8.** the steady, driving motion of something: *the sweep of the wind.* **9.** a swinging movement, as of the arm or an oar. **10.** a continuous stretch: *a long sweep of empty road.* **11.** CHIMNEY SWEEP. —**Idiom. 12. sweep (someone) off one's feet,** to cause (someone) to fall in love or otherwise be overwhelmed. —'**sweep•er,** *n.* [*count*]

sweep•ing /'swiypɪŋ/ *adj.* **1.** of wide range: *sweeping change.* **2.** [*before a noun*] very vague: *sweeping generalizations.*

sweet /swiyt/ *adj.*, **-er, -est,** *adv.*, *n.* —*adj.* **1.** having the taste or flavor of sugar or the like: *The coffee is too sweet.* **2.** not salted: *sweet butter.* **3.** pleasing to the senses: *sweet music; her sweet, soft voice.* **4.** pleasing or agreeable: *Our neighbors were so sweet, looking after our apartment while we were away.* —*adv.* **5.** in a sweet manner; sweetly. —*n.* [*count*] **6. sweets,** [*plural*] very sweet foods, as pie, cake, or candy. **7.** *Brit.* **a.** a piece of candy. **b.** a sweet dish or dessert. **8.** a beloved person. —'**sweet•ly,** *adv.*: *She smiled sweetly at him.* —'**sweet•ness,** *n.* [*noncount*]

sweet•en /'swiytn̩/ *v.* [~ + *obj*] **1.** to (cause to) become sweet: *Add some brown sugar to sweeten the mix.* **2.** to make (the breath, air, etc.) sweet or fresh. —'**sweet•en•er,** *n.* [*count*]

sweet•heart /'swiyt,hɑrt/ *n.* [*count*] **1.** either of a pair of lovers in relation to the other. **2.** *Informal.* a generous, friendly person.

'**sweet po,tato,** *n.* [*count*] the sweet root of a Central American trailing vine, used as a vegetable.

'**sweet ,tooth,** *n.* [*count; singular*] a liking for sweets.

swell /swɛl/ *v.*, **swelled, swol•len** /'swowlən/ or **swelled, swell•ing,** *n.*, *adj.* —*v.* **1.** to (cause to) increase in size, amount, etc.: [*no obj*]: *Her foot swelled (up) where the bee had stung her.* [~ + *obj*]: *Such a sting could swell the foot (up) to twice its size; to swell (up) the foot.* **2.** [*no obj*] to rise in waves, as the sea. —*n.* [*count*] **3.** the act of swelling, or the condition of being swollen. **4.** a wave, esp. when long and unbroken. —*adj.* *Informal.* **5.** excellent; fine: *a swell prize.*

swell•ing /'swɛlɪŋ/ *n.* [*count*] a swollen part: *The swelling on his head still hasn't gone down.*

swel•ter /'swɛltər/ *v.* [*no obj*] to suffer from too much heat.

S

swept /swɛpt/ v. pt. and pp. of SWEEP.

swerve /swɜrv/ v., **swerved, swerv·ing,** n. —v.
1. to turn aside suddenly: [no obj]: He swerved to
avoid hitting the child. [~ + obj]: She swerved
the car to avoid the dog. —n. [count] **2.** the act of
swerving.

swift /swɪft/ adj., **-er, -est,** n. —adj. **1.** moving
with great speed: a swift boat. **2.** happening or
performed quickly: a swift decision. —n. [count]
3. a long-winged, swallowlike bird. —'**swift·ly,**
adv.: She ran swiftly ahead of the others.
—'**swift·ness,** n. [noncount]

swig /swɪg/ n., v., **swigged, swig·ging.** Informal. —n. [count] **1.** an amount of liquid taken in
one large swallow. —v. [~ + obj] **2.** to drink in
a large swallow or greedily.

swill /swɪl/ n. [noncount] **1.** partly liquid food
for animals, esp. kitchen garbage given to pigs.
—v. [~ + obj] **2.** to drink a great deal of (something), esp. in a greedy manner: swilling beer.

swim /swɪm/ v., **swam, swum, swim·ming,**
—v. **1.** [no obj] to move the body through water
by using arms, legs, fins, tail, etc. **2.** [~ + obj]
to move along in or cross (a body of water) this
way: to swim the English Channel. **3.** [no obj] to
be covered or filled with a liquid: eyes swimming
with tears. **4.** [no obj] to be dizzy: My head began to swim. —n. [count] **5.** an act, instance, or
period of swimming. —'**swim·mer,** n. [count]

swim·suit /swɪm,suwt/ n. BATHING SUIT.

swin·dle /swɪndl/ v., **-dled, -dling,** n. —v. [~
+ obj] **1.** to cheat (someone) out of money or
other valuable things: They swindled us (out of
thousands of dollars). —n. [count] **2.** a scheme
involving swindling. —'**swin·dler,** n. [count]

swing /swɪŋ/ v., **swung** /swʌŋ/, **swing·ing,** n.,
adj. —v. **1.** to (cause to) move back and forth, as
something hanging from above, or to (cause to)
move in a curve: [no obj]: The door swung open.
[~ + obj]: She swung her arms as she walked.
2. to move (the hand or something held) back
and forth, or round and round: [~ + obj]: He
swung the bat back and forth and waited for the
next pitch. [no obj]: He swung (at the pitch) and
missed. **3.** to (cause to) move in a curve: [~ +
obj]: I swung the car into the driveway. [no obj]:
The car swung into the driveway. **4.** to (cause to)
be changed: [no obj]: Public opinion swung in his
favor. [~ + obj]: She hopes to swing public opinion in her favor. —n. **5.** [count] the act or manner of swinging. **6.** [count] a moving of the body
with a free, swaying motion: walking with a
swing. **7.** [count] a stroke with the hand or an
object grasped in the hands, as in baseball: a
smooth, effortless swing. **8.** [count] a change in
attitude, opinion, etc.: mood swings. **9.** [non-
count] movement forward: to get into the swing
of things. **10.** [count] a seat hung by a rope from
a rod, on which one may swing. **11.** [noncount]
a style of jazz. —**Idiom. 12. in full swing,** in
full operation: The company was back in full
swing when sales improved.

swipe /swayp/ n., v., **swiped, swip·ing.** —n.
[count] **1.** a strong, sweeping blow. —v. **2.** [no
obj] to strike with a sweeping blow: swiping at
the ball. **3.** [~ + obj] Informal. to steal.

swirl /swɜrl/ v. **1.** to move with a whirling motion; whirl: [no obj]: The water swirled down the
drain. [~ + obj]: She swirled the wine in her
glass. **2.** [no obj] to be dizzy: Riding the roller
coaster made my head swirl. —n. [count] **3.** a
swirling movement. **4.** any curving, twisting line,
shape, or form.

swish /swɪʃ/ v. **1.** [~ + obj] [no obj] to move
with or make a hissing or whistling sound, as a
whip. **2.** to rustle, as silk. —n. [count] **3.** a
swishing movement or sound.

Swiss /swɪs/ n., pl. **Swiss,** adj. —n. [count] **1.** a
person born or living in Switzerland. —adj. **2.** of
or relating to Switzerland.

switch /swɪtʃ/ n. [count] **1.** a device for turning
on or off an electric current. **2.** a track structure
for directing trains from one track to another. **3.**
a change: We had to make a switch in our plans.
4. a slender, easily bent rod or stick. —v. **5.** [~
+ obj] to transfer (a train, car, etc.) from one set
of tracks to another. **6.** to change: [~ + obj]: to
switch the subject. [no obj]: Let's switch to another subject. **7. switch on** or **off,** to turn on (or
off) (an electric device) by operating a switch:
Switch on the light, please. Switch the light off,
please. —'**switch·er,** n. [count]

switch·board /swɪtʃ,bɔrd/ n. [count] an electronic unit with switches used to connect telephone calls.

swiv·el /swɪvəl/ n., v., **-eled, -el·ing** or (esp.
Brit.) **-elled, -el·ling.** —n. [count] **1.** a device
that allows parts attached to it to move around
easily. —v. **2.** to (cause to) turn around on or
like a swivel: [~ + obj]: He swiveled his chair
around. [no obj]: He swiveled around to see what
was behind him.

swol·len /swowlən/ v. a pp. of SWELL.

swoop /swuwp/ v. [no obj] **1.** to rush or sweep
down suddenly. —n. [count] **2.** a swooping
movement.

sword /sɔrd/ n. [count] a weapon having a long,
sharp-edged blade attached to a handle.

sword·fish /sɔrd,fɪʃ/ n. [count], pl. **-fish·es,**
(esp. when thought of as a group) **-fish.** a large
saltwater fish with a bladelike upper jaw.

swore /swɔr/ v. pt. of SWEAR.

sworn /swɔrn/ v. pp. of SWEAR.

swum /swʌm/ v. pp. of SWIM.

swung /swʌŋ/ v. pt. and pp. of SWING.

syl·lab·i·fy /sɪ'læbə,fay/ v. [~ + obj], **-fied,**
-fy·ing. to form or divide into syllables. —**syl·**
lab·i·fi·ca·tion /sɪ,læbəfɪ'key∫ən/, n. [noncount]

syl·la·ble /sɪləbəl/ n. [count] a unit, usually
containing a vowel, into which a word can be divided: "Dog," "eye," and "sixths" are English
words of one syllable; "doghouse" has two syllables.

syl·la·bus /sɪləbəs/ n. [count], pl. **-bus·es, -bi**
/-,bay/. an outline of the main points of the
contents of a course at school, etc.

sym·bol /sɪmbəl/ n. [count] something that represents something else: The ring was a symbol
of his love. —**sym·bol·ic,** adj.

sym·bol·ism /sɪmbə,lɪzəm/ n. [noncount] the
practice of representing things by symbols.

sym·bol·ize /sɪmbə,layz/ v. [~ + obj], **-ized,**
-iz·ing. to be a symbol of: The fox often symbolizes slyness and cunning.

sym·met·ri·cal /sɪ'mɛtrɪkəl/ also **sym'met·**
ric, adj. characterized by or showing symmetry.
—**sym'met·ri·cal·ly,** adv.

sym·me·try /sɪmɪtriy/ n. [noncount] exact likeness in size or shape of two halves on opposite
sides of each other: the symmetry of the human
body; the symmetry of a snowflake.

sym·pa·thet·ic /,sɪmpə'θɛtɪk/ adj. **1.** having,
showing, or feeling sympathy: He was a sympathetic listener, willing to help whenever someone
had a problem. **2.** agreeing with one's tastes,

mood, or nature: *a sympathetic companion.* —,**sym•pa'thet•i•cal•ly,** *adv.*

sym•pa•thize /'sɪmpə,θayz/ *v.* [*no obj*], **-thized, -thiz•ing.** to feel or show sympathy: *Believe me, I can sympathize with your situation.* —'**sym•pa,thiz•er,** *n.* [*count*]

sym•pa•thy /'sɪmpəθiy/ *n., pl.* **-thies. 1.** [*noncount*] harmony of or agreement in feeling, as between two persons: *There was instant sympathy between the two leaders when they met at the hotel.* **2.** [*noncount*] the ability to share the feelings of another, esp. in times of sorrow or trouble: *Thank you for your kind expression of sympathy.* **3. sympathies,** [*plural*] feelings of compassion or support.

sym•pho•ny /'sɪmfəniy/ *n.* [*count*], *pl.* **-nies.** a long musical composition for a large orchestra, usually having four parts or movements.

symp•tom /'sɪmptəm/ *n.* [*count*] **1.** a physical condition that results from an illness and is a sign of it: *The symptoms of flu are aching joints, high fever, and stomach pains.* **2.** any condition that arises from something else and serves as evidence of it: *the symptoms of economic inflation.* —,**symp•to'mat•ic** /,sɪmptə'mætɪk/, *adj.*

syn•a•gogue /'sɪnə,gɒg, -,gɔg/ *n.* [*count*] a Jewish house of worship.

syn•chro•nize /'sɪŋkrə,nayz/ *v.* [~ + *obj*], **-nized, -niz•ing. 1.** to cause to show the same time, as one clock or watch with another: *Let's synchronize our watches and meet in an hour.* **2.** to cause to move, etc., at the same rate or exactly together: *The skating couple had to synchronize their movements perfectly.*

syn•di•cate /n.'sɪndɪkɪt; v. -,keyt/ *n., v.,* **-cat•ed, -cat•ing. —n.** [*count*] **1.** a group of individuals or organizations that combine to engage in business transactions: *A syndicate is buying up all the stock of that business firm.* —*v.* [~ + *obj*] **2.** to publish at the same time in a number of newspapers or periodicals: *Her column is syndicated in many daily newspapers.* —**syn•di•ca• tion** /,sɪndɪ'keyʃən/, *n.* [*noncount*]

syn•drome /'sɪndrowm, -drəm/ *n.* [*count*] **1.** a group of symptoms that together are signs of a certain illness or condition: *a baby suffering from Down's syndrome.* **2.** a predictable pattern of behavior that occurs under certain circumstances:

the retirement syndrome of endless golf games and card games.

syn•o•nym /'sɪnənɪm/ *n.* [*count*] a word having the same or nearly the same meaning as another, as *joyful* in relation to *glad.* —**syn'on•y•mous,** *adj.*

syn•op•sis /sɪ'nɒpsɪs/ *n.* [*count*], *pl.* **-ses** /-siyz/. a summary of the plot of a novel, play, etc.

syn•tax /'sɪntæks/ *n.* [*noncount*] the way in which sentences and phrases are formed from words. —**syn•tac•tic** /sɪn'tæktɪk/, **syn'tac•ti•cal,** *adj.*

syn•the•sis /'sɪnθəsɪs/ *n., pl.* **-ses** /-,siyz/. **1.** [*noncount*] the combining of the basic elements of separate components into a single or unified thing (opposed to *analysis*). **2.** [*count*] a whole formed by this combining: *His theory was a synthesis of different ideas.*

syn•the•size /'sɪnθə,sayz/ *v.* [~ + *obj*], **-sized, -siz•ing.** to make or form (something) by combining.

syn•the•siz•er /'sɪnθə,sayzər/ *n.* [*count*] a computerized device for creating or modifying the sounds of musical instruments.

syn•thet•ic /sɪn'θɛtɪk/ *adj.* **1.** of or relating to compounds, materials, etc., made by a chemical process, as opposed to those of natural origin: *synthetic fabrics.* —*n.* [*count*] **2.** something made by a synthetic, or chemical, process. —**syn'thet• i•cal•ly,** *adv.*

sy•ringe /sə'rɪndʒ, 'sɪrɪndʒ/ *n.* [*count*] a small tube with a needle for injecting fluid into the body.

syr•up /'sɪrəp/ *n.* [*noncount*] a thick, sweet liquid: *She poured some syrup on her pancakes.*

sys•tem /'sɪstəm/ *n.* [*count*] **1.** a collection or combination of parts that work together: *an improved transportation system.* **2.** an organized set of methods or a plan of procedure: *a system of government.* **3. a.** a combination of organs or tissues in the body concerned with the same function: *the digestive system.* **b.** the entire human or animal body considered as a unit.

sys•tem•at•ic /,sɪstə'mætɪk/ also ,**sys• tem'at•i•cal,** *adj.* having, showing, or involving a system: *a systematic campaign to change the law.* —,**sys•tem'at•i•cal•ly,** *adv.*: *She systematically went through the pile of mail on her desk.*

S

T

T, t /tiy/ *n.* [count], *pl.* **Ts** or **T's, ts** or **t's.** the 20th letter of the English alphabet, a consonant.

T., an abbreviation of: **1.** tablespoon. **2.** Tuesday.

t., an abbreviation of: **1.** teaspoon; teaspoonful. **2.** temperature. **3.** time. **4.** ton. **5.** transitive.

tab /tæb/ *n.* [count] **1.** a small flap, strap, or loop used for opening, hanging, or decorating (something): *tabs on the jacket collar.* **2.** *Informal.* a bill; check: *She promised to pick up (= pay) the tab for dinner.* —*Idiom.* **3.** **keep tab(s) on,** to keep a watch over: *Keep tabs on what he spends.*

tab•by /'tæbiy/ *n.* [count], *pl.* **-bies. 1.** a cat with a striped coat. **2.** a domestic cat, esp. a female one.

ta•ble /'teybəl/ *n.* [count] **1.** a piece of furniture with a flat top supported on one or more legs. **2.** people seated at a table: *He had the whole table laughing at his jokes.* **3.** an orderly arrangement of information in columns or rows: *the periodic table (of the chemical elements).* —*Idiom.* **4.** **turn the tables,** to reverse a bad situation, esp. by gaining the advantage over an opponent. **5.** **under the table,** secretly, and often dishonestly: *He slipped the customs officials some money under the table.*

ta•ble•cloth /'teybəl,klɔθ, -,klɑθ/ *n.* [count] a cloth for covering a table, esp. during a meal.

ta•ble•spoon /'teybəl,spuwn/ *n.* [count] **1.** a large spoon used in serving food. **2.** a cooking measure equal to ½ fluid ounce (14.8 ml). —'**ta•ble•spoon,ful,** *n.* [count], *pl.* **-fuls.**

tab•let /'tæblɪt/ *n.* [count] **1.** a small, flat piece of medicine: *two tablets of aspirin.* **2.** a number of sheets of paper fastened together at the edge; pad. **3.** a flat piece of material, esp. stone, used as a surface for writing: *clay tablets with hieroglyphics.*

'table ,tennis, *n.* [noncount] a game played on a table using paddles to hit a small light ball across a net.

tab•loid /'tæblɔyd/ *n.* [count] a newspaper with small pages, many pictures, and sensational stories.

ta•boo /tə'buw, tæ-/ *adj., n., pl.* **-boos.** —*adj.* **1.** forbidden by society because improper or unacceptable: *taboo words.* —*n.* [count] **2.** a thing or an act forbidden by common custom: *It was once a taboo to discuss pregnancy on television.*

tab•u•lar /'tæbyələr/ *adj.* [before a noun] or arranged in a table, as in columns and rows: *This appendix contains information in tabular form.*

tab•u•late /'tæbyə,leyt/ *v.* [~ + *obj*], **-lat•ed, -lat•ing.** to arrange (numbers, facts, etc.) in tabular form.

tac•it /'tæsɪt/ *adj.* understood without being expressed; implied: *He gave his tacit approval.*

tack /tæk/ *n.* **1.** [count] a short, sharp-pointed nail with a broad, flat head: *Hammer a few tacks into the rug.* **2.** a course of action, esp. one differing from another course: [noncount]: *to change tack and try something else.* —*v.* **3.** [~ + *obj*] to fasten with tacks. **4.** [~ + *obj*] to secure by temporary fastening, as before sewing. **5.** to attach as something extra: [~ + *on* + *obj*]: *He tacked on a conclusion to his paper.* [~ + *obj*]: *to tack it on at the end.*

tack•le /'tækəl; *for 2* 'teykəl/ *n., v.,* **-led, -ling.**

—*n.* **1.** [noncount] equipment for certain sports: *fishing tackle.* **2.** a device using pulleys, ropes, and blocks to raise or lower heavy objects: [count]: *a tackle for lowering cargo.* [noncount]: *moving tackle into position to bring the gear aboard.* **3.** [count] an act of tackling, as in football. —*v.* [~ + *obj*] **4.** to work with or begin work on (something), so as to handle or solve it: *to tackle a problem.* **5.** to seize and throw down (a football player holding the ball): *Smith was tackled on the play.* **6.** [~ + *obj*] to seize (someone) suddenly, esp. in order to stop: *He tackled the thief.*

tack•y /'tækiy/ *adj.,* **-i•er, -i•est.** not tasteful or fashionable; cheap-looking: *a tacky outfit.*

ta•co /'tɑkow/ *n.* [count], *pl.* **-cos.** a fried, folded tortilla filled with chopped meat, tomatoes, cheese, lettuce, and hot sauce.

tact /tækt/ *n.* [noncount] a skill in speaking or acting without giving offense: *Sometimes she has no tact.* —'**tact•ful,** *adj.* —'**tact•less,** *adj.*: *a few tactless remarks.*

tac•tic /'tæktɪk/ *n.* [count] a course of action to achieve a goal: *a smart tactic to get the job.*

tac•tics /'tæktɪks/ *n.* [noncount; *used with a singular verb*] the purposeful moving and arranging of forces against an opponent: *Tactics has always been their strong point in making war.*

tac•tile /'tæktɪl, -tayl/ *adj.* of or relating to the sense of touch.

tad•pole /'tædpowl/ *n.* [count] the immature form of frogs and toads, living in water.

taf•fy /'tæfiy/ *n.* [noncount] [count], *pl.* **-fies.** a chewy candy made of sugar or molasses boiled down.

tag¹ /tæg/ *n., v.,* **tagged, tag•ging.** —*n.* [count] **1.** a piece of paper, etc., attached to something as a marker: *a price tag.* —*v.* **2.** [~ + *obj*] to provide with a tag. **3.** [~ + *obj*] to attach as an addition or afterthought. **4.** [*no obj*] to follow closely: *The child always tagged along behind his big brother.*

tag² /tæg/ *n.* [noncount] a children's game in which one player chases the others in an effort to touch one of them, who then becomes the pursuer.

tail /teyl/ *n.* [count] **1.** a distinct, flexible body part that extends from the trunk at the rear of an animal: *The dog wagged its tail.* **2.** something suggesting this: *the tail of a comet.* **3.** Also, **tails.** [plural] the side of a coin that does not have a face of a person on it; the side opposite to the *head.* **4.** **tails,** [plural] men's formal clothing. —*v.* [~ + *obj*] **5.** to follow closely and in secret in order to observe the activities of someone: *The FBI tailed the suspect to his home.*

tail•gate /'teyl,geyt/ *n., v.,* **-gat•ed, -gat•ing,** *adj.* —*n.* [count] **1.** a gate at the back of a wagon, truck, etc., that can be removed or lowered for loading or unloading. —*v.* **2.** to drive dangerously close to the rear of another vehicle: [*no obj*]: *Some jerk behind us is tailgating.* [~ + *obj*]: *The truck tailgated the little car.*

tai•lor /'teylər/ *n.* [count] **1.** a person who makes, mends, or alters clothes. —*v.* **2.** to make by doing tailor's work: [~ + *obj*]: *to tailor the garment to fit.* [*no obj*]: *to make a living at tailoring.* **3.** [~ + *obj*] to change something according to specific needs or conditions: *He tailored the facts and figures for his own ends.*

taint /teynt/ *n.* [*count*] **1.** a trace of something bad or offensive: *a taint of scandal.* **2.** a trace of infection or decay. —*v.* [~ + *obj*] **3.** to infect or spoil: *This meat is tainted.* **4.** to ruin or damage (a person's name, etc.): *Rumors of bribery tainted his good name.*

take /teyk/ *v.*, **took** /tʊk/, **tak•en** /'teykən/, **tak•ing,** *n.* —*v.* [~ + *obj*] **1.** to bring into one's possession by voluntary action: *She took a pen and began to write.* **2.** [~ + *obj*] to hold or grip with the hands: *She took my hand and shook it.* **3.** [~ + *obj*] to seize or capture: *to take a prisoner.* **4.** [~ + *obj*] to pick or choose from a number of alternatives: *She'll take white wine with her dinner.* **5.** [~ + *obj*] to receive or accept (a person) into some relation, as marriage: *Do you take her to be your lawful wedded wife?* **6.** [~ + *obj*] to receive or react to in a certain manner: *She took his death hard.* **7.** [~ + *obj*] to obtain from a source; derive: *The book takes its title from a song by Franz Schubert.* **8.** [~ + *obj*] to receive into the body, as by swallowing: *to take a pill.* **9.** [~ + *obj*] to do, perform, etc.: *She took a hot bath. She took a walk.* **10.** [~ + *obj*] to undergo or endure: *to take a heat treatment.* **11.** [~ + *obj*] to remove by death; to end (a life): *The flood took many victims.* **12.** [~ + *obj*] to subtract or deduct: *to take 2 from 5.* **13.** [~ + *obj*] to carry with one: *Are you taking an umbrella?* **14.** [~ + *obj*] to carry from one place to another; transport: *Can you take the kids to school?* **15.** [~ + *obj*] to go into or enter: *Take the road to the left.* **16.** [~ + *obj*] to lead or escort: *Her talent and ambition took her to the top.* **17.** [~ + *obj*] to attack or affect with or as if with a disease: *He was taken with a fit of laughter.* **18.** [~ + *obj*] to require; call for; need: *This wood takes three coats of paint. It takes courage to do that.* **19.** [~ + *obj*] to proceed to occupy: *Take a seat.* **20.** [~ + *obj*] to use up; consume: *I took just ten minutes to solve that problem. Solving the problem took (me) only ten minutes. It took (me) only ten minutes to solve the problem.* **21.** [~ + *obj*] to make (a picture, video, etc.) (of): *to take a photograph.* **22.** [~ + *obj*] to write down: *to take notes.* **23.** [~ + *obj*] to apply oneself to; study: *to take a history course.* **24.** [~ + *obj*] to deal with: *He promised to take the matter under consideration.* **25.** [~ + *obj*] to have or experience (a feeling, etc.): *She took pride in her appearance.* **26.** [~ + *obj*] to grasp mentally: *Don't take the remark as an insult. I take your silence to mean that you agree.* **27.** [~ + *obj*] to assume as a fact: *I take it that you won't be there.* **28.** [~ + *obj*] to regard or consider: *I took them to be Frenchmen; weren't they? I took them to be wealthy.* **29.** [~ + *obj*] to be used with (a certain grammatical form, case, etc.): *This verb takes an object.* **30.** [*no obj*] to fall or become: *He took sick.* **31. take after, a.** to resemble (another person), as in appearance, behavior, etc.: *My daughters take after my wife.* **b.** to follow or chase: *The police took after him.* **32. take back, a.** to regain possession of: *The army took back the town; to take it back.* **b.** to admit that (a statement) is wrong: *to take back an insult; What did you call her? You'd better take it back!* **33. take down,** to write down; record: *to take down a speech; to take it all down.* **34. take in, a.** to change (a garment) so as to make smaller or tighter: *to take in a dress; to take it in a few inches.* **b.** to understand the meaning of: *Do you think he took in everything we said? Did he*

take it all in? **c.** to deceive; trick: *She took us in with that scheme. Has she taken in anyone else with it?* **35. take off, a.** to remove: *Take off your coat or Take your coat off.* **b.** to leave the ground and rise into the air: *The plane took off.* **c.** to depart; leave: *The man took off before we could ask him who he was.* **d.** to achieve sudden, noticeable growth, etc.: *Sales took off just before Christmas.* **36. take on, a.** to hire; employ: *to take on new workers or to take new workers on.* **b.** to undertake; begin (work): *She took on extra work to pay the bills. How can he take so much extra work on?* **c.** to assume, as a form or quality: *In the sunset, the lake took on a special beauty.* **37. take out, a.** to withdraw; remove: *She took out several library books. The doctor took my appendix out.* **b.** to buy or obtain by applying: *to take out insurance on a house or to take insurance out on a house.* **c.** to escort, as on a date: *He took her out on a couple of dates. He took out several girls last summer.* **38. take (something) out on (someone),** to cause (another) to suffer for (one's own misfortune, etc.): *He took out his frustration on his children. I know you're upset, but don't take it out on the kids!* **39. take over,** to assume management of or responsibility for: *Who will take over when you retire? Who will take over the company when you retire? Can they take the company over without losing any business?* **40. take (something) upon oneself,** to assume (something) as a responsibility: *Dad took it upon himself to visit her in the hospital.* —*n.* [*count*] **41.** the act of taking. **42.** something taken. **43.** *Informal.* money taken in, esp. profits: *a take of at least $5,000.* **44.** a view or a response to (something): *What's your take on his deciding not to run for office?* —*Idiom.* **45. take place,** to happen; occur: *When will the wedding take place?*

take•off /'teyk,ɔf, -,ɒf/ *n.* **1.** the action of leaving the ground, as in beginning an airplane flight: [*count*]: *a smooth takeoff.* [*noncount*]: *Five minutes after takeoff the plane flew into bad weather.* **2.** [*count*] a funny imitation or parody: *a hilarious takeoff of his nosy neighbor.*

take•out /'teyk,awt/ *adj.* intended to be taken from the point of sale and eaten elsewhere: *takeout meals.*

take•o•ver /'teyk,owvər/ *n.* [*count*] **1.** the act of seizing authority or control. **2.** the taking over of a corporation through the purchase or exchange of stock.

talc /tælk/ *n.* TALCUM POWDER.

'talcum ,powder /'tælkəm/ *n.* [*noncount*] a fine, dry powder for the body, usually perfumed.

tale /teyl/ *n.* [*count*] **1.** a story or an account, either fictional or true, of something that happened: *the scary tale of Count Dracula.* **2.** a lie, esp. against another: *She's telling tales again.*

tal•ent /'tælənt/ *n.* **1.** a special, often creative natural ability or skill: [*count*]: *a talent for drawing.* [*noncount*]: *to show talent in drawing.* **2.** [*count*] a person with special ability, esp. in a particular field: *the local talent.* —'**tal•ent•ed,** *adj.*: *a very talented actress.*

talk /tɔk/ *v.* **1.** [*no obj*] to communicate information by or as if by speaking: *Sometimes we just sit and talk.* **2.** to discuss or chat about (a topic): [~ + *about* + *obj*]: *We talked about the movies.* [~ + *obj*]: *to talk politics.* **3.** [~ + *obj*] to express in words: *Now you're talking sense.* **4. talk back,** to reply disrespectfully: *to talk back (to one's parents).* **5. talk down to,** to speak as if

T

better than someone: *A good teacher won't talk down to the students.* **6. talk out,** to try to clarify or resolve by discussion: *to talk out the problem; Don't just walk away; let's talk it out.* **7. talk (someone) out of (something),** to convince (someone) not to do (something): *I talked him out of quitting.* **8. talk over,** to consider; discuss: *Let's talk it over instead of getting angry. Let's talk over the problem with your teacher.* —*n.* **9.** [count] an act of speaking (with someone); a conversation: *We had a short talk before class.* **10.** [count] an often informal speech or lecture: *She gave a little talk on her research.* **11.** [count] a conference or session: *peace talks.* **12.** [noncount] rumor; gossip: *He's not going to quit; that's just talk.* —**'talk•er,** *n.* [count] —**Usage.** See SPEAK.

talk•a•tive /'tɔkətɪv/ *adj.* willing or ready to talk a great deal.

'talk ˌshow, *n.* [count] a radio or television program in which someone interviews interesting or famous guests.

tall /tɔl/ *adj.,* **-er, -est,** *adv.* —*adj.* **1.** having great height: *a tall man.* **2.** [*after a noun*] having the height that is specified: *a man six feet tall.* **3.** [*before a noun*] giving an appearance of being greater or better than what is really true; overstated: *a tall tale.* —*adv.* **4.** in a proud, erect manner: *to stand tall.*

tal•ly /'tæliy/ *n., pl.* **-lies,** *v.,* **-lied, -ly•ing.** —*n.* [count] **1.** a number counted or recorded. —*v.* **2.** [~ + *obj*] to record; count: *to tally the results of the election.* **3.** to (cause to) correspond or agree: [*no obj*]: *Both accounts tally.* [~ + *obj*]: *to tally the accounts.*

ta•ma•le /təˈmɑliy/ *n.* [count], *pl.* **-les.** chopped and seasoned meat packed in cornmeal dough, wrapped in corn husks, and steamed.

tam•bou•rine /ˌtæmbəˈriyn/ *n.* [count] a small drum with several pairs of metal jingles attached, played by striking with the knuckles and shaking.

tame /teym/ *adj.,* **tam•er, tam•est,** *v.,* **tamed, tam•ing.** —*adj.* **1.** changed from the wild or savage state; gentle: *a tame bear.* **2.** not very exciting; dull: *a tame party.* —*v.* [~ + *obj*] **3.** to make tame: *to tame wild animals for the circus.* **4.** to use and control: *to tame the power of the atom.* —**'tame•ly,** *adv.* —**'tame•ness,** *n.* [noncount] —**'tam•er,** *n.* [count]: *a lion tamer.*

tamp /tæmp/ *v.* [~ + *obj*] to force in or down tightly using repeated light strokes: *to tamp tobacco into a pipe.*

tam•per /'tæmpər/ *v.* [no obj] **1.** to change, esp. without permission: *to tamper with a lock.* **2.** to make changes, esp. to falsify: *to tamper with official records.*

tam•pon /'tæmpɒn/ *n.* [count] a plug of cotton or the like placed inside the vagina during menstruation.

tan /tæn/ *v.,* **tanned, tan•ning,** *n., adj.,* **tan•ner, tan•nest.** —*v.* **1.** [~ + *obj*] to change (the skin of an animal) into leather, esp. by soaking in a special bath. **2.** to (cause to) become brown by reaction to the rays of the sun: [~ + *obj*]: *The sun had tanned his skin.* [*no obj*]: *Her skin had tanned to a golden brown.* —*n.* **3.** [count] a brown color appearing on the skin after exposure to the sun. **4.** [noncount] yellowish brown; light brown.

tan•dem /'tændəm/ *n.* [count] **1.** a bicycle for two riders. —*Idiom.* **2. in tandem,** together; in partnership: *The two worked in tandem to increase their sales.*

tang /tæŋ/ *n.* [count] a strong taste, smell, or flavor: *the tang of the salty sea air.* —**'tang•y,** *adj.,* **-i•er, •-i•est.**

tan•gent /'tændʒənt/ *n.* [count] **1.** a straight line that touches but does not cross through a curved line. —*Idiom.* **2. off on** or **at a tangent,** suddenly changing from one course of discussion to another: *He has gone off on a tangent and forgotten his main idea.*

tan•ge•rine /ˌtændʒəˈriyn, 'tændʒəˌriyn/ *n.* [count] a kind of small, loose-skinned orange.

tan•gi•ble /'tændʒəbəl/ *adj.* **1.** that can be touched. **2.** definite; not vague; clear: *There was no tangible reason to be afraid.*

tan•gle /'tæŋgəl/ *v.,* **-gled, -gling,** *n.* —*v.* **1.** to (cause to) be brought together into a mass of confused parts or strands: [~ + *obj*]: *The wind tangled the girl's long hair.* [no obj]: *Those puppet strings tangle too easily.* **2.** [~ + *obj*] to catch in or as if in a net: *She was tangled in a web of lies.* **3.** [no obj] to fight or argue: *I don't want to be around when those two tangle.* —*n.* [count] **4.** a tangled situation; a tangled mass: *The deer was caught in a tangle of vines.* **5.** a conflict; disagreement: *I got into a tangle with the manager.*

tan•go /'tæŋgow/ *n., pl.* **-gos,** *v.,* **-goed, -go•ing.** —*n.* [count] **1.** a ballroom dance from Latin America. **2.** music for this dance. —*v.* [no obj] **3.** to dance the tango.

tank /tæŋk/ *n.* [count] **1.** a large container for holding a liquid or gas: *a full tank of gas.* **2.** an armored combat vehicle, moving on a belt of treads and usually armed with a cannon.

tank•er /'tæŋkər/ *n.* [count] a ship, airplane, or truck used to carry liquids or gases, as for fuel: *an oil tanker.*

'tank ˌtop, *n.* [count] a sleeveless pullover shirt with shoulder straps.

tan•ta•lize /'tæntlˌayz/ *v.* [~ + *obj*], **-lized, -liz•ing.** to torment (someone) by offering something desirable but not giving it; to tease (someone) by raising hopes that cannot be met: *He tantalized her with dreams of a promotion.*

tan•trum /'tæntrəm/ *n.* [count] an outburst of anger or bad temper: *a two-year-old child having a tantrum.*

tap¹ /tæp/ *v.,* **tapped, tap•ping,** *n.* —*v.* **1.** to strike with a light blow or blows: [~ + *obj*]: *He tapped my shoulder and winked.* [no obj]: *A stranger tapped on the window.* **2.** [no obj] to tapdance. —*n.* [count] **3.** a light, soft blow: *He gave the window a tap.* **4.** the sound made by such a blow. **5.** a piece of metal attached to the toe or heel of a shoe to make the tapping of a dancer more easily heard.

tap² /tæp/ *n., v.,* **tapped, tap•ping.** —*n.* [count] **1.** a faucet: *a hot-water tap.* —*v.* [~ + *obj*] **2.** to draw liquid from (a vessel, a tree, etc.): *to tap a maple tree for sap.* **3.** to draw upon; begin to use: *to tap their financial resources.* **4.** to connect into (a communications device) secretly so as to listen to or receive what is being sent: *to tap a telephone line.* —*Idiom.* **5. on tap,** ready to be drawn and served, as liquor from a container.

'tap ˌdance, *n.* [count] a dance in which rhythmic sounds are produced by a dancer wearing shoes fitted with metal taps. —**'tap,dance,** *v.* [no obj], **-danced, -danc•ing.** —**'tap-ˌdancer,** *n.* [count]

tape /teyp/ *n., v.,* **taped, tap•ing.** —*n.* **1.** [count] a long, narrow strip of fabric, paper, metal, etc. **2.** [noncount] material in the form of narrow strips, with a sticky surface, used for

taunt

sealing, etc.: *a piece of adhesive tape.* **3. a.** [*non-count*] a long strip of plastic able to record and play back sounds or images: *The tape must have broken inside the VCR.* **b.** [*count*] a length of this tape with recorded sounds or images; an audio-tape, cassette tape, or videotape. —*v.* [~ + *obj*] **4.** to tie up, bind, or attach with tape: *to tape the bows to the packages.* **5.** to record on specially treated tape: *to tape the concert.*

'**tape ,measure,** *n.* [*count*] a long, flexible strip marked in inches, feet, centimeters, and meters, etc., for measuring distances.

ta•per /'teypər/ *v.* **1.** to (cause to) become thinner or narrower toward one end: [*no obj*]: *The shirt tapered at the waist.* [~ + *obj*]: *to taper the shirt at the waist.* **2. taper off,** to decrease gradually in force or size; diminish: *The snow will taper off at about midnight.*

'**tape re,corder,** *n.* [*count*] an electrical device for recording, or for playing back something recorded, on magnetic tape.

tap•es•try /'tæpəstriy/ *n., pl.* **-tries.** a decorative fabric with a picture or design woven into it: [*noncount*]: *examples of careful tapestry.* [*count*]: *tapestries depicting medieval life.*

tap•i•o•ca /,tæpiy'owkə/ *n.* [*noncount*] a substance obtained from a kind of plant and used for making pudding or for thickening soups.

taps /tæps/ *n.* [*noncount; used with a singular verb*] a bugle signal played in a camp or military post at night as an order to turn off all lights: *Taps is played every night at dusk.*

tar /tɑr/ *n., v.,* **tarred, tar•ring.** —*n.* [*noncount*] **1.** a dark, thick, sticky substance that can be poured when hot to make roads, etc.: *hot tar smeared on the highways.* **2.** solid material produced when tobacco burns: *cigarette tar.* —*v.* [~ + *obj*] **3.** to smear or cover with or as if with tar.

ta•ran•tu•la /tə'ræntʃələ/ *n.* [*count*], *pl.* **-las, -lae** /-,liy/. a large, hairy spider having a painful but not poisonous bite.

tar•dy /'tɑrdiy/ *adj.,* **-di•er, -di•est. 1.** late; coming or happening after the desired time; not on time. **2.** moving or acting slowly; sluggish. —'**tar•di•ness,** *n.* [*noncount*]

tar•get /'tɑrgɪt/ *n.* [*count*] **1.** an object to be aimed at in shooting practice or contests. **2.** any object fired at. **3.** a goal to be reached; aim: *a target of $25,000 for the charity drive.* **4.** one who is the object of abuse, scorn, etc.: *a target of abuse.* —*v.* [~ + *obj*] **5.** to use or set up as a target: *The pilots targeted the bridge for their first bombing run.* **6.** to direct toward a target: *The pilots targeted their bombs on the bridge.*

tar•iff /'tærɪf/ *n.* [*count*] taxes charged by a government on imports or exports: *a fifty-percent tariff on rice imports.*

tar•nish /'tɑrnɪʃ/ *v.* **1.** to (cause a metal surface to) be dull; (cause to) be discolored: [~ + *obj*]: *The salty ocean air tarnished her silver teapot.* [*no obj*]: *Silver tarnishes easily in salty air.* **2.** [~ + *obj*] to destroy the good name of: *The charge of fraud tarnished the company's reputation.* —*n.* [*noncount*] **3.** a tarnished coating. **4.** tarnished condition; discoloration.

tar•pau•lin /tɑr'pɔlɪn, 'tɑrpəlɪn/ *n.* [*count*] a sheet of waterproofed canvas used as a protective covering against weather: *He covered the car with a tarpaulin.*

tart¹ /tɑrt/ *adj.,* **-er, -est. 1.** sharp to the taste; sour or acid: *tart apples.* **2.** sharp in character, spirit, or expression; cutting: *a tart reply.* —'**tart•ly,** *adv.* —'**tart•ness,** *n.* [*noncount*]

tart² /tɑrt/ *n.* **1.** [*count*] [*noncount*] a small, shallow pie, sometimes without a top crust, filled with fruit, etc. **2.** [*count*] a prostitute.

tar•tar /'tɑrtər/ *n.* [*noncount*] a hard substance made up of saliva, salts, and food particles that forms on the teeth.

'**tartar ,sauce,** *n.* [*noncount*] a sauce made of mayonnaise and containing chopped pickles, olives, etc., served esp. with fish and seafood.

task /tæsk/ *n.* [*count*] **1.** a piece of work assigned to a person: *a boring task.* —**Idiom. 2. take (someone) to task,** to scold or reprimand: *The boss took him to task for being late.*

tas•sel /'tæsəl/ *n.* [*count*] **1.** decorative threads or cords tied together at one end and hanging from something such as a hat or curtain. **2.** something resembling this, as at the top of a stalk of corn.

taste /teyst/ *v.,* **tast•ed, tast•ing,** *n.* —*v.* **1.** [~ + *obj*] to test the flavor or quality of by taking some into the mouth: *She tasted the wine.* **2.** [~ + *obj*] to notice the flavor of: *I can't taste the wine in that sauce.* **3.** [~ + *obj*] to experience, esp. to only a slight degree: *She had tasted freedom and would no longer wait for it.* **4.** to have a particular flavor: [~ + *adjective*]: *The coffee tastes bitter.* [~ + *of/like + noun*]: *The coffee tastes like lead.* —*n.* **5.** [*noncount*] the physical sense by which the flavor of things is felt or noticed: *He has no sense of taste when he has a cold.* **6.** [*count*] a sensation noticed by this sense; flavor: *foods that have a sweet taste.* **7.** [*count*] a small quantity tasted: *a little taste of wine.* **8.** [*count*] a liking for something: *a taste for classical music.* **9.** [*noncount*] a sense of what is fitting or pleasing in appearance; or of what is polite, correct, etc., to say or do socially: *She always dressed in good taste.*

'**taste ,bud,** *n.* [*count*] one of many small sites along the lining of the tongue that function as the organs for the sense of taste.

taste•ful /'teystfəl/ *adj.* having, showing, or in accordance with good taste. —'**taste•ful•ly,** *adv.*: *a room tastefully decorated in muted colors.*

taste•less /'teystlɪs/ *adj.* **1.** having no taste; lacking a taste or flavor: *Water should be tasteless.* **2.** lacking good taste; lacking a sense of what is proper, harmonious, fitting, etc.: *tasteless jokes.*

tast•y /'teystiy/ *adj.,* **-i•er, -i•est.** good-tasting; savory. —'**tast•i•ness,** *n.* [*noncount*]

tat•ter /'tætər/ *n.* [*count*] **1.** a piece torn away and hanging from something; a shred. **2. tatters,** [*plural*] torn or ragged clothing: *dressed in tatters.* —*v.* [*no obj*] **3.** to tear or wear to tatters: *Their clothes were tattered.*

tat•tle /'tætl/ *v.,* **-tled, -tling. 1.** [*no obj*] to tell something secret about another out of spite: *Don't tattle; it's not friendly.* **2. tattle on,** to betray by tattling: *Why did you tattle on me?* —'**tat•tler,** *n.* [*count*]

tat•tle•tale /'tætl,teyl/ *n.* [*count*] one who tattles on another; one who makes a habit of tattling.

tat•too /tæ'tuw/ *n., pl.* **-toos,** *v.,* **-tooed, -too•ing.** —*n.* [*count*] **1.** a design, picture, or figure put on the skin using dyes. —*v.* [~ + *obj*] **2.** to mark with tattoos, as a person or a part of the body: *Her back was tattooed with a butterfly.* **3.** to put (a design, etc.) on the skin: *A butterfly was tattooed on her back.*

taught /tɔt/ *v.* pt. and pp. of TEACH.

taunt /tɔnt, tɑnt/ *v.* [~ + *obj*] **1.** to make fun

of or insult: *They taunted him with shouts of "Coward!"* —*n.* [*count*] **2.** a mocking remark, made as a challenge or an insult.

taut /tɔt/ *adj.*, **-er, -est.** tightly drawn; tense; not slack: *His muscles were taut as he strained to lift the weights.* —**'taut•ly,** *adv.* —**'taut•ness,** *n.* [*noncount*]

tav•ern /'tævərn/ *n.* [*count*] **1.** a place where alcoholic drinks are served. **2.** a public house for travelers and others; inn.

taw•ny /'tɔniy/ *adj.*, **-ni•er, -ni•est.** of a yellowish brown color; golden brown. —**'taw•ni•ness,** *n.* [*noncount*]

tax /tæks/ *n.* **1.** a sum of money paid to a government for its support, based on income, etc.: [*noncount*]: *an annual income tax.* [*count*]: *to rebel against paying new taxes.* —*v.* [~ + *obj*] **2.** (of a government) to put a tax on (a person or business): *The government taxes its citizens.* **3.** to make serious demands on (someone); strain: *Putting the children through college taxes our financial resources.* —**tax'a•tion,** *n.* [*noncount*]: *Higher taxation is necessary to increase government spending on education.*

tax•i /'tæksiy/ *n.*, *pl.* **tax•is** or **tax•ies,** *v.*, **tax•ied, tax•i•ing** or **tax•y•ing.** —*n.* [*count*] **1.** a taxicab: *I'll call for a taxi to send you home.* —*v.* **2.** [*no obj*] to ride or travel in a taxicab. **3.** (of an airplane) to (cause to) move on the ground at slow speed before flying: [*no obj*]: *The plane was taxiing on the runway.* [~ + *obj*]: *The pilot taxied the plane to the center of the runway.*

tax•i•cab /'tæksiy,kæb/ *n.* [*count*] a car with a driver who is paid to carry one or more passengers somewhere.

tax•pay•er /'tæks,peyər/ *n.* [*count*] one who pays a tax or taxes.

tbs. or **tbsp.,** an abbreviation of: **1.** tablespoon. **2.** tablespoonful.

tea /tiy/ *n.* **1.** [*noncount*] the dried and prepared leaves of an Asian shrub, used to make a drink. **2.** a bitter drink prepared by adding tea leaves to boiling water: [*noncount*]: *a cup of tea.* [*count*]: *I'll have two teas with sugar and lemon, please.* **3.** a light meal, usually including tea, sandwiches, and cakes, eaten in the late afternoon: [*noncount*]: *They had us over for tea.* [*count*]: *a lovely afternoon tea.*

teach /tiytʃ/ *v.*, **taught** /tɔt/, **teach•ing. 1.** to give knowledge of or skill in (some subject, etc.) to students; give instruction in (some topic): [~ + *obj*]: *She teaches mathematics.* [~ + *that clause*]: *The Koran teaches that hostages should not be mistreated.* **2.** to give knowledge of or skill in some subject, etc., to (students); give instruction to: [~ + *obj*]: *He teaches a large class of high school students.* [~ + *obj* + *to* + *verb*]: *He taught his daughter (how) to drive.* **3.** [*no obj*] to give knowledge, or instruction, esp. as one's profession: *He has been teaching for over twenty years.*

teach•er /'tiytʃər/ *n.* [*count*] one who teaches, esp. as a profession; instructor.

teach•ing /'tiytʃɪŋ/ *n.* **1.** [*noncount*] the job or activity of one who teaches. **2.** Often, **teachings.** [*plural*] something taught, esp. a belief or doctrine: *One of his teachings was that people who are humble will be rewarded.*

tea•cup /'tiy,kʌp/ *n.* [*count*] a cup in which tea is served.

tea•ket•tle /'tiy,kɛtl/ *n.* [*count*] a covered metal pot with a spout and handle, used for boiling water.

team /tiym/ *n.* [*count*] **1.** a group of people playing against another group in a game or contest: *a basketball team; a debating team.* **2.** a group of people meeting for an action or activity: *A team of experts visited the crash site.* **3.** two or more horses or other animals working together to pull a vehicle, plow, etc. —*v.* **4.** to join together in a team: [~ + *obj*]: *He teamed them (together) on the project.* [*no obj*]: *The two teamed up to work on the project.*

team•mate /'tiym,meyt/ *n.* [*count*] a member of the same team.

team•work /'tiym,wɜrk/ *n.* [*noncount*] effort on the part of a group acting together as a team.

tea•pot /'tiy,pɒt/ *n.* [*count*] a covered container with a spout and handle, used for making and pouring tea.

tear¹ /tɪər/ *n.* [*count*] **1.** a drop of salty, watery liquid formed in the eye when one cries: *Tears wash away dirt and dust in the eye.* **2. tears,** [*plural*] an act of weeping: *She burst into tears.* —*v.* [*no obj*] **3.** (of the eyes) to fill up with tears: *His eyes teared whenever he thought of his late father.* —*Idiom.* **4. in tears,** weeping: *I found her in tears.* —**'tear•ful,** *adj.* —**'tear•y,** *adj.*, **-i•er, -i•est.**

tear² /tɛər/ *v.*, **tore, torn, tear•ing,** *n.* —*v.* **1.** to (cause to) be pulled apart or in pieces by force: [~ + *obj*]: *He tore the fabric.* [*no obj*]: *This fabric tears easily.* **2.** [~ + *obj*] to pull or take violently: *She tore the book from my hands.* **3.** [*no obj*] to act very quickly or with great energy: *The wind tore through the trees.* **4. tear down,** to pull down: *They're tearing the old library down* or *They're tearing down the old library.* **5. tear into,** to attack hard and quickly: *The army tore into the enemy.* **6. tear up,** to tear completely into small pieces: *He tore up the message* or *He tore the message up.* —*n.* [*count*] **7.** the act of tearing. **8.** a place where something is or has been torn or pulled apart.

tease /tiyz/ *v.*, **teased, teas•ing,** *n.* —*v.* **1.** to irritate or bother (someone or an animal) with jokes, playful words or actions, etc.: [~ + *obj*]: *She teased me about my girlfriends.* [*no obj*]: *Don't tease; it's cruel to animals.* **2.** to cause someone to want (something) without intending to give it: [*no obj*]: *She thought he really liked her, but he was just teasing.* [~ + *obj*]: *He was just teasing her.* **3.** [~ + *obj*] to treat hair by holding it at the ends and combing toward the scalp so as to give body to a hairdo. —*n.* [*count*] **4.** a person who teases: *She's such a tease.*

tea•spoon /'tiy,spuwn/ *n.* [*count*] **1.** a small spoon used to stir tea and coffee, eat dessert, etc. **2.** a cooking measure equal to ⅙ fluid ounce (4.9 ml). —**'tea,spoon ful,** *n.* [*count*], *pl.* **-fuls.**

teat /tiyt, tɪt/ *n.* [*count*] a nipple through which young animals get milk.

tech•ni•cal /'tɛknɪkəl/ *adj.* **1.** of or relating to an art, science, profession, trade, etc.: *technical journals; technical experts.* **2.** of, relating to, or showing technique: *The skaters were judged on their technical ability.* **3.** according to a strict interpretation of rules: *a technical violation of the law.* —**tech•ni•cal•i•ty,** *n.* [*count*], *pl.* **-ties.** —**'tech•ni•cal•ly,** *adv.*: *Technically we are thirty seconds late, but no one will care.*

tech•ni•cian /tɛk'nɪʃən/ *n.* [*count*] **1.** one trained or skilled in technical parts of a field of study or work. **2.** a person skilled in the technique of an art, as music or painting.

tech•nique /tɛk'niyk/ *n.* **1.** [*noncount*] the manner with which an artist, athlete, performer, etc., uses technical skills in a particular art, field of study, etc.: *The diver showed perfect technique in entering the water.* **2.** [count] any method used to do something: *a simple technique for backing up my disks.*

tech•nol•o•gy /tɛkˈnɒlədʒiy/ *n., pl.* **-gies. 1.** [noncount] the study of science for practical use. **2.** [count] a technological process or invention: *new technologies for computer chip manufacturing.* —**tech•no•log•i•cal** /ˌtɛknəˈlɒdʒɪkəl/, *adj.* —ˌ**tech•no'log•i•cal•ly**, *adv.* —**tech'nol•o•gist,** *n.* [count]

'**teddy** ˌ**bear** /ˈtɛdiy/ *n.* [count] a stuffed toy bear.

te•di•ous /ˈtiydiyəs, ˈtiydʒəs/ *adj.* having the character of tedium: *a tedious book; a tedious lecture.* —'**te•di•ous•ly**, *adv.* —'**te•di•ous•ness,** *n.* [noncount]

te•di•um /ˈtiydiyəm/ *n.* [noncount] the quality or state of causing someone to feel tired and bored.

tee /tiy/ *n., v.,* **teed, tee•ing.** —*n.* [count] **1. a.** Also called **teeing ground.** the area on a golf course where the game begins. **b.** a small structure on which a golf ball is placed at the beginning of each hole. —*v.* **2. tee off,** to strike a golf ball from a tee: *They finally teed off at eleven o'clock.*

teem /tiym/ *v.* [no obj] to have plenty of: *The lake was teeming with fish.*

teen /tiyn/ *adj.* [before a noun] **1.** teenage: *teen fashions.* —*n.* [count] **2.** a teenager. See TEENS.

teen•age /ˈtiynˌeydʒ/ *adj.* also '**teen,aged,** *adj.* of, relating to, or characteristic of people in their teens. —**teen•ag•er,** *n.* [count]

teens /tiynz/ *n.* [plural] **1.** the numbers 13 through 19: *Temperatures will fall into the teens tonight.* **2.** the ages of 13 to 19 inclusive: *two sons in their teens.*

tee•ny /ˈtiyniy/ *adj.,* **-ni•er, -ni•est.** TINY.

'**tee ,shirt,** *n.* T-SHIRT.

tee•ter /ˈtiytər/ *v.* [no obj] to move back and forth unsteadily: *The ladder teetered, then fell.*

teeth /tiyθ/ *n.* pl. of TOOTH.

teethe /tiyð/ *v.* [no obj], **teethed, teeth•ing.** to grow teeth.

tele-, a combining form meaning: at or over a distance (*telegraph*); of, by or television (*telecast*).

tel•e•cast /ˈtɛlɪˌkæst/ *v.,* **-cast** or **-cast•ed, -cast•ing,** *n.* —*v.* **1.** to broadcast by television: [~ + *obj*]: *to telecast a show live.* [no obj]: *to telecast live.* —*n.* [count] **2.** a television broadcast. —'**tel•e,cast•er,** *n.* [count]

tel•e•com•mu•ni•ca•tions /ˌtɛlɪkəˌmyuwnɪˈkeyʃənz/ *n.* [noncount; used with a singular verb] Sometimes, **telecommunication.** the science and technology of sending information over great distances, in the form of electromagnetic signals, as by telegraph or television.

tel•e•gram /ˈtɛlɪˌɡræm/ *n.* a message sent by telegraph: [count]: *He received a telegram yesterday.* [noncount; often: by + ~]: *The message came by telegram.*

tel•e•graph /ˈtɛlɪˌɡræf/ *n.* [noncount] **1.** a system or a device for sending messages to a distant place by means of connected wires: *to send by telegraph.* —*v.* **2.** to send or transmit (a message) by telegraph to (someone): [~ + *obj*]: *They telegraphed a message to her.* [~ + *obj*]: *They telegraphed her the message.* [~ + *obj*]: *They tele-*

graphed that they would arrive early. [no obj]: *They telegraphed ahead with the news.*

tel•e•mar•ket•ing /ˈtɛləˌmɑrkɪtɪŋ/ *n.* [noncount] selling or advertising by telephone.

te•lep•a•thy /təˈlɛpəθiy/ *n.* [noncount] communication between minds using some means beyond the ordinary or normal senses: *In the story the aliens spoke to humans by mental telepathy.* —**tel•e•path•ic** /ˌtɛləˈpæθɪk/, *adj.*

tel•e•phone /ˈtɛləˌfown/ *n., v.,* **-phoned, -phon•ing.** —*n.* **1.** Also called **phone.** a device, system, or process using electricity to send sound or speech to a distant point: [count]: *There were no telephones on the highway.* [noncount; often: by + ~]: *See if we can reach him by telephone.* —*v.* **2.** to send (a message) by telephone to (someone); phone: [~ + *obj*]: *They telephoned her with the news. They telephoned her the message.* [~ + *that clause*]: *She telephoned that there had been an accident.* [no obj]: *They telephoned ahead with the news.*

'**telephone ,tag,** *n.* [noncount] See PHONE TAG.

tel•e•pho•to /ˈtɛləˌfowtow/ *adj.* of or relating to camera equipment that can take pictures over long distances: *a telephoto lens.*

tel•e•scope /ˈtɛləˌskowp/ *n., v.,* **-scoped, -scop•ing.** —*n.* [count] **1.** a device for making distant objects appear nearer when viewed. —*v.* **2.** to slide or force together (the parts of something), one into another: [no obj]: *Her music stand telescoped into a six-inch stick.* [~ + *obj*]: *to telescope the music stand.* —ˌ**tel•e'scop•ic,** *adj.*

tel•e•thon /ˈtɛləˌθɒn/ *n.* [count] a long television broadcast, usually designed to aid a charity or cause.

tel•e•vi•sion /ˈtɛləˌvɪʒən/ *n.* **1.** [noncount] the broadcasting of images by means of radio waves projected onto a picture tube: *the powerful influence of television.* **2.** [count] Also, **television set.** a device or set for receiving television broadcasts: *He bought a new television.* —'**tel•e•vise,** *v.* [no obj] [~ + *obj*], **-vised, -vis•ing.**

tell /tɛl/ *v.,* **told** /towld/, **tell•ing. 1.** to narrate (a story, etc.) to (someone): [~ + *obj*]: *He told a story to the children. He told the children a story.* [no obj]: *The story tells of the life of King Arthur.* **2.** [~ + *obj*] to make known (a fact, news, etc.) to (someone); communicate: *He told us the news of her death. He told us about her death. He told us that she had died.* **3.** [~ + *obj*] to utter (the truth, etc.); speak: *He wasn't telling the truth to his wife. He wasn't telling his wife the truth.* **4.** to reveal to others by speaking to them about (something private): [~ + *obj*]: *I just told her a secret. I told a secret (to my wife).* [no obj]: *Will you hate me if I tell?* **5.** to be able to see clearly; identify; know: [~ + *obj*]: *to tell twins apart; to tell if it is night or day.* [no obj]: *Don't ask me how I know; I can just tell.* **6.** [~ + *obj*] to order or command: *Tell her to stop. I told her (that) she should pull the car over and stop.* **7.** [~ + *obj*] to give a sign or signal of (something) to (someone): *The light on the dashboard tells you if you're driving too fast.* **8. tell off,** to express anger at: *It was about time somebody told him off. He told off the whole class because no one was finishing assignments.* **9. tell on,** to tattle on: *Don't tell on your sister.* —*Usage.* See SAY.

tell•er /ˈtɛlər/ *n.* [count] a bank employee who receives or pays out money over the counter.

tell•ing /ˈtɛlɪŋ/ *adj.* **1.** effective: *a telling blow.* **2.** revealing: *a telling analysis.* —'**tell•ing•ly,** *adv.*

tell•tale /ˈtɛl,teyl/ *adj.* [*before a noun*] revealing something not meant to be known: *a telltale fingerprint.*

temp /tɛmp/ *n.* [*count*] **1.** a temporary worker. —*v.* [*no obj*] **2.** to work in this way: *She was temping for a detective agency.*

temp., an abbreviation of: **1.** temperature. **2.** temporary.

tem•per /ˈtɛmpər/ *n.* **1.** [*count*] a state of mind or feelings: *in a bad temper; a sweet temper.* **2.** [*noncount*] a tendency to get angry easily. **3.** [*noncount*] calm state of mind: *to lose one's temper.* —*v.* [~ + *obj*] **4.** to soften or tone down: *to temper justice with mercy.* **5.** to strengthen by heating and cooling: *to temper steel.*

tem•per•a•ment /ˈtɛmpərəmənt, -prəmənt/ *n.* the character of a person as shown by the way he or she usually acts or feels: [*noncount*]: *differences in temperament between the twins.* [*count*]: *The child has an angry temperament.*

tem•per•ate /ˈtɛmpərɪt, ˈtɛmprɪt/ *adj.* **1.** moderate in behavior, as in the use of alcoholic drinks. **2.** moderate in respect to temperature: *the more temperate mountainous regions of Kenya.*

tem•per•a•ture /ˈtɛmpərətʃər, -,tʃʊr, -prə-/ *n.* **1.** a measure of the warmth of an object: [*count*]: *very cold temperatures this winter.* [*noncount*]: *a sudden change in temperature.* **2.** [*count*] **a.** the degree of heat in the human body, normally about 98.6°F (37°C): *The nurse took my temperature.* **b.** a fever: *The baby has a temperature.*

tem•pered /ˈtɛmpərd/ *adj.* **1.** having a specified temper or disposition: *a bad-tempered child.* **2.** made less intense or violent: *justice tempered with mercy.*

tem•pest /ˈtɛmpɪst/ *n.* [*count*] **1.** a violent windstorm. **2.** a loud argument or disturbance. —*Idiom.* **3. tempest in a teacup** or **teapot,** a great argument or disturbance concerning something small or unimportant. —**tem'pes•tu•ous,** *adj.*

tem•plate /ˈtɛmplɪt/ *n.* [*count*] a pattern used in producing copies of a thing or a shape.

tem•ple¹ /ˈtɛmpəl/ *n.* [*count*] **1.** a place for the service or worship of a deity. **2.** a synagogue.

tem•ple² /ˈtɛmpəl/ *n.* [*count*] the part of the face on either side of the forehead.

tem•po /ˈtɛmpow/ *n.* [*count*], *pl.* **-pos, -pi** /-piy/. **1.** the rate of speed of a musical passage or work. **2.** any normal rate or rhythm: *the fast tempo of city life.*

tem•po•rar•y /ˈtɛmpə,rɛriy/ *adj., n., pl.* **-rar• ies.** —*adj.* **1.** lasting or effective for a limited time only; not permanent: *The new bill will create 75,000 temporary jobs.* —*n.* [*count*] **2.** an office worker hired for a short period of time and paid every day. —**tem•po•rar•i•ly** /,tɛmpə'rɛərəliy/, *adv.*: *Work with us temporarily and see if you'd like to stay.*

tempt /tɛmpt/ *v.* [~ + *obj*] **1.** to attract (someone) to do something, esp. something wrong: *The devil tempted him to sin.* **2.** to attract, appeal strongly to, or invite: *I'm tempted to take a job in the U.S.* —**temp'ta•tion,** *n.* [*count*] [*noncount*]

ten /tɛn/ *n.* [*count*] **1.** a number, 9 plus 1, written as 10. —*adj.* **2.** amounting to 10 in number.

ten•an•cy /ˈtɛnənsiy/ *n.,* *pl.* **-cies. 1.** [*noncount*] a holding or use by a tenant. **2.** [*count*] the length of time of a tenancy.

ten•ant /ˈtɛnənt/ *n.* [*count*] one who rents and occupies land, a house, etc., from another.

tend¹ /tɛnd/ *v.* [*no obj*] **1.** to be likely to do something; to happen often: *Things tend to hap-*

pen fast in the city. **2.** (of a person) to begin to move in a direction or toward a state (of being), etc.: *She tends to be happy.*

tend² /tɛnd/ *v.* [~ + *obj*] to watch over and take care of: *to tend a fire; Who will tend to the baby?*

ten•den•cy /ˈtɛndənsiy/ *n.* [*count*], *pl.* **-cies.** a natural likelihood: *He has a tendency to be impatient.*

ten•der¹ /ˈtɛndər/ *adj.,* **-er, -est. 1.** soft in material or substance: *a tender steak.* **2.** weak in structure: *a tender spot on the baby's head.* **3.** full of gentle feelings: *He gave her a tender glance.* **4.** painfully sensitive. —**'ten•der•ize,** *v.* [~ + *obj*], **-ized, -izing:** *To tenderize the meat, the cook pounded it and then spread on a sauce.* —**'ten•der•ly,** *adv.*: *She held the kitten tenderly in her arms.* —**'ten•der•ness,** *n.* [*noncount*]

ten•der² /ˈtɛndər/ *v.* [~ + *obj*] **1.** to present or offer: *to tender one's resignation from a job.* —*n.* [*noncount*] **2.** something tendered, esp. money.

ten•don /ˈtɛndən/ *n.* [*count*] a dense, tough cord or band of fiberlike tissue connecting a muscle with a bone or another body part: *He tore a tendon in his leg.*

ten•e•ment /ˈtɛnəmənt/ *n.* [*count*] Also called **'tenement ,house.** an apartment house in bad condition and often overcrowded.

ten•et /ˈtɛnɪt/ *n.* [*count*] an opinion, principle, etc., held to be true: *the basic tenets of democracy.*

ten•nis /ˈtɛnɪs/ *n.* [*noncount*] a game in which players use rackets to hit a ball back and forth across a low net.

ten•or /ˈtɛnər/ *n.* **1.** [*count*] the general meaning or direction of something written or spoken: *The tenor of the meeting was one of hopefulness.* **2. a.** [*noncount*] the adult male voice between the bass and the alto. **b.** [*count*] a singer with such a voice.

tense¹ /tɛns/ *adj.,* **tens•er, tens•est,** *v.,* **tensed, tens•ing.** —*adj.* **1.** stretched tight, as a cord, etc.; stiff: *tense muscles.* **2.** of or relating to a state of nervous strain: *a tense moment.* —*v.* **3.** to make or become tense: [*no obj*]: *Her neck muscles tensed in the sudden cold.* [~ + *obj*]: *He tensed (up) his muscles when he heard the guard open his prison cell.* —**'tense•ly,** *adv.*: *They watched tensely through the whole movie.* —**'tense•ness,** *n.* [*noncount*]

tense² /tɛns/ *n.* a verb form indicating time of action or state of being: [*count*]: *How many verb tenses are there in English?* [*noncount*]: *how different languages express tense.*

ten•sion /ˈtɛnʃən/ *n.* **1.** [*noncount*] the state of being stretched: *the tension of her leg muscles as she performed on the balance beam.* **2.** [*noncount*] emotional strain, esp. great nervousness: *a lot of tension in his job.* **3.** a strained relationship between individuals, countries, etc.: [*noncount*]: *Tension increased along the border.* [*count*]: *Tensions sprang up between the two nations.*

tent /tɛnt/ *n.* [*count*] a movable shelter of cloth, etc., placed over a frame of poles and held down by stakes in the ground.

ten•ta•cle /ˈtɛntəkəl/ *n.* [*count*] a slender, easily bent body part like a limb used by certain animals for grabbing or feeling things.

ten•ta•tive /ˈtɛntətɪv/ *adj.* not definite; serving as a test; hesitant: *a tentative smile.* —**'ten•ta• tive•ly,** *adv.* —**'ten•ta•tive•ness,** *n.* [*noncount*]

tenth /tɛnθ/ *adj.* **1.** next after ninth. **2.** being one of ten equal parts. —*n.* [*count*] **3.** a tenth part, esp. of one (¹/₁₀). **4.** the tenth member of a series.

ten•u•ous /'tɛnyuwəs/ adj. lacking a sound basis: a tenuous argument.

te•pee /'tiypiy/ n. [count], pl. **-pees.** an Indian tent made from animal skins placed on a cone-shaped frame of long poles.

tepee

tep•id /'tɛpɪd/ adj. moderately warm: tepid water.

term /tɜrm/ n. [count] **1.** a word or group of words having meaning in a particular field: Define the term atom as it is used in physics. **2.** a fixed period of time: a one-year term of office. **3.** a division of a school year, during which there is regular instruction: It's the start of a new term. **4. terms,** [plural] **a.** conditions of payment, etc.: The car dealer promised reasonable terms. **b.** conditions of proposed agreement: The terms of the treaty were clear. **c.** relations: She's on good terms with everyone. —v. [~ + obj] **5.** to give a particular name to; call: He termed the agreement "ridiculous." —**Idiom. 6. come to terms,** to reach an agreement. **7. in terms of,** with regard to; concerning: In terms of pay, the job is terrible. **8. in the (short** or**) long term,** in a (short or) long while from the present: In the short term—say, a few months—interest rates will go up.

ter•mi•nal /'tɜrmənl/ adj. **1.** located at or forming the end of something: a terminal bud of a flower. **2.** occurring at or causing the end of life: a terminal disease. —n. [count] **3. a.** a point at the end of a transportation system, as a railroad line, or any important meeting point within the system. **b.** the site of a terminal: The new terminal has good restaurants. **4.** any device, such as a keyboard and a video screen, for connecting with a computer in order to send and receive information: The terminal was hooked up to the mainframe. —'ter•mi•nal•ly, adv.: terminally ill patients.

ter•mi•nate /'tɜrmə,neyt/ v., **-nat•ed, -nat•ing.** to (cause to) come to an end; cease: [~ + obj]: The countries vowed to terminate hostilities. [no obj]: When will hostilities terminate? —,ter•mi'na•tion, n. [noncount] [count]

ter•mi•nol•o•gy /,tɜrmə'nɒlədʒiy/ n., pl. **-gies.** the terms or system of terms used in a particular field: [noncount]: A certain amount of terminology has to be defined before we can talk about computers. [count]: a terminology that confuses learners.

ter•mite /'tɜrmayt/ n. [count] a soft-bodied insect that eats wood.

ter•race /'tɛrəs/ n., v., **-raced, -rac•ing.** —n. [count] **1.** a flat, raised area of land with sharply rising sides, or a series of such areas rising one above another. **2.** an open area connected to a house and serving as an outdoor extension; patio or balcony.

ter•ra cot•ta /'tɛr'ə kɒtə/ n. [noncount] a hard, brownish red clay used for ornaments in buildings and in pottery.

ter•rain /tə'reyn/ n. [noncount] an area of land, esp. with reference to its natural features: hilly terrain.

ter•res•tri•al /tə'rɛstriyəl/ adj. **1.** of or relating to the earth as distinct from other planets: terrestrial atmosphere. **2.** of or relating to land as distinct from water: Cats are terrestrial animals. —n. [count] **3.** an inhabitant of the earth, esp. a human being.

ter•ri•ble /'tɛrəbəl/ adj. **1.** distressing; severe: a terrible battle. **2.** horrible; awful: We had a terrible time at their party. **3.** very great: a terrible responsibility.

'ter•ri•bly, adv. **1.** in an awful manner: He played terribly in the game yesterday. **2.** extremely; very: It's terribly late.

ter•ri•er /'tɛriyər/ n. [count] a breed of usually small dogs, used originally to drive wild animals out of their burrow.

ter•rif•ic /tə'rɪfɪk/ adj. **1.** extraordinarily great: They left with terrific speed. **2.** extremely good; wonderful: We had a terrific vacation. —**ter'rif•i•cal•ly,** adv.

ter•ri•fy /'tɛrə,fay/ v. [~ + obj], **-fied, -fy•ing.** to fill with terror: The horror movie terrified the child.

ter•ri•to•ri•al /,tɛrɪ'tɔriyəl/ adj. of or relating to territory or land: territorial claims.

ter•ri•to•ry /'tɛrɪ,tɔriy/ n., pl. **-ries. 1.** [noncount] an area of land, esp. with regard to its geographical features; terrain: mountainous territory. **2.** [noncount] [count] the land and waters belonging to a state, etc. **3.** [count; usually Territory] **a.** a region of the U.S. not yet a state but having its own legislature and governor. **b.** a similar district elsewhere, as in Canada. **4.** [noncount] [count] an area considered by a person, animal, group, etc., to belong to it alone.

ter•ror /'tɛrər/ n. **1.** [noncount] intense, sharp fear: She was filled with terror at the thought of death. **2.** [count] a person or thing that causes such fear: the terrors of the night. **3.** [noncount] violence or threats used as a means to force others to do something: the use of terror to achieve political aims. —**'ter•ror•ism,** n. [noncount] —**'ter•ror•ist,** adj., n. [count]: The terrorists used bombs to force their political demands on the people. —**'ter•ror•ize,** v. [~ + obj], **-ized, -iz•ing.**

ter•ry /'tɛriy/ n. [noncount] Also called **'terry ,cloth.** a fabric with tiny loops on its surface, often used for towels.

terse /tɜrs/ adj., **ters•er, ters•est.** using no extra words; brief: Her response was a terse rejection. —**'terse•ly,** adv. —**'terse•ness,** n. [noncount]

TESOL /'tiysɔl, 'tɛsɔl/ **1.** teaching English to speakers of other languages. **2.** Teachers of English to Speakers of Other Languages.

test /tɛst/ n. [count] **1.** a set of problems, questions, etc., for evaluating a person's abilities, skills, or performance: a driver's test. **2.** the means by which the presence, quality, or genuineness of anything is judged: a pregnancy test; a test of a new product. —v. **3.** to (cause someone to) undergo a test of any kind: [~ + obj]: The school has to test you on your writing ability. [no obj]: The hospital wants to test for diabetes.

tes•ta•ment /'tɛstəmənt/ n. [count] something that shows or proves the existence of something else; a proof: a testament to his hard work.

tes•ti•cle /'tɛstɪkəl/ n. [count] a testis.

train terminal

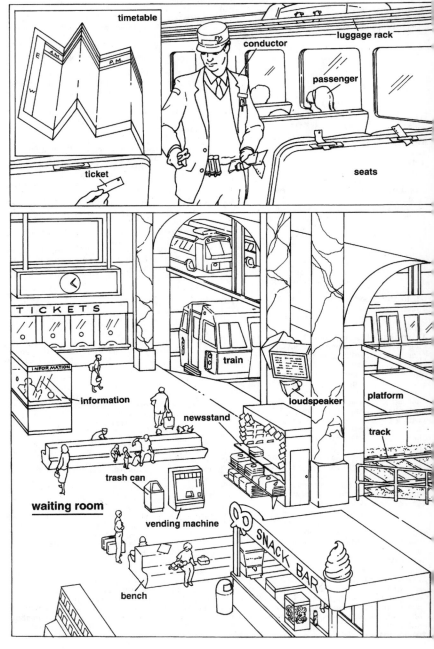

timetable

conductor

luggage rack

passenger

seats

ticket

TICKETS

INFORMATION

information

train

loudspeaker

platform

newsstand

track

trash can

waiting room

vending machine

bench

SNACK BAR

tes•ti•fy /'tɛstə,fay/ v., **-fied, -fy•ing. 1.** to state or declare something formally, usually in court: [no obj]: The witness was afraid to testify. [~ + obj]: She testified that she had seen him fleeing from the scene of the crime. **2.** [no obj] to give evidence about something: This excellent book testifies to the author's ability.

tes•ti•mo•ni•al /,tɛstə'mowniyəl/ n. [count] **1.** a formal written statement affirming a person's good character, conduct, etc.: a very favorable testimonial praising her excellent work. **2.** something given or done to express admiration: They gave her a testimonial at her retirement.

tes•ti•mo•ny /'tɛstə,mowniy/ n., pl. **-nies. 1.** [noncount] the sworn statement of a witness: The judge took testimony from the next witness. **2.** evidence that supports a fact or statement: [noncount]: an improvement that was testimony to his good judgment. [count]: a testimony to his good judgment.

tes•tis /'tɛstɪs/ n. [count], pl. **-tes** /-tiyz/. the male reproductive gland that produces sperm.

'test ,tube, n. [count] a thin glass tube for holding laboratory chemicals, specimens, etc.

tes•ty /'tɛstiy/ adj., **-ti•er, -ti•est.** irritable; impatient; touchy: a testy reply. **—tes•ti•ly** /'tɛstļiy/ , adv. **—'tes•ti•ness,** n. [noncount]

tet•a•nus /'tɛtnəs/ n. [noncount] a disease often resulting from a cut, in which muscles, esp. of the lower jaw and neck, become stiff.

teth•er /'tɛðər/ n. [count] **1.** a rope, etc., used to tie an animal so as to limit its range of movement. **—v.** [~ + obj] **2.** to tie or confine with or as if with a tether. **—Idiom. 3. at the end of one's tether,** at the limit of one's resources, patience, or strength: She's at the end of her tether and explodes with anger often.

text /tɛkst/ n. **1.** [noncount] the main body of matter in a manuscript, book, etc., as distinguished from headings, notes, appendixes, illustrations, etc: Did you look at the pictures or did you actually read the text? **2.** [count] the actual, original words of an author or speaker, as opposed to a summary or a translation: We could send away for a copy of the text of the interview. **3.** [count] a textbook: The texts haven't arrived for the class yet.

text•book /'tɛkst,bʊk/ n. [count] a book used by students in a particular branch of study.

tex•tile /'tɛkstayl, -tɪl/ n. [count] cloth or fabric produced by weaving, knitting, etc.

tex•ture /'tɛkstʃər/ n. [count] **1.** the characteristic physical structure of a material or an object: soil of a sandy texture. **2.** the appearance and feel of a textile fabric: wool of a coarse texture.

-th, a suffix used to form ordinal numbers (fourth).

Thai /tay/ n. **1.** [count] a person born or living in Thailand. **2.** [noncount] the language spoken in Thailand. **—adj. 3.** of or relating to Thailand. **4.** of or relating to the language spoken in Thailand.

than /ðæn, ðɛn; unstressed ðən, ən/ conj. **1.** (used after adjectives and adverbs and other words such as other, more, etc., to introduce the second part of a comparison): an increase of more than fifty dollars a week; The rabbit runs faster than the turtle. **2.** (used after some adverbs and adjectives such as other, otherwise, else, anywhere, different, etc., to introduce a choice or to name or show a difference): We had no choice other than to return home. I'd rather walk there than drive.

thank /θæŋk/ v. [~ + obj] **1.** to express grati-

tude to (someone): We thanked him for his generosity. **2.** to hold responsible: We have him to thank for this lawsuit. **—n.** [plural] **3. thanks,** an expression of gratitude for a kindness, etc.: Let us give thanks for this meal. **—interj. 4. thanks,** (used as a way of saying "I thank you.") **—Idiom. 5. Thank God** or **thank goodness,** (used to express relief or gratitude that a result is better than expected, or that harm or danger is avoided): Thank God we have our health. **6. thanks to,** because of; owing to; due to (sometimes used ironically): We were late thanks to the bad weather. **7. thank you,** (used as a common expression of gratitude, as for a gift or favor): She gave him a gift and he said, "Thank you." **—'thank•ful,** adj.: She was thankful for her job. **—'thank•ful•ly,** adv. **—'thank•less,** adj.: It was a hard and thankless job.

thanks•giv•ing /,θæŋks'gɪvɪŋ/ n. **1.** [noncount] the act of giving thanks. **2.** [count] an expression of thanks, esp. to God. **3.** a public celebration for giving thanks, esp. a holiday in the United States and Canada.

that /ðæt; unstressed ðət/ pron. and adj., pl. **those,** adv., conj. **—pron. 1.** (used to refer to a person or thing pointed out or present, mentioned before, or supposed to be understood by the speaker and the listener, or to give emphasis): That is her mother (= the woman we have just pointed to or spoken about). After that we never saw each other (= after some event we have just described,...). **2.** (used to indicate one of several people or things already mentioned, the one that is more distant or that is contrasted with another): This is my sister and that's my cousin (= The one next to me or near me is my sister, and the one farther away is my cousin). Here, I'll take this and you take that (= I'll take a particular one of the two, and you take the one near you or the other one). **3.** (used to introduce a relative clause, which defines or says something to pinpoint the person or thing referred to): We saw the house that collapsed. **—adj. 4.** (used before a noun to indicate a person, place, thing, or degree as indicated, mentioned before, present, well-known, or characteristic: That woman is her mother (= the one we were talking about). **5.** (used before one noun from a group to indicate the one more distant from the other or others already mentioned; in contrast with this): This room is his and that one is mine (= The one near us or near me is his, and the other one is mine). **6.** (used before a noun to indicate one of several people or things already mentioned and to imply that there is a contrast between the two; opposed to this): not this house, but that one. **—adv. 7.** (used with adjectives and adverbs of quantity or amount) to the extent or degree shown; so; as much as: Don't take that much (= Don't take as much as you have taken, or as much as my hand points to). **—conj. 8.** (used to introduce a clause that functions as the subject or object of the principal verb, and that gives necessary additional information as to cause, reason, purpose, etc.: I'm sure that you'll like it. I'm sorry that you were sick. She worked so quickly that she finished early. **—Idiom. 9. that is,** to speak more accurately: I read the book; that is, I read most of it. **10. that's that,** Informal. that's final; there is no more to be said or done: I'm not going, and that's that! **11. with that,** following that; thereupon: She said, "I quit!," and with that she left.

thaw /θɔ/ v. **1.** to change from a frozen to a liq-

T

uid or soft state: [*no obj*]: *The snow is thawing.*
[~ + *obj*]: *Use the microwave to thaw the meat.*
—*n.* [*count*] **2.** the act or process of thawing.

the¹ /stressed ðiy; *unstressed before a consonant*
ðə, *unstressed before a vowel* ðiy/ *definite article.*
1. (used before a noun that is known to both the
speaker and the listener, or that is about to be
made known by means of a clause which speci-
fies it or makes it definite): *Please close the window* (= *There is a window in the room that you
and I both know about, and it is open*). *Here is
the book you gave me* (= *Here is a book, and
now you know which one I mean*). *Come on into
the house for a drink* (= *We are standing near a
house, and we both know which house I am referring to*). **2.** (used before certain place names having the plural ending -*s*, or when the place name
is short for a longer name, or before certain other
place names that are well known): *the Alps; the
Mississippi* (= *short for the Mississippi River*); *the
Bronx* (= *a borough of New York City*). **3.** (used
to mark a noun as the best known, most approved, etc., of its kind): *Butternut Mountain was
considered the place to ski.* **4.** (used before a
count noun to indicate its generic sense, including all such examples of it): *The dog is a four-
legged animal* (= *All dogs are four-legged*). *The
tiger is a fierce animal* (= *All tigers are fierce*).
5. (used before certain adjectives to stand for a
class or number of individuals, or for an abstract
idea): *to visit the sick* (= *to visit sick people*);
Only the good die young (= *Only good people die
young*).

the² /*before a consonant* ðə; *before a vowel* ðiy/
adv. **1.** (used to modify an adjective or adverb
that means or has the meaning "more") on that
account or in some or any degree: *He's been on
vacation and looks the better for it.* **2.** (used before an adjective or adverb that means or has the
meaning "most"): *She is the tallest girl in her
class.*

the•a•ter or **thea•tre** /'θiyətər, 'θiyə-/ *n.* **1.**
[*count*] a building or an outdoor area for the
presentation of plays or motion pictures. **2.** [*noncount*] **a. the theater,** drama as a branch of art,
esp. as a profession. **b.** a particular type, style, or
category of this art: *Elizabethan theater.* **3.**
[*count*] an area of military operations: *He fought
in the Pacific theater in World War II.*

the•at•ri•cal /θiy'ætrɪkəl/ *adj.* Also, **the•at'ric.**
1. of or relating to the theater. **2.** suggestive of
the theater and therefore not real; artificial;
showy: *theatrical temper tantrums.*

theft /θɛft/ *n.* **1.** [*noncount*] the act of stealing;
larceny. **2.** [*count*] an instance of this.

their /ðɛər; *unstressed* ðər/ *pron.* (used before a
noun to indicate that the noun is possessed by,
owned by, or related in some way to a word that
can be replaced by THEY) of them; of the people
or things mentioned: *their home* (= *the home
owned by them*); *their rights as citizens* (= *the
rights they have as citizens*).

theirs /ðɛərz/ *pron.* **1.** (used after the verb *be* to
indicate that the subject is possessed by, owned
by, or related in some way to someone known or
mentioned): *Are you a friend of theirs? That car
is theirs.* **2.** (used to mean that the thing referred
to belongs to the people already mentioned or
understood): *Theirs is the white house on the corner.*

them /ðɛm; *unstressed* ðəm, əm/ *pron.* **1.** the
form of the pronoun THEY used as a direct or indirect object of a verb, or as the object of a prep-

osition: *We saw them yesterday. I gave them the
books. I ran toward them.* **2.** *Informal.* (sometimes used instead of the pronoun *they* after the
verb *to be*): *It's them, across the street. It isn't
them.*

theme /θiym/ *n.* [*count*] **1.** a subject of a talk, a
thought, or a piece of writing; topic: *He returned
to the theme of American values.* **2.** a short, informal essay, esp. a school composition.

them•selves /ðəm'sɛlvz, ˌðɛm-/ *pron.* [*plural*]
1. the reflexive form of the pronoun THEY, used
when the object of a verb or preposition names
the same noun as the subject: *The boys washed
themselves quickly.* **2.** (used to emphasize a plural noun): *The authors themselves left the theater.*
3. their normal or usual selves: *After a few hours'
rest, they were themselves again.*

then /ðɛn/ *adv.* **1.** at that time: *Prices were lower
then.* **2.** immediately or soon afterward: *The rain
stopped and then started again.* **3.** next in order
of time or place: *We ate, then we started home.*
4. since that is so; therefore: *If the car is out of
gas, then it won't start.* —*adj.* [*before a noun*] **5.**
existing or being at the time indicated: *In 1967,
the then prime minister visited the United States.*
—*n.* [*noncount*] **6.** that time: *We haven't been
back since then.*

thence /ðɛns/ *adv.* from that place: *I went to
Paris and thence to Rome.*

the•ol•o•gy /θiy'ɒlədʒiy/ *n., pl.* **-gies. 1.** [*noncount*] the study of religious beliefs; the study of
God (or gods). **2.** [*count*] a particular form or
branch of this study.

the•o•rem /'θiyərəm, 'θiərəm/ *n.* [*count*] *Math.*
a statement that can be shown to be true by the
use of other statements.

the•o•ret•i•cal /ˌθiyə'rɛtɪkəl/ *adj.* existing only
in theory; not practical. —,**the•o'ret•i•cal•ly,**
adv.

the•o•ry /'θiyəriy, 'θiəriy/ *n.* [*count*], *pl.* **-ries.**
1. a group or collection of general ideas held as
an explanation for certain facts or events: *Dar-
win's theory of evolution.* **2.** an explanation for
some fact or behavior claimed to be true but not
yet proven: *He has a theory about why so many
students have trouble with the word the in English.* —**Idiom. 3. in theory,** under normal
conditions; according to reasoning; theoretically:
In theory everyone has certain equal rights.

ther•a•py /'θɛrəpiy/ *n.* [*noncount*] **1.** the treatment of disease, injury, or disability by medical
or physical methods, as exercise or massage,
without the use of surgery: *physical therapy;
speech therapy.* **2.** PSYCHOTHERAPY. —,**ther•a'peu•
tic,** *adj.*: *a therapeutic drug.* —'**ther•a•pist,** *n.*
[*count*]

there /ðɛər; *unstressed* ðər/ *adv.* **1.** in, at, or to
that place (opposed to *here*): *Is there now.
We lived there* (= *in some place just mentioned
or otherwise understood*) *for about a year.* **2.** at
that point in an action, speech, etc.: *He stopped
there for applause.* **3.** (used, with some stress, to
call attention to something or someone): *There
they go. There's the man I saw.* —*pron.* **4.** (used
in place of a subject, and followed by the verb *be*
and some other verbs to indicate that something
exists): *There are two windows in this classroom.
There appears to be something wrong.* **5.** (used in
place of a name to address or greet a person):
Hello, there. —*n.* [*noncount*] **6.** that place or
point: *I come from there, too.* —*adj.* **7.** (used for
emphasis, esp. after a noun modified by a demonstrative adjective): *Ask that man there.*

—*interj.* **8.** (used to express satisfaction, relief, etc.): *There! It's done* (= *I'm glad it's done*). *There, there, don't cry* (= *I'm sorry you feel bad*). *There you go* (= *Well done!*). — *Usage.* When *there* is used as the subject (as in definition 6), the person or thing that exists is usually not definite and comes after the verb, while the verb (such as *be*) agrees with that person or thing. In such sentences, the word *there* carries very little stress and more attention is paid to what comes after it.

there•a•bout /'ðɛərə,bawt/ *also* **'there• a,bouts,** *adv.* near that place, time, or number, etc.; approximately there or then: *last June or thereabout.*

there•af•ter /,ðɛər'æftər, -'af-/ *adv.* after that in time or sequence; afterward; subsequently.

there•by /,ðɛər'bay, 'ðɛər,bay/ *adv.* by that; by means of that: *He started his lawn mower at dawn, thereby enraging the whole neighborhood.*

there•fore /'ðɛər,fɔr/ *adv.* as a result; for that reason; consequently: *The new computer has more memory and is therefore more costly than the old one.*

ther•mal /'θɜrməl/ *adj.* **1.** of, relating to, or caused by heat or temperature: *thermal energy.* **2.** designed to help retain body heat: *thermal underwear.*

ther•mom•e•ter /θər'mɒmɪtər/ *n.* [count] a device used for measuring temperature.

ther•mos /'θɜrməs/ *n.* [count] a container used for keeping liquids hot or cold. Also called **'ther• mos ,bot•tle.**

ther•mo•stat /'θɜrmə,stæt/ *n.* [count] a device that measures and also controls temperature: *The thermostat in the furnace didn't work properly.*

the•sau•rus /θɪ'sɔrəs/ *n.* [count], *pl.* **-sau• rus•es, -sau•ri** /-'sɔray/. a book that lists words similar in meaning and words opposite in meaning.

these /ðiyz/ *pron., adj.* pl. of THIS.

the•sis /'θiysɪs/ *n.* [count], *pl.* **-ses** /-siyz/. **1.** a statement for consideration, esp. one to be argued for or against: *The politician's thesis was that big government spent too much money wastefully.* **2.** a formal paper showing original research on a subject, esp. one written by a candidate for an advanced degree, as a master's degree.

they /ðey/ *pron. pl., poss.* **their** *or* **theirs,** *obj.* **them. 1.** (used when the speaker and the listener know the people or things the speaker is referring to) the plural of HE, SHE, and IT: *Do you see those two girls? They are staring at us.* **2.** (used to refer to people in general): *They say he's rich.* **3.** (used after a word or phrase like *anyone, someone, a person,* or *whoever* to refer back to that singular person without mentioning the sex of the person, in place of *he* or *she*): *Whoever is of voting age, whether they are interested in politics or not, should vote. Anyone who says they're not afraid of dying is lying.*

they'd /ðeyd/ **1.** contraction of *they would*: *They'd like to see you now.* **2.** contraction of *they had*: *They'd gone before we got there.*

they'll /ðeyl/ contraction of *they will*: *They'll probably be late.*

they've /ðeyv/ contraction of *they have*: *They've already left.*

thick /θɪk/ *adj. and adv.,* **-er, -est,** *n.* —*adj.* **1.** having a great distance between opposite surfaces or sides; not thin: *a thick slice of bread.* **2.** [*after a noun or phrase of measurement*] measured between opposite surfaces: *a board one inch*

thick. **3.** made up of objects close together; dense: difficult to see through: *The planes couldn't land in the thick fog.* **4.** easy to notice; obvious: *I have a thick Russian accent.* **5.** heavy; not easily poured: *thick soup.* **6.** mentally slow; stupid: *Sometimes he can be a little thick.* —*adv.* **7.** in a thick manner. —*n.* [*noncount*] **8.** the densest or most crowded part: *in the thick of the fight.* —*Idiom.* **9. through thick and thin,** under both good and bad conditions; faithfully: *They stayed friends through thick and thin.* —'**thick•en,** *v.* [~ + *obj*] [*no obj*] —'**thick•ly,** *adv.* —'**thick•ness,** *n.* [*noncount*]

thick•set /'θɪk'sɛt/ *adj.* heavily or solidly built; stocky: *a thickset wrestler.*

'thick-'skinned, *adj.* not easily offended by criticism.

thief /θiyf/ *n.* [*count*], *pl.* **thieves** /θiyvz/. one who steals secretly.

thieve /θiyv/ *v.* [*no obj*], **thieved, thiev•ing.** to steal. —'**thiev•er•y,** *n.* [*noncount*]

thigh /θay/ *n.* [*count*] the part of the leg between the hip and the knee.

thim•ble /'θɪmbəl/ *n.* [*count*] a cover for the fingertip to protect it when pushing a needle through cloth.

thin /θɪn/ *adj.,* **thin•ner, thin•nest,** *adv., v.,* **thinned, thin•ning.** —*adj.* **1.** having a small distance between opposite surfaces or sides; not thick: *a thin sheet of paper; a thin strip of cloth.* **2.** having little flesh; lean; not fat: *She had become thin after her hospital stay.* **3.** widely separated or scattered; sparse: *thin vegetation; hair getting thin on top.* **4.** easily poured; not dense: *thin soup.* **5.** lacking firmness, solidity, or volume; weak or insincere: *thin ice; a thin excuse; a thin smile.* —*adv.* **6.** in a thin manner. —*v.* **7.** to make thin or thinner: [~ + *obj*]: *Thin the gravy by adding more water.* [*no obj*]: *The gravy will thin if you add too much water to it.* He wants to *thin down before summer.* **8.** [*no obj*] to become lower in number or less: *The crowd thinned (out) as the rain poured down.* —'**thin•ly,** *adv.* —'**thin•ness,** *n.* [*noncount*]

thing /θɪŋ/ *n.* [*count*] **1.** an object, usually not a person or animal: *A noun is the name of a person, place, or thing.* **2.** anything that is an object of thought or discussion: *another thing I want to talk to you about.* **3. things,** matters; affairs in general: *How are things?* **4.** an achievement or accomplishment: *I expect great things from our team.* **5. things,** possessions that one owns: *Pack your things and leave!* **6.** a task; chore: *I've got things to do.* **7.** *Informal.* a special or strong attitude about something: *She has a thing about cats* (= *She likes/dislikes them*). *He has a thing for Irish music* (= *He likes it*). —*Idiom.* **8. do one's thing,** *Informal.* to follow a way of life that allows one to express oneself: *Let the kids do their own thing.*

think /θɪŋk/ *v.,* **thought** /θɔt/, **think•ing,** *n.* —*v.* **1.** [*no obj*] to use one's mind to decide or to judge (something) in a reasoning way: *Think carefully before you act.* **2.** to have a certain thing as the subject of one's thoughts: [*no obj*]: *I was thinking about college the other day.* [~ + *obj*]: *I was thinking that our college days were the best years of our lives. Think nice thoughts and go to sleep.* [*used with quotations*]: *"That's odd," Alice thought.* **3.** [~ + *obj*] to call something to one's conscious mind: *to think of others less fortunate than we are.* **4.** [~ + *obj*] to have a belief or opinion: *I think (that) she is funny.* **5.** [~ + *obj*]

T

to consider a person or thing as indicated: *I only think well of her. He thought me unkind. She thought him a total fool.* **6. think over,** to consider carefully before making a decision: *Think the deal over and call me. Think over her offer.* **7. think through** or **out,** to solve by thinking; come to a conclusion by thinking: *to think through a problem* or *to think a problem through.* **8. think up,** to invent; create: *I couldn't think up a better excuse; to think something up.* —*Idiom.* **9. think better of,** to change one's mind: *He was ready to yell at her, but then he thought better of it and kept quiet.* **10. think little** or **nothing of,** to believe (something) to be without value or importance: *He thinks nothing of bicycling 20 miles.* **11. think the world of,** to like or admire greatly: *Her father thinks the world of her.* **12. think twice,** to consider carefully before acting: *I urged him to think twice about going to Hanoi.* —'**think•er,** *n.* [count]

'**thin-'skinned,** *adj.* sensitive to criticism.

third /θɜrd/ *adj.* **1.** next after the second. **2.** being one of three equal parts. —*n.* [count] **3.** a third part, esp. of one (¹/₃): *Cut it into thirds.* **4.** the third member of a series. —*adv.* **5.** in the third place; thirdly.

'**third 'person,** *n.* [count; usually singular; usually: the + ~] the grammatical form used to indicate the person or thing spoken of: *The pronouns* he, she, it, *and* they *are in the third person.*

'**Third 'World,** *n.* [noncount; usually: the + ~; sometimes: third world] the underdeveloped or developing nations of Africa, Asia, and Latin America.

thirst /θɜrst/ *n.* **1.** a dry feeling caused by the need to drink (something): [count]: *He had developed quite a thirst after working in the hot sun all day.* [noncount]: *to quench thirst.* **2.** [count] an eager desire for something: *a thirst for knowledge.* —*v.* [~ + obj] **3.** to have a strong desire for something. —'**thirst•y,** *adj.,* -**i•er, -i•est.**

thir•teen /'θɜr'tiyn/ *n.* [count] **1.** a number, 10 plus 3, written as 13. —*adj.* [before a noun] **2.** amounting to 13 in number. —'**thir'teenth,** *adj.*

thir•ty /'θɜrtiy/ *n.,* pl. -**ties,** *adj.* —*n.* [count] **1.** a number, 10 times 3, written as 30. —*adj.* [before a noun] **2.** amounting to 30 in number. —'**thir•ti•eth,** *adj., n.* [count]

this /ðɪs/ *pron.* and *adj.,* pl. **these** /ðiyz/, *adv.* —*pron.* **1.** (used to refer to a person, thing, idea, or event present or near or just mentioned or understood, or to give emphasis): *This is my coat.* **2.** (used to refer to one of two or more persons, things, etc., pointing to the one that is nearer in place, time, or thought; opposed to *that*): *This is Liza and that is Amy.* **3.** (used to mean "what is about to follow," before some thing, action, or event): *Do it like this: Put a quarter in the slot and press the button.* —*adj.* **4.** (used before a noun to indicate presence, nearness, or identity): *This book is mine.* **5.** (used to indicate nearness in time, place, or thought; opposed to *that*): *This dress fits you better than that one.* **6.** (used to suggest a contrast; opposed to *that*): *this book, not that one.* —*adv.* **7.** (used with adjectives and adverbs of amount) as much as indicated: *We've come this far; why turn back now?*

thong /θɔŋ, θɒŋ/ *n.* [count] **1.** a narrow strip, esp. of animal hide, used for fastening something. **2.** a shoe or slipper held on the foot by a strip of leather between the first two toes.

thorn /θɔrn/ *n.* [count] a hard, sharp, pointed growth projecting from a plant: *Roses have thorns.* —'**thorn•y,** *adj.,* -**i•er, -i•est.**

thor•ough /'θɜrow, 'θʌrow/ *adj.* **1.** done or accomplished fully: *a thorough search.* **2.** careful as to accuracy and detail: *a thorough worker.* —'**thor•ough•ly,** *adv.* —'**thor•ough•ness,** *n.* [noncount]

thor•ough•bred /'θɜrow,brɛd, -ə,brɛd, 'θʌr-/ *n.* [count] a horse or other animal of pure breed.

thor•ough•fare /'θɜrow,fɛər, -ə,fɛər, 'θʌr-/ *n.* [count] a major road or highway.

those /ðowz/ *pron., adj.* pl. of THAT.

though /ðow/ *conj.* **1.** in spite of the fact that; although: *Though we tried hard, we lost the game.* —*adv.* **2.** however: *Though fast, he wasn't fast enough.*

thought[1] /θɔt/ *n.* **1.** [count] a single act or product of thinking; an idea: *to collect one's thoughts.* **2.** [noncount] the act or process of thinking; mental activity: *He was deep in thought and didn't hear me come in.* **3.** [noncount] consideration, attention, or care: *He gave no thought to his appearance.*

thought[2] /θɔt/ *v.* pt. and pp. of THINK.

thought•ful /'θɔtfəl/ *adj.* **1.** showing consideration or care for others; considerate: *How thoughtful of you to remember my birthday!* **2.** showing careful thought: *a thoughtful essay.* **3.** thinking a great deal: *a thoughtful mood.* —'**thought•ful•ly,** *adv.* —'**thought•ful•ness,** *n.* [noncount]

thought•less /'θɔtlɪs/ *adj.* **1.** lacking in or not showing care or consideration for others: *a thoughtless remark about her weight.* **2.** not thinking enough; careless: *He was thoughtless about his health.* —'**thought•less•ly,** *adv.*

thou•sand /'θawzənd/ *n., pl.* -**sands,** (as after a numeral) -**sand,** *adj.* —*n.* [count] **1.** a number, 10 times 100, written as 1000. —*adj.* **2.** amounting to 1000 in number. —'**thou•sandth,** *adj.*

thrash /θræʃ/ *v.* **1.** [~ + obj] to beat soundly; flog. **2.** [no obj] to move about wildly or violently: *She was thrashing around in bed, having a nightmare.* **3. thrash out,** to talk over thoroughly to reach a decision or understanding: *They decided to thrash out an agreement.*

thread /θrɛd/ *n.* **1.** a thin, fine cord of fiber spun out to great length: [noncount]: *I need some thread to sew a button back on.* [count]: *Some threads are coming off your sleeve.* **2.** [count] the raised line on the long part of a screw: *The threads had been stripped and the screw was useless.* **3.** [count] something that runs through the whole course of a thing, as a narrative, connecting parts in sequence: *I lost the thread of the story in all the confusion.* —*v.* **4.** [~ + obj] to put a thread through the eye of (a needle). **5.** [~ + obj] to fix or attach (beads, etc.) upon a thread; string. **6.** [~ + obj] to put (tape, etc.) through or into a narrow opening: *He threaded the film into the projector and started the movie.* **7.** to move past or around things or people blocking the way: [~ + obj]: *He threaded his way through the crowd.* [no obj]: *He threaded through the crowd.*

thread•bare /'θrɛd,bɛər/ *adj.* having the top surface, as of a fabric, worn away: *a threadbare jacket.*

threat /θrɛt/ *n.* **1.** a warning that someone intends to harm another: [count]: *Death threats were made against the witnesses.* [noncount]: *under threat of death.* **2.** [count] a person or thing that threatens (peace, safety, etc.).

threat•en /'θrɛtṇ/ *v.* **1.** [~ + obj] to make a

statement or promise that one will punish or harm (another): *The gangsters threatened him with the execution of his family if he didn't cooperate.* **2.** [~ + *obj*] to promise to inflict punishment or harm on someone: *They threatened swift retaliation if their demands were not met.* **3.** to be dangerous to: [~ + *obj*]: *to threaten one's peace of mind.* [*no obj*]: *We wondered what to do if danger threatened.* **4.** [~ + *obj*] to give a warning of (something bad or unfortunate): *The clouds threaten rain.*

three /θriy/ *n.* [*count*] **1.** a number, 2 plus 1, written as 3. —*adj.* [*before a noun*] **2.** amounting to three in number.

'three-di'mensional, *adj.* having, or seeming to have, depth, width, and height.

thresh /θrɛʃ/ *v.* to separate the grain from (a cereal plant), as by beating with a tool: [~ + *obj*]: *to thresh the wheat.* [*no obj*]: *They spent all day in the fields threshing.*

thresh•old /'θrɛʃowld, 'θrɛʃhowld/ *n.* [*count*] **1.** the bottom part of a doorway. **2.** any point of beginning: *He was on the threshold of a new career.*

threw /θruw/ *v.* pt. of THROW.

thrift /θrɪft/ *n.* [*noncount*] economical management of property. —'**thrift•y,** *adj.*, **-i•er, i•est.**

thrill /θrɪl/ *v.* **1.** to (cause to) feel a sudden wave of emotion or excitement: [~ + *obj*]: *The good news thrilled him.* [*no obj*]: *to thrill at the thought of Paris.* —*n.* [*count*] **2.** a sudden wave of strong emotion: *He felt a thrill go through him when she arrived.* **3.** something that produces such a sensation: *It's certainly a thrill to meet the president.* —'**thrill•er,** *n.* [*count*]: *a horror thriller.*

thrive /θrayv/ *v.* [*no obj*], **thrived** or **throve** /θrowv/, **thrived, thriv•ing. 1.** to prosper; be successful: *The business is thriving.* **2.** to grow or develop well: *The plants will thrive in such a climate. He thrives on challenges.*

throat /θrowt/ *n.* [*count*] **1.** the top of the passage from the mouth to the stomach and lungs: *I drank water to soothe my dry throat.* **2.** the front of the neck below the chin. —*Idiom.* **3. jump down someone's throat,** to attack suddenly and unexpectedly with words. **4. ram something down someone's throat,** to force someone to accept something.

throat•y /'θrowtiy/ *adj.*, **-i•er, -i•est.** (of sound) husky; hoarse.

throb /θrɒb/ *v.*, **throbbed, throb•bing,** *n.* —*v.* [*no obj*] **1.** to pound, pulse, or beat with increased force or speed, as the heart does when one feels emotion. —*n.* [*count*] **2.** a violent beat, as of the heart.

throne /θrown/ *n.* [*count*] **1.** the chair used by a king or queen. **2.** the rank or office of a king or queen: *to assume the throne.*

throng /θrɔŋ, θrɒŋ/ *n.* [*count*] **1.** a great crowd of people: *A throng of people surrounded the Pope.* —*v.* **2.** [*no obj*] to assemble in large numbers; crowd: *A huge crowd thronged outside to see the accident.* **3.** [~ + *obj*] to fill with a crowd: *The protesters thronged the hallways.*

throt•tle /'θrɒtl/ *n.*, *v.*, **-tled, -tling.** —*n.* [*count*] **1.** the valve that controls the amount of fuel entering an engine. —*v.* [~ + *obj*] **2.** to choke (someone) by squeezing the throat; strangle.

through /θruw/ *prep.* **1.** in at one end, side, or surface and out at the other: *to pass through a tunnel.* **2.** past; beyond: *She drove through a red light.* **3.** from one to the other of: *monkeys swing-*ing through the trees. **4.** throughout: *We worked through the night.* **5.** done with: *What time are you through work?* **6.** to and including: *He lived there from 1935 through 1950.* **7.** by means of: *I found out through him.* **8.** from the first to the final stage of: *Somehow he managed to get through the performance.* —*adv.* **9.** in at one end, side, or surface and out at the other: *to push a needle through.* **10.** all the way: *This train goes through to Boston.* **11.** throughout; completely: *She was soaked through.* **12.** from beginning to end: *I read the letter all the way through.* —*adj.* **13.** [be + ~] finished, completed, as of an action: *Please be quiet until I'm through.* **14.** [*before a noun*] proceeding to a destination, etc., without a change, break, or turning away: *a through flight.*

through•out /θruw'awt/ *prep.* **1.** in, to, or during every part of: *I looked throughout the house for the book.* —*adv.* **2.** in every part or during the whole period of time: *The apple is rotten throughout.*

throw /θrow/ *v.*, **threw** /θruw/, **thrown** /θrown/, **throw•ing,** *n.* —*v.* **1.** to propel from the hand: [~ + *obj*]: *She threw the ball (to me). She threw me the ball.* [*no obj*]: *The pitcher's arm hurt so much he could hardly throw.* **2.** [~ + *obj*] to move (a part of the body) suddenly, as in reaction to an emotion: *He threw up his hands in despair.* **3.** [~ + *obj*] to direct or send forth: *Soon they were throwing angry insults at each other. He threw her a dirty look.* **4.** [~ + *obj*] to put into some place or state forcefully: *The explosion threw him to the floor.* **5.** [~ + *obj*] to cause to fall off: *The horse threw him.* **6.** [~ + *obj*] to give or host: *We threw a big party (for them); to throw them a big party.* **7.** [~ + *obj*] to amaze or confuse: *His answer really threw me.* **8. throw away, a.** to dispose of; get rid of; discard: *to throw away the garbage; Throw that junk away!* **b.** to waste (something, as time, value, or potential): *Why throw your money away on a bad car? Why throw away your money?* **9. throw in,** to add (something extra) as a bonus: *The car dealer promised to throw in new seat covers. They threw meals in for the cost of the hotel room.* **10. throw off,** to free oneself of; cast aside: *He had some trouble throwing off that uneasy feeling; to throw her clothes off.* **11. throw out, a.** to discard; reject: *We threw out your letter. We threw it out.* **b.** to remove from a place, esp. with or as if with force; to remove from (a club, organization, etc.): *The Democrats voted to throw him out of the party. The security guards threw out anyone without a pass.* **12. throw together,** to make or produce hurriedly and not carefully: *He threw together a quick meal; to throw a meal together.* **13. throw up,** to vomit: *Suddenly she grabbed her stomach and threw up. She threw up her lunch.* —*n.* [*count*] **14.** an act or instance of throwing. —*Idiom.* **15. throw in the towel (or the sponge),** to admit defeat; give up: *He threw in the towel and telephoned his opponent to congratulate her.* **16. throw oneself at,** to try hard to attract the affections of: *He threw himself at his teacher every chance he got.* **17. throw oneself into,** to do (something) with enthusiasm: *After the death of his wife, he threw himself into his work.*

thru /θruw/ *prep.*, *adv.*, *adj.* an informal, simplified spelling of THROUGH.

thrush /θrʌʃ/ *n.* [*count*] a usually dull-colored songbird found in most parts of the world.

thrust /θrʌst/ *v.*, **thrust, thrust•ing,** *n.* **1.** to push forcefully; shove: [~ + *obj*]: *He thrust his*

T

way through the crowd. [no obj]: *She thrust through the crowd until she was next to him.* —n. **2.** [count] an act or instance of thrusting; a sudden forward drive or stab, as with a sword. **3.** [noncount] a force produced by a propeller, etc., to move a missile, ship, etc.: *The ice-coated engine failed to develop enough thrust.* **4.** [count; usually singular] the main point: *the thrust of his argument.*

thru•way /'θruw,wey/ n. [count] a wide principal highway or expressway bearing high-speed automobile traffic over long distances.

thud /θʌd/ n., v., **thud•ded, thud•ding.** —n. [count] **1.** a dull sound, as of a heavy object hitting or falling on a surface. —v. [no obj] **2.** to strike or fall with a thud.

thug /θʌg/ n. [count] a vicious or violent criminal.

thumb /θʌm/ n. [count] **1.** the short, thick, inner finger of the hand, next to the forefinger and set apart from the other four. —v. [~ + obj] **2.** to turn through pages quickly: *She thumbed through the magazine.* **3.** (of a hitchhiker) to ask for a ride by signaling with the thumb to oncoming drivers: *to thumb a ride.* —**Idiom. 4. be all thumbs,** to be very awkward or clumsy: *When it comes to car repairs he's all thumbs.*

thumb•nail /'θʌm,neyl/ n. [count] the nail of the thumb.

thumb•tack /'θʌm,tæk/ n. [count] a short nail or pin with a large, flat head, to be pushed into a board by the pressure of the thumb.

thump /θʌmp/ n. [count] **1.** a blow with a heavy object. **2.** the dull, heavy, blunt sound made by or as if by such a blow. —v. **3.** [~ + obj] to (cause to) be struck with a heavy object, so as to produce a dull sound: *He thumped the side of the barrel.* **4.** [no obj] to beat or pulse violently, making a loud noise, as the heart.

thun•der /'θʌndər/ n. [noncount] **1.** a loud, rolling noise following a flash of lightning. **2.** any loud, resounding noise: *a thunder of applause.* —v. [no obj] **3.** to produce thunder: *It thundered all night.* **4.** to make a loud, rolling, rumbling noise like thunder: *Cannons thundered in the hills.* **5.** to speak intensely at a loud volume; shout: [used with quotations]: *"Watch out,"* the boss thundered about the company's losses. *the officer thundered, "get out of here now!"* —'**thun• der•ous,** adj.: *thunderous applause.*

thun•der•bolt /'θʌndər,bowlt/ n. [count] a flash of lightning followed by thunder.

thun•der•clap /'θʌndər,klæp/ n. [count] a crash of thunder.

thun•der•storm /'θʌndər,stɔrm/ n. [count] an intense, usually brief storm with lightning and thunder.

Thurs., an abbreviation of: Thursday.

Thurs•day /'θɜrzdey, -diy/ n. the fifth day of the week, following Wednesday: *I'll meet you on Thursday.* [count]: *Thursdays we have sales meetings.*

thus /ðʌs/ adv. **1.** in the way just indicated; in this way: *Managed thus, the business will succeed.* **2.** accordingly; as a result; for this reason: *Your interest rates will go down; thus, you'll save money.* **3.** to this extent or degree: *thus far.* **4.** as an example; for instance.

thwart /θwɔrt/ v. [~ + obj] to oppose successfully: *The general thwarted his opponent by making a brilliant defense of his city.*

'thy•roid ,gland, n. [count] a gland at the base

of the neck that secretes hormones regulating metabolism and growth.

tic /tɪk/ n. [count] a sudden, unconscious muscular movement, as of the face: *a nervous tic.*

tick¹ /tɪk/ n. [count] **1.** a slight, sharp click or beat, as of a clock. **2.** a small dot or mark used to check off items on a list. —v. **3.** [no obj] to make the sound of a tick, like that of a clock: *The clock ticked loudly.* **4.** [~ + obj] to sound or announce by a tick or ticks: *The clock ticked the minutes.* **5.** [~ + obj] to mark with a tick; check: *to tick off the items.* **6. tick off,** Slang. to make angry: *His bullying really ticked me off. He managed to tick off everyone in the office.* —**Idiom. 7. what makes one tick,** one's basic motives, needs, etc.

tick² /tɪk/ n. [count] a bloodsucking insectlike creature, related to but larger than a mite.

tick•et /'tɪkɪt/ n. [count] **1.** a printed piece of paper or cardboard showing that the holder has paid to ride, enter, or obtain some service: *a train ticket.* **2.** an official written notice of a traffic violation: *his fifth ticket for speeding.* **3.** a tag attached to something to show its price, contents, or owner. **4.** a list of people from one political party who are candidates in an election: *He voted a straight Democratic ticket.* —v. [~ + obj] **5.** to attach or give a ticket to.

tick•le /'tɪkəl/ v., **-led, -ling,** n. —v. **1.** [~ + obj] to touch or stroke part of the body lightly, esp. so as to cause laughter. **2.** [no obj] to have or be affected with such a sensation: *The hairs on his face tickled.* **3.** [~ + obj] to amuse or delight: *The clown's antics tickled the kids.* —n. [count] **4.** an act or feeling of tickling.

tick•lish /'tɪklɪʃ/ adj. **1.** sensitive to tickling: *She was very ticklish on the soles of her feet.* **2.** calling for or needing delicate, careful handling: *a ticklish situation.*

tick-tack-toe or **tic-tac-toe** /,tɪktæk'tow/ n. [noncount] a simple game played on a surface divided into nine squares, with one player marking X's and the other one marking O's, toward a goal of completing a row of three squares.

tid•bit /'tɪd,bɪt/ n. [count] **1.** a delicate bit of food. **2.** an esp. pleasing or interesting bit of anything, as gossip: *Here's a little tidbit: The boss and the secretary are dating.*

tide /tayd/ n., v., **tid•ed, tid•ing.** —n. **1.** the regularly occurring rise and fall of the waters of the ocean: [count]: *a study of the periods of the tides.* [noncount]: *at high tide.* **2.** [count] anything that increases and decreases: *the tides of unemployment.* —v. **3. tide over,** to help in getting over or through a difficult period: *This money will tide you over until you get a new job.* —'**tid•al,** adj.

ti•dy /'taydiy/ adj., **-di•er, -di•est,** v., **-died, -dy• ing.** —adj. **1.** neat and orderly, as in appearance or dress: *a tidy bedroom.* **2.** [usually: before a noun] fairly large in amount: *That car must have cost you a tidy sum.* —v. **3.** to make tidy: [no obj]: *I'll just tidy up a little before I go.* [~ + obj]: *He tidied (up) the office before he left.* —'**ti• di•ness,** n. [noncount]

tie /tay/ v., **tied, ty•ing,** n. —v. **1.** [~ + obj] to bind or fasten with a cord, etc.: *to tie a bundle.* **2.** to fasten by tightening and knotting (the strings or ends of): [~ + obj]: *He stopped to tie his shoes.* [no obj]: *Her dress tied in the back.* **3.** [~ + obj] to bind or join firmly: *Great affection tied them.* **4.** [~ + obj] to confine or restrict: *The weather tied us to the house.* **5.** to make the same score (as another); be equal (to) in a con-

test: [*no obj*]: *The two teams tied and had to play an extra period.* [~ + *obj*]: *Suddenly the other team tied the score.* **6. tie down,** to restrict the freedom or actions of (someone); confine: *The desk job ties him down; to tie down his workers.* **7. tie up, a.** to secure by binding with rope or cord so as to restrict movement: *The hijackers tied up all the hostages. They tied them up.* **b.** to hinder or bring to a stop; impede: *The accident tied up traffic.* **c.** to occupy or use (something) to such an extent that it is unavailable to others: *She tied up the phone all morning.* **d.** to be completely occupied with something: *The boss is tied up till noon.* —*n.* [*count*] **8.** a cord, string, or the like, used for tying, fastening, or wrapping something. **9.** a necktie: *Your tie is crooked.* **10.** a bond, as of affection: *family ties.* **11.** a state in which the same number of points has been scored, etc., among competitors; also, a competition that ends in such a state: *The game ended in a tie.*

tier /'tɪər/ *n.* [*count*] one of a series of rows that rise one behind or above another, as of seats in a theater.

ti•ger /'taygər/ *n.* [*count*], *pl.* **-gers,** (*esp. when thought of as a group*) **-ger.** a large, powerful, brownish-orange cat with black stripes.

tight /tayt/ *adj.* and *adv.,* **-er, -est.** —*adj.* **1.** firmly fixed in place; secure: *a tight knot.* **2.** drawn or stretched tense: *tight muscles.* **3.** fitting closely, esp. too closely: *This tight collar is choking me.* **4.** allowing little space, time, etc., between parts; full: *a tight schedule.* **5.** nearly even; close: *a tight race.* **6.** not generous with money: *a tight boss who never gives raises.* **7.** *Slang.* drunk; tipsy. —*adv.* **8.** in a tight manner: *Shut the door tight.* **9.** soundly or deeply: *to sleep tight.* —'**tight•en,** *v.* [~ + *obj*]: *He could feel his chest tighten with anxiety.* [*no obj*]: *to tighten rules regarding immigration.* —'**tight•ly,** *adv.*: *The dress fit too tightly.* —'**tight•ness,** *n.* [*noncount*]: *He complained of tightness in his chest.*

tight•rope /'tayt,rowp/ *n.* [*count*] a cable, stretched tight, on which acrobats balance.

tights /tayts/ *n.* [*plural*] a skintight garment that covers the lower part of the body, from the waist to the ankles; a similar garment that covers the feet as well.

tile /tayl/ *n., v.,* **tiled, til•ing.** —*n.* [*count*] **1.** a piece of baked clay used in forming covering for roofs, walls, etc.: *cracked and dirty tiles on the wall.* —*v.* [~ + *obj*] **2.** to cover with or as if with tiles: *a tiled roof.*

till[1] /tɪl/ *prep.* **1.** up to the time of; until: *to fight till death.* **2.** (used with a negative word or phrase) before; until: *They didn't come till today.* **3.** before; to: *My watch says ten till four.* —*conj.* **4.** until: *Till we meet again, I'll be thinking of you.* —*Usage.* TILL and UNTIL are used interchangeably in speech and writing: *It rained till (or until) nearly midnight.* TILL is not a shortened form of UNTIL and is not spelled '*till.* 'TIL is usually considered a spelling error, though commonly used in business and advertising: *Open 'til ten.*

till[2] /tɪl/ *v.* [~ + *obj*] to work on (land), as by plowing; to raise crops; cultivate.

tilt /tɪlt/ *v.* **1.** to (cause to) lean, slant, or incline: [*no obj*]: *The room tilted during the earthquake.* [~ + *obj*]: *He tilted his head to one side.* —*n.* [*count*] **2.** an act or instance of tilting. **3.** the state of being tilted; a sloping position.

tim•ber /'tɪmbər/ *n.* **1.** [*noncount*] the wood of

trees used for construction. **2.** [*count*] a single piece of wood forming part of a structure: *A timber fell from the roof.*

time /taym/ *n., v.,* **timed, tim•ing.** —*n.* **1.** [*noncount*] a relational system in which events, following from one to another, can be measured; the passing of minutes, hours, days, or years: *Einstein's conception of time.* **2.** [*noncount*] a system of measuring the passage of time: *six o'clock Greenwich Mean Time.* **3.** [*count*] a limited period, as between two events: *a long time.* **4.** Often, **times.** [*plural*] a period in history, esp. one covering the same years as (the life of) a famous person: [*count*]: *prehistoric times.* [*noncount*]: *in Lincoln's time.* **b.** [*count*] a period identified with reference to its conditions: *hard times.* **5.** [*count*] a period experienced in a particular way: *Have a good time.* **6.** [*noncount*] *Informal.* a term of forced duty or imprisonment: *She had to do time for her crime.* **7.** a definite point in time: [*noncount*]: *breakfast time.* [*count*]: *at evening times.* **8.** [*count*] each occasion or instance of a repeated action: *to do something five times.* **9. times,** [*plural*] the number of instances a quantity or factor are taken together: *Two goes into six three times.* **10.** [*noncount*] *Music.* **a.** tempo; the speed of movement in a piece of music; its meter or rhythm. **b.** proper rhythm or tempo: *The drummer couldn't keep time.* See *keep time* below. —*v.* [~ + *obj*] **11.** to measure or record the speed or rate of: *The judges timed the race.* **12.** to choose the moment or occasion for: *He timed the attack perfectly.* —*Idiom.* **13. ahead of one's time,** in advance of others in one's thinking, etc.: *Those ancient astronomers were way ahead of their time.* **14. ahead of time,** before the time due; early: *We arrived ahead of time and had to wait.* **15. at one time,** once; formerly: *At one time she was the chairman of the board.* **16. at the same time,** nevertheless; yet: *He's young; at the same time, he's quite responsible.* **17. at times,** occasionally: *The car seems to stall at times.* **18. behind the times,** old-fashioned; out-of-date: *She complained that her father's taste in music was behind the times.* **19. for the time being,** temporarily; for now; for a while: *For the time being we'll let you stay on the job.* **20. from time to time,** occasionally: *From time to time she'd let me watch as she painted.* **21. in no time,** in a very brief time: *She was ready to go in no time.* **22. in time, a.** early enough: *Come in time for dinner.* **b.** in the future; eventually: *In time he'll understand.* **c.** in the correct rhythm or tempo: *The drummer isn't in time.* **23. keep time, a.** to record time, as a watch does: *Does your watch keep good time?* **b.** to mark the correct tempo, as with rhythmic movements. **24. kill time,** to busy oneself to make time seem to pass more quickly: *He killed time by watching TV.* **25. make time,** to move or travel quickly: *We made very good time on the highway.* **26. on time,** at the specified time: *For once the train was on time.* **27. take one's time,** to act without hurry. **28. the time of one's life,** a very enjoyable experience: *We had the time of our lives at the seashore.* **29. time after time,** again and again; repeatedly: *Time after time he'd try to get over the wall.* **30. time and (time) again,** often.

'**time-,honored,** *adj.* respected because for a long time it has been done this way: *a time-honored custom.* Also, *esp. Brit.,* '**time-,honoured.**

time•less /'taymlɪs/ *adj.* **1.** without beginning or

end; eternal. **2.** referring or restricted to no particular time: *timeless beauty.*

time•ly /'taymliy/ *adj.,* **-li•er, -li•est.** occurring at a good time: *a timely warning.*

time•piece /'taym,piys/ *n.* [*count*] a device for measuring and recording the progress of time, as a clock.

tim•er, *n.* [*count*] **1.** a device that measures the passage of time. **2.** a device that gives a signal or causes something to happen at a set time: *The timer turned the lights on and off while we were on vacation.*

time•ta•ble /'taym,teybəl/ *n.* [*count*] a list of times at which railroad trains, etc., are set to arrive and depart.

'time ,zone, *n.* [*count*] one of the 24 regions of the earth where time is said to be ahead or behind a standard hour set at Greenwich, England.

tim•id /'tɪmɪd/ *adj.,* **-er, -est.** lacking in boldness: *a timid child.* —**ti•mid•i•ty** /tɪ'mɪdɪtiy/, *n.* [*noncount*] —**'tim•id•ly,** *adv.*

tin /tɪn/ *n., adj., v.,* **tinned, tin•ning.** —*n.* **1.** [*noncount*] a metal element with a silvery color: *Tin is used in alloys.* **2.** [*count*] any container made of or plated with tin. **3.** [*count*] *Chiefly Brit.* a sealed can containing food: *tins of soup.*

tin•der /'tɪndər/ *n.* [*noncount*] any dry material that burns easily, esp. such a substance used in starting fires.

tinge /tɪndʒ/ *v.,* **tinged, tinge•ing** or **ting•ing,** *n.* —*v.* [~ + *obj*] **1.** to give a slight degree of color to; tint: *walls tinged with brown from the rusty pipes.* **2.** to give a slight trace of (some) feeling or emotion to: *praise tinged with envy.* —*n.* [*count*] **3.** a slight trace, as of coloring.

tin•gle /'tɪŋgəl/ *v.,* **-gled, -gling,** *n.* —*v.* [*no obj*] **1.** to have a slight stinging sensation on the skin, as if from cold or from a slap: *His arm tingled when he hit his elbow.* —*n.* [*count*] **2.** the tingling action of cold, excitement, etc. —**tin•gly** /'tɪŋgliy/, *adj.,* **-gli•er, -gli•est:** *He gets a tingly feeling when she walks in the room.*

tin•ker /'tɪŋkər/ *n.* [*count*] **1.** a person who travels from place to place working at mending pots and pans. —*v.* [*no obj*] **2.** to spend time aimlessly and uselessly fixing or adjusting something: *She likes to tinker with the car.* —**'tin•ker•er,** *n.* [*count*]

tin•kle /'tɪŋkəl/ *v.,* **-kled, -kling,** *n.* —*v.* **1.** to (cause to) make light ringing sounds, as a small bell: [*no obj*]: *A bell tinkled in the background.* [~ + *obj*]: *He tinkled the bell.* —*n.* [*count*] **2.** a tinkling sound. **3.** an instance of tinkling.

tin•ny /'tɪniy/ *adj.,* **-ni•er, -ni•est. 1.** of or like tin; containing tin. **2.** lacking in a deep or solid sound: *a tinny piano.*

tin•sel /'tɪnsəl/ *n.* [*noncount*] a thin sheet or thread of shiny, glittering metal, used to produce a sparkling effect in threads and decorations: *hanging pieces of tinsel on the Christmas tree.*

tint /tɪnt/ *n.* [*count*] **1.** a variety of a color; a hue. **2.** a delicate or pale color. —*v.* [~ + *obj*] **3.** to color slightly; tinge: *He tinted his hair light brown.*

ti•ny /'tayniy/ *adj.,* **-ni•er, -ni•est.** very small; little: *a doll house with tiny chairs and tables.* —**'ti•ni•ness,** *n.* [*noncount*]

-tion, a suffix meaning: action or process (*convention*); result of action (*reflection*); state or condition (*affliction*).

-tious, a suffix added to roots to form adjectives, some of which are related to nouns, as in: *fiction: fictitious; ambition: ambitious.*

tip¹ /tɪp/ *n., v.,* **tipped, tip•ping.** —*n.* [*count*] **1.** a pointed end: *the tips of the fingers.* **2.** the top; apex: *the tip of a steeple.* **3.** a small piece covering the end of something: *a cane with a rubber tip.* —*v.* [~ + *obj*] **4.** to mark the tip of.

tip² /tɪp/ *v.,* **tipped, tip•ping,** *n.* —*v.* **1.** to (cause to) be in a slanting position; tilt: [*no obj*]: *The whole room tipped as the earthquake rocked the region.* [~ + *obj*]: *He tipped his hat in greeting.* **2.** to overturn; upset: [~ + *obj*]: *to tip the basket (over); He tipped (over) the basket.* [*no obj*]: *The lamp tipped (over).* —*n.* [*count*] **3.** the act of tipping. **4.** the state of being tipped.

tip³ /tɪp/ *n., v.,* **tipped, tip•ping.** —*n.* [*count*] **1.** a voluntary payment for a service; a gratuity: *a tip for the waiter.* **2.** a useful hint or idea: *tips on gardening.* —*v.* **3.** to give a voluntary payment for a service: [~ + *obj*]: *tipping a waiter.* [*no obj*]: *She tipped generously.* **4. tip off,** to give secret information: *Someone must have tipped off the cops. Someone must have tipped him off.* —**'tip•per,** *n.* [*count*]: *She's not a big tipper.*

tip•sy /'tɪpsiy/ *adj.,* **-si•er, -si•est.** slightly drunk.

tip•toe /'tɪp,tow/ *n., v.,* **-toed, -toe•ing.** —*n.* **1.** the tip or end of a toe: [*count*]: *She stood on her tiptoes.* [*noncount*]: *She walked in on tiptoe.* —*v.* [*no obj*] **2.** to go on tiptoe, so as to be quiet or to remain unnoticed: *I tiptoed into the room while he was sleeping.*

tire¹ /tayᵊr/ *v.,* **tired, tir•ing. 1.** to make or become weary or fatigued: [~ + *obj*]: *The exercise tired him.* [*no obj*]: *As he grew older he tired easily.* **2.** [*no obj*] to have one's interest or patience exhausted: *The children tired of playing games.* **3.** tire out, to make (someone) completely weary: *The exercise tired him out.* —**'tire•some,** *adj.:* *a tiresome person who talks too much.*

tire² /tayᵊr/ *n.* [*count*] a ring of rubber over the rim of a wheel on cars, trucks, etc.

tired /tayᵊrd/ *adj.* **1.** needing sleep or rest; weary: *I'm too tired to go to the movies.* **2.** bored with or annoyed with: *I'm tired of this stupid TV show.*

tis•sue /'tɪʃuw/ *n.* **1.** a group of cells forming a structural part of a living thing: [*noncount*]: *living tissue; soft tissue.* [*count*]: *The virus invaded the body's tissues.* **2.** tissue paper. **3.** soft paper used for various purposes: [*noncount*]: *toilet tissue.* [*count*]: *He took a tissue and wiped his nose.* **4.** [*count*] a connected series or mass: *a tissue of lies.*

'tissue ,paper, *n.* [*noncount*] very thin paper used for wrapping, packing, etc.

tit for tat /'tɪt fər tæt/ *n.* [*noncount*] the countering of an offense with a matching response.

tit•il•late /'tɪtl,eyt/ *v.* [~ + *obj*], **-lat•ed, -lat•ing.** to excite agreeably or pleasantly: *to titillate one's curiosity.*

ti•tle /'taytl/ *n., v.,* **-tled, -tling.** —*n.* **1.** [*count*] the name of a work, as a book, play, painting, etc. **2.** [*count*] a name describing rank or office: *He was given the title of "Lord Mayor."* **3.** [*count*] a championship: *to win a tennis title.* **4.** [*noncount*] an established right to something, as to (possessing) land or property: *He has title to the farm his parents owned.* —*v.* [~ + *obj*] **5.** to furnish with a title; entitle: *What will you title your book?*

tit•ter /'tɪtər/ *v.* [*no obj*] **1.** to giggle or laugh in a silly or nervous way: *At first the audience tittered at his jokes.* —*n.* [*count*] **2.** a tittering laugh.

TM, an abbreviation of: trademark.

TN, an abbreviation of: Tennessee.

TNT, *n.* [*noncount*] a chemical substance that is a strong explosive.

to /tuw; *unstressed* tʊ, tə/ *prep.* **1.** (used to express motion or direction toward a place, person, or thing approached and reached): *Come to the house.* **2.** (used to express motion in a direction): *from north to south.* **3.** (used to express an extent of movement or growth): *He grew to six feet.* **4.** (used to express the destination of a journey or process): *He was sentenced to jail.* **5.** (used to express a resulting condition): *He tore it to pieces.* **6.** (used to express the object of hope): *They drank to her health.* **7.** compared with: *This year's harvest is inferior to last year's.* **8.** in accordance with: *They promised us a room to our liking.* **9.** with respect to; with reference to: *What will he say to this?* **10.** (used to introduce the indirect object of a verb): *Give it to me. Show the book to the girl.* **11.** (used as the ordinary marker of the infinitive): *They left early (in order) to catch their flight. It's too late to try calling now.* —*adv.* **12.** toward a point, person, place, or thing. **13.** into a state of consciousness: *After he came to, he remembered everything.* —*Idiom.* **14. to and fro,** back and forth: *trees swaying to and fro in the wind.*

toad /towd/ *n.* [*count*] an animal like a frog, living mostly on land and having short legs and a rough, dry, warty skin. Compare FROG.

toad•stool /'towd,stuwl/ *n.* [*count*] a kind of mushroom with an umbrellalike cap.

toast¹ /towst/ *n.* [*noncount*] **1.** sliced bread browned by dry heat. —*v.* **2.** (of bread, etc.) to (cause to) become brown by means of dry heat: [~ + *obj*]: *to toast a few slices of bread.* [*no obj*]: *This bread doesn't toast well.* **3.** [~ + *obj*] to heat or warm thoroughly at a fire, as one's hands or feet.

toast² /towst/ *n.* [*count*] **1.** a few words of welcome, congratulations, etc., said just before drinking (usually, an alcoholic beverage) to honor a person, event, etc.: *I propose a toast to all our good friends gathered here tonight.* **2.** a person, event, etc., honored with raised glasses before drinking. —*v.* [~ + *obj*] **3.** to propose or drink a toast to or in honor of: *They toasted the newlyweds.*

toast•er /'towstər/ *n.* [*count*] an appliance for toasting bread, muffins, etc.

toast•y /'towstiy/ *adj.*, **-i•er, -i•est.** cozily warm: *She hopped back into her toasty bed.*

to•bac•co /tə'bækow/ *n.*, *pl.* **-cos, -coes. 1.** [*noncount*] a plant whose leaves are prepared for smoking or chewing or as snuff. **2.** [*noncount*] [*count*] the prepared leaves of this plant, as used in cigarettes, cigars, and pipes.

to•bog•gan /tə'bɒgən/ *n.* [*count*] **1.** a long, narrow, flat-bottomed sled curved up at one end. —*v.* [*no obj*] **2.** to coast or ride on a toboggan.

to•day /tə'dey/ *n.* [*noncount*] **1.** this present day: *What's today? Today is Thursday.* **2.** this present age: *the songs of today.* —*adv.* **3.** on this present day: *Call me today.* **4.** at the present time; in these days: *There are many changes in offices today.*

tod•dle /'tɒdl/ *v.* [*no obj*], **-dled, -dling.** to move with short, unsteady steps, as a young child learning to walk. —'**tod•dler,** *n.* [*count*]

toe /tow/ *n.*, *v.*, **toed, toe•ing.** —*n.* [*count*] **1.** one of the five fingerlike parts at the end of the foot. —*Idiom.* **2. on one's toes,** alert; ready:

Competition will keep you on your toes. **3. step on someone's toes,** to offend a person by intruding on his or her rights or responsibilities. **4. toe the line,** to follow a rule; obey orders: *You'll have to toe the line with the new boss.*

TOEFL /'towfəl/ Test of English as a Foreign Language.

toe•nail /'tow,neyl/ *n.* [*count*] the nail of a toe.

tof•fee /'tɔfiy, 'tɒfiy/ *n.* [*noncount*] [*count*], *pl.* **-fees** or **-fies.** a brittle candy made by boiling brown sugar, butter, and vinegar.

to•fu /'towfuw/ *n.* [*noncount*] a soft, cheeselike food made from curdled soybean milk.

to•geth•er /tə'gɛðər/ *adv.* **1.** into or in one mass or body: *Call the people together.* **2.** into or in union, as two or more things: *to sew things together.* **3.** considered as a group: *This one computer costs more than all the others together.* **4.** at the same time; simultaneously: *We left together.* **5.** in cooperation; with united action; jointly: *to undertake a task together.* —*adj.* **6.** *Informal.* stable in one's emotions: *a very together person.* —to'geth•er•ness, *n.* [*noncount*]: *The family showed its togetherness by helping anyone who needed it.*

toil /tɔyl/ *n.* [*noncount*] **1.** hard or exhausting work. —*v.* [*no obj*] **2.** to work or labor with great difficulty: *to toil on the project night and day.*

toi•let /'tɔylɪt/ *n.* **1.** [*count*] a large bowl with a water-flushing device for receiving and carrying away body wastes. **2.** [*count*] a bathroom or washroom; lavatory. **3.** [*noncount*] the act or process of grooming oneself.

'**toilet ,paper,** *n.* [*count*] a soft, thin paper, usually in a roll, used for cleaning oneself after defecation or urination. Also called '**toilet ,tissue.**

toi•let•ry /'tɔylɪtriy/ *n.* [*count*], *pl.* **-ries.** any article, substance, or preparation used in washing, cleaning, or grooming oneself, as soap or deodorant.

to•ken /'towkən/ *n.* [*count*] **1.** something serving to represent a particular feeling or event: *a token of my esteem.* **2.** a stamped piece of metal used in place of money, as for bus fares: *He dropped his token in the slot.* —*adj.* [*before a noun*] **3.** hired for a job, admitted into a school, etc., to cover minimum requirements of antidiscrimination laws: *a token male on an all-female staff.* **4.** slight; minimal; not showing much effort or effect: *He received a token salary.*

told /towld/ *v.* **1.** pt. and pp. of TELL. —*Idiom.* **2. all told,** counting everyone or everything; in all: *All told, there were thirty students in the class.*

tol•er•a•ble /'tɒlərəbəl/ *adj.* **1.** capable of being tolerated: *The pain was tolerable.* **2.** fairly good; not bad: *a tolerable acting performance.*

tol•er•ance /'tɒlərəns/ *n.* **1.** [*noncount*] a fair, open attitude toward people whose race, religion, practices, etc., differ from one's own: *tolerance toward the beliefs of others.* **2.** the act of enduring or the capacity to endure; endurance: [*noncount*]: *My tolerance for noise is limited.* [*count*]: *a weak tolerance for the drug.* —'**tol•er•ant,** *adj.*

tol•er•ate /'tɒlə,reyt/ *v.* [~ + *obj*], **-at•ed, -at•ing. 1.** to allow, without interference, the presence of a disliked person or condition. **2.** to endure; put up with: *I cannot tolerate the heat.* —tol•er•a•tion /,tɒlə'reyʃən/ *n.* [*noncount*]

toll¹ /towl/ *n.* [*count*] **1.** a fee demanded by an authority for some right or privilege, as for driving along a road. **2.** the extent of loss, damage,

tools

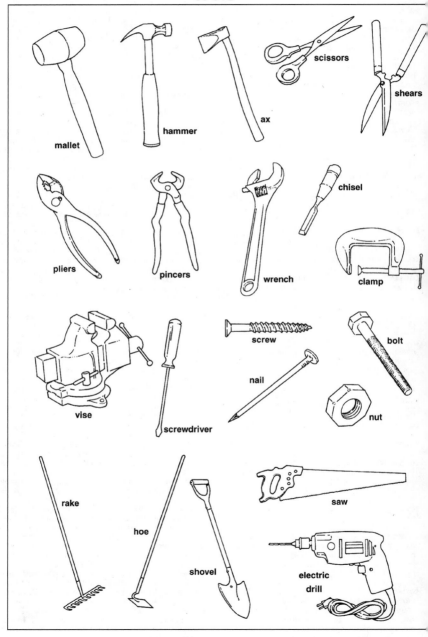

mallet

hammer

ax

scissors

shears

pliers

pincers

wrench

chisel

clamp

vise

screwdriver

screw

nail

bolt

nut

rake

hoe

shovel

saw

electric drill

or suffering resulting from some action: *The toll from the earthquake was 300 persons dead.* **3.** a payment made for a long-distance telephone call.

toll² /towl/ *v.* to (cause a large bell) to sound repeatedly and slowly: [~ + *obj*]: *to toll a bell.* [*no obj*]: *Bells tolled in the distance.* —*n.* [*count*] **2.** the act or sound of tolling a bell.

tom /tɒm/ *n.* [*count*] **1.** the male of some animals, as the turkey. **2.** a tomcat.

tom•a•hawk /ˈtɒməˌhɔk/ *n.* [*count*] a light ax used by American Indians as a weapon or tool.

to•ma•to /təˈmeytow, -ˈmɑ-/ *n.* [*count*], *pl.* **-toes.** a large, edible, mildly acid, pulpy fruit, red to red-yellow when ripe.

tomb /tuwm/ *n.* [*count*] a large burial chamber or grave.

tom•boy /ˈtɒmˌbɔy/ *n.* [*count*] a lively girl who is said to play and act like a boy: *As the neighborhood tomboy, she could wrestle any of the boys her age.*

tomb•stone /ˈtuwmˌstown/ *n.* [*count*] a stone marker, usually with writing on it, on a tomb or grave.

tom•cat /ˈtɒmˌkæt/ *n.* [*count*] a male cat.

to•mor•row /təˈmɒrow, -ˈmɒrow/ *n.* **1.** [*noncount*] the day following today: *Tomorrow is another day.* **2.** a future period or time: [*noncount*]: *the exciting world of tomorrow.* [*count*]: *There were no tomorrows left for the condemned man.* —*adv.* **3.** on the day following today: *I'll see you tomorrow.* **4.** at some future time.

ton /tʌn/ *n.* [*count*] **1.** a unit of weight, equivalent to 2000 pounds (0.907 metric ton) **(short ton)** in the U.S. and 2240 pounds (1.016 metric tons) **(long ton)** in Great Britain. **2.** Often, **tons.** [*plural*] a great quantity; a lot: [~ + *a plural noun*]: *a ton of pencils.* [~ + *a noncount noun*]: *tons of money.*

tone /town/ *n.*, *v.*, **toned, ton•ing.** —*n.* **1.** [*count*] any sound considered in terms of its quality, pitch, strength, source, etc.: *shrill tones.* **2.** [*count*] a particular quality or intonation of the voice: *From the tone of her voice I knew she was angry.* **3.** [*count*] a quality of color; a tint, hue, or shade. **4.** [*noncount*] the normal, healthy condition of the organs, muscles, or tissues of the body: *He had fine muscle tone after weeks of exercise.* **5.** [*noncount*] general character or quality: *the liberal tone of the 1960s.* —*v.* [~ + *obj*] **6.** to make strong or properly healthy: *to tone the body with exercise.* **7. tone down,** to (cause to) become softened; to (cause to) be reduced in force: *to tone down the harsh colors; to tone the harsh colors down by using different lighting.*

tongs /tɒŋz, tɒŋz/ *n.* [*plural; usually used with a plural verb*] a tool made of two movable arms joined at one end, used for picking up an object.

tongue /tʌŋ/ *n.* **1.** [*count*] an organ in the mouth used for tasting, eating, and speaking. **2.** [*noncount*] [*count*] the tongue of an animal, as an ox, beef, or sheep, used for food. **3.** [*noncount*] the power or ability to speak: *What's the matter, lost your tongue?* **4.** [*count*] the language of a particular people, region, or nation. **5.** [*count*] a strip of leather under the lacing of a shoe. —*Idiom.* **6. on the tip of one's** or **the tongue,** about to be recalled into conscious memory. **7. hold one's tongue,** to remain silent. **8. (with) tongue in cheek,** as a joke; ironically: *His sarcasm and insults were all offered tongue in cheek.*

'tongue-,tied, *adj.* unable to speak, as from shyness, embarrassment, or surprise.

'tongue ,twister, *n.* [*count*] a phrase or sentence that is difficult to pronounce quickly, because of its dense structure of similar sounds, as "She sells seashells by the seashore."

ton•ic /ˈtɒnɪk/ *n.* **1.** [*count*] a medicine that increases mental or physical strength, health, or well-being. **2.** soda water with quinine: [*noncount*]: *some gin and tonic.* [*count*]: *two tonics.*

to•night /təˈnayt/ *n.* [*noncount*] **1.** this present or coming night; the night of this day: *Tonight is the night I (will) propose to her.* —*adv.* **2.** on this night; on the night of this day: *See you tonight about six.*

ton•sil /ˈtɒnsəl/ *n.* [*count*] a mass of tissue on each side of the throat at the back of the mouth.

ton•sil•li•tis /ˌtɒnsəˈlaytɪs/ *n.* [*noncount*] inflammation of a tonsil or the tonsils.

too /tuw/ *adv.* **1.** in addition; also; furthermore: *She's young, clever, and rich, too.* **2.** to a degree beyond normal or proper: *She's too sick to travel.* **3.** (used to emphasize disagreement with something said): *"You're not ready to go."* —*"I am too!"* (= *Actually, I am ready to go*). **4.** (used with a negative word or phrase) extremely; very: *The boss was none too pleased with the results.*

took /tʊk/ *v.* pt. of TAKE.

tool /tuwl/ *n.* [*count*] **1.** an implement, esp. one held in the hand, as a hammer, for doing something mechanical: *The carpenter laid out his tools and began to work.* **2.** anything used to accomplish a task: *Education is a tool for success.*

toot /tuwt/ *v.* **1.** to (cause a horn or whistle to) make a short sound: [~ + *obj*]: *He tooted his horn.* [*no obj*]: *The foghorn tooted in the distance.* —*n.* [*count*] **2.** an act or sound of tooting.

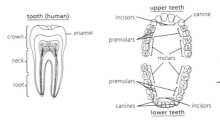

tooth (def. 1)

tooth /tuwθ/ *n.* [*count*], *pl.* **teeth** /tiyθ/. **1.** one of the hard white bony structures in the mouth, serving to bite and chew food or, esp. in animals, as weapons. **2.** any part of something that sticks out and resembles a tooth, as a part of a comb, etc. —*Idiom.* **3. set** or **put one's teeth on edge,** to cause a feeling of irritation in one: *The supervisor always sets my teeth on edge.* **4. sink one's teeth into,** to work on (something) with enthusiasm: *At last he found a project he could sink his teeth into.* —'**tooth•y,** *adj.*, **-i•er, -i•est:** *a toothy smile.*

tooth•ache /ˈtuwθˌeyk/ *n.* [*count*] a pain in or around a tooth. —'**tooth,ach•y,** *adj.*

tooth•brush /ˈtuwθˌbrʌʃ/ *n.* [*count*] a small brush with a long handle, for cleaning the teeth.

tooth•paste /ˈtuwθˌpeyst/ *n.* [*noncount*] a substance in the form of paste, for cleaning the teeth.

tooth•pick /ˈtuwθˌpɪk/ *n.* [*count*] a small, pointed piece of wood, plastic, etc., for removing food particles from between the teeth.

T

top¹ /tɒp/ n., adj., v., **topped, top•ping.** —n. **1.** [count] the highest point, part, etc., of anything: *the top of the mountain.* **2.** [count] a lid of a container. **3.** [count; usually singular] the highest or leading position: *She's always ranked at the top of the class.* **4.** [count] a garment for the upper body: *a skirt and a matching top.* —adj. [before a noun] **5.** of or relating to the top; highest: *to pay top prices.* **6.** chief or principal: *The best salaries are paid to the top players.* —v. [~ + obj] **7.** to furnish with a top; put a top on: *She topped the sundae with a cherry.* **8.** to be at, form, or make up the top of: *Ice cream topped the cake.* **9.** to surpass or outdo: *I've seen some weird things before, but this tops everything.* **10. top off,** to complete, esp. in a pleasing manner; finish: *On their anniversary they topped off the evening with champagne. And to top it off, they won some money in the lottery.* —*Idiom.* **11. at the top of one's lungs** or **voice,** as loudly as possible. **12. off the top of one's head,** without thought or preparation: *Off the top of my head I would say we've lost 12% of our sales force.* **13. on top of, a.** in addition to; over and above: *They lost their jobs, and on top of that their children got sick.* **b.** in control: *The firefighters seem on top of the problem and will put out the fire soon.*

top² /tɒp/ n. [count] a toy that spins on a point at its end.

'top ,hat, n. [count] a tall hat with a small brim, worn by men on formal occasions.

'top-,heavy, adj. too heavy at the top: *The car is top-heavy and could roll over easily.*

top•ic /'tɒpɪk/ n. [count] the subject of a discussion, speech, or piece of writing.

top•i•cal /'tɒpɪkəl/ adj. **1.** of current or local interest. **2.** on the skin or external surface: *a topical ointment.*

top•less /'tɒplɪs/ adj. **1.** lacking a top. **2.** nude above the waist: *topless dancers.*

to•pog•ra•phy /tə'pɒɡrəfiy/ n. [noncount] [count], pl. **-phies.** the surface features of an area, such as its hills and rivers.

top•ping /'tɒpɪŋ/ n. **1.** [count] a part forming a top to something. **2.** a sauce placed on food before serving: [noncount]: *whipped topping on the dessert.* [count]: *a choice of toppings for the ice cream.*

top•ple /'tɒpəl/ v., **-pled, -pling. 1.** to (cause to) fall forward: [no obj]: *He suddenly toppled to the sidewalk.* [~ + obj]: *The champion toppled the challenger with one punch.* **2.** [~ + obj] to remove from power, as from a position of authority: *to topple a king.*

top•soil /'tɒp,sɔyl/ n. [noncount] the upper part of the soil, usually the best for growing things.

top•sy-tur•vy /'tɒpsiy'tɜrviy/ adv. **1.** with the top where the bottom should be; upside down: *The waves turned the boat topsy-turvy.* **2.** in or into a state of confusion: *Things went completely topsy-turvy when the new boss arrived.* —adj. **3.** turned upside down: *a topsy-turvy reflection.* **4.** confused or disorderly: *a topsy-turvy classroom.*

To•rah /'tɔrə/ n. [noncount] In Judaism, the first five books of the Bible.

torch /tɔrtʃ/ n. [count] **1.** a light consisting of a wood stick with fire at the upper end. **2.** something thought of as a source of knowledge or guidance: *the torch of learning.* **3.** Chiefly Brit. FLASHLIGHT. —v. [~ + obj] **4.** to destroy by means of fire: *Before the police arrested him he had torched five buildings.*

tore /tɔr/ v. pt. of TEAR².

tor•ment /v.tɔr'mɛnt, 'tɔrmɛnt; n. 'tɔrmɛnt/ v. [~ + obj] **1.** to cause (someone) to feel severe suffering: *The disease tormented him.* **2.** to worry or annoy greatly; keep bothering: *She constantly tormented me with her schemes.* —n. **3.** [noncount] a state of suffering; agony; misery. **4.** [count] a source of much trouble or worry. —**tor'men•tor,** n. [count]: *He punched his tormentor in the nose.*

torn /tɔrn/ v. pp. of TEAR².

tor•na•do /tɔr'neydow/ n. [count], pl. **-does, -dos.** a violent, destructive windstorm having a long, funnel-shaped cloud that extends to the ground.

tor•pe•do /tɔr'piydow/ n., pl. **-does,** v., **-doed, -do•ing.** —n. [count] **1.** a tube-shaped underwater bomb, usually sent from a submarine or other warship against a surface vessel. —v. [~ + obj] **2.** to attack or destroy with or as if with torpedoes: *The battleship was torpedoed and sunk.*

tor•rent /'tɔrənt, 'tɒr-/ n. [count] **1.** a quick-flowing, violent stream of water. **2.** a rushing, violent stream of anything: *a torrent of abuse.* —**tor•ren•tial** /tɔ'rɛnʃəl, tə-/, adj.

tor•rid /'tɔrɪd, 'tɒr-/ adj. **1.** extremely hot or burning, as climate or air: *a torrid summer day.* **2.** passionate: *a torrid love affair.*

tor•so /'tɔrsow/ n. [count], pl. **-sos, -si** /-siy/. the trunk of the human body.

torte /tɔrt/ n. [count] a rich cake made with eggs, ground nuts, and usually no flour.

tor•til•la /tɔr'tiyə/ n. [count], pl. **-las.** a thin, round, unleavened bread made from cornmeal or wheat flour, and baked on a griddle or stone.

tor•toise /'tɔrtəs/ n. [count] a turtle, esp. a slow-moving land turtle.

tor•toise•shell /'tɔrtəs,ʃɛl/ n. [noncount] Also, **'tortoise ,shell. 1.** the horny yellow and brown outer surface of a turtle shell, used for making combs and decorative objects. **2.** a synthetic substance resembling natural tortoiseshell.

tor•tu•ous /'tɔrtʃuwəs/ adj. **1.** full of twists, turns, or bends: *a tortuous path.* **2.** not direct or straightforward, as in behavior or speech: *tortuous reasoning.*

tor•ture /'tɔrtʃər/ n., v., **-tured, -tur•ing.** —n. **1.** [noncount] the act of causing great pain, as punishment, for getting a confession or information, or for cruelty's sake. **2.** [count] a method of causing or giving such pain: *different tortures, like whipping and electric shocks.* **3.** [noncount] a cause of pain or anguish: *It was torture for him to see his old girlfriend with another guy.* —v. [~ + obj] **4.** to force to suffer torture: *The guards tortured the prisoner for hours.* **5.** to cause to suffer great physical or mental pain.

toss /tɔs, tɒs/ v., **tossed** or **tost, toss•ing,** n. —v. **1.** [~ + obj] to throw, esp. lightly or carelessly: *She came in and tossed her coat on the chair.* **2.** [~ + obj] to throw from one to another, as in play: *to toss a ball back and forth.* **3.** to move or pitch with irregular motions; jerk about: [no obj]: *I was tossing and turning all night.* [~ + obj]: *The storm tossed the ship about.* **4.** to make a chance decision by throwing a coin into the air and seeing which side lands facing upward: [~ + obj]: *The official tossed a coin and it came up heads. We can't decide who should go first.* [no obj]: *We can't decide who should go first; let's toss for it.* **5.** [~ + obj] to mix (a salad) lightly in order to coat with dressing. —n. [count] **6.** an act or instance of tossing.

toss•up /'tɔs,ʌp, 'tɒs-/ n. [count] an even choice or chance: *The election is a tossup at this point.*

tot /tɒt/ n. [count] **1.** a small child. **2.** a small portion, as of liquor.

to•tal /'towtl/ adj., n., v., **-taled, -tal•ing** or (*esp. Brit.*) **-talled, -tal•ling.** —adj. **1.** [before a noun] of or relating to the whole of something; entire: *the total expenditure.* **2.** [usually: before a noun] complete in extent or degree; utter: *a total failure.* —n. **3.** [count] the total amount; sum: *That brings the cost to a total of $50,000.* **4.** [noncount; in + ~] the whole: *There were several thousand people there in total.* —v. [~ + obj] **5.** to bring to a total; add up: *He totaled the three columns.* **6.** to reach a total of; amount to: *The money totaled over $50,000.*

to•tal•i•tar•i•an /tow,tælɪ'tɛəriyən/ adj. of or relating to a single-party government that does not allow differing opinion: *the totalitarian system of George Orwell's novel* 1984.

to•tal•i•ty /tow'tælɪtiy/ n. [noncount], pl. **-ties.** the state of being total; entirety.

to•tal•ly /'towtəliy/ adv. completely; entirely: *You're totally crazy to think like that.*

tote /towt/ v., **tot•ed, tot•ing,** n. —v. [~ + obj] **1.** to carry, as in one's arms: *toting bags of groceries.* **2.** to carry on one's person: *to tote a gun.* —n. [count] **3.** an open shopping bag, used for carrying small items.

'totem ,pole /'towtəm/ n. [count] a pole carved and painted with totems (symbolic images of ancestors), built by Native Americans of the NW coast of North America.

tot•ter /'tɒtər/ v. [no obj] **1.** to walk or go with clumsy, unsteady steps: *After the blow to the head he tottered and fell.* **2.** to sway or rock, as if about to fall: *During the earthquake the building tottered, then crashed to the ground.*

touch /tʌtʃ/ v. **1.** to put the hand, finger, etc., on or into contact with (something) so as to feel it: [~ + obj]: *He touched the stove cautiously.* [no obj]: *You may look at it but don't touch.* **2.** [~ + obj] to bring (the hand, etc., or something held) into contact with something: *He touched a match to the papers.* **3.** to come into contact with; be next to: [~ + obj]: *My shoulder was touching hers.* [no obj]: *Our shoulders were touching on the crowded elevator.* **4.** [~ + obj] to move (someone) to feel sympathy: *Your kindness touched me deeply.* **5.** [~ + obj] to use or consume: *He won't touch another drink.* **6.** to be equal with; compare with: *Her apple pie doesn't touch my mother's.* **7.** **touch down,** (of an aircraft or spacecraft) to land. **8. touch off, a.** to cause to ignite or explode: *The flame touched off the explosion. What touched it off?* **b.** to start, esp. suddenly: *The incident touched off a debate. That's what touched the debate off.* **9. touch on** or **upon,** to mention (a subject) casually: *Her speech touched on the subject.* **10. touch up,** to make minor changes in the appearance of: *The artist touched up the painting. She touched it up.* —n. **11.** [count] the act of touching; state or fact of being touched: *a light touch on his shoulder.* **12.** [noncount] that sense by which anything material is felt by physical contact: *a well-developed sense of touch.* **13.** [noncount] a coming into or being in contact with another: *Over the years we lost touch. Let's keep in touch.* **14.** [noncount] ability or skill; a knack for doing something: *He seems to have lost his touch in dealing with people.* **15.** [count] a slight attack, as of illness: *He's had a touch of the flu.* **16.** [count] a slight added effort

in completing any piece of work: *She put some finishing touches on the painting.* **17.** [count] a slight amount of some quality, emotion, etc.: *a touch of sadness in her voice.*

touch•down /'tʌtʃ,dawn/ n. [count] **1.** an act of scoring six points in football by being in possession of the ball on or behind the opponent's goal line. **2.** the act of a Rugby player who touches the ball on or to the ground behind his own goal line. **3.** the act or the moment of landing, as of an aircraft.

touch•ing /'tʌtʃɪŋ/ adj. causing tender emotion: *a touching story about a girl and her dog.*

touch•y /'tʌtʃiy/ adj., **-i•er, -i•est. 1.** likely to take offense for some slight reason; irritable: *She's sort of touchy about her weight.* **2.** requiring caution, careful handling, or tact; risky: *It's a touchy situation.*

tough /tʌf/ adj. **-er, -est,** adv., n. —adj. **1.** strong and long-lasting: *tough plastics.* **2.** difficult to chew; not tender: *a tough steak.* **3.** capable of great endurance: *tough troops.* **4.** difficult to perform or deal with: *a very tough exam; It's tough to get a good grade from him.* **5.** hard to bear or suffer through; severe: *a tough struggle to succeed.* **6.** rough; violent: *a tough neighborhood.* —adv. **7.** in a tough manner: *They play tough, but not dirty.* —n. [count] **8.** a rough person who attacks others; a rowdy. —'**tough•en,** v. [~ + obj]: *The union toughened its stance.* [no obj]: *This metal toughens under higher temperatures.* —'**tough•ness,** n. [noncount]

tou•pee /tuw'pey/ n. [count], pl. **-pees. 1.** a man's wig. **2.** a patch of false hair for covering a bald spot.

tour /tʊr/ n. [count] **1.** a long journey including visits to a number of places: *a tour of the Greek islands.* **2.** a brief trip through a place to view or inspect it: *an inspection tour.* **3.** a period of duty at one place or in one job: *I'll be back in New York after a year's tour in England.* —v. **4.** to travel from place to place: [~ + obj]: *They toured the Greek islands.* [no obj]: *They toured for a few seasons.* —'**tour•ism,** n. [noncount]: *He got a good hotel room through the office of tourism.* —'**tour•ist,** n. [count]: *Many American tourists go to Europe in the summer.*

tour•na•ment /'tʊrnəmənt, 'tɜr-/ n. [count] a trial of skill in some game, in which players play a series of contests: *a chess tournament.*

tour•ni•quet /'tɜrnɪkɪt, 'tʊr-/ n. [count] any device for slowing or stopping bleeding by pushing down with force on a blood vessel: *He applied a tourniquet above the wound.*

tou•sle /'tawzəl, -səl/ v. [~ + obj], **-sled, -sling.** to make a little untidy: *The wind tousled our hair.*

tout /tawt/ v. [~ + obj] Informal. to advertise boastfully: *The owners touted their new restaurant.*

tow /tow/ v. [~ + obj] **1.** to pull or haul (a car, etc.) by a rope, chain, etc.: *They towed my car to the garage.* —n. [count] **2.** an act or instance of towing. —**Idiom. 3. in tow,** following behind: *The movie star walked down the street with reporters in tow.*

to•ward /tɔrd, twɔrd/ prep. Also, **to•wards'. 1.** in the direction of: *to walk toward the river.* **2.** with a view to having; for: *They're saving money toward a new house.* **3.** turned to; facing: *She turned toward me.* **4.** shortly before; close to: *The moon came out toward midnight.* **5.** as a help or contribution to: *to give money toward a person's* *expenses.* **6.** with respect to; as regards: *What are your feelings toward gun control?*

tow•el /'tawəl, tawl/ *n.*, *v.*, **-eled, -el•ing** or (*esp. Brit.*) **-elled, -el•ling.** —*n.* [*count*] **1.** a cloth or paper that absorbs liquids, used for wiping and drying. —*v.* [~ + *obj*] **2.** to wipe or dry with a towel: *She toweled her hair dry.*

tow•er /'tawər/ *n.* [*count*] **1.** a tall, narrow structure, either standing alone or extending upward from a building: *a television tower.* —*v.* [*no obj*] **2.** to rise or extend far upward or above, as a tower: *The mountains towered above us.*

town /tawn/ *n.* **1.** [*count*] a thickly populated area, usually smaller than a city and larger than a village, having fixed borders and its own government. **2.** the people living in a town: *The whole town supports the high school football team.* **3.** [*noncount*] the particular town or city in mind or referred to: *to be out of town.* —*Idiom.* **4. go to town,** *Informal.* to do something with unrestrained interest and energy: *They really went to town on that contracting job.* **5. on the town,** *Informal.* looking for entertainment in a city's nightclubs, etc.; out to have a good time: *The company took us out for a night on the town.*

tox•in /'toksın/ *n.* [*count*] any poison formed from living matter. —**'tox•ic,** *adj.*: *a toxic drug.*

toy /tɔy/ *n.* [*count*] **1.** an object for children to play with. —*v.* [~ + *with* + *obj*] **2.** to play with something or flirt with someone without serious purpose: *to toy with one's food; She's just toying with him.* **3.** to think about or consider lightly: *I'm toying with the idea of buying a new computer.*

trace /treys/ *n.*, *v.*, **traced, trac•ing.** —*n.* [*count*] **1.** a mark, sign, or piece of evidence of the existence of someone, something, or some event: *Those statues are the only traces of a once-great civilization.* **2.** a small amount: *a trace of sadness in her smile.* —*v.* [~ + *obj*] **3.** to follow the footprints, tracks, or traces of: *The FBI traced the van back to the rental company.* **4.** to follow the course or development of. **5.** to copy the lines of a drawing or picture onto a transparent cover sheet: *She traced the picture of the dog onto her notebook paper.* —**'trac•ing,** *n.* [*count*]

track /træk/ *n.* **1.** [*count*] a pair of parallel lines of rails on which a railroad train, trolley, or the like runs. **2.** [*count*] Usually, **tracks.** [*plural*] marks left by an animal, person, or vehicle: *You can see the tracks where the deer crossed the stream.* **3.** [*count*] a path made by the feet of people or animals; trail: *a track through the woods to the river.* **4. a.** [*count*] a course laid out for running or racing: *The school spent millions on a new track.* **b.** [*noncount*] the various sports performed on such a course. **5.** [*count*] one of the pieces of music on a CD or record. —*v.* [~ + *obj*] **6.** to follow or pursue the track of: *The dogs tracked the fox to its hole.* **7.** to make a trail of footprints with (dirt, etc.): *to track mud on the floor.* **8. track down,** to pursue until caught or captured; follow: *I promised to track him down. I promised to track down the traitor.* —*Idiom.* **9. keep track,** to remain aware; take notice: *There are too many things to do; I can't keep track. I can't keep track of all those employees.* **10. lose track,** to fail to stay aware: *I keep losing track; are we on page 1055 or 1056? I lost track of how many disks my computer destroyed.* —**'track•er,** *n.* [*count*]

tract¹ /trækt/ *n.* [*count*] **1.** an area of land, water, etc.: *a five-acre tract of land.* **2.** a definite re-

gion or area of the body, esp. a system of parts or organs: *the digestive tract.*

tract² /trækt/ *n.* [*count*] a brief pamphlet, usually on a religious or political topic.

trac•ta•ble /'træktəbəl/ *adj.* easily managed or controlled.

trac•tion /'trækʃən/ *n.* [*noncount*] the friction of an object that causes it to stick on some surface, as a tire on a road: *These tires provide good traction.*

trac•tor /'træktər/ *n.* [*count*] **1.** a powerful motor-driven vehicle with large, heavy treads, used for pulling farm machinery, etc. **2.** a short truck with a driver's cab but no body, designed for hauling a trailer.

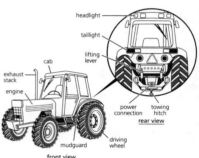

tractor (def. 1)

trade /treyd/ *n.*, *v.*, **trad•ed, trad•ing,** *adj.* —*n.* **1.** [*noncount*] the act or process of buying, selling, or exchanging goods: *domestic trade; foreign trade.* **2.** an occupation that is one's business or livelihood: [*count*]: *He's in the tourist trade.* [*noncount; by* + ~]: *She's a carpenter by trade.* **3.** [*noncount*] the people who work in a particular business or industry: *The whole trade is talking about his new invention.* —*v.* **4.** to buy and sell: [*no obj*]: *to trade in silver and gold.* [~ + *obj*]: *They trade silver and gold.* **5.** to exchange: [~ + *obj*]: *I traded my dessert for his. I'll trade you my dessert for yours.* [*no obj*]: *I'll trade for it.* **6. trade in,** to give (an article) as payment for or toward a purchase of something: *to trade in one's old car for a down payment on a new one; to trade your old car in and get a new one.* —**'trad•er,** *n.* [*count*]

trade•mark /'treyd,mɑrk/ *n.* [*count*] **1.** a name, symbol, etc., adopted by a manufacturer to separate their products from others: *A trademark must be registered with a government patent office.* —*v.* [~ + *obj*] **2.** to register the trademark of: *to trademark the name of his product.*

tra•di•tion /trə'dıʃən/ *n.* **1.** [*noncount*] the handing down of statements, beliefs, etc., esp. by word of mouth or by practice: *In Jewish tradition, learning is highly valued.* **2.** [*count*] something handed down in this way: *the traditions of the Eskimos.* **3.** [*noncount*] a long-established way of thinking or acting: *They followed an unbroken tradition.* —**tra•di•tion•al,** *adj.*: *The folkdancers wore traditional dress.* —**tra•di•tion•al•ly,** *adv.*

traf•fic /'træfık/ *n.*, *v.*, **-ficked, -fick•ing.** —*n.* [*noncount*] **1.** the vehicles, persons, etc., moving in an area or over a route: *heavy traffic.* **2.** trade; buying and selling; commerce: *the traffic in illegal drugs.* —*v.* [*no obj*] **3.** to trade in a commod-

                 transform

ity or service, often of an illegal nature: *to traffic in opium.*

'traffic ˌlight, *n.* [count] a set of signal lights used to direct traffic at intersections.

trag•e•dy /'trædʒɪdiy/ *n.* [count], *pl.* **-dies.** **1.** a sad or terrible event; disaster: *a family tragedy.* **2.** a play with a sad ending: *Shakespeare's tragedies.* —**trag•ic** /'trædʒɪk/ *adj.*: *a tragic accident.* —**'trag•i•cal•ly,** *adv.*

trail /treyl/ *v.* **1.** to (cause to) be dragged along the ground; (cause to) be drawn behind: [~ + obj]: *She trailed her little toy wagon along behind her.* [*no obj*]: *Her long hair trailed down her back.* **2.** [~ + obj] to follow the track or scent of: *The agents trailed him to his cabin.* **3.** [~ + obj] to follow (another), as in a race: *For most of the race he trailed the front-runners.* —*n.* [count] **4.** a path worn away through an area of land by the passing of people or animals: *They followed the trail through the woods.* **5.** the track or scent left by an animal, person, or thing: *The police lost the trail of the killer.*

trail•er /'treylər/ *n.* [count] **1.** a large van or wagon pulled by an automobile, truck, or tractor, used esp. in hauling freight by road. **2.** a closed vehicle pulled by an automobile and used as a mobile home: *They stay in a trailer when they go away on weekends.*

train /treyn/ *n.* **1.** a connected group of railroad cars: [count]: *a long freight train of about 100 cars.* [*noncount; by* + ~]: *She only travels by train or bus.* **2.** [count] a line or procession of persons, vehicles, etc. **3.** [count] something drawn along, as a part of a long dress: *The bride wore a white dress with a long train.* **4.** [count] a course or path in thinking or reasoning: *I've lost my train of thought.* —*v.* **5.** [~ + obj] to teach or discipline (a child) in regard to habits, thoughts, or behavior: *to train him to be kind to animals.* **6.** to (cause to) become skilled in some work by teaching or practice: [~ + obj]: *His father trained him to fix cars.* [*no obj*]: *She trained as an accountant.* **7.** [~ + obj] to discipline or teach (an animal): *She trained her dog (to obey commands).* **8.** [~ + obj] to bring (a plant, etc.) into a particular shape or direction. —**'train•er,** *n.* [count]

train•ee /trey'niy/ *n.* [count], *pl.* **-ees.** a person in training for some job, skill, etc.

train•ing /'treynɪŋ/ *n.* [*noncount*] the act of someone who trains; the state of being trained: *He received no formal training in the new technology. He's in training for the big tennis match.*

trait /treyt/ *n.* [count] a quality, esp. of one's nature, that sets one apart from others: *his bad character traits.*

trai•tor /'treytər/ *n.* [count] one who betrays.

tram /træm/ *n.* [count] **1.** *Brit.* a streetcar. **2.** a car on rails, esp. one that moves by means of an overhead cable, as to carry skiers at a ski lodge.

tramp /træmp/ *v.* **1.** to walk with a firm, heavy step (on or through); march; trudge: [*no obj*]: *soldiers tramping through the streets.* [~ + obj]: *to tramp the streets.* **2.** [*no obj*] to walk continuously, over a long distance or period of time: *He tramped through the streets looking for a job.* —*n.* **3.** [*count; usually singular*] the act of tramping. **4.** [count] one who travels about on foot, taking occasional jobs or gifts of money or food. **5.** [count] a woman regarded as behaving immorally, esp. a prostitute.

tram•ple /'træmpəl/ *v.,* **-pled, -pling. 1.** to step heavily or carelessly on (something): [~ + obj]:

The cowboy was nearly trampled by the wild horses. [*no obj*]: *Don't trample on the grass.* **2.** [*no obj*] to control (another) harshly; crush: *They claimed that the police trampled on their rights.*

tram•po•line /ˌtræmpə'liyn, 'træmpə,liyn, -lɪn/ *n.* [count] a canvas sheet stretched onto a frame above the floor, used in acrobatic tumbling.

trance /træns/ *n.* [count] a mental state between sleeping and waking, esp. a state produced by hypnosis: *The music was so powerful that it put him into something like a trance.*

tran•quil /'træŋkwɪl/ *adj.* free from commotion; peaceful; quiet; calm: *a tranquil village.* —**tran• quil•li•ty, •tran•quil•i•ty** /træŋ'kwɪlɪtiy/, *n.* [*noncount*]

tran•quil•ize or **tran•quil•lize** /'træŋkwə,layz/ *v.* [~ + obj], **-ized** or **-lized, -iz•ing** or **-liz•ing.** to make tranquil, as by giving a drug to: *The veterinarian tranquilized the dog with an injection.* —**'tran•quil,iz•er** or **'tran• quil,liz•er,** *n.* [count]: *He was so upset that he needed to take a tranquilizer.*

trans-, a prefix meaning: across, through, or on the other side (*transatlantic*); changing thoroughly (*transform*); beyond or surpassing (*transnational*).

trans•act /træn'sækt, -'zækt/ *v.* [~ + obj] to conduct (some business, etc.) to completion: *to transact a business deal before lunch.*

trans•ac•tion *n.* **1.** [*noncount*] the act of transacting. **2.** [count] something transacted; a piece of business.

tran•scend /træn'sɛnd/ *v.* [~ + obj] to go beyond; exceed: *That strange tale about men from Mars transcends belief.*

trans•con•ti•nen•tal /ˌtrænskɒntn̩'ɛntl̩/ *adj.* extending across a continent: *a transcontinental railroad.*

tran•scribe /træn'skrayb/ *v.* [~ + obj], **-scribed, -scrib•ing. 1.** to make a written or printed copy of (something spoken): *to transcribe a lecture.* **2.** to write out in another language or alphabet; translate. —**tran'scrip•tion,** *n.* [*noncount*] [count]

tran•script /'trænskrɪpt/ *n.* [count] **1.** a written or printed copy; something made by transcribing. **2.** an official school report on a student, listing subjects studied, grades received, etc.

trans•fer /*v.* træns'fɜr, 'trænsfər; *n.* 'trænsfər/ *v.,* **-ferred, -fer•ring,** *n.* —*v.* **1.** [~ + obj] to move or bring from one place, person, or position to another: *She transferred laundry from one arm to the other; The company transferred him to Texas.* **2.** to cause to pass (thought, power, etc.) from one person to another: [~ + obj]: *On the death of the king, power was transferred to his son.* [*no obj*]: *Power then transferred to the king.* **3.** [*no obj*] to remove oneself or be moved from one place, position, etc., to another: *He transferred from Yale to Harvard.* —*n.* **4.** [count] a means or system of transferring. **5.** [*noncount*] the fact of being transferred. **6.** [count] a place for transferring. **7.** [count] a ticket that allows a passenger to continue a ride on another bus, train, or the like. **8.** [count] one who has transferred, as from one college to another.

trans•fix /træns'fɪks/ *v.* [~ + obj], **-fixed** or **-fixt, -fix•ing.** to paralyze (someone) because of amazement, terror, etc.: *He stood transfixed with horror.*

trans•form /*v.* træns'fɔrm; *n.* 'trænsfɔrm/ *v.* [~ + obj] to change in condition or character: *to* *transform sunlight into electrical power.* **—trans•for•ma•tion** /ˌtrænsfər'meyʃən/, *n.* [count]

trans•fusion /træns'fyuwʒən/ *n.* [count] a medical process of providing blood by means of injection into an artery or vein: *The nurse gave the accident victim a blood transfusion.*

trans•gress /træns'grɛs, trænz-/ *v.* **1.** [~ + obj] to go beyond (a limit, etc.): *She transgressed the bounds of good sense.* **2.** to go beyond the limits set by (a law, etc.); violate: [no obj]: *to have transgressed against God and nature.* [~ + obj]: *to have transgressed the laws of God and nature.* **—trans•gres•sion** /træns'grɛʃən, trænz-/, *n.* [count]: *He was punished for his transgressions.* [noncount]: *transgression of common sense.*

tran•sient /'trænʃənt, -ʒənt, -ziyənt/ *adj.* **1.** staying, lasting, or remaining only for a short time: *a transient illness.* **—n.** [count] **2.** a person or thing that is transient: *The hotel near the bus station was always filled with transients.*

tran•sis•tor /træn'zɪstər/ *n.* [count] **1.** a small device for controlling electric current, usually in a radio. **2.** Also called **tran'sistor 'radio.** a small radio that uses transistors.

tran•sit /'trænsɪt, -zɪt/ *n.* [noncount] **1.** passage of people or goods from one place to another; transportation: *The airline advised that our clothes were still in transit.* **2.** a system of public transportation, esp. in an urban area: *mass transit.*

tran•si•tion /træn'zɪʃən, -'sɪʃ-/ *n.* [noncount] movement or change from one position, state, stage, etc., to another: *The company is still in transition from one boss to another.* **2.** [count] a period during which such change takes place.

tran•si•tive /'trænsɪtɪv, -zɪ-/ *adj.* of or relating to a verb that takes a direct object: *The verbs* deny, put, *and* elect *are transitive verbs.* **—tran•si•tiv•i•ty** /ˌtrænsɪ'tɪvɪtiy, -zɪ-/, *n.* [noncount]

tran•si•to•ry /'trænsɪˌtɔriy, -zɪ-/ *adj.* brief by nature; not lasting long: *a transitory illness.*

trans•late /træns'leyt, trænz-, 'trænsleyt, 'trænz-/ *v.,* **-lat•ed, -lat•ing. 1.** to rewrite or restate in another language: [~ + obj]: *to translate his speeches into Arabic.* [no obj]: *She translates at the UN.* **2.** [~ + obj] to change the form, condition, or nature of; transform: *to translate thought into action.* **—trans'la•tion,** *n.* [noncount] [count] **—trans'la•tor,** *n.* [count]

trans•lu•cent /træns'luwsənt, trænz-/ *adj.* permitting light to pass through but not allowing the objects on the far side to be clearly visible: *Frosted window glass is translucent.* **—trans'lu•cence,** *n.* [noncount]

trans•mis•sion /træns'mɪʃən, trænz-/ *n.* **1.** [noncount] the act or process of transmitting; the fact of being transmitted: *transmission of radio signals.* **2.** [count] something transmitted: *Our transmissions aren't getting through.* **3.** a system of gears in an automobile that transfers power from the engine to the wheels: [noncount]: *This car has automatic transmission.* [count]: *They replaced our transmission.*

trans•mit /træns'mɪt, trænz-/ *v.,* **-mit•ted, -mit•ting. 1.** to send (a radio signal, a dispatch, etc.) to someone receiving, or to a destination: [~ + obj]: *He transmitted his instructions to us by special messenger.* [no obj]: *The submarine was transmitting, but there was no one to receive the signal.* **2.** [~ + obj] to send or pass from one person or place to another. **3.** [~ + obj] to cause or allow (light, heat, etc.) to pass through

a medium: *Glass transmits light.* **—trans'mit•ter,** *n.* [count]

trans•par•en•cy /træns'pɛərənsay, -'pær-/ *n., pl.* **-cies. 1.** [noncount] the state of being transparent. **2.** [count] something transparent: *The art teacher projected some transparencies on the wall.*

trans•par•ent /træns'pɛərənt, -'pær-/ *adj.* **1.** allowing light to pass through its substance so that objects on the far side can be clearly seen. **2.** so thin or sheer as to permit light to pass through: *a transparent blouse.* **3.** easily seen through or recognized: *a transparent lie.*

tran•spire /træn'spayər/ *v.* [no obj], **-spired, -spir•ing.** to occur or take place: *What transpired next is not known exactly.* **—tran•spi•ra•tion** /ˌtrænspə'reyʃən/, *n.* [noncount]

trans•plant /v.træns'plænt *n.* 'trænsˌplænt/ *v.* [~ + obj] **1.** to remove (a plant) from one place and plant it in another. **2.** to transfer (an organ, etc.) from one person or animal to another: *to transplant a human heart.* **—n.** [count] **3.** the act or process of transplanting: *a successful transplant.* **4.** a transplanted plant, organ, etc. **—trans•plan•ta•tion** /ˌtrænsplæn'teyʃən/, *n.* [noncount]

trans•port /v.træns'pɔrt, *n.* 'trænspɔrt/ *v.* [~ + obj] **1.** to carry (goods or people) from one place to another: *to transport food from the countryside to the cities.* **2.** to carry away by strong emotion: *He was transported by his feelings for her.* **—n.** [noncount] **3.** the act of transporting; transportation: *the days of really cheap air transport.* **4.** a means of transporting, as a truck, ship, or plane: *military transport by helicopters.*

trans•por•ta•tion /ˌtrænspər'teyʃən/ *n.* [noncount] **1.** the act of transporting or the state of being transported. **2.** the means of transporting; transport.

trans•pose /træns'powz/ *v.* [~ + obj], **-posed, -pos•ing.** to change or reverse the order of; interchange: *to transpose the third and fourth letters of a word.*

trans•verse /træns'vɜrs, trænz-; 'trænsvɜrs, 'trænz-/ *adj.* extending across: *a transverse beam.*

trap /træp/ *n., v.,* **trapped, trap•ping. —n.** [count] **1.** a device for catching birds or other animals: *several traps to catch mice.* **2.** a trick for catching a person by surprise: *When the thief tried to sell the stolen goods, he fell right into the trap.* **3.** *Slang.* mouth: *Keep your trap shut.* **—v. 4.** to catch in or by a trap: [~ + obj]: *to trap beavers for their fur.* [no obj]: *They hunted and trapped for several years.* **—'trap•per,** *n.* [count]

trap•door /'træp'dɔr/ *n.* [count] a hinged or sliding door in a floor, ceiling, or roof.

tra•peze /træ'piyz, trə-/ *n.* [count] a short horizontal bar hanging from two ropes, on which a gymnast or acrobat swings.

trap•e•zoid /'træpəˌzɔyd/ *n.* [count] a four-sided figure having two sides that are parallel and two sides that are not parallel.

trash /træʃ/ *n.* [noncount] **1.** anything worthless or thrown away; rubbish. **2.** anything of low, inferior, or offensive quality: *His campaign speech was mostly trash.* **—'trash•y,** *adj.,* **-i•er, -i•est.:** *trashy books.*

'trash ˌcan, *n.* [count] a container for the disposal of waste articles.

trau•ma /'trawmə, 'trɔ-/ *n., pl.* **-mas, -ma•ta** /-mətə/. **1. a.** [count] a wound or injury to the body, as from an attack: *multiple traumas.* **b.** [noncount] the condition produced by this: *Check for signs of trauma on the victim.* **2.** [count]

very painful shock, esp. one causing lasting emotional harm. —**trau•mat•ic** /traw'mætɪk, trɔ-, trə-/, *adj.*

trav•el /'trævəl/ *v.,* **-eled, -el•ing** or (*esp. Brit.*) **-elled, -el•ling,** *n.* —*v.* **1.** to go from one place to another, as by car, train, plane, or ship: [*no obj*]: *They traveled all night.* [~ + *obj*]: *They traveled the world.* **2.** to proceed (at a certain speed or distance): [*no obj*]: *The car was traveling at sixty miles an hour.* [~ + *obj*]: *We traveled nearly six hundred miles.* **3.** [*no obj*] to pass or be transmitted, as light or information: *The news traveled quickly.* —*n.* **4.** [*noncount*] the act of traveling, esp. to distant places: *She enjoys theater and travel.* **5. travels,** [*plural*] journeys; wanderings: *In all my travels I never saw anything as beautiful as this.* —'**trav•el•er,** '**trav•el•ler,** *n.* [*count*]

tray /trey/ *n.* [*count*] a flat, shallow container, used for carrying or displaying articles: *He carried his lunch tray to the table.*

treach•er•ous /'trɛtʃərəs/ *adj.* **1.** of or relating to treachery: *the treacherous spy.* **2.** unstable or insecure; dangerous: *treacherous footing on the icy slope.*

treach•er•y /'trɛtʃəriy/ *n., pl.* **-er•ies. 1.** [*noncount*] betrayal of trust; disloyalty; treason. **2.** [*count*] an act of treason.

tread /trɛd/ *v.,* **trod** /trɒd/, **trod•den** /'trɒdṇ/ or **trod, tread•ing,** *n.* —*v.* **1.** to set down the foot in walking; step: [*no obj*]: *to tread softly on the stairs.* [~ + *obj*]: *Many pilgrims have trod this same street to the holy shrine.* **2.** [~ + *obj*] to step or walk, esp. so as to press or injure something; crush; trample: *The boys trod on the flowers carelessly.* —*n.* [*count*] **3.** the action of treading. **4.** the sound of footsteps: *We heard her quiet tread.* **5.** the part of a wheel or tire that touches the road, rail, etc.: *worn treads.*

tread•mill /'trɛd,mɪl/ *n.* [*count*] an exercise device consisting of moving steps or a moving belt used for continuous walking.

trea•son /'triyzən/ *n.* [*noncount*] the act of destroying one's government or of being disloyal to it. —'**trea•son•a•ble,** '**trea•son•ous,** *adj.*

treas•ure /'trɛʒər/ *n., v.,* **-ured, -ur•ing.** —*n.* **1.** [*noncount*] a mass of wealth, esp. in the form of precious metals, money, or jewels. **2.** [*count*] any thing or person greatly valued. —*v.* [~ + *obj*] **3.** to think of (someone or something) as precious; cherish: *We treasured the few moments we spent together.* —'**treas•ur•er,** *n.* [*count*]

treas•ur•y /'trɛʒəriy/ *n., pl.* **-ur•ies. 1.** a place where government revenue is stored and then set apart to be spent. **2.** the funds or revenue of a government, a private business, etc.

treat /triyt/ *v.* **1.** [~ + *obj*] to act or behave toward (someone or something) in some way: *to treat all people with respect.* **2.** [~ + *obj*] to use an agent on (something) or put (something) through a process to bring about a change: *to treat a substance with an acid; a new way to treat AIDS.* **3.** to provide with food, entertainment, etc., at one's own expense: [~ + *obj*]: *The boss treated me to dinner.* [*no obj*]: *Put your money away; I'll treat.* —*n.* [*count*] **4.** entertainment, food, etc., given or paid for by someone else, as an expression of friendliness, as a professional courtesy, etc. **5.** any special form of enjoyment: *It was a real treat to have steak for dinner.* —'**treat•ment,** *n.* [*noncount*]: *Her treatment of you was unkind.* [*count*]: *Heat treatments will relieve your back pain.*

trea•tise /'triytɪs/ *n.* [*count*] a formal piece of writing on a subject.

trea•ty /'triytiy/ *n.* [*count*], *pl.* **-ties.** a formal agreement between countries in regard to peace, friendship, etc.: *a new treaty to allow more trade.*

tre•ble /'trɛbəl/ *adj., n., v.,* **-bled, -bling.** —*adj.* **1.** threefold; triple. **2. a.** of the highest pitch or range, as a voice part or instrument. **b.** high in pitch; shrill. —*n.* **3.** [*count*] **a.** the treble part. **b.** a treble voice or instrument. **4.** [*count*] a high voice or sound. **5.** [*noncount*] the upper range of audio frequencies: *She turned up the treble on her stereo.* —*v.* **6.** to (cause to) become three times as much or as many; triple: [~ + *obj*]: *We'll treble our profits.* [*no obj*]: *Our profits will treble.*

tree /triy/ *n.* [*count*] **1.** a plant having a permanently woody trunk and branches. **2.** something that resembles a tree in form: *a coat tree.*

trek /trɛk/ *v.,* **trekked, trek•king,** *n.* —*v.* [*no obj*] **1.** to travel, esp. slowly or with difficulty: *to trek across the desert.* —*n.* [*count*] **2.** a long journey, esp. one involving hardship.

trem•ble /'trɛmbəl/ *v.* [*no obj*], **-bled, -bling. 1.** to shake with short, quick movements, as from fear or cold: *His hands trembled from fear.* **2.** (of things) to shake or vibrate with slight motion: *After the explosion the whole house trembled.* **3.** to be unsteady, as sound: *His voice trembled.*

tre•men•dous /trɪ'mɛndəs/ *adj.* **1.** very great in size, amount, or intensity: *a tremendous ocean liner.* **2.** extraordinary; excellent: *a tremendous movie.* —**tre'men•dous•ly,** *adv.*

trem•or /'trɛmər, 'triymər/ *n.* [*count*] **1.** an uncontrolled shaking of the body or limbs, as from disease, fear, or excitement: *As the fever struck, tremors shook his body.* **2.** a vibration: *the tremors following an earthquake.* **3.** an uncertain sound, as of the voice: *She asked, with a tremor in her voice, if he was going to be all right.*

trench /trɛntʃ/ *n.* [*count*] a long, narrow area dug out of the ground.

trend /trɛnd/ *n.* [*count*] **1.** the way or direction things tend to go: *the trend of current events.* **2.** style; vogue: *the new trend in women's clothing.* —'**trend•y,** *adj.,* **-i•er, -i•est.**

tres•pass /'trɛspəs, -pæs/ *n.* [*count*] **1.** an act of entering the home or property of another without permission. **2.** an offense or sin: *Forgive us our trespasses.* —*v.* [*no obj*] **3.** to commit a trespass. **4.** to commit an offense; sin. —'**tres•pass•er,** *n.* [*count*]

tri-, a combining form meaning: three (*triangle*).

tri•ad /'trayæd, -əd/ *n.* [*count*] a group of three. —**tri'ad•ic,** *adj.*

tri•al /'trayəl, trayl/ *n.* **1.** the examination of the facts of a case before a court of law, in order to decide on a person's guilt or innocence: [*noncount*]: *on trial for murder.* [*count*]: *He is entitled to a trial before a jury.* **2.** [*count*] the act of testing to find out if someone or something is useful, valuable, etc.: *We gave the new worker a trial of six weeks.* **3.** [*count*] an ailment or trouble: *His blindness was a great trial to him.* **4.** [*count*] a troublesome thing or person: *That disobedient child is a trial to his parents.*

'**trial and 'error,** *n.* [*noncount*] coming to a result or a solution by making repeated tests and rejecting methods that were unsuccessful.

tri•an•gle /'tray,æŋgəl/ *n.* [*count*] a geometrical figure having three sides and three angles. —**tri•an•gu•lar** /tray'æŋgyələr/, *adj.*

tribe /trayb/ *n.* [*count*] a group of people de-

T

scended from the same ancestor, having similar customs and traditions. —'**trib•al,** *adj.*

trib•u•la•tion /,trɪbyə'leyʃən/ *n.* **1.** [*noncount*] severe trial or suffering: *He had much tribulation in his life.* **2.** [*count*] an instance of this.

tri•bu•nal /tray'byuwn], trɪ-/ *n.* [*count*] a court of justice.

trib•u•tar•y /'trɪbyə,tɛriy/ *n.* [*count*], *pl.* **-tar• ies.** a stream that flows to a larger stream: *The river system and its tributaries extend for hundreds of miles.*

trib•ute /'trɪbyuwt/ *n.* a gift, speech of praise, etc., given in gratitude toward another: [*count*]: *They gave the retiring president a tribute.* [*noncount*]: *They paid tribute to his outstanding talents.*

trick /trɪk/ *n.* [*count*] **1.** a sneaky plan to deceive or cheat: *He played a nasty trick on me.* **2.** a silly or mischievous act; a practical joke. **3.** a clever act done to entertain, amuse, etc.: *some clever card tricks.* —*v.* [~ + *obj*] **4.** to deceive: *They tricked me into giving them my money.* **5.** to cheat (someone), forcing someone to lose something: *He was tricked out of his inheritance by dishonest lawyers.* —*Idiom.* **6. do the trick,** to produce the desired effect: *Give me that screwdriver—that should do the trick.* —'**trick•er•y,** *n.* [*noncount*]

trick•le /'trɪkəl/ *v.,* **-led, -ling,** *n.* —*v.* **1.** to (cause to) flow by drops: [*no obj*]: *Tears trickled down her cheeks.* [~ + *obj*]: *She trickled some water into his mouth.* **2.** [*no obj*] to pass in small amounts or slowly: *The guests trickled out of the room.* —*n.* [*count*] **3.** a trickling flow or stream. **4.** a small or slow amount of anything proceeding.

trick•y /'trɪkiy/ *adj.,* **-i•er, -i•est. 1.** willing to use deceitful tricks: *a tricky salesman.* **2.** difficult; requiring clever thought or action: *a tricky dance step.*

tri•cy•cle /'traysɪkəl, -,sɪkəl/ *n.* [*count*] a vehicle, esp. one for children, having one large front wheel and two small rear wheels, propelled by foot pedals.

tried /trayd/ *v.* pt. and pp. of TRY.

tri•fle /'trayfəl/ *n., v.,* **-fled, -fling.** —*n.* [*count*] **1.** something of very little value: *buying little trifles for the kids.* **2.** a small amount; a bit: *He's still a trifle angry.* —*v.* [~ + *with* + *obj*] **3.** to treat (someone) without seriousness or respect: *Don't trifle with me!*

trig•ger /'trɪgər/ *n.* [*count*] **1.** a small lever in a gun that, when pressed by the finger, fires the gun. **2.** anything that causes a reaction: *a trigger for the fight.* —*v.* [~ + *obj*] **3.** to cause or begin (a chain of events): *Inflation triggered unemployment.*

trill /trɪl/ *n.* [*count*] **1.** a rapid alternation between two nearby musical tones. **2.** a similar quavering sound, as that made by a bird. —*v.* **3.** to sing, pronounce, or play with a trill: [~ + *obj*]: *to trill a few notes.* [*no obj*]: *birds trilling in the morning.*

tril•lion /'trɪlyən/ *n., pl.* **-lions,** (*as after a numeral*) **-lion,** *adj.* —*n.* [*count*] **1.** a number written in the U.S. as 1 followed by 12 zeros, and in Great Britain as 1 followed by 18 zeros. —*adj.* [*after a number and before a noun*] **2.** amounting to one trillion in number: *one trillion dollars.* —'**tril•lionth,** *n.* [*count*], *adj.*

tril•o•gy /'trɪlədʒiy/ *n.* [*count*], *pl.* **-gies.** a series or group of three plays, novels, etc., closely related in characters, theme, etc.

trim /trɪm/ *v.,* **trimmed, trim•ming,** *n., adj.,* **trim•mer, trim•mest.** —*v.* [~ + *obj*] **1.** to make neat or orderly by cutting, paring, etc.: *to trim a hedge.* **2.** to cut down; reduce: *to trim the sales force.* **3.** to decorate with something; esp., to decorate a store window: *to trim the windows for Christmas.* —*n.* **4.** [*noncount*] the condition, order, or fitness of a person or thing for action, etc.: *The boxer was in fighting trim.* **5.** [*noncount*] material used for decoration. **6.** [*count*] a trimming by cutting, clipping, or the like: *He didn't want a full haircut, just a (quick) trim.* —*adj.* **7.** neat or smart in appearance: *trim lawns.* **8.** (of a person) in excellent physical condition: *Swimming is a good way to keep trim.*

trim•ming /'trɪmɪŋ/ *n.* **1.** [*noncount*] anything used for decoration: *the trimming on a uniform.* **2.** Usually, **trimmings.** [*plural*] something that goes with a main dish: *They had roast turkey with all the trimmings.*

Trin•i•ty /'trɪnɪtiy/ *n., pl.* **-ties** for 2. **1.** in Christian doctrine, the union of three divine persons (Father, Son, and Holy Ghost). **2.** [*count; trinity*] a group of three; triad.

trin•ket /'trɪŋkɪt/ *n.* [*count*] a small ornament, etc., of little value: *a few trinkets for the kids.*

tri•o /'triyow/ *n.* [*count*], *pl.* **tri•os. 1.** any group of three. **2.** a musical composition for three voices or instruments. **3.** a company of three singers or players.

trip /trɪp/ *n., v.,* **tripped, trip•ping.** —*n.* [*count*] **1.** a short journey: *my weekly trip to the bank.* **2.** a misstep, as by catching one's foot. **3.** *Slang.* **a.** an instance of being under the influence of a drug that produces hallucinations, esp. LSD. **b.** an exciting or unusual experience. —*v.* **4.** to (cause to) stumble: [*no obj*]: *to trip on one of the toys.* [~ + *obj*]: *He stuck out his foot and tripped her.* **5.** to (cause to) make a slip or mistake, as in conversation or conduct: [~ + *obj*]: *The lawyer tried his best to trip up the witness; to trip him up.* [*no obj*]: *During his speech he tripped up when he confused the two ambassadors.*

tri•ple /'trɪpəl/ *adj., n., v.,* **-pled, -pling.** —*adj.* [*before a noun*] **1.** threefold; consisting of three parts. **2.** three times as great: *triple profits.* —*n.* [*count*] **3.** an amount, number, etc., three times as great as another. —*v.* **4.** to (cause to) become triple: [~ + *obj*]: *Our company tripled its profits.* [*no obj*]: *Profits tripled last year.*

tri•plet /'trɪplɪt/ *n.* [*count*] one of three children born to the same mother at one time.

tri•pod /'traypɒd/ *n.* [*count*] a three-legged stand, as for a camera.

trite /trayt/ *adj.,* **trit•er, trit•est.** (of a word, phrase, or expression) lacking in originality and freshness because of constant use; uninteresting.

tri•umph /'trayəmf, -ʌmf/ *n.* **1.** [*count*] great victory; success or achievement: *some medical triumphs in the war against cancer.* **2.** [*noncount*] joy resulting from victory or success: *a feeling of triumph.* —*v.* [*no obj*] **3.** to gain a victory or be highly successful: *The Allies triumphed over the Axis in World War II.* —**tri'um•phant,** *adj.*: *They were triumphant when they got the building contract.* —**tri'um•phant•ly,** *adv.*

triv•i•a /'trɪviyə/ *n.* matters or things that are unimportant; meaningless facts or details; trifles: [*noncount; used with a singular verb*]: *Trivia is what you need to know to do well in some games.* [*plural; used with a plural verb*]: *studying numerous trivia.*

triv•i•al /'trɪviyəl/ *adj.* of or relating to trivia.

—**triv•i•al•i•ty** /ˌtrɪviy'ælɪtiy/, *n.*, *pl.* **-ties.** [*noncount*]: *the triviality of considering what clothes to wear after an earthquake.* [*count*]: *the trivialities of daily living.*

trod /trɒd/ *v.* a pt. and pp. of TREAD.

trod•den /'trɒdn̩/ *v.* a pp. of TREAD.

troll[1] /trowl/ *v.* to fish in (a body of water) by trailing a line behind a slow-moving boat: [~ + *obj*]: *trolling the lake for trout.* [*no obj*]: *trolling for trout.*

troll[2] /trowl/ *n.* [*count*] (in Scandinavian folk stories) a supernatural being, usually hostile to humans, who lives underground or in caves.

trol•ley /'trɒliy/ *n.* [*count*], *pl.* **-leys** or **-lies. 1.** TROLLEY CAR. **2.** a small truck or car operated on a track, as in a factory. **3.** a serving cart, as for desserts.

'trolley ˌcar, *n.* [*count*] a streetcar propelled electrically by means of an overhead wire.

trom•bone /trɒm'bown, 'trɒmbown/ *n.* [*count*] [*noncount*] a brass musical instrument having valves or a sliding tube for varying the tone.

troop /truwp/ *n.* [*count*] **1.** a group of persons or things; a band of people. **2. troops,** [*plural*] a body of soldiers, police, etc. —*v.* [*no obj*] **3.** to walk, as if in a march: *The kids came trooping down to breakfast.*

troop•er /'truwpər/ *n.* [*count*] a member of a state police force.

tro•phy /'trowfiy/ *n.* [*count*], *pl.* **-phies.** an object for display, won or awarded as a sign of victory, etc.; an award or prize: *a football trophy.*

trop•ic /'trɒpɪk/ *n.* [*count*] **1.** either of two parallel lines of latitude on the earth's globe, about 23½° N and about 23½° S of the equator. **2. the tropics,** the regions lying between these, having a hot climate. —**'trop•i•cal,** *adj.*

trot /trɒt/ *v.*, **trot•ted, trot•ting,** *n.* —*v.* **1.** (of a horse) to (cause to) go at a pace between a walk and a run: [*no obj*]: *The horse trotted along.* [~ + *obj*]: *The rider trotted his horse for the competition.* **2.** [*no obj*] to go at a quick, steady pace: *He trotted along behind his big brother.* —*n.* [*count*] **3.** the pace of a horse or person when trotting.

trou•ble /'trʌbəl/ *v.*, **-bled, -bling,** *n.* —*v.* [~ + *obj*] **1.** to disturb the calm and contentment of; worry: *The sufferings of the poor troubled him.* **2.** to put to inconvenience, bother, or the like: *May I trouble you for a match? May I trouble you to shut the door?* —*n.* **3.** [*noncount*] difficulty or annoyance: *He loves to make trouble for me.* **4.** an unfortunate occurrence; misfortune: [*noncount*]: *He's in a bit of financial trouble at the moment.* [*count*]: *He's had some financial troubles lately.* **5.** [*noncount*] a physical disease, etc.: *heart trouble.* **6.** [*count; singular*] effort or inconvenience in accomplishing some deed, etc.: *I don't want you to go to any trouble over this.* —*Idiom.* **7. in trouble,** in danger or difficulty: *He was in big trouble with the police.* —**'trou•bled,** *adj.*: *a troubled look.* —**'trou•ble•some,** *adj.*

trou•ble•mak•er /'trʌbəlˌmeykər/ *n.* [*count*] one who causes trouble for others.

trough /trɔf, trɒf/ *n.* [*count*] a long, boxlike container, used chiefly to hold water or food for animals.

troupe /truwp/ *n.* [*count*] a company of actors, esp. one that travels.

trou•sers /'trawzərz/ *n.* [*plural*] PANTS. —**'trouˌser,** *adj.*

trout /trawt/ *n.* [*count*], *pl.* (*esp. when thought of as a group*) **trout,** (*esp. for kinds or species*)

trouts. a usually speckled freshwater game fish of the salmon family.

trow•el /'trawəl/ *n.* [*count*] **1.** a tool having a flat blade with a handle, used for spreading and smoothing out mortar, etc. **2.** a similar tool with a curved blade, used in gardening.

tru•ant /'truwənt/ *n.* [*count*] a student who stays away from school without permission. —**'tru•an•cy,** *n.* [*noncount*]

truce /truws/ *n.* [*count*] a period of time in which all fighting is stopped, by agreement of all those involved; a cease-fire: *to declare a truce for Christmas.*

truck /trʌk/ *n.* [*count*] **1.** a motor vehicle for carrying goods and materials. **2.** a platform or open cart with wheels used for transporting heavy objects. —*v.* [~ + *obj*] **3.** to transport or deliver (articles, etc.) by truck. —**'truck•er,** *n.* [*count*]

trudge /trʌdʒ/ *v.*, **trudged, trudg•ing,** *n.* —*v.* **1.** to walk (along or over), esp. wearily: [*no obj*]: *He trudged back to his house.* [~ + *obj*]: *to trudge the streets.* —*n.* [*count; usually singular*] **2.** a long, tiring walk: *a slow trudge to the gas station.*

true /truw/ *adj.*, **tru•er, tru•est,** *adv.* —*adj.* **1.** being in accordance with reality or fact: *a true story.* **2.** [*before a noun*] real; genuine; authentic: *true gold.* **3.** loyal; faithful; steadfast: *a true friend; He was true to his principles.* **4.** exact; precise; accurate; correct: *a true copy.* —*adv.* **5.** in a true manner; truly; truthfully. —*Idiom.* **6. come true,** (of a wish, etc.) to become a reality: *All your dreams will come true when you make this change in your life.*

tru•ly /'truwliy/ *adv.* **1.** in accordance with truth; truthfully: *Mozart was truly a brilliant composer.* **2.** really; genuinely: *I'm truly sorry I hurt your feelings.* **3.** (used at the end of a letter) sincerely: *Yours truly, Jane and Michael Banks.*

trum•pet /'trʌmpɪt/ *n.* **1.** a brass musical instrument having a long curved tube that widens into a bell-shaped end: [*count*]: *a beautiful trumpet.* [*noncount*]: *He plays trumpet for the band.* **2.** [*count*] a sound like that of a trumpet. —*v.* **3.** to give out a loud cry: [~ + *obj*]: *The elephant trumpeted a cry of warning.* [*no obj*]: *elephants trumpeting.* **4.** [~ + *obj*] to announce loudly or widely: *The president trumpeted his new plan.*

trunk /trʌŋk/ *n.* [*count*] **1.** the main stem of a tree. **2.** a large sturdy box for clothes, personal possessions, etc. **3.** a large area in the rear of an automobile, for holding luggage, etc. **4.** the body of a person or an animal not including the head and limbs; torso. **5.** the long, flexible nose of the elephant. **6. trunks,** [*plural*] shorts worn by men, as for swimming.

trust /trʌst/ *n.* **1.** [*noncount*] strong belief or faith in the goodness, honesty, or ability of a person or thing: *trust in government.* **2.** [*noncount*] the duty of a person in authority: *The president occupies a position of trust.* **3.** [*noncount*] charge, care, or guardianship: *We left our valuables in her trust.* **4.** a legal relationship in which a person holds title to money, property, etc., for another: [*noncount*]: *The money was held in trust for her.* [*count*]: *Her parents set up a trust for her.* —*v.* [~ + *obj*] **5.** to have trust or confidence in: *He didn't trust the psychologist.* **6.** to expect confidently; hope: *I trust that the job will soon be finished.* —**'trust•ful,** *adj.* —**'trust,wor•thi•ness,** *n.* [*noncount*] —**'trust•wor•thy,** *adj.* —**'trust•y,** *adj.*, **-i•er, -i•est.**

T

trust•ee /trʌ'stiy/ n. [count], pl. **-ees.** one whose job is to manage a trust.

truth /truwθ/ n., pl. **truths** /truwðz, truwθs/. **1.** [noncount] the actual state (of something): Do you promise to tell the truth? **2.** [noncount] the condition of being factual or real: The detective attempted to check the truth of the witness's statement. **3.** [count] a fact, statement, etc., proven to be correct: mathematical truths. —'**truth•ful**, adj. —'**truth•ful•ly**, adv. —'**truth•ful•ness**, n. [noncount]

try /tray/ v., **tried, try•ing,** n., pl. **tries.** —v. **1.** to attempt to do (something): [~ + obj]: Try running a mile a day. [no obj]: You must try harder if you want to succeed. **2.** [~ + obj] to test or sample: He tried each button, but nothing worked. He tried (out) a new recipe for chicken. He tried it (out). **3.** [~ + obj] to examine facts and decide on something, as in a court of law, esp. to affirm the guilt or innocence of (a person): The state tried him for murder. **4.** [~ + obj] to put to a severe test: She is trying my patience with her chatter. **5. try on,** to put on an article of clothing to judge how well it fits: Try this jacket on. She tried on every jacket in the store. **6. try out,** to compete for a role, as by taking part in a test or trial: She tried out for the swim team. —n. [count] **7.** an attempt or effort.

try•ing /'trayɪŋ/ adj. straining one's patience and goodwill; irritating: He found her very trying.

try•out /'tray,awt/ n. [count] a trial or test to see if something is strong enough or in good enough condition for some purpose: a good tryout for the car.

tryst /trɪst/ n. [count] an appointment for a meeting, esp. one made secretly by lovers.

tsar /zɑr, tsɑr/ n. CZAR.

T-shirt or **tee shirt** /'tiy,ʃɜrt/ n. [count] a lightweight, short-sleeved pullover shirt.

tsp., an abbreviation of: **1.** teaspoon. **2.** teaspoonful.

tub /tʌb/ n. [count] **1.** a bathtub. **2.** a broad, round, open container. **3.** any of various small, usually round containers: a tub of butter.

tu•ba /'tuwbə, 'tyuw-/ n., pl. **-bas.** a brass musical instrument with valves, having a deep sound: [count]: Tubas are quite large. [noncount] He plays tuba in the symphony orchestra.

tub•by /'tʌbiy/ adj., **-bi•er, -bi•est.** short and fat.

tube /tuwb, tyuwb/ n. **1.** [count] a hollow, rounded, narrow piece of metal, glass, etc., used esp. for carrying liquids or gases: a short rubber tube. **2.** [count] a small, soft container closed at one end, with a capped opening at the other end, from which a substance, as toothpaste, may be squeezed. **3. the tube,** [singular] Informal. television: What's on the tube tonight? **4.** Brit. SUB-WAY (def. 1). —'**tu•bu•lar,** adj.

tu•ber /'tuwbər, 'tyuw-/ n. [count] a thick, fleshy underground stem, as a potato.

tu•ber•cu•lo•sis /tʊ,bɜrkyə'lowsɪs, tyʊ-/ n. [noncount] an infectious disease that usually affects the lungs. Abbr.: TB

tuck /tʌk/ v. [~ + obj] **1.** to put into a small, close place: Tuck the money into your wallet. **2.** to push in the loose ends or edges of so as to hold closely in place: Tuck in your blouse. Tuck your shirt in. **3.** to cover snugly or tightly in this manner: She tucked the children into bed. She tucked in the children at bedtime. She tucked the children in and read to them. —n. [count] **4.**

something tucked or folded in. **5.** a fold sewn into cloth, as to make a tighter fit.

tuck•er /'tʌkər/ v. [~ + obj] Informal. **tucker out,** to tire; exhaust: All this skiing will tucker the children out. That long climb would tucker out anyone.

-tude, a suffix added to roots, esp. adjectives, to form nouns that refer to abstract ideas: aptitude; gratitude; altitude.

Tues. or **Tue.,** an abbreviation of: Tuesday.

Tues•day /'tuwzdey, -diy, 'tyuwz-/ n. the third day of the week, following Monday: See you on Tuesday. [count]: Let's meet on the 23rd; that's three Tuesdays from today.

tuft /tʌft/ n. [count] a group of hairs, feathers, or leaves gathered close together at one end.

tug /tʌg/ v., **tugged, tug•ging,** n. —v. [~ + obj] **1.** to pull at with force or effort: He tugged his beard while he thought; to tug at his beard. **2.** to move (something) by pulling with force: She tugged the trunk into the closet. —n. [count] **3.** an act or instance of tugging; pull. **4.** TUGBOAT.

tug•boat /'tʌg,bowt/ n. [count] a small, powerful boat for pulling ships, barges, etc.

'tug of 'war, n. [count] a contest between two teams at opposite ends of a rope, each team trying to pull the other over a line.

tu•i•tion /tuw'ɪʃən, tyuw-/ n. [noncount] the charge or fee for instruction: tuition for college.

tu•lip /'tuwlɪp, 'tyuw-/ n. [count] a plant of the lily family, having large, showy, bell-shaped flowers.

tum•ble /'tʌmbəl/ v., **-bled, -bling,** n. —v. **1.** to (cause to) fall helplessly down: [no obj]: She tumbled down the stairs. [~ + obj]: She tumbled the boxes down the stairs. **2.** to roll end over end, or to flow over and down: [no obj]: The water tumbled down the waterfall. [~ + obj]: The army tumbled rocks on top of the enemy. **3.** [no obj] to fall or decline rapidly; drop: Prices on the stock exchange tumbled. **4.** [no obj] to go, come, etc., in a fast, disorderly way: Tourists came tumbling out of the bus. —n. [count] **5.** an act of tumbling. **6.** a movement in gymnastics. **7.** an accidental fall; spill.

tum•bler /'tʌmblər/ n. [count] **1.** one who performs acrobatic movements. **2.** a part of a lock that allows the bolt to move. **3.** a stemless drinking glass having a flat, often thick bottom.

tum•my /'tʌmiy/ n. [count], pl. **-mies.** Informal. the stomach or abdomen.

tu•mor /'tuwmər, 'tyuw-/ n. [count] an abnormal growth of cells in animal or plant tissue. Also, esp. Brit., '**tu•mour.**

tu•mult /'tuwmʌlt, -məlt, 'tyuw-/ n. **1.** [count; usually singular] a noisy disturbance caused by a mob: a loud tumult in the street. **2.** [noncount] a condition of confusion and disorder: a state of tumult following the war. —tu'mul•tu•ous, adj.

tu•na /'tuwnə, 'tyuw-/ n. [count], pl. **-na** (esp. when thought of as a group) **-nas,** (esp. for kinds or species) a large sea-dwelling food fish.

tune /tuwn, tyuwn/ n., v., **tuned, tun•ing.** —n. **1.** [count] a series of musical sounds forming a melody: She whistled a happy tune. **2.** [noncount] relationship that is harmonious or agreeable: Her ideas were not in tune with mine. —v. **3.** [~ + obj] to adjust (a musical instrument) to a pitch: to tune a guitar (up) or to tune (up) a guitar. **4.** [~ + obj] to adjust (a motor, etc.) so as to make it work properly: to tune the engine (up) or to tune (up) the engine. **5. tune in,** to adjust a radio or television so as to receive (signals, etc.):

Tune in to our station next week. Tune in your favorite station; to tune it in. **6. tune out,** *Slang.* to stop paying attention to: *Whenever her parents ask her about school, she just tunes out. She just tunes them out; to tune out her parents.* —*Idiom.* **7. change one's tune,** to reverse one's opinions.

tu•nic /ˈtuwnɪk, ˈtyuw-/ *n.* [count] **1.** an outer garment resembling a long, loose shirt worn by the ancient Greeks and Romans. **2.** a straight upper garment, extending to the hips.

tun•nel /ˈtʌnl/ *n., v.,* **-neled, -nel•ing** or (*esp. Brit.*) **-nelled, -nel•ling.** —*n.* [count] **1.** an underground passage, esp. one for trains or automobiles. —*v.* **2.** to make or dig out (a tunnel) through or under (something): [~ + *obj*]: *to tunnel one's way out of prison.* [*no obj*]: *to tunnel out of prison.*

tur•ban /ˈtɜrbən/ *n.* [count] a man's headdress worn chiefly by Muslims in S Asia, made of a long cloth of silk, cotton, etc., wound around the head.

tur•bine /ˈtɜrbɪn, -baɪn/ *n.* [count] an engine or motor driven by a moving fluid, as steam or water, by hot gases, or by air: *the helicopter's turbines.*

tur•bu•lence /ˈtɜrbyə ləns/ *n.* [noncount] **1.** a state of confusion or disorder: *the turbulence of the revolution.* **2.** swirling motion in water or air: *The aircraft flew into turbulence.* —ˈtur•bu•lent, *adj.*

Turk /tɜrk/ *n.* [count] a person born or living in Turkey.

tur•key /ˈtɜrkiy/ *n., pl.* **-keys,** (*esp. when thought of as a group*) **-key. 1.** [count] a large North American bird of the pheasant family. **2.** [noncount] the flesh of this bird, used as food. **3.** [count] *Slang.* a person or thing of little attractiveness or value.

Turk•ish /ˈtɜrkɪʃ/ *adj.* **1.** of or relating to Turkey. **2.** of or relating to the language spoken by many of the people in Turkey. —*n.* [noncount] **3.** the language spoken by many of the people in Turkey.

tur•moil /ˈtɜrmɔɪl/ *n.* a state of commotion, disorder, or disturbance: [count; usually singular]: *Without her, the house has been in a turmoil.* [noncount]: *a factory in turmoil since the strike.*

turn /tɜrn/ *v.* **1.** to (cause to) move around a central point; rotate: [~ + *obj*]: *to turn a wheel.* [*no obj*]: *The wheel wouldn't turn.* **2.** to (cause to) move around or partly around: [~ + *obj*]: *to turn a key in a door.* [*no obj*]: *The key turned in the lock.* **3.** to change or reverse the position or placement of: [~ + *obj*]: *to turn a page.* [*no obj*]: *The suspect turned and ran.* **4.** to change the nature or appearance of; to (make something) become something else: [~ + *obj*]: *Worry has turned his hair gray. The heat turned the ice to water.* [*no obj*]: *The neighborhood has turned into a slum. The milk turned sour.* **5.** to (cause to) be affected with nausea, as the stomach: [~ + *obj*]: *Violence turns her stomach.* [*no obj*]: *My stomach turned at the terrible thought.* **6.** to give attention to (doing something): [~ + *obj*]: *He turned his mind to more practical matters.* **7.** to go around: [~ + *obj*]: *He turned a corner and disappeared from sight.* [*no obj*]: *He turned to the left and walked away.* **8.** [~ + *noun*] to reach (a certain age, etc.): *He turned sixty last week.* **9.** [~ + *obj*] to cause to go; send; drive: *She turned him away.* **10.** to (cause to) be angry (with) or be-

tray: [~ + *obj*]: *to turn children against their parents.* [*no obj*]: *They turned against their parents.* **11.** to twist out of position: [~ + *obj*]: *He turned his ankle when he fell.* [*no obj*]: *His ankle turned when he fell.* **12.** [*no obj*] to depend: *The whole question turns on this point.* **13.** [*no obj*] to go to someone for help or information: *to turn to a friend for a loan.* **14. turn down,** to refuse, deny, or reject (a person, etc.): *They turned down your request for promotion. She asked him to marry her, but he turned her down.* **15. turn in, a.** to give (something) to someone in authority: *Turn in your keys and report to the office. He turned his keys in.* **b.** to go to bed; retire: *I'm exhausted; I think I'll turn in.* **16. turn off, a.** to stop the flow of (water, etc.), as by closing a valve (or a faucet): *The electrician turned off the electricity to the house. The plumber turned the water off.* **b.** to put out or extinguish (a light): *Turn off the lights and go to bed. Turn the light off.* **c.** *Slang.* to disgust; to cause a feeling of dislike: *Her manners turn me off. She turned off every dinner guest with her bad manners.* **17. turn on, a.** to cause (water, etc.) to flow, as by opening a valve (or a faucet): *to turn on the gas; to turn the gas on again.* **b.** to put on or switch on (a light): *Turn on a light. Turn the lights on.* **c.** *Slang.* to (cause to) feel pleasure or excitement: *Architecture really turns her on.* **18. turn out, a.** to put out or extinguish (a light): *Turn out the light. Turn the lights out.* **b.** to produce as the result of labor: *The factory turns out fifty computers every hour. Our factory can turn them out quickly.* **19. turn over,** to transfer; give: *He went to the police and turned over the gun. He turned the gun over to the police.* **20. turn up, a.** to (cause to) be noticed, uncovered, or found: *Some new facts have just turned up. He turned up some new leads in the investigation. Did the detective turn anything up yet?* **b.** to intensify or increase, as volume or pressure: *to turn up the radio or to turn the radio up.* **c.** to appear; arrive; happen: *She always believed that "something (good) will turn up."* —*n.* **21.** [count] the act of turning or rotating: *a turn of the handle.* **22.** [count; usually singular] a chance or right time (to do something): *It's my turn to speak.* See *in turn* and *out of turn* below. **23.** [count] an act of changing or reversing course or direction. **24.** [count] a change in condition or circumstances: *Her battle with cancer has taken a turn for the worse.* **25.** [count] the point or time of change: *at the turn of the century (= when the century changed, as from 1899 to 1900).* —*Idiom.* **26. in turn,** in order of one following another: *We shook hands in turn with each of the people on line.* **27. out of turn,** out of proper order: *He went out of turn and tried to push his way to the front.* **28. take turns,** to follow one another in alternating order: *We took turns making breakfast.* **29. turn one's back on,** to abandon, ignore, or reject: *She turned her back on her boyfriend and left him for another.*

ˈturning ˌpoint, *n.* [count] a point at which an important change takes place: *We reached a turning point in our relationship.*

tur•nip /ˈtɜrnɪp/ *n.* [count] the thick, edible, fleshy root of certain plants of the mustard family.

turn•out /ˈtɜrnˌawt/ *n.* [count] the number of persons who come to an exhibition, party, etc.; attendance: *There was a huge turnout at their first concert.*

turn•o•ver /ˈtɜrnˌowvər/ *n.* [count] **1.** the

T

amount of business done in a given time. **2.** the rate at which workers are replaced: *a high rate of turnover.* **3.** a baked pastry in which half the dough is folded to cover and seal in the filling.

turn•pike /'tɜrn,payk/ n. [count] a high-speed highway or expressway that charges a fee for its use.

turn•stile /'tɜrn,stayl/ n. [count] a bar or similar structure that blocks passage until a charge is paid, or that allows people to enter one at a time: *He put his token in the turnstile.*

turn•ta•ble /'tɜrn,teybəl/ n. [count] the rotating disk that spins the record on a phonograph.

tur•pen•tine /'tɜrpən,tayn/ n. [noncount] a strong-smelling resin taken from trees, used for removing or thinning paint.

tur•quoise /'tɜrkɔyz, -kwɔyz/ n. **1.** [count] [noncount] a mineral of copper and aluminum, colored greenish blue and cut as a gem. **2.** [noncount] a greenish blue or bluish green.

tur•tle /'tɜrtl/ n. [count], pl. **-tles,** (*esp. when thought of as a group*) **-tle.** any of various water- and land-dwelling reptiles having the body enclosed in a shell.

tur•tle•neck /'tɜrtl,nɛk/ n. [count] **1.** a high, close-fitting collar, appearing esp. on pullover sweaters. **2.** a garment with such a neck.

tusk /tʌsk/ n. [count] a long, pointed tooth, usually one of a pair, of an animal, such as an elephant or a walrus.

tu•tor /'tuwtər, 'tyuw-/ n. [count] **1.** one employed to instruct another, esp. privately. —*v.* **2.** to act as a tutor to: [~ + obj]: *She tutored several Japanese ladies in English.* [no obj]: *She tutored as often as she could.*

tu•tu /'tuw,tuw/ n. [count], pl. **-tus.** a short, full skirt, usually made of several light layers, worn by ballerinas.

tux /tʌks/ n. [count] Informal. a tuxedo.

tux•e•do /tʌk'siydow/ n. [count], pl. **-dos. 1.** a man's jacket for semiformal evening dress. **2.** a complete outfit of men's semiformal clothing, including this jacket and dark trousers: *The groom wore a fancy tuxedo.*

TV or **tv,** an abbreviation of: television.

tweak /twiyk/ v. [~ + obj] to pinch and pull with a jerk and twist: *to tweak someone's ear.*

tweed /twiyd/ n. [noncount] a rough, coarse wool cloth produced esp. in Scotland.

tweet /twiyt/ n. [count] **1.** a chirping sound, as that made by a small bird. —*v.* [no obj] **2.** to chirp.

tweez•ers /'twiyzərz/ n. [plural; used with a singular or plural verb] a small tool made of two pieces of metal joined at one end, used for pulling out hairs, etc.

twelfth /twɛlfθ/ adj. **1.** next after the eleventh. **2.** being one of 12 equal parts. —*n.* [count] **3.** a twelfth part, esp. of one (1/12). **4.** the twelfth member of a series.

twelve /twɛlv/ n. [count] **1.** a number, 10 plus 2, written as 12. —*adj.* [before a noun] **2.** amounting to 12 in number.

twen•ty /'twɛnti, 'twʌn-/ n., pl. **-ties,** adj. —*n.* [count] **1.** a number, 10 times 2, written as 20. —*adj.* [before a noun] **2.** amounting to 20 in number. —**'twen•ti•eth,** adj., n. [count]

twice /tways/ adv. two times: *Our class meets twice a week.*

twid•dle /'twɪdl/ v., **-dled, -dling.** to play idly with the fingers, esp. circling the thumbs around each other; twirl: [~ + obj]: *He sat and twiddled*

his thumbs while he waited. [no obj]: *Quit twiddling.*

twig /twɪg/ n. [count] a small, thin piece of a wooden branch or stem.

twi•light /'tway,layt/ n. [noncount] the faint light that appears just after sunset, or sometimes just before sunrise; the period of time when this light can be seen.

twill /twɪl/ n. [noncount] a fabric made from cotton cloth.

twin /twɪn/ n. [count] **1.** either of two offspring born at one birth: *identical twins.* **2.** either of two persons or things that appear very similar. —*adj.* [before a noun] **3.** being one of a pair; identical: *twin towers.*

twine /twayn/ n., v., **twined, twin•ing.** —*n.* [noncount] **1.** a strong string composed of several strands twisted together. —*v.* **2.** to twist or wind: [~ + obj]: *She twined her fingers in her hair.* [no obj]: *The weeds had twined around the fence.*

twinge /twɪndʒ/ n. [count] **1.** a sudden, sharp pain: *He felt a twinge in his side.* **2.** a sudden, sharp feeling of distress: *He felt a twinge of guilt.*

twin•kle /'twɪŋkəl/ v., **-kled, -kling,** n. —*v.* [no obj] **1.** to shine on and off again continuously with quick flashes of light; sparkle: *Stars twinkled in the night sky.* —*n.* **2.** [count] a flash or flicker of light. **3.** [count; usually singular] a bright shining or sparkle in the eyes, showing amusement or pleasure.

twirl /twɜrl/ v. **1.** to (cause to) rotate rapidly: [~ + obj]: *The cheerleader twirled a baton.* [no obj]: *The baton twirled in the cheerleader's hands.* **2.** to turn quickly so as to face in another direction: [no obj]: *She twirled around and faced her partner.* [~ + obj]: *He twirled her around on the dance floor.* —*n.* [count] **3.** an act or instance of twirling.

twist /twɪst/ v. **1.** [~ + obj] to combine, as several strands, by winding together: *She twisted her sister's hair into a braid.* **2.** to change in shape, as by turning the ends in opposite directions: [~ + obj]: *to twist a paper clip.* [no obj]: *Paper clips twist easily.* **3.** to turn so as to face in another direction: [no obj]: *He twisted around to see who it was.* [~ + obj]: *He twisted his head around to see who was there.* **4.** to turn (something) from one direction to another, as by rotating: [~ + obj]: *He slowly twisted the doorknob.* [no obj]: *He watched as the doorknob slowly twisted.* **5.** to turn sharply or (cause to) be suddenly pulled out of place; sprain: [~ + obj]: *He fell and twisted his ankle.* [no obj]: *His ankle twisted when he fell.* **6.** to change the appearance of (the face, etc.) into something unnatural; contort: [~ + obj]: *She twisted her face into a smile.* [no obj]: *His face twisted into a frown.* **7.** [~ + obj] to alter so as to misstate the usual or correct meaning of: *He accused us of twisting his remarks.* **8.** [no obj] to bend or turn in different directions: *The road twisted and turned for about a mile.* —*n.* [count] **9.** a sudden change in direction; turn: *several twists in the road.* **10.** anything formed by or as if by twisting. **11.** the act or process of twining strands together. **12.** a sudden change of course, as of events in life or a literary work: *the twists of fate.* —*Idiom.* **13. twist someone's arm,** to use force or persuasion on someone: *I didn't want to go along with the idea, but they twisted my arm.*

twist•er /'twɪstər/ n. [count] Informal. a tornado.

twitch /twɪtʃ/ v. **1.** [no obj] [~ + obj] to (cause

to) move with a sudden, jerking motion, or a series of such motions, as a part of the body. **2.** to tug or pull at with a quick, short movement: [~ + *obj*]: *Someone twitched my coat sleeve.* [*no obj*]: *Someone twitched at his coat sleeve.* —*n.* [*count*] **3.** a quick, jerky, uncontrolled movement of the body or of some part of it, as a muscle.

twit•ter /'twɪtər/ *v.* [*no obj*] **1.** to make a number of short, quick, high-pitched sounds, as a bird does: *birds twittering in the trees.* **2.** to talk lightly and rapidly, in an excited, trembling manner; chatter. —*n.* **3.** [*count*] a twittering sound. **4.** [*count; usually singular*] a state of trembling excitement: *They were all in a twitter at his visit.* —'twit•ter•y, *adj.*

two /tuw/ *n.*, *pl.* **twos**, *adj.* —*n.* [*count*] **1.** a number, 1 plus 1, written as 2. —*adj.* [*before a noun*] **2.** amounting to two in number. —*Idiom.* **3. in two,** into two separate parts, as halves: *The cake was cut in two.* **4. put two and two together,** to reach the correct and obvious conclusion by considering certain facts: *Putting two and two together, they found out who the murderer was.*

two•some /'tuwsəm/ *n.* [*count*] two together; a couple.

'two-'way, *adj.* [*before a noun*] **1.** moving or allowing movement in opposite directions: *two-way traffic.* **2.** involving two groups or participants: *a two-way political race.* **3.** demanding that duties be shared by both parties: *Marriage is a two-way street.* **4.** capable of both receiving and sending signals: *a two-way radio.*

TX, an abbreviation of: Texas.

-ty, a suffix meaning: state or condition (*certainty*).

ty•coon /tay'kuwn/ *n.* [*count*] a businessperson of great wealth and power.

ty•ing /'tayɪŋ/ *v.* pres. part. of TIE.

tyke or **tike** /tayk/ *n.* [*count*] a small child.

type /tayp/ *n.*, *v.*, **typed, typ•ing.** —*n.* **1.** [*count*] a class or category of things or persons sharing characteristics: *people of a criminal type.* **2.** [*count*] a person, animal, or thing thought of as a member of a class or group; a kind; a sort: *This dog is a type of terrier. What is your blood type: A, B, O, or AB?* **3.** [*count*] a person thought of as being a perfect example of: *a civil service type.* **4. a.** [*count*] a block with a raised surface used in printing a letter or a character on paper. **b.** [*noncount*] such blocks thought of as a group. **c.** [*noncount*] a printed character or printed characters: *a headline in large type.* —*v.* **5.** to write on a typewriter: [*no obj*]: *She can type very fast.* [~ + *obj*]: *She typed the whole paper by herself. She typed the paper up and sent it off. I'll type up*

the report. **6.** [~ + *obj*] to figure out the type of (a blood or tissue sample). —*Idiom.* **7. be not one's type,** to be the kind or sort of (person) one does not enjoy: *She's pretty in a glamorous sort of way, but she's just not my type.*

type••cast /'tayp,kæst/ *v.* [~ + *obj*], **-cast, -cast•ing.** to cast (an actor) in a role that matches the actor's body type, personality, etc., esp. to do so repeatedly: *He was typecast as the villain in a dozen or more films.*

type••writ•er /'tayp,raytər/ *n.* [*count*] a machine for writing in characters similar to printer's types by pressing the letters of a keyboard.

ty•phoid /'tayfɔyd/ *n.* [*noncount*] Also called **'typhoid 'fever.** a disease with high fever and diarrhea, spread by means of food or water.

ty•phoon /tay'fuwn/ *n.* [*count*] a cyclone or hurricane of the tropical areas of the W Pacific and the China seas.

ty•phus /'tayfəs/ *n.* [*noncount*] a serious infectious disease carried by lice and fleas, causing exhaustion, headache, and a sudden appearance of reddish spots on the body. Also called **'typhus 'fever.**

typ•i•cal /'tɪpɪkəl/ *adj.* **1.** of or relating to a type; being an example of a type: *a typical family.* **2.** having the character or qualities of a person or group of persons, animals, or things: *his typical behavior; It was typical of him to give a twenty-minute speech.* —'**typ•i•cal•ly,** *adv.*

typ•i•fy /'tɪpə,fay/ *v.* [~ + *obj*], **-fied, -fy•ing.** to serve as a typical example of: *a hero who typified courage.* —**typ•i•fi•ca•tion** /,tɪpəfɪ'keyʃən/, *n.* [*noncount*]

typ•ist /'taypɪst/ *n.* [*count*] one who operates a typewriter.

ty•po /'taypow/ *n.* [*count*], *pl.* **-pos.** *Informal.* an error, such as a misspelled word, made when typing.

ty•ran•ni•cal /tɪ'rænɪkəl, tay-/ also **ty'ran• nic,** *adj.* of or relating to tyranny; oppressive: *a tyrannical king.* —**ty'ran•ni•cal•ly,** *adv.*

tyr•an•nize /'tɪrə,nayz/ *v.*, **-nized, -niz•ing.** to rule tyrannically: [~ + *obj*]: *to tyrannize the citizens.* [*no obj*]: *to tyrannize over the country.*

tyr•an•ny /'tɪrəniy/ *n.*, *pl.* **-nies. 1.** [*noncount*] the use of unlimited power; abuse of power: *the tyranny of totalitarian government.* **2.** [*count*] the government or rule of a tyrant: *tyrannies of dictators through the years.* **3.** [*noncount*] a condition of severe or harsh authority: *the tyranny of nature.*

ty•rant /'tayrənt/ *n.* [*count*] one who uses power cruelly or unjustly.

tzar /zɑr, tsɑr/ *n.* CZAR.

T

U

U, u /yuw/ *n.* [*count*], *pl.* **U's** or **Us, u's** or **us.** the 21st letter of the English alphabet, a vowel.

u.c., an abbreviation of: uppercase.

ud•der /'ʌdər/ *n.* [*count*] a baggy gland on female goats and cows from which milk is produced.

UFO /'yuw'ɛf'ow; *sometimes* 'yuwfˌow/ *n.* [*count*], *pl.* **UFOs, UFO's.** unidentified flying object: any unexplained moving object seen in the sky, esp. one believed to be from beyond the Earth.

ug•ly /'ʌgliy/ *adj.*, **-li•er, -li•est. 1.** very unattractive or displeasing in appearance. **2.** disagreeable; unpleasant: *ugly weather.* **3.** hostile; quarrelsome: *an ugly mood.* —'**ug•li•ness,** *n.* [*noncount*]

u•ku•le•le or **u•ke•le•le** /ˌyuwkə'leyliy, ˌuw-/ *n.* [*count*], *pl.* **-les.** a small, guitarlike musical instrument often used in Hawaiian music.

ul•cer /'ʌlsər/ *n.* [*count*] a sore, as on the skin, mouth, or stomach lining.

ul•te•ri•or /ʌl'tɪəriyər/ *adj.* [*before a noun*] intentionally kept hidden: *His ulterior motive was to enrich himself.*

ul•ti•mate /'ʌltəmɪt/ *adj.* [*before a noun*] **1.** last; furthest or farthest; final: *his ultimate destination.* **2.** decisive; highest: *the ultimate authority.* **3.** most extreme: *the ultimate sacrifice.* **4.** unequaled; best: *the ultimate vacation.* —*n.* [*noncount; the* + *~*] **5.** the final point or result. **6.** the finest or most superior of its kind; the best: *This apartment is the ultimate in luxury.* —'**ul•ti•mate•ly,** *adv.*

ul•ti•ma•tum /ˌʌltə'meytəm, -'mɑ-/ *n.* [*count*], *pl.* **-tums, -ta** /-tə/. a final demand issued by one side in a dispute, that if rejected will, it is threatened, lead to the ending of talks, the use of force, or some other undesirable outcome or action.

ul•tra•son•ic /ˌʌltrə'sɒnɪk/ *adj.* of, being, or using ultrasound.

ul•tra•sound /'ʌltrəˌsawnd/ *n.* [*noncount*] **1.** sound with a frequency that is close to the upper limit of human hearing. **2.** the application of ultrasonic waves to methods of medical diagnosis or healing.

ul•tra•vi•o•let /ˌʌltrə'vayəlɪt/ *adj.* relating to light having wavelengths shorter than visible light but longer than x-rays.

um•bil•i•cal cord /ʌm'bɪlɪkəl/ *n.* [*count*] a cordlike structure that connects an unborn baby to the mother and carries nourishment to the baby.

um•brel•la /ʌm'brɛlə/ *n.* [*count*], *pl.* **-las.** a light, circular cover for protection from rain, snow, or sometimes hot sun, made of a frame of fabric supported by thin ribs that come out of the top of a handle.

um•laut /'umlawt/ *n.* [*count*] a mark (¨) used as a marker over a vowel, as *ä, ö, ü,* to indicate a vowel sound different from that of the vowel without the mark, esp. as used in German.

um•pire /'ʌmpayᵊr/ *n., v.,* **-pired, -pir•ing.** —*n.* [*count*] **1.** a person who rules on the plays in a game, esp. baseball. —*v.* [*~* + *obj*] [*no obj*] **2.** to act as umpire in (a game).

un-¹, a prefix meaning: not (*unseen*); the opposite of (*unrest*).

un-², a prefix meaning: reversal of an action (*unfasten*); removal or depriving (*unclog*); completely (*unloose*).

UN or **U.N.,** an abbreviation of: United Nations.

un•a•ble /ʌn'eybəl/ *adj.* [*be* + *~* + *to* + *verb*] lacking the necessary power, ability, time, etc., to accomplish some act: *He's unable to swim.*

un•ac•cus•tomed /ˌʌnə'kʌstəmd/ *adj.* **1.** not used to: *unaccustomed to hardships.* **2.** uncommon; unexpected: *an unaccustomed delay.*

un•a•dorned /ˌʌnə'dɔrnd/ *adj.* not decorated; plain.

un•a•dul•ter•at•ed /ˌʌnə'dʌltəˌreytɪd/ *adj.* **1.** not mixed with other elements; pure. **2.** complete; utter: *unadulterated nonsense.*

u•nan•i•mous /yuw'nænəməs/ *adj.* being in or showing complete agreement: *a unanimous vote.* —**u•na•nim•i•ty** /ˌyuwnə'nɪmɪtiy/, *n.* [*noncount*] —u'**nan•i•mous•ly,** *adv.*

un•armed /ʌn'ɑrmd/ *adj.* being without weapons or armor: *an unarmed police officer.*

un•as•sum•ing /ˌʌnə'suwmɪŋ/ *adj.* modest; not pretentious: *an unassuming manner.*

un•at•tached /ˌʌnə'tætʃt/ *adj.* not engaged, married, or involved with another.

un•at•tend•ed /ˌʌnə'tɛndɪd/ *adj.* [*leave* + *obj* + *~*] alone; not supervised: *They blamed the parents for leaving the children unattended all day.*

un•a•ware /ˌʌnə'wɛər/ *adj.* **1.** [*be* + *~*] aware; not knowing about (something): *I was unaware of your problem. I was unaware that you were sick.* —*adv.* **2.** unawares.

un•a•wares /ˌʌnə'wɛərz/ *adv.* without warning; unexpectedly; without being prepared: *The attack caught the enemy unawares.*

un•bal•anced /ʌn'bælənst/ *adj.* lacking steadiness and soundness of judgment; mentally disturbed: *unbalanced behavior.*

un•bear•a•ble /ʌn'bɛərəbəl/ *adj.* that cannot be endured, suffered through, or tolerated: *unbearable pain.* —**un'bear•a•bly,** *adv.*

un•be•com•ing /ˌʌnbɪ'kʌmɪŋ/ *adj.* taking away from one's appearance, character, or reputation; unattractive or unseemly: *an unbecoming hat.*

un•be•liev•a•ble /ˌʌnbɪ'liyvəbəl/ *adj.* **1.** too unlikely to be believed: *Your story is unbelievable.* **2.** extraordinary; impressive: *unbelievable good luck.*

un•bend•ing /ʌn'bɛndɪŋ/ *adj.* refusing to give in, yield, or compromise: *an unbending attitude during the negotiations.*

un•bro•ken /ʌn'browkən/ *adj.* **1.** not interrupted or disturbed: *unbroken sleep.* **2.** not exceeded, as a record in sports.

un•called-for /ʌn'kɔldˌfɔr/ *adj.* not right or fair: *uncalled-for criticism.*

un•can•ny /ʌn'kæniy/ *adj.* having or seeming to have a supernatural or unexplained basis; extraordinary: *to shoot with uncanny accuracy.*

un•cer•tain /ʌn'sɜrtn/ *adj.* **1.** not known or determined precisely; not fixed: *The amount of the loss is uncertain; a manuscript of uncertain origin.* **2.** not confident or assured; hesitant: *an uncertain manner.* **3.** likely to change; unstable: *The weather pattern for the next few days is uncer-*

tain. —**un'cer•tain•ly,** *adv.* —**un'cer•tain•ty,** *n.* [*noncount*] [*count*], *pl.* **-ties.**

un•civ•i•lized /ʌn'sɪvə,layzd/ *adj.* not civilized or cultured: *an uncivilized tribe.*

un•cle /'ʌŋkəl/ *n.* [*count*] **1.** a brother of one's father or mother. **2.** an aunt's husband.

un•clean /ʌn'kliyn/ *adj.,* **-er, -est.** not clean or pure: *unclean thoughts.*

un•com•fort•a•ble /ʌn'kʌmftəbəl, -'kʌmfərtə-/ *adj.* **1.** causing discomfort or distress; irritating; painful: *uncomfortable shoes.* **2.** experiencing discomfort; uneasy: *uncomfortable with the idea of fame.* —**un'com•fort•a•bly,** *adv.*

un•com•mon /ʌn'kɒmən/ *adj.,* **-er, -est. 1.** not common; unusual. **2.** exceptional; outstanding. —**un'com•mon•ly,** *adv.*: *an uncommonly good student.*

un•com•pro•mis•ing /ʌn'kɒmprə,mayzɪŋ/ *adj.* unwilling to make concessions or give in, as with respect to positions in a dispute, political or religious principles, etc.

un•con•scious /ʌn'kɒnʃəs/ *adj.* **1.** having lost consciousness: *was unconscious from the blow.* **2.** not noticed at the level of awareness: *an unconscious impulse.* **3.** done unintentionally: *an unconscious insult.* —*n.* [*noncount; the* + ∼] **4.** the part of the mind that a person is rarely aware of but that has an important influence on behavior. —**un'con•scious•ly,** *adv.* —**un'con•scious•ness,** *n.* [*noncount*]

un•con•sti•tu•tion•al /,ʌnkɒnstɪ'tuwʃənḷ, -'tyuw-/ *adj.* not constitutional; not authorized by, or consistent with, a constitution, esp. the U.S. Constitution.

un•couth /ʌn'kuwθ/ *adj.* rude: *uncouth language.*

un•cov•er /ʌn'kʌvər/ *v.* [∼ + *obj*] **1.** to remove the cover or covering from. **2.** to lay bare; disclose; reveal: *He uncovered a deadly plot.*

un•daunt•ed /ʌn'dɔntɪd, -'dɑn-/ *adj.* not discouraged; not held back or worried by danger; unafraid.

un•de•cid•ed /,ʌndɪ'saydɪd/ *adj.* **1.** having the result in doubt: *The contest was still undecided.* **2.** not having one's mind made up: *undecided about where to shop.*

un•de•ni•a•ble /,ʌndɪ'nayəbəl/ *adj.* **1.** clearly true or real: *undeniable evidence of arson.* **2.** obviously excellent: *her undeniable artistic talent.*

un•der /'ʌndər/ *prep.* **1.** beneath and covered by: *She stood under a tree.* **2.** at a point lower than: *He got a bump just under his eye.* **3.** below in degree, amount, etc.; less than: *I purchased that book for under ten dollars.* **4.** working for; controlled by the authority, influence, or guidance of: *She studied violin under a great master.* **5.** in accordance with; following; bound by or subject to: *already under contract to a publisher; under the provisions of the law; under the influence of alcohol.* **6.** in the state or process of: *a bridge under repair; It's under discussion* (= *It's being discussed*). —*adv.* **7.** below or beneath something: *Go over the fence, not under.* —*adj.* **8.** lower in position, degree, amount, rank, etc.: *Children under five get in free.*

under-, a prefix meaning: place or situation below or beneath (*underbrush*); lower in grade or dignity (*understudy*); of lesser degree, extent, or amount (*undersized*).

un•der•age /,ʌndər'eydʒ/ *adj.* below the age required by law to engage in a given activity, as drinking alcoholic beverages.

un•der•brush /'ʌndər,brʌʃ/ *n.* [*noncount*] shrubs, small trees, bushes, low vines, etc., growing under the large trees in a wood or forest.

un•der•clothes /'ʌndər,klowz, -,klowðz/ *n.* [*plural*] UNDERWEAR.

un•der•cov•er /,ʌndər'kʌvər, 'ʌndər,kʌv-/ *adj.* [*before a noun*] secret: *an undercover investigation.*

un•der•cur•rent /'ʌndər,kɜrənt, -,kʌr-/ *n.* [*count*] **1.** a current, such as of air or water, that flows below the upper currents or surface. **2.** a hidden tendency or feeling that is typically the opposite of what is expressed on the surface: *an undercurrent of suspicion beneath the kind words.*

un•der•de•vel•oped /,ʌndərdɪ'vɛləpt/ *adj.* **1.** improperly developed; not developed enough, as a part of the body. **2.** DEVELOPING (def. 2): *underdeveloped countries.*

un•der•dog /'ʌndər,dɔg, -,dɒg/ *n.* [*count*] a person who is expected to lose in a contest or conflict.

un•der•es•ti•mate /,ʌndər'ɛstə,meyt/ *v.* [∼ + *obj*], **-mat•ed, -mat•ing.** to estimate at too low a value, rate, or the like: *to underestimate the costs.*

un•der•foot /,ʌndər'fʊt/ *adv.* under the foot or feet: *felt the thorns underfoot.*

un•der•gar•ment /'ʌndər,gɑrmənt/ *n.* [*count*] an article of underwear.

un•der•go /,ʌndər'gow/ *v.* [∼ + *obj*], **-went, -gone, -go•ing.** to experience or endure: *He has undergone surgery.*

un•der•grad•u•ate /,ʌndər'grædʒuwɪt/ *n.* [*count*] a college-level student who has not received a first, esp. a bachelor's, degree.

un•der•ground /*adv.* 'ʌndər'grawnd; *adj.,* *n.* -,grawnd/ *adv.* **1.** beneath the surface of the ground. —*adj.* **2.** existing, situated, or operating beneath the surface of the ground. **3.** hidden or secret; not open: *underground political activities.* **4.** published or produced by political or social radicals: *an underground newspaper.* —*n.* [*count*] **5.** a secret organization fighting the established government or occupation forces: *the French underground of World War II.* **6.** *Brit.* a subway system.

un•der•growth /'ʌndər,growθ/ *n.* UNDERBRUSH.

un•der•hand•ed /'ʌndər'hændɪd/ *adj.* not open and honest; secret and crafty: *an underhanded deal.*

un•der•lie /,ʌndər'lay/ *v.* [∼ + *obj*], **-lay, -lain, -ly•ing.** to form the foundation of.

un•der•line /'ʌndər,layn/ *v.* [∼ + *obj*], **-lined, -lin•ing. 1.** to mark with a line or lines underneath: *to underline the paragraph.* **2.** to indicate the importance of; emphasize: *She underlined the need for caution.*

un•der•mine /,ʌndər'mayn/ *v.* [∼ + *obj*], **-mined, -min•ing.** to weaken or destroy by degrees: *Her health was undermined by the stress of her job.*

un•der•neath /,ʌndər'niyθ, -'niyð/ *prep.* **1.** below or under. —*adv.* **2.** on the underside.

un•der•pants /'ʌndər,pænts/ *n.* [*plural*] shorts worn under outer clothing, usually next to the skin.

un•der•pass /'ʌndər,pæs/ *n.* [*count*] a passage running underneath, esp. a passage for pedestrians or vehicles under a railroad or street.

un•der•priv•i•leged /'ʌndər'prɪvəlɪdʒd, -'prɪvlɪdʒd/ *adj.* denied the normal rights enjoyed by members of a society because of low economic and social status: *underprivileged children.*

un•der•score /'ʌndər,skɔr/ *v.* UNDERLINE.

U

un·der·shirt /ˈʌndərˌʃɜrt/ n. [count] a collarless, usually pullover undergarment for the upper body, usually of lightweight fabric.

un·der·stand /ˌʌndərˈstænd/ v., **-stood,** **-stand·ing.** **1.** to see or perceive the meaning of; comprehend: [~ + obj]: to understand a poem; He doesn't understand that he's not welcome. [no obj]: Don't say a word to anyone, understand? **2.** [~ + obj] to be familiar with; have a thorough knowledge of: She understands the needs of businesspeople. **3.** [~ + obj] to learn or hear: I understand that you were ill. —**un·der'stand·a·ble,** adj.: My French was barely understandable. It's understandable that you are upset. —**un·der'stand·a·bly,** adv.

un·der·stand·ing /ˌʌndərˈstændɪŋ/ n. **1.** [count] the result of an act or process of comprehension; an interpretation: My understanding of the word does not agree with yours. **2.** [count] a mutual agreement, esp. of a private or unspoken kind: to have an understanding that each would pay a share. **3.** [noncount] sympathy and compassion: He showed real understanding toward those in trouble.

un·der·state /ˌʌndərˈsteyt/ v. [~ + obj], **-stat·ed, -stat·ing.** to state or represent (some result, finding, etc.) less strongly than the facts would indicate; make (something) seem less important than it really is: The report understates the magnitude of the disaster. —**un·der·state·ment** /ˌʌndərˈsteytmənt, ˈʌndərˌsteyt-/, n. [count]: Claiming that the hurricane was "inconvenient" is an understatement.

un·der·stood /ˌʌndərˈstʊd/ v. **1.** pt. and pp. of UNDERSTAND. **2.** implied but not said in words: It was understood that I wasn't welcome to return.

un·der·stud·y /ˈʌndərˌstʌdiy/ n. [count], pl. **-stud·ies.** a performer who learns the role of another in order to serve as a replacement if necessary.

un·der·take /ˌʌndərˈteyk/ v. [~ + obj], **-took, -tak·en, -tak·ing.** **1.** to take upon oneself, as a task or performance; attempt: He undertook the job of answering the mail. **2.** to promise or state as a promise (to do something): He undertook to finish the job ahead of schedule.

un·der·tak·er /ˈʌndərˌteykər/ n. [count] a person whose job is to arrange or direct funerals.

un·der·tak·ing /ˌʌndərˈteykɪŋ, ˈʌndərˌtey-/ n. [count] a task, enterprise, etc., that is undertaken or begun.

un·der·tone /ˈʌndərˌtown/ n. [count] **1.** a low or quiet tone of voice. **2.** an underlying quality or element; undercurrent: There is an undertone of regret in his voice.

un·der·tow /ˈʌndərˌtow/ n. [count] the current of water toward the sea and usually under the surface, from waves breaking on a beach and flowing back.

un·der·wa·ter /ˈʌndərˈwɔtər, -ˈwɒtər/ adj. **1.** existing or occurring under water. **2.** designed to be used under water: underwater cameras and lights.

un·der·wear /ˈʌndərˌwɛər/ n. [noncount] clothing worn next to the skin under outer clothes.

un·der·world /ˈʌndərˌwɜrld/ n. [count; usually singular; usually: the + ~] **1.** the criminal world of gangs or organized crime. **2.** (in the religious beliefs of various cultures, esp. the ancient Greeks and Romans) a place below the surface of the earth in which the spirits of the dead live on.

un·do /ʌnˈduw/ v. [~ + obj], **-did, -done, -do·ing.** **1.** to reverse the doing of; repair or erase: to undo the damage. **2.** to untie; unfasten: She undid her straps.

un·do·ing /ʌnˈduwɪŋ/ n. [count; usually singular] a cause of destruction or ruin: Drinking was his undoing.

un·done /ʌnˈdʌn/ adj. [be + ~] **1.** not finished: work that was still undone. **2.** loose; not fastened: His shirt buttons were undone. **3.** ruined: She was undone by greed.

un·doubt·ed /ʌnˈdawtɪd/ adj. not doubted or disputed; accepted as true or authentic. —**un'doubt·ed·ly,** adv.

un·dress /ʌnˈdrɛs/ v. to take the clothes off (oneself, a person, etc.): [no obj]: He undressed and went to bed. [~ + obj]: She undressed the child and put him to bed.

un·due /ʌnˈduw, -ˈdyuw/ adj. too much; excessive: undue haste.

un·du·ly /ʌnˈduwliy, -ˈdyuw-/ adv. too much; excessively: unduly anxious.

un·dy·ing /ʌnˈdayɪŋ/ adj. lasting forever: undying fame.

un·earth /ʌnˈɜrθ/ v. [~ + obj] **1.** to dig out of the earth: to unearth the ancient city of Troy. **2.** to bring to light; make known: to unearth an old rumor.

un·earth·ly /ʌnˈɜrθliy/ adj. **1.** supernatural; ghostly; weird: an unearthly cry. **2.** unreasonable or absurd: to get up at an unearthly hour.

un·eas·y /ʌnˈiyziy/ adj., **-i·er, -i·est.** not comfortable in body or mind; worried or nervous: I was uneasy about the upcoming exam. —**un·eas·i·ly** /ʌnˈiyzəliy/, adv. —**un'eas·i·ness,** n. [noncount]

un·em·ployed /ˌʌnɛmˈplɔyd/ adj. **1.** not employed; having no job. —n. **2. the unemployed,** [plural; used with a plural verb] persons without jobs. —**un·em'ploy·ment,** n. [noncount]

un·e·qual /ʌnˈiykwəl/ adj. **1.** not equal; not of the same measurement, quantity, or status: unequal portions; unequal rank. **2.** [be + ~ + to + obj] not adequate or sufficient, as in amount, power, or ability: He's unequal to the task. —**un'e·qual·ly,** adv.

un·e·ven /ʌnˈiyvən/ adj. **1.** not level or flat; rough: an uneven surface. **2.** not uniform; varying; inconsistent: a novel of uneven quality.

un·e·vent·ful /ˌʌnɪˈvɛntfəl/ adj. routine; normal: an uneventful day.

un·ex·pect·ed /ˌʌnɪkˈspɛktɪd/ adj. surprising because not expected. —**un·ex'pect·ed·ly** adv.

un·fail·ing /ʌnˈfeylɪŋ/ adj. never ceasing; always reliable: her unfailing love.

un·fair /ʌnˈfɛər/ adj. not fair; not conforming to or following common standards of justice, honesty, or the like: The students claimed that the test was unfair. [be + ~ + obj]: It was very unfair (of the teacher) to give the students so much homework on a holiday weekend. —**un'fair·ly,** adv.

un·faith·ful /ʌnˈfeyθfəl/ adj. not sexually faithful to a spouse or lover.

un·fa·mil·iar /ˌʌnfəˈmɪlyər/ adj. **1.** not acquainted with: to be unfamiliar with modern art. **2.** different; unusual: an unfamiliar treat.

un·fas·ten /ʌnˈfæsən/ v. [~ + obj] [no obj] to (cause to) be undone or opened.

un·feel·ing /ʌnˈfiylɪŋ/ adj. not sympathetic; hardhearted: an unfeeling remark.

un·fit /ʌnˈfɪt/ adj. **1.** [be + ~] not adapted or suited; not suitable: Her office is unfit for more than two occupants; food that is unfit to eat. **2.** not qualified; incompetent: *unfit parents.*

un•fold /ʌn'fowld/ *v.* **1.** to (cause to) come out of a folded state; (cause to) be spread or opened out: [~ + *obj*]: *The bird unfolded its wings and flew off.* [*no obj*]: *The flower petals unfolded in the sun.* **2.** [*no obj*] to be revealed or displayed; become clear: *The movie's plot gradually unfolded.*

un•fore•seen /ˌʌnfɔr'siyn/ *adj.* not foreseen; happening unexpectedly: *unforeseen difficulties.*

un•for•get•ta•ble /ˌʌnfɔr'gɛtəbəl/ *adj.* staying in one's memory: *an unforgettable adventure.* —ˌun•for'get•ta•bly, *adv.*

un•for•tu•nate /ʌn'fɔrtʃənɪt/ *adj.* **1.** suffering from or characterized by bad luck; unlucky: *an unfortunate series of bad investments; an unfortunate fellow.* **2.** unsuitable; not appropriate: *He made an unfortunate remark about your weight.* —**un'for•tu•nate•ly,** *adv.*

un•gain•ly /ʌn'geynliy/ *adj.,* **-li•er, -li•est.** not graceful; awkward; clumsy: *an ungainly dancer.*

un•hap•py /ʌn'hæpiy/ *adj.,* **-pi•er, -pi•est. 1.** sad; miserable. **2.** unfortunate; unlucky: *to meet an unhappy fate.* **3.** not suitable or appropriate: *an unhappy choice of words.* —**un•hap•pi•ly** /ʌn'hæpəliy/, *adv.*: *unhappily married.* —**un'hap•pi•ness,** *n.* [*noncount*]

un•health•y /ʌn'hɛlθiy/ *adj.,* **-i•er, -i•est. 1.** not in a state of good or normal health: *He has been unhealthy for years.* **2.** showing signs of, or resulting from, bad health: *skin with an unhealthy paleness.* **3.** not healthful; bad for one's health: *an unhealthy diet.* **4.** morally harmful; unnatural: *an unhealthy interest in violence.*

un'heard-ˌof, *adj.* not seen or known before; shocking: *an unheard-of salary for a ball player.*

u•ni•form /'yuwnəˌfɔrm/ *adj.* **1.** identical, the same, or consistent, as from example to example or place to place: *a uniform building code.* **2.** without changes in detail; constant; not changing: *a uniform surface, without dents.* —*n.* **3.** dress of distinctive style worn by the members of a given profession, organization, or rank: [*count*]: *nurses wearing white uniforms.* [*noncount*]: *He wasn't in uniform.* —**u•ni•form•i•ty** /ˌyuwnə'fɔrmɪtiy/, *n.* [*noncount*] —**'u•ni,form•ly,** *adv.: products of uniformly high quality.*

u•ni•fy /'yuwnəˌfay/ *v.* [~ + *obj*], **-fied, -fy•ing.** to cause to become a single unit; unite; merge: *set out to unify the country.* —**u•ni•fi•ca•tion** /ˌyuwnəfɪ'keyʃən/, *n.* [*noncount*]

u•ni•lat•er•al /ˌyuwnə'lætərəl/ *adj.* undertaken or done by or on behalf of one side, party, or group only; not mutual: *a unilateral decision.*

un•in•ter•est•ed /ʌn'ɪntərəstɪd, -trəstɪd, -təˌrɛstɪd/ *adj.* not interested; not taking an interest: *seemed uninterested in others' problems.* —**Usage.** See DISINTERESTED.

un•ion /'yuwnyən/ *n.* **1.** [*noncount*] the act of uniting or the state of being united. **2.** [*count*] an instance of this, esp. a marriage. **3.** [*count*] a number of persons, states, etc., joined or associated together for some common purpose: *a labor union.* **4.** [*count; often used in a proper name; often: the* + ~; *Union*] a uniting of states or nations into one political body: *the Union of South Africa.* **5.** [*the Union*] the United States, in the time of the American Civil War.

u•nique /yuw'niyk/ *adj.* **1.** existing as the only one of its kind or type, or as the only example: *a unique copy of an ancient manuscript.* **2.** having no like or equal: *a unique individual.* **3.** [*be* +

~ (+ *to*)] limited in occurrence to a certain class, situation, or area: *The kangaroo is unique to Australia.* **4.** extraordinary; remarkable: *She has a unique ability to inspire people.* —**u'nique•ly,** *adv.* —**u'nique•ness,** *n.* [*noncount*] —**Usage.** UNIQUE is an adjective representing an absolute state that cannot exist in degrees. Therefore, it cannot be sensibly used with a limiting or comparative adverb such as "very," "most," or "extremely": *She has a unique* (not "*very unique*" or "*most unique*") *style of singing.*

u•ni•sex /'yuwnəˌsɛks/ *adj.* designed or suitable for both sexes: *unisex clothes.*

u•ni•son /'yuwnəsən, -zən/ *n.* [*noncount*] —*Idiom.* **in unison, 1.** in perfect agreement or accord: *My feelings are in unison with yours.* **2.** at the same time and in the same way: *to march in unison.*

u•nit /'yuwnɪt/ *n.* [*count*] **1.** a single thing; one person or thing. **2.** any group of things or persons thought of as a single thing: *The team finally played like a unit.* **3.** a machine, part, or system of machines having a specified purpose, often an apparatus or piece that is part of a bigger piece: *a heating unit.* **4.** a specified amount of a quantity, as of length, volume, or time, by comparison with which any other quantity of the same kind is measured: *a unit of measurement (as an inch).*

u•nite /yuw'nayt/ *v.,* **u•nit•ed, u•nit•ing. 1.** to (cause to) be joined so as to form a single whole or unit: [~ + *obj*]: *united all the states into one country.* [*no obj*]: *The states united into one country.* **2.** to (cause to) come together in agreement on an issue, or to pursue a common goal: [*no obj*] *They united around the opposition candidate.* [~ + *obj*]: *They united their forces.*

u•ni•ty /'yuwnɪtiy/ *n.,* [*noncount*], *pl.* **-ties.** the state of being one or united, or of being in agreement: *a unity of purpose; In unity there is strength.*

u•ni•ver•sal /ˌyuwnə'vɜrsəl/ *adj.* of, affecting, or characteristic of all members of a group or of the whole; applying everywhere: *A universal characteristic of language is the ability to form questions; universal truths about the human condition.* —**u•ni'ver•sal•ly,** *adv.*

u•ni•verse /'yuwnəˌvɜrs/ *n.* [*noncount; usually: the* + ~] all the known or imagined objects, matter, and events throughout space; the cosmos: *the secrets of the universe.*

u•ni•ver•si•ty /ˌyuwnə'vɜrsɪtiy/ *n.* [*count*], *pl.* **-ties.** an institution of learning of the highest level that is allowed to award both undergraduate and graduate degrees.

un•kempt /ʌn'kɛmpt/ *adj.* messy: *an unkempt appearance.*

un•kind /ʌn'kaynd/ *adj.,* **-er, -est.** lacking in kindness or mercy; severe: *an unkind remark; He's unkind to animals.* —**un'kind•ness,** *n.* [*noncount*]

un•known /ʌn'nown/ *adj.* **1.** not within the range of knowledge, experience, or understanding; unfamiliar. **2.** not discovered, explored, identified, or figured out: *an unknown amount; an unknown continent until the twentieth century.*

un•less /ʌn'lɛs/ *conj.* except under the circumstances that: *We'll be there at nine, unless the train is late.*

un•like /ʌn'layk/ *adj.* **1.** different; not alike: *They gave unlike accounts of the incident.* —*prep.* **2.** different from: *She is unlike my sister.* **3.** not typical of: *It is unlike him to forget a name.*

U

un•like•ly /ʌn'laykliy/ adj., -li•er, -li•est. 1. not likely to be or occur; doubtful: an unlikely outcome. [It + be + ~ + obj]: It is unlikely that she knows him. She is unlikely to know him. 2. [before a noun] having little chance of success; not promising: an unlikely candidate for the job.

un•load /ʌn'lowd/ v. 1. [~ + obj] to take the load or cargo from: to unload a ship. 2. to remove or discharge (cargo, passengers, etc.): [~ + obj]: The sailors began to unload the cargo. [no obj]: The ship can't unload now. 3. [~ + obj] to remove the bullets from: to unload a gun.

un•lock /ʌn'lɒk/ v. to undo the lock of; open: [~ + obj]: to unlock a car; to unlock a door. [no obj]: The door unlocks easily.

un•manned /ʌn'mænd/ adj. without the physical presence of people in control: an unmanned spacecraft.

un•mis•tak•a•ble /,ʌnmɪ'steykəbəl/ adj. clear; obvious: unmistakable evidence of guilt. —,un•mis'tak•a•bly, adv.

un•moved /ʌn'muvd/ adj. not affected emotionally: He was unmoved by her plea.

un•nat•u•ral /ʌn'nætʃərəl, -'nætʃrəl/ adj. 1. contrary to the laws or course of nature; different from or opposite from the normal or expected character or nature of a person, animal, or plant. 2. not genuine or natural; artificial: a forced, unnatural smile.

un•nerve /ʌn'nɜrv/ v. [~ + obj], -nerved, -nerv•ing. to take courage, strength, or confidence away from (someone); upset: Fear unnerved him.

un•oc•cu•pied /ʌn'ɒkyə,payd/ adj. 1. lacking occupants: unoccupied houses. 2. not held or controlled by invading forces: unoccupied territory. 3. not busy or active; idle: unoccupied hours.

un•par•al•leled /ʌn'pærə,lɛld/ adj. without equal; unmatched.

un•prec•e•dent•ed /ʌn'prɛsɪ,dɛntɪd/ adj. never before known or experienced: an unprecedented victory.

un•pre•pared /,ʌnprɪ'pɛərd/ adj. not prepared; not expecting something: I was unprepared for visitors.

un•pro•voked /,ʌnprə'vowkt/ adj. not provoked; having no apparent cause or reason: an unprovoked attack.

un•qual•i•fied /ʌn'kwɒlə,fayd/ adj. 1. lacking the necessary qualifications. 2. not limited: unqualified praise. 3. [before a noun] complete; total: an unqualified disaster.

un•rav•el /ʌn'rævəl/ v., -eled, -el•ing. 1. to separate or (cause to) be disentangled, as the threads of a fabric, rope, etc.: [~ + obj]: to unravel the thread. [no obj]: The thread unraveled. 2. to (cause to) be free from complications; (cause to) be solved: [~ + obj]: to unravel a mystery. [no obj]: The mystery was slow to unravel.

un•re•al /ʌn'riyəl, -'riyl/ adj. not real or actual; imaginary.

un•rea•son•a•ble /ʌn'riyzənəbəl, -'riyznə-/ adj. 1. not guided by reason or good judgment. 2. too great; excessive: an unreasonable demand. —un'rea•son•a•ble•ness, n. [noncount] —un'rea•son•a•bly, adv.

un•re•quit•ed /,ʌnrɪ'kwaytɪd/ adj. not felt in return: unrequited love.

un•rest /ʌn'rɛst/ n. [noncount] dissatisfaction or turbulence: political unrest.

un•ri•valed /ʌn'rayvəld/ adj. having no equal; superb: poetry unrivaled for its beauty.

un•ruf•fled /ʌn'rʌfəld/ adj. 1. not flustered or nervous; calm: She remained unruffled by the confusion. 2. not ruffled; smooth: unruffled fabric.

un•ru•ly /ʌn'ruwliy/ adj., -li•er, -li•est. not cooperative or well-behaved; disorderly: an unruly gang of troublemakers.

un•scathed /ʌn'skeyðd/ adj. not harmed; unharmed: They escaped the explosion unscathed.

un•scru•pu•lous /ʌn'skruwpyələs/ adj. dishonest: unscrupulous business dealings.

un•sea•son•a•ble /ʌn'siyzənəbəl/ adj. abnormal, for being out of season: unseasonable weather. —un'sea•son•a•bly, adv.

un•seat /ʌn'siyt/ v. [~ + obj] 1. to remove from a seat, esp. to throw from a saddle. 2. to remove (someone) from political office: In the last election the mayor was unseated by her opponent.

un•seem•ly /ʌn'siymliy/ adj., -li•er, -li•est. not in keeping with accepted standards of taste or proper form; inappropriate.

un•set•tle /ʌn'sɛtl/ v. [~ + obj], -tled, -tling. to disturb or upset.

un•sight•ly /ʌn'saytliy/ adj., -li•er, -li•est. distasteful or unpleasant to look at; unattractive; ugly: unsightly old furniture.

un•sound /ʌn'sawnd/ adj., -er, -est. 1. unhealthy or diseased, as the body or mind. 2. not firm or secure, as the foundations of a building. 3. not based on fact: an unsound argument.

un•speak•a•ble /ʌn'spiykəbəl/ adj. too terrible to be described: unspeakable crimes.

un•spo•ken /ʌn'spowkən/ adj. implied or understood being spoken or uttered.

un•sure /ʌn'ʃʊr/ adj. [often: be + ~ (+ of)] 1. not certain: She was unsure of her feelings. 2. lacking confidence: He was unsure of himself.

un•swerv•ing /ʌn'swɜrvɪŋ/ adj. strong; firm: unswerving loyalty.

un•think•a•ble /ʌn'θɪŋkəbəl/ adj. too terrible to be considered: an unthinkable crime.

un•tie /ʌn'tay/ v. [~ + obj], -tied, -ty•ing. 1. to loose or unfasten by undoing a knot: to untie a prisoner. 2. to undo the string or cords of: to untie (the strings of) a package.

un•til /ʌn'tɪl/ conj. 1. up to the time that or when; till: Wait until it starts getting dark. 2. [usually used with a negative word or phrase] before: I didn't remember it until the meeting was over. —prep. 3. onward to or till (a certain time or occurrence): to work until 6 P.M. 4. [usually used with a negative word or phrase] before: He did not go until noon. ——Usage. See TILL[1].

un•time•ly /ʌn'taymliy/ adj., -li•er, -li•est. 1. not occurring at a suitable time: an untimely interruption. 2. premature: an untimely death.

un•to /'ʌntuw/ unstressed -tə/ prep. to: Do unto others as you would have them do unto you.

un•told /ʌn'towld/ adj. [usually: before a noun] too great or extreme to count, calculate, or express: untold suffering; untold wealth.

un•to•ward /ʌn'tɔrd/ adj. 1. unfavorable or unfortunate: Untoward circumstances forced him into bankruptcy. 2. improper: untoward social behavior.

un•truth /ʌn'truwθ/ n. [count] something untrue; a lie: spreading untruths.

un•used /ʌn'yuwzd for 1; ʌn'yuwst for 2/ adj. 1. never having been used: unused dishes stored *in the attic.* **2.** [*be* + ~ + *to*] not accustomed: *I'm unused to cold winters.*

un•u•su•al /ʌn'yuwʒuwəl/ *adj.* not usual or ordinary: *an unusual day.* [*It* + *be* + ~ + *adj*]: *It was unusual that she was late. It was unusual (for him) to be at work before ten o'clock.* —**un'u•su•al•ly,** *adv.*: *He was unusually early.*

un•veil /ʌn'veyl/ *v.* [~ + *obj*] **1.** to remove a veil or other covering from: *The artist unveiled the sculpture at the dedication ceremony.* **2.** to reveal or make known: *She unveiled the new plan at the meeting.*

un•wield•y /ʌn'wiyldiy/ *adj.*, **-i•er, -i•est.** used, handled, or managed with difficulty because of size, shape, weight, or complexity: *an unwieldy load of scrap iron; an unwieldy bureaucracy.*

un•will•ing /ʌn'wɪlɪŋ/ *adj.* not willing; reluctant: *an unwilling partner in the crime.* [*be* + ~ (+ *to* + *verb*)]: *He's unwilling to testify.* —**un'will•ing•ly,** *adv.*: *He came to the party unwillingly.*

un•wind /ʌn'waynd/ *v.*, **-wound, -wind•ing. 1.** to (cause to) be undone or loosened from or as if from a coiled or wound condition; untwist: [~ + *obj*]: *He unwound the coil of electric wire.* [*no obj*]: *The rope began to unwind.* **2.** to (cause to) be relieved of tension; relax: [*no obj*]: *I needed to unwind after a hard day at work.* [~ + *obj*]: *a little soft music to unwind your tense nerves.*

un•wit•ting /ʌn'wɪtɪŋ/ *adj.* unintentional; accidental; not on purpose: *an unwitting victim.*

un•wor•thy /ʌn'wɜrðiy/ *adj.*, **-thi•er, -thi•est. 1.** lacking worth or excellence; not deserving: *an unworthy sinner.* [*be* + ~ + *to* + *verb*]: *I am unworthy to marry her.* **2.** [*be* + ~ + *of*] beneath the dignity: *behavior unworthy of a true leader.* —**un'wor•thi•ness,** *n.* [*noncount*]

up-, a combining form meaning up (*upheaval*).

up /ʌp/ *adv.*, *prep.*, *adj.*, *n.*, *v.*, **upped, up•ping.** —*adv.* **1.** to, toward, or in a higher position: *to climb up to the top of a ladder; rolled the car windows up.* **2.** to or in an erect position: *to stand up; He straightened up.* **3.** out of bed: *Come on, time to get up!* **4.** above the horizon: *The moon came up.* **5.** to or at a higher point or degree, as of rank, size, value, volume, or strength: *Prices went up. Speak up!* **6.** to or at a point of equal advance: *He caught up with her.* **7.** into existence, notice, or consideration: *The lost papers turned up.* **8.** in a state of continuing awareness or knowledge: *She kept up with the latest developments in her field.* **9.** to the final point; to an end; entirely: *to be used up.* **10.** (used with a verb to express additional emphasis on the action of the verb, or to suggest more thoroughness, or completion, of the action): *Go wake your brother up. Drink up! Eat up!* —*prep.* **11.** to, toward, or at a higher place on or in: *to go up the stairs.* **12.** to, toward, or in a higher station, condition, or rank on or in: *She's well up the social ladder.* **13.** at or to a farther point or higher place on or in: *The store is up the street.* **14.** toward the source, origin, etc., of: *to float up a stream.* **15.** Baseball. being the player or team batting; at bat. —*adj.* **16.** [*before a noun*] moving in or related to a direction that is up or that is thought of as up: *the up elevator.* **17.** [*be* + ~ + *on/in*] informed; familiar with; aware: *I'm not up on current events.* **18.** [*be* + ~] concluded; ended; finished: *Your time is up.* **19.** [*be* + ~] going on or happening: *What's up (with you)?* **20.** [*be* + ~] in an erect, vertical, or raised position: *The tent is up.* **21.** [*be* + ~] (of heavenly bodies) risen above the hori-

zon: *The sun is up.* **22.** [*be* + ~] awake or out of bed: *It was morning, but I wasn't up yet.* **23.** [*be* + ~] higher than formerly in amount or degree: *The price of meat is up.* **24.** [*be* + ~] considered or under consideration: *up for reelection.* —*n.* [*count*] **25.** a time of good fortune, prosperity, etc.: *the ups and downs of a career.* —*v.* [~ + *obj*] **26.** to make larger; step up; increase: *to up the rent.* —**Idiom. 27. up against,** confronted with; faced with: *We came up against a number of problems.* **28. up and around** or **about,** recovered from an illness; able to leave one's bed. **29. up to, a.** as far as: *I am up to the eighth chapter.* **b.** as many as; to the limit of: *This car can hold up to five persons.* **c.** capable of; equal to: *Is he up to the job?* **d.** being one's responsibility: *It's up to you to tell her.* **e.** engaged in; doing: *What have you been up to lately?*

'up-and-'coming, *adj.* likely to succeed; bright and industrious: *an up-and-coming young executive.*

up•beat /'ʌp,biyt/ *adj.* optimistic; happy; cheerful: *an upbeat report on the economy.*

up•bring•ing /'ʌp,brɪŋɪŋ/ *n.* [*count; usually singular*] the care and training of children or a particular type of such care and training: *He had a religious upbringing.*

up•com•ing /'ʌp,kʌmɪŋ/ *adj.* [*usually before a noun*] about to take place, appear, or be presented: *the upcoming spring fashions.*

up•date /'ʌp,deyt; *v. also* ,ʌp'deyt/ *v.*, **-dat•ed, -dat•ing,** *n.* —*v.* [~ + *obj*] **1.** to bring (a publication, a person, etc.) up to date; incorporate new information in or for: *to update a report; She updated her coworkers.* —*n.* [*count*] **2.** an act or instance of updating.

up•grade /*n.* 'ʌp,greyd; *v.* ʌp'greyd, 'ʌp,greyd/ *n.*, *v.*, **-grad•ed, -grad•ing.** —*n.* [*count*] **1.** a new, usually improved model or version of something, as computer software. —*v.* [~ + *obj*] **2.** to raise in rank, position, importance, etc.: *She was upgraded to senior vice president.* **3.** to improve or enhance the quality, value, or usefulness of: *to upgrade our computers.*

up•heav•al /ʌp'hiyvəl/ *n.* strong or violent change or disturbance, as in a society: [*noncount*]: *War brought social upheaval to the country.* [*count*]: *an upheaval caused by war.*

up•hill /'ʌp'hɪl/ *adv.* **1.** up or as if up the slope of a hill or other slope; upward. —*adj.* **2.** going or tending upward on or as if on a hill: *an uphill road.* **3.** very tiring or difficult: *an uphill struggle to earn a living.*

up•hold /ʌp'howld/ *v.* [~ + *obj*], **-held, -hold•ing. 1.** to support or defend, as against criticism: *to uphold the family's good name.* **2.** to confirm or approve (a verdict or decision).

up•hol•ster /ʌp'howlstər, ə'powl-/ *v.* [~ + *obj*] to fit with upholstery: *to upholster a chair.* —**up'hol•ster•er,** *n.* [*count*]

up•hol•ster•y /ʌp'howlstəriy, -striy, ə'powl-/ *n.* [*noncount*] the materials used to cushion and cover furniture, as chairs and sofas.

up•keep /'ʌp,kiyp/ *n.* [*noncount*] **1.** the care, repairs, etc., necessary for the proper functioning of a machine, building, household, etc. **2.** the cost of this: *Upkeep is one quarter of our budget.*

up•lift•ing /ʌp'lɪftɪŋ/ *adj.* providing emotional or spiritual encouragement: *an uplifting speech.*

up•on /ə'pɒn, ə'pɔn/ *prep.* **1.** up and on; upward so as to get or be on: *She climbed upon her horse.* **2.** in a higher or elevated position on: *a flag upon the roof.* **3.** in or into proximity with in time or space: *The holidays will soon be upon us.* **4.** on the occasion of; at the time of: *The kids shouted with joy upon hearing the news.*

up•per /'ʌpər/ *adj.* [*before a noun*] higher in place or position: *the upper stories of a house.*

up•per•case /'ʌpər'keys/ *adj.* (of an alphabetical character) capital: *uppercase characters like A, B, and C.*

'upper 'class, *n.* [*count*] a class of people above the middle class, characterized by wealth and social prestige. —**'upper-'class,** *adj.*

up•per•most /'ʌpər,mowst/ *adj.* Also, **up•most** /'ʌp,mowst/. highest in place, order, rank, or position: *a subject of uppermost concern.*

up•pi•ty /'ʌpɪtiy/ *adj. Informal.* tending to be haughty; snobbish; arrogant.

up•right /'ʌp,rayt, ʌp'rayt/ *adj.* **1.** straight, erect, or vertical, as in position or posture: *upright posture.* **2.** being fair, right, honest, and just: *an upright citizen.* —*n.* [*count*] **3.** something standing straight up, as a piece of timber. **4.** an object designed to stand upright: *This piano is an upright.*

up•ris•ing /'ʌp,rayzɪŋ, ʌp'rayzɪŋ/ *n.* [*count*] a revolt; an act of revolt against authority.

up•roar /'ʌp,rɔr/ *n.* [*noncount*] a state of noisy disturbance, as of a crowd; turmoil.

up•roar•i•ous /ʌp'rɔriyəs/ *adj.* **1.** very funny: *an uproarious joke.* **2.** very loud or noisy: *uproarious laughter.*

up•root /ʌp'ruwt, -'rʊt/ *v.* [~ + *obj*] **1.** to pull out by or as if by the roots: *The wind uprooted the trees.* **2.** to displace or remove (people) violently, as from a home, country, or way of life.

up•scale /'ʌp,skeyl/ *adj.* of, relating to, or suitable for relatively wealthy people: *an upscale restaurant.*

up•set /*v.*ʌp'sɛt; *n.* 'ʌp,sɛt/ *v.*, **-set, -set•ting,** *n.* —*v.* [~ + *obj*] **1.** to overturn: *to upset a glass of milk.* **2.** to disturb completely; throw into disorder: *to upset the plans.* **3.** to disturb mentally or emotionally; distress: *The accident upset her.* **4.** to disturb physically: *The food upset his stomach.* **5.** to defeat (an opponent that is favored), as in politics or sports. —*n.* [*count*] **6.** the unexpected defeat of an opponent that is favored.

up•shot /'ʌp,ʃɒt/ *n.* [*count; usually singular*] the final outcome; result: *The upshot of the disagreement was that they broke up the partnership.*

'upside 'down, *adv.* **1.** with the upper part at the bottom. **2.** in or into complete disorder: *They turned the room upside down in their search for her ring.*

up•stage /'ʌp'steydʒ/ *v.* [~ + *obj*] **1.** to draw attention away from (another actor). **2.** to outdo professionally or socially.

up•stairs /'ʌp'stɛərz/ *adv., adj., n., pl.* **-stairs.** —*adv.* **1.** up the stairs; to or on an upper floor: *I walked (her) upstairs.* —*adj.* [*before a noun*] **2.** of, relating to, or located on an upper floor: *an upstairs apartment.* —*n.* [*count; singular; used with a singular verb*] **3.** an upper story or stories; the part of a building or house above the ground floor.

up•stand•ing /ʌp'stændɪŋ/ *adj.* honorable; upright: *an upstanding member of the community.*

up•start /'ʌp,stɑrt/ *n.* [*count*] a person who has risen suddenly from a humble position to wealth, power, or importance, esp. one who is arrogant.

up•state /'ʌp'steyt/ *n.* [*noncount*] the part of a state that is farther north or away from a large city.

up•stream /'ʌp'striym/ *adv.* **1.** toward or in the higher part of a stream; against the current. —*adj.* **2.** directed or located upstream.

up•tight /'ʌp'tayt/ *adj. Informal.* tense or nervous.

'up-to-'date, *adj.* **1.** keeping up with the times; modern: *up-to-date fashions.* **2.** including the latest information or facts: *an up-to-date report.*

up•town /*adv.*'ʌp'tawn; *adj.* -,tawn/ *adv.* **1.** to, toward, or in the upper part of a town or city, usually the part away from the main business section. —*adj.* [*before a noun*] **2.** moving toward, situated in, or relating to the upper part of a town or city: *Take the uptown bus; an uptown nightclub.*

up•ward /'ʌpwərd/ *adv.* Also, **up'wards. 1.** toward a higher place or position: *birds flying upward.* —*adj.* **2.** moving or tending upward; directed at or situated in a higher place or position: *an upward motion.*

u•ra•ni•um /yʊ'reyniyəm/ *n.* [*noncount*] a white, shining, radioactive, metallic element, used in atomic and hydrogen bombs and as a fuel in nuclear reactors.

ur•ban /'ɜrbən/ *adj.* of, relating to, or making up a city or town: *urban areas.*

ur•bane /ɜr'beyn/ *adj.* polished in one's manner or style; sophisticated.

ur•chin /'ɜrtʃɪn/ *n.* [*count*] a poor and dirty child.

urge /ɜrdʒ/ *v.*, **urged, urg•ing,** *n.* —*v.* [~ + *obj*] **1.** to try to persuade (someone), as by asking or imploring: *She urged us to reconsider.* **2.** to argue for; insist on as a course of action: *to urge caution.* —*n.* [*count*] **3.** an impelling influence, force, or drive: *an urge for traveling.* **4.** an instinctive drive: *the sex urge.*

ur•gent /'ɜrdʒənt/ *adj.* requiring immediate action or attention: *an urgent message.* —'**ur•gen•cy,** *n.* —'**ur•gent•ly,** *adv.*

u•ri•nal /'yʊrənl/ *n.* [*count*] a wall fixture used by men for urinating.

u•ri•nar•y /'yʊrə,nɛriy/ *adj.* of or relating to urine or to the organs that secrete and discharge urine.

u•ri•nate /'yʊrə,neyt/ *v.* [*no obj*], **-nat•ed, -nat•ing.** to discharge urine. —,**u•ri'na•tion,** *n.* [*noncount*]

u•rine /'yʊrɪn/ *n.* [*noncount*] the waste matter sent out of the body by the kidneys through the bladder, in mammals as a slightly acid, yellowish liquid.

urn /ɜrn/ *n.* [*count*] **1.** a large or decorated vase. **2.** a large metal container with a spout, used for making or serving tea or coffee in large amounts.

us /ʌs/ *pron.* **1.** the form of the pronoun WE used as a direct or indirect object: *They took us to the circus. She asked us the way.* **2.** *Informal.* (sometimes used in place of the pronoun *we* after the verb *to be*): *Who's there? —It's us!*

U.S. or **US,** an abbreviation of: United States.

U.S.A. or **USA,** an abbreviation of: United States of America.

us•a•ble or **use•a•ble** /'yuwzəbəl/ *adj.* **1.** available or convenient for use. **2.** capable of being used. —**us•a•bil•i•ty** /,yuwzə'bɪlɪtiy/, *n.* [*noncount*]

us•age /'yuwsɪdʒ, -zɪdʒ/ *n.* **1.** [*noncount*] a customary way of doing something; a custom or practice. **2.** [*noncount*] the customary manner in which a language or a form of a language is spoken or written. **3.** [*count*] a particular instance of this: *a usage borrowed from French.*

use /*v.*yuwz *or, for pt. form of* 4 yuwst; *n.* yuws/

v., **used, us•ing,** *n.* —*v.* **1.** [~ + *obj*] to employ for some purpose: *to use a knife to cut the meat.* **2.** [~ + *obj*] to consume, expend, or exhaust: *We've used (up) the money. We've used the money (up).* **3.** [~ + *obj*] to take unfair advantage of; exploit: *She was just using him for his money.* **4.** [*past tense of use* + *to* + *verb*] to be customarily found doing (expresses habitual or customary actions in the past): *He used to go to school every day.* —*n.* **5.** [*noncount*] the act of using or the state of being used. **6.** [*count*] an instance or way of using something: *a painter's use of color.* **7.** [*noncount*] the power, right, or privilege of using something: *We gave her the use of our car; to lose the use of an eye.* **8.** [*noncount*] usefulness; service: *of no practical use.* **9.** [*noncount*] gain or advantage: *What's the use of complaining?* **10.** [*noncount*] occasion or need to use: *Have you any use for another calendar?* —*Idiom.* **have no use for, a.** to have no need for. **b.** to feel intolerant of: *I have no use for lazy people.* **11. in use,** being used: *The laboratory is in use.* **13. make use of,** to use, esp. effectively; employ: *He makes good use of his time.* **14. put to use,** to find a function for; utilize: *He puts his computer to good use.* —**'us•er,** *n.* [*count*]

used /yuwzd *or, for 2,* yuwst/ *adj.* **1.** previously owned: *a used car; used books.* —*Idiom.* **2. used to,** accustomed to: *He's still not used to life in the city.*

use•ful /'yuwsfəl/ *adj.* being of use or service: *a useful member of society; a useful resource, like timber.* —**'use•ful•ness,** *n.* [*noncount*]

use•less /'yuwslɪs/ *adj.* **1.** of no use; not serving a given purpose or any purpose: *useless information.* [*It* + *be* + ~ + *to* + *verb*]: *It was useless to complain.* **2.** without useful qualities; of no practical good: *He's useless at solving problems.*

'user-'friendly, *adj.* easy to operate, understand, etc.: *a user-friendly computer.*

ush•er /'ʌʃər/ *n.* [*count*] **1.** a person who escorts people to seats in a theater, church, etc. —*v.* **2.** to act as an usher (to): [~ + *obj*]: *She ushered them to their seats.* [*no obj*]: *He got his brother to usher at the wedding.* **3. usher in,** to precede or herald: *ushering in a new age of prosperity.*

u•su•al /'yuwʒuwəl/ *adj.* **1.** expected to be found or in evidence; commonly encountered or ob-served; ordinary: *She accomplished the job with her usual skill.* [*It* + *be* + ~ *(for* + *obj) + to* + *verb*]: *It's not usual (for him) to be so late. We'll have dinner at the usual time.* **2.** commonplace; everyday: *all the usual things of life.* —*Idiom.* **3. as usual,** in the customary or usual way: *As usual, I forgot something on my way out.* —**'u•su•al•ly,** *adv.*

u•surp /yuw'sɜrp, -'zɜrp/ *v.* [~ + *obj*] to seize and hold (a position, office, power, etc.) by force or without legal right: *to usurp the throne.*

UT *or* **Ut.,** an abbreviation of: Utah.

u•ten•sil /yuw'tɛnsəl/ *n.* [*count*] **1.** an instrument, container, or other object commonly used, esp. in a kitchen: *eating utensils.* **2.** any instrument, container, or tool serving a useful purpose: *farming utensils.*

u•ter•us /'yuwtərəs/ *n.* [*count*], *pl.* **u•ter•i** /'yuwtə,ray/, **u•ter•us•es.** a hollow organ of certain female mammals in which the fertilized egg develops during pregnancy; the womb.

u•til•i•ty /yuw'tɪlɪtiy/ *n., pl.* **-ties. 1.** [*noncount*] the state or quality of being useful; usefulness. **2.** [*count*] a company or government agency providing a public service, as electricity or water.

u•ti•lize /'yuwtḷ,ayz/ *v.* [~ + *obj*], **-lized, -liz•ing.** to put to use, esp. to profitable or practical use: *How can we best utilize our limited resources?* —**u•ti•li•za•tion** /,yuwtḷə'zeyʃən/, *n.* [*noncount*]

ut•most /'ʌt,mowst/ *adj.* **1.** of the greatest or highest degree, quantity, etc.: *of the utmost importance.* —*n.* [*noncount; often: the* + ~] **2.** the greatest degree or amount: *the utmost in comfort.*

ut•ter[1] /'ʌtər/ *v.* [~ + *obj*] to make (a sound) with the voice: *to utter a few words.*

ut•ter[2] /'ʌtər/ *adj.* [*before a noun*] complete; total: *utter abandonment to grief.* —**'ut•ter•ly,** *adv.: That book is utterly boring.*

ut•ter•ance /'ʌtərəns/ *n.* **1.** [*count*] something uttered; a verbal or written statement. **2.** [*noncount*] an act of uttering.

U-turn /'yuw,tɜrn/ *n.* [*count*] **1.** a U-shaped turn made by a vehicle so as to head in the opposite direction from its original course. **2.** a reversal of policy, tactics, etc., resembling such a turn.

U

V

V, v /viy/ *n.* [*count*], *pl.* **Vs** or **V's, vs** or **v's.** the 22nd letter of the English alphabet, a consonant.

V, *Symbol.* [*sometimes:* v] the Roman numeral for five.

v., an abbreviation of: volt.

VA, an abbreviation of: Virginia.

Va., an abbreviation of: Virginia.

va•cant /'veykənt/ *adj.* **1.** having no contents; empty. **2.** having no occupant; unoccupied: *a vacant seat.* **3.** lacking in intelligence: *a vacant expression.* —'**va•can•cy,** *n.* [*noncount*] [*count*], *pl.* -**cies.**

va•cate /'veykeyt/ *v.* [~ + *obj*], -**cat•ed, -cat•ing.** to give up occupancy of: *to vacate an apartment.*

va•ca•tion /vey'keyʃən, və-/ *n.* **1.** a period during which one does not have to report to one's regular work, school, or other activity, usually used for rest, recreation, or travel: [*count*]: *went on a long vacation.* [*noncount*]: *They're on vacation.* —*v.* [*no obj*] **2.** to take or have a vacation: *We vacationed in Spain.* —**va'ca•tion•er,** *n.* [*count*]

vac•ci•nate /'væksə,neyt/ *v.* [~ + *obj*] [*no obj*], -**nat•ed, -nat•ing.** to inject a vaccine into (a person or animal). —**vac•ci•na•tion** /,væksə'neyʃən/, *n.* [*noncount*] [*count*]

vac•cine /væk'siyn/ *n.* [*count*] a preparation introduced into the body to prevent a disease by causing the body to produce antibodies against it, usually a weakened substance containing the virus causing the disease.

vac•il•late /'væsə,leyt/ *v.* [*no obj*], -**lat•ed, -lat•ing.** to be unsure in one's mind or opinion; be indecisive about what action to take: *to vacillate before deciding.* —**vac•il•la•tion** /,væsə'leyʃən/, *n.* [*noncount*]

vac•u•um /'vækyuwm, -yəm/ *n.*, *pl.* -**u•ums** for 1–3, -**u•a** /-yuwə/ for 1, 2; *v.* —*n.* [*count*] **1.** an enclosed space from which matter, esp. air, has been partially removed so that the matter or gas remaining in the space exerts less pressure than the atmosphere. **2.** any space not filled or occupied; emptiness; void: *The loss of his son left a vacuum in his life.* **3.** VACUUM CLEANER. —*v.* **4.** to clean with a vacuum cleaner: [~ + *obj*]: *to vacuum the rug.* [*no obj*]: *I vacuum on Fridays.*

'**vacuum ,cleaner,** *n.* [*count*] an electrical device for cleaning carpets, floors, etc., by suction.

vag•a•bond /'vægə,bɒnd/ *n.* [*count*] a person, usually without a permanent home, who wanders from place to place.

va•gi•na /və'dʒaynə/ *n.* [*count*], *pl.* -**nas, -nae** /-niy/. the passage leading from the uterus to the outer sex organs in female mammals. —**vag•i•nal** /'vædʒənəl/, *adj.*

va•grant /'veygrənt/ *n.* [*count*] a person who wanders about idly and has no permanent home or employment; a vagabond. —'**va•gran•cy,** *n.* [*noncount*]

vague /veyg/ *adj.*, **va•guer, va•guest. 1.** not clearly stated or expressed: *vague promises.* **2.** not clear or definite in thought, understanding, or expression: *was vague when I asked his plan.* —'**vague•ly,** *adv.* —'**vague•ness,** *n.* [*noncount*]

vain /veyn/ *adj.*, -**er, -est. 1.** overly proud of or concerned about one's own appearance, qualities, achievements, etc. **2.** unsuccessful; useless: *vain efforts.* —*Idiom.* **3. in vain, a.** without effect; to no purpose: *All the work was in vain.* **b.** in an improper or irreverent manner: *to take God's name in vain.* —'**vain•ly,** *adv.*

val•en•tine /'vælən,tayn/ *n.* [*count*] **1.** a card or message, usually expressing love or affection, sent by one person to another on a holiday called Valentine's Day, February 14. **2.** a sweetheart chosen or greeted on this day.

val•et /væ'ley, 'vælɪt, 'væley/ *n.* [*count*] **1.** a male servant who attends to the personal needs of his employer, as by taking care of clothing. **2.** an attendant who parks cars for guests at a hotel, restaurant, etc.

val•iant /'vælyənt/ *adj.* boldly courageous; brave: *valiant soldiers.* —'**val•iant•ly,** *adv.*

val•id /'vælɪd/ *adj.* **1.** sound; reasonable: *a valid argument.* **2.** that can be used legally or properly: *a valid driver's license.* —**va•lid•i•ty** /və'lɪdɪtiy/, *n.* [*noncount*]

val•i•date /'vælɪ,deyt/ *v.* [~ + *obj*], -**dat•ed, -dat•ing. 1.** to make legally valid or binding: *to validate a passport.* **2.** to confirm: *The incident validated our suspicions.* —**val•i•da•tion** /,vælɪ'deyʃən/, *n.* [*noncount*]

va•lise /və'liys, -'liyz/ *n.* [*count*] a small piece of hand luggage; suitcase.

val•ley /'væliy/ *n.* [*count*], *pl.* -**leys. 1.** a long, narrow area that is lower than surrounding lands, hills, or mountains. **2.** a wide, more or less flat, and relatively low region drained by a river system.

val•or /'vælər/ *n.* [*noncount*] boldness or determination in facing danger. Also, *esp. Brit.,* '**val•our.**

val•u•a•ble /'vælyuwəbəl, -yəbəl/ *adj.* **1.** worth a great deal of money. **2.** of considerable use, importance, or value: *a highly valuable player; valuable information.* —*n.* [*count*] **3.** Usually, **valuables.** [*plural*] personal articles, as jewelry, of great value.

val•ue /'vælyuw/ *n.*, *v.*, -**ued, -u•ing.** —*n.* **1.** [*noncount*] relative worth or importance; significance: *the value of a college education.* **2.** [*noncount*] monetary or material worth (of land, inventory, artwork, etc.), as in business. **3.** Often, **values.** [*plural*] the ideas of what is right, worthwhile, or desirable according to a person, society, etc.; principles or standards. —*v.* [~ + *obj*] **4.** to calculate or estimate the monetary value of: *They valued the painting at over one million dollars.* **5.** to regard highly; think of (someone or something) greatly: *We value your friendship.*

valve /vælv/ *n.* [*count*] **1.** any device for stopping or controlling the flow of something, as a liquid, through a pipe or other passage. **2.** a structure in the body that permits the flow of a fluid, as blood, in one direction only: *a heart valve.*

vam•pire /'væmpayᵊr/ *n.* [*count*] a corpse believed to come alive and leave the grave, typically in order to suck the blood of sleeping persons at night.

van /væn/ *n.* [*count*] a covered vehicle, usually a large truck or trailer, used for moving goods or animals, or that can house passengers for traveling and camping.

van•dal /'vændl̩/ *n.* [*count*] a person who maliciously destroys or damages public or private property.

van•dal•ize /'vændl̩,ayz/ *v.* [~ + *obj*], **-ized, -iz•ing.** to destroy or deface (property). —'**van•dal•ism,** *n.* [*noncount*]

vane /veyn/ *n.* [*count*] WEATHER VANE.

van•guard /'væn,gɑrd/ *n.* **1.** [*count*] the front part of an advancing army. **2.** [*count; usually singular; often: the* + ~] the forefront in any political movement, field of study, etc.

va•nil•la /və'nɪlə/ *n., pl.* **-las. 1.** [*count*] a tropical orchid with fragrant flowers. **2.** [*count*] Also called '**vanil•la ,bean.** the fruit or bean of this orchid. **3.** [*noncount*] the juice squeezed or pressed out of this fruit, used in flavoring food and in perfumes: *ice cream made with vanilla.*

van•ish /'vænɪʃ/ *v.* [*no obj*] **1.** to disappear suddenly: *The magician made the coin vanish before our eyes.* **2.** to cease to exist; come to an end: *The pain vanished when he relaxed and listened to some soothing music.*

van•i•ty /'vænɪtiy/ *n., pl.* **-ties. 1.** [*noncount*] too much pride in oneself or one's appearance. **2.** [*count*] a table topped with a mirror, used while dressing or grooming.

van•quish /'væŋkwɪʃ, 'væn-/ *v.* [~ + *obj*] to conquer or defeat; overcome: *to vanquish their foes.*

va•por /'veypər/ *n.* **1.** a visible mass of tiny particles, as fog, mist, or smoke, floating or hanging in the air: [*count*]: *the vapors rising from the bog.* [*noncount*]: *clouds of vapor.* **2.** [*noncount*] a substance that has been made into the form of a gas: *water vapor.*

var•i•a•ble /'vɛəriyəbəl/ *adj.* **1.** apt to vary; changeable; not staying the same: *a cloudy day with variable winds.* —*n.* [*count*] **2.** something that may or does vary: *a situation with many variables.* —**var•i•a•bil•i•ty** /,vɛəriyə'bɪlɪtiy/, *n.* [*noncount*]

var•i•ant /'vɛəriyənt/ *adj.* [*before a noun*] **1.** showing variety or variation. **2.** differing, esp. from something of the same kind. —*n.* [*count*] **3.** a person or thing that varies. **4.** a different spelling, pronunciation, or form of the same word.

var•i•a•tion /,vɛəriy'eyʃən/ *n.* **1.** [*noncount*] the act or process of varying or differing from what is normal or usual: *Those prices are subject to much variation.* **2.** [*count*] an instance of this: *a variation in quality.* **3.** [*count*] amount or degree of change: *a temperature variation of 20°.*

var•ied /'vɛəriyd/ *adj.* characterized by or showing variety; diverse: *varied species of plants.*

va•ri•e•ty /və'rayɪtiy/ *n., pl.* **-ties. 1.** [*noncount*] the state of being varied or various: *He needed variety in his diet.* **2.** [*count; usually singular*] a number of different types of things, esp. ones in the same general category: *a large variety of foods to choose from.* **3.** [*count*] a kind, sort, or type: *different varieties of apples.*

var•i•ous /'vɛəriyəs/ *adj.* [*usually: before a noun*] **1.** of different kinds; differing one from another: *various cheeses for sale.* **2.** several; many: *We stayed at various hotels along the way.*

var•nish /'vɑrnɪʃ/ *n.* [*noncount*] [*count*] **1.** a preparation for coating surfaces, as of wood, made of the resin of trees dissolved in oil, alcohol, or the like. —*v.* [~ + *obj*] **2.** to coat with varnish: *to varnish the wood table.*

var•y /'vɛəriy/ *v.,* **var•ied, var•y•ing. 1.** to alter, as in form, appearance, or substance; to change so as not to be constantly the same; diversify: [~ + *obj*]: *to vary one's diet.* [*no obj*]: *Her diet never varied.* **2.** [*no obj*] to be different: *to vary from the norm.*

vase /veys, veyz, vɑz/ *n.* [*count*] a container or vessel, as of glass or porcelain, usually higher than it is wide, used to hold cut flowers or for decoration.

vast /væst/ *adj.,* **-er, -est. 1.** of very great area or size: *a vast continent.* **2.** very great in quantity or amount: *vast wealth.* —'**vast•ly,** *adv.* —'**vast•ness,** *n.* [*noncount*]: *the sheer vastness of space.*

vat /væt/ *n.* [*count*] a large container, as a tank, used for holding liquids: *a wine vat.*

VAT /væt/ an abbreviation of: value-added tax.

vault¹ /vɔlt/ *n.* [*count*] **1.** an arched structure, usually of stones, concrete, or bricks, that forms a ceiling or roof. **2.** a room or compartment for the safekeeping of valuables, usually with a locked door and thick walls. **3.** a burial chamber.

vault² /vɔlt/ *v.* **1.** to jump, as to or from a position or over something: [*no obj*]: *He vaulted over the tennis net.* [~ + *obj*]: *She vaulted the fence.* —*n.* [*count*] **2.** the act of vaulting.

V-chip /'viy,tʃɪp/ *n.* [*count*] a computer chip or other electronic device that blocks television reception of programs with violent or sexual content.

VCR, *n.* [*count*] videocassette recorder: an electronic device for recording television programs or playing back videotapes.

VD, an abbreviation of: venereal disease.

veal /viyl/ *n.* [*noncount*] the flesh of a calf used for food.

veer /vɪər/ *v.* [*no obj*] to change direction or course or turn aside; shift or change from one course, position, etc., to another: *The car veered to the right.*

veg•e•ta•ble /'vɛdʒtəbəl, 'vɛdʒɪtə-/ *n.* [*count*] **1.** any plant whose fruit, seeds, roots, tubers, bulbs, stems, leaves, or flower parts are used as food. **2.** any part of a plant that is usually eaten: *Eat all the vegetables on your plate.*

veg•e•tar•i•an /,vɛdʒɪ'tɛəriyən/ *n.* [*count*] **1.** a person who does not eat, or does not believe in eating, meat, fish, fowl, or, in some cases, any food made from animals. —*adj.* **2.** relating to this diet or philosophy: *a vegetarian cookbook.* —,**veg•e'tar•i•an•ism,** *n.* [*noncount*]

veg•e•tate /'vɛdʒɪ,teyt/ *v.* [*no obj*], **-tat•ed, -tat•ing.** to lead an inactive life without much physical, mental, or social activity.

veg•e•ta•tion /,vɛdʒɪ'teyʃən/ *n.* [*noncount*] the plants or plant life of a place.

ve•he•ment /'viyəmənt/ *adj.* showing or characterized by strong feeling: *vehement opposition.* —'**ve•he•mence,** *n.* [*noncount*] —'**ve•he•ment•ly,** *adv.*

ve•hi•cle /'viyɪkəl or, sometimes, 'viyhɪ-/ *n.* [*count*] **1.** a conveyance moving on wheels, runners, or the like, such as an automobile; a device by which someone or something is carried: *a motor vehicle.* **2.** any means or medium of expression, communication, or exhibition: *The play was a powerful vehicle for her talents.*

veil /veyl/ *n.* [*count*] **1.** a piece of material worn over the face to hide or protect, to enhance the appearance, or to be part of an outfit or costume: *a bride's veil.* **2.** anything that covers or hides: *a veil of secrecy.*

vein /veyn/ *n.* [*count*] **1.** one of the branching vessels or tubes carrying blood from various parts of the body to the heart. **2.** one of the thin lines forming the framework of a leaf or the wing

V

of an insect. **3.** a clearly separated layer or mass of mineral deposit in rock: *a rich vein of copper.* **4.** a temporary attitude, mood, or temper: *He spoke in a serious vein.* **—veined,** *adj.*

Vel•cro /'vɛlkrow/ *Trademark.* [*noncount*] a fastening tape consisting of opposing pieces of nylon fabric that interlock when pressed together, used to attach or close garments, pieces of luggage, etc.

ve•loc•i•ty /və'lɒsɪtiy/ *n.* [*count*], *pl.* **-ties.** quickness or speed of motion, action, or operation: *the velocity of light.*

vel•vet /'vɛlvɪt/ *n.* [*noncount*] a fabric of silk, nylon, rayon, etc., with a thick, soft pile. **—'vel•vet•y,** *adj.*

'vending ma,chine, *n.* [*count*] a coin-operated machine for selling small articles, as candy bars or soft drinks.

ven•dor /'vɛndər/ *n.* [*count*] a person or agency that sells.

ve•neer /və'nɪər/ *n.* **1.** [*noncount*] a thin layer of wood or other material for covering a surface of wood. **2.** [*count*; *usually singular*] an apparently good or pleasing appearance: *a veneer of respectability.*

ven•er•a•ble /'vɛnərəbəl/ *adj.* worthy of respect or reverence, because of great age, high office, noble character, or the like.

ven•er•ate /'vɛnə,reyt/ *v.* [~ + *obj*], **-at•ed, -at•ing.** to regard or treat with reverence: *to venerate a saint.* **—ven•er•a•tion** /,vɛnə'reyʃən/, *n.* [*noncount*]

ve'nereal dis,ease, *n.* [*noncount*] [*count*] any disease transmitted by sexual contact. *Abbr.:* VD

ve'netian 'blind /və'niyʃən/ *n.* [*count*] a window blind having overlapping horizontal slats that may be opened, closed, or set at an angle, and which may be raised or lowered by pulling a cord.

Ven•e•zue•lan /,vɛnə'zweylən, -'zwiy-/ *adj.* **1.** of or relating to Venezuela. **—n.** [*count*] **2.** a person born or living in Venezuela.

venge•ance /'vɛndʒəns/ *n.* [*noncount*] **1.** the act of injuring, harming, or humiliating in return for an injury or offense; revenge. **2.** the desire for revenge: *to be full of vengeance.* **—Idiom. 3. with a vengeance,** with extreme energy: *He set to work with a vengeance.*

venge•ful /'vɛndʒfəl/ *adj.* characterized by or showing a mean spirit that is eager for revenge.

ven•i•son /'vɛnəsən, -zən/ *n.* [*noncount*] the flesh of a deer or similar animal used for food.

ven•om /'vɛnəm/ *n.* [*noncount*] **1.** the poisonous fluid that some animals, as certain snakes and spiders, give off and inject into the bodies of their victims by biting, stinging, etc. **2.** something suggesting poison in its effect, as hatred, malice, or jealousy. **—'ven•om•ous,** *adj.*: *a venomous attack.*

vent /vɛnt/ *n.* **1.** [*count*] an opening, as in a wall, that serves as an outlet for air, fumes, or the like. **2.** [*noncount*] expression; utterance; release: *giving vent to one's emotions.* **—v.** [~ + *obj*] **3.** to give free play or expression to (an emotion): *He vented his frustration.*

ven•ti•late /'vɛntl,eyt/ *v.* [~ + *obj*], **-lat•ed, -lat•ing.** to provide (a room, mine, etc.) with fresh air. **—ven•ti•la•tion** /,vɛntl'eyʃən/, *n.* [*noncount*]

ven•tri•cle /'vɛntrɪkəl/ *n.* [*count*] either of the two lower chambers of the heart that receive blood from other chambers and in turn force it into the arteries.

ven•tril•o•quism /vɛn'trɪlə,kwɪzəm/ *n.* [*noncount*] the art or practice of speaking with little or no lip movement so that the voice does not appear to come from the speaker but from another source, as a puppet or dummy. **—ven'tril•o•quist,** *n.* [*count*]

ven•ture /'vɛntʃər/ *n., v.,* **-tured, -tur•ing. —n.** [*count*] **1.** an activity or undertaking involving risk or uncertainty, as a business enterprise in which something is risked in the hope of profit. **—v. 2.** to take the risk of; undertake or embark: [~ + *obj*]: *to venture an ocean voyage.* [*no obj*]: *We ventured deep into the jungle.* **3.** to offer or attempt to express (an idea, opinion, or guess), despite possible opposition or resistance: [~ + *obj*]: *She ventured an opinion.* [~ + *to* + *verb*]: *I venture to say we'll need help.*

ve•ran•da /və'rændə/ *n.* [*count*], *pl.* **-das.** a porch, usually roofed, often extending across the front and sides of a house.

verb /vɜrb/ *n.* [*count*] a member of a class of words that typically express action or condition or a relation between two things and are often formally distinguished, as by being marked for tense, aspect, voice, mood, or agreement with the subject or object. *Abbr.:* v.

ver•bal /'vɜrbəl/ *adj.* **1.** of or relating to words: *verbal ability.* **2.** spoken rather than written; oral; involving words rather than action: *verbal communication; a verbal protest.* **3.** of or derived from a verb. **—'ver•bal•ly,** *adv.*

ver•bal•ize /'vɜrbə,layz/ *v.,* **-ized, -iz•ing.** to express or communicate in words: [~ + *obj*]: *I can't verbalize my feelings.* [*no obj*]: *to verbalize at an early age.* **—ver•bal•i•za•tion** /,vɜrbələ'zeyʃən/, *n.* [*noncount*]

'verbal 'noun, *n.* [*count*] a noun derived from a verb, as the *-ing* form in *Smoking is forbidden.*

ver•bose /vər'bows/ *adj.* expressed in or characterized by the use of too many words: *a verbose report; a verbose speaker.*

ver•dict /'vɜrdɪkt/ *n.* [*count*] **1.** the finding of a jury in a court of law. **2.** any judgment or decision.

verge /vɜrdʒ/ *n., v.,* **verged, verg•ing. —n.** [*count*; *usually singular*] **1.** the limit or point beyond which something begins or occurs; brink: *He's on the verge of a nervous breakdown.* **2.** the edge, rim, or margin of something; a border of something: *the verge of a desert.* **—v.** [*no obj*] **3.** to be on the edge or margin; border: *Our property verges on theirs.* **4.** to come close to; approach: *a talent that verges on genius.*

ver•i•fy /'vɛrə,fay/ *v.* [~ + *obj*], **-fied, -fy•ing.** to prove the truth of, as by evidence or testimony; confirm: *Several witnesses verified his alibi.* **—ver•i•fi•ca•tion** /,vɛrəfɪ'keyʃən/, *n.* [*noncount*]: *We'll need verification of your signature.*

ver•i•ta•ble /'vɛrɪtəbəl/ *adj.* being truly or very much so: *a veritable genius.*

ver•mil•ion /vər'mɪlyən/ *n.* [*noncount*] a brilliant scarlet red.

ver•min /'vɜrmɪn/ *n.* [*plural*; *used with a plural verb*] **1.** harmful or unwanted animals thought of as a group, as flies, lice, cockroaches, and rats. **2.** offensive persons thought of as a group.

ver•nac•u•lar /vər'nækyələr, və'næk-/ *adj.* **1.** expressed or written in the language or dialect characteristic of a particular area, or using that language. **2.** using plain, ordinary language. **—n.** [*count*] **3.** the native speech or language of a place, esp. the particular language of a place. **4.**

the plain variety of language in everyday use by ordinary people.

ver•sa•tile /'vɜrsət̬l, -ˌtayl/ *adj.* **1.** capable of turning easily from one thing to another: *a versatile teacher.* **2.** having or capable of many uses: *a versatile tool.* —**ver•sa•til•i•ty** /ˌvɜrsə'tɪlɪtiy/, *n.* [*noncount*]

verse /vɜrs/ *n.* **1.** [*count*] a part of a poem or song. **2.** [*noncount*] poetry.

versed /vɜrst/ *adj.* [*be* + ~ (+ *in*)] experienced or knowledgeable: *versed in Latin.*

ver•sion /'vɜrʒən, -ʃən/ *n.* [*count*] **1.** a particular account or telling of some matter or event, esp. as contrasted with some other account: *There were two different versions of the accident.* **2.** a particular variant of something, as a song or machine: *an updated version of a computer program; the King James version of the Bible.* **3.** a modified form of something, a literary work, made suitable for another medium: *a movie version of her life story.*

ver•sus /'vɜrsəs, -səz/ *prep.* **1.** as compared or contrasted with: *traveling by plane versus traveling by train.* **2.** against (esp. used in sports contests or court cases): *Ali versus Frazier; Roe versus Wade. Abbr.:* v., vs.

ver•te•bra /'vɜrtəbrə/ *n.* [*count*], *pl.* **-brae** /-ˌbriy, -ˌbrey/, **-bras.** a bone or segment of the spinal column.

ver•te•brate /'vɜrtəbrɪt, -ˌbreyt/ *adj.* **1.** having vertebrae; having a backbone or spine. —*n.* [*count*] **2.** a vertebrate animal: *Vertebrates include mammals, birds, snakes, frogs, and fishes.*

ver•ti•cal /'vɜrtɪkəl/ *adj.* upright; pointing straight up from the ground. —**'ver•ti•cal•ly,** *adv.*

verve /vɜrv/ *n.* [*noncount*] liveliness; enthusiasm or vigor: *Her novel lacks verve.*

ver•y /'veriy/ *adv., adj.,* **-i•er, -i•est.** —*adv.* **1.** in a high degree; extremely: *a very clever person.* **2.** This word is sometimes used to show the speaker's intense feeling, or to emphasize or stress something: *the very best thing; in the very same place.* —*adj.* [*before a noun*] **3.** precise; particular: *That is the very item we want.* **4.** mere: *The very thought of losing the game makes me feel nervous.* **5.** extreme; utter: *to the very end.*

ves•sel /'vɛsəl/ *n.* [*count*] **1.** a craft for traveling on water, esp. a fairly large one; a ship or boat. **2.** a hollow utensil, as a cup, bowl, or pitcher, used for holding liquids or other contents. **3.** a tube or duct, as an artery or vein, containing or carrying blood or some other body fluid.

vest /vɛst/ *n.* [*count*] **1.** a fitted, waist-length, sleeveless garment with buttons down the front, usually worn under a jacket. —*v.* [~ + *obj*] **2.** to give powers, rights, etc., to: *They vested him with full authority.*

ves•ti•bule /'vɛstəˌbyuwl/ *n.* [*count*] a passage, hall, or small chamber between the outer door and the interior parts of a house or building.

ves•tige /'vɛstɪdʒ/ *n.* [*count*] a trace of something that is no longer in existence: *the last vestiges of a once great empire.*

vest•ment /'vɛstmənt/ *n.* [*count*] an official or ceremonial robe, esp. one of the garments worn by priests, ministers, and their assistants.

vet¹ /vɛt/ *n.* [*count*] *Informal.* a veterinarian.

vet² /vɛt/ *n., adj. Informal.* VETERAN.

vet•er•an /'vɛtərən, 'vɛtrən/ *n.* [*count*] **1.** a person who has had long service or experience in an occupation, office, or the like. **2.** a person who has served in a military force, esp. during a war.

vet•er•i•nar•i•an /ˌvɛtərə'nɛəriyən, ˌvɛtrə-/ *n.* [*count*] a person whose work is the medical treatment of animals.

vet•er•i•nar•y /'vɛtərəˌnɛriy, 'vɛtrə-/ *adj.* [*before a noun*] of or relating to the medical and surgical treatment of animals: *veterinary medicine.*

ve•to /'viytow/ *n., pl.* **-toes,** *v.* **-toed, to•ing** —*n.* **1.** [*noncount*] the power given to one branch of a government to cancel or postpone the decisions or actions of another branch, esp. the right of a president or other chief executive to reject bills passed by the legislature: *the power of the veto.* **2.** [*count*] a use or exercise of this power: *Another presidential veto was overridden by Congress.* **3.** [*count*] a strong forbidding of something. —*v.* [~ + *obj*] **4.** to reject by exercising a veto. **5.** to forbid: *His parents vetoed that idea.*

vex /vɛks/ *v.* [~ + *obj*] **1.** to irritate; annoy: *She was told to stop vexing the dog.* **2.** to trouble; distress: *He was vexed by many problems.* —**vex•a•tion** /vɛk'seyʃən/ *n.* [*noncount*] [*count*]

vi•a /'vayə, 'viyə/ *prep.* by means of or by way of: *They came to Tangiers via Casablanca.*

vi•a•ble /'vayəbəl/ *adj.* **1.** having the ability to grow, develop, or live: *a viable seedling.* **2.** that can be used or made useful; practical; workable: *a viable plan.* —**vi•a•bil•i•ty** /ˌvayə'bɪlɪtiy/, *n.* [*noncount*]

vi•a•duct /'vayəˌdʌkt/ *n.* [*count*] a bridge for carrying a road, railroad, etc., over a valley or the like, consisting of a number of short spans.

vi•al /'vayəl, vayl/ *n.* [*count*] a small container, as of glass, for holding liquids or medicines.

vi•brant /'vaybrənt/ *adj.* alive with vigor and energy; lively: *the vibrant life of a large city; a vibrant personality.* —**'vi•bran•cy,** *n.* [*noncount*] —**'vi•brant•ly,** *adv.*

vi•brate /'vaybreyt/ *v.,* **-brat•ed, -brat•ing.** to (cause to) move to and fro or up and down quickly and repeatedly; quiver; tremble: [*no obj*]: *The whole house vibrated when the heavy truck went by.* [~ + *obj*]: *to vibrate a tuning fork.* —**vi•bra•tion** /vay'breyʃən/ *n.* [*noncount*] [*count*]

vic•ar /'vɪkər/ *n.* [*count*] a parish priest in the Anglican Church.

vice /vays/ *n.* [*count*] an immoral or evil habit or practice: *His vices include drinking and gambling.*

vice-, a combining form meaning in place of (*vice-president*).

'vice 'president or **'vice-'president** /vays/ *n.* [*count*] **1.** [*often: Vice President*] a governmental officer next in rank to a president, who serves as president in the event of the president's death, illness, removal, or resignation. **2.** an officer who serves as a deputy to a president or oversees a special division or function, as in a corporation. —**'vice 'presidency,** *n.* [*noncount*]

vi•ce ver•sa /'vay'sə vɜrsə, 'vays/ *adv.* in reverse order from that of a preceding statement: *She likes me, and vice versa* (= *She likes me and I like her).*

vi•cin•i•ty /vɪ'sɪnɪtiy/ *n.* [*noncount*] **1.** the area or region near or about a place; neighborhood. —*Idiom.* **2. in the vicinity of,** almost; approximately: *It cost in the vicinity of a thousand dollars.*

vi•cious /'vɪʃəs/ *adj.* **1.** dangerously hateful and ready to do violence; savage: *a cruel, vicious dictator; a vicious temper.* **2.** spiteful; nasty: *vicious gossip.* —*Idiom.* **3. vicious circle,** a situation in which an effort to solve a given problem only

V

makes the problem worse. Also, **vicious cycle.** —'**vi•cious•ly,** adv. —'**vi•cious•ness,** n. [noncount]

vic•tim /'vɪktəm/ n. [count] **1.** a person who suffers from destruction or an injury: war victims. **2.** a person who is deceived, betrayed, or cheated: the victims of a fraudulent scheme.

vic•tim•ize /'vɪktə,mayz/ v. [~ + obj], **-ized, -iz•ing.** to make a victim of. —**vic•tim•i•za•tion** /,vɪktəmə'zeyʃən/, n. [noncount]

vic•tor /'vɪktər/ n. [count] a winner in any struggle or contest.

vic•to•ry /'vɪktəriy, 'vɪktriy/ n., pl. **-ries.** a success or superior position achieved against any opponent, competitor, opposition, difficulty, etc.: [count]: We gained a moral victory. [noncount]: celebrating victory. —**vic•to•ri•ous** /vɪk'tɔriyəs/, adj.

vid•e•o /'vɪdiy,ow/ n., pl. **-e•os. 1.** [noncount] the parts of a television program, broadcast, or script that relate to the sending or receiving of a visual image (distinguished from audio). **2.** [count] a program, movie, or the like recorded on videotape.

'**videocassette re,corder,** n. VCR.

vid•e•o•disc /'vɪdiyow,dɪsk/ n. [count] [noncount] an optical disc on which a motion picture or television program is recorded for playback on a television set.

'**video ,game,** n. [count] **1.** a game played with a microcomputer on a video screen or television set. **2.** a game played on a microchip-controlled device, as an arcade machine.

vid•e•o•tape /'vɪdiyow,teyp/ n., v., **-taped, -tap•ing.** —n. **1.** [noncount] magnetic tape on which a television program, motion picture, etc., can be recorded. **2.** [count] the usually plastic cassette in which this tape is contained: I made a videotape of last night's episode. —v. [~ + obj] **3.** to record (programs, etc.) on videotape.

vie /vay/ v. [no obj], **vied, vy•ing.** to struggle or compete with another in a game or contest: vying for the championship.

Vi•et•nam•ese /viy,ɛtnɑ'miyz, -'miys, -nə-, ,vyɛt-, ,viyɪt-/ n., pl. **-ese. 1.** [count] a person born or living in Vietnam. **2.** [noncount] the language spoken by many of the people of Vietnam.

view /vyuw/ n. **1.** [count] an instance of seeing or beholding, or of visual inspection or examination: a good view of the painting. **2.** [noncount] range of sight or vision: objects in view. **3.** [count] a sight of a landscape, the sea, etc.: a room with a beautiful view. **4.** a personal attitude; opinion; judgment: [count]: the scientist's view of evolution. [noncount]: a strange (point of) view. **5.** [count] aim, intention, or purpose: with a view toward reducing the budget. —v. [~ + obj] **6.** to see; watch; look at: to view an art collection; Thousands viewed the parade. **7.** to think about; consider: How do you view the current crisis? —Idiom. **8. in view of,** because of; considering: In view of the poor state of the economy, investment seems risky. **9. on view,** in a place for public inspection; on exhibition: a new exhibit of paintings on view. **10. with a view to,** with the aim or intention of: She worked hard with a view to getting promoted. —'**view•er** n. [count]

view•point /'vyuw,pɔynt/ n. [count] **1.** a place providing a view of something. **2.** an attitude of mind; a point of view.

vig•il /'vɪdʒəl/ n. a watch or period of watchful attention maintained at night or at other times: [count]: a peace vigil. [noncount]: to keep vigil for someone.

vig•i•lant /'vɪdʒələnt/ adj. watchful; wary; alert: a vigilant watchdog. —'**vig•i•lance,** n. [noncount]

vig•or /'vɪgər/ n. [noncount] **1.** great force; intensity; energy: He pursued his new career with great vigor. **2.** healthy physical or mental energy or power; vitality: He rowed with vigor.

vig•or•ous /'vɪgərəs/ adj. full of vigor: a vigorous effort to finish on time. —'**vig•or•ous•ly,** adv.

vile /vayl/ adj., **vil•er, vil•est. 1.** uncomfortably bad: vile weather. **2.** highly offensive or unpleasant: a vile odor; vile language. **3.** very evil: vile acts of murder.

vil•la /'vɪlə/ n. [count], pl. **-las.** a country home or estate, esp. a large, impressive one.

vil•lage /'vɪlɪdʒ/ n. [count] a small rural community, usually smaller than a town. —'**vil•lag•er,** n. [count]

vil•lain /'vɪlən/ n. [count] **1.** a cruel or evil person; a scoundrel. **2.** a character in a play, novel, or the like who commits cruel and evil deeds. —'**vil•lain•ous,** adj.

vil•lain•y /'vɪləniy/ n. [noncount] [count], pl. **-lain•ies.** the actions or conduct of a villain; terrible wickedness or evil.

vim /vɪm/ n. [noncount] lively or energetic spirit; enthusiasm; vitality: full of vim and vigor.

vin•di•cate /'vɪndɪ,keyt/ v. [~ + obj], **-cat•ed, -cat•ing. 1.** to clear, as from an accusation or suspicion: to vindicate someone's honor. **2.** to prove to be right or correct: His theory was vindicated by laboratory tests. —**vin•di•ca•tion** /,vɪndɪ'keyʃən/, n. [count]: a vindication of the theory. [noncount]: He wanted vindication.

vin•dic•tive /vɪn'dɪktɪv/ adj. eager for revenge; vengeful: a vindictive loser.

vine /vayn/ n. [count] a plant with a long stem that grows along the ground or that climbs a support by winding or by clinging to it.

vin•e•gar /'vɪnɪgər/ n. [noncount] a sour liquid obtained from sour wine, cider, or the like and used on food, in cooking, as a preservative, etc.

vine•yard /'vɪnyərd/ n. [count] a plantation of grapevines, esp. one producing grapes for winemaking.

vin•tage /'vɪntɪdʒ/ n. **1.** [count] the wine from a particular harvest or crop, esp. a very fine wine from the crop of a good year. **2.** [noncount] the output (of a given object) of a particular time or year; a collection of things manufactured or in use at the same time: a car of 1917 vintage. —adj. [before a noun] **3.** representing the high quality of a past time; classic: those old, vintage movies.

vi•nyl /'vaynl/ n. [noncount] a firm plastic that can be slightly bent, used for making floor coverings, furniture coverings, phonograph records, etc.

vi•o•la /viy'owlə/ n. [count], pl. **-las.** a musical instrument of the violin family, slightly larger than the violin. —**vi•o•list,** n. [count]

vi•o•late /'vayə,leyt/ v. [~ + obj], **-lat•ed, -lat•ing. 1.** to break or infringe (a law, a promise, instructions, etc.): to violate the law by stealing; She violated her oath of office. **2.** to break in upon or disturb rudely: to violate someone's privacy. —**vi•o•la•tion** /,vayə'leyʃən/, n. [noncount] [count]

vi•o•lent /'vayələnt/ adj. **1.** acting with or characterized by uncontrolled, strong, rough force: a violent attack with a kitchen knife. **2.** characterized or caused by very harmful or destructive force: *a violent death.* **3.** intense in force, effect, etc.; severe; extreme: *violent pain; a violent tornado.* —**'vi•o•lence,** *n.* [*noncount*] —**'vi•o•lent•ly,** *adv.*

vi•o•let /'vayəlɪt/ *n.* **1.** [*count*] a low, stemless or leafy-stemmed plant having purple, blue, yellow, white, or differently colored flowers, as an African violet. **2.** [*noncount*] a reddish blue color.

vi•o•lin /ˌvayə'lɪn/ *n.* [*count*] a four-stringed instrument played with a bow and held nearly horizontal by the player's arm under the chin. —**ˌvi•o'lin•ist,** *n.* [*count*]

VIP or **V.I.P.** /'viy'ay'piy/ *n.* [*count*] *Informal.* a very important person.

vi•per /'vaypər/ *n.* [*count*] **1.** a poisonous snake having a pair of hollow fangs that, once erect, can bite and inject venom. **2.** a vicious, spiteful, or treacherous person.

vi•ral /'vayrəl/ *adj.* of, relating to, or caused by a virus.

vir•gin /'vɜrdʒɪn/ *n.* [*count*] **1.** a person who has not had sexual intercourse. —*adj.* [*before a noun*] **2.** pure; untouched: *the virgin snow.* **3.** not having been used or made use of: *a virgin forest.* —**'vir•gin•al,** *adj.* —**vir'gin•i•ty,** *n.* [*noncount*]

vir•ile /'vɪrəl/ *adj.* **1.** having or showing masculine strength or qualities; manly. **2.** vigorous or forceful. **3.** capable of having sex. —**vi•ril•i•ty** /və'rɪlɪtiy/, *n.* [*noncount*]

vir•tu•al /'vɜrtʃuwəl/ *adj.* **1.** [*before a noun*] being (the condition, thing, or person stated) in force or effect, though not actually or expressly such: *They were reduced to virtual poverty.* **2.** temporarily simulated or extended by computer software: *virtual memory on a hard disk.* —**'vir•tu•al•ly,** *adv.*

vir•tue /'vɜrtʃuw/ *n.* **1.** [*noncount*] the practice of behaving or living one's life according to moral and ethical principles; moral excellence: *a life of virtue.* **2.** [*count*] a particular quality that reflects such moral excellence: *His virtues include honesty and integrity.* **3.** [*noncount*] chastity, esp. in a woman. **4.** [*count*] any desirable quality or property: *Being able to ride a bike to work was one of the virtues of living in a university town.* —*Idiom.* **5. by** or **in virtue of,** by reason of; because of: *By virtue of his office, the vice president decides a tie in the Senate.*

vir•tu•o•so /ˌvɜrtʃuw'owsow/ *n.* [*count*], *pl.* **-sos, -si** /-siy/. a person who has special knowledge or skill in a field, esp. a person who is excellent in music. —**vir•tu•os•i•ty** /ˌvɜrtʃuw'ɒsɪtiy/, *n.* [*noncount*]

vir•tu•ous /'vɜrtʃuwəs/ *adj.* **1.** following moral and ethical principles; morally excellent. **2.** pure; chaste: *a virtuous young woman.* —**'vir•tu•ous•ly,** *adv.*

vir•u•lent /'vɪryələnt, 'vɪrə-/ *adj.* **1.** extremely poisonous; harmful or deadly: *a virulent strain of bacteria.* **2.** violently hostile: *virulent hatred.* —**'vir•u•lence,** *n.* [*noncount*]

vi•rus /'vayrəs/ *n.* [*count*], *pl.* **-rus•es. 1.** a very small living thing causing infection, which reproduces only within the cells of living hosts, mainly bacteria, plants, and animals. **2.** a disease caused by a virus: *was ill from a virus.* **3.** a part of a computer program that is planted illegally in another program, often to damage or shut down a system or network.

vi•sa /'viyzə/ *n.* [*count*], *pl.* **-sas.** an official stamp or mark made on a passport, which per-

mits the holder to enter the country: *a tourist visa.*

vise /vays/ *n.* [*count*] a device usually having two jaws adjusted by means of a screw, lever, or the like, used to hold an object firmly while work is being done on it.

vis•i•ble /'vɪzəbəl/ *adj.* **1.** capable of being seen. **2.** apparent; obvious: *no visible means of support.* —ˌvis•i'bil•i•ty, *n.* [*noncount*] —**'vis•i•bly,** *adv.*: *He was visibly upset.*

vi•sion /'vɪʒən/ *n.* **1.** [*noncount*] the act or power of sensing with the eyes; sight. **2.** [*noncount*] the act or power of anticipating that which will or could come to be; foresight; imagination: *prophetic vision; a man of vision.* **3.** [*count*] a vivid, imaginative idea or conception of something that could come to be: *visions of a world at peace.* **4.** [*count*] something seen in or as if in a dream or trance, often thought to come from God.

vi•sion•ar•y /'vɪʒəˌnɛriy/ *adj., n., pl.* **-ar•ies.** —*adj.* **1.** showing or having vision or imagination, as the ability to see things that will or could be. **2.** too idealistic; impractical: *an impractical, visionary scheme.* —*n.* [*count*] **3.** a person of unusually keen foresight.

vis•it /'vɪzɪt/ *v.* **1.** to go to and stay with (a person or family) or at (a place) for a short time: [~ + *obj*]: *We visited our friends in Greece.* [*no obj*]: *Come visit with us for a few hours.* **2.** [~ + *obj*] to inflict or afflict: *The plague visited London in 1665.* —*n.* [*count*] **3.** the act of or an instance of visiting: *a long visit.* —**'vis•i•tor,** *n.* [*count*]

vis•it•a•tion /ˌvɪzɪ'teyʃən/ *n.* a formal visit, as one granted by a court to a divorced parent to visit a child in the custody of the other parent. [*noncount*] [*count*]

vi•sor /'vayzər/ *n.* [*count*] **1.** the projecting front brim of a cap. **2.** a flap inside a car that shields the eyes from glaring sunlight. **3.** the movable front piece on a medieval helmet.

vis•ta /'vɪstə/ *n.* [*count*], *pl.* **-tas.** a view, esp. one seen through a long, narrow passage, as between rows of trees or houses.

vis•u•al /'vɪʒuwəl/ *adj.* of or relating to seeing or sight: *a visual image.* —**'vis•u•al•ly,** *adv.*

vis•u•al•ize /'vɪʒuwəˌlayz/ *v.* [~ + *obj*], **-ized, -iz•ing.** to form a mental image of: *I tried to visualize what it would be like to live there.* —**vis•u•al•i•za•tion** /ˌvɪʒuwələ'zeyʃən/, *n.* [*noncount*]

vi•tal /'vaytl/ *adj.* **1.** energetic, lively, or forceful: *a vital leader.* **2.** necessary for life or existence: *vital supplies.* **3.** of great importance: *vital decisions.* —**'vi•tal•ly,** *adv.*

vi•tal•i•ty /vay'tælɪtiy/ *n.* [*noncount*] **1.** lively physical or mental vigor or strength: *a person of great vitality.* **2.** ability to survive or endure or to carry on a meaningful or purposeful existence: *the vitality of an institution.*

vi•ta•min /'vaytəmɪn/ *n.* [*count*] any of a group of substances that are essential to the body in small quantities for normal metabolism, found in very small amounts in foods and also produced artificially.

vi•va•cious /vɪ'veyʃəs, vay-/ *adj.* lively; spirited: *a vivacious, outgoing personality.* —**vi'va•cious•ly,** *adv.* —**vi•vac•i•ty** /vɪ'væsɪtiy, vay-/, *n.* [*noncount*]

viv•id /'vɪvɪd/ *adj.* **1.** (of color, light, etc.) strikingly bright or intense; brilliant: *a vivid red.* **2.** presenting the appearance, freshness, spirit, etc., of life; very realistic or lifelike: *a vivid recollection*

V

of the wedding. —'**viv•id•ly**, adv. —'**viv•id•ness**, n. [noncount]

vix•en /'vɪksən/ n. [count] **1.** a female fox. **2.** a bad-tempered woman.

vo•cab•u•lar•y /vow'kæbyə,lɛriy/ n. [count] [noncount], pl. **-lar•ies.** the stock of words used by, known to, or peculiar to a particular person, group, language, or profession.

vo•cal /'vowkəl/ adj. **1.** of, relating to, or produced with the voice: vocal sounds. **2.** inclined to express oneself in words, esp. in many words or insistently; outspoken: a vocal advocate of reform. —'**vo•cal•ly**, adv.

'**vocal ,cords**, n. [plural] either of two pairs of folds of membrane stretched across the larynx, the lower pair of which produces sound or voice as it is made to vibrate by the passage of air from the lungs.

vo•cal•ist /'vowkəlɪst/ n. [count] a singer.

vo•cal•ize /'vowkə,layz/ v., **-ized, -iz•ing.** to make vocal; to make or produce sounds: [~ + obj]: to vocalize one's objections. [no obj]: dolphins and chimpanzees vocalizing. —**vo•cal•i•za•tion** /,vowkələ'zeyʃən/, n. [noncount] [count]

vo•ca•tion /vow'keyʃən/ n. [count] the particular occupation, business, or profession which one feels called to pursue.

vo•ca•tion•al /vuw'keyʃənl/ adj. of or related to training or preparation for a job or a certain skill: a vocational school for carpentry.

vod•ka /'vɑdkə/ n. [noncount] a colorless, distilled alcoholic spirit made esp. from rye or wheat mash.

vogue /vowg/ n. the current or popular fashion at a particular time: [count]: a vogue for long hair. [noncount]: Some of that slang is no longer in vogue.

voice /vɔys/ n., v., **voiced, voic•ing.** —n. **1.** [count] sound uttered through the mouth of living creatures, esp. of human beings in speaking, singing, etc. **2.** [noncount] the ability to utter sounds through the mouth by controlling the air sent out; speech: He had such a sore throat that he lost his voice. **3.** [count; usually singular] an expressed opinion, choice, or desire: the voice of the opposition. **4.** [count] the right to present and receive consideration of one's desires or opinions: to have a voice in company policy. —v. [~ + obj] **5.** to express by words or utterances; declare; proclaim: They voiced their disapproval.

'**voice ,mail**, n. [noncount] a computerized system that answers telephone calls and records phone messages for later playback, used esp. in offices.

void /vɔyd/ adj. **1.** having no legal force or effect: This law has been declared null and void. **2.** [be + ~ + of] empty; lacking: His life was void of meaning. —n. [count] **3.** empty space; emptiness: to disappear into the void. **4.** a state or feeling of loss: His death left a great void in her life. —v. [~ + obj] **5.** to make invalid; nullify: to void a check.

vol•a•tile /'vɑlət/, -,tayl/ adj. **1.** passing off quickly in the form of vapor. **2.** having or showing sharp or sudden changes; unstable: a volatile stock market. —**vol•a•til•i•ty** /-'tɪlɪtiy/, n. [noncount]

vol•ca•no /vɑl'keynow/ n. [count], pl. **-noes, -nos.** a mountain or hill, usually having a cuplike crater at the top, that was formed around a vent in the earth's crust through which lava, steam, ashes, etc., were, or continue to be, forced out. —**vol•can•ic** /vɑl'kænɪk/ adj.

vo•li•tion /vow'lɪʃən, və-/ n. [noncount] the act of willing, choosing, or deciding to do something: She left of her own volition.

vol•ley /'vɑliy/ n., pl. **-leys,** v., **-leyed, -ley•ing.** —n. [count] **1.** the shooting of a number of missiles or firearms at the same time. **2.** a burst or outpouring of many things at once or in quick succession: a volley of protests. **3. a.** the return of a ball, as in tennis, before it hits the ground. **b.** a series of such returns; a rally. —v. **4.** [~ + obj] to shoot in or as if in a volley. **5.** [no obj] [~ + obj] to return (a ball) before it hits the ground.

vol•ley•ball /'vɑliy,bɔl/ n. **1.** [noncount] a game in which two teams volley a large ball back and forth over a high net. **2.** [count] the ball used in this game.

volt /vowlt/ n. [count] a standard unit of measure for electrical force. Abbr.: V

volt•age /'vowltɪdʒ/ n. electrical force expressed in volts: [count]: different voltages. [noncount]: measuring voltage.

vol•ume /'vɑlyuwm, -yəm/ n. **1.** [noncount] the amount of space, measured in cubic units, that an object or substance occupies. **2.** [count] a mass, amount, or quantity: a volume of mail. **3.** [noncount] the degree of sound intensity: to turn up the volume. **4.** [count] **a.** a book. **b.** the books of a set: a three-volume history of Europe. —**Idiom. 5. speak volumes,** to be very expressive or meaningful: Her silence spoke volumes.

vo•lu•mi•nous /və'luwmənəs/ adj. **1.** very productive: a voluminous writer. **2.** of great volume: a voluminous briefcase.

vol•un•tar•y /'vɑlən,tɛriy/ adj. **1.** done, made, brought about, or performed through or by one's will or one's own free choice: a voluntary contribution. **2.** depending on or supported by the work of volunteers: voluntary hospitals. —**vol•un•tar•i•ly** /,vɑlən'tɛərəliy, 'vɑlən,tɛr-/, adv.

vol•un•teer /,vɑlən'tɪər/ n. [count] **1.** a person who voluntarily offers himself or herself for a service or undertaking, or who performs a service willingly and without pay. —v. **2.** to offer oneself for some service or undertaking: [no obj]: eager to volunteer. [~ + obj]: He volunteered to write the report. **3.** [~ + obj] to say, tell, or communicate (something) freely or willingly: to volunteer an explanation.

vo•lup•tu•ous /və'lʌptʃuwəs/ adj. shapely in a way that is sexually pleasing or attractive: a voluptuous body. —**vo'lup•tu•ous•ness**, n. [noncount]

vom•it /'vɑmɪt/ v. **1.** to throw up the contents of the stomach through the mouth: [no obj]: He feared he might vomit. [~ + obj]: to vomit one's dinner. —n. [noncount] **2.** the undigested food thrown up when vomiting.

voo•doo /'vuwduw/ n. [noncount] a religion practiced chiefly by West Indians, derived principally from African cult worship and incorporating elements of sorcery and witchcraft.

vo•ra•cious /vɔ'reyʃəs, və-/ adj. **1.** wanting or eating large quantities of food: a voracious appetite. **2.** very eager: a voracious reader. —**vo'ra•cious•ly**, adv. —**vo•rac•i•ty** /vɔ'ræsɪtiy/, n. [noncount]

vote /vowt/ n., v., **vot•ed, vot•ing.** —n. **1.** [count] a formal expression of one's choice, opinion, or decision, usually either for or against someone or something, as a policy or proposal, by an individual or a body of individuals. **2.** [count; usually singular] the right to such expression: gave citizens the vote. **3.** [count; usually singular] the total number of votes cast: *The vote was 55,000 in favor, 22,000 against.* —*v.* **4.** to express or show one's will or choice in a matter, as by casting a ballot: [*no obj*]: *Did you vote?* [~ + *obj*]: *We voted to go on strike. I vote that we all go on strike.* —'**vot•er,** *n.* [*count*]

vouch /vawtʃ/ *v.* [~ + *for* + *obj*] **1.** to provide proof, supporting evidence, or assurance: *Her record vouches for her integrity.* **2.** to give a guarantee: *I can vouch for his reliability.*

vouch•er /'vawtʃər/ *n.* [*count*] a document, receipt, stamp, etc., that gives evidence of money spent or received.

vow /vaw/ *n.* [*count*] **1.** a solemn promise, pledge, or personal commitment: *marriage vows; a vow of secrecy.* —*v.* [~ + *obj*] **2.** to make a vow of; promise by a vow; pledge or declare solemnly: *to vow revenge; He vowed to be on time. He vowed that he would never drink and drive again.*

vow•el /'vawəl/ *n.* [*count*] **1.** a speech sound, as /iy/, /ʊ/, or /æ/, produced without stopping, blocking, or changing the path of the flow of air from the lungs. **2.** a letter or other symbol that represents a vowel sound, as, in English, *a, e, i, o, u,* and sometimes *y.*

voy•age /'vɔyɪdʒ/ *n.* [*count*] a course of travel or a journey, esp. a long journey by water to a distant place. —'**voy•ag•er,** *n.* [*count*]

VP, an abbreviation of: vice president.

vs. or **vs,** an abbreviation of: versus.

VT or **Vt.,** an abbreviation of: Vermont.

vul•gar /'vʌlgər/ *adj.* **1.** characterized by or showing one's lack of refinement or good taste; crude; coarse. **2.** indecent; obscene: *a vulgar gesture; vulgar language.* —**vul•gar•i•ty** /vʌl'gærɪtiy/ *n.* [*noncount*] [*count*]

vul•ner•a•ble /'vʌlnərəbəl/ *adj.* **1.** capable of being or easily being wounded or hurt physically or emotionally. **2.** open to or defenseless against criticism or moral attack. —**vul•ner•a•bil•i•ty** /ˌvʌlnərə'bɪlɪtiy/, *n.* [*noncount*]

vul•ture /'vʌltʃər/ *n.* [*count*] **1.** a large bird of prey that feeds on dead animal flesh. **2.** a greedy and immoral person who preys on others.

vy•ing /'vayɪŋ/ *v.* pres. part. of VIE.

V

W

W, w /'dʌbəl,yuw, -yʊ/ *n.* [*count*], *pl.* **Ws** or **W's, ws** or **w's.** the 23rd letter of the English alphabet, serving as either a vowel or a consonant.

W, an abbreviation of: **1.** watt. **2.** west. **3.** western.

w/, an abbreviation of: with.

WA, an abbreviation of: Washington.

wack•y /'wækiy/ *adj.,* **-i•er, -i•est.** *Slang.* odd or slightly crazy. —**'wack•i•ness,** *n.* [*noncount*]

wad /wɒd/ *n.* [*count*] **1.** a small mass, as of cotton, used esp. for padding and packing, filling a hole, etc. **2.** a roll of bank notes. **3.** a small mass of substance for chewing: *a wad of chewing tobacco; a wad of gum.*

wad•dle /'wɒdl/ *v.,* **-dled, -dling,** *n.* —*v.* [*no obj*] **1.** to walk with short steps, swaying from side to side in the manner of a duck. —*n.* [*count*] **2.** a waddling way of walking.

wade /weyd/ *v.,* **wad•ed, wad•ing. 1.** [*no obj*] to walk through a substance, as water or snow, that interferes with one's motion: *They waded through the mud.* **2. wade through,** to struggle or make one's way through (some task or job) with effort or difficulty: *to wade through a pile of bills to be paid.*

wa•fer /'weyfər/ *n.* [*count*] a thin, crisp cake, cookie, biscuit, or candy.

waf•fle¹ /'wɒfəl/ *n.* [*count*] a batter cake baked in a hinged appliance **(waf/fle i'ron)** that imprints a gridlike pattern on each side.

waf•fle² /'wɒfəl/ *v.* [*no obj*], **-fled, -fling.** to speak or write without taking a definite stand.

waft /wɑft, wæft/ *v.* to (cause to) be carried or float lightly and smoothly through or as if through the air: [*no obj*]: *The smell of fresh bread wafted in.* [~ + *obj*]: *The smells were wafted along the hallway.*

wag /wæg/ *v.,* **wagged, wag•ging. 1.** to move up and down or from side to side: [*no obj*]: *The dog's tail wagged.* [~ + *obj*]: *The dog wagged its tail. Don't wag your finger (in rebuke) at me!* **2.** to move (the tongue) in talking idly: [~ + *obj*]: *Quit wagging your tongue and listen!* [*no obj*]: *Local tongues are wagging over this latest scandal.*

wage /weydʒ/ *n.,* *v.,* **waged, wag•ing.** —*n.* **1.** Often, **wages.** [*plural*] money paid or received for work or services: [*count*]: *My wages are too low.* [*noncount*]: *a decent wage.* —*v.* [~ + *obj*] **2.** to begin or carry on: *to wage war.*

wa•ger /'weydʒər/ *n.* [*count*] **1.** something risked or bet on an uncertain event; a bet: *I made him a wager (that) he couldn't finish on time.* —*v.* [~ + *obj*] **2.** to bet; gamble: *She wagered fifty dollars. She wagered (fifty dollars) (that) he wouldn't finish on time.*

wag•on /'wægən/ *n.* [*count*] a four-wheeled vehicle, esp. one for the movement or carrying of heavy loads; also, a child's toy of this kind, designed to be pulled.

waif /'weyf/ *n.* [*count*] a homeless child: *caring for orphans and waifs.*

wail /weyl/ *v.* **1.** to express sorrow with a long, loud cry: [*no obj*]: *The child wailed unhappily.* [~ + *obj*]: *She wailed a warning.* [*used with quotations*]: *"I want to go home!" she wailed.* —*n.* [*count*] **2.** a wailing cry or sound.

waist /weyst/ *n.* [*count*] **1.** the narrow part of the human body between the ribs and the hips. **2.** the part of a garment covering the waist.

waist•band /'weyst,bænd/ *n.* [*count*] a band, as on a skirt, that goes around the waist.

waist•coat /'wɛskət, 'weyst,kowt/ *n.* *Chiefly Brit.* **VEST** (def. 1).

waist•line /'weyst,layn/ *n.* [*count*] **1.** the distance around the body at the waist. **2.** the seam where the skirt and body of a dress are joined; the narrowest section of a dress.

wait /weyt/ *v.* **1.** to remain in a place and not do anything until something expected happens: [*no obj*]: *We waited until the bus came. We've been waiting for the bus.* [~ + *obj*]: *We waited a week for your letter. We've waited three hours to see you!* **2.** [*no obj*] to be available or in readiness: *A letter is waiting for you on your desk.* **3.** to (cause to) be postponed or delayed: [*no obj*]: *Your vacation will have to wait until next spring.* [~ + *obj*]: *to wait another year before buying a house.* **4.** [~ + *for* + *obj*] to look forward to eagerly: *to wait for a chance to get even.* **5. wait on, a.** to serve food or drink to. **b.** to attend to the needs of (a customer): *Is someone waiting on you?* **6. wait out,** to postpone or delay action until the end of: *We decided to wait out the storm.* **7. wait up,** to postpone going to bed in order to await someone's arrival. —*n.* [*count*] **8.** an act or period of waiting.

wait•er /'weytər/ *n.* [*count*] a person, esp. a man, who waits on tables, as in a restaurant.

'waiting ,list, *n.* [*count*] a list of persons waiting, as for reservations or admission.

'waiting ,room, *n.* [*count*] a room for the use of persons waiting, as in a railroad station or doctor's office.

wait•ress /'weytrɪs/ *n.* [*count*] a woman who waits on tables, as in a restaurant.

waive /weyv/ *v.* [~ + *obj*], **waived, waiv•ing. 1.** to give up (a right) on purpose or willingly: *He waived his right to appeal the decision.* **2.** to decide not to enforce or insist on (a rule or regulation): *The department waived the normal requirements.*

waiv•er /'weyvər/ *n.* [*count*] the deliberate or intentional giving up of a right.

wake¹ /weyk/ *v.,* **waked** or **woke** /wowk/, **waked** or **wok•en** /'wowkən/, **wak•ing,** *n.* —*v.* **1.** to (cause to) become roused from sleep; awake: [*no obj*]: *to wake (up) from a nightmare.* [~ + *obj*]: *The noise woke him (up). Please wake (up) the children.* **2.** to (cause to) become aware of something: [*no obj*]: *You'd better wake (up) to what's happening.* [~ + *obj*]: *The energy crisis woke us (up) to the need for conservation. The crisis failed to wake (up) the public.* —*n.* [*count*] **3.** (in some religious traditions) a vigil held in the presence of the body of a dead person before burial.

wake² /weyk/ *n.* [*count*] **1.** the track of waves left by a moving ship or boat. **2.** the path or course of something that has passed or gone before: *The hurricane left ruin in its wake.* **—Idiom. 3. in the wake of,** after; following: *In the wake of the snowstorm the schools closed.*

wake•ful /'weykfəl/ *adj.* unable to sleep; sleepless.

wak•en /'weykən/ v. [~ + obj] to awake; awaken: The noise wakened them.

walk /wɔk/ v. **1.** [no obj] to move on foot at a moderate pace or speed, usually naturally and normally: He walks to work every day. **2.** [~ + obj] to proceed along, through, or over on foot: We walked the streets for several miles. **3.** [~ + obj] to cause or help to walk: She walked the old man back to his seat. **4.** [~ + obj] to go with or accompany (someone) on foot: I'll walk you to the elevators. **5. walk off** or **away with, a.** to steal: Someone walked off with my money. **b.** to win, esp. with ease: She walked away with the prize for best essay. **6. walk out on,** to desert; leave behind: He walked out on his family. —n. [count] **7.** an act or instance of walking: a short walk for exercise. **8.** a distance walked or to be walked: a ten-minute walk from here. **9.** a path or route taken in walking, esp. a habitual or customary one. **10.** a profession, line of work, or position in society: people from all walks of life.

walk•er /'wɔkər/ n. [count] **1.** a framework on small wheels for supporting a baby who is learning to walk. **2.** a similar device but without wheels, usually a waist-high, four-legged framework of lightweight metal, for use by an injured, elderly, or disabled person as a support while walking. **3.** one who walks or likes to walk.

walk•ie-talk•ie /'wɔkiy'tɔkiy/ n. [count], pl. **-talk•ies.** a small portable radio that allows two-way communication.

walk•out /'wɔk,awt/ n. [count] a strike by workers.

walk•way /'wɔk,wey/ n. [count], pl. **-ways.** a passage for walking, esp. one that is enclosed.

wall /wɔl/ n. [count] **1.** a vertical, upright structure used to form part of a shelter, to divide an area into rooms, or to protect or enclose an area. **2.** something not physical that is like a wall in that it forms a barrier between people or keeps people apart: a wall of silence between them. —v. [~ + obj] **3.** to enclose, separate, form a border around, or surround with or as if with a wall: to wall a town; The workers walled off the area with bricks. —**Idiom.** **4. climb the walls,** Informal. to be overly nervous or worried. **5. drive up the wall,** Informal. to make emotionally tense or out of control. **6. off the wall,** Slang. **a.** unreasonable; crazy. **b.** very strange or odd.

wal•la•by /'wɔləbiy/ n. [count], pl. **-bies, -by.** a small- to medium-sized animal of the kangaroo family.

wal•let /'wɔlɪt, 'wɔlɪt/ n. [count] a flat, folding case with compartments for carrying paper money, credit cards, and other items.

wal•lop /'wɔləp/ v. [~ + obj] **1.** to strike hard; sock: He walloped them with his stick. —n. [count] **2.** a hard blow.

wal•low /'wɔlow/ v. [no obj] **1.** to roll around, as in mud: The pigs were wallowing in the mud. **2.** to indulge oneself; remain in a given state or condition for a long time: to wallow in self-pity.

wall•pa•per /'wɔl,pæpər/ n. [noncount] **1.** paper, usually with decorative patterns, for covering walls or ceilings in a house. —v. [~ + obj] **2.** to put wallpaper on or in; cover with wallpaper.

'wall-to-'wall, adj. covering the entire floor: wall-to-wall carpeting.

wal•nut /'wɔl,nʌt, -nət/ n. [count] an edible, meaty nut with a hard, wrinkled shell.

wal•rus /'wɔlrəs, 'wɒl-/ n. [count], pl. **-rus•es, -rus.** a large mammal of arctic seas, having large tusks and a tough, wrinkled hide.

waltz /wɔlts/ n. [count] **1.** a ballroom dance in moderately fast triple meter. **2.** a piece of music in this rhythm, often intended to accompany dancing. —v. **3.** to dance a waltz (with): [no obj]: learning to waltz. [~ + obj]: to waltz her around the floor.

wam•pum /'wɒmpəm, 'wɔm-/ n. [noncount] beads made of pierced and strung shells, once used by North American Indians as a medium of exchange.

wan /wɒn/ adj., **wan•ner, wan•nest.** unnaturally pale, esp. on account of ill health or fatigue.

wand /wɒnd/ n. [count] a slender rod, esp. one used by a magician.

wan•der /'wɒndər/ v. **1.** [no obj] to move around without a definite purpose or plan; roam: wandering through the mall. **2.** [no obj] to stray, as from a path or subject: Your thoughts are wandering. **3.** [~ + obj] to travel about, on, or through: to wander the countryside. —'wan•der•er, n. [count]

wane /weyn/ v. [no obj], **waned, wan•ing. 1.** to decrease, as in strength or intensity: His influence in the company had waned. **2.** (of the moon) to decrease in brightness and roundness after the full moon, in regular periods. Compare WAX^2 (def. 2).

want /wɒnt, wɔnt/ v. **1.** [~ + obj] to feel a need for (or to); wish or desire; feel inclined; long for: The baby wants his dinner; I want to be alone. I want you to leave. **2.** [~ + obj] to request, demand, or desire the presence, affection, or company of: You are wanted in the manager's office. I want you, I need you, I love you. **3.** [~ + obj] to require: The room wants cleaning. **4.** [~ + obj; usually: be + ~ -ed] to have an arrest warrant for, or seek in order to question in connection with a criminal investigation: He is wanted for armed robbery. **5.** [no obj] to have a need: to want for money. —n. **6.** [count] something wanted or needed: My wants are simple. **7.** [noncount] a state of need: to be in want of an assistant.

wan•ton /'wɒntṇ/ adj. **1.** without motive; unprovoked: a wanton attack. **2.** sexually loose. **3.** extravagant or excessive: wanton luxury.

war /wɔr/ n., v., **warred, war•ring.** —n. **1.** armed conflict or fighting between nations or factions: [count]: Wars keep breaking out. [noncount]: a state of war. **2.** any conflict or struggle: [count]: a war against poverty. [noncount]: to wage war against poverty. —v. [no obj] **3.** to make or carry on war: They warred among themselves.

war•ble /'wɔrbəl/ v., **-bled, -bling,** n. —v. **1.** to sing or whistle with trills or melodies that vary quickly: [no obj]: to warble happily. [~ + obj]: to warble a tune. —n. [count] **2.** a warbled song or trill.

war•bler /'wɔrblər/ n. [count] a small songbird, esp. one that is brightly colored.

ward /wɔrd/ n. [count] **1.** an administrative division of a city or town, or a division for voting purposes. **2.** a division of a hospital: the children's ward. **3.** a division of a prison. **4.** a person, esp. a child or person under eighteen, who is under the care of a legal guardian or a court. —v. **5. ward off,** to turn aside; avert: to ward off a blow; to ward it off.

-ward, a suffix meaning in or toward a certain direction in space or time (backward). Also, **-wards.**

war•den /'wɔrdṇ/ n. [count] **1.** a person whose

W

job is the care and custody of something; keeper. **2.** the chief administrative officer of a prison.

ward•robe /'wɔr,drowb/ n. [count] **1.** a collection of clothes or costumes, as of a person or a theatrical company. **2.** a piece of furniture or closet for keeping or storing clothes.

ware /wɛər/ n. **1.** Usually, **wares.** [plural] merchandise; goods: a peddler selling his wares in the market. **2.** [noncount] a particular kind of merchandise: glassware.

ware•house /n.,'wɛər,haws; v. -,hawz, -,haws/ n., v., **-housed, -hous•ing.** —n. [count] **1.** a building for the storage of goods or merchandise. —v. [~ + obj] **2.** to deposit or store in a warehouse.

war•fare /'wɔr,feyr/ n. [noncount] **1.** armed conflict between enemies; the activity of war. **2.** a particular type of armed conflict: chemical warfare.

warm /wɔrm/ adj., **-er, -est,** v. —adj. **1.** having or giving out moderate heat: a warm climate; a warm oven; a warm bath. **2.** conserving warmth: warm clothes. **3.** suggestive of warmth, as by being friendly, affectionate, or sympathetic: a warm heart; warm friends. **4.** close to a correct answer, as in a game. —v. **5.** to (cause to) become warm or warmer: [~ + obj]: warmed himself (up) by the fire. [no obj]: I just couldn't warm up. **6. warm to** or **toward,** to grow more enthusiastic about or sympathetic toward: gradually warming to the subject; My heart warmed toward him. **7. warm up, a.** to prepare for strong exercise by performing mild or moderate exercise. **b.** to become friendlier or more receptive. —'**warm•ly,** adv. —'**warm•ness,** n. [noncount]

'**warm-'blooded,** adj. having a relatively constant body temperature in spite of varying temperatures in the surrounding environment: Mammals are warm-blooded animals.

'**warm-'hearted** or '**warm'heart•ed,** adj. having or showing emotional warmth.

warmth /wɔrmθ/ n. [noncount] **1.** the quality or state of being warm, or of being intimate, friendly, or caring. **2.** enthusiasm; intensity.

warn /wɔrn/ v. [~ + obj] **1.** to give advance notice to, esp. of danger or possible harm: The authorities warned (the residents) of the approaching storm. I warned you (that) she was crazy, didn't I? **2.** to advise (someone to do or not to do something): I warned you not to take such chances. —'**warn•ing,** n. [count]

warp /wɔrp/ v. **1.** to (cause to) be bent or twisted out of shape: [no obj]: The door hinges warped. [~ + obj]: The high humidity will warp those wooden door hinges. **2.** [~ + obj] to turn away from what is right or proper; distort: Prejudice warps the mind.

war•rant /'wɔrənt, 'wɒr-/ n. [count] **1.** a document that gives authority to an officer to make an arrest or to search or seize property. —v. [~ + obj] **2.** to be sufficient reason for; justify: The invasion warranted a strong response.

war•ran•ty /'wɔrəntiy, 'wɒr-/ n., pl. **-ties.** a written guarantee given to a purchaser that the manufacturer, dealer, etc., will make repairs or replace defective parts free of charge for a stated period of time: [count]: a one-year warranty. [noncount]: This computer is under warranty.

war•ren /'wɔrən, 'wɒr-/ n. [count] a place where rabbits breed.

war•ri•or /'wɔriyər, 'wɒr-/ n. [count] a person engaged or experienced in warfare; soldier.

war•ship /'wɔr,ʃɪp/ n. [count] a ship armed for combat.

wart /wɔrt/ n. [count] a small, often hard growth on the skin, usually caused by a virus. —'**wart•y,** adj., **-i•er, -i•est.**

war•y /'wɛəriy/ adj., **-i•er, -i•est.** being on guard; watchful; cautious: was wary of the danger. —'**war•i•ly,** adv. —'**war•i•ness,** n. [noncount]

was /wʌz, wɒz; unstressed wəz/ v. 1st and 3rd pers. sing. past indic. of BE.

wash /wɒʃ, wɔʃ/ v. **1.** to cleanse by dipping, rubbing, or scrubbing in liquid, esp. water: [~ + obj]: to wash the dishes. [no obj]: You wash and I'll dry. **2.** [no obj] to wash oneself: He always washes before eating. **3.** [no obj] to undergo washing without damage, as shrinking or fading: These clothes wash well in hot water. **4.** to (cause to) be carried away or worn or eroded by the continual action of water: [no obj]: The bridge washed away during the storm. [~ + obj (+ away)]: The floods washed the bridge away. **5.** [no obj] Informal. to be found or judged true or valid upon consideration or examination: That excuse won't wash with me. **6. wash down,** to make the swallowing of (food or medicine) easier by drinking liquid: Wash down the pill with some water. Wash it down with water. **7. wash out,** to (cause) to be removed by washing: trying to wash out the stains or trying to wash the stains out; Will the stains wash out? —n. [count] **8.** an act or process of washing. **9.** items, as clothes, to be washed at one time. —Idiom. **10. come out in the wash, a.** to finally be revealed or become known. **b.** to finally come to a good or satisfactory result. **11. wash one's hands of,** to renounce further responsibility for or involvement in: He washed his hands of the problem. **12. (all) washed up** or **washed-up,** no longer successful or popular: She was all washed up as a singer. —'**wash•a•ble,** adj.

Wash., an abbreviation of: Washington.

wash•bowl /'wɒʃ,bowl, 'wɔʃ-/ n. [count] a large bowl for washing the hands and face. Also called '**wash,ba•sin.**

wash•cloth /'wɒʃ,klɔθ, -,klɒθ, 'wɔʃ-/ n. [count] a cloth for washing the face or body.

wash•er /'wɒʃər, 'wɔʃər/ n. [count] WASHING MACHINE.

'**washing ma,chine,** n. [count] an apparatus, esp. a household appliance, for washing clothing, linens, etc.

wash•room /'wɒʃ,ruwm, -,rʊm, 'wɔʃ-/ n. [count] a room with sinks and toilets.

was•n't /'wʌzənt, 'wɒz-/ contraction of was not.

wasp /wɒsp/ n. [count] a slender winged insect with a narrow abdomen and a powerful sting.

waste /weyst/ v., **wast•ed, wast•ing,** n. —v. **1.** [~ + obj] to use up or spend to no profit; squander: wasting money; wasting time. **2.** [~ + obj] to fail to use: Never waste an opportunity. **3.** to (cause to) become feeble, weak, or thin: [~ + obj]: He was wasted by disease. [no obj]: Every day the patient seemed to waste away. —n. **4.** an act or instance of wasting: [count; usually singular]: a waste of money. [noncount]: to cut down on waste. **5.** [count] a ruined area, or one that is unsuitable or considered unsuitable for living, as a desert. **6.** something left over, esp. after some process has been performed and something more valuable removed: [count]: factory wastes. [noncount]: the disposal of radioactive waste. **7.** [often: wastes] matter discharged from the body, as feces. —*Idiom.* **8. go to waste,** to be wasted, rather than used: *This food will go to waste if you don't eat it.* —'**waste•ful,** *adj.*

waste•bas•ket /'weyst₁bæskɪt/ *n.* [*count*] an open container for trash. Also called '**wastepaper ₁basket.**

waste•land /'weyst₁lænd/ *n.* uncultivated or barren land, or land that has been ruined, as by war: [*count; usually singular*]: *a radioactive wasteland.* [*noncount*]: *wide areas of uninhabited wasteland.*

waste•pa•per /'weyst₁peypər/ *n.* [*noncount*] paper thrown away as useless.

watch /wɒtʃ/ *v.* **1.** to look (at) with attention, observe: [*no obj*]: *The children watched carefully as the magician removed a rabbit from a hat.* [~ + *obj*]: *He had a feeling that he was being watched. We watched the magician remove a rabbit from a hat.* **2.** [~ + *obj*] to view with attention or interest: *to watch TV.* **3.** [*no obj*] to wait with attention: *We watched for the signal.* **4.** [*no obj*] to be careful or cautious: *Watch (out) when you cross the street.* **5.** [~ + *obj*] to guard or take care of: *Watch the baby while I go to the store.* **6. watch over,** to safeguard; protect: *He watched over her and protected her from harm.* —*n.* **7.** [*count; usually singular*] close, continuous observation or guard: *We kept a close watch on the patient.* **8.** [*count*] a portable timepiece, as a wristwatch. **9. a.** [*noncount*] a period of time, usually four hours, during which a part of a ship's crew is on duty. **b.** [*count*] the crew on duty during this time.

watch•band /'wɒtʃ₁bænd/ *n.* [*count*] a bracelet or strap for holding a wristwatch on the wrist.

watch•dog /'wɒtʃ₁dɒg, -₁dɔg/ *n.* [*count*] **1.** a dog kept to guard property. **2.** a watchful guardian, such as against illegal or unethical conduct: *environmental watchdogs.*

watch•ful /'wɒtʃfəl/ *adj.* alert; observant. —'**watch•ful•ly,** *adv.* —'**watch•ful•ness,** *n.* [*noncount*]

watch•man /'wɒtʃmən/ *n.* [*count*], *pl.* **-men.** a person who keeps watch, esp. at night.

wa•ter /'wɒtər, 'wɔtər/ *n.* **1.** [*noncount*] an odorless, tasteless liquid compound of hydrogen and oxygen that makes up rain, oceans, lakes, and rivers: *Water is essential to life.* **2.** a body of water, such as an ocean: [*noncount*]: *sailing on the water.* [*count; usually plural*]: *the waters of the Atlantic.* —*v.* **3.** [~ + *obj*] to sprinkle with water: *to water the plants.* **4.** [*no obj*] to fill with or give off water or liquid: *Her eyes watered.* **5.** [~ + *obj*] to supply (animals) with drinking water. **6. water down,** to weaken or dilute with or as if with water: *She watered down her criticism.* —*Idiom.* **7. above water,** out of trouble or difficulty, esp. financial. **8. hold water,** to be capable of being defended or proven correct: *Your theory doesn't hold water.* **9. in deep** or **hot water,** in trouble or difficulty. **10. like water,** lavishly; abundantly: *spending money like water.* **11. make one's mouth water,** to inspire a desire or appetite for something: *a sports car that can make your mouth water.* **12. throw cold water on,** to discourage by criticism or indifference.

'**water ₁buffalo,** *n.* [*count*] an Asian buffalo with large, curved horns.

wa•ter•col•or /'wɒtər₁kʌlər, 'wɒtwr-/ *n.* [*count*] a picture painted with pigments mixed with water rather than oil.

wa•ter•cress /'wɒtər₁krɛs, 'wɒtər-/ *n.* [*non-*

count] a plant that grows in clear, running streams, whose leaves are used for salads, soups, and in cooking.

wa•ter•fall /'wɒtərfɔl, 'wɒtər-/ *n.* [*count*] a steep fall of water from a height, as over a cliff.

wa•ter•front /'wɒtər₁frʌnt, 'wɒtər-/ *n.* [*count*] a part of a city or town on the edge of a body of water, esp. an ocean.

'**water ₁lily,** *n.* [*count*] a plant that grows in the water, with large, disklike floating leaves and showy flowers.

wa•ter•logged /'wɒtər₁lɒgd, -₁lɔgd, 'wɒtər-/ *adj.* so filled with water as to be heavy or unmanageable.

'**water ₁main,** *n.* [*count*] a main pipe for carrying water.

wa•ter•mel•on /'wɒtər₁mɛlən, 'wɒtər-/ *n.* [*noncount*] [*count*] a large melon with a hard, green rind and sweet, juicy, usually red pulp.

wa•ter•proof /'wɒtər₁pruwf, 'wɒtər/ *adj.* **1.** that does not allow water to pass through: *a waterproof raincoat.* —*v.* [~ + *obj*] **2.** to make waterproof.

'**water-re₁pellent,** *adj.* repelling water but not entirely waterproof.

wa•ter•shed /'wɒtər₁ʃɛd, 'wɒtər-/ *n.* [*count*] **1.** a region or area drained by a river or stream. **2.** an important point of division or transition between two phases or conditions; a turning point: *a watershed in relations between the two countries.*

'**water ₁ski,** *n.* [*count*] one of a pair of short, broad skis on which to glide over water while being towed by a motorboat. —'**water-₁ski,** *v.* [*no obj*], **-skied, -ski•ing.** —'**water-₁skier,** *n.* [*count*] —'**water-₁skiing,** *n.* [*noncount*]

wa•ter•tight /'wɒtər₁tayt, 'wɒtər-/ *adj.* **1.** constructed or fitted so tightly as to prevent water from passing through. **2.** not subject to evasion or misunderstanding; without loopholes: *a watertight contract.*

wa•ter•works /'wɒtər₁wɜrks, 'wɒtər-/ *n.,* *pl.* **-works.** a system, as of reservoirs, pipelines, and the like, by which water is collected, purified, stored, and pumped to urban users: [*count; used with a singular verb*]: *The waterworks is old and decrepit.* [*plural; used with a plural verb*]: *Those old waterworks are falling apart.*

wa•ter•y /'wɒtəriy, 'wɒtə-/ *adj.* **1.** of, consisting of, or full of water. **2.** containing too much water: *watery gravy.*

watt /wɒt/ *n.* [*count*] a unit of electrical power. *Abbr.:* W, w

watt•age /'wɒtɪdʒ/ *n.* [*noncount*] electrical power measured in watts.

wave /weyv/ *n., v.,* **waved, wav•ing.** —*n.* [*count*] **1.** a moving ridge or swell on the surface of water: *The ocean waves crashed against the rocks.* **2.** a movement of the hand, as in greeting: *She gave us a wave and a smile.* **3.** a movement or part resembling a wave: *a wave in her hair.* **4.** a sudden surge or rush, as of a feeling; esp., a widespread, typically surging feeling, attitude, tendency, belief, activity, etc.: *He felt a wave of nausea; a crime wave.* **5.** a period of unusually hot or cold weather: *a heat wave.* **6.** *Physics.* a disturbance sent out or across from one point to another in a medium or space, without progress or advance by the points themselves, as in the transmission of sound or light: *a sound wave; a light wave; electromagnetic waves.* —*v.* **7.** to (cause to) move back and forth or up and down: [*no obj*]: *flags waving in the wind.* [~ + *obj*]:

W

They waved their arms in distress. **8.** to signal, esp. in greeting, by raising the hand and moving the fingers: [*no obj*]: *He waved to us in greeting.* [~ + *obj*]: *He waved his hand in greeting.* —*Idiom.* **9. make waves,** to disturb the existing state or condition. —**'wav•y,** *adj.*

wave•length /'weyv,lɛŋkθ, -,lɛnθ/ *n.* [*count*] **1.** the distance, measured in the direction of the progression of a wave; between two successive points in the wave. —*Idiom.* **2. on the same wavelength,** in agreement or accord; having a common way of thinking.

wa•ver /'weyvər/ *v.* [*no obj*] **1.** to feel or show doubt or indecision: *He wavered in his loyalty. When she heard the news of the defeat, her courage wavered.* **2.** (of things) to vary: *Prices wavered.*

wax¹ /wæks/ *n.* [*noncount*] **1.** Also called **beeswax,** a solid, yellowish substance made by bees when building their honeycomb. **2.** any of various similar substances, esp. ones made up of fats or oils: *a candle made of wax.* **3.** a yellowish, waxy secretion in the canal of the outer ear. —*v.* [~ + *obj*] **4.** to rub, polish, or treat with wax: *to wax the wooden floors.* —**'wax•y,** *adj.*

wax² /wæks/ *v.* [*no obj*] **1.** to increase, as in amount, size, or intensity. **2.** (of the moon) to increase gradually in brightness and roundness. Compare WANE (def. 2).

'wax ,bean, *n.* [*count*] a kind of string bean having yellowish, waxy pods.

'wax ,paper, *n.* [*noncount*] paper that resists moisture because of a waxlike coating.

way¹ /wey/ *n.* [*count*] **1.** a path or course: *the shortest way to town.* **2.** a direction: *He went that way.* **3.** distance, as between two points in space or time, or as a measure of progress: *a long way to San Francisco; He's come a long way since his college days.* **4.** manner, mode, or fashion; also, a characteristic or habitual manner of acting, living, etc.: *a nice way of saying thanks; That's just his way of being friendly.* **5.** a method or means for gaining something or achieving a goal: *We found a way to save money.* **6.** a respect or particular: *This plan is defective in several ways.* —*Idiom.* **7. by the way,** apart from the main subject; incidentally. **8. go out of one's way,** to make an extra or unusual effort, as to do someone a favor. **9. have a way with,** to have an effective manner of dealing with: *He has a way with children.* **10. have it both ways,** to benefit from two opposing beliefs or courses of action, without having to choose between them. **11. in a way,** to some extent; from one point of view: *I miss her in a way.* **12. make way,** to remove things that block passage, as by standing aside. **13. under way,** in progress; proceeding: *You're late; the meeting is well under way.*

way² /wey/ *adv.* to a great degree or at quite a distance: *That trunk is way too heavy for you to lift. The house is way down the road.*

'way-'out, *adj. Informal.* very unusual: *some way-out theories on UFOs.*

-ways, a suffix meaning in a specific direction, manner, or position (*sideways*).

way•ward /'weywərd/ *adj.* stubborn; disobedient: *a wayward son.*

we /wiy/ *pron.pl., poss.* **our** *or* **ours,** *obj.* **us. 1.** the plural of I, used as the subject of a sentence when the speaker wishes to refer to himself or herself and another or others: *I met her last night and we attended a concert.* **2.** (used after some form of BE with the same meaning): *It is we who*

should thank you. **3.** Also called the **editorial we.** (used by editors, writers, etc., to avoid the personal *I* or to represent a collective viewpoint).

weak /wiyk/ *adj.,* **-er, -est. 1.** liable to give way under pressure or strain: *A weak wall.* **2.** lacking in bodily strength: *He's weak from hunger.* **3.** lacking in force or effectiveness: *a weak president; a weak argument.* **4.** lacking in moral strength. **5.** not having enough ability or skill: *He's weak in math.* **6.** not great in amount, volume, intensity, etc., or in a characteristic property or essential ingredient: *a weak electrical current; a weak pulse.* —**'weak•ly,** *adv.*

weak•en /'wiykən/ *v.* to (cause to) become weak or weaker: [*no obj*]: *The animal weakened and eventually died.* [~ + *obj*]: *A lack of resources will weaken our efforts.*

weak•ling /'wiyklɪŋ/ *n.* [*count*] a person who is physically or morally weak.

weak•ness /'wiyknɪs/ *n.* **1.** [*noncount*] the state or quality of being weak. **2.** [*count*] a fault or defect: *several weaknesses in the plan.* **3.** [*count*] a special fondness or liking: *He has a weakness for sweet, strong coffee.*

wealth /wɛlθ/ *n.* **1.** [*noncount*] a great deal of money, property, or possessions. **2.** [*count*] a large amount of something; an abundance: *a wealth of information.* —**'wealth•y,** *adj.,* **-i•er, -i•est.**

wean /wiyn/ *v.* [~ + *obj*] to cause (a child or young animal) to become accustomed to or used to food other than the mother's milk.

weap•on /'wɛpən/ *n.* [*count*] **1.** an instrument or device used for attack or defense: *guns and other weapons.* **2.** anything used against an opponent or enemy: *Her sharp wit is an important weapon in debating opponents.*

weap•on•ry /'wɛpənriy/ *n.* [*noncount*] weapons thought of as a group.

wear /wɛər/ *v.,* **wore** /wɔr/, **worn** /wɔrn/, **wear•ing,** *n.* —*v.* **1.** [~ + *obj*] to have on the body as clothing, covering, or ornament: *He wore his best suit to the funeral.* **2.** [~ + *obj*] to bear or have in one's aspect or appearance: *She wore an angry expression on her face.* **3. a.** to (cause to) worsen in quality by a constant or repeating action: [~ + *obj*]: *Foot traffic wore the carpet.* [*no obj*]: *The carpet began to wear after a few years.* **b.** [~ + *obj*] to produce by such action: *He wore a hole right through his shoe.* **4.** [*no obj*] to last, stay strong, or withstand much use or strain: *That strong fabric wears well.* **5. wear down, a.** to make or become shabbier, smaller, etc., by wearing: *to wear down the heels of his shoes; to wear the heels down.* **b.** to overcome (opposition) by persistence; prevail: *Gradually she wore her father down until at last he consented to the marriage.* **6. wear off,** to become less slowly or gradually: *The effects of the drug began to wear off.* **7. wear on,** to irritate; annoy: *That noise really wears on me.* **8. wear out, a.** to make or become unfit or useless through hard or extended use: *She wears out clothes quickly* or *She wears clothes out quickly. Those clothes will wear out in no time.* **b.** to cause (someone) to be tired: *That long bicycle ride wore me out.* **9. wear thin, a.** to weaken; diminish: *My patience is wearing thin.* **b.** to become less appealing, tolerable, etc.: *childish pranks that soon wore thin.* —*n.* [*noncount*] **10.** clothing of a particular kind: *winter wear; men's wear.* **11.** the quality of resisting the effects of use; durability: *still a lot of wear in this old jacket.* **12.** gradual condition of falling apart, as from use: *The carpet is beginning to show wear.* —**Idiom. 13. wear the pants,** to exercise controlling authority in a household. —'**wear•a•ble,** *adj.* —'**wear•er,** *n.* [*count*]

wea•ri•some /'wɪəriysəm/ *adj.* causing tiredness or annoyance: *his wearisome complaints.*

wea•ry /'wɪəriy/ *adj.,* -**ri•er,** -**ri•est,** *v.,* -**ried,** -**ry•ing.** —*adj.* **1.** physically or mentally exhausted: *He was weary from staying up all night.* **2.** impatient or dissatisfied: [*often*: ~ + *of*]: *I am weary of your excuses.* —*v.* **3.** to (cause to) become tired or weary: [*no obj*]: *The patient wearied quickly from even a short walk.* [~ + *obj*]: *The long hours of work wearied him.* **4.** [~ + *obj*] to (cause to) grow impatient or dissatisfied with something: *Living in hotel rooms wearied him. He wearied of living in hotel rooms.* —**wea•ri•ly** /'wɪərəliy/, *adv.* —'**wea•ri•ness,** *n.* [*noncount*]

wea•sel /'wiyzəl/ *n.* [*count*], *pl.* -**sels, -sel.** a small, meat-eating animal having a long, slender body and short legs.

weath•er /'wɛðər/ *n.* [*noncount*] **1.** the state or condition of the atmosphere with respect to wind, temperature, moisture, etc. —*v.* **2.** to (cause to) be exposed to or affected by exposure to the weather: [~ + *obj*]: *to weather lumber so that it dries out.* [*no obj*]: *rocks weathered by rain and wind.* **3.** [~ + *obj*; *often*: ~ + *through*] to come safely through: *to weather a storm; to weather through a difficult time.* —**Idiom. 4. under the weather,** slightly ill.

'**weather-,beaten,** *adj.* **1.** worn or damaged by having been exposed to the weather. **2.** tanned and toughened by having been exposed to the weather.

weath•er•man /'wɛðərˌmæn/ *n.* [*count*], *pl.* -**men.** a meteorologist; a person who studies and forecasts the weather.

'**weather ,vane** or '**weath•er,vane,** *n.* [*count*] a rod to which a freely spinning pointer is attached that moves in the wind and shows the direction of the wind.

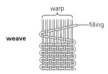

weave /wiyv/ *v.,* **wove** /wowv/ or (*esp. for* 5) **weaved, wo•ven** /'wowvən/ or **wove, weav•ing,** *n.* —*v.* **1.** to lace together (threads, strands, etc.) so as to form a fabric: [*no obj*]: *to knit and to weave.* [~ + *obj*]: *to weave the threads together.* **2.** [~ + *obj*] to form by weaving: *to weave a basket.* **3.** [~ + *obj*] (of a spider or similar small creature) to spin (a web or cocoon). **4.** [~ + *obj*] to combine into a connected whole: *to weave a story from all the little events in his life.* **5.** to (cause to) move by winding or zigzagging: [*no obj*]: *The bicycle weaved through traffic.* [~ + *obj*]: *He wove his way through the crowd.* —*n.* [*count*] **6.** a pattern of or method for weaving. —'**weav•er,** *n.* [*count*]

web /wɛb/ *n.* [*count*] **1.** a fabric formed by weaving. **2.** a cobweb. **3.** any intricate or network or pattern of elements, esp. one that traps or entangles: *a web of intrigue; a web of lies.* **4.** a piece of skinlike material connecting the digits of an animal, as a bird living in water. **5.** [*the Web*]

the World Wide Web. —**webbed,** *adj.*: *the webbed feet of a duck.*

'**Web ,site,** *n.* [*count*] a connected group of pages on the World Wide Web, dealing with a particular subject, product, etc.

wed /wɛd/ *v.,* **wed•ded** or **wed, wed•ding.** to marry: [~ + *obj*]: *They were wed in July.* [*no obj*]: *They wed in July.*

we'd /wiyd/ contraction of *we had, we should,* or *we would.*

Wed., an abbreviation of: Wednesday.

wed•ding /'wɛdɪŋ/ *n.* [*count*] the act or ceremony of marrying.

wedge /wɛdʒ/ *n.,* *v.,* **wedged, wedg•ing.** —*n.* [*count*] **1.** a triangular piece of hard material used for raising, holding, or splitting objects: *He put a wedge under the door to prop it open.* **2.** something that serves to part, split, or divide: *She tried to drive a wedge between the two friends by whispering rumors.* —*v.* [~ + *obj*] **3.** to fix firmly with a wedge: *to wedge a door open.* **4.** to pack tightly into a narrow space: *to wedge clothes into a suitcase.*

wed•lock /'wɛdˌlɒk/ *n.* [*noncount*] the state of being married; matrimony.

Wednes•day /'wɛnzdey, -diy/ *n.* the fourth day of the week: *I'll see you on Wednesday.* [*count*]: *We always met on Wednesdays.*

wee /wiy/ *adj.* [*before a noun*], **we•er, we•est. 1.** very small; tiny. **2.** very early: *the wee hours of the morning.*

weed /wiyd/ *n.* [*count*] **1.** an unwanted plant growing wild, esp. one that takes food or nourishment from a crop, lawn, or flower bed. —*v.* **2.** to free from weeds: [~ + *obj*]: *to weed a garden.* [*no obj*]: *She was weeding in the garden.* **3. weed out,** to remove as being unwanted or unneeded: *The coach had to weed out the inexperienced players. He had to weed them out.*

week /wiyk/ *n.* [*count*] **1.** a period of seven days following one after the other, usually beginning with Sunday. **2.** the working portion of a week, usually (in the U.S.) not including Saturday and Sunday: *a 35-hour work week.*

week•day /'wiykˌdey/ *n.* [*count*] any day of the week except Saturday and Sunday.

week•end /'wiykˌɛnd, -'ɛnd/ *n.* [*count*] **1.** the end of a week, esp. the period between Friday evening and Monday morning. **2.** this period with one or more days added immediately before or after: *a three-day holiday weekend.*

week•ly /'wiykliy/ *adj., adv., n., pl.* -**lies.** —*adj.* **1.** done, happening, or appearing once a week. **2.** computed or determined by the week: *the weekly exchange rate.* —*adv.* **3.** once a week: *We pay our employees weekly.* —*n.* [*count*] **4.** a publication, as a newspaper or magazine, that appears once a week.

weep /wiyp/ *v.,* **wept** /wɛpt/, **weep•ing.** to shed (tears) because of strong emotion: [*no obj*]: *They wept for days over his sudden death.* [~ + *obj*]: *He wept bitter tears.* —'**weep•er,** *n.* [*count*]

'**weeping 'willow,** *n.* [*count*] an Asian willow tree having drooping branches.

weep•y /'wiypiy/ *adj.,* -**i•er,** -**i•est.** easily moved to tears.

wee•vil /'wiyvəl/ *n.* [*count*] a beetle with a long snout, destructive to nuts, grain, fruit, and plants (as cotton).

weigh /wey/ *v.* **1.** to have weight or a certain weight: [~ + *obj; no passive*]: *He weighs sixty pounds.* [*no obj*]: *How much do you weigh?* **2.** [~ + *obj*] to determine the heaviness of (some-

W

thing), esp. by use of a scale: *The butcher weighed the meat.* **3.** [~ + *obj*] to think about or consider carefully: *I weighed the advantages against the disadvantages.* **4. weigh down,** to lower the spirits of; depress: *These burdens weighed him down.* —*Idiom.* **5. weigh on,** to cause worry or anxiety to: *His mounting debts weighed on him.*

weight /weyt/ *n.* **1.** the amount something weighs: [*noncount*]: *He wants to lose weight.* [*count; usually singular*]: *at a weight of over one hundred pounds.* **2.** [*count*] a system of units for expressing heaviness or mass: *a table of weights and measures.* **3.** [*count*] a heavy object used to hold something open or down. **4.** [*count*] a heavy piece of equipment lifted or held for exercise or body building or in athletic competition. **5.** [*count*] a burden, as of responsibility: *The debts were a weight on his mind.* **6.** [*noncount*] importance, significance, or influence: *His opinion carries great weight with the boss.* —*v.* [~ + *obj*] **7.** to add weight to; make heavier, so as to prevent easy movement: *to weight (down) the papers on his desk; to weight them (down).* —*Idiom.* **8. pull one's (own) weight,** to contribute one's share of work to a job. **9. throw one's weight around,** to exercise one's power or influence, esp. in an arrogant or offensive way.

weight•less /ˈweytlɪs/ *adj.* being without apparent weight. —**'weight•less•ness,** *n.* [*noncount*]: *periods of weightlessness in the space capsule.*

weight•lift•ing /ˈweytˌlɪftɪŋ/ *n.* [*noncount*] the lifting of heavy weights for exercise or in a competitive event. —**'weight,lift•er,** *n.* [*count*]

weight•y /ˈweytiy/ *adj.,* **-i•er, -i•est. 1.** burdensome or troublesome: *weighty matters on his mind.* **2.** important.

weird /wɪərd/ *adj.,* **-er, -est. 1.** suggesting the supernatural; unearthly: *a weird sound in the night.* **2.** strange; odd: *a weird costume; a weird neighbor.* —**'weird•ly,** *adv.* —**'weird•ness,** *n.* [*noncount*]

weird•o /ˈwɪərdow/ *n.* [*count*], *pl.* **-os.** *Slang.* an odd or strange person.

welch /wɛltʃ, wɛlʃ/ *v.* WELSH.

wel•come /ˈwɛlkəm/ *interj., n., v.,* **-comed, -com•ing,** *adj.* —*interj.* **1.** (used as a greeting, as to one whose arrival gives pleasure): *Welcome, stranger!* —*n.* [*count*] **2.** a kindly greeting or reception: *We gave her a warm welcome.* —*v.* [~ + *obj*] **3.** to greet with pleasure or courtesy: *We welcomed her into our home.* **4.** to invite or accept with pleasure or courtesy: *I welcome your comments.* —*adj.* **5.** gladly received: *a welcome visitor.* **6.** agreeable: *a welcome rest.* **7.** [*be* + ~ + *to* + *verb*] willingly permitted: *You are welcome to try it.* **8.** (used in the phrase *You're welcome* as a response to thanks: *"Thank you."* —*"You're welcome."*

weld /wɛld/ *v.* **1.** to unite (metal or plastic pieces) by hammering or squeezing them together, esp. after applying heat: [~ + *obj*]: *He welded the steel doors shut.* [*no obj*]: *The engineer is still welding.* —*n.* [*count*] **2.** a joint that has been welded. —**'weld•er,** *n.* [*count*]

wel•fare /ˈwɛlˌfɛər/ *n.* [*noncount*] **1.** health, happiness, and prosperity; well-being. **2.** assistance given by government to those in need; public relief: *He is receiving welfare. He is on welfare.*

well¹ /wɛl/ *adv., adj., comparative* **bet•ter,** *superlative* **best,** *interj.* —*adv.* **1.** in a good or satis-

factory manner: *Our plans are going well.* **2.** thoroughly or carefully: *Shake the bottle well before using.* **3.** in a proper manner: *That child behaves well in school.* **4.** with justice or reason: *I couldn't very well refuse.* **5.** with favor or approval: *My family thinks well of her.* **6.** comfortably or prosperously: *to live well.* **7.** to a considerable degree: *These grades are well below average.* **8.** in a close way; intimately: *I've known them well.* **9.** without doubt; certainly: *I cry easily, as you well know.* **10.** with good nature; without anger: *He took the joke well.* —*adj.* **11.** in good health: *not a well man; He's not well.* **12.** [*be* + ~] satisfactory or good: *All is well.* —*interj.* **13.** (used to express surprise, a mild scolding, or the like:) *Well! I didn't know you felt so strongly about it.* **14.** (used to introduce a sentence, resume a conversation, etc.:) *Well, it's time to go home.* —*Idiom.* **15. as well,** in addition; also: *She wanted to produce the play and to direct it as well.* **16. as well as,** and not only (what is known or assumed): *She's smart as well as beautiful.* **17. leave well enough alone,** to avoid changing something that is satisfactory the way it is. **18. well up on,** very knowledgeable about.

well² /wɛl/ *n.* [*count*] **1.** a hole drilled into the earth to obtain a natural deposit, as water or petroleum: *an oil well.* **2.** a natural source of water, as a spring. —*v.* [*no obj*] **3.** to rise, spring, or gush, as from a well: *Tears welled (up) in my eyes.*

we'll /wiyl; *unstressed* wɪl/ contraction of *we shall* or *we will.*

'well-be'haved, *adj.* showing good behavior or manners.

'well-'being, *n.* [*noncount*] a state of health, happiness, comfort, or prosperity.

'well-'bred, *adj.* showing good breeding, as in behavior.

'well-'done, *adj.* **1.** performed accurately and skillfully. **2.** (of meat) thoroughly cooked.

'well-'groomed, *adj.* **1.** clean, neat, and dressed with care. **2.** carefully cared for: *a well-groomed lawn.*

'well-in'formed, *adj.* having a great deal of knowledge, as of a subject or of a variety of subjects.

'well-'known, *adj.* **1.** fully or thoroughly known: *a well-known fact.* **2.** widely known; famous: *a well-known rock star.*

'well-'meaning, *adj.* having or based on good intentions.

'well-'off, *adj.* [*be* + ~] well-to-do.

'well-'read /ˈrɛd/ *adj.* having read a great deal.

'well-'rounded, *adj.* having desirably varied or different abilities or talents: *a well-rounded personality.*

'well-'spoken, *adj.* speaking well or in a way that pleases; polite in speech.

'well-to-'do, *adj.* comfortably prosperous; wealthy.

welsh /wɛlʃ, wɛltʃ/ *also* **welch,** *v.* [~ + *on* + *obj*] *Sometimes Offensive.* **1.** to fail to pay what is owed: *He welshed on his debts.* **2.** to go back on one's word.

Welsh /wɛlʃ, wɛltʃ/ *adj.* **1.** of or relating to Wales. **2.** of or relating to the language spoken by many of the people in Wales. —*n.* **3.** [*plural; the* + ~; *used with a plural verb*] the people born or living in Wales. **4.** [*noncount*] the language spoken by many of the people in Wales.

welt /wɛlt/ *n.* [*count*] a ridge or raised mark like a cut on the surface of the body, as from a blow.

wench /wɛntʃ/ n. [count] **1.** a girl or young woman. **2.** a sexually loose woman.

wend /wɛnd/ v. [~ + obj] to travel or proceed on (one's way): to wend his way home.

went /wɛnt/ v. pt. of GO¹.

wept /wɛpt/ v. pt. and pp. of WEEP.

were /wɜr; unstressed wər/ v. a 2nd pers. sing. past indic., pl. past indic., and past subj. of BE.

we're /wɪər/ contraction of we are.

were•n't /wɜrnt, 'wɜrənt/ contraction of were not.

west /wɛst/ n. **1.** [noncount] one of the four main points of the compass, the direction toward which the sun goes down. **2. a.** a region in the west of a country, esp. of the U.S. **b.** the countries of Europe and the Western Hemisphere. —adj. **3.** lying toward or located in the west. **4.** coming from the west: a west wind. —adv. **5.** to, toward, or in the west: to head west.

west•er•ly /'wɛstərliy/ adj., adv. toward or from the west: a westerly wind; The wind turned westerly.

west•ern /'wɛstərn/ adj. **1.** of, toward, or in the west: a western migration. **2.** [usually: Western] of the West: That country has resisted Western influence for centuries. —n. [count; often: Western] **3.** a story, movie, or radio or television program about the U.S. West in the 19th century. —'west•ern•er, n. [count]

west•ward /'wɛstwərd/ adj. **1.** moving, facing, or located toward the west. —adv. **2.** Also, 'west•wards. toward the west.

wet /wɛt/ adj., wet•ter, wet•test, v., wet or wet•ted, wet•ting. —adj. **1.** moistened, covered, or soaked with liquid: Wipe this with a wet cloth. **2.** in a liquid state: wet paint. **3.** rainy or misty: a cold, wet day. —v. [~ + obj] **4.** to (cause to) become wet or moistened: Wet the cloth with warm water. **5.** to urinate on or in: The dog had wet the carpet. —Idiom. **6.** all wet, Informal. completely mistaken. —'wet•ness, n. [noncount]

wet•land /'wɛt,lænd/ n. [count] Often, wetlands. [plural] land with wet and spongy soil.

we've /wiyv/ contraction of we have.

whack /hwæk, wæk/ v. **1.** to strike or hit with or as if with a strong, loud blow: [~ + obj]: She whacked the stick against the table. [no obj]: He whacked at the ball and missed. —n. [count] **2.** a strong, loud blow: She gave him a whack on the knuckles. **3.** an attempt: He took a whack at the job. —Idiom. **4. out of whack,** not working correctly or properly.

whale /hweyl, weyl/ n., pl. whales, whale. **1.** [count] a very large mammal that lives in the sea, having a fishlike body. **2.** [count; usually singular] something great or fine of its kind: I had a whale of a time in Europe.

whal•er /'hweylər, 'wey-/ n. [count] a person or ship in the business of whaling.

whal•ing /'hweylɪŋ, 'wey-/ n. [noncount] the work or industry of capturing whales.

wham /hwæm, wæm/ n., v., whammed, wham•ming. —n. [count] **1.** the sound of a sharp, forceful hit, blow, punch, kick, explosion, etc. —v. [~ + obj] **2.** to hit forcefully, esp. so as to produce a loud sound.

wharf /hwɔrf, wɔrf/ n. [count], pl. wharves /hwɔrvz, wɔrvz/ wharfs. a large dock or similar structure next to which ships are attached at shore to load or unload.

what /hwʌt, hwɒt, wʌt, wɒt; unstressed hwət,

wət/ pron. **1.** (used in questions as a request for information): What is your phone number? What is the matter? **2.** (used in questions to ask for a repetition of words or information not fully understood): You need what? **3.** (used in questions) how much?: What does it cost? **4.** (used to introduce a clause) that which; whatever; as much or as many as: I will send what was promised (= I will send the thing that was promised). We will stay together come what may (= whatever happens). **5.** (used to introduce an exclamation, or to make stronger the next word or noun): What luck! What an idea! —adj. **6.** (used to signal a question): What time is it? **7.** whatever; whichever: Take what supplies you need. —adv. **8.** to what extent or degree?: What does it matter? —interj. **9.** (used to show shock or surprise, and may then be followed by a question or phrase): What, no kiss? —Idiom. **10. so what,** (used to express indifference or contempt): They're rich, so what? **11. what for,** why: What did you do that for? **12. what have you,** other things of the same kind: tissues, cosmetics, keys, and what have you in her handbag. **13. what if,** what would be the outcome if; suppose that: What if we get lost? **14. what with,** because of; in light of: What with all I've had to do, I haven't had time to relax. **15. what's what,** the true situation: Let's find out what's what around here.

what•ev•er /hwʌt'ɛvər, hwɒt-, hwɑt-, wʌt-, wɒt-, wət-/ pron. **1.** anything that: Do whatever you like. **2.** any quantity or amount (of an understood or specified item): Take whatever you like of these. **3.** no matter what: Do it, whatever happens. **4.** Informal. anything else of the sort (often a deliberately vague reference): I'll go swimming, see a movie, take a walk, whatever. —adj. **5.** in any amount; to any extent: whatever merit the book has. **6.** no matter what kind, degree, number, etc.: Whatever problems you might have, we will help. **7.** being what or who it may be: Whatever the reason, she refuses to go. **8.** of any kind (used following the noun it modifies): I've given no thought whatever to my future plans. —adv. **9.** (used to introduce a question but with extra emphasis): Whatever were you thinking?

what's /hwʌts, hwɒts, wʌts, wɒts/ contraction of what is, what has, or what does.

what•so•ev•er /,hwʌtsow'ɛvər, ,hwɒt-, ,wʌt-, ,wɒt-/ pron., adj. (used to add greater emphasis to a preceding negative word or phrase) whatever: She has no friends whatsoever.

wheat /hwiyt, wiyt/ n. [noncount] **1.** the grain of a cereal grass used in the form of flour. **2.** the plant itself.

whee•dle /'hwiydḷ, 'wiydḷ/ v. [~ + obj], -dled, -dling. to influence or try to persuade (a person), esp. by charming or flattering him or her, in order to gain (something): I was trying to wheedle her into lending me the car. He tried to wheedle some more money from her.

wheel /hwiyl, wiyl/ n. [count] **1.** a circular frame or disk that can revolve or spin around an inner frame or on an axis, allowing an object to which it is attached to move. **2.** something like a wheel in shape or function. **3.** the steering wheel of a vehicle. **4. wheels,** [plural] **a.** the forces, institutions, etc., propelling or driving action or activity: the wheels of commerce. **b.** Informal. an automobile, esp. one's personal automobile. **5.** someone powerful and influential: a big wheel in the oil business. —v. **6.** [~ + obj] to move or carry on wheels: They wheeled him off to the emergency room. **7.** [no obj] to turn, rotate, or revolve; change direction: *She wheeled around to see who was calling her.* —*Idiom.* **8. spin one's wheels,** to waste one's effort. **9. wheel and deal,** to make deals or conduct business in a boldly forceful way. —**wheeled,** *adj.*

wheel·bar·row /ˈhwiylˌbærow, ˈwiyl-/ *n.* [*count*] a small cart for carrying and moving a load, supported at one end by a wheel and pushed at the other by two handles.

wheel·chair /ˈhwiylˌbeys, ˈwiyl-/ *n.* [*count*] a chair mounted on wheels for use by persons who cannot walk.

wheeze /hwiyz, wiyz/ *v.,* **wheezed, wheez·ing,** *n.* —*v.* [*no obj*] **1.** to breathe with difficulty and with a whistling sound. —*n.* [*count*] **2.** a wheezing breath or sound.

whelp /hwɛlp, wɛlp/ *n.* [*count*] the young of such mammals as the dog or the wolf.

when /hwɛn, wɛn; *unstressed* hwən, wən/ *adv.* **1.** (used to introduce a question) at what time or period?: *When will they arrive?* **2.** (used to introduce a question) under what circumstances?: *When is an apology in order?* —*conj.* **3.** at what time: *He knows when to be silent.* **4.** at the time that: *when we were young.* **5.** whenever: *The dog barks when the doorbell rings.* **6.** as soon as: *Stop the car when the light turns red.* **7.** whereas; although; while on the contrary: *Why are you here when you should be in school?* —*pron.* **8.** what or which time: *Since when have you been teaching?* —**Usage.** WHEN and WHERE are not interchangeable: *Weekends are occasions when* (not "*where*") *we have a chance to spend time with the family.*

whence /hwɛns, wɛns/ *adv.* **1.** from where; from what place. **2.** to the place from which.

when·ev·er /hwɛnˈɛvər, wɛn-, hwən-, wən- / *adv., conj.* at whatever time; when: *I'm ready whenever you are.*

where /hwɛər, wɛər/ *adv.* **1.** (used to introduce a question) in, at, or to what place?: *Where is he? Where are you going?* **2.** (used to introduce a question) in what position, circumstances, respect, or way?: *Where do you stand on this question?* **3.** (used to introduce a question) from what source?: *Where did you get such a notion?* —*conj.* **4.** in or at what place, part, or point: *Find where the trouble is.* **5.** in or at the place, part, or point in (or at) which: *The cup is where you left it.* **6.** in a position or situation in which: *He's useless where tact is needed.* **7.** to what or whatever place: *Where you go, I will go.* **8.** in or at which place: *They stopped at a motel, where they spent the night.* —*pron.* **9.** (used to introduce a question) what place?: *Where are you from?* **10.** the place in or point at which: *This is where the boat docks.* —**Usage.** See WHEN.

where·a·bouts /ˈhwɛərəˌbawts, ˈwɛər-/ *n.* the place where a person or thing is: [*plural; used with a plural verb*]: *His whereabouts are still unknown.* [*noncount; used with a singular verb*]: *His whereabouts is still unknown.*

where·as /hwɛərˈæz, wɛər-/ *conj.* **1.** while on the contrary; although: *One student arrived promptly, whereas the others came late.* **2.** it being the case that; since: *Whereas we wish to get married, we must apply for a license.*

where·by /hwɛərˈbay, wɛər-/ *conj., adv.* by which; according to which: *a contract whereby he retained all rights to his work.*

where·in /hwɛərˈɪn, ˈwɛər-/ *conj.* in which; in what.

where·of /hwɛərˈʌv, -ˈɒv, wɛər-/ *adv., conj.* of what, which, or whom.

where·up·on /ˌhwɛərəˈpɒn, -ˈpɔn, ˌwɛər-; ˈhwɛərəˌpɒn, -ˌpɔn, ˈwɛər-/ *conj.* upon or after which; as a consequence of which: *He'll surely try to get in touch with her, whereupon she'll fall in love with him again.*

wher·ev·er /hwɛərˈɛvər, wɛər-/ *conj., adv.* **1.** in, at, or to whatever place or circumstance: *Wherever you go, I'll follow.* —*adv.* **2.** (used to introduce a question but with extra emphasis): where?: *Wherever did you find that?*

whet /hwɛt, wɛt/ *v.* [~ + *obj*], **whet·ted, whet·ting. 1.** to sharpen by grinding or friction. **2.** to make eager; stimulate: *The smell of food whetted his appetite.*

wheth·er /ˈhwɛðər, ˈwɛð-/ *conj.* **1.** (used to introduce the first of two or more choices or possibilities; the second one is preceded by the word *or*:) *I don't care whether we go or stay.* **2.** (used to introduce a single choice, while the second choice is understood or implied to be the negation of the first): *See whether she has come.* —*Idiom.* **3. whether or not** or **whether or no,** under whatever circumstances; in any case; regardless: *He tends to insist on his views whether or not the facts support them.*

whey /hwey, wey/ *n.* [*noncount*] the liquid that separates from the curd in milk that has become solid.

which /hwɪtʃ, wɪtʃ/ *pron.* **1.** (used in questions) what one or ones: *Which of these do you want?* **2.** whichever; the one that: *Choose which appeals to you.* **3.** (used in relative clauses to refer back to a word that has already been mentioned): *This book, which I read last night, was exciting.* **4.** (used in a relative clause that starts with a preposition): *That's the house in which I lived.* —*adj.* [*before a noun*] **5.** what one or ones of a number or group: *Which book do you want?*

which·ev·er /hwɪtʃˈɛvər, wɪtʃ-/ *pron.* **1.** any one that: *Take whichever you like.* **2.** no matter which: *Whichever you choose, some in the group will be offended.* —*adj.* [*before a noun*] **3.** no matter which: *whichever ones you choose.*

whiff /hwɪf, wɪf/ *n.* [*count*] **1.** a slight gust or puff, as of wind or smoke. **2.** a slight trace, as of an odor; hint: *a whiff of onions.* **3.** a single act of breathing in, as of tobacco smoke.

while /hwayl, wayl/ *n., conj., v.,* **whiled, whil·ing.** —*n.* [*count; singular*] **1.** an amount, period, or interval of time: *a long while ago.* —*conj.* **2.** during the time that: *He read the paper while he waited.* **3.** even though; although: *While they are related, they don't get along.* —*v.* [~ + *obj*] **4. while away,** to cause (time) to pass, esp. pleasantly: *whiling away the hours; to while the hours away.* —*Idiom.* **5. worth one's while,** worth one's time, trouble, or expense.

whim /hwɪm, wɪm/ *n.* [*count*] a sudden idea, thought, or wish to do something without a good reason: *I decided on a whim to leave early.*

whim·per /ˈhwɪmpər, ˈwɪm-/ *v.* [*no obj*] **1.** to cry with or utter in low, sad, weak sounds: *The dog whimpered with fear.* —*n.* [*count*] **2.** a whimpering sound.

whim·si·cal /ˈhwɪmzɪkəl, ˈwɪm-/ *adj.* **1.** given to playful or fanciful notions, ideas, or behavior. **2.** odd or strange; unpredictable.

whim·sy or **-sey** /ˈhwɪmziy, ˈwɪm-/ *n.* [*noncount*], *pl.* **-sies** or **-seys.** playful or fanciful humor.

whine /hwayn, wayn/ *v.,* **whined, whin·ing,** *n.* —*v.* **1.** [*no obj*] to make a long, complaining sound, often high-pitched: *The dog whined at the*

whole

door. **2.** to complain in a self-pitying way: [~ + *that clause*]: *The children whined that they wanted to stay up late.* [*no obj*]: *Don't whine.* —*n.* [*count*] **3.** a whining word, sound, or complaint. —'**whin•er,** *n.* [*count*] —'**whin•y,** *adj.,* **-i•er, -i•est.**

whin•ny /'hwɪniy, 'wɪniy/ *n., pl.* **-nies,** *v.,* **-nied, -ny•ing.** —*n.* [*count*] **1.** a low, gentle neigh of a horse. —*v.* [*no obj*] **2.** to utter a whinny.

whip /hwɪp, wɪp/ *v.,* **whipped, whip•ping,** *n.* —*v.* [~ + *obj*] **1.** to beat with a flexible piece of rope or leather, as a lash, esp. as punishment: *to whip the slaves; The child was whipped for telling a lie.* **2.** to defeat; overcome: *Their team whipped us, 30-0.* **3.** to (cause to) move, pull, or seize suddenly: *She whipped out her camera* or *She whipped her camera out.* **4.** to beat to a froth: *to whip cream.* **5. whip up, a.** to prepare quickly: *to whip up a meal; I'll whip a meal up.* **b.** to urge to action: *to whip up the crowd; to whip them up into a frenzy.* —*n.* [*count*] **6.** a flexible rod, as of rope or leather, used for whipping. **7.** a kitchen utensil for whipping; whisk.

whir or **whirr** /hwɜr, wɜr/ *v.,* **whirred, whir•ring,** *n.* —*v.* [*no obj*] **1.** to move or spin quickly with a humming sound: *The helicopter whirred overhead.* —*n.* [*count*] **2.** an act or sound of whirring.

whirl /hwɜrl, wɜrl/ *v.* **1.** to (cause to) turn around or aside very fast, or to spin quickly: [*no obj*]: *The plane's propellers whirled.* [~ + *obj*]: *He whirled the rope around his head.* **2.** [*no obj*] to feel dizziness: *My head is whirling after that roller coaster ride.* —*n.* [*count*] **3.** a whirling movement or act of whirling. **4.** a rapid succession of events: *a whirl of parties.* **5.** an attempt; trial: *He promised to give that new diet a whirl.*

whirl•pool /'hwɜr,puwl, 'wɜrl-/ *n.* [*count*] water moving quickly in a circular motion, often producing a downward spiraling action.

whirl•wind /'hwɜrl,wɪnd, 'wɜrl-/ *n.* [*count*] **1.** a small mass of air that spins very quickly, as a tornado. **2.** something resembling a whirlwind, as in violent or destructive force. —*adj.* **3.** like a whirlwind in speed or force: *a whirlwind visit.*

whisk /hwɪsk, wɪsk/ *v.* [~ + *obj*] **1.** to move with a rapid brushing or sweeping stroke: *The waiters whisked away the trays and plates.* **2.** to whip or blend (eggs or egg whites, cream, etc.) with a whisk. —*n.* [*count*] **3.** an act of whisking. **4.** a tool, usually of wire, for beating or whipping food.

whisk•er /'hwɪskər, 'wɪs-/ *n.* [*count*] **1.** Usually, **-kers.** [*plural*] the hair growing on a man's cheeks and chin. **2.** a single hair of the beard. **3.** one of the long bristlelike hairs growing near the mouth of an animal, as a cat. —'**whisk•ered,** *adj.*

whis•key or **whis•ky** /'hwɪskiy, 'wɪs-/ *n., pl.* **-keys** or **-kies.** [*noncount*] [*count*] a strong alcoholic drink made from a grain, such as barley.

whis•per /'hwɪspər, 'wɪspər/ *v.* **1.** to speak or say with soft, quiet, hushed sounds, esp. with little or no vibration of the vocal cords: [*no obj*]: *He whispered softly in her ear.* [~ + *obj*]: *She whispered a secret to me.* [*used with quotations*]: *"Quiet, someone will hear us!" she whispered.* —*n.* [*count*] **2.** an act or instance of whispering: *They spoke in whispers.* **3.** a soft rustling sound: *the whisper of the wind.*

whis•tle /'hwɪsəl, 'wɪs-/ *v.,* **-tled, -tling,** *n.* —*v.* **1.** to make a high, clear sound by forcing the breath through stretched lips or through teeth: [*no obj*]: *He whistled happily to himself.* [~ + *obj*]: *He whistled a happy tune.* **2.** [*no obj*] to produce a sound or call resembling a whistle: *The birds were whistling in the trees.* **3.** to signal or call for by or as if by whistling: [*no obj*]: *He whistled for her to come down and see him.* [~ + *obj*]: *She whistled her dog to her side.* **4.** [*no obj*] to move with a whistling sound, as a bullet. —*n.* [*count*] **5.** an instrument for producing whistling sounds: *The police officer blew her whistle.* **6.** a whistling sound. —*Idiom.* **7. blow the whistle on,** to expose (a crime or the person who commits it): *The accountants blew the whistle on the dishonest employee.*

white /hwayt, wayt/ *adj.,* **whit•er, whit•est,** *n.* —*adj.* **1.** of the color of pure snow. **2.** light in color; pale: *I prefer white wine. His face turned white at the terrible news.* **3.** having a light-colored skin. **4.** snowy: *a white Christmas.* —*n.* **5.** [*noncount*] a color without hue that is the opposite of black. **6.** [*count*] a person who has a light-colored skin. **7.** [*count*] the white or light-colored part of something, as an egg after cooking.

'**white 'blood ,cell,** *n.* [*count*] a nearly colorless blood cell that fights disease-carrying organisms.

'**white-,collar,** *adj.* pertaining to office or professional, non-manual, workers.

'**White ,House,** *n.* **1.** the official home or residence of the president of the U.S. **2.** the executive branch of the U.S. government.

'**white 'lie,** *n.* [*count*] a harmless lie, often one told to avoid hurting someone's feelings.

whit•en /'hwaytən, 'wayt-/ *v.* to (cause to) become white: [~ + *obj*]: *He poured bleach into his laundry to whiten the clothes.* [*no obj*]: *The ground slowly whitened as the snow fell.* —'**whit•en•er,** *n.* [*count*]

whit•tle /'hwɪtl, 'wɪtl/ *v.,* **-tled, -tling. 1.** to cut, trim, or shape (wood) by carving off bits with a knife: [~ + *obj*]: *to whittle wood.* [*no obj*]: *She likes to whittle.* **2.** [~ + *obj*] to form by whittling: *to whittle a toy soldier from a block of wood.* **3.** [~ + *obj*] to reduce the amount of gradually: *to whittle down expenses; to whittle away one's inheritance.*

whiz or **whizz** /hwɪz, wɪz/ *v.,* **whizzed, whiz•zing,** *n.* —*v.* [*no obj*] **1.** to make or move with a humming, buzzing, or hissing sound, as of an object flying quickly through the air: *A cloud of hornets whizzed by.* —*n.* [*count*] **2.** *Informal.* a very skillful person; expert: *She's a whiz at math.* **3.** a whizzing sound: *the whiz of the traffic passing by.*

who /huw/ *pron., possessive* **whose,** *objective* **whom. 1.** (used to introduce a question, as the subject or, in informal conversational use, the object of a verb) what person or persons: *Who is he? Who is at the door?* **2.** the person or persons that: *Do you know who called?* **3.** (used in relative clauses to refer to a person): *The woman who called this morning is here.* **4.** (used in questions to ask about the character or importance of someone): *Who does she think she is?*

whoa /hwow, wow/ *interj.* (used as a command, esp. to an animal, to stop).

who'dun•it /'huw'dʌnɪt/ *n.* [*count*] a story about the solving of a crime; a detective story.

who•ev•er /huw'ɛvər/ *pron.* whatever person; anyone that: *Whoever did it should be proud.*

whole /howl/ *adj.* **1.** [*before a noun*] making up

W

the full amount, number, or extent; entire; complete: *He ate the whole pie. She ran the whole distance; a whole set of china; the whole truth.* **2.** not broken or damaged; not injured or hurt: *Thankfully, the vase arrived whole.* **3.** (used to emphasize how much an amount is): *I'd feel a whole lot better if you'd point that gun somewhere else.* —*n.* [count] **4.** the entire amount, number, or extent: *the whole of the amount you owe.* **5.** a thing complete in itself, as an assembly of parts or elements thought of as one thing: *We combined the elements of the theory into a unified whole.* —*Idiom.* **6. as a whole,** as a unit; considered together. **7. on the whole,** everything considered; in general: *On the whole, I agree with you.*

whole•heart•ed /'howl'hɑrtɪd/ *adj.* completely sincere or enthusiastic: *He gave his wholehearted approval to the plan.* —'**whole'heart•ed•ly,** *adv.*

whole•sale /'howl,seyl/ *n., adj., adv., v.,* **-saled, -sal•ing.** —*n.* [noncount] **1.** the sale of goods in quantity, as to retailers. —*adj.* **2.** large in amount or scale: *wholesale layoffs.* —*adv.* **3.** on wholesale terms: *I can get it for you wholesale.* **4.** in a wholesale way: *The company began firing people wholesale.* —*v.* [~ + *obj*] [no *obj*] **5.** to sell by wholesale. —'**whole,sal•er,** *n.* [count]

whole•some /'howlsəm/ *adj.* **1.** bringing about a condition of well-being; healthful. **2.** having a good effect, esp. on the morals of someone: *wholesome family entertainment.* **3.** suggesting health, esp. in appearance: *a fresh, wholesome look.*

'**whole-'wheat,** *adj.* prepared with the complete wheat kernel: *whole-wheat flour.*

who'll /huwl/ contraction of *who will* or *who shall: Who'll drive?*

whol•ly /'howliy, 'howlliy/ *adv.* entirely; totally; completely: *wholly satisfied.*

whom /huwm/ *pron.* the form of the pronoun WHO used as the object of a verb or a preposition: *Whom did you call? To whom should I send this? The man whom you called has returned.*

whom•ev•er /huwm'ɛvər/ *pron.* the form of the pronoun WHOEVER used as the object of a verb or a preposition: *She was gracious with whomever she spoke.*

whoop /hwuwp, hwʊp, wuwp, wʊp; *esp. for* huwp, hʊp/ *n.* [count] **1.** a loud cry or shout, as of excitement. —*v.* [no *obj*] **2.** to utter with, or make, a loud cry or shout: *The kids whooped at the good news.*

whop•per /'hwɒpər, 'wɒp-/ *n.* [count] *Informal.* **1.** something uncommonly large: *That fish was a whopper.* **2.** a big lie.

whop•ping /'hwɒpɪŋ, 'wɒp-/ *adj. Informal.* **1.** very large; unusually large: *a whopping inflation rate.* —*adv.* **2.** extremely: *a whopping big lie.*

whore /hɔr; *often* hʊr/ *n.* [count] PROSTITUTE.

whorl /hwɜrl, hwɔrl, wɜrl, wɔrl/ *n.* [count] a circular arrangement of similar parts, as of leaves; anything shaped like a coil or spiral. —**whorled,** *adj.*

who's /huwz/ contraction of **1.** *who is: Who's on first base?* **2.** *who has: Who's received a paycheck?*

whose /huwz/ *pron.* **1.** the form of the pronoun WHO or WHICH used to show that something is owned, appearing before a noun: *someone whose faith is strong; a word whose meaning escapes me.* **2.** This word is used in questions to mean "the one or ones belonging to what person or persons": *Whose umbrella is that?*

why /hway, way/ *adv.* **1.** (used to introduce a question) for what cause or reason or purpose?: *Why do you ask? Why are you here?* —*conj.* **2.** for what cause or reason; on account of which: *I don't know why he left; the reason why she refused.* **3.** the reason for which: *That is why he returned.*

WI, an abbreviation of: Wisconsin.

wick /wɪk/ *n.* [count] a twist of soft threads that in a candle or oil lamp draws up the liquid to be burned.

wick•ed /'wɪkɪd/ *adj.* **1.** morally bad; evil: *a wicked witch.* **2.** *Slang.* wonderful; great: *She has a wicked tennis serve.* —'**wick•ed•ly,** *adv.* —'**wick•ed•ness,** *n.* [noncount]

wide /wayd/ *adj.* and *adv.,* **wid•er, wid•est.** —*adj.* **1.** of great size or extent from side to side; broad: *the wide lands of the prairie.* **2.** having a certain measurement from side to side: [*after a noun*]: *The doorway was three feet wide.* [*before a noun; after a number of measurement*]: *a three-foot-wide doorway.* **3.** of great range or scope: *a wide selection of videos.* **4.** fully opened: *He stared at the teacher with wide eyes.* **5.** [*usually: be + ~*] far from an aim or goal: *That remark is wide of the truth.* —*adv.* **6.** to the most; fully: *The door was wide open.* **7.** away from a target or objective: *The shot went wide.* **8.** over a large area: *The friends were scattered far and wide after high school.* —'**wide•ly,** *adv.*: *She is widely known as an expert in management.*

-wide, an adjective suffix meaning extending or applying throughout a certain area or space (*countrywide; worldwide*).

'**wide-a'wake,** *adj.* fully awake.

wid•en /'waydn/ *v.* to (cause to) become wide or wider: [~ + *obj*]: *The highway crew is widening the road up ahead.* [no *obj*]: *This narrow road needs widening.*

wide•spread /'wayd'sprɛd/ *adj.* **1.** spread over a wide area: *widespread destruction.* **2.** occurring or found in many places or among many persons: *a widespread belief.*

wid•ow /'wɪdow/ *n.* [count] a woman whose husband has died and who has not remarried. —'**wid•ow,hood,** *n.* [noncount]

wid•owed /'wɪdowd/ *adj.* being a widow through the death of a husband.

wid•ow•er /'wɪdowər/ *n.* [count] a man whose wife has died and who has not remarried.

width /wɪdθ, wɪtθ/ *n.* the size or amount of something measured from side to side; breadth: [count]: *a width of sixty feet.* [noncount]: *sixty feet in width.*

wield /wiyld/ *v.* [~ + *obj*] **1.** to exercise, use, or control: *They wielded the real power in the government.* **2.** to use (a weapon, instrument, etc.) effectively; handle: *to wield a sword.*

wie•ner /'wiynər/ *n.* FRANKFURTER.

wife /wayf/ *n.* [count], *pl.* **wives** /wayvz/. a married woman considered in relation to her husband. —'**wife•ly,** *adj.*

wig /wɪg/ *n.* [count] a covering of natural or artificial hair for the head.

wig•gle /'wɪgəl/ *v.,* **-gled, -gling,** *n.* —*v.* **1.** to move with quick, irregular, side-to-side movements: [~ + *obj*]: *He wiggled his hips while he danced.* [no *obj*]: *Her toes wiggled while she slept.* —*n.* [count] **2.** a wiggling movement or motion.

wig•wam /'wɪgwɒm, -wɔm/ *n.* [count] a North American Indian dwelling, often like a rounded tent in shape.

wild /wayld/ *adj.*, **-er**, **-est**, *adv.*, *n.* —*adj.* **1.** living in a state of nature and not tamed: *wild animals.* **2.** growing or produced without being grown and cared for by humans, as flowers; not cultivated. **3.** not inhabited; undeveloped: *wild country.* **4.** not civilized: *a wild tribe.* **5.** marked by violence or intensity: *a wild storm.* **6.** marked by violent feelings or excitement: *a wild look; a wild party.* **7.** out of emotional control: *to drive someone wild.* **8.** not disciplined; unruly: *a gang of wild boys.* **9.** wide of the mark; missing the target: *a wild pitch.* —*adv.* **10.** in a wild manner: *The gangs were running wild in the streets.* —*n.* [*count*] **11.** Often, **wilds.** [*plural*] an area of land that has not been cultivated; wilderness or wasteland. —'**wild•ly,** *adv.* —'**wild•ness,** *n.* [*noncount*]

wil•der•ness /'wɪldərnɪs/ *n.* [*count; usually singular*] a wild, uncultivated region, usually where humans do not live.

wild•flow•er or **wild flow•er** /'wayld,flawər/ *n.* [*count*] the flower of a plant that grows wild, or the plant itself.

wild•life /'wayld,layf/ *n.* [*noncount*] animals living in the wild: *to protect the wildlife of a region.*

wile /wayl/ *n.*, *v.*, **wiled**, **wil•ing.** —*n.* [*count; usually: wiles*] **1.** a trick meant to fool, trap, or lure another. —*v.* **2. wile away,** to while away (time): *to wile away the hours; wiling the days away.*

will¹ /wɪl/ *auxiliary v.* and *v.*, *pres.* **will;** *past* **would.** —*auxiliary*, *modal verb.* This word is used before the root form of the next verb **1.** to indicate that the action of that verb is going to take place in the future: *I will be there tomorrow.* **2.** to express willingness: *I will do whatever I can. Nobody will help us.* **3.** to express a command: *You will report to the principal at once.* **4.** to express probability or to show what is likely: *They will be asleep by this time, don't you think?* **5.** to express customary action: *She will write for hours at a time. Boys will be boys.* **6.** to express capability: *This couch will seat four.* —*v.* [~ + *obj*] **7.** to wish; like: *Take what you will.*

will² /wɪl/ *n.* **1.** [*noncount*] the ability to do actions that one is conscious of and that one chooses to do deliberately: *free will.* **2.** [*noncount*] purpose or determination: *the will to succeed.* **3.** [*count*] the power of choosing or deciding: *a strong will.* **4.** [*count; usually singular*] wish or desire: *He went against his mother's will.* **5.** [*noncount*] feelings, emotions, or regard toward another: *She still felt a lot of ill will toward her old boss.* **6.** [*count*] a legal document stating what will happen to one's possessions or property after one's death. —*v.* [~ + *obj*] **7.** to decide upon or bring about by an act of the will: *He willed himself to get out of bed.* **8.** to leave (one's possessions or property) to (someone) by a will; bequeath: *She willed the silver tea set to her daughter. She willed her the silver tea set.* —*Idiom.* **9. at will,** as one desires; whenever one chooses: *The kids were free to wander at will.*

will•ful /'wɪlfəl/ or **wil•ful,** *adj.* **1.** deliberate; intentional: *willful negligence.* **2.** unreasonably stubborn, determined, or headstrong. —'**will•ful•ly,** *adv.* —'**will•ful•ness,** *n.* [*noncount*]

will•ing /'wɪlɪŋ/ *adj.* **1.** [*be* + ~; *often:* ~ + *to* + *verb*] consenting; agreeing; inclined: *I was willing to go along with the plan.* **2.** cheerfully enthusiastic about doing something; ready: *a will-*

ing *student.* —'**will•ing•ly,** *adv.* —'**will•ing•ness,** *n.* [*noncount*]

wil•low /'wɪlow/ *n.* [*count*] a tree or shrub with lance-shaped leaves and tough twigs.

will•pow•er or **will pow•er** /'wɪl,pawər/ *n.* [*noncount*] self-control and determination: *It takes willpower to train for a marathon race.*

wilt /wɪlt/ *v.* to (cause to) become limp and drooping, as a flower: *The plants began to wilt in the hot sun.* [~ + *obj*]: *The hot sun will wilt the plants.*

wil•y /'wayliy/ *adj.*, **-i•er,** **-i•est.** full of wiles; clever in a dishonest way.

wimp /wɪmp/ *n.* [*count*] *Informal.* a weak or timid person. —'**wimp•y,** *adj.*, **-i•er,** **-i•est.**

win /wɪn/ *v.*, **won** /wʌn/, **win•ning,** *n.* —*v.* **1.** to finish first, as in a race or contest; achieve by effort or luck: [~ + *obj*]: *She won the marathon. He won the prize.* [*no obj*]: *We never seem to win.* **2.** [~ + *obj*] to be victorious in (a battle, war, etc.): *They won the war.* **3.** [~ + *obj*] to gain, as by one's good qualities, hard work, or influence: *She won the respect of her coworkers.* **4. win over,** to gain the favor, consent, or support of: *Her arguments won us over. She could win over even the most stubborn opponents.* —*n.* [*count*] **5.** a victory, as in a game, a horse race, etc.

wince /wɪns/ *v.* [*no obj*], **winced, winc•ing.** to draw back slightly, as in pain, embarrassment, or fear.

wind¹ /*n.*wɪnd, *Literary* waynd/ *v.* wɪnd/ *n.* **1.** air in natural motion, esp. strong motion: [*count*]: *high winds.* [*noncount*]: *occasional gusts of wind.* **2.** [*count; singular*] breath or breathing; breathing capacity: *to catch one's wind.* **3.** [*noncount*] a hint: *They caught wind of a scandal.* —*v.* [~ + *obj*] **4.** [*usually passive*] to make short of breath: *He was winded after the long race.* —*Idiom.* **5. in the wind,** about to occur. **6. second wind,** ability to make another effort.

wind² /waynd/ *v.*, **wound** /wawnd/, **wind•ing,** *n.* —*v.* **1.** to have or take a curving or twisting course or direction: [*no obj*]: *The road winds a bit and then straightens out.* [~ + *obj*]: *He wound his way down the path.* **2.** [~ + *obj*] to wrap, coil, or twine around (something): *to wind thread on a spool.* **3.** [~ + *obj*] to tighten the spring of: *She wound the clock.* **4. wind down, a.** to bring or come to a gradual end: *After a busy week, the conference began to wind down.* **b.** to calm down; relax: *to wind down at the end of the day.* **5. wind up, a.** to (cause to) come to an end or conclusion: *The meeting wound up at about 4:30. Let's wind this meeting up.* **b.** to arrive in a place or situation as a result of a course of action: *to wind up in jail.* **c.** to make tense or nervous; excite: *All the excitement wound up the kids; wound them up so much (that) they couldn't sleep.* **d.** (in baseball) to prepare to pitch. —*n.* [*count*] **6.** a single turn, twist, or bend.

Wind•break•er /'wɪnd,breykər/ *Trademark.* [*count*] a light outer jacket worn to protect against the wind.

wind•ed /'wɪndɪd/ *adj.* out of breath.

wind•fall /'wɪnd,fɔl/ *n.* [*count*] an unexpected gain or piece of good fortune.

'**wind ,instrument** /wɪnd/ *n.* [*count*] a musical instrument played by forcing the breath through it, classified as either a brass instrument, as the trombone or trumpet, or a woodwind, as the flute or clarinet.

wind•mill /'wɪnd,mɪl/ *n.* [*count*] a machine for grinding or pumping, usually a building with a

W

structure of four sails on the outside that is spun and driven by the wind acting on the sails.

win•dow /'wɪndow/ n. [count] **1.** an opening in a building, vehicle, etc., for letting in air or light. **2.** such an opening with its frame, sashes, and panes of glass. **3.** a period of time available or favorable for doing something: a window of opportunity.

win•dow•pane /'wɪndow,peyn/ n. [count] a pane of glass for a window.

'window-,shop, v. [no obj], **-shopped, -shop•ping.** to look at articles in store windows without making purchases.

win•dow•sill /'wɪndow,sɪl/ n. [count] the sill under a window.

wind•pipe /'wɪndpayp/ n. [count] the tube through which air passes from the throat to the lungs.

wind•shield /'wɪnd,ʃiyld, 'wɪn-/ n. [count] a shield of glass above the dashboard of an automobile.

'wind-,swept /wɪnd/ adj. open or exposed to the wind: a windswept beach.

wind•y /'wɪndiy/ adj., **-i•er, -i•est. 1.** accompanied by or having wind: a windy March day. **2.** characterized by or using pompous, empty talk: a long, windy speech.

wine /wayn/ n. [noncount] [count] the fermented juice of grapes, or sometimes of other fruits, used esp. as an alcoholic beverage.

win•er•y /'waynəriy/ n. [count], pl. **-er•ies.** an establishment where wine is made.

wing /wɪŋ/ n. [count] **1.** either of the two limbs or similar parts of birds, insects, and bats that are specially designed for flight. **2.** one of a pair of usually long, flat parts of an aircraft that stick out from its body and provide lift. **3.** a part of a building that sticks out from a central or main part. **4.** an often extreme group or faction within an organization: the radical wing of the party. **5.** Usually, **wings.** [plural] the space at the side of a stage, usually not seen by the audience: We stood in the wings. —v. **6.** to travel on or as if on wings: [~ + obj]: Birds wing their way south during the winter. [no obj]: birds winging south.

wink /wɪŋk/ v. **1.** to close and open (one eye) quickly, often as a hint or signal: [no obj]: She winked at me to let me know she understood. [~ + obj]: He winked his eye. —n. [count] **2.** an act of winking. **3.** an instant: in the wink of an eye. **4.** the least bit: She didn't sleep a wink.

win•ner /'wɪnər/ n. [count] one that wins; victor.

win•ning /'wɪnɪŋ/ n. **1.** [noncount] the act of one that wins. **2.** Usually, **winnings.** [plural] something won, esp. money. —adj. [usually: before a noun] **3.** pleasing or pleasant: a winning personality.

win•o /'waynow/ n. [count], pl. **-os.** a person who is addicted to wine.

win•some /'wɪnsəm/ adj. sweetly or innocently charming: a winsome child; a winsome smile.

win•ter /'wɪntər/ n. **1.** the cold season between autumn and spring: [noncount]: to ski all winter. [count]: harsh winters. —v. [no obj] **2.** to spend the winter: to winter in Florida.

win•ter•ize /'wɪntə,rayz/ v. [~ + obj], **-ized, -iz•ing.** to prepare (a house, car, etc.) to withstand cold weather: to winterize the house by adding insulation.

win•ter•time /'wɪntər,taym/ n. [noncount] the season of winter.

win•try /'wɪntriy/ also **wintery** /'wɪntəriy/ adj., **-tri•er** also **-i•er, -tri•est** also **-i•est.** of or like winter: a cold, wintry day.

wipe /wayp/ v., **wiped, wip•ing,** n. —v. [~ + obj] **1.** to clean or dry by patting or rubbing: to wipe the furniture clean; to wipe the dishes. **2.** to remove by or as if by rubbing: She wiped the tears from her eyes. **3. wipe out,** to destroy completely: They wiped out the supply depots. The crews wiped them out. —n. [count] **4.** an act of wiping. —'**wip•er,** n. [count]

wire /wayᵊr/ n., adj., v., **wired, wir•ing.** —n. **1.** a thin, slender, threadlike piece of metal: [noncount]: a piece of wire. [count]: copper wires. **2.** [count] a length of such metal used to conduct current in electrical, cable, telegraph, or telephone systems. **3. a.** [count] a telegram: Send him a wire. **b.** [noncount] telegraph: Send the message by wire. —v. [~ + obj] **4.** to equip or furnish with wire: to wire a building with new electrical outlets. **5.** to send (a message) to (someone) by telegraph: to wire a message to headquarters; to wire her the news. —Idiom. **6. down to the wire,** to the very last moment or the very end. **7. under the wire,** just within the limit or deadline.

wire•less /'wayᵊrlɪs/ n. [count] Chiefly Brit. a radio.

wire•tap /'wayᵊr,tæp/ n., v., **-tapped, -tap•ping.** —n. [count] **1.** an act or instance of making a secret connection to a telephone or telegraph wire in order to intercept conversations and gain information. —v. **2.** to listen in on by means of a wiretap: [~ + obj]: to wiretap a conversation; to wiretap a telephone. [no obj]: The detectives were busy wiretapping.

wir•y /'wayᵊriy/ adj., **-i•er, -i•est.** (of a person's body) lean, supple, and strong.

Wis. or **Wisc.,** an abbreviation of: Wisconsin.

wis•dom /'wɪzdəm/ n. [noncount] the quality or state of being wise.

'wisdom ,tooth, n. [count] the third molar, a tooth in the back of the mouth, on each side of the upper and lower jaws.

wise /wayz/ adj., **wis•er, wis•est,** v., **wised, wis•ing.** —adj. **1.** having or showing understanding and good judgment, or deep knowledge and learning: a wise decision; a wise proverb; a wise teacher. It was not very wise of him to be rude. —v. **2. wise up,** Slang. to (cause to) become informed: He finally wised up to their scheme. [~ + obj]: They wised him up finally. —'**wise•ly,** adv.

-wise, a suffix meaning: in a particular manner, position, or direction (clockwise); with reference to (timewise).

wise•crack /'wayz,kræk/ n. [count] a clever, sarcastic, or impolite remark.

'wise ,guy, n. [count] Informal. a person who annoyingly pretends to know more than he or she does.

wish /wɪʃ/ v. [~ + obj] **1.** to want; desire; express a desire for: I wish to stay here. I wish him to obey. She wished for peace in the world. **2.** to desire (a person or thing) to be as stated: We wished the matter (to be) settled. We wished that the matter would be settled. **3.** to bid, as in greeting, or to express a desire with respect to another's circumstances: I wished her a good morning. We wished her well. **4. wish on,** to desire to convey (something unwanted or bad) to another: I wouldn't wish this awful weather on my worst enemy. —n. [count] **5.** an act or instance of wishing. **6.** something wished: *Her last wish was to see her home country.*

wish•ful /'wɪffəl/ *adj.* based on a wish rather than reality: *wishful thinking.*

wish•y-wash•y /'wɪʃiy,wɒʃiy, -,wɔʃiy/ *adj.* lacking strength or character: *a wishy-washy leader.*

wisp /wɪsp/ *n.* [*count*] **1.** a thin lock of hair. **2.** a thin puff or streak, as of smoke. **3.** a person or thing that is small or delicate. —'**wisp•y,** *adj.,* -i•er, -i•est.

wist•ful /'wɪstfəl/ *adj.* having or showing thoughtful, sometimes sad, wishing or longing: *a wistful look.* —'**wist•ful•ly,** *adv.* —'**wist•ful• ness,** *n.* [*noncount*]

wit /wɪt/ *n.* **1.** [*noncount*] keen intelligence. **2.** [*noncount*] the ability to be clever in an amusing way. **3.** [*count*] a person having or noted for this ability. **4.** Usually, **wits.** [*plural*] **a.** powers of intelligent observation or perception: *to live by one's wits.* **b.** normal mental powers: *She was scared out of her wits.* —**Idiom. 5. at one's wit's** or **wits' end,** drained of all ideas or mental resources. **6. keep (** or **have) one's wits about one,** to be able to think clearly, as in an emergency.

witch /wɪtʃ/ *n.* [*count*] **1.** a person who is believed to practice magic, esp. black magic. **2.** an ugly or nasty woman.

witch•craft /'wɪtʃ,kræft/ *n.* [*noncount*] the art or practices of a witch; magic, esp. evil magic; sorcery.

with /wɪθ, wɪð/ *prep.* **1.** accompanied by: *I will go with you.* **2.** characterized by or having; in a manner showing: *a person with initiative; He worked with diligence.* **3.** by means of; using: *I'll cut the meat with a knife.* **4.** in comparison to: *How does their plan compare with ours?* **5.** in regard to; in (some) relation to: *They were very pleased with the gift. She has already dealt with the problem.* **6.** owing to; because of: *He was shaking with rage.* **7.** from: *She hated to part with her book when it was bedtime.* **8.** against: *Don't fight with your sister.* **9.** in the keeping of: *We left our cat with a friend during our vacation.* **10.** in the judgment of: *Her argument carried weight with the trustees.* **11.** at the same time as or immediately after: *With that last remark, she left.* **12.** of the same opinion as or, in any case, supporting: *Are you with me on this issue?* **13.** in the same household as: *He lives with his parents.*

with•draw /wɪð'drɔ, wɪθ-/ *v.,* -drew, -drawn, -draw•ing. **1.** to draw back, away, to the side, or aside: [~ + *obj*]: *The general withdrew his army.* [*no obj*]: *He withdrew to another room.* **2.** [~ + *obj*] to remove, retract, or recall: *I withdraw my objection to your proposal.* **3.** to remove oneself from participation, as in an activity: [*no obj*]: *He withdrew from the contest.* [~ + *obj*]: *He withdrew himself from the contest.* **4.** [~ + *obj*] to take (money) from a place of deposit.

with•draw•al /wɪð'drɔəl, wɪθ-/ *n.* **1.** the act of withdrawing or state of being withdrawn: [*count*]: *a sudden withdrawal.* [*noncount*]: *a feeling of emotional withdrawal.* **2.** [*count*] something that is withdrawn, as a sum of money from a bank account. **3.** [*noncount*] the process of ceasing to use of an addictive drug: *suffering from symptoms of withdrawal.*

with•drawn /wɪð'drɔn, wɪθ-/ *v.* **1.** pp. of WITH-DRAW. —*adj.* **2.** shy: *a quiet, withdrawn child.*

with•er /'wɪðər/ *v.* to (cause to) shrivel or fade: [*no obj*]: *The plants are withering in the heat.* [~

+ *obj*]: *The heat has withered the entire corn crop.*

with•hold /wɪθ'howld, wɪð-/ *v.* [~ + *obj*], -held, -hold•ing. to hold back; keep from giving or granting: *He withheld his support of the project.*

with•in /wɪð'ɪn, wɪθ-/ *prep.* **1.** in or into the interior of; inside: *The noise came from within the house.* **2.** subject to the limits of; not beyond: *to live within one's income.* **3.** in the field, sphere, or scope of: *Keep that within the family. It's not within my power.* —*adv.* **4.** in or into an interior or inner part: *They proceeded within.* **5.** in the mind, heart, or soul; inwardly: *to listen to the voice within.*

with•out /wɪð'awt, wɪθ-/ *prep.* **1.** with no or none of; lacking: *He did it without help.* **2.** not accompanied by: *Don't go without me.* **3.** at, on, or to the outside of: *both within and without the city.* —*adv.* **4.** outside. **5.** outdoors. **6.** lacking something implied or understood: *For years they were too poor and simply had to do without.*

with•stand /wɪθ'stænd, wɪð-/ *v.* [~ + *obj*], -stood, -stand•ing. to resist or oppose, esp. successfully: *I could hardly withstand the pain.*

wit•ness /'wɪtnɪs/ *v.* [~ + *obj*] **1.** to see, hear, or know on account of personal presence and experience: *to witness a crime.* **2.** to be present at and show this by writing one's signature: *He witnessed her will.* —*n.* **3.** [*count*] a person who has witnessed something, esp. one who is able to declare what has taken place: *a witness to the accident.* **4.** [*count*] a person who gives testimony, as in a court of law. **5.** [*noncount*] something serving as evidence: *His lined, gray face is witness (*or *bears witness) to his suffering.*

wit•ti•cism /'wɪtə,sɪzəm/ *n.* [*count*] a witty, clever, or funny remark.

wit•ty /'wɪtiy/ *adj.,* -ti•er, -ti•est. having or showing wit; amusingly clever: *a witty fellow; a witty remark.* —**wit•ti•ly** /'wɪtḷiy/, *adv.* —'**wit• ti•ness,** *n.* [*noncount*]

wives /wayvz/ *n.* pl. of WIFE.

wiz•ard /'wɪzərd/ *n.* [*count*] **1.** a magician or sorcerer. **2.** a person of amazing skill, ability, or accomplishment: *She's a wizard at chemistry.* —**wiz•ard•ry** /'wɪzərdriy/, *n.* [*noncount*]

wk., an abbreviation of: week.

w/o, an abbreviation of: without.

wob•ble /'wɒbəl/ *v.,* -bled, -bling, *n.* —*v.* **1.** [*no obj*] to move unsteadily with a side-to-side motion: *The unbalanced car wheel wobbled.* **2.** to (cause to) be unsteady; (cause to) tremble: [*no obj*]: *The table wobbled on its uneven legs.* [~ + *obj*]: *You're wobbling the table.* —*n.* [*count*] **3.** a wobbling movement. —'**wob•bly,** *adj.,* -bli•er, -bli•est.

woe /wow/ *n.* **1.** [*noncount*] great distress or trouble: *a life of woe.* **2.** [*count*] a cause of such distress or trouble; an affliction: *the woes of life.*

woe•ful /'wowfəl/ *adj.* **1.** full of woe; wretched: *a woeful situation.* **2.** of poor quality; terrible: *a woeful bunch of job applicants.* —'**woe•ful•ly,** *adv.: a woefully inadequate diet.*

wok /wɒk/ *n.* [*count*] a large, bowl-shaped pan used esp. in cooking Chinese food.

woke /wowk/ *v.* a pt. of WAKE[1].

wok•en /'wowkən/ *v.* a pp. of WAKE[1].

wolf /wʊlf/ *n., pl.* **wolves** (wʊlvz), *v.,* **wolfed, wolf•ing.** —*n.* [*count*] **1.** a meat-eating animal resembling and related to the dog. —*v.* [~ + *obj*] **2.** to eat very greedily or quickly: *He wolfed (down) his food.*

W

wom·an /'wʊmən/ *n., pl.* **wom·en** /'wɪmɪn/. **1.** [*count*] an adult female person. **2.** [*noncount*] women thought of as a group; womankind. —*adj.* [*before a noun*] **3.** female: *a woman plumber; a woman astronaut.*

-woman, a combining form of WOMAN: (*chairwoman; spokeswoman*).

wom·an·hood /'wʊmən,hʊd/ *n.* [*noncount*] the state or time of being a woman.

wom·an·ize /'wʊmə,nayz/ *v.* [*no obj*], **-ized, -iz·ing.** to pursue or chase after women regularly. —**'wom·an,iz·er,** *n.* [*count*]

wom·an·kind /'wʊmən,kaynd/ *n.* [*noncount*] women thought of as a group and as distinguished from men.

wom·an·ly /'wʊmənliy/ *adj.* having qualities traditionally thought of as being typical of women; feminine.

womb /wuwm/ *n.* [*count*] UTERUS.

'women's liber'ation, *n.* [*noncount*] a political movement to gain rights and opportunities for women equal to those of men.

won /wʌn/ *v.* pt. and pp. of WIN.

won·der /'wʌndər/ *v.* **1.** to think about and ask oneself about something; to be curious about: [*no obj*]: *He says he didn't do it, but I still wonder.* [*~ + clause*]: *I wonder what she's doing tonight.* **2.** [*no obj*] to be filled with awe or amazement; marvel: *I have often wondered at her cleverness.* **3.** [*~ + clause*] This word is sometimes used to introduce a request: *I wonder if you would help me.* —*n.* **4.** [*noncount*] a feeling of amazement, awe, or reverent admiration: *We were filled with wonder when we saw the great cathedral.* **5.** [*count*] a cause or source of surprise, awe, or admiration: *one of the wonders of the ancient world; a wonder he wasn't killed.*

won·der·ful /'wʌndərfəl/ *adj.* **1.** excellent; marvelous: *a wonderful day; a wonderful time at the party.* **2.** causing wonder; extraordinary: *a scene wonderful to behold.* —**'won·der·ful·ly,** *adv.*

won·drous /'wʌndrəs/ *adj.* wonderful; remarkable.

won't /wownt/ contraction of *will not.*

woo /wuw/ *v.* [*~ + obj*] **1.** to seek the love of, esp. with a view to marriage: *He wooed his lady love.* **2.** to seek to persuade (a person, group, etc.), as to do something: *to woo the voters with promises.*

wood /wʊd/ *n.* **1.** [*noncount*] [*count*] the hard, fiberlike substance that makes up most of the stem and branches of a tree or shrub beneath the bark. **2.** [*count*] Often, **woods,** [*plural*] a thick growth of trees; forest. —*Idiom.* **3. out of the woods,** no longer in a dangerous or difficult situation; safe.

wood·chuck /'wʊd,tʃʌk/ *n.* [*count*] GROUNDHOG.

wood·en /'wʊdn/ *adj.* **1.** made of wood: *a large wooden crate.* **2.** stiff, ungainly, or awkward: *walking with slow, wooden steps.*

wood·land /'wʊd,lænd, -lənd/ *n.* [*noncount*] [*count*] land covered with woods or trees.

wood·peck·er /'wʊd,pɛkər/ *n.* [*count*] a climbing bird with a bill like a chisel that it hammers repeatedly into the wood of trees in search of insects.

wood·wind /'wʊd,wɪnd/ *n.* [*count*] **1.** a musical wind instrument, as a flute, clarinet, oboe, or bassoon. **2. woodwinds,** [*plural*] the section of an orchestra or band comprising these instruments.

wood·work /'wʊd,wɜrk/ *n.* [*noncount*] **1.** ob-

jects or parts made of wood, as furniture. **2.** interior wooden fittings, as doors or moldings, in a house.

wood·y /'wʊdiy/ *adj.*, **-i·er, -i·est.** having many woods or a great deal of wooded area; wooded.

woof /wʊf/ *n.* [*count*] **1.** the bark of a dog, esp. when gruff and low-pitched. —*v.* [*no obj*] **2.** to make this sound.

wool /wʊl/ *n.* [*noncount*] **1.** the fine, soft, curly hair that forms the fleece of some animals, esp. sheep. **2.** yarn, a fabric, or a garment of wool.

wool·en /'wʊlən/ *adj.* **1.** of, made of, or consisting of wool. —*n.* **2. woolens,** [*plural*] wool cloth or clothing.

wool·ly or **wool·y** /'wʊliy/ *adj.*, **-li·er** or **-i·er, -li·est** or **-i·est.** **1.** of or resembling wool. **2.** unclear; confused: *woolly thinking.*

word /wɜrd/ *n.* **1.** [*count*] a meaningful unit of a language, consisting of one or more spoken sounds or their written representation: *"A," "bicycle," and "speedy" are words in English.* **2.** [*count*] something said; an expression or utterance: *a word of warning.* **3.** [*count*] a short talk: *May I have a word with you?* **4.** [*one's + ~*] assurance or promise: *He gave his word (that) he'd be on time. She keeps her word.* **5.** [*noncount*] news; information: *When did you receive word of his death?* **6.** [*count*] a command that has authority: *When the sergeant gives the word, begin firing.* —*v.* [*~ + obj*] **7.** to express in words: *See if you can word this statement more clearly.* —*Idiom.* **8. eat one's words,** to acknowledge error in a previous statement, esp. with humility. **9. from the word go,** from the beginning. **10. in so many words,** in clear, exact terms; explicitly: *She didn't say so in so many words, but I think she likes you.* **11. put in a (good) word for,** to speak favorably on behalf of. **12. take the words out of someone's mouth,** to say exactly what another person was about to say.

word·ing /'wɜrdɪŋ/ *n.* [*count*] choice of words; phrasing: *The wording of the law is unclear.*

'word of 'mouth, *n.* [*noncount*] oral communication as opposed to written: *The rumor spread rapidly by word of mouth.*

'word ,processing, *n.* [*noncount*] the automated production and storage of documents using computers, electronic printers, and text-editing software. —**'word ,processor,** *n.* [*count*]

word·y /'wɜrdiy/ *adj.*, **-i·er, -i·est.** showing or making use of too many words: *a wordy speech; a wordy speaker.*

wore /wɔr/ *v.* pt. of WEAR.

work /wɜrk/ *n., v.*, **worked** or (*Archaic except in some senses, esp.* 13) **wrought** /rɔt/, **work·ing.** —*n.* **1.** [*noncount*] the use of effort or action to produce or accomplish something; labor: *Cleaning the whole house is a lot of work.* **2.** [*noncount*] a task or something to do or be done: *The students finished their work in class.* **3.** [*noncount*] productive activity, esp. a job or employment: *He's been looking for work ever since he graduated.* **4.** [*noncount*] a place of employment: *Don't phone me at work.* **5.** the result of exertion, labor, or activity, as a building, book, work of art, etc.: [*count*]: *the collected works of Robert Louis Stevenson; Bach's musical works.* [*noncount*]: *a shoemaker who takes pride in his work.* —*v.* **6.** [*no obj*] to do work: *The mechanic had to work for two hours on the car.* **7.** to be employed (at): [*no obj*]: *She works at a factory.* [*~ + obj*]: *He's working two jobs.* **8.** [*~ + obj*] to cause to work: *That new boss works his employees hard.*

9. [*no obj*] to be functional, as a machine; operate: *He got the machine to work again.* **10.** [*no obj*] to prove effective: *This plan works.* **11.** to (cause to) come to be, as by repeated movement: [*no obj*]: *The nails worked loose.* [~ + *obj*]: *The nails worked themselves loose.* **12.** to have an effect (on), as on a person's feelings: [*no obj*]: *Don't try crying; that doesn't work on him.* [~ + *obj*]: *Diet and exercise worked wonders on him.* **13.** [~ + *obj*] to make or fashion by work: *to work a piece of sculpture with one's hands.* **14.** [~ + *obj*] to make (one's way) with effort: *We worked our way slowly through the crowd.* **15.** [~ + *obj*] *Informal.* to greet and make conversation with a group of people, so as to make a good impression or develop friends, contacts, or supporters: *She worked the crowd. He's good at working the (people in the) room.* **16. work in** or **into,** to include after some effort: *Try to work me into your schedule.* **17. work off,** to get rid of: *to work off a few pounds by exercising* or *to work a few pounds off.* **18. work out, a.** to solve, as a problem: *to work out a problem between friends; We can work it out.* **b.** to prove effective or suitable: *Their marriage just didn't work out. Things have a way of working themselves out.* **c.** to exercise or train, esp. in an athletic sport. **19. work through,** to deal with successfully: *to work through one's problems.* **20. work up, a.** to stir the feelings of; excite: *to work up the crowd into a frenzy; to work the crowd up.* **b.** to develop by exercise, effort, or exertion: *to work up a sweat.* —*Idiom.* **21. in the works,** in preparation: *His new book is still in the works.*

work•a•ble /'wɜrkəbəl/ *adj.* that can be made use of; practical: *a workable plan.*

work•a•hol•ic /ˌwɜrkə'hɔlɪk, -'hɒlɪk/ *n.* [*count*] a person who has a powerful need to work.

work•er /'wɜrkər/ *n.* [*count*] **1.** one that works. **2.** a laborer or employee.

work•ing /'wɜrkɪŋ/ *n.* [*count*] **1.** operation; activity: *the complicated workings of his mind.* —*adj.* **2.** doing or engaged in work for a living; employed: *working men and women.* **3.** related to or organized for conducting work: *a working lunch.* **4.** adequate for usual or customary needs: *a working knowledge of Spanish.*

work•man /'wɜrkmən/ *n.* [*count*], *pl.* -men. a man employed or skilled in manual, mechanical, or industrial work.

work•man•ship /'wɜrkmənˌʃɪp/ *n.* [*noncount*] **1.** the art or skill of a workman. **2.** the quality of work done: *Look at the excellent workmanship of this desk.*

work•out /'wɜrkˌawt/ *n.* [*count*] a session of practice designed to keep up or improve one's physical ability.

work•shop /'wɜrkˌʃɒp/ *n.* [*count*] **1.** a room or building in which work, esp. mechanical work or the work of a craftsperson, is carried on. **2.** a seminar or similar meeting designed to explore a subject or develop a skill or technique: *a workshop to improve language skills.*

world /wɜrld/ *n.* **1.** [*singular; the* + ~] the earth when it is considered as a planet: *the happiest man in the world.* **2.** [*singular; the* + ~] a particular part or division of the earth: *the Western world; the ancient world.* **3.** [*singular; the* + ~] people in general; human society generally: *The world watched with sorrow. That's not the way the world works.* **4.** [*count*] a class or group of people with common interests: *the literary world.* **5.** [*count*] an area, sphere, realm, or do-

main of activity or existence: *the world of dreams; the world of sports.* **6.** [*count*] one of the general groupings of physical nature: *the animal world.* **7.** Often, **worlds.** [*plural;* ~ + *of* + *noncount noun*] a great deal: *a world of trouble on my mind.* —*Idiom.* **8. in the world,** (used to intensify a question): *How in the world will you get home?* **9. out of this world,** extraordinary; wonderful: *The dinner was out of this world.*

world•ly /'wɜrldliy/ *adj.,* **-li•er, -li•est. 1.** of or concerned with this (material) world rather than heaven, an afterlife, or spiritual life in general. **2.** experienced; sophisticated: *a worldly diplomat and traveler.*

world•wide /'wɜrld'wayd/ *adj.* **1.** throughout the world: *a worldwide oil shortage.* —*adv.* **2.** everywhere in the world: *The shortage was felt worldwide.*

'World 'Wide 'Web, *n.* [*noncount*] a system of linked documents, being a branch of the Internet.

worm /wɜrm/ *n.* [*count*] **1.** a long, soft-bodied, legless creature without a backbone, as the earthworm. **2.** a low, worthless, contemptible person. —*v.* [~ + *obj*] **3.** to creep, crawl, or move slowly, as into a tight or small space: *She wormed herself through the tunnel.* **4.** to get by persistent or indirect effort: *He wormed the secret out of his sister.*

worn /wɔrn/ *v.* **1.** pp. of WEAR. —*adj.* **2.** lessened or lowered in value or usefulness because of wear or use: *an old, worn jacket.*

'worn-'out, *adj.* **1.** worn or used beyond repair. **2.** having no more energy or strength; exhausted.

wor•ried /'wɜriyd, 'wʌr-/ *adj.* having or showing worry; concerned; anxious.

wor•ri•some /'wɜriysəm, 'wʌr-/ *adj.* **1.** causing worry: *worrisome unemployment.* **2.** often worrying: *worrisome parents.*

wor•ry /'wɜriy, 'wʌr-/ *v.,* **-ried, -ry•ing,** *n., pl.* **-ries.** —*v.* **1.** to (cause to) feel or be uneasy or anxious: [*no obj*]: *He worries about his kids.* [~ + *obj*]: *The high cost of college worries them. It worries me that you might not pass the test. It worries me to think of your going home alone every night.* —*n.* **2.** [*noncount*] uneasiness or anxiety. **3.** [*count*] a cause of worry: *Money is their biggest worry.* —*'wor•ri•er, n.* [*count*]

worse /wɜrs/ *adj.,* *comparative of* **bad** *and* **ill. 1.** bad or ill to a greater extent; inferior: *Your score is worse on this test than on yesterday's.* **2.** in poorer health: *The patient is worse today.* —*n.* [*noncount; usually: the* + ~] **3.** something that is worse: *a turn for the worse.* —*adv.* **4.** in a worse manner. **5.** to a greater degree.

wors•en /'wɜrsən/ *v.* to (cause to) become worse: [*no obj*]: *The economy has worsened.* [~ + *obj*]: *Those measures will worsen the situation.*

wor•ship /'wɜrʃɪp/ *n., v.,* **-shiped** or **-shipped, -ship•ing** or **-ship•ping.** —*n.* [*noncount*] **1.** reverence offered to or expressed for God, a sacred personage, or a sacred object, as at a religious service or in a devotional exercise. **2.** a feeling of strong, adoring reverence or regard: *hero worship.* —*v.* **3.** to give worship (to): [~ + *obj*]: *to worship God.* [*no obj*]: *They worship at church.* **4.** [~ + *obj*] to adore or idolize, as a person or celebrity. —*'wor•ship•er, n.* [*count*] —*'wor•ship•ful, adj.*

worst /wɜrst/ *adj.,* *superlative of* **bad** *and* **ill. 1.** bad or ill in the most extreme degree: *the worst repair job I've ever seen; the worst drivers in the country.* —*n.* [*noncount; usually: the* + ~] **2.** something, as a circumstance or outcome, that is the most unsatisfactory or unpleasant possible: *Prepare for the worst.* —*adv.* **3.** in the worst manner. **4.** to the greatest degree. —*Idiom.* **5.** at **(the) worst,** under the worst conditions. **6.** **worst comes to worst,** if the very worst happens.

worth /wɜrθ/ *prep.* **1.** good or important enough to justify: *That place is definitely worth visiting.* **2.** having a value of: *That vase is worth 20 dollars.* —*n.* [*noncount*] **3.** excellence, as of character; merit: *a man of worth.* **4.** usefulness or importance, as to the world, to a person, or for a purpose. **5.** value, as in money. **6.** a quantity of something of a specified value: *He bought 50 cents' worth of candy.*

worth•less /'wɜrθlɪs/ *adj.* without worth; having no value: *Those promises were worthless.* —'**worth•less•ly,** *adv.* —'**worth•less•ness,** *n.* [*noncount*]

worth•while /'wɜrθ'hwayl, -'wayl/ *adj.* worthy of the time, work, trouble, or money spent.

wor•thy /'wɜrðiy/ *adj.,* **-thi•er, -thi•est. 1.** having merit, character, or value: *a worthy opponent.* **2.** deserving: *an effort worthy of praise.* —'**wor• thi•ness,** *n.* [*noncount*]

-worthy, an adjective suffix meaning: deserving of or fit for: (*newsworthy; trustworthy*); capable of travel in or on: (*seaworthy*).

would /wʊd/ *unstressed* wəd/ *auxiliary (modal) verb* [~ + *root form of a verb*] **1.** the past tense of WILL[1]. **2.** (used to express the future when a past tense verb appears in a clause before it): *He said (that) he would go tomorrow.* **3.** (used in place of *will* to soften a statement or question): *Would you be so kind as to move your bag?* **4.** (used to express an action that was habitual in the past): *Years ago, we would take the train every morning.* **5.** (used to express the wish or intention of someone): *Health experts would have us all eat whole grains.* **6.** (used to express lack of certainty): *It would appear that he is guilty.* **7.** (used to show that an action, etc., depends or depended in the past on a condition (having) been fulfilled): *He would come if he had enough money. I would have been on time if the train had not been late.* **8. would like,** (used to express one's desire to do something): *I would like to go next year.*

would•n't /'wʊdnt/ contraction of *would not.*

wound[1] /wuwnd/ *n.* [*count*] **1.** an injury, usually involving the cutting or tearing of skin or tissue. **2.** an injury or hurt to feelings, emotions, or reputation. —*v.* [~ + *obj*] **3.** to inflict a wound upon; injure.

wound[2] /wawnd/ *v.* a pt. and pp. of WIND[2].

wove /wowv/ *v.* a pt. and pp. of WEAVE.

wo•ven /'wowvən/ *v.* a pp. of WEAVE.

wow /waw/ *interj.* (used to show surprise, wonder, or pleasure): *Wow, what a beautiful sunset!*

wran•gle /'ræŋgəl/ *v.,* **-gled, -gling,** *n.* —*v.* [*no obj*] **1.** to argue or quarrel, esp. noisily or angrily: *The kids wrangled over who should get to sit near the window.* —*n.* [*count*] **2.** a noisy or angry quarrel.

wrap /ræp/ *v.,* **wrapped, wrap•ping,** *n.* —*v.* **1.** [~ + *obj* + *on/around* + *obj*] to wind, fold, or bind (something) around as a covering: *He wrapped a bandage around his finger.* **2.** [~ + *obj*] to enclose and make fast within a covering, as of paper: *She wrapped the gifts and put them under the Christmas tree.* **3.** [~ + *obj*] to surround, envelop, or hide: *He wrapped her in his*

arms. —*Idiom.* **4. wrapped up in,** totally absorbed in: *He was wrapped up in his work.*

wrap•per /'ræpər/ *n.* [*count*] something in which a thing, as candy or a newspaper, is wrapped.

wrap•ping /'ræpɪŋ/ *n.* [*count*] Often, **wrappings.** [*plural*] the covering in which something, as a gift, is wrapped.

wrath /ræθ, rɑθ/ *n.* [*noncount*] fierce anger; rage. —'**wrath•ful,** *adj.*

wreak /riyk/ *v.* [~ + *obj*] to bring about; cause: *The storm wreaked damage on the whole coastline.*

wreath /riyθ/ *n.* [*count*], *pl.* **wreaths** /riyðz, riy θs/. a circular band, as of flowers, used for decoration.

wreathe /riyð/ *v.* [~ + *obj*], **wreathed, wreath•ing. 1.** to make a circle around (something) or decorate with or as if with a wreath. **2.** to surround or envelop: *a face wreathed in smiles.*

wreck /rɛk/ *n.* [*count*] **1.** a building, vehicle, or object that has been destroyed or greatly damaged. **2.** a person of ruined physical or mental health. —*v.* [~ + *obj*] **3.** to destroy; ruin: *I wrecked the car.*

wreck•age /'rɛkɪdʒ/ *n.* [*noncount*] the remains of something that has been wrecked.

wren /rɛn/ *n.* [*count*] a small songbird with streaked or spotted brown-gray coloring.

wrench /rɛntʃ/ *v.* [~ + *obj*] **1.** to pull, jerk, move, or force with or as with a violent twisting motion: *He wrenched the door open.* **2.** to injure (the ankle, knee, etc.) by a sudden, violent twist. **3.** to twist or distort the meaning of (words, facts, etc.).: *The reporter wrenched my words out of context.* —*n.* [*count*] **4.** a sudden, violent twist: *a wrench of the ankle.* **5.** a sharp, distressing feeling of anguish or pain, as one caused by separation: *Her death was a wrench to the family.* **6.** a tool for gripping and turning or twisting a bolt, nut, etc.

wres•tle /'rɛsəl/ *v.,* **-tled, -tling. 1.** to compete (with) in the sport of wrestling: [*no obj*]: *He wrestled for his high school team.* [~ + *obj*]: *She wrestled the best opponents in each school.* **2.** to fight or struggle (with) by holding, throwing, or forcing an attacker to the ground: [~ + *obj*]: *He wrestled the mugger to the ground.* [*no obj*]: *They wrestled until one of them fell.* **3.** [*no obj*] to struggle (with) in order to overcome: *He wrestled with the problem.* —'**wres•tler,** *n.* [*count*]

wretch /rɛtʃ/ *n.* [*count*] a very unfortunate or unhappy person.

wretch•ed /'rɛtʃɪd/ *adj.* **1.** characterized by or causing misery and sorrow: *living in wretched conditions.* **2.** miserable or unhappy: *She felt wretched for having betrayed her friends.*

wrig•gle /'rɪgəl/ *v.,* **-gled, -gling,** *n.* —*v.* **1.** to twist from one side to the other: [*no obj*]: *The child was wriggling in his seat.* [~ + *obj*]: *to wriggle one's toes.* **2.** to move along by twisting and turning the body, as a worm: [*no obj*]: *The worm wriggled in the dirt.* [~ + *obj*]: *He wriggled his way through the narrow tunnel.* **3. wrig• gle out of,** to escape from or avoid: *He tried to wriggle out of doing the work.* —*n.* [*count*] **4.** the act or motion of wriggling.

wring /rɪŋ/ *v.* [~ + *obj*], **wrung** /rʌŋ/, **wring• ing. 1.** to squeeze or twist (esp. the neck) forcibly. **2.** to twist, squeeze, or compress (something) in order to force out (a liquid): *to wring (out) the wet washcloth; to wring the washcloth (out); to wring (out) the water from the towel; to* *wring the water out of the towel.* **3.** to force out as if by squeezing: *They captured the spy and wrung the secret password out of him.* **4.** to hold or clasp tightly, as one's hands or another's hand(s), usually with a twisting motion in distress or in greeting: *She wrung her hands in anxiety.*

wrin•kle /'rɪŋkəl/ *n., v.,* **-kled, -kling.** —*n.* [*count*] **1.** a small crease in the skin, as from aging. **2.** a slight ridge in a fabric, as from folding. —*v.* **3.** to (cause to) become full of wrinkles: [*no obj*]: *This fabric wrinkles easily.* [~ + *obj*]: *He wrinkled his forehead by frowning.* —'**wrin•kly,** *adj.,* **-kli•er, -kli•est.**

wrist /rɪst/ *n.* [*count*] the joint between the forearm and the hand.

wrist•watch /'rɪst,wætʃ/ *n.* [*count*] a watch attached to a strap or band worn about the wrist.

writ /rɪt/ *n.* [*count*] a court order directing a person to do or not do something.

write /rayt/ *v.,* **wrote** /rowt/, **writ•ten** /'rɪtn̩/, **writ•ing.** —*v.* **1.** to form (letters, words, etc.), esp. on paper, with a pen or pencil: [~ + *obj*]: *He learned to write his name.* [*no obj*]: *to learn to read and write.* **2.** to express or compose in writing, as an essay, play, musical work, etc.: [~ + *obj*]: *to write a short story.* [*no obj*]: *She writes for magazines.* **3.** to communicate with (someone) by (a letter): [~ + *obj*]: *I wrote her about your troubles. She wrote me a thank-you note. I wrote (her) that you were ill. She wrote (me) to say thank you.* [*no obj*]: *I wrote to her.* **4.** [~ + *obj*] to fill in the blank spaces of (a printed form) with writing: *to write a check.* **5. write down,** to set down in writing; record; note: *He wrote down his ideas. He writes his ideas down.* **6. write in,** to vote for (a candidate not listed on the ballot) by writing his or her name on the ballot: *to write in the name of the candidate; to write the name in on the ballot.* **7. write up,** to put into writing, esp. in full detail: *to write up a report of the incident; He knew he had to write it up before lunch.*

writ•er /'raytər/ *n.* [*count*] a person engaged in writing, esp. as an occupation.

writhe /rayð/ *v.* [*no obj*], **writhed, writh•ing.** to twist and turn, as in pain.

writ•ing /'raytɪŋ/ *n.* **1.** [*noncount*] the act of one who writes, or the profession of one who writes books, newspaper articles, etc. **2.** [*count; usually: writings*] written matter, esp. a literary work: *a collection of her writings.* **3.** [*noncount*] written form: *Put the agreement in writing.* **4.** [*noncount*] handwriting.

writ•ten /'rɪtn̩/ *v.* pp. of WRITE.

wrong /rɔŋ, rɒŋ/ *adj.* **1.** being in error; mistaken; not correct: *a wrong answer; a wrong (telephone) number.* **2.** [*be* + ~] not in agreement with what is morally right; evil; bad: *Telling a lie is wrong.* [*It* + *be* + ~ + *to* + *verb*]: *It's wrong to tell a lie.* **3.** not proper; unsuitable: *Those are definitely the wrong shoes for that dress.* —*n.* [*count*] **4.** something improper, immoral, unjust, or harmful: *many wrongs committed against them.* —*adv.* **5.** in a wrong manner: *I did it all wrong. Did I pronounce your name wrong?* —*v.* [~ + *obj*] **6.** to do wrong to; harm. —*Idiom.* **7. go wrong, a.** to go badly; fail: *Everything went wrong with my computer after I installed that new program.* **b.** to follow an undesirable or evil course: *Bad friends caused him to go wrong.* **8. in the wrong,** at fault; in error. —'**wrong•ly,** *adv.*: *She was wrongly accused.*

wrong•do•er /'rɔŋ,duwər, -'duw-, 'rɒŋ-/ *n.* [*count*] a person who does wrong, esp. a sinner or a criminal. —'**wrong,do•ing,** *n.* [*noncount*]

wrong•ful /'rɔŋfəl, 'rɒŋ-/ *adj.* not just or legal. —'**wrong•ful•ly,** *adv.*: *wrongfully accused.*

wrote /rowt/ *v.* pt. of WRITE.

'**wrought** '**iron,** *n.* [*noncount*] a form of iron that is easily shaped.

wrung /rʌŋ/ *v.* pt. and pp. of WRING.

wry /ray/ *adj.,* **wri•er, wri•est. 1.** twisted out of shape or contorted, as the facial features when expressing displeasure: *a wry grin.* **2.** bitingly or bitterly ironic or amusing: *a wry tale about the loss of innocence.* —'**wry•ly,** *adv.*

WV or **W.V.,** an abbreviation of: West Virginia.

W.Va., an abbreviation of: West Virginia.

WWW, an abbreviation of: World Wide Web.

WY or **Wy.,** an abbreviation of: Wyoming.

Wyo., an abbreviation of: Wyoming.

W

XYZ

X, x /ɛks/ *n.* [*count*], *pl.* **Xs** or **X's, xs** or **x's.** the 24th letter of the English alphabet, a consonant.

X, *Symbol.* (*sometimes* x) the Roman numeral for 10.

Xe•rox /ˈzɪərɒks/ *n.* **1.** [*noncount*] *Trademark.* a machine for making photocopies. **2.** [*count; sometimes:* xerox] a copy made on such a machine. —*v.* [~ + *obj*] [*no obj*] **3.** [*sometimes:* xerox] to copy by means of such a machine.

Xmas /ˈkrɪsməs/ *often* ˈɛksməs/ Christmas.

x-ray or **X-ray** /ˈɛksˌreɪ/ *n., v.,* **-rayed, -ray• ing.** —*n.* [*count*] Also, **x ray, X ray. 1.** radiation capable of passing through solids. **2.** a photograph made by means of x-rays: *a chest x-ray.* —*v.* [~ + *obj*] **3.** to photograph or treat with x-rays: *The technician x-rayed my knee.*

xy•lo•phone /ˈzaɪləˌfoʊn/ *n.* [*count*] a musical instrument consisting of a series of bars of different sizes, usually played by striking with a small hammer.

Y, y /waɪ/ *n.* [*count*], *pl.* **Ys** or **Y's, ys** or **y's.** the 25th letter of the English alphabet, serving as either a vowel or a consonant.

-y¹, an adjective suffix meaning: characterized by or like (*cloudy*); tending to (*squeaky*).

-y², a noun suffix meaning: dear (*granny*); little (*kitty*).

-y³, a noun suffix meaning: action of (*inquiry*); quality or state (*victory*); goods or business establishment specified (*bakery*).

yacht /yɒt/ *n.* [*count*] a large, expensive boat used for private cruising or racing.

yak /yæk/ *n.* [*count*] a large, shaggy-haired ox of Tibet.

yam /yæm/ *n.* [*count*] **1.** the starchy root of a climbing vine resembling the sweet potato, eaten as a vegetable. **2.** SWEET POTATO.

yank /yæŋk/ *v.* **1.** to pull or tug sharply: [~ + *obj*]: *Yank the doorknob.* [*no obj*]: *He yanked on the doorknob.* **2.** [~ + *obj*] to remove quickly and sharply: *He was yanked out of school.* —*n.* [*count*] **3.** a sharp, sudden, strong pull; jerk.

Yank (yangk), *n.* [*count*] *Informal.* Yankee.

Yan•kee /ˈyæŋkiy/ *n.* [*count*] **1.** a native of, or a person living in, the United States. **2.** a native of, or a person living in, a Northern state, esp. in New England. **3.** a Federal soldier in the Civil War.

yard¹ /yɑrd/ *n.* [*count*] a unit of measure in English-speaking countries, equal to 3 feet or 36 inches (0.9144 meter).

yard² /yɑrd/ *n.* [*count*] **1.** the ground next to or surrounding a house, public building, etc. **2.** an outside area used for work or business (often used in combination): *a shipyard; a navy yard.*

yard•stick /ˈyɑrdˌstɪk/ *n.* [*count*] **1.** a stick that is a yard long, often marked with smaller divisions, used for measuring. **2.** any standard of measurement: *Tests are a yardstick of academic achievement.*

yarn /yɑrn/ *n.* **1.** [*noncount*] thread made of natural or artificial fibers and used for knitting and weaving. **2.** [*count*] a tale, esp. a long story of adventure.

yawn /yɔn/ *v.* [*no obj*] **1.** to open the mouth and breathe in deeply, often from sleepiness or boredom. **2.** to open wide: *a cavern entrance yawned*

before them. —*n.* [*count*] **3.** an act or instance of yawning.

yd., an abbreviation of: yard.

yeah /yɛə/ *adv., n.* [*count*] *Informal.* yes.

year /yɪər/ *n.* [*count*] **1.** a period of 365 or 366 days, divided into 12 calendar months, beginning Jan. 1 and ending Dec. 31. Compare LEAP YEAR. **2.** a period or space of 12 calendar months counting from any point: *We expect to finish in a year from now.* **3.** a period, usually less than 12 months, that is spent in a certain activity or the like: *The academic year lasts from September to June.* **4. years,** [*plural*] **a.** age: *She's very active for her years.* **b.** an unusually long time: *We haven't spoken in years.* —*Idiom.* **5. year in and year out,** regularly through the years; continually. Also, **year in, year out.**

year•ly /ˈyɪərliy/ *adj.* [*before a noun*] **1.** done, occurring, appearing, etc., once each year; annual: *a yearly report.* —*adv.* **2.** once a year; annually.

yearn /yɜrn/ *v.* [*no obj*] to have a strong desire; long: *He yearned for her love. They yearned to return to their village.* —ˈyearn•ing, *n.* [*noncount*] [*count*]

'year-'round, *adj.* [*before a noun*] **1.** continuing, available, used, etc., throughout the year: *a year-round vacation spot.* —*adv.* **2.** throughout the year.

yeast /yiyst/ *n.* [*noncount*] [*count*] a fungus, usually in the form of dry powder, used in brewing alcoholic beverages and to make bread rise.

yell /yɛl/ *v.* **1.** to cry out; shout: [*no obj*]: *kids yelling in the schoolyard.* [~ + *obj*]: *to yell (out) insults.* —*n.* [*count*] **2.** a shout.

yel•low /ˈyɛloʊ/ *n.* [*noncount*] **1.** a color like that of egg yolk, lemons, etc. —*v.* **2.** to (cause to) become yellow: [*no obj*]: *The papers yellowed with age.* [~ + *obj*]: *The years had yellowed the pages of his diary.*

'yellow ˌjacket, *n.* [*count*] a wasp with black and bright yellow stripes.

yelp /yɛlp/ *v.* [*no obj*] **1.** to give a sharp, high-pitched cry: *All the dogs were yelping.* —*n.* [*count*] **2.** a quick, sharp bark or cry.

yen¹ /yɛn/ *n.* [*count*], *pl.* **yen.** the unit of money of Japan.

yen² /yɛn/ *n.* [*count*] a desire; craving: *She had a yen for ice cream.*

yes /yɛs/ *adv., n., pl.* **yes•es.** —*adv.* **1.** (used to express agreement with or to emphasize a previous statement): *Do you want that? Yes, I do.* **2.** (used to show a willingness to follow a request): *Could you bring us some water? Yes, in just a minute.* **3.** (used to express disagreement with a negative statement or command): *You can't do that! Oh yes I can!* **4.** (used to express uncertainty, curiosity, etc.): *"Yes?" he said after the police officer called his name.* —*n.* [*count*] **5.** a reply or vote that shows acceptance or approval.

yes•ter•day /ˈyɛstərˌdey, -diy/ *adv.* **1.** on the day before this day: *I got home late yesterday.* **2.** in the recent past: *Yesterday your money went further.* —*n.* [*noncount*] **3.** the day before this day: *in yesterday's paper.* **4.** the recent past: *the customs of yesterday.*

yet /yɛt/ *adv.* **1.** at the present time; now: *Are they here yet?* **2.** (used with negative words or phrases, or in questions) up to a particular time; so far: *They had not yet come. Haven't they come yet?* **3.** in the time remaining; still: *There is yet time.* **4.** to the present moment; as previously; still: *He came this morning, and he is here yet.* **5.** in addition; again: *The mail brought yet another reply.* **6.** in addition; even: *We'll have to use yet greater strength.* **7.** nevertheless: *The story was strange and yet true.* —*conj.* **8.** though; still; nevertheless: *The essay is good, yet it could be improved.*

yew /yuw/ *n.* [*count*] an evergreen tree or shrub having needles and seeds enclosed in a fleshy pod.

yield /yiyld/ *v.* **1.** [~ + *obj*] to give forth or produce by a natural process or after cultivation: *to yield 40 bushels to the acre.* **2.** [~ + *obj*] to produce (profit). **3.** to give in or surrender, as to superior power or authority: [~ + *obj*]: *The army yielded the fort to the enemy.* [*no obj*]: *to yield to temptation.* —*n.* [*count*] **4.** the act of yielding or producing. **5.** the quantity or amount yielded or produced: *a high yield.* **6.** the income produced by a financial investment, usually given as a percentage of cost: *a low yield on government bonds.*

YMCA, an abbreviation of: Young Men's Christian Association.

YMHA, an abbreviation of: Young Men's Hebrew Association.

yo•del /'yowdl/ *v.* [*no obj*] [~ + *obj*], **-deled, -del•ing,** or (*esp. Brit.*) **-delled, -del•ling.** to sing or call out with frequent changes from a low voice to a high voice and back again, in the manner of mountaineers in the Swiss Alps. —'**yo• del•er,** *n.* [*count*]

yo•ga /'yowgə/ *n.* [*noncount*] a system of physical and mental activities done to gain control of the body and mind and become relaxed

yo•gurt or **yo•ghurt** /'yowgərt/ *n.* [*noncount*] a tart, custardlike food made from milk that has turned thick and sour from the action of bacteria.

yoke /yowk/ *n.*, *v.*, **yoked, yok•ing.** —*n.* [*count*] **1.** a wooden frame for joining together a pair of animals, esp. oxen, that pull a plow, wagon, etc. **2.** a burden or cause of enslavement, oppression, etc.: *the yoke of tyranny.* —*v.* [~ + *obj*] **3.** to join with or as if with a yoke; unite.

yo•kel /'yowkəl/ *n.* [*count*] an unsophisticated country person.

yolk /yowk, yowlk/ *n.* [*noncount*] [*count*] the yellow substance of an egg, as distinguished from the white.

yon•der /'yɒndər/ *adj.* [*before a noun*] **1.** being in that place or over there: *Do you see yonder hut?* —*adv.* **2.** at, in, or to that place; over there: *Look yonder!*

you /yuw; *unstressed* yu, yə/ *pron., poss.* **your** or **yours,** *obj.* **you,** *pl.* **you;** *n., pl.* **yous.** —*pron.* (used as the subject of a verb, or as the object of a verb or preposition) **1.** the pronoun of the second person singular or plural used to refer to the person or persons being spoken to: *You are the winner. I sent it to you.* **2.** one; anyone; people in general: *a tiny animal you can't even see.* —*n.* [*count*] **3.** the nature or character of the person addressed: *After our exercise program, your friends will see a new you!*

young /yʌŋ/ *adj.*, **young•er** /'yʌŋgər/, **young• est** /'yʌŋgɪst/, *n.* —*adj.* **1.** being in the first or early stage of life, growth, or development: *two young children; a young science.* **2.** having the appearance, freshness, vigor, or other qualities of youth: *I feel young again!* —*n.* [*plural; used with*

a plural verb] **3.** [*the* + ~] young persons. **4.** young offspring: *a mother hen protecting her young.*

young•ster /'yʌŋstər/ *n.* [*count*] a young person.

your /yur, yɔr, *unstressed* yər/ *pron.* **1.** (used before a noun to mean possessed or owned by you; of or relating to you; belonging to you): *I like your idea. The library is on your left.* **2.** (used to indicate all members of a group, occupation, etc.); some, any, or one: *He's just your average factory worker.* —**Usage.** Do not confuse YOUR and YOU'RE. YOUR is the possessive form of "you": *Your book is overdue at the library.* YOU'RE is the contraction of "you are": *You're just the person we need for this job.*

you're /yur; *unstressed* yər/ contraction of *you are*: *You're right!* —**Usage.** See YOUR.

yours /yurz, yɔrz/ *pron.* (used to mean possessed or owned by you; of or relating to you; belonging to you): *Which cup is yours? Yours was the first face I recognized.*

your•self /yur'self, yɔr-yər-/ *pron., pl.* **-selves** /-'selvz/. **1.** a reflexive pronoun, used to show that the subject of the sentence and this pronoun refer to the same person: *You can think for yourself.* **2.** (used to give emphasis to the word YOU): *Here is a letter that you yourself wrote.* **3.** (used in place of YOU in certain constructions): *a small gift for your mother and yourself.* **4.** your usual, normal, or customary self: *After some rest you'll be yourself again.*

youth /yuwθ/ *n., pl.* **youths** /yuwθs, yuwðz/. **1.** [*noncount*] the condition or time of being young. **2.** [*the* + ~] young persons thought of as a group: *the youth of today.* **3.** [*count*] a young person, esp. a young man.

youth•ful /'yuwθfəl/ *adj.* young or seeming young. —'**youth•ful•ness,** *n.* [*noncount*]

yo-yo /'yowyow/ *n.* [*count*], *pl.* **-yos.** a spoollike toy that is spun and reeled in by means of a string that loops around the finger.

yr., an abbreviation of: **1.** year. **2.** your.

yuck /yʌk/ *interj. Slang.* (used to express disgust): *Oh, yuck, the pond is slimy.*

yuck•y /'yʌkiy/ *adj.*, **-i•er, -i•est.** *Slang.* very unappetizing or disgusting: *a yucky mess.*

yup•pie /'yʌpiy/ *n.* [*count*], *pl.* **-pies.** a young, ambitious city dweller who has a highly paid professional job.

YWCA, an abbreviation of: Young Women's Christian Association.

YWHA, an abbreviation of: Young Women's Hebrew Association.

Z, z /ziy/ *n.* [*count*], *pl.* **Zs** or **Z's, zs** or **z's.** the 26th letter of the English alphabet, a consonant.

za•ny /'zeyniy/ *adj.*, **-ni•er, -ni•est.** very silly; absurdly comical: *a zany comedian.* —'**za•ni• ness,** *n.* [*noncount*]

zap /zæp/ *v.*, **zapped, zap•ping.** *Informal.* —*v.* [~ + *obj*] **1.** to attack, defeat, destroy, or kill with sudden speed and force. **2.** to bombard with electrical current, radiation, laser beams, bullets, etc. —*n.* [*count*] **3.** a jolt or charge, as of electricity. **4.** a forceful and sudden blow.

X

Y

Z

zeal /ziyl/ n. [noncount] strong feeling, enthusiasm, or desire for a person, cause, or object. —**zealous,** adj.

zeal•ot /'zɛlət/ n. [count] a person who shows too much zeal.

ze•bra /'ziybrə/ n. [count], pl. **-bras,** (esp. when thought of as a group) **-bra.** a horselike African mammal having a pattern of black stripes on a whitish background.

ze•nith /'ziynɪθ/ n. [count] **1.** the point in the sky directly overhead. **2.** the highest point or state; peak: the zenith of his career.

ze•ro /'zɪərow/ n., pl. **-ros, -roes,** v., **-roed, -ro•ing.** —n. **1.** [count] the figure or symbol 0, which stands for the absence of quantity or amount; a cipher. **2.** [noncount] a beginning point on a scale from which values are measured, as on a temperature scale: twelve degrees below zero. **3.** [noncount] nothing: I had gained zero after all that hard work. —v. **4. zero in on,** to aim directly at: to zero in on a target.

zest /zɛst/ n. hearty enjoyment; enthusiasm: [noncount]: full of zest. [count; usually singular]: a zest for life. —'**zest•y,** adj., **-i•er, -i•est.**

zig•zag /'zɪg,zæg/ n., adj., adv., v., **-zagged, -zag•ging.** —n. [count] **1.** a line or course having sharp turns first to one side and then to the other. —adj. **2.** moving or formed in a zigzag: zigzag stitches. —adv. **3.** in a zigzag manner. —v. [~ + obj] [no obj] **4.** to (cause to) be in a zigzag direction, form, or course; move in a zigzag direction.

zilch /zɪltʃ/ n. [noncount] Slang. zero; nothing.

zil•lion /'zɪlyən/ n. [count], pl. **-lions,** (as after a numeral) **-lion.** Informal. an extremely large number or amount that is not made definite: a zillion thanks.

zinc /zɪŋk/ n. [noncount] a bluish-white metallic chemical element used in some mixtures of metals.

zin•ni•a /'zɪniyə/ n. [count], pl. **-ni•as.** a plant having dense, colorful flower heads.

zip[1] /zɪp/ n., v., **zipped, zip•ping.** —n. [noncount] **1.** energy; liveliness: That boring book needs some zip. —v. [no obj] **2.** to move with a sudden, brief hissing sound: Bullets zipped through the air. **3.** to move with speed: The car zipped ahead.

zip[2] /zɪp/ v., **zipped, zip•ping. 1.** to (cause to) be fastened or unfastened with a zipper: [~ + obj]: He zipped (up) his jacket. [no obj]: The jacket won't zip. **2.** [no obj] [~ + obj] to close or open (a zipper).

'ZIP ,code, n. [count] a series of numbers written directly after the address on a piece of mail to specify the postal delivery area.

zip•per /'zɪpər/ n. [count] a device for fastening clothing, luggage, etc., consisting of two parallel tracks of teeth that can be interlocked or separated by the pulling of a slide between them.

zith•er /'zɪθər, 'zɪð-/ n. [count] a musical instrument made up of a flat box with numerous strings stretched over it.

zo•di•ac /'zowdiy,æk/ n. [count; singular] **1.** an imaginary belt in the heavens representing the apparent paths of the sun, moon, and planets, divided into 12 divisions, each named after a constellation. **2.** a diagram representing the zodiac.

zodiac (def. 2)

zom•bie /'zɒmbiy/ n. [count] **1.** the body of a dead person that is magically filled with what seems to be life and set to perform tasks as a slave. **2.** a person whose behavior or responses are slow, mechanical, or without feeling; automaton.

zone /zown/ n., v., **zoned, zon•ing.** —n. [count] **1.** an area that differs in some respect, or is distinguished for some purpose, from nearby areas: a work zone; a danger zone. **2.** any of five divisions of the earth's surface, bounded by lines parallel to the equator and named according to the temperature that is common there: the temperate zone; the torrid zone. —v. [~ + obj] **3.** to divide into zones.

zoo /zuw/ n. [count], pl. **zoos.** a parklike area in which live animals are kept in cages or large, closed-off areas so that the public can view them.

zo•ol•o•gy /zow'ɒlədʒiy/ n. [noncount] the scientific study of animals and their behavior. —**zo•o•log•i•cal** /,zowə'lɒdʒɪkəl/, adj. —**zo'ol•o•gist,** n. [count]

zoom /zuwm/ v. **1.** to move quickly or suddenly, esp. with a loud humming or buzzing sound: [no obj]: The plane zoomed across the sky. [~ + obj]: He zoomed the car ahead. **2.** [no obj] to increase or rise suddenly and sharply: Prices zoomed.

zuc•chi•ni /zuw'kiyniy/ n. [count], pl. **-ni, -nis.** a cucumber-shaped squash having a smooth, dark green skin.

Nations of the World

Nation	Pronunciation	Capital
Afghanistan	/æf'gænə,stæn/	Kabul
Albania	/æl'beyniyə/	Tirane
Algeria	/æl'dʒɪəriyə/	Algiers
American Samoa	/ə'mɛrɪkən sə'mowə/	Pago Pago
Andorra	/æn'dɔrə/	Andorra la Vella
Angola	/æŋ'gowlə/	Luanda
Argentina	/ˌɑrdʒən'tiynə/	Buenos Aires
Armenia	/ɑr'miyniyə/	Yerevan
Australia	/ɔ'streylyə/	Canberra
Austria	/'ɔstriyə/	Vienna
Azerbaijan	/ˌazərbay'dʒɑn, ˌæzər-/	Baku
Bahamas, The	/bə'hɑməz, -'hæməz/	Nassau
Bahrain	/bɑ'reyn/	Manama
Bangladesh	/ˌbɑŋglə'dɛʃ, ˌbæŋ-/	Dhaka
Barbados	/bɑr'beydows/	Bridgetown
Belarus	/ˌbyɛlə'rus, ˌbɛl-/	Minsk
Belgium	/'bɛldʒəm/	Brussels
Belize	/bə'liyz/	Belmopan
Bermuda	/bər'myuwdə/	Hamilton
Bhutan	/buw'tɑn/	Thimphu
Bolivia	/bə'lɪviyə/	La Paz
Bosnia & Herzegovina	/'bɒzniyə ænd hɜrtsəgow'viynə/	Sarajevo
Botswana	/bɒt'swɑnə/	Gaborone
Brazil	/brə'zɪl/	Brasilia
Brunei	/bru'nay, -'ney/	Bandar Seri Begawa
Bulgaria	/bʌl'gɛəriyə/	Sofia
Burkina Faso	/bər'kiynə 'fɑsow/	Ouagadougou
Burundi	/bʊ'rʊndiy/	Bujumbura
Cambodia	/kæm'bowdiyə/	Phnom Penh
Cameroon	/ˌkæmə'ruwn/	Yaoundé
Canada	/'kænədə/	Ottawa
Cape Verde	/ˌkeyp 'vɜrd/	Praia
Central African Republic	/'sɛntrəl 'æfrɪkən rɪ'pʌblɪk/	Bangui
Chad	/tʃæd/	N'Djamena

Nation	Pronunciation	Capital
Chile	/'tʃɪliy/	Santiago
China	/'tʃaynə/	Beijing
Colombia	/kə'lʌmbiyə/	Bogotá
Comoros	/'kɒmə,rowz/	Moroni
Congo, People's Republic of the	/'kɒŋgow/	Brazzaville
Congo, Democratic Republic of the	/'kɒŋgow/	Kinshasa
Costa Rica	/'kɒstə 'riykə/	San José
Cote d'Ivoire	/kowt diy'vwar/	Yamoussoukro
Croatia	/krow'eyʃə/	Zagreb
Cuba	/'kyubə/	Havana
Cyprus	/'sayprəs/	Nicosia
Czech Republic	/'tʃɛk rɪ'pʌblɪk/	Prague
Denmark	/'dɛnmɑrk/	Copenhagen
Djibouti	/dʒɪ'buwtiy/	Djibouti
Dominica	/,dɒmə'niykə, də'mɪnɪkə/	Roseau
Dominican Republic	/də'mɪnɪkən rɪ'pʌblɪk/	Santo Domingo
Ecuador	/'ɛkwə,dɔr/	Quito
Egypt	/'iydʒɪpt/	Cairo
El Salvador	/ɛl 'sælvə,dɔr/	San Salvador
Equatorial Guinea	/,iykwə'tɔriyəl 'gɪniy, ,ɛkwə-/	Malabo
Eritrea	/,ɛrɪ'triyə/	Asmara
Estonia	/ɛ'stowniyə/	Tallinn
Ethiopia	/,iyθiy'owpiyə/	Addis Ababa
Federated States of Micronesia	/'fɛdə,reytɪd 'steyts əv ,maykrə'niyʒə/	Palikir
Fiji	/'fiydʒiy/	Suva
Finland	/'fɪnlənd/	Helsinki
France	/fræns/	Paris
Gabon	/ga'bɔ̃/	Libreville
Gambia, The	/'gæmbiyə/	Banjul
Georgia	/'dʒɔrdʒə/	Tbilisi
Germany	/'dʒɜrməniy/	Berlin
Ghana	/'gɑnə, 'gænə/	Acara
Greece	/griys/	Athens
Grenada	/grɪ'neydə/	St. George's
Guatemala	/,gwɑtə'mɑlə/	Guatemala City
Guinea	/'gɪniy/	Conarky
Guinea-Bissau	/'gɪniybɪ'saw/	Bissau
Guyana	/gay'ɑnə, -'ænə/	Georgetown
Haiti	/'heytiy/	Port-au-Prince
Honduras	/hɒn'durəs, -'dyʊr-/	Tegucigalpa
Hungary	/'hʌŋgəriy/	Budapest
Iceland	/'ayslənd/	Reykjavik
India	/'ɪndiyə/	New Delhi
Indonesia	/,ɪndə'niyʒə/	Jakarta

Nation	Pronunciation	Capital
Iran	/ɪˈræn, ɪˈrɑn/	Teheran (or Tehran)
Iraq	/ɪˈræk, ɪˈrɑk/	Baghdad
Ireland	/ayˈərlənd/	Dublin
Israel	/ˈɪzriyəl, ˈɪzrey-/	Jerusalem
Italy	/ˈɪtḷiy/	Rome
Jamaica	/dʒəˈmeykə/	Kingston
Japan	/dʒəˈpæn/	Tokyo
Jordan	/ˈdʒɔrdṇ/	Amman
Kazakhstan	/ˌkazakˈstɑn/	Akmola
Kenya	/ˈkɛnyə, ˈkiyn-/	Nairobi
Kuwait	/kʊˈweyt/	Kuwait
Kyrgyzstan	/ˌkɪərgɪˈstɑn/	Bishkek
Laos	/ˈlɑows, ˈleyɒs/	Vientiane
Latvia	/ˈlætviyə, ˈlɑt-/	Riga
Lebanon	/ˈlɛbənən, -ˌnɒn/	Beirut
Lesotho	/ləˈsuwtuw, -ˈsowtow/	Maseru
Liberia	/layˈbɪəriyə/	Monrovia
Libya	/ˈlɪbiyə/	Tripoli
Liechtenstein	/ˈlɪktənˌstayn/	Vaduz
Lithuania	/ˌlɪθuwˈeyniyə/	Vilnius
Luxembourg	/ˈlʌksəmˌbɜrg/	Luxembourg
Macedonia	/ˌmæsɪˈdowniyə/	Skopje
Madagascar	/ˌmædɪˈgæskər/	Antananarivo
Malawi	/məˈlɑwiy/	Lilongwe
Malaysia	/məˈleyʒə/	Kuala Lumpur
Maldives	/ˈmɔldiyvz, ˈmældayvz/	Malé
Mali	/ˈmɑliy/	Bamako
Malta	/ˈmɔltə/	Valletta
Marshall Islands	/ˈmɑrʃəl ˈayləndz/	Dalap-Uliga-Darrit
Mauritania	/ˌmɔrɪˈteyniyə/	Nouakchott
Mauritius	/mɔˈrɪʃəs/	Port Louis
Mexico	/ˈmɛksɪˌkow/	Mexico City
Moldova	/mɔlˈdowvə/	Chișinău
Monaco	/ˈmɒnəˌkow, məˈnɑkow/	Monaco
Mongolia	/mɒŋˈgowliyə/	Ulan Bator
Morocco	/məˈrɒkow/	Rabat
Mozambique	/ˌmowzæmˈbiyk/	Maputo
Myanmar (Burma)	/ˈmyɑnmɑr, -mɑ/	Yangon
Namibia	/nəˈmɪbiyə/	Windhoek
Nepal	/nəˈpɔl, -pɑl/	Katmandu
Netherlands	/ˈnɛðərləndz/	Amsterdam & The Hague
New Zealand	/ˌnuw ˈziylənd, nyu/	Wellington
Nicaragua	/ˌnɪkəˈrɑgwə/	Managua
Niger	/ˈnaydʒər/	Niamey
Nigeria	/nayˈdʒɪəriyə/	Abuja
North Korea	/ˈnɔrθ kəˈriyə/	Pyongyang
Norway	/ˈnɔrwey/	Oslo

Nation	Pronunciation	Capital
Oman	/ow'mɑn/	Muscat
Pakistan	/'pækə,stæn, ,pɑkə'stɑn/	Islamabad
Panama	/'pænə,mɑ/	Panama City
Papua New Guinea	/'pæpyuwə ,nuw 'gıniy, ,nyuw, 'pɑpuw,ɑ/	Port Moresby
Paraguay	/'pærə,gway/	Ascunción
Peru	/pə'ruw/	Lima
Philippines	/'fılə,piynz, ,fılə'piynz/	Manila
Poland	/'powlənd/	Warsaw
Portugal	/'pɔrtʃəgəl/	Lisbon
Qatar	/'kɑtɑr, kə'tɑr/	Doha
Réunion	/riy'uwnyən/	St. Denis
Romania	/row'meyniyə, rə-/	Bucharest
Russian Federation	/'rʌʃən ,fɛdə'reyʃən/	Moscow
Rwanda	/ruw'ɑndə/	Kigali
Saint Kitts-Nevis	/,seynt 'kıts'niyvıs, -'nɛvıs/	Basseterre
Saint Lucia	/,seynt 'luwʃə, 'luwsiyə/	Castries
Saint Vincent & the Grenadines	/,seynt 'vınsənt ænd ðə ,grɛnə'diynz, 'grɛnə,diynz/	Kingstown
San Marino	/,sæn mə'riynow/	San Marino
São Tomé & Príncipe	/,saw tʊ'mey ənd 'prınsəpə/	São Tomé
Saudi Arabia	/,sawdiy ə'reybiyə, ,sɔdiy/	Riyadh
Senegal	/,sɛnı'gɔl, -'gɑl/	Dakar
Seychelles	/sey'ʃɛl, -'ʃɛlz/	Victoria
Sierra Leone	/siy'ɛrə liy'owniy, liy'own/	Freetown
Singapore	/'sıŋgə,pɔr/	Singapore
Slovakia	/slow'vɑkiyə, -'vækiyə/	Bratislava
Slovenia	/slow'viyniyə/	Ljubljana
Solomon Islands	/'sɒləmən 'ayləndz/	Honiara
Somalia	/sow'mɑliyə/	Mogadishu
South Africa	/,sawθ 'æfrıkə/	Pretoria & Cape Town
South Korea	/'sawθ kə'riyə/	Seoul
Spain	/speyn/	Madrid
Sri Lanka	/,sriy 'lɑŋkə, ʃriy-/	Colombo
Sudan	/suw'dæn/	Khartoum
Suriname	/,sʊrə'nɑm, -'nɑmə/	Paramaribo
Swaziland	/'swɑziy,lænd/	Mbabane
Sweden	/'swiydn̩/	Stockholm
Switzerland	/'swıtsərlənd/	Bern
Syria	/'sıəriyə/	Damascus
Tajikistan	/tə'dʒıkə,stæn, -stɑn/	Dushanbe
Tanzania	/,tænzə'niyə/	Dodoma
Thailand	/'tay,lænd, -lənd/	Bangkok
Togo	/'towgow/	Lomé
Trinidad & Tobago	/'trını,dæd ən tə'beygow/	Port-of-Spain

Nation	Pronunciation	Capital
Tunisia	/tuw'niyʒə, tyuw-/	Tunis
Turkey	/'tɜrkiy/	Ankara
Turkmenistan	/ˌtɜrkmɛnə'stæn, -'stɑn/	Ashgabat
Uganda	/yuw'gændə, uw'gɑn-/	Kampala
Ukraine	/yuw'kreyn/	Kiev
United Arab Emirates	/yuw'naytid 'ærəb 'ɛmərɪts/	Abu Dhabi
United Kingdom	/yuw'naytid 'kiŋdəm/	London
United States	/yuw'naytid 'steyts/	Washington, D.C.
Uruguay	/'yʊrəˌgwey/	Montevideo
Uzbekistan	/ʊz'bɛkəˌstæn, -ˌstɑn/	Tashkent
Vanuatu	/ˌvɑnuw'ɑtuw/	Vila
Venezuela	/ˌvɛnə'zweylə/	Caracas
Vietnam	/viyˌɛt'nɑm, -'næm/	Hanoi
Western Samoa	/'wɛstərn sə'mowə/	Apia
Yemen	/'yɛmən/	Sanaa
Yugoslavia	/ˌyuwgow'slɑviyə/	Belgrade
Zambia	/'zæmbiyə/	Lusaka
Zimbabwe	/zɪm'bɑbwey, -wiy/	Harare

Irregular Verbs

Note: If more than one form is shown, the most frequent one is listed first.

Root Form	Past Tense	Past Participle
arise	arose	arisen
awake	awoke, awaked	awoke, awaked, awoken
be	was	been
bear	bore	borne
beat	beat	beaten, beat
become	became	become
begin	began	begun
bend	bent	bent
beseech	besought, beseeched	besought, beseeched
bet	bet, betted	bet, betted
bid	bade, bid	bidden, bid
bind	bound	bound
bite	bit	bitten
bleed	bled	bled
blow	blew	blown
break	broke	broken
breed	bred	bred
bring	brought	brought
broadcast	broadcast, broadcasted	broadcast, broadcasted
build	built	built
burn	burned, burnt	burned, burnt
burst	burst	burst
buy	bought	bought
cast	cast	cast
catch	caught	caught
choose	chose	chosen
cling	clung	clung
clothe	clothed, clad	clothed, clad
come	came	come

Root Form	Past Tense	Past Participle
cost	cost	cost
creep	crept	crept
cut	cut	cut
deal	dealt	dealt
dig	dug	dug
dive	dived, dove	dived
do	did	done
draw	drew	drawn
dream	dreamed, dreamt	dreamed, dreamt
drink	drank	drunk
drive	drove	driven
dwell	dwelt, dwelled	dwelt, dwelled
eat	ate	eaten
fall	fell	fallen
feed	fed	fed
feel	felt	felt
fight	fought	fought
find	found	found
flee	fled	fled
fling	flung	flung
fly	flew	flown
forget	forgot	forgotten
forgive	forgave	forgiven
forsake	forsook	forsaken
freeze	froze	frozen
get	got	gotten
give	gave	given
go	went	gone
grind	ground	ground
grow	grew	grown
hang	hung, hanged	hung, hanged
have	had	had
hear	heard	heard
hide	hid	hidden, hid
hit	hit	hit
hold	held	held
hurt	hurt	hurt
keep	kept	kept

Root Form	Past Tense	Past Participle
kneel	knelt, kneeled	knelt, kneeled
know	knew	known
lay	laid	laid
lead	led	led
leap	leaped, leapt	leaped, leapt
leave	left	left
lend	lent	lent
let	let	let
lie	lay	lain
light	lit, lighted	lit, lighted
lose	lost	lost
make	made	made
mean	meant	meant
meet	met	met
mistake	mistook	mistaken
misunderstand	misunderstood	misunderstood
outdo	outdid	outdone
overcome	overcame	overcome
overdo	overdid	overdone
overhear	overheard	overheard
overrun	overran	overrun
oversee	oversaw	overseen
oversleep	overslept	overslept
overtake	overtook	overtaken
overthrow	overthrew	overthrown
partake	partook	partaken
pay	paid	paid
prove	proved	proved, proven
put	put	put
read	read	read
relay	relayed	relayed
rid	rid, ridded	rid, ridded
ride	rode	ridden
ring	rang	rung
rise	rose	risen
run	ran	run
say	said	said
see	saw	seen
seek	sought	sought

Root Form	Past Tense	Past Participle
sell	sold	sold
send	sent	sent
set	set	set
sew	sewed	sewn, sewed
shake	shook	shaken
shave	shaved	shaved, shaven
shed	shed	shed
shine	shone	shone
shoot	shot	shot
show	showed	shown, showed
shrink	shrank, shrunk	shrunk, shrunken
shut	shut	shut
sing	sang	sung
sink	sank, sunk	sunk, sunken
sit	sat	sat
slay	slew	slain
sleep	slept	slept
slide	slid	slid
sling	slung	slung
slink	slunk	slunk
slit	slit	slit
smell	smelled, smelt	smelled, smelt
sow	sowed	sown, sowed
speak	spoke	spoken
speed	sped, speeded	sped, speeded
spend	spent	spent
spill	spilled, spilt	spilled, spilt
spin	spun	spun
spit	spit, spat	spit, spat
split	split	split
spoil	spoiled, spoilt	spoiled, spoilt
spread	spread	spread
spring	sprang, sprung	sprung
stand	stood	stood
steal	stole	stolen
stick	stuck	stuck
sting	stung	stung
stink	stank, stunk	stunk
stride	strode	stridden

Root Form	Past Tense	Past Participle
strike	struck	struck, stricken
string	strung	strung
strive	strove, strived	striven, strived
swear	swore	sworn
sweep	swept	swept
swell	swelled	swollen, swelled
swim	swam	swum
swing	swung	swung
take	took	taken
teach	taught	taught
tear	tore	torn
tell	told	told
think	thought	thought
thrive	thrived, throve	thrived
throw	threw	thrown
thrust	thrust	thrust
tread	trod	trodden, trod
undergo	underwent	undergone
understand	understood	understood
undertake	undertook	undertaken
undo	undid	undone
unwind	unwound	unwound
uphold	upheld	upheld
upset	upset	upset
wake	woke, waked	woken, waked
wear	wore	worn
weave	wove, weaved	woven, wove
wed	wedded, wed	wedded, wed
wet	wet, wetted	wet, wetted
win	won	won
wind	wound	wound
withdraw	withdrew	withdrawn
withhold	withheld	withheld
withstand	withstood	withstood
wring	wrung	wrung
write	wrote	written